THE NEW OXFORD
COMPANION TO
LAW

THE NEW OXFORD COMPANION TO LAW

EDITED BY

Peter Cane

Joanne Conaghan

OXFORD
UNIVERSITY PRESS

OXFORD
UNIVERSITY PRESS

Great Clarendon Street, Oxford OX2 6DP

Oxford University Press is a department of the University of Oxford.
It furthers the University's objective of excellence in research, scholarship,
and education by publishing worldwide in

Oxford New York

Auckland Cape Town Dar es Salaam Hong Kong Karachi
Kuala Lumpur Madrid Melbourne Mexico City Nairobi
New Delhi Shanghai Taipei Toronto

With offices in

Argentina Austria Brazil Chile Czech Republic France Greece
Guatemala Hungary Italy Japan Poland Portugal Singapore
South Korea Switzerland Thailand Turkey Ukraine Vietnam

Oxford is a registered trade mark of Oxford University Press
in the UK and in certain other countries

Published in the United States
by Oxford University Press Inc., New York

British Library Cataloguing in Publication Data

Data available

Library of Congress Cataloging in Publication Data

Data available

Typeset by Newgen Imaging Systems (P) Ltd., Chennai, India
Printed in Great Britain
on acid-free paper by
MPG Books Ltd, Bodmin, Cornwall

ISBN 978–0–19–929054–3

10 9 8 7 6 5 4 3 2 1

Contents

The Companion: A–Z   1

Introduction and Reader's Guide

This is a book about law designed first and foremost for non-lawyers. Your first reaction might be that a law book for the non-lawyer is a contradiction in terms. After all, isn't law boring, complicated and—worse still—remote and irrelevant to most people's lives most of the time? We don't think so, and we hope that this book will convince you that we're right. Think of how many items of daily news have a legal angle. Besides the regular diet of serious and not-so-serious crime, we hear every day of transport accidents and environmental disasters, elections and wars, national disputes over territory and natural resources, scandals involving sporting celebrities, performers, and movie stars, broken marriages, workplace stress and injury, racial and ethnic conflict, corporate collapses and major financial deals, dangerous pharmaceuticals, genetic and medical breakthroughs. Events such as these all have legal aspects and implications, and many of them directly involve law, lawyers, and the legal system. Indeed, it's hard to think of any public event or aspect of social life that doesn't involve law in one way or another.

Law is everywhere—not only in Parliaments, courts, police stations, and lawyers' offices but also on TV and the internet, in the Press and at the cinema, in workplaces and schools, in art galleries and airport bookshops, and even in the home. In recent decades law has become a much more prominent and central feature of our personal, social, economic, and cultural lives. Fifty years ago, for example, if someone lost their job, people might have thought them unlucky or hard-done-by, but they would be unlikely to have seen them as legally wronged. Now, when someone is fired, the legality of their treatment is an integral aspect of our assessment of the employer's conduct. Fifty years ago did parents ever stop to question the lawfulness of smacking their children or imagine that one day their children's truancy might result in their own imprisonment? Fifty years ago the Race Relations Act did not exist, homosexual activity in private between consenting males was still a crime, a husband could rape his wife without legal sanction, Britain had not 'joined Europe', the Human Rights Act was not even a glint in the legal eye, no one had thought of civil partnerships or the International Criminal Court, and no one foresaw the 'compensation crisis', mass asbestos litigation, or Guantanamo Bay.

All these and any number of other changes affecting the lives of all of us have made knowledge about law, lawyers, and the legal system much more important than they have ever been for understanding and successfully negotiating the world around us. Law, like morality, religion, and politics, is a ubiquitous and pervasive feature of our lives, a crucial dimension of private and public discourse, encroaching upon even the most intimate aspects of our daily existence. To navigate the complex, fragmented, and highly regulated environment we now occupy, a knowledge and understanding of law's operations and effects is increasingly necessary and valuable.

The New Oxford Companion to Law is specifically designed to offer the curious and concerned non-lawyer a lively and accessible, vivid and informative account of law, legal institutions, legal processes, and legal actors. It aims to give the ordinary reader a real sense of the importance of law in everyday life, to remove some of its mystique and, above all, to show that law is much, much more interesting and relevant than most people ever imagine. This book will help you to appreciate what law is and what it is for. It explains what lawyers, courts, and law-makers do. It explores law's history and the extraordinary variety of the world's legal systems and traditions. It introduces you to great lawyers, famous trials, and leading court cases. And much, much more.

The first *Oxford Companion to Law* was published in 1980. It was entirely the work of a single author—Professor David Walker, then Regius Professor of Law in the University of Glasgow. It was an extraordinary achievement, and over the years it has provided pleasure and edification to many. But if a week is a long time in politics, twenty-eight years is a very long time indeed in the law, and a great deal has changed in the past quarter of a century. The legal system has grown in size and complexity and the sheer volume of written law—legislation and case law—has grown and continues to grow apace. This should not surprise us. After all, law tends to reflect and respond to wider social and political change, and the period since the first *Companion* was penned has witnessed a transformation of the social and political landscape: from Thatcherism to New Labour; from inner city race riots to the celebration of multiculturalism; from the nine-to-five job to the 24/7 global marketplace. But law is no mere barometer of social change; it also produces it. Increasingly law significantly shapes social experience and personal lives.

Several years ago, John Louth, Senior Law Editor at OUP, wisely judged that the time had come to produce a *New Oxford Companion to Law*. It was immediately clear that the task was far too large and demanding to be undertaken by any one—or even a few—individuals. In fact, this volume is the product of the work not only of the two Editors, but also of some forty Editorial Consultants and Advisers and more than 700 authors. As Editors, we are extremely grateful to them all for offering their knowledge and skills for this project. The result is a cornucopia of diverse contributions from an ensemble of legal experts—judges, practitioners, and scholars; a veritable chorus of legal voices of varying pitch, timbre, and resonance, capturing the frequently contested nature of knowledge of and about law. Law is many-faceted and extremely diverse; and no account, however long and detailed, can hope to capture it definitively or uncontroversially. There is a widespread misconception that law is a matter of facts not opinions, rules not argument—in short, a collection of cut-and-dried dos and don'ts. Our hope is that by representing the law in all its variety and colour, this book will provide an alternative to this misconception and give the reader a much richer understanding of what law is and of why it matters.

Because law is a product and reflection of society more broadly, it varies in significant ways as between different countries and different 'jurisdictions'. It would be practically impossible in a single volume to give an account of all the world's legal systems with any claim to depth or comprehensiveness of coverage. Nevertheless, although *The New Oxford Companion to Law* is published in the UK, it contains a great deal that will be of value and interest to non-UK readers, especially those in jurisdictions with legal systems that are historically derived from English law, which are sometimes collectively referred to as 'the common law world' (a concept discussed in the entry on 'common law' in this book). Because authors were asked to focus on general concepts rather than technical detail, a high proportion of the entries have relevance beyond the UK because legal systems in the common law world share many basic features. For readers outside the common law world, *The New Oxford Companion to Law* will provide a valuable introduction to many aspects of this major family of legal systems. In addition, many entries in areas such as Biography, Legal Theory, and World's Legal Systems and Traditions are of universal relevance.

To the extent that *The New Oxford Companion to Law* has a 'jurisdictional focus' it is on the law of the United Kingdom. However, it is important to understand that although the United Kingdom is (in terms of international law) a single nation state, it contains three different, geographically-based legal systems or 'jurisdictions': England

and Wales (which—leaving aside complexities resulting from devolution—together constitute one jurisdiction), Scotland, and Northern Ireland. There is no such thing as 'UK law'. For instance, each of the UK jurisdictions has its own court system and, since devolution, its own legislature. Even before devolution, there were significant variations between the three legal systems within the UK, and these are likely to increase in the years to come. Furthermore, because the origins of Scots law are different from those of English law, there are many differences of legal terminology between these two systems. Nevertheless, because England and Wales is the largest of the three UK jurisdictions, and England is the politically dominant element of the UK, there is a tendency for 'English law' to figure most prominently in discussions of law in the UK. Such 'Anglo-centrism' is disrespectful and can be seriously misleading; and we have gone to considerable lengths in this volume to give due recognition to jurisdictional variation within the UK. However, lawyers are typically expert in the law of only one jurisdiction, and we have not always been able to ensure that relevant differences between the laws of the various UK jurisdictions have been recorded.

The New Oxford Companion to Law does not aim to provide, and indeed does not offer, advice about legal rights and obligations. In this sense, it is a book *about* law rather than a book *of* law. Although a significant proportion of the entries deal with the law and legal institutions as they currently operate, it has not been written as a practical guide to the law. Authors were asked, as far as possible, to avoid legal jargon and technicality, and to *explain* legal concepts and ideas rather than to focus on their practical deployment by courts, legal advisers, and so on. Moreover, the book deals with many topics other than the law as it currently operates—legal history and legal theory, for instance, as well as political, sociological, and cultural aspects of law's content and application. It also covers important legal topics that are unlikely to have a direct or immediate impact on the day-to-day life of the typical reader—international law and different legal traditions, for instance. The purpose of *The New Oxford Companion to Law* is to introduce readers to the fascinating richness and diversity of legal phenomena, not to provide them with a legal 'how-to' manual.

There are various ways of accessing the material in this book. The entries are arranged alphabetically. However, the list of entries was not compiled in this way. Instead, we constructed a list of about forty subject headings that together provide reasonably comprehensive coverage of legal knowledge. Each subject heading was given a word allocation and Editorial Consultants and Advisers were asked to construct a list of entries ('headwords') of various lengths relating to one or two subject areas within their expertise. Towards the end of the book there is a list of entries arranged by subject area. This will enable the reader to locate cognate entries. Some entries appear in more than one subject area. In addition to substantive entries, there are 'zero-word' entries that cross-refer to other substantive entries. These cross-reference headwords appear in the appropriate place in the A–Z section of the book and also in the lists of entries arranged by subject area where they are indicated by the use of bold type. At the end of many substantive entries will be found a list of one or more 'related entries'. These direct the reader to cognate entries that may or may not be within the same subject area as the entry of which they are part. Within the text of substantive entries bold type indicates that the emboldened word is also itself a substantive or cross-reference headword. Such words have not been emboldened in all instances but only when reference to the appropriate entry would add significantly to understanding of the entry in which the emboldened word appears. Towards the beginning of the book there is a List of Cases and a List of Legislation referred to in the various entries. Finally, towards the end of the book will be found a List of Names of persons mentioned in the various entries.

By following these various ways into *The New Oxford Companion to Law* the reader should be able not only to indulge their occasional curiosity or need for information but also to pursue themes, ideas, and concepts more systematically, and in that way to build up a more coherent picture of some part of the legal tapestry. In addition, at the end of some entries there are one or two suggestions for further reading to help those who want more discussion and analysis.

Although *The New Oxford Companion to Law* is arranged alphabetically, it is not a legal dictionary. The entries in the book range in length from 250 words to 1,500 words. Although authors were asked to write as non-technically as possible, inevitably entries may contain words and concepts that are unfamiliar or puzzling to the typical reader. For this reason, we strongly recommend the reader to use *The New Oxford Companion to Law* in conjunction with a legal dictionary such as the *Oxford Dictionary of Law* (2006) edited by Elizabeth Martin and Jonathan Law. A legal dictionary will provide concise definitions of many common legal words and phrases.

Finally, we must emphasize that law is in a constant state of flux. This does not mean that many aspects of the law and the legal system do not remain constant over significant periods of time; but the life of the law is as much one of change as of stability. One result is that books of and about law tend quite quickly to go out-of-date in significant respects as courts and legislatures engage in the ongoing task of fashioning the law to meet changing social needs and demands. As we have already said, the entries in this book generally focus on general principles rather than specific details, and this approach slows the ravages of time. However, no guarantee can be given that everything said in *The New Oxford Companion to Law* about the technical content of the law will be correct at the time it is read; and inevitably some entries may not provide an entirely accurate account of the contemporary state of the law. This is one important reason why this book should not be used as an advice manual. Nevertheless, we are confident that the account provided in the entries in this volume will continue to be useful and substantially accurate for a significant number of years.

The project of producing *The New Oxford Companion to Law* has been complex and time-consuming. It is no exaggeration to say that this book could not have been completed (or even begun) without the extraordinary and unfailing efficiency, patience, and good humour of Ros Wallington, Editorial Executive to the *Companion* project. We shudder to think how many hours of her life she has devoted to the *Companion* over the past few years and we thank her sincerely for her cheerful tolerance of our many quirks and demands. We owe Ros a debt of gratitude that we cannot adequately discharge. Special thanks are also due to Gwen Booth and the other members of the production team at OUP who undertook the many and varied jobs that are inevitably generated by a project of this size.

We are extremely grateful to Sarah Carter who, at a rather late stage in the life of the project, enthusiastically and expertly undertook the large task of collecting and collating the marvellous set of illustrations that grace this book. They can do no more than hint at the under-appreciated visual aspects of law. A note by Sarah about the illustrations and the process of finding them appears immediately after this introduction.

Our hope and expectation is that *The New Oxford Companion to Law* will instruct, challenge, and entertain, and that it will provide readers with a much better understanding of the significance of law and the legal system, and of why they are a source of deep fascination and concern to those of us who have been privileged to be part of the *Companion* project.

PETER CANE AND JOANNE CONAGHAN

A Note about the Illustrations

Finding illustrations for the *New Oxford Companion to Law* was a fascinating and frustrating task. It was fascinating because once you get away from the traditional images of men in wigs and the law courts you find the law everywhere. It would be impossible to illustrate everything, and so I chose to concentrate on a limited number of topics and some of these generated a whole library of pictures, many of which I was unfamiliar with. It was frustrating because an initial collection of around 300 pictures had to be cut down to 200, and again to around 120. Time and again I found a whole series of images from which I had to select an exemplary two or three.

With such a large number of entries in the book it would have been impossible to cover the subject matter comprehensively. I chose, therefore, to concentrate on topics which were visually arresting, keeping a balance of contemporary and historical images and selecting topics which offered a narrative context for the images wherever possible. Some things don't change: it would have been possible to fill the book with wonderful cartoons of rapacious lawyers from the eighteenth century onwards (lawyers have always been the most hated profession). Cartoons proved a fertile source for many topics, although I reluctantly rejected many brilliant ones because of the complexity of the contemporary events to which they referred, which might be obscure to modern readers. Other choices were dictated by the image itself. So when I had to whittle down my original selection of lawyers I chose interesting portraits rather than to rely on a hierarchy of eminence. How hard it was to decide between Jeremy Bentham's embalmed body (in the possession of University College, London!) and the delightful painting by G.F. Watts. And how could we resist Edward Carson on a cigarette card!

Trawling through the databases I was briefly surprised at the paucity of images of certain legal milestones. The passing of key legislation is not usually reflected in pictures, of course, and although there were references in cartoons to the liberalization of abortion and sex offences laws in the sixties, or the Human Rights Act, for example, these do not find their way into documentary images as a rule. On the other hand, we remember 'events' as a series of iconic images: some of which are shown here. I have tried to get away from the best known of these, although some will be very familiar from press coverage. It is probably self-evident that there would be hundreds of photographs of protests and strikes, since the very purpose of these is to generate publicity, but the effect of seeing image after image of people holding placards pleading their cause is very moving. The Troubles in Northern Ireland and, to a lesser extent, the transition of South Africa from apartheid to multi-racial state are imprinted on our minds in a series of powerful photographs. The growth of image databases in recent years has given access to a huge range of visual imagery of the law which allowed for accidental discoveries and a far broader conceptualization of the law than would have been possible with only paper resources. I hope the reader will find as many surprises in the images presented here as I did when collating them.

SARAH CARTER

List of Contributors

DR CAROLYN ABBOT   Lecturer in Law, University of Manchester

PROFESSOR RICHARD ABEL   Connell Professor of Law, University of California, Los Angeles

MR STUART ADAM   Senior Research Economist, Institute for Fiscal Studies

MR DAPO AKANDE   University Lecturer in Public International Law and Yamani Fellow, St Peter's College, University of Oxford; Visiting Associate Professor Yale Law School (08/09)

DR ALBERTINA ALBORS-LLORENS,   University Senior Lecturer and Fellow and Director of Studies in Law, Girton College, University of Cambridge

PROFESSOR JOHN ALDER   Emeritus Professor of Law, Newcastle University

TREVOR ALDRIDGE QC

PROFESSOR T R S ALLAN   Professor of Public Law and Jurisprudence, University of Cambridge

PROFESSOR TOM ALLEN   Professor of Law, Durham University

PROFESSOR PHILIP ALSTON   John Norton Pomeroy Professor of Law, Law School, New York University

PROFESSOR STUART ANDERSON   Faculty of Law, University of Otago

DR TANYA APLIN   Senior Lecturer in Law, King's College London

MS MARIA ARISTODEMOU   Senior Lecturer, School of Law, Birkbeck College, University of London

PROFESSOR ANTHONY ARNULL   Professor of European Law and Head, Birmingham Law School, University of Birmingham

PROFESSOR ROSEMARY AUCHMUTY   School of Law, University of Reading

DR SIMON AUERBACH   Employment Judge, London Central Employment Tribunal

DR JOHN AVERY JONES   Special Commissioner of Income Tax

MR RODERICK BAGSHAW   Tutor and Fellow in Law, Magdalen College, University of Oxford

DR ANDREW BAINHAM   Fellow of Christ's College Cambridge, Reader in Family Law and Policy, University of Cambridge

PROFESSOR JOHN BALDWIN   Professor of Judicial Administration, Birmingham School of Law, University of Birmingham

PROFESSOR ROBERT BALDWIN   Professor of Law, Law Department, London School of Economics and Political Science

DR ANETTE BALLINGER   Lecturer in Criminology and affiliated to the Research Institute for Law, Politics and Justice, School of Criminology, Education, Sociology and Social Work, University of Keele

NICHOLAS BAMFORTH   Fellow in Law, The Queen's College, University of Oxford

PROFESSOR ERIC BARENDT   Professor of Media Law, University College London

MR ANTHONY BARKER   formerly Reader in Government, University of Essex

MS NICOLA BARKER   Lecturer in Law, University of Keele

PROFESSOR ANNE BARLOW   Professor of Family Law and Policy, University of Exeter

PROFESSOR LIZZIE BARMES   Professor of Labour Law, Queen Mary, University of London

DR CATHERINE BARNARD   Trinity College, Cambridge; Reader in EU Law, Cambridge; Jean Monnet Chair of EU Law

PROFESSOR BRENDA BARRETT   Emeritus Professor of Law, Middlesex University

JOHN BATES   Barrister, Old Square Chambers, London

PROFESSOR UPENDRA BAXI   Professor of Law in Development, University of Warwick

PROFESSOR CHRISTINE BELL   Director, Transitional Justice Institute, Professor of Public International Law, University of Ulster

PROFESSOR JOHN BELL   Professor of Law, Pembroke College, Cambidge

PROFESSOR MARK BELL   Professor of Law, University of Leicester

PROFESSOR STUART BELL   Professor of Law, University of York

MISS CATHERINE BELOFF   Solicitor, DLA Piper UK LLP

THE HONOURABLE MICHAEL J BELOFF QC   Barrister of Blackstone Chambers, The Temple

RUPERT BELOFF   Barrister, No 5 Chambers, Fountain Court, Birmingham

PROFESSOR PAUL BENJAMIN   Professor, School of Law, University of Cape Town, South Africa

PROFESSOR TOM BENNETT   Professor in the Department of Public Law, University of Cape Town

DR SARAH BERESFORD   Lecturer in Law, University of Lancaster

PROFESSOR SANDRA BERNS   Professor of Law, Griffith Law School, Nathan Campus, Griffith University

DR BRENNA BHANDAR   Kent Law School, Eliot College, University of Kent

STEPHEN BICKFORD-SMITH   Barrister, Landmark Chambers, London

PROFESSOR HAZEL BIGGS   Professor of Medical Law, Lancaster University

LORD (TOM) BINGHAM OF CORNHILL   Senior Lord of Appeal in Ordinary, House of Lords

PROFESSOR JOHN BIRDS   Professor of Commercial Law, School of Law, University of Manchester

PROFESSOR PATRICK BIRKINSHAW   Professor of Public Law and Director of the Institute of European Public Law, University of Hull

PROFESSOR BRIAN H BIX   Frederick W. Thomas Professor of Law and Philosophy, University of Minnesota

PROFESSOR ROBERT BLACKBURN   Professor of Constitutional Law, King's College London

PROFESSOR IAN BLACKSHAW   International Sports Lawyer and Fellow of The International Sports Law Centre, The TMC Asser Instituut, The Hague, The Netherlands.

MS ANN BLAIR   Senior Lecturer, School of Law, University of Leeds

PROFESSOR MICHAEL BLAKENEY   Herchel Smith Professor of Intellectual Property Law at Queen Mary, University of London

PROFESSOR NICHOLAS BLOMLEY   Department of Geography, Simon Fraser University, Canada

MS ALISON BONE   Principal Lecturer, Brighton Business School, University of Brighton

PROFESSOR DAVID BONNER   Dean of Law, University of Leicester

PROFESSOR ANDREW BOON   Dean, University of Westminster School of Law

DR FRANCIS N BOTCHWAY   Reader In Law, Hull Law School, University of Hull

MS ANNE BOTTOMLEY   Senior Lecturer, Kent Law School

JOHN BOWERS QC   Littleton Chambers; Honorary Professor, University of Hull

PROFESSOR BENJAMIN BOWLING   Professor of Criminology & Criminal Justice and Associate Head of School, School of Law, King's College, London

PROFESSOR A W BRADLEY   Research Fellow, Institute of European and Comparative Law, University of Oxford

PROFESSOR ANTHONY BRADNEY   Professor of Law, Keele University

MR RICHARD BRAGG   Senior Lecturer in Law, University of Manchester

DR PAUL BRAND   Senior Research Fellow, All Souls College, University of Oxford

PROFESSOR MICHAEL BRIDGE   Professor of Law, London School of Economics and Political Science

MS JO BRIDGEMAN   Senior Lecturer in Law, Sussex Law School, University of Sussex

PROFESSOR SUSAN BRIGHT   Lecturer and McGregor Fellow in Law, New College, University of Oxford

PROFESSOR DOUGLAS BRODIE   Professor of Employment Law, and Head of School, School of Law, Edinburgh University

PROFESSOR SIMON BRONITT   ANU College of Law, The Australian National University

PROFESSOR ROGER BROWNSWORD   Director of TELOS and Professor of Law, King's College London

PROFESSOR TREVOR BUCK   Professor of Socio-Legal Studies, De Montfort University, Leicester

PROFESSOR RICHARD BUCKLEY   Professor of Law, University of Reading

DR MELISSA BULL   Lecturer, School of Crimininology and Criminal Justice, Griffith University

ASSOCIATE PROFESSOR DORIS BUSS   Associate Professor, Law Department, Carleton University

PROFESSOR WILLIAM BUTLER   John Edward Fowler Distinguished Professor of Law, Dickinson School of Law, Pennsylvania State University; Emeritus Professor of Comparative Law, University of London

PROFESSOR PETER BUTT   Professor of Land Law and Legal Drafting, University of Sydney

PROFESSOR JOHN W CAIRNS   Professor of Legal History, University of Edinburgh

MR ANDREW CAMPBELL   Director of the Centre for Business Law and Practice and Reader in International Banking and Finance Law, School of Law, University of Leeds

MS MAIA CAMPBELL Research Fellow, Indigenous Peoples Law and Policy Program, University of Arizona

PROFESSOR TOM CAMPBELL Director, Centre for Applied Philosophy and Public Ethics (CAPPE), Charles Sturt University

PROFESSOR PETER CANE Distinguished Professor of Law, John Fleming Centre for Advancement of Legal Research, The Australian National University College of Law

PATRICK CANNON Barrister, Tax Chambers, 15 Old Square

DR EUGENIA CARACCIOLO DI TORELLA Lecturer in Law, University of Leicester

HELEN CARR Senior Lecturer, Kent Law School. University of Kent

PROFESSOR PETER CARTWRIGHT Professor of Consumer Protection Law, School of Law, University of Nottingham

MS HAZEL CARTY Reader in Law, Manchester University

DR PAUL CAVILL Lecturer in Early Modern History, Bangor University

PROFESSOR RUTH CHADWICK Distinguished Research Professor, Cardiff University

PROFESSOR HILARY CHARLESWORTH Australian Research Council Federation Fellow, Australian National University

PROFESSOR BRIAN CHEFFINS SJ Berwin Professor of Corporate Law, Faculty of Law, University of Cambridge

PROFESSOR BEN CHIGARA Research Professor of International Laws, Brunel Law School, Brunel University

PROFESSOR CHRISTINE CHINKIN Professor of International Law, London School of Economics and Political Science; Matrix Chambers

DR RYSZARD CHOLEWINSKI Labour Migration Specialist, Migration Policy, Research and Communications, International Organization for Migration (IOM)

PROFESSOR EMILIOS CHRISTODOULIDIS Professor of Legal Theory, School of Law, University of Glasgow

PROFESSOR ROBIN CHURCHILL Professor of International Law, University of Dundee

DR ANDREW CLARK Senior Lecturer, School of Law and Social Science, University of Plymouth

PROFESSOR DAVID S CLARK Maynard and Bertha Wilson Professor of Law, Willamette University, Salem, Oregon, USA

CHRIS CLARKE Consultant, Environmental Law & Policy, Faculty of Laws, University College, London

MR PETER CLARKE Fellow and Tutor in Law, Jesus College, University of Oxford, and Barrister

PROFESSOR LUKE CLEMENTS Cardiff Law School

MARK COATES Head of Legal and Business Affairs, Music and Brands Ltd, London

PROFESSOR RAYMOND COCKS Professor of Law, University of Keele

DR RICHARD COLLIER Professor of Law, University of Newcastle

PROFESSOR HUGH COLLINS Professor of English Law, London School of Economics and Political Science

PROFESSOR JOANNE CONAGHAN Professor of Law and Head of Kent Law School, University of Kent

DR MATTHEW CONAGLEN   Lecturer, University of Cambridge

CLARE CONNELLY   Senior Lecturer, School of Law, University of Glasgow

DR ANTHONY J. CONNOLLY   Senior Lecturer, Law School, Australian National University

PROFESSOR ELIZABETH COOKE   Solicitor; Professor of Law, University of Reading

DR NEIL COOKSON   Director, North East Archaeologcal Research

PROFESSOR DAVINA COOPER   Professor of Law & Political Theory, University of Kent

PROFESSOR BRENDA COSSMAN   Professor of Law, Faculty of Law, University of Toronto

DR KEVIN COSTELLO   Lecturer in Law, Faculty of Law, University College, Dublin

PROFESSOR ROGER COTTERRELL   Anniversary Professor of Legal Theory, Queen Mary and Westfield College, University of London

PROFESSOR DAVID COWAN   Professor of Law and Policy, University of Bristol, and Barrister, Arden Chambers, London

PROFESSOR FIONA COWNIE   Professor of Law, Keele University

DR NEVILLE COX   Senior Lecturer in Law, Trinity College Dublin

MS LETITIA CRABB   Senior Lecturer, School of Law, The University of Reading

PROFESSOR PAUL CRAIG   Professor of English Law, St John's College, University of Oxford

PROFESSOR IAN CRAM   Professor of Comparative Constitutional Law, School of Law, Leeds University

ROSS CRANSTON FBA   Judge, High Court; Visiting Professor, London School of Economics and Political Science

DR RACHAEL CRAUFURD SMITH   Senior Lecturer, Europa Institute, University of Edinburgh

PROFESSOR ADAM CRAWFORD   Director of the Centre for Criminal Justice Studies & Chair of Criminology, University of Leeds

PROFESSOR JAMES CRAWFORD   Whewell Professor of International Law, University of Cambridge

PROFESSOR FRANÇOIS CRÉPEAU   Professor of International Law, Canada Research Chair in International Migration Law, Scientific Director, Centre for International Studies (CÉRIUM) University of Montreal

PROFESSOR MARY E CROCK   Professor of Public Law, Faculty of Law, The University of Sydney

PROFESSOR ROBERT CRYER   Professor of International and Criminal Law, Birmingham Law School, University of Birmingham

MS HOLLY CULLEN   Reader in Law, Durham University

MR PETER CUMPER   Senior Lecturer, Law School, University of Leicester

PROFESSOR CHRIS CUNNEEN   New South Global Chair in Criminology, The University of New South Wales

MAHER M DABBAH   Barrister and Director, ICC, School of Law, Queen Mary, University of London

PROFESSOR TERENCE DAINTITH   Professorial Fellow, Institute of Advanced Legal Studies, University of London

PROFESSOR GERHARD DANNEMANN   Professor of English Law, British Economy and Politics at the Humboldt-Universität, Berlin

PROFESSOR CATHERINE DAUVERGNE   Canada Research Chair in Migration Law, University of British Columbia

DR ANNE C L DAVIES   Reader in Public Law, University of Oxford; Fellow and Tutor in Law, Brasenose College, Oxford

PROFESSOR MARGARET DAVIES   Professor of Law, Flinders University

ADVOCATE GORDON DAWES   Partner, Ozannes, Advocates and Notaries Public, Guernsey

PROFESSOR NORMA DAWSON   Professor of Law, Queen's University, Belfast

LUDOVIC DE WALDEN   Litigation Partner, Lane & Partners LLP

DR RONAN DEAZLEY   Reader in Law, Birmingham Law School, University of Birmingham

BARONESS RUTH DEECH   Independent Adjudicator for Higher Education

MARIE DEMETRIOU   Barrister, Brick Court Chambers, London

PROFESSOR EILEEN DENZA   Visiting Professor of Law, University College London

PROFESSOR SARAH DERRINGTON   Professor of Law, University of Queensland

PROFESSOR JOHN DEWAR   Deputy Vice Chancellor (Academic), Griffith University

PROFESSOR BRICE DICKSON   Professor of International and Comparative Law, Queen's University Belfast

MS ALISON DIDUCK   Reader in Law, University College London

DR ALAN DIGNAM   Reader in Corporate Law, School of Law, Queen Mary, University of London

PROFESSOR ROBERT DINGWALL   Director, Institute for Science and Society, University of Nottingham

PROFESSOR DAVID DIXON   Dean, Faculty of Law, University of New South Wales, Sydney, Australia

DR MARTIN DIXON   Reader in the Law of Real Property, University of Cambridge

DR CHERYL DOLDER   Law Lecturer, Kent Law School, University of Kent

PROFESSOR MICHAEL DOUGAN   Professor of European Law and Jean Monnet Chair in EU Law, Liverpool Law School, University of Liverpool

PROFESSOR GILLIAN DOUGLAS   Head of Cardiff Law School, Cardiff University.

PROFESSOR LAWRENCE DOUGLAS   James J Grosfeld Professor of Law, Jurisprudence and Social Thought, Amherst College, USA

PROFESSOR COSTAS DOUZINAS   Department of Law, Birkbeck College, London

PROFESSOR DAVID DOWNES   Professor Emeritus of Social Policy, Mannheim Centre for Criminology and Criminal Justice, London School of Economics and Political Science

PROFESSOR PETER DRAHOS   Director of the Centre for the Governance of Knowledge and Development, RegNet, Australian National University

PROFESSOR GAVIN DREWRY   Professor of Public Administration, Royal Holloway, University of London

PROFESSOR SARAH DROMGOOLE   Professor of Maritime Law, University of Nottingham

PROFESSOR R A DUFF   Professor, Department of Philosophy, University of Stirling

DONALD DUGDALE Barrister, Auckland

DR RUTH DUKES Lecturer in Employment Law, University of Glasgow

DR ALISON DUNN Senior Lecturer, Newcastle Law School, Newcastle University

DR PAUL DU PLESSIS Lecturer, School of Law, Edinburgh University

PROFESSOR NEIL DUXBURY Law Department, London School of Economics and Political Science

PROFESSOR GERALD DWORKIN Distinguished Professor of Philosophy, University of California, Davis

PROFESSOR DAVID DYZENHAUS Professor of Law and Philosophy, Toronto

PROFESSOR KIM ECONOMIDES Professor of Legal Ethics, University of Exeter

MS SANDRA EDEN Senior Lecturer, University of Edinburgh

BRENDAN EDGEWORTH Head of School, Associate Professor, Faculty of Law, University of New South Wales, Australia

ASSOCIATE PROFESSOR BRENDAN EDGEWORTH Head of School and Associate Professor, Faculty of Law, University of New South Wales

DR GARY EDMOND Associate Professor, School of Law, The University of New South Wales, Australia

PROFESSOR EVELYN ELLIS Professor of Public Law, Birmingham Law School, University of Birmingham

PROFESSOR CLIVE EMSLEY Professor of History and Director of the ICCCR at the Open University

PROFESSOR RICHARD ERICSON formerly Professor of Law and Sociology at the University of British Columbia

DR LAURENCE ETHERINGTON Lecturer and Director of Professional Liaison, York Law School, The University of York

PROFESSOR CHRIS EVANS Professor of Taxation, Australian School of Taxation (Atax), Faculty of Law, The University of New South Wales

DR GAIL E. EVANS Reader in International Trade and Intellectual Property Law, Queen Mary, University of London, Centre for Commercial Law Studies

PROFESSOR JIM EVANS Emeritus Professor, Auckland University

PROFESSOR MALCOLM D EVANS Professor of Public Interntaional Law and Dean, Faculty of Social Sciences and Law, University of Bristol

MR PAUL EVANS Principal Clerk, House of Commons

PROFESSOR RICHARD J EVANS Professor of Modern History, University of Cambridge

PROFESSOR KEITH EWING School of Law, King's College London

MR DAMIAN FALKOWSKI Bencher of Gray's Inn, 4–5 Gray's Inn, Gray's Inn Square, London

PROFESSOR LINDSAY FARMER Professor of Law, University of Glasgow

PROFESSOR JOHN FARRAR Dean, School of Law, University of Waikato, New Zealand

PROFESSOR DAVID FELDMAN, QC, FBA Faculty of Law, University of Cambridge and Judge of the Constitutional Court of Bosnia and Herzegovina

PROFESSOR PAUL FENN Norwich Union Professor of Insurance Studies, Nottingham University Business School

PROFESSOR PHIL FENNELL   Professor of Law, Cardiff Law School

PROFESSOR HELEN FENWICK   Professor of Law, University of Durham

DR SONYA FERNANDEZ   Lecturer in Law, Canterbury Christ Church University

DR JEFF FERRELL   Professor of Sociology, Texas Christian University, USA, and Visiting Professor of Criminology, University of Kent

PROFESSOR MATTHEW FESTENSTEIN   Professor of Political Philosophy, Co-editor, Political Studies, Politics Department, University of York

PROFESSOR VANESSA FINCH   Law Department, London School of Economics and Political Science

PROFESSOR ROBERT FINE   Professor of Sociology, University of Warwick

PROFESSOR MARK FINNANE   ARC Australian Professorial Fellow, ARC Centre of Excellence in Policing and Security, Griffith University, Brisbane, Australia

PROFESSOR ALISON FIRTH   Professor of commercial law, Newcastle Law School, Newcastle University

PROFESSOR RICHARD MICHAEL FISCHL   Professor of Law, University of Connecticut School of Law

DR LIZ FISHER   Fellow in Law, Corpus Christi College, University of Oxford

DR DANIEL FITZPATRICK   College of Law, Australian National University

PROFESSOR JOHN FITZPATRICK   Director Kent Law Clinic, University of Kent

PROFESSOR PETER FITZPATRICK   Anniversary Professor of Law, School of Law, Birkbeck, London

DR TATIANA FLESSAS   Lecturer in Law, London School of Economics and Political Science

PROFESSOR JOHN FLOOD   Professor of Law and Sociology, University of Westminster, and Visiting Professor of Law, University of Miami School of Law

DR CHRISTINE FORSTER   Law Faculty, University of New South Wales

PROFESSOR CHRISTOPHER FORSYTH   Professor of Public Law and Private International Law, University of Cambridge

PROFESSOR NIGEL FOSTER   Jean Monnet Professor of European Law, and Deputy Vice Chancellor, The University of Buckingham

DR SARA FOVARGUE   Lecturer, Law School, Bowland North, Lancaster University

DR DAVID FOX   University Lecturer in Law; University of Cambridge

LADY HAZEL FOX CMG QC   4/5 Grays Inn Square, Grays Inn, London

PROFESSOR MARIE FOX   Professor of Law, School of Law, Keele University

PROFESSOR MARK FREEDLAND   Tutorial Fellow in Law, St John's College, University of Oxford

PROFESSOR JUDITH FREEDMAN   KPMG Professor of Taxation Law, University of Oxford

PROFESSOR MICHAEL FREEMAN   Professor of English Law, University College London

DR SANDRA FRISBY   Baker & McKenzie Associate Professor and Reader in Corporate and Commercial Law, School of Law, University of Nottingham

PROFESSOR MARK FURSE   Professor of Competition Law and Policy, University of Glasgow

PROFESSOR MICHAEL GAGARIN   James R Dougherty, Jr. Centennial Professor of Classics, Department of Classics, University of Texas

MR RICHARD GARDINER, PROFESSOR JOHN GARDNER   Professor of Jurisprudence, University of Oxford

DR MALCOLM GASKILL   Reader in Early Modern History, University of East Anglia

PROFESSOR JAMES THUO GATHII   Governor George E. Pataki Professor of International Commercial Law, Albany Law School, USA

PROFESSOR CONOR GEARTY   Professor of Human Rights Law, London School of Economics and Political Science

ASSOCIATE PROFESSOR ANDREW GEDDIS   Faculty of Law, University of Otago, New Zealand

DR MARKUS GEHRING   Lecturer in International Law, Centre of International Studies, Robinson College, Cambridge

DR JOSHUA GETZLER   Fellow in Law and Reader in Legal History, St Hugh's College and University of Oxford

NAVRAJ SINGH GHALEIGH   Lecturer in Public Law, Edinburgh Law School, University of Edinburgh

PROFESSOR THOMAS GIBBONS   Halliwells Professor of Law, University of Manchester

DR MATTHEW J GIBNEY   University Reader in Politics and Forced Migration, University of Oxford

PROFESSOR GEOFF GILBERT   Professor of Law, Human Rights Centre, University of Essex

PROFESSOR PAULA GILIKER   Professor of Comparative Obligations Law, University of Bristol

DR DAVID W J GILL   Reader in Mediterranean Archaeology, Swansea University

DR MARK GODFREY   Lecturer in Scots Law, University of Glasgow

DR RICHARD GOLDBERG   Reader in Law, School of Law, University of Aberdeen

PROFESSOR PHYLLIS GOLDFARB   Jacob Burns Foundation Professor of Clinical Law and Associate Dean for Clinical Affairs, George Washington University Law School

PROFESSOR ANDREW GOLDSMITH   Professor of Law and Criminal Justice, Flinders University

PROFESSOR PETER GOODRICH   Director of the Program in Law and Humanities, Cardozo School of Law, New York

PROFESSOR GUY S GOODWIN-GILL   Senior Research Fellow, All Souls College, University of Oxford

PROFESSOR JAMES GORDLEY   W R Irby Distinguished University Professor, Tulane Law School

PROFESSOR WENDY GORDON   Professor of Law and Paul J Liacos Scholar in Law, Boston University School of Law, USA

MS EMILY GRABHAM   Research Fellow, Centre for Law, Gender and Sexuality, Kent Law School

PROFESSOR NIGEL P GRAVELLS   Professor of English Law, School of Law, University of Nottingham

PROFESSOR CHRISTINE GRAY   Dean of Trinity College, Cambridge, Professor of International Law, University of Cambridge and National University of Singapore

PROFESSOR KEVIN GRAY   Professor of Law, Trinity College, Cambridge

MS ANNA GREAR   Senior Lecturer in Law, Bristol Law School, University of the West of England, Bristol

MR DANIEL GREENBERG   Parliamentary Counsel, Office of the Parliamentary Counsel

PROFESSOR CAROL J GREENHOUSE   Professor and Chair, Department of Anthropology, Princeton University

DR REBECCA GREENLAND   Kent Law School, Eliot College, University of Kent

PROFESSOR NICHOLAS GRIEF   Head of the Law Department and Steele Raymond LLP Professor of Law, Bournemouth University

PROFESSOR STEPHEN GRIFFIN   University of Wolverhampton

PROFESSOR JOHN GRIFFITHS   Emeritus Professor ofSociology of Law, University of Groningen

MR LYNDEN GRIGGS   Senior Lecturer, Faculty of Law, University of Tasmania

PROFESSOR JOHN O HALEY   Wiley B. Rutledge Professor of Law, School of Law, Washington University in St Louis

PROFESSOR MICHAEL HALEY   Professor of Property Law, Keele University

PROFESSOR SIMON HALLIDAY   Professor of Law, Strathclyde University

DR PHIL HANDLER   Lecturer in Law, Keele University

MR IVAN HARE   Barrister, Blackstone Chambers, Temple

PROFESSOR JOHN HARRINGTON   Professor of Law, University of Liverpool

DR NATHAN HARRIS   Fellow, Regulatory Institutions Network (Regnet), Australian National University

PROFESSOR NEVILLE HARRIS   Professor of Law, School of Law, The University of Manchester

PROFESSOR COLIN HARVEY   Head of School of Law, Queens University Belfast

PROFESSOR KEITH HAWKINS   Professor Emeritus of Law and Society, University of Oxford, and Fellow Emeritus of Oriel College, Oxford

PROFESSOR STEVE HEDLEY   Faculty of Law, University College Cork

PROFESSOR FRANCES HEIDENSOHN   Visiting Professor, Department of Sociology, London School of Economics and Political Science

PROFESSOR R H HELMHOLZ   Ruth Wyatt Rosenson Distinguished Service Professor, University of Chicago Law School

MR JONATHAN HERRING   Fellow in Law; Exeter College, University of Oxford

PROFESSOR TAMARA HERVEY   Professor of Law, The University of Sheffield

DR VEERLE HEYVAERT   Lecturer in Law, London School of Economics and Political Science

MR ROBIN HICKEY   Lecturer in Law, Queen's University Belfast

PROFESSOR JENNIFER HILL   Professor of Corporate Law, Sydney Law School

PROFESSOR CHRIS HILSON   Professor of Law, University of Reading

PROFESSOR CHRISTOPHER HIMSWORTH   Professor of Administrative Law, University of Edinburgh

MS BRONAGH HINDS   Senior Practitioner Fellow, Institute of Governance, Public Policy and Social Research, School of Law, Queens University Belfast

DR MERCEDES S HINTON   Nuffield Research Fellow, London School of Economics and Political Science

PROFESSOR LESLEY HITCHENS   Professor of Law, University of Technology Sydney, Australla

DR CHRISTOPHER HODGES   Head, Research Programme on Civil Justice Systems, Centre for Socio-Legal Studies, University of Oxford

DR JANE HOLDER   Reader, Faculty of Laws, University College London

PROFESSOR SØREN HOLM   Professorial Fellow in Bioethics, Cardiff Law School & Professor of Medical Ethics II, University of Oslo

JOSHUA HOLMES   Barrister, Monckton Chambers, Raymond Buildings, Gray's Inn London

PROFESSOR ROSS HOMEL   Professor of Criminology and Criminal Justice; Director, Strategic Research Program for the Social and Behavioural Sciences; Deputy Director, Key Centre for Ethics, Law, Justice & Governance, Griffith University, Australia

DR SIMON HONEYBALL   Senior Lecturer in Law, Faculty of Law, University of Exeter

PROFESSOR TONY HONORÉ   All Souls College, University of Oxford

MR DAVID HOOD   Guest Lecturer, London School of Economics and Political Science

PROFESSOR ROGER HOOD   Professor Emeritus of Criminology, University of Oxford, and Emeritus Fellow, All Souls College, Oxford

DR PETER P HOUTZAGER   Fellow, Institute of Development Studies (IDS), University of Sussex

LAURA HOYANO   Fellow & Tutor in Law, Wadham College, University of Oxford

DR CAROLYN HOYLE   Reader in Criminology, Centre for Criminology, University of Oxford

DR ANTHEA HUCKLESBY   Senior Lecturer in Criminal Justice, University of Leeds

PROFESSOR JOHN HUDSON   Professor of Legal History, University of St Andrews

PROFESSOR ROSEMARY HUNTER   Professor of Law, University of Kent

PROFESSOR DENNIS HUTCHINSON   William Rainey Harper Professor and Senior Lecturer in Law, The University of Chicago

PROFESSOR DAVID IBBETSON   Regius Professor of Civil Law; University of Cambridge

PROFESSOR PADDY IRELAND   Professor of Law, Kent Law School

DR RICHARD W IRELAND   Senior Lecturer, Department of Law and Criminology, Aberystwyth University

DR VENKAT IYER   Senior Lecturer in Law, The University of Ulster, Northern Ireland, and Editor of The Commonwealth Lawyer

DR SYBIL M JACK   Department of History, The University of Sydney, Australia

PROFESSOR BERNARD JACKSON   Alliance Professor of Modern Jewish Studies, University of Manchester

PROFESSOR EMILY JACKSON   Professor of Law, London School of Economics and Political Science

PROFESSOR JOHN JACKSON   School of Law, Queen's University Belfast

MR JUSTICE RUPERT JACKSON   Royal Courts of Justice

JOSEPH JACOB   Reader in Civil Justice, Law Department, London School of Economics and Political Science

DR MARK JAMES   Reader in Law, Salford Law School, University of Salford

MS SUHRAIYA JIVRAJ   PhD candidate/Researcher/Teacher in Public Law, Kent Law School, University of Kent

DR ANDREW JOHNSTON   Senior Lecturer, University of Queensland

MR ANGUS JOHNSTON   University Lecturer in Law, Faculty of Law, University of Cambridge; and Trinity Hall, Cambridge

PROFESSOR CAROL JONES   Professor of Law, Law School, University of Glamorgan

DR NEIL JONES   Uniiversity Senior Lecturer in Law, University of Cambridge

DR WALTER KÄLIN   Professor of Constitutional and International Law, Institute of Public Law, University of Bern, Switzerland

MS FELICITY KAGANAS   Reader, Brunel Law School, Brunel University

PROFESSOR EVANCE KALULA   Professor of Law and Director, Institute of Development and Labour Law, University of Cape Town

PROFESSOR ANDREW KEAY   Professor of Corporate and Commercial Law, School of Law, University of Leeds

PROFESSOR FERGUS KELLY   Director, School of Celtic Studies, Dublin

ASSOCIATE PROFESSOR ANDREW KENYON   Director CMCL-Centre for Media and Communications Law, Melbourne Law School, University of Melbourne

PROFESSOR JOHN KEOWN   Professor of Christian Ethics, and Visiting Professor of Law, Jurisprudence and Bioethics, Kennedy Institute of Ethics, Georgetown University, Washington

PROFESSOR BRUCE KERCHER   Emeritus Professor of Law, Macquarie University

DAVID KERSHAW   Law Department, London School of Economics and Political Science

DR MARY KEYES   Associate Professor, Griffith Law School, Griffith University, Queensland

KIRSTY KEYWOOD   Senior Lectuer in Law, School of Law, The University of Manchester

DR SHANE KILCOMMINS   Senior Lecturer, University College Cork, Ireland

PROFESSOR MICHAEL KING   School of Law, University of Reading

PROFESSOR HEINZ KLUG   Evjue-Bascom Professor of Law, University of Wisconsin Law School, Madison, WI, USA and Senior Honorary Research Associate in the School of Law, University of the Witwatersrand, Johannesburg, South Africa

DR AUDREY KOBAYASHI   Professor and Queen's Research Chair, Department of Geography, Queen's University

DR KHALID KOSER   Fellow, The Brookings Institution

PROFESSOR MARTTI KOSKENNIEMI   Academy Professor, University of Helsinki

PROFESSOR MARTIN KRETSCHMER   Director, Centre for Intellectual Property Policy & Management Bournemouth University

PROFESSOR BERT KRITZER   Professor of Law, William Mitchell College of Law and Professor of Political Science and Law emeritus, University of Wisconsin

DR JENNY KUPER   Research Fellow, Law Department London School of Economics and Political Science

PROFESSOR NICOLA LACEY   Professor of Criminal Law and Legal Theory, London School of Economics and Political Science

DR ROBERT LANE   Senior Lecturer, School of Law, University of Edinburgh

CHIEF JUSTICE PIUS LANGA   Constitutional Court of South Africa

DR BETTINA LANGE   Lecturer in Law and Regulation, University of Oxford

PROFESSOR SANDRA LAVENEX   Professor of International Politics, University of Lucerne, Switzerland

MS ANNA LAWSON   Senior Lecturer, School of Law, University of Leeds

DR ELLIE LEE   Senior Lecturer in Social Policy, University of Kent

PROFESSOR NATALIE LEE   Professor of Tax Law and Head of School, School of Law, University of Southampton

PROFESSOR IAN LEIGH   Professor of Law and Co-Director of the Durham Human Rights Centre, University of Durham

PROFESSOR ANDREW LE SUEUR   Professor of Public Law, Queen Mary, University of London

DR FIONA LEVERICK   Senior Lecturer in Law, University of Glasgow

PROFESSOR MICHAEL LEVI   Professor of Criminology, Cardiff University, School of Social Sciences

PROFESSOR DAVID LEWIS   Professor of Employment Law, Middlesex University Geoffrey Lewis

PROFESSOR PENNEY LEWIS   Professor of Law, King's College London.

MR PHILIP LEWIS   Associate Research Fellow, Centre for Socio-Legal Studies, University of Oxford

PROFESSOR RICHARD LEWIS   Professor of Law, Cardiff University

PROFESSOR SANDRA LIEBENBERG   H F Oppeheimer Professor in Human Rights Law, Department of Public Law, Stellenbosch University, South Africa

MR CRAIG LIND   Senior Lecturer in Law, School of Law, University of Sussex

PROFESSOR DOUGLAS LINDER   University of Missouri-Kansas City School of Law

PROFESSOR IAN J LLOYD   Professor of Information Technology Law, University of Strathclyde

PROFESSOR MICHAEL LOBBAN   Professor of Legal History, School of Law, Queen Mary, University of London

PROFESSOR EVA LOMNICKA   Professor Of Law, King's College London; and Barrister, Four New Square Chambers

DR ARLIE LOUGHNAN   Lecturer, Faculty of Law, University of Sydney, Australia

MR GLEN LOUTZENHISER   Career Development Fellow in Tax Law, Christ Church, University of Oxford

PROFESSOR VAUGHAN LOWE QC   Chichele Professor of Public International Law, University of Oxford

PROFESSOR JOHN LOWRY   Vice Dean, Faculty of Laws, University College London

PROFESSOR WILLIAM LUCY   School of Law, University of Manchester

MS LAURA LUNDY   Barrister at Law, School of Law, Queen's University Belfast

MARK LUNNEY   Associate Professor of Law, University of New England, Armidale, Australia

PETER LUTHER   Senior Lecturer, Department of Law, University of Essex.

PROFESSOR GEOFFREY MACCORMACK   Emeritus Professor of Jurisprudence, University of Aberdeen

SIR NEIL MACCORMICK   Professor Emeritus of Public Law and the Law of Nature and Nations, University of Edinburgh

MR ANGUS MACCULLOCH   Senior Lecturer, Lancaster Univeristy

PROFESSOR RONNIE MACKAY   Professor of Criminal Policy and Mental Health De Montfort University Law School, De Montfort University, Leicester

ROBIN MACKENZIE   Director of Medical Law and Ethics, Kent Law School, University of Kent

RUTH MACKENZIE   Principal Research Fellow and Assistant Director, Centre for International Courts and Tribunals, Faculty of Laws, University College London

PROFESSOR AUDREY MACKLIN   Faculty of Law, University of Toronto, Canada

MAVIS MACLEAN CBE   Director, Oxford Centre for Family Law and Policy, Department of Social Policy and Social Work, University of Oxford

MS CATHARINE MACMILLAN   Senior Lecturer, Queen Mary, University of London.

PROFESSOR FIONA MACMILLAN   Corporation of London Professor of Law, Birkbeck, University of London

DR M R T MACNAIR   Tutor in Law, St Hugh's College, University of Oxford

PROFESSOR IAIN MACNEIL   Alexander Stone Professor of Commercial Law, University of Glasgow

DR WILLIAM MACNEIL   Associate Professor of Law, Griffith Law School, Nathan Campus, Australia

PROFESSOR HECTOR L MACQUEEN FBA FRSE   Professor of Private Law, Edinburgh Law School, University of Edinburgh

PROFESSOR RICHARD MACRORY QC   Professor of Environmental Law, Faculty of Laws, University College London

DR ALEX MAGAISA   Senior Lecturer, Kent Law School, Eliot College, University of Kent

DR TOVE H MALLOY   Senior Researcher, Institute for Minority Rights

PROFESSOR COLIN MANCHESTER   Professor of Licensing Law, University of Warwick

PROFESSOR DESMOND MANDERSON   Canada Research Chair in Law and Discourse, Faculty of Law, Mcgill University

PROFESSOR WADE MANSELL   Professor of Law, University of Kent

PROFESSOR SUSAN MARKS   Professor of Public International Law, King's College London

PROFESSOR ANDREI MARMOR   Maurice Jones Jr, Professor of Law and Professor of Philosophy, Center of Law and Philosophy, University of Southern California, USA

PROFESSOR SHADD MARUNA   Professor of Justice and Human Development, School of Law, Queen's University Belfast

PROFESSOR JUDITH MASSON   Professor of Socio-Legal Studies, University of Bristol

PROFESSOR PAUL MATTHEWS   Visiting Professor, King's College London and HM Coroner, City of London

CAROLINE MAUGHAN   Principal Lecturer in Law, Bristol Law School, University of the West of England.

DR ALLYSON N MAY   Assistant Professor, Department of History, University of Western Ontario

PROFESSOR LARRY MAY   Professor of Philosophy, Washington University in St Louis, and Strategic Research Professor, Centre for Applied Philosophy and Public Ethics (CSU) in Canberra

DR JANE MCADAM   Senior Lecturer and Director of International Law Programs, Faculty of Law, University of New South Wales

PROFESSOR RICHARD H MCADAMS   Bernard D. Meltzer Professor, Professor of Law, University of Chicago Law School

PROFESSOR PATRICK MCAUSLAN   Professor of Law, School of Law, Birkbeck College, University of London

MR NICHOLAS MCBRIDE   Fellow, Pembroke College, Cambridge

PROFESSOR STEPHEN MCCAFFREY   Distinguished Professor and Scholar and Professor of Law; and Counselor, Institute for Sustainable Development, McGeorge School of Law, University of the Pacific, USA

MS JULIE MCCANDLESS   Research Student, Keele University

PROFESSOR AILEEN MCCOLGAN   Professor of Human Rights Law, King's College London

KIRSTEN MCCONNACHIE   Researcher, Queen's University Belfast, School of Law

PROFESSOR GERARD MCCORMACK   School of Law, University of Leeds

PROFESSOR ROBERT MCCORQUODALE   Director of the British Institute of International and Comparative Law, and Professor of International Law and Human Rights at the University of Nottingham

DR CLAIRE MCDIARMID   Senior Lecturer in Law, University of Strathclyde

PROFESSOR JOHN MCELDOWNEY   Professor of Law and Director of LLM in EU Law in the World Economy, School of Law, The University of Warwick

PROFESSOR KIERAN MCEVOY   Professor of Law and Transitional Justice, School of Law, Queens University Belfast

JEAN MCFADDEN   was Senior lecturer in Law University of Strathclyde

MR BEN MCFARLANE   University Lecturer in Property Law & Trusts, University of Oxford, and Fellow of Trinity College, Oxford

MR DONALD MCGILLIVRAY   Senior Lecturer, Kent Law School

PROFESSOR CLARE MCGLYNN   Professor of Law, Durham University

PROFESSOR JEAN MCHALE   Professor of Law, University of Leicester

DR P G MCHUGH   University Reader, Sidney Sussex College, Cambridge

PROFESSOR JOHN MCLAREN   Emeritus Professor of Law, University of Victoria, British Columbia

DR LARA MCMURTRY   Lecturer in Law, Keele University

ASSOCIATE-PROFESSOR SHAUN MCVEIGH   Academic, Melbourne Law School, Melbourne Universitty

DR ROSE MELIKAN   Fellow, St Catharine's College, Cambridge

DR EMMANUEL MELISSARIS   Lecturer in Law, Law Department, London School of Economics and Political Science

MAURICE MENDELSON QC   Barrister, Blackstone Chambers London, and Emeritus Professor of International Law in the University of London

PROFESSOR CARRIE MENKEL-MEADOW   AB Chettle Jr. Professor of Law, Dispute Resolution and Civil Procedure Georgetown University Law Center

PROFESSOR DR WERNER MENSKI   Professor of South Asian Laws, School of Law, The School of Oriental and African Studies, University of London

DR PAUL MEREDITH   Reader in Law, University of Southampton

PROFESSOR ALAN MERRY   Head of Department, Department of Anaesthesiology, Faculty of Medical and Health Sciences, University of Auckland and Auckland City Hospital

MR JOHN MESHER   Social Security and Child Support Commissioner; Professor Associate, University of Sheffield

DR GEORGE MESZAROS   Associate Professor, School of Law, University of Warwick

PROFESSOR DENISE MEYERSON   Professor of Law, Division of Law, Macquarie University

PROFESSOR DAVID MIERS   Professor of Law, Cardiff Law School

PROFESSOR CHRIS MILLER   Professor of Environmental Law, School of Environment and Life Sciences, Salford University

PROFESSOR JOHN MILLER   Emeritus Professor of Law, University of Birmingham

PROFESSOR SUSAN MILLNS   Professor of Law, University of Sussex

PROFESSOR DAVID MILMAN   Professor of Law, Lancaster University

DR M C MIROW   Associate Professor of Law, Florida International University College of Law

JONATHAN MOFFETT   Barrister, Inner Temple

PROFESSOR NIAMH MOLONEY   Professor of Capital Markets Law, University of Nottingham

MR GIORGIO MONTI   Senior Lecturer, Law Department, London School of Economics and Political Science

DR CLAIRE MOON   Lecturer, Department of Sociology/Centre for the Study of Human Rights, London School of Economics and Political Science

PROFESSOR RICHARD MOORHEAD   Deputy Head of School, Cardiff Law School, Cardiff University

PROFESSOR LESLIE J MORAN   School of Law Birkbeck College, London

PROFESSOR MAYO MORAN   Dean and James M Tory Professor of Law, University of Toronto, Faculty of Law

MS JILL MORGAN   Reader in Property Law, Swansea University

MR JONATHAN MORGAN   Fellow in Law, Christ's College, Cambridge

PROFESSOR JOHN MORISON   Professor of Jurisprudence, Queen's University Belfast

PROFESSOR GILLIAN MORRIS   Barrister, Matrix Chambers; Professor Associate, Brunel University; Honorary Professor, Warwick Business School, University of Warwick

PROFESSOR BRADFORD W MORSE   Professor of Law, Common Law Section, University of Ottawa

DR STEWART MOTHA   Senior Lecturer in Law, Kent Law School, University of Kent, Canterbury

MS HELEN MOUNTFIELD   Barrister, Matrix Chambers

PROFESSOR ALASTAIR MOWBRAY   Professor of Public Law, School of Law, University of Nottingham

PROFESSOR PETER MUCHLINSKI   Professor in International Commercial Law, The School of Law, The School of Oriental and African Studies, University of London

MISS JANE MULCAHY   Barrister, Blackstone Chambers

DR SIOBHÁN MULLALLY   Co-Director Centre for Criminal Justice and Human Rights, and Senior Lecturer, Faculty of Law, University College Cork, Ireland

PROFESSOR DAVID MULLAN   Professor Emeritus, Faculty of Law, Queen's University, Kingston, Ontario, Canada

MR NICHOLAS MULLANY   Barrister, 3 Serjeants' Inn, London

THE HONOURABLE SIR JAMES MUNBY   High Court Family Division, Royal Courts of Justice, London

DR RODERICK MUNDAY   Reader in Law, University of Cambridge

PROFESSOR VANESSA MUNRO   Professor of Socio-Legal Studies, University of Nottingham

PROFESSOR THERESE MURPHY   Professor of Law & Critical Theory, School of Law, University of Nottingham

PROFESSOR TIM MURPHY   Law Department, London School of Economics and Political Science

MR ANDREW MURRAY   Reader in Law, London School of Economics and Political Science

PROFESSOR ANTHONY MUSSON   Professor of Legal History, University of Exeter

PROFESSOR NGAIRE NAFFINE   Law School, The University of Adelaide, Australia

MISS URVASI NAIDOO   Senior Counsel & Company Secretary, International Cricket Council

PROFESSOR DELPHINE NAKACHE   Faculty of Law, University of Alberta, Canada

SIBONGILE NDASHE   Lawyer, Equality Programme, INTERIGHTS

PROFESSOR TIM NEWBURN   Professor of Criminology and Social Policy, London School of Economics and Political Science

PROFESSOR CHRISTOPHER NEWDICK   Professor of Health Law, University of Reading

PROFESSOR RICHARD NOBLES   Professor of Law, Queen Mary, University of London

MR R C NOLAN   Reader in Corporate & Trust Law, University of Cambridge, and Fellow & Director of Studies in Law, St John's College, Cambridge

MS HEATHER NORTON   Barrister, QEB Hollis Whiteman

DR TONIA NOVITZ   Reader in Law, University of Bristol

MR COLM O'CINNEIDE   Senior Lecturer in Law, Faculty of Laws, University College London

DR OKEOGHENE ODUDU   Herchel Smith Lecturer and Deputy Director, Centre for European Legal Studies; Fellow in Law, Emmanuel College, Cambridge

DR GBENGA ODUNTAN   Law School, Eliot College, University of Kent

PROFESSOR ANTHONY OGUS   Professor of Law, School of Law, University of Manchester

PROFESSOR PATRICK O'KEEFE   Adjunct Professor, Research School of Pacific and Asian Studies, Australian National University and Honorary Professor, School of English, Media Studies and Art History, University of Queensland

DR ROGER O'KEEFE   Lecturer in Law, University of Cambridge and Fellow, Magdalene College, Cambridge

PROFESSOR JAMES OLDHAM   St. Thomas More Professor of Law and Legal History, Georgetown University Law Centre

MR JOHN O'LEARY   Senior Lecturer in Law, Anglia Ruskin University

PROFESSOR KEN OLIPHANT   School of Law, University of Bristol

PROFESSOR FRANCES OLSEN   Professor of Law, University of California at Los Angeles

PROFESSOR PAT O'MALLEY   University Professorial Research Fellow, Sydney Law School, The University of Sydney

DR ALEXANDER ORAKHELASHVILI   Junior Research Fellow, Jesus College, University of Oxford

DR ADA ORDOR   Post-doctoral Fellow, Institute of Development and Labour Law, University of Cape Town

PROFESSOR ANNE ORFORD   Australian Professorial Fellow and Chair of Law Melbourne Law School University of Melbourne

DR FEDERICO ORTINO   Lecturer in International Economic Law, School of Law, King's College London

MRS JANET O'SULLIVAN   Senior Lecturer, Faculty of Law, Cambridge University, and Fellow, Selwyn College, Cambridge

PROFESSOR MARGARET OTLOWSKI   Professor of Law and Deputy Head of School, Faculty of Law, University of Tasmania

MR PAUL OZIN   Barrister, 23 Essex Street, London

MRS NICOLA PADFIELD   Senior Lecturer, University of Cambridge; Fellow of Fitzwilliam College, Cambridge; and Recorder

ASSOCIATE PROFESSOR SUNDHYA PAHUJA   Co-Director, Law and Development Research Programme, Institute for International Law and the Humanities, Melbourne Law School, University of Melbourne

MR DAVID PALFREYMAN   Bursar & Fellow, New College, University of Oxford; and Director, Oxford Centre for Higher Education Policy Studies (OxCHEPS)

PROFESSOR ABDUL PALIWALA   Professor of Law and Director, Law Courseware Consortium and Electronic Law Journals, University of Warwick

DR MARC PALLEMAERTS   Professor of European Environmental Law, University of Amsterdam; Professor of International Environmental Law, Université Libre de Bruxelles

DR STEPHANIE PALMER   Senior Lecturer in Law, Faculty of Law, University of Cambridge; Fellow, Girton College

DR CHRISTINE PARKER   Associate Professor and Reader, and ARC Australian Research Fellow, Melbourne Law School, University of Melbourne

MRS DEBORAH PARRY   Independent Consultant on Consumer Law

DR REENA PATEL   Associate Professor, School of Law, University of Warwick.

PROFESSOR ALAN PATERSON   Director of the Centre for Professional Legal Studies, Strathclyde University

DR SHAUN D PATTINSON   Reader in Law, Durham University

PROFESSOR GEORGE PAVLAKOS   Research Chair in Globalisation and Legal Theory Universiteit Antwerpen, Belgium; and Professor of Globalisation and Legal Theory, University of Glasgow

PROFESSOR KEN PEASE   Visiting Professor and Fellow, University College London

PROFESSOR MARKKU PELTONEN   Professor of Intellectual History, University of Helsinki

PROFESSOR JAMES PENNER   Faculty of Laws, University College London

WARREN PHELOPS   Partner and Head of Sports Group, K&L Gates

PROFESSOR GAVIN PHILLIPSON   Professor and Director of Undergraduate Studies, Department of Law, University of Durham

DR MARK PHILP   Fellow and Tutor in Politics, Oriel College, University of Oxford

PROFESSOR ROB PICKARD   Professor of Built Environment and Heritage Conservation, School of the Built Environment, Northumbria University

DR JUSTINE PILA   University Lecturer in Intellectual Property and Fellow, St Catherine's College, University of Oxford

PROFESSOR CHRISTINE PIPER   Professor, Brunel University

PROFESSOR PASCOE PLEASENCE   Professor of Empirical Legal Studies, University College London

PROFESSOR PATRICK POLDEN   Professor of Law, Law School, Brunel University

ALAIN POTTAGE   Law Department, London School of Economics and Political Science

PROFESSOR EMERITUS WILFRID PREST   Law School and School of History and Politics, University of Adelaide

NICOLETTE PRIAULX   Senior Lecturer, Cardiff Law School, Cardiff University

PROFESSOR DAVID PRICE   Professor of Medical Law, De Montfort University School of Law, Leicester

MS REBECCA PROBERT   Senior Lecturer, University of Warwick

DR CHARLES PROCTOR   Partner, Bird & Bird, London

PROFESSOR TONY PROSSER   Professor of Public Law, University of Bristol

PROFESSOR WESLEY PUE   Nathan T Nemetz Professor of Legal History, Faculty of Law, University of British Columbia

PROFESSOR MICHAEL PURDUE   Professor of Law, Department of Law, City University London

MR RAY PURDY   Deputy Director of the Centre for Law and the Environment, Faculty of Laws, University College London

DR OLIVER QUICK   Senior Lecturer in Law, University of Bristol

PROFESSOR DR ASIF QURESHI   Professor of International Economic Law, University of Manchester

DR ERIKA RACKLEY   Lecturer in Law, Durham University

DR PETER RADAN   Associate Professor of Law, Macquarie University, Australia

PROFESSOR FRANCES RADAY   Director, Concord Research Center for Integration of International Law in Israel, College of Management Academic Studies; Visiting Professor, University College London

PROFESSOR FIONA RAITT   Professor of Law, University of Dundee

PROFESSOR IAIN RAMSAY   Professor of Law, Kent Law School, Eliot College, University of Kent

PROFESSOR CATHERINE REDGWELL   Professor of International Law, University College London

PROFESSOR MIKE REDMAYNE   Professor of Law, London School of Economics and Political Science

MS HELEN REECE   Reader in Law, Birkbeck College, University of London

PROFESSOR CHRIS REED   Professor of Electronic Commerce Law, Queen Mary University of London

PROFESSOR JAVAID REHMAN   Professor of International Law, Brunel University

DR EMILY REID   Lecturer in European Law, University of Southampton

PROFESSOR KENNETH REID   Professor of Property Law, University of Edinburgh

PROFESSOR ROBERT REINER   Professor of Criminology, Law Department, London School of Economics and Political Science

PROFESSOR COLIN RENFREW   (Lord Renfrew of Kaimsthorn), Senior Fellow, McDonald Institute for Archaeological Research, and Emeritus Disney Professor of Archaeology in the University of Cambridge

PROFESSOR F M B REYNOLDS   Retired, Formerly Professor of Law at Worcester College, University of Oxford

PROFESSOR ROD RHODES   Professor of Government, University of Tasmania, and Distinguished Professor of Political Science, Australian National University

PROFESSOR GENEVRA RICHARDSON   Professor of Law, School of Law, King's College London

DR JANICE RICHARDSON   Senior Lecturer in Law, University of Exeter

PROFESSOR KERRY RITTICH   Faculty of Law, University of Toronto, Canada

PROFESSOR SIMON ROBERTS   Law Department, London School of Economics and Political Science

PROFESSOR ANDREW ROBERTSON   Professor of Law, University of Melbourne

PROFESSOR GEOFFREY ROBERTSON QC   Doughty Street Chambers, 10–11 Doughty Street, London

PROFESSOR O F ROBINSON   Honorary Research Fellow, School of Law, University of Glasgow

PROFESSOR PAUL H ROBINSON   Colin S Diver Professor of Law, University of Pennsylvania Law School

PROFESSOR PAUL ROCK   Emeritus Professor of Sociology at the London School of Economics and Political Science and Visiting Professor at the University of Pennsylvania

PROFESSOR CHRISTOPHER RODGERS   Professor of Law, and Director of Research, Newcastle Law School, University of Newcastle

MR HORTON ROGERS   Senior Fellow, School of Law, University of Nottingham

PROFESSOR CHRISTOPHER ROOTES   Professor of Environmental Politics and Political Sociology, and Director of the Centre for the Study of Social and Political Movements, University of Kent, Canterbury

PROFESSOR FREDERICK ROSEN   Professor Emeritus of the History of Political Thought, and Honorary Research Fellow, the Bentham Project, University College London

MS ANDREA ROSS   Senior Lecturer, School of Law, University of Dundee

MR PHILIP ROSTANT   Employment Judge, Employment Tribunal

PROFESSOR CRAIG ROTHERHAM   Professor of Law, School of Law, University of Nottingham

PROFESSOR JEREMY ROWAN ROBINSON   Solicitor and Legal Associate of the Royal Town Planning Institute and Emeritus Professor of Law, Aberdeen University

MR JACOB ROWBOTTOM   Lecturer in Law, University of Cambridge

PROFESSOR PETER ROWE   Lancaster University Law School

DR IAN ROXAN   Lecturer in Law and Director of the Tax Programme, London School of Economics and Political Science

PROFESSOR KIM RUBENSTEIN   Director, Centre for International and Public Law, ANU College of Law, Australian National University

PROFESSOR GERRY R RUBIN   Professor of Law, Kent Law School, Kent University Canterbury

PROFESSOR BERNARD RUDDEN   Emeritus Professor of Comparative Law, and Fellow of Brasenose College, University of Oxford

PROFESSOR WILFRID E RUMBLE   Professor Emeritus and Adjunct Professor of Political Science, Vassar College, Poughkeepsie, New York

DR JUDITH RUMGAY

PETER D RUSH   Director of Sovereignty and Jurisdiction Research Program, Melbourne Law School, University of Melbourne

DR MEG RUSSELL   Senior Research Fellow, University College London

PROFESSOR BART RWEZAURA   Advocate, The High Court of Tanzania

DR BERNARD RYAN   Reader in Law, University of Kent

DR MAGNUS RYAN   Peterhouse, Cambridge

PROFESSOR JAMES SALZMAN-SAMUEL MORDECAI   Professor of Environmental Law, Duke Law School

PROFESSOR GEOFFREY SAMUEL   Kent Law School, Eliot College, University of Kent

PROFESSOR ANDREW SANDERS   Professor of Criminal Law and Criminology, School of Law, University of Manchester Ralph Sandland Associate Professor, Faculty of Social Sciences, Law and Education, University of Nottingham

PROFESSOR DAN SAROOSHI   Professor of Public International Law, University of Oxford; and Member, World Trade Organization Dispute Settlement List of Panellists

DR BEN SAUL   Director, Sydney Centre for International Law, Faculty of Law, The University of Sydney

PROFESSOR CHERYL SAUNDERS   Director, Centre for Comparative Constitutional Studies, Melbourne Law School

PROFESSOR DAVID SCHIFF   Professor of Law, Queen Mary, University

PROFESSOR PIERRE SCHLAG   Byron R White Professor of Law

PROFESSOR ULRIKE SCHULTZ   Akademische Oberrätin, Fern Universität in Hagen

PROFESSOR IAIN SCOBBIE   Law Department, School of Oriental & African Studies, London

PROFESSOR ANDREW SCOTT   Professor of European Union Studies School of Law, University of Edinburgh

PROFESSOR COLIN SCOTT   Professor of EU Regulation and Governance, University College Dublin School of Law

MRS JANYS M SCOTT QC   Faculty of Advocates, Edinburgh

PROFESSOR LEN SEALY   S J Berwin Professor Emeritus of Corporate Law and Fellow of Gonville and Caius College, University of Cambridge

PROFESSOR MARY SENEVIRATNE   Director of Research, Nottingham Law School, Nottingham Trent University

DR DAVID M SEYMOUR   Lecturer in Law, School of Law, Lancaster University

PROFESSOR MICHAEL SHANKS   Violet Andrews Whittier Faculty Fellow, Stanford Humanities Center, Stanford University

ROBERT J SHARPE   Justice, Court of Appeal for Ontario

PROFESSOR MALCOLM SHAW QC   Sir Robert Jennings Professor of International Law, University of Leicester; and Barrister, Essex Court Chambers

WILLIAM R SHEATE   Reader in Environmental Assessment, Centre for Environmental Policy, Imperial College London

MR DONALD SHELL   Senior Lecturer in Politics, University of Bristol

PROFESSOR AVROM SHERR   Director, Institute of Advanced Legal Studies

MR ADRIAN SHIPWRIGHT   Barrister, Pump Court Tax Chambers; Visiting Professor at King's College, London; Special Commissioner and VAT Tribunal Chairman

PROFESSOR ROBERT SHOEMAKER   Professor of Eighteenth-Century British History, University of Sheffield

PROFESSOR STEPHEN SHUTE   Professor of Criminal Law and Criminal Justice, Birmingham Law School, University of Birmingham

PROFESSOR SUSAN S SILBEY   Leon and Anne Goldberg Professor of Humanities; Professor of Sociology and Anthropology, and Department Head, Massachusetts Institute of Technology

PROFESSOR JOE SIM   Professor of Criminology, Liverpool John Moores University

PROFESSOR A P SIMESTER   Professor of Law, National University of Singapore; Fellow, Wolfson College, Cambridge

PENELOPE SIMONS   Associate Professor Faculty of Law Common Law Section, University of Ottawa

PROFESSOR A W BRIAN SIMPSON QC, FBA and FAAAS   Charles F and Edith J Clyne Professor of Law at the University of Michigan Law School

MR EDWIN SIMPSON   Barclay's Bank Lecturer in Tax Law, Christ Church, University of Oxford

PROFESSOR GERRY SIMPSON   Professor of International Law, London School of Economics and Political Science, and Chair of Law, University of Melbourne Law School

MR ROBERT SIMPSON   Reader in Law, London School of Economics and Political Science

PROFESSOR BOUDEWIJN SIRKS   Regius Professor of Civil Law, University of Oxford

PROFESSOR LOANE SKENE   Professor of Law, Melbourne Law School, University of Melbourne, Australia

PROFESSOR A T H SMITH   Pro Vice Chancellor and Dean, Faculty of Law, Victoria University of Wellington, New Zealand

PROFESSOR LIONEL SMITH   James McGill Professor of Law and Director, Quebec Research Centre of Private and Comparative Law, McGill University, Canada

MR PETER SMITH   Reader in Property Law, University of Reading

MR ROGER SMITH   Director, JUSTICE

MR ROGER SMITH   Fellow and Tutor in Law, Magdalen College, University of Oxford

PROFESSOR STEPHEN SMITH   Faculty of Law, McGill University

MR JOHN SNAPE   Associate Professor, School of Law, University of Warwick

PROFESSOR RUTH SOETENDORP   Professor Emerita, Centre for Intellectual Property Policy & Management, Bournemouth University

DR HILARY SOMMERLAD   Professor of Law & Society, Director Centre for Research into Diversity in the Professions, Leeds Metropolitan University

PROFESSOR ANN SOMMERVILLE   Head of Medical Ethics Department, British Medical Association

PROFESSOR PETER SPARKES   Professor of Property Law, University of Southampton

DR ELEANOR SPAVENTA   Reader in Law and Director of the Durham European Law Institute, Department of Law, Durham University

PROFESSOR JOHN RASON SPENCER   Professor of Law, University of Cambridge

PROFESSOR ST JOHN BATES   Director of the Centre for Parliamentary and Legislative Studies, University of Strathclyde Law School

PROFESSOR MARK STALLWORTHY   Co-Director of the Centre for Environmental and Energy Law and Policy, Department of Law, Swansea University

PROFESSOR JANE STAPLETON   Professor of Law, John Fleming Centre for Advancement of Legal Research, The Australian National University College of Law; and Ernest E. Smith Professor of Law, University of Texas School of Law

PROFESSOR JENNY STEELE   Professor of Law, York Law School, University of York

MS ANN STEWART   Reader in Law, School of Law, University of Warwick

PROFESSOR RICHARD STONE   Head of Department of Law , University of Lincoln

DR TIM STRETTON   Associate Professor, History Department, Saint Mary's University, Canada

PROFESSOR CARL STYCHIN   Professor of Law and Social Theory, University of Reading

PROFESSOR BRENDA SUFRIN   Professor of Law, University of Bristol

PROFESSOR DAVID SUGARMAN   Professor of Law and Founding Director, Centre for Law and Society, Lancaster University, Lancaster University Law School

PROFESSOR ROBERT SULLIVAN   Professor of Law, University College London

PROFESSOR MAURICE SUNKIN   Professor of Law, University of Essex

PROFESSOR RICHARD SUSSKIND   Honorary Professor, Gresham College, London

DR ADAM SUTTON   Associate Professor, APC Coordinator, and Deputy Head, Department of Criminology, The University of Melbourne, Australia

DR WARREN SWAIN   Lecturer in Law, Department of Law, Durham University

PROFESSOR VICTOR TADROS   Professor of Criminal Law and Legal Theory, University of Warwick

PROFESSOR MICHAEL TAGGART   Alexander Turner Professor of Law, Faculty of Law, The University of Auckland, New Zealand

DR STEFAN TALMON   Reader in Public International Law, St Anne's College, University of Oxford

PROFESSOR DR JUR & PHIL DITLEV TAMM   Law Researcher and Teacher, University of Copenhagen, Faculty of Law

DR CAROL TAN   Senior Lecturer, Newcastle Law School

PROFESSOR ROBERT TAVERNOR   Professor of Architecture and Urban Design, Cities Programme, London School of Economics and Political Science

JONATHAN TAYLOR   Partner, Bird & Bird Solicitors

PROFESSOR HARVEY TEFF   Professor Emeritus, Durham University

PROFESSOR ANDREW TETTENBORN   Bracton Professor of Law, University of Exeter

MS MERYL THOMAS   Reader in Law, Birmingham City University

PROFESSOR PETER THOMAS   Emeritus Professor of History, University of Aberystwyth

BRIAN THOMPSON   Senior Lecturer, University of Liverpool

PROFESSOR MARK P THOMPSON   Professor of Law and Pro-Vice-Chancellor, University of Leicester

MR ALAN THOMSON   Lecturer in Law, The University of Kent

PROFESSOR MICHAEL THOMSON   Professor of Law, Keele University

PROFESSOR MARGARET THORNTON   Professor of Law, Australian National University

DR ROSY THORNTON   Fellow and Lecturer in Law, Emmanuel College, Cambridge

PROFESSOR JOHN TILEY   Professor of Tax law, University of Cambridge

PROFESSOR MICHEL TISON   Financial Law Institute, Ghent University

HELEN TONER   Associated Professor, School of Law, University of Warwick

MRS JOYCEY TOOHER   Barrister at Law, Victorian Bar, Melbourne, Australia

PROFESSOR PAUL TORREMANS   Professor of Intellectual Property Law, School of Law, University of Nottingham

PATRICIA TUITT   School of Law, Birkbeck College, London

MR RICHARD TUR   Senior Law Fellow, Oriel College, University of Oxford

DR VOLKER TÜRK   Director for Organizational Development and Management, UNHCR Headquarters, Geneva

MR COLIN TURPIN   Emeritus Reader in Public Law, University of Cambridge.

PROFESSOR MARK TUSHNET   William Nelson Cromwell Professor of Law, Harvard Law School

DR CHRISTIAN TWIGG-FLESNER   Reader, Law School, University of Hull

PROFESSOR WILLIAM TWINING   Quain Professor of Jurisprudence Emeritus, University College London and Visiting Professor, University of Miami School of Law

PROFESSOR STEVE UGLOW   Professor of Criminal Justice, Kent Law School, University of Kent

MR JAMES UPCHER   DPhil Candidate in Law, University of Oxford

PROFESSOR JOHN USHER   Professor of European Law and Head of the School of Law, University of Exeter

PROFESSOR MARIANA VALVERDE   Director, Centre of Criminology, University of Toronto

V V VEEDER QC   Essex Court Chambers

DR ELLIOT VERNON, BARRISTER   9 King's Bench Walk, Temple, London

PROFESSOR RUSS VERSTEEG   Professor of Law, New England School of Law

DR SOPHIE VIGNERON   Lecturer, Kent Law School

PROFESSOR CHARLOTTE VILLIERS   University of Bristol

PROFESSOR GRAHAM VIRGO   Professor of English Private Law and Lecturer, University of Cambridge

PROFESSOR DANIEL VISSER   Advocate of the High Court of South Africa, Department of Private Law, Faculty of Law, University of Cape Town

PROFESSOR STEFAN VOGENAUER   Professor of Comparative Law and Fellow of Brasenose College, University of Oxford

PROFESSOR ANDREW VON HIRSCH   Emeritus Honorary Professor of Penal Theory and Penal Law, University of Cambridge; Honorary Fellow, Wolfson College, Cambridge, and Honorary Professor, Faculty of Law, Johann Wolfgang Goethe University, Frankfurt am Main, Germany

PROFESSOR STEPHEN WADDAMS   Goodman/Schipper Professor of Law, University of Toronto

PROFESSOR LISA WADDINGTON   European Disability Forum Chair in European Disability Law, Maastricht University (NLs)

DR CHARLOTTE WAELDE   Senior Lecturer and Co-Director SCRIPT, AHRC funded research Centre, University of Edinburgh

DR ROBERT WAI   Associate Professor, Osgoode Hall Law School, York University, Toronto, Canada

PROFESSOR CLIVE WALKER   School of Law University of Leeds

PROFESSOR JANET WALKER   Emeritus Professor, Strategic Research Adviser, Institute of Health and Society, Newcastle University

DR JULIE WALLBANK   Senior Lecturer, University of Leeds

PROFESSOR ADRIAN WALTERS   Professor of Corporate and Insolvency Law, Nottingham Trent University

PROFESSOR COLIN WARBRICK   Barber Professor of Jurisprudence, Birmingham Law School

PROFESSOR JEAN WARBURTON   Professor of Law, University of Liverpool

PROFESSOR KATE WARNER   Director, Tasmania Law Reform Institute, Faculty of Law, University of Tasmania

PROFESSOR MARTIN WASIK   Professor of Criminal Justice, Keele University

MR GARY WATT   Reader in Law, University of Warwick

SIR ARTHUR WATTS KCMG QC   formerly of Essex Court Chambers

PROFESSOR PETER WATTS   Law Faculty, The University of Auckland

DR MATTHEW WEAIT,   Senior Lecturer in Law and Legal Studies, Birkbeck College, University of London

PROFESSOR JULIAN WEBB   Professor of Legal Education and Director of the UK Centre for Legal Education, University of Warwick

DR LISA WEBLEY   Reader, University of Westminster School of Law

PROFESSOR TODD GRIERSON WEILER   Adjunct Professor, University of Calgary, Faculty of Law and the University of Western Ontario Faculty of Law; Senior Editorial Advisor, OUP Investmentclaims.com

DR RIVKA WEILL, LECTURER   Radzyner School of Law, Interdisciplinary Center (IDC) Herzliya, Israel

ROGER WELCH   Principal Lecturer, School of Law, University of Portsmouth

MARC WELLER   Reader in International Law and International Relations in the University of Cambridge; Fellow of the Lauterpacht Research Centre for International Law and of Hughes Hall

PROFESSOR SALLY WHEELER   Director, Institute of Governance, School of Law, Queens University Belfast

SIR MICHAEL WHEELER-BOOTH   Special Lecturer in Politics, Magdalen College, University of Oxford

PROFESSOR STEPHEN WHITTLE, OBE, PHD, MA, LLB, BA   Professor of Equalities Law, Manchester Metropolitan University

JOHN WIGHTMAN   Senior Lecturer in Law, Kent Law School, Eliot College, University of Kent

PROFESSOR NICK WIKELEY   John Wilson Chair in Law, School of Law, University of Southampton

MRS CATHERINE WILLIAMS   Reader in Law, Sheffield University

PROFESSOR SIR DAVID WILLIAMS   Emeritus Vice-Chancellor, Cambridge University

DR DAVID WILLIAMS   Social Security and Child Support Commissioner and Part time Special Commissioner of Income Tax

DR GLENYS WILLIAMS   Lecturer; Aberystwyth University

MS KATHERINE S WILLIAMS   Lecturer, Department of Law and Criminology, Aberystwyth University

ASSOCIATE PROFESSOR CHRISTIAN WITTING   Melbourne Law School

SIR MICHAEL WOOD   Senior Fellow Lauterpacht Centre for International Law, University of Cambridge

PROFESSOR DIANA WOODHOUSE   Pro Vice-Chancellor (Research) and Assistant School Dean, School of Social Sciences & Law, Oxford Brookes University

PROFESSOR GORDON R WOODMAN   Emeritus Professor of Comparative Law, Birmingham Law School, University of Birmingham

PROFESSOR SARAH WORTHINGTON   Pro Director and Professor of Law, London School of Economics and Political Science, and Barrister, 3–4 South Square, Gray's Inn, London

PROFESSOR JANE WRIGHT   Department of Law, University of Essex

DR TONY WRIGHT MP   House of Commons

PROFESSOR KAREN YEUNG   Professor of Law, School of Law, King's College London

DR ALISON L YOUNG   Lecturer, University of Oxford; Fellow and Tutor in Law, Hertford College

PROFESSOR RICHARD YOUNG   Professor of Law and Policy Research, School of Law, Bristol University

PROFESSOR LUCIA ZEDNER   Professor of Criminal Justice, University of Oxford

PROFESSOR LESLIE ZINES   Emeritus Professor, Visiting Fellow, John Fleming Centre for Advancement of Legal Research, Australian National University

List of Abbreviations

A A A	American Anthropological Association
ABA	American Bar Association
ABS	access and equitable benefit sharing
ACAS	Advisory, Conciliation, and Arbitration Service
ACHPR	African Charter on Human and Peoples' Rights
ACHR	American Convention on Human Rights
ACLU	American Civil Liberties Union
ADR	Alternative Dispute Resolution
AGAI	Army General Administrative Instructions
AGM	annual general meeting
AHD	*Ad Hoc* Division
ALI	American Law Institute
AMAA	Ancient Monuments and Archaeological Areas Act 1979
ANC	African National Congress
ANH	artificial nutrition and hydration
AP	Additional Protocol
APR	annual percentage rate
ARVs	antiretrovirals
ASA	Advertising Standards Authority
ASBO	anti-social behaviour order
ASEAN	Association of South East Asian Nations
ASN	Additional Support Needs
ATCA	Alien Tort Claims Act
ATE	after the event
ATS	alternative trading system
AU	African Union
AWIA	Adults with Incapacity (Scotland) Act 2000
BBC	British Broadcasting Corporation
BBFC	British Board of Film Classification
BCS	British Crime Surveys
BCSB	Banking Code Standards Board
BGB	Burgerliches Gesetzbuch
BIRPI	Bureaux internationaux réunis pour la protection de la propriété intellectuelle
BITs	bilateral investment treaties
BME	Black and Minority Ethnic
BPBU	Bar Pro Bono Unit
BROs	Bankruptcy Restriction Orders

BSI	British Standards Institute
BT	British Telecom
BVC	Bar Vocational Course
BWIs	Bretton Woods Institutions
C-Mec	Child Maintenance and Enforcement Commission
CABx	Citizens Advice Bureaux
CAC	Central Arbitration Committee
CAG	Comptroller and Auditor General
CAS	Court of Arbitration for Sport
CAT	Competition Appeal Tribunal
CBD	Convention on Biological Diversity 1992
cc	creative commons
CCRC	Criminal Cases Review Commission
CCT	compulsory competitive tendering
CDDA	Company Directors Disqualification Act 1986
CDPA	Copyright Designs and Patents Act 1988
CEDAW	Convention on the Elimination of All Forms of Discrimination Against Women
CEHR	Commission for Equality and Human Rights
CEO	Chief Executive Officer
CERD	Convention on the Elimination of All Forms of Racial Discrimination
CFA	conditional fee arrangement
CFASS	Committee on Freedom of Association
CFC	Controlled Foreign Company
CFI	European Court of First Instance
CFSP	Common Foreign and Security Policy
CGT	capital gains tax
CHOGM	Commonwealth Heads of Government Meeting
CIPA	Chartered Institute of Patent Attorneys
CIS	collective investment scheme
CITES	Convention on the International Trade in Endangered Species 1973
CJA	Criminal Justice Act 1988
CJSNI	Criminal Justice System Northern Ireland
CLES	Community Legal Service
CLS	Critical Legal Studies
CNR	cell nuclear replacement

CNVs	copy number variants		DMA	Direct Marketing Association
CO	commanding officer		DORA	Defence of the Realm Acts
COBS	Conduct of Business		DPA	Data Protection Act 1988
COCOS	comparative constitutional studies		DPPR	Data Protection Principles
CoE	Council of Europe		DPP	Director of Public Prosecutions
CORE	Comment on Reproductive Ethics		DPS	designated premises supervisor
COREPER	Committee of Permanent Representatives		DRC	Disability Rights Commission
CPC	club premises certificate		DRIP	Declaration on the Rights of Indigenous Peoples
CPD	Continuing Professional Development		DRO	Debt Relief Order
CPE	Common Professional Examination		DS	data subjects
CPR	Civil Procedure Rules 1998		DSM	Diagnostic and Statistical Manual of Mental Disorders
CPS	Crown Prosecution Service			
CRD	Citizens' Rights Directive		DSM-IV-TR	American Psychiatric Association's Diagnostic and Statistical Manual of Mental Disorders, Fourth Edition, Text Revision
CRE	Commission for Racial Equality			
CSA	Child Support Agency			
CSCE	Conference on Security and Cooperation in Europe			
CSID	Convention on the Settlement of Investment Disputes between Convention States and Nationals of Other States		DSP	Director of Service Prosecutions
			DSS	Department for Social Security
			DSs	developing societies
			DTB	digital terrestrial broadcasting
			DTCD	duty to confirm or deny
CSR	corporate social responsibility		DWA	decent work agenda
CST	European Union Civil Service Tribunal		DWP	Department for Work and Pensions
CT	Constitutional Treaty 2004			
CTC	child tax credit		EA	Enterprise Act 2002
CTM	Community Trade Mark		EAL	economic analysis of law
CUKC	Citizens of the UK and Colonies		EAW	European Arrest Warrant
CVA	Company Voluntary Arrangement		EC	European Community
CVL	creditors' voluntary liquidation		ECA	Electronic Communications Act 2000
CVS	chorionic villus sampling			
			ECB	European Central Bank
DAB	digital audio broadcasting		ECHR	European Convention on Human Rights
DA Notices	Defence Advisory Notices			
DBERR	Department of Business, Enterprise, and Regulatory Reform		ECMH	Efficient Capital Market Hypothesis
			ECNI	Equality Commission for Northern Ireland
DC	data controllers			
DCA	Department for Constitutional Affairs		Ecofin	Economics and Finance Council
			ECOSOC	Economic and Social Council
DCMS	Department for Culture, Media, and Sport		ECtHR	European Court of Human Rights
			ECJ	European Court of Justice
DCSF	Department for Children, Schools, and Families		ECN	European Competition Network
			ECNI	Equality Commission for Northern Ireland
DDA	Disability Discrimination Act 1995			
DDR	Demobilization, Disarmament, and Reintegration		ECSB	European System of Central Banks
			ECU	European currency unit
DENI	Northern Ireland Department of Education		EEC	European Economic Community
			EEZ	exclusive economic zone
DERR	Department of Enterprise and Regulatory Reform		EGM	extraordinary general meeting
			EHRC	Equality and Human Rights Commission
DG Competition (or DG COMP)	Directorate-General for Competition			
			EIA	Environmental Impact Assessment
DISS	Dispute Settlement System		EIR	regulations allowing access to environmental information
DLA	disability living allowance			

EMAS	environmental management standards
EMEA	European Agency for the Evaluation of Medicinal Products
EMI	Electronic Money Institution
EMS	European Monetary System
EMU	Economic and Monetary Union
EN	European Standard Mark
ENE	Early Neutral Evaluation
EOC	Equal Opportunities Commission
EP	European Parliament
EPC	European Patent Convention 1973
EPO	European Patent Office
ER	Environmental Report
ERA	Employment Rights Act 1996
ERM	Exchange Rate Mechanism
ESC	European Social Charter
ESRC	Economic and Social Research Council
ETMs	environmental trading markets
EU	European Union
Europol	European Police Office
FAPL	Football Association Premier League
FCSC	Financial Services Compensation Scheme
FDI	Foreign Direct Investment
FGM	female genital mutilation
FIA	Federation Internationale de L'Automobile
FIFA	International Federation of Football Associations
FII	fabricated or induced illness
FINRRAGE	Feminist International Network of Resistance to Reproductive and Genetic Engineering
FOI	freedom of information
FOIA	Freedom of Information Act 2000
FOS	Financial Ombudsman Service
FRC	Financial Reporting Council
FRU	Free Representation Unit
FSA	Financial Services Authority
FSAP	Financial Services Action Plan
FSAVC	Free Standing Additional Voluntary Contributions
FSMA	Financial Services and Markets Act 2000
GA	General Assembly
GAD	gender and development analysis
GAERC	General Affairs and External Relations Council
GATS	General Agreement on Trade in Services
GATT	General Agreement on Tariffs and Trade

GBH	grievous bodily harm
GCHQ	Government Communications Head Quarters
GDL	Graduate Diploma in Law
GDP	gross domestic product
GER	group exemption regulation
GHS	Globally Harmonized System of Classification and Labelling of Chemicals
GLO	Group Litigation Order
GLS	Government Legal Service
GMOs	genetically modified organisms
GNP	gross national product
GOQ	genuine occupational qualification
GP	general practitioner
GST	goods and services tax *or* general sales tax
GTC	General Teaching Council
GWR	Great Western Railways
HACCP	Hazard Analysis at Critical Control Points
HC	High Courts
HEA	Higher Education Act 2004
HEFCE	Higher Education Funding Council for England
HEI	higher education institution
hES cells	human embryonic stem cells
HFEA	Human Fertilization and Embryology Authority
HIPC	Heavily Indebted Poor Countries
HLA	Human Leukocyte Antigen
HMI	Her Majesty's Inspector of Education, Children's Services, and Skills
HMIe	Her Majesty's Inspectorate of Education
HMRC	Her Majesty's Revenue and Customs
HPC	Health Professions Council
HRA	Human Rights Act 1998
HRP	home responsibility protection
IAT	Immigration Appeal Tribunal
IBRD	International Bank for Reconstruction and Development
IC	Information Commissioner
INC	integrated circuit
ICAS	Independent Complaints Advocacy Service
ICASP	International Council on Arbitration for Sport
ICC	International Criminal Court
ICCPR	International Covenant on Civil and Political Rights

ICD	International Classification of Diseases	IPPC	Integrated Pollution Prevention and Control Directive 1996
ICD 10	World Health Organization's International Statistical Classification of Diseases and Related Health Problems, 10th Revision	IPRs	intellectual property rights
		ISA	International Seabed Authority
		ISAC	individual savings account
ICESCR	International Covenant on Economic, Social, and Cultural Rights	ISO	International Standard Mark
		ISOP	Insolvency Practitioner
ICJ	International Court of Justice	ISP	Internet Service Provider
ICOM	International Council of Museums	ISSP	intensive supervision and surveillance programme
ICOMOS	International Council on Monuments and Sites	IT	Information and Communications Technologies
ICRC	International Committee of the Red Cross	ITC	Independent Television Commission
ICSID	International Centre for the Settlement of Investment Disputes	ITLOS	International Tribunal for the Law of the Sea
ICSL	Inns of Court School of Law	ITU	International Telecommunications Union
ICSTIS	Independent Committee for the Supervision of Standards of the Telephone Information Services	IVA	Individual Voluntary Arrangement
		IVF	*in vitro* fertilization
ICTR	International Criminal Tribunals for Rwanda	JAC	Judicial Appointments Commission
ICTY	International Criminal Tribunals for the Former Yugoslavia	JHA	Justice and Home Affairs
		JP	justice of the peace
ICVC	investment companies with variable capital	JV	joint venture
		KFI	Key Facts Illustration
IDA	International Development Association	LACORS	Local Authorities Coordinators of Regulatory Services
IDD	Initial Disclosure Document	LBA	Planning (Listed Buildings and Conservation Areas) Act 1990
IDPs	internally displaced persons		
IEL	international economic law	LCAD	Legal and Constitutional Affairs Division
IFA	Independent Fostering Agency		
IFC	International Finance Corporation	LEA	local education authority
IFI	International Financial Institution	LEI	legal expenses insurance
IFT	Information Tribunal	LGTB	Lesbian, Gay, Transgendered, and Bisexual
IGO	international organization		
IHT	inheritance tax	LGO	Local Government Ombudsman
IIAC	Industrial Injuries Advisory Council	LLP	limited liability partnership
		LPA	local planning authority
ILC	International Law Commission	LPAT	lasting power of attorney
ILO	International Labour Organization	LPC	Legal Practice Course
ILOC	intended learning outcome	LPM	Landless Peoples' Movement
IMF	International Monetary Fund	LRC	law reform commission
IMT	International Military Tribunal	LSE	London Stock Exchange
IMTFE	International Military Tribunal for the Far East	LTIPs	Long Term Incentive Plans
IOC	International Olympic Committee		
IOM	International Organization for Migration	MA	Museums Association
		MACA	military aid to the civil authority
IP	intellectual property	MAPPAs	Multi-agency Public Protection Agencies
IPC	integrated pollution control		
IPCC	Independent Police Complaints Commission	MCA	Matrimonial Causes Act 1973
		MD	managing director
IPOFF	initial public offering	MDRI	Multilateral Debt Relief Initiative
IPOs	Income Payment Orders	MENCA	Mental Capacity Act 2005

MFN	most-favoured-nation
MHRT	Mental Health Review Tribunal
MiFID	Markets in Financial Instruments Directive 2004
MIGA	Multilateral Investment Guarantee Agency
MNCs	Multinational Corporations
MNEs	Multinational Enterprises
MOTA	Mail Order Traders' Association
MPC	Monetary Policy Committee
MTIC	missing trader intra-community
NA	Narcotics Anonymous
NAACP	National Association for the Advancement of Colored People
NAFTA	North America Free Trade Agreement
NAO	National Audit Office
NATO	North Atlantic Treaty Organization
NAV	net asset value
NCAs	national administrative competition authorities
NCC	National Consumer Council
NCCUSL	National Conference of Commissioners on Uniform State Laws
NCT	New Control Total
NDPBs	Non-Departmental Public Bodies
NED	non-executive director
NEPA	National Environmental Policy Act 1969
NFA	no further action
NGOs	non-governmental organizations
NGRI	not guilty by reason of insanity
NHS	National Health Service
NHSLA	NHS Litigation Authority
NI	Northern Ireland
NICs	national insurance contributions
NICE	National Institute for Health and Clinical Excellence
NICtS	Northern Ireland Court Service
NIHRC	Northern Irish Human Rights Commission
NINo	national insurance number
NIns	National Insurance
NIO	Northern Ireland Office
NIPS	Northern Ireland Prison Service
NMT	Nuremberg Military Tribunals
NMW	national minimum wage
NOMS	National Offender Management Service
NT	National Treatment
NTA	Native Title Act 1993
NVQs	National Vocational Qualifications
OBSP	Old Bailey Session Papers

OCSE	Organization for Cooperation and Security in Europe
ODA	Olympic Delivery Authority
ODR	Online Dispute Resolution
OECD	Organization for Economic Cooperation and Development
OEIC	open-ended investment company
Ofcom	Office of Communications
OFFA	Office for Fair Access
Ofsted	Office for Standards in Education, Children's Services, and Skills
OFT	Office of Fair Trading
OFTEL	Office of Telecommunications
OHIM	Office for Harmonization in the Internal Market
OIA	Office of the Independent Adjudicator
OISC	Office of the Immigration Services Commissioner
OJC	Office for Judicial Complaints
OLAF	European Anti-Fraud Office
OPEC	Organization of Petroleum Exporting Countries
OSCE	Organization on Security and Cooperation in Europe
OTC	over-the-counter
PA	public authority
PAC	Public Accounts Committee
PACE	Police and Criminal Evidence Act 1984
PAFT	Policy Appraisal and Fair Treatment
PAT	pensions appeal tribunal
PAYE	Pay as You Earn
PBL	problem-based learning
PBNI	Probation Board for Northern Ireland
PCA	Permanent Court of Arbitration
PECA	Personal Capability Assessment
PCAT	Primary Care Trust
PCC	Press Complaints Commission
PCIJ	Permanent Court of International Justice
PCT	Patent Cooperation Treaty
PDO	Protected Designation of Origin
PET	potentially exempt transfer
PFI	private finance initiative
PGD	pre-implantation genetic diagnosis
PGI	Protected Geographical Indication
PII	public interest immunity
PIL	public interest litigation
PIN	personal identification number
PLHA	people living with HIV and AIDS
PLO	Popular Front for the Liberation of Palestine
PPC	Pollution Prevention and Control

PPG 15	Planning Policy Guidance Note 15—Planning and the Historic Environment (1994)	SGO	Special Guardianship Order
		SIB	Securities and Investments Board
		SIS	Schengen Information System
PPG 16	Planning Policy Guidance Note 16: Planning and Archaeology 1990	SNPs	single nucleotide polymorphisms
		SPA	Social Policy Agreement
PPOs	Periodical Payment Orders	SPAB	Society for the Protection of Ancient Buildings
PPR	persons, papers, and records		
PPS	Public Prosecution Service	SPBG	Solicitors' *Pro bono* Group
PRSPs	Poverty Strategy Reduction Papers	SSP	statutory sick pay
PSB	public service broadcasting	SSSI	Site of Special Scientific Interest
PSLA	pain and suffering and loss of amenity	STV	single transferable vote
PSNI	Police Service of Northern Ireland		
PSU	Public and Commercial Services Union	TAG	The Accident Group
PTSD	Post-traumatic Stress Disorder	TAS	Tribunal Arbitral du Sport
PVS	persistent vegetative state	TCF	Treating Customers Fairly
		TCPA	Town and Country Planning Act 1990
QAA	Quality Assurance Agency	TCP/IP	Transmission Control Protocol/Internet Protocol
RAPEX	Rapid Exchange	TCSC	Treasury and Civil Service Select Committee
RATE	Regulatory Authority for Tissue and Embryos		
		TDA	Training and Development Agency for Schools
RCEP	Royal Commission on Environmental Pollution		
		TEC	Treaty establishing the European Community 1987
RDA	Registered Designs Act 1949		
RE	Religious Education	TEN	temporary event notice
REACH	Regulation 1907/2006 on the Registration, Evaluation, and Authorization of Chemicals	TEU	Treaty on European Union
		TINA	there is no alternative
		TNCs	Transnational Corporations
REP	Register of Exercise Professionals	TPO	tree preservation order
RSFSR	Russian Soviet Federated Socialist Republic	TPS	Telephone Preference Service
		TRC	Truth and Reconciliation Commission
RSPB	Royal Society for the Protection of Birds	TRIPs	World Trade Organization Agreement on Trade Related Aspects of Intellectual Property Rights
RTA	road traffic accident		
		TSol	Treasury Solicitor's Department
SA	Sustainability Appraisal	TWF	Television Without Frontiers
SAC	Summary Appeal Court	TULRCA	Trade Union and Labour Relations (Consolidation) Act 1992
SACEM	Société des Auteurs et Compositeurs et Editeurs de Musique		
		TUPE	Transfer of Undertakings (Protection of Employment) Regulations
SAL	social action litigation		
SAPs	structural adjustment programmes		
SBS	Southall Black Sisters	UCC	Universal Copyright Convention
SC	Security Council	UC Code	Uniform Commercial Code
SCI	Supreme Court of India	UCDR	unregistered community design right
SDGRR	Sex Discrimination (Gender Reassignment) Regulations 1999	UCITS	Undertaking for Collective Investment in Transferable Securities
SDRT	stamp duty reserve tax	UCPD	Directive on Unfair Commercial Practices
SEA	Strategic Environmental Assessment		
SEN	special educational needs	UCTA	Unfair Contract Terms Act 1977
SENDA	Special Educational Needs and Disability Act 2001	UDHR	Universal Declaration on Human Rights 1948
SENDIST	Special Educational Needs and Disability Tribunal	UEFA	Union of European Football Associations
SGBs	sports governing bodies	UET	Universal Expenditure Tax

UK	United Kingdom	UTCCR	Unfair Terms in Consumer Contracts Regulations 1999
UK UDR	UK unregistered design right		
UN	United Nations	VAC	Video Appeals Committee
UNCITRAL	United Nations Commission on International Trade Law	VAT	value added tax
		VFM	value-for-money
UNCRC	United Nations Convention on the Rights of the Child	VOIP	Voice Over Internet Protocol
UNCT	United Nations Convention against Torture	WB	World Bank
		WHM	working holiday maker
UNCTAD	United Nations Conference on Trade and Development	WHO	World Health Organization
		WHS	World Heritage Status
UNEF I	United Nations Emergency Force I	WID	Women in Development
UNESCO	United Nations Educational, Scientific and Cultural Organization	WIPO	World Intellectual Property Organization
UNFCCC	United Nations Framework Convention on Climate Change	WMD	weapons of mass destruction
		WPPT	WIPO Performances and Phonograms Treaty
UNHCR	United Nations High Commissioner for Refugees	WRA	Water Resources Act 1991
UNICEF	United Nations' Children's Fund	WTC	working tax credit
UNSG	United Nations Secretary-General	WTO	World Trade Organization
UPOV Convention	International Convention for the Protection of New Varieties of Plant	YJA	Youth Justice Agency
		YJB	Youth Justice Board
US	United States	YOTs	Youth Offending Teams
USSR	Union of Soviet Socialist Republics		
USTR	US Trade Representative		

Tables of Cases

European Court of Justice and Court of First Instance

Alphabetical

Chronological

France

Germany

International Court of Justice

United States of America

Tables of Legislation

Regulations

Statutory Instruments

United States of America

Table of Conventions and Treaties, etc

A

A v Secretary of State for the Home Department
see Liversidge v Anderson

Aarhus Convention On 25 June 1998, the United Nations Economic Commission for Europe adopted the Convention on Access to Information, Public Participation in Decision-Making and Access to Justice in Environmental Matters (the Aarhus Convention). The Convention entered into force on 30 October 2001. Unlike many international environmental agreements, the Convention is not concerned (directly) with substantive environmental issues, but with procedural constraints on environmental decision-making. The three pillars of the Convention—access to information, public participation and access to justice—are inextricably linked, for participation without adequate information and the availability of effective remedies if the outcome is unsatisfactory, would be ineffective.

Under the Convention, the public (individuals and their organizations) are afforded certain rights to which public authorities must give effect. The access to environmental information provisions are the most clearly defined of the three pillars. The public has the right to request and receive environmental information held by public authorities, including information on the state of the environment, policies, and cost-benefit analyses, within one month of request, without having to state an interest. Public authorities are also required actively to disseminate certain types of environmental information, including a national report on the state of the environment. The public participation pillar requires ratifying states to promote effective participation in environmental decisions. Broadly speaking, the affected public and environmental **non-governmental organizations** ('NGOs') must be given the opportunity to comment on specific activities (such as those subject to an **Environmental Impact Assessment**), and the preparation of plans, programmes, policies, and executive regulations relating to the environment. The outcome of the participatory procedures must be taken into account in decision-making,

and reasons must be given for the final decision. The third pillar on access to justice gives the public concerned, including NGOs promoting environmental protection, the right to challenge, before a court or other independent and impartial body, decisions that have been made without complying with the Convention's information and participation provisions, and strengthens the enforcement of domestic environmental law more generally.

The ratification of the Convention by both the EU and the UK in February 2005 represents an undoubted political commitment to its contents. EU Directives pertaining to the first two pillars have been adopted and the UK government (including the devolved administrations) has gone some way to implementing the European (and therefore the Convention's) provisions. Radical changes to existing EU and domestic legislation have not, however, been necessary.   CAROLYN ABBOT

S Stec and S Casey-Lefkowitz, *The Aarhus Convention: An Implementation Guide* (New York and Geneva: United Nations/Economic Commission for Europe, 2000)

Aboriginal law *see* **indigenous law**

Aboriginal peoples *see* **indigenous peoples**

abortion An often overlooked point about abortion law in Britain is that while abortion is legal it is not de-criminalized. Criminal law still governs the provision of abortion through the Offences against the Person Act 1861, ss 58 and 59. This Act made the attempt to 'procure a miscarriage' by a woman or any other person a criminal offence which could be punished by imprisonment, at that time setting the harshest penalties yet to be introduced in the western world to punish abortionists and women who sought abortion.

This Act is still in place so that abortion remains a criminal offence. The major subsequent reform was the Abortion Act 1967, under the terms of which doctors authorising the performance of an abortion or performing an abortion themselves have a legal defence against its criminality in specified circumstances. The 1967 Act has only been revised once, in the Human Fertilisation and Embryology Act 1990, the main innovation of which was to specify an upper legal time limit for abortion in some circumstances.

According to the 1967 Act, s 1(1), the current law states:

Subject to the provisions of this section, a person shall not be guilty of an offence under the law relating to abortion when a pregnancy is terminated by a registered medical practitioner if two registered medical practitioners are of the opinion formed in good faith—

(a) that the pregnancy has not exceeded its twenty-fourth week and that the continuance of the pregnancy would involve risk, greater than if the pregnancy were terminated, of injury to the physical or mental health of the pregnant woman or any existing children of her family; or

(b) that the termination is necessary to prevent grave permanent injury to the physical or mental health of the pregnant woman; or

(c) that the continuance of the pregnancy would involve risk to the life of the pregnant woman, greater than if the pregnancy were terminated; or

(d) that there is substantial risk that if the child were born it would suffer from such physical or mental abnormalities as to be seriously handicapped.

The Abortion Act 1967 is often referred to as a 'liberal law' passed in the context of the 'swinging sixties', but some argue that liberal ideas about 'rights over one's body' are in fact not reflected in it. The veteran campaigner for abortion law reform, Madeline Simms, for example, remarked of the years preceding the 1967 Act:

Few people at that period thought of anything as unrealisable and extravagant as A Woman's Right to Choose. That came many years later. People sometimes forget that abortion law reform preceded the Women's Movement.

Women are given no right to abort a pregnancy through the 1967 Abortion Act. The statute frees *doctors* from the threat of criminal prosecution where they believe 'in good faith' that an abortion should be performed in line with the prescribed grounds. Thus, in legal terms, decision-making power in abortion rests with the medical profession.

This Abortion Act regulates termination of pregnancy procedures in England, Scotland and Wales. The Act does not apply to Northern Ireland, where abortion remains to all intents and purposes illegal. About 2,000 Northern Irish women each year terminate pregnancies privately in British abortion clinics.

Factors leading to the 1967 Abortion Act are numerous. One over-arching pressure was the perceived gap between law and practice. Despite its legal prohibition, abortion was commonplace before 1967, provided by clandestine 'backstreet' abortionists and by some doctors prepared to run the risk of prosecution. Marie Stopes, the famous pioneer of birth control noted, for example, that at her birth control clinic established in the 1930s she had 'in three months . . . as many as 20, 000 requests for criminal abortion'. Illegal abortionists were protected by community secrecy and popular support. Over 25,000 people attended the 1939 funeral of one doctor who aborted many women, routinely flouting the law and (successfully) defending himself against prosecution.

Given this gap between highly restrictive laws and the relatively commonplace practice of abortion, something had to give. Prior to 1967, this 'giving' took the form of opening up 'legal loopholes'. One such loophole was created by the *Bourne* ruling in the 1930s. Alec Bourne, a doctor, deliberately provoked his own prosecution by aborting a 14-year-old girl raped by soldiers. His defence was that the girl was a mental wreck because of what had happened, and was therefore deserving of abortion. Through his acquittal of all charges, this case made it clear that there *was* such a thing as legal abortion, and further that it could be carried out for wider reasons than risk to the mother's life.

Following *R* v *Bourne*, while some doctors were prepared to take the opportunity presented by this ruling of carrying out abortions on wealthy women for high fees on 'mental health grounds', the number of doctors prepared to abort remained small. *Bourne* did prefigure the major reform of the 1960s, however, in bringing to law the idea that there are wider reasons for legal abortion than risk to the mother's life.

By the 1960s, the impetus to widen the 'loophole' still further came to influence public and political life. One reason for this was emerging concern with 'social justice'. Lena Jeger, Labour MP and early parliamentary advocate of legal abortion, asserted that, 'Abortion is like equal pay. The women who are best off get it'. Some argued it was the poor who needed legal abortion *most*. They could be assisted to lead a better life, it was thought, were they able to prevent 'over large families', as one MP, supportive of legal change, put it. Legal abortion thus came to be viewed as a way of addressing harms to society and the issue moved as a result into the realm of public debate.

The most notable feature of the Abortion Act 1967 is, perhaps, its enduring and widespread social acceptance. This law has been the subject of often heated controversy. Fifteen anti-abortion bills were introduced to Parliament between 1967 and 1989. Yet none were successful, and there is no significant body of opinion in British society that that seeks to restore the illegality of abortion. Further, legal access to abortion on the part of increasing numbers of women appears tolerated.

The Abortion Act 1967 could be interpreted in a restrictive or facilitative manner by doctors. Potentially, legal abortion could be provided to relatively small numbers of women, were it the case that doctors chose to form opinions 'in good faith' that risks posed by continued pregnancy to the health of women and their families should be defined narrowly. On the other hand, where abortion is viewed by medical professionals (at least those who opt to be involved in abortion provision) as preferable to the continuation of unwanted pregnancies, they can opt to make it easily accessible to women on mental and physical health grounds. For example, doctors can define 'threat to mental health' as the woman feeling stressed by the pregnancy and the prospect of unwanted **motherhood**.

The abortion rate for England and Wales—abortions per 1,000 female residents aged 16–45—stood in 1976, 1986, 1991, 1996, 2000, and 2003 at 10.2, 13.0, 15.0, 16.0, 17.0, 17.5 respectively, and at 18.3 for resident women aged 15–44 for 2006, with an increase in absolute numbers from 129,700 to 193,700 over this time. This suggests a relatively permissive interpretation of the law is adopted by abortion providers at present.

While this increasing abortion rate is the subject of some debate and controversy, it is striking that abortion controversy today tends to be focused on the relatively small proportion of abortions carried out at late gestational stages. This focus within the abortion debate can be interpreted to mean that 'early' abortions are considered an unfortunate but inevitable 'fact of life'.

In relation to the current debate about the law and 'late abortion', it should be noted that the scale of women's requests for abortion that result in legal terminations follows gestation. The vast majority of abortions occur in early pregnancy with over 90 per cent performed before 12 weeks' gestation. The proportion dwindles as pregnancies proceed to less than 1.5 per cent at 20+ weeks. It is not the law that shapes this pattern of demand. Relatively few women terminate pregnancies late, not because the law discourages this, but because their own feelings about their pregnancies lead women to want abortion as early as possible. Evidence suggests that the small proportion of women who do seek late abortion include those who are young and inexperienced, abandoned by their partner and desperate, or have been unable to get an abortion earlier.

While debate about the ethical issues associated with 'late abortion' will continue, its legality needs to be considered in relation to the alternative, which is that often desperate pregnant women have no legal option but to continue their pregnancy to term and give birth.   ELLIE LEE

See also: **Roe v Wade**

absolute territorial protection   Absolute territorial protection is a concept used in European Community ('EC') **competition law**. It refers to the situation where a distributor or reseller will be shielded from competition and as a result may be the only firm operating in the relevant territory. Absolute territorial protection may be possible to achieve in a situation where the supplier of a particular product appoints a distributor in a particular territory to handle the resale of its product exclusively in that territory. The producer may grant the distributor additional rights, such as intellectual property rights, which effectively prevent other firms from handling the product in that territory. The producer may even go further and impose an export ban on the distributor effectively preventing it from selling outside the territory. The result in this case will be an isolation of the relevant territory.

Absolute territorial protection is highly objectionable under EC competition law because it can have the effect of defeating one of the main aims behind the EC Treaty, namely the creation of a single market throughout the Member States of the EC. Therefore where the absolute territorial protection applies along national borders, ie where the relevant territory is a Member State of the EC, such protection may be considered to have an object restrictive of **competition** in the EC.   MAHER DABBAH

See also: **EC competition law, modernization of; intellectual property rights, European harmonization of**

abuse of a dominant position   This concept relates to the behaviour of a dominant undertaking which, through the use of methods different from those that condition normal **competition**, has the effect of hindering maintenance of the level of competition existing in a market or the growth of competition in that market (Case 85/76 *Hoffmann-La Roche v Commission* (1979)). Both Article 82 EC and Chapter II of the UK Competition Act prohibit the *abuse* of a **dominant position**, not the holding of such a position. The fact that a company is dominant merely entails that it has a 'special responsibility' to behave in a way that would not undermine competition in a given market. Only abuses of that position of economic strength are outlawed by EC and UK competition legislation. While these provisions do not provide a definition of abuse, they do set out a non-exhaustive list of examples of abusive practices: imposition of unfair purchase or selling prices or other unfair trading conditions; limitation of production, markets, or technical development to the prejudice of consumers; application of dissimilar conditions to equivalent transactions with other trading parties; and imposition of tying obligations. Academic commentators distinguish two broad categories of abuse: exclusionary and exploitative abuses.

Exclusionary abuses

Exclusionary abuses consist of behaviour by a dominant company which seeks to harm the position of its competitors by completely or partially preventing them from profitably having access to or expanding in the relevant market. This type of abuse may not directly and immediately harm consumers, but is invariably detrimental to them in the long term. The most common forms of exclusionary abuse are predatory pricing, imposition of exclusive dealing obligations, application of certain types of rebates and discounts, tying practices, and refusals to supply by a dominant company.

Predatory pricing is a strategy by which a dominant company lowers its prices dramatically or incurs losses in the short run in order to eliminate a rival or rivals or prevent their entry into the market. After competitors have been successfully expelled, the dominant company will generally try to recoup its losses by raising its prices. In **European Community ('EC') law**, prices below average variable cost are presumed to be predatory, as are prices above variable cost but below average total cost when there is evidence of 'predatory intent' on the part of the dominant company to eliminate a competitor. There is no need to *prove* recoupment of losses by the dominant company in order to find this form of abuse. It suffices to show that the pricing strategy is likely to eliminate the firm's competitors.

Exclusivity obligations, such as requirement contracts, oblige the customers of a dominant company to buy all or most of their requirements exclusively from the company and will be classified as abusive when they have the actual or potential effect of foreclosing the market.

Some discounts and rebates applied by dominant companies will also fall foul of Article 82 EC as exclusionary practices. These include loyalty rebates—which normally reward customers for buying supplies exclusively from the dominant company;

target rebates—where customers are granted discounts once they have reached a particular sales target; and top-slice rebates—given to entice customers who still purchase a small portion of their requirements from companies other than the dominant company.

All these forms of discounting are objectionable when pursued by a dominant company because of their potential tying effect on customers, who will be discouraged from buying from rivals of the dominant company. Tying consists of a company making the sale of one product or service (the tying product or service) conditional upon the purchase of another product or service (the tied product or service). This practice may be abusive when a company dominant in the market of the tying product tries to foreclose the tied market by reducing the number of customers available to its rivals in the tied market.

A refusal to supply by a dominant company may be classified as abusive where it prevents a customer from getting access to goods, services, or necessary information and, as a result, the customer is either driven out of or prevented from entering the market. A finding of abuse will be made only if it can be shown that the refusal to deal is likely to have an anti-competitive effect that is ultimately detrimental to consumer welfare.

Exploitative abuses

Exploitative abuses involve a dominant company exploiting its market power in order to harm consumers directly. The main forms of exploitative abuse are imposition of unfair or excessive prices; limitation of production, markets, or technical development; and certain discriminatory pricing practices. The European Court of Justice has not yet provided a clear test to decide what is meant by excessive prices other than stating that they are prices that bear no reasonable relation to the economic value of the product supplied. Equally, the imposition of unfair trading conditions may be abusive. However, other than in obvious circumstances, the criteria to determine the unfairness of trading conditions remain unclear. Discriminatory pricing practices based on nationality and, more controversially, geographical price discrimination have also been held to contravene Article 82 EC.

In contrast to the position under Article 81 EC (dealing with certain anti-competitive agreements and concerted practices) there is no provision for exemptions under Article 82 EC. Article 82 EC appears to be drafted as an absolute prohibition of abuses of market power by dominant undertakings, and no escape routes are formally provided. Nevertheless, some decisions of the **European Commission** and of the European Community judicature have developed an analysis of Article 82 EC, based on the notions of justification and proportionality, which has instilled some flexibility into the application of this provision. A 2005 Commission Discussion Paper specifically endorsed the principle that exclusionary conduct by a dominant company can sometimes be objectively justified and that behaviour, which at first sight may seem abusive, can be justified on account of the general efficiencies it achieves.   ALBERTINA ALBORS-LORENS

abuse of court process This term refers to improper use of legal process. Examples in civil proceedings include: claims that are vexatious, scurrilous, or obviously ill-founded; attempts to re-litigate, in another guise, issues already judicially determined; seeking redress through a claim in private law when **judicial review** proceedings are appropriate; denying in a claim a matter admitted in previous proceedings; having an ulterior motive in taking proceedings.

A court has the 'inherent power to prevent its procedure being used for the purpose of oppression and with the result of working injustice' (Lord Justice Kennedy, 1908). The inherent jurisdiction includes the power to stay proceedings that are an abuse of process. It is invoked only in exceptional circumstances and employed with caution. The **Civil Procedure Rules** 1998 give the court the power to strike out a statement of case if it appears to the court that it is an abuse of the court's process or is otherwise likely to obstruct the just disposal of the proceedings.

Examples of abuse of process in criminal proceedings include: prosecution delay rendering fair trial impossible; deliberate interference with a suspect's privileged communications with his or her solicitor; other conduct by police or state prosecutors which threatens or undermines the integrity of the justice system and the **rule of law**. The Crown Court can stay proceedings on indictment for an abuse of process where it considers either that the defendant could not receive a fair trial, or that it would be unfair for the defendant to be tried.   JOHN FITZPATRICK

abuse, civil liability for When we talk of physical, sexual, or emotional abuse, we generally seek to denote abuse in a relational settling, for example, between intimates or within a relationship of trust and power—doctor/patient, teacher/student, etc. Such acts of abuse generally take place in private rather than public settings and often violate social and moral taboos. Until the late twentieth century, for example, there was widespread unwillingness to acknowledge or address abuse within the family. As a consequence, although many of the acts which constitute abuse may be criminal—assault, battery, sexual offences—the **criminal justice system** has struggled—and indeed still does struggle—to redress them.

In recent years there has been increasing interest in bringing civil suits against perpetrators of abuse, often as a direct consequence of perceived failings of the criminal justice system. Witness, most notably, the successful civil suit brought against American football star, OJ Simpson, by the families of his alleged **victims**. The direct failings of criminal justice aside, there are other reasons why victims of abuse might seek a civil **remedy**: the burden of proof is lower in the civil system (the allegation must be proved 'on the balance of probabilities' rather than 'beyond reasonable doubt'); the victim has formal standing in the civil court as 'the claimant' (in criminal cases, the victim is technically only a witness while the **Crown** is effectively the claimant); there may also be the possibility of substantial **compensation** in a civil case (although that does depend on whether the abuser or other party sued in relation to the abuse has the wherewithal to pay). Finally, some people argue that civil suits provide a better therapeutic context for victims to have their 'day in court' and that, regardless of the remedy, the civil trial serves better as a form of cathartic release than the criminal trial.

For all those reasons and perhaps many more, civil claims in the context of physical, sexual, and emotional abuse are on the rise. Such claims have been brought against perpetrators—husbands, fathers, brothers, doctors, teachers, priests—and against third parties who, while not themselves abusers, are alleged to be responsible in some way for failing to detect, prevent, or stop the abuse. Typical targets for such third party claims include local councils, health trusts, education authorities, social services, churches, etc. In both contexts, the claims are most likely to lies in **tort law**; against perpetrators, most typically, **trespass** to person (for acts of assault, battery, and/or false imprisonment) and against third parties, most often in negligence (for breach of a duty of care in relation to the claimant). Third parties may also be vicariously liable if the perpetrators are their employees acting in the course of employment.

Civil claims may also fall within the **common law** (from which tort law is mostly comprised) or within the ambit of statute. For example, the Protection from Harassment Act 1997 provides civil and criminal remedies for **harassment.** This includes kinds of behaviour associated with 'stalking' which may not necessarily fall within the strict parameters of traditional torts. In some cases, claimants have sought to use tort law creatively to deploy an existing cause of action to a new abuse-related situation. In *Khorasandjian v Bush* (1993), for example, (decided before the 1997 Act was enacted), a claimant successfully invoked the rule in a relatively obscure case, *Wilkinson v Downton* (1897) (dealing with a practical joker who injured a woman by telling her, falsely, that her husband had been seriously harmed in an accident), to secure an injunction against a stalker who was telephoning her repeatedly. The difficulties the claimant faced in *Khorasandjian* highlight one of the limits of tort law in relation to abuse claims: because tort struggles to recognize and provide redress for **psychiatric damage** (as opposed to physical damage), abuse taking a primarily emotional or psychological form is less likely to attract liability. Although *Wilkinson v Downton* provides the basis for the development of an action in relation to intentional intention of emotional distress, it has rarely been followed in the UK although, in the US, it forms the base of an independent tort.

Notwithstanding a potential range of civil actions and defendants, abuse suits are far from easy to sustain. A number of common problems are associated with such suits. First there are doctrinal problems hinted at above. It is not always easy to 'fit' what we now understand as acts of abuse into the frame of traditional torts. Trespass to the person, for example, relies on establishing lack of consent, a murky area in the context of relationships, particularly where issues of trust and power are involved. Negligence (of third parties) is far harder to establish in relation to omissions, ie failures to act, as it is too in relation to liability for the criminal acts of another. There are also difficulties of evidence and credibility: the abuse may have taken place without witnesses, a long time prior to the claim being made, and the claimant may have been very young when the alleged abuse took place. The remedial reach may be limited with the practical reality of compensation depending on whether the defendant is solvent. This is particularly problematic in suits against perpetrators who are unlikely to have taken out insurance against liability for their abusive acts! It is also one of the main reasons why claimants seek to sue institutional third parties who are more likely to have deeper pockets from which compensation may be paid.

However, by far the greatest difficulty that has faced claimants bringing civil suits for acts of abuse has been limitation periods. In UK law, tort actions, including actions for trespass to person, must be brought within six years of the tort being committed (Limitation Act 1980, section 2). (In the case of torts against **minors**, the period runs from when they reach their majority.) Thus, a claimant who was sexually abused as a **child** must bring the claim within six years from when they have turned eighteen. The difficulty is that many abuse victims do not fully confront the harm they have sustained until well after that. They may be in their thirties by the time they feel sufficiently able to bring a claim and in some cases it may only be then that the harm (in the form of post-traumatic distress) displays itself or indeed that the abuse itself is recognized/recalled.

In 1993, in *Stubbings v Webb*, the **House of Lords** declined a claim brought by a victim of **child abuse** outside the limitation period. The adult claimant who had been sexually abused as a child by her stepfather and stepbrother had sought to avoid the restrictiveness of section 2 by invoking section 11 of the 1980 Act. This imposed a three-year limitation period in relation to 'actions for damages for negligence, nuisance and breach of statutory duty', *but*, crucially, time ran 'from the date of knowledge . . . . of the person injured' where 'knowledge' required that the claimant knew that 'the injury in question was significant'. The claimant argued that she did not know the significance of harm she had sustained until well into adulthood. In addition (should that argument fail) she relied on a judicial discretion to extend the limitation period conferred by section 33, *but only in relation to section 11 and not section 2*. The House of Lords rejected her arguments and insisted that the section 2 limitation period applied; her claim failed as did a subsequent claim to the **European Court of Human Rights** (*Stubbings v UK* (1996)). In 2001, a **Law Commission** report on limitation periods recommended a uniform regime for personal injuries whatever the basis of the claim. However, no legislative action was taken. The situation continued until *A v Hoare* (2008). *Hoare* was a combined decision (what is known as a 'conjoined appeal') involving a number of suits by abuse victims, mainly against institutional defendants including local councils and a church organization. In some of these cases the claimants had sought to establish 'systemic negligence' by the defendants in relation to abusive acts by their employees rather than alleging **vicarious liability** for the employees' acts of trespass, in order to ensure the claims fell within section 11 and section 33, rather than section 2. In other words, the limitation rules were affecting the kinds of claims being made, often requiring distorted arguments based on tenuous tortious liability in negligence where a more straightforward tortious route in trespass existed. This was not a desirable situation as the House of Lords acknowledged. The facts in *Hoare* itself were slightly different, Hoare being a private rather than institutional defendant who, having been convicted for rape in 1989, won the lottery (£7million) in 2004, as a result of which his victim sued him. Inevitably, the claim failed in the lower courts because of *Stubbings* but on appeal to the House of Lords, the claimant asked their Lordships to overturn *Stubbings* which, remarkably (but not before time) they did, holding that the action against Hoare (in trespass) could constitute a 'breach of duty' for purposes of section 11, thus triggering the judicial discretion to extend the limitation period in section 33.

It is interesting that their Lordships took a step that the legislature had hitherto declined. *Hoare* is a good example of judicial law-making (albeit disguised as a straightforward interpretation of prior cases) and inevitably raises questions about the appropriateness of such judicial activism. On the other hand, as their Lordships observed, the situation as it stood was bringing the law into disrepute, both by forcing the distortion of legal arguments and failing to do justice to tort victims. Many difficulties remain for abuse victims seeking civil redress. And there are still issues to be debated about whether litigation is really the best way to address these kinds of social ills. However, at the individual level, the injustice wrought by the harshness of *Stubbings* appears for the time being to have been alleviated.

JOANNE CONAGHAN

D Fairgrieve and S Greene (eds), *Child Abuse Tort Claims against Public Bodies* (Aldershot: Ashgate Publishing, 2004)

J Conaghan, 'Tort Litigation in the Context of intra-familial Abuse' (1998) 61 *Modern Law Review* 132–181

See also: **acts and omissions; negligence in civil law**

academic freedom *see* **universities and higher education**

ACAS ACAS is the acronym by which the Advisory, Conciliation, and Arbitration Service is known. Originally established as the Conciliation and Arbitration Service in 1974, it has been a statutory body since 1976. As its full name suggests, it provides 'third party' services to employers and their associations on the one hand, and workers and trade unions on the other. These include the appointment of arbitrators or mediators and the provision of conciliation services in collective disputes where both sides agree to this. ACAS itself employs conciliation officers who have a legal duty to try to resolve disputes between individual workers and employers which involve workers' legal rights—such as the right not to be unfairly dismissed or discriminated on various grounds including sex or race—without these issues going to an **employment tribunal** for adjudication. ACAS has also issued 'codes of practice' which explain how certain legal rights for workers and trade unions should be implemented in practice. The best known of these is that on Disciplinary and Grievance Procedures. While much of ACAS's work in the 1970s and 1980s concerned collective disputes in which strikes were threatened or taking place, by the early twenty-first century, in addition to the work of its conciliation officers, ACAS had become more focused on its advisory role through the provision of helpline services and published guidance on good industrial relations practice and research. In Northern Ireland, the Labour Relations Agency has functions similar to those of ACAS in Great Britain.

BOB SIMPSON

See also: **codes of practice in employment law; discrimination in employment**

access, child *see* **children and divorce**

Accident Line *see* **legal advice and assistance**

accountability Accountability is a principle which requires public authorities to explain their actions and be subject to scrutiny. It may also entail sanctions, such as resignation from office or censure. Effective accountability depends on a commitment to open government and rights to **freedom of information**. The news media and pressure groups also play vital roles in ensuring accountability is achieved.

In a **democracy**, the ultimate form of public accountability is through **elections.** In the UK, for example, MPs sit in the **House of Commons** and councillors serve on local authorities. However, elections can only provide periodic and partial opportunities for calling those in power to account because much public sector activity is carried out by unelected officials and appointees.

Political accountability between elections is therefore important. In systems of parliamentary government, ministers are members of parliament and hold office individually and collectively for only so long as they enjoy the confidence of their fellow members. Ministers are held to account on a day-to-day basis through parliamentary questions (written and oral), in debates on the floor of the parliamentary chambers, and through the work of policy scrutiny committees (called **'select committees'** in the UK).

Courts too may be regarded as mechanisms for securing accountability. Individuals, groups, and businesses may use **judicial review** procedures to challenge the lawfulness of action taken by public authorities. Especially where human rights are at stake, there is a growing 'culture of justification' in which government must present cogent explanations for its actions to the courts. Yet, *quis custodiet ipsos custodies?*—'who will watch the watchmen'? It is sometimes said that the principle of **judicial independence** prevents **judges** being held to account for their decisions. Certainly it would be constitutionally wrong for government to impose sanctions on courts which made politically unpalatable decisions. However, judges and **courts** are subject to accountability insofar as they must explain and justify their decisions (for example, by giving reasoned judgments in public).

A range of other bodies also seek to secure accountability. In England, the **Audit Commission** seeks to improve economy, efficiency, and effectiveness in **local government** and the **National Health Service** through inspections and audit; similar commissions exist in the other parts of the UK. The National Audit Office audits the financial statements of many public bodies and reports to Parliament on 'value for money'.

Some commentators complain that the 'accountability revolution' has gone too far. Rather than promoting the legitimacy of public institutions, it now risks undermining public confidence in them. Others express different concerns, for example, that changes in the way we are governed have created an accountability deficit. Globalization has shifted decision-making in some spheres to international institutions—such as the European Union, **World Trade Organization**, and **United Nations**. Privatization has resulted in some public functions being carried out by non-governmental bodies (including businesses and charities). In both these contexts, it is open to question whether adequate accountability arrangements have been established.

ANDREW LE SUEUR

D Oliver, *Constitutional Reform in the UK* (Oxford: Oxford University Press, 2003), ch 3

M W Dowdle, *Public Accountability: Designs, Dilemmas and Experiences* (Cambridge: Cambridge University Press, 2006)

See also: **courts; parliaments; Westminster Parliament**

accusatorial system   *see* **criminal justice system: England and Wales, Northern Ireland; criminal justice system: Scotland**

acquis communautaire The *acquis communautaire* represents the total body of European Union law. It includes: the European Community Treaty (to be renamed the 'Treaty on the functioning of the European Union' if the Treaty of Lisbon is ratified) and the Treaty on European Union, as amended; **European Community laws** such as Regulations and Directives; international agreements entered into by the European Union; general principles developed by the **European Court of Justice**; measures adopted by Member States on 'justice and home affairs' and 'common foreign and **security** policy'; and 'soft' laws such as declarations and resolutions. The *acquis communautaire* is a constantly evolving body of principles, policies, laws, practices, obligations, and objectives that have been agreed within the European Union.

Countries seeking to join the European Union must adapt their national laws and administrative practices in order to comply with the *acquis communautaire*. In the negotiations for the 2004 accession round, the *acquis communautaire* was divided into substantive 'chapters'. The chapters covered: **free movement** of goods, persons, services, and capital; **company** law; competition policy; agriculture; fisheries; transport policy; taxation; **economic and monetary union**; statistics; social policy and employment; energy; industrial policy; small and medium-sized enterprises; science and research; education and training; telecommunication and information technologies; culture and audio-visual policy; regional policy; environment; **consumers** and health protection; cooperation in justice and home affairs; customs union; external relations; common foreign and security policy; financial control; financial and budgetary provisions; and institutions. This list gives a good idea of areas covered by the *acquis communautaire*.   TAMARA HERVEY

See also: **European Community law; European treaties**

act of state doctrine   This term may be used to describe three different principles of law suggesting restraint by **courts** in the area of foreign affairs. The first of these doctrines (the UK act of state doctrine) is the principle laid down in *Buron v Denman* (1848) that the courts will not entertain a claim relating to injury caused to an alien by an act of the **Crown**, or an agent of the Crown, done abroad. The second (the foreign act of state doctrine) refers to the principle that the courts will not adjudicate on the legality of acts of foreign governments that take place within the territory of the foreign state. The third principle, set out in *Buttes Gas v Hammer* (1982), states that UK Courts will not adjudicate on the transactions of foreign states. The first of these doctrines is based on UK constitutional law and regulates the relationship between the courts and the domestic executive. The second and the third principles were inspired, in part, by domestic constitutional considerations but reflect principles of **international law** preventing intervention by states in the affairs of other states.

The operation of these doctrines has been restricted in recent years. The UK act of state doctrine has not been relied on in recent cases even in cases where it has appeared applicable, such as claims by foreign nationals that the actions of British troops abroad violated their **human rights**. Also, the courts will, on grounds of **public policy**, refuse to recognize foreign governmental acts where the act constitutes a flagrant breach of fundamental principles of international law and where international law requires such non-recognition.   DAPO AKANDE

acts and omissions Law commonly divides human conduct into two categories: acts (things we actively do or cause) and omissions (things we fail to do or prevent). As a general principle, legal liability flows from a person's acts, and not from omissions. This general principle cuts across the entire legal system. For example, it is a crime deliberately to drown someone, but not to stand by and watch while that person drowns. Likewise, there is no civil liability in **tort law** if Pauline sees Victor about to walk into danger and does not shout a warning. This is so even though an act causing equivalent injury would be unlawful. The former is 'non-feasance', and generally of no legal significance; the latter is 'misfeasance', and actionable. Much the same holds in **contract law**. If Peter offers to buy Sarah's car for £5,000, Sarah's failure to refuse the offer cannot constitute its acceptance. The contract can only be formed by Sarah's active communication. Silence will not do. Similarly, in international law, treaties bind only those states actively assenting to them.

That is the general position. It is subject to certain exceptions, which mainly occur when someone has a specific legal duty to intervene. Such ('positive') duties can arise in diverse ways. For example, if a person has created a particular danger, say by accidentally igniting a fire, she may become under a duty to prevent it from spreading. Alternatively, a duty may be attached to some more general activity, such as the duty on drivers to report accidents involving another vehicle. One can also volunteer for a duty, as when one becomes a lifeguard. Other duties arise when one person is responsible for another's welfare: thus an on-duty doctor has responsibility for patients, and parents are responsible for their children. In such cases, to stand by while one's child starves to death, or one's patient dies from treatable injuries, may be a **homicide**. Even though a **stranger** can refuse to help with impunity, one who owes a legal duty cannot. Instead, he must make reasonable efforts to prevent the harm from occurring.

The positive duty requires only 'reasonable' efforts to save, thereby allowing doctors to discontinue treatment no longer in a patient's best interests. This includes switching off life support, at least where the patient is in a persistent vegetative state without hope of recovery. In law, such conduct is a permitted omission, whereas deliberate killing by lethal injection would be murder. The analysis is controversial, however, since *switching off* machinery seemingly involves an act, and would be murder if done by a stranger.

More generally, the law's basic differentiation between acts and omissions is itself controversial. It has been attacked on the basis that more should be required of us: as citizens, we have altruistic moral obligations that the law should recognize. Thus it has been argued in the law of **restitution** that a **person** who knowingly permits another to confer an unasked-for benefit, say by washing her windows, should be legally bound to pay for the service; and various writers have advocated a crime (existing in many European jurisdictions) of failing to undertake reasonable steps to rescue someone in peril.

These are arguments for the creation of fairly specific duties, and it is easy to be diverted from the underlying issue by the power of selected examples in which, say, James rubs his hands gleefully while the toddler next door drowns in the swimming pool. Perhaps there should be a duty to rescue in such cases. But too many arguments for law reform rely on graphic examples that skew our instincts—a one-off situation in which life is at stake and there is no serious inconvenience to the rescuer, etc. By their nature, such examples are incapable of establishing the case for general law reform. The primary question is whether the law should distinguish between acts and omissions *in general*. Should deliberate silence be enough to generate contractual and restitutionary obligations? Should the omission to prevent minor harm to another's property (or person) be criminal damage (or assault)? It is only once the basic case is established for distinguishing omissions from acts that the argument for extending liability in particular contexts can intelligibly be addressed.

At the general level, there does seem reason to separate omissions from acts. First, albeit not always, they are *on average* morally less serious than actions. Positive acts that cause harm usually manifest a greater level of hostility than do omissions, and we tend to feel very differently about the actual harm-doer than about the non-savers. Omissions are often incidental to the defendant's motivations—they disclose a lesser fault, of limited imagination or empathy, rather than direct malice. There is also the point that we are normally entitled to prefer the interests of family and those near us to the interests of strangers (which is partly why we are not obliged to donate all our savings to charitable causes). The act-omission distinction arguably provides a rough-and-ready line by which the law can reflect these differences, with specific duties operating in contexts where a more refined approach is appropriate.

Secondly, attaching legal consequences to omissions is much more intrusive than attaching them to actions. Suppose that Sarah wishes to avoid incurring legal liability, and knows that liability results from a particular *act*: say, of injuring Peter or accepting Peter's offer to buy her car. All Sarah has to do is refrain from attacking Peter or accepting his offer. She can simply ignore him and get on with whatever else she was doing. One way of thinking about this is to ask: if we know that Sarah is obeying the instruction not to attack Peter, how much do we know about her actual behaviour? In essence, nothing. Refraining from an act thus still leaves her plenty of options.

Contrast omissions. Suppose that legal liability instead resulted from an omission: say, of not preventing injury to Peter or failing to reject Peter's offer to buy the car. Now, in order to avoid liability, Sarah must interrupt whatever else she is doing and actively save Peter or communicate rejection of his offer. Instead of being free to do other things, her immediate options are down to one.

This is, no doubt, not a great difficulty if the prospect of liability arises only occasionally and in a narrow context, especially where the interests at stake are vital (as in easy rescue cases). But it is a good reason, when considering all the possible varieties and sources of legal liability, to differentiate acts from omissions, and to hesitate before extending liability to the latter. Making Sarah's legal status turn primarily on her acts rather than her omissions allows her greater freedom and control of her own life. By comparison, if liability in restitution turned, as proposed, on omissions, it would become easy for others to control Sarah's actions, for example by inundating her with unsolicited services which she must actively reject lest she became liable to pay for them. It is no surprise that such 'passive selling' activities are themselves unlawful. Like being required to reject unsolicited services, treating acts

and omissions generally as equal sources of liability would impose far too many burdens on citizens.

ANDREW SIMESTER

See also: **negligence in civil law**

Acts of Parliament   The UK famously possesses no written Constitution or formal document conferring law-making powers or establishing a hierarchy of laws. Some laws are enacted by Parliament and are known as Acts of Parliament, statutes or 'primary legislation'. In other areas, law develops through the decisions of judges of the higher courts who recognize a system of binding precedent; this is the process which has resulted in the creation of the **common law**.

Acts of Parliament are either Public (affecting the public as a whole), or Private (determining the rights of a limited group of people).

Since the Union with Scotland in 1707, the Parliament of the UK has had its seat at Westminster. However, at the end of the twentieth century, a process of regional devolution took place. Today, the most powerful of the devolved authorities is the **Scottish Parliament**, which was given extensive although limited power to legislate for Scotland by the Scotland Act 1998; its instruments are known as Acts of the Scottish Parliament. The Northern Ireland Act 1998 makes provision for the introduction of a similar system in that Province. The **Welsh Assembly** currently has somewhat lesser powers and cannot enact its own legislation.

There is a vital distinction between Acts of the **Westminster Parliament**, on the one hand, and Acts of the devolved Parliaments and other legislative acts on the other. The Westminster Parliament is recognized by the courts as possessing its own inherent power to enact law. No other body possesses such power. Parliament at Westminster can, however, delegate authority to other institutions and empower them to legislate within a limited sphere; the resultant laws are known as 'secondary', 'subordinate', or 'delegated' legislation.

In the absence of a hierarchy of laws, all law from whatever source is of theoretically equal weight. Thus, primary legislation is of the same weight as secondary legislation and rules of the common law are of the same importance as legislative rules. However, chaos would result if there was no mechanism for deciding which rule is to be enforced in the event of a conflict between laws springing from different sources. The modern rule is that law in the form of Acts of the Westminster Parliament constitutes the highest form of legal authority and cannot be challenged by the judges or by any other authority. This is one of the ways in which democracy is reflected in the UK constitution. It is usually referred to as the principle of parliamentary 'sovereignty'. Nonetheless, courts have power, pursuant to the Human Rights Act 1998, to declare an Act 'incompatible' with the European Convention on Human Rights. They may also apply a provision of European Union law in preference to an Act of Parliament where there is a conflict between the two; this is a necessary consequence of membership of the **European Union** and is given legislative blessing by the European Communities Act 1972.

Acts of Parliament must be made in accordance with the procedures currently prescribed by Parliament itself. The House of Lords made clear in *Pickin v British Railways Board* (1974) that the courts will not investigate whether these procedures have been complied with. Most Bills emanate from the government of the day but a small number are introduced by Private Members. Bills normally require the consent of both Houses, in addition to the Royal Assent, to become Acts. However, an exceptional procedure was introduced by the **Parliament Act** 1911, amended by the Parliament Act 1949. This enables Money Bills and most kinds of Public Bill to become law without the consent of the **House of Lords**. As regards Public Bills, this can occur where the Bill has been passed by the Commons but rejected by the Lords in two successive sessions, a year having elapsed between the Second Reading in the Commons in the first of those sessions and the date when the Bill passed the Commons in the later session. In *R (Jackson) v Attorney-General* (2005), the House of Lords confirmed the lawfulness of this procedure and thus the formal validity of the Hunting Act 2004, which banned hunting with dogs and was enacted despite the opposition of the House of Lords.

EVELYN ELLIS

See also: **bills (parliamentary); House of Commons; legislative drafting; legislative processes; Northern Ireland Assembly; parliamentary sovereignty; soft law**

administrative law Lawyers divide the law up into 'subjects' or 'areas' or 'categories', partly to make the jobs of understanding and teaching law more manageable, and partly in a search for 'general principles' or 'theories' that underpin, and can explain and justify, large sets of legal rules. **Criminal law** and **contract law**, for instance, are legal categories known to many non-lawyers. This process of legal categorization began in earnest in the late nineteenth century, when academic study of law in universities began to flourish. But in the UK, at least, administrative law did not emerge as a distinct legal subject until the mid-twentieth century. One of the main concerns of administrative law is control of government decision-making and the exercise of governmental power. In the late nineteenth century the very influential Victorian jurist, Albert Venn **Dicey**, denied that there was a distinct set of legal rules about holding public officials to account; and although Dicey's view was widely considered to be wrong, it is generally thought to have delayed for more than half a century the development and recognition of administrative law as a distinct legal category. The 1950s and 1960s witnessed not only a flowering of academic interest in the subject but also, more significantly, a new willingness on the part of courts to exercise firm control over government activity. A series of important decisions of the **House of Lords** were seen as establishing a new dispensation in which the legal **accountability** of government would be considerably strengthened—a development thought by many to provide a necessary counterweight to the enormous growth of governmental involvement in and regulation of social and economic life in the previous half-century.

The basic nature of administrative law can best be understood in terms of the concept of **separation of powers**. It is traditional to distinguish between three different types of governmental power: legislative, administrative (or 'executive'), and judicial; and three branches of government: the legislature, the executive, and the judiciary. In the British system, the principle of **parliamentary sovereignty** more-or-less completely prevents the judiciary from controlling the exercise of legislative power by the **Westminster Parliament**. By contrast, the concept of the **rule of law** has been widely thought to justify and require judicial control of the exercise of power—whether administrative, legislative, or judicial—by the executive branch at both central and local levels of government. Viewed in this framework, administrative law is the area of law concerned with judicial control of the executive. It also encompasses various types of non-judicial control of executive power, notably by **tribunals**, public-sector **ombudsmen**, the **Auditor-General**, parliamentary **select committees**, and so on.

Some people insist that in addition to rules about government accountability, rules about the creation and conferral of powers on organs of executive government are also part of administrative law; but in this regard, the boundary between administrative law and **constitutional law** is somewhat blurred, and its precise location is a matter of little or no significance.

Administrative law is part of public law. Public law is contrasted with private law. Traditionally understood, private law is law about relations between private citizens, whereas public law is law about relations between governors and the governed, and between various organs of **governance**. But this understanding of the distinction is flawed because private law (**tort law** and **contract law**, for instance) applies to governors as well as to the governed. There is no special *public law* of tort or contract. Nevertheless, private law rules may operate differently according to whether they are applied to governors or governed, and many books on administrative law include treatment of the tort and contract liability of government bodies. The distinction between public law and private law is much more sharply drawn in French law, partly because of the existence in France of a special system of public-law courts (notably the *Conseil d'Etat*) that handle claims against government.

Leaving such 'private law' liability aside, the main principles of administrative law are as follows. Powers must be exercised in accordance with the procedural rules of **natural justice**: the rule against bias and the fair-hearing rule. Officials and agencies must not exceed the legal limits of their powers as defined by statutes and **common law**. They must respect **human rights**. Decisions must be based on true facts and correct legal principles. As a general rule, officials and agencies must not 'delegate' their powers to any other official or agency. They must act in good faith, consistently, and in accordance with any 'legitimate expectation' their conduct has raised. Duties must be performed as prescribed. **Discretion** must be exercised 'reasonably', 'for proper purposes', and flexibly on the basis only of 'relevant considerations'. A decision that breaches any of these principles is said to be 'illegal' and can be 'quashed'—which means that it has no legal effect and will typically have to be made again in compliance with the principles. Officials and agencies can be ordered to perform their duties and prohibited from acting illegally. These are the principles according to which *courts* exercise control over the exercise of administrative power through what is called **judicial review**. Tribunals are less concerned with whether decisions are 'legal' and more with whether they are fair and appropriate in the circumstances of the case. If not, the tribunal can change the decision. Ombudsmen (who can only recommend, not require, remedial action) root out '**maladministration**', which is considered to be less serious than illegality.

Until the 1980s, administrative law was thought of as law about the conduct of governmental bodies. However, the Thatcher government began a process (continued by New Labour) of **privatization** of publicly-owned enterprises (such as utility companies),

contracting-out of the provision of 'public services' (such as residential care for the sick and elderly), private financing of public infrastructure projects (such as motorways), and so on. These developments raised the important question of whether administrative law rules would apply to private entities performing functions that had previously been performed by government. This question has been answered by redefining administrative law as applying to the performance of 'public functions', whether by governmental or private actors. But whereas it is relatively easy to decide whether an agent is part of government or not, it is much harder to classify functions as public or private without ideological commitment. As a result, the scope of application of administrative law has become increasingly unclear and the role of the courts, in developing and applying it, is controversial.   PETER CANE

See also: **legal rules, types of; local government; prerogative orders; public bodies, liability of; writs**

administrative rule-making   *see* **legal rules, types of**

admiralty courts   *see* **civilian courts**

admiralty law   The Admiralty jurisdiction was traditionally, and is still today, considered to be exceptional. Its most significant feature is the action *in rem*, or action against property, most usually a ship. In such an action, a warrant for the arrest of a ship may be issued by the Admiralty Marshal of the High Court upon an application being made by a claimant who asserts that the claim is within the Admiralty jurisdiction of the Court and who offers an undertaking to pay the Marshal's costs and expenses of the arrest. The Marshal will then arrange to have the warrant affixed to a prominent place on the vessel, thereby placing the vessel into the Marshal's custody and beyond the control of the ship's owner unless and until the owner provides security for the amount of the claim which has been commenced against the ship.

The arrest of the ship or other property, usually cargo or freight, pursuant to an action *in rem* has threefold significance. First, and most importantly, it creates in the claimant (or gives effect to) a 'security interest' in the property. Secondly, it often has the effect of securing the appearance of the owner of (or others interested in) the ship or other property to answer the claim. Thirdly, it may provide a basis for jurisdiction: the arrest of a ship within the territorial waters of England or Wales will usually give the High Court jurisdiction to determine the claim even if the circumstances giving rise to the claim are wholly unconnected with England or Wales. If the claimant is ultimately successful, the security interest, which has been created by the action *in rem*, is enforceable by judicial sale of the arrested property or against the security which has been given in its place. Where the fund generated by the sale of the arrested property, or the security given in its place, is insufficient to meet all the judgments obtained against the ship, the Admiralty Court will rank the claims in order of priority in accordance with well-established doctrines and principles.

The Supreme Court Act 1981 (to be renamed the Senior Courts Act) provides for Admiralty jurisdiction to be exercised by the High Court and distinguishes between actions commenced *in personam*, or 'against another person' and those commenced *in rem*, thus permitting the arrest of a ship as security for the claim. If the claim is of a type that must be commenced *in personam*, the defendant must be able to be served with the originating process and it is not possible to commence the action against the ship which is the subject of the claim.

Four main categories of claim may be commenced *in rem*. The first category encompasses claims which relate to the ownership or possession of a ship, including a claims relating to the **mortgage** of a ship. The second category comprises what are known as 'maritime liens'. Originally, only the existence of a maritime lien would entitle a claimant to arrest a ship; and even today the existence of a maritime lien gives the claimant priority over most other types of claim against the ship, including priority over a mortgagee. A maritime lien arises in respect of damage done by a ship, salvage, a claim by the master of the ship for wages or disbursements, and a claim by the crew for wages. The third category consists of the claims which have been agreed by international convention (The International Convention on the Arrest of Sea-going Ships 1952, and its 1999 successor) to found a right to arrest. In addition to the claims which give rise to a maritime lien, that list includes claims for: damage to goods carried in or on a ship; claims arising out of an agreement relating to the carriage of goods or to the use or hire of a ship; claims for towage or pilotage; claims for the supply of necessaries; claims relating to the construction, repair, or equipment of a ship; claims arising out of general average; and claims relating to bottomry (now obsolete). In the fourth category are claims relating to the towage or pilotage of an aircraft.   SARAH DERRINGTON

SC Derrington and JM Turner, *The Law and Practice of Admiralty Matters* (Oxford: Oxford University Press, 2007)

See also: **admiralty courts; mortgages of chattels**

adoption   Adoption is a process for conferring parental rights and is currently governed by the Adoption and Children Act 2002. Unsurprisingly, it is difficult to find a consensus on adoption law. An adoption order is draconian: **parental responsibility** is transferred to the adoptive parents so that, for the adopted **child**, it is as if, legally, the previous family had not existed. Further, the legal framework is a response to a host of contentious issues, for example, the circumstances in which parental opposition to the adoption of their child may be surmounted, the weight given to the welfare of the child and the qualifications for would-be adopters.

Adoption law reform must also take account of changing socio-economic patterns and moralities. The background to the Adoption Act 1926 was pressure from childless couples seeking babies of their own. Such needs could be met, given a lack of access to reliable contraception and widespread social disapproval of 'single mothers'. More recently the focus has shifted to finding homes for children who, for whatever reason, cannot live with their birth families. Inevitably such children are likely to be older, may have been 'damaged' by abuse and neglect, and have a personal history which includes relationships with members of their birth families.

This trend has had several implications. Children can be adopted up to the age of 19 (unless married) but older children and those with special needs are less attractive to 'traditional' adopters and their care may have resource implications. Further, psychologists now consider it to be potentially harmful for children to terminate all contact with 'significant others' in their birth families or to deny children any knowledge about their 'roots' and genetic make-up. Recent **legislation** has responded to these issues.

Adoption can only proceed with the consent of each birth parent (or guardian) with parental responsibility. However, there are legal criteria for 'dispensing with consent'. Under previous law the crucial test was whether parents were withholding consent 'unreasonably'. Now there are only two grounds for dispensing with consent: that the parents are 'incapable' (or cannot be found) or that 'the welfare of the child requires consent to be dispensed with' (2002 Act, s 52). At the same time the **welfare principle** has been made determinative: instead of the child's welfare being 'the first consideration', the child's welfare 'throughout life' must now be the 'paramount consideration' (2002 Act, s 1(2)). The child herself does not have a veto to the adoption although such a provision was included in a previous draft of the 2002 Act.

Courts must now consider whether there should be arrangements for contact with members of the birth family before an adoption order can be made (s 46(6)) although positive attitudes towards, and case examples of, 'open' adoption have developed from the 1980s. Subject to exceptions, adopted persons over 18 have more opportunities to access information about their birth families. An adopted person can obtain a copy of the original birth certificate, search the index of the Adopted Children Register (and obtain a copy of the entry), and register their interest in making contact with birth relatives by requesting an entry in the Adoption Contact Register. In addition the 2002 Act, ss 55–65 contains new provisions governing the disclosure of information held by adoption agencies.

The qualifications for adopters have also changed. Unmarried couples and homosexual couples 'living as partners in an enduring family relationship' over the age of 21 can now adopt whilst the 2002 Act, ss 2–8 deal with access to the post-adoption support for adoptive parents which has become necessary in relation to 'hard to place' children. Both these measures are likely to increase the pool of potential adopters.

The 2002 Act also introduces new legal statuses short of adoption, notably special **guardianship** which ends when the child becomes an adult. Recent cases make clear that guardianship is more appropriate than adoption for grandparents and other kin where adoption would 'skew' familial relationships. Similarly, a step-parent can now make a sole application to adopt but can, alternatively, seek a parental responsibility order or agreement (Children Act 1989, amended s 4).

The Hague Convention on the Protection of Children and Cooperation in Respect of Inter-country Adoption has been applied in the UK since 2003. Inter-country adoptions are subject to the same procedures as domestic adoptions but there are further restrictions in relation to particular foreign countries (see Adoption and Children Act 2002, s 83 and the Children and Adoption Act 2006, Pt 2).

CHRISTINE PIPER

D Cullen, 'Adoption – a (fairly) new approach' (17/4 *Child and Family Law Quarterly* (2005) 475–486).
A Diduck and F Kaganas, *Family Law, Gender and the State* (Oxford: Hart Publishing, 2006), 129–152.

adoptive leave   *see* **parental leave**

advance directives   An advance directive ('directive') is an anticipatory refusal of **consent to medical treatment** by an adult of sound mind which remains effective notwithstanding subsequent loss of **capacity**. Directives were created by the **common law** but are now regulated in England and Wales by sections 24–26 of the Mental Capacity Act 2005 which is in large part declaratory of the **common law**.

At common law a directive derives its efficacy from the interaction of three principles: first, that any touching (and every medical procedure involves some degree of touching) is, without consent, both a crime and a civil wrong; secondly, that an anticipatory refusal of consent by a person with **capacity** remains effective notwithstanding subsequent loss of capacity (temporary, indefinite, or permanent); and, thirdly, that the doctrine of necessity (which permits medical treatment in the absence of consent if, in the circumstances, it is reasonably required in the best interests of the patient) cannot be relied upon if the treatment is known to be contrary to the previously expressed wishes of the patient. These same principles mean, however, that a directive operates purely negatively. A patient can by a directive refuse particular forms of treatment but cannot require a doctor to provide treatment which, on clinical or ethical grounds, the doctor is unwilling to provide.

No particular formalities are required for a valid directive at common law, but the court needs to be satisfied that the words relied upon (which may be expressed in lay terms) were more than a mere off-hand remark and really were intended to be binding for the future. Where there is nothing in writing the court requires clear and convincing proof. Under the Act, a directive refusing consent to life-sustaining treatment is not valid unless it is verified by a statement by the patient that it is to apply even if life is at risk and is in writing signed both by the patient and, in the patient's presence, by a witness.

A directive is applicable in such circumstances and in relation to such treatment(s) as it specifies. It is not applicable to treatment if, at the material time, the patient has capacity to give or refuse consent or if the treatment is not that specified in the directive, if any circumstances specified in the directive are absent, or if there are reasonable grounds for believing that circumstances exist which the patient did not anticipate at the time of the directive and which would have affected his decision had they been anticipated.

A directive is revocable and can be withdrawn at any time while the patient retains capacity. Withdrawal need not be in writing. (Provisions to the contrary are void on grounds of **public policy**.) A directive may be withdrawn by express words or if the patient has done anything else clearly inconsistent with the directive remaining his fixed decision.

Thus, a directive refusing blood transfusions made by a Jehovah's Witness ceased to be operative upon her subsequent conversion to Islam.

JAMES MUNBY

adventure sports *see* safety in sport

adversary system This term is a general description of the approach to dealing with claims in civil legal proceedings that is followed in England and Wales and many other **common law** legal systems (such as the USA, Canada, and Australia). A distinction is often drawn between adversarial and **inquisitorial system**s. There are parallels between the adversarial system for civil claims and the **accusatorial system** in the criminal process, as both share several common assumptions about the nature of court proceedings.

To understand the nature of the adversary system, we need to look at the function of the court, the role of the legal profession, that status of the parties to the proceedings, and views about how best to determine the truth of conflicting factual accounts. Lord Devlin, a prominent English judge, said: 'The English say that the best way of getting at the truth is to have each party dig for the facts that help it; between them they will bring it all to light.... Two prejudiced searchers starting from the opposite ends of the field will between them be less likely to miss anything than the impartial searcher starting in the middle' (*The Judge* (Oxford: Oxford University Press, 1979), 61).

In an adversarial system, the court takes on the role of a neutral umpire. Legal proceedings are viewed as a contest between opposing views rather than as an independent inquiry into the truth. The court is not involved in the preparation of a case—that is a function of the parties and their legal advisers. Each party sets out the gist of their view of the legal and factual dispute on a claim form (or 'pleadings') lodged with the court and assembles the evidence necessary to prove their case.

Each party has freedom to present their case as they think best. Judges need not say much during adversarial proceedings. They call each party in turn to present their case and to respond to the other side. Judges may need to rule on the admissibility of a piece of evidence but it is for each party (or their legal representative) to choose what evidence to put before the court. Rarely will a judge take a leading role in questioning a witness directly—and when they do, it will generally be for the limited purpose of seeking to clarify something that has been said.

The role of each party's lawyer is therefore vital. As well as selecting what issues of law and fact to put before the court, the legal representative seeks to challenge the other party's evidence—by cross-examining their witnesses and seeking to undermine any **expert evidence** produced by the opposing side. Lawyers are champions of their client's case rather than state officials charged with finding out the truth. **Legal professional ethics and values**, as well as the law, prohibit lawyers from deliberately misleading the court by presenting evidence on behalf of their client that they know to be untrue; but they have no duty to seek out and disclose evidence that is unfavourable to their client's case. In some circumstances, fairness requires that all parties have access to an independent lawyer, and so legal aid provides funds to pay for representation for people who cannot afford to pay for this themselves.

The core elements of the adversary system described above are often modified to ensure fairness. Adversarial systems assume that there is an 'equality of arms' between the two opposing parties which is often not reflected in the reality. In situations where one of the parties is not legally represented at the trial, the judge will need to take a more active role in questioning the other side's witnesses in order to ensure that the proceedings are fair. A corollary of freedom to pursue a claim as a party thinks best is that a party may also agree to settle and withdraw a claim or defence before the trial is concluded; but where the party is a minor or a vulnerable adult the court may have a role in approving the proposed settlement.

Adversarial systems may also be modified for reasons of efficiency and cost-saving. In England and Wales, the **Civil Procedure Rules**, introduced in 1999, seek to encourage a less adversarial approach by measures such as according to judges new roles in managing the conduct of litigation. This has involved departure from some features of a 'pure' adversarial system. Emphasis is now placed on presentation to the court of mutually acceptable evidence rather than separate evidence from each side. 'Trial by ambush', in which many of the key points of evidence are not revealed to the opposing side until the trial, is being replaced by obligations to disclose evidence at an early stage of the process and, where possible, to reach agreement on contested issues. Parties are now encouraged to use **alternative dispute resolution** methods, such as mediation, which are generally less adversarial. In all these ways, the freedom of parties to pursue their claim as they think best is now balanced against other goals, including saving time and expense.

ANDREW LE SUEUR

JA Jolowicz 'Adversarial and inquisitorial models of civil procedure' (2003) 52 *International and Comparative Law Quarterly* 281

J McEwan, *Evidence and the Adversarial Process: the Modern Law* (Oxford: Hart Publishing, 2nd edn, 1998)

See also: **civil trials; criminal trials; evidence (civil); evidence (criminal)**

adverse possession   This term refers to the acquisition of ownership of land by possession adverse to the true owner for twelve years. Consent of the owner is fatal to adverse possession, but it does not matter that the owner has no present use for the land. The underlying theory is that adverse possession gives rise to a **fee simple estate** at a very early point, but it is inferior to the true owner's fee simple estate. By statute, the title of the true owner terminates after the twelve years.

Adverse possession is particularly important in relation to unregistered land. Purchasers see title deeds to the land covering only the relatively short period of fifteen years. This is viable only because any earlier estates in the land are likely to have been extinguished by adverse possession. Its role in relation to registered land is more controversial. It was argued that, as it operated before reforms in 2002, it constituted a taking of property without compensation for no sufficient policy reason. However, a majority of the **European Court of Human Rights** has held adverse possession to be consistent with Convention rights.

The Land Registration Act 2002 has greatly limited the future scope of adverse possession as regards registered titles. It can be claimed after ten years, but the claim fails unless the true owner makes no claim to the land (the claim must be backed up by taking proceedings within the next two years) or the two parties are neighbours. The requirement of a claim ensures that land can be efficiently used when the true owner effectively abandons it. As for neighbours, the position on the ground is allowed to prevail because plans are commonly inaccurate.

ROGER J SMITH

See also: **human rights and property; registration of title; trespass**

advertising   The development of mass production in the early twentieth century created a problem for producers who found that local and traditional markets were inadequate to sell all that they could produce. The development of sophisticated techniques of mass marketing provided the means by which producers could persuade consumers to consume more of their products. In contrast with a more traditional understanding of consumers demanding from producers what they need, an understanding of consumer behaviour linked to marketing suggests that the key purpose of advertising is to persuade consumers to buy what producers need to sell. This key role for advertising in the contemporary consumer society is accommodated rather poorly by the law. Advertising law, to the extent that it exists, is a blend of **common law** (**contract law** and **tort law**), statutory regulation and enforcement and self-regulatory practices.

A key reason why the law adapts with difficulty to modern advertising practice is that much marketing activity is the responsibility of producers, who rarely have a direct contractual relationship with consumers. Accordingly the chief mechanisms through which consumers might hold producers to account for misleading advertising claims, based in contract, are rarely available. The leading court case, *Carlill v The Carbolic Smoke Ball Company* (1893), is authority for the proposition that a contract between a producer and consumer is only likely to be generated by an advertisement where the advertisement makes a specific offer with requirements that are met by the consumer. A well-known example of such contractual expectations being created in the early 1990s turned on a promise from the vacuum cleaner manufacturer, Hoover, to give free flights to consumers who bought Hoover products over a specified value. (Hoover under-estimated the demand for their offer and struggled to meet demand both for their products and for free flights, with consequential adverse public-relations consequences). But in most instances the claims made in print, broadcast, or internet advertisements do not give rise to such specific expectations and would generally give disappointed consumers no contractual rights against the producer. Marketing material may affect contractual expectations between consumers and sellers.

This gap in the enforceability of advertising claims is partly addressed through the criminal law regime established under the Trade Descriptions Act 1968 and the Consumer Protection Act 1987, Part III. This legislation addresses, amongst other things, claims made in advertisements concerning the nature and qualities of goods and services, and claims relating to prices. More specific legislation in particular sectors requires, in addition to accuracy in claims, that particular information is supplied in advertising material. The most widespread examples of these positive 'disclosure rules' are found in consumer credit legislation which requires disclosure of such things as interest rates to be charged for credits and risks associated with taking loans secured on property (such as mortgages).

The criminal law regime was supplemented by the introduction of administrative procedures for enforcing rules on misleading advertisements implemented in the UK in 1988 as a result of a European directive. The Control of Misleading Advertisements Regulations 1988 (as amended) target misleading claims which are likely to adversely affect the economic position of consumers (for example because they buy a product which does not live up to the claims made). Responsibility for enforcement lies with a central agency, the **Office of Fair Trading**, which is empowered to advise businesses to desist from making misleading claims and to seek a court order (an injunction) requiring the misleading conduct to be stopped. In practice this system is linked to the self-regulatory regime established by the industry itself (discussed in the next paragraph) and provides a mechanism for official enforcement against an advertiser who fails to follow the rules of the self-regulatory regime insofar as these relate to misleading claims.

The advertising industry itself has long had concerns that the legal framework concerning advertisements is inadequate for maintaining the reputation and credibility of the industry. In the face of sustained attack on the questionable methods of advertising the Advertising Standards Authority ('ASA') was established by the industry in 1962 to develop and enforce a code of good conduct for advertisers, which requires advertisements to comply with legal rules, but goes considerably beyond such legal requirements. This wide scope is captured in the ASA slogan 'Is it legal, decent, honest and truthful?'. The Code of Advertising Practice contains both general principles and more detailed rules governing such things as advertising to children and problematic products such as slimming aids. The rules embrace a principle of substantiation, according to which factual claims should only be made when backed up with evidence. The ASA offers 'copy advice' to advertisers unsure whether a proposed advert is in compliance with the rules, but operates chiefly through published adjudications on complaints made by consumers and competitors. An indicator of the confidence of government in the value of regime is that the statutory responsibility of the government agency, the Office of Communications, to regulate broadcast advertising, has recently been delegated to the ASA as a supplement to its traditional responsibility for print and internet advertising.

COLIN SCOTT

See also: **Advertising Code; advertising standards and complaints; Consumer Credit Act; mortgages of chattels; mortgages of law; quality of products; trading standards**

Advertising Code   *see* **codes of practice in consumer Law**

advertising standards and complaints
see **advertising**

advice centres   *see* **Citizens Advice Bureaux**

Advice Services Alliance   *see* **legal advice and assistance**

advisory opinions in international law   *see* **international courts and tribunals**

advocacy   *see* **lawyering skills**

Advocate General   *see* **European Court of Justice**

advocates, famous   Advocacy, the art of persuasion, is a talent deployed in many spheres of life, but is most closely associated with the **courts**. It has flourished in that context, more in the **common law** than in civilian jurisdictions, because of the emphasis traditionally placed in the former on adversarial rather than inquisitorial litigation, and on oral rather than written presentation. Not all famous advocates were great lawyers; and there are many great lawyers who were not famous advocates.

As a discipline advocacy dates back to classical times: **Cicero,** (106 BC–43 BC) the best known of the Ancient Roman advocates, was himself reared in the Greek tradition of rhetoric, although it appears that the hallmark of advocacy at that time was personal abuse of one's opponent (*vituperatio*). Cicero's first major case was his defence of Sextus Roscius in 80 BC on a charge of parricide, and he made his name by his successful prosecution of Gaius Verres, former Governor of Sicily, although Verres was represented by Hortensius, previously reckoned to be Rome's greatest lawyer.

In England, advocacy as an art is a relatively recent phenomenon. One scholar wrote 'our early lawyers were not eminent for their eloquence and there was little to encourage the graces of address'. Only a few names stand out before what is generally recognized to have been the golden age of advocacy—the early twentieth century. **Erskine** (1750–1823) started as a seaman and ended up as **Lord Chancellor**; he is celebrated for his defence of Tom **Paine**, charged with treason in 1793 for his work, 'The Rights of Man'. Brougham (1778–1868) also a future Lord Chancellor defended another unpopular figure, Queen Caroline, in 1820. The roll call of the renowned contains names such as Charles Russell (1832–1900) who defended Charles Parnell in charges brought against him by the British Government in 1888, exposing in an eight-day cross examination the forgeries of the main witness, Pigot; Marshall Hall (1858–1929), known as 'the Great Defender' for saving notorious alleged murderers from the gallows; **Edward Carson**, a future Law Lord who destroyed Oscar Wilde in cross-examination and, for his political sympathies, was dubbed 'the Uncrowned King of Ulster'; Rufus Isaacs (1860–1935), a future **Lord Chief Justice** and Viceroy of India, who successfully prosecuted Seddon, the poisoner; FE Smith (1872–1930), a future Lord Chancellor, who secured the conviction of **Sir Roger Casement** in 1916 where he was opposed by Sergeant Sullivan (1871–1959), the last of the sergeants who built a successful practice on the Munster circuit; and of later vintage, Patrick Hastings (1880–1952), a libel expert and Norman Birkett (1883–1962) a future Lord Justice of Appeal and member of Marshall Hall's Chambers, and, like Hall, a criminal defence specialist.

An amalgam of reasons contributed to their fame. The timetable of the law courts and the **House of Commons** permitted many of the above to prosper in both, the reputation in one feeding off but also feeding their reputation in the other. **Capital punishment** still remained the ultimate sanction for murder; advocates in criminal courts battled for their clients' lives, not only their property or good name. Drama not being then available through the multimedia, assiduous court reporting, especially in actions for **libel**, **slander**, or breach of promise, provided a form of mass entertainment. The role of **juries**, not only in major criminal but also civil cases, encouraged a more flamboyant style of advocacy, sometimes, as with Marshall Hall and his scented inhaler, trespassing on the theatrical.

The post-war era saw the decline in that florid form of advocacy: it was in fiction rather than fact that the hyperbolic tradition persisted, as with John Mortimer's comic creation, Rumpole of the Bailey. Only George Carman (1919–2001), the libel lawyer with the soubriquet 'the Silver Fox', caught the popular imagination in the same way. A quieter more cerebral type of advocacy became the attribute of the modern fashionable silk. Hartley Shawcross (1902–2003), in his time the youngest KC in history, burnished his name in his presentation in the **Nuremberg trials**; and another leading Labour politician, Gerald Gardiner (1900–1990), again a future Lord Chancellor, defender of *Lady Chatterley's Lover* in a seminal **obscenity** prosecution was also recognized as the actual, and not only the titular head of the Bar.

It was in the USA, where, unlike in England, juries were still prevalent in civil litigation that more popular, even populist, advocacy continued on display, from Clarence Darrow (1857–1938), who overthrew another famous advocate and three times Democrat Presidential candidate, William Jennings Bryan (1860–1925) in the 'Scopes' trial in 1925 pitting Darwinism against creationism; Melvin Belli (1908–1996), the self-styled King of Torts, whose celebrity clients included Jack Ruby, Mae West, Sirhan Sirhan, and Zsa Zsa Gabor; Marvin Mitchelson (1928–2004) who developed a practice in palimony, a state he described as 'marriage with no rings attached'; through to Johnnie Cochrane (1932–2005) who achieved the improbable acquittal of **OJ Simpson**.

On the international stage Sidney Kentridge (1921–), who starred in the inquest of radical black leader Steve Biko and represented Nelson Mandela in his native South Africa, and then became an outstanding constitutional and commercial lawyer in England, demands mention.

It was not only the diminution in the jury's role which explains why the best advocates, if not inferior to their better known predecessors in terms of ability, retain less fame. There are now forms of popular entertainment other than court reports. Accession to the European Community in 1972 and the domestication of the **European Convention on Human Rights** from 2000, introduced to the English legal system an exposure to forms of litigation where oral advocacy was more of an epilogue than the central act. **Case management** restricted the freedom previously enjoyed by the advocate to dictate the pace of litigation. The removal of the Bar's monopoly of pleading diluted the quality of presentation. There was a move in favour of arbitration, a private function, and to other forms of dispute resolution such as mediation which gave no scope to public persuasive arts. The battles between Tom Bingham (1934–) (subsequently **Master of the Rolls**, Lord Chief Justice and Senior Law Lord, a unique treble) and Bob Alexander (1934–2005) resonated around the Temple but excited little recognition in a wider sphere. It is safe to say that while advocacy will continue to be an admirable and admired quality, the golden age of the advocate lies not in the future, but in the past.

MICHAEL BELOFF

See also: **adversary system**

affirmative action   *see* **positive discrimination**

African Charter on Human and Peoples' Rights
The African Charter on Human and Peoples' Rights, also known as the Banjul Charter, was adopted by

the Organization of African Unity, the predecessor to the African Union ('AU'), on 27 June 1981. To date every member of the AU has ratified the Charter (Morocco is the only African country that is not a member of the AU).

The Charter was adopted to serve as a **human rights** instrument that reflected the values of, and dealt with issues relevant to, the African continent. It covers a wider range of rights than its European and American counterparts; it contains protections for civil, political, and socio-economic rights. As its name suggests, it is concerned with peoples' rights to social, cultural, and economic development; **self-determination;** and free disposition of natural resources.

Unlike its European and American counterparts, the Charter contains a number of duties that bind individuals, in keeping with the traditional African philosophy that, since individuals live in and are part of **communities**, they cannot expect to enjoy rights without, at the same time, also fulfilling certain duties or **responsibilities**.

Individuals and NGOs can hold state parties accountable for violations of the Charter and the Protocol by bringing complaints to the African Commission on Human and Peoples' Rights. Plans are well underway for the activation of an African Court on Human and Peoples' Rights.

The Charter is supplemented by a Protocol on the Rights of Women in Africa which came into force on 25 November 2005. PIUS LANGA

African customary law This useful, albeit disputed, term denotes a body of largely unwritten laws that have been derived from social practices regarded as obligatory by the communities concerned. The account below is confined to the indigenous laws of sub-Saharan Africa. Given the variety of different cultures in Africa, generalizing about this subject is far from easy. Nevertheless, there are sufficient similarities in social and economic conditions to produce a group of related legal forms.

For much of the colonial period, African customary law was treated as unimportant, because, from a Western perspective, it lacked features thought essential for law 'properly so called': a class of professionals, a source in sovereign commands and the backing of institutionalized force. Study of the subject was accordingly relegated to anthropologists. Lawyers developed an interest only when customary law became applicable in the colonial courts.

In spite of the vagueness, lack of uniformity and apparently conservative values of customary law, it continues to be accepted as part of the legal systems of nearly all post-colonial African states. Even so, it remains in a subordinate relationship to imported European laws, and is entirely excluded in matters of public law. Hence, customary law is applied mainly by lower courts, in domestic disputes and where the parties retain an attachment to a notionally traditional African culture.

The ascertainment of unwritten law is bound to be a problem for courts working in a Western legal tradition. Thus, from an early date, colonial authorities sought to capture customary law in written forms (whether codifications, restatements or instruction manuals) amenable to use in legal practice. These texts cast the law in European languages and legal categories, thereby transforming what had originally been undifferentiated repertoires of principles, maxims and proverbs—which are typical of oral traditions—into systematic sets of rules. The result was clearly not an exact representation of earlier traditions or, thereafter, contemporary social practices. Thus, today, the only truly authentic version of customary law is generally considered to be the 'living law', namely, the law in fact being observed by its subjects.

Even now, however, texts on customary law tend to describe it in terms of pre-colonial traditions, when most societies were composed of small, self-contained settlements, each inhabited by closely related families supporting themselves by subsistence agriculture. In the absence of central state authorities, kin performed the critical tasks of rearing children, caring for the sick and attending to religious rites. On the basis of fieldwork in Zambia, Max Gluckman, a leading theorist on customary law, described (*The Ideas in Barotse Jurisprudence* (Manchester: Manchester UP, 1972 reprint)) how such a society generated certain distinctive forms and legal institutions. He noted the overriding importance of family relationships and the duty to support kin. As a result, the claims of kinfolk tended to supersede any individual rights to property, so that a person could not be said to 'own' food, livestock or land absolutely. Gluckman concluded that, instead of exclusive rights in economically productive property, customary law allowed a number of people to hold different interests concurrently.

From this conception of family and property rights, it followed that various institutions considered central to Western law were of minor importance in customary law. Wills and contracts were examples. The disposal of a deceased man's assets, for instance, was of no particular concern. (Except in certain West African societies, women had limited control over property, and so succession to female estates was seldom an issue.) Instead, customary law concentrated on the transmission of support obligations, and the control of family estates, to suitable heirs, whose status was predetermined by their positions in the kinship system.

Commercial contracts, too, were of marginal concern, due mainly to the fact that, in most parts of pre-colonial sub-Saharan Africa, trade was neither regular nor widespread. Promises, however, were taken very seriously. Ritual pledges of brotherhood, for example, had a sacramental quality. They were sworn by members of age grades at the end of an initiation ceremony to mark the creation of long-term bonds of support, comparable to family ties. Otherwise, customary law considered bare promises, in the absence of an appropriate ritual or the conveyance of property, unenforceable.

Where societies had no central state authority to register birth, initiation, **marriage** or death, these major rites of passage were marked by the families concerned. Marriage, in particular, was a private affair requiring, principally, the approval of the spouses' guardians, and, in most cultures, payment of bridewealth. Thereafter, the validity of the union was progressively strengthened, as the spouses discharged their duties and children were born.

For a proper understanding of the legal cultures of Africa, it must be appreciated that rules were less important than finding solutions to disputes acceptable to both the parties and the wider community. When courts could not rely on organized force to sanction their judgements, they tended to mediate or arbitrate. These procedures did not require the impartial application of predetermined rules in order to legitimate the final decision, as is the case with adjudication. Instead, rules served as a flexible basis for discussion, during which litigants were persuaded to accept compromise settlements.

While the measure of an effective court in Africa was the thoroughness of its inquiry, the scope of this process was qualified by the court's purpose: the more distant the parties' relationship, the more likely that the purpose was straightforward adjudication, and thus the less detailed the court's investigation. Hence, if a person suffered injury at the hands of a stranger, the inquiry was more likely to be aimed at assessing **compensation**, without considering the parties' overall relationship. Conversely, where a court sought to reconcile kinfolk, the immediate 'legal' issues that precipitated litigation had little significance for the eventual outcome. The court then had to consider the parties' full relationship over a period of time.

Much of the above account is in the past tense, reflecting the fact that most of the major texts on customary law were written during the early to mid-twentieth century. In view of the social, political and economic upheavals in Africa, not to mention a long association with dominant European laws and values, there is clearly a need for modern fieldwork (such as that conducted by AMO Griffiths, *In the Shadow of Marriage* (Chicago: Chicago UP, 1997)). The shortage of current information is especially disturbing in light of Africa's growing urban population. In these heterogeneous communities, people's lives are being shaped by diverse forces, whether work, religion, new patterns of residence or **HIV/Aids**, and the traditions of the past are being recast, abandoned or made over into more appropriate forms. No doubt, people's lives have also changed as a result of legal reforms, and, indeed, throughout Africa, bills of rights now challenge the long-established privileges enjoyed by senior males and traditional authorities. The full implications of these changes, however, await further investigation.   TOM BENNETT

TW Bennett, *Human Rights and African Customary Law under the South African Constitution* (Cape Town: Juta & Co, 1995)
AO Obilade & GR Woodman (eds), *African Law and Legal Theory* (Aldershot: Dartmouth, 1995).

See also: **colonialism; common law in the colonies; customary law; family law in developing countries; gender and development**

after-the-event-insurance   *see* **conditional fee arrangements**

age and crime   A significant proportion of crime is committed by young people. Indeed, this has led two American criminologists, Hirschi and Gottfredson, to argue that the age–crime distribution 'represents one of the brute facts of criminology'. Young people are also the focus of considerable adult concern—concern which has focused on terms like 'delinquency' and more recently '**anti-social behaviour**'.

In the UK, official statistics suggest that at least one-fifth of all those cautioned or convicted annually are aged between ten and seventeen and well over one-third are under twenty-one. Self-report studies confirm that offending in the teenage years is relatively common. Estimates of the peak age of offending vary but generally place it somewhere between fifteen and eighteen and show it to be higher for men than women. In terms of patterns of offending, it is also important to note that there is considerable evidence to show that males from lower socio-economic groups are disproportionately involved in criminal activity compared with other social groups.

Frequency of offending varies markedly and there is now a considerable literature looking at persistent offending by juveniles. Early research by Wolfgang and colleagues found that 'chronic offenders'—representing just over 6 per cent of the cohort being studied—accounted for more than half of the **arrests** experienced by the whole group, and similar findings have been regularly replicated. There has been considerable policy interest in such offenders for a decade or more and a substantial body of longitudinal and cross-sectional research has examined the backgrounds and offending histories of such 'frequent' or 'life course persistent' offenders.

Another area of youthful behaviour that has come in for close scrutiny in recent years has been drug use. Data on the incidence and prevalence of drug use among young people are now available and survey data have charted both the pattern of usage among people of different ages and the patterning of drug use over time. In many jurisdictions, increases detected in the 1980s and 1990s have now stabilized somewhat. What seems undeniable is the now fairly embedded role that illicit drugs now play in youth subcultures.

When the words 'age' and 'crime' are linked, the picture in most minds is generally of the young person as an offender. Given the frequency and prevalence of offending by young people this is perhaps not surprising. Such a view hides the high levels of victimization experienced by the young, and the particular vulnerability—in terms of impact rather than frequency—of the elderly. Most victimization surveys do not routinely collect information on young people under sixteen. Where there are exceptions they have found, for example, that twelve to fifteen-year-old boys and girls are at least as much at **risk** of victimization as adults, and for some types of crime, more at risk than adults and older teenagers; and that young people are more likely to be the **victim** of personal crimes (assault, robbery, theft from the **person,** and other personal theft) than those in older age groups.   TIM NEWBURN

DJ Smith 'Crime and the Life Course', in M Maguire, R Morgan, and R Reiner (eds), *Oxford Handbook of Criminology* (Oxford: Oxford University Press, 2007)

See also: **drugs and crime; young offenders**

age discrimination   *see* **protected grounds**

agency workers   An agency worker is supplied by an employment agency to work for an individual or firm often labelled the 'user'. There are two types of employment agency. One recruits workers for employment by the user. The other hires workers itself and supplies them to the user.

Employment agencies are regulated by the Employment Agencies Act 1973 and the Conduct of Employment Agencies and Employment Businesses Regulations 2003. There is no system of licensing for agencies, though there are exceptions in sectors such as nursing and agriculture. The main principle of the **legislation** is that agencies may not in general charge workers a fee.

Problems can arise in employment law where the agency supplies workers to the user. The workers will have an ongoing 'triangular' relationship with both the agency and the user, but they may find it difficult to determine who their employer is for the purposes of claiming statutory employment protection. There will usually be a contract between the worker and the agency but although this may be a **contract of employment,** it may instead be a contract for services in which case the worker will count as self-employed and will have few rights against the agency. The court may imply a contract of employment between the worker and the user but this is rare in practice (see *Dacas v Brook Street Bureau* (2004)).

As a result of these uncertainties, special provision is made for agency workers in legislation on tax, **national insurance**, the **minimum wage**, working time, and discrimination.   ANNE DAVIES

agent   Agency is a concept in **contract law** which enables one **person** to enter a contract on behalf of another. The relationship of agency arises where a principal authorizes an agent to enter a contract with a third party on the principal's behalf; for example, the principal asks the agent to buy goods from a seller. The result is a fully binding contract of sale between the principle and the seller. The agency device enables organizations and individuals to depute others to deal on their behalf where it is not practical for them to do so, for example because the agent is present in a remote location, or because the agent can provide specialist knowledge. It is an important way in which contract law, traditionally based on an agreement between two parties, adapts to the practicalities of more complex commercial relationships.

The agency relationship is normally created where the principal gives express authority to the agent to make the contract. It can also arise in three situations where there is no express authority. The first situation is where the agent has been asked to carry out a task and entering a particular contract is a necessary part of it: this is known as 'implied' authority. The second is where a principal creates the impression that someone is entitled to act as their agent, even though this is not actually the case. For example, where a person has acted as agent in previous dealings between the principal and a third party, and the principle revokes the authority without notifying the third party, an agency relationship could still arise in a subsequent transaction. This is known as 'ostensible authority', although it cannot arise merely by the 'agent' holding themselves out as acting on another's behalf. The third case of agency without express authority is where the agent acts without the principal's authority, but the principal later ratifies the action.

English law is unusual in recognizing the creation of an agency situation even where the principal is undisclosed. This means that a seller can believe they are contracting to sell goods to one person, when, in fact, there is a binding contract between the seller and an undisclosed principal who is in fact the buyer. This will not apply, however, where it reasonable for the other party to infer that the agent could only be contracting in a personal **capacity**. Even if an agency relationship does arise with an undisclosed principal, the agent will remain liable on the contract personally at least until the principal is disclosed. After disclosure, the third party can elect to sue either the agent or principal.

The agency device was developed in the nineteenth century and remains a central part of commercial life; **consumers** also deal with agents quite commonly. Where one is dealing through an intermediary, such as an insurance broker, it is important to be clear whose agent they are. Thus, an insurance broker will typically be regarded as the agent of the customer in dealings with the **company**, and the result may be that the company will deny any liability based on the actions or statements of the broker. However, for certain purposes, the broker will also be treated as acting as the company's agent, for example, when arranging temporary or immediate cover.

One traditional reason for the creation of agency relationships was to enable organizations to deal with suppliers, clients, etc in locations remote from their main place of business. Electronic communications have removed some of the practical need to use agents in these circumstances.   JOHN WIGHTMAN

aggregates levy   *see* **environmental taxes**

aggression   *see* **use of force**

Agreement Reached in the Multiparty Negotiations, 10 April 1998   'The Agreement Reached in the Multi-party Negotiations, 10 April 1998' is the full title of what is more often referred to as either the 'Good Friday Agreement', (reflecting the day on which it was finally reached), or the 'Belfast Agreement' (reflecting the city in which it was reached). The Agreement was the culmination of nearly four years of stop-start negotiations between Northern Ireland's political parties and the British and Irish governments, on how to end the conflict in Northern Ireland. This conflict involved primarily, the British State, the Provisional Irish Republican Army, and Loyalist paramilitary groupings such as the Ulster Defence Association and the Ulster Volunteer Force.

The Agreement had eleven sections. The first set out a Declaration of Support, in which all the parties committed to values such as equality, democratic and peaceful means of resolving political differences, and the Institutions provided for by the agreement. The second section entitled 'Constitutional Issues' spoke of self-determination. Three strands then provided for: democratic institutions in Northern Ireland—primarily a **Northern Ireland Assembly** (strand one); a North-South Ministerial Council with North-South implementation bodies (strand two); and a British-Irish Council and British-Irish Intergovernmental Conference (strand three). The Agreement next provided extensive human rights and equality protections under the heading 'Rights, Safeguards and Equality of Opportunity'. The remainder of the Agreement dealt with: Decommissioning; Security; Policing and Justice; Prisoners; and Validation, Implementation, and Review. The Agreement included an Annex agreed between the British and Irish governments to 'support, and where appropriate implement the provisions' of the Agreement.

As provided for in the Agreement, on 22 May 1998, it was subject to a referendum in the North and the South, which was carried in both jurisdictions, by 71.12 per cent and 94.4 per cent respectively. The agreement's broad institutional framework was put into place by the Northern Ireland Act 1998, which complemented that of the Government of Wales Act 1998 and Scotland Act 1998. Many aspects have been implemented, but this has taken new rounds of negotiation and new supplementary agreements. The process of implementation and development of the agreement continues.   CHRISTINE BELL

C Bell, *Peace Agreements and Human Rights* (Oxford: Oxford University Press, 2003), 51–65, 134–143, 213–220
'Analysis of the Northern Ireland Peace Agreement: dedicated to George J. Mitchell, David Trimble and John Hume', (1999) 22(4) *Fordham International Law Journal* 1136–1906

agricultural tenancies   Until the end of World War II farm tenants had very little legal protection. The Agricultural Holdings Act 1948 gave tenants security of tenure, control of rents, and more extensive rights than they previously had to compensation for improvements. The landlord of an agricultural holding can only compulsorily obtain possession of the land if the tenant is in breach of the tenancy agreement, or in limited other circumstances (for example if planning permission has been granted). The tenant can refer the rent to an arbitrator, who will fix the rent payable by reference to (among other things) the earning and productive capacity of the holding. These rights were further expanded by the Agriculture (Miscellaneous Provisions) Act 1976, which conferred two-generation succession rights on farm tenants, enabling them to pass the farm on to their children or widow. These rights are now contained in the Agricultural Holdings Act 1986, which applies to all farm tenancies granted before 1 September 1995. The law was reformed in 1995 to introduce more flexibility into the market for let farmland. The Agricultural Tenancies Act 1995 introduced a new type of tenancy—the farm business tenancy—under which farm tenants enjoy no security of tenure beyond the contractually agreed term of the tenancy, subject only to the requirement that the landlord must give at least twelve months' notice to terminate and pay compensation for improvements. There is also no rent control for farm business tenancies, although the tenant can ask an arbitrator to adjudicate what is an appropriate free market rent for the holding.

CHRIS RODGERS

J Muir Watt and J Moss, *Agricultural Holdings* (London: Sweet & Maxwell, 14th edn, 1998)
CP Rodgers, *Agricultural Law* (London: Butterworths, 2nd edn, 1998), chs 1 and 3–10

air and space law   Air law is mostly contained in international agreements ('conventions') which aim to enable safe, orderly, and efficient use of national and international airspace by civil aircraft. Because uniform rules are the only effective way of achieving these aims, virtually all states are parties to these agreements and give effect to the international rules in their own laws. The Chicago Convention (1944) provides the main framework for use of airspace. It set up the International Civil Aviation Organization to develop more detailed rules which are set out in eighteen Annexes, such as the 'Rules of the Air' (avoidance of collisions), 'Personnel Licensing' (competence of crews), 'Aircraft Nationality', 'Airworthiness of Aircraft', 'Aeronautical Telecommunications', 'Air Traffic Control', 'Accident Investigation', 'Environmental Protection', 'Security', etc. Other agreements establish the international crimes of hijacking and sabotage of aircraft, and determine which state's laws apply to keep order on board aircraft and for prosecution of crimes committed in the air. The right to operate commercial air transport within a single state is usually reserved for airlines of that state (though different arrangements sometimes apply as in the **European Union**).

In international air transport different rules apply to non-scheduled flights (including charter flights) and scheduled international air services. The Chicago Convention establishes rights to operate non-scheduled international air services. The right to operate scheduled international air services is mostly provided by a large network of agreements between pairs of states, though progressive deregulation has somewhat reduced their complexity. The Warsaw Convention (1929) and the Montreal Convention (1999) have provided standard terms for relations between air carriers and their passengers and shippers of cargo. These international agreements have enabled passengers and cargo to use different air carriers successively without having to treat each sector of a journey as a separate venture, and have placed on a uniform footing claims which passengers and shippers may have against the carriers, which could otherwise be subject to the vagaries of different laws of the states whose airports or airspace have been used in a journey. The International Air Transport Association, an association of airlines, has had a significant role in facilitating the operation of such air services, for example enabling use of one set of documents for extensive itineraries.

Air law applies to aircraft at whatever height but the boundary with outer space has not been clearly defined. Space law governs activities in outer space and on celestial bodies. There is a general principle of non-appropriation by claims of sovereignty, a principle which has been significant in ensuring equitable allocation of slots (designated places) for satellites in the geostationary orbit, the area of space where satellites keep a fixed relationship with the earth. This is of key importance for broadcasting and telecommunications; but the international agreements on specific subjects such as liability for damage caused by space objects, registration of space objects, rescue of astronauts, and a regime for the moon and other celestial objects have not yet become so generally accepted as those in air law

RICHARD GARDINER

IHPh Diederiks-Verschoor, *An Introduction to Air Law* (Deventer, Netherlands: Kluwer, 8th edn, 2006)
RK Gardiner, *International Law* (London: Pearson/Longman, 2003) ch 10

airspace   *see* **territory trespass**

alcohol and liquor licensing   Retail sale of alcohol, previously licensed as 'intoxicating liquor' by **justices of the peace**, is licensed by local authorities under the Licensing Act 2003 and extends to both indoor and outdoor sales. (There is a comparable scheme in Scotland and one is proposed for Northern Ireland.) Most businesses selling alcohol for consumption on or off the premises, or both, need a premises licence; there must be a 'designated premises supervisor' ('DPS') for the premises who is an individual holding a personal licence and having day-to-day control of the premises (and who can, but need not, be the premises licence holder); and all sales of alcohol have to be made or authorized by a personal licence holder. Personal licence holders are individuals aged 18 or over who normally have a recognized personal licence holder qualification. A personal licence is 'portable', a holder can sell or authorize sales in any premises with a premises licence and it is renewable after ten years. Only the police can object to the grant of a personal licence where an applicant has convictions for licensing and other specified (generally serious) offences on the ground that grant would undermine prevention of crime and disorder, and the authority can refuse to issue a licence on this ground. Clubs run for the benefit of their members (eg British Legion) can supply alcohol to members and sell to members' guests by obtaining a club premises certificate ('CPC') instead of a premises licence. No DPS or a personal licence holder is needed to make or authorize supply or sales under a CPC.

Premises licences and CPCs are normally of unlimited duration and do not require renewal. They must be granted if there are no objections from responsible authorities (eg police, fire authority) or interested parties (residents and businesses in the vicinity of the premises). They must be granted subject to conditions consistent with the applicant's operating schedule, which indicates how the premises will operate. Any objections must be about the likely effect of grant on the licensing objectives, which are prevention of crime and disorder, public safety, prevention of public nuisance and protection of children from harm (and, in Scotland, public health). If there are objections, the authority must hold a hearing to consider them and can take various steps considered necessary to promote the licensing objectives. These include grant with modified conditions, rejection of the application or, for premises licences, refusal to specify the named person as the DPS. Applications for grant, and for variation, must be advertised in a newspaper and by notice on the premises.

For temporary events, provided certain requirements are met (eg events do not exceed ninety-six hours and less than 500 persons are present when alcohol is sold), a person using the premises can issue a temporary event notice ('TEN') to the authority indicating that the event is taking place. No licence or authorisation is needed and only the police can object on the ground that, if the event went ahead, this would undermine prevention of crime and disorder. If the police object the authority must decide whether to issue a counter notice on this ground preventing the event going ahead. The authority can also issue a counter notice where specified limits for TENs (for each calendar year) are exceeded. These limits apply to premises where events take place (twelve events not exceeding fifteen days in total) and to persons giving TENs (fifty for personal licence holders, otherwise five).   COLIN MANCHESTER

C Manchester, S Poppleston and J Allen, *Alcohol and Entertainment Licensing Law* (2nd edn, London: Routledge-Cavendish, 2008)

alcohol duties   *see* **excise duties**

alien   An 'alien' is someone who owes no allegiance to the **Crown.** Historically, alien status affected the ability to enter and remain in Britain, the rights enjoyed once admitted, and liability to expulsion. Whereas subjects enjoyed the right to enter and remain permanently, aliens were subject to the Crown's **prerogative** discretion, and the rights of aliens have waxed and waned according to the prevailing political, economic, and security climate. When the term originated in the thirteenth century, aliens enjoyed few rights in medieval England (as when all Jews were arbitrarily expelled from England in 1290), while at other times aliens have enjoyed the freedom to enter Britain and rights in property, contract, and to sue, although political rights have always been limited. Even by 1870, the Naturalization Act left unregulated the entry and exit of aliens and liberalized their rights within Britain.

Alien immigration was regulated more closely from the late nineteenth century, as Britain expanded its colonies and fought in revolutionary, Napoleonic, and world wars between 1870 and 1918. Detailed **legislation** gradually displaced prerogative powers, although statutory **discretion** remained. The Aliens Act 1905 was the first modern law to regulate aliens, in response to public anxiety about Jewish immigrants from eastern Europe after 1880, and permitted the exclusion of 'undesirable' aliens who could not support themselves or were diseased or infirm. Control over aliens expanded during the First World War under the Aliens Restriction Act 1914, effectively extended to peacetime in 1919, while further restrictions on enemy aliens (including internment) were imposed in the Second World War.

Aliens were subsequently defined under the British Nationality Act 1948 as those who are not British subjects (also known as Commonwealth citizens), British protected persons, or Irish citizens. Following concerns that many Commonwealth citizens might migrate to Britain, restrictions were later imposed on Commonwealth citizens who were not born in Britain or lacked a British passport (Commonwealth Immigrants Act 1962). In practice, the law discriminated between whites and non-whites, particularly East African Asians who had British passports but lacked a British-born parent as required by the Commonwealth Immigrants Act 1968.

Until 1971, the distinction between British subjects and aliens determined who could enter Britain. After the Immigration Act 1971, the main distinction was between patrials and non-patrials. A right to enter and remain was accorded only to patrials—British and Commonwealth citizens born or naturalized in Britain or who had a parent born or naturalized there, or British citizens with a grandparent so born or naturalized. Henceforth, British subjects and Commonwealth citizens who lacked a parentage tie could be treated much like an alien, while over time European Union citizens gained new rights to enter and remain in Britain.

As a result, the term 'alien' is increasingly anachronistic. Modern immigration and nationality law instead focus on parentage, **nationality/citizenship,** and birth place, rather than on **subject**-hood and alienage. By contrast, alienage is still significant in international law, since a country has a discretionary right to exclude or expel any alien from its territory (subject to its **human rights** obligations), as well as to define who are nationals (and thus aliens).

BEN SAUL

Alien Tort Claims Act The Alien Tort Claims Act ('ATCA'), also known as the Alien Tort Statute, is a US federal law that reads: 'The district courts shall have original jurisdiction of any civil action by an alien for a tort only, committed in violation of the law of nations or a treaty of the United States'. Originally adopted in 1789, the ATCA lay largely dormant until the landmark decision in *Filartiga v Pena-Irala* (1980) in which the US Court of Appeals held that under the ATCA the district courts had jurisdiction to hear civil claims by aliens for damages for **torture**

and other **human rights** violations. The perpetrator must be served court papers in the US, but neither the victim nor the perpetrator need reside in the US, and the violation must not have taken place there. Since 1980, alien plaintiffs have sought to hold states, government officials, multinational corporations, and international terrorists liable for human rights violations in more than 100 cases. The ATCA has proven a controversial tool for the private enforcement of human rights and led to some embarrassment for the US Government in its foreign relations. In *Sosa v Alvarez-Machain* (2004) the **United States Supreme Court** affirmed the exercise of universal tort jurisdiction (which is not (yet) part of **international law**) but limited its application to the violation of universally accepted, clearly defined rules of **customary international law**. While hailed as a powerful human rights tool, claims under the ATCA often fail because of the defendant's **sovereign immunity**.

STEFAN TALMON

JJ Paust, 'The History, Nature, and Reach of the Alien Tort Claims Act' (2004) 16 *Florida Journal of International Law* 249

RG Steinhardt and A D'Amatao (eds), *The Alien Tort Claims Act: An Analytical Anthology* (Ardsley, NY: Transnational Publishers, 1999)

Allcard v Skinner (1887) In 1870 Miss Mary Allcard joined a Church of England sisterhood called the Sisters of the Poor. Organizations of this kind, devoted to good works, were on the rise in the second half of the nineteenth century, attracting a great deal of public and parliamentary concern. The rules of the Sisterhood included a rule of poverty, although they did not require that Sisters should give their property to the Sisterhood. Allcard transferred money and securities amounting to several thousand pounds to Miss Skinner, the Superior of the Sisters and also its co-founder. Allcard left the Sisters in 1879, and converted to Roman Catholicism. In 1885 she demanded the return of some of her gifts. The claim being refused, she brought legal proceedings later that year.

There was no suggestion that the Sisterhood was not a legitimate organization, nor that Allcard had been defrauded, tricked, or threatened. The case was argued as one of '**undue influence**'. The basis of this kind of claim is that the claimant, in making a will or a gift or some other legal disposition, was not freely exercising her own will. Instead, she was under the influence of another person. Mr Justice Kekewich rejected the claim, holding that Allcard fully understood what she was doing when she made the gifts. Allcard appealed in respect of some of the gifts, and the Court of Appeal allowed the appeal. The court held that in some cases, a claimant has to prove undue influence; but in some circumstances, undue influence will be presumed, and the burden will be on the defendant to prove that the claimant's decision was a free one. A gift from a member of a religious order to the head of the order fell into this class. Lord Justice Cotton said that in such cases, 'the Court interferes, not on the ground that any wrongful act has in fact been committed by the donee, but on the ground of public policy, and to prevent the relations which existed between the parties and the influence arising therefrom being abused'.

This decision continues to resonate in the modern law. It remains true that in certain situations, undue influence will be presumed. Undue influence is presumed as between parent and child, guardian and ward, trustee and beneficiary, solicitor and client, spiritual advisor and follower, and medical adviser and patient. Many recent cases have arisen between married or cohabiting parties. For example, a husband carries on a business and needs to borrow money. He persuades his wife to grant a guarantee, or a mortgage over her share in the matrimonial home, so that he can borrow more money. Later, when the bank tries to enforce the security, the wife may say that the husband exercised undue influence over her. The relationships of marriage and cohabitation do not raise a presumption of undue influence, but the courts require banks to be careful to ascertain that people in these relationships understand the nature and consequences of such legal transactions.

LIONEL SMITH

Allen v Flood (1898)   In the late Victorian period there was disagreement within the judiciary about what role **tort law** should play in cases where economic harm was deliberately inflicted by one person on another in the course of trade competition or as a result of the use of trade union power or the application of collective pressure ('combination'). Some judges preferred that tort law should play a narrow role, based on a requirement that the harm be the result of an unlawful act, whereas others favoured a broader role, based on a requirement that the harm be caused maliciously (even if not unlawfully). The **House of Lords** was presented with the opportunity to resolve the disagreement in 1898. In *Allen v Flood* (1898) the defendant, a trade union official, informed an employer that his workers would cease to work unless the plaintiffs were dismissed. Neither the dismissal nor the cessation of work would have been unlawful: there was no evidence of unlawful conduct such as conspiracy, intimidation, or **breach**

of contract. However the defendant was motivated by malice: the aim of the action was to punish the plaintiffs for previous 'misconduct' in relation to a demarcation dispute. The central policy issue for the House of Lords was whether the defendant—who clearly sought to cause economic harm to the plaintiffs—could be liable on the basis of malice alone for their dismissal. The majority of the House of Lords decided that bad motive by itself was not a permissible basis for imposing tort liability for deliberately inflicted economic harm. Lord Watson said that 'the law of England does not . . . take into account motive as constituting an element of civil wrong . . . the existence of a bad motive, in the case of an act which is not of itself illegal, will not convert that act into a civil wrong'. This holding prevented creation of what is often called a 'general tort' of unjustifiable interference with trade. The court accepted that there was a 'chasm' between intentional harm done by lawful means and such harm effected by the 'violation of a legal right'. The key ingredient for liability would be the presence of unlawful means, used (either personally by the defendant or through a third party) against the claimant. However it should be noted that there were dissenting judgments and some uncertainty about the implications of the decision. As a result, the door was left open for a subsequent House of Lords decision in *Quinn v Leathem* (1901) to reject the full implications of *Allen v Flood*. The facts of *Quinn v Leathem* were similar to those of *Allen v Flood*, but the House of Lords distinguished the latter case on the basis that in *Quinn* there was a combination and threats were used. These additional factors allowed Lord Halsbury to impose liability by establishing the economic tort of 'simple conspiracy', where the 'magic of plurality' renders a combination to injure tortious, despite the lack of unlawful means. Though rarely of practical use (because there is a wide defence of justification), the existence of this anomalous tort creates tension within the common law in this area.   HAZEL CARTY

See also: **conspiracy and trade union activity**

alternative dispute resolution   Alternative Dispute Resolution ('ADR'), sometimes called 'Appropriate' Dispute Resolution, is a general term referring to modes of conflict resolution other than those associated with courts and tribunals. ADR includes a mixed bag of activities ranging from adjudication and formal, binding arbitration to informal, open-door policies, with intermediate possibilities including mediation, conciliation, and ombudsman schemes. Some of the better recognized ways of using ADR as a dispute management mechanism are detailed below.

Adjudication is a binding determination made by an appointed neutral, either by deciding a dispute on the basis of submitted documents, or after convening a hearing. In the strictest sense, there seems to be little to distinguish adjudication from litigation. However, an important example of adjudication used as an alternative method of dispute resolution can be found under the Housing Grants, Construction and Regeneration Act 1996, Part II of which confers on parties to construction contracts the statutory right to insist upon the adjudication of disputes. Prior to the Act's commencement, parties to construction contracts were obliged to use either court-based litigation or arbitration to resolve their disputes. Indeed, one of Parliament's main aims for introducing 'statutory' adjudication was to reduce the number of construction and engineering disputes that ended up in litigation or arbitration. In contrast to either of these methods, construction adjudication tends to be quicker than other methods of dispute resolution and not as disruptive, as the process requires an independent party to be selected within one week and to make a decision within twenty-eight days. In addition, the informality of statutory adjudication—for example, the facts that strict rules of evidence do not apply and that a hearing is seldom required—has meant that parties to a construction contract increasingly find themselves opting for the adjudication alternative while the contract subsists. Since either party has the right to have the same dispute litigated, statutory adjudication does not necessarily achieve final settlement. Nevertheless, due to the speed, simplicity, and flexibility of the process, statutory adjudication has overtaken arbitration to become the principal means of resolving disputes in the construction industry.

Arbitration involves an impartial, independent third party, chosen by the disputants, hearing both sides of a disagreement, then issuing a binding decision to achieve resolution of the dispute. The arbitrator's final award may be based on 'good practice' and 'reasonableness' as well as legal precedent. Under the Arbitration Act 1996, there is very limited scope for appeal to a court against an arbitrator's award. The arbitration process dates back to ancient Greece and has been used in the UK for at least three centuries, although recent years have seen a significant revival in its use as a form of dispute resolution. It is now utilized widely in a number of settings, including: international disputes, disputes between major corporations, employment rights, and consumer disputes. Arbitration is conducted within a legal framework, but the process and decision are not as rigidly defined as litigation by, for example, strict rules of evidence. However, due to its legal framework, arbitration proceedings can be slow and expensive. Like adjudication, arbitration is sometimes not considered to be as 'pure' an ADR process as conciliation or mediation.

Conciliation is a loosely defined term ambiguously applied to a number of different dispute resolution processes, including negotiation and mediation. In fact, it overlaps, in many respects, with mediation, with the result that the two terms are used indiscriminately, even though there are important differences. In the National Health Service complaints procedure, for example, it is suggested that health trusts and boards adopt a 'conciliation' stage, but 'mediation' and 'conciliation' are used interchangeably in this context. A conciliator, like a mediator (see below), is an independent, impartial third party who helps parties resolve a dispute. However, a conciliator will often take a more active role in making suggestions, or advising on the best route to resolution of a dispute. The conciliator listens to the parties and may examine statements made by the parties, subsequently delivering an opinion about the likely outcome of the case. This is the model of conciliation used by many trade associations and some professional bodies dealing with complaints about their member organizations. In this sense, the conciliator's role is more closely akin to that of an *evaluative mediator* or an *early neutral evaluator* (see below). Another difference between conciliation and mediation is that in conciliation the parties often do not meet, but the neutral works with them separately, usually restricting contact to the telephone. Confusingly, the initial stage of some internal **complaints procedures** is also referred to as 'conciliation'. In such cases, the conciliator is not an independent person at all, but a representative of the organization involved in the dispute.

In *Early Neutral Evaluation* ('ENE') an independent third party evaluates the claims made by each side and issues an opinion, either on the likely outcome, or on a particular point of law. The opinion, though non-binding, can be used by parties when considering how they might proceed with their case. Likewise, the opinion can form the basis for settlement. ENE can help narrow the issues and focus parties' minds on realistic outcomes by giving them an objective view of their arguments. Often the evaluator has been chosen because of his or her expertise in the subject matter of the dispute, but just as often the evaluator is a lawyer with litigation experience. This experience can be particularly valuable when the purpose of using ENE is either to obtain an opinion on a point of law, or to moderate parties' unrealistic views of their chances of success at trial.

Mediation is a voluntary, guided, and informal process whereby a neutral third party meets with disputants in order to help them negotiate the resolution of their claims. Mediation is the most wide-ranging ADR process in that it is used in a variety of dispute arenas, including divorce and separation, small disputes, medical negligence, workplace, community care, education, youth crime, and housing, as well as international and cross-border disputes. Mediation can be used in cases involving two parties, for disputes involving a large number of parties, or even entire communities. Mediation is a non-binding process, although a signed mediated agreement—the product of mediation—is a contract and could, in theory, be legally enforceable if breached. Nevertheless, parties do tend to keep to mediated agreements. The explanation for this lies in the nature of the process; because it is consensual, parties will have determined the terms of their settlement voluntarily. Thus, the goodwill engendered by voluntary mediation will lead to a commitment by parties to honour their arrangements.

There are a number of different models of mediation, each of them reflecting different approaches and roles taken by mediators. The two most common approaches are facilitative mediation and evaluative mediation. In the former, the mediator conducts the session using a structured, but non-directional, format. One way of describing this style of mediation is that the mediator is in charge of the process, while the parties are in charge of the content. This is also sometimes called 'interest-based' mediation and is used in the majority of contexts in this country. In evaluative mediation the mediator tends to take a more interventionist role by making suggestions, or issuing opinions as to the likely outcome of a dispute. Parties with the expectation that a mediator will direct them towards an appropriate resolution will probably be more satisfied with an evaluative approach than a facilitative one.

Negotiation involves direct dealing between the parties to a dispute, or their representatives. When negotiating, the complainant, or her representative or advocate can approach the 'other side' with details of the complaint and suggestions for how it can be resolved. The respondent/defendant does not need to agree to participate before a complainant/representative makes the approach. The process is non-binding, although parties can agree to make a negotiated agreement into a binding contract or order. Importantly, it should be recognized that negotiation resolves the majority of disputes in

this country. Negotiation differs from conciliation, mediation, and arbitration in that any third party is acting *on behalf of* the client and advocating for his or her interests. The negotiator is not impartial, as in mediation, and may also have a role in advising the client as to the best course of action, which conciliators and mediators generally do not.

Ombudsmen are impartial referees who adjudicate on complaints about public and private organizations. The ombudsman (or ombuds) role originated in Sweden in the nineteenth century to investigate wrongdoing by public officials. The first British ombudsman was the Parliamentary Commissioner for Administration, established in 1967. Subsequent public-sector ombudsmen have been established over the past thirty years or so. Generally, ombudsmen serve as a last resort when complaints fail to be resolved through the internal complaints procedure of the organization complained about. Although ombudsman schemes were initially set up in order to rectify the power imbalance between individual consumers and large institutions, they do not act on behalf of individuals. Thus, it can happen that the ombudsman finds that something has gone wrong, but that it did not cause injustice. Needless to say, it can be highly frustrating for complainants to be told they have been treated badly, or that a flawed decision has been made, but that they have not suffered injustice as a result. Some ombudsmen have slightly wider remits; for example, private-sector ombudsmen can generally consider whether an organization's decision-making was fair and reasonable, taking into account industry standards of good practice.

Online Dispute Resolution ('ODR'), sometimes known as e-ADR, uses electronic media to assist in the resolution of a dispute, usually without the parties meeting or speaking directly. ODR generally involves one of two options: blind bidding, based on a mathematical process, or the use of a real person who operates as a neutral over the internet.

CHERYL DOLDER

alternative trading system   One of the most striking recent developments in financial markets is the sharp increase in competition for **securities** trading (or execution) business in the **secondary markets**. Traditionally, **stock exchange**s, such as the London Stock Exchange and the New York Stock Exchange, were the main providers of trading services. Securities were generally traded on formal stock exchanges, which also listed securities (or in effect, provided securities with a quality mark by imposing disclosure and other requirements) and frequently performed a quasi-regulatory function with respect to issuers who admitted securities to their markets. Outside the stock exchanges, trades tended to be bilateral, based on telephone trades between sophisticated investors.

Developments in technology have seen the rise of alternative trading systems (or 'ATSs'), which now provide competition in trading services. They generally take the form of automated, screen-based trading systems built on computer networks. Some investment firms also 'internalize' trades, or execute trades for their investor clients against their own book of securities (their proprietary trading book) rather than sending the trade for execution on a stock exchange or other ATS. These new venues have drawn considerable business away from stock exchanges by reducing trading costs and providing specialized services for particular securities and investors. The growth in ATSs has also partly driven the worldwide wave of stock exchange mergers as stock exchanges have consolidated to meet this new business model.

ATSs generate a range of challenges for regulators. Where the venues for trading a security proliferate, liquidity in that security can fragment, as opposed to being concentrated on a stock exchange. It can, therefore, become difficult to assess the security's price and the most appropriate trading venue. ATSs may also exclude retail investors. They have the advantage, however, of providing professional investors, in particular, with a choice of trading venues, mechanisms, and degrees of transparency. ATSs have also centralized liquidity in areas where trades were previously fragmented, particularly in the bond market. The issues faced by regulators include: how to ensure fair access; how to ensure overall market stability; how to protect liquidity and the transparency of securities pricing; how to protect investors, particularly where conflict-of-interest risks exist; and how to ensure that ATSs do not become vulnerable to market manipulation—all without damaging competition or interfering with market innovation. A threshold question concerns whether to regulate ATSs as stock exchanges, which are generally subject to high levels of regulation given their central role in the financial markets.

The regulation of ATSs in the UK is driven by the EU under the Markets in Financial Instruments Directive 2004. This Directive is designed to liberalize trading services and promote **competition** between trading venues in order to generate efficiencies. It provides for trading by 'internalizing' investment firms on ATSs (termed multilateral trading facilities) and on 'regulated markets'. A graduated regulatory regime applies which is designed to address risks related to market stability and integrity, securities pricing, conflict of interest, and investor protection, which may arise on each venue, while promoting competition between trading venues.

NIAMH MOLONEY

See also: **disclosure in financial markets; transparency of securities trades**

ambulance chasing   *see* **compensation culture**

American Civil Liberties Union ('ACLU') The ACLU is a non-profit, non-partisan organization dedicated to defending the United States Bill of Rights. The organization boasts over 500,000 members and maintains a fifty-state network of staffed affiliate offices. The ACLU calls itself the 'nation's largest public interest law firm' and handles approximately 6,000 cases annually through the collaboration of 100 ACLU staff attorneys and 2,000 volunteer attorneys. The ACLU appears before the **US Supreme Court** more than any other organization with the exception of the federal government.

The ACLU was founded in 1920 by American civil libertarian Roger Baldwin, and others. During the first two decades, much of its work was dedicated to defending working class and labour union rights. Baldwin viewed the championing of civil rights as essential to social reform. At the same time, the ACLU adopted a policy of impartiality in the defence of civil liberties and, over time, it has defended all kinds of extremist groups and individuals against the government, including, for instance, Nazis.

Between 1930 and 1960, the ACLU shifted from an organization on the radical fringes to one in the liberal political mainstream. President Roosevelt's New Deal, a series of social programmes initiated between 1933 and 1938, interested liberals in the ACLU and during this period, the ACLU was involved in several landmark constitutional cases including *Powell v Alabama* (1932) and ***Brown v Board of Education*** (1954). In the 1960s, the ACLU filed *amicus curiae* in cases including *Gideon v Wainwright* (1963), *Griswold v Connecticut* (1965), and ***Miranda v Arizona*** (1966).

In recent times, the ACLU has been a target of right-wing pundits and politicians who cast it as an extreme liberal/left organization. Whether such charges are accurate or a reflection of far right rhetoric is difficult to assess. One thing is clear: ever since its foundation, the ACLU has experienced internal disagreement about whether it should be defending any and all civil rights as an end in itself or whether the defence of civil rights should be understood to be in service of the achievement of social reform. It is safe to say that this is a question which would produce different responses within the ACLU membership itself.

PIERRE SCHLAG AND KIMBERLY C DIEGO

S Walker, *In Defense of American Liberties: A History of the ACLU* (New York: Oxford University Press, 1990)

American Law Institute *see* **Model Penal Code; restatements of the law (USA); Uniform Commercial Code**

American legal realism *see* **legal realism**

amnesty (criminal justice) Amnesty (from the Greek *amnestia*, 'oblivion') refers to a sovereign act of reprieve usually issued by the executive branch of the state, granting a release from punishment to groups or certain individuals for a specific, usually political, offence such as treason. Amnesties are usually granted in advance of a trial or conviction and are conditional upon a cessation of the offences for which amnesty is granted.

Key historical examples include some of the earliest recorded amnesties granted in the fifth century BC by Athens to ostracized enemies of the city-state who were pardoned, returned to Athens, and restored as citizens, and, in the wake of the English Civil War in 1682, Charles II granted amnesty to Cromwell's supporters.

Political amnesty achieved special prominence in the post-Cold War era, providing a central mechanism by which states managed a) political transitions and democratization in the 1980s and 1990s, for example, Argentina and Chile; and b) the resolution of civil conflict, in which negotiated peace settlements contained amnesty agreements between conflicting parties, for example, South Africa (1991) and Sierra Leone (1999). Amnesties are a controversial feature of **transitional justice** which curbs criminal justice, balancing punishment against the pragmatic demands of democratization and peace in the name of other objectives such as **reconciliation** and nation-building. However, it is important to note that amnesty takes different forms in different states at different times, reflecting the balance of political forces and the tactical or strategic considerations that key parties might have at the time of its deployment.   CLAIRE MOON

amnesty (immigration) In the migration context, amnesty describes a government policy whereby the state formally elects not to deport non-status migrants who entered or remained in the country without legal authorization. Instead, eligible persons are 'regularized' through the conferral of some form of temporary or permanent lawful immigration status. Amnesties usually apply only to a subset of non-status migrants, for example, failed **asylum** seekers, persons who arrived before a certain date, those who have been continuously employed, etc. An amnesty may be presented as a one-time event to clear an inventory of outstanding removal orders, or it may be available on an ongoing basis for those who meet the eligibility criteria. Why do states offer amnesties? Political, legal, and practical impediments render it impossible for states of the Global North to execute **deportation** orders against non-status migrants in numbers that make a dent in the backlog. In many cases, certain sectors of the economy are dependent on the cheap labour of migrants who, fearing detection and deportation, 'work hard and work scared'. While the native population may oppose illegal immigration in general, they may react with greater sympathy when confronted with the sight of their neighbours or children being apprehended, detained, and expelled.

Opponents complain that amnesties reward law-breaking and surrender sovereign control over borders. The immediate prospect of an amnesty creates surges of irregular migration by those wanting to enter before an announced deadline, and encourages irregular migration over time by creating an expectation of future amnesties. Proponents claim that amnesties (or regularization) recognize that over time and regardless of legal status, migrants contribute to, and integrate into, the economy and the broader community. They contend that amnesties ought to be regarded as akin to statutes of limitations in other legal domains, namely as a time limit after which it is unfair and inefficient for the state to pursue someone for commission of a non-violent legal infraction.   AUDREY MACKLIN

See also: **migrant workers**

anarchism Anarchism means 'without rulers' and refers to both a scholarly theory and a form of political organization. Anarchism was influential in the late nineteenth and early twentieth centuries, but still attracts scholars and activists who believe that it is necessary to envisage a society without formal authority such as that enshrined in a state. There is no single authoritative form of anarchist thought. Generally though, anarchists argue that the institutionalization of power leads to unnecessary **violence**, corruption, social inequality, and apathy. Traditionally, anarchists have aimed to replace the state with an alternative method of **governance** in which society as a whole would be run cooperatively by its members using a form of consensus-based or participatory politics. Realizing the futility of overthrowing the entire state, modern anarchists have moved away from the idea of wholesale **revolution**. They instead argue that anarchist principles can and often should be used on a local scale, for instance in running **community** organizations.

Anarchism is often aligned with other forms of emancipatory politics such as feminism or socialism. However, anarchists are not exclusively associated with left-wing political beliefs. Anarcho-capitalism argues for a minimization of state power, but as a way of enhancing individual liberty and private property, rather than as a means of ensuring social solidarity and **equality**.

Anarchism has not been influential in mainstream legal theory, perhaps because it is assumed that anarchism requires the abolition of law. However, anarchism is arguably consistent with concepts of law which do not rely on the existence of a state.

MARGARET DAVIES

See also: **emancipation; state, concept of**

ancient egyptian law   *see* **ancient Middle Eastern law**

ancient Middle Eastern law   This entry covers Mesopotamia and Egypt. The principal sources for law in ancient Mesopotamia are law collections, king's edicts (*misharum* edicts), and contemporaneous public and private legal documents, such as letters, contracts, adoption memoranda, boundary markers, administrative texts, and international agreements. The law collections are the most important of these various sources. Scholars have long debated the historical character of the law collections. Some have argued that they were actually written laws, or statutes. Others have posited that they were summaries of cases that had been decided by a king or court. Others have suggested that they were merely abstract expressions of a king's judicial principles and aspirations. Today most scholars agree that at the very least, they reflect fundamental policies and accurate statements of legal principles that governed law and society in an ancient Mesopotamia.

The most significant law collections are the Laws of Ur-Nammu (c. 2100 BCE); the Laws of Lipit-Ishtar (c. 1930 BCE); the Laws of Eshnunna (c. 1770 BCE); and the Law of Hammurabi (c. 1750 BCE).

The Laws of Ur-Nammu contain about forty provisions. These laws protect interests such as property and family. Admittedly, they seem to be particularly concerned with protecting the interests of the wealthy. But they also give some protection to the poor and disadvantaged. There are about fifty laws in the collection of Lipit-Ishtar. His laws primarily concern securing rights to and protecting property. Some defend the rights of children. Others punish persons who bring unsubstantiated lawsuits, thus discouraging frivolous litigation. The Laws of Eshnunna (over sixty laws) especially promote the interests of upper class citizens. There are many laws protecting property owners and many relating to commercial transactions. One of their significant features is that they treat persons differently, depending upon their social class. The *awilum* (upper class) receives preferential treatment. The *mushkenum* (commoner) receives fewer benefits but fares far better than slaves. Nevertheless, the Laws of Eshnunna do foster family values and the rights of the individual, whether rich or poor.

The Laws of Hammurabi are the most famous and complete of the ancient Mesopotamian law collections. There are 275–300 laws in Hammurabi's collection; the traditional number is 282. The famous copy of Hammurabi's Laws is carved on a cone-shaped black diorite stela that stands over two metres tall in the Louvre in Paris. The Babylonian god of justice, Shamash, is seated at the top of the stela, dictating the laws to Hammurabi. The laws appear in vertical columns that encircle the stela. In addition to the laws themselves, there is a poetic prologue, recounting Hammurabi's accomplishments and articulating his desire to establish justice, and an epilogue, explaining his purpose and cursing those who might deign to disobey his laws or deface his stela. The laws are arranged by topic. It is convenient to categorize them into eleven groups: procedure, property, military, land and agriculture, miscellaneous gap provisions, principal and agent, debts and **bailment,** family law, personal injury, professional wages and liability, and sale of slaves.

Hammurabi's procedural laws promoted truth as a value, by punishing false witnesses and unsubstantiated claims. His property laws promoted an individual's interest in protecting his property, including slaves. Certain contracts were invalid unless there were witnesses and other formalities such as writing and seals. Such formal contract requirements protected both buyers and sellers. Several laws protected children. Other laws promoted public safety and welfare by making allowances for military service. Landowners received preferential treatment. For example, the laws punished tenants who failed to produce crops on schedule. The laws also punished defaulting debtors and their families. Still, some laws did protect the rights of debtors against unfair practices by creditors. Hammurabi's **marriage** laws reflect a strong desire to preserve families and to promote fidelity and the institution of marriage itself. These and other laws even demonstrate an interest in protecting the rights of women.

The prologues and epilogues of these law collections evince the jurisprudential foundations of ancient Mesopotamian law. They suggest that there were at least eight predominant elements that defined 'justice' for the Mesopotamians: freedom (especially for the weak and the poor, freedom from oppression by the strong and the rich), public safety, economic prosperity, order, family security (ensuring that family members cared for one another), truth, and the existence of a dispute resolution process.

Ancient Egyptians generally used common, everyday words, not technical legal vocabulary, to deal with legal matters. The Egyptian word closest to 'law' was *hp*. A nascent legal system existed as early as the Old Kingdom (c. 3150–2700 BCE). Because the kings of that era were thought to have received their power from the gods, and were actually considered gods themselves, a king's decrees had the force of law. It is unlikely that there were any written laws at this time. The king and his chief judicial official, the vizier, based their decisions on the divine concept of justice, *ma'at*. *Ma'at* was both a goddess and an abstract concept. As a goddess, the daughter of the solar deity, Re, her iconographic symbol was an ostrich feather. As a concept, *ma'at* was the central, controlling principle of law, representing natural order, truth, justice, and the harmonic balance of life. *Ma'at* concerned religion, ethics, and morality. Egyptian law reflected other jurisprudential principles, such as adherence to tradition, recognition of the rights of the weak and disadvantaged, fostering of impartiality and social justice, and natural law.

The particulars of the judicial structure during the Old and Middle Kingdoms are somewhat obscure. During the New Kingdom, the pharaoh Horemhab (c. 1323–1295 BCE) reorganized the court system, establishing two Great Courts, one in Upper Egypt and one in Lower Egypt. In addition to the Great Courts, Horemhab founded smaller, local courts to serve the needs of towns and villages. The local court in the village at Dier El-Medina (home to labourers constructing tombs for the pharaohs of the New Kingdom) handled contract disputes and theft cases. Pharaohs also appointed special courts to investigate and try exceptional crimes. The sixth Dynasty King Pepi I (c. 2325 BCE) appointed a special tribunal to investigate a conspiracy to assassinate him. A similar conspiracy arose under Ramses III (c. 1186–1154 BCE). A special court also adjudicated

the Great Tomb Robberies that occurred during the reign of Ramses IX (c. 1125–1107 BCE).

The Egyptians developed sophisticated laws relating to numerous topics. Although there were distinct social classes (including slaves), women enjoyed a legal status nearly equal to men. Women could buy, sell, and own property. Because agriculture was so important, and because the annual Nile flood required property boundaries to be redrawn and surveyed systematically, viziers maintained records regarding the sale, lease, taxation, and ownership of real estate. The nuclear family was important, and specialized family laws promoted stability in marriage and protected the interests of women and children. Laws pertaining to wills and inheritance ensured an orderly division of property among a deceased's family and heirs. **Criminal law** and **tort law** imposed punishments on those who injured others or damaged or stole property. Because merchants were very active, business laws developed which protected the rights of contracting parties. A specialized document called the *imyt-pr* served as a written contract for transactions such as funeral services, slave sales, slave rentals, donkey rentals, and sales of both houses and goods. Eventually, as a result of conquest first by Alexander the Great and then by the Romans, ancient Egyptian law and procedure were gradually absorbed into Greek and then Roman law.

J RUSSELL VERSTEEG

***Anderson v Gorrie* (1895)**   By the early 1890s British judges had erected an almost impregnable barrier to protect themselves from lawsuits brought by litigants disgruntled by judges' actions or (more often) by words spoken from the bench. The principal rationale for this immunity was the risk that the judge might go 'in daily and hourly fear of an action being brought against him' (Kelly CB in *Scott v Stansfield* (1868)), which would imperil the judge's independence. This immunity extended to colonial judges who, as recent instances had demonstrated, could not all be trusted not to abuse it. For those who suffered at their hands there was possibly one gap in the immunity still left open: in *Thomas v Churton* (1862) Lord Chief Justice Cockburn had said that he would be reluctant to decide that it extended to words uttered maliciously and without reasonable and probable cause.

What Robert Anderson endured went well beyond slanders. A planter and doctor in Tobago, Anderson repeatedly fell foul of the local chief justice, Sir John Gorrie. Gorrie had constituted himself a champion of the non-whites, encouraging them to bring free law suits against the whites and delivering his idiosyncratic version of social justice—conduct which caused a commission of inquiry to be sent from England. Anderson's attempt to appeal an adverse decision predictably failed, since the appeal court comprised Gorrie and two puisne judges, one weak (Lumb), the other a disreputable crony (Cook). When Anderson sought to bring the matter before the **Privy Council** in London, Gorrie and Cook commenced against him what the eminent jurist Sir Frederick **Pollock** denounced in an official report as a course of 'judicial persecution'. The report led to Cook being dismissed, Lumb transferred and Gorrie suspended. Anderson, facing ruin through the judges' actions, sued them for damages in England.

Gorrie died before the trial and though the jury awarded Anderson £500 against Cook, Coleridge LCJ—trying his last case—entered a verdict for Cook as a matter of law, obliging Anderson to go to the Court of Appeal. Even as presented by the plaintiff in person, Anderson's case for excluding maliciously motivated acts and words from the protection of judicial immunity seemed strong, but it did not persuade the judges. Lord Esher MR held that public policy required judicial protection to be absolute, and in argument he did not shrink from the extreme logic of that position: even if a judge shot dead a litigant in court, he would probably not be liable for murder, he said. Kay and Smith LJJ agreed with his reasoning. Anderson could not afford an appeal to the **House of Lords**, and this decision settled the scope of judicial immunity for a century.

The decision certainly caused injustice to Anderson, since the **Crown** declined to pay **compensation** for its servants' wrongs. The comprehensive scope of judicial immunity did not escape criticism, but judges of the period were faced with an increasing number of actions brought by **vexatious litigants**, and were anxious to deny them further opportunities.

PATRICK POLDEN

P Polden, 'Doctor in Trouble: *Anderson v Gorrie* and the Extension of Judicial Immunity from Suit in the 1890s' (2001) 22 *Journal of Legal History* 37–68

See also: **judges; judicial independence**

Anglo-Saxon law and custom The Anglo-Saxon period, particularly from the end of the ninth century, has a very important place in the development of English law. Our knowledge of its law and custom is derived primarily from sets of laws, some surviving anonymously, others in the names of kings from Æthelberht of Kent in c. 600 to Cnut in the first half of the eleventh century; from charters recording land grants; from various other documents including writs (letters, generally royal letters) and wills; and from accounts of disputes in other sources including chronicles, and saints' lives and miracles. Even so, our knowledge of many aspects of pre-1066 law is very patchy compared with that of the period after 1066.

The judicial was only one way of pursuing and settling disputes in Anglo-Saxon England. At least until the tenth century, feud and related settlement practices were a recognized alternative method, accepted by kings even if they sometimes sought to restrict the disruption caused. Other, more peaceful methods, including **mediation**, were also probably of considerable importance, as they would continue to be in later periods.

Various courts offered justice in Anglo-Saxon England. The king's court might deal with the most serious cases and particularly those between the most important people of the realm. Below that, in the earlier part of the period, there were courts held by the king's reeves. By later in the tenth century these had come to be more clearly defined into two types of court, those for the county or shire, and those for the sub-division of the shire known as the hundred in English areas, the wapentake in areas of Danish settlement. There may also have been lesser courts for villages, and there certainly were courts for boroughs. There is no clear evidence that lords had courts simply as a result of lordship, and ecclesiastical cases appear to have been heard in the hundred and shire courts.

If an offence of violence or theft was committed, the normal form of prosecution would be by the harmed individual or, particularly if that individual had been killed, by their family. Many offences would be paid for with monetary **compensation** to the victim or his family, but were also penalized by a monetary fine payable to the king or to a person to whom the king had delegated the fine. Increasingly, however, serious offences appear to have been punished by death, normally by hanging. The death penalty could most effectively be imposed on those caught in or soon after the act. Otherwise the catching of offenders might be difficult, and the main penalty against them would be outlawry.

Historians have generally distinguished three types of land in Anglo-Saxon law. The first is bookland, that is land originally granted by royal charter (in Old English, *boc*). Initially, it appears, bookland was only granted to monasteries, although Bede's *Letter to Egbert* in 734 shows lay nobles setting up supposed religious houses and thus benefiting from the advantages of bookland. From the late eighth century, laymen themselves received grants of bookland. Bookland was desirable because of the evidence of title that the charter could provide, because its tenure was to be perpetual, because for laymen it carried the right to alienate or bequeath, and because it was free from most secular dues. The second type of land is referred to as loanland, land held by lease. Most surviving leases were for one or three lives and were granted by churches. It is likely, however, that laymen also granted leases, and that there were leases for shorter terms of years. The third type of land is folkland. This is very rarely mentioned in the sources and its nature is unclear. The term may cover all land that was not bookland, or just land in some way associated with the office of king.

The period's major contribution to the later development of the **common law** was the degree of power exercised by the late Anglo-Saxon kings. In particular, their control of serious offences laid the foundation for later **criminal law**. The law of landholding would be more dramatically changed by the aristocratic customs introduced by the Normans after the Conquest of 1066.   JOHN HUDSON

animals, liability for The law has provided **remedies** for those injured by animals from earliest times, no doubt a reflection of the widespread practice of keeping animals and the propensity of certain animals to do damage if they escaped from their keeper's control. Apart from allowing claims for injury where the keeper has been negligent, a special liability regime, instituted by the Animals Act 1971 (UK), also applies to animals. This regime traces its history to the old action of *scientia* whereby the keeper of certain types of animal was strictly liable (that is, without fault) for damage caused by that animal, and to the action for cattle trespass whereby the owner of cattle was strictly liable for any damage to property caused by cattle trespassing on another's land. In the *scientia* action a distinction was made between animals dangerous by virtue of their breed, such as lions and elephants (*ferae naturae*), and animals of a breed not considered dangerous (*ferae manseuto*). In the case of animals *ferae naturae* the keeper was strictly liable for any damage done by the animal, but for animals *ferae mansueto* the keeper was only liable if the particular animal had a propensity to be dangerous and the keeper had knowledge of this propensity. Another liability regime applied to dogs which, broadly, made the keeper of a dog strictly liable for any injury caused by the dog to cattle or poultry. Conversely, the law provided an immunity for owners of livestock straying onto the highway and causing damage to highway users, by refusing to recognize a duty to fence.

The Animals Act 1971 now provides a statutory basis for all these actions under one statute as well as making some changes to the previous law. Based on the *scientia* action, the Act draws a distinction between dangerous and non-dangerous animals, although the statutory conditions which must be satisfied before the keeper of the latter is strictly liable have given rise to difficulties of interpretation. The action for cattle trespass has been extended to all trespassing livestock, and the power of the landholder on whose land the livestock has trespassed to sell the livestock is strictly regulated. The keeper of a dog that kills livestock is strictly liable, and a person who kills a dog worrying livestock is given a defence to any civil claim for killing or injuring the dog. There are a number of defences to these actions, an important thread amongst these being a reluctance to impose strict liability where a person or livestock has strayed onto land where an animal is regularly housed. However, the owner of land adjacent to a road cannot now leave livestock to stray freely onto the highway with impunity: the question now is whether it was careless not to fence, with the Act directing that in certain circumstances it is not careless. The immunity only remains in a number of Commonwealth jurisdictions (that is, Queensland, Western Australia), presumably as it is thought the requirement to consider fencing is incompatible with the size of many landholdings.

MARK LUNNEY

See also: **negligence in civil law; strict civil liability**

animals, rights of The 1970s witnessed the inauguration of the animal liberation movement, since when activists and academics have posited arguments rooted in the discourse of animal rights. Peter Singer's *Animal Liberation* (1975) is frequently portrayed as the bible of the animal liberation or animal rights movement, although it eschews rights-based arguments in favour of a utilitarian approach, which includes animal interests in calculations of plain and pleasure. From **Bentham** onwards, utilitarian philosophy has contributed significantly to enlightened thinking on the treatment of animals. His declaration that:

The day *may* come when the rest of the animal creation may acquire those rights which never could have been withholden from them but by the hand of tyranny . . . the question is not, can they *reason?*, nor, can they *speak,* but, can they *suffer?*

has been lauded by animal welfarists as the appropriate criterion to apply to our treatment of animals. Bentham stipulated that each person's interests were to count equally and that the interests of animals were to be weighed in any calculus of pain and pleasure. To counter the objection that crude versions of utilitarianism fail to attach sufficient importance to the **capacity** of each **person** to decide for herself on her conception of the good life, Singer adopts a modified version of preference utilitarianism according to which one seeks to maximize the extent to which each person can attain her own preferences. Applying this to animals, Singer contends that, since they have a preference to carry on living and not to suffer or experience pain, this makes killing or infliction of pain a wrong done to individual animals, and that the moral principle of equal consideration applies to animals just as it does to humans. Singer's theory is thus grounded, not in according moral or legal rights to animals but in a combination of preference utilitarianism and the principle of **equality** of treatment.

A significant disadvantage of this approach is that it denies the animal any intrinsic value, leading Singer to conclude that vegetarianism is not morally obligatory. Rather what is necessary is that the animal must have been well-reared, humanely killed, and lack self-consciousness. Similarly, in relation to animal experimentation, he contends that while vivisection should be replaced as soon as possible by alternative methods, and animals should in the meantime be anaesthetized and humanely killed to ensure that they do not suffer pain, clinical trials involving animals are permissible provided they are not painful. Critics suggest that this reformist, welfare-oriented approach fails adequately to protect the interests of animals and that a more robust, rights-based approach is necessary.

A full-blown and intellectually defensible theory of animal rights was first articulated in Tom Regan's *The Case for Animal Rights* (1984). Regan proposes that to safeguard animals from **human** oppression, it is essential to accord rights to animals, on the basis that rights are moral claims which affirm that certain treatment is owed or due. To the extent that animals are similar to humans, consistency demands that rights are attributed to both. Regan's argument is that we have good reason to believe that 'mammalian animals are not only sentient and conscious, but also have beliefs, desires, memory, a sense of the future, self awareness, and an emotional life, and can act intentionally'. Thus, as subjects of a life, such animals at least are possessors of inherent value and should be accorded rights. For Regan, the basic right which humans and animals are owed is the right to be respectfully treated—any harm done to them must be consistent with **recognition** of their inherent

value and equal *prima facie* right not to be harmed. He concludes that adherents of animal rights theory require the total abolition of harmful uses of animals in medical science or for food because it violates the rights of those animals regardless of anyone else's utility. In this sense, animal rights theory is significantly stronger than utilitarianism—it gives animals a privileged moral status and rules out treatment based on the assumption that they are reducible to the best possible utility of others.

Both Singer and Regan, in common with other animal advocates, have sought to locate animal liberation within a genealogy and discourse of earlier liberation movements for slaves, **women,** and **minority** groups, pointing to the operation of similar dynamics of power, domination, and supremacy. Clearly, in such contexts, rights arguments have a strong rhetorical and political appeal and have proven influential in terms of political and legal strategizing. To date, the most prominent animal rights campaign has been the 'Great Ape Project', which draws on scientific developments in evolution and genetics to argue for a rethinking of the place of humans and apes in the moral universe. Its thirty-four contributors demand 'the extension of the community of equals to include all great apes: human beings, chimpanzees, gorillas and orang-utans'. They contend that the basic moral principles or rights which govern relations within this 'community of equals' might include the **right to life**, the protection of individual liberty, and the prohibition of **torture**. Acknowledging the limited, and politically strategic nature, of the project, its authors state that '[t]he Great Ape Project aims at taking just one step in this process of extending the community of equals'.

Notwithstanding its symbolic value, such rights-oriented campaigns have severe limitations, especially the fact that they do little to destabilize the species boundary itself. Given the historical role of law in shoring up and defending this boundary, it may be that adopting rights-based arguments will prove even more contentious in the context of animal liberation than in relation to women's rights. In this context, it is arguable that rights arguments are ultimately incapable of settling meaningful conflicts, instead perpetuating a system of adversarial claims. Thus, they seem particularly ill-equipped to resolve the sort of conflicts that bedevil the animal-human relationship, such as the clash between the right of animals to a life free from human interference and the right of humans to putative benefits of animal research, or the assertion of rights to hunt animals that are couched as cultural claims. Arguably, once claims are framed in such terms it is inevitable that animals will lose out, since the concept of rights originates in human social relationships built on power, and of necessity they are articulated by humans. On this view, rights for animals would be productive only if the power basis of society is changed, so that what is needed for animal liberation is a change in the conditions that make rights seem necessary.

MARIE FOX

See also: **animal welfare**

annual accounts of corporations   A major feature of the 'disclosure philosophy' in the context of **company** law is the requirement for companies to produce audited accounts and to make these available to their members and debenture holders and also to the public by delivering them to the registrar of companies. The Companies Act 1985 requires all limited and unlimited companies to keep accounting records and to send their accounts to the Registrar. If they are eligible and wish to, medium-sized, small, very small and dormant companies may prepare and file 'abbreviated accounts'.

The annual accounts of companies have a number of purposes. They assist shareholders in monitoring the performance of managers; they provide information about the company's financial position and performance including details about available profits for distribution of dividends; and they assist creditors and potential investors and creditors in making decisions about financing the company. In an important case about the scope of liability of auditors the **judges** indicated that the purpose of annual accounts is to enable members 'to question the past management of the company, to exercise their voting rights if so advised and to influence future policy and management'. In the same case the judges stressed that 'advice to individual shareholders in relation to present or future investment in the company is no part of the statutory purpose of the preparation and distribution of the accounts' (*Caparo Industries plc v Dickman & Others* (1990)).

A company's accounts must include: a profit and loss account (or income and expenditure account if the company is not trading for profit); a balance sheet signed by a director; an auditors' report signed by the auditor (if appropriate); a directors' report signed by a director or the secretary of the company; notes to the accounts; and group accounts (if appropriate). The accounts must be approved by the company's board of directors and signed before they are sent to Companies House.

The fundamental requirement of the Companies Act 1985 (and 2006) is that the accounts give a true and fair view. Compliance with accounting standards issued by the Accounting Standards Board will generally be necessary to meet the true and fair view requirement. The Companies Act lays down the details of the information required to be disclosed in the accounts although there is a choice of formats. The Act also contains a number of accounting principles that must be complied with in drawing up the accounts including a requirement of consistency in accounting policies from one year to the next, a presumption that the company is carrying on business as a going concern, and prudence.

A problem widely recognized with financial accounts is that their emphasis on historical rather than forward-looking information means that they fail to meet the needs of all potential users. However, the Accounting Standards Board has identified the following characteristics as a key to quality accounts: materiality, relevance, reliability, comparability, and understandability.

CHARLOTTE VILLIERS

See also: **auditor liability**

annual general meeting, corporations
   see **shareholder meetings**

Antarctica   *see* **territory**

anthropology and law   From an early stage 'law' was recognized—alongside economics, kinship, politics, and religion—as one of the large compartments into which modern social anthropologists divided up their subject; but the constellation we have come to associate with law in the West—a compartmentalized, self-conscious, governmental structure; a specialized judiciary; the differentiation of legal norms; the emergence of a legal profession—is without easily recognizable counterparts in many of the societies anthropologists have traditionally studied. The confident self-understandings and robust institutional forms of law in the West have therefore been the source of long-term uncertainties as to what the anthropology of law might plausibly be. These uncertainties have not prevented the growth of a vigorous field to which both anthropologists and lawyers have contributed; but the durable label of 'law' has provided an appearance of continuity linking a succession of otherwise disparate conversations.

The anthropology of law is widely recognized as being inaugurated by Bronislaw Malinowski's monograph *Crime and Custom in Savage Society* (1926). There he announced an explicit break with the evolutionary studies of 'primitive law' that proliferated from the mid-nineteenth century following the work of Johann Jacob Bachofen (*Das Mutterrecht,* 1861) and Sir Henry Maine (*Ancient Law,* 1861).

Recognizing also the need for legal ethnography to escape the overbearing 'folk' understandings of state law, but equally skeptical of the Durkheimian view that 'order' could primarily be understood in terms of commitment to norms, Malinowski daringly shifted focus to explore the elaborate networks of reciprocal economic obligation that, he argued, ensured compliance with core normative understandings among the Trobrianders.

Malinowski's work appeared at the moment when local communities were being recognized and incorporated in British colonial polities under an emergent policy of 'indirect rule'. This process of encapsulation generated a range of applied studies, an early example being Isaac Schapera's classic, *A Handbook of Tswana Law and Custom* (1938), sponsored by the government of the Bechuanaland Protectorate. The *Handbook* was a rule-centred study; but in the period following World War II, under the inspiration of oral histories of North American Indian dispute processes collected earlier by Karl Llewellyn and Adamson Hoebel in *The Cheyenne Way* (1941), attention shifted primarily to the processes through which disputes were managed at local levels. Two closely observed studies, Max Gluckman's *The Judicial Process among the Barotse* (1955) and Paul Bohannan's *Justice and Judgement among the Tiv* (1957), launched this work, generating a celebrated argument around the theoretical problems that the linguistic, conceptual, and institutional categories of Western law continued to represent for anthropological studies (see Nader, *Law and Culture in Society,* 1969). Subsequent field studies sought to develop clear analytic boundaries between negotiation, mediation and adjudicative modes of decision-making (PH Gulliver's *Social Control in an African Society,* 1963) and searched for reconciliation between normative and processual paradigms (John Comaroff and Simon Roberts, *Rules and Processes: The Cultural Logic of Dispute in an African Context,* 1981).

These studies of dispute processes tended to focus upon small, local communities, cut away from the larger colonial context. This excision was a conscious choice, taken because recovery of the unique features of the community in question was the central objective. But from the l970s this fiction was increasingly dropped, the implications of 'contact' were underlined and the points of intersection of small local communities with the larger encapsulating colonial order became the explicit focus of interest. Thus an historical dimension and an interest in change were restored to legal anthropology. This work explored links between the governmental arrangements and normative understandings of the pre-colonial world and those prevailing in the post-colonial present (FG Snyder, *Capitalism and Legal Change: An African Transformation,* 1983). In doing so, it examined the extent to which 'customary law' was a construct of the colonial project rather than a survival of the pre-colonial past (M Chanock, *Law, Custom and Social Order,* 1985).

These studies of colonial domination posed some important questions, which ultimately resolved themselves into a single problem: with the imposition of a centralized legal system upon the pre-existing orders of indigenous communities, how can we best conceptualize the ensuing 'plural' scene? In *Kapauku Papuans and their Law* (1958), Leopold Pospisil had proposed that we should describe these conditions as a 'hierarchy of legal levels', a situation for which Franz von Benda-Beckmann later coined the term '**legal pluralism**' (*Rechtspluralismus in Malawi,* 1970). Sally Falk Moore subsequently argued for a more fluid conceptualization under which normative orders, including the national legal system, are better represented as partially discrete, but overlapping and interpenetrating social fields.

In the 'post-modern' period, pluralist conceptualizations of law have become virtually universal. At the same time, scholars have shown a growing freedom to draw on detailed local studies for the purposes of comparative speculation. For example, under an emergent fashion for interrogating the West from the perspective of 'the **Other**', Marilyn Strathern uses her constructions of various Papuan cosmologies to clarify Western conceptions of personhood thrown into disarray through innovations in biotechnology (*Property, Substance and Effect: Anthropological Essays on Persons and Things,* 1999).

Obviously, the compartments constituted by these successive anthropologies of law were never watertight. Further, the sediments of each remain reflected in different strands of contemporary anthropological work, increasingly carried out at local levels within the polities of the West.

SIMON ROBERTS

I Hamnett (ed), *Social Anthropology and Law* (London: Academic Press, 1977)

A Pottage and M Mundy (eds), *Law, Anthropology and the Constitution of the Social: Making Persons and Things* (Cambridge: Cambridge University Press, 2004)

See also: **colonial administration and law; Colonialism; historical jurisprudence; indigenous peoples; indigenous law**

anti-dumping measures   *see* **World Trade Organization**

antiquities and looting Antiquities, unless of intrinsically valued materials (such as gold or silver), were not considered valuable until the Renaissance, when 'ancient marbles'—sculptures from Greek and Roman times—became prized collectibles. 'Finders, keepers' has often been the rule, certainly until the nineteenth century, except for finds of valuables although, increasingly, it has been realised that a nation's antiquities form part of the national heritage and most countries now have laws protecting nationally important monuments and archaeological sites. However, the international market for antiquities sought by private collectors and museums has meant that looting—the illicit excavation of archaeological sites to provide saleable antiquities—was already widespread in the nineteenth century in countries like Greece and Italy. It has since become a worldwide problem with the increase in interest (and value) of antiquities from other lands.

In England, as early as the thirteenth century, the customary law of Treasure Trove made finds of gold or silver the property of the **Crown**, although, from the 1930s, the finder was entitled, following a coroner's inquest, to receive the value of the finds if the Crown exercised its **prerogative** of retaining them. In practice, important finds of early gold and silver, including coins, usually went to the British Museum or a local museum. The Treasure Act (1996) codified these procedures, requiring that landowners as well as finders receive compensation, and widening the category of 'treasure' to include prehistoric bronze objects. Since the first Ancient Monuments Act of 1882, officially designated ('scheduled') sites and monuments in England and Wales have been protected against unauthorized excavation: comparable legislation exists for Scotland and Northern Ireland.

The increased scale of looting and the growing international market in illicit antiquities led many nations to subscribe in 1970 to the UNESCO Convention on the Means of Prohibiting and Preventing the Illicit Import, Export and Transfer of Ownership of **Cultural Property**, ratified by the UK in 2001. Increasing public concern over the London antiquities market, prompted in part by a scandal at Sotheby's (a prominent auctioneering firm), led to the Dealing in Cultural Objects Offences Act (2003) which now makes it a criminal offence to deal in 'tainted' objects—ie antiquities illicitly excavated after 2003 or subsequently illegally exported. The US, in implementing the UNESCO Convention, enacted provision for bilateral agreements between the US and individual governments to prevent illicit import of their antiquities to the United States. The more restrictive UNIDROIT Convention on the International Return of Stolen or Illegally Exported Cultural Objects (1995) has not yet been ratified by the UK or US.

Despite these provisions, looting continues on a worldwide scale, with Mesoamerica, South America, China, and South-East Asia as notable source areas, alongside the traditionally rich lands of Greece, Italy, Turkey, Egypt, Iraq, and Iran. There is increased understanding that the main concern is damage to archaeological sites, with consequent loss of information about the past. For that reason many museums now decline to acquire antiquities which have appeared on the market since 1970. The University Museum of Pennsylvania at Philadelphia was the first to adopt such an acquisition code and was followed in 1998 by the British Museum. The J. Paul Getty Museum in Los Angeles, previously one of the worst offenders, adopted a clear and comparable acquisition code in 2006. Nevertheless, many of the world's prominent museums, such as the Metropolitan Museum of Art in New York, the Boston Museum of Fine Arts, and the Miho Museum in Japan, have refused to publish an acquisition code conforming with the 1970 UNESCO Convention, and the Musée du Louvre in Paris has continued to acquire illegally exported African antiquities.

Recently a number of national governments (including Turkey, Italy, and Greece) have been more pro-active in demanding the return of recently looted antiquities—with the Metropolitan Museum returning to Italy the notorious 'hot pot', a Greek vase with a depiction by the painter Euphronios of the Death of Sarpedon—for which it paid a million dollars in 1972. These advances have been welcomed by the archaeological community (although not by all museum directors).

The issue of the **restitution** of antiquities removed in earlier times, such as the Parthenon Marbles, taken from the acropolis in Athens in 1806 by Lord Elgin, often during times of colonial rule, is a different and more complex one. Whatever the merits of restitution claims seeking to right earlier wrongs, there is general recognition that further measures are needed to restrict the widespread and continuing looting of archaeological sites.

COLIN RENFREW

C Renfrew, *Loot, Legitimacy and Ownership: the Ethical Crisis in Archaeology* (London: Duckworth, 2000)
N Brodie and KW Tubb (eds), *Illicit Antiquities: The Theft of Culture and the Extinction of Archaeology* (London: Routledge, 2002)

anti-social behaviour Governmental impatience with the perceived shortcomings of traditional criminal justice processes lay behind the introduction of a raft of measures to deal with relatively low level but persistent, 'troublesome', nuisance-type behaviour. Of these measures, the most prominent (and contentious) is the Anti-Social Behaviour Order or ASBO. Not least of the criticisms is that there is no widely accepted understanding in Britain of what constitutes anti-social behaviour; and the Crime and Disorder Act 1998, which introduced the ASBO, is itself framed in such broad terms that it is capable of being applied to the behaviour of the socially unpopular as opposed to conduct deserving or requiring regulation, ultimately through criminal sanctions.

The 1998 Act, the first measure designed to combat social incivilities, provides that a civil restraining order can be made by magistrates against a person over the age of ten who is shown to have engaged in conduct which caused or was likely to cause alarm, **harassment,** or distress to one or more persons not of the same neighbourhood as himself. Orders can be couched in remarkably broad terms, forbidding their subjects from engaging in conduct or going to specified areas. The order and the proceedings themselves are civil as opposed to criminal in nature, and may be made at the behest of the police or other individuals and enforcement agencies (the British Transport Police, registered social landlords, Housing Action Trusts, and County Councils), using hearsay evidence and on the civil standard of proof. Failure to comply with the order, on the other hand, is treated as being criminal in character, and can be punished by imprisonment for up to five years. Amendments to the original legislation widened the ambit of the jurisdiction considerably, giving the courts powers to use the mechanism following conviction for a criminal offence.

Critics of the law say that the measures adopted are offensive in principle, criminalizing what might be otherwise lawful behaviour; that the definition is unacceptably vague and includes a great deal of conduct (vandalism, theft, abusive conduct, and harassment) that is already criminalized by other legislation; that the measures constitute an attempt to outflank the protections that the criminal law system would otherwise provide; and, finally, that the evidence shows that orders made under the legislation do not work to a degree that justifies their use, since they are regularly flouted with impunity. Supporters of the orders (which include the Anti-Social Behaviour Unit established by the Government in the Home Office in 2003) say that despite undoubted difficulties of application, the use of ASBOs has sometimes been successful in suppressing the behaviour of those who have made the lives of their neighbours (particularly on housing estates) completely intolerable.

Whichever view one takes as to their desirability and compatibility with principle, ASBOs are undoubtedly one manifestation of the belief that social discord can be resolved and social control imposed through the use of the law, and ultimately the criminal law.   A T H SMITH

antitrust   This is the American term for **competition law**. The basic provision of US antitrust is the Sherman Act of 1890. Section 1 states: 'Every contract, combination in the form of trust or otherwise, or conspiracy, in restraint of trade or commerce among the several States, or with foreign nations, is hereby declared to be illegal. Every person who shall make any contract or engage in any combination or conspiracy hereby declared to be illegal shall be deemed guilty of a felony . . .'. Section 2 states: 'Every person who shall monopolize, or attempt to monopolize, or combine or conspire with any other person or persons, to monopolize any part of the trade or commerce among several States, or with foreign nations, shall be deemed guilty of a felony . . .'.

The term 'antitrust' adverts to one of the reasons for passing the Sherman Act, which was to combat the power of the 'trusts' set up by the railroad companies. It had become common for the owners of stocks held in competing companies to transfer them to trustees who then controlled the activities of the competitors and consequently lessened competition between them. 'Antitrust' is often used throughout the world as a synonym for competition law. In Europe, however, the Competition Directorate-General of the EU Commission uses 'antitrust' to denote the areas of competition law which do not deal with mergers or state aids.   BRENDA SUFRIN

ET Sullivan (ed), *The Political Economy of the Sherman Act* (Oxford: Oxford University Press, 1991)

RA Posner, *Antitrust Law* (Chicago: University of Chicago Press, 2nd edn, 2001)

Anton Piller orders   *Anton Piller* (or 'search') orders are made by civil courts where a wrongdoer is likely to defeat justice by destroying evidence: *Anton Piller KG v Manufacturing Processes Ltd* (1976). They are distinct from criminal search warrants.

The applicant for an *Anton Piller* order is commonly the claimant in an intellectual property infringement case. The person to whom the order is addressed must allow search of identified premises. The addressee may take legal advice, but must comply with the order on pain of being in **contempt of**

court. Those executing the order may record evidence found and take away identified material.

Applicants for *Anton Piller* orders must show an extremely strong *prima facie* case and a real possibility the person against whom the order is sought will destroy material evidence in their possession. The application is heard in closed court without notifying the addressee. The court looks for clear evidence of serious harm to the applicant and considers likely harm to the addressee. In England (but not Scotland) the applicant must give a cross-undertaking in damages (ie undertake to compensate the addressee for damage resulting from execution of an improperly obtained order) and show proper arrangements for supervision, conduct and reporting of the search.

UK courts have inherent jurisdiction to grant such orders as well as jurisdiction under the Civil Procedure Act 1997 (section 7)). There must be a named addressee and the premises to be searched must usually be specified, although 'roving' *Anton Piller* orders have been granted.

The order may be discharged if improperly obtained, and any evidence recorded during an improper search will be excluded.

Anton Piller searches impinge upon professional or private life, but may be justified under **European Convention on Human Rights**, Article 8(2): *Chappell v UK* (1990). Privilege against self-incrimination cannot usually be claimed in order to resist an application for an *Anton Piller* order.   ALISON FIRTH

S Gee, *Commercial Injunctions* (London: Sweet & Maxwell, 2004)

See also: **search and seizure**

apartheid   A system of institutionalized racial segregation and discrimination enforced in South Africa by white minority governments from 1948 to 1994. The term means 'separateness' in Afrikaans and Dutch and its first recorded use is in 1917 in a speech by Jan Smuts, South Africa's Prime Minister for much of the period between 1919 and 1948.

The roots of apartheid lie in the patterns of social, economic, and political segregation established in the colonial era. The establishment by an Act of the British Parliament of the Union of South Africa in 1910 transferred power to white voters. The 1913 Native Land Act entrenched the geographical separation of racial groups by restricting black land ownership to 7 per cent of the country. This law destroyed the thriving African agricultural sector and resulted in massive forced removals. Legislation in the first quarter of the twentieth century established industrial colour bars that restricted blacks

from occupying positions of skill and responsibility and prohibited racially mixed **trade unions**.

Under the National Party government which came to power in 1948, the South African Parliament legislated extensively to strengthen and formalize segregation and discrimination. All citizens were required to register and be allocated one of four racial identities (African, Indian, Coloured, and White). Inter-racial sexual relations and marriages were outlawed. Public amenities such as restaurants, beaches, parks, and cinemas were segregated. The Group Areas Act of 1953 restricted land ownership on racial grounds and led to the forced removal of some two million people. Influx control legislation prohibited Africans from residing in urban areas without a permit and required African South Africans to carry passes (identity documents). In 1960, a protest against the pass laws led to the Sharpeville massacre in which sixty-one protestors were killed. A security state was introduced after 1948 to crush opposition to apartheid and the major political representatives of black South Africans, most notably the African National Congress ('ANC'), were outlawed.

The Bantu Education Act 1953 established a separate and inferior system of education for Africans and state subsidies to mission schools were reduced and later scrapped, resulting in the closure of most of these schools. The ironically named Extension of Universities Act implemented segregation within universities.

From 1958 the government established nominally independent homelands (Bantustans) for black people which covered 13 per cent of the country and sought to restrict the **citizenship** rights of Africans to these homelands. Separate legislatures were created for people classified as being Coloured (mixed race) or of Indian descent. Political opposition groups organized highly effective boycotts of the **elections** to these institutions.

In 1973 the **United Nations** General Assembly adopted the International Convention on the Suppression and Punishment of the Crime of Apartheid which provided a legal framework within which member states could apply sanctions to press the South African government to change its policies. The Convention defines the term 'the crime of apartheid' to include policies and practices of racial segregation and discrimination similar to those practised in Southern Africa, committed for the purpose of establishing and maintaining domination by one racial group over persons of any other racial group and systematically oppressing them. In 1971, the International Court of Justice condemned apartheid as a form of systemic racial discrimination that violated the essential principles of international law.

Economic and political pressure led to the dismantling of the apartheid edifice from the late 1970s onwards. In 1979 labour relations **legislation** was desegregated. During the 1980s a number of the social aspects of apartheid were loosened and the pass laws were scrapped. In 1990, the ANC and other banned political organizations were unbanned, leading to a negotiated transition to **democracy**. In April 1994 South Africa held its first democratic elections. A **Truth and Reconciliation** Commission was established to investigate human rights abuses committed between 1960 and 1994.

PAUL BENJAMIN

See also: **racialization**

appeals An appeal is the reconsideration of a judicial or similar decision by a higher court. This entry focuses on the position in England and Wales, but the general principles are applicable to other jurisdictions in the UK.

Civil appeals In civil proceedings appeals are regulated by Part 52 of the **Civil Procedure Rules**. An appeal usually lies to the level of judge immediately above the one who made the relevant decision. Thus an appeal lies from a district judge to a circuit judge, from a circuit judge to a High Court judge and from a High Court judge to the civil division of the Court of Appeal. There are exceptions to this scheme, the most important of which is that if a circuit judge gives a final decision in a multi-track case any appeal goes to the Court of Appeal.

Some statutes provide (subject to a variety of restrictions) for appeals to the courts from decision-making bodies which are not themselves courts. For example, appeals may be brought, in homelessness cases, from certain local authority decisions to the county court; appeals may be brought from decisions of the Fitness to Practise Panel of the General Medical Council to the High Court; appeals may be brought from decisions of the Asylum and Immigration Tribunal to the Court of Appeal; the courts may hear appeals from awards of arbitrators; and so forth.

Where an appeal is brought from one court to a higher court, in most cases permission to appeal is required. Permission may be granted either by the lower court or by the appeal court. The criteria for granting permission are (a) that the appeal has a real prospect of success; or (b) that there is some other compelling reason for the appeal to be heard.

An appeal from a decision which was itself made on appeal is known as a 'second appeal'. A second appeal must be made to the Court of Appeal and (except in arbitration matters) only the Court of Appeal can give permission for a second appeal. The Court of Appeal will only give such permission if (a) the appeal raises an important point of principle or practice; or (b) there is some other compelling reason for the Court of Appeal to hear it.

An appeal usually proceeds by way of review. In other words the appeal court scrutinizes the findings of fact and the reasoning process of the lower court and determines whether the lower court fell into error. This involves some examination of the documents before the court below and possibly the transcript of any oral evidence, but falls far short of a re-run of the original hearing. The appeal court usually accepts any findings of primary fact, especially when those findings were based upon the evidence of witnesses who gave oral evidence in the court below. The appeal court is less reluctant to interfere with inferences made from those findings of primary fact.

In certain specified cases, and also when it would be 'in the interests of justice', the appeal proceeds by way of re-hearing, rather than review. This does not literally mean that the appeal court starts afresh or hears the evidence of the witnesses all over again. A re-hearing does, however, involve a rather fuller scrutiny of the evidence before the court below and the conclusions reached by that court.

An appeal court has the power to receive evidence which was not before the court below. The appeal court will not exercise this power unless there is some good reason to do so.

An appeal will be allowed if the decision of the lower court was (a) wrong; or (b) unjust because of a serious procedural or other irregularity. In that event the appeal court may set aside or vary the decision of the lower court, or refer any matter for determination by the lower court, or order a new trial or hearing before the lower court.

Criminal appeals A defendant may appeal against his conviction or sentence from the magistrates' court to the Crown Court. The appeal is heard by a circuit judge or recorder, who must normally sit with two magistrates. Such an appeal is a genuine re-hearing (unlike a 're-hearing' in civil appeals). The witnesses are called to give evidence afresh. Neither party is limited to the evidence adduced in the magistrates' court.

Either the prosecution or defence may appeal from the magistrates' court on a question of law by 'case stated' to the Divisional Court of the Queen's

Bench Division. In order to facilitate this procedure the magistrates' court states a 'case', setting out the facts and identifying the question of law which is the subject of appeal.

A defendant who has been convicted or sentenced in the Crown Court may appeal against conviction or sentence to the criminal division of the Court of Appeal. Such an appeal may only be brought if the Court of Appeal gives leave or (in rare cases) if the trial judge certifies that the case is fit for appeal. The Court of Appeal proceeds on the basis of the evidence before the Crown Court and investigates whether there was any error of law or procedure (for example, the admission of inadmissible evidence or a misdirection in the summing up). In rare cases, if there is good reason to do so, the Court of Appeal may hear limited oral evidence. The Court of Appeal will allow an appeal against conviction, if it thinks that the conviction was unsafe. The Court of Appeal will allow an appeal against sentence, if the sentence was wrong in law, wrong in principle or manifestly excessive.

Appeals to the House of Lords The **House of Lords** is the final appellate court for England, Wales, Scotland, and Northern Ireland. The House of Lords hears appeals from the English Court of Appeal, in civil or criminal cases, which raise a point of law of general public importance. Such an appeal may only be pursued with the leave of the House of Lords or (in certain cases) of the Court of Appeal. Appeals to the House of Lords are usually heard by five law lords (ie judges of the court).   RUPERT JACKSON

See also: **courts; criminal justice system: Scotland; judges; Scottish law after 1900**

appeals service (social security)   *see* **tribunals**

approximation of laws in the EU   The approximation (or harmonization) of laws refers to the European Union's ability to adopt binding legislative measures setting out common regulatory standards across Member States. When the EU carries out approximation, national laws remain in place, but must conform to the regulatory standards prescribed by the EU, so that the Union's policy objectives are achieved within the framework of the domestic legal systems. In this sense, approximation is not as intensive as the unification of national laws; the latter implies the wholesale integration of domestic legal orders, effectively replacing national law with Union **legislation**.

Although the approximation of laws may take many forms, it is possible to identify two principal types, distinguished according to the impact of the relevant Community measure upon the exercise by the Member State of its own regulatory powers. First, exhaustive or total harmonization refers to Community legislation which effectively binds Member States to a given regulatory standard; they cannot lawfully and unilaterally adopt divergent national rules. Exhaustive harmonization does not exclude some degree of difference between domestic laws: for example, it is common for Community legislation to contain derogations, defining specific situations in which Member States are permitted to deviate from the otherwise exhaustively harmonized Community standard.

Secondly, partial harmonization refers to Community legislation which imposes certain obligations on Member States as to how they must exercise their own regulatory competences, but nevertheless leaves the national authorities a margin of discretion to make their own independent policy choices, even within the regulated field. This is most common with Community legislation which provides for only minimum harmonization: the Community act establishes a regulatory 'floor of rights', and the Member State may not enact rules which fall lower than that common standard; but the Member State does remain competent to enact higher standards of protection (for example) in favour of consumers, workers, or the environment—provided such standards do not breach obligations contained in the EU Treaty itself, such as the free movement of goods, persons, and services.

In some policy fields, the treaty determines that only partial harmonization by the Community institutions is legally possible. This is true, for example, in fields such as environmental and consumer law; the relevant treaty provisions in each case expressly state that the approximation of national laws will result in only minimum standards of protection. In other policy fields, however, the treaty does not specify which type of harmonization is possible; it is thus left to the legislative practice of the Community institutions to determine the degree of approximation (total or partial) suitable for any given regulatory measure.

The harmonization of national laws takes place in many contexts and for often very different purposes under **European Community law**. In this regard, one of the most important provisions is Article 95 of the Treaty of Rome, which empowers the Community to adopt the measures for the approximation of Member State rules which have as their object the establishment and functioning of the internal market. On that basis, the Community adopts legislation which promotes the free movement of goods and services by removing obstacles to cross-border trade and / or distortions of competition between undertakings. As the **European Court of Justice** held in its *Tobacco Advertising* judgment (*Germany v Parliament and Council* (2000)), Article 95 does not confer upon the Community a general power to regulate in the public interest; it confers only the power to adopt approximation measures which remove genuine trade obstacles and / or appreciable competitive distortions (though in doing so, the Community institutions will inevitably have to take into account all relevant public interest objectives, so as to reach an appropriate common standard of market regulation).

Article 95 was introduced into the Treaty of Rome by the Single European Act 1986, whose primary purpose was to accelerate the process of economic integration between Member States, in particular, by permitting harmonizing legislation to be adopted by the **Council of Ministers** through majority voting rather than unanimity. In this regard, the introduction of Article 95 EC was complemented by an important change in the *style* of approximation pursued by Community institutions. Before, the Community was often accused of adopting overly detailed legislation on goods and services. It was often difficult to reach agreement on such measures within the Council of Ministers; they also drew accusations of excessive uniformity that suppressed market variety and consumer choice. Under the so-called 'new approach' to harmonization, introduced in the mid-1980s, Community legislation restricts itself to approximating only the essential features of a policy field (for example, **safety standards** for cars or toys). National law must conform to those particular harmonized standards, but each Member State will remain competent to regulate for itself all other aspects of (say, car or toy) manufacturing and marketing. However, Member States are then required to grant mutual recognition to each others' non-harmonized rules: provided a good or service complies with the Community's harmonized standards governing its essential features, as enforced in its country of origin, other Member States cannot then impede its importation and sale on the grounds that the relevant good or service does not comply with their own non-harmonized regulations governing other aspects of manufacturing and marketing.

Being easier to negotiate within the Council of Ministers, this 'new approach' to approximation both increased the volume of Community harmonizing activity and accelerated the removal of obstacles to economic integration between Member States. In effect, the harmonization of essential regulatory standards facilitates the mutual recognition between Member States of any remaining differences between their national laws. Since countries are meant to trust that imported goods and services satisfy the regulatory standards necessary to protect the public interest, those countries should not impede the free movement of goods and services on any other grounds. At the same time, the 'new approach' makes clear that the approximation of national laws need not lead to the unappetizing spectre of 'Euro-sausages' or 'Euro-beers'. In fact, the internal market is constructed around a careful balance between the harmonization of, and continued divergence / mutual recognition between, domestic regulatory regimes.

The approximation of national laws is possible not only in the field of the internal market, but also in other policy areas entrusted to Community institutions: for example, environmental protection and social policy. In such sectors, however, approximation is not aimed at, or dependent upon, facilitating free movement for goods and services; and the style of the 'new approach' to harmonization is less relevant or appropriate. The exercise of Community competence is instead intended to promote substantive policy objectives within the relevant regulatory field: for example, high standards of environmental protection as regards waste management and habitat conservation; or just and fair conditions of employment as regards issues such as working time and equal treatment on grounds of sex.

The approximation of national laws is also possible under the Third Pillar of the European Union concerning police and judicial cooperation in criminal matters. In particular, Articles 29 and 31 of the EU Treaty state that the Union is empowered to adopt approximation measures establishing minimum rules relating to the constituent elements of criminal acts and to penalties in the fields of organized crime, terrorism, and illicit drug-trafficking.

In certain fields of Community policy, the Treaty expressly precludes legislative action aimed at the approximation of national laws. Instead, Community action is limited to supporting or supplementing national policies; it cannot curtail the exercise by Member States of their own inherent regulatory competences. This is true, for example, in fields such as educational policy, macro-employment policy, and cultural policy. In such fields, Community intervention is often aimed at coordinating national decision-making: for example, by identifying and encouraging voluntary convergence by the Member States around certain common policy objectives; and/or by identifying and disseminating among

Member States information about best practice in addressing a particular problem. In sectors such as macro-employment policy and the modernization of social protection systems, such Community action has become highly formalized and is now termed the 'open method of coordination'.

MICHAEL DOUGAN

See also: **European Community legal instruments; European Community powers; European treaties; Pillars of the European Union**

Aquinas, Thomas (1224/5–1274)   Aquinas joined the Dominican Order, studying under leading scholar, Albertus Magnus, and taught at Cologne and Paris. He was canonized in 1323.

In writing about law, as in writing about theology and philosophy, Aquinas's task was to reconcile Christian teaching with Greek philosophy, and, in particular, with Aristotle's newly available works, such as the *Politics* and the *Ethics*. He also had to reconcile the Christian and Greek traditions with that of Roman law.

The *Ethics* was concerned with virtue defined as a capacity to live a distinctively human life which was man's end and in which all human potentialities were realized. Aquinas explained that to live as virtue prescribed was to live in accord with 'natural law' and therefore to act in accord with God's plan—the 'eternal law'—by which man was created with a certain nature and end. But to realize his end, man needed, not virtue alone, but God's help: grace, supernatural virtues of faith, hope and charity, and 'divine law'. Divine law contained precepts that man could not know naturally or could know only with difficulty. Finally, man needed secular or 'human law'. It laid down a clear rule when natural law was obscure and a single rule when several different ones would be consistent with natural law. There were, then, many types of law, each with its proper place. It was not a world in which all normative authority belonged to the virtuous; or morality rested on an inscrutable divine plan; or right conduct was known only by revelation; or laws were human contrivances resting on no higher moral authority.

Aquinas also used Aristotle's concept of **justice** to explain rules of **Canon** and Roman law. For Aristotle, distributive justice secures each citizen a fair share of resources; commutative justice preserves the share of each. Commutative justice is violated if one person deprives another of resources without consent. Aquinas explained in Aristotelian terms, why, as Roman and Canon law recognized, such a person might have done so wrongfully either intentionally or through negligence. Aquinas added that if he

did not act wrongfully, he must still make compensation if he was enriched, thereby recognizing what modern lawyers call a claim in unjust enrichment. Commutative justice in exchange requires that the parties exchange resources equivalent in value, so that neither is enriched at the other's expense. Aquinas used this principle to explain Roman remedies for unjust prices and undisclosed defects. His work had little influence on the medieval lawyers whose attention remained fixed on their legal authorities. Centuries later, however, scholars such as Domingo de Soto (1494–1560), Luis de Molina (1535–1600), and Leonard Lessius (1554–1623) self-consciously synthesized Aristotle and Aquinas's ideas with Roman law. They thereby gave Roman law a systematic structure it previously lacked. Many of their conclusions were borrowed by the influential seventeenth- century jurists Hugo Grotius (1583–1645) and Samuel Pufendorf (1632–94), and thence passed into modern law, long after their foundation in the thought of Aristotle and Aquinas had been forgotten.

JAMES GORDLEY

See also: **natural law theory; Roman-dutch law**

arbitration   *see* **alternative dispute resolution**

arbitration, consumer   Throughout the post-war period, there has been a worldwide search for simpler, cheaper, and speedier alternatives to court adjudication in resolving consumer disputes. Since court action may well prove costly, consumers are well advised to consider alternative procedures. Taking the simple example of the consumer who has a complaint against a travel agent about delayed flights or substandard accommodation, it might well be worthwhile considering whether the matter might be resolved by arbitration.

Arbitration involves adjudication by a neutral third party—the arbitrator—whose decision is binding on the parties. This may be done at a hearing but it is more common for consumer disputes to be resolved on a 'documents only' basis. Arbitration more closely resembles court adjudication than other forms of **alternative dispute resolution** such as mediation and conciliation. The differences lie primarily in the specialized nature of the arbitrator's jurisdiction; the fact that parties voluntarily submit to arbitration; the adaptability of procedures, especially adjudication based on documents; the less adversarial character of proceedings; and the limited avenues of appeal.

Being relatively inexpensive, arbitration often suits commercial organizations as well as consumers. A range of arbitration schemes for consumers exists, many of which are run on behalf of trade associations, companies, and other organizations by the Chartered Institute of Arbitrators, which has more than 11,000 members in over 100 countries. While thousands of consumer disputes are resolved annually through such schemes, public awareness remains low and confused, and the schemes are in consequence often under-used.   JOHN BALDWIN

See also: **arbitration, international; small claims**

arbitration, international   *see* **international courts and tribunals**

archaeological heritage   A working definition of 'heritage' is provided by the expression 'that part of a nation's past which is of public interest and concern'. Of necessity this invokes the public law of the relevant jurisdiction(s), and in the UK, it is fair to say that not just the heart, but virtually the entire body and function of that law are the product of **legislation,** primary or otherwise.

Legislation focuses on protecting sites and buildings from destruction or other undesirable activities. The two main statutes are the Ancient Monuments and Archaeological Areas Act 1979 ('AMAA') and the Planning (Listed Buildings and Conservation Areas) Act 1990 ('LBA').

The AMAA empowers the government to 'schedule' any monument considered by them to be of national importance, including the remains of 'any structure, work, cave or excavation'. There are over 30,000 scheduled monuments in the UK, including prehistoric earthworks, sites detected from aerial photography, medieval ruins, and industrial structures. Groups of scheduled monuments may cluster to provide protection of a landscape, for example, on Salisbury Plain or the castles of Edward I in Gwynedd. Yet the sole measure in the AMAA specifically designed to cater for 'areas of archaeological importance' was introduced only on an experimental basis (in Canterbury, Chester, Exeter, Hereford, and York), and has not been pursued at all outside England. Some principal scheduled monuments are 'World Heritage Sites' (UNESCO World Heritage Convention (1972)), but this does not provide any additional legal protection. Sites within UK territorial waters may be scheduled, but historic wreck sites (designated under the Protection of Wrecks Act 1973) are separately regulated.

In contrast to the AMAA, the LBA provides the framework for the protection of buildings in use. The list is of buildings which the government considers 'of special architectural or historic importance', numbering about 400,000 nationally, including,

for example, timber-framed houses, stately homes, banks, railway stations, churches, and town halls. Each is classified by non-statutory grades (I, II* and II), the bulk falling into Grade II (the lowest importance). Grade I—and some grade II*—buildings have similar importance to scheduled monuments.

Conservation areas designated under the LBA aim to preserve or enhance a locality's special architectural or landscape character, but are not specifically archaeological.

The AMAA and the LBA impose consent regimes, whereby operations will only be legally carried out if prior consent is obtained from the relevant authority. Without such consent, operations will usually constitute an offence, punishable by a substantial fine. An 'enforcement notice' can also be served by the authorities in listed building cases, but not on scheduled monuments. Under both the AMAA and the LBA, public authorities are empowered to purchase important monuments or buildings compulsorily; under the LBA after first serving a 'repairs notice' on the owner, which specifies steps to be taken if such acquisition is to be avoided.

Archaeological remains in general are also protected under the land use planning regime (Planning Policy Guidance Note 16: Planning and Archaeology 1990 ('PPG 16')). PPG 16 and its philosophy represent a watershed in protection of the archaeological heritage in the UK, crystallizing a tendency within late 1980s public policy to preserve 'archaeological resources' when planning permission is granted by the planning authority under the Town and Country Planning Act 1990 ('TCPA'). The doctrine is one of 'preservation *in situ*' (where planning permission will not be granted) or 'preservation by record' (where archaeologically damaging works can go ahead provided that suitable mitigation, usually by excavation, is carried out beforehand). Other designations may be significant when deciding whether planning permission should be granted, for example, World Heritage Status ('WHS'), national park policy, local development plans, or English Heritage's non-statutory list of battlefields, or list of parks and gardens. The 'developer' has become the major source of funding for archaeological work, and knowledge of contract and procurement law is now another key skill for many archaeologists.

The AMAA, the TCPA, and the LBA do not specifically restrict any searching for or removal from the ground of archaeological finds, except in 'protected places' (mainly scheduled monuments)— where use of metal detectors is prohibited by the AMAA. However, the Treasure Act 1996 (not applicable to Scotland), with a wide definition of 'treasure', provides a reporting and investigation framework for found objects, whereby archaeological finds can in appropriate cases be acquired by a public museum (following detailed valuation and payment of a reward to the finder). In Scotland, all items recovered from the ground—whether or not they could be defined as treasure under the Act—vest in the **Crown** under the enduring doctrine of *bona vacantia*. All finds must therefore be reported (often under standing arrangements). In Northern Ireland, the Historic Monuments and Archaeological Objects (Northern Ireland) Order 1995 enacts a different regime from that in the rest of the UK. Here a government licence is required to undertake any archaeological excavation and the Order and conditions of licences provide for all finds to be reported and surrendered for analysis. NEIL COOKSON

See also: **UNESCO World Heritage Centre**

architectural conservation The desirability of conserving past architectures and their settings has its roots in antiquarianism, a fascination with architectural antiquity and the Italian Renaissance. From the sixteenth century onwards, the careful science of archaeology gradually superseded antiquarianism, and the detritus of **time** was scraped away to reveal ever more about ancient civilizations. By the mid-nineteenth century in France, Viollet-le-Duc, the architect-restorer of Notre Dame de Paris and the fortified town of Carcassone, set out the principles of restoration in his influential *Dictionnaire raisonné de l'architecture française du XIe au XVIe siècle*. Viollet-le-Duc believed it was essential to determine the exact age and character of each portion of a building and to write a factual report based upon historical documents, notes, sketches, photography, and observation. It was the duty of the architect to recognize the different periods of construction, and the building was to be viewed as a totality of evolution aesthetically and structurally. Once these facts were recorded physical changes could be introduced to sustain or bring new life to a building.

In England, a different form of rationality was at play as the nation's Gothic monuments were reappraised. The Cambridge Camden Society, founded in 1839 to promote 'the study of Gothic Architecture and of Ecclesiastical Antiques', advocated the return to a 'purer' medievalism in church architecture. A counter-view was set out by John Ruskin in his *Seven Lamps of Architecture* published in the mid-nineteenth century. In 'The Lamp of Memory', Ruskin argued that the greatest glory of a building was its display of the patina of age, and there should be no attempt to 'improve' the appearance of an ancient building except to ensure its survival. This view was to prevail for the next eighty years, particularly as augmented by the manifesto of the Society for the Protection of Ancient Buildings ('SPAB') written and issued in 1877 by William Morris and other founder members, in response to the interventionist conservation approaches of the nineteenth century. Ruskin and SPAB were 'anti-scrape', the stripping—or scraping back—of the interior distemper and the relaying of the floor throughout the church. By limiting restoration work to what is essential, and using well-proven repair methods, they sought to protect the characteristics that make each old building unique and special, and to leave them physically unharmed for the benefit of future generations.

National responses to architectural conservation were internationalized in 1933 with the First International Congress of Architects and Technicians of Historic Monuments, held in Athens in 1931. The so-called Athens Charter established some key principles: to abandon restorations *in toto* and to avoid initiating a system of permanent preservation. In the spirit of the SPAB, it recommended that the historic and artistic work of the past should be respected, without excluding the style of any given period. The International Council on Monuments and Sites ('ICOMOS') was founded in 1965 on the good work initiated by the Athens Charter of 1931 and the subsequent Venice Charter of 1964, the Second Congress of Architects and Specialists of Historic Buildings. ICOMOS was created by UNESCO to advise on World Heritage Sites. The Venice Charter adopted thirteen resolutions, which includes the concept (Article 1) that an historic monument embraces not only the single architectural work but also its urban or rural setting, and that this concept applies not only to great works of art but also to more modest works which have acquired cultural significance with the passing of time. Also (Article 13) that additions will not be allowed if they detract from the interesting parts of the building, its traditional setting, the balance of its composition, and its relation with its surroundings. ICOMOS subsequently formulated the Burra Charter in 1979, which was amended most recently in 2004 and remains its definitive statement on building conservation.

In England and Wales, following the physical devastation of World War II, the Town and Country Planning Act 1947 was introduced to regulate rebuilding and protect the historic buildings that had survived. The **legislation** introduced the requirement of planning permission for land development, and stipulated that historic buildings of note should be placed on a Statutory List and graded according to their national, architectural, or historic interest. The Statutory List was supplemented by the concept of conservation areas, which was initiated in 1967 through the Civic Amenities Act. This placed a duty on Local Planning Authorities to designate 'areas of special architectural or historic interest the character or appearance of which it is desirable to preserve or enhance'. There are now over 8,000 conservation areas across England and Wales and listing currently protects around 500,000 buildings.

There is a general government commitment to preserve the historic environment and the Planning (Listed Buildings and Conservation Areas) Act 1990, issues directions on Listed Buildings and Conservation Areas such that 'special attention shall be paid to the desirability of preserving or enhancing the character or appearance' of the historic environment (section 73.1). Related to this *is Planning Policy Guidance Note 15—Planning and the Historic Environment* (1994), better known as PPG 15, which provides a full statement of government policies for the identification and protection of historic buildings, conservation areas, and other elements of the historic environment at present. The practice of architectural conservation in Britain must adhere to these legal directives as well as following the guidance of consultative bodies established by the government—such as English Heritage—to advise on such issues. The character of a listed building or conservation area, and so the aspects of a building worthy of conservation, is defined by national and regional planning authorities and advisory bodies. Nonetheless, the legal requirement of 'enhancement' in proposals affecting buildings identified as being worthy of preservation continues to be contested in public planning inquiries.   ROBERT TAVERNOR

armed conflict, law of   *see* **international humanitarian law**

armed forces   The armed forces of the **Crown**, that is, the Royal Navy, the British Army, the Royal Air Force, the Royal Marines and both the reserve and territorial forces of those services derive their legal authority and existence from the Armed Forces Act 2006 and the Reserve Forces Act 1996 (though the Royal Navy is arguably based on the royal prerogative). The prohibition in the **Bill of Rights (1689)**, Art 6 of a standing army in peacetime unless with the approval of Parliament is thereby overcome.

Parliament controls the numbers of the armed forces, and matters of supply and maintenance, including funding, and conducts reviews of the provisions of the military discipline system. The Crown commissions officers and is responsible for military deployment and disposition of forces. Decisions on such matters involve exercise of the **royal prerogative,** and are traditionally 'non-justiciable'—ie not subject to review by courts. However **human rights** law and EU directives impact on exercise of prerogative powers in relation to such issues, thus allowing more expansive judicial review.

Military law is commonly conceived of as the rules of conduct contained in the Armed Forces Act 2001 and its subordinate legislation. However regard must also be had, inter alia, to the 'administrative' and employment provisions in the Act, such as enlistment rules, to Queen's Regulations issued under the prerogative, and to the services' administrative and managerial instructions governing day-to-day activities. The Army's rules, known as AGAI (Army General Administrative Instructions), have authorized, since January 2005, the imposition of low-level punishments for minor disciplinary infractions.

There are distinct military offences which have no counterpart in civilian law, such as the offences of mutiny, desertion, misconduct in action, disobedience to standing orders and conduct prejudicial to good order and service discipline. Service personnel are, however, also subject to the provisions of English criminal law and therefore could face prosecution before military courts for such offences as theft and assault, amongst others. Regular soldiers as well as all officers are subject to the service discipline laws wherever they serve, even if off-duty, both at home and abroad.

Proceedings may be taken against service personnel at different levels. Apart from the use of AGAI within a unit for the most minor breaches, summary dealing (or 'CO's orders') is conducted before the commanding officer or his second-in-command for lesser offences. The procedure is relatively informal, there is no legal representation, the prosecution is conducted by a battalion officer, the accused is assisted, but not represented, by an 'accused's adviser', and punishments are limited.

While it appears that most servicemen are satisfied with the expeditious system of summary dealing, an appeal from the award and/or sentence can be made to the Summary Appeal Court ('SAC'), chaired by an experienced judge advocate (of equivalent status to a circuit judge). The SAC was introduced by the Armed Forces Discipline Act 2000 to ensure that summary dealing was compatible with Article 6 of the **European Convention on Human Rights** ('ECHR'), which guarantees the right to trial by an 'independent and impartial tribunal'.

The accused, nonetheless, has the right to opt for trial by court martial. The structure, organization and personnel of the latter court were significantly altered in April 1997 following a ruling under the ECHR that courts martial breached Article 6 (*Findlay v United Kingdom* (1997)). Prosecutions are now determined and conducted by service prosecution authorities independent of the chain of command. Moreover, the judge advocate, previously only advisory during the trial, effectively directs the court as in a civilian trial. An independent body appoints the members of the court.

The Armed Forces Act 2001 has created standing tri-service courts martial, replacing separate ad hoc courts. It is considered that this will significantly enhance the independence of such courts and their personnel from command influence, though others believe that such a problem did not exist. Appeals go to the civilian Courts-Martial Appeal Court (a branch of the Court of Appeal, Criminal Division) created in 1951.

Apart from the defence of the realm, or participating in peace support operations abroad or engaging in defence diplomacy, which are matters primarily falling within the royal prerogative, the armed forces may also be called upon to provide, within the United Kingdom, military aid to the civil authority ('MACA'). Apart from supporting the police in respect of law enforcement, the armed forces may be called upon (for instance) to move essential goods during strikes, assist the agriculture ministry during a foot and mouth disease outbreak or engage in flood rescue. Legal authority for the exercise of 'emergency powers' is contained in Pt 2 of the Civil Contingencies Act 2004. However, the constitutional principle of civilian supremacy prevails.   GR RUBIN

***Armory v Delamirie* (1722)**   To a certain extent the law seems to recognize the well-known maxim 'finders keepers'. A finder of any goods who takes possession of them acquires a property right which will be protected by the legal system. (Compare *Asher v Whitlock* (1865) on **adverse possession** of land.)

In *Armory v Delamirie*, a chimney sweep's boy found a jewel ring and took it to a local goldsmith to have it valued. The goldsmith's assistant pretended to weigh the stone, and the goldsmith offered the boy a trivial amount of money for it. The boy declined the offer, but the goldsmith refused to redeliver the stone, returning to the boy only the empty socket. Later the boy brought legal proceedings against the goldsmith and recovered damages to compensate for the value of the stone. The court found that, although the boy was not the owner of the jewel, yet he had acquired 'such property as [would] enable him to keep it against all but the rightful owner'.

This statement from the court in *Armory* requires some qualification. First, it is clear that an owner of goods almost always will be able to recover them from a finder. The owner's property rights in his goods are unaffected by the acquisition of right by the finder, and so if the finder refuses to redeliver the goods to the owner, the owner can sue the finder in the same way he could sue a thief or any other unlawful possessor. In this sense, a finder of goods has no right to keep them against their owner. In the same way, secondly, a finder's right will not avail against anyone with prior possession of the goods, such as the occupier of the land where the goods are found. A finder is answerable to a non-owning prior possessor for the value of the goods in the same way as a subsequent possessor like the goldsmith is answerable to the finder for the value of the goods.

It follows, then, that a finder has such property as will enable him to keep his find against all but those with a prior right to it. This allows the finder to restrain subsequent interference with the find, but not to 'keep' it in any sense greater than that. Some recent cases additionally have sought to impose on the finder certain obligations to reacquaint the find with its owner, and to care for it in the meantime, since the policy of the law is always to protect the property interests of owners. These obligations are easily discharged by reporting any find to the police, and to do as much is still the best legal advice to finders. Any attempt to keep a find without making such enquiries risks occasioning a civil liability for wrongful interference with goods, and perhaps, if the finder is dishonest, a criminal conviction for theft.   ROBIN HICKEY

See also: **finding of property**

arms control   This term describes the international cooperative management of the production, testing, transfer, possession and use of weapons and related know-how and technology. Arms control recognizes that arms will always exist and is accordingly distinguished from 'disarmament' or 'general and complete disarmament', which aim towards the total abolition of certain types of weapons.

Arms control encompasses different kinds of arms regulation. These include agreed ceilings on, and numerical reductions of, certain classes of arms (eg under the Strategic Arms Limitation Treaty 1972); reduction of arms and their total removal from certain regions (eg under the Treaty on the Elimination of Intermediate-Range and Shorter-Range

Missiles 1987); restrictions on the proliferation and possession of arms (eg Nuclear Non-Proliferation Treaty 1968); and inhibitions on the use (under the Conventional Weapons Convention 1981) and testing (under the Comprehensive Nuclear Test Ban Treaty 1996) of certain weapons. Arms control obligations address both conventional weapons (troop numbers, artillery, tanks, and so on) and weapons of mass destruction (nuclear, chemical, biological, radiological).

Strategic arms control was first attempted in the limitations of battleships during the inter-war years (Washington Naval Conference 1921–1922). With the dawn of the nuclear age, the focus shifted to stabilizing the strategic relationship between the USA and the then USSR. Nuclear arms limitation treaties sought to ensure that both sides would be guaranteed a secure second-strike capacity, rendering a nuclear first strike an irrational act ('mutually assured destruction'). Since the termination of the Cold War, both sides have agreed to 'de-target' their nuclear weapons away from the territories of their former opponents and to limit further the number of operationally deployed strategic nuclear warheads (Treaty on Strategic Offensive Reductions 2002).

Most arms control regimes are based on international treaties, although informal political are also undertaken where a formal treaty appears inappropriate or impossible. In view of the requirement of Senate ratification of formal treaties in the US, its arms control commitments sometimes take the form of agreed understandings or executive agreements.

Arms control agreements often contain a withdrawal clause, permitting states to denounce when circumstances change. In 2002 the US exercised this option, withdrawing from the Anti-Ballistic Missile Treaty 1972 in preparation for the deployment of its defensive missile shield. In response the Russian Federation threatened to withdraw from offensive arms limitation agreements.

Many arms control arrangements provide for a verification mechanism. Previously, in the strategic realm, such mechanisms mostly consisted of 'national technical means' (satellite monitoring). As arms control has increasingly come to address weapons of mass destructions other than nuclear weapons, which cannot be remotely monitored, derogations from state sovereignty so as to permit on-site inspections are now often provided for. There may also be country-specific restrictions and monitoring mechanisms, such as the invasive measures and on-site inspections imposed on Iraq at the conclusion of the

Iraq conflict through Security Council Resolution 687 (1991).

While arms control has traditionally been treated as the preserve of high governmental politics, the Ottawa Land Mine Ban Convention 1997 was obtained as the result of strong civil-society campaigns operating in coalition with certain governments.

MARC WELLER

arrest   Arrest 'is not a legal concept . . . Whether a person has been arrested depends . . . on whether he has been deprived of his liberty to go where he pleases' (*Lewis v Chief Constable South Wales* (1991)). Before the creation of **police** forces, most law enforcement was done by victims, if it was done at all. The **common law** had evolved to allow ordinary citizens to 'arrest' people where there was strong evidence of serious crime. But this 'deprivation of liberty' was allowed for one purpose only—to bring suspects before the criminal courts speedily. Magistrates decided whether or not those suspects should be prosecuted and, if so, whether they should be bailed or held in custody pending trial. This is the origin of 'citizens' arrests', which are still common, as when suspected shoplifters and suspected burglars are detained by stores and security staff. But the people whom these citizens arrest are handed over to the police rather than to magistrates.

The police were originally given no specific arrest powers: they could arrest on the same basis as other citizens, or they could act on a warrant which would have been granted by a magistrate only after considering evidence presented by them. Either way, they also had to bring arrestees before the magistrates. But gradually they have been given ever greater arrest powers, both by the **judges** through development of the common law, and by the legislature. Thus warrants are now used only occasionally—eg if someone skips bail or escapes from prison—almost eliminating judicial control of the police power to arrest.

The police can now arrest anyone reasonably suspected of committing a crime (or of being about to do so) or who is reasonably suspected of having done so in the past. Police can arrest in circumstances where, were they private citizens, the arrest would be unlawful. For instance, police may lawfully arrest a person if, despite reasonable suspicion, no crime has actually been committed; whereas arrest in such circumstances by a private citizen would be unlawful and the arrestee would be able to sue the arrester in tort for 'unlawful imprisonment'. The Police and Criminal Evidence Act 1984 ('**PACE**') had originally restricted arrests to relatively serious offences in most circumstances. For minor offences a summons had to be secured from the magistrates, which told suspects when to appear in court. But the Act was amended in 2005 to allow the police to arrest on suspicion for almost any offence. Thus, like warrants, use of summons is diminishing. This is despite the Royal Commission on Criminal Procedure, in 1981, recommending that arrest be used *less* often, since 'Arrest represents a major disruption to a suspect's life . . . Police officers . . . fail at times to understand the sense of alarm and dismay felt by some of those who suffer such treatment'.

The police also decide *how* they will arrest. Frequently they make arrests in the small hours, suspects and their families sometimes even being woken by the sound of their front doors being broken down. 'Reasonable force' may be used to effect arrest, and the premises searched.

Following arrest, the police usually detain suspects in custody in order to investigate further— including searching them (sometimes intimately) and their houses, and interrogating them. Again, while PACE gave the police more power to detain than they had previously had, this power was further extended in 2005, to up to thirty-six hours without charge. The police also decide whether arrestees who are charged will be bailed or will have to remain in the cells until they can be brought to court. No wonder so many people feel 'alarm and dismay' when they are arrested!

So, arrest has been transformed. No longer simply a means of bringing likely offenders to court, it is now a means of bringing suspects to police stations. Little over half of all arrestees are prosecuted. In some ways this is a good thing, as most of the remainder are either released with no further action, or are cautioned. But a less authoritarian system would require the police to reach many of these decisions without the coercive process of arrest. There are around 1.5 million arrests every year, and the socially marginal (young, poor, ethnic minority) suffer this indignity disproportionately. This may be because the police have complete discretion whether or not to arrest. Some social groups could be favoured because decisions not to arrest do not have to be justified to anyone; and they only have to justify arrests to police station 'custody officers'—usually sergeants—in the very broad 'reasonable suspicion' terms of PACE. To whom are the police accountable for the exercise of their coercive powers?

ANDREW SANDERS

A Sanders and R Young, *Criminal Justice* (Oxford: Oxford University Press, 3rd edn, 2007), ch 3

art and law *see* **heritage markets**

Article 14 Article 14 of the **European Convention on Human Rights** provides that: 'The enjoyment of the rights and freedoms set forth in this Convention shall be secured without discrimination on any ground such as **sex**, **race**, colour, language, **religion**, political or other opinion, national or social origin, association with a national minority, property, birth or other status'. It is a parasitic right rather than a free-standing prohibition on discrimination, regulating as it does only discrimination in the 'enjoyment of the rights and freedoms set forth in this Convention'. By contrast, the recently adopted Protocol 12 to the Convention regulates discrimination (on the same grounds as Article 14) in 'the enjoyment of any right set forth by law', and prohibits discrimination on these grounds by any public authority. Protocol 12 has not been ratified by the UK government and is thus not binding on it.

The approach of the **European Court of Human Rights** to Article 14 is not always very clear, but it is broadly correct to say that the Court will find a breach of the provision only where it is satisfied that there has been less favourable treatment on a **protected ground.** Such characteristics are not limited to those specifically listed but also, through the term 'other status' have included, *inter alia*, age, **disability**, sexual orientation and, on occasion, less personal characteristics such as property ownership. Less favourable treatment may consist of differential treatment associated with a protected ground, or of treating different groups of people the same where this results in disadvantage associated with a protected ground. The latter form of discrimination (generally known as **indirect discrimination** or disparate impact) is very under-developed in Article 14 jurisprudence but the decision in *Thlimmenos v Greece* (2001) is an example of such discrimination being found to breach Article 14.

Less favourable treatment on a protected ground will not breach Article 14 if it is justifiable (*Belgian Linguistic Case (No 2)* (1968)). Different standards of justification appear to apply to different protected grounds, the European Court of Human Rights tending to require 'very weighty reasons' for discrimination on grounds of sex, sexual orientation, religion, etc, while adopting a much less rigorous approach in respect, for example, of discrimination between different categories of landowners, or members of large and small **trade unions** (contrast *Abdulaziz v United Kingdom* (1985); *L & V v Austria* (2003); and *Hoffmann v Austria* (1993); with *Chassagnou v France* (1999); and *National Union of Belgian Police v Belgium* (1979)). Having said this, the

Court is frequently less than clear in its reasoning in Article 14 cases and it has not developed explicit distinctions such as those drawn by the **US Supreme Court** between grounds in relation to which 'strict scrutiny', 'intermediate scrutiny', and 'rational review' will be applied.   AILEEN MCCOLGAN

articles of association   see **memorandum and articles of association**

asbestos   see **diseases, liability for group action**

ASBOs   see **anti-social behaviour**

Asher v Whitlock   see *Armory v Delamirie*

assault   see **crime and violence**

assessment in legal education   Legal education in the UK, like any other form of education, is driven to a great extent by assessment. Law may be studied in school or college at GCSE and GCE Advanced level, as well as at university through undergraduate (LLB—Bachelor of Laws) to postgraduate level (LLM—Master of Laws). Many will study law intending to enter the legal profession and for this it is necessary to undertake a qualifying law degree in which seven 'core subjects' (Contract, Public Law, Torts, European Union Law, Criminal Law, Land Law and Equity, and Trusts) are studied and assessed. For those who have a degree (or equivalent) in another subject, there is a shorter Common Professional Examination course ('CPE') which covers the same ground.

Because of the great influence of the law professional bodies (the Law Society and the Bar Council in England and Wales and their equivalents in Scotland and Northern Ireland) most universities assess the core subjects by means of a traditional examination. The abilities to recall knowledge, analyse situations, and put together a coherent argument under time pressure are not of course unique to lawyers but they are skills that are necessary for those seeking to practise. Other skills such as the ability to conduct legal research and communicate in writing effectively are assessed by coursework which may take the form of an essay or a legal problem which requires 'advice'.

The law degree or CPE both satisfy the 'academic stage' of the law professional bodies, but, in order to practise, it is necessary to undertake a vocational course geared towards qualifying either as a solicitor or a barrister. Whereas law undergraduates may study law for a variety of purposes and so (apart from the core subjects mentioned above) assessment may take different forms, the vocational courses are geared towards the needs of the relevant profession and assessed accordingly. Basic knowledge and understanding of a wider range of topics are tested—often by a traditional examination, sometimes by multiple choice tests—but so are a wide range of relevant skills such as negotiation, advocacy, legal drafting, and interviewing. Skills' testing is carried out under controlled conditions which attempt to simulate the work environment and involve practical exercises, sometimes videoed for assessment purposes.

Although there are regular reviews of the nature and purposes of assessment by course providers and—less frequently—by the professional bodies, change is rare, at least in relation to the core subjects. Modern technology has meant that it is possible to test knowledge online by using computers, but the availability of so much information through the internet has given rise to problems of plagiarism. The ability of students to download information and paste it into assessed work while claiming it as their own has led to a greater reluctance by course providers to move away from examination where conditions can be controlled.

In addition to completing the relevant courses of study, barristers (advocates in Scotland) and solicitors must complete a period of 'on-the-job' training. This is not formally assessed but the trainee needs to be signed off as competent in various skills. This training is supported by short courses on various topics, for example, finance which must be completed and are sometimes assessed depending on the subject.   ALISON BONE

assimilation   The term 'assimilation' in contemporary public debate is often used to refer to the absorption of minority groups into the mainstream majority culture of a particular state. 'Assimilationist' public policies attempt to ensure that ethnic, cultural, and religious minorities, and, in particular, more recently arrived immigrant communities, come to share the language, values, world view, and shared common **identity** of the majority. Advocates of such assimilation policies argue that they encourage communal bonds, foster a common sense of **citizenship,** and reduce inter-group tension. France is often cited as an example of a state that adopts an explicit assimilationist approach towards minority groups: considerable emphasis is placed on attempting to ensure that migrants absorb French culture and accept French social norms.

Assimilation strategies have been subject to criticism, on the basis that they require minority groups to conform to the dominant majority culture and discourage group diversity. Critics also argue that demands for minority groups to adhere to mainstream values often cloak racist attitudes. Since the 1960s, public policy in the UK has tended to avoid the language of assimilation in favour of an emphasis on **multiculturalism**, whereby public policy aims to accommodate a diversity of different minority cultures within a shared concept of equal citizenship. Since the events of the 11 September 2001, there has been a greater emphasis on ensuring that minority communities integrate more fully within UK society, which can be seen as an attempt to find a halfway house between assimilationist and multicultural approaches. COLM O'CINNEIDE

See also: **minority rights**

assisted conception   The birth of Louise Brown, the first baby created by *in vitro* fertilization ('IVF'), in July 1978 was one of the most important scientific breakthroughs of the twentieth century. Following the publication of the Warnock Report in 1984, which considered the ethical issues arising from assisted conception, the **Human Fertilization and Embryology Act 1990** was passed. The Act set up a regulatory Authority, **the Human Fertilization and Embryology Authority** ('HFEA'), to offer advice to clinicians and government, and to administer a licensing and inspection regime for clinics performing licensable treatments, including IVF, **preimplantation genetic diagnosis** ('PGD'), treatment involving donated sperm and eggs (**gamete donation**), and **embryo research**. The HFEA is due to be replaced in 2008–2009 when the government intends to merge it with the Human Tissue Authority to form RATE (the Regulatory Authority for Tissues and Embryos).

Although the statute sets out the basic framework within which assisted conception services are to be provided, much of the detail comes from HFEA guidance and policies. The Authority issues guidance on the implementation of the Act through its regularly updated Code of Practice, which can accommodate this fast-moving area of clinical practice more quickly and efficiently than primary **legislation**. The rules in the Code set out matters such as how many embryos can be replaced in each treatment cycle. While the Code is not legally binding, failure to follow it might be taken into account by licence committees when deciding whether to grant, renew, or revoke a centre's licence.

The Human Fertilization and Embryology Act 1990 contains strict consent provisions. Unlike most medical treatment, consent to the use of one's gametes (sperm or eggs) in fertility treatment *must* be in writing. Both gamete providers must give their consent to the use of embryos created with their gametes, and it is possible for them to withdraw this consent at any time until the embryos are used in treatment (or research). Once either gamete provider has withdrawn consent to the embryos' use or continued storage, they must be destroyed or allowed to perish. If the couple's relationship has broken down, whichever partner does not want the embryos to be used in treatment effectively has a right of veto, even if the embryos in storage now represent the other gamete provider's only opportunity to have genetically-related offspring.

Some countries place restrictions upon access to fertility treatment. Common examples might include only treating heterosexual couples, or setting an upper age limit for female patients. In the UK there are no statutory limits upon who can lawfully receive treatment in licensed clinics, but that does not mean that anyone who wants fertility treatment will be able to receive it. Access to treatment is, in fact, restricted in two ways: first, through a **child** welfare filter, which enables clinicians to weed out 'unsuitable' parents; and, second, through restrictions upon NHS funding.

First, the Act provides that treatment services must not be provided unless account has been taken of the welfare of any child who might be born as a result of treatment (including that child's need for a father). This is a rather oddly worded provision: it is, after all, difficult to base a decision not to bring a child into the world upon an assessment of that child's best interests, unless their life would be so appalling that it would be better for them if they never existed. The HFEA issues guidance on the interpretation of this child welfare filter and currently advises clinicians that it should assess whether potential patients pose a risk to any child they might conceive, rather than whether they would be good or ideal parents. Factors which might be relevant to this assessment are:

- previous convictions relating to harming children;
- **child protection** measures taken in relation to existing children;
- serious **violence** or discord within the family;
- mental or physical conditions;
- drug or alcohol abuse;
- any other circumstances likely to cause serious harm to the child or any existing child of the family.

The requirement to consider the child's need for a father is a product of the political landscape in which the 1990 Act was passed, when the Thatcher government had been pursuing policies designed to promote 'traditional family values'. It is now out of step with recent **adoption** legislation, which permits same sex couples to adopt children, and with the Human Rights Act, which proscribes discrimination on grounds of sexual orientation in the exercise of rights under the **European Convention of Human Rights**, including the 'right for respect for private and **family life**' (Article 8), and the 'right to found a family' (Article 12).

Secondly, there are financial restrictions upon access to treatment. NHS funding is patchy, and private treatment is expensive. Following guidance from the National Institute for Heath and Clinical Excellence (NICE), Primary Care Trusts are now supposed to fund (at least) one cycle of treatment per couple, but since IVF has an average success rate of around 25 per cent, access to the repeated treatment cycles which may be necessary to achieve a successful pregnancy is often contingent upon a person or couple's ability to fund their own treatment.

EMILY JACKSON

assisted suicide Assited suicide—intentionally helping another die—is controversial. Ordinarily **suicide** is perceived as morally wrong, and any potential suicide as misguided. We seek to dissuade, frequently with success: 'To how many has it not seemed, at some one period of their lives, that all was over for them, that to them in their afflictions there was nothing left but to die! And yet they have lived to laugh again, to feel the air was warm and the earth fair, and that God in giving them ever-springing hope had given everything' (Trollope, *Orley Farm*). Accordingly, we tend more to oppose than assist suicide, unless persuaded that it is rational. This is classical liberalism. We are entitled to stop others doing as they choose until sure that they are fully informed. Nonetheless, the onus is on those who seek to justify decriminalizing assisted suicide. Beyond these general principles, additional specific considerations apply to physician-assisted suicide.

One possible example of rational choice, featured in the press, concerned a fifty-seven-year-old man, suffering advanced motor neurone disease and already a threefold unsuccessful suicide. He considered, but rejected on financial grounds, ending life in Switzerland, where assisted suicide is lawful. He died at home, after an emotional day with his family. The coroner said, '...we all deplore suicide . . . [but] . . . in these exceptional circumstances one can only have the greatest respect for the way . . . [he] . . . coped with this appalling problem'. Another press example reported Liverpudlian relatives accompanying a disabled man, suffering unbearably, to Switzerland for assisted suicide, returning with his body for the funeral. The legal issue related to possible **prosecution** for assisted suicide but ultimately it was accepted that no crime had been committed or attempted in either England or Switzerland.

Unusually, but not uniquely, assisted suicide criminalizes aiding what is not itself unlawful. The Suicide Act 1961 decriminalized suicide as follows: 'The rule of law whereby it is a crime for a person to commit suicide is hereby abrogated' but also enacted that '[a] person who aids, abets, counsels or procures the suicide of another, or an attempt by another to commit suicide, shall be liable . . . for a term not exceeding fourteen years'.

Ordinarily one is free to do that which is not prohibited. Therefore those subject to the Act have a legal *right* to voluntary suicide. This is fortified by the principle of **autonomy** and classical liberal assumptions. On this approach, the criminalizing of assistance calls for justification. This justification is said to be based on two considerations: (i) suicide is morally wrong; and (ii) there is a **risk**, difficult empirically to quantify, that the weak and vulnerable may be overreached by those with an interest in their early death. However, the Act is open to an alternative interpretation as a concession to **human** frailty, generating an immunity rather than a right. This is fortified by the principle of **sanctity of life** and the law's adverse policy towards suicide. Whichever overarching interpretation one favours, the Act has proved increasingly troublesome and controversial. At the time of writing, the Act is approaching its half century and moral views as to end-of-life decisions have moved on. Worldwide, births now exceed deaths by 74 million annually. Many appear to be kept alive far longer than was possible even a generation ago by the miracles of modern medical science. In such circumstances there is a question about officiously striving to keep alive those who, rationally, prefer to die at a time and in a manner of their own choosing but need assistance to do so.

The Act applies harshly in limited circumstances. Ordinarily, one can legally take one's own life without the assistance of anyone else. That is the theory but in practice a degree of pharmaceutical expertise might be called for; yet such advice is outlawed by the Act. Attempted suicides are left to their own devices, sometimes with bad outcomes all round. However, those who are paralysed even if they have the means, need the physical assistance of another, and that **person** is liable to prosecution under the 1961 Act, a further peculiarity of which is that a prosecution for assisted suicide may only proceed with the consent of the **Director of Public Prosecutions**. This raises the problem that those willing to assist in such tragic circumstances may not be able to ascertain in advance whether their conduct is or is not liable to prosecution. This bears heavily upon close family members and invokes '**Rule of Law**' concerns.

Some had hoped that there was interpretative room for judicial reform. Litigation failed and attention turned to legislative reform. The reformers took a narrow approach in the Patients (Assisted Dying) Bill 2003, seeking merely to empower physicians to assist the terminally ill end their lives if competent, fully informed, suffering unbearable pain, and consenting. Yet the Bill was defeated. The Assisted Dying for the Terminally Ill Bill 2004 also failed, even though it tried to defuse all objections to its predecessor.

Physicians are in a special position and will not ordinarily face prosecution if they adhere to normal medical practice. However were a physician to bring about death intentionally, even with the consent of the patient, that would be murder. Similarly, providing a lethal potion on a 'take it or leave it basis' would be contrary to the Act. Moreover, the healthcare profession is not united. A significant proportion regard saving—not ending—life as paramount.

Reformers are critical of what they see as religious groups imposing their values but that is not the only difficulty. The principle of autonomy applies more widely than to the aged and terminally ill. There is understandable reluctance to extend to younger, healthier individuals any *right* to assisted suicide. Moreover, the hospice movement argues with some justification that a great deal can be achieved by palliative care. However, in a small number of tragic cases, the law as it is imposes unnecessary burdens. In a humane society surely a legislative solution could be implemented?   RICHARD TUR

M Battin, R Rhodes, and A Silvers (eds), *Physician Assisted Suicide* (New York and London: Routledge, 1998)
RHS Tur, 'Legislative Technique and Human Rights: The Sad Case of Assisted Suicide' (2003) *Criminal Law Review* 5–12

See also: **assisting crime; euthanasia in Belgium and The Netherlands; Pretty, Diane**

assisting crime   Much crime is committed by people acting in concert, and this creates problems for the criminal law. A stabs V, intending to kill V, and V dies. A can obviously be convicted of murder, but what about B, who was nowhere present when the stabbing occurred, but did play some role in it? B may have plotted the murder with A, or lent A the knife,

or told A where V could be found. In the first of these scenarios B obviously has murder in mind, so we may find little problem in holding him responsible for the murder committed by A. But in the other two scenarios B might merely suspect that A wants to kill someone, or might think that A only wants to cause minor harm, or might think that A will only use the knife to slash V's car tyres. And what if B lends A the knife believing that it will be used to kill V, but at the last moment A desists and gives up his criminal plan? Or what if at the last moment A cannot find the knife and beats V to death with a brick instead? It should be obvious from the foregoing that the law of criminal complicity—the rules governing when one person is responsible for a crime committed by another—deals with a complex area. There are so many ways in which one person can assist another to commit a crime, and so many degrees of culpability associated with that assistance, that general rules will have to cover a lot of ground. There are difficult questions here about how far criminal liability should extend: the examples above where B merely suspects that A intends to commit a crime probably result in no liability under current English law, though the difficulty of the question has left the case law unclear.

When it comes to general principles, English and Scots law adopt a derivative approach to B's liability, deriving B's liability from A's. Thus, in the examples above, B will be convicted of, if anything, murder. There is currently no independent offence of 'assisting murder' (although the Law Commission for England and Wales is currently proposing reform along these lines). This means that in the example where A unexpectedly desists, B has committed no crime at all, even though his culpability is no different from that in the scenario where A does kill V and B gets convicted of murder. The derivative approach is convenient: it does not matter if it cannot be proved whether A or B was the one who actually stabbed V. So long as it can be shown that they were in it together, both can be convicted of murder. However, in cases where B's culpability seems very much less than A's, the derivative approach may appear crude, and this has led to some tensions in the case law. When it comes to the conduct by B which will trigger liability, the law is wide: any causal contribution may suffice. In the example above, where A uses a brick rather than the knife lent by B, B may still be liable if his loan of the knife is found to have encouraged A to kill V. If B comes upon A committing a crime, and stands and watches, there may again be liability if his presence is found to have encouraged A.

Within the law on complicity, there is generally thought to be a sub-set of cases where slightly different principles apply. Where A and B form a joint enterprise to commit a particular crime, B will be liable for any crimes committed during the joint enterprise which B foresaw as possible results thereof. Thus if A and B agree to commit burglary, and A unexpectedly kills the householder, B will be liable for the death if he foresaw it as possible: no more demanding *mens rea*, such as foresight of death being a likelihood, is required. While this is controversial, the courts often justify it on instrumental grounds: given the dangers posed by criminal gangs, it is said that the law should provide strong disincentives to embarking on joint enterprises.

MIKE REDMAYNE

KJM Smith, *A Modern Treatise on the Law of Criminal Complicity* (Oxford: Oxford University Press, 1991)

Associated Provincial Picture Houses Ltd v Wednesbury Corporation (1948)

To lawyers the name 'Wednesbury'—an otherwise unexceptional West Midlands town—is synonymous with the principle that no public authority has the power to act unreasonably. This principle is an ancient one, but the case of *Associated Provincial Picture Houses Ltd v Wednesbury Corporation* (1948) is (in)famous for the considerable degree of deference the judges said they would afford decisions by elected public authorities.

Although the *Wednesbury* case became an emblem of judicial restraint and the most cited decision in **administrative law** in the second half of the twentieth century, it concerned a rather ordinary dispute over who could attend the local cinema on Sundays. In 1946, the people of Wednesbury had, by postal ballot, voted in favour of Sunday cinema opening. The cinema licensing authority was the local council, leading members of which had unsuccessfully opposed Sunday cinema on religious grounds. Pursuant to a statutory power to impose such conditions as it thought fit, the council banned children under 15 years of age, whether or not accompanied by an adult. The local Gaumont theatre challenged this decision as unreasonable.

The Court of Appeal rejected the challenge on the ground that the Corporation had stayed within the 'four corners' of its power and had not acted unreasonably in the relevant, 'special' legal sense. The ground of unreasonableness was defined tautologously as acting as no reasonable authority would act. The Court illustrated the concept by way of an example from a 1926 decision that said it would be unreasonable in the relevant sense to dismiss a redheaded schoolteacher on the ground of her hair colour (overlooking the fact that at that time and for some time thereafter women lost such jobs when they married—illustrating that as society changes so do the values law protects).

While a close study of the context suggests strongly that the upper class councillors tried to snatch a partial victory for their religious objection to Sunday cinema from the jaws of electoral defeat at the hands of the predominantly plebeian electors, the Court refused to see it that way and simply asserted that the physical and moral (including religious) well-being of the children were proper considerations for the local authority to take into account.

The case became a leading one and over the years since 1948 '*Wednesbury* unreasonableness' has been restated in many ways, including absurdity, perversity, irrationality and simply 'losing one's marbles'. The doctrine has been criticized on all sides for its opacity and for leaving too much discretion in the hands of the judiciary to intervene (or not) in administrative decision-making.

Currently influential opinion favours consigning '*Wednesbury* unreasonableness' to the scrap heap of history, preferring instead the more structured and overtly human rights-respecting doctrine of 'proportionality', drawn from continental European sources. But as long as judges accept that there are some limits on their inherent power to judicially supervise governmental action then something like the unreasonableness principle articulated in the *Wednesbury* case will survive, with or without the geographical epithet.

MIKE TAGGART

J Laws, 'Wednesbury' in C Forsyth and I Hare (eds), *The Golden Metwand and the Crooked Cord: Administrative Law Essays in Honour of Sir William Wade QC* (Oxford: Clarendon Press, 1998)

M Taggart, 'Reinventing Administrative Law' in N Bamforth and P Leyland (eds), *Public Law in a Multi-Layered Constitution* (Oxford: Hart Publishing, 2003)

assumpsit Until the early fourteenth century, the action of covenant provided a general remedy for enforcing informal agreements—those not contained in a **deed**—in the Royal Courts. However, once a deed was made a condition of success in covenant, the action withered. Several other remedies for informal contracts took covenant's place. An entitlement to a specific sum of money or goods could be enforced by actions called 'debt on a contract' and 'detinue'. The Statute of Labourers provided a remedy for contracts of employment. Another solution was to bring a claim in what modern lawyers call tort—the actions of trespass and trespass on the case.

The basis of these claims was that by mis-performing the agreement the defendant committed a wrongful act. The maxim that 'not doing is no trespass' meant that contractual non-performance was more troublesome. The objections fell away at the end of the fifteenth century; trespass on the case could be used for nonfeasance, and assumpsit soon began to break off as a separate sub-form of trespass on the case.

The action of assumpsit took its name from the wording of the count (ie the allegation in the claim): the defendant 'assumed and faithfully promised'—*assumpsit et fideliter promisit*—to do something for the plaintiff. The count stressed that the obligation rested on a promise or contract. It may have been inspired by claims for breach of faith in the **Ecclesiastical Courts**. The tortious origins of assumpsit left a mark because the count also drew attention to the defendant's breach (wrongful act). From around 1570, in order to bring a successful claim in assumpsit, the plaintiff was also required to show that the promise was supported by good consideration. Consideration was based on the idea that the plaintiff had given something in exchange for the promise.

Assumpsit was good at plugging gaps in the older remedies. It could be used for agreements for the sale of land and for services, and against executors where debt on a contract was unavailable. Plaintiffs also began to use assumpsit even where an action of debt could be brought. Assumpsit had two main advantages. It allowed recovery of consequential damages: recovery was not limited to the fixed sum of money owed, which was all that was available in debt. Damages might be a larger amount than the sum owed. Also, jury trial was available. Jury trial was more attractive to plaintiffs than wager of law, which was used in debt. Wager of law, which allowed the defendant to bring oath helpers before the court to swear that no money was owed, gave rise to fears that it was too easy for a defendant to avoid obligations.

Some judges were still disinclined to allow a new form of action when there was an existing remedy. But from the 1530s, it was possible to bring assumpsit in the place of debt provided an acceptable method of pleading was used. In effect this meant that, once more, there was a general remedy for informal contracts. The most enduring of these pleading devices was the indebitatus assumpsit count. The count alleged that the defendant was indebted to the plaintiff and had promised to pay. By focusing on the subsequent promise rather than the underlying debt, the count was designed to defeat the objection that assumpsit stood in place of debt. By the 1580s, judges of the two main Royal Courts, the King's Bench and the Common Pleas, were divided about whether an express promise had to be proved. For a period in the 1590s, the position of the more conservative Common Pleas judges began to harden to the extent that they were unwilling to countenance assumpsit in place of debt. Matters came to a head in *Slade's Case* (1602), where a decision of all the judges in the Court of Exchequer Chamber favoured the King's Bench position. With the death of the traditionalist judges in the Common Pleas, a general remedy for informal contracts was available once more.

Once assumpsit was a general remedy for informal contracts, the older actions were, for practical purposes, obsolete. By the late eighteenth century, assumpsit was synonymous with the law of contract. But assumpsit was not confined to contract. By the seventeenth century, a number of common indebitatus counts, covering frequently occurring situations, had developed. Over time, some of the common counts came to be used where the underlying debt was not created by a contract. For a brief period following *Moses v Macferlan* (1760), one of these counts, for money had and received, had the potential to develop into a broader remedy. By borrowing from Equity, Lord Mansfield tried to develop a general remedy for recovering money which *ex æquo et bono* the defendant ought to refund. By the early nineteenth century, judges had become hostile to such a potentially broad action. Money had and received was stifled and it would take the rise of **unjust enrichment** in the twentieth century before non-contractual claims outside of tort would have anything like the same importance again.

WARREN SWAIN

DJ Ibbetson, *A Historical Introduction to the Law of Obligations* (Oxford: Oxford University Press, 1999)

AWB Simpson, *A History of the Common Law of Contract The Rise of the Action of Assumpsit* (Oxford: Clarendon Press, 1987)

See also: **contract law; equity as a system of law; trespass, case and negligence**

assumption of risk   *see volenti non fit injuria*

asylum   Historically, 'asylum' meant sanctuary offered by the Church, but it is now used to describe a place of refuge and the right of the state to give protection in the exercise of its sovereign power over territory and regarding the admission and removal of foreign nationals. The 1948 **Universal Declaration of Human Rights** provides that everyone has 'the right to seek and to enjoy' asylum from persecution. However, asylum as an individual right was not included in later **human rights** instruments, such as the 1966 **International Covenant on Civil and Political Rights**. While they continue to provide protection more or less consistently with the 1951 Convention/1967 Protocol relating to the Status of Refugees, states generally resist admitting any obligation to grant asylum. Asylum is nevertheless referred to in many **United Kingdom** statutes adopted since the early 1990s, and the Nationality, Immigration and Asylum Act 2002 and the Immigration Rules identify an asylum application as arising whenever a foreign national in the country or at the border claims that it would be contrary to international obligations either to remove or exclude him or her. All such applications are decided by the **Home Secretary** (subject to certain rights of appeal), who will 'grant asylum' (and leave to enter or remain in the UK) if satisfied that the person concerned is a refugee as defined in the 1951 Convention/1967 Protocol Relating to the Status of Refugees, and that refusal of admission or permission to remain would entail that individual going to a country in which he or she has a well-founded fear of persecution. In accordance with European human rights and **European Union** requirements, provision is also made for a form of asylum ('subsidiary protection') for those who, while not **refugees** in the strict sense, nevertheless have good human rights-based grounds for not being required to return to their own country.

GUY S GOODWIN-GILL

asylum seeker   *see* **asylum**

Atkin, James Richard   (Baron Atkin of Aberdovey, 1867–1944) James Richard Atkin had an Irish father and Welsh mother. He was born in Australia, his parents having decided within months of their marriage to make their life in Queensland, sheep farming. But his father died, full of promise, at the age of thirty, when Atkin was only three, and his mother brought him and his two brothers home to her family in Merioneth, Wales, where Atkin was brought up and educated.

Atkin's attachment to Merioneth was strong. The influence of his Welsh grandmother was perhaps the most important in his life. She detested pretence of rank or religion always, and so did he. 'The greatest woman I have ever met,' he wrote of her, 'I thank God for every memory of her'.

Atkin made his way from Oxford to the Bar, where, as a young married man, he did not escape the customary penury of the early years of practice. His bride was Lucy Elizabeth (Lizzie) Hemmant. Her father had been a friend of Atkin's father in Australia, and when Hemmant returned to England, he made

Atkin welcome at his splendid house in Sevenoaks, and helped him by steering legal work his way. Lizzie Atkin was a strong character as were all the women in Atkin's life, and she bore him eight children, six girls and two boys.

Atkin was appointed to the High Court bench in 1913. He was promoted to the **Court of Appeal** in 1919 and to the **House of Lords** (the final appeal court) in 1928. The Court of Appeal in which he sat as a member with Lords Justices Bankes and Scrutton became a legend and, in the opinion of many, the best equipped commercial court that ever sat in an appellate capacity. Bankes presided like a calm country squire. On one side was the rugged, irascible, and bearded figure of Sir Thomas Scrutton; on the other, Atkin sat for the most part quietly. They were an awesome trio, Atkin and Scrutton disagreeing constantly, but they sliced through their business with great speed and delivered short, usually extempore, judgments, which were framed in language of terse precision. Their decisions have stood the test of time.

Atkin's most celebrated decisions from his time in the House of Lords were *Donoghue v Stevenson* (1932) and *Liversidge v Anderson* (1942). The circumstances which gave rise to *Donoghue's* case were humble enough. A young woman claimed **compensation** from the manufacturer of ginger beer which she had drunk when visiting a café, and then discovered that the bottle contained the decomposing remains of a snail. A direct claim by the consumer against the manufacturer had never before succeeded. By a majority consisting of Atkin and two Scottish judges, Lords Macmillan and Thankerton, the Law Lords ruled that such a claim could be made. In his leading judgment Atkin chose the parable of the Good Samaritan as his text. His question, who then in law is my neighbour? has become one of the most famous judicial expressions ever coined. 'I doubt,' he said, 'whether the whole law of tort could not be comprised in the golden maxim to do unto your neighbour as you would that he should do unto you'.

Liversidge's case was a very different one. Liversidge had been detained under the notorious Defence Regulation 18B during the Second World War. Churchill had described the power of the Executive to lock a man up without trial (which 18B gave the power to do) as 'in the highest degree odious'. Atkin would have agreed but thought that in time of war it was probably necessary. But in his dissenting judgment he protested against the strained meaning given by the majority to the plain words of the regulation. He employed language which was strong and emotive, including a quotation from 'Alice in Wonderland' to scorn the majority view. Lord Maugham, the **Lord Chancellor** and leader of the majority, was offended and wrote to *The Times*. But Atkin would have nothing to do with such public controversy.

The great judge was a very private person who believed that the public side of his life should be kept inside the court room. There was too a humane spirit which pervaded his work as a judge. He was convinced, with all the force he could bring to his striking prose, that the law should be based on morality, but also that it must be a sensible thing and should measure itself against the expectations of the plain man.   GEOFFREY M LEWIS

attempts, conspiracy, and incitement The criminal law defines and punishes such offences as homicide, fraud, and criminal damage. These are, in form and substance, 'complete' or 'consummate' offences: they are defined in terms of the completion of a specified action (killing; obtaining goods fraudulently; damaging property); such actions constitute the mischief with which the criminal law is concerned. The law also includes offences that are in form or substance 'incomplete' or 'nonconsummate'.

The most general of these are attempt, conspiracy, and incitement. If it is criminal to do something, it is generally also criminal to attempt to do it, to conspire with others to do it, or to incite others to do it. Such offences are nonconsummate in form: they are defined in terms of a complete offence towards which they are directed, but which need not be committed; what makes me guilty of attempting, inciting, or conspiring to commit criminal damage is not that property is damaged, but that my action is directed towards such damage. They are also nonconsummate in substance: we criminalize attempt, conspiracy, or incitement only because of their connection to the complete crime towards which they are directed; their commission does not itself constitute the mischief that ultimately concerns the criminal law. (There are also specific offences which are in substance or form nonconsummate: these include offences of endangerment, such as dangerous driving; and offences of preparation, for instance having or acquiring materials that are intended to be or could be used for a crime.)

Why should the law include such offences: why not just criminalize complete offences? One answer focuses on wrongdoing and culpability. If it is wrong to kill, defraud, or damage, it is wrong to attempt, or to conspire with others, or to incite another, to do these things. If we, and the law, should condemn such completed actions, we should also condemn attempts, conspiracies, or incitements to commit them. Another answer focuses on prevention. A law

that did not criminalize such nonconsummate conduct would be less efficient in preventing complete crimes. First, if people knew that they would face criminal liability only if the complete crime was committed, they would be more likely to embark on attempts to commit it, or to conspire with or to incite others to do so; and some would then complete the crime. Second, if the police intervened to prevent the commission of the complete crime, they would save the would-be criminal from criminal liability—thus leaving him free to try again.

There are three harder questions. One concerns the proper scope of such nonconsummate offences. The criminal law supposedly should not punish mere thought or intention, until it is translated into action that impinges on the world: for criminal intentions might not be firm or determinate enough to warrant criminal liability before they are put into action; and a liberal state should leave its citizens as free from the law's coercive attentions as is possible—which includes leaving them the chance to change their own minds about going through with their criminal intentions. But at what stage in an intended criminal enterprise should the agent become criminally liable? Should the law of attempts wait, as English law does, until a person has taken some 'more than merely preparatory' step; or only, as American law does, until she has taken a 'substantial step'? How precise are these ideas? What kind of encouragement should constitute incitement? How far must discussion of the contemplated crime proceed before it constitutes a conspiracy? **Common law** courts might hope to answer such questions on a case-by-case basis, but there remains a tension between permitting early intervention in criminal enterprises, and a due liberal respect for freedom. Incitement and conspiracy are especially problematic, since they can easily be stretched to cover, and oppress, political activity.

Another question concerns the significance of intention. These general nonconsummate offences all require an intention that the relevant complete offence be committed; why should the law not also include a similarly general offence of endangerment, involving the creation of a serious risk of criminal harm, but without the intention that that harm occur?

A final question concerns punishment. Why should attempts, whose failure might be a matter of luck, be punished less severely than they would have been had they succeeded? How should sentences for incitement and conspiracy compare to those for the relevant complete crime?   RA DUFF

AP Simester and GR Sullivan, *Criminal Law: Theory and Doctrine* (Oxford: Hart Publishing, 3rd edn, 2007), ch 9

See also: **fault-based criminal liability; criminalization, rationale of**

Attorney-General   The Attorney General is at the intersection of law and politics, a position which, on the one hand, requires independence from the government and, on the other, allegiance to it. The Attorney is a government minister with responsibility for the Treasury Solicitor, **Crown Prosecution Service**, Serious Fraud Office, and Customs Prosecution Group, and senior legal adviser to the government. Whether the advice given to ministers is confidential became a matter of dispute in 2004 when the government was pressed to release in full the Attorney's advice on the legality of invading Iraq.

The Attorney also helps progress some Bills through Parliament; advises the parliamentary Committee of Standards and Privileges; is leader of the English bar; and leads for the **Crown** in major prosecutions (particularly those involving state security) and civil actions in which the Crown is a party. Additionally, the Attorney's consent is required for some prosecutions, such as those under the Official Secrets Act, and the Attorney has the power to stop, and give immunity from, prosecution. Prosecution decisions must be made in the public interest, independently of ministers. This, according to Sir Hartley Shawcross' classic statement in 1951, does not prevent Attorneys consulting with ministerial colleagues about the public policy implications of a prosecution; but the Attorney must not yield to political pressure. Given the fineness of this distinction, it is not surprising that from time to time allegations are made that the Attorney's decision has been politically influenced. This leads some to argue that the prosecution and executive responsibilities of the Attorney-General should be separated.   DIANA WOODHOUSE

Attorney-General v De Keyser's Royal Hotel Ltd (1920)   This case established that where both statute and the **royal prerogative** address essentially the same subject matter, the former 'abridges' (that is, supplants) the latter. Some might see the decision as echoing the seventeenth century constitutional struggle between the **Crown** and Parliament, now projected into the twentieth century. But at the time it was simply about money.

The case concerned an elegant hotel on London's Embankment, which had gone into receivership in June 1915. Following its requisitioning by the military authorities in April 1916, the Crown sought to justify the takeover on the legal authority of the royal prerogative. Alternatively the Crown argued

that the requisitioning was authorised under the Defence of the Realm Acts ('DORA'). In either case, it urged (unsuccessfully, as is shown below), not only would there be no *legal* obligation on the Crown to make payment for the occupancy but any *ex gratia* payments made from a scheme already established under the royal prerogative would be calculated on the basis of the actual loss of profits (which, in the case of an insolvent business, would not amount to very much).

The receiver, a distinguished accountant, Sir Arthur Whinney, was not fobbed off. Nor was he deterred by a Court of Appeal decision in a similar case in 1915, which had upheld the Crown's arguments (see *In Re a Petition of Right* (1915) concerning the requisitioning of Shoreham Aerodrome). He therefore took his case for full market compensation to the courts where the **Law Lords** unanimously found in favour of the hotel owners (as indeed had the Court of Appeal). Their Lordships determined that since a series of pre-twentieth century Defence Acts, with their arrangements for military requisition, were applicable in wartime as well as during peacetime, they abridged prerogative powers exercisable for the same purpose. More importantly for Whinney, he would not be forced to accept lesser compensation under the parsimonious royal prerogative scheme.

Furthermore, their Lordships also observed that market value compensation had always been paid in previous centuries even when the prerogative power to requisition had been invoked; and that silence regarding compensation in the relevant wartime Defence Regulation issued under DORA did not mean that claimants had lost their legal right to compensation under the earlier Defence Acts.

Yet the Crown was probably not unduly worried by the outcome. For although the hotel, through the receiver, benefited financially by the ruling, Parliament soon passed the Indemnity Act 1920 to enshrine in statute the less generous actual loss basis of compensation for future claimants and to prohibit the re-opening of cases settled on that basis prior to the *De Keyser* ruling.

The case is still cited in important litigation today. For example in 1995 it was held that the Home Secretary was not legally entitled to rely upon the prerogative to replace an existing statutory compensation scheme for firemen with a less generous non-statutory scheme, notwithstanding that he possessed (unexercised) statutory power to introduce a new scheme (*R v Home Secretary, ex parte Fire Brigades Union* (1995).   GR RUBIN

GR Rubin, *Private Property, Government Requisition and the Constitution, 1914–1927* (London: Hambledon Press, 1994)

See also: **insolvency, corporate**

Attorney-General's references   When the Criminal Appeal Act 1907 for the first time allowed defendants the right to appeal against both conviction and sentence, reciprocal rights were not given to the **prosecution**. This remained true until section 32 of the Criminal Justice Act 1972 gave the Attorney-General the right to refer to the Court of Appeal any point of law arising from an acquittal of a defendant tried on **indictment**. The Court of Appeal's role was confined to clarifying the relevant law; it was not entitled to quash the acquittal itself.

The Attorney-General's reference powers were extended by section 36 of the Criminal Justice Act 1988 to include sentences passed for indictable-only offences—and later a limited range of triable-either-way but not summary-only offences—considered by the Attorney-General to be 'unduly lenient'. In contrast to section 32, section 36 allowed the Court of Appeal to quash a referred sentence and replace it with any other sentence that the **Crown** Court had the power to pass. The expression 'undue lenience' was not defined in the **legislation** but was held in *Attorney General's Reference No. 4 of 1989* (1989) to mean any sentence which lies 'outside the range of sentences which the judge, applying his mind to all the relevant factors, could reasonably consider appropriate'. A 1994 article by this author reviewed the working of the sentence reference scheme and concluded that it had largely fulfilled the hopes of those who supported its introduction.

Part 9 of the Criminal Justice Act 2003 recently granted the prosecution further limited rights to appeal against certain termination and evidentiary rulings made in a trial.   STEPHEN SHUTE

S Shute, 'Prosecution Appeals against Sentence: The First Five Years' (1994) 57 *Modern Law Review* 745

Audit Commission   The Audit Commission was established in 1982 with the primary function of undertaking audits of local authorities in England and Wales. It should not be confused with the National Audit Office, the body responsible for the audit of central government expenditure. Since 2005 in Wales both functions have been performed by the Auditor General for Wales. In 1990 the remit of the Audit Commission was extended to cover health service bodies. The Commission conducts both certification audits and value-for-money audits.

The Audit Commission is an independent public body with corporate status employing more than 2,500 people. The Chief Executive is responsible for day-to-day operations under the direction of a governing body. According to the Commission's mission statement, its role is 'to be a driving force in the improvement of a public service'. Five themes dominate the Commission's Strategic Plan published in 2006:

- to raise standards of financial management and financial reporting;
- to challenge public bodies to deliver better value for money;
- to encourage continual improvements in public services so that they meet the changing needs of diverse communities and provide fair access for all;
- to promote high standards of governance and accountability;
- to stimulate significant improvement in the quality of data and the use of information by decision-makers.

The Audit Commission publishes annual reports and accounts. However, the Commission is not directly accountable to any parliamentary committee responsible for the scrutiny of its activities and reports. Its audit reports are published and made available to the public. The Commission may appoint an auditor to consider whether to issue a public interest report on any significant matter that requires the attention of the public. Examples are reports into several National Health Service Trusts in September 2006. Since its inception in 1982, the Audit Commission has helped reshape the working of local government. Its pro-active role has helped improve the day-to-day working of local authorities, and it helps to ensure that public money is spent wisely, avoiding waste. The Audit Commission observes very high professional standards in its reports and encourages good value and efficient administration.

JOHN MCELDOWNEY

See also: **Auditor General**

auditor liability   It is the function of auditors to scrutinize the company's accounts and as they are well paid for this service, it follows that a negligent audit will expose auditors to liability. In determining what constitutes negligence, auditors are expected to act 'as watchdogs and not bloodhounds'; they should be alert to suspicious practices, but cannot always be expected to unearth sophisticated fraud. They must visit the company's premises and make sample checks (e.g. of stock). If suspicions have been aroused, their obligation to investigate becomes more stringent. Reliance upon professional accounting/ financial reporting standards may establish that auditors have not been negligent.

The relationship between the **company** and its auditors is based on contract. A negligent performance of contract will render the auditors liable in damages to the company. Such a claim may be pursued in circumstances where, as a result of the negligent audit, the company erroneously has paid out a dividend. The company's right to sue its auditors will pass to a liquidator, receiver or administrator if the company has become insolvent.

Can an auditor be sued in negligence by a third party (such as an investor who has bought shares in the company or a person who has extended credit to the company) who has relied on the audited accounts? Such a claim must necessarily be founded upon tort and will be governed by **common law**. The rule here, laid down by the **House of Lords** in *Caparo v Dickman* (1990), is that auditors are not liable to such parties unless there are special circumstances. This is a policy decision developed from a concern that auditors may be exposed to indeterminate liability. There are exceptions. So, if the third party made it known to the auditors that he intended to rely upon the audit before investing or lending that may trigger liability since a duty of care has arisen. However, in any case based upon negligence, even if it can be shown that the auditors owed the claimant a duty of care, it must also be proven that the claimant's loss was *caused* by the auditors' negligence.

Auditors who fail to discharge their responsibilities may be disciplined by their own professional body.

In response to the threat of auditor liability most auditors' firms have switched from **partnership** to **limited liability** partnership structure. They have also persuaded the government to allow them to 'cap' their liability under reforms introduced in the Companies Act 2006. Auditors can also seek a judicial pardon under the Companies Act in response to any claim by the company that they have been in breach of duty, but this facility is not available where a third party bases the claim upon tort. Moreover, it is rare for the court to grant such a pardon as the preconditions that have to be met are stringent.

DAVID MILMAN

See also: **contract law; negligence in civil law; tort law**

Auditor-General The Comptroller and Auditor-General ('CAG') is head of the National Audit Office ('NAO') and an independent officer of the **House of Commons** responsible for auditing public expenditure on behalf of Parliament. There are separate Auditors General for Scotland, Wales, and Northern Ireland under devolution arrangements. The office of Auditor General is of great antiquity. From earliest times to the present the Auditor General has had the jobs of checking that all revenue is correctly paid into the Consolidated Fund and National Loans Fund, that the limits set by Parliament on payments out of the Bank of England are strictly observed, and that expenditure is duly authorized. Certification audits check that expenditures are correctly authorized, while value-for-money ('VFM') examinations are concerned with whether departments have achieved economy, efficiency, and effectiveness in their expenditure, and may provide advice on how the management of public money can be improved.

The CAG's remit includes all central government departments and, since 1994, the Security Services, the National Health Service, and other public bodies such as universities. The government may also seek the advice of the CAG in drawing up public spending plans and on general matters involving economic issues that are relevant to the government expenditure. However, CAG's remit does not extend to commenting on the merits of government policy.

The CAG reports to the Public Accounts Committee ('PAC') of the House of Commons and may be invited to attend and give evidence at the Committee's hearings. The CAG with the support of the PAC provides strong accountability for public expenditure. The PAC's reports are the subject of regular debate and the government normally gives a written response to any recommendations it makes.

The CAG's high reputation for quality and independence are largely due to the work of the NAO, which is staffed by accountants and public expenditure experts. The NAO has a worldwide profile and its work on VFM examinations is a model of its kind. Particular areas of concern are the evaluation of large capital projects and the use of public funds in public/private partnerships.

JOHN MCELDOWNEY

See also: **Audit Commission**

auditors and whistleblowing External auditors must scrutinize the company's accounts to attest to their integrity. In so doing they should display reasonable care. If anything irregular is uncovered by the audit, auditors are in a dilemma in that, as **fiduciaries** with access to sensitive data, they are expected to preserve client confidentiality; but the law imposes an overriding obligation in the public interest to 'whistleblow' in defined circumstances. Auditors' obligations here are governed by the Companies Acts, as supplemented with guidance from professional regulators.

Auditors should draw any concerns they have to the directors' attention as they may have an explanation for the discrepancy. As the accounts must be approved at the **annual general meeting** of shareholders the auditors should alert them by 'qualifying' the accounts. In their report to shareholders they should state whether the accounts have been prepared both in accordance with the Companies Acts and accounting/financial reporting standards and should indicate whether they give a 'true and fair' view. It may be necessary to refer suspicious cases to the attention of regulatory authorities. There are professional guidelines that are of assistance in this context.

Auditors who have suspicions about the accounts cannot evade responsibility by quietly resigning—when they leave office they must give a written explanation of the reasons for their departure. Where auditors resign, they may require the company to convene an extraordinary general meeting of shareholders to discuss the departure.

Special **whistleblowing** rules apply to auditors of different types of institution beyond the paradigm of the limited liability **company**, for example financial institutions, higher education institutions, etc.

The Public Interest Disclosure Act 1998 applies to protect employees who act as in-house 'internal auditors'.   DAVID MILMAN

Austin, John (1790–1859)   Although Austin eventually became a major figure in English jurisprudence, he did not live to see it. The muted reception of his legal philosophy was but one of the many disappointments and failures of his life. Called to the bar by the Inner Temple in 1818, he attracted only a few clients and quit the practice of law in 1825. He fared little better as a teacher. He was appointed in 1826 to the Chair in Jurisprudence and the Law of Nations at the newly founded University of London. Enrollment in his course dwindled to such a low level, however, that he resigned his Chair in 1835 and never taught again. Even his most notable achievements were not unalloyed triumphs. For example, his book, *The Province of Jurisprudence Determined* (1832), consisting of the introductory lectures in his course, although in general enthusiastically reviewed, was ignored by the two leading journals of the day. Austin concluded that he was 'born out of time and place' and wrote nothing more about his

'philosophy of positive law'. Overall, he published only the one book, four articles and a pamphlet, *A Plea for the Constitution* (1859), an unrelenting critique of attempts to reform Parliament.

Austin's stature rose substantially after his death in 1859. The catalyst for this development was his wife Sarah's decision to produce a new edition of *The Province* (1861). In 1863 she also edited the remaining lectures in his course and his *Lectures on Jurisprudence* underwent three subsequent editions. Their publication marked the start of a process that would transform Austin from a minor figure into a major force in nineteenth-century English jurisprudence (and, to a lesser extent, that of certain other countries, such as the United States). The lectures themselves reflected his conception of jurisprudence as the analysis of fundamental and necessary, or at least widespread, legal principles, notions, and distinctions. They included such matters as the nature of a law 'properly so-called', the meaning of legal rights and duties, the notion of **sovereignty**, 'judiciary' law, codification, and the classification of the *corpus juris*. Austin called this approach 'general' jurisprudence in order to distinguish it from 'particular' jurisprudence, or the exposition of the law of a specific nation or nations. He also insisted that the subject matter of the science of jurisprudence is positive law, or the law as it is rather than as it ought to be, which is the focus of the related science of **legislation**. The legal validity of a positive law, ie the command of a sovereign, a person, or body of persons of legally unlimited power, does not depend on whether it is ethically or morally good. Evil or unjust laws exist and may be enforced.

Although Austin's doctrines were frequently, sometimes harshly, criticized in the twentieth century, some continue to be influential. The most important examples are his 'analytical' conception of jurisprudence and his sharp distinction between law and morality. In short, he remains a figure to be reckoned with in the study of jurisprudence.

WILFRID E RUMBLE

L and J Hamburger, *Troubled Lives: John and Sarah Austin* (Toronto: University of Toronto Press, 1985)

WE Rumble, *Doing Austin Justice: The Reception of John Austin's Philosophy of Law in Nineteenth-Century England* (London: Continuum, 2005)

See also: **legal positivism to 1970**

Australian law   *see* **Commonwealth law**

aut dedere' aut judicare   *see* **extradition**

authors' rights   *see* **copyright moral rights**

autonomy The concept of autonomy has assumed increasing importance in contemporary political and legal philosophy. Philosophers such as John Rawls, Robert Paul Wolff, Thomas Scanlon, and Joseph Raz have employed the concept to ground principles and illuminate issues such as the choice of principles of **justice**, the justification of political authority, the limits of free speech, the nature of the liberal state, and the justification of **democracy**.

The fact that different theorists may use the same word should not, however, lead one to assume they are all referring to the same thing. One reason for supposing they are not is that different philosophers are worrying about different problems. Perhaps the same concept is useful in thinking about the nature of political obligation, whether the state can be neutral, and issues of distributive justice, but this cannot be assumed to be the case. It is more likely that one has to fashion different concepts in light of the nature of the problems.

There is also a tendency to use the concept in a broad fashion. It is sometimes used as equivalent to liberty, sometimes to free will, sometimes identified with rationality, or **sovereignty**. It is applied to very different entities: to actions, **persons**, the will, desires, principles, thoughts, values, and dispositions.

However, it does seem to be the case that the concept of autonomy is almost always linked to something or other being the agent's own—to being *hers*. Whether it is the agent's actions, character, life, or motivations, there is a distinction between those which are authentic to the agent and those which are foisted upon her or manipulated or coerced.

One way of spelling out this contrast is by way of the idea of an agent reflecting upon her life or motivations or actions and either identifying with them and affirming them, or rejecting them and trying to change them. On this conception an agent is autonomous with respect to some aspect of her life if she reflects upon that aspect and either affirms or seeks to alter it.

The most important task for which autonomy has been harnessed in contemporary legal and political philosophy is to argue for a certain ideal of the liberal state: that of neutrality. The idea of neutrality is itself complex and has different formulations. The root idea is that the state must recognize and acknowledge the autonomy of persons, that is, the **capacity** of persons to stand back from their current ends and ideals, to question their value, and to attempt to change them if necessary. In order to recognize this ideal of autonomy the state must not justify its actions on the basis that some ways of life are intrinsically better than others; the state does not rank

various ways of living and attempt to promote some rather than others. This does not mean that the state is neutral in any stronger sense. Its policies may differentially favour different conceptions of the good, in that the *consequences* of its policies may promote a more favourable environment for some conception of the good at the expense of others. But it does place a limitation on the grounds or reasons that the state puts forward to justify its policies.

The neutral state is opposed to various perfectionist theories, that is, theories which believe the state ought to promote certain ways of living, and discourage others, because some ways of living are better, more valuable than others. Theorists of the neutral state believe perfectionism ought to be resisted, not because they are sceptical about ranking ways of life, but because they believe that the political sphere must always honour the capacity of individuals to change their views about what kind of life is worth living, and that only if we are free to form and revise such ideas can we be said to be *leading* a good life, as opposed to simply *having* one

The legal philosopher, Joseph Raz, uses the concept of autonomy to consider a related problem: the legitimacy of state coercion. He wants to derive principles which will determine what kinds of behaviour the state may seek to limit by means of the criminal law. Like Mill, he believes that harm to others (the harm principle) is the only legitimate reason for justifying criminal sanctions. Unlike Mill, he believes a certain amount of paternalism may be justifiable—justified by the harm principle but the harm in question being that to the person who is being restricted.

Raz does not seek to derive the harm principle from utilitarian considerations. Instead he believes it is derivable from a principle of autonomy. He defines autonomous persons as 'those who can shape their life and determine its course . . . creators of their own moral world'. There are certain conditions which are necessary for a person to be autonomous—adequate options, sufficient mental abilities, and freedom from coercion and manipulation. Finally, Raz interprets autonomy so that its value is dependent on being directed at good options. A person may be autonomous even if he pursues what is bad, but his autonomy only has value if he chooses the good.

A third important use of autonomy is to object to various kinds of paternalism and legal moralism in criminal law. Legal moralism is a family of views that share the idea that certain acts may be criminalized, not because they cause any physical or emotional harm to persons without their consent, but simply because the acts are part of a way of life that is immoral. If one relies on a notion of autonomy which is defined in terms of the person choosing for themselves the kind of life they regard as valuable or good, and if that requires that the person must recognize or accept that a certain form of life is good, it can be argued that various forms of legal moralism and paternalism are unacceptable. Whether or not autonomy as just defined is something that is truly desirable is an open question. If one thinks that agents can be seriously mistaken in their failure to recognize the evil nature of certain ways of life, and that they can be benefited by making it more difficult or impossible to choose those ways of life, then it will not seem illegitimate for the state to promote the agent's good at the expense of his autonomy.

GERALD DWORKIN

J Raz, *The Morality of Freedom* (Oxford: Clarendon, 1986)

B

Babylonian law   *see* **ancient Middle Eastern law**

Bacon, Francis   Viscount St Alban (1561–1626), **Lord Chancellor**, politician, and philosopher. Studied at Trinity College, Cambridge 1573–1575, was entered at Gray's Inn in 1576, but spent the years 1576–1579 in France, accompanying Sir Amias Paulet, English ambassador to France. Resuming his legal studies in 1579, he was admitted to the bar in 1582, became bencher in 1586 and was elected as a reader in 1587.

Throughout his life Bacon pursued a career in law and politics, becoming an MP in 1581 and serving in every Parliament until 1621. He failed in his bids for office during Elizabeth I, but was more successful with James I, becoming **solicitor-general** in 1608, **attorney-general** in 1613, a privy councillor in 1616, **Lord Keeper** in 1617 and Lord Chancellor in 1618. He was knighted in 1603, raised to the peerage and created Baron Verulam of Verulam in 1618, and Viscount St Alban in 1621.

Bacon was impeached by Parliament in 1621 for taking bribes, but his **impeachment** was an indirect attack against **patents** and monopolies. He was thus a victim of a campaign against James's favourite, Buckingham. Thereafter Bacon dedicated the last five years of his life to his philosophical and literary pursuits.

He is most famous for his natural philosophical projects, the earliest evidence of which comes from the 1590s. His first publication in natural philosophy (and the only one in English) is *The Advancement of Learning* (1605). Although many of his writings in natural philosophy remained unfinished (a reflection of the limited time he could dedicate to them) he published extensively towards the end of his life, most importantly in 1620 a volume which consisted of the preliminary material for his grand philosophical plan (the *Instauratio magna*), and of the incomplete methodological part (*Novum organum*). An expanded Latin translation of *The Advancement of Learning*, entitled *De dignitate & augmentis scientiarum* came out in 1623. Bacon also published several volumes of natural history and his utopian writing, *New Atlantis*, came out posthumously in 1627.

Bacon's natural philosophical work aimed at forming a novel view of natural philosophy—replacing the Aristotelian idea of contemplative science with a more active conception of natural philosophy. Human science (*scientia*) should be linked with human power (*potentia*). Bacon also developed a new methodology where scientific inference should start from empirical experience and proceed along a strict hierarchy of increasing generality until the fundamental laws of nature have been reached. From these laws new experiments could then be derived by practical deduction. Both views proved to be extremely influential.

Bacon also wrote *The Essays* (1597, 1612, 1625), and *The Historie of the Raigne of King Henry the Seuenth* (1621). In law, he had a life-long idea of the reformation of the English laws. He emphasized the role of the Roman law in the reformation of the English law. This did not mean that he wanted England to adopt the Roman civil law. The importance of the Roman law was a means to find universal legal axioms which would facilitate the removal of ambiguity from the positive law.   MARKKU PELTONEN

bail   Bail is granted when criminal cases are adjourned and suspects and defendants are released from custody pending the outcome of an investigation, trial, or appeal or whilst awaiting sentence after conviction. Bail decisions are taken by different criminal justice agencies/institutions at various stages of the criminal justice process namely, by the police, before and after charge and by the **courts**, before conviction, after conviction but prior to sentence, and whilst awaiting appeal outcomes. Most bail decisions are taken when suspects/defendants are legally innocent. Consequently, they are a reflection of the fairness and legitimacy of the criminal justice process. This is particularly pertinent when bail decisions vary between courts and between different groups of suspects/defendants. Bail decisions are also crucial because they impact upon the size of the prison remand population and subsequent decisions, including **pleas** and **sentencing**.

Police bail is regulated by Police and Criminal Evidence Act 1984 ('**PACE**') but in practice, the law is similar to that which relates to court bail. The law governing court bail decisions is the Bail Act 1976. This Act has been amended considerably since it was enacted, primarily to make the granting of bail more difficult for defendants who have allegedly committed serious offences and/or who have allegedly committed offences on bail. Consequently, the presumption of bail enshrined in law has been diluted. Nevertheless, in most cases, a presumption of bail exists unless certain circumstances apply. The main circumstances in which bail may be refused relate to potential risks in relation to defendants absconding, committing offences, or interfering with witnesses. Weighing up these risks involves an assessment of likely future behaviour and consequently, decisions are open to a considerable degree of error. In cases where the court believes that defendants committed the offence whilst on bail the presumption of bail is reversed unless there is no significant risk of offences being committed on bail (Bail Act 1976, Schedule 1, part 2A). This legislation was recently introduced to tackle the problem of offending on bail which has been highlighted as making a significant contribution to the crime problem despite a lack of systematic evidence or agreement about how to measure it.

Both the police and the courts may grant bail with or without conditions in most circumstances. Conditions may be attached to bail on similar grounds to those which enable bail to be refused (Bail Act 1976, section 3(6)). No guidance exists about which conditions may be applied although they should relate to the grounds on which bail was refused and the police are unable to use certain conditions. In practice, a limited range of conditions is usually applied by the police and courts including residence, **curfews**, exclusion zones, and no contact conditions. Concerns exist about the purpose, effectiveness, and necessity of conditional bail, especially in light of its increased use and variations in its use between courts. Breaching conditions is not an offence but may result in bail being refused whereas failing to appear in court to answer bail is an offence.

ANTHEA HUCKLESBY

A Hucklesby, 'Bail in Criminal Cases' in M. McConville and G. Wilson (eds), *The Handbook of the Criminal Justice Process* (Oxford: Oxford University Press, 2002)

bailment   Bailment is the legal relationship which arises when one party, a bailee, takes possession of goods knowing that another party, the bailor, has a prior right to possession of those goods. Bailments often arise within a contractual relationship, as when you hire a car, or leave a coat with a dry cleaner, but they need not. For example, if you lend an umbrella to a friend, a bailment arises: you are the bailor of the umbrella and your friend its bailee. If your friend then lends the umbrella to a colleague this creates two further bailments: one between your friend and his colleague (a sub-bailment), and a second between you and the colleague. That second bailment can arise even if you are not aware of, and did not consent to, the transfer of possession to the colleague. There is no need for the bailee to be aware of the identity of the bailor: all that is required is that the bailee knows that someone else has a prior right to possession. As a result, if the colleague leaves the umbrella on a bus and I later find it and take possession of it, I too become its bailee.

Where there is a contractual relationship between bailor and bailee, that contract will usually regulate the rights of each party against the other. In the absence of such a contract, the basic rules of bailment become crucial. The bailee must take reasonable care of the goods. This duty goes beyond the universal duty to take care not to damage another's property. In particular, if the goods are lost or damaged whilst in the bailee's possession, then the burden is on the bailee to show that he was not at fault, not on the bailor to show that bailee was. So if your friend is unable to return the umbrella, he is liable to you unless he can show that it was lost without his being at fault. In general, this is so even if the bailor was not the owner of the goods: it is no defence for your friend to argue that the umbrella you lent him did not in fact belong to you. A bailee is also *prima facie* liable for damage occurring during a sub-bailment: it is no defence for your friend to say that the umbrella was lost after he lent it to his colleague.

A bailment only arises if the bailee has possession. So, if you visit a friend and leave your umbrella by the front door then, during your visit at least, no bailment arises. Because a bailee has possession, he has certain rights against third parties: if a third party carelessly damages bailed goods, the bailee may claim damages. It is no defence for the third party to say that the goods in fact belonged to the bailor. However, if asked, the bailee will have to pass the damages on to the bailor, although the bailee can keep a proportion to compensate him for his own loss.

BEN MCFARLANE

NE Palmer, *Bailment* (North Ryde, NSW: Law Book Co, 2nd edn, 1991)

ballots   *see* **strikes**

bank accounts The essence of banking can be seen as receiving money in order to lend it to others or to finance activity. Central to this is the idea of accepting deposits. A deposit is a sum of money received on the basis that it will repaid either on demand or as agreed by the parties. When a deposit is made, the bank is entitled to mix the money paid in by its customers with its general funds and use that money. The obligation on the bank is to repay the equivalent amount. The relationship between bank and customer is thus similar to that of debtor and creditor, although not identical. For example, unlike an ordinary creditor, a bank customer cannot demand repayment at any time or place. It has been necessary to adapt the debtor-creditor relationship to reflect the practical reality of the banker-customer relationship.

Deposit accounts are a form of interest-bearing account, and have historically been distinguished from current accounts on a number of bases. First, current accounts typically did not pay interest. Secondly, there is no practice permitting the drawing of cheques on the balance of an interest-bearing account. Thirdly, the law recognizes an overdrawn current account, but not an overdrawn interest-bearing account. Although changes in banking practice—in particular the willingness to pay interest on current accounts—have eroded this distinction, it may still be indicative of the differences between different types of account. Current accounts are usually seen as the principal means by which most customers carry out their main financial transactions, while deposit accounts are primarily used for savings.

Consumers have recently seen the introduction of basic bank accounts, which typically allow payments such as salaries, benefits, and pensions to be paid in, cash to be withdrawn, direct debit payments to be made and money to be transferred. Some basic bank accounts also provide debit cards, cheque books, and standing order facilities. However, basic bank accounts do not allow the customer to overdraw. More than 5 million basic bank accounts have been opened in the UK. Under the Banking Code, banks now undertake to assess consumers to see whether their needs are suited to a basic bank account and, if they are, to offer this product. The British Bankers' Association regards this as the UK's equivalent to the French statutory right to a bank account.

PETER CARTWRIGHT

EP Ellinger, E Lomnicka and RJA Hooley, *Ellinger's Modern Banking Law* (Oxford, Oxford University Press, 4th edn, 2006), chs 6–9

see also: **consumer protection in retail banking**

Bank of England The Bank of England was founded in 1694 and rapidly became the government's bank. It is one of the best known and most respected central banks in the world. It is often affectionately called 'The Old Lady of Threadneedle Street', referring to its location in the City of London. The Bank has two primary functions: to maintain monetary stability and to support the economic policies of the government of the day. Although legally separate from HM Treasury, the Bank remained under its *de facto* influence and control until 1997, when the Chancellor of the Exchequer gave the Bank an independent role in setting interest rates. The Monetary Policy Committee ('MPC') of the Bank is given an inflation target by the government and expected to meet the target through adjustments to interest rates whenever necessary. The creation of the MPC was intended to remove direct government influence in the setting of interest rates. Necessarily, however, the Bank works closely with the Treasury in supporting the government's economic policies.

The task of supervising the Bank's activities falls mainly to the Treasury and Civil Service Select Committee ('TCSC') of the **House of Commons**. Great importance is attached to the process of confirmation of the members of the MPC by the TCSC. There is a regular turnover of the external economists on the MPC to ensure that its advice is broadly based and that no single opinion can dominate over the long term. In the House of Lords, the Select Committee on Economic Affairs was appointed in 2001 to monitor the MPC and the framework for its work.

The Bank has four main operational areas: monetary policy and statistics; markets; financial stability; and banking services. The Bank publishes an annual report that contains strategic priorities determined by the Bank's Court. It also regularly publishes an Inflation Report, which contains authoritative analysis of economic data; a Financial Stability Report, which surveys areas of risk and seeks to promote and maintain a stable financial system; and a Quarterly Bulletin, which provides commentary on market developments and the UK's monetary policy.

JOHN MCELDOWNEY

see also: **public finances; Treasury**

bank runs and capital adequacy The banking industry depends heavily on the trust and confidence of all its participants. The principal reason for this is that banks operate on the basis of fractional reserves. This means that banks are not able to meet all their liabilities when they fall due. Where customers lose trust and confidence in their own banks (or in other banks) they have an incentive to withdraw their deposits. Deposits are repayable on a first-come, first-served basis, so a customer who is able to withdraw funds swiftly will not lose out. However, a customer who attempts to withdraw after the bank's funds have dried up will obviously be disappointed. There may be good reasons for customers to withdraw their deposits even if they believe that their own bank is soundly run. A wise, self-interested depositor will have an incentive to withdraw if he or she fears that other depositors are likely to withdraw. In this way, the risk of a run becomes self-fulfilling. There are several ways to reduce the likelihood of bank runs. One is to establish **deposit protection** schemes. Another is for regulators to require banks to hold certain levels of capital. Capital acts as a buffer, or cushion, to absorb losses, and can therefore reduce the risk of insolvency. Furthermore, capital adequacy requirements ensure that the cost of failure is borne primarily by the bank's owners, who this have an incentives to monitor the behaviour of the bank's management.   PETER CARTWRIGHT

see also: **insolvency; corporate**

banking and investment services industry The banking and investment services industry has increasingly become a target for **regulation**, not least as pressure grows for individuals to take greater responsibility for long-term savings and for pension provision and as the investment advice industry becomes increasingly sophisticated.

Investment firms essentially act as market intermediaries. Through a range of services, they act as a bridge between companies seeking market finance and investors seeking a return on their capital. Investment firms provide companies with corporate finance advice, steer companies through **securities** issuances and **stock exchange** admission, underwrite securities (by taking on the initial risk of a securities offering in the **primary markets** and subsequently selling the securities), and act as corporate broker. They will also provide brokerage services to investors (retail and professional), investment advice services, and asset management or portfolio management services under which a firm manages a portfolio of investments for an investor on a discretionary basis but in accordance with a mandate agreed with the investor (by comparison with the non-discretionary collective investment services provided by **collective investment schemes**). Firms (fund managers) will often, however, also design, market, and operate collective investment schemes. Increasingly firms are beginning to compete with

stock exchanges by building trading platforms or providing trading services. Investment firms will also engage in 'dealing' or proprietary trading for the firm's own profit and on its own account. Boutique investment firms may specialize in one or other of these activities, particularly with respect to retail investment advice. A range of intermediaries may sell investments, insurance, or mortgages, singly or in combination. The dominant firms in the industry are large multi-service firms providing a range of wholesale and retail market services. All of these services are regulated on a functional basis.

Traditionally, banking business is associated with taking deposits, making personal and home loans, and, in the commercial market, making large bilateral (one bank) and syndicated (multiple bank) loans. Increasingly, however, banks are entering into insurance and investment business. The multi-service bank or financial institution is now a common business model and a major feature of the European financial landscape. (These are called financial conglomerates where more than one of banking, insurance, and investment services activities are carried out within the same group. The term 'universal bank' reflects the banking and investment services model and, in particular, the German model, while the term 'banc-assurance' refers to banking and insurance groups.) Although each business line is subject to sector-specific regulation, particular rules apply to financial conglomerates. Financial conglomerates raise particular risks for effective supervision as risks in particular business units can generate contagion risks which impact on the group as a whole. Specific regulation is imposed to ensure that clear reporting lines to different supervisors, where relevant, are established, that an overall risk profile is developed, and to support the stability of the group as a whole. The **Financial Services Authority** assesses the overall direction of and risks posed by the UK financial services industry in its annual Financial Risk Outlook.

NIAMH MOLONEY

see also: **alternative trading system**

bankruptcy *see* **insolvency, individual; insolvency, corporate**

Barbie, Klaus Klaus Barbie was born in Bad Godesberg, Germany, in 1913. Barbie advanced to the rank of Captain in the SS while serving as head of the Information Section of the Gestapo in Lyon from 1942 until 1944. Reviled as the 'Butcher of Lyon', Barbie was blamed for the death of 4,000 persons, including the resistance leader Jean Moulin and forty-four Jewish children deported to Auschwitz from the French orphanage at Izieu. By the war's end, Barbie appeared on a United Nations' list of war criminals, but eluded capture, in part because of his work for the US Army's Counter-Intelligence Corps in Germany. In 1951, using the assumed name of Klaus Altmann, Barbie fled to Bolivia where he spent the next three decades. Tracked down by Beate Klarsfeld, the French hunter of Nazis, Barbie arrived on French soil in 1982 to stand trial for crimes against humanity, the first such proceeding in French history.

This was not Barbie's first trial, however. Twice during his years of hiding, in 1952 and again in 1954, Barbie had been tried *in absentia* and sentenced to death for war crimes. At the time, post-war French trials for war-related crimes fell into one of two categories. Frenchmen were tried as collaborators under laws of treason, while non-Frenchmen, such as Barbie, were tried as war criminals. It was not until the mid-1960s that crimes against humanity gained an independent status in French law.

Barbie's prosecution raised a host of difficulties. Because the limitation period for war crimes had already expired, and because the death sentences from his first two convictions had lapsed, Barbie could only be tried for crimes essentially different from those for which he had already twice been condemned. The legal case against Barbie thus raised the question: how did crimes against humanity differ from war crimes?

On 20 December 1985, the Cour de Cassation, the highest French appeal court, answered this question, declaring that crimes against humanity constitute only those 'inhumane acts and persecutions' perpetrated by a state 'practising a hegemonic political ideology'. This decision was criticized in many circles. By linking crimes against humanity with a state practicing a 'hegemonic political ideology,' the court's decision appeared designed to render French conduct in Algeria, already shielded from prosecution by the statute of limitations for war crimes, immune from prosecutions as crimes against humanity.

Barbie's trial ran from 11 May until 4 July 1987. Viewed by the government as a pedagogic exercise that would teach the nation about Nazi occupation and Vichy policies, the trial was filmed under a new French law that permitted cameras to record trials for historical purposes. Barbie's defence counsel, Jacques Vergès, launched a 'defense of rupture' designed to unmask hypocrisy and to turn the pedagogic purpose of the trial to the defendant's advantage. Vergès tried, largely unsuccessfully, to reveal the pervasive complicity of ordinary Frenchmen in the crimes attributed to Barbie.

Convicted on 4 July 1987, Barbie was sentenced to life in prison where he died in 1991.

LAWRENCE DOUGLAS

Alain Finkielkraut, *Remembering in Vain: The Klaus Barbie Trial and Crimes Against Humanity* (New York: Columbia University Press, 1992)

Barcelona Traction Case   *see* nationality

Bates' Case (or *Case of Impositions*) (1606)

Bates' Case (An Information against Bates or Case of Impositions) raised a fundamental question of constitutional law concerning the power of the monarch to raise revenue using the **royal prerogative**, without parliamentary approval. Some monarchs had sought to do this by ordering impositions on goods imported to or exported from England, but from the end of the reign of King Edward III to the reign of King Henry VIII monarchs had been content to rely on parliamentary grants of subsidies to supplement their normal income. The cash-strapped Tudor queens, Mary and Elizabeth, facing increasingly obstreperous Parliaments, had resorted once more to impositions under the prerogative, and the early Stuart kings continued to rely on them.

Bates' Case was one of the leading occasions on which the legality of prerogative impositions was tested in the courts. Bates, an English merchant trading with the Levant, had imported currants from Venice. An Act of Parliament had recently provided for King James to receive poundage (a duty assessed by reference to the quantity of different kinds of goods imported) of 2s. 6d. on every hundredweight of currants imported. The King sought to use the royal prerogative to require an additional payment of 5s. per hundredweight. Bates refused to pay the additional sum, arguing that the imposition was unlawful as being contrary to common law and custom without parliamentary approval.

No earlier judicial decision or statute settled the point, so it had to be decided by inference and analogy, and by attempting to reconstruct the historical circumstances surrounding various grants by Parliament of subsidies to monarchs over several hundred years. Bates argued that the common law allowed merchants to come and go freely, and any limitation of that by imposing restrictions on the free movement of people or goods required specific legal authority, either from common law (which, it was said, had long allowed certain impositions on staples such as wool) or Parliament. There was no such authority in relation to the supplementary duty on currants.

The judges of the Court of Exchequer whose opinions are reported (Baron Clark and Chief Baron Flemming) rejected this. Clark B thought that questions concerning the prerogative depended not on common law but on the previous practice (or 'presidents') of the Crown. The **monarch** could use the prerogative to facilitate trade, for instance by granting privileges to corporations, and could profit from them. He could also impose duties on commodities as a matter of royal policy, which the courts could not question and for which the King need not give reasons. Flemming CB distinguished between the ordinary and absolute power of the King. The ordinary power allowed him to dispense justice and apply private common law for the benefit of individuals. The absolute power allows him to benefit the people as a whole. The King could not use his absolute power to alter the common law without an Act of Parliament, but could use it to make war and peace, alliances and treaties, and regulate trade. The King could restrain subjects from going beyond the sea (using the prerogative writ of *ne exeat regno*) or carrying or sending goods beyond the sea, because such actions might harm the commonwealth of England. He could a *fortiori* use the absolute prerogative power to impose a duty on the export of domestic commodities such as wool or prohibit or impose a duty on the importation of foreign commodities such as currants.

Flemming CB said that only the King could judge what was necessary for the public good. The absolute prerogative's governing principle was not one of personal right but of public good—*salus populi suprema lex est*—and courts and subjects could not question the King's judgment as to what would best contribute to the common welfare.

This judgment against Bates was a victory for the King not only over the commercial interests of merchants but also over those members of the **House of Commons** who claimed **parliamentary supremacy** in revenue matters. The case dealt only with imposition of indirect taxation under the prerogative; but in 1637 a similar conclusion was reached (by a bare majority) in the *Case of Ship Money*. As a matter of strict law, one cannot confidently say that *Bates' Case* was wrongly decided. Even parliamentary radicals were disinclined to deny that duties could properly be imposed on purely commercial activities. But the judgment was out of line with political trends. When the government exploited the decision in 1608 to extend impositions to a very wide range of imported commodities, lawyers and parliamentarians reflected on the political implications of the decision.

In 1610 there was an extensive debate in the House of Commons on the matter of impositions. The House was swayed by Hakewill, who argued that the precedents did not support the decision: every attempt by a monarch to impose such duties had provoked a challenge from Parliament, and the absolute character of the prerogative was inconsistent with Magna Carta and with common law liberties. Following the debate, the House addressed a petition against impositions (*inter alia*) to King James. He reduced them, but he and his son King Charles I continued to impose them and relied on them increasingly to reduce their dependence on Parliament.

In 1641 the Long Parliament passed a Tunnage and Poundage Act, imposing penalties on anyone who in the future would collect tonnage and poundage without parliamentary authority, and declared and enacted that 'it is and hath been the ancient right of the subjects of this realm that no subsidy, custom, impost or other charge whatsoever ought or may be laid or imposed upon any merchandise exported or imported by subjects, denizens or aliens, without common consent in Parliament'. After the Civil War, the Protectorate, the Restoration, and the Glorious Revolution, the matter was authoritatively laid to rest by Article IV of the **Bill of Rights 1689**, which provided 'That levying money for or to the use of the Crowne by pretence of prerogative without grant of Parlyament for longer time or in other manner then the same is or shall be granted is illegal'.

Bates' Case was thus only part of a long struggle for mastery in fiscal matters between the Crown and Parliament. Part of its significance lies in the reaction it provoked in the constitutional struggle of which it formed part. However, the statement of Fleming CB that judges could not review the exercise of prerogative powers remains influential, although its scope has been severely limited since the 1984 decision of the House of Lords in *Council for Civil Service Unions v Minister for the Civil Service*.

DAVID FELDMAN

battered wife syndrome   *see* **syndrome evidence**

***Beatty v Gillbanks* (1882)**   This case is important in the law of public order. Particular prominence was given to the decision in AV Dicey's *Introduction to the Study of the Law of the Constitution* (London: Macmillan, 1885, ch. vii) where it is stated that 'a meeting which is not otherwise illegal does not become an unlawful assembly solely because it will excite violent and unlawful opposition, and thus may indirectly lead to a breach of the peace'.

The case arose from the activities of the Salvation Army which, in the later nineteenth century, was in the forefront of outbreaks of public disorder in many parts of the United Kingdom. Disorder arose in particular because the Army's vigorous campaign against alcohol drew often-violent opposition from people who adopted the mocking title of the Skeleton Army. There had been several clashes in Weston-super-Mare in early 1882 and eventually local magistrates, acting on advice originating from the Home Office, issued a public notice directing all and sundry to abstain from 'assembling to the disturbance of the public peace'. Despite the notice, a number of Salvationists led by William Beatty processed on Sunday 26 March; there was opposition, and, after a further warning from a police sergeant, he and two colleagues were arrested. Some days later they were jailed for three months in default of agreeing to be bound over to keep the peace. They were released on bail pending appeals to the Queen's Bench Division. The appeals were successful, and one of the two judges spoke of the 'lawful and laudable purpose' of the Salvation Army, of the absence of any force or violence shown by the appellants, of the lawful nature of processions as the exercise of a right to pass and re-pass on the highway, and of the actions of the Skeleton Army in 'entirely' causing the disturbance.

Beatty v Gillbanks has been cited in many cases and was recently approved of in *Redmond-Bate v Director of Public Prosecutions* (2000). However it has often been distinguished—for instance, where there is deliberate provocation of opponents—and in *R v Chief Constable of Sussex, ex p International Trader's Ferry Ltd* (1999) the **House of Lords** recognized that the manpower and financial resources available to the police are highly relevant in determining the scale of support that can be offered in protecting lawful activities. In addition there has been extensive legislation limiting the range of lawful activities on the highway and elsewhere.

Yet, despite suggestions that *Beatty v Gillbanks* was 'an aberration' or 'somewhat unsatisfactory' or even 'notorious', it has shown a remarkable vitality and resilience. The underlying importance of the case is that it presumes in favour of those going about their lawful business and acts as a reminder of the desirability of achieving a sensible balance between public order and freedom of expression. Both the presumption and the reminder are strengthened by the incorporation of the **European Convention of Human Rights**, especially Article 10 (**freedom of expression**) and Article 11 (**freedom of assembly**) under the Human Rights Act 1998.

SIR DAVID WILLIAMS

D Feldman, *Civil Liberties and Human Rights in England and Wales* (Oxford: Oxford University Press, 2nd edn, 2002), ch 18

see also: **breach of the peace; binding over; criminal regulation of public order**

Beck, Adolf The case of Adolf Beck (1841–1909) was one of the most notorious miscarriages of justice of the late nineteenth century, as he was twice wrongly convicted on the basis of mistaken identification. His case (along with that of Florence **Maybrick**) was central to the acceptance of the need for the establishment of a Court of Criminal Appeal in 1907.

Beck was a Norwegian sailor and businessman who had lived in London since 1885. In 1896 he was convicted at the Central Criminal Court of defrauding eleven women of their jewellery in 1895, and was sentenced to seven year's penal servitude. The prosecution had believed the frauds to be similar in character to those of a convicted fraudster, known as Smith, who had been sentenced to five year's penal servitude in 1877, and much of their case was based on this assumption. Beck claimed mistaken identification and could prove that he was in Peru in 1877 when Smith had been convicted for the original frauds; but he was prevented from leading crucial evidence on this point at his trial.

A public campaign raised doubts about the conviction in relation to three points: first, the identification of Beck as the fraudster. Although Beck was identified by the victims in a police line-up, he was the only person in the line-up with the physical characteristics—grey hair and a moustache—of the fraudster. Evidence of other distinguishing marks, such as the style of moustache or scar on the fraudster's neck, were disregarded. Secondly, the trial judge, Sir Forrest Fulton, wrongly refused to allow the defence to lead the evidence of a handwriting expert—which would have established that the 1877 and 1895 fraudster were the same person—on the basis that it would have revealed the previous conviction, evidence of which he believed could not be placed before the court until after the jury had returned its verdict. This error was compounded by his failure to reserve the point of law for discussion by the whole body of **common law** judges. Third, the prison authorities had initially assumed that Beck was Smith and had allocated the same convict number. In 1898 they recognized that, as Beck was uncircumcised, he could not be Smith; and this fact was reported to Fulton. Fulton acknowledged that they were not the same person, but maintained that Beck was still the impostor of 1895, and so nothing was done with the case.

Beck was released on licence in 1901, but was again convicted of similar charges in 1904. By chance, before sentence could be passed, the real Smith was arrested and confessed to all the frauds. Beck was pardoned and received £5,000 compensation.

An inquiry into the miscarriage of justice censured the various participants in the case for their failure to recognize and act on the errors that had been made. The more lasting impact of the case was in the recognition of the need for a Court of Criminal Appeal, for which legal reformers had unsuccessfully campaigned throughout the previous century. The new court was empowered to hear appeals on matters of both fact and law. This allowed a means of redress to those who had been wrongly convicted or harshly sentenced.   LINDSAY FARMER

before-the-event insurance   *see* **legal expenses insurance**

Belfast Agreement   *see* **Agreement Reached in the Multiparty Negotiations, 10 April 1998**

***Bell v Lever Brothers Ltd* (1932)**   This decision is the leading English authority on the effect of mistake on the formation of a contract. Bell and Snelling, who were senior officers in a Lever Brothers' subsidiary, secretly and in breach of their employment contracts bought on their own behalf cocoa in which their company traded. Lever Brothers later paid both men generous compensation for termination of their employment contracts. Upon discovering the trades, Lever Brothers sought return of the compensation. The resulting legal trial was a sensation because Lever Brothers alleged that the pair's conduct had been fraudulent. While these claims of fraud could not be sustained (because it was found that by the time of the termination contracts, Bell and Snelling had forgotten about their earlier breaches), the jury found in Lever Brothers' favour on the alternative claim that the termination contracts were void because they had been entered into on the basis of a belief that the employment contracts were still binding—which was a mistake because of the breaches by Bell and Snelling. Lever Brothers was therefore entitled to recover the compensation. The Court of Appeal upheld this result.

The **House of Lords** allowed the appeal by the narrowest of margins. In the leading judgment, Lord **Atkin** sought to establish a basis for mistake in

contract law. He held that where parties contracted under a sufficiently fundamental mistake, the mistake operated to negative or nullify their consent to contract with the result that there was no contract. Lord Atkin outlined particular types of circumstances in which a mistake could operate: mistake as to the existence of the subject matter of a contract; mistake as to the identity of a contracting party; or a mistake as to title. Another type was a mistake as to quality of the subject matter of the contract, provided that the mistake was shared by the parties and concerned the existence of some quality which made the subject matter, without that quality, essentially different from what it was believed to be. In this case, the relevant mutual mistake as to quality was that the employment contracts were still binding at the date they were terminated. Lord Atkin held that this was not a sufficiently fundamental mistake to avoid the termination contracts. Lever Brothers received what they had sought: a release from the employment contracts. It was immaterial that they had unnecessarily paid compensation to secure that release.

The decision was unfortunate for two reasons. First, the contemporary importance of the case, namely its relevance to concerns about the appropriate conduct of senior employees, was obscured. Indeed, the decision allows **directors** to compete with their companies and means that directors' fiduciary duties do not include a duty to disclose their own misconduct. Secondly, the doctrine of mistake expounded by Lord Atkin has proven largely unworkable. If this mistake was not sufficiently fundamental to render the contract void, it is hard to see that there could ever be such a mistake. Lord Atkin was right to say that Lever Brothers received what it bargained for. However, this overlooks the reason Lever Brothers sued. Atkin's decision is illogical: he based contract on consensus but he also denied the relevance of a fact that, if known, would have removed Lever Brothers' consent to the termination contracts, a factor that a jury recognized would have removed such consent. The decision has served to stymie the later development of the law in this area.   CATHERINE MacMILLAN

belligerency   *see* **international humanitarian law; war and armed conflict**

benchmarking in legal education   *see* **learning outcomes of legal education**

benefits in kind, taxation of   *see* **employment tax**

Bentham, Jeremy   Jeremy Bentham (1748–1832), the utilitarian philosopher and reformer, is also regarded as one of Britain's greatest jurists. According to JS Mill, he not only (like Francis **Bacon**) prophesized the creation of a science of law and **legislation**, he 'made large strides' towards its realization ('Remarks on Bentham's Philosophy' (1833)). Though he studied law and was admitted to Lincoln's Inn, he never practised law. As a young man he attended the lectures of William **Black-stone** (later published as *Commentaries on the Laws of England* (1765–1769)), and, while he owed much to the systematic arrangement that Blackstone gave to English law, Bentham developed a lifelong antipathy to the principles of law (particularly 'judge-made law') expounded there.

As a critic of the **common law** and the **corruption** that surrounded the judicial system administering it, Bentham conceived of a vast system of law and judicial procedure to replace it in the form of a series of legal codes. The most important of these codes were concerned with penal, civil, and **constitutional law**, and **evidence**, judicial procedure and organization. In penal law he drew on Montesquieu and Beccaria to develop their insights into the connections between crime, punishment, and liberty. *An Introduction to the Principles of Morals and Legislation* (1789), written as an introduction to a penal code, emphasized the importance of a proportion between crimes and punishments to avoid both undue severity and sentences too lenient to prevent future crimes. In the famous chapter on 'Offences' Bentham used his hedonistic utilitarian philosophy to construct a map of all possible offences. This map was partly designed to question the validity of those offences (for example, of a sexual or religious nature) that tended to be severely punished but caused little or no actual harm to other individuals.

Although written in the 1770s, Bentham's initial work on the civil law was first published in Étienne Dumont's recension of his writings, *Traités de législation civile et pénale* (1802). Bentham emphasized here the importance of subsistence, abundance (meaning future subsistence), security (a form of liberty where individuals and the state are restrained by law and punishment from harming other individuals), and **equality**. These ideas formed the objects of the civil law in numerous fields (for example, property, contract, tort, etc) to which the penalties of the penal law would then be attached. The main work in the field of evidence and judicial procedure, the *Rationale of Judicial Evidence* (1827), edited by the young Mill, attacked the technical system of evidence and adjective law, which, in Bentham's opinion, led to unnecessary delay, vexation, expense, and corruption. Bentham favoured a 'natural' system of procedure, where all parties were heard, all evidence admitted, cross-examination encouraged, and increased powers given to the courts to obtain evidence.

In constitutional law Bentham's thought evolved from a critical, though cautious, examination of Blackstone's largely Lockean views in the early *A Fragment on Government* (1776), to the advocacy of a complex system of representative **democracy** with popular **sovereignty**, near-universal suffrage, frequent **elections**, **freedom of information**, widespread influence of public opinion. and publicity on government—all designed to appeal to those professing 'liberal opinions'—in *Constitutional Code* (1830). Although Bentham's epicurean philosophy was radical in the sense of returning to the roots of philosophical problems, he only tentatively flirted with radical politics at the time of the French Revolution (despite being made an honorary citizen of France in 1792). He began to write on parliamentary reform in 1809–1810 although the first publication of his radical political views was delayed until the publication of *Plan of Parliamentary Reform* in 1817.

Bentham's *pannomion* (from the Greek meaning 'all the laws') reflected his analysis of law and, additionally, included other elements of his philosophy, such as the theory of fictions in language and the system of classification and logical division. Many of these ideas have been taken up by thinkers in numerous fields from economics to psychology. In addition, his work as a practical reformer from the early comment on the Penitentiary Act of 1779 to the Anatomy Act of 1832, including the Panopticon prison scheme and **poor law** reform, are too numerous to chronicle here. A team of scholars on the Bentham Project at University College London have now published twenty-six of a projected sixty-five volume edition of his works and correspondence. They are joined by Bentham himself, who, after public dissection and the creation of his 'Auto-Icon', eventually came to reside in the south cloisters of the college.

FREDERICK ROSEN

J Bentham, *An Introduction to the Principles of Morals and Legislation*, JH Burns and HLA Hart (eds), with a New Introduction by F Rosen (Oxford: Clarendon Press, 1996).
F Rosen, 'Jeremy Bentham (1748–1832)' in *Oxford Dictionary of National Biography* (Oxford: Oxford University Press, 2004), v 221–234.

Berlin (1945–1991)   *see* **occupation, belligerent**

Berne Convention for the Protection of Literary and Artistic Works   Prior to the conclusion of The Berne Convention for the Protection of Literary and Artistic Works of 1886 the enforcement of copyright internationally was governed by bilateral and minor multilateral agreements. The Berne Convention, now administered by the **World Intellectual Property Organization** ('WIPO'), was the first major multilateral agreement, establishing an international regime for the protection of copyright. It establishes the Berne Union of signatory states, within which the provisions of the Convention protecting the rights of authors of literary and artistic works applies.

The main principle governing the Berne Union is that of national treatment, under which each member of the union affords the same copyright protection to the nationals of other members as it affords to its own nationals. Two further principles underpin the national treatment principle. One is the principle of automatic protection under which members may not make national treatment subject to any formality. The other requires that the protection granted by the principle of national treatment must be independent of the existence of protection in the country of origin.

The Convention also sought to introduce a degree of harmonization into the copyright law of the members of the Berne Union. It lays down minimum standards of protection that members of the Union are obliged to introduce into their copyright laws. These include provisions on the minimum range of rights to be afforded to authors and to users of copyright works, and minimum requirements with respect to duration of rights. In general, the Convention sought to follow existing copyright law in the founder members of the Union. However, the need to take into account the varying practices in common law and continental European countries meant that members were obliged to implement some new rights. In particular, in its Article 6*bis* the Convention requires members of the Union to introduce the moral rights of paternity and integrity.

The Berne Convention has been subject to multiple revisions, the most recent of which was the Paris Revision of 1971. This revision added the Appendix to the Convention, which establishes a special regime for developing countries. The significance and standing of the Berne Convention was affected by the coming into force in 1995 of the **World Trade Organization Agreement on Trade Related Aspects of Intellectual Property Rights ('TRIPs')**, which moved the focus of international copyright protection into the domain of the **World Trade Organization ('WTO')**.

TRIPs obliges members of the WTO to comply with Articles 1 to 21, except Article 6*bis*, and the Appendix of the Berne Convention. TRIPs extends the obligations under the Berne Convention with respect to computer programs, rental rights, and the protection of performers, producers of sound recordings and broadcasting organizations. In an attempt to regain some of the ground lost to TRIPs, the WIPO Copyright Treaty was concluded in 1996 as a special agreement under the Berne Convention. However, this treaty, which seeks to address issues raised by digitization of copyright works, only binds those members of the Berne Union that have acceded to it.

FIONA MACMILLAN

A Ilardi and M Blakeney, *International Encyclopaedia of Intellectual Property Treaties* (Oxford: Oxford University Press, 2004)

S Ricketson, *The Berne Convention for the Protection of Literary and Artistic Works: 1886–1986* (London: Kluwer, 1987)

best interests of patients   The 'best interests' test is used to determine what medical treatment should be given to children and to adults who lack **capacity**.

With regard to children, the **courts** will apply the 'best interests' test whenever there is some dispute as to the treatment which a **child** should receive. Most commonly, such a dispute arises when the parents disagree with the child's doctors, and refuse to give consent to the treatment which the doctors believe to be in the child's best interests. In such cases, the child's welfare is the paramount concern, and the court's task is to decide what treatment will be in his or her best interests. In practice, the courts will very seldom permit parents to take a different view from the child's doctors about where a child's best interests lie. The courts have been willing to override parental refusals whenever a child's life or health might be endangered. In one of the most dramatic cases of recent years, *Re A (Children) (Conjoined Twins: Separation)* (2000), the Court of Appeal authorized the separation of **conjoined twins** in order to save the stronger twin's life, despite the parents' refusal to consent to the operation.

In relation to the treatment of incompetent adults, the courts have fashioned a 'best interests' test out of the doctrine of necessity. This is now given statutory effect by the Mental Capacity Act 2005. Once it has been determined that an adult patient lacks capacity, the doctors involved in their care must treat them in their best interests. Where there is any doubt about a proposed treatment's legality, an application can be made to the court, which will apply the best interests test in order to determine how the patient should be treated. It seems clear that the best interests test not only takes into account the patient's immediate clinical needs, but also accommodates their emotional or psychological interests. For example, in *Re Y (Mental Incapacity: Bone Marrow Transplant)* (1996), the court decided that acting as a bone marrow donor to her desperately ill sibling was in the best interests of a severely mentally handicapped woman, because it would be to her 'emotional, psychological and social benefit'.

The Mental Capacity Act 2005 introduces a statutory 'checklist' of factors which should be taken into account when determining how a patient who lacks capacity should be treated. These include whether and when a **person** is likely to regain capacity. This means that if the person's incapacity is temporary, it would not be in their best interests for decisions to be taken which could wait until they regain capacity, and can decide for themselves. The 'checklist' also specifies that efforts should be made both to encourage the patient to participate, and to improve their ability to participate in any decision which affects them. The decision-maker is instructed to take into account the person's past wishes and feelings, and any written statement they made when they had capacity, as well as their beliefs and values. To this end, the decision-maker should consult anyone involved in caring for the patient as to what the patient themselves would have wanted. The Act therefore makes it clear that the patient's best interests are not to be judged objectively, on purely clinical grounds, but must take into account the individual patient's own perspective.   EMILY JACKSON

Bilateral Investment Treaties   *see* **investment protection**

Bill of Rights (1689)   *see* **parliamentary sovereignty**

Bills (parliamentary)   *see* **Acts of Parliament; Private Bills; Private Members' Bills**

bills of rights, international and supranational
Treaties, such as those against the slave trade in the nineteenth century and those protecting minorities and religious groups affected by the redrawing of the political map of Europe after World War I, have long protected **human rights**. Nevertheless, states were reluctant to compromise the principle of non-intervention in each other's internal affairs. It was shock at the scale of atrocities revealed at the end of World War II that led the newly-formed **United Nations** Organization ('UN'), influenced by Eleanor

Roosevelt's campaigning, to treat the drafting of a codified statement of fundamental human rights as a high priority.

The General Assembly of the UN adopted the **Universal Declaration of Human Rights** in 1948. Its preamble asserted the link, between human dignity, rights, the rule of law, peace, and justice, which has since become a key justification for taking international action to protect people's human rights against states. The Declaration listed twenty-five rights ranging from individual rights such as life, freedom from torture and slavery, to rest and leisure, and social and economic matters such as rights to work, an adequate standard of living, and a social and international order in which the other rights can be fully realized. Rights were to be limited only by law and for restricted purposes.

Whilst the Declaration did not impose legal obligations on states, it reflected the opinion of nearly all states in the world at the time, and it formed the basis for negotiations on binding human rights treaties. However, ideological divisions emerged between collectivist states, which feared that strong protection for individuals' rights would impede central economic and social planning and the sovereignty of the people, and liberal states which resisted recognition for economic and social rights, arguing that they were achievable, if at all, only by restricting individual freedom and the free market. Some other peoples, particularly in Asia and Africa, considered the imposition of human rights on traditional cultures to be a form of cultural imperialism. These tensions were only partially resolved.

It took the UN negotiators eighteen years to finalize the text of the **International Covenant on Civil and Political Rights ('ICCPR')** and the **International Covenant on Economic, Social and Cultural Rights ('ICESCR')**, which can together be called an international bill of rights. The ICCPR includes individual rights such as the rights to life, freedom from torture and slavery, freedom of expression, belief and association, and freedom from discrimination. It also requires states to legislate against propaganda for war and advocacy of much national, racial, or religious hatred. Many rights may be restricted on certain limited grounds, but subject to those the rights are to be given effect at once and in full. The ICESCR covers a range of social and economic rights but requires their progressive rather than immediate achievement in accordance with each state's level of economic strength and development. Severing the two kinds of rights allowed states to decide whether and to what extent to accept obligations in relation to each separately, thus accommodating rather than overcoming ideological divisions. Both Covenants open with the right of peoples to self-determination, which has proved highly controversial in practice.

Enforcement under the UN Covenants depends on committees of experts, which receive and critically examine periodic reports from state's parties on their compliance with their obligations, bringing moral, political, and diplomatic pressure to bear to encourage states to improve their performance. The committee for the ICCPR can exercise an adjudicative function in respect of complaints from alleged victims of violations only if the state concerned has ratified a protocol giving the committee jurisdiction.

In western Europe there were fewer ideological divisions, so the Council of Europe was able to broker agreement on the first attempt to cast a body of international human rights in a legally enforceable form. The text of the **European Convention on Human Rights** ('ECHR') was agreed in 1950 and entered into force in 1953. It covered individual rather than collective rights, and included innovative enforcement mechanisms: victims of alleged violations were able to lodge petitions against states which accepted the procedure, and these would be examined by a Commission (now defunct), which had a mediating and fact-finding role, and if necessary by the **European Court of Human Rights**, which had final authority to adjudicate on alleged violations. Today all member states of the Council of Europe are required to accept the right of individual petition to the Court. A European Social Charter ('ESC')—first version finalized in 1961, with a revised and more demanding version in 1996—operates alongside the ECHR protecting social and economic rights. Whilst the ESC's enforcement mechanisms are weaker than those under the ECHR, a 1995 Protocol to the ESC makes provision for collective complaints against states to be adjudicated if the state has ratified the Protocol.

Other regional bills of rights have followed, including the American Convention on Human Rights (1969) and the **African Charter on Human and People's Rights** (1981). Each one now has a system to adjudicate on alleged violations by states parties. Since 1989 there has also been a UN **Convention on the Rights of the Child**, adapting the provisions of the International Covenants to the special needs and circumstances of children and providing a monitoring arrangement through an expert committee.

More recently bills of rights or their equivalent have started to appear among the instruments establishing supranational regional organizations established for other purposes. The **European Union** ('EU'), originally a free-trade association (the European Economic Community), adopted a Charter of Fundamental Rights in 2000. This was expressed to be non-binding, but is used as an aid to interpreting the legally binding provisions of EU law and might at some stage become part of a constitutional treaty for the EU.

As human rights instruments have multiplied, issues arise as to the relationship between states' human rights obligations and their sometimes competing obligations under UN Security Council resolutions or in other organizations such as the EU or the **World Trade Organization**.

DAVID FELDMAN

bills of rights, national The term 'bill of rights' covers a range of legal instruments. A minimal definition of a bill of rights is a document that sets out a series of individual or collective rights; this definition, however, does not address either where the responsibility to protect the rights lies or the methods by which rights are to be protected, both of which can vary greatly. The efficacy of bills of rights depends on the legal culture in which they are embedded.

As a set of demands made by the English Barons against the monarch, forcing him to recognize some constraints on his power, **Magna Carta** 1215 is often considered an early bill of rights. The right to demand *habeas corpus* is one enduring legacy of Magna Carta. William and Mary accepted a Declaration of Rights, later enacted as the **Bill of Rights 1689**, as a condition of being offered the English throne. The Bill of Rights recognized rights such as freedom from royal interference in the courts, the right to petition the sovereign, and the right to be free from cruel and unusual punishment. Some clauses of the Bill of Rights are still part of British law.

The United States Bill of Rights, the first ten amendments to the United States Constitution, was adopted in 1791 and it has shaped modern discussions of the value of such instruments. The US Bill of Rights covers a range of individual rights expressed in terse language without qualification, including the right to freedom of speech and religion, the right to keep and bear arms, the right to due process in criminal trials, and the right to be free from cruel and unusual punishment. Its constitutional, or entrenched, status means that American judges can assess legislation to determine if it is consistent with the Bill of Rights; if laws are judged inconsistent, they become invalid.

Bills of rights are now found in all types of legal systems; indeed in 2007 Brunei and Australia are the only countries with civilian governments that do not have some form of national bill of rights. Most bills of rights include a catalogue of civil and political rights, such as the right to life, the right to privacy, freedom from torture and slavery, freedom from arbitrary arrest and detention, due process rights, freedom of thought, speech, and religion, the right to non-discrimination, and the right to participate in government. Some bills of rights, for example that contained in the Iraq Constitution of 2005, accord priority to religious laws over civil and political rights. The Indian Constitution of 1947 includes a section entitled 'Directive Principles of State Policy' covering economic and social rights; but these rights, unlike the protected civil and political rights, cannot be directly enforced in the courts. By contrast, under the 1996 South African Constitution economic and social rights, such as access to housing, health care, food, water, and security, as well as civil and political rights, are enforceable. The South African Constitutional Court's decisions implementing economic and social rights, such as the right to health care, indicate that there is no inherent legal difference between the two categories of rights.

Constitutional bills of rights generally accord great weight to judicial interpretation of rights guarantees and this feature has led to intense debate about interpretative methods. For example, should judges, when interpreting a bill of rights, adhere to the intention of the drafters of the right in question (possibly centuries previously), or should judges interpret rights to be relevant to modern conditions? Moreover, whatever interpretative method is used, a democratic question remains about the legitimacy of judicial interpretation: should unelected judges be able to strike down legislation adopted by an elected legislature?

These questions influenced the drafting of the Canadian Charter of Rights and Freedoms, adopted in 1982, as part of the Canadian Constitution. The Charter sets out various categories of rights drawn from national and international sources: fundamental freedoms including conscience and religion, thought, expression, and association; democratic rights; mobility rights; legal rights; official language rights and the educational rights of minority language groups. The Charter also affirms existing aboriginal and treaty rights of the Indian, Inuit, and Métis peoples. While the Charter's rights have constitutional status, they are qualified in two ways: first, the rights and freedoms are subject 'to such reasonable limits prescribed by law as can be demonstrably justified

in a free and democratic society'. The second limitation on the scope of the Canadian Charter allows national and provincial legislatures, by enacting a 'notwithstanding clause', to exclude legislation from most of the Charter's operation by express declaration for (renewable) five-year periods. Such a clause has been enacted by provinces on several occasions, but not so far by the federal government.

More recently, at least in the **common law** world, there has been a move away from constitutional bills of rights to statutory instruments. In 1990, the New Zealand Parliament adopted the Bill of Rights Act. The Bill of Rights covers a range of civil and political rights, largely modelled on international law guarantees. The major enforcement mechanism of the New Zealand Bill of Rights is its requirement that courts must, where possible, interpret legislation to be consistent with the designated rights and freedoms. The courts have no power to invalidate any law that is inconsistent with these rights. The New Zealand government thus is not constrained from enacting legislation inconsistent with the designated rights and freedoms; but it is required to inform Parliament on the introduction of such a law.

The **United Kingdom** drew on the New Zealand example when it adopted the Human Rights Act in 1998, but it also added new features to the statutory model. The Human Rights Act implements rights set out in the **European Convention on Human Rights** of 1950 ('ECHR'), to which the UK is a party. The Act employs a range of mechanisms to import the international standards into national law. First, it requires that all laws are, so far as is possible, to be read and given effect to in a way that is compatible with the ECHR. There has, of course, been much debate about the meaning of the word 'possible'. Secondly, if courts find that legislation is incapable of being interpreted compatibly with the ECHR, they have no power to invalidate the statute, but they may make a 'declaration of incompatibility' with respect to the legislation. However, the declaration 'does not affect the validity, continuing operation or enforcement of the provision'; rather it exerts pressure on Parliament to amend or at least closely scrutinize and reconsider the legislation. It has been said that the scheme of the Human Rights Act establishes a dialogue between the judiciary, Parliament, and the executive about the scope and nature of human rights in contrast to the more conversation-stopping mechanism of judicial striking-down of legislation, as occurs in the United States. The UK law leaves Parliament as the final arbiter on the protection of human rights, thus avoiding the objection that the Human Rights Act illegitimately transfers power from the legislature to the judiciary. Some have argued that the Human Rights Act is not a truly UK bill of rights because it implements the rights set out in the European Convention; and proposals have been made for a UK Bill of Rights, which would go beyond the ECHR rights and include rights such as the right to trial by jury.

Whatever their form, bills of rights tend to create controversy because they assert that a particular set of rights should have either moral or legal priority over legislative action. The charge that bills of rights undermine democratic structures, based on legislative majorities, has been constant. One response to this 'anti-majoritarian' criticism is that bills of rights serve the interests of the community in the long-term, pressuring legislators not to breach human rights for short-term political gain. Another response is to distinguish between the 'strong' form of judicial review required by a constitutional bill of rights and the 'weak' form available under a statutory human rights scheme. The latter leaves final decisions on rights to elected legislators, but allows courts to consider the particular circumstances of individual cases.   HILARY CHARLESWORTH

P Alston (ed), *Promoting Human Rights Through Bills of Rights* (Oxford: Oxford University Press, 1999)
C Gearty, *Principles of Human Rights Adjudication* (Oxford: Oxford University Press, 2004)

See also: **Constitutional Court, South Africa; interpreting constitutions; interpreting legislation;** *Marbury v Madison* (1803)

binding over   The power to bind over to keep the peace and/or to be of good behaviour is a form of preventive justice which can be exercised by **justices of the peace**. It is frequently invoked in England and Wales, especially in the area of public order. Binding over involves the making of an order requiring a person formally to agree to forfeit a sum of money to the **Crown** in the event of failure to keep the peace and/or be of good behaviour. A person who does not so agree could be jailed, even though to be bound over is not technically the equivalent of a **criminal conviction**.

The origins of binding over lie in the **common law** and in the Justices of the Peace Act 1361. Several recent judicial decisions, however, have raised issues of definition and **natural justice**, and there are recent statutes affecting procedure and rights of appeal. A striking feature of the law is that, in addition to a statutory procedure applicable where a person is brought by complaint before a magistrates' court with the intention from the outset of seeking to have the respondent bound over, the power to bind over may be exercised during or at the conclusion of

ordinary criminal prosecutions or where proceedings have been discontinued, and those affected may include defendants, even when acquitted, and witnesses.

There are several areas of uncertainty. The higher courts have of late provided some clarification of the term '**breach of the peace**' but 'good behaviour' remains very vague. These and other uncertainties raise additional problems of compatibility with the **European Convention on Human Rights** and of the desirability of retaining the binding over power when there has been so much recent legislation on anti-social behaviour.   SIR DAVID WILLIAMS

Report of the Law Commission on *Binding Over* (Cm 2439 of 1994, Law Com No 222)

See also: **ASBOs**

biodiversity   The legal significance of biodiversity is largely derived from the 1992 Convention on Biological Diversity ('CBD'), which establishes a global regime for the preservation of ecosystems and for the sustainable exploitation of genetic resources. The definition of biodiversity as 'the variability among living organisms from all sources' (CBD 1992, Article 2) describes an ecological phenomenon; namely, the ongoing enhancement of genetic diversity that results from interactions between species and between species and environments. Whereas seed banks conserve biodiversity only in isolated form, as the genetic potential of particular plants, the CBD seeks to promote the conservation of the complex ecological and cultural networks within which evolutionary variations emerge. Given that the inventive capacities of evolution still precede and outstrip those of science, enhanced genetic diversity is of obvious value to agricultural and pharmaceutical science; indeed, as global agriculture becomes increasingly standardized, artificial selection makes a diminishing contribution to the enhancement of diversity, which reinforces arguments for the conservation of ecological networks. In the CBD, conservation encompasses measures of preservation, as exemplified in programmes for the prevention of deforestation or desertification, and measures of sustainable use, which are articulated in a *sui generis* regime of access and equitable benefit-sharing ('ABS'). ABS is the most the significant legal initiative of the CBD because it develops a complex and innovative framework for the integration of **sovereignty**, ownership, and rights to **political participation**. Starting from the premise that conservation is best encouraged by giving relevant constituencies clear incentives to respect or enhance biodiversity, the

ABS regime attempts to give legal form to the various ways in which ecology is socialized by cultural, technological, and economic processes. In particular, the CBD's recognition of the unique connection between **indigenous peoples** and biodiversity (Article 8j) has become a significant factor in the evolution of this complex regime and has become a basis for the assertion of the political and cultural agency of indigenous peoples in spheres extending beyond the conservation of biodiversity. ABS is in effect a regime for the regulation of bio-prospecting. In one direction, plants and micro-organisms sourced in diversity-rich states are exported towards laboratories in technologically-advanced states, where potentially interesting molecular traits are identified and ultimately developed into patented agricultural or pharmaceutical commodities. In the other direction, some of the benefits of this research process flow back to the states in which the genetic resources originated. These benefits usually take the form of capacity-building initiatives directed towards local **communities** or research bodies that are particularly closely involved in the conservation of biodiversity. This requires, first, a contractual form that can link diverse parties (states, corporations, universities, indigenous communities) and establish schedules and forms of payment that recognize both the commercial risks of natural products research and the principle that benefits should be linked to the conservation of biodiversity and, secondly, an overarching regime of domestic permitting and international 'user measures' (notably customs controls and patent office regulations). Much of the work of the institutions of the CBD focuses on the development of these legal forms.   ALAIN POTTAGE

biological weapons and warfare *see* **arms control; international humanitarian law**

biotechnology   Modern biotechnology originated with the elaboration of the structure of DNA by Watson and Crick in 1953, which provided the conceptual basis for the isolation and manipulation of DNA to modify existing organisms. Genetic engineering, which is the generic term given to all the techniques which are used to isolate DNA from one organism and introduce it into another, has made very significant innovations in both agricultural and medicine possible.

These technologies have become the subject of intellectual property protection, as a consequence of the favourable decisions of courts, as well as of supportive legislation in the USA and Europe. The basis for the patentability of biotechnological innovations was the decision of the **United States Supreme Court** in *Diamond v Chakrabarty* (1980), which allowed the patentability of a bacterium genetically engineered to degrade crude oil.

The European response to this US development was the Directive on the Legal Protection of Biotechnological Inventions. Article 1 of the Directive requires Member States to protect biotechnological inventions under their national patent laws. Article 3(1) provides that a product consisting of or containing biological material, or a process by means of which biological material is produced, processed or used, is patentable. Article 3(2) indicates that biological material which is isolated from its natural environment or produced by means of a technical process is deemed to be an invention even if this material previously occurred in nature.

Patent laws have traditionally excluded from patentability items which would offend against conventional morality. Opponents of the patentability of biotechnological inventions have argued that tampering with 'God's creation' is precisely an example of an immoral invention. The Biotechnology Directive had attempted to anticipate this argument by identifying and excluding from patentability a number of inventions considered immoral, namely: processes for cloning human beings; processes for modifying the germ line genetic identity of human beings; uses of human embryos for industrial or commercial purposes; and processes for modifying the genetic identity of animals which are likely to cause them suffering without any substantial medical benefit to man or animal, as well as animals resulting from such processes.

This list of exclusions did not satisfy the opponents of biotechnological patenting and in October 1998, the Netherlands, among other countries, requested that the **European Court of Justice** ('ECJ') should annul the Biotechnology Directive on grounds which included the argument that it was in breach of the fundamental right to respect for **human dignity**. The European Court of Justice declined this annulment request on the ground that Article 5(1) of the Directive provides that the human body at the various stages of its formation and development cannot constitute a patentable invention. The ECJ stated that: 'It is clear from the directive that, as regards living matter of human origin, the directive frames the law on **patents** in a manner sufficiently rigorous to ensure that the human body effectively remains unavailable and inalienable and that human dignity is thus safeguarded'.

MICHAEL BLAKENEY

bisexuality   *see* homosexuality

black-letter law   *see* doctrinal legal research

Blackstone, William (1723–1780)   Blackstone's fame rests on his *magnum opus*, the *Commentaries on the Laws of England*, first published in four volumes between 1765 and 1769, thereafter continuously in print down to the present day. More than twenty English and Irish editions had appeared by the middle of the nineteenth century; the work's North American bibliographical footprint is still larger, likewise its cultural and educational influence, together with its authoritative role in representing the **common law** as it stood before nineteenth-century reforms.

Born in 1723, the posthumous younger son of a financially distressed London silk merchant, William had the further misfortune to lose his mother when he was 12 years old and a student at London's Charterhouse school. He nevertheless went on to Oxford University's Pembroke College three years later, gaining a coveted All Souls fellowship before he had turned 21. By then he had composed a 400-line verse essay on comparative theology, issued anonymously in 1747 under the imprint of London's leading literary publisher, Robert Dodsley, besides drafting a summary outline of the rules of architecture as laid down by the classical author, Vitruvius, which remains in manuscript. Blackstone also applied himself tirelessly to matters of college and university business, taking effective responsibility for the completion and fitting-out of All Souls' new Codrington Library, later serving as assessor in the Chancellor's court, and promoting the successful electoral campaign of one of the university's two MPs.

These and other Oxford distractions, even more than his lack of patronage, connections, and oratorical skills, explain Blackstone's initial failure to establish a London practice following his call to the bar at the Middle Temple in 1746. Hopes of further academic preferment led him to announce simultaneously in July 1753 his abandonment of the London bar and a forthcoming year's course of lectures for fee-paying undergraduate students on the 'Municipal Laws'—a subject not previously taught at either English university.

The success of this venture made him the prime candidate for Oxford's newly-established Vinerian Chair in the Laws of England, to which he was elected in 1758. His inaugural professorial lecture, published that same year, argued for 'making an academical education a previous step to the profession of the common law, and at the same time making the rudiments of the common law a part of academical education'. Blackstone could hardly have expected either the **Inns of Court** or the unreformed universities to adopt these sweeping proposals immediately and in their entirety; but they pointed the way to the future, albeit first in North America rather than England. Meanwhile their author resumed his London practice, while still continuing his law lectures and other Oxford involvements (not least the rehabilitation of the university press, which in 1759 issued his elegant scholarly edition of *Magna Charta*).

Although he never won renown as a courtroom advocate, Blackstone's second venture at the bar proved more rewarding, with his chamber advice and written opinions in some demand and the tangled affairs of the aristocratic Bertie family providing a source of income through the 1760s. He also served in Parliament, as member successively for two Wiltshire pocket boroughs, following an independent political line both there and at Oxford which did not endear him to Lord Bute, who had put up the purchase price for the first seat. Relative inexperience and ministerial instability made it difficult for Blackstone to obtain the professional preferment he now sought with increasing urgency, following the compulsory resignation of his college fellowship when he married in 1761. The enthusiastic reception of the *Commentaries*, essentially a much-polished version of his Oxford lectures, may have helped ease financial pressures, but did not perceptibly hasten his ascent to the judicial bench. That promotion finally came in 1770, together with a knighthood, both very likely reflecting the personal intervention of King George III.

Blackstone spent the last decade of his relatively brief life as a conscientious and hardworking judge. Despite ill-health he enjoyed family life, maintained his literary interests, and promoted various schemes for 'improvement', notably the establishment of 'penitentiaries' as a more humane penal alternative to transportation or **capital punishment**. His posthumous reputation was long overshadowed by Jeremy **Bentham**'s unrelenting attacks on the *Commentaries* and their author as muddled defenders of the status quo and enemies of all reform. But a more balanced verdict has emerged over the past century, with better appreciation and fuller documentation of Blackstone's innovative achievement.

WILFRID PREST

SFC Milsom, *The Nature of Blackstone's Achievement* (London: Selden Society, 1981)

W Prest (ed), *The Letters of Sir William Blackstone, 1744–1780* (London: Selden Society, 2006)

Bland, Tony Tragedy struck a Sheffield soccer stadium on 15 April 1989. Tony Bland, then eighteen, was one of many seriously injured in a mass crush, his rib and lung injuries temporarily preventing oxygen reaching his brain, resulting in permanent and irreversible brain damage which left him in a '**persistent vegetative state**' ('PVS').

In such a condition there is no awareness. The patient is wholly insensate, experiencing neither pain nor pleasure. Bland's EEG and CT scans revealed no evidence of any cortical activity whatsoever, nor of a 'working mind'. Photographs 'showed more space than substance' in the relevant part of his brain and, in such circumstances 'there is no hint nor hope of any prospect of improvement' and 'no medical procedure or treatment can bring about any beneficial change in his condition' (Sir Stephen Brown, P, *Airedale NHS Trust v Bland* (1993)).

Bland was more 'kept alive' than 'living' in any normal sense of the term. He was fed artificially and mechanically by means of a nasogastric tube; all bodily functions required nursing assistance. He required a catheter which caused infection necessitating surgical intervention which could be carried out without any anaesthetic, so complete was the absence of feeling. Bland's was as extreme and clear a form of PVS as is possible to imagine. No complaint was raised by the Health Trust as to the allocation of substantial resources. Rather, the moral and medical issues related to **autonomy** and benefit.

The medical team concluded as early as August 1989 that sustaining 'life' in the circumstances was of no benefit to the patient. Bland's parents agreed and expressed their opinion as to what he would have wished. The practical issue was whether artificial feeding and hydration should be withdrawn, leading to death by starvation. Alternatively, there was a suggestion that, when inevitable infection next occurred, antibiotics should not be prescribed and administered, with the same consequence. It was with some shock that the doctors received advice that this might constitute murder, not least because what was contemplated was a medical practice acceptable to a responsible body of medical opinion (*Bolam v Friern Hospital Management Committee* (1957)).

At the time, the law on non-treatment had not moved beyond newborn babies (*Re J (a minor) (wardship: medical treatment)* (1990); and *R v Arthur* (1981)) and did not provide either clarity or comfort for doctors contemplating withdrawing treatment from an adult, although the underlying principles that decisions should be made in the best interests of the **child** and that there should be prospects of a reasonable quality of life were clearly capable of generalization. It is trite law that any competent adult can refuse medical treatment, even though the consequence is death (*Re B (Adult: Refusal of Medical Treatment)* (2002)). It is also accepted that, by a so-called 'living will', an adult when competent can make forward provision for later incompetence or inability to communicate. None of these circumstances prevailed here and the Health Trust sought declaratory relief in the **courts**, which was granted at first instance and upheld both by the Court of Appeal and **House of Lords**, primarily on the basis that the continuation of treatment was of no conceivable benefit to the patient, but secondarily on the less plausible grounds that the withdrawal of treatment was an omission and not an act. Moreover, more soundly, the cause of death was deemed to be the underlying injury, rather than the medical treatment. Tony Bland died on 3 March 1993, the ninety-sixth fatal victim of the 'Hillsborough Disaster', his life celebrated and his death mourned by family, friends, and football fans; and his name immortalized in a landmark legal decision.

That decision was highly controversial and characterized by some as permitting 'murder' (as was unsuccessfully argued by the Official Solicitor) or involuntary **euthanasia** and opposed on religious or moral grounds. Others welcomed the decision as humane and rational. Clearly views are polarized and this might explain but not excuse the absence of **legislation**, fifteen long years later (at the time of writing). Some Law Lords expressed the sound opinion that 'it is imperative that the moral, social and legal issues . . . should be considered by **Parliament**'. Others expressed the equally sound opinion that, until established practice emerges, application should be made to the Family Division in such cases. One wonders why, after so long, it remains necessary, absent special circumstances, to refer all such cases (see *An NHS Trust v J* (2006)) to the court, the principles being clear and the practice now well-established.   RICHARD TUR

JM Finnis, 'Bland: Crossing the Rubicon?' (1993) 109 *Law Quarterly Review* 329–337

P Lewis, 'Withdrawal of Treatment from a Patient in a Permanent Vegetative State: Judicial Involvement and Innovative Treatment' (2007) *Medical Law Review* 392–399

See also: **acts and omissions; advance directives; withdrawing/withholding life-sustaining treatment**

Blandy, Mary Mary Blandy (1718–1752) was tried at the Oxford Assizes in March 1752 for the murder of her father, Francis, by poisoning. The case sharply divided public opinion at the time because of Mary's good breeding and supposed good character, many believing that she was manipulated by her greedy and exploitative lover.

In 1746 Blandy fell in love with Captain William Henry Cranstoun, an impecunious Scot. He was refused her hand in marriage by her father, who believed that he was merely a fortune hunter and subsequently also discovered that he already had a wife and child in Scotland. The pair continued to correspond, and in June 1751 she began putting powders in her father's food and drink, later claiming that she believed the powder to be a love potion, sent by Cranstoun, that would make her father look more favourably on their union. After a short period of illness, her father died of poisoning in August 1751. Following an inquest at which arsenic was discovered in the corpse, she was apprehended and put on trial for his murder. The trial lasted only a single day, and turned on the question of her intent to kill. After only five minutes deliberation the jury found her guilty of murder. She was executed on 6 April 1752.

Aside from the huge amount of public interest that it generated, the trial was notable as an example of the early use of scientific evidence and the use of circumstantial evidence to establish guilt.

LINDSAY FARMER

blasphemy In England and Wales blasphemy is a **common law** criminal offence, the statutory counterpart having been abolished in 1967. In Scotland the last successful prosecution for blasphemy was in 1843 and some writers argue that the offence now no longer exists; whilst in Northern Ireland there has never been a successful prosecution for blasphemy. Blasphemy is notoriously difficult to define. In *R v Ramsay and Foote* (1883) Lord Coleridge said that blasphemy requires '[a] wilful intention to pervert, insult, and mislead others, by means of licentious and contumelious abuse applied to sacred objects, or by wilful misrepresentations or wilful sophistry, calculated to mislead the ignorant and unwary'. However, one does not need to intend to blaspheme to commit the offence. The maximum penalty is imprisonment for life and a fine. Blasphemy protects only the Christian religion and is probably limited to protecting the beliefs of the Church of England. There were only two successful prosecutions for blasphemy in England and Wales in the twentieth century—the last, in 1979, being that of *Gay Times* for publishing James Kirkup's poem 'The Love That Dares to Speak Its Name'. There are, however, a number of instances where publishers have refused to publish something because of fear that the work might constitute a blasphemy. In 1989 the British Board of Film Classification refused Nigel Wingrove's 'Visions of Ecstasy' on the ground, amongst others, that it was blasphemous. In 2003 the House of Lords Select Committee on Religious Offences observed that, following the passage of the Human Rights Act 1998, because blasphemy was discriminatory and uncertain in its nature, any future prosecution for blasphemy would be likely to fail.

TONY BRADNEY

See also: **freedom of religion and belief; freedom of speech; religion; religion in the media; strict criminal liability**

blood sports This is a term commonly used to describe entertainment or sport involving animal suffering. It is a fluid term and various activities have been historically so described. However the activities referred to can be broadly divided into three types. These are hunting, such as coursing or fox hunting; baiting, such as badger baiting; and fighting, such as cock fighting or dog fighting.

Fighting and baiting sports are now subject to a total ban under section 8 of the Animal Welfare Act 2006. This legislation also includes wide provisions banning the promoting of or profiting from such activities. Fights between animals and humans are covered by the ban.

The Hunting Act 2004 banned hunting wild mammals with dogs, including hare coursing, subject to certain exemptions. These allow the stalking or flushing out of wild mammals with dogs provided that the hunting is for food or to prevent serious damage to property or livestock, and that the mammal is shot or caught by a bird of prey. There is also a narrow exemption for the use of a dog below ground for the purpose of protecting bred or wild birds that are being kept to be shot. The hunting of rabbits or rats is exempted on a person's own land.

Other activities such as bird shooting or fishing are legal provided they do not breach provisions prohibiting cruelty contained in the Animal Welfare Act 2006 and do not involve the hunting of animals protected by the Wildlife and Countryside Act 1981.

RUPERT BELOFF

Bloody Assizes The Bloody Assizes followed in the wake of the failed rebellion of James, Duke of Monmouth in June 1685. Monmouth, who was the oldest, but illegitimate, son of Charles II sought to cause a rebellion in the south-western counties of England whilst the Duke of Argyll would do likewise in Scotland. The target of Monmouth's rebellion was to seize the throne from his uncle, the Roman Catholic James II and to rule as a

Protestant king. Although Monmouth was popular, his raggle taggle army of clothworkers and non-conformists did not attract support from the gentry and nobility and was no match for James' forces led by Major-General John Churchill, later the Duke of Malborough. Argyll was captured and executed before he could muster his troops. Monmouth was defeated at the battle of Sedgemoor in Somerset; he was captured, and beheaded at Tower Hill on 15 July 1685.

With the defeat of Monmouth, James II ordered the Lord Chief Justice George Jeffreys, 1st Baron Jeffreys of Wem, and four other judges to travel to the Western Circuit to try the rebels. Jeffreys had been one of the leading criminal barristers of his day, acting as counsel for the Crown in prosecuting treason and sedition trials. As a judge he maintained steadfast loyalty to the crown in crimes of state, but had built a good reputation in the legal profession as a fair judge in matters of civil litigation.

Jeffreys travelled from Winchester through the Western Circuit in September 1685 hearing the treason trials of the rebels and those who harboured them. As was common for the period, the judicial process was short but many of the accused were represented by counsel, notably Henry Pollexfen. Approximately 2,600 people were detained on charges linked to the uprising and nearly half of these confessed, hoping to receive pardon or clemency. Jeffreys acted in close confidence with James II, recommending those whom he felt should be granted clemency. James, whose crown had long been rendered insecure by Whig and Protestant opponents, took vengeance against his enemies by denying clemency in the majority of cases. In all, 1,381 people were tried and between 200 and 300 people were executed. The most infamous execution was that of the octogenarian Lady Alicia Lisle, whose crime was to harbour some of the rebels. The majority of those not executed were transported to the West Indies to serve as penal labourers.

The term 'Bloody Assizes' derives from James Tutchin's book entitled '*The Protestant Martyrs, or the Bloody Assizes*' (1688). The title of this work of Whig/Williamite propaganda, echoed that of the perennially popular Foxe's *Book of Martyrs* and immediately captured the popular imagination. On its front page, Tutchin's book referred to Jeffreys as 'that bloody and cruel judge'. Although modern historians contend that the sentences meted out by Jeffreys were unexceptional for early modern English rebellions, his reputation has been for ever besmirched as a result of his role in the trials of Monmouth's rebels.   ELLIOT VERNON

Bloody Sunday inquiries   'Bloody Sunday' refers to the events in Derry/Londonderry, Northern Ireland, on Sunday 30 January 1972 when members of the parachute regiment of the British Army opened fire on a civil rights demonstration, killing thirteen participants and injuring a further fourteen. One of the wounded subsequently died as a result of his injuries.

Widespread domestic and international condemnation led to the creation of an official **inquiry**, chaired by Lord Widgery (at the time, **Lord Chief Justice** of England and Wales). The final Report of the Widgery **Tribunal** largely exonerated the Army and suggested there was 'strong suspicion' that a number of those killed had been bombers or were handling weapons. This conclusion was reached following an investigation which was widely criticized as partial and incomplete: the entire process was concluded in less than eleven weeks, key witnesses were not called (including some of those injured during the events), and a number of eye-witness accounts given to the inquiry were not incorporated into the final report.

The events of Bloody Sunday—combined with the perceived cover-up of the Widgery Tribunal—had a cataclysmic impact on the course of political events in Northern Ireland, hardening Nationalist and Republican attitudes towards the British state and bolstering the case of those who believed that non-violence was futile. For decades, the families of those killed and injured on Bloody Sunday campaigned to clear the names of their loved ones. Finally, in January 1998, a new public inquiry was announced by then British Prime Minister, Tony Blair. The Bloody Sunday Tribunal—also known as the 'Saville Inquiry'—became the largest, most complex, and most expensive public inquiry in British legal history. The Tribunal was created under the Tribunals of Inquiry (Evidence) Act 1921, which granted powers to compel evidence equivalent to those of the English High Court. Statements were taken from around 2,500 individuals over a five-year period (March 2000 to January 2005). Although part of the trial was held in London—following a Court of Appeal ruling that it would be unsafe for soldiers to give evidence in Derry/Londonderry—deliberations were held in public and daily updates of proceedings were made available online.

Despite initial optimism that this investigation would finally provide the definitive explanation of events which has been so long overdue, the Saville Inquiry has been increasingly criticized, in particular for its exorbitant costs (a total of more than £180 million, around half of which was paid in legal fees) and a failure punctually to release the Inquiry's findings. The Inquiry concluded its investigations in 2005 and publication of its Report was scheduled for summer 2006. At the time of writing (January 2008), public release of the Report has been postponed until at least summer 2008. As a result, through the Saville Inquiry, Bloody Sunday continues to exert a significant role in shaping public and political opinion, this time regarding the appropriate role for truth recovery and historical inquiry in Northern Ireland.

KIRSTEN MCCONNACHIE

A Hegarty 'Truth, Law and Official Denial: The Case of Bloody Sunday' (2004) 15 *Criminal Law Forum* 199–246

board of directors   Companies can only operate through the agency of their human participants. In modern companies, extensive powers to manage and oversee the company's business are vested by the articles of association in the **directors** acting collectively as a board. It is therefore the board of directors, rather than the members, which has authority to act and transact in the company's name and on its behalf. It does not follow that the **company** can *only* act and transact through the board. The board is free to authorize individual directors or employees below board level to act on the company's behalf, either generally or in relation to particular areas of the company's business. Similarly, the board may delegate some or all of its powers to a managing director or chief executive. The wide scope that the board has to tailor the company's operational arrangements reflects the diversity of companies in terms of size, business, and organizational structure.

Given the extensive nature of board power, there is a need to ensure that it remains properly accountable to the company's members. Legal mechanisms designed to ensure **accountability** include the power of the members to remove the directors from office and **directors' duties**. In addition, companies whose shares are listed on the stock exchange are required to appoint independent non-executive directors from outside the company onto the board to monitor the activities of the executive directors.

ADRIAN WALTERS

Board of Inland Revenue v Haddock   Under the Bills of Exchange Act 1882 a cheque must be 'in writing.' Usually such writing is on paper, but the words in their ordinary meaning do not so require: a lapidary inscription, for example, is plainly 'in writing'.

Yet when Albert Haddock tendered to the Collector of Taxes a cheque stencilled in red ink on the back and sides of a white cow the Collector declined to accept delivery and Haddock found himself sued

for the unpaid tax and charged with various public order offences. The Court rejected both the claim and the charges, accepting Haddock's submission that 'an order to pay is an order to pay, whether it is made on the back of an envelope or on the back of a cow'.

Penning cheques on the hides of living animals seems not to have become a widespread custom, but *Haddock's* case should not on this ground be dismissed as obsolete. Its reasoning has never been challenged. Even after the adoption of clearing mechanisms reliant on numerals printed in magnetic ink on the cheque forms they supply to customers, English banks have shrunk from stipulating for contractual terms compelling customers always to use those forms in drawing cheques. The continuing significance of *Haddock* lies in the Court's refusal to construe a statutory prescription so expansively as to impede innovation in banking practice. The Automatic Teller Machine and the giro system should be acknowledged as the progeny of Albert Haddock's cow.

(This fictitious case, created by the barrister, Parliamentarian and writer AP Herbert, has passed into popular culture as a real case and is legally correct as a statement of banking law.)   D F DUGDALE

body parts   Human body parts may be removed during surgery and other human material during diagnostic or therapeutic procedures, research, and forensic testing (to establish identity or relationships). Hospitals and laboratories often retain excised human material for re-testing, other forensic use, research, or quality assurance. Human material, or genetic information derived from it, may be used in developing pharmaceutical products.

Unlawful removal of body parts or other human material from a person is a trespass and compensation may be awarded without proof of fault or loss. Removal is lawful with consent from the person or legally authorized surrogate; under statutory authority (eg post-mortem examinations; blood tests for alcohol or drugs after road accidents); or under a court order (eg for paternity testing). Excised tissue may be used in research with the person's consent or, in some circumstances, approval from an ethics committee.

At **common law** excised human material is not legally the 'property' of the person from whom it came; and people do not 'own' their bodies, excised body parts, or bodily material. However, an institution or person lawfully acquiring excised human material has a right to possession that entitles them to protect their interest against others (eg by legal proceedings if the material is removed without authority; or by insurance). Those who apply skill in refining excised human material (eg developing cell lines) may gain rights in the material and information from it that enable commercialisation.

Legislation (eg the Human Tissue Act 2004) commonly prohibits buying and selling human material, subject to limited exceptions.   LOANE SKENE

body samples   *see* **crime investigation by police**

body, law and the   The modern body politic is based on the masculine body. It embodies fantasies about that body, its capacities, and value. The imagined bounded, impermeable, and invulnerable male body is a general referent for both public policy and law. Much academic work has explored the place of the body in law; particularly the bodies that do not mirror the privileged male body. Attention has been paid to the role of corporeal specificity in determining social and political participation. At different times slaves, women, children, and the working classes have all been excluded from political participation on the basis of their bodily specificity. Feminist analysis in particular has explored the body as both subject and object of legal discourse. Such analysis has, *inter alia*, highlighted the role of the body in excluding women from the public sphere in terms of both political participation and areas of employment. Law has constructed very different relationships for men and women towards (re)production with women constructed as passive and reproductive but to a large extent unproductive. At the same time, the female body is at times narrated within reproduction as dangerous and volatile; sanctioning a higher degree of medico-legal surveillance and control. Whilst feminist work has done much to uncover the particularity of the female body of law, the male body has been a more recent focus for scholarship. The imagined invulnerable male body has left the health interests of this body at times unarticulated and under-protected.

MICHAEL THOMSON

M Gatens, 'Corporeal Representation in/and the Body Politic', in R Diprose and R. Ferrell, *Cartographies: Poststructuralism and the Mapping of Bodies and Spaces* (Sydney: Allen and Unwin, 1991), 79 at 84

C Daniels, *Exposing Men: The Science and Politics of Male Reproduction* (New York: Oxford University Press, 2006)

Bolton v Stone (1951)   Few cases in the history of the **common law** are as well known as that of *Bolton v Stone* (1951). On an afternoon in August 1947,

members of the Cheetham and Denton St Lawrence 2nd XI were playing cricket at Cheetham's ground in Manchester when a batsman hit a cricket ball over the fence. The ball hit Miss Bessie Stone, a resident of a street adjoining the ground. The ball struck Miss Stone in the head, and caused bleeding, but the wound later became infected and Miss Stone suffered significant pain and disablement as a result of the incident. She commenced proceedings, probably with the aid of solicitors acting *pro bono*, against three members of the management committee of the Cheetham Cricket Club, alleging, essentially, that the cricket club had been careless in allowing cricket to be played in circumstances where a ball could be hit out of the ground and cause injury to a pedestrian or home owner. In May 1951 the **House of Lords** found for the cricket club, although it seems the club allowed Miss Stone to keep the damages she was awarded by winning the earlier appeal to the Court of Appeal.

The legal significance of *Bolton v Stone* lies in its recognition that a finding of carelessness requires an assessment of the probability that the risk created by the defendant's conduct will result in injury. In *Bolton* the evidence suggested that a cricket ball had been hit out of the ground less than ten times in nearly thirty years. Given the remote possibility that a ball would be hit out of the ground, and the even more remote possibility that it might hit someone, the cricket club was not careless in continuing to allow cricket to be played at the ground without expending money to take additional precautions (such as raising the height of the fences) to prevent balls escaping from the ground. More generally, suggestions, made by the club to the press, that a decision against it would prevent or limit the opportunities for the cricket to be played, demonstrate the strength of the rhetoric that portrayed cricket as embodying all that was best about being English, a point emphasized by the MCC's decision to fund the club's appeal to the House of Lords. In fact, a simpler, more equitable solution to denying liability was available: cricket clubs could insure against the liability. It is now clear that such liability insurance was available at the time and it was only through an oversight that the Cheetham Cricket Club did not have this insurance. It is, perhaps, no surprise that no reported case has since reached the same result as *Bolton*. Even at the time, concern was expressed both judicially and in the press as to why Bessie Stone should suffer injury without recompense in the wider public interest of playing cricket, and later commentators have seen it as the paradigm case where **compensation** should be paid irrespective of fault.   MARK LUNNEY

See also: **negligence in civil law; pro bono legal services**

bona fide purchaser The principle of *bona fide* purchase determines the priority of competing claims to property. It allows a new proprietor to take the property free of the rights of another person who could have enforced some claim to it. It is an exception to the general rule that existing claims to property normally bind a new proprietor to whom it is transferred.

The rule developed in the Court of Chancery where it was applied to resolve disputes over the priority of equitable claims to many different kinds of property. The classic instance was of a trustee who wrongfully transferred land subject to a trust. The new proprietor took the land free of the trust beneficiary's claim, if he or she purchased it for valuable consideration, in good faith and without notice of the trustee's breach of duty. The Court regarded the conscience of a *bona fide* purchaser for value as completely clear. There was no equitable justification for enforcing the trust against the purchaser. In land transfers, the rule has now largely been replaced by the priority rules of the land title registration system.

Outside equity, the rule occasionally applies to determine the priority of competing **common law** claims to property. So a *bona fide* purchaser of stolen money will take it free of the original owner's surviving legal claim. Here the rule facilitates the free circulation of money as a medium of exchange by removing the need for the payee to inquire into the payer's title.   DAVID FOX

See also: **breach of trust; Chancery court; contract law; equity as a system of law; registration of title; trusts**

bonus pay   *see* **wages and deductions**

border control of intellectual property One of the major innovations introduced by the **World Trade Organization Agreement on Trade Related Aspects of Intellectual Property Rights ('TRIPs')** was provision for the enforcement of intellectual property rights by customs authorities at national borders. The Declaration of Trade Ministers which launched the Uruguay Round of the **General Agreement on Tariffs and Trade ('GATT')** in 1986 was precipitated by the perception that the trade in goods which infringed intellectual property rights was of such a large scale that it diverted a significant volume of trade away from legitimate traders. The USA estimated in 1986 that its losses to counterfeiters of trade-marked products and to pirates of **copyright** goods was in the vicinity of $60 billion annually,

involving a loss of employment for 200,000 of its workers. Similarly, as the EC Green Paper, *Combating Counterfeiting and Piracy in the Single Market* (1998) observed: 'since the early 1980s counterfeiting and piracy have grown considerably to a point where they have now become a widespread phenomenon with a global impact'.

The reasons for growth in counterfeiting and piracy are various. They include developments in reprographic technologies, where digitization has facilitated the rapid and extensive production of copies at a minimal cost, the growth in world demand for branded items, as well as economic and political developments, such as the growth of international trade, the internationalization of the economy, the expansion of means of communication and the opportunism of organized crime following the collapse of the political systems in central and eastern Europe and in the former Soviet Union.

In addition to trade diversion and its employment implications the trade, in infringing goods results in losses of State revenue (taxes and customs duties). There may also be infringements of labour legislation where the counterfeit or pirated goods are made in sweatshops by undeclared workers. The phenomenon is a serious threat to economies in general as it may destabilize markets, including such fragile markets as that in textiles, and clothing. Counterfeiting and piracy likewise have damaging consequences for consumers. They generally involve deliberately deceiving the consumer about the quality to be expected from products bearing well-known **trade marks**. Counterfeiting and piracy also has an adverse effect upon public security, where profits from this trade are appropriated by organized crime, which uses them as a means of recycling and laundering the proceeds of other unlawful activities (trading in arms, drugs, etc).

Given the concern about the trade in pirated and counterfeit goods which precipitated the interest of the GATT in intellectual property protection, it was probably to be expected that the architects of TRIPs would look to the customs authorities to assist in the interdiction of this trade. It is obviously more effective to seize a single shipment of infringing products while they are in transit than to await their distribution in the market. Section 4 of Part III of TRIPs establishes a scheme for suspension of the release into circulation of 'counterfeit trademark goods' or 'pirated copyright goods'. Release may be suspended on the application of a right holder or as a result of *ex officio* action by border authorities.

The key border control provision of TRIPS is Article 51 which requires Members to:

adopt procedures to enable a right holder, who has valid grounds for suspecting that the importation of counterfeit trademark or pirated copyright goods may take place, to lodge an application with competent authorities, administrative or judicial, for the suspension by the customs authorities of the release into free circulation of such goods.

As a footnote to this provision, the term 'counterfeit trademark goods' is defined to mean 'any goods, including packaging, bearing without authorization a trademark which is identical to the trademark validly registered in respect of such goods, or which cannot be distinguished in its essential aspects from such a trademark, and which thereby infringes the rights of the owner of the trademark in question under the law of the country of importation'. The term 'pirated copyright goods' is defined to mean 'any goods which are copies made without consent of the rights holder in the country of production and which are made directly or indirectly from any article where the making of that copy would have constituted an infringement of a copyright or a related right under the law of the country of importation'.

In addition to the suspension of release of goods bearing a suspected counterfeit trade mark, or which are pirated copyright goods, Article 51 also provides that an application for suspension may also be made in respect of goods suspected of infringing other intellectual property rights, such as goods carrying ornamentation which infringes a registered design or the production of which involved a patented process.

Article 58 of TRIPs envisages that Members may permit the competent authorities to act upon their own initiative in suspending the release of goods where they have *prima facie* evidence that an intellectual property right is being infringed. In these circumstances the Article permits the competent authorities to 'seek from the right holder any information that may assist them to exercise these powers'.

The border control provisions of TRIPs have been implemented by WTO Members in their national legislation and in the EU by Council Regulation 3295/94 (amended by Council Regulation (EC) 1383/2003). The World Customs Organization, which is the key collaborating body of national customs offices, has drafted a model border control law for national implementation.

A survey conducted by the **World Intellectual Property Organization ('WIPO')** in 2002 indicated that the principal barriers to eliminating counterfeiting and piracy did not reside in the substantive law, but rather in the remedies and penalties available (or not available) to stop and deter counterfeiting and piracy. The ineffectiveness of enforcement systems was attributed, in many cases, to a lack of human resources and funding and of practical experience in intellectual property enforcement on the part of relevant officials, including the judiciary; insufficient knowledge on the part of right holders and the general public concerning their rights and remedies; and systemic problems resulting from insufficient national and international coordination, including a lack of transparency.   MICHAEL BLAKENEY

See also: **designs; excise duties; patents**

boundaries in international law   *see* **territory**

boundaries in land law   The boundaries of an owner's property, whether freehold or leasehold, are recorded in the title documents. By agreement, a holding's size may be reduced by sub-division or increased by amalgamation. If the documentary definition is imprecise, and without other evidence, certain presumptions can apply, eg property bounded by a non-tidal river extends to the centre of the stream. The title plan of registered property does not generally show precise boundaries, although there is a procedure for fixing precise boundaries. Those plans are based on the Ordnance Survey, whose mapping conventions—eg showing boundaries running down the centre line of hedges and fences—can differ from traditional presumptions and from what neighbouring landowners intended.

Vertical boundaries can also be defined, eg by describing part only of a building or by separating ownership of the surface of land from the minerals underneath. If there is no restriction, ownership in Scotland extends infinitely upwards and downwards, but in England and Wales it goes only so far as required for the satisfactory use of the land.

A landowner has no general duty to fence boundaries. In some circumstances, it is required: eg by agreement with neighbouring owners and to prevent access to dangerous places. A wall dividing two properties is a party wall. In England and Wales, the adjoining owners have extensive statutory rights and obligations to use the wall, extend it, repair it and not to damage it. In Scotland, a wall is normally a joint responsibility only if it straddles the boundary.

                    TREVOR ALDRIDGE

See also: **registration of title**

boycotts   *see* **strikes**

Bracton, Henry de   Henry de Bracton was probably born at Bratton Fleming in Devon. By 1238 he had entered the service of the senior royal justice, William Raleigh, as one of his clerks; Raleigh had been rector of Bratton Fleming since 1212. Bracton became a royal justice in the mid-1240s but his judicial career was brief. He served as a junior justice for two county eyre visitations in 1245 and as a junior justice of King's Bench from 1247–1251 and from 1253–1257. Bracton also pursued a parallel clerical career. By 1249 he had become a canon of Wells Cathedral. He was appointed archdeacon of Barnstaple in 1264 and held the chancellorship of Exeter Cathedral from 1264 till his death in 1268. The treatise that bears his name is the most ambitious English legal work of the Middle Ages, conceived on a grand scale as a survey of the whole of the English **common law**, with supporting citations of decided cases. What now survives is only part of the work as originally envisaged. Even so, the book is around ten times the length of the only previous general English common law treatise, *Glanvill*. Its main topics are the acquisition and transmission of property rights, the criminal law and the working of the different kinds of real action for the assertion of rights over land, and other forms of real property. *Bracton* is clearly the work of an author with knowledge of Roman and **canon law** as well as common law, but just how expert he was in the 'learned laws' remains controversial. The belief that Henry de Bracton was the author of *Bracton* can be traced back to within a few years of his death. It remained unchallenged until 1977 when SE Thorne, its latest editor and translator, argued that Bracton can only have been the reviser of the book, not its original author, for parts of the treatise must have been written prior to the mid-1230s and this does not fit what is known of Henry de Bracton's life and career. Thorne's view is now generally, though not universally, accepted. A more plausible candidate for authorship is the senior royal justice whom Bracton had served as clerk. Raleigh's authorship would explain the author's knowledge of what Martin of Pattishall, a judge of an earlier generation, had said and done in court and his occasional use of the great justice's first name. Raleigh had served Pattishall as a clerk before becoming a justice. The manuscript of the treatise was evidently entrusted to Bracton to revise and update. He made some revisions but seems to have abandoned work on the treatise by the mid-1250s, more than a decade before his own death. This apparent abandonment of work on the treatise by its author has always seemed puzzling. It is much less so if it was a reviser who was giving up the unequal struggle to update a book written by another.   PAUL BRAND

breach of contract   *see* contract law

breach of statutory duty   *see* statutory duty, civil liability for breach of

breach of the peace   A form of misbehaviour which is a criminal offence in Scotland and which, though not a criminal offence as such in England and Wales or in Northern Ireland, may justify the summary **arrest** of a person in order to prevent its commission, and in respect of which the person responsible may also be 'bound over'—ie required to promise to abstain from it in future, on pain of forfeiting a sum of money known as a 'recognizance'. If the legal consequences of committing a breach of the peace are clear, less certain are the types of behaviour that potentially amount to one. In Scotland, the criminal offence exists 'at **common law**' and, in the absence of a statutory definition, originally meant virtually any conduct of which the court disapproved: including, famously, a man parading around the red light area of Aberdeen clad in woman's clothing (*Stewart v Lockhart* (1990)); but modern Scottish case law limits it to behaviour 'severe enough to cause alarm to ordinary people, and threaten serious disorder to the community' (*Smith v Donnelly* (2001)). In England, the Court of Appeal in *Howell* (1982) said that 'there is a breach of the peace whenever harm is actually done or is likely to be done to a person or in his presence to his property or a person is in fear of being so harmed through an assault, an affray, a riot, unlawful assembly or other disturbance'; a definition later approved by the House of Lords in *R (Laporte) v Chief Constable of Gloucestershire* (2006). But wider definitions can be found in other cases: notably from the Court of Appeal in *R v Chief Constable of Devon and Cornwall, ex p Central Electricity Generating Board* (1982).   JOHN SPENCER

See also: **Beatty v Gillbanks** (1882); binding over; criminal regulation of public order

breach of trust   A trustee commits a breach of trust whenever he or she acts, or fails to act, in a way that is contrary to the duties of a trustee. Common forms of breach of trust include: (a) failure to comply with the obligations imposed by the terms of the trust instrument; (b) acting in an unauthorized manner outside of the trustee's powers; and (c) failure to meet the obligations of care and loyalty imposed on trustees in the conduct of their trusteeship. A trustee must account for his or her stewardship of the trust property, and so the trustee can be held personally liable for his or her breach of trust.

Where more than one trustee is liable for a breach of trust, their liability is joint and several.

Where trust property has been disposed of in breach of the terms of the trust, the breach of trust can potentially be remedied by a court forcing the recipient to re-transfer the trust property back to the trustee. However, such an order cannot be made against someone who has purchased legal title to the trust property in good faith without any notice of the breach of trust. If the trust property cannot be restored to the trust, the trustee is liable, at his or her own personal expense, to restore the trust fund to the state in which it would have been had there been no breach of trust (eg by replacing the original trust property with equivalent property from another source, or by payment of monetary **compensation** for the property which has been lost); otherwise the trustee is unable to comply with his or her obligation to distribute the trust property at the relevant time.

Similarly, if the trustee has acted imprudently in his or her management of the trust fund (eg by investing trust property in authorised but imprudent investments), the trustee is liable to repair any damage done, by placing the trust fund in the position in which it would have been had the trustee acted prudently.

Where a trustee has personally profited as a result of a breach of trust, the beneficiaries have a right to claim that profit for the benefit of the trust fund, thereby stripping it from the trustee. The obligation to account for profits extends to any property into which the trustee may have invested the illegitimate profit, and the trustee holds such property on constructive trust for the beneficiaries.

Third parties who are not trustees can also be held personally liable for participating in a breach of trust, but only in limited circumstances. Primary among these circumstances are those where the third party has dishonestly assisted the trustee in committing the breach of trust, and where the third party has dissipated trust property, so that it cannot be restored to the trust fund *in specie*, despite having received it with knowledge that makes retention of the benefit of the property unconscionable.

MATTHEW CONAGLEN

See also: **bona fide purchaser; constructive trusts; equity as a system of law; joint liability; restitution; trusts**

Brehon law The early Irish had a distinctive legal system, which in English was called 'Brehon law' from the Irish word *breitheamh* ('judge'). The documents which describe this system date mainly from the seventh and eighth centuries CE, but it is clear that it continued in use in parts of Gaelic Ireland until the subjugation of the native lords by the English monarch at the beginning of the seventeenth century. About fifty law texts survive in late copies, mainly in fourteenth to sixteenth century manuscripts now held in the libraries of Trinity College, Dublin, the Royal Irish Academy and the Bodleian Library, Oxford. Many short fragments also survive from other lost texts.

The law texts cover a wide range of subjects, ranging from general topics such as injury, theft, suretyship, **marriage**, evidence, **theft**, contracts, etc, to highly specialized treatments of the legal aspects of bee-keeping and ownership of watermills. Throughout the law texts there is great emphasis on rank. A person's rank is reflected in his 'honour-price', the sum payable to him (or to his relatives) in the event of any offence against his honour, ranging from insult to murder. The honour-price of a dependant is a proportion of that of his or her legal superior. Thus, the honour-price of a chief wife is half that of her husband, whereas that of a subsidiary wife or concubine is only one third. In general, the evidence of a high-ranking person outweighs that of one of lower rank. The texts also lay great stress on the legal obligations attached to membership of the kin. If a person failed to fulfil these obligations he could be ejected from the kin, thereby losing his rights in society.

Crime was normally punishable by a heavy fine, usually of cattle. If the culprit was unable to pay the fine from his own or his kin's resources, he could be enslaved. The death penalty was only employed as a last resort. No case law has survived from the early period, but it is clear that cases were commonly heard in open-air courts. The advocate for each party entered a plea, and evidence was heard from witnesses. The judgment was pronounced by one or more judges. If necessary, it was enforced by sureties. An appeal could be made to a superior court, but if it was rejected, the appellant had to pay a heavy fine to the original judge.

The basic character of early Irish law can be traced back into the prehistory of the Celtic-speaking peoples, as there is a good deal of agreement in the terminology employed in early Irish, Welsh and Breton legal material. However, there was also strong influence from Canon law, and the law texts recognized the central position of the church in early Irish society, and assigned special status and privileges to the clergy.

FERGUS KELLY

F Kelly, *A Guide to Early Irish Law* (Dublin: Dublin Institute for Advanced Studies, 1988)

Liam Breatnach, *A Companion to the Corpus Iuris Hibernici* (Dublin: Dublin Institute for Advanced Studies, 2005)

See also: **common law in Ireland; Welsh law**

brides in the bath   *see* **Smith, George Joseph**

British Broadcasting Corporation   *see* **public service broadcasting**

British citizenship   British **citizenship** is a complex legal web reflecting Britain's imperial era in intricate detail. The complexity of British citizenship law distinguishes it from that of most similarly situated nations. At the height of the British Empire, British **subjects** were permitted entry throughout the empire. This freedom was significant in establishing migration patterns through the twentieth century as migration became increasingly regulated. It also provided a sure migration route from former colonies to Britain itself until such time as the former imperial power also sought to shut it down. This animated the law reform which remains the basis of British citizenship law.

The British Nationality Act 1981 came into force on 1 January 1983. It set out three separate citizenships: British citizenship, British Dependent Territories citizenship, and British Overseas citizenship. Each of these categories represents a different set of rights and entitlements, with the status of British citizen having the highest value.

British citizenship corresponds most directly with the use of the term 'citizenship' around the world. People became British citizens on 1 January 1983 if they were previously citizens of the United Kingdom and Colonies and had unrestricted rights to enter and live in Britain under immigration **legislation**. British citizens can generally pass on this status to their children, whether the children are born in Britain or elsewhere. There are some exceptions to this, notably, if the parent citizen has British citizenship solely on the basis of descent and the **child** is also born abroad, or if a British father is not married to the child's non-British mother.

The status of British Dependent Territories citizenship was largely abolished in 2002, but its logic and demise are an illustration of the colonial recasting of British citizenship. People who, in 1983, had close connections to British Dependent territories, but not to Britain itself, acquired this status. In general, people would lose the status when the territory they lived in (or were closely connected to) became an independent country, or, in the case of Hong Kong, merged with an existing independent country. The 2002 legislative change transformed British Dependent Territories citizens into British Overseas Territories citizens for a few months, and

then into British citizens. There is a minor exception for people whose sole connection is with sovereign bases in Cyprus, and for some children of British Overseas citizens. These people remain British Overseas Territories citizens. The 2002 changes were a significant step in aligning British citizenship law more closely with the citizenship law of other liberal democracies.

British Overseas citizenship is the status that was accorded to people who were citizens of the United Kingdom and Colonies at the end of 1982, but who did not qualify as either citizens or dependent territories citizens. British Overseas citizens cannot generally pass their citizenship on to children. However exceptions to this rule apply if the child was born in British territory or would otherwise be stateless. British Overseas citizens can apply for British Citizenship after five years residency in the UK.

In addition to these principal categories of British citizenship, British law also recognizes the categories of British subject, Commonwealth citizen, and British national, which adds further confusion to this terrain.

The category of British subject encompasses people who held that status prior to the 1948 creation of citizenship of the United Kingdom and Colonies. In 1948, those ineligible for Citizens of the UK and Colonies ('CUKC') status, and similarly ineligible for citizenship in another Commonwealth country, remained British subjects. This residual category was preserved in the 1981 law reform, and, like the status of British Overseas citizen, provides one route towards British citizenship if supplemented by a period of residency in the UK.

Commonwealth citizenship refers simply to citizenship in any country which is a member of the Commonwealth. It does not confer any rights separate or additional to the rights of citizenship in member states. It is therefore not functionally similar to **citizenship of the European Union.**

The category of British national acquired a unique meaning during the negotiations surrounding the end of British rule in Hong Kong. When Hong Kong was returned to the People's Republic of China in 1997, British Dependent Territories citizens there generally lost this status. However, special rules were created in 1986 allowing registration in the newly created category of British National (Overseas). This is somewhat misleading as the category of 'national' is for most countries simply the international equivalent of 'citizenship'. Like British subjects, British Nationals (Overseas) can apply for British citizenship after a period of residency.

Despite these intricacies, British citizenship now conforms in broad brush strokes with the major trends in citizenship laws of Western liberal democracies: birthright citizenship is available only to the children of those with citizenship or permanent migration status; citizenship by descent is limited to one generation; dual citizenship is permitted (although British subjects who become citizens in another country lose their subject status).

CATHERINE DAUVERGNE

See also: **nationality**

British Commonwealth   *see* **Commonwealth of Nations**

British Standards Institution   *see* **safety standards quality of products**

British Transport Police   *see* **crime investigation other than by police**

broadcasters' rights   *see* **neighbouring rights**

broadcasting   *see* **media, regulation and freedom of**

Brown v Board of Education (1954)   *Plessy v Ferguson* (1896) upheld the constitutionality of state laws requiring the separation of the races on private railroads. The decision, asserting that segregation was permissible if the separate facilities were otherwise equal in quality, validated and encouraged the spread of the US system of 'Jim Crow', segregating whites and African Americans in public as well as private institutions.

In the 1930s the National Association for the Advancement of Colored People ('NAACP') began to challenge the 'separate but equal' doctrine in lawsuits successfully demonstrating that the educational facilities available to African Americans were markedly inferior from those available to whites. The cases effectively undermined the foundations of the 'separate but equal' doctrine, and in 1950 the NAACP's lawyers decided to seek a ruling overturning the doctrine itself in its application to elementary and secondary education.

Five lawsuits from different areas of the nation were consolidated for decision in *Brown v Board of Education*, which involved the segregated schools in Topeka, Kansas. Because of the justices' inability to come up with a rationale for overruling *Plessy*, the Court deferred decision after the cases were initially argued. Before they were re-argued Chief Justice Fred Vinson, who was sympathetic to the claim that

overruling *Plessy* would disrupt the Southern social order, died and was replaced by Earl **Warren**, who led the fractious justices to a unanimous decision.

Warren wrote the Court's short opinion, hoping to make it accessible to readers who were not lawyers. The legal issue was whether the Fourteenth Amendment's guarantee of equal protection of the laws permitted racial segregation by law. Finding the original understanding of the guarantee unclear, the Court emphasized the role of education in contemporary society, concluding that '[s]eparate educational facilities are inherently unequal'. Directing attention to modern psychological studies, Warren wrote that separating children 'solely because of their race generates a feeling of inferiority as to their status in the community that may affect their hearts and minds in a way unlikely ever to be overcome'.

Segregated education prevailed throughout the American South, and displacing it proved difficult. The Court put off for a year deciding what it should order states with segregated systems to do, eventually holding that states should begin to desegregate immediately and then should implement desegregation plans 'with all deliberate speed'. Border states with segregated schools generally did so, but the states of the deep South, including Mississippi, Alabama, and South Carolina, engaged in a programme of 'massive resistance', erecting legal barriers to desegregation and encouraging violent resistance. That resistance delayed desegregation in the deep South for more than a decade.

Ambiguously successful as a matter of social policy, *Brown* is nonetheless a central symbol of the American constitutional commitment to racial equality even as the precise meaning of racial equality remains contested. It is also the decision routinely used to demonstrate the value to the United States of the Supreme Court's power to invalidate legislation on constitutional grounds.   MARK TUSHNET

See also: **race discrimination; United States Supreme Court**

bugging   *see* **surveillance, surreptitious**

bullying at work   *see* **harassment**

burden of proof   *see* **evidence (civil); evidence (criminal)**

business organization, forms of   For anyone thinking about setting up a business in the UK, there are several types of business organization from which one could select. There are two important distinctions to consider when determining what type of organization is best suited to the endeavour the person forming the organization has in mind. First, is the form of business organization a separate legal **person**, that is, a corporate body which is recognized by the law to be a legal person with rights similar to that of a real person, for example, the ability to own property? Second, does the form of organization provide that the members are responsible for the debts of the organization or are those members shielded from liability for such debts?

In this regard one might distinguish between, on the one hand, the organizational form of a **company**, which is a separate legal person and, one would typically assume, has **limited liability** so that its members are not liable for the company's debts, and, on the other hand, the organizational form of a **partnership** which is not a separate legal person and whose partners are indeed liable for the partnership's debts. Whilst there is much truth in this distinction, a closer look at business organization forms reveals greater complexity.

All companies formed in accordance with the Companies Act 1985 and the Companies Act 2006 (expected to be fully in force in Autumn 2009) are separate legal persons (bodies corporate) that may, amongst others, own property, enter into contracts, sue, and be sued. However, a company can be formed with limited liability or with unlimited liability (where the members are responsible for the company's debts). Typically, a company is formed with limited liability. The company may be a company limited by shares or by guarantee. The former provides that members (shareholders) are liable to pay only what they agreed to pay for the shares, the latter the amount set forth in the guarantee. Typically companies are limited by shares. Companies limited by guarantee are often used for bodies carrying out governmental functions.

A further distinction must also be made between whether the company is a **public company** or a **private company**. A public company must have the words 'public limited company' or Plc after its name. A private company has to have 'limited' or 'Ltd' after its name. A public company may, although need not, issues its shares to the public at large. A private company may not do so. It is possible, however, to convert a private company into a public company and vice versa.

General partnerships, on the other hand, are not bodies corporate; they are merely associations of individuals carrying on business together to make a profit (see Partnership Act 1890). The partnership itself, for example, does not own property; rather 'its' property is owned in by its partners as tenants in common. Its partners are liable for the debts of the partnership. However, if a partnership is a limited partnership it is possible to have limited partners, sometimes colloquially referred to as silent partners, who are not liable for any amount in excess of what they agreed to invest in the partnership. They lose this protection, however, if they directly undertake to manage or control the partnership business (Limited Partnerships Act 1907).

The separate legal person and limited liability distinctions between companies and partnerships has been recently unsettled by the introduction of the **limited liability partnership**, that is both a separate legal person and provides for limited liability for the partners (Limited Liability Partnerships Act 2000). It is probably best to ignore the word 'partnership' to understand this entity. It is really a form of company which is treated as a partnership for tax purposes and is subject to only certain aspects of the detailed regulation of the Companies Acts.

DAVID KERSHAW

See also: **corporate personality**

business rates   National non-domestic rates, or business rates, are a tax levied on non-residential properties, including shops, offices, warehouses, and factories. Companies pay a fixed proportion (44.4 per cent in England and Scotland and 44.8 per cent in Wales in 2007–2008) of the officially estimated market rent ('rateable value') of properties they occupy. Northern Ireland operates a slightly different system of regional rates and locally varying district rates, with an average combined rate of 49.5 per cent in 2007–2008.

Properties are revalued every five years. A revaluation took effect in April 2005, based on April 2003 rental values. Major changes in business rates bills caused by revaluation are phased in through a transitional relief scheme. Some types of property qualify for reductions, including unoccupied buildings, small rural shops, and agricultural land and associated buildings. Reduced rates apply to businesses with a low rateable value.

Business rates were transferred from local to national control in 1990. Rates are set by central government, with local authorities collecting the revenue and paying it into a central pool. Formally, this revenue is then redistributed back to local authorities; but since this amount is simply deducted from the grant that central government would have made to local authorities in any case, local authorities' income need not bear any relation to the amount that business rates bring in. However, the

Government proposes to allow English local authorities to levy a supplementary business rate of up to 2 per cent of rateable value on large properties under certain conditions from 2010–2011. Business rates were expected to raise £21.9 billion in 2007–2008, 4.0 per cent of total government revenue.

STUART ADAM

business taxation There are two key questions arising in relation to the taxation of a business. First, who should be taxed and secondly, what should be the tax base?

In relation to the first question, who is taxed depends upon the legal form of the business. The self-employed or sole trader, and partnerships will be subject to **income tax** charged to the individuals engaged in the business activity. Incorporated businesses are subject to **corporation tax,** although this tax is actually borne by the shareholders, consumers, and employees, the corporation being an artificial person which cannot in fact bear the tax itself. The corporation owners also pay **dividend tax** on profits distributed to them. This can bring problems of integrating the personal and corporate taxes to avoid double taxation. Approaches to this are discussed in the entry dealing with **corporation tax**. If the corporation tax rate is lower than the income tax rate, as is currently the case in the UK, business owners can incorporate, pay corporation tax at this lower rate and extract profits from the company through dividends, which carry a tax credit, so that the overall tax bill is lower that it would be for an unincorporated firm.

Businesses with premises in the UK pay **business rates,** as well as **stamp taxes** on land and shares, and securities and taxes on capital gains (although there are substantial exemptions from **capital gains tax** for businesses, and for business owners when they sell their business assets).

Businesses act as tax collectors for certain taxes. In the UK, employers are required to withhold income taxation from employees' wages under the Pay as You Earn ('**PAYE**') system and also to collect **national insurance** contributions (social security taxes), which are levied in part as deductions from employees' wages or salaries and in part as additional payments by employers. The **value added tax** ('VAT') is collected by businesses and the sums due are paid over to the government; but this is an indirect tax—that is, it is not borne by the person who pays it (the business) but is passed on to another (the ultimate consumer). Nevertheless, there may be a VAT cost to business where exemptions mean that costs cannot be passed on or reclaimed. In relation to

all these taxes, the compliance cost of tax gathering for business is considerable.

As regards the business tax base, in the UK income and corporation taxes on businesses are levied on business profits. For the individual, the business income is calculated separately from other income, and there are restrictions on the extent to which business losses for tax purposes can be set against taxable income from other sources. It is now provided by statute, following years of evolution through the case law, that taxable profit arising from business is calculated in accordance with generally accepted accounting practice, subject to any adjustment required or authorized by law in computing profits for those purposes. There are statutory adjustments often related to the different treatment of capital and income for tax purposes (for example, there are statutory depreciation provisions which override accounting practice). There are also special provisions in complex areas such as the taxation of financial instruments. In the past there have also been case law differences, but as commercial accounting standards become more professional and sophisticated, the courts seem to be increasingly likely to follow these for tax purposes, unless there is an express statutory direction to do otherwise. Profit definition can be problematic and the issue of timing of profits can be particularly difficult.

It would be possible to move away from profit as a tax base altogether and to move to a cash-flow basis of taxation of businesses, especially corporations. This would remove some of the problems of profit definition but, arguably, would introduce others (see **expenditure tax**).

JUDITH FREEDMAN

See also: **financial instruments, taxation of; tax administration and compliance costs**

business tenancies A lease of commercial property, such as a warehouse, car park, public house, and corner shop, is often described as a 'business tenancy'. While all types of tenancy share the same fundamental characteristics, major differences arise as to the statutory protection offered to the different types of tenant and the policy motivations underlying parliamentary intervention. Part II of the Landlord and Tenant Act 1954 is designed to protect business tenants from exploitation by their landlords. The policy is that business tenants should not, at the end of their leases, have to choose between renewal at a highly inflated rent, or business closure and associated loss of goodwill. The Part II provisions offer those tenants within its reach a qualified right to obtain a new lease at a market rent or, in certain circumstances, to obtain flat-rate compensation in lieu of renewal. During the interim period, the tenant is allowed to remain in occupation of the same premises essentially on the same terms as before. In recognition that the relationship is between commercial parties, however, there is no further erosion of the landlord's rights and there exists a generous facility which allows the parties to contract out of the legislative code before the lease is granted. This can be done by private agreement, following advance notice. The ability to contract out of the scheme makes it optional at the behest of the parties and also explains why this area of landlord and tenant law has proved immune to deregulation.

MICHAEL HALEY

See also: **leasehold estate**

Bywaters, Frederick and Thompson, Edith
Frederick Bywaters (1902–1923) and Edith Thompson (1893–1923) were tried in London in December 1922 for the murder of Thompson's husband Percy. The case was one of the most sensational in the post-war period, attracting enormous levels of press coverage and public interest, raising concerns about the regulation of the media and access to the courtroom. It also raised issues of evidence of common purpose.

Bywaters was a merchant seaman who had served in the navy during the war. He began a passionate affair with the older Edith Thompson in the summer of 1921, and was invited by an unsuspecting Percy Thompson to become a lodger in the couple's home in Ilford shortly afterwards. The affair continued throughout the following year, notwithstanding the periods when he was away at sea. On 3 October 1922 Percy Thompson was stabbed to death by a young man as he and Edith returned to their home following a night at the theatre. Edith Thompson, who was visibly distressed, identified Bywaters to the police as the assailant and referred to their relationship. Bywaters was then arrested, and after the police

discovered letters from Edith declaring her love and her willingness to do anything, even murder, to escape her husband, they also arrested her. Both were charged with murder.

At the trial the prosecution argued that Edith Thompson was the controlling figure in the relationship, influencing the younger, impressionable Bywaters, and that she had conceived and planned the crime. To prove this they relied on incriminating statements in the letters, in which Thompson claimed to have fed her husband broken glass and urging Bywaters to 'do something desperate'. There was, however, no physical evidence linking Thompson to the attack, and Bywaters consistently maintained that she knew nothing about it. The defence position that Thompson was merely a romantic dreamer was undermined when she insisted on giving evidence on her own behalf, as permitted following the Criminal Evidence Act 1898, apparently in a misguided attempt to save the life of Bywaters. Her testimony was confused and self-contradictory, and she was unable to explain why she had made certain statements in the letters. Both were found guilty and, in spite of a considerable public campaign for clemency, both were executed in January 1923.

The trial was one of the last major trials before the Criminal Justice Act 1925, section 41 prohibited the use of photography in court, and the press coverage contained a number of photographs of the defendants and jurors either in or entering the courtroom. Concerns were also raised following the trial about the practice of overnight queuing outside the courtroom, and the selling of places obtained by this means. Most importantly the trial, with its representation of Thompson as alternately a scheming adulteress and an innocent dreamer, generated extensive debate about the position of women and the institution of marriage. The events which led to the trial continue to inspire fictional representations in books and film.   LINDSAY FARMER

C

Cabinet   The Cabinet may be defined as a 'regular meeting of **Ministers of State**'. Neither the membership of the Cabinet nor its functions are specified by law. It usually consists of about twenty-three members, including the **Prime Minister**, the Home Secretary, the Foreign Secretary, the Chancellor of the Exchequer, the Lord President of the Council, the Lord Privy Seal, the **Lord Chancellor**, the Leaders of the **House of Commons** and the **House of Lords**, and other ministerial heads of government departments. The **Attorney-General**, as the senior **Crown** law officer, attends Cabinet meetings when required to do so. The Cabinet Secretary (the most senior civil servant) is also the Head of the **Civil Service**. The Cabinet Office, headed by the Cabinet Secretary, has around 1,800 staff and plays a key role in coordinating the work of government departments.

The work of the Cabinet has become progressively more complex and has generally expanded in recent times. Its main function is the formulation of policy at the highest level. Since the beginning of the twentieth century, the use of cabinet committees has increased. In 2005 there were around twenty-eight. The use of committees may cause tension within the main Cabinet as a result of a small, closely-knit group of ministers becoming more influential. The role and operation of the Cabinet in the conduct of government business depends largely on the mode of government preferred by the Prime Minister.

In principle, members of the Cabinet are bound by strict rules of secrecy and confidentiality. Cabinet papers are even unavailable to an incoming government of a different political party. In practice, however, members of the Cabinet may authorize 'leaks' to gain public support for the adoption of a political initiative or for some other purpose. Increasingly, too, ex-Cabinet ministers publish autobiographies and memoirs that purport to reveal the inner workings of Cabinet.

The 'cabinet system of government' is underpinned by the principle of collective **ministerial responsibility**. This means that all cabinet members are obliged to support the decisions reached by the cabinet. In the event that this is not possible they are expected to resign. There is a complex system of Cabinet committees that allows decisions to be taken outside the meeting of the whole Cabinet. This system is based largely on the desirability of specialization and the need for effective decision-making by smaller groups of ministers. Critics point to the existence of such committees as evidence of Prime Ministerial dominance, allowing the Prime Minister to bypass the full cabinet. This is also seen as the reason for the growth in Prime Ministerial power. A further criticism of the cabinet system is that it has become an ineffective means of controlling the work of the various government departments because of the volume and complexity of government business.

JOHN MCELDOWNEY

cable tv   *see* **digital television and radio regulation**

Calvo Doctrine/Calvo Clause   *see* **investment protection**

Canadian Charter of Rights and Freedoms   The Canadian Charter of Rights and Freedoms is part of the Canadian Constitution. It was a central element of constitutional renewal embarked upon by then Prime Minister, Pierre Trudeau, following his return to power in 1980. It was enacted as part of the Constitution Act 1982, and it was controversial in part because Trudeau failed to secure agreement from the government of the province of Quebec. However, the Charter applies to the federal and all provincial governments. It dramatically altered the principle of the supremacy of Parliament and the legislatures, because it empowers the **courts** to strike down **legislation**. But the drafters of the Charter made explicit that rights were subject to 'such reasonable limits prescribed by law as can be demonstrably justified in a free and democratic society'. The Charter also allows Parliament or a legislature to expressly declare that legislation 'shall operate notwithstanding' certain Charter rights, which was an attempt to answer concerns regarding the power of unelected **judges** to invalidate legislation. Charter rights include freedom of conscience and religion, expression, association, **equality**, language, and democratic rights, and 'life, liberty and security of the person'. Canadian courts have applied the Charter proactively in some fields (particularly the criminal law as well as equality rights), and more deferentially in those cases concerning economic policy choices. Some are critical of judicial activism by the Supreme Court of Canada in areas such as **abortion** and gay rights. Others argue that courts have been too reluctant to protect positive socio-economic rights.   CARL STYCHIN

Canadian law   *see* **Commonwealth law**

Cannibalism   *see* **Dudley and Stephens (R v)**

canon law   Canon law is the law of the church—so called because it is contained in canons, a word of Greek origin meaning measures, or norms, of right conduct. Such measures, enacted in ecclesiastical assemblies, have been a part of the life of the church from its first centuries, and even before the establishment of Christianity in the Roman Empire, norms were extracted from the writings of church fathers, secular law, and the Bible itself in order to provide guidance to the church's leaders—as for example the *Dicaché* (c. 100) and the *Didascalia Apostolorum* (c. 250–300). Early ecumenical councils, like that of Nicaea (325) or Chalcedon (451), also enacted canons regulating church government, religious practice, and moral conduct—even to the point of attempting to settle a controversy over whether worshippers should kneel or stand while praying. It is undeniable that over the centuries, antinominianism has been a temptation for spiritually minded men and women, but most Christian thinkers have regarded the creation of law as a necessary part of the life of the church. Today Orthodox, Catholic, and most Protestant churches have adopoted codes of canon law.

Despite its early start, before the twelfth century canon law played a relatively minor role in governance of the church. Promulgation of canons was local and occasional. No instruction in canon law was offered to the clergy. No system of courts existed to enforce its decrees. Canons were enacted and collected together throughout the early Middle Ages, but their authority was unclear, their invocation infrequent, and their coverage incomplete. There were ups and downs, but it was the arrival of the

movement for reform of the church led by the papacy and the revival of learning in the twelfth century that set the church's law on a more ambitious course. A signal event in the process was Gratian's compilation of the *Concordia canonum discordantium* (c. 1140). This collection of canons, apparently designed for use in teaching at the nascent university of Bologna, adopted the dialectic method of Abelard's *Sic et Non*. It set forth the basic laws of the church, and where the authorities were contradictory, Gratian added his own comments and distinctions to reconcile the inconsistencies. Few books, saving the Bible, have been as influential in church history. Although never adopted officially by the papacy, or indeed any other ecclesiastical body, it influenced the way the law was understood and taught for centuries.

Gratian's *Decretum*, as it was called, was followed by two developments of immediate and lasting importance. The first was the rise of the papal decretal as the primary source for the church's law. This was capped by the promulgation in 1234 of the *Liber extra*, a collection of decretals commissioned by Pope Gregory IX and edited for clarity and consistency by St Raymond of Peñaforte. He organized them according to subject matter into five books, each divided into titles and chapters. The first book dealt with the constitution and organization of the church; the second with jurisdiction and procedural rules; the third with regulation of the clergy, the sacraments, and ecclesiastical obligations; the fourth with marriage, divorce, and domestic relations; and the fifth with the criminal law of the church. The *Liber Extra* built upon the *Decretum*, not diverging from it on most points, but enlarging it and filling gaps in the coverage of the earlier work. It also reflected changes in the church's law (as in the law of **marriage**) between 1140 and 1234. The same pattern was followed by the other collections of papal decretals, primarily the *Liber sextus* (1298) and the Clementines (1317). Together, all the various collections of decretals made up the *Corpus iuris canonici*. This *Corpus* remained the basic law of the (Roman) Catholic church until 1917, and it influenced the law of churches that threw off the Roman yoke during the Reformation.

The second development that followed upon Gratian's *Decretum* was the inception of academic commentary on the law. The texts were glossed almost at once, just as theologians glossed the Bible. The earliest efforts simply clarified the meaning of the texts, but glossing soon led to the creation of a separate body of writing on the canon law. Together with commentaries on **Roman law**, this literature would give rise to the so-called *ius commune*, a body of learned commentary and juristic thought that dominated legal education and influenced legal practice in Western Europe throughout the Middle Ages and into the era of the Enlightenment and Codification.

The canon law contained in the *Corpus iuris canonici* always stood somewhat apart from secular law. Though it shared much of its procedure and substance with Roman law and though it assumed (and depended upon) the existence of secular law in many particulars, canon law was always different—different in jurisdiction, sanctions, and ultimate purposes. Its coverage was partial, never seeking to regulate all human life. For instance, it governed the clergy with a comprehensive set of regulations, but it touched the laity only in areas of life where the church claimed special competence, as in marriage, charitable bequests, and religious opinions. Its sanctions too differed from those of the temporal law. Excommunication, the separation of individuals from the life of the church, was its principal and most serious penalty. When more severe sanctions were thought necessary, as they were in the medieval church, the ecclesiastical courts invoked what the canonists called 'the secular arm' to execute them. And the ultimate goals of the canon law always differed from those of secular law. Its function was to lead men and women to God. This could entail minute regulation of many aspects of human life—**usury**, sexual relations, and false swearing, for example. One must be taught to avoid missteps on the path towards God. However, the canonists never wholly lost sight of the law's ultimate goal. Today, when anything but voluntary observance of canon law would be contrary to accepted views of religious freedom, that goal is even more salient than it was at the time Gratian taught.

RICHARD H HELMHOLZ

JA Brundage, *Medieval Canon Law* (London: Longman Press, 1995)

RH Helmholz, *The Spirit of Classical Canon Law* (Athens, GA: University of Georgia Press, 1996)

See also: **marriage and divorce, history of**

capacity The term 'capacity' refers to those skills considered essential for acts and decisions to be valid in law. Many legal acts and decisions presuppose the possession of mental capacity on the part of the actor, for example, in making a will, undertaking financial and property transactions, or making decisions about health and welfare. Significantly, the law operates on the presumption that adults have capacity to make such decisions and that these may be overturned only if evidence is established, on a balance of probabilities, that an individual lacks the capacity to make the decision in question. This presumption thereby gives effect to the ethical principle of **autonomy**, that is, to the principle that individuals have the right to make meaningful decisions about their property, health, and welfare even though others might disagree with these decisions or consider them unjust or irrational. Historically, the ancient *parens patriae* jurisdiction provided the legal basis for managing the property and welfare of those termed 'lunatics' and 'idiots'. The modern law of incapacity is found in the Mental Capacity Act 2005 and the Adults with Incapacity (Scotland) Act 2000. These legislative frameworks brought much-needed codification and elaboration of a range of **common law** principles that had evolved in the absence of a coherent statutory schema.

The statutes each provide a definition of incapacity which will be applied to a range of different situations and scenarios. Although the two Acts adopt different definitions of incapacity, they identify common aptitudes pertinent to decision-making. In order to give effect to the presumption of capacity (see above), **legislation** provides a definition of incapacity which must be determined in connection with a particular decision. Thus, a **person** may lack capacity to make a particular decision but will otherwise be presumed capable of making decisions in law. A finding of incapacity will be made if a person is unable to: understand information relating to the decision; weigh or use the information to reach a decision; retain information; or communicate the decision. The legislative frameworks acknowledge the dynamic nature of capacity determinations, such that a person's ability to make or communicate a particular decision can be significantly affected by external influences (for example, attitudinal or institutional factors or the level of support provided to the decision-maker) and does not derive from a set of inherent (in)abilities in the decision-maker. To this end, legislation and supporting guidance in Codes of Practice make clear that steps must be taken to assist capacity through the provision of alternative communication methods, for example, or other steps to enable the person to make a capacitous decision.

A decision made by a person who lacks capacity in relation to the matter in question will not, as a general rule, be legally binding. However, where necessary goods or services are supplied to a person who lacked capacity to make the transaction in question, that person is obliged to pay a reasonable price for receipt of these. In other contexts, decisions will be set aside and assistance provided to the person lacking capacity on the basis of their best interests. Where a person lacks capacity, assistance may be provided by those involved in their care and support under a general authority conferred by legislation. Alternatively, a specific individual may be nominated by the court to act as a proxy (a 'deputy' in English Law or 'guardian' in Scots law). In addition, a person anticipating future incapacity may nominate another to make particular decisions on her behalf through the execution of a power of attorney. Under English legislation, such a power can only be executed by a person aged eighteen or over. In all such cases, decisions made in connection with the person lacking capacity must be made in their best interests. Moreover English legislation outlines the circumstances in which persons aged eighteen and over with capacity may issue advance refusals of health care (**advance directives**) to become effective in the event of their incapacity. (In Scotland, the effectiveness of advance refusals of health care continue to be determined by common law.)

There are important restrictions on the decisions that can be made in connection with a person lacking capacity. Decisions concerning, for example, **marriage**, **adoption**, or voting cannot be made on behalf of a person lacking capacity. Decisions concerning admission into hospital for mental disorder have been subject to particular discussion in recent years, following the ruling of the **European Court of Human Rights** in *HL v United Kingdom* (2005). Here the Court held that the use of the English common law doctrine of necessity to authorize the hospital admission of a compliant patient who lacked capacity to make a decision about his admission, was in breach of procedural guarantees required by Article 5 ECHR in relation to liberty and security of person To this end, the Mental Health Act 2007 is amending the Mental Capacity Act 2005 to provide a detailed statutory framework, complete with reviews at twelve-monthly intervals, to govern the detention of such patients. The amendments have attracted criticism for failing to provide the same review mechanisms and safeguards that apply to patients who are formally detained under the Mental Health Act 1983. Whether they will ensure ECHR compliance provide remains to be seen.

The English and Scottish statutory frameworks extend to people aged sixteen years and over. The common law continues to regulate decision-making in connection with children under the age of sixteen in England and Wales, whilst the Age of Legal Capacity (Scotland) Act 1991 confers power on the competent **minor** under sixteen to **consent to medical treatment** (and dental treatment). In practice, children seem to be expected to demonstrate a higher level of understanding of information than

is required of adults under mental incapacity legislation, at least where children are seeking to make decisions that others consider to be against their best interests. Thus, minors refusing life-sustaining medical treatment are often deemed to lack capacity to refuse treatment because they contemplate death merely as a theoretical possibility or because they lack sufficient insight into the manner of their death and the impact it will have on others. The obligation to develop and facilitate capacity among this age group has not been acknowledged by the **courts**, who have found a minor to lack sufficient understanding of the nature of her death in circumstances where she had information concerning this had been withheld from her.

Even where children are found to have capacity, however, English law has firmly established that decisions made by them which are not in their best interests may be overridden by the courts or by those with **parental responsibility**. Whilst a child with capacity in relation to a particular decision may consent to treatment, s/he possesses no corresponding right to refuse. In consequence, the child with capacity enjoys merely the right to make decisions that others deem to be in his or her best interests. At best, this is a qualified right to autonomy which has been the subject of considerable academic criticism and some judicial dissent in Scotland. In the Scottish case of *Re Houston* (1996), Sheriff McGowan found the distinction between accepting and refusing treatment to be illogical and suggested that a child with capacity who refused admission to psychiatric care could not have his wishes overridden by parental consent. Significantly, the parental power to consent on behalf of a child with capacity is set to be limited when the Mental Health Act 2007 comes into force. Under English law at present, a parent may consent to the admission to hospital for psychiatric care on behalf of her child who is expressing a competent refusal to being so admitted. The Mental Health Act 2007 will preclude the use of parental consent to detain a child aged sixteen or seventeen with capacity and who is refusing admission to hospital for treatment of a mental disorder. Similarly, parental consent to electro-convulsive therapy in relation to an informally detained child under the age of eighteen will be invalid, as will parental consent to treatment for mental disorder in respect of children subject to a community treatment order. Under the Mental Health (Safeguards for Certain Informal Patients) (Scotland) Regulations 2005, child patients admitted to hospital informally under the age of sixteen who have capacity to make a decision and refuse treatment cannot be compelled to have treatments which are regarded as having particularly serious consequences for the patient. Currently, these include electro-convulsive therapy, transcranial magnetic stimulation, and vagus nerve stimulation.

KIRSTY KEYWOOD

See also: **best interests of patients; children and medical treatment; withdrawing/withholding life-sustaining treatment**

capital allowances   *see* **business taxation**

capital gains tax   Capital gains tax ('CGT'), first introduced in 1965, is best understood as an adjunct to the taxation of income, charging those who receive returns from capital transactions rather than (or, more likely, in addition to) income. In 2006–2007 it contributed a little under £4,000 million to the total receipts of Her Majesty's Revenue and Customs ('HMRC') of nearly £425,000 million (ie rather less than 1 per cent). By contrast, income tax contributed nearly £145,000 million (ie almost 35 per cent). CGT is a tax on the difference in value of chargeable assets between their date of acquisition and their disposal, levied on gains (less allowable losses) accruing in a year of assessment during any part of which a person is resident or ordinarily resident in the **United Kingdom**. The tax applies to individuals, trustees, and personal representatives but not to companies, which are instead charged to corporation tax on receipts of both an income and a capital nature.

Chargeable assets for the purposes of the tax are widely defined and include not only straightforward objects of ownership but also options, debts, and incorporeal property generally; any currency other than sterling; and any form of property created by the person who disposes of it (for example, paintings, crops, **patents,** and **copyright**), or otherwise coming to be owned without being acquired (for example, goodwill). The legislation does not define the central concept of 'disposal', but makes clear that it includes the destruction of an asset, a part disposal, or the receipt of a capital sum in return for the surrender or forfeiture of any rights. Assets disposed of by way of gift are deemed to be disposed of and acquired at market value. Bargains not at arm's length, and transactions between 'connected persons'—such as husband and wife, trustee and settler, or company and shareholder—are treated in the same way. A certain amount of capital gains made by an individual in any year is completely exempt (in 2006–2007, £8,800); above this limit chargeable gains are added to a taxpayer's income and charged at the appropriate marginal rate (ie between 10 and 40 per cent).

There are significant exemptions, most notably in respect of a person's only or main private residence, and (somewhat less generously, given that the disposal will usually involve a loss) in respect of a private car. Furthermore there is no liability to CGT on death (although there may, of course, be liability to **inheritance tax**); those on whom the deceased's property devolves are deemed to acquire it at its then market value, so exempting from the tax entirely any gains which accrued during the deceased's period of ownership. Various other significant reliefs are available, particularly in connection with business and agricultural assets, notably holdover relief, which reduces the gain crystallized by a donor to nil, but leaves the donee with a correspondingly reduced acquisition cost; and rollover relief, which enables those carrying on a trade to defer a charge until a subsequent disposal of the asset into which a gain is rolled.

Although certain expenditure is allowed against chargeable gains (in addition to any original acquisition cost) without more particular provisions the tax would be levied upon purely inflationary effects. For disposals on or after 5 April 1998, of an asset held since 31 March 1982, legislation now provides that the relevant acquisition cost for the purposes of calculating the capital gain will be the asset's value at that earlier date. This 'rebasing' of the tax is supplemented by an 'indexation allowance' which takes account of the increase in the retail prices index in determining the acquisition cost allowable against the value of an asset at the time of its disposal (although this allowance does not extend so far as to turn a gain into a loss). The indexation allowance has, however, been frozen at its April 1998 level. For disposals after 5 April 1998, the allowance is replaced by a taper relief whereby a chargeable gain is progressively reduced according to the length of time the asset has been held, with more generous relief for certain business assets than for assets generally. Further reform was foreshadowed on 9 October 2007 when the Chancellor of the Exchequer announced an intention to sweep away indexation and taper relief, and replace them with a single rate of 18 per cent applicable to all disposals after 5 April 2008. This would undoubtedly simplify CGT, but arguably at the risk of intellectual incoherence and unfairness.   EDWIN SIMPSON

capital import/export neutrality   *see* **international tax**

capital punishment   The death penalty was the appointed punishment for every felony, with the exception of petty larceny and maiming, in eighteenth-century Britain, although many persons sentenced to death were not in fact executed. Cesare Beccaria's famous treatise, *Dei Delitti e delle Pene* (*On Crimes and Punishment*, 1764), which declared that capital punishment was both inhumane and ineffective, inspired a movement for reform of this 'bloody code'. In 1810 there had been at least 223 offences punished by death, but so successful was the campaign against capital punishment that from the early 1840s onwards persons were only executed, by hanging, for murder. In 1861 it was abolished for all ordinary offences except murder (but retained for **piracy**, arson in HM Dockyards and **treason**). Public executions ceased in 1868. Efforts made in the 1860s and 1870s to define more precisely which types of murder merited capital punishment produced no consensus. Instead, the **Royal Prerogative** of Mercy was widely employed by **Home Secretaries**. Between 1900 and 1949 40 per cent of males and 90 per cent of females mandatorily sentenced to death had their sentences commuted to life imprisonment.

A Select Committee of the House of Commons in 1929 produced no clear consensus on abolition and the issue remained so politically divisive that in 1949 the Labour government established a **Royal Commission** to review whether 'liability to suffer capital punishment for murder . . . should be limited or modified, and if so, to what extent and by what means'. Its report, in 1953, stated bluntly that 'the quest is chimerical and must be abandoned', and concluded that 'the real issue is now whether capital punishment should be retained or abolished'. The infamous cases of Derek Bentley (later exonerated), executed in 1953 as an accessory to a shooting of a policeman even though he was in police custody at the time, and of Ruth Ellis, executed in 1955 for a crime *passionel* because she used a pistol, combined with the concern that an innocent man, Timothy Evans, had been executed in 1950 (also later exonerated), led to a National Campaign for the Abolition of Capital Punishment. Instead, the Conservative government introduced the Homicide Act 1957, in an attempt to define a narrow group of mandatory 'capital murders'. They were murders committed in the course or furtherance of theft or robbery, by using firearms or explosives, of **police** or prison officers, or multiple murders. Under this formula, most killers of young children for sexual purposes were spared, as were most who committed violent crimes, unless they used a firearm. This gave rise to so many anomalies that the judges were ready to support full abolition. With the election of a Labour government, and on a free vote led by Sidney Silverman MP (with a Commons majority of 355 to 170 and a

Lords' majority of 100) capital punishment was abolished for murder in England, Wales, and Scotland in 1965 (the last execution was in 1964) for a trial period of five years. Abolition was confirmed in December 1969 and, in 1973, in Northern Ireland (where the last execution was in 1961). Attempts to reintroduce it—thirteen times in all—for certain categories of murder, such as **terrorism** or the murder of a child were defeated for the same reasons that the Homicide Act was scrapped. But an end to these debates came after a shocking spate of wrongful and unsafe convictions for just such offences—the most notable being the 'Birmingham Six', the 'Guildford Four' and the Price Sisters, all wrongfully convicted of murder through 'terrorist bombings', and Stefan Kisko, a man of limited intelligence, wrongfully convicted of a child sex murder. This persuaded many previous supporters of hanging to change their minds: the most prominent being the Conservative Home Secretary, Michael Howard. On the last occasion—in 1994—that the question was debated in the **House of Commons**, the motion was defeated by a very large majority. Subsequently, an amendment, introduced in the **House of Lords**, to the Crime and Public Order Act 1998 abolished capital punishment for piracy with violence (last execution, 1860) and treason (William **Joyce**, 'Lord Haw Haw', was the last to be executed in 1946). The same year it was abolished for all offences under **military law**.

The UK subsequently ratified Protocols No 6 and 13 of the **European Convention of Human Rights** and the Second Optional Protocol to the **International Covenant on Civil and Political Rights** ('**ICCPR**'), confirming its commitment not to reintroduce the death penalty for any offences. By the end of August 2007, 91 countries had abolished the death penalty completely and a further 10 for all crimes in peacetime. Article 2 of The Charter of Fundamental Rights, adopted by all countries of the EU in Nice in December 2000, states that 'No one shall be condemned to the death penalty or executed'. It also prohibits **extradition** of persons charged with a capital offence to retentionist countries unless a firm guarantee is given that the death penalty will not be imposed.   ROGER HOOD

Victor Gatrell, *The Hanging Tree. Execution and the English People 1770–1868* (Oxford: Oxford University Press, 1994)
Roger Hood and Carolyn Hoyle, *The Death Penalty. A Worldwide Perspective* (Oxford: Oxford University Press, 4th edn, 2007)

capital transfer tax   *see* **inheritance tax**

capitulations   *see* **states**

Cardozo, Benjamin Nathan (1870–1938)
Benjamin Cardozo was an American jurist, the
most widely known and influential state court judge
of his era. Although he briefly served at the end of
his career on the **United States Supreme Court**, his
importance lies in the opinions he wrote on tort—
particularly **product liability**—and **contract law**
while on the highest court of New York State.

Cardozo was born to a family of Sephardic Jews
that had emigrated to the US in the mid-eighteenth
century. His father was a state judge who resigned
to avoid **impeachment** over his involvement with
the New York City political machine, an event later
said to have shaped the son's determination to live a
life of modest rectitude and achievement. Cardozo
was tutored at home before attending Columbia College where he graduated top of his class. He attended
Columbia Law School and then practiced law for 23
years before being elected to the New York Supreme
Court, then, as now, the state trial court of general
jurisdiction. A few months later, he was promoted to
the highest court, the New York Court of Appeals,
where he served for eighteen years—the last five as
chief judge.

During that period, Cardozo wrote opinions for
the court that reshaped numerous aspects of contract and tort law, especially in relation to **damages**. His most revolutionary opinion allowed the
purchaser of a defective automobile to sue the manufacturer instead of having his relief limited to the
retail seller by the privity doctrine (*MacPherson v
Buick Motor Co* (1916)). Most of Cardozo's significant opinions were more modest and drew their
importance from adapting old doctrines to new
states of facts or in applying practical business perspectives to what had become highly doctrinaire
sub-fields.

His opinions were memorable for their rhetorical
flourishes (occasionally ornate), scholarly citations,
and masterful control of authority.

When Oliver Wendell **Holmes**, Jr, retired from
the US Supreme Court, President Herbert Hoover—
forcefully urged by the bar—named Cardozo to succeed him and he became only the second Jew ever
to sit on the Court. The transition from **common
law** to federal and **constitutional law** was not congenial to Cardozo, and the political atmosphere of
Washington led him to refer to his service there as
'homesick exile'. He aligned himself with those on
the Court who read Congress's constitutional powers broadly and generally upheld President Franklin D Roosevelt's 'New Deal' recovery programme.
Cardozo wrote the opinions in 1937 sustaining the
constitutionality of the Social Security Act 1935.

Cardozo never married and lived with his sister
until her death in 1929. He died of heart disease in
1938.

Before moving to Washington, Cardozo often
accepted invitations to deliver occasional lectures,
the most prominent of which resulted in a highly
discreet attempt to explain the scope of a common
law judge's power in deciding cases, *The Nature of
the Judicial Process* (1921). Although extremely dated
and not as revealing as advertised, the work continues to be in print and to sell widely.

DENNIS J HUTCHINSON

Andrew L Kaufman, *Cardozo* (Cambridge: Harvard UP,
2000)
Richard A Posner, *Cardozo: A Study in Reputation*
(Chicago: U Chicago Press, 1993)

care, duty of   *see* **negligence in civil law**

care, standard of   *see* **negligence in civil law**

Carlill v Carbolic Smoke Ball Co Ltd (1893)   This
is probably the most famous case in the English law
of contract. The Carbolic Smoke Ball was a patented
device designed to puff carbolic acid dust into the
nostrils. It was widely advertised with extravagant
claims that it would ward off as well as cure many
ailments, including influenza. The advert included
a '£100 reward' if the Smoke Ball did not work.
Mrs Carlill bought a Smoke Ball, used it, and still got
'flu' she sued and was successful in her claim for the
reward.

The main reason the case is still recalled lies in the
way the court modified the idea of agreement, which
had come to dominate thinking about contract law
during the nineteenth century. The dominant idea
was that a contract needed an agreement, which
could be broken down into an offer (containing the
proposal) and acceptance of the proposal. This agreement comprised the contract, and was quite separate
from the performance. In *Carlill* there was no such
agreement here—the first the company knew of Mrs
Carlill was when she claimed the reward (she had
bought the Smoke Ball from an intermediary). The
court was clear she should succeed, and found the
requisite 'acceptance' in her act of buying the ball,
using it and getting the 'flu'.

This case recognized the 'unilateral contract': a
contract under which the resulting obligation is one-
sided. Mrs Carlill was never under a legal obligation,
only the company. This differs from the dominant
bilateral model, which imposes obligation on both
sides. A bilateral contract can be analysed as a promise

in return for a promise, while a unilateral contract is a promise in return for an act. Although the bilateral model predominates, the unilateral contract has been a useful supplement, providing a legal basis for a contract in cases where the parties do not come into any contact (as in cases of reward), although a unilateral contract is not limited to such cases. It still does not fit neatly within the orthodox concepts of offer and acceptance, and the question of whether a unilateral offer can be revoked once someone has embarked on the specified act continues to be conceptually (but not practically) troublesome.

Carlill is also notable as one of the very earliest cases of what we now regard as consumer protection—the litigation took place at a time of heightened concern about quack remedies. However, its legal significance hardly justifies its fame. It is one of the first cases that law students encounter; and its renown is perhaps owed to the unusually memorable facts and possibly the fact that it offers an uplifting narrative of the manufacturer of a quack remedy getting their just deserts. Few contract cases involve so clear a moral contest.   JOHN WIGHTMAN

AWB Simpson, *Leading Cases in the Common Law* (Oxford: Clarendon Press, 1995), ch 10

Caroline, The   *see* self-defence in international law; use of force

carrier sanctions   Carrier sanctions are penalties imposed by a country on transport operators for facilitating the entry of a person into that country where the person is not entitled to enter under immigration law, or where the person possesses inadequate or fraudulent travel documents (such as a **visa** or **passport**). Sanctions commonly apply to airlines but also to shipping, rail, and road transport, and typically entail a fine for each unlawful entrant and often the cost of accommodating and repatriating the person.

The US pioneered carrier sanctions in 1952 and many European and Western countries have followed suit, particularly since the late 1980s in response to large increases in unlawful entrants by air. The UK adopted carrier sanctions laws in 1987 and the Immigration and Asylum Act 1999 now imposes a fine of £2,000 per passenger on carriers which bring into the UK passengers who lack valid visas or travel documents. Over £120 million in fines has been levied since 1987. EU laws have also harmonized carrier sanctions within the EU, with a minimum penalty of EUR 3,000 per unlawful entrant.

Two central criticisms are made of carrier sanctions. First, there is the danger that they restrict access to **refugee** protection by **asylum** seekers fleeing persecution. International law requires countries not to return a person to a place where they are at risk of persecution (see the 1951 Refugee Convention and the 1950 **European Convention on Human Rights**) or **torture** or inhuman or degrading treatment (see the 1984 Convention against Torture and the ECHR), also known as *non-refoulement*.

Asylum seekers and those fleeing torture often travel in an urgent, unplanned, or irregular manner. Their own governments may refuse to provide travel documents or permission to travel, necessitating the use of fraudulent documents. They may also be unable to obtain a visa, because it would be refused or because they cannot safely apply for one. Carrier sanctions may deter carriers from transporting asylum seekers to safe countries, and thus breach a country's refugee law and human rights obligations, although UK law does not penalize carriers if a passenger receives asylum. Sanctions may actually encourage **illegal migration**, since people desperate to find safety may resort to dangerous, exploitative people smugglers.

The second criticism is related to the first. On one view, carrier sanctions amount to a 'contracting out' or privatization of government immigration procedures, shifting the burden and costs onto carriers. The contrary view is that carrier sanctions are a legitimate measure to protect a country's borders and are merely a regulatory cost of doing business. What is certain is that airline employees must now assess passengers' immigration status and the validity of their travel documents. Unlike immigration officers, airline employees are not usually trained in immigration law and do not enjoy the same legal rights. There is a risk that carriers—motivated by profit not humanitarianism—will decide whether to carry a passenger based on racial or nationality profiling, resulting in discrimination.   BEN SAUL

See also: **immigration security screening; migrant smuggling**

Carson, Edward   Sir Edward Carson was an advocate who had the Irish gift for histrionics. But, unlike most Irish advocates of the day, he was absolute master of the detailed facts. His preparation left him with as much knowledge of the case as his client, sometimes more.

These qualities were seen to advantage in his celebrated defence of the odious Marquess of Queensbury in the libel action brought by Oscar Wilde. Carson allowed Wilde to run rings of epigram round him in cross-examination, knowing that Wilde, gradually becoming more unwary in his peacock display of cleverness, would eventually trap himself by giving something away about his disreputable life style–as he did. It proved fatal, and Wilde destroyed himself. An eye-witness newspaper reporter of the trial described it as 'a duel of thrilling interest'. When Carson became angry his face 'assumes the immovability of a death mask'; and when he scored a point, 'he smiles a grim smile to his junior . . . his self- possession is absolute'.

The 'Winslow Boy', to use the title of Terence Rattigan's dramatization, was another case in which Carson showed his consummate qualities as advocate. Carson here acted for a 13-year-old naval cadet, George Archer-Shee, against the Admiralty, who had dismissed the boy from the Naval College at Osborne on the accusation of stealing a postal-order for five shillings (25p). The Admiralty argued that the cadet had no case because servants of the **Crown** held their position at the King's pleasure. Carson persuaded the Court of Appeal that justice required that the facts should be looked at first. The whole thing depended on the post-mistress's identification of the cadet who cashed the postal-order. She was transparently honest, but, by gentle probing, Carson elicited the answer that she couldn't be quite sure. So the boy, who had protested his innocence throughout, was vindicated. The *Observer* published an editorial which paid Carson a great compliment. His whole conduct of the case had been one of the finest things in the annals of the Bar, it said. 'Even law may be dead and impotent without personality.'

GEOFFREY M LEWIS

See also: **Wilde, Oscar**

cartel   Cartel is a situation in which market operators collude together in a way that harms competition. This collusion can be the result of an agreement or of another form of coordination such as concerted practice. Forming a cartel is not particularly easy. Among other things, it requires setting up a strong and workable operational structure. Normally, this requires a single firm to act as instigator or ringleader so as to provide a bond between the various participants. Cartels vary in structure and the number of firms participating. At one end of the spectrum, a cartel may have only a few participants and its policies may be produced at one level, typically that of the chief executives of the firms concerned. At the other end of the spectrum, a large number of firms may be involved and the operation of the cartel may be handled through different committees established at different levels: from the level of

chief executives all the way down to the level of sales managers. Also, the cartel may concern one product or market, or a number of products or markets; in the latter case, effectively the cartel will include a number of 'sub-cartels'. The more firms involved in the cartel and the more products falling within its scope, the harder it is to run the cartel. Additionally, of course, there is always the risk that one of the participants may choose to 'cheat' and deviate from the agreed cartel behaviour. For this reason, a cartel requires policing and an effective mechanism to punish such cheating or deviation. Punishment typically takes the form of retaliation against the cheating participant by other participants. For this reason, success in forming and running a cartel is not guaranteed and there is always the risk that the cartel may fail. Indeed, in many situations cartels may fail even before they begin operation; and in many situations they may fail during their operation. However, many cartels successfully begin operation and they may exist for many years without being detected or punished.

Cartels are treated very seriously under competition law because they are viewed as harmful to consumers and competition in the market. Many competition authorities view cartels as the cancer of the free economy. Cartels can have different aims. The most common types of cartels are those aimed at fixing prices, sharing markets, and limiting output. Firms engage in cartels because they desire to maximize their own profits and benefits while having a quiet life through removing the uncertainty of competition. This will be achieved at the expense of consumers. Worldwide, defeating cartels is one of the top priorities of competition authorities. Where a competition authority detects a cartel, punishment may follow in the form of a hefty fine and/or imprisonment for individuals found guilty of a cartel offence. This includes company directors. In some countries, such as the UK, a person found guilty of a cartel offence may even be disqualified from acting as director of any firm for a period of time. The harsh attitude towards cartels is reflected in the fact that under the competition rules of many countries, a firm can be held liable of a cartel offence merely for being present at and participating in a cartel meeting without implementing what was agreed at the meeting.

Uncovering cartels may not be easy or even possible. A cartel is a secretive operation and sometimes it can be virtually impossible for a competition authority to obtain necessary evidence of the existence of the cartel. Cartel participants are normally very careful in making sure that all incriminating documents are destroyed and that no records of their cartel meetings will be kept. Furthermore, cartels have become increasingly international and a competition authority in one jurisdiction may not be able to obtain documents located in other countries. Because of these and other difficulties, many competition authorities have developed what is called a leniency or amnesty programme. This programme involves encouraging firms that participate in cartels to come forward and confess to the relevant competition authority in return for leniency in the punishment which the competition authority would otherwise impose. Leniency may take the form of a total immunity from fine and/or any other penalty or a reduction in the level of the fine and/or other penalty. This is a sound and desirable policy because the interests of consumers and the economy will be better served by the eradication of as many cartels as possible than by imposing fines and/or other penalties, however heavy these may be.

MAHER DABBAH

See also: **horizontal agreement**

case management   Case management is the process by which the court itself manages the conduct of civil cases by the parties. It is a key innovation of the **Civil Procedure Rules** 1998.

First, the court allocates cases to one of three tracks. The 'small claims track' is for claims with a value of £5,000 or less, for any claims for damages for personal injuries of £1,000 or less (where the total value of the claim is not more than £5,000), and for small housing disrepair cases. The 'fast track' is for claims with a value of £15,000 or less, but only if the trial is likely to last no more than a day, and **expert evidence** will be limited. The 'multi-track' is for all other claims.

When the court allocates a case to the fast track it gives directions to the parties, for example on disclosure of documents, service of witness statements, and expert evidence, and sets a timetable for compliance. It later requires the parties to complete a 'listing questionnaire' to check readiness for trial. On the fast track, this normally takes place within thirty weeks of the directions. In multi-track cases the court will, in addition, usually fix a case management conference or pre-trial review.

A key objective of case management is the early identification of the issues between the parties, their cooperation with each other in their conduct of the case, the encouragement of alternative dispute resolution procedures and settlements where appropriate, and the maintenance of control generally of the progress of the case.   JOHN FITZPATRICK

Casement, Sir Roger   Sir Roger Casement (1864–1916) was tried and convicted of treason for his support for a plot to enlist German support for the Irish nationalist rebellion in 1916.

Born in Ireland in 1864, he had served as a diplomat for the British government in Africa and Latin America between 1892 and 1913, being knighted for his services in 1911. He had a longstanding interest in Irish nationalism, which crystallized in his efforts to organize an Irish Volunteer Force to defend the cause of home rule. With the outbreak of the First World War, Casement's efforts to support the cause of Irish nationalism were increasingly manifested in support for Germany against Britain, and he spent much of the early part of the war in Berlin. In 1916 the Germans agreed to contribute arms for an Irish rebellion, and Casement returned to Ireland on a German submarine in April 1916. There he was arrested by the Irish police, acting on information from British intelligence. He was returned to London and charged with treason in May 1916. His trial began on 26 June 1916. One issue in the trial concerned whether the crime of treason could extend to acts committed outside Britain. It was mainly notable, however, because Casement's private diaries, which contained detailed accounts of his homosexual activities, were released to the press—apparently with official collusion—in order to discredit his character.

He was found guilty of treason and executed on 3 August 1916, following an unsuccessful public campaign for a reprieve.   LINDSAY FARMER

cash flow tax   *see* **corporation tax**

casual workers   The term 'casual workers' is not defined in law. It refers to workers who are called in to work by an employer when they are needed. Some casual workers may work for a succession of different employers on a series of short-term contracts. Others may work for the same employer, sometimes over a period of years, but always on an 'as required' basis.

Casual work is often thought of as 'atypical'. In the typical employment relationship, the employer takes the risk of a downturn in the business and continues to pay the employee even when there is little work to do. A casual worker would be laid off in this situation. Firms which use casual workers commonly have a 'core' of typical employees who work continuously and provide stability, and a 'periphery' of casual workers who can be called in at busy times.

Casual workers are not well protected by employment law. Access to statutory employment rights depends on having a **contract of employment** or a worker's contract. In a contract of either type, there must be 'mutuality of obligation'. This means that the employer must promise to provide work in the future, and the individual must promise to accept it (*O'Kelly v Trusthouse Forte* (1984)). It is inherent in the concept of casual work that the employer makes no such promise. Although there are signs in recent cases that the **courts** may be relaxing this test, casual workers have a precarious status in the law at present. ANNE DAVIES

causation For legal purposes, it is often necessary to determine whether a particular factor, be it an act or an omission, was historically involved in an event, such as a person's death, or in the persistence of a state of affairs, such as the continuing **nuisance** of a tree that overhangs a neighbour's property. The law's purpose in making such determinations may not be to decide whether legal **responsibility** for the event or state should be allocated to that factor. Rather it may be concerned simply to determine how to avoid the event or state in future. Modern lawyers therefore tend to include within the law's notion of a 'cause' any factor that was historically involved in the occurrence of the event or the persistence of the state. For example, suppose that hunters often carelessly shoot into forests where their bullets hit and kill hikers. The presence of the hikers in the forest is a factor that is historically involved in their own deaths. The recognition that all such historically involved factors are 'causes' of such fatal hunting accidents helps to alert regulatory authorities to the fact that the most effective strategy to reduce the number of such deaths may be to ban hiking in areas where shooting is permitted rather than to attempt to regulate or ban hunting.

Historical involvement is most easily established if the relevant factor bears a 'but-for' (ie necessity) relation to the event or state. Returning to the example of the hunters and the hikers, we can see that the presence of a hiker at a particular place in the forest at a particular time is historically involved in the hiker's death because but for that presence, the hiker would not have died.

Sometimes a factor does not satisfy the but-for test but is, nevertheless, historically involved in the event. This requires the but-for test to be supplemented. For example, suppose two hunters each simultaneously shoot one bullet into the forest and both bullets hit a hiker. Suppose, too, that the medical evidence shows that either bullet would have been sufficient to kill the hiker instantly. It cannot be said that but-for the shot fired by hunter No 1 the hiker would not have died where and when he did. Equally, it cannot be said that but-for the shot fired by hunter No 2 the hiker would not have died where and when he did. Yet it is clear that each hunter is historically involved in the death, and that only if neither had been involved would the death have been avoided. In order correctly to identify the historical involvement of each hunter the law needs to use a more sophisticated approach than the but-for test. In *Causation in the Law* (Oxford: Oxford University Press, 1959) HLA Hart and T Honoré formulated the required algorithm in what later became known as the 'NESS test'. Under that test, a factor is historically involved in an event or state if it is a 'necessary element for the sufficiency of a sufficient set' of factors. In this way we can correctly identify the historical involvement of hunter No 1. Consider the set of all the factors present when the hiker died, except for hunter No 2. That set was sufficient for the death, and hunter No 1 was necessary for that sufficiency. It follows that hunter No 1 was historically involved in the hiker's death, and in that sense a 'cause' of the death. The historical involvement of hunter No 2 in the hiker's death can be similarly established.

Whether a factor is a cause of—ie historically involved in—an event or state is a question of objective fact, not a matter that is affected by considerations of **justice** or policy. However, there are legal rules governing how facts—including causation—must be *proved*. For example, to establish a defendant's liability in a civil claim (as opposed to a criminal prosecution), the claimant must normally prove all elements of the claim on the balance of probabilities. There are exceptions to this rule. One such exception applies to cases of liability for causing a person to contract mesothelioma. Mesothelioma is a cancer caused by the inhalation of asbestos, but the precise causal mechanism is unknown: it may be caused by a single asbestos fibre or by a certain accumulation of fibres. Suppose that a worker inhales asbestos during consecutive periods of employment, first with employer No 1 and subsequently with employer No 2. Because the precise mechanism by which mesothelioma is contracted is not known, the worker cannot show that but-for the first period of exposure he would not, on the balance of probabilities, have contracted mesothelioma. In other words, the worker cannot show that the exposure during the period of employment with employer No 1 was a but-for cause of his disease. Nor, for identical reasons, can the worker show that the exposure during the period of employment with employer No 2 was a cause. The dilemma posed by such 'evidentiary gaps' recently prompted the **House of Lords** to relax the requirements of proof in such cases, allowing proof (on the balance of probabilities) that the defendant's conduct contributed to the *risk* that the claimant would contract mesothelioma to satisfy the requirement of proof (on the balance of probabilities) that the defendant's conduct contributed to the *injury*—ie the mesothelioma itself. The scope of this new rule (eg its application to conditions other than mesothelioma) is unclear.   JANE STAPLETON

See also: **burden of proof; scope of liability**

cause lawyering   Cause lawyering, a variant of the term 'public interest lawyering', refers to practising law in furtherance of the lawyer's moral and political commitments. It is a category of lawyering distinct from the traditional practice of law in which the lawyer's work serves goals that are determined exclusively by the client.

The leading proponents of cause lawyering, as a category distinguishable from conventional law practice, are Austin Sarat and Stuart Scheingold, two American academics who have been studying the phenomenon since the 1990s. These professors have popularized the 'cause lawyer' label to denote lawyers who use law as an instrument of political struggle. Sidestepping intractable ideological disagreements about what constitutes the public interest, the cause lawyer concept has sufficient breadth to incorporate not only lawyering on behalf of politically progressive causes, but also the recent emergence of lawyering on behalf of politically conservative causes.

While conservative cause lawyering and progressive cause lawyering may be politically antagonistic, they are conceptually similar. Both sets of politically motivated lawyers share an image of law as a means to broader social objectives, unlike conventional lawyers who are acculturated to view themselves as neutral and non-partisan, and to view law as an end in itself. Indeed, it is generally the vision of lawyering as a moral and political endeavor that attracts cause lawyers, because within such a vision, personal values and professional activity can be made mutually sustaining and reinforcing.

Cause lawyering is a cross-cultural and transnational phenomenon, visible in nearly every region of the world. Cause lawyers address a variety of causes, working on a range of issues such as the environment, immigration, reproductive freedom, civil rights, poverty, education, racial equality, religious freedom, animal rights, human rights, the death penalty, and countless others. These attorneys work in diverse professional settings, such as non-profit agencies, solo practice, law school clinics, small law firms, and the pro bono projects of large private firms. In some instances, cause lawyers practice with significant resource constraints, low compensation,

and considerable personal risk. They may represent individuals, classes, organizations, or communities, but what unites cause lawyers is their motivation to represent a cause that transcends the particular interests of their clients.

The most widely identified ethical dilemma for cause lawyers has been named by philosopher David Luban as the 'double agent' problem. Cause lawyers may experience a conflict of interest between the needs of the clients they formally represent and the needs of the multiple clients who comprise the cause they serve. One of the best solutions to the double agent problem is found in full disclosure and open communication with the client, who may consent to representation under these conditions. Although limited, the existing empirical research suggests that cause lawyers generally work diligently and effectively on behalf of their clients.

The connection between the personal and the professional that makes cause lawyering a satisfying choice for some, is also what makes it controversial to others. From the standpoint of conventional practice, cause lawyers threaten and destabilize the ideal of disinterested professional service and undivided fealty to the client's lawful interests. On the other hand, cause lawyers bring legitimacy to a legal profession that seeks to overcome its public image as a bastion of hired guns who sell their technical expertise to those who can afford high-priced services. Consequently, cause lawyers and conventional lawyers are simultaneously oppositional to and dependent on one another, allied in a fragile and tenuous relationship.

The strategies realistically available to cause lawyers depend in part on the political contexts in which they operate. In authoritarian regimes, cause lawyers may work in solidarity with social movements, often in an effort to strengthen the rule of law as a restraint on the exercise of governmental power. In countries where institutional structures embody liberal legalism, cause lawyers may choose to work within established legal institutions, using strategies such as litigation, which can function paradoxically both to oppose and to legitimate state power.

The more transformative their aims, the less comfortable cause lawyers may be in deploying the tools of mainstream legality. Yet the more overtly political and transgressive the strategies they adopt, the less acceptance these cause lawyers find within the legal profession as a whole. Globalization's new political configurations create fresh possibilities and impediments for cause lawyers who in some contexts may find that the state is an ally in efforts to constrain global capital. As structures and conditions evolve, so too will the methods that cause lawyers devise in their quest to promote a more just society.

PHYLLIS GOLDFARB

A Sarat and S Scheingold (eds), *Cause Lawyering: Political Commitments and Professional Responsibilities* (Oxford: Oxford University Press, 1998)

S Scheingold and A Sarat, *Something to Believe In: Politics, Professionalism, and Cause Lawyering* (Stanford, CA: Stanford University Press, 2004).

See also: **pro bono** legal services

cautioning **Criminal justice systems** generally provide for suspected offenders to be warned—ie 'cautioned'—instead of being prosecuted. Enforcement agencies cannot arrest and prosecute everyone, and **prosecution** would often be an over-reaction that might do more harm than good. The **police** used to give many instant verbal informal warnings as part of normal policing. However, this 'low visibility' process opens officers to bribes from suspects, and suspects to pressure (eg to inform) from officers, in exchange for no formal action. This opens the way for serious offences to be inappropriately cautioned.

Regulation is therefore important, and has been done since the 1960s via instructions from the Home Office (or, for Scotland, from the Scottish Executive). These are revised periodically, and law enforcement agencies adapt them to their own circumstances. Oddly, cautions are not regulated by **legislation** apart from some isolated instances noted later. There is some relevant case law related to the exercise of executive **discretion** as cautions can be cited in **court** and are a form of administrative **justice** without any other judicial oversight.

The more serious the offence the less likely it is that a caution will be appropriate. Cautions will usually be inappropriate if there are previous prosecutions and/or cautions, depending on what happened before. Very young and very old offenders are treated relatively generously and the views of **victims** are taken into account. Since a caution is a warning not to re-offend, it is important that the suspect really did commit the alleged offence. Consequently, cautions should not be administered unless there is enough **evidence** to prosecute and the suspect confesses. To ensure that these criteria and conditions are followed, instant cautions have been largely replaced (excepting minor motoring offences and possession of cannabis, for example) by formal cautions administered by senior officers.

Cautioning is often seen as a 'slap on the wrist', and if the crime in question is a symptom of a problem, a mere warning does nothing to address it. Thus, the Youth Justice and Criminal Evidence Act 1999 provides for formal warnings for juveniles (where a less formal caution is inappropriate) with a **restorative justice** element. This approach was extended to adults in the Criminal Justice Act 2003 with the creation of 'conditional cautions' administered by the **Crown Prosecution Service**. There are similar provisions in Scotland.

Around half of all under-eighteens, and one-quarter of adults, who commit or admit to offences are now cautioned. However, this is fewer than the mid-1990s; research shows that the criteria and conditions are not always followed; sometimes a caution may be an alternative, not to prosecution, but to no action at all. This apparently benevolent development could therefore be seen as an erosion of open justice, and extended state intervention. Unfair and possibly discriminatory practices—particularly disadvantaging socially marginal and ethnic **minority** groups—remain hidden. Finally, the number of crimes not prosecuted by the police is insignificant compared with that of most non-police agencies, eg HM Revenue and Customs, the Health and Safety Executive, and **pollution** agencies, who prosecute very rarely, almost always using alternatives like cautions and the legislative innovations of 1999 and 2003.

ANDREW SANDERS

R Evans and K Puech, 'Reprimands and warnings: populist punitiveness or restorative justice?' (2001) *Criminal Law Review* 794

A Sanders and R Young, *Criminal Justice* (Oxford: Oxford University Press, 3rd edn, 2007), 344–372

caveat emptor The principle of *caveat emptor* (or buyer beware) underpins UK financial market regulation and regulation internationally. Financial market regulation generally seeks to ensure that an investor is provided with sufficient information to make an informed investment choice. It does not intervene paternalistically in that choice or attempt to direct investment decisions. Regulation rarely prevents an individual investor from making a particular decision, such as buying a risky, unregulated product; although it may prevent an investment from being offered to the public at large. Disclosure, which assumes investor competence and investor autonomy, is at the heart of financial market regulation.

The principle is particularly strong in the lightly regulated wholesale or professional markets, where sophisticated investors are regarded as expert and able to demand any protections they deem necessary from those with whom they are transacting. Accordingly, the debt or bond markets are generally less heavily regulated than the equity markets in which retail investors are active.

The principle is also, however, applied to the retail markets and is embedded in the **Financial Services and Markets Act 2000**, which governs the UK's financial markets. The **Financial Services Authority** ('FSA') is required to act in accordance with the Act's regulatory objectives which include, under section 2, the protection of consumers. The *caveat emptor* principle is expressly referred to in section 5, which provides that, in considering the appropriate degree of consumer protection, the FSA must have regard to the general principle that consumers should take responsibility for their actions.   NIAMH MOLONEY

See also: **disclosure in financial markets; information disclosure**

cctv   *see* **surveillance, surreptitious**

CEDAW (Convention on the Elimination of all Forms of Discrimination against Women) The 1979 Convention on the Elimination of all Forms of Discrimination against Women—ratified by 185 countries, though not by the United States—aims to rectify 'extensive discrimination against women', which 'hampers the growth of the prosperity of the society and the family'. States parties must take all appropriate measures to end discrimination against women, incorporate the principle of **equality** of men and women in their legal systems, establish machinery for the effective protection of women against discrimination by public or by private agents, and achieve *de facto* equality, including by temporary special measures.

All major spheres of human activity are regulated by the Convention. Women are entitled to rights and access, on equal terms with men, in political and public life, **nationality,** education, employment, social security, health care, credit facilities, and rural development. They are entitled to equality in all matters relating to **marriage** and family relations and to proper reproductive care. The Convention prohibits trafficking and exploitation of prostitution. The CEDAW Committee clarified, in General Comment 19, that states must take action to prevent rape, **sexual harassment**, or **domestic violence**.

Beyond requiring equal opportunity under existing social norms, CEDAW addresses structural disadvantage, requiring a proper understanding of **maternity** as a social function and education to the common parental responsibilities of men and women. It requires states to modify cultural patterns which involve **stereotyping** or discrimination.

Enforcement methods include: country reporting to the CEDAW Committee; and individual complaints against those states which have ratified CEDAW's Optional Protocol.   FRANCES RADAY

F Raday, 'Culture, Religion and Gender' (2003) 1 *International Journal of Constitutional Law* 663
Ineke Boerefijn *et al* (eds), *Temporary Special Measures – Activating de facto Equality of Women under Article 4(1) CEDAW* (Oxford, New York: Intersentia Antwerp, 2003), 35

censorship   Censorship commonly refers to the determination by a public official that certain material is unsuitable for publication or performance on grounds such as morality, religion, politics, or **national security**. The material may be banned outright or its circulation restricted to those thought less susceptible to its influence. Beyond these administrative decisions, the concept can encompass many forms of penalty after publication, such as laws of sedition, racial hatred, and **obscenity**. These limits vary greatly with national approaches to freedom of speech.

Changes in communications technologies have frequently prompted debates about censorship, with sharply divergent views on the power, if any, of new media forms to cause harm. The internet offers a contemporary example, but belief in the libertarian potential of communication and the difficulty of regulating it has recurred since the emergence of printing.

Wider cultural practices and resources affecting the ability of people to speak, or ideas to circulate, can also be debated in terms of censorship. This has been prominent following the reformulation of politics, especially in the later twentieth century, with demands for greater recognition of gender, racial, and sexual diversity. Through these changes, censorship can be understood less as an external force than as something which constitutes social practices themselves.

Historically, opposition to censorship has been important in developing free speech and political dissent. For almost all the sixteenth and seventeenth centuries, for example, licenses were required for printing presses, notwithstanding significant resistance, as John Milton's *Areopagitica: A Speech for the Liberty of Unlicensed Printing* illustrates. After the licensing system lapsed in 1694, print media was limited through specific taxation policies and the law of sedition was used frequently against publishers who breached norms of political or social propriety.

During the twentieth century, much censorship focused on sexuality and literature with, for example, DH Lawrence's **Lady Chatterley's Lover** constrained by obscenity law until the early 1960s (*R v Penguin Books* (1961)). UK law treats material as obscene if it would 'deprave and corrupt' a significant portion of its probable audience, while allowing publications 'for the public good' in the interests of science, literature, education 'or other objects of general concern' (Obscene Publications Act 1959).

Traditional concepts of censorship remain significant for audiovisual material. In the UK, films are subject to censorship by the British Board of Film Classification and local authorities, although authorities can allow films to be exhibited contrary to Board decisions or ban films which have received Board approval. The Board also has responsibility for classifying videos, where a stricter approach is taken due to the domestic context in which videos can be viewed. The Board's decision in the 1990s to ban 'Visions of Ecstasy', which depicted a nun's erotic fantasies, as being potentially blasphemous was upheld by the **European Court of Human Rights**. The censorship came within the room given to national authorities under the **European Convention of Human Rights** to restrict free speech on grounds such as national security, public safety, morality, and the rights of others (*Wingrove v UK* (1997)).   ANDREW KENYON

See also: **film censorship; freedom of expression; media regulation and freedom of**

Central Arbitration Committee   *see* **collective bargaining**

Central London Property Trust Ltd v High Trees House Ltd (1947)

In the *High Trees* case **Denning** J (as he then was) creatively interpreted a series of earlier cases to establish a new principle of law, which has become known as promissory estoppel. The influence of the decision has been remarkable, given that the relevant statements of principle were made by a single judge, by way of obiter dicta (observations not essential to the decision, and therefore less authoritative), in a short extempore judgment.

In 1937, the plaintiff landlord leased to the defendant a block of London flats for ninety-nine years for a rent of £2,500 per year. As a result of wartime conditions, the defendant was unable to let all of the flats. The landlord therefore agreed in writing in 1940 to reduce the rent to £1,250. The flats were fully let by early 1945. The landlord demanded the full arrears, but then sued only with respect to the last two quarters of 1945. The claim was successful. Denning J interpreted the 1940 agreement as intended to operate only while wartime conditions continued. It had

ceased to operate when the flats became fully let in early 1945, and therefore had no effect on the landlord's claim.

Under orthodox principles of contract law the 1940 promise was not binding because it was gratuitous: the landlord had received no consideration in return for the promise. But Denning J held that, as a result of a series of earlier decisions, it could now be said that a promise that was 'intended to be binding, intended to be acted on and in fact acted on is binding' even though no consideration had been given for it. The 1940 agreement was therefore binding and, if the landlord had sued for the amount foregone prior to 1945, the defendant could have resisted the claim.

The principle established in the *High Trees* case can only be used to prevent the person who made the promise from asserting rights that are inconsistent with it. In the United States and Australia the courts have taken promissory estoppel further, allowing it to be used as an independent cause of action, or basis for suing, to enforce a promise. The English courts have remained cautious. In a later case in the Court of Appeal, Denning LJ himself refused to allow promissory estoppel to be used to create a new cause of action, noting that the principle must 'not be stretched too far, lest it should be endangered'.

The *High Trees* case exemplifies Lord Denning's commitment to the rectification of injustices in the law, particularly those resulting from the inflexible rules of **contract law** developed during the nineteenth century. It also exemplifies his technique of doing so through the creative development of broad and flexible principles. Denning J noted in *High Trees* that a Law Revision Committee report had recommended legislative reform to allow the enforcement of a promise which has been relied upon by the promisee to his or her detriment. This result, he said, 'has now been achieved by the decisions of the courts'.   ANDREW ROBERTSON

E Cooke, *The Modern Law of Estoppel* (Oxford: Oxford University Press, 2000)

See also: **precedent**

CERD (Convention for the Elimination of Racial Discrimination)

Ratified by 173 states, the 1965 Convention for the Elimination of Racial Discrimination was based on the 'conviction that any doctrine of superiority based on racial differentiation is scientifically false, morally condemnable, socially unjust and dangerous . . . repugnant to the ideals of any human society'.

Racial discrimination is defined as 'any distinction, exclusion, restriction or preference based on **race**, colour, descent, or national or ethnic origin which impairs the enjoyment, on an equal footing, of human rights in the political, economic, social, cultural or any other field of public life'. States parties undertake to eliminate racial discrimination and guarantee the right to equal treatment in judicial proceedings, political rights, public affairs, public service, **freedom of movement**, residence, **nationality, marriage**, ownership of property, inheritance, employment, trade union membership, **housing,** medical care, social security, education and training, participation in cultural activities, and access to any place or service for use by the general public.

States parties must provide effective protection and **remedies** against any acts of racial discrimination, as well as the right to seek adequate reparation for any damage suffered as a result of such discrimination. They must introduce effective measures, particularly in the fields of education, culture, and information, to combat prejudices. Special measures, to ensure the 'adequate advancement' of certain racial groups, are required when warranted.

Enforcement measures include reporting to the CERD Committee by state's parties, an early-warning procedure and examination of inter-state and individual complaints against those states which have ratified CERD's Optional Protocol.

FRANCES RADAY

M Banton, *International Action against Racial Discrimination* (Oxford: Oxford University Press, 1996)

certainty and flexibility in law   One of the functions of law is to guide behaviour and to provide frameworks within which individuals can plan. For this, certainty is a high value. For example, in planning the disposal of property after her death, a person wants to be clear what property she can freely dispose, who may have entitlements to share in the estate, and what will be the consequences of particular dispositions in a will or intestacy, particularly in relation to taxation. Certainty is particularly important in criminal law and taxation, where the consequences can affect a person's liberty or property. Typically law provides certainty through rules that are clear and precise, either in legislation or in individual contracts or wills. On the other hand, there are limits to the powers of human foresight, either of individuals or legislators. To achieve **justice**, it may well be necessary to examine a particular situation on a case-by-case basis and decide the correct solution, taking all its features into account. For example, it is hard to plan in advance to deal with the situation

in which a divorce may occur. The personal and financial situation of the parties will vary at different moments of a particular marriage; and so it is hard to foresee what will be a fair way of solving issues such as the division of property or the arrangements for the care of children. Giving a flexible discretion to a decision-maker or encouraging the parties to agree in advance may well be the most appropriate way of achieving a just outcome at the moment of divorce.

These competing ideas of certainty and flexibility create a tension that pervades the law. The demand for certainty creates a pressure for clear and precise rules, so that everyone knows where they stand. The need for flexibility is met by giving discretion to individuals or officials to take decisions in the light of all the circumstances of particular situations. The law creates frameworks in which discretionary decisions can be taken. The positive side of such flexibility is the ability to adjust the legal outcome to the needs of individuals. The potential negative side is that this leaves considerable power in the hands of the decision-maker, which could be abused in an arbitrary fashion. In order to control this, the law usually tries to stipulate the procedures by which decisions are made, eg who has to be consulted, what information is needed, and by what process the decision is to be reached. In addition, the law will set out a number of measures to make the decision-maker accountable, such as duties to give reasons, to hear objections, and to give publicity to decisions.

Legal certainty has become a recognized principle of law. One manifestation is the rejection of the retrospective application of rules or decisions where this will undermine established legal positions. For example, a ban on imports that affects supply contracts already made is equivalent to an expropriation and might well be held unlawful, unless it can be justified by some imperative public interest. Even when no existing rights are affected, a citizen may have legitimate expectations based on past practice or assurances of being allowed to continue with an activity (eg trading in a Sunday market) or of being granted a permit to do so by a public authority. In such cases, before the public authority can depart from past practice or assurances it has already given, it would typically be expected to consider representations (oral or in writing) from the person affected about whether the expectation should be overridden and what impact this might have. It would also be expected to give reasons for doing so that are serious and take due account of the impact of the decision on her.

An obvious application of this idea is the doctrine of **precedent**. Courts are concerned not to overrule longstanding rules or interpretations on which people may have relied, unless there is a clear need to do so. Legal certainty is also an increasingly important influence on how administrative and legislative rules are drafted. Rules that are intelligible and clear are more likely to provide the security on which citizens rely in operating their affairs.   JOHN BELL

chance, loss of When, in a legal context, it is necessary to answer a question about what would have happened, what has happened, or what will happen in circumstances of uncertainty, one approach that may be adopted is to accept statistical estimates. As an example of the uncertainty about what would have happened, suppose that a transport provider, in breach of obligation to a finalist in a beauty competition, fails to convey her to the final of the competition, in which there is a total of five finalists. It is unclear whether, had she been able to compete, the woman would have won the contest. One possible way of conceptualizing the woman's grievance against the transport provider is to say that the breach of obligation caused her to lose a 20 per cent chance of winning the competition and to award her damages against the transport provider of 20 per cent of the value of the prize. Where this approach is adopted, it is accepted that a grievance, for which a legal remedy may be available, can relate to 'damage' constituted by loss of a chance of an advantageous outcome, even if the outcome was statistically improbable.

Next, consider uncertainty about what would have happened at some future time. For example, the basic legal rule for the calculation of **compensation** for injury caused by torts and breaches of contract is that the injurer should pay the injured claimant sufficient money to restore the claimant, as far as money can, to the position he would have been entitled to be in had the injury not occurred, including the position in which he would have been in the future. But we cannot be sure what *would have happened* had the claimant not been injured. Suppose a defendant carelessly runs over a stranger whose leg must be amputated as a consequence. If the stranger had been a trainee ballet dancer, the orthodox rule would require assessment of the chance that the trainee would have succeeded as a ballet dancer. Even if the chance of this is small, say 10 per cent, the injured trainee is entitled to a sum representing this lost chance.

Consider also uncertainty about what *will actually happen* in the future. For example, there may be a remote chance, say 5 per cent, that our trainee ballet dancer may develop cancer as a result of the amputation of her leg. Under the basic legal rules for assessment of damages she would be entitled to a sum representing this risk, technically the lost chance of remaining cancer-free.

Finally, when there is uncertainty about what *has actually happened* in the past, the loss-of-a-chance approach may be adopted. As an example of this type of uncertainty, suppose a boy accidentally falls out of a tree and injures his hip. When he arrives at hospital his condition is such that medical knowledge only allows a crude assessment that even if the hospital treated him appropriately, he would have only a 25 per cent chance of avoiding the development of necrosis in his injured hip. In breach of legal obligation the hospital fails to treat the boy and he develops necrosis. According to the medical evidence, of 100 boys with such an injury from a fall, 75 were doomed to develop necrosis whatever the hospital did or did not do. Medical science is unable to say whether this particular boy was one who would have avoided necrosis had he been treated. If the boy alleges that the hospital was a cause of his necrosis he will fail because, statistically, but-for the hospital's failure it is more likely than not that he would have developed the necrosis anyway. However, the boy may be allowed to argue that, at the best approximation, all boys in his position presenting at the hospital had a 25 per cent chance of avoiding necrosis, that the conduct of the hospital had deprived him of this chance, and that he should be allowed to recover damages proportional to that deprivation.

The law tends to embrace loss-of-a-chance concepts far more readily when applied to matters in the future: what would have occurred post-trial had the wrong behaviour not occurred, and what will in fact occur after trial. The deployment of the concept in cases of uncertainty about what actually happened in the past is viewed with caution because, among other things, it appears to undermine the orthodox approach to proof, which is based on an all-or-nothing standard.   JANE STAPLETON

See also: **burden of proof; causation**

Chancery Court The Chancery was in origin the King's writing office for issuing and filing documents, headed by the King's Chancellor, more recently Lord Chancellor. Though some authors have suggested Anglo-Saxon origins, the currently dominant view is that it was a Norman import after 1066.

The regularization of the writ system from the reign of Henry II onwards gave the Chancery a specific role in the legal system as the body which issued

writs. Occasional reports exist of legal argument before the Chancellor as to which writ (if any) should issue on the basis of the claimant's allegations. Its character as the office for the issue of royal documents also gave the Chancellor a jurisdiction in relation to the validity and enforcement of documents enrolled in Chancery (both royal grants by letters patent, and some private contracts); and in proceedings in connection with the Crown's feudal rights over its tenants in chief. Like most public bodies in the pre-modern legal regime, the Chancery also had a privilege jurisdiction over cases involving its officials. These aspects of the Chancery's jurisdiction are called the 'Latin side' of the Chancery because the proceedings, like those at **common law** at the time, were recorded in Latin.

In the late fourteenth or early fifteenth century, the Chancellor acquired responsibility for dealing in a summary way with petitions complaining of injustices in the regular legal system. By the 1450s, this was coming to be thought of as a specific jurisdiction, called 'conscience'. The jurisdiction could also—until modern times—be called the 'English side' of the Chancery, because the proceedings were in English; from the late sixteenth or early seventeenth century it began to be called the equity jurisdiction.

The typical issues in 'conscience' identified by reporters and writers in the early period were uses (**trusts**) of land; contracts incompletely recorded by documents, including penalties and mortgages, and those vitiated by mistake, impossibility, or fraud; and cases more generally where relevant documents were lost or in the hands of the adverse party.

Procedure on the English side of Chancery ('bill procedure') was distinguished by three main features. The first was that while common law 'original' writs of summons made very specific claims (the 'forms of action'), the summons (the subpoena) gave the defendant no notice at all of the basis of the claim; and the petition or bill was a single form which could contain a variety of claims. The second was that, in place of common law pleadings, the defendant was required to answer the claimant's claims in detail and on oath. Admissions in the defendant's answer were the main form of proof in Chancery. The third, less practically important, feature was that jury trial was not used: witness evidence, so far as it was used, was taken down in writing by court officials or local commissioners.

Before the Civil War, the English bill jurisdiction of the Chancery was one among a large number of jurisdictions using similar procedures. However, these procedures were episodically politically controversial from 1415 (at the latest), and down to the American Revolution, on the ground that they denied 'due process'. The Civil War and Restoration Settlement saw the abolition of many of the bill jurisdictions. Chancery's equity jurisdiction survived. This was probably because, on the one hand, it was largely limited to contract, property, and succession matters, and did not pose a global political alternative to common law; and on the other, incorporating the subjects it dealt with into the common law would have required such major reform as to amount to codification.

In the seventeenth and eighteenth centuries the jurisdiction of the Chancery expanded in some directions and contracted in others. The Latin side largely withered away, leaving jurisdiction in relation to the guardianship of infants and the mentally disordered, and a few other odd elements, as relics which became absorbed into the equity side. The simpler parts of the equity contract jurisdiction, especially relief against penalties, were absorbed into common law.

On the other hand, the Chancellor's statutory powers to issue commissions in relation to bankruptcy and charities gave rise to a supervisory jurisdiction in equity. The inconvenient common law rule that the church courts had no jurisdiction to probate wills of land led to an 'estate' jurisdiction in Chancery, created at first by inserting express trusts in the will, and later through implied trusts. The jurisdiction over mortgages led to the elaboration of rules of priority in relation to multiple mortgages.

The consequence of these developments was that by the late eighteenth and early nineteenth century the Chancery's caseload was skewed towards complex long-term multi-party litigation. Its staffing was insufficient for the purpose, and its procedures allowed too great a facility for appeals. The result were the notorious delays of the unreformed Chancery made famous by Charles Dickens' *Bleak House*. A series of attempts to improve the situation culminated in the incorporation of Chancery and its powers in the single Supreme Court of Judicature by the Judicature Acts 1873–1875.

MICHAEL MacNAIR

GW Spence, *The Equitable Jurisdiction of the Court of Chancery* (London: V&R Stevens & GS Norton, 1846), vol i

J Baker, *An Introduction to English Legal History* (London: Butterworths, 4th edn, 2002), ch 6

Channel Islands law   The Channel Islands comprise two 'Bailiwicks', namely Jersey and Guernsey. The former comprises the Island of Jersey, the latter the Islands of Alderney, Brecqhou, Herm, Guernsey, and Sark. Geographically they are much closer to France than to England. While both Bailiwicks are Crown Dependencies (of the English Crown) they are each separate jurisdictions, with their own laws, customs, and institutions.

The Islands owe their unique status to the fact that, historically, they formed part of the Duchy of Normandy. When Duke William conquered England in 1066, the government of both duchy and kingdom came under the same King or Duke, with interruptions, until the year 1204 when King John, great-great-great grandson of the Conqueror, was dispossessed of continental Normandy by the French King. The Channel Islands remained loyal to the English Crown, but retained their identity as vestiges of Normandy without ever becoming incorporated into the Kingdom of England or the United Kingdom.

Each Bailiwick has its own Royal Court with a Bailiff at its head. Each evolved a parliamentary assembly, known respectively as the Assembly of the States of Jersey and the States of Deliberation in Guernsey. The reference to 'States' relates to the early composition of the assemblies comprising the various 'États', as in France. The Bailiff in each Bailiwick occupies the position of both senior judge and presiding officer of the assembly. Appeals from the Royal Courts of both Islands are to their respective Courts of Appeal, although the Courts' members comprise the same body of eminent United Kingdom judges and lawyers. Appeal from the Court of Appeal is to the Judicial Committee of the Privy Council. Alderney and Sark have their own legislatures and courts but are, essentially, dependencies of Guernsey.

After 1204, Norman laws and customs were maintained in the Islands. Royal privileges were granted and confirmed in a succession of Charters. Channel Island law continued to look to Norman **customary law**, itself first collated in the mid-thirteenth century and elaborated in later commentaries, principally Guillaume Terrien's *Commentaires du Droict Civil tant public que privé, observé au pays & Duché de Normandie*, 1574. In 1583 Guernsey law was defined by reference to Terrien. Jersey law retained a greater fluidity, although partly codifying its law in 1771. However, customary law itself had a fairly narrow purview. Its chief concerns related to questions of jurisdiction, feudal rights, and obligations and, above all, the law of succession. Narrow customary law was supplemented by legislation and court decision. The French *Code civil* of 1804 marked the end of continental Norman customary law. The *Code* influenced Channel Island law, while at the same time English law came

to have an increasingly profound influence as the Islands themselves became more Anglicized in the nineteenth and twentieth centuries.

Although the United Kingdom claims the theoretical right to legislate directly for the Bailiwicks, in practice it would only do so after consultation and by agreement. It is more common that UK legislation will be expressed as capable of being extended to the Islands with such amendments as might be necessary. In fact the vast majority of Islands legislation is made by the Bailiwicks themselves. In the case of Laws (statutes) these are subject to Royal Assent by way of Order in Council. It is very rare that an Assenting Order would not be granted. Increasingly commonly, such primary legislation permits subsequent amendment or law making in the relevant area by local ordinance or regulation. Both Bailiwicks have power to make more purely local or police regulations without the need for an Order in Council in any event.

Both Bailiwicks are within the European Community free trade area without being members of the Union. The relationship is governed by Protocol 3 to the United Kingdom's Act of Accession to the Community, containing a series of articles imposing limited obligations relating to free movement of industrial and agricultural goods, and identical treatment of Community nationals. Both Bailiwicks have taken powers to implement Community legal provisions either when they perceive themselves as being obliged to under Protocol 3 or because it is convenient to do so. Channel Island law remains an amalgam of Norman customary law, **Roman law** and **French law**, and is strongly influenced by English case law. English statute is often used as a template for legislative drafting. Modern Channel Island law occupies an interesting position between the Anglo-American and Continental traditions, leaving it, perhaps, better placed to adjust to the increasing Europeanization of law than, say, English law.

GORDON DAWES

channels 3, 4 and 5   *see* **public service broadcasting**

character merchandising   Character merchandising may be defined as the exploitation of the names and images of famous personalities and fictional characters (the 'character') in connection with the manufacture and distribution of a wide variety of mass-market merchandise from T-shirts and toys to food and soft drinks. Today, merchandising programmes involve many fields of cultural activity ranging from sporting events to art exhibitions, providing a means by which both profit and non-profit organizations can raise significant revenue. The character will normally be the subject of licensing agreements enabling one or more third parties to be regarded as authorized users of the character.

Where the character is not the subject of a registered **trade mark**, in the **United Kingdom** the 'owner' of the character may seek to prevent its unauthorized use by means of the **common law** action for **passing off**. However, there are difficulties with passing off, as courts in the UK have tended to draw back from effectively licensing the use of unregistered marks or of material **copyright** in which is not owned by the licensor. To succeed in an action for passing off the claimant has the burden of proving not only that there is an operative misrepresentation but also damage to the goodwill or reputation of the business. While the courts recognize that goodwill may attach to the activities of sportsmen, writers, and performers or to the licensing of a character's image or name, proving misrepresentation tends to be the stumbling block.

While there is no requirement, in a passing-off action, that the claimant and the defendant be involved in a common field of activity, without a common field it will be difficult for the claimant to establish that the defendant falsely represented that its goods are connected with the business of the claimant. It will also be more difficult for the claimant to demonstrate consumer confusion and, therefore, damage to goodwill. Without copyright in the name, it is insufficient for the claimant to show that the public would assume (a) that there was a licensing arrangement between the parties and; (b) that the licensed goods would be of a certain quality.

Recently, the courts have recognized that an individual celebrity, who is falsely depicted as having endorsed a product or service, may succeed in claiming damages for passing off. The claimant needs to prove, first, that he or she had a significant reputation or goodwill at the date of the conduct complained of and; secondly, that the actions of the defendant gave rise to a false message, which would be understood by a significant section of the public, that its goods had been endorsed or recommended, or are approved of, by the claimant.

While the primary remedy sought in a passing-off action is usually an injunction to stop the defendant's conduct at the first opportunity, if passing off is proved, available remedies include delivery up of offending merchandise and compensation for loss of sales and loss of fees and royalties.   GAIL EVANS

charities Charities are organizations established for public purposes which the law considers to be entitled to special protection and benefits. A generally accepted list of purposes regarded as charitable appeared in the Preamble to the Statute of Charitable Uses 1601. Over the years the courts expanded the type of purpose accepted as charitable, not necessarily with method or logic, until it was difficult to determine with ease which purposes were charitable and which were not. The Charities Act 2006 now provides a list of charitable purposes which is based on the previous case law. A similar, although not identical, list is provided for Scotland by the Charities and Trustee Investment (Scotland) Act 2005.

The following purposes are listed in the 2006 Act: the prevention or relief of poverty; the advancement of education; the advancement of religion; the advancement of health or the saving of lives; the advancement of citizenship or community development; the advancement of the arts, culture, heritage, or science; the advancement of amateur sport; the advancement of human rights, conflict resolution, or reconciliation or the promotion of religious or racial equality and diversity; the advancement of environmental protection or improvement; the relief of those in need, by reason of youth, age, ill-health, disability, financial hardship, or other disadvantage; the advancement of animal welfare; the promotion of efficiency of the armed forces of the Crown or of the efficiency of the police, fire, and rescue services or ambulance service; and other purposes recognized as charitable under existing law. Whilst the list does make it easier to see which purposes are charitable and which are not, it can still be difficult at times to determine if a particular organization is charitable. For example, although the 2006 Act states that 'religion' includes a religion which involves belief in more than one god and one that does not involve belief in a god, there is considerable debate as to what is a 'religion' for the purposes of charity law. It is also far from clear when purposes are political rather than charitable.

The 2006 Act recognizes that views as to what is charitable will change as social circumstances change. The list is not set in concrete. Provision is made in the Act for the courts to add to the list of charitable purposes if new purposes are within the spirit of existing purposes.

Even if an organization has a purpose which is regarded as charitable, it will not be a charity in law if it is not for the public benefit; charities are public, not private, bodies. Thus an organization set up to provide scholarships will not be charitable if the only children who can benefit are the children of employees of a particular company. Similarly, an art collection will not be a charity if there is only very limited public access. The 2006 Act removes all presumptions of public benefit and no organization can be a charity if it does not pass the public benefit test. The Charity Commission is charged with producing guidance as what is necessary for the public benefit requirement to be satisfied for particular types of charity.

The law has always looked favourably on charities and tries to ensure that property intended for charitable purposes is gained and retained for charity. The usual rules of certainty of object do not apply with the same rigour to charitable **trusts** as to non-charitable trusts, and the court will always apply construe charitable gifts benignly. Charitable trusts are not subject to the rules against perpetuity; and charities still exist today which were founded in the eleventh century. If a charity fails for any reason, the law applies its property 'cy-pres', that is, for other charitable purposes as near as possible to the original ones. Once property is in the hands of charity it stays with charity; property is not returned to donors.

The most important benefits of charitable status are now fiscal. Charities themselves have major reliefs from taxation and there are valuable tax reliefs to encourage donation to charity. Charities do not enjoy a blanket relief from tax, but specific provisions do exempt charities from the majority of direct taxes. For example, subject to anti-avoidance provisions, charities do not pay tax on investment income nor do they pay **capital gains tax**. There is only limited relief from income tax on trading income so charities often have to set up a separate trading company to get maximum tax relief. There are also some exemptions from value added tax for fundraising events. Individuals giving to charity by Gift Aid receive relief from **income tax** on the amount of the gift. Regular donors through payroll giving also receive relief from income tax. There are reliefs from income tax on gifts of shares and land and reliefs from capital gains tax and **inheritance tax** for gifts of capital assets to charity.

Somewhat surprisingly, there is no one designated legal structure for charities. They can take a number of legal forms for their governing instrument. Many charities are trusts or unincorporated associations but concerns about personal liability of trustees has lead more recently-formed charities to incorporate as a company limited by guarantee. Some larger, more important charities are corporations by Royal Charter or by Act of Parliament. The Charities Act 2006 contains provision for a new incorporated body for charities, the Charitable Incorporated Association, to be registered with the Charity Commission.

The Charity Commission is the regulatory body for charities. With few exceptions, charities must register with the Commission and the register is open to public inspection and on the Charity Commission website. Charities have to send accounts and a report on activities annually to the Commission. The Charity Commission provides advice for charities and has a variety of powers, such as the power to update governing instruments, which can assist charities to operate more effectively. In the case of mismanagement or misappropriation of property the Charity Commission has power to intervene in a charity and can, for example, freeze bank accounts, suspend trustees, and put in a receiver and manager.

Many charities depend on funds raised from the public. There is considerable potential for abuse and not just of the public; individual charities can be abused if they are dependent on particular fundraisers. The law controls fundraising in a number of ways. Anyone who wishes to carry out a public charitable collection must have a certificate from the Charity Commission and also a permit from the relevant local authority for each collection. A professional fundraiser cannot solicit funds for a charity unless there is a contract between the fundraiser and the charity which deals with specified matters such as the amount of remuneration and methods of fundraising to be used. The fundraiser must also tell potential donors which charity he or she is raising funds for and how he or she is to be paid. Much fundraising is now the subject of self-regulation through the Fundraising Standards Board.

This entry assumes that all the provisions of the Charities Act 2006 are in operation (although not all were at the time of writing). JEAN WARBURTON

See also: **tax avoidance; trusts, taxation of**

Charter of Economic Rights and Duties of States *see* international economic law

Charter of Fundamental Rights (EU)

The Charter of Fundamental Rights of the European Union is a written catalogue of rights which was 'solemnly proclaimed' in Nice on 7 December 2000 by the **European Commission**, the **Council of Ministers,** and the **European Parliament**. It was then reproduced, with some amendments, in Part II of the Constitutional Treaty. Whilst the Charter is, for the time being, not legally binding, it would acquire treaty status should the Constitutional Treaty enter into force.

The Charter was drafted by a Convention composed of representatives of national Parliaments, national governments, the European Parliament, and the Commission; its mandate was to codify 'existing' rights, drawing from a number of sources, from common constitutional traditions to international **treaties,** so as to make rights protected at EU level more visible to citizens.

The Charter departs from the traditional division between **civil and political rights** on the one hand and **economic and social rights** on the on the other. Instead, the Charter adopts a 'horizontal approach' to fundamental rights aimed at underlining their indivisibility. Accordingly, it is divided into chapters along six fundamental values: Dignity, Freedom, **Equality**, Solidarity, **Citizenship,** and **Justice**. The rights listed in the Charter comprise traditional rights (for example, **freedom of expression**) as well as 'new generation' rights (for example, bioethics rights). Furthermore, the Charter also contains a number of 'inspirational' values. Those are referred to as principles and are aimed at directing, as well as constraining, legislative **discretion**. They are not however free-standing rights. For instance, environmental protection is one such principle: whilst individuals do not have a free-standing right to a high level of environmental protection, the EU legislature always has to take into account such a principle when legislating and failure to do so might entail the annulment of Union legislation.

Charter rights are not absolute, and can be limited for the pursuance of public interest objectives. Any such limitation, however, must respect the 'essence' of the right at stake, must be proportionate and necessary. In any event, the level of protection granted by the Charter cannot fall below that afforded by the **European Convention on Human Rights** and the Charter cannot be interpreted as negatively affecting rights recognised by the other sources of general principles of Union law, including national **constitutions**.

The Charter was intended as a solution to the lack of a catalogue of rights for the European Union: it is therefore primarily directed at Union institutions. However, it also binds Member States when they are adopting regulatory measures to implement Union law since in those cases Member States are acting as the Union's delegated powers and must therefore comply with the Union's constitutional system. Although the Charter is not at present legally binding, this does not mean it is a legally insignificant document. The European Parliament and the Commission have already declared themselves bound by the Charter regardless of its official legal status and the European courts have referred to it in several rulings.   ELEANOR SPAVENTA

See also: **European treaties; horizontal application of human rights**

Charter of the Fundamental Social Rights of Workers   *see* Social Chapter

chartered companies in international law   *see* territory

chattels and fixtures
The legal definition of land includes all fixtures attached to the land. A fixture is an item that has become so attached to the land that it forms part of the land. By contrast, a chattel is a thing that never loses its status as personal property. In deciding whether an item is a fixture or a chattel, it is relevant to consider the degree of annexation to the land and the purpose of annexation; but the purpose or intent of annexation is the more important consideration. Purpose and intent are judged 'objectively' rather than 'subjectively'. The question is whether an observer would conclude that the item was intended to be placed on or annexed to the land permanently and thus to constitute a lasting improvement to the land, or (on the contrary) that it was placed or attached merely to facilitate enjoyment of the item itself. The owner of a chattel may remove the item at any time, whereas generally, a fixture may only be removed by the landowner, or by someone with the landowner's authority. However, by way of exception to this rule, a tenant may remove fixtures which were affixed for trade, domestic, ornamental, or, in limited circumstances, agricultural purposes.

LYNDEN GRIGGS

R Abbs, 'The Law of Fixtures: Informed Principle or Independent Predilection' (2004) 11 *Australian Property Law Journal* 31.

P Luther, 'Fixtures and Chattels: A Question of More or Less' (2004) 24 *Oxford Journal of Legal Studies* 597.

chemical weapons and warfare   *see* arms control

chemicals regulation
Chemicals regulation aims to control the health and environmental risks posed by the production, use, and/or disposal of chemical substances and preparations. Moreover, as chemicals are valuable commodities, harmonized rules affecting their marketing facilitate trade.

A first challenge confronting the effective regulation of chemicals is the scarcity of sufficient and reliable information on chemical risks. In response, chemicals regulation imposes information supply duties on producers, importers and, in areas such as the European Union ('EU'), users of chemicals. The stringency of information supply duties differs significantly between countries. For instance, since late 1981, the EU preconditions the marketing of new chemicals on the submission of detailed technical data, including toxicity and eco-toxicity data. Information duties under the US Toxic Substances Control Act 1976 are more limited, and in principle do not cover toxicology test results. Chemicals information is used by regulatory authorities (or private parties acting on their behalf) to perform an assessment of the chemical risks. Hence, chemicals regulation includes standarized **risk** assessment rules.

Another challenge for chemicals regulation is to develop and enforce strategies to manage and reduce identified risks. Regulatory techniques range from facilitating ones, such as the classification of dangerous chemicals in hazard categories, and packaging and labelling rules, to more interventionist measures, including marketing and use restrictions for dangerous substances, bans, and authorization requirements. Classification is pivotal since, once classified as dangerous, chemicals can be subjected to additional **safety** requirements, within but also outside the chemicals regulatory framework, such as in the context of an **environmental impact assessment**, or in transport regulation. A Globally Harmonized System of Classification and Labelling of Chemicals ('GHS') has been developed internationally and should be fully operational by 2008. Authorization requirements are rare for general categories of chemicals, but are commonly found in the regulation of chemicals for a specific use, such as pesticides and pharmaceuticals.

The EU has the most precautionary and restrictive approach to chemicals control. Regulation 1907/2006 on the Registration, Evaluation and Authorization of Chemicals ('REACH') conditions production or trade of all chemicals, whether old or new, on their registration with the **European Commission**, which is itself conditioned on the supply of chemical data. High volume production chemicals are subjected to a risk evaluation, and limited categories of very dangerous chemicals, such as carcinogens, must obtain authorization prior to (continued) marketing. The REACH Regulation also demands that, where feasible, highly dangerous chemicals should be substituted by less dangerous ones. REACH entered into effect in June 2007.   VEERLE HEYVAERT

cheques   *see* **negotiable instruments**

Chicago Convention   *see* **air law**

Chicago School   'Chicago' is a school of monetarist and free-market economics, called after the University where many of its originators (such as Milton Friedman) and adherents worked. Chicago School scholars, such as George Stigler, developed a distinctive view of **competition law** ('**antitrust**') which first came into the ascendant in the US during the 1970s and 1980s and has since had a profound influence on competition law thinking throughout the world. For example, it revolutionized the antitrust analysis of vertical restraints. The Chicago School questioned the conclusions of the 'Harvard School' that the market structure is of prime importance and that concentration in general leads to monopoly profits. Its approach was rigorously theoretical rather than empirical and was based on neoclassical price theory.

The Chicago School holds that most markets are competitive, even with relatively few suppliers; monopoly tends to be self-correcting and government **regulation** provides the only real barriers to entry; economies of scale are present in more industries than previously thought; firms are profit-maximizers; and vertical restraints should not usually be regulated. This leads to a belief in minimal intervention by antitrust law and confidence that imperfections in the market will ultimately be corrected by the forces of **competition**. The fundamental Chicago view is that the pursuit of efficiency, by which is meant allocative efficiency as defined by the market, should be the *sole* goal of competition law. Other concerns, of a 'socio-political' nature such as those to do with employment, 'fairness', the protection of small businesses, and the economic freedom of competitors, should play no role in competition law. Original Chicago School thinking has more recently been tempered by new insights, particularly in respect of the importance of strategic behaviour and dynamic competition, leading to what is known as the 'Post-Chicago' approach.   BRENDA SUFRIN

RH Bork, *The Antitrust Paradox: A Policy at War with Itself* (New York: Basic Books, 1978; reprinted with a new Introduction and Epilogue, 1993)

RA Posner, *Antitrust Law* (Chicago: University of Chicago Press, 2nd edn, 2001)

See also: **efficiency in competition law**

child   In law a child is a **person** under the age of majority, which in the UK is now eighteen. The definition of 'child' in the **Children Act 1989** and the Children (Scotland) Act 1995 is also a person under the age of eighteen, as is the definition in the **United Nations Convention on the Rights of the Child 1989**, to which the UK is a signatory. Obviously a child is a legal person in law and the bearer of (some) rights, but he or she also labours under some legal disabilities. Most of these end at age eighteen, but for some legal purposes, the age at which 'childhood' ends varies according to specific context. The age at which children in England and Wales may be employed by someone other than a parent (fourteen, under the Children and Young Person's Act 1933) is different, for example, from the age at which they may be deemed legally responsible for crimes (ten, under the Crime and Disorder Act 1998). And in some situations, the age at which children may have legal **capacity** varies with the individual child, such as in the context of capacity to give **consent to medical treatment** (*Gillick v West Norfolk and Wisbech Area Health Authority* (1986)). The definition of child, then, is not fixed; it has changed over the years and is still changeable. To that extent, 'child' may be said to be a socially constructed concept.

Historically, children were of only marginal concern to law; they were treated virtually as the property of their fathers. The law began to be interested in the welfare and protection of children in the nineteenth century and, since then law and policy have focused on promoting and protecting children's welfare. The Children Act 1989 (for England and Wales) and the Children (Scotland) Act 1995 both state that the welfare of the child is the paramount consideration in determining questions about children's upbringing. A legal focus on welfare means that decision-makers rely upon professionals such as child psychologists and social workers to help them determine not only what is 'good' for children generally, but also what is 'good' for the particular child involved. Perhaps unsurprisingly, understandings of children's welfare have changed over the years, and one of the most significant recent shifts is that toward some notion of respect for their rights.

Children's rights are contentious, but the move towards respecting them might be one which simply gives teeth to law's demand to ascertain children's views or 'wishes and feelings' about proceedings concerning them. In any event, courts are beginning to pay more attention to The UN Convention on Children's Rights and to children's rights claims under the Human Rights Act 1998. Some commentators have argued that legal focus on children's rights is misguided both philosophically and legally because it frustrates or disregards law's responsibility to protect and promote children's welfare. Others argue that children should be accorded all the rights of adults. Courts tend to take account of children's rights, but to make them subject always to welfare.

ALISON DIDUCK

See *also*: **children and medical treatment; child protection**

child abduction   It is a criminal offence to abduct a **child** from the UK without 'appropriate consent' (for example, of a parent with **parental responsibility**). If it is suspected a child is about to be removed from the jurisdiction it is possible to apply to a court for an order preventing the removal of the child. A parent wishing to remove the child permanently from the jurisdiction should obtain the consent of all those with parental responsibility for the child or seek a court order approving the removal.

The UK is a signatory to the Hague Convention on the Civil Aspects of International Child Abduction 1980. The Convention applies where a child who is habitually resident in a contracting state is wrongfully removed and brought to another contracting state. The presumption is that a dispute over a child's residence should be heard by the courts of the country where the child is habitually resident. Normally, therefore, an abducted child will be returned to their country of origin unless, for example, it can be shown that there is a grave risk of physical or psychological harm to the child. If the child has been removed from a country which is not signatory to the Convention to the UK, then the courts will decide whether to return the child to their country of origin based on what is in the welfare of the child.

JONATHAN HERRING

child abuse   The maltreatment of children has, since the nineteenth century, justified law's intervention in the parent–child relationship, overriding the principle of parental authority. However, it was not until the 'discovery' of 'battered child syndrome' in the 1960s, by the American paediatrician, CH Kemp, that 'child abuse' took on significance for policymakers and **courts**. Since then, several different types of **child** abuse have been identified by psychiatrists and the caring professions—physical abuse, sexual abuse, emotional or psychological abuse, and, most recently, ritual abuse. A succession of child abuse scandals and subsequent public **inquiries**, starting with the Maria Colwell Inquiry in 1974, put enormous pressure on governments to protect children and promote their welfare. As a result, legislative measures aimed at combating child abuse left a wide **discretion** to the courts in determining whether abuse had or had not occurred and in authorizing social workers and **police** to take compulsory measures to protect children by removing them from the family or supervising the family.

In England and Wales, the statute governing the principles for legal intervention is the **Children Act 1989**, while for Scotland it is the Children (Scotland) Act 1995. The major difference between these jurisdictions lies in the fact that in Scotland these decisions are made, not by courts, but by lay people sitting as Children's Panels.

In both jurisdictions the decisions often involve difficult assessment of **expert evidence** and the balancing of the risks of allowing the child to remain in a potentially harmful family situation against the obvious disadvantages of institutional or uncertain substitute care. In recent years the decision-making process has been made more complex by the need to respect the rights of the child, and in particular, to obtain and take into account the child's views. In England and Wales this is achieved by the appointment of a Children's Guardian and, on occasions, a lawyer to represent the child's interests. The result is often lengthy contested hearings with as many as four or five lawyers representing the interests of the parties. The Scottish Children's Panels have avoided this situation by involving parents directly in the Panel's decision and by introducing lay 'Safeguarders' to represent the child's interests.

There is no evidence to suggest that the lengthy, complex and costly decision-making process undertaken by the English and Welsh courts results in better outcomes for children than the Scottish Children's Panels or, indeed, than the French system of children's judges, who take direct responsibility for protecting children and where lawyers play little part. It is suggested that these outcomes are likely to depend upon matters over which the court has no control, such as the availability of resources, the efficiency of social services, police and other agencies and events affecting the child which occur after the legal decision. One could justifiably argue, therefore, that the present system operating in England and Wales owes more to the self-generated demands of lawyers, judges and court administrators than to any firm evidence-based assessment of the effectiveness of legal decision-making.   MICHAEL KING

See also: **guardianship and children; Children's rights**

child labour   A combination of the idea of childhood as an age of innocence and nurture and the need for a more numerate and literate workforce has led to legislative restrictions on work by children of school age since the late nineteenth century in Britain and other advanced economies. EU Directive 94/33 on the Protection of Young People at Work fixes a minimum working age of 15, and places detailed restrictions on the type of work and conditions of employment for adolescents between the ages of 15 and 18. The Children and Young Persons Act 1933, as amended, establishes criminal offences in the UK for breach of similar rules, but it also creates a complex body of regulations that permit exceptions to be made for certain kinds of child labour, such as acting, work in the family, and light work. These regulations and local authority by-laws achieve only patchy compliance owing to their intricacy and weaknesses of local authority enforcement. The abolition of child labour is a core standard of the **International Labour Organization** ('ILO') of the **United Nations**, but in developing economies this principle is frequently rejected because in subsistence agriculture and crafts children's work is often vital to a family's wellbeing. The ILO has more recently concentrated its attention on a campaign to eliminate forced labour, including military service, child prostitution and pornography, drug trafficking, and work likely to harm the health, **safety**, and morals of children.   HUGH COLLINS

child offenders   The law concerning **child offenders** varies between countries, and is also shaped by binding international treaties to which any particular country is party (eg the **Convention on the Rights of the Child** (1989, 'UNCRC') and by 'good practice' norms articulated in international policy (for example, the UN Standard Minimum Rules for the Administration of Juvenile Justice). Further, there can be variations of practice within one country—eg in the UK, between the jurisdictions of England and Wales on the one hand and Scotland on the other. The focus here is on the pertinent international treaty rules, all of which apply throughout the UK.

Regarding the term 'child offender', UNCRC (Article 1) defines a child as someone under eighteen 'unless under the law applicable to the child, majority is attained earlier', and many countries including the UK do set the age of majority at eighteen. Countries also specify different ages (eg ten years old) as the applicable 'minimum age of criminal **responsibility**'—the age below which children are deemed to lack **capacity** to commit a crime. Further, there may be different rules for the treatment of child offenders in other specified age categories (eg between ten to thirteen, and fourteen to seventeen).

The widely ratified UNCRC provides a summary of the main norms applicable to child offenders. It also incorporates other rules via its Article 41, stating that this treaty's provisions will be trumped by others 'more conducive to the realisation of the rights of the child' contained in relevant national or **international law** binding on that country.

The UNCRC rests on key measures that inform the application of its other substantive articles. These include: (a) that the 'best interests' of children shall be a primary consideration in actions concerning them (Article 3); and (b) that children, according to their capacity, shall be entitled to express their views on matters affecting them (Article 12).

Certain articles of the UNCRC are more specifically pertinent to child offenders. Article 37, on the deprivation of liberty and the prohibition of **torture** and analogous treatment, prohibits the death penalty or life imprisonment without possibility of release. Further, deprivation of liberty must not be arbitrary or unlawful, and should be a last resort and for the shortest possible time. Children deprived of liberty must be treated with '**humanity** and respect' and appropriately for their age. They should generally be separated from adults, and allowed to maintain family contact.

Article 40, on the administration of juvenile justice, states that children should be treated in a manner that promotes their 'sense of dignity and worth', reinforces their respect for others, and takes into account their age and the desirability of promoting their social reintegration. It specifies a right to legal assistance and other due process measures, while also urging governments to make provision, eg for informal proceedings and non-custodial sentences.

Further relevant articles include Article 38, which, *inter alia*, makes clear that, even in situations of armed conflict, children should benefit from due process safeguards and the prohibition of the death penalty.   JENNY KUPER

See also: **young offenders**

child protection Society assumes that parents are naturally responsible for the care and upbringing of their children. When a **child** is born and parentage established, both parents will be given **parental responsibility** for the child. In a minority of cases the identity of the father is not established or he is not registered as the father. Here the mother alone, if the parents are unmarried, will have parental responsibility for the child. In some instances prescribed by law, someone other than a parent may acquire parental responsibility. Parental responsibility gives to the parent the legal powers to take decisions about the child's upbringing. It also places duties on the parent to satisfy the child's basic needs, such as feeding, clothing, and shelter. Parents must also arrange for their child to be educated. The law however allows

them to determine the precise manner in which their child is raised. It is, for example, for them to decide whether the child should be immunized, which school the child should attend or where the child is to be taken on holiday.

Where parents appear to have failed to discharge their minimum responsibilities, the local authority may act to protect the child. The primary statutory responsibility for the support and protection of children rests with local authorities. Following concern that local services for children should be properly coordinated and information effectively shared between the various agencies involved with children and families, each local authority is now responsible for establishing a Local Safeguarding Children Board. The Children Act 2004 requires each Children's Services Authority to appoint a Director of Children's Services.

There are two major aspects to the statutory responsibilities of local authorities under the Children Act 1989. First, they are required to provide support and services to children who are 'in need'. One of the most important services is to 'accommodate' a child where the parents are either dead or unable to look after the child themselves because of illness or some other reason. The majority of children accommodated in this way are looked after by the local authority for only a matter of weeks. These children are *not* in care. The arrangement involves voluntary cooperation with the parents who have a right to take the child home at any point.

Sometimes, however, there may be more serious concern that a child is being abused, neglected, or at risk. Here the authority may need to use its compulsory powers under the Children Act 1989 to protect the child. The authority must investigate the circumstances of any child in its area thought to be suffering significant harm, or at risk of suffering significant harm if action is not taken. In an emergency, the authority may act immediately under an emergency protection order. The **police** also have **emergency powers** designed to prevent significant harm to children. This may result in a child being removed from the parents for up to eight days while consideration is given to what further action needs to be taken. Where the concern, although serious, is not considered an emergency the authority will, after investigating the circumstances, hold a conference involving relevant professionals involved with the family at which the parents will usually be allowed to participate. This may result in the child being placed on the child protection register and his or her position will then be monitored through a child protection plan and the appointment of a key worker.

There are on average just under 30,000 children on the child protection register in England and Wales in recent years.

In some cases the concern about possible abuse or neglect may lead to the authority seeking a court order authorizing the care or supervision of the child. Abuse and neglect are difficult to define but they must be 'significant' before compulsory action by the local authority is warranted. There are four recognized categories, namely physical abuse, sexual abuse, neglect, and emotional abuse. The largest proportion of children on the child protection register (roughly 50 per cent of the total) are there in relation to concerns about neglect. In a substantial number of cases, there are issues about more than one form of abuse. Corporal punishment of children may constitute abuse if it results in 'actual bodily harm' to the child. Serious cases of abuse or neglect may lead to criminal prosecution as well as to care proceedings.

Before a care or supervision order may be made, it is not sufficient, as in private law, that the court considers this to be in the child's best interests. It must also be proved that a minimum 'threshold' of significant harm, or risk of significant harm, to the child is crossed. It must also be proved that this risk is attributable to the child not receiving, or being at risk of not receiving, a reasonable standard of parental care or being beyond parental control. The courts have held that this test should be satisfied when the authority first takes its protective action in relation to the child. The principal facts on which the authority is relying must be proved—suspicion is not enough. Where there is doubt as to which parent or other carer may have been responsible for a child's injuries, the courts have held that it is not necessary to prove which person it is as long as it is clear that one of them is responsible. Where the child is in care, the authority must continue to consult and work in partnership with parents and must endeavour to reunite them even though this may ultimately prove impossible in some cases. At all stages of child protection the state must comply with the requirements of the **European Convention on Human Rights**. What this means is that the action it takes to protect the child must be proportionate to the risk and not excessive. It must however also take sufficient action to protect the child since failure to do so may lead to a violation of the child's convention right to be protected.

ANDREW BAINHAM

See also: **child abuse**

child support The child support scheme seeks to ensure that parents who do not live with their children make a financial contribution to their maintenance. Before the Child Support Act 1991, and in the absence of agreement between the parents, there were three main mechanisms for obtaining an order for child maintenance. First, the High Court and the County Court had various powers to award child maintenance. Second, magistrates' courts had more restricted powers to make such orders. Third, the then Department for Social Security ('DSS') could negotiate an agreement with, or obtain a court order against, the parent who was responsible for supporting the child (the 'liable relative'), a power originally derived from the **Poor Law**. The result was that orders for child maintenance were typically for modest and inconsistent amounts, and were seldom increased or enforced effectively.

The then Conservative government's concern was that these problems undermined the personal responsibility of parents to support their children, resulting in an increasing burden on the taxpayer in the form of social security payments to lone parents. Having examined responses to similar problems in both Australia and the United States, Mrs Thatcher's government introduced reforms to reduce the role of the courts in making child maintenance orders. The Child Support Act 1991 imposed a duty on all parents, whether or not they were married to each other, to support their children. For those parents, known as 'absent parents', not living with their children (or for whom they were not the primary carer, where there was shared care) this responsibility had to be met by payment of child support in accordance with the legislation. This liability related only to natural and adopted children, not to step-children.

The child support scheme introduced by the 1991 Act was different from the previous arrangements in two important respects. First, the amount of child support in any case was to be fixed by a formula, rather than being a matter of broad discretion. The original formula sought to identify the cost of bringing up children by reference to social security rates, and then to allocate that cost as between the parents in proportion to their respective incomes. Second, the Child Support Agency ('CSA') was charged with the responsibility for assessing, collecting, and enforcing child support payments. Appeals against the CSA's assessment decisions were to **tribunals** modelled on the **social security appeals** system. The courts' powers were limited to making orders where the parents either agreed on the amount payable, and the recipient was not on benefit, or where there were special circumstances (such as a child with a disability, or the fact that the child or one of the parents was not habitually resident in the United Kingdom).

The CSA was given the exclusive power to enforce its child support assessments in court where other collection methods (such as a deduction from earnings order) had proved unsuccessful.

The 1991 Act came into force in April 1993 and immediately provoked considerable public controversy. The complexity of the formula led to long delays in making assessments, which were exacerbated by widespread non-cooperation with the CSA, especially on the part of 'absent parents'. Parents with care who were in receipt of income support, and who were required to apply for child support, saw no direct financial benefit even if payments were made, because of the rules governing means-tested benefits, and so had little incentive to cooperate. The CSA was also plagued with operational problems, particularly with its computer systems, and proved to be as slow and inefficient as the courts in dealing with non-payment. The Conservative government made a series of adjustments to the child support scheme, principally designed to meet complaints from absent parents, but these changes (such as introduction of a very limited degree of discretion to depart from the formula in special cases under the Child Support Act 1995) merely added to its complexity.

The Labour government elected in 1997 brought forward more radical proposals to reform the child support scheme; and these were enacted in the Child Support, Pensions and Social Security Act 2000. They included the introduction of a new, simpler formula with the only variables being the number of children and income of the 'non-resident parent' (the new term for absent parent). To encourage compliance by both parents, parents with care who were on income support were to be allowed to keep the first £10 a week in child support by way of a 'child support premium' without affecting their benefit. The CSA was given new enforcement powers and a more efficient and personalized service was promised. However, owing to ongoing problems with both its old and new computer systems, the CSA was unable to start operating the new child support scheme until March 2003. As a result, the CSA is still running two different formula-based schemes in parallel—applications since March 2003 are handled under the 'new scheme', whereas those made between April 1993 and March 2003 remain subject to the 'old scheme'. The IT problems are such that there is no immediate prospect of these old scheme cases being transferred to the new scheme.

These continuing operational problems in the CSA led the government to launch an independent review of the child support scheme in 2006. The Henshaw Report made recommendations for a (further) redesigned child support scheme, with the aim of encouraging parents so far as possible to reach private agreements for payment of child support. The Henshaw Report also proposed that the child support premium be increased as a means of tackling child poverty. The Report envisages the gradual phasing out of the CSA and its replacement by a successor body with a lower caseload, designed to act as a back-up service for those parents who cannot agree on the level of child support to be paid. The existing old and new scheme caseloads will not automatically transfer to the successor organisation, raising difficult questions about how the substantial amounts of arrears that have accrued will be handled in the future.   NICK WIKELEY

N Wikeley, *Child Support Law and Policy* (Oxford: Hart Publishing, 2006)

child, capacity of   *see* capacity; minor

Children Act 1989   The Children Act 1989 which came into force on 14 October 1991 was the culmination of a ten-year reform process involving the **House of Commons** Social Services Committee, central government, and the Law Commission. Lady Hale, then a Law Commissioner, was a major force in its development. Unlike the previous statutes, the Act covers private law (legal relationships between children and their parents or guardians) and public law (local authority powers and duties relating to children).

The Act introduced new concepts and terminology: '**parental responsibility**', a term which covers all the legal powers and duties held by parents replaced 'parental rights' (section 3); **residence** replaced 'custody' and '**contact**' replaced '**access**'. It set out the principles to be applied by the courts considering disputes about children's upbringing. Paramount consideration must be given to the welfare of the **child**, delay is prejudicial to children's welfare and orders should only be made where this is better for the child than no order. **Courts** are given further guidance in the form of a 'welfare checklist' (section 1) and powers to make 'section 8' orders—orders relating to residence, contact, or the exercise of parental responsibility in any family proceedings.

New powers were given to local authorities to support 'children in need' and their families (section 17). Powers to commit children to care were simplified; local authorities had to apply for care orders and prove that children are suffering or at **risk** of 'significant harm' (section 31). The Act also regulates the care of children away from home.

                        JUDITH MASSON

children and divorce There are approximately 165,000 divorces each year in the United Kingdom, roughly 55 per cent of which involve children under the age of sixteen. The highest percentage of these children consistently comprises those between the ages of five and ten. Not surprisingly, there is widespread public concern about the large numbers of children caught up in the 'adult' process of divorce and about what the legal system might be able to do to ameliorate any harm to them.

There is now a substantial body of research evidence both in Britain and in North America which establishes an association between parental divorce and negative outcomes for children. Children of divorced parents, when compared with children whose parents remain married, on average do less well at school or in terms of psychological development and social relations. This research is however unable to establish cause and effect. Other factors apart from parental separation or divorce are also associated with poor outcomes for children. There is clear evidence, for example, that exposure to parental conflict is bad for children and this conflict may be present while the **marriage** is intact as well as carried on in some cases after separation. Children in high-conflict marriages may, therefore, actually benefit from parental separation and divorce.

There has been a considerable shift in official thinking on the issue of maintaining a relationship with the 'non-resident' parent, usually the father. This has been reflected in changes to the law and legal practice. It used to be thought that the most important consideration for the child's welfare was the child's relationship with the so-called 'psychological parent', usually the mother, who would be the child's primary caretaker following divorce. A very high proportion of sole 'custody' orders in favour of mothers were traditionally made, usually with 'reasonable access' only to the respective fathers. The view now most widely held and endorsed in various ways by family **legislation** is that children are likely to fare best, in the absence of special factors such as **domestic violence**, if they maintain as good a relationship with both parents as is possible in the circumstances.

The law tries to give effect to this central philosophy in a number of ways. First, the **Children Act 1989** abolished the polarizing ideas of 'custody' and 'access' and replaced these with the principle that parents remain parents despite divorce. Hence they continue to share **parental responsibility**. This was coupled with the notion that court orders should no longer be routine, but made only where it could be shown that they were necessary in order to promote the child's welfare. In the great majority of divorce cases there is therefore no need for any court order in relation to children. Parents are however required, as part of the process of divorce, to file a detailed statement of arrangements for the children. This statement covers such matters as where the children will live, what contact they are to have with the 'non-resident' parent, their education, health, financial support and so on. The statement will be scrutinized by a district judge before the divorce is granted and the court has powers, seldom used, to delay the divorce decree if there are unanswered concerns about the children.

The court must also give explicit consideration to whether it needs to exercise any of its powers to make orders. In a small minority of cases there will be a significant dispute over children. Orders in relation to contact with children, for example, account for only about 10 per cent of divorces in which children are involved. In the first instance these parents will be encouraged to reach agreement through in-court conciliation. Some may already have been trying to reach agreement through **mediation.** Where agreement is not reached the court may make a range of orders. In doing so it will be guided by the central principle that the best interests of the child concerned is the court's *paramount* consideration. The court must have regard to the views of the children themselves bearing in mind their age and understanding. These views will normally be conveyed in a welfare report but in a minority of cases, where there may be a serious conflict of interest between the child and the parents, the child may be separately represented. A **residence** order may regulate where the child is to live; a **contact** order may govern with whom the child is to have contact and when; a specific issue order may be made to resolve an area of dispute over upbringing, such as the choice of school or whether the child should have an operation; and a prohibited steps order may prevent something being done in relation to a child such as taking the child out of the country. Despite the law's support for the child's continuing relationship with both parents, there is no presumption that the child should spend an equal amount of time with each, despite pressure from some fathers' rights groups for this to be introduced. The Children and Adoption Act 2006 has however introduced a number of measures designed to facilitate contact and prevent disputes. The same legislation has increased the powers of the courts to enforce contact in the minority of cases in which a parent, without good cause, refuses to comply with the orders of the court.

The law and practice in the UK governing the position of children and parents following divorce, must now comply with the **European Convention on Human Rights**. The principal effect of this is that in relation to divorce, as in relation to other family issues, the state must uphold the rights of *both* parent and child to respect for their private and **family life**. What this means in the context of separation and divorce is that the relationship of parent and child must be maintained and fostered, and in particular contact must be allowed, unless to do so would be clearly contrary to the best interests of the child.

ANDREW BAINHAM

children and medical treatment The legal duty to seek medical assistance for a child under the age of sixteen is imposed upon the child's parents. Failure to do so—where it can be established that the person responsible knows that medical treatment is required but decided not to secure it or did not care whether the child needed medical assistance—may amount to the criminal offence of child neglect.

A central issue for the law has been the role of parents, fulfilling their '**parental responsibility**', in making decisions about the medical treatment of their child. The **European Court of Human Rights**, in a decision concerning the treatment of a severely disabled child, David Glass (*Glass v United Kingdom* (2004)), made it clear that it is parents who make decisions about the medical treatment of young and dependent children. In the event of disagreement between parents and professionals, the matter must be referred to court for resolution—doctors are not permitted to treat contrary to the wishes of the child's parents. Both parents and the court must reach a decision according to the best interests, or welfare, of the child.

The 'best interests' principle applies to all decisions about children's health from the everyday—childhood immunization, treatment of minor accidental injury, administration of antibiotics—through to those concerning the treatment of children with chronic or acute conditions, or physical and mental disabilities. For cases brought under the **Children Act 1989**, the **legislation** provides a checklist of relevant factors. In other cases, the court is encouraged to draw up a balance sheet of benefits against disadvantages to assist in determination of the best interests of the child.

Despite criticism, the courts continue to be heavily influenced by medical opinion: giving **consent to treatment** recommended by doctors in all but one case where parents were refusing it; and, refusing to order doctors to treat against their professional judgment by declaring the legality of withdrawal or withholding of further medical treatment from children with life-limiting conditions. However, differences of opinion between doctors and parents about the quality of life of children with life-limiting conditions occur within the context of advances in medical treatment and nursing care which can extend their lives. Issues about the future treatment and care of Charlotte Wyatt, born prematurely with severe physical and mental impairments, were resolved by the court on at least eleven occasions as her doctors and parents failed to agree about the extent to which her impairments were reversible and to which she experienced pain or pleasure, her ability to develop her capacities and her interaction with those caring for her and, consequently, her best interests (the circumstances are detailed in the Court of Appeal judgement of October 2005, *Re Wyatt*). For much of the time she spent in hospital a court order permitted doctors to withhold aggressive artificial ventilation in the event, which her doctors considered inevitable, that she suffer a respiratory arrest. Against medical expectations, Charlotte survived and was discharged from hospital at the age of three.

Older children will form their own views about medical treatment, participate in decisions, assent to treatment, and eventually make decisions for themselves. The Family Law Reform Act 1969, section 8, creates a presumption that children aged sixteen and over have the capacity to make decisions about surgical, medical, and dental treatment (but not, for example, **organ donation**). In the case of *Gillick*, the question before the court was whether children under the age of sixteen could give a valid consent to medical treatment (*Gillick v West Norfolk and Wisbech AHA and another* (1985)). This case, which originated with a mother who did not want her daughters to be provided with contraceptive or **abortion** treatment or advice without her knowledge, had implications far beyond medical treatment to the decision-making **capacity** of young people more generally (and their **autonomy, self-determination,** and rights). The **judges** were split on the issue with the House of Lords eventually deciding by a majority of three to two that young people can give valid consent to medical treatment as long as they have, in the words of Lord Scarman, 'sufficient understanding and intelligence to enable him or her to understand fully what is proposed'. What a child must understand in order to be competent to decide will differ depending upon the nature of their condition and treatment.

Most teenagers will accept the advice of their doctors and consent to recommended treatment. In a series of cases, young people have refused to consent to treatment for a serious or life-threatening condition. Inevitably, these are difficult situations, exacerbated by either the mental health of the child or where their judgments are determined by religious beliefs (for example, Jehovah's Witnesses refusing consent to treatment involving the administration of blood products). Where the court concludes that the young person does not have sufficient understanding of what is involved (for example, the nature of dying from their condition) the court decides according to their judgment of best interests. Furthermore, even if the young person does have sufficient understanding, doctors can treat as long as they have the consent of anyone with parental responsibility or the court.

The ability of young people to consent to medical treatment raises a further issue of the confidentiality of medical consultations, most particularly in relation to those aspects of their lives, or health, about which they may not want their parents to know, such as contraception or the termination of pregnancy. Rejecting the argument that to extend the duty of confidentiality to young people would compromise the ability of parents to fulfil their responsibilities to them, the law is clear that competent young people who refuse to inform or permit the professional to inform their parents, are owed the same duty of confidentiality as adults—the decision to involve or seek the advice and support of their parents is one for the young person to make. JO BRIDGEMAN

See also: **welfare principle**

children's rights Children's rights have been a preoccupation of policymakers and academic commentators in western jurisdictions for at least a century. However, the twentieth-century fascination with children's rights is really only the most recent reformulation of an old tradition of thinking of children as vulnerable and in need of some legal protection (the Romans, for example, developed a series of legal devices to prevent children from being overreached by adults).

One important development taken in relation to thought about children's rights does appear to be a peculiarly twentieth-century one; In the late 1960s the children's liberationist movement began to assert rights for children, not simply to protect them from adults, but to empower them like adults. The children's liberationists suggested that children, like adults, should be able to assert their rights under subsisting fundamental rights doctrines (described in such instruments as the **United Nations** Declaration of **Human Rights**). Traditionally these had been

thought to protect the rights of adults. Liberationists reminded us that children were also people to whom these doctrines of rights applied.

Although their desire to see rights comprehensively extended to children was not universally shared (because it ignored the vulnerability of children and the **capacity** of adults to overreach them and to exploit their 'rights'), it did ignite a debate on the place of children in a world order that regarded individual rights as fundamental; rights thinking had a renaissance in relation to children. What the liberationists had demanded prompted commentators and policymakers to formulate their own visions of the moral worth of children and the fundamental rights that childhood demanded.

This reformulation involved a move from autonomy rights to a reconceptualized enunciation of specifically children's rights which acknowledged their more common inability to assert rights. Wills theories of children's rights gave way to interests theories. John Eekelaar, for example, conceived of children's rights as a rhetorical device which would foster a better childhood and improve life chances for children. But because autonomy could not be at the centre of children's rights he categorized the interests of children that a doctrine of children's rights should serve. He argued that children had basic interests (like food and shelter), developmental interests (like education) and autonomy interests (like the need to develop the capacity to act alone) which a doctrine of children's rights should capture (it is noteworthy that this formulation includes an autonomy element). If these interests could be asserted in the guise of rights his ambitions for an enhanced childhood would be met.

Of course, children's rights were never likely to attract universal acclaim. Onora O'Neil, for example, argued that the rhetoric of rights narrowed our concern for the wellbeing of children. Instead of focusing our minds on their general moral worth, rights talk concentrated only on those moral requirements which could be met by rights assertions. Rights could not encapsulate the much more wide-ranging good that we should pursue for children. The 'imperfect' obligations that were owed to children (like affection) could not be reduced to rights. She suggested, therefore, that we should concentrate instead on developing a theory of obligations owed to children. That process would allow us to determine what adults (both individually and in society) should do for children. In particular a theory of obligations would demand mechanisms for implementing the obligations owed to children.

By the end of the twentieth century it was clear that a rights' doctrine for children, which focused on children's interests, had been established in the institutional framework of the international community and was being promoted nationally across the world. The UN Convention on the Rights of the Child 1989 came into force in 1990 and it was no longer unusual to see children (or those representing them) using rights' doctrines to protect them.　　CRAIG LIND

J Fortin, *Children's Rights and the Developing Law* (Cambridge: Cambridge University Press, 2nd edn, 2003)

children's rights and education Children's rights are given only limited protection under English education law. Local education authorities have a duty under the Education Act 1996 to provide sufficient primary and secondary schools; and parents must ensure that their children of compulsory school age receive efficient full-time education. Children may be said to have rights co-relative to those duties, but their content is unclear. Provision is made for the content of education in the Education Act 2002, which requires provision of a basic curriculum for all maintained schools comprising the national curriculum for pupils from the age of three to sixteen, religious education for all registered pupils (subject to a parental right of withdrawal), and, for secondary pupils, sex education (again, subject to a parental right of withdrawal). Sex education may be provided in primary schools.

The difficulty of enforcing children's rights in education is a recurrent theme, as is the possibility of conflict between children's and parental rights. Such rights as exist tend to be vested in parents, as in such contexts as choice of school, provision for children with special educational needs, and the right of parents to withdraw their children from religious or sex education. There is some recognition of children's educational rights under international conventions, including Articles 28 and 29 of the UN **Convention on the Rights of the Child**, and Article 2 of the First Protocol to the **European Convention of Human Rights**, the first sentence of which provides that no person shall be denied the right to education.

PAUL MEREDITH

See also: **education and human rights; parental choice of school**

Chinese law Chinese law, historically considered, has undergone a number of incarnations. First and foremost, we have the law applied by the imperial government in the administration of the country for a period of over two thousand years from the third century BC to the first decade of the twentieth century. This law had two important aspects: administrative and penal. The penal codes of the great imperial dynasties defined offences and prescribed punishments, while the administrative corpus of rules, of increasing complexity over time, defined the organs of central and local government, as well as the duties and jurisdiction of the officials staffing them. The penal law is of particular interest because it possessed certain distinctive features that endured, despite changes in the content of the laws, throughout its long history. The continuity of law in traditional China, even with respect to details of the specific offences, is a remarkable legal phenomenon. We can still, for example, detect similarities in the rules on homicide and physical injury contained in the Qin laws of the third century BC and the code of the Qing dynasty in the nineteenth century AD.

The distinctive features of the penal code as a whole, often, although misleadingly, attributed to the influence of Confucianism, are derived from the respect paid to the hierarchies, deemed to be given in nature, which characterized both the structure of the family and the organization of society. The family is structured according to the division between senior and junior relatives (by age as well as generation) and the distinction between male (superior) and female (inferior), while the organization of society is based both on the distinction between the emperor and his subjects and on the division of the population into three distinct classes: the officials, free persons, and persons belonging to servile groups. Senior relatives and political or social superiors were owed respect and obedience by juniors or inferiors. This duty manifested itself in the criminal law in the form of discrimination in the treatment of offences. It was a more serious offence for a junior or inferior to injure a senior or superior than vice versa; and the punishment was correspondingly more severe.

Status was also important in other ways. On the basis of their connection with the emperor, officials were granted various privileges that in many cases enabled them to escape normal punishments. Other classes of person were also given privileges on the ground of pity. The young (those aged fifteen or under), the old (those aged seventy or over), the disabled, and women were given significant concessions with respect to the operation of the criminal law, often leading to reduced (or even no) punishment. Thus the law was not the same for everyone. Its application to an individual depended upon a variety of factors reducible to the 'status' he or she occupied in the family and society.

The 'five punishments' utilized in the penal codes were in ascending order of severity: beating with the light stick, beating with the heavy stick, penal servitude (not imprisonment, but forced labour in a fixed place) for periods ranging from one to three years, exile (to various distances), and death (strangulation, decapitation). Other kinds of punishment might in addition be prescribed by imperial decree for particular offences. Although numerous offences theoretically attracted the death penalty, a complex system of review led to many reprieves and commutations.

A person accused of a crime appeared to have few rights. There was no legal representation. His fate was entirely in the hands of the magistrate before whom he appeared. The latter investigated the facts and, if convinced of the accused person's guilt, sought to compel a confession. For this purpose torture (generally beating) might be employed subject to the conditions specified in the code. Only after the accused had confessed, could sentence be passed. All sentences, other than beatings, were subject to review by a higher authority.

What is now termed civil law, that is, matters concerning land, contract, inheritance, or **marriage**, was regulated only sparsely by the codes. Contrary to what was once thought, people frequently brought civil disputes before the magistrate's court. The magistrate primarily sought to resolve them through the application of the law.

After the collapse of the empire in 1911 and the establishment of the Republic, the movement to reform the law, already initiated in the last years of the Qing dynasty, accelerated. Essentially, the aim of the new rulers was to modernize China along Western lines and remove grounds for Western interference. New criminal, civil, and commercial codes were introduced, derived, through the medium of Japan, from continental models, especially the German and Swiss codes. Nevertheless, the Republican civil codes still preserved certain elements of the old imperial land and family law. During the Republic, law schools were introduced and, for the first time in China, a legal profession emerged. The new legislation proved largely ineffective, given the turbulent conditions of the time, but had greater success after transplantation to Taiwan with the Kuomintang in 1949. In Hong Kong, until 1971, Qing customary law was still applied in matters of marriage, inheritance, and adoption. The customary land law even now remains relevant in some situations.

The triumph of communism entailed the creation of a new socialist legal system in the People's Republic of China, influenced at first by Soviet models and later, particularly after the Cultural Revolution, by Western systems of civil and **common law**. The criminal law totally abandoned the traditional emphasis on status, but still preserved some principles of the old law, such as the reliance on confession and the review of death sentences. During the Cultural Revolution both law and the legal profession suffered an eclipse but, since the 1980s, there has been an enormous proliferation of civil and commercial legislation as well as a move towards the implementation of individual rights in the criminal process. These changes have been given impetus by China's desire to renounce isolationism and become part of the international community of nations.

GEOFFREY MacCORMACK

KG Turner, JV Feinerman and RK Guy (eds), *The Limits of the Rule of Law in China* (Seattle and London: University of Washington Press, 2000)

CS Hsu, *Understanding China's Legal System: Essays in Honor of Jerome A. Cohen* (New York and London: New York University Press, 2003)

See also: **civil law systems**

chose in action   Also known as 'thing in action', chose in action is a form of personal (as opposed to real) property, largely corresponding to the notion in **civil law systems** of intangible moveable property. It was originally so called because its enjoyment was dependent on its owner's right to bring a personal action against someone else. Typical choses in action are debts, rights to sue for damages, rights under insurance policies, intellectual property rights and **shares** in a company. For some purposes the term is extended to cover a beneficiary's right arising under a **trust** or will (often here called a 'chose in equity').

Although a form of property, choses in action were—subject to a few exceptions—regarded as non-transferable at **common law**. However, equity quickly recognized the assignability of choses in equity. From the seventeenth century it also gave effect to the assignment of other choses in action by the expedient of forcing the assignor to lend his name to litigation at common law for the benefit of the assignee (and, after the fusion of law and equity, by allowing the assignor to be joined as a nominal defendant). In addition, by the nineteenth century it was clear that a contract for value to assign a chose in action had the effect of assigning it in equity on the basis of the equitable maxim that equity regards as done that which ought to be done.

Subsequently, the Supreme Court of Judicature Act 1873, s 25(6) (since re-enacted as the Law of Property Act 1925, s 136(1) of) provided that the assignment of any 'debt or other legal thing in action' vested that chose in the assignee, provided that the transfer was in writing, signed by the assignor, absolute, and notified in writing to the defendant or obligor. This supplemented the old equitable assignment process, but did not supplant it. Hence assignments not satisfying the statute can still be given effect as equitable assignments.

In addition, specific statutory means of transfer are provided for certain choses in action, such as company securities, insurance policies and intellectual property rights.

English law is generous in allowing assignment of choses in action. Debts and choses in equity can be transferred virtually without restriction (unless the contract creating the debt prohibits assignment). The assignment of rights to recover damages for tort or breach of contract is more restricted in that the assignee must have a genuine commercial interest—that is, some interest over and above mere speculation—in taking the assignment.

Where a chose in action is assigned, the assignee can generally be in no better position than the assignor. Matters that would have affected the assignor's title to sue will also affect the assignee, whether or not the latter was aware of them. In addition, there are relatively complex rules concerning cases where a counterclaim or right of set-off available to the debtor against the assignor will also be good against the assignee.

ANDREW TETTENHORN

See also: **equity as a system of law**

Church of England   The Church of England's unique status arises by virtue of the fact that it is the established church. Establishment is seen in the fact that the Archbishops of Canterbury and York, the Bishops of London, Durham, and Winchester, plus twenty-one senior bishops of the Church sit in the House of Lords, the Sovereign is the head of the church as well as being head of state, and its ecclesiastical law and ecclesiastical courts form part of the English legal system. Moreover the creation of the Church is the result, at least in part, of legislative acts by the state. The monarch appoints persons to episcopal office within the church and the church has power to enact some types of legislation, although these must be submitted to Parliament for approval. Church and state are thus closely intertwined and the Sovereign takes an oath to 'maintain ... the Protestant reformed religion established by law'. However

the Church of England cannot be seen as being the national church of the United Kingdom. First there is no general duty on the part of citizens to support the Church in any manner. Secondly, with the exception of those matters noted above, there is no general legal preference given to the Church of England over other faiths. Thirdly, the **Church of Scotland**'s position in Scotland is protected by the Act of Union and is recognized in statute.   TONY BRADNEY

N Doe, *The Legal Framework of the Church of England* (Oxford: Oxford University Press, 1996)

See also: **House of Lords reform**

Church of Scotland   A fundamental condition of the Anglo-Scottish Union was that each country retain its own religious establishment. The kingdom of Great Britain came into existence in 1707 with two established Churches, of which the Church of Scotland is one. The government of the Church is Presbyterian in form. A Kirk Session in each parish comprises Minister and Elders, is responsible for the local discipline and worship of the Church, and elects representatives to the Presbytery comprising the several parishes of a district. The highest judicial and legislative body of the Church is the General Assembly, normally meeting annually in May, under the presidency of a Moderator, elected by the Commissioners of Assembly to serve for one year. The Monarch (whose coronation oath includes a promise to preserve it) is not the Church's head, but, when in Scotland, an ordinary member of it.

The right of each congregation to call its own minister without lay patronage, and the independence of the church in 'matters spiritual', have been controversial issues since the Patronage Act of 1712, passed in violation of the Union. This led to the Disruption of 1843, when the Church divided into Free and Established Churches. The split was healed (but incompletely) through the Church of Scotland Act 1921 under which the Church recognizes the propriety of the state's temporal jurisdiction, but is assured of its own right of self-government in matters spiritual. Final authority on the extent of 'matters spiritual' belongs to the ordinary courts.

NEIL MacCORMICK

R Black *et al* (eds), *The Laws of Scotland: Stair Memorial Encyclopaedia*, vol 3 (Edinburgh: Law Society of Scotland/Butterworths, 1994) paras 1501–1609

F Lyall, *Of Presbyters and Kings: Church and State in the Law of Scotland* (Aberdeen: Aberdeen University Press, 1980)

See also: **Treaty of Union**

Cicero, Marcus Tullius Born in Arpinum in central Italy in January 106 BC, Cicero was educated in Rome. In 91 BC, he embarked on a brief military career followed by an informal training in law under two members of the Scaevola family, the most distinguished lawyers of the Republic. During this time he also enhanced his study of philosophy by spending six months in Athens attending lectures. In 77 BC, he embarked upon a senatorial career and, as a practising advocate, quickly rose to prominence. His willingness to prosecute and defend influential people gave him powerful enemies in the world of late-Republican politics. In 63 BC, while holding the consulship, he suppressed the Catilinarian conspiracy, but his botched handling of the case forced him into exile in 58 BC. After returning to Rome in 57 BC, he continued to engage in politics. He had a troubled relationship with Julius Caesar and, although the two were reconciled after the battle of Pharsalus, he openly rejoiced upon hearing the news of his assassination. Cicero believed that with Caesar's death, the Republic would be restored and spoke out publicly against Marc Anthony, who he felt undermined this ideal. With the formation of the second triumvirate in 43 BC, he was proscribed at the insistence of Marc Anthony. He was killed near his villa in Formiae while trying to escape.

Cicero's contribution to the development of law extends to three areas. First, his letters and courtroom speeches provide an invaluable snapshot of the orator's profession in late-Republican Roman law. These works also demonstrate the fluid state of the law during this period and the relationship between Roman jurists and orators. Secondly, his philosophical works, on topics such as diverse as the state and the ideal orator, provide an interesting account of the interplay between law and philosophy and were used with great effect in the Renaissance to shape the broad outlines of legal philosophy. Finally, Cicero's writings on the nature of forensic oratory and his exposition of the modes of argumentation have proven to be extremely valuable in modern jurisdictions where courtroom oratory still plays an active role.

PAUL DU PLESSIS

J Powell and J Paterson, *Cicero the Advocate* (Oxford: Oxford University Press, 2004)

J Harries, *Cicero and the Jurists – From Citizen's Law to the Lawful State* (London: Gerald Duckworth, 2006)

circuit judges *see* **courts; judges**

circulars *see* **legal rules, types of**

Citizens Advice Bureaux Citizens Advice Bureaux ('CABx') fulfil the invaluable function of serving as the first—and often the last—port of call for millions of people who face legal and other difficulties. A network of some 3,000 CABx operates in large towns and cities throughout the UK. They are charitable bodies which provide advice to members of the public about a very wide range of personal and social problems. Their services are offered free of charge, regardless of the means of clients. With a huge caseload of about 5.5 million cases in 2005–2006, no other advice agency in the UK provides a service on anything like this scale. The provision of legal advice is a relatively minor part of the overall work of CABx although it is still highly significant, particularly since public funds for legal advice and assistance have greatly diminished in recent years.

In some of the larger CABx, full-time lawyers (and other experts) are employed and local lawyers volunteer their services in many others. But CABx rely very heavily upon a small army of unpaid voluntary workers—over 20,000 in number—who use their commonsense and experience, reinforced by a modicum of training, in providing advice and assistance to those who consult them. This will often involve completing forms, writing letters, conducting negotiations, and the like. Some clients are referred to solicitors, law centres, local government departments, and other agencies, but the aim as far as possible is to deal with problems on the spot.

JOHN BALDWIN

Citizen's Charter A citizen's charter is a commitment to improving standards of public service, informing the consumers of services about the level of service they are entitled to expect, and encouraging them either to complain or to seek another provider if the promised standards are not met. Such a charter does not, generally speaking, confer any legally enforceable entitlements. Charters are nowadays found in many countries around the world, bearing a variety of different names, but the prototype was the UK Citizen's Charter, launched by John Major's Conservative Government in July 1991. Its main themes were:

- *Higher standards*: publication, in clear language, of standards of service; tougher, independent inspectorates; a 'Charter Mark' scheme to commend bodies that abided by the terms of the Charter.
- *Openness*: elimination of secrecy about organizational arrangements, costs of service, etc. Staff were to be identified by name badges.
- *Information*: regular publication of information about performance targets, and how well they had been met.

- *Choice*: 'the public sector should provide choice wherever practicable'.
- *Non-Discrimination*: services to be available regardless of race or sex; leaflets to be printed in minority languages where there was a need.
- *Accessibility*: 'services should be run to suit the convenience of customers, not staff'.
- *Proper redress when things go wrong*: 'at the very least the citizen is entitled to a good explanation, or an apology'; better machinery for redress of grievances; adequate remedies, including compensation where appropriate.

There was also a value for money message: 'the Charter programme is about finding better ways of converting the money that can be afforded into even better services'.

Driven by the personal backing of the **Prime Minister**, charters were quickly launched in every part of the public service—eg a Taxpayers' Charter, a Courts Charter, a Patients' Charter (the NHS), a Parents' Charter (Education) and a Passengers' Charter (railways). Those familiar performance league tables, regularly published in the newspapers, based on such indicators as the lengths of hospital waiting lists, school exam results, and police crime clear-up rates, are enduring by-products of the charter initiative.

After the election of Tony Blair's Government in 1997, the Charter was repackaged as 'Service First' and its message later became subsumed in a broader New Labour 'modernisation of government' agenda. The change of nomenclature answered one important criticism of charterism: that 'citizenship' is not just about *entitlements*, it is also about civil *obligations*; and later versions of charters have tended to reflect this. Another criticism has been that that the promise of 'choice' is often, in practice, illusory: some public services are monopolies; parents in rural areas who are dissatisfied with their local school often find that the only alternatives are too far away to offer a practical alternative.

The basic charter message is now an accepted part of the landscape of UK public administration. The generic charters that emerged from the 1991 initiative have now largely been fragmented into a much larger number of decentralized mini-charters: the word 'charter' itself lives on in the continuing Chartermark scheme, run by the Cabinet Office.

GAVIN DREWRY

citizenship Within the disciplinary confines of law, citizenship is deployed in two ways: first, it refers to formal membership status within a political unit, usually a territorial state. This is the specifically juridical meaning of citizenship. The term **nationality** is preferred to citizenship in **international law**, but is essentially synonymous. Within the national frame of reference, the opposite of 'citizen' is '**alien**'. In international law, the concept of nationality covers the position of aliens as well as of citizens, and the stateless person embodies the absence of nationality within a global order of sovereign states. An emergent third locus of legal citizenship is the supranational political unit of the **European Union**. Although EU citizenship denotes a distinct status and confers certain rights, it remains dependent on state citizenship insofar as only citizens of Member States of the EU are eligible for EU citizenship.

A relatively small but crucial set of legal rights and duties are usually reserved to legal citizens. These are the right to exit, enter, and remain in the country of citizenship, the franchise, conscription, and full access to civil service employment. In some states, inheritance, investment, and property laws discriminate between citizens and non-citizens. Citizenship in the formal, legal sense is 'absolute'—one is either a citizen or one is not.

A second way in which citizenship figures in legal discourse is as a description of the full expression of membership in a community. The rights, entitlements, benefits, and duties associated with this conception of citizenship extend far beyond the abbreviated list of rights formally reserved to those holding legal citizenship. In this context, the (full) citizen stands in contrast to the 'second-class citizen'. **Equality** among all citizens is an implicit norm; inequality between citizens is presumptively unjust. While jurists may invoke citizenship in this broader, substantive sense, it is not a specifically juridical concept or status.

People acquire legal citizenship at birth and through **naturalization**. Birthright citizenship is conferred in two ways: by descent from a citizen (*jus sanguinis*) or by birth on the territory of the state (*jus soli*). Virtually all states confer citizenship by descent from a citizen mother or father, and countries such as Ireland require only a citizen grandparent. A few states still discriminate on the basis of sex in the application of *jus sanguinis*. For example, Saudi Arabia permits male citizens to pass Saudi nationality to their children, but a Saudi woman can pass Saudi citizenship to her child only if the father is unknown or stateless. Some states take an expansive and ethnicized view of 'descent'. For instance, Germany long regarded all persons who could demonstrate German ancestry as automatically entitled to German citizenship. This automatic acquisition of citizenship has since been terminated for those born after 1993. The Israeli Law of Return grants citizenship to any person who has a Jewish grandparent. Several states extend preferential access, to members of an ethnic diaspora, to the status of permanent residence. Examples include Finland, India, and Japan.

A smaller number of states also confer birthright citizenship according to *jus soli*. Among these, Canada does so by statute, while in the United States and Mexico the constitution confers the right to citizenship on anyone born on state territory. On 1 January 2005, the Republic of Ireland amended its constitution to abolish unconditional *jus soli* citizenship. France has long provided what is known as 'double *jus soli*', whereby citizenship is conferred at birth on a child whose non-citizen parent was also born in France. France also has a form of delayed *jus soli*, whereby children born in France to foreign-born parents may opt for French citizenship at the age of majority. This model of acquisition combines the ascriptive quality of birthright citizenship with the element of choice characteristic of naturalization.

In 2000, Germany supplemented its existing citizenship law by granting automatic citizenship to children born in Germany to at least one parent who had legally resided in Germany for at least eight years. Some states that previously had unrestricted *jus soli* laws, such as Australia and Britain, have also imposed a requirement that at least one parent be legally resident as a condition precedent to the attribution of citizenship to a child born on the territory. Opposition to citizenship for children of non-status ('illegal') migrants best accounts for this latter trend. Ascribing citizenship only to children born to a legally residing parent might best be understood as combining elements of both *jus soli* and *jus sanguinis*, since eligibility requires both birth on territory and descent from a parent with a designated legal status.

Various theories are offered to account for the fact that the citizenship laws of most countries recognize the transmission of citizenship only by descent, while others recognize both *jus sanguinis* and *jus soli*. One explanation is grounded in distinct forms of nationalism: states that embrace ethnic nationalism, in which membership is determined by a common ethnicity that determines the boundaries of 'the people', will insist on an exclusively descent-based citizenship regime. States that subscribe to an ethos of civic citizenship endorse a model of citizenship grounded in allegiance to the state and adherence to a common set of practices, norms, rights, customs, and values (sometimes encapsulated by a national constitution). The classic exposition of this theory posits Germany

as an example of ethnic nationalism and France as an example of civic nationalism (R Brubaker, *Citizenship and Nationhood in France and Germany* (Cambridge: Harvard University Press, 1992)). However, critics have responded that history does not bear out the hypothesis (P Weil, 'Access to Citizenship: A Comparison of Twenty-Five Nationality Laws', in TA Aleinikoff and D Klusmeyer (eds), *Citizenship Today: Global Perspectives and Practices* (Washington DC: Carnegie Endowment for International Peace, 2001)). Germany passed its *jus sanguinis* law in the mid-nineteenth century, when *jus sanguinis* was the norm for all European states (including France). Nazi Germany represents the ultimately horrific consequences of an ethnically exclusionary conception of the nation, and it is certainly the case that citizenship laws were manipulated in the service of that regime. But it does not follow that the adoption of a *jus sanguinis* citizenship regime as such was a strong causal factor, pre-requisite, or even harbinger. Nor is the history of *jus soli* rooted in civic nationalism. *Calvin's Case* (*Calvin v Smith* (1608)) established *jus soli* in Britain with a feudal framework based on ligeance to the feudal lord, or sovereign. *Jus soli* citizenship permanently and irrevocably secured the subject's duty of allegiance to the sovereign who ruled the territory at birth.

A more plausible explanation for contemporary trends in citizenship laws across states examines the extent to which a state is—or sees itself as—a country of immigration or emigration. States which are self-consciously and normatively committed to an identity as 'countries of immigration' will opt for *jus soli* citizenship. Ascribing citizenship automatically to anyone born on state territory facilitates and accelerates the process of state-building and integration. There will be no second or third generation 'immigrants', because these children and grandchildren of immigrants will be citizens by virtue of birth on the territory. States of emigration who desire for sentimental, political, or economic reasons to maintain links with their diaspora will be inclined toward a *jus sanguinis* model as a means of ensuring continuity across space and time. The adoption of actual or modified *jus soli* citizenship by European states such as Germany may be viewed as concession to the reality that they are, in fact, countries of immigration. Some states of emigration that previously prohibited dual citizenship, are either abandoning the prohibition or granting preferential access, to their ethnic diaspora, to the status of permanent residence.

Naturalization refers to the process by which an immigrant acquires legal citizenship. Not coincidentally, the choice of terminology tracks the analogy between birth as a naturally occurring bond between parent and child and adoption as an artificial bond that must be made natural. The requirements for naturalization vary from state to state. Applicants must demonstrate residence in the state for a specified number of years, and satisfy one or more of the following prerequisites: competence in at least one official language, basic knowledge of the history, culture, and political organization of the state, and the swearing of an oath of allegiance to the sovereign, the constitution, or the state itself. Criminal convictions or allegations that the applicant poses a security risk may disqualify applicants. The ease of naturalization depends on the minimum length of residence and the stringency of the language and civic knowledge tests. The introduction of new or more demanding criteria is usually read as evidence of a relative increase in anti-immigrant sentiment. Recent proposals (and even some attempts) to test applicants on their attitudes regarding social, political, and cultural issues have brought debates about **multiculturalism** and **integration** to bear on the specific content of naturalization law.

Typically, a citizen by naturalization is equal to a birthright citizen before the law in all respects but one: many states reserve the right to strip a naturalized citizen of citizenship if the status was obtained by fraud or misrepresentation. Some states retain the right indefinitely. While in most states birthright citizens may renounce their citizenship voluntarily, stripping birthright citizens of their citizenship is legally impossible in virtually all states, although Britain amended its nationality law in 2006 to enable the revocation of birthright and naturalized citizenship on grounds of **national security**.

International law does not stipulate or explicitly limit the content of states' citizenship laws. However, this does not mean that all citizenship attributions will be recognized for purposes of international law. Thus, in the *Nottebohm Case* (*Liechtenstein v Guatemala* (1955)), the **International Court of Justice** held that where a person asserts that he or she is a citizen of a state for purposes of asserting rights under international law, the fact that the state considers the person a citizen is not determinative. The International Court of Justice declared that under international law, 'nationality is a legal bond having as its basis a social fact of attachment, a genuine connection of existence, interests and sentiments, together with the existence of reciprocal rights and duties. It may be said to constitute the juridical expression of the fact that the individual upon whom it is conferred, either directly by the law or as the result of an act of the authorities, is in fact more closely connected with the population of the State conferring nationality than with that of any other State'

International and European legal instruments prohibit the creation of statelessness. The capacity of states to revoke the citizenship of a person who does not possess another nationality is thereby limited, except in the case of citizenship obtained by fraud or misrepresentation.   AUDREY MACKLIN

L Bosniak, 'Citizenship', in P Cane and M Tushnet (eds), *The Oxford Handbook of Legal Studies* (Oxford: Oxford University Press, 2003)

JGA Pocock, 'The Ideal of Citizenship since Classical Times', in G Shafir (ed), *The Citizenship Debates: A Reader* (Minneapolis: University of Minneapolis Press, 1998)

See also: **dual/multiple citizenship; illegal migration**

citizenship education   *see* **secular curriculum in schools**

citizenship of the European Union   While a desire to create a 'People's Europe'—as a way of connecting the EU with its people—dates back to the early 1970s, it was not until the Spanish pressed the issue at Maastricht that the idea of Union **citizenship** took concrete form. The question facing the EU was what should **European Union** citizenship look like? The literature was full of suggestions—market citizenship (focusing on the rights of economic actors), social citizenship (emphasizing the social-welfare elements of citizenship), republican citizenship (based on active citizen participation). The transnational nature of the EU raised yet further problems: should EU citizenship aim to replicate citizenship of a nation state or should the EU aim to create a new, 'postnational' form of citizenship based on multiple-level associations and identifications at regional, national, and European level?

The citizenship provisions included in the new Part Two by the Maastricht Treaty were something of a mish-mash and did not really answer these questions. Article 17(1) provides that 'Citizenship of the EU is hereby established'. Citizenship is, however, confined to those people holding the **nationality** of one of the Member States. Thus, the Member States are the gatekeepers to EU citizenship. Articles 17(2)–21 then list a number of specific rights which citizens can enjoy: the right to move and reside freely in another Member State, subject to the limitations and conditions laid down by the Treaty (Article 18(1)); the right to vote in local and European elections in the host state (Article 19); the right to diplomatic and consular protection from the authorities of any Member State in third countries (Article 20); and the right to petition the **European Parliament** and the right to apply to the ombudsman in any one of the official languages of the EU (Article 21).

However, it would be a mistake to look at the four substantive rights listed in Part Two in a vacuum because Article 17(2) makes clear that 'Citizens of the Union shall enjoy the rights conferred by this Treaty and shall be subject to the duties imposed thereby'. Therefore, migrant citizens can enjoy the right to non-discrimination on the ground of nationality found in Article 12 EC, and all citizens (and not just those who have exercised their rights of free movement) can enjoy the right to equal treatment, originally on the ground of **sex**, now on other grounds, along with other social, environmental, and consumer rights. These rights were made more visible by the **Charter on Fundamental Rights** which was signed in 2000, bringing together both civil and political rights and economic and social rights in a single, non-binding text. The Reform Treaty, if ratified by all twenty-seven Member States, is due to give the Charter legal effect.

The importance of the citizenship provisions in the Treaty was emphasized by the **European Court of Justice** in *Grzelczyk* (2001):

Union citizenship is destined to be the fundamental status of nationals of the Member States, enabling those who find themselves in the same situation to enjoy the same treatment in law irrespective of their nationality, subject to such exceptions as are expressly provided for.

But is this anything more than rhetoric? Most of the case law has concentrated on the 'primary' right, Article 18(1) on the right of free movement and residence. While the case law is neither consistent nor altogether clear, it seems that the ECJ is prepared to use 'citizenship' to extend rights to free movement and equal treatment to those who are not economically active (children, the unemployed), to expand existing rights, and to justify imposing limits on the limits (such as **derogations**) laid down by Community law.

The rights laid down by the Treaty must now also be viewed in the context of the Citizens' Rights Directive ('CRD') 2004/38 which is premised on the idea that the longer an individual resides in the host state the more rights they enjoy. In particular, it distinguishes between three groups of migrants:

(1) those entering the host state for up to three months;
(2) those entering for up to five years; and
(3) those resident beyond five years.

In essence the first group enjoy a 'right of residence' but are not subject to the requirement of being economically active nor are they subject to any conditions (for example, as to adequate resources, medical insurance) or formalities other than holding a valid identity card or **passport**. They also enjoy equal treatment with nationals in the host state but not in respect of social assistance or student benefits.

The second group also have a 'right of residence' but only if they are engaged in gainful activity in the host state as a worker or a self-employed **person,** or they have sufficient medical and financial resources for themselves and their family members, or they are students with comprehensive sickness insurance and sufficient resources for themselves and their family members, or they are family members (including third country nationals, that is, those not holding the nationality of one of the twenty-seven Member States) accompanying or joining a Union citizen. These individuals enjoy the right to the same treatment as nationals of the host state, including in respect of social assistance. However, there is no right to equal treatment in respect of **maintenance** aid for studies, including vocational training to persons other than workers, the self-employed persons and members of their families.

The third group are those with a *'right of permanent residence'*. After five years, Union citizens do not need to show they are workers, self-employed, students, or adequately resourced. As with the second group, the third group also enjoy the **right to work** and to equal treatment. In addition, they can enjoy equal treatment not only in respect of social assistance but also in respect of student maintenance in the form of grants or loans. Thus, after five years' **residence**, migrants—whether they are economically active or not—are treated by the Directive as being sufficiently assimilated into the host state that in respect of all of their rights they should be treated as in the same way as—and should be viewed as—a national. This is a dramatic change in perspective, a change which serves to underline just how far the EU has moved from its common market origins.

CATHERINE BARNARD

civil and political rights   The Universal Declaration of **Human Rights** set down a large number of rights, amongst which are the civil and political rights that were afterwards to be fleshed out in the **International Covenant on Civil and Political Rights ('ICCPR')**. This document took eighteen years to agree (1966) and another ten years to come into force (1976). Its first optional protocol provides for an oversight mechanism whereby individuals take complaints of breaches of the Covenant before a specialist **United Nations** body with a view to securing strong (albeit non-binding) decisions. This is a jurisdiction that has never been made compulsory, with the result that, on one view, we have a neat 'Catch 22': the countries committed enough to submit themselves to the jurisdiction are by definition those that do not need to. This may be an overly cynical view: the number of states signing up is growing, over 100 at the most recent count, and it may be that as **democracy** takes hold in the post-Cold War world, the Covenant's quasi-judicial oversight of freedom will bite to an increasing extent.

The civil and political rights set out in the Covenant reflect a division of labour in the **human** rights field, between those rights that are personal and those that connect with the body politic. As far as the former is concerned, the civil rights that appear include the **rights to life**, liberty, privacy, and a fair trial as well as the right to marry. The political rights encompass the right to vote and also those various **freedoms (of expression**, of assembly and of association) that are essential if the voting process is to have credibility. It was this linkage to democratic forms of government that made the Covenant so difficult to agree and then to embed in the international community: the embers of this controversy can be seen in the continued ambiguity of China's approach to the Covenant, signed up certainly but currently not seeming to be inclined to do very much else.

The ICCPR establishes a Human Rights Committee to monitor the implementation of its terms among those countries that have submitted to its requirements. Composed of independent experts, its most important function is to review on a periodic basis the record of the states subject to its remit. To facilitate this, each state has to submit reports and even if they do not do so, the Committee now proceeds nevertheless with its review. Drawing on evidence from **non-governmental organizations** and other sources, committee members often take strong and not uncritical lines when inviting government representatives to explain themselves. The system now also allows for follow-up submissions after it has made its general observations, and for the appointment of a special rapporteur (from among the membership) to oversee this. These meetings, at which states are scrutinized on their human rights records, have become a high point of the human rights calendar, a way of keeping the importance of civil and political rights at the top of the international agenda.

CONOR GEARTY

civil disobedience   Sometimes the term 'civil disobedience' is used broadly to cover any principled disobedience of the law. More commonly, the term is used narrowly to cover public disobedience of the law done with the purpose of changing the law. By way of context, one must note the ongoing debate about whether and when there is a moral obligation to obey the law. Most who argue for the existence of such an obligation restrict it to just laws or to legal systems that are generally just. Civil disobedience presents the flipside of the question: when or under what conditions is public disobedience of the law, with the purpose of changing the law, morally authorized, or perhaps even morally required?

One must recall that while a number of prominent theorists, for example, **Aquinas,** seemed to accept that one could morally disobey an unjust law, at least where the disobedience would not have other significant negative consequences, other theorists, for example, Socrates in Plato's *Crito*, Kant (1724–1804), and **Bentham** ('what is the motto of a good citizen? To obey punctually; to censure freely'), assumed or asserted that one could object to unjust laws, but must obey them nonetheless.

Much of the modern theoretical (and popular) writing on civil disobedience can be traced back to three sources: Henry David Thoreau (1817–1862) and his pamphlet, *Resistance to Civil Government* (1849); the writings and actions of Mohandas Karamchand ('Mahatma') Gandhi (1869–1948), who used non-violent resistance to law (*Satyagraha*) as a central tactic in the struggle for Indian independence from Britain; and the writings and actions of Martin Luther King, Jr (1929–1968), who expressly relied on a version of the non-violent resistance practiced by Gandhi, in the protests he led as part of the American Civil Rights Movement.

Some theorists argue that there are strict rules that must be followed for civil disobedience to be morally legitimate: that it must be public and non-violent, and that those practising civil disobedience must be willing to accept the legal punishment (imprisonment or otherwise). Adherence to these rules is sometimes said to show that those practising civil disobedience accept the legal system in general as legitimate, and wish only to change particular unjust rules. However, this characterization seems descriptively inaccurate for the modern paradigm cases of civil disobedience: Gandhi did not accept the general legitimacy of British colonial rule, and King did not accept the general legitimacy of the American society of his time, given its pervasive, severe **racism**.

Critics of civil disobedience argue that it is contrary to the principles of **democracy** (where, it is said, legal change should occur through democratic channels, not be forced by the disruptive actions of a few); that disobedience, however high the moral motives, only works to encourage unlawful actions by those less high-minded; or that civil disobedience is simply contrary to our moral obligations to obey the law (as noted, whether there is any such obligation, even for generally just legal systems, remains highly controversial).   BRIAN BIX

MK Gandhi, *Non-Violent Resistance (Satyagraha)* (Mineola, NY: Dover, 2001)

HD Thoreau, *Civil Disobedience and Other Essays* (Mineola, NY: Dover, 1993) (*On the Duty of Civil Disobedience* first published in 1849, under the title, *Resistance to Civil Government*)

civil law systems 'Civil law systems', 'civilian systems' and 'the civil law' are general terms used to denote those jurisdictions belonging to the Western world which are neither part of the Anglo-American **common law** tradition nor 'mixed' legal systems, ie systems combining civilian and common law elements. The civilian tradition comprises all European jurisdictions apart from English, Scots and Irish law, as well as Central and Latin American systems, and some African and Asian jurisdictions which modelled their law on Western lines.

Sometimes the civilian systems are also called 'Romano-Germanic' jurisdictions. This points to the fact that the civil law tradition is fairly heterogeneous. Thus civilian lawyers hardly use the term 'civil law systems'; instead they distinguish three legal families. The 'Romanist' family comprises the legal systems which were strongly influenced by French law. The 'Germanic' family includes the jurisdictions which were decisively shaped by German law. The 'Nordic' legal family encompasses the Scandinavian systems. Even within one and the same family, civilian systems often differ substantially as to the outcome of similar cases and as to their more general outlook.

But despite their significant differences, civil law systems share a distinctive heritage based on antique **Roman law** and its peculiar interaction in the Middle Ages with local, mainly Germanic, customs and with **canon law**, ie the law of the Roman Catholic church. The sources of Roman and canon law were studied, ordered, refined, and taught by medieval jurists in the first universities in Northern Italy to which students flocked from all over Europe. These students returned to their home countries and served as judges, advisors and administrators for secular and spiritual rulers. By virtue of their common background they shared the knowledge of a common legal language, a common body of law and

legal literature, and a common method of rationalizing and organizing legal materials.

Roman-canon law was thus received in the different European territories and became the 'common law', or *ius commune*, of Continental Europe. This process of 'reception' was not only due to the qualitative superiority of the *ius commune* to the local laws and customs. It also rested on the inherent authority of Roman law as ancient 'written reason'. Moreover, it was facilitated by the absence of centralized court systems and strong legal professions which might have resisted the implementation of a foreign law.

Nowhere did the *ius commune* wholly supersede the local laws. It mixed and fused with them to different degrees. Thus the intensity and the extent of the reception varied considerably between different parts of Europe. It was, for instance, particularly strong in Germany where it fitted in well with the claim of the rulers of the Holy Roman Empire to be successors of the Roman Caesars. During the sixteenth and seventeenth centuries other local variants of the *ius commune* emerged, such as 'Roman-Dutch law'. Factors contributing to this development were the schism of the church and the increased use of the vernacular languages, but most importantly the rise of the modern nation state together with the corresponding idea that sovereign rulers should exert their will through legislation applicable throughout their territory and with the creation of powerful national court hierarchies.

Thus, ultimately, the unity of the *ius commune* was substantially weakened and national legal traditions with different substantive and procedural laws, national legal literatures and national court systems prevailed. Like the reception of Roman-canon law, the nationalization of European laws advanced at different speeds and with varying force in different jurisdictions, depending on how quickly legal unity was achieved in different countries.

In France, for instance, the law was unified and the court system centralized immediately after the revolution. The early nineteenth century saw five major codifications governing general private law, commercial law, civil procedure, criminal law, and criminal procedure. As a consequence of the Napoleonic wars, this model was imposed on Belgium, Luxembourg, the Netherlands, some parts of Italy and Poland and the western regions of Germany and Switzerland. But the new French legislation held wider cultural attractions. With its clarity, rationality, elegance of style, and its determination to break the fetters of aristocratic feudalism, church power, and restrictions on commerce, it seemed to embody the ideals of the enlightenment and commended itself to legislators in Portugal, Spain, and the emerging nations in Central and Latin America. The development of this Romanist family was facilitated by the similarities of the Romance languages.

German legislation and its court hierarchy were only unified in the last third of the nineteenth century. This period also saw the enactment of five codes covering the same subject matters as the earlier French codifications. However, they differed both in substance and in style from the French model because they drew heavily on nineteenth century German legal scholarship, which had continued to refine the *ius commune*. The German codes and German legal scholarship made a strong impact on Austrian, Swiss, and Greek law. They influenced the Eastern European laws and, indirectly, the law of Turkey, which adopted large parts of Swiss law. The Germanic approach to law also had a bearing on Italian and Dutch law reforms in the twentieth century.

In Scandinavia, the influence of the *ius commune* had never been as strong as in other parts of the Continent. Moreover, strong and centralized states with major codifications developed there at a relatively early stage. Today, they differ from other European countries because of their emphasis on social welfarism. Nevertheless, the inclusion of the Nordic family in the civil law tradition can be justified by the fact that throughout the nineteenth and twentieth centuries, German legal thinking exerted a strong influence in Scandinavia.

Despite the diversity of civil law systems, there are a number of characteristic features setting them apart from the non-Western traditions, such as **Islamic law**, **Hindu law**, **Chinese law**, **Japanese law** and many other legal systems in Africa and Asia which are largely based on customary law. All civil law systems are secular and capitalist. They rely almost exclusively on written sources of law. Their conception of law is rationalist and state-centred. Law is seen as a means of settling disputes authoritatively, and its administration and enforcement is primarily dealt with by professional lawyers. Civil law systems are based on the **rule of law** in the sense that government authority is constrained by legal rules and procedures. They accord great importance to personal autonomy and individuality and acknowledge some form of **human rights**.

All these characteristics are shared by the common law systems, so it might be argued that the civil law and the common law together constitute a single Western legal tradition. Indeed, most comparative lawyers agree that the traditional distinction between the two traditions tends to diminish.

Some have even argued that it is outdated. Nevertheless, the civilian systems are linked by a number of features related to their common historical origin. These relate mainly to the relative importance of the sources of law and of the groups of persons responsible for their development.

Whilst legislation is today the principal source of law in both traditions, common law jurisdictions have larger areas of law which are primarily based on case law. Such areas exist in civilian systems as well, such as French administrative law or German employment law, but they are more exceptional. Furthermore, the paradigm case of legislation in the civil law is that of codification. The civilian codes have the ambition to make comprehensive provision for an entire area of law, such as private law, or for a major branch of it, such as consumer law, and to supersede all pre-existing law in that area. Statutes in common law systems have a much narrower ambit and are usually meant to fit into the existing case law.

Civilian systems have traditionally denied that judges make law. Case law is still not accepted as a binding source of law, so there is no system of **precedent** as in Britain. Today, civilians are more conscious of the law-making function of the judiciary, and they accord strong persuasive authority to court decisions, but the force of precedent is still weaker than in the common law. Neither do they confer special prestige on their **judges**.

In the civil law tradition, the central actor of the legal system is the legal scholar. Under the *ius commune*, in the absence of powerful national legislators and courts, they were responsible for systematizing and updating the ancient Roman law. Law professors were also influential in creating major codes and, later, in interpreting, criticising, and developing them. Their enhanced position is also due to the fact, in contrast to the position in England, that legal education on the Continent has always been the preserve of the universities rather than of the professions. A scholarly approach therefore shapes the mindset of all future lawyers. As a consequence, civilians tend to be less pragmatic than common lawyers. They pay less attention to facts of particular cases and think and rather argue in abstract categories and systematic contexts. However, these differences in legal reasoning are also diminishing.

STEFAN VOGENAUER

See also: **codes and codification in national law; common law of Europe; custom as a source of law; legal education; mixed jurisdictions**

civil liability, theories of   When we speak of 'civil law' in an English law context, we may mean one of two things. First, we may be contrasting our 'common law' system with the continental 'civil law' system derived from **Roman Law.** Secondly, we may be talking about civil as opposed to criminal law. Civil law in this sense means the body of law concerned with delineating the individual 'civil' obligations we owe to one another, as opposed to the obligations we owe to the state (eg to refrain from murder, etc). In this context, theories of civil liability address the rationale, foundation, or justification for imposing legal obligations on people in relation to each other. These obligations may be property-based, contractual, or may arise from standards enshrined in law about how we should conduct ourselves in relation to the concerns and interests of others. The latter area is terrain largely occupied by **tort law** and it is in this particular terrain that views about the basis and scope of legal obligations may differ.

Early accounts of the development of tort law emphasize its role in settling disputes between people which otherwise might escalate and create public disorder. For this reason, the emphasis was on developing a procedure–the **writ** system—for the parties to follow, rather than articulating substantive principles of liability. With early industrialization and, in particular, with the rise of industrial and transport-related accidents, the basis upon which liability should be imposed became more important: strict liability for accidents, ie without the need to prove fault, would impose greater costs on industrial entrepreneurs while a fault standard would limit liability to accidents where fault was in evidence. It is for this reason, scholars such as Morton Horwitz argue, that fault emerged as the primary standard of tort liability in the late nineteenth and early twentieth centuries. That said, pockets of strict liability remained and indeed still do so (eg in relation to **liability for animals**). However, for the most part, theories of civil liability are preoccupied with the fault principle although certain liability rationales are more likely to favour a stricter liability standard.

A number of justifications can be offered for **fault-based civil liability.** Fault, it is argued, is retributive, ie it facilitates retribution corresponding with the function of early forms of tort action to channel retributive impulses in an orderly way. Fault is also corrective: it 'makes good' the relational imbalance created by the wrongful act by requiring the wrongdoer (hereafter 'tortfeasor') to pay for his harmful acts; finally fault is normative; it sets a standard of behaviour, a norm, which regulates how people *ought* to conduct themselves in relation to one another (a moral imperative, if you like). As a regulatory standard it is desirable because it strikes the right balance

between the need to encourage people to be enterprising and to take risks (eg start up a business, build a railway) and the need to discourage careless and unreasonable behaviour. It is thus economically *efficient* (balances costs against benefits) and *deters* conduct which is socially (as well as economically) undesirable.

However, as is too often the case in the real world, theory and practice do not so neatly cohere. With regard to the **tort system** in particular, the presence and operation of **liability insurance**, substantially undermines many of the claims made in defence of fault. Retributive **justice** is hardly satisfied if an insurance company rather than the tortfeasor bears the cost of wrongdoing; nor is corrective justice effected if the loss is not shifted but spread via insurance premiums among a wide number of people. With respect to efficiency and/or deterrence, the counter-arguments are more complex but the essential thrust of them is to suggest that fault neither strikes the right balances between cost and benefits (in part because property rules ensure that many costs are externalized and not borne by those who generate them) nor deters undesirable behaviour. (If the tortfeasor does not in fact pay, he is hardly likely to be deterred.)

Some people have argued that, to be 'true to tort', liability insurance should be abolished or at least radically curtailed. However, the problem with this is that people would only get **compensation** where they were injured by someone who could afford to pay. An awful lot of people would receive little or no compensation, no matter how great the tortfeasor's fault.

This suggests that, at least to some extent, tort liability is about *compensating* people. Indeed, the principle of tort compensation is to put people back in the position they would have been in had the tort not been committed (insofar as this is possible through an award of **damages**). Such a perspective on tort liability as concerned with accident compensation is particularly associated in UK tort theory with the 1960s and 1970s. However, if accident compensation is a primary purpose of tort liability, then fault is not a suitable standard. After all, why should accident victims only get compensation if someone else is at fault? Surely, those who are injured by accidents which are not the result of fault (accidents which are truly 'accidental') are just as much in need of compensation. A broken limb is a broken limb, howsoever caused.

A related argument here highlights and draws upon the loss-spreading effects of liability insurance. With a liberal liability standard and liability insurance, the effect of tort is to spread risks as widely as possible. If I am injured in a car accident and receive compensation by suing the person whose car caused the injury, then, through their liability insurance, the costs of my injury are spread, via premiums, among all car users. Thus, tort serves both a compensation and a loss-spreading function; it effects a form of *distributive justice*.

But, it is argued, if compensation and loss-spreading are the goals, there are other ways in which this might be done, for example, through first party insurance or through a state-based social insurance scheme (which would have the advantage of ensuring that compensation is not limited to those who can afford to take out insurance). At this point, the justification for imposing tort liability seems to disappear; moreover, fault appears to operate as an arbitrary and restrictive principle which denies people compensation when they need it. Far from a theory of civil liability, one is left with the question of why the imposition of liability and the availability of compensation are contingent upon one another in the first place.

In addition to articulating principles for the imposition of tort liability, theories of civil liability are often concerned with delineating the boundaries of tort and distinguishing it from other kinds of civil obligation, particularly those derived from **contract law**. Thus, it is typically asserted that while torts are obligations imposed on individuals whether or not they consent to them, contractual obligations derive from agreement; they are the product of an exchange of promises between the contracting parties. In principle, this is very clear; in practice far less so, not least because many of the obligations which arise through contract are state-imposed, whether through the legislature (eg the Unfair Contracts Terms Act 1977) or the courts (eg the common law terms implied in every **contract of employment**). Likewise, some tort obligations are triggered by agreement or at least by voluntary undertaking (eg the occupier's undertaking with regard to visitors under the **Occupiers Liability** Act 1957). Moreover, sometimes the same conduct may give rise to tortious and contractual liability simultaneously (eg where a worker is injured on the job or a defective product caused injury) although the conditions for and extent of liability may well vary.

Another area of law which is the source of civil obligations and which may be difficult to distinguish between tort and contractual liability is **restitution**. Restitution is concerned with situations where someone is unjustly enriched at another's expense; it creates a civil obligation on the part of the person so

enriched to make restitution to the person who has lost out. This is not quite the same as tort liability although, very often, the activities which generate tort claims are activities carried out by the tortfeasor with a view to commercial benefit (eg building railways).

What all three areas of civil liability, ie tort, contract, and restitution, have in common is that they are concerned with regulating conduct within the context of an individualistic, market-oriented view of social relations. For this reason, civil liability cannot be so burdensome as to inhibit entrepreneurship. Inevitably, then, there will be situations where the acts of some impact upon and cause loss to others without a right of redress or a means of securing compensation. To remedy this situation would require a radical rethink of how we envisage civil society, ie not as a collection of atomistic individuals bumping into one another in pursuit of our own self-interest but as a **community** with shared **responsibility** for the welfare of those of whom the community is comprised, whether in the general context of wealth and resource distribution or in the particular context of bearing the costs of individual injury or misfortune.   JOANNE CONAGHAN

P Birks, 'The Concept of a Civil Wrong' in D Owen (ed), *Philosophical Foundations of Tort Law* (Oxford: Oxford University Press, 1995)

J Stapleton. 'Tort, Insurance, and Ideology' (1995) 58 *Modern Law Review* 520

See also: **negligence in civil law; strict civil liability**

civil liberties   *see* **human rights and civil liberties**

civil partnership   Civil partnership is a status created in United Kingdom law by the Civil Partnership Act 2004. This Act, which came into force in late 2005, allows adult same-sex couples to gain formal legal recognition of their relationships. Couples gain access to a range of rights and responsibilities, which resemble the status of **marriage**. The **legislation** was introduced by the Labour government, and was justified on the basis of **equality** and dignity. It has proven extremely popular, and take up has exceeded the government's expectations.

The Act consists of 429 pages, much of which mirrors the legislative provisions which govern marriage. It specifies different rules for England and Wales, Scotland, and Northern Ireland, and it also deals with the formation and termination of **same-sex relationships** abroad. The Act avoids the creation of an institution called same-sex marriage. Unlike marriage, civil partnership is a legal status which is entirely the creation of statute with no presumption of a lifetime commitment. The Act makes provision for dissolution, which is similar to **divorce** proceedings.

Although the Act transplants much of the substantive law of marriage, there are some differences. At the formation stage, partnership is achieved through the signing of the civil partnership document, but there is no exchange of vows. Nor may a religious service be used at the time of the signing, and registration may not take place in religious premises. Two concepts which have been historically central to marriage—consummation and adultery—are absent.

Despite avoiding the language of marriage, civil partnership has become commonly known as same-sex marriage. In large part, this is because of the similarity of the institutions. Furthermore, it is noteworthy that there has been no attempt to create a substantively new legal relationship form that would be available to all couples as an alternative to marriage. Unlike some earlier proposals which sought to produce a universally available model open to same-sex and opposite-sex couples alike, civil partnership is limited to two people of the same-sex, and it replicates virtually the entire package of rights and responsibilities associated with marriage.

The Act also makes provision for the unregistered to have their relationships governed by law in some circumstances. With respect to social security, the Act states that two people of the same sex who are not civil partners of each other but are living together as if they were civil partners can be treated as a couple for the purposes of means tested benefits and **tax credits**. As a consequence, it might be argued that civil partnership favours wealthy couples who will receive exemption from **inheritance tax** on the **death** of one partner (like married people), but disfavours the poor.

Despite its apparent popularity, some have been sceptical of civil partnership because of its similarity to marriage. These critics include (from very different perspectives) religious conservatives, **lesbian** feminists, and **queer** activists. For example, critics have argued that civil partnership excludes many relationships of care from its purview and that it privileges the privatization of care within couples.

CARL STYCHIN

Civil Procedure Rules Following the publication in 1996 of Lord Woolf's final report into the civil justice system (*Access to Justice*), the Civil Procedure Act 1997 gave effect to many of his recommendations. It established the Civil Procedure Rule Committee which made, and continually updates, the Civil Procedure Rules 1998; and also the review body, the Civil Justice Council, which is charged with considering how to make the civil justice system more accessible, fair, and efficient.

The Civil Procedure Rules govern procedure in all non-criminal cases filed in the County Court, the High Court, and the Court of Appeal in England and Wales. The first of the new Rules states: 'These Rules are a new procedural code with the overriding objective of enabling the court to deal with cases justly'. This bold declaration represented a decisive break from the past, emphasizing that the old civil procedural law is now of persuasive rather than binding authority, and that the old ways would not be allowed to rule the new regime from their graves.

Rule 1 goes on to state that 'Dealing with a case justly includes, so far as is practicable – (a) ensuring that the parties are on an equal footing; (b) saving expense; (c) dealing with the case in ways which are proportionate – (i) to the amount of money involved, (ii) to the importance of the case, (iii) to the complexity of the issues, and (iv) to the financial position of each party; (d) ensuring that it is dealt with expeditiously and fairly; and (e) allotting to it an appropriate share of the court's resources, while taking into account the need to allot resources to other cases'. The court is required to further these overriding objectives by actively managing cases.

Active case management is stated to include: (a) encouraging the parties to cooperate with each other in the conduct of the proceedings; (b) identifying the issues at an early stage; (c) deciding promptly which issues need full investigation and trial and disposing summarily of the others; (d) deciding the order in which issues are resolved; (e) encouraging the parties to use alternative dispute resolution if appropriate; (f) helping the parties to settle the whole or part of the case; (g) fixing timetables or otherwise controlling the progress of the case; (h) considering whether the likely benefits of a particular step justify the cost; (i) dealing with as many aspects of the case as it can on the same occasion; (j) dealing with the case without the parties needing to attend at court; (k) making use of technology; and (l) giving directions to ensure that the trial of a case proceeds quickly and efficiently.

The Rules require the court to allocate cases to an appropriate trial track—'small claims', 'fast track', or 'multi-track' either from the information available from the claim form and defence or by requiring the parties to complete an allocation questionnaire. The objective is to tailor the time, attention, and formality applied to the case in a way that is proportionate to the nature and financial value of the claim.

On the 'small claims track', for example, the court may adopt any method of proceeding at a hearing that it considers to be fair; hearings will be informal; the strict rules of evidence do not apply; the court need not take evidence on oath; it may limit cross-examination; it may allow lay persons to represent litigants. The court has very limited powers to order a party to pay a sum to another party in respect of that other party's costs. This is to discourage the parties in small claims from retaining lawyers.

Directions (for example, as to disclosure, witness statements, and **expert evidence**) and timetables are imposed in 'fast track' and 'multi-track' cases, and also case management conferences in the latter. 'Listing questionnaires' require the parties to declare their readiness for trial. This normally takes place within thirty weeks of directions being given. The parties are not allowed to proceed at their own chosen speed.

The court is given wide powers to take a robust approach to hopeless or unmeritorious claims or defences. It may strike out a statement of case if it appears to the court that it discloses no reasonable grounds for bringing or defending the claim; or give default judgment where no acknowledgement of service or defence is entered in time; or give summary judgment against a party on the whole of a claim or on a particular issue if it considers that the party has no real prospect of succeeding on the issue; and there is no other compelling reason why the case or issue should be disposed of at a trial.

JOHN FITZPATRICK

See also: **case management**

civil service   The civil service is the body of officials—about half a million in the Home Civil Service, some 6,000 in the Diplomatic Service—whose task it is to administer the government of the **United Kingdom** under the control and direction of Ministers. Teams of Ministers come and go according to the results of general elections and the consequent composition of the **House of Commons**, whose support they must command in order to govern. Civil servants do not owe their employment to political allegiance; they are restricted as to the political activities in which they may engage, and remain in post notwithstanding changes of government. This fundamental division among the personnel of central government, often recognized in foreign constitutions in a distinction between 'government' and 'administration', is in the United Kingdom essentially a matter of politics, not law.

In law both Ministers and civil servants are 'servants of the **Crown**', a term crucial to an understanding of the legal regulation of the civil service. **Common law**, in maintaining the fiction that the Queen, institutionalized as 'the Crown', is the head of government, grants her the power to organize and manage the executive branch without reference to Parliament, as part of her **royal prerogative**. Since, constitutionally, the Queen acts only on the advice of Ministers, this means that the executive is in principle free to organize itself without parliamentary intervention. Though the Northcote-Trevelyan Report of 1854, which gave the service its modern shape, recommended that the service be put on a statutory basis, the proposed reforms lacked sufficient parliamentary support and were effected by means of the prerogative. Since that time, successive governments have preferred to continue to rely on prerogative power as the vehicle for civil service reform and for control of the service as a whole. In consequence, the rules relating to the organization, tenure, and discipline of the service are not normally made by or under parliamentary legislation, but promulgated in Orders in Council issued under prerogative power and in codes made under their authority. Public and parliamentary pressure led the government in 2004 to prepare a draft Civil Service Bill for consultation, but this Bill was never presented to Parliament.

The Cabinet Office, which today oversees the Home Civil Service under the authority of the **Prime Minister** in his or her capacity as Minister for the Civil Service, has stated that the aim of the rules is to maintain 'a non-political, permanent Civil Service which sets high value on integrity, impartiality and objectivity, which serves loyally the Government of the day . . . and which recruits on the basis of fair and open competition on the basis of merit'. The crucial instruments, dating from 1996, follow from and respond to the transfer in 1992, to departments and agencies, of functions of recruitment and management, which for a century had been centrally discharged. The Civil Service Management Code sets out the key principles which apply to the recruitment, management, and conduct of staff across government. The Recruitment Code deals with recruitment issues in more detail and is produced by the Civil Service Commissioners, an independent body appointed directly by the Crown by Order in Council.

A further document of 1996, the Civil Service Code, was prompted by parliamentary concern that ministers might press civil servants to act inappropriately, and aims to state clearly and briefly the constitutional framework within which civil servants work—notably, their duty of loyalty to their minister—and the values they are expected to uphold. Should ministerial instructions appear in conflict with the general obligations deriving from these values, civil servants may, after exhausting departmental channels, appeal to the Civil Service Commissioners. A separate code regulates the activities of special advisers, directly appointed by ministers outside normal recruitment arrangements, restricted as to the functions they may perform, and holding office only for the duration of the government under which they were appointed.

The status of Crown servant was long thought to preclude any contractual relationship between civil servants and their employer, but since 1996, members of the Senior Civil Service, comprising the 3,000 or so most senior posts across departments, are employed under individual contracts of employment; and decentralization of management and other recent developments—such as the opening of staffing decisions under the prerogative to judicial review in *Council of Civil Service Unions v Minister for the Civil Service* (1985)—have largely assimilated the employment of civil servants generally to employment under contract.   T DAINTITH

T Daintith and A Page, *The Executive in the Constitution: Structure, Autonomy and Internal Control* (Oxford: Oxford University Press, 1999), ch 3

See also: **departments of state; ministers of state**

civil service code *see* **civil service**

civil service reform *see* **civil service**

civil trials The civil trial is a procedure for the just determination of disputes, primarily between private persons (including companies); but public authorities and the **Crown** may also be parties. The civil trial may concern duties, rights, and **remedies** in either private law, for example in contract or tort matters, or in public law, but not in criminal law. It is part of, and is controlled by, civil law which comprises the whole matrix of rules and procedures which regulate all legal relations in society (other than those relating to the criminal law) with a view to justice being done between citizens.

In England and Wales civil trials are primarily conducted in the County Courts and the High Court, with appeals to the Court of Appeal (Civil Division) and the **House of Lords** (from 2009 the **Supreme Court (UK)**), although a similar process is conducted in many **tribunals**. The party bringing a claim is called the 'claimant' (formerly 'plaintiff') and the other party the 'defendant' or 'respondent'. In Scotland civil trials are primarily conducted in the Sheriff Court and the **Court of Session** with appeals to the Inner House of the Court of Session and the House of Lords (from 2009 the Supreme Court (UK)), and the parties are called 'pursuer' and 'defender'.

The distinction between civil and criminal process rests ultimately on whether the primary aim is to provide redress to the party found to have been wronged or to punish the party found to have committed the wrong in question. The objective of a civil trial is to achieve the former. The court does this by requiring the person held liable for the wrong to give effect to the rights of the wronged party. This is done by ordering the wrongdoer to pay **compensation**, to take action to discharge their legal duties, to desist from acting in an unlawful way, or to make other acts of satisfaction and **restitution**.

The **United Kingdom** has obligations under Article 6 of the **European Convention on Human Rights** with respect to civil process: 'In the determination of his civil rights and obligations . . . everyone is entitled to a fair and public hearing within a reasonable time by an independent and impartial tribunal established by law'. In this country in order to obtain such a hearing a person must first have 'a cause of action': 'A cause of action is simply a factual situation the existence of which entitles one person to obtain from the court a remedy against another person' (Lord Justice Diplock).

If the law does offer a remedy for any given factual situation then a person can ask the court to issue a claim. In England and Wales, civil procedure (including the civil trial) is governed by the **Civil Procedure Rules** 1998. The overriding objective of the Rules is to enable the court to deal with cases justly. The pre-trial procedures are designed to enable the parties and the court to identify as early as possible the precise questions in issue between the parties and the strength of each party's case in relation to those questions.

The civil trial itself must generally be conducted, and judgment given, in public, but there are various circumstances, for example where children or national security are concerned, in which the court is entitled to exclude both press and public.

The trial is conducted in accordance with the **adversary system** in which each party, subject to the Rules, has the right to present its own case and to test and comment upon the case of the other party. Parties may be represented by a solicitor or barrister, or assisted by another person (called 'a McKenzie Friend') who does not address the court. Lay representatives may sometimes be allowed.

The claimant bears the burden of proving to the court that they are entitled to the remedy that they seek. The standard of proof that they have to satisfy is the 'preponderance (or balance) of probability'. In theory, this is a lower standard than the 'beyond reasonable doubt' standard in criminal proceedings, but in practice, in the case of very serious allegations satisfying the civil standard is not dissimilar to satisfying the criminal standard.

Civil trials are normally conducted by **judges**. However, a person charged with (civil) fraud may apply for a trial with judge and jury, and where the claim is **libel, slander**, malicious prosecution, or false imprisonment any party may apply for the trial to be held with judge and jury. There are limited grounds for refusing such applications.

JOHN FITZPATRICK

V Williams, *Civil Procedure Handbook* (Oxford: Oxford University Press, 2007)

AWB Simpson, *Leading Cases in the Common Law* (Oxford: Clarendon Press, 1995)

See also: **evidence, civil**

civil war *see* **war and armed conflict**

civilian courts From the middle of the twelfth century, the earliest time at which it becomes realistic to speak of the **common law** at all, practically all litigation in England took place within **common law courts**, applying the common law. A few courts, however, remained outside the normal system and applied civil law. Some, like the university courts of Oxford and Cambridge, were of very limited significance; but two groups had considerable importance: the ecclesiastical courts and the Court of Admiralty. They had three things in common: first, and most obviously, the law they applied was a version of civil law, the pan-European system derived from **Roman law**; secondly, they followed the written Romano-canonical procedure rather than the oral procedure characteristic of the common law; thirdly, the lawyers who practised in them were not common lawyers (who were members of the **Inns of Court**), but civilians with their own 'Inn', known as Doctors' Commons.

A hierarchy of ecclesiastical courts distinct from secular ones dates back to the latter part of the twelfth century. At the bottom were archdeacons' courts, where offences against good morality were prosecuted; above these were the bishops' courts, which heard appeals from the archdiaconal courts and exercised original jurisdiction over civil matters falling under ecclesiastical jurisdiction. Appeal from bishops' courts lay to the courts of the two archbishops, the Chancery Court of York in the northern province and the Court of Arches in the southern, and from these there was a final appeal to the highest court in the Western Christian church, the papal Rota. The appeal to Rome was abolished in 1534, as the Church of England separated itself from the Roman Catholic Church.

The boundaries of the ecclesiastical courts' jurisdiction were loosely defined by the pseudo-statute *Circumspecte Agatis* (1285); they were policed by the (common law) writ of prohibition. Their jurisdiction over marriage and questions of personal status was unquestioned, though there was a troublesome boundary with the secular courts when issues of the legitimacy of children arose in the context of the inheritance of land. Their jurisdiction over wills of personal property was equally unchallenged; as a matter of theory this did not extend to debt claims against testamentary executors, but in practice these were heard by the ecclesiastical courts in the Middle Ages without any objection being raised. Offences prosecuted in the ecclesiastical rather than the secular courts ranged from minor breaches of morality, in particular sexual misconduct, right up to the most serious of mortal sins. Alongside this, after 1222, the ecclesiastical courts heard claims of **defamation**. Above all, the ecclesiastical courts exercised a jurisdiction over the clergy, whether in matters of tithes and other church property or disciplinarily over allegations of misconduct.

From the early years of the sixteenth century the ecclesiastical jurisdiction was slowly eroded away. Defamation claims were the first victims: the courts of common law began to exercise a jurisdiction over them just after 1500, and by 1600 most cases of any degree of seriousness were being heard there, leaving the ecclesiastical courts with a mass of low-grade claims against—primarily—sharp-tongued women. The archdiaconal jurisdiction over moral offences disappeared in the seventeenth and eighteenth centuries, together with a substantial proportion of cases concerning tithes. Most of the rest of the courts' business disappeared in 1857, and marriage and testamentary causes were transferred to the common law courts. After this little remained other than the disciplinary jurisdiction over the clergy and the oversight of the sale or alteration of church property.

The Court of Admiralty emerged in the fourteenth century to deal with cases arising at sea, which in theory fell outside the jurisdiction of the common law. As well as dealing with claims to prize resulting from the taking of foreign ships, it had a significant role in hearing disputes relating to overseas trade. From the middle of the sixteenth century it had to fight for business against the common law courts, which in practice exercised a concurrent jurisdiction over such claims by using a fiction that overseas contracts had in fact been made in England. By the end of the seventeenth century, it had lost most of its business. It was abolished as a separate court in 1857, when it became a division of the High Court; and in 1970 it was finally absorbed completely by the Court of Queen's Bench.

DAVID IBBETSON

See also: **admiralty law; civil law systems**

civilian population in armed conflict   *see* **international humanitarian law**

claims assessors   *see* **legal advice and assistance**

claims management companies   *see* **legal advice and assistance**

class action   *see* **group action**

class and crime   Since the jurist Dicey outlined what he regarded as the key aspects of the **rule of law** in 1885, the **criminal justice system** has laid claim to encompass the principles of due process and **equality**, as well as predictability, consistency, and equanimity in the application of law. For liberals, these principles, coupled with the ideology of neutrality, objectivity, and fairness, symbolized by the blindfolded Justicia, have combined to create a consensus around the criminal justice process. However, Marx, also writing in the nineteenth century, argued that a capitalist society consists of unequal social classes, notably the bourgeoisie and the proletariat. Hence, power itself, as well as access to it, is differentiated by class; consequently different social classes do not share the same interests. For example, the owners of the means of production—the bourgeoisie—are uniquely placed to influence definitions of both crime and law, thus ensuring their interests dominate through the defence and protection of private property. Through the ideology of the free market, the fact that the means of production and the vast majority of property are owned by a tiny fraction of the population is obscured while through the ideology of 'due process' and '**rule of law**', the legal system is able to present itself as independent of both economic and political interests, capable of allocating fair **justice** and **punishment** to all, regardless of social class. In reality however, this arrangement serves to perpetuate existing inequalities between the powerful and the powerless.

The Marxist perspective was developed by Steven Box during the early 1980s when he observed that official crime statistics are highly selective—concealing crimes committed by the powerful whilst exaggerating crimes committed by the powerless. In support of his claim, Box noted that only 0.05 per cent of the **prison** population had a university degree. Meanwhile, at a time when the rate of unemployment was 14 per cent, 40 per cent of those imprisoned came from this category. Moreover, conventional forms of crime identified in official statistics represent only a fraction of the total offences committed. Yet, such crimes—mainly committed by the powerless—receive intense focus while relatively little attention is paid to crimes committed by the powerful. For example, Levi noted that in 1985 the total cost of *reported* fraud was £2,113 million—twice the cost of theft, burglary, and robbery combined in that year. Hence, crimes by the powerful are *at least* as harmful as those committed by the powerless, yet remain largely invisible.

This *in*visibility of white collar and corporate criminality and—conversely—the *visibility* of working class criminality, can be explained through the concept of the social construction of criminal law categories. Some acts—for example burglary—are constructed as criminal, and therefore a threat to law and order and require imprisonment. Other acts—despite carrying the potential to cause serious injury or even death, for example, failure to comply with health and safety regulations—are constructed as 'violations', and therefore perceived to be less serious. Box termed this process 'mystification', noting that these legal categories are 'ideological constructs' since they are designed to criminalize only victimizing behaviours carried out by the powerless, whilst rendering victimizing behaviour committed by the powerful invisible.

Official crime statistics and the prison population therefore do not present a complete or accurate picture of the crime problem. Instead, they represent only a fraction of the types of crimes committed and the type of people committing it. Those crimes and criminals captured within official statistics are socially differentiated from those with the power to define what counts as crime, and who are consequently able to define themselves out of the criminal statistics. The social and ideological construction of those who are rendered punishable serves the interests of the powerful by legitimizing the intensification of their social control agencies such as the **police** and the prison system. In this way, the established class differentiation is reinforced and maintained and the dominant social and economic order perpetuated along existing unequal class divisions.

ANETTE BALINGER

See also: **crime and social differentiation**

clausula rebus sic stantibus/**fundamental change of circumstances**   *see* **treaties**

clemency   *see* **pardons**

climate change   Atmospheric concentrations of carbon dioxide (CO_2) and other greenhouse gases trap infrared radiation emitted from the earth's surface. Although part of a natural greenhouse effect, scientists believe that the earth's climate system is being thrown out of balance by significantly increased emissions from **human** activities. Human-induced climate change is occurring through our reliance and consumption of fossil fuels such as coal and oil and activities like deforestation. This is causing potentially irreversible impacts to our climate and ecosystems that could have profound implications for our way of life. Studies such as the UK Treasury Stern Review in 2006 warn of this harming long-term UK economic growth, and suggest that, worldwide, hundreds of millions could suffer hunger, water shortages, and flooding.

As the world's most pressing environmental challenge, solutions underpinned by laws continue to gather apace. Legal controls over atmospheric emissions and air quality have long existed at national level, but there has been a growing recognition that the climate system is a shared resource affecting all the international community. The first international response to these concerns was the **United Nations** Framework Convention on Climate Change ('UNFCCC') in 1992. The UNFCCC is a framework law requiring contracting parties to adopt policies aimed at the stabilization of greenhouse gases in the atmosphere, at levels that prevent dangerous interference to the climate system. Stabilization may be achieved by preventing greenhouse gas emissions from entering into the atmosphere or removing them once emitted.

The UNFCCC placed a non-binding commitment on Annex 1 industrialized countries to reduce their greenhouse gas emissions to 1990 levels by 2000. The Kyoto Protocol to the UNFCCC, adopted in 1997, provides for binding commitments. Entry into force of the Protocol was delayed because it required countries responsible for 55 per cent of industrialized emissions to approve it. The USA, responsible for approximately a quarter of all global emissions had signed the agreement but refused to ratify it, largely because they considered it unfair that non-Annex 1 Parties were not assigned binding targets. The Protocol finally entered into force in 2005 after ratification by Russia. The UK is a party to Kyoto and the UNFCCC. Under Kyoto, developed countries agreed to reduce their emissions by an average of five per cent below 1990 levels over the period 2008–2012. The EU and its Member States agreed to an eight per cent reduction of emissions, but this target can be redistributed between Member States to reflect national circumstances and under EU law the UK's binding target is 12.5 per cent below 1990 levels. Compliance is monitored by registries and annual inventory reports. These tracked amounts reveal that many of the largest countries are failing to meet Kyoto targets. Countries continue to participate in annual international meetings to negotiate on issues related to the Convention, such as future commitment periods.

As well as setting targets, Kyoto established flexible mechanisms, enabling Annex I Parties to reduce emissions or remove carbon from the atmosphere in other countries and count them towards their own targets. Projects carried out in countries without Kyoto targets (non-Annex I Parties) operate under the Clean Development Mechanism adopted in 2005. Projects carried out in territories of other Annex I Parties operate under the Joint Implementation mechanism, launched in 2006. These mechanisms allow for wind farms and carbon sink forestry projects, and the logic behind them is that although the cost of combating climate change varies globally the atmospheric benefit is the same wherever the action is taken. International committees oversee the approval of these projects and participants must meet a number of eligibility requirements relating to registries and reporting. Businesses, **non-governmental organizations** and other entities can participate in these mechanisms under the authority and responsibility of national governments.

A third Kyoto mechanism allows for emissions trading between Annex I Parties. The UK launched the world's first voluntary economy-wide emissions trading scheme in 2002. This scheme, with final reconciliation in 2007, was overtaken by a multi-country CO_2 emission trading scheme in Europe, established under EU law in 2005. Emission caps and allowances for installations covered by the scheme are set down in national allocation plans and licensed trading of allowances takes place during specified periods. Operators of installations are placed under a legal duty to annually surrender allowances equal to their total verified emissions during the preceding calendar year. Registries and transactions are overseen by national regulators and EU administrators. The first phase of the scheme ran until 2007. The second phase (2008–2012) expands the greenhouse gases covered, and sectors such as aviation were included. The EU Linking Directive also allows emission credits from the Clean Development Mechanism and Joint Implementation mechanisms to be legally used by operators of national installations covered by the EU trading scheme. Countries outside the EU are also developing domestic trading schemes, and links between these and the EU scheme could be established under future legal agreements.

RAYMOND PURDY

climate change levy   *see* **environmental taxes**

clinical judgement   *see* **medical negligence**

clinical legal education   Clinical legal education entails the learning and teaching of law through students undertaking practical legal work alongside more traditional forms of study, generally in a university or a postgraduate vocational training institution. It can be done in many ways. For example it can be done by students, under the supervision of academic staff who are also practising lawyers, providing legal advice and **representation** to members of the public, as part of a service provided by a university. Or it can be done by students doing similar work but on placement in the office of a solicitor or advice agency, supervised by those staff but reporting back to a university. Another approach involves students role-playing the work of practising lawyers in simulated casework exercises within a university, or students, under the supervision of academic staff, may give talks and classes on legal subjects to members of the public in voluntary organizations, schools, and **prisons**. It can be a voluntary or compulsory, assessed for degree purposes or an extra-curricular activity. Key features are the supervision and scrutiny by academic staff of the work undertaken by students, and the structured reflection by students on their practical work in the context of their study of law. A long-established feature of US law schools, it only developed extensively in the UK from the 1990s, encouraged by the increasing emphasis in education generally on experiential learning, vocational relevance, the acquisition of skills, the importance of ethical awareness, and in the legal profession, of *pro bono* activity by solicitors and barristers.

JOHN FITZPATRICK

H Brayne, N Duncan, and RH Grimes, *Clinical Legal Education: Active Learning in Your Law School* (London: Blackstone Press, 1998)

See also: **pro bono** **legal services**

clinical negligence   *see* **medical negligence**

Clinton impeachment trial   President William J Clinton was impeached on two charges by the House of Representatives in December 1998, and tried and acquitted the following month by the Senate. The trial marked only the second time in United States history that the Senate tried a president. House prosecutors succeeded in winning 50 of 100 votes on one article of impeachment, and just 45 votes on the other, far short of the two-thirds vote required for conviction under the Constitution. The vote closely followed party lines, with all Senate Democrats voting 'Not Guilty' on both charges.

The two articles of impeachment approved by the House concerned a sexual affair that President Clinton had with Monica Lewinsky beginning in 1995 when she was a 21-year-old intern working in the White House. The Republican-controlled House charged Clinton with lying to a federal grand jury about his relationship with Lewinsky, and with obstructing the investigation of the Lewinsky affair conducted by the Office of Independent Counsel, headed by Kenneth Starr.

The impeachment trial had its roots in a sexual harassment lawsuit brought against President Clinton by Paula Jones, who claimed that Clinton, while serving as governor of Arkansas in 1991, made unwanted sexual advances towards her in a hotel room. Tips led Jones's lawyers to question Clinton about Lewinsky, whom he denied ever seeing 'alone'. Lewinsky's decision to preserve a semen-stained blue dress established the falsity of Clinton's denial of a sexual relationship, and eventually led to the impeachment charges.   DOUG LINDER

closed shop   The closed shop is a practice in employment relations whereby a worker is required to be or to become a member of a trade union in order to secure or retain employment. In the United Kingdom the term is used generically to cover a situation where someone is required to be a member of a trade union as a condition of employment (sometimes referred to as a pre-entry closed shop), as well as a situation where someone is required to join a trade union after commencing employment with a particular employer (sometimes referred to as a post-entry closed shop). In the United States and Canada in contrast, the closed shop refers to a situation where existing union membership is a condition of obtaining employment with a particular employer, with the union shop or agency shop being the terms used to define the situations where a worker must join the union after commencing employment (union shop) or pay a fee to the union in lieu of union dues (agency shop) for the services the union provides.

The closed shop creates conflict between (a) those who believe that workers should not be required to join or pay towards an organization to which they are opposed; and (b) those who believe that workers should not enjoy the benefits of trade union organization without contributing to its costs. Closed shop arrangements operated formally and informally in the UK for many years, with the agreement or acquiescence of employers. Although such arrangements were seen to have benefits for both employers and **trade unions**, concerns about individual liberty rather than collective **security** were ultimately to prevail. In *Young, James and Webster v United Kingdom* (1982) the **European Court of Human Rights** held in an important decision that the closed shop arrangements then operating in the railway industry violated the right to **freedom of association**, to the extent that the workers in question were required to join one of three prescribed trade unions, on pain of dismissal.

Closed shop arrangements were once widespread. Indeed, it has been estimated that in 1980, some five and a quarter million workers were employed in a situation where a closed shop operated, accounting for some 25 per cent of the labour force at the time. Although closed shop agreements are not unlawful, they are now largely unenforceable, following **legislation** introduced by the government of Mrs Thatcher, which Labour governments since 1997 have undertaken not to repeal. Under the Trade Union and Labour Relations (Consolidation) Act 1992, it is automatically unfair for an employer to dismiss someone because of his or her non-membership of a trade union, and it is unlawful to refuse to employ someone because he or she is not a member of a trade union. Even agency shop arrangements of the kind operating in North America are unenforceable in British law, and, moreover, an employee cannot be required to make a payment to charity in lieu of either union membership or the payment of trade union dues.   KEITH EWING

closer cooperation in the EU   Closer cooperation is provided for and regulated under Title VII of the Treaty on European Union ('TEU'). It provides that Member States may use the institutions, procedures and mechanisms of the European Union ('EU') and European Community ('EC') Treaties to pursue enhanced cooperation, which other states do not wish to enter into. This is subject to certain conditions; first, enhanced cooperation can only be entered into as a last resort (that is, where it is not possible to achieve its objectives within the framework of the Treaties). Secondly, the cooperation must be consistent with the objectives and legal order of the EU and EC. Thirdly, the pursuit of enhanced cooperation requires a minimum of eight Member States and must be open to all Member States (initially it required the participation of a majority of states, under the proposed Constitution for Europe this would have become one-third of Member States). The core EU provisions on closer cooperation are supported by specific provision for enhanced cooperation in relation to each of the EU's three pillars.

Closer cooperation specifically permits a group of states to use the institutional mechanisms and procedures of the EC to pursue the development of policies in areas in which not all Member States are prepared to proceed. This is significant because traditionally the EC was premised on the development of uniform policies and measures: closer cooperation, in contrast, permits the development of difference across the EC—giving rise to references to 'variable geometry' or 'multi-speed' Europe. Although these terms have not been clearly defined, 'variable geometry' may be distinguished from the notion of 'multi-speed' Europe, since 'multi-speed' could indicate all states progressing ultimately in the same direction, but at different rates of progress, whereas 'variable geometry' suggests quite clear difference in direction, cooperation with which other states will not subsequently join.

The origins of closer cooperation lie in the opt-outs developed during the negotiation of the Maastricht Treaty, notably in relation to the development of social policy which the majority of states supported. The UK, however, was immovably opposed to it, creating an impasse. The solution to this was the UK opt-out, under which the other eleven states 'borrowed' the Community institutions to develop social policy which did not apply to the UK. The opt-out has also been used in relation to monetary union and the area of Freedom Security and Justice.

The opt-out in Maastricht was viewed simply as a way out of a particular deadlock. Since then, however, the development of closer cooperation, while still only to be used as a last resort, has become recognized as a necessity for the development of policy in the EU, particularly in view of enlargement and the increasing difficulty of obtaining a consensus among all the Member States. Acceptance of the opt-out, and closer cooperation itself has given rise to a suggestion (or fear) of 'Europe a la Carte'—according to which states would pick and choose which policies they would participate in—as yet this has not materialized.   EMILY REID

See also: **European constitution; European treaties**

closure of business   *see* **redundancy; transfer of business; insolvency, corporate**

Coase, Ronald   The work of economist Ronald Coase (1910–) transformed legal scholars' approaches to social policy, and spurred economists to focus attention on how institutions function. When Coase received the Nobel Prize for Economics in 1991, the Nobel Committee cited two key articles concerning Coase's pioneering notion of 'transaction cost'.

In 'The Nature of the Firm', Coase pointed out when an entrepreneur decides between purchasing a factor of production through the market, or making the needed item himself, the decision will turn on the comparative costs of transacting. That is, an entrepreneur who goes the market route must bear transaction costs such as searching for sources of supply, comparing and verifying qualities of goods, and negotiating contracts. If instead an entrepreneur goes the route of creating a firm to manufacture the factor in-house, she must bear costs such as searching for potential employees and monitoring their performance. Understanding these transaction costs can both help us understand the size, shape and nature of firms, and make recommendations as to institutional structures that will facilitate economic growth.

In 'The Problem of Social Cost', Coase examined the problem of intersecting activities that cause harm to each other. Economist Arthur Pigou suggested that the government should impose a tax or damages on the active party (for example, on the factory emitting the pollution) to make that party's private costs equal the social costs. The liable party would then purportedly choose a socially optimal path as it compared the social costs of its activity with the profits it anticipated. Coase showed that in many circumstances—depending on transaction costs—this rigid Pigovian rule would not achieve maximum productivity: that harms are the consequence of two activities interacting, and that the optimal route might involve a combination of changed activities by all parties.

Coase argued that in a world without transaction costs, it would not matter who bore the legal liability: for example, if the factory bore the liability but its neighbours could better lower costs, the factory would pay the neighbours to take the needed action. However, in the real world, where transaction costs are everywhere, the party bearing the liability might find it too costly to negotiate contracts with its neighbours, and might instead respond to the legal rule by curtailing production in a way that was socially inefficient.

The latter discussion gave rise to the so-called 'Coase Theorem' (so named by co-Laureate, George Stigler). It postulates that in the absence of transaction costs, parties will bargain to an efficient solution regardless of which parties receive rights through law. Coase is sometimes misunderstood as suggesting that law is unimportant. To the contrary: the point of Coase's exploring how resources would flow in a world without transaction costs was to underline the crucial role that transaction costs play in understanding how law's effects play out.

Coase suggested that **judges** could legitimately seek to foster the flow of resources to their most productive uses. Notably, judges could deploy the allocation of rights for purposes such as placing resources initially in productive hands, and lowering transaction costs so that misplaced and undervalued resources can be easily transferred. Law can do these things directly, and by affecting the shape of institutions.

For lawyers, Coase's work functioned as if to strip the social world to its elemental atoms. Scholars could track the way different legal rules affected resource use and the shape of institutions, and seek to affect the 'chemical reactions' directly. The resultant intoxication rewrote the history of law schools for the next fifty years, under the rubric of 'Law and Economics'. Others responsible for the growth of the field include Guido Calabresi and Richard Posner.

                    WENDY J GORDON

See also: **economic analyses of law; civil liability, theories of**

Code Napoléon   The Code Napoléon (as the French Civil Code was known) is the most influential European legal document since **Justinian**'s Digest of 532 AD. Promulgated in 1804, it created the unity of French private law. Previously, the private law of France had consisted in a set of customs established and enforced by regional *parlements*, which had limited similarities one to another. Some were based on local customary law and some on **Roman law**, together with canon law influences. The result was that private law varied from one part of France to another.

The political unity of the French created by the Revolution required a legal unity. Beginning in 1793, a number of drafts failed to gain approval before Napoleon personally took over the project. In 1800, a commission of Tronchet and Bigot de Préameneau, from the customary law tradition, and Portalis and Maleville from the Roman law tradition, produced a draft within four months, which eventually became a code of 2,279 articles. The Code represented a political settlement after the turbulence of the revolutionary period, settling areas such as family and property law.

The Code aims to be exhaustive. Portalis argued that it should set out general principles the implications of which could be determined by the judges. All the same, some of the provisions on property are very detailed and specific.

The Code was adopted in the regions which France had conquered under Napoleon (notably Belgium, The Netherlands, Austria, Spain, and parts of Italy and Germany), before they created their own codes many years later. It served as a model for the development of civil codes in Latin America and Quebec.

JOHN BELL

co-decision procedure   *see* **European Parliament**

codes and codification in national law   Codes aim to present the law on a particular area in a coherent and consistent way. At its most ambitious, a code can attempt to offer a complete statement of the rules and principles that apply to a particular aspect of life. This was the ambition of the **Code Napoléon** and the German *Burgerliches Gesetzbuch* ('BGB') of 1900 in civil law. Many countries, notably Switzerland (1907) and The Netherlands (1992) have achieved similar kinds of codification. The Napoleonic suite of codes also included civil procedure, criminal procedure, and commercial law. A number of countries also have codes in these areas. Once such a code has been promulgated, there is no need to refer to the preceding legislation or previous interpretations offered in judicial case law and academic doctrinal writing. Other codes are less ambitious. They seek to consolidate the current state of the legislation in a single document for ease of use. The modern French *Commission de la Codification* has undertaken this kind of codification and produced a significant simplification of the body of texts that lawyers have to use.

The process of codification can be very long, particularly where an exhaustive code is being produced. Such a code will contain a clear statement of the basic principles, followed by more detailed set of provisions dealing with specific issues. In terms of drafting, its provisions will typically use general language, aiming to provide a broad orientation for interpretation, rather than very detailed rules. As Portalis put it in 1803, it is for the legislator to set out the general principles and leave the judge as interpreter to fill in the details. Because such a code aims to be a foundation document, there will be much debate on general issues, and that can last a long time. (For example, work began on the New Dutch Civil Code in 1947, but remains incomplete.) The production of the French Criminal Code of 1994 involved the question of whether to introduce provisions that made corporations liable for criminal offences, and such a debate illustrates the kind of matter of principle that makes an exhaustive code a slow process.

By contrast, the production of a consolidating code is more technical and can proceed more quickly. Since the purpose is to make existing provisions more coherent and consistent, the essential task is to arrange the rules drawn from different sources in a more systematic way. The process occurs without much need for debate on policy and can proceed rapidly by subordinate legislation. Common lawyers would not consider such documents to be codes, but rather consolidating legislation. Certainly the style is typically more detailed than the general provisions of exhaustive codes.

Different countries adopt distinct methods of producing exhaustive codes. In Germany, the major revisions of the BGB in 2000 were produced by a committee of academics. Combinations of academics and practitioners produced the French criminal code and the new Dutch Civil Code. It is clear that the process of formulation needs to take place away from political debate. But the process of adoption by a parliament needs to avoid complexity. In order to have a code adopted, there needs to be either a decisive political moment or political pressure. The Code Napoléon was written in four months under political pressure; the German Code of Civil Procedure of 1878 was adopted because there was an urgent need for common court procedure within a recently unified country.

Since 1923, The American Law Institute has offered an alternative to codification, namely restatement. A *Restatement* has no formal legal status, but offers guidance. The authority comes from the care and independence with which the different solutions adopted in the various states have been examined, and by the authority of the academic organization that produced it. There is no need for adoption by a political process, but the text can serve as a benchmark for courts in individual states. Many of the models of draft codes for a European contract law and delict (tort) law are operating in this way.

The other approach is to attempt some form of harmonization. That will focus on problem areas and seek to resolve those, without fundamentally changing the shape of the law. Such a process has advantages in trying to achieve similarity in several jurisdictions, since obtaining assent to a comprehensive change is almost impossible. In this approach, the systematization of the rest of the law with the harmonized parts falls to courts and academic writers.

The movement for codification began as an expression of the ideals of the eighteenth century Enlightenment, seeking to introduce rationality and order into established ways of conducting government. The idea was to produce a simple and comprehensive statement of principles that required no further interpretation. Early examples were the Danish code of 1683 and the Swedish private law code of 1734. The Prussian General Land Law of 1794 was comprehensive and excessively detailed. They provided lessons for the more principled approach of the nineteenth-century codes. The attempt to ban judicial interpretation of the Prussian Code failed, as did attempts in France and Austria to insist that judges should refer difficulties of interpretation to the Parliament. Once a code has been operating for some time, its meaning is overlaid by a body of judicial interpretation that transforms it, sometimes almost completely. A good example is the law of delict in French law, contained originally in six articles, but which now requires books of over 500 pages to explain subsequent interpretations and applications. As a result, in practice codes cannot be the sole source from which the law can be found.   JOHN BELL

See also: **civil law systems; restatements of the law (USA)**

codes of conduct in international law   Codes of conduct are principles of, or guidelines for, behaviour. They are voluntary non-binding instruments that cannot usually be legally enforced. The voluntary aspect of such a code pertains both to their adoption and to compliance with their principles. Such codes have been developed by States, international organizations and other non-State actors such as transnational corporations, non-governmental organizations and multi-stakeholder initiatives.

Voluntary codes of conduct are currently the key means for regulating the social and environmental impacts of corporate conduct in the absence of international legal obligations and host-State capacity or willingness to regulate these entities. Examples of such codes include company business codes and policies as well as international initiatives such as the Global Compact, the OECD Guidelines for Multinational Enterprises, the Global Sullivan Principles of Social Responsibility, and the Voluntary Principles on Security and Human Rights. The effectiveness of these types of codes in regulating corporate behaviour has been the subject of much debate.

Within the international legal system, codes of conduct form part of the corpus of **soft law**. Although such codes are not legally binding, in certain circumstances they can have legal effect where they interact with binding rules of international law. For example, a code, such as the UN Food and Agricultural Organisation's *Voluntary Guidelines to Support the Progressive Realization of the Right to Adequate Food in the Context of National Food Security* (adopted by the 127th Session of the FAO Council, November 2004), may provide further guidance on the content of international legal obligations of States and could subsequently be used by international dispute-settlement bodies or domestic courts in the interpretation of such obligations.

PENELOPE SIMONS

codes of practice in consumer law   A code of practice is a form of self-regulation, which is an alternative to adopting binding legislation on specific matters of consumer protection. For example, the Advertising Codes are administered by the Advertising Standards Authority ('ASA'), and require that all advertising (whether broadcast or non-broadcast) must be legal, decent, honest, and truthful. Advertisements which fail to comply may have to be amended or withdrawn.

A code will set out how a business should treat consumers and will not only include a commitment to respect consumers' legal rights, but also offer a benefit above and beyond what is required by law. It may, for example, offer a quick procedure for resolving disputes when something has gone wrong, or seek to address concerns about practices in a particular sector. A code is usually drafted by a trade or industry association for a specific business sector, and members of such an association are expected to comply with the relevant code.

The **Office of Fair Trading** ('OFT') has been given the power to approve codes of practice. An approved code has to comply with a range of criteria regarding the body preparing the code, the drafting process, content, complaints handling, monitoring, enforcement, and publicity. It is also necessary to demonstrate that these criteria are followed on a day-to-day basis. Once that has been done, the OFT will formally approve the code, and the code may carry the OFT-approved logo. Approved codes exist for the motor trade, estate agents, direct selling, and car repairs.   CHRISTIAN TWIGG-FLESNER

OFT, *Consumer Codes Approval Scheme* (OFT 390, November 2006)

Codes of Practice in employment law   Codes of Practice are statements issued with the aim of describing and encouraging desirable behaviour—'best practice'—in particular areas or circumstances. Often they are designed to accompany a piece of **legislation**, in which case a Code may be intended as a guide to interpretation of the legal provisions. Alternatively, the Code may require something over and above the behaviour prescribed by law. Codes of Practice are not binding in a legal sense—breach of a Code does not, of itself, constitute grounds for legal proceedings. They are sometimes referred to in legislation, however, and may be admissible in evidence in proceedings before a court or **employment tribunal**. **Tribunals** and **courts** are obliged, at times, to take into account any provisions of a Code which seem relevant to an issue before them. For these reasons, Codes can have a significant influence on the outcome of legal proceedings. In some cases their recommendations have come to be regarded, in practice, as essentially obligatory.

Codes of Practice are issued by authorized bodies in accordance with set procedures. In the employment law sphere, a number of individuals and bodies are empowered by statute to publish Codes within their areas of competence, including the Secretary of State for Employment, **ACAS** (Advisory, Conciliation, and Arbitration Service), and the **Commission for Equality and Human Rights** (a competence formerly held by the Equal Opportunities Commission, the Commission for Racial Equality, and the Disability Rights Commission). One prominent example of a Code currently in force is the ACAS Code of Practice on Disciplinary and Grievance Procedures.   RUTH DUKES

codes of practice, administrative guidance and circulars   *see* **legal rules, types of**

codification and progressive development of international law   *see* **customary international law**

cohabitation   'Cohabitation' has become the accepted term used in family law to refer to couples in intimate relationships who are living together in the same household but are not formally married or, in the case of same-sex couples, have not registered a **civil partnership** in accordance with the Civil Partnership Act 2004. Whilst in England and Wales, legal recognition for informal '**common law marriage**' was abolished by the Clandestine Marriages Act 1753, Scotland, in contrast, retained a form of common law marriage known as **marriage** by cohabitation with habit and repute, which allowed those who held themselves out to be formally married, to apply to be legally recognized as married. However, this too was abolished for future relationships by the Family Law (Scotland) Act 2006 which introduced other remedies for those cohabiting.

As a social phenomenon, heterosexual cohabitation, colloquially known as common law marriage, has risen steeply since the 1980s and has gained widespread social acceptance as a partnering and parenting choice, constituting for some an alternative and for others a preliminary to marriage. National Statistics' data published in 2005–2006 confirm that UK-wide whilst the number of marriages has been in decline since 1972, over a quarter of all children are now born to cohabiting couples and over a quarter of all couples under sixty (treble the 1986 figure) now cohabit. These trends are predicted to continue to increase.

The law has responded to these changing social norms in a piecemeal fashion and has also struggled to find appropriate terminology to describe such *de facto* as opposed to *de jure* couples. The phrase 'unmarried wives', was originally chosen in the Unemployment Insurance Act 1927. Later, whilst other jurisdictions such as Australia, preferred the term *de facto marriage* (see for example New South Wales De Facto Marriages Act 1980), in the UK the word 'cohabitation' was adopted to describe the phenomenon of unmarried (and originally just heterosexual) couples who lived together 'as husband and wife'. This can be traced to the so-called 'cohabitation rule' in the National Assistance Act 1948 which withdrew entitlement to means-tested benefits from women living together in the same household with a man 'as his wife'. The expectation was that the man would financially support her from his earnings or by claiming state benefits for them as a couple rather than two individuals. Whilst the term 'cohabitee' is used in general language to describe cohabiting partners, this is considered ungrammatical and so the term 'cohabitant' is now used in **legislation** having been first adopted by the Law Commission in their 1992 report *Domestic Violence and Occupation of the Family Home* (Law Com No 207).

There is currently no universal legal definition of cohabitation which is defined by statute and case law in specific contexts. Whilst research undertaken in the nationally representative British Social Attitudes Survey 2000 showed that most people falsely believe cohabiting couples have a 'common law marriage' giving them the same legal rights as married couples after a period of time, the law is in fact inconsistent in its treatment of cohabitants, although it no longer discriminates between heterosexual and same-sex couples. In some areas, such as succeeding to the tenancy of the rented family home on a partner's death, **domestic violence** protection, eligibility for means-tested benefits or some **tax credits**, they are treated identically to married couples. In others, such as making a claim against a deceased partner's estate or for **compensation** following the wrongful death of a partner, they are treated as family members inferior to married couples, entitled to a lower award. In yet other situations, they are treated as completely unrelated individuals. Thus in contrast to spouses, a partner is ignored for pension entitlement purposes; there is no **Inheritance Tax** exemption when one partner dies leaving the other property; there is no automatic succession to any part of their partner's estate if no will is made. Perhaps most significantly, outside Scotland where such a remedy was introduced in 2006, there is no family law claim for financial provision on cohabitation breakdown, leaving property law rather than family law to govern how assets are to be distributed and providing no **maintenance** rights. The Law Commission for England and Wales made recommendations for reform in their report published in July 2007 *Cohabitation: The Financial Consequences of Relationship Breakdown* (Law Com No 307) which must now be considered by government. It proposes eligible cohabitants should have a remedy for financial hardship on relationship breakdown or death where one partner has retained a benefit or suffered economic disadvantage as a consequence of the relationship. The Northern Ireland Office for Law Reform has indicated it will await the response to the English review.   ANN BARLOW

cohabitation rule   In the schemes relating to some social security benefits a distinction is made between couples and single people. A couple for this purpose comprises two persons who are either married to each other or are 'living together as husband and wife' (the cohabitation rule). The quoted phrase is not defined in legislation but has been judicially interpreted. The courts and the Social Security Commissioners have confirmed that the factors that are relevant to this status include: membership of the same household; permanency of the relationship; shared care for any children; financial contributions to household expenditure; 'public acknowledgement' of the couple's relationship; and (although a contentious issue) whether the couple have a sexual relationship. The cohabitation rule has been adapted to apply also to gay and lesbian couples, who (as members of a civil partnership or living together as though civil partners) will be treated in an analogous way to heterosexuals affected by it. In relation to means-tested benefits, the rule reflects an assumption, which also underlies the level of benefit provision to be made, that persons living together as a couple will pool their resources to meet their needs and that shared living costs, including food and fuel costs, will be smaller than the total for two single individuals. If one member of a couple is in full-time employment, one effect of being caught by the cohabitation rule could be that neither member may qualify for a means-tested benefit at all. The rule can also affect entitlement to bereavement benefits.

NEVILLE HARRIS

Coke, Sir Edward   Sir Edward Coke (1552–1634) was a lawyer of enormous ability and energy. He, more than any other, set English **common law** on to its modern footing, building on its medieval foundations. As Chief Justice of the Court of Common Pleas and then of the Court of King's Bench, he took the lead in a series of decisions which set the boundaries of the power of the King and of other **courts**; as an active parliamentarian in the first years of Charles I, he was a focus of opposition to the King, protecting constitutional propriety as he understood it; and as the author of a host of legal works, in particular his Reports and Institutes, he interpreted medieval law, reconstructed it, and transmitted it for the benefit of future generations.

Called to the Bar in 1578, Coke was rapidly marked out as a lawyer of very great promise. He combined an encyclopaedic knowledge of the medieval common law with a facility for inventive argument, and was hence able both to undermine an opponent's position by showing that it was built on flimsy foundations and to construct a framework within which his own position could appear to have an inevitable logic to it. At the same time, he built on his political connections. In 1592 he was elected to **Parliament** and made **Solicitor-General**; in 1593, he became Speaker of the Commons; and in 1594 he was appointed **Attorney-General**, a position which he held for twelve years. In the last of these capacities he played a prominent role in the putting into execution of **Crown** policies; in particular he had the primary responsibility for the treason trials of the last years of Elizabeth and the first years of James, including those of the Earl of Essex and Sir Walter Ralegh.

In 1606, he was made Chief Justice of the Common Pleas and in 1613 translated to the Chief Justiceship of the King's Bench, holding that office until his dismissal in 1616. In this ten-year period he led the **judges** in establishing the dominance of the common law over its rivals. Central to this was the attack on the ecclesiastical Court of High Commission, which had been set up by statute in 1559. The common lawyers' opposition, visible long before Coke's involvement, focused not so much on the existence of the court as on the powers which it claimed to exercise: Coke's view, supported by other lawyers, was that they should be limited to those which had been granted by Parliament and could not be extended by the King in the exercise of the royal **prerogative**. The assault on the High Commission, therefore, implicitly involved an attack on the King himself. Coke did not shy away from this conclusion. In the case known as *Prohibitions del Roy* (1608), it was held that the King himself could not sit in judgment in any case: lawsuits, both criminal and civil, were to be decided by proper legal process according to the law of the realm. Three years later, in the *Case of Proclamations*, the royal prerogative was similarly constrained: the King did have the power to issue proclamations, but the limits of that power were determined by the common law. Other courts too, most notably the Court of Admiralty, were attacked on the same basis: the extent of their powers was a matter of common law, and it was for the judges of the common law courts to say what this was. Ambiguous remarks in *Doctor Bonham's Case* in 1610 suggest that he may have been willing to contemplate the common law—and hence the judges—having the power to control parliamentary **legislation**. Coke's final battle was with the **Chancery Court**, which had for many decades issued injunctions in appropriate cases to prevent the enforcement of judgments given at common law. This brought matters to a head between Coke and King James, and in 1616 the King dismissed him from his office.

In 1621 Coke returned to the **House of Commons**. His learning and experience pushed him into a position of prominence, and he played an active part in all types of parliamentary work, apparently taking an especial interest in economic and commercial matters. In addition, though he was at first by no means a consistent opponent of Crown policy, he continued to give voice to the constitutional theory which he had developed and expressed as a judge. Inevitably, this led him into difficulties with the King, and for

several months in 1622 he was imprisoned by royal order. His anti-royalist position hardened after the accession of Charles I, and in the Parliament of 1625 he was a persistent critic of the King's policy on taxation, **religion,** and foreign affairs. In his final Parliament, that of 1628, he was at his most active. His focus here was on the protection of the rights of citizens against all forms of royal incursion. He led the demands for a substantial elaboration of **Magna Carta**, resulting in the King's reluctant acceptance of the Petition of Right. At the same time, he articulated afresh his own constitutional position, this time effectively one of unlimited parliamentary supremacy.

Above all, though, Coke was a lawyer. His voluminous legal writings, in particular his *Reports* and *Institutes*, can be seen as marking a new beginning for the common law. The *Reports*, of which eleven volumes appeared in his lifetime and two volumes posthumously, were not—and did not purport to be—faithful reproductions of decisions and the reasons which the judges had given for them. At this time, judges were not expected to give formal reasons for their decisions, so the reasons articulated by Coke were an amalgam of the arguments of counsel and judges and his own explanations. Each case reported, therefore, can be seen as an essay explaining the result in terms of the medieval **precedents**, and, in so doing, replacing the authority of those precedents with the authority of Coke's explanations of them. In consequence, the *Reports* represent a disorderly heap of great learning, pointing to a view of the common law which was more dependent on the authority of the past than on moral principle. The four volumes of the *Institutes*, written after his retirement from Parliament and consciously or unconsciously reflecting the four books of **Justinian**'s *Institutes*, are superficially better structured, but no more than the *Reports* do they follow any abstract framework. The *First Institute*, the *Commentary on Littleton*, dealt with the law of real property. Littleton's work provided the framework for the volume, but Coke's commentary ranged far and wide around the subject matter. The *Second Institute*, a commentary on the most important statutes since Magna Carta, is again crammed with learning; it can be seen as the counterpart of the *Reports*, updating the medieval law at the same time purporting to reproduce it. The *Third Institute* dealt with criminal law, analysing each significant crime in turn; and the *Fourth Institute* described the jurisdiction and operation of all the various courts.

What Coke's legal works do not contain is any respectable theory of the common law. Unless he was to say that it was largely made by judges, a difficult position to adopt at the same time as he was denying the law-making power of the King, he was probably committed to saying that it had always existed except in so far as it had been altered by parliamentary legislation. He got very close to saying this in the preface to his *Fourth Report* (1602), but it demanded a good deal of historical credulousness. His own approach, ultimately, was to duck the issue and to take the way out of the legal practitioner, describing and analysing the law as it was without enquiring too deeply into its theoretical bases.   DAVID IBBETSON

collective agreements A collective agreement is the term used to describe the successful outcome of **collective bargaining** between **trade unions** and employers; if the parties fail to agree there will be no—or no new—collective agreement. The term has been legally defined since the 1970s, but the legal definition now in section 178 of the Trade Union and Labour Relations (Consolidation) Act 1992 is a reflection of actual practice. In general terms it is an agreement between one or more trade unions and one or more employers or employers' associations on substantive and/or procedural issues concerning the employment of workers in respect of whom the union or unions were bargaining, and their employers. Those issues include pay, working time, and other conditions of employment, procedures relevant to employment including negotiating procedures, disciplinary and grievance procedures, and rights of trade union officials at the workplace.

A distinctive feature of the law in Britain and Northern Ireland is that collective agreements are not normally legally enforceable contracts between the parties negotiating them. While there has been a statutory provision to this effect since the mid-1970s, in Britain now in section 179 of the 1992 Act, in this case the **legislation** is only a reflection of the parties' wishes. It was accepted in the High Court in England in the case of *Ford Motor Co v AUEFW* (1969) that collective agreements are not legally binding as between employers and trade unions because the parties had no intention to enter into legally binding agreements. A collective agreement will only be legally binding if it expressly states that this is what the parties intend; this rarely, if ever, happens.

It is, however, possible for some of the provisions of collective agreements to be legally enforced as expressly or impliedly incorporated terms of the **contract of employment** of individual workers. An extensive body of case law has established that, in broad terms, 'substantive' provisions in collective agreements—for example, those relating to pay and working time—will normally be incorporated into the employment contracts of individual workers on whose behalf the unions were negotiating, whether or not they are **trade union members**. On the other hand, 'procedural' issues, such as, for example, provisions relating to the selection of workers for **redundancy**, are not usually regarded as being 'apt' or 'appropriate' for incorporation into and enforcement as terms of individual workers' contracts. There are, however, some inconsistencies in the case law on this issue and it is often difficult to be certain where the line will be drawn between provisions in collective agreements which can be enforced as terms of the individual employment contracts and those which cannot be enforced because they are not incorporated into the workers' contracts.   BOB SIMPSON

collective autonomy   *see* **autonomy**

collective bargaining Collective bargaining is the process by which terms and conditions of employment are determined by negotiations between employers and **trade unions**. The scope of collective bargaining varies from negotiations between a single employer and a particular trade union over the terms of employment of a specified group of workers employed by that employer, to industry or service wide negotiations in which several trade unions and employers, or possibly employers' associations, take part. There has been a decline in such multi-employer bargaining since the 1970s. While this is part of a general decline in the incidence of collective bargaining and the numbers of workers whose terms of employment are determined in this way, it also reflects a shift towards more—though not necessarily all—terms of employment being settled, whether by collective bargaining or some other process—at the level of the individual workplace. Sector-wide collective bargaining has remained important in some areas of the public sector, although even here there has been increased devolution of some issues to local level. Where collective bargaining does take place, the trade unions concerned are said to be 'recognized' by the employers. Most trade union recognition has been established on a voluntary basis, but there is a legal procedure which independent trade unions can use in order to secure a limited right to recognition by an employer for the purposes of collective bargaining.

The substance of collective bargaining can be divided into two parts: substantive issues and procedural matters. The most important and certainly the most publicized item on bargaining agendas is pay. While collective bargaining may not determine the amount of pay that any particular worker will receive from their employer, it will normally be concerned with the pay scale for particular jobs and may determine the extent to which progression up a pay scale by any worker is automatic, subject to satisfying specified criteria or within the exercise of management **discretion**. Working time and any premium payments for working at specified times, such as nights or weekends, are also normally negotiated where pay is part of the collective bargaining agenda.

The procedural issues determined by collective bargaining normally cover the procedure for the bargaining process itself, which may include specifying what should happen in the event of a failure to agree, for example the use of third party services such as mediation or arbitration. Disciplinary and grievance procedures may also be the subject of collective bargaining. More far-reaching bargaining agendas covering, for example, employers' future investment plans, have been rare.

Independent trade unions which are recognized for the purposes of collective bargaining do, however, have a legal right to disclosure of information by employers for that purpose. A **Code of Practice** prepared by **ACAS** provides guidance on the sort of information which a union might be entitled to ask for. The enforcement procedure for this right provides that where an employer refuses to provide information which the Central Arbitration Committee ('CAC') has decide should be disclosed, the union may make a claim for improved terms and conditions for the workers on whose behalf it is negotiating, and the CAC award on this claim is legally binding and enforceable by the workers concerned.

BOB SIMPSON

See also: **collective agreements**

collective investment schemes A collective investment scheme ('CIS') is an arrangement which allows investors to access the markets through a pooled investment vehicle which invests in a range of assets according to the investment criteria adopted by the particular CIS. A CIS will pool investors' funds, spread risk across a range of investments, allocate returns among its investors, and will usually be subject to stringent regulation addressing in particular asset allocation, risk management, and the redemption or withdrawal of the investor's investment.

The benefits of a CIS include wide diversification from a small investment, access to expert investment management, wider investment opportunities than those available to retail investors and economies of scale resulting from the fact that a CIS, as an institutional investor, is in a position to reduce trading costs.

There are two dominant types of CIS in the UK. In the first, the corporate form, the scheme assets are owned by a company in which investors own shares, which represent their investment. In the second, the **unit trust**, the CIS does not have a separate legal personality in the form of a company; rather, the assets are held by a trustee, and the stake of investors in the scheme is represented by 'units'. Both structures have an 'open-ended' form in that they can issue shares or units (as the case may be) in accordance with investor demand and, conversely, can redeem the shares or units continuously (at a value linked to the net asset value ('NAV') of the fund) whenever an investor wishes to withdraw the investment. As a result, a corporate CIS must take the special form of an 'open-ended investment company' ('OEIC') because under UK company law, companies not in this form (as the typical company is not) have a fixed share capital and are subject to strict rules when they issue shares or reduce their capital by buying back shares. The typical company cannot redeem or re-purchase their shares continuously.

The close **regulation** of CISs reflects the risks inherent in the transfer of funds to the control of a CIS manager, the marketing risks arising from the possibility that inappropriate and fraudulent schemes may be marketed to the public, and the high levels of retail participation in CISs. Regulation typically addresses: management of the scheme—to ensure that assets of the CIS are managed in the best interests of investors and in accordance with the CIS' objectives, and to minimize risks associated with issues of competence and conflict of interest; the structure of the scheme (in a CIS, asset custody and management are separated); asset protection; valuation—to ensure that the investor can redeem the investment at a value related to NAV; redemption; and diversification requirements in the form of investment limits and asset allocation rules.

In the UK, regulated CISs, which may be marketed to the public, take the form of authorized unit trusts or investment companies with variable capital ('ICVCs'), both of which are closely regulated by the **Financial Services Authority** ('FSA') under the **Financial Services and Markets Act 2000** and the FSA's Collective Investment Scheme Sourcebook. Additional rules apply to ICVCs, reflecting their exceptional status under UK company law as companies with variable capital (OEICs). Unregulated collective investment schemes include **hedge funds**, which may not be marketed to the public.

The design and regulation of authorized CISs under the FSA regime strongly reflect the influence of the EU Undertaking for Collective Investment in Transferable Securities ('UCITS') Directive (1985). The UCITS Directive provides a pan-EU regulatory passport for CISs that conform to its requirements, which relate to authorization, structure, disclosure, asset allocation and so on. The asset allocation rules were originally very restrictive and were designed, in the interests of investor protection, to restrict the UCITS to conservative investments. They prevented a CIS in the form of a UCITS from investing in derivatives (for example) or from tracking an index of **securities**, such as the FTSE 100 (because the rules restricted the proportion of fund assets which a particular security could represent in the fund). These restrictions have now been loosened. Authorized UCITSs may be freely marketed across the EU. The UK rules are designed to allow authorized unit trusts and ICVCs to qualify as UCITSs and benefit from the pan-EU passport.

An authorized ICVC must be approved by the FSA and is subject to the CIS Sourcebook. The requirements include: that the ICVC has a separate 'authorised corporate director' responsible for the management of the assets, and a depositary responsible for the custody of the assets and for ensuring the scheme is managed in accordance with the FSA rules; pricing and redemption requirements; and diversification and risk-pooling rules designed to ensure that the assets can be easily valued for redemption purposes and to provide appropriate asset diversification.

Similar rules apply to authorized unit trusts. Particular disclosure rules also apply to the prospectus issued by an authorized CIS. This is a key document, which sets out the terms under which the CIS operates. A summary prospectus must also be provided which covers investment information, including the CIS's objectives, its investment policy, a brief assessment of its risk profile, and a profile of the CIS's typical investor.

The term 'investment trust' does not refer to a trust but to a listed public company which manages investments. Unlike the opened-ended authorized unit trust and the ICVC, an investment trust is 'closed-end.' Because an investment trust is a company with a fixed share capital and not an OEIC, it cannot continuously issue and redeem its shares. Investors in an investment trust therefore take market risk and can only trade their shares with other investors on the market, as is the case with investors in all publicly-traded companies. As a result, a share in an investment trust may trade at a discount relative to the value of the assets held by the trust, whereas authorized CISs must redeem their shares at a value related to the scheme's NAV. Unlike unit trusts and ICVCs, investment trusts in the UK are not regulated as authorized CISs under the FSA regime, but they are subject to the rules applied by the London Stock Exchange and the **UK Listing Authority** (which include diversification requirements) when they seek admission to the exchange. Overall, investment trusts are more a creature of company law than financial market regulation, although the regime under the Financial Services and Markets Act 2000 applies to investment advice offered in respect of trusts.   NIAMH MOLONEY

See also: **investment diversification**

collective ministerial responsibility   *see* **ministerial responsibility**

collective punishment in international law   *see* **international humanitarian law**

collective rights   *see* **human rights in the workplace**

collective self-defence   *see* **self-defence in international Law**

collective worship in schools   *see* **religious education and worship in schools**

College of Law   *see* **vocational legal education**

colonial administration and law   Sir William Blackstone and Lord Mansfield sought to reduce colonial governance and law in the eighteenth-century British Empire to a formal pattern of order by distinguishing conquered and ceded colonies in which the previous law remained in effect until changed by the **Crown** from settled, uninhabited colonies in which British settlers took their law and legal institutions with them. However, this attempt at rationalization was belied by the complex pattern of **colonialism** within the Empire. Considerations of timing, place, and strategic, political, economic, and cultural factors complicated both the form and substance of colonial governance and law. Even in its own terms the pattern was insufficient because of the difficulty experienced with classifying 'discovered' territories with indigenous, 'uncivilized' populations.

During the first Empire (1497–1780) varied methods of founding colonial government—mercantile charters, proprietary deeds, internal religious covenants between inhabitants, and direct royal rule—were employed. In royal colonies a governor appointed by London often co-existed with elected and appointed legislative bodies. Law applied within colonies included a potpourri of English law, remembered or invented local customs, and local legislative initiatives. The institutions of **justice** ranged from formal **court** structures, through corporate and proprietary adjudicative bodies, to informal and mediatory systems. In conquered or ceded territories previously held by other colonial powers or by non-European rulers with identifiable and developed governmental institutions, local law might be retained, for example Spanish or French civil law in several Caribbean islands and Quebec, and Muslim and **Hindu Law** in India. The attitude to 'uncivilized' **indigenous law** was more ambivalent. Local legislated law in all colonies was subject to disallowance in London. Appeals from colonial courts to the **Privy Council** were available but distance and cost precluded it in most cases.

Domestic and international politics, as well as strained imperial resources, meant that London's control of its colonies was loose. Consequently, colonies were able to experiment with their own institutions, for instance, the town meeting and local selection of **judges** in New England. By the 1760s there were two empires: the theoretical one entertained by some British statesmen in which the centre ordered and controlled the parts, and, the working empire that compromises, inefficiency, and ignorance had allowed to develop in which a dynamic local role in policymaking was possible.

After the American Revolutionary War, fought in part around this clash of imperial visions, attempts were made by the British government to exercise closer control of its remaining colonies and to induce greater dependency. William Pitt the Younger's strategy was to grant settler colonies a full range of legislative bodies and superior courts, as in Lower and Upper Canada, while ensuring that the Crown's representative possessed important overriding political powers (such as that of proroguing assemblies at will) and a degree of fiscal independence from the elective body. From the late eighteenth century in non-settler colonies with multi-racial populations or those founded in frontier areas, the model of the Crown colony was increasingly utilized in which the Governor enjoyed extensive plenary powers. The law applied across British colonies continued to represent a patchwork quilt ranging from predominantly English law, through mixed systems, to informal or **customary law**. From the late eighteenth into the twentieth century, indigenous governance and laws which were not 'civilized' were widely ignored or submerged, for example by invocation of the **terra nullius** doctrine. Several African territories provided exceptions to this policy of erasure.

Two developments were to assist in producing an imperial **common law** more consciously reflecting English law. The Colonial Office was founded in 1801 as the department of state responsible for the colonies. Active powers of disallowance and of seeking the opinion of the Law Officers on colonial laws were vested in that body. More important in engendering consistency in law across the Empire was the establishment of the Judicial Committee of the Privy Council in 1833. In time this body became consciously directive of imperial common law and **statutory interpretation**.

The failure of Pitt's counter-revolutionary experiment in colonial governance in the Canadas consummated in the Rebellions of 1837–1839, and reformist enthusiasm in Britain and its settler colonies led to moves to end colonial dependency in those territories, and to create a new constitutional relationship with the metropolis. The result was the grant of responsible government from 1848 and later dominion status in the 'white Empire' allowing for greater freedom in local development of governance and law with a corresponding decrease in imperial control. In the 'non-white Empire' much closer colonial rule with its inherent threat of imperial **violence** against resistance to British rule continued well into the twentieth century until the 'winds of change' began to engulf and subvert the imperial project from the late 1950s.   JOHN MCLAREN

colonialism   Initially, at least, European colonial activity was motivated by trade and the need to protect trade routes. In almost all cases, trade preceded the introduction of colonial government. And it was trade that first shaped the introduction of European law into colonial (or pre-colonial) territories. European law created enclaves for European commercial activity. Private law applied to legal relations among resident Europeans and to commercial trading contracts with non-Europeans. European public law and administration did not apply in the early stages of colonialism, other than through criminal justice for resident Europeans.

Trade and its private law enclaves could not last long as the defining characteristic of colonial activity. Resident Europeans demanded law and order, public services, and recognizable rights to their residential land. Within European enclaves, there were inevitable demands for European forms of public administration. Colonial traders also became local political actors, allies in indigenous conflicts, and armed guarantors of commercial contracts. Opportunities arose not just to trade but to secure direct control of valuable resources. Over time a race to claim resources, in part to preempt claims by other colonial powers, led to extension of military and political control beyond European trading enclaves.

For states to claim resources there must be a constitutional or public law justification. This justification was found through European concepts of state **sovereignty**. The sovereign authority of a state, as applied to a defined area under European state control, allowed the lawful exercise of power through colonial forms of administration. In the colonial era, sovereign authority could be acquired through a variety of legal mechanisms including conquest, treaty, cession, settlement, or establishment of a protectorate. In all cases, the concept of sovereignty not only legalized **colonial administration** as the highest authority in a hierarchical system of government, it also territorialized colonial power by reference to lines on a map that could be asserted against other colonial powers. Needless to say, these maps often bore little resemblance to the historical or actual facts of control on the ground.

The acquisition of sovereignty had various implications for the introduction of private European law. For the British, the **common law** followed sovereignty. From the moment that sovereignty was established, the new territorial **subjects** of the British Crown were entitled *prima facie* to the rights and privileges of the common law. For the French, colonial subjects became citizens of France and thereby entitled to the rights and privileges of French municipal law. In contrast, there was no presumptive notion that Dutch law extended to Dutch colonial subjects. The application of Dutch law to indigenous colonial subjects was governed by **legislation** rather than any *a priori* notion of sovereignty or **citizenship**.

For all colonial powers, the validation of political control through concepts of sovereignty did not resolve the day-to-day difficulties of extending control across large territorial areas. In many cases, direct government by colonial authorities was neither desired nor practicable. As a result, the British largely pursued a model of indirect rule through tribal chiefs and indigenous rulers (often with assistance or supervision from British district offices). The Dutch adopted a similar approach in large colonies such as Indonesia. But the French were less willing to clothe indigenous rulers with constitutional authority, generally because of their philosophy that only one law—French municipal law—is applicable to all

French citizens. Nevertheless, even in French colonies, indigenous rulers continued to exercise *de facto* authority in areas beyond direct French control.

The challenges of territorial control created a degree of pluralism in colonial public law and administration. It also affected the application of private European law. While in theory the common law applied to all British colonial subjects, the demands of indirect rule led to qualified legislative recognition of '**customary law**' in most British colonial systems. The Dutch also recognized customary forms of private law, although they relied less on expert evidence of custom through the judicial process, and more on compilations of customary law by academic Dutch lawyers. For their part the French were less inclined to recognize customary law, but traditional arrangements continued their *de facto* application in the fields of **marriage**, inheritance, and the like.

All forms of colonial **legal pluralism** involved some degree of contestation between indigenous systems and European rule. The very notion of customary law subordinated indigenous norms to European institutions and classificatory schemes. Hence, for example, the recognition of customary law relating to land did not extend to all indigenous rights to land. All colonial systems appropriated valuable land, without adequate compensation to indigenous occupiers or users, by manipulating European legal classifications to define certain areas as state land or land without an owner. Unowned land included common property are as essential for livelihoods (eg forests, pastureland, and fringing reefs).

In sum, resident Europeans were subject to European laws in colonial systems. They held rights to land that were defined in European terms. Indigenous inhabitants were subject to European criminal law, in order to 'keep the peace'; and European forms of public administration (including elements of indirect rule). They had qualified access to customary law, particularly in basic social fields such as marriage, inheritance, and land. They also had highly qualified access to European commercial law if they submitted (voluntarily or presumptively) their rights and transactions to European law.

According to some developmental economists, this colonial legacy of legal pluralism led to chronic underdevelopment because indigenous inhabitants were unable to access modern forms of contracting and credit. But, in many colonial systems, there was little option other than to recognize **indigenous law**, because non-recognition did not prevent the continuation of local practices. Hence the application of French private law to its colonial subjects did not prevent *de facto* legal pluralism, and has not led to different development outcomes in former French colonies. A more telling criticism of colonial laws is that they failed to facilitate the evolution of indigenous institutions, and allowed post-colonial elites to maintain exploitative arrangements through legal means.   DANIEL FITZPATRICK

colonialism and the legal profession   If only because empires require at least rudimentary legal and administrative structures, lawyers are always present. Their work products—contracts, leases, dispute resolution, property arrangements, financial instruments, official documents, and records— form part of all but the most rudimentary of military adventures. Beyond this, however, the diversity of empire defies generalization, a point well illustrated in the British Empire from the eighteenth to the twentieth centuries.

Powerful mythologies of law infected the English and their Empire. Constitutionalism, the **common law**, regularity in the administration of justice, and the **rule of law**, each secured by the Glorious Revolution's constitution settlement, were believed to be Britain's peculiar contribution to the world. Though the exigencies of Empire produced frequent violations, principle tugged in these directions. Tensions emerged.

Individuals engaged in colonial service expected their rights as British subjects to be respected and, as permanent colonies were established, British settlers carried the full panoply of rights with them. In settled colonies, such as those in North America and the Antipodes, considerable effort was invested in creating institutional structures analogous the United Kingdom's. The first Lieutenant Governor of Upper Canada (Ontario), John Graves Simcoe, expressed pride in establishing 'the very image and transcript' of the British constitution in the colony. This, amongst much else, implied the creation of courts, the existence of an independent legal profession, and the fullest possible application of common law and British customary expectations. Lawyers had a central role to play in British imperialism's political and cultural mission.

Key features of English legal professionalism, however, could not be readily reproduced in places lacking the dense, long-established networks and structures of the United Kingdom. The English Bar, for example, expressed professionalism through self-governing guilds that were of ancient origin and created independently of statute or royal grant, operating under conventions and practices shaped over centuries (the **Inns of Court**). No colonial equivalent was possible

and colonial lawyers struggled mightily to create substitutes. In Upper Canada this produced the British Empire's oldest Law Society (older than that of England and Wales), an early effort to create an Inn-like centre for law in Toronto's Osgoode Hall and an elaborated vision of legal professionalism that was self-consciously developed and articulated in ways that were both unusual and largely unnecessary in the United Kingdom. To greater or lesser degree, lawyers in all settler colonies sought to replicate British ways through innovative schemes of professional regulation, legal education, and associational activities.

These projects had political and cultural objectives: lawyers frequently viewed themselves as transmitting solid British values to the diverse, often non-British, populations of colonies. In the early twentieth century leading groups of legal professionals in both Canada and Australia viewed themselves as having a 'missionary' role to play in converting non-British subjects to the virtues of British law. This became central to the professionalizing projects of the Canadian Bar Association.

It is important to note that lawyers' ideological commitments were most often to constitutionalism rather than to political 'liberalism' or '**democracy**' as such. Though this could make lawyers enemies of change, constitutionalism is Janus-faced: when propriety was violated in practice—as often happened— they became champions of reform, and sometimes of **revolution**. Lawyers played pivotal roles in the 1770s revolution in the American colonies, in India's Congress movement, in Canada's 'rebellions', and in the cause of revolution or independence movements in countless sites around the world.

'Native' populations lived in ambiguous relationships to British law and, hence, to British colonial lawyers. Some colonies instituted complex formal legal pluralism where different individuals were governed under different 'personal law' (eg India), while others developed formal or informal zoning of areas into which British law did not intrude (Nigeria; North America). For a period in the twentieth century Canada's First Nations peoples were prohibited from employing lawyers to advance their causes. Similarly, British authorities attempted to keep lawyers out of 'Native' areas of Nigeria for fear of the consequences. Where lawyers did become involved in 'Native' causes, as in causes célèbres involving the Emir of Kano and the Eleko of Lagos, Imperial authority invariably came away bloodied.

In the twentieth century's decades of decolonization, lawyers frequently came to the forefront as national leaders. A profession that advanced the cause of Imperialism often championed the causes of national independence and Imperial disassembly. Not infrequently, lawyers and their professional associations played heroic roles in sustaining constitutional propriety and defending the rule of law in the face of the many challenges that independent **nationalism** brought in the wake of Empire.

WESLEY PUE

C Oguamanam and WW Pue, 'Lawyers' Professionalism, Colonialism, State Formation and National Life in Nigeria, 1900–1960: 'the fighting brigade of the people' (2007) *Social Identities* 769–785

WW Pue, 'Planting British Legal Culture in Colonial Soil: Legal Professionalism in the Lands of the Beaver and Kangaroo', in L Cardinal and D Headon (eds), *Shaping Nations: Constitutionalism and Society in Australia and Canada* (Ottawa: Institute of Canadian Studies and University of Ottawa Press, 2002)

combat sports Combat sports are sports that simulate hand-to-hand combat either with or without the use of weapons. They include boxing, fencing, wrestling, and numerous other martial arts. It is in the nature of most combat sports that participation will include activities that might amount to offences against the person, such as assault. Whether the sport involved is a legitimate one and therefore whether willing participation provides a defence to such offences is a matter of public policy. There is no specific legal precedent legitimizing boxing or other similar contact combat sports. A distinction has long been drawn between prize fighting and sparring. The latter is legitimate, the former is not. Professional boxing appears to be allowable due to public tolerance.

The staging of combat sports competitions requires a licence. Certain martial arts disciplines are recognized by Sport England and The Sports Council of Wales. The presence of this recognition and licensing may be seen as indicative of public policy approval.

The commission of criminal offences may arise in any event if a participant's actions fall outside what might reasonably be expected of one undertaking the sport or outside of the rules. Civil liability in negligence may also arise if the participant's actions fall below a reasonable standard. Certain martial arts' equipment is banned outright, other types are only allowed for use in martial art participation.

RUPERT BELOFF

combatants During the course of an armed conflict between two or more states the members of their armed forces have a right to take part in hostilities as combatants. Should they be captured they are to be treated as prisoners of war (Geneva Convention III 1949; Additional Protocol I 1977). Combatants may attack enemy combatants and military objectives (defined as objects which by their nature, purpose or use make an effective contribution to military action and whose destruction would offer a definite military advantage). If combatants confine themselves to such targets they will not commit any offence under the national law of the state in which they are operating or under the laws of war (**international humanitarian law**) unless they do so by a prohibited means, such as by wearing civilian clothes when carrying out an attack.

Individuals who take part in hostilities during an international armed conflict and who are not members of the armed forces of a state engaged in the conflict have no right under international law to do so; and, if captured, they are not entitled to be treated as prisoners of war. They may be subject to the national law of the state which captures them and treated as 'unlawful combatants'. In *Military Prosecutor v Kassem* (1971) a person fighting for the Popular Front for the Liberation of Palestine ('PLO') was not entitled to be treated as a lawful combatant since the PLO was not a state. The activities of 'non-state actors' have become more common. Members of al Qaeda are unlikely to be acting as members of (or as an organized group belonging to) the armed forces of a state, and cannot be categorized as lawful combatants.

States party to Additional Protocol I are required to presume that those whom they have captured on the battlefield are lawful combatants and entitled to be treated as prisoners of war unless their status is decided otherwise by a competent tribunal. A state which is not a party to this treaty but is bound by Geneva Convention III 1949, such as the USA, is required to set up a competent tribunal if any doubt arises as to whether an individual is entitled to prisoner-of-war status. Issues which arose from the detention by the USA of individuals in Guantanamo Bay included whether the detainees were entitled to be treated as prisoners of war and whether they could be lawfully detained without some form of judicial proceedings.

Mercenaries are not entitled to be combatants or to be treated as prisoners of war on capture. A mercenary is someone who is recruited (usually from abroad) in order to fight in an armed conflict and who takes a direct part in the hostilities whilst not being a member of the armed forces of a state engaged in that conflict (Additional Protocol I).

There is no concept of the lawful combatant in a civil war or in any situation which falls short of an international armed conflict.

PETER ROWE

Comitology   Under the EC Treaty the implementation of **legislation** can be delegated to the **European Commission** (Commission). Comitology is the system through which committees of Member States' representatives review the exercise of delegated powers. This system was developed by the **Council of Ministers** (Council) and formalized by the adoption of the Comitology Decision (the Decision).

Under the Comitology system, when exercising a delegated power the Commission must submit a draft of the proposed measure to a committee and obtain that committee's approval. Traditionally there have been three standard committee types: Advisory, Management, and Regulatory, each giving rise to particular implications concerning both the procedure to be followed and the impact of the committee's opinion. Since July 2006 a fourth has been added—Regulatory Procedure with Scrutiny.

The criteria for the choice of committee type are laid down in the Decision. Advisory Committees are used where a matter is not particularly politically sensitive, the Commission must 'take the utmost account of' the Committee's opinion'. Management Committees are used for measures managing Community common policies and action programmes (for example the Common Agricultural Policy). In these cases if the Committee does not agree with the Commission proposal the Commission must refer the matter to the Council.

The Regulatory Committee procedure is now the standard. Under this procedure if the Committee does not agree with the Commission the Commission must submit a proposal to Council and inform the **European Parliament** (Parliament). In certain cases (dependent on Parliament's role in the adoption of the initial legislation) if **Parliament** is of the view that the proposal exceeds the implementing powers laid down, it informs Council of that view. If Council opposes the proposal the Commission has to re-examine it. Under the 'Regulatory Procedure with Scrutiny' if Parliament opposes a proposal it cannot be adopted. This reflects the increased role of Parliament in the adoption of legislation under the co-decision procedure and is used in relation to acts adopted under that procedure.

Delegated powers are crucial, not least to facilitate swift regulatory responses to changing circumstances, as in sectors such as agriculture. Comitology ensures states' involvement, and the representation of their interests, in the decision-making process, even where the development of norms has been delegated to the Commission. However, despite the pragmatic arguments in favour of delegated powers and Comitology itself, the system has been criticized for giving rise to a democratic deficit, by-passing elected **representation** and **accountability** (the Parliament was originally excluded from the process). The Parliament has criticized the process's lack of transparency, arising from the fact that committees generally meet 'behind closed doors', minutes of the proceedings are not published and votes remain secret.

Recent amendments, however, have gone some way towards addressing the legitimacy concerns traditionally raised in relation to the Comitology system. For example, under the 'Regulatory Procedure With Scrutiny', Parliament's role is equal to that of the Council, the Regulatory procedure is now standard and there is increased information on the workings of Committees both to Parliament and the public.

EMILY REID

comity   Comity is the vague and amorphous body of rules and principles which are not legally binding but which are regularly applied in dealings between states and their authorities as a matter of courtesy or on the basis of reciprocity and convenience, and whose essence lies in mutual respect and accommodation between states and their interests. Sometimes established practices, such as the deployment of red carpets and twenty-one gun salutes, are referred to as prescribed by rules of comity; but these are better regarded as ceremonial rules and the term comity reserved for non-binding rules that bear upon legal relationships between states.

One of the clearest instances of comity is the principle of deference applied by courts when they refrain from exercising jurisdiction over a case in which some other legal system, with jurisdiction over the case, has a substantially greater interest. This principle is associated particularly with the line of US jurisprudence developed in *Hartford Fire Insurance v California* (1993), in which competing claims to exercise jurisdiction are subjected to a 'balancing of interests' test. Another instance of restraint based upon comity rather than law is the practice of states in refraining from exercising jurisdiction over inter-crew crimes and other internal affairs of foreign ships in their ports unless they are requested to intervene or the crime is particularly serious.

VAUGHAN LOWE

command and control regulation   Most public law regulatory regimes involve behavioural requirements imposed by primary **legislation**, secondary legislation, or a public agency, backed up by the threat of the imposition of a sanction in the event of non-compliance; hence 'command and control'. The required behaviour may involve the prohibition of certain activities, the use of pre-scribed methods or materials to avoid harm ('spec-ifications standards'), the fulfilment of conditions of quality or **safety** ('performance standards') or simply the provision of information, concerning, for example, the risks involved in the regulated product or activity.

Regulation of this kind has been used to control vast areas of market and non-market activity to protect, notably, health and safety, and the environ-ment, but also consumers in relation to financial and professional services. Enforcement is invariably undertaken by a specialist agency, although victims of harm-creating contraventions and other third parties may be allowed to intervene. The threatened sanction might be administrative but, in the **com-mon law** world, it has almost always been penal. At the same time, to facilitate enforcement, regulatory offences are generally ones of **strict liability**, thus distinguishing them from mainstream crime.

The phrase 'command and control' became in the 1970s and 1980s rather a modish term, with depreca-tory overtones, as this traditional approach to regu-lation was increasingly criticized. In the first place, it tended to be highly prescriptive, leading therefore to complex and bulky sets of rules. Secondly, the fact that firms and individuals were given little or no alternative as to how the regulatory goal might be achieved was problematic since in most cases industry was more knowledgeable than government bureaucracies on the best ways of dealing with the problem; in consequence command and control approaches tended to inhibit technological innov-ation. Thirdly, a significant degree of uncertainty attached to the enforcement process. Only a small proportion of detected contraventions resulted in court prosecutions. While this might be rationalized on the basis that persuasion was effective in securing compliance, it nevertheless was seen as compromis-ing the coercive character of command and control.

Increasing awareness of these problems inspired much discussion and some experimentation with alternatives to command and control, notably with use of financial instruments such as taxes. More sig-nificant have been modifications to the command and control approach itself. Instruments retain the characteristic of obligations backed by threat-ened sanctions, but behavioural requirements have become more general, leaving some latitude on how they might be achieved. Or '**due diligence**' has been allowed as a defence, enabling firms and individu-als to show that the measures they had taken were equally adept at meeting the regulatory goal. The relationship between those who command and those who are commanded has indeed been trans-formed in many areas, leading to the phenomenon of so-called 'co-regulation', in which industry plays a complementary role to that of government: while the latter lays down broad principles, industry can devise and formulate its own 'rule book' to concre-tize those principles.   ANTHONY OGUS

N Gunningham, 'Beyond Compliance: Next Generation Environmental Regulation' in R Johnstone and R Sarre (eds), *Regulation: Enforcement and Compliance* (Can-berra: Australian Institute of Criminology, 2004), ch 4

A Ogus, 'New Techniques for Social Regulation: Decen-tralisation and Diversity' in H Collins, P Davies and R Rideout (eds), *Legal Regulation of the Employment Relation* (London: Kluwer Law International, 2000), 83–98

command papers   *see* **White papers**

command responsibility   *see* **war crimes**

commercial arbitration, international   Inter-national commercial arbitration has become indispensable to the global economy. It has long been regulated by a network of multilateral treat-ies, beginning with the League of Nations' Geneva Protocol (1923) and Geneva Convention (1927) and culminating with the UN New York Convention (1958), currently ratified by more than 170 coun-tries. The Model Law of Arbitration (1985) (UNCI-TRAL) has also produced significant harmonization between different national traditions. Arbitration starts with the parties' written agreement to submit past or present disputes to the binding decision of an arbitration tribunal. Arbitrators, chosen by or on behalf of the parties, are required to be impartial and independent. A valid arbitration agreement ousts (or stays) the jurisdiction of state courts to decide the dispute and, conversely, confers exclusive jurisdic-tion on the arbitration tribunal. Parties may choose their own procedure, subject only to the operation of mandatory laws. That choice is usually exercised by agreeing institutional rules providing for either administered arbitration (ie arbitration managed by a third-party provider of arbitration services) or non-administered arbitration (ie arbitration organ-ized by the parties themselves) in a neutral place. Arbitral procedure is generally marked by flexibility suited to the particular dispute, free from nation-al court procedures. The state court at the place of arbitration may assist the arbitral process and also exercise a supervisory function. The arbitration ends with a reasoned award legally binding on the parties. It can be enforced by state courts both at the place of arbitration and in other countries—in the latter case an arbitration award can usually be enforced with less difficulty than a foreign court judgment.

VV VEEDER

commercial exploitation of intellectual property Intellectual property ('IP') is a valuable asset in the hands of the originator, assignees, and licensees. For example, through registration, **patents**, industrial **designs**, **trade marks**, and plant varieties are granted a statutory period of exclusivity during which those rights can be exploited. Through registration and renewal, the protection of trade marks can extend for an unlimited period, during which the value of marks can grow to become the principal asset in a rights-holders books. Thus for example, the value of trade marks such as COCA COLA and MARLBORO are given book values in excess of $US 40 billion. Similarly, **copyright**ed works, such as books, music, films, and computer programs, which are protected for periods in excess of fifty years, can become significant assets in the hands of their owners.

The value of IP has enabled its securitization, such that increasingly, IP is being used as the basis of raising finance. For this reason, part of the due diligence, which is conducted prefatory to corporate acquisition, will involve the identification and valuation of IP. As an asset that valuation will be related in large part to the revenue flows which will be generated by that IP. On the other side of the ledger will be the costs associated with securing, maintaining, and defending that IP.

Part of the justification for IP protection is to compensate the innovator for the research and development costs incurred in generating the IP, and to provide a profit incentive to secure further innovation and to secure the disclosure of the innovation.

Securing IP rights carries a number of costs in addition to research and development. Filing and renewal fees are payable to the IP offices in each of the countries in which the IP is protected. These will typically be the principal markets of the IP owner. Additionally, there are the larger costs of obtaining IP representation from lawyers and patent and trade mark attorneys.

The statutes which create IP rights provide for the ways in which they might be exploited. There are various modes of commercial exploitation of IP, the most common of which are assignment and licensing. In the first instance, the IP right itself can be assigned to a purchaser by its creator or owner. Alternatively, the IP can be divided up and assigned to a variety of purchasers, or only assigned in part.

The assignment of IP is not a common commercial transaction, but in some situations it can be justified. For example, a university research centre which obtains a patent over an invention, may, in the absence of any commercial expertise in the exploitation of inventions, assign the invention to a business enterprise, in order to recoup the investment in research and development. In this way the university is spared the trouble of getting involved in something beyond its commercial competence. Alternatively, if IP is generated for one purpose, it might be assigned where other applications are more feasible. For example, a molecule might be developed and patented by an animal sciences business as an animal treatment, but it may turn out that its application for the treatment of humans is more profitable, in which case it might be assigned to a human life sciences business. Increasingly, universities are developing some commercial expertise, in which case its IP might be assigned to a spin-off company, operated as a joint venture between the university and a commercial partner.

A more common option is the licensing of IP, which enables the rights holder to exploit the IP without relinquishing ownership. This enables the rights holder to exploit the widest possible range of markets by taking advantage of the particular expertise and contacts of the licensee. This is especially important in the case of licensing outside the rights holder's home country, but it also includes licensing outside the sectors of the economy occupied by the rights holder. For example, a patentee in one industry can license applications of the patent in other industries; or licensing can occur across different functional markets, for example a manufacturer can licence wholesalers or retailers.

The commercial exploitation of IP is often bundled up with other items. For example in a number of different technology transfer transactions, the IP may be but one ingredient in the technology package. Other items may include the supply of raw materials or other products and technical consultancy services and know-how. Of course, the IP rights are often a commercial device which is used to tie-in the supply of the other items, subject to competition laws.

In situations where ownership of the IP is retained by the rights holder, a commercial expense will be the maintenance of the IP, through the filing of registration renewals, where appropriate. Also, there will be the expense of monitoring the IP to identify infringing conduct by others. Where infringing conduct occurs, there will also be the expense of anti-infringement litigation.

Another way in which IP might be commercialized is through the trading of IP portfolios. In the area of patenting in high technology industries the development of 'patent thickets' has been noted. These are defined as an overlapping set of patent rights requiring that those seeking to commercialize new technology obtain licenses from multiple patentees. Dealing with the owners of the thicketed patents will often involve prohibitive transaction costs and will impose research hold-ups as patent owners are identified and dealt with. But patent thickets provide an incentive for firms to patent defensively, because a firm's bargaining power is raised by having more patents to trade in patent disputes. Even in situations where there are no transaction costs or research holdups, some companies aggressively seek to build large patent portfolios for the purpose of extracting benefits from competitors. These companies negotiate on the basis of their portfolios rather than on the basis of individual patents. An alternative to cross-licensing as a means of negotiating patent thickets is the creation of patent pools. This is an arrangement among multiple patent holders to aggregate their patents, which are shared by members of the pool and made available on standard terms to non-members of the pool. These arrangements are, of course, subject to **competition** laws.

MICHAEL BLAKENEY

Commission for Equality and Human Rights ('CEHR') *see* **Equality and Human Rights Commission**

Common Agricultural Policy *see* **single market**

common but differentiated responsibility, principle of   The principle of 'common but differentiated responsibility' is an important principle of **international environmental law**. The principle recognizes historical differences in the contributions of developed and developing countries to global environmental problems, and differences in their respective economic and technical capacity to tackle these problems. It was given express recognition in Principle 7 of the 1992 Rio Declaration. The principle consists of two basic elements: states have a common responsibility for a shared environmental problem, and states have differentiated responsibility depending on their abilities to address the problem.

Common responsibility of states for a natural resource was recognized as early as 1949 in a treaty concerning tuna fishing, and differentiated responsibility is contained in treaties such as the 1972 London Convention, which emphasized that measures needed to be adopted by the parties 'according to their scientific, technical and economic capabilities'.

The essence of the combined principle was first included in the Stockholm Declaration of 1972, which recognized that standards of developed countries would impose a disproportionate burden on developing countries. Today it is explicitly included in important conventions such as the 1992 UN Framework Convention on Climate Change, the 1992 Convention on Biological Diversity and more recently in the 2001 Stockholm Convention on Persistent Organic Pollutants.

Given the amount of state practice and *opinio iuris* the principle can now be seen as forming part of **customary international law**. Its sister principle is that of special and differential treatment, which is part of the law of the **World Trade Organization ('WTO')** and the **General Agreement on Tariffs and Trade ('GATT')**. The two principles are not identical because in their trade relations, developed countries in the world trading system are hesitant to acknowledge a special responsibility relative to developing countries.

The principle of common but differentiated responsibility has its basis in the notion of general equity in international law and the '**common heritage of mankind**' as well as in the polluter-pays principle. Conventions usually give effect to the principle through 'grace periods', delayed implementation, technical assistance, or less stringent commitments for developing countries. For example, the 1987 Montreal Protocol for the protection of the ozone layer allowed certain countries to delay their implementation and make it dependent upon financial assistance from the Montreal Protocol Fund.

MARKUS GEHRING

common heritage of mankind   The common heritage of mankind is a concept which captures the idea that not all jurisdictional competencies recognized by **international law** are to be exercised by states or by international organizations, whether acting unilaterally or multilaterally, in their own self-interest, but are to be exercised, in respect of those areas or subject matters to which that concept applies, for the benefit of mankind as a whole. The origins of the common heritage lay in the desire to prevent the more powerful states from taking advantage of their greater technological capacities to appropriate for themselves resources outside of areas of national jurisdiction. The concept is best known for its application to areas of the seabed and subsoil of ocean space which lie beyond the outer limits of the Exclusive Economic Zone and/or continental shelves of coastal states.

However, the manner in which the 'common heritage' approach is applied in practice does not necessarily reflect the underlying assumptions. The 1982 Convention allowed for the resources of the 'Deep Seabed' (also known as 'the Area') to be exploited both by states and corporations for private gain (under license from an international regulatory agency (The International Seabed Authority ('ISA')) whilst also establishing an 'operational entity' (known as 'the Enterprise') which was to exploit the area on behalf of the international community as a whole, with revenue generated from both sources being distributed as appropriate to the international community by the Authority. Many industrialized states were dissatisfied with the terms of the 1982 Convention and were instrumental in 1994 in negotiating the so-called 'Implementation Agreement', which took effect at the same time as the Convention itself entered into force. The 1994 Agreement had the practical effect of modifying the Deep Seabed Regime to better secure the interests of states and corporations, resulting in the 'common heritage' being manifested through the regulatory mechanisms of the ISA, rather than through 'international exploitation' for the benefit of all.

The Common Heritage idea (or its analogues) has also been applied to Antarctica and to Outer Space (particularly in the 1979 'Moon Treaty'). It remains to be seen whether the application of the concept in these contexts is similarly re-oriented in favour of the state and corporate entities rather than the international community as a whole when the practical opportunities for exploitation increase. The concept is also increasingly canvassed as having a relevance to more general questions, such as the protection of the environment, and it may be that its future potency will lie in its role as a framework principle in relation to such questions, rather than as an operational tool.   MALCOLM EVANS

common land   The right of non-owners to exercise rights over a piece of land may lead to its being termed 'common land'. Under the Norman system, a manor could include waste land: land belonging to the lord but subject to the right of each of his tenants to benefit from its natural products by, for example, grazing cattle. These rights and their modern equivalents, belonging to specific individuals and not to the general public, are known as 'rights of common'.

Their presence ensured that waste land remained unfenced, allowing common access. In England and Wales, a statutory right for the general public to use manorial waste land for 'air and exercise' was conferred in 1925. In 1965 registration of land subject to rights of common, of manorial waste land, and of town and village greens, was made compulsory by the Commons Registration Act. As a result, registers maintained by local authorities, and open to the public, list virtually all common land in England and Wales: it makes up about 4 per cent of the total land area. Under the Commons Act 2006, commons councils can be set up to coordinate the management and preservation of common land.

In Scotland, commonties were the closest equivalent to common land; but following the 1695 Act for the Division of Commonties they were enclosed and lost to common use. However, crofting common grazings, land over which local crofting communities enjoy rights, remain in the Highlands and Islands and make up around 7 per cent of Scotland's land area.   BEN MCFARLANE

common law   The common law is the name given to the legal tradition which evolved in England after the Norman Conquest, and which has become one of the major world legal traditions. Most states use legal traditions which, either in whole or in part, have been borrowed from elsewhere; they rely on what have been called legal transplants. The common law, however, did not originate in such a process of cultural diffusion; it was an indigenous English legal tradition, though it has been considerably influenced by the other major Western European legal tradition, the **Roman law** (or 'civil law') tradition.

Like all such indigenous traditions, the common law evolved out of a practice of dispute resolution; this indeed is how Roman Law originally evolved back in the ancient world. The history of law and the resolution of disputes in England is a long one, and can be traced back to the reign of Aethelbert of Kent, a paramount chief in whose reign, in about 603, a code of written laws was promulgated, long before a unified realm of England had come into existence. However, historians tend to think of the common law as having assumed a characteristic institutional form at a much later date, during the reign of Henry II (1154–1189), when an unknown royal clerk was able to write a treatise (nominally associated with a Royal official called Ranulf de Glanvill) which gave a coherent account of the procedures followed by the King's officials in adjudication.

At this time there existed in England a multiplicity of customary laws—laws of manors and towns, laws of particular industries, like the stannary law of Cornwall, and laws which applied to particular persons, such as churchmen. The common law was one such body of law, but it was royal law, and this was the basis for its superior authority. It was royal not in the sense that it had been laid down by the monarch, but because it was administered by royal officials, amongst whom the judges possessed their authority as deputies for the King. The King's law was 'common' in the sense that it was not local or personal, but was, like a common prostitute, available, or at least applicable, to everyone throughout the realm; this was the primary sense in which this body of law was said to be 'common'.

In the early middle ages the scope of royal adjudication was very limited, being concerned only with important property disputes relating to the landholdings of freeholders, and to the graver crimes. It was also largely concerned with the procedures which brought disputes to a point of decision. The actual decision was originally submitted to mechanisms the legitimacy of which depended on some form of divine intervention, such as ordeals, or ritualized battles. But in the twelfth century some disputes were being adjudicated upon by juries of neighbours, and in the following century the lay jury came to be the typical common law mode of trial. With the rise of the jury came the expansion of the common law not only to regulate the procedures to be followed, but also to impose conformity to substantive law, ie law which prescribes how the dispute ought to be decided. With this evolved the notion that questions of law were the responsibility of the professional judges, whilst questions of fact were for decision by the lay jurors under professional supervision.

In the course of the thirteenth century there developed a common law legal profession, distinct from the Church, administering a secular body of royal law in three distinct courts—the Common Pleas for civil disputes, the King's Bench for matters specially concerning the monarch, and the Exchequer for tax disputes. Over the centuries, these various courts acquired overlapping jurisdiction in civil matters, though only the King's Bench handled crime. They survived as distinct institutions until reforms of the nineteenth century. In a second sense 'common law' meant the law used by these three courts. Though primarily based in London, the law which they used became ubiquitous as the result of a system in which trials took place locally before royal judges who travelled around the country on established circuits, and before local juries. But issues of law arising out of trials were largely handled in London. Until modern times, very few professional judges were needed to run this system, since lay juries did most of the work.

In the fifteenth century the King's Chancellor began to adjudicate on complaints brought by petitioners, who alleged that their complaints were inadequately addressed by the common law courts. Soon there evolved a regular court, the Court of Chancery, to deal with such petitions. The body of doctrine applied in the Court of Chancery could not be common law, for that was the concern of the common law courts. It came to be called 'equity'. This term is derived from Aristotelian thought, according to which there needs to exist a power to vary the application of legal rules and make exceptions to them when following the rule would produce injustice. It was this power which the Court of Chancery was thought to be exercising. So it is that sometimes, in a third sense, the expression 'common law' is used to differentiate the body of doctrine to which reference is being made, that is the law administered by the common law courts, from 'equity' administered in the Court of Chancery.

Although, from an early time, the royal courts used writing, for example to formally record the proceedings, the common law was for long primarily an oral tradition, transmitted from the past to the present through practice and memory. But from the late thirteenth century lawyers came to compile unofficial notes of what had been said in court, and to use what had been done in the past as an argument for what should be done in the present. Reliance on precedents is indeed integral to any system of governing tradition, and common lawyers from an early time came to treat what had been done in earlier cases as a principal source of law, though legislative texts were also an important source of law. So when Chaucer in the Prologue to the *Canterbury Tales* gave a picture of a common lawyer, the Serjeant at Law, he said that he possessed law reports going back to the time of William the Conqueror. The term 'common law' came, in a fourth sense, to have the connotation of law based on cases, or law evolved through adjudication in particular cases, as opposed to law derived from the analysis and exposition of authoritative texts. Indeed sometimes 'common law' is more or less synonymous with the expression 'case law'. Since the common law was developed by the judges, interacting with barristers engaged in litigation, the expression 'common law' came, in a related fifth sense, to mean law made by judges. A body of law developed in this way tends to be strong on detailed illustration and pragmatic sense, and weak on general principle; and this has often been remarked about the common law.

With the expansion of English power, first to Wales and Ireland, and later to the overseas empire, the territorial reach of the common law expanded. In territories where there existed a resilient local culture with its own legal arrangements, normally of a customary nature, these were normally respected; but Britain also exported aspects of its own legal system, which co-existed in complicated ways with indigenous law. Thus there might be an introduced code of contract law or of criminal law, based on the English system, as was the case, for example, in British India. Where overseas territories were settled, and the culture of the indigenous inhabitants was wholly or partially destroyed, British settlers took with them so much of the common law as was appropriate to their condition. This all created a common law world—that is to say a world in which the common law tradition was exported. Thus Australia and most of Canada became part of this world, as in part did British colonies in Africa and elsewhere. Even after de-colonization the common law tradition remains as a permanent legacy of British imperialism.

Attempts have been made by scholars to identify basic values thought to be embodied in the common law tradition, such as a respect for personal liberty, or a commitment to the pursuit of economic efficiency. There are numerous rival theories, often of a romantic or speculative nature. Some, derivative of Marxist thinking, are derogatory, viewing the common law as an instrument of oppression. Exploration of such theories lies outside the scope of this entry.

AW BRIAN SIMPSON

JH Baker, *An Introduction to English Legal History* (London: Butterworths, 2002)

CK Allen, *Law in the Making* (Oxford: Oxford University Press, 1964)

See also: **civil law systems; common law in the colonies; equity as a system of law**

common law courts   It is an axiom of **common law**, so deeply rooted and well established as to need no specific authority, that 'justice should not only be done but manifestly and undoubtedly be seen to be done'. The first meaning of this maxim is that officials of the court, and the judge in particular, must act in a manner that cannot reasonably be viewed as anything but impartial. There must be no hint of a suggestion of interest or of the judge deciding in his or her own cause. Implicit in this particular rule is a second and broader principle, namely that the appearance of justice, the open and publicly accessible dispensation of justice is 'so precious a feature' of common law as to be 'the salt of the constitution'

(*Macpherson v Macpherson* (1936)). The **courts** of common law are precisely the open face and manifest public theatre of justice both seen and being seen to be done.

The requirement that, as Lord Haldane once put it, 'Every Court of Justice be open to every subject of the [Queen]' (*Scott v Scott* (1913)) bears with it a panoply of further rules of visible propriety and solemnized process. The courts are sites of legal decorum and of theatrical ceremony. They are the primary social space of serious speech and as such, require elaborate manifestations of obedience and of respect expressed through architecture and furnishings, as well as through elaborate rhetorical requirements, reverential forms of address, restrained modes of response, appropriately dull clothing, wigs and gowns for judges and barristers, and deference in both speech and behaviour throughout all proceedings. Common law rules of **contempt of court**, reinforced by statute, subject those who act in an offensive manner, who disrespect or threaten to lower the standing of the judge, or the court, in the eyes of the public, to summary imprisonment, meaning incarceration on the spot. The root of that rule of contempt goes back to the laws of Henry I and to the power of the **Crown**, through its sheriff, to imprison those who acted in contempt of royal writs. The royal roots of the rules governing court procedure provide interesting clues as to the derivation and function of what is now called the court service, meaning most broadly the hierarchy of **tribunals** and courts.

The original court of common law was simply the King's (or occasionally Queen's) court, his or her suite, meaning place of habitation and following. It was to the Royal court and then, later, to its itinerant royal delegates that disputants would come and air their grievances. When the hierarchy of common law courts was later established, each court bore with it some element, vicarious or delegated though it be, of majesty or sovereign power. Even after the Civil Procedure Act 1997 and the Civil Procedure Rules 1998 revamped civil litigation, and the more recent passage of the Constitutional Reform Act 2005, which replaces the House of Lords as final court of appeal with a Supreme Court, the Oath of Allegiance and Judicial Oath, as set out in the Promissory Oaths Act 1868, remain in force and require that all judges swear allegiance to the Crown and fidelity to the divinity. The Lord Chancellor's Oath is set out anew in section 17 (1) of the 2005 Act and after requiring 'respect for the rule of law' ends with the traditional invocation 'So help me God'.

Historically the highest court of common law was Parliament, properly speaking the Crown in

Parliament, which through legislation would determine disputed issues and promulgate new rules. Parliament remains the supreme source of law, although the legislature is no longer conceived to be a court. There are also limits to its powers. After entry into the **European Union**, parliamentary sovereignty has been subjected to the restraint of **European law**, and now also to the review of the **Supreme Court (UK)**. Where legislation conflicts with European law or the **European Convention on Human Rights**, the Supreme Court may disapply it. In practice this means that the House of Lords and its successor (the Supreme Court (UK)) will interpret legislation so as not to conflict with European directives or Convention rights; but there is now, with the advent of the Supreme Court, a further and more formal separation of powers along the lines of the United States constitutional framework in which the eponymous Supreme Court can review and restrain legislative enactments on constitutional grounds.

The symbolic importance of the establishment of the Supreme Court lies in the creation of a third and formally independent branch of government. The court system, represented here by its pinnacle, gains thus an even more visible role as bearer of rights, reviewer of government, and dispenser of justice. Without a written constitution the exact parameters of the Court's power to limit parliamentary sovereignty is open to case-by-case interpretation; but recent decisions already suggest that 'rights inherent and fundamental to democratic civilised society' (*R v Secretary of State for the Home Department, ex p. Pierson* (1998)) will be recognized and protected by the courts as inherent in precedent and immune to executive or legislative intrusion. As one judge recently put it: 'The rule of law enforced by the courts is the ultimate controlling factor on which our constitution is based' (*Jackson v Attorney General* (2006)).

The Supreme Court is simply the most visible exemplum of the court system. It is the final court of appeal and last arbiter of disputes. It is also the exception in that it deals with final appeals in what is necessarily a very small number of cases within a court system that itself deals with only approximately 1 per cent of all civil disputes and a slightly higher percentage of criminal indictments. Negotiation, compromise, agreement, and non-legal sanction in civil cases, and guilty pleas in criminal cases, resolve the overwhelming bulk of disputes but such resolution nonetheless takes place in the shadow of the courts; and where lawyers are involved, as they often are, the shade cast is structured by the relevant court pronouncements, the precedents and other rules of

law. It is again the symbolism, the exceptional character of court decisions, the rare and solemn theatre of the court term and determination that is of greatest significance. What happens in court is a matter of record and must be seen and heard outside of court, first by other lawyers and legislators, latterly and less often by the public at large.

The formality and the technicality of court procedure grows according to the place in the hierarchy that any particular court holds. At the bottom of the hierarchy are the magistrates' courts. These are technically inferior courts of first instance, and are usually presided over by lay magistrates unimpeded by legal qualifications. They hear in the main the less serious criminal cases. Appeals from their decisions go to the Crown Court and from thence to the Court of Appeal. The Court of Appeal is in reality the final court of appeal in most cases, it being very rare indeed for a case to go on from there to the House of Lords/Supreme Court. In civil cases the County Court is the usual tribunal of first instance and appeals from there go first to one of the three divisions of the High Court, and from thence to the Court of Appeal and ultimately to the Supreme Court.

PETER GOODRICH

A Bradney, F Cownie, and M Burton, *English Legal System in Context* (Oxford: Oxford University Press, 4th rev edn, 2007).

P Haldar, 'The Function of the Ornament in Quintilian, Alberti, and Court Architecture', in C Douzinas and L Nead (eds), *Law and the Image* (Chicago: Chicago University Press, 1999)

common law courts, history of   As part of his reforms which would result in the birth of the **common law**, Henry II appointed judges on an *ad hoc* basis to pronounce judgment in cases brought under his new writs. By the 1190s, a fixed central court at Westminster, with its own records, had emerged, thanks to the growing specialization of the royal administration. The court did not require the king's presence, or follow him, though matters pertaining to the royal interest continued to be heard before the king himself. When the king wanted more proceedings to be brought before himself—as John did after the loss of Normandy—the fixed court at Westminster stopped sitting. This angered the barons, who inserted into Magna Carta a clause that common pleas should not follow the itinerant king. After John's death in 1216, and his succession by an infant king, the fixed court accordingly developed strongly. However, after reaching his majority in 1234, Henry III revived the practice of hearing cases with a royal interest in his own court—the King's Bench—leaving suits between other subjects to another venue, the Common Pleas. At the same time, a third court, the Exchequer of Pleas, emerged, when the royal Exchequer began to keep records of its legal business. In this way, three separate common law courts emerged in the thirteenth century, each with its own records and staff. By the fifteenth century, all three courts were settled at Westminster Hall, sharing the space with the new court of Chancery.

Each common law court was made up of four judges (known as Barons in the Exchequer), one of whom was chief. These men were able to handle a vast workload, since the common law system required litigants to refine the precise point at issue between them through a system of pleading before trial and left all matters of fact to be determined by **juries** at trial. By the thirteenth century, cases would be formally commenced in one of the three courts at Westminster, and would then be sent for trial before a local jury presided over by any one of the twelve judges on circuit. The system was known by the words *nisi prius*, since juries were formally summoned to come to Westminster 'unless before then' (*nisi prius*), the judges should have visited their county of residence. Since this was habitually done, verdicts were given in the locality by the jury. However, judgments would be given by the court from which the cases originated, with any further legal issues being discussed by the judges *in banc*. Errors made by the Common Pleas judges could be corrected by the King's Bench. Errors from the Exchequer and King's Bench were referred to two distinct Exchequer Chambers, set up under legislation dating from 1357 and 1585. In 1830, these bodies were replaced by a single Exchequer Chamber, which heard errors from all three courts. In this court, errors from one of the three courts would be heard by the judges of the other two.

Each court had in theory a distinct jurisdiction. The Exchequer was in its origins a court dealing with revenue disputes. In contrast to the other two, it was also a royal office issuing its own **writs**, and so was able to develop its own distinct equity jurisdiction, which survived until 1841. As Magna Carta made clear, the Common Pleas was the main court for civil litigation between subjects, dealing mainly with property disputes. The King's Bench was a court for criminal matters and civil wrongs 'against the king's peace'. However, by the end of the fifteenth century, the courts were competing with each other for business, and in practice their caseloads overlapped. The King's Bench in particular began to encroach on the workload of the Common Pleas, by devising a cheap and attractive procedure, the Bill of Middlesex. Using the fiction that the defendant had committed a trespass in the county of Middlesex (where the court sat), plaintiffs were able to get their adversary into court without using the costly writ procedure, since the King's Bench had always allowed the use of bills to commence cases arising in the county where it was sitting. The fact that the defendant was in a different county was no impediment, for the court acted on a fictitious claim that the he had fled from Middlesex and was 'lurking' (*latitat*) elsewhere and issued a writ to arrest him. Having secured the defendant, the plaintiff could then abandon the trespass claim and proceed to seek a remedy for matters (such as debts) which should otherwise have gone to the Common Pleas. The result was to encourage a dramatic increase in suits in the court. The Exchequer also expanded its jurisdiction (notably in the seventeenth century) by allowing the use of a procedural fiction, by which litigants claiming to be debtors to the king could bring any case before this court.

Despite being unable to match these procedural innovations, the Common Pleas managed to maintain the largest share of business in the early modern era, at a time when the volume of civil litigation grew dramatically. But when litigation rates dropped drastically in the eighteenth century, this court was affected most, and by mid-century, its caseload was for the first time smaller than that of the King's Bench. It also lagged behind when rates of civil litigation revived, and by the 1820s, over two-thirds of all common law business went to the King's Bench, and only one-fifth to the Common Pleas. The imbalance was redressed by the mid-nineteenth century, thanks to reforms in the 1830s and 1840s which instituted a common procedure for commencing cases and which removed the restrictive practices of the Exchequer and Common Pleas. In addition, each court obtained a fourth judge in 1830 and a fifth in 1868. Although the overall caseload of the Superior Courts did not increase significantly in second half of the nineteenth century, this was largely because of the creation in 1846 of a new system of county courts, where the vast bulk of litigants took their cases.

The first half of the nineteenth century also saw a reform in the internal organization of the courts. A series of reports on the officials of the courts, issued between 1818 and 1822, led in the 1820s to the abolition of a large number of sinecure offices. Further reforms of the offices of the courts followed, with payment of officers by fees being gradually replaced by payment by fixed salaries. Similarly, judicial salaries were increased, and their income from fees was removed. The mid-nineteenth century also saw significant reforms of common law procedure, aimed at making litigation simpler and cheaper. By the 1850s, it was increasingly apparent that a legal system which required litigants to seek their remedies in two distinct courts —those of law and equity— needed more substantial reform, and pressure grew to unite all judicatures in one body. In 1875, the three common law courts were duly merged with the court of Chancery into a single High Court of Justice. By 1880, the Exchequer and Common Pleas Divisions of this court were abolished, leaving the Queen's Bench Division as the only 'common law' division of the new court.   MICHAEL LOBBAN

JH Baker, *An Introduction to English Legal History* (London: Butterworths, 4th edn, 2002)

CW Brooks, *Lawyers, Litigation and English Society since 1450* (London: Hambledon, 1998)

See also: **Chancery court; courts; equity as a system of law**

common law in Ireland   The transmission of the **common law** into Ireland began with the arrival of the first Anglo Norman settlers in 1169. The process was formalized when, in 1210, King John (1167–1216) promulgated a charter requiring the observance of the common law in the lordship of Ireland, and later in the same year sent a register of writs to Ireland (and thereby the means to administer in Ireland the principal processes of the common law for initiation of proceedings). A single 'king's court' functioned in Ireland in the early thirteenth century. That was superseded by two courts: the Dublin Bench, a court staffed by three or four justices based at Dublin for hearing civil pleas (a court equivalent to the Westminster Bench, whose existence was first recorded in the 1240s), and by the Court of the Justiciar (an analogue of the English king's bench, whose existence was first recorded in the 1280s). By end of the thirteenth century the Irish exchequer was also exercising a restricted common pleas jurisdiction. The Court of Chancery was a much later development, probably not coming into existence in Ireland until the late fifteenth century.

However, during the medieval period the common law only operated within the geographical area under royal control: the Lordship of Ireland. Within the greater part of Ireland, Ulster, Connaught, and the South west of the country, the legal system remained the native Irish system of jurisprudence, **Brehon law**. Indeed, the area under common law jurisdictional control contracted severely after 1300, and by 1450 consisted of just four counties around Dublin. The volume of work processed by the central common law courts shrunk to a quarter of what it had been in the reign of Edward 1.

Legislation as a source of law commenced in the early thirteenth century with some items of English legislation being sent to Ireland with instructions that it be adopted in Ireland. Later in the thirteenth century an Irish Parliament began to meet and issue ordinances. In 1494 the Irish Parliament, sitting in Drogheda, enacted Poynings's Act, which adopted into Irish law all public acts enacted by the English Parliament. It also significantly restricted the sovereignty of Parliament by requiring that no enactment of the Irish Parliament could become law without the approval of the king in council. This conciliar veto upon the law making capacity of the Irish Parliament remained until 1782 when Yelverton's Act deprived the British and Irish council of the power to veto Irish parliamentary legislative measures.

The reach of the common law extended with the Tudor re-conquest of Ireland. In the period 1570–1610, in particular, the process, of establishing the common law system and constructing in Ireland a judicature along English model, was completed. In 1571 a Court of Castle Chamber (equivalent to the court of Star Chamber) was established. Shortly thereafter Ireland had its own court of admiralty (and a further prerogative court was established when in 1622 the court of ward and liveries was constituted). In 1569 and 1571 Sir Henry Sidney established presidential courts of Connaught and Munster in order to provide accessible, local, common law tribunals which would 'withdraw the people from their liking or using of their accustomed Brehon laws'. Popular access to justice was increased by the institution of courts of assize which operated, from the beginning of the seventeenth century, throughout the country. These courts offered litigants the facility of simple civil bills (in place of common law pleadings) for the recovery of small debts. (In 1796 this small claims' civil bill jurisdiction was transferred to the courts of quarter sessions presided over by assistant barristers).

By the end of the eighteenth century the Court of Exchequer had emerged as the most widely used of the central common law courts followed by the Courts of King's Bench and Common Pleas. By the early nineteenth century the number of processes issued by the courts of common law numbered about 12,000 per annum, about one-third of the level of activity conducted in the English courts of common law. Common law procedure and the nature of litigation (primarily contractual) did not differ significantly from that heard by the central courts in England (although the common law procedure acts of 1850 instigated innovations unique to Irish law in the form of writs and the equalisation of business among the courts of common law). In 1877 a Judicature Act equivalent to the English Act of 1871 consolidated the four superior courts into a unitary court.

A legal nationalist tendency, associated with lawyers allied to the Independence movement of the early twentieth century, promoted the revival of Brehon law jurisprudence as a supplement or even substitute for English common law. However, the post-Independence Constitutions of 1922 (Article 73) and 1937 (Article 49) both re-adopted common law as the legal system of the Irish Free State, and of Ireland (as the state became known in 1937).

The study of Irish legal history has been severely restricted by a catastrophic explosion which occurred in June 1922 during a siege of the Four Courts building, and in which most of the court records then deposited in the Public Records Office of Ireland were destroyed.   KEVIN COSTELLO

common law in the colonies   How did the **common law** spread from England to its colonies, and what shape did it take once it reached there? The answer is not generally found in imperial (ie English) statute law. Few imperial statutes explicitly imposed English common law on any of the colonies. Instead, the theories and practice of the spread of the common law were developed through judge-made law in England and its colonies, and through the actions of the Crown in its metropolitan and colonial guises. Eventually, some colonial legislatures adopted English law by colonial, not imperial, statute.

The imperial theory of the reception of English common law developed from the early seventeenth century onwards. The American colonies analogized from Sir Edward Coke's judgments (including *Calvin's Case* (1608)) and other writings, from which they assumed that the same basic legal principles applied in the colonies as in England. The underlying theory was one of interlocking personal allegiance and protection, under which the common law travelled with a subject of the Crown. This developed into the colonial birthright theory, the common law being the subject's inheritance even for subjects born in the colonies.

In the first edition of his *Commentaries on the Laws of England* in 1765, William Blackstone drew a distinction between conquered or ceded colonies on the one hand, and settled colonies in unoccupied lands on the other. In conquered or ceded colonies, laws already existed and remained in force until altered by the King. In settled colonies, 'all' the English laws were the birthright of British subjects. In later editions Blackstone qualified this, stating that the settled colonies received only those parts of English law which were applicable to the conditions of the colony concerned. For Newfoundland and some of the Australian colonies, this was later placed into statutory form, under which English law was received in the colonies 'so far as the same can be applied' there.

In many cases, English common law was simply assumed to apply through the actions of the Crown and sometimes the **Westminster Parliament**. Royal charters of the seventeenth century created colonial legislatures or granted land in the colonies, and with that, it was assumed, ran the common law. Something similar applied in the eighteenth century, when legislation and letters patent were used to create courts for newly established colonies. From many of these, there was an appeal to the **Privy Council** in London.

The mechanism of an appeal to the Privy Council might seem to have had the potential to achieve uniform common law around the empire. But the Privy Council's appeals committees were not explicitly concerned about uniformity of law until well into the nineteenth century. Not until the middle of the nineteenth century did the Judicial Committee (as the appeals committee was called from 1833) give recorded reasons for its decisions, holding the colonial courts to an explicit imperial standard.

Those who study the law of the British colonies from the seventeenth to the nineteenth century usually reach a similar conclusion: that the common law, the judge-made law, of any colony was not simply a copy of the common law of England with minor variations. Colonial common law was marked by pluralism, especially in the first generation or two of new colonies. Colonial law did contain a large slab of inheritance, through the habits of colonists and colonial judges. That inheritance included the common law of the superior courts of London, but it also included many local laws and customs of England. Popular attitudes to law flowed upwards into the formal laws of the colonies. New laws also developed locally to match local circumstances. The imperial government appointed the colonial judges, who often travelled from one colonial appointment to the next. Especially among those who were legally trained, they carried the traditions of English law, and often a determination to apply those traditions, but they met with new conditions and varying attitudes among colonial people. Through these interactions came patterns of acceptance and resistance to English common law. In many cases, an English lawyer visiting a colony would have recognized the colonial courts' language and procedures, but on some matters he would as likely have been struck by difference as much as similarity.

Some patterns emerged in colonial common law that distinguished it from that of England, largely due to circumstances common to the colonies but absent in England. There are many examples of this, including the law of attaint and basic tort law. English debt recovery law, for instance, was not adopted as our visiting lawyer might have expected. Land had a different social meaning in the colonies from that in England. It was more readily available, and valued less. English law resisted remedies against land holders in favour of unpaid creditors, while colonial law was more relaxed about it. And the lack of sterling in the colonies often meant that debts had to be paid in kind, in cattle or pigs, or even labour, rather than cash. The colonial courts sometimes recognized this and made formal orders for payment in kind.

The colonies also had to deal with the presence of indigenous people in ways long forgotten in Britain. Would indigenous evidence be accepted in the courts? Were indigenous people subject to the common law when one indigenous person killed another? Would indigenous land rights be recognized by colonial common law? The answers to these questions varied from one colony to the next, and English law gave little assistance.

As time passed in the nineteenth century, especially with the appointment of barristers as colonial judges, the common law of the colonies became more orthodox in an English sense. There was always a tension between local conditions and the inheritance, but the balance tipped further towards the inheritance. Eventually the Judicial Committee of the Privy Council decided that the common law ought to be uniform. In 1879 it declared that it was 'of the utmost importance that in all parts of the empire where English law prevails, the interpretation of that law by the Courts should be as nearly as possible the same' (*Trimble v Hill* (1879)). This came about both as a matter of imperial policy and as a consequence of a change in the nature of judicial reasoning. From the second half of the nineteenth century, the notion of **precedent** became much stricter, more 'scientific'. What had often before been a form of loose analogous reasoning, a dipping into the past for useful principles, became instead a search for the one right answer found in the words of previous judges. Courts of appeal were there to correct errors. And by 1879, correctness meant English correctness, as determined by the Judicial Committee sitting in Downing Street, London. This was the high water mark of the spread of supposedly uniform English common law into the colonies. This peak was reached just as the Canadian

and Australian colonies were seeking to unite into two new federations, and to begin their separation from England, which was finally completed in the twentieth century.   BRUCE KERCHER

P Karsten *Between Law and Custom: 'High' and 'Low' Legal Cultures in the Lands of the British Diaspora, 1600–1900* (Cambridge: Cambridge University Press, 2002)

See also: **colonialism; colonial administration and law; indigenous law; indigenous peoples; native title**

common law marriage   The term 'common law marriage' bears multiple meanings and has been the subject of much misunderstanding. Many modern cohabitants mistakenly believe that by living together they have a 'common law marriage' that gives them the same rights as if they were legally married. The term is also used in a historical context to refer to marriages celebrated according to the **canon law** that governed marriage prior to the Clandestine Marriages Act of 1753, and also to marriages celebrated overseas under circumstances in which compliance with the local law is not possible. It is widely assumed that before 1753 all that was required for a valid marriage was the exchange of consent by the parties, and that a **common law** marriage may today take place overseas with similarly attenuated formalities. In fact, while a simple exchange of consent was binding on the parties prior to 1753, it was neither legally nor socially the equivalent of a marriage celebrated in church. It was not until the early nineteenth century that the concepts of a binding promise and a legally valid ceremony became elided, first in the American case of *Fenton v Reed* (1809) and then in the English **courts**. This misunderstanding has coloured the subsequent history of common law **marriage** on both sides of the Atlantic, forming the basis of the distinctive American concept and leading the English courts to uphold marriages celebrated overseas with minimal formalities and historians to assume that marriage was virtually unregulated in the past.   REBECCA PROBERT

common law of Europe   When jurists speak of a 'common law of Europe' they are either speaking of a *ius commune* that was once in force in much of continental Europe, or of an aspiration to escape from the nationalized law that replaced it.

The *ius commune* was the name that medieval jurists gave to the **Roman law** and **Canon law** that was the staple of continental university education. Around 1100, Irnerius began systematic lectures in Bologna on the so-called *Corpus iuris civilis*, a compilation of Roman legal texts made under the

Emperor Justianian in the early sixth century and neglected in the intervening years. His successors, the 'Glossators', wrote notes (*glossae*) to these texts, culminating in the mid-thirteenth century *Glossa ordinaria* of Accursius which contained nearly 100,000 notes. The later medieval jurists, known as 'Commentators', wrote more elaborate expositions of Roman texts and tried to reconcile them where possible with local custom. The greatest of these were Bartolus of Saxoferrato and his pupil Baldus degli Ubaldis.

The systematic study of Canon law began around 1140 when Gratian, about whom we know little, collected excerpts from the Fathers, Church councils, and other sources regarded as authoritative for medieval Christians, in a work known as the *Decretum* or *Concordance of Discordant Canons*. Over time, it was supplemented by letters written by popes to settle particular controversies. A collection of these letters, the Decretals of Pope Gregory IX, was compiled by St. Raymond of Penafort. It and the *Decretum* became known as the *Corpus iuris canonici*, which was taught in law schools along with the *Corpus iuris civilis*. Ambitious students sought the 'double doctorate' in 'both laws'.

The law of the *Corpus iuris canonici* was also called *ius commune*, and in two senses. First, it was the common law of the Church applied in ecclesiastical courts everywhere, as distinguished from local custom. Secondly, for the medieval jurists, Canon and Roman law together formed a whole which they sometimes called the *ius commune*. The Canon lawyers applied the Roman law when no particular rule of Canon law was in point. The Roman lawyers accepted rules that had been forged by the Canonists: for example, the rule that no promise was binding if circumstances had changed sufficiently since it was made.

One can exaggerate the extent to which the *ius commune* of the *Corpus juris civilis* was a common law of Europe if by that one means a law that is uniformly applied or uniformly understood. The medieval jurists claimed that in principle the Holy Roman Emperor ruled the entire world, and hence his law was applicable everywhere. In fact, it was accepted in some territories but not others: at first, in northern Italy and southern France, and only centuries later, in Germany and The Netherlands. In territories that accepted it, the *ius commune* was still a law *in subsidium*, which governed only in the absence of some local custom or statute.

It was based on a common system of instruction. But the Glossators and Commentators themselves often disagreed, as did the judges who applied the law. Moreover, with the passing of the Middle Ages, new schools arose which took different approaches, so that the unity of the university tradition was broken. In the Renaissance, humanists used the methods of philology to discover the original meaning of Roman texts, unlike the medieval jurists who had merely tried to reconcile them in a logical and practical fashion. From the sixteenth to the eighteenth century, the so-called natural law schools explained Roman law by philosophical principles, dismissing the rules they could not explain as mere Roman positive law. In the seventeenth and eighteenth centuries, commentaries on the *Corpus iuris civilis*, often called the *Usus modernus pandectarum*, were written by a school of northern European lawyers. Their object was to produce works that were simple, practical, and avoided the subtleties of the Glossators and Commentators.

Nevertheless, the fact remains that for centuries, jurists from much of Europe were trained on the same texts (albeit in different ways) and shared common reference points and common concepts. Moreover, because of the work of university trained jurists, the influence of the *ius commune* extended beyond the territories that had expressly accepted it. Provisions of local customary law as interpreted or described by such jurists often reflected those of the *ius commune*. Branches of Roman law were sometimes impressed into service when customary law was sparse, and were declared to be part of custom. An example was the acceptance of Roman rules of tort and contract in northern France. English law proved exceptionally resistant to infiltration. But in the nineteenth and twentieth centuries, some scholars believe, English law was rationalized by borrowing a large number of ideas from the continental civil law and declaring them to be English.

Beginning in the eighteenth century, the Roman texts were replaced by codes: in Bavaria (1756), in Prussia (1794), in France (1804), in Austria (1811), in Italy (1865), in Spain (1888), in Germany (1900)—despite Friedrich Karl von **Savigny**'s defence of the old Roman texts—and in Switzerland (1907/1912). Codes were understood as an exclusive source of law. The study of one's national code became, and still remains, the prime object of legal education and academic commentary. The old *ius commune* based on transnational study of common texts ceased to exist.

Some say we should still speak of a 'common law of Europe' and, indeed, recognize it as the basis for a European-wide study of law. Every code is an amalgam of rules descended from the old *ius commune*, often differing because the old rules happened to be understood differently when particular codes were enacted. As mentioned, even much of English law was shaped by continental rules. Some think that these resemblances could serve as a common basis for legal studies and perhaps for gradual harmonization of laws. Some want to go further: to enact a common code whose texts would form a new *ius commune*.   JAMES GORDLEY

See also: **civil law systems; codes and codification in national law**

common market   *see* **single market**

common prostitute   *see* **prostitution**

commonholds   The traditional method favoured by English property developers to create apartments in a sub-divided building, to be disposed of to third party purchasers, is that of long leases. This method fell into disrepute. There were a number of reasons for this. Apartment leaseholders resented the fact that they did not own the freehold in their units. A long lease is a wasting asset. The management of some long leasehold schemes was criticized.

Following the Report of the Aldridge Committee (*Commonhold, Freehold Flats* (1987)) and subsequent consultations over some fifteen years, the Commonhold and Leasehold Reform Act 2002 was enacted. The Act creates commonhold—ie freehold property in sub-divided units in a freehold building. Title to the land must be registered with a commonhold title following an application from the developer in the prescribed form. Commonhold may be used for residential as well as for business use, or a mixture of both. Conversion from existing long-lease units is only possible if all the long leaseholders agree to the registration application. This is not likely to happen except in the case of small schemes.

The basic structure of commonholds is as follows. Unit holders are compulsory members of a commonhold association, a company limited by guarantee under which the liability of members is limited to £1. There are standard-form articles of association for this company. The management of commonhold is governed mainly by a standard-form commonhold community statement. Long leases can be individually negotiated and may vary in quality, but major variations in the management structure of commonholds are impossible. The commonhold association is responsible for the maintenance and repair of the common parts of the relevant buildings (such as the roof, entrances, and gardens) and its directors must, in particular, fix an annual budget. Each unit holder must pay regular assessments towards the running costs of the common parts. The unit holder is granted statutory powers of sale and mortgage of the unit. However, because of hostility to leases within a freehold system, no lease of a residential unit can be granted for longer than seven years. While a commonhold association cannot be broken up at the whim of any individual unit holder, provision is made both for the voluntary winding up of an association and for its winding up by court order in the event of insolvency.

Existing long lease schemes cannot be easily converted to commonhold. As a result, the new tenure is likely to be available for only new-build schemes, and may take time to be adopted on a wide scale. Even so, as from 27 September 2004, a workable scheme for freehold ownership of flats and other units now exists, and this is welcome.   PETER SMITH

DN Clarke, 'The Enactment of Commonhold – Problems, Principles and Perspectives' [2002] *Conveyancer* 349

L Crabb, 'The Commonhold and Leasehold Reform Act 2002 A Company Law Perspective' (2004) 25(7) *Company Law* 213

commons   *see* **creative commons**

Commonwealth law   The Commonwealth (known formerly as the 'British Commonwealth') is a voluntary association of fifty-three independent states spread over the Americas, the Caribbean, Europe, Africa, Asia, and the Pacific. Most of the states have historic links with Britain, many having been under British rule before becoming independent. Direct constitutional ties with Britain are, however, not a requirement of Commonwealth membership, as is evidenced by the examples of South Pacific countries such as Samoa and Nauru (which were previously administered by Australia or New Zealand), Namibia (which was governed by South Africa), and Mozambique (which was a Portuguese colony with no links to Britain at all before its admission to the Commonwealth in 1995). The Commonwealth's membership accounts for nearly a third of the world's countries and for about a quarter of the world's population.

The reigning monarch is the titular head of the Commonwealth. The main decision-making body is the Commonwealth Heads of Government Meeting ('CHOGM') which is held once every two years. The day-to-day administration of the organization is conducted from a secretariat in London, headed by the Commonwealth Secretary-General.

Unlike, say, the European Union or the Organization of American States, the Commonwealth does not have a legal structure or a legal adjudicatory mechanism binding all its member states.

English **common law** is widely recognized and used throughout the Commonwealth, and it is a prominent aspect of the shared legacy of values and institutions enjoyed by member states. The common law is, however, far from universal. A number of other laws and legal systems are also in vogue, including Roman Dutch law (eg in South Africa and Sri Lanka), European civil law (in Mauritius and Seychelles), **Islamic law** (in Pakistan and Malaysia), and **Hindu law** (in India). Many of these laws exist alongside the common law to form mixed legal systems.

The ubiquity of English common law can be traced back to the practice, developed at the height of the British Empire, under which legal measures enacted from London—whether in the form of royal proclamations, charters. and commissions, or (in later years) statutes passed by the Westminster Parliament—began supplanting local laws in the colonies, so that the common law eventually assumed a position of paramountcy throughout the colonies and dependant territories. This practice nevertheless made occasional exceptions for indigenous laws and customs—usually in relation to matters such as succession or marriage—which continued to remain in force and enjoy full legal recognition. A further measure of autonomy for local law-making was provided by the Colonial Laws Validity Act 1865 under which certain domestic statutes (called 'dominion laws') were allowed to exist alongside law made in London.

Another legacy of the paramountcy of the common law was the Judicial Committee of the **Privy Council** which became the highest court of appeal for the colonies and which also exercised exclusive powers to determine questions concerning the compatibility of dominion laws with legislation of the **Westminster Parliament**. The Privy Council's jurisdiction has declined significantly since the middle of the twentieth century: it now exercises appellate functions in relation to only a handful of Commonwealth territories, including Antigua and Barbuda, Bahamas, Barbados, Belize, Cook Islands and Niue, Grenada, Jamaica, St. Christopher and Nevis, St. Lucia, St. Vincent and the Grenadines, Tuvalu, Anguilla, Bermuda, British Virgin Islands, Cayman Islands, Falkland Islands, Gibraltar, Monserrat, Pitcairn Islands, St. Helena and dependencies, Turks and Caicos Islands, Trinidad & Tobago, Dominica, Kiribati, and Mauritius. By a special arrangement with the Sultan of Brunei, the Privy Council also hears civil appeals from that country, on the understanding that the Judicial Committee's report would be addressed to the Sultan, rather than the British Monarch, as is customary.

The Commonwealth does not have a constitution. Its core values are, however, articulated in a number of declarations, statements of principles, and decisions of the Heads of Government handed down over the years. These have acquired the status of a 'code of principles' which is binding on member states. Among the foremost of the shared values is a commitment to the **rule of law**, the elements of which have been identified and expressed in various multilateral documents issued by the organization since the early 1970s.

The first of the major declarations, issued at Singapore in 1971, stressed, among other things: the liberty of the individual; equal rights for all citizens regardless of race, colour, creed, or political belief; the citizen's right to participate in free and democratic political processes; and representative political institutions. It saw racial prejudice as a 'dangerous sickness' and urged all member states to work towards its elimination. The next important declaration, issued at Harare in 1991, affirmed the organization's belief in the 'rule of international law' and reiterated its abhorrence of racial prejudice. The Harare Declaration also listed distributive justice, respect for the environment, and sound economic management as objectives which member states should strive to promote. The principles in that Declaration were reiterated at a CHOGM held in New Zealand in 1995, which issued a document entitled the 'Millbrook Commonwealth Action Programme on the Harare Declaration'; that document, *inter alia*, called upon the Commonwealth Secretariat to provide an increased level of advice, training, and other forms of technical assistance to governments with a view to 'strengthening the rule of law and promoting the independence of the judiciary'.

Recent years have seen an increasing emphasis by the Commonwealth on the promotion and protection of human rights values. To this end, a Human Rights Unit was set up in the Secretariat and it has been active in conducting educational and training programmes on internationally recognized human rights principles throughout the Commonwealth. Although the organization has expressed its interest in establishing a 'Commonwealth code of human rights' since at least the 1970s, it has repeatedly failed to reach a consensus on the contents of such a code.

A tangible outcome of the focus on human rights has been an increasing scrutiny by Commonwealth leaders of the record of member governments in this area, and the imposition of sanctions on those found wanting. Sanctions—in the form of suspension of membership—have been imposed on Nigeria (1995),

Sierra Leone (1997), Pakistan (2000), Zimbabwe (2002) and Fiji (2006), among others, for gross violations of democratic principles and human rights. Zimbabwe withdrew from the organization in 2003 after its suspension was extended indefinitely for continuing human rights violations.

The Commonwealth has launched a number of initiatives for legal cooperation among its members, which have led to the development of a growing body of '**soft law**' in several areas. Examples include: a Commonwealth Model Law on the Civil Recovery of Criminal Assets including Terrorist Property; a Model Bill on Competition and Consumer Protection; and a Scheme Relating to Mutual Assistance in Criminal Matters within the Commonwealth. These initiatives are usually the result of action at the level of Commonwealth Law Ministers who meet periodically to discuss matters of mutual interest and concern. A number of non-official Commonwealth bodies are also engaged in mutual cooperation and assistance. These include the Commonwealth Association of Law Reform Agencies, the Commonwealth Lawyers' Association, the Commonwealth Legal Education Association, the Commonwealth Magistrates' and Judges' Association, and the Commonwealth Human Rights Initiative. Some of them were responsible, in 1988, for the development of the 'Commonwealth (Latimer House) Guidelines on the Accountability of and Relationship Between the Three Branches of Government', which was endorsed by the Heads of Government in 1993.

Other areas of activity which have engaged the attention of the Commonwealth include international humanitarian law, criminal defamation, proliferation of small arms and light weapons, terrorism, justice for victims of crime, protection of personal information, and private international law. Exchange of information between member states on legal developments, including case law from national courts, is facilitated by the *Commonwealth Law Bulletin*, published on a quarterly basis by the Legal and Constitutional Affairs Division ('LCAD') of the Secretariat. The LCAD also produces and disseminates a wide array of legal materials relevant to governments. Direct legal advice, mainly to the less-developed member states, is provided by the Economic and Legal Advisory Services Division. The Commonwealth Fund for Technical Cooperation extends financial support to small and developing countries which lack the resources to follow or implement developments in international law.

A number of non-official bodies affiliated to the Commonwealth also facilitate legal capacity-building. Foremost among these is the Commonwealth Legal Advisory Service, based in the British Institute of International and Comparative Law, which offers advice and expertise to governments on such matters as legislative reform. Among private non-governmental organizations, the London-based Interights disseminates information on comparative jurisprudence across the Commonwealth through a free online database. The Commonwealth Law Conference, held every two years, provides a forum for lawyers and judges from member states to exchange information and ideas on legal developments across jurisdictions. Together, these bodies and initiatives have led to the growth of an increasingly influential and harmonious corpus of Commonwealth law and jurisprudence.   VENKAT IYER

See also: **civil law systems; common law in the colonies; mixed jurisdictions**

Commonwealth of Nations The Commonwealth of Nations grew out of the British Empire. It had its origins in meetings of ministers of **Great Britain** and the self-governing colonies (later known as 'dominions'), which were first held in 1887 and 1897 on the occasions of Queen Victoria's golden and diamond jubilees. The meetings continued to be held every few years, and were known as 'Colonial Conferences' and, after 1907, as 'Imperial Conferences'.

As a result of the contribution of the dominions to the allied cause during the Great War they were made members of the League of Nations and were given charge of territories under League of Nations mandates. At the Imperial Conference of 1926 it was declared that Britain and the dominions (Canada, Australia, New Zealand, South Africa, the Irish Free State, and Newfoundland) were equal in status in all aspects of their internal and external affairs 'though united by a common allegiance to the **Crown** and freely associated as members of the British Commonwealth of Nations'. The Statute of Westminster 1931 gave some statutory recognition to this status.

In 1949 Ireland chose to become a republic and thereby ceased to be a Commonwealth member because it no longer satisfied the criterion of allegiance to the Crown. Shortly afterwards, however, the Government of India, which was about to become a republic, said it wanted to continue its association with the Commonwealth. This was achieved by the London Declaration of April 1949 at a meeting of Commonwealth Prime Ministers. By virtue of this Declaration, acceptance of the King as symbol of the free association of Commonwealth members, and as such Head of the Commonwealth, replaced allegiance to the Crown as the criterion of membership. In the decades that followed many British dependencies, on achieving independence, became republics or had their own monarchs (such as Malaysia) and, under the formula agreed to in the case of India, became or remained members of the Commonwealth.

The Commonwealth of Nations is now an association of fifty-three independent states which (with one exception, Mozambique) were part of the British Empire or had a special relationship (for example, as protectorate or UN trusteeship territory) with Britain or another Commonwealth country.

Queen Elizabeth II is recognized by each state as the symbol of their association and Head of the Commonwealth. She is, however, **monarch** of only sixteen of those states. Of the others, thirty-one are republics and six have their own monarchs.

Since 1965 the Commonwealth has had a secretariat stationed in London with a secretary-general as chief executive officer. The secretariat's chief function (among many others) is to organize, every two years or so, the Commonwealth Heads of Government Meeting (known as 'CHOGM'). The members at those meetings discuss international affairs that concern the members as a whole.

In 1971 at the Singapore Conference a declaration described the Commonwealth as a voluntary association of independent sovereign states, consulting and cooperating in the common interests of their people and the promotion of international understanding and world peace. In 1991 the heads of government issued the Harare Commonwealth Declaration, which declared their commitment to democratic processes, human rights, and the rule of law.

The Commonwealth has suspended members from 'the Councils of the Commonwealth' for failure to conform to its principles, usually because of the overthrow of democratic government. Fiji was suspended between 2000 and 2001 and again in 2006, following military coups. For similar reasons Pakistan was suspended from 1999 to 2004 and Nigeria from 1995 to 1999. Zimbabwe was suspended as a result of the electoral and land policies in 2002. It left the association in 2003.

Where a realm of Queen Elizabeth II becomes a republic it automatically ceases to be a member of the Commonwealth and must apply to retain membership. This occurred in the case of South Africa in 1961, but it was forced to withdraw its application for continued membership because of hostility to its apartheid policy. It was readmitted in 1990. Similarly the creation of a republic in Fiji in 1987, as the result of a military coup, meant its membership had lapsed. Application for membership was successful in 1997.

In addition to CHOGM there are regular meetings of Commonwealth ministers concerned with many specific areas of government, such as health, finance, and law.

There is a vast number of Commonwealth non-governmental associations and organizations covering many aspects of society and human endeavour. These include groups of universities, lawyers, doctors, journalists, teachers, nurses, business organizations, sporting bodies, and many others. The Commonwealth Games, held every four years, is probably the most widely known Commonwealth event. LESLIE ZINES

See also: **Commonwealth law**

communications regulation Until recently, different forms of electronic communication were associated with distinct regulatory approaches. The sectors of broadcasting, telecommunications, and wireless telegraphy each had their own statutory frameworks and regulatory bodies, which were intended to reflect their particular needs. However, those sectors are increasingly convergent, enabling the same content to be delivered to viewers or consumers on a variety of platforms. The digitalization of signals means that audiovisual material can almost equally be broadcast through an aerial, carried down a traditional telephone line, sent across a cable or a mobile telephone network, or made available on the internet; and this applies whether the content is packaged for mass audiences or is interactive, and whether it is made available free or by subscription. As a response to these developments, the UK's Communications Act 2003 is a bold attempt to rationalize communications regulation by providing a unified statutory framework to be implemented by a single regulator, the Office of Communications ('Ofcom'). The legislation attempts to be 'future-proof' by giving Ofcom flexible powers to deal with new technological and business developments.

Ofcom replaces the previous regulators for particular media sectors: the Independent Television Commission ('ITC'), the Radio Authority, the Office of Telecommunications ('OFTEL'), the Radiocommunications Agency, and the Broadcasting Standards Commission. Its principal duty, consisting of two equal components, is to 'further the interests of citizens in relation to communications matters; and to further the interests of consumers in relevant markets, where appropriate by promoting competition'. In doing that, it must secure the following: an optimal use of the wireless spectrum; the widespread availability of electronic communications services (covering telecommunications and the internet); the availability of a wide range of television and broadcasting services; the maintenance of a sufficient plurality of different television and radio providers; and the application of appropriate standards to prevent the inclusion of offensive and harmful content in programmes, and to prevent intrusions into privacy and unfair treatment. Other aims include securing various aspects of public service broadcasting, promoting competition, and encouraging self-regulation. However, the list of functions does not include the **regulation** of the internet. Generally, Ofcom's brief is to regulate with a light touch.

As a response to fears that the new super-regulator would allow matters of economic regulation to dominate those of content regulation, Ofcom has a special committee, the Content Board. Whilst this has a majority of external members, it has no independent power. It is responsible only for making representations to Ofcom about the public interest in: the nature and quality of television and radio programmes, the reflection of national or regional perspectives, and the development of media literacy. However, its influence on Ofcom's deliberations is not transparent and the regulator's approach often appears to be weighted towards market concerns. Ofcom also has an independent Consumer Panel, which advises about aspects of service delivery and issues such as price, quality, safety, and the handling of complaints; again, it has no power to determine policy.

In terms of substance, the overall effect of the Communications Act 2003 has been to deregulate and liberalize the communications industry. In relation to electronic communications, it has transposed a bundle of **European Union** directives, agreed in 2002, which cover both radio and wired systems, and which introduce a regime of general competition regulation with limited sector-specific exceptions for the public interest. Telecommunications licensing is replaced with a scheme of general authorization, under which companies are entitled to provide networks and services without prior approval, provided that they keep Ofcom informed of their activities and comply with its conditions dealing, for example, with consumer interests, the allocation and adoption of telephone numbers, universal service (enabling basic services to all, at an affordable price), open access to networks, and limiting the exercise of significant market power by large operators. In addition, the Act enables Ofcom to manage the radio spectrum, including arrangements for spectrum trading and auctions. At the same time, the intensity of **digital television and radio regulation** has been relaxed. Whilst all providers have to comply with some basic standards, only a few (ITV, Channel 4, S4C and Five) have additional public service obligations, and advertising is self-regulated.

Reflecting the increasingly open market in the production and supply of programming and content, Ofcom has powers to ensure fair and effective competition in the provision of audiovisual services. It also exercises general competition powers concurrently with the **Office of Fair Trading** (the normal competition regulator) in respect of commercial activities in the communications industry.

TOM GIBBONS

Department of Trade and Industry & Department of Culture, Media and Sport, *A New Future for Communications* (2000) (Cm 5010)

See also: **telecommunications regulation**

communitarianism This term is used to refer to a plethora of philosophical doctrines loosely connected by the core idea that linguistic meaning is a function of the activities of members of a particular **community**. Communitarian readings of the late philosophy of Wittgenstein highlight the prominence of communal practice in the constitution of meaning by arguing that what fixes the content of our thought and language is the actual fact of convergence of behaviour or agreement amongst members of a community, instead of any objective or universal standards of truth and correctness.

Hostility to universal standards is a prominent communitarian theme in political and social philosophy—an area in which, more than any other, communitarian ideas have flourished. Here communitarianism began as a sharp criticism of liberal theorizing on **justice** and the **person**, put forward especially in the work of John Rawls. Contrary to Rawls' arguments, communitarians such as Alasdair McIntyre, Michael Sandel, Charles Taylor, and Michael Walzer have argued that it is not possible to locate universal principles that establish the priority of a universal ideal of justice (the 'Right') over conceptions of the good life ingrained in the local practices of particular communities (the 'Good'). The main argument adduced is that liberal principles of justice are caught in a dilemma: either they are too 'thin' and fall short of providing appropriate solutions to problems of distribution; or, when they manage to do so, they cease to be universal. The dilemma is taken by communitarians to demonstrate the 'thick' character of principles of justice and their constitutive dependence on practices of particular political communities. From this flows a second reason for rejecting liberal justice as an ideal that is universally shared: principles of justice, in being incommensurable with one another, cannot be combined into a coherent universal scheme of justification of political authority; instead they require a pluralist model of reasoning that accommodates their dependence on the 'thick' political values of a particular community.

This line of argument is underpinned by a contextualist understanding of the concept of person or self as one that is embedded in the community in a constitutive sense. A main shortcoming of liberal thought is that it conceives individuals as conceptually prior to communities. Building on traditional forms of community, such as the Greek *polis*, communitarians have argued that liberal adherence to choice and **autonomy** is not inherently valuable, for there are communal values and attachments that may override principles arrived at through a process of rational deliberation. The fact that we are 'thrown into a community' may provide an horizon for thought and action which is far more fundamental than our critical ability as autonomous beings to reflect upon the conditions of our existence from an uncommitted or impartial point of view. Consequently, community membership and the conception of the good it promotes are deemed more important than any universal, context-independent standards that may challenge our allegiance to community values.

Finally, in law and jurisprudence, the ideas of communitarianism are particularly relevant with respect to the theory and application of **human rights** as legally enshrined norms. Interpretation and enforcement of rights, both at national and international level, turns largely on balancing the interests of individuals against those of communities. Substantive views on justice and the self aside, communitarian reasoning has also led to distinctive legal constructions which may influence the weight assigned to the various claims involved in judicial or policy-related acts of balancing. One influential variant of communitarianism is legal pragmatism, according to which the content and scope of a legal right is grounded on predictions about what the community of lawyers will treat as a legal standard. Another variant builds on **legal positivism**: here rights are defined by reference to a complex social rule (the rule of recognition) which operates as a general formula of validity by identifying a set of facts that must obtain for a legal right to come into force. The kinds of facts which usually count include acts of officials, procedures in Parliament, and the case law of higher **courts**. Either of these variants encourages an understanding of rights that renders them dependent on the agreement or consensus of a community rather than some moral ideal of inviolability of persons.

In a nutshell, far from having scored a definitive theoretical victory over liberalism, say by demonstrating the viability of some non-liberal vision of society, communitarianism has decisively contributed to a critical reassessment and recasting of the main tenets of contemporary liberal thinking. An increased awareness of issues of inequality, discrimination and **identity**, the reinvigoration of political participation and **social movements**, as well as the refinement of rigid liberal ideals in the light of the challenges presented by globalization, are only some of the most obvious amongst the contributions of communitarianism's critical acumen.

GEORGE PAVLAKOS

S Mulhall and A Swift, *Liberals & Communitarians* (Oxford: Blackwell, 2nd edn, 1996)

community Community denotes commonality, fellowship, sharing. At a general level community expresses a plurality of individuals who are held together by some common initiative or enterprise. However, community is much more than an instrumental enterprise of individuals. At a normative level community is the space where individuals might cohere or be drawn together by shared values, principles, norms, common objectives, or a sense of fraternity. While community can have normative purchase it is far from benign. Communalism, often based on **ethnicity** or **religion,** is regularly the source of **violence** inflicted on one community by another. Fraternity, rooted in the phallocentric union of brothers, has been a site of violent exclusion as much as it is also an expression of common and sometimes revolutionary values (such as in the French Revolution of 1789).

In liberal political theory a debate has ensued for many years about whether the individual can be an **agent** forming her conception of the 'good' as an autonomous **subject**, or whether she is a being whose life-ends are determined by being embedded in a particular community (liberalism v **communitarianism**). State-based policies of **multiculturalism** were often informed by a communitarian ethic—while critics of multiculturalism have tended to privilege individual rights over community or group rights. Political theories about community have thus been a basis for challenging the fundamental basis of liberal political thought—the autonomous individual.

Community can be the site and source of norms. In sociological investigations community as a source of norms has been distinguished from state-based or wider societal norms. The German sociologist, Ferdinand Tönnies, provided an influential distinction between community (*Gemeinschaft*) and society (*Gesellschaft*). His book *Gemeinschaft und Gesellschaft* published in 1887 elaborated these ideal types in a manner that suggested an evolution from community to society. However, Tönnies acknowledged that both forms of social grouping can co-exist in modern social formations. In post-colonial contexts for instance, struggles by **indigenous people** have often involved attempts to assert the importance of communal rights based on **customary law** over the state's attempt to be the hierarchically privileged source of rights for a society that stands over and above community.

Numerous other sociologists such as Émile Durkheim, Max Weber, Talcot Parsons, and more recently, Niklas Luhmann, have developed comprehensive accounts of the relationship between community, social formations, and law. While there is not the scope to elaborate all of their ideas here—it is worth pointing out that sociological theories about community and social dynamics has been central to the elaboration of modern law. Community has been explained through the distinction between mechanical and organic forms of solidarity—and these notions influenced how individual **transgressions** of norms (crimes) would be punished (Durkheim). The division of labour, forms of rationality based on social organization, and social and economic class have also been central to understanding the relationship between modes of production and law's role in sustaining social divisions (Marx and Weber). Society as a functional system that is comprised of various sub-systems, of which law is one, has been central to understanding an increasingly complex society (Parsons and Luhmann). Luhmann famously proposed that law is a 'cognitively open but normatively closed' sub-system which interacts with other sub-systems such as the economy.

At a more philosophical level the study of community has involved a contemplation of *being* as such. The notion of Being, 'being there', or 'existence', was comprehensively articulated by the German philosopher, Martin Heidegger—radically departing from the earlier theories of Hegel and Marx who proposed inter-subjective or socio-historical accounts of being and subjectivity. Towards the end of the twentieth century the French philosopher Jean-Luc Nancy drew on Heidegger to develop a theory of the relationship between being and community. Nancy explained that all beings are finite—they are born and they die—but each being cannot experience their own non-being, their death. A singular being can only experience the finiteness of their existence, and thus the very limits of their being, by being in relation with others. Community is thus central to the very sense one has of existence. However, noting the totalitarian formations of commonality from Fascism to ethno-nationalism which plagued the twentieth century, Nancy proposed a radically anti-essentialist account of community. The key to this is that community must not be *operative* as such. Community is made operative when it is based on some essence such as **race**, ethnicity, **nationality**, **sex/gender**/sexuality, or class. Nancy's account of community has profound implications for all political enterprises that are based on group membership.   STEWART MOTHA

T Murphy, *The Oldest Social Science: Configurations of Law and Modernity* (Oxford: Clarendon Press, 1997)
J-L Nancy, *The Inoperative Community* (trans P Connor) (Minneapolis: University of Minnesota Press, 1991)

community care Community care law is concerned with rights of disabled, elderly, ill, and otherwise vulnerable people to social care support services. The National Assistance Act 1948 laid the foundations of the modern scheme, purportedly repealing the previous Poor Law regime. However, community care law bears many of its traits, being means tested and local in its administration. Major reform occurred in 1990 with the NHS (Community Care) Act, which introduced the requirement that (except in emergencies) before services could be provided there should be a 'community care assessment' by the local authority to establish the extent of 'need'. In *R v Gloucestershire County Council, ex p Barry* (1997) the House of Lords held that authorities could (to a limited degree) take available resources into account in determining the extent of an individual's 'need'.

Many of the more radical community care legal developments have resulted from legislation originating as Private Members Bills. For instance, the Chronically Sick and Disabled Persons Act 1970 (sponsored by Alf Morris MP) gave individually enforceable rights to disabled people in relation to non-residential services and the Carers (Recognition and Services) Act 1995 (sponsored by Malcolm Wicks MP) introduced the right of 'unpaid carers' to an assessment.

Now the emphasis is moving away from authorities providing or arranging for the provision of services and towards a 'Direct Payments' scheme under which money is paid in lieu of services to enable the recipient to purchase services for themselves (often by employing a personal care assistant).

LUKE CLEMENTS

L Clements and P Thompson, *Community Care & the Law* (London: Legal Action Group, 2007)

community order   *see* **probation**

companies and the outside world   A **company**, as an artificial **person**, can only transact with outsiders through its **board of directors** either acting collectively or through those to whom this task has been delegated, for example a particular director or other corporate officer. The board, or its delegate, acts as an agent of the company. The question that arises is what is the position where a company's constitution restricts its contractual capacity and a transaction either falls outside such restriction or, if within its capacity, is outside the authority conferred on its agent? The capacity of a company to enter into contracts depends upon its 'objects clause' found in its constitution (the **articles of association**). Although its capacity may be unrestricted, the articles may provide otherwise. For example, if a company has a restrictively framed objects clause which declares it, without more, to be in the business of manufacturing railway carriages, any contract which falls outside the scope of this activity, unless it is reasonably incidental, will be beyond the company's capacity. On the other hand, the authority of the company's agent will depend upon the terms of the mandate. For example, an upper financial limit may be imposed on the agent's authority to contract on behalf of the company.

An outsider can enforce the contract against the company notwithstanding that it is beyond its constitution. However, the directors who caused the company to enter into the agreement will be in breach of their duty to act within their powers and will, therefore, be liable to the company for any loss or damage.

Where agents exceed their mandate, outsiders are protected provided they acted in good faith. This is presumed and there is no duty to enquire either into the agent's authority or, as to whether the company's constitution placed some procedural limitation on authority, for example where it stipulates for a minimum number of directors for a board meeting and the transaction was decided upon by an board which was not quorate. Similarly, where outsiders believe that they are dealing with the company's managing director, it will be reasonable to assume that he or she has authority to bind the company and the fact that the managing director was never formally appointed as such will not affect the outsider's position where the co-directors have acquiesced in this state of affairs. The consequence is that a transaction entered into by the board or its delegate in these circumstances will nevertheless bind the company. To avoid liability, the company will need to prove bad faith on the part of the outsider. Mere knowledge of the irregularity is not sufficient; something more is required such as collusion. The directors themselves will, however, be personally liable to compensate the company for any losses it suffers as a result of their breach of authority in exceeding any constitutional limitations on their powers although they may be relieved from liability by an ordinary resolution of the company's members.

JOHN LOWRY

company   The term 'company' was first used to denote an association for business purposes in the fourteenth and fifteenth centuries. The kinds of business association to which the term has since been attached, however, have changed over time. The first English organizations to which the term 'company' was generally applied were merchant guilds, such as the Company of Merchant Adventurers which brought together London's leading overseas merchants and received its royal charter in 1407. It was a 'regulated company', a trading franchise which extended the guild principle into the foreign sphere. Within a regulated company, members traded not in **partnership** but on their own individual accounts, subject to the rules of the company. Regulated companies sought corporate status not to facilitate joint trade but to obtain monopolistic privileges for their members over particular trades or regions.

Over time, however, the members of these regulated companies began to trade in partnership with a joint stock. Eventually, individual trading was prohibited in many companies, completing their transformation from trade protection associations to joint commercial enterprises, from 'regulated' to 'joint stock' companies. By the eighteenth century, the term 'company' had become shorthand for 'joint stock company', referring to a relatively impersonal business association based around a capital fund composed of more or less freely transferable **shares** owned by a relatively large and fluctuating body of shareholders. Joint stock companies were distinguished from 'ordinary' partnerships based around a small and specific group of people; in contemporary parlance, they were 'public' rather than 'ordinary' or 'private' partnerships.

Ideally, joint stock companies needed corporate status to give them a separate legal existence from their relatively large and fluctuating memberships, but for many years they did not find corporate privileges, which were available only from Parliament or the **Crown**, easy to obtain. This was in part because of their association with monopoly and with speculation (after the South Sea Bubble of 1720), and in part because of what was seen as their inherent inefficiency. Because of their separation of ownership from management, Adam Smith famously argued, joint stock companies were bound to be characterized by 'negligence and profusion', and were inherently inferior to individual enterprises and small partnerships. They should only be formed and granted corporate privileges in special circumstances: where they were necessary in the public interest because the capital required in a particular sector was beyond the reach of an 'ordinary' partnership (as with canals) and where their operations could be reduced to 'routines', minimizing the problems associated with non-owning managers. As a result, many joint stock companies in the eighteenth and early nineteenth centuries were forced to operate as *un*incorporated concerns in seeming contravention of the Bubble Act 1720. During this period, therefore, the term '(joint stock) company' conveyed nothing about a business association's legal status–incorporated or unincorporated–it merely connoted that it was a large partnership with certain economic characteristics which distinguished it from an ordinary, private partnership. Indeed, at this time all joint stock companies, incorporated and unincorporated, were thought in principle to be subject to the law of partnership, corporate status and privileges merely taking them outside the law of partnership in certain limited respects. One consequence of this was that companies were closely identified with their members and conceptualized as aggregations of people: a company was a 'they' rather than an 'it'. Under the Joint Stock Companies Act 1856, people 'formed themselves' into a company.

As the number and size of joint stock companies grew during the course of the nineteenth century, the **courts** and legislature gradually began to modify the principles of the law of partnership as they applied to joint stock companies, mainly in order to accommodate and protect the growing number of *rentier* shareholders. Central to this process were the Joint Stock Companies Acts of 1844–1862 which introduced free incorporation and general limited liability. Initially, the growing body of 'joint stock company law' which resulted from these changes was regarded as a mere branch of the law of partnership (Nathanial Lindley's seminal partnership text,

which first appeared in 1860, was entitled *Treatise on the Law of Partnership, including its application to Joint Stock Companies*) but by the end of the century this body of law had come to be recognized as a conceptually distinct legal category in its own right: 'company law', the body of law regulating joint stock companies. By now much larger, joint stock companies were less closely identified with their increasingly *rentier* shareholders and people came to be seen as 'forming companies', objects external to them. The company had become an 'it'. This reification of the company paved the way for the development of the doctrine of separate **corporate personality** in its modern form.

As (joint stock) company law emerged as a separate legal category, however, the meaning of the term 'company' changed once more. The Great Depression of the late nineteenth century prompted a growing number of firms of all kinds–one-man firms and small partnerships as well as joint stock companies—to incorporate under the Companies Acts to get the protection of limited liability. Many questioned the legality of these new 'private' (non joint-stock) companies, arguing that the Acts had been intended only for use by joint stock companies. For this reason, in the celebrated case of *Salomon v Salomon & Co Ltd* (1894–1897) both the Court of Chancery and the Court of Appeal held Salomon liable for the debts of his company. When the **House of Lords** overturned these decisions and pronounced Salomon's company legitimate, however, there was a flood of incorporations. By 1914, the great majority of significant business enterprises—one-man companies and 'ordinary' partnerships as well as joint stock companies—had become incorporated, limited liability companies. The term 'company' thus came to acquire its modern meaning as shorthand for 'incorporated, limited liability company'. Today, the term 'company' communicates nothing about the economic nature of a firm, unless the epithet 'public' or 'private' is attached, merely connoting an enterprise with a particular legal status. Indeed, in common parlance 'company' is now often used as a synonym for 'firm'.   PADDY IRELAND

See also: **private companies; public companies; unincorporated association**

company law, sources of   Company law is derived from a range of sources. These include statute, case law, and the company's constitution. The most important current statutes are the Companies Act 1985 and the Companies (Audit, Investigation and Community Enterprise) Act 2004. The Companies Act 2006 received Royal Assent in October 2006 and should be fully in force by Autumn 2008. The 2006 Act is the largest Act ever to make its way through Parliament, consisting of 1,300 provisions in 760 pages. It restates much of the existing law and reforms the law in certain key areas, particularly with respect to when shareholders can bring a legal action in the name of the **company**, but is particularly significant for its codification of the law relating to **directors' duties**, which was previously largely governed by case law. **Public companies** are subject to more extensive statutory regulation including the Financial Services and Markets Act 2000, the Listing Rules issued by the UK Listing Authority which apply only to companies listed on a stock exchange, and the Takeover Code.

Case law remains an important source of company law in two noteworthy respects. First, several areas of company law still rely exclusively on case law. Second, with respect to the newly codified area of **directors' duties**, the 2006 Act makes clear that it is not possible to understand the meaning of the new regime without reference to and reliance upon prior case law.

Many of the rules governing how the company acts, the rights attached to its **shares**, and who may act on its behalf are not found in the Companies Acts. English law gives considerable flexibility to the parties who form the company to operate it as they wish. These privately-agreed rules are set forth in the company's constitution (once the Companies Act 2006 comes into force these rules will be contained in the articles of association in relation to which the 2006 Act also sets out model articles).

DAVID KERSHAW

See also: **memorandum and articles of association**

comparative criminal justice policy It has regularly been noted that much criminology is strikingly uncomparative. Even when it attempts to look beyond a single jurisdiction, much English-language theorizing about criminal **justice** policy takes most of its assumptions from the nature of and developments in 'Anglo-American' legal culture. Cross-jurisdictional study in criminal justice is inherently difficult and much of the work in this area has had little to say about the actual process of comparative research. Work by Nelken is probably the main exception to this and he outlines three main ways of undertaking comparative work, summarizing them as 'virtually there', 'researching there', and 'living there' and advocates the latter wherever possible as providing the basis for the deepest understanding.

Although criminal justice research has been extraordinarily ethnocentric, it appears that one impact of globalization has been to begin to change this, with new comparative studies appearing with increasing regularity. Arguably the most influential thesis in this general area in the past decade—although its focus is more on similarity than difference—has been advanced by David Garland in *The Culture of Control* (2001). This new culture of control, visible in America and Britain, he argues, is characterized by two major strategies: the first is pragmatic and adaptive and the second is primarily expressive and seeks to denounce the crime and reassure the public. In seeking an explanation for the emergence of these strategies, an approach to crime control he identifies as occurring in both America and Britain, and most likely elsewhere, Garland argues that they were driven by the social, economic, and cultural characteristics of 'late modernity' on the one hand, and by the political realignments and policy initiatives that emerged in response to these social, economic, and cultural developments, on the other. The latter he describes as a combination of free market '**neo-liberalism**' and social conservatism.

A recent, and highly persuasive argument, and one which is compatible with Garland's though it places even greater emphasis on political economy in explaining trends in penal policy, has been outlined by Cavadino and Dignan (*Penal Systems*, 2006). In their comparative analysis, they identify four general models of political economy, which they relate to important differences in penal policy and practice. In brief, they argue that 'social democracies' such as Sweden and Finland tend to have the lowest rates of incarceration along with the one 'oriental corporatist' state—Japan—that they study. Although 'conservative corporatist' countries, such as Germany and The Netherlands, have somewhat higher incarceration rates, it is the 'neo-liberal' countries that are the heaviest users of imprisonment. By 'neo-liberal' they mean states that adopt free market economic policies, have high levels of income inequality, and have a pronounced tendency toward social exclusion. In this category they include America, South Africa, New Zealand, England and Wales, and Australia.

What authors such as these appear to argue is that recent trends in liberal democracies such as America, Britain, and elsewhere suggest that there is something of an elective affinity between neo-liberal economic and social policies and populist punitiveness in the penal sphere. Important elements in this elective affinity include: the spread and growing influence of **risk**-oriented, managerialist discourses and mentalities in the economic, social, and penal spheres; the gradual formalization of social control as informal means are eroded by the marketization of the economy and other areas of public life; and the need to develop systems to regulate and discipline those left marginalized and excluded by the residualization of welfare and the rise of the new economy.

Although such analyses are enormously persuasive, a degree of caution is necessary. While there is much that links the trajectories in the penal policies of the US, the UK, and other 'neoliberal' economies, it is also possible to identify a number of very substantial differences, not least in the scale and intensity of the changes taking place. Thus, there is a further body of work which focuses much more on the local, particular, and contingent nature of criminal justice policy development. In this vein, it is possible to identify striking differences in penal policy interventions between countries with different historical and cultural traditions. For scholars working in this field it is the fact that systems of *punishment* and control are embedded in local political cultures that helps explain the continued existence of often quite profound differences despite the apparently homogenizing effects of globalization. TIM NEWBURN

D Garland, *The Culture of Control* (Oxford: Oxford University Press, 2001)

D Nelken, 'Comparing Criminal Justice' in M Maguire, R Morgan, and R Reiner, (eds), *Oxford Handbook of Criminology* (Oxford: Oxford University Press, 4th edn, 2007)

comparative law Comparative law involves a process of drawing lessons from a confrontation of two or more legal systems. Comparison is a method which can serve a number of purposes. It can illuminate the researcher's understanding of their own legal system by highlighting features that are distinctive or those that are shared by many legal systems. It can be a way of approaching a new legal system, seeking to understand its distinctive features; and it is used as a method of law reform—examining how other systems tackle a problem within the home system.

There is considerable debate about how far this method can be used legitimately. At a basic level, not all societies separate out 'law' from other normative orders. For comparison to be meaningful, the systems need to be sufficiently similar in their differentiation of law from other social systems. A typical approach, the functionalist approach, identifies a problem—eg 'compensation for road accidents'—and then sees how the different legal systems handle it. This approach raises three issues. First, the formulation of the problem makes a number of assumptions about how society is organized. For example, it assumes that road accidents are identified as a distinct subset of 'personal injuries'. Secondly, the problem may not necessarily be handled by the law in both systems. For example, some solutions are provided by the practices of insurance companies rather than by legal regulation. Thirdly, the terminology used may not capture the way the problem is perceived in the system that is being compared to that of the researcher. Certainly, the problem cannot be formulated simply in the language familiar to the researcher's own system. Although there is no 'neutral' terminology, the comparison has to be undertaken with an awareness of the potential dangers of simple comparison.

What can be compared? Many authors, such as Zweigert and Kötz (K Zweigert and H Kötz, *An Introduction to Comparative Law* (Oxford: Oxford University Press, 3rd edn, 1998), ch 2) and Markesinis (B Markesinis, 'Unity or Division. The Search for Similarities in Contemporary European Law' (2001) *Current Legal Problems* 591) focus on comparing the outcomes for individuals that result from the different legal systems—eg how much does a wife receive on a divorce? But this is contested. Others would argue that way in which the law operates is as significant as the outcomes. Law has a major symbolic importance in many societies, and the concepts used to justify a result and the processes by which it is reached reveal much about the nature of the outcome. For example, a divorce reached after a full court hearing based on the fault of the parties is different from a divorce order made by an official on receipt of a joint letter from the spouses.

Since Montesquieu it has been argued that law is a manifestation of a particular culture, and that law cannot be understood without reference to its social and cultural context. Looking simply at specific legal rules or outcomes is deeply misleading. By contrast, others point to the way in which rules taken from one legal system are transplanted into other legal systems—eg China borrowing the German Civil Code and Turkey the Swiss Civil Code. They argue that the legal community has its own dynamic and can develop the law sometimes in advance of social and economic trends and sometimes lagging behind. These contrasting views show that there is no simple correlation between economic, social, and cultural development on the one hand and development of the law on the other. At the same time, these features cannot be ignored in any comparison.

In order to study another legal system, it is therefore necessary not just to focus on particular rules or outcomes. One needs to be aware of how these fit within the broader conceptual framework of the legal system. Each legal community has its own set of concepts and values within which it situates problems to be resolved. The foreign comparatist needs to learn this concept map and appreciate how the local lawyer sees the problem. The foreign comparatist also has to situate the problem within the matrix of legal and non-legal institutions and arrangements. These features require a significant element of immersion in the system as a whole, before trying to draw lessons from any specific comparison. This is particularly important when considering law reform, because it is important to understand why a specific solution works in its home system in order to evaluate whether it could work elsewhere.

In the interlocking systems of national and supranational laws, it is essential to be able to draw out common standards and approaches to be applied within many jurisdictions. But this must be undertaken critically and with sensitivity to the distinctive features of the individual legal and social systems studied.   JOHN BELL

M Reimann and R Zimmermann (eds), *The Oxford Handbook of Comparative Law* (Oxford: Oxford University Press, 2006), chs 9–13
W Van Gerven, 'Comparative Law in a Regionally Integrated Europe' in A Harding and E Örücü, *Comparative Law in the 21st Century* (London: Kluwer Law International, 2002), ch 9

comparator 'Discrimination' is regularly conceptualized as being concerned with comparisons. While some commentators point out that this can result in a situation whereby a disadvantaged **person** or group can continue to be denied the benefits enjoyed by the more fortunate unless and until they emulate the characteristics or behaviour of the advantaged, some comparison is inevitable even if only to demonstrate and challenge relative disadvantage. Demanding that in order to prove **sex** discrimination a woman must prove that she is exactly similar to a particular man in every factor except the bare difference of sex is a very narrow approach to sex discrimination. But even a generous approach which permits challenge to indirect as well as **direct discrimination** requires some kind of comparison.

Indirect discrimination occurs where people are treated the same regardless of sex (in a sex discrimination claim), **race** (in a race discrimination claim) or other **protected ground**, but where characteristics associated with membership of one sex or race, etc have the effect that persons of that sex or race are disadvantaged in practice by the treatment (a classic example is a requirement to work full-time with

which, typically, fewer women than men are able to comply). The very point of recognizing discrimination in its indirect form is to remove the requirement that men and women, or persons of different racial groups, sexual orientations, religions, etc be precisely similar in order to permit challenge to rules, practices, etc serving to perpetuate disadvantage associated with these grounds. Even in the case of indirect discrimination, however, comparators are necessary in order to demonstrate the relative effect that these rules or practices have on different groups. This can only be done by selecting groups of comparators (real or hypothetical) between which comparisons can be made.

Comparators are required in UK discrimination claims whether those claims arise under the **Equal Pay** Act 1970, the other discrimination legislative provisions, or **Article 14** of the **European Convention on Human Rights**. The various discrimination regimes differ, however, as regards the requirements which a comparator must fulfil in order to establish actionable discrimination. Under the Equal Pay Act 1970, for example, a woman (or man) can only challenge a pay differential which arises between her (or him) self and a person of the opposite sex who is engaged in comparable work for the same employer in the same or a similar establishment. No claim can succeed under that Act by reference to a hypothetical comparator (this would be the case where a woman wished to complain that she would have been paid more had she been a man, but there is no man actually engaged in comparable work and paid more).

By contrast, all the other discrimination **legislation** in the UK allows claims by reference to real or hypothetical comparators. So, for example, a Muslim who wishes to challenge a refusal to allow him, as a Muslim, access to accommodation would not have to show that an actual non-Muslim had been treated differently. It is sufficient for him to say that a non-Muslim *would have been* treated differently had he sought access to the accommodation. Comparison is at the heart of the discrimination question, but the existence of an actual non-Muslim who has been treated more favourable than the claimant is relevant only to *proof* of discrimination; among the best evidence which the claimant could put forward would be that an otherwise very similar non-Muslim had been granted access to the accommodation. Equally, however, if the person who refused the claimant accommodation was witnessed stating that the refusal was because of the claimant's religion, or if he or she displayed a 'no Muslims here' sign, the existence or not of an *actual* comparator would be unnecessary for evidential purposes.

Comparators frequently give rise to difficulties in practice because **courts** regularly lose sight of their purpose, which is essentially to demonstrate less favourable treatment (or, in indirect discrimination cases, less favourable outcomes) related to a protected ground. In Article 14 cases, in particular, the courts have blocked claims on the basis that, irrespective of the claimant's ability to establish that s/he has been subjected to less favourable treatment than another, and that the treatment has been by reason of a protected ground, *nevertheless* the differences between claimant and comparator are such that no comparison can be made between them (*R (Carson) v Secretary of State for Work and Pensions* (2006); *R (Al Rawi and Ors) v Secretary of State for Foreign and Commonwealth Affairs & Anor* (2006)). This is wrong in principle. While the existence of such differences may lead a court to the conclusion that the disputed difference in treatment was not the protected ground, they are irrelevant to a discrimination claim where it has been established in fact that the treatment complained of is on the protected ground. Thus, for example, if a council denied planning permission to an Asian applicant who wished to extend his house, and did so *because* he was Asian (and, for example, this caused the decision-makers to assume that the extension would be used to house extended family members currently resident abroad, in circumstances in which it wanted to preserve the ethnic 'balance' of a council ward), it would be no answer to a race discrimination claim that the council could have dismissed the application on other grounds. The existence of differences other than that of race between the unsuccessful applicant and a neighbour granted planning permission for a similar extension will make his race discrimination allegation more difficult to *prove*, but if race was *in fact* the reason for the impugned decision these differences are irrelevant to the question whether the comparator is an appropriate one even in a case in which the comparator requirement is legislatively imposed.

AILEEN MCCOLGAN

compellable witnesses   *see* evidence (criminal)

compensation   In English law, as with many other legal systems, the idea that compensation should be required under some circumstances for harm or loss caused by one party to another is central. What is more variable are the circumstances under which such compensation should be required and the assessment of the level of compensation that is appropriate.

Before considering compensation itself it is important that the concept be distinguished from that of **restitution** for, as will be shown, the distinction has substantial implications. Restitution is intimately connected with restoration, the act of restoring that which was lost. It involves replacing what has been lost or taken, with something that is either the thing itself or something identical or indistinguishable. After restitution the party receiving it should be in the exact position she would have been in had the act leading to the need for restitution or restoration not occurred.

By contrast, unless compensation is simply money paid for money lost, the idea of compensation always implies that what is lost is replaced with something not identical to the loss. Most often it will be money that is intended to make up for what has been lost. This of course requires an assessment of the amount of money required to make good the loss at the required level (whatever that level might be). While the assessment process is usually asserted to be an objective one, the sheer impossibility of accurately valuing in money terms losses which may be to **person** or property contradicts such an assertion. If restitution concerns replacing like with like, at best compensation provides a subjectively determined approximation of the value of thing or person affected or lost.

To exemplify this point it is necessary only to consider compensation (money damages) payable in **tort law** for personal injury. Theoretically the level of compensation to be paid is full compensation—that is, as nearly as possible the tort **victim** should be returned to the state she would have been in but for the tort. While there are well established tables suggesting the value to be placed upon the loss of almost every part of the body which might be injured or destroyed (the value modified by any special considerations), the fact is that it is not possible to replace flesh with money (a point well understood by Shakespeare's Shylock). But while an approximation is attempted, there are other losses where money compensation makes little sense, and indeed somewhere, in the words of Adam Bede, 'There's a sort o' damage, sir, that can't be made up for' (G Eliot, *Adam Bede*, ch 48).

The problem is well described by Staughton LJ when he said in *Lancashire County Council v Municipal Mutual Insurance Ltd* (1996) that:

The word "compensation" when used by lawyers, in connection with the recovery of damages from a wrongdoer, usually means a sum of money designed to repair or make good the loss that the victim suffered. Of course there is always the proviso: so far as money can do that. Where the wrong is loss of reputation, or **pain and suffering** and loss of amenity, it cannot in reality be repaired or made good by money. But the law has the fiction that it can.

The 'fiction' in fact extends beyond the proviso. The usual principle of compensation is that of 'full compensation', meaning that the person given a right to compensation should have her losses made good. While this may be possible in calculating the value of the loss of a bargain in **contract law**, or the value of land upon **compulsory purchase**, in fact so extensive are the limitations upon losses deserving of compensation in other areas of law such as tort that the centrality of 'full compensation' must be doubted. In the tort of negligence even if some losses are directly caused by the person committing the tort they will be irrecoverable if they are deemed to be 'too remote', otherwise defined as 'unforeseeable'. The effect of this ruling in *Overseas Tankship (UK) Ltd v The Miller Steamship Co Pty Ltd The Wagon Mound (No 2)* (1967) means that many innocent victims in the tort of negligence will suffer uncompensated loss which will lie where it falls simply because a **court** would hold that the particular damage could not reasonably have been foreseen by the negligent actor at the time of her negligence. From the point of view of the person committing the tort, this no doubt seems reasonable and just, but the innocent victim is certainly not receiving 'full compensation'. Indeed the effect is that not only will some victims receive less than full compensation for the harm they have been caused but some entirely innocent victims will receive no compensation at all if their particular loss is held to be unforeseeable. Further, compensation of any kind will be irrecoverable if the victim is merely one of a class of those suffering loss from negligence that amounts to public nuisance.

But if the concept of full compensation is a fiction, so too is the very justification for compensation in the tort of negligence. This is said to rest upon the moral principle that it is right that a party carelessly causing loss to another should be obliged to compensate that other. In other words it is thought right that the loss should be shifted from the innocent victim to the wrongdoer. Theoretically this is not unattractive but in fact of course this is almost never the outcome. It is seldom worth suing the actual person who has caused the tort and almost all actions will actually be concerned with compensation from an insurance company, or else against a defendant who may be held to be vicariously liable for the harm caused (as for example when an employer is held vicariously liable for the tortious acts of an employee). This contradiction means that far from the burden

of compensation falling upon the careless actor, it falls in fact upon the shoulders of all those insurance policyholders who have elected to spread the **risk** of committing a negligent act but are not in fact themselves negligent. The loss is thus, in reality, not shifted but redistributed. Much the same holds true with **vicarious liability** where almost all employers will be insured against losses caused by negligent employees.

One further feature of compensation in tort aggravates the problems with the justification of tort compensation. It arises from the principle of 'joint and several liability'. Under this doctrine, where more than one party has some **responsibility** for the negligent act, each of those parties will be liable for the full compensation payable. The advantage of this principle is that a victim need only bring an action against one defendant, leaving that defendant to seek a share of the compensation she must pay from the other joint tortfeasors. The doctrinal disadvantage is that often a joint tortfeasor whose part in the negligence was small, will be called upon to pay for all of the damage—and often without hope of recovery from others who may be poor, uninsured, bankrupt, or liquidated. A not untypical factual example of this is to be found in *Anns v Merton London Borough Council* (1978).

Not surprisingly, dissatisfaction with negligence as a means of compensating accident victims has been widely expressed and the facts of the matter most clearly exposed in the many editions of Patrick Atiyah's *Accidents Compensation and the Law*. In New Zealand a decision was taken to provide compensation to accident victims irrespective of cause and the focus of compensation calculation was to be based upon the needs of the victims rather than the cause of the harm. While the level of compensation is lower than would result from a successful English tort action there is arguably a more equitable distribution of the resources available for accident compensation. Such a scheme as that in New Zealand requires what is in essence compulsory and universal insurance of all. Recognizing that such government 'interference' was probably incompatible with the current English political climate, Patrick Atiyah argued for a move to encouraging individuals to take out comprehensive first party insurance.

One final point should be remembered. Because compensation is almost always a money payment arising from insurance, in reality it protects the wrongdoer and the social world she inhabits from having to face any of the non-financial results of the harmful act. Money is all that is required, regardless of the social or physical **disability** that may result for the victim. Law may place a price on loss of amenity but it does little to redress the true harm that has been caused. Perhaps it reflects the view of the English Metaphysical poet, Francis Quarles (1592–1644), who observed of compensation: 'As there is no worldly gain without some loss, so is there no worldly loss without some gain. If thou hast lost thy wealth, thou hast lost some trouble with it. If thou art degraded from thy honour, thou art likewise freed from the stroke of envy. If sickness hast blurred thy beauty, it hath delivered thee from pride. Set the allowance against the loss and thou shalt find no great loss'!

WADE MANSELL

J Conaghan and W Mansell, *The Wrongs of Tort* (London: Pluto Press, 2nd edn, 1999)

P Atiyah, *The Damages Lottery* (Oxford: Hart Publishing, 1997)

See also: **joint liability**

compensation culture 'Compensation culture' is the shorthand label commonly used to describe a cluster of perceived social phenomena, particularly the perceived increase in the number of claims for compensation being made in contexts where 'victims' might previously have been expected to have remained stoical or to have accepted that they were themselves responsible for their injuries or losses. The development of 'compensation culture' is commonly blamed in public discourse for a catalogue of social ills, such as a reduction in the willingness of schoolteachers to supervise extra-curricular activities and trips, additional time spent by businesses and other entities on risk assessment and risk management, and increases in the cost of liability insurance. In a speech in May 2005, the then Prime Minister, Tony Blair, set out plans for leading the United Kingdom away from 'the compensation culture' back to 'a common sense culture', and illustrated his theme with examples involving the unnecessary removal of 'unsafe' playground equipment and over-cautious instructions given to employees to reduce the risk of injuring themselves.

One of the most difficult issues surrounding 'compensation culture' is whether the social phenomena for which it provides a label are real or merely imaginary. There is very little evidence of an expansion in the number of claims for compensation in England and Wales during the period when 'compensation culture' supposedly took hold. Moreover, it seems that many of the examples of 'compensation culture' invoked in public debate are either wholly fictional events or involve gross simplification or exaggeration. However, although there is very little evidence

of an increasing number of claims there is stronger evidence of an increase in the amount of precautionary behaviour being taken in the attempt to avoid claims, and, relatedly, an increase in the *perceived* threat of being sued.

Because of the wide the range of phenomena associated with 'compensation culture' and the difficulty of determining to what extent these phenomena are real, it is difficult to give an exhaustive answer to the question of who is responsible for the development. Many of those who regard the phenomena as real blame the legal profession and, in particular, the adjunct businesses that marshal small claims (sometimes, derogatorily, referred to as 'claims farmers'). Others, however, point to those bodies which draft precautionary regulations and guidance, and those officials and private professionals who assist with their interpretation and application. By contrast, many of those who regard the phenomena as illusory might identify the media as responsible for changing public perceptions by peddling misleading anecdotes and unsupported opinions about imaginary 'trends'. Others suggest that insurance companies have played a role in establishing the myth in order to explain away rising premium costs. Those more prone to cynicism might also point to the political advantages that businesses can gain in disputes about regulation by invoking concerns about 'promoting' compensation culture.

RODERICK BAGSHAW

See also: **claims management companies**

compensation neurosis Compensation neurosis was once defined as 'a state of mind, born out of fear, kept alive by avarice, stimulated by lawyers, and cured by a verdict'. Such a definition while clearly facetious does reflect the considerable cynicism felt by many (especially lawyers) towards a defined medical condition. Nevertheless it is indisputable that the prospect of receiving **compensation** for personal injury can and does affect the mental state of some victims. Such effects can lead to the unconscious exaggeration of the symptoms of the injury, or to the prolongation of the symptoms, the disappearance of which could reduce the compensation to be received. As in the case of other psychosomatic conditions, the genuineness of the symptoms is difficult either to prove or disprove; but it is clear that there is a factual distinction between what might be better termed 'malingering', involving conscious and voluntary production of symptoms aimed at achieving a recognizable goal or at least enhanced compensation, and compensation neurosis.

The concept of compensation neurosis was originally formulated when a study in the 1960s seemed to show clearly that men seeking compensation for head injuries had more prolonged complaints than did men, with at least equally severe but comparable injuries, who were not anticipating compensation. Although the motivation may seem obvious those in the former group were apparently unaware of any compensation-driven effect on their suffering. A further result of the study was that upon settlement of the compensation claim the aggravated symptoms usually disappeared (although this finding has been disputed in subsequent studies).

Perhaps feeding into legal scepticism of medical definitions of compensation neurosis, at least one neuro-psychologist has suggested that the above apparently clear distinction (between malingering and compensation neurosis) is actually specious. The claim is that simulation of symptoms for whatever reason, deserves 'mental health attention, understanding, analysis, and treatment' because, it is argued, simulation of symptoms is never purely for compensation but really 'to solve complex psychological and interpersonal issues'—a perspective unlikely to find favour with defence counsel.

Leaving such extreme views aside, it is hardly surprising that the indeterminate amount of unliquidated **damages** payable to a victim suffering bodily injury, which it is claimed arose from a tortious act, creates genuine stress. Further, while the process of claim and calculation continues, whether consciously or not, the plaintiff has some incentive not to minimize the harm that has been done.

It should be stressed in conclusion that there are no objective criteria for distinguishing genuine stress disorders associated with traumatic events from symptoms that contain a purposive conscious element directed to compensation enhancement. There may well be disagreement both between legal experts and medical experts. Ironically, such expert disagreement may in itself aggravate the stress disorder.   WADE MANSELL

G Hutchinson, *Disorders of Simulation: Malingering, Factitious Disorders, and Compensation Neurosis* (Madison, CT: Psychosocial Press, 2001)

Compensation Recovery Unit   *see* **compensation**

competition   Competition is the bedrock of the market economy, an economic system in which the allocation of resources is determined solely by supply and demand in free markets. States which adopt the model of the free market economy do so because, on the basis of neo-liberal economic theory, they consider it to be the form of economic organization which brings the greatest benefits to society. The basis of a free market is competition between firms because such competition is believed to deliver efficiency, low prices, choice, and innovation. This is said to maximize '**consumer welfare**'.

Traditional theory of the economics of competition contrasts the model of a market where there is 'perfect competition' with one where there is a monopoly producer. A perfectly competitive market is one in which there are a large number of buyers and sellers (so that firms with very small market shares can operate at minimal cost because the minimum efficient scale is small in comparison to the size of the market), the product is homogeneous, all the buyers and sellers have perfect information (they know of every change in price or demand and so respond immediately to such changes), and there are no barriers to entry or exit. Sellers can come into, and leave, the market freely. Each seller is insignificant in relation to the market as a whole and has no influence on the product's price. This results in allocative and productive efficiency (goods are produced in the quantities valued by society and at the lowest possible cost), which produces consumer welfare.

At the opposite end of the spectrum from the competitive market is the monopoly, a market in which there is only one seller. Economic theory predicts that as the firm is not constrained by any competitors it will set its price as high as it possibly can by restricting output, leading to a loss in efficiency. Many monopolies are created and maintained by government **regulation** (statutory monopolies); and others are 'natural', which means that the minimum efficient scale of production is so large that there is room for only one firm to operate efficiently in the market.

Recently, great importance has been accorded to 'dynamic efficiency' in maximizing consumer welfare and it is recognized that in some markets (those in the 'new economy' of high technology markets) competition may focus on innovation rather than price. In such markets competition may not be *in* markets but *for* markets, as markets may 'tip' towards one firm whose products become the standard, rendering the firm dominant, and competition will be aimed at replacing that firm. In reality, perfectly competitive markets are very rare indeed and many markets are oligopolistic—that is, they are highly concentrated, consisting of a number of big players but no singly dominant firm. The central concept in modern theories of competition is that of 'market power', which broadly means the power of a firm to raise prices above the competitive level and keep them there for a significant period of time. It is generally recognized that the maintenance of a competitive market economy requires a system of **competition law**.   BRENDA SUFRIN

DW Carlton and JM Perloff, *Modern Industrial Organization* (Boston: Pearson Addison Wesley, 4th edn, 2005)
S Bishop and M Walker, *The Economics of EC Competition Law: Concepts, Application and Measurement* (London: Sweet & Maxwell, 2nd edn, 2002)

See also: **natural monopoly**

Competition Appeal Tribunal ('CAT')   The Competition Appeal Tribunal ('CAT') was created by the Enterprise Act 2002. It consists of a president and members appointed to form a panel of chairmen (judges of the Chancery Division of the High Court or similarly qualified senior lawyers, appointed by the **Lord Chancellor**) and members appointed (by the Secretary of State) to form a panel of ordinary members. Cases are heard by three members: the president or a member of the panel of chairmen and two ordinary members. The CAT sits as a tribunal in England and Wales, in Scotland, or in Northern Ireland, the choice of forum depending upon the centre of gravity of the parties and matters before it.

The function of the CAT is essentially that of **judicial review**, primarily of decisions taken by the **Office of Fair Trading** ('OFT') or an industry regulator under the Competition Act 1998; and decisions made by the OFT, the **Competition Commission** and the Secretary of State in respect of various references under the Enterprise Act 2002. It also hears actions for damages brought by parties injured by the conduct of other undertakings, which conduct is prohibited by UK or EC **competition law**s. It has wide powers, and may dismiss an application or set aside a decision in whole or in part; refer the matter back with a direction to reconsider and decide anew; and impose penalties and revoke or vary the amount of any penalty. Appeal on penalties imposed or damages awarded, or on a point of law, lies to the Court of Appeal or, in Scotland, the **Court of Session**.
                                        ROBERT LANE

See also: **competition**

Competition Commission   The Competition Commission is a body corporate established by the Competition Act 1998, replacing the Monopolies and Mergers Commission. It consists of members appointed by the Secretary of State to form panels to discharge the functions assigned to it by, primarily, the Enterprise Act 2002. There are at any given time around fifty panel members, with specialist panels for utilities, telecommunications, water, and newspaper matters. Except for the Chairman, they are part-time posts.

The Commission responds to references made to it by the **Office of Fair Trading** ('OFT'), an industry regulator or, exceptionally, the Secretary of State, where the referring authority takes the view that (a) a completed or anticipated merger has resulted, or may be expected to result, in a substantial lessening of **competition** within a UK market for goods or services (a 'merger investigation'); or (b) the features of a particular market in the UK for goods or services are such that there is an adverse effect upon competition (a 'market investigation'). There are special rules for media and water mergers. The tests are purely competition-based, unlike their predecessor, which was based on the much more malleable formula 'against the public interest'. A group, usually of four or five panel members, investigates and reports upon the matter referred as it sees fit. It may compel production of documents and witnesses to attend and give evidence. It determines whether there is a substantial lessening of or adverse effect upon competition (as the case may be); and if so what, if any, action should be taken to remedy, mitigate or prevent it. It may accept undertakings from the parties about their future conduct or make appropriate orders.
                                        ROBERT LANE

competition law   Competition law (in American terminology 'antitrust') is concerned with ensuring that firms operating in the free market economy do not act in a way that harms competition so preventing the market operating to its optimal effect. Competition laws normally deal with restrictive agreements between independent firms; the unilateral conduct of firms that have a monopoly or a substantial degree of 'market power'; the behaviour of oligopolies; and the control of mergers. **European Union** competition law also deals with state aids, where Member States intervene in the market by giving favourable treatment to particular firms or business sectors.

There is much controversy about the objectives which competition law should aim to achieve because it is possible for systems of competition law to be used to pursue objectives other than the economic ones of welfare and efficiency. For example, the aim may be to protect competitors rather than the competitive process itself because of the importance attached to the dispersal of economic power and the notion of economic freedom. Competition law may also be used as a tool to advance sociopolitical policies in fields such as employment and the environment. The prevailing consensus amongst competition authorities in the UK and the EU at present is that the objective of competition law is to promote **consumer welfare** by securing low prices, high quality, choice, and innovation. EU competition law has, historically at least, been used a major instrument in integrating the **single market**. There are now nearly 100 states with systems of competition law.

BRENDA SUFRIN

R Whish, *Competition Law* (Oxford: Oxford University Press, 6th edn, 2008)
A Jones and B Sufrin, *EC Competition Law* (Oxford: Oxford University Press, 3rd edn, 2007)

See also: **merger control; state aid (in EC law)**

competition: restriction, prevention and distortion of

Article 81 EC and the Chapter I Prohibition in the Competition Act 1998 provide mechanisms whereby agreements (or other forms of multilateral activity) entered into by undertakings are subject to the strictures of **competition law**. These provisions apply only to situations in which the agreement in question may be expected to, or does, 'prevent, restrict or distort competition'. Where an agreement is found to prevent, restrict or distort **competition** (and meets the other relevant criteria for condemnation) it will only survive legal scrutiny if it satisfies the exception criteria set out in Article 81(3) EC or s 9 of the Competition Act 1998.

The clarification of the meaning of the phrase, 'prevent, restrict or distort competition' is therefore central to the operation of this part of competition law, and as such forms a substantial part of the analysis carried out in decisions and case law. In essence, any agreement between undertakings may be argued in some way to prevent, restrict, or distort competition. In practice, such an approach would be untenable, and it has been necessary to draw boundaries between conduct which is clearly detrimental to competition, conduct which may harm competition but which also produces benefits, and conduct which, while being *restrictive*, cannot be argued to harm competition in any meaningful sense of the word. This process has been to some extent influenced by US practice in relation to its antitrust law. In particular, certain agreements may be considered to be *per se* illegal by virtue of the fact that by their very nature they are more than likely to have a harmful affect on competition. Such would be the case, for example, in relation to a horizontal price fixing **cartel**. Other agreements (eg an agreement relating to research and development) are more likely to be considered as lawful unless they contain certain restrictive

terms. Substantial guidance as to the approach to be taken may be found in relevant guidelines published by the **European Commission** and, in the UK, by the **Office of Fair Trading** ('OFT'). In its *Guidelines on the applicability of Article 81 of the EC Treaty to horizontal cooperation agreements* (2001) the EC Commission recognizes explicitly that some agreements may 'lead to competition problems' while others 'can lead to substantial economic benefits'.

In the leading case of *Gottrup-Klim v Dansk Landbrugs Grovverselskab* (1994) the **European Court of Justice** held that it would be wrong to consider the terms of agreements in the abstract in determining the legality of the agreement, and that regard had to be paid to the content of the agreement, and to the relevant economic conditions in the relevant market. In this case there existed an agreement relating to the functioning of a cooperative association, which in part excluded members from joining other such associations. Whilst this clearly imposed a restriction on the competitive activity of the members, without such a term the association might not have been viable, and its overall effect was considered to be pro-competitive.

The point was made more generally in *European Night Services v Commission* (1998). Here the European Commission had condemned an agreement between several operators in the passenger rail industry, and on appeal its decision was roundly attacked by the European Court of First Instance ('CFI'). The CFI held that in assessing any agreement, full account must be taken of the way in which it operated, and the economic conditions in which it operated. The analysis must, the Court held, be based 'not only on existing competition . . . but also on potential competition'. In this case the Court held that, were the relevant joint venture to function at all, there was no alternative to the restrictive terms of the arrangements made between the parties, and that no other such joint venture could in fact function. In other words, although the agreement contained restrictions within it, there was no other way to achieve a pro-competitive outcome, as a result of which the agreement could not reasonably be said to 'prevent, restrict or distort competition'. The CFI here drew a clear distinction between agreements 'containing obvious restrictions of competition such as price-fixing, market sharing or the control of outlets', which would be presumed to fall within the prohibition of Article 81(1) (and by extension, the Chapter I Prohibition), and other agreements which must be subject to the more sensitive analysis demanded by the court.

Elsewhere in EC competition law the Commission and the courts have taken a restrictive approach to the meaning of 'prevent, restrict or distort competition'. This is most noticeable in the treatment accorded to vertical agreements, which is stricter than that applied, for example, in the US. In the leading case of *Consten and Grundig v Commission* (1966) the ECJ found that a distribution agreement between a German manufacturer of electrical goods and a French distributor infringed Article 81(1) EC. It may be argued with some conviction that the agreement was, as a whole, pro-competitive. It contained within it restrictions which prevented others from distributing Grundig's goods into the territory assigned to Consten, but in doing so gave the latter the incentive to take the economic risk entailed in trying to develop the German brand in France. In making its determination the ECJ was heavily influenced by an overriding objective—as then understood—of creating a common market, within which territorial restrictions were to be condemned.

MARK FURSE

complaints procedures Complaints procedures allow customers who feel that service providers have failed to achieve satisfactory standards to approach them with details of their shortcomings. In general, such procedures or policies are provided to dissuade individuals from taking further action, possibly of a legal nature; and most seek to resolve disputes as early in the life of a complaint as possible, with a minimum of formality and resources. Often, an organization will publicise its complaints procedure as evidence of a commitment to provide good quality services, and as an opportunity for complaining customers to receive an apology, or other acceptable response to their concerns. It is usual for service providers to require dissatisfied users to negotiate a number of informal stages before their complaints are dealt with. This may enable angry complainants to regain their composure and complain more competently. However, the protracted time scales that characterize many complaints management schemes may have the effect of encouraging the abandonment of more complex complaints.

National Health Service (NHS) Complaints Procedure

There is now a standard complaints procedure which is used throughout the NHS in order to pursue rectification for perceived shortcomings of NHS treatment and services, other than through the courts. It is now accepted that, in some cases, a patient may not be looking to receive financial compensation, but would prefer an apology, or an explanation of why something went wrong, along with the assurance that improvements will follow. In other cases, making use of the complaints procedure is a precursor to the commencement of legal proceedings.

Anyone who is receiving, or has received, NHS treatment or services from, for example, a hospital, general practitioner, dentist, or optician, can complain using the standard complaints procedure. If patients are unable to complain themselves, someone else, such as a relative or close friend can complain for them. The time limit for complaints is normally six months, but primary care practitioners and complaints managers in NHS organizations have discretion to waive this time limit if there are good reasons why a patient or advocate was unable to complain earlier.

The first step in the complaints procedure is to contact the organization the patient is unhappy about in order to try to resolve the complaint effectively at a local level. This informal approach to complaints handling reflects the view that complaints are the responsibility of all those involved in patient care. At this juncture, patients are informed that they may wish to access the services of the Independent Complaints Advocacy Service ('ICAS'). Section 12 of the Health and Social Care Act 2001 places a duty on the Secretary of State for Health to make arrangements to provide independent advocacy services to assist individuals making complaints against the NHS. As a result, ICAS was launched in 2003 to support patients and members of the public wishing to make a complaint about their NHS care or treatment.

ICAS aims to ensure that complainants have access to the level of support they need to identify key issues and manage their own complaints, thereby maximizing the chances of avoiding misunderstandings and resolving complaints quickly and capably. It is a patient-centred service, delivering support ranging from provision of self-help information to the assignment of a dedicated, specialized advocate able to assist individuals with more complex needs. Statistics from ICAS are shared with various bodies involved in improving patients' experience, such as the Patients Forum, and others whose function is to influence decision-makers for the benefit of NHS users. In this way ICAS provides an additional layer of information which can help alert the NHS to potential problem areas, also ensuring that lessons from users' experiences of the NHS are fed back into the service. In addition, twice a year, ICAS generates a Complaints Outcome

Register for each NHS Trust giving details about Trusts' commitments to change, made as a result of patients' use of the NHS complaints procedure.

If this attempt at local, less formal, resolution is unsuccessful, a dissatisfied complainant can approach the Healthcare Commission to request an independent review of their case. When a complaint is received by the Healthcare Commission, an initial review is carried out to determine whether or not it is possible, or appropriate, for the complaint to be scrutinized further. The Commission may then recommend additional exploration under local resolution, or inform the complainant that it believes the complaint to have been investigated sufficiently, or agree to set up an Independent Review Panel to consider the complaint anew. If an Independent Review is denied, that decision may be referred to the Health Service Ombudsman, who will look at the process of consideration of the request for a Review, but not the merits of the complaint. Where an Independent Review Panel is convened, it must produce its final report and send it to the complainant within one month of the hearing. The report will include statements of fact and the Panel's comments and recommendations for future action. Ultimately, if complainants remain unhappy with the outcome of the Independent Review, they can go on to complain to the Health Service Ombudsman.

Police complaints procedures

Another area in which a complaints procedure has become standardized is where members of the public wish to register complaints regarding unsatisfactory treatment by the police. Complaints about police behaviour and conduct are dealt with in a variety of ways. A complaint can be submitted: directly to any police station; via a Citizens Advice Bureau, Racial Equality Council, Neighbourhood Warden, Youth Offending Team or Probation Service, a solicitor, or Member of Parliament; in writing to the Chief Constable of the force concerned; or directly to the relevant independent watchdog, the Independent Police Complaints Commission ('IPCC'). The IPCC formally began operations on 1 April 2004, replacing the Police Complaints Authority as the guardian of the complaints procedure about police behaviour. The legal framework for the investigation of complaints arises from the Police Reform Act 2002, which includes measures to ensure that complaints against the police are properly handled, and that complainants have a right of appeal under certain circumstances, such as if the police refuse to record their complaint, if they are unhappy with the process of Local Resolution to

which they agreed for their complaint, or if they are unhappy with the outcome of the investigation into their complaint.

An individual can make a complaint to the IPCC if he or she has been the victim of misconduct by a person serving with a police force. An example of misconduct might include: a police officer or member of police staff being rude, or using excessive force. It could also include unlawful arrest or an abuse of a person's rights. Others may complain if they were present when the alleged misconduct took place, or were close enough to see or hear the misconduct, and as a result suffered loss, damage, distress, or inconvenience, or were put at risk of danger. A member of the public may also complain, with written consent, on behalf of another.

Ombudsman schemes

Ombudsman schemes are set up as 'last chance' complaints procedures allowing for independent, impartial officials to provide a free complaints handling service to those who wish to take a complaint further, when it has not been resolved internally by the organization complained against. There is a wide range of Ombudsman schemes in the United Kingdom, with different methods of operation, which have been designed to meet the needs of specific client groups. Some are concerned with state-owned organizations, while others deal with the private sector. Some are statutory, and some non-statutory; some schemes have compulsory membership, whilst others are voluntary. All are designed to be easily accessible to unassisted complainants. In this way, ombudsman schemes offer advantages over legal action, which would provide an alternative course of action in some cases.

Ombudsmen investigate complaints of maladministration; examples might include unreasonable delay, rudeness, failure to follow proper procedures, bias, knowingly giving advice which is misleading or inadequate, and refusing to answer reasonable questions. For instance, the Estate Agents Ombudsman Scheme covers most of the large chains owned by banks, building societies, and insurance companies, and offices under the management of members of the National Association of Estate Agents, and the Royal Institution of Chartered Surveyors. The ombudsman in this area deals with complaints from private individuals as actual or potential buyers or sellers of residential property in the United Kingdom, made within twelve months of the event.

When a complaint is found to be justified, the ombudsman can usually recommend redress by way of compensation, if this is appropriate. A key feature of ombudsman schemes as a method of complaint handling is that ombudsmen can take account of what is fair and reasonable in all the circumstances. Thus, their recommendations are not bound by a strict analysis of the law, or by precedent.

CHERYL DOLDER

See also: **ombudsmen**

complaints: internet information   Internet usage is increasingly prevalent. The volume of internet information explaining people's rights and dispute resolution processes is also expanding. It is no surprise, therefore, that a growing number of people are turning to the internet to obtain information about legal rights and process.

The growth has been substantial over the last few years. The 2001 English and Welsh Civil and Social Justice Survey indicated that around 5 per cent of people facing problems involving rights sought information from the internet. By 2004 the figure was 10 per cent. By 2006 it was closer to 15 per cent.

This is mirrored by a substantial growth in the number of users of websites providing information about people's rights and dispute-resolution processes. Dedicated not-for-profit rights information websites, such as *adviceguide.org.uk*, run by **Citizens Advice Bureaux**, *CLSdirect.org.uk*, run by the **Legal Services Commission**, and *advicenow.org.uk* and *ADRnow.org.uk*, run by the **Advice Services Alliance**, now assist many millions of people each year. Each continues to extend its reach. For example, between 2004/5 and 2005/6, *adviceguide.org.uk* saw an 83 per cent increase in users, from 2.4 to 4.3 million. *Adviceguide.co.uk* and *CLSdirect.org.uk* both offer wide-ranging information in multiple languages and provide adviser directories. *Advicenow.org.uk* acts primarily as a gateway to information produced by Advice Services Alliance members, government bodies, and specialist organizations, including solicitors' firms. *ADRnow.org.uk* sets out details of the broad set of options for the resolution of disputes and complaints outside of formal legal process.

A number of commercial websites also supply free general legal information, along with various forms of charged online legal advice. Some are operated by solicitors' firms, others simply represent independent commercial ventures. Broader based information websites, such as *direct.gov.uk* and *bbc.co.uk* also present extensive information on rights and processes.

Reflecting the many types of rights-based dispute that can arise, a multitude of websites provide more narrowly based information on rights and processes. Some are dedicated rights-information services, such as *consumerdirect.gov.uk* and *tradingstandards.gov.uk*. Some are operated by consumer representative bodies, such as *energywatch. org.uk* and *passengerfocus.org.uk* (rail travel). Some are operated by national charities, such as *shelter.org.uk*, *ageconcern.org.uk* and *which.co.uk*. Others are operated by **regulatory agencies**, such as *ofcom.org.uk* and *ofwat.gov.uk*. Yet others are operated by **ombudsmen,** such as *ombudsman. org.uk* (central government and the NHS in England) and *ni-ombudsman.org.uk* (public bodies in Northern Ireland). A small number, such as *ippc. gov.uk* (police complaints) are operated by independent complaints commissions. Government departments and other public bodies also provide a considerable amount of information on their responsibilities and dispute resolution processes on their websites.

For complaints about legal services, the websites of the regulatory bodies of the legal professions all set out details of how to proceed, as do the websites of the Legal Services Ombudsmen in England and Wales, and Scotland.

Finally, dispute resolution services (such as **ACAS**), along with courts and tribunals services around the United Kingdom, provide information on how to utilize their processes on their websites. Some even allow claims to be originated online (see, for example, **Money Claims On Line**).

PASCOE PLEASENCE

comprehensive income tax   *see* **income tax**

compromise   *see* **international dispute settlement**

Comptroller and Auditor-General   *see* **Auditor-General**

compulsory purchase   From time–to-time land is required for public purposes. It may be required, for example, for a major road, for urban regeneration, or for the provision of a new school. Such land is often acquired through the normal operation of the market. However, to avoid public purposes being frustrated by the resistance of a landowner, powers are commonly conferred on public authorities and others to acquire land compulsorily.

The origins of the power to acquire land compulsorily probably lie in the sovereignty of the state. Today, however, the power is vested in Parliament and in the devolved administrations, although case law indicates that there remains with the **Crown** a

prerogative power to take and destroy a subject's property in time of war. Parliament and the devolved administrations, in turn, confer conditional powers of compulsory purchase through legislation for specified purposes on various government agencies and on others. The compulsory acquisition of land will not infringe the **European Convention on Human Rights** provided the acquisition can be shown to be in the public interest and a proportionate measure in the circumstances.

In the nineteenth century, compulsory purchase powers to support the construction of railways, canals, harbours, and so on were mainly conferred for specific projects through private bills. While private legislation is still a means of securing compulsory powers, the growth of municipal government in the twentieth century resulted in the conferring of general powers on local and other authorities to acquire land compulsorily. Such powers are exercised in particular cases by the making of a compulsory purchase order subject to approval by the appropriate Minister.

The compulsory purchase of land is one of the harshest impositions by the state upon its citizens. The loss to the individual is justified by the gain to the wider community of which the individual is a part. The history of the development of compulsory purchase powers has been one of striving to achieve a balance between retaining adequate safeguards for the interests of the individual on the one hand and the importance of not delaying schemes which are to serve a much needed public purpose on the other. This balance has been adjusted over the years according to the dictates of public policy.

At present, the safeguards for individuals are contained in a standard procedure set out in the Acquisition of Land Act 1981, and in its Scottish counterpart, which applies to the exercise of most compulsory purchase powers. The key safeguards comprise notice of the making of a compulsory purchase order, an opportunity to object and the right to be heard in support of an objection.

A further important safeguard is a statutory entitlement to compensation in the event of the compulsory acquisition of an interest. Complex rules have been formulated to give claimants a measure of financial compensation that is broadly equivalent to their loss, which is generally determined as the market value of their interest plus disturbance and, in some cases, a home or additional loss payment.

JEREMY ROWAN ROBINSON

compulsory treatment of patients with mental disorders Throughout the nineteenth century and for the first half of the twentieth century the assumption was made that patients who had been certified and were detained could be given treatment for their mental disorder without their consent. Whilst mechanical restraint such as the use of straitjackets and seclusion (supervised solitary confinement) were regulated, drug treatments were not subject to any special regulation. Many powerful sedatives were used over the period from 1850–1950, including opium, morphine chloral hydrate, and barbiturates. Powerful laxatives were also used as a way of controlling patients who 'misbehaved'. The invention of the hypodermic syringe in the second half of the nineteenth century enabled drugs to be administered more efficiently without consent. The 1930s and 1940s were great periods of experimentation with new and radical treatments including shock treatments, coma treatments using insulin or barbiturates, and psychosurgery. In the 1940s and 1950s, there was extensive use of psychosurgery on both sides of the Atlantic, and very often this was given without the patient's consent. The treatment then used was the prefrontal lobotomy which detached the frontal lobes from the rest of the brain. Use of the lobotomy declined with the advent of antipsychotic medication and nowadays psychosurgery is only used as a last resort, and in England and Wales requires the patient's true consent.

Since the 1950s, the landscape of psychiatric treatment has been dominated by pharmaceutical approaches to mental disorder, with the development of powerful drugs which can act on the central nervous system. These can address the symptoms of mental disorders more directly rather than simply providing a sedative effect. For examples, neuroleptic drugs block the receptors in the brain which receive the signals causing hallucinations or delusions, and by the early 1960s these were seen as the first effective antipsychotic drugs. Antipsychotics also have a sedative effect. They can produce adverse side effects, including neuroeptic malignant syndrome, Parkinsonian symptoms in the case of the old style antipsychotics, and obesity and diabetes in the case of the newer 'second generation' antipsychotics. Because of these side effects, service users may discontinue their medication leading to relapse. Treatment without consent engages the right of respect for physical integrity and effective supervision and review of such decisions is necessary in order to meet international **human rights** requirements. Accordingly, during the second half of the twentieth century there has been increasing recognition of the need to provide safeguards to ensure that where drug treatments or Electro-Convulsive Therapy are given without a patient's consent that these are clinically necessary according to accepted medical opinion.

Over the past half century there has been a policy shift across the **common law** world away from treating mentally disordered people in institutions towards **community** care, with detention being reserved for patients who, without compulsory in-patient treatment, would pose a risk to themselves or to others. The arrival on the scene in the 1960s of depot antipsychotics meant that a patient could be given an injection once every week or ten days, hence ensuring compliance, allowing greater possibilities for care in the community. Following concerns about **homicides** and **suicides** by patients in the community, a primary goal of mental health policy has been securing compliance with medication. This has led to the introduction in many jurisdictions (including England and Wales) of community treatment orders whereby patients may be subjected to a legal requirement to accept medication in the community on pain of recall to detention in hospital if they fail to comply. As long as they consent to medication they may remain in the community. If they refuse they may be recalled to hospital.   PHILLIP FENNELL

P Fennell, *Treatment without Consent: The Treatment of Mentally Disordered People since 1845* (London: Routledge, 1994)

See also: **mental health law**

concentration   Under EC **competition law** a concentration arises where two or more previously independent undertakings merge, or where one or more persons, already controlling one undertaking or one or more undertakings, acquire direct or indirect control over the whole or parts of one or more undertakings. Creation of a joint venture performing on a lasting basis all the functions of an autonomous economic entity also constitutes a concentration. The EC Merger Regulation regulates concentrations under EC law and clarifies that the acquisition of control means the acquisition of rights, contracts, or any other means that confer the possibility of exercising decisive influence over an undertaking. Concentrations that have a Community dimension, which would significantly impede **competition** in the **Common Market** or in a substantial part of it, in particular as a result of the creation or strengthening of a dominant position, are declared incompatible with EC law by the EC Merger Regulation. A concentration has a Community dimension when it satisfies either the primary or the residual thresholds set out in Article 1 of the EC Merger Regulation. These thresholds are calculated on the basis of the Community-wide and worldwide turnover of the undertakings concerned. Consequently, non-Community

undertakings can come within the scope of the EC merger regulation even when a concentration is concluded outside the **European Union** if the merger has the effect of significantly impeding competition in the Common Market or in a substantial part of it.

ALBERTINA ALBORS-LORENS

conception, assisted   *see* **assisted conception**

concerted practice   The concept of concerted practice is not one that appears in all **competition law**s in the world. In some regimes, the equivalent notion is that of a 'conspiracy'. Essentially, the concept is used by **competition** authorities as a tool to prove the existence of anti-competitive behaviour (usually a **cartel**) on the part of several firms where doing so by relying on the existence of a **horizontal agreement** is not possible. In a situation where a competition authority is able to demonstrate coordination in the behaviour of the firms which is short of an agreement but which shows that the firms have clearly stopped competing and have chosen to collude instead, the concept makes it possible for harmful anti-competitive behaviour to be caught without the need to rely on the existence of agreement.

Proof of the existence of a concerted practice may be difficult because it depends on circumstantial evidence. Suppose that the prices charged by several firms suddenly increase by the same rate and at the same time. The explanation may be that the chief executives of the firms concerned happened to be skiing at the same resort immediately before the price increase. Moreover, market conditions may result in firms behaving as if they are engaged in a concerted practice. For example, in a transparent market a firm may be able easily to observe the behaviour of its competitors and to adapt its behaviour to that of those competitors. In this case, although the firms will be behaving in parallel, it would be wrong to conclude that their behaviour was the result of a concerted practice. Faced with parallel behaviour a competition authority would normally ask whether there was a plausible explanation for the behaviour other than that of a concerted practice. If such an explanation exists, the concept of concerted practice would not apply.   MAHER DABBAH

conciliation   *see* **alternative dispute resolution**

conciliation, family   *see* **mediation, family**

conciliation, international   Conciliation is a well-established mode of third-party international dispute settlement, combining elements of inquiry and mediation. It is listed in Article 33.1 of the UN Charter as one of the modes by which states who are parties to a dispute are bound to seek a solution.

Conciliation may be entrusted to a single person or to a commission of two or more (usually three) persons. Essentially, conciliation involves the conciliator(s) making an impartial enquiry into the facts of the dispute and then making a report containing non-binding proposals for a settlement.

Recourse to conciliation requires the agreement of both parties to a dispute. In addition to *ad hoc* agreement between the parties (as in the case of the 1980 Iceland–Norway agreement concerning Jan Mayen Island), conciliation may also be provided for either in a general treaty establishing standing dispute-settlement arrangements (eg the Pact of Bogotá 1948, the European Convention for the Peaceful Settlement of Disputes 1957, and the Convention on Conciliation and Arbitration within the CSCE (Conference on Security and Cooperation in Europe) 1992) or in a bilateral or multilateral treaty dealing with a particular subject and providing for conciliation as a mode of settling disputes arising under that treaty (eg the UN Convention on the Law of the Sea 1982, Annex V).

Conciliation featured in a number of bilateral and multilateral treaties after World War I, and continues in practice to retain its utility as a mode of settlement of disputes between states as well as international commercial disputes (under the UNCITRAL (United Nations Commission on International Trade Law) Conciliation Rules 1980). SIR ARTHUR WATTS

Handbook on the Peaceful Settlement of Disputes (United Nations, 1992), 45–55

JG Merrills, *International Dispute Settlement* (Cambridge: Cambridge University Press, 3rd edn, 1998), 62–87

See also: **mediation of international disputes**

conditional fee arrangements　*see* **legal aid; no-win, no-fee arrangements**

condominium and coimperium　*see* **territory**

conduct of business regulation　Those providing financial services have to be licensed or 'authorized' and, once authorized, are subject to conduct of business regulation. The purpose of this regulation is primarily to protect the interests of those dealing with authorized firms. The **Financial Services Authority** ('FSA') has power under the **Financial Services and Markets Act 2000** both to authorize and then to impose conduct of business rules on firms in the financial services sector. These rules are found in the FSA Handbook. In consequence of 'MiFID' (the Markets in Financial Instruments Directive 2004), which seeks to establish a 'single market' in investment business in the EU, many of the conduct of business rules for investment firms are harmonized throughout the EU.

The FSA has set out eleven 'Principles for Business' which are intended to be a general statement of the fundamental obligations imposed on authorized firms under the regulatory system. So, for example, they require a firm to conduct its business with 'integrity' and with 'due skill, care and diligence' as well as to observe 'proper standards of market conduct'. A firm must 'arrange adequate protection for clients' assets' and communicate with clients in a way that is 'clear, fair and not misleading'. In addition, the FSA has made more detailed rules to deal with particular circumstances, but these are stated to be without prejudice to the Principles, which apply in so far as specific provision is not made. These detailed rules are mainly contained in that part of the FSA Handbook that is designated 'COBS' (the acronym for Conduct of Business) and COBS applies primarily to investment firms. COBS has limited application to banks and there are more specific rules for firms with (non-investment) insurance business customers in 'ICOB' and with mortgage business customers in 'MCOB'.

In 2005 the FSA decided on a change of approach to conduct of business regulation. It took the view that such regulation should be 'principles-based', rather than too reliant on detailed rules. Hence it has rewritten COBS so that it contains more high-level statements of principle and fewer detailed rules. This approach is intended to give more flexibility (and responsibility) to authorized firms themselves and their trade associations in complying with the regulatory regime. In the retail sector, the FSA has introduced the 'TCF' (the acronym for 'Treating Customers Fairly') initiative which requires firms to demonstrate that the 'fair treatment' of consumers is central to their corporate culture and that firms are committed to a number of 'outcomes' which ensure such fair treatment.

Authorized firms may deal with a wide variety of persons and provide a wide variety of services. When it imposes conduct of business obligations on authorized firms, the FSA differentiates between those with whom a firm deals ('clients' as they are called in the FSA Handbook). The FSA rules now divide clients into three categories: 'retail clients', 'professional clients', and 'eligible counterparties'. The terminology and dividing line changed when MiFID was implemented in October 2007, but the principle remained the same. Much more onerous obligations are imposed on authorized firms when they deal with retail clients than with the other two types of client. This reflects the relative lack of expertise of retail clients and the greater reliance they place on the firm. Thus COBS is largely disapplied to so-called 'inter-professional business', where authorized firms deal with eligible counterparties. Before an authorized firm deals with any client, it must classify the client by determining which category the client falls within so that the appropriate protections apply.

As far as investment firms are concerned (to which the bulk of COBS applies), they are subject to a number of general conduct of business requirements when they deal with customers. For example, firms are required to manage 'fairly' any conflict of interest arising, whether between itself and its customers or between a customer and another client. One of the methods permitted, subject to strict requirements, is the establishment of so-called 'Chinese Walls', which are internal arrangements in a firm that restrict the movement of information within it. Moreover, so-called 'inducements', that is, incentives which might cause a conflict between the firm's interests and those of its customer, are also strictly controlled. COBS also limits the extent to which a firm may exclude or restrict liability to its customers. When it comes to advertising and other forms of financial promotion, COBS lays down detailed control, which is at its most onerous as far as retail clients are concerned. Depending on the investment service or product involved, firms are also required to provide clients with specific information (especially about the risks involved) and, in certain cases, a cooling-off period, during which the retail client may cancel the agreement. If a firm gives advice or makes discretionary decisions for any client who is entitled to rely upon its judgment, it must take reasonable care to ensure the suitability of its advice and decisions. To help monitor compliance with all these obligations, a firm is required to keep records and make periodic reports to the FSA.

If a firm breaches the conduct of business rules, a number of consequences follow. First, the FSA has a variety of disciplinary powers, ranging from a public reprimand or unlimited financial penalties and culminating in a revocation of authorization. The FSA may also require the authorized firm to disgorge profits made or to compensate for losses caused. Secondly, most rule breaches enable a private client to bring a civil claim in the courts for breach of the duty imposed and recover for any loss suffered. Such claims are particularly useful when the firm is insolvent and the client makes a claim against the Financial Services Compensation Scheme. Although a client may have the usual **common law** claims against the firm and hence the Scheme, this claim for breach of a conduct of business rule is easier to establish. An alternative avenue which private clients have for redress against authorized firms is the Financial Ombudsman Scheme. EVA LOMNICKA

See also: **European Union, influence of on financial markets; financial regulation; investment firm licensing; investor compensation schemes; ombudsmen**

conference presentation   *see* **lawyering skills**

confidential information Confidential information, along with trade secrets, know-how, and reputation, are sometimes referred to as 'quasi-intellectual property'. This is because they are often generated alongside intellectual property rights ('IPRs') and like IPRs they have a commercial value. It is important in a company that confidential information is recognized as soon it comes into existence. If you or your colleagues, employees, or consultants do not realize that certain knowledge should be regarded as confidential, it will be difficult to afford it the protection needed for its exploitation in the future. Confidential information and trade secrets are vulnerable where technology allows information to be replicated swiftly and without expense by disaffected staff members or competitors.

The difference between 'secrecy' and 'confidentiality' is difficult to establish. A trade secret tends to have independent, legitimate, commercial value in and of itself, whereas confidential information may or may not have commercial value. For example, the secret formula for a popular soft drink would be considered a trade secret, whilst the menu choices for a film star's wedding breakfast would be confidential information. In a case where someone, without permission, photographed an 'installation' put together to be photographed for a record sleeve, and sold that photograph for commercial publication, a court decided that there was no possibility of an action for breach of **copyright** because the 'installation' was not an artistic work. Instead, an action for breach of confidence was successful. When the *Daily Mail* published extracts of the Prince of Wales' diaries, both his copyright and confidentiality were infringed.

A legal claim for breach of confidence will succeed only if efforts have been made to ensure the secrecy or confidentiality of the information. There need not necessarily be a confidentiality or non-disclosure agreement in place to ensure that information will be treated as confidential. However, whenever commercial dealings involve confidential information or trade secrets, it would be good practice to have one in place. Often, a clear understanding of whether or not information is defined as a trade secret emerges only as the result of a judicial decision.

In a dispute about confidentiality, the court considers a number of factors, which point to the importance of 'good housekeeping' in respect of confidential information. One is the extent to which the information is known outside the owner's business, and the extent to which it is known inside to employees and others. In negotiations, confidential information should be disclosed in the context of a non-disclosure agreement which spells out the exact and specific nature of the information being disclosed, the purposes for which it might used, and the people entitled to have access to it. The court also takes account of provision made by the owner to protect the secrecy of the information and procedures put in place to minimize risk, eg computer screen savers, shredders, signing-in sheets for visitors. Good practices will not protect against abuse but absence of good practice will make it more difficult to challenge an abuse successfully. In addition, the court will consider the value of the information to its owners and to competitors. Value comes from consideration of the amount of effort or money invested in developing the information and whether or not that information could be easily replicated or obtained by other people.

The **World Trade Organization Agreement on Trade Related Aspects of Intellectual Property Rights ('TRIPs')** sets down minimum standards for many forms of IP regulation. It was negotiated at the end of the Uruguay Round of the **General Agreement on Tariffs and Trade ('GATT')** in 1994. It contains requirements that must be met by laws dealing with IPRs and undisclosed or confidential information. It provides for protection of undisclosed information where such information is secret, has a commercial value because it is secret, and where the person lawfully in control of the information has taken reasonable steps under the circumstances to keep it secret. TRIPs remains the most comprehensive international agreement on intellectual property to date, although there is no obligation under TRIPs to provide for criminal procedures in respect of abuse of trade secrets and confidential information by espionage, for instance. All states which are members of the World Trade Organization are signatories to the TRIPs agreement.

TRIPs lays down a benchmark for respect of confidential information in all signatory states, but if secret information which is owned, say, in Germany has been made public in France, the secrecy is lost. The US Supreme Court has said 'once secrecy is lost the property interest is lost forever'. UK law regarding confidential information has been described as 'a shield and not a sword', which suggests how difficult it is to assert the right through the courts and achieve restitution. Both comments emphasize the importance of concentrating effort in protecting secret information. In most common law jurisdictions confidentiality and trade secrets are regarded as an equitable right rather than a property right.

Confidentiality of trade secrets is difficult to maintain over time or in relation to a large number of people—but not impossible, as Coca Cola's secret recipe shows. Confidentiality may be at risk when employees, privy to a secret, leave. Whilst there may be situations where relying on confidentiality is preferable to public disclosure in a patent application, it is invariably more difficult to prove a breach of confidence than infringement of a patent.

There are various practical measures that can be taken to protect confidential information. An express undertaking of confidentiality can be written in to the contracts of all staff, support workers, consultants, casual workers, and students on placement. Visitors to your premises can be asked to sign a visitors book in which they undertake an obligation of confidence in respect of everything they see and hear during their visit; and they can be invited to leave their electronic communication equipment at reception. People who expect to talk about the company's trade secrets outside the company need to know what type of non-disclosure agreement is appropriate in the circumstances. People at any level in a company should know to whom to take their bright idea. If they do not, or if the designated person does not know how to respond appropriately, the bright idea might be lost to the company, along with its value.   RUTH SOETENDORP

See also: **equity as a system of law; patents**

confidentiality (work)   A duty of confidentiality is implied into all **contracts of employment** if not expressly agreed. During employment the employee must keep confidential all that an employer might reasonably regard as confidential. A narrower duty of confidentiality remains after employment (*Faccenda Chicken Ltd v Fowler* (1984)), applying only to 'trade secrets' and similar: not only secret formulae but also customer information which, if disclosed to a competitor, would be liable to cause significant harm to the employer, and the widespread publication of which is limited or at least not encouraged or permitted (*Lansing Linde Ltd v Kerr* (1991)).

It is not always clear what will be regarded as confidential. In *Faccenda Chicken* customer information which employees necessarily carried away in their heads was not protected by the implied term of confidentiality. However, in *Lansing Linde* it was suggested that the implied term relating to confidentiality could cover customer information even if it was inevitably carried away. Any action taken during employment to gather information about an employer's customer base in order to facilitate subsequent **competition** would breach the implied duty of confidentiality (*Roger Bullivant Ltd & Ors v Ellis & Ors* (1987)).

An employer faced with a threatened breach of an implied or express term relating to confidentiality can sue for an **injunction** to stop the breach and/or **damages** for loss resulting from it. In rare cases an employee or former employee may have to account to the employer for profits made (as distinct from damages caused to the employer) as a result of the breach of confidence (*Attorney-General v Blake & Anor* (2001)). AILEEN MCCOLGAN

confidentiality, medical *see* **medical confidentiality**

conflict of interest and corporations *see* **corporate governance and conflict of interest**

conflict of laws *see* **transnational civil litigation**

conflicting rights Rights can be seen to conflict in a multitude of contexts. For example, the right to **freedom of expression** of the media (and the allied right of viewers, listeners, and readers to receive such expression) may conflict with a **person**'s right to **privacy** where the latter does not wish certain personal information to be published by the media. A key responsibility of the legal system is to determine how rights will be prioritized and conflicts resolved. Sometimes, particularly where the topic has become a matter of public or political controversy, Parliament will seek to give express guidance as to how conflicting rights should be balanced. Take, for example, the Racial and Religious Hatred Act 2006, which controversially extends the criminal law to prohibit the use of threatening words or behaviour intended to stir up religious hatred. This new offence was designed, in large part, to protect the right to religious freedom. However, critics of that Act contended that it would significantly limit the right to freedom of expression of those who criticized or ridiculed specific religious beliefs. Consequently, after major amendments during the legislative process, the final Act includes a provision which states that the Act is not to be applied in a way which, *inter alia*, restricts discussion, criticism, or expressions of antipathy, dislike, or ridicule of particular religious beliefs. Hence, only extreme forms of religious expression will be prohibited. Ultimately, it is up to **judges** to determine the precise balance between rights in specific cases. Under the **Human Rights Act 1998** our judges are guided in balancing protected **human rights** by the extensive jurisprudence of the **European Court of Human Rights** ('ECtHR'). These judgments disclose a sophisticated collection of principles for balancing conflicting rights. If we take our earlier example of the clash between personal privacy and freedom of expression, the ECtHR prioritizes the latter when it is disclosing matters of public interest (for example, significant criminal convictions of a politician's spouse). This is because democratic societies rely on the media to inform the public of these matters so that governments and politicians can be held accountable via electoral and other processes. However, where the media is merely seeking to give publicity to personal matters which have no legitimate public interest (for example, pictures of a member of a royal family engaging in routine shopping) the ECtHR will safeguard the right to privacy. In areas of social policy where national **parliaments** have reached democratic decisions to advance the rights of certain groups over the rights of others, such as the **Westminster Parliament**'s decision to enable long leasehold tenants to purchase their freeholds against the wishes of their landlords, the ECtHR has accorded states a wide discretion to determine the correct balance between groups' opposing rights. This clearly demonstrates the judiciary recognizing that broad cultural, economic, and political considerations can play an important role in the balancing of conflicting rights.

ALASTAIR MOWBRAY

A Mowbray, *Cases & Materials on the European Convention on Human Rights* (Oxford: Oxford University Press, 2nd edn, 2007)

See also: **freedom of religion and belief; hate speech**

conflicts of interest in financial markets Management of conflicts of interest has always been a major preoccupation of financial market **regulation**. It has, however, become an acute and high profile concern following the series of financial scandals that emerged in Europe and the US following the end of the dotcom boom, of which **Enron** is now the paradigm example. In particular, Enron and similar collapses suggested that financial market 'gatekeepers', typically auditors, credit rating agencies, and investment analysts, were subject to conflict-of-interest risks which damaged their ability to assess **securities** and companies independently. A recent wave of regulation in the US, the UK, and Europe, including best-practice initiatives by the International Organization of Securities Commissions (the umbrella body of market regulators), has sought to address such conflicts of interest.

Market 'gatekeepers' perform a key function in financial markets. They are so-called because they provide important verification services for investors by using their reputation as independent reviewers to provide objective assessments of companies and securities. Auditors provide an opinion on the financial disclosure provided by a company. Investment analysts provide recommendations on equity investments in particular. Credit rating agencies 'rate' an issuer's debt securities, and are important in bond markets.

In the aftermath of the dotcom collapse, it is now argued that a range of factors intensified conflicts of interest and damaged the ability of gatekeepers to provide independent services and to warn the investing public of imminent insolvencies, fraud, and poor financial performance. Such factors included exuberant stock markets, which may have reduced investor caution and awareness of conflicts of interests. They also included the payment of company executives through share options, which may have given executives incentives to manipulate financial information and to exert pressure on auditors in order to increase company share prices (resulting in compromised financial information). Growth in the provision of lucrative non-audit services (such as consulting services) by audit firms, which provided companies with a mechanism for exerting pressure on auditors, also heightened conflicts of interest. Finally, links between investment analysts and corporate finance, trading, and other divisions within firms (including links between analysts' pay and the performance of other divisions) generated severe conflicts of interest bcause a positive recommendation from an analyst on a particular security could help the firm's broking and trading divisions in selling those securities to investors and in securing corporate finance business from the issuer, particularly as prices reached dizzying heights

A range of reforms have now been adopted in the UK and internationally. These include: stronger public supervision of the auditor; more extensive disclosure requirements in relation to the meaning of investment recommendations and the possibility that investment analysts may face conflicts of interest (including disclosure of the relationship between the investment firm and the company and securities examined); clearer separation and insulation of analysts from other investment banking divisions in an investment firm; and fuller disclosure by credit rating agencies of potential conflicts of interest.

Although conflicts of interest confronting gatekeepers have recently been a major preoccupation of financial market regulation, financial markets themselves are subject to a range of conflicts which are addressed by regulation. An issuer faces a fundamental conflict of interest in issuing securities in primary markets and has an incentive to conceal poor financial performance. This is why strict disclosure requirements are imposed on securities offerings. Market intermediaries may also face conflicts of interest as a result, for instance, of providing various different services such as broking, trading, investment advice and corporate finance. This is particularly the case in the multi-service investment firm, which is now the dominant model in the UK and Europe, where numerous investment activities are carried out within the same firm. For example, investment advisers and asset managers in an investment firm may face conflicts of interest where the firm holds a proprietary position in (or owns) securities which are underperforming, and wishes to offload the securities.

Risks associated with conflicts of interest do not necessarily result in prejudice to the investor so long as the risk is appropriately disclosed and managed. Regulation is therefore generally directed towards the identification of the conflict, the management of the conflict and, if the conflict cannot be managed without potential prejudice to the investor, disclosure of the conflict to the investor or requiring the the firm not to act in the particular circumstances. Management of a conflict, which typically requires a firm to maintain all necessary operational and organizational arrangements, may include a separation of functions through, for example, 'Chinese Walls', which prevent the flow of information between divisions of an investment firm that may have conflicting interests. The existence of the conflict and its source should be clearly disclosed to the investor. Risks of conflict will often be addressed by a network of rules. For example, the potential conflict which arises where an investment firm acting as broker executes a client trading order against its own proprietary trading book ('internalization') is addressed by a series of rules, including disclosure rules and best execution rules, which require a broker, when executing orders, to take all reasonable steps to obtain the best possible result.

The **common law** relating to **fiduciaries** requires investment firms, which owe a fiduciary duty to their clients, to manage conflicts of interest. This regime of fiduciary law is extended by the **Financial Services and Markets Act 2000** and the rules made under it by the **Financial Services Authority**. For example, at present, Principle 8, one of the eleven high-level Principles for Business to which all investment firms are subject, requires a firm to 'manage conflicts of interest fairly both between itself and its customers and between a customer and another client'. More detailed Conduct of Business rules address the identification, management, and disclosure of conflict of interests in investment business (and include a fair treatment obligation), while particular rules apply to investment research and investment analysts and to conflicts which arise with respect to corporate finance advice, and, in particular, advice on the issuance of securities by a company.   NIAMH MOLONEY

conformity with contract   *see* **sale of goods; quality of products**

conjoined twins   The case of Maltese conjoined twins (*Re A* (2001)) is one of the most controversial decisions of recent years. It raises profound legal and ethical questions. The weaker of the twins (Mary) was dependent on the stronger (Jodie).She would die immediately upon separation from her sister. Jodie could, on separation, be expected to live a near normal life. If no action were taken both would die in a matter of months. The parents, who are Roman Catholics, wanted nature to take its course. The court accepted that sincerely held views of parents were an important incident of **parental responsibility**. The parents were overruled by the **courts**. Some have questioned whether 'in a finely balanced judgment' the overruling of parental choice can be justified. However, once the court had insisted on the final say, it had to apply the paramountcy principle. It was clearly in the **best interests** of Jodie for the separation to take place. But what about Mary, whose welfare was also paramount? The trial judge and one judge in the Court of Appeal thought it was not in Mary's best interests to be maintained alive given the quality of life she could expect. The majority in the Court of Appeal saw benefit to Mary in giving her 'bodily integrity and dignity', although Ward LJ admitted this was a 'wholly illusory goal because she will be dead before she can enjoy her independence'. Mary was not receiving treatment which could be passively withdrawn, and so positive action that would terminate her life had to be justified. There was understandable anxiety lest this justification

were to countenance **euthanasia**. It was held that the separation could be performed even though it would result in Mary's death because the surgeons would be acting in Jodie's defence against her sister who was killing her. It would not be murder because the doctor would be acting in quasi-self-defence or with the defence of **necessity**.   MICHAEL FREEMAN

connected loan   *see* **credit cards**

conquest   *see* **territory**

conscientious objector   The term 'conscientious objector' is usually taken to refer to service personnel who refuse to serve or to continue to serve in the armed forces on grounds of conscience. As the United Kingdom currently deploys all-volunteer forces, the issue is of lesser significance than in those countries retaining conscription. Conscription legislation may make provision, qualified or otherwise, for exemption from compulsory military service on grounds of conscience, as Britain did during the two world wars.

There is currently no express right of conscientious objection to military service in **international human rights law** (let alone in domestic law) despite the guarantee of freedom of belief, conscience and religion under Article 9 of the **European Convention on Human Rights**. Consequently, a court held that a Royal Air Force reservist medical assistant recalled to non-combatant duty in the United Kingdom in order to release regular airmen for deployment to the Iraq war in 2003 could not rely on Article 9 as a defence when he went absent without leave before manifesting to the authorities a conscientious objection to military service which entailed fighting against fellow-Muslims.

This case is also interesting inasmuch as the question posed to the court was in terms of a genuine conscientious objection, 'general or particular'. This might suggest that conscientious objection may cover not only pacifists or those religiously opposed to violence, but also both servicemen refusing to support or participate in military action against co-religionists and those with a moral or political objection to a particular conflict.

Service personnel claiming a conscientious objection may make an internal application to leave the service and must provide supporting evidence of their genuine belief. If the application is rejected, an appeal may be made to an independent civilian board, the Advisory Committee on Conscientious Objection, chaired by a Queen's Counsel, for a final decision. Hearings are in public, the procedure is informal and the applicant is entitled to be represented.   GR RUBIN

consent to treatment Consent to treatment is said to be the legal expression of **self-determination** and, at **common law**, a legally valid consent to or refusal of medical treatment by an adult must take priority over the **sanctity of human life**. To this end, an adult patient's right to refuse consent to medical treatment must be respected, even if the consequence of that decision is that s/he will die. A number of challenges to the primacy of self-determination are evident in recent case law. They have been advocated by clinical staff wishing to give effect to their ethical duty to preserve the life of the patient or in order to safeguard the life of the **foetus** in cases where a pregnant woman is refusing medical care. They have also been suggested by **judges** concerned that patient autonomy has been given too much weight in English law and that other ethical values have been relegated to a lesser status. Notwithstanding these challenges, the higher **courts** have reiterated a commitment to the primacy of patient **autonomy** and the right to refuse treatment.

An effective consent to treatment provides justification for the legal administration of medical care. In the absence of consent, the tort of battery, which is the direct application of force to another person, will have occurred. To be valid, consent must be given by a person with **capacity** to make that decision; and it must be voluntary and sufficiently informed.

The voluntariness of a patient's consent will be determined by reference to the impact of external influences on the patient's decision. Thus, institutional or familial pressures may invalidate consent where the patient's will has been sufficiently overborne and the patient's consent is in form only and not in substance. To what extent such pressures invalidate consent will be determined on the facts of each case.

The level of information to be imparted to and understood by the patient has been the subject of considerable academic and judicial comment. The courts have declined to give full effect to the ethical doctrine of informed consent, which demands recognition of the patient's right to be informed of **risks** inherent in medical treatment, side effects, and alternatives to the proposed treatment. Instead, the law requires simply that the patient must be informed in broad terms the nature of what is proposed for consent to be valid. Whilst the courts have interpreted the 'nature' of the procedure as requiring also an understanding of its 'purpose', a failure to be informed of risks, side effects, and alternative treatments will not usually give rise to an action in

battery, since these do not necessarily impede an understanding of the nature of what is intended.

However, failures in information disclosure relating to the risks, side effects, and alternatives to treatment may give rise to an action in **negligence** if claimants can overcome the difficulties in establishing a breach of the duty to inform the patient. Such difficulties were compounded by the courts' determination in the landmark judgment of the House of Lords in *Sidaway v Board of Governors of the Bethlem Royal Hospital and the Maudsley Hospital and Others* (1985) that the appropriate level of information disclosure was primarily a matter of clinical judgment. *Sidaway* rejected the doctrine of informed consent as developed and endorsed in other jurisdictions, including the US, Canada, and Australia. That doctrine was premised on the notion that patients rather than doctors had the right to determine the amount and quality of information provided to them, in order to assist them to make decisions about health care. To this end the doctor's duty to provide information to patients should be determined according to whether the risk would be considered 'material' by the reasonably prudent patient. In English law, however, the amount and quality of information provided to patients is determined by reference to the '*Bolam*' principle, which requires professionals to disclose information according to what is considered acceptable by responsible medical practice (*Bolam v Friern Hospital* (1957)). A practitioner who fails to disclose information will not be found liable in negligence provided the decision to withhold information can be supported by a responsible body of medical opinion. Subsequent judgments have applied the *Bolam* principle to failures of information disclosure in cases involving non-therapeutic medical treatment, and even to situations where the patient has specifically demanded information of the practitioner. Courts in the UK have shown greater willingness in recent years to challenge failures in information disclosure by ruling that withholding information may not be considered 'responsible' in certain cases. More recently they have ruled that doctors should exercise their skills in information disclosure by having regard to the risks that would be deemed significant by the reasonable patient. Moreover, the Court of Appeal has confirmed that a doctor's duty extends to providing a truthful answer to questions specifically posed by the patient. To this end, there has been a rapprochement with, if not an unqualified endorsement of, the legal doctrine of informed consent.

The impact of fraud on the validity of consent has given rise to conflicting views in the courts.

One view advanced by the judiciary suggests that withholding or misrepresenting information in bad faith will automatically vitiate consent. Other judgments are more circumspect, however, advising only that those fraudulent statements by clinicians which impede the patient's understanding of the nature of the procedure will invalidate consent. Thus, the courts have ruled that patients who agreed to treatment in the belief that interventions were medically indicated, when in fact they were not, should be successful in their claims for battery.

The law relating to consent to treatment for patients detained under mental health **legislation** may be contrasted with the common law. Under the Mental Health Act 1983 (as amended by the Mental Health Act 2007) and the Mental Health (Care and Treatment) (Scotland) Act 2003, patients receiving treatment for their mental disorder do not enjoy the same rights to refuse medical treatment as their common law counterparts. Aside from the performance of neurosurgery for mental disorder, the surgical implantation of hormones to reduce male sex drive or the provision of electro-convulsive therapy, detained and informal patients under English mental health legislation have no enforceable right to refuse treatment. Under Scots law, capable but refusing detained patients have the right to refuse neurosurgery, deep brain stimulation, transcranial magnetic stimulation, vagus nerve stimulation treatment, and electro-convulsive therapy.

Challenges to the appropriateness of administering treatment without consent under mental health legislation have hinged on the potential incompatibility with the **European Convention on Human Rights**, in particular Articles 3 (the right not to subject to inhumane and degrading treatment) and 8 (the right to privacy and family life). Domestic courts have reiterated their confidence that treatment of capable, refusing patients detained under mental health legislation will not be in breach of the ECHR, provided such interventions can be said to constitute a 'therapeutic necessity' are in the **'best interests' of patients**. Nevertheless, concerns about the ethical legitimacy of forcible medical treatment on detained psychiatric patients persist.

Children have the legal right to consent to medical treatment, provided they have sufficient capacity and their consent is voluntary and informed. Their refusal of medical treatment may be overridden in English law by the courts or those with **parental responsibility** if treatment is considered to be in their best interests.   KIRSTY KEYWOOD

conservation *see* **nature conservation**

consolatory payments Consolatory payments are financial awards that are paid for non-financial loss to those who have suffered injustice as a result of maladministration by a public body. Complaints about maladministration by public bodies are investigated by **ombudsmen**, and where maladministration is found, the ombudsmen recommend an appropriate remedy to be provided by the public body concerned. The recommendation indicates the appropriate action that the public body should take in order to rectify the injustice caused by the maladministration. The remedies recommended can include apologies, rectification of mistakes, and reviews of procedures. The ombudsman can also recommend that compensation be paid to cover actual financial loss suffered as a result of the maladministration. However, even where no actual financial loss has been incurred, the ombudsman can recommend a consolatory payment, that is, a financial award to compensate for the stress and anxiety that may have been caused as a result of the maladministration, and also for the time, trouble, and inconvenience, and general 'botheration' associated with pursuing a complaint. These consolatory payments can also be awarded in addition to an award for compensation for actual financial loss.

Consolatory payments, sometimes known as 'solace' payments, are meant to console an individual and offer some recompense for the stress and anxiety that has been caused as a result of maladministration. They are not intended to put a value on the distress an individual has actually suffered, but are meant to offer some consolation, and are often given in addition to an apology. Typical awards are fairly modest, ranging from £50 to £200, although they can be larger, and awards of £1,000 have been given, where there has been gross inconvenience or severe distress. For example, one government agency has paid £850 for severe distress, inconvenience, and gross embarrassment. Consolatory payments are also given to compensate for the time and trouble taken by a complainant in pursuing a complaint, where this is over and above the time and trouble routinely expected in doing so. Again, the awards are usually modest, at around £50, but they can be larger.

It is now accepted that public bodies should consider making consolatory payments, in addition to other forms of redress, to individual complainants. Government departments, agencies, and other public bodies now normally have well-defined rules about when such payments should be made, and the appropriate amount. For example, in exceptional circumstances, payments of between £25–£250 will be made for gross inconvenience resulting from persistent error. Similar amounts will be paid for severe distress, with the possibility of payments between £1,000 and £2,000, in the most severe cases.

It should be borne in mind that all these payments are discretionary, and that they are paid in the absence of legal liability or statutory provision. It should also be noted that the ombudsmen's recommendations are not awards that are enforceable by the courts, but that public bodies normally comply with them.   MARY SENEVIRATNE

conspiracy and trade union activity   Early **trade unions** ran a gauntlet of statutory restriction and **common law** liability. The Combination Acts of 1799 and 1800 made trade unionism illegal, and although the Acts were repealed in 1824, further **legislation** in 1825 declared various forms of trade union action unlawful. These controls addressed conduct deemed to constitute threats, molestation, intimidation, and obstruction, and were not repealed until 1871 when they were replaced with less red-blooded restraints. In *R v Bunn* (1872), however, it was held that there continued to be common law liability in conspiracy for taking **strike** action. This liability would arise even though the action was not unlawful if done by an individual acting alone: the collective nature of the action turned what was lawful into a crime. The decision in *Bunn's* case was reversed in the Conspiracy and Protection of Property Act 1875, providing immunity from criminal conspiracy for acts done in contemplation or furtherance of a trade dispute, if the act in question was not punishable as a crime if done by one person acting alone. The criminal route thus having been blocked, further legislation was necessary to reverse the **House of Lords** decision in *Quinn v Leathem* (1901) that the mere act of taking or threatening industrial action could constitute an actionable conspiracy in *civil* law, exposing defendants to the risk of liability in **damages** for losses caused. There continues to be protection in modern labour law statutes to protect trade unionists from criminal and civil liability for conspiracy.
                                                KEITH EWING

conspiracy, civil   *see* **economic torts**

conspiracy, criminal   *see* **economic torts**

Constantine v Imperial Hotels Ltd (1944)   During World War II, cricket provided catharsis for service personnel and the English civilian population. A limited schedule was maintained throughout.

On 2–3 August 1943, England played the Dominions at Lords. The Dominions included Learie Constantine, the famed West Indian, born in Trinidad but then an English resident and Labour Ministry employee. Before the game, the Imperial Hotel in London denied Constantine and his family accommodation because of his colour. He had booked for four nights but was told that they could stay only one. Protesting, he relocated to another hotel under the same ownership. Management feared the reaction of American forces guests to the Constantines' presence.

On 28 June 1944, Constantine gained some vindication. With flying-bombs overhead, Birkett J held that the hotel had violated the **common law** duty of innkeepers, arising from 'custom of the realm', not to deny accommodation unreasonably. This was not achieved easily. Constantine neither pleaded nor led evidence of any particular damage. Was an essential component of this rare cause of action proof of actual damage? There was no binding precedent. Ultimately, Birkett J favoured Constantine. He applied the principle in the iconic case of *Ashby v White* (1703) of no right without a remedy. In such instances, he held, the law should presume damage. Birkett J awarded five guineas' nominal damages and costs but, on the basis of the pleadings and absence of precedent, refused to award punitive or substantial damages for the humiliation and distress that Constantine had obviously suffered.

The judgment was a qualified personal triumph for Constantine and his barristers, Sir Patrick Hastings and Rose Heilbron. It also exemplifies the adaptive qualities of the common law. Ultimately, however, it was too thin a sliver for evolution into a claim for discrimination. Legislation proved essential in the law's battle against racism.   DAVID MULLAN

constituencies   A fundamental characteristic of voting and elections for political office in Britain has been the idea of territorial representation combined with equality of electors per representative. For the purpose of electing our political representatives and leaders, therefore, the area of government concerned is divided up into geographical units known as constituencies.

In the case of the **House of Commons**, there are currently 646 constituencies, each returning one Member. The boundaries of each constituency are periodically reviewed by the Electoral Commission (formerly the Boundary Commissions) to ensure broad parity of electoral quotas, being the number of the UK's total electorate divided by the number of constituencies for the time being.

The outcome of every boundary review is politically sensitive because such reviews almost always produce a result that favours one political party's electoral prospects. In the past the process of constituency review was criticized for being open to gerrymandering or, in other words, manipulation for political advantage by those in power. This was because formerly the legislative measures (Orders) needed to give effect to a constituency boundary review were presented to the Home Secretary, who had the power to vary the Orders and choose the time to lay them before Parliament for implementation. There have been some notable political controversies on such matters in the past, especially in 1969.

However, under the terms of the Political Parties Elections and Referendums Act 2000, the Electoral Commission will in future present its report on constituency boundary changes directly to Parliament.

ROBERT BLACKBURN

Constitution for Europe Following concerns about the disconnection of European citizens from the European Union, allegations of a lack of **democracy**, legitimacy, and **accountability**, incomprehensibility of its legal instruments, and the prospect of future EU enlargement, the European Council meeting in Belgium in December 2001 adopted a text known as the 'Laeken Declaration'. This Declaration proposed setting up a Convention to debate the Future of the Union. Presided by former French President, Valérie Giscard d'Estaing, and comprising 105 persons (drawn from the governments and **parliaments** of Member States and candidate countries, **European Parliament,** and Commission), the Convention met from February 2002 until July 2003. Its discussions were divided between a number of focused Working Groups and, following this eighteen-month period, the Convention agreed upon a draft Treaty establishing a Constitution for Europe (the Constitutional Treaty).

This text (in slightly amended form) was approved by the intergovernmental conference in June 2004 and signed in Rome on 29 October 2004 by the Heads of State and government of all twenty-seven Member States and the three then candidate countries (Bulgaria, Romania, and Turkey). The Constitution, comprising some 448 articles, proposed to reorganize and simplify the various existing Treaties upon which the European Community and European Union were based and to consolidate their provisions in one single text. The Constitution also contained some key institutional changes, such as the introduction of an elected President of the Union, a new post of Union Minister for Foreign Affairs, a cap on the number of Commissioners, and a revised system of qualified majority voting. It also gave full legal effect to the EU's **Charter of Fundamental Rights**.

Following signature, however, the Constitution still had to be ratified through the national constitutional procedures (referendum or parliamentary approval) of the twenty-five Member States. It was projected to enter into force on 1 November 2006.

Ten states had approved the Constitution when, in the early summer of 2005, the people of France and the Netherlands both rejected it in national referenda. Reasons for the rejection were wide-ranging, including concerns that the Constitution was too liberal and insufficiently social, fears that it would prompt increased immigration, worries about a further loss of national **sovereignty**, and discontent over unfavourable national economic performance.

As a result of this blow to the prospects of entry into force of the new Treaty, the European Council meeting in June 2005 called for a period of reflection, explanation, and discussion during which a wide-ranging debate was to take place in each country (whether or not they had ratified the Treaty) on the future of the Constitution. Two years later, in June 2007, and following a report prepared by the German Presidency on the way forward, the European Council decided to convene an intergovernmental conference in July 2007. Its task was to agree the text of a new EU Reform Treaty designed to amend the EU's two core treaties (The European Community Treaty and the Treaty on European Union) with the aim of securing ratification of the Reform Treaty before the European Parliament elections in June 2009.

SUSAN MILLNS

constitutional conventions A constitutional convention is a representative body, brought together to draft a new constitution or to design or approve changes to an old one.

Use of a convention as a constitution-making body can be traced to the Federal Convention of 1787 that met in Philadelphia to draw up the United States Constitution. The concept of a convention itself, however, has a longer history in the **United Kingdom**, which helps to explain its subsequent evolution. In both England and Scotland the term was used at various times to refer to meetings of the estates of the realm that were distinct from meetings of the Parliament. The term resurfaced for use during the revolutionary period and in particular in 1689, to describe a Parliament that was legally flawed because of the absence of a monarch. During the American Revolution it was adapted again to describe colonial assemblies and other bodies that met without the consent of the governor. Gradually, it became accepted that a convention might more perfectly embody the popular will, in a manner peculiarly suited to constitution-making. The device of a convention thus contributed to the understanding of a constitution as more authoritative than ordinary law.

Since 1789, conventions have been used for a variety of other constitution-making moments. Examples include the Scottish Constitutional Convention 1989–1995, the European Convention on the Future of Europe 2001–2003 and the Conventions of 1891 and 1897–1898 that drew up the Australian Commonwealth Constitution.

While terminology is not always used consistently, a constitutional convention usually can be distinguished from a constituent or constitutional assembly in several ways. First, a convention generally deals only with constitutional issues and not with other business of government. Second, a convention typically has insufficient authority to give its constitutional proposals legal effect. By contrast, both the Constituent Assembly of India and the Constitutional Assembly of South Africa also acted as legislatures during the constitution-making period and adopted the Constitutions that they had designed.

Differences in the constitutional and political context in which conventions are held mean that no two are likely to be the same. There are at least four sets of variables. The first is the authority by which a convention is brought together, which may range from a procedure in an existing Constitution (United States Constitution Article V), to the agreement of participating polities that a new Constitution would unite, acting individually or collectively (USA, Europe, Australia), to a claim by the convention itself, on behalf of the people (Scotland). The second is the composition of the convention and the associated, vexed question of the extent to which delegates are bound by their constituencies. The third is the role of the convention—although, as the Philadelphia Convention shows, a convention may sometimes exceed its formal mandate. The fourth and final variable is the manner in which the proposals of a convention become law. Here also the options vary widely, between enactment by a legislature; approval by referendum; or ratification by representative organs of participating polities.   CHERYL SAUNDERS

Gordon Wood, *The Creation of the American Republic 1776–1787* (New York: W W Norton & Company, 1972)

Georges Lefebvre, *The French Revolution* (tr. Elizabeth Moss Evanson) (London: Routledge Classics, 2001)

Constitutional Court of South Africa The Constitutional Court is the highest court in all cases concerning South Africa's Constitution. It was born out of the 1993 negotiated settlement between the white **apartheid** government, the liberation movements, and various other groupings. The new Constitution was a drastic departure from the past. From being an authoritarian, repressive, and racially-divided country, the new Constitution ushered in a non-racial and non-sexist democratic dispensation in which the system of **parliamentary sovereignty** was replaced with **constitution** supremacy.

The new Court became the guardian of the new Constitution which is founded on the values of **human dignity**, the achievement of **equality** and the advancement of **human rights** and freedoms, non-racialism, non-sexism, and the **rule of law**. New appointment procedures for **judges** were instituted to reflect this change; judicial officers are now drawn from all sectors of the legal profession and not solely from the white section of the population and from the ranks of senior advocates. This is in keeping with the constitutional imperative for the judiciary to reflect broadly the racial and gender composition of the country.

The judges to the Court are appointed for a maximum period of fifteen years by the President from a list determined by the Judicial Services Commission. There are eleven Judges, which include the Chief Justice and the Deputy Chief Justice. Although there is a quorum of eight, they sit *en banque* on every matter.

The Court sits in new premises in a striking new building in Johannesburg. It occupies a site of an old Afrikaaner fort which was later converted to a prison which housed many noted political activists including Albert Luthuli, Nelson Mandela, and Mahatma Gandhi. The Court now stands side-by-side with the old disused prison, which has been turned into a heritage site. The symbolism of a transition from a place of incarceration and oppression to an institution that stands for hope and freedom is stark. Many bricks from the demolished sections of the prison have been incorporated into the building of the courtroom and serve to remind everyone of the past which the Court was established to reject. As a building, the institution strives to emulate the ideals of openness, accessibility, and transparency.

The Court's decisions have to reflect the new ethic of a democratic state which lays emphasis on **accountability**, responsiveness, and openness in all spheres of government. It has made many decisions which have had an impact on every aspect of life in

South Africa. **Capital punishment** in South Africa was abolished as a result of the first case heard by the Court. This momentuous decision set the tone for the Court's later jurisprudence in its robust defence and protection of fundamental **human** rights. It also signalled the Court's determination not to be swayed by public opinion when difficult decisions have to be made. There have been a number of these, for example on issues relating to corporal punishment, gay **marriages**, the constitutionality of traditional practices, **prostitution**, selling liquor on Sundays, access to healthcare, access to housing, the rights of citizens abroad, and the rights of non-citizens in South Africa. The Court has generally received great public support for its decisions; it has also been criticized for not reflecting the views of the majority of South Africans in other instances. It has constantly emphasized that the Constitution is the foundation of all of South Africa's law and that all law must now be considered with the Constitution in mind. Its emphasis on government accountability and upholding the founding values of dignity, equality, and freedom has brought about a **revolution** in the way South African law works and is perceived. PIUS LANGA

constitutional law Constitutional law deals with the structure and powers of government. In most countries, key features of the constitution are set out in a document referred to as 'the constitution', which normally has a status superior to any other law. Such a document may set out a number of objectives and guiding principles, though few do so quite as opaquely as the Canadian Constitution, which seeks to establish 'a Constitution similar in principle to that of the **United Kingdom**'. At the core of a constitution, however, will be (i) provision for the different institutions of government—the executive, the legislature and the judiciary; along with (ii) the manner of their composition and the powers they each possess; as well as (iii) the powers they possess in relation to one another. The UK does not have a constitution in the sense of a single document with a superior legal status, making British constitutional law an unusual subject when compared with its equivalent in other jurisdictions. Nevertheless, with its deep roots, constant evolution, and extraordinary flexibility, British constitutional law has facilitated radical constitutional change without revolution, at least since the seventeenth century when Parliament wrestled power from the **Crown**. Perhaps because of the absence of a 'constitutional' text, it is a notable feature of British constitutional law that its boundaries have been set and its contours shaped

by influential scholars—including AV **Dicey** and Sir Ivor Jennings—perhaps to a greater extent than other countries.

It was famously said by Professor JAG Griffith that the UK has a 'political constitution', in contrast to the 'legal **constitutions**' found elsewhere. This, however, is not to under-estimate the extent to which constitutional government in the UK is grounded in principles acknowledged by the courts. The first is the **rule of law**, the second the legal sovereignty of Parliament, and the third responsible government in the sense that ministers are responsible to Parliament for the conduct of their departments. In recent years, the first of these principles has been strengthened by the development of **judicial review**, the introduction of the Human Rights Act 1998, and the enactment of the Constitutional Reform Act 2005 designed to enhance **judicial independence**. The second principle (**parliamentary sovereignty**) was consolidated as a revolutionary act in the Bill of Rights 1689, though some constitutional lawyers now suggest that it exists as a judicial indulgence, a rule of the **common law** capable of being changed. The principle has, however, been challenged (but not eclipsed) by British membership of the EC (and the competing principle of the supremacy of European law); and more recently (but to a much lesser extent) by the Human Rights Act 1998, whereby certain provisions of the **European Convention on Human Rights** may be enforced in the domestic courts. The principle of responsible government has more clearly been diluted by recent practice, with ministers now claiming to be 'accountable' rather than 'responsible' to Parliament for their departments.

Yet although constitutional lawyers can point to important constitutional principles which are applied by the courts, it is nevertheless the case that the core institutions of British government have developed as a matter of constitutional practice rather than constitutional law. So, while the monarchy is recognized and regulated by the Act of Settlement 1701, there is no law that says that there must be a **Prime Minister** or a **Cabinet**, or that the Prime Minister must be a member of the **House of Commons**. These are required as a matter of convention, a term used to describe the many non-legally binding rules, principles, and practices of the constitution, which help to ensure that ancient institutions now serve democratic ends. And just as core institutions of the constitution are the creatures of conventions, so too conventions regulate the way in which the legal powers of governing institutions are exercised. So, although the **monarch** has legal authority under the **royal prerogative** (another name for the **common law** powers of the Crown) to appoint the Prime Minister, there are no legal rules to determine who should be appointed to that office. But here again, conventions prescribe how the monarch's powers are to be exercised, in a way that best commands the confidence of Parliament. Yet it is not only the case that these conventions are created by constitutional practice rather than constitutional law: once created they are not, as a matter of constitutional law, legally enforceable and must rely on the political process for their observance.

While British constitutional law thus operates in part to preclude the legal enforceability of constitutional rules, it would be a mistake to convey the impression that the British constitution operates in a legal vacuum. Legislation has been necessary to introduce universal suffrage (with the legal principle of parliamentary sovereignty being the vehicle for the construction and carriage of the political principle of popular sovereignty), and to reduce the power and alter the composition of the **House of Lords** (in order to ensure the legislative and fiscal supremacy of the popularly elected House of Commons). It is also the case that it is constitutional law in the form of legislation rather than constitutional practice in the form of convention that established the devolved legislatures in Scotland, Wales, and Northern Ireland, as well as many (though not all) of the other constitutional changes since 1997, including the removal of the bulk of hereditary peers from the House of Lords. Yet while the constitutional scales have thus moved, it would be premature to see the balance now tilting in the direction of a 'legal' rather than a 'political' constitution: it continues to be a remarkable feature of British constitutional law that it has neither created nor defined the limits of the principal institutions of the British constitution, which nevertheless must act in accordance with the law. The British constitution is thus still principally about empowering rather than restraining government, an important and often overlooked dimension of constitutional law in a democracy.

KEITH EWING

See also: **conventions of the constitution; devolution; Parliament Acts**

constitutional monarchy This is a term used to describe the link between democratically elected elements of government and the **monarch** as a symbol and head of state and as a link with the past. The movement towards republicanism in the eighteenth and nineteenth centuries replaced many monarchies with democratically elected institutions. In countries such as the United Kingdom, with a strong tradition of monarchy (England has the oldest surviving monarchy in Europe), the monarchy has been preserved even though the monarch's powers are limited and constrained. In the UK the main working principles that regulate the monarch's relationship with the government of the day are as follows. In exercising constitutional functions the monarch is bound to accept and act on the advice of **ministers of state.** The Monarch has the duty to 'counsel, encourage and warn' the government. The Monarch must treat all communications with the Prime Minister of the day as confidential. The attraction of a constitutional monarchy is the time-honoured dignity that surrounds the office of monarch. A further strength is that monarchy sits above day-to day politics.

In the UK, reform of the system of constitutional monarchy is not high on the political agenda. There is a desire that the monarchy change sufficiently to remain in tune with the needs of the nation, but this falls short of demands for abolition and replacement by an elected head of state. Various problems associated with an elected head of state are seen by many as providing good reason to maintain the hereditary constitutional monarchy in its present form. This partly explain the failure of a referendum held in Australia in 1999 to abolish the monarchy and elect a head of state.

JOHN MCELDOWNEY

constitutional reform The Victorian constitution was lauded for the strength of government it produced in **Great Britain** and its Empire, and for the qualities of tolerance and freedom it secured for its citizens. From the Reform Act 1832 through to the cessation of war in 1945, evolutionary constitutional changes took place on an ad hoc basis. These were invariably to resolve constitutional conflicts or groundswells of new ideological opinion. They included, for example, the Parliament Act 1911 to curtail the power of the aristocracy in the **House of Lords** over the progressive social policies of the Liberal Government in the **House of Commons**, and the successive extensions of the franchise down to the Representation of the People Act 1918 granting universal adult suffrage.

In the second half of the twentieth century the British constitution proved remarkably immune to reform, due in part to a deeply ingrained pride in the traditional institutions and processes of its system of government. Nonetheless, serious political and intellectual interest in constitutional change emerged in the 1960s and 1970s. There were some notable failures in government reform initiatives, such as the doomed attempt at **House of Lords reform** by the Wilson

Government in 1969 (stymied by cross party back bench opposition in the Commons), and the debacle over Scottish and Welsh **devolution** by the Callaghan Government in 1978 (withdrawn after post-legislative referendums to endorse the measures failed to secure the required level of electoral support).

Membership of the European Community (now Union) took place under the Conservative Government in 1973, despite being deeply divisive across the party political spectrum. The later, long period of Conservative rule between 1979 and 1997 was then remarkable for the government largely ignoring constitutional reform whilst revolutionizing public sector management. The most significant reform of a constitutional nature in this period was the establishment of the Select Committee system in the Commons in 1979, set up to scrutinize the administration, expenditure, and policy of **departments of state**.

Public opinion in favour of radical constitutional reform gathered momentum in these years. Lectures, books, and reports were published on the subject, among them *Elective Dictatorship* in 1976 by Lord Hailsham (London: British Broadcasting Corporation), *Arguments for Democracy* in 1981 by Tony Benn (London: J Cape), and *A Written Constitution for the United Kingdom* in 1991 by the Institute for Public Policy Research (London: Mansell). Membership bodies lobbied for general or particular reforms, the most prominent of which being Charter 88.

The Labour Party under Tony Blair's leadership was elected into government in 1997, committed to a wide-ranging programme of constitutional reform. A series of major reforms began, starting with the Human Rights Act 1998 incorporating the **European Convention on Human Rights** into UK domestic law; and the Scotland Act 1998 and Government of Wales Act 1998 establishing the **Scottish Parliament** and **Welsh Assembly**. There followed the creation of a London mayor and assembly (Greater London Authority Act 1999); the first stage of reconstituting the House of Lords by removing all but ninety-two hereditary peers (House of Lords Act 1999); and the Freedom of Information Act 2000.

In the early years of the twenty-first century, formal machinery was established for keeping the constitutional arrangements of the UK under review, and for bringing forward proposals for modernization. In 2001, a Select Committee on the Constitution was established in the House of Lords, having both an investigative function in carrying out inquiries into broad constitutional issues and a scrutiny function in examining public bills for matters of constitutional significance.

In 2003 a new department of state was created, the Department for Constitutional Affairs ('DCA'), which subsumed the earlier **Lord Chancellor**'s Department and acquired new formal functions that included constitutional reform. The mission statement of the DCA, written by the first Secretary of State for Constitutional Affairs, Lord Falconer, stated that the department was 'the reformer and guardian of the constitution'. It said the DCA would 'embed fundamental political and constitutional change to achieve better government for the public, and to strengthen their democratic rights'. The present Ministry of Justice replaced the DCA in 2007, taking over responsibility for constitutional reform. Shortly afterwards, a newly appointed Prime Minister (Gordon Brown) launched a major government initiative on constitutional reform, set out in a consultative document *The Governance of Britain* that described itself as a 'route map' towards a new constitutional settlement. The proposal for a written constitution was to be considered, and two fundamental questions addressed which the Prime Minister stated to be 'to hold power more accountable and to uphold and enhance the rights and responsibilities of the citizen'.
ROBERT BLACKBURN

See also: **constitutional law**

constitutionalism   Constitutionalism, as political theory and practice, posits that the powers of government must be structured and limited by a binding constitution incorporating certain basic principles if the protection of values like human liberty and dignity is to be assured. This is the vision expressed in the first 'modern' constitutions, those of the United States (1789), and of France (1789, 1791), in contradistinction to the notion of the constitution—previously dominant, but still commanding some support in the United Kingdom—as merely describing how the state's functions are allocated and organized at any given time.

Today, the great majority of states are 'constitutionalist' in that they have codified constitutions which proclaim themselves as supreme law; are based on popular sovereignty; incorporate the principles of limited, representative, and accountable government, and the separation of powers; guarantee judicial independence; protect human rights; and require special procedures for amendment. Many also accept the principle that the constitution, as a binding legal document, can be authoritatively interpreted only by the courts, or by a specialist constitutional court. Constitutionalism so enhanced appeals to lawyers, since it places law above politics and makes judges, not legislators or governments, the custodians of the fundamental values of society.

The fact that the United Kingdom constitution, though departing in important respects from the precepts of constitutionalism, nonetheless secures its values, while many 'constitutionalist' states fail in this, is attributed by constitutionalists not to any weakness of their theory but to unusual features of our national character and political development.

TERENCE DAINTITH

C McIlwain, *Constitutionalism, Ancient and Modern* (Ithaca, NY: Cornell University Press, rev edn, 1947)

constitutions   In the broadest sense, a nation's constitution is the set of arrangements that organize the nation's governing institutions. At the heart of a constitution are the institutions to create laws, such as legislatures or parliaments, the institutions to administer them, such as executive ministries and departments, and the institutions to enforce them, such as courts. In addition, modern constitutions also identify what the nation's people regard as fundamental human rights.

More narrowly the term *constitution* can refer to a single written document such as the United States Constitution, originally adopted in 1789 and currently the world's oldest such document. Influential modern constitutions include those of Germany, Canada, and South Africa. A few nations, most notably the United Kingdom, New Zealand, and Israel, continue to organize their governing institutions under a so-called unwritten constitution. Such constitutions ordinarily consist of a collection of basic statutes that could in theory be modified but that are protected against actual modification by strong social and political norms. Such norms, and others, are sometimes described as **constitutional conventions**. Written and unwritten constitutions can also identify important governing institutions that are less universally used than legislatures, executive ministries, and courts, such as offices of **ombudsmen**, budget offices, and **political parties**.

Unwritten constitutions develop gradually. In contrast, written constitutions are created at specific moments, and then can be periodically amended or replaced. Most commonly, a nation creates or replaces a constitution in a situation of national crisis, such as military defeat, collapse of a prior regime, or success in an independence struggle. Because constitutions organize a nation's governing institutions, constitution-makers usually find it important to provide some basis for the claim that the nation's people

has endorsed their work. The ways in which they do so vary. Classically, constitutions were developed by constituent assemblies, representative bodies of constitution-makers brought together for the sole purpose of proposing a new constitution. More recently, the replacement of one constitution by another has sometimes been negotiated in 'round table' processes, in which representatives of competing factions in divided societies work out proposals and then submit them to some wider ratification process. There appears to be a modern norm, which some scholars have suggested is becoming a legal requirement, that fundamental changes in a nation's constitution be endorsed through a national referendum.

Occasionally, existing legislatures propose new constitutions, although this is rare for practical and theoretical reasons. New constitutions ordinarily seem valuable when the existing governing institutions have visibly failed, which makes constitutional revision by those very institutions unlikely to gain wide acceptance; and many theorists have questioned whether a legislature chosen under existing constitutional arrangements to enact ordinary legislation has the authority to establish an entirely different set of arrangements.

Written constitutions typically prescribe methods by which they can be amended. Amendments usually deal with matters of detail, with provisions that have become outdated, or with matters that have come to be regarded as fundamental in ways that were not appreciated earlier. Some scholars and constitutional courts have argued that some truly basic constitutional provisions cannot be amended even by following to the letter the forms prescribed in the constitution itself. The Supreme Court of India has held that constitutional amendments cannot alter the nation's 'basic structure,' a position asserted as well by the German Constitutional Court. Precisely which provisions are thought to be unamendable is rarely clear, but strong candidates are provisions dealing with core aspects of freedom of speech and core guarantees of the right to vote.

The fact that one constitution can be replaced by another raises questions about the proposition that some constitutional provisions cannot be amended. The questioned amendment might be seen as a provision in a new constitution, the remaining provisions of which are identical to those in the old constitution. This might be a merely theoretical point, except that it exposes an important feature of constitution-making generally. New constitutions usually are not created according to the forms prescribed in the constitutions they replace. The US Constitution replaced the Articles of Confederation, which stated that they could be amended only by unanimous agreement among the nation's component states, but the new Constitution stipulated that it would take effect when nine of the thirteen states ratified it. Constitution-making so frequently breaks the bonds of existing legality for the same reason that legislative constitution drafting is rare. Crisis conditions discredit the existing constitution, and may seem to require action that the existing constitution makes impossible.

Constitutions are usually understood to be a higher law than ordinary legislation, in the sense that laws inconsistent with the constitution are invalid. That is why a constitutional amendment can be adopted only after some process more difficult than the one used to enact ordinary legislation. In systems with unwritten constitutions, this follows as a matter of course from the fact that constitutional change occurs gradually. The procedures for amending written constitutions vary from the relatively easy, such as enactment by ordinary legislative majorities in successive legislative sessions, to the extremely difficult, as in the United States, which requires adoption by two-thirds of both legislative houses and ratification by legislatures in three-quarters of the nation's states.

When legislatures move to adopt, or actually do adopt, laws that some contend are inconsistent with the constitution, how can the constitution's higher-law status be preserved? Some systems rely on political mechanisms, such as party competition or a separation of power between the executive and the legislature, to make it difficult for legislatures actually to enact unconstitutional laws. Many systems rely on such mechanisms with respect to some matters, designated in the United States as 'political questions', which are least controversially invoked in connection with foreign affairs.

Increasingly, though, constitutional systems give courts the power to determine whether a proposed or enacted law is consistent with the constitution. Sometimes, as in the United States, the power is lodged in the regular courts, those that decide ordinary criminal and civil cases and interpret statutes as well as the constitution. Influenced by the ideas of Austrian legal theorist Hans Kelsen, other nations give the power of constitutional review to specialized constitutional courts. Such courts are particularly attractive in **civil law systems**, where judges in the regular courts are not trained to consider the mixed questions of constitutional law and public policy that arise whenever courts exercise the power to invalidate statutes. Judges who serve on specialized constitutional courts can be chosen with an eye to their ability to blend legal and policy analysis, a trait that one might not want in judges on ordinary courts.

Constitutional review is effective only when a nation's leaders or its people regularly accede to judicial determinations of unconstitutionality. The traditional mode of constitutional review had courts making a final decision that a statute was unconstitutional, unrevisable except by constitutional amendment. Since the 1980s, other modes of constitutional review have developed. Some courts make a provisional determination that legislation is incompatible with the constitution, but that determination can be overridden by ordinary legislation. Canada's Charter of Rights pioneered this technique, and the British Human Rights Act 1998 adopts a variant by authorizing the courts to issue declarations that parliamentary legislation is incompatible with certain important provisions of the **European Convention on Human Rights**. These techniques are said to create the possibility of a desirable dialogue between courts and legislatures, although the extent to which such dialogues actually occur is open to question.

There is no necessary connection between constitutions and **constitutionalism**, the normative idea that government power should be limited and exercised pursuant to law. The Soviet Constitution of 1936 is regularly offered as an example of a sham constitution, whose terms were routinely belied by the rules' actual practices. Contemporary written constitutions serve many purposes other than limiting government power. For a newly independent nation, the adoption of a written constitution signals its presence as a sovereign nation in world affairs. Yet, many scholars believe that true constitutions must comply with basic principles of constitutionalism. Some connection between constitutions and constitutionalism seems essential at least with respect to nations with unwritten constitutions, which might otherwise be difficult to distinguish from mere anarchy or a state of nature.

Are constitutions necessarily tied to nations? In one sense, clearly not. We can speak of the constitution of a private association, or of a sub-national entity such as one of the states in the United States. Yet there does seem to be some important connection between nationhood and constitutions. The nature of that connection was important in early twenty-first century discussions of whether the **European Union** had or could have a constitution. If the term refers only to the fact that there are governing institutions, the European Union clearly had something fairly described as a constitution, in the arrangements set out in the treaties creating the Union. If a 'true' constitution exists for a nation, the claim that Europe had a constitution was more questionable because few believed that there was a European 'nation' or people that could have a constitution in that sense.

MARK TUSHNET

constructive dismissal *see* **unfair dismissal**

constructive trusts *see* **trusts**

consuls *see* **diplomatic relations, immunities and privileges**

consultation by government Consultation is generally required within government when proposals or items of legislation are being developed. Thus, Cabinet approval will depend on the appropriate inter-departmental consultations having taken place. Consultation with outside interests, however, tends to take place at the discretion of the government and is not legally mandatory. The exception is where a statutory power is being exercised and the provision conferring that power stipulates that consultation of a designated kind must precede the exercise of the power.

In practice, governmental departments and agencies tend to consult widely before taking decisions or making new policies and rules. **Green Papers** are often issued by Ministers and are consultative in nature. (They are thus distinguishable from **White Papers**, which state the Government's policy on a matter.) **Common law** notions of fairness demand that bodies taking administrative decisions should consult affected parties where this is reasonable; but the common law imposes no general duty to consult parties who may be affected by an item of legislation or an administrative rule. (Primary legislation and Statutory Instruments are published but there is no general duty to publish tertiary rules or 'soft laws'). If, however, a body undertakes to engage in consultation with certain parties before making a decision, policy or rule, that undertaking may create a legally enforceable expectation of consultation.

In cases where the law does demand that consultation takes place, the courts have indicated that there must be a genuine invitation to give advice and a genuine undertaking to give consideration to any representations made. This means that sufficient information must be supplied to the consulted party to enable it to give helpful advice. In addition, the consulted party must be given enough time to give informed and considered advice. Whether any representations that have been made have been properly considered may often, however, be difficult for the consulted party to discern since the law imposes no comprehensive obligation on decision or rule-makers to give reasons for their actions.

ROBERT BALDWIN

See also: **legal rules, types of**

consultation with workers Consultation with workers is a form of worker involvement in managerial decision-making distinct from **collective bargaining**. Consultation has no fixed legal definition but refers, essentially, to the communication by management to the workers of information such as planned **redundancies** or restructuring, and to the consideration and criticism of that information by the workers, as communicated back to management. Consultation can take various forms, for example, individual consultation, which involves the employer and individual workers, or collective consultation, which takes place between the employer and workforce as a whole, either directly or through worker representatives. Consultation can proceed with a view to agreement, in which case, it might be argued that all that ultimately separates collective consultation from collective bargaining is the possibility of the sanction of industrial action.

Legal obligations to consult with workers regarding specific subject matter have been present in UK law since the 1940s. In the post-war **legislation** which nationalized key industries, a provision was included which placed the various management boards under an obligation to consult with the relevant **trade union** regarding the establishment and maintenance of joint machinery for consultation regarding *inter alia* safety, health, and welfare issues (see eg Coal Industry Nationalization Act 1946, section 46). For the most part, however, consultation, like collective bargaining, was not regulated by legislation in the years before 1971. In the Royal Commission on Trade Unions and Employers Associations 1965–1968 ('the Donovan Report'), very little mention was made of consultation with workers and no consideration was given to the idea of regulating consultation by means of legislation. Consultation of workers, either individually or collectively, through shop stewards, was regarded by Donovan as something which occurred, 'at the discretion of management' (paragraph 102).

Beginning in the 1970s, legal duties to consult employees in connection with specific matters such as collective redundancies and **transfers of business** were introduced pursuant to **European Community law**. In 1994 and 2002, directives were adopted which seek to encourage the institution of consultation machinery in workplaces throughout the Community in order that workers might be consulted regularly on a variety of matters. With regard to implementation in the UK, one of the most controversial issues has been that of whom exactly management must consult. Both the Labour government of 1974–1979 and the Conservative government of 1979–1983 provided, in line with the existing single channel system, that consultation should proceed exclusively with the representatives of trade unions recognized for the purposes of collective bargaining. Where no trade union was recognized, there was no requirement for consultation. Following a decision of the **European Court of Justice** in 1992, which found the UK to be in breach of the directives (*Commission of the European Community v UK* (1994)), the relevant legislation was amended so that where, in a given workplace, there was no recognized trade union, alternative employee representatives had to be elected from within the workforce. Later legislation has not guaranteed any priority to trade union representatives: regardless of whether or not a union is recognized for purposes of collective bargaining, employers are directed to arrange the **election** by employees of 'information and consultation' representatives.   RUTH DUKES

consumer   The term 'consumer' has various legal meanings. It can be used broadly, to mean citizens who 'consume' or use goods or services, ranging from plumbing to health services and education. Usually it is used in a more restrictive way.

Many statutory provisions, designed to protect purchasers of goods and services, contain specific measures applicable only to consumers. The statutory definitions of 'consumer' often contain slight variations, but there are certain common core features.

'Consumer' normally means a private individual acquiring goods or services. In some instances, in addition to natural persons, it can also include businesses such as sole-traders and partnerships, for example, under consumer credit measures. Occasionally, even companies come within the definition, if acting outside their normal business activities—for example a manufacturing company buying a car for a director.

A further requirement, often found in consumer protection measures emanating from the **European Union**, is that a consumer must be acquiring the goods or services otherwise than for business, trade, or professional purposes, that is, for their own private use and consumption.

Frequently, the consumer must be dealing with someone who *is* acting in the course of a trade or business. Deals between two private individuals will usually fall outside the definition of a consumer transaction.

'Consumer' need not be limited to contractual situations but may also cover people who ultimately use products and who, perhaps, have been injured by them, for example the person drinking the ginger beer in the famous case of *Donoghue v Stevenson* (1932).   DEBORAH PARRY

Consumer Credit Act   *see* **hire purchase; credit cards**

consumer protection in retail banking   In the UK, the **Financial Services Authority** ('FSA') is given responsibility under the **Financial Services and Markets Act 2000** ('FSMA') for the regulation of most forms of financial services. It has the statutory objective of securing the appropriate degree of protection for consumers, which it undertakes alongside its other objectives of maintaining confidence in the financial system, promoting public understanding of the financial system, and reducing the extent to which it is possible for business to be carried on for a purpose connected with financial crime. There will be overlaps between these objectives. For example, the existence of financial crime may lead to a reduction in market confidence as well as harm to the consumer.

It is possible to draw a distinction between two main types of consumer protection **regulation** where banking and, to an extent, other forms of financial services, are concerned: prudential regulation and **conduct of business regulation**. Prudential regulation aims to reduce the chance of individual institutions becoming insolvent. There is an argument that the authorities should minimize the likelihood of institutions failing, not just because of the effect that this has on market confidence and, ultimately, the safety and soundness of the economy as a whole, but also because of the harm it would cause to consumers. There is an economic rationale for this. If markets worked perfectly, banks would be under an incentive to run their affairs with prudence because this is so highly valued by consumers. However, consumers are generally not in a strong position to judge such matters. There may be some indicators of the soundness of an institution that can be disclosed prior to entering a contract, but it is doubtful that a regime based on disclosure will enable consumers to make appropriately informed choices. Furthermore, a bank's soundness depends on the conduct it undertakes after a consumer has entered a relationship with it. We might argue that consumers could, in theory, monitor the behaviour of banks once those consumers have entered a contract with their banks, but this seems far-fetched in practice.

For these reasons, there is a strong consumer-protection argument for regulation to minimize some (though, of course, not all) of the risks that banks confront. This does not mean that banks will never fail. The FSA has made it clear that it would be undesirable to expect that. The FSA has stated that it aims to maintain a regime which 'ensures as low an incidence of failure of regulated firms and markets (especially failures which would have a material impact on public confidence and market soundness) as is consistent with the maintenance of competition and innovation in the markets'.

Conduct of business regulation is concerned with how banks conduct business with consumers. It is carried out in a variety of different ways. Consumers receive protection under the criminal law from fraudulent activities, and have common law rights which enable them, for example, to sue for breach of contract, misrepresentation, or negligence. Furthermore, general consumer protection legislation, such as that dealing with **unfair contract terms** and trade descriptions applies to banking as well as to other business. In addition, there is now a body of more specialist law which controls how banks deal with consumers. However, it is interesting to observe that while the FSA regulates the majority of financial services activity, much conduct of business regulation in the area of retail banking is carried out through a voluntary code of practice known as the Banking Code. The first Code came into effect in 1992 and the latest version of the Code was published in 2005. The Code aims to set standards of good banking practice for firms dealing with consumers (in the words of the Code 'personal customers') in the UK. As well as banks, building societies, credit card companies, and National Savings and Investments are also eligible to join the Scheme.

The Code is based largely on principles. Indeed, it is underpinned by six, very general 'key commitments'. For example, subscribers to the Code promise: 'we will make sure that our advertising and promotional literature is clear and not misleading and that you are given clear information about our products and services'. There is a clear overlap between some of the provisions of the Code and the obligations imposed on banks by the FSA. Many of the provisions of the Code are designed to provide consumers with information. For example, under section 10 which deals with cards and personal identification numbers ('PINs'), paragraph 10.7 states: 'before you become a customer, we will give you the main features of the credit card in a summary box'. In some cases, the Code provides specific benefits to consumers beyond that required by law. For example, paragraph 7.1 allows consumers who are not happy with a choice of current or savings account to cancel it within 14 days of the day the contract is entered, or the day on which the consumer receives the terms and conditions, whichever is later.

The Banking Code has been broadly supported. Since 1999 it has been monitored and enforced by a body called the Banking Code Standards Board ('BCSB'). In addition, the Code is regularly and independently reviewed. Voluntary codes such as the Banking Code have some potential advantages over legislation. Their provisions can be changed relatively quickly, they are flexible, and can contain general principles that might be difficult to include in legislation. However, some concerns remain. One such concern is the relationship between codes and the law. It could be argued that where banks state that they adhere to the code, its provisions could be treated as implied terms in the banking contract. However, express terms in contradiction of the Code would have to take precedence. It might also be argued that some provisions of the Code are so rooted in trade usage that they become terms of a contract on that basis. If this is so, then the term would presumably be binding on non-subscribers as well as subscribers. This leads to a related point. One difficulty with voluntary regulation is that one can, to an extent, opt out of it. Banks are not obliged to subscribe to the Code, although the vast majority do. The BCSB is able to discipline errant firms on the basis of the contractual relationship it has with them. Disciplinary powers include the ability to name and shame banks that commit material breaches of the Code, to issue directions as to future conduct and to recommend the payment of compensation. However, if the firm chooses to leave it is able (so far as the provisions are not binding in other ways) to operate outside the provisions of the Code.

Where there has been breach of a provision of the Code and a consumer has suffered loss, one would expect the consumer to be compensated by the firm. However, as noted above, the BCSB only has powers to recommend the payment of compensation, and is not, primarily, a vehicle for providing consumer redress. That role is performed by the Financial Ombudsman Service ('FOS').

The FOS was established by FSMA as a statutory form of **alternative dispute resolution** ('ADR'). The FOS entertains complaints from consumers, small businesses, and charities about a number of matters, including virtually all areas of retail banking.

Particularly interesting is the approach to decision-making taken by the ombudsman (it is customary to talk of decisions or approaches of 'the ombudsman' rather than the FOS). In contrast to the courts, the ombudsman adopts an inquisitorial rather than adversarial approach. This gives the flexibility to obtain whatever information is necessary to resolve a complaint. Furthermore, the ombudsman will determine a complaint by reference to what is, in his of her opinion, fair and reasonable in all the circumstances of the case. In forming this judgment, the ombudsman will take into account a variety of matters, including law, regulatory guidance, codes of practice and, where appropriate, what he or she believes to have been good industry practice at the time. This means that the ombudsman can go beyond the strict legal requirements placed upon firms in providing redress. This is controversial, and might be criticized as favouring flexibility above certainty. However, although the ombudsman is not bound by **precedent**, he or she aims for consistency, and it seems that the ability to transcend strict legal requirements in favour of the consumer brings considerable benefits including, in some cases, changes in law or practice. The scheme is free to the consumer, decisions are binding on firms (though not on the consumer, who is free to ignore it and pursue a claim by other means), and can make awards of up to £100,000.

One of the key issues in banking (and other financial services) regulation is that of the balance between detailed rules and guidance and more general principles. The FSA has had eleven 'Principles for Businesses' since 2001 and describes these as providing the backbone of its regulatory regime. The FSA has also set out its determination to move firmly towards more principles-based regulation in the future.

PETER CARTWRIGHT

See also: **codes of practice in consumer law; deposit protection; disclosure in financial markets; financial regulation; investor compensation schemes; ombudsmen**

consumer welfare   It is noted in the definition of **efficiency in competition law** that the various types of efficiency can move in different directions. There may, for example, be an increase in productive efficiency, but a reduction in allocative efficiency. A standard is required in order to determine whether the conduct is positive, negative, or neutral. The consumer welfare standard takes the view that competition is protected for the benefit of consumers and that consumers benefit from low prices. According to this standard, which focuses on allocative efficiency, the

law should prohibit conduct that results in increased prices. The consumer welfare approach is subject to a number of criticisms. First, allocative efficiency is not necessarily a good measure of welfare. For example, reducing the price of cigarettes is welfare enhancing according to this standard, even though it has harmful effects on the consumer. Secondly, it assumes that consumers are a discreet and homogeneous section of society that all benefit in the same way. Thirdly, other efficiencies are sacrificed and these might outweigh the benefits to consumers.

OKEOGHENE ODUDU

contact, family   Contact with a **child**, or deciding with whom a child ought to have contact, is one of the incidents of legal **parenthood**, but contact can also be ordered or agreed between a child and any other **person**. 'Contact' is used in the Children Act 1989 and the Children (Scotland) Act 1995 both in cases of family breakdown (such as separation or **divorce**) and where the child is separated from family or carers by the state (such as when he or she is in the care of a local authority). The concepts of **residence** and contact in UK family law replace those of 'custody' and 'access' and are meant to highlight their child- rather than adult-centredness. Contact can be supervised or unsupervised, direct, including staying or overnight contact, or indirect, such as by telephone, email, or post. If the child is aged sixteen years or under and the parties cannot agree contact arrangements, the court has jurisdiction to make orders regulating, specifying, or even prohibiting contact between a child and any person including a parent or other relative, if it is in the child's welfare to do so.

All decisions about contact must be made with the welfare of the child being the court's (and ideally, the parents') paramount consideration. Understandings of a child's welfare have varied over the years, some research in the 1970s and 1980s suggesting that in the interests of stability, decisions about contact ought to be made by the child's primary carer, that contact may provoke divided loyalties in the child, and that while regular good quality contact was beneficial, infrequent or unpredictable contact was damaging for the child. Other research suggests that contact provides for the child a sense of approval and warmth, allows for developing or maintaining meaningful relationships, provides information and knowledge of personal **identity**, and helps repair distorted relationships. In the context of parental separation, most research confirmed that conflict between separated parents was harmful for children. The current interpretation of welfare is unequivocal about contact: not only is contact with a non-resident parent deemed to be beneficial for children, its denial is thought to jeopardize the child's welfare. Combined with the admonition against conflict, this understanding of welfare has meant that in practice, **mediation**, negotiation, and court-based investigations of post-separation contact disputes begin with the assumption that contact will occur and the parent who wishes to deny contact must make a case for why that denial is in the best interests of the child. It has also meant that most parents do make their post-separation child care arrangements outside court. In addition, it has meant that whether parents reach agreement or whether the case is one of the minority that go before a court, the outcome is usually contact in some form except where there is some serious problem such as **violence** or potential violence. Finally, it has lent support to the government's commitment to contact, where it is 'safe', as a general 'good' for children and has directed legislative and policy initiatives to facilitate, encourage and sometimes coerce contact. These initiatives include expansion of the use of contact centres and, in England and Wales, permitting the court to make orders requiring parents to attend information, advice, or counselling sessions about contact and to make a wide range of contact enforcement orders (Children and Adoption Act 2006).

Children's views on contact are sometimes sought by mediators and ought normally to be sought by **courts** in disputed cases. **Legislation** and now, the **Human Rights Act 1998** demand that children's views be obtained where the child is old enough to give them, but even the views of very young children can be heard by the court. Usually, children's views are presented through reports made by court (or privately appointed) welfare professionals. But, while the courts (and, ideally but not always, mediators and negotiating parties) must ascertain the wishes and feelings of children who are the subjects of contact disputes, those views will not be decisive; the welfare of the child may demand they be overridden.

Contact with non-resident parents is also said to be a child's right. The first judicial statements to this effect were made, arguably, to highlight the child-centredness of contact and distinguish it from rights claims made by non-resident fathers to contact with their children. Recently, however, successful claims for contact have been made by both adult family members and children under the **Human Rights** Act 1998 as respecting their **private** and **family life** under Article 8 of the **European Convention on Human Rights**. Courts in these cases have been careful to say, however, that Article 8 cannot establish a relationship between a family member and

a child; it can only protect an existing one. So, for example, a biological father or grandparent with no existing relationship with a child may not use Article 8 to create one by demanding contact, but he or she or a child may use it to protect an already existing 'family life' together. While these cases may acknowledge that contact is a right both of a child and parent or other family member, courts will always consider such claims in the light of the child's welfare.

The pro-contact culture in law, psychology, and social work is most influential in cases of parental separation, but it has also influenced the presumption in favour of contact in cases of local authority involvement with children and has influenced policy in favour of open **adoptions**. While some applaud it, particularly in parental separation cases, others suggest that it does not go far enough and that law should go further and include a presumption of shared residence of children. Still others argue that the pro-contact assumption goes too far and too often permits contact in cases where it is harmful for the children and their carers, such as in cases of **domestic violence**. They argue that such an assumption of general application leaves little room for considering the interests of individual children and their parents.   ALISON DIDUCK

See also: **child protection; welfare principle**

contaminated land and soil conservation
Despite being a non-renewable source, soil has been the subject of much less legal attention than that given to the other environmental media of air and water. The reasons for this include the fact that problems may be hidden within the ground; may take a substantial amount of time to become apparent; and that setting standards for a medium which can be used for many different purposes can be very difficult. For example, the level of various contaminants which we might consider acceptable for land used for heavy industrial processes is likely to be very different to that considered acceptable for agriculture, or for playing fields. There are also difficulties in conserving the amount or quality of something which is usually privately owned, in contrast with the other media.

For many years legal rules influencing the condition of land were restricted to general **common law** provisions, such as **nuisance**, **public health legislation**, and policy controls through the **Town and Country Planning** system. More recently, environmental regulations, such as the **Waste** Management Licensing and Pollution Prevention and

Control regimes, have attempted to prevent further **pollution** of land, with the Planning system continuing to play an important role in both the clean-up and prevention of soil pollution. The lack of effective control in the past resulted in the need to introduce a new regulatory system aimed at the clean-up of historically contaminated land through Part 2A of the Environmental Protection Act 1990. This provides powers for local authorities and the **Environment Agency** to require the clean-up of land, or to recover the costs of their own clean-up actions. Land is identified as 'contaminated' by reference to risks of harm to **human** health, ecological systems, or property, and to water pollution. There are complex provisions regarding the identification of clean-up actions and of the polluters and landowners who can be made liable for these. The number of sites which have been the subject of enforcement under Part 2A has been much lower than anticipated. This might reflect one of the main aims of the system which is to provide clarity as to potential liability in order to encourage voluntary clean-up actions and to assist with the allocation of liability in commercial transactions.

Strategic action to preserve and enhance soil quality has been even more limited, though a recent European Soil Strategy provides a focus for legal and policy developments.   LAURENCE ETHERINGTON

contempt of court   Contempt of court has been aptly described as 'the Proteus of the legal world, assuming an almost infinite diversity of forms' (see J Moskovitz, 'Contempt of Injunctions, Civil and Criminal' (1943) 43 *Columbia Law Review* 780). Its central concern is not, as might be assumed, to protect the dignity of individual judges or courts but, rather, to assist the due administration of justice and to safeguard it against improper interference. In the United Kingdom this protective jurisdiction benefits not only the traditional **courts** of law, but also any other body (including employment **tribunals** and mental health review tribunals) which exercises the judicial power of the state. A broadly similar jurisdiction exists in other **common law** countries, for example, Australia, New Zealand, and Canada, and some functional equivalents are to be found in **civil law systems**.

An initial distinction is made between 'civil' and 'criminal' contempt. Civil contempt plays an essential role in underpinning the effectiveness of such court orders as injunctions whereby a court requires a person to desist from a particular activity or to act in a specified way. It seems obvious that such orders must carry the threat of a sanction if they are disobeyed; and in the United Kingdom this is provided by the law of contempt. Thus, on proof of disobedience, the 'contemnor' may be fined or imprisoned for a fixed term which, in the case of a superior (higher) court, may be for as much as two years. Moreover, the penalty may be imposed not only coercively and to secure future compliance, but also to punish past disobedience. Although any such contempt is 'civil' in character, the alleged contemnor is entitled to the safeguards associated with criminal proceedings. For example, breach of the injunction must be proved beyond reasonable doubt and the rules of evidence applicable to criminal proceedings usually apply. This is entirely understandable in that a person's liberty is at stake.

The most obvious form of criminal contempt occurs within the body or in the face of the court. Typical cases involve disruptive, threatening, or insulting behaviour (and there have been numerous colourful examples over the years) or any equivalent conduct which seriously disrupts court proceedings, such as using mobile phones or cameras in the public gallery. For similar reasons, witnesses may commit a contempt by refusing without just cause to be sworn or to answer questions. Although the need to control such disruptive behaviour seems self-evident, certain aspects of its use have been controversial. In particular, the procedure which is adopted is 'summary' in the sense that it does not follow the usual pattern of investigating and trying offences. Rather, contempt is often dealt with by the presiding judge who witnessed the events. Although this may be convenient, there are dangers in 'instant justice', and care needs to be taken to ensure that the alleged contemnor has received a fair trial before an independent and impartial tribunal. Indeed, a failure to do so would infringe the minimum rights associated with Article 6 of the **European Convention on Human Rights**.

A criminal contempt of court may also be committed where material is published (whether in a newspaper, on television, or elsewhere) which has the potential to interfere with the administration of justice in a current or forthcoming trial. The common law has long since controlled trial by the media and this was evident in the well-known *Sunday Times* case (*Attorney-General v Times Newspapers Ltd* (1974)), where the background was newspaper comment on the alleged responsibility of a pharmaceutical company for abnormalities caused by the drug thalidomide. However, nowadays, the principal source of control is the 'strict liability rule' of the Contempt of Court Act 1981. This form of statutory contempt will start to apply once proceedings are 'active' which, in the case of criminal proceedings, will typically be when a suspect has been arrested or charged or a warrant for arrest has been issued; and they will remain 'active' until the conclusion of any appeal.

Since liability for contempt is strict, it does not depend on any intent to prejudice a fair trial. What is required, rather, is that the publication should have created a substantial risk of seriously impeding or prejudicing the proceedings. Such a risk may exist if, for example, a newspaper were to publish material which was highly prejudicial but unlikely to be admissible in evidence at any subsequent trial. So, in one modern example (*Attorney-General v Morgan* (1998)) a newspaper was fined £50,000 for contempt when it described an accused as a 'veteran villain' with a 'long criminal record for fraud, deception, car crime, drug offences and burglary'. Whether any given publication is adjudged to have caused a substantial risk of serious prejudice will depend on a variety of factors, including its circulation, timing, form, and—depending on the facts—judicial perceptions of the effectiveness of any warnings which the trial court judge issued to the jury to ignore matters that were not evidence in the case. In principle, the risk of prejudice would usually be lower if the publication appeared soon after the suspect was arrested, since future jurors may never have seen it or may have forgotten it. Conversely, it would usually be higher if it appeared towards the end of the trial when the force of its impact might lead to the jury being discharged. However, this distinction will not invariably apply since future trials may be irreparably compromised from the very start of the criminal process, as when a photograph of the principal suspect is published (perhaps on television or in a national newspaper) in advance of an identity parade. In such cases, potential witnesses would then know who had been arrested and whom they were expected to pick out.

Although these examples of statutory contempt represent the typical or paradigm case, a contempt may occasionally be committed by creating a serious risk of prejudice to civil proceedings, perhaps through subjecting witnesses or parties to intensive public pressure to modify their evidence or withdraw. Whether the context be criminal or civil proceedings, any restriction imposed by the law of contempt must be consistent with the right to freedom of expression enshrined in Article 10 of the European Convention on Human Rights and necessary for maintaining the authority and impartiality of the judiciary and of the judicial process.

The concern of statutory contempt of court under the 'strict liability rule' of the 1981 Act is to safeguard the administration of justice in particular criminal or civil proceedings. However, contempt of court has a similarly important (but less obvious) role to play in safeguarding the administration of justice as a continuing or ongoing process. Three examples illustrate the point. First, it is contempt to victimize a witness for evidence given on an earlier occasion. Leading examples have involved trade union officials, landlords, and even the RSPCA. As Lord Denning noted in a leading case (*Attorney-General v Butterworth* (1963)), if there were no effective sanction to prevent such conduct potential witnesses would be unwilling to come forward in future. Similar reasoning applies to others who have a role to play in judicial proceedings, for example, as parties or even judges.

Second, and more controversially, it may also be a contempt of court to 'scandalize' a court or judge whether by general abuse or invective or by imputing corruption, bias or some improper motive to them. Although the rationale is understandable, in that such comment may undermine public perceptions of the integrity of judicial decision-making, this aspect of contempt has fallen into desuetude within the United Kingdom. The problem is that it can easily be characterized as being concerned with safeguarding the dignity of judges, rather than with protecting the administration of justice.

The third example is the general prohibition contained in the 1981 Act against disclosing such matters as statements made, opinions expressed, or votes cast by members of a jury during their deliberations. The confidentiality of jury deliberations promotes the open exchange of views and the finality of verdicts, although it may also mask indications that jurors were in dereliction of their duties to such an extent as to create the risk of a miscarriage of justice.

Although the above instances represent the most typical examples of criminal contempt of court, they are by no means the only ones. For example, it is also contempt to obstruct persons who are officially connected with the court or its process or to interfere with persons who are under the special protective jurisdiction of the court. Indeed, the breadth of the concept is well illustrated by the relatively modern development known as the *Spycatcher* principle. In the case which gave its name to this principle (*Attorney-General v Times Newspapers Ltd* (1992)), the House of Lords held that even though a newspaper or any other body is not bound by an injunction (and so cannot commit a civil contempt in relation to it), nonetheless it commits a criminal contempt if it acts in a way which is intended to thwart the very purpose for which the injunction was granted. Such conduct falls within the general unifying principle that the law of contempt is concerned to protect the due administration of justice, whether in relation to particular legal proceedings or more generally.

CJ MILLER

CJ Miller, *Contempt of Court* (Oxford: Oxford University Press, 3rd edn, 2000)

D Eady and ATH Smith, *Arlidge, Eady and Smith on Contempt* (London: Sweet & Maxwell, 3rd edn, 2005)

See also: **freedom of expression; freedom of speech; juries; media reporting of courts and tribunals, restrictions on**

contiguous zone   *see* **law of the sea**

continental shelf   *see* **law of the sea**

contingency fee arrangements   *see* **no-win, no-fee arrangements**

contraband   *see* **neutrality**

contract law   The law of contract is that part of the civil law that governs the enforceability of agreements. It consists of general rules, which apply to all kinds of contract, and specialist rules which are restricted to particular kinds of contract.

A striking feature of the legal obligations which arise from contracts is that, at least in theory, they are self imposed. Most other legal obligations which relate to individuals' conduct exist independently of their volition, notably the criminal law and the law of tort. An individual or organization, by entering a contract, undertakes obligations, typically to act for another's benefit—for example by paying money, rendering services, or delivering goods. The result is that the law of contract has to identify when such obligations arise, the contents of such obligations and the legal consequences of their breach.

Although it is commonly believed that an agreement in writing is needed for a contract to exist, this is not in fact the general rule. A contract may be found in oral exchanges or even mere conduct, as well as in durable forms such as writing or electronic storage. However, writing is necessary for some types of contract, most notably those concerning land. Also necessary (unless the promise is contained in a **deed**) is the presence of *consideration*. This has a technical meaning, the gist of which is that something has to be given in return for a promise if it is to be legally enforceable. Most market exchanges will easily clear this hurdle, but it means that a gratuitous promise (for example a promise of a gift) is made without consideration and so will not be enforced. A binding contract will typically arise out of an agreement before any actual transfer of goods or services takes place.

Where a contract is not performed as agreed, one party may request a court to enforce the agreement. Unless the contract concerns land (where a court may compel a transfer of the land to the purchaser by an order of **specific performance**), the remedy will almost invariably consist of the payment of money. Whilst the most common claim is for the price due under a contract, monetary **compensation** (**damages**) can also be claimed where goods or services are not provided as agreed. Damages are based on the loss suffered by the claimant, and this is measured by comparison with the position the claimant would have been in if the contract had been properly performed. However, the claimant is expected to take reasonable steps to 'mitigate' losses, and is limited to compensation for losses which could have been foreseen as likely. In addition, a party may 'rescind' (ie put an end to) a contract where agreement was procured by wrongdoing (such as a misrepresentation or duress), although the circumstances where this is possible are limited. Where one party's performance (eg building work) is seriously deficient, the other may refuse further performance and terminate the contract.

It is a paradox of the law of contract that, whilst agreement between the parties has been regarded as foundational of the contract, contract law itself has mainly emerged from cases where the agreement has been incomplete or imperfect. Cases where the parties have negotiated all the terms are relatively exceptional: it is much more usual for negotiation to focus on key issues such as price, leaving much of the substance to be filled out by 'standard terms' applicable to many contracts of the type in question. This means that, as a matter of practicality, the law has had to work out how to deal with standard terms which could (for example) be in a notice, on the back of an order form, or referred to on a ticket. Such terms are often one-sided, having been drafted by one party to further their interests and offered to the other party on a 'take-it-or-leave-it-basis'. The **common law**'s first answer was to include such terms as part of the contract: under the 'objective' approach to interpreting agreement, parties were bound by an appearance of agreement even if, subjectively, they had not agreed. Thus, a person who signed a contract could be bound by standard terms inserted by the other party even if these had not been read or understood.

This robust expectation that contracting parties would look after their own interests was dignified by appeal to the value of freedom of contract. However, this did not really explain why the common practice of signing a set of standard terms without any real understanding of them should result in parties—particularly **consumers**—being bound by unusual or unfair terms. Standard terms thus posed a question of contractual morality about how parties to a contract should be expected to treat one another. The individualism of nineteenth- and early twentieth-century contract law meant that there were few limits on taking advantage of others; examples of this included very limited recognition of factors which might undermine consent (such as mistake and duress), and a reluctance by the courts to interfere with the parties' bargain, resulting in a literal interpretation of contract terms.

The general rules of the common law, applying to all contracts, did not adapt well to the emerging need for more protective rules in consumer and other contracts. The modern law has seen the qualification of those general rules—mainly by legislation—for specific kinds of contract. Contracts which individuals enter into in a personal rather than business capacity—mainly consumer and employment contracts, and residential tenancies—now contain obligations which are effectively compulsory in that they cannot be excluded by agreement between the parties. The Sale of Goods Act 1979, for example, provides minimum standards for the quality of goods and their fitness for purpose. **European Union** directives have played an increasing role here, and the Unfair Terms in Consumer Contracts Directive ('UTCCD') of 1993 introduced a general test of fairness for all non-negotiated terms in consumer contracts, other then those defining the basic price and performance. This directive applies to a wide range of situations including financial contracts, such as mortgages as well as tenancies. It has the effect that the old common law rule that a person is bound by their signature on a document no longer applies if the terms in a consumer contract are unfair.

Commercial contract law (ie the law applying between businesses) has also seen development of situation-specific rules, although they have generally not been of a protective character. The EU has not yet embarked on the harmonization of commercial contract law. However, a Principles of European Contact Law project was initiated in 1993 by leading contract scholars, designed to restate the principles underlying the contract law of the various EU Member States. These principles may be incorporated into contracts by the agreement of the parties, but are not otherwise binding. The Common Frame of Reference is a harmonization project of the EU Commission. This has focused on consumer law, and, although it

has the potential to apply much more widely, it seems unlikely it will cover the whole field of contract law in the foreseeable future. The UK has resisted such a move, in part because of the position English contract law has attained as the preferred law of much international trade. Nevertheless, some UK protective legislation does apply to commercial contracts, notably the Unfair Contracts Terms Act 1977, which imposes a test of reasonableness on clauses which seek to exclude the basic obligations in contracts for the sale of goods and the provision of services.

Although the function of commercial contract law has been regarded as facilitative rather than protective, there has been a significant change in the way in such contracts are interpreted. Traditionally, the literal approach meant the terms of a contract were given meaning in isolation from the surrounding circumstances. A much more contextual approach has now been adopted by the House of Lords, the effect of which can be to reject a clear literal meaning when, taking account of the context, this does not reflect what the parties are likely to have intended.

While contract law has adapted to fulfil a protective function in relation to categories such as consumers, the fact it is only mobilized in private litigation limits its effect. Regulation by an official agency (which forms the bulk of consumer protection) is generally a more effective mechanism than private law, and an important innovation of the UTCCD was to give the **Office of Fair Trading** power to intervene to prevent the continued use of unfair terms. This is a far more effective means of eradicating such terms than depending on private litigation to test whether or not particular terms are unfair.

The rise of electronic communication has widely transformed contracting practice, although this has not resulted in large changes in contract law. The EU Directive on Electronic Commerce (2000) sought to ensure that contracts can be made in electronic media, and the Electronic Communications Act 2000 contains provisions to ensure that legal requirements of writing can be met by an electronic equivalent. The bulk of contract law, however, seems to have remained unscathed.

Although part of modern contract law still consists of rules of general application, the most striking feature has been the emergence of different legal regimes for different categories of relationship. From the earlier position where the law was underpinned by an individualism which left parties pretty much to fend for themselves, the law has embraced a mixture of protective and facilitative purposes, which are worked out differently in various contracting contexts. Much of the recent impetus has come from the

EU, and the future of a body of distinctively English contract law remains uncertain.

JOHN WIGHTMAN

J Adams and R Brownsword, *Understanding Contract Law* (London: Sweet & Maxwell, 5th edn, 2007)

H Collins, *Law of Contract* (Cambridge: Cambridge University Press, 4th edn, 2004)

See also: **sale of goods; tort law; unfair contract terms**

contract of employment In English law, and in the laws of the United Kingdom more generally, the contract of employment is a central organizing concept, many would say *the* central organizing concept, for labour and employment law, and indeed for the legal representation and regulation of the individual employment relationship more generally. It is easy for English common lawyers to imagine that this is a universal proposition for all legal systems, but that would be something of a misconception; for example, the US labour law system analyses the basic employment relationship in the absence of an express contract as 'employment at will', the contractual status of which is very debatable, at least according to the way in which the contract of employment is constructed in English law. In continental European legal systems, although there is no single clear alternative to the contract of employment as the prevailing category in the legal analysis of employment relationships, it nevertheless seems that the contract of employment is not such a dominant paradigm as it is in English law. In most such systems, it is perceived as less of a necessity to understand the employment relationship as a primarily contractual one.

Where and to the extent that the employment relationship is legally analysed in the form of the contract of employment, such analyses tend to have a number of key features in common. The legal analysis of the employment relationship in the form of the contract of employment is very strongly associated with a binary legal analysis of all personal work relationships whereby those relationships are regarded as being either ones in which the worker is subordinated to an employer or employing enterprise or ones in which the worker remains independent of an employer or employing enterprise. The contract of employment is *par excellence* the legal expression of the subordinate or dependent work relationship, and this is very apparent as a constant theme of the doctrine and case law which has developed in different legal systems to distinguish it from the 'contracts for services' under which independent or autonomous workers are employed. This binary analysis tends to persist despite the considerable difficulties of applying it in practice to the immense variety and complexity of personal work relations which modern labour economies evolve and support.

This is by no means the only sense in which the legal analysis of the dependent work relationships in the form of the contract of employment, instead of being straightforwardly reflexive of the social and economic features of those relationships, imposes a particular vision or construction of those relations which quite strongly shapes their realities, sometimes in ways which are anachronistic or otherwise distorting. In English law, at least, that particular vision includes the features of: (1) a strong commitment to an understanding of the employment relationship as a bilateral one with a single employer, making it difficult to deal with the realities of multilateral employment relations, for example in the case of employment via the intermediation of an employment agency; (2) a set of default terms and default rules which accord very wide powers of disciplinary dismissal to the employing enterprise, largely unqualified powers of dismissal with notice, and very limited remedies for the employee in respect of **wrongful dismissal**; and (3) a limiting condition or defining requirement of continuing mutuality of obligation, making it difficult for **casual workers** to establish that they are employed under continuing contracts of employment, and so limiting their access to many statutory employment rights.

In an even more general sense, the primacy of the contract of employment in the analysis of the employment relationship in English law has the effect of representing that relation as being mainly derived from individual agreement between the worker and the employer, as shaped and interpreted by the **common law courts**. When treated as more than a convenient legal fiction, this analysis is apt to obscure a reality in which the normative bases of employment relations are not generally derived from genuine bargaining with individual workers. Although the late Sir Otto Kahn-Freund ingeniously developed a convincing rationale for the incorporation of the substantive terms of **collective agreements** into individual contracts of employment, this was not free of the cost of some reduction in the legal effectiveness of **collective bargaining**. And, today even more significantly, the contractual construct tends to understate the extent to which the employment relation is regulated by **legislation**, whether emanating from **European Community law**, domestic statute law, or governmental measures of various kinds. In continental European employment law systems, a much less contractually-oriented view tends to be taken of the nature of the hierarchy of sources of the law and norms of the employment relationship, a view most fully reflected by the French *Code du Travail* and the doctrinal treatment of it by authorities on employment law.

Moreover, any analysis of the treatment of the employment relationship even in English law has to acknowledge the crucial role of legislation not only in prescribing minimum hourly remuneration, paid **holidays**, standards of provision for health and safety and requirements of **equality** of treatment between various groups of workers, but also in closely controlling the duration and termination of those relationships. Sometimes indeed those prescriptions or controls are expressed by the relevant legislation precisely as mandatory terms in contracts of employment, and sometimes as overriding provisions from which those contracts cannot derogate. However, the foregoing account should not be seen as depicting a wholly sclerotic legal institution. It forms the reasonably dynamic heart of processes of evolution in the legal treatment of the personal work relation in most employment law systems, and figures largely in the development of associated institutions and concepts such as those of 'employee', 'personal work contract', 'worker', '**good faith performance in employment law**', and '**redundancy**'.   MARK FREEDLAND

contracting out   In the private sector, contracting out or 'outsourcing' is a common technique for the provision of goods or services which can be furnished by another enterprise more efficiently than it can be provided in-house. As such, it does not raise any particular legal problems apart from those of general **contract law**, though there is controversy about the desirability of outsourcing core activities or those which involve direct contact with the public because of difficulties in quality control. The use of contracting out has been much more controversial in the public sector, where it has been used by central and **local government** and the **National Health Service** as a means of passing the provision of services to the private sector. Initially it was used for ancillary services such as cleaning and catering, but in some areas has grown to encompass core activities.

In the case of central government, an important form of contracting out has been through the process of market testing, by which the costs of internal public and external private provision of services are compared through competitive tendering. The result determines whether provision is retained in-house subject to conditions set out in a service level agreement (a legally unenforceable internal 'contract') or provided by an outside firm under a legally binding contract. Examples include the management of some prisons and the provision of information technology services. To facilitate this process, some legal changes had to be made, notably to permit the removal of the presumption that a minister could not delegate his/her functions outside the civil service (Deregulation and Contracting Out Act 1994, section 69).

Contracting out has also played a major part in the National Health Service; indeed the NHS has been largely redesigned as a system of purchasing authorities and trusts providing services (the 'purchaser/provider split') linked by 'NHS contracts' which are not legally enforceable. This process started in the 1980s under Conservative governments, but has been given further momentum in England from 2003 with the establishment of Foundation Trusts, which have a separate legal identity from the health service in general and which do enter into legally enforceable contracts with purchasing authorities. There has also been a large increase in the contractual provision of public health services by the private sector. The aims are to increase efficiency of provision and to permit more patient choice. However, previous attempts at contractualization of the service have been criticized as fragmenting it and reducing cooperation; the reforms have not been fully adopted by the devolved administrations in Scotland and Wales.

It is in relation to local authorities that contracting out of services was most fully developed and proved most controversial. Throughout the 1980s and early 1990s compulsory competitive tendering ('CCT') legislation was used to compel authorities to put key services out to tender; for example, construction and maintenance work, refuse collection, cleaning, and catering. Where the local authorities themselves wished to bid to retain the service provision, this had to be accomplished through a distinct Direct Service Organization separate from the authority's purchasing role. The Minister had power to enforce competitive tendering, and issued voluminous guidance dealing with such issues as the avoidance of unfair competition in the tendering process. The CCT regime was widely perceived as having become over-technical and legalistic, and was replaced by the incoming Labour government with the 'Best Value' regime under the Local Government Act 1999. This gives greater autonomy to local government to review and improve its own service provision; however, major powers of central government **regulation** are included and local authorities are encouraged to contract out service provision as one means of securing improvement in the delivery of services.

The result of the contracting out process is that it is no longer a simple matter to point to the distinction between the public and private sectors, and this has led to legal complexities. An important example is the extent to which a private body to which service provision has been contracted out is covered by the Human Rights Act 1998. According to the courts, the Act will not apply to such a body in most circumstances, thus creating a gap in the protections afforded by the legislation. In some cases, a body to which a service is contracted may also not be subject to the process of **judicial review**, whilst the doctrine of privity of contract may prevent those receiving services from relying on the terms of the contract between the public authority and the service provider.

TONY PROSSER

contributory negligence Contributory negligence is a (partial) defence which can be pleaded in **tort law**. It is normally raised in claims of **negligence** or **breach of statutory duty**. It addresses situations where the person bringing a claim is partly at fault in relation to the loss for which she is seeking to be compensated. In these circumstances, it will usually be possible for the defendant to raise a defence of contributory negligence. The effect of doing this will be to permit a court to reduce the amount of **compensation** payable to the claimant in accordance with how much she was to blame for the loss, as compared with the defendant. So, for example, the defence will be available in a case where a driver sues for compensation for injuries she sustained in a car accident caused by the defendant's negligence, if it can be shown that the driver's failure to wear a seat belt at the time of the accident contributed to the extent of her injuries. It cannot be raised against the **victim** of fraud, no matter how foolish she may have been to believe the lies told to her. Nor can the defence be raised against a claimant who has carelessly allowed someone else to steal his goods. It is an open question whether the defence can be raised against a claimant who provoked the defendant to assault him physically. In cases where a claimant sues a defendant for committing a breach of contract, the defence can only be raised where the breach of contract involved a failure to act carefully. The defence cannot be raised against the victim of an equitable wrong.

Originally a defence of contributory negligence, if successfully established, barred a claim altogether. This arguably resulted in unjust outcomes in which the defendant, while overwhelming responsible for the claimant's harm, could avoid liability altogether by establishing that the claimant shared even the smallest degree of responsibility for what had happened to her. This problem was addressed in the Law Reform (Contributory Negligence) Act 1945 in which an apportionment system was adopted.

NICHOLAS MCBRIDE

contributory principle *see* **national insurance**

controlled foreign companies *see* **international tax**

Convention for Elimination of Racial Discrimination *see* **CERD**

Convention for the Elimination of all Forms of Discrimination against Women *see* **CEDAW**

Convention on Access to Information, Public Participation in Decision-Making and Access to Justice in Environmental Matters *see* **Aarhus Convention**

Convention on the Rights of the Child The **United Nations** Convention on the Rights of the Child ('UNCRC') was adopted by the General Assembly on 20 November 1989 and came into force in 1990. By December 2006 all member states had ratified the convention except the United States of America and Somalia (which had only signed the convention by that date).

The Convention was the third of its kind; in 1924 the League of Nations adopted the Geneva Declaration on the Rights of the Child. This was followed by the UN Declaration on the Rights of the Child in 1959. These declarations were significant in promoting the idea that children were important and deserved protection. However, they were aspirational, imposing no enforcement mechanism on states.

The UNCRC, on the other hand, recognized that children deserved more than simply protection. It created a more powerful tool which children (or their advocates) could use to assert and achieve their individual rights. It inscribed into international law a measure of the **autonom**y rights that had, hitherto, been exclusively within the province of adults (see, for example, Articles 12 and 13 (expression), 14 (conscience), 15 (association), and 16 (**privacy**)). In doing this it did not, however, neglect the protective rights that children also required (see, for example, Article 19 (protection from harm)). Perhaps most importantly, it was enforceable. It established a policing mechanism for the rights it defined. Signatory states were now under an obligation to protect and promote **children's rights**, tested by a UN administered inspection and reporting system.

CRAIG LIND

conventions of the constitution Conventions are non-legal constitutional rules established by custom and practice, precedent, and prescription. In the British context, where there is no basic constitutional document, they are particularly important in filling gaps, mediating the application of the law, and regulating discretion. Conventions govern the relationships between most constitutional actors including the Queen and the government, **Cabinet** and the **prime minister**; the government and Parliament; the two Houses of Parliament; ministers and the judiciary; and ministers and the **civil service**. Conventions may be more important in constitutional terms than the law.

Some conventions are precise and specific; others are formulated in more general terms. In the precise category are the rules that the Queen assents to all laws duly passed by both Houses of Parliament and acts only on the advice of ministers; and the rule that stipulates that ministers, not the Queen, exercise the prerogative of the **Crown**. It was these conventions that AV **Dicey**, a constitutional lawyer writing in the nineteenth century, considered to be particularly important, because they transferred legal power from the monarch to elected politicians without the need for contentious legislation. Thus, while in law the Queen is an equal partner with Parliament in the law-making process, and under the prerogative chooses the government and her ministers, the conventional position is very different.

A further important group of conventions are those concerning the responsibility of ministers to Parliament. These are formulated in more general terms. They stipulate that ministers are individually responsible to Parliament for their own actions and those of their departments, and collectively responsible to Parliament for government policies. However, what this responsibility requires is open to dispute. There is, for instance, little agreement—other than in cases of deliberate lying to Parliament, financial impropriety or refusing to support government policy—on the circumstances in which a minister should resign. Many other conventions are similarly formulated in general terms, and this may explain why many questions related to them remain unsettled. Thus, the broad rule that the **House of Lords** should not obstruct the policy of an elected government with a majority in the **House of Commons** leaves room for disagreement over whether it applies to any policy or is limited to manifesto pledges on which the government was elected.

The imprecision of constitutional conventions does not argue against their existence or utility.

Imprecision allows adjustment to practicality and constitutional development without the need to amend the law which, in the constitutional context, may be controversial. Hence conventions provide constitutional flexibility. However, imprecision and flexibility work to the advantage of those in positions of power, for it is difficult to determine, and thus appeal to, the constitutional position and constitutional limitations.

This raises the question of why politicians feel obliged to comply with constitutional conventions or, if they are accused of not doing so, to argue for a particular interpretation of a convention. Sir Ivor Jennings wrote that conventions were obeyed 'because of the political difficulties which follow if they are not' (*The Law and the Constitution* (London: Hodder & Stoughton, 1959), 134). These may be significant when a government has a small majority. Fear of losing office at the next election may also be a factor in which case the system of responsibility to Parliament and indirectly to the electorate helps to ensure good behaviour. However, problems arise when a government is in office for a long time and challenges to it are ineffectual, for it may come to see conventions as irrelevant or insubstantial. Their authority in such instances depends on 'what ministers think they can get away with' and the political security of party-supported governments means they can get away with most things, including ignoring or paying lip service to conventions.

Conventions are not enforced by the **courts**, although **judges** may use them to interpret the law. However, for constitutionalists the obligatory force of conventions goes to the heart of the constitutional morality which underlies the legitimacy and stability of a political system; and the ultimate sanction for conformity to constitutional conventions resides in the constitution itself. Geoffrey Marshall and Graham Moodie argued that 'the crucial questions must always be whether or not a particular class of action is likely to destroy respect for the established distribution of authority and whether or not it is likely to maintain respect for the constitutional system of changing or (sustaining) the distribution of authority' (*Some Problems of the Constitution* (London: Hutchinson, 1971), 32). Conventions may not have the force of laws; but given their importance, a consistent failure to recognize their obligatory nature could undermine the current constitutional system and result in constitutional change.

DIANA WOODHOUSE

See also: **ministerial responsibility; Parliament Acts; royal prerogative**

conversion In English law, conversion is a tort which protects a person's interests in goods. It is most commonly committed by wrongfully taking or disposing of another's goods or refusing to return them on demand. Lesser acts inconsistent with the owner's rights (such as temporarily moving the goods) are not conversion but trespass to goods. A person who has the 'immediate right to possession' can sue; and this may include people other than the owner. However, where more than one person has an interest in the goods, there is machinery to allow the different interests to be dealt with in one set of proceedings.

Conversion does not require dishonesty or even knowledge that another's rights are being infringed. So that the basic rule is that an innocent purchaser from a thief is liable, though there are a number of situations in which a person, who innocently purchases goods from someone who had no right to sell, gets a good title. Where the converter no longer has the goods, the remedy is a judgment for (normally) the value of the goods. Even where the converter still has them, he or she will not normally be ordered to return them unless they have some unique qualities, but may be given the choice between returning them and paying their value. The largest conversion claim in history is probably *Kuwait Airways v Iraqi Airways* (2002) where Kuwait Airways claimed $800 million damages in the English courts for the conversion of ten airliners by Iraqi Airways during the Gulf War.

WVH ROGERS

See also: **tort law**

conveyancing This is the process of creating and transferring interests in land, most commonly applied to transfers of the fee simple, and grants and assignments of leases. Conveyancing is undertaken by solicitors and licensed conveyancers.

The conveyancing process is divided into three stages. The first stage operates from the time of agreement between vendor and purchaser and lasts until there is a formal contract. It has to be established that the purchaser knows enough about the land to undertake a legal commitment to purchase. This means that checks need to be made with bodies such as local authorities, a survey needs to be carried out, and finance for the purchase put in place. Detailed inquiries will be made of the purchaser in an attempt to avoid any difficulties. The introduction of 'home information packs' (Housing Act 2004) makes much of the relevant information available by the time the sale is advertised.

The contract is usually in a standard form (generally the Standard Conditions of Sale), with the addition of details relevant to the particular purchase. The contract has to be written and signed. It is usual for it to be in duplicate parts which the parties exchange to show that the contract has come into force. Completion is the final stage: the formal transfer of the interest, with the purchaser paying the vendor. The transfer document (a deed) is frequently quite short. Many implications are made by legislation, for example 'covenants for title' which specify the liability of the vendor if a defective title is given.

Much of this procedure has in the past been the same whether title is registered or not. For registered titles, however, the purchaser looks at the registered title and not at title deeds to confirm that the seller owns the land free from proprietary claims. In addition, the transfer has to be registered before it is effective to transfer a legal interest.

This changes with the introduction of electronic conveyancing by the Land Registration Act 2002, expected to start in 2008. Registered titles are already held electronically. All dealings with the land will be made electronically by communication with the Land Registry, for which the seller's representative must be a member of the Land Registry Network. There will be no need for the contract to be in writing or for the transfer to be by deed. Electronic creation will not only act as a document between the parties, but will directly change the register. The system requires the involvement of the Land Registry prior to completion to ensure that all is in order. The Land Registry will operate a 'chain matrix', whereby the progress of the sale will be recorded, together with any related sales (for example the sale of the purchaser's present house to provide funds for the purchase).

A few years after electronic conveyancing is introduced on a voluntary basis, it will be made compulsory so that transactions will be effective only if created electronically. Writing or a deed will not suffice.

ROGER J SMITH

See also: **registration of title**

convoy *see* **neutrality**

cooling-off periods A cooling-off period, also known as a 'withdrawal' or 'cancellation' period, permits a **consumer** to withdraw from a contract within a short period after it has been concluded. A contract is binding from the moment it is made, but in circumstances where a cooling-off period is made available, a consumer is entitled to withdraw from a contract without incurring any form of penalty for doing so. Goods which have been supplied must be returned (sometimes, a charge for this may be made), and any prepayments have to be refunded by the trader.

A cooling-off period is only made available in particular circumstances (often under EC legislation), including **doorstep-selling**, distance selling (**mail order**), consumer credit agreements, timeshare contracts, and extended warranties. Apart from these, there is no general entitlement to withdraw from a contract. Many retailers offer a 'returns policy', which permits customers to return goods for a full refund within a fixed period of purchase; but this is not a cooling-off period.

A cooling-off period is designed to provide protection in circumstances where the consumer is not able to assess fully whether the contract is suitable. Thus, contracts concluded on the doorstep often involve an element of surprise, and where goods are supplied by mail order, a consumer will not have been able to inspect the goods before purchasing them.

The length of cooling-off periods varies (seven days for doorstep-selling; forty-five days for extended warranties), and it is debatable whether there should be a single period of fixed duration.

CHRISTIAN TWIGG-FLESNER

cooperation procedure   see **European Parliament**

co-ownership   There is no law which requires persons living in a property to share ownership of it. The simple fact that a person lives with a spouse, lover, or friend does not entitle them to ownership. Ownership of land needs to be established under normal principles of property law or it may arise because of the exercise of some power given by Act of Parliament.

In many cases, the family home is deliberately co-owned. This means that ownership of the property is split between the persons living in it and this may be so irrespective of whether the owners are married, unmarried, in a **civil partnership,** or in no formal relationship at all (eg parent and child or four friends buying a house together). This deliberate (or 'express') co-ownership will have arisen when the property was first purchased and it will be the result of a choice made at that time by the purchasers. In such cases, the names of the owners will appear on the title deeds, or more usually on the register of title held at the Land Registry.

Express co-ownership may take two forms: the 'joint-tenancy' and the 'tenancy in common'. A choice as to which form to adopt will be made at the time of purchase. These two forms do not mean that the owners have a lease, but describe the way the co-owners enjoy ownership. The main consequence arises on the death of one of the co-owners. If the co-owners are joint tenants, the survivors automatically become owners of the 'share' of the deceased. This is so even if the deceased has tried to leave his 'share' by will to someone else. The will cannot change the 'right of survivorship' because it is automatic. This has advantages (such as no paperwork, ease of transfer to partner) and disadvantages (unintended consequences, tax complications). During the lifetime of the co-owners, a joint-tenancy can be turned into a tenancy in common by 'severance' and this often occurs on relationship breakdown. A tenancy in common does not have the right of survivorship, so the deceased is free to leave his or her share by will to whomsoever (s)he chooses.

Even if a person does not appear on the title deeds and so appears not to own a share in the land, it is possible to claim a share because of events that have taken place after the land was purchased. The issue may arise on relationship breakdown, but also in other circumstances. This is known as implied co-ownership and results in the owners being tenants in common. A person may claim a share on the basis of a promise of ownership made by the owner, or by reason of a contribution in money or in kind to the acquisition of the land. Necessarily, this claim must be supported by evidence of the promise or of the contributions made (such as contribution to the deposit, mortgage payments, undertaking of domestic responsibilities so that the owner may work), but a court would look at the totality of the parties' relationship in respect of the land. It is important to realize that the court is not doing what seems fair, or ordering one person to give land to another: the court is applying property law principles to discover who is the true owner, and in what share.

Irrespective of express or implied co-ownership courts have a wide discretion to order property re-adjustment on the break up of a **marriage** or civil partnership. This power is not based on who owns the land, but on the needs of the parties and any children. The court may enlarge or diminish any ownership share, and may award ownership to a person who could not make out a claim under express or implied co-ownership. The parties are encouraged to agree a solution, rather than have one imposed by the court. At present, no such power exists in relation to unmarried couples living together. Unmarried couples must establish express or implied co-ownership. A proposal exists for legislation to give the court powers in relation to certain types of unmarried couples, but it is not clear when, if at all, this will become law. MARTIN DIXON

See also: **fee simple estate**

co-parenting Neither English, Welsh, nor Scottish law confers equal parental rights and responsibilities on mothers and fathers. All mothers have parental rights and responsibilities for their **child**. The father will if he is married to the mother, is registered on the child's birth certificate as the father, if he has entered a **parental responsibility** agreement with the mother which has been lodged at court, or if the court has made an order granting him parental responsibility. If a father is applying to court for parental rights and responsibilities it will take into account the degree of commitment that he has shown towards the child and the relationship between the father and child.

If a child's mother and father both have parental responsibility for a child then they have (at least formally) equal rights and responsibilities. Even if they separate this does not affect their parental rights and responsibilities. Parents with parental responsibility are required to consult with any other parent with parental responsibility before making an important decision in relation to the child (for example, whether to change the child's school or surname). If an agreement cannot be reached then either party can take the matter to court seeking an order resolving the dispute. The court will make the order which best promotes the welfare of the child.

If the mother has parental rights and responsibilities for the child, but the father does not, then she is free to make decisions about the child, without involving the father. However, the father could seek to challenge her decision by an application to the court. When deciding what order to make, the court will be governed by the principle that it should make the order which best promote the child's welfare.

When a couple separate one key issue is with whom the children should live. Many couples resolve the issue without recourse to the court, most commonly by agreeing that the children will remain with the mother. If no agreement can be reached then the court will resolve the dispute, based on what is in the best interests of the child. The courts draw no distinction between whether the parent is the mother or father, although in the case of very young children the courts seemed prepared to assume that normally mothers are more suited to care for them. In practice, following parental separation, children generally reside with their mother.

It is possible for a court to order that **residence** be shared between the mother and father. However, this will only be feasible where the parents live close together and are able to cooperate, as necessary, in the child's upbringing. In practice such 'joint residence' orders are not made very often although in recent years the **courts** have been increasingly willing to make them.

Where it has been determined that the child shall live primarily with one parent it is very common for the other to be given a **contact** order. This requires the parent with whom the child lives to allow the child to see the other parent. In cases where the non-resident parent poses a threat to the child, the court may prefer to order 'indirect contact' where the contact will not be face-to-face, but rather through telephone or email. Another option is to require supervised contact where the time the non-resident parent spends with the child will be monitored by a social worker.

The court will decide whether or not to make a contact order based on what is in the welfare of the child. Although the courts have denied there is a right to contact, the courts will readily assume that it is in the best interests of the child to maintain contact with both parents. Even where there has been **domestic violence** the court may well be willing to grant contact, although it will take into account the danger that contact visits could be used to perpetuate abuse.

The courts have faced great difficulty in enforcing contact orders. Where the resident parent has refused to allow contact, the options of fining her or sending her to prison are unattractive because they are likely to harm the child. The English courts can now require parents who are in dispute over contact to attend classes or meetings designed to persuade or enable them to react an amicable agreement.

JONATHAN HERRING

copyright Copyright is a transmissible property right to prevent certain acts in relation to particular types of works. In the United Kingdom, copyright law is governed by the Copyright Designs and Patents Act 1988 ('CDPA'), as amended, and by a large body of case law. As with other intellectual property rights, there is a substantial similarity in copyright law around the world as a result of the harmonizing effects of the major multilateral treaties, in particular, the **Berne Convention for the Protection of Literary and Artistic Works**, the **Rome Convention** and the **World Trade Organization Agreement on Trade Related Aspects of Intellectual Property Rights ('TRIPs')**. Further harmonization has also taken place in the European Union as a result of a range of directives. However, despite similarities, some differences of approach remain between the **common law** countries and continental jurisdictions, the latter of which are known as *droit d'auteur* systems.

Copyright in a work arises automatically as soon as the work is reduced to a material form, such as writing or a recording. Accordingly, there is no registration requirement with respect to copyright. The works in which copyright is protected fall into two classes, reflecting copyright's concern with encouraging both creativity and the dissemination of that creativity. The first class comprises works of primary creativity: literary, dramatic, and musical works; artistic works, including works of visual art; works of artistic craftsmanship; and buildings. The second class of protected works consists of entrepreneurial works: sound recordings; broadcasts; and typographical arrangements of published editions. Straddling these two classes are films, which reflect elements of both classes.

This division between works of primary creativity and entrepreneurial works is reflected in the identity of the first owner of copyright. For works of primary creativity, the first owner is the original creator or 'author'. For entrepreneurial works, the first owner of copyright is the person who has made the investment necessary to produce the work. For films, the first ownership of copyright is shared between the producer and the director. The ownership of copyright may be transferred to another person. As transfer of ownership is a common practice, it is often the case that the ownership of copyright does not rest with the original author or investor. The other circumstance in which the original author does not own copyright in the work is where the work has been produced pursuant to a contract of employment, in which case the employer is the first copyright owner.

The copyright interest has a fixed duration. For literary, dramatic, musical, and artistic works this period runs from the time of creation of the work until seventy years after the death of its author. If the author is unknown, then copyright lasts for seventy years from the date of creation or publication, whichever is the later. For films, the copyright period lasts from the time of making until seventy years after the death of the principal director, screenplay author, dialogue author, or soundtrack composer, whichever is the latest. If the identity of all of these people is unknown, then copyright in a film runs for seventy years from the making or release of a film, whichever is the later. Copyright in sound recordings lasts

for fifty years from their making or release, whichever is later. Similarly, for broadcasts copyright lasts for fifty years from the first broadcast. Publishers' copyright in the typographical arrangements of published editions lasts for twenty-five years from first publication.

The protection of copyright is subject to two important limitations. One is that copyright is only protected to the extent that the work is 'original', meaning that it has not been copied from another work. Second, copyright protects only the actual expression of the work, not its underlying idea. Subject to these limitations, the exclusive rights that the copyright owner enjoys with respect to the work, or a substantial part thereof, are to do the following: copy it; issue copies of it to the public; rent or lend it to the public; perform, show or play it to the public; communicate it to public, including by broadcasting it or making it available on the internet; and, adapt it or do any of the foregoing in relation to an adaptation. The copyright owner also has the exclusive right to authorize, or 'license', a person to do any of these acts in relation to the work. Thus, a person doing any of these acts, or purporting to authorize somebody else to do any of these acts, without the authorization of the copyright owner will infringe copyright in the work.

In addition to acts of direct infringement and the authorization of infringement, described above, the CDPA also lays down acts of secondary infringement. Acts of secondary infringement involve certain dealings with either an infringing copy or an infringing performance. An infringing copy includes a copy made by an act of direct infringement, and a copy imported or proposed to be imported into the UK if its making in the UK would have amounted to infringement. Knowingly importing, possessing or dealing with, or providing the means for making, an infringing copy all constitute acts of secondary infringement. So far as infringing performances are concerned, permitting premises to be used for an infringing performance of a literary, dramatic, or musical work is an act of secondary infringement unless the person who gave such permission had reasonable grounds to believe that the performance would not infringe copyright. Knowingly providing the necessary apparatus for an infringing performance is also an act of secondary infringement.

Actions for breach of copyright are subject to a wide range of defences and exceptions that are intended to ensure that copyright does not become an instrument for the suppression of creativity or the free flow of ideas and information. However, there is considerable debate over whether the existing exemptions and defences meet this objective.

Arguably, the most important defences are the fair dealing defences, which provide that copyright is not infringed as a result of a fair dealing with certain copyright works for certain purposes. These defences cover (a) fair dealings with literary, dramatic, musical, and artistic works, and with typographical arrangements of published editions, for the purposes of non-commercial research or private study, provided that where the fair dealing is for non-commercial research, the work and its author are identified; (b) any work used for the purpose of criticism or review, provided the work and its author are identified and the work had already been made available to the public; and (c) works, other than photographs, used for reporting the news, provided the work and its author are identified (unless the news report takes place in a sound recording, film, or broadcast, and such identification would not be practicable). The word 'fair' places important limitations on the availability of this defence since dealings involving the use of more of the work than is necessary in relation to the exculpatory purpose, or dealings involving publication of confidential material, have been held to be unfair and thus outside the scope of the defence.

Other important defences relate to: incidental inclusion of a copyright work in an artistic work, sound recording, film, or broadcast; certain acts undertaken by educational institutions, and by libraries and archives; acts undertaken for the purposes of public administration, including judicial, parliamentary, and royal commission proceedings; and certain acts undertaken in relation to computer programs and databases. There is some debate over the extent to which acts that can be justified on the ground of public interest constitute a defence to infringement of copyright.

Where an infringement of copyright takes place and the infringer is unable to rely on any defence then, assuming the standard requirements for the grant of such remedies are met, the copyright owner is entitled to a range of civil remedies. These include an injunction and a pecuniary remedy in the form of either damages or an account of profits. A copyright owner also has a right to an action for delivery up of infringing copies, as well as a right, subject to certain constraints, to seize or detain infringing copies that are being offered for sale or hire. Copyright piracy, where infringement takes place on a commercial scale, is also subject to criminal sanctions.

Concerns about the impact of digital technology on the enforceability of copyright have led to the inclusion in the CDPA of two new forms of rights' infringement, which are associated with copyright. One of these is a prohibition on the circumvention of technological measures designed to protect copyright works from infringement, and the other is a prohibition on tampering with electronic rights-management information embedded in a copyright work. The regime governing these prohibitions is, however, distinct from that governing copyright generally. One important effect of this is that the broad range of defences and exceptions to actions for copyright infringement are not available in this context. In relation to the prohibition on circumvention of technological measures, this has led to concerns that this right may be used by copyright owners unjustifiably to restrict access to and use of copyright works.

FIONA MACMILLAN

copyright collecting societies Copyright collecting societies have proliferated. In Europe alone, there are more than 150 organizations collecting licensing fees for public performances, broadcasting, online use and copying of music, literary, artistic, and audiovisual works. The largest societies, such as Germany's GEMA or the UK's MCPS/PRS Alliance, have an annual turnover exceeding £500 million. Despite their economic importance, very few people understand the complicated mandate under which these societies operate. They have been criticized as ossified bureaucratic structures that exploit a dominant position (see **abuse of a dominant position**), and they have been hailed as facilitators of an information society. The rationale of collecting societies can only be understood in historical perspective.

Copyright has been conceived as an exclusive property right for about 200 years. Initially, it covered only printed matter. Towards the end of the eighteenth century, copyright began to shift towards abstract authored works that should be protected in all their forms, including public performances (previously outside the scope of exclusive rights).

The first statutes to reflect this new view were the French revolutionary Acts of 1791 (regarding performances of theatre and musical drama) and 1793 (regarding the sale and dissemination of artistic works of any genre). However, widening the scope of copyright posed an enforcement problem that became most acute in the field of music. How could right owners trace all uses made of copyright works? In practice therefore, the right to public performance was widely ignored until a day in 1847 when Ernest Bourget, a composer of popular *chansons* and *chansonettes comique*, entered the Paris café *Ambassadeurs*. Live music was being played, and Bourget recognized his own tunes. As he had not received any payment, Bourget refused to settle the bill for his drink of sugared water (at the time a fashionable beverage). Bourget won the resulting dispute before the *Tribunal de Commerce de la Seine*. With fellow composers and a publisher, he founded an agency that became in 1851 the *Société des Auteurs et Compositeurs et Editeurs de Musique* ('SACEM').

SACEM became the model for all modern collecting societies. Where the transaction costs of individual licensing are too high, it appears advantageous for copyright owners to inject exclusive rights into a collective organization that monitors use, issues licenses, and distributes royalties to its members. Almost inadvertently, collective licensing can also deliver important benefits to users: licensed public venues and broadcasters get easy access to the world repertoire of music; libraries may offer generous dissemination arrangements. However, troubles start here. Market prices for these licenses cannot be fixed because there is only one supplier; royalty distribution is contested between authors and publishers; bureaucratic overheads are high. In short, governance of these societies is a nightmare.

The growing digital use of copyright works has changed the incentives of large right owners to use collective administration (they prefer to administer individually), while new providers of online services often are unhappy with the licensing terms offered. Policymakers have identified the collective management of copyright as an area that may need intervention.　　　MARTIN KRETSCHMER

M Kretschmer, 'The Failure of Property Rules in Collective Administration: Rethinking Copyright Societies as Regulatory Instruments' (2002) 24 *European Intellectual Property Review* 126

The Collective Management of Rights in Europe: The Quest for Efficiency, KEA Report commissioned by the European Parliament (2006)

COREPER　*see* **Council of Ministers**

coroners　Over 800 years ago royal officials were appointed in each county to look after the king's financial interests in the local **courts**. Their title was 'Keeper of the Pleas of the Crown'; in Latin, *custos placitorum coronae*. Their functions were at first administrative, but later judicial. Coroners nowadays have just two functions left: (1) inquiry into unnatural death; and (2) inquiry into treasure that is found (rarely necessary).

Before 1926 the coroner always sat with a **jury**. Since then only a small minority of cases are so heard: deaths in prison, in **police** custody or through police

action, reportable to a government department or agency under other **legislation**, or in circumstances possibly prejudicing **public health** or safety. The law and practice today are governed mainly by the Coroners Act 1988 and the Coroners Rules 1984 (both based on much earlier legislation), and, for treasure cases, the Treasure Act 1996.

Coronial jurisdiction in death cases today still depends largely on the presence of a body within a coroner's district, and not where the death took place. Hence bodies brought back from abroad may be the subject of an inquest. There is power to inquire only where there is reason to suspect that the death: (i) was violent or unnatural; (ii) was sudden and of unknown cause; or (iii) occurred in prison. Usually the coroner will direct an autopsy to be carried out to establish the precise medical cause of death. In a case within category (ii), where the autopsy finds the cause of death to be natural, the coroner may dispense with an inquest. There is limited power to transfer jurisdiction between coroners.

Deaths are usually reported to the coroner by doctors and by the emergency services, although the registrar of deaths must do so in some cases. Coroners' 'officers' (often serving or retired police officers) make preliminary inquiries and deal with the paperwork. In 2007, of about 499,000 deaths in England and Wales, 234,504 were reported to coroners, 81,860 (34.9 per cent) of these being dealt with by autopsy without inquest, and 30,979 (13.2 per cent) resulting in inquests. In about 121,571 cases (51.8 per cent), there was neither autopsy nor inquest.

In 2007 there were about 110 coroners in England and Wales, 70 per cent part time, and 30 per cent full time. The qualification is five years either as a lawyer or as a medical practitioner (in 2007 nearly 90 per cent were lawyers). Coroners are appointed, financed, and paid by, but are independent from, local authorities. This patchwork system is chronically underfunded, with wide local variations in practice. What little **responsibility** central government has for coroners was transferred in May 2005 from the Home Office to the Department of Constitutional Affairs (now the Ministry of Justice). Complaints against coroners personally (as opposed to their decisions) are dealt with by the **Office for Judicial Complaints**. The **Lord Chancellor** and the **Lord Chief Justice** may remove coroners from office for inability or misbehaviour.

Inquests find facts, rather than attribute **responsibility**. Procedure is thus inquisitorial, not accusatorial. They try to answer four questions (*who* the deceased was, and *when*, *where* and *how* the deceased came by his or her death) and to find the death registration particulars. They must not express opinions on any other matters, and verdicts must not be expressed so as to appear to determine questions of liability. Article 2 of the **European Convention of Human Rights** requires an enhanced level of inquiry where the state is involved in the death. Coroners' decisions are not subject to appeal as such, but instead to two different kinds of review by the High Court: (i) **judicial review** (the general public law remedy); (ii) review under the Coroners Act 1988, section 13 (specific to coroners' inquests).

The coroner institution was exported to former British colonies (including the USA). In some it remains largely as in England and Wales. Elsewhere it has been modified. In parts of the USA and Canada, the coroner has been replaced by the medical examiner, a forensic pathologist who administers the system. In civil law countries there are no coroners at all. The investigation of unnatural death takes place, if at all, only as part of the investigation of crime. In Scotland, a mixed system, there are similarly no coroners, and deaths are reported to the procurator fiscal, who may direct an autopsy. In comparatively few cases, a public inquiry must be held by the sheriff under the Fatal Accidents and Sudden Deaths Inquiry (Scotland) Act 1976.

The government has proposed reforms to the system, but these have been criticized, as they do not go as far as recent independent Reports have recommended, probably on resources grounds.

PAUL MATTHEWS

P Matthews, *Jervis on Coroners* (London: Sweet & Maxwell, 12th edn 2002)
C Dorries, *Coroners' Courts* (Oxford: Oxford University Press, 2nd edn, 2004)

See also: **deaths in custody; inquisitorial system**

corporal punishment *see* **punishment, history of**

corporal punishment in schools *see* **school discipline and exclusion of pupils**

corporate authority *see* **companies and the outside world**

corporate capacity *see* **companies and the outside world**

corporate conglomerates and groups A corporate conglomerate describes a cluster of businesses generally operating in different industries which are controlled from a central point. In the UK and the US, conglomerates reached their high point in the 1960s and have been in decline since as businesses began to focus on a single industry. In the US one of the few surviving conglomerates is the General Electric Company while in the UK the most famous conglomerate, Hanson PLC, split into four separate companies in 1997. Outside the UK and US conglomerates are common. For example Germany's Siemens AG, Korea's Samsung, Japan's Mitsubishi, and India's Tata Group are all conglomerates. Conglomerates are organized legally either as one **company** with a number of divisions or departments operating in differing industries or through a Group structure where each division is a separate company (called a subsidiary company) which is ultimately controlled by another company (the parent company) through its shareholding in the subsidiary. Organizing a business through a Group structure has significant advantages. If the business is organized through a single company then the collapse of one of the divisions of the company can cause the collapse of the whole company. If however the division that collapses is a subsidiary company then because the shareholders (in this case the parent company) have limited liability for the debts of the subsidiary the losses do not affect the rest of the Group. As a result the loss is contained and the overall business of the Group survives.

ALAN DIGNAM

corporate creditors Companies incur debts in a variety of ways. Their trading operations will often involve those acquiring supplies or services from other companies or individuals, or they will borrow money, often from banks or other institutional lenders, to finance their business. Other corporate creditors include the **Crown,** for corporation and other forms of taxes, and the company's employees, whose salary will usually be paid in arrears.

The important point to appreciate is that wherever the **company** becomes liable in debt to one of its creditors, it is *only the company* to which that creditor can look for repayment. Once a company is formed and registered it acquires its own legal personality, which is entirely separate from that of its shareholders. Thus, where a party enters into a transaction with a company which gives rise to a debt, only the company is liable for the repayment of that debt (*Salomon v A Salomon & Co Ltd* (1897)).

The company's shareholders are also protected by the closely related principal of **limited liability** (Insolvency Act 1986, section 74(2)(d)): they are only liable to contribute to the company the amount they have agreed to pay for their **shares** and no more. If the company is unable to pay its debts, the shareholders cannot be pursued by its creditors.

SANDRA FRISBY

BR Cheffins, *Company Law: Theory, Structure and Operation* (Oxford: Oxford University Press, 1997), 69–82
E Ferran, *Company Law and Corporate Finance* (Oxford: Oxford University Press, 1999), 457–481

corporate criminal liability Companies are legal **persons** in their own right. Whether the **company** is a large, multi-national entity or runs the smallest of family businesses, it has a legal personality of its own, quite separate and apart from its **directors,** shareholders, and employees. The company owns its own property and assets and pays its own taxes.

It also commits its own crimes. In the mid-nineteenth century, the early days of the statutory, registered company, there was some resistance to the idea that a company could commit crimes. The sense of guilt and wrongdoing associated with crimes seemed out of place in the case of companies. As was famously said, a company has 'no soul to be saved and no body to be kicked'. However, that reluctance could not long survive the rapidly achieved predominance of the limited company as a business medium. It was essential that regulatory criminal law—that part of the criminal law which enforces minimum standards of **safety**, hygiene, and environmental protection on industrial, pharmaceutical, and food production, construction, extractive, and transportation activities—be applied to businesses using the corporate form. Many regulatory offences are offences of strict liability requiring no proof of culpability. For instance, the Clean Air Act 1993 proscribes smoke emissions exceeding prescribed levels of carbon. The offence is committed if excess levels are present; the **prosecution** need not establish that the owner of the business was in any way at fault. Proof of guilt requires establishing the same facts, whether the defendant owner is a limited company or an individual. The corporate form does not make for any kind of complication when enforcing this type of offence. **Courts** and regulators regularly resolve in the case of corporations such questions as whether it was reasonably practicable to provide a safe system of work, whether food sold to the public was fit for human consumption, whether the vehicle complied with standards imposed by the construction and use regulations and so forth. Conceptually, the imposition on companies of liability for strict liability offences is straightforward and, in terms of policy, largely uncontroversial.

Questions of law and policy become considerably more complex and debatable when companies are charged with offences requiring proof of culpability. Following appellate decisions made in 1944, it has been possible to convict companies of offences requiring proof of forms of culpability such as intent to defraud the revenue, a dishonest intention to appropriate the property of another, a grossly negligent failure to comply with a duty of care. The legal device used to attribute culpability to limited companies is what used to be called the *alter ego* principle, which is now better named the doctrine of identification.

The informing principle behind the doctrine is simple, indeed simplistic. Members of the senior management of a company may be considered something more than directors or employees connected to the company. If they have sufficient authority within the company, they can be identified with the company. If a person can be identified, his or her conduct and state of mind can be regarded for certain legal purposes as the conduct and state of mind of the company itself. Through this reasoning the company, in legal theory, can be made *directly* rather than vicariously responsible for crimes or civil wrongs. The facts of a leading civil case (*Lennard's Carrying Company Limited v Asiatic Petroleum Co Ltd* (1915)) clearly demonstrate the nature of the identification principle. The Lennards Carrying Company was sued for the entirety of the loss sustained by the cargo owners, following the sinking of a vessel owned by Lennards. Under the statutory compensation scheme for such losses, **damages** meeting the entirety of the loss were obtainable only if the defendant shipowner was 'at fault' in respect of the loss of cargo. Previous case law established that the fault had to be personal to the shipowner. It was not enough that someone employed by the owner was at fault. The managing director ('MD') of Lennards knew of the unseaworthy condition of the vessel and was at fault in allowing the ship to sail. Unlimited damages were recoverable as it was ruled that the fault of the MD was the fault of the defendant company itself. It was not vicariously responsible on the basis of the MD's personal fault. The personal fault of the managing director was the corporate fault of the company.

The identification principle was transplanted to criminal law, allowing direct corporate liability for crimes requiring proof of culpability. For instance, a dishonest scheme conceived by the chief executive to evade the payment of **corporation tax** was held to constitute the company's intention to defraud the revenue. Who besides the **board of directors** and the MD may be identified with the company? At one time a flexible approach prevailed. Besides the chief executive, finance directors, company secretaries, and in one case a mid-management transport manager were considered eligible for identification. Of course, the more persons eligible for identification, the easier it is to make companies liable for crimes requiring proof of culpability. By the same token, the more likely it becomes that well run and socially responsible companies may find their reputation damaged by implication in serious crimes which were essentially the product of aberrant individuals.

Whatever the merits or otherwise of a flexible approach to identification, a very narrow doctrine now prevails following the House of Lords decision in *Tesco Supermarkets Ltd v Nattrass* (1972). The contention that the manager of a supermarket ('one of hundreds') could be identified with the company was emphatically rejected. Those persons who could be identified were limited to the board of directors when acting as a board, a chief executive with the board's full authority to manage the company and, possibly, a director/executive with full authority for a significant area of the company's activities. The limiting effect of *Tesco* can be seen in the failure of two prosecutions for corporate manslaughter following, respectively, the Zeebrugge ferry disaster (1987) and the Southall rail crash (1997). Conviction of the defendant companies required proof that deaths were caused by a grossly negligent failure on the part of the companies to fulfil a duty of care owed to the persons who had died. In both cases it was held that a finding of gross negligence against the company required a finding of gross negligence against persons sufficiently senior to be identified with the company. Although P&O Ferries plc ('a company infected with the disease of sloppiness') and South Western Trains plc were subjected to swingeing official criticism in matters of **safety**, the lack of direct involvement of very senior management in safety concerns ensured, perversely, the failure of the charges of corporate manslaughter.

Dissatisfaction with the outcomes in these cases largely explains the enactment of the Corporate Manslaughter and Corporate Homicide Act 2007. This Act seeks to capture a truly *corporate* form of culpability for corporate manslaughter, a culpability that may be present even in the absence of any individual associated with the company possessing the culpability the offence requires. The proposed offence requires a death caused by a gross breach of a duty of care owed by the company. However, that, of itself, will not suffice. A company will only be guilty of the offence only if 'the way in which its activities are managed or organized by its senior management is a substantial element in the [gross breach of duty]'.

A gross breach of duty will arise if the performance of senior management 'falls far below what can be reasonably expected in the circumstances'. A senior manager is defined in the Act as a person with a significant role in making decisions about how the whole or a substantial part of the company's activities are to be managed or organized or who actually manages the whole or a substantial part of the company's activities. Only the company may be liable for corporate manslaughter. The Act provides that individuals, however much at fault, are not to be implicated in the company's crime.

The culpability concerned is truly corporate in that a company may be found liable on the basis of the inadequate team performance of senior management even if no given individual within senior management exhibits the culpability for the offence. Yet the culpability involved is complex; it will give rise to many issues of degree and evaluation. A simpler model suggests itself, a beefed up version of regulatory law. Instead of tackling difficult issues of corporate culpability it could be asked whether it was 'reasonably practicable' (a familiar phrase from the Health and Safety at Work Act 1974) for the company to have devised a safe system for its activities which would have avoided causing [a particular] death or serious injury. Further, in the interests of deterrence, it could be inquired whether one or more individuals associated with the company was at serious fault in not ensuring that the company took reasonably practicable steps which would have avoided causing [a particular] death or injury. If the first question is answered in the affirmative, the company should be criminally liable for an aggravated form of corporate safety offence. If the second question is answered affirmatively against any given individual, he or she will be criminally liable for an aggravated safety offence but only if at serious fault.

BOB SULLIVAN

Celia Wells, *Corporations and Criminal Responsibility* (Oxford: Oxford University Press, 2nd edn, 2001)
Peter Glazebrook, 'A Better Way of Convicting Businesses of Avoidable Deaths and Injuries?' [2002] *Cambridge Law Journal* 405

corporate debt and registration of charges The consequences of corporate **insolvency** may be to some extent avoided by debt financiers by the taking of security. Taking security is described in *Bristol Airport v Powdrill* (1990) as the obtaining of 'rights exercisable against some property in which the debtor has an interest in order to enforce the discharge of the debtor's obligation to the creditor'.

Security may be **possessory security** (where the lender takes possession of the property) or non-possessory security (where the property remains in the possession of the borrower), and non-possessory security is far more appropriate in the case of lending to companies, as the borrowing **company** will be able to use the secured asset in its business in order to generate cash to repay the underlying indebtedness.

The most common form of non-possessory security is the equitable charge. In return for an advance (or the granting of an overdraft facility) the borrowing company confers upon the lender rights over some or all of its assets (both tangible and intangible). This right entitles the lender to have recourse to the charged asset (sometimes termed the collateral) in the event of the borrower failing to repay the advance or discharge the overdraft. This right takes priority over the claims of unsecured creditors of the company to the charged assets. Whilst the lender cannot claim to *own* the charged asset, his right to recourse is recognized as a **property right** in that asset (*Re BCCI (No 8)* (1997)) which persists until the borrower discharges its indebtedness or the lender releases the property from the charge. It is legally possible to grant a charge over *future* assets of the company, so that where a company agrees to grant a charge over, say, its 'present and future machinery', and machines are acquired at a later date, those machines are immediately subject to the charge (*Holroyd v Marshall* (1862)).

Because a charge is a non-possessory form of **security**, those considering advancing credit to the company might be misled into over-estimating its creditworthiness because of its possession of valuable assets which are, in fact, subject to a charge. This problem is addressed by requiring company charges to be registered, thus allowing parties to check the register to see whether assets in the company's possession, which would otherwise be available to meet their debts, are in fact subject to a charge which would give its holder priority over their claims. Section 395 of the Companies Act 1985 (to be replaced by section 874(1) of the Companies Act 2006 when that provision is brought into force, probably in autumn of 2008) provides that if a charge is not registered within twenty-one days of its creation it is void against a **liquidator**, administrator, or creditor of the company. The effect of this provision is that the charge holder can no longer claim priority in relation to the charged asset and will, in effect, find himself unsecured.   SANDRA FRISBY

See also: **corporate creditor; debt finance**

corporate disclosure   Corporate disclosure is a key aspect of **company** law, and is widely regarded as the consequence for companies and their members of benefiting from the privileges of separate personality and **limited liability**. The disclosure philosophy is prevalent in statutory requirements, codes of practice and in the rule books of various institutions with which many corporate actors are connected. Disclosure, as a **corporate governance** tool, serves as a mechanism for **accountability** through which the managers answer to their shareholders for their activities during the previous year. The disclosure system also has the objective of protecting investors and others from fraud by managers and **directors**, as well as enhancing **democracy** by improving corporate decision-making processes, resulting in more effective capital allocation within and outside the company.

The disclosure regime consists of a three-tiered regulatory structure, comprising legislative mandatory rules, self-regulatory mandatory requirements, and voluntary codes and conventions. Many of the legislative and self-regulatory requirements originate from European directives, recently modernized to take into account international standards created by the International Accounting Standards Board. Disclosure is regarded as a hybrid between self-regulation and more demanding mandatory requirements.

The legislative provisions within the Companies Act 1985 (and now 2006) include requirements to make disclosures to the registrar of companies, who, via the registry at Companies House, acts a main source of information on registered companies. Under **legislation**, companies are also required to keep accounting records which are sufficient to show and explain the company's transactions and which will enable the directors to disclose with reasonable accuracy, at any time, the financial position of the company and to ensure that the profit and loss account and balance sheet will comply with legislative requirements. Directors must prepare for their shareholders each financial year company accounts, a directors' report and, for all but small companies, an enhanced business review, and, for quoted companies, a directors' remuneration report. Auditors must prepare an auditors' report. As well as sending these documents to members, debenture holders, and **persons** entitled to receive notice of general meetings, the documents must be laid before the meeting and also delivered to the companies registrar. The legislation contains general principles relating to the preparation and disclosure of the company's accounts and reports, as well as the requirement that the accounts must give a true and fair view of the state of the affairs of the company and its profit and loss for the financial year. The legislation also sets out the required form and contents of the accounts.

Additionally, the Financial Reporting Council sets accounting and auditing standards, oversees their enforcement and monitoring, and oversees the major professional accountancy bodies. An operating body of the Financial Reporting Council is the Accounting Standards Board with the role of establishing and improving standards of financial accounting and corporate reporting in collaboration with the International Accounting Standards Board.

The **Financial Services and Markets Act 2000** sets out the principle that listing rules may provide that certain specified securities may not be admitted to the official list unless listing particulars have been submitted to and approved by the competent authority and published. The Act requires disclosure in listing particulars of all such information as investors and their professional advisers would reasonably require and expect for the purpose of making informed assessments. The Act also requires publication of a prospectus approved by the competent authority for new securities to be offered to the public for the first time before admission to the official list. The rules on preparation and publication of a **prospectus** are supplemented by detailed rules set out by the **Financial Services Authority**, the UK's competent authority for listing arrangements.

To supplement the legislative and self-regulatory mandatory requirements there exist also a number of non-mandatory but authoritative provisions issued by professionally experienced committees and bodies. In particular, the Combined Code on Corporate Governance contains several 'comply or explain' rules on different aspects of corporate governance, including disclosure.

Many non-mandatory provisions appear in the area of social and environmental reporting. Typically, they appear as recommendations, guidance, codes, and process frameworks and they are developed by a wide variety of different organizations, including international bodies and multisector alliances such as Social Accountability International and SA8000. Such instruments are largely unenforceable, and diverse treatment by different companies means that their disclosures are not easily comparable, making assessments difficult to accomplish.

The more recent trend towards recognizing corporate social responsibility has instigated the introduction of a new enhanced business review requirement in the Companies Act 2006. The focus is increasingly on providing information that will be useful for decision-making. Under the new legislative provisions all but small companies will be required to publish a balanced and comprehensive analysis of (a) the development and performance of the company's business during the financial year; and (b) the position of the company's business at the end of that year, consistent with the size and complexity of the business. In the case of a quoted company the business review must, to the extent necessary for an understanding of the development, performance or position of the company's business, include (a) the main trends and factors likely to affect the future development, performance, and position of the company's business; and (b) information about: (i) environmental matters (including the impact of the company's business on the environment); (ii) the company's employees; and (iii) social and community issues, including information about any policies of the company in relation to those matters and the effectiveness of those policies; and (c) information about persons with whom the company has contractual or other arrangements which are essential to the business of the company, unless such information would put such persons at serious risk of danger.

Accounting and corporate disclosure is an evolving process with objectives that change over time as the economic, legal, political, and social environments change. Modern views indicate three new challenges facing the disclosure environment: globalization, technological developments, and the growing importance of intangible assets to the creation of shareholder wealth. These aspects will continue to lead to changes in the requirements and the resulting contents and character of corporate reporting.   CHARLOTTE VILLIERS

corporate governance   The webpage on corporate governance on the website of the Department of Enterprise and Regulatory Reform ('DERR') defines corporate governance as being concerned with the systems by which **companies** are directed and controlled. This definition was first formulated in a 1992 report issued by the Committee on the Financial Aspects of Corporate Governance under the chairmanship of Sir Adrian Cadbury. Corporate governance, a rather obscure subject prior to this point, generated in the wake of the Cadbury Report much academic debate, considerable press coverage, and a series of follow-up reports on UK corporate governance, namely, the Greenbury Report 1995, the Hampel Report 1998, and the Higgs Report in 2003. Corporate governance has also been in the limelight elsewhere, with an important catalyst being the widely publicized 2002 collapse of Enron, a US energy company.

Some take a '**stakeholder**'-oriented view of corporate governance, assuming the topic relates to the entire network of constituencies with a 'stake' in how companies are run, including employees, customers, and local communities. Others treat the proper domain of corporate governance as being the relationship between managers and investors, with particular emphasis on promoting managerial **accountability** to shareholders in companies with publicly traded shares. The Cadbury, Hampel, and Higgs reports used this narrower conception as their departure point and, in the UK, debates on corporate governance have generally followed the same pattern.

In the UK, publicly quoted companies are managed by a small team of executives led by the chief executive officer. The senior executives will typically own only a small percentage of the **shares**, meaning they receive only a tiny fraction of the returns generated by their efforts. Executives thus have incentives to further their own interests at the expense of shareholders, potentially imposing what economists refer to as 'agency costs' on investors.

If a company's executives are lazy or corrupt, over time net earnings will suffer and the share price will decline. If matters deteriorate far enough, a hostile **takeover** bid or corporate bankruptcy is likely to result. Either way the incumbent executives will be out of work and their chances of managing another quoted company will be remote. A desire to avoid such an outcome provides executives with incentives to run companies honestly, competently, and diligently.

While market forces serve to reduce agency costs, periodic corporate governance scandals illustrate they do not constrain agency costs perfectly. The **board of directors** can potentially play a major role in addressing gaps in managerial accountability. In publicly quoted companies the board is typically composed of a number of senior executives and a number of 'non-executive' or 'outside' **directors**. Outside directors can potentially serve as corporate governance 'watchdogs' by evaluating management's performance from a detached perspective and taking corrective action where necessary if matters are going awry.

The Cadbury, Hampel, and Higgs reports on corporate governance each made numerous recommendations concerning boards, with key themes being that non-executives should be well represented on the boards of publicly quoted companies and that board committees made up primarily or entirely of non-executives should be established to deal with topics where independent judgement is most crucial, such as nomination of future **directors**, supervision of accounting and auditing issues, and setting **executive pay**. Recommendations in these reports have been implemented in the 'Combined Code on Corporate Governance', an annex to listing rules with which companies quoted on the London Stock Exchange must comply. Companies may depart from the Combined Code's principles and provisions so long as they explain their reasons for so doing. This 'comply or explain' model, an innovation of the 1992 Cadbury Report, has been widely imitated around the world since it provides a way to encourage better corporate governance without imposing a restrictive 'one size fits all' set of mandatory rules on companies that vary widely.

Following on from recommendations made in the Cadbury and Hampel Reports, the Combined Code puts shareholders under an onus to take seriously their responsibilities as 'owners' of companies and to insist on high standards of corporate governance. In the typical UK publicly-quoted company, share ownership is divided chiefly among a sizeable number of institutional investors, such as **pension** funds and insurance companies. UK institutional shareholders have generally adopted a passive approach to the companies in which they own shares, believing they lack sufficient information and expertise to take a 'hands-on' role and fearing they might incur the bulk of the costs of activism and receive only a tiny fraction of the benefits. Due to Combined Code guidance and numerous warnings from the government that institutional passivity is inappropriate, activism has been on the increase recently, manifested most obviously by institutional shareholders using their voting rights much more regularly than in the past.

Executive pay is a topic where institutional shareholders have proved willing to step forward. Theoretically, managerial remuneration can be used to reduce agency costs, since executives can be expected to place a high priority on creating value for shareholders when their remuneration is linked closely to corporate performance. In practice, there has traditionally been little correlation between pay and performance in UK quoted companies, with an example being the awarding of generous severance packages to executives fired for poor performance. Institutional investor pressure, in tandem with Combined Code guidelines introduced to implement the Greenbury Report, prompted most quoted companies to cut the duration of managerial services contracts, thereby reducing the leverage of dismissed executives to negotiate a generous settlement. The government sought to prompt further shareholder activism in 2002 by giving shareholders an annual advisory vote on executive pay policy, but investors have thus far proved reluctant to vote against what companies have proposed.

Could the attention devoted to corporate governance be too much of a good thing? Many senior executives, weary of growing corporate governance **responsibilities**, reportedly would be happy to leave the quoted sector and buy-out activity by private equity firms has created an exit option. However, private equity buy-outs are insufficiently common to herald any immediate wholesale changes to the UK's corporate governance arrangements.

BRIAN R CHEFFINS

See also: **agent; corporate governance and conflicts of interests; institutional investor activism; shareholder power**

corporate governance and conflicts of interest

In *The Wealth of Nations*, Adam Smith noted the problems caused by the separation of ownership and management in joint stock **companies**, the forerunners of today's public corporations. Observing that most joint stock company shareholders were passive recipients of **dividends**, he commented disapprovingly on the scope that this created for less-than-vigilant or opportunistic managerial behaviour: joint stock companies, Smith believed, were inevitably characterized by 'negligence and profusion'. During the century which followed, as companies increased in size and came increasingly to be populated by passive *rentiers*, the 'agency problem' (as it is now called) grew. What was to stop **directors**, the **agents** of the shareholders to whom more and more discretionary power had been delegated, from acting in their own rather than the shareholder interest?

The judiciary responded, by applying to company directors, rules developed by the courts of equity for application to trustees and **fiduciaries**. The result was the gradual development of an elaborate set of common law **directors' duties**. These fiduciary duties sought to deal with potential conflicts of interest by obliging directors to act in the shareholder interest. Thus, when exercising the discretionary powers vested in them, directors were bound to act *bona fide* in (what they thought to be) the best interests of 'the company', interpreted to mean the best interests of the shareholders. These general **common law** duties were eventually supplemented by statutory rules dealing with specific types of self-dealing (such as where a director contracts with his or her company; or where a company

enters into a contract with a third party in which a director has an interest). These provisions, contained until recently in Part X of the Companies Act 1985, prohibited some sorts of transactions and subjected others to approval by either the board or the shareholders in general meeting. Certain forms of self-dealing (such as **insider dealing**) were criminalized. In recent decades, attempts have been made further to minimize the 'agency problem' by constructing performance-related executive remuneration packages (incorporating things like **share** options) which align the interests of managers and shareholders. For many, however, the staggering growth in **executive pay** suggests that self-dealing is still alive and well.

Following a review of company law, the law on directors' duties was overhauled by the Companies Act 2006. Part X of the Companies Act 1985 was replaced and to some extent rewritten, and the general duties of directors were 'codified' (sections 171–177), although the language used differs from that of the common law. Directors are now obliged to act in the way they consider in good faith 'would be most likely to promote the *success* of the company for the benefit its members [shareholders] as a whole'. Although the close identification of the interests of 'the company' with those its shareholders has thus been retained, however, the Act states that in promoting the success of the company, directors must 'have regard to' the long-term consequences of their decisions, the interests of employees, the need to foster relationships with suppliers and customers, and the impact of their operations on the environment and **community**.

This manifestation of what the *Company Law Review* called 'enlightened shareholder value', with its nod in the direction of interest groups other than shareholders, highlights the controversies which have surrounded the conceptualization of the large corporation and the wider conflicts of interest with which, arguably, corporate governance should be concerned. For much of the nineteenth century, joint stock companies were very closely identified with their shareholders, so much so that they were conceptualized as those shareholders merged into a separate corporate entity, hence the regular references to companies as 'theys', a collection of individuals. However, as shares became fully paid-up (turning **limited liability** into *de facto* no liability) and as increasingly passive shareholders relinquished most of the rights traditionally associated with ownership, understandings of the nature of 'the company' changed. Companies came to be conceptualized as entities completely separate from, and cleansed of, their shareholders, hence the emergence of the modern reified conception of the company as an 'it'. It was soon being argued that separate **corporate personality** should be taken more seriously and that large joint stock corporations should be regarded not as purely 'private' enterprises to be run exclusively in the interests of their (liability-, obligation- and responsibility-free) shareholders, but as social institutions whose directors should be obliged balance a range of competing interests. From this perspective, now associated with '**stakeholding**' conceptions of the corporation, **corporate governance** involves more than a mere 'agency problem' involving managers and shareholders, the conflicts of interest involved encompassing not only shareholders but employees, creditors, customers, and the community at large. In a modest way, the language of the 2006 Act recognizes these wider conflicts of interest—suppressed in much of the contemporary literature—despite its rejection of an overtly 'pluralist', stakeholding model of the corporation.

PADDY IRELAND

corporate governance, Combined Code on   The closing years of the Thatcher era saw a series of corporate collapses and scandals (Polly Peck, Coloroll, Bank of Credit and Commerce International, Maxwell) characterized by directorial financial malpractice and the misuse of corporate assets. These prompted the establishment in 1991 of a committee—chaired by Sir Adrian Cadbury under the auspices of the Financial Reporting Council ('FRC'), the London Stock Exchange ('LSE') and the accountancy profession—charged with examining the financial aspects of **corporate governance.** The committee produced a Code of Practice and recommended that listed **companies** state whether they complied with the Code and give reasons for any areas of non-compliance. In 1995, following further public outcries over directors' remuneration, not least in the newly privatized utilities ('rewards for failure'), another committee, chaired by Sir Richard Greenbury, was established and another Code of Practice produced. Areas of non-compliance now not only had to be identified but justified. Shortly after, the FRC asked yet another committee, chaired by Sir Ronnie Hampel, to review the existing recommendations in light of the issues raised by corporate governance as a whole. The final report of the Hampel Committee recommended the creation of a Combined Code on Corporate Governance which was duly established in 1998. The Combined Code is an appendix to, but does not actually form part of, the LSE Listing Rules.

Following more corporate scandals, particularly in the US, still more high-profile committees were set up (Turnbull on internal control requirements; Myners on institutional investors; Higgs on non-executive directors; Smith on audit committees) and further reports produced. The result was the publication of a revised code by the FRC (the independent regulator responsible for the statutory oversight of auditors and the professional accountancy and actuarial bodies) in 2003. The Code's provisions on the role of independent non-executive **directors** in large public companies, in particular, did not meet with City approval. The Code was updated again in 2006 and the FRC began yet another review in 2007 to check that it was working effectively and 'not having an adverse effect'. Under the Code's 'comply or explain' mechanisms, all companies incorporated in the UK and listed on the main market of the LSE are now required under the Listing Rules to report on how they have applied the Combined Code in their annual reports and accounts.

The Code, which is firmly rooted in a shareholder-oriented model of the corporation and which cements the unitary board in the UK, sets out standards of good practice in relation to issues such as board composition, remuneration, **accountability** and audit, and relations with shareholders. It is based on principles rather than rules; on 'soft' rather than 'hard' law. The production and constant revision of the Code is a reflection of the ongoing concerns surrounding corporate financial malpractice and executive excess, and of the desire of the City, corporate executives, and the professions to stave off legislative interference in corporate governance. As such, it is illustrative of the growing trend, characteristic of contemporary **neo-liberalism**, towards voluntary self-regulation and self-policing, and governance by experts and elites insulated from democratic pressures.   PADDY IRELAND

corporate manslaughter   *see* **corporate criminal liability**

corporate personality   The essential attribute of corporate personality is that on **incorporation** the **company** becomes a legal **person** distinct from its members (shareholders). As a result the company can sue and be sued in its own name, it does not cease to exist if its members die and, crucially, it has its own debts for which its members are not liable. **Human** beings are generally legal persons—that is they are subject to and have rights within the legal system in which they find themselves. While that legal system imposes obligations on the legal person it also confers rights. When dealing with humans it is often assumed that people have a full range of rights and obligations within a legal system simply by virtue of being human. This is however incorrect; children for example, while they are human beings, are commonly excluded from having full legal personality until they cease being children. In essence humanity is a state of nature and legal personality is an artificial construct which may or may not be conferred by the state. So, if humanity is not necessary for legal personality it follows that it is possible for legal personality to be conferred on non-humans. Some societies for example attribute legal personality to religious icons. The icon itself is therefore treated as having rights and obligations within the legal system. A logical extension of this separation of humanity from legal personality is that groups of humans who are engaged in a common activity could attempt to simplify their joint activity by gaining legal personality for the venture. This is the origin of corporate personality.

The most successful groups to attain legal personality were religious orders. Their motive was relatively simple. If a religious order could obtain legal personality, the complications that regularly arose when an Abbot died, over the passing of the order's land to the new Abbot, would fall away. The conferring of legal personality would mean that the religious order as a legal personality would hold the lands in its own name and as it was not human and therefore not subject to weaknesses of the flesh, such as death; the death of an individual head of the order had no effect on the life or lands of the corporate legal personality of the order. As the main beneficiary of these land disputes with religious orders was the **Crown** (through death taxes levied on what the Crown deemed to be the Abbot's lands), the conferring of legal personality was necessarily tied directly to a concession from the Crown, in the form of a charter incorporating (from the Latin meaning to 'form a body') the order. Over time the process of incorporation through Charters, statute, and finally registered companies, extended to local authorities and commercial organizations.

One of the best examples of how this legal concept operates is the case of *Lee v Lee's Air Farming* (1961). Mr Lee incorporated a company in which he was effectively the only shareholder, director, and employee (he was the chief pilot). Mr Lee was killed while at work for the company. The company as part of its statutory obligations had been paying an employee insurance policy. His widow claimed she was entitled to **compensation** as the widow of a 'worker' under the relevant statute. The issue went to the New Zealand Court of Appeal. It found that Mr Lee was not a 'worker' within the meaning of the Act because he was not capable of being commanded to work by the company, as he was in effect the company. It followed that no compensation was payable. The case was further appealed to the Privy Council in London. The **Privy Council** emphasized that the company and Mr Lee were distinct legal personalities. Therefore, the company, through its managing director (Mr Lee), was capable of commanding its chief pilot (also Mr Lee) to go out to work. As one can see, the court's concern was to map out the interaction of the legal personalities in this situation regardless of the fact that when Mr Lee went to work that day he was unlikely formally to have commanded himself to go out to work. Nevertheless, in the legal world the corporate personality is commanding Mr Lee's legal personality to go to work that day, which he did. It was therefore a master and servant relationship and as such fitted the definition of 'worker' under the Act. The widow was therefore entitled to compensation.

ALAN DIGNAM

P Ireland, I Grigg-Spall and D Kelly 'The Conceptual Foundations of Modern Company Law' (1987) 14 *Journal of Law and Society* 149

corporate rescue Companies may become insolvent for many reasons, and it may be the case that **winding up** is an unnecessarily terminal procedure, as it will inevitably lead to the dissolution (a statutory version of 'death') of the **company**. Yet, in certain cases, the company's business may be inherently viable and a process of rehabilitation might lead to the recovery of the corporation. Much depends on the individual circumstances, but it has long been accepted that a good system of **insolvency** law will make provision for what is known as 'corporate rescue'. Corporate rescue involves an intervention whereby the company is restored to financial viability, with its workforce intact, its operations or activities substantially the same, and in the ownership of the same people. The UK government has recently legislated with a view to increasing the incidence of corporate rescue in the UK.

Corporate rescue may take place informally (usually via the intervention of the company's main lender, who will work with its management to devise a rescue strategy) or formally under one of two procedures in the Insolvency Act 1986. The first of these is the Company Voluntary Arrangement ('CVA': see Part I of the Insolvency Act 1986). In essence, a CVA involves the company's directors devising a set of proposals to be put to its creditors with a view to allowing the company to 'trade out' of its difficulties. The directors must identify a 'nominee' who will supervise the operation of the arrangement and will call meetings of the creditors to discuss and to vote on the proposals. Where the proposal is approved, all creditors (including those who voted against its terms) are bound by its terms and may no longer commence individual enforcement actions against the company.

The second 'rescue-orientated' procedure in the Insolvency Act is administration (see Schedule B1 to the Insolvency Act 1986). An administrator may be appointed by the company, its **directors,** or a creditor holding a floating charge. Only qualified insolvency practitioners are eligible to act as administrators. The administrator must formulate proposals in relation to the company, and, in doing so, must have as his objective the rescue of the company as a going concern (paragraph 3(a) of Schedule B1), *unless* he thinks that it is not reasonably practicable to achieve that objective *or* that the interests of the company's creditors would be better served by not attempting to rescue the company (and, perhaps, attempting instead to sell its *business* as a going concern). The administrator's proposals are then put to the company's creditors who may vote that they should be implemented, modified, or rejected (paragraphs 49, 51 and 53 of Schedule B1). In order that administrators can effectively manage the administration, they are given considerable powers, equivalent to, and in many cases exceeding, those of the company's original directors (Schedule 1 to the Insolvency Act 1986).   SANDRA FRISBY

R Goode, *Principles of Corporate Insolvency Law* (London: Sweet & Maxwell, 3rd edn, 2005), ch 10

corporate social responsibility ('CSR')   The idea that corporations should act in a socially responsible manner can be traced at least as far back as the early twentieth century. The sheer size and market power of the giant joint-stock corporations which emerged during this period endowed their activities with a social significance which made it much harder to see them as purely 'private' in nature. In the 1920s and 1930s, this, together with the increasingly functionless, *rentier* nature of their shareholders and the growing separation of ownership and control highlighted by Adolf Berle and Gardiner Means in their celebrated *The Modern Corporation and Private Property* (1932), led many commentators to argue that corporations should be conceptualized not as 'private' enterprises 'owned' by their shareholders but as social or quasi-social institutions with wider **responsibilities.** In the UK, views of this sort figured

prominently in the work of Fabian intellectuals such as RH Tawney (*The Acquisitive Society* (1921)) and Harold Laski (*Grammar of Politics* (1925)). In the US, they were implicit in much of the work of Thorstein Veblen (see, eg *Absentee Ownership* (1923)) and found famous expression in the concluding chapters of Berle and Means' book and in Merrick Dodd's contributions to his debate with Berle in the *Harvard Law Review* (1931–1932). As Dodd made clear, views of this sort also had some support within the business community.

In the post-war years, these ideas crystallized into the 'managerialist' view that corporations—increasingly thought to be dominated by managers free from the control of passive, dispersed, investor-shareholders—should be regarded as quasi-social institutions whose managers should balance the different interests of employees, customers, creditors, and the **community** at large (what we now call '**stakeholders**'). Some thought that to reflect these changed realities the rights of corporate shareholders (particularly their voting rights) should be pared down and that other groups should have a say in corporate affairs, especially employees, hence the many proposals to introduce worker participation. In the 1950s and 1960s, many thought that management-controlled corporations had indeed become significantly more 'socially responsible' and that this was contributing to a radical transformation of capitalism itself. In the UK, this view was exemplified by the Labour Party intellectual, Anthony Crosland; in the US by the work of Berle and JK Galbraith.

The idea of the 'socially responsible corporation', with its transformative aspirations, began to fade in the 1970s as the power of finance and influence of neo-liberal ideas grew. In the 1980s and 1990s the principle of shareholder primacy was restored with a vengeance, with so-called 'nexus-of-contract' theories providing new efficiency (rather than 'ownership') based justifications for shareholder-orientated corporations. Amidst a dramatically changed corporate culture, the maximization of shareholder value emerged as the overriding goal of managers. It is now widely believed that stock markets and the 'market for corporate control', supported by performance-related executive remuneration packages (**share** options) and **independent directors**, ensure that corporate managers act in the shareholder interest; and that the principle of shareholder primacy, by ensuring allocative efficiency, operates for the benefit of society as a whole.

CSR in its contemporary form, promoted initially by **non-governmental organizations** and other campaign groups emerged as a defensive reaction to these changes. Unlike the earlier, more radical idea of the socially responsible corporation, contemporary CSR is ameliorative, rather than transformative, in aspiration, seeking to remind corporations of their ethical and social responsibilities to a broader range of stakeholders and trying to effect modest changes in the way they make profits (thereby distinguishing itself from old-fashioned philanthropy) without challenging the principle of shareholder primacy or the policy tenets of **neo-liberalism**. Thus, although rhetorically it promotes a shift in focus from the 'bottom line' to the 'triple bottom line' (people, planet, and profits), CSR in its contemporary form essentially endorses neo-liberal rhetoric about the limited economic role of states by emphasizing voluntary self-regulation by corporations rather than mandatory, coercive **regulation** and by relying on 'soft' rather than 'hard' law. It seeks to persuade corporations to do more than that required by law. Its typical mechanisms are thus the voluntary code of conduct and the public–private partnership. Indeed, in recent years, CSR has been embraced by much of the corporate world, despite continued opposition from those who, like David Henderson (author of *Misguided Virtue*), support Milton Friedman's claim that the responsibility of business is to make profits. Its rise to prominence has been remarkable.

Views on the effectiveness and potential of CSR vary. Some think it is genuinely making corporations more socially, environmentally, and ethically responsible, and that it is generating new ideas about corporate **accountability** involving a complex array of legal and extra-legal mechanisms; others see it as an important tool for fostering economic and social progress, particularly in the developing world. Many, however, remain deeply sceptical, seeing the corporate adoption of CSR as evidence of its unthreatening nature, highlighting its use by corporations as a branding device in what David Vogel has called the 'market for virtue'. From this perspective, CSR is not only capable of being commodified but is a modest price for financial interests to pay to maintain their hegemony. PADDY IRELAND

corporation tax Corporation tax is a tax on companies and corporations. In the United Kingdom not only are **limited liability** companies subject to corporation tax, but unincorporated associations such as clubs are also liable. **Partnership**s (including **Limited Liability Partnerships**) are specifically excluded, as are local authorities and local authority associations.

The major design difficulty for a corporation tax is dealing with the fact that a corporation is a legal construct with a separate legal personality, while economically the only persons who can benefit from it are investors in the corporation. Other fiscal intermediaries, such as **trusts** and partnerships, may be transparent for tax purposes and credit may be given for tax paid by the underlying entity. Various approaches can be taken to taxation of corporations:

- No tax on the Company. This has been advocated in the past but has not been favoured by governments.
- The Classical System. This was the system introduced in the UK in 1965. Here, both the company and the shareholder are taxed. This effectively makes distributed income liable to a higher tax. Some argue this system helped the 'German Economic Miracle' of the mid-twentieth century.
- The Imputation System. Under this system, payment of tax by the company is treated as payment of the tax (or part of it) payable by the shareholder. This was the approach of the system in the UK from 1973 till the late 1990s. On paying a dividend a company paid part of its tax bill early, called Advance Corporation Tax. This 'franked' or gave a credit to the shareholder, which reduced the shareholder's tax bill. This system reduces the bias against distributions.
- Hybrid: tax may be levied on a combination of the above systems and/or others. The present UK system is probably best described as hybrid.

UK corporation tax is charged on 'profits', ie income plus chargeable (capital) gains. Companies resident in the UK are chargeable on their worldwide profits. Companies carrying on a trade in the UK through a permanent establishment are chargeable on the profits attributable to the permanent establishment in the UK. A company incorporated in the UK is always a UK resident for UK purposes. Other companies are treated as UK residents if their centre of management and control is in the UK.

The rate of tax payable by companies is not necessarily the same as that payable by individuals or trustees. Currently in the UK, the former is lower than the latter; and in the past it has been considerably lower than it is now. This led to special measures being introduced to deal with 'money box' companies, ie closely held companies. At one time their income was deemed to be distributed even if it was not.

There are special rules for groups of companies which are economically one entity. This allows certain payments to be made within the group without attracting tax, and for losses to be surrendered and assets transferred on a no gain/no loss basis for **capital gains tax** purposes. There are similar rules about payments and losses for consortium companies that do not fall within the group provisions. These benefits have been limited in many cases to UK resident companies. This has led to difficulties under **European law** with respect to Freedom of Establishment and Movement of Capital. This has also been the case with anti-avoidance legislation aimed at offshore money box companies (Controlled Foreign Companies ('CFCs')).   ADRIAN SHIPWRIGHT

See also: **corporate personality; dividend tax**

corrective justice *see* **civil liabilities, theory of justice**

corruption Defined as a *quid pro quo* in which private gain is secured at public expense, corruption is a broad term, describing a range of activities. From bribery to win contracts, to electoral malpractice, to offering inducements to public servants, the term is necessarily capacious. It is similarly venerable. No less a figure than Moses' father-in-law urged that judicial selection should 'look for men who are trustworthy and hate dishonest gain' (Exodus 18:21). The Sale of Offices Act 1551 penalized 'corruption in offices of justice or places of trust' and bribery itself has been a **common law** offence since at least the eighteenth century.

As a consequence of the expansion of the franchise and growth of the state, with the attendant expansion of opportunity structures, the late nineteenth and early twentieth centuries saw repeated attempts to criminalize corruption. In the electoral context, the Corrupt and Illegal Practices Act 1883 penalized hitherto commonplace conduct such as treating electors and paying them to display election materials. More important was the Act's imposition of local limits on the election expenditure of parliamentary candidates. This early instantiation of the principle of political equality proved to be one of the pillars of United Kingdom's party funding law in the twentieth century, although it was not expanded to include national expenditure limits for political parties until the Political Parties Election and Referendum Act 2000.

Perhaps the most notorious example of political corruption in the United Kingdom—Maundy Gregory's expert selling of peerages at Lloyd George's behest—generated one of Parliament's more ineffectual statutes. The Honours (Prevention of Abuse) Act 1925, introduced as a direct response to Gregory's actions, makes the sale of honours illegal. The fact that only one person has ever been successfully prosecuted under the Act—Gregory himself in 1933—is less a testament to the flawless character of British politics than the tortuous drafting of the Act. In mid-2007, after a fourteen-month police investigation, the **Crown Prosecution Service** announced that it would not bring charges under the 1925 Act against anyone involved in the 'Cash For Peerages' affair which implicated the then **Prime Minister**'s chief fundraiser.

At the multinational level, the OECD (Organization for Economic Cooperation and Development) Convention on Combating Bribery (1997) has proved to be a significant instrument, for the first time penalizing the offeror rather than the recipient of the bribe. Signatories are required to put in place domestic legislation that criminalizes bribery by their citizens of public officials from other countries, even if the events take place outwith the signatory's national boundaries. Further, the OECD itself has notable monitoring powers, which enable it to review domestic implementing legislation so as to assess its adequacy and also to assess the effectiveness with which the legislation is implemented. This process led to terse criticism of the British Government's decision in 2007 to discontinue the Serious Fraud Office's investigation concerning BAE Systems and the Al Yamamah defence contract with the government of Saudi Arabia, with the OECD expressing 'serious concerns as to whether the decision was consistent with the OECD Anti-Bribery Convention'.

Whilst further instruments have been initiated at various regional levels, such as the Council of Europe's Corruption Conventions (1999), it can be anticipated that the United Nation's Convention Against Corruption (2003) will be a major focus of future legal attention.   NAVRAJ SINGH GHALEIGH

M Pieth, LA Low and P Cullen (eds), *The OECD Convention On Bribery : A Commentary* (Cambridge: Cambridge University Press, 2007)
C O'Leary, *The Elimination of Corrupt Practices in British Elections, 1868–1911* (Oxford : Clarendon Press, 1962)

cosmopolitanism The idea of the 'cosmopolis' has a long history in social and political thought and has played a significant role as a standard of judgment in traditional **natural law theories**. Since 1989, a 'new cosmopolitanism' has evolved into a vibrant, interdisciplinary movement in the social sciences. This cosmopolitan research agenda has revolved around three shared intuitions: the overcoming of national presuppositions and prejudices within social scientific disciplines, the recognition that society has entered an era of mutual interdependence on a world scale, and the development of normative theories of world **citizenship**, global justice, and cosmopolitan **democracy**.

One important aspect of this larger movement concerns the increasing centrality of **international law** and its transformation over time. In the field of international law cosmopolitanism has displayed a logic that extends the scope of the discipline. International law is conventionally conceived as a form of law which recognizes the nation state as its basic unit of analysis and advances national **self-determination** and non-interference in the internal affairs of other states as its guiding principles. It imagines a world of sovereign states with relatively few international rules to constrain the behaviour of governments either towards other states or towards their own citizens. Cosmopolitanism seeks to extend the reach of international law beyond issues of state **sovereignty** and concern itself with the rights and **responsibilities** of world citizens.

One of the key problems cosmopolitanism addresses is that some of the worst violators of **human rights** can be states or state-like formations. Whilst international law has traditionally developed according to the principle that every state is sovereign within its own territory, cosmopolitanism endorses legal limitations on how rulers may behave towards the ruled; and whilst international law leaves it mainly to states to protect the rights of individuals, cosmopolitanism looks also to the formation of international legal bodies, such as the UN or UN authorized **courts**, to perform this function. For this reason the creation of 'crimes against humanity' in international law is seen as a key cosmopolitan moment in developing a legal response to changing forms of state **violence**.

A formative expression of the development of a cosmopolitan perspective on law is to be found in John Rawls's *The Law of Peoples* (1999), where Rawls makes the case that a constitutional regime must establish an effective 'Law of Peoples' in order to realize fully the freedom of its citizens. He argues that 'Peoples' are bound to honour **human** rights and that the principle of non-intervention may be suspended in the case of major human rights abuses. A more radical version is to be found in Jürgen Habermas's *The Divided West* (2006) where Habermas develops the idea of the 'constitutionalisation of international law', partly to defend the legitimacy of international law despite its expanded scope and increasing distance from the consent of states, and partly to justify its involvement not only in conflicts *between* states but also in conflicts *within* states. The further development of the cosmopolitan paradigm is highly responsive to controversial political issues,

such as the legitimacy of humanitarian military interventions. ROBERT FINE

U Beck, *Cosmopolitan Vision* (Cambridge: Polity, 2006)
R Fine, *Cosmopolitanism* (London: Routledge, 2007)

costs of complaining and claiming When people think about the costs associated with bringing legal actions, they tend to focus on the cost of engaging the services of a solicitor or barrister for advice or assistance, although the range of costs associated with legal action is much wider. At an early stage in a complaint, it may be necessary to instruct other professionals to provide an expert opinion to establish the strength of one's claim. For example, if a person lives in rented accommodation and the house is in a state of disrepair, which the landlord refuses to rectify, the tenant may need to instruct a surveyor to assess the disrepair and take photographs of the problems to demonstrate their extent. It may be necessary to pay court fees in order to begin formal legal proceedings. And, if legal action is unsuccessful, the claimant may also be liable to pay the cost of the other party's legal fees. Legal proceedings or negotiations via solicitors may not be the only way to complain or claim. It may be possible to make use of an industry or statutory ombudsman scheme, some of which are free of charge. Other forms of **alternative dispute resolution** such as **mediation**, or arbitration may also be available. Finally, it may be possible to seek advice and assistance from a one of several free, **pro bono legal services**.

The costs associated with complaining and claiming may be paid by the individual herself, or may be met through **legal aid**, or legal expenses insurance or through trade union or work-based legal assistance schemes. It is, perhaps, useful to begin by considering the main mechanisms for claiming and complaining and their costs, if any, before considering some of the ways in which the cost may be met—whether this be through legal aid, insurance or other mechanisms.

Cost of Legal Advice, Legal Assistance and Legal Proceedings

Many people instruct a solicitor to assist them in their complaint or claim. Most solicitors calculate their fees on the basis of an hourly rate, many charged in five, six or ten minute intervals. Costs range widely, from the relatively modest fees charged by some high street practices to very high fees charged by City and large commercial law firms. Barristers often charge a fee for the brief (the case), rather than an hourly rate. The cost of legal advice is a concern to many considering a complaint or a claim. Surveys have found that the perception that legal advice is prohibitively expensive is one of the greatest barriers to justice.

However, there are mechanisms for challenging the level of legal fees, in the event of a dispute, through the legal professional's firm, the professional body, or the courts using a process called 'court assessment'.

Some solicitors and barristers work within not-for-profit organizations, which do not charge the public for legal advice and assistance, but instead receive funding from local authorities, other direct grants, or charities that meet the cost of running the service. Some of these organizations operate within the legal aid scheme as well: Law Centres, **Citizens Advice Bureaux** and some other specialist agencies that provide money, debt, immigration, and housing legal advice and help. There are also some pro bono advice clinics and advice schemes that provide help with complaints and claims, free of charge.

Cost of Ombudsman Schemes & Alternative Dispute Resolution Mechanisms

Investigations by **ombudsmen** of complaints that fall within their jurisdiction may lead to a finding being made against the body that is the subject of the complaint along with a (non-legally enforceable) recommendation of a remedy. There are two main forms of ombudsman scheme. Statutory schemes, such as those of the Parliamentary Ombudsman and the NHS Ombudsman, have a public service mission. They are free of charge to complainants being funded by the taxpayer. Industry schemes are usually supported by industry members who have joined an accredited scheme or membership organization. These, too, are usually free, although in some instances a small fee may be payable to access the ombudsman. Some industry schemes are true ombudsman services, whereas others are closer to alternative dispute resolution mechanisms that facilitate negotiations between the disputing parties. Other forms of alternative dispute resolution, such as mediation and arbitration, may involve solicitors, barristers, or former judges, or they may be operated by other professionals with expert knowledge of that type of dispute. Although some are free, most attract a fee—from the small to the very high, depending on the professionals involved and the nature of the service they provide.

Meeting Costs—Legal Aid

Legal aid is funded by the state, through the tax system, to ensure access to justice in a range of social welfare matters as well as family law and criminal law matters. Costs associated with legal advice and assistance and, in some instances, legal proceedings, may be met through the scheme if the individual meets the merits test in relation to their legal problem and they meet any financial means test. The legal aid system does not necessarily meet the full legal and associated costs of the dispute, nor does it operate like the NHS, which is free at the point of delivery and thereafter. Individuals benefiting from legal aid are likely to have to contribute to the cost of the case, and may also have to repay some legal aid costs from any money they recover through the action. Consequently, in many instances legal aid is more like a loan to pay for legal costs than a free system of legal advice and assistance.

As the cost of legal aid has increased, each successive government has sought ways to keep the legal aid budget under control while attempting to retain access to justice. To this end, the ways in which legal and other professionals are paid through the scheme have been subject to greater scrutiny and increased regulation and restriction in recent years. However, it is widely acknowledged both in the UK and abroad that our system is one of the best resourced, most far reaching and most respected legal aid systems in the world, even if there are difficulties associated with it.

Meeting Costs—Legal Expenses Insurance

There are other ways of meeting the costs of claiming and complaining, other than through private finance or through legal aid. Legal expenses insurance ('LEI') covers the cost of specified legal claims. Sometimes it covers the cost of legal advice only, whereas more extensive policies may also cover the cost of litigation. Some LEI policies are similar to standard insurance policies—the individual pays in advance for cover and thereafter she is insured against future costs that fall within the terms of the agreement. This type of 'before-the-event' cover is often sold as part of general household insurance policies. Another form of LEI is 'after-the-event insurance', which an individual takes out after the legal problem has occurred. After-the-event insurance has been most closely associated with **conditional fee arrangements**. Although it costs more than before-the-event LEI, it generally only covers the cost of meeting the other party's legal costs in the event that the insured loses the case and is required to pay the other side's costs.

Meeting Costs—Conditional Fee Arrangements

Conditional fee agreements ('CFAs'), often popularly referred to as a no-win-no-fee agreements, are arrangements under which a solicitor does not charge her client if the client does not 'win' the case;

but if the claim is successful, the lawyer may charge a 'success fee' in addition to her basic fees. Our legal system operates on a 'costs follow the event' principle, which means that the loser usually pays the legal costs of the winner—hence the development of after-the-event LEI, which is designed to cover the risk of losing and having to pay the other side's costs. The result of entering a CFA coupled with before-the-event LEI should be that the client pays nothing if she wins, as her costs are met by the other side, and nothing if she loses: the LEI insurer will pay the winner's costs. There may be no clear 'winner' or 'loser', if the case does not go to court and there is a negotiated settlement. In that situation, the client may have to pay a portion of her own legal costs, depending on the terms of the agreement.   LISA WEBLEY

costs of litigation   *see* **costs of complaining and claiming**

***Council of Civil Service Unions v Minister for the Civil Service* (1985)**   The Government Communications Head Quarters ('GCHQ') is a branch of the public service whose task is to ensure security of UK official and military communications and to provide signals intelligence. Self-evidently much of its work is vital to national security. However, industrial action had been taken at GCHQ on seven occasions in the early years of the Thatcher Government in support of national trade unions in disputes having nothing specifically to do with conditions of employment at the GCHQ. On one occasion, the operations of GCHQ were virtually shutdown. There was a long established practice of consulting with the trade unions before conditions of employment were changed. But in 1983, without any consultation with the trade unions, it was decided by the Government that employees at GCHQ would no longer be permitted to belong to national trade unions but could only belong to an approved departmental staff association. This decision was challenged by **judicial review** by the trades unions.

The unions clearly had a legitimate expectation of being consulted, and in the normal course that expectation would have been protected. But the power to determine the conditions of employment of civil servants was considered a **prerogative** power. The royal prerogative consists of the **common law** powers of the **Crown**. As was the case here, prerogative powers are frequently delegated to Ministers. It had been established since 1611 that judges could determine whether a prerogative power existed. But it had been equally clear that judicial scrutiny would

not extend to the way in which those powers were exercised.

The breakthrough in the *GCHQ* case was to establish that where the exercise of the prerogative power in question is justiciable, it can be judicially reviewed. Since *GCHQ* applicants have succeeded in subjecting a wide range of prerogative powers to judicial review, most prominently the power to issue passports and to grant pardons.

Thus there appeared to be no reason why the decision to deny trade union membership should not have been subject to judicial review. But the House of Lords accepted that Government had feared that prior consultation might have precipitated industrial action that would have threatened national security. And in that case the requirements of fairness gave way to considerations of national security. Once it was clear that the executive had acted out of concern for national security, judicial scrutiny was at an end. Ministers had to be the judge of what national security required. Consequently, the unions' appeal failed. In 1997 the incoming Labour Government restored trade union rights at GCHQ.

One of the most influential aspects of the case has not yet been mentioned. In a dictum that immediately became canonical, Lord Diplock summarized the grounds of judicial review in a threefold formula. A court might set aside a decision because of 'illegality', 'procedural impropriety' or 'irrationality'. Each of these concepts is the subject of complex elaboration in case law and scholarly writing.

                CHRISTOPHER F FORSYTH

See also: **administrative law**

Council of Ministers   Article 203 EC provides that the Council shall consist of a representative of each Member State at ministerial level, who is authorized to commit the government of that state. The members of the Council are, therefore, politicians as opposed to civil servants, but the politician can be a member of a regional government where this is appropriate. The Council meets when convened by the President of the Council on his or her own initiative, or at the request of one of its members, or at the request of the **European Commission**. There are approximately eighty Council meetings per year, most of which take place in Brussels, although in April, June, and October they are held in Luxembourg. The Council has its own General Secretariat, under the responsibility of a Secretary-General, which provides direct administrative support to it.

Council meetings are arranged by subject matter with different ministers attending from the Member States, and are regulated by the Council's Rules of Procedure. There are at present nine such Council configurations, having been reduced from the much larger number of twenty-two prevailing in the 1990s. The General Affairs and External Relations Council ('GAERC'), normally attended by foreign ministers, deals with external relations and many matters concerning general Community policy. The Economics and Finance Council ('Ecofin') is concerned with matters such as the budget, **Economic and Monetary Union,** and financial markets; finance ministers from the Member States attend this Council. There is a Council dealing with matters concerning Justice and Home Affairs. The other Council configurations deal with sectoral issues: Transport, Telecommunications, and Energy; Employment, Social Policy, Health, and Consumer Affairs; Agriculture and Fisheries; Competitiveness; Environment; and Education, Youth, and Culture. The ministers responsible for these matters within Member States will attend such meetings. They will be supported by their own delegations of national officials who have expertise in the relevant area. The Commission is invited to attend Council meetings.

The Presidency of the Council is held by each Member State in turn for six months. The position of President of the Council has assumed greater importance in recent years. Strong central management has become more necessary in order to combat centrifugal tendencies within the Council. The growing complexity of the Community's decision-making structure has necessitated more coordination between the institutions. The scope of EU power has increased, demanding greater leadership in the Council. The Council's wish to take a more proactive role in the development of Community policy has required initiatives which the President can help to organize. The President will, seven months before taking office, set the dates for Council meetings in consultation with the Presidencies preceding and following its term of office. Every eighteen months the three Presidencies due to hold office prepare, in consultation with the Commission, a draft programme of Council activities for that period, which has to be endorsed by the GAERC. The incoming Presidency establishes, at least one week before taking office, indicative provisional agendas for Council meetings for the next six-month period, based on the eighteen-month programme and after consulting the Commission. Part A of the agenda covers matters that can be approved without discussion, Part B deals with those matters that require deliberation.

The President may also develop policy initiatives within areas which are of particular concern either to the Council as a whole or to the Member State which currently holds the Presidency. The President will have an important liaison role to play with the Presidents of the Commission and the Parliament, and will represent the Council in discussions with institutions outside the Community.

The work of the Council is prepared by the Committee of Permanent Representatives (COREPER), which is staffed by senior national officials. COREPER II is the more important and consists of permanent representatives of ambassadorial rank. It deals with the more contentious matters such as economic and financial affairs, and external relations. It also performs an important liaison role with national governments. COREPER I is composed of deputy permanent representatives and is responsible for issues such as the environment, social affairs, the internal market, and transport. COREPER plays an important part in EC decision-making, because it considers draft legislative proposals from the Commission, and because it helps to set the agenda for Council meetings.

The powers of the Council are described in Article 202 EC. This states that the Council is to ensure coordination of the general economic policies of Member States; have power to take decisions; and that it can confer, albeit subject to conditions, implementation powers on the Commission. This does little to convey the reality of the Council's powers. The Council exercises an important role in the decision-making process in six ways.

First and foremost, the Council has to vote its approval of virtually all Commission legislative initiatives before they become law. The vote will be by unanimity, qualified, or simple majority depending upon the particular Treaty Article. Secondly, the Council has become more proactive in the legislative process through the use of Article 208 EC, which allows the Council to request that the Commission undertake studies which the Council considers desirable for the attainment of the Community's objectives. The Council has used this power to frame specific proposals which it wishes the Commission to shape into concrete **legislation**.

Thirdly, the Council can delegate power to the Commission, enabling the latter to pass further regulations within a particular area. It is now common for such delegations of power to be subject to the condition that the Commission action is acceptable to committees staffed by national representatives. This operates as a mechanism whereby the Council can ensure that the detail of the delegated legislation is in conformity with its own wishes. Fourthly, the Council, together with the European Parliament, plays a major role in relation to the EU's budget, on which many initiatives depend.

Fifthly, it will be the Council that will normally conclude agreements on behalf of the EC or the EU with third states or international organizations. Finally, in addition to its powers under Pillar 1, the EC Treaty, the Council also has significant powers under Pillar 2, dealing with the Common Foreign and Security Policy, and under Pillar 3, concerned with Police and Judicial Cooperation in Criminal Matters.   PAUL CRAIG

See also: **Pillars of the European Union**

Council on Tribunals   *see* **ombudsmen**

council tax   Council tax was introduced in April 1993 to replace the community charge ('poll tax'). It is Britain's only significant local tax, providing 15 per cent of local authorities' income. Council tax is a largely property-based tax: domestic residences are banded according to an assessment of their market value. Individual local authorities determine the overall level of council tax, while the ratio between rates for different bands is set by central government (and has not changed since council tax was introduced). Northern Ireland operates a different system of regional rates and locally variable district rates; since April 2007, these have been charged as a percentage (averaging 0.64 per cent in 2007–2008) of the assessed value of properties as at 1 January 2005.

In England and Scotland there are eight council tax bands, with the highest (Band H) charged three times as much as the lowest (Band A); almost two-thirds of properties are in the lowest three bands. Property bandings are currently based on assessed market values as at 1 April 1991. In Wales, a revaluation took effect in April 2005 based on April 2003 property values, and a ninth band (Band I) was introduced. A similar revaluation in England, due to take effect in April 2007, was cancelled.

There is a range of exemptions and reliefs from council tax, most notably a 25 per cent reduction for properties with only one resident adult. Low-income families can have their council tax bill reduced or eliminated by claiming council tax benefit. Council tax, net of council tax benefit, was expected to raise £23.7 billion in 2007–2008, 4.3 per cent of total government revenue. The average household bill in England and Wales for 2007–2008 was £1,088.

STUART ADAM

counterfeit goods   *see* **misleading product descriptions**

counterfeiting   *see* **border control of intellectual property; trade marks**

counter-measures   *see* **sanctions**

countervailing measures   *see* **World Trade Organization**

countryside, access to   *see* **rights to roam**

court fees   *see* **costs of litigation**

Court of Arbitration for Sport   The Court of Arbitration for Sport ('CAS') —also known by its French acronym ('TAS') (Tribunal Arbitral du Sport)—was established in 1983 and began operating in 1984. Governed by the International Council on Arbitration for Sport ('ICASP'), CAS and ICASP have a permanent President and a Secretary General who heads up the CAS Office at Chateau Bethusy in Lausanne, Switzerland.

CAS can decide any dispute relating to sport and is the final 'court of appeal' under the Anti-Doping Code of the World Anti-Doping Agency. Since 1999, CAS offers a mediation service, and also gives non-legally binding Advisory Opinions. There are 300 arbitrators and 65 mediators, drawn from lawyers around the world with expertise in arbitration or mediation relating to sport. CAS proceedings are governed by the Code of Sports-Related Arbitration (2004). During the Summer and Winter Olympic Games, CAS operates an Ad Hoc Division ('AHD'), which handles disputes arising during the Games. AHD proceedings are free and decisions must be rendered within 24 hours.

CAS awards are enforceable under the New York Convention of 10 June 1958. CAS awards may be challenged in the Swiss Federal Tribunal on limited grounds under Article 190(2) of the Swiss Federal Code on Private International Law of 18 December 1987.   IAN BLACKSHAW

IS Blackshaw, RCR Siekmann and J Soek (eds), *The Court of Arbitration for Sport 1984–2004* (The Hague: TMC Asser Press; Cambridge: Cambridge University Press, 2005)

Court of Criminal Appeal   *see* Beck, Adolf;
Maybrick, Florence

Court of First Instance (CFI)   *see* European
Court of Justice

Court of Session   The Court of Session is Scotland's supreme civil court. Its jurisdiction is subject only to an appeal to the **House of Lords**. Its functions mirror those carried out by the High Court of Justice and the Court of Appeal in England and Wales, neither of which has jurisdiction over Scottish cases. Like all United Kingdom courts, it is subject to references to the **European Court of Justice** on the interpretation and validity of European Union law and to the adjudication of the Judicial Committee of the **Privy Council** if disputes about devolved powers arise. Such disputes may arise because the powers of the devolved **Scottish Parliament** and Executive created in 1999 are limited by the Scotland Act 1998 and the **European Convention on Human Rights**.

The Court of Session is the only significant part of Scottish central governance which survives from before the Union of 1707, alongside the High Court of Justiciary, Scotland's supreme criminal court. The pre-union Scottish Parliament had exercised a central jurisdiction as a sovereign court of law in the medieval period, but this was yielded gradually to the late medieval King's Council, whose judicial 'sessions' constituted the Court of Session in its earliest form. By the late fifteenth century the Session, as it was first known, developed its historic role as a regular central tribunal alongside Parliament, followed ultimately (in 1532) by its establishment, by James V and the Scottish Parliament, as a College of Justice. Although there had been a hundred years or so of prior experiment, with significant consolidation from the 1490s, it was only in 1532 that the court reached a decisive level of institutional and jurisdictional development.

The statute concerning the institution of the College gave as its main basis the desire of James V for a permanent order of justice for the common good of his subjects, and its fundamental jurisdiction and institutional form have since remained remarkably unchanged. To this day its judges continue to be technically both Senators of the College of Justice and Lords of Council and Session. Since 1887, in addition, all hold office concurrently as criminal judges in the High Court of Justiciary. The main discontinuity has been the disruption caused by the Cromwellian occupation of Scotland in the 1650s, which saw the Court of Session temporarily cease to sit between 1650 and 1661. Following the Restoration, the Court of Session was revived in 1661; and under the terms of the Union of 1707 its authority, constitution and location in Scotland were declared inviolable, subject only to such 'regulations for the better administration of justice' as might be made by the post-union Parliament of Great Britain.

The Court of Session is a court of first instance as well as appeal, with a generally unlimited civil jurisdiction. Its competence is exclusive in certain areas, such as **judicial review**. Its structure has always been collegiate. Until 1808 its (then) full complement of fifteen judges sat together to decide cases in the 'Inner House', with preliminary work performed by individual nominated judges in the 'Outer House'. In 1808, the current separation of the Inner House into two 'Divisions' of equal authority was first adopted. In modern times an *ad hoc* 'Extra Division' often sits too, constituted from the Outer House or from retired judges. Exceptionally a full court may still be convened. The functions of the Outer House are performed by single judges of the court sitting as a 'Lord Ordinary' at first instance, responsible for preliminary procedural decisions on a case as well as for giving final decree after hearing evidence in a 'proof' or legal argument about a claim in a 'debate'. Normally a proof is decided alone by a judge, but some actions can go to a civil jury trial.

The Court of Session Act 1988 now provides for thirty-four judges in total, of whom five should sit in each Division of the Inner House. The Lord President of the Court of Session presides over the First Division and is the most senior civil judge in Scotland, also holding concurrently the office of Lord Justice-General of Scotland, the most senior criminal judge in Scotland. The Lord Justice-Clerk presides over the Second Division. Each Division acts principally as an appeal court, hearing appeals from the Outer House, as well as from the Sheriff Court and various statutory tribunals such as the Employment Appeal Tribunal. Rights of audience in the Court of Session are exclusively held by those practising as 'advocates' in the Faculty of Advocates, though under legislation enacted in 1990 solicitors may also appear if qualified as 'solicitor advocates'. The court sits in Parliament House in Edinburgh, originally completed in 1639 to house the Scottish Parliament and Privy Council as well as the Court of Session.   MARK GODFREY

*The Laws of Scotland: Stair Memorial Encyclopaedia,
   Volume 6 (Courts and Competency)* (Edinburgh: Lexis-
   Nexis UK, 1988), paras 896–937

See also: **courts; criminal justice system: Scotland;
   judges**

court proceedings—starting a claim The effect of starting a claim is to subject the parties involved to the court's processes. As with other aspects of procedure, the history has been of the procedures for starting a claim becoming encrusted with technicalities, followed by reform measures, with the cycle being repeated.

Before the courts of England and Wales, starting a claim has always been a relatively formal process. That contrasts with how claims are started in some courts elsewhere (eg a letter will do to institute public interest litigation before courts in India) and before other bodies providing access to justice, such as **ombudsmen**. For eight centuries claims before the higher courts in England and Wales were commenced by issue of a writ; but the last writs were issued in 1999. As part of recent procedural reforms (the so-called 'Woolf reforms' after Lord Woolf, the chair of the inquiry that preceded the changes), one aspect of which was to simplify court procedures, claims are now typically commenced by the issue of a claim form.

At one time (and in local courts this continued for much longer) responsibility for summoning a party so as to start a claim before a court fell upon the plaintiff personally, who might have to take witnesses to the defendant to do so. Then in the Middle Ages, and especially during and after the reign of Henry II, a claimant would pay for a writ to be issued which ordered a defendant to come before the King's judges. A defendant who failed to appear could be fined. When Glanvill wrote the first book on the **common law** of England in the 1180s he distinguished original writs, issued under the Chancellor's great seal to commence proceedings, and judicial writs issued by judges for purposes such as compelling attendance at court.

With time, the forms of various original writs became specialized, depending on the nature of the claim. Choosing the appropriate writ became crucial because otherwise a plaintiff would have the action dismissed and would have to commence proceedings anew. The technicalities and fictions associated with choosing the right writ led to complexity. To an extent this was ameliorated by the growth of the equitable jurisdiction of Chancery, where actions were commenced by filling a bill, which would lead to a subpoena being issued to compel the defendant to attend court. Over time Chancery procedure became rigid as well.

The nineteenth century was an important period of reform of procedure. After 1832 all personal actions were commenced by a single common form of writ, in which the nature of the action was stated.

Legislation in 1875 meant that it was not necessary to state the precise ground of complaint or the precise relief the plaintiff claimed in a writ in the High Court. It also became possible to commence certain actions—eg one concerning construction of a written document or statute—by an 'originating summons'; and proceedings in the Chancery division could be commenced by motion, petition, or summons. The county court had its own method for commencing proceedings.

Lord Woolf, in considering reform of rules of procedure in the mid 1990s, identified the fact that there were four different ways of starting proceedings in the High Court and another four in the county court as a prime aspect of the complexity of the rules. One aspect of his reforms to simplify procedure was the introduction of a single claim form, which could be used in all cases to commence proceedings. The existing position was preserved, in that the claimant can choose whether to include the particulars of the claim on the claim form or to provide them later. The time of commencement of proceedings, which is important for limitation purposes, is the date entered on the form by the court. In the case of money claims, the claim form may be issued electronically at the **Money Claims On Line** website (www.moneyclaim.gov.uk). Public utilities and financial institutions can issue claim forms for debts in bulk through the Production Centre in Northampton. In both cases the claims are limited to £100,000 and are brought in the County Court.

Critics have pointed out that despite the Woolf reforms, it is still possible to commence claims in the civil courts in twelve different ways other than by the issue of a claim form. These cover special situations and in some cases are for convenience (eg there is a special claim form for use where there are no substantial, factual disputes) and in others are prescribed by statute (eg by petition for divorce, the winding up of a company, or bankruptcy). Overall the procedure for commencing a claim is now more straightforward than it has ever been, although history teaches that this position is not guaranteed forever.

ROSS CRANSTON

See also: **courts; equity as a system of law; limitation of actions**

courts The term 'court' is used to describe such a wide variety of institutions in a legal system that it is difficult to identify common features beyond saying that most (but not all) courts consist of legally qualified **judges** and that courts are involved in making binding determinations of fact and law to resolve disputes through a process of adjudication. Some tribunals share many of the characteristics of courts (for example, **Employment Tribunals** in Great Britain might as well have been called 'Employment Courts').

The huge variety of courts means that many different procedures are used in the task of decision-making. The majority of courts have some form of oral hearing, at which individuals or their legal representatives address the judge. Some courts proceed mainly by way of written submissions. The principle that 'justice must not only be done but must also be seen to be done' is recognized in many national **constitutions** and international human rights treaties, so courts are generally expected to sit in public when hearings are held and when giving judgments.

National courts generally operate within a single legal system; it is quite common for a country to have more than one legal system. In federal systems, each constituent part of the federation (state, province, länd) will have its own court system, with another serving the distinct legal system at the federal level. The UK is not a federal system, but there are three separate legal systems, each with its own set of courts: one for England and Wales; another for Scotland; and a third for Northern Ireland.

Principal courts of England and Wales

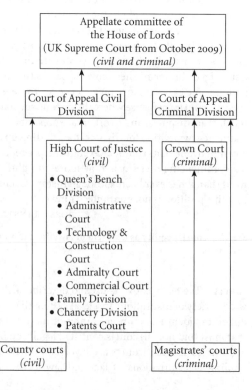

Principal courts of Scotland

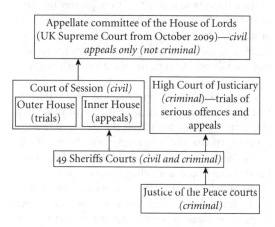

Principal courts of Northern Ireland

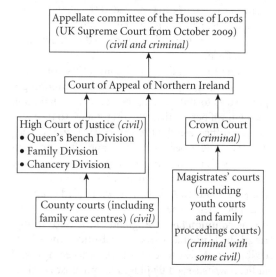

In hearing any particular appeal, the UK Supreme Court (and its predecessor up to 2009, the Appellate Committee of the **House of Lords**) sits as a court of the legal system from which the appeal is brought—a decision 'is to be regarded as the decision of a court of that part of the United Kingdom' (Constitutional Reform Act 2005, section 41). The UK Supreme Court will also deal with 'devolution issues' about the limits of powers of the Scottish, Welsh, and Northern Irish executive bodies and the **Scottish Parliament**, National Assembly for Wales, and the Northern Ireland Assembly; here it sits (like the Judicial Committee of the **Privy Council**, which hears these cases prior to 2009) as a court of the whole United Kingdom.

The 'jurisdiction' of a court defines the types of case it may hear.

- *Trial courts and appeal courts.* Most courts operate as part of a court system, with lower courts making 'first instance' decisions at trials and the possibility of an appeal to a higher appellate court. In England and Wales, trial courts include magistrates' courts, county courts, the Crown Court, and the High Court. At trial level, courts obtain and assess written and oral evidence upon which findings of fact are made, and legal rules and principles are applied, to determine the issues before the court. The role of appeal courts is generally to ensure that errors of law or fact-finding have not occurred. Trials are usually conducted by a single judge and appeal courts often consist of three or more judges.

- *Civil courts and criminal courts.* Most legal systems have separate courts—dealing with civil matters, such as contract disputes, family matters, and negligence claims, and criminal courts—determining innocence and guilt and sentencing those convicted.

- *Inferior courts and superior courts (or 'courts of record').* In some **common law** legal systems, a distinction is made between the lower courts (such as magistrates' courts and county courts in England and Wales) and higher courts (the Crown Court, High Court, and Court of Appeal, together known as the Supreme Court of Judicature or, after 2009, the 'Senior Courts') in which a permanent record is made of the court's proceedings, kept by the court or in a national archive.

- *Special jurisdictions.* Some legal systems have ear-marked some kinds of subject matter as requiring adjudication by special courts outside the normal system. Many countries have established separate courts for dealing with military discipline and crime (as in the United Kingdom, the District Court-Martial, the General Court-Martial, and the Courts-Martial Appeals Court). Special courts may also exist for church-related matters (in England and Wales, known as **Ecclesiastical Courts**). Coroner's courts (consisting of a legally or medically qualified coroner sitting with a jury) conduct inquests into causes of death. In the United Kingdom, many fields involving disputes with public authorities and in relation to employment have been hived-off to tribunals.

- *National courts and international courts.* National legal systems have for centuries been served by courts but in more recent times there has been a proliferation of international courts. These include the **European Court of Justice** and **Court of First Instance** (serving the **European Union**), the **European Court of Human Rights** (adjudicating on individual complaints of violations of the **European Convention on Human Rights**), the **International Court of Justice** and the **International Criminal Court**.

The day-to-day work of most courts has little impact on people beyond the individual litigants and criminal defendants in particular trials and appeals. However, some courts have broader functions. In some countries (notably in continental Europe) a constitutional court, separate from the ordinary court system, adjudicates on issues of constitutional law arising from their codified constitutions. These may include questions about 'division of powers' between the different governments of federal systems and on fundamental or human rights guaranteed by the national constitution. The German Federal Constitutional Court (the Bundesverfassungsgericht) and the Constitutional Court of South Africa are notable contemporary examples, but the idea of a specialist constitutional court can be traced back to the Austrian Constitutional Court established in 1920 following recommendations by the jurist Hans Kelsen. Some constitutional courts permit individuals to petition the court; other cases come to the court on references from the ordinary courts or other state institutions. Constitutional courts typically have powers to strike down legislation passed by a national Parliament on the grounds that it is unconstitutional. The court systems in countries with a specialist constitutional court have a 'dual apex'—the constitutional court dealing with issues of constitutional interpretation and a supreme court as the highest of the ordinary courts. Tensions have sometimes developed between the two courts as the division between what is a constitutional issue and what an ordinary question of law is not always clear cut.

In predominantly common law legal systems, constitutional and fundamental rights questions are generally dealt with by the ordinary courts and will often end up being determined by the final court of appeal in the legal system, often called the 'supreme court'. Such courts include the High Court of Australia, the Canadian Supreme Court, the Supreme Court of India, and the **United States Supreme Court**. In the legal systems of the United Kingdom, the top-level court for most purposes will, from October 2009, be the UK Supreme Court; and until then the Appellate Committee of the House of Lords and (for devolution issues) the Judicial Committee of the Privy Council. Some of the rulings of these top-level courts have engendered political controversy, dealing as they do with divisive issues such as gay rights, abortion (***Roe v Wade*** in the USA), the balance between individual liberty and counter-terrorism (***A v Secretary of State for the Home Department*** in the UK), and aboriginal land rights (***Mabo v The Commonwealth*** in Australia). Inevitably, the role of the top-level courts has prompted questions about judicial appointments. Some, but by no means all, supreme courts have power to strike down legislation as unconstitutional (see in relation to the US Constitutional Court, ***Marbury v Madison***). Although it is issues of constitutional law that most often generate public controversy, top-level courts in common law systems give judgment across a wide range of cases, including commercial, family, and criminal law.

The work of national courts is generally funded out of general taxation, though in some systems (including that of England and Wales) fees charged to litigants in civil cases contribute a large proportion of the budget. Courts have varying degrees of autonomy in relation to practical arrangements. Some courts are responsible for administering their own affairs, have their own support staff, and have a high degree of autonomy in setting their budgets (among them the US Supreme Court). Other court systems are dependent on the funding decisions taken by the national government and are staffed by civil servants (eg Her Majesty's Courts Service, an executive agency of the Department for Constitutional Affairs). These practical arrangements give rise to issues of **judicial independence**.

ANDREW LE SUEUR

See also: **admiralty courts; Chancery Court; civilian courts; common law courts; Constitutional Court, South Africa; Court of Arbitration for Sport; Court of Criminal Appeal; Court of Session; courts martial; criminal courts; Crown Court; Environmental Court; international courts and tribunals; international military tribunals; International Prize Court; Mental Health Review Tribunals; magistrates' courts; Permanent Court of Arbitration; Supreme Court (UK); tribunals**

courts martial   *see* **military law**

Courvoisier, François Benjamin   Courvoisier, a servant, was charged in May 1840 with the murder of his master, Lord William Russell. His three-day trial in the following month attracted enormous publicity because of the social status of the victim and the circumstances of the crime: Russell was a member of one of England's leading aristocratic families; he was aged and infirm, and his throat

had been savagely cut in his own home, in his own bed, while he slept. Extra seating had to be provided for the spectators who flocked to London's Central Criminal Court; and the judges presiding over the case found themselves sharing the bench with His Royal Highness the Duke of Sussex and various aristocratic ladies.

The evidence against the Swiss valet at first appeared entirely circumstantial, and some of it had clearly been manufactured by police officers keen to share in the substantial reward (£400) offered for a conviction. On the second day, however, a genuine link between crime and suspect was revealed: a woman came forward to claim that prior to the murder Courvoisier had left with her a parcel containing property belonging to Russell. When this new evidence was made known to the accused he summoned his two counsel and confessed to the murder, but insisted that they continue to defend him.

Courvoisier's trial took place only four years after defendants had been granted the right to full professional representation; and his leading counsel, Charles Phillips, was placed in a very difficult position. The duty owed to a client who confesses his guilt had not formed part of the discussion leading up to the Prisoners' Counsel Act 1836, no formal guidelines for professional conduct were in place, and no informal consensus existed as to acceptable practice in these circumstances. Reluctantly, after consulting the bench and his own conscience, Phillips continued. Courvoisier was convicted and hanged (6 July 1840) despite his efforts, but when news of the confession reached the public the case acquired a new notoriety. Phillips himself was now in the dock, accused at length in the press of having attacked witnesses whose evidence he knew to be true and widely condemned for continuing in the defence of a man he knew to be guilty as charged.

The *Courvoisier* case provoked a sustained debate in both the lay and professional press about the consequences of a confession of guilt for legal representation. During the course of that debate, moral wrong was reconciled with legal right: a guilty client, the bar concluded, was entitled to a legal defence and it was the barrister's duty to ensure that the client was convicted according to law. By 1850, that is, a professional distinction had been made between 'truth' and 'justice'. A confession of guilt did, however, place limits on advocacy. Phillips was widely believed to have transgressed those limits and his professional reputation was permanently tarnished by the trial. He gave up criminal practice in 1842.

ALLYSON MAY

couverture   *see* **woman**

covenants affecting freehold land   A covenant is technically defined as a promise contained in a deed, but in the present context the term is use to denote any enforceable promise affecting the use of freehold land.

Covenants provide a private law means of regulating the use of land, operating in parallel with the public law system of land use planning and development control. However, covenants can regulate matters beyond the scope of planning law; and they are an additional means of control that can prevent the development of land even where the planning authority has granted permission for the development.

Covenants are commonly used where an owner of freehold land sells part of that land and, as part of the transaction, the purchaser promises not to do certain things on the land that has been purchased. Such negative covenants, for example not to use the land for commercial purposes, are usually intended to preserve the residential amenity value of the land retained by the seller; and, in theory, the restrictions on the use of the purchaser's land are reflected in a lower purchase price. (Covenants sometimes require positive action or the expenditure of money on the part of the purchaser, but such positive covenants are less common because of the difficulties of on-going enforcement: see below.)

If the purchaser covenants with the seller to restrict the use of the land, and later reneges on the promise, the seller can take legal action against the purchaser for breach of contract. However, as a simple contract, the promise would normally be enforceable only between the original parties. In fact, the courts allowed a subsequent owner of the seller's retained land to enforce the promise against the original purchaser (and statute has extended the right of enforcement to others); but a promise that could not be enforced against a subsequent owner of the purchaser's land was of limited value. Consequently, following the classic case of *Tulk v Moxhay* **(1848)**, the courts allowed enforcement against a subsequent owner of the original purchaser's land, subject to certain conditions. Most importantly, such enforceability applies only to restrictive (negative) covenants: it has never extended to positive covenants. In addition, such covenants are enforceable against subsequent owners only where they had notice of the covenant at the time they purchased the land—although notice is now provided by registration of the covenant.

Covenants of the type discussed above are one-sided, enforceable by the original seller (and subsequent owners of the land retained) against the original purchaser (and subsequent owners of the land sold). However, covenants are also be used in the context of new building developments in such a way that the covenants are enforceable as a form of local law both by and against all the present and subsequent owners of plots on the development.

The unenforceability of positive covenants against subsequent freehold owners has long been criticized, but reform of the law is still awaited. In the meantime, such covenants can only be generally enforced as terms of leases or as terms regulating a **commonhold** development.   NIGEL GRAVELLS

See also: **town and country planning**

covenants over leasehold land   Leases invariably contain undertakings between landlord and tenant imposing various rights and obligations on the parties. Because leases are generally made by deed these undertakings are assumed, in the absence of clear evidence to the contrary, to take the form of covenants. However, leases for less than three years do not have to be made by deed and are often made simply in writing. Strictly speaking, the terms of such leases should be described as 'contractual rights and obligations' but the term 'covenant' is commonly extended to embrace all promises the landlord and tenant make to each other, including those created in writing and those that are implied. In some circumstances, leasehold covenants will be binding on (and enforceable by) not only the original parties but also their successors in title (ie subsequent lessors and lessees).

Express covenants are those the parties have agreed between themselves. In practice, they will depend upon the duration of the lease, the nature and location of the property, and the strength of the parties' bargaining positions. Express covenants by the tenant will typically include a covenant to pay rent, covenants as to the use of the premises, and a covenant not to assign or sub-let either at all or without the landlord's prior consent. Express covenants by the landlord will commonly include a covenant to allow the tenant quiet enjoyment of the premises, and a covenant to keep the premises insured.

Implied covenants are those implied by **common law** or by statute. Generally, an express covenant will override a covenant implied by the common law with which it conflicts; but statutorily implied covenants cannot usually be overridden by express agreement unless the statute itself allows otherwise.

Where the parties enter into a contract to grant a lease but fail to specify the terms the actual lease will contain, a term will be implied into the contract that the lease, when granted, will contain 'the usual covenants'. What is 'usual' will again depend on the nature and location of the premises and the duration of the lease. 'Usual' covenants by the tenant include covenants to pay rent and taxes, to keep and deliver up the premises in good repair, and (if the landlord has covenanted to repair) to allow reasonable access to allow the landlord to do so. The 'usual covenants' on the part of the landlord are to allow the tenant quiet enjoyment and not to derogate from grant, and a covenant giving the lessor the right to recover possession if the tenant defaults on the rent.

Breach of a leasehold covenant does not by itself allow either party to treat the lease as being at an end; but it will give rise to a cause of action (ie a right to sue the party in breach). The basic common law remedy for breach of covenant is **damages**; but if the court considers that damages would be insufficient, it may order either an **injunction** or **specific performance**. In addition, if the lease gives the landlord a right of re-entry for breach of a tenant's covenant, the landlord can exercise that right and forfeit the tenancy, although the tenant may apply for and obtain relief against forfeiture.   JILL MORGAN

See also: **deeds**

CR v UK *see* **R v R**

creative commons   Creative commons ('cc') is a non-profit organization based in the US. Founded in response to the complexities and cost surrounding licensing of works protected by **copyright**, it provides a simple method for authors to license works and though which users can determine whether a work can be used for specified purposes. cc makes available modularized licences in human and machine readable forms: options include attribution, non-commercial, derivative, and share-alike. Originally written with US copyright law in mind, there are now over thirty-six jurisdiction-specific licences. Statistics suggest that many millions of works are licensed using cc licences, with well over 200,000 works under the cc licences covering England and Wales, and Scotland in early 2007. cc now encompasses a number of different projects including science commons (for scholarly works and scientific data) and ccMixter (for music). There have been few court cases in which the enforceability of

the licences has been tested. In 2006 a Dutch court confirmed that the licences bind users even where there is no express agreement or knowledge of the terms; while a Spanish court held that a bar which played cc music on its premises did not owe a royalty to a collecting society. Academic critics of the movement focus attention on the irony of the reliance on property rights and viral contracts to promote free culture, and the absence of an ethical standard of freedom in information in the licence terms. Others, including content industries, re-emphasize the role of copyright law in promoting and sustaining innovation.   CHARLOTTE WAELDE

credit business   *see* **licensing as consumer protection**

credit cards   Credit cards are now a common method of making payments and borrowing money. In 1971 there was only one type of credit card in the UK; by 2003 there were 1,300 and the amount owing on credit cards had increased from £32 million to over £49 billion. Credit cards are a lightning rod for discussion of the 'credit society' in the UK. The media often report unfavourably on aggressive credit card marketing and lending practices, the high costs and charges of credit cards, and the perceived connection between credit card borrowing and increasing over-indebtedness and insolvency in the UK.

Credit cards provide consumers with several benefits: an interest free period, reduction of the necessity for carrying cash, and the possibility of borrowing variable amounts without having to seek approval each time from a lender. They may also offer other benefits such as air miles or affinity benefits. Credit cards offer the possibility of income smoothing if individuals have a period of reduced income. Credit card purchases also provide consumers in the UK with the possibility of holding a credit card company liable should something go wrong with a purchase financed by the card. These UK protections (the Consumer Credit Act 1974) are the strongest in the world. It is unlikely that they would have been as strong but for the fact they were enacted at a time when the credit card industry was a nascent phenomenon in the UK.

The credit card industry is now dominated by a small number of international card networks comprised of the banks that issue the brands. These operate as a form of private government, setting and enforcing standards on the business institutions and consumers which use the network.

A major social cost of credit cards is that they can result in over-indebtedness for some consumers and this is related to the distinct form of borrowing on a credit card, which differs from traditional forms of lending. Repayment schedules are not fixed at the outset beyond the minimum payment, the total credit available is potentially variable, and the debt is incurred in small amounts over a period of time. Research suggests that individuals may underestimate at the time of obtaining a card, the amount that they will subsequently borrow on the card or the possibility that they may make a late payment or miss a payment. At the same time individuals are sensitive to the immediate short-term costs of using a card such as annual fees. These factors may partly account for the structure of contemporary credit card pricing, with short-term costs such as annual fees or transaction fees often being minimal, and contingent costs, such as interest rates on borrowing and late payment fees, very high. Institutions issuing credit cards derive the great majority of their income from interest charged to consumers who borrow on cards. They also earn profits on penalty charges and the 'interchange fee'—that is the fee set by the card network and charged by the acquirer bank to the issuer bank. This pricing structure means that those who do not borrow are subsidized by those who borrow, a potentially regressive pricing structure.

Critics have pointed to the high interest charges on credit cards and it is alleged that credit cards earn excessive profits for issuers. The **Competition Commission** found that store credit cards generated such profits from 1999–2004. Why should there be excessive profits in an apparently competitive industry? The answer, it is suggested, lies primarily in the consumer irrationality noted above: individuals wrongly estimate the likelihood that they will borrow on a card, or the likely extent of borrowing, when they obtain the card.

Regulation of credit card contracts in the UK is primarily through required disclosures and the application of general contract norms. Disclosure is required in advertising and when a consumer obtains the card. Many of these disclosures are limited in their effect because they are not made at the relevant time, when the consumer is thinking of borrowing on the card. Regulators have also required 'wealth warnings' on credit card statements about the dangers of making a minimum payment on the card. But it is not clear whether consumers pay much attention to standardized warnings. There is a reluctance to use price control of credit in the UK; but the **Office of Fair Trading** challenged

late payment fees charged by credit card companies in the UK as contravening the penalty doctrine in **contract law** and the Unfair Terms in Consumer Contracts Regulations. As a consequence, all credit card issuers agreed to reduce their fees by approximately 50 per cent. Given the standardized nature of many subsidiary terms in credit card contracts and the absence of competition in relation to many of these terms, there may be a case for the introduction of a standardized contract.

IAIN RAMSAY

See also: **usury**

crime   *see* **crime and social differentiation, crime and the media; crime rates; politics of crime control, rationale of criminalization**

crime and communities   The meaning of **community** is intimately linked with the ambitions and **capacity** of the nation state and often defined in contrast to formal institutions of state authority. In jurisdictions where the nation state occupies a dominant symbolic and authentic role—eg contemporary France—the concept of community is perhaps a misnomer. Allegiance to the nation state, and the bonds of **citizenship** that it affords, marginalizes the recognition of other ties of **identity**—along the lines of culture, **ethnicity,** and **religion**. The contemporary acknowledgement of the limitations of state action has provoked community-based developments that recognize the role of informal institutions and social control in sustaining order and promoting conformity. **Public policy** increasingly emphasizes governing crime through community-based institutions. Crimes that fuel public anxieties are highly concentrated within communities. Most offenders do not travel far to commit crimes. Much inter-personal **violence** occurs in familiar or familial relationships and the values that foster criminality are often sustained by peers and community members.

The decline of communal bonds is identified as both symptom and cause of rising crime and perceptions of increased disorder. Crime impacts adversely on community well-being, whilst fractured communities allow crime to flourish. Hence, reviving community cohesion is a prerequisite for crime prevention. Interventions that work through informal systems of control can exploit local capacity and knowledge in ways that reduce the harm caused by crime. According to communitarians, communities assert moral authority. They allow the policing *by* rather than *of* communities. Consequently, 'community safety' has become the dominant discourse, institutionalized through the Crime and Disorder Act 1998, giving rise to an infrastructure of local preventive partnerships.

This shift has occurred when communities have become harder to find. Social and cultural trends appear to be loosening and undermining traditional social ties. Accordingly, there is often a slippage between community as a sense of something lost (tradition) and as a focus for building modern democratic institutions. There is confusion between what communities *are* or *ought to be*. The ideals of community—reciprocity, intimacy, and trustworthiness—sit awkwardly with contemporary concerns for individuality, freedom, and mobility. These ideals do not necessarily equate with an absence of crime. 'Community' and its shared values may be criminogenic. Social ties and networks sustain organized crime and gang cultures. Inversely, low crime areas are not necessarily structured around tightly organized informal control. The moral order of suburbia does not conform to ideals of community affiliation. The structural attributes of communities—how they connect with, and are situated within, sources of power and resources in the wider environment— may be more important than community as a sense of belonging. One implication of the crime-community nexus is that offenders frequently are perceived as 'outsiders' against whom communities should protect themselves. This 'ideology of unity' perpetuates homogeneity. It evades understandings of offenders as members of communities and of crimes committed by intimate insiders—**domestic violence** and corporate crime. Fundamentally, it questions the extent to which 'community' and 'the social' are complementary aspects of the same rationality of government or potentially competing levels of government. ADAM CRAWFORD

crime and punishment, 900–1600 In the Middle Ages 'crime' was primarily identified with 'sin'. Notions of divine law and heavenly justice informed contemporary understanding of punishable behaviour. God's judgment was depicted in representations of the Last Judgment and invoked in early methods of proof of innocence (such as the ordeal and trial by combat). An influence on moral behaviour was maintained through religious teachings and the (post-Conquest) church courts. By the end of the sixteenth century, previously acceptable activities were condemned by the Puritans seeking to impose on communities their ideals of godly behaviour.

While the meaning of crime remained flexible, by the thirteenth century offences (other than treason) were being classified as felonies or trespasses. Felony (originally equated with disloyalty) constituted serious violence against the person and violation of property: homicide (including secret killing or 'murder' as later defined), robbery, burglary, larceny (goods worth over a shilling), rape, and arson. The categorization was not absolute: mayhem (serious assault) and rape/ravishment could equally be charged as trespass. Felony included receiving stolen goods, illegal purveyance, prison breach (until 1295), forgery (though counterfeiting the king's coin became treason in 1352), and (amongst other fifteenth-century additions) procuring removal of the legal record to secure reversal of the judgment.

During the Tudor period numerous statutory felonies were created covering such diverse areas as religious doctrine and observance, sorcery/witchcraft, illegal assemblies, vagabonds, deserting/demobilized soldiers, hunting/poaching (in disguise), dangerous prophecy, and sexual offences (notably sodomy and rape of a girl under 10). Criminal trespasses (misdemeanours), less serious offences committed in breach of the king's peace, could constitute 'enormous' trespasses (concerted actions and threatening behaviour intended to undermine the judicial process) or 'light' ones (against person or property). Statutory trespasses penalized various forms of conduct of an economic and social nature.

The notion, that serious wrongdoing was an infringement of both God's peace and of (his representative on earth) the king's authority and interests, developed during the tenth and eleventh centuries. However, the idea that it was in the public interest to punish offences committed by individuals and deter future wrongdoing did not emerge until Anglo-Norman times. Before then, persons found guilty of homicide or robbery could be punished by death, but as a means of compounding or compensating a victim (their kin or lord) for a wrong committed (and achieving an equivalent measure of honour and respect) there operated a formal system of tariffs (*wer* and *bot*) enforced in court by the threat of outlawry. This system continued after the Conquest, co-existing with punishment by loss of life or limb. In later years, although death or physical chastisement predominated, the compensation culture endured; and even in the mid-sixteenth century homicide could still be regarded as a private wrong requiring settlement and compensation.

Theoretically capital punishment was the preserve of the King; but in reality, various towns and lords exercised the right to carry out judgments of death, notably on thieves caught red-handed (*infangentheof*). Death by hanging on local gallows was the usual method of execution for felons, notorious criminals being strung up (in chains) at or near the scene of their misdeeds. Men guilty of the heinous crime of treason also provided a public spectacle, being drawn, hanged and quartered, each symbolically reflecting elements of their criminous behaviour. Noble traitors were decapitated, their head displayed on London Bridge, the quartered body parts sent to specific locations as a deterrent. Women or servants found guilty of petty treason (killing their husband or master) were burned, as were sorcerers. Before 1275 rapists could be blinded and castrated.

Regional variations in punishment survived into the fifteenth century: counterfeiters of coin were boiled alive (Channel Islands), thieves were taken out to sea and marooned on a rock (Scilly Isles), homicides were buried alive (Sandwich in Kent), convicted felons were thrown from the cliffs (Dover). By mutual agreement of church and state, punishment was attenuated for felons who claimed sanctuary or benefit of clergy. For trespasses, punishment was normally financial, though a brief spell in prison was ordained by some statutory offences. Ecclesiastical, manorial, and urban jurisdictions commonly employed corporal punishment: confinement in publicly visible stocks/pillory, whipping, and public penance (parading barefoot in underclothes). Petty thieves could lose an ear or a hand or, imaginatively, could be branded on the forehead with the church key if they broke in and stole ecclesiastical items. Rituals of humiliation (such as riding backwards on a horse or being pulled on a hurdle), imposed for sexual indiscretion or fraud, date from medieval times.

Levels and patterns of crime during the Middle Ages and Tudor period are hard to assess. Quantification is problematic since the records themselves do not comfortably yield to statistical analysis. Case material is limited (especially before the thirteenth century) and there are few continuous runs of extant proceedings for the plethora of courts and jurisdictions. Only the most dramatic and serious wrongs appear in the early records of the royal courts; minor assaults and lesser injuries were either brought in lower courts or were accepted as part and parcel of everyday life. Equally, the records do not include out-of-court settlements or crimes that went undetected or un-prosecuted owing to perennial difficulties of deliberate concealment and in identifying and capturing offenders. High profile examples of 'fur-collar' crime and the activities of gentry gangs such as the Folvilles and Coterels (who in the early fourteenth century murdered one royal judge and kidnapped and ransomed another) have coloured and reinforced popular perceptions deriving from the corpus of imaginative literature relating the exploits of gangs of outlaws (ballads of medieval origin, added to in the Tudor period). Chroniclers sometimes elaborate on specific criminal incidents, but tend towards impressionistic overviews of law and order, reflecting (like the records) temporal variations in law enforcement.　ANTHONY J MUSSON

crime and punishment, 1600–1900　In the seventeenth and eighteenth centuries the English criminal justice system depended upon local amateur officials, informal procedures, and severe, exemplary punishments. Justice was administered through royal courts but there was room at every stage of the process for the exercise of local discretion. **Common law** judges regularly travelled around the country to try serious crimes (felonies) at assizes, whilst the **Crown**'s local representatives, the justices of the peace ('JPs'), held regular sessions to try lesser offences. The Court of King's Bench in Westminster had a general supervisory criminal jurisdiction but the Old Bailey's regular sessions for London and Middlesex cases made it more important in practice.

The dominance of royal law and its local application gave the system strength and flexibility. Crime was perceived in local, rather than national, terms and the law was enforced selectively. If a particular area experienced high levels of crime, exemplary punishments could be enforced to restore order. Most felonies were punishable with death. Alternative punishments included transportation, the pillory, the stocks, whipping, branding, fines, or short periods of imprisonment.

The law comprised a heterogeneous collection of common law crimes such as homicide, burglary, robbery, arson, rape, and larceny and an increasing number of statutory offences, many of which were capital. The fault required for these offences was usually defined by broad terms, such as malice, whereas the act required was often set out in unwieldy, technical detail. The lack of clear guidelines meant that much of the law's content was determined at the point of application. The volume of prosecutions fluctuated over the period, but theft accounted for the majority and young men were the most common offenders. Assaults were usually treated as misdemeanours, reflecting the high tolerance of violence in society.

Most victims of crime chose not to prosecute. In the seventeenth century they had to do their own detective work and provide the impetus for prosecutions. This involved trouble and expense, so offenders either went free or settled the matter with the victim privately. Many cases in which a formal prosecution was initiated did not proceed beyond the informal preliminary hearing with the JP, who frequently brokered a settlement. JPs also had jurisdiction to try minor offences summarily, alone or in pairs at petty sessions.

Prosecutions for more serious charges proceeded by indictment. This bill of accusation was presented by a grand jury, made up of local gentry, which had to be satisfied that the prosecution case was strong enough to go forward for trial at the assizes or quarter sessions. Seventeenth and eighteenth-century trials were informal and short, often lasting only minutes. The judge presided over an unstructured debate between jury, prosecutor, and accused. **Juries** commonly acquitted against the evidence or committed 'pious perjury' by undervaluing stolen goods to convict on a lesser charge. Convicts could not appeal but they could petition for a royal pardon or a reduction in sentence. **Judges** routinely reprieved capitally convicted offenders after each assize, leaving only a few to hang as an example.

This discretionary, personal style of justice was well suited to the pre-industrial structure of English society. Social change, particularly urban growth, brought a shift in direction towards more professional, formal, and structured processes. Policing was traditionally the preserve of local, amateur constables who did little preventive or detective work. Concern with the problem of crime in eighteenth-century London prompted successful efforts to coordinate the law enforcement activities of JPs, constables, watchmen, beadles, and reward-seeking thief-takers. In the nineteenth century the creation of professional, uniformed police forces signalled the state's increased commitment to law enforcement. Summary jurisdiction expanded rapidly to include a wide range of minor and public order offences.

In trials for serious offences, the arrival of lawyers from the mid-eighteenth century eventually worked a transformation to an adversarial procedure. Rules of evidence evolved, and by 1900 the trial had become a much more formal, rule-governed process. Post-trial processes remained dependent on private applications for clemency. There was a shift away from public, corporal punishments. JPs became more likely to use fines or short periods of imprisonment, whilst transportation to the colonies provided a crucial alternative to hanging from the early eighteenth until the mid-nineteenth century. The collapse of the 'bloody code' in the 1830s practically confined the death penalty to murder and public executions were abolished in 1868. The prison emerged as the principal form of punishment, replacing the public terror of the scaffold with strict, disciplinary regimes.

The nineteenth century witnessed the first sustained attempts to rationalize the criminal law. It was consolidated rather than codified, with the result that much of the old law and terminology was retained. New fears about violence prompted stricter laws on assault, but property offences continued to account for the majority of prosecutions. **Common law** development was enhanced by the increased presence of lawyers in trials but, although the trial judge had discretion to reserve a point of law for further consideration by the judges, there was no right of appeal until 1907.

By 1900 a formal, impersonal system of justice had emerged in which milder penal laws were enforced with greater consistency. Crime had become a major social problem that required national solutions. The inevitable result was a growth in state power, but the system remained full of the paradoxes and local variations that were the consequence of centuries of piecemeal development. These discretionary practices ensured that the law continued to be shaped by a wide range of people across society.

PHIL HANDLER

JA Sharpe, *Crime in Early Modern England 1550–1750* (London: Longman, 2nd edn, 1999)
C Emsley, *Crime and Society in England 1750–1900* (Harlow: Pearson/Longman, 3rd edn, 2005)

crime and sexual integrity   In relation to crime, sexual integrity may be seen to have both a positive and a negative dimension. The negative dimension posits crime as a violation of sexual integrity, a harm perpetrated by others, from which criminal law protects and safeguards individuals. This dimension may be labelled negative in that it connotes a freedom *from* harmful acts. Offences such as **rape,** sexual assault, **sexual harassment** and incest violate victims' sexual integrity, just as offences such as assault and battery violate victims' bodily integrity. A sexual offence may violate a victim's physical **security**, his or her trust of persons in authority or loved ones, as well as his or her sexual integrity. The positive dimension of sexual integrity posits crime as a demarcation of proscribed sexual activity, thereby sanctioning and legitimating those sexual activities that fall into the category of non-criminal. This dimension may be labelled positive because it connotes a freedom *to* engage in certain acts. The positive dimension of sexual integrity shifts the focus away from particular offences to the process of criminalizing certain conduct. While criminal offences may violate sexual integrity, the process of criminalization may also circumscribe or even violate individuals' sexual integrity. Thus, to understand the topic of crime and sexual integrity, it is necessary to consider both these dimensions.

Historically, the concept of sexual integrity—in either its negative or positive dimension—has not been central to the legal construction of acts as criminal. In relation to the negative dimension of sexual integrity, freedom from harmful acts, patriarchal social institutions, together with the origins of the criminal law in the principles and practices of private law, meant that sexual offences were conceptualized as violations of a property right (such as that of a husband or father in relation to his wife or daughter) or as offences against public order (flashing, for example). Similarly, in relation to the positive dimension of sexual integrity, freedom to engage in particular acts, legal sanction for particular sexual behaviour was less a product of an individualized concept of sexual integrity than the result of collective norms and values about social morality, health, and order. Social, moral, religious, and legal norms combined to naturalize certain behaviour and denaturalize (and criminalize) other behaviour. Thus, the core wrongfulness of sexual offences—as harmful actions and legally proscribed behaviour—was located in the social space between a single **person** and his or her family or the **community** more generally rather than with the individual him or herself. The rise of the individual as a social and legal **subject**, the development of a discourse of **human rights** and freedoms, as well as changing social mores, have together pushed the concept of sexual integrity to the fore.

Sexual integrity is both a socially constructed and historically contingent concept, like crime itself. Social attitudes to sex and sexuality, and thus to the concept of sexual integrity, have changed markedly over the course of the last century. With respect to the post-war era, change has been particularly profound, with, for example, changes in attitudes to same-sex sexual activity, **marriage** and reproduction. Over the same period, problems such as sexual violence, including **domestic violence** and **child abuse**, have come to attract a significant amount of social and governmental consternation. Thus, growing liberalization of values related to sex and sexuality has been accompanied by growing anxiety about the enforcement of laws and the protection of vulnerable people. This has resulted in an uneven development of the concept of sexual integrity in relation to crime. A survey of some of the changes in the law on sexual offences reveals the increasing prominence of sexual integrity as an important legal precept when it comes to freedom from harm, but also reveals that sexual integrity has not had such an impact in relation to freedom to engage in particular acts.

Two changes in the law on sexual offences serve to illustrate the increasing importance of the concept of sexual integrity in relation to freedom from harm. The first change is the legal position on rape in marriage. Until 1991, it was not possible to hold a husband criminally liable for the rape of his wife. In the case of *R v R* (1992), the **House of Lords** upheld the conviction of R for the attempted rape of his estranged wife. The Lords criticized the position that a husband could not be held liable for the rape of his wife, labelling it inapplicable in modern times in which men and women are equal parties in a marriage. In Lord Keith's words, the idea that a woman gives her irrevocable consent to sexual intercourse on marrying was 'unacceptable' (at 616). A second change in the law that illustrates the increasing importance of sexual integrity is provided by the courts' treatment of the transmission of sexually transmitted diseases. As a result of decisions such as *R v Clarence* (1888), in which it was held that a husband could not be convicted of assault occasioning grievous bodily harm when he infected his wife with venereal disease, individuals could not be charged with a criminal offence relating to the transmission of a disease during sexual activity. Recently, however, in the decision of *R v Dica* (2004), the court concluded that Dica could be liable for assault occasioning grievous bodily harm for recklessly transmitting **HIV** to two women who had been his sexual partners, although their consent to sexual intercourse had to be taken into account. Arguably, this change in the criminal law must be seen against the background of the spread of AIDS and other sexually transmitted diseases. In addition, this change, like the abrogation of marital immunity from rape charges, reflects the growing significance of the concept of sexual integrity to the criminal law.

Turning to the positive dimension of sexual integrity—freedom to engage in certain acts—the profile of the concept of sexual integrity is more mixed. On the positive side, sexual integrity may be regarded as an ingredient in the decriminalization of private and consensual homosexual sex in the 1960s and the much more recent abolition of homophobic sexual offences such as buggery and gross indecency (see Sexual Offences Act 2003). On the other, negative side, the concept of sexual integrity seems to have little substantive force in relation to at least some specific sexual practices. In the decision of *R v Brown* (1993), the House of Lords upheld the convictions of a group of men who were charged with offences of assault and wounding in relation to consensual sado-masochistic homosexual activity. By a majority, the Lords upheld the Court of Appeal and first instance decisions that the men's consent was not a valid defence to these offences. The intimate connection between sex and **violence** inherent in sado-masochistic sexual activity seemed to disgust the Law Lords. Viewed from the perspective of sexual integrity, the decision in *Brown* marks a clear limitation on the sexual integrity of the individuals concerned. The power of the law to circumscribe or even violate sexual integrity by defining certain acts as criminal is the flipside of crime and sexual integrity.

There is a tension between freedom from harm and freedom to engage in particular acts, the negative and positive dimensions of the concept of sexual integrity as it relates to crime. This tension is evident in the regulation of the sexual activity of young people. Criminal law in this arena may be seen to chart a fine line between protection and freedom. The provisions in the Sexual Offences Act 2003 relating to sex offences committed by children seemed designed to protect younger children from manipulation by older children, but also criminalize consensual sexual activity between two 16-year-olds, for example. Thus, in this respect, the negative dimension of sexual integrity seems to have trumped the positive dimension, with protection from harm judged more important than freedom to engage in particular sexual acts. The tension between protection on the one hand and freedom on the other in relation to sexual integrity reflects broader tensions in the criminal law in a democratic social system. With regard to sexual integrity, the precise way in which this tension plays itself out depends on social norms and values, which inform legal decisions to criminalize certain behaviour. In this sense, the rise of the concept of individual sexual integrity may be best understood as evidence of a reconfiguration of the current legal construction of crime rather than a profound paradigm shift.   ARLIE LOUGHNAN

J Bridgeman and S Millns, *Feminist Perspectives on Law: Law's Engagement with the Female Body* (London: Sweet & Maxwell, 1998)

N Lacey, C Wells and O Quick, *Reconstructing Criminal Law: Text and Materials* (London: Butterworths, 3rd edn, 2003)

crime and social differentiation   The concept of crime and social differentiation has been developed by those adopting a critical perspective when analysing the **criminal justice system** and, as such, stands in contrast to liberal perspectives which regard the legal system as being based on due process and **equality**. The main categories of social differentiation are those of social class, **gender**, and **race**. All three categories involve some form of structural inequalities which, in some cases, are shared between categories. For example, both male and female **prison** populations contain disproportionate numbers from **minority** ethnic backgrounds and economically marginalized social classes. On the other hand, the added dimensions of patriarchy and racism to the issue of differentiation and social class mean that other forms of structural inequalities are unique to specific groups. For example, working class **women** can be understood to experience social differentiation on two levels—through class and patriarchy, while minority ethnic working class women may experience social differentiation on three levels—through class, patriarchy, and **racialization**. Conversely, even if it were possible to replace such differentiation with total equality between all parts of the human population, the *impact* of criminality would still be experienced differentially due to broader cultural factors. The impact of imprisonment, for example, may cause more pain to women who are mothers than men who are fathers, since women are more likely to have been the main carers prior to conviction. Therefore, from a critical perspective, the state in general, and the criminal justice system in particular, contrary to liberal theories of **justice**, engages in processes and practices which criminalize the behaviour of particular groups whose structural location has been generated by broader patterns of social inequality. It is these groups who are labelled and targeted as potential sources of disruption and deviance, in other words, as different from the acceptable norms of the wider society.   ANETTE BALLINGER

See also: **class and crime; ethnicity and crime; gender and crime; race and crime**

crime and the media   Anxiety about possible harmful consequences of media representations of crime has been a perennial counterpoint to the development of mass media. They have frequently been said to portray deviance seductively. Conversely, they have been accused of creating a climate of fear by exaggerating risks of crime. These concerns have generated a vast library of research on how the media portray crime and criminal justice, and the consequences and determinants of these representations.

Given the wide variety of studies analysing the content of media representations of crime, both purportedly 'factual' and fictional, ranging across many places and periods, and using a variety of methods, what is most remarkable is the broad convergence of results. News and fiction crime stories have been prominent in all media, throughout media history. There are clear variations, however, in the prominence given to crime stories by different media (television as opposed to radio for example), and according to the level of the market aimed at (popular newspapers typically have more stories of murder and **violence**, and fewer about complex frauds, than the 'quality' press).

The pattern of **representation** of crime by the media follows what the American criminologist Ray Surette has called 'the law of opposites'. The characteristics of crime in the media are almost entirely the obverse of what official statistics show. The media concentrate largely on serious violent crime, especially murder, and downplay property crimes. **Victims** and offenders portrayed by the media are disproportionately older and higher status. The image of the effectiveness and integrity of policing and criminal justice is overwhelmingly positive. Most cases are cleared-up, and few stories feature **police** corruption or abuse (although an increasing proportion now do so).

A huge volume of research has probed the influence of the media on crime and violence. The bulk of this has comprised social psychological studies in which experimental and control groups are exposed to media content representing deviance, usually violence, and are measured before and after for 'effects'. Most studies do show some overall effects in the expected direction, ie that exposure to 'anti-social' images increases propensities to deviance, and vice versa for 'pro-social' representations. However, the measured 'effect' is usually small, and varies considerably. Experimental studies of this kind are testing a somewhat unlikely hypothesis: that exposure to media representations has invariable, immediate effects. The media are more plausibly complexly intertwined with wider enculturation processes: influencing patterns of behaviour in interaction with many other factors, which in turn feed back to shape media representations.

The media are the principal source of information about crime and criminal justice for most people. They frame debate about '**law and order**', together with politicians' campaigning and broader shifts in culture, social structure, and political economy. Public concern about crime is more closely related to media campaigns than trends in crime, as shown by research such as Katherine Beckett's *Making Crime Pay* (1997).

The pattern of media representation of crime, broadly embodying a law and order perspective, is ultimately related to the predominantly conservative political ideology of those who own and control media corporations. But it is more immediately informed by the sense of what constitutes a 'good story', shared by journalists and producers of popular fiction: drama, vivid human interest, novelty, salaciousness, moral clarity, closure. It is also shaped by a variety of structural and organizational pressures on news production. The police and the **courts** are reliable sources of regular stories, and crime reporters' dependence on them gives the police much power to define the news.

The prominence of crime stories has grown sharply since the late 1960s. Crime is portrayed as increasingly threatening and out of control, ever more pervasive and serious, symptomatic of wider social crisis. Greater individualism underpins media narratives: crime is seen as problematic not because it violates the law but because it hurts sympathetic individual victims with whom audiences are invited to identify. Offenders are portrayed as pathologically evil individuals. Attempts to understand them are castigated as insensitive to victims' pain: offenders and victims' interests are constructed as a zero-sum game. Changing media representations of crime are inter-related with broader transformations: the rise of **neo-liberalism** and increasing individualism since the 1970s, shaping a harsher politics of law and order. ROBERT REINER

R Reiner 'Media-Made Criminality' in M Maguire, R Morgan, and R Reiner (eds), *The Oxford Handbook of Criminology* (Oxford: Oxford University Press, 4th edn, 2007).

R Reiner, S Livingstone, and J Allen 'From law and order to lynch mobs: crime news since the Second World War', in P Mason (ed), *Criminal Visions: Media Representations of Crime and Justice* (Cullompton: Willan, 2003)

crime and violence Crime and violence are broad concepts which reflect the cultural, economic, moral, and political forces at work in society. Although images in the press and popular culture suggest that crime is largely about **violence**, in reality violent crime only represents around 15 per cent of the total number of crimes processed by the **criminal justice system** annually. Around 800,000 violent crimes are recorded by the **police** each year, which is considered to be a major underestimate given the large amount of unreported incidents. Most non-fatal violent crime is committed by and against young men. In terms of fatal violence, there are around 700 homicides recorded by the police in England and Wales annually, the vast majority of which are committed by men. Whilst there has been surprisingly little agreement about definition, images of violence revolve around street fights and muggings between **strangers**. However, most violent crime involves individuals known to each other and in recognition of this there has been increasing awareness of the problem of less visible (but more prevalent) forms of sexual and '**domestic**' violence. There has also been attention towards violence caused by the transmission of serious infectious diseases or the unsafe practices of corporations, as well as to non-physical, 'psychological' violence. This broader understanding of violence is now reflected in official government definitions which extend its reach to include 'physical and emotional abuse'.

Although the term 'violence' is rarely found in criminal statutes, it informs and underlies the practice of criminal law. In terms of crimes of non-fatal violence, the Offences against the Person Act 1861 sets out a ladder of offences. However, reflecting its origins in the Victorian era, contemporary society is left with a somewhat rotten ladder in need of constant repair and renovation by judicial interpretation. Much is left to the **discretion** of police, prosecutors, and **juries**, and a relatively high number of appeals. This has led to critical comment, producing related and more recently enacted statutes to deal with problems such as 'stalking' (Protection from Harassment Act 1997) and 'domestic' violence (Domestic Violence, Crime, and Victims Act 2004). Crimes of sexual violence have also been rewritten in the Sexual Offences Act 2003. Fatal violence is dealt with by the law of homicide.

Assault

Assault is the main non-fatal offence of violence. The term is often used generically to include the two separate offences of 'common' or 'technical' assault and battery. The essence of common assault is that the **victim** should apprehend immediate violence whereas a battery involves non-consensual and thus unlawful touching. Whilst these offences are now charged under section 39 of the Criminal Justice Act 1988, the definitions are contained in **common law**. In terms of common assault, the notion of immediacy has been generously interpreted to accommodate instances where a defendant embarks on a course of conduct such as stalking: *R v Ireland; R v Burstow*

(1997). This decision of the **House of Lords** also established that mere words, or indeed heavy breathing telephone calls, are capable of constituting assault. Common assault and battery may be tried in the Magistrates or **Crown** Court and are punishable by a **fine** of up to £5,000 and/or up to six months imprisonment. In practice, **community** penalties are common. The 1861 Act also includes three aggravated assaults listed here in ascending levels of seriousness: assault occasioning actual bodily harm (section 47), unlawfully and maliciously wounding or inflicting grievous bodily harm (section 20), and unlawfully and maliciously wounding or causing grievous bodily harm with intent to do so (section 18); the first two carrying a maximum punishment of five years and the latter of life imprisonment. Tougher penalties may be imposed where the assault is racially or religiously aggravated. The police and **Crown Prosecution Service** work with what are called 'charging standards' which list various forms of physical harm and the appropriate associated assault charge. In practice, it is common for charges against defendants to be downgraded at trial as a result of negotiation between **prosecution** and defence, or for a jury to convict of a less serious assault.

Consent may act as a 'defence' to violent offences where the harm is not serious and there are good reasons for engaging in the conduct, for example surgical or sporting activity. However, judges have struggled to set the lines of legitimacy here, as seen in the case of *R v Brown* (1993) where a majority of the **House of Lords** denied that consent could render consensual sado-masochistic acts as lawful yet failed to deliver a workable general principle of the legal relevance of consent to physical harm. The Court of **Appeal** has also affirmed that intentional or reckless infliction of a serious sexually transmitted infection is contrary to the aggravated assault offences. In this situation, consent can only apply as a defence where the victim specifically consented to the risk of such infection: *R v Dica (Mohammed) No 2* (2005). The reluctance to label as criminal dangerous conduct on the sports field continues: *R v Barnes* (2005). Proposals by the **Law Commission** of England and Wales in 1993 to rebuild this ladder of offences led to a draft bill being drawn up by the Home Office in 1998. This proposed a neater ladder of offences consisting of 'intentionally causing serious injury', 'recklessly causing serious injury', and 'intentionally or recklessly causing injury'. This bill also proposes to fill another gap in the current law whereby threatening to commit violence is not a crime. The government has showed little interest in implementing these reforms and it remains an unlikely prospect for the foreseeable future.

Manslaughter

Manslaughter is a broad offence category catching most unlawful killings falling below that of murder. It is classified into voluntary and involuntary manslaughter. Voluntary manslaughter means that the defendant voluntarily intended to kill the victim (which would ordinarily constitute murder) but this conduct is 'partially' excused on the grounds of **provocation** or **diminished responsibility**. This is partial in the sense that it only applies to murder prosecutions, and only has the effect (if successful) of leading to a conviction for manslaughter. Involuntary manslaughter is a broad category covering a wide range of unintentional killings. Liability may be established by proving that the defendant was reckless or grossly negligent to the risk of death, or committed an unlawful and dangerous act such as an assault, which consequently caused the death of the victim. Involuntary manslaughter has been heavily criticized for being an overly inclusive offence category which unfairly labels a diverse range of killing under the same name. **Judges** have discretion in relation to punishing manslaughter, although there is a maximum penalty of life imprisonment.

Murder

The traditional definition of murder is **homicide** committed with 'malice aforethought'. In more modern times, this means an intention to kill or cause grievous bodily harm to the victim. Surprisingly for the most serious criminal offence, the boundaries of the law of murder have been fairly broad. In a series of murder cases since the 1950s, judges struggled to pin down the proper meaning of the term intention, sometimes veering off course into the realm of recklessness. However, it is accepted that intention has two meanings: both the purposes and virtually certain consequences of one's conduct. Scots criminal law has charted a different course by basing the crime of murder on the notion of 'wicked recklessness'. The boundaries of murder are broad in another sense in that defendants may be guilty even if they only intended to cause serious bodily injury rather than death; in fact, most murder cases involve no intention to kill. After the abolition of **capital punishment** in 1965, a murder conviction has carried a mandatory life sentence. This has led to tension between the legislature and the judiciary over the issue of who should determine the length of the **prison** sentence which resulted in legislative reform which sets out a structured system for sentencing in relation to the seriousness of the murder. In 2005, the Law Commission of England and Wales

proposed a new Homicide Act which would create a three-tiered approach to homicide with offences of first degree murder, second degree murder, and manslaughter, designed to offer a simple and jury-friendly structure. Whether the government will support these reforms through the parliamentary process is another matter. The history of trying to reform the legislation of non-fatal violent offences does not afford much room for optimism.

OLIVER QUICK

N Fielding, *Courting Violence: Offences against the Person Cases in Court* (Oxford: Oxford University Press, 2006)

S Jones, *Understanding Violent Crime* (Maidenhead: Open University Press, 2000)

crime control, politics of   *see* **politics of crime control**

crime, definitions of   There is no simple and universally accepted definition of crime in the modern criminal law, a feature that probably reflects the large and diverse range of behaviours that have been criminalized by the modern state. It is now widely accepted that crime is a category created by law—that is, that most actions are only criminal because there is a law that declares them to be so—so this must be the starting point for any definition.

The main modern definitions of crime fall into two different categories, the moral and the procedural. Moral definitions of crime are based on the claim that there is (or should be) some intrinsic quality that is shared by all acts criminalized by the state. This quality was originally sought in the acts themselves—that all crimes were in an important sense moral wrongs, or *mala in se*—and that the law merely recognized this wrongful quality. The weakness of this approach was that it could not extend to certain actions which seemed morally neutral (often referred to as *mala prohibita*), such as speeding or failing to register the birth of a **child**, which have been made crimes by statute. Accordingly, it is argued crimes are such because criminal law recognizes public wrongs as violations of rights or duties owed to the whole **community**, that is, that the wrong is seen as the breach of the duty owed to the community to respect the law. This definition can covers a broader range of offences, as well as recognizing the sociological fact that many acts are criminal only by virtue of being declared so by law. The strength of this type of definition is less as a description of the object of criminal law, than as an account of the principles which should limit the proper scope of the criminal law.

Procedural definitions, by contrast, define crimes as those acts which might be prosecuted or punished under criminal procedure. The most influential definition of this type was produced by legal theorist, Glanville Williams, in 1955. He sought a purely formal definition of crime. For him, a crime is:

an act capable of being followed by criminal proceedings having a criminal outcome, and a proceeding or its outcome is criminal if it has certain characteristics which mark it as criminal.

This is undeniably circular (something is criminal if it is criminal), and seems to avoid definition of the term 'criminal' and so might appear to be of little use. However, it arguably reflects more accurately the reality of the modern criminal law, where the scope of the law has extended to include large numbers of regulatory offences tried under criminal proceedings, the content of which go far beyond conduct which can easily be regarded as moral or even public wrongs. However, given the diverse range of sanctions and procedures which can be adopted, from forms of treatment or reparation to mediation or **restorative justice**, it is not obvious that this definition alone can help to determine what is or is not a criminal proceeding.

The definition does, however, have an important practical application, something which has become even clearer following the incorporation of the **European Convention on Human Rights** as part of the law in the United Kingdom. Under Article 6 of the Convention certain 'due process' protections are available in criminal, but not civil, proceedings, and this has reopened the question of when a particular proceeding is or is not to be regarded as criminal. The question has arisen particularly in relation to certain new forms of 'hybrid' offences which combine elements of civil and criminal proceedings, exemplified by the **Anti-Social Behaviour** Order ('ASBO'). These new offences were specifically designed to avoid certain legal protections, in terms of the burden of proof or the types of **evidence** that might be admissible. However, in view of the heavy penalties which might attach to their breach, an important issue has become that of whether or not they are properly to be regarded as criminal proceedings. Addressing this question, the **House of Lords** held that they were civil, though in view of the penalties the civil court should apply a criminal standard of proof (*McCann* (2002)). The question may fall to be addressed by the **European Court of Human Rights** which has tended to define criminal proceedings in terms of the severity of the penalty which might be applied by the **courts**.   LINDSAY FARMER

See also: **criminalization, rationale of**

crime investigation by the police Investigating crime is seen by the public as a primary function of the **police**. This is reactive, with the police responding to the demands made on them by the public. When an offence is reported by a member of the public, the police record and, resources permitting, investigate the incident and, if successful, take some form of action against the perpetrator. The public dictate not only the amount and nature of crime brought to the attention of the police. There is a 'dark figure' of unreported crime which includes much serious crime, especially **violence** against women and children, racial assaults, and white-collar crime. Demand policing is not an adequate mechanism to cope with such problems

An alternative approach is proactive policing. This means that the police take the initiative in crime reduction. For example, intelligence-led policing utilizes the gathering of intelligence, the analysis of that information and of crime patterns with the purpose of targeting specific, 'criminally-active', individuals to monitor their activities and obtain evidence for a successful **prosecution** rather than relying on 'accidental' convictions of such people for offences which happen to come to police attention. Proactivity also implies strategic initiatives against particular categories of offences that are identified as problematic in a particular area.

The police are successful in about one-quarter of their investigations. This figure has declined from about one-half in the past fifty years, a decline attributed to a steep rise in the volume of property crime. Detection rates vary dramatically from offence to offence—while there is a high clear-up rate for serious violence, it is very low for burglary and criminal damage. The high clear-up rate for **homicide** reflects the effort and resources put into such investigations but for all offences of violence, the assailant is likely to be known to the **victim**. Clear-up rates are more to do with the factors surrounding particular offences and owe much to the public.

Police powers in the investigation of crime, namely to intervene, detain, and **arrest** without judicial supervision, were traditionally those of a private citizen. There were no special powers for the constable and no special immunities. There are now powers, especially under the Police and Criminal Evidence Act 1984 ('PACE') and the Regulation of Investigatory Powers Act 2000 which can be exercised only by police officers. These powers are regulated by Codes of Practice promulgated under the **legislation**.

The most basic power is to stop people on the street, question them, and to conduct a search. This power was exercised *de facto* prior to 1984 but formal **stop-and-search powers** came in with section 1 of PACE allowing an officer with reasonable suspicion that a person was carrying prohibited items to stop that person and conduct a superficial search. Forces vary considerably in their use of section 1 power but in metropolitan areas, such searches generate hostility towards the police in ethnic and **minority communities** who regard police practice as discriminatory. At this stage, there is no obligation for a suspect to identify themselves or to answer questions except in road traffic and terrorist cases. However a failure to answer police questions at this point may have adverse consequences at any subsequent trial.

Most other powers of investigation rest upon arrest—a lawful arrest consists of telling the suspect that they are under arrest and of informing them of the essential legal and factual grounds of the arrest. The person arrested can be detained against their will and to escape from arrest is an offence in itself. An officer can, under section 24 of PACE, amended by section 110 of the Serious Organised Crime and Police Act 2005, arrest for any offence, whether summary or indictable, if the officer has reasonable grounds for believing it is necessary. Those grounds are where it is necessary to identify the name or address of the suspect, to prevent the suspect from causing or suffering injury, from causing loss or damaging property, from committing an offence against public decency, or from obstructing the highway. The old **common law** power to arrest for **breach of the peace** still exists. On arrest a suspect must be taken to a police station.

On arrest, the police can search the suspect's person—initially this is limited but at the police station the custody officer can authorize full searches of detained persons, including a strip search, an intimate search without the **consent** of the suspect. There is also a power to take intimate samples (including blood, saliva, or semen). An arrested person can be fingerprinted without consent. The National Automated Fingerprint Identification System is operational in all English and Welsh police forces. The national DNA database has proved of significant value, not least in solving 'cold cases'.

Searching premises for evidence is an important stage of criminal investigation, particularly in serious crimes, the forensic examination by crime scene investigators. The search of private premises can be undertaken under a warrant issued by **justices of the peace** under sections 8–16 of PACE. Officers also have the power to enter and search premises without warrants—at common law, this can be done 'to deal with or prevent a breach of the peace'. Under section 17, a constable has the power to enter and search premises to make an arrest or to protect people from serious injury or prevent serious property damage. Having made an arrest, under section 32, after an arrest for an arrestable offence, an officer can lawfully enter and search premises in which the person was when arrested or immediately before he or she was arrested. When the suspect has been taken to a police station, under section 18, a senior officer can authorize a search where there is a reasonable belief that there is evidence of the immediate offence or other offences on the premises.

The interview of a suspect is also likely to produce significant evidence. At the police station, the arrested person is taken before the custody officer who must decide whether sufficient evidence exists either to charge the person or to warrant further detention for the purpose of obtaining evidence through interview—in practice, detention is almost never refused. The custody officer is initially responsible for the length of time that a person is detained in a police station. That detention must be periodically reviewed and normally will not exceed four days. The police still rely on detention and interrogation as the interview under caution is the essential investigative tool for gathering incriminating evidence—Code C governs the detention, treatment, and questioning of suspects. There are substantial safeguards, with access to legal advice at all times and an audio recording of the interview. The suspect has the right to remain silent, although a 'no comment interview' has risks as a failure to mention matters which are later relied upon at **court** may be used as part of the **prosecution** case. Such safeguards are not observed in taking witness statements—there will be no independent scrutiny or formal legal procedures. Such statements may be admitted into evidence at trial.

Cases are often resolved as a result of information from the public, who were present at the scene and who detain or identify the offender. **Juries** can place substantial probative weight on a confident identification but such evidence can be of variable quality. The investigating officers can use various identification procedures—identification parades, video identification, group identification, or confrontation. There are detailed protocols, laid down in Code D of PACE, as to when these should be used and the safeguards to be observed.

Intelligence-led policing can involve the targeting by the police of individuals suspected of involvement in criminal activities. The purpose is often to acquire evidence to be used in subsequent prosecution. Where the police undertake their own proactive investigations, they may use informants, surveillance techniques, undercover agents, or other special inquiries. Modern technology has brought in its wake sophisticated mechanisms for observing people's lives or listening in on their communications.

At common law, the police were not required to demonstrate specific legal powers for such actions and any investigative technique was permitted as long as it was not forbidden by law. There were no general principles protecting individuals from intrusive surveillance such as the right to privacy. However Article 8 of the **European Convention on Human Rights** requires that such techniques must be authorized by law, that the intervention must be necessary and proportional to the offence under investigation, and that there are proper systems of **accountability**. The European Convention jurisprudence allied to the **Human Rights Act 1998** has led to the passage of legislation which specifically authorizes and regulates such investigative techniques. Where the police enter property to place recording devices, authority must be given under Part III of the Police Act 1997. The Regulation of Investigatory Powers Act 2000 deals with the interception of communications through the telephone system and mail deliveries but also the use of directed surveillance, intrusive surveillance, and covert **human** intelligence sources. It introduced a framework for primary authorization and subsequent monitoring of such surveillance.　　　　STEVE UGLOW

See also: **surveillance, surreptitious**

crime investigation other than by police　Investigation and prosecution of crime is not only undertaken by the **police.** In theory, any individual citizen has the power to investigate crime and initiate a private **prosecution**. In the area of regulatory crime, the police have neither the resources nor the specialist knowledge to investigate effectively. Reliance in these cases is instead on a wide range of agencies, such as **trading standards** departments, the health and safety executive, the **environment agency**, revenue and customs, the DVLA, or non-governmental bodies such as the NSPCC or RSPCA. The breadth of such agencies responsibilities is often considerable—trading standards offices were once known as '**weights and measures**' but are now responsible for enforcing over eighty Acts of **Parliament** and 200 statutory instruments.

These **regulatory agencies** often use powers of prosecution as a last resort. Agencies prefer persuasion and advice as a mechanism for securing their primary objectives, such as preventing illegal tipping, improving the safety of the workplace, or collecting tax. Whether regulating waste management or **health and safety in the workplace,** officers see their role as advisory with letters and visits as standard practice. They are reluctant to prosecute businesses for oversights or temporary breakdowns. In a similar vein, research for local education authorities shows that prosecuting parents has limited impact on truancy and that the objective of ensuring school attendance is more likely to be achieved by working with truants and their parents. For agencies, prosecution is less a matter of routine and more a symbolically important act, to be used sparingly for public education and general deterrence or where it is necessary to provide a clear and visible resolution to a case. While the agencies enforce the criminal law, the enforcement philosophy underpinning them is very different from those in mainstream criminal law.

In the investigation of offences, enforcement personnel may not be able to rely on powers given to police officers in the Police and Criminal Evidence Act 1984 but often possess specific powers in the relevant **legislation**. Her Majesty's revenue and Customs ('HMRC') is an example of this—it is the principal revenue-raising department and is also the biggest prosecuting agency after the **Crown Prosecution Service**. It is not only concerned with a wide variety of tax offences but also matters such as import control offences (including drug and arms offences). It conducts large investigations and prosecutions, which included surveillance and undercover investigation, with international dimensions. Officers can exercise standard powers such as making **arrests**, detaining, and interviewing, although those powers vary as to whether they are investigating customs and excise issues rather than Inland Revenue matters. The exercise of other routine powers can be cumbersome—for example, the ex-Revenue powers require two Commissioners for HMRC to personally authorize an application before a **judge** can be asked to consider issuing a warrant. However, HMRC has specific wide powers—for example to apply for production orders requiring a person to provide information. They are generally used to obtain information from a third party, for example a bank, rather than the suspect. HMRC also has more specialized powers used to protect frontiers, powers under the Proceeds of Crime Act 2002, and various surveillance powers.　　　　STEVE UGLOW

crime prevention   *see* **early intervention; risk and criminal justice policy; situational crime prevention**

crime rates   Crime rates have become increasingly central to public debate and to criminal justice policy, as 'law and order' has became politicized over the last thirty-five years. The 'crime rate' usually refers to the national statistics compiled by the Home Office since 1857, based on data provided by police forces. The latest are in Walker, Kershaw, and Nicholas, *Crime in England and Wales 2005/6* (London: Home Office; available online at *www. homeoffice.gov.uk/rds/crimeew0506.html*).   Since 2001–2002 this annual publication has included both 'police recorded crime' and 'British Crime Survey' figures. There are also briefer quarterly updates, as well as similar reports for Scotland and for Northern Ireland.

The statistics recorded by the **police** have long been known to suffer from many problems. Although commonly referred to as the 'crime rate' by journalists and politicians, the Home Office labels them more cautiously as 'crimes recorded by the police'. The problem is how accurately they reflect rates and patterns of offending. The police recorded statistics are both incomplete and biased, as analysis of their process of construction shows. For an event to be recorded as crime it must overcome two hurdles. It must: (1) literally become known to the police; and (2) be recorded as such by the police, using particular technical procedures. Criminologists and statisticians have always realised that there is a 'dark figure' of unrecorded crime, which is either not known to police, or not recorded by them.

Crimes may become known to the police in two possible ways: (1) **victims** may decide to report a crime to the police—but many do not; and (2) crimes may be discovered through proactive policing, finding the offence together with the offender (eg patrol, surveillance of 'hot spots', undercover work, raids on pubs or clubs for drugs, analysis of financial transactions to identify frauds). This is particularly significant for offences in which there is no aware victim who could report the occurrence (eg crimes against the public at large such as tax or customs evasion; against people who may not realize the nature of what they have suffered, such as children or people who have been successfully conned; or with consensual offences such as drug-taking where participants do not regard themselves as victimized).

Even if crimes become literally 'known to the police' they may not be recorded. The police inevitably exercise some **discretion** not to record offences, and also about what offences should be recorded in specific cases. This discretion may be exercised for reasons varying from benign (genuine doubt about the truthfulness or accuracy of victim reports, for example) to corrupt (such as taking bribes to overlook offences). Most commonly, however, offences may not be recorded in order to ease organizational pressures: cases that are unlikely to be successfully detected, for example, may be 'cuffed' or recorded as more minor offences in order to boost clear-up rates and meet performance targets.

Police recorded crime rates are not just incomplete, but biased. Some crimes and some criminals are much more likely to be counted than others. Because they depend entirely on discovery by the police, offences without aware victims (such as corporate crime or consensual offences) are far less likely to be recorded than those that are reported by victims. Most likely to be reported and recorded are 'street' crimes such as thefts of and from cars, burglary, criminal damage, assaults, or robbery. An enormous volume of **socio-legal research** over the last half-century has documented that the **criminal justice system** processes primarily crimes committed by the socially disadvantaged and relatively powerless, for a variety of reasons including discrimination. Victimization surveys and other evidence also suggests that poorer and less powerful groups suffer more from many types of crime, but that these offences are less likely to be recorded or cleared up. The result is summed-up by the title of Jeffrey Reiman's classic text of critical criminology: *The Rich Get Richer and the Poor Get Prison* (Harlow: Allyn & Bacon, 8th edn, 2006).

The incompleteness and bias of official crime statistics means that apparent trends and patterns may be quite misleading. A rise in crime may result from higher reporting and/or recording rates, and/or more successful proactive policing, rather than actual changes in offending (and vice versa for falls). A variety of new measures have developed over the last forty years in response to the limitations of police-based crime rates in a context of greater concern about law and order. The most significant for tracking crime trends are victim surveys. Another development has been self-report studies, which ask samples of the population, who are guaranteed confidentiality, about their own offending behaviour. They are not a measure of overall crime rates or trends, although they shed valuable light on the extent to which the officially recorded rates of crime of different social groups correspond to the differences in self-reported offending or result from systematic biases in recording.

Victim surveys originated in the 1960s in the US and the 1970s in the UK. The regular Home Office *British Crime Surveys* ('BCS'), conducted since 1982, allow comparison of trend data, as well as analysis of non-reporting and many other features of victim experience. The BCS does not claim to provide a complete index of crime rates, however. It only purports to measure crimes with individual victims, who are able and willing to tell interviewers about their experiences. It excludes offences against organizations, or the public at large. It also omits consensual crimes, such as drug-taking or vice offences. Like any survey, it is subject to sampling and other methodological problems. Its samples do not include children under sixteen, for example, or the homeless. The results also depend on the accuracy and honesty of the respondents interviewed. Despite the state-of-the-art methodological scrupulousness of the BCS, therefore, it does not claim to provide a definitive calculation of crime rates. But triangulating the BCS with police statistics does allow much greater confidence in judging trends.

There also many technical issues involved in interpreting official crime rates. The police record crimes according to counting rules issued by the Home Office to achieve reliability and comparability of data. These determine the overall coverage of the statistics, and provide guidance on issues such as how many and which crimes to count when several occur in one incident, and how to deal with related series of offences. There is no 'right' answer to these issues, but altering the rules to accord with shifting policy agendas has introduced problems of comparison. There have been two major recent changes: (1) considerably revised Counting Rules were issued in 1998, expanding the range of recordable offences; and (2) in 2002 a National Crime Recording Standard became operational, intended to structure the recording practices of local forces more consistently. This mandated a *prima facie* standard whereby an offence should be recorded according to the perspective of the reporting victim. This was distinguished from the 'evidential' approach that Home Office research had found to be used in many forces, whereby crimes were only recorded if further evidence supported the victim's claims. Both changes had the effect of increasing recorded crime rates.

The trajectory of official crime rates since their inception in 1857 falls into two broad phases. For a century after 1857 the crime rate was not seen as a significant issue. During the later nineteenth century the overall rate fell, and then remained on a rough plateau for some decades (it has been argued that this was partly because of Home Office policy,

for example the encouragement of a strict 'evidential' approach to recording crimes). In the inter-war years there was a rising trend, but this was reversed in the post-war decade.

A sharp break occurred after the mid-1950s, when crime rates began to rise spectacularly. It is impossible to be certain how much of this was due to shifts in reporting and recording, as opposed to offending, until the 1980s when the regular BCS provided an alternative measure, less subject to short-term vicissitudes. Until 1992 the BCS broadly confirmed the sharp rise indicated by police statistics. But since then the two series have diverged. The police rate fell from 1992 until 1995, whilst the BCS continued to rise, because victim reporting and police recording of offences both decreased. Since 1997 the series have diverged in the opposite way. The BCS indicates a substantial fall in crime overall, but the police recorded rate rose substantially for most of the late 1990s and early 2000s, largely because of the reformed counting procedures. This has generated some politicization of the hitherto arcane issue of how to measure crime rates, as the BCS makes New Labour's record look good, whilst the police recorded figures portray the 1990s Conservative performance more favourably.

ROBERT REINER

M Maguire 'Crime Data and Statistics' in M Maguire, R Morgan, and R Reiner (eds), *The Oxford Handbook of Criminology* (Oxford: Oxford University Press, 4th edn, 2007)

R Reiner, *Law and Order: An Honest Citizen's Guide to Crime and Control* (Cambridge: Polity Press, 2007), ch 3

crimes against humanity   *see* **Demjanjuk, Ivan; Milosevic, Slobodan; war crimes**

crimes against peace   *see* **war crimes**

crimes of passion   *see* **provocation**

criminal appeals   *see* **appeals**

Criminal Cases Review Commission   The Criminal Cases Review Commission ('CCRC') was set up in 1995 to investigate possible **miscarriages of justice** in England, Wales, and Northern Ireland. It started operating in 1997 and a Scottish version was set up two years later. Its establishment represented a substantial (nine fold) increase in expenditure to remedy miscarriages of justice from that committed by its forerunner, the Home Office's C3 Division. It also represented a significant attempt to increase public confidence in the **criminal justice system** following acknowledged high profile miscarriages

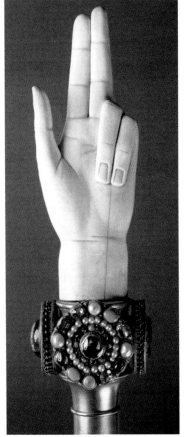

Top left: Bronze figurine of the goddess Ma'at, ancient Egyptian personification of truth and justice, Late Dynastic Period, *c.* 600–400 BC.

Top right: Two figures of jurisdiction, one male and one female, to be stuck in the ground to the right and left of the 'Oba' or king of Benin when he was sitting in judgement, 17th century.

Left: The Hand of Justice, ivory and precious stones, made for the coronation of Napoleon in 1804.

Above: Justice, terracotta roundel, by Luca della Robbia, 15th century.

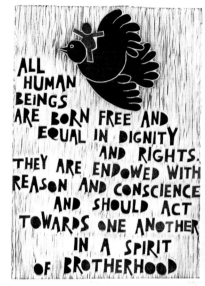

Left: La Déclaration des Droits de l'Homme et du Citoyen, 1789. Coloured wood engraving at the Musée de la Révolution Française, Vizille, France.

Above: Article 1 of the Universal Declaration of Human Rights. Artwork by Brazilian artist Octavio Roth.

The Declaration of Independence of the United States of America. Third paragraph: 'We hold these Truths to be self-evident, that all Men are created equal . . .'. From the original manuscript of a draft by Thomas Jefferson.

18th century cartoon from a postcard produced by Wildy & Sons.

Cartoon by Clive Collins, *The Sun*, 21 November 1969.

Cartoon by Peter Brookes, *The Times*, 16 July 1997.

Cartoon of Judge Francis Butler by Thomas Rowlandson, Butler ruled that a man was allowed to beat his wife, providing that the stick was no thicker than his thumb, 1782.

'The Cat and Mouse Act' 1913 (Prisoner's Temporary Discharge for Ill-Health Act). Suffragette poster depicting the Act, which allowed prisoners on hunger strike to be released on licence, only to be re-arrested when their health improved.

Indian suffragettes in the Women's Coronation Procession in London, 12 June 1911.

'When we get women on juries', cartoon by WK Haselden, Daily Mirror, 18 March 1920.

Sir Francis Bacon, 1st Baronet (1561–1626), by Paul van Somer, 17th century.

Jeremy Bentham, by George Frederick Watts, 1835.

Lord Alfred Thomson ('Tom') Denning, by Bryan Organ, 1982.

Friedrich August von Hayek, by Rodrigo Moynihan, 1982.

Marcus Tullius Cicero, Roman, 1st century BC.

Earl Warren, Chief Justice of the US Supreme Court, 1965.

Oliver Wendell Holmes (1841–1935), engraving, American School.

HLA Hart, photograph by Steve Pyke, 1990.

Dame Brenda Hale, the first woman Law Lord, on a visit to New Delhi.

Dame Cornelia Sorabji, 1866–1954. After graduating in India, she was the first woman to sit for the examination of Bachelor of Civil Law at Oxford in 1892. She was called to the Bar in 1922.

Dame Rosalyn Higgins, President of the International Court of Justice.

Helena Normanton KC and Rose Heilbron KC, the first women to be appointed King's Counsel in 1949.

Advertisement for the Carbolic Smoke Ball, 1892, (*Carlill v Carbolic Smoke Ball Co.*).

A popular print of the ginger beer bottle containing the snail in *Donoghue v Stevenson*.

Daniel M'Naghten's trial at the Old Bailey, 1843, M'Naghten's case.

in the late 1980s and early 1990s. The CCRC has a number of **responsibilities.** In particular, they refer applications they receive, after investigation, to the relevant appeal **court** (usually the Court of Appeal, Criminal Division) where they feel there is a 'real possibility' of a successful appeal. Such a possibility may exist in any of the following circumstances: where complainants are not factually guilty of the crimes for which they were convicted; where a conviction occurred after errors in trial procedure or serious errors in pre-trial processes; where the sentence was unfair or inappropriate. The Commission receive roughly 900 applications a year, from those convicted of crimes who have had previous **appeals** turned down, or from who did not appeal within the normal time limits (often longstanding miscarriage allegations). They refer about 4 per cent of these.

The premise for the creation of the CCRC, like the Criminal Court of Appeal set up ninety years earlier in 1907, is that confidence is better maintained by identifying and admitting to mistakes, than by pretending they have not happened. Against the background of a loss in confidence prior to its creation, the CCRC has helped to restore confidence in the ability of the current system of appeals to rectify miscarriages of justice. However, in the light of the history of miscarriages over the last century it remains to be seen how long such confidence can be maintained.

RICHARD NOBLES AND DAVID SCHIFF

Criminal Cases Review Commission, *http://www.ccrc.gov.uk/* and Scottish Criminal Cases Review Commission, *http://www.sccrc.org.uk/*

R Nobles and D Schiff, 'The Criminal Cases Review Commission: Reporting Success?' (2001) 64 *The Modern Law Review* 280–299

criminal charge   *see* **crime investigation by police**

criminal compensation orders   Compensation orders may be made by a criminal **court** in England and Wales or in Scotland as part of or as the only sentence that it imposes on a convicted offender. The current law was introduced in 1972, and is now governed by sections 130–34 the Powers of Criminal Courts (Sentencing) Act 2000. They require the offender to pay compensation to the **victim** or to anyone else who has sustained any personal injury, loss, or damage as a result of the offence or of one taken into consideration, and are most commonly used in cases of property damage. Where the offender is a **child** or young **person**, the parents can be ordered to pay, and the court must give reasons why it does not make an order where it has power to do so.

Compensation orders are not available for road traffic offences or for **homicide**. In the latter case, dependants will usually be eligible under the **Criminal Injuries Compensation Scheme**, applicable in both jurisdictions. In deciding whether to make an order, the court must take account of the offender's means. Where these are limited it must give priority to the compensation order over a **fine**. As criminal courts are not well equipped to assess compensation in complex cases, orders are typically made where the loss is simple to calculate. As the majority of offenders are not wealthy, payments tend to be much lower than would be available under the Scheme or in a civil action against the offender, less than £300 on average.

DAVID MIERS

criminal contempt   *see* **contempt of court**

criminal conviction   Conviction is the key decision in the criminal process. Coming from the Latin *convincere,* it is the act of demonstrating that a **person** is guilty of an offence before a legal **tribunal**. In the narrowest sense of the word, a person is convicted when they plead not guilty but are found guilty by the trier of fact—that is, the magistrates or the **jury**. But conviction normally covers both finding of guilt and guilty **pleas**. The latter are common in all **courts**.

Recently the concept of 'conviction' has become less clear, as **police** and prosecutors are able to dispose of cases away from the courts: for example, reprimands and final warnings for **young offenders** or cautions for adults require recognition by the person that they committed the offence and the fact of the reprimand or caution may be recorded and used in subsequent proceedings. Similarly there are on-the-spot **fines** for various offences, including drunkenness as well as road traffic offences.

Where guilt is contested, the decision to convict must be reached on the basis of relevant and reliable **evidence** being presented to the trier of fact, supported by the necessary procedural safeguards such as effective legal **representation** or the exclusion of illegally obtained evidence. Both sides have the opportunity to examine witnesses and address the court on the law and the facts. At the conclusion of a contested case, the trier of fact must decide whether to convict.

A major safeguard against wrongful conviction is the right of appeal. The **Crown** Court is primarily responsible for reviewing magistrates' courts decisions and does so on the basis of reviewing the substance of the evidence. **Appeals** from the Crown Court go to the Court of Appeal which does not substitute its view of the evidence for that of the jury. It is instead a review of process to ensure that, by section 2 of the Criminal Appeals Act 1995, that the conviction was 'safe'.

A conviction allows the court to proceed to sentence. There are a range of penalties, from discharges, to fines, to **community** penalties, to imprisonment. There are some mandatory minimum sentences but normally the statute creating the offence specifies a maximum penalty. Magistrates' courts cannot imprison anyone for more than one year.

The impact of a conviction goes beyond the sentence itself—the fact of conviction will be stored in the criminal records system. If the offence is sexual, the offender will be placed on the Sex Offenders' Register and required to comply with its requirements. If an individual is prosecuted for subsequent offences, the fact of conviction may be used as part of the **prosecution** case, if it is relevant to the charge. It certainly will be used to inform any subsequent **sentencing** process. Furthermore the fact of conviction may be required to be disclosed in applications for employment —this will inevitably be the case where a criminal records certificate is required and the consequences in terms of employment or housing may well be severe.   STEVE UGLOW

See also: **sex offenders, treatment of**

criminal courts   *see* **courts**

criminal defences   *see* **justification, excuse, and mitigation in criminal law; mental incapacity and crime**

Criminal Injuries Compensation Appeals Panel   *see* **criminal injuries compensation schemes; tribunals**

criminal injuries compensation schemes Compensation schemes to compensate **victims** of crime emerged in the legal systems of many Western jurisdictions around the world during the 1960s. Despite the recent emergence of the schemes in modern statutory frameworks, the concept of providing **compensation** for victims of crime is centuries old and can be traced to ancient Babylonian, Greek, Jewish, and Germanic law. New Zealand was the first country to introduce a criminal injuries compensation scheme (Criminal Injuries Compensation Act 1963 (NZ)). The scheme was established by statute and state-funded. It was soon followed by the United Kingdom which operated a non-statutory scheme

for two decades until enacting the Criminal Justice Act 1988, later superseded by the Criminal Injuries Compensation Act 1995. New Zealand and the UK were followed by the United States, Australia, Canada, and some European countries.

The schemes provide compensation to victims of crime for personal injury and consequent financial loss and are typically created by statute and state-funded. The schemes do not generally require the specific identification of a perpetrator but all uniformly require proof of a breach of the national criminal law and proof of an injury or loss of some kind. The schemes typically limit the amount of compensation payable to each claimant. In some jurisdictions there is a maximum amount attached to each criminal event regardless of the extent of injury, and in other jurisdictions there is a maximum amount attached to each injury, which is specified in a table of injuries. In some schemes, compensation is extended to secondary victims, for example those who witness a crime and suffer injury (usually psychological) as a result. In most jurisdictions a successful claim under a criminal injuries compensation scheme does not preclude the right of the claimant to pursue **common law** proceedings.

The schemes came into being in part because of the failure of other previous methods of compensating victims of crime. **Restitution** awards by the court at the time of **sentencing** payable by the perpetrator to the victim had proven ineffective because many perpetrators of crimes are unidentified, or, if identified, have few or no resources. Civil litigation was equally ineffective primarily because the process of litigation is costly, lengthy, and involves the satisfaction of complex legal rules. The underscoring rationale of the schemes is the notion that criminal **violence** is a communal **responsibility**. Because of this responsibility, the state, as representative of the **community,** has a legal duty to compensate victims of crime because it has failed to prevent the crime. Alternatively, the responsibility arises because the state has created the conditions that produced the perpetrator and has accepted liability under a 'social contract' to protect citizens from injuries caused by criminal activities. Another perspective is that all citizens should bear the costs of crime since it is an unavoidable feature of the modern state. Compensation paid out under the schemes is therefore a monetary expression of the state and community's sympathy and concern for those who suffer unjustifiable invasions of their personal integrity resulting in injury or loss as a result of crime.

                                CHRISTINE FORSTER

criminal justice policy in developing countries
The welfare of **human** beings is inevitably affected by the ability of the state to enforce its laws and punish violations of its codes. Central to such state authority are policing, penal, and adjudication systems. These institutions, however, are highly controversial and subject to frequent public criticism and review. If this is true even in advanced industrialized **democracies**, what can be said of the legitimacy and efficacy of **criminal justice systems** in the far more populous developing-country context, where socio-economic and political conditions are more difficult?

An example from Brazil, one of the world's largest and most powerful developing countries, is illustrative. In May 2006, Brazil's most economically important state, São Paulo, was paralysed by simultaneous prison uprisings in forty-five jails. Aggravating matters further, these prison rebellions were coordinated with a series of lethal drive-by attacks on **police** officers, bus hijackings, and shootings at bank branches and police stations. This criminal offensive, and the deadly police retaliation that followed, paralysed much of São Paulo for over a week, leaving scores of police officers, prison guards, prisoners, criminals, and innocent bystanders dead and causing over US$1 billion of damage.

Certainly, everyday patterns in Brazil and other developing countries are not always so extreme. In the developing world the crime situation varies significantly by country and city, level of economic development, degree of urbanization, extent of societal cohesion, and penetration of organized crime, among other factors. Nevertheless, the Brazilian example is evocative of many broader patterns.

Generally speaking, developing countries are characterized by high levels of poverty, inequality, and urban crime, social dislocation, and large informal economies. The **rule of law** is characteristically weak, **citizenship** rights are precarious, corruption and white collar crime are widespread, and society is often affected by an authoritarian legacy and patterns of intrusion and extraction by foreign powers.

Policing, **punishment**, and dispute resolution are highly contentious in such societies. Legal rules are often drafted with particularistic or repressive purposes and may be applied harshly by undertrained, underpaid, heavy-handed, and often corrupt agents of the criminal justice system. **Courts** are inaccessible to most citizens, are severely backlogged, and are slow at handing down judgment, while prisons are characterized by severe overcrowding, scarce food, **torture**, and routine prison breaks and revolts.

Finally, the police are viewed as authoritarian **agents** who predominantly engage in political and social repression while providing scant protection to the citizenry. Not surprisingly, the affluent attempt to insulate themselves from crime by means of private security guards, gated **communities**, and other expensive adaptations, while the poor live and work in a pervasive climate of insecurity.

All these factors impinge heavily on the state's ability in a developing country to protect life and property, provide for basic needs, and shape the patterns of behavior of the population. This undermines the social wellbeing of the majority of the world's population and even the wellbeing of those living far from the centres of poverty. Processes of transnational migration, organized crime, environmental degradation, and the spread of disease and pandemics are all interlinked phenomena in today's globalized environment and thus make further comparative criminal justice policy research and study exceedingly important.   MERCEDES S HINTON

MS Hinton, *The State on the Streets: Police and Politics in Argentina and Brazil* (Boulder and London: Lynne Rienner Publishers, 2006)

M S Hinton and T Newburn, *Policing Developing Democracies* (London: Routledge/Taylor & Francis Publishers, forthcoming 2008)

criminal justice policy, comparative   *see* comparative criminal justice policy

criminal justice rights   *see* due process rights

criminal justice system: England and Wales, and Northern Ireland   An analysis of the criminal justice system could focus on any of the words in the title. The breadth of the concept of 'crime' in England and Wales, and Northern Ireland is considered elsewhere in this volume (see especially '**criminalization, rationale of**'). Suffice it to say, that in recent years the number of offences has been vastly increased, adding to the burdens on the 'system'. And the concept of '**justice**' is fundamental. Those of us who like to think of justice as fairness have been deeply depressed by the misappropriation of the term by the current UK government when they speak, for example, of 'narrowing the justice gap', which means simply convicting more suspects. But the focus of this piece is a discussion of whether or not there is a criminal justice 'system', a question which has long been debated in criminal justice circles. For this reason, many commentators prefer to describe a criminal justice 'process'. But both terms imply something rather 'smoother' than that which actually exists. This commentator would also suggest that the criminal justice 'system' should in any case not function too 'smoothly', for due process, or justice, reasons.

From the government's perspective, there is clearly a system, made up of certain key players, such as the **police**, **courts**, Prison Service, **Crown Prosecution Service** ('CPS'), and the National **Probation** Service. Indeed, the government provides an excellent guide on the web, designed primarily for those who have come into contact with the criminal justice system, whether as **victim**, witness, juror, or as someone who has been accused or convicted of a crime (see *www.cjsonline.gov.uk*). There is a similar website for the criminal justice system in Northern Ireland (*www.cjsni.gov.uk*). This announces that the Criminal Justice System Northern Ireland ('CJSNI') is made up of seven main statutory agencies:

- Northern Ireland Court Service ('NICtS')
- Northern Ireland Office ('NIO')
- Northern Ireland Prison Service ('NIPS')
- Police Service of Northern Ireland ('PSNI')
- Probation Board for Northern Ireland ('PBNI')
- Public Prosecution Service ('PPS')
- Youth Justice Agency ('YJA')

The precise borders of this criminal justice system can of course be debated. How does the Youth Justice Board (of England and Wales) or the Youth Justice Agency (of Northern Ireland) fit in? Why is the National Offender Management Service ('NOMS') not on the Government's list for England and Wales? Part of the difficulty in identifying a 'system' is the different (and often controversial) status of the various players. For example, the tension between local and national control of policing bodies is discussed under the entry on '**police**'. And the CPS was created in 1985 to provide an 'independent' check on police decision-making: yet, the latest reorganizations have sought to get the CPS more closely connected with the police to 'smooth' the decision to prosecute. And the criminal justice bodies responsible for prisons and probation are being privatized and fragmented. The Prison Service is the body which runs only public sector prisons: but there are now eleven private ('contracted out') prisons in England and Wales, managed by private companies such as GSL, Serco, and G4S Justice Services. The latest plans for **community** punishments also includes greater use of private providers. Already electronic monitoring in England and Wales is delivered by private **security** companies under contract to the Home Office. Three companies operated in four regions until April 2005; now two companies (Group4Securicor, and Premier

Monitoring Services Ltd) cover England and Wales in five contract areas. Constant change results in difficulties in coordination, and makes it more difficult to speak of a 'system'. The Offender Management Bill 2006, if enacted, will allow the Home Secretary to commission services for dealing with offenders from public or private providers, and we can therefore expect greater fragmentation of service providers.

Perhaps the most controversial member of the government's list of criminal justice agencies is the courts. Are the courts part of the 'system'? The courts provide a check on the abuse of powers held by the executive and other bodies. To what extent should they be seen as part of the government's 'system'? Should courts face government-imposed targets? Should **judges** and magistrates take into account the costs of particular disposals when **sentencing**? Or to give another perhaps minor but topical example, should the courts be required to limit their requests for pre-sentence reports in order to save money?

There are other bodies for which a case can be made that are part of the criminal justice system: for example, health, education, and other local authorities all have statutory roles in both MAPPAs and crime and disorder strategies. The first example, MAPPAs, are Multi-agency Public Protection Agencies, created by the Criminal Justice and Courts' Services Act 2000, to manage sexual and violent offenders in the community. As well as police, prison, and probation services, youth offending teams, Jobcentre Plus, local education authorities, local housing authorities, registered social landlords, social services, strategic health authorities, Care Trusts, NHS Trust, and electronic monitoring providers may all be involved. To move to the second example, section 5 of the Crime and Disorder Act 1998 listed the authorities which must develop local Crime and Disorder strategies, giving the **Home Secretary** the power to prescribe by order which bodies should have the duty to cooperate. The current list includes the governing bodies of schools, the proprietors of independent schools, and the governing bodies of further education institutions. Known as Crime and Disorder Reduction Partnerships in England, and Community Safety Partnerships in Wales, these bodies develop and implement strategies to tackle crime and disorder in their area. Are all these bodies part of the 'system'?

What is the role of defence lawyers within the system? To the astonishment of many, when the Crime and Disorder Act 1998 enacted a 'principal aim' of the youth justice system (to prevent offending: see section 37), this was to apply to 'all **persons** and bodies carrying out functions in relation to the youth justice system', and this seems to include a suspect's legal representatives. It is thus abundantly clear that it is difficult to delineate the 'boundaries' of the criminal justice system.

So our first challenge was to identify the key players within the 'system'. But now we move to explore how and in what sense the system is indeed a 'system'. Clearly the various players work together, and many of the links and inter-dependencies are self-evident. What one criminal justice agency does has important implications for other players. Thus in 2005, the police cautioning rate for indictable offences (excluding motoring offences) rose another 4 percentage points to an extraordinary 38 per cent (see *Criminal Statistics 2005* (HOSB 19/06)). If the police decide to caution more offenders rather than prosecute, there is less pressure on the subsequent stages. Or, to give another example, if the probation service has fewer resources targeted at pre-trial **bail** support, it is unsurprising if the prison remand population goes up.

'Systems talk' is an obvious facet of modern 'managerialism', driven by the desire to improve performance throughout the 'system' (or to save money, or as a political article of faith). Key performance indicators drive performance. The budget of one organization has direct impact on the performance of another. Thus, probation budgets have 'squeezed' community penalties, which may indirectly explain the increasing use of imprisonment as a sentence. Sentencers have little faith in probation as a 'robust' sentence. The prison population grows, and probation budgets get further squeezed. From the government's point of view, a case can be seen as progressing smoothly though the system or process: a crime is reported, the police investigate, the CPS make the decision to charge, the courts convict and sentence, and the probation and prison authorities carry out the **punishment**. Thus the system can be seen as something of an assembly line, as one agency passes the offender on to the next. This is reminiscent of what Packer (1968) identified as the crime control model of criminal justice: as a result of the decisions made by police and prosecutors early in the process, determination of probable guilt or innocence emerges. The suspect is then 'processed' through the system. Packer contrasted this crime control model with a due process model (more obstacle course than assembly line), which puts greater value on preventing and eliminating mistakes. A 'smooth' process is not necessarily a fair or just one. Thus, for example, whilst the government has put great emphasis on the need to reduce the number of days from arrest to sentence (particularly for persistent **young offenders**), others point out that some delays may be essential

or even inevitable. Or, another example, the government continues to oppose decisions of courts to allow prisoners greater access to oral hearings to challenge important release decisions: whilst the courts put great emphasis on due process, the Home Office puts greater emphasis on speedy and cheaper decision-making processes.

The government has sought to bring the 'system' together by creating an 'umbrella' National Criminal Justice Board, and forty-two local criminal justice boards. These have key targets to meet on such 'measures' as bringing more offences to 'justice', reducing the number of ineffective trials, reducing the time between **arrest** and sentence and better enforcing fines.

A final word on the question of funding. There has been a significant shift in the last thirty years or so in the funding of this 'system'. Thirty years ago, it would have been accepted that this 'system' was publicly financed: even most defence work was paid for out of public money through the legal aid system. Now, there have been significant shifts in the privatization of criminal justice. As the 'system' becomes more fragmented, so it will become more difficult to speak of a criminal justice 'system'.

NICOLA PADFIELD

H Packer, *The Limits of the Criminal Sanction* (Oxford: Oxford University Press, 1968)

criminal justice system: Scotland Although it shares many features with that of England and Wales, Scotland has its own criminal justice system, with distinct procedural rules (contained mostly in the Criminal Procedure (Scotland) Act 1995). Scottish criminal procedure is a predominantly accusatorial system.

Prosecution of crime in Scotland is the responsibility of the procurator fiscal. The procurator fiscal decides whether or not to bring charges in a particular case and, in the event that charges are not brought, whether any of a number of alternatives to prosecution should be used (such as a warning letter). There is a *very* limited right of private prosecution in Scotland but it has only been used twice in the last 100 years.

Criminal cases in Scotland can be prosecuted under either 'solemn' or 'summary' procedure. Solemn procedure is used for the more serious cases and trials are conducted in front of a **jury** (presided over by a professional **judge**, who plays no role in the adjudication of the case). If the case is prosecuted under solemn procedure, it can be brought in either the High Court (where the maximum penalty available is life imprisonment) or the sheriff court (where the maximum penalty available is five years imprisonment).

If the case is prosecuted under summary procedure, the case can be brought in either the sheriff court or the district court. Summary proceedings are reserved for less serious cases and there is no jury. Trials are conducted in front of either a single sheriff (a professional judge) if proceedings are taking place in the sheriff court or one or more lay justices if proceedings are taking place in the district court. The lay justice is assisted by a legally qualified clerk, whose role is to provide legal advice, rather than to make any adjudication on the outcome of the case.

Where the accused is charged with murder, **rape,** or treason, he must be prosecuted under solemn procedure in the High Court. Likewise, there are some crimes which cannot be tried in the district court, such as robbery, culpable **homicide,** or serious **assaults.** Other than this, the choice between solemn or summary procedure (and thus whether a jury will hear the case) is made by the procurator fiscal. The accused cannot elect to be tried by a jury in Scotland, as he can in certain circumstances in England and Wales.

Trial by jury in Scotland has two distinctive features. First, the jury has fifteen members and a majority verdict will be accepted. Secondly, there are three verdicts available: guilty, not guilty, and not proven. The not proven verdict has the same effect as a verdict of not guilty, in that the accused is acquitted.

Like other accusatorial systems, the vast majority of cases in Scotland do not even reach the trial stage because the accused tenders a guilty plea. In order to encourage guilty pleas, a sentence discount of around one-third is normally offered to those who plead guilty at the earliest possible stage in the process (see *Du Plooy v HM Advocate* (2005)).

FIONA LEVERICK

criminal law   *see* **acts and omissions; assisting crime; attempts, conspiracy and incitement; causation; corporate criminal liability; criminal liability without fault; fault-based criminal liability; homicide; justification, excuse and mitigation in criminal law; mental incapacity and crime; rape**

Criminal Law Revision Committee   Historically, English criminal law was judge-made, supplemented from time to time by parliamentary 'intervention' in the form of statutes. The resulting law became progressively unwieldy and difficult to know or to state. Attempts were made throughout the nineteenth century to reform it and reduce it into the form of a Criminal Code. The Offences Against the Person Act 1861 and the Larceny Act of the same year represented steps in that direction. Attempts by Sir James Fitzjames **Stephen** to revive the codification movement resulted in a major draft code, but nothing came of it in England (as opposed to the colonies, in several of which it was enacted). The Criminal Law Revision Committee was established as a standing committee in February 1959 'to examine such aspects of the criminal law . . . as the Home Secretary may from time to time refer to the Committee, to consider whether the law requires revision and to make recommendations'. The body was to consist of **judges** and legal practitioners, civil servants, and academics. It is believed to be the first reform agency to consult by the use of **green papers**.

Successive Home Secretaries did make references, on seventeen occasions, and on subjects as diverse as suicide (which informed the enactment of the Suicide Act 1961) and larceny (which resulted in the Theft Act 1968). Many of the Committee's recommendations concerning evidence and procedure saw the light of day only many years later and after much further inquiry, in the Police and Criminal Evidence Act 1984. The utility of the Committee was much reduced when the Law Commission, established in 1965, decided in 1968 to begin working on a criminal law codification project. Several references were made to the Committee following this, and the Committee has never been formally abolished; but is has been inactive since its 1986 Report on Conspiracy to Defraud.

ATH SMITH

criminal liability without fault   A defendant can normally be convicted of a serious criminal offence if he was at fault for perpetrating that offence. At least since the nineteenth century it has been regarded a fundamental principle of criminal law that there should be no crime without fault. However, many criminal offences do not adhere to this principle, or adhere to it only partially. Liability without fault ranges from **health and safety** legislation to environmental **legislation** to some very serious criminal offences.

For some criminal offences, there is no fault element at all. The defendant, in such cases, can be convicted if the relevant criminal act is perpetrated even if she had no reason to believe that she was committing a criminal offence. These are commonly called offences of 'strict liability'. For other offences, there is fault element which may not be commensurate with the gravity of the offence for which the defendant may be made liable. For example, if the defendant intentionally commits a minor **assault** on the **victim** and the victim unfortunately dies, the defendant may be found guilty of manslaughter even though no reasonable **person** would think that death was a foreseeable consequence of the defendant's conduct. Such offences are sometimes called offences of 'constructive liability': a major criminal offence is constructed out of the fault element of a more minor offence.

Offences of strict and constructive liability are becoming increasingly common in the criminal law of England and Wales, despite concerted criticism by academic commentators. There are two main criticisms that have been put forward. First these offences fail properly to respect the **autonomy** of citizens. They do not allow citizens a full opportunity to ensure that their behaviour conforms to the criminal law, and through that to avoid criminal convictions and **punishments**. Secondly, these offences fail to ensure that it is only those defendants who deserve moral condemnation for their conduct that are punished. Defendants may be punished by chance. For many, the purpose of punishment is to censure the defendant for his conduct, and offences which do not include a fault element, or with an insufficient fault element, make punishment possible where no such censure is appropriate.

It is sometimes suggested that strict liability offences are acceptable as long as the offences concerned are 'regulatory' rather than 'truly criminal'. The distinction between true criminal offences and regulatory offences is notoriously difficult to draw, however, and, unlike some continental jurisdictions, there is no formal separation between true crimes and regulatory offences in the law of England and Wales. There are some very serious criminal offences that are offences of strict liability, including, for example, **rape** of a **child** below the age of thirteen.

Some offences appear to be strict liability defences on their surface, but in fact introduce a weak fault element by making available to defendants a defence of due diligence. If the defendant can show that he did what could reasonably be expected of him in ensuring that his conduct conformed to the requirements of the law, such defences provide, he will not be convicted of the offence. Controversially, it is quite common for **Parliament** to impose some burden of proof on the defendant in respect of such defences.

Many offences that are created by statute do not indicate on their surface that there is a requirement on the **prosecution** to prove fault. They simply state the acts that are prohibited. In that case, the **courts** have had a role in deciding whether to interpret those offences as having a fault element or not. It is sometimes stated that there is a general presumption in favour of interpreting offences as including a fault element where parliament has not made this clear. However, that principle has not consistently been followed by the courts, and some ambiguous pieces of **legislation** have been interpreted as offences of strict liability.

The courts and academic commentators have debated whether criminal liability without fault violates the right to be presumed innocent until proven guilty as protected by Article 6(2) of the **European Convention of Human Rights**. The domestic courts have, in general, been reluctant to find breach of the right in respect of such offence definitions, suggesting that the presumption of innocence only ensures that proper evidential standards are met by criminal trials rather than restricting how criminal offences can be defined. The **European Court of Human Rights** has suggested that offences of strict liability are acceptable within reasonable limits.

VICTOR TADROS

criminal libel   In English, but not Scots, law the publication of a serious **libel** amounts to a **common law** criminal offence as well as a civil wrong. (But **slander** is only a civil wrong.) Criminal proceedings can only succeed if the libel is sufficiently grave to justify a prosecution. There is no need, as there is for the civil wrong, for the libel to be published to a third party. In a criminal libel case it is not enough for the defendant to prove the truth of the defamatory allegations; he must also show that they were published for the public benefit. Otherwise the defences are broadly the same as they are in civil proceedings. A prosecution against the owner or editor of a newspaper can only be brought with the consent of a judge, who will consider whether the alleged libel was serious and whether the public interest requires a charge to be brought.

Prosecutions for criminal libel are now very rare. It is often argued that the offence should be abolished as incompatible in principle with **freedom of expression**; moreover, civil libel proceedings and other remedies are almost always adequate to safeguard individuals. But in exceptional circumstances a prosecution may be justified, for example, when defamatory attacks are repeatedly circulated about someone unable to afford the costs and risks of civil proceedings. Comparable offences exist in many European countries, and it is unlikely that the **European Court of Human Rights** would hold the common law infringes the **European Convention on Human Rights**.

ERIC BARENDT

criminal offences   *see* **crime and sexual integrity; crime and violence; criminal regulation of property relations; criminal regulation of public order; fraud, honesty and markets; regulatory offences**

criminal records   *see* **crime investigation by police; evidence (criminal)**

criminal regulation of property relations   Most Western jurisdictions criminalize violations of **property rights**. Those 'offences against property', as they are traditionally regarded and referred to, cover acts ranging from petty shoplifting to complex and serious cases of corporate fraud. Property offences broadly conceived include: theft, ie the dishonest appropriation (or, in some jurisdictions, taking away or mishandling) of property belonging to another; robbery, ie theft with the use or threat of **violence** at some point before, during, or after the act; burglary, ie trespassing and stealing or trespassing merely with the intention of stealing; criminal damage; fraud, that is, deceiving in order to obtain property. Furthermore, property is indirectly involved in other offences or defences. For example, the use of reasonable force in self-defence is legally allowed for the protection of one's property. In such instances property becomes commensurable with goods and values such as life and bodily integrity subject to the principle of proportionality, according to which there must be a reasonable symmetry between the threat and the response. The central place occupied by property offences in the doctrine of criminal law seems to be reflected in our everyday lives as well. **Criminological research** suggests that property offences are consistently among the most common offences committed and that they crucially determine people's sense of **safety** or fear of crime. Such empirical evidence should always be read with the necessary caveat concerning the circularity in the definition of crime (is an act criminal *prior to* or *because of* its inclusion in the criminal law?) and the distinction between *mala in se* and *mala prohibita*, but it is still indicative of the significance of property offences in law and everyday life.

At least two questions are thrown open by the so-called 'offences against property', namely those of justification and coherence. Does property have a sufficient moral weight so as to justify the intervention of the criminal law? Precious little has been written on this. It seems to be almost universally but tacitly accepted that violations of individual property are the business of criminal law as a matter of course but the ubiquity and sheer scope of property offences as well as their significance in our everyday lives make it imperative that we provide a more careful account of their justification.

The issue of coherence is directly related to that of justification. The lack of an obvious justificatory ground makes it difficult to understand all property offences as protecting the same good. Establishing the internal coherence of property offences is not simply a pragmatic, technical question of legal drafting but has important substantive extensions. What is at stake is the placement of property offences in the grid of criminal offences in a coherent and consistent way as well as the fairness of the response of the criminal law to specific acts. This need becomes even more pressing when we consider the way that the category of criminality is constructed and how the law of property offences is enforced. As has been forcefully shown in the literature, the category of the criminal has been so constructed as to include shoplifters and burglars whereas corporate interference with other people's property is often regarded as justified common practice which simply entails a higher degree of **risk**, despite the fact that the stakes and the effect of such practices on people's lives are significantly more serious. This inconsistency is read by many critics, in a Marxist vein, as an indication of the fact that property offences are nothing but instruments of oppression or ideological apparatuses and are accordingly rejected as altogether unjustifiable.

Let us however take a more charitable view and try to see whether liberal theories of private property can help us reconstruct the justificatory basis and normative coherence of property offences. What cannot be overemphasized is that any reconstruction of the justificatory basis of property offences must have just as much explanatory as normative force. In other words, it must be such that it explains current institutions and practices while, at the same time, shedding a critical light on them from an external perspective.

The obvious starting point in this, inevitably selective and brief, exploration would be the strand of liberalism, which is genealogically linked to John Locke's labour or first occupancy theory of property. According to this, property is intrinsically valuable and therefore gives rise to an inalienable right. One acquires an exclusive property right over a thing once she mixes her labour with a natural resource and produces an artefact or appropriates things, which, in a state of nature, are common to all, eg crops and raw material. The problem with this theory is that it fails to make the necessary conceptual or moral transition from the transformation of nature with one's labour to the grounding of private property. Even if we accept that in a state of nature all we own is our **person** and labour and everything else is common to all, it is not clear at all how picking an apple or making a chair out of a piece of wood creates an exclusive entitlement to those things. In order for such an entitlement to be established, there must be some other connection between the person and the resource, one that pre-exists the process. It also does not take seriously the social dimension of property. Resources can only be exploited and enjoyed in cooperation and not in isolation. But even if we turn a blind eye to the analytical and moral problems of first occupancy theory, a further step is required in order to establish the moral wrongfulness and criminalization of violating one's property rights. Otherwise, it is difficult to see why civil law remedies would not be enough to redress violations of private property or, more importantly, why the criminal law does not or should not intervene in all cases, in which property relations are disrupted such as in breaches of contractual agreements or tortious acts. Finally, the first occupancy theory does not sit comfortably with current legal arrangements, not least because, in most jurisdictions, the entitlement of the **victim** to the thing bears no relevance to the criminal **responsibility** of the defendant.

One possible way of lending private property a thick moral content would be to establish its connection with personhood. The argument, which can be traced back to Hegel, is that our dominion over things provides a real, material extension to our abstract subjectivity and consciousness. It is especially those things to which we are emotionally attached because of their place in our personal histories, such as family heirlooms, gifts from people we love, and so forth, are parts of who *we are* as persons. This idea carries a certain intuitive appeal and, indeed, justificatory potential for the moral wrongfulness of interfering with others' property. But note how it shifts the justificatory focus from property to personhood. What is being violated by property offences is no longer a property right but the victim's personality. Not only does this not square with current law but it also contradicts the fundamental and inescapable legal principles of universality and generality. Modern Western law can only make sense of its **subjects** in terms of universal characteristics and impartiality becomes the cornerstone of justice. Thus the law is incapable of being attentive to the particularity of personhood and its materialization in and through property.

Liberal theories of distributive justice may provide a more convincing justification. This is how the argument roughly goes: everyone has intrinsic worth as an autonomous, free **human** being. It follows that substantive **equality** and fairness ought to be regarded as overarching principles guiding our civil constitution. Therefore, the resources, which are necessary for us to be able to flourish as autonomous human beings, ought to be distributed fairly with regard to the particular needs of each individual. Such theories do not go as far as to question market economy, although if they are pressed to their extremes they will have to concede that the market is inherently unjust, they do approach property simply as an institution safeguarding the distribution of resources. Thus, property is recast as instrumental and acquires a social texture marking a departure from its libertarian conception as bound to the individual and her dominion over the physical world in direct antagonism with others. The criminal law is then called to regulate by way of coercion this arrangement. If all this holds, it becomes evident that what is really protected by the criminal law is not property, which ceases to be a right in itself as it is reducible to other values, but rather the principle of fair distribution and the values of **autonomy**, liberty, and equality underlying it.

This conception of property seems to cohere more smoothly, although not seamlessly, with current institutional arrangements. Property offences such as theft, fraud, and burglary, seem to be directed at safeguarding the fair distribution of resources. The reason for criminalizing them can be reconstructed as the violation of fundamental principles of distributive justice and the disruption of a by and large fair state of affairs. To be sure, this conception of the grounds of property offences would leave unaccounted for crimes, most notably robbery, in which the violation of property is accompanied by violence. But, on the other hand, it sheds new light on such offences, makes us aware of their different nature and urges us to rethink the contours of criminal liability for such acts. Similarly, a distributive justice conception of property offences calls for a reassessment of the criminal nature of various violations of property rights as well as corporate practices. It also emphasizes the need for introduction of defences, akin to the well established defences such as duress and, in some jurisdictions, necessity, with regard to the personal circumstances of defendants.

EMMANUEL MELISSARIS

See also: **criminalization, rationale of; fraud, honesty, and markets**

criminal regulation of public order By comparison with the interests that are protected by the various criminal offences against the **person** such as assaults and **homicides**, and offences against property such as theft and burglary, the values that are at stake in the preservation of public order through the use of the criminal law are much less clear, more inchoate, and more remote from the harms they are designed to prevent. Ultimately, the justification for punishing people who cause public alarm by disturbing the public peace is that outbreaks of public disorder, if left unchecked, might eventually threaten others' bodily integrity and the **safety** of their property, and the state is justified in intervening to protect itself where those outcomes seem likely or even possible.

Historically, offences against public order were associated with (and arguably derived the justification for their existence from) a power of dispersal which was to be found in the Riot Act. The **common law** gradually devised a series of offences which, in escalating order of seriousness, might be employed as criminal sanctions, namely unlawful assembly, affray (derived from the Norman French *effrayer*, to frighten, and aimed at gangs circulating in public brandishing weapons), rout, and riot. Riot involved a group of twelve or more who were acting for a common purpose and were using **violence** or the threat of violence in order to do so. In cases of serious outbreaks of disorder, the Justices could literally 'read the Riot Act' (which was formulated in the reign of Queen Anne in 1714) requiring all those present at the scene to disperse to their homes, upon pain that should they remain for an hour after the Act had been read, their unlawful assembly would be converted from a misdemeanour to a felony. The significance of this point was that fatal force could be used to prevent the commission or continuation of felony. The Riot Act was last read in the course of the Campaign for Nuclear Disarmament marches in the 1960s and has since been abolished (consequent upon the more general abolition of the distinction between felony and misdemeanour in 1967).

In 1986, as part of the ongoing project of ridding the criminal law of its common law origins and replacing the old (and sometimes ill-defined) offences with clear statutory provisions, **Parliament** (on the advice of the **Law Commission**) enacted the Public Order Act 1986. Shortly before that measure was formulated and adopted, Lord Scarman, in his Report on the Brixton disorders (1981), had recommended against the reinstatement of any sort of general dispersal power or order as a way of controlling widespread disorder, largely because of the practical difficulties that might be associated with its implementation. The view was taken by the Law

Commission that the non-dispersal rationales for the use of criminal law specifically against public disorder were nevertheless sufficiently strong to justify the replacement of the old common law with offences of some seriousness, and the statutory offences of affray (carrying imprisonment for three years), violent disorder (five years), and riot (ten years) were enacted.

As anticipated at the time of its enactment, riot is very rarely employed, but the other two offences are the mainstays of public order law. In practice, both affray and violent disorder are sufficiently widely defined that they are frequently to be found employed by prosecutors in the same **indictments** as offences against the person and offences against property, and in relation to the same incidents. It is probably fair to conclude (after a period of some twenty plus years of its operation) that this aspect of the Public Order Act has been a successful exercise in statutory law reform.

The serious offences are supplemented by somewhat lesser offences of causing fear or provoking violence (six months) and using threatening, abusive, or insulting language or behaviour which causes or is likely to cause **harassment**, alarm, and distress (initially three months, but later increased to six where the conduct is intentionally threatening, etc). In addition to the contribution that the existence and **prosecution** of such offences might make in their own right, these latter offences have been employed by legislators as base models for the proscription of the highly controversial offences of inciting racial hatred and, more recently, inciting religious hatred. These are 'controversial' in the sense that there is no general agreement that it is appropriate to use the criminal law to suppress the freedom of speech that they necessarily entail, particularly where (for example) the subject of discussion is the religious make-up of the nation and the wisdom or otherwise of imposing constraints upon immigration.

Preserving the Queen's Peace has long been one of the functions of the law in this area, but the related concept of '**breach of the peace**' should not be translated as being a concern to preserve mere tranquillity. Although the precise scope of that concept was for many years uncertain, it became understood by the 1980s that: there cannot be a breach of the peace unless there has been an act done or threatened to be done which either actually harms a person or, in his presence, his property, or is likely to cause such harm, or which puts someone in fear of such harm being done. In short, the concept involves a fairly immediate (imminent) outbreak of violence directed at persons or property.

Where a breach of the peace has occurred, or is reasonably feared, a constable may take such measures as are reasonably necessary (up to and including **arrest**, if necessary with force) to prevent it or its recurrence. Lesser steps might include requiring a provocative speaker to desist where the audience was hostile to the message being imparted, or preventing a group of protesters from travelling to a particular destination. In view of the fact that freedoms of speech and assembly are now protected by the incorporation of the **European Convention of Human Rights** under the **Human Rights Act 1998**, **courts** will be vigilant to ensure that any such use of the powers must be shown by the state to be proportionate to the aim that is being pursued, and in consequence the **police** themselves must be astute to ensure that any such use of their powers is Convention compliant.

Before the development of modern police forces, the task of preserving the peace was a function of the **Justices of the Peace**, the Magistrates, who could call where necessary upon the assistance of the military. Since the preservation of public order is now very much the preserve of the police, their powers have been increased considerably in recent years to enable them to undertake this task. They have been given the power to levy on-the-spot **fines** for minor acts of loutishness and incivility, and the power of summary arrest for criminal offences has been extended to any criminal offence, so long as the officer arresting judges it 'necessary' to do so rather than, as hitherto, only offences of a sufficiently high degree of seriousness.

The last decade or so has seen a considerable rise in what has been termed 'the culture of control', the phenomenon which describes how governments seek to use the law to enforce compliance with social norms; in part, this is the product of the spiralling political rhetoric that promises that governments (and oppositions) will be 'tough on crime, tough on the causes of crime'. Nowhere is this more evident than in the spate of **legislation** that has been devised to preserve public order. Branding those who engage in behaviour which is a social nuisance as 'yobs', the Labour government elected in 1997 has sought relentlessly to employ the criminal law to force such people to 'respect' the forces of law and order. As part of this effort, there has been a considerable increase in the use of preventive **justice** measures available to the courts and the police, and increasingly to other agencies such as local authorities. At common law, there was a power in the courts to bind a person over not to commit a breach of the peace upon pain of penalty in the event of a breach. These have been supplemented with **anti-social behaviour** orders, 'parenting orders', and 'child **curfew** schemes'. Other measures whose titles ('dispersal orders', 'closure orders', 'removal orders', 'reparation orders', 'referral orders', 'dog control orders', and so forth) give some indication of the powers that they contain, but the power to make them is vested in the police and other enforcement agencies rather than in the courts. Failure to comply with any of these orders is generally backed by the threat of the use of the criminal sanction. This proliferation and the general escalation of the use to which the criminal law is put, not to mention the problems associated with the enforcement of compliance with these orders, does little to enhance the view of the criminal law as a mechanism of social control that punishes those who commit acts that are seriously blameworthy. It has become, instead, a mechanism of early rather than last resort.

ATH SMITH

See also: **hate speech; law and order debates**

criminal responsibility *see* **assisting crime; attempts, conspiracy and incitement; corporate criminal liability; criminal liability without fault; fault-based criminal liability; justification, excuse and mitigation in criminal law; mental incapacity and crime**

criminal trials In criminal procedure, a 'trial' is the formal procedure by which, where an accused **person** contests his guilt by pleading 'not guilty', the accusation brought against him is 'tried', ie tested to see if it is valid. In the early history of the **common law**, the usual test was an appeal to God in the form of an ordeal. After ordeals were condemned by the Church at the Lateran Council in 1215, the resulting gap was filled in England and in Scotland by putting the question to a **jury** drawn from the area where the offence allegedly took place; a procedure which gradually developed into the modern form of adversarial trial once it had been decided that, in cases where the jury knew nothing about the facts, it could be informed by witnesses. A modern criminal trial resembles its mediaeval counterpart to the extent that it is oral, public, and—like a cricket match—divided into two parts, in each of which one side has its 'innings': first the **prosecution** case, in which the **evidence** of guilt is examined, and then the defence case, in which evidence is called to rebut it. But in matters of detail the procedure has hugely changed over the centuries—in particular as a result of the greater involvement of lawyers, a process that began around the middle of the eighteenth century.

Most of the changes were intended to provide safeguards against the risk of wrongful conviction; but their combined effect has been to slow the trial process down, to the point where it is now no longer possible (as it once was) for trials to be the normal method by which criminal cases are disposed of. To meet this difficulty, three main stratagems have been evolved. First, the traditional form of trial, known as 'trial on indictment', has been supplemented (and in practice, now largely replaced) by a simplified form, called summary trial, in which the jury is replaced by a bench of lay magistrates, or by a single professional **judge**, and in which defendants who fail to appear may often be tried in their absence. Secondly, and more radically, trials are increasingly avoided by the use of guilty pleas, which nowadays are officially encouraged by offering '**sentencing** discounts' to those defendants who will renounce their right to trial. Thirdly, and still more radically, new procedures have been developed, like cautions and on-the-spot **fines**, by means of which an ever-widening range of criminal offences can be handled by the **police** without the involvement of the **courts** at all. Although criminal trials still grip the attention of the public, statistically they have become relatively rare events. In fact, it is scarcely an exaggeration to describe the history of criminal procedure in the UK over the last 150 years as the story of the attempt to suppress the trial.   JOHN SPENCER

JH Langbein, *The Origins of the Adversary Criminal Trial* (Oxford: Clarendon Press, 2003)

criminalization, rationale of   In a society which conceives itself as liberal, criminalization—the proscription of conduct through the mechanism of criminal law—bears a heavy burden of justification. Criminal **punishment** represents one of the most draconian forms of state force; its exercise over individuals conceived as free and responsible **agents**— as citizens rather than **subjects**—requires robust defence. It is therefore no surprise that there have been many attempts to provide an overall theory of criminalization: an account which organizes in a systematic way the bewildering diversity of actual criminal prohibitions, ranging from minor road traffic offences and licensing infractions to serious interpersonal **violence** and sexual abuse via a terrain as diverse as corporate fraud, property violations, and tax evasion. Whilst such theories differ in the extent to which they purport to be explanatory or normative, even the primarily explanatory theories are informed by implicit ideas of the values which criminal justice processes seek to promote

and which constrain the exercise of criminal **justice** power. Conversely, the normative theories are informed by an implicit descriptive understanding of criminal justice. Among these theories, two sets of ideas stand out and call for specific consideration.

On the first view, criminal justice is indeed all about 'doing justice' and 'justice' in a distinctive sense. The background idea is that members of a society owe each other reciprocal obligations to forbear from breaking criminal laws—laws which are assumed to be in the antecedent interest of all, because they protect some of the most important interests of individuals and of the polity itself. On this view, the practice of attempting to identify and punish offenders is integral to the pursuit of just social relations, for only through criminalization of those who have taken an unfair advantage by breaking the law can the just relations of the pre-existing moral equilibrium be restored, and the interests of both **victim** and society given due **recognition**. This argument is associated with theories which emphasize the symbolic or expressive features of criminalization, and which seek to explain the value of punishment in terms of relationships of justice structured around retribution, desert, or reparation. As far as the criminal process is concerned, such a view tends to be associated with a commitment to the importance of 'due process'—that is, of procedural safeguards such as the presumption of innocence and the requirement that offenders have some substantial element of **responsibility** for their breaches of criminal law, which can thus be meaningfully conceived as 'unfair' advantages.

Whilst the 'justice' approach does conceive criminal justice as a relatively discrete sphere, it also contains seeds which undermine this separateness. For the idea that the justice of criminalization is independent of broader social justice is called into question by the obvious fact that the weight of the burden of complying with criminal law is directly related to the social situation of the offender. To take an example, the starving **person** who steals a loaf of bread cannot meaningfully be said to have taken the same kind of unfair advantage as the wealthy fraudster. This account therefore raises in an acute form the question of how criminalization in an unjust society can contribute social justice in a broader sense.

The continuity of criminal justice and broader social justice is more explicit in the other main approach to theorizing criminalization. On this view, criminalizing power is legitimated in terms of its capacity to secure beneficial consequences. The most influential version of this view is the utilitarian theory according to which the sole motivation and good of **human** beings is the pursuit of pleasure or preference-satisfaction and the avoidance of pain or preference-frustration; crime is conceived as harmful conduct in this sense. Whilst both punishment itself and the costs of the criminal process are, on this view, *prima facie* evils, criminalization may be justified wherever it counterbalances those evils and maximizes human happiness overall. This is typically by reducing the level of pain-producing offending, whether by individual or general deterrence, incapacitation, reform of offenders, moral education, prevention of resort to less utility-maximizing methods such as private vengeance, the satisfaction of victims' grievances, or general inculcation of utility-serving norms.

On this view, the pursuit of criminal justice is essentially an instrumental enterprise: whilst criminalization may be seen as a distinctive means of pursuing social good, the terms in which that good is to be measured are the same as those to be applied to, say, the education system or the handling of the economy. Notably, in terms of the criminal process, the commitment of such consequence-oriented approaches to procedural safeguards such as the presumption of innocence will be entirely contingent upon their contribution to the effectiveness of the process as a whole. This does not mean that utilitarian approaches eschew procedural safeguards. For procedural safeguards sometimes contribute directly to utility. Furthermore, efficacy is dependent on a baseline of legitimacy, and the latter is in turn dependent on certain procedural principles which have an important place in the social conscience. Thus, whilst a hard-nosed utilitarian might dream of educating the citizenry out of such 'prejudices', utilitarian systems must learn to accommodate them as long as they exist.

When read as explanatory theories about the criminal process, each of these general approaches has a place. The notion that criminal processes are geared to 'doing justice' is one which helps to account for both a number of actual features of criminal processes and the social meaning—the symbolic and practical significance for members of a society—of having a **criminal justice system**. In the case of many kinds of offence (murder, **assault**, theft, driving while intoxicated) and many penal practices (imprisonment, fining), it does seem plausible to say that what might be called a 'moral analogy' holds. In other words, criminalization and punishment reflect a collective *judgment* about what is not acceptable, and enunciate a general standard of social behaviour which is assumed at some level to be shared and which constitutes a significant

expression of the **identity** of the social order. Conversely, the utilitarian view helps to account for the sense in which criminal justice both is and is seen as a set of practices which responds to a certain set of social 'problems', generating an array of relatively morally neutral offences regulating issues such as health and safety and activities such as driving. The success or failure of these regulatory offences is to be judged (at least in principle) in primarily instrumental terms such as relative costs and impact on levels of offending and re-offending.

Equally obviously, however, even some combination of these two approaches fails to give a complete account of what 'criminal justice' is all about. In order to fill the gaps, we need to know a great deal more about how the 'wrongs' or 'harms' associated with 'crime' are defined in a society. This means having not merely a normative theory of criminalization, teasing out general rationales such as the proscription of harm to others, of harm to self, of offence to others, or of violation of conventionally valued moral norms, but also a sense of how the 'crime problem' is constructed in particular societies; about the social, political, and economic conditions which obtain; and about the more detailed practices and the values, goals, and occupational culture of those who administer social practices relevant to criminal justice. We need, too, to know about the social distribution of offending behaviour which meets with official response, for this is likely to have an impact on the meaning which criminalization can have. If criminalizing power is consistently invoked in relation to certain groups within the population—for example, young members of certain ethnic groups—in ways which systematically benefit other groups to a far greater extent, this will have clear implications for both the legitimacy and the efficacy of criminal justice. In particular, it will affect whether criminalization can have any socially re-integrative effects, drawing offenders back into the group of those who regard criminal justice power as legitimate as opposed to marking and reinforcing their exclusion. It is the challenge of how to link up our very general theoretical understandings with these and other realities of social practice which has so often eluded those committed to seeking a general rationale for criminalization.

Perhaps the most fruitful approach is to conceive criminalization, in the sense of the practices of identifying and responding to offenders, as a related but not entirely coordinated set of practices geared to the construction and maintenance of social order. At a general level, criminalization may be seen as an instrumental and expressive regulatory practice which is legitimated, in a broadly liberal society, by its avowed commitment to the protection of certain interests which are regarded as of fundamental importance to all members of society, and which operates by means of a relatively distinctive but in important respects porous set of procedures and publicly endorsed coercive apparatuses. This is not to say that criminal justice practices actually do fulfill these liberal-egalitarian functions, nor even that they are intended to do so by those with most influence over their development and exercise. It is rather to identify this conception as the core of criminal justice's capacity to *present itself* as legitimate. In other words, criminalization is concerned with social order not exclusively or even primarily in any instrumental, straightforwardly empirical sense, but rather with social order in a symbolic sense: with a society's sense of itself as a cohesive, viable and ethical entity.   NICOLA LACEY

Nicola Lacey, Celia Wells and Oliver Quick, *Reconstructing Criminal Law* (Cambridge: Cambridge University Press, 3rd edn, 2003)
Mike Maguire, Rod Morgan and Robert Reiner (eds), *The Oxford Handbook of Criminology* (Oxford: Oxford University Press, 4th edn, 2007)

criminological research   Research into the phenomena of criminal behaviour and the cause(s) of crime has been ongoing at least since the eighteenth century. Early approaches, taken by Cesare Beccaria, Jeremy **Bentham**, and others of the so-called 'classical school' of criminology, assumed that offenders were rational **persons** who had chosen to break the law for their own advantage. It was the state's responsibility to punish those offenders, to deter them and others, and to reinforce the social contract between the state and its citizens. During the nineteenth century a wide range of alternative explanations of crime emerged, largely as a result of scientific developments. The 'positivist school' of criminology focused on the pathology of offenders as a distinct group, and emphasized the importance of empirical research (although much of the methodology would now be regarded as suspect). Early theories proposed that criminals differed from the law-abiding in having different head shapes, or body types, and later theories suggested that offenders had distinct chromosomal differences, anti-social personalities, or mental dysfunction. Psychologists attempted to explain criminal behaviour by trait of intelligence and psychoanalysts explored the relationship between personality traits and criminal behaviour. Taken together, these positivist approaches diverged sharply from the classical school in depicting crime as a function of individual pathology, and therefore dependent on factors over which offenders might have little or no control. Studies of identical twins brought up separately from birth ultimately proved inconclusive in establishing whether 'nature' or 'nurture' held the key to deviant behaviour.

In the twentieth century the search for a single cause of crime, or a single theory that might explain criminal behaviour, was abandoned but the old theories have continued to provide important insights. Sociology became the dominant element in the discipline. The theory of 'anomie' and 'strain', proposed by Emile Durkheim and developed by Robert Merton and others, explored the extent to which crime is the product of the push by all individuals for personal success, and the frustrations of those who lack the life opportunities to achieve those goals legitimately. Criminology also became more focused on the phenomenon of crime itself, building on Edwin Sutherland's pioneering work on 'white-collar crime'. It asked why only some forms of deviant behaviour were defined as criminal (using cannabis rather than tobacco), and questioned the social and political processes by which crime is defined and regulated. 'Critical criminology' drew attention to the different ways in which similar crimes are treated in different contexts (tax evasion as against benefit fraud, or 'crime in the suites' as against 'crime in the streets). 'Labelling theory', developed by Howard Becker and others, stressed the importance of researching not just offending behaviour, but also the manner in which society reacts to it, stigmatizing individuals and groups, and often perpetuating criminal lifestyles. There has developed a much greater interest in differential treatment of **minority** groups by the **criminal justice system** (offenders of Afro-Caribbean descent, but not other minority groups, are greatly over-represented in **prison**), and in **gender** differences. Low levels of female offending prompt questions about why people conform to the law, as well as why they infringe it.

Criminological research has focused on crime 'hot-spots', the disadvantaged parts of major towns, associated poverty and unemployment, and offenders who belong to a gang, a sub-culture, or an underclass with values different from and antithetical to the mainstream, or who, according to David Matza, 'drift' back and forth between the conventional and the marginal. Most recently, the interest in crime and the environment has led to massive growth in practical techniques of 'situational crime prevention'. A range of strategies has developed to 'design out crime', by providing better street lighting, safer environments, better housing design, neighbourhood watch schemes, traffic cameras, and CCTV surveillance. Protection against crime has been improved by 'target hardening', through better security of homes, vehicles, and non-cash means of payment for goods and services. On this model, crime is increasingly seen as a fact of life, an inevitable social problem which has to be contained and **risk**-managed.

We know that, typically, offending starts between the ages of eight and fourteen, that offending peaks between fifteen and nineteen, that the peak age for desistance from crime is the mid-twenties, and that the earlier the onset of crime the more likely it is to persist into adult life. Longitudinal studies, such as those designed by David Farrington, which follow up a cohort of individuals throughout their lives, is a key research tool in this context. We know that a wide range of factors can be relevant here. Crime tends to run in families, and is affected by large family size, parental discipline or lack of it, **child abuse** and neglect, and conflict and disruption within the family. It is also associated with low educational attainment (including lack of basic literacy and numeracy skills), low intelligence, and low social status. Also important is peer group influence, unemployment, poor accommodation or rootlessness, lack of meaningful close relationships, and dependency on drink or drugs. Many of these risk factors coincide in people's lives, and are often inter-related. If criminal behaviour is viewed with the benefit of hindsight, we see that 'career criminals' often have several of these identified predictive factors present in their lives. We sometimes say that a person was 'destined' to become a criminal, or 'never had a chance'. The problem with this approach, however, is that these factors greatly over-predict future offending. Many people, even with multiple disadvantages, do not go on to have criminal lifestyles. The majority of young offenders 'grow out of trouble' and do not go on to be adult criminals. Conversely, some people break the law despite having had the benefit of advantages in life.

Research shows that desistance from offending is associated with gaining employment, forming significant life partnerships, and moving from a fragmented lifestyle to one involving regular and routine activities (to put it crudely, finding a job and a good woman). Where these factors come together at the same time, and especially where an offender is maturing in age, they are likely to have most effect. Sometimes, it seems, we have to wait for people to 'grow out of crime'. It remains an open question how far **punishment** through the **courts** and the use of criminal justice 'programmes for offenders', are effective in changing behaviour. General programmes, available

in custody or as part of community-based sentences, include 'enhanced thinking skills', 'controlling anger', and 'addressing substance misuse', and those targeted on particular offender groups include those for women, drink-impaired drivers, sex offenders, and those convicted of **domestic violence**. There is now some renewed optimism, after a forty-year period during which rehabilitative programmes were largely dismissed: 'nothing works'. We now know that carefully designed and targeted programmes, delivered by skilled and enthusiastic professionals, and involving offenders open to change, can make a difference. Recent Home Office research, however, which matches reconviction rates of offenders who have, or have not, benefited from such programmes, offers only limited encouragement.

MARTIN WASIK

S Titus Reid, *Crime and Criminology* (Maidenhead: McGraw-Hill, 11th edn, 2006)
M Maguire, R Morgan, and R Reiner (eds), *The Oxford Handbook of Criminology* (Oxford: Oxford University Press, 4th edn, 2007)

Crippen, Dr Harvey Hawley   Dr Harvey Hawley Crippen (1862–1910) remains one of the most celebrated of English criminals, the archetypal suburban poisoner. He was tried and found guilty for the murder of his wife in October 1910.

When Crippen's wife, Cora, disappeared in January 1910, he told friends that she had left him to return to the US, later maintaining that she had died there. The suspicion of her friends was aroused when Crippen's mistress, Ethel le Neve, moved into his house and was seen in public wearing Cora's jewels and clothing. When the police began to make inquiries Crippen panicked and fled, and the police subsequently discovered human remains buried beneath the cellar of the house. Newspaper descriptions of the fugitives led to Crippen being identified by the captain of the ship on which they were travelling. He telegraphed the police in London, who were able to arrest the pair as they arrived in Quebec. He was returned to London and charged with murder.

The case is notable for a number of reasons. In the absence of a body, the prosecution case rested on proof that human remains that were found beneath the floor of the cellar of his house were those of his wife, and that she had died as a result of poisoning. This was established through the careful use of forensic evidence. Crippen consistently denied the murder, even throughout a cross-examination lasting over a day. His very coolness and imperturbability under intense pressure was taken as evidence of his callousness and capacity to commit cold-blooded murder, and the jury found him guilty. He was executed in Pentonville Prison in November 1910.

LINDSAY FARMER

critical legal studies   The intellectual movement known as Critical Legal Studies ('CLS') emerged in the United States in the late 1970s, and quickly spread to Europe. The movement was united rather more by a set of progressive political attitudes than agreement on a particular theoretical perspective. The political orientation was leftist, but not Marxist, and, as the movement evolved, it increasingly stressed issues concerning minorities and identity politics, until it dissolved into these other streams, such as critical race theory, in the 1990s. In its distinctive views about legal theory and the function of law in society, the CLS movement drew upon the earlier American progressive movement in legal theory known as **Legal Realism**, but it modified in significant ways that earlier instrumentalist and pragmatic account of legal thought.

The central claim of CLS with respect to legal thought is the ultimate incoherence and indeterminacy of legal reasoning. Despite the apparent certainty and predictability achieved by the judicial application of legal rules to factual circumstances, this legal method, even when practised and explained in a sophisticated way, in fact concealed the chaotic character of the legal materials. For every principle or rule in the legal system, it is possible to find a rival contradictory rule or principle. Although mainstream lawyers believe that it is possible, though difficult, to reconcile these competing principles into a coherent body of law, the CLS movement insisted that these rival principles merely revealed the presence of deeper contradictions in liberal legal thought that had never been resolved. Duncan Kennedy, a leading thinker of the movement, suggested that at the root of these contradictions lay the unresolved problem of liberal political theory that relations with others are both necessary to and incompatible with our freedom.

Yet the CLS movement was not crudely sceptical about legal reasoning. It accepted that for the most part legal decisions, though in their view ultimately not resting on coherent foundations, were usually predictable and justified by reference to legal rules and precedents. For the most part, one legal principle would be widely accepted as dominant over its rivals, so that the counter-principle would not be mentioned or recognized as relevant. This avoidance of consideration might be achieved by the construction of boundaries or compartments between aspects of the law. For instance, principles of public law could be restricted to disputes involving the government, thereby excluding them from consideration in relation to private disputes. Procedural due process or **natural justice** would be confined to actions of government such as a criminal trial, but due to the boundary between public law and private law, would not be applied to the exercise of power by private bodies, such as a business dismissing an employee.

Another way in which counter-principles could be marginalized in legal reasoning was by viewing the facts of a case from a particular perspective, excluding from consideration events that might bring the rival principle to attention. The effect of avoiding consideration of the counter-principle by one of these routes, or some other technique, was to give the appearance that a legal decision was justified by reference to the legal rules. The CLS movement insisted, however, that this justification was illusory, because it was always possible, by using a different account of the facts of the case or by invoking marginalized principles, to justify a different outcome. The existence of this alternative result reflected the constant presence of more fundamental conflicts of principle in the foundations of legal reasoning.

To this critique of the indeterminacy of legal reasoning, the CLS movement added that the privileged principle in contemporary legal discourse was invariably one that favoured conservative viewpoints. As Mark Kelman, another leading writer put the point in his excellent introductory book *A Guide to Critical Legal Studies* (Cambridge, Mass: Harvard University Press, 1987), the dominant principles described a political programme of a remarkably right-wing, quasi-libertarian order. Much of the published work of the CLS movement sought to expose both the indeterminacy of legal reasoning and the political orientation of the dominant legal discourse in the context of the whole range of legal subjects, from constitutional law principles to the details of equitable proprietary interests.

The CLS movement was a deeply political movement, because it insisted that every aspect of legal rules and doctrine was imbued with controversial and contestable political ideologies. The work of members of the movement in 'trashing' the work of others who sought to find coherence in the law earned them many opponents. Those scholars who continued with traditional **doctrinal legal research** could be tarred with the brush of either being deeply confused about the coherence of their work or of being part, probably unconsciously, of a right-wing conspiracy. For a brief period in the 1980s, the controversies and divisions within the faculty became so heated in some leading American law schools that it became difficult to reach agreement on any matters at all, especially the appointment of new professors.

The CLS movement was criticized for being negative, critical, and merely disruptive, without having a positive agenda. It is true that the movement lacked a concrete political programme and was suspicious about grand theories, whether on the Marxist left or the libertarian right. Instead, what members of the movement tended to emphasize was the need for experimental challenges to the settled order, and the capacity to question hierarchies and limitations, whether in the legal system or the university, with a view to discovering progressive possibilities. Perhaps the member of the movement with the most sweeping vision was Roberto Unger, whose multi-volume treatise entitled *False Necessity* (London: Verso, 2001; first published in 1987) argued that liberal democratic institutions could remake themselves in many radical ways, and that there was no logical or determinate pattern—contrary to what was often assumed by liberals and conservatives—between the institutions of **democracy**, free markets, and the **rule of law**. With respect to the law, Unger saw possibilities for change in the form of deviationist doctrinal writing, in which hitherto suppressed principles were permitted to flourish. Yet Unger also regarded the agenda of debating legal rules as ultimately too narrow: what was required for an effective progressive movement was a more fundamental questioning of the institutions of society, the ability to challenge them through legal rights that might disrupt fundamental arrangements such as property rights and government institutions. He despaired of the continuing rationalizing legal analysis conducted in courts and law schools as a possible vehicle for radical change.

The gradual fading of the influence of the CLS movement raises timeless questions about whether law can ever be an instrument for radical change and whether it is possible to be both a progressive person in politics and a good lawyer. HUGH COLLINS

D Kairys, *The Politics of Law: A Progressive Critique* (New York: Basic Books, 3rd edn, 1990)
I Grigg-Spall and P Ireland, *The Critical Lawyers Handbook* (London: Pluto Press, 1992)

critical race theory Critical race theory is a movement and body of literature which evolved out of the **critical legal studies** movement in the US. The absence in critical legal studies of an analysis of how **race** and **racialization** are imbricated within legal doctrines and liberal legal frameworks were (and remain) prime objectives of critical race theory as it emerged in the 1980s and 1990s. Critical race theory offers analyses of the social and legal construction of race in a wide variety of contexts. Rather than taking 'race' as a given biological or natural category, critical race theorists take as their starting point the socially constructed nature of race. The ways in which law and legal apparatuses rely upon and further entrench socially constructed notions of race is a prime focus of critical race theory.

Much of the scholarship in this field examines contemporary racial formations in their historical contexts. Some of the key writings have focused on the legacies of **slavery**, the civil rights movement, the landmark decision of ***Brown v Board of Education*** (1954), issues of socio-economic and racial segregation in historic and contemporary forms, histories of migration, and constitutional politics. Constitutional, property, contract, tort, commercial, anti-discrimination, and criminal law, among other fields, have been the focus of critical race analyses.

Critical race theory addressed a significant lacuna in critical legal studies and feminist theory by rendering critiques of the intersections of various forms of oppression. Rather than viewing **gender** and race, for instance, in categorical terms that cannot account for the experiences of **women** of colour, critical race theorists developed the concept of **intersectionality** to account for the ways in which race, gender, sexuality, and class combine in different ways to produce particular experiences of oppression and marginalization. This critical perspective illustrated the racial bias that was pervasive in Western feminist discourses. Kimberle Crenshaw, Patricia Williams, and Angela Harris, among other feminist legal scholars, emphasize the need for a multi-layered approach to understand and undo the machinations of discrimination in the study of legal cases. The concept of intersectionality has subsequently become a major theme for feminist theorists and other critical legal scholars.

Critical race theory is a movement insofar as it addresses itself to questions of social **justice** in a wide variety of contexts. It takes as it subject everyday experiences of marginalized **communities**; broader political and social issues within the US such as **hate speech**, hate crimes, and anti-discrimination law; legal practice; and legal education and issues of pedagogy. Critical race theory seeks to render the abstract and universal objectivist epistemological framework of legal studies into one grounded in the social and material.

Another key feature of the critical race scholarship is the rich diversity of methodologies employed. These include the use of personal and historical narratives, storytelling, utilizing critical epistemological strategies, and standpoint theory. By drawing on this range of methodologies, critical race theory has developed techniques that upset positivist conceptions of law as being founded on an objective and universal principles.

Originating in the work of African American legal scholars, critical race theory has widened its focus to include the work of Latino and Latina scholars ('Latcrit'), Indigenous and Native American scholars, and also Asian scholars. Key theorists include Derrick Bell, Kimberlé Crenshaw, Richard Delgado, Mari Matsuda, Kendall Thomas, Patricia J Williams, amongst many others.   BRENNA BHANDAR

K Crenshaw (ed), *Critical Race Theory: The Key Writings that Formed the Movement* (New York: New Press, 1995)

R Delgado (ed), *Critical Race Theory: The Cutting Edge* (Philadelphia: Temple University Press, 1995)

cronyism   *see* **corruption; public appointments**

Crown   The expression 'The Crown' has institutional and symbolic meanings. Institutionally it refers to both the monarch and the executive branch of government, and it symbolizes the formal location of authority within the UK's constitution. In both these senses the Crown presents difficulties for commentators and much disagreement exists as to its precise meaning. These disagreements can have important practical constitutional implications, not least because the Crown (in its institutional sense) possesses significant privileges and immunities, including from judicial process.

First, then, the Crown in its institutional sense: Lord Diplock said that 'the Crown' means 'the government' and includes 'all of the ministers and parliamentary secretaries under whose direction the administrative work of government is carried on': *Town Investments Ltd v Department of the Environment* (1978). Professor Sir William Wade considered this 'extraordinary'. He wrote that '[I]n truth, "the Crown" means simply the Queen, though the term is usually confined to her political or constitutional capacity' (M Sunkin and S Payne (eds), *The Nature of the Crown* (Oxford: Oxford University Press, 1999), 24). There can be no doubt that 'the Crown' extends to the monarch in her official capacity, but it is impossible to confine the Crown to the Queen. In particular, this is because circumstances exist in which the Crown's powers are exercised by ministers as agents of the Crown, so that their decisions are decisions of the Crown. Examples include the exercise of the prerogative of mercy by the Home Secretary and the disposition of the armed forces by the Prime Minister and the Secretary of State for Defence. However, such situations are comparatively rare and

most powers exercised by ministers are not Crown powers but powers conferred upon ministers specifically, usually by statute. In such situations ministers are members of Her Majesty's Government and serve the Crown: but they do not act as the Crown itself. For this reason, while Lord Diplock's statement may be colloquially correct, it is almost certainly inaccurate from a strictly legal perspective.

Turning to the Crown in its symbolic sense: in their leading textbook on Constitutional Law, Professors Bradley and Ewing say that: 'It is still formally the case that executive power in the United Kingdom is vested in the Crown however little this may reflect the reality of modern government' (AW Bradley and KD Ewing, *Constitutional and Administrative Law* (London: Pearson, 14th edn, 2007), 242). In reality executive power is vested not in the Crown but in the government by virtue of its ability to command the political support of Parliament that derives from electoral success. So what sense is there in saying that formally executive power vests in the Crown? The essential answer is rooted in the fact that the monarch is the longest established source of power in the UK. While over the centuries its powers to dispense justice, to legislate, and to govern have been transferred to other institutions, the Crown continues to symbolize the continuity of a system in which those who exercise power do so because they have constitutional authority to do so.   MAURICE SUNKIN

Crown Court   *see* **courts**

Crown Prosecution Service   Until the creation of the Crown Prosecution Service ('CPS') by the **Prosecution** of Offences Act 1985 almost all prosecutions in England and Wales were handled by the **police**. The Royal Commission on Criminal Procedure (1981) recommended an independent prosecution body because it believed that it would (by comparison with the police) prosecute fewer weak cases, and handle potentially strong cases more effectively. The aims were more consistent decisions, better conviction rates and fewer suspects dragged through the **courts** unnecessarily. Headed by the **Director of Public Prosecutions** ('DPP'), the internal organization of the CPS has changed several times, but broadly there is a local CPS area corresponding to each police force area.

For many years the CPS mainly led to police decisions to prosecute being reviewed and, if appropriate, discontinued (ie reversed) at an early stage and to all prosecutions being prepared and prosecuted by professionals. Perhaps inevitably, prosecution patterns hardly changed. Weak cases were still being prosecuted; few cautionable cases were being discontinued and inconsistency remained rife (eg caution rates varied greatly from force to force). At the same time as the CPS was criticized by some for being too close to the police, others regarded the 'Criminal Protection Society' as insufficiently robust—particularly with regard to types of offence such as **rape,** where prosecution and conviction rates remained low.

The dilemma facing the CPS is clear. Its *raison d'etre* is to be first, an independent agency since the police are too close to their own cases to make objective and fair decisions enough of the time; and secondly, a prosecuting agency *for* the police to improve conviction rates. These two objectives are often incompatible. The Criminal Justice Act 2003 attempts to square the circle. Initial prosecution decisions were taken from the police and given to the CPS. Although the police retain no-action and caution powers, some prosecutors now work in police stations to expedite prosecution decisions. Advice can be given on whether to prosecute, caution, 'no further action' ('NFA'). or investigate further; and cases that the police want prosecuted can be handled differently if appropriate. Further, this **legislation** gives the CPS an additional power to issue conditional cautions, requiring some form of **restorative justice** if the offender is to escape prosecution.

The CPS has had to come to terms with several new challenges. For example, planning and facilitating special provisions for vulnerable witnesses, such as children, **victims** of sexual and **domestic violence**, and people with mental illness or **disability**. Another is dealing with victims—taking their interests and views into account, and (in serious cases) explaining their decisions to them. It is evident that the CPS is becoming more like continental prosecuting bodies and the Scottish procurator fiscal service: it is more central to criminal justice than was originally conceived. But while the CPS remains totally dependent on the police for the information on which it makes its decisions, it will never be truly independent.

Scotland and Northern Ireland have their own distinct **prosecution** bodies, in Scotland the procurator fiscal, and in Northern Ireland, the Public Prosecution Service.　　ANDREW SANDERS

I Brownlee, 'The statutory charging scheme in England and Wales: towards a unified prosecution system?' (2004) *Criminal Law Review* 896

A Sanders and R Young, *Criminal Justice* (Oxford: Oxford University Press, 3rd edn, 2007), ch 7

cultural anthropology and law　The cultural dimensions of law constitute a speciality within anthropology as well as across the interdisciplinary 'law and society' field. Specialists may be found on every continent—with journals, professional associations, and literatures in many languages.

Recounting the story of Anglophone anthropology's engagement with law would require a history of academic law, its 'scientification' alongside the emergence of the social sciences, and positioning as both the means and ends of the public interest. It would also take us to myriad locations where legality emerged fully independently of the west, and indeed, apart from states—its force contingent on other ideals, canons, authorities, and social practices. We would necessarily consider the zones of encounter—in coloniality, empire, war, travel, trade, legal education and law practice, the media, and other forms of transnationalism—where legalities confront and influence each other.

For anthropologists, law's cultural dimensions are inherent in its social character—its context, content, meaning, and expression in (and through) social relationships. Specialized topics are diverse as to theme, locale, and scale. To risk an overgeneralization: we look for the nature and limits of law's cultural significance in its ethical force, its warrants of obligation and freedom, its calls for interpretation and expertise, its enhancement (or encumbrance) of social exchange, its repertoires of expression, its overlays and confrontations with other systems of social ordering (whether in the public or private sector)—or of disorder. Cultural analysis tends to blur the distinction between law and custom, except as modes of formality. Classically, anthropologists emphasized the mutuality of law and **identity**; however, this is no longer assumed, and contemporary scholars study how cultural **communities** rally to demand relief and redress on the basis of rights. Above all, it rides distinctions between norms in action and legal rules, and between what the law 'says' and what it 'does' (or does not do).

While culture, as anthropological *argot*, dates only to the 1870s, it has travelled widely across the disciplines of the **human** sciences as a field of study, and into many types of communities, institutions, and organizations as a framework for self recognition. Thus, what it means to refer to law as a cultural question can never be defined theoretically in advance. Law is conventionally understood as the purview of states, but anthropologists are also engaged with non-state authority and delegations of state power to the private sector. Thinking of law as cultural complicates questions of state power in another way by drawing hegemonic and counter-hegemonic practices into a single framework.

To say that law is cultural does not by itself answer fundamental questions of **justice** or the relationship between state and society, nor does it provide assurance that law is inevitably democratic, fair, or non-violent. **Violence,** too, is cultural in its means, ends, and targets. Cultural analysis situates law's meanings in its makings and maintenance, its challenges and retrenchments—but assumes neither its merits as a moral project nor its instrumental efficacy. In short, to say that law is everywhere cultural is to stipulate that law's meanings constantly escape its texts, and that law's power is never its own.

CAROL J GREENHOUSE

cultural heritage　There is growing interest at national and international levels in developing legal means to afford protection to evidence of the human past which is regarded as worthy of preservation. The term 'cultural heritage' is generally used to denote such evidence. The word 'heritage' is suggestive of an inheritance: we have inherited something of value that we should preserve and pass on to future generations. The word 'cultural' indicates that this heritage pertains to humankind and provides evidence of human intellectual development. Cultural heritage is of value both as a means of expanding the general body of knowledge about the past and for public education and enjoyment. Exactly what should be encompassed by the term is a matter of opinion and, over time, notions of the nature and extent of what should be preserved have tended to broaden. Factors such as age and rarity clearly play some part. A flint tool from the Palaeolithic era is part of the cultural heritage; a musical instrument made today, using skills that are dying out, may also be part of the cultural heritage. A mobile phone, while a commonplace item today, may form part of the cultural heritage in 100 years time. The preservation of context is also important. A flint tool, by itself, is of little interest unless we know something about where it was found, who it was used by and what it was used for.

Cultural heritage is commonly divided into two categories: tangible and intangible. Tangible cultural heritage comprises remains of human existence that are material, in the sense that we can touch them. Tangible remains can be sub-divided into movable objects, such as paintings and antiquities, and immovable buildings, monuments and sites. Intangible cultural heritage, sometimes referred to as 'living heritage', cannot be touched, but might be seen (a dance, or performance of a play or ritual) or heard (music, or a spoken language). These divisions derive from property law, and the term 'cultural property' is sometimes used synonymously with 'cultural heritage'. Tangible cultural heritage tends to be particularly associated with the monuments and works of art of Western civilization; intangible cultural heritage with the traditional ways of life, values and beliefs of the world's **indigenous peoples**.

The United Nations Educational, Scientific and Cultural Organization ('UNESCO') has been the leading force internationally in developing the field of cultural heritage protection. It has adopted a number of important international instruments, most notably the Hague Convention 1954 which is designed to protect cultural heritage threatened by armed conflict; the 1970 Convention which seeks to regulate illicit trade and transfer of ownership of cultural heritage; and the World Heritage Convention 1972, which provides protection for cultural heritage of 'outstanding universal value'. More recent UNESCO instruments have dealt with underwater cultural heritage (2001) and intangible cultural heritage (2003). The development of UNESCO's programme of work in this field reflects changing societal values and perceptions about the nature of cultural heritage, and the extent to which it warrants legal protection.

SARA DROMGOOLE

LV Prott and PJ O'Keefe, '"Cultural Heritage" or "Cultural Property"?' (1992) 1 *International Journal of Cultural Property* 307–320

D Gillman, *The Idea of Cultural Heritage* (Leicester: Institute of Art and Law, 2006)

cultural property　This term refers to artifacts considered to be of significant cultural or historical value. Typically these are monuments, archives, archaeological finds and sites, works of art and craft, and items of ethnological interest. Their value is related to claims that they have a special connection with a community, such as a nation or ethnic group, that they are integral to the identity of such a group, and that they provide significant information about a group or about humanity. '**Cultural heritage**', and its close cognate 'patrimony', are collective terms for such objects and sites. For example, an ancient Mayan sculpture may variously be valued as cultural property because Mayan civilization is claimed as ancestral precursor to some contemporary communities in central America, because it is part of a history of human artistic achievement and can thereby command a significant price in the art market, because academics study the artifact as evidence of the history and workings of Mayan society, or because such items are collected by museums.

There is disagreement over how old objects and sites need to be to qualify as cultural property. The terms 'cultural property' and 'cultural heritage' also include and frequently refer to *intangible* artifacts such as historical events and narratives, myths, and legends. Nor is the definition of what *particularly* constitutes cultural property at all static; the field of cultural heritage is characteristically one of competing claims to significance, value, and ownership. For example, a Mayan sculpture legally acquired by a European museum and held in their collections may become subject to a claim of ownership by a community or state in central America, with demands for the repatriation of the work to its claimed place origin or indigenous home.

The most significant recent international instruments dealing with cultural property are the 1970 UNESCO Convention on the Means of Prohibiting and Preventing the Illicit Import, Export and Transfer of Ownership of Cultural Property, which has 100 signatory nations, and the 1972 Convention Concerning the Protection of the World Cultural and Natural Heritage.

Pressing issues regarding cultural property include:

- the loss of ancient sites because of development or deliberate destruction;
- the looting of ancient sites and the associated illicit trade in antiquities;
- repatriation claims for cultural property to be returned to its place or people of origin;
- protective and regulatory legislation dealing with imports and exports of cultural property.

There is considerable disagreement around some key questions such as:

- ownership of cultural property—can anyone own the past?
- sovereignty—is there a place for state involvement and ownership?
- is collective ownership of cultural property defensible?
- stakeholder interests—who can claim ownership and on what grounds?
- cultural identity—how is identity connected with cultural property?
- (professional) ethics and responsibilities—how should museums deal with claims for repatriation or with the art market?

In competing claims to access and ownership, five arguments are used to justify the possession of an item of cultural property:

- identity—where the property is claimed to be part of cultural, religious, or other identity;
- origin—the item is argued to belong where it was made or comes from;
- ownership—the item is claimed as legal property;

- curation—in the absence of any other care, possession is claimed by those who have looked after an item.;
- academic expertise—a party may claim an item on the basis that they can make the most of its educational value to inform people of their heritage.

These various arguments are based on different views about the rights and responsibilities of interested parties and imply different regulatory mechanisms. Such views include:

- that collectors have a right to own pieces of the past;
- that the past should be in the care of officially sanctioned stewards or custodians (not private individuals);
- that people generally should have a protected right to preserve, foster and enrich those aspects of culture that represent their identity;
- that it is right and responsible to maximize the retention and transmission of information about the past and about culture.

The difficulty in achieving settlement of competing claims to cultural property on the basis of clear definition and regulation of such rights, responsibilities, interests, and arguments has led to the treatment of cultural property in terms of conflict resolution, with a focus not upon a specific kind of artifact or property but upon diverse local relationships with the remains of the past that beg negotiation around shared human values, such as the significance of the past for the present. MICHAEL SHANKS

cultural relativism For the cultural relativist, culture is the source of validity of all or most moral values, rules, and principles. There are and cannot be any trans-cultural or transcendent ideas of right and wrong. Premised on the belief in the incommensurability of values, in its extreme form, cultural relativism denies the possibility of external critiques of cultural practices or beliefs. This denial has particular implications for **international law**. Of contemporary relevance, and the subject of much debate at an international level, is the cultural relativist denial of the applicability of international **human rights** standards to culturally diverse societies. The defence of culture is invoked to justify opting out of or limiting the application of international standards to diverse **communities**, groups, or states.

As an anthropological doctrine, cultural relativism came to the fore in the early twentieth century, through the work of German anthropologist, Franz Boas (*Race, Language and* Culture (1940)) and later, through the work of his students, anthropologists Ruth Benedict (*Patterns of Culture* (1934)), and Melville Herskovits (*Cultural Relativism: Perspectives in Cultural Pluralism* (1972)).

Herskovits noted that where criteria to evaluate different ways of life were proposed, the question immediately arose: 'Whose standards?'. The need for a cultural relativistic point of view became apparent, he said, because of the realization that there was 'no way to play this game of making judgments across cultures except with loaded dice'.

In its early incarnations, cultural relativism was asserted as a profoundly egalitarian claim to counter beliefs in a hierarchy of '**races**'. One of the most well known assertions of cultural relativism is to be found in the American Anthropological Association's Statement on Human Rights, adopted in 1947, in opposition to the then draft Universal Declaration of Human Rights. The Statement argues that universal standards defining **human** rights were neither possible nor desirable. Standards and values were relative to the culture from which they derive. This position was motivated by a concern to respect differences, to challenge imperialist expansion, and to avoid what the Association described as the 'demoralization of human personality and the disintegration of human rights' amongst **indigenous peoples**'.

The egalitarian and anti-imperialist impulse underpinning early articulations of cultural relativism are often forgotten today. Today, cultural relativism is criticized as leading to a paralysing relativism. Critics such as Donnelly warn against cynical manipulations of 'a dying, lost, or even mythical cultural past'. Appeals to culture, it is noted, may serve to shield arbitrary exercises of power by states or powerful groups. The problem of who defines culture is also raised. Cultural relativists are criticized for their conception of culture as bounded, hermetically sealed, static. Some of the strongest criticisms of cultural relativism have come from Third World human rights activists, who reject cultural claims that seek to justify discriminatory practices.

Weaker forms of cultural relativism accept the universal validity of some norms and values (including the value of equal concern and respect), while emphasizing the need for greater sensitivity to differences in the interpretation and implementation of international standards.

In 1999, the American Anthropological Association ('AAA'), reversing its earlier position, adopted a Declaration on Anthropology and Human rights, which 'builds on' the Universal Declaration on Human Rights and principles of respect for difference.   SIOBHAN MULLALLY

See also: **universalism**

J Donnelly, 'Cultural Relativism and Universal Human Rights', in id, *Universal Human Rights in Theory and in Practice* (Ithaca, NY: Cornell UP, 1989)

S Tamale and J Oloka-Onyango, '"The Personal is Political" or Why Women's Rights are Indeed Human Rights: An African Perspective on International Feminism' (1995) 17 *Human Rights Quarterly* 691–731

curfews The curfew is a form of house arrest, designed to incapacitate offenders and prevent crime. The Curfew Order was introduced under the Criminal Justice Act 1991, section 12 and requires an offender to remain at home during specified hours. Carefully targeted, it has the power to restrain offenders at times when they are most likely to offend. By keeping them away from sources of temptation and places of risk, it has the potential to reduce opportunistic crimes such as assaults after pub-closing hours or night time burglaries. Given that curfews can only be applied for limited periods, this incapacitative effect applies only where offending is to some degree time-specific. Whether the curfew has penal qualities beyond its incapacitative effects is open to doubt. It is only minimally punitive; the degree of public censure it conveys is slight; and the pain it inflicts relatively small. Nor does the curfew have any positive reformative effect. It does not address the problems that led to the offending behaviour and may leave the offender as likely to offend at its conclusion as before. Devoid of rehabilitative content, the curfew maintains control over offenders, in the name of risk reduction and protecting the public, but does little more.

Seen positively, the curfew order is a sensible, parsimonious means of dealing with non-dangerous offenders within the community. It achieves a potentially effective form of containment at relatively little personal, social, or financial cost. Offenders remain in free society, avoid the contamination effects and stigma of imprisonment, and can maintain their home, their ties with family and friends, and their employment. They are restricted only during periods set by the court and are otherwise free to go about their life as usual. Moreover the order is extremely flexible: it can be combined with other programmes, used at any stage in the penal process from pre-trial remand to parole, and readily altered to fit changing circumstances. It has the potential to reduce the prison population and to avoid the contaminating effects of sending offenders, particularly first offenders, to prison. Under the Crime (Sentences) Act 1997 curfews became available as an alternatives to custody for fine defaulters and have greatly reduced imprisonment on default for offences that were not, in the first instance, sufficiently serious to merit a custodial sentence.

Regarded negatively, however, it is a gross invasion of personal freedom and a threat to civil liberties. Civil libertarian concerns are exacerbated by the fact that the curfew order is generally imposed in conjunction with its handmaiden, the electronic tag. If applied to those who would not otherwise have been sent to prison, then the claim that it is less intrusive and less costly is dubious. The curfew can even be said to transform the offender's home into a prison since the privacy of the home is undermined and state control intrudes. The curfew affects not only the offender but also other members of the household, turning them into fellow inmates or even quasi-warders and putting family relations under pressure.   LUCIA ZEDNER

custody of children   *see* **children and divorce**

custom as a source of law   Custom operates as a source of law in two very distinct ways, sociologically and analytically.

Sociologically, legal rules will very frequently reflect the values or social practices of the society in which they are applied. These values and practices can be described as customary insofar as they are adopted unreflectively or where their validity is justified in terms of 'the way in which we have (always) done things in the past'; and to this extent the law can be described as customary too. Also, in highly developed legal systems, many rules identified according to formal criteria may have their historical roots in social practice, and in this sense it can be said that custom is the source of the law. This is particularly the case with uncodified systems, such as the English **common law**; although since the sharp detail of the rules will rarely reflect the genuine practices of the society in any meaningful sense, it is often said that their true source is the custom of lawyers rather than the custom of society as a whole.

Analytically, highly-developed legal systems commonly recognize custom as a formal source of law alongside legislation and the like, though its role tends to be minor. The basic criteria for its recognition, found already in **Roman law**, are that there should be a long-standing practice, perhaps even an immemorial one, and that it should not be contrary to reason. In general custom is only a subsidiary source, though from time to time it has been argued that it should prevail even over express legislation to the contrary. In its most frequent manifestation in modern legal systems, as the basis of the

recognition of local practices inconsistent with the normal rules of a system or supplementary to them, there is always a degree of tension between custom and the general law. If justification for its inclusion as a source of law is needed, it is usually based on some idea of the tacit agreement of the people who are governed by it, though this is little more than a rhetorical flourish.

It is rarely possible to know in advance whether a custom will in fact be recognized as law. How long-standing the practice must be is often indeterminate, and even if it is fixed it may not be necessary to prove it. As a matter of theory, in modern English law a custom will be recognized only if it has existed continuously since 1189; but in the absence of clear contrary evidence this may be presumed, and courts are sometimes willing to adopt such a presumption on the flimsiest of bases. Equally, the requirement of reasonableness, or consonance with reason, is exceedingly vague, effectively giving to the courts a wide discretion to reject an alleged custom should they wish to do so.   DAVID IBBETSON

customary international law   Once, customary law was the most important source of law in most parts of the world—including Europe; more important than either legislation or case law. The underlying principle is that, through regular practice, what is normally done becomes not just morally or socially required, but legally binding—normative. It has been said that the greatest achievement of customary law—and certainly its most important surviving manifestation—is in the field of public international law. Customary international law is the law that emerges from the constant and uniform practice of states. For example, the practice of according immunity to foreign diplomats came to be regarded as a matter of legal obligation, not just of good manners or prudence. Not all customs date from time immemorial; the right of states to claim an 'exclusive economic zone' beyond their territorial waters crystallized within the last quarter-century or so.

In the past, customary rules developed quite slowly; but no particular time is specified for a customary rule to be formed, and it can happen quite quickly. For instance, the rule that foreign aircraft do not, in general, have a right to fly over a state's territory emerged almost immediately upon the outbreak of World War I. What is required, first of all, is that the practice should be constant and uniform. If the same state, or different states, do significantly different things, no general customary rule can emerge: thus, the fact that, in the past, some states claimed a territorial sea of three nautical miles in breadth, others of four, others of ten, and so on, prevented a general rule from emerging.

Mostly, customary rules are created by one or a few states claiming a right, and others either following suit or acquiescing in the claim, either expressly or tacitly, until there is a sufficiently widespread and representative practice—as with the exclusive economic zone, for instance. Unanimity is not required: if some states simply do nothing, perhaps because they do not have a particular interest in the activity concerned, a rule will still emerge. Furthermore, it will be binding on them, even though they did nothing. However if, whilst the practice is in the process of developing, some states (or even a single state) who are significant actors in the particular field oppose the rule, then it will not come into being. This is what might be called the strong form of the 'persistent objector rule'. A weaker form is that, even if the objecting state is not sufficiently significant in the field to prevent the general rule emerging, that state can exclude itself, by its protests, from the scope of the rule. It is important to note that the persistent objection, in both cases, must take place whilst the rule is emerging: after it has crystallized, it is too late.

It is noticeable that some of these criteria are lacking in precision: no specific time is required for a customary rule to emerge; it depends on there being a 'substantial and sufficiently representative' number of participants, and so on. But this is the nature of the customary process: unlike legislation or adjudication, for instance, where specific majorities and procedural steps are stipulated.

It is often said that, as well a practice that meets the criteria already described, there must also be a 'subjective element' in the form of acceptance or recognition: the so-called *opinio juris sive necessitatis*. Often it is indeed present: an established rule is recognized as such. But it is more doubtful that this is a necessary ingredient. The subjective element can play a negative role, however: if a practice is regarded as just being one of politeness or morality, for instance, it will not be legally binding.

What has been described above is general customary law, binding on all states (subject to the 'persistent objector' exception). But it is also possible, as the **International Court of Justice** has recognized, for particular customary rules to exist, which bind only some states. Thus a bilateral customary rule was held to exist concerning a right of passage over Indian territory to reach Portuguese enclaves; and it was also recognized—at least in principle—that there could be regional customary rules peculiar to Latin-American states. Particular customary rules need not be geographically localized: it is also possible for groups of states with, say, a political or economic affinity, to adopt a practice amongst themselves that diverges from a more general rule.

Largely for political reasons, it has been incorrectly argued by some that resolutions of the **United Nations** General Assembly can create a sort of 'instant customary law'. They can (but do not necessarily) declare existing law; and sometimes, they can influence the direction in which state practice evolves, so that they are indirectly an historic source of a customary rule. Some of the most well-known General Assembly declarations, such as that on Friendly Relations between States, or Self-Determination, fall into one or both categories. But whether one either of these processes has occurred can only be determined by examining the evidence in each case; and certainly there have been major resolutions, such as those on the 'New International Economic Order', that have not had this effect.

The same is true of **treaties**. A treaty can be declaratory of existing customary law; but not necessarily, and indeed not usually. Again, it can happen that even non-parties to a treaty develop a practice along the same lines as what is required by the treaty, so that a new customary rule emerges. This happened, for example, in the case of the abolition of privateering (a type of state-licensed piracy). But it would be a serious mistake to assume that what is in a treaty is necessarily customary law, for very often, it is not.

As a general rule, if a treaty is concluded covering the same ground as an existing customary rule, the treaty will prevail. Compared to the position from the seventeenth to nineteenth centuries, the importance of customary international law has diminished as treaties have occupied the field to an increasing extent. Sometimes this is because the subject matter is new and no (or few) relevant customary rules have emerged. Examples are international trade; human rights; and the regime of outer space. Secondly, even where there is an established body of customary law, states (either states generally, or just some states) may agree on a different regime: for instance, the various treaties of the **European Union**, and (to some extent) the provisions of the United Nations Charter on the use of force. Sometimes, too, existing customary law has been 'codified' in a multilateral treaty, often drawn up in the first instance by the **International Law Commission** of the United Nations. Examples include conventions on the law of treaties and on diplomatic relations. It is naturally rare for codification to be attempted where the customary law is already clear and uncontroversial: the effort would be unnecessary. But it can happen that parts of the law are unclear; or that parts need 'progressive development', even if others are uncontroversial. So, for instance, the Law of the Sea Convention 1982 in part restated existing customary law; in part restated existing treaty (but not customary) law; and in part made wholly new (treaty) law.

Despite the increasing role of treaties in the modern world, customary international law is still important. First, it is rare for all states to accede even to treaties with a universal vocation: and if a state is not party to the relevant treaty, what will prevail between it and other non-parties, and equally between it and the parties, is customary law, not the treaty (which can only bind parties to it). Secondly, it sometimes happens that a practice grows up as to how a treaty is to be applied or interpreted—the new rule can be regarded as a (type of) customary rule. It occasionally also happens that, by practice, as treaty provision is in effect amended or repealed—though this is rare. Finally, there remain important areas of international law that still remain uncodified by treaty. Cases in point include the rules relating to international legal personality; recognition; sovereignty over territory; state jurisdiction; and **state responsibility**.

Furthermore, customary international law plays an important role in domestic law. In numerous national legal systems, treaties are only part of the law if they have been specifically incorporated through legislation. By contrast, in very many countries customary international law is automatically part of the law of the land, and is applied as such by the courts. Usually, this is subject to there not being any conflicting national legislation; but in some systems customary international rules are on a par with, or occasionally even superior to, legislation. There have been numerous important cases in domestic courts in recent years that have turned wholly or in part on customary international law.

In short, this ancient source of international law is still alive and well.　　　MAURICE MENDELSON

See also: **custom as a source of law**

customary law　Customary law arises when the members of a **community** adopt habitual forms of conduct in social life and these customs become generally regarded as obligatory in that community. Customary law, also referred to as 'folk law' and 'living law', exists as social fact, the subject matter of legal anthropology. It may be contrasted with **legislation**, which is formally created, usually in writing, by a specific **person** or a body of persons with law-making power. Customary law does not necessarily accord with the common interests of all members of the community. Some classes, such as older men or aristocratic lineages, may have disproportionate influence on its content. It differs also from religious law, which is believed to rest on divine authority.

Customary law existed before states and state laws. The legal institutions of some states, such as those of Western Europe, sought initially to enforce this independently existing customary law, although later laws made by state institutions replaced much customary law. In regions outside Europe colonizing European powers required the state administrations which they had created to apply their laws (or, in British colonies, English law). In territories where the indigenous populations outnumbered European settlers, these colonial state legal systems were also required to enforce the customary laws of the local ethnic and religious groups in some areas of social life such as **marriage** and land tenure. Especially in British colonies, including a large part of Africa and South Asia, 'native laws and customs' became parts of state law, and have generally remained so after Independence. In territories where the indigenous populations were smaller than the colonial settler populations, such as North America, Australia, and Latin America, indigenous customary laws were largely ignored by the state until, in the past half-century, these states also came to recognize 'native', 'First Nation', 'Aboriginal', or **indigenous laws**. 'Recognized' customary laws have been subject to re-interpretation, adjustment, and amendment by **judges** and other state officials. Thus there have emerged 'lawyers' customary laws' which differ from the popularly observed customary laws. State legal doctrine has sometimes asserted that the only true customary law is that recognized by the state, but this is hardly sustainable empirically.

The usual understanding of customary law, as arising from social practices within a community, suggests that there are many different bodies of customary law in the modern world in addition to those of indigenous ethnic communities. Even legal doctrine recognizes some customary law as a component of **international law**, as well as a transnational *lex mercatoria*. There are also customary laws of immigrant ethnic groups, medical and various other professions, corporate groups ranging from commercial corporations to religious institutions and **trade unions**, various transnational communities, communities of prison inmates, participants in various sports (again often transnational), and military formations. Religious laws may often be derived only in part from religious doctrine and partly from custom. **Legal pluralism** is thus ubiquitous. In cases of conflict, people may often follow non-state customary law in preference to state law.

Further, the state and non-state law dichotomy may need reconsideration. Not all state law is legislation. Even in state law, **precedent**, and the elaborate techniques of interpreting and applying precedent and legislation, are generally not explicitly set out, but are rather determined by customary practices of the legal professions. Beyond this, even a formal legislature can be effective only if **subjects** of the state observe a customary 'rule of **recognition**' defining valid law. Thus arguably state law rests ultimately on customary law.   GORDON WOODMAN

E Ehrlich, *Fundamental Principles of the Sociology of Law*, trans. W L Moll, (Cambridge Mass.: Harvard University Press, 1936)

A Dundes Renteln and A Dundes (eds), *Folk Law: Essays in the Theory and Practice of Lex Non Scripta* (New York: Garland, 1994)

customary law and the treatment of criminals
Customary law is the complex of law-like norms and sanctions considered to influence the behaviour of **indigenous peoples** in colonized settings. As such it is the product of colonialism rather than the written-down forms of law of the peoples whose lands British colonists came to occupy. While indigenous (or First) peoples in the settler societies of North America and Australasia were commonly treated as British **subjects** after declarations of **sovereignty**, their liability for **prosecution** for offences committed between themselves (*inter se*) was often uncertain. Even where jurisdiction was clear, the consequences of making indigenous offenders liable frequently produced uncertainty in criminal justice procedure. A common result was under-policing and infrequent prosecution.

The rise of anthropology and the refinement of colonial administration into an art of government contributed to more consistent prosecution of *inter se* offences during the twentieth century. Anthropological knowledge made accessible a greater understanding of the cultural context of some offending. Innovative jurists and policy-makers responded by proposing the use of 'tribal assessors' (as, for example, in the subordinate **courts** in colonial Africa), advisers chosen from among indigenous elders to counsel the court on the contexts of offending and the relevance of sanctions, as well as recommending the mitigation of conventional penalties. In much altered form each of these changes has remained influential in contemporary criminal justice policy in many jurisdictions.

While often misinterpreted in popular media as an excuse for crime, the invocation of customary law as a context for offending has most commonly taken place in **sentencing** policy. In the Australian territories of Papua and New Guinea, in the early twentieth century, the mandatory sentence of death for murder was usually commuted to a short term of imprisonment, in acknowledgement of the 'payback' context of many killings. A similar principle informed the statutory amendment in Australia's Northern Territory in 1934 relieving the Court, 'where an Aboriginal native is convicted of murder', of the obligation to pronounce a sentence of death and allowing it to consider evidence of 'any relevant native law or custom' in determining an appropriate penalty.

Insisting on the authority of a single sovereign law, superior courts nevertheless continue to acknowledge the relevance of other legal obligations and contexts affecting the lives of those brought before the criminal courts. Consequently sentencing argument may refer to the need to consider the relevance of customary law to an estimation of the gravity of the offence charged. Such law may include practices such as promised **marriage**, prohibitions on access to places or knowledge considered secret or sacred, and the obligation to carry out physical **punishment** of offenders against custom. Mitigation of penalty has also taken place in circumstances where evidence was adduced of the defendant having already (or being likely to in the future) suffered a customary punishment for the offence.

While juridical pronouncements in the course of sentencing decisions and appeals judgments make up much of the contemporary understanding of customary law, some governments have investigated ways of recognizing forms of customary law, subject to the repugnancy condition that these be consistent with the rights of individuals at **common law** and, increasingly, **international law**. The development of the 'restorative justice' movement has highlighted the contribution that can be made to developing alternative sanctions from the cultural traditions of indigenous peoples in common law countries.

MARK FINNANE

M Chanock, *Law, Custom, and Social Order: the Colonial Experience in Malawi and Zambia* (Cambridge and New York: Cambridge University Press, 1985)

H Douglas, 'Customary Law, Sentencing and the Limits of the State' 20/1 *Canadian Journal of Law and Society* (2005) 141–156

customs union   *see* **free movement in the EU**

D

damages Damages are a monetary remedy awarded by the court to a successful claimant, eg in an action in tort or for a breach of contract. Strictly speaking, the term does not extend to other monetary court awards in which the claim is for a liquidated (ie fixed) amount, eg claims for the repayment of a debt, unpaid wages or salary, or the purchase price of goods that have been returned to the seller. These are frequently referred to as 'money claims'. Damages, by contrast, are in an amount determined by the court, normally as an assessment of the claimant's losses, and not a sum specified by the claimant.

Damages are usually compensatory, designed to make good a loss suffered by the claimant as the result of conduct for which the defendant is responsible. The aim is to put the claimant in the position he or she would have been in if the conduct had not occurred. The losses that may be compensated vary according to the nature of the defendant's liability, but typically include the cost of repairing damaged property, and/or diminution in its value, and losses consequent upon personal injury, eg **pain and suffering**, loss of amenity, loss of earnings and medical costs. As can be seen, economic loss consequential upon property damage or personal injury may also be included in the typical award of damages. But where damages are sought for pure economic loss (ie economic loss not consequent upon property damage or personal injury) much more depends on the nature of the liability, with (eg) damages for breach of contract routinely extending to such loss and damages in tort routinely excluding them.

A distinction frequently employed by practitioners is between special and general damages. In this context, special damages are financial losses suffered by the claimant before trial or such other time at which the damages are to be assessed. Special damages are deemed to be capable of precise calculation and must normally be specifically itemized in the claimant's schedule of damages. General damages refer to all other losses for which the claimant seeks compensation, which can be divided into non-pecuniary losses (eg pain and suffering) and future pecuniary losses (eg post-trial loss of earnings). General damages are not capable of precise calculation and do not have to be itemized in the initial schedule of damages because they are presumed to flow from the conduct for which the defendant is liable.

Exceptionally, the measure of damages may be other than compensatory. The following alternative measures of damages may also on occasion be applied: (1) nominal damages—these acknowledge that the claimant has suffered a legal wrong or the infringement of his or her right in a case where no resulting loss can be established; (2) contemptuous damages—these are similar to nominal damages except that they carry the implication that the claimant, though technically in the right, ought not to have pursued his or her claim, and the award is typically expressed to be in the amount of 'the smallest coin in the realm'; (3) punitive or exemplary damages—these are designed to punish misconduct by public officials, the calculated commission of a legal wrong in circumstances where the defendant reckoned on making a profit in excess of any liability in compensatory damages, and other wrongdoing specified by statute; (4) aggravated damages—these are awarded where the claimant's loss is increased by the defendant's misconduct, including his or her misconduct during the course of the litigation, and for that reason are considered by some to be partly compensatory in nature and partly punitive; and (5) restitutionary damages—these are awarded to make the defendant give up some advantage gained at the claimant's expense (**unjust enrichment**). Use of the last-mentioned term is disputed: some writers prefer the term 'disgorgement damages', and others question whether a gain-based remedy can properly be called 'damages' at all. At the present time, the award of restitutionary damages is exceptional in cases of both tort and breach of contract.

Damages are normally assessed on a once-and-for-all basis and paid in a single lump sum. Where the claimant's loss is continuing, the court must estimate its likely extent in the period after judgment. There is generally no opportunity to revise the assessment if the estimate proves to be wrong, and the award therefore turns out to be either too great or too small. However, three exceptional types of award must be noted. (1) Interim damages represent a reasonable proportion of the likely final award, and may be awarded in a case where the defendant's liability has been established or is clear to the court's satisfaction, provided the claim is against an insured person or a public body. (2) Provisional damages may be awarded in exceptional cases where there is a chance that the claimant will develop a serious disease or suffer a serious deterioration in his physical or mental condition after the end of proceedings. The procedure is for the court to award damages in two stages: first, on the hypothesis that the specified disease or deterioration will not take place, and, secondly, if the specified disease or deterioration occurs. (3) Periodical Payment Orders ('PPOs'): since 2005, courts have been empowered to award damages for personal injury in the form of periodical payments, and indeed must consider whether periodical payments would be preferable to the traditional lump sum where it awards damages for future pecuniary loss arising from personal injury. In making this decision, the claimant's needs are paramount. This new power reflects the existing practice in respect of structured settlements (agreements between the parties that damages should be paid on a periodical basis) but the court now has the power to require periodical payments even if the parties object. Periodical payments may be awarded for duration of the claimant's life or some other period ordered by the court, and may continue after the claimant's death, usually at a reduced rate, for the benefit of his or her dependants. Variable PPOs may be made in the same circumstances as an award of provisional damages. The reform reduces the possibility that the award will turn out to be too great or too small because of events after the close of proceedings, but does not eliminate all the uncertainties associated with traditional lump sums.   KEN OLIPHANT

McGregor on Damages (London: Sweet & Maxwell, 17th edn, 2003)

See also: **contract law; remedies; tort law**

data protection The increase in the amount of personal information held in electronic form by public and private bodies is a threat to personal privacy. In the modern world, vast amounts of data including payroll details, medical files, taxation information, credit, social security, and criminal records are processed and held by corporations and public authorities. In the United Kingdom, the Data Protection Act 1998 ('DPA') regulates the processing (obtaining, holding, transferring) of such information as well as its use and disclosure. The issue of **privacy** and free movement of personal data across borders has been the subject of concern to both the Council of Europe and the **European Union** for some time. Indeed, the catalyst for the DPA 1998, which replaced earlier UK legislation, was the EC Data Protection Directive 1995, which imposes a duty upon Member States 'to protect the fundamental rights and freedoms of natural persons and, in particular, their right to privacy with respect to the processing of formal data'. More recently, the European Union has addressed the protection of data and privacy in the advanced digital technologies such as the internet and mobile telephone networks in the Directive on Privacy and Electronic Communications 2002.

Subject to a number of qualifications and exemptions, the DPA gives individuals a right of access to personal data or information held about themselves. Such data must be communicated to the individual in a form that is capable of being understood. Personal data is defined widely and may include computerized or paper records. An individual can prevent or require the cessation of processing of data, which is causing, or is likely to cause, damage or substantial distress. Where personal information held is shown to be inaccurate a court may order correction or erasure of the offending material. Compensation may be recovered if an individual suffers damage resulting from a breach of the DPA by a data controller (the person who determines the purpose for processing the personal data).

The 'data protection principles' of the DPA consist of obligations with which any data controller must comply. These principles are set out in a detailed manner and provide that personal data shall be: fairly and lawfully processed; obtained for a specified and limited purpose and the individual concerned notified; adequate, relevant, and not excessive given its purpose; accurate and kept up-to-date; retained for no longer than necessary; processed in line with the individuals' rights; secure; and not transferred to other countries without adequate protection. Stricter restrictions apply where 'sensitive personal data' are being processed. Information about race, political opinions, religion or philosophical beliefs, trade union membership, health, sexual life, and criminal proceedings against the individual are 'sensitive data' and subject to special rules. There are many exemptions from the administrative machinery that the DPA has established to ensure that the 'data protection principles' are observed. They include exemptions from particular provisions in order to protect national security, to prevent crime, to assess or collect tax. Further exemptions allow processing for journalistic, literary, and artistic purposes: an attempt to reconcile the tension between the right to privacy and freedom of expression.

The Information Commissioner oversees the 'data protection principles' and, if satisfied that any are being breached, may issue an 'enforcement notice' requiring the data processor (any person who processes the data on behalf of the data controller) to take remedial action. The Commissioner also has the power, on the request of an individual affected by an unlawful processing of data, to require the data processor to provide the information necessary to assess whether or not there has been a breach; but this is restricted where the journalistic, literary, and artistic purposes exemption is engaged. There is a right of appeal to the Information Tribunal and a further appeal to the High Court on a point of law.

Significant protection for individuals and their personal information is contained in the technical and complex DPA. New technologies, however, continue to emerge and the DPA has failed to keep up with the reality of present day data processing. **CCTV** data remains largely unregulated even though the UK has over four million cameras in operation. The National DNA Database has been expanded: samples can be taken and retained following **arrest** for any recordable offence. These samples are retained regardless of whether there is any conviction or charge. New concerns about mass data retention and the creation of 'data trails' have emerged from government proposals on ID cards and road pricing. Processes such as 'data mining' (mass automated data is processed to see whether any characteristics or behaviours are exposed) are utilized to justify specific and more intrusive surveillance. Further legislation is needed to protect the right to privacy and data protection.

STEPHANIE PALMER

See also: **personal information, access to**

databases Collections of information in hardcopy form, such as business directories, have long been protected by **copyright** law as 'compilations', ie a type of original literary work. The development of information technology enabled vast collections of information to be electronically stored and processed. These types of collections became known as 'databases', and it was uncertain whether they would qualify for protection as 'compilations'. The distribution of databases initially occurred via tangible media, such as CD-Roms and DVD-Roms, but increasingly databases were distributed via digital networks, such as the internet. As a result, it became harder for database producers to prevent third parties from copying and re-using data without permission.

To provide clear and strong protection for databases, and in order to stimulate investment in database production within the Europe, the European Union ('EU') adopted a Directive on the Legal Protection of Databases ('Database Directive'). This legislation had to be implemented within EU Member States by 1 January 1998, a deadline which the UK met.

The Database Directive sought to achieve two objectives. The first was to harmonize copyright law protection of databases within the **European Union**. This was thought necessary because EU Member States took varied approaches to copyright protection of databases, particularly in relation to the originality requirement. For example, the UK adopted an originality test of 'labour, skill and judgment', whereas Germany applied a higher test of 'personal intellectual creation'. The second objective was to establish a new *sui generis* (ie unique) right for databases to protect against misappropriation of the investment involved in their making.

Although the Directive deals with two separate rights—copyright and the *sui generis* right—the definition of 'database' is common to both and refers to 'a collection of independent works, data or other materials arranged in a systematic or methodical way and individually accessible by electronic or other means'. This is an extremely broad definition, however, it does not include computer programs, nor does it include individual films, literary works, or musical works.

In the UK, copyright protection now extends to 'databases' as a type of literary work. The database must satisfy an originality requirement of 'author's own intellectual creation'. This standard is higher than 'labour, skill and judgment' and probably excludes from protection mundane compilations, such as telephone directories. Protection extends to prohibiting third parties from copying, adapting, or distributing or renting the whole or substantial part of the database without permission. When it comes to assessing infringement, it is important to note, however, that protection extends only to the selection or arrangement of the database contents, and not to the contents themselves. Thus, the headings and order of a yellow pages directory would be protected as part of the database, but not the individual entries. Protection lasts for seventy years after the author's death.

A *sui generis* right arises where there has been substantial investment in obtaining, verifying, or presenting the contents of a database. Investment can include financial resources and intellectual effort. However, investment in creation of database materials is excluded from consideration. The database maker, ie the person who takes the initiative in obtaining, verifying, or presenting the database contents and assumes the risk of investment, can prevent third parties from extracting or re-utilizing all or a substantial part of the database contents. Extraction refers to the permanent or temporary transfer of contents to another medium by any means or in any form, and is not limited to the first removal of data. Re-utilization covers most forms of communication to the public and is not limited to first publication of data. A substantial part of the database contents can be either a large amount (quantitatively substantial) or a part reflecting significant investment (qualitatively substantial). Repeated and systematic extraction or re-utilization of insubstantial parts of the databases contents may also infringe where the purpose is to reconstitute the whole or a substantial part of the database contents. Protection lasts for fifteen years from the time the database was completed or made available to the public, although new investment resulting in a substantial change to the database may trigger a further fifteen-year term. Lawful users of a database may extract a substantial part of the database contents where it is for non-commercial teaching or research purposes and the source is indicated.　　　　TANYA APLIN

death duties　*see* **inheritance tax**

death in the family, legal consequences　Once a death certificate has been issued the recipient can arrange burial or cremation. Normally only spouses, civil partners, or other relatives can deal with the body of the deceased. Except when appointed as an executor, a cohabitant has no right to arrange for the burial or cremation of a partner. Family members can overrule the wishes of the deceased to be an organ donor.

Parents with **parental responsibility** can appoint a guardian in the event of death. However, if there is a surviving parent with parental responsibility the appointment will only come into effect after the death of both parties. In Scotland the appointment comes into effect straight away and parent and guardian share responsibility.

The deceased is under no obligation to make specific provision for anyone in a will. However, if he has left a will without providing for a family member, application for provision can be made under the Inheritance (Provision for Family and Dependants) Act 1975. There is no **legislation** corresponding to this in Scotland. **Divorce** or the dissolution of a **civil partnership** does not automatically revoke a will.

Applicants must apply within six months of grant of probate if claiming under the Inheritance (Provision for Family and Dependants) Act 1975. Spouses, civil partners, and dependants can all make a claim. Cohabitants can only claim if they have been living in the same household as the deceased for at least two years. All applicants must show that they have not received reasonable financial provision from the estate. Spouses and civil partners have to show what provision it would be reasonable to receive in all the circumstances, whether or not it is required for their maintenance. However, to be successful, all other applicants can only show they require provision for their **maintenance** alone. Able-bodied adult children will normally have to show the deceased owed them an obligation or **responsibility** in order to succeed.

Where the family home is jointly owned, the survivor will automatically inherit it, but if it is in the sole name of the deceased then it is subject to the rules of intestacy. If a person dies intestate, the Administration of Estates Act 1925 provides that where there is a spouse or civil partner and children, the survivor has the right to a statutory legacy of £125,000 plus a life interest in half the remainder. The rest goes to direct descendants. If there are no direct descendants, the legacy increases to £200,000 and an absolute interest in half the remainder, the rest to other family members. If there is no spouse or civil partner, the Act lists who inherits in order. Cohabitants are not included in any of the intestacy provisions. In Scotland the amounts are more generous and there is a broad **discretion** to award cohabitants reasonable provision under the Family Law (Scotland) Act 2006.

If the home is a private tenancy, the tenancy agreement with the landlord will dictate what happens. If it is a council tenancy a spouse, civil partner, or cohabitant who had a settled relationship with the deceased, can apply for the tenancy to be transferred into her own name.　　　　CATHY WILLIAMS

death penalty　*see* **capital punishment**

deaths in custody　A 'death in custody' denotes a situation where a **person** dies in **police** or **prison** custody. Most deaths occur in prison custody and most are self-inflicted. A death in prison custody includes deaths that occur in prison or in juvenile detention facilities, and deaths that occur during transfer to and from such facilities or while in medical facilities under the prison authority. A death in police custody may involve a situation where the deceased was arrested or detained by police. These are referred to as deaths in institutional settings (such as deaths in police stations, police vehicles, or during transfers to or from hospitals or other settings). Deaths in police custody may also occur during custody-related police operations. These include situations such as sieges, clandestine operations, stop and search operations, or police pursuits.

The issue of whether the person was in custody when they died will be uncontentious in many cases. However, it is also important to acknowledge a grey area around deaths in custody, particularly in relation to police operations, or where the custody is illegal, or in cases where a person is out of custody at the time of death but dies from injuries received whilst in custody. There is also the question of whether to define deaths in custody narrowly in terms of policy or prison custody or broadly, to encompass deaths in mental hospitals, military prisons, and immigration detention facilities. For example nearly 100 deaths of prisoners occurred in US military custody in Iraq and Afghanistan between the end of 2002 and early 2006.

Deaths in custody are subject to a public inquest by a **coroner**. The coroner is required to determine the medical cause of death, to draw attention to particular circumstances surrounding the death, and to make recommendations where appropriate to prevent future deaths. There are also other investigations conducted depending on the nature of the death. For example in Britain, the Independent Police Complaints Commission is responsible for investigations into deaths in police custody.

Why is there particular concern about deaths in custody? The UK Parliamentary Committee on **Human Rights** (2004) succinctly stated the issue: 'When the state takes away a person's liberty, it assumes full **responsibility** for protecting their **human** rights. The most fundamental of these is the **right to life**'. When people lose their liberty they are by definition placed in a vulnerable situation. State authorities have a particular duty of care in these situations. International human rights standards guarantee a right to life and freedom from **torture** and cruel, inhuman, and degrading treatment. There is a positive obligation to prevent deaths in custody and to protect people from **violence** and serious neglect.

There are many issues arising from deaths in custody which need addressing, including the over-representation of racial and ethnic minorities and people with mental illnesses, and problems with substance abuse. There are basic questions about prison overcrowding and the provision of adequate health care. There is also research which suggests the quality of prison life can have an important influence on reducing deaths in custody. Organizations involved in monitoring deaths in custody include Inquest (UK) and Amnesty International.

CHRIS CUNNEEN

debt and structural adjustment Between 1970 and 1999, there was a thirty-fold increase in the debt owed by sovereign developing countries, from $56 billion in 1970 to $1.6 trillion in 1999. The increase was even greater for the International Financial Institutions ('IFIs') including the World Bank (*www.worldbank.org*) and the International Monetary Fund ('IMF') (*www.imf.org*), with IMF debt increasing 100-fold. Some developing countries, especially the Asian 'Tigers' such as Taiwan and Singapore, and more recently, China and India, escaped debt and developed at rapid rates. However, even relatively rich countries such as Argentina have not escaped crises. The worst affected have been predominantly African 'Heavily Indebted Poor Countries' ('HIPC'). The burden of servicing debts had grown enormously and, for some, consumed more than half export earnings, making it impossible to escape balance of payments crises and poverty.

While bad government, corruption, and mismanagement undoubtedly bore **responsibility**, spiralling debt resulted from oil price rises and recycling through injudicious lending by Western Banks of deposited oil country wealth. Other factors included the worsening of commodity prices, enormous increases in interest rates, and activities of financial speculators.

Massive global public protests signified by campaigns such as *Jubilee 2000* (*www.jubileedebtcampaign.org.uk*) pressured developed country governments and international institutions to respond, but slowly and fitfully through structural adjustment programmes ('SAPs') and debt rescheduling measures. SAPs involve new loans and lowering of interest rates on existing loans by the IFIs. In return, countries agree to 'conditionalities' which require them to reduce trade and investment barriers, privatize state enterprises, deregulate, concentrate on export led growth, substitute indirect for direct taxes, reduce state social expenditure, and balance budgets. These had mixed success and provoked substantial criticism. From the 1990s, greater emphasis was placed on 'good **governance**' reforms including improvement of legal and anti-corruption machinery. Continuing criticisms led to a remodelled

IMF **Poverty Reduction** and Growth Facility and the World Bank's Poverty Reduction Strategy Credits. To be eligible, governments are required under Bank guidance to develop Poverty Reduction Strategy Papers ('PRSPs') (*www.worldbank.org/prsp*) in consultation with civil society. However, in practice, there has been no change in the fundamental global market orientation, and while PRSPs emphasize 'local ownership', in practice they involve intrusive IFI involvement in social and economic policy.

It was assumed that 'structural adjustment' would lead to economic growth and finance debt repayment. In the meantime, temporary debt relief measures emphasized 'debt rescheduling'. This involves increasing the repayment period and reducing the rate of interest on existing loans and new money lent to service debts. Western creditors are the main beneficiaries of debt rescheduling as they continue to get repayment on loans which would be lost through inability or refusal to pay.

Another response to debt is 'forgiveness' or cancellation. The HIPC initiative which was extended in 2005–2006 to the Multilateral Debt Relief Initiative ('MDRI') involves practical recognition that the debt burden of the HIPCs undermined their development potential. The MDRI provides for 100 per cent debt forgiveness of IMF, World Bank, and African Development Bank debts of HIPC countries which meet conditionalities.

While much of the poorest countries' debt is owed to donor governments of the 'Paris Club' and the IFIs, other countries owe large debts to private corporations who reschedule debts through the 'London Club'. Countries cannot declare insolvency, but developing countries as 'sovereign' governments are reluctant to default on debts. However, in 2004, when Argentina after a major crisis proposed unilateral rescheduling of its enormous debt burden, most of the creditors agreed a settlement which effectively forgives 60 per cent of debts.   ABDUL PALIWALA

Jubilee 2002, *Beginner's Guide to Debt Crisis* (London: Jubilee, *http://www.jubileeresearch.org/analysis/reports/beginners_guide/debt.htm*)
N Woods, *The Globalizers: The IMF, the World Bank and their Borrowers* (Ithaca: Cornell UP, 2006)

debt finance   Borrowing money is a tax-efficient way of raising capital for companies. Debt finance is available from a number of sources, and should be distinguished from equity finance, which can be described as the contribution shareholders make to companies in return for the issue to them of **shares** in the **company**. Equity holders receive a return on their investment through **dividends**, whereas debt

financiers are entitled to repayment of the capital sum plus an amount representing interest, so that, unlike shareholders, there is a 'ceiling' on the amount a debt financier can expect to receive from the company. Freedom of contract allows the lender and borrower to decide the terms of any loan and the **courts** tend not to interfere in such agreements.

Methods of raising debt finance vary enormously, from traditional lending or overdraft facilities from a single source (usually a bank), to syndicated loans, where a number of finance providers collaborate to offer what is often a very large loan (a common source of project finance). An important question in relation to debt finance is whether the loan in question is secured or unsecured. An unsecured creditor must rely on the corporate debtor's promise to repay the principal sum and any interest, whereas a secured creditor bargains for rights enforceable against assets owned by the company. In the event of corporate **insolvency**, secured creditors can assert these rights in priority to unsecured creditors.

SANDRA FRISBY

E Ferran, *Company Law and Corporate Finance* (Oxford: Oxford University Press, 1999), 457–481

deception   *see* **criminal regulation of property relations; fraud, honesty and markets**

decolonization   For many centuries a number of mainly European countries controlled a different territory from their own, with that territory being known as a colony. This control usually began by force and then continued by the administration of the territory and people from a distance, with a governor (or a similar official), appointed by the colonial power, having legal power in that territory. Particularly after the founding of the **United Nations** in 1945, colonial powers came under increasing pressure to allow the people of the colonies to decide for themselves how they wished to be governed. This became known as the right of self-determination for peoples.

In 1960 the United Nations agreed on a Declaration on the Granting of Independence to Colonial Territories and Peoples, in which 'the necessity of bringing to a speedy and unconditional end colonialism in all its forms and manifestations' was proclaimed, and by which it was declared that 'the subjection of peoples to alien subjugation, domination and exploitation constitutes a denial of fundamental human rights, is contrary to the Charter of the United Nations and is an impediment to the promotion of world peace and co-operation'. This

Declaration, together with other international actions, added political and legal weight to the growing demands within colonies for self-government. The process by which the colonies became self-governing, which was usually by independence, is known as decolonization. One clear consequence of decolonization has been that about 100 states have come into existence from what were once colonies.

ROBERT MCCORQUODALE

deductions from pay *see* **wages and deductions**

deed A deed is a formal document which is commonly used to transfer property or to record an agreement between people. Many transactions, eg transfers of freehold land, legal mortgages, and leases for more than three years, are required by statute to be contained in a deed. Historically, deeds would often be written on vellum or parchment, though the use of paper became common by the nineteenth century. To have legal force, a deed must be validly executed. In English law this meant (until 1991) that it must have been signed, sealed, and delivered. In Scots law most deeds did not require to be sealed, but instead had to be signed in the presence of witnesses. Historically there were two types of deed: the indenture (a deed between two or more parties) and the deed-poll (a deed executed by one person—still used today when a person wishes to announce a change of name).

The requirement of English law that a seal was necessary was changed (for deeds executed by individuals) by the Law of Property (Miscellaneous Provisions) Act 1989, which provided that a deed must (a) make it clear on its face that it is intended to be a deed, and (b) must be signed, witnessed, and delivered. Seals may still be used for some deeds executed by corporations.

The use of deeds to transfer land will change dramatically when electronic **conveyancing** is introduced: electronic documents bearing electronic signatures will be regarded as 'deeds'.

PETER LUTHER

defamation *see* **criminal libel; libel; libel trials; slander**

default judgment A default judgment is a procedure to meet the situation where the defendant simply does not respond to a claim. It relieves the claimant of any more process or delay before obtaining judgment. In the **Civil Procedure Rules 1998 (CPR)** Part 12 it is defined as 'judgment without trial where a defendant (a) has failed to file an acknowledgment of service; or (b) has failed to file a defence'.

A defence must generally be filed within fourteen days after service of the particulars of claim, which must be served on the defendant within fourteen days after the service of the claim form; but if the defendant has filed an acknowledgement of service then the defence may be filed within twenty-eight days after service of the particulars.

A default judgment is not available on a claim for delivery of goods subject to an agreement regulated by the Consumer Credit Act 1974, nor where the claimant uses the alternative (simpler) claims procedure under CPR Part 8, nor in any case where default judgment is precluded by a specific practice direction (for example in contentious probate proceedings).

A default judgment is also unavailable if the defendant has applied to have the claimant's statement of case struck out or for summary judgment and any such application has not been disposed of, nor if the defendant has satisfied the whole claim (including any claim for costs), nor in a claim for money if the defendant has filed an admission together with a request for time to pay.

JOHN FITZPATRICK

defence of claims Defendants tend to get a bad press in civil litigation. It is, of course, entirely understandable that an aggrieved party thinks that they have a conclusive case that should be conceded without dispute, so that any delay or questioning is merely time-wasting or pettifogging. However, it is of the essence of the **adversarial system** of justice in the United Kingdom that the person who is making a claim must prove their case. Defendants are not only entitled to test this: they may have competing obligations or interests that require them to do so.

The civil justice system is like an iceberg: 90 per cent of it is invisible because it consists of claims that collapse or settle. This tendency has become even more marked in the UK since the implementation of the Woolf procedural reforms (which are so-called because Lord Woolf chaired the inquiry that led to their introduction in 1999). However, law is made by the cases that come to court, go to judgment, and are recorded in **law reports**. It is important to realize that these cases do not define the system: they are cases that the system has been unable to deal with because they raise some novel point of law or evidence that means they cannot be dealt with in the normal fashion. For the most part, lawyers prefer to settle than to go to court. Trials increase costs, introduce uncertainty about outcomes, and may lead to decisions that destabilize well-established arrangements for negotiating settlements.

The defence of claims reflects an interaction between claimant and defendant. Claims between individual and individual are uncommon, although they may be very bitter because of their emotional content, as in the case of neighbour disputes. Even where individuals are involved in the event that leads to a claim, such as a workplace or road traffic accident, their cases are normally managed by corporate actors, such as insurance companies and trades unions. When this happens, claims cease to be considered as unique events affecting individuals and are managed in accord with an economic rationality. This often frustrates individuals with a strong sense of grievance or with a reputation at stake, but is the inevitable result of their claim being taken over by professionals who see it as one of a class, to be dealt with according to corporate rather than individual priorities.

Typically, for example, insurers are concerned about efficiency. While they have a responsibility to the people they insure, they also have a responsibility to their shareholders, the people who have subscribed the capital that makes their business possible. Even where the company has a mutual form of ownership—so that there are no shareholders—there is a responsibility to all the people who have paid into the insurance fund, not just to the one that is making the claim. An insurer needs to be convinced that there is a proper basis on which to pay out; but once this is established, there is no point in taking the case further. Delays and trials simply raise the insurer's costs when they are going to have to pay out anyway. However, it is the job of the claimant and their representatives to lay a proper basis of evidence for their claim and their valuation of it. Negotiation cannot begin until the insurer has been presented with the right documentation. Before 1999, this often did not happen until close to a trial date. The parties would not do serious work on the file until a court date was at hand, would then settle the case, or realize that the claim was unsubstantiated, and cancel the hearing. The Woolf reforms have encouraged the parties to do this work at a much earlier stage and they now often find they can avoid any of the costs of litigation by preparing a standard set of documentation and negotiating around this.

Not every case can be settled, of course. Some claims raises raise difficult questions of fact or novel issues of law. This is often the case with claims against pharmaceutical companies, for example, where the relationship between a drug and adverse events may be unclear. Another example might be indirect discrimination, where the scope of equality legislation may not have been defined in a sufficiently unambiguous fashion. More rarely, one side or the other may wish to prove a point by going to trial. Over a period of time, for example, either claimants or defendants may feel that they have yielded too much in negotiation and may wish to use a trial to set a benchmark. Occasionally a defendant may wish to deter other claims: this appears to be a factor in some of the sex discrimination cases in the City of London, for example, where large financial institutions have been prepared to spend a lot of money resisting well-founded cases. However, the pure defence of reputation is rarely accomplished in civil litigation, outside the very specialized field of defamation. This often frustrates the individuals who are being defended. A doctor may accept that she made an honest mistake that has injured a patient but see her insurer concede negligence in order to save the legal expenses of resisting a claim. Her reputation is not part of the package. Conversely, of course, claimants may be frustrated that they have not had a day in court, where they can seek to humiliate the party who has damaged them. Civil claims deal with economic losses not emotions.

A particularly difficult category of cases are those where individuals are defending claims made against them by corporate bodies. This is the case with many consumer debts for example. In order to minimize costs, the corporate body uses automated processes to issue claims in bulk. Once initiated, this process may be difficult to check and individuals may not be able to determine whether they have reasonable grounds for defending themselves. The decay of civil legal advice services in the UK has aggravated this problem. On the other hand, individuals can often use the cost structures of large organizations to their advantage: where they file a small claim under the simple procedures available in the UK, it can be uneconomic for a corporate body to defend, whether the claim has merit or not.   ROBERT DINGWALL

See also: **legal aid; money claim on line; small claims**

defences, criminal   *see* **justification, excuse and mitigation in criminal law**

delegated legislation   *see*   **see legal rules, types of**

demilitarization   *see* **arms control**

Demjanjuk, John (Ivan)   Born in the Ukraine in 1920, John (Ivan) Demjanjuk emigrated to the United States in 1952; he settled in Cleveland and became a naturalized citizen in 1958. In the late seventies, prosecutors working for the Immigration and Naturalization Service began investigating Demjanjuk as a suspected war criminal. American policy has never been geared toward trying suspected Nazis living in the United States as war criminals; instead it has sought to deport resident aliens or naturalized citizens (such as Demjanjuk) as persons who lied on their emigration forms.

In 1977, the Justice Department requested that Demjanjuk's citizenship be revoked, and in 1983 Israel requested his extradition. Demjanjuk was the first perpetrator since Adolf **Eichmann** to be tried under the Nazi and Nazi Collaborators Law of 1950. Like the Eichmann trial, the Demjanjuk trial was staged, in part, for didactic reasons: to familiarize a younger generation of Israelis with the history of the Holocaust and the tales of survivors. Yet a trial meant to showcase the importance of memory came to reveal its vulnerabilities.

The trial, which lasted from 17 February 1987 until 18 April 1988, was one of the longest in Israel's history. The prosecution case claimed that Demjanjuk had served as the operator of the Treblinka gas chamber, earning the sobriquet *Ivan Grozny,* Ivan the Terrible, for his unusual cruelty. These allegations were based almost entirely on the identifications and testimony of Treblinka survivors. On 25 April 1988, the three-judge tribunal convicted Demjanjuk and sentenced him to death. The court's judgment discounted evidence suggesting that the initial identification parades conducted by Israeli police fell short of satisfying normal police practice, and dismissed the relevance of the testimony of defence witness Willem Wagenaar, an experimental psychologist from the University of Leyden and a leading expert on memory problems.

During the process of appeal, mandatory in such cases, a slow but steady stream of information began to emerge from the collapsing Soviet Union suggesting that Ivan the Terrible had been one Ivan Marchenko, a Ukranian guard who, as the German war effort collapsed, had last been seen serving with Yugoslavian partisans. While none of this information entirely exculpated Demjanjuk—on the contrary, it appeared to prove that Demjanjuk had served at Sobibor, another death camp—it did cast doubt on whether Israeli justice was about to execute the right man as Ivan the Terrible. In July 1993, the Israeli Supreme Court overturned Demjanjuk's conviction.

Demjanjuk's legal odyssey was far from over. After his release, he returned to the United States, where his citizenship was restored in light of evidence that the US Justice Department's Office of Special

Investigations had known of the misidentification at the time of the Jerusalem trial. In 1999, the Justice Department again sought to revoke Demjanjuk's citizenship, now relying on the evidence of his service at Sobibor. In 2004, a federal court panel supported the revocation and in 2005 Demjanjuk was slated for deportation to the Ukraine, an order upheld in December 2006. LAWRENCE DOUGLAS

L Douglas, *The Memory of Judgment: Making Law and History in the Trials of the Holocaust* (New Haven: Yale University Press, 2001)

democracy Democracy involves inverting the long-standing idea that the ruler's job is to govern, and the people's role is to obey. It suggests instead that everyone affected by a decision has a right to participate in the decision-making process. In the words that are often attributed to Abraham Lincoln, democracy is government of the people, by the people, for the people.

The idea of democracy has its origins in ancient Athens of two-and-a-half thousand years ago where small units of (male and free) citizens debated openly on the public good. Now the idea of democracy is widespread with more than two thirds of countries in the world claiming to have the basic elements of democracy in place, and a whole range of international bodies, from the World Bank to the group of industrialized countries known as G8, endorsing the values of democracy and setting out conditions of democratic sufficiency to countries that wish to join their club. But the actual content of democracy remains uncertain and the term has a range of elusive meanings.

In part this uncertainty results from the fact that democracy is, fundamentally, a struggle over power, and as such, it provides an entirely different experience for those who hold power and those who do not. Viewed from the centre of institutions of power, democracy appears as a set of structures where interests are represented and participation enabled through institutionalized channels and by means of voting systems. This is incumbent democracy: it is a justificatory and legitimizing idea. Democracy here relates to a single political project to which all can be safely harnessed through the development and refinement of a set of electoral institutions that are to be valued, protected, and, perhaps indeed, incrementally improved. Viewed from another perspective, at the periphery of the institutions of government, the powerless see democracy as a response to exclusion. Here democracy is critical, and opposed to the top-down orientation of formal democracy. It is personal and developmental, located at the margins, and involves resistance to elite government. From this perspective, democracy becomes a means of challenging the orderly management of decision-making and instead demanding that a whole range of power relationships be democratized as excluded voices are empowered in wider participatory processes.

In part this distinction relates also to the idea that with formal, incumbent democracy, the focus is on *frameworks* for decision-making while more radical democracy is concerned with *process*. This connects to the distinction between the 'market' and the 'forum'. With liberal, representative, or incumbent democracy there is a market for choices, and the most popular policy or political party will win the competition for votes. Participation here is primarily instrumental. It is not about producing or shaping preferences but about a system for aggregating them, and giving effect to the most popular. In such representative systems the issues are about who is given the right to vote, and who will be chosen as the representative charged with making public decisions. In contrast a more deliberative approach may well be concerned more with *preference building*. The emphasis here is on 'voice', and which argument is most persuasive in the forum of ideas and deliberation. It is an integrative as opposed to aggregative approach which moves beyond simply counting votes. Instead it reinforces the idea of society as a collectivity where people decide things together and a particular value of **empowerment** results from participation in collective decision-making about the actual substance of public action.

In any society democracy will exist in both forms but its official expression will tend towards the creation and maintenance of structures for translating a political process into a mechanism for government through the counting of votes. Certainly in the United Kingdom the history of formal democracy is one that stresses a struggle over eligibility to vote. The story here is one of incremental development where the right to vote gradually extended across property qualifications, age, sex, residence, and, most recently to the homeless, as popular, democratic politics comes to inhabit the traditional structures of the British **constitution**. More recently however, in the UK as elsewhere, there is concern over citizen disengagement with the formal electoral process. This has given impetus to attempts to develop not only e-voting but also more informal ideas about mechanisms for enhanced consultation over policy developments. This emphasis on participation through widespread consultation over the details of government perhaps signals a return to more deliberative forms, even within a formal representative system. JOHN MORISON

See also: **democracy and human rights**

democracy and human rights The relationship between **democracy** and **human rights** has gone through many phases when the shared outlook of each has been complicated by the appearance of conflict. In analysing the two terms, much depends both on the level of abstraction at which they are being explored and the geographic remit—global, regional, or national—in which such a discussion is taking place.

The idea at the core of both democracy and **human** rights is **equality** of esteem, the notion that each individual has a right to respect as a **person** independently of his or her status, wealth, **community** connections, or natural ability. Readily understood as one of the fundamental building blocks of human rights, it is less often appreciated that it is also exactly this insight that makes modern democracy possible: long gone are the days when wealth, **gender**, **ethnicity** or literacy set limits to the register of electors. The triumph of the democratic principle is due in large part to the breakthroughs made on its behalf by the proponents of human rights in earlier eras of struggle. The English revolution of the seventeenth century was rooted in an idea of individual freedom which saw government as a voluntary concession rather than a despotic imposition and the representative assembly that resulted grew over time into that paradigmatic democratic institution, the British **House of Commons**. In continental Europe, the incendiary writings of, among others, Rousseau provided intellectual ballast for **revolutions** both at home (France) and abroad (the United States of America) and these produced a rights-based form of government in both countries. By 1800, democracy and human rights stood confidently together, as two sides of the same radical coin.

The connection between the two was not to last. An early assumption was that a truly representative body was not capable of violating the rights of individuals; that democratic government could not help but be just. Even Rousseau had talked of forcing people to be free however, and the upsurge in nationalistic and racialist thinking that accompanied the rise of democracy at the end of the nineteenth and the first third of the twentieth century made both individuals and **minority** groups vulnerable to majoritarian excess. The gulf between democracy and human rights widened to a chasm when the Nazi regime took power in Germany not in defiance of the democratic form of government that preceded it but through astute deployment of its legitimizing potential.

Since the end of the Second World War, it has become normal to think of democratic government as necessitating some kind of control in the name of human rights. Theorists like Ronald Dworkin have reconfigured the meaning of democracy so as to build into its very fabric a set of guarantees against the oppression of individuals which have been most often and most readily described in terms of fundamental human rights. In practical terms, the same trend has led to oversight by international organizations (eg the Human Rights Committee at the **United Nations**) and/or regional authorities (the Council of Europe) as well as a further, more embedded set of controls, at home (eg a **Supreme Court** with power to invalidate **legislation**). The first of these levels, that of the international, sees the human rights jurisdiction being applied generally, to all the states across the world regardless of whether or not they are democratic (though there have been recent moves to establish an **international law** right to democratic **governance**). The stresses that arise here are between human rights and sovereign power, not solely between human rights and democracy. The latter tension explicitly emerges only where there is a presumption in favour of democracy in a region or state that also commits itself to human rights.

Returning to an already-mentioned regional example to elaborate this latter point, the Council of Europe is a continental-wide association of sovereign states that are by definition of their membership committed not only to democracy but also to human rights. What this entails is acceptance of the jurisdiction of the **European Court of Human Rights**, with a promise both to allow individuals to take the authorities to that **Court** for breach of rights and also to implement in their own law any ruling that that Court might issue. This jurisdiction does provoke controversy from time to time though the Court seeks to minimize the potential for this by using specially-adapted international law concepts like the margin of appreciation to give a greater degree of leeway to state parties than the relevant rights charter (the **European Convention on Human Rights**) might itself seem to suggest. (It remains to be seen whether the European Union's increasingly assertive human rights jurisdiction will turn out over time to be very much more intrusive, at least for those states that belong to this inner European grouping).

It is at the state level that the tension between democracy and human rights (sometimes called constitutional or basic or civil rights) has been most evident. As indicated above, government organized on the representative principle generally accept these days that a commitment to the **rule of law** involves not just the sanctity of legislation but also of the rights regime that polices the content of such legislation for breach of fundamental human rights. This does not mean that the issue does not produce great controversy from time to time. The ongoing argument over **abortion** rights in the US is testimony to the still unsettled question of whether the inclusion of a right to terminate a pregnancy as part of a right to **privacy** to be implied into the US **constitution** was a legitimate exercise of the judicial function (*Roe v Wade* (1973)). More recently, the decision of the British **House of Lords** to declare the detention of suspected international terrorists a breach of the European Convention on Human Rights was very controversial, despite the fact that UK law did not enable the courts to proceed to strike the law down. Elected representatives dislike being told that their policy choices are impossible because they infringe a set of principles over neither the implied content nor enforcement of which they have any control.

CONOR GEARTY

democracy, right to in international law The idea that there is a right to democracy in international law entails three things: that international law prescribes the basis of legitimate authority; that what is required for legitimate authority is democratic government; and that democratic government is accordingly not simply an option, but an entitlement. Though it has earlier antecedents, this idea began to take root in the 1990s in connection with the demise of state socialism and the establishment of international procedures for monitoring multiparty elections. In some accounts it belongs with the right to self-determination and certain political and civil rights; in other accounts the right to democracy appears as a synthesis of human rights in their entirety. Its justification is linked with the 'democratic (or liberal) peace', ie the claim that democratic governments can be expected to maintain peaceful relations with one another.

For all its considerable appeal, the right to democracy is not unproblematic, as commentators have been quick to observe. Most obvious perhaps is the danger of weakening the prohibition of force in international affairs by authorizing 'pro-democratic' intervention. Linked to this is an anxiety that the democratic peace may be less a matter of promoting peace within the democratic zone than of shifting or even exacerbating violence outside it. Finally, there is concern at the risk of treating periodic elections and civil liberties as exhausting the meaning and implications of democracy. A right to democracy must be a right to inclusive decision-making—and not only at national level but in global governance as well.

SUSAN MARKS

democratic deficit   *see* **European Parliament**

demonstrations   *see* **processions and demons-trations**

denial of justice   *see* **state claims**

Denning, Alfred Thompson Lord Denning (1899–1999) was the most renowned English judge of the twentieth century. His fame rested on an irresistible combination of qualities. He had a quick forensic and analytical mind. He was a master of **precedent** and could wield the case law creatively to justify the policies and results he favoured. He was a marvellous stylist whose short, simple sentences and folksy cadences veiled a sophisticated legal mind. He expressed himself with enormous sympathy for the common people in times when class deference was more prevalent and lawyers tended to social elitism. He would confidently push beyond hampering precedents in order to bring the law into line with modern values, to clarify muddled rules, or to correct individual injustices. He was pragmatic and adventurous in applying the policy of statutes during the burgeoning era of post-war legislation. One of his greatest achievements was to help develop judicial controls for wrongful exercise of public powers in the 1960s. Perhaps the *leitmotif* of his career was a strong aversion to arrogant abuse of power whether by big business, government, or labour. He was thus seen by the legal profession and the general public as a defender of the vulnerable individual in modern mass society. Whenever a 'settled rule' of the law seemed unjust to Denning, he would research the legal roots of the doctrine and begin storing ideas of how the contending precedents could be used to reach more practical or just solutions. His famous decision in *Central London Property Trust Ltd v High Trees House Ltd* (1947), allowing a serious promise that had been relied upon to shift rights in the absence of fresh payment, was a case in point. Denning revived the obscure equitable doctrine of promissory **estoppel** in order to outmanoeuvre the **common law** rule that no promise could be enforced without a separate consideration. Shortly afterwards he identified the potential of the law of negligence to give a remedy for economic harms caused by misstatements outside contract. In a dramatic

case in public law, he held that ministers would not be allowed to keep evidence from court based on an assertion of executive privilege (**public interest immunity**) without the court testing this claim. Not all his judicial innovations worked; his theory that unfair terms cutting back contractual remedies were themselves cancelled when a contract was breached, was never accepted; and his invention of an equitable test of factual unfairness, allowing the cancellation of contracts based on shared mistakes, never made sense and eventually was overruled. His attempts to reallocate property in failed marriages so as to protect 'deserted wives' introduced unwanted uncertainty into property law and also was not followed. Denning accepted such casualties as the price of creativity. His critics argued that he grasped for a power to legislate from the bench and unnecessarily unsettled the law. Denning dominated the Court of Appeal which he headed as **Master of the Rolls** for many decades. He resigned from judicial office in 1982 following controversy caused by his statements about the lack of impartiality of jurors from immigrant communities. But despite the undercurrents of legal and political controversy, Denning's towering judicial achievements across the gamut of English law stand undiminished. It is impossible to imagine the common law of our time with his contributions subtracted.

JOSHUA GETZLER

See also: **contract law; negligence in civil law**

departments of state   This is a general term referring to the various ministries and government departments used to govern the country. A remarkable feature of the UK's constitutional arrangements is the relative informality of the departmental system, which has a long history of organic growth. Many aspects of the system are regulated by exercises of **royal prerogative** powers rather than by statute. That said, the Ministers of the Crown Act 1975 provides mechanisms for the transfer of ministerial functions from one department to another. Modernization strategies adopted in 1997 have resulted in considerable movement of functions from one department to another. One notable recent innovation has been the creation of the Department of Constitutional Affairs as a result of reforms to the ancient Office of **Lord Chancellor**. The departmental system has been significantly changed in recent times by the creation of various executive agencies, otherwise known as **Next Steps Agencies**.

Responsibility for the policies of a department rests with the relevant **minister of the Crown**. In relation to policy, the function of civil servants is to provide politically neutral advice and guidance to ministers. Since 1997 there has been a marked increase in the numbers, variety, and roles of specialist ministerial policy advisers. Concern is often expressed about the extent of the influence of such advisers and their relationship with civil servants within the department. Day-to-day administrative and operational decisions are in the hands of senior civil servants.

Ministers are accountable to Parliament for the working of their departments, and may be questioned by select committees. Civil servants may also be called upon to give evidence. Select Committees have the power to summon a civil servant against the wishes of the relevant minister. In practice, civil servants normally appear with ministerial agreement.

JOHN MCELDOWNEY

See also: **civil service; ministerial responsibility**

deportation   Deportation may be defined as the expulsion of non-citizens by a state through the (threatened or actual) use of force. The right of states to deport has traditionally been seen as flowing from the state's right to control immigration. Just as states are entitled to prevent non-citizens from entering their territory, so they claim a correlative entitlement to expel non-citizens who have entered or remain on their territory in breach of immigration laws. Some countries, like Germany, do not use the term deportation because of its negative historical associations with the Nazi period; others, like the **United Kingdom**, refer to the 'removal' as well as the deportation of non-citizens. However, notwithstanding its different appellations, the practice of deportation remains a feature of all contemporary liberal democratic states.

The origins of contemporary deportation power are to be found in the emergence of restrictive immigration controls in the period between 1880 and the beginnings of World War I. In the UK, deportation power derives from the **Crown**'s prerogative to control the entry and residence of aliens. Statute law relating to deportation stems from the Aliens Act of 1905, developed partly to control the entrance of Russian Jews. Because the **royal prerogative** power applied to aliens only, **Commonwealth** citizens were not deportable from the UK until specific legislation was passed in the 1960s. Both the nature of regulation and the practical ability of states to deport expanded during World War I, as a way of dealing with 'enemy aliens', specifically Germans. But it was on the continent that the association between deportation and specific ethnic

groups reached its nadir with the mass deportation of European Jews to concentration camps by the Nazis during World War II. In the War's aftermath, international law responded by prohibiting, in the 1949 Geneva Conventions on the Protection of Victims of War, 'individual or mass transfers, as well as deportation of protected persons from occupied territory'.

Mass deportation, whether carried out for reasons of race, ethnicity, or political ideology, is only loosely related to the current operation of deportation power in democratic states. Legitimate deportation power is exercised only against non-citizens and most states face tight legal constraints on their ability to strip citizenship. Moreover, contemporary deportation orders are the consequence of individual violations of immigration (or other state) laws. There are three primary ways that someone may become eligible for deportation: by entering the state illegally (eg using fraudulent documentation); by breaching the terms specified for the legal entrance and residence of foreigner (eg committing a crime); or by gaining entrance to or continued residence in a state on the basis of a claim to be a refugee that has been rejected.

Even though contemporary deportation power is exercised on an individual basis, it is still a lightening rod for controversy. Deportation shows in a clear and unambiguous way the force that lies behind contemporary immigration controls. While the public may ignore the hardships inflicted upon foreigners by policies that prevent arrival, they find it harder to ignore images of distraught families being bundled onto airplanes by government officials, even more so when those being removed are friends, neighbours, or colleagues who may have resided in the state for many years.

Controversy is heightened further by the fact that those being removed may have very limited ability to challenge their expulsion. In the United States (and many other countries), 'classical immigration law holds that deportation is a civil, administrative proceeding, not a criminal prosecution' (PH Schuck, *Citizens, Strangers and In-Betweens* (Boulder: Westview, 1998), 34–35). Thus the range of protections available to those subject to deportation are, despite the extreme hardships involved, much more limited than those available to someone who has violated criminal law. In the UK, an individual may appeal against a decision to deport by the Home Secretary. By contrast, those subject to a removal order, including most illegal migrants and asylum seekers, are often able to appeal only from abroad. The development of **human rights** and refugee law has mitigated this situation only partly. International instruments such as the **United Nations** Convention Against Torture and other Cruel, Inhuman, or Degrading Treatment or Punishment, the UN Convention Relating to the Status of Refugees and, for European countries, the **European Convention on Human Rights** protect individuals against return to countries where they would face serious human rights violations. MATTHEW GIBNEY

G Clayton, *Textbook on Immigration and Asylum Law* (Oxford: Oxford University Press, 2nd edn, 2006)

MJ Gibney and R Hansen, 'Deportation and the Liberal State', in *New Issues in Refugee Research*, 77 (Geneva: UNHCR, 2003)

deposit protection Deposit protection (sometimes called deposit insurance, depositor protection, or deposit guarantee) schemes are a major tool in bank **regulation** and consumer protection. A deposit protection scheme provides a payout to depositors in the event of certain circumstances (usually, a bank's becoming unable to meet its liabilities towards its depositors).

Such schemes have two main objectives. The first is consumer protection. Bank customers find it difficult to make informed judgments about whether an institution is likely to be able to meet its obligations to them in the future because the information available about this is difficult to assess, and because the ability of a bank to meet its obligations depends in part on the behaviour of bank management after the customer has entered a contract with the bank. Deposit protection schemes compensate for the difficulty in making an informed choice. Furthermore, less affluent customers are likely to have a high proportion of their wealth in the form of simple deposit accounts, and so may be disproportionately affected by a bank's failure. There is therefore a strong social dimension to deposit protection. The second objective of deposit protection schemes is the maintenance of confidence and, in particular, the avoidance of bank runs which might have a damaging effect upon the financial system at large. By reducing the incentive for customers to initiate bank runs, deposit protection schemes contribute towards the stability of the financial system.

Deposit protection schemes may take different forms. One distinction that is sometimes drawn is between explicit and implicit schemes. Implicit schemes involve no formal structure but merely an expectation that depositors will be protected in the event of a bank failing. While they have the strengths of low administration costs and flexibility, they may not be sufficient to dissuade depositors

from initiating runs because they are premised on an expectation rather than a guarantee of protection. Furthermore, implicit protection may take the form of a bank rescue, which provides 100 per cent protection across the board. It must be doubted whether this provides appropriate incentives.

Explicit schemes are those that are formally established, funded (usually in advance) and the rules of which are set out from the start. The strengths of such schemes are that funding is available when needed (provision usually being made for further funding if necessary), and certainty is provided for all stakeholders. The main criticism levelled against explicit deposit protection schemes is that they create **moral hazard**. Because depositors and bankers know that protection will be provided in the event of bank failure, they are under less incentive to take care than if no protection were in place. This might provide incentives to engage in imprudent conduct. Responses to these concerns include the use of co-insurance, where depositors have only a proportion of their deposits protected, and rules that prevent those who are in some way at fault in a bank's collapse benefiting from the scheme's protection.

PETER CARTWRIGHT

See also: **bank accounts; bank runs and capital adequacy; consumer protection in retail banking; financial regulation**

deposits A deposit is a sum of money paid when making a contract, to show commitment to the deal. It may take the form of a specified amount or a percentage of the total contract price, for example 10 per cent. Deposits are commonly required in sales of land and property, holiday contracts, when goods are specially ordered or adapted for a customer and when, in a contract for goods and services, materials are purchased before work commences. Deposits may also be required when goods are being hired, as a method of ensuring their return.

If a person, having paid a deposit, cancels the contract, the other party may retain the deposit, whether or not they incur losses following the cancellation. Deposits are, thus, normally non-refundable, unless the parties have agreed otherwise. If the deposit is a substantial percentage of the total price, it could be considered a part payment and not a deposit; the supplier then would only be entitled to retain his actual losses and not necessarily the whole amount.

A deposit cannot be retained if there is a statutory right of cancellation which has been properly exercised, or if the supplier has broken the contract. Deposits can also be recovered if the contract has been cancelled (rescinded) due to a misrepresentation by the supplier.

It is possible to challenge the requirement of a non-returnable deposit as an unfair term in a consumer contract if there is no similar provision to compensate the consumer for a supplier's failure to perform the contract.   DEBORAH PARRY

See also: **unfair contract terms**

deregulation   see **regulation**

derogation in EU law   Individuals and companies enjoy the rights of **free movement in the EU**. States (and sometimes private parties) can legitimately obstruct that free movement by invoking a 'derogation', that is, a 'good' reason identified in the EC Treaty to obstruct trade. The derogations differ according to the freedom concerned. For example, the grounds on which Member States can restrict the free movement of goods appear quite generous (**public policy** and **security**, health (animal, human, and plant), public morality, protection of intellectual property rights, and protection of national treasures). However, because reliance on these derogations obstructs the functioning of the **single market**, the ECJ has laid down a number of rules restricting their use. States must produce evidence why they are invoking the derogation; the derogation cannot serve an economic purpose (that is, protecting national industry); states must also show that the steps taken are proportionate and respect fundamental rights. In the field of free movement of persons, the derogations are more limited (public policy, public security, and public health, together with a specific derogation about employment in the public service). The detail of how states can invoke these 'persons' derogations has been fleshed out by the Citizens' Rights Directive 2004/38.

The derogations, unamended since 1957, are an exhaustive list and do not include interests regarded as important today such as **consumer** and environmental protection. This has led the ECJ to supplement the express derogations by a non-exhaustive list of judicially recognized 'justifications' to cover these matters. These justifications can be invoked only where the barrier to trade is not overtly discriminatory.   CATHERINE BARNARD

See also: **citizenship of the European Union; free movement in the EU**

derogations in human rights law   Human rights law acknowledges that in certain exceptional circumstances, such as armed conflict, it may be necessary to derogate from some **human rights** obligations in order to deal with an emergency situation which is threatening the life of the nation. Article 4 of the **International Covenant on Civil and Political Rights** ('ICCPR') refers to a 'public emergency which threatens the life of the nation and the existence of which is officially proclaimed' and which allows the state to take certain measures 'to the extent strictly required by the exigencies of the situation' and 'provided the measures are not inconsistent with their other obligations under **international law** and do not involve discrimination solely on the ground of **race**, colour, **sex**, language, **religion** or social origin'. Some **human** rights are non-derogable; for example, no derogation is permitted from the **right to life**, and the prohibition against **torture**. This general position is also reflected in instruments such as the **European Convention on Human Rights** ('ECHR'), Article 15. The UK has used Article 15 to derogate from Article 5 in relation to Northern Ireland as well as in relation to more recent measures addressing 'international **terrorism**'.

Derogation from human rights standards is a serious step and intended to be exceptional to address a public emergency of particular severity. The standards which provide for derogation set boundaries and limits, and it is not the case that every emergency situation a state has to deal with should justify a derogation. Is there a threat of sufficient severity to justify derogation? Are the measures taken strictly required by the situation? This is an area where **courts**, for example, can demonstrate considerable reluctance to interfere in relation to what constitutes a 'public emergency which threatens the life of the nation' and the **European Court of Human Rights** has granted states a wide margin of appreciation in making this assessment (*Brannigan and McBride v UK* (1993)). It has never held that an Article 15 derogation was unjustified.

For the purposes of counter-terrorism law and policy, the UK derogated from Article 5(1) of the ECHR—and Article 9 of the ICCPR—in 2001, in order to put in place a system of potentially indefinite **detention without trial** for 'suspected international terrorists'. The government's policy was successfully challenged in the **House of Lords** (*A and others v Secretary of State for the Home Department* (2004)). The majority of the Law Lords could accept that there was a public emergency threatening the life of the nation, but the court was not persuaded that the measures could overcome the hurdle of strict proportionality laid down in Article 15, and concluded that they amounted to discriminatory treatment on grounds of **nationality** and immigration status (Articles 14 and 5, read together). Although the majority of the Law Lords were not prepared to interfere with the assessment of whether there was an emergency, they were willing to subject the measures taken to scrutiny to decide whether they were proportionate to 'the exigencies of the situation' and consistent with other provisions of international law. This confirms the general position that derogations are exceptional measures which have established boundaries and limits in law.   COLIN HARVEY

See also: **proportionality in human rights law**

designs The registered design system, which dates back to 1839, was introduced by Parliament in order to encourage the production of aesthetically appealing industrial articles. Protection in the UK is now governed by the Registered Designs Act 1949 ('RDA'), as substantially amended in 2001 to implement EC law harmonizing this area (the EC Designs Directive).

Protection under the RDA is obtained through registration, by making an application to the Design Registry in the UK Patent Office. A design must relate to 'the appearance of the whole or a part of a product resulting from the features of, in particular, the lines, contours, colours, shape, texture or materials of the product or its ornamentation'. Excluded, however, from consideration are features that are solely dictated by the product's technical function or those that depend on the features of another article with which the article in question is to be connected. A design must also be 'new' and have 'individual character'. A design will qualify as 'new' if no identical design, or only a design differing in immaterial details, has been made available to the public before the date of application. What constitutes having been made available to the public is broadly defined; but there are important limitations. For instance, a design will not have been made available to the public where the disclosure has been made by the designer in the twelve months before the application date or where there has been disclosure but not such that the design could reasonably have become known to specialists in the design sector operating in the European Economic Area. A design will have 'individual character' if the overall impression it produces on the informed user differs from the overall impression produced on such a user by any other designs which have previously been made available to the public before the application date. In determining this requirement, the freedom of the designer in creating the design is taken into account.

If an applicant (who is usually the person who creates the design but may be an employer, commissioner

of a design, or an assignee of a design) is successful in registering their design, the proprietor (ie owner) of the registered design right is given the exclusive right to use the design, along with any design which does not produce on the informed user a different overall impression. A person 'uses' the design if they make, offer, place on the market, import, export, or use a product in which the design has been incorporated or applied. The proprietor's right to use the design can be infringed by use regardless of whether the infringer actually copies the design (in other words, even if they independently produced and used the same design as the one that is registered). A few minor defences are available to a claim of infringement, such as that the use was private and non-commercial or was for experimental purposes. The registered design right lasts for five years initially, renewable for up to a total of twenty-five years.

The registered design system operating in the UK is mirrored at the EU level. In other words, there is available an EU community registered design right. This was created by the Community Designs Regulation 2002, which became effective in April 2003. The requirements for obtaining a community registered design right are the same as under the RDA. Applications for registration can be made to a Community institution, the Office of Harmonization in the Internal Market, or to offices of Member States. The scope of protection is similar to that under the RDA, with the important difference that protection is not limited to the territory of the UK but extends to the entire **European Community**.

Designs are also protected by unregistered design-right systems, at both UK and EU levels. Apart from the superficial similarity that the unregistered design right arises automatically once the threshold requirements are satisfied (ie without the need for registration), the registered and unregistered design rights are vastly different from one another. The UK unregistered design right ('UK UDR') was introduced in 1988 (by the Copyright Designs and Patents Act 1988) and deals with designs relating to the shape or configuration of the whole or part of any article. Thus, unlike the registered design right, it is not concerned with aesthetic features. Protection arises if the design is 'original' and 'not commonplace'. 'Originality' means that the design must originate with the designer and not be slavishly copied from a pre-existing design. The courts have elaborated less on when a design is 'not commonplace', mainly stressing that the term does not mean 'new'. The owner of the UK UDR has the exclusive right to reproduce the design for commercial purposes by making articles to that design. Thus, persons will infringe the right where they produce articles exactly or substantially to the design; but, importantly, only where they have copied the design. Protection endures for up to fifteen years.

The unregistered community design right ('UCDR') is a recent addition to the armory of protection available to designers of industrial and functional articles, introduced pursuant to Community Designs Regulation 2002. There must be a design relating to the appearance of a product resulting in particular from lines, contours, colours, shape, texture, materials, or ornamentation. The design must also be 'new' and have 'individual character'. Because there is no application process, these requirements are assessed as of the date when the design is made available to the public, and will usually be assessed by a court in an infringement action as part of a defendant's counterclaim that the alleged UCDR does not exist. The UCDR gives the owner the exclusive right to use the design and to prevent the use of the design by third parties. In this context, use involves copying the design. The UCDR lasts only for three years.

As may be apparent from the above discussion, the protection available for designs is a complicated mixture of registered and unregistered rights, national (UK) rights and EU rights. It has been remarked before that this is an area that could do with some streamlining.   TANYA APLIN

See also: **European harmonization of intellectual property rights**

desistance   *see* **recidivism**

detention centres   *see* **immigration and emigration**

detention without trial   The detention of **persons** without trial has long been viewed as one of the most serious of **human rights** abuses. It represents both a flight from due process and a possible journey in the direction of even grosser violations, in the form of **torture** and inhuman and degrading treatment. Prohibited by all the key international human rights texts, the subject has attracted the specific concern (since its establishment in 1991) of the **United Nations** ('UN') working group on arbitrary detention, charged among other duties with oversight of the UN Body of Principles for the Protection of All Persons under Any Form of Detention or Imprisonment (1988).

Until recently, discussion of detention without trial was regarded as a topic mainly for consideration in the context of authoritarian or totalitarian states. This was not to say that democratic governments did not from time to time deploy the tool as a means of countering rebellion or potential subversion at a time of war: the United States authorities had famously detained persons of Japanese origin in special camps during the Second World War, and the British forces in Northern Ireland had used the power in the context of countering Republican separatist **violence** in the early 1970s (leading to a ruling in the **European Court of Human Rights** in 1978 that detainees had been subjected to inhuman treatment). This exceptional status in democratic states has begun to erode in recent years, under pressure from the US reaction to attacks on it by the group Al Qaida on 11 September 2001. The US response has involved the initiation of what the Bush administration has described as a 'war on terror'. The creation of camps outside the territory of the state at which 'unlawful combatants' have been held indefinitely has become one of the great human rights scandals of the Bush presidency, with the torture at Abu Ghraib coming to symbolize the kind of ill-treatment to which detainees of this nature can be so easily exposed. In the United Kingdom in contrast, the detention of suspected international terrorists under Pt IV of the Anti-terrorism, Crime and Security Act 2001 was declared to be incompatible with the **rights to liberty** and non-discrimination in the **European Convention on Human Rights**, and this has led to the power being replaced by a new system of control orders. (No effort was made by the UK to locate its detained persons outside the reach of UK law.)

An emerging question is the extent to which detention before charge can be characterized as detention without charge (and therefore without trial as well). The point arises because democratic governments increasingly argue for long period of detention with a view to securing the evidence necessary to bring criminal **prosecutions**—but say in doing so that they are not introducing detention without charge or (to give it its highly charged label) **internment**. The Blair administration in the UK unsuccessfully sought to obtain a ninety day period of this sort and the current limit—twenty-eight days for this sort of suspect—remains under challenge for being allegedly too short. There must come a time when this kind of detention merges into *de facto* detention without trial, at least so far as its impact on those subject to it is concerned.   CONOR GEARTY

deterrence (civil)   *see* **civil liability, theories of**

deterrence (criminal)   *see* **punishment, theories of**

development   *see* **gender and development**

Devlin, Patrick Arthur Baron Devlin (1905–1992), son of an architect, enjoyed debating at Stonyhurst and Christ's College, Cambridge. He joined Gray's Inn in 1927 and was taken on as a devil by Jowett, the Attorney-General, who appointed him a **judge** in 1948 at the early age of forty-two. He showed himself a sound commercial lawyer with a gift for close but intelligible reasoning. He became known in 1957 for his conduct of the trial of Dr Bodkin Adams, accused of murdering a patient for a legacy, a trial of which Devlin after retirement wrote a controversial account in *Easing the Passing* (1985). In 1959 he chaired an **inquiry** into an alleged plot to murder the governor, his officials, and all Europeans in Nyasaland (now Malawi). He concluded that the plot was a figment of an informer's imagination. The Attorney-General, Manningham-Buller, ridiculed this conclusion. Devlin was nevertheless promoted to the **House of Lords** in 1961. Disliking the dreary work and poor facilities in the Lords, he resigned in 1964.

Thereafter he flourished as an arbitrator and was the first non-journalist to be chairman of the Press Council. His informal manner and sense of humour in these spheres was appreciated. **Justice**, 'the root of which is the love of an order that moves the universe' was, for him, the highest value. He wrote about it in *Trial by Jury* (1956), *Samples of Lawmaking* (1962), and *The Enforcement of Morals* (1965). The power of **juries** to decide questions of fact and of guilt or innocence in **criminal trials** should be respected. This led him to join with Lord Scarman and others in pressing for a review of the convictions in the *Luton post office* case (1969) and that of the Guildford four (1975). In the end, though in the *Guildford* case only in 1989, the campaigns were successful. On morality he clashed with HLA Hart in a famous controversy in which Devlin defended a more conservative, Hart a more libertarian, view about the right of a **community** to enforce strongly held moral opinions. At the end he returned to the rites of the Catholic church of his youth. His fascinating autobiography, *Taken at the Flood*, was published posthumously. Of the small number of twentieth-century English judges who addressed a wider public, his rigorous conscience, clarity, and eloquence made him the most impressive writer.   TONY HONORÉ

devolution 'Devolution' is the term used to express the idea of the decentralization of government within a unitary state. Although sometimes described as 'quasi-federal' in character, devolution stands well short of the classic forms of federalism with their constitutionally entrenched division between federal and territorially-based state or provincial institutions. Thus 'devolution' described the form of government designed for Northern Ireland between 1922 and 1972 under the Government of Ireland Act 1920 with its (Stormont) Parliament and Government. Today, it is the term used to describe the arrangements established under the Scotland Act 1998, the Government of Wales Act 1998 and, though its full implementation was delayed, the Northern Ireland Act 1998. No part of England currently enjoys devolved government although the Greater London Authority has some devolved characteristics and, if regional government were, in due course, to be set up across other parts of England, this would be regarded as an extension of the devolution process.

Evident from this account is that devolution in the United Kingdom is asymmetric in its impact. Scotland at present represents the strongest model, with the devolution of substantial law-making powers (in relation to education, health, planning etc) to the Scottish Parliament. The Northern Ireland model is similar. For Wales, however, devolution is often described as 'administrative' or 'executive' in that the National Assembly for Wales does not have 'primary' law-making powers but instead exercises administrative and subordinate law-making powers formerly exercised by the Secretary of State for Wales and other UK Ministers. Recently, though, the Government of Wales Act 2006 has anticipated the eventual transfer of law-making powers to the National Assembly.

Politically, the creation of devolved institutions provides new opportunities for the injection of additional representative democracy into government, new possibilities for national and regional accountability, experimentation in institutional design (such as the use of proportional representation in the voting systems for the Scottish Parliament and the National Assembly for Wales), and a greater diversity of politics and policy in decision-making. In addition, new inter-institutional questions arise in the relationship between Whitehall and the devolved administrations, concerning the provision of central funding, the statutory powers available to UK ministers to control the actions of the devolved bodies, and the non-legal relationships created by the Memorandum of Association and concordats concluded between them. Overarching all these inter-institutional relationships is the retained competence of the UK Parliament to legislate not only in reserved (ie non-devolved) but also in devolved fields across the entire United Kingdom. In relation to Scotland this competence is tempered by an undertaking to legislate in relation to devolved matters only with the consent of the Scottish Parliament (the 'Sewel convention'). Also important is the availability of special judicial procedures for the resolution of 'devolution issues' touching on the competence of the devolved bodies, with ultimate recourse to the Judicial Committee of the **Privy Council** (in due course, the UK Supreme Court).   CHRIS HIMSWORTH

See also: **Supreme Court (UK)**

Dicey, Albert Venn (1835–1922) Albert Venn Dicey served as the Vinerian Chair Professor of English Law at Oxford for twenty-seven years and reached a level of legal prominence such that many still characterize the British constitution as 'Diceyan'. Dicey was born at Claybrook Hall in Leicestershire to a Whig, Evangelical, middle-class, intellectual family that made its fortune printing and editing the *Northampton Mercury,* a regional newspaper. His early education was conducted at home by his mother. At seventeen, he attended King's College in London and two years later matriculated at Balliol College Oxford, graduating in 1858 with first class honours. Dicey earned a fellowship at Trinity College, Oxford in 1860 and held it until he married Elinor Mary Bonham-Carter in 1872, a union that lasted half a century but bore no children. Dicey served as junior counsel to the Commissioners of Inland Revenue from 1876 until 1890.

In the face of competition from recognized scholars like William Anson and Frederick **Pollock,** Dicey won the Vinerian Chair in 1882 based largely on his already published works: *A Treatise on the Rules for the Selection of the Parties to an Action* (1870) and *The Law of Domicil as a Branch of the Law of England, Stated in the Form of Rules* (1879). During his tenure, Dicey successfully revived the prestige of the Vinerian Chair, which had been inaugurated by Sir William **Blackstone**, with his three major scholarly contributions: *Introduction to the Study of the Law of the Constitution* (1885); *A Digest of the Law of England with Reference to the Conflict of Laws* (1896); and *Lectures on the Relation between Law and Public Opinion in England during the Nineteenth Century* (1905).

In *Law of the Constitution*, Dicey enumerated three principles of British **constitutional law**: **parliamentary sovereignty**; the **rule of law**; and conventions of the **constitution**. In a country lacking a formal constitution, Dicey articulated the main characteristics affecting the development of the non-formal constitution, and he did so in a signature style that was accessible to scholars as well as the general public. These principles have become so strongly identified with Dicey that later scholarship assesses whether and to what extent the British constitution ever was or still is 'Diceyan'. Since the British constitution has served as a model for other countries to either follow or reject, Dicey's work has been widely cited worldwide and is still discussed.

While his constitutional work was 'born under a lucky star', Dicey found the work on *Conflict of Laws* tedious, spending fourteen years writing it. But it was time well spent, as Dicey succeeded in influencing the very development of the then emerging field of private **international law**. Many consider the book his *magnum opus*. In *Law and Public Opinion,* which originated in lectures he gave at Harvard Law School in 1898, Dicey tried to trace the history of ideas, dividing the nineteenth century to three main periods: Old Toryism (1800–1830); Benthamism (1825–1870); and Collectivism (1865–1900). The book has been the most severely criticized of his enduring contributions, though it is still studied in connection with the rise of the welfare state and the 'revolution in government' controversy.

Originally, Dicey's political creed included liberalism, support of free trade, and enfranchisement for women. He was willing, however, to sacrifice all these beliefs to preserve the Union between England and Ireland. Once Home Rule became a real threat in 1885–1886, Dicey joined the Unionist ranks. When the Unionists were torn between free trade and protectionism, Dicey advocated compromise or even acceptance of protectionism for the sake of the Union. Women's enfranchisement could no longer be risked mainly because it might stoke Irish nationalism. Scholars have even suggested that Dicey contradicted his constitutional dogma in his fervour for unionism.

From 1886 until near his death, Dicey wrote prolifically against Home Rule, trying to influence politicians and public opinion in support of the Union. He did not treat the Irish as a separate nation. He believed Irish despair was economic in nature, and regardless, Home Rule was worse than complete separation, since it compromised parliamentary **sovereignty**. Dicey would not accept the constitutionality of any statute establishing Home Rule until it had been first submitted for the verdict of the people at **election** or **referendum**. He was one of the ardent advocates of the referendum, viewing it as 'honestly democratic in theory and conservative in practice'. Although parliamentary sovereignty is identified as Diceyan, Dicey himself may be viewed as supporting popular sovereignty although the relevant populace for him was that of the United Kingdom, not Ireland alone.   RIVKA WEILL

RA Cosgrove, *The Rule of Law: Albert Venn Dicey, Victorian Jurist* (Chapel Hill: University of North Carolina Press, 1980)

R Weill, 'Dicey was not Diceyan' (2003) 62 *Cambridge Law Journal* 474

difference and discrimination The justification for 'difference' as a basis for discriminatory treatment was explained by Aristotle: 'things that are alike should be treated alike, while things that are unalike should be treated unalike in proportion to their unalikeness'. Anti-discrimination law has struggled with this issue and, in particular, the extent to which **equality** of treatment can be demanded in the face of 'essential' differences between people. The most frequently cited example is pregnancy. Courts had great difficulty in finding that pregnancy discrimination was a form of **sex** discrimination because there was no direct male comparator to the discriminated-against pregnant woman. In recent years, though, there has been a greater willingness to reach this conclusion under **European Community law**.

The strategic issue of whether pregnancy should be understood as a form of incapacity comparable to other **disabilities** (sameness) or whether it should be understood as a sex specific condition (difference) gave rise to the 'sameness/difference debate' within feminist legal theory. However, both positions leave maleness as the undisturbed norm against which women must either be found similar or provided with 'special' treatment and 'protection'. Neither approach may be conducive to the achievement of genuine equality. A more radical approach examines the specific context and effects of discrimination. Particular attention is given to whether difference in treatment is a result of **stereotyping** and prejudice, and therefore whether it is the manifestation of the historical disadvantage of a group. This nuanced approach was developed by the Supreme Court of Canada.   CARL STYCHIN

C MacKinnon, 'Reflections on Sex Equality in Law' (1991) 100 *Yale Law Journal* 1281

GC More, ' "Equal Treatment" of the Sexes in European Community Law: What Does "Equal" Mean?' (1993) 1 *Feminist Legal Studies* 45

See also: **feminist theories of law; substantive equality**

digital television and radio regulation Until the 1980s, radio and television programmes were disseminated to mass audiences by analogue broadcasts from terrestrial transmitters. Following the introduction of cable and satellite, viewers have the opportunity to subscribe to bundles of programming that enable them to be more selective about what they obtain. However, the introduction of digitalization has transformed the ways that audiovisual content can be made and distributed and, in the UK, it is planned to replace analogue television broadcasting completely by 2012. Digitalization offers improvements in technical quality, it enables the same content to be marketed in a variety of ways (for example, television, DVDs, or the internet), and it is possible for the audience to interact with producers and suppliers to choose what they want to receive. These developments challenge the assumption underlying traditional broadcasting **regulation** that there is a public interest in controlling the use of scarce broadcasting frequencies to ensure that programme content is appropriate for a large and undifferentiated audience. The UK's approach to regulation accepts that television and radio channels will continue to exist and to provide 'linear' streams of programming, some of which will have public service remits; but it also recognizes that audiences will increasingly be able to pick which elements they desire and to construct their own schedules of what to see or hear. However, consistent with the approach in European broadcasting, there is no regulation of 'non-linear', or on-demand, services, including those available through the internet.

The Communications Act 2003 retains but modifies the basic licensing structure that was created by the Broadcasting Act 1990 for the traditional broadcasting sector. In television, Channel 3 (ITV) is a network of regional companies, funded by advertising and sponsorship, with various public service obligations. Channel 5 (Five) is a national commercial television service, with a lesser public service remit. Channel 4, provided by a public corporation, is also funded by advertising and sponsorship, but has a duty to provide public service television programming that complements ITV and Five. There is a Welsh language counterpart to Channel 4, S4C (Sianel Pedwar Cymru). Under the digital terrestrial broadcasting ('DTB') scheme established by the Broadcasting Act 1996, provision was made for these services to be broadcast digitally (via set-top boxes) alongside their analogue format. However, the 2003 Act has replaced that complex structure with a simpler system of digital licences for ITV, Five, Channel 4, and S4C Digital. The 1996 DTB scheme also made provision for additional digital broadcast services to be established, but the company which secured the franchise (OnDigital, which later became ITV Digital) was unsuccessful. Its licences were obtained by Freeview in 2002, and the latest legislation preserves that position whilst again making simpler provision for any expansion of DTB.

The Communications Act 2003 also replaces the former separate licences for satellite services and cable programming, which had already evolved into digital services for commercial reasons, with new, light-touch 'television licensable content service' licenses. Those are defined to include traditional linear television programmes, together with electronic programme guides, but are not intended to cover the internet or pure video-on-demand services. In respect of radio, the basic structure is that established in 1990, with three national services (one to be devoted to non-pop music and the other to the spoken word) and provision for licensing a large number of local stations. A scheme for digital audio broadcasting ('DAB') was introduced in 1996, and the Communications Act 2003 simplifies its regulation. It also makes provision, for the first time, for community radio services.

Although the licensing of television and radio services continues, controls over content regulation have been reduced under the Communications Act 2003. Provision for **programme standards and complaints** has been retained in a revised form. For the public service channels (ITV, Channel 4, and Five) their general remit continues to be to disseminate information and to provide for education and entertainment. In doing so, the services as a whole (not every programme) must deal with, for example, current affairs, the UK's cultural diversity, educational matters, a wide range of knowledge and interests, religion, and high quality material suitable for children. However, the statute contains detailed rules only about objectively measurable requirements, such as quotas for European and independent productions, and the amount of time devoted to news and current affairs and to regional programmes. More qualitative public service obligations and aspirations, relating to the range of programming and its production values, are now implemented through a system of co-regulation, relying on televisions companies' promises to the regulator. The BBC's Charter and Agreement make separate but similar provision for its services. However, **Ofcom** is required to review the general provision of all **public service broadcasting** every five years, with a view to enhancing it.

The Communications Act 2003 does not regulate the BBC directly. The BBC is established under Royal Charter, the latest one being in force from 2007 to 2016, which recognizes the BBC's editorial independence and sets out its public purposes. But the BBC's Agreement with the Government makes it subject to most of Ofcom's general powers to regulate standards in television and radio, including the power to exact penalties and levy charges.

One area of traditional regulation, which is substantially relaxed by the Communications Act 2003, relates to media ownership. The Act has abolished the former restrictions on foreign control of television and radio licences and on accumulations of control greater than 15 per cent of total audience share. Instead, a special **competition law** regime for media mergers has been introduced. The rationale is that this, together with the existing diversity of channels and content regulation, can better protect media pluralism. Only some limits on cross-ownership are retained: principally, a proprietor of a newspaper that has more than 20 per cent of national circulation cannot hold an ITV licence. In addition, local radio rules are also retained to ensure that there will be at least two local radio stations (in addition to the BBC) in any one market.   TOM GIBBONS

Department of Trade and Industry & Department of Culture, Media and Sport, *A New Future for Communications* (2000) Cm. 5010

Joint Committee on the Draft Communications Bill (Chair: Lord Puttnam), *Volume I – Report* (2001–02) July 2002, HL Paper 169 – I, HC 876 – I

See also: **British Broadcasting Corporation; communications regulation; European broadcasting obligations; media concentration**

dignity and discrimination   The concept that all **persons** should be treated equally is widely recognized to be an important philosophical, moral, and legal value. However, defining exactly what it means to treat persons equally is difficult. Distinctions are constantly being made between different individuals and groups in almost every area of life: for example, different people pay different levels of tax, go to different educational institutions, and are recruited to do different jobs. Which of these distinctions between individuals and groups are acceptable, and which are not?

It is now widely accepted that certain forms of discrimination, especially **sex** and **race** discrimination, should be prohibited. However, complex issues remain. Should all distinctions based on **gender**, sexual orientation, age, **religion,** and other 'equality grounds' be prohibited? Should the emphasis in law and public policy be placed on treating individuals as much as possible in the same manner, known as an 'equality as sameness' or a '**formal equality**' approach? Or should the differences between individuals and social groups be recognized, with special support given to **minority** groups with particular disadvantages and special needs, an approach often referred to as 'equality as difference'? Whichever approach is adopted may lead to different results, especially in controversial areas such as positive action, **disability** rights, and accommodating religious difference. As the Chief Justice of Canada has commented, equality is in many ways 'the most difficult right'.

In recent years, attempts have been made to define exactly what treating people equally should mean in practice. In particular, many academics and **judges** now suggest that respecting equality should mean that all individuals should be treated as having the same right to be treated with equal dignity and respect. In the case law of several constitutional **courts**, in particular the German Constitutional Court, the Canadian Supreme Court, and the **South African Constitutional Court**, **human dignity** is a core constitutional value which requires individuals to be treated in a manner that respects their **autonomy**, self-respect, and equality of status. Unfair discrimination is seen as violating this concept of human dignity, as it deprives those affected by discrimination of equality of respect and status and treats them as second-class persons.

This link between the idea of human dignity and the right of freedom from unfair discrimination has been used to reinforce the importance of equality as a right. For example, the South African and Canadian courts have repeatedly insisted that the right to equality must be given due weight and respect in law, as respect for this right is essential to protect the human dignity of all persons. The link between dignity and discrimination is also used as a means of deciding which forms of discrimination the law should concern itself with. The South African and Canadian courts, along with the **European Court of Human Rights**, the **US Supreme Court,** and other leading judicial bodies, often give public authorities considerable freedom to make distinctions between different individuals and social groups in areas such as taxation and **pension** arrangements, if these issues are not seen as involving issues of individual dignity. For example, teachers and nurses living in London can be paid more than teachers and nurses living outside of London, due to the high cost of living in the capital: however, the courts will usually not be concerned with this type of difference of treatment, as this distinction would not be regarded as involving discrimination based on a denial of equal dignity. However, discrimination that denies or threatens individual autonomy, integrity, and equality of respect will be treated with much greater seriousness. For example, the Canadian courts have extended constitutional protection to individuals that suffer discrimination based on their sexual orientation or disabled status, on the grounds that these types of inequality usually involves a process of **stereotyping** disadvantaged groups which undermines their right to equality of respect.

The concept of dignity is also sometimes used to identify when the treatment of individuals and groups has crossed the threshold of acceptability. In South Africa and Canada, the courts have struck down **legislation** that discriminated against **homosexuals** and same-sex partners, and other laws that discriminated against women in family law and the **criminal justice system**, on the basis that these laws treated the affected groups as being 'second-class citizens' and therefore denied their right to be treated with dignity as equal members of society. The development of legal protection against sexual and other forms of **harassment** has also been based on the need to make sure that individuals are treated with appropriate respect.

A dignity-based approach can also prevent 'levelling down', ie where, in order to make sure everyone is treated the same, benefits given to one group are taken from them and not extended to any others. Respecting human dignity may require that special assistance is given to all that may require it, and that differences of **capacity**, belief, and **identity** are accommodated if necessary. This is particularly important when it comes to disability: a failure to make **reasonable accommodation** for the needs of many disabled persons may result in their autonomy and **self-determination** being severely eroded.

The advantage of using the concept of human dignity in these ways is that it gives some substantive content to the often uncertain idea of equality. However, some criticisms can also be made of the link increasingly made between dignity and equality. Some academics have argued that dignity is too vague a concept to give clear guidance to judges and policymakers. Also, there is the danger that some forms of unfair discrimination which are not regarded as affecting human dignity will be ignored. The UK courts are slowly developing a concept of human dignity in how they are interpreting and applying the **European Convention on Human Rights**. However, in contrast to developments in Canada and South Africa in particular, this new approach has been slow, tentative, and cautious. It remains to be seen whether a strong concept of dignity emerges in UK law and how it might affect questions of discrimination and equality. COLM O'CINNEIDE

Dimes v The Proprietors of the Grand Junction Canal (1852) In order to preserve public confidence in the judiciary it is important that decision-makers, including judges, should not be, or appear to be, biased or, in other words, to exhibit an improper tendency to decide for one side or the other in a dispute.

Dimes's case is a foundation stone of this principle. It concerned a dispute over the ownership of certain land over which ran the Grand Junction Canal. Injunctions had been made restraining William Dimes, who claimed an interest in the land, from impeding navigation. But he placed a chain across the canal and dug a trench across the tow path; and was in due course committed to prison.

Lord Chancellor Cottenham had affirmed the injunction made by the Vice-Chancellor in favour of the canal company. But it turned out that Lord Cottenham was a shareholder in the company to the extent of several thousand pounds. His decrees were set aside by the **House of Lords** on account of his pecuniary interest: a direct financial interest in the outcome of a decision disqualifies the decision-maker.

But this did not avail William Dimes. The House then dealt with the appeal on its merits, and affirmed the decrees of the Vice-Chancellor. But Lord Campbell said: 'No one can suppose that Lord Cottenham could be, in the remotest degree, influenced by the interest that he had in this concern; but, my Lords, it is of the last importance that the maxim, that no man is to be a judge in his own cause, should be held sacred . . . And it will have a most salutary influence on [inferior] tribunals when it is known that this High Court of last resort, in a case in which the Lord Chancellor of England had an interest, considered that his decree was on that account a decree not according to law, and was set aside'.

It has recently become clear that the principle of automatic disqualification extends beyond the pecuniary and proprietary interests in play in *Dimes*. It applies equally where the judge is himself a party or has a relevant interest in the subject matter of the litigation, even if he has no financial interest in its outcome. This was the result of *R v Bow Street Metropolitan Stipendiary Magistrate, ex p Pinochet Ugarte (No 2)* (2000). This case concerned the validity of extradition warrants made against a former head of state. Amnesty International were given leave to intervene in the proceedings before the House of Lords. One of the Law Lords (Lord Hoffmann) was the (unpaid) chairman of another company under the control of Amnesty International. The Law Lord had no financial interest in the outcome and was not formally a party to the proceedings. Even so, his close association with a party was enough automatically

to disqualify him; and the matter was reheard before a differently constituted Appeal Committee.

CHRISTOPHER F FORSYTH

See also: **natural justice**

diminished responsibility   *see* **mental incapacity and crime**

diplomatic immunity   *see* **immunity, diplomatic and state**

diplomatic protection   *see* **state claims**

diplomatic relations, immunities and privileges

The law on diplomatic relations provides the procedures and rules under which independent sovereign states do official business with each other to protect and further their own interests. Establishment and maintenance of diplomatic relations require the consent of both states. If either one breaks off relations, the two states no longer have diplomatic relations. In modern times, states maintain diplomatic relations with almost all other States which they recognize, but the sending of permanent–or even special–ambassadors and missions is much more limited. The framework for the modern law is the 1961 Vienna Convention on Diplomatic Relations ('the Vienna Convention') to which almost all states are parties. Because of the reciprocity underlying diplomatic relations there is a high degree of compliance with its rules.

The key functions of ambassadors and other diplomatic agents are to protect the interests of their own state ('the sending state') and of its nationals, to negotiate on its behalf with the government of the state where they are posted ('the receiving state') and to provide confidential reporting on conditions and prospects in the receiving state. These functions have remained unchanged over the many centuries that states have maintained relations among themselves on a basis of sovereign equality; only techniques have changed in the light of modern methods of travel and communications. To enable diplomats to carry out their functions effectively they are protected by special rules—immunities and privileges—which enable them to act without fear of coercion or harassment through enforcement of local laws, and to communicate freely and securely with their sending governments.

Except where diplomats are given a privilege or special exemption—for example in regard to most direct taxes, social security contributions, and customs duties—local laws apply to diplomats; but because of diplomatic immunities they cannot be enforced by local police or courts. Where there is abuse, political pressure may be exercised through the ministry of foreign affairs for the sending state to waive immunity; and an individual diplomat in breach of local law may be declared *persona non grata* and required to leave. Breaking off of diplomatic relations—the most extreme sanction—is reserved for cases of flagrant abuse, such as the shooting of a policewoman from the premises of the Libyan mission in London in 1984 or complicity by the Syrian mission in London in attempted sabotage of an Israeli airliner in 1986.

Premises of the Mission

Under the Vienna Convention the premises of a diplomatic mission (an embassy or, among states of the **Commonwealth**, a High Commission) are inviolable. Inviolability means, first, that no form of law enforcement such as police entry, search or official requisition may take place without consent of the head of mission and, second, that the receiving state has a special duty to protect the premises from intrusion or damage and to prevent any disturbance of the peace or impairment of dignity. In policing demonstrations outside embassies a balance must be struck between these duties and rights of protesters to freedom of speech and assembly. To qualify for inviolability, premises must be 'used for the purposes of the mission'; and in borderline cases such as cultural institutes, sending and receiving states must agree on application of this definition. A receiving state may impose procedures when new premises are acquired, provided that it does not obstruct the sending state in its search for suitable premises.

Archives and Communications

Under the Vienna Convention, archives and documents of a mission in whatever form (including modern forms of information storage) are inviolable wherever they may be, and the receiving state may not seize, detain or inspect them or permit their use in legal proceedings. Documents released by or under the authority of the mission, whether to a third party or into the public domain, are no longer inviolable.

The Convention guarantees the mission a right to free and secure communication with the sending state, although operation of a wireless transmitter requires consent of the receiving state. The diplomatic bag, used for transmission of documents and official articles between the mission and the sending state, may not be opened or detained. Electronic screening of the bag is generally not permitted—modern technology enables identification of contents and even deciphering of letters, which would violate the right to secure communication.

Diplomatic Agents

Diplomatic agents have personal inviolability—they may not be arrested, searched, or compulsorily tested. The sanctity of the person of an ambassador is the oldest established rule of international law. If a diplomat declines to submit voluntarily to pre-flight screening, a carrier may refuse to permit the person to travel. Widespread kidnapping of diplomats followed by demands for ransom or prisoner release declined when it became generally accepted that the Vienna Convention did not require receiving states to comply with unlawful or unreasonable demands. Diplomats are immune from criminal jurisdiction and, subject to three exceptions, from civil jurisdiction. They are exempt from the obligation to give evidence as a witness.

Any of these immunities may be waived—but waiver must be express and authorised by the sending state. Waivers have become more common—particularly for drugs charges—in recent years; but sending states usually prefer to withdraw a diplomat rather than risk his conviction and imprisonment in the receiving state. When a diplomat returns, the immunity lapses for personal matters, but continues to cover official acts. Full diplomatic immunities and privileges extend to members of a diplomat's family (spouse and minor children at the least) living with the diplomat. The Vienna Convention contains complex rules for different categories of junior staff and for diplomats and junior staff who are nationals or permanent residents of the receiving state. Diplomats in transit to or from post are entitled in third states to inviolability and such other immunities as are required to secure their transit or return.

EILEEN DENZA

J Salmon, *Manuel de Droit Diplomatique* (Brussels: Bruylant, 1994)

E Denza, *Diplomatic Law* (Oxford: Oxford University Press, 3rd edn, 2008)

direct applicability of EU law   Direct applicability (or direct effect) is one of the fundamental legal doctrines of the European Community (the 'First **Pillar**' of the European Union). Article 249 of the Treaty of Rome describes regulations adopted by the Community as being 'directly applicable' within the national legal systems: regulations become an integral part of the Member State's legal order, without necessarily being transposed into a domestic legal instrument (such as an Act of **Parliament**). The Treaty of

Rome was silent as to the legal effects of other forms of **European Community law**, but in *van Gend en Loos* (1963), the **European Court of Justice** ('ECJ') held that provisions of the Treaty itself may also have 'direct effect': they may act as an autonomous source of rights and obligations within the national legal system, which must be recognized and enforced as such by the domestic **courts.** Although some authors draw a conceptual distinction between 'direct applicability' and 'direct effect', the ECJ treats the terms interchangeably in practice. Since *van Gend en Loos*, other binding instruments of Community law (directives, decisions, and general principles) have also been recognized as capable of having direct effect. According to the principle of **supremacy of EC law**, directly effective Community law must take precedence over all conflicting provisions of purely national law.

For any provision of Community law to have direct effect, it must satisfy certain threshold criteria. First, the relevant provision must be sufficiently clear, precise, and unconditional: it should be possible accurately to identify the content of the rights and obligations created by Community law on the basis of the relevant provisions themselves, without any significant **discretion** being left in this regard to the Member States or the Community legislature. These criteria are applied flexibly, on a case-by-case basis. Even if direct effect is excluded on this particular ground, the national courts are under a duty to interpret domestic law, so far as possible, to comply with the objectives sought by the relevant Community provisions. Secondly, the deadline (if any) for transposition of the relevant Community provisions into national law must have expired. This is most commonly the case with directives, which set out certain objectives to be achieved by the Member States, but grant the latter time within which to adopt the necessary measures under national law. Once that deadline passes, if the Member State has not complied with its Community obligations, then direct effect becomes possible.

Assuming these threshold criteria are satisfied, the question then arises: who may rely on directly effective Community law? In many cases, the relevant provisions will create rights (eg to non-discrimination on grounds of **nationality** or **sex**) which are intended to benefit an identifiable class of individuals. However, certain provisions of Community law are intended to protect the public (rather than any private) interest; this is the case with many environmental protection measures. Such provisions may still have direct effect, acting in a manner akin to *locus standi* under English administrative law:

Community law may be invoked before the national courts by interested parties, so as to require public authorities (and natural / legal **persons**) to respect the obligations imposed upon them by Community law in the general interest.

The converse question also arises: who may be bound to observe directly effective Community law? In the case of the Treaty itself, regulations, decisions, and general principles, the ECJ has established that the relevant Community provisions may, in principle, be enforced against both public authorities and private parties (though whether this is the case in practice depends on the particular provision at issue). The position is more complex as regards directives. Failure by the Member State to fulfil its duty to implement a directive into national law within the prescribed deadline can justify permitting individuals to enforce that directive against public bodies. However, the ECJ has ruled that, since private parties are not the direct addressees of any obligations contained in Community directives, such measures cannot of themselves be enforced against individuals. While this distinction has a certain internal logic, it gives rise to anomalous results: for example, if a Member State fails to implement the Community directive on sex **equality** as regards employment within its deadline, **victims** of sex discrimination may rely upon the directly effective provisions of that directive against their employer *only* if the latter happens to be a public authority, *not* a purely private undertaking.

There are various ways of mitigating this limitation on the direct effect of directives. First, the national courts remain bound to interpret national law, so far as possible, in accordance with Community law; this might result in the relevant directive binding the private party indirectly, ie through the medium of domestic law, without amounting to direct effect *per se*. Secondly, the Member State may be found liable, in accordance with the principles established in the case of *Francovich* (1991), to make reparation to individuals who are unable to enforce their rights under an unimplemented directive. This depends on the Member State having committed a 'sufficiently serious breach' of its obligation to implement the directive into national law.

The situation is rather different as regards the 'Third Pillar' of the European Union: **police** and judicial cooperation in criminal matters. Here, the Treaty on European Union explicitly states that the two main legislative instruments available to the Union institutions—framework decisions and decisions (similar to First Pillar directives and decisions, respectively)—are not capable of having direct effect. Nevertheless, the ECJ has established that the national courts remain bound, as regards Third Pillar instruments, by the same duty as applies in the field of First Pillar law, ie to interpret domestic rules, so far as possible, in compliance with Union law. It remains to be settled whether the *Francovich* principle will also apply to the Third Pillar, allowing individuals adversely affected by a Member State's failure to implement a framework decision or decision to seek **compensation** for their losses. It seems safe to assume that the doctrine of direct effect does not apply to measures adopted pursuant to the Second Pillar concerning the Union's common foreign and **security** policy.   MICHAEL DOUGAN

direct discrimination   The concept of 'direct discrimination' includes some of the most obvious and everyday examples of discrimination. For example, if a **person** is refused a job because of their ethnic origin, this would be direct discrimination on grounds of **ethnicity**. Alternatively, if a club does not permit entry to persons under twenty-five, this would be direct discrimination on grounds of age. In these examples, direct discrimination is overt, but it can also be covert. If a woman is refused a promotion, she may suspect that it was connected to her **gender**. However, the employer might explain the decision by reference to other criteria, such as experience and work performance. Indeed, as employers and service-providers have become familiar with the requirements of anti-discrimination **legislation**, overt instances of discrimination appear to have declined. This has been recognized by the **courts**: 'it is important to bear in mind that it is unusual to find direct evidence of racial discrimination. Few employers will be prepared to admit such discrimination even to themselves. In some cases the discrimination will not be ill-intentioned but merely based on an assumption "he or she would not have fitted in"' (Lord Justice Neill in *King v Great Britain-China Centre* (1992)). Therefore, one of the main challenges encountered by law is establishing **causation** in alleged cases of direct discrimination.

Three steps can be identified in the conventional approach of courts to locating direct discrimination. First, the courts often begin by searching for an appropriate **comparator** for the individual complainant. Therefore, if a **woman** is claiming direct **sex** discrimination, the courts will seek to identify a similarly situated man in order to compare their treatment. This reflects the theoretical underpinning of direct discrimination, which is often described as '**formal equality**'. In essence, this is the idea that **equality** means the same treatment of

persons in the same situation: like should be treated alike. Once a comparator has been identified, then the next step is to ask whether the complainant has been treated less favourably than her comparator. If a man has been appointed to a vacancy and a female complainant is alleging direct sex discrimination in that decision, then the less favourable treatment will be the act of not appointing the woman to the job. Where less favourable treatment is established, then the final step is to determine the reason for this treatment. The fact that a man has been appointed to a job vacancy rather than a woman might be because of direct sex discrimination, but equally it might be because of non-discriminatory reasons, such as performance in the job interview.

The process described above for identifying direct discrimination has, though, proven controversial and difficult to apply in all cases. Problems often arise surrounding who is the appropriate comparator. A good illustration can be found in the case of *Grant v South West Trains* (1998). Workers for a train company were entitled to free travel for their spouses or cohabiting opposite-sex partners. Ms Grant claimed a free travel pass for her same-sex partner, but this was refused. She argued that this was direct sex discrimination; a man living with a woman was granted the pass, whereas a woman living with a woman was not. The **European Court of Justice** decided that this was the wrong comparison to make and that the correct comparison was between the treatment of a woman living with a woman and a man living with a man. As in both situations male or female employees with same-sex partners were refused the travel pass, then there was no sex discrimination. The difficulty with such cases is that the courts often fail to explain the principled basis for why one type of comparator should be preferred to another. The outcome of the entire case turns on the preliminary question of selecting the appropriate comparator, but at times this choice seems rather arbitrary. As a consequence, some **judges** have proposed a more flexible approach, where identification of the correct comparator does not always need to take place before considering the other elements. In particular, it has been suggested that some cases of direct discrimination might be more easily resolved by focusing on the final step; what was the *reason* for the less favourable treatment?

Aside from the mechanics of how to analyse complaints of direct discrimination, there is a more deep-seated critique of the comparator approach. Sandra Fredman has argued that the comparator test tends to reinforce **assimilation** to the existing norm, rather than creating space for diversity.

Specifically, complainants will often be comparing themselves to the treatment of someone who is male/white/able-bodied/heterosexual/etc. It may be the norm for employees to have **holidays** at Christmas and Easter, but simply being treated in the same way will not address the situation of non-Christian employees who may wish to enjoy holidays around other religious festivals, such as Eid or Diwali. Challenges to such practices will typically be brought as complaints of **indirect discrimination**.

The conventional approach in UK **legislation** has been that direct discrimination cannot be justified. This means that the motive of an employer or service-provider is not relevant to determining whether unlawful direct discrimination has occurred. This principle has been particularly advantageous in combating stereotypes. For example, a publican cannot justify refusing entry to a bar to a Traveller on the basis that the other customers might object.

Whilst direct discrimination normally cannot be justified, this is balanced by the inclusion within legislation of narrow statutory exceptions. Here, actions that would otherwise constitute unlawful direct discrimination can be permitted. These exceptions vary according to the ground of discrimination, but a common exception is for 'genuine occupational requirements'. This covers situations where the prohibited ground actually can be relevant to the context in which a person performs a job. For instance, in making a film of the life of Martin Luther King, it would be a genuine occupational requirement to stipulate that the lead actor shares a similar ethnic origin to the role he was playing. Clearly, a white actor could play the role, but given the centrality of Martin Luther King's ethnicity to his life story, a white actor might seem unconvincing and inappropriate to audiences. Other areas where statutory exceptions are permitted to direct discrimination include sex requirements in relation to modelling or religious requirements for some posts within an organization with a religious ethos (such as faith schools).

Finally, it is worth noting that the introduction in 2006 of legislation on age **discrimination in employment** has challenged the conventional model where direct discrimination cannot be justified. Direct discrimination on grounds of age can be justified if it pursues a legitimate aim and it is a proportionate means of achieving that aim. Therefore, an employer who imposed medical checks on employees over fifty-five using dangerous machinery could mount the argument that this was justified by reasons of health and safety. By permitting the justification of direct discrimination, there is a risk that this will diminish the capacity of the law to tackle age-based

stereotypes. Furthermore, it places greater control into the hands of the judiciary to determine when direct age discrimination should or should not be allowed. MARK BELL

See also: **stereotyping**

S Fredman, *Discrimination Law* (Oxford: Oxford University Press, 2002), ch 4

A McColgan, *Discrimination Law—Text, Cases and Materials* (Oxford: Hart Publishing, 2nd edn, 2005), ch 2

direct effect of EU law *see* **direct applicability of EU law**

Directives *see* **European Community Legal Instruments**

Director of Public Prosecutions The Director of Public Prosecutions ('DPP') is the head of the **Crown Prosecution Service** ('CPS'), which is responsible for prosecuting those criminal cases which the **police** desire to be taken to **court**. The DPP can also bring a **prosecution** in person, take over private prosecutions brought by members of the public, and terminate any prosecution under his or her control. The DPP is appointed and supervised by the **Attorney General**, who is a government Minister, answerable to **Parliament** for the DPP's actions.

The 'system' of prosecutions in England and Wales has developed haphazardly and the office of the DPP reflects this. The office was created by **legislation** in 1879 to supplement existing arrangements whereby senior government lawyers (including the Attorney-General and the **Solicitor General**) controlled prosecutions of particular importance or complexity. Vestiges of the historical role of the DPP can be seen in the fact that, for certain offences, his or her consent is required before a prosecution can be commenced. The long list of these offences is replete with anomalies and absurdities. It includes, for example, the offence of purporting to act as a medium with intent to deceive.

The modern form of the DPP was brought about by the Prosecution of Offences Act 1985 which created the CPS. Crown Prosecutors were given all of the powers of the DPP but must exercise those powers under the latter's direction. The DPP issues a Code for Crown Prosecutors on the general principles to be applied when deciding whether to start, amend, or terminate a prosecution, and also provides more detailed guidance on specific offences and decisions (all of which can be found on the internet at *http://www.cps.gov.uk/*).

In 2003 the formal police power to initiate prosecutions was transferred to the CPS other than in minor cases. Even following this change it would be misleading to say that the DPP directs all significant public prosecutions. There are many other **regulatory agencies** which handle their own prosecutions, such as the **Environment Agency**, the Health and Safety Executive, and Her Majesty's Revenue and Customs. In addition, the DPP can do nothing about cases in which the police decide to take no further action, or to impose a penalty which does not require the involvement of prosecutors or the courts, such as a fixed-penalty notice, a reprimand or a warning (for youths), or police cautions (for adults).

It is accordingly impossible for the DPP to ensure that offences of similar gravity are treated similarly. For example, nearly all offences committed by **companies** are dealt with by non-police agencies (which have a presumption against prosecution even for fairly serious offences), whereas most offences committed by individuals are dealt with by the police and the CPS (which broadly share a presumption in favour of prosecution regardless of seriousness). Since the DPP's glossy, self-congratulatory annual reports to Parliament cover only CPS prosecutions, the huge disparities of approach remain largely hidden. Until the DPP is made responsible for all prosecution policies and agencies, the system of prosecution is likely to remain productive of injustice.

RICHARD YOUNG

Directorate-General for Competition The Directorate-General for Competition ('DG Competition' or, in internal Commission jargon, 'DG COMP') is one of the twenty-three Directorates-General which make up the bulk of the 'services' of the **European Commission**. Its stated mission is to enforce Community **competition** rules in order to ensure that competition in the **internal market** is not distorted, thereby contributing to the welfare of consumers and the competitiveness of the European economy. In UK terms, it is a hybrid of a government department and the **Office of Fair Trading**. Its principal activities are in the areas of:

- **antitrust**: the application and enforcement of Community rules on **cartels**, abuse of monopoly or near monopoly market strength, and restrictive practices. These matters lie at the core, and form the bulk, of its work;
- control of mergers and takeovers (in Community terms, '**concentration**s');
- control of state intervention: ensuring that public authorities and publicly owned and operated

undertakings are not allowed to distort the processes of competition and, related to that, the liberalization of markets; and

- state aids.

It also plays the pivotal role in the decentralized enforcement of the antitrust rules within the **European Competition Network**. It enforces, within the Community, the competition rules of the European Economic Area and deals with the (rapidly expanding) international dimension of competition policy in dealing with equivalent authorities in third countries.

DG Competition has its own Director-General and (normally) three deputy Directors-General. It is divided into ten directorates. Two are responsible for administrative and central services (strategic planning and resources; policy and strategic support). Four are sector specific (energy, basic industries, chemicals, and pharmaceuticals; information, communications and media; services; industry, consumer goods, and manufacturing). One is devoted to cartels, and three to state aids (cohesion and competitiveness; network industries, liberalized sectors, and services; policy and strategic coordination). Each directorate is headed by a director, who assumes responsibility for the file in a case investigation. It used to include a Merger Task Force but this was dissolved in 2003 and integrated into the sector directorates. That year also saw the appointment of a 'chief competition economist' with overall advisory responsibilities, assisted by teams of specialist economists. In 2006 the DG had a staff of about 750, most trained in law and/or economics.

DG Competition is politically responsible to the Commissioner for competition, there always being a dedicated Commissioner with the competition 'portfolio'. Formal decisions are taken by the college of Commissioners, but all preliminary and preparatory work—fact finding (investigation, examination), the compulsory hearing of parties (under the authority of the Hearings Officer who is, for reasons of impartiality, attached to the Commissioner's office and not the DG), drafting of any formal decision—is done by DG Competition. It liaises with other interested DGs, particularly as regards state aids, and works most closely and constantly with the Commission's legal service both in formulating action and in dealing with the frequent challenges to it by disgruntled parties before the Community courts, in which proceedings the Commission as litigant party is represented by an 'agent' from the legal service with support from DG Competition.

RICHARD LANE

See also: **abuse of dominant position; state aid (in EC law)**

directors   Directors decide the strategic direction and oversee the management of a **company**'s business. Company law contemplates that they will act collectively as a **board of directors**. The role and functions of directors are not prescribed by **legislation** but are left to be fleshed out by company participants according to business need. Every company must have directors. **Private companies** may operate with a sole director. Directors are not automatically managers or employees although, in practice, they will often be employed under service contracts. Listed companies are required to appoint non-executive directors from outside to provide an independent voice on such matters as the appointment and remuneration of the executive directors.

Directors formally appointed in accordance with the procedures in the company's articles of association and who have consented to act are *de jure* directors. *De jure* directors are subject to **directors' duties**. **Persons** who are not *de jure* directors may be treated as such in law so as to render them liable for breach of directors' duties and/or to bring them within the scope of the disqualification regime. There are two such categories: (i) *de facto* directors: persons who act as if they were *de jure* directors although not appointed as such; (ii) shadow directors: persons in accordance with whose directions or instructions the *de jure* directors are accustomed to act. Those involved in directing the company's business cannot therefore evade liability for **governance** failings on the pretext that they were not formally appointed.

ADRIAN WALTERS

See also: **independent directors**

directors and shareholders   Companies have two decision-making bodies or organs: the **board of directors** and the members in general meeting. In the case of companies limited by shares, the members are the shareholders. Articles of association commonly confer extensive powers of management on the **directors** whilst reserving certain matters such as the appointment of directors and the approval of **dividends** to the shareholders for determination by majority vote. The Companies Acts also reserve a number of fundamental matters for decision by the shareholders such as changes to the articles, the removal of directors from office, and the entry of the company into voluntary liquidation. This division of powers between directors and shareholders has been reinforced by **court** rulings establishing the principle that shareholders cannot interfere in matters which fall within the directors' remit as defined by the articles. Thus, in theory, as long as the matter is not reserved to the shareholders by the Companies Acts or the articles, the directors may take decisions and pursue business strategies that are against the wishes of the shareholders. In these circumstances, unless it can be said that the directors have breached their duties, the only sanction available to the shareholders is to exercise their powers to remove the incumbents and replace them with new directors who may be more inclined to act in accordance with their wishes. Where the board cannot function properly (for example, because the directors have fallen out and are refusing to meet so that the quorum requirements of the articles are not satisfied), the courts have ruled that the board's powers revert to the shareholders by way of exception to the general principle.

The division of powers principle reflects the workings of **public companies**. These companies are mechanisms through which entrepreneurs can raise finance on the capital markets from a wide pool of investors. As a result, the owners (shareholders) and managers (directors) of public companies will typically be different people. This pattern of business organization in which the functions of investment and management are differentiated has exerted a powerful influence on the evolution of company law, much of which is concerned with the **accountability** of the directors to shareholders through a variety of means such as **directors' duties** and the promotion of shareholder democracy. However, the rigid distinction between directors and shareholders which functions well in the context of public companies has proved less helpful for small **private companies** many of which are owner-managed (ie the directors and shareholders are the same people) and which are run with considerably less formality in practice. In particular, it is inconvenient for directors of owner-managed private companies to be forced to convene general meetings where they need to take decisions in their **capacity** as shareholders. The blurring of the distinction between directors and shareholders that can be observed in private companies and the greater informality with which they are run has led to the legislative streamlining of decision-making procedures for these companies and the removal of other regulatory burdens.   ADRIAN WALTERS

See also: **shareholder power**

directors, appointment and removal of   The Companies Acts require **companies** to have **directors**, to maintain a register of directors, and to notify the registrar of companies of any change to its directors but does not prescribe the manner of their appointment. The first directors are the **persons** named in the company's **incorporation** documents. Thereafter, the appointment process is determined by the company's participants and is usually set out in the articles of association. Articles commonly provide for directors to be appointed by members' resolution and/or by the **board of directors** subject to subsequent confirmation by the members. Persons must be at least sixteen before taking office but otherwise are not required to have any particular training or qualifications. At least one director must be a natural person. Disqualified persons cannot take office without the **court**'s permission.

The Companies Acts provide that directors can be removed from office by members' resolution. A general meeting must be held to consider the resolution. Directors have the right to protest against their removal. Removal does not affect the director's rights arising from any service contract. The position of directors who are also shareholders can be entrenched by providing in the articles that they will have additional voting rights on a resolution to remove them from office. Articles commonly provide for directors to retire periodically (forcing them to stand down or put up for re-election) and to vacate office in the event of disqualification or other legal disability (for example, under mental health **legislation**). ADRIAN WALTERS

directors, disqualification of   *see* **disqualification of directors**

directors' duties   Directors have extensive legal duties which can be categorized as follows: (i) fiduciary duties; (ii) duty of care and skill; (iii) statutory duties. As a general rule, **directors**' civil law duties are owed to and are enforceable by the **company** as a legal **person** acting through its board, general meeting, or (in the event of insolvent liquidation) **liquidator**. Individual members cannot generally bring proceedings for breach of these duties against wrongdoing directors.

First, let us consider fiduciary duties. Directors are *agents* of the company and are treated as **fiduciaries**. Accordingly, they are subject to the category of legal obligations known as fiduciary duties which were developed historically by the **courts** of equity to regulate the conduct of trustees. Fiduciary duties are concerned with concepts of honesty and loyalty rather than competence or negligence. They seek to ensure that directors pursue the company's interests rather than their own personal interests. In an attempt to make the law more accessible, the underlying equitable principles have been distilled and the duties set out in statutory form in the Companies Act 2006.

The main fiduciary duties are as follows:

(i) A director must act in accordance with the company's constitution. Directors who enter into contracts, dispose of company property, or otherwise act beyond the scope of the company's **capacity** or the directors' powers as set out in the articles of association are said to act in excess of their powers. Failure to comply with the constitution may affect the validity of the relevant transaction although there are extensive statutory provisions that allow such transactions to be enforced against the company in order to protect third parties. The directors are liable to make good any losses that the company suffers as a result of the breach of duty.

(ii) A director must only exercise powers for the purposes for which they are conferred. As well as acting within the scope of their powers, directors must exercise them for 'proper purposes'. To do otherwise is an abuse of power. In order to evaluate whether this duty has been breached the court must construe the articles to ascertain objectively the purposes that the relevant power was designed to serve and then review the exercise of the power to establish whether it was used for its proper ends. Several of the cases in which the duty has been considered have concerned the allotting of shares for the improper purpose of seeking to block a **takeover**. Transactions or dealings entered into by the directors in abuse of power may be subject to challenge. The directors are also liable to make good any losses that the company suffers as a result.

(iii) A director must act in the way he considers, in good faith, would be most likely to promote the success of the company for the benefit of its members as a whole. As Lord Greene, then **Master of the Rolls**, put it in *Re Smith & Fawcett Ltd* (1942) directors, 'must exercise their **discretion** *bona fide* in what they consider—not what a court may consider—is in the interests of the company'. Under the statutory reformulation of this duty 'the interests of the company' are equated with the collective interest of the members. However, in discharging the duty the directors must also have regard to a number of factors set out in the statute which include the likely long-term consequences of any decision, the interests of the company's employees, the need to foster the company's business relationships with suppliers, customers, and others, and the impact of the company's operations on the **community** and the environment. The requirement to consider these factors has provoked controversy. Business leaders fear that the scope of the duty is too ill-defined and will increase the risk of legal liability resulting in a more defensive management culture. However, it is clear from the statutory language that the court cannot substitute its own judgment for commercial judgments made in good faith by the directors. Breach of the duty is an abuse of power and has similar legal consequences to a breach of the 'proper purposes' duty.

(iv) A director must exercise independent judgment. This reflects the former equitable rule barring directors from fettering their discretion by binding themselves to exercise their powers in the future in a particular way. The problem with such fetters is that they prevent the directors from exercising an independent judgment as to what is in the interests of the company at the relevant point in time. However, the duty is not infringed if directors act in accordance with an agreement restricting the future exercise of their discretion that itself was entered into in good faith or in a way authorized by the company's articles.

(v) A director of a company must avoid a situation in which he has, or can have, a direct or indirect interest that conflicts, or possibly may conflict, with the interests of the company. Liability under the 'no conflict' duty is triggered where a director is representing both himself and the company on either end of the same transaction. The concern is that the director's duty to act in the interests of the company may be compromised by his self-interest in these circumstances. The conflict may be actual or potential. To illustrate, let us say that ABC Ltd enters into a contract to sell some land to one of its directors, X. Even if X agrees to pay the full market value, the fact that he is on the other side of the transaction gives rise to the possibility of a conflict of interest and duty. The director's interest may be direct or indirect. By contracting in his own name to buy the land from ABC Ltd, X has a direct interest. If instead ABC Ltd contracted to sell the land to another company owned by X, X's interest would be indirect. Where a director is in any way, directly or indirectly, interested in a proposed transaction or arrangement with the company, he is also obliged to declare the nature and extent of that interest to the other directors before the company enters into the transaction or arrangement. Conflicts of interest are remedied by reversing the effect of the tainted transaction and restoring the parties as far as is practicable to the *status quo ante*. The duty applies equally where a director exploits for his own benefit any property, information or opportunity which, by virtue of his office, he ought to exploit for the benefit of the company. Here the director will be liable to account to the company for his personal gains. As a general rule, actions that would otherwise breach the 'no conflict' duty may be authorized in advance or ratified after the event by the members where the director has made full and frank disclosure of his interest. This mirrors the position in the law of **trusts** where the beneficiaries may consent to actions by the trustees that would otherwise be in **breach of trust**. The Companies Act 2006 allows the general rule to be modified by the company's articles to enable the board (acting through the other directors) to authorize or ratify transactions caught by the duty.

The second category of directors' duties encompasses duties of care and skill. As well as acting with honesty and propriety, directors must also exercise reasonable care, skill, and diligence: in other words they must be reasonably competent. The standards of competence expected of directors by the courts have not traditionally been high. This is partly because directorship is not an established profession and may also reflect the fact that the members have it in their power to replace directors who are not up to the task. Modern company law, however, imposes a more professional standard. Directors are now required as a minimum to perform their functions to the standard of a reasonably diligent person with the general knowledge, skill, and experience that may reasonably be expected of a person carrying out the functions which they carry out in relation to the company. This is a flexible objective standard which enables the court to benchmark a director's conduct against what would be expected of a hypothetical director performing comparable functions in a comparable company. It follows that the level of competence expected of a director of a small family company will not be the same as that expected of a director of a large FTSE 100 company. More exacting standards can be imposed on directors through their service contracts. As with other forms of negligence liability, directors who breach the duty will be liable to compensate the company for any loss caused by the breach.

Finally, as well as the duties referred to above, the Companies Act 2006 imposes additional statutory controls on directors' conflicts of interest. There are also obligations relating to the preparation and approval of the company's annual accounts. Company law is far from being the only source of directors' duties. Directors have statutory obligations in other fields including insolvency law, environmental law, and health and safety law.   ADRIAN WALTERS

disability Legislation in the United Kingdom has been concerned with disability, and specifically disabled people, for many years. In the nineteenth century, disabled people who were unable to work were given **Poor Law** Relief—namely a place in the workhouse or money from public funds. They were regarded as the 'worthy poor'—as opposed to the work-shy 'unworthy poor', who were treated less favourably. By the early twentieth century **legislation**, such as the Mental Deficiency Act 1913, led to the increased institutionalization and segregation of disabled people. This occurred not only with regard to places of residence, but in other areas of life such as education and employment.

The approach to disability that provided the basis for such legislation was highly medicalized. The medical model of disability, which still influences legislation and policymakers, perceives disability as resulting from a physical or intellectual impairment, and the disadvantages which disabled people experience—such as lack of employment opportunities and access to education—are caused directly by the impairment. The disadvantages are therefore largely unconnected to the surrounding environment. Where medical intervention cannot remove the impairment, thereby enabling the individual to adapt to the prevailing norms and standards of society, legislation (and charity) provides for a system that meets the most basic needs of those people who are not able to support themselves through work. For example, in the sphere of employment, this model leads to an almost exclusive focus on rehabilitation—a medicalized approach to removing the impairment and its impact—with income support and sheltered employment being provided for those who are unable to compete in the open labour market, or even to work at all.

This model can be contrasted with the social model of disability, which has come to the fore in the UK and globally within the last twenty years or so. The social model is based on a socio-political approach which argues that disability stems primarily from the failure of the social environment to adjust to the needs and aspirations of people with impairments, rather than from the inability of people with impairments to adapt to the environment. The argument here is that it is discrimination, in both the physical and attitudinal environment, prejudice, stigmatization, segregation, and a general history of disadvantage associated with impairment—but which need not be associated with impairment—which is the major problem for disabled people. According to this perspective the difficulties confronting disabled people arise from the disabling environment rather than from impairment. An acceptance of the social model implies that society has the responsibility to adapt to meet the needs of people with impairments. At its most extreme, this model holds that disability is purely a social construction.

In spite of **recognition** by the UK government and policymakers of the importance and relevance of the social model of disability, there has been a failure to develop a legal definition of disability which is based on the social model, and the medicalized approach—defining disability in terms of impairment and in terms of what individuals cannot do—is still dominant in UK legislation. Nevertheless, the social model of disability has had an impact on UK disability legislation and policy and this is most evident with regard to the adoption of Disability Discrimination Act 1995.

Whilst the medicalized approach still determines the definition of disability found in UK legislation, even with regard to the Disability Discrimination Act, this is not to say that there is a single legal definition of disability within British law. Indeed, such a definition would not be desirable. This is because the definition of disability contained in any statute determines eligibility for the protection or benefit provided by that statute. Some statutes, such as those providing financial disability-related benefits, distribute scarce resources and should only be received by those who are most in need—which usually correlates to the degree of severity of disability. For example, incapacity benefits which are designed to provide a regular income to disabled people should only be available to those individuals whose degree of disability is so severe that they are unable to carry out any paid employment and thereby support themselves. In contrast some statutes—and the Disability Discrimination Act 1995 is a particularly good example—do not distribute scarce resources, and could potentially include a very wide definition of the protected group. Indeed, in countries such as The Netherlands, one does not even need to be disabled in order to claim protection under the disability non-discrimination statute, as the law protects both disabled people from disability-related discrimination, and non-disabled people from discrimination on the grounds that they do not have a disability. However, this is not the case in the United Kingdom, and only disabled people are entitled to make a claim that they have been the victim of disability discrimination.

Irrespective of the statute concerned, definitions of disability under UK law frequently consist of two elements—a reference to the origin and length of the impairment and the requirement that the impairment restricts the individual in carrying out certain activities. In the case of income support instruments, such as incapacity benefits, the requirement is that the disability results in an inability to work, and this must be confirmed by a member of the medical profession. In contrast, with regard to non-discrimination legislation relating to employment, the impairment must affect certain named 'day-to-day' activities, such as mobility or manual dexterity. Therefore, in order to claim protection under the Disability Discrimination Act an individual must first prove that they have a reduced ability to carry out certain basic activities (in order to qualify as disabled and fall under the scope of the Act), to be allowed to subsequently prove that they are able to carry out the employment or employment-related tasks (and therefore that they should not be treated adversely [discriminated against] on the grounds that they are less qualified than others, or even unqualified for the position). In practice this means that **courts** must first establish whether a complainant actually has a disability, and only if the court is satisfied that this is the case, will they consider the issue of whether discrimination has occurred.

The impairment which contributes to the disability can originate in a variety of ways. Impairments can be physical, intellectual, sensory, neurological, or have multiple causes and can include conditions as wide-ranging as heart disease, Down's syndrome, blindness, and Parkinson's disease. However, in order to qualify as a disability the condition must be permanent, long-lasting, or recurring (such as a series of episodes of depression) and have the required impact on the ability to function. This recognition of the medical origin of impairment should not, however, obscure the fact, that much of the disadvantage and difficulties experienced by disabled people result from the interaction between the impairment and the attitudinal and physical environment.

LISA WADDINGTON

See also: **incapacity for work**

disability benefits   The two main disability benefits in the social security system are attendance allowance and disability living allowance ('DLA'). These are both non-contributory benefits, so there is no requirement for a claimant to have paid **national insurance** contributions or to satisfy a means test. There is no direct linkage between the severity of a person's disability and the level of benefit to which they are entitled. Instead, both benefits use care needs (and also, in the case of DLA, mobility needs) as a proxy indicator for the level of disability experienced by an individual.

Attendance allowance is a benefit for disabled people who claim when they are aged sixty-five or over and who have care needs. A higher rate is paid to those with day and night time care needs and a lower rate for those whose care needs arise in the day, or at night, but not both. DLA, a benefit for those aged under sixty-five, including children, is a more complex benefit and consists of two components, a care component and a mobility component. Claimants may qualify for either or both components. The care component is paid at either the highest, middle, or lowest rates. The highest and middle rates of the care component are equivalent to the higher and lower rates of attendance allowance respectively in terms of both the entitlement criteria and the amount of benefit paid. The criteria for both day and night time needs are defined in terms of either how much help with personal functions or supervision the individual reasonably requires. The lowest rate care component, which has no equivalent in attendance allowance, is payable where an individual cannot prepare and cook a main meal for one person. The mobility component of DLA is paid at a higher and lower rate, depending on the nature and severity of the mobility needs. There is no mobility component to attendance allowance. DLA is the only social security benefit for which children may qualify in their own right, although they are subject to special rules.

The rather generalized entitlement criteria for attendance allowance and for both components of DLA are difficult to apply in practice. For example, the higher rate mobility component of DLA is payable where a person is virtually unable to walk. This requires consideration of the distance, speed, time, and manner of their walking, disregarding any walking which is achieved only with severe discomfort. This test, as with the criteria for the care component, inevitably gives rise to difficult questions of judgment. As a result, DLA claims tend to generate a substantial number of appeals before tribunals.

If a person receives either attendance allowance or the highest or middle rate of the DLA care component, another individual who looks after them may qualify for carer's allowance, also a non-contributory benefit. The **industrial injuries** and **war pensions** schemes make special and sometimes more generous provision for those who have been disabled as a result of either work or service in the armed forces.

NICK WIKELEY

See also: **means-tested benefits; non-contributory benefits**

disability discrimination *see* **disability; protected grounds; reasonable accommodation**

Disability Rights Commission *see* **Equality and Human Rights Commission**

disabled persons in the workplace *see* **disability**

disarmament *see* **arms control**

discipline in schools *see* **school discipline and the exclusion of pupils**

discipline in the workplace Disciplinary action can take a variety of forms including warnings, demotion, suspension, or dismissal, but an employer's right to take such action is not unfettered. Employers have an implied duty of trust and confidence, which has been defined as an obligation on the part of the employer not to 'conduct [himself] in a manner calculated or likely to, destroy or seriously damage the relationship of trust and confidence between employer and employee' (*Woods v WM Car Services (Peterborough) Ltd* (1981)).

This implied duty impacts upon the employer's right to take disciplinary action. For example, an employer who issues an employee with a final warning for reasons that are capricious will have acted in breach of the duty and therefore unlawfully. The written terms of the **contract of employment** may also limit the employer's disciplinary powers. For example, some contracts prescribe the grounds upon which certain disciplinary outcomes can be justified (eg 'theft will result in instant dismissal'). In most workplaces however all written disciplinary processes (eg 'disciplinary action must be preceded by a meeting with the employee to discuss the allegations') are contained in an employee handbook that will rarely have contractual force. Any failure by the employer to follow such processes will not be unlawful unless that failure amounts to a breach of the duty of trust and confidence, or it renders a dismissal non-compliant with the statutory protection against **unfair dismissal.**

The employer's ability to discipline its employees is also restricted by **legislation**, including the various statutes prohibiting discrimination. For example, an employer will act unlawfully if its reason for taking disciplinary action is based on the fact that the employee is a woman (Sex Discrimination Act 1975). In addition, the right to dismiss an employee as a form of disciplinary action is, as mentioned above, regulated by the law of unfair dismissal, including the statutory disciplinary procedure contained in Schedule 2 to the Employment Act 2002, although at the time of writing the government has just announced its intention to revoke this statutory procedure and replace it with a voluntary one.

DAVID HOOD

disclaimers *see* **exclusion clauses**

disclosure *see* **insurance contracts/policies; unfair commercial practices**

disclosure in civil litigation Disclosure in civil litigation is the process which enables the parties to discover evidence relevant to the issues between them which is or has been in the control of the other party. It can be crucial in assisting a party in proving or resisting a claim, and also in revealing the strength of the other party's case.

Part 31 of the **Civil Procedure Rules** 1998 ('CPR') deals with disclosure and inspection of documents. The Rules state, 'A party discloses a document by stating that the document exists or has existed'. A document is defined as 'anything in which information of any description is recorded'. That includes, for example, a video film.

Under the CPR an order for standard disclosure requires a party to disclose the documents which are or have been in his control (a) on which he relies; (b) which adversely affect his own case, adversely affect another party's case, or support another party's case; and (c) the documents required by a relevant practice direction. Control includes physical possession, a right to possession, or a right to inspect or take copies of it. A reasonable search must be conducted. That depends upon the number of documents, the ease and expense of their retrieval, the complexity of the proceedings, and the significance of any document likely to be located. The duty to disclose continues until the end of the proceedings.

Each party serves on the other a concise list of documents in a convenient order, indicating those in respect of which the party claims a right or duty to withhold inspection; and those documents which are no longer in the party's control; and what has happened to those documents.

A party to whom a document has been disclosed has a right to inspect that document unless the document is no longer in the control of the disclosing party or that person has a right or a duty to withhold inspection of it. A party may also inspect a document mentioned in a statement of case, a witness statement, a witness summary, an affidavit, or an expert's report. This right includes an entitlement to receive a copy of that document within seven days on giving an undertaking to pay a reasonable copying fee.

A person may apply for permission to withhold a document from disclosure on the ground that disclosure would damage the public interest. A party wishing to withhold a document must state their grounds, which could include: **legal professional privilege**, the privilege against **self-incrimination**, the requirements of **public policy**, disproportion between the difficulty of disclosure and the importance of the question in issue, a statutory requirement of secrecy, or a contrary agreement between the parties.

Documents disclosed in proceedings may be used only for the purposes of those proceedings unless the disclosing party agrees, the court gives permission, or the document has been read or referred to at a public hearing in the case. Even then the court may ban any other use of the document on application by either a party or the owner of the document.

JOHN FITZPATRICK

See also: **public interest immunity**

disclosure in criminal cases   *see* **evidence (criminal)**

disclosure in financial markets   Investors in financial markets cannot make a proper investment decision, whether buying or disposing of financial instruments, such as **shares**, bonds, or derivatives, unless they are adequately informed about the assets considered for investment. A sufficient level of transparency regarding relevant information is important not only from the point of view of an individual investor, but also for the orderly functioning of the markets generally: the absence of a system of timely disclosure of relevant information, or the lack of equal access by investors to this information, will either discourage investors from effecting transactions or distort the pricing mechanism of securities, as investors will discount the lack of information in their bid and ask prices. More fundamentally, a low degree of transparency of information will negatively impact on the ability of financial markets to function as an adequate source of finance for business entities.

From a regulatory point of view, an optimal system of disclosure of information in the financial markets should ensure (1) that all information which investors generally consider to be relevant to make their investment decision is disclosed; (2) that the information is disclosed in a timely way; and (3) that all investors are give equal access to information, thus preventing insiders taking advantage of information asymmetries.

The UK regulatory system is based to a large extent on a still-increasing number of European directives aimed at integrating capital markets in the **European Union**. First, the European Prospectus Directive 2003 mandates the publication of a **prospectus**, approved by a supervisory authority (in the UK the **Financial Services Authority**) for every **public offer** of **securities**, and for the admission of securities to trading on a regulated market (such as the London **Stock Exchange**). Under European and UK law, a 'public' offer is one made to at least 100 investors in each EU Member State. A private placement of securities does not attract statutory disclosure requirements. Nor do EU securities law directives regulate the disclosure regime applicable to companies whose securities are listed on a securities market that does not qualify as a 'regulated market'. This matter is left to regulation by Member States.

Under EU law and UK law, the prospectus for a public offer must contain all the information needed to enable an investor to make an informed assessment of the financial situation and the prospects of the issuer, and of the rights attached to the securities. In approving the prospectus, the main task of the supervisory authority is to assess the quality and comprehensiveness of the information contained in the prospectus, not to make a judgment on the quality of the opportunity provided by the public offer made by the issuer.

Once the securities are admitted to trading on a regulated market, the listed company is bound to disclose relevant information on a continuing basis. First, all listed companies must make available at least an annual and a half-yearly financial report. These reports contain not only the key financial figures of the issuer, but should also include a management report describing the possible risks and uncertainties facing the issuer. The latter requirement is consistent with the generally accepted view that the value of securities, unlike regular consumer goods, is highly contingent on the prospects and future performance of the issuer of the securities. In some markets there is an obligation to make more frequent periodical reports (eg on a quarterly basis).

Beside the periodical disclosure requirements, listed companies must disclose as soon as possible any inside information which directly concerns them. Inside information is any and all non-public information which, if made available, would be likely to have a significant effect, whether positive or negative, on the price of the securities. Immediate disclosure should ensure that insiders cannot take advantage of non-public information, to the detriment of other investors who lack the inside information, by buying securities (where the information is positive) or selling securities (where the information is negative). However, an issuer is allowed to defer the disclosure of inside information in order to protect its legitimate interests provided adequate procedures are put in place to guarantee the confidential character of the information. For instance, a company may have an interest in delaying for some time the disclosure of information on acquisition talks it is engaged into, in order not to frustrate the success of the ongoing negotiations.

Finally, the system for regulation of disclosure of information provides for transparency regarding the ownership structure of listed companies. Pursuant to the European Transparency Directive 2004, persons acquiring or disposing of a 'major shareholding' in a listed company should notify that company of the number of its voting rights when they exceed or fall below certain thresholds. The listed company should in turn publicly disclose the notifications it has received. To companies that fall under its jurisdiction, UK law applies a stricter regime with lower thresholds, thus providing a more detailed picture of the ownership structure of listed companies.

From an EU perspective, the harmonized disclosure regime operates under a system of 'home country control' and mutual recognition, thus avoiding the multiplication of disclosure requirements and the need to comply with multiple supervisory regimes when a company makes a multi-jurisdictional securities offering or seeks securities listing in several jurisdictions. Under this system, only one prospectus needs to be filed with and approved by the competent home-state supervisory authority for a multi-country public offer, and that approved prospectus must be recognized as a valid prospectus in the other countries where the public offer is made. Likewise, a company whose securities are traded in regulated markets in different EU Member States will only be subject, as concerns its ongoing disclosure obligations, to the supervisory system of the country which is designated under the EU regime as its home country. This mutual recognition and home country control system is generally perceived as an essential feature of the creation of integrated capital markets in the European Union.   MICHEL TISON

See also: **insider dealing; listing; transparency of securities trades**

discretion   We tend to think of law as a structure of authoritative rules intended to affect behaviour. But legal rules must be translated into action, involving processes of interpretation and choice in the exercise of discretion. Discretion is all-pervasive in legal systems. The meaning and relevance of rules must be defined, and facts need interpreting. This also means characterizing the present problem and judging whether it is addressed by the rule. The significance of discretion is that the everyday decision-making of **judges**, public officials, lawyers, and others distributes the burdens and benefits of law, provides answers to questions, and solutions to problems. Sometimes discretion is exercised collectively, with several people (panels, **tribunals**, **juries**) sharing decision-making, but it is frequently exercised by individuals, though legal decisions are not often the work of individuals behaving independently of others.

Discretion is central to law; indeed, legal systems increasingly rely on grants of authority to officials to attain legislative purposes. The growth of the state has meant more dependence on bureaucracies to advance public order and welfare, health and safety, planning, environmental protection, the **regulation** of business, and so on. Society has become more complex, the legislative task has expanded, and specialist, technical, or scientific knowledge and expertise are now essential. Sometimes lawmakers want to avoid controversial or complex matters of **public policy**; passing discretion to bureaucracies allows them to duck or fudge problems.

Discretion, whether formally granted or assumed, has its advantages. Legal rules are sometimes clumsy where complex policy goals are concerned, not working as intended, creating injustice, leaving gaps, or colliding with other rules. Over-inclusive rules penalize too widely, requiring flexibility in their application; they may be difficult to formulate precisely, or impede the conduct of a task, demanding adaptation. Discretion can individualize the implementation of the law, softening the harshness or injustices that sometimes arise from rules dispassionately applied.

Discretion, ironically, is sometimes needed to promote the purpose of a rule. It brings functional benefits, like avoiding costly formal procedures or obscuring ambiguities or lack of consensus in policy. The **common law** is hospitable to discretion, and in its pursuit of the conflicting goals of continuity and change, judges exercise discretion in adapting legal doctrines and expressing conceptions of justice where rules fall short. Yet **courts** occupy a modest place in the realities of legal life.

But discretion is controversial. It challenges conceptions of legitimacy. In the liberal state, law must be applied consistently, openly, and dispassionately. Discretion represents the opposite: subjective **justice** where rules represent formal justice, prompting concern that its subjectivism facilitates arbitrariness or inconsistency. Discretion is power, with its corrupting implications, allowing an individual to act as that individual chooses, on the basis of improper considerations, substituting personal standards for public, legal standards. It is conducive to apparent inconsistencies of outcome, which can occur even if decisions are made according to approved procedures. Negotiated determinations may permit legal standards to be bargained away, while lack of procedural protections may disadvantage the weak. For decision subjects, discretion can lead to uncertainty and insecurity.

The potential for abuse has prompted interest in the control of discretion by legal means such as rules, procedures, methods of accountability, or rights granted to decision subjects or the parties to a legal case. Another constraint is the power to appoint—deciding who is to decide—which may lead to discretion being exercised in ways desired by those appointing. Disciplinary or budgetary controls on decision-makers are a further constraint, as are policies and general principles; this is true of policies embodied in the law itself, and the policies which bureaucracies devise to guide their junior officials. One consequence of control efforts can be that discretionary play in the system may be transposed elsewhere, possibly to less visible sites, suggesting that reformers need to think holistically about legal systems to understand the interplay of constraints on discretion.

But, significantly, non-legal constraints also operate: moral, economic, political, and organizational forces work upon legal decision-makers to shape their discretion. Decision-makers often claim that they judge matters 'on the merits of the individual case', implying that a case exists as a discrete entity, decided about independently of wider forces. But discretion seemingly exercised by an individual, such as a **police** officer, is almost always shared with others in a sequence of decisions, a serial process. A decision made at one point may profoundly affect subsequent decisions owing to the structural position of the individual exercising prior discretion, as subsequent decision-makers can only act on the basis of cases supplied by others. Decisions by gatekeepers to the legal system (eg police, regulatory inspectors, social security staff) may close off discretion afforded to subsequent decision-makers entirely (by discarding the case) or partially (by narrowing choice). Plea-bargaining frequently restricts, as is intended, how judges may sentence. Effective power to decide is frequently assumed by actors other than those allocated formal authority. Those deciding about the creation and handling of cases wield substantial power, since they command access to the law in generally less visible, less controllable, settings. Equally, those supplying information or assessment can influence the handling of a case enormously.

Legal organizations shape discretion powerfully. Organizational decisions are not usually made independently of each other but take account of the implications of deciding about the present case in a particular way for the handling of others. Sequence effects, arising from the order in which cases are decided, can determine an individual decision. Here previous decisions, or the anticipation of a future decision shape the outcome in the present case. Knowledge of the past allows people to predict: the past instructs not only common law judges, but also legal officials whose regular working practices harden into organizational precedent. Inertia discourages departures from earlier decisions, **precedent** leading to matters being decided in ways 'normally' adopted in 'cases of this kind'. Such practices crystallize into occupational subcultures, with informal rules of decision emerging—customs, conventions, routine practices. Such approaches appeal as efficient, for exercising less constrained discretion takes more time and effort. Discretion is often exercised in routine and repetitive ways; and the frequency with which legal actors make decisions is important, as repetitive decision-making is more likely to be stable, consistent, and therefore predictable. It conveys information about the decision-making proclivities of others; and such familiarity permits a high degree of mutual predictability, allowing decisions in anticipation of what others to whom cases will be handed on will do, facilitating practices such as plea-bargaining or out-of-court settlements, by enabling decisions in anticipation of how 'the other side' will react.

A problem may be decided about in a particular way for reasons that have little to do with intrinsic features in the case, but much with pressures upon the decision-maker. Decision-makers simplify the complexities involved, even though a decision may be officially portrayed as very complicated. They do not see a unique world of distinctive events, problems, and people, but look for pattern, or draw on past experience to align present with past. Simple decision rules can be employed to allow a matter to be categorized readily, with reflection only needed when a new problem arises, or the possible implications of a course of action seem serious. Those legal actors, like judges, who make decisions relatively infrequently probably adopt a more complex approach, taking more time and considering more information.

Research into law enforcement discretion shows that rules are often not enforced as lawmakers might have intended. In bureaucracies such as the police, discretion is squeezed out to, or effectively assumed by, the periphery, where it may be exercised largely invisibly and immune from organizational control. Bargaining is prevalent and formal enforcement often avoided. Assessments of moral character are especially pervasive in shaping discretion: moral disreputability tends to prompt more punitive responses by law enforcers. In handling cases, both criminal and civil, much turns on the credibility of the individuals involved, whether as complainants, defendants, or witnesses. Legal rules are valuable when discretion suspends their enforcement: they are an important resource to be surrendered by rule-users in pursuit of some broader goal of social order or the public interest. Order is often attained more efficiently by forbearing from enforcing rules. This is a paradox of legal control, for attainment of the broad mandate is sought by suspending formal enforcement as part of a bargain to achieve compliance. Discretionary power not only permits the realization of the law's broad purposes, but allows or even encourages officials sometimes to distort or ignore the word or spirit of the law. And sometimes officials assume a legal authority they do not in fact possess, or deny an authority they do.

Discretion in practice is much more constrained than it might appear. From a policy point of view the important question is whether the constraints acting on discretion serve the interests of justice and the broad legal purpose.   KEITH HAWKINS

K Hawkins (ed), *The Uses of Discretion* (Oxford: Clarendon Press, 1993)

K Hawkins, *Law as Last Resort. Prosecution Decision-making in a Regulatory Agency* (Oxford: Oxford University Press, 2002)

discretion in the criminal justice system   *see* discretion

discrimination in employment Since 1975, UK law has begun to regulate discrimination on a number of grounds in the employment context. The **Equal Pay** Act 1970, which aimed to remove discrimination in pay between men and women, came into force in 1975. In the same years the Sex Discrimination Act 1975 prohibited **sex** discrimination in employment more generally (as well as discrimination against married persons). 'Discrimination' can be direct (less favourable treatment on grounds of sex) or indirect (facially neutral treatment which in practice disfavours men or women and is not justified on a proportionality assessment). The Race Relations Act 1976 made similar provision in relation to discrimination on grounds of **race**: 'colour, race **nationality** or ethnic or national origins'; and the **Disability** Discrimination Act 1995 prohibited unjustified less favourable treatment for reasons related to disability (narrowly defined), and imposed duties on employers to make reasonable adjustments to meet the needs of staff and prospective staff.

The Sex Discrimination Act was amended in 1999 to regulate discrimination against transgendered people in the employment context and, in 2003, significant improvements were made to the race and disability **legislation** to reflect the requirements of **European Community law** (Directives 2000/43 and 2000/78). For the same reasons, the Employment **Equality** (Sexual Orientation) and Employment Equality (**Religion** or Belief) Regulations were enacted. These provisions, which (unlike sex, race, and disability legislation) applied only to employment and third level education, and prohibited direct and **indirect discrimination** and **harassment** connected with sexual orientation, religion, or belief, or lack of religion or belief. Harassment also became a separate head of discrimination under the race and disability provisions. 2006 saw the amendment of the Sex Discrimination Act to bring it into line with the requirements of amended EC law (Directive 76/207 as amended by Directive 2003/73) and the introduction of the Employment Equality (Age) Regulations.

The present law is complex and at times lacks coherence. It is very difficult for claimants to negotiate their way around the many pieces of legislation and the extensive case law, yet legal funding is not available in employment **tribunals** in Great Britain (where employment discrimination cases are heard). The position is particularly unsatisfactory where people experience 'intersectional' discrimination: that is, discrimination on grounds of (say) sex *and* race *and* religion, as might be experienced by an Asian Muslim woman subjected to less favourable treatment by virtue of her **identity** as an Asian Muslim woman. Success rates in discrimination claims are relatively low, though awards are on occasion very large, especially where discrimination results in severe injury to feelings and psychiatric injury, or in very significant loss of earnings and/or **pension** entitlements.

Some of these problems may be ameliorated by single equality legislation which at the time of writing is still at planning stage, with detailed provisions yet to be published. Meanwhile, the Equality Act 2006 has provided for a single **Commission for Equality and Human Rights** which will have responsibility for all grounds on which discrimination is now regulated.

AILEEN MCCOLGAN

See also: **comparators; direct discrimination; multiple discrimination; protected grounds**

diseases, liability for   Except under a few statutes, the law does not formally distinguish between liability for traumatically-caused personal injuries and liability for diseases. Nonetheless, features inherent in the process by which a person suffers disease introduce special difficulties for that person when they seek to establish that someone was liable for the disease. For example, while the victim who suffers, say, a broken leg in a car crash will immediately be aware of having been injured and will be able to pinpoint the time and place where the injury occurred, this is typically not the case where the victim suffers a disease. Indeed, the disease may be 'latent' and may not manifest itself for many years after contact with the pathogen. This raises many problems for the law.

First, there may be doubt about whether the alleged pathogen was capable of causing the relevant disease (this is often termed 'general **causation**'). For example, for many years the tobacco industry disputed the hypothesis of epidemiologists that cigarettes could cause lung cancer in users. Even where such a general causal link is accepted, there may be problems in determining whether the particular claimant's disease was caused by the alleged pathogen (this is often termed 'specific causation'), rather than some other background source of risk of that disease. For example, even if it is accepted that the operation of a nuclear power plant increases the risk of childhood leukemia in the surrounding district from 2 per cent to 3 per cent, no local child with leukemia will be able to establish that, more likely than not, her leukemia was caused by the plant, even though it actually causes the leukemia of a third of such children.

Another set of problems arises where, even though there is no doubt about the type of physical agent responsible for the disease, it is not possible to determine which exposure or exposures to that agent were responsible for the disease of the particular victim. A classic example here is the fatal disease of mesothelioma. At present it is thought that the only agent that can cause this cancer is asbestos. Although it is known that each exposure to asbestos increases the risk of contracting mesothelioma, the severity of the disease, once contracted, is not determined by the extent of the victim's exposure to asbestos. The mechanism by which the disease comes about is unknown: it may be caused by a single asbestos fibre or by a certain accumulation of fibres. Under orthodox rules of proof of causation, this creates an evidentiary gap. Suppose that a worker inhales asbestos during consecutive periods of employment with employer No 1 and then with employer No 2. The worker cannot show that but-for the first period of exposure he would not, on the balance of probabilities, have contracted mesothelioma. The **House of Lords** has created a special doctrine to assist such claimants (see **causation**).

In the past, the statutory rules governing the **limitation of actions**—ie the fixed period of time within which a claimant must sue—created grave problems for many disease victims. This was because, according to those rules, the limitation period 'began to run' at the moment the claimant's cause of action 'accrued'. A cause of action 'accrues' when all elements of that cause of action are in place; and in personal injury cases this moment is when the victim has suffered 'actionable damage' caused by the breach of obligation owed to her by the defendant. But in a disease case, what is 'actionable damage'?

The problem was exposed in mid-twentieth century in litigation concerning claims by workers suffering from a latent industrial disease: *Cartledge v E. Jopling & Sons Ltd* (1963). In that case the workers' disease had not become manifest until many years after their exposure to the deleterious agent. Only if it were accepted that the workers did not suffer 'actionable damage' until their disease was 'discoverable' would their claims have been made within the time limit. However, the House of Lords refused to date 'damage' from the point of discoverability; and so it remains the case that a cause of action may accrue before the discoverability or manifestation of physical changes or symptoms and before diagnosis—and, therefore, well before the victim has reason to know that they have a cause of action. However, the outcry that followed the rejection of the workers' claims in *Cartledge* prompted a change to statutes governing limitation of actions to allow an action to be brought either within a certain period dating from the accrual of the cause of action or within a certain period starting when the 'damage' became reasonably discoverable by the claimant.

The workers in *Cartledge* were clearly gravely disabled by the time their cases came to court. But another issue raised by disease cases is what can constitute 'damage' sufficient to enable a person to sue. For example, exposure to asbestos can produce pleural plaques on the lung that can be seen with X-rays. Typically these are not associated with any symptoms or lack of function. Nor, it seems, are they the precursors of asbestos cancers or of asbestosis. This raises the question of whether such benign physical changes to the lung are legally cognizable 'damage' entitling those with such plaques to sue. In a recent decision the House of Lords gave a negative answer to this question.   JANE STAPLETON

dismissal   *see* **unfair dismissal; wrongful dismissal**

disparate impact   *see* **indirect discrimination**

displaced persons   Displaced persons are individuals or groups who are forced to leave their homes and habitual places of residence and find refuge elsewhere. If they flee to another country there they are considered **refugees**. If they find refuge within their own country, they are called IDPs ('IDPs').

'Displaced persons' camps after World War II encompassed both refugees and IDPs. At the same time, a more specific notion of displaced person was used by the then International Refugee Organization to designate individuals who were deported by Nazi Germany or its allies to another country, eg as forced labourers (Constitution of the 15 December 1946). The Convention on the Status of Refugees 1951 (and the Organization of African Union Convention on Refugees 1969) gave the word 'refugee' its specific definition. Since that time, usage of the term 'displaced person' has usually connoted IDPs.

The 1998 **United Nations** Guiding Principles on Internal Displacement describe the internally displaced as 'persons or groups of persons who have been forced or obliged to flee or to leave their homes or places of habitual residence, in particular as a result of or in order to avoid the effects of armed conflict, situations of generalized **violence**, violations

of **human right**s or natural or human-made disasters, and who have not crossed an internationally recognized state border'. **Victims** of forced relocation by development projects (eg high dams) may also qualify as IDPs. It is the element of coercion in their movement that distinguishes IDPs from economic migrants; because their movement takes place within national borders, they are not—in legal terms—refugees.

IDPs can be found in more than fifty countries all over the world. The number of those displaced by armed conflict has been estimated between 23 and 25 million for most of the present decade, a figure double or even triple that of refugees during the same period. About half of them can be found in Africa, the others in the Americas, Asia, Europe, and the Middle East, with between 2 and 4 million in each of these regions. The numbers of those displaced by natural disasters reaches millions as is evidenced by events such as the 2004 tsunamis in the Indian Ocean or in 2005 the earthquake in the Himalayas and Hurricane Katrina in New Orleans and the Gulf Coast.

What are the rights of IDPs? Unlike refugees who are protected by the 1951 Convention, there is no international convention on IDPs, and none of the innumerable provisions of international human rights and humanitarian law explicitly addresses their plight. Although their fate is similar to that of refugees, IDPs cannot invoke the guarantees of refugee law which only protect those who were able to flee to another country. Nevertheless, because they have not left their own country, they remain entitled to enjoy the full range of **human** rights as well as those guarantees of **international humanitarian law** that are applicable to the citizens of that country.

However, the internally displaced have many special needs: unlike the non-displaced population, they are in need of shelter, may face the dangers of **gender**-based violence in overcrowded camps or settlements, be denied access to schools and health services, or suffer other forms of discrimination, are often allowed to vote only in their original residences to which they cannot return, and face difficulties in regaining their property upon return. Because of their particular vulnerabilities, the protection of their human rights requires a specific approach.

The Guiding Principles on Internal Displacement, presented in 1998 to the (former) UN Commission on Human Rights by the then Representative of the UN Secretary General on Internally Displaced Persons, Dr Francis Deng, set forth the rights of IDPs and the obligations of national authorities and non-state actors towards them. Its thirty principles cover all phases of displacement: (i) protection during the pre-displacement phase where the right not to be arbitrarily displaced, ie protection against orders to leave one's home and residence that cannot be justified by serious and legitimate reasons, is of particular importance (Principle 6); (ii) protection during displacement where many economic, social, and cultural rights as well as **civil and political rights** acquire special significance for the displaced; and (iii) protection during the post-displacement phase where IDPs are entitled to freely choose between return, local integration at the place of displacement, or resettlement and reintegration in another part of the country as durable solutions (Principle 28). The Guiding Principles emphasize that the primary responsibility to provide protection and humanitarian assistance to IDPs lies with national authorities (Principle 3), but underline, at the same time, that international humanitarian assistance must be accepted by countries whose authorities are unwilling or unable to provide the required aid and support (Principle 25).

The Guiding Principles, although not a legally binding instrument, draw their authority from the binding law upon which they are based and the wide international acceptance they have received. The heads of state and government who assembled in New York for the 2005 World Summit explicitly and unanimously recognized them 'as an important international framework for the protection of internally displaced persons' (UN Doc A/61/L.1, paragraph 132).

At the institutional level, there is no dedicated UN agency for the assistance and protection of IDPs. However, the Office of the High Commissioner for Refugees has been designated, in 2005, as agency responsible for the protection of persons displaced by armed conflict. In situations of disasters, responsibility for protecting the human rights of the displaced lies with the Office of High Commissioner for Human Rights and the International Federation of the Red Cross/Red Crescent Societies. The present representative of the UN Secretary-General for the Human Rights of Internally Displaced Persons, Dr Walter Kalin, is tasked with entering into dialogue with governments to improve the protection of the human rights of IDPs.   WALTER KALIN

disqualification of directors Directors and others who act improperly in the course of managing **companies** in the UK may face disqualification under the Company Directors Disqualification Act 1986 ('CDDA') or the Company Directors Disqualification (Northern Ireland) Order 2002. The disqualification regime operates alongside the general law as an additional public interest sanction for managerial misconduct and breach of **directors' duties**.

The CDDA creates a series of powers of disqualification which give rise to a civil prohibition restraining the disqualified **person** from taking part in the management of **companies** without the **court's** permission and from acting as an insolvency practitioner, for up to a maximum of fifteen years. Disqualified persons acting in breach of the prohibition face criminal penalties and personal liability for the debts of companies in the management of which they have been unlawfully involved. CDDA disqualification triggers further statutory restrictions under **charities, pensions,** and a wide range of other **legislation**.

The policy underlying the CDDA is that those who fall below the standards of probity and competence expected of company directors should be disqualified in order to protect the public from their misdeeds and to promote good **corporate governance**. The usual applicant is the Secretary of State for Business, Enterprises and Regulatory Reform. The main legal ground for disqualification is that a person's conduct as regards a company that has become insolvent or been subject to statutory investigation makes him or her unfit to be concerned in the management of companies generally. Undischarged bankrupts are also automatically disqualified.   ADRIAN WALTERS

A Walters and M Davis-White QC, *Directors' Disqualification and Bankruptcy Restrictions* (London: Sweet & Maxwell, 2005)

distribution of assets   When a **company** is subject to **winding up** (in liquidation) one of the most important actions that has to be undertaken is the distribution of the company's assets. If the company is insolvent, ie not able to pay all of its debts, the shareholders of the company will get nothing, not even the money they paid into the company. If the company is solvent, then once the debts of the company have been paid in full, the remaining assets of the company are distributed to the shareholders, according to the terms of the company's constitution. Unless the constitution provides to the contrary, the assets are distributed equally. In fact, if those entitled to the assets so wish and can agree amongst themselves, the actual assets can be distributed. Such pay-outs are known as '**dividends**'.

Distribution causes the most problems where insolvent companies are concerned, mainly because there are simply not enough assets to go around; most creditors are not going to get what they are owed. Any assets that are the subject of security, such as a mortgage, will be sold for the benefit of the creditor who is entitled to the security. Assets that are not subject to any security are sold and the resulting proceeds are distributed amongst the unsecured creditors equally and rateably. This means that creditors will receive the same percentage pay-out, but the amount paid will depend on how much creditors were owed. So, a creditor who is owed £50,000 will get twice as much as a creditor who is only owed £25,000. However, the upshot is that they will both only get part of what they were owed. In some liquidations, creditors receive nothing at all because the proceeds from the sale of unsecured assets are used up in paying the remuneration and expenses of the **person** who administers the liquidation, namely the **liquidator**.

There is an important exception to the rule that the proceeds of unsecured assets are distributed equally and rateably. **Legislation** provides that some unsecured creditors are to be paid before others. These creditors are known as preferential creditors as they are granted priority when it comes to payment. The primary preferential creditors in the United Kingdom are employees of the company. They can each be paid up to £800 before the other creditors share in the assets. Until recently, the revenue authorities who were owed money in relation to **income tax** and **VAT** were also preferential creditors, and this state of affairs continues to exist in many countries around the world.

Before anyone can share in a distribution of the assets they must prove to the liquidator that they are in fact owed a debt by the company. This is usually done by submitting what is known as a 'proof of debt' setting out the basis for the debt with any proof to support the claim.   ANDREW KEAY

A Keay, *McPherson's Law of Company Liquidation* (London: Sweet & Maxwell, 2001), chs 13 and 14

See also: **insolvency, corporate; liquidator; winding up**

distributive justice   *see* **civil liability, theories of; Justice**

district judges   *see* **courts judges**

diversionary programmes   Diversion refers to the direction of offenders away from the formal **criminal justice system** by providing a means of dealing with them outside of traditional criminal **justice** processes. Recently, alternative institutions within the criminal justice system have also engaged in the process. For example, problem-solving **courts**—like US drug courts—provide an alternative to imprisonment. Diversion can occur at different stages in the justice process. **Police cautioning** before **arrest** prevents offenders from having any formal involvement with the criminal justice system. **Prosecution** of an offence may be deferred while a defendant undertakes some type of action (like drug treatment or reparation). On completion the matter is referred back to the prosecutor and a decision is made to withdraw or dismiss the charge. Diversion at the time of **sentencing** occurs when the matter is adjourned pending participation in some type of activity: like **community** service or a vocational programme. The offender returns to court after a specified time and a sentence decision is made that may result in a lessor conviction or having the matter dismissed. Early release programmes reduce the amount of time offenders spend incarcerated, diverting offenders away from **prison**. **Alternative dispute resolution** processes also divert people from more formal legal procedures and sanctions. They can include basic 'self-help' strategies (do-it-yourself legal kits and advice); out-of-court settlement, mediation, and specialized courts and **tribunals**. Many of these approaches focus on civil disputes of various kinds.

The rationale for diversion is linked to factors including: the failure of prison to reduce repeat offending, growing prison populations, the costs of formal courtroom processes and of maintaining prison building and programmes, as well as the negative impact of conventional methods of conflict resolution and **punishment** on both offenders and **victims**.

The point of diversion is to decrease the impact of the formal criminal justice system on offenders' and victims' lives while achieving the same or better effects than traditional structures. Critics argue that the opposite is often the case. People are diverted away from formal agencies into less formal, but no less bureaucratic organizations rather than away from the system altogether. Some people who would normally have avoided custodial options, as a result of diversionary programme are drawn more deeply into the system. Stanley Cohen (*Visions of Social Control*, 1985) calls this 'net-widening'. There is an increase in the overall intensity of intervention with offenders being subject to levels of intervention that they might not have previously received; and new agencies and services add to, rather than replace, the original set of control mechanisms. Diversion can increase the number of people and range of behaviours subject to official control, when the idea was to reduce them. However, we should not automatically disregard the possibilities diversionary programmes offer. Not every initiative amounts to further net-widening. Alternative interventions do not necessarily result in negative social control. Moreover, if community-oriented programmes are simply criticized in total then we are left with only much harsher and socially unredeeming measures like prison.   MELISSA BULL

diversity in legal education   *see* **gender issues in legal education; legal academics**

dividends   A dividend is a distribution of profit by a **company** to its members. It is different from a return or distribution of capital.

There is a complex statutory system for determining what profits are available for lawful distribution (Companies Act 2006, Pt 23). This system exists for the protection of the company's creditors. It requires the company to have up-to-date accounts before payment of a dividend which show that the company can pay the dividend without prejudice to its creditors.

A shareholder's entitlement to a dividend depends on the rights attaching to his **shares** under the company's constitution. Thus, it is possible to create different classes of shares in the same company which carry different entitlement to dividends. Equality between shares is presumed unless the contrary is stated (*Birch v Cropper* (1889)).

So, for example, some shares (commonly called 'ordinary shares') have a right to dividends as and when declared. Dividends are declared by the body within a company given the authority to do so by the company's constitution—the board or the general meeting. Other shares (commonly called 'preference shares') have the right to receive a fixed dividend on a regular basis, so long as a dividend can lawfully be paid at the time. Where a share carries a right to a preferential dividend, it carries no further rights to dividends unless the contrary is stated (*Will v United Lankat Plantations Co Ltd* (1914)).

                    RICHARD NOLAN

dividend tax   Dividends are paid by companies. In the paradigm case, dividends are a share of the company's profits and are treated as income of the shareholder, taxable as such. The issues that this raises are whether dividends should be taxed, if so at what rate and what constitutes a dividend for these purposes.

If a company has paid tax on the profit why should a dividend from those profits be taxed again? Many tax systems take a more pragmatic approach. In the UK the dividend is taxable in an individual shareholder's hands but a non-recoverable tax credit

(currently 10 per cent) is allowed and a special rate applied. Thus, a higher-rate taxpayer who receives a dividend of 90 is treated as receiving 99 (90 + a credit of 9). This is taxed at a special rate. However, where a UK resident company receives a dividend from another UK resident company the dividend is not liable to UK corporation tax as income of the recipient.

Payment of a dividend is not the only way that benefits can be extracted from a company for the benefit of investors. For example, a company could pay up bonus redeemable shares for its shareholders, which are later redeemed. Without more, this would not usually be categorized as a dividend but as a capital payment, notwithstanding that it has the same economic effect as a dividend for the recipient. Accordingly, many countries adopt an extended definition of dividend for these purposes. In the UK, any transfer of assets by a company to its members otherwise than for new consideration is treated as a taxable distribution—ie a dividend. There are also complex rules for bonus issues, redeemable shares, and payments by group companies.

Distribution payments are not usually deductible in computing taxable profits. Accordingly, there are anti-avoidance provisions treating certain payments, which might otherwise be deductible, as distributions.

There are also special rules for stock or scrip dividends and share reorganizations, etc. Problems can arise with determining whether enhanced scrip dividends are income or capital, particularly when received by trustees. Accordingly, there are special rules in the legislation.

The tax on dividends may be collected by withholding tax or in the usual way, such as by self-assessment.

There are special rules for distributions in the course of liquidation which, in the UK, fall within the **capital gains tax** rules.   ADRIAN SHIPWRIGHT

See also: **corporation tax; shares**

divorce   A divorce is the legal dissolution of a **marriage** usually requiring an order of the **court**. While divorces obtained in the UK are valid only by order of a court, the court retains **discretion** to recognize as valid divorces granted in other jurisdictions where no court proceedings were taken. So, for example, a *talaq* divorce, if valid in the place of the parties' domicile, might be recognized as valid in English law.

Divorce is governed in England and Wales by the Matrimonial Causes Act 1973 and, in Scotland, by the Divorce (Scotland) Act 1976 as amended, most recently by the Family Law (Scotland) Act 2006. Unsurprisingly, divorce law in the UK has gone through a number of reforms since the first laws were passed, and each reform generally can be said to have exhibited a move towards a more liberal policy. While divorce has been available at **common law** in Scotland since 1560 and by statute since 1573, before 1857 judicial divorce was not available in England and Wales at all. There, the Ecclesiastical Courts could pronounce only decrees of nullity of marriage and decrees that we would know now as judicial separation, relieving spouses of the obligation to cohabit. Only **Parliament** could dissolve a marriage. Even after statutes were passed in the UK permitting courts to dissolve marriages, however, divorce was difficult to obtain; it was only available from the superior courts, was expensive, and could be granted only upon very restricted grounds which required culpability on the part of the guilty spouse and complete innocence on the part of the wronged spouse. For a time, adultery (and in Scotland, desertion) was the only ground for divorce, but even as the number of grounds increased to include facts such as cruelty, divorce was still thought to be a remedy for a matrimonial offence, and only a limited number of matrimonial offences were sufficiently serious to justify the termination of a marriage.

In each period of public and political debate about divorce, including the most recent debates in Scotland, reformers were preoccupied with the question whether, in the interests of promoting marriage, divorce ought to be made 'easier' or more 'difficult' in law. Reform initiatives in the 1960s and 1970s in particular were concerned with the degree to which divorce ought to remain based upon fault or the matrimonial offence. It was questioned for example, whether marriage breakdown could ever be attributed to the 'fault' of one spouse only and the idea of the matrimonial offence was also said to increase hostility and acrimony between the parties. As in other jurisdictions, reformers in the UK periodically explored seriously the idea of no-fault divorce by consent. The resulting **legislation** created a basis for divorce that was a compromise between matrimonial fault and no-fault. That legislation (amended most recently in 2006 in Scotland, but still in effect in England and Wales) states that there is only one ground for divorce: irretrievable marriage breakdown. But it goes on to say that a court may not hold that a marriage has broken down unless one or more facts are proved, some of which retain the notion of fault. The two fault-based facts common to both jurisdictions are that one spouse has committed adultery and the

other finds it intolerable to continue to live with him or her, and that one spouse has behaved in such a way that the other cannot reasonably be expected to live with him or her. In England and Wales there is an additional fault-based fact: that the respondent has deserted the petitioner for a continuous period of two years. The other facts upon which a court may find that a marriage has broken down irretrievably are based on the separation of the parties. Where the spouse not seeking the divorce consents to it, the court may grant the divorce after the parties have lived separately for a continuous period of two years in England and Wales and, since 2006, one year in Scotland. Where there is no consent, the separation must be for five years in England and Wales and, since 2006, two years in Scotland. If the court is satisfied as to one or more of these facts and as to the irretrievable breakdown of the marriage, it must grant a decree of divorce. This, however, is only a conditional decree, called a Decree Nisi in England and Wales. Then, after a further six weeks if there are no objections, the petitioner is entitled to apply to the court for the Decree Absolute of Divorce. Only on the grant of the Decree Absolute are the parties divorced. In Scotland, a divorce decree obtained under the ordinary rules is not final until the Extract Decree of Divorce is issued by the court. The Decree is extracted automatically after twenty-one days if no objections are filed. It is only once the decree is extracted or made absolute that the parties' legal status changes and they become free once again to marry or register a **civil partnership** with another **person**.

While reform of the substantive divorce law has been relatively slow in the UK, reform of the procedure has been more far-reaching. In both England and Wales, and Scotland, 'special procedures' have been created to expedite undefended divorces. In these cases, one spouse will complete a set of forms outlining the facts relied upon to establish the ground for divorce (in Scotland only the separation facts can be relied upon), provide written evidence of those facts, and submit them to the appropriate court. If the other spouse does not contest the divorce, or consents where required, the court is satisfied that the facts have been made out and that the marriage has broken down irretrievably, it will issue the decree of divorce without requiring the parties to attend court. In Scotland the extracted decree will issue simultaneously, while in England and Wales the parties must wait the ordinary six week period before applying for the Decree Absolute. By far the majority of divorces in the UK adopt this 'special procedure'.

Divorce procedure has also been transformed since the 1980s with the advent of **mediation** and other forms of **alternative dispute resolution**. Family law solicitors in the UK have long pursued a policy of negotiation and settlement in divorce cases, but government policy is now to use law directly to encourage divorcing spouses to settle their financial, property, and **child**-related issues outside court, initially by mediation. Public funding for the divorce itself is not available in the UK; it is only available for issues 'ancillary' to the divorce such as the post-divorce care of children or the re-ordering of the parties' property and finances. Spouses are encouraged, sometimes required, to attend a meeting with a mediator to determine if their case is suitable for mediation of these disputes, which may then be paid for by public funds.

Even where funding is not an issue, because on granting a decree of divorce the court has the power to adjust the financial circumstances of the parties to achieve fairness between them, parties often attend mediation to attempt to resolve these matters by consent. Parents also tend to reach their own agreements about the post-divorce care of children. Current policy begins with the belief that contact with a non-resident parent is in the interests of children and extends to the idea that cooperation and consensus between parents promotes children's welfare. Both mediation and negotiation are pursued with these imperatives in mind and only a minority of disputes ends up before the courts.

Divorce has always been a political and social issue as much as a personal one, and divorce law reflects these political and social dimensions. The rate of divorce is thought to demonstrate the rate at which marriages are either 'failing' or 'stable', which in turn is linked to the health of society. While these links are contentious (does the rate of divorce accurately measure marriage breakdown? Is the legal end of unhappy marriages a sign of health or pathology in society?), divorce law tries to strike a balance between encouraging the spouses to facilitate a cooperative transition to a 'post-divorce relationship' while at the same time not making divorce too 'easy'. And so, because divorce is a matter of both public and private concern, the law attempts to protect the interests of both the individuals and society. Policy in the UK aims to promote and support marriage and so divorce by consent of the parties without the required period of separation is not permitted. One spouse still must pursue the divorce, which the other can choose to defend or not. On the other hand, policy also aims to assist divorcing parties to re-order their lives with a minimum of acrimony

and so divorce law and procedure encourage the spouses to settle issues about finances, property, and children outside of court.   ALISON DIDUCK

divorce, history of   *see* **marriage and divorce, history of**

doctors, complaints against   *see* **complaints procedures; ombudsmen**

doctrinal legal research   How do lawyers go about researching their subject? Scientists tend to research by experiment and investigation to explain and predict how the natural world works. But law is artificially constructed and cannot be researched in the same way. The raw materials are cases and statutes rather than chemicals and elements and there are no laboratories, just libraries and the internet. However, the methodology of legal research does have much in common with scientific research. Indeed, the study of law is sometimes described as legal science.

The nature of legal research depends on the objectives of the researcher. The object may be to investigate the policy the law should be seeking to implement. This type of research tends to be more theoretical and may require engagement with other disciplines, such as sociology, history, economics, and philosophy. But a different type of research focuses on the legal rules themselves, to work out what the law says on a particular issue and why it says it. This is doctrinal research. This focus on the content of legal rules is sometimes described as 'black-letter law'.

If we are trying to work out what the law says on a particular point, two distinct approaches can be adopted. One is pragmatic and involves the researcher surveying the law on a particular topic and concluding from this what the rules are. This might be a difficult process depending on the nature of the issue. The relevant law might be statutory and may be easy to interpret, but where the statute is ambiguous it will be necessary to consider any judicial decisions which have sought to resolve the ambiguity. In other areas there may be no relevant statute at all. Instead, the researcher will only have recourse to judicial decisions which may be contradictory or may not provide a complete answer to the problem. Reading a lot of cases can take a long time, so the researcher may rely on textbooks to identify the state of the law. These books take a variety of forms. Some deal with very specific topics, whereas others provide a comprehensive statement of the law in a much larger area. A number of these books, known as treatises, were first written in the nineteenth century when a systematic approach to legal exposition was becoming popular. For example, *Chitty on Contracts* was first published in 1826 and *Clerk and Lindsell on Torts* was first published in 1889. This pragmatic approach to legal research is particularly adopted by legal practitioners, who need to know what the law says on a particular point and then apply that law to the particular problem to be able to advise a client.

The other approach to doctrinal legal research is more academic but it too can be of real benefit to the practice of the law. Here the researcher seeks to identify the principles underpinning a mass of rules to explain the function of those rules. This is done through the recognition of maxims of the law which are generalizations and distillations of complex bodies of law and are known as principles. This process of generalization is a bit like looking at a television screen. If you get very close to the screen you can see loads of individual pixels, but you cannot make out a picture. For that, you need to step back, to put the pixels together to see the big picture. In the same way, the search for principle requires you to step back to see the bigger picture. This process of identifying principles makes the study of law similar to the study of mathematics. Mathematicians try to identify general principles which accurately explain specific phenomena. Lawyers also need constantly to check the principle which they have identified to ensure that it accurately explains the detailed rules. If it does not, the principle may need to be rejected or, more likely, qualified by the creation of another subordinate principle.

The doctrinal researcher who searches for principle is faced with a dilemma as to whether a 'top down' or 'bottom up' approach should be adopted. 'Top down' research starts with the identification of a principle and then considers whether the case law is consistent with it. If not, the law may be considered to be wrong. 'Bottom up' research, on the other hand, seeks to identify the principle from the decided cases. This approach may still result in criticism of the law, but shows greater respect for the decided cases. The significance of 'bottom up' research to the evolution of the law is illustrated by two significant developments in the law of obligations in the twentieth century. One concerns the creation of the modern tort of negligence. That body of law developed in the nineteenth century through the recognition of many different rules to determine when the defendant was liable to compensate the claimant for harm suffered as a result of the defendant's negligence. In *Donoghue v Stevenson* (1932) the **House of Lords** examined all of these different rules and synthesized them to create a new general tort of negligence which has been the touchstone against which all negligence claims have subsequently been determined. Another example is the law of **unjust enrichment**. For over 200 years the law has recognized a lot of different situations where the defendant is liable to pay something back to the claimant. In *Lipkin Gorman (a firm) v Karpnale Ltd* (1991) the House of Lords recognized that all these different situations could be explained by the unjust enrichment principle. This principle enabled lawyers to have a much better understanding of how the law operated, what needed to be proved, and what the underlying rationale was.

This principled approach to doctrinal research is of particular relevance to legal education. Many textbooks on legal subjects which are written for students seek to identify the principles which underpin the detailed rules to enable students to gain a better understanding of the rules themselves. But this principled approach is also of real benefit to legal practitioners and to researchers who are concerned with policy questions, since often analysis of the policy objectives of law is informed by a prior understanding of the applicable principles, even if this is only with a view to criticize those principles and suggest alternatives.

The distinction between pragmatic and principled approaches to doctrinal research is not absolute, because the identification of principles must depend on a prior understanding of the detailed rules themselves. However, the distinction is worth drawing because the methodology of the researcher is different depending on which approach is being followed. The methodology of the researcher who adopts a pragmatic approach is essentially to find a solution in the law to a particular problem. For example, if you enter into a contract to buy a vase and you pay the full purchase price in advance, but the vase is not delivered to you, you will want to recover your money. There are a number of questions which need to be considered before we can determine whether the money can be recovered. First, what is the cause of action on which your claim can be based and what do you need to prove to establish that cause of action? Secondly, does the defendant have any defences to your claim? Finally, if you can establish the cause of action and there are no defences, what *remedy* will be available to you? The answers to these questions will depend on careful consideration of what the cases say. If the solution is not clear or if the matter has never been considered by the *courts* before then it may be necessary to provide a solution through litigation or the researcher may need to suggest their own solution.

If, however, the same problem is viewed from the perspective of a principled analysis of the law, different questions would be asked. The starting point will be to determine what the relevant cases decide. After that the researcher will determine whether any relevant principles can be distilled from those cases, then identify the policy which underpins the principle and finally consider whether the law is right. If the principle does not accurately reflect the policy then the law may be wrong and the researcher will consider alternative solutions to the problem. This is a much more academic approach to doctrinal research, since it looks beyond the mere solution of the problem to the identification of a defensible rationale underpinning the detailed rules.

Whichever approach is adopted there are a number of distinct and complementary aims to of such research. First, the research seeks to *describe* the state of the law. Secondly, such research seeks to *interpret* the law, to resolve ambiguities and inconsistencies. Thirdly, where there is no law on a particular point, doctrinal research seeks to *predict* what the law should be. Fourthly, there is the process of *generalization*, when the principles underpinning the law are identified. Finally, doctrinal research places the researcher in a position to *criticize* the law and to suggest alternative legal rules which are consistent with principle as well as policy.

GRAHAM VIRGO

Lord Goff, 'The Search for Principle', reprinted in *The Search for Principle: Essays for Lord Goff* (ed WJ Swadling and GH Jones) (Oxford: Clarendon Press, 1999)
C Barnard, J O'Sullivan, and G Virgo (eds) *Foundations of Law* (Oxford: Hart Publishing, 2007), ch 1

doctrine of double effect The 'doctrine' or 'principle' of double effect is an integral part of a tradition of common morality which holds that while it is always wrong intentionally to bring about a bad consequence it is not always wrong merely to foresee that one's conduct will produce a bad consequence. The principle identifies when conduct which produces a 'double effect'—a good consequence and a bad consequence—is nevertheless morally permissible.

The principle sets out four requirements which must be satisfied. First, the action itself must be ethically sound or at least neutral: it cannot be evil in itself. Secondly, the bad effect which results from the action must not be part of the **agent's** intention (in the word's ordinary sense of aim or purpose). Thirdly, the bad effect must not be a means to the good

effect. Finally, there must be a proportionate reason for allowing the bad effect to occur.

The principle is of general application, though it is most frequently invoked in the contexts of medicine and warfare. A medical scenario will illustrate its application. 'Is it ethical for a doctor to administer palliative drugs to a cancer patient who is close to death in order to ease the patient's pain even if the doctor knows that the drugs will also hasten the patient's death?' The principle of double effect would produce an affirmative response, provided its four conditions were fulfilled. First, there is nothing immoral in administering drugs to ease pain; indeed it is part of the doctor's moral duty. Secondly, if the doctor's intention is to ease the patient's pain and the doctor merely foresees the hastening of death, then the second condition is fulfilled. Thirdly, the bad effect of shortening the patient's life is not a means of alleviating the pain, so the third condition is fulfilled. Finally, given that the patient is close to death, the palliation of the patient's pain is a sufficient justification for incidentally bringing about a brief shortening of life.

The extent to which English law embraces the principle is unclear. Although there is authority that the law incorporates the principle to insulate a doctor in the above scenario from liability for **homicide** (*R v Cox* (1992)) there is also authority which appears to conflate intention and foresight (*R v Woollin* (1999)) and thereby to reject a distinction central to the principle.   JOHN KEOWN

TA Cavanaugh, *Double-Effect Reasoning. Doing Good and Avoiding Evil* (Oxford: Clarendon Press, 2006)
P A Woodward (ed), *The Doctrine of Double Effect. Philosophers Debate a Controversial Principle* (Notre Dame: University of Notre Dame Press, 2001)

domain names   *see* **internet regulation**

domestic accidents   *see* **tort system**

domestic jurisdiction   Under traditional international law a state's national sovereignty extends over all matters subject to its legislative, executive, and judicial powers within its territory, matters that are within its exclusive domestic jurisdiction. Intervention into these affairs by another state or international institution would violate the state's **sovereignty**.

After World War I states started entering into **treaties** on matters previously considered as within domestic jurisdiction, for example treatment of national minorities and workers' rights. By so doing, they internationalized these issues, thereby accepting the right of other states to intervene, for example through diplomatic protest, debate, making claims, or other action within international institutions. The **United Nations** Charter 1945, Article 2(7), reiterates the principle by clarifying that nothing in the Charter authorizes 'the United Nations to intervene in matters which are essentially within the domestic jurisdiction of any state', although this is without prejudice to the Security Council's enforcement powers for the maintenance of international security.

The trend of narrowing the scope of domestic jurisdiction has continued as more issues have become subject to international regulation including human rights and environmental standards, foreign investment, requirements of the International Financial Institutions relating to good governance, and trade regulations. However, the principle still retains significance in international law, as shown by the fact that a number of states have made the exclusion of questions within their domestic jurisdiction a condition of their acceptance of the jurisdiction of the **International Court of Justice**.

CHRISTINE CHINKIN

domestic violence Domestic violence has been variously defined over the years although most current definitions now extend beyond physical **violence**. Types of behaviour identified as constituting domestic violence range through murder, **rape**, **assault**, indecent assault, and destruction of property to threats, belittling, isolation, deprivation of money, and **harassment**. Domestic violence affects opposite sex, same sex, and transgender partners as well as family members other than intimate partners. However it is within heterosexual intimate relationships that domestic violence is most prevalent. And while there are instances of women abusing their male partners, it is overwhelmingly women who suffer domestic violence and it is their male partners and former partners who perpetrate it.

Research shows that domestic violence involves a pattern of abusive behaviour which can worsen over time and which can persist or even escalate after separation. This pattern is associated with efforts to exert power and control over the **victim**. The **gender** difference is attributed to longstanding hierarchical notions about relationships between men and women, Until the late nineteenth century, men had a right of reasonable chastisement over their wives and it was only in 1991 that the law changed so that men could be prosecuted for raping their wives (*R v R (Rape: Marital Exemption)* (1991)). Contemporary accounts of abuse offered by abusers themselves

reveal feelings of sexual jealousy and possessiveness, and a sense of male entitlement to **family finances** and to sexual and domestic services.

It is largely through the work of feminists since the 1970s that domestic violence has come to be seen as a serious social problem affecting many women and children. Feminist definitions and analyses have gained widespread acceptance but these are challenged by some researchers and by men's groups. They claim that women are as likely as men to be perpetrators. However these researchers fail to consider the context, motive, or severity of the acts they measure. Women designated violent tend to be acting in self-defence and women's behaviour is not characterized by a pattern of violence and control. It is primarily women who are subjected to frightening, serious, and life-threatening assaults. It is mainly women who experience sexual abuse, repeat violence, multiple abuse, and post-separation violence. In contrast, most men who report victimization tend to regard this as relatively unimportant and do not feel threatened.

Many of the behaviours classified as domestic violence constitute criminal offences, whether in terms of the Domestic Violence, Crime and Victims Act 2004 or the Protection from Harassment Act 1997 or under **common law**. In the past those working within the **criminal justice system** perceived domestic violence as a private matter and intervened only exceptionally. However practice has changed. **Police** forces now have Domestic Violence Officers/ Co-ordinators to help victims. The police are instructed to **arrest** unless there is good reason not to, and, in order to address the problem that victims often withdraw their complaints, officers are expected to investigate such cases to determine whether the victim was pressurized. They are also expected to collect forensic evidence to avoid the need to rely on victim testimony. If a victim withdraws, the **Crown Prosecution Service** ('CPS') is supposed to consider proceeding without her. They are also supposed to improve victim care. Nevertheless, police and CPS practice are still criticized and only a small proportion of cases result in **prosecution** and conviction. There is a high rate of acquittal, frequent use of **binding over,** and lenient **sentencing** on the part of the **courts**. Consequently, specialist courts are being piloted.

Remedies in the civil courts are provided under the Family Law Act 1996. Non-molestation orders (s 42) afford personal protection to victims. They are available to associated **persons**, defined to include current and former spouses, civil partners, cohabitants, and those in intimate relationships (s 62(3)).

'Molestation' is wide in scope and refers to behaviour that involves a serious degree of harassment. Occupation orders regulate occupation of the home and empower the court to exclude an abuser. They can be sought by associated persons who are 'entitled'. These are people have a legal interest in the home (s 33) and spouses and civil partners who are entitled by virtue of having 'home rights' (s 30). Also eligible for orders are non-entitled former spouses and civil partners as well as cohabitants and former cohabitants. The criteria for obtaining orders and the duration of orders varies, depending on the category into which the applicant falls. In any event, courts are reluctant to grant occupation orders because they consider it a draconian step to exclude people from their homes. Sometimes, it is the work of extra-legal services, like the refuge movement, that proves more helpful for victims.   FELICITY KAGANAS

See also: **feminism and law reform**

dominant position   A dominant position is a position of economic strength enjoyed by an undertaking which enables it to prevent effective **competition** being maintained in the relevant market by affording it the power to behave to an appreciable extent independently of its competitors, its customers, and ultimately of the consumers. Virtually the same definition has been applied in cases under Article 82 EC and in cases under Chapter II of the UK 1998 Competition Act. Single dominance is that of one undertaking, while collective (or 'joint') dominance is that of two or more undertakings together. There are two stages involved in determining whether or not an undertaking is dominant. First, and given that dominance cannot exist in the abstract but only in reference to particular products and geographical areas, it is necessary to identify the relevant market where the supposed dominance exists. Secondly, the market power of the undertaking(s) needs to be determined.

The relevant market has a product-related and a geographical dimension. In general terms, the relevant product market is constituted by the range of products and services which are interchangeable or close substitutes for one another. In defining the product market, the **European Commission** and the **European Court of Justice** principally consider demand substitutability. In other words, products or services that are interchangeable from the point of view of consumers will be deemed to belong to the same product market. Economic indicators, such as cross-elasticity of demand, but also product characteristics, price, and intended use, are used to measure demand substitutability. In some cases, the Commission and the Court have also considered supply interchangeability. There, the breadth of the market depends on whether competitors can easily penetrate an identified market by straightforward adaptation of their production plant and facilities.

The geographical market will be formed by a clearly defined geographical area where the conditions of competition are sufficiently homogeneous for the effect of the economic power of an undertaking to be evaluated. Transport costs have an important impact on the determination of the relevant geographical market. Where these costs are relatively low, geographical markets will tend to be wide. Conversely, where these costs are high, the markets are likely to be narrower.

Once the relevant market has been defined, the dominance of the undertaking in that market must be assessed. Ultimately, it needs to be demonstrated that the undertaking or undertakings in question have a position of economic strength that allows them to behave to a certain extent independently of competitive pressures. The market share of the allegedly dominant undertaking relative to the market shares of its competitors, the existence of barriers to expansion and entry, and the position of buyers in the relevant market are key factors in proving dominance. The holding of a very large market share by a single undertaking for some time will be generally taken as a reliable indicator of dominance, so long as the market shares of other players in the market appear to be significantly smaller. A market share of 50 per cent or more will be considered as a very large market share in the absence of exceptional circumstances. Market shares between 40 per cent and 50 per cent can frequently indicate dominance, as sometimes can market shares between 25 per cent and 40 per cent, depending on the strength and number of competitors of the dominant undertaking.

Barriers to entry and expansion are a second important element used in the assessment of dominance. If the relevant market has low barriers to entry or expansion, the fact that one undertaking has a large market share may not automatically indicate that it is dominant because any attempts to obtain monopoly profits may be rapidly frustrated by entry of new competitors into the market. Barriers to entry or to expansion include legal barriers—such as intellectual property rights or the concession of exclusive rights—and large-scale production or a high degree of vertical integration by the allegedly dominant undertaking. Finally, the existence of strong buyers in the market can be a relevant factor to counteract a finding of dominance only if these are able to protect the market whenever the ostensibly dominant supplier tries to raise prices above the competitive level.

Although most cases concern instances of single dominance by a dominant supplier (monopolist) or by a dominant buyer (monopsonist), Article 82 EC and Chapter II of the UK Competition Act also refer to abuses of dominant position by one or more undertakings, that is, to situations of collective or joint dominance. According to the case law of the EC judicature, collective dominance exists when two or more independent undertakings united by economic links are able to adopt a common policy in the market and act to a considerable extent independently of their competitors and customers, and ultimately of their consumers. The case law once provided a broad definition of the concept of economic links that encompassed agreements and links in law, but also connecting factors resulting from economic assessment and from market structure. This approach caused some difficulties in the consideration of oligopolies, which are highly transparent markets in which there are only a few producers with similar market shares that are naturally interdependent and hence may be able to tacitly coordinate their behaviour without having to resort to concluding agreements for **concerted practice**s. In particular, it was feared that a finding of collective dominance could be made too readily in this type of market.

Recent case law, however, has clarified that a position of collective dominance will only be found in such markets when three factors are cumulatively satisfied. First, each undertaking must be able to monitor whether or not the other undertakings are adhering to the common policy. Therefore, there must be sufficient market transparency for all undertakings to be aware, sufficiently and quickly, of the market conduct of the others. Second, the common policy must be sustainable over time, and hence incentives must exist for the market players not to depart from that policy. Third, the competition enforcement authority must establish that the foreseeable reaction of current and future competitors, as well as of consumers, would not jeopardize the implementation of the common strategy.

ALBERTINA ALBORS-LORENS

See also: **abuse of dominant position**

Donaldson v Beckett (1774) The passing of the Statute of Anne in April 1710 marked a historic moment in the development of **copyright** law. The world's first copyright statute, it conferred exclusive rights of publication and sale upon the author of an unpublished literary work for a period of fourteen years (and if the author was still alive at the end of that time, for an additional fourteen years), as well as providing a twenty-one-year protection for works already in print. When these statutory periods of protection began to expire the metropolitan publishers who dominated the book trade sought to safeguard their position against a newly emerging and predominantly Scottish reprint industry. Throughout the mid-eighteenth century the general concept of literary property and the specific right to reprint works falling outside the protection of the Statute were repeatedly examined in the **common law** courts. In essence, the Scottish booksellers argued that no copyright existed in an author's work at common law. By contrast, the London booksellers suggested that the Statute of Anne simply functioned to supplement a pre-existing common law copyright that was otherwise perpetual in duration. This battle of the booksellers culminated in the landmark decision of the **House of Lords** in *Donaldson v Beckett* (1774).

While *Donaldson* confirmed that the duration of copyright protection an author enjoyed in his published literary works was solely determined by the Statute of Anne, the wider meaning and significance of the case remains contested. A traditional interpretation of the decision suggests that the House of Lords affirmed the existence of copyright at common law while at the same time holding that that natural right was nevertheless circumscribed by the Statute. Yet recent research has demonstrated that this reading is based on misreporting of the true opinions of the judges and Law Lords. In the light of the corrected record, it can be cogently argued that the House of Lords actually rejected the arguments in favour of common law copyright. In the context of the broader contemporary debate as to whether copyright as a phenomenon is best understood as a natural authorial property right or no more than an institutional mechanism evidencing the existence of a state sanctioned privilege, the general argument from history, and from *Donaldson* in particular, allows for no definitive conclusions.

RONAN DEAZLEY

R Deazley, *On the Origin of the Right to Copy: Charting the Movement of Copyright Law in Eighteenth Century Britain, 1695–1775* (Oxford: Hart Publishing, 2004)

M Rose, *Authors and Owners: The Invention of Copyright* (Cambridge, Massachusetts, and London: Harvard University Press, 1993)

Donoghue v Stevenson (1932) Arguably the most famous personal injury compensation case ever, amongst UK and **Commonwealth** lawyers at least, is *M'Alister (or Donoghue) v Stevenson* (1932). The case involved the purchase of a jar of Stevenson's Ginger Beer at a restaurant in Paisley. It was consumed on the premises not by the purchaser but by her friend, May Donoghue, a 30-year-old woman, married but separated from her husband, and bringing up a son then aged 12. The allegation was that the ginger beer was putrid, containing as it did the rotted remains of a snail; the stink and the sight of the snail's corpse made May Donoghue ill, and in consequence she raised a claim for damages in the (Scottish) Court of Justiciary.

A paying customer would have had a clear case in contract against the restaurant itself in those circumstances, but it was not obvious that the recipient of mere generosity had any claim against anyone. Her solicitor, one Walter Leechman, cannot have had high hopes for the claim, as a similar case he had taken only weeks before (involving a dead rat) had been refused. Nonetheless he took the case, suffering several early reverses (including a hopeless attempt to join the restaurant's owner as party), followed by defeat of the main action before the Court of Justiciary. He then appealed to the **House of Lords**. By that stage May Donoghue's lack of funds was even more severe, and Leechman used this to secure public funding to pay counsel's fees, under the *in forma pauperis* procedure. While the facts of the case were never determined by any court, May Donoghue's victory in the House of Lords proved a valuable bargaining chip in later negotiations: Stevenson died soon after the ruling, and his executors settled the claim for £100 (it is believed—though the evidence is indirect), a considerable amount in the circumstances. While little is known of May Donoghue's life after the case, it is certain that she survived Stevenson, being divorced in 1945 and eventually dying in 1958, aged 59.

While on its precise facts the importance of the case was minimal, nonetheless the significance of the issue of principle did not escape the members of the House of Lords. Were consumer claims (and, perhaps, all negligence claims) involving goods or services supplied under a contract to be determined solely by that contract, or was there a possibility in addition of claims in negligence going beyond contract? By a bare majority, it was held that the claim could succeed if May Donoghue's story was true, and it was no answer to it that contractual issues arose, or might have arisen, on the same facts.

The most familiar reference point here is Lord Atkin's opinion, with its rhetorical invocation of a 'neighbour principle', under which a defendant owes a duty to all those foreseeably affected by the defendant's conduct. The principle itself was no novelty, and Atkin did not claim that it was; but his reformulation of the duty had considerable power, and is treated by many today as the very foundation of **tort law**. There has been some discussion down the years of whether it can be said to represent an infusion of Christian values into the **common law**. Some argue that it is, noting how readily Atkin incorporated the parable of the good Samaritan into the legal discourse. Others, by contrast, suggest that the opinion entirely subverts the Christian message, taking the lawyer's view that 'neighbourliness' must be strictly defined and limited, rather than the biblical view that it should not. Whatever may be the truth of this, clearly Atkin was advocating a more pro-plaintiff view than the legal system had adopted hitherto, and his opinion chimed well with the general expansion of negligence liability that has followed the case.

In fact, all five opinions in the case have their merits, reflecting very modern concerns about the manner and frequency with which judges should be prepared to expand negligence liability in the light of new fact-situations. Given modern complaints of a '**compensation culture**', it is hard not to sympathize with the two dissenting opinions, which argued that allowing the claim in this case would be the prelude to a succession of pro-plaintiff arguments which would prove equally hard to resist. While such 'slippery slope' arguments do not always convince, in this instance the dissenters' claim turned out to be exactly right.

The great impact that the case, and especially Lord Atkin's opinion in it, was to have on the common law world was hardly visible at first. Consumer law and **product liability** was then, and is now, a relatively unimportant aspect of negligence litigation in common law systems (with the exception of the United States). But its importance was stressed by law teachers to cohort after cohort of their students, and by the 1960s its pre-eminent status was axiomatic.

STEVE HEDLEY

PT Burns (ed), *Donoghue v Stevenson and the Modern Law of Negligence* (Continuing Legal Education Society of British Columbia, 1991)

doorstep selling The term 'doorstep selling' is a shorthand way of referring to consumer contracts which are concluded anywhere apart from proper business premises, usually at the home of a consumer, but also at the consumer's place of work or on an outing organized by a trader. In this situation, a consumer will usually be surprised by the trader, and will not have the same degree of choice as he or she would have had when visiting retail premises, because of inability to compare products and prices. Moreover, the consumer may not know anything about the trader's reputation, and may feel somewhat coerced into agreeing to buy goods or services to get the trader to leave.

In order to reduce these problems, the Consumer Protection (Cancellation of Contracts concluded away from Business Premises) Regulations 1987, implementing a corresponding EU directive, provide a consumer with a seven-day **cooling-off period** where a contract has been concluded away from retail premises, provided that the consumer did not expressly ask the trader to visit him at the consumer's home or place of work (although the government has announced reforms that would extend the legislation to contracts made in such circumstances). In addition, the consumer must be informed by the trader about the cooling-off period. If this is not done, any contract concluded cannot be enforced against the consumer, and the trader could face criminal penalties. A consumer needs to notify the trader of his or her decision to cancel a contract, and will have to return any goods supplied for a full refund.

CHRISTIAN TWIGG-FLESNER

double effect, doctrine of   *see* **doctrine of double effect**

double jeopardy   *see* **justification, excuse and mitigation in criminal law**

double taxation treaties   *see* **international tax**

drafting   *see* **lawyering skills**

drafting of legislation   Legislative drafting is like brick-laying in that it seems to the casual observer to be such an easy and simple process as not to demand any special knowledge or skill; and the more expertly it is performed, the more likely it is to give that impression. Indeed, the product of the inexperienced practitioner may be superficially serviceable, but it will not withstand the extreme rigours of analysis routinely applied by those with an interest in challenging, circumventing, or undermining the law. An expert insolvency lawyer is no more likely to be competent to draft a new law about bankruptcy than is a teacher to build a school. It is essential, however, for the drafter to be instructed by those with expert knowledge of the precise purpose for which the provisions are required, and to be fully briefed on the political, social, and legal context. The drafter can temper the legislation by reference to its purpose and context; but drafting expertise can no more

compensate for inherent weakness in the instructions or underlying policy than building expertise can remedy inherent faults of design.

The principal objectives in legislative drafting are clarity and simplicity. The use of plain English is therefore neither a luxury nor a fad, but a fundamental necessity. It is good modern legislative drafting practice to use short and simple sentences, and to avoid archaisms and jargon so far as possible. But legislation still often fails to be either simple or clear. This is sometimes the result of poor drafting. But it is often an inevitable reflection of the complex or technical nature of the subject matter or the policy (for example, a provision about the taxation of hedging derivative contracts); or for political reasons a provision may have had to be produced unreasonably quickly, or may have been amended structurally during its passage through Parliament. Shorter legislation is not necessarily better legislation: the insertion of a few extra words may avoid the need for a point to be litigated in the courts.

In the case of most **Acts of Parliament**, Ministers set the broad policy objectives, departmental administrative civil servants develop the detailed policy, and then departmental lawyers determine precisely how the law needs changing to reflect that policy, at which point they instruct **Parliamentary Counsel**, a separate office of civil service lawyers, who draft. The draft is discussed with and between departmental lawyers and administrators and adjusted as necessary, following which it is approved by the appropriate Minister and introduced into Parliament in the form of a Bill. For Scotland, Wales, and Northern Ireland, legislation to be made by the devolved legislatures is handled similarly within the devolved administrations. Secondary legislation—principally orders, rules, and regulations made by Ministers under powers conferred by Act—is mostly drafted by departmental lawyers, taking instructions from their administrative colleagues.

DANIEL GREENBERG

Renton Committee Report, *The Preparation of Legislation*, May 1975, Cmnd 6053

D Greenberg, *Craies on Legislation* (London: Sweet & Maxwell, 8th edn, 2004)

See also: **legal rules, types of**

dress codes in the workplace   Employers may want to regulate the appearance of their staff for many different reasons, eg to secure uniformity, for health and safety reasons, or to project a particular corporate image.

In principle, the employer may impose such dress requirements as part of the implied contractual duty of employees to comply with reasonable instructions. Disobedience in these circumstances will usually be treated as a breach of discipline and may result in a fair dismissal. For example, in *Singh v RHM Bakeries (Southern) Ltd* (1977), it was held that a dismissal for hygiene reasons was fair when the employee, who handled food, refused to shave off his beard. If the employee objects to the rule because it causes discomfort or ill health, then dismissal may be unfair unless the rule can be justified. Dismissal for breach of a rule that men had to be clean shaven was held to be unfair in *FME Ltd v Henry* (1986) where the applicant suffered from a rash if he shaved every day.

In addition to issues of discipline, dress codes may also give rise to claims of discrimination. In particular, where the dress code imposed is different for men and women, **sex** discrimination may be alleged. In *Smith v Safeway plc* (1996), differences in dress code requirements for men and women which, *inter alia*, prohibited men but not women from wearing ponytails, were held not to be sexually discriminatory; the code merely laid down a requirement for conventional appearance and did not result in men being treated less favourably than women. In *Department of Work and Pensions v Thompson* (2004), the Department announced that all staff had to dress 'in a professional and business like way'. This required men to wear a collar and tie and, when an employee refused, he received a formal warning. The Employment Appeal Tribunal said the relevant question, given the overarching requirement to dress in a professional and business-like way, was whether the level of smartness which the employers required, applying contemporary standards of conventional dress, could only be achieved for men by requiring them to wear a collar and tie.

Certain ethnic groups may have religious or cultural requirements for clothing or appearance so that dress rules which disallow such clothing or appearance may lead to discrimination under the Race Relations Act 1976. It may be that such a requirement can be justified, eg on health and safety grounds (see *Panesar v Nestle Co Limited* (1980)). The employer will have to show a good reason why it is imposing a rule if it serves to exclude certain **minorities** from employment.

There may also be a breach of the Employment Equality (Religion or Belief) Regulations 2003. Certain clothing or appearance requirements may have been adopted for religious reasons and an employer who insists that clothing rules be followed may be in breach of the regulations if there is no sound reason

for the rule. It may be that the employer can justify the rules on the basis of health and safety but clearly employers cannot simply impose a blanket rule without sound reasons. In *R (on the application of Begum (by her Litigation Friend Sherwas Rahman)) v Denbigh High School Headteacher & Governors* (2006) a school's refusal to allow a pupil to wear a jilbab at school was held not to interfere with her right under Article 9 of the **European Convention of Human Rights** to manifest her religion and, even if it did, the school's decision was objectively justified under Article 9(2). In the circumstances, the pupil had not been denied access to education in breach of Protocol 1, Article 2 of the ECHR.   JOHN BOWERS

See also: **religious affiliation and school dress**

dress in schools   *see* **religious affiliation and school dress**

Dreyfus, Captain Alfred   Captain Alfred Dreyfus (1859–1935) was a Jewish artillery officer in the French Army. In 1894 he was convicted of treason for passing military secrets to Germany and sentenced to life imprisonment on Devil's Island. In June 1899 the case was reopened, but he was reconvicted of the crime and sentenced to ten years in prison. Following widespread popular protest he was pardoned by President Loubet and released from prison. He was not fully exonerated until the Court of Cassation annulled the second conviction in July 1906.

Dreyfus was apparently scapegoated by the army because of his Jewish and Alsatian background. The main evidence against him was a handwritten note (*bordereau*), containing details of French artillery plans, discovered in the waste basket of a German military attaché. This was wrongly identified as Dreyfus' handwriting, and though the overall evidence against him was weak the prosecution pressed on for fear of antagonizing the right-wing press and to protect the careers of senior army officers. The conviction of Dreyfus precipitated a storm of anti-Semitic propaganda.

Dreyfus' guilt was questioned almost from the start. The most significant role in uncovering the miscarriage of justice was played by Major Georges Picquart who worked in the office of military intelligence. Picquart concluded that the *bordereau* had actually been written by one Major Esterhazy, a French-born infantry officer of Hungarian descent. He was court-martialled in 1898, but acquitted, a move which provoked the novelist Emile Zola to publish his famous open letter, 'J'Accuse'. Although Zola was subsequently prosecuted and convicted of **libel**, his intervention helped further to mobilize public opinion against the government and in favour of a retrial. The significance of the Dreyfus Affair, as it came to be known, extended well beyond the legal process, exposing anti-Semitism in France, and precipitating a major political crisis for the Third Republic that was only resolved with the formal separation of church and state in 1905.   LINDSAY FARMER

drug testing in employment   *see* **human rights in the workplace**

drugs and crime   Many commentators assume a causal link between drug use and crime. This is reinforced by media accounts of drunken brawls in and around hotels and other licensed premises, and defence lawyers' claims that dependency on heroin or some other drug caused their client to offend. What is the research evidence?

Of all psychotropic (mood altering) drugs, alcohol shows the strongest and most consistent relationship to crime. For decades, research in the United States, Canada, the United Kingdom, Sweden, Australia, New Zealand, and other countries has been showing that a high percentage of offenders consumed alcohol before breaking the law. Consistent with alcohol's effects in depressing the central nervous system and reducing inhibitions, associations are higher for assaults and other offences that stem from loss of self-control than for property crimes. Alcohol's status as the drug most often associated with crime is consistent with its larger user base in contemporary societies.

Evidence of links between crime and illicit drug use is less pervasive, and the relationship is more complex. Eight countries, including the United States, England and Wales, Australia, Scotland, and South Africa, test whether people arrested for a criminal offence have consumed illegal drugs. Quite high proportions (between 48 per cent and 78 per cent) yield positive returns. Cannabis is detected more frequently than 'harder' drugs such as the opiates and cocaine.

That an arrestee has traces of an illicit drug is not proof that the substance caused them to offend. Cannabis, for example, generally reduces aggression and the likelihood of predatory behaviour. A more plausible hypothesis is that dependent users of drugs like heroin, cocaine, and metamphetamine resort to shop theft, breaking and entering, and even armed robbery to raise funds to finance their habit. Consistent with this theory, specialist drug **courts** in the United States and Australia focus on addressing the defendant's drug

problems, and treat property and other offending as symptomatic.

Not all researchers accept this approach. They point out that in many instances criminal activity predates illicit drug use. Rather than drug use causing crime, the relationship may be in the opposite direction. Because it provides additional funds, offending can facilitate increased consumption. Opponents of drug courts argue that use of alcohol and other mood altering drugs is normal in complex societies, and that even chronic users of illicit drugs can manage and take responsibility for associated behaviours.

Belief that there is a direct causal relationship between illicit drug use and crime helps justify laws and policies aimed at keeping supplies to a minimum. However as United States experience with attempts to ban alcohol has shown, prohibitionism also can be criminogenic. Placing a lucrative industry outside the law gives an advantage to operators who can threaten or use **violence** to protect turf and ensure contracts are honoured. More research is needed, on the relationship between drug policies and organized crime.   ADAM SUTTON

G Dingwall, *Alcohol and Crime* (Devon: Willan Publishing, 2006)

A Stevens, M Trace, and D Bewley-Taylor, *Reviewing Drug Related Crime: An Overview of the Global Evidence*, Report five (Surrey: The Beckley Foundation, 2005)

drugs in sport   Although doping has been used in sport since the times of the ancient Greeks, it has been identified as a problem only since the mid-twentieth century, when it became viewed by sporting authorities and governments as contrary to the essence of sport. Originally, each governing body took responsibility for its own anti-doping regulation. It has been held that the relationship between sports men and women and their governing bodies is a contractual one, the terms of which include, inter alia, the doping regulations of that particular sport.

Because insufficient thought was given to the compatibility of anti-doping regulation between various sports and of failure on the part of governing bodies to amend the rules in a logical, coherent manner, this early regulation proved vulnerable to legal challenge. As a result of this, sport has attempted to harmonize the doping regulations of the various national and international governing bodies. In the vanguard of this movement is the World Anti-Doping Agency. Its World Anti-Doping Code, a document of some legal complexity, was introduced in 2003 as a benchmark minimum standard for all sports. The only sports now resisting compliance are the professional sports peculiar to the United States (this is due largely to the system of collective bargaining that underpins agreements between players and the governing bodies in that country).

Three important principles characterise modern anti-doping regulation:

- The strict liability definition of doping. Strict liability allows a governing body to ban an athlete without showing that the athlete intended to take the substance—a positive test is sufficient. This standard was approved by the High Court in 1988 even though it results in the application of stricter standards than the corresponding criminal law provisions contained in s 28(2) of the Misuse of Drugs Act 1971.
- A list of banned substances. The positive test must be for a substance listed (or a related one such as a metabolite or a masking agent) in the banned list. For a substance to be included on the list it must satisfy two of the following three requirements: it enhances sporting performance; it is a risk to health; and it violates the spirit of sport. Legally, all three requirements lack satisfactory definitions and such nebulous expressions may in future form the basis of legal challenge.
- A system of fixed minimum penalties for offenders typically a two-year ban for a first violation with a lifetime ban for a further contavention. Fixed-term bans have been criticized for their failure to take into account their disparate impact depending on the sport in question.

JOHN O'LEARY

J O'Leary (ed), *Drugs and Doping in Sport* (London: Cavendish, 2000)

J Soek, *The Strict Liability Principle and the Human Rights Of Athletes in Doping Cases* (The Hague: TMC Asser Press, 2006)

dual/multiple citizenship   Multiple citizens possess the legal citizenship status (or nationality) of two or more separate states. Multiple citizenship may arise through various combinations of birthright citizenship and naturalization (for explanations of these terms see the entry on **citizenship**). The following non-exhaustive list illustrates some of the ways in which dual and multiple citizenship can arise:

- A citizen of state X, which confers birthright citizenship by *jus sanguinis* (descent), gives birth to a child in state Y, which recognizes *jus soli* (territory). The child is a dual citizen of states X and Y.
- A citizen of state X, and a citizen of state Z, both of which transmit birthright citizenship by *jus*

sanguinis, have a child in state X. The child is a dual citizen of states X and Z.

- A citizen of state X and a citizen of state Z, both of which transmit birthright citizenship by *jus sanguinis*, have a child in state Y, which recognizes *jus soli*. The child is a citizen of states X, Y, and Z.
- A citizen of state X migrates to state Y and naturalizes as a citizen of state Y while retaining citizenship of state X. The individual is a dual citizen of states X and Y.

Until relatively recently, individual states and the international community regarded dual citizenship as aberrant and undesirable, a condition akin to 'political polygamy'. Now, an uneven but seemingly inexorable trend toward tolerance of dual citizenship prevails worldwide, in practice if not always in principle. States that have reconciled themselves to the permanence of large immigrant populations have an interest in promoting the incorporation of immigrants into the political community. States with significant emigrant populations (especially states that depend on foreign remittances) have an interest in encouraging their nationals to retain cultural and economic links to the state of origin. Thus, both sending and receiving state have a disincentive to prohibit dual citizenship, lest the individual choose the citizenship of the other state. Technical hurdles, such as competing conscription obligations, voting rights of non-resident citizens, and the potential for 'divided loyalty' between two enemy states of citizenship, have proven manageable through unilateral or multilateral legal arrangements.

AUDREY MACKLIN

Dudley and Stephens (R v)   Captain Tom Dudley and three sailors were sailing the yacht 'Mignonette' from Southampton to Sydney. The yacht foundered in a gale, and all escaped in an open boat, but with no water, and virtually no food. In desperation Dudley and the Mate, Edwin Stephens, agreed to kill Richard Parker, the youngest member of the crew, who was by now the weakest member. Dudley killed him, with Stephen's assistance, and they and the other sailor, Ned Brooks, ate him. Not long after they were rescued. Dudley and Stephens were tried for murder, Brooks acting as a prosecution witness.

The practice of acting in the way Dudley and Stephens did, sometimes preceded by drawing of lots, was well established in nautical circles, being called 'the custom of the sea'. The jury was encouraged to agree the facts, and leave to the judges responsibility for deciding whether it was lawful in a case of such dire necessity for a person to kill another person, who was presenting no threat, in order to save their life. In convoluted legal proceedings the judges in *R v Dudley and Stephens* (1884) ruled that this was no defence; Dudley and Stephens were sentenced to death, but the sentence was commuted to six months imprisonment.

The case was viewed as involving the relationship between law and ethical values; the decision was controversial at the time, and has continued to be widely used as the basis for exploring issues as to the functions and proper limits of the criminal law. Cases in which a defence of 'necessity' is put forward continue to arise in the courts. As for 'the custom of the sea', it is still sometimes observed in desperate survival situations, but with discretion.

AW BRIAN SIMPSON

AWB Simpson, *Cannibalism and the Common Law. A Victorian Yachting Tragedy* (London: Hambledon Press, 1994)

due diligence defence   Due diligence defences are a common feature of **regulatory offences** of **strict criminal liability**—eg where the objective is **consumer** protection or employee health and safety. A common form of the defence permits a defendant to be acquitted if it can prove that the contravention resulted from the act or default of another person and that the defendant had taken all reasonable precautions and exercised due diligence to prevent the occurrence of the offence. These defences recognize that it may not serve the instrumental objective of the legislation—eg the avoidance of misleading pricing—to impose liability where a business has taken all reasonable care to avoid committing the offence. Central questions are how far such a defence should permit a corporation to escape liability for acts committed by employees and whether the corporation's compliance system both in theory and practice meets the test of all 'reasonable precautions'. Leading cases such as *Tesco v Nattrass* (1972) have been criticized for restricting corporate criminal

liability to the 'directing mind' of the corporation so that actions of employed managers are not identified with the corporation but constitute the acts of 'another person' for the purposes of a due diligence defence. It may also be difficult for a court *ex post facto* to determine whether a corporation's system of organizational control constitutes an effective system of supervision. Although the higher courts have warned against the acceptance of 'paper' schemes of supervision, distinguishing between form and substance may not always be easy. More recent cases suggest a sceptical attitude towards due diligence defences pleaded by corporations, and the courts require a higher standard of conduct to establish such a defence when pleaded in answer to an offence involving protection of consumer safety than when pleaded in answer to one concerned with protection from economic loss.

In recent years strict criminal liability has been criticized as unfair because it does not differentiate between companies that unintentionally contravene a law and those that flout the law. But this criticism does not take account of the existence of statutory due diligence defences to most regulatory offences. Studies of enforcement agencies indicate that they take these defences into account in making decisions on enforcement. Do the defences create general incentives for corporations to establish proper compliance systems and thus encourage **self-regulation** by business? There is little evidence on this issue but Australian research in relation to trade practices offences suggests that any such effect has been rather modest.

IAIN RAMSAY

due process rights   *see* **fair trial, right to**

duress   *see* **justification, excuse and mitigation in criminal law**

duty solicitor scheme   *see* **legal advice and assistance**

E

Earl of Oxford's Case (1615) *The Earl of Oxford's Case* (1615), which is reported on the first page of the first volume of the Chancery Reports, is the foundation stone of Equity in modern English law. The case is notable for Lord Chancellor Ellesmere's robust defence of the specialist equity court, the Court of Chancery, at a time when the head of the **common law** Courts, Sir Edward Coke, Chief Justice of the Court of King's Bench, was seeking to curtail its power. The essence of Coke's complaint was that the Chancellor's practice of granting injunctions in Chancery to prevent the enforcement of common law judgments was in breach of statutes designed to prevent appeals from the common law courts.

The case was hewn from the bedrock of modern England. It concerned land in London which Henry VIII had gifted to Thomas, Lord Audley, as a reward for such work as procuring the trial and execution of Anne Boleyn. By his will, Audley left the land to Magdalene College, Cambridge, but the college subsequently sold the land and some of it was acquired, indirectly, by the Earl of Oxford. Magdalene College challenged Oxford's title on the basis of a statute which prohibited the disposition of College lands; but against this was the fact that, as part of the original sale, Magdalene College had made an intermediate transfer to Queen Elizabeth with the deliberate intention of bypassing the statute. The battle lines were drawn. Coke was committed to upholding the wording of the statute and to denying exceptions based upon Royal **prerogative**. Ellesmere was committed to ensuring that the College did not take unconscionable advantage of the strict letter of the law by denying Oxford's right to proper compensation for loss of title; and he was committed to upholding Royal prerogatives, not least because the Court of Chancery had itself developed from the ancient Royal prerogative of mercy.

It is clear from Ellesmere's speech that Equity does not seek to overrule the common law, but only to prevent a party from enforcing a common law right where it would be unconscionable to do so in the particular case. Equity does not act against the law, but against the party: 'The Cause why there is a Chancery is, for that Mens Actions are so divers and infinite, That it is impossible to make any general Law which may aptly meet with every particular Act, and not fail in some Circumstance. The Office of the Chancellor is to correct Mens Consciences for Frauds, Breach of Trusts, Wrongs and Oppressions, of what Nature so ever they be, and to soften and mollify the Extremity of the Law'.

In 1616, the jurisdictional dispute between Ellesmere and Coke was referred to King James I. Keen to preserve his Royal prerogatives in the face of Coke's campaign against them, the King determined the matter in favour of the Court of Chancery and thereby established the rule which maintains equity's preeminent status to the present day: *where equity and law conflict, equity shall prevail.*   GARY WATT

See also: **common law; equity as a system of law**

early intervention   Early intervention involves the organized provision of resources to individuals, families, schools, or **communities** to forestall the later development of crime or other problems. Doing something about crime early, preferably before the problem becomes entrenched, strikes most people as a logical approach to crime prevention.

There is a growing body of scientific evidence that supports this common sense view. Evidence comes from two kinds of studies: those that identify 'risk factors' for crime and related problems from longitudinal studies that measure samples of children and young people over many years; and studies that use the results about risk factors to implement and evaluate interventions. Strictly speaking 'early intervention' is focused on individuals who show the early signs of an identified problem. It is therefore a form of what is known as 'indicated prevention', in contrast to approaches designed for entire populations ('universal prevention') and approaches designed for those at risk but not yet exhibiting a problem ('selective prevention').

A famous study cited by proponents of early intervention or prevention is the Perry Preschool Project, which was designed in the USA in the early 1960s to enhance intellectual development and school achievement in about sixty disadvantaged three- and four-year-old children. A daily pre-school programme was provided in addition to weekly home visits by teachers. Although cognitive gains for children in the programme were not maintained, the programme participants' school achievement and behaviour were significantly better than those of control children, and they were more likely to graduate from high school and continue to further education. By ages twenty-seven and forty, they had higher incomes and were more likely to be home-owners, and by age forty the programme group had significantly fewer lifetime arrests than the no-programme group.

There have been dozens of more recent interventions using a variety of methods such as home visiting to young pregnant women and education of parents on how to deal with children's behaviour problems that yield results nearly as impressive as the Perry Preschool Project, although few have measured such a wide range of outcomes over such a long time period.

There is much debate in the field about how 'early' intervention should take place. On the basis of evidence on the development of aggression and other problems from longitudinal studies of infants, one influential group argues that if intervention does not take place in early childhood, before the age of five, it may be too late to repair damage caused by problems like **child abuse** or family **violence**. Others argue that not all problems have their genesis in early childhood and that in any case it is not too late to repair damage after the age of five. This group argues for interventions early in the developmental pathway that leads to problems, which may not necessarily mean early in life. For example, there is good evidence that intensive interventions with juvenile offenders and their families through what is known as 'multisystemic therapy' can change the directions of many offenders' pathways away from crime.

ROSS HOMEL

easement   An easement generally takes the form of a right attached to one piece of land (the dominant land) to use another piece of land (the servient land) in a particular way. Examples include the right to walk or drive over the servient land, to lay drains across it, or to use it for storage. Occasionally, however, an easement will take the form of a right enjoyed by owners of the dominant land to restrict the manner in which the servient land can be used. The prime example of this 'negative' type of easement is a right to light (which prevents the servient owner allowing their land to obstruct the flow of light to the dominant land).

Easements may be created between neighbours at any time. They are often created when the owner of a piece of land sells off part of it and retains the rest. In such circumstances, even if the easement is not explicitly mentioned in the relevant documentation, the law may imply it if this appears to be what the parties intended. An easement may also come into being if the particular right has in practice been exercised by the dominant owner over the servient land for a period of twenty years.

If an easement exists, it generally runs with the land. This means that it will benefit future owners of the dominant land, the value of which may consequently be increased. It will also burden future owners of the servient land and therefore potentially reduce its value. The courts have been particularly mindful of the need to avoid imposing excessive burdens on the servient land in developing rules as to the types of rights which may give rise to easements. Agreements may be made between neighbouring land owners to create other types of right but (unless they amount to a different type of substantive property right such as a lease or a restrictive covenant) these are likely to be mere contractual arrangements which will bind only the people making the agreement.

A right will be capable of amounting to an easement (and thereby running with the land) only if it benefits the dominant land. This means that it must be of benefit to any owner of that land, present or future, as opposed to being of benefit only to the current owner. It must therefore be connected in some way with the normal enjoyment of land and not simply relate to the interests or lifestyle of a particular individual.

Before a right can give rise to an easement it must also be similar in nature to rights already accepted as easements. It must therefore generally not impose expense on the servient owner. Neither must it confer exclusive use of the servient land and thereby prevent the servient owner from using it. Thus, although rights to park or to store goods may amount to easements, they will not do so if they would effectively prevent the servient owner from using their own property.

ANNA LAWSON

EC competition law, modernization of   In the period from 1999 to 2004 EC competition law went through a process of reform which became better known as the modernization process. The modernization process focused on the role played by the **European Commission** in the enforcement of EC competition law. In the **competition law** regime which existed from 1962 until May 2004 the **Directorate General for Competition** within the European Commission played a central role in enforcement of competition law by developing policy, taking enforcement action against those who violated the prohibitions, and issuing exemptions from the prohibition of anti-competitive agreements under Article 81(3) EC. In the early years of the system the central role of the Commission was useful in developing policy, but the Commission's workload quickly became unmanageable. The Commission's workload issues would have no doubt also been exacerbated by the imminent enlargement of the European Union.

The modernization process began in 1999 with the publication of the Commission *White Paper on the Modernization of the Rules Implementing Articles 85 and 86 of the EC Treaty*. The White Paper highlighted the problems with the existing regime and suggested a number of options for reform, which became the focus of a lengthy consultation process. In the process that followed the Commission's preferred option became a 'directly applicable' system. Under such a system the Commission would give up its exclusive power to grant exemptions from the prohibition of anti-competitive agreements under Article 81(3) EC. The main effect would be to increase the power and effectiveness of the National Competition Authorities (the competition enforcement agencies in each Member State) and the domestic legal systems. As the national authorities would be able to fully apply both prohibitions in the EC Treaty, Article 81 EC prohibiting anti-competitive agreements and Article 82 EC prohibiting **abuse of a dominant position**, the European Commission would be in a position to focus its efforts on policy development and particularly important cases with a 'Community interest'.

The political negotiations leading up to the adoption of the new competition enforcement regulation were difficult, but a new settlement between the Commission and the Member States was agreed in 2003. The most important innovation was the extension of the use of Article 81(3) EC to the National Competition Authorities and the domestic Courts. The Commission and the National Competition Authorities now form the **European Competition Network** which coordinates competition enforcement activity across the **European Union**. The Network has a case allocation system under which a single 'well-placed' authority leads each investigation. The European Commission will only act where it is well-placed because the investigation spans three or more Member States, or raises novel legal issues which need to be settled at the Community level. The majority of day-to-day enforcement is now to be undertaken by the National Competition Authorities cooperating with each other to share information and evidence.

ANGUS MACCULLOCH

ecclesiastical courts   *see* **civilian courts**

ecclesiastical law   *see* **canon law**

ecological heritage   *see* **biodiversity**

ecological law   The law protecting wildlife distinguishes between the direct protection of individual animals, plants, and birds, and the protection of wildlife habitats. Under Part 1 of the Wildlife and Countryside Act 1981 it is a criminal offence to kill, injure, or take a wild animal or bird unless it is categorized as a 'pest', is a species of game bird or animal, or its killing or capture is licensed by the authorities. Legal protection is conferred on species of bird, animal, and plant listed in Schedules to the 1981 Act that give differing levels of protection. Endangered bird species are listed in Schedule 1 and are given enhanced protection. In these cases it is also an offence to disturb a member of the species when it is building or near its nest, or to intentionally disturb the young of the species. The Schedules to the Act are reviewed periodically, and species can be added to the list of endangered bird species in Schedule 1 if necessary, thus bringing them within the fullest protection offered by the law. Certain indiscriminate methods of killing wildlife are banned in all circumstances, even if the animals or birds killed are classified as pests—for example the use of gin traps and poison is absolutely prohibited.

Wildlife habitats are protected by designating protected areas in which damaging land use practices are legally controlled. The primary wildlife designation is the Site of Special Scientific Interest ('SSSI'). SSSIs are designated under Part 2 of the 1981 Act. On designation, the owner of an SSSI is given a list of operations likely to damage the conservation interest of the site. It is a criminal offence to carry out any of these operations without the written consent of Natural England, the Countryside Council for Wales, or Scottish Natural Heritage, otherwise than under a management agreement. Strict rules apply to planning permission for development in these sites, and in some circumstances permitted development rights are also withdrawn. Some important habitats are also designated 'European Sites' under the Conservation (Natural Habitats & C) Regulations 1994. These host wildlife habitats or endangered species of European significance for which protection is required under the EC Wild Birds Directive of 1979 or the EC Habitats and Species Directive of 1992. All European Sites will also be SSSIs protected by Part 2 of the 1981 Act, but they are subject to additional—and more stringent—restrictions on land use. There is a presumption against granting planning permission for development in a European site. In the case of both planning permission, and operational consent from Natural England or SNH for other activities, the authorities can only give permission if there are overriding reasons of public interest for the development or operation. Under European law, if the site hosts a 'priority' habitat or species identified in the EC Habitats Directive these reasons cannot be economic or social in nature.   CHRIS RODGERS

CT Reid, *Nature Conservation Law* (London: Sweet & Maxwell, 2nd edn, 2002)
C Rodgers, 'Planning and Nature Conservation: Law in the Service of Biodiversity?' in C Miller (ed), *Planning and Environmental Protection* (Oxford: Hart Publishing, 2001)

e-commerce   'E-commerce' is a collective term for three forms of transaction: (i) the use of electronic media for information gathering and the electronic ordering of goods and services delivered in physical form (e-tailing); (ii) the electronic delivery of digital goods and services; and (iii) the trade in telecommunication and internet services.

Electronic commerce is a key plank of UK economic growth. Recent surveys of e-retailing show that in 2005 £80 billion of UK consumer spending was either on or influenced by the internet, accounting for 10 per cent of all retail sales for that year. Further, while retail spending grew by 1.5 per cent, spending online surged ahead by 28.9 per cent. Such economic development can only flourish where the necessary legal framework to provide certainty and efficiency in online transactions is in place. This means the law of e-commerce has had to develop rules on electronic contracting, consumer protection, and electronic payments similar to those found in the real world.

The foundation of any commercial transaction is the contract. Without the legal protections offered by **contract law** transactions would need to be formed on trust alone. Online contracts take two forms: informal or formal. Informal contracts may be concluded in writing or orally, electronically or physically. Such contracts, which are the vast majority of

all contracts, may safely be concluded by means of electronic communication. Formal contracts, such as contracts regulated by the Consumer Credit Act 1974 required to be in writing, and signed, both of which posed problems for electronic communications. The issue of contract formality has now been dealt with by the EC Electronic Commerce Directive 2000 and the Electronic Signatures Directive 1999 and subsequent national legislation (the Electronic Communications Act 2000 ('ECA') in the UK). These provisions make electronic communications effective in relation to all contractual agreements.

The (potential) anonymity of any counterparty to an electronic contract, and the difficulty of verifying their domicile, can undermine consumer confidence in the contract. To remedy this consumer protection is offered by the Distance Selling Directive 1997. This provides the consumer with a suite of rights including the right to be informed of the identity of the supplier and the characteristics of the goods or services; and a 'cooling-off period' during which time the consumer may withdraw from the contract. These provisions have both been implemented in the UK by the Consumer Protection (Distance Selling) Regulations 2000. A consumer will usually have a seven day cooling-off period, with a three-month period in exceptional circumstances.

Finally payment must be made. Although most online transactions are settled using credit or debit cards, the development of alternate payment systems has proven popular in relation to transactions between **consumer**s where neither party has a pre-existing agreement with banking institutions. The most popular of these is eBay's PayPal system. PayPal is an account-based payment scheme which is recognized by the UK **Financial Services Authority** as an Electronic Money Institution ('EMI') under the Electronic Money Directive 2000 and the Electronic Money (Miscellaneous Amendments) Regulations 2002. This allows PayPal to issue Electronic Money, which is 'value stored on an electronic device, issued on receipt of funds accepted as a means of payment'. Although the value of treating account-based systems like PayPal as money issuers has been questioned, the recognition of PayPal as an EMI in a world where card-based electronic payment schemes are faltering towards extinction, while account-based schemes are the fastest growing sector of e-payments, perhaps points the way to the future of e-payments.

                              ANDREW MURRAY

L Edwards (ed), *The New Legal Framework for E-commerce in Europe* (Oxford: Hart Publishing, 2005)
J Dickie, *Producers and Consumers in EU E-Commerce Law* (Oxford: Hart Publishing, 2005)

economic analysis of law The use of economics to criticize law is as old as economics itself. Adam Smith criticized laws that impeded trade in his book *The Wealth of Nations*. But the beginning of sustained application of economic theory to legal topics dates from the 1960s, and occurred in the US, where today it is probably the dominant form of legal critique. Prior to that date, the use of economics to criticize law was limited to commercial and market-oriented laws. Thereafter, economic critique was progressively extended to all forms of law, including such apparently non-market topics as family, criminal, and constitutional law.

The beginnings of law and economics as a movement can conveniently be traced to the writings of Ronald **Coase**, who in 1960 wrote a seminal work on the interaction of the market and the distribution of legal rights. The particular problem that he addressed was the problem of social cost: the inefficiencies which result when, for example, enterprises pollute without paying compensation to parties who bear the costs of pollution. He challenged the conventional view, which informed the law of **nuisance**, that **pollution** involves one person causing cost to another. Instead, he argued that pollution arises where two persons compete for the use of a resource, such as clean air, or water. Thus it is not a question of imposing costs on one party or the other, but of designing rules of liability such that the shared use of resources occurs at an optimally efficient level. He provided a model that could be used to design such rules and pointed out that if one applied economic assumptions about the behaviour of individuals (that they act rationally to maximize their utility), and if one assumed that there were no impediments to trading (zero transaction costs), then from the standpoint of efficiency it does not matter how one allocates the right to pollute (or to be free from pollution). If the right were not allocated to the person who valued it the most, then that person would sell it to the person who did.

This model has lessons for those who wish to use economics to study the effectiveness of laws (alerting them in the dynamic manner in which individuals may alter their behaviour in response to laws) particularly through the formation of a market (black or otherwise) in legal entitlements. But it also forms the basis for economics to provide a normative critique of law, because where there are impediments to trading (transaction costs are not zero) the allocation of legal entitlements may lead to a less than optimal allocation of legal entitlements (resources would remain with persons who would prefer to exchange them for other things on which they place

a higher value). Much of economic analysis of law can be understood as attempts to reduce transaction costs (so that any initial misallocation of legal entitlements can be corrected through markets); or allocating resources to the party who would have ended up with them, if trading (with zero transaction costs) had been possible.

Normative economic analysis of law ('EAL') is based on the assumption that it is better to give people more of what they desire or prefer than less. As such it has much in common with utilitarianism: increasing utility is good, and actions are assessed in terms of their contribution to this good (so goodness is based on the consequences of actions, not their inherent quality). But whereas utilitarianism has no method for measuring an individual's utility, or what might increase it, EAL looks to market behaviour to provide indices. Individuals demonstrate what they desire, and how much, in terms of what they are willing to pay in order to acquire or keep any particular item. 'Pay' here has a wide meaning, which covers everything that an individual might receive or forgo (time, opportunity, possessions, etc) in order to acquire or keep any particular entitlement. Where exchange is possible, individuals can actually demonstrate their preferences amongst alternative entitlements by (not) exchanging what they have, for alternatives. Where exchange is not possible, preferences can only be measured by extrapolating from the evidence of value provided from situations (such as markets) where exchange is possible.

The assumption central to both positive (predictive) and normative economics, that the individual is a rational utility maximizer, has been questioned. If this assumption is taken to imply that the individual is concerned only with their own utility, then it fails to account for altruistic behaviour. In addition, it ignores the difficulties facing individuals in making choices, due to their limited access to information, the problems of processing such information, the psychological difficulties of choosing between alternatives, and the strategies adopted by individuals when confronting these difficulties. In response some versions of economics and economic analysis of law have incorporated more realistic assumptions of human behaviour (theories based on 'bounded rationality').

Another and more sustained critique of economic analysis of law has focused on the goal of normative economics: efficiency. There are actually two versions of efficiency used by economists. The first, Pareto efficiency, regards a change as an improvement if it makes no person worse off, and at least one person better off, in terms of their willingness to pay. In a world without transaction costs, such improvements (Pareto superior moves) would occur through trading. (Anyone who had an entitlement that was worth less to them than what someone else would pay for it would exchange that entitlement for the offered alternative.) The second version of efficiency is maximum social wealth. This is a situation in which resources are owned by those who value them most in terms of willingness to pay. In a zero transaction cost world, the two operate together. Trading occurs until no-one can be made better off by exchanging what they have for something else. But in the real world, the two standards of efficiency diverge. Entitlements may be owned by people who value them far less than others, but the costs of achieving trades prevent re-allocation.

Pareto efficiency, especially where there are few impediments to exchange (low transaction costs), combines aspects of utilitarianism (Pareto superior moves will increase utility) with some of the features of liberalism, particularly anti-paternalism. Individuals are assumed to be capable of identifying what is good for them (what they desire). Where they act to achieve what they desire, and make no other person worse off (in terms of their respective desires) then there is no justification for interfering with their actions.

However, efficiency has been criticized as a normative standard on the basis that our willingness to pay is a function of our ability to pay. This is most obvious when purchasing items: the maximum that could be paid for any single item is all one's wealth. But this also operates if one considers what people need to be paid in order to forgo an entitlement. For example, poor people would be expected to be more willing to exchange medicines for alcohol than the rich. (But such exchanges still show that poor people value alcohol more than medicine, so that a law prohibiting such exchanges will make them worse off in terms of their own expressed preferences).

The response to this problem within EAL is to argue for redistribution of wealth as something separate from the pursuit of efficiency. If one starts with an equality of initial resources, it is even more illiberal to seek to prevent consensual Pareto superior behaviour. Redistribution of wealth also serves to strengthen the connection between EAL and utilitarianism, due to a phenomenon known as the diminishing marginal value of wealth. The utility that is derived from £1 by a poor person is generally accepted to be higher than that of a wealthy person. As such, if wealth were redistributed, the overall level of utility achievable through Pareto superior behaviour could be expected to be higher than that

possible if one started from an unequal distribution of wealth. (Though, this concession to the benefits of redistribution ignores any disincentives resulting from the experience or expectation of wealth redistribution.)

Whilst Pareto efficiency has a normative appeal based on its connection to utilitarianism and liberalism, it has little application as a basis for legal reform, tending on almost all occasions to favour the status quo. Few (if any) legislative programmes leave no person worse off (even reforms reducing transaction costs, such as the introduction or improvement of markets, are likely to make at least one person worse off). Adjudication which alters the law also produces losers, leaving only decisions which establish new law in situations where no party had a prior entitlement (hard cases) as candidates for resolution by reference to the pursuit of Pareto efficiency.

In the face of these difficulties, the standard of efficiency more commonly applied is maximum social wealth. Wealth is increased whenever resources are moved from persons who value them less, in terms of willingness to pay, to those who value them more. Those who lose out from such changes need not be compensated. (Such changes are known as 'potential' Pareto moves, on the basis that the winners gain enough to compensate the losers. Their other name is 'Kaldor-Hicks' moves.) Whilst this standard has more practical applications, it lacks the normative appeal of Pareto efficiency, being likely to produce changes that are neither utilitarian nor liberal. Changes that produce losers are unlikely to be consensual (the rational utility-maximizer would be expected to resist them) and if reforms are coerced, one cannot be sure that resources have been transferred to those who value them more in terms of willingness to pay (value can only be extrapolated from situations where consensual exchange does occur). Moreover, changes that increase social wealth do not necessarily increase utility, given the presence of diminishing marginal returns from wealth (transferring resources to a rich man who values them at £15 from a poor man who values them at £10 does not increase utility if £10 generates more utility for a poor man than £15 does for the rich man).

RICHARD NOBLES

A Leff, 'Economic Analysis of Law: Some Realism about Nominalism' (1974) 60 *Virginia Law Review* 451–492

R Posner, *Economic Analysis of Law* (Boston: Little Brown, 6th edn, 2002)

Economic and Monetary Union Economic and Monetary Union ('EMU') within the European

Union began on 1 January 1999, and as of 1 January 2008 comprises fifteen of the twenty-seven Member States of the Union: Germany, France, Italy, Spain, Portugal, The Netherlands, Belgium, Luxembourg, Ireland, Austria, Finland, Greece, Slovenia, Cyprus, and Malta. It is characterized by the use of a single currency, the euro, with a single monetary policy set by the **European Central Bank**. Its Member States remain free to set their own budgets, subject to Treaty rules about budgetary deficits and accumulated government debt, which have evolved into the **Stability and Growth Pact**, policed not by the European Central Bank but by the **European Commission** and Council It is also the prime example of differentiated integration within the EU: Member States may only be admitted to EMU if they meet the convergence criteria set out in the Treaty; furthermore it will be seen that certain of these criteria are effectively voluntary, and in any event there are specific opt-outs for the UK and Denmark, who will only be considered for membership if they so request. It may therefore be suggested that membership of EMU is only for those Member States both able and willing to participate.

An understanding of EMU involves tracing three major elements: the antecedents of the euro and the legal consequences of its introduction; the political and legal evolution of the concept of EMU; and the application and continuing relevance of the convergence criteria. The euro can be linked back to the unit of account initially used under the European Coal and Steel Community Treaty. This unit of account happened to be the gold value of the US dollar, against which all Member States had official parities under the Bretton Woods system. The use of this unit of account continued after the entry into force of the EEC Treaty in 1958, and it was used for example, to fix common agricultural prices from 1962.

It was against this background that, in 1969, a committee was set up under the chairmanship of the Luxembourg Prime Minister, M Werner, to look at the question of economic and monetary union. The Werner Committee's Report in 1970 reached the fundamental conclusion that in such a union 'the Community currencies will be assured of total and irreversible mutual convertibility free from fluctuations in rates and with immutable parity rates, or preferably they will be replaced by a sole Community currency'. However, the Werner Report was drafted in a world of fixed exchange rates, and the assumptions underlying it were therefore destroyed when the US dollar was decoupled from gold, and world currencies began to float in 1971.

The fact that the US dollar had decoupled from gold meant that a gold-based unit of account ceased to provide uniformity, but it was not until 1975 that a new unit of account was created for the purposes of development aid in the context of the Lome Convention with African, Caribbean, and Pacific countries. This unit of account was a basket of fixed sums of the currency of each Member State, weighted so as to reflect economic performance, and its overall value was declared to be the same as that of the basket created by the International Monetary Fund in 1974 for the purposes of calculating its drawing rights—a value again derived from the dollar. This basket unit of account gradually became used for all Community financial purposes, and at the end of 1978 it was adopted as the criterion of value for the exchange-rate mechanism of the European Monetary System ('EMS'), being renamed the 'European currency unit', or ECU. With hindsight, the major feature of the EMS was that membership of its exchange rate mechanism was voluntary, but each participating currency had a central rate against the ECU, and participants undertook to maintain bilateral exchange rates against other participating currencies within a band of either +/-2.25 per cent or +/-6 per cent; and the central rate against the ECU enabled participants to determine whether their currency had increased or decreased in value.

The EMS brought relative currency stability, and a Committee chaired by Jacques Delors, then President of the Commission, was set up in June 1988, reporting back in April 1989. The Delors Committee took as a starting point the view that the development of the **single market** necessitated a more effective coordination of economic policy between national authorities, pointing out that with full freedom of capital movements and integrated financial markets, incompatible national policies would quickly translate into exchange rate tensions and put an increasing and undue burden on monetary policy—a prediction which was subsequently proved correct in 1992 and 1993. With regard to the mechanisms for achieving economic and monetary union, the Delors Committee recommended a three-stage process. The first stage did not require any Treaty amendments, and in fact the European Council meeting in June 1989 decided that it should start on 1 July 1990, which happened also to be the date by which the free movement of capital was due to be achieved. In that stage it was suggested that it would be important to include all Community currencies in the EMS exchange rate mechanism subject to the same rules; even the UK did in fact join the exchange rate mechanism in 1990, but unfortunately in 1992 both the UK and Italy had to leave the system, although Italy rejoined in November 1996 during the second stage of economic and monetary union. In stage two, which the Maastricht Treaty defined as beginning on 1 January 1994, a fundamental recommendation was that the institutional structure should be established. However, perhaps its most important feature was the establishment of the criteria determining whether progress may be made towards the third stage. Finally, it was foreseen that in the third stage, which began, as required under the final deadline set by the Maastricht provisions, on 1 January 1999, the irrevocably locked exchange rates would begin, to be replaced by a single currency, and the relevant monetary and economic competences would be transferred to Community institutions.

The Maastricht Treaty largely followed the Delors recommendations, although the price of including provisions on EMU in the legally binding European Community pillar of the Union was that the UK and Denmark were given opt-outs. The Delors Committee and the Masstricht Treaty envisaged that the basket ECU would be transformed into the new single currency. However, there are obvious problems with printing or stamping 'European Currency Unit' in multiple languages on notes and coins, and at the Madrid European Council in December 1995 it was decided to use terms which could be the same in every language, subject to differences of alphabet: 'euro' instead of ECU, and 'cent' for the subdivisions of the euro. When EMU commenced in 1999, there were clearly no euro notes and coins, and it was agreed that they would be introduced in 2002. However, speculation between the participating currencies during that period was prevented by **legislation** which declared the euro to be the currency of the participant Member States, and the legacy currencies were declared legally to be subdivisions of the euro. They could only be exchanged at the rates set by EC legislation for each former currency against the euro; this meant the banks could not have differential buying and selling rates, and the only way they could profit was by openly charging commission. However, countries which have joined EMU after the introduction of euro notes and coins have all so far opted for their immediate use.

There are four convergence criteria which must be met in order to join EMU. The third and fourth of these criteria expressly relate to membership of the European Monetary System:

- the observance of the normal fluctuation margins provided for by the Exchange Rate Mechanism ('ERM') of the European Monetary System, for at least two years, without devaluing against the currency of any other Member State;
- the durability of convergence achieved by the Member State and of its participation in the Exchange Rate Mechanism of the European Monetary System being reflected in the long-term interest rate levels.

Sweden, which joined the Community in 1995, had not participated at all in the ERM, and was known politically not to wish to participate in stage three of EMU, but did not have the benefit of a special protocol like the UK or Denmark. It was concluded that Sweden, by not participating in the ERM, did not fulfil the third criterion. While these criteria have not been interpreted literally, it would appear that a Member State which does not participate at all in the ERM will not be regarded as meeting the criterion, at least if it has suffered currency fluctuation (which is highly likely to be the case). The practical consequence therefore is that to the extent that membership of the ERM was and is voluntary, participation in the third stage of Economic and Monetary Union was and is also voluntary, even though no new Member State has been offered the special treatment given to the UK and Denmark.

The first of the convergence criteria requires the achievement of a high degree of price stability. This is stated to be apparent from a rate of inflation which is close to that of, at most, the three best performing Member States in terms of price stability. Closeness is defined in terms of not exceeding the rates of the best three states by more than 1.5 per cent. However, the second of the convergence criteria, relating to the sustainability of the government financial position, is not simply a hurdle to be passed in order to gain entry to the Eurozone but reflects a continuing obligation and requirement. Sustainability is stated to be apparent from having achieved a government budgetary position without a deficit that is excessive: government deficit must not exceed 3 per cent of GDP, and government debt must not exceed 60 per cent of GDP, although these criteria are not absolute. This requirement is the background to the Stability and Growth Pact.

All these criteria must still be met by any new states wishing to join EMU. However, since the basket ECU has evolved into the euro, a new version of the European Monetary System was created in 1997, under which participating currencies have a central rate against the euro, and must remain within a defined band of fluctuation in relation to that central rate. At the end of 2007, Denmark, Lithuania, Estonia, Latvia, and Slovakia were participating in this exchange rate mechanism, and Greece, Slovenia, Cyprus, and Malta had graduated from this exchange rate mechanism to participation in EMU.

JOHN A USHER

economic and social rights   Economic and social rights broadly include rights relating to participation in the economy, particularly the rights of workers such as the right to fair working conditions, and rights to social goods, notably food, water, health care, housing, and welfare. They are often considered to be a distinct category of **human rights**, different from **civil and political rights** such as **freedom of expression** or the **right to a fair trial**. Influenced by the political conflicts of the Cold War, early international **human** rights treaties tended to cover either civil and political rights or economic and social rights. However, more recent human rights treaties such as the **Convention on the Rights of the Child** contain both categories of rights. It is possible to argue, furthermore, that these supposedly distinct categories are nothing of the sort. Some rights may be found in treaties covering either type of rights. Examples of rights which have been included in both civil and political rights treaties and economic and social rights treaties are **freedom of association**, rights of families to protection, **property rights**, and the right to education. The **European Convention on Human Rights**, and, therefore, the **Human Rights Act**, includes versions of all four rights. In addition, since the 1990s, it is more common to talk about the indivisibility of human rights and to minimize the distinction between categories (sometimes called 'generations') of rights.

Some critics have gone so far as to argue that economic and social rights are not really human rights but merely represent social goals. They argue that civil and political rights merely require states not to interfere with their citizens, whereas economic and social rights require **positive action** by governments, usually through complex institutions and programmes. However, in counter-argument, the same can be said for the right to a fair trial, a typical civil and political right. States must maintain systems of investigation, **prosecution**, and adjudication in order to guarantee a fair trial, just as they have to maintain hospitals and a network of health care professionals in order to guarantee the right to health care.

A related argument is that economic and social rights are not justiciable, meaning that they cannot be the subject matter of a legal dispute before a **court**. This argument is justified on the ground that deciding whether or not a state has violated an economic or social right involves deciding whether it has used its resources wisely, which is not an appropriate question for a court to answer. Despite these concerns about expanding the scope of **judicial review** of government action, some states do include economic and social rights in their **constitutions** and allow individuals to bring cases before courts concerning these rights. South Africa and India are notable examples amongst **common law** states. In addition, the **United Nations** is currently drafting a procedure which would allow individuals to bring complaints under the **International Covenant on Economic, Social and Cultural Rights**.

HOLLY CULLEN

D Beetham, *Democracy and Human Rights* (Cambridge: Polity Press, 1999), Chapter 6

A Eide, C Krause, and A Rosas, *Economic, Social and Cultural Rights: A Textbook* (Dordrecht: Martinus Nijhoff, 2001)

economic coercion   *see* **use of force**

economic duress   *see* **contract law**

economic refugees   From an international law perspective, the phrase 'economic **refugee**' has long been out of favour, both among states and in the practice of the **United Nations High Commissioner for Refugees** ('UNHCR'). Insofar as they were ready to accept obligations towards refugees, states ensured that the range of beneficiaries was clearly delimited in favour of those outside their own country who no longer enjoyed its protection and/or who had a well-founded fear of persecution. Those who left 'voluntarily' for reasons of 'personal convenience' were therefore outside the refugee protection regime, and considered as economic migrants, not refugees. In common with other countries, the UK's Immigration Act makes no provision for 'economic refugees' and, unlike refugees strictly so-called or family members or skilled migrants, they are not identified in the Immigration Rules as a category either entitled or eligible to be admitted to the UK. In practice, for example in the process of determining refugee status and eligibility for **asylum**, the distinction between the voluntary migrant and the involuntary refugee from persecution, has never been that simple to apply. Its value is also now often called into question in certain forums, given that a certain level of economic deprivation can push people to move, just as more egregious examples of **human rights** violations or the effect of armed conflict. Internationally, the combined effects of globalization, demographic factors, and underdevelopment will likely see migratory flows continuing, and in the search for solutions, the phrase 'economic refugee' may well come into its own.

GUY S GOODWIN-GILL

economic sanctions   *see* sanctions

economic torts   English law does not have a 'general' tort of unfair **competition**. Rather, an aggrieved party must identify a specific tort or torts that cover the harm done. The causes of action most appropriate where unfair competition is the gist of the complaint are the so-called 'economic torts'. This term refers to the torts of simple conspiracy, unlawful conspiracy, inducing breach of contract, intimidation, unlawful interference with trade, and malicious falsehood. The list also includes the important tort of **passing off**. Passing off differs from all the other economic torts in that it can be committed without the intention of causing harm.

The economic torts are often divided into those that require a misrepresentation (passing off and **malicious falsehood**) and those that do not. The prime reason for the existence of the economic torts is the protection of economic interests, particularly in three-party settings where aggressive competition involves targeting the commercial partners or customers of the rival.

Most of these torts had their origins in the early **common law**; but their real development took place from the late Victorian era onwards. The agenda for these torts was set by the important decision of the **House of Lords** in *Allen v Flood* (**1898**). In this case, a 'general' tort of unjustifiable interference with trade was rejected and it was decided that the key ingredient for liability would be the use of unlawful means. However uncertainty has dogged the operation of the economic torts even into the twenty-first century, and key aspects, such as the meaning of 'intention' and 'unlawful', and the precise relationship between the various torts, are still being debated in the courts.

The two main economic torts are inducing breach of contract (dating from the decision in *Lumley v Gye* (1853)) and the 'genus' economic tort of unlawful interference with trade, which was acknowledged by the House of Lords in *Merkur Island Shipping Corp v Laughton* (1983)—although there had been earlier indications of its existence. The genus tort has been defined as interference with a person's trade by unlawful means with the intention of injuring that person. In essence the tort enables a person (the claimant) to complain of harm intentionally done to them as the result of the use of unlawful means by a second person against a third person. This genus tort encompasses the tort of unlawful conspiracy (conspiring to do something unlawful to harm the claimant) and intimidation (threatening to do something unlawful to harm the claimant).

By contrast with the tort of unlawful conspiracy, the tort of *simple* conspiracy can (anomalously) be committed by the concerted action of more than one person with the intention of injuring another, even though such action would not be unlawful if engaged in by a single individual.

The tort of inducing breach of contract requires an intentional procurement by one person of a breach of contract by another person's co-contractor. In essence it enables the victim of the breach to sue in tort the party that procured the breach, as an alternative to suing the contract breaker. The tort may be committed by persuading the co-contractor to breach the contract or by engaging in unlawful action that precipitates the breach. The tort may also be committed by engaging in unlawful conduct that prevents the co-contractor performing the contract properly, even if such non-performance does not amount to a breach. Whereas the gist of the original (persuasion) version of the tort is the breach of contract itself, the gist of the various extensions is unlawful conduct. For this reason, the precise relationship between these varieties of the tort of inducing breach of contract and the genus tort is a matter of debate.

In addition there are economic torts of which the gist is misrepresentation: malicious falsehood and passing off. Malicious falsehood commonly involves a disparagement of a person's trade or business. It is a tort of limited application, demanding as it does that the victim prove malice, defined as either spite or lies. The contrast with the tort of passing off could not be more stark. Here the standard case involves a trader misrepresenting to third parties that its own goods are the goods of the another—ie passing one's own goods off as being those of another. A successful claim for passing off provides relief not to those confused as a result of the misrepresentation (the customers or consumers) but to the trader harmed by the misrepresentation. It has been a dynamic cause of action since late Victorian times, with judges acknowledging it should be developed 'to meet changing conditions and practices in trade'. Though in theory the boundaries of the tort are clear, involving the 'classic trinity' of a misrepresentation, the existence of goodwill (or, in other words, a 'customer base'), and harm to that goodwill, at present it stands at the edge of becoming a more general remedy again unfair competition, preventing a person reaping the benefit of the another's reputation.   HAZEL CARTY

H Carty, *An Analysis of the Economic Torts* (Oxford: Oxford University Press, 2001)

See also: **conspiracy and trade union activity; tort law**

ECU   *see* **Economic and Monetary Union**

education and human rights   There are education rights under various international **human rights** instruments to which the UK is a signatory, including the United Nations **Convention on the Rights of the Child** and the European Convention for the Protection of Human Rights and Fundamental Freedoms ('ECHR'). The ECHR, which alone is justiciable in the UK **courts**, requires (under the first sentence of Article 2 of the First Protocol) that no-one shall be denied the right to education and (in the second sentence) for the state, in exercising its education functions, to respect the right of parents to ensure that the education and teaching of their children conforms to 'their own religious and philosophical convictions'. The UK has entered a reservation: it guarantees the right in the second sentence only to the extent that doing so is compatible with 'the provision of efficient instruction and training and the avoidance of unreasonable public expenditure'.

The case law on the Convention, including that of the **European Court of Human Rights**, indicates that the right to education applies to school and tertiary education and does not require the state to fund education to a particular degree or guarantee any particular form of provision requested by the parent. In only very limited circumstances is there a right to mother tongue teaching. The right of parents to have their religious and philosophical convictions upheld is aimed primarily at preventing children's indoctrination. Therefore, in a case where the state (Denmark) made **sex** education compulsory for pupils, parents' objections did not hold sway because the education was provided objectively, critically, and in a pluralistic manner, while, in another case, the participation of children in Greece in school parades commemorating war did not infringe the right of parents who, as Jehovah's witnesses, were pacifists. Generally the UK courts have found the Convention to give the state considerable latitude over education decisions and policies, particularly those that are resource-sensitive. However, parental objections on philosophical grounds to the use of corporal punishment in school have been upheld.

The **right to a fair trial** in the determination of civil rights and obligations (Article 6) has been held not applicable to various adjudications concerning education (for example, the exclusion appeal process), on the basis that the right to education is not a 'civil right' but one based on public law. The right to respect for **privacy** and **family life** (Article 8) has been invoked, unsuccessfully, in relation to various education decisions, such as a local authority's placement of siblings at different schools or a child's exclusion from school, separating him/her from his/her peers. Generally the courts regard parents as relinquishing some aspects of family **autonomy** and privacy when they place their **child** within the education system.

The right to freedom of thought, conscience, and religion, including the right to manifest one's religion or beliefs (Article 9), has been the subject of some important recent cases in the UK. They have demonstrated how, in the context of education, interference with this right may be justified by the limitations to the right contained in the Article itself, including where interference is 'necessary in a democratic society . . . for the protection of the rights and freedoms of others'. In one case, in 2005, the **House of Lords** held that although the legislative ban on corporal punishment interfered with the right of **persons** with fundamentalist Christian views who saw its use as consistent with their religious beliefs, the **legislation** had a legitimate aim of protecting the right of children not to be subjected to corporal punishment and was a proportionate means of achieving it. In another important case, in 2006, the House held that a Muslim girl, barred from attending her school wearing the jilbab because the school's policy on uniform did not permit it, had not had her right to manifest her religion interfered with, as she could attend a different school. However, the **judges** concluded that even if her right had been interfered with, it was justified, in particular because the restriction was intended to prevent pupils from being subjected to undue pressure from others to wear this more strict form of religious dress.

The legitimacy of, for example, **censorship** of school textbooks or curbs on expressions of view in the classroom may be judged with reference to Article 10, protecting **freedom of expression**. All of the articles cited above may be read with **Article 14**, which provides for a right to enjoy the Convention rights without discrimination on various grounds, including **race**, **religion**, sex, and political opinion.

NEVILLE HARRIS

See also: **religious affiliation and school dress; religious education and worship in schools**

education under devolved government: Northern Ireland   Northern Ireland's education system reflects the wider divisions in Northern Irish society. Schools are almost completely religiously segregated in terms of their pupil profile: Protestant children generally attend state-owned controlled schools (managed by local education authorities) and Catholic pupils generally attend state-funded voluntary schools which are in the ownership and management of the Catholic Church. Only 5 per cent of children attend 'integrated' (mixed **religion**) schools and a smaller number still attend Irish medium schools—schools in which instruction is provided mainly through the Irish language (a language associated mainly with the Catholic **community**).

For most of the last thirty years, Northern Ireland has been governed by a system of direct rule from the **Westminster Parliament**. Under this, the Department of Education (headed by a British Minister for Education) has had the main responsibility for securing elementary and secondary education within Northern Ireland, including policy development and the implementation of programmes of legislative change. Primary **legislation** was made at Westminster, a process which was thought to inhibit both debate on the substance of the legislation and the influence of local politicians. One consequence of this is that educational reforms have often been modelled on previous legislative initiatives in England and Wales. For instance, Northern Ireland has inherited a series of statutory provisions that were designed originally for England and Wales in an effort to increase parental rights and raise educational standards (for example, a statutory curriculum). However, there are several areas in which the law is distinctively different. These often reflect Northern Ireland's distinct social and educational context and can, in many instances, be attributed to the influence of religion in general, and the local churches in particular, on the education system. One example of this is a legal obligation on the Department of Education to take advice from those with an interest in religious education (in practice, the four main Christian churches) as to the content of the core syllabus for religious education.

The high level and varying types of segregation within schools has meant that Northern Ireland's education system has provided a venue in which the jurisdiction's complex religious, social, and political divisions find a public outlet and therefore a setting in which claims that **human rights** are being infringed arise frequently. Although much of the litigation has been unsuccessful, the government has made a number of concessions in response to ongoing campaigns from the Catholic Church (eg permitting an option of full funding for capital costs in Catholic schools) and the Irish Language movement (eg the introduction of a statutory obligation on the Department of Education to facilitate Irish Medium education). Moreover, a series of innovative **human** rights and **equality** provisions, negotiated as part of the Belfast Agreement in 1998 and implemented by the Northern Ireland Act 1998, has provided further scope for litigation. Of these, the proposed Bill of Rights has the most potential for human rights-based litigation in the context of education and could, if implemented, distinguish Northern Ireland from its neighbouring jurisdictions.

LAURA LUNDY

See also: **agreement reached in the multiparty negotiations, 10 April 1998; religious education and worship in schools**

education under devolved government: Scotland

Scotland has a long-established and unique system of education. The structure of the modern system is found in the much-amended Education (Scotland) Act 1980. The Scotland Act 1998 entrusts oversight of education in Scotland to the Scottish Ministers, who are responsible for policy and for making regulations and issuing guidance. Education authorities must secure adequate and efficient provision of school education for their area, including teaching of Gaelic in Gaelic-speaking areas. Nursery education must be available for children between the ages of about 3 and 5. State schools in Scotland are known as 'public schools'. They are comprehensive. There is no academic selection. Education at a public school is generally free. Denominational schools are public schools which have particular links with a church or religious body. There are also independent fee-paying schools and one grant-aided school. Scottish Ministers and education authorities are required to have regard to the general principle that pupils should be educated in accordance with the wishes of their parents.

It is the duty of every parent to provide education for his or her **child**, by causing the child to attend a public school, or by other means. The term 'parent' covers all those with **parental responsibilities**, persons liable to maintain the child and **persons** with care of the child. A parent may chose to educate a child at home. If a child of school age does not attend school regularly, and is not being provided with efficient education at home, then the parent may be prosecuted. Parents have the right to make placing requests for children at public schools of their choice and may appeal against a refusal of a place to an appeal committee, with the possibility of further appeal to the sheriff court. Education authorities are required to consult parents in relation proposals for material changes to schools.

The Standards in Scotland's Schools etc. Act 2000 recognizes the **United Nations Convention on the Rights of the Child**. Every child of school age has a right to be provided with education by, or arranged by, an education authority. Children are of school age between the ages of about 5 and 16. Pupils over the age of 16 are designated 'young persons'. Public school education should be directed to the development of the personality, talents, and mental and physical abilities of the child or young person to their fullest potential. Education authorities should have due regard to the views of children or young persons in decisions that significantly affect them, so far as reasonably practicable and taking account of their age and maturity. Pupils, as well as parents, may challenge exclusion from school.

The Education (Additional Support for Learning) (Scotland) Act 2004 requires education authorities to make provision for the additional support required by each child and young person in a public school, provided this does not result in unreasonable public expenditure. In more serious cases, authorities should prepare a coordinated support plan. Disputes in relation to coordinated support plans may be referred to the Additional Support Needs **Tribunals** for Scotland.   JANYS SCOTT

S McGuire & I Nisbet, *A-Z of Scots Education Law: a Guide for Parents* (Scottish Consumer Council, 2004)
J Scott, *Education Law in Scotland* (Edinburgh: W Green, 2003)

education under devolved government: Wales   Under schedule 2 of the Government of Wales Act 1998, the National Assembly for Wales has devolved secondary legislative powers in relation to aspects of education and training. The National Assembly for Wales (Transfer of Functions) Order 1999 (as amended 2000), transfers to the Assembly Government many powers which, under already existing education **legislation**, were held by the Secretary of State for Wales. To prevent any diminution of devolved powers all new Westminster legislation needs to transfer secondary legislative powers to the Assembly.

This system is complex and cumbersome. Following the Richards Commission Report (*The Report of the Commission on the Powers and Electoral Arrangements of the National Assembly for Wales*, 2004) and a resolution from the National Assembly, the Secretary of State for Wales published a White Paper (*Better Governance for Wales* (2005) Cm 6582) proposing, among other things, to enhance the legislative powers of the Assembly. Part 3 and Schedule 5 of the Government of Wales Act 2006 do not confer additional powers on the

Assembly; rather they provide a mechanism (Orders in Council) whereby such powers can be conferred on a case-by-case basis (at the moment these are being passed weekly). Some Orders in Council have been passed in relation to education: most emanate from Westminster, these tend to confer narrow legislative powers to Wales, e.g. Matter 5.1 'provision about the categories of school that may be maintained by local authorities.' Where the Assembly has requested powers, these are for primary legislative powers in broad areas of education. e.g. Matter 5.17 (not yet conferred as of January 2008) would transfer all primary legislative functions for the education of those with **disabilities** or learning difficulties to the Assembly. As with the devolution of secondary legislation the powers transferred are fragmentary. Far from simplifying the situation of devolved powers in Wales it has led to further complexity. More primary legislative powers have been conferred in education than in other devolved matters. Despite this, primary legislation from the Assembly on education matters is not likely to emerge quickly; they need to consult (to ensure inclusive government), set policy, and then draft legislation.

In Wales education and training is channelled through the Education and Lifelong Learning Committee. Their policies until 2010 are set out in 'The Learning Country'. Whilst on the face of it education in Wales still looks similar to that in England the Assembly has used its secondary legislative powers to alter its delivery, assessment, content, language base and cost.

For example:

- As well as the normal compulsory elements of education, pupils are required to study the Welsh language to 16 and education at all levels (though not in all disciplines at HE level) is available through the medium of Welsh.
- Starting with the pathfinder areas, Wales is working towards more integration between traditional education and work-related training. There is a genuine focus on lifelong learning such as literacy and numeracy classes and delivery of computer skills to farmers.
- In the area of **special educational needs** ('SEN'), both the codes of practice and the regulations are different from those pertaining to England and whilst these differences are minor, it seems likely that they will diverge more as time progresses, especially as there is a separate SEN and Disabilities **tribunal** in Wales facilitate further diversion in this area.
- The Assembly has set up new assessment systems such as the Welsh Baccalaureate and is streaming higher and further education into a system of levels to permit school, further, and higher education

to fit together logically and smoothly, so allowing greater movement between these systems and reflecting achievements at each level.

- Welsh schools do not use Standard Assessment Tests. Pupils are assessed at key stages but these assessments are low key and designed to test skills in numeracy, reading, and problem-solving and to inform learning needs.

- The Assembly provides funding for university fees and a means-tested Education Maintenance Allowance for post-sixteen education in universities, schools, and in the **community**. It has also set up Student Finance Wales which provides a unified service for the delivery of student finance for students normally living in Wales. This is delivered by the Assembly in partnership with the Student Loans Company and the Welsh Local Education Authorities.

- The Assembly and the Assembly Government will use the primary legislative functions to further these differences ensuring an education system which meets the needs of Wales, culturally, socially, linguistically and in terms of the economy.

KATE WILLIAMS

See also: **devolution**

educational charities   *see* **independent schools**

educational failure   It is well established that statutory duties obliging education authorities to provide education, for example under the Education Acts, cannot themselves form the basis of a claim for **compensation**. These statutory duties are far too broad and general to be relied upon in this way. They are purely 'public law' duties concerned with social welfare, and their breach does not give rise to an award of **damages**. It is therefore a matter of some controversy that important steps have been taken in recent years towards compensating individuals for the consequences of educational failure. The applicable principles are those of the tort of negligence (and potentially the law of contract in circumstances, such as private schooling, where there is a contract between the parties).

The tort of negligence awards compensation only where a duty to take care is owed, and breached. In the education context, such duties are based on a close analogy with 'private' relationships such as those between a solicitor and client, or between a surveyor and purchaser of a home. The duties, where they are recognized, are generally owed by individual education professionals, and only rarely by education authorities in their own right. Liability of the education authority will typically be on the basis of **vicarious liability** for the torts of employees.

In the leading case of *Phelps v Hillingdon* (2001), a duty of care was owed by an educational psychologist in respect of the claimant's undiagnosed dyslexia. The relationship between the parties was interpreted as being similar to other professional relationships involving advice or services. In another appeal heard together with *Phelps*, it was considered arguable that the local education authority might itself owe a duty of care where it offered an education psychology service, but only because this too might be analogous to offering professional services. Importantly, it was held that actions taken or decisions made under statute are not immune from actions in tort, unless they relate to issues (such as resource allocation) which it is not appropriate for a **court** to judge. But it must still be established positively in each case that a duty of care is owed on ordinary principles of private law.

In *Phelps*, it was made plain that duties to take care could not be restricted to educational psychologists assessing special educational needs. Teachers must also, as a matter of principle, be potentially subject to such duties. They would not, it was said, be liable simply for 'bad teaching'. But in the case of a plain and identifiable mistake, such as teaching the wrong syllabus for a public examination, a duty might be owed. More recently, it has been held that an 'education officer' may owe a duty of care when making (or failing to make) an assessment of special educational needs, despite not belonging to a recognized 'profession'. The existence of the duty depends on the professional nature of the *relationship* with the claimant. It does not depend on whether the employee in question is to be categorized as a 'professional' **person.**

Even if a duty of care is owed by the authority or (more likely) by an individual employee, a successful claimant must also show that the duty was breached through a failure to take reasonable care. To satisfy this criterion, it must be shown that there was manifest incompetence, or something plainly and obviously wrong. It is not enough to show that the defendant should 'arguably' have acted differently. A number of claims since *Phelps* have failed partly because negligence in this sense was not established. Equally, individuals will not be thought to have breached their duties if their decisions are reasonable, taking into account resource constraints.

A further key requirement is that the claimant must have suffered a form of 'damage' which the tort of negligence will compensate. This damage will have to be quantified, since the aim of compensation is to make good losses suffered as a consequence of the breach. Significant issues have arisen concerning the sort of 'damage' which forms the basis of the claim in such actions. In *Phelps* itself, it was considered that an undiagnosed condition such as dyslexia was capable of amounting to 'personal injury', and could therefore be compensated in its own right. A more recent **House of Lords** decision (*Adams v Bracknell* (2004)) confirms this as a sensible solution, even if it is to some extent a fiction. The undiagnosed learning difficulty is treated as analogous to an untreated physical injury. Damages may also be awarded for feelings of frustration and loss of self-confidence and self-esteem, but this is because such feelings (which cannot on their own form the basis of a claim in negligence) are the consequences of an undiagnosed condition.

An award of damages was also made in *Phelps* for lost earnings. Since there was little evidence of what income would have been achieved 'but for' the failure to diagnose, this award was very speculative. Despite the apparent potential for large losses to be caused by educational failure, the awards will reflect many uncertainties and will therefore tend to be relatively low. In *Phelps* itself the award for lost earnings was set at £25,000; and for 'general damages' (all other losses) at £12,500. As such, the greatest problem posed for education authorities is not so much exposure to huge liability in any given case, but exposure to many claims. It is therefore important to note that the House of Lords in *Adams v Bracknell* tightened its interpretation of the law relating to **limitation of actions**, defining the period of **time** within which a civil claim may be brought. The avoidance of stale claims will be a further important element in protecting education authorities from excessive litigation—which is just as important as excessive liability—arising from past errors.   JENNY STEELE

See also: **contract law; statutory duty, civil liability for breach of**

Edwards v Attorney-General for Canada (1930)

On 18 October 1929 the then Lord Chancellor, Lord Sankey, in deference to the importance of the occasion, broke with tradition and read the whole of the Privy Council's advice in *Edwards v Attorney-General for Canada* (1930) to the packed chamber before him.

The Judicial Committee of the **Privy Council** had been asked to consider whether the term 'persons' contained in section 24 of the British North American Act 1867, allowing the Governor General to summon 'qualified persons' to the Canadian Senate, included 'female persons'. Overruling a Canadian Supreme Court decision to the contrary and a significant body of British case law, their Lordships rejected 'the exclusion of women from all public offices [as] a relic of days more barbarous than ours', and held that '[t]he word 'person' . . . may include members of both sexes . . . to those who ask why the word should include females the obvious answer is why not?'.

The tenacity of five women from Alberta, Canada had serendipitously combined with changes in judicial personnel and political moves towards female emancipation in the UK—including the extension of the vote to women on the same terms as men and the appointment of the first-ever female **cabinet** minister—to bring about the resolution of an issue that had dogged the British judiciary for almost sixty years. No longer aligned alongside imbeciles, bankrupts, or horses, women were, at last, persons in the eyes of the law.   ERIKA RACKLEY

A Sachs and JH Wilson, *Sexism and the Law* (Oxford: Martin Robertson & Co Ltd, 1978), ch 1

efficiency defence in competition law It is noted in the definition of **efficiency in competition law** that the various types of efficiency can move in different directions. There may, for example, be an increase in productive efficiency, but a reduction in allocative efficiency. A standard is required in order to determine whether the conduct is positive, negative, or neutral. The efficiency defence in **competition law** is part of a claim that the total welfare standard be adopted and is based on work originally carried out by Oliver Williamson. Under the total welfare standard, any loss in any type of efficiency can be offset by a gain in another type of efficiency. Whilst the **consumer** welfare standard requires nobody to be worse off, the total welfare standard simply requires those that gain to be *able* to compensate those that lose and still be better off themselves. Society as a whole is better off as long as the sum of the efficiencies is positive, thus the existence of countervailing efficiencies should be a defence.

Implicit in the total welfare standard is a view that the identity of the winners and losers is unimportant. However, some object that it is consumers who lose out as a result of allocative inefficiency while it is producers who gain from productive efficiency; and that the law ought to protect the first group against the second group. Another critique is that the total welfare standard ignores marginal utility. Marginal utility describes the additional benefit derived from an additional unit of wealth, which, after a point, diminishes with each additional unit. Those who are comparatively rich value an additional unit of wealth less than those who are relatively poor, which justifies a more detailed assessment of the identity of the winners and losers from a particular course of conduct. Both the first and second objection can be countered by adding a pass-on requirement to the total welfare standard. This specifies that not only must the gains be sufficient to outweigh the losses, but also that those who that gain must pass-on some of the gain to those that lose. Determining how this redistribution is to occur or how to know when it occurs is difficult. In any event, it is true to say that whether an efficiency defence does or should exist in competition law remains controversial.

OKEOGHENE ODUDU

efficiency in competition law   Use of law to promote **competition** is usually justified on the ground that competition increases efficiency. Efficiency has numerous dimensions. First, productive efficiency refers to the relationship between the output of goods and the input of resources used to make them. It occurs when a producer maximizes the number of outputs that can be produced from a fixed quantity of inputs, or minimizes the number of inputs used to produce a fixed quantity of output, using the best methods of transforming inputs into outputs. Except in the special case of **natural monopoly**, it is thought that firms operating in a market that is competitive are more likely to achieve productive efficiency because an important way competitor firms gain an advantage over their rivals is by reducing production costs. If one firm can lower its costs (and therefore its price), all firms must follow suit or they will lose customers and be eliminated from the industry. In the absence of this pressure for survival and the need to win more business, firms will fail to maximize productive efficiency.

Second, allocative efficiency refers to the situation where goods or services cannot be transferred from one party to another without making one of the parties worse off. Competitive markets are allocatively efficient because firms can only add to profit by becoming productively more efficient and by making more sales. Producers find it profitable to produce until the marginal cost (the cost of producing one additional unit of output) is equal to price. All consumers willing and able to pay at least the cost of production will be supplied and so the goods, services, and resources required to produce them end up in the hands of those that value them the most.

Third, and finally, dynamic efficiency refers to the incentives for and the rate at which markets produce new and better goods. It is considered important because living standards are dependent not simply on more and cheaper goods, but also on new and better goods. New and better goods result from investment in research and development. It is uncertain whether competitive markets encourage more or less investment in innovation than non-competitive markets. However, it is felt that innovation would not occur if marginal-cost pricing (allocative efficiency) were enforced in relation to the ideas produced. Once produced, an idea can be used by an infinite number of people indefinitely with little or any additional cost. If marginal-cost pricing were enforced in relation to ideas, the cost of producing the idea could never be recovered and there would be no incentive to produce the idea.

Competition law is concerned with efficiency because efficiency, whether productive, allocative, or dynamic, affects the quantity, quality, and price of the goods and services produced. The different types of efficiency do not need to move in the same direction, so that increasing allocative efficiency may reduce dynamic efficiency and vice versa. It is then a policy question as to which species of efficiency is favoured.

OKEOGHENE ODUDU

See also: **consumer welfare; efficiency defence in consumer law**

efficient markets hypothesis   see **rational markets and regulation**

Eichmann, Adolf   Born in Austria in 1906, Adolf Eichmann served in the Gestapo from 1939 to 1945. He rose to the rank of Lieutenant-Colonel, becoming the agency's leading expert on Jewish affairs. From 1942 to 1945, he directed section 'IV-B-4' specifically responsible for 'Evacuations and Jews.' In this function, Eichmann organized and oversaw the deportation of Jews to death camps and concentration camps. After the war, he fled to Argentina, where the Israeli secret service captured him in 1960 and smuggled him to Israel to stand trial. His trial remains the most important legal proceeding to focus attention specifically on the Nazis' systematic persecution and extermination of European Jewry.

Eichmann's trial lasted from 11 April until 15 August 1961. The trial was staged in Jerusalem's *Beit Ha'am* (House of the People), a community theatre remodelled to serve as a courtroom that could accommodate 750 spectators. The court claimed jurisdiction over Eichmann, relying in part on a theory of universal jurisdiction. Reasoning analogically from international law's treatment of pirates and slave traders, the court concluded that Eichmann was an enemy of humanity who could be tried by whomever laid hands on him.

The prosecution's fifteen-count indictment included crimes against humanity perpetrated against gypsies and Poles; but the gravamen of the complaint accused Eichmann of 'Crimes against the Jewish People'. These charges arose under the 'Nazi and Nazi Collaborators (Punishment) Law' passed by the Knesset (Parliament) in 1950, two years after Israel's declaration of statehood. With the exceptions of Eichmann and Ivan **Demjanjuk**, only Jewish collaborators have been prosecuted under this law.

In a tactical rejection of Nuremberg's documentary approach, Israeli Attorney-General, Gideon Hausner, structured the prosecution's case around survivor testimony. The testimonial approach was designed to personalize the victims of genocide. It also challenged the collective image of the victims as having gone 'like sheep to the slaughter', replacing it with an image of the victim as heroic resister. An outstanding example of a trial used to honour anguished memory and define collective memory, this view became powerfully embedded in Israeli public consciousness through the retransmission of accounts and images of the trial.

Eichmann's German attorney, Robert Servatius, argued that his client was a mere cog in a bureaucratic machine. Hannah Arendt, who famously insisted that the trial failed to perceive that terrifyingly normal bureaucrats could commit acts of radical evil, advanced a variation of this argument. The prosecution, however, was able to submit substantial evidence indicating Eichmann's individual initiative, in particular in organizing the deportation of the Jews from Hungary in the summer of 1944.

Israel abolished the death penalty in 1953 for all criminals except those convicted under the Nazi law of 1950. The three-judge panel, presided over by Moshe Landau, sentenced Eichmann to death on 11 December 1961. After the Israeli Supreme Court upheld his conviction, Eichmann was hanged on 31 May 1962. He remains the only person to have been executed by the Israeli justice system.

LAWRENCE DOUGLAS

H Yablonka, *The State of Israel vs. Adolf Eichmann* (New York: Schocken Books, 2004)
L Douglas, *The Memory of Judgment: Making Law and History in the Trials of the Holocaust* (New Haven: Yale University Press, 2001)

See also: **Nuremberg trials**

election broadcasts   *see* **elections**

election financing   *see* **elections**

elections

Elections are held in Britain to determine the composition of most, though not all, of our governing institutions. Those whose membership are subject to elections include the **House of Commons**, the **Scottish Parliament**, the **Welsh Assembly**, the **Northern Ireland Assembly**, British membership of the **European Parliament**, and a number of local authorities (London boroughs, metropolitan and non-metropolitan councils, and district councils). In Britain, no strict **separation of powers** exists, so one set of national elections (a UK general election) determines the composition of both the legislature and the executive government, the **Prime Minister** being the majority party leader in the Commons.

The role of elections in British political life has traditionally revolved around the idea of **accountability** rather than pure representation. This is reflected in its 'first past the post' electoral system, which produces a wide deviation from proportionality between votes cast for a party's candidates and the seats the party wins in the Commons.

Any adult person may stand as a candidate for election to political office except those falling within certain categories of legal disqualification at **common law** or in statute. In parliamentary elections, residency in the constituency where the candidate is standing is not required. Foreign nationals (except citizens of a **Commonwealth** country or the Republic of Ireland) are disqualified.

The universal adult right to vote was granted by statutes passed in 1918 and 1928. For parliamentary elections, a voter must be a British or Commonwealth citizen and on the electoral register as being resident in a constituency. There are a number of disqualifications such as membership of the **House of Lords** and being a person convicted of corrupt or illegal practices at elections. In local and European elections, resident EU citizens may also vote.

The Prime Minister and governing party have a discretion over the timing of UK general elections. Within a five-year time frame set by the Parliament Act 1911, the Prime Minister may request the **monarch** to call an election under the authority of the **royal prerogative** of dissolution. In the past, this power of dissolution has sometimes been exercised to allow the electorate to express its support or otherwise for the government over some major national issue, as in 1910 (reform of the Lords), 1923 (tariff reform), and 1974 (trade union power). In 2007 the Prime Minister announced that in future the House of Commons' approval would be sought before a dissolution and UK general election. Other elections in Britain (local, regional, and European) take place at fixed intervals.

ROBERT BALDWIN

See also: **electoral systems**

elections and multi-party democracy

Since the end of the Cold War, liberals have argued multi-party **democracy** is the best antidote to alternative political arrangements including totalitarianism, dictatorships, military rule, and one-party governance. Multi-party democracy is also argued to epitomize the victory of liberalism over communism and other left-leaning ideologies. Under this argument, **elections** are the quintessential hallmark of a multi-party democracy. In the early 1990s, the World Bank argued that multi-party democracy was a necessary counterpart to its prescription of market **governance** and its attendant commitment to individual rights. In perhaps the best exemplification of this policy, the World Bank suspended its loan programmes to Kenya in 1991. Resumption of the loan programmes was conditioned on then President, Daniel Arap Moi, ending one-party rule and ushering in multi-party democracy. Shortly thereafter, President Moi ended his refusal to introducing multi-party democracy and Kenya became a multi-party democracy.

International law does not define what a multi-party democracy is. Neither the Universal Declaration of Human Rights nor the **International Covenant on Civil and Political Rights** prescribe multi-party democracy as the ideal political system that every country should adopt. Instead, under these rules of international law, individuals are guaranteed a right to political participation within a democratic society. However, international law does not define a democratic society.

In a multi-party democracy, several political parties participate in regular free and fair elections. A primary feature of a multi-party process therefore is a procedure for the competitive selection of leaders in an election. Each political party fields its candidates in the electoral districts or constituencies. The voters elect the candidates of their choice based on their belief that the candidate and their political party will represent their interests effectively. Where a multi-party democracy has also adopted a parliamentary system, the party that wins the most parliamentary seats forms a government led by a Prime Minister. Canada and Australia are good examples of parliamentary systems. In a Presidential system like the United States, the political parties nominate a candidate of their choice and the candidates compete in a popular election for the Presidency.

Many Latin American and African countries have very strong Presidential systems where the President is not only directly elected but has almost unimpeachable authority over other branches of government. In such contexts, there is often a dominant political party headed by the President that overshadows minority political parties. In some of the largest multi-party democracies like India and Mexico, it was not until very recently that dominant political parties suffered electoral defeat.

Free and fair elections have come to symbolize a country's journey in consolidating democracy particularly where a dominant political party is thrown out of power in a peaceful election and transition of power. Political scientists have argued that the period beginning in the early 1990s witnessed a third wave of democracy because of the large number of countries that held multi-party elections for the first time in their history or after long periods. The significance of elections as a measure of democracy is evidenced by the coinage of the term 'free and fair elections'. Free and fair elections are a short form of the international standards elections are required to conform to such as: uninhibited voter participation or universal suffrage; electoral competition among various candidates and parties; the absence of restrictions on the **freedoms of assembly**, association, and expression in the period prior to the election; and an impartial system of conducting and verifying election results.

In many multi-ethnic societies, elections have a propensity to divide people along ethnic lines since politicians find it convenient to mobilize political support through ethnic affiliation rather than on the basis of party programme or political ideology. **Violence** has followed electoral disputes where politicians have exploited ethnic sensitivities while conveniently using the language of **human rights**, including in the former Yugoslavia and in many African countries.

In general terms, elections often result in polyarchies or elite-dominated governments since they do little to involve or encourage mass aspirations for addressing inequality and the undemocratic character of international and national decision-making beyond the ballot box. At the end of the day, multi-party democracy is nothing more than political democracy. It does or says little about the social and economic challenges and inequalities in a country. In fact, some argue that by failing to address itself to social and economic inequalities, multi-party democracy legitimizes these inequalities and is therefore an inherently unstable political experiment in the absence of institutions and mechanisms of stabilization.   JAMES GATHII

electoral commission   *see* **constituencies**

electoral systems   Whilst there are innumerable ways of organizing any system of **elections**, there are four broad models that have been adopted for electing political representatives in the democracies of the world: 'first past the post' (the simple plurality system), the alternative vote, the single transferable vote, and the party list system.

For elections to the **House of Commons** (that also determine which party forms the government), the system remains 'first past the post'. Under this electoral system, the **United Kingdom** is divided into geographical areas known as **constituencies**, currently numbering 646, each of which returns one Member of Parliament. A relative majority of votes in each constituency produces the winning candidate, ie the candidate who receives more votes than any other candidate standing for election in the constituency.

The alternative vote system, used for example in Australia, utilizes a preferential voting system, so that the winner always receives over 50 per cent of all votes cast in the constituency. Thus if no candidate attains over 50 per cent of first preferences of all persons voting, then the second preferences of the candidate coming last are distributed as votes to the others (and if that fails to achieve a majority winner, then the second preferences of the next bottom candidate).

The single transferable vote ('STV') and the list systems are processes designed to achieve proportional representation, ie close correlation between votes cast for candidates of a particular party and number of seats won for that party. STV operates in the Republic of Ireland and within the UK in the electoral process of the **Northern Ireland Assembly**. STV uses multi-member, large constituencies, enabling voters to rank their preferences and distinguish between different candidates belonging to the same party.

Under a list system, winning candidates are taken from lists drawn up by the parties, the relative numbers of winning candidates being determined by votes cast for each party. A regional list system is used in UK elections of its Members of the **European Parliament**. A list system is often incorporated as an additional part of an electoral process, working alongside a constituency system of elections. This 'mixed' or 'additional member' type of system operates in New Zealand and German legislative elections, and in elections to the **Scottish Parliament**, **Welsh Assembly**, and London Assembly.

In 1997 the Prime Minister appointed an Independent Commission on the Voting System, chaired by Lord Jenkins, to recommend an alternative to the existing system for parliamentary elections to be put before the British people in a referendum. Its report (1998) recommended a system of 'AV Top-Up', under which most seats were determined through the alternative vote, with a list system being used to return around one-fifth of Members in a manner to achieve more representative proportionality.

ROBERT BLACKBURN

R Blackburn, *The Electoral System in Britain* (London: Macmillan, 1995), chapter 8.

electronic conveyancing   *see* **conveyancing**

email monitoring   *see* **human rights in the workplace**

emancipation   Modern emancipation can be defined as drive for individual **autonomy**. It is this autonomy that is expressed in and becomes the content of juridical rights. The origin of critical philosophy and critical thinking turned on this notion of emancipation and its independence from external constraint. This is the meaning and significance of Kant's (1724–1804) aphorism in 'What is Enlightenment?'—*Sapere Aude*! (dare to know); 'Have courage to use your own understanding!'. That is the motto of enlightenment, a motto at first aimed against religious institutions, developing into a rejection of God and theology.

Emancipation was actualized politically through the French and American Revolutions. The emancipation from the constraints of the *ancien regime*—the move from **subjects** to citizens and from chattels to 'man'—and the autonomy of the individual this implied was expressed through the juridical concepts of the Rights of the **Citizen** and the Rights of Man. The substance of this emancipation was criticized from two directions. Karl Marx (1818–1883) illustrated the limited and yet to be completed goal of emancipation by showing that the 'rights of man' were in fact, the rights of the private property owner; a right that conflated autonomy with conflict and **competition**. Joseph de Maistre (1753–1821) argued that the very idea and ideal of emancipation, and its rejection of heavenly and earthy authority, was nothing other than an act of hubris. De Maistre believed that 'the Terror' into which the French **Revolution** degenerated was divine punishment for the crime of usurpation.

At a different level, the French and American Revolutions also contained the seeds of the idea that emancipation and autonomy could apply to 'peoples' as well as 'people'. This development was expressed in the idea of '**self-determination**'; the rights of peoples to emancipate themselves from their colonial 'masters'. The autonomy that arises from such emancipation is expressed through the juridical concept of 'equal **sovereignty**'.

The optimism of emancipation at both the individual and national level was severely shattered (*inter alia*) by the Holocaust. In more recent times, this **trauma** has expressed itself in the thought that Nazism and anti-semitism, far from being the antithesis of emancipation and juridical rights are, rather, the indirect (Lyotard (1924–1998)) or direct (Agamben (b. 1942)) consequence of the connection between the theological and political dimensions of emancipation. Returning to the tradition of de Maistre, this negation of critical thinking has led to demands for emancipation from emancipation.

DAVID SEYMOUR

embryo   *see* **foetus**

embryo research   The regulatory story of research on **human** embryos in the United Kingdom starts with the Report of the Warnock Committee (Cmnd 9314, 1984). Controversially, Warnock took the view that research on human embryos was morally permissible; and some members of the Committee (in fact, just a majority) were prepared to sanction the creation of embryos for research. However, as a counterweight, it was emphasized that the human embryo has a special status and should not be regarded simply as a ball of cells.

Despite considerable parliamentary unease, the Government took forward the main thrust of Warnock's recommendations when it enacted the Human Fertilization and Embryology Act 1990. Accordingly, the **legislation** seeks to declare quite explicitly (for the guidance of scientists and funders as well as for the reassurance of the public) when embryo research is lawful and when it is not; and it establishes a dedicated regulatory body (the **Human Fertilization and Embryology Authority** (the 'HFEA')) to license and monitor such research activities.

Crucially, the legislation puts in place three limiting principles: first, that, in no circumstances, should research on human embryos run beyond fourteen days or the appearance of the primitive streak; secondly, that the HFEA should license the use of human embryos for research only if it is necessary (in the sense that the research cannot be done without using human embryos); and, thirdly, that if the HFEA is satisfied that such research is necessary, then a licence should be granted only if the particular activity is judged to be necessary or desirable in relation to one of the approved statutory purposes.

In the 1990 Act, five purposes are listed as approved. These are:

(a) promoting advances in the treatment of infertility;
(b) increasing knowledge about the causes of congenital disease;
(c) increasing knowledge about the causes of miscarriages;
(d) developing more effective techniques for contraception; [or]
(e) developing methods for detecting the presence of gene or chromosome abnormalities in embryos before implantation.

In 2001, these purposes were extended to pave the way for **therapeutic cloning** and human embryonic **stem cell** research.

The contrast between the UK's relatively permissive regulatory environment and that found in much of Europe is highlighted by the restrictive terms of Article 18 of the Council of Europe's Convention on Human Rights and Biomedicine. According to Article 18(2), the *creation* of human embryos for research is categorically prohibited; and, Article 18(1) provides that, where the law permits research on human embryos (such embryos having been created for some other purpose, as in an IVF programme), then 'it shall ensure adequate protection of the embryo'. If the UK is to sign up to the Convention without entering a reservation for embryo research, it might argue that domestic law complies with Article 18(1) by sufficiently protecting those embryos that are used for research; but there is no such easy way round Article 18(2).

ROGER BROWNSWORD

Emergency leave   *see* **Parental leave**

emergency powers   During the past decade, emergencies have arisen in connection with floods and droughts, fuel price protests (in 2000), Foot and Mouth disease (in 2001), and terrorism on the devastating scale witnessed in 2001 and 2005. For the future, there loom deadly influenza pandemics and climate change. Consequently, risk assessment and resilience against the impact of emergencies have become important themes in political debate and social action in the modern 'risk society'.

According to Marcus Tullius **Cicero**, 'Salus populi suprema est lex' ('The safety of the people is the highest law'). The core response is the Civil Contingencies Act 2004. To ensure flexibility and adaptability, the Act sets out a highly inclusive definition of 'emergency', which encompasses threats to human welfare, the environment, and security.

Part I of the Act covers local arrangements for civil emergency planning. Schedule 1 lists those persons and bodies—called 'Responders'—which are subject to duties imposed under Part 1. Local bodies such as the local authority and police ('Category 1 responders') must assess risks, maintain response plans, and provide advice and warnings. Other bodies such as utility providers ('Category 2 responders') must cooperate with Category 1 responders. All must work together in local resilience forums. By contrast, the Act is virtually silent about the roles of regional resilience forums, of lead government departments, and of the Cabinet Office.

Part II delineates the extensive lists of permissible powers to issue regulations in response to the occurrence of emergencies. Safeguards are included which reflect the 'triple lock' principles—that restraints will be imposed by reference to seriousness, necessity, and geographical proportionality. There are also strong political imperatives against future usage which have conduced against the invocation of powers of this kind since the 1970s.

As well as the 2004 Act, many other emergency provisions respond to emergencies on a sector-by-sector basis. Most prominent in recent years has been legislation about terrorism. Other legislation has addressed industrial hazards, power and water supply shortages, and food chain hazards. There also remain broad **common law** powers to respond to threats to security and order.

Despite the dire situations in which they may emerge, the rule of law demands that emergency powers should be subject to constitutional control. As Lord Mansfield declared in *R v Wilkes* (1770): 'Fiat justitia, ruat caelum' ('Though the heavens fall, let justice be done'). Yet, the judges generally show restraint in reviewing the emergency decisions of the executive. **Judicial review** is unlikely to halt any other than disastrously and patently ill-founded or ill-argued cases, such as where detention without trial was found to be evidently discriminatory under Article 14 of the **European Convention on Human Rights** in *A v Secretary of State for the Home Department* (2004). It should also be noted that Article 15 of the European Convention on Human Rights allows for derogations from normal rights entitlements when there exists a public emergency threatening the life of the nation.   CLIVE WALKER

U Beck, *Risk Society* (London: Sage, 1992)
C Walker and J Broderick, *The Civil Contingencies Act 2004: Risk, Resilience and the Law in the United Kingdom* (Oxford: Oxford University Press, 2006)

emergency services, liability of   *see* **acts and omissions**

émigré lawyers   While émigré lawyers are both migrants and lawyers, the term is normally understood more narrowly. Unlike 'emigrant', the French term 'émigré' is usually limited to those who have migrated under some pressure, in particular fear of persecution on ethnic, political, or religious grounds, and who regard themselves as being in exile. This will naturally include a large group of lawyers who left Germany for the UK after 1933. But it may be less obvious what was, for example, on the mind of two young men who left **apartheid** South Africa on Rhodes scholarships to Oxford, went back to South Africa to practice, returned to the UK, and eventually became the Law Lords, Steyn and Hoffmann.

Those who look at the impact of émigré lawyers (see below) may therefore be less concerned with motives for migration, but are likely to restrict this group to **persons** who were trained in a different legal system before they migrated, thus excluding, eg Lord Justices Kerr and Schiemann, or Professor Sir Guenther Treitel, who left their native Germany as children. The converse restriction may apply to foreign trained lawyers who did not work as lawyers in the UK, thus excluding, eg the later German Constitutional Court judge, Gerhard Leibholz. Furthermore, the present entry deals only with lawyers who migrated to the UK rather than from the UK, or within the UK, thus excluding Scots migrating to England and vice versa.

Among the first émigré lawyers on record are Protestants who fled to England around 1600 in order to avoid religious persecution. This includes the well-known Italian lawyer and author of *De jure belli* (On the law of war, 1598), Alberico **Gentili** (1552–1608), who became Professor of **Roman Law** at the University of Oxford in 1581, and Regius Professor in 1587. Similar motives may have driven Adam Reuter (†1626), a Silesian scholar of civil and **canon law**, to move to Oxford in 1608, where he became affiliated with New College. His work takes side with the King and the Anglican Church, and he wrote a treatise *De consilio* (On counsel, 1626).

Little is known about émigré lawyers between then and the end of the nineteenth century, when law faculties developed at the Universities, became more outward looking, and occasionally sought to attract continental lawyers. Erwin Grueber from Munich was thus in 1882 appointed Reader in Roman Law at Oxford, and held this position until 1906. Paul Vinogradoff, a Russian historian and lawyer who had also studied at Berlin, was in 1903 elected to the Oxford Chair in Jurisprudence, which he held until his death in 1925; he received a knighthood in 1917. In 1895, the German lawyer, Lassa Oppenheim, left a chair in Basle, Switzerland, to become an academic gentleman of independent means in London, where he wrote his influential book, *International Law*. In 1923, the Polish born Austrian lawyer, Hersch Lauterpacht, enrolled for studies at the London School of Economics; he was eventually made Professor there and became a towering figure of Public **International Law**. While Grueber was definitely, and Oppenheim and Lauterpacht were arguably, more emigrants than émigrés, Vinogradoff, having clashed with Russian authorities, had pressing political reasons for moving to the UK.

The trickle of foreign lawyers turned into a stream from 1933, when scholars and practitioners alike were persecuted in National socialist Germany for racist and political reasons. Many found their way into UK academia and legal practice, including some twenty well-known persons (see below). The vast majority of them were Jewish or had Jewish ancestors. By comparison, those who fled Hungary after the 1956 uprising, or Czechoslovakia after the 1968 invasion, or political circumstances in various African, Asian, or Latin American countries, appear to have arrived in the UK in substantially smaller numbers.

Little research has been conducted on émigré lawyers in the UK, apart from the German refugees, so that few figures exist on countries of origin. Records available for 1933–1956 from the archives of the UK-based Society for the Protection of Science and Learning show not only some 100 German or Austrian, but also sizeable groups of Italian and Spanish, lawyers (some fifteen each) who at some time sought refuge or help, but it appears that they never arrived in the UK, or went on to some other place, or else left few traces. From 1944 until 1947, the University of Oxford hosted a Polish Faculty of Law in exile, which included many well-known scholars, such as the administrative law expert, Ludwig Bar. Their task was to educate Polish students who should take over legal positions in Poland after the war. Most staff and students did indeed return to Poland, with two notable exceptions: faculty member, Leon Radzinowich (see below) and student, Janusz Grodecki, who became Professor of Law in the University of Leicester in 1965. Some émigré (or emigrant) lawyers from Italy, Russia, Hungary, Poland, and South Africa are mentioned above or below.

The vast majority of émigré lawyers whose fate has been documented took residence in England, and most in Oxford, London, or Cambridge. As **Scottish law** is closer to continental legal systems than English law, it is surprising how few went to Scotland. A rare exception is the German émigré, Julius Fackelheim, who between 1947 and 1954 was a part-time lecturer at the University of Aberdeen. Another German émigré, Josef Unger, spent 1942–1949 as Lecturer at the University of Wales at Aberystwyth before moving on to Birmingham.

The majority of twentieth century émigré lawyers came from legal practice, and perhaps half of them found work as legal practitioners in the UK. Their fates are generally less well documented than those of their academic colleagues. Best known amongst the practitioners are three German émigrés, Francis Mann, Rudolf Graupner (both solicitors), and Ernst Cohn (a barrister), and the Hungarian, Andrew Martin (born Neugröschel), also a barrister. All four were also prolific writers of textbooks, commentaries, or articles and thus also count on the academic side; two of them were even made professors in England (Ernst Cohn at King's College London, Andrew Martin at Southampton). Few émigré lawyers went on to become judges; Lords Steyn and Hoffmann have been mentioned above. Some, including Richard Fuchs and Bernhard Wolff, became UK civil servants (both working in post-war Germany), and many more acted as government advisors.

The group of twentieth century émigré academic lawyers (origin German unless indicated otherwise) concentrated on areas of law which rise above, do not form part of, or had previously been largely ignored by English Law. They include Comparative (Private and Commercial) Law (Ernst Cohn, Wolfgang Friedmann, Otto Giles (born Prausnitz), Sir Otto **Kahn-Freund**, Clive Schmitthoff, Martin Wolff), Conflict of Laws (Sir Otto Kahn-Freud, Kurt Lipstein, Francis Mann, Clive Schmitthoff, Martin Wolff), Criminology (Hermann Mannheim, Max Grünhut, and Sir Leon Radzinovic, from Poland), European Law (Rudolf Graupner, Kurt Lipstein), Labour Law (Sir Otto Kahn-Freund), Legal History (Walter Ullmann, from Austria), Legal Philosophy (Wolfgang Friedmann, Hermann Kantorowicz), Public International Law (Francis Mann, Georg Schwarzenberger; see also above for Oppenheim and Lauterpacht), and Roman Law (David Daube, Fritz Pringsheim, Fritz Schulz).

As Peter North has put it, émigré lawyers brought 'an international breadth of scholarship, coupled with a real breadth of vision' to the UK, and they worked in areas where their talents could be put to best use. They introduced Criminology, Labour Law and (through Gentili) Public International Law as areas of academic study, strongly influenced and almost dominated Public International Law during parts of the twentieth century, made significant contributions to Legal History, were amongst the first to write on European Law, and developed Comparative Private Law, Conflict of Laws, Legal Philosophy and the study of Roman law in the UK. That they also influenced teaching is evidenced by the fact that Vinogradoff introduced the seminar as a form of teaching to the Oxford Law Faculty. And it is perhaps not a coincidence that it was another émigré lawyer, Andrew Martin, who formulated the need for a Law Commission as an independent body for monitoring the **common law** and for proposing legislative development, and who even wrote the first draft for the Law Commissions Act 1965.

It is difficult to tell whether émigré lawyers gave law in the UK (and particularly English law) a different direction, or whether they mostly accelerated developments which would have occurred at any rate. But they helped to make English law more systematic, principled, modern, and outward looking, and thus prepared it for the increased exposure to other legal systems which occurred when the UK joined what now is the European Union, and which continues until today.   GERHARD DANNEMANN

J Beatson and R Zimmermann (eds), *Jurists Uprooted* (Oxford: Oxford University Press, 2004)
M Jabs, *Die Emigration deutscher Juristen nach Großbritannien* (Osnabrück: Rasch, 1999)

empirical legal research   *see* **socio-legal research**

employee   *see* **contract of employment**

employee participation   *see* **consultation with workers; collective bargaining**

employee share ownership   It has become increasingly popular in recent years for employees to own **shares** in their employer's business. It is thought that this promotes bilateral loyalty and the common interests of capital and labour, saves the employer salary costs, and can be a method of raising capital. Employees can find share ownership attractive because participation in an approved scheme has **income tax** advantages, and means they benefit over and above their salary in the commercial success of their **company**. On the other hand, too great a use of this in a business can result in proportionate reduction in share value. Additionally, through making employee rewards directly dependent on the commercial success of the company, they will also be clearly affected by downturns. Employers will also bear additional administration costs both in running the scheme and (if desired) obtaining HM Revenue and Customs ('HMRC') approval.

There are many types of scheme. Some target key employees while others are open to all. Some amount to options only to purchase shares, while others are part of the employees' remuneration package or are free. Some have particular eligibility requirements such as length of service. Some apply only if the company is sold or floated on the **Stock Exchange**. Each has particular tax implications both for the employer and employees depending on whether the scheme is approved by HMRC or not. The following are approved schemes—Share Incentive Plan, Save As You Earn schemes, Enterprise Management Incentives, and Company Share Option Plans.

SIMON HONEYBALL

employers' liability   *see* **negligence in civil law; vicarious liability**

employment agencies   *see* **agency workers**

employment tax   Employment tax is an important source of government revenue, accounting for about 90 per cent of total receipts from income tax in the UK. The three key elements of employment tax are: (i) the subject of the tax; (ii) the tax base; and (iii) collection.

(i) Subject: Whether a UK worker is an 'employee' and thus subject to employment tax on his or her earnings is determined under **common law** tests aimed at distinguishing a contract of' service (employment) from a contract 'for' service (self-employed). The courts will weigh a number of factors, including the intention of the parties to the engagement, the degree of control exercised over the worker, whether the worker is able to provide a substitute, and whether the worker is carrying on business on his or her own account and open to the prospect of profit and risk of loss. In addition, a worker who is employed through an intermediary (such as a 'one-man' company owned by the worker) may be subject to employment tax on payments received by the intermediary for the worker's services where the relationship between the worker and the intermediary's clients would satisfy the common law tests for a contract of service.

(ii) Base: Earnings from employment subject to tax in the UK are broadly defined, encompassing any salary, wages, or fee, any gratuity, or other profit or incidental benefit of any kind obtained by the employee, if it is money or convertible into money. Nearly any payment or benefit provided to an employee for acting as or being an employee will be caught. Even payments made to an employee by a third party (such as a customer of the employer) are potentially taxable. However, payments made by way of present or testimonial on grounds personal to the recipient may escape tax.

Originally, non-cash benefits (sometimes called 'perquisites' or 'perks') were subject to tax in the UK only if convertible into money, and then only at their conversion value. However, the scope for taxing perks has been expanded for almost all employees, with the result that most perks are taxable, normally on the basis of the cost to the employer. Special rules apply for determining the taxable amount of some perks, including living accommodation, employee share schemes, and the private use of an employer-provided vehicle. Some benefits are specifically exempted from tax, in whole or in part, such as workplace canteen meals, work-related training, and employer-provided childcare.

Employees are permitted to claim deductions from their taxable employment earnings for certain specified employment-related costs incurred, including professional memberships and travel in the performance of employment duties. Other expenses may be deductible under a general statutory test if the employee is obliged to incur and pay them as holder of the employment, and the amount is incurred wholly, exclusively, and necessarily in the performance of the duties of the employment. However, this test is notoriously difficult to satisfy in practice.

(iii) Collection: Earnings from employment are taxed in the UK when received. Tax is collected primarily at source by employers. Unusually, the UK operates a cumulative withholding system—Pay As You Earn ('PAYE')—with the result that most employees have the correct amount of tax withheld each pay period and do not have to file a year-end tax return. Employee and employer **national insurance** contributions ('NICs') are also levied at source on most forms of employment income. Strictly NICs are not a 'tax' since contributions give rise to entitlement to state benefits. However, the link between contributions made and entitlement has been weakened over the years, and NICs generally are viewed as simply another employment tax.

GLEN LOUTZENHISER

employment tribunals   Employment **tribunals** were first established under the Industrial Training Act 1964 to hear appeals from assessments of Industrial Training levies. Gradually, under many different statutes, their jurisdiction was extended and the major part of tribunal work now comprises **unfair dismissal**, **redundancy** payments, **working time**, and **discrimination in employment** claims. Claims are normally brought by a worker against his employer but in some cases a **trade union** may pursue a claim and, in contractual disputes arising or outstanding on dismissal, an employer may bring a counter claim against a claimant employee. In most cases a grievance must be presented to the employer about the particular matter before a claim may be made to the tribunal.

Generally, three members sit as the tribunal, one derived from the employers' panel, one from an employees' panel (appointed for renewable terms of three years) and a legally qualified chair. Where the tribunal members cannot agree, the decision may be made by a majority. The Chairman sits alone on **case management** discussions, and on pre hearing reviews unless there are 'one or more substantive issues of fact . . . likely to be determined'. Further there are certain jurisdictions such as unauthorized deductions from wages and the right to a written statement of terms where the Chairman sits alone.

The procedure is generally governed by the Employment Tribunals Act 1996 and the Employment Tribunals (Constitution and Rules of Procedure) Regulations 2004. The original vision of the Donovan Commission on Trade Unions and Employers' Associations 1965–1968 was that they should be 'easily accessible, informal, speedy and inexpensive'. The Rules now provide that the tribunal, so far as it appears to be appropriate, should seek to avoid formality in its proceedings and conduct hearings in such manner as it considers appropriate for the clarification of the issues before it, and generally to the just handling of the proceedings (rule 14(2)-(3)).

Most jurisdictions have limited timescales for claims to be made, typically three months from the relevant event subject to a discretionary extension. The employer must respond to the claim within 28 days. The Advisory Conciliation and Arbitration Service ('**ACAS**') has a duty to promote the settlement of most disputes presented to a tribunal. Tribunals are expected actively to case manage claims and have many powers to do so, eg to order that answers are given to questions posed by the other side, witness and disclosure orders. In extreme circumstances claims and responses may be struck out.

There is no restriction on who may represent parties in tribunals. Costs are rarely awarded, and in most cases the tribunal may only do so if a party has, in bringing or conducting the proceedings, acted vexatiously, abusively, or otherwise unreasonably.

The overall head of Employment Tribunals is the President, and there are eleven regions of Tribunals in England and Wales. Appeals on points of law are heard by the Employment Appeal Tribunal.

JOHN BOWERS

empowerment   Empowerment entails the process of enabling persons or groups to participate more fully as rights-bearing entities within a society and state. Empowerment is closely tied to the exercise of full **citizenship** rights without any impediments. As such it has been particularly significant in the context of historical marginalization of **persons** or groups that have been subject to systemic oppression or subordination due to cultural, religious, or political factors. The process of empowerment entails efforts to overcome such enduring marginalization through creating and sustaining political, legal, and institutional change. Empowerment processes must necessarily engage with the requirement of fostering individuals' and groups' agency, while simultaneously seeking to create structures which will best allow the expression of such agency. To a large degree, therefore, empowerment is ultimately about participation, participatory decision-making, and democratic processes.

The focus of empowerment strategies may be economic, social, political, legal, or all of these, to address identified issues with respect to particular groups with specific experiences and subject to particular structures of exclusion. For example, civil and political empowerment for **women** has been the focus within the legal-political arena in most countries around the world at different times in establishing equal voting rights for women. This process has empowered women by directly affecting their role and participation within modern political processes. Another example of targeted efforts at empowerment for women construed around particular goals is that of micro-credit provision to overcome women's lack of independent earning capacity in many societies. To the extent that such schemes are created for the purpose of giving women a greater ability to engage in economically productive activities, they are potentially empowering for women through increased economic participation, which in turn contributes to higher earning capacity, lesser dependence, enhanced status within the family and society, and enhanced agency.

Empowerment mechanisms must address root issues in a multifaceted and integrated way to bring about systematic enhancement of the group identified. This is borne out by the recognition that systematic subordination and exclusion is rarely the product of a single practice or idea but a complex interplay of multiple practices, norms, values, and structures which work together. Law can play a very important role as the process as well as the locus of empowerment. As the experience of many societies has shown, the process of bringing about legal change, located, as it must be, within wider political agreement, itself contributes to empowerment by making visible the hierarchies, norms, and processes of exclusion. In the case of untouchables in India for example, the wider debates surrounding the role of **religion** and religiously sanctioned exclusionary practices prior to and during independence from British colonial rule supported legal change. The explicit prohibition of the practice of untouchability in the Constitution can be seen as a defining moment for the whole class of people hitherto subject to this inhuman practice, whence they become legally empowered to resist continued marginalization resulting from the practice. The example of equal rights for black Americans, born out of the Civil Rights struggles in the United States, provides another example of empowerment through engagement with law and legal change. Legal developments through various stages, from the abolition of **slavery** to the full protection of citizens' enjoyment of civil rights, show that empowerment through law requires constant review to accommodate recognition and redressal of different aspects of exclusion and marginalization on an ongoing basis.

Struggles for empowerment can be constructed around greater access to economic resources, political participation, or the right to define cultural **identity**. In the current multicultural context of many jurisdictions, one important aspect is to obtain equal respect for group practices and rights against compulsory conformity with the majority within law and the wider political economy. However, claims for greater empowerment of the group in such cases must be critically assessed in terms of possibilities of empowerment of individual members of the group itself. The very real possibility of greater marginalization on vulnerable members within the **minority** group alongside greater power of the group to regulate its members has to be recognized and overcome.

Where legal changes create new rights and obligations to enable full citizenship, it may nevertheless not be sufficient to bring about empowerment in the everyday lives of people so empowered. This is to recognize that legal change by itself is insufficient to guarantee enduring non-subordination and exclusion. Legal change is critical for the provision of a publicly-agreed framework to create the necessary rights and enforcement mechanisms were such rights to be violated. Legal empowerment to fulfil its promise, however, needs adequate social, economic, and political engagement as well. Any campaigns specifically focused upon legal reforms must take on board that law reforms can only be the start of a wider, perhaps renewed process of empowerment rather than its culmination. This is particularly relevant in the context of empowerment strategies which seek to overcome historical exclusion based on prejudicial attitudes. As experiences across societies have made clear in a variety of contexts, attitudes cannot be changed merely through non-recognition within law, but require a deeper social transformation.

Law can provide important inputs and support mechanisms to the ongoing empowerment project. Further to wider legal and constitutional empowerment guarantees, targeted affirmative action as positive measures to further the empowerment of marginalized groups have also been part of legal development. Positive or affirmative action around the rights and protections of Native Americans in North America, the Aborigines in Australasia, Scheduled Castes and Scheduled Tribes and Other Backward Castes and women's political representation in India are some examples of continued legal engagement. Law's power to recognize, define, and sanction, and its corresponding power to exclude from state protection is fundamental to struggles over **recognition** and redistribution which inform empowerment struggles and campaigns. Engagement with law as part of these wider empowerment campaigns must therefore be on a reflexive and critical basis. Empowerment is about enabling **equality**, **autonomy**, and non-discrimination in relation to the identity of any marginalized person or group.

REENA PATEL

See also: **feminism and law reform; positive action**

enemy subjects and enemy property *see* **international humanitarian law; war and armed conflict**

enforcement of court orders More than any other factor, the ineffective enforcement of court orders undermines the credibility and the integrity of the courts. It is axiomatic that, if public confidence in the machinery of justice is not to be eroded, court orders must be honoured. Where enforcement fails, those affected inevitably feel frustrated, disillusioned, angry, even betrayed, and the courts are derided for peddling idle threats. Enforcement poses serious difficulties for both the criminal and civil courts yet it has always been regarded as a peripheral part of the justice system and, until the recent past, largely neglected.

As far as the criminal courts are concerned, the issue of enforcement arises mainly in relation to non-payment of financial penalties and failure to comply with the conditions of a community penalty. **Fines** are by far the most commonly used of penal sanctions in the UK, being imposed in almost three-quarters of all criminal cases, and it is fine defaulters who, numerically at least, present the principal problem of enforcement. The criminal courts wield much stronger powers in enforcing their orders than do the civil courts, and severe penalties can be imposed on those who fail to comply. Many millions of pounds are lost annually through non-payment of fines and, although the imprisonment of fine defaulters is viewed as a last resort, it can be used where the

original offence was punishable by imprisonment. A large number of the defendants who are fined each year—as many as 10 per cent in Scotland, though lower elsewhere in the UK—are sent to prison for non-payment of fines. Great unease has, however, been voiced about whether imprisonment is appropriate for them when the original offence was not itself deemed to merit a prison sentence. Imprisoning fine defaulters also contributes to prison overcrowding and, while most defaulters stay in prison for only a matter of days, they nevertheless make up a significant minority of prison receptions and their rapid turnover places considerable administrative burdens on the prison authorities.

With such considerations in mind, a search for alternatives to imprisonment for fine defaulters (and others who fail to comply with criminal court orders) has gathered momentum in recent years. The range of the available alternatives to prison is wider in England and Wales than in other parts of the UK, and the Crime (Sentences) Act 1997 extended the range still further so that it now includes community service orders, curfew orders with electronic monitoring, and driving disqualification. The early signs suggest that these measures are proving popular with courts and resulting in a reduction in the numbers of fine defaulters sent to prison.

On the civil side, the situation surrounding enforcement of orders is much bleaker. The stark reality is that a majority of civil court judgments fail to result in full payment in the timescale ordered by the court. More often than not, enforcement action also proves ineffective. The picture is so grim that it is scarcely an exaggeration to say that debtors who are knowledgeable and unscrupulous enough can, with relative ease, frustrate enforcement processes and evade payment of a civil court judgment if they are so minded. The dispiriting truth for claimants is that securing a civil court judgment is merely the first step in what may prove a lengthy process of obtaining payment and one that may ultimately prove fruitless.

Several court-based options are available to claimants who seek to enforce a judgment, although they are often baffled by the arcane terminology that is used. The legal terminology surrounding enforcement has a distinctly medieval ring to it, and measures such as 'warrants of execution', 'writs of *fieri facias*', and 'charging orders' mean little to most lay people. Even more familiar terms like 'bailiff', 'sheriff', 'impound', and 'warrant' are still confusing. The corresponding terminology in Scotland is different but no less obtuse. It is only in Northern Ireland, where there is an Enforcement of Judgments

Office, that much help is given to claimants in making decisions about the enforcement action to take. This Office assumes responsibility in enforcement and takes all the key decisions on the claimant's behalf. In other parts of the UK, it remains the claimant's own responsibility, not the court's, to take the initiative. This generally suits the interests of large business creditors, but it places individual claimants at a disadvantage since most have no idea about how to go about enforcing a court judgment. As a consequence, the choice of mechanism for enforcing judgment is often a hit-and-miss business. Claimants are obliged to pay further court fees if they wish to pursue one of these court-based options, and this merely aggravates their difficulties.

The problems that have dogged enforcement in this country have been recognized by governments for many years and, after completing the most detailed review of enforcement procedures ever undertaken in this country, a draft Tribunals, Courts and Enforcement Bill was published in July 2006. Parts 3 and 4 of the Bill propose several measures to assist claimants in enforcing judgments, the most important of which is a court-based mechanism that will help courts gain access to information about the financial circumstances of debtors. This will help courts distinguish between debtors who are unable to pay and those who refuse to do so. Provisions of this kind are important although it is probably unwise to anticipate dramatic change to result. As anyone who has studied the subject of enforcement soon realizes, there are no quick-fix solutions. The problems are deep rooted, have occurred for decades, and are found on a comparable scale in many other jurisdictions.

No one seriously questions the proposition that those subject to court orders should honour them and a tough approach to the enforcement of court orders is generally seen as appropriate. However, care needs to be exercised in ensuring that those who are unable to make payment are adequately protected from methods of enforcement that are unfair, intrusive, or oppressive. Striking the right balance between competing interests is exceedingly difficult.

JOHN BALDWIN

See also: **curfews**

enforcement order An enforcement order is an order made by a court which compels a trader to act in accordance with **consumer** protection laws. Although an individual consumer can take action if he or she has suffered harm because a trader has not complied with the law, the majority of consumers do not take legal action because the costs involved do not make it worth their while. Traders who repeatedly breach consumer protection legislation are likely to cause significant detriment.

Following an EU Directive, the Enterprise Act 2002 created enforcement orders. These can be used when a trader infringes consumer laws and where this harms the collective interests of consumers. An order will require the trader to stop the infringement, and not commit further breaches in the future. These orders can be applied for by enforcers, of which there are general enforcers (such as the **Office of Fair Trading**, Trading Standards Departments, and the Northern Irish Department of Enterprise, Trade, and Investment), Community enforcers (enforcers from another EU Member State authorized by that state to take action), and designated enforcers (allowed to take action when specific consumer laws are breached). Before an enforcer can apply to court for an order, it is necessary to consult with the trader concerned to persuade it to stop breaching the law, but if this is not successful, an order can be requested. If a trader subsequently fails to comply with that order, it may be prosecuted for contempt of court, which may result in a prison sentence.

CHRISTIAN TWIGG-FLESNER

enforcing human rights Unlike most states, the United Kingdom has not adopted a codified written **constitution** (ie a constitutional document of the highest legal status) with an entrenched (specially protected) set of fundamental **human rights**. Instead, our uncodified constitution has traditionally relied upon **Acts of Parliament** and judgments of the **courts** to provide legal protection for basic **human** rights. However, from the 1970s, a number of leading **judges**, lawyers, and **non-governmental organizations** began to argue for enhanced legal protection of fundamental human rights within domestic law. By the 1990s the focus of reform had concentrated upon securing enforcement of the basic **civil and political rights** enshrined in the **European Convention on Human Rights** ('ECHR') within domestic law. Our highest court (the House of Lords) ruled that this major development required the approval of **Parliament** through **legislation**. Subsequently, the Labour Party manifesto for the general election of 1997 proposed incorporating ECHR rights into domestic law. Following that party's election victory the government published a policy paper (*Rights Brought Home*: 1997) which set out the arguments for giving qualified domestic effect to specified rights within the ECHR. However, the historic constitutional doctrine of the legislative supremacy of Parliament was to be maintained. This meant that the courts would not be empowered to strike down Acts of Parliament that violated rights guaranteed under the ECHR. In 1998, Parliament enacted the **Human Rights Act**. The Act specifies which rights under the ECHR, called 'Convention rights', can be given effect by domestic courts. British courts are subject to a new duty to interpret legislation 'so far as it is possible to do so' in a way that is compatible with Convention rights. This empowers the courts to engage in considerable manipulation of statutory language. In rare cases where it is not possible for the higher courts to interpret an Act in a manner compatible with Convention rights then they can issue a 'declaration of incompatibility'. The issuing of such a declaration does not affect the validity of the Act, but it is a public notification to the government, Parliament, and the media that a piece of legislation violates fundamental human rights. In such circumstances, the Human Rights Act authorizes a Minister to issue an amending Order. Alternatively, Parliament may decide to enact amending legislation.

Where **persons**' rights under the ECHR have not been protected by domestic courts they can make a formal complaint to the **European Court of Human Rights**. There are strict admissibility criteria (about 95 per cent of applications fail to satisfy them). Admissible cases will be subject to a judgment by the Court, applying its detailed case law in respect of the interpretation of ECHR rights to the facts of the complaint. If the Court finds a breach it can order the relevant state to pay financial **compensation** to the successful applicant. During 2005, the Court gave judgment in 994 cases where it found at least one violation of the applicants' rights (in 48 cases no violations were found). The major challenge facing the Court is determining the ever increasing number of applications (45,000 applications were lodged in 2005). ALASTAIR MOWBRAY

D Feldman, *Civil Liberties and Human Rights in England and Wales.* (Oxford: Oxford University Press, 2nd edn, 2002)

M Amos, *Human Rights Law* (Oxford: Hart, 2006)

English Heritage *see* architectural conservation

enlargement of the EU The enlargement of the European Union has progressed steadily since the six founding Member States (France, Germany, Italy, and the Benelux countries) agreed the Treaty of Paris setting up the European Coal and Steel Community in 1951 and the Treaties of Rome establishing the European Economic Community and the European Atomic Energy Community in 1957; thus providing the basis for a lasting peace in Europe and building a prosperous common market premised upon the abolition of customs duties and the free movement of goods, persons, services, and capital. Now totalling twenty-seven members, the Union has widened progressively over half a century to extend the benefits of European integration from Western Europe across to Central and Eastern European states. The story of EU enlargement is one of sporadic growth, some of it of a somewhat controversial nature. Inevitably, the controversy continues today with questions continually being raised about the geographic, political, and cultural borders of the Union and the adequacy of the original institutional framework to cope with the pressure of more and more members.

The first enlargement of the Communities from six to nine members came in 1973 when Denmark, Ireland, and the United Kingdom joined (the UK having had two previous applications refused following opposition from France's President de Gaulle). Norway, which had also made an application, did not proceed to ratify the Treaty of Accession due to a negative result in a national referendum. This first enlargement was followed in 1981 by the accession of Greece and in 1986 by Spain and Portugal, bringing the total number of members to twelve. Following the introduction of the Treaty on European Union which came into force in 1993, three more countries, Austria, Finland, and Sweden joined in 1995 (Norway again having applied but returning a negative result in a national referendum), taking the total membership to fifteen.

It was the fall of Communism in Central and Eastern Europe in the late 1980s and early 1990s which led to the greatest expansion yet of the Union. This wave of enlargement was generated by membership applications received from twelve countries (six former Soviet bloc countries—Bulgaria, the Czech Republic, Hungary, Poland, Romania, and Slovakia; three Baltic States that were also once part of the Soviet Union—Estonia, Latvia, and Lithuania; one of the republics of the former Yugoslavia—Slovenia; and two Mediterranean countries—Cyprus and Malta). Criteria (named the 'Copenhagen criteria' after the summit at which they were agreed) had been introduced in June 1993 to measure the compliance of the applicants with the standards expected for EU membership. Notably, the criteria included a political condition (candidate countries must have stable institutions guaranteeing **democracy**, the **rule of law**, **human rights**, and respect for and protection of **minorities**); an economic condition (candidates must have a functioning market economy which would be robust enough to deal with competitive pressure and market forces); and a third condition requiring candidate states to be in a position as to take on the obligations of EU membership including the *acquis communautaire* (the body of existing EU law) and adherence to the aims of political, **economic, and monetary union**. Such conditions of membership had, of course, not been applied to previous applicants generating some concerns that double standards were being adopted for present and future members. Nevertheless, negotiations with ten of the twelve candidate countries were concluded in Copenhagen in December 2002 and the momentous decision to accept these states into the Union on 1 May 2004 was taken. This increased the number of members to twenty-five and permitted the historic political and economic reunification of Eastern and Western Europe with considerable financial assistance being provided to the new countries for structural and regional projects, and support for farming and rural developments, thus helping their economies to catch up with those of the older member states. Bulgaria and Romania were found not yet to meet the qualifying conditions and had to wait a further three years to join, being admitted eventually on 1 January 2007, thereby taking the present membership of the Union to twenty-seven and nearly 500 million people.

The question of Turkey's adhesion to the Union has been much debated. Turkey has had an association agreement with the EU since 1964 and has been an applicant for membership since 1987 with formal accession negotiations being opened in October 2005. Its membership of the Union would add a new dimension to the EU, promoting in particular the religious diversity of the peoples of Europe. There is, inevitably, considerable opposition to Turkish membership from some Member States such as France, Germany, and Austria which have suggested instead the possibility of some sort of 'partnership' between the EU and Turkey, an arrangement falling well short of full membership. The reasons for this cautious approach are not hard to grasp. Turkey lies at the geographical limits of the continent of Europe and its application for membership raises the thorny question of the finality of the boundaries of the Union, not only geographically but also in socioeconomic and cultural terms.

Besides Turkey, other countries continue to knock at the door of the Union. Accession negotiations were opened with Croatia in October 2005 and the Former Yugoslav Republic of Macedonia was recognized as a candidate country in December 2005. Other countries of the western Balkans such as Albania, Bosnia-Herzogovina, Serbia, and Montenegro have also expressed their interest in applying once they meet the Copenhagen conditions of political and economic stability. The continued enlargement of the EU has inevitably resulted in new neighbours for the Union, including Belarus, Russia, and Ukraine. Cross-border cooperation with these states in fields such as security, the environment, and transport has been made a necessity as a result. Above all, the expansion of the EU's borders raises continuing questions about what it means to be European, the values that this entails and, most importantly, the present and future purposes of European integration.   SUSAN MILLNS

Enron   *see* **conflicts of interest in financial markets**

entertainment law   Although the expression 'entertainment law' is not uncommon, it is doubtful whether the title merits classification as a distinct area of law. The subject can more accurately be regarded as the application, in its own particular context, of a number of separate areas of law. The common theme that unites each area is control of rights—for example, the right to print copies of a novel, the right to adapt it as a screenplay or film script, or the right to the services of the actor who will bring that script to life on screen.

The foundation of entertainment law is intellectual property and, most often, **copyright**. In general terms, the law of copyright gives the author of a creative work a number of exclusive rights over his creation. For example, if I write a book, then you may not copy or sell that book without my permission. In theory, this means that a novelist, or scriptwriter, or composer, can do what he likes with the work. In order to create a hit entertainment product, however, a great deal of additional input will be required. How deals are structured depends a great deal on the entertainment genre in question—so a book publishing deal will be different to a film development agreement. But the common idea behind every agreement of this sort is that the creative party is selling some or all of his or her rights (primarily copyright and moral rights) in a creative work, and the other party agrees to use its financial and other resources to develop, release, and distribute the product.

So, for example, the holy grail for many aspiring bands is to secure a record deal. The band supplies the talent and, if they write their own material, the songs themselves. The record company supplies the state-of-the-art recording equipment, funds the band while they record their songs (since at this point they will have no income of their own), and uses its substantial marketing and distribution clout to generate interest in the band and to get the recordings into the shops. The parties share the spoils: usually the record company takes the proceeds and pays the band its share by way of a royalty. The legal basis for this sort of arrangement is that the creation has value protected by the law of intellectual property, and can be sold or licensed usually in return for help in making the most of that creation.

Although this may give the gist of a typical deal in the entertainment sector, in fact entertainment law is a patchwork of a whole range of other laws: contract, **trade marks**, **passing off**, **privacy**, confidence, **defamation**, employment law, broadcast **regulation**, **freedom of speech**, **agency**, corporate law, in fact any area of law insofar as it is relevant to the entertainment industries. The term 'entertainment law' has probably emerged in practice because entertainment is big enough business to demand lawyers who understand not only the law, but also the industry in which their clients work.   MARK COATES

entertainment licensing 'Regulated entertainment', covering provision of various forms of entertainment and entertainment facilities, is licensed by local authorities under a single scheme in the Licensing Act 2003 (although separate schemes for entertainments operate in Scotland and Northern Ireland). The forms of entertainment include performance of a play, exhibition of a film; an indoor sporting event, a boxing or wrestling entertainment; performance of live music, playing of recorded music, performance of dance; and entertainment of a similar description to the three previously-mentioned types. In all instances the entertainment is licensable only if it takes place in the presence of an audience and is provided for purposes which include entertaining the audience. The forms of entertainment facilities include facilities for enabling persons to take part in making music, dancing, and entertainment of a similar description to either of these activities. No audience need be present.

Regulated entertainment is licensable whether it takes place indoors or outdoors (except for indoor sporting events). There are various exemptions from licensing. Some relate only to certain types of entertainment (eg morris dancing, film exhibitions in museums and art galleries, and music incidental to other activities), although most have general application (eg regulated entertainment at garden fetes, in religious meetings or services, or at places of public religious worship).

There is only 'provision' of regulated entertainment where it is made available to certain categories of persons and premises are made available for a purpose which includes enabling the entertainment to take place. It needs to be made available to the public or a section of the public (eg persons over 21); or in the case of a club run for the benefit of its members, exclusively for club members and guests; or in any other case only if a charge is made by those organizing or managing the entertainment and it is with a view to profit.

Where regulated entertainment is licensable, various forms of authorization can be obtained, including a premises licence, club premises certificate, and temporary event notice. The position for granting these authorizations is the same as for sale of alcohol (also licensable under the 2003 Act scheme). For entertainment, unlike sale of alcohol, no personal licence is required nor is any designated premises supervisor needed under a premises licence.

COLIN MANCHESTER

C Manchester, S Poppleston and J Allen, *Alcohol and Entertainment Licensing Law* (London: Routledge-Cavendish 2nd edn, 2008)

See also: **alcohol and liquor licensing**

Entick v Carrington **(1765)**   On 6 November 1762, the Secretary of State, the Earl of Halifax, issued a general warrant to Nathan Carrington, the senior King's messenger, to arrest John Entick and Arthur Beardmore and seize their papers. These men were the proprietors of the *Monitor,* a weekly paper which had been a thorn in the side of Bute's ministry, particularly when it began to publish material by John Wilkes, an MP. Another general warrant was issued in April 1763, after Number 45 of Wilkes's own *North Briton* was published, ordering the arrest of its printers and publishers. Forty-eight printers and journeymen were arrested in one day, and Wilkes was confined in the Tower. Although general warrants like these had long been used, it was a political gamble to issue one against an MP with a flair for manipulating public opinion and an eye for using the law to his advantage.

Wilkes immediately challenged his arrest. He obtained a writ of **habeas corpus** in the Common Pleas, where the Pitt-ite chief justice, Charles Pratt, ordered his release. Although the legality of the warrant was not directly raised in the judgment, Pratt privately expressed his view that such warrants were legally indefensible. Once released, Wilkes encouraged the arrested printers and publishers to bring civil actions in the Common Pleas against Halifax and his messengers for **trespass** and false imprisonment. These actions, financed by another Pitt-ite, Richard Grenville, Earl Temple, were very successful. By June 1764, fourteen printers had won damages. These actions, which focused attention on the conduct of the messengers, did not directly question the legality of general warrants. But when Dryden Leach (printer of the *North Briton*) sued John Money for false imprisonment, he not only won £400, but in a writ of error taken to the King's Bench obtained a dictum from Lord Mansfield against the legality of general warrants authorizing arrests (*Money v Leach* (1765)). The question whether general warrants could authorize searches of property was subsequently addressed in *Entick v Carrington*. In his judgment of November 1765, Pratt, who had become Earl Camden in July, aimed to settle many of the broader arguments raised in earlier cases about the legality of general warrants and the extent of the Secretary of State's powers.

First, he rejected the contention that the officers were protected by a statute of 1751, designed to secure justices of the peace and constables from suits when acting under flawed warrants. For Camden, neither the messengers, nor their principal, the Secretary of State, were **common law** magistrates with the power to commit prisoners. Secondly, he held that the warrant was itself unlawful, and that the messengers were therefore guilty of trespass. Camden noted that the power claimed—to search and seize a person's private papers before he had been convicted of any crime—was not found in any law book. Continued practice since 1688 did not settle the matter, since one could not prove 'the ancient immemorable law of the land, in a public matter . . . by the practice of a private office'. Nor could the court now declare the power to issue general warrants lawful, since that would be an act of legislation. Moreover, he felt that to do so would subvert the security of property which people had entered political society to protect. Instead, he held that every invasion of private property was a trespass, for which the perpetrator was liable, unless he could show a statutory or common law justification. No justification could be found in state necessity, for 'the common law does not understand that kind of reasoning'. His view was confirmed by a resolution of the House of Commons in April 1766.

Entick v Carrington soon entered the canon as one of the great constitutional cases of the common law. It was taken by subsequent constitutional lawyers to affirm the principle that the **Crown** and its officers were bound by the **rule of law**. For AV **Dicey**, it demonstrated the supremacy of regular law over arbitrary power. It revealed that the constitution was the product of the ordinary law, for the principles of private law determined the Crown's position. Citizens and officials, Dicey stressed, were equal at common law, since officials were personally liable for acts done in their official character without lawful authority. But in fact, it was the Crown, rather than its agents, which paid out the large sums which were awarded in the cases brought by the printers in the 1760s.   MICHAEL LOBBAN

RR Rea, *The English Press in Politics, 1760–1774* (Lincoln: University of Nebraska Press, 1963)
PDG Thomas, *John Wilkes: A Friend to Liberty* (Oxford: Oxford University Press, 1996)

entrapment   Entrapment is a method of gathering **evidence** which intentionally involves the use of deception to procure the commission of an offence. This method is not limited to targeting individuals suspected of committing serious crime (see *Nottingham City Council v Amin* (2000)). Proactive investigative methods raise a number of legal and ethical issues concerning the participation of **police** and informers in criminal behaviour, including the incitement of others to commit crime. Historically, English **courts** placed no limits on the use of entrapment, which could be raised only after conviction as a matter relevant to sentence mitigation (*Sang* (1979)). By contrast, in the United States, entrapment by state officials bears on the guilt of the accused, providing a complete criminal defence (*Jacobson v US* (1992)). Modern approaches to entrapment recognize that the illegality or impropriety involved in these practices, while not necessarily affecting the reliability of evidence, may adversely impact upon public confidence in the administration of **justice**, as well as an accused's right to a fair trial. In *Looseley* (2001) the **House of Lords** held that in cases of entrapment, **judges** have a **discretion** to exclude evidence, or to halt proceedings as an abuse of process in extreme cases. In order to apply these **remedies**, the **common law** has developed principles to assist the determination of unfairness in this context. These principles have been derived, in part, from *Teixeira de Castro* (1998). In that case, the **European Court of Human Rights** held that the **right to a fair trial** under Article 6 of the **European Convention on Human Rights** would be violated where police did not confine themselves to investigating criminal activity in an essentially passive manner, but actively incited the offence. While *Looseley* broadly accepted this approach, caution was expressed against applying the active/passive distinction in a mechanical or formalistic fashion, noting that active instigation and persistence might be legitimate to overcome the wariness of street criminals who were acquainted with undercover police tactics. Their Lordships' preferred approach was that entrapment should be determined by a 'cluster of factors' including: the reason for the operation; whether police action was based on reasonable suspicion and subject to proper supervision; the nature of the offence; and the extent of police participation in the crime. Consideration of a **person**'s underlying predisposition to commit the offence remains controversial. Denying a remedy in this situation, as occurs in the United States, has the effect of forever rendering convicted persons 'fair game' for police entrapment. As Lord Nicholls noted in *Looseley*, 'Predisposition did not negative the misuse of state power'. Lord Hoffmann also suggested that consideration of the nature of the offence should not extend to its 'seriousness' since this may produce a position where the 'ends justify the means'. In the absence of legislative codification, the definition and boundaries of entrapment will continue to be the subject of common law development over time.

SIMON BRONITT

A Ashworth, 'Re-Drawing the Boundaries of Entrapment' (2002) *Criminal Law Review* 161

S Bronitt, 'The Law in Undercover Policing: A Comparative Study Of Entrapment and Covert Interviewing in Australia, Canada and Europe' (2004) 33/1 *Common Law World Review* 35

entrenched rights   These are legal rights which have a special status, so that they cannot be removed or curtailed by the ordinary process of changing the law. They are thus protected from change even by democratic process. Typically, national **constitutions** entrench fundamental **human rights**, such as **freedom of expression**, personal liberty, the **right to life**, etc. Even entrenched rights may be changed or removed, however, by amendment of the constitution that guarantees them. The extent of their entrenchment varies, therefore, depending upon how easy or difficult it is to amend the constitution in which they are set out. The very highest level of protection is represented by certain rights in the German Basic Law, which cannot lawfully be removed at all. More typically, the US Constitution provides for its own amendment by a two-thirds majority in each House of Congress and the consent of three quarters of the states.

In the UK, there are, strictly speaking, no entrenched rights, since **Parliament** may lawfully repeal any statute it has previously passed. Thus, the domestic protection for the rights set out in the **Human Rights Act** may be removed by the Act's repeal. UK citizens enjoy certain rights under **European Community law**, which has superior status over ordinary Acts of Parliament. However, it is generally believed that such rights could be overridden either by express words in an Act of Parliament, or, if necessary, by prior express repeal of the European Communities Act 1972, which gives domestic effect to EU law.   GAVIN PHILLIPSON

entrenchment of constitutions and legislation
Entrenchment subjects the constitution or legislation to which it applies to an alteration procedure that is more difficult than that for ordinary laws. In extreme cases, it may prevent alteration altogether. Mechanisms for entrenchment typically range from requirements for special parliamentary majorities to use of the **referendum**. Typically, the provision that prescribes the special alteration procedure is itself entrenched, to prevent it from being altered by ordinary law, thus circumventing the effect of entrenchment.

There is no constitutional obstacle to entrenchment in states in which prevailing political theory accepts that the people is sovereign and can confer a system of government on itself. Difficulty may arise, however, where, as in the **United Kingdom**, theory assigns legal **sovereignty** to the parliament. There are at least two possible understandings of what sovereignty involves in this context. First, it might mean that the legislative authority of the current parliament can never be constrained by legislation of an earlier parliament, making entrenchment impossible. Secondly, it might mean that the authority of a current parliament extends even to protecting its own legislation from future change, albeit at cost to the authority of later parliaments. In *The Concept of Law* (Oxford: Oxford University Press, 1961), HLA **Hart** described the distinction as being between 'continuing' and 'self-embracing' sovereignty.

The former remains the orthodox understanding in the United Kingdom, favoured by AV **Dicey** and some early twentieth century case law. The latter applies in most other countries in the British constitutional tradition. Comparison is complicated by the colonial origins of the constitutional arrangements in these states. Nevertheless, it is increasingly difficult to reconcile continuing sovereignty with actual practice in the United Kingdom, and the question should be regarded as unsettled.

Its resolution is affected by various factors. First, an entrenching provision that prescribes the manner or the form in which amending legislation must be passed can be understood as altering the composition or the procedures of a future parliament for this purpose, rather than limiting parliamentary authority. This line of thought reconciles the possibility of entrenchment with the continuing view of parliamentary sovereignty, although in a highly artificial way. Secondly, the **Parliament Acts** of 1911 and 1949 have already altered the composition of parliament for some purposes. While these Acts make legislation easier, rather than more difficult, it has been held that they create an additional primary legislation-making procedure, and some judicial comments offer further encouragement to the possibility of entrenchment. Thirdly, the manner in which the United Kingdom gives effect to its obligations under **European law** in the European Communities Act 1972 appears to have settled that one parliament can constrain a later parliament at least in relation to the form in which alterations to its legislation are made. Finally, acceptance of entrenchment would have implications for the rule that courts will not look behind an Act of Parliament to examine the procedure by which it was made.   CHERYL SAUNDERS

See also: **constitutions**

entrepreneurialism and company law   The word 'entrepreneur' was originally an old French word meaning 'to undertake', adopted into the English language by economists in the eighteenth century to mean a general risk taker in business. Later the phrase became synonymous with a risk taker who founds and manages a business. **Company** law is the area of law which focuses on the creation and regulation of companies. The extent to which it encourages entrepreneurialism is unclear. In theory it should encourage entrepreneurialism as it is relatively easy to form a company and has the advantage of **limited liability** which allows the entrepreneur to protect his or her personal assets should the company collapse. However, most entrepreneurs need a bank loan to found their business and banks require entrepreneurs to secure loans with their personal assets. As a result most entrepreneurs do end up risking their personal assets to found the business. Additionally company law is not designed for small entrepreneurial companies and has a raft of technical requirements that are burdensome for these companies. Indeed the conclusion of the UK company law reform process in 2006 was that company law needed to think small first. On the other hand company law is said to allow managers of companies to act in a more entrepreneurial risk-taking way as they know that the shareholders' personal assets are protected by limited liability. However, when all is said and done, the first industrial revolution occurred in the UK driven by entrepreneurs before company law existed.   ALAN DIGNAM

See also: **shareholder risks and residual claims**

J Freedman, 'Small Businesses and the Corporate Form: Burden or Privilege?' (1994) 57 MLR 555–584

Environment Agency   The Environment Agency was established under the Environment Act 1995 as a non-departmental body responsible for a wide range of environmental functions in England and Wales, including the implementation of a number of core areas of environmental regulation. The background to its creation was an increasing policy concern for a more coherent and integrated approach towards **pollution** control, a number of official reports highly critical of the ability of local authorities to handle **waste** regulation, and the perceived economic efficiencies to be gained from a 'one stop' shop.

The core **responsibilities** of the Agency include waste management, radioactive waste regulation, the regulation of around 6,000 industrial sites under the integrated pollution control regimes, a supervisory role in emissions trading regimes, the management of contaminated land on special sites, water pollution and water abstraction control, fisheries and navigation, and flood defence and management. The Agency, headed by a board of between eight and twelve members appointed by the Secretary of State, employs almost 12,000 staff and an overall budget of around £900 million a year. Its income is based on three main sources—charges and fees from licences and permits, grant-in-aid from the Department of the Environment and the Welsh Assembly, and capital grants and levies for flood defence.

Although the Environment Act gives reserve powers to the Secretary of State to give the Agency binding directions on both general and specific matters, in practice the Agency has established an environmental profile independent from government. In 2000, a House of Commons **Select Committee** called for the Agency to be more of a 'champion for the environment' than simply a regulatory arm of government, and in 2002, Government Statutory Guidance acknowledged for the first time that the Agency had a key role as an independent advisor on environmental matters affecting policy-making both with government and more widely.

In contrast to equivalent agencies in Scotland and Northern Ireland and many other countries, the Environment Agency has the power to undertake its own **prosecutions** for environmental offences under its areas of responsibility. It was one of the first UK environmental agencies to publish an enforcement and prosecution policy, indicating the circumstances when it was likely to exercise its **discretion** to prosecute for regulatory breaches. In more recent years, it has developed systems that reflect more of a **risk**-based approach to regulation, allowing it to focus resources more closely on sites that are likely pose greater environmental risk.

RICHARD MACRORY

environment, legal definition of   This is difficult to encapsulate in a few words. Just as Einstein came to realize that the universe was continually expanding, the same can be said for our **human** understandings of our environment. It will be variously defined, depending on the disciplinary perspectives from which definitions come. Thus the idea of environment can be separated neither from ecological notions of oneness and inter-dependence of species, nor from the related idea of ecosystems, expressing the dynamics of existence, especially as to how life forms react with one another.

A definition should reflect the range of problems facing human sustainability, arising from strains upon those natural resources and processes on which survival depends. Having moved from an apparently balanced and self-regulating natural world, by virtue of increasing intensities of exploitation, society has undergone a wide range of regulatory responses as we have sought to alleviate environmental degradation. Yet paradoxically as we discover more about our impacts on the environment (and solving some of the problems) we have also seen new and unintended consequences (with potentially greater intensity and impact): such as **climate change**. Humankind is therefore moving into a new phase, in which we will need to explore alternative reactions as certain environmental limits are reached, in terms of natural resources and the survival of ecosystems that have nurtured species that have evolved and survived to the present day.

Law generally focuses on anthropocentric priorities (rights, duties), and in the environmental context upon **pollution**, **waste**, and activities harmful to human health. **Legislation** generally defines working terms, and an illustration (in the context of pollution control, under the UK's Environmental Protection Act 1990) is of an environment consisting 'of all, or any, of the following media, namely, the air, water and land' and environmental pollution being that which is 'due to the release (into any environmental medium) from any process of substances which are capable of causing harm to man or any other living organisms supported by the environment' (section 1(2), (3)).

Legal definitions must also now engage with more intractable environmental problems, such as the impacts of certain pesticides, lead and sulphur pollution (including acid rain) in the atmosphere, and CFCs in the stratosphere. Concerns increasingly focus on the impact of man-made climate change, brought about by the enhanced greenhouse effect as certain gases (especially carbon dioxide and methane) become trapped in the atmosphere. With such a challenge now in mind the succinct definition of environment once offered in a European Community document (Council Regulation 1872/84, *Action by the Community Relating to the Environment*, 1984) appears increasingly apt: namely that 'combination of elements whose complex inter-relationships make up the settings, the surroundings and the conditions of life of the individual and of society as they are and as they are felt'.

MARK STALLWORTHY

U Beck, *Risk Society: Towards a New Modernity* (London: Sage, 1992)

B Commoner, *The Closing Circle – Nature Man and Technology* (New York: Alfred A Knopf, 1971)

environmental agreements   An environmental agreement is an agreement between a regulator and those being regulated that governs the environmental **responsibilities** of those being regulated. Such agreements may take a variety of legal forms and range from being legally binding contracts to more informal arrangements. Likewise, such agreements may vary in their subject matter of application. While these agreements can be predominantly seen in relation to **pollution** emissions, they can also be seen in the context of natural resource management and the design of products as to be environmentally friendly. Another variation in such agreements is whether they are with a specific legal actor or with an entire industry. Depending on the actual nature of a specific agreement, it can vary from a form of voluntary self regulation to a more tailored form of traditional **command and control regulation**.

While arguably such agreements are not new, environmental agreements gained popularity in the 1990s as part of the promotion of more flexible, less command and control approaches to environmental regulation. Such agreements were seen as a way of implementing **sustainable development**—that is economic development that meets the needs of current generations without sacrificing the needs of future generations. In particular, such agreements were a means of encouraging fruitful cooperation between government and the private sector. A key aspect of environmental agreements is the negotiations that occur between the regulator and those being regulated, although these negotiations may involve other interested actors including local **communities** and **non-governmental organizations**.

The strength of environmental agreements, it is believed, is that they result in environmental protection objectives being better integrated with other objectives of a commercial operator. As such, these agreements are also understood to promote more effective environmental problem solving as they encourage consensus solving among public and private actors, the sharing of information and ideas, and the development of innovative techniques for addressing environmental problems. The promotion of environmental agreements is thus often understood in environmental law in terms of **environmental governance**.

Most examples of environmental agreements in practice are in small-scale regulatory programmes, usually in relation to a specific set of firms or a specific set of industries. A number of examples can be found across all jurisdictions but they have been particularly promoted within the European Union as part of a more flexible approach to environmental regulation.   LIZ FISHER

environmental   assessment Environmental assessment describes a process of predicting the likely effects of a project, plan, or policy on the environment prior to a decision being made about whether these should proceed. It evolved as a response to the increasing recognition of the harmful impacts of post-war development schemes such as dams and motorways, and an upsurge in public environmental activism. In legal terms, environmental assessment originated in the United States' National Environmental Policy Act 1969 ('NEPA') which has since provided a template for environmental assessment regimes the world over. NEPA required federal agencies formally to document how they considered the environment when making decisions to authorize works and pursue policies. The European Union's form of environmental assessment basically followed this pattern, although the first piece of **legislation** on the subject, Directive 85/337 on the assessment of the effects of certain public and private projects on the environment ('the EIA Directive'), restricted its scope to environmental impact assessment or the assessment of projects (rather than policies).

Environmental assessment generally involves the following stages. The first is screening, to differentiate between projects and policy proposals that should be made subject to a full assessment process on the basis of the likelihood of significant harm to the environment. Secondly, a scoping exercise is carried out to identify potential receptors, impacts, alternatives, and mitigation measures (as well as relationships between these), and to help decide which methodologies to use and who to consult. Thirdly, the developer or proponent provides information about the likely environmental effects of a proposed project or policy in the form of an environmental statement. The next stage of the process is the consultation of a larger audience, in recognition of the public interest nature of activities with environmental effects. Comments on the environmental statement and any other information arising from the assessment process may be provided by, for example, statutory consultees, and also members of the public, especially those living near to a proposed project. Finally, when deciding whether or not to grant planning permission for a project, or whether or not to advance a particular policy, the decision-maker must take into account all the information gathered in the course of the environmental assessment process. To do otherwise is to provide grounds for challenging the decision.

Importantly, environmental assessment procedures regulate the manner in which decisions are made, by seeking to ensure that the decision-maker is availed of all the information derived from the procedures and that this is taken into account prior to reaching a decision. Environmental assessment does not pursue a particular objective or standard, so that, for example, a project likely to be extremely destructive in environmental terms may still be granted development consent, so long as the assessment procedures have been complied with. However, there is a school of thought that the carrying out of an assessment procedure inculcates environmental protection values amongst those taking decisions, bringing about changes in attitude towards the need for and design of new development and thereby furthering a new administrative logic which prioritises environmental concerns. In the case of the environmental impact assessment of projects, there is some evidence that it has fostered cultural changes amongst decision-makers, and that decisions have been 'reoriented' towards environmental protection as a result. But, equally, developers have been found to be capable of using the environmental statement as a means of publicizing their proposed development in a favourable light.

Although environmental assessment is clearly a procedural mechanism, in the US the procedures have had certain substantive effects. The high water mark of a substantive approach to environmental assessment is seen in the judgment of Judge Skelley

Wright in *Calvert Cliffs Coordinating Committee v Atomic Energy Commission* (1971) which, although it ultimately turned its face to a review of administrative decisions on their merits, suggested that environmental assessment requires a thorough cost/benefit assessment of federal projects, so as to take into account their previously neglected environmental costs. A more substantive reading of *Calvert Cliffs*, suggesting the need for merits review, failed to stick—although the US courts have since required fairly stringent consideration of alternatives—and it soon became clear that the courts regarded the impact assessment provisions of NEPA as purely procedural in nature (see, for example, *Strycker's Bay Neighborhood Council Inc v Karlen* (1980); and *Robertson v Methow Valley Citizens Council* (1989)). In the EU, the **European Court of Justice** has consistently upheld the need for close compliance with the EIA Directive and a purposive reading of its provisions (*Kraaijeveld* (1996)). The Court has also made clear that a failure to consider alternative options to the proposed development may invalidate the assessment (*Commission v Portugal* (2006)).

The main problem with environmental impact assessment is that decision-making at the project level is often superseded by higher level policy decisions, for example the proposed expansion of a port, having potentially local impacts, may in practice be determined by transport and trade policies made at the national, EU, and, increasingly, international, level. In theory, the development of **strategic environmental assessment** (the assessment of plans, programmes, and policies) overcomes this problem by requiring environmental assessment at a high level of decision-making. In the EU, a diluted form of strategic environmental assessment was adopted with the passing of Directive 2001/42 (the 'SEA Directive') which requires the environmental assessment of certain plans and programmes (*not* policies) in order to provide a framework for the future development consent of projects. The procedure for strategic environmental assessment under the SEA Directive is basically the same as that set out in the EIA Directive.

The development of strategic environmental assessment represents the logical expansion of environmental assessment, beyond a concern with an individual project or site usually representing the interests of a developer, to encompass the assessment of policies and legislative proposals of more general interest. The scope of environmental assessment has now been further broadened to encompass sustainability criteria of social and economic impacts, of the sort now commonplace in the EU

as 'sustainability analysis', and located in a broader movement of 'better **regulation**' initiatives. Both of these developments are a product of the '**mainstreaming**' of environmental assessment in policy-making, in an effort to incorporate environmental concerns and considerations into everyday, and wide-ranging, decision-making.

Environmental assessment procedures are now required in a variety of legal and social settings, such as **pollution** controls and water resources, conservation of biological diversity, and development assistance. The procedure has also been recognized and strengthened in **international law**, with instruments negotiated by the United Nations Economic Commission of Europe on transboundary environmental assessment (the Espoo Convention (1991)), strategic environmental assessment (the Kiev Protocol (2003)) and on participation, public access to environmental information, and access to justice in environmental matters (the **Aarhus Convention** (1999)). The **International Court of Justice** has also recognized environmental assessment as a principle of environmental law (*New Zealand v France* (1995)), affirming its importance as an instrument of environmental regulation.　　　　JANE HOLDER

environmental citizenship Citizenship, in a state-context, typically involves membership of a political **community**, with members identifying with one another (and their political institutions) and sharing common duties and rights, including rights to participate in political decision-making for the community. It thus involves issues of membership, **identity**, rights/duties, and participation. Just as different political theories, such as **communitarianism** and **cosmopolitanism**, are likely to disagree over such issues in the context of 'normal' citizenship, so too will they be contested within environmental citizenship. Rights are often the starting point for analyses of environmental citizenship. The question inevitably arises of whether there is or ought to be a substantive **human right** to a clean environment within national **constitutions** and international treaties such as the **European Convention on Human Rights** ('ECHR'). While cosmopolitans may support such a right, republicans question the wisdom and feasibility of allowing essentially political decisions to be judicialized in this way, supporting instead legislative rights such as (European) Community environmental rights that are often the correlatives of obligations owed by Member States in EU directives. Certainly in Europe, procedural environmental rights are more prominent than substantive ones, as illustrated by the **Aarhus Convention**, which provides procedural rights of access to information, to public participation in decision-making, and access to **justice** in environmental matters. There is less often a focus on duties, although authors such as Andrew Dobson have made a convincing case for environmental duties (such as composting or recycling) to be seen as a key part of environmental citizenship. Such duties will often be located within the private sphere as opposed to the public sphere more often associated with traditional citizenship. On this view, environmental citizenship has much in common with feminist approaches to citizenship where the personal *is* political.

With rights, there is also the question of who should enjoy **environmental rights** and what should be the object of their protection. Some have claimed that within ecological citizenship, citizenship rights should be extended to non-humans. And similarly, others have questioned the legitimacy of a human rights approach to environmental protection (as adopted, for example, within ECHR case law) on the basis that it protects only **humans** and not (or only incidentally) the wider environment. Even within anthropocentric accounts, this issue of membership is crucial to environmental citizenship. The question of who to include counts not only in relation to substantive rights but also in relation to the procedural Aarhus rights of access to information, justice (in terms of standing), and public participation in decision-making. In this respect, the all-affected or affectedness principle may be brought into play to argue that all those who are affected by a particular issue should have a say. Given that many environmental problems are trans-boundary in nature and produce extra-territorial effects, this provides environmental citizenship with a distinctly post-national flavour. It also, finally, raises the issue of environmental identity: if someone is not physically affected but psychologically identifies with a 'foreign' environment, are they to be legitimately regarded as affected by a decision made about it?

CHRIS HILSON

environmental civil liability Environmental liability is about who has to pay when damage to the environment occurs or is imminently threatened. In some circumstances, immediate responsibility to prevent, contain, or remedy the harm is treated separately from ultimate legal liability for the costs involved. Since the 1980s, as society has become increasingly sensitive to environmental harm, this has become one of the most controversial areas of environmental law, because of the sheer scale of environmental costs, which can run into millions or even hundreds of millions of pounds (dollars, euros, etc) at a single site.

The most highly contested issues have concerned whether liability should be imposed for historic damage (which originated before the relevant statute was passed), whether the liability standard should be strict or fault-based, how liability is to be apportioned in cases involving multiple responsible parties, and the defences or other protections afforded to defendants under strict liability regimes. Other key questions have included: the clean-up standards imposed; the value to be put on injured natural resources like habitats and species; the rights of environmental or other citizens groups to bring legal actions against polluters; and any rules requiring economic actors to hold insurance or other financial security before they engage in potentially damaging activities.

Civil, as opposed to criminal, liability may arise under either civil/private law or public/**administrative law**. Both are referred to as 'civil liability' in Anglo-Saxon, **common law** countries. However, only the former is given that title within continental Europe's civil code traditions, where public/administrative law is treated entirely separately, with different **courts** and rules. This difference has produced considerable muddle over twenty years of EU debates on the subject, which resulted in 2004 in an EC Directive on environmental liability (2004/35).

Under civil/private law, liability rules primarily concern claims for monetary **damages** in response to personal injury or damage to property, or for **injunctions** (court orders to stop a harmful act occurring or continuing). In recent years, there have been attempts by environmental and **victims'** groups to find ways to hold someone liable for damage to **public health** allegedly caused or exacerbated by various types of **pollution**. There have also been attempts to broaden standing for environmental groups or private claimants to bring civil claims against polluters on behalf of the general environment. So far, such initiatives have not proved particularly successful. In most countries, although rights of standing have eased somewhat, personal injury claims still require proof of fault on the part of the defendant and, even in countries which have introduced strict liability in this field, major obstacles remain for claimants in relation to proving **causation**. Property damage claims, which may be subject to strict liability under traditional rules, such as **nuisance** or the rule in *Rylands v Fletcher* (safe keeping of dangerous substances), have generally had more success.

The main focus of environmental liability law since the 1980s has been on public/administrative law, where regulatory authorities bring enforcement actions under specific statutes to require particular parties to repair or prevent harm. The majority of these initiatives have concerned contaminated land (including groundwater), pollution of surface waters, air pollution, **waste** or, most recently, harm to protected species and habitats. Most of the statutes involve a strict liability standard, although its severity may be softened by various defences. Liability generally falls on the party which caused or knowingly permitted the offending substances to be released into the environment, but may also be imposed, either equally or secondarily, on owners and occupiers of the damaged site, or even on producers of the waste or pollutants whose presence has caused the harm. Rules requiring restoration of damaged habitats and species have introduced new issues which are as yet relatively little understood.

Some specific fields, such as marine pollution and nuclear activities, are subject to international convention regimes, which involve strict liability and compulsory financial security, but set financial caps on the amount of liability in each incident.

CHRIS CLARKE

See also: **strict civil liability**

V Fogleman, *Environmental Liabilities and Insurance in England and the United States* (London: Witherbys, 2005)

US Environmental Protection Agency, *Superfund: 20 Years of Protecting Human Health and the Environment* (Washington DC: USEPA, 2000) (available at: *http://www.epa.gov/superfund/action/20years/index.htm*)

environmental court   Forms of specialist environmental court have been established in a number of **common law** jurisdictions, notably the Environment Court in New Zealand, and various courts in Australian States, such as the New South Wales Environment Courts established in 1979, and the Queensland Planning and Environment Court established in 1990. A number of specialist **courts** or **tribunals** exist in Europe, the most developed being five regional environmental courts and an Environmental Court of Appeal established under the Swedish Environment Code in 1999. The State of Vermont in the United States has an environment court handling a broad range of administrative appeals against environmental decisions.

In the United Kingdom, along with many other countries, environmental legal disputes, whether involving criminal, civil, or public law, have been handled by the ordinary courts responsible for those

areas of jurisdictions. Administrative appeals concerning environmental licences and other regulatory decisions have been routed to a number of different bodies, including, in England and Wales, the planning inspectorate, county courts, and local magistrates courts. From the early 1990s, there have been calls for a specialist environmental tribunal or court to be set up in the UK. It is argued that the current fragmented nature of the legal fora employed is ill-equipped to handle the complexity of contemporary environmental **legislation**, and fails to reflect interconnections across environmental policy challenges. A specialist environmental court or tribunal could adjudicate across a range of environmental disputes and subjects, and with a greater sensitivity to environmental law and emerging core principles such as **sustainable development** and the **precautionary principle**.

Conflicting views over the jurisdiction of any proposed environmental court or tribunal, coupled with the cost implications of setting up a new body, have held back its establishment to date. The concept also raises some difficult questions. The boundaries of environmental law are not precise. If criminal jurisdiction is included, it may suggest that environmental offences are to be considered different from other criminal offences, a proposition that many would disagree with. Legal and evidential issues in areas such as health and safety or personal injury litigation may be as challenging as those arising in environmental disputes, and argues against the environment being treated so differently from other areas of law. An approach which is rather less ambitious than setting up a distinct court or tribunal is to ensure greater specialist training for the judiciary and magistrates handling environmental cases, and to consolidate environmental administrative appeals within the tribunal system.

RICHARD MACRORY

environmental crime and enforcement   The criminal law can be used directly to punish **acts or omissions** which cause environmental harm or indirectly in a ancillary and complementary role within a detailed regulatory system. In general it is used in this second way because the main purpose of the criminal law is to punish behaviour which is considered to be socially or morally unacceptable. Many criminal offences do not consist of committing a direct act of **pollution** or environmental damage, but instead of breaching the conditions of a regulatory permit or ignoring an order from a regulatory body. This distinction between the direct and indirect use of the criminal law to sanction environmental harm mean that there is no generally accepted definition of 'environmental crime' primarily because there is no necessary connection between environmental harm and criminal behaviour.

Activities which cause harm to the environment are, in many situations, considered to be acceptable or even desirable either because they are directly associated with economically beneficial activities or they represent a trade-off between personal benefits and any harm that is caused. The key to defining environmental crime in such circumstances depends largely upon the acceptability of the activity in question. Such questions are much more suited to political processes and the establishment of a coherent system of environmental regulation which defines the framework for determining whether such benefits outweigh the harm caused. The criminal law is a rather blunt instrument in terms of balancing different factors to determine whether something is acceptable and thus is mainly used to address activities or omissions which are clearly unacceptable (eg deliberate acts of environmental vandalism), or to reinforce the regulatory system and the manner in which it defines 'unacceptable' behaviour (eg by defining breaches of environmental authorizations or permits as crimes).

In such circumstances, criminal offences are viewed as being secondary to the regulatory system, since the administrative enforcement agencies are responsible for both setting the limits of what is acceptable and in enforcing them. Consequently, and subject to a few notable exceptions, environmental crimes can be seen as classic regulatory offences which are not 'evil in themselves'. Offences are linked to administrative processes rather than the environmental harm caused. In turn, this creates a moral ambiguity which has consequences in terms of how 'environmental crime' is viewed by those who might be termed 'environmental criminals', by enforcement agencies with responsibilities for monitoring and policing the regulatory system, and the **courts** which have the ultimate **responsibility** for imposing sanctions for environmental crimes.

The ancillary nature of the criminal law is also illustrated by the range of sanctions for breach of the regulatory system. The use of **prosecution** and criminal penalties are only a small part of the environmental enforcement tool box. Indeed, historically, prosecution rates for environmental crime are very low in relation to the number of breaches of environmental law. This is partly explained by the use of non-criminal enforcement mechanisms. Many areas of environmental regulation provide for the variation or revocation of licences or for the

enforcement against anticipated or actual breaches of licences without any reference to criminal law.

In addition there are other informal measures and practices which are used as part of an enforcement process in which **regulatory agencies** attempt to secure compliance with the regulatory system and thereby prevent or rectify environmental harm. These might include educating and advising the ignorant operator; imposing deadlines for the improvement of environmental performance; increased monitoring or inspection visits; or issuing verbal and written 'last warnings' prior to more formal enforcement action.

The use of this range of measures to secure compliance links to the use of particular enforcement styles. In circumstances where environmental harm is deliberate or where negligence is clear the decision to prosecute is normally the only suitable option which will send out a punitive and deterrent message. In addition to these sorts of situations, however, there is a range of breaches which may be characterized as part of an ongoing pattern of behaviour. Thus breaches of licence conditions or accidents which have varying degrees of culpability may require enforcement responses. The enforcement of environmental law in these cases is primarily concerned with the prevention of harm. A key element of prevention is in trying to secure compliance with the regulatory system. Thus enforcement practices in the context of ongoing operations are best seen from a perspective where regulatory agencies balance cooperation and deterrence.

This blend of cooperation using education and administrative tools and deterrence using prosecution and severe measures has been termed 'responsive regulation' in that different types of enforcement tools will be used depending upon how well operators respond to the level of enforcement adopted. Under 'responsive regulation' increasingly formal enforcement measures will be adopted in the absence of a willingness to comply with legal obligations. Thus regulatory agencies use responsive regulation in order to achieve compliance using the minimum amount of formal enforcement. The majority of operators are looking to comply, and persuasion and education will secure the necessary compliance. Beyond this majority there may be others who are unable or unwilling to comply and will only respond to more formal enforcement measures such as variation or enforcement notices. Finally, there is a tiny minority of operators who are reluctant to comply with such measures and will only respond to the severest sanctions such as prosecution or revocation notices. In many ways, the use of responsive regulation is just a theoretical framework for describing the use of the right blend of enforcement and sanctions in relation to environmental crime. In practice, enforcement agencies are merely seeking to identify the optimal level of enforcement to secure compliance.

This idea of optimality in enforcement raises the issue of the right level of **punishment** for environmental crimes. In recent years there has been a growing dissatisfaction with the courts' approach to **sentencing** for environmental offences. It has been argued that levels of **fines** are too low to act as a sufficient deterrent, particularly in relation to large **companies** who might prefer to break the law in situations where profits from polluting activities would be many times higher than the average fine imposed. Efforts have been made to promote the use of civil or administrative penalties as a supplement to criminal sanctions. Thus, in the case of minor breaches of the regulatory system, it may be more suitable for a regulator to respond with civil or administrative penalties which would better reflect the ancillary nature of the enforcement process. This would then leave severe criminal sanctions for true environmental crimes, where deliberate or reckless actions or omissions have caused serious environmental harm or where the risk of such harm was high. Such an approach would establish a clear boundary between the enforcement of the regulatory system and those acts which would generally be considered to be socially or morally unacceptable. Thus the changing nature of society's attitudes to environmental protection would be reflected in the idea that there were clearly identifiable environmental crimes. This approach might also encourage the development of alternative criminal sanctions on the basis that different offenders respond to different penalties. Although such proposals have been the subject of detailed discussion, no new alternatives to criminal sanctions have been introduced.   STUART BELL

environmental disputes and dispute resolution
Environmental disputes arise in all sorts of different contexts. These can feature commercial organizations such as buyers and sellers of contaminated land, or local, neighbour disputes involving private or statutory **nuisances,** or on an international scale between different nation states dealing with questions of natural resource use or trans-boundary **pollution.** Most typically environmental disputes feature land use planning issues based around the suitability of often hazardous or 'risky' development. Such disputes have led to the coining of the acronym NIMBY—'Not In My Back Yard', reflecting the situation in which local residents oppose a development as inappropriate for their own locality, but by implication do not oppose such development in other areas.

The idea of NIMBY-ism illustrates the significant overlap between the public and private interest in environmental disputes. Many people are concerned because of impacts upon private property interests but a distinguishing feature of environmental disputes is that they often feature a public interest element. Thus although private disputes can feature environmental factors (eg in relation to private nuisances), environmental disputes are characterized by their broader application. This public interest element extends to the depletion of common resources, the protection of the unowned environment, including the nature conservation interest, and the consideration of the welfare of future generations. The incorporation of this public interest element raises questions about who has 'standing' in a dispute. In other words it is often difficult to identify who has the right to be involved on behalf of the public interest and how that right should be recognized in law.

Typically private disputes feature a small number of parties representing their own interests which are resolved through the use of the **courts** finding in favour of one party by determining answers to yes/no questions. On the other hand, environmental disputes often feature many parties representing different interests, including those who represent their own private interests (eg house owners or industrial operators), those who represent collective interests (eg **community** groups), and those who claim to represent the 'public interest'. These can be governmental bodies (eg the **Environment Agency**), or **non-governmental organizations** (eg Greenpeace). This wide variety of participants also raises the issue of access to **justice** and the disparity in funding and resources available to different parties to argue cases.

In addition to this idea of overlapping public and private interests, environmental disputes can be characterized as involving questions which are technically and scientifically complex in situations where the environmental consequences are, for practical purposes, irreversible. The issues which lie at the heart of environmental disputes are often multi-faceted and involve the resolution of competing values about what is considered to be important in terms of priorities for environmental protection. It is a common theme in such disputes that each of the parties believe very strongly that they alone represent the public interest and that they possess the 'right' solution to the problems posed. This often means that there is a tension between individual 'rights', local concerns, and the wider public interest. This is because environmental decisions are mostly concerned with what is 'acceptable'.

Defining what is 'acceptable' in terms of **environmental risk** or pollution often raises difficult questions which require the balancing of different types of evidence such as complicated scientific arguments about whether something is 'safe' or whether the benefits which accrue from a project outweigh the costs. Ultimately, though, these methods are not determinative and simply provide different ways of trying to give a decision-maker more information upon which to make a decision. Thus there is no scientific or economic evidence which, on its own account, can provide an answer to such questions as to where hazardous developments should be situated.

The resolution of the tension between competing values is difficult to achieve through the classic adversarial methods adopted in most legal systems. Determining acceptable trade-offs involves the balancing of difficult policy questions. In this sense there is no 'perfect' answer and diametrically opposed interests cannot be fully accommodated within the legal system or any dispute resolution mechanisms. Typically, therefore, environmental decisions are made 'in the public interest' or 'on balance weighing various considerations'.

Traditional methods of environmental dispute resolution through procedures such as public **inquiries** still leave some parties as 'winners' and others as 'losers' which provides a fertile ground for continuing disputes. As a response to the dissatisfaction with legalistic methods of resolving environmental disputes, there has been some developments in methods which emphasize participation and collaborative decision-making. The aim here is to use mediation to work towards consensual solutions which reinforce the legitimacy of the decision-making process and provide more satisfying long-term outcomes. Such approaches tend to work best at the margins where there is no fundamental clash of competing values (e.g. on matters such as siting or design).

STUART BELL

environmental ethics The main concern of environmental ethics is whether duties should be owed to anything other than existing **human** beings. For example do entities such as plants, habitats, and landscapes have value for their own sake? Do we have obligations to future generations? Environmental ethics also concerns whether we should value environmental interests exclusively in economic as opposed to the aesthetic and emotional dimensions?

Protagonists claim to present a new ethic by rejecting the traditional belief that the human **capacity** to reason makes us morally superior, or by emphasizing the collective rather than the individual. However, their main strategy is to extend familiar ethical principles to non-humans. Ethics is portrayed as a widening historical process. Just as we have rejected racism and sexism, so we should now reject 'speciesism'.

Protagonists disagree as to what features should attract ethical concern. Utilitarians focus on suffering, thus favouring sentient creatures and permitting us to cause suffering to avoid greater suffering. Liberals favour **autonomy** and would override the interests of a purposive animal only where we would those of an innocent human being in similar circumstances, thus confining moral status to the higher animals. These approaches have been criticized both for their apparent indifference to nature conservation and for favouring creatures attractive or similar to ourselves.

The 'biocentric' ethic regards all life-forms as interdependent and of equal value. It is based on the teleological assumption that each life has an essential 'purpose'. Inter-species disputes are resolved by stipulating a hierarchy of interests and freedoms in a manner analogous to **human rights** law. Interference with another species is permitted only proportionately. Basic interests are preferred and, where they conflict, minimum harm must be caused. Genetic modification, for example, is suspect. If we interfere with another being other than in self-defence, **restitution** must be made which may involve protecting the species.

The above are primarily individualistic. Aldo Leopold's influential 'land ethic' favours *collective* life-sustaining entities such as habitats and ecosystems. Its idea of right is the' integrity, stability, and beauty of the biotic **community**' which it believes is best served by encouraging natural processes. It has been described as 'environmental fascism' because it seems to subordinate and instrumentalize the individual. In the end, all these approaches may fail because, whatever moral solvent is used, humans seem to have the largest share.

Environmental ethics also concerns duties to future generations as reflected in the internationally recognized concepts of **sustainable development** and the **precautionary principle**. Inter-generational equity has many inherent problems of which the following are examples. First, it is impossible to know what the needs of the future will be so that any sacrifice we make may be wasteful and unfair to known present needs. Secondly, should we discount future interests as we discount postponed enjoyment? Without such discounting, the interests of future generations would overwhelmingly outweigh our own. On the other hand, if discounted, the value of future generations eventually becomes nothing. Third, our present acts determine *who* exists in the future. If, for example, we think it is right to produce a relatively small population in a better environment, we thereby deny the possibility of life to others albeit in a worse environment. Why is the first option better? Is there any ethical imperative to produce future generations at all? On the other hand it is often argued that human beings have a deep psychological need to be located in a narrative which links generations.

The role of law concerns how far legal institutions and processes can accommodate environmental ethical interests. International treaties, notably the Biodiversity Convention (1992), sometimes announce that nature is of value irrespective of human interests, but no operational machinery is provided. **Charity** law provides the mechanism for a perpetual **trust** but human benefit is required. The ethical concern of preventing cruelty to animals has been held to justify state action under the **Human Rights Act** (*R (Countryside Alliance) v AG* (2006)). However, it is not clear whether bodies such as local councils can take ethical matters into account without specific statutory authority (*R v Somerset CC, ex p Fewings* (1995)). The **courts** have at least accepted that matters can be raised beyond those susceptible to strict scientific rationality although the limits of this are obscure (see *Berkeley v Secretary of State* (2000)).

Non-human entities or future beings could be given rights to participate in processes such as **environmental impact assessment** or challenges to government decisions in the courts (eg *Minors Oposa v Secretary of Department of the Environment* (1994)). They would be represented by human agents as is the case with **companies** or people without capacity, such as babies. This can be considered either as directly embodying radical ethical perspectives or pragmatically, as a convenient fiction to give environmental issues a higher profile.   JOHN ALDER

J DesJardins, *Environmental Ethics: an Introduction to Environmental Philosophy* (Belmont, CA: Wadsworth, 4th edn, 2006)

C Stone, *Should Trees Have Standing and other Essays* (New York: Harper and Rowe, 1998)

environmental governance   This is a term referring to the fact that the regulation of an activity to promote environmental protection often involves a network of interrelated public and private actors who are operating at the sub-national, national, and international levels of government. The interrelationships between these different actors can be both formal and informal and vary in terms of their legally binding nature. In some cases environmental **governance** may involve legally enforceable obligations and in other cases may be more voluntary and diplomatic in character. Public actors include governments at the local, regional, and national level, as well as international and supranational institutions. Private actors include industry, local **communities**, and **non-governmental organizations**. Environmental governance regimes may operate in relation to a specific environmental issue, industry, or community or may involve a series of different environmental issues that operate across a wide range of different industries and communities.

Political scientists were first to recognize these networks. Studying environmental regulation in the international context, they identified examples of environmental governance networks in regional settings such as the European Union but also in relation to specific environmental issues such as **biodiversity**. The role of environmental governance has been increasingly recognized in other areas and other settings, including in sub-national contexts. Moreover, since the mid 1990s, environmental governance has been promoted as a desirable way of thinking about environmental regulation and, in particular, as an alternative to **command and control regulation**. This is because thinking of the protection of the environment in terms of environmental governance arguably promotes better problem solving, cooperation, better integration of environmental issues into mainstream decision-making, and a more flexible approach to addressing environmental problems. What this means is that environmental governance is a descriptive term used to describe how environment regulation works in some contexts and a prescriptive term used to promote a certain form of regulatory decision-making.

While there is considerable variation over how environmental governance is defined and how it operates, environmental governance regimes tend to have three main features. First, environmental governance requires a significant role for private actors in the making of decisions. Private actors are empowered in such contexts and a significant aspect of developing environmental governance is promoting public participation. Two lingering questions for many commentators are how democratic such regimes are, and how democratic they should be.

These questions reflect a more general ambiguity over the legitimate and democratic nature of governance. Secondly, environmental governance regimes invariably operate across jurisdictional borders and involve non-hierarchical forms of government cooperation. Thus, for example, environmental governance regimes may involve a group of national governments cooperating on a trans-boundary problem such as the **pollution** of a regional sea, or may involve a more geographically spread group of sub-national, national, and international bodies, coordinating their actions in relation to a specific problem such as trade in endangered species. It is for this reason that environmental governance is understood as to be a departure from approaches to environmental law they are based on traditional ideas of state **sovereignty**, such approaches being at odds with the global and trans-boundary nature of environmental problems. Thirdly, environmental governance regimes usually involve flexible forms of regulation including **environmental agreements**, economic regulatory instruments, and other more innovative forms of regulation. As such, the recognition and promotion of environmental governance tends to part of the recognition that environmental protection issues needs to be integrated with the market and other aspects of social and political life. In particular, environmental governance emphasizes the importance of promoting cooperation between those involved in the decision-making process. Thus the creation of punitive sanctions is eschewed in favour of more consensual models of decision-making.

Many examples of environmental governance regimes can be seen in operation particularly in relation to issues where the relevant groups of actors are well identified and easily mobilized. In recent years a major focus for recognizing and promoting environmental governance has been the international **sustainable development** debate which began with the Bruntland Report on Sustainable Development in 1987. In 1992, in Rio, the **United Nations** Agenda 21 programme was set up which is a far-reaching plan of action which involves a role for all levels of government and public and private actors. Agenda 21 involves not only many areas of environmental protection but also includes a programme for the production and dissemination of information and frameworks that promote cooperation in relation to environmental issues. The programme was reaffirmed and added to at the World Summit on Sustainable Development in Johannesburg in 2002. Another area where environmental governance regimes have been recognized is in the context of the European Union. Understanding and promoting regulatory frameworks in environmental governance terms is understood to be recognizing the importance of **subsidiarity** and the integration of environmental issues into other areas of decision-making.

LIZ FISHER

environmental heritage Environmental heritage comprises all that surrounds us. However, policy and law have evolved by dealing piecemeal with particular facets of it. Only recently has there been an attempt at a comprehensive approach.

Monuments—the built remains of past ages—were the first to be protected by prohibiting alteration or destruction of their sites. Then people realized that many buildings were at risk of destruction and so provision was made for listing of individual buildings of heritage value. But often part of the value of a building lies in its surrounds. These came to be regulated under planning laws for the benefit of the building as, for example, by prohibiting development which would detract from the heritage value of the protected building. It was also realized that in some cases a building and its associated land are integrated and should be treated as a unit with both being subject to the same controls. Finally, some buildings have no particular heritage value in themselves but do as a group. These are protected since 1967 as a totality through the concept of conservation areas.

At the same time as the above was evolving, land and nature began to be protected as 'environmental heritage'. Action in relation to these was regulated in order to preserve unique values that made them of benefit to the public. For example, **legislation** was passed in 1949 to establish a system of national parks with the objective, among other things, of preserving and enhancing their natural beauty. Another programme involved Environmentally Sensitive Areas which sought to promote farming sensitive to the traditional countryside. Gradually it was accepted that the cultural and natural heritage were both environmental heritage.

But these two aspects of protection had been evolving independently of each other. They came together with the concept of the cultural landscape where the values are drawn from the combined effect of human activity and nature. An example of this in England is the Royal Botanic Gardens, Kew, which was inscribed as a World Heritage Site in 2003 in accordance with the Convention concerning the Protection of the World Cultural and Natural Heritage 1972. This instrument was the first attempt internationally to apply the same principles to both cultural and natural heritage. Part of the justification for inscribing

Kew Gardens on the World Heritage List was that the landscape gardens together with the buildings 'reflect the beginning of movements which were to have international influence'.

However, the European Landscape Convention 2000, to which the UK is a party, has a much broader scope: applying to the entire territory of the parties and concerning landscapes that might be considered outstanding as well as those which are 'everyday or degraded' landscapes. How the UK implements this remains to be seen but any legislation will need to be carefully drawn to comply with human rights legislation and obligations contained in the **European Convention on Human Rights,** particularly the right to property and respect for a person's home.

PATRICK O'KEEFE

See also: **environmental governance; heritage, international dimensions; heritage legislation**

environmental impact assessment *see* **environmental assessment**

environmental justice Environmental justice represents the idea of social equity in the face of the impact of environmental harms and risks of harm. It has an awkward place in the environmentalist canon, in similarly ambivalent territory to the propounding of environmental **human rights** arguments. Environmental justice informs social and political discourse concerning the need for fair and systematic review of the **human** dimensions of both environmental threats and related societal adjustments. It offers a normative framework for measuring distributive impacts of the associated risks and costs. Aside from its ethical perspective, the idea also serves functional ends: by ensuring debate over burden allocation with a view to seeking equitable conflict resolutions. Such conflicts arise both in present and future time, raising issues of both intra- and inter-generational justice.

The roots of the environmental justice movement lie in the development in the last decades of the twentieth century of organized responses to inequitable treatment of vulnerable **communities** across the United States. From the first, a synonymous term, 'environmental racism', was commonly ascribed. The idea, drawing strength from political conflicts over social inequalities, focused on the preponderant siting in particular locations (and conversely non-siting elsewhere) of harmful activities such as **waste** facilities and other polluting operations. Key complaints were that in such circumstances risks of harms to health and damage to surroundings were self-reinforcing. Thus a cycle of deprivation and

deterioration was created in areas with clusters of toxic installations, further resulting in 'flight' on the part of those inhabitants aspiring (and able) to relocate. This resulted in further increases in concentration of noxious activities, in step with downwards adjustment of relative property values, whilst further pressing economically disadvantaged populations: with reduced capacity to harness political and legal processes in their self-defence, and often desperate for related employment opportunities on whatever terms. A notable contribution of the movement has been to encourage community **empowerment** in seeking wider **recognition** of environmental justice considerations within mainstream US policymaking.

Environmental justice concerns, reflecting the incidence of environmental harm itself, are not necessarily restricted either temporally or geographically. In illustrating the former, environmental justice in relation to intergenerational equity can be traced to the 1987 World Commission for Environment and Development (Brundtland) Report, *Our Common Future*. This defined '**sustainable development**' as being 'that which meets the needs of the present without compromising the ability of future generations to meet their own needs'. This broadly challenged what has been a generally unregulated exploitation of natural resources on which economic wealth (mainly of developed nations) has been built. Sustainable development, bundling together environmental, social, and economic strands of policymaking, can be seen as fundamentally about environmental justice in the intergenerational context, challenging the heavy discounting of future needs in favour of shorter-term priorities.

Considering such questions geographically, in a global economy environmental injustice can be exported with as much facility as can capital, as threats from hazardous wastes and toxic industrial processes are spatially displaced. A tragic instance of such displacement is the aftermath of a lethal gas leak (methyl isocyanate) from a tank at the Union Carbide pesticide plant in the Indian city of Bhopal. This is reported to have resulted directly in upwards of 4,000 deaths; severe health problems such as breathing disabilities, gynaecological disorders, and blindness, affecting perhaps tens of thousands; and further legacies such as **pollution** migration into water supplies. Inequalities can also have multijurisdictional effects. In negotiating global carbon emissions reductions under the Kyoto Protocol (of the UN Framework Convention on **Climate Change**) I and II, environmental justice arguments concerning differentiated responsibility (and also for contraction and convergence) as between developed and developing states emphasize not only **responsibility** for past emissions linked to a right to develop, but also the sharing of the environmental implications of the synchronous industrializing and de-industrializing of states now taking place within the global economy.

In the further, specific context of climate change risks, communities most exposed to the consequences of, for instance, sea level rise over the coming century are those in developing countries situated along low-lying island (especially in the Indian and Pacific Oceans) or sub-continental shorelines (such as Bangladesh) with least capacity to mitigate and adapt. The contribution of environmental justice analysis to addressing such environmental risks lies in its urging of a sharing of burdens, whether in relation to harms threatened or the consequences of mitigation or adaptation. MARK STALLWORTHY

RD Bullard, *Dumping in Dixie: Race, Class and Environmental Quality* (Boulder, CO: Westview Press, 3rd edn, 2000, 1st edition published in 1990)

A Dobson, 'Social Justice and Environmental Sustainability: Ne'er the Twain Shall Meet', in J Agyeman, RD Bullard, and B Evans, *Just Sustainabilities – Development in an Unequal World* (London: Earthscan, 2003)

Environmental Pollution, Royal Commission on

The Royal Commission on Environmental Pollution ('RCEP') was established in 1970 as a permanent, independent UK advisory body with broad terms of reference 'to advise on matters, both national and international, concerning **pollution** of the environment; on the adequacy of research in the field, and the future possibilities of dangers to the environment'. Members are formally appointed by the Queen on recommendation of the **Prime Minister**, and, although the RCEP has always been chaired by a distinguished scientist, membership has been drawn from a wide range of disciplines, including law and economics. The RCEP, which is supported by a small secretariat, has been described as a committee of experts rather than an expert committee, and is currently the only standing Royal Commission in the UK. Its wide-ranging reports, covering such areas as transport, energy, fisheries, and agriculture, have provided an important source of authoritative and independent assessment of policy challenges in the environmental field. The choice and timing of its studies are determined by the RCEP, and while its recommendations are not formally binding on government, its reports have frequently been extremely influential. UK legislative initiatives concerning areas such as the release of genetically manipulated organisms, integrated pollution control, and greater public access to environmental information can be directly traced to analysis contained in previous RCEP reports. Although the RCEP is formally a UK body, its reports have international standing, and in recent years the RCEP has engaged in closer cooperation with equivalent advisory bodies in other European countries. RICHARD MACRORY

environmental rights The term 'environmental rights' is perhaps best understood as a diverse group of legal **remedies** which apply when either a **person** suffers harm which originates in the environment (anthropocentric), or the environment, including non-human species, is harmed (ecocentric). The boundaries of this collection are not well-defined, but what we conventionally term '**animal rights**' clearly fall within the ecocentric sub-group and 'a right to clean air' would be a founder member of the anthropocentric branch.

Many would argue that it is meaningless to talk of animals (far less, plants) having legal rights because they cannot possibly invoke those rights in **court**. But neither can a **human** baby (or a mentally incapacitated adult) and, in England and Wales, the Family Division of the High Court regularly hears cases in which a **child**'s best interests are determined. When Christopher Stone posed the question '*Should trees have standing?*' (1974, Los Altos, California), he meant 'legal standing' and, in effect, he was asking 'should the courts recognize a person or an organization whose duty it is defend the interest of trees when threatened by, to cite the obvious example, commercial logging?'. But how, the sceptics will respond, can a court know what the interests of plants and animals are? When we observe our genetically closest neighbours—the great apes—it is not difficult to infer that, like us, they simply want to reproduce their kind and live out their lives with plentiful food and minimal threats from predators. Insofar as a tree 'wants' anything, it would appear to be to exist long enough to spread its progeny over a wide area. But a lion's '**right to life**' entails the denial of that right to antelopes or similar prey species. The recognition that evolution has required the vast majority of animals and plants to be parts of long food chains has led to the emergence of a notion of environmental rights which concentrates, not on individual species, but on ecosystems themselves. Holistic thinkers, like Aldo Leopold, point with awe at the integrity of an ecosystem and the complex interdependencies of its animate and inanimate components. But whatever our motivation in seeking to protect, for example, peregrine falcons, provided that there are laws which offer sanctions against those who cause these birds, their eggs, or their nests harm, and if these sanctions are effectively enforced, then it is not fanciful to speak of these birds having a right to an undisturbed existence.

Ecocentric rights, if they exist, are a recent phenomenon. But for centuries, the law treated the environment, or rather, land and its non-human inhabitants, as 'property'. Riparian rights (such as the right of the owner of a riverbank to receive water unpolluted by upstream users) and the more general right of property owners to take action in **nuisance** are 'environmental' in that they relate directly to our physical surroundings. The '**right to roam**' (over land made accessible under the Countryside and Rights of Way Act 2000) is also environmental in a similarly obvious way. But over the past forty years or so, the environmental movement has given rise to a notion of an 'environmental right' which, whilst clearly anthropocentric in that it is concerned with human welfare, is independent of property and ownership. The following can be found in (a recent addition to the French Constitution) the *Charter of the Environment*: 'Every person has the right to live in a balanced environment that does not harm his or her health'. A similar 'right to a healthy environment' can be found in the constitutions of Spain and Portugal (as well as those of Ecuador, Peru, and Brazil). And, in *Our Common Future* (1987), the World Commission on Environment and Development claimed that: 'All human beings have the fundamental right to an environment adequate for their health and well being'.

It is not difficult to point to various bodies of **international law** and to the written **constitutions** of a number of nation states which include a 'right to healthy environment'. **European Community law** contains a number of provisions which can be interpreted as establishing certain rights in regard to environmental quality. In addition to what might be described as *explicit* statements of this right, it is also possible to identify other sources of international law from which a comparable right may be derived or inferred. Under this 'inferred' category, those of most relevance to the United Kingdom are rights which derive from the **European Convention on Human Rights** ('ECHR').

Mrs Lopez Ostra lived with her family in the Lorca, Spain. Her home was situated very close to a tannery and the odours arising from the processing of leather was the source of considerable nuisance to the family. Eventually they were rehoused but only after a delay during which, Mrs Lopez Ostra argued, the local authority had failed adequately to regulate the tannery and to protect her family's health. Unable to persuade any Spanish court to find in her favour, she eventually sought justice at the **European Court of Human Rights** at Strasbourg. Here, in 1990, she was more successful and was awarded some £20,000 for what was adjudged to have been an unjustified infringement of her Article 8 (of the ECHR) 'right to respect for [her] private and **family life**, [her] home and [her] correspondence'.

The ruling in *Lopez Ostra v Spain* (1995) led many observers to believe that Article 8 could create what amounted to a right to a healthy environment, which could be invoked whenever **pollution** posed a threat to domestic felicity. *Lopez Ostra* assisted other victims of environmental harm to enjoy success at the Strasbourg court. However, the case of *Hatton v UK* (2003) was to expose a major hurdle which others will have to overcome if they are to use ECHR to protect their domestic life from environmental threats. Article 8 (2) recognizes that some intrusions into the family home are an inevitable feature of daily life in a developed economy, and the state must be accorded a certain 'margin of appreciation'. Aviation, or more precisely, sleep disturbance by aircraft landing at Heathrow Airport around 6 am, is one such example. Since Mr Hatton *chose* to locate his family in house beneath the flight path, and since the early morning flights were not (unlike the source of Mrs Lopez Ostra's complaint) unlawful, he was unable to secure redress under the European Convention.

The *Hatton* case raises an issue which is common to both the explicit and inferred categories of (anthropocentric) environmental rights. Given the existence of a free market in housing, it will inevitably be the poor who occupy houses in areas most blighted by noise and pollution. Yet they are as much the **victims** of their poverty as their environment. And the extent to which their relative deprivation should be reduced, being a matter of social and economic policy, is for **Parliament** to decide, not the courts. **Judges** may occasionally award **compensation** to those who have been the victims of incompetence or maladministration by state agencies charged with environmental protection. However, such payments should not be seen as clear proof of the existence of an effective right to a clean and healthy environment for everyone.   CHRIS MILLER

environmental risk regulation   The very idea of 'environmental risk regulation' is ambiguous. On the one hand, it might be thought to refer to hazards posed to the environment ('environmental risks'), which require regulation. On the other hand, it might be thought to refer to a particular way of regulating activities in order to enhance environmental protection, that is, through use of the concept of '**risk**'. It is the second interpretation that is closer to the truth. 'Risk regulation' is a term of art which implies particular methods of approaching problems and identifying hazards. The **Environment Agency** for example adopts a 'risk based' approach to regulation, in the sense that it seeks to set regulatory priorities in the light of assessment of risks. Risk analysis and risk management have been embedded alongside other techniques in the modernization of environmental regulation. But 'risk' is certainly not an uncontested term and there are major variations in the way that risk regulation is understood.

In particular, there is a division between *quantitative* and *evaluative* approaches to risk. On one view, risk assessment—particularly through the use of statistical methods—is the best way to generate reliable information about potential outcomes, identifying the greatest risks to health and environment, and setting regulatory priorities for reducing them. Public perceptions about risk, and the priorities expressed in the public's response to various hazards, are seen as irrational and as probably formed on the basis of distorted information (or on the basis of little information of any sort). 'Risk assessment' is therefore the best guide to regulatory action.

An opposing view declines to ascribe deviations between public and expert perceptions to irrationality or ignorance on the part of lay people. Rather, such divergent views are equally likely to show that experts neglect the evaluative element which ought to be central to the treatment of risks. Public responses may also reflect valuable ideas about legitimacy and fairness, for example.

Some years ago, these approaches seemed to be irreconcilably in conflict. A Royal Society Report in 1992 on 'Risk: Analysis, Perception and Management' failed to reach any reconciliation between these two views. There is some hope however that these divergent views could be reconciled, at least in principle. Sound risk assessments are important to the transparency and rationality of decision-making, but in the final analysis all decisions about risk-taking are evaluative. Inevitably, once quantification of risks and benefits has been carried out, it must be determined whether projected benefits justify taking (or leaving unregulated) the risk in question or, in the alternative, whether regulatory costs justify minimising or avoiding the risk. The answers to such questions will require assessment of risks and benefits—including value foregone by *not* taking a risk. But the answers will also depend on other factors including 'risk aversion': different individuals take a different view of the value of a given risk in the light of its potential benefits.

The existence of 'risk aversion' is entirely recognized in the context of individual decision-making but is much more difficult to incorporate into a social decision-making framework. In a social context, decisions about risk involve judgments not only about one's own exposure to potential harm but also about the harm that may be foisted on others, since risks are not evenly distributed. The risks associated with global warming for example appear to be common to all nations but it is generally accepted that they disproportionately affect low-lying countries such as Bangladesh. Equally, many environmental risks created by current activities (for example, the risks associated with nuclear waste) are imposed on the generations of the future. These examples display an important feature of environmental risks, which is that they are not necessarily placed with those who benefit most from the activities which give rise to them. Risk aversion on the part of the public is also open to manipulation and the current vilification of health and safety in the popular press, for example, could be said to demonstrate a quite successful celebration of productive social risk-taking on the part of the UK government in recent years.

If the public seems to be overly sensitive to particular risks (such as nuclear power), whilst remaining unduly nonchalant about others (such as, historically, smoking), one possible strategy for overcoming the shortcomings of both technical and populist approaches to environmental risk is to engage in deliberative decision-making processes. Here, members of the public are able to participate in reasoning processes, rather than simply having their preferences taken into account. This sort of process has the advantage of fostering closer reflection on risks and benefits on the part of lay participants, as well as potentially making regulators more aware of the reasons behind different responses to relevant risks.

JENNY STEELE

environmental self-regulation The term 'environmental self-regulation' covers a range of voluntary actions which are designed to bring about environmental improvement. In recent years, such voluntary measures have been seen as complementary to traditional direct methods of environmental regulation. Thus, a contrast can be drawn between what is often referred to as **command and control regulation** which focuses largely on mandatory requirements or prohibitions through licensing systems and the flexible, voluntary nature of self-regulation. In practice, however, very few self-regulatory mechanisms are truly voluntary and they are often arranged under the threat of compulsion or are parasitic upon existing regulatory frameworks. Even in situations where no parallel regulatory system exists, some element of compulsion may remain. This may be based around collective initiatives (eg through industry-wide arrangements), or where there is a economic basis for action, such as a clear commercial benefit (eg eco-labelling which heightens market differentiation and thus increases product sales).

The obvious attraction of self-regulation is that voluntary mechanisms are quick and easy to produce and flexible so that they can be adapted to specific circumstances. For example, the use of management agreements between statutory nature conservation bodies and landowners to manage sites positively to preserve habitats can focus on the detailed management of individual sites. In some circumstances, voluntary mechanisms can go beyond normal regulatory systems and yet still impose fairer obligations because they reflect what people are willing to adopt. On a much deeper level, they can promote a progressive attitude to environmental performance which is based not upon a reaction to regulation but to a genuine desire to improve. This can encourage regular incremental improvements which would not be otherwise achieved under legislative initiatives.

On the other hand the disadvantages of self-regulatory mechanisms stem from their strengths, ie the fact that they tend to be voluntary and flexible in nature. By definition, voluntary commitments rarely have any enforcement tools and they tend to be set at levels which can be achieved using reasonable amounts of effort. In addition, there is the problem of an uneven application of self-regulation. Unless measures are adopted comprehensively there is a danger of so-called 'free-riders', ie people or companies gaining an advantage over competitors by not agreeing to or simply not implementing self-regulatory measures. In this sense, they are 'rewarded' for using lower environmental standards. Finally, it is common for the terms of any self-regulatory mechanisms to be finalized in private. Public participation is limited and consequently there is a lack of transparency and **accountability**.

Although the exact nature of environmental self-regulation is diffuse and dependent upon individual circumstances, three broad categories of self-regulatory instruments can be identified, namely agreements or contracts to secure environmental improvements; the use of environmental management standards ('EMAS'); and the voluntary provision of environmental information and educational initiatives.

The use of contracts and covenants to secure environmental improvements can be formal and backed by statutory powers (eg nature conservation management agreements); ancillary to regulatory systems (eg **Climate Change** Agreements which link energy efficiency with tax reductions); or much more informal and sometimes aspirational agreements which have been negotiated between government or the regulator and individual **companies** or industry sectors. Some agreements, particularly those made under statutory powers, are drafted as contracts with enforceable obligations. In many others, the exact legal status of agreement provisions is uncertain since they are not private contracts nor made subject to any statutory powers. In such circumstances, any agreement is symbolic and often made with the background threat that failure to meet the obligations under the agreement may result in formal regulation on the issue. Experience has shown that such agreements have been used to set targets which at best are the same as would have been imposed under direct regulation but with the disadvantage of delaying the introduction of such regulation. For example, the **European Commission** and international car manufacturers agreed to reduce average CO_2 emissions from new cars to 140 g/km by 2009 at the latest with an overall reduction target to 120 g/km by 2012. Although partially successful, the pace of the reduction was considered to be too slow and the European Commission was forced to propose **legislation** in early 2007—some twelve years after the initial discussions over the voluntary agreements.

EMAS promote voluntary corporate environmental improvement through the adoption of quality control systems which set basic environmental performance standards. Although environmental improvement is a primary goal, the achievement of the objectives is also intended to result in business benefits such as cost savings, efficiency gains, and a competitive advantage based upon an enhanced public perception of a company's activities. Typically, an EMAS is based around specific environmental objectives which are measured against a publicly produced environmental policy. This includes a minimum commitment of compliance with all legal standards whilst attempting to improve environmental performance in areas as diverse as energy consumption, a reduction in the use of raw materials, **waste** minimization and transport.

The adoption of an EMAS requires a company to assess and understand the environmental impacts associated with all of the company's products, services, and activities (not just those connected with production) and then to set up an active programme for managing those impacts and general environmental performance in the context of pre-established targets. Once adopted, the continuing achievement of the EMAS is subject to verification by independent accredited auditors. The most widely adopted standard, ISO 14001, has an international presence as a result of supply chain management and pressure brought about by corporate customers to ensure high levels of environmental performance from suppliers. Although EMAS provide a good illustration of one of the benefits of self-regulation in that they are designed to encourage continuous improvement beyond the basic requirement of legal compliance, they also illustrate the weakness that truly voluntary goals are subjective in nature. Thus at its lowest an EMAS may merely be a statement of what should be a given, ie compliance with all environmental laws.

The voluntary use of environmental information as a method of self-regulation should be distinguished from mandatory requirements for monitoring and reporting information subsequently held on public **pollution** control registers. For example, the voluntary disclosure of environmental performance in a company annual report can give **consumers**, investors, and other interested parties (eg insurers and trade customers) a picture of any improvements or deterioration in performance as part of a wider dissemination of **corporate social responsibility** policies. One of the weaknesses of such self-regulation is the potential for the selection of and emphasis upon 'success stories' rather than under-performance.

In addition, the use of market-orientated information, including eco-labelling or environmental certification, can provide information on the environmental impacts of goods and products. An eco-label is attached to a qualifying product to signify that it has been produced in accordance with certain environmental standards. This information can send important signals to consumers in relation to the true environmental costs of products enabling 'environmentally friendly' preferences to be exercised. A general eco-label (which resembles a flower) has been agreed at a European level (eg see Regulation 1980/00) with product specifications for different consumer products as well as a separate eco-label for fishery products.   STUART BELL

environmental taxes Most taxes, historically, have been imposed to finance government expenditure. There are, however, long-standing economic arguments in favour of taxes the primary purpose of which is to discourage certain types of behaviour.

Rational people, so the argument goes, will avoid types of behaviour that are taxed more highly, and are therefore more expensive, than others. Environmentally harmful behaviour is an obvious candidate for such taxation. So greenhouse gas emissions, waste pollution, and the unsightly and noisy use of land, have all been the targets of environmental taxes. The argument also applies to behaviour such as excessive car use, where congestion, as well as emissions, imposes a significant societal cost.

Translating theory into practice has nonetheless been difficult. Environmental arguments do not guarantee political acceptability. When, in 2001, the climate change levy, a business tax designed to help reduce greenhouse gas emissions, was introduced, it had to be matched by offering British industry the opportunity to qualify for incentive payments under a national emissions trading scheme.

Again, technical constraints, imposed by EU or international law, or by market structures (such as the electricity and gas markets, or the market in waste management), or even by the type of environmental harm involved, often make it difficult for the consumer to see the link between the tax imposed and its environmental benefit. Such constraints mean that the climate change levy is a tax on energy inefficiency, rather than on emissions; that landfill tax, a tax on waste pollution from 1996, affects local authorities and businesses more directly than individuals; and aggregates levy, a 2002 tax on mineral extraction, relies on rather opaque economic assessments of the environmental damage caused by mineral extraction.

Moreover, with the possible exception of vehicle excise duty ('road tax' or 'vehicle tax'), which imposes differential rates of duty based on emissions, it can be difficult to judge the environmental effectiveness of a particular environmental tax where, like landfill tax and climate change levy, it is only one of a range of policy instruments in a particular field.

The Stern review of autumn 2006 has tended to underline critical scepticism of energy taxes by placing the emphasis on emissions trading. Enabling industrial polluters to purchase pollution allowances, at a level fixed by the market rather than by the state, may yet eclipse the concept of the environmental tax. Similar market arguments may ultimately lead to the replacement of vehicle excise duty with a national road-pricing scheme.   JOHN SNAPE

J Snape and J de Souza, *Environmental Taxation Law: Policy, Contexts and Practice* (Aldershot: Ashgate, 2006)

K Määttä, *Environmental Taxes: An Introductory Analysis* (Cheltenham: Edward Elgar, 2006)

environmental trading   Over the last decade, there has been a growing interest in policy approaches that explicitly commodify environmental impacts by creating markets for their sale. These environmental trading markets ('ETMs') now operate in a range of regulatory settings where parties exchange credits to emit air pollutants, extract natural resources, and develop habitat.

Dating from the first trading programme in 1974, ETMs have reduced emissions of a wide range of pollutants (including acid rain, lead from gasoline, nitrogen oxides, chlorofluorocarbons, etc), managed fisheries and lobster harvests (through so-called individual transferable quotas), and channelled habitat development (through tradable development rights, wetlands mitigation banking, endangered species habitat trading, etc).

Despite the myriad ETMs and the many differences among them, their basic structure is similar. The basis for trading environmental commodities is a regulatory proscription of behaviour followed by regulatory permission of the behaviour under controlled conditions. In establishing a market, the government first creates a new form of property—legal entitlements to emit pollutants, catch fish, develop habitat—and then imposes a set of rules governing their exchange.

In the typical 'cap and trade programme' for pollution, policymakers establish a socially desirable level of aggregate emissions for a given pollutant. Regulators then determine a formula or mechanism (such as an auction) for initial allocation of emissions among sources and issue permits to members of the regulated community that entitle each bearer to emit a given quantity of that pollutant. In sum, the total quantity of emissions allowed by those permits should equal the aggregate level set by policymakers. Similarly, in the context of scarce natural resources, permits cap the bearer's right to take a specified amount of the resource and the total quantity of permits is equal to the aggregate extraction or harvest level set by policymakers. All trading programmes therefore take place within carefully constructed markets. Absent legal restrictions on pollutant emissions, fish landings, or wetlands development, and the creation of alienable entitlements to these activities, few if any trades would take place.

Proponents of trading programmes argue that such arrangements increase efficiencies. In the case of air pollutant trades, for example, by letting the market rather than regulators determine individual actors' impacts, profit-motivated agents who can control pollution at low cost will reduce more emissions than needed to comply with permit limits. They can then sell surplus allowances at a profit to higher-cost agents. Thus, the greatest share of reductions will come from agents who can do so at the cheapest cost, allowing each polluter to weigh the marginal cost of abatement against the cost of buying credits and make an efficient individual decision.

These enthusiastic claims have not gone unchallenged, however. Recent scholarship has contended that in many cases trading has not delivered the same or better protection at less cost, and has proven overly complex to administer and enforce. Strong normative critiques contend that trading programmes legitimize pollution, weakening the environment's special claim to public protection. And both environmental justice and economics scholarship clearly recognize that certain air pollutant trading may lead to hot spots and distributional inequities.

JAMES SALZMAN

environmental trusts   Trust concepts and mechanisms have an increasingly important role to play in environmental protection in harnessing the strength of private property rights in the communal interest for environmental protection purposes. The essence of the trust concept is the separation of legal and beneficial ownership of property. Trust mechanisms may be used flexibly to ensure environmental protection of trust assets, such as a park or wildlife reserve, or to provide long-term financing of environmental projects through trust funds. The latter are generally established as a separate investment account to provide a dependable and long-term source of revenue. When publicly administered and controlled, trust funds may be established to recompense future generations for resource loss through present use, and/or to ensure that the benefits of future exploitation of public resources are employed to broader public benefit. The device is one found both in national and international law. Well-known examples of the former are trust funds whose purpose is to finance the clean-up of pollution damage such as the Oil Spill Liability Trust Fund established pursuant to the US Oil Pollution Act 1990 which combines the use of a trust fund with the appointment of trustees to recover for damage to, *inter alia*, natural resources.

Internationally there are now a wide range of financial mechanisms labelled 'trust fund' which operate in the environmental field, such as the World Bank/UNDP/UNEP administered Global Environmental Facility with its Global Environmental Trust Fund which serves as the financial mechanism for the 1992 Climate Change Convention and the 1992 Biodiversity Convention. It provides new and additional grant and concessional funding to meet the agreed incremental costs of measures to achieve agreed global environmental benefits. Access to such funds may also be used as a tool to encourage compliance with environmental treaty obligations, such as the World Heritage Fund established under the 1972 World Heritage Convention and the Small Wetlands Conservation Fund established under the 1971 Ramsar Convention on Wetlands of International Importance. These last examples have a further feature, however, and it is the compensation element whereby the environmental trust fund is, in essence, compensating the 'host' countries of world heritage sites or wetlands of importance for wild birds for their conservation efforts on behalf of the international community. The trust mechanism is also increasingly used in private/public partnerships to mobilize funding to establish sustainable financing mechanisms such as trust funds for selected sites of outstanding biodiversity.

C Redgwell, *Intergenerational Trusts and Environmental Protection* (Manchester: Manchester University Press, 1999)

PH Sand, 'Trusts for the Earth: New International Financial Mechanisms for Sustainable Development' in W Lang (ed), *Sustainable Development and International Law* (London: Kluwer, 1995)

Equal Oportunities Commission   *see* **Equality and Human Rights Commission**

equal pay   Pay disparities between women and men are endemic in the UK and elsewhere, full-time women earning around 83 per cent of the full-time male hourly average rate while almost 50 per cent of women who work part-time earn a figure closer to 60 per cent. The Equal Pay Act 1970, which came into force in 1975, aims to prohibit discrimination between men and women in relation to the contractual terms of employment including (but not limited to) pay. In its earliest incarnation it prohibited such discrimination only between men and women doing jobs which were essentially the same or which the employer itself had recognized as equivalently valuable by virtue of a job evaluation scheme. This left a significant gap in relation to women working in generally underpaid, predominantly female, occupations who, for the most part, were unable to point to appropriate male '**comparators**' for the purposes of pay claims. In 1984 the Act was amended after a decision by the **European Court of Justice** that it failed properly to implement Council Directive 75/117 (the Equal Pay Directive), which requires equal pay 'for the same work or for work to which equal value is

attributed'. The Act now entitles a woman (or a man) to equal contractual terms (including pay) with a person of the opposite **sex** who performs 'like work', 'work rated as equivalent', or 'work of equal value'.

'Equal value' claims are complicated to establish, generally requiring that an employment **tribunal** appoint and receive a report from an independent expert on the question of value. All claims require that the comparator be employed by the same employer in the same workplace or at one in which generally similar terms and conditions apply. A defence is provided to employers who can establish that the disputed pay differential was the result of a 'material factor' which was not the difference of sex. This has been interpreted to mean that a pay-related factor which is genuinely sex-neutral establishes the defence if, in fact, it underpinned the differential treatment. One which distinguishes directly between men and women (as would be the case with a 'male breadwinner' bonus) would be incapable of providing the employer with a defence. In practice, no employer would put forward such a defence, though an employer might try to attribute to a non-discriminatory reason a pay differential which was *in fact* based on sex. The third, and most common, type of factor is one which does not distinguish *directly* between men and women, but which nevertheless advantages one sex (usually men) over the other. Such factors include the reward of seniority (men generally have longer service because they have fewer child and family-related career breaks); ability to work full-time (women tend to shoulder a disproportionate amount of childcare responsibilities); ability to accept a mobility clause (because women generally earn less than male partners they are less likely to be in a position to move in order to retain a job); or pay practices which reflect external salaries, and therefore frequently perpetuate previous pay discrimination. Such factors will only provide the basis of a defence to an equal pay claim where the employer can justify relying on them *notwithstanding* their unequal impact.

The Equal Pay Act cannot be considered in isolation from Article 141 of the Treaty establishing the European Community and from the Equal Pay Directive. To the extent that the Equal Pay Act does not properly implement these provisions, claimants may rely on Article 141 regardless of whether they are employed by the state or by a private body. An Article 141 claim could, for example, be brought where a woman and her comparator have different employers (hence blocking an Equal Pay Act claim) but where a single 'source' governed pay (see *Lawrence & Ors v Regent Office Care* Case (2002); and Case C-256/01

Allonby v Accrington & Rossendale College & Anor (2004)).

Equal pay cases are in practice slow, cumbersome, and expensive to bring and individual claims would have to be brought even if many women were in exactly similar positions in relation to an appropriate male comparator. The government has thus far resisted all calls to permit class actions, much less to impose positive obligations on employers to eradicate pay discrimination. A number of other jurisdictions impose such positive (or 'proactive') obligations requiring employers, generally in conjunction with appropriate **trade union** or other representatives, to analyse pay structures to determine whether any gaps between the average wages of men and women within the organization are attributable, whether directly or indirectly, to sex. This type of **legislation** is generally referred to as 'pay equity' legislation and it has been adopted most notably in many Canadian jurisdictions. Also characteristic of the approach taken in a number of Canadian jurisdictions is 'employment equity' legislation which imposes positive obligations on employers to analyse the composition of their workforces by reference, typically, to sex, ethnicity, and disability, and to take steps to overcome significant disparities between workers defined by reference to these factors in terms of access to jobs, promotion, etc.

AILEEN McCOLGAN

equal protection clause 'Equal protection clauses' are provisions in written **constitutions** or **human rights** treaties that require a state to treat all **persons** within its jurisdiction as having **equality** of status and respect. **Courts** have often interpreted equal protection clauses as prohibiting many forms of discrimination. However, the interpretation and application of equal protection clauses is often a source of controversy and dispute.

Perhaps the most famous equal protection clause is the Fourteenth Amendment to the US Constitution. Introduced in the aftermath of the US Civil War, this Amendment was intended to prevent states from denying equal **citizenship** rights to Afro-Americans. The **US Supreme Court** has developed in recent decades an extensive, complex, and often controversial case law on equality issues. The Court will find discrimination by federal and state authorities against 'discrete and insular minorities' which is based on 'suspect' classifications such as **race** to be unconstitutional, unless the justification for the measures in question can survive close and exacting judicial scrutiny. Controversy continues as to how the Court should apply this approach to issues such

as affirmative action, gay **marriage,** and **women**'s rights.

Similar equal protection clauses now exist in most national constitutions. However, UK law has at present no full equivalent to an 'equal protection clause'. **Article 14** of the **European Convention on Human Rights** ('ECHR') only guarantees equality 'in the enjoyment of' other Convention rights. Protocol 12 of the ECHR makes it possible for states to accept a full equal protection clause, but the UK has not as yet agreed to accept this Protocol.

COLM O'CINNEIDE

See also: **interpreting constitutions; United States Bill of Rights**

equality Equality is a concept which can be applied in many fields of human activity; but as a principle of law it is most commonly encountered in the context of status. In this sense it means that people have the right to be regarded as equals as regards access to positions and facilities. This is often viewed by courts as an application of the fundamental human right to autonomy.

If complete equality were to be guaranteed to all people, all decisions about access to positions and facilities would have to be justifiable and could be challenged if they were not. However, in practice, this would bring day-to-day transactions to a halt. The law has therefore opted for a compromise: those belonging to certain groups are acknowledged to experience disadvantage by reason of their membership of the relevant group. Remedies are therefore provided to members of these groups in relation to particular types of disadvantage. The most important types of disadvantage must then be identified by the law. The approach taken is to fasten on situations which are peculiarly apt to influence a person's life chances; current law opts for the fields of employment, education, the provision of goods, services, and facilities, including social security and other services provided by public bodies. The grounds on which discrimination is currently prohibited in the UK include gender, race, religion or belief, sexual orientation, disability, and age.

One apparent paradox is that, despite the fact that the reason for the law existing in the first place is the perceived disadvantage encountered by certain sections of the population, the legal protection afforded generally extends to all. For example, discrimination on the ground of sex is forbidden, even though disadvantage is experienced to a greater degree by women than by men; race is similarly targeted, although certain ethnic minorities have certainly experienced more disadvantage than others. The only current exception to this symmetrical approach is in relation to disability. The law merely forbids discrimination against those who are disabled, so that an able-bodied person may not complain of receiving less favourable treatment than someone who is disabled.

Equality law emanates from various sources: domestic legislation, law made by the **European Union**, and that flowing from the **European Convention on Human Rights**, which is enforceable by UK courts pursuant to the Human Rights Act 1998. The consequences of infringing these laws are civil, rather than the criminal; thus, the victim will frequently seek damages for the legal wrong done. The aim of the law is compensatory, deterrent, and educative; it is not essentially punitive.

A very difficult legal and philosophical question is the substantive content of the notion of equality. The US Supreme Court concluded in *Plessy v Ferguson* in 1896 that the separate but allegedly equal treatment of blacks and whites by a railroad company satisfied the Constitutional guarantee of equal protection of the laws, despite the limitation that such treatment involved for individual liberty. However, in 1954, a unanimous Supreme Court in **Brown v Board of Education** rejected the 'separate but equal' doctrine, holding that separate educational facilities for blacks and whites are 'inherently unequal'. If all human beings are of fundamentally equal worth, then arguably the desired goal for the legal system should be equality of outcome or results. However, in practice, of course, people possess vastly differing aptitudes and an efficient society requires these to be effectively harnessed. Today, therefore, it is generally accepted that equality means in essence equality of opportunity, the right to compete with others on equal terms.

Another way of expressing this is through the so-called 'merit' principle: individuals should be treated according to their individual merit and not according to stereotyped assumptions made about them on account of group membership. However, this principle sounds deceptively simple; there is much room for subjectivity in the judgment that the abilities of two people are either the same or different. For example, men and women often perform different kinds of work in industry, with women doing work requiring manual dexterity and men doing jobs which demand physical strength. Pay systems traditionally reward physical strength more generously than dexterity, but this surely masks a highly controversial and gender-biased assessment of value. There are also other downsides

to the law's choice of the merit principle. One is that, since people possess different aptitudes, it does not result in the equal distribution of wealth, power, and other prizes. Therefore, further mechanisms, in particular social welfare provision, are required to even out the imbalances which continue to manifest themselves.

Modern equality law adopts a two-pronged approach. First, it reflects in legal terms the principle expressed by Aristotle that like things should be treated alike and unlike things treated differently, unless there is good reason to depart from this basic logic. The law's expression of this principle is the concept of '**direct discrimination**', often also referred to as '**formal equality**'. It means that, within the areas governed by the law, it is unlawful to base a decision about a person on a prohibited classification, such as being a woman or being black. It is unnecessary to demonstrate that the alleged discriminator intended to cause a disadvantage to the victim. The test adopted is the so-called 'but-for' test used to gauge **causation** generally in the civil law; if the victim would have received more favourable treatment but for their membership of a particular group, direct discrimination has occurred. Thus, in *James v Eastleigh Borough Council* (1990), it was established that the sixty-two-year-old Mr James experienced unlawful discrimination on the ground of his being a man when he was charged 75p for entry to a council swimming pool, in circumstances where his sixty-two-year-old wife was admitted free. The council operated a free entry scheme for those over the state pension age (then sixty for women, but sixty-five for men) and it intended no harm; however, but-for their policy, Mr James would have been able to swim free-of-charge. There are certain defences which are allowed to those alleged to have discriminated directly, but their ambit is strictly limited. The most important applies where it is essential to choose someone from a particular group in order to perform the relevant task, for example, the choice of Muslim for a position of imam.

The second approach taken by the law is an acknowledgement of the fact that it is not sufficient to treat people identically at the formal level, since certain groups experience such disadvantage that they are unable to compete in the race in the first place. The law also therefore strives for 'substantive' equality, which it tries to achieve via the concept of '**indirect discrimination**'. Although there are a number of different ways in which this notion is expressed technically, in essence it means that the courts must scrutinize practices which are operated by those making the kinds of decisions which are within the purview of equality law. If their practices impact adversely on a protected group, anyone belonging to that group who is in fact so disadvantaged has a legal claim. The only escape for the decision-maker is to justify the practice by showing that it was necessary and was not disproportionate.

The area in which this principle has found most application is that of part-time work. It has been customary to extend less generous employment rights to part-time workers than to full-timers, in particular in relation to pay and related benefits. On its face, such treatment is group neutral since it affects the position of anyone who works part-time. However, in practice, it impacts adversely on the situation of women as a group, because the practical division of domestic labour means that some 90 per cent of the part-time workforce is female. Any such practice must then be justified by the employer as necessary for the business and as achieving a goal which could not be attained by another, non-discriminatory route.

However, even prohibition of indirect discrimination fails to produce complete substantive equality in practice. Amongst the reasons, this is because it is a non-dynamic concept; it takes on board the practical situation of groups such as women, but it does nothing to alter their situation. The legal system therefore acknowledges that some further 'positive' acts are necessary to make the playing field more level in society. However, no consensus has yet clearly emerged as to the permissible limits of such action. Though many would agree that it is acceptable to undertake non-discriminatory action designed to encourage groups into areas not traditionally occupied by them, there is little or no agreement about more invasive mechanisms, such as the setting of goals or quotas. Still less is there agreement about the permissibility of reverse discrimination. However, Northern Ireland legislation is acknowledged to have been practically effective. This requires employers to record the participation rates of different groups within their organizations and thus alerts them to possible inequalities which it is within their ability to redress.   EVELYN ELLIS

equality and discrimination Although 'equality' and 'discrimination' are terms frequently invoked in public and political discourse, there is little consensus on what they mean. For some, **equality** is about people being treated in the same way, yet for others equality means the **recognition** of difference. **Legislation** has tended to focus on the prohibition of specific acts of discrimination. However, in recent years, public authorities have been placed under legal duties to promote 'equality'. This conveys the idea that equality is the ultimate objective, whereas actions or behaviour which obstruct the achievement of equality constitute discrimination. The difficulty lies in pinning down the contours of this end goal of equality; how would we know when and if it had been achieved? Academic literature has conventionally distinguished between two principal concepts of equality: **formal equality** and **substantive equality**.

Formal equality is premised on the notion that 'likes should be treated alike'. If two **persons** are in a comparable situation, then they should be treated in the same way, with no regard to irrelevant characteristics, such as **religion** or sexual orientation. In the employment context, this means that it constitutes discrimination to take into account such characteristics when making decisions on whom to hire, promote, or dismiss. Decisions should be fair and rational, based on merit. The simplicity of this concept makes it attractive and it tends to coincide with popular ideas of what amounts to unfair discrimination. Nevertheless, there are certain weaknesses with the formal equality concept, two of which are highlighted below.

First, formal equality is a relative concept based on being treated in the same way as another person. Therefore, it depends on identifying another person in a similar situation who has been treated more favourably and who has different personal characteristics (for instance, comparing the treatment of a **woman** with that of a man). In some circumstances, it may be very difficult in practice to locate an appropriate **comparator**. A woman seeking to make a claim for **equal pay** will find this impossible if no male comparator performing work of equal value works for the same employer. Moreover, formal equality assumes that the way in which the comparator is treated is a neutral standard. An employer whose uniform requirement forbids the wearing of any headgear by all employees will not infringe the concept of formal equality even though this may have the effect of excluding persons whose religious beliefs require them to cover their heads (eg certain Sikhs, Jews, and Muslims).

A second criticism of formal equality is that it focuses on the treatment of individuals. In the employment field, it supposes that fair procedures for allocating jobs and wages are sufficient. Yet, more than thirty years of legislation on **sex** and **race** discrimination in Great Britain has not resulted in labour market equality for women or ethnic **minority** communities. There are still large gaps in areas such as pay or employment rates. Whilst the reasons for the persistence of inequality are complex, it seems clear that there are structural factors affecting certain groups in society which go beyond the treatment of any given individual. For example, the unequal distribution of caring responsibilities between women and men is evidently linked to women's overrepresentation in part-time employment. Even if fair procedures are in operation, the organization of work is often based around a male norm. In particular, senior executive positions tend to be associated with long working hours that may be impossible to reconcile with childcare responsibilities.

Substantive equality aims to move beyond the emphasis on the 'sameness' of treatment found in the formal equality concept. Instead, it focuses on addressing the structural causes of inequality. In particular, there is an acknowledgement that socially entrenched forms of disadvantage undermine the ability of certain groups to compete on an equal basis. This implies that it is not sufficient to enact a prohibition on discrimination; instead, specific measures may be needed to redress past and present disadvantages. An example would be allowing greater flexibility in working hours for persons with caring responsibilities. This could assist women's participation in the labour market.

A range of tools may be used in pursuing substantive equality. A crucial distinction is between **positive action** and **positive discrimination**. Positive action is the term most commonly used to designate measures that seek to assist particular groups without providing unconditional preferential treatment. For instance, outreach schemes are used to encourage presently under-represented groups to apply for university places. Positive action would not, though, extend to preferential treatment in selection for university on the basis of sex, **ethnicity**, etc. Individual decisions must still be based on an objective assessment of the best qualified candidate. Measures that permit forms of preferential treatment are better described as positive discrimination. This would occur, for example, if a university decided to give a place to a suitably qualified disabled applicant, even if there was a better qualified applicant without a **disability**. In its strongest form, positive discrimination can result in quotas for specific groups in society.

The distinction between positive action and positive discrimination reveals a tension within the concept of substantive equality as to its ultimate goal. *Equality of opportunity* is consistent with the idea of compensatory measures in order to put disadvantaged groups in a position to compete on the same basis (for example) in the labour market. *Equal results* goes further, implying that substantive equality will only be achieved when all groups are fairly represented and enjoy a proportionate distribution of resources (such as jobs, housing, university places, etc). Strong forms of positive discrimination, notably quotas, clearly aim to achieve equal results rather than simply equality of opportunity. On the one hand, equal results is an inevitable benchmark for assessing whether equality exists within society. If some groups receive lower pay, poorer educational outcomes and live in worse housing, then that will be difficult to reconcile with the idea of equality. On the other hand, equal results in its most absolute form, that is, proportionate **representation** of all groups in all social goods, is a highly ambitious goal. Indeed, equal results is ultimately difficult to reconcile with a market-based economy.

In recent years, increasing emphasis has been placed on the impact of diversity on concepts of equality and discrimination. Namely, characteristics such as **gender**, ethnicity, and age are not experienced in isolation, but frequently combine in multiple **identities**. Such **persons** are vulnerable to 'multiple discrimination', that is, where disadvantage stems from a combination of **protected grounds**. This poses challenges for both formal and substantive equality. In terms of formal equality, the comparison of persons in like situations has in practice meant comparing women with men, disabled and non-disabled persons, etc. Where discrimination occurs on more than one ground, for example, against Asian women, then the process of comparison becomes more complex; should it be Asian men, non-Asian women, or non-Asian men? Similarly, substantive equality with its focus on group inequalities can lead to an assumption of distinct homogeneous groups (such as 'women', 'Muslims', or 'disabled people'). This tends to downplay diversity within such groups. For instance, Pakistani women in Britain are currently four or five times more likely to be unemployed than White women. Another challenge posed by diversity is the conflicts than can arise between grounds. A frequent example is religion and sexual orientation. In such circumstances, it may be difficult to find any consensus on what equality demands. Instead, the task may be to balance competing equality claims.

MARK BELL

S Fredman, *Discrimination Law* (Oxford: Oxford University Press, 2002) ch 1

J Squires, 'Equality and Difference' in J Dryzek, B Honig, and A Phillips (eds), *The Oxford Handbook of Political Theory* (Oxford: Oxford University Press, 2006) 470–487

equality and diversity The relationship between **equality**, diversity, and law raises fiendishly difficult questions of many kinds. While many would agree that **recognition** of the equal worth of individuals is one of the most important tenets of a civilized society, the depth of consensus on this point is perhaps only matched by the depth of disagreement about what it actually means. It would not be hard to characterize the great ideological battles of the last centuries as contests between differing conceptions of what is required and justified in pursuit of equality.

The contentious issues are legion. What does an individual's status as an equal entitle them to? To put it another way, what degree of material and symbolic inequality is sustainable in a **community** of equals? These questions have particular poignancy for systems claiming to be democratic, since the extent to which any polity is democratic depends on how far its members come to the political process as equals. The difficulties appear only more forbidding when the dramatic disparities in the innate **capacities** and propensities of **human** beings are acknowledged, and it is remembered that it is a constant of history that a **person's** life chances are arbitrarily distorted by irrelevant features of their **identity**.

In the face of such intractably difficult and deeply contested questions, it is unsurprising that the role of public policy, and hence of law, in delivering equality, is hotly debated. Discussion of diversity has played an increased role in recent years. This has its roots in the US, in judicial musings about affirmative action and in the thinking of management theorists. The important shift is to the idea that equality entails differences of all kinds being celebrated. This has not, of course, made the deep philosophical questions about equality go away; but it has highlighted that inclusiveness may be intrinsic to the more effective pursuit of that goal.

Turning to ways that the law has responded, it is difficult to know where to begin or, indeed, to end. Each time the law intervenes, or doesn't, it structures power relations, whether by bolstering or by altering the pre-existing position. This makes it arguable that there is as much, or more, reason for a discussion of equality and diversity to consider, for example, tax, property, or electoral law, as to look at laws that deal explicitly with this topic.

It is from this vantage point that any law that purports to work towards equality should be evaluated. In particular, it is dangerous to see any given legal intervention as saying the last word. Not only would such complacency fail to take underlying theoretical debates seriously, it is likely to obscure weaknesses in the existing approach.

There is no doubt that UK law which explicitly engages with equality, and increasingly diversity,

evidences an ongoing process of experimentation and revision. This has been influenced in important ways by EU law. But home-grown initiatives have been as significant. The **Race** Relations Act 1976, which built on 1960s **legislation,** addresses inequality based on colour, ethnic origin, **nationality**, national origin, and race. The **Equal Pay** Act 1970 and the **Sex** Discrimination Act 1975 jointly tackled inequality between the sexes. Protection for **transsexuals** was added more recently. These statutes have in fact continuously been updated. An important recent development, inspired by the Stephen Lawrence **Inquiry**, is that public authorities are under the duty to promote racial equality in various ways, with similar duties enacted in relation to **gender** and disability.

The Disability Discrimination Act 1995 concerns equality for people with disabilities. Only the disabled, as defined, are protected, whereas, for example, the Sex Discrimination Act 1975 protects both sexes. There is also now a duty on public authorities to promote equality for people with disabilities.

Northern Ireland has for some time had specific legislation on religious discrimination. More recently, the Employment Equality (**Religion** or Belief) Regulations 2003, the Employment Equality (Sexual Orientation) Regulations 2003, and the Employment Equality (Age) Regulations 2006, were passed regarding, respectively, religion, belief, sexual orientation, and age discrimination. These laws all initially focused on working life, but the Equality Act 2006 has now led to the laws on religion, belief, and sexual orientation having a broader ambit.

A major review of anti-discrimination legislation is under way, with plans for a Single Equality Act in the near future. Apart from anything else, this allows for consideration of the legal issue that is arguably the most contentious, ie how far the law should either permit or require organizations to take **positive action**, including **positive discrimination**, in the quest for equality or diversity.

LIZZIE BARMES

See also: **equality and discrimination**

Equality and Human Rights Commission ('EHRC')

The Equality and Human Rights Commission (originally called Commission of Equality and Human Rights) was established in 2007. Its purpose is to act as an independent body to champion respect for **human rights** and anti-discrimination principles, and to help ensure that the Human Rights Act 1998 and UK anti-discrimination **legislation** are enforced. In the field of **human** rights, it will work with the recently established Scottish Human Rights

Commission, which has exclusive responsibility for human rights matters that relate to Scottish devolved functions. However, the EHRC retains responsibility for promoting **equality** and enforcing compliance with anti-discrimination legislation throughout Britain. In Northern Ireland, the Equality Commission for Northern Ireland ('ECNI') carries out these functions, while the Northern Irish Human Rights Commission ('NIHRC') has responsibility for promoting and securing respect for human rights.

The EHRC replaces and absorbs the three previous existing British equality commissions, the Commission for Racial Equality ('CRE'), the Equal Opportunities Commission ('EOC', which had responsibility for **gender** equality) and the **Disability** Rights Commission ('DRC'). The CRE and the EOC had been established in the late 1970s for the purpose of promoting and enforcing compliance with the new **race** and **sex** discrimination legislation. The DRC was established later, in 1999. All three commissions have played a prominent role in promoting equality of opportunity, through media campaigns, the provision of advice and guidance, and the use of their legal enforcement powers.

The decision to merge these three commissions into a single unified commission, announced by the Government in the White Paper, *Fairness for All,* in May 2004, was initially controversial. The CRE, DRC, and some other campaigning organizations expressed strong concern that a monolithic single commission would ignore or overlook the special needs and perspectives of disadvantaged groups, and could also be more vulnerable to government interference. However, the Government argued that it made more sense to have a single commission working across the full range of equality issues than to maintain separate commissions, especially as a single commission would be better able to maximize resources and target overlapping, cross-strand and **multiple discrimination**. The decision was therefore taken to go ahead and establish the new EHRC by means of the Equality Act 2006, which also conferred some extended powers and functions on the new body to assuage some of its critics.

The EHRC is headed by a Chief Commissioner and between nine and fourteen other commissioners. These commissioners working together direct the work of the staff of the EHRC and set its policies and goals, with specialist Scottish, Welsh, and Disability Committees coordinating strategy in particular areas of activity. As was the case with the three previous equality commissions, the new body's commissioners are to be appointed by a government minister and will remain accountable to that

minister for how they spend public money. However, the Commission is to act as an independent body in deciding how it should perform its functions.

A similar organizational structure is in place for the Northern Irish Commissions and for the Scottish Human Rights Commission, except that the Scottish Commission is directly accountable to the **Scottish Parliament** and not to a particular government minister. During the passage of the Equality Act 2006 through Parliament, it was widely suggested that the status and independence of the new EHRC should be reinforced by making it also directly accountable to the **Westminster Parliament**, which would itself appoint the commissioners and decide the budget that the Commission should have. However, the Government rejected this suggestion, arguing that the EHRC would have sufficient independence under the existing arrangements that had also been in place for the CRE, EOC, and DRC.

When it comes to equality and anti-discrimination issues, the EHRC has similar functions as and marginally greater powers than those possessed by the CRE, EOC, and DRC. It can commission research on equality issues, promote good **community** relations, and campaign for greater equality of opportunity. The Commission can prepare codes of practice to give guidance on how to comply with the legislation, and can also give financial and legal support to anti-discrimination claims brought by individual claimants (within the limits of its resources). Due to the limited availability of **legal aid** for discrimination cases, this latter power is very important: it allows the Commission to ensure that ground-breaking or particularly significant cases are heard that might otherwise never be brought forward before the courts.

The Commission may enter into legally enforceable agreements with parties to avoid discriminatory treatment. It will also be able to carry out formal investigations into whether public authorities, employers, or providers of goods and services are complying with anti-discrimination law. In carrying out these investigations, the Commission can summon witnesses and conduct formal hearings. If it concludes that there has been a breach of the legislation, it can issue notices requiring the offending body to take specific steps to comply with the law: if necessary, these notices may be enforceable through the courts. The CRE, EOC, and DRC had similar powers but experienced great difficulty in carrying out investigations, due to complex procedural requirements. It remains to be seen whether the EHRC will be able to make better use of its streamlined and enhanced investigative powers.

The EHRC's powers in respect of human rights matters are more restricted. The Commission will be able to promote compliance with domestic and international human rights standards. It will also be able to carry out general **inquiries** into issues such as the treatment of **asylum** seekers that raise issues of relevance to human rights and/or anti-discrimination principles. It can also intervene in court cases that touch on human rights and/or anti-discrimination issues and seek **judicial review** against bodies performing public functions to enforce the **Human Rights Act** and anti-discrimination rules. However, the Commission will not be able to conduct formal investigations into alleged breaches of human rights law, and can only provide legal support to individual cases that raise human rights issues when they also are linked to anti-discrimination arguments. The Scottish Human Rights Commission has similar powers.

In contrast, however, both the NIHRC and the ECNI, while possessing powers equivalent to those of the EHRC, also have significant additional powers. For example, the NIHRC can provide support to individuals bringing human rights cases, while the ECNI has the power to assess compliance with the positive equality duties which have been imposed on public and private sector bodies in Northern Ireland. The EHRC lacks these additional powers. However, it will nevertheless play a crucial role in defending human rights and anti-discrimination principles in Britain, and its success will depend on whether it can make best use of the powers and resources that are available to it.   COLM O'CINNEIDE

equality duty   *see* **positive action**

equitable utilization of shared resources   *see* **international waterways and watercourses**

equity as a system of law   Equity lies at the heart of the **common law** legal system, yet experienced common lawyers still dread the question, What is equity? A short, intelligible answer is difficult. We know 'equity' is a body of law, and the word 'equity' evokes ideas of fairness and justice. But what sets equity apart?

The tag that equity is the conscience of the law reflects the history of equity's development. In medieval times, English 'common law' was administered in royal courts established by the king. The law in these courts was 'common law' because, in theory, it applied universally. But individuals dissatisfied with the outcome in these courts could petition the King, alleging that the rules had worked an injustice in their case. Since the King was regarded as the fount of justice, these pleas needed a considered response. The task was delegated to the Chancellor, the King's most powerful minister. He could order individuals not to act upon their common law rights but, instead, to act in some other more fair or just way. The precise form of the order was at the Chancellor's discretion. 'Equity' is the body of law that grew out of this delegated function.

The King's early reliance on the Chancellor had an important impact on equity's development. In medieval times the Chancellor was usually an cleric, familiar with **ecclesiastical law** and notions of **natural justice**, and instinctively concerned about matters of conscience. This recourse to 'conscience' is a hallmark of equity.

As the volume of Chancery business grew, and successive Chancellors saw the advantages of consistent decisions, so equity grew. Equity was clearly never an independent system of law, but an appendix and complement to the common law, and unintelligible apart from it. Even so, until the late nineteenth century, common law and equity judges operated from separate courts, adopting and applying different practices to meet the demands placed upon them. Even when the administration of the courts was finally fused, the substantive distinctions between the two bodies of law were retained.

Explained in this way, it might seem to be no more than an historical accident that common law and equity exist as two distinct bodies of law. Had the circumstances been different, the common law courts might themselves have masterminded the necessary evolutionary changes. The real issue, then, is whether equity's distinctive development has produced a distinctive product?

Certainly equity's approach is different. Initially, equity was only called upon to intervene when the common law rules were seen as inadequate. If equity reacted at all, it necessarily reacted differently from the common law. Its procedures, substantive rules, remedies, and enforcement techniques all differed from the common law's. At the substantive level, equity might declare a contract not binding even though it was binding at common law, or declare that a party owed obligations of confidentiality not recognized by the common law. When it came to **remedies**, equity largely ignored the common law practice of money remedies, and typically ordered the defendant to *do* something, to hand over an item of property, perform a contract, cease creating a nuisance, or sign a document. And if enforcement of these orders was needed, equity did not follow the common law practice of stripping wrongdoers of assets to the extent necessary to pay the damages owed, but instead regarded it as contempt of court to refuse to comply with equity's order. Historically, defendants could be thrown into prison for such contempt; this was powerful persuasion to comply. Indeed, in one of equity's most valuable developments, equity slowly took this idea of specific performance and specific enforcement to its logical extreme: if equity thought the claimant was entitled to certain property, then it would order the defendant to deliver the property to the claimant on pain of imprisonment for failure to do so. Because these orders *had* to be carried out, and the claimant *had* to receive the property, the orders were eventually seen as giving the claimant ownership of the property 'in equity' even before physical delivery by the defendant, and, eventually, even before the court had made its order. This technique effectively converted personal remedial obligations into property, and so the trust was born.

But none of these developments, however inspired, suggest an unbridgeable divide between the philosophy and jurisprudence of the two bodies of law. Yet this is what is often advanced as justification for maintaining the separation. The arguments invariably come down to two core assertions. Equity is said to be conscience-based, moral, and discretionary in ways that the common law is not. The argument has waged for years, and until it ends equity will remain distinct, and needing to be explained by common lawyers. SARAH WORTHINGTON

See also: **trusts; uses and trusts, history of**

equity finance and stock exchange listing *see* **listing; prospectus; public offer**

equity in pay and employment *see* **equal pay**

erga omnes obligations *see* **customary international law**

Erskine, Thomas Thomas Erskine, first Baron Erskine (1750–1823), barrister and **Lord Chancellor**, was born in Edinburgh, but left Scotland at the age of fourteen. After brief stints in both the Navy and the Army he was admitted to Lincoln's Inn and called to the bar in 1778. Success came quickly. In November of the same year he established himself as a powerful orator in a libel case involving a naval officer. In 1781 he secured the acquittal of Lord George Gordon, indicted for high treason. In 1783 Erskine was elected (Whig) MP for the Admiralty borough of Portsmouth. While his parliamentary career

suffered from regular (and almost immediate) interruption he continued to thrive in the courtroom, especially before a jury. Throughout the politically charged 1790s he championed freedom of the press and defended the radicals inspired by the French revolution, among them Thomas Hardy and John Horne Tooke, becoming something of a public hero in the process. Apart from seditious libel and treason trials his practice encompassed commercial cases and those of 'criminal conversation' (ie adultery). In Parliament, the flamboyant oratory and political radicalism of 'Counsellor Ego' were less appreciated; and Erskine endured various political humiliations. His appointment as Lord Chancellor in 1806 was controversial and his conduct in that briefly held office—he resigned in April 1807—timid. Erskine is remembered as an advocate rather than a politician or judge, for his persuasive ways with a jury, and for his vigorous defence of constitutional principles.

ALLYSON MAY

estate agents *see* **property misdescriptions**

estate duty *see* **inheritance tax**

estoppel The word 'estoppel' comes from medieval legal French. To 'estop' meant to close up, or to put a stopper in (eg a wine bottle). It denotes rules that prevent someone from saying or doing something he or she would normally be free to say or do.

Today we can identify two main forms of the doctrine. On the one hand there are rules which prevent a case or issue, once tried by a court, from being tried again. These are relatively formal rules aimed at enabling people to rely on the decisions of courts without having to re-litigate matters which have been brought to a close.

On the other hand, estoppel regulates statements and, in some restricted circumstances, promises. In relation to statements, estoppel operates as a rule of evidence. If A has made a statement of fact and B has relied on that statement, A cannot then contradict that statement in proceedings against B. In a nineteenth-century case (but with numerous obvious modern parallels) some horses were carried by rail, and their owner signed an insurance form confirming that they were worth less than £10. The horses were injured in transit. Their owner was estopped from claiming their true value of £40, because the railway company had carried them on the basis that they were worth £10.

The enforcement of promises is regulated by the law of contract, and by the rule that requires consideration in the form of a bargain between the parties.

By contrast, the mere fact that someone has relied on my promise (without bargaining for it) does not, in English law, mean that I have to keep it. If A promises to give B £2,000, and in reliance on that promise B buys a piano, A still does not have to keep the promise to make the gift. This means that it is not normally possible to enforce a promise using estoppel.

There are two exceptions. One concerns a promise not to enforce an already existing contractual obligation. In a case from the 1940s, a landlord told tenants that they need pay only half of their rent for the duration of the war. Later the landlord tried to go back on that promise and recover the rent arrears, but was estopped from doing so because the tenants had relied on the promise. This is known as promissory estoppel. In English law, unlike US law, it cannot be used to create new obligations.

The other exception concerns a promise to grant an interest in land. This is known as proprietary estoppel, and can create new rights. Where A promises B that land will be B's, and B spends money or does work in reliance on that promise, A will be estopped from going back on the promise and will be ordered to put it into effect. This works in a range of contexts. The promise might be to share a house with a partner; to make a gift by will or, in a more commercial context, to allow a tenant to renew a lease when not formally entitled to do so. Proprietary estoppel is a fast-developing area of the law.

ELIZABETH COOKE

See also: **contract law**

ethnic cleansing   *see* **international humanitarian law**

ethnic minorities   *see* **minorities**

ethnicity   Ethnicity or ethnic identity is based on an assumed common ancestry or genealogy. Ethnic groups or **communities** are usually identified on the basis of common linguistic, cultural, religious, behavioural, or biological traits. Ethnicity is also often a defining criterion in conflicts between various national or racial groups—indeed 'ethnocide' and 'ethnic cleansing' are terms devised to explain cultural **genocide** and physical extermination of specific groups. **International law** and domestic **constitutional laws** have struggled to advance acceptable definitions of ethnicity. In its initial phase, international instruments preferred to use 'race' as criterion for non-discrimination. The **United Nations** Universal Declaration of **Human Rights** (1948) did not mention 'ethnicity' as a ground for non-discrimination. Nor is the concept of 'ethnicity' referred to in the Council of Europe's **European Convention on Human Rights** (1950). However, over a period of time, a growing consensus emerged within the UN that 'ethnicity' was a more appropriate word since it referred to all historical, cultural, and biological traits, in contrast to 'race' which was limited to inherited physical characteristics. The concept of ethnicity has been increasingly deployed in the UN **human** rights instruments. The Genocide Convention (1948) uses the term 'ethnicity' to cover cultural, physical, and historical characteristics of a group. Article 27 of the **International Covenant on Civil and Political Rights** (1966) which is the main provision in international law aimed at the provision of direct protection of **minorities**, protects ethnic (as well as religious and linguistic) minorities. The **International Convention on the Elimination of All forms of Racial Discrimination** (1965), as its title confirms, focuses on the elimination and prohibition of racial discrimination. In defining 'racial discrimination' the Convention nevertheless prohibits distinctions based, *inter alia*, on race or ethnic origin attempting a comprehensive prohibition.

In the United States, related groups from Latin America or Black and 'African-Americans' are accorded a collective ethnic identification. In the United Kingdom, the classification of ethnic groupings has proved controversial. Within the legislative framework of Race Relations Act 1976, discrimination is impressible on grounds which include ethnic or national origin. English **courts** have established that while Sikhs, Jews, and Gypsies are regarded as ethnic groups, Christians and Muslims are too diverse to be identified on the basis of ethnicity. The UK national statistics classification contains the terms White, Mixed, Asian, Black, and Chinese as broad categories with which to define ethnicity. Countries with much larger populations such as China and India also have had difficulties in defining and providing rights for distinct ethnic groups. The Peoples Republic of China officially recognizes fifty-six ethnic groups, constitutionally recognizing them as **nationalities**. In India, ethnicity is reflected in such varied forms as religious distinctions and from within the caste-system prevalent amongst majority Hindus. India's neighbour, Pakistan, has always (even prior to the secession of East Pakistan in 1970) refused officially to recognize the existence of any ethnic or racial groups—the constitutional position being that the state only contains a Muslim majority and a small (currently 3 per cent) non-Muslim religious minority.

JAVAID REHMAN

ethnicity and crime Ethnicity and crime are often linked in the public imagination. In nineteenth-century England, the belief that Irish people were responsible for rising crime led pundits to coin the term 'hooligan' to describe a newly discovered anti-social type. In the twentieth century, high levels of criminality were attributed first to Jews, Irish, Cypriots, and Maltese, later to West Indians, Turks, and Russians and, most recently, to Eastern Europeans and 'foreign criminals' in general. Criminological theorists too have long been preoccupied with ethnicity, from Cesare Lombroso's 'criminal anthropology' to the ecological theories of the **Chicago School** and contemporary cultural criminology.

Debate in this criminological sub-field has focused on criminal behaviour, but ethnic differences in patterns of victimization have also been examined. Victimologists have found that people from ethnic minority **communities** tend to be at greater risk of property and violent crime. However, once social and demographic factors such as area of residence and social class have been accounted for, the differences between groups tend to diminish. That is, high rates of crime within ethnic **minority** communities result largely from their concentration into urban areas with high rates of poverty and income inequality.

Much crime is intra-ethnic. The vast majority of UK **homicides,** for example, are 'white on white' killings and in most other cases **victim** and offender are from the same ethnic group. The most obvious exception is racist **violence** targeted specifically at minorities. Violence motivated or aggravated by racism has a long history in the UK with attacks directed against ethnic minority groups common at points throughout the twentieth century. The problem became an increasing focus of public debate during the 1970s and 1980s and reached the top of the political agenda during the *Stephen Lawrence Inquiry* (Cmnd 4262–1, HMSO (1999)) when the extent of the problem and the failure of the **police** and **courts** to provide an effective response were revealed.

Discussions of **ethnicity** and crime are closely linked with issues of racism and discrimination in the **criminal justice system**. In many countries, people from ethnic minority communities are over-represented in police, court, and **prison** statistics. In the UK, for example, black people are six times more likely to be stopped and searched by the police than would be expected from their numbers in the general population; they are three times as likely to be arrested and five times as likely to be imprisoned. Among the most frequently asked questions in this field is how far do these disparities reflect differences in patterns of crime and to what extent are they the result of discrimination in policing, the courts, and prisons?

In a world of growing global mobility, ethnic segregation, social inequality, and anxiety about crime, **terrorism,** and insecurity, talk about ethnicity and crime seems set to continue. The challenge for the future is to ensure that this discussion yields policies that protect ethnic minorities and include them fully in economic and social life rather than entrench long-standing patterns of social exclusion and criminalization.   BEN BOWLING

G Pearson, *Hooligan* (London: Macmillan, 1983)
B Bowling and C Phillips, *Racism, Crime & Justice* (Harlow: Longman, 2002)

See also: **racial and ethnic minorities in the criminal justice system**

Euro *see* **Economic and Monetary Union**

europe 'a la carte' *see* **closer cooperation in the EU**

European arrest warrant *see* **extradition**

European broadcasting regulation Two international organizations, the Council of Europe ('CoE') and the European Community ('EC'), have been active in regulating the broadcast media at the European level. Neither institution, however, has a specific mandate in relation to broadcasting. The basis for CoE intervention stems from its commitment to safeguarding **democracy**, fundamental **human rights**, in particular **freedom of expression**, and cultural diversity. The CoE is able to influence the policies of its sixty-four Member States by facilitating the adoption of **treaties** and passing non-binding recommendations. It has worked closely with a number of Central and East European countries in reforming their media laws. The EC, with twenty-seven members, has instead relied primarily on the economic and industrial objectives set out in its founding Treaty. Its main priority has been to facilitate the creation of a pan-European market for television services and to foster the development of Europe's broadcasting industry. Implementation of these objectives has been facilitated by recourse to regulations, directives and decisions that can create directly enforceable rights and obligations. Although the EC originally had no remit to promote cultural objectives—the present article on culture in the EC Treaty was added only in 1992—it has throughout regarded broadcasting as important, not only as a means to reflect Europe's cultural diversity, but also, and more contentiously, as a tool to foster European identity. Commercial initiatives have thus been tempered, to varying degrees, by cultural considerations.

CoE and EC **regulation** of television broadcasting can be traced back to political and technical changes that took place in Europe during the 1980s. The period was characterized by, on the one hand, a commercialization of domestic broadcasting markets, with private operators increasingly competing with established public service broadcasters; and, on the other, the development of direct-to-home satellite and cable services, facilitating the transmission of television channels across borders. Attempts by states to prevent their citizens receiving these foreign services were challenged by commercial operators before the **European Court of Human Rights** as an unlawful restriction on freedom of expression under the **European Convention on Human Rights** ('ECHR'), and before the **Court of Justice**, as an unwarranted restriction on freedom to provide services under the EC Treaty. These cases confirmed that states could lawfully restrict foreign services in order to pursue certain public interest objectives such as media pluralism, provided such measures were proportionate; but that restrictions designed simply to protect the economic interests of their domestic broadcasting industry would be unacceptable.

Given that states retained some freedom to restrict foreign broadcasts, there was a risk that cross-border television services might continue to be obstructed. In 1989 the CoE and EC cooperated in responding to this risk by adopting the Transfrontier Television Convention and Television Without Frontiers ('TWF') Directive respectively. These measures, amended in the late 1990s, are broadly similar in content and approach. The Convention and Directive seek to ensure that broadcasters are regulated by one country only: that in which they are established. They also set out minimum content standards which all broadcasters are required to meet. These comprise quotas for European and independent programmes; restrictions on the amount, placement, and content of advertising, sponsorship, and teleshopping; prohibitions on programmes damaging to children and hate speech; and a requirement that broadcasters provide a right of reply.

The European quota provisions, which require states 'where practicable and by appropriate means' to ensure that broadcasters under their jurisdiction allocate a majority proportion of their transmission time to European programmes, illustrate some of the difficulties in realizing the industrial and cultural objectives underpinning the Convention and Directive. The quota was primarily a response to the success of US programmes, such as 'Dallas', on television stations across Europe. The scale of the US market enables producers to recoup most of the cost of high-quality productions domestically and then to offer these programmes at competitive prices on European markets. Although data supplied by the **European Union** Member States suggest that on average the quota is comfortably met, compliance remains variable, with, for example, less than 50 per cent of relevant channels in the UK meeting the quota threshold. Cultural and linguistic barriers continue to impede the circulation of European programmes across Europe, with limited transmission of non-domestic European programmes, particularly in the larger European markets such as Germany and the UK.

The Convention and Directive apply solely to 'television broadcasting', which covers the transmission of television programmes, by air or wire, according to a schedule fixed by the broadcaster. Services that enable the viewer to select television programmes from a catalogue 'on-demand' are not included. In the EC context such services are covered by the 2000 Electronic Commerce Directive. The Electronic Commerce Directive, whose main objective is to regulate the liability of intermediary internet service providers, does not establish minimum standards in the fields covered by the TWF Directive. With the facility to manipulate television broadcasting schedules using personal video recorders and the growing availability over the internet of previously scheduled programmes, the distinction between scheduled and on-demand television services has began to look unconvincing. In December 2005 the European Commission consequently proposed a new Audiovisual Media Services Directive, designed to extend certain basic requirements in the TWF Directive to on-demand television programme services, available over the internet or on mobile phones. Also envisaged is a relaxation of the existing advertising restrictions, allowing, for example, spot advertising in unscheduled breaks in football matches, and some product placement.

The European Community has increasingly emphasized the role of self-regulation and co-regulation (self-regulation with a degree of public oversight) in the communications sector. This is reflected in its approach to child protection, set out in its Safer Internet Plus Programme (2005–2008). The Programme supports the establishment and coordination of hotlines across Europe for the reporting of illegal content, and the development of rating and filtering systems that can be used by parents to block their children's access to unsuitable programme material.

Both the CoE and EC have sought to influence the structure of European broadcasting markets, as well as the content of broadcasting services. In 2002 the EC introduced an ambitious package of five directives governing electronic communications networks and services. In particular, the package provides digital television and radio broadcasters with rights to access key technical facilities needed to make contact with the audience. The EC has also supported the development by industry of technical standards, notably regarding television transmission systems, and has become increasingly active in coordinating Member State policies regarding the use of the radio spectrum.

The EC has been less successful in its attempts to address concerns over growing concentration in media ownership. The political sensitivity of the issue, diverse national markets and divergent national regulations made agreement on a directive impossible. Instead, interest groups and frustrated broadcasters have employed **human rights** to highlight the lack of diversity in certain media markets. The EC does not have a mandate to directly protect human rights, but respect for human rights is one of the founding principles of the **European Union**, and the EC has become increasingly active in monitoring member state compliance. Freedom of expression and media pluralism are explicitly recognized in the European Union's Charter of Fundamental Rights. Although the European Court of Human Rights held (in *Informationsverein Lentia and others v Austria* (1994)) that Austria's total broadcasting monopoly contravened the right to freedom of expression under the ECHR, it subsequently afforded states considerable latitude in determining how much competition to allow in their broadcasting sectors.

Though the EC was unable to agree a media ownership directive, it has reviewed a number of major media mergers in Europe through the application of its **competition** rules and the Merger Regulation. European Commission competition decisions reveal a concern to ensure that media markets remain open to new entrants and that ownership of distribution networks and intellectual property rights, in particular rights to popular music, sporting events, and films, are not exploited in order to exclude competitors.

The EC's commitment to open and competitive markets has brought it into conflict with Member States over their funding of public service broadcasting. All forms of public finance, including licence fees, potentially constitute illegal **state aid**. Such aid can, however, be justified if it pursues certain public interest objectives and is proportionate. Community review of the financing of a number of European public service broadcasters, including the **British Broadcasting Corporation**, has encouraged the Member States to introduce clearer remits for their public service broadcasters, to ensure that such broadcasters do not use public funds to subsidize their commercial activities, and do not foreclose competing commercial services without a convincing public interest rationale. With public service broadcasters diversifying to provide new internet and mobile services, however, continuing tensions with commercial operators can be expected.

RACHAEL CRAUFURD SMITH

European Central Bank   The European Central Bank ('ECB') in Frankfurt sets the monetary policy of the Eurozone, the EU countries that participate in **Economic and Monetary Union**, and it sits at the head of the European System of Central Banks ('ESCB'), which also includes the national central banks of those countries. The primary objective of the ESCB is to maintain price stability. The basic tasks are to define and implement the monetary policy of the Community; to conduct foreign exchange operations; to hold and manage the official foreign reserves of the Member States; and to promote the smooth operation of payment systems. Within the Eurozone, the ECB has the exclusive right to authorize the issue of bank notes, which are issued by the ECB and participating national central banks. With regard to coins the participating Member States may issue coins subject to ECB approval of the volume of issue.

The ECB and its members are subject to a strong requirement of independence. When exercising the powers and carrying out the tasks and duties conferred upon them by the Treaty and the Statute of the ESCB, neither the ECB, nor a national central bank, nor any member of their decision-making bodies may seek or take instructions from Community institutions or bodies, from any government of a Member State or from any other body. Conversely, the Community institutions and bodies and the governments of the Member States undertake not to seek to influence the members of the decision-making bodies of the ECB or of the national central banks in the performance of their tasks.

The Treaty goes on to require that the statutes of the national central banks should provide that the term of office of a Governor of a national central bank shall be no less than five years. Furthermore, a Governor may be relieved from office only if he no longer fulfils the conditions required for the performance of his duties or if he has been guilty of serious misconduct. Such a dismissal may be referred to the **European Court of Justice** by the Governor concerned, or the Governing Council of the ECB—a unique example of a national official becoming subject to Community jurisdiction.

There are limits to this independence: when the ECB claimed that its independence under the **EC Treaty** meant that it was not subject to an European Parliament ('EP') and Council Regulation concerning investigations conducted by the European Anti-Fraud Office ('OLAF'), it was held that while the ECB had independence in relation to the exercise of its specific powers, that did not have the consequence of separating it entirely from the EC and exempting it from every rule of Community law.

The ESCB is governed by the decision-making bodies of the ECB which are the Governing Council and the Executive Board. However, as long as there are non-participant Member States, the General Council of the ECB forms a third decision-making body, involved only in matters such as accession to the Eurozone. The Governing Council of the ECB comprises the members of the ECB Executive Board and the Governors of the national central banks of participating Member States. The Executive Board comprises the President, the Vice-President, and four other members by common accord of the governments of participating Member States at the level of heads of state or of government. Their term of office is eight years and may not be renewed. The initial appointments were staggered, so members would not all be replaced at the same time. The Governing Council formulates the monetary policy of the Community, and the Executive Board implements monetary policy in accordance with the guidelines and decisions laid down by the Governing Council.

JOHN A USHER

European Commission   The European Commission is one of the major institutions of the European Union, together with the **European Parliament**, the Council, and Court of Justice. The European Commission is a political institution which means that is involved in the legislative process.

Although often described as the Executive of the EU, the Commission's role cannot be compared to traditional domestic institutions. It has three main tasks. First, it supervises the implementation of the internal market by ensuring the application of the Treaty and secondary **legislation** (Article 211 EC);

for this purpose it will initiate infringement procedures against Member States (Article 226 EC) and will accordingly issue **fines** (Article 228 EC). Secondly, the Commission has a legislative role: it proposes policy directions and in this respect is arguably the driving force behind EU integration. Thirdly, the Commission can also enforce competition rules, a task that it shares with the domestic National Competition Authorities.

Following the 2004 EU enlargement to twenty-five countries, the Commission is formed by twenty-five Commissioners, one from each Member State: a President, five vice-presidents, and nineteen other Members. They are appointed every five years. The Commissioners have normally held political positions in their countries of origin, often at ministerial level. This composition will change in 2014 when the Commission will be composed of a number of Commissioners corresponding to two thirds of the number of Member States. Commissioners will be chosen on a equal rotation basis. Although appointed by their national governments, Commissioners represent the interests of the EU rather than those of their Member States. The Commission operates under a principle of collective **responsibility** and is politically answerable to the European Parliament, which has the power to dismiss it by adopting a motion of censure. This happened in 1999 when the whole Commission was forced to resign following the publication of a powerful report initiated by the European Parliament investigating corruption. This affair prompted the publication of a blueprint for reform of the Commission in the form of a White Paper as well as more general discussion of the role of the institutions in a changing EU. In 2004 the Commission was again in the spotlight when the European Parliament objected to the proposed appointment of the Italian nominee, Rocco Buttiglione, for the Freedom, **Security** and **Justice** portfolio on the grounds that he had expressed personal opinions that conflicted with his function as Commissioner with prime responsibility for fundamental rights. As a consequence, Buttiglione was replaced and his nomination withdrawn by Italian government.

EUGENIA CARRACCIOLO DI TORELLA

J Temple-Lang, 'How much do the Smaller Member States Need the European Commission? The Role of the Commission in a Changing Europe' (2002) 39 *Common Market Law Review* 315

European communities   *see* **European treaties**

European Community law   The 'European Community' is the legal successor to the 'European

Economic Community', which was set up by the **EC Treaty** (or Treaty of Rome) 1957, to secure peace in Europe, by bringing together ('integrating') the economies of its Member States into a common or **single market**. In order to achieve this, the Member States agreed (in the EC Treaty) to be bound by European Community law, as interpreted by European Community institutions, in particular the **European Court of Justice**, which sits in Luxembourg.

European Community Law is found in the EC Treaty (primary EC law) and in various Regulations, Directives, and Decisions (secondary EC law) adopted by the **Council of Ministers**, the **European Parliament,** and the **European Commission**, which, acting together, comprise the European Community legislature. Regulations are intended to be generally binding in Member States, without further action on the part of national **Parliaments.** They become part of the 'law of the land' automatically. Decisions apply to specific actors, or categories of actors, such as importers or exporters. According to the EC Treaty, directives are supposed to place an obligation to achieve a particular regulatory result on the governments of Member States, but leave to Member States the choice of form and method in so doing. However, in practice, many directives are framed in quite specific terms.

If the Lisbon Treaty 2007 is ratified, the EC Treaty will be renamed the Treaty on the Functioning of the European Union, and the EC will become the European Union, or 'the Union'. Most of European Community law is concerned with trade. It covers provisions to ensure that goods and services may be freely traded across the single European market; that **companies** and professionals may carry out their business in any Member State; that capital is able to move freely between Member States; and that anti-competitive practices are prohibited. However, it also concerns wider policies such as those relating to agriculture, transport, the environment, **consumer** protection, and employment.

A special feature of European Community law is that—unlike ordinary **international law** which essentially consists of agreements between states—it confers rights and obligations on individuals within the Member States of the European Union. It is a condition of membership of the EU that national **courts** and **tribunals** must uphold these rights and enforce these obligations. Moreover, European Community law applies in priority over conflicting rules of national law. These principles of European Community law are controversial, because they are not found explicitly in the EC Treaty (agreed by the governments of the Member States), but were 'discovered' therein by the European Court of Justice (*Van Gend*

en Loos (1963)). However, they have been accepted by courts in Member States, including in the UK by the **House of Lords**. 'Under the terms of the [European Communities] Act of 1972, it has always been clear that it was the duty of a United Kingdom court, when delivering final judgment, to override any rule of national law found to be in conflict with any directly enforceable rule of Community law' (Lord Bridge of Harwich in *R v Secretary of State for Transport, ex p Factortame* (1991)).   TAMARA HERVEY

See also: **European Community legal instruments**

European Community legal instruments   A novel feature of the EU legal system is the **capacity** of its institutions, acting independently of Member States, to adopt binding instruments. The EU institutions cannot make use of that capacity whenever they wish but only when expressly or impliedly given the power to do so. Provisions granting the institutions such powers are called legal bases and may be contained in the **Treaties** themselves or in existing instruments adopted under the Treaties. Legal bases typically specify the institution empowered to act, the procedure it must follow in order to do so, and the type of instrument that must be used (although sometimes the institution is allowed to choose the instrument). Where an institution is alleged to have acted outside the scope of the legal basis on which it relied, the legality of the resulting instrument may be challenged in the **European Court of Justice** or the Court of First Instance.

In practical and legal terms, the most significant instruments are regulations, directives, and decisions adopted under the EC Treaty.

- Regulations have general application and produce legal effect on their own terms from the moment they are adopted. They may impose obligations on public bodies and private parties which, if sufficiently clear, can be enforced before the national **courts** of Member States.

- Directives are addressed to Member States and require them to achieve a given result within a fixed deadline. In theory, Member States are free to choose how this is done, but in practice directives have become increasingly prescriptive, so the choice available to the national authorities may be limited. The obligations imposed by a directive on Member States and public bodies may, if they are clear enough, be enforced before the national courts, particularly where the directive has not been implemented within the deadline laid down in it. Directives cannot be directly enforced in the national courts against private bodies or individuals. However, national rules which overlap with a directive must be interpreted as far as possible in a way which renders them consistent with it. Moreover, private bodies and individuals may not rely in the national courts on a breach by a Member State of its own substantive obligations under a directive. Directives may therefore have an indirect effect in national litigation between private parties.

• Decisions are binding in their entirety on those to whom they are addressed, against whom they may be enforced in the national courts.

Like the EC Treaty itself, binding instruments adopted under it may take precedence over inconsistent provisions of national law, regardless of the domestic legal status of such provisions or their date of adoption.

Different types of instrument may be adopted under the EU Treaty, but their legal effects are more limited than those of instruments adopted under the EC Treaty. If the Treaty of Lisbon enters into force, all instruments adopted by the EU institutions will take the form of those adopted under the EC Treaty (to be renamed Treaty on the Functioning of the European Union).   ANTHONY ARNULL

Sacha Prechal, *Directives in EC Law* (Oxford: Oxford University Press, 2nd edn, 2005)

See also: **European Community law**

European Community powers   The subject matter areas in which the EC has power to act have increased over time. The core remains the four freedoms: free movement of workers, goods, and capital, and freedom of establishment and the provision of services. There also titles of the Treaty according the Community power in areas as diverse as: agriculture; transport; **visas**, **asylum**, and immigration; **competition**; tax; **economic and monetary union**; employment; common commercial policy; customs cooperation; environment; **public health**; social policy, education and vocational training, and youth; consumer protection; culture; economic and social cohesion; development cooperation; and economic cooperation with third countries. In addition the EU has power under Pillar 2 in relation to Common Foreign and Security Policy, and in Pillar 3 in relation to Police and Judicial Cooperation in Criminal Matters.

The EU only has the powers attributed to it. It can therefore only act within the limits of its power as laid down by the relevant Treaty article. Thus Article 5 EC states that the Community shall act within the limits of the powers conferred upon it by the Treaty and of the objectives assigned to it therein. A regulation, decision or directive will therefore always stipulate the Treaty article on which it is based. It can nonetheless be difficult to discern the limits of the EU's power for a number of reasons.

First, Treaty articles may be drafted relatively specifically, or they may be framed in more broad open-textured terms, and thus there may be disagreement about the ambit, scope, or interpretation of the relevant Treaty article, more especially so when it is cast in broad terms, as exemplified by the *Working Time Directive* case (*United Kingdom v Council* (1996)). The **European Court of Justice** has generally been disinclined to place limits on broadly worded Treaty articles. It can however do so, as exemplified by the *Tobacco Advertising* case, in which the ECJ held that a directive relating to tobacco advertising could not be based on Article 95 EC (*Germany v European Parliament and Council* (2000)). Subsequent case law on related subject matter has nonetheless shown that the ECJ will accept the use of Article 95 as the legal basis for the enacted measure (*R v Secretary of State for Health, ex p. Swedish Match* (2004)) and the ECJ has interpreted the Community's competence in broad terms (*Germany v European Parliament and Council* (2006)).

Secondly, the Treaty has not traditionally contained a neat list demarcating which competences are exclusive to the EC, and which are shared with Member States. The reality is that many of the competences are shared rather than exclusive, and in some instances the non-exclusive nature of these powers is made express, especially in relation to the newer competences granted to the EC. The precise division of competence between the EC and Member States varies in different subject matter areas, and is often drawn in imprecise terms. It may therefore be contestable whether a measure falls within the sphere allocated to the Community or to the Member States. This question is decided ultimately by the ECJ.

Thirdly, the ECJ has accepted a doctrine of implied power, whereby the existence of a given power implies the existence of any other power that is reasonably necessary for the exercise of the former. Moreover the existence of a given objective or function implies the existence of any power reasonably necessary to attain it (*Fédération Charbonnière de Belgique v High Authority* (1956); *Germany v Commission* (1987)).

The fourth reason why delineation of Community powers can be difficult is because of Article 308 EC, which provides that 'if action by the Community should prove necessary to attain, in the course of the operation of the common market, one of the objectives of the Community and this Treaty has not provided the necessary powers, the Council shall, acting unanimously on a proposal from the Commission and after consulting the **European Parliament**, take the appropriate measures'. Thus Article 308 was used to legitimate Community **legislation** in areas such as the environment and regional policy, before these matters were dealt with through later Treaty amendments.

A fifth reason why demarcation of the scope of Community power has become more difficult is because of the existence of the Three Pillars. There is an increasing overlap between the Pillars, and measures may be adopted under the Community Pillar where the primary objective is to support action taken under the Second or Third Pillars. This can lead to claims that the Community measure did not properly fall within the sphere of the relevant Treaty article.

The final reason for difficulty in discerning the limits to Community power relates to the Community's external competence. The rules concerning when the Community has power to make a Treaty with another international organization, or with a non-Member State, are complex, and this is even more so in relation to whether such Community competence is exclusive, thereby precluding Member States from making such agreements in their own name.

The Constitutional Treaty (2004) ('CT') attempted to provide greater clarity through provisions that dealt more systematically with the scope of Community competence. The CT retained the central principle that the EU operates on the basis of attributed competence. It then set out different categories of competence and assigned subject matter areas to each category: the EU could have exclusive competence; it could share competence with the Member States; the EU could be limited to taking supporting/coordinating action; and there were special categories for EU action in the sphere of economic and employment policy, and the CFSP. The CT also attached concrete consequences in terms of EU and state power to legislate in relation to each head of competence.

The CT did not become a reality because of the negative referenda in France and the Netherlands. The great majority of the CT's provisions, including those on the division of competence, were however taken into the Lisbon Treaty, on which the Member States reached agreement in December 2007. The Treaty must be ratified in an all Member States, and if this occurs it will enter into force in January 2009.

PAUL CRAIG

See also: **pillars of the European Union; Constitution for Europe**

European Community taxation The European Community ('EC') has, subject to some limited exceptions, no power to levy taxes on businesses, individuals, or consumption within the Member States; and it is clear that, at present, the chance that such a power will be created is politically extremely remote. This means that the subject of EC taxation is largely concerned with the ways in which the taxing powers of each Member State are constrained or influenced by the rules of the EC.

The abolition of customs duties within the European Economic Community ('EEC') and the introduction of common tariffs with the rest of the world was one of the cornerstones of the **Treaty of Rome**, which established the EEC in 1957. Since then, the thrust towards the single market has had a significant impact on the internal tax systems of Member States, although domestic taxation remains an important symbol of national sovereignty, and Member States have often strongly resisted proposals for greater harmonization across the EC.

Within the EC, indirect and direct taxation have followed rather different patterns. Indirect taxation, in the form of consumption taxes and customs duties, forms a very visible barrier to cross-border trade; and, from the very start, a common system of consumption tax in the form of **value added tax** ('VAT') was imposed on Member States of the EC. The details of VAT are contained in directives and regulations, and whilst each Member State has a limited leeway over its implementation, its introduction has reduced the economic distortions of cross-border trade to a significant extent. The structure and base of the tax, and the treatment of cross-border transactions, are fundamentally the same in each Member State. A residual freedom over the rate of VAT remains, although the main rate must be between 15 per cent and 25 per cent. However, the different administrative requirements in each Member State continue to be a hindrance to cross-border trade, especially for smaller businesses. **Excise duties**, the other main form of indirect taxation, are significantly less harmonized, creating incentives for individuals to shop across borders and, of course, for smuggling.

In contrast, direct taxation, in particular **corporation tax** and **income tax**, were not tackled at the birth of the EC for two reasons. First, whilst the existence of very different tax systems in each Member State undoubtedly forms a barrier to the single market, this barrier is much less visible than that created by indirect taxes; and it was therefore, less urgently addressed. Secondly, whilst there was consensus that VAT was the appropriate system for taxing consumption, there was no such consensus over many important areas of direct taxation, for example as to whether the taxpayer's jurisdiction should give relief for foreign tax paid by way of credit or whether foreign income should simply be exempt from taxation. Similarly, there was no consensus over the appropriate taxation of payments between companies and their shareholders. As a result, there was virtually no reference to direct taxation in the Treaty of Rome.

Since then, the **European Commission** has been active in putting forward proposals for EC legislation to deal with direct tax problems generated by cross-border activities, although with limited success. One continued difficulty is the 'veto' in relation to direct taxation: no legislation may be passed unless all Member States are in favour. This has led to suggestions that a 'two-speed' tax Community may eventually develop.

In contrast, the **European Court of Justice** has indirectly had more impact on the tax systems of Member States. It was noted above that the Treaty of Rome contained little on direct taxes; but it does provide for the four freedoms (freedom of movement of goods, persons, services, and capital), and hindrances to these freedoms have formed the basis of many successful challenges to the domestic tax systems of Member States.   SARAH EDEN

European Competition Network In 2004 a 'modernization programme' for the enforcement of EC **competition** rules came into effect, introducing a new decentralized regime in which the rules are enforced by the **European Commission**, which retained a degree of pre-eminence, but also by its fellow national administrative competition authorities ('NCAs') and by national courts. Uniformity, or harmony, of enforcement is sought by a system of compulsory 'close cooperation' between the Commission and NCAs, involving exchange of documents, information, allocation of work (to the authority, or authorities, best placed effectively to act), and the provision of assistance to and from the Commission and amongst the NCAs themselves.

Underpinning this extensive collaboration is the European Competition Network ('ECN'), initiated at the time of the adoption of the modernization Regulation by a joint statement of the EU Council and the Commission; it therefore has no formal basis and creates neither rights nor obligations. The ECN comprises the Commission and the principal NCAs in each of the twenty-seven Member States (for example, the **Office of Fair Trading** in the UK, the *Bundeskartellamt* in Germany). Within its framework there is now an annual meeting of the Director-General of the **Directorate-General for Competition** and the heads of all NCAs to discuss important policy issues, plenary meetings for discussion of general issues, working groups, and thirteen sectoral subgroups (banking, securities, insurance, food, pharmaceuticals, professional services, healthcare, environment, energy, railways, motor vehicles, telecoms, and media). It has begun to develop pan-network programmes, for example a 2006 model leniency programme for **cartel** whistleblowers.   ROBERT LANE

See also: **EC competition law, modernization of**

European Constitution   *see* **Constitution for Europe**

European Convention on Human Rights The European Convention on Human Rights ('ECHR') has created the most sophisticated and successful international system of guaranteeing fundamental rights so far developed in the world. The origins of the ECHR lay in the desires of European politicians and civic leaders to proclaim and protect such rights in the aftermath of the gross rights violations by the Nazis and their allies, together with the subsequent threats posed by totalitarian communist regimes in central and eastern Europe. The ECHR, a treaty, was drafted by the Council of Europe (an older and larger organization of European states than the European Union) during 1949–1950. The ECHR sets out basic **civil and political rights** including the **right to life**, prohibition of **torture**, **slavery**, and forced labour, liberty, fair trial, respect for private/**family life**, freedom of thought/religion, and **freedom of assembly** and association. These rights have subsequently been expanded by additional Protocols to the Convention which states can also choose to ratify (eg to abolish the death penalty). States which become parties to the Convention (today all forty-seven members of the Council of Europe are bound by the ECHR) undertake to guarantee these rights to all **persons** within their jurisdiction. If such persons fail to have their ECHR rights protected by national legal systems they can now bring a formal complaint against the relevant state before the **European Court of Human Rights**.   ALASTAIR MOWBRAY

D Harris *et al*, *Law of the ECHR* (Oxford: Oxford University Press, 2nd edn, 2008)

European Court of Human Rights The European Court of Human Rights ('ECtHR') is a permanent court entrusted with monitoring the compliance of European States with their obligations under the

European Convention on Human Rights ('ECHR'). The forty-six member states of the Council of Europe are signatories to the ECHR. The Court was set up in 1959 and is located in Strasbourg.

Initially, the determination of applications was the shared responsibility of the European Commission on Human Rights, the ECtHR, and the Committee of Ministers of the Council of Europe. A dramatic increase in the number of applications to the Convention institutions made it impossible to keep the length of proceedings within an acceptable time limit. In 1998, Protocol 11 came into force and established a new institutional system for deciding applications brought under the ECHR. Its aim was to simplify the ECHR's supervisory machinery, to fuse the ECtHR and the Commission into a single, full-time Court with mandatory jurisdiction and to abolish the Committee of Ministers' adjudicative role. The reform of the institutional structure has strengthened the judicial character of the system but the ECtHR is a victim of its own success: the Court's caseload continues to grow at an unprecedented rate.

The structure and procedure of the ECtHR is laid down in Section II of the ECHR, Articles 19–51. The Court is made up of forty-six judges, a number equal to that of the contracting states. The Parliamentary Assembly of the Council of Europe elects the judges from a shortlist of three nominated by governments. Judges do not represent their states: they serve in their individual capacity for a renewable six-year period and must retire at the age of seventy. The ECtHR has four components: the Plenary Court, Committees, Chambers, and the Grand Chamber. The Plenary Court has overall procedural control in adopting rules and setting up the Chambers. Each judge is assigned to one of five sections taking into account geographical and gender balance and the different legal systems of the state parties. Within each section there are Committees of three judges to review the admissibility of applications and Chambers comprising seven judges. The Chambers deliver the great majority of judgments of the ECtHR. In circumstances where a case raises a serious question of interpretation or an issue of general importance, the Chamber may relinquish its jurisdiction in favour of the Grand Chamber, composed of seventeen judges. Parties may also request referral to the Grand Chamber after the judgment of a Chamber. If the request is successful, the whole case is heard again. The judge from the state party concerned is always a member of the Chamber or Grand Chamber hearing the application.

There are two institutional mechanisms provided by the ECHR for its enforcement. Individual victims, non-governmental organizations, and groups of individuals (including trade unions and corporations) may petition the ECtHR alleging a breach of the ECHR by a state party. In addition, a state party may bring to the ECtHR a case against any other state party that is alleged to have violated the ECHR. Although there have been few inter-state applications, some have been of great significance. For example, in *Ireland v United Kingdom* (1978) Ireland alleged violations of Article 3 (prohibiting torture) in the treatment of suspected IRA members in Northern Ireland.

The ECtHR has been a successful regional human rights court. It has handed down hundreds of judgments and many have had far-reaching implications. Judgments are legally binding and for the most part states bring in measures to give effect to the judgments. There is growing concern, however, that the systemic violations of human rights and unacceptable delays in the implementation of ECtHR decisions in some of the new member states of the Council of Europe, especially the Russian Federation, threaten the efficacy of the ECHR system.

STEPHANIE PALMER

European Court of Justice The European Court of Justice ('ECJ') is the main judicial organ of the European Union. Based in Luxembourg, it should not be confused with the **European Court of Human Rights**, which sits in Strasbourg and applies the **European Convention on Human Rights**, or the International Court of Justice, which sits in The Hague and is the main judicial organ of the **United Nations**. The ECJ has played a major role in shaping the legal framework in which the EU operates. It has sometimes been criticized for pursuing an agenda of its own about Europe's political settlement, although it seems to be motivated principally by the need to uphold the **rule of law** in accordance with the **European Treaties** upon which the EU is based.

The ECJ consists of one judge per Member State (although it is rare for them all to sit in individual cases). It is assisted by eight Advocates General, whose status is equal to that of **judges**. There is always one Advocate General from France, Germany, Italy, Spain, and the United Kingdom, while the remaining posts rotate among the smaller Member States. (Following the Treaty of Lisbon, it is likely that Poland will acquire a permanent Advocate General and that the total number will be raised to eleven.) One Advocate General is assigned to each case. His or her function is normally to present to the judges an independent and impartial opinion containing a recommendation as to how it should be decided. The

Advocate General's opinion is generally (though not always) followed by the judges and Advocates General have made a major contribution to the coherence and accessibility of the ECJ's case law. However, straightforward cases may now be decided without an Advocate General's opinion. Judges and Advocates General are appointed by Member States, acting together, on the basis of national nominations for six-year terms which are in principle renewable. They are assisted by *référendaires*, or legal secretaries, generally early- to mid-career lawyers who help with drafting, research, and other tasks.

An important category of case brought before the ECJ comprises so-called direct actions. These start and finish in Luxembourg. Examples are actions by the **European Commission** against Member States for infringement of their Treaty obligations and challenges to the legality of **European Community legal instruments**. Direct actions may be contrasted with references for preliminary rulings. These represent an interlude in proceedings which started—and will finish—in a national court of a Member State. When a national **court** is called upon to decide a question of European law before giving judgment that question may—and sometimes must—be referred to the ECJ for an answer called a preliminary ruling, which the national court applies to the facts of the case. The purpose of this procedure is to ensure that the law based on the Treaties has the same effect throughout the Member States. This is essential to the proper functioning of the internal market but would be hard to achieve if the national courts were left to their own devices. The preliminary rulings procedure gives the ECJ a vital role in the application of European law at the national level and has enabled it to deal with important questions it might not otherwise have had an opportunity to address. Examples include the doctrine of direct effect, according to which European law may give litigants rights they can enforce in the national courts; the doctrine of primacy, according to which such rights may take precedence over inconsistent provisions of national law; and the principle of state liability, according to which Member States breaching their Treaty obligations may have to pay damages to those who suffer loss as a result.

The ECJ sits at the top of a three-tiered judicial structure. Immediately below it is the Court of First Instance ('CFI'), set up in 1988 partly to reduce pressure on the ECJ resulting from its growing case load. Also based in Luxembourg, the CFI consists of one judge per Member State, all appointed for renewable terms of six years by the Member States acting together. The CFI normally sits in chambers of five or three judges. There are no full-time Advocates

General in the CFI. A judge may be asked to perform the function of Advocate General in difficult or complex cases, but in practice this is rarely done. The CFI hears all direct actions brought by private parties, including challenges by businesses to the way the European Commission has applied the European Community competition rules. It also hears some direct actions brought by Member States. Its decisions in all such cases are subject to a right of appeal to the ECJ on points of law only, which means that on questions of fact they are final. The CFI has no jurisdiction at present to hear infringement actions against Member States, disputes between EU institutions, or references from national courts for preliminary rulings.

The bottom tier of the EU's judicial hierarchy comprises the judicial panels, of which only one has so far been created. The European Union Civil Service Tribunal ('CST') was established in 2004 to handle disputes between Union institutions and their staff, which were previously dealt with by the CFI. Again based in Luxembourg, the CST consists of seven judges appointed for renewable terms of six years by the Council of the EU, acting unanimously after consulting an advisory committee. The Council must ensure as far as possible that the composition of the CST is geographically balanced and that it reflects the national legal systems. The decisions of the CST are subject to a right of appeal to the CFI on points of law only. (This renders the title of the CFI a misnomer. The Treaty of Lisbon will, if it enters into force, rechristen it the General Court.) The decisions of the CFI in such cases are subject, in exceptional cases only, to review by the ECJ. The establishment of a further judicial panel, to deal with disputes arising out of the proposed European Community patent, has been suggested by the European Commission.

ANTHONY ARNULL

See also: **preliminary reference**

Anthony Arnull, *The European Union and its Court of Justice* (Oxford: Oxford University Press, 2nd edn, 2006)
L Neville Brown and Tom Kennedy, *Brown and Jacobs' The Court of Justice of the European Communities* (London: Sweet & Maxwell, 5th edn, 2000)

European harmonization of intellectual property rights   The creation of a single European market based on the principle of free competition required a further substantial harmonization of intellectual property provisions. This was not apparent right from the start, but once the customs barriers had been removed the widely diverging national provisions on intellectual property started to interfere with the free movement of goods and with

competition law. The harmonization effort that aimed at ironing out these problems took different forms, depending on the right involved

Patents: A supranational patent system was added to the existing national patent systems. The European Patent Convention 1973 ('EPC') provides a system comprising a single patent application and search. This is carried out by the European Patent Office in Munich, which started working on 1 June 1978. At the end of the procedure the applicant is granted a bundle of national patents, one for each Member State indicated in the application, rather than a single unitary patent. The EPC is not an initiative of the **European Union**: other European countries such as Switzerland, Turkey, and Liechtenstein adhere to it as well. The Convention also harmonized the provisions of national patent law, and a revised version, signed in 2000, entered into force on 13 December 2007.

The European Community wanted to go further and replace the bundle of national patents at the end of the granting procedure by a single Community patent. This was the aim of the Community Patent Convention 1975. The Convention never entered in force. At present attempts are under way to revive the project as a **European Union** Regulation. The European Patent Office would administer the new scheme, but a final agreement is held up by issues concerning the use of languages and the creation of a form of European Patent Court.

Other initiatives of the Community relate to pharmaceutical inventions and inventions relating to plant protection products where the term of protection was extended by means of the introduction of a Supplementary Protection Certificate for Pharmaceutical Products and a Supplementary Protection Certificate for Plant Protection Products and there is a special directive dealing with patents for biotechnological inventions.

The European Union has also adopted a special registration system for plant varieties that operates separately from the patent system and is in line with the international UPOV Convention.

Trade marks: The Community acted on two levels. The national trade mark laws of the Member States have been harmonized by means of a directive, and a Community Trademark has been created by means of a regulation. This latter system has been in force since 1996, with far greater success than expected, and provides a single trade mark for the Community as a whole. The Community Trade Mark Office, which is officially called the Office for Harmonization in the Internal Market (trade marks and designs), is located in Alicante, Spain.

Designs: The Community undertook the same action in this area as the one taken in relation to trade marks: harmonization of the national design laws by means of a directive and a single Community Design Right by means of a regulation. The difficult issue of spare parts and a repair clause made negotiations very cumbersome, but eventually a directive was agreed in October 1998. Shortly afterwards agreement on a regulation on Community Design was reached and the Alicante Office (OHIM) was able to extend its role from a mere Community trade mark office to a Community trade mark and design office in January 2003.

Copyright: The Community has up to now refrained from attempting to harmonize copyright as a whole. Only certain aspects of copyright, such as the term of copyright protection have been harmonized.

A number of areas have received special attention: computer programs, rental rights and lending rights, satellite broadcasting and cable re-transmission, and databases. And a latest directive in that series is harmonizing certain aspects of copyright and related rights in the information society. The implementation of that directive should enable the EU to accede to the **World Intellectual Property Organization ('WIPO')** Copyright Treaty and the WIPO Performances and Phonograms Treaty, especially as Member States have undertaken to legislate in a timely fashion to meet the provisions on moral rights for performers, which are not retained in the directive.

Although not of the same importance and dealing with a small point in copyright law, agreement on the Directive to harmonize the provisions on the artist's resale right was only reached after heated debates.

At the time of writing the Commission was focusing its attention on the management of copyright and related rights on the one hand and on a review of the *acquis communautaire* in the area of copyright and related rights. Both are the subject of consultation procedures, but no new legislative initiatives have yet emerged, apart from a recommendation addressed to the collecting societies.

Enforcement of intellectual property rights: Moving away from individual intellectual property rights, a Directive of the European Parliament and of the Council (2004) on the enforcement of intellectual property rights attempts to streamline the enforcement mechanisms of the Member States and to achieve a common minimum standard. The directive covers all intellectual property rights and Member States are bringing their national legislation into line with it.

The Community has also adopted measures in the areas of comparative advertising, for the purposes of which trade marks of competitors can be used; and electronic commerce, which may involve a substantial intellectual property content. A special regime of protection has been put in place for topographies of semiconductor chips and a scheme to protect against piracy and counterfeiting, involving the assistance of customs departments, has been added to the range of measures and tools available. And finally, a short directive dealing with the legal protection of conditional access services was also adopted in 1998.

This harmonization effort has already achieved substantial progress, but whilst further progress may well be a bit slower, there are no signs that the process has been completed or come to an end. Further initiatives are therefore to be expected.

PAUL TORREMANS

See also: **single market**

European law   *see* **common law of Europe; European Community law**

European Parliament   The European Parliament is one of the major institutions of the European Union, together with the **European Commission**, the Council, and the Court of Justice. Amongst the EU institutions, the European Parliament is the one which has changed the most over the years, thanks, in particular to the contribution of the **European Court of Justice**. Crucially, the case law of the Court in this area has been progressively codified in the EC Treaty.

The European Parliament is closely linked to the debate on the EU democratic deficit. Indeed, although it is the only EU institution that, since 1979, is democratically elected, it is also the one with least powers. Originally, the European Parliament was not intended to perform the duty of a parliament in the traditional sense. It was indeed conceived as an Assembly: a mere consultative organ with limited powers as highlighted in the case of *Roquette Frères* (1980). Things have changed, however. Today the EC Parliament has strengthened its important functions: advisory, legislative, supervisory, budgetary, and to pronounce upon certain matters relating to the Union's external relations. Furthermore, the Parliament represents the interests of the citizens of the EU Member States.

In its advisory role, the Parliament is entitled to advice on any question concerning the Communities and to adopt relevant resolutions. As part of the legislative process, although the Parliament still cannot pass **legislation** independently, thanks to the co-decision procedure established in 1992 by the Treaty of Amsterdam, it shares legislative competence with the Council in a vast range of areas. The co-decision procedure implies that both institutions are involved in drafting a piece of legislation which requires the signatures of the two institutions. The Court of Justice has emphasized on several occasion that the Parliament is an essential actor in the legislative process (*Maizena v Council* (1980)). Complementing its involvement in the decision-making process is the right of the Parliament to bring acts of the other institutions before the Court of Justice for the purpose of **judicial review** in order to protect its prerogative. This was established through the Court of Justice's case law such as *Parliament v Council (Chernobyl)* (1990). These important changes have been codified in subsequent amendments to the EC Treaty.

In its supervisory role the Parliament can set up a temporary committee of enquiry. In this context, in 1999 it scrutinized the activity of the Commission. This led to a censure motion and, as a consequence, the Commission resigned. The Parliament has also the last word as far as non-compulsory expenditures are concerned and may reject the budget in its entirety. Finally, whilst the Commission represents the interests of the EU and the Council those of the Member States, the Parliament is the institution that represents the interests of the EU citizens. For this purpose, it can appoint an **Ombudsman** who provides citizens with a opportunity of informing about institutional maladministration which s/he had suffered.

The EU Treaty states that the Parliament is composed of 'representatives of the peoples of the States brought together in the Community' and it is elected by direct universal suffrage which gives it democratic legitimacy. Regrettably, the turnout for its elections is usually disappointing and might cast doubts on its legitimacy. Yet, the European Parliament remains an important political institution. Through representative **democracy** it provides the EU with a degree of democratic legitimacy and has contributed to the 'parliamentarization' of the EU.

EUGENIA CARACCIOLO DI TORELLA

European Patent Convention   The European Patent Convention ('EPC') establishes 'a system of law, common to the Contracting States, for the grant of **patents** for inventions' and an organization, the European Patent Organization, to administer it. A patent granted under the EPC is called a European patent but takes effect as a bundle of national patents under the laws of the contracting states in which protection is sought.

The European Patent Organization comprises a European Patent Office ('EPO') and Administrative Council. Under the EPC, applications are determined at first instance by the EPO's five first-tier administrative and legal arms—its Receiving Section and Search, Examining, Opposition, and Legal Divisions—and in the event of a dispute, its Technical and Legal Boards of Appeal. There also exists an Enlarged Board of Appeal responsible for determining points of law referred by an individual Board and giving opinions on points of law referred by the EPO President.

The EPC is a document of enormous and under-studied legal significance, not only for intellectual property but also for the wider contemporary project of European private law harmonization. Its immediate roots lie in the failed attempt of the six original members of the European Economic Community to create a unitary patent for the Common Market in pursuance of the trade objectives of their founding 1957 Treaty. However, it also has deeper roots in the 1949 proposal for a regional patent system that was made by French senator Longchambon to the Council of Europe barely a month after its creation. While Longchambon's proposal was rejected, belief in the need for a patent office and supporting laws to facilitate the early stage of post-war integration was overwhelming, and led to the submission of a string of further proposals to the same end during the 1950s. While each proposal failed, in combination they helped set the agenda for the creation of a European patent.

Since the 1950s that agenda has all but defined European patent reform, and while its ultimate goal remains elusive, significant milestones on the path to it have been reached. Of those milestones the EPC is the most important. It was signed in 1973 and today has a membership close to that of the **European Union** itself.

Still, the EPC is divisive as well as unifying, and in this sense represents the difficulty, if not the futility, of contemporary efforts to harmonize European private law. The main reason for its divisiveness is its failure to have displaced the corresponding legal and administrative infrastructure of its contracting states. Thus there exists in Europe a network of differently constituted and oriented legal and administrative bodies which operate in parallel and have joint responsibility for construing and applying the same principal text. The inevitable result has been inconsistent interpretations of that text between the national patent offices and courts of EPC contracting states, and also between those offices and courts

and the EPO, creating fractures in a regime founded on its contracting states' political and legal commitments to harmonious decision-making.

JUSTINE PILA

European treaties The main treaties, or agreements between states in **international law**, between European countries, fall under the purview of two regional organizations: the Council of Europe, and the European Union. The older of the two, the Council of Europe, has forty-six Member States (countries belonging to it), and is broadly concerned with the protection of **human rights**, parliamentary **democracy**, and the **rule of law**. The European Union has twenty-seven Member States, and is the successor to the 'European Economic Community', the purpose of which is to achieve peace and stability in Europe through economic integration.

Probably the best known of European Treaties is the European Convention for the Protection of Human Rights and Fundamental Freedoms 1950, which entered into force in 1953. Part of the Council of Europe's body of treaties, this Treaty covers **civil and political rights**, such as the **right to life**, freedom from **torture**, the right to liberty and **security**, the **right to a fair trial**, respect for private and **family life**, freedom of conscience and **religion,** and **freedom of assembly**. It includes the important non-discrimination principle, guaranteeing equal protection of these rights, regardless of status, such as **race**, class, or **gender**.

The **European Convention on Human Rights** is recognized in UK law through the **Human Rights Act 1998**, which provides that national law must be interpreted to be consistent with the Convention as far as possible. If this is not possible, then the **House of Lords,** the Judicial Committee of the **Privy Council,** the Courts-Martial Appeal Court, in Scotland, the High Court of Justiciary sitting otherwise than as a trial court or the Court of Session, or in England and Wales or Northern Ireland, the High Court or the Court of Appeal, may declare the law to be incompatible with the Convention. Such a judicial declaration is likely to prompt legislative reform. Furthermore, the Convention is unusual in international law in that it may be enforced, after domestic remedies have been exhausted, by an individual, **non-governmental organization**, or group of individuals bringing a claim before the **European Court of Human Rights**, which sits in Strasbourg.

The Council of Europe is also responsible for the European Social Charter 1966 (Revised version 1996), which guarantees various **economic and social rights**, such as the **right to work**, the right to organize and bargain collectively, the right to social security, the right to housing, and the right to health. A large number of further European treaties have been agreed by Council of Europe Member States, covering matters as diverse as social security arrangements between Member States; cooperation in matters of criminal justice such as **terrorism, human trafficking**, and money laundering; cross-frontier audio-visual policies; and intellectual property.

The European Union was established by the Treaty on European Union 1992 (sometimes known as the Treaty of Maastricht), which entered into force on 1 November 1993. The aim of the European Union is promote 'European integration'—the bringing together initially of the economies, but subsequently of other matters of common interest, of its Member States. The European Union includes, as one of its three 'pillars', the European Community, which is the successor to the European Economic Community, originally established by the EC Treaty 1957 (sometimes known as the Treaty of Rome). If the Treaty of Lisbon 2007 is ratified, the EC Treaty will be renamed the Treaty on the Functioning of the European Union, and the EC will become the European Union, of 'the Union'. The EC Treaty, as amended, establishes the '**single market**' within which the factors of production (goods, services, workers, and capital) may move freely. It also sets up common policies, in the fields of agriculture, transport, **competition, economic and monetary union**, employment, external trade, health and safety at work, **equal pay** for men and women, education and vocational training, culture, **public health, consumer** protection, economic and social cohesion of the regions, research, the environment, and overseas development, in order to promote the process of integration of the economies of the Member States.

The other elements of the Treaty on European Union cover a common foreign and security policy among European Union Member States, and cooperation in the field of **justice** and home affairs, such as judicial cooperation and policing. This latter field includes treaties such as the Convention establishing a European **Police** Office (Europol) 1995, which aims to improve police cooperation between Member States to combat terrorism, illicit traffic in drugs, and other serious forms of international crime; and the Convention on mutual assistance and cooperation between customs administrations 1997. The European Union is also responsible for Treaties on the conflict of laws, where a legal dispute involves parties from two different countries, such as the Brussels Convention on jurisdiction and enforcement of judgments in civil and commercial matters 1968.

The EC Treaty and the Treaty on European Union have been amended several times, in particular by the confusingly named 'Single European Act' 1986 (a Treaty which entered into force 1 July 1987) and by the Treaties of Amsterdam 1997 (which entered into force 1 May 1999) and Nice 2001 (which entered into force on 1 February 2003). The Treaty of Lisbon 2007, if ratified, will be the next amending Treaty. The Treaties are also amended by an accession treaty each time a new Member State or group of Member States joins the European Union.

TAMARA HERVEY

European Union   *see* **European treaties**

European Union environmental law   European Union environmental law is that body of law emanating from the European Union ('EU') concerning environmental protection. Technically speaking this body of law is Community environmental law in that it operates pursuant to the first pillar of the European Union rather than the other two pillars. As an area of law it covers most areas of environmental protection and consists of laws on specific subjects such as **waste**, water quality, and air quality as well as laws which regulate a range of decision-making processes such as laws relating to access to environmental information and strategic environmental assessment.

As a body of law it is made up of two overlapping sets of law and policy—harmonized law and policy and laws limiting the power of Member States to pass environmental laws. EU environmental law is the product of two catalysts. First, the development of EU environmental law was a spill-over from the process of market integration between the Member States. This is because having different environmental laws in different Member States creates barriers to free movement of goods due to such national law distorting **competition** and/or acting as measures equivalent to quantitative restrictions on free movement of goods. Secondly, EU environmental law is the product of an explicit policy on the part of Member States to develop EU environmental law which originated from the Paris Summit in 1972 when the EU Member States decided to commit to an obligation of environmental protection. An explicit environmental Treaty competence (Articles 174–176) was only added to the Treaty establishing the European Community ('TEC') in 1987 as part of the Treaty amendment process brought about by the Single European Act 1986. Even before that time, however, Community institutions had been proactive in relation to environmental protection and passed at least 100 directives on the issue.

The bulk of EU environmental law is in the form of directives which are required to be implemented by Member States although there are some regulations on the topic as well. This means that there is in a significant role for Member State governments in interpreting, implementing, and enforcing environmental law. Moreover, the TEC allows Member States to take more protective environmental measures in certain limited circumstances, thus meaning that EU harmonization is often understood as minimum harmonization.

The early directives of the 1970s tended to operate on a command and control basis and set very strict standards for **pollution** discharges and environmental quality. These directives, while aspirational, were not well implemented by Member States and by the 1990s it was recognized that EU environmental law had one of the worst implementation records of any area of EU law. This, alongside the promotion of **sustainable development** and **subsidiarity**, was one of the catalysts for promoting more flexible approaches to regulation from the early 1990s onwards. These approaches gave a greater role to private actors and, in some cases, utilized market-based regulatory techniques. Indeed, the EU has led the world in the development of innovative regulatory techniques, in particular those that are more non-legal in form including **environmental agreements**, environmental management systems, and different forms of information provisions. Moreover, cooperation between different Community, national and sub-national institutions has been encouraged. This has meant it has become popular to talk about EU environmental law in terms of **environmental governance**.

Alongside directives and different regulatory techniques there has also been a significant role for policy. Since its commitment to environmental protection in 1972 the Community institutions have produced an action programme in relation to the environment every five years or so which sets out their key objectives and which forms the basis for a legislative and more detailed policy agenda. Another significant aspect of EU environmental law is the role of environmental principles. Article 174(2) of the TEC lists a number of principles that 'Community policy on the environment shall be based on' including the preventive principle, the polluter pays principle, the **precautionary principle**, and the principle that damage will be rectified at source. As well, the Treaties make reference to the concept of sustainable development. These principles are understood to have an important jurisprudential role to play in environmental law and are increasingly being referred to by the **European Court of Justice**, particularly the precautionary principle.

There are many different institutions that play a role in EU environmental law including the main Community institutions and governments at both the national and sub-national level. The European Environment Agency began operation 1996 to provide information about environmental issues. As well there is a growing role for private actors, **communities**, and those operating in the public interest. There has been an increasing focus on the involvement of the latter two in recent years, due to a more general concern with the democratic deficit and encouraging participation in the EU and/or because in 1998 the Community and the Member States signed the UN Economic Commission for Europe **Aarhus Convention** on access to information, public participation in decision-making, and access to **justice** in environmental matters.

The ECJ has played a significant role in developing EU environmental law. This is both in relation to harmonized community law as well as regularly ruling on the ability of Member States to take unilateral action in relation to environmental issues in cases where there is, and is not, a harmonized Community regime.

One example of where the ECJ has had a role to play is hearing challenges to the legal competence of Community institutions to pass **legislation** in relation to environmental issues. These cases are not about whether Community institutions have no competence but under which Treaty competence a provision should be passed. Thus, for example, there has been litigation concerning whether a measure should be based under the internal market competence or the environmental competence (*Commission v Council* (1991)) and litigation concerning whether a measure should be based under the common commercial policy competence or the environmental competence (*Opinion 2/00 on Cartagena Protocol* (2002)). The reasons for these cases have been largely technical but they highlight two key issues. First, in these cases the Court has stressed the importance of environmental protection. In 1985, even before the Treaty amendment, the ECJ described environmental protection as one of the 'Community's essential objectives' (*ABDHU* (1985)). The importance of environmental protection in the operation of the Community has been continually affirmed by the Court and by further Treaty amendments. As such, a fundamental feature of EU environmental law and policy is that numerous Treaty articles require that both 'aim at a high level of protection'. Secondly, the fact that an environmental measure can also be an internal market measure, a common agricultural measure, or a common commercial policy measure reflects the fact that Community action in relation to the environment is closely interrelated with other Community goals and activities. The importance of integrating these different areas can be seen in Article 6 TEC which requires 'environmental protection requirements must be integrated into the definition and implementation' of other Community policies.

LIZ FISHER

L Kramer, *EC Environmental Law* (London: Sweet & Maxwell, 6th edn, 2007)

European Union, influence on financial markets
Although the **Financial Services Authority** supervises UK financial markets, the regulatory structure under which it operates is now driven, almost entirely, by European Union requirements. The EU financial market regime provides the most advanced example of regional harmonization of financial market rules (although the International Organization of Securities Commissions—the umbrella organization for market regulators—promotes the adoption of harmonized best practice internationally through its Codes and Principles). For example, the rules for **collective investment schemes** are governed by the EU's Undertaking for Collective Investment in Transferable Securities Directive 1985; the rules on public offers of **securities** and prospectuses by the Prospectus Directive 2003; the rules on insider dealing and market manipulation by the Market Abuse Directive 2003; and the rules on investment firms, investment services, stock exchanges, alternative trading systems, and trading by the Markets in Financial Instruments Directive 2004. These major 'level 1' directives are supplemented by more detailed 'level 2' directives. All of these measures must be implemented by the UK as national rules. Together they amount to a detailed regulatory scheme, which governs the UK and all other EU financial markets.

This regime derives from the Financial Services Action Plan ('FSAP'). Since 1999, the EU has been engaged in a massive and wide-ranging reform project to upgrade the architecture of its financial markets and its regulatory framework under the FSAP, an ambitious reform agenda completed in 2005. The FSAP extends from the issuing of securities and issuer disclosure, through to trading in securities (including trade execution and transparency rules) and the supply of investment services, to credit rating agencies and investment analysts, and on to market infrastructure, in particular clearing and settlement systems. Although the FSAP is a regulatory reform agenda, it operates in the context of the EU's wider market integration agenda. It is closely linked to monetary union and seeks to maximize the benefits of the Euro. The FSAP pre-dates the **Enron** series of scandals and subsequent reforms, although it incorporated Enron-related reforms in its later stages. It is more closely associated with the 'dotcom' period and exuberant financial markets. It is also allied to the EU's political agenda (Lisbon 2000) to make the EU the world's leading knowledge-based economy by 2010. Efficient EU financial markets were regarded as a key element of this agenda.

The FSAP is designed to liberalize investment services and securities markets across the EU and to support an integrated, deep, and liquid financial market across the Member States. To achieve this, the FSAP is based on a home Member State control model: issuers, investment firms, and other market actors can operate across the EU financial market on the basis of authorization and regulation in their home Member State (essentially the Member State in which the actor is registered or has its head office). To support home Member State control of pan-EU operations, a detailed harmonized regulatory regime applies across the EU under the FSAP. Supervision remains at Member State level. A single, central EU financial market supervisor remains highly controversial.

NIAMH MOLONEY

See also: **regulation**

European Union migration Traditionally, the European Union's approach to international migration was limited to the facilitation of internal **freedom of movement** for nationals of Member States. Thus, the Treaty of Rome included the free movement of workers as one of the four freedoms of the **Single Market** (along with free movement of goods, services, and capital). Subsequently, the range of **persons** benefiting from these rights has expanded to encompass all EU citizens, including the economically non-active. The abolition of controls at the internal borders of the EU through the first **Schengen Agreement** of 1985 added a symbolic dimension to this internal process of liberalization, while, at the same time, spurring cooperation on extra-European immigration from so-called third country nationals. In contrast to internal migration policy, freedom of movement, which has firm roots in the Treaties and enjoys supranational decision-making procedures and a vigilant jurisdiction by the **European Court of Justice**, external migration policies have developed incrementally and through inter-governmental cooperation, before being slowly brought into the ambit of supranational decision-making procedures. The transfer of **asylum** and immigration matters from the inter-governmental third pillar of the Maastricht Treaty to the supranational first pillar was realized with the Amsterdam Treaty 1997. Nevertheless, whereas significant progress has been made in the development of common European policies on external border controls, **visas**, and asylum, the approach towards immigrant integration and economic immigration remains very much in the competence of Member States. Likewise, national **citizenship** and naturalization policies are not affected by European **legislation**. Articles 62 and 63 of the EU Treaty lay down a list of measures for the **European Council** to adopt within five years after the entry into force of the Amsterdam Treaty in 1999. These provisions have since been specified and extended through the (legally non-binding) Hague Programme of 2004.

With regard to the crossing of external borders, this includes a harmonized visa policy for stays of no longer than three months and common standards and procedures for checks at external borders. Many relevant provisions on the control of the EU's external borders were included in the Second Schengen Agreement of 1990 and developed in subsequent deliberations of the Schengen Executive Committee. Its Handbook on Controls at the External Borders as well as the 'Schengen-*acquis*' were translated in EU legislation through the Amsterdam Treaty. The management of the external border involves in the first place the promotion of operational cooperation through intergovernmental coordination between the border control authorities of Member States. In 2005, Frontex, the European Agency for the Management of Operational Cooperation at the External Borders of the Member States of the EU took up its functions in Warsaw. Although responsibility for the control and surveillance of external borders lies with Member States, the Agency facilitates the application of existing and future Community measures relating to the management of these borders through the coordination of operational cooperation between Member States, integrated risk assessment, training for border guards, and research and assistance for Member States in difficult circumstances, including support for joint return operations. First common operations have focused on the Mediterranean and the Canary Islands.

Next to cooperation on the crossing of external borders, asylum policy is the area where European integration is most advanced. Compared to the former, integration in this field takes the form of more supranational structures and focuses on the development of harmonized European legislation. The goal is the realization of a common asylum system. This consists in common regulations on the state responsible for the examination of an asylum claim (Dublin Convention 1990 and the corresponding 1997 Regulation as well as the Eurodac fingerprint system); directives on a common definition of the eligibility for **refugee** status; the asylum procedure; reception conditions; and cooperation with third countries, including the promotion of regional protection programmes. Because progress on restrictive measures has been much stronger than for the **human rights** and procedural law aspects of asylum policy, the Commission published a green paper in 2007 setting out a more balanced and comprehensive plan of action with a view to realizing a common European asylum system by the end of 2010. In addition, common measures have been adopted to deal with the temporary protection of refugees not qualifying for asylum status. Despite strong asymmetries in the degree to which different Member States are affected by refugee flows, efforts to devise a system of burden-sharing and to establish a refugee fund to compensate for eventual inequalities have hitherto produced little tangible results.

Progress on immigration policy proper and the rights of third country nationals residing legally in the EU has been more mixed. Common directives have been adopted after long negotiations on the right to family reunification and the rights of long-term resident third country nationals. Both directives only lay down minimum standards and leave a large degree of **discretion** to Member States with regard to implementation. Efforts to devise common admission criteria for third country nationals have met particularly strong resistance from some Member States. Whereas in recent years directives could be adopted on the admission of self-employed persons and students, Member States have hitherto opposed the idea of developing supranational rules on economic immigration. This is also manifest in the refusal to establish supranational decision-making procedures (in particular, qualified majority voting rather than unanimity) in recent Treaties and the draft Constitutional Treaty, which contrasts with other areas covered by Articles 61–63 TEC.

Another area where integration is promoted but where Member States are reluctant to develop binding European legislation is immigrant integration policy. Given the wide disparity of experiences with immigration in old and new Member States, the historical legacies and questions of national **identity** linked to the issue, the development of a common approach in these matters is promoted through non-legal mechanisms such as dialogue and exchange of best practices. The main tangible outputs in this respect are the production of Annual Reports on Immigration and Integration by the **European Commission**, in which it synthesizes the results of open coordination among Member States, a Handbook on Integration for Policy-Makers and Practitioners, and the mobilization of funds for promoting local integration initiatives.

Finally, the fifth and currently most dynamic area of cooperation is the development of an external dimension to EU asylum and immigration policies. This involves acceding and candidate countries' adjustment to the *acquis*; cooperation with the countries included in the European Neighbourhood Policy, the negotiation and conclusion of re-admission agreements with countries of transit and countries of origin, as well as, since 2007, the development of a comprehensive approach towards African countries. Based on an ambitious process of deliberation, this initiative shall help to devise mutually beneficial solutions between countries of origin, transit, and destination. In this respect, EU external migration policies have moved closer to broader attempts to develop an international normative framework for managing migration in the context of the **United Nations**.

Summing up, originally limited to measures seen as necessary to compensate for the loss of control instruments emanating from the decision to abolish checks at internal borders, EU asylum and immigration policies have seen a considerable expansion in scope and depth. Nevertheless, the European integration of these fields is marked by persisting tensions between human rights aspects and repressive prerogatives on the one hand, and between the principle of territorial **sovereignty** and supranational integration on the other. In the light of expanding migration flows, these tensions maintain the momentum for more integration, and are likely to co-exist for the foreseeable future.

SANDRA LAVENEX

See also: **European treaties; free movement in the EU**

Europhile *see* **Eurosceptic**

Europhobe *see* **Eurosceptic**

Eurosceptic Although its origins are unclear, the term 'Eurosceptic' has come to depict national political movements that fundamentally oppose—in part or in whole—the process of European integration as manifest in the ongoing development of the **European Union**. In that sense the label 'sceptic' to describe the views of individuals subscribing to this movement is something of a misnomer; the view that characterizes and unites Eurosceptics is outright opposition to European integration. Eurosceptics see integration as a Treaty-based process to create a European 'super state' by progressively eroding the constitutional **sovereignty** and law-making powers of the EU Member States. Legislative competence over an ever expanding range of national policies is being transferred to the EU level of governance, further empowering the EU's supranational institutions (the **European Commission**, the **European Parliament,** and the **European Court of Justice**) with national governments increasingly becoming subservient to these institutions. Euroscepticism is driven by the imperative of stemming this flow of power to the EU level and instead reasserting the primacy of the (EU) nation state in order, Eurosceptics assert, to protect the underlying democratic principles that regulate the activities of all governments. Eurosceptics argue that the EU institutions are profoundly undemocratic, and that consequently the EU—both as an institutional arrangement and as a legislature—lacks any political or social legitimacy.

Intellectually Euroscepticism can be linked to deep-seated concerns about the democratic credentials of the EU and, by extension, the legitimacy of its legislative activity. Issues such as the persistently low turnout at EU elections, seemingly widespread popular opposition to specific Treaty reforms (certainly from the Treaty on European Union onwards), allegedly burdensome EU regulations, improper use of EU finance, and the emergence of the EU as a distinctive and pre-eminent legal order undeniably are sources of discontent with the process of integration that deserve serious attention by advocates of 'deeper' European integration. The difficulty is that in their opposition to further integration (and, in some variants, in their support for withdrawal from the EU), Eurosceptics instead appeal to populist anxieties and concerns which either have little basis in empirical evidence ('scaremongering') or which are thinly disguised attacks on the allegedly improper influence of non-nationals ('foreigners') in what they deem to be issues of solely national concern. Unsurprisingly, therefore, Eurosceptics usually tend to lie towards the far right of the political spectrum, although this is not the case in all Member States.

The popularity of Eurosceptic parties has tended to rise since the early 1990s, although it remains very much a minority interest in all EU Member States. Euroscepticism is most popular in the UK where ten of the UK's seventy-eight Members of the European Parliament represent the UK Independence Party, which campaigns for withdrawal from the EU. There is also an emerging Eurosceptic movement in some of the Member States that have joined the EU since 2004. Elsewhere the strength of Euroscepticism tends to fluctuate according to domestic politics and EU initiatives, rising during periods when further EU treaty reform is being discussed. However there is no indication that Euroscepticism will emerge as a serious political movement across the EU.

ANDREW SCOTT

euthanasia Euthanasia can be defined as the deliberate taking of life of a suffering patient. It also constitutes the crime of murder at **common law** and under the legal systems of most countries around the world. The term euthanasia is usually discussed in the clinical context of health care professionals assisting a patient to die, as distinct from family 'mercy killings'.

A number of distinctions are frequently drawn in the discussion on euthanasia including that between active/passive euthanasia, between voluntary/involuntary or non-voluntary euthanasia, and also the distinction with doctor-**assisted suicide**. Active euthanasia describes conduct by a doctor involving provision of active assistance for the patient to die, for example, by administration of a lethal injection. In contrast, passive euthanasia denotes assisting death by omission such as the non-provision of life-sustaining treatment. Given that withholding or withdrawing treatment is regarded as legitimate medical practice, there is considerable debate as to whether this should even be described as euthanasia which is more typically associated with the provision of active assistance to die. Although the criminal law does not presently differentiate between euthanasia which is performed with or without the request of a patient , or indeed, against the patient's express wishes, the difference between 'voluntary' euthanasia on the one hand, and involuntary and non-voluntary euthanasia on the other is significant. What lies at the heart of the voluntary/involuntary or non-voluntary distinction is whether the patient has requested such intervention. Voluntary euthanasia is euthanasia performed at the explicit request of the patient. Euthanasia is involuntary where it is performed without the consent, or against the will of, a competent patient. Euthanasia is non-voluntary where it is performed on a **person** who is incompetent and therefore incapable of giving consent. Finally, the distinction between euthanasia and doctor-assisted suicide should be noted: euthanasia involves active assistance by the doctor in bringing about death, such as the administration of a lethal injection, whereas doctor-assisted suicide entails the doctor providing advice and/or drugs to the patient to enable the patient to take his or her own life.

Although there has been much agitation for reform of the law, the current legal status of euthanasia in the form of active assistance is illegal, amounting to the crime of murder. This is the case, even where euthanasia is performed at the request of the patient, and the patient is in the terminal phase of their illness. This is because criminal law does not recognize as valid a person's consent to their death, and the health status of the **victim** (whether healthy or near death) is similarly irrelevant for the purposes of establishing criminal liability. Nor does the criminal law have regard to the benevolent motive or *bona fides* of the doctor who performs euthanasia (namely, to relieve the patient's suffering, at their request), focusing instead on whether the *actus reus* (here the act causing death) and *mens rea* (or the mental element for murder, which includes an intention to cause death) can be established. In circumstances where there is deliberate and intentional intervention for the purpose of ending life, these matters are not usually at issue. Notwithstanding empirical data which indicates that a not insignificant minority of doctors have performed euthanasia at the request of a terminal patient, in practice, there are very few **prosecutions** of doctors for deliberately taking the lives of their patients. This is, in large part, due to the fact that the present unlawfulness of the practice drives the conduct underground; furthermore, prosecuting authorities have shown little interest in such actions, even where doctors have made public admissions about providing such assistance to their patients.

Whilst the criminal laws of most countries prohibit euthanasia, it has been legalized in a number of European jurisdictions, in particular, The Netherlands and, more recently, Belgium. Since the 1970s, euthanasia has been a topic of interest and discussion. Although Article 293 of the Dutch Penal Code 1867 prohibits the taking the life of another at that person's express and serious request, through a series of decisions, the Dutch **courts** developed certain exceptions to this prohibition by defining guidelines for its practice. In doing so, the courts have resorted to another provision of the Dutch Penal Code dealing with *force majeure* or 'necessity' which has become known as the *noodtoestand* or 'emergency' defence, in which the defendant faces an irreconcilable conflict of duties. The recognition of this defence has played a central role in the development of Dutch law on euthanasia, and ultimately has provided a means by which doctors in The Netherlands can perform voluntary euthanasia without incurring criminal sanction despite the prohibition in Article 293. More recently, **legislation** has been passed amending the Dutch Penal Code, to give statutory protection to doctors who adhere to the requirements of careful practice in performing euthanasia on request. The requirements of careful practice, originally developed by the courts and endorsed by the Royal Dutch Medical Association, are now specified in this legislation (Termination of Life on Request and Assisted Suicide (Review Procedures) Act 2001). They focus on the need for voluntary and informed choice by the patient, careful consideration of the patient's medical circumstances, whether there are alternatives, and the need for consultation with an independent doctor. These legislative changes have formalized the *de facto* legal **recognition** already given to the practice of voluntary euthanasia in The Netherlands. The criminal law in neighbouring Belgium has also recently undergone reform through the Belgium Act on Euthanasia 2002 to permit voluntary euthanasia performed by a doctor.

In many other countries around the world, there has been longstanding debate about the permissibility of euthanasia and the appropriate role for law and policy. There are both doctrinal as well as practical arguments presented against legalization of euthanasia. Prominent amongst doctrinal arguments are religious objections which invoke the **sanctity of human life**, the prohibition against intentional killing, and the value of human suffering. Practical arguments against the legalization focus on concern about long-term consequences if the practice of euthanasia is legalized. One of these is the so-called **'slippery slope' argument** or the 'thin edge of the wedge'; namely, that legalization of voluntary euthanasia would, through incremental steps, eventually result in the legal permissibility of euthanasia for patients who are not competent.

Amongst the main arguments advanced in support of reform, are the importance of upholding the **self-determination** of competent patients, and the resulting **empowerment** that this delivers for the terminally ill. Another key argument in support of legalization is that the criminal prohibition is ineffective in practice in preventing the occurrence of euthanasia. Indeed, on the basis of empirical research

into doctors' practices undertaken in a number of jurisdictions, there are strong grounds to suggest that a policy of prohibition does not impact significantly on the incidence of voluntary euthanasia (rates being quite comparable as between jurisdictions where euthanasia has been prohibited, namely Australia and Belgium (up until recently), and The Netherlands where there has been legal tolerance of the practice for decades). Significantly, however, the countries investigated with a policy of prohibition have recorded a higher incidence of euthanasia performed without the explicit request of the patient. This suggests that a restrictive policy on euthanasia as currently prevails in most countries around the world, may in fact be less protective of the rights of patients than a policy such as in The Netherlands which aims to control and regulate the practice with the specification of guidelines for careful practice which must be adhered to in order for doctors to escape liability.

Over the years, numerous initiatives have been brought to introduce legislation permitting euthanasia, including the introduction of **private member's bills** in many jurisdictions. This push for reform has been supported by a groundswell of public opinion in favour of legalization. Surveys of doctors' attitudes indicate growing backing within the medical profession for a more open and permissive policy on euthanasia. In the Australian Northern Territory, legislation permitting doctors to perform voluntary euthanasia subject to stringent safeguards was, for a short time, successfully introduced (Rights of the Terminally Ill Act (NT) 1995), but this was subsequently overridden by the Australian Commonwealth Parliament (The Euthanasia Laws Act (Cth) 1997). Although ostensibly a private member's Bill, it received strong support from the government, including the Prime Minister, and was ultimately passed by the Federal Parliament in a virtually unprecedented exercise of overruling the validly enacted legislation of an Australian territory.

Euthanasia remains a contentious issue. There appears to be wide recognition that it does occur. Although prohibited by the criminal law, it does not attract the same moral condemnation as other unlawful taking of life: indeed, it is widely viewed as acceptable in exceptional cases. Consensus is lacking, however, as to how the law, as a matter of policy, should respond to this issue: whether to retain what is an ineffectual prohibition, or to embrace legal change, acknowledging the reality of the practice and seeking to control and regulate it through the imposition of safeguards to enhance protection for both patients and their doctors.

MARGARET OTLOWSKI

euthanasia in The Netherlands and Belgium   The term 'euthanasia' has been used to refer to a wide variety of different conceptions of or ways of achieving a 'good death'. In The Netherlands and Belgium it has come to have a much narrower legal definition: behaviour that causes the death of another **person** at that person's request. Closely related to euthanasia in this narrow sense is **assisted suicide**. In The Netherlands and Belgium, euthanasia is legal if carried out by a doctor at the request of a patient who is unbearably suffering from a serious medical condition with no prospect of improvement; the doctor must consult a second independent doctor and comply with a variety of other procedural requirements, including reporting what he has done. Legalization took place in The Netherlands through court decisions in the mid-1980s, confirmed ultimately in **legislation** in 2002. In Belgium, legalization took place through legislation in 2002.

Dutch public opinion has been surveyed repeatedly over the years and strongly supports legal euthanasia: only about a tenth of the population is opposed under all circumstances and support in The Netherlands is the highest in Europe, although it is also strong in Belgium, Denmark, France, Sweden, and the United Kingdom. Politically speaking, euthanasia has become non-controversial in The Netherlands (although some small Christian political parties are still opposed), and there is no significant political support for fundamental change in current policy. In Belgium, political support seems equally strong. During the parliamentary proceedings leading to the law of 2002, only one political group was opposed to legalizing euthanasia.

The Dutch medical profession has supported legal euthanasia by doctors since the mid-1980s. More than half of Dutch doctors have performed euthanasia at least once and only about 10 per cent would be unwilling to do so. Stated support for the patient's right to choose is almost equally strong among Belgian doctors, although during the legislative procedure the medical association did not seem enthusiastic about the prospect of legal regulation of a medical practice it did not regard as giving rise to problems. Professional support is weaker in all other European countries except Switzerland. However, the situation there is not entirely comparable with that in other European countries because assisted suicide—but not euthanasia—without direct involvement of a doctor is a legal and institutionalized practice.

The frequency of euthanasia as a cause of death in The Netherlands has been estimated in national surveys beginning in 1990. The methodology of these surveys has become the international standard. The results indicate that the euthanasia rate in The Netherlands (about 2 per cent of all deaths in 2005) is quite a bit higher than in other European countries (including Belgium before legalization), but that the total of all deaths due to something a doctor does or does not do (withdrawing or withholding treatment and pain relief being by far the most important categories) is no higher in The Netherlands (a little over 40 per cent of all deaths) than in several other Western European countries.

Euthanasia is subject both in The Netherlands and Belgium to a specific control regime. Since the 2002 legislation, the report filed by a doctor who performs euthanasia is reviewed by an interdisciplinary review committee. If the committee finds that the doctor has complied with all the legal requirements, the case ends there; if not, the case is forwarded to the prosecutorial authorities. The number of reported cases per year in The Netherlands since 2002 has been just below 2,000, of which an average of fewer than five per year result in an adverse judgment (none of these cases has been prosecuted, but several have lead to medical disciplinary proceedings and sanctions). In Belgium, the number of reported cases has risen from 24 in 2002 to 393 in 2005; through 2005 there has been no adverse judgment.

The effectiveness of the control regime is dependent upon the willingness of doctors to report what they have done. The rate of reporting in The Netherlands has risen from zero before about 1980 (when doctors began reporting, despite the risk of **prosecution**) to about 80 per cent. The conclusion drawn from this, that doctors are willfully concealing a large part of the euthanasia they actually perform, has led to repeated efforts to encourage fuller reporting (of which the above-mentioned review committees are the most important example). However, this policy conclusion assumes that doctors classify behavior as 'euthanasia' in the same way as the national researchers who calculate the reporting rate. It has recently become clear that there is in fact a significant difference between classifications made by doctors and those made by researchers. The data has been re-analysed, leading to an estimated reporting rate of about 70 per cent in 1995 and 2001 and 99 per cent in 2005.

In considering the relative effectiveness of legal control in The Netherlands and Belgium it should be remembered that, while euthanasia certainly occurs in other countries, the rate of reporting elsewhere remains zero. Apart from the rapid increase over the years in the rate of reporting in both countries, other indications of the effectiveness of the control system (in particular in The Netherlands) are the relatively large number of criminal prosecutions and medical disciplinary cases over the years (almost all of this concerning the exact boundaries of legal euthanasia), and in recent years the very large number of judgments of the review committees, and the resulting enormous growth of law in the area (to which the active regulatory efforts of professional associations must be added).   JOHN GRIFFITHS

J Griffiths, A Bood, and H Weyers, *Euthanasia and Law in the Netherlands* (Amsterdam: Amsterdam University Press, 1998)
J Griffiths, H Weyers, and M Adams, *Euthanasia and Law in Europe* (Oxford: Hart Publishing, 2008)

eviction   *see* **unlawful eviction**

evidence, civil   The law of evidence emerged fairly late in legal history, only taking shape as a system of rules in the eighteenth century. For much of its history, no distinction was drawn in evidence law between the rules applied in civil and criminal trials. Only in the twentieth century did we start to see two distinct laws of evidence emerging, as the rules applying in civil litigation began to be relaxed. If this process meant that we could talk of a distinct law of civil evidence, the relaxation of evidentiary rules in civil courts has today gone so far that we might wonder if there is a law of civil evidence at all, as opposed to a wide discretion given to judges to admit and weigh evidence as they see fit.

The characteristics of civil evidence are best appreciated in light of comparison with criminal evidence. Criminal trials involve putting a defendant at jeopardy of conviction with its associated stigma. They also involve the application of the criminal law, which many believe makes the moral context of the criminal trial a pertinent factor, leading to calls to exclude improperly obtained evidence. While the stakes may be high in a civil case, the moral context is less apparent, and it is usually considered that the parties are on an equal footing to the extent that a mistaken verdict for a claimant is as serious as a mistaken verdict for a defendant. The more serious criminal cases are still tried by a jury, while jury trial only takes place in a handful of civil cases a year.

These differences lead to a number of distinctions between the rules governing civil and criminal trials. Most obvious is the standard of proof: the civil standard of proof 'on the balance of probabilities' (as opposed to the criminal standard 'beyond reasonable doubt') reflects the equality of the parties in a civil case. While the criminal courts have a discretion to exclude improperly obtained prosecution evidence, historically the civil courts have not recognized such a discretion: their role is not to keep the parties to high standards of morality. The more or less complete absence of juries from civil courts is one reason for the relaxation of the most significant **common law** rules of evidence in civil courts. Hearsay evidence will no longer be excluded from a civil trial, and evidence of bad character will be admissible so long as it is relevant.

It is not quite true, however, to say that civil litigation is governed by a principle of free proof under which all relevant evidence is admissible. Evidence may still be excluded on grounds of public policy if, for example, **public interest immunity** applies, as in situations where information is kept secret on grounds of national security. **Legal professional privilege** means that communications between lawyers and their clients are inadmissible. These principles might be said to deal with issues extrinsic to civil evidence, for they reflect wide policy objectives rather than the ends of civil litigation itself. When it comes to rules dealing with matters intrinsic to civil litigation, the shift to free proof is very significant. It might, however, be questioned. The absence of a jury can be said to justify the relaxation of rules governing character and hearsay evidence; but this suggests that the rationale for those rules was that we do not trust juries to reason properly about evidence. But do we really have grounds for such mistrust that do not apply equally to judges?

While highlighting the distinctive nature of the law of civil evidence, the foregoing sketch needs to be qualified in some respects. Recent reforms to civil procedure in England and Wales have given judges more power over civil litigation than they previously had, including new powers to exclude evidence. The courts have recognized the possibility that judges may use such powers to exclude improperly obtained evidence, though it is unlikely that this will happen often. A further qualification is that civil litigation covers a broad range of procedures and tribunals dealing with various different types of case: 'civil' simply means all that is not criminal. Where civil courts consider matters which could have serious consequences for a defendant, such as disqualification from a profession or deportation, the criminal standard of proof beyond reasonable doubt has been held to apply. Indeed, some **tribunals** which deal with matters of professional discipline have been held to be bound wholesale by the rules of criminal evidence.   MIKE REDMAYNE

HM Malek *et al*, *Phipson on Evidence* (London: Sweet & Maxwell, 2005)

Frederick Schauer, 'On the Supposed Jury-Dependence of Evidence Law' (2006) 155 *University of Pennsylvania Law Review* 165

See also: **evidence, criminal**

evidence, criminal   In a criminal trial, the fact-finder (who may be a lay **person**, such as a juror or magistrate, or a professional **judge**) must decide whether to find the defendant guilty. This is a decision which has serious repercussions: a mistaken guilty verdict will brand an innocent person a criminal, and may result in loss of liberty. The rules of criminal evidence govern the way in which the fact-finder's decision is made and, given what is at stake, it is not surprising that the rules are generally stricter than those governing civil trials. Criminal trials require a high standard of proof: the fact-finder should generally not return a verdict of guilty unless convinced beyond reasonable doubt of the defendant's guilt. This high standard of proof is justified by the need to protect defendants from the risk of false conviction; various other rules of criminal evidence are best thought of as promoting accurate decision-making by excluding from the trial, or regulating the use of, evidence to which the fact-finder may give too much weight. But accuracy is not the only value in the criminal trial: it is generally thought that the moral resonance of the criminal verdict requires high standards of procedural propriety. Evidence may therefore be excluded from the trial even if it could promote accurate decision-making: if, for example, the evidence was obtained in breach of the suspect's rights. On the basis of these brief observations, it is tempting to think that the rules of evidence can be divided into two groups: those promoting accurate decision-making, and those concerned more generally with fairness. But things are not this simple, for particular rules of evidence often have more than one justification. This complication is becoming increasingly important in an environment where the traditional rules of evidence are being questioned and, especially in England and Wales, radically reformed.

In the Anglo-American tradition, the best known exclusionary rules are those which exclude hearsay evidence and evidence of bad character. Evidence is hearsay if it is evidence of a statement made before the trial, and the person who made the statement is not available in court to be cross-examined about it. It is often said that fact-finders will give too much weight to hearsay evidence, but most commentators now agree that, if not completely baseless, this justification for the hearsay rule is simplistic. In recent times, there has been interest in justifying something like the hearsay rule on grounds of procedural fairness: a criminal defendant is said to have a right to confront the witnesses against him. While confrontation is a constitutional right in the United States, and receives some **recognition** in the **European Convention on Human Rights**, British **courts** have been reluctant to interpret it as a strong right. This reluctance may reflect a burgeoning recognition of the importance of the rights of **victims** and witnesses in the criminal process: the courts are aware that the process of giving evidence may be stressful, and that in some cases witnesses face threats and intimidation. The rule against evidence of bad character paradigmatically protects defendants from having their previous convictions revealed in court. In England and Wales, this aspect of the rule has been substantially reformed (as has the hearsay rule) by the Criminal Justice Act 2003, which has weakened the presumption against the admissibility of the defendant's previous convictions. In general the exclusion of evidence is a drastic step, for it denies the fact-finder relevant information. Even if there is well-grounded concern that the fact-finder will put too much weight on the fact that the defendant has previous convictions, it is not obvious that denying the fact-finder this evidence altogether will promote accuracy. An alternative strategy is to alert the fact-finder to the dangers of relying on a particular type of evidence. This is how the courts deal with eye-witness evidence, and, in some cases, with evidence from the defendant's associates. The Scottish courts go further, stipulating that in the vast majority of criminal cases a defendant cannot be convicted on uncorroborated evidence.

Underlying the rules of evidence are more general principles, about which the law has little to say. Only relevant evidence is admissible, but what is it that makes evidence relevant? This is in part an empirical matter: a failure to respond to an accusation of wrongdoing is only relevant to the question of guilt if the guilty are more likely to stay silent than the innocent. At times such questions of relevance are controversial, as in debates about whether a rape complainant's previous sexual history is relevant to the issue of consent in a **rape** trial.

MIKE REDMAYNE

P Roberts and A Zuckerman, *Criminal Evidence* (Oxford: Oxford University Press, 2004)

ex aequo et bono   *see* **international dispute settlement**

excise duties The *Shorter Oxford English Dictionary* definition of 'excise duties' provides a good working description. It defines an excise duty as 'a duty levied on goods produced or sold within a country and on licences granted for certain activities' (eg vehicle excise duty). Excise duties are to be contrasted with customs duties, which are generally levied on the importation of goods. Excise duties seem to have originated in the charge levied by a feudal lord on goods being taken to market, which was then taken over by the **Crown**. These days, levying of excise duties, particularly on alcohol, hydrocarbon oils, and tobacco products, is regulated to a considerable degree by **European law**.

The rate of duty is set separately for each product within European limits. Goods subject to excise duty include beer, wine, spirits, and other alcoholic drinks; hydrocarbon oils (including fuel oil); and tobacco goods. In the past duty has been levied on such things as wigs, dogs, and maid servants. In the UK, excise duty is administered by Her Majesty's Revenue and Customs ('HMRC'), the successor to the Board of Excise set up in the seventeenth century. The HMRC website provides further practical and detailed information.

'Drawbacks', which figured in discussions leading to the Act of Union in the early eighteenth century, are still a feature of the law of excise duties. Drawback allows repayment of excise duty paid on goods that have not been and will not be consumed in the UK. There are also arrangements for duty suspension that allow goods which will not be consumed in the UK to be traded without the duty having to be paid. Bonded warehouses are warehouses authorized by HMRC for the deposit, without payment of duty, of such goods. There are special rules for the storage of oil.

Payment of duty is sometimes designated by marks and stamps (eg the recent introduction of stamps for liquor).   ADRIAN SHIPWRIGHT

exclusion clauses An exclusion clause, also known as an 'exception' or 'exemption clause', or a 'disclaimer', is a term in a contract (often a **standard form contract**) which purports to exclude the liability of one of the parties to the contract for failure to perform or for performance otherwise than as agreed in the contract. Such a clause can be expressed straightforwardly (eg 'Any liability for non-performance is excluded'), but it may also be phrased in such a way as to require more careful analysis in order to identify its exclusionary nature. Although inclusion in the contract of an exclusion clause may be agreed by the parties, perhaps for reasons of cost, such clauses are often imposed by the party which has greater economic strength and/or better information about the particular transaction. The use of such clauses is of particular concern in consumer contracts.

A number of legal tools for controlling the impact of exclusion clauses have been developed, including the Unfair Contract Terms Act 1977 ('UCTA') and regulations dealing specifically with consumer contracts. A party seeking to rely on an exclusion clause will first have to establish that this forms part of (has been 'incorporated into') the contract, and that its terms covers the circumstances of the particular case. The clause will be incorporated into the contract if it is in a document which has been signed by the parties, or if the party against whom the clause is relied upon knew that the contract included such a clause. A clause can also be incorporated if reasonable notice is given of the clause's existence. Such notice must be given before the contract is made, and it must be reasonably sufficient to draw the other party's attention to the clause. A particularly onerous clause would have to be clearly drawn to the other party's attention.

If incorporated, the clause will be interpreted restrictively against the party seeking to rely on it (*contra proferentem*) and in favour of the other party. Even if the clause, so interpreted, is apt to exclude liability, it may be rendered ineffective by UCTA. Certain exclusion clauses will always be ineffective; other clauses will be ineffective if contained in a contract between a business and a consumer, but may be effective as between two businesses, if 'reasonable' within the meaning given to this term by UCTA. So a clause excluding liability for death or personal injury caused by negligence will always be ineffective. A clause that purports to exclude the rights of a buyer under the legislation on the **sale of goods** will always be ineffective where the buyer is a consumer, but ineffective only if unreasonable where the buyer is a business. UCTA provides guidelines to be used in establishing the reasonableness of a term. This is determined by reference to the context of the particular contract, leaving judges applying the guidelines with a significant amount of discretion.

UTCA also applies to notices which are not part of a contract. For example, signs displayed in car parks excluding liability for damage to cars are ineffective unless damage caused by negligence on the part of the car-park operator is expressly removed from the scope of the notice.   CHRISTIAN TWIGG-FLESNER

See also: **unfair contract terms**

exclusion from school   *see* **school discipline and the exclusion of pupils**

exclusive economic zone   *see* **law of the sea**

excuse (criminal)   *see* **justification, mitigation and excuse in criminal law**

executive agencies   *see* **next steps agencies**

executive agreements   *see* **treaties**

executive pay   In the last two or so decades, there has been a manifest and steady increase in the remuneration of leading corporate executives. It is estimated (by Income Data Services) that between 1993–2003, in a period when average earnings rose by about 45 per cent, the average earnings of leading executives of the FTSE 100 companies increased by 288 per cent. A survey of executive remuneration (Guardian/RTF) revealed that in 2006 the average pay of the directors of Britain's leading **companies** had risen by 37 per cent. Although still some way behind CEO earnings in the US, the earnings of CEOs in the UK are now almost 100 times those of their average employee. What we are seeing, some argue, is a 'globalization (or Americanization) of executive pay'. Even European executive compensation, while still only at levels one-third of those in the US, is beginning to rise.

The issue has become entwined with increasingly widespread concerns about the effects of growing income and wealth inequality: it is estimated that the richest one per cent of the British population increased its share of overall income from 6.5 per cent in 1980 to 13 per cent in 1999. In this context, executive pay has come to symbolize the polarization of income and wealth, and become an increasingly controversial and politically charged issue, exemplified by regular references to 'fat cats'. Thus far, the government has declined to intervene. Indeed, in 2001 Tony Blair expressly ruled out state intervention to set limits on how much people could earn. This may explain why the UK Company Law Review in 2005 was conspicuously silent on the issue.

Executive pay is composed of a number of basic components: salary, annual bonuses (which have themselves attracted much recent media attention), share options, and LTIPs (Long Term Incentive Plans), to which are often added retirement plans and, in the event of departure (even for alleged failure) 'golden handshakes'. The relative mix varies between jurisdictions: executives in the US and UK, for example, tend to receive a higher proportion of

their remuneration in the form of options. It was recently suggested that a modern British executive can expect to make nearly five times as much from bonuses, **share** awards, share options, incentive schemes, and **pension** contributions as from basic salary. For some, rising executive pay benefits shareholders. 'Optimal contracting theory', for example, suggests that pay practices promote the maximization of shareholder wealth by balancing the separate costs of contracting, monitoring, and potential 'shirking' by managers so as to minimize costs. More prosaically, it is also argued that should levels of executive remuneration fall in Britain, talent would migrate. For others, however, spiralling executive pay is simply a reflection of the growing power of the managerial elite, an example of 'rent extraction'. Although formally delegated to remuneration committees made up of allegedly 'independent' non-executive directors, they argue, executive remuneration is effectively in the hands of the managerial elite. In support, they cite evidence suggesting both that these committees lack genuine 'independence' and that the increased use of remuneration committees has had little effect on either the level or sensitivity of executive pay. Even 'failure', it is argued, is being richly rewarded. 'A CEO salary', JK Galbraith once remarked, 'is not so much a reward for achievement as a warm personal gesture by the individual to himself'. Written of the US some believe this has now become true of Britain.

PADDY IRELAND

B Wedderburn, *The Future of Company Law: Fat Cats, Corporate Governance, and Workers* (London: Institute of Employment Rights, 2004)

See also: **independent directors**

exhaustive harmonization   *see* **approximation of laws in the EU**

expenditure tax   An expenditure tax is a tax on an individual's spending on goods and services, that is to say a tax on the individual's consumption. The term 'expenditure tax' is generally used in place of 'consumption tax' to describe a tax on consumption imposed in the form of a direct tax on individuals. Consumption can also be taxed through various forms of taxes on businesses and through a general sales tax such as retail sales tax or a **value added tax**.

An expenditure tax calculates consumption indirectly by taxing income minus net saving. All of an individual's income is, by definition, spent, saved, or used to repay money borrowed in the past. If we regard borrowing as a sort of negative saving, it follows that we can measure consumption expenditure as income less net saving. Because a tax on consumption does not tax savings, it has the advantage over the other principal 'ideal' tax, a comprehensive income tax, that a consumption tax does not distort the rate of return on savings, and thus does not distort individuals' choices between consumption and savings. However, both consumption and income taxes affect the choice between working and not working (the choice between consumption and leisure).

On the negative side it is argued that consumption taxes tend to be regressive in terms of income, notably because those with higher incomes are in a position to save a considerably larger proportion of their incomes. In response, it is argued that from a lifetime perspective, a tax on consumption does not favour the better off because, in principle, a consumption tax taxes all consumption eventually.

The principal advantage of an expenditure tax over other consumption taxes is that it makes it possible to calculate the total expenditure of each individual. As a result it is possible to implement it with progressive rates on higher levels of expenditure if desired. In particular, this provides a response to the concern that consumption taxes tend to be regressive. Higher rates of tax on higher levels of consumption may also be desired in themselves on grounds of inter-personal equity.

In principle, it would be possible to calculate expenditure for an expenditure tax by adding up all incomings (such as wages and salaries, dividends, interest, withdrawals of savings, the proceeds of selling capital assets, and borrowings) and subtracting all outgoings other than consumption (such as amounts saved, interest paid, amounts lent or repaid, and the cost of purchasing capital assets). In practice, however, expenditure can be calculated much more simply by identifying the key elements of net savings using a concept of registered assets. In calculating expenditure the taxpayer would get a deduction for deposits into registered accounts or purchases of registered assets. These would then be treated in the same way as pension fund contributions are treated in many income tax systems: any income or gains on registered assets would be ignored, but the full proceeds of any sales of registered assets or net withdrawals from registered accounts would be added to taxable expenditure for the year, unless reinvested in other registered assets or accounts. Amounts borrowed would be treated as withdrawals, but repayments (including interest thereon) would be deductible in the same way as registered savings. When a registered asset was purchased using borrowed money,

the borrowing would offset the purchase price, so only the deposit, if any, would be deductible as saving; but in future years repayments of the loan would also count as saving. This treatment could be used for the purchase of housing.

Various forms of consumption taxation, including expenditure taxes, have been proposed since the early twentieth century. An important proponent of expenditure tax was the economist Nicholas Kaldor, who influenced the introduction of taxes on this principle in India and Ceylon in the 1950s. These taxes ran into practical and political difficulties and did not long survive. In the UK, the Meade Committee proposed a registered-asset form of progressive expenditure tax, which the Committee called Universal Expenditure Tax ('UET'). It also proposed a system under which a progressive registered-asset expenditure tax, applied only to higher levels of expenditure, would be combined with a flat-rate tax, such as a value added tax ('VAT'). The Committee called this a Two-Tier Expenditure Tax ('TTET').

IAN ROXAN

expert evidence Expert evidence, also known as 'expert opinion evidence', forms an exception to the opinion rule. The opinion rule prevents witnesses from testifying about matters of opinion or drawing inferences beyond those necessary for the understanding of their testimony. The exception allows expert witnesses to testify about matters of opinion and inferences based upon facts which they did not personally experience. Provided they restrict themselves to their area of specialization, experts are conventionally granted considerable testimonial latitude.

Determinations of the admissibility of expert evidence and assessments of expertise tend to be concerned with assuring the foundations (or basis) of the evidence and the reliability of the expert's opinions. This usually involves some assessment of the training, competence, and experience of the expert as well as an evaluation of his or her knowledge, methods, techniques, and assumptions. Admissibility determinations tend to be least controversial where there is an established discipline or profession (eg obstetrics or accounting) and a skilled exponent intends to give evidence based on knowledge, methods, techniques, and assumptions widely accepted among the practitioners in that field. Where, however, the field is new or controversial (eg polygraphy) or the expert intends to present opinions not widely accepted, judges tend to act more cautiously. Always the prerogative of the trial judge, admissibility determinations tend to be more restrictive where expert evidence will go before a jury.

To be admitted, expert evidence should be relevant to the disputed facts and help the fact finder (whether judge or jury) to decide the case. It is generally limited to specialized knowledge beyond the ken of the average juror. Notwithstanding the continuing use of lay judges and jurors as fact finders, there are no rules requiring fact finders to accept uncontroverted expert evidence. In practice, however, it may be difficult for fact finders, and institutionally unsettling for courts of appeal, to resist uncontested and apparently credible expert evidence.

The rationale for the reception of expert evidence was expressed by Saunders J in *Buckley v Rice Thomas* (1554): 'we [lawyers] do not despise all other sciences . . . but we approve of them and encourage them as things worthy of commendation'. Indexing legal practice to exogenous expertise is intended to enhance the legitimacy of legal institutions by helping fact finders to make accurate as well as just decisions. Despite these aspirations, expert evidence and procedures associated with its admissibility and assessment have been controversial for centuries. Perhaps the most interesting aspect of the continuing controversy is the pervasive, though empirically questionable, attribution of a range of socio-legal problems to unreliable expert evidence. In recent decades this disquiet has stimulated a range of procedural reforms.

In England, changes to the Civil Procedure Rules ('CPR') in 1998, following the Woolf Report, have encouraged managerial trial judges to streamline legal processes by: requiring greater pre-trial disclosure of expert reports; promoting the use of written reports so that experts are not required to testify in person; reducing the number of experts; and, empowering judges to compel opposing parties to agree upon a single joint expert. The CPR impose on expert witnesses an overriding duty to the court and create an expectation that they will adhere to idealized norms of independence, impartiality, and cooperation. Some of these changes have been mimicked in Commonwealth jurisdictions (eg Australia). In the US, where jury trials are constitutionally guaranteed, empirically unfounded anxieties about the prevalence of so-called junk science, increases in litigation rates and damages awards, and juror incompetence have, in the wake of a few important Supreme Court decisions, led to the imposition of more demanding admissibility thresholds and revision of the Federal Rules of Evidence (1975). Onerous pre-trial admissibility hearings have been used to pre-empt tort and **product liability** litigation by excluding plaintiffs' expert evidence.

Recent reforms have not responded to changes in the way modern scientific research is organized and funded. Striving for illusive ideals such as independence and objectivity, contemporary rules and procedures seem indifferent to the changing relations between the sciences and commerce as well as their implications for litigation and proof. Rather than developing procedures capable of accommodating expert disagreement or trying to address the complexity of modern forms of expertise, **common law** judges have developed rules designed to limit expert disagreement (eg requiring the use of a single joint expert) and have prevented expert evidence from entering courts. Ostensibly intended to improve access to justice by reducing costs and enhancing the reliability of expert evidence, recent reforms have conferred procedural efficiencies (predominantly on judges) and reduced institutionally destabilising controversies; but the fairness of the procedures and the reliability of decisions remain uncertain.

GARY EDMOND

See also: **evidence, civil; evidence, criminal**

expropriation Expropriation occurs where state conduct results in a substantial deprivation of a person's rights in, or enjoyment of, property. Expropriation is also known as 'taking'. It is generally accepted that **customary international law** recognizes the right of persons to hold, and enjoy the use of, property, and to receive prompt, adequate, and effective compensation for its expropriation by a foreign state. Expropriation is not prohibited under international law. Expropriation is a concept found in most of the world's legal systems. Property rights regimes differ widely from state to state, however, and expropriation can only occur where it has been established that a particular right was granted or enjoyed under the relevant regime.

The right to hold property is found in **international human rights law**. However, international law also recognizes the sovereign right of states to interfere with individual property rights, including those held by foreign nationals. This recognition is based on the theory that each state is responsible for establishing and regulating a system of property rights within its territorial jurisdiction. Customary international law does not regulate the conditions on which states allow foreigners to acquire or enjoy property rights within their territory. Such conduct may be regulated by economic treaty.

Often codified by treaty, the customary international law of expropriation regulates whether and when compensation is due should expropriation occur. The expropriation analysis focuses on the effects of state conduct. Expropriation does not occur if state conduct does not substantially interfere with the right to hold, or enjoy the use of, property. Severity of interference depends upon several factors, including: the temporal nature of the interference, its impact upon the rights holder, and its impact upon the property right itself. Interference need not be permanent, or total, for expropriation to occur. Expropriation can take place by direct or indirect means. Expropriation can occur by means of a nationalization decree or through regulation. It can take place through conduct that has an immediate impact or through the imposition of a series of measures (known as: 'creeping expropriation'), including confiscatory tax increases. A finding of expropriation is not based upon whether property has been physically taken or whether property rights have been officially transferred.

'Prompt, adequate and effective' compensation means compensation that is paid in a convertible currency as soon as is practicable, and which constitutes the fair market value of that which has been expropriated. Fair market value is the amount a notional investor would have paid to acquire that which was taken, excluding any decrease in value attributable to the state conduct that resulted in such taking.

The expropriation analysis is highly contextual, although tribunals commonly draw analogies to past cases. Relevant factors include: the conditions under which the property right was granted; the nature and extent of the conduct at issue; and whether any treaty rights otherwise condition such conduct.

Historically, a distinction was made between 'legal' and 'illegal' takings, where only the latter required compensation on a prompt, adequate, and effective basis. Factors that contribute to a finding of illegal expropriation included: whether state conduct was discriminatory; whether it was in accordance with principles of fairness and due process; and whether the taking was for a public purpose. These factors are still relevant to the overall analysis but it is generally accepted that all takings require prompt, adequate, and effective compensation.

Some commentators believe that an expropriation does not occur where state conduct constitutes a *bona fide* exercise of the 'police power' (ie the power to regulate in the public interest). The better view is that a claimant must prove that it held a legitimate expectation to enjoy its property rights, given the totality of the circumstances. Such circumstances include the nature of the legal regime under which the rights were granted and the reasonableness of any state conduct that alters it. Where such expectation is not established, prompt, adequate, and effective compensation may be withheld.

TODD WEILER

expulsion　*see* **refugees**

external protections　The concept of an 'external protection', as it is considered here, arises in the legal and political theory of **multiculturalism**, particularly **liberal multiculturalism**. The latter idea argues that the state should grant rights to certain groups that would otherwise be disadvantaged, such as exemptions from laws which generally apply, rights to group **representation** in government, and rights of legal and political **self-determination**. For a liberal proponent of group rights (such as Will Kymlicka, who has probably done the most to develop and clarify this position, and who coined the term 'external protection'), these are justified since they allow members of a group to pursue a way of life, culture, or religion on an equal footing with the rest of society. So, for example, a minority language group may claim that equality of educational opportunity requires that this language be used as a medium of instruction in schools. Defenders of these group rights characterize them as external protections, that is, as ways in which a group may protect its identity from the impact of the economic and political decisions of the wider society. Without such protections, the argument runs, control over a minority group's **identity** is taken out its hands, in a way damaging to the members of this group. A group right understood as an external protection contrasts with a group right that acts as an **internal restriction**, compelling members to follow traditional practices and suppressing dissent. The latter is far more problematic for a liberal multiculturalism concerned to protect a traditional 'bundle' of liberal rights for individuals. However, it is not always easy to prise apart the function of a right as an external protection and its internally restrictive consequences. For example, if a province (such as Wales or Quebec) is granted the right to impose its own language policy, in order to protect a minority language, this can entail restricting the options available to members of that group. In order to protect French in Quebec, for example, the right to public education in English is barred to the children of Francophone parents. It is only through some internal restriction that the minority language can be protected against English.

MATTHEW FESTENSTEIN

extortionate credit bargains   *see* **usury**

extradition   Extradition and **deportation** are popularly confused. Deportation is a process whereby the authorities order that someone leave the country; extradition, however, is the process whereby a person who is accused or, more rarely, has been convicted of a crime in another state is returned to a state asserting jurisdiction to prosecute or punish that person. A person who is deported may face trial on return to their country of nationality, but that is not the object of deportation.

Extradition usually requires some form of international arrangement between the requesting and requested states—a bilateral treaty or, more often now, a regional multilateral treaty, such as the Council of Europe's European Convention on Extradition 1957. A state can ratify such a multilateral treaty and thereby obviate the need for negotiating individual bilateral treaties. The London Scheme for Extradition within the [British] Commonwealth 2002 resembles a treaty in form, but relies on domestic implementation without any need to ratify the Scheme. Some states have close relationships and they adopt simplified schemes without the need for diplomatic relations. Australia and New Zealand, for example, have a procedure under which arrest warrants issued by one are recognized by the other. There is no diplomatic request and the executive is not involved. Extradition is conducted solely at the level of the police and courts.

Similar schemes once operated between the Benelux countries and between Ireland and the UK. However, the European Arrest Warrant ('EAW') has now implemented a warrant-based system that is being introduced across the **European Union**'s Member States. The EAW will allow extradition between the twenty-seven Member States without requiring diplomatic intervention and without having to prove double criminality (see below). Previously, neighbouring states have established simplified schemes, whereas the EAW's remit stretches from the Baltics to Ireland and from the Arctic Circle down to Malta. Finally, *ad hoc* extradition is also possible for certain states without any general arrangement. The **United Kingdom** can extradite *ad hoc*, but has an obligation to ensure that adequate safeguards are imposed for the protection of the alleged fugitive offender. The alternative is that a serious criminal might escape punishment for lack of an arrangement between the requesting and requested states.

Traditionally, extradition should commence with a diplomatic request for the fugitive's surrender, which, if authorized, is passed to the courts to execute. Normally, however, the prosecuting authorities send a provisional request to their counterparts in the requested state, the diplomatic niceties being concluded later. Of course, in simplified schemes, it is solely a matter for the prosecutor, courts, and the police. In the UK, the Extradition Act 2003 governs the process. It divides requesting states into Categories 1 and 2: Category 1 states are those to which the EAW applies; Category 2 contains all other states.

Regardless of the process under which the person is detained in the requested state, the court hearing is reasonably similar. The extradition court will require proof of identity, that the request is for an extradition crime (usually determined by the possible sentence for such a crime in the requested state), double criminality, and, possibly, a *prima facie* case against the accused. Double criminality is the requirement that the facts reveal the commission of a crime recognized by the law of the requesting state and that courts of the requested state would have jurisdiction in similar circumstances. Ordinarily this is no problem: if, for instance, Canada requested extradition of someone for a robbery in Ottawa, an English court would have jurisdiction over a robbery in London. Difficulties arise where the requesting state is asserting extraterritorial jurisdiction, particularly over failed attempts or conspiracies. In the **Pinochet case**, the Spanish request for Pinochet's extradition turned on whether the UK would, in similar circumstances, have been able to prosecute the former head of state for torture of Chileans in Chile.

Assuming the requesting state meets its obligations, the fugitive can prevent extradition by relying on various 'defences'. One defence is that surrender to the requesting state would leave the UK in breach of its obligations under the **European Convention on Human Rights** ('ECHR'), particularly freedom from torture. In one case, the **European Court of Human Rights** held it would breach Article 3 of the ECHR (on torture) to return someone to the 'death row phenomenon' in the USA. A flagrant denial of fair trial should also prevent extradition. Civil law states (eg in continental Europe) usually refuse to extradite their own nationals, although the EAW does not permit this limitation.

The distinctive extradition defence is the political offence exemption. Most states, but—since 2003—not the UK, refuse extradition where the request relates to a political offence. It is not enough that the crime was politically motivated: the offence must have been part of and in furtherance of a political disturbance; it must not have been too remote from the ultimate goal of the fugitive's organization, it must have been political vis-à-vis the requesting state, and it must be proportionate to the organization's goal. The so-called 'Swiss predominance test' has been adopted by most states, excluding terrorist crimes because they are disproportionate. The Genocide Convention 1948, the European Convention for the Suppression of Terrorism 1977, and certain recent **United Nations** multilateral treaties have excluded the political offence defence with respect to stipulated crimes.

Certain anti-terrorist treaties require the requested state either to surrender a fugitive or prosecute: *aut dedere, aut judicare*. Refusal is usually predicated on human rights or due process grounds, but that should not mean that the fugitive enjoys impunity. It is unclear whether the obligation to surrender or prosecute is triggered without a rejected extradition request.

Finally, related to extradition, although different, is surrender to the various international criminal tribunals. Special arrangements were needed so that the UK could surrender persons to the Yugoslav and Rwanda Tribunals and to the **International Criminal Court** ('ICC'). The Security Council established the *Ad Hoc* Tribunals which had, as a consequence, primacy; but the ICC has complementary jurisdiction with the result that states and the ICC could submit competing requests for the same person.

GEOFF GILBERT

extraordinary general meeting   *see* **shareholder meetings**

F

Factortame case: R v Secretary of State for Transport, ex p Factortame (No 2) (1991) This case concerned the relationship between the legislation of the UK's 'sovereign' **Westminster Parliament** and **European Community law**. The decision clarified that relationship: when EC law conflicts with UK legislation, the UK courts will disapply the UK legislation and apply the EC law. However, questions about the theoretical basis of the decision remain.

The case concerned whether it was lawful for Spanish-owned trawlers, registered in the United Kingdom, to fish under the British EU fishing quota. The trawlers had been registered in Britain and fished under the British quota for several years before the Merchant Shipping Act 1988 was passed, which prevented foreign-owned trawlers from benefiting in this way. The trawler owners considered that their rights under EC law had been violated. In the UK courts they challenged the application of the 1988 Act by the Secretary of State.

A crucial issue was whether the trawler owners could obtain interim relief to continue fishing while the courts decided the case. The House of Lords eventually held that English law precluded the award of an interim injunction against a Secretary of State. Was this sufficient to protect the alleged rights of the claimants under Community law pending the final decision of the court? The House of Lords referred this question to the **European Court of Justice**, which held that the maintaining of the effectiveness of Community law required that a national law that precluded interim relief to protect such rights should be set aside.

The House of Lords now had to decide whether to grant interim relief. It held that it would not restrain a public authority from enforcing an Act of Parliament unless the challenge to the Act was 'sufficiently firmly based to justify the exceptional course [of imposing interim restraint] being taken'. However, under relevant EC law the applicants' challenge to the validity of the 1988 Act was 'strong'. Accordingly interim relief was granted.

Thus the 1988 Act was disapplied; and EC law prevailed over the legislation of the 'sovereign' Westminster Parliament. Lord Bridge 'with a sublime detachment from constitutional dogma' held that there was nothing 'novel' about this.

The European Communities Act 1972 indeed says that Community law prevails over conflicting **Acts of Parliament** 'passed or to be passed', and the disapplication of the 1988 Act seemed to follow from that. But this means that Parliament in 1972 had effectively bound Parliament in 1988 not to legislate contrary to Community Law. Constitutional dogma had long held that Parliament could not bind its successors. To hold otherwise would deprive the later parliament of its **sovereignty**.

Views differ on whether the resulting supremacy of EC law should be considered a constitutional **revolution** or simply an alteration of the rule of interpretation that later statutes prevail over earlier ones. All are agreed, though, that at present Parliament retains the power to repeal the 1972 Act and bring an end to all Community Law in the UK.

CHRISTOPHER F FORSYTH

See also: **entrenchment of constitutions and legislation; interpreting legislation**

failing schools and local education authorities   *see* **school standards and the inspection of schools and LEAs**

fair access to higher education   *see* **universities and higher education**

fair reporting by media   Fair reporting may refer broadly to the overall balance of media content. In that sense, there is no requirement that the press should report fairly; and while journalistic ethics may encourage objectivity, the law allows editors to be as selective as they choose about what is published. However, broadcasters are prohibited from editorializing and must report news, and matters of political and industrial controversy and of public policy, with due impartiality.

Fair reporting also includes the way that the media treat individuals and organizations in obtaining and publishing information about them. Under Ofcom's Fairness Code, broadcasters must avoid unjust and unfair treatment in programmes. Whilst there may be public interest justifications for withholding information or practising deception (including surreptitious recording), contributions should normally be based on informed consent, which entails that relevant persons should be told the nature and purpose of the programme, and how they and others will feature in it, and should be kept aware of significant changes in its development. Editing should ensure that all contributions, including past and re-used material, are represented fairly, and that guarantees of anonymity or confidentiality are honoured. Opportunities to contribute or to respond to allegations should be given to those affected by the programme, before it is broadcast, and their absence or refusal to participate should be explained fairly. By contrast, fairness, including such a right of reply, is not required in the **Press Complaints Commission**'s code, which concedes only a fair opportunity for reasonable requests to reply to inaccuracies.

TOM GIBBONS

See also: **programme standards and complaints**

fair trial, right to   The right to a fair trial is recognized in every significant international document protecting **human rights**. It is a standard by which a state's commitment to **democracy** and the **rule of law** is measured. As with other **human** rights, its development can be traced to the individualistic philosophy of the Enlightenment. The **common law** has long recognized two minimum fair trial guarantees, known as the principles of **natural justice**: *nemo judex in causa sua* ('nobody can be a judge in their own cause') and *audi alteram partem* ('the right to be heard'). Over the years, the right has evolved to encompass a number of other elements including a right of access to the courts, a public hearing, a hearing within a reasonable time, and an obligation on **judges** to give reasons for decisions.

The right to a fair trial has been given further significance in recent years by the incorporation of the **European Convention on Human Rights** into UK domestic law under the Human Rights Act 1998. The constituent rights that comprise the right to a fair trial under Article 6 of the Convention have been given an enhanced status under the Act which requires that courts must do all they can to resolve any conflict between a Convention right and a provision of primary legislation in favour of the Convention.

Furthermore direct reliance can now be placed on those rights in domestic court proceedings.

Article 6(1) of the Convention states that in the determination of their civil rights and obligations or of any criminal charge against them, everyone is entitled to a fair and public hearing within a reasonable time by an independent and impartial tribunal established by law. A number of principles have been developed by the **European Court of Human Rights** to give content to a 'fair' hearing, including the need for proceedings to be 'adversarial' and the need for 'equality of arms', although the Court's notion of 'adversarialism' does not include all the attributes of the common law adversarial trial.

Article 6(2) and (3) provide for certain specific minimum rights in criminal cases including the presumption of innocence, information as to the accusation, adequate time and facilities to prepare a defence, a right to defend oneself in person or through legal assistance, the right to examine witnesses, and the assistance of an interpreter. These minimum rights must be read together with Article 6(1), as a criminal trial could still be unfair even if they have been respected. The European Court has also recognized other rights which lie at the heart of the right to a fair trial but are not explicitly provided for under the Article, such as the right of access to the courts (*Golder v UK* (1975)) and the privilege against self-incrimination (*Saunders v UK* (1997)).

There are a number of uncertainties about the scope and application of Article 6. It is unclear to what extent 'civil rights and obligations' extend beyond private rights into the realm of public law and to what extent unfairness at an earlier stage of the proceedings can affect fairness at the trial. In criminal proceedings Article 6 protections are only triggered once a 'criminal charge' is being determined and there is some uncertainty as to when this occurs. Although Article 6 cannot be qualified in any way under the Convention, another uncertainty relates to the extent to which the constituent rights within Article 6 may be balanced against other interests. The European Court has held that these rights are not themselves absolute and may be qualified in certain circumstances. In *Doorson v Netherlands* (1997) the Court went so far as to say that the principles of fair trial require that in appropriate circumstances the interests of the defence are balanced against those of witnesses or **victims** called upon to testify. However, it has been argued that despite certain British decisions indicating the contrary (see *Brown v Stott (Procurator Fiscal)* (2001)), it is not legitimate to permit the general interests of the **community** to outweigh the interests of the individual. While the right to a fair trial is fundamental, there is scope for considerable debate as to how entrenched the various elements of a fair trial ought to be.

JOHN JACKSON

R Clayton and H Tomlinson, *Fair Trial Rights* (Oxford: Oxford University Press, 2001)

B Emmerson, A Ashworth, and A Macdonald, *Human Rights and Criminal Justice* (London: Sweet & Maxwell, 2007)

See also: **adversarial system; criminal trials**

fairness in broadcasting　*see* **fair reporting by media**

faith schools　*see* **school admissions**

family finances　The obligations arising from a **marriage** are mutual, both parties owe each other the same duties, but as it is usually the wife who is economically the weaker party the discussion below assumes this is so.

When a marriage breaks down the wife may be in need of immediate financial assistance. Husbands are under a duty to maintain their wives and if the husband fails to do so the wife can apply to the magistrates' or county **court** for an order for **maintenance**. If the husband fails to pay maintenance as required, the wife can claim social security benefits. However, the Benefits Agency can then recover that money from the husband. Cohabitants are not under any duty to maintain each other, but any couple who are living together will find that their income is aggregated for the purpose of assessing any claim for means-tested benefits. If money is needed for the children then an application has to be made by the **woman** to the **Child Support** Agency ('CSA'). From 2008, most parents will be encouraged to agree payments between themselves, with the new Child Maintenance and Enforcement Commission ('C-Mec') taking over the difficult cases.

Also after breakdown, if the marital home is owned and is solely in the name of the husband it is important that the wife consider registering her right to live in the house. If she does not, the husband can enter into a transaction with a third party without her knowledge or consent and subsequently the wife may find that she loses her home to the third party. If there has been **domestic violence** the wife can apply for an order to exclude the husband. He will remain liable to pay the rent or mortgage, or the wife can seek an order for payments to herself to cover the cost of the accommodation.

If the parties decide to **divorce** the Matrimonial Causes Act 1973 provides guidelines for deciding what should happen between the parties. Courts take into account a list of factors, with the welfare of the children coming first. It thereafter depends on the facts of each individual case which factors are crucial. The issues the courts consider are: the parties income and earning capacity; needs and **responsibilitie**s; standard of living; age and length of marriage; any **disability** suffered; contributions to the family, including domestic and caring; conduct if particularly bad; and loss of **pension**.

In relation to income, the first call on the husband's income is payment for any dependent children. The CSA works to a formula and the husband will be expected to pay whatever figure the CSA stipulates. A small portion of the CSA payment is regarded as money belonging to the wife as carer. However, as it is characterized as **child** support the wife no longer receives it when the child support ceases. If he has any money left over after paying for the children, the husband is likely to be expected to make payments to maintain the wife at least initially.

Unlike orders in relation to property, an order for maintenance to the wife is not a final order and can be varied at any **time** until the order comes to an end. There is a general principle that where possible there should be a clean break between the parties after divorce. So, even if maintenance payments are thought appropriate, how much the wife should be seeking and for how long is very relevant. Thus although, eg women with small children can expect payments to begin with, there is an expectation that in time they will go out to work and their support will cease. However, where the marriage has been a very long one and the wife has been financially dependent on the husband he may have to maintain her for the rest of her life.

There are a number of options available in deciding what should happen to the family home and the fact that only one person is named as the legal owner does not make any difference, there is complete **discretion** as to how to deal with it. The house could be given entirely to the wife, or she could be given a life interest in it, the husband only being allowed to deal with it after her death or in his will. This would be unusual and will normally only happen if the husband can be properly compensated in some other way, the marriage has been fleeting and it was the wife's property, or the behaviour of the husband has been so atrocious that this is a fair outcome. Alternatively, the house could be sold and the proceeds divided, in whatever proportion is thought appropriate, between the parties. Particularly if there are no dependent children living at home and there will be enough money from the sale for both parties to be re-housed, this is a sensible option. However, if there are still children living at home then a more usual option is that the home will be transferred to the wife for the time being and the husband will get his share at a later date when a specified event or events occurs. The usual events are ones based around either the children or the wife. The age of the children is often chosen, for example when the youngest child reaches eighteen years or finishes full-time education. If based around the wife, the choice could be when she moves, remarries, dies, or cohabits. The last choice can cause difficulties both in determining whether **cohabitation** has actually occurred and its length. When the earliest of the specified events has occurred the husband is then entitled to his share in the property. The wife can then either try to buy the husband out, or the house will have to be sold and the proceeds split in the designated proportions.

It is very important to try and make the correct decision about how the proceeds from the property should be divided at the outset, as once agreement has been finalized or a court order has been made concerning property, that decision is final and cannot subsequently be altered even though things may have changed substantially in the meantime. Ultimately, what should be sought is a fair outcome and on this basis a reasonable starting point is equal division between the parties. However, in England and Wales, there is no presumption of equal sharing, which is in marked contrast to Scotland, where there is a statutory presumption of a 50/50 split.

The Scottish have a system of separate property and the law is more 'rule-based' than in England, favouring legal certainty over discretion. Criteria are laid down dealing with a variety of situations. Thus, although there is a presumption that household goods are jointly owned, money and cars are expressly excluded. Consequently, unlike in England where all assets are normally put into a common pool for division, there is a presumption that a car belongs to its registered owner, not necessarily the **person** who drives it, and that money placed in a sole named account belongs to that person. Similarly any property acquired as a gift from a third party or as an inheritance is separately owned. In England whether property acquired through inheritance should go into the general melting pot for distribution is much more difficult to decide. Where there are not many assets to go around it is likely to be added in with everything else, provision for any children and the needs of the parties taking priority.

However, where more wealthy parties are involved the view may be taken that the beneficiary should keep all the inheritance.

In Scotland there is a duty to aliment, ie maintain, the wife, but this obligation ceases on divorce, when Scotland has the underpinning philosophy of aiming for a clean break. On divorce there is a statutory presumption under the Family Law (Scotland) Act 1985 that fair sharing is equal sharing. However, courts can depart from this principle if justified by special circumstances. These circumstances include where one party suffers an economic disadvantage in the interests of the family, although, unlike England, payment of any periodical allowance is restricted to a maximum period of three years. Most importantly, where there are children who need a home, the court can order that the home be transferred to the wife and although her share of the rest of the property may be reduced proportionately, this might still not compensate the husband for his loss of half the value of the home.

Those who have entered into a **civil partnership** are treated in exactly the same way as married couples in both jurisdictions. However, it is very important to note that none of the rules about the distribution of property and money on divorce apply to cohabitants. They have to rely on the ordinary rules of **trusts** and property law for the division of assets and although a man is always liable to support his children, he is under no duty to maintain a cohabitant.

CATHY WILLIAMS

See also: **family property; property, family**

Family Law Act 1996 The Family Law Act 1996 was a radical and controversial landmark in family law in England and Wales. It sought to address public concerns about the rising number of **divorces** and the detrimental consequences, particularly for children. The existing **legislation** had long been regarded as confusing, misleading, discriminatory, and unjust, and as provoking hostility and bitterness. The new Act attempted to save **marriages** wherever possible, to change the dominant adversarial culture of divorce, and to promote cooperative post-divorce parenting. Consequently, it laid out a process of divorce over time, did away with fault, and introduced a period of reflection involving mandatory attendance at an information meeting and an optional meeting with a marriage counsellor.

These meetings were tested, but the government was unconvinced that they would meet the twin objectives of saving marriages and helping couples resolve conflicts with the minimum of acrimony, and so has never implemented the reformed process of divorce. Nevertheless the Act has provided public funding for family **mediation**, and **remedies** to protect family members from harm when relationships end. It also provides the framework for family law policy and practice. This supports marriage, encourages conciliatory divorce, and helps divorced parents maintain their responsibilities to their children.

Attempts to reform divorce legislation always generate heated debate about moral and cultural values and the role of law in **family life**, and the Family Law Act was no exception. It did, however, provide the impetus to find better ways of managing marriage breakdown and supporting families within existing legislation.   JAN WALKER

J Walker (ed), *Information Meetings and Associated Provisions Within the Family Law Act 1996: Final Evaluation Report* (Lord Chancellor's Department, 2001)

J Walker, P McCarthy, C Stark, and K Laing, *Picking Up the Pieces: Marriage and Divorce Two Years after Information Provision* (Department for Constitutional Affairs, 2004)

family law in developing countries The primary function of family law, whether in developed or developing countries, is to provide a legal framework for the establishment and regulation of family relationships. Family law also seeks to protect the interests of weaker family members such as **women** and **children** during **marriage** and on its termination. Although family relationships fall in the private domain and are therefore assumed to be largely beyond state regulation, it is now widely accepted that public interest requires certain forms of state intervention in the family. The family is now well recognized as the building block of society and the predominant site for the care and upbringing of children. It is largely because of its significance to society that the family is viewed as deserving legal protection. The question remains, however, as to what is meant by the term 'family'. This question arises because during the past century there has been a major increase in the diversity and variety of family forms, especially in developed countries. This development has greatly expanded not only the scope of family law but has also thrown up new challenges for policymakers and family lawyers.

In the specific case of developing countries, one finds certain features of family law which, while not unique to these regions, are more closely associated with the developing countries. Some of these features are by-products of many years of colonial rule. They are also a consequence of an imposition, upon these states, of non-indigenous family law systems. Moreover, the introduction of new **religions** such as Islam, Buddhism, and Christianity into these regions also added another option to existing religions and local cultures. The result was the rise of plural systems of family law operating alongside one another in a single state legal system. In some of these countries one finds not only state **courts** but also religious courts presiding over family disputes and applying religious law to members of their **communities**. In others, a frequent occurrence is that within the same country, traditional courts are also empowered to apply local customary family laws to members of their community.

Although the inclusion of differing family law systems in a single state might be commended for its flexibility and ostensible respect for other non-state systems, it has a number of negative side effects. One of these is the problem of double standards with some citizens appearing to enjoy better protection and superior forms of **justice** than others. For example, in states where local cultures and religious organizations are politically strong, there is a tendency for these non-state systems to legitimize and enforce forms of spousal inequality and practices such as dowry, **polygamy**, child marriages, **female genital mutilation**, and son preference. The weakness of the state systems in these developing countries, particularly the shortage of **human** and economic resources, has contributed significantly to the state's inability to protect vulnerable family members against various forms of injustice and victimization.

Many developing countries have tried, with varying degrees of success, to integrate the religious and indigenous systems of family law into one national system. Others, fearing to antagonize vested interests of powerful elements in these communities, have either avoided significant reforms or merely provided for umbrella **legislation** under which all the existing systems freely operate. This situation, however, has not remained static. In recent years a number of developing countries have become parties to major international and regional treaties dedicated to the promotion and protection of the rights of women and children. The most prominent of these are the 1979 UN **Convention on the elimination of all forms of discrimination against women** ('CEDAW'); the 1989 UN **Convention on the rights of the child** ('UNCRC'), the 1990 African Charter on the rights and welfare of the child, and the African Women's Protocol (2003).

Moreover, a small albeit growing number of developing countries have amended their national **constitutions** to outlaw **gender** discrimination and to provide for the protection of children's rights. This new initiative, while it remains to be fully implemented, has important implications for the future development of family law in the developing countries.

Areas where future policy initiative is urgently required include the elimination of child marriages; better protection of the child from sexual exploitation and abuse; control of **child labour** and child trafficking; protection of the child from discrimination and marginalization; better protection of women from **domestic violence** including spousal **rape**; the right of married women to family planning services; the regulation of the legal consequences of **divorce** including post-divorce **maintenance,** division of family assets, **custody of children;** and the protection of the land rights of former wives and widows. The final challenge, which some may erroneously believe to be less urgent, include the protection of the rights of same-sex couples and those of trans-national families; provision and regulation of reproductive technology; and the protection of elderly members of family groups.

BART RWEZAURA

family law solicitors Family law problems are more likely than many other problems people experience to be taken to a solicitor. Family law practice, however, is regarded as low status, due to the nature of its clientele (generally individuals who do not generate repeat business) and its association with the less rational side of **human** behaviour. It is also a relatively highly feminized area of the legal profession, which appears to be both a cause and a consequence of its perceived low status.

International studies have consistently found, contrary to assertions by policy-makers and proponents of 'alternative' forms of family dispute resolution, that family law solicitors tend not to behave adversarially. Rather than creating or aggravating conflict between their clients, they prefer to take a non-litigious approach, expecting matters to settle and using **court** proceedings, if at all, as an aid to negotiations. Such shared norms can be seen to arise from the 'communities of practice' in which family lawyers participate. Client management is thus a key element of their role—negotiating with the client in order to arrive at a 'reasonable' position within the parameters of existing law and practice. Male clients tend to begin with more unrealistic expectations which need to be reduced. Solicitors are also more likely to attempt to minimize than to run up costs for their clients, which may involve delegating some tasks to the client, particularly direct negotiation

with the other party over **child** contact arrangements and division of household property. The studies suggest some variation in the extent to which solicitors will deal with the 'emotional' as opposed to the 'legal' divorce, and provide forms of non-legal support and assistance.

In many countries, at least some of the work of family law solicitors is publicly funded. This work is often poorly remunerated, and may involve high transaction costs and levels of regulation. As a consequence, studies suggest a divergence between the nature of **legal aid** or low income family law practice (characterized by high caseloads and reactive case handling, and focused on quick resolutions) and higher end divorce practice (in which the solicitor may have greater ability to act strategically and the client may be given greater scope to 'drive' the process). There is also evidence that law firms are increasingly choosing to exit from legal aid work, creating potential problems of access for low income clients.

ROSEMARY HUNTER

J Eekelaar, M Maclean, and S Beinart, *Family Lawyers: The Divorce Work of Solicitors* (Oxford: Hart Publishing, 2000)

L Mather, CA McEwen, and RJ Maiman, *Divorce Lawyers at Work: Varieties of Professionalism in Practice* (New York: Oxford University Press, 2001)

family life The right to respect for family life is protected by Article 8 of the **European Convention on Human Rights**, now given effect in the **United Kingdom** by the machinery of the Human Rights Act 1998. The Article 8 right is not absolute and may be subject to interferences by the state, provided that such interference is in accordance with the law and necessary to protect the interests that are set out in Article 8(2). Thus, removing a child into the care of local authority will be an interference with the right to respect for family life of both the child and its parents, but will be justified if done to protect the child.

The concept of family life has evolved since the European Convention on Human Rights was drafted; and its existence does not depend on marriage or legitimacy. The existence of family life is essentially a question of fact which depends upon the existence of close personal ties. It may include a very broad range of relationships, extending to grandparents and grandchildren, siblings, adoptive parents and their children, cousins, homosexual and lesbian, as well as transsexual, couples and their children. It is not necessary for the members to live together permanently. English courts have held that the right to respect for family life is engaged where adoptive parents and child have never lived together permanently. However, there is no right to enjoy family life in the place of your choosing.   JANE WRIGHT

family life and human rights   *see* **human rights and family life**

family property   English law has no coherent regime of family or matrimonial property comparable to community property regimes in **civil law systems**. The relevant legal rules must be picked out from the law of **conveyancing**, real property, **trusts** and contract, and from statutes dealing with **divorce**, children, **domestic violence**, **insolvency**, trusts of land, tenancies, and creditor protection.

English law starts from the principle of separation of property. This means that family members are treated as strangers to each other in terms of their capacity to acquire and own property, and neither **marriage** nor **cohabitation** of themselves confer property rights in jointly-used property. However, English law has consistently sought to avoid the consequences of this strict doctrine, and has created much complexity in doing so.

There are two ways in which this has occurred. The first is the 'familialization' of the doctrines of real property and trusts, which is the process by which both **judges** and the legislature have modified general principles of land law or trusts to accommodate the specific needs of family members. The doctrines of resulting, implied, and constructive trusts, and of proprietary **estoppel**, have been pressed into service in this context, and have together evolved into a specialist sub-branch of equity jurisprudence. By these means, judges have sought to extend the basis on which informal claims to family property can be made, while preserving the security interests of third parties, such as mortgage lenders. We have now reached the stage at which these doctrines have no application outside the context of the family home. However, this process has been an uneven one, with some significant disagreements emerging between judges about what the approach should be.

The second tendency has been the slow accretion of legislation singling the family home out for special treatment, as the pre-eminently significant item of family property. For example, there is now a detailed statutory code governing occupation of the family home; there are statutory criteria for sales of family homes in bankruptcy; and statutory provisions for resolving disputes over co-owned land. There are also extensive provisions allowing courts to distribute property on divorce; and similar legislation is under consideration for the unmarried. However,

the applicability of each legislative provision turns on status (married, unmarried, a parent, bankrupt) or on the procedural context (divorce or separation, bankruptcy or the enforcement of security). The prescribed criteria differ. There is little evidence of a coherent framework.

Much of the focus in this area has been on real property—most of the cases, for example, involve a family home. Yet as economies evolve, and as the population ages, the sources of financial security for family members will change, and the law can be expected to adapt accordingly. For example, superannuation entitlements and **pensions** are rapidly increasing in significance as items of family property. The legal techniques for addressing the proper allocation of these resources are still rudimentary; yet their importance to ensuring the financial security of men and women in retirement will continue to grow.   JOHN DEWAR

See also: **property rights, impact of marriage civil partnership on**

family taxation   Since 1997, there has been a sea change in the impact of taxation on the family unit. Mortgage interest relief, the child's tax allowance, and tax allowances for married couples (with one exception) have given way to tax credits, introduced to reduce poverty in families, particularly amongst children, and to provide an incentive to work by making work pay. Another major change is the parity of treatment (from the 5 December 2005) between married couples and civil partners.

The equitable principle that underlies the UK tax system is 'ability to pay', meaning that those who have greater amounts of income or capital are in a position to pay more tax than those who have less. However, the important question is what unit of taxation should be used to determine ability to pay; should it be husband and wife, the nuclear family, the extended family, or the individual? Until the tax year 1990–1991, the unit for income tax purposes comprised husband and wife. This had a number of repercussions. First, the wife's income was aggregated with that of her husband with the result that, despite an extra allowance being given to the husband in recognition of the marriage, a married couple sometimes paid more income tax than an unmarried couple with the same income. Secondly, a husband was responsible for the couple's tax, meaning that a wife could have no privacy in her financial affairs. That the then Inland Revenue kept files only in the name of husbands and, consequently, would undertake no correspondence with married women, further exacerbated an already difficult situation.

Following a review in 1980 by the Equal Opportunities Commission, and the publication of two **Green Papers** (*The Taxation of Husband and Wife*, 1980 and *The Reform of Personal Taxation*, 1986), independent taxation was finally introduced for the tax year 1990–1991 and subsequent years. Independent taxation means that individuals (including children) have their own personal allowance and are responsible for their own tax affairs. The married couple's allowance, anomalously retained after the introduction of independent taxation, was partly abolished from the tax year 2000–2001, and is now available only where at least one of the parties to the marriage attained the age of 65 on or before 5 April 2000.

There exist exceptions to the principle of independent taxation. First, marriage continues to be a relevant factor in certain anti-avoidance provisions, particularly those which prevent a settlor *or his spouse* from benefiting from a settlement created by him. Secondly, the child tax credit and the working tax credit, which are administered by Her Majesty's Revenue and Customs and which were hailed as a step towards securing the integration of the tax and social security systems, are modelled on the social security system, so that qualification for a tax credit award is based upon the income of a 'couple' (provided the claimant is not single) rather than the individual.

It has always been the case that husband and wife have, to a large extent, been treated as individuals for **capital gains tax** ('CGT') and **inheritance tax** ('IHT') purposes, each being able to enjoy the use of exemptions for both taxes, including the annual exempt amount of chargeable gains in the case of the former, and their own nil rate band in the case of the latter. However, their status as a married couple is not overlooked, with the result that gifts between husband and wife escape a CGT charge that might otherwise have arisen, and transfers between spouses both during lifetime and on death, are exempt from IHT.

Following the Civil Partnership Act 2004, which gave same-sex couples in the **United Kingdom** the opportunity of acquiring a legal status for their relationship, the tax system has been duly amended so that tax charges and reliefs, together with the various anti-avoidance rules, now apply to married couples and civil partners alike. Heterosexual couples who choose to live together without marriage continue to be treated as two individuals for all tax purposes apart from tax credits—denying them, amongst other things, the right to take advantage of the IHT spouse exemption. It has been held that the difference in the tax treatment of married and unmarried heterosexual couples is not a breach of the **European Convention on Human Rights.**   NATALIE LEE

farmers' rights   *see* **genetic resources, access to**

fatherhood   At **common law** the presumption that the husband of a married woman is the genetic father of any **child** she bears can be rebutted by proof that the husband could not be the genetic father. Blood tests and DNA fingerprinting mean that **paternity** can now be established with a high degree of accuracy and it is rare in law for it to be in the best interests of a child not to know their 'true' father. The question of 'who is a legal father' has been complicated both by 'new' family forms, marked by multiple parent–child bonds and relationships, and by developments in reproductive technology. The law is moving to a position in which a mixture of genetic links, marital ties, and demonstrated intention to create and care for a child can each be relevant in determining who is father. This has been described as an attempt to accommodate the social and technical fragmentation of fatherhood. There is a recognition that different men may share the legal rights, **responsibilities,** and status of fatherhood and play important roles in a child's life. Historically fatherhood has entailed ideas of men as breadwinners and providers for families rather than as nurturers and carers of children. Some research suggests this may be changing and, as many men seek a more 'involved' relationship with children, the rights and responsibilities of fathers has become an increasingly contested issue in law reform debates, in particular in the area of post-**divorce** contact and residence arrangements.

RICHARD COLLIER

R Collier and S Sheldon, Fragmenting Fatherhood: a Socio-legal study (Oxford: Hart Publishing, 2008)

See also: **contact, family; co-parenting; parental responsibility**

Fathers' Rights Movement   Discussion of the legal status, **responsibilities,** and rights of men who are fathers—whether married or unmarried, cohabiting or separated, genetic or social—has a long history. In recent years, however, Western societies have witnessed a heightening of concern about the extent to which families need fathers. Internationally, the fathers' rights movement has sought to advance **equality** claims on behalf of fathers. The relationship between **fatherhood** and law has become particularly contested in the areas of *child support* and post-**divorce** contact and residence arrangements. Research suggests that the continuation of a meaningful relationship between non-resident fathers and **children** in the period after separation can, in some cases, be extremely difficult to establish and maintain. A central claim of the fathers' rights movement is that, within the present law, there is no legal *presumption* to contact. It is argued that the law is out of step both with social changes in parenting and the declared aims of policymakers themselves in promoting co-parenting after divorce. The government in the Children and Adoption Act 2006, is committed to ensuring that non-residential parents, in the majority of cases the father, have contact with their children provided that the arrangements made are safe and in the best interests of the child. They have rejected, however, the call for a legal presumption to such contact.

There has occurred a significant shift in the tactics of law reform campaigning with some fathers' rights groups embracing a form of direct action politics best represented in the UK context by the pressure group *Fathers 4 Justice*. In contrast to a group such as *Families Need Fathers* the protests of *Fathers 4 Justice* have been highly visible and aimed at drawing the attention of politicians, policymakers, and the public to the plight of fathers. They have included physical attacks on government offices, protests outside the homes of solicitors, barristers, and **judges** and a series of confrontations with senior government figures. *Fathers 4 Justice* is most well-known, however, for a series of protests involving men dressed as comic book characters scaling public buildings. Despite the extensive media coverage the campaign has received, the success of the fathers' rights movement in influencing law reform debates has been limited. The observations of members of the judiciary suggest that the form of the protest has made it unlikely that politicians will accord them a 'place at the table.' There are signs, however, that the fathers' rights movement has, to degrees, shaped the wider cultural context in which debates about fatherhood and law reform are now taking place. Critics of fathers' rights groups suggest that, far from fathers being the 'new **victims**' of laws relating to the family, fathers have become so central to a new contact culture in family law that it is the interests of mothers which, if anything, have been downgraded. RICHARD COLLIER

R Collier and S Sheldon (eds) *Fathers' Rights Activism and Law Reform in Comparative Perspective* (Oxford: Hart Publishing, 2006)

fault-based civil liability Civil liability is contrasted with criminal liability. Civil liability can be either for fault or regardless of fault ('strict'). In civil law (**tort law** and **contract law**, for instance), fault means either **intention** or negligence. In criminal law intention is further distinguished from (less culpable) **recklessness**; but in civil law, 'intention' is typically used to include recklessness. Criminal law's finer discrimination makes allowance for the special stigma that attaches to liability and punishment for serious crime as opposed to civil law liability to compensate for harm. A person intends to do something (does it 'deliberately') or intends to produce some state of affairs if it is their purpose or aim to do the thing or produce the state of affairs, as the case may be. A person behaves recklessly (or 'knowingly') if they are actually aware that their behaviour creates a risk of some adverse outcome. Intention and recklessness are said to be 'mental states'. In civil law, anyway, negligence is not the mental state of being 'careless' or 'inadvertent', but rather failure to measure up to a standard (or 'fulfil an obligation') of (careful) conduct established by law. In abstract terms, that obligation is to take the precautions that a 'reasonable person' would take against risks which are 'foreseeable' in the sense that a reasonable person would foresee (ie anticipate) them. Because **negligence in civil law** is not a mental state but a quality of conduct, a person can be negligent even if they behave intentionally or recklessly and, conversely, even if they try their hardest to be careful.

PETER CANE

See also: **criminal liability without fault; fault-based criminal liability; negligence in civil law; strict civil liability**

fault-based criminal liability Criminal lawyers often regarded it as a fundamental principle of criminal law that a defendant should not be convicted of a criminal offence if he was not at fault, or not sufficiently at fault, for committing that offence. Imposing criminal liability on the defendant normally involves moral condemnation of his behaviour and punishment for it. It is commonly thought that such condemnation and punishment is appropriate only if the defendant was sufficiently morally blameworthy for what he did.

For this reason, most serious criminal offences have two main aspects. The first is a description of the relevant action, conduct, or circumstances (the *actus reus*) and the second is the fault element that must be proved by the prosecution for the defendant to be criminally liable for that action (the *mens rea*). For example, in respect of the offence of murder in England and Wales, a defendant will be convicted of the offence only if the prosecution prove that two elements of the offence were present beyond a reasonable doubt: first, that the defendant caused the death of the victim (the *actus reus*); and secondly, that she caused that death either intentionally, or with at least an intention to do grievous bodily harm ('GBH'). The second element is known as the fault element (or *mens rea*) of murder.

Different criminal offences have different fault elements. So whereas the defendant will be convicted of murder only if the prosecution prove beyond reasonable doubt that he intended to kill or to cause GBH to the victim, he can be convicted of the lesser offence of manslaughter if it is proved that he was either reckless or grossly negligent with respect to the killing. In general, the more serious criminal offences have stricter fault elements. So the fault element for murder (intention to kill or do GBH) is more difficult for the prosecution to establish than the fault element for manslaughter (gross negligence with respect to the killing). The most common fault elements are intention and recklessness, but knowledge, belief, wilful blindness, and dishonesty are also are also commonly found in the criminal law.

Some circumstances surrounding the defendant's conduct are irrelevant to the offence of which he will be convicted, even if they seem to affect the defendant's degree of fault. The most important of these is the defendant's motive. In general, in establishing whether the defendant is guilty of an offence, his motivation for committing it is irrelevant. So, if the defendant caused the death of the victim with the intention to kill or do GBH to him, it does not matter whether the killing was done in order to inherit from the victim, out of revenge, or to prevent the victim from continued suffering from a terminal illness. The defendant will be convicted of murder regardless of the motive.

There is a debate amongst criminal law scholars about whether it should be a requirement that, for the defendant to be convicted, he was aware at least of the possibility of committing the *actus reus* of the offence. Those that think that it should be are called 'subjectivists'; those that do not are called 'objectivists'. Objectivists think that standards of reasonableness, or comparison with the **reasonable man**, should form the basis of criminal liability. Some serious criminal offences, including **rape**, have objective standards of *mens rea*.

In order to ensure that the defendant is convicted of a criminal offence only if he is at fault for his conduct, the criminal law includes a range of defences. Some defences provide exceptions to the principle that the defendant's motive is irrelevant to establishing criminal liability. For example, it is a defence to murder that the defendant was acting in self-defence. And that is to ensure that defendants who use reasonable force in defending themselves, and so are not at fault for the killing, will not be convicted of murder. These are known as *justification* defences. Other defences indicate that the defendant is not fully responsible for the conduct, for example if he was heavily intoxicated against his will or if he suffered from a mental disorder. These are known as *excuse* defences.

For some criminal offences, the prosecution does not need to prove that the defendant was at fault, or needs only to prove that he was at fault with regard to a lesser form of conduct than the offence specifies in the *actus reus*. These are known as offences of strict liability and constructive liability respectively.

VICTOR TADROS

See also: **criminal liability without fault; justification, excuse and mitigation in criminal law**

federalism   Federalism is an organization of government in which the authority to govern is divided between a central (national) government on the one hand, and a number of constituent regions, provinces, states, or other territorially distinct political authorities on the other hand. Federal systems are therefore characterized by a division of policy competences between the different levels of government that comprise the federation, some of which are exercised at the central—federal—level and others at the sub-central level. While no two federations will have an identical division of competences between the central and sub-central governments, a feature common to all federations is that the assignment of competences will be set out in relevant articles of a written constitution and may only be changed in accordance with the provisions of that constitution. Disputes between levels of government within a federation with respect to the exercise of competences typically are resolved by an absolute constitutional authority such as a constitutional (or supreme) court.

Federalism is underpinned by two opposing political presumptions. The first is that a sufficient number of shared interests exist between the constituent parts and peoples within a federation to warrant the exercise of some powers by a central government. The second is that excessive concentration of governing authority at the centre should be avoided lest it gives rise to a situation of the 'tyranny of the majority' and the effective disenfranchisement of peoples and territories who are in the minority. Clearly there is an inherent tension between these presumptions, and this explains why the term federalism has been construed by some as meaning the decentralization of government whilst by others as describing the centralization of government. In practice there is no prescribed model of federalism: the division of powers between federal and sub-state units of government depends largely on the specific historical circumstances surrounding the establishment of the federation and subsequent events. For instance, in the USA the nature and scope of federal powers established in the late eighteenth century changed sharply following the Civil War of the nineteenth century; and in Germany, the Basic Law of 1949 re-established federalism following the usurpation of the Weimar Constitution by Hitler in 1933. Similarly the nature of contemporary Russian federalism and the recent federations in the Western Balkans are rooted in the particular national and international circumstances in which they have emerged.

While the principle of federalism as a system of shared power between different levels of government within a single polity is one that has endured over centuries, in practice it is not immune to challenge. Today many federations face a wide range of challenges from internal and external developments. Internally, federalism is susceptible to challenge by entities that seek either a greater measure of self-determination within the federation (including by **secession**) or enhanced representation at the federal level. Both issues are rooted in discontent with the prevailing division of powers (including decision-making power) between central and sub-central governments—discontent that might in turn reflect a diminishing of 'shared interests' between the peoples and the states of the federation with regard to distributional issues, for instance. Externally the effects of increasing international economic and social integration ('globalization') not only undermine the capacities of all national governments unilaterally to defend the multifarious interests of their peoples and states. Globalization also offers alternative **governance** structures in which sub-national political territories might participate even though they are not nation states in their own right. An important example of this latter trend is the **European Union** where nationalist movements in a number of EU Member States (federal and unitary) are prospering on the basis that the EU is emerging as a federation within which nation states are not necessarily the optimal constituent elements.

The internal and external challenges to current federations reveal three fundamental questions that contemporary federalism has to answer, namely 'who does what'—how are powers to be divided between the levels of government; 'who decides'—which level of government is the ultimate arbiter on the division of powers; 'on what grounds'—what is the rationale for any particular division of powers, and on what basis should revisions to the current divisions be determined? One part of the answer to these questions is found in the principle of subsidiarity, which is very much a live issue in the context of European integration. This principle asserts that wherever possible, policy competence should be assigned to the level of government that is closest to the citizen. Moreover, competence should only be re-assigned to an 'upper' level of government when there are demonstrable benefits from so doing—that is, where the objectives of the policy are better achieved by re-assigning policy authority to that level. Application of the principle of subsidiarity ensures that as far as practicable, 'local' preferences are taken into account in the design and delivery of public policies, making them consistent with the principle of federalism. Additionally it is arguable that by ensuring that policies are devised and implemented as close to the citizen as possible, application of the principle of subsidiarity to the three issues noted above will maximize both the political accountability and political legitimacy of public policy decisions.

As a form of political organization of a cohesive territory, federalism stands in counterpoint to unitary government. In comparison to unitary government it has conceptual strengths—such as accommodating divergence and addressing local circumstances; and weaknesses—such as absence of simple majoritarianism and complex rules of representation. Moreover, in practice there is no single model of federal governance: each federal state devises its own federal system. In practice, however, it is arguable that federalism as a model of governance is better equipped than unitary government to meet the challenges of contemporary politics, challenges that elevate the individual over the collective and the 'region' over the nation state. The organizational flexibility inherent to federalism as a model of governance may ultimately be its greatest strength, capable as it is of re-assigning policy authority 'upwards' and 'downwards' as required to address the ever-changing internal and external environment of domestic politics. ANDREW SCOTT

fee simple estate Also called 'estate in fee simple' or 'fee simple', this is the largest estate in land known to the **common law**. The term is often used in the sense of 'freehold ownership' [of land]. This usage is technically incorrect, as 'ownership' of land is strictly not possible in countries which retain the doctrine of tenures.

To understand the term 'fee simple estate' we must understand two foundational doctrines of medieval land law: the doctrine of tenures and the doctrine of estates. Under the doctrine of tenures, the **Crown** granted rights 'to hold' (*tenere* in Latin) land in return for performing services to the Crown. That holder in turn could, by a process known as 'sub-infeudation', grant rights to others to hold from him or her in return for performing services. The doctrine of tenures determined the terms on which land was held. The other doctrine—the doctrine of 'estates'—determined the duration for which land was held. In essence, an 'estate' was (and still is) an interest in land of a given duration.

The common law knew three estates: the 'fee simple', the 'fee tail' (now obsolete in most countries), and the 'life estate'. Of these, the interest of the largest potential duration was the fee simple. The word 'fee' denoted an estate of inheritance. The word 'simple' denoted that the estate would pass to 'heirs' generally (that is, blood relations and their heirs) rather than to lineal descendants only (as in the case of a 'fee tail').

In medieval times, a fee simple estate would last for as long as the grantee lived and was survived by 'heirs'. This was reflected in the formula needed to create or convey a fee simple estate: 'to [the grantee] and his [or her] heirs'. In this formula, 'and his [or her] heirs' were 'words of limitation': they marked out (we might say 'delimited') the extent of the grantee's interest—a fee simple estate—and gave no present interest to the grantee's heirs (for strictly speaking a living person has no heirs). The fee simple estate would come to an end ('determine') if, for example, the grantee died without leaving heirs; indeed, it would determine even if that grantee had since conveyed the estate to a purchaser who was alive. However, by 1306 it was established that a fee simple estate would continue for as long as the holder from time to time survived and had heirs, even though the original grantee had died without heirs.

In modern times, when land is freely traded as a commodity, the concept of an interest that lasts for as long as the holder from time to time lives and is survived by heirs may seem dysfunctional; but the law wears its medieval mantle to the extent that if the holder at a given time dies intestate and without next of kin who can inherit, ownership 'escheats' (reverts) to the Crown (in modern understanding, the state).

PETER BUTT

female genital mutilation/surgery The various names given to this practice reflects its contentious nature: circumcision, harmful traditional practice, genital cutting, or surgery, to female genital mutilation ('FGM'). Presently the practice is most commonly described as FGM.

The World Health Organization identifies different levels of severity. The most common form (80 per cent) excises the clitoris and the labia minora; infibulation which is the most extreme, less common form (15 per cent), removes the clitoris, labia minora, and part of the labia majora which are then sewn up. FGM is usually performed on girls between four and eight.

It is estimated that up to 130 million **women** and girls have been mutilated and that about two million are at risk each year. FGM is practised in twenty-five countries in Africa and a few countries in the Middle East and Asia. In Somalia, 98 per cent of women will have experienced FGM. In Eritrea 44 per cent are performed on infants under one year. It is also practiced by diasporic communities in Europe, Canada, and the United States.

The origins of the practice are unclear. Some give reasons based on **sex**: a desire to exercise sexual control or to reduce female sexuality. Others provide a socio-cultural explanation: an initiation for girls into womanhood to ensure social integration. Some cite hygiene and aesthetic reasons: female genitalia are considered dirty and unsightly. Others believe erroneously that it is a religious requirement.

Interventions in beliefs and practices sincerely held by women and men which others consider deeply harmful raise highly sensitive issues. Initially African women found the Western focus on this one practice a new form of imperialism, reinforced by the use of FGM as the staple example of the 'clash between culture and rights' in legal texts.

More recently, women with direct experience of FGM have contributed to the development of a better understanding of the issues involved. The practice is increasingly understood as a violation of a range of **human rights**: life and health; discrimination on grounds of sex; bodily integrity and **violence** against women; and particularly as violating the rights of children. In addition, Western women have now recognized that their cultures produce forms of self-mutilation such as cosmetic surgery, cutting, and eating disorders.

FGM is recognized in a wide range of international human rights instruments. It is included in the right to health in the **International Covenant on Economic and Social Rights** (1966). It is a violation of women's rights within the **Convention on the Elimination of All Forms of Discrimination against Women** 1979 and covered by the Declaration on Violence against Women 1993. It violates a number of **children's rights** within the **Convention on the Rights of the Child** 1989. Importantly, FGM is recognized as violation of children rights in the African Charter on the Rights and Welfare of the Child 1990 and as a harmful practice within the 2003 Protocol to the **African Charter on Human and Peoples' Rights on the Rights of Women in Africa.** The European Union passed a resolution in 2001 making FGM a violation of fundamental human rights. While not necessarily directly enforceable within specific countries these measures provide a positive framework for intervention. In 2003 representatives from twenty-eight African and Arab countries adopted the Cairo Declaration on Legal Tools to Prevent FGM which recognized the need for legal strategies to be set within a wider multidisciplinary approach.

Many African countries have adopted specific, often criminal **legislation**, to outlaw the practice although some, such as Somalia, have not. Even in countries with longstanding laws, FGM is widespread. Legal measures work best to reinforce educational programmes.

In the UK, legislation passed in 1985 was updated in 2003. The Female Genital Mutilation Act 2003 makes procuring, assisting, or performing FGM a criminal offence wherever committed. Thus, taking a **child** overseas to carry out the procedure is also illegal. The maximum penalty on conviction is fourteen years. There have been no **prosecutions** under the law despite increasing evidence of the practice obtained primarily through health professionals and women's support groups.

The Metropolitan Police, working with African women's organizations, focus on raising awareness of the law, seeking to change attitudes and supporting those who wish to resist. Health professionals have developed specific policies relating to FGM and undertaken training for staff. The British Medical Association has a code of practice for doctors which opposes medicalization: enabling the practice to be carried out by trained medical staff. Two doctors who performed FGM have been struck off the medical register.

Scandinavian countries have adopted similar legal measures to the UK. Sweden obtained its first two convictions in 2006. ANN STEWART

feminism and law reform Law reform has long been a key focus of feminist political strategy. This is because law is simultaneously and, perhaps, somewhat contradictorily, both a key site of **women's** oppression and a primary feminist tool for pursuing equality-seeking social change. As such, the history of feminism is awash with examples of feminist-inspired law reform, from the struggles to secure female suffrage and access to the professions in the late nineteenth and early twentieth centuries to the campaigns to procure legal access to **abortion** and the prohibition of **sex** discrimination which characterized the period of 'second-wave feminism' in the 1960s and 1970s. Since then, the degree and level of feminist influence on law and law reform initiatives has only intensified, particularly in key areas of feminist concern. These include: issues relating to **violence** against women (radical reform of the law and practices around **rape** and **domestic violence** and the development of new legal rights in relation to **sexual harassment**); women's participation in paid work (introduction and extension of anti-discrimination protection, maternity, paternity, and parental rights, access to **flexible working**); reproductive regulation (in addition to abortion there has been considerable feminist activity around issues of access to reproductive treatments); and family issues (as well as developments in the fields of **divorce**, maintenance, and **child** custody which are broadly to women's benefit, the emergence of a gay and lesbian reform agenda around notions of what counts as 'family' for legal purposes is in many ways a result of feminist arguments and strategies). In all these areas, what is detectable is not just, in some cases, radical legal change but also a heightened legal awareness of gender (in)equality issues.

That said, not all feminists agree that engagement with law reform is positive or desirable. Indeed, within feminist legal scholarship, a number of arguments have been levelled against feminist reliance on law as a tool of egalitarian transformation. For some feminists, law is simply too deeply entrenched in patriarchal norms and practices to be effective in pursuing feminist objectives. This view has been fuelled by growing feminist disillusion with the capacity of law to law truly to tackle core problems such as rape and domestic violence. Notwithstanding a tranche of legal reforms stemming back to the 1970s, the conviction rate for rape is at its lowest ever (between 5 and 6 per cent of reported rapes); similarly, a range of initiatives designed to tackle domestic violence appears to have produced little in the way of results, with law and society still struggling to cope with the impact and effects of widespread domestic violence, particularly with regard to women and children. As the twenty-first century has progressed many feminists are asking: why has law failed here? And the process of formulating answers to this question has encouraged a reflectiveness among feminists with regard to the promises and pitfalls of law reform strategy.

Yet another feminist concern—and one which perhaps applies more widely within progressive social movements—is that over-reliance on law may have a disabling effect on political drive, legitimacy, and momentum. As political ideals become translated into 'acceptable' legislative demands, resulting in turn in rather more limited legal rights than originally envisaged, the passion which energized an effective political campaign can become diffused and fragmented. The 'problem' is perceived to be recognized and resolved by law; but, in fact, it may simply be contained and/or displaced by it. Take, for example, equal pay—the focus of huge political energy in the late 1960s, resulting in the Equal Pay Act 1970. Yet some thirty years after the introduction of the Act, there remains a marked gender pay gap in relation to which, extensive analysis has revealed, the current provisions are wholly inadequate. Indeed, from a socio-legal perspective, one can almost trace the reach and outer limits of the Equal Pay Act right to that point where the pay gap ceases to narrow. In this sense, the legislation *contains and displaces* the problem of equal pay but it does not resolve it. Moreover, the problem of equal pay emerges as a problem of law which law (in turn) can best resolve. The result is continued political effort into legal reform, perhaps at the expense of other political strategies and approaches.

A further difficulty with law reform is the risk of backlash. Perhaps there is nothing peculiarly legal about this risk but it is certainly detectable in the context of feminist law reform initiatives. A good example here is family law. Over the last 150 years, law has come from a position where women's legal personality was absorbed in that of their husbands on **marriage** and mothers had virtually no rights with regard to their children, to one in which law now recognizes and actively seeks to secure the separate interests of wives/mothers particularly in the event of family breakdown. However, because gender equity is now so embedded a discourse in family law, it has also been deployed by fathers' rights groups to challenge family law reforms which are perceived to have benefited women. What is striking about the arguments and strategies of such groups is the way in which they draw on—often very effectively—feminist legal discourse and rhetoric, discourse around equality, for example, and access to children. From a feminist perspective, what is problematic here is the way in which a formal egalitarian legal approach can be effectively deployed by men notwithstanding a context in which the deleterious consequences of family breakdown continue to borne most heavily by women (and children). More generally, the example illustrates yet again the risks inherent in traversing legal terrain in search of feminist-inspired solutions.

Within current legal scholarship, the focus is increasingly on law not as a tool by which to effect legal change but as a site for the production and transformation of gendered social norms, attitudes, and practices. Law, it is argued, offers a way of thinking about, conceiving of, and engaging with questions of sex and gender; it is an ongoing source of meaning and value, and an increasingly important one too as its reach becomes ever more expansive and intrusive. Law is a very big part of defining, shaping, and producing everyday understanding with, *inter alia*, gendered social effects. Therefore, if we want to transform everyday understanding, law is *a* place (although not the only place) for doing this.

Now what all this means in terms of feminism and law reform is that feminist strategic engagement with law need not be wholly or even mainly about bringing about practical legal change; to engage with law, for example by bringing feminist-inspired claims into court, making feminist arguments through the legislative process, feeding feminist perspectives into legal policymaking, is to use law as a space, an opportunity to transform the way we think about and act in relation to issues of **sex** and **gender,** whether these be social attitudes to rape, social perceptions of what constitutes a 'family', or the 'proper' social roles of women and men. Indeed, at its most ambitious, feminist legal engagement seeks to challenge and disrupt the very notions of sex and gender as fixed and meaningful concepts which define and demarcate who and how we should be.

JOANNE CONAGHAN

H Samuels, 'Feminism, Activism. Third Part Intervention and the Courts' (2005) 13 *Feminist Legal Studies* 1–14

V Munro, *Law and Politics at the Perimeter: Re-Evaluating Key Debates in Feminist Theory* (Oxford: Hart Publishing, 2007), ch 3

See also: **fathers' rights movement; feminist theories of law**

feminism and reproduction Reproduction has long existed as a site of contestation and resistance for feminists. While some theorists, such as Adrienne Rich, celebrate reproduction, birth, and motherhood as distinctively feminine spheres, others, such as Simone de Beauvoir, view women's ties to reproduction as a form of biological tyranny that must be transcended to allow women to realize their full potential. What unites these opposing viewpoints is a consensus that the different situation of **women** and men with regard to reproduction significantly impacts on their status in society.

During the second wave of the feminist movement in the late 1960s/early 1970s, campaigns focused on **abortion** and contraception, with demands for reproductive freedom encapsulated in assertions of 'a woman's right to choose'. The advent of the oral contraceptive pill and legal recognition of abortion in certain situations seemed to offer the potential to free women from the tyranny of reproduction, although assumptions about the biological foundations of reproduction have persisted. Moreover, law has proven resistant to full recognition of women's reproductive rights. Thus, the 1967 Abortion Act positioned doctors as gatekeepers to control access to lawful abortion. This medicalization of reproduction, which also characterizes regulation of and access to reproductive technologies under the Human Fertilization and Embryology Act 1990, has been a constant target of feminist critique for denying women's **autonomy** and legitimizing state intervention in their lives. The potential of reproductive technologies to sever the connection between **sex** and reproduction and to fragment understandings of parenthood and families has further complicated the relationship between feminism and reproduction. Feminist interventions in the 1980s, exemplified by FINRRAGE (the Feminist International Network of Resistance to Reproductive and Genetic Engineering), were characterized by hostility to medically assisted reproduction. Such accounts portrayed reproductive technologies as a mechanism for patriarchal medicine to entrench its control over women's bodies. By contrast, Shulamith Firestone heralded reproductive technologies as a means to liberate women from the dictates of pregnancy and **motherhood**.

Although debates continue as to whether such technologies enhance women's freedom or are simply a technological fix designed to mask underlying causes of infertility, reproductive technologies have been normalized since the 1980s. For those with the means to fund treatment privately, **assisted conception** now enables single women and **lesbians** to bear and rear children with minimal involvement from men. Anticipated future developments, including the creation of artificial gametes and wombs, suggest that biotechnologies will continue to open up new reproductive choices while further destabilizing natural or biological understandings of masculine and feminine roles.

With an expanding menu of reproductive choices, questions about the state's role in funding such technologies become more acute and, as with related debates about whether reproduction is best regarded as a private or public matter, have prompted disagreement amongst feminists. Construing reproductive rights as private supports arguments that the state should leave such decisions to individuals free of state intrusion; yet meaningful access to abortion and reproductive technologies is crucially dependent on public funding of such services. Reproduction is thus at the centre of debates about what constitute core feminist values and a classic illustration of the multitude of feminist perspectives with regard to matters such as bodily autonomy, **privacy**, just distribution of resources, and **equality**.

MARIE FOX

feminist analyses of crime During the late 1960s and early 1970s, when ideologies associated with Marxism enjoyed relatively high levels of support, feminist writers observed that even within such supposedly revolutionary movements, women remained subordinate to men who dominated decision-making positions. Second-wave feminism thus arose out of women's increasing awareness that they were oppressed as a category due to their **gender,** and regardless of their social class. The movement challenged both Marxism and male power through the concept of patriarchy, arguing that women's subordinate role within the family, as well as in Western capitalist societies more generally, serves the interests of men. Hence, the operation of power must be understood through an analysis of gender relations as well as class relations. The concept of patriarchy thus identified women as a social category in their own right who have different interests to men.

The arrival of second-wave feminism also caused a fundamental challenge to traditional, male-centred explanations of female criminality and victimization which had hitherto been understood largely through biological determinism and victim-blaming respectively. Feminists pointed out that femininity is socially constructed, not biologically determined, and this construction has a major impact on how both female offenders and **victims** are perceived. While both men and women living within a class-divided society are subject to material, repressive, and ideological forms of social control, women are affected *differentially* and *specifically* as a result of their domestic role within the private sphere. In particular, women's behaviour is socially controlled through deeply ingrained cultural expectations, especially in relation to **motherhood**, domesticity, respectability, and sexuality. A 'good' **woman** is caring, demure, and respectable, aspiring to motherhood and domesticity through her maternal 'instinct', whilst a 'bad' woman goes against 'nature' by pursuing her own selfish desires and interests at the expense of motherhood and domestic responsibilities. In turn, this social construction has serious consequences for the way criminal women are perceived, since the mere fact they have committed a crime, ensures they are understood as having failed to conform to dominant expectations of acceptable female conduct and respectable femininity.

Feminism had thus identified the 'double standard' operating when criminal women enter the legal system, resulting in them being regarded as 'doubly deviant' because they have failed to behave according to dominant ideals of appropriate femininity. Consequently, female offenders are judged not only according to their crimes, but according to how they have performed as *women*. For example, Pat Carlen's extensive research on criminal women has led her to conclude that the majority of sentences given to female prisoners do not reflect the seriousness of their crimes, but the court's assessment of them as wives, mothers, and daughters. In turn, their failure to act according to the rules of acceptable femininity helps to explain the disciplinary regimes within women's prisons. Offending women are perceived to be in need of discipline and control to help re-feminize and 'normalize' them—teaching them how to become 'good' women. Yet, research demonstrates that the vast majority of women offenders commit crime as a direct result of poverty, more prevalent amongst women as a result of their subordinate position within a capitalist, hetero-patriarchal society. Indeed, statistics indicate that only 4 per cent of women imprisoned have been convicted of violent offences. Hence, the female prison population confirms Box's thesis in relation to **class and crime**, ie it is overwhelmingly the poor and powerless who are imprisoned. Indeed such women can be understood as doubly disadvantaged since they are located within a subordinate position according to both social class and gender.

In contrast, female victimization is prevalent within all social classes. The biggest success of second-wave feminism has been its achievement in uncovering the extent of **violence** against women. In particular, **rape** and **domestic violence** have become matters of public concern requiring national policy responses as a direct result of feminist pressure and demands. Since the 1970s, the sheer extent of violence against women taking place within the private sphere has gradually become uncovered and has confirmed that such violence takes places within all social classes, lending support to the feminist claim

of unequal power relations between men and women within a patriarchal society.   ANETTE BALLINGER

See also: **crime and social differentiation; feminist theories of law**

feminist legal research   *see* **feminist theories of law**

feminist theories of law   Feminists have always been ambivalent about law. On the one hand, they view law as deeply implicated in women's oppression; on the other hand, they also see it as a potential tool to be deployed on women's behalf. Feminist legal theory attempts to navigate this tension between the positive and negative possibilities of law, within the context of a broader exploration of the relationship between sex/gender and wider society.

Until the late twentieth century, there was little in the way of feminist theoretical engagement with law although there was an established tradition of feminist writing within liberal political theory which endeavoured to harness the progressive elements of liberal political thought—democracy, freedom, and equality—to the cause of women's rights (see eg Mary Wollstonecraft's *A Vindication of the Rights of Woman* (1798); and Harriet and John Stuart Mill's *The Subjection of Women* (1869)).

The rise of social theory in the twentieth century, and in particular, the influence of Marxism, also engaged feminist theoretical attention. By the 1970s, 'materialist' feminists were probing the relationship between women's oppression and the broader social, political, and economic ordering, particularly with regard to the organization of labour under capitalism. The same period also witnessed the publication of key radical feminist texts—eg Kate Millett's *Sexual Politics* (1970) and Shulamith's Firestone's *The Dialectic of Sex* (1970)—in which the primary theoretical focus was on how sexual rather than labour relations produced women's subordination to men.

Within this diverse theoretical landscape, feminist legal theory emerged with key texts by Frances Olsen and Catharine MacKinnon appearing in US law journals in the early 1980s. Around the same time, in the UK, Katherine O'Donovan published *Sexual Divisions in Law* (1985) and thereafter, in the US and UK, as well as, independently, in countries as far flung as Norway and Australia, a lively and burgeoning feminist legal literature evolved. By the turn of the millennium, few legal texts were left unmarked by the impact of feminist legal scholarship (although the degree to which feminism is acknowledged in this context varies considerably).

What then is the nature and significance of feminist legal theory? There are many conflicting and contested accounts of what feminist legal theory entails. However, it is not really productive to offer any definitive account. This is part because, as with theory generally, feminist legal theory is always in a process of evolution. (In fact, in general terms, it is probably easier to understand theory in terms of process rather than production, ie as something we *do* rather than something we *make*.) That said, there are some features which are common or recurring in much feminist legal scholarship. These include (i) excavating the gendered content of what often appear to be gender-neutral legal rules and regimes; (ii) exploring law's content and operation from the perspective of women's needs and concerns (sometimes called a 'woman-centred' approach); and (iii) holding law to account through the application of norms and values, eg **justice**, **equality**, **autonomy**, **community** and so forth.

The first element entails moving feminist critical scrutiny beyond explicit **gender** classifications in law (eg only men may vote) to look at the impact of legal rules on people's lived experience. Feminists have demonstrated how property law rules have traditionally favoured men's interests in the context of relationship breakdown; how labour law has extended greater protection to male rather than female workers by privileging the full-time, long-term worker; and how criminal law, notwithstanding gender-neutrality on its face, has systematically worked to the detriment of women victims of male violence. There are limits to this strategy. Sometimes (although not that often) law works the other way; this is a point, much contested but constantly reiterated by the fathers' rights movement. A more important limitation is that by focusing solely on how law impacts differentially on men and women, other, cross-cutting, legally produced forms of disadvantage—based perhaps on race, sexuality, disability, or class—may be ignored and feminism may end up serving the interests of a narrow group of women who are privileged, middle-class, and white. Recognizing this, feminist legal theory is increasingly focused on identifying the many ways in which gender disadvantage is entangled with other inequality forms, combating what feminists legal theorists have characterized as intersectional inequality.

A second common feature of feminist legal theorizing is a woman-centred approach. In many ways this is an extension of the first because it relies for its effectiveness as a form of critique on the fact (or contention) that law reflects and reinforces male experience. Returning to labour law, for example, it is only

when we look at the legal rules from women worker's point of view that we see how women—who are more likely to be part-time, short-term, or casual workers—are ill-served by them Similarly, it is only when we look at rape law from the female victim's point of view that we recognize the absurdity of a rule which states that a man who honestly—if entirely unreasonably—believes that the woman with whom he is having sex is consenting, is not guilty of rape. Of course there are many who would argue that law is not supposed to have a point of view, that it should be neutral, and that feminism, by adopting a woman's point of view, is therefore partial and distorted. Perhaps. However, the whole point of woman-centredness is not to install women's perspective as the 'correct' way of seeing and judging law, but simply to show that other perspectives, often male (and middle-class, white, heterosexist, etc), are already inscribed there. In other words, a woman-centred approach challenges law's claim to neutrality and objectivity. It is part of a broader critique of the idea of 'objective' knowledge. However, one of the difficulties with woman-centredness is that it tends to turn on itself. Once epistemological foundations come under siege, the very tools feminists use, the very categories they deploy—categories such as 'woman' for example—lose much of their normative and critical purchase. In feminism, this realization has resulted in the anti-essentialist debate, in which gender categories have been critiqued for their claims to an 'essential' content or character. Anti-essentialism, like **intersectionality**, threatens understandings of feminism in which gender difference is presented as relatively unproblematic. It encourages the 'troubling' of gender categories, the disruption of gender norms, practices, and performances (as, for example, in the work of Judith Butler). Within a legal context this has yielded a focus how law contributes to the production of 'women' and 'men' as we know and understand them: what is the role of law in bringing sex and gender differences into effect?

This leads to a third recurring feature of feminist legal theory, its normative or ethical aspirations. It is true that this third aspect is not particularly feminist; norms such as equality, justice, etc lurk behind many legal theoretical approaches. Moreover, some feminist legal theorists, particularly those influenced by postmodernism, purport to eschew norms by adopt a 'norm-free' approach (ie an approach which does not invoke, prescribe, or rely upon a particular norm or set of norms. Invariably however, these theorists tend to fall on their own swords; it is difficult to escape the prescriptive dimensions of an injunction against prescription!). That said, a primary feminist concern is with law's transformative potential; feminism is in large part a transformative discourse in which the object is to criticize the way things are and work out how to make them better. Norms are crucial in this context; one cannot get far in the business of transformation without some vision or plan to inspire and direct it. Feminist legal theorists are thus very interested in norms or values which inform and infuse law. For example, feminist legal theory is very concerned with debating the merits and demerits of equality: does equality require that men and women should be treated in the same way or should it acknowledge differences between them? How should these differences be conceived in law? Can law move beyond **formal equality** ('treat like alike') towards some notion of **substantive equality** or equality of results?

Other concepts attracting feminist scrutiny in a legal context include (human) rights (are rights any good to women? Does human really mean 'male'?); autonomy (are there ways of understanding autonomy other than in terms of the individual, bounded self?); responsibility (is the legal allocation of responsibility unnecessarily circumscribed to reflect the relative irresponsibility of men's lives (as opposed to women's) with regard to the care of others?): and, of course, justice which feminists frequently contrast with notions of care to highlight how different ethical frames are at work in law. These many conceptual and normative projects remain ongoing, while the overall parameters of feminist legal theory continue to shift and change as they encounter new challenges and concerns.   JOANNE CONAGHAN

fertility industry   *see* **reproduction business**

fiduciaries   In certain circumstances, one person owes a duty of loyalty to another person. This duty was first recognized and enforced in the context of **trusts**, and so it is called a 'fiduciary' (or 'trust-like') duty. By extension, the person who owes such a duty is often (if inelegantly) called 'the fiduciary'. By extension from trust law, the person to whom the duty is owed is often called the 'beneficiary', even in cases where there is not a trust as such.

The duty of loyalty generally requires the fiduciary to act in what he or she perceives to be the best interests of the beneficiary. The duty of loyalty is usually protected by strict 'prophylactic' rules, so called because they are designed to prevent fiduciaries from being in certain situations where they might be tempted to sacrifice the interests of the beneficiary. There is a 'no-conflict' rule, which forbids the fiduciary from being in a situation where his or her self-interest might conflict with the duty

of loyalty. For example, a trustee is not allowed to purchase, for his or her own interest, trust property that he or she is selling in his or her capacity as trustee. The no-conflict rule also forbids the fiduciary from being in a situation where one duty of loyalty might conflict with another, as in the case where a lawyer tries to act for two clients who have opposing interests.

The other prophylactic rule is the 'no-profit' rule, which states that in the absence of express authority from the beneficiary, or the governing instrument, or the general law, fiduciaries may not derive any profit from their office (although there is a right to recover proper expenses). There is some debate as to whether the no-profit rule is merely an application of the no-conflict rule, or whether they are analytically distinct.

The prophylactic rules are very easy to violate. The reason is that by their nature, they do not require the beneficiary to prove that the fiduciary actually made a badly-motivated decision in managing the affairs of the beneficiary; still less that any harm was actually caused to the beneficiary's interests. It is only necessary to show that the fiduciary is in one of the prohibited situations. Those situations are prohibited on the basis that they are ones where the fiduciary *might* be badly motivated. If the fiduciary has placed himself or herself in one of the prohibited situations, then the beneficiary can require the fiduciary to disgorge any gain that the fiduciary acquired, even if the latter was acting in perfect good faith. It is also possible for the beneficiary to recover losses that can be shown to have resulted from breach of one of the prophylactic rules.

Fiduciary duties are owed by trustees to beneficiaries, and by the executor of the estate of a deceased person to the beneficiaries of the estate. They are owed by corporate directors and officers to their corporation. They are also owed by agents to principals, and by partners in a **partnership** to one another. They are owed by solicitors to their clients. In some jurisdictions, it has been held that fiduciary duties exist between parent and child, doctor and patient, and in other relationships that involve decision-making power. The UK courts have been somewhat more conservative, and have confined these duties to their roots in the property-holding context. But regardless of whether the facts fall into a recognized category of fiduciary relationship, a claimant can always attempt to argue that the particular facts of the relationship are such as to justify a fiduciary obligation. Speaking generally, the claimant will succeed if he shows that he placed his confidence in the other and the other undertook to act in the claimant's interests.

Exactly when fiduciary obligations should be imposed is a difficult and contested question, mainly because the normative foundations of the fiduciary duty of loyalty are contested. One view is that the fiduciary obligation is simply part of the law of contract, arising by implication out of the dealings between the parties. Another view is that while there may be a role played by consent, the basic idea is that when the law allows or recognizes that one person holds powers on behalf of another, it requires that those powers be exercised for the sole benefit of that other. This view shows why there are undeveloped but recognizable threads of fiduciary thinking in public law. If a town councillor takes money from a land developer, or if a judge decides a case involving a member of his own family, everyone feels there is something wrong. Both cases involve powers held by a public figure on behalf of the public, and the presence of a conflict between self-interest and public duty provokes the same uneasiness as it would in the case of a true fiduciary.   LIONEL SMITH

film and law   Since its inception, film has been intimately involved with the law. On both sides of the Atlantic, lawyers were instrumental in establishing the film industry, incorporating the studios (Paramount, Pinewood), drafting staff contracts (for writers, directors, actors), and setting up movie theatre/cinema franchises. But even more than facilitate, law has *regulated* film: in the 1930s, by developing standards of 'decency' with the Hollywood 'Hays Code'; in the 1940s, by applying **antitrust** law against the studios, and their tie-in with movie theatre/cinemas; and, more recently, in the 1960s (as well as up to and including the present), by rating films with a potpourri of alphabetic codes (X, R, PG13, G, and so on). Breach of contract (for instance, Bette Davis and Olivia de Havilland both challenged their studio contracts) and **libel** (for instance, in the case of Prince Felix **Yussupov**, 'slandered' in the film, *Rasputin and the Empress*) are just some of the legal doctrines that have been raised and rendered against the film industry. Film, for its part, has repaid, many times over, the dubious compliment of law's obsession with it; indeed, film has exceeded that obsession, returning over and over again to the law for its setting (the courtroom), cast of characters (lawyers, clients, juries, judges) and plot-lines (whodunit?!). From *Adam's Rib* to *Witness for the Prosecution*—and all the letters in between: *Breaker Morant, The Caine Mutiny, Legally Blonde, The Verdict*—film *loves* the law. That 'love affair' between law and film has been inspirational for lawyers, many citing as their professional ideal

the example of the screen's Atticus Finch as played by Hollywood stalwart, Gregory Peck, in Horton Foote's poignant filmic adaptation of Harper Lee's now classic novel, *To Kill A Mockingbird.*

Mention of Atticus Finch raises the growing spectre of academic and legal professional commentary on law and film; for that cinematic character has attracted a host of competing law review analyses—as heroically ethical or patronizingly incompetent. This sort of debate is only a small part of a larger discussion going on in university law faculties and bar societies about the value of film as a *pedagogic* device: that is, training better lawyers for tomorrow through the use of law-on-film today in the law school classroom. This project of 'legal *reel*ism' underlies the scholarship of legal academics on both sides of the Atlantic concerned principally with *instruction*. In their work, they précis films, codify character types, and articulate thematic topics, as if providing a teacher's lesson plan that will structure a Law and Film course and embed it as a 'respectable' (and permanent) fixture of the law school curriculum (*not* a bad thing). Their joint efforts appear to be working, with 'law and film' courses proliferating in the American law school and elsewhere; and 'law and film' studies, attracting the attention of specialist symposia and themed journal issues. In this, lawyers and legal academics are contribute to a deeper understanding of 'the images of law in everyday life', including film.

Missing here, however, is a sense of film's possibilities not only to instruct, but to critique and, thereby, represent alternative forms of law, legal process, and legal theory. Not for nothing has Melbourne criminologist Alison Young called for a study that examines 'cinema as jurisprudence'; that is, for an analysis of 'law's moving image' in terms of its portrayal of legal philosophical *ideas*. Such ideas might include **justice**, rights, or law's morality; all jurisprudential staples which figure not only in Hollywood vehicles such as *Judgment at Nuremberg* but much more elliptically in, for example, Derek Jarman's avant-garde *Blue,* Shyamalan thriller *The Sixth Sense,* and even Aussie comedy *The Castle.* Pride of place, however, for properly introducing contemporary and critical *theory* to Law and Film must belong to Austin Sarat, a socio-legal scholar turned cultural legal critic. For example, his 'deconstruction' of Egoyan 'indie' film, *The Sweet Hereafter* is a model of this theory-driven method. For Sarat actually *reads* the texts of law *and* film, and is attuned to the ambiguities of both, as well as the indeterminacies within each. This 'close reading' of Law and Film has become a distinctive trade mark of what might be called the 'Amherst

School' that Sarat has gathered around him. Theory, however, is not the only kind of current commentary law and film attracts; **identity**, particularly in terms of **race** and **gender**, provides an alternative interpretive frame, and sophisticated studies have appeared of late examining the screen representation of women and the law, homosexuals and the law, and race and law. The actual *material* conditions of law and film have not been overlooked either, especially the overarching question of intellectual property: that is, who owns the screen image? Courts and commentators continue to grapple with that issue in an era of digitalization and downloading, video piracy, and extended **copyright** control. All of which suggests a persistent and ongoing intimacy between law and film, so much so that one might well wonder if the prompt on cinema sets is now, 'Lights, Camera, Litigate!' .

WILLIAM MacNEIL

film and video recordings regulation   Video recordings, on cassette or DVD, are subject to the normal laws relating to obscene publications. In addition, a system of classification controls their distribution. The system was introduced in the mid-1980s in the wake of a 'moral panic' based on research which suggested that a high proportion of young children had viewed one or more very violent videos. The accuracy of this research has subsequently been doubted, but the result was the Video Recordings Act 1984. This put in place a system of pre-censorship for most videos, operated by the British Board of Film Classification ('BBFC', a body originally set up by the film industry to deal with cinema films). Videos which deal solely with education, sport, religion, or music, do not need to be classified, as long as they do not include any sexual or violent material. All other videos must have a classification from the BBFC before they can be legally supplied to the public.

The BBFC currently uses the following categories for classification of videos:

- U Universal: Suitable for all
- Uc Universal: Particularly suitable for pre-school children
- PG Parental guidance: Some scenes may be unsuitable for young children
- 12 May only be sold, etc, to persons of 12 or over
- 15 May only be sold, etc, to persons of 15 or over
- 18 May only be sold, etc, to persons of 18 or over
- 18R May only be sold in specially licensed premises to which no-one under the age of 18 is admitted

It is also possible for a video to be refused a classification altogether, in which case it will be illegal to supply it to anyone.

The legislation directs the BBFC in applying these categories to have regard to the harm that may be caused to viewers, or through their behaviour, to society, by material concerned with sex, violence, drugs, or the depiction of criminal behaviour (though this is not an exclusive list of factors which can be considered). It also has to have special regard to the likelihood of the video being viewed in the home. This enables it to take account of the fact that in the home, as opposed to the cinema, particular scenes can be replayed, slowed down, or frozen, and so have a different impact from a 'one-off' viewing.

The person who submitted the video for classification, generally the distributor, has a right of appeal against a decision of the BBFC. This goes to the Video Appeals Committee ('VAC'), an independent tribunal. The VAC has been prepared in some cases to overturn a BBFC classification. At the end of the 1990s, for example, the VAC overturned a BBFC decision refusing a certificate to certain videos depicting actual, as opposed to simulated, sexual intercourse.

The UK's system of classification is more intrusive than exists elsewhere in Europe, but does not currently seem to be a matter of significant controversy in the industry or more widely.   RICHARD STONE

See also: **obscenity**

film censorship   Responsibility for the control of cinemas lies, as it has always done, with local authorities—currently by virtue of the Licensing Act 2003. The Act imposes a duty on the local authority, when licensing a cinema, to impose conditions prohibiting the admission of children to films unsuitable for them. It also gives a power to impose similar conditions in relation to adult audiences. In practice, local authorities generally adopt the classifications of the British Board of Film Classification ('BBFC'). This is an independent body, established by the film industry in 1912, but now given statutory recognition. It currently uses the following classifications:

- U Universal: Suitable for all
- Uc Universal: Particularly suitable for pre-school children
- PG Parental guidance: Some scenes may be unsuitable for young children
- 12A Persons under 12 may only be admitted if accompanied by an adult
- 15 No persons under 15 may be admitted
- 18 No persons under 18 may be admitted

• 18R Only to be shown in specially licensed premises to which no-one under the age of 18 is admitted

Classifications may be the subject of negotiation, but there is no appeal. Local authorities will sometimes refuse to accept a BBFC classification. This happened in 1997, in relation to *Crash*, a film based on JG Ballard's novel exploring the connections between car crashes and sex. Several local authorities banned the film, despite the fact that it had been granted an 18 classification by the BBFC.   RICHARD STONE

financial instruments, taxation of   *see* **business taxation**

financial regulation   Intervention in financial markets is generally regarded as appropriate as financial markets are thought to have a wider economic impact in efficiently allocating a scarce resource, namely capital (which is essential for financing and growth). Empirical evidence also suggests that the strength and size of a country's financial infrastructure (including the growth and size of banks, investment firms, and **stock exchange**s) is related to overall economic growth.

There are often said to be three objectives of financial **regulation**, and particularly financial market regulation: investor protection; systemic stability, or the avoidance of market-wide financial crises; and ensuring that the trading markets on which investors trade securities are efficient, fair, and transparent. Banking regulation is also heavily concerned with depositor protection. In justification of intervention in support of these objectives, financial regulation theory typically draws on the more general market failure doctrine. This theory suggests that regulation, which can be costly and carry risks, should be imposed only to correct a 'failure in the market'. A market is regarded as 'failing' when it does not allocate resources between producers and suppliers efficiently. But market failure alone is not sufficient to justify regulation. The costs of intervention must also be taken into account.

Lack of information causes particular problems in financial markets and, in theory at least, may trigger market failure and remedial regulation. Information is regarded as a public good in that it is shared by the public as a whole. While information is costly to supply, the supplier does not recover all the benefits of supplying the information because once the information is in the public domain, the supplier cannot charge all those who use it. As a result, incentives to supply information are poor while conflicts

of interest may further reduce incentives to supply accurate information. In theory, therefore, banks and companies that issue securities to investors on the markets in order to raise finance, and investment firms supplying investment services, may not supply sufficient or accurate information. This may lead to market failure because investors and consumers do not have sufficient information to make decisions which will lead to efficient allocation of resources, particularly given the information imbalance or asymmetry between suppliers of financial services or investments and consumers or investors, the complexity of the products and the fact that the decisions involved often have long-term consequences.

Market failures also exist in financial markets in the form of 'externalities', ie the impact of the wider third-party effects of a particular transaction. In theory, if a producer's good affects a third party in a way not reflected in the good's price, an inefficient allocation of resources will occur as the purchaser is not paying for the good's true costs given the impact on other parties. The classic externality in financial markets is the risk of systemic stability, where a problem or risk in one market, or one market sector, causes a cascade effect across markets. This is regarded as a particular risk in the banking sector. Linkages also exist in the securities and investment services markets, however, particularly as markets become international, as new products are developed, and as new trading venues are developed, which pose systemic risks if one key link in an investment chain becomes insolvent or unstable. Fraud is also regarded as a market failure justifying regulatory intervention.

Financial regulation is typically designed so that burdensome rules are not imposed on professional markets. Retail investors and consumers benefit from the highest level of regulation. Sophisticated professional investors (such as pension funds, banks, and investment firms) are typically expert, have a large asset base for investment, invest in very large volumes, and are able to protect themselves. They are frequently active in investments and on markets where trading is exclusively between professional investors. As a result, they are often excluded from certain protections, although professional investors are generally given the option to 'opt in' to higher levels of regulatory protection. In the absence of regulation, professional investors can engage in private ordering or enter into contracts which provide appropriate protections. Market-based constraints, such as reputation pressures, industry guidelines and codes, and self-regulation also form part of the overall matrix of standards which govern the financial markets.

Regulatory intervention can take a number of forms. Disclosure mechanisms are often regarded as the least interventionist form of regulation, although disclosure can be costly and investors and consumers may not be in a position to decode complex information. Regulation may also take the form of initial licensing or authorization systems, which control access to the markets and to consumers and investors, and ongoing conduct standards, which are particularly important in the banking and investment services sectors. Portfolio shaping rules address the nature of the investments a market actor may undertake and are particularly important in the insurance, pension, and asset management sectors. Finally, prudential, or stability-based measures are designed to cushion financial intermediaries against particular risks and, ultimately, manage the effects of an insolvency in an orderly manner. These measures are a key element of bank regulation.

A range of actors produce the standards which govern the financial markets. In addition to government rules, standards are produced by regulators such as the UK **Financial Services Authority** and the US Securities and Exchange Commission. Internationally, standards of best practice, designed to promote international convergence as markets increasingly interact, are produced by a range of international bodies including the International Organization of Securities Commissions (the umbrella body for market regulators), the Basel Committee on Banking Supervision (concerned with banking matters), and the International Accounting Standards Board (which sets the financial reporting standards which are essential for company disclosure). Trade associations also play an important role, particularly in the professional markets, in setting standards of best practice and adopting standard form contracts.

NIAMH MOLONEY

See also: **bank runs and capital adequacy; depositor protection; disclosure in financial markets; financial regulation, costs of; investor protection in securities markets**

financial regulation, costs of   In designing effective **regulation**, the benefits of intervention must be weighed against the costs of regulation. Financial market regulation carries a number of costs. Direct costs include the compliance costs borne by regulated entities and the cost of regulatory bodies. Indirect costs can also be significant. These include moral hazard, or the risk that investors may take less care than they otherwise would, notwithstanding the principle of **caveat emptor**. Innovation, which

is critical for efficient financial markets, and choice may also be damaged by over-regulation. Particular markets may become unattractive to issuers and uncompetitive if they are perceived as over-regulated. The reforms to financial markets and corporate governance introduced by the controversial US Sarbanes-Oxley Act, adopted in 2002 as part of the US response to the Enron scandal, are now widely regarded as weakening the attraction of the US markets, and particularly the New York Stock Exchange, for non-US companies, given the compliance burden imposed by the Act.

More generally, financial market regulation is subject to the generic 'capture risk' faced by regulators who may become overly close to the regulated industry and to the risk of over-regulation by regulators who may seek to increase their power by adopting onerous rules. Financial regulation is also prone to risks of over-reaction. For example, the major US financial market measures, which have strongly influenced the shape of regulation internationally, followed in the wake of the 1929 Wall St Crash (the Securities Act 1933 and the Securities Exchange Act 1933), the Enron insolvency and the series of scandals which followed the collapse of the dotcom boom (the Sarbanes-Oxley Act 2002). Similarly, the Financial Services Act 1986 (the precursor of the **Financial Services and Markets Act 2000**), which was the first sustained attempt at regulating investment services in the UK, grew from a series of financial scandals.

Regulatory costs can be diluted by effective cost-benefit analysis. Section 2 of the Financial Services and Markets Act 2000 requires the UK **Financial Services Authority** to follow principles of good regulation in carrying out its activities. These include: use of its resources in the most efficient and economic way; that burdens should be proportionate to benefits; that innovation in regulated activities and competition should be supported. In meeting its statutory objectives and these requirements, the FSA conducts a cost-benefit analysis of new measures. It adopted a Better Regulation Agenda in 2005, which includes a commitment to an increased use of principles, to the removal of rules where the costs cannot be justified by the benefits, and to supporting firms in complying with FSA requirements. In particular, a strategic shift towards less detailed, principles-based regulation is occurring under the Better Regulation Agenda. The current FSA Handbook of rules (made under the Financial Services and Markets Act 2000) contains 11 Principles but over 5,000 rules and related guidelines. The FSA is concerned that this imbalance between principles and rules might dilute the clarity of its objectives and reduce senior management's sense of responsibility; and it is moving toward greater reliance on high-level principles.

NIAMH MOLONEY

Financial Services and Markets Act 2000 The Financial Services and Markets Act 2000 provides a framework for the **regulation** of financial services in the **United Kingdom**. The Act superseded the Financial Services Act 1986, which represented the beginning of the modern era of financial regulation in that it introduced a wide-ranging scheme of statutory regulation for financial services. Prior to the 1986 Act there was no such regulation, the tendency being to rely on market practitioners regulating their own activities. While the 1986 Act retained some elements of self-regulation by market practitioners, that approach was ended by the 2000 Act, which placed regulatory responsibility in the hands of a statutory body, the **Financial Services Authority** ('FSA').

The objectives of the Act are to maintain confidence in and promote public understanding of the financial system, protect consumers, and reduce financial crime. The scope of the Act is broad: the 'regulated activities' cover a wide range of services such as banking, insurance, mortgage-lending, managing investments, operating stock exchanges, and providing financial advice. It also extends to the promotion (eg by advertising) of financial services before a transaction has been concluded.

The Act established a licensing system for those engaged by way of business in financial services and authorizes the FSA to supervise the structure and operation of their business. To become authorized to conduct 'regulated activities' a firm (including individuals and companies) must show that it is fit and proper to engage in the relevant activity and have adequate financial resources. The first consideration encompasses the experience and qualifications of the firm's management and the second the scale of its activity and operating procedures. Firms established in other EU states, which have been authorized by the relevant regulator in that state, are permitted by the Act to engage in similar regulated activity in the UK.

The Act authorizes the FSA to make rules governing authorized persons. The FSA's 'Handbook of Rules and Guidance' comprises both high-level statements of principle and detailed rules. The former focus on generalized objectives such as treating customers fairly, managing risk, and safeguarding customers' assets. The latter provide in considerable detail for the practical implementation of the objectives. In most instances the rules apply to authorized firms rather than directly to individuals within firms, but the rules applicable to 'approved persons' apply directly to individuals who have contact with customers or their property.

The Act provides several means by which the FSA can enforce the Act and the rulebook. It can publicly censure a firm (damaging its reputation); impose a financial penalty; vary or cancel authorization to engage in regulated activities (forcing the firm to close or retrench); or prohibit individuals from performing regulated activity (effectively ending their employment). The FSA is also empowered in some instances to bring a criminal prosecution against individuals for offences under the Act: these include carrying on regulated activity without authorization and using misleading statements and practices to induce another person to enter into an investment agreement. There is also the possibility in some circumstances of a civil action for damages to be brought by a person who suffers loss as a result of a contravention of a regulatory rule.   IAN MACNEIL

Financial Services Authority The Financial Services Authority ('FSA') is empowered to carry out the regulatory functions conferred on it by the **Financial Services and Markets Act 2000** ('FSMA'). These functions include those transferred to the FSA from the Chief Registrar of Friendly Societies, the Friendly Societies Commission, and the Building Societies Commission; and the regulatory functions previously carried out by the **Treasury** in respect of insurance. The FSA had already taken over responsibility for banking supervision from the Bank of England as a result of the Bank of England Act 1998. The Treasury and the Bank of England do, however, retain a significant role in the system of financial **regulation** established by the FSMA. A memorandum of understanding agreed between the three organizations in 1998 set out the respective role of each as follows:

(a) The Bank of England is responsible for the overall stability of the financial system. This remit includes monitoring payment systems and broad overview of the financial system as a whole.

(b) The FSA has statutory responsibility for authorization and prudential supervision of banks, building societies, insurers, and investment firms, supervision of financial markets and associated clearing and settlement systems. Prudential supervision focuses primarily on solvency and the protection of deposits and assets of customers.

(c) The Treasury is responsible for the overall institutional structure of regulation and the legislation which governs it. It has no operational responsibilities for the activities of the FSA or the Bank of England, but does nevertheless have considerable influence on regulatory policy through oversight and order-making powers granted by the FSMA.

The FSA existed prior to the Act, having been created in 1997 as result of a change in the name of the Securities and Investments Board ('SIB'), the regulator created by the Financial Services Act 1986. As was the case with SIB, the FSA is a private company limited by guarantee, subject to the provisions of the Companies Act 1985. Its constitution must comply with the FSMA which provides, *inter alia*, for organizational structure, the maintenance of monitoring and enforcement arrangements in respect of rules imposed by or under the Act, investigation of complaints against the FSA, and the Authority's immunity from liability in respect of the exercise of its functions. The Authority must have a chairman and governing body appointed by the Treasury, and a majority of the members of the governing body must be non-executives.

While the FSA was established with the intention of creating an independent regulator, the FSMA does provide for a degree of accountability to government ministers, Parliament, and stakeholders. The most significant form of ministerial control is the power of the Treasury to appoint and remove the chairman and members of the governing body of the FSA. This gives the Treasury a significant role in influencing the manner in which the FSA approaches its regulatory remit. It is possible for the Treasury to require the FSA to alter its rules but only when they have a significantly adverse affect on competition or in order to comply with the UK's EC or international obligations. Probably of greater long-term significance for the structure and operation of financial markets is the Treasury's power to make regulations setting out the requirements to be met by exchanges and clearing houses seeking 'recognized' status. That power has the potential effectively to bring the major exchanges under the regulatory control of the Treasury rather than the FSA. It is also possible for the Treasury to commission value-for-money audits and to arrange independent inquiries into regulatory matters of serious concern.

Some measure of parliamentary scrutiny of the FSA is made possible by the requirement that its annual report be laid before Parliament. The FSA is also in principle subject to **select committee** scrutiny but serious doubts have been expressed about the effectiveness of such oversight. The main mechanism for securing accountability to stakeholders has been the requirement that the FSA establish Consumer and Practitioner Panels. The FSA must consider representations made by either Panel and if it disagrees with it, must give the Panel a statement in writing of its reasons for disagreeing.

As regards the potential liability of the regulator for losses suffered by investors as a result of regulatory failures, the FSMA provides that neither the FSA nor any person who is, or is acting as a member, officer, or member of staff of the Authority, is to be liable in damages for anything done or omitted in the discharge, or purported discharge, of the Authority's functions. This provision does not apply to acts or omissions shown to have been in bad faith or acts or omissions which are unlawful as a result of contravening the **European Convention on Human Rights**. Even without the statutory exclusion of liability, it would be difficult to establish a claim for negligence as the courts have been reluctant to recognize that regulators owe a **duty of care** to the customers of regulated firms. However, the FSA is in principle subject to **judicial review**. It was established in the context of the Financial Services Act 1986 that in principle, SIB (the FSA's predecessor) was amenable to judicial review; and therefore the same principle would appear to apply to the FSA. However, the relatively narrow grounds on which judicial review can be sought means that in most instances it does not provide a realistic basis for challenging acts or decisions of the FSA.

The FSA operates what it refers to as a 'risk-based' system of regulation. This means that regulation is based on the risk, posed by particular firms, to the realization of the objectives of the FSMA. The FSA undertakes risk assessments of individual firms, other than those that are viewed as posing minimal risk, and then links the result with the statutory objectives. The outcome is a risk score which determines the intensity of supervision to which a firm becomes subject. While there is some common ground, the FSA's approach to risk is, in principle, different from that of regulated firms because it measures risk to regulatory objectives and not simply risk to the economic interests of the firm.

IAN MACNEIL

Financial Services Ombudsman   *see*
  Ombudsmen

finding of property   The finder of lost or abandoned property, such as goods or money, acquires possessory rights by taking physical control of the property, but will not necessarily be allowed to keep it. Unlike 'lost' property, 'abandoned property' generally means property over which the owner has intentionally relinquished all rights of ownership. The finder of lost or abandoned property must take reasonable steps to locate the owner or risk being charged with theft. For example, honest finders generally leave their contact details at the place of discovery, hand in the property to police, or advertise their finding in a local newspaper or in some other way. The finder's possessory rights protect against interference by anyone who cannot show a better right to possession. Priority is based on possession: the finder's possessory title is measured against the relative strength of the possessory title of rival claimants. Thus, the possessory title of the finder might be tantamount to full ownership or merely transitory, depending on whether a rival claimant successfully claims a superior and better right to possession. Rather than being the original owner, the typical rival claimant is usually the current or former occupier of the land where the property was found or, where property was found in the course of employment, the finder's employer. The law generally favours occupiers and owners of land ahead of finders who are trespassers. Where property was attached to the land or embedded in the soil, the occupier is generally deemed to have a prior, superior possessory interest.   JOYCEY TOOHER

fines   The fine is the most common penalty imposed by the criminal **courts**. It requires offenders to pay a specified sum to the court within a set period. Its success lies in that it is flexible, readily calibrated, minimally intrusive, and followed by fewer reconvictions than other penalties. It is primarily punitive, inflicting the pain of financial deprivation upon an offender in proportion to the wrong done. It may have a deterrent effect both on the individual offender and the public more generally but it does not seek to reform or intrude into offenders' lives. It is thus a juridical penalty in the sense that, once paid, the offender is said to have discharged his debt to society. One problem with fines is that the same sum may have a very different impact depending on the relative wealth of the offender. Recognition of this basic unfairness led to the introduction of Unit Fines under the Criminal Justice Act 1991 which took account of an offender's financial means, but these were abolished by the Criminal Justice Act 1993 after much political controversy. Another problem is that there is nothing to stop the offender from getting others to pay the fine on his behalf (indeed in respect of **young offenders** it is assumed parents will do so). Offenders may also refuse to cooperate or to prefer to go to **prison** for default than pay. High levels of default have led to a decline in the use of the fine in recent years.   LUCIA ZEDNER

fingerprinting   *see* **crime investigation by police**

fitness for purpose   *see* **sale of goods quality of products**

fixed-term workers   Fixed-term work is a form of atypical work. The term refers to 'a person with a **contract of employment** which is due to end when a specified date is reached, a specified event does or does not happen, or a specified task has been completed'. Indeed, a fixed-term contract comes to an end automatically once it has reached its agreed end point without the need for the employer to give notice. A worker can be employed on a fixed-term contract as a specialist, such as a consultant, to complete a project, as additional staff taken on during a peak period, or as someone employed to cover during another's **maternity** leave. A fixed-term contract can be beneficial to both employer and employee: employers can bring in people with special skills or employ extra labour when needed; workers retain their flexibility and at the same time gain broader experience.

Sometimes, fixed-term employees are paid more than permanent staff either because of their special skills, or to compensate for the temporary nature of the job. Yet, it is easy to see how fixed-term workers can be exploited. In order to avoid this, many European countries have regulated the position of fixed-term workers with relevant l**egislation**.

The kernel of the legislation is that fixed-term workers must have the same minimum rights as permanent workers doing the same, or largely the same, job, unless there is a good reason for not doing so. An employee on a fixed-term contract who is being treated less favourably than colleagues on permanent contract can raise the matter before a national **tribunal**.   EUGENIA CARACCIOLO DI TORELLA

fixtures   *see* **chattels and fixtures**

flat tax   *see* **tax, ability to pay**

flexible work   Flexibility is a key characteristic of many contemporary industrialized labour markets. It emerged as a phenomenon of significance in the early 1970s in response to the perceived exigencies of increasingly globalized commodity markets and a corresponding need to address labour markets, labour allocation, and investment rigidities. From the perspective of employers, flexibility was considered necessary to enable an efficient response to the '24-hour' world market and to more intense market fluctuations. Flexible working practices allowed for the decentralization of the workplace and the reconstruction of the workforce via a bipolarization of 'typical' 'standard' employees and less contractually secure, 'atypical' 'non-standard' workers (also labelled by mainstream labour theorists in terms of 'core' and 'peripheral' workers). An organization offering limited permanent employment with its accompanying rights and entitlements was better able to lay workers off in a cost-efficient manner when demand for labour is low—as is more likely in a flexible, short-termist production system (often referred to as 'numerical flexibility'). At the same time, technological change and market fluctuations created a need for flexibility with regard to tasking functions ('functional' flexibility). Thus, working arrangements which had hitherto been regarded as atypical and were more likely characterize work carried out by women became much more widely practised, while the pronounced **gender** stratification also raised the possibility of encouraging flexible working not just to benefit employers but also to facilitate the balance of work and family responsibilities by workers. In this way, flexibility which was primarily employer-driven became harnessed to a public policy agenda for the promotion of family-friendly working practices

Today, modes of flexible working offered by employers are more nuanced and multitudinous than the stark dichotomy between typical and atypical work suggests. Such arrangements include: compressed hours (permitting employees to undertake work over a shorter but more intense period of time), flexitime (which operates by allowing employees effectively to select their time at work outside certain core working hours), job-sharing, term-time working, shift working, staggered hours (which involves employees starting and finishing work at different times of the day), and annualized hours (in which employees are obliged to work a certain number of hours per year, rather than per week). Such arrangements can and do offer benefits to workers, particularly those seeking to balance work and family life. However, the greater use by employers of casual work and contracts of a fixed duration has caused contingency and insecurity for workers, leading to pressure, both at a UK and European level, to extend the scope of protective employment regulation beyond standard workers. In Europe, a proliferation of directives in

recent years had sought to improve the employment status of flexible workers, including the Part-Time Workers Directive (1998) and the Fixed-Term Workers Directive (1999). At the time of writing (March 2008), a draft Temporary (Agency) Workers Directive is still in the process of being worked out through negotiation among Member States. In the UK, the introduction of delegated legislation in response to European Directives, eg the Part Time Workers (Prevention of Less Favourable Treatment) Regulations 2000 and Fixed Term Workers (Prevention of Less Favourable Treatment) Regulations 2002, has been complemented by judicial decisions extending the scope of employment protection to home-workers (*Nethermere v Gardiner* (1984)) and agency workers (*Cable & Wireless plc v Muscat* (2006)) at least in some circumstances, although equally, there have been a number of decisions were courts have resisted pressure from litigants to extend protection (eg *Carmichael v National Power plc* (1999)).

One issue which has arisen in a judicial and statutory context is the extent to which workers have a right of *access* to flexible work. In the early days of sex discrimination law, the Court of Appeal upheld a decision that a failure by an employer to permit an employee returning from work after having a baby to work part-time, might, in some instances amount to **indirect discrimination** (eg *Home Office v Holmes* (1981)). However, this proved to be an insufficient legal basis to found a stable general right of access to flexible work, generating, *inter alia*, frequent problems around the marshalling of adequate evidence to establish discrimination, (see eg the long drawn process of litigation culminating in the decision in *London Underground v Edwards (No 2)* (1999)). As a result, the government enacted **legislation** introducing a right to request flexible working arrangements (Employment Act 2002 and the Flexible Working (Eligibility, Complaints and Remedies) Regulations 2002). Strictly speaking, this did not enact any right of access but only a right to *request* flexible work in some circumstances (which, one might suppose, one was hardly previously prohibited from doing). The 'right' originally applied only to parents of children under six (in the case of a disabled child, under eighteen) but in 2006 it was extended to employees with caring responsibilities for sick, disabled, or elderly adults. In essence, the right conferred is one of access to a procedure whereby the employer is required to consider a request for flexible working; in substance, it places very limited obligations on employers. In consequence, some people argue that the flexible work provisions are too insubstantial to effect any real change in employment practices in workers' favour. Others argue that the provisions have had important symbolic effect and have contributed to gradual change in workplace culture around the reconciliation of work and family needs. Only time will tell whether the provision are robust enough to deliver any real benefit to working parents and carers.

JOANNE CONAGHAN AND REBECCA GREENLAND

J Fudge and R Owens, *Precarious Work, Women and the New Economy: The Challenge to Legal Norms* (Oxford: Hart Publishing, 2006)

See also: **agency workers; casual workers; part-time workers**

flotation   *see* **public offer**

foetus   There will never be agreement among philosophers, theologians, and ethicists on the moral status of the foetus. At one extreme, there are those who believe that a newly fertilized egg should have the same status as an adult **human** being, and at the other extreme, some people believe that personhood is in fact acquired some time after birth when a baby acquires self-awareness and some rudimentary reasoning ability. It is obviously important for the law to be able to tell when a legal **person** comes into being, and in the UK, this is the moment at which the baby has an existence separate from his or her mother, that is, at birth. Before that, the foetus has certain interests but it does not have any legally enforceable rights.

It is, of course, possible that a foetus might be harmed before birth, perhaps because of another's negligence. The Thalidomide tragedy, in which children were born with serious limb deformities as a result of a drug which had been prescribed to their mothers as a cure for morning sickness, raised the problem of whether a **child** can receive **damages** if they were born disabled as a result of something that happened to them while they were still *in utero*. Because a foetus is not a legal person it cannot be owed a duty of care. The law's solution to this problem has been to say that the duty of care 'crystallizes' at birth when the child acquires legal personhood, and 'inherits' his or her damaged body. It would still have been difficult for the Thalidomide children to sue, however, because they would have to have proved fault on the part of the drug's manufacturers.

A child might also be injured as a result of criminal behaviour, most probably an assault upon their mother. Analogously, criminal law will allow **responsibility** for acts which took place before a child's birth to 'crystallize' once the child is born, so if a child dies as a result of injuries inflicted and which had been inflicted while they were still *in utero*, a conviction for manslaughter is possible.

Within Europe there is considerable disagreement over the protection which should be afforded to the foetus *in utero*. In Ireland, for example, the Constitution provides that the 'unborn child' has a **right to life** equal to that of the pregnant **woman**. In contrast, an English **judge** has held that 'there can be no doubt that in England and Wales the foetus has no right of action, no right at all, until birth'. Article 2 of the **European Convention of Human Rights** (incorporated into UK law by the **Human Rights Act 1998**) protects the 'right to life'. Does this extend to foetal life? The **European Court of Human Rights** has generally taken the view that the foetus is not a person, and that any rights it might have are implicitly limited by the mother's rights and interests: hence legal **abortion** does not contravene Article 2. However, because there is no European consensus on the moral or legal status of the foetus, the question of when the right to life begins is said to lie within the 'margin of appreciation' which states enjoy in this sphere.   EMILY JACKSON

See also: **fault-based civil liability; negligence in civil law**

folk law   Folk law is a type of **customary law**. The term is most commonly used when the law arises from the customs of an ethnic group. Folk law is thus not created by institutions of the modern state, which may recognize and endorse it, but may alternatively ignore or seek to suppress it.

The German jurist, von **Savigny**, was one of the first legal scholars to use the term folk law (in German *Volksrecht*). He argued that in the early history of a people their law consisted of customs which had by repetition become laws, and were an emanation of their distinctive 'common consciousness'. As a people's culture developed they would be elaborated and developed into technical forms in written **legislation** and juristic doctrine, but would continue to manifest their common spirit (in German *Volksgeist*).

Much of the more recent literature on folk law has concerned the customary laws of indigenous ethnic groups who have become **minorities** as a result of colonial settlement in their countries. Other terms which refer to these folk laws include **indigenous law**, tribal law, traditional law, and Aboriginal law. Earlier, there were references to 'primitive law', and 'native law' also had for a time a derogatory undertone. The inception in 1982 of the Commission on

Folk law and Legal Pluralism of the International Union of Anthropological and Ethnological Sciences contributed to the acceptability of the term 'folk law'. This type of non-state law has been investigated principally by anthropologists and other social scientists.

Increasing scientific interest in the latter half of the twentieth century coincided with a growing acceptance by state laws of a right of indigenous minorities to govern themselves by their folk laws. In the USA, there was increased study and some **recognition** of the laws of native peoples. In Canada, Indian and Inuit populations gained rights and, in some cases, a measure of **self-government**. In some South American states, **indigenous peoples** gained some communal rights, as did Aborigines in Australia, especially with respect to land, while, in New Zealand, there was a growth of state recognition of Maori rights. These are the principal but not the only examples.

Legal scholars of the positivist tradition have often denied that folk law is law properly so called, seeing it as mere 'positive morality'. They have claimed that true law is enacted and enforced by state institutions, is written, and carries exclusive legal authority. All of these claims seem to be of questionable validity, and many peoples continue to observe their folk laws rather than state law.

Although much scholarly and political activity has been directed to the folk laws of indigenous ethnic minorities, the term has continued to be used of the normative orders of other ethnic groups, especially immigrant groups. It has been further argued that the folk laws of ethnic groups are of a character which is in principle indistinguishable from that of other types of customary law. It is arguable that folk law should be regarded as a universal synonym for customary law. GORDON WOODMAN

food labelling Food labelling is dealt with under the Food Safety Act 1996 and the Food Labelling Regulations 1996. There are hundreds of detailed requirements in this area, all of which have to be marked on the packaging.

In general terms, there is a requirement to list the ingredients of a product in descending order of weight This includes water if that constitutes over 5 per cent of the weight. With some exceptions, the product must have a 'Best Before' or 'Use By' label. The label must specify special conditions or requirements for use. The label must contain the name and address of at least one of the manufacturer, packer, or retailer. The country of origin of the product must be stated where failure to do so might mislead.

There must be instructions for use in appropriate circumstances.

The product must be given a name, which is either that prescribed by law (which may include varieties) or the customary name, or a name which describes its true nature. It cannot merely be labelled with a brand name. There are special rules for the labelling of flavourings, sweeteners, and additives. There are special labelling rules for products that may cause an allergenic reaction.

There are special rules for particular products. For example alcoholic products must be labelled with the strength of the alcohol by volume. Untreated milk must be labelled with warnings. Most natural products require no labelling.

The regulations also ban from a product's labelling many claims about the product. There are particular rules about slimming products and vitamins. Breach of the regulations is a criminal offence.

RICHARD BRAGG

food safety The sale and consumption of food has always involved risks to human health. The adulteration of basic food products in thirteenth-century England was not only a source of unfairness to buyers (who did not get what they were paying for), but also risked contamination of the food with injurious substances, and was targeted by the Statute of Bread and Ale 1266. More modern legislative initiatives have frequently been developed in response to particular incidents of food poisoning. The first modern legislation dates from 1860 and arose out of scares concerning food poisoning from unsafe food. Much of more recent food safety legislation similarly has arisen out of public concerns related to such matters as salmonella in eggs, in the 1980s, and the public policy disaster arising out of BSE (known as 'mad cow disease') in the 1990s, which led to the establishment of a judicial inquiry chaired by Lord Phillips.

The basic substantive requirements, found in the Food Safety Act 1990, are that food should be safe, should not be injurious to health, should be of the 'nature, substance, and quality' demanded and, where labelled, should be labelled accurately. More specific requirements, introduced in regulations made under the Food Safety Act and under the European Communities Act 1972 (which empowers ministers to make regulations to implement the requirements of EC food law), apply both to specific products and to particular activities, such as labelling of food products. Breach of any of these requirements constitutes a criminal offence which, in common with **trading standards** offences, are generally offences of strict liability, meaning that the prosecution need not prove intent or even knowledge on the part of the business which committed the offence in order to secure a conviction. However, the legislation does offer a defence based on the claim that the defendant exercised due diligence to avoid committing the offence. The availability of this defence encourages businesses to implement quality assurance procedures, and in particular Hazard Analysis at Critical Control Points ('HACCP') regimes so that even where standards are breached they may be able to demonstrate that they exercised sufficient due diligence to avoid conviction.

The substantive requirements of food safety legislation are supported by a variety of institutional and procedural arrangements. The main responsibility for enforcement lies with local authority environmental health or regulatory services officers. The enforcement officers have statutory powers to test food products and inspect premises and, in recent years, have been encouraged to link the frequency of their inspections to the risk associated either with the food sector involved and/or the particular premises.

The scandals of the 1990s generated a lack of confidence in the Ministry of Agriculture Fisheries and Food, and in particular a perception that it was too closely allied to the interests of farmers and food producers and was insufficiently concerned with the interests of consumers. The institutional response from the new Labour government, elected in 1997, was to establish an independent Food Standards Agency to take on responsibility of steering of food policy in the UK, coordinating enforcement, and advising ministers, industry, and consumers in matters relating to food. The Meat Hygiene Service, established to inspect slaughterhouses and meat processing plants, in the wake of the BSE crisis, was subsumed within the Food Standards Agency, and provides an example of central, as opposed to local, government enforcement in this domain.

COLIN SCOTT

forced labour *see* **slavery**

forced marriage Forced marriage is a **marriage** obtained without the free and full **consent** of both parties, and is distinct from an arranged marriage where the parties exercise free choice as to solemnization. The UK government has sought to tackle the problem through a series of proposed legislative initiatives, including criminalization. However, this was met with much criticism, and eventually shelved and replaced with the Forced Marriage (Civil Protection) Act 2007 which introduces protection orders for **victims** and potential victims.

Tackling forced marriages is not unproblematic. First, individuals may not wish to involve the authorities, for the majority of forced marriages occur at the instigation of close family members. Secondly, the legal construction of consent in English law is premised upon an understanding of consent based upon individual choice, which ignores the complex familial, communal, and cultural interactions at play within many of the **communities** in which forced marriages occur. Finally, the legal requirement of duress is tricky when one considers the range of behaviour which may exert pressure, such as emotional blackmail, socialization, and familial expectations. Accordingly, it is not always obvious or easy to ascertain the point at which an arranged marriage becomes forced. This has a twofold effect—first, victims may find that the duress alleged is not sufficient under law to render the marriage voidable; and secondly, there is the potential for abuse, whereby individuals may falsely allege that a marriage was forced, by playing to cultural stereotypes which the **courts** unwittingly reinforce.

SONYA FERNANDEZ

forced migration Traditional typologies characterize migrations by the degree of choice involved in the decision to leave home: 'voluntary' migrants choose to look for new economic opportunities, 'involuntary' migrants are forced to flee and seek refuge elsewhere. However, migration is increasingly caused by a variety of interrelated factors, including elements of both compulsion and choice in the decision-making of almost all migrants. Although forced migrants are often called '**refugees**', most flee for reasons not explicitly recognized in international refugee law, and many are displaced within their own country. The categories of forced migrants most often discussed are: (1) Refugees: under Article 1 of the 1951 Convention Relating to the Status of Refugees, a refugee is a **person** outside her home country, who cannot return because of a 'well-founded fear of persecution on account of **race, religion**, **nationality**, membership in a particular social group, or political opinion'. Regional instruments in Africa and Central America enlarged this definition to include armed conflict, occupation, and massive violations of **human rights**. The key elements are the crossing of an international border and **violence** as a causal factor; (2) **Asylum** seekers, ie people who have moved across an international border in search of protection but whose claim for refugee status is as yet undecided; (3) Internally **Displaced Persons**

('IDPs'): under the 1998 UN Guiding Principles on Internal Displacement, IDPs are 'persons who have been forced (...) to leave their homes (...) in order to avoid the effects of armed conflict, situations of generalized violence, violations of human rights or natural or human-made disasters, and who have not crossed an internationally recognized state border'. IDPs are still subject to their countries' **sovereignty** and laws; (4) Development displacees: people compelled to move by large-scale development projects (dams, airports, mining, conservation parks); (5) Environmental and disaster displacees: people displaced by natural disasters (floods, volcanoes, landslides, earthquakes), environmental change (deforestation, desertification, land degradation), and human-made disasters (industrial accidents, radioactivity, water **pollution**); and finally, (6) Trafficked persons: under the 2000 UN Protocol to Prevent, Suppress and Punish Trafficking in Persons, Especially Women and Children, these are persons transported using violence, coercion, or by providing misleading information, in order to exploit them sexually or economically. Trafficking should be distinguished from the smuggling of migrants through borders.

People often do not fit readily into these categories and they are not mutually exclusive. Whereas international refugee law carries a clear legal status and the protection of the **UN High Commissioner for Refugees**, other forced migrants benefit from only fragmented forms of protection regime. Lack of a coherent set of rules and institutional responsibilities implies an urgent need to identify human rights protection and gaps in material assistance, and work towards more effective solutions.

DELPHINE NAKACHE AND
FRANÇOIS CRÉPEAU

N Van Hear, *New Diasporas: The Mass Exodus, Dispersal and Regrouping of Migrant Communities* (London: UCL Press, 1998)
S Castles, 'Global perspectives on forced migration' (2006) 15/1 *Asian and Pacific Migration Journal* 7–28

foreign tax credit   *see* **international tax**

foreseeability   *see* **negligence in civil law**

formal equality   The idea of '**equality**' appears, at first glance, very simple. Equality means treating likes alike. However, the meaning of equality has been the subject of considerable legal debate over time and particularly in the past three decades. In jurisdictions such as the United Kingdom, the European Union, and Canada, legal definitions of

equality have been (very) broadly split into two types: (1) formal equality; and (2) **substantive equality**.

Formal equality refers to the 'commonsense' understanding mentioned above. Individuals should be treated alike, no matter what their differences are in terms of **sex**, **race**, sexuality, or any other characteristic. In making job appointments, for example, an employer should aim to give the job to the best qualified **person**, adopting the 'merit principle'. Any discrimination against, or in favour of, a candidate is deemed to be unlawful. The application of the formal equality principle has particular consequences in law and has been subject to considerable criticism. Such legal consequences and the criticisms that flow from them will now be examined.

The first legal consequence of formal equality is that it entrenches the concept of 'symmetry' in equality law. Symmetrical **legislation** requires that any anti-discrimination enactment must apply both ways, ie in the case of sex discrimination legislation, to prohibit discrimination against men as well as women. A man might argue that a swimming pool's policy of awarding a concessional rate to people of pensionable age discriminates against him because he has to wait until 65 to claim the rate, whereas a woman can claim the rate from age 60 (see *James v Eastleigh Borough Council* (1990)). In this way, symmetrical legislation works for relatively privileged groups in society, as well as for relatively disadvantaged groups. Much of the equality legislation in the UK and in **European Community law** stems from a symmetrical model. The problem with symmetry, as Nicola Lacey has pointed out, is that it does not acknowledge the specific, and socially embedded, consequences of discrimination against women, and her analysis could equally be applied in the context of race, sexual orientation, **disability**, age, and religious discrimination. As Lacey observes, abandoning formal equality would 'acknowledge that sex discrimination against men is not a social phenomenon of the same order, does not involve comparably damaging and oppressive effects as does sex discrimination against women, and that this clear social difference justifies, and indeed, calls for a totally different legal response'.

The second legal consequence of formal equality concerns '**positive action**' measures. Because formal equality frowns on any type of discrimination, it also outlaws many types of affirmative action or 'positive action' measures, from 'outreach' programmes aimed at under-represented groups, to quotas for particular groups of people in employment. Many people would agree with this: there is a great deal of unease in wider society about so-called 'reverse' or

positive discrimination. The issue of 'reverse discrimination' goes to the very heart of the distinction between formal and substantive equality. Whereas there is a presumption with formal equality that positive action measures are unlawful or need to be justified, the presumption under a substantive equality model is that wide-ranging **institutional discrimination** should be addressed by positive measures, and that such measures are integral to equality law. Indeed, the **Canadian Charter of Rights and Freedoms** ('the Charter') contains a provision explicitly endorsing positive or 'ameliorative' action. The main equality provision in section 15(1) of the Charter sets out the right of every individual to equal treatment and equal benefit under the law, and section 15(2) states that this 'does not preclude any law, program or activity that has as its object the amelioration of conditions of disadvantaged individuals or groups…'.

Despite the fact that much of UK discrimination law operates in accordance with formal equality principles, there has been a recent shift towards accepting the need for positive action strategies due to a number of high profile reports on embedded, institutional discrimination throughout UK society: see, for example, the *The Stephen Lawrence Inquiry*, published in 1999, acknowledging institutional racism in the Metropolitan Police Force. Public authorities in the UK are now under positive duties to promote race, disability, and **gender** equality. At the European level, and against a similar background of formal equality legislation, there has also been a growing acceptance of positive action measures. The position of the **European Court of Justice** at present is that measures giving priority to under-represented groups can be lawful under European Union equality law as long as: (1) they do not automatically grant priority to a member of one group (for example, women) where a member of the other group (men) is equally qualified; and (2) the specific circumstances of each candidate are taken into consideration (*Badeck v Landesanwalt beim Staatsgerichtshof des Landes Hessen* (2000)).

Apart from problems of symmetry and the restrictions on ameliorative measures, it is possible to discern three further criticisms of formal equality in the socio-legal literature. First, formal equality presumes that the law is neutral, and that applying the law equally to different individuals will, itself, lead to equality. This overlooks the instrumental role of the law in centuries of systemic oppression, including **slavery**, **apartheid,** the subordination of women, and the outlawing of **homosexuality**. Examples of laws that have supported and enabled discrimination in

the past include US anti-miscegenation laws (prohibiting inter-racial **marriages**), criminal laws against homosexual sex in the US and the UK, and the 'pass laws' in apartheid South Africa which regulated and restricted the movement of black Africans. Applying these laws 'equally' does not provide us with a mechanism of criticizing, and remedying, the oppression that led to the law in the first place.

The second criticism of formal equality is that it presumes that the state is neutral. Formal equality is based on an ideology that favours minimal state involvement in the lives of individuals and in the way that businesses are run. In this sense, it does not look to interfere with how employers and other decision-makers are running their organizations, and it will prioritize 'voluntary' schemes over 'compulsory' legislation. The problem here is that the theory of state neutrality ignores the inherent distributive function of the state. As Sandra Fredman puts it: '(e)ven a non-interventionist strategy favours some groups by supporting the status quo'. If the status quo consists of wide-ranging social inequalities, then it is arguably incumbent on the state to implement measures addressed at eliminating disadvantage.

This leads to the third, and final, point: formal equality implies that when discrimination happens, it is the result of one individual holding a negative stereotypical view and applying that view, in an obvious and clear manner, to another. All that the wronged individual has to do is go to **court,** explain the discrimination, and obtain a legal **remedy** tailored to their own personal circumstances. But discrimination rarely happens in this way. It is typically systemic, wide-ranging, and institutionally embedded. Organizations can have policies that look neutral, but which impact negatively on particular groups. For example, in the US case of *Griggs v Duke Power Co* (1971), it was held that a requirement that applicants achieve a certain score in an IQ test or had passed their high school diploma had an adverse effect on black applicants and was therefore unlawful. For this reason, equality laws should have the capacity to look at the impact of apparently neutral policies, and to deliver remedies to all individuals who are affected by discriminatory policies, not merely the people who bring the claims.

EMILY GRABHAM

N Lacey, 'Legislation against Sex Discrimination: Questions from a Feminist Perspective' 14 *Journal of Law & Society* (1987) 420

S Fredman, *Women and the Law* (Oxford: Oxford University Press, 1997)

formalism *see* **doctrinal legal research**

fostering Foster care is frequently the preferred way of providing for children who cannot live with their own families. Individuals and couples provide day-to-day care for children in state care in return for an allowance paid by the local authority. Fostering arrangements may be short term, lasting for days or weeks, or long term/indefinite until the **child** is able to return to their family or live independently. Specialist foster carers care for children and young people who would otherwise be in custody. Approximately 40,000 children and young people live in foster placements, arranged directly by a local authority children's services department or by an Independent Fostering Agency ('IFA'). A few parents also make arrangements directly with private foster carers who agree to look after their children for payment. Foster carers do not have **parental responsibility**; the foster placement agreement should state the arrangements for **consent to medical treatment**, school trips, etc.

The care of children by anyone other than close relatives (parents, step-parents, grandparents, aunts and uncles, or siblings) is highly regulated to ensure the well-being of children separated from their families. Local authorities have responsibilities for making and supervising placements for children they look after, and for the welfare of children fostered privately; those arranging private fostering must notify the local authority. Fostering Services, provided by local authorities or IFAs are inspected by the Commission for Social Care Inspection. The Children Act 1989 and the Fostering Services Regulations 2002 contain the main provisions relating to fostering children in state care; private fostering is regulated in the Children (Private Arrangements for Fostering) Regulations 2005.

Local authorities owe a duty of care to children they place in foster care and to foster carers. A local authority may be liable to compensate a child or carers who are harmed because of its negligent failure to assess a carer's suitability or to provide information about the child's behaviour. The local authority is not responsible just because a child is injured in a foster home, even if the carers were negligent. Foster carers also owe a duty of care to children they look after and the standard of care required is the same as for parents.

Local authorities may remove children from foster homes whenever they consider that this is in the child's interests. Foster carers who wish to continue to care for a child can seek a residence order. If they have cared for a child in state care for less than a year they must have the consent of the local authority to apply for the court's permission to make an application. Foster carers who have looked after a child for a year, or who have the permission of everyone with parental responsibility, can apply directly to **court**. A person who obtains a residence order acquires parental responsibility and ceases to foster. The local authority may continue the allowance (Children Act 1989).

The Fostering Network provides information about fostering (*www.fostering.net*).

JUDITH MASSON

See also: **negligence in civil law; residence in family law**

franchise *see* **elections**

franchising *see* **commercial exploitation of intellectual property**

Frankfurter, Felix Felix Frankfurter (1882—1965), a justice of the **United States Supreme Court**, was born in Vienna, emigrating with his family to the United States in 1894. He excelled academically at the City College of New York and Harvard Law School. While a member of the Harvard faculty, Frankfurter wrote for the influential weekly, *The New Republic*, and advised liberal politicians, eventually becoming one of Franklin D Roosevelt's most influential advisers.

Roosevelt appointed Frankfurter to the Supreme Court in 1939, where he served until he suffered a severe stroke in 1962. Frankfurter believed that **judges** should be restrained in exercising their power to invalidate **legislation** as unconstitutional. Yet, he enthusiastically enforced the Constitution's ban on establishments of **religion**, perhaps because of his reflections on the meaning of being Jewish in the United States; in one of his most famous dissents, Frankfurter specifically mentioned his religion in explaining why governments could promote **assimilation** and patriotism by requiring all school children, even religious objectors, to salute the American flag.

Frankfurter's philosophy of judicial restraint was consistent with American liberalism in the 1930s and 1940s, but it became marginalized as liberalism itself changed. Although his colleagues on the Supreme Court often found him difficult to deal with, Frankfurter developed a cadre of scholarly disciples, who briefly made him one of the central figures in American constitutional scholarship. His influence rapidly faded after his death, and his work did not play a significant role in the criticisms of judicial activism that flourished in the late twentieth century.

MARK TUSHNET

fraud and misrepresentation In civil (as opposed to criminal) law, a remedy may be available for the innocent victim who suffers injury, harm, or loss as the result of the making of a false statement ('misstatement') or a false representation ('misrepresentation').

In a narrow sense, the term 'misrepresentation' refers to a situation where a person is induced to enter into a contract entirely or partly by an assertion made by the other contracting party. In this sense, a misrepresentation is made prior to contracting and is an assertion of fact, not of opinion or intention. Claims that can be described as 'puffery' or sales talk—eg many advertising slogans—are not 'misrepresentations'. A misrepresentation that induces a contract may or may not 'be incorporated into' the contract as a term. If it is incorporated, it may form the basis of an action for breach of contract and the awarding of contractual remedies. If not, the person to whom the misrepresentation was made may be able to 'rescind' the contract (ie effectively, withdraw from it) or obtain damages under **tort law**.

Remedies for misrepresentation are provided both by the **common law** and under the Misrepresentation Act 1967. In particular, the 1967 Act creates remedies for negligent misrepresentation (see below). The rules governing liability for negligent misrepresentation under the Act are different from their common law counterparts in several respects.

The term 'misstatement' is generally used to refer to a false assertion that causes injury, harm, or loss to the person to whom it is made other than by inducing that person to enter a contract. Whether a remedy will be available to that person depends on the rules of tort law.

Under tort law (but not under **contract law**) the remedy, if any, available to the victim of a misstatement or misrepresentation depends in part upon whether the misstatement or misrepresentation was made fraudulently, negligently, or non-negligently (innocently). A misstatement or misrepresentation is made fraudulently if the maker knows that it is false or knows that it may be false but makes it anyway without honestly believing in its truth. It is often difficult to establish fraud. A person makes a misstatement or misrepresentation negligently if they fail to take reasonable care to ascertain its truth. A misstatement or misrepresentation that was made neither fraudulently nor negligently is termed 'innocent'.

Under tort law, fraudulent misstatement or misrepresentation can attract a remedy for what is called 'deceit'. Because the law considers deceit to be more serious than negligence, the damages available in an action for deceit may be greater than those available in an action for negligence. In particular, whereas in an action for negligence damages will be recoverable only for 'foreseeable' injury, harm, or loss resulting from the tort, in an action for deceit damages may be recoverable for injury, harm, or loss that is a 'direct' result of the tort, even if not foreseeable. Except in the case of false statements that are defamatory, no remedy is available under tort law for an innocent misstatement or misrepresentation. A party may be entitled to rescind a contract induced by an innocent misrepresentation and, if the misrepresentation has become part of the contract, recover damages for breach of contract. Under the Misrepresentation Act 1967 a person who is entitled to rescind a contract because it was induced by an innocent misrepresentation may be required to accept damages instead if the court considers this to be fairer.

DEBORAH PARRY

See also: **defamation**; *Hedley Byrne & Co Ltd v Heller & Partners Ltd*; **negligence in civil law; remedies**

fraud trials *see* **Orton, Arthur**

fraud, honesty, and markets The principal focus of the criminal law is upon the discrete actions of individuals: stealing from and/or physically injuring other people; or damaging property. Fraud is mainly about getting goods, money, or services by 'dishonestly' deceiving other people or institutions who would not supply them (at least on those terms) if they knew the truth; but it can also involve causing losses without any obvious benefit to self (other than keeping one's job or getting a performance bonus that otherwise one would not get). However, as in some violent and dramatic property crimes, the ego satisfaction of being 'in control' of others is itself a driver of harmful behaviour. As in cases where traders falsify financial business to avoid their bosses realizing that they have lost money and dismissing them, claims of apparent disinterest are sometimes argued in criminal trials. Causing harm *wrongfully* implies *both* that the conduct is regarded as harmful (to individuals, business, and/or to general social interests) *and* that we believe that there has been some level of mental awareness on the part of the suspect that makes them blameworthy. This involves (a) the setting of legal rules, eg determining whether or not to criminalize recklessness which entails seeing a **risk** of non-consensual harm to another and ignoring it—see, eg the Fraud Act 2006 and the Financial Services and Markets Act 2000 ('FSMA'); and (b) the judgment of legal gatekeepers (**police** and prosecutors) and 'fact-finders' (**juries**, magistrates, and

Sheriffs in Scotland) that the potential accused or defendants had the mental element required by law. Markets are a set of contexts in which some financial crimes can take place: situational opportunities for fraud and for 'market abuses' such as insider trading.

It is unambiguously fraud if someone 'steals' (or, more accurately, borrows/duplicates) someone else's identity and uses it to obtain credit facilities; uses stolen credit cards pretending to be the cardholder; offers substantial amounts of goods for sale on e-Bay which are paid for, but never sends them; takes moneys from clients and friends for investment but instead spends the funds at casinos and on plush holidays, or merely hides them in overseas accounts. The plea of innocent mistake or carelessness might work on the first occasion, but is implausible to explain away a pattern of events. However, compared with 'ordinary' property crimes, some people accused of serious frauds in a business or financial market context benefit from the greater opportunities for constructing ambiguity about 'what happened': the **prosecution** must prove that what was done was done by or with the connivance of the accused; was dishonest by the ordinary standards of honest and reasonable people; and that the defendant realized this at the time (*R v Ghosh* (1982)). Sometimes, when looking at how people react in **securities** and other financial markets, the dividing line between fraud and cleverness in taking advantage of informational/market asymmetries can be a fine one. The attribution of culpability is part imaginative empathy (of a situation that may be alien to most jurors), part morality play; our construction of what fair dealing constitutes and how harmful fraud is varies over time and place. Stereotypes of whether the actual/potential defendant is or is not 'a criminal type' may also impact on the decision not to prosecute, influenced (as per the Code for Crown Prosecutors) by the second guessing of jury reactions: jurors may be reluctant to conclude that people in prestigious jobs with much to lose would be dishonest, or alternatively may impose retrospective moral evaluations.

Whatever the theoretical ambit of the criminal law, decisions may be taken by regulators that it is pragmatically more efficient in **restorative justice** terms to treat financial institutions and their staff as if they were 'mis-sellers' of financial services rather than fraudsters, even though they may have lied to clients about the appropriateness of investments in order to gain bonuses for themselves and profits for their shareholders. The result of this is that someone who steals a bar of soap from a shop can become a 'thief' with a criminal record, whereas business people who cause millions of pounds in losses may escape any criminal sanction. Other bodies also act (conscious or not of these fairness issues) as gatekeepers who often divert possible frauds away from the criminal justice process. These include HM Revenue and Customs, the Department of Work and Pensions, the **Financial Services Authority** ('FSA'), and even the Electoral Commission, or the **House of Commons** Standards and Privileges Committee (eg if MPs make inappropriate payments to their families 'for research' or fail to declare political donations). The pragmatic benefits of not prosecuting corporations for other than 'strict liability' offences are particularly strong, given problems of attribution in the UK of **corporate criminal liability**, and of showing the actual role of individuals in corporate or other bureaucratic chains of command. Some *de facto* 'decisions' about what is to be treated as criminal and what is not may be made by default, through resource shortages or abundance. Those resources may in turn be the product of popular sentiment and governmental tradition—one reason for the greater cultural appetite for corporate and individual business criminalization in the US compared with the UK, which goes back to the early twentieth century. It took the UK almost a century after the US Sherman Anti-Trust Act to enact similar provisions in the Enterprise Act 2002 and to give the Serious Fraud Office substantial extra resources to prosecute cartels; the first FSA prosecution for insider trading in seven years was begun in 2008, whereas they are relatively commonplace in the US, eg the six-year jail sentence in 2007 for the former CEO of Qwest. A rare FSMA prosecution occurred in 2005, when two **directors** of call-centre software firm, AIT, had issued a statement to the market stating that the turnover and profit of the **company** were in line with expectations, but many contracts did not exist. Both were found guilty of recklessly making a misleading statement to the market, but acquitted of knowingly making misleading statements.

People can 'know' that they have been defrauded without being able to show that the person(s) who did them harm possessed the required level of 'wrongfulness'. Sometimes, there may be disputes about whether ATM payments were made through customer carelessness with PINs or by technological compromise; whether insurance claims have been deliberately exaggerated; or whether those running insolvent companies have continued to trade when they knew or suspected they would not be able to repay debts: such suspicions of 'first party fraud' are seldom prosecuted.

In England and Wales, 'fraud' was redefined in the Fraud Act 2006, which created a new general offence of fraud and introduced three possible ways of committing it—by false representation (section 2), failure to disclose information when there is a legal duty to do so (section 3, eg by a solicitor to a client), and abuse of position (section 4) (see *http://www.cps. gov.uk/legal/section8/chapter_d.html#16*). In each case, the defendant's conduct must be dishonest and his intention must be to make a gain, or cause a loss or the risk of a loss to another. The offence of false representation is entirely offender-focused and is complete as soon as the defendant makes one with 'dishonest' intent, irrespective of how it is communicated (eg on the internet or in person, and explicitly or implicitly by the mere fact that one pretends to be someone else). It differs from 'deception' in that it makes no difference whether or not any one is aware of the representation, is deceived, or any property is actually gained or lost. Thus, it avoids the arguments over whether electronic devices can properly be viewed as 'deceived'. However, the Act has come in for severe criticism for (over)criminalizing lying. As one commentator observes: 'The wrong seems to be the act of lying or misleading with intent to gain or cause loss; the harm might be construed as one of destabilizing society's processes of property and financial transfers' (Ormerod (2007)). It remains to be seen how such provisions will affect conduct as varied as market traders selling 'soccer shirts as worn by Beckham'; friends who obtain a loan by falsely saying that they will repay you when their pay comes in at the end of the week; investment analysts who tell their clients that stocks held by their firm are a good 'buy', while informing their firm that the stocks are of poor quality; and directors who make reassuring statements about the health of their company while selling their own shares because of their pressing need to purchase a mansion in Florida (where forfeiture of homes is difficult) or in the non-extraditable Turkish Republic of North Cyprus. In all cases, the statements may be false and intended to cause gain or avoid loss: but are they all dishonest? Ironically, because of the reputational/financial impact of the allegation of fraud, even civil fraud and regulatory 'market abuse' cases must meet a quasi-criminal standard of proof.   MICHAEL LEVI

D Ormerod, 'The Fraud Act 2006 – Criminalising lying?' (2007) *Criminal Law Review* 193–219

S Green, *Lying, Cheating and Stealing* (Oxford: Oxford University Press, 2006)

free movement in the EU   At the heart of the EEC—and now EC—Treaty is the creation of the common, now single or internal, market, an area without frontiers in which the so-called 'four freedoms' can be ensured. The four freedoms concern the free movement of goods (Articles 23–25, 28–30 and 90 EC), **persons** (Article 39 on workers (essentially employed persons) and Article 43 on establishment (the self-employed and **companies**)), services (Articles 49 and 50 EC) and capital (Articles 56–58). Some might add an additional category: the free movement of citizens (Article 18(1) EC). The idea behind the four freedoms is that it should be as easy to trade or move between London and Budapest as it is between London and Birmingham. The aim is market integration, ie the removal of barriers to trade and migration between states. This is what the Treaty provisions aim to do, and this is what is sometimes referred to as *negative integration*.

The advantages of free movement are various. In the case of **persons**, there are benefits for both individual **migrant workers** and the 'host' state where they go to work. Workers coming from other Member States often take up jobs which cannot be filled from the pool of national workers. The migrants might also bring new talents and skills which the national workforce cannot offer. For individual migrants, moving to a new job in another Member State means escaping from possible unemployment at home, bettering their personal circumstances, and broadening their range of experience. So far: so win-win. When times are good, workers from other Member States do help to fill a skills gap. But when times are bad, migrant workers are seen to threaten jobs for nationals and it is then that host governments, bowing to domestic political pressure, may decide to make life more difficult for migrant workers. This is where **European Community law** comes into play: Article 39 can be invoked to challenge the barriers; while Member States can invoke '**derogations**' to restrict the movement of the migrants, their attempts will be unsuccessful because the derogations cannot be used to serve 'economic' purposes (ie protecting national industry).

The principle of non-discrimination on the grounds of **nationality** is the cornerstone of the four freedoms. The principle prohibits not only direct or overt discrimination on the ground of nationality against out-of-state goods, persons, services, and capital but also unjustified **indirect discrimination**. Indirect discrimination prohibits national rules which, on their face, apply to domestic and imported goods/persons/capital, but in fact particularly disadvantage the imported good/service/capital or migrant. According to the orthodox case law, states can defend directly discriminatory rules only by invoking one of the express derogations laid down by the Treaty; by contrast indirect discrimination can be saved by an express derogation or a judicially developed justification.

The advantage of the non-discrimination model approach is that it allows Member States to regulate the way that, for example, goods are produced and services provided. The problem is that the non-discrimination approach sometimes does not produce the desired effect of opening up the market because the imported good or migrant person still has to comply with non-discriminatory rules laid down by the host state. This has led the **European Court of Justice** ('ECJ'), in the famous case of *Cassis de Dijon* (1979), to develop the rule of mutual recognition. According to this rule, goods lawfully produced and marketed in France can be marketed in Germany without further restriction. The burden then shifts to the host state to justify that restriction. The principle of mutual recognition has the effect of putting the different legal systems in **competition** with one another. The benefit of mutual recognition is that German consumers now have the choice of buying French goods or German goods, both produced according to different standards. The disadvantage of mutual recognition is that it might prompt German business to take advantage of the free movement of capital and/or freedom of establishment rules, flee to France to set up business there and produce fruit liqueur according to the 'lower' French standards, with serious implications for German jobs. Alternatively, if capital does not move but German consumers buy the cheaper French Cassis, this outcome will also be detrimental to German jobs. One response would be for German producers to lobby their government for lower standards. If successful, this might prompt French producers to request their government to lower standards still further, leading to a race to the bottom and a convergence (rather than a diversity) of standards at this low level. The so-called 'mandatory requirements' recognized by the ECJ in *Cassis* (ie the open-ended justifications like **consumer** protection) are intended to place a brake on any such race to the bottom.

So far we have concentrated on the non-discrimination model. As we have seen, the problem with that model is that it allows host states to maintain barriers to inter-state trade, provided they are non-discriminatory. Such barriers might impede access for out-of-state goods or people to the host state's market. For this reason, some advocate that a broader market access test should be applied: national rules preventing or hindering market access are unlawful, irrespective of whether they actually discriminate against imports or migrants. There is evidence in the case law, particularly in the field of persons, services, and capital, that the ECJ increasingly favours this approach. For example, in *Gebhard v Consiglio dell'Ordine degli Avvocati e Procuratori di Milano* (1995), a case concerning a German lawyer wishing to set up business in Italy under Article 43 but finding that he could not use the Italian title 'avvocato', the ECJ abandoned the language of discrimination and talked instead of national measures 'liable to hinder or make less attractive the exercise of fundamental freedoms guaranteed by the Treaty'. According to the ECJ, the Italian rules on titles breached Article 43 unless they could be justified and were proportionate.

The advantage of the market access approach is that it goes a long way towards building a **single market** by removing any unjustified obstacles to trade; the disadvantage is that it is far more intrusive into individual states' freedom to enact their own laws since Community law requires such laws to be struck down, even though they may not discriminate against the non-national, unless they can be justified and the steps taken proportionate. This has serious implications for national **legislation** adopted by democratically elected governments, not least because a case can be made that almost any national rule has some effect on inter-state trade, even if that was never the intention of the rule and the effect on inter-state trade is very slight. There is some evidence that the ECJ has recognized this problem and has experimented with different legal techniques to draw the line between those rules which should be caught by Community law and those which should fall outside it. The most famous example is the case of Joined Cases C-267 & 268/91 *Keck and Mithouard* (1993) where the Court ruled that national rules governing 'certain selling arrangements' (essentially rules concerning the time, place, and manner of sale, such as rules limiting shops' ability to trade on Sunday) which apply to all traders in the state and which do not discriminate in law or in fact, and do not breach the rules on the free movement of goods (Article 28 EC). This case suggests that, in the field of free movement of goods the Court has reverted to the non-discrimination model in preference to the market access approach.

Whether the non-discrimination or the market access approach is applied, states can legitimately interfere with inter-state trade if they have good reasons to do so and those good reasons fit into one of the derogations laid down by the Treaty or one of the justifications developed by the Court. These (legitimate) barriers to inter-state trade of course still interfere with free movement. It is here that *positive integration* plays a role: legislative measures (such as Regulations and Directives) adopted by the institutions of the European Community help facilitate free movement by drawing up common harmonized standards which apply across the EU.

CATHERINE BARNARD

See also: **derogation in EU law**

freedom of assembly Despite the willingness with which the British have taken to the streets and public places to protest against grievances and to celebrate momentous events in the life of the nation, British law did not historically recognize a right of assembly. The enormously influential constitutional lawyer Professor AV **Dicey** once famously remarked that a man has as much right to hold a public meeting as he does to eat a bun. In practice the use by the **police** of their wide discretionary powers dictated the extent to which the public were permitted to assemble; and in practice the degree to which there was a freedom to assemble varied in accordance with such matters as social conditions and the public mood. With the enactment of the **Human Rights Act 1998**, containing as it does a recognition of the right to assemble, the default position is arguably different, and there is a presumption in favour of a right to assemble.

There is certainly a right to assemble in private places, but public assemblies are more problematic because there is no right to use public property on which to exercise the right. An assembly on the highway is regarded as a **trespass** to the highway; but (following an important decision of the **House of Lords** in 1999) there is a right of reasonable use of the highway, which will include use of the highway for purposes of demonstration provided that is done in a way that does not unduly hinder the rights of others to pass and re-pass.

The law regulating freedom of assembly is not to be found in a neatly structured package. It consists of a hotch-potch of legislation and regulatory instruments, of judicial decisions regulating such apparently unconnected matters as the obstruction of the police in the execution of their duty and the related concept of a **breach of the peace**, and of Home Office circulars. Legislation introduced in 1968 for the first time gave the police powers to impose conditions upon assemblies, which were defined as gatherings of twenty or more persons in a public place which is wholly or partly open to air. The conditions could relate to the place of the assembly, the maximum number of persons who might constitute it, or its duration. Astonishingly, the number twenty was subsequently reduced to two by legislation aimed primarily at **anti-social behaviour**. It may well be that such a small group would never trigger a situation in which such conditions might be imposed, namely one in which the police reasonably fear serious public disorder, serious damage to property, or serious disruption to the life of the community, or in which the police reasonably believe that the purpose of the persons organizing the gathering are intimidatory. But the knock-on effect of the legislation is to give the police an enormous amount of discretion in policing assemblies.

ATH SMITH

freedom of association Freedom of association has come to be understood as an essential aspect of citizenship. This form of freedom can be understood as a civil liberty, a political right, and a socio-economic entitlement. It also can be regarded as a 'third generation' cultural right. However, each of the different ways in which freedom of association can be viewed as significant for citizenship has important consequences for its content and the scope of its application. Not surprisingly, given the diversity of this term's usage, its definition is disputed. Fundamentally, there remains tension between the element of individual freedom associated with the concept and the collective aspect of its exercise.

Freedom of association can be regarded as a civil liberty insofar as it contemplates the ability of persons to form associations without intervention by the state. The notion emerged from early assertions of religious liberty, and can be traced back to the protestant movement, which emerged in Europe from the sixteenth century onwards. It is also a freedom utilized by an emergent capitalist class who sought to associate in incorporated bodies for commercial purposes. Freedom of association can further be understood in political terms as the right to organize political parties aimed at challenging the power of the ruling elite. Its significance therefore grew with the spread of democratic government, initially through revolution, in the seventeenth and eighteenth centuries.

Notably, the notion of freedom of association did not prevent governments from labelling and banning certain organizations which were commonly regarded as 'seditious' or 'subversive', and nor does it do so today. However, it is to this concept that we owe our freedom to form and join political parties and to assert common interests through **non-governmental organizations** ('NGOs').

Moreover, the freedom to associate in a trade union, strongly asserted by workers in the nineteenth century, has come to be recognized by law. Insofar as **trade unions** are understood to play a substantial role in improving terms and conditions of employment through collective bargaining and workplace representation, freedom of association has thereby acquired a socio-economic dimension. Finally, in the twentieth century there has been burgeoning recognition of the cultural entitlements particularly of **indigenous peoples** and their entitlements as 'groups'. In this way, freedom of association has come to be understood less as an aspect of individual choice and more a collective assertion of values.

Article 16 of the American Convention on Human Rights ('ACHR') is interesting insofar as it reflects this historical development, stating that: 'Everyone has the right to associate freely for ideological, religious, political, economic, labor, social, cultural, sports or other purposes'. However, there is interesting diversity in the treatment of freedom of association within national constitutional documents and international instruments. For example, the US Constitution does not specifically mention freedom of association, but the constitutional jurisprudence of the US Supreme Court has invoked this freedom in the context of intimate relationships and freedom of speech. By contrast, the guarantee of freedom of association is explicitly recognized in a provision of the German constitution, which has been interpreted by German courts for the benefit of workers seeking to exercise the right to strike.

We also see differences between, on the one hand, the texts of Article 22 of the **International Covenant on Civil and Political Rights ('ICCPR')** and Article 11 of the **European Convention on Human Rights** ('ECHR'), which both refer explicitly to the notion that freedom of association includes 'the right to form and join trade unions' and, on the other, Article 20 of the Universal Declaration on Human Rights 1948 ('UDHR') and the **African Charter on Human and Peoples' Rights** ('ACHPR'), both of which make no such explicit connection. Nevertheless, freedom of association was the foundational value of, and continues to possess prominent constitutional importance within, the **International Labour Organization** by virtue of its significance to workers, and it is in this context that one can find most frequently find complaints relating to violations of freedom of association that affect trade unions.

There are at least two compelling controversial issues which currently arise in relation to freedom of association. The first is whether this freedom encompasses not only the positive entitlement to become part of an organization, but also the negative entitlement to refuse to do so. The second is whether freedom of association extends beyond the mere ability to form and join an organization without state interference, to the ability to act collectively as an organization assisted by the state. The answer to these questions arguably lies in whether one characterizes this entitlement primarily as a civil liberty, as a political right, as a socio-economic entitlement, or as being of fundamental cultural importance.

If one views freedom of association as a civil liberty involving primarily individual choice and autonomy from the state, protection of what has been called negative freedom of association may be deemed appropriate. This is the position explicitly set out in both the UDHR and the ACHPR, which state that 'no one may be compelled to join an association'. Also, while the drafters of the ACHR and the ECHR did not adopt such a formulation, both the **European Court of Human Rights** and the Inter-American Court of Human Rights have subsequently done so. This approach has also been taken by the **European Court of Justice**. However, simple equation of a right to join a trade union and the right not to join a trade union is problematic because the effect of the two choices on other people may be quite different. In the European context, the approach of the European Court of Human Rights has led to abolition of the closed shop and compulsory trade union membership, arguably exacerbating the 'free-rider' problem for trade unionists engaged in collective bargaining.

However, while a civil liberties view has prevailed in relation to negative freedom of association, the position in relation to collective action is more complex. This was an issue highlighted in the case of *Wilson and the NUJ v UK* (2002) before the ECtHR. Formerly the UK **House of Lords** had reached the conclusion that, as long as there was state protection of the bare right to form and join trade unions, there was no necessity to protect trade union activities *per se*, such as collective bargaining. In this instance, the ECtHR disagreed, for without the potential to carry out such activities there is little point in trade union membership. If freedom of association can be regarded as having a strong positive dimension, collective action must not be illegal *per se* or otherwise easily thwarted by private third parties. There may thus be a case for the state to facilitate the activities of lawful associations through recognition of legal personality, for legislative intervention to regulate the conduct of private actors, and even for the devotion of state resources to realization of the achievement of collective objectives.   TONIA NOVITZ

See also: **human rights and civil liberties; third generation rights**

freedom of expression Freedom of expression is often regarded as the most important civil liberty or constitutional right because of its role in the working of an effective democracy. Without freedom to debate political issues, a liberal democracy would soon degenerate into an authoritarian state. But there are other justifications for freedom of expression, notably John Stuart Mill's argument that it enables the discovery of truth and social progress, and the argument that it is essential to the self-fulfilment of individuals. The term 'freedom of speech' has generally been used in the **common law**, and is also used in the First Amendment to the US Constitution: 'Congress shall make no law . . . abridging the freedom of speech, or of the press . . .'. But the **European Convention on Human Rights** ('ECHR') and other international instruments guarantee the 'right to freedom of expression'. Article 10(1) of the ECHR, now part of United Kingdom law under the Human Rights Act 1998, provides that the right includes 'freedom to hold opinions and to receive and impart information and ideas without interference by public authority . . .'.

Freedom of expression (or speech) obviously includes the right to disseminate information and ideas verbally, in writing, or by other means of communication, such as broadcasting and the new electronic media. One aspect of the freedom is press freedom or media freedom. Some forms of expressive conduct, such as desecration of a national flag or the burning of a draft or identity card in protest against the government, may be treated as an exercise of freedom of expression. But apart from those cases, the distinction between expression and conduct is important. It would be wrong to treat an act of violence, for instance, as an exercise of freedom of expression, even though the perpetrator intended to communicate a message in this way.

Freedom of expression is primarily a liberty against state interference. It does not confer positive rights, for example, that the state provide premises for speech or subsidize, say, the theatre or art exhibitions. Nor does the right to receive information and ideas, recognized by the ECHR, give members of the public a right to compel a public authority to provide it. That right is often conferred by a **freedom of information** law, but it is quite distinct from freedom of expression. However, a few positive rights are recognized, for example, the right of candidates to use public halls for election meetings. Freedom of expression is particularly strongly guaranteed against **censorship**, often described as 'prior restraint' because it is applied prior to publication. This applies most clearly in the case of the print media and theatre; press censorship was abolished in England as long ago as 1694, although scrutiny of stage plays existed until 1968. But censorship of films and videos by independent agencies still exists in the **United Kingdom** and in many other countries, particularly to stop the showing of unsuitable matter to children.

Political speech lies at the heart of the freedom, and is the type of expression most strongly protected against the restrictions imposed by either criminal or civil law. Consequently, courts are reluctant to uphold limits on the expression of views on any matter which engages the attention of the public, whether it is an issue of electoral and political debate or one of general social concern—for example, whether the abortion laws should be relaxed or tightened. But freedom of expression in many jurisdictions has been extended far beyond the realm of political speech. It may include literature, artistic expression (including painting and other works of art), pornography, and commercial speech (including advertising). But extreme hardcore pornography is generally not regarded as 'expression'; so a law can ban or restrict its dissemination without the prospect of a legal challenge that it contravenes the freedom. Also excluded from the scope of freedom of expression are those types of speech which have no value at all: blackmail, bribery, perjury, and direct incitement to someone to commit a specific crime. Equally, statements made during the course of commercial or other transactions are not covered by freedom of expression: contractual promises, representations inducing a contract, or the exchange of marriage vows.

It is unusual to treat freedom of expression as an absolute right, although the First Amendment to the US Constitution, on a literal understanding of its words, appears to preclude any abridgement of the freedom by Congress. Even in the United States where freedom of speech is very strongly protected, exercise of the right may be limited, provided the restriction is necessary to protect some vital public interest. The ECHR allows states to impose restrictions on the exercise of freedom of expression, provided they are necessary to further one of the stated aims, for example, national security, public order, morality, the reputation and rights of others, and the authority of the courts. But they cannot penalize expression on the ground either that it communicates shocking or offensive ideas or that it uses unpleasant or vulgar language. Freedom of expression gives speakers the right to choose their own vocabulary.

In most countries, including the United Kingdom, the law imposes significant restrictions on expression. For example, it is generally an offence to disclose official secrets; courts will rarely uphold an argument that official secrets statutes infringe freedom of expression. Other restrictions are imposed by criminal laws penalizing sedition, **blasphemy**, obscenity, **contempt of court**, and the encouragement of **terrorism**. Sometimes it is successfully argued that these laws, or their application to the particular circumstances, infringe exercise of the freedom of expression, so that the speaker or publisher cannot be prosecuted. Courts are very sympathetic to that argument when the publication concerns a matter of political or social controversy, but much less so if the publication is, say, pornographic. One matter of great controversy now is whether laws penalizing **hate speech**—a publication intended or likely to stir up hatred against a racial or religious group—should be upheld or whether they infringe freedom of expression. These laws would be regarded as infringing freedom of speech in the United States, but in the United Kingdom and Europe are usually considered compatible with freedom of expression. Holocaust denial is not proscribed in the United Kingdom, but it is in France, Germany, and some other countries.

Other restrictions are imposed by the civil law, in particular the law of **libel** and laws protecting personal **privacy**. In these circumstances, freedom of expression has to be balanced against the competing rights of individuals to safeguard their reputation or privacy. In the United States greater importance is attached to the former; under the rules established by the Supreme Court in *New York Times v Sullivan* (1964) and subsequent decisions, public officials and figures can only win a libel action if they prove that the libel was published with knowledge that it was false or with indifference to whether it was true or not. In contrast UK courts treat freedom of expression on the one hand, and the right to reputation or privacy on the other as equally important; neither right has pre-eminence. Freedom of expression will prevail if the particular publication has great importance because it concerns, say, politics, rather than celebrity gossip. In contrast to their approach in privacy cases, the courts attach little importance to broad freedom of expression arguments in **copyright** and other intellectual property cases; when a reporter or satirist infringes copyright, he or she must argue that the infringement was covered by a specific statutory defence in order to avoid liability.

In addition to the restrictions imposed by law, the exercise of freedom of expression may be limited by the rules of a professional association. These rules significantly restrict commercial or professional advertising, a type of expression which enjoys less protection than political or literary discourse. Employers, school, and university authorities may impose tighter restrictions on the expression of their staff or students than those imposed by the law. An employee, for instance, may be disciplined if he comments adversely on the conduct of his employer, even though the comments concern a matter of public importance such as the management of a hospital. Freedom of expression arguments sometimes succeed in such contexts; but speech at work or on a university campus does not usually contribute to general debate and it is therefore reasonable to give it less protection than public discourse.

The scope of freedom of expression has widened considerably over the last few decades; it covers much more than the expression of opinion on topics of political interest. For example, it has been argued, sometimes successfully, that restrictions on nude dancing or on the amount of money that can be spent on election campaigns engage freedom of expression. The same argument was made when the government denied the leader of a militant organization permission to enter the country. As a result, freedom of expression law is now far from simple; with the ingenuity of civil liberties lawyers, it is likely to become even more complex.   ERIC BARENDT

E Barendt, *Freedom of Speech* (Oxford: Oxford University Press, 2nd edn, 2005)

See also: **film and video recordings regulation; film censorship; media, regulation and freedom of**

freedom of expression in developing countries Freedom of expression is a fundamental **human right** guaranteed under major international human rights treaties, notable regional human rights instruments, as well as national **constitutions** and laws. The multi-layered protection referred to here describes the situation in both developing and developed states. Many African constitutions, for instance, entrench freedom of expression along with other human rights guarantees in the substantive provisions of their national constitutions. The location of these provisions in the various national constitutions determines not only the legal nature of the rights but also the extent to which they are justiciable.

In many cases the very constituencies that ought to protect freedom of expression cannot in themselves adequately express this important right for the very reasons that prevent the realization of freedom of expression by other sectors in the society or state. The level of the freedom of expression of journalists in developing states is generally considered unsatisfactory but the particular experiences of the concerned states differ considerably. The variables that operate to ameliorate the curtailment of the rights to expression of journalists may include the availability of a strong, diverse, and vibrant print and electronic press in states like Nigeria, India, and Malaysia. Whereas wherever the major print and electronic press is government-controlled, press **censorship** becomes easier for sitting governments. Military regimes and dictatorial governments are particularly prone towards curtailment of human rights to free expression and conscience. Similarly, states leaning towards theocracy impose laws on **blasphemy** that journalists and other vocal elements in society, such as artists, find very stifling of their self-expression. The freedom of expression enjoyed by parliamentarians and lawyers in some developing states is also severely curtailed and serves as a reminder of the interconnectedness of civil rights and the need to secure rights for the benefit of all sectors in society. In 2007, Pakistani lawyers protesting against the arbitrary removal of the Chief Justice as well as the imposition of a state of emergency (martial law) were infamously beaten, arbitrarily arrested, and detained by security operatives.

The pattern of abuses of the right to free expression prevalent in many developing states include press censorship, proscription of publications, closure of television and radio stations, **arrest** and detention of journalists, assassinations, internet censorship, and monitoring of website content and web-surfing activities. Censorship of editorial content has been achieved in many developing countries under the guise of anti-**terrorism legislation** developed after the terrorist events of 11 September. The right of foreign journalists to gather news material, broadcast, and express views from within certain developing states is severely curtailed. Foreign journalists face increasingly stringent **visa** restrictions and outright bans. The British Broadcasting Corporation ('BBC') was banned from entering and operating within Zimbabwe in 2001. Significant issues of **sovereignty**, jurisdiction, and legitimate exercise of governmental powers over national **territory** surround such decisions. Whereas issues surrounding the legal **responsibility** of states may become paramount after incidents such as the fatal shooting by police of a Japanese photojournalist while covering a riot in Burma in October 2007.

Censorship of internet publication is rife in states such as Egypt and China. Abdel Karim Suleiman, in February 2007 became the first blogger to be convicted in Egypt for internet writings in connection with eight online articles he wrote since 2004. Chinese authorities have, since 1995, implemented at least sixty sets of regulations aimed at establishing control over internet content. In broadly-worded regulations which human right groups claim violate the right to freedom of expression, publication of materials over the internet is heavily censored. In January 2001, the communication of 'secret' or 'reactionary' materials over the internet became a capital offence. Up to the present, however, the use of the internet in such illegal ways has attracted no more than imprisonment for been between two and four years.   GBENGA ODUNTAN

freedom of information Freedom of information ('FOI') means access to government-held documents by requesters as a presumptive right in whatever format the documents are held. In some regimes, the right is restricted to those in residence in the relevant jurisdiction or to citizens of the relevant country. The modern freedom of information movement began in the USA in 1966, although the origins go back to eighteenth-century Sweden. The **United Kingdom** and Germany were two of the last liberal democratic regimes to legislate for FOI, but the UK regime is broader than many.

The right of access is invariably subject to exemptions and exclusions, and disputes concerning access are determined by independent bodies. In the UK, the Freedom of Information Act 2000 ('FOIA') exists alongside other access legislation, including regulations allowing access to environmental information ('EIR'), which operate in tandem with the FOIA but which have a wider reach. Like the regulations allowing re-use of public sector information, enactment of EIR is a requirement of compliance with EU directives. Data Protection laws ('DPA') are likewise an EU requirement and operate closely with the FOIA (see below).

Under the FOIA, where a public authority ('PA') holds information that is requested and described in writing (including email), a PA has to inform the requester in writing of that fact. This is known as the duty to confirm or deny ('DTCD'). A private body may be designated as a PA by the Secretary of State. A PA may request further information to enable it to identify and locate the information. An address must be supplied by the requester. The DTCD will not apply where compliance would lead to the disclosure of exempt information. A PA must, as far as reasonably practicable (eg subject to cost), communicate the information to the requester by the latter's preferred means. PAs have to provide appropriate advice and assistance to applicants.

'Exemption' refers to the situation where a document is notionally covered by access provisions but a claim is made to exempt it from access on stated grounds. These might involve national security, security and intelligence, foreign affairs, personal privacy, and other sources of sensitivity. Under the FOIA, exemptions are either discretionary and based on a public interest test—is the public interest best served by secrecy or disclosure?—or absolute. Where the public interest test applies, if the scales are evenly balanced between secrecy and disclosure, the information must be disclosed. Under absolute exemptions (there are eight), there is no discretion to disclose and the Information Commissioner ('IC') cannot order disclosure. In some cases, exemption is absolute because another access regime, such as the DPA, governs access or because information is protected by the law of confidentiality. In the case of national security, ministerial certificates classifying information as exempt are appealable to the Information Tribunal ('IFT'). Some exemptions are class-based—ie the information belongs to a class of documents which require protection. Other exemptions are content-based—ie disclosure of the contents of the particular document would or would be likely to cause damage to a specified interest.

Technically, the FOIA gives a right of access to *information*; but public authorities should, the IC advises, grant access to a *document* where this is the easiest way of facilitating the request. A request can be made for a specific document. Information is excluded from the operation of the FOIA where it is held by a body not named as a PA in the Act, including the Queen and members of the Royal family, MI5, and MI6.

At present, over fifty nation states, as well as supranational organizations such as the **European Union**, possess some form of freedom of information legislation. The UK enacted its FOIA in 2000 although it was more than four years before it came into effect. The UK regime introduced 'publicity schemes' whereby public bodies covered by the Act are required to publish certain classes of information independently of any application for access. These schemes have to be approved by the IC.

The IC has responsibility for administering both the FOIA and DPA regimes. The relationship between the two regimes is complex; but basically information about a data subject sought by the subject is requested under the DPA regime. Information about another individual sought by a third party is requested under the FOIA, with certain of the DPA safeguards for processing (using) information applying. The IC acts as a sort of ombudsman for requesters, and the IC enjoys wide powers of investigation and review. The IC may issue Decision Notices, Enforcement Notices, and Information Notices. From the IC's decision there is a very wide right of appeal to the IFT and from there to the High Court (or its equivalents in Scotland and Northern Ireland) on a point of law. Scotland has its own FOIA, which is more liberal in certain respects than the UK version. The UK legislation applies in Northern Ireland and in Wales. A Code of Practice supplements the UK FOIA.

Fees may be charged for supply of information. As of writing, fees of up to £600 are waived for information held by central government and the UK Parliament, and of up to £450 for information held by other public bodies. Above these figures, the authority has a discretion to disclose, but it may request the additional cost involved. By the end of 2006, the Lord Chancellor, following an independent review, announced a plan to increase fees considerably to cover the time taken to search for documents and the true labour cost of senior management and Ministers. It was reported that the Home Secretary personally examined sensitive requests twice a week. The revised fees will cover examination of documents, consultation, and time taken in considering exemption. Costs will be aggregated in cases where requesters act in concert or as a campaign. There was also discussion of the possibility of limiting the number of institutional requests to four a year per institution because of the heavy use of the law by media outlets.

Under the UK scheme 'an accountable person' has a veto power to override the IC's decision that a PA should, *inter alia*, disclose information. This only applies in the case of discretionary disclosures and not in the case of information covered by an absolute exemption. The government has decided that such a veto would only be exercised by the Cabinet. To date, it has not been exercised. There was wide expectation that it would be exercised to prevent disclosure of the **Attorney-General**'s advice on the legality of the war in Iraq. In the event, the advice was disclosed before the general election in 2005 and the IC in 2006 issued an Enforcement Notice ordering disclosure of some of the information relating to the advice. Many disclosures are on routine matters of little interest except to the requester. Among the more important or sensational disclosures have been: the Attorney-General's advice just mentioned; information about payment of EU subsidies to landowners and members of the Royal family, the number of patients who die in operations carried out by individual surgeons, lobbying of Ministers, the results of restaurant hygiene inspections by local authorities, details of contracts of public authorities, and reasons for inquiries under the Companies Acts.

There have been other non-statutory developments affecting the operation of the Act. A clearing house was established in the Department for Constitutional Affairs (now Ministry of Justice) to receive and monitor more sensitive requests including those from the press and media and MPs. The role of the clearing house is to ensure consistency across central government in the way the access laws operate. The clearing house works closely with the Cabinet Office, which takes the lead in those cases intrinsic to the operation of collective **ministerial responsibility** and the **Cabinet,** and to the role of ministers; and those cases in which the **Prime Minister** takes a personal interest.   PATRICK BIRKINSHAW

P Birkinshaw, *Freedom of Information: the Law, the Practice and the Ideal* (Cambridge: Cambridge University Press, 3rd edn, 2001)

P Birkinshaw, *Government and Information: the Law Relating to Access, Disclosure and their Regulation* (London: Butterworths, 3rd edn, 2005).

freedom of movement The freedom to travel within and between countries has always been important to trade, and has progressively become more significant for ordinary people as economic and social developments have demanded greater mobility. Some international human rights instruments, such as Article 2 of the Fourth Protocol to the **European Convention on Human Rights**, protect liberty of movement and freedom to choose one's residence within a state and to leave the state. The **United Kingdom** has not ratified the Fourth Protocol or protected the right under the Human Rights Act 1998, but is bound in international law by the equivalent provisions of Article 12 of the **International Covenant on Civil and Political Rights**. In practice, interstate travellers require travel documents including, typically, passports and visas from states to enter or (sometimes) leave states.

Historically freedom to travel was limited. Even when feudal ties relaxed, travellers were, and sometimes still are, liable to be penalized as vagrants. Merchants have long enjoyed travel privileges for economic reasons, but rulers restricted movements of people and goods in and out of their countries to prevent damaging flows of people or commodities. Sovereign states now enjoy the same right under international law, subject to interstate agreements on freedom of establishment of businesses and movement of people and goods as in the European Union. Special restrictions on interstate travel are increasingly important politically as part of states' policies to control immigration and combat terrorism.

In the former USSR, and in South Africa under apartheid, restrictions on people's movement within the state were a powerful tool of government oppression and social control. Restrictions on the freedom within the UK are aimed more at controlling the behaviour of identified individuals, including anti-social behaviour orders ('**ASBOs**'), sexual offences prevention orders, **binding-over** orders, football banning orders, and **bail** conditions.

DAVID FELDMAN

freedom of religion and belief Religious discrimination has received much less attention than discrimination on most other grounds in **Great Britain**. (Northern Ireland differs from other parts of the **United Kingdom** in historically having religious discrimination as a serious problem.) This is largely because religion is not an important matter for the majority of the British population. Whilst the last census showed that 71 per cent of the population described themselves as being Christian, the proportion of the population regularly attending a place of religious worship has dropped over the years, and in England is now in single percentage points. For most people their religious beliefs, insofar as they have any, are a personal and private matter. Most people cannot, therefore, experience religious discrimination because they have no value or pattern of behaviour that they would identify as being religious and to which they strongly hold. However, alongside the majority of the population who take little interest in religion, there is a minority for whom religion is an important matter and may even be the defining feature of their lives. This minority is mainly, though not wholly, to be found in ethnic minority communities. Questions of religious discrimination thus become mixed up with questions of racial discrimination.

At the same time as levels of attendance at places of religious worship have dropped, the number of religions with membership of noteworthy size in the UK have grown. Islam is now the second largest religion in the UK after Christianity, and there are considerable numbers of Hindus and Sikhs. Moreover, these religions, new to the UK, tend to be concentrated in particular areas. Thus, for example,

Leicester is the first city in the United Kingdom in which Christians are in a minority. The issue of religious discrimination is therefore one that is more likely to arise in some parts of the country rather than others.

A number of judgments made by courts have asserted that the courts are neutral towards questions of religious belief. Freedom of religion and belief might therefore be thought to be protected under the law. In fact, the issues, of whether the law is in fact neutral towards religion and the degree to which religion and belief are protected, have always been deeply problematic. Indeed even the notion of what constitutes a religion for legal purposes has long been unclear. The most widely quoted definition of religion, taken from the law of charities, states that religion involves a belief in a god or gods; but then it immediately goes on to note that Buddhism, which does not necessarily involve such a belief, is also a religion. The status of a range of other belief systems, such as the Sea of Faith movement, universalist Quakers, and Pagans, which do not necessarily involve belief in a god or gods, is unclear.

It is plain that particular religious values permeate some parts of the law. Thus, for example, the prohibited degrees of relationship, which prevent marriage between certain close family members, find their origins in Judaeo-Christian beliefs. However, it is usually only Christian religious values that are reflected in the law. Polygamy, for example, is not normally recognized under British law. Some legal rules actively promote religion. Thus the Education Reform Act 1988, although widely ignored in practice, legally requires compulsory religious education to reflect the 'fact' that the religious traditions of Great Britain are Christian; and it requires schools to perform acts of worship of a 'broadly Christian character'. One of the heads of charity is the advancement of religion; and, because of this, religions can be the beneficiary of significant tax advantages. Equally some religious believers receive special treatment under the law because of their religion. Thus, for example, two Archbishops and twenty-four bishops of the Church of England are members of the House of Lords by virtue of their ecclesiastical office. Quakers have a special marriage ceremony that is recognized by law, whilst Sikhs are exempt from both crash-helmet legislation for motor cyclists and construction-site legislation about the wearing of hard hats. Many other examples could be given.

The special treatment accorded to religions can sometimes appear capricious or arbitrary. Rastafarians are not exempt from either crash-helmet or construction-site legislation. Jews received special treatment under legislation that prevented Sunday trading, but Muslims did not. Christians are more likely to find their values reflected in the law than non-Christians, and they are also more likely to receive special treatment from the law. Special treatment under the law is not, however, limited to religious believers. Upon occasion, although more rarely than in the case of religion, conscience also receives specific protection in legislation. Thus, for example, the Abortion Act 1967 gives people the right to refuse to participate in abortions on grounds of conscientious objection. Similarly, in wartime conscientious objection to military service has been recognized.

Even where the law makes no specific reference to religion, some believers may find that their faith causes the courts to make a decision it otherwise would not have. Thus, for example, the courts have sometimes refused parents custody of their children following divorce because they believed a parent's religion would mean that they were socially isolated. In such instances, the courts would distinguish between the mere fact of belief and the consequences attendant on belief and purport to be concerned only about the latter; but the distinction may seem a matter of sophistry to the parent. Courts, and sometimes legislatures, make a distinction between belief and the practice of that belief, holding that the former is to be respected but the latter can be restricted. However, such a distinction may not be accepted by believers, who would feel that a right to believe without a right to practice that belief is illusory.

From the above it is clear that the law does pay attention to questions of religion and conscience, sometimes promoting religion and sometimes seeking to protect the special position of those for whom either their religion or their personal conscience is of particular consequence. Piecemeal legislation, however, carries with it the risk that, as much as it prevents discrimination in particular instances, it may also exacerbate discrimination. Where one religion is protected others that are not protected feel themselves to be doubly discriminated against. Where a religion's needs receive attention in one part of the law but not in another there is again a perception of discrimination. Similarly where religion but not conscience receives specific legislative attention, there is a perception of discrimination. Thus there is an argument for the general protection of religious belief and conscience rather than the traditional case-by-case approach taken by British law.

In England and Wales, and in Scotland, religion and belief were not accorded general legal protection until the passage of the Human Rights Act 1998. Under this Act the right to freedom of thought, conscience, and religion, found in Article 9 of the **European Convention on Human Rights**, is written into UK law. The courts must therefore interpret legislation where possible in such a way as to be consistent with Article 9 and should not themselves do anything which is inconsistent with the Article. Moreover, following this Act, where a court's determination might affect a religion's right to freedom of thought the courts, before making their determination, must have regard to the importance of that right. Because of the relatively recent implementation of the Act it is not yet clear what impact these provisions will have. Another recent general provision is the Employment Equality (Religion or Belief) Regulations 2003, which prohibit both **direct dicrimination** and **indirect discrimination** on grounds of religion or belief.

The situation in Northern Ireland as regards religious discrimination is radically different from that in the rest of the UK. First, religion has had and continues to have a much more important role in public life there than has come to be the case in the rest of the UK. Secondly, religion has been divisive there to a degree that has not been generally true of the rest of the country. As a result, Northern Ireland saw the introduction of legislation intended to prevent religious discrimination at a much earlier date than in Great Britain. The Fair Employment Act, which was first introduced in 1976, made discrimination on grounds of religious belief or political opinion illegal. It also introduced procedures for monitoring employment patterns. This legislation was strengthened by its replacement, the Fair Employment (Northern Ireland) Act 1989, which, amongst other things, made indirect discrimination illegal.

TONY BRADNEY

R Ahdar and I Leigh, *Religious Freedom in the Liberal State* (Oxford: Oxford University Press, 2005)

P Edge, *Legal Responses to Religious Difference* (The Hague: Kluwer Law International, 2002)

See also: **race discrimination**

freedom of speech   *see* **freedom of expression**

freedom of the press   *see* **media, regulation and freedom of**

freeview TV   *see* **digital television and radio regulation**

French law   French law is one of the most distinctive and influential of the European legal systems. Directly or indirectly, it has influenced national laws in all continents of the world, as well as supranational legal systems.

Modern French law has a number of distinctive features. The most important is the distinction between public law (constitutional law and administrative law) and private law (civil law and commercial law) to which should also be added criminal law.

French public law has its origins mainly in **canon law** and in the law developed by the King's Council (*Conseil du Roi*), but some of the principles have their origins in **Roman law**. The main catalyst for the modern development of public law was the creation of the *Conseil d'Etat* in 1799. This body combined the functions of legal adviser to the government and an institution offering redress for wrongs committed by it. It acquired a more formal, independent status as a court in 1872, but it continues to be the main legal adviser to the government, through its administrative sections. The principles of government according to the law (*l'état de droit*) were developed during the liberal Third Republic (1870–1940) by the *Conseil d'Etat*, and these included the principles both of judicial review of administrative action and government liability. That Republic did not have a written constitution, and there was no code of administrative law or administrative procedure. It was left thus to the *Conseil d'Etat*, supported by academic writers and specific pieces of legislation, to develop both the principles and the procedures of administrative law. It was at its most active in this regard between 1879 (when it was purged of anti-republican elements) and World War I. The *Conseil d'Etat* also developed 'general principles of law', which provided a basic list of fundamental rights in the period 1930 to 1960. The idea of an independent judicial control of the administration was influential not only in French colonies, but also as a reference point for the development of administrative law by other European countries. The distinctive character of French administrative law lies not only in these principles developed by the *Conseil d'Etat*, but also in the separate character of the administrative judiciary. Administrative judges are recruited and trained separately from private law judges, and their careers remain distinct. The distinctiveness of the law and the judiciary is reflected in the strong separation of public lawyers from private lawyers in doctrinal writing and in the universities. Many of the most influential public law writers are judges.

Since the 1970s, French public law has developed a strong constitutional law tradition. Although commentary on constitutions has been longstanding, the impact of binding constitutional rules and principles has depended on the creation of an independent

Conseil Constitutionnel under the Constitution of the Fifth Republic of 1958. It was not conceived as a court and it was not integrated into the judicial hierarchy. The full development of judicial review had to await a decision of 1971 by the *Conseil Constitutionnel* in which it struck down legislation for breach of fundamental rights (here the right of association) and a 1974 constitutional amendment, which gave opposition parliamentarians the power to refer legislation to that *Conseil*. The *Conseil Constitutionnel* has developed a substantial body of constitutional law that is applied by the ordinary courts and is the subject of lively doctrinal commentary.

French private law has its origins in both Roman law (as revived in the medieval period) and in the customary laws of the local *parlements*. It was only brought together into a single national system by the **Code Napoleon** in 1804. Unlike public law, private law has at its centre codes (the Civil Code and the Commercial Code of 1807), and doctrinal writing produced by university academics is highly influential in their interpretation. Family law (including the law on succession and matrimonial property) have changed radically since 1804, and most of these provisions in the Civil Code have been amended. Among the influential modern developments has been the PACS (*pacte civil de solidarité*), a civil union for heterosexual and homosexual couples alike that provides an alternative to marriage. But most of the provisions on property law and the law of obligations remain unamended. Among the influential areas of the law of obligations has been the law of civil wrongs (delict). In the face of accidents caused first by machines and then by cars and products, French doctrinal writers and courts developed principles of no-fault liability for the acts of things which a person has under his control. Although the text of Article 1384, paragraph 1, was originally only an introduction, it became a principle in its own right and spawned a major area of liability. (One writer called the law in this area 'a skyscraper built on a pinhead', so substantial is the case law built around a mere dozen words of the Code.) Contract law also managed to develop strict liability in fields such as passenger transport and liability for products through a distinction between where a contracting party undertakes an 'obligation to achieve a result' and an 'obligation to do one's best'. The law in these areas has often been replaced by legislation, but the general provisions of the Code have proved flexible and adaptable to changed social circumstances through a combination of innovation by doctrinal writers and expansive interpretation by the courts.

French criminal procedure is distinguished by its judge-led investigative method. Following arrest by the police, the criminal process in serious cases is directed by a judge (either the prosecutor or, in the most serious cases, the *juge d'instruction*). The judge ensures that the evidence is gathered and assessed before a decision is made to send an accused to trial. This pre-trial evidence gathering may include interviewing the accused and witnesses and even organizing a face-to-face confrontation between those giving conflicting testimony. As a result of this preparation, those cases selected for trial are highly likely to lead to a conviction.

Civil and criminal judges are mainly recruited from those graduating from law school. They are trained and serve within the civil and criminal courts (unless on secondment to the Ministry of Justice). The highest court in this hierarchy is the *Cour de Cassation* in Paris.   JOHN BELL

See also: **civil law systems; inquisitorial system**

friendly relations, declaration   *see* **customary international law**

fuel duties   *see* **excise duties**

Fuller, Lon L   Lon Luvois Fuller (1902–1978) was an important figure in American contracts law and **alternative dispute resolution**, but he is probably best known for his 'procedural natural law theory', made famous in a 1958 debate with HLA **Hart** in the *Harvard Law Review*, and later elaborated in Fuller's book, *The Morality of Law* (1964).

Fuller characterized law as 'the enterprise of subjecting human conduct to the governance of rules'. Law is a way of governing people, to be contrasted with other forms of governance, for example, managerial direction. Law is a particular means to an end, a particular kind of tool.

In contrast to legal positivist analyses of law based on power, orders, and obedience, Fuller offered an analysis based on the 'internal morality' of law. The internal morality of law consists of a series of requirements which, Fuller asserted, a system of rules must meet—or at least substantially meet—if that system is to be called 'law'. The requirements are: (1) laws should be general; (2) they should be promulgated so that citizens might know the standards to which they are being held; (3) retroactive rule-making and application should be minimized; (4) laws should be understandable; (5) laws should not be contradictory; (6) laws should not require conduct beyond the abilities of those affected; (7) they should remain relatively constant through time; and (8) there should be a congruence between the laws as announced and as applied.

Critics have argued that Fuller's 'principles of legality' are merely amoral solutions to problems of efficacy, such that one could just as easily speak of 'the internal morality of poisoning'. However, such criticisms arguably misunderstand the extent to which our perceptions of **justice** incorporate procedural elements. BRIAN BIX

LL Fuller, *The Morality of Law* (New Haven: Yale University Press, 1964, rev edn 1969)

Robert Summers, *Lon L Fuller* (Stanford: Stanford University Press, 1984)

G

gambling The Gambling Act 2005, which came into force on 1 September 2007, provides the legislative and regulatory framework for gambling in **Great Britain**. After several years of consultation and review, the Act provides a significant legislative update to the previous legislative regime (such as the Betting Gaming & Lotteries Act 1963 and the Gaming Act 1968) to take account of advances in technology (such as the advent of online gambling) and the liberalization in society's attitude towards gambling.

For most forms of gambling to be lawful in Great Britain, they must be conducted in accordance with the provisions of the Act and its associated regulations, licence conditions, and codes of practice. At the heart of the new gambling regulatory regime are the three statutory licensing objectives set out in section 1 of the Act. These are: (a) preventing gambling from being a source of crime or disorder, being associated with crime or disorder or being used to support crime; (b) ensuring that gambling is conducted in a fair and open way; and (c) protecting children and other vulnerable persons from being harmed or exploited by gambling.

The Act defines 'gambling' as 'gaming', 'betting' or 'participating in a lottery'. 'Gaming' is playing a game of chance for a prize. 'Betting' is making or accepting a bet on the outcome of a race, competition, or other event or process; on the likelihood of anything occurring or not occurring; or on whether or not something is true. A 'lottery' is an arrangement where persons are required to pay in order to participate in the arrangement; in the course of the arrangement one or more prizes are allocated to one or more members of a class; and the prizes are allocated by a process which relies wholly on chance (or where there are a series of processes, the first of those processes relies wholly on chance).

Gambling, therefore, includes fixed odds betting, pool betting, certain lotteries, bingo, gaming machines, and gaming (such as casino games including poker, roulette, and blackjack). It does not include prize competitions based on skill or knowledge, or free prize draws. The National Lottery is subject to the National Lottery Act 1993 and regulated by the National Lottery Commission. Spread betting (a higher-risk form of betting, common in the financial industry), is subject to the **Financial Services and Markets Act 2000** and is regulated by the **Financial Services Authority**.

The 2005 Act introduced a new regulatory body for gambling in Great Britain—the Gambling Commission—which replaces the old Gaming Board for Great Britain. The Gambling Commission is the Government's principal independent advisory body for issues relating to gambling. It is also responsible for advising local licensing authorities on how they exercise their functions under the Act.

There are two main offences in relation to gambling: the provision of facilities for gambling, or using premises for gambling, without the appropriate authorization. There are also a number of offences involving the participation of children and young people in gambling.

Gambling operators based in Great Britain will often require one or more of a range of statutory licences, permits, and registrations which can be obtained from the Gambling Commission or the local licensing authority depending on what type of gambling is involved and by what manner it is conducted. The Gambling Commission has issued Licence Conditions, which attach to each type of licence, as well as Codes of Practice with which all licensed operators must comply.

There are restrictions on **advertising** of gambling in Great Britain. The Act contains a wide definition of advertising, and creates two key offences—advertising of 'unlawful' gambling, and advertising of 'foreign' gambling (which means gambling which is not subject to the laws of a state within the European Economic Area, Gibraltar, or any other jurisdiction on the Government's 'White List' (in 2007 only Alderney and the Isle of Man were included on that list)). The content of advertising is subject to the advertising industry's self-regulatory Codes of Practice (issued by the Committee of Advertising

Practice and enforced by the Advertising Standards Agency). As with gambling generally, the overriding objective of the regulation of gambling advertising is the protection of children, young people and vulnerable people.   WARREN PHELOPS

gamete donation Most people undergoing fertility treatment in the UK use their own gametes (sperm and eggs), but in some circumstances, treatment with donated gametes will be necessary. All egg donation in the UK takes place in licensed clinics, which are subject to the Human Fertilization and Embryology Act, and regulated by the **Human Fertilization and Embryology Authority** ('HFEA'). Unlike egg donation, informal sperm donation is comparatively straightforward. A woman might obtain sperm from a friend or acquaintance, or via the internet, and she can then inseminate herself at home with no need for medical intervention. As a result, these informal arrangements are not subject to any regulatory control. There is, for example, no compulsory **HIV** screening, as there is for donors in licensed clinics, and the HFEA's rules relating to the donor's consent and the need to consider the welfare of the **child** do not apply. In addition, with no reporting requirements, we have little information about the incidence of informal gamete donation. Unlike sperm donors who donate in licensed clinics, the informal sperm donor will, if identified, be the child's legal father, and may have to pay **child support** throughout the child's minority.

Until April 2005, unless a relative or friend was donating their sperm or eggs to a named patient, most gamete donation in licensed clinics was anonymous. Children could be given access to non-identifying information such as the donor's occupation or **religion**, and they could find out, once they reached the age of eighteen, whether had been conceived as a result of gamete donation, and if they are genetically related to a prospective spouse. Regulations which came into force in April 2005 removed anonymity for donations after that date. Children born following non-anonymous donation will have access to identifying information about the donor once they reach the age of eighteen.

One potential problem with this shift towards identifiable donors is that a child will obviously only be able to apply to the HFEA for identifying information if she knows, or suspects, that she was conceived using donated gametes. Unless her parents have given her some reason to believe that she was not conceived naturally, the child will have no reason to make an application to receive identifying information about her genetic origins. This is especially important given that the evidence indicates that the majority of parents do *not* tell their donor-conceived offspring that they were conceived using donated gametes. The removal of anonymity will only make a difference to children's access to information about their origins if it *also* promotes a new culture of openness about the use of donated gametes.

Unlike some other countries, such as the US, where egg donors, in particular, can be paid considerable sums for 'donating' their eggs, gamete donors in the UK are not paid, although they can compensated for any financial losses associated with donation, such as travel expenses and loss of earnings. Egg-sharing schemes are lawful in the UK. These involve women who need access to IVF themselves agreeing to donate half of the eggs retrieved during one cycle in return for reduced price, or even free treatment. This might be said to represent substantial, albeit indirect, payment for gametes.

Each gamete donor can create no more than ten families, which in practice may mean somewhere between ten and thirty children. This applies principally to sperm donors, since it is very unlikely that an egg donor would donate sufficient eggs to come anywhere near the upper limit set for gamete donors. Donors are entitled to set a lower limit. In part, it may be the prospect of being contacted eighteen years later by a large number of children which has led to the reported shortages of sperm in the UK since the removal of anonymity.

                                        EMILY JACKSON

See also: **assisted conception**

gangmasters The term 'gangmaster' refers to **persons** who organize the employment of **casual workers**. Gangmasters are a long-established phenomenon in the United Kingdom, particularly in agriculture. From the early 1990s, gangmaster activity became more common in other sectors, and increasingly involved foreign nationals both as gangmasters and workers. These changes led to growing calls for the regulation of gangmasters from 1997 onwards to ensure greater compliance by gangmasters and 'user undertakings' with labour, tax, and related laws, while reducing irregular migration. Public and political concerns in relation to gangmaster activity were confirmed in the tragedy of 5 February 2004, when twenty-three Chinese irregular migrants are thought to have drowned while cocklepicking on Morecambe Bay.

The February 2004 tragedy led to the enactment of the Gangmaster (Licensing) Act 2004. The Act provides a licensing system for persons who act as gangmasters in agriculture, the gathering of shellfish, as well as in related food processing activities. The Act covers three categories of organization in all cases: employment agencies (which introduce workers and user undertakings), employment businesses (which employ workers and loan them to user undertakings), and sub-contractors (where an employer carries out works at a user undertaking's work place). The Act also covers direct employers who enter a lease or similar arrangement in agriculture, or who use workers to gather shellfish.

Under the Act, it is a criminal offence for a person who acts as a gangmaster not to possess a licence. It is also a criminal offence to be supplied with workers or services by an unlicensed gangmaster, unless the purchaser of the services has taken 'all reasonable steps' to ensure the gangmaster has a valid licence. The Gangmasters Licensing Authority defines the conditions for licences, issues licences, and enforces compliance with licences. Within the licensing system, rules previously applicable to employment agencies and businesses are applied to all gangmasters. These rules include a prohibition on gangmasters charging workers; a requirement that gangmasters check a worker's **identity**, qualifications, and authorization to work; a requirement that the terms of the relationship between gangmaster and worker be agreed in advance and in writing; and, a prohibition on the imposition of detriment on a worker who takes work with another employer.

The wider significance of the gangmaster licensing system lies in its potential to uphold labour standards. That is the result of the requirement upon the Authority to 'have regard to' two principles: 'avoidance of any exploitation of workers as regards their recruitment, use or supply' and 'compliance with any obligations imposed by or under any enactment...'. This aspect of the gangmaster licensing system means a reversal of official reluctance to develop labour inspection systems in the UK. It is also a new departure for the authorities to seek to discourage irregular migration through worker protection, rather than through the punishment of illegal behaviour.   BERNARD RYAN

B Ryan, 'The Evolving Legal Framework on Unauthorized Work by Migrants in Britain' (2005) *Comparative Labor Law and Policy Journal* 27–58

Garrow, William   William Garrow (1760–1840), barrister, judge, and member of Parliament, held the post of **Solicitor-General** (1812–1813) and **Attorney-General** (1813–1817) and was appointed a puisne baron of the Exchequer in 1817. Neither his political career nor his tenure as a judge were in the least distinguished, however, and he is now remembered for

his practice at the Old Bailey. Although defendants would not win the legal right to a full professional defence until 1836, a criminal bar emerged in London in the 1780s. Between 1783, the year of his call to the bar, and 1793, when he was made a King's counsel and gave up regular attendance at the Old Bailey, Garrow was its undisputed leader.

Like many criminal barristers, Garrow was no lawyer; and contemporaries remembered him as profoundly ignorant: 'There have probably been few more ignorant men in the profession than this celebrated leader. To law, or anything like law, he made no pretence ... his ignorance of all beside, of all that constitutes science, or learning, or indeed general information, nay even ordinary information, was perfect' ('Memoir of Mr. Baron Garrow,' *Law Review* 1 (1844–1845): 318–28 at 319). But as Henry Brougham acknowledged, Garrow was 'a great, a very great advocate' (ibid, 320). He had both a beautiful voice and an extraordinary talent for cross-examination, the ability to elicit from a witness a clear story that skirted around any potentially damaging information. While he was not the first barrister to undertake criminal practice, in the eighteenth century Garrow was easily the most famous.   ALLYSON MAY

gay   *see* **homosexuality**

gay and lesbian legal research   *see* **queer theory**

gender   The term gender is closely related to that of **sex**. A traditional understanding of the sex–gender distinction is that sex refers to innate biological and physiological differences between men and women. In contrast, gender refers to the socially constructed roles, behaviour, attributes, and attitudes that societies culturally associate with one sex or the other. Male and female are understood as categories of sex, whilst masculinity and femininity are gender categories. Gender is relevant across many areas of law. The question has arisen, for example, as to what legally determines whether someone is male or female. In most cases this may appear obvious. The matter is complicated, however, in the case of transgender or intersex individuals. The legal implications of assigning a legal **identity** to sex at birth have been far reaching, encompassing questions of criminal, family, and employment law amongst others. In the UK, the Gender Recognition Act 2004 gives legal **recognition** to **transsexual** people and allows them to acquire, subject to certain criteria, a new birth certificate, and to be able to marry, as well as affording full recognition in law for other purposes. In some jurisdictions certain sexual offences can only be committed by men.

Gender has been a central concern for feminist legal scholars concerned with how law regulates, constructs, and embodies beliefs about sex difference. Studies concerned with the 'hidden gender' of law (Graycar and Morgan (2002)) have explored diverse aspects of institutions and practices of law. In accounts of the work of solicitors, barristers, and **judges**, the administration of criminal and civil **justice,** and in legal education, the presence of a distinctive gendered (masculine) culture has been seen as problematic for **women**. It has been argued that women in law have been historically judged against a male norm which corresponds to qualities culturally associated with men.

In the UK, as elsewhere, there has been a move towards equalizing the position of men and women in law. The incorporation of the **European Convention on Human Rights** through the **Human Rights Act 1998** has further entrenched ideas of gender **equality** in law. Law has been used to encourage and/or reinforce gendered behaviour in a number of ways. In family and employment law, for example, measures have been introduced to foster a 'work-life balance' by encouraging both sexes to contribute to **child** care, and attempts have been made to facilitate co-parenting following **divorce**. Attempts to tackle men's **violence** in the field of criminal justice, meanwhile, has been explicitly informed by research on gender. The politics of gender has become a key element in many law reform debates and diverse groups have sought to address what they see as unfairness in law between the sexes. Others, meanwhile, have questioned whether the distinction between sex and gender is a useful analytic tool in understanding law, suggesting that it is far from clear to what extent gender is a social as opposed to biological construct.

RICHARD COLLIER

R Graycar and J Morgan, *The Hidden Gender of Law* (Annandale: Federation Press, 2nd edn, 2002)

gender and crime Men commit more crimes, especially serious and violent crimes, than **women;** a difference largely accounted for by **gender** socialization rather than biological **sex** differences. Men commit approximately four-fifths of all offences, a higher proportion of violent crimes and almost all sexual crimes reported (the only offences committed more by women are prostitution and television license evasion). Hence, of the current 80,000 prisoners in England and Wales, less than six per cent are women, most of whom are convicted of drug or theft offences (the proportion of women

in Scottish prisons is five per cent and in Northern Ireland, three per cent). Self-report studies show that the gap between male and female offending is narrower than indicated by official statistics, suggesting that the data may partially reflect differential policing practices.

Marginal increases in women's crime rates in the UK over the past decade have encouraged 'gender-convergence' theses, suggesting girls in particular are becoming more violent and copying the criminal behaviour of delinquent boys. However, academic scrutiny of the data confirms only limited increases in women's crime rates, primarily for property offences.

National **victim** surveys in Britain, Scotland, and Northern Ireland show that men are more likely to be victims of violent crime, especially **stranger violence**, than women, with young men most at risk. Men constitute the majority of victims, as well as perpetrators, for murder. Yet the data show that men are much less afraid of crime and disinclined to modify their behaviour to prevent it. Women are more likely to be victims of severe **domestic violence** resulting in injuries. Nearly half of female **homicide** victims are killed by a partner, compared to only a few men. However, family conflict studies indicate gender symmetry for less serious domestic abuse, resulting from the more typical conflict couples experience.

Studies of crime focused largely on males until the 'second wave' of feminism when seminal works by feminist academics and activists rendered female criminals visible (eg Carol Smart, *Women Crime and Criminology* (1977)) and alerted practitioners and policymakers to the widespread abuse of women by men (eg Erin Pizzey, *Scream Quietly or the Neighbours Will Hear* (1973)). Recently, the influence of post-modern and socialist feminism has encouraged intersectional approaches, exploring how structural inequalities such as racism, class privilege, and heterosexism intersect with gender oppression and discrimination, and how women's experiences of crime and criminal justice are mediated through these sites of structural inequity.

With the development of feminist scholarship has come a growing body of theoretical literature on 'masculinities' and empirical studies of men's experiences as perpetrators and victims, including studies of male victims of **rape** and domestic violence. Much of this work is similarly stratified by age, **race**, social class, and sexuality. Experiences of men in the criminal process are understood in terms of societal constructions of masculinity and the unequal power relations between different groups of men and boys. It is now considered evidence of careless research and theory-building to refer to female or male victims or offenders as if these were homogenous groups.   CAROLYN HOYLE

S Walklate, *Gender, Crime and Criminal Justice* (Cullompton: Willan, 2nd edn, 2004)

F Heidensohn, *Gender and Justice: New Concepts and Approaches* (Cullompton: Willan, 2006)

gender and development   The phrase 'gender and development' is associated with the academic discipline of development studies and the related pursuit of public policy. The broad objective of development is to improve the chances of many millions of people who are unable to access the resources needed to provide themselves with a decent life. Gender is singled out not only to focus on the differential effect of development policies on **women** and men but also to highlight the ways in which gender relations underpin development.

The concept of development emerged as an area of theory and practice in the mid-twentieth century when many former colonies became independent states in the immediate aftermath of World War II and the onset of the Cold War. The deep ideological divide between the socialist and Western capitalist worlds had a profound effect on the way in which development policy was promulgated.

Western countries established two key development institutions at the Bretton Woods Conference in 1944: the World Bank and the International Monetary Fund ('IMF'). These bodies were set up to promote fiscal security and to foster the growth of world trade and thereby counter the claims of socialism and the activities of the Soviet bloc. The two blocs fought for influence in countries newly emerging from **colonialism**. Despite very different ideologies and methods, both championed economic growth and development through industrialization and urbanization.

Three worlds emerged: a first world of Western market economies, a second world constituted by the Soviet socialist bloc, and a third world of non-aligned countries which were trying to develop their own models of development. The last became identified by their status as post-colonial states and occupation of a particular position within the world economic system: low Gross National Products per head.

The first world provided aid in poor countries for capital intensive investments and to mechanize agriculture in order to expand markets and to develop export-oriented economies. It was assumed that the benefits of growth would 'trickle-down' to citizens.

Women were not singled out except in relation to population control policies. However, as third world states became increasingly identified by the Bretton Woods institutions as underdeveloped or undeveloped, development agencies began to target welfare-focused policies on 'poor and hapless' women.

By the 1970s, feminism started to have an impact through the Women in Development ('WID') movement which argued that the prevailing **equality** and efficiency model was based on Western gender stereotypes which misunderstood or ignored the gender relations and status issues which underpinned third world agricultural production. Women were essential to successful development policies and required access to the processes of modernization such as education, training, and loans. WID was, and remains, associated with liberal market approaches which characterize much international development policy.

The trickle-down theory was challenged by the International Labour Organization which saw the objective of development as the fulfilment of basic **human** needs, not growth. Amartya Sen in the 1980s argued that poverty was an indication of the inability of people to meet their basic needs and the aim of development was to ensure that individuals had the opportunities to fulfil their capabilities. By shifting the focus to all members of society not just those in the productive economy, the interests of individual women, as distinct from households, emerged.

Another trenchant critique of liberal market development emerged from ecofeminism which argued strongly for **sustainable development** based upon women's particular, and close, relationship with nature.

Socialist approaches championed the alternative models of state-led development in China and Cuba while Marxist theorists argued that the third world became undeveloped as a result of incorporation in the international capitalist system, leading to dependent development and exploitation. Marxist feminists developed their own critique which focused on the unvalued but essential socially reproductive activities of women characterized as 'housework'.

With the collapse of the Soviet bloc, neo-liberal market development policies championed by the IMF and World Bank burgeoned. Feminists shifted the focus from women to gender relationships within the home, in waged work, or in access to and control over resources and benefits. A gender and development analysis ('GAD') also considers gender as socially constructed between men and women and explores the relationship between gender and power relationships in specific contexts. It recognizes that other relationships, based on class, **ethnicity**, caste, or sexual orientation, interact with gender divisions to create specific forms of gendered subordination. In contrast to WID, GAD seeks to redefine development in order to take account of the often ignored but unequal gender divisions which underpin both analysis and practice.

The GAD approach figures less than WID in development planning and in the work of development agencies, although recently much development practice has been couched in terms of empowering disadvantaged women (and men) to participate fully in decision-making, whether in political, social, or economic institutions. **Empowerment** is linked increasingly to a rights approach to development which harnesses the language of **human rights** to the struggle for development.

GAD has tended to focus less on the gendered relations of production in the global market place. The contemporary challenge is to understand the complex effects of the processes of globalization on gender relations worldwide, whether through mass migration, insecurity, and **violence**, or rapidly changing relationships between work and family life, which are producing profound inequalities and injustices. To tackle these, GAD must tackle the way in which globalization is governed at local, state, and transnational levels.   ANN STEWART

gender issues in legal education   Gender issues in legal education are discussed here in relation to three distinct but related areas: the law school curriculum, **legal academics** and, finally, law students. It is generally accepted that **gender**, together with **race**, sexuality, class, and other cross-cutting **identity** influences, plays a significant part in the lived experience of legal academics and students.

The idea that gender might be an appropriate (or even necessary) lens through which to study and understand law began to appear in some law school curricula in the 1970s. Focusing on the perspectives and experiences of **women**, early 'women and law' courses and texts largely concentrated on 'woman-centred' issues, for example, **sex** discrimination in the workplace, **pornography**, and **rape**. A more developed notion now recognizes that these should be conceptualized as gender issues and, as such, part of a larger project which questions the apparent objectivity and rationality of law and legal reasoning across all aspects of law, legal institutions, and processes. This understanding of gender in law teaching also works to trouble the possible marginalization of gender issues as separate (and usually optional) courses by encouraging the incorporation and/or

recognition of gender perspectives and issues into mainstream legal education.

Like their counterparts in the professions and the university as a whole, female legal academics continue to be largely under-represented at senior levels of the academic hierarchy and fare little better in relation to other equal treatment issues, for example research and teaching evaluation, pay, and the allocation of administrative responsibilities. In response, some point to a 'credibility gap' which, it is argued, works to ensure that personal achievements or academic practices which depart from the white-male-straight-upper/middle class norm go largely unacknowledged and/or unrewarded. Given the evidence suggesting that colleague and student expectations of male and female legal academics differ, doing things 'differently' (whatever that might mean), may even be detrimental.

Finally, the tacit assumption that law, masculinity, and authority are somehow synonymous—or at the very least intimately entwined—and the subsequent marginalization of female academics (as well as members of other '**minority**' groups) and their scholarship has an inevitable impact on the undergraduate and postgraduate student's experience of legal education. Despite increasing numbers and **representation** of women within the student body, the process of learning to 'think like a lawyer' can be an alienating and dissatisfying encounter for students unable or unwilling to identity with the hegemonic norm. In the groves of the legal academy 'feminine' traits are simultaneously designated and devalued and, as a result, the would-be lawyer to a large extent emerges from the taken-for-granted of the law school experience and culture speaking a new language—male—fluently.   ERIKA RACKLEY

C McGlynn, *The Woman Lawyer: Making the Difference* (London: Butterworths, 1998)
R Graycar and J Morgan, *The Hidden Gender of Law* (Sydney: The Federation Press, 2nd edn, 2002)

gender mainstreaming   *see* **mainstreaming**

genealogical approaches to law   Genealogy has an ambitious agenda: to undermine and replace conventional forms of knowledge. It is an 'anti-science' and a 'counter-history'. It aims to reveal that the political or philosophical rationality of the age, however benevolent or neutral it may appear, is actually always an expression of domination. And yet every dominating structure—of ideas, of practices—is also fundamentally unstable, shot through with fault lines, itself ever at risk of being usurped by different species of domination. For example,

Thomas Jefferson was able simultaneously to believe 'that all men are created equal' and to keep slaves, because for Jefferson 'all men' meant white men. The US Constitution may have been characterized by principles of liberty, but it also promoted racial (and gendered) domination. Some time later, however, the fault-lines in Jefferson's position were exposed, and the ideas of constitutionally guaranteed equality that he espoused were deployed precisely to challenge the domination of white men.

A genealogist would note from this example that ideas like 'equality' and 'justice' do not speak a universal truth, but rather tend to be coopted by contemporary structures of domination for very specific, non-universal purposes. For this reason, genealogy eschews the use of such big ideas, claiming, rather, to be avowedly empirical: descriptive not prescriptive. It focuses on the details of everyday interactions, and on how they are structured by dominating sets of ideas and practices. A major target for genealogy has been 'history'. History charts continuities, lines of development, through time: this renders historical discourse teleological, having a tendency to legitimize the present arrangements of power by 'normalizing' or 'naturalizing' their operation. For the genealogist the problem with this is that highlighting one line of development through time reduces other histories to the level of background interference. Historical truth and historical distortion, therefore, amount to the same thing. Genealogy seeks to correct this, by bringing those other histories into greater focus. The picture presented is a good deal messier, a mass of contradictions, accidents, and reversals, which in the randomness of their interaction, in their inability to be reduced to clear 'lines' of development, bring both the legitimacy and the stability of present forms of domination radically into question.

For example, a historian might chart the lineage of the **Monarch**. In this there will be some decisive shifts (as when one 'house' replaces another), but in general an unbroken line will be demonstrated by reference to births, marriages, and deaths, which reveal the authenticity of the lineage, and hence the claim to rule, of the current incumbent. A genealogist might chart a different history, or rather set of historical trajectories or stories, of births, marriages, and deaths unrecorded or suppressed in the authorized version, of bastards and bigamists, of manipulations, discontinuities, and breaks rather than continuities, which radically question rather than confirm the authenticity of the lineage. Moreover, such a 'counter-history' undermines the very concept of 'lineage', to reveal a fragile, cobbled together assemblage of claims and denials. Now, the superiority of

the monarch is shown to have only ever been product of the play of dominations, won and lost through violence, accident as much as design; and stories such as the 'Divine Right' to rule were only ever a ruse. There was nothing special about the monarch after all: it was all a case of the Emperor's New Clothes.

The key point here is that this critique of our hypothetical ruler speaks a general truth about all rules: 'Humanity does not gradually progress from combat to combat until it arrives at universal reciprocity, where the rule of law finally replaces warfare; humanity installs each of its violences in a system of rules and thus proceeds from domination to domination' (M Foucault, 'Nietzsche, Genealogy, History' in P Rabinow (ed), *The Foucault Reader* (London: Penguin, 1984), 85). If politics is war carried on by another name, then so too is law. As such, a genealogical approach to law involves exploring the 'violences' which are supported by the rule of law. These may be physical acts of legitimate violence, or they may be metaphorical: violence at the level of ideas, practices, norms, etc, which constitute and limit the field of possible ways of being human. Consider, for example, the role of law in slavery and apartheid, or the criminalization of homosexuality: it is the humanity of those affected which is at stake.

Genealogy offers new foci for investigation, most significantly the body. The body is the site on which dominations, manifesting less as physical violence and more in the form of ideas, discourses, practices, rituals—collectively 'the disciplines' or 'disciplinary power'—are played out. Domination, in other words, works, fundamentally at the level of individual bodies, by reference to a list of dos and don'ts drawn up by reference to particular historical norms. The body, accordingly, has a history and a politics. Although the 'disciplines' most frequently cited are non-legal: medicine, social work, penology, and psychiatry, this insight has important consequences for lawyers, and there has been much research in recent years which takes 'the legal construction of the body' as its topic.

The reference to power and discipline, however, raises particular issues regarding the very possibility of a genealogical approach to law. This is because genealogy is conceptualized—at least in the influential writings of Michel Foucault—as being timely because it attends to the operations of disciplinary power, seen as the characteristic form of power in the modern era. Law is what discipline (sometimes called 'counter-law') has replaced. Power can no longer be characterized in terms of the prohibitions and top-down edicts of law. Instead, disciplinary power—which does not have an ultimate source or seat of authority, but operates out of many sites—works not by prohibiting but by inculcating a certain, historically specific, set of norms as just that, normal. On this reading, law belongs to a bygone age. It was the main mechanism of power when power was in fact unitary and top-down in its operation, such as in a feudal society or an absolute monarchy. These days, however, law is to be viewed in much the same way as one might view a medieval castle.

There is something in this. For instance, in UK constitutional law the monarch has the power to veto any law passed by Parliament, but the constitutional reality is very different: the monarch has negligible political power. So, law can mislead or act as a distraction when the real power is operating elsewhere. But it is also reasonable to argue that law can itself be seen as a modern 'discipline'. Genealogy can exaggerate the redundancy of law, and this is probably because its model of law, as a series of negative prohibitions, is deficient. As already suggested, law can and does operate as a constructive force, as a body of authorized truths and essences, elaborating and enforcing norms (rather than rules) of behaviour.

Genealogy is not immune to criticism. Its anti-essentialism sits uncomfortably alongside its insistence on the endless play of dominations, which it posits as a sort of essential feature of all human interaction. Presumably—or why intervene at all?—there is an optimum method of interaction between competing dominations, but genealogy has little to say on this, or how to judge the merits of competing modes of domination. For this, we must look to conventional political or ethical ideas. But genealogy also has much to offer in understanding law that is novel and important, especially in terms of how law works and the sites of its operation.

RALPH SANDLAND

See also: **body, law and the**

General Agreement on Tariffs and Trade (GATT)   *see* World Trade Organization

General Agreement on Trade in Services (GATS)   *see* World Trade Organization

genetic databases   Genetic **databases** involve the long-term storage of samples of human material—typically blood and also personal information including medical history and lifestyle information—taken from a population or sub-group within a population. Such databases may be valuable in determining the relationship between genes, disease, and the environment. In addition they can identify groups of individuals who may be susceptible to certain diseases. They can also assist in determining the reasons for different reactions by different groups of people to pharmaceutical drugs. The legal regulation of such databases is complex because it is drawn from a diverse range of statutory and **common law** principles raising a range of legal and ethical issues. For example, use of samples of human material is regulated under the **Human Tissue Act 2004** but also by the common law as it concerns ownership of human material. Use of personal information stored in databases is regulated under the Data Protection Act 1984, the common law concerning breach of confidence and, in addition, is increasingly impacted by developments under Article 8 of the **European Convention of Human Rights**. While such databases have considerable potential for scientific advancement they have not been free from controversy. Some concerns have been expressed as to the basis on which the information and material is obtained and used over what may be some ten to twenty years. Uncertainties which remain relate to, for example, how much information should be given to participants regarding the purposes for which it is proposed to use the information. Is a general 'one-off' consent sufficient or is it necessary for researchers to obtain specific consent for each research project they intend to conduct using the database? Who should be able to access information obtained in the databases and should individuals be able to profit commercially from their use? One response to the general concern to ensure good governance for such databases has been the establishment of related regulators/advisory bodies. So for example, one major UK population genetic database, UK Biobank, which intends to collect samples and information from some 500,000 people over a twenty-year period, has established an Ethics and Governance Council to provide advisory guidance to UK Biobank.

JEAN MCHALE

See also: **consent to treatment; data protection**

genetic resources, access to   The possibility of obtaining intellectual property rights in relation to biological materials has inevitably conferred economic value upon nations' genetic resources. A plethora of incidents of 'biopiracy' or the unauthorized patenting of these resources has led to calls for the establishment of an international legal regime governing the access to genetic resources. The first step in this direction occurred at the Rio Earth Summit in June 1992 at which was promulgated the Convention on Biological Diversity ('CBD'). The CBD represented an attempt to establish a programme for the preservation of the world's biological resources.

Article 1 declared the objectives of the Convention to be 'the conservation of biological diversity, the sustainable use of its components and the fair and equitable sharing of the benefits arising out of the utilization of genetic resources'. The Convention noted in Article 3 the sovereign right of nations 'to exploit their own resources pursuant to their own environmental policies', but Article 15 requires contracting parties to 'endeavour to create conditions to facilitate access to genetic resources for environmentally sound purposes' by other contracting parties on mutually agreed terms and conditions on the basis of 'prior informed consent'. A detailed code of access to biotechnology is prescribed in Article 16. Access and transfer is stated to be 'provided on terms which recognize and are consistent with the adequate and effective protection of intellectual property rights'. Article 19.2 provides for the grant of access on a fair and equitable basis and on mutually agreed terms, to contracting parties, 'particularly developing countries, to the results and benefits arising from biotechnologies based upon genetic resources provided by those contracting parties'.

A problem with the CBD is that it has not been ratified or implemented by the USA, which is a leading bio-prospecting country. To deal with this political problem, attempts have been made to include the guarantees of permitted access and equitable benefit sharing ('ABS') within international agreements which the USA has implemented, such as the **World Trade Organization Agreement on Trade Related Intellectual Property Rights ('TRIPs')**, or to promulgate new international instruments which contain an access and benefit sharing regime. The **World Intellectual Property Organization ('WIPO')** is currently considering a Substantive Patent Law Treaty, proposed by a number of developing countries, under which patent applications concerning biological material would identify source countries. The response of a number of industrialized countries is that ABS should be a matter of private contractual negotiation.

The identification of useful biological resources is often assisted by the **traditional knowledge** of indigenous communities. WIPO has been called upon to formulate an international code to recognize its contribution to securing access to genetic resources.

In 2001 the Food and Agricultural Organization promulgated an International Treaty on Plant Genetic Resources for Food and Agriculture, which creates an access regime in relation to the biological resources conserved by the international agricultural research community. This Treaty also recognizes the rights of farmers arising from their conservation of plant varieties.   MICHAEL BLAKENEY

See also: **patents**

genetically modified organisms   *see* GMOs

Geneva Conventions I–HIV (1949)   *see* international humanitarian law

genocide   Raphael Lemkin coined the term 'genocide' when he forced together a Greek term for people and a Latin term for killing. In this way the term 'genocide' was coined to mean the killing of a group, just as homicide is the killing of an individual person. Genocide has come to be seen as the 'crime of crimes'. In popular discussions, genocide is associated with massive killing. In **international law**, genocide has a specialized meaning that is not necessarily consonant with that of the public's understanding of genocide.

Article II of the Convention on Genocide defines genocide as 'any of the following acts committed with the intent to destroy, in whole or in part, a national, ethnical, religious, racial or religious group, as such'. The acts that follow include 'killing members of the group; causing serious bodily or mental harm to members of the group; deliberately inflicting on the group conditions of life calculated to bring about its physical destruction in whole or in part; imposing measures intended to prevent births within the group; and forcibly transferring children of the group to another group'.

The formulation of genocide in the Genocide Convention, which has been followed in many other legal instruments, provides many puzzles. How are social groups to be identified, and why are only four types of group subject to genocide? What is the harm of destroying a social group, and why is this harm thought to be worse than killing many people who are not part of the same social group? Such matters are the subject of much of contemporary debate in international law about genocide.   LARRY MAY

R Lemkin, *Axis Rule in Occupied Europe, Laws of Occupation, Analysis of Government, Proposals for Redress* (Washington: Carnegie Endowment for World Peace, 1944)

Gentili, Alberico   Alberico Gentili (1552–1608), born in San Ginesio (near Macerata, Italy), graduated as doctor of law in 1572 at the University of Perugia. His father Matteo, a physician, was forced as a Protestant to leave San Ginesio around 1579 with his sons Alberico and Scipio; in 1580 Alberico fled to London. At the recommendation of Robert Dudley he was received as member of the University of Oxford where, in 1581, he was appointed professor of **Roman Law** and on 8 June 1585, Regius Professor of Civil Law. In 1590 Gentili moved to London, where he was more and more to work at the Admiralty Court (he was admitted in 1600 to Gray's Inn), hardly returning to Oxford.

Gentili published several works, amongst which his *De legationibus libri tres* (1585), the first systematic treatise on ambassadorial rights. His next great work was *De jure belli libri tres* (1598). In it he disentangled international law from theology. For him international law was the *ius inter gentes*, the law between all nations, and as such a kind of positive natural law of which the law of war was part. Gentili also defined the legitimate conduct of warfare, staying close to the practice of his days; but he pleaded for moderation and peace as well. These books established him as the founder of the modern concepts of international law and of international relations. For that he was already praised by Hugo Grotius who borrowed much from him.   BOUDEWIJN SIRKS

GHJ van der Molen, *Alberico Gentili and the Development of International Law* (HJ Paris: Amsterdam 1937; AW Sijthoff: Leiden 1968 (2nd edn rev))

geographical indications Marks indicating the geographical origins of goods were the earliest types of **trade mark**. In the competition to earn revenues from developing international trade, it became apparent that the products of particular regions were more saleable than comparable products from other regions, because of their superior quality. This superior quality resulted from natural geographic advantages, such as climate and geology (eg Seville oranges, Kentish hops, Burgundy wine); recipes and food processing techniques local to a region (eg Melton Mowbray pies, Malmesbury mead, Frankfurter sausages); or indigenous manufacturing skills (eg Toledo steel, Delft ceramic ware, Westphalian linen).

A geographical indication is a generic description which is applicable by all traders in a particular geographic location to goods which emanate from that location. The right to protect a geographical indication from wrongful appropriation is enjoyed by all traders from the particular geographical location, whereas a trade mark is protected from wrongful appropriation only at the suit of the registered proprietor of that mark. Generally, geographic indications are monitored and protected by producer associations from the relevant region.

The concept of geographical indications includes the following categories of designation: 'Indication of Source'—a sign that indicates that a product originates in a specific geographical region; 'Appellation of Origin'—a sign that indicates that a product originates in a specific geographic region when the characteristic qualities of the product are due to the geographical environment, including natural and human factors.

The protection of geographical indications is mandated by the **World Trade Organization Agreement on Trade Related Aspects of Intellectual Property Rights ('TRIPs')**. Member States are obliged to prohibit the deceptive use of geographical indications and the Agreement envisages the establishment of a multilateral register of geographical indications for wines. Discussion is underway to extend this register to agricultural products and handicrafts.

The EU has the most developed system for the registration of geographical indications. A series of regulations deal with designations for wines and spirits and for agricultural products and foodstuffs. These regulations provide for the registration of a Protected Designation of Origin ('PDO'), which is the name of a locality used to describe a product originating in that locality, the quality or characteristics of which are essentially or exclusively due to 'inherent natural and human factors', and the 'production, processing and preparation of which' take place in that locality. The regulations also provide for the registration of a Protected Geographical Indication ('PGI'), where one or other of the production, processing, and preparation take place in that locality.

The following are among the geographical indications protected by the EU:

Wines & spirits: Beaujolais, Bordeaux, Bourgogne, Chablis, Champagne, Chianti, Cognac, Grappa di Barolo del Piemonte di Lomardia del Trentino del Friuli del Veneto dell'Alto Adige, Graves, Liebfrau(en)milch, Malaga, Marsala, Médoc, Moselle, Ouzo, Porto, Rhin, Rioja, Saint-Emilion, Sauternes, Jeres Xeres.

Other products: Asiago, Azafràn de la Mancha, Comté, Feta, Fontina, Gorgozola, Grana Padano, Jijona y Turrón de Alicante, Manchego, Mortadella Bologna, Mozarella di Bufala Campana, Parmigiano Reggiano, Pecorino Romano, Prosciutto di Parma, Prosciutto di San Daniele, Prosciutto Toscana, Queijo São Jorge, Reblochon, Roquefort.

A number of these designations have become generic descriptions of goods, predominantly in New World countries. In 2005 the USA and Australia successfully objected to the discriminatory way in which its registration system operated – vis-à-vis non-EU countries, and the EU has undertaken to modify its procedures accordingly.   MICHAEL BLAKENEY

German law The distinctive features of German law arise from comprehensive and rapid assimilation of **Roman law** in the middle ages, nineteenth-century codification, and changes introduced following WWII. At the turn of the nineteenth century, a vast difference existed between German law and the law of England and Wales. Due to the increasing importance of case law in Germany and of statute in the UK, and as a result of membership of the **European Union**, the legal systems are growing closer together.

German Law belongs to the central European family of legal systems, broadly classified as **civil law systems**. At least in theory and in basic principles, such systems contrast strongly with the UK legal system. The core of civil law systems, such as German law, typically consists of five 'codes' dealing respectively with civil law, criminal law, civil procedural law, criminal procedural law, and commercial law.

German law recognizes a sharper division between private and public law than English law does. Public law (*Öffentlichesrecht*) is concerned with the legal relationships between the citizen and the state. Areas of law within public law are constitutional law and administrative law and criminal law; procedural law, as applicable in both public and civil jurisdictions; international law; law governing the public authorities, courts, and public professions; social law; the law of elections and political parties; and revenue law. Private law (*Privatrecht*) is the body of laws which regulates affairs between individuals. It includes the law of obligations (contract and tort), succession, family law, property law, commercial law, company law, and labour law. However, labour law now contains so many public law elements that it is difficult to strictly regard it any longer as private law. As a result of the greater power of the state, public law was traditionally more rigid than private law and insisted on a stricter relationship of rights between the state and the citizen. Private law, concerned with equals, could afford to be based on much more flexible foundations and left it very much to the parties to determine exactly how their relations should be governed.

The greater emphasis in German law on the classification or division of the law into private and public areas had and still has an influence on the organization of the courts, the form and style of legal education and the legal professions Germany. New areas of law overlap the two divisions, as in the case of the Law of Economic Administration (*Wirtschaftsverwaltungsrecht*), which is entirely concerned with the state's intervention in the economy and, thus, the private and commercial affairs of individuals. Environmental law is another area of law which, although having its roots firmly in public law, nevertheless has significant impact on private relations. Consumer law, essentially a private law development, is now subject to increasing state and international legislative intervention.

The fact that German law is largely contained in codes and statutes originally distinguished it from the **common law**. The process of codification involves more than mere compilation or consolidation of a number of statutes in particular areas of law. It also entails presentation of these laws in a complete and systematic form, free from contradiction and complete with general and specific principles. The very many statutes and case decisions that exist in a particular area of law are completely reviewed, and the general principles they contain are distilled and presented at the beginning of the code with the specific rules in following sections. Codification involves the attempt to present an area of law as a unified whole containing not only specific rules but also general and abstract rules and principles which apply to all of the specific circumstances. Thus the codes contain broad legal concepts which can be applied to new legal problems to resolve particular cases. The codes can be used to interpret everyday problems and agreements without the need for going into great detail in the agreement itself. To a limited extent, the process of codification continues, with additions to the social law code and various proposals being made for codification of environmental and labour law.

In the German legal system, only two sources of law are formally recognized—statute and customary law; although other influences do without doubt have an impact. Statute (*Gesetz*) includes the German Constitution (the *Grundgesetz*), the comprehensive codes, and amending or additional statutes made by both the Federation (*Bund*) and individual States (*Länder*). The term also encompasses any general secondary legislation (mainly regulations and by-laws (*Verordnungen and Satzungen*) of the Federation, ministries of the Federation, the Länder and other law making bodies recognised by public law.

Custom (*Gewohnheitsrecht*) includes all regular and general public practice recognized as binding. Custom is now a very limited source of new law in Germany.

Although not formally acknowledged as such, case law and the law of the European Communities are also sources of law in the German system. In theory, courts are supposed only to apply law and not to create it. However the role the judges play as interpreters and developers of law is clearly far greater than legal theory permits. In theory, too, there is no system of binding precedent, and judges are completely free to decide every case on its merits, unhindered by previous decisions. In practice, however, previous decisions of higher courts are studied carefully and consistency is maintained wherever possible. Indeed major or radical changes to principles of law, proposed by the courts, must be sanctioned by special senates of the Federal Court of Justice. German courts have adopted the practice of giving greater respect to more recent decisions. Additionally, the writings of academics and jurists command considerable persuasive authority especially if a dominating opinion (*herrschende Meinung*) appears to exist.

NIGEL FOSTER

NG Foster and S Sule, *German Legal System and Laws* (Oxford: Oxford University Press, 3rd edn, 2002)

NG Foster, *Austrian Legal System and Laws* (London: Cavendish Publishing, 2003)

See also: **codes and codification in national law; common law; customary law**

gerrymandering   *see* **constituencies**

gift taxes   *see* **inheritance tax**

gifts *inter vivos*   All types of property may be the subject of an *inter vivos* (lifetime) gift. A gift is a gratuitous, consensual transfer of ownership from the giver (donor) to the recipient (donee). An intention to give, however clearly expressed, is not in itself enough to transfer ownership since the donor may have a change of mind. The law also requires some action by the donor to make the gift effective. The type of action required depends on the nature of the property being given. Gifts of land are made by the same methods of **conveyancing** as for the sale of land. For gifts of chattels, the common method is delivery of possession, where the property is physically handed over to the donee. Where, however, the chattel is already in the possession of the intended donee, perhaps on loan, the donor's intention to make a gift of it is enough to transfer ownership to the donee. If the donor and donee are members of the same household, it may be difficult to prove a change of possession of a chattel, especially where the donor continues to use it. In all cases where the effectiveness of a gift becomes an issue, it is for the donee to prove that a gift was intended and that effective delivery has occurred. An alternative method of making a gift of chattels is by **deed.** Gifts of land or chattels may also be made by declaring a **trust** of the property in favour of the donee as beneficiary under the trust.

If a donor attempts but fails to make an effective outright gift of land or chattels, it is unlikely that a court will intervene: thus, the donee gets nothing. But a donee who, with the donor's knowledge, has acted in the belief that a failed gift is effective may be able to rely on **estoppel** to overcome the imperfections of the gift. Also, the eccentric rule in the case of *Strong v Bird* (1874) automatically cures any defect in a gift where the intended donee becomes executor under the donor's will or administrator of the donor's estate on death.

Gifts made under duress or **undue influence**, or with the intention of defeating the claims of creditors on the donor's insolvency, or the claims of relatives or dependants on the donor's estate at death, may be declared invalid. Conditions attached to gifts will be enforced if they are not ambiguous, illegal or contrary to public policy.

A hybrid between lifetime gifts and gifts by will is the *donatio mortis causa*: a gift of any type of property, made in contemplation of the donor's death. Here, the donor, contemplating death, hands property (or title documents) over to the donee on condition that ownership is only to be transferred if the donor dies. If the death occurs, the gift takes effect, but if the donor does not die, or revokes the conditional gift before death, the donee must return the property.

NORMA DAWSON

See also: **succession**

global civil society   From Seattle to Gleneagles, Scotland, the mass street protests accompanying meetings of the **World Trade Organization**, the G8, and other international gatherings of heads of state are the public face of 'global civil society'. More commonly, global civil society refers to the individuals and organizations operating separately from state governments to shape, resist, and implement **international law** and policy. Is it possible that international law and relations, historically the rarified world of tight-lipped bureaucrats and secretive Foreign Office ministers, might give way to the loud, eclectic, and insistent voices of **human rights** advocates, anti-globalization protestors, and **climate change** campaigners? The dramatic growth in individuals and organizations active in contesting issues from world trade to **women**'s rights, suggests a global civil society may be unfolding.

What makes civil society *global* and why should we care? Global civil society, unlike its national—or 'domestic'—equivalents, focuses on issues having international effect—human rights, trade, the environment—connecting local with global concerns. And the locations in which non-governmental actors work are generally international; the **United Nations**, the World Trade Organization, the **World Bank**. The involvement of **non-governmental organizations** ('NGOs') in international institutions is nothing new; from the International Labour Organization to the structure of the UN, most international institutions bear the imprint of non-governmental activism. However, the sheer number of non-governmental actors, and the breadth of political and social interests they represent, suggests that something distinctive is unfolding. This is a civil society marked by its presumed grassroots, plural, and independent character. Its radical potential lies in offering an alternative to the 'democratic deficit' of an international realm based on state **sovereignty** and seen as elitist, unaccountable, opaque, and inaccessible.

Global civil society, for **international lawyers**, is a paradox. International law by definition governs relations between *states*. It presumes the nation state represents the interests of its citizens. But, NGOs raise the interests and issues states ignore, and they provide expertise and flexible and immediate action where states are slow to act. By challenging the exclusive focus of international law and relations on inter-state matters, NGOs strengthen **democracy** and human rights. Or do they?

The potential of global civil society as a work in progress remains indeterminate. Is global civil society necessarily a force of good? With a history enmeshed in Western imperialism, might civil society in global form be just a new incarnation of old **colonialism**? And what of the non-governmental actors comprising global civil society? Potentially, this civil society includes not only Amnesty International but also Al Qaeda. Who decides who and what counts as a non-governmental actor? Finally, are non-governmental actors any more accountable—and to whom—than the inter-state institutions they criticize? Does global civil society represent something politically and legally new, or is it merely a spectacle without substantive impact? And, what real prospect is there for global civil society with the war in Iraq and a sole super-power seemingly opposed to the (international) **rule of law**?

DORIS BUSS

globalization and crime   Globalization is generally understood to describe a process of change whereby networks of activity (whether economic, social, legal, ideological, etc) have become more widespread geographically speaking, reaching out to and involving more people in more places than previously was the case. It involves also an intensification of these contacts and networks, facilitated by modern forms of communication and transportation. While there have been international networks and exchanges of various kinds dating back for centuries, the reach and intensity (and hence significance) of these contacts has changed markedly in the last thirty years.

While globalization can be seen in respect of legitimate activities (eg new trading relationships, mass tourism), it has also become evident in illegitimate practices. In the past, crime has mostly been viewed and experienced as a domestic phenomenon. The perpetrator and the **victim** have usually lived close to one another and the crime committed has taken place in a particular location where the perpetrator and the victim have both been present at the same time. Crime now more frequently occurs across national borders and between countries. The term 'transnational crime' is widely used in this context. The principal examples in recent times have been drug trafficking, people smuggling and trafficking, arms smuggling, and money-laundering. More recently, greater concern has emerged around **terrorism** and cyber-crime. In addition, the establishment of the International Criminal Court to deal with humanitarian crimes (**genocide**, **war crimes,** etc) indicates a growing willingness to recognize certain categories of international crime.

Transnational crime and humanitarian crime are widely viewed as threats to legitimate government, **security**, and trade. The significant wealth and power associated with an activity such as the trafficking of heroin, if concentrated in the hands of a single or a few non-state organizations, can quickly undermine the effectiveness of government and displace economic activity from legitimate to illegitimate forms. A subsistence farmer in Afghanistan, for example, fares better economically if he cultivates opium poppy rather than a feed crop for grazing animals. Post 9/11, terrorism-related crimes have further reinforced awareness of the globalized threat from some crimes.

The globalization of crime has affected how it is regulated. Once**, communities** either dealt with crime as an internal matter themselves or their governments took action on their behalf. Governments have acted against offending behavior, mainly by first criminalizing the behavior and then putting in place procedures to bring alleged offenders to **justice** in accordance with those laws and procedures. Today, in the absence of an international **police** force and with only limited capacity to prosecute matters in the International Criminal Court, governments must rely upon harmonization of domestic criminal law and cooperation between respective law enforcement agencies to tackle these kinds of crimes. These needs are increasingly reflected in the policy positions taken by regional governments (eg the European Union) and international organizations (especially, the **United Nations**). The UN Convention against Transnational Organized Crime (which entered into force on 29 September 2003) is a key international convention that seeks to coordinate governmental responses to transnational crime.

ANDREW GOLDSMITH

P Andreas and E Nadelmann, *Policing the Globe: Criminalization and Crime Control in International Relations* (New York: Oxford University Press, 2006)

globalization and large law firms Large law firms have been one of the most successful institutions of the twentieth and twenty-first centuries. They have grown hugely in number and size. Each year *The Lawyer Top 100* and the *Am Law 200* chart the successes and failures of this particularly Anglo-American elite. Those at the top of this group now generate a £1 billion a year in revenues, have offices in thirty countries with 3,000 lawyers spread among them. Their expertise and reach enable them to counsel on the big transactions that are the mainstay of globalization. They are the architects of globalization because they provide the infrastructure and certainty of expectations that wire together all the different parties in wide-ranging jurisdictions and make global business possible.

Within the major jurisdictions of the UK and the US the vast majority of the legal profession is composed of small law firms of between one and five lawyers. Yet this majority is shrinking as firms consolidate and merge. The significant growth is in law firms of more than 100 lawyers. However, *The Lawyer Global 100 2005* shows the range for large law firms to span from 400–500 lawyers at the bottom, to the top twelve where each firm has each more than 1,000 lawyers.

The remainder of this entry presents a brief history of the large law firm and its structure, with examples of work that shows how it is implicated in globalization.

The second half of the nineteenth century saw the birth of the corporate law firm. The industrial revolutions of the UK and the US were in full swing, railways were expanding (and collapsing), global trade was increasing, and stock markets were floating many companies. London and New York were being established as the centres of the world's capital markets. Corporate law firms were small ventures with two or three partners and a large number of managing clerks (**paralegals**). At the height of the railway boom, some firms had leverage ratios of one partner to seventy managing clerks. These partners were as much entrepreneurs as their clients; in fact it could be difficult to distinguish them apart. Depending on the nature of their clients' business, UK lawyers could find themselves travelling as far afield as the United States or Argentina. During this period the law firms established strong ties with investment and merchant banks.

In the first part of the twentieth century the blueprint for the modern large law firm was drawn by Paul Cravath. His model was simple in its design and execution but radically different from what had gone before. Instead of taking into practice sons of friends and relatives, Cravath proposed that the best-qualified students graduating from law school should be hired. They would be paid a good salary to prevent them from taking on other work. Instead of being assigned their own docket of cases, they would collaborate with a partner or senior associate, who would dissect a case into its constituent parts and give them to a range of associates. Over time, say seven or eight years, an associate would be considered for partnership. If he met the expectations of the firm, he would be promoted. If he was not selected, the firm would place him in another firm or in the legal department of a client, thereby strengthening links through alumni networks. There were always more associates than openings for partnership, which created a tournament between associates for these coveted positions. The tournament discouraged associates from taking their expertise away from the firm too early in their probationary periods. A problem with the tournament strategy is that it is predicated on unlimited growth, which has become unrealistic. The presence of hundreds of partners within the modern large law firm has made governance among equals very difficult. The result is increased stratification, with the introduction of two-tier and multi-tier partnerships, which effectively extends probationary periods and reduces the numbers of equity holders (partners).

For much of the twentieth century, partnership was a stable marriage, for life. But from the 1980s on law firms became more entrepreneurial and business-oriented, leading to lawyers moving between firms more often and taking clients with them. Law firms now resemble interlocking networks of specialisms held together by competition for resources, especially associates. They have become managed professional businesses, with the prospect of evolving into corporate structures as governments relax their regulatory hold over professional organizations.

Large law firms have always looked out beyond their jurisdictional borders. The rapid growth in capital markets has meant that the demand for New York and English law has risen dramatically. Through a process that enables legal instruments to be created via contract for the particular deal, large law firms have exported their legal technology throughout the world. When, for example, the largest Chinese automobile manufacturer had to be restructured to provide access to Japanese joint-venture investment, despite the existence of Chinese corporate law firms, an American large law firm was used for the task as it provided global legitimacy for the transaction.

Even where statutes provide solutions for legal problems, large law firms can create alternative structures through transactions that are better than the statute-based one. In Germany a successful mortgage-backed bond, *Pfandbriefe*, exists by statute. In the UK there was no equivalent. The investment banks and City of London law firms were able to fashion an English-based counterpart that provided greater returns than the original *Pfandbriefe* by joining together various elements of English law in documents that created a legitimating structure without the need for a statute. Sometimes domestic laws can contradict each other, thus preventing satisfactory resolutions, as many insolvency laws do. Transnational companies experiencing financial problems turn to large law firms to engineer informal restructurings that satisfy markets without incurring the penalties imposed by formal laws.

As long as **international law** remains unable to cope with the demands of globalization, the gaps will be filled by creative lawyering from large law firms.

JOHN FLOOD

globalization and law The term 'globalization' is much contested and its impact on law remains relatively unclear. Twining defines 'globalization' as 'those processes which tend to create a unified world economy, a single ecological system, and a complex network of communications that covers the whole globe, even if it does not penetrate to every part of it'. Lawyers do a great deal in fields relevant to globalization as defined by Twining such as, for example, international business law, EU law, **human rights**, comparative law, and public and private **international law**. But these may be little more than studies of the policies, technical rules, and practical

skills needed to conduct *international* interactions, whether between states, non-state actors or both, in an essentially *territorial* legal world. The question remains whether globalization should generate new approaches to law that go beyond such a strictly territorial conception of legal action, and which may capture something new about law in a world that is increasingly characterized by 'globalization'.

The most significant areas of existing legal thought that are of relevance to the issue of law and globalization include: public international law, private international law or 'conflict of laws', and comparative law. These may be said to represent the fields that cover the legal issues arising out of the operation of the traditional international legal order. This is founded on the independent nation state, the **sovereignty** of which derives from its control over territory and the legal status of which is equal to that of every other sovereign state, regardless of size or power. On the other hand, as a result of pragmatic responses by lawyers to the challenges of globalization, a new type of legal order and methodology may be being created. This has led to the relocation of certain regulatory functions outside the traditional domain of the territorial nation state towards regional and multilateral organizations. Furthermore, informal or 'unofficial' transnational regulatory orders are emerging based on such things as business practices, shared communal values, and professional perceptions of problems and their solution, all of which give rise to order outside 'official' law. Both kinds of developments cast doubt on exclusively territorial theories of legal order and sovereignty.

These factors have led to developments in legal research along a number of identifiable and complementary lines. First, there are approaches that seek to create a new alignment between state sovereignty and other sources of sovereign power in evolving regional and global institutions, what can be called 'revisionist approaches to state and legal sovereignty'. These approaches cover at least three main issues: first, the relationship between law and **territory** as the traditional building block of state sovereignty and national legal order; secondly, the relationship between law and economic power in the emergent global economy; and, thirdly, how to preserve and further **human dignity** and democratic **accountability** in the emergent global economy and society. They draw on political science perspectives which question the continuing validity of a world order based on independent sovereign states, but they can vary in intensity between positions that effectively negate the importance of the territorial state, to those that see its role as being transformed rather than undermined by the process of globalization.

Secondly, there are approaches that build on the possibility of new legal orders developing beyond the sovereign state through the activities of significant non-state actors and groups, what may be called 'supra-territorial legal approaches'. These include approaches based on **systems theory** and post-modernist reconsiderations of legal rationality and state forms in the light of globalization. An important empirical issue for this perspective is the existence of a so-called 'New *Lex Mercatoria*', a system that develops new contract regimes and dispute settlement systems outside formal state laws in response to the need for international business to regulate its activities in the absence of formal law. Another example might be the internal management systems of **multinational corporations** which may be used to determine the resolution of internal disputes and issues without reference to outside laws. Beyond the economic sphere other such orders may be found in, for example, the globalized discourse on human rights or in the increasingly global educational sphere. The key to this new level of law is its distance from the existing centres of law-making—national **Parliaments**, global legislative institutions, and intergovernmental agreements.

Thirdly, there are approaches which build on the spatial organization of **regulation** in the global system and which consider that globalization, particularly in its economic dimensions, can generate new kinds of '**legal pluralism** in globalization'. In this context 'legal pluralism' is used as a socio-legal concept, stressing the concurrent operation of multiple orders of law on cross-border transactions. The emphasis is on the variety of regulatory 'sites' that globalization has created, in response to the increasing global integration of economic and social activity. These 'sites' include informal self- regulation, local, sub-national, and national regulation, and regional and multilateral regulation. This approach is inclusive in that it does not privilege formal state-centred regulation, or informal non-state based order creation, as the definitive form of law in globalization. Rather it permits a comprehensive and eclectic view of the interactions between these various sites of regulation as they work to generate new forms of regulatory organization aimed at giving functional effect to the process of globalization. In particular it does not diminish the significance of existing territorial, in addition to supra-territorial, sources of legal rules and practices as an input into legal globalization. Furthermore, it allows for a consideration of the power relations between the principal players and the sites of global legal pluralism by stressing the interactions between them.

The future development of ideas about law and globalization is hard to predict. However it may be unwise to abandon the view that law is essentially a territorial phenomenon, notwithstanding the tendency in social science and legal literature to stress the supra-territorial character of globalization as evidenced by the growth of global business chains, informal orders of self-regulation, and the alleged resultant decline of the nation state.

PETER MUCHLINSKI

PT Muchlinski, 'Globalisation and Legal Research' (2003) 37 *The International Lawyer* 221
W Twining, *Globalisation and Legal Theory* (London: Butterworths, 2000)

glossators and post-glossators The scholars of the early twelfth century who first specialized in the study and teaching of **Roman law** in the medieval West are known as glossators. This is because so much of their teaching survives as marginal and interlinear glosses in manuscripts of the Roman law or *Corpus iuris civilis*. The term also describes scholars of **canon law** in the same period, whose principal sources were Gratian's *Decretum*, or *Concord of Discordant Canons*, and the various compilations of papal decretal letters. By the later thirteenth century, these normative sources had been provided with such a depth of glossing that new work tended to take a different literary form. Moreover, teaching genres had to change in response to the emergence of standard or 'ordinary' apparatuses of glosses which were routinely copied into the margins of the normative texts as the foundation for all teaching. The eventual result was the more detailed, free-standing, lengthy commentary; hence the name 'commentators', which refers to law teachers from the last years of the thirteenth century onwards.

The distinction between glossators and commentators is a little arbitrary and admitted to be so; the early commentators, for example, are often referred to as post-glossators, and even the glossators of the twelfth century wrote free-standing commentaries (often entitled *Summa*, meaning 'summary' and often doing a great deal more than this term suggests). The usual cut-off point between glossators and commentators/post-glossators of the Roman law is the acceptance in the 1260s of Accursius' gloss to all components of the *Corpus iuris civilis* as the standard gloss (*Glossa ordinaria*); in the case of the canonists, whose basic texts were rather different in format from those used by the Romanists (often called 'civilians' after the 'civil law' or *ius civile* they taught), there is no such commonsense dividing line.

The point of departure for legal argument, whether in gloss or commentary, was historically and logically the explanation of terms. This rapidly burgeoned into detailed contextual analysis of different passages in the normative sources, frequently with the purpose of resolving apparent contradictions in what were regarded as internally consistent bodies of law. The outcome of this process might very properly be called the power tool of all medieval jurisprudence, the distinction; lists of *distinctiones* in fact constituted one of the most popular genres of twelfth and early thirteenth-century legal education. The very arrangement of many glosses on the page often reflects the broader method of pro-and-contra analysis which was central to juristic as to all scientific method in the later middle ages: a column of minutely written references for the pro, another for the contra. These references ranged all over the relevant sources. In the twelfth century and for the first half of the thirteenth century, Roman lawyers tended to cite only Roman law, whereas canonist work is filled with references to Roman law as well as canon law. This initial resistance on the part of the Romanists to external sources of law gradually receded, such that by the late thirteenth century it is common to find dense blocks of canon law citations in Romanist work, fully justifying the term *utrumque ius* or 'both laws', the amalgam of Roman and canon law which was the substrate of legal practice across wide areas of later medieval Europe.

Historians used to attribute chiefly textual or purist-exegetical and doctrinal interests to the glossators, whereas their successors the commentators were supposed by contrast to have been animated by the desire to put into practice what their books contained. Again, this is a distinction which makes more sense of the civilians than the canonists, but even here it is exaggerated. The glossators of the twelfth and thirteenth centuries have left behind hundreds of transcripts or re-workings of their public disputations (*quaestiones diputatae*) which often indicate, by their circumstantial detail, the growing importance as early as the late twelfth century of forensic experience in teaching. Thanks to changes in diocesan administration, especially the introduction of the legally trained Official (*officialis*), at different times in different areas of medieval Europe, the university-trained practising lawyer had become an inevitable fact of life by the middle of the thirteenth century and had indeed been hard to avoid for a century before that. Glossators, then, were every bit as anxious to apply the law as the commentators

would be. It is certainly true, however, that the average fourteenth-century commentator spent more teaching time on practical questions than the average glossator did.

A discussion of these practical issues in fact formed an integral part of any full and formally satisfactory commentary on a particular law or paragraph of a law, usually coming after a resumé of its contents, the resolution of textual difficulties arising from it, very often a critique of the relevant section of the Standard Gloss, and a defence of the interpretation offered against likely criticisms. The list of practical *quaestiones* (as they were usually called) could stretch for column after column. One genre which well illustrates the difference in weighting between glossatorial and commentatorial literature is the collection of professional opinions for litigants, courts, and rulers, known as *consilia*. Such opinions do survive in small numbers from the glossators, whereas many thousands survive from the commentators of the fourteenth and fifteenth centuries, covering a vast panoply of medieval experience.

Late medieval Roman and canon law were not, therefore, autonomous texts, but were mediated and experienced via their accompanying literature of gloss and commentary. The works of the medieval jurists themselves constituted a source of law in all but name; received opinion (*communis opinio*) was itself a recognized authority in legal argument and was often cited as such. The works of the glossators and commentators therefore constituted much more of medieval Roman and canon law than those of today's lawyers do of modern law, such that a familiarity with their teaching is indispensible for an understanding of the origins of modern legal culture of the West and those other countries which have imported or been forced to accept it.

MAGNUS RYAN

GMOs The increasing ability to genetically modify crops and other organisms, and the polarization of public opinion on the desirability of introducing these genetically modified organisms ('GMOs') into the environment, presents significant legal challenges. Broadly, these challenges relate to the regulatory procedures in place to authorize the release of GMOs into the environment, and to the liability regime that governs damage caused by the deliberate release of GMOs. In the United Kingdom, the regulatory regime for the deliberate release of GMOs is governed by a European Union Directive, implemented in the UK by Part VI of the Environmental Protection Act 1990 and the Genetically Modified Organisms (Deliberate Release) Regulations 2002.

The legislative framework requires that a **risk** assessment relating to **public health** and the environment be carried out and that the public be given the opportunity to comment on the proposal before any consent is given to release a GMO for commercial purposes (such as a farmer growing a crop). Other Member States and the European Commission are also entitled to raise objections. Other EU **legislation** imposes similar requirements before approval is granted for a GMO to be used in food and feed products, and labelling requirements have been imposed for food products consisting of, containing, or produced from GMOs.

In contrast to the regulatory regime, there has been little legislative activity dealing with liability for damage caused by the deliberate release of GMOs. EU legislation imposes **strict civil liability** for environmental damage but it is clear that the legislation does not give private parties a right to sue for environmental damage, nor does it apply to claims for personal injury, damage to private property, or any economic losses. Individuals who suffer losses as a result of the release of GMOs into the environment may bring actions under the law of negligence and private **nuisance**, but to succeed some type of fault on the part of the **person** being sued must generally be established, which presents insuperable difficulties where losses may be caused—eg through a GM crop cross-pollinating the crops of an organic farmer—without any fault on the part of the farmer growing the GM crop. One solution is to impose strict liability either on the farmer or, as has been attempted in several states in the United States, on the producer of seeds for GM crops. An alternative, adopted in Denmark, is to establish a **compensation** fund from which individuals who have suffered loss from the unintended presence of GM material in non-GM crops may claim, funded by levies on either growers of GM crops, producers of GM seeds, or a combination of both. Although such a solution has been recently rejected in Australia, it seems likely that any long-term plan for co-existence between GM and non-GM crops will have to address the issue of unintentional presence, and in this context the idea of a compensation or 'redress' fund has been mooted, eg by the Department for Environment, Food, and Rural Affairs (*Consultation on proposals for managing the coexistence of GM, conventional and organic crops*, July 2006).   MARK LUNNEY

See also: **fault-based civil liability; negligence in civil law**

good faith (*bona fides*) in international law   Good faith is a central principle of public **international law**. It is among the 'general principles of law' referred to in Article 38 of the Statute of the **International Court of Justice**, which lists the sources of law to be applied by the World Court. As one leading authority puts it, '[t]he significance of this principle touches every aspect of international law'.

The principle that all international obligations are to be interpreted and applied in good faith is expressly recognized in treaties and in the decisions of international courts and tribunals. Article 2 of the Charter of the **United Nations**, which sets out the Principles of the Organization, provides that '[a]ll Members, in order to ensure to all of them the rights and benefits resulting from membership, shall fulfil in good faith the obligations assumed by them in accordance with the . . . Charter'. Article 26 of the Vienna Convention on the Law of Treaties of 1969, which sets out the fundamental principle of the law of treaties (*pacta sunt servanda*), states that '[e]very treaty in force is binding upon the parties to it and must be performed by them in good faith'. Article 31 of the Vienna Convention provides that '[a] treaty shall be interpreted in good faith'. The same principle extends beyond the law of treaties to the interpretation and application of all obligations under international law (for example, those arising under the decisions of international courts and tribunals, Security Council resolutions and unilateral declarations by states).   MICHAEL WOOD

good faith performance in employment law   The idea of 'good faith performance' does not, generally speaking, figure as a technical concept or term of art in employment law (although arguments have been advanced for the recognition of a general implied obligation of 'fair management and performance' in personal employment contracts in English law); but nevertheless this notion of 'good faith performance' does identify a significant element in the legal construction of personal work relations in most systems of employment law. There seem to be three main ways in which notions of good faith performance or associated notions such as obligations of cooperation or loyalty may present themselves in employment law systems. First, they may come into play as general clauses or default terms for contracts at large which apply equally to **contracts of employment** (and for that matter other personal work contracts), as happens with the doctrine of *bonne foi* in French law or that of *treu und glauben* in German law. Secondly, they may operate as obligations which are declared or enacted to be inherent in employment relationships; for example, obligations of cooperation are pronounced to be characteristic of employment relationships which fall within the scope of the German Works Councils **legislation**. Thirdly, in legal systems which do not import notions of good faith into contracts at large, such doctrines may nevertheless be applied to contracts of employment. For example in English law there is no general implied obligation of good faith in contracts; but a strong notion of contractual cooperation developed in the context of contracts of employment; and in recent years this has transmuted into an implied obligation of mutual trust and confidence which applies to contracts of employment and which may extend to other personal work contracts. There is nothing very novel in regarding employees, indeed workers at large, as being subject to such obligations; the main significance of that recent development has been to elaborate reciprocal obligations of or in the nature of good faith on the part of employing enterprises. Those obligations may come to encapsulate ideas of fair dealing in employment relations, at least in the sense of requiring even-handedness of treatment on the part of managers as between individual workers. Since employing enterprises are often in a position to prescribe the terms of employment contracts, one very live issue in employment law is the extent to which obligations in the nature of 'good faith performance' are capable of modification or exclusion by express contract terms. One might expect that such obligations, once recognized, would be seen as intrinsic and fundamental to the employment relations to which they apply; but it is far from being automatically assured that these guarantees of a certain quality of behaviour in employment relations will not be undermined by contracts which confer very broad prerogatives or **discretions** upon management.   MARK FREEDLAND

See also: **mutual trust and confidence**

Good Friday Agreement   *see* **Agreement Reached in the Multiparty Negotiations, 10 April 1998**

good offices   *see* **international dispute settlement**

governance   In much present-day use, governance refers to: a *new* process of governing; or a *changed* condition of ordered rule; or the *new* method by which society is governed. Of course, nothing is ever that simple. Kjær's (2004) excellent introduction distinguishes between governance in public administration, governance in international relations, European Union governance, governance in comparative politics, and good governance as extolled

by the **World Bank**. The several uses have little or nothing in common, leading Don Watson to include it in his *Dictionary of Weasel Words, Contemporary Clichés, Cant & Management Jargon* (2005). Like Humpty-Dumpty, whoever uses this term must assert that 'when I use a word it means what I choose it to mean - neither more nor less'.

Wearing public administration spectacles, the discipline most cognate to constitutional and administrative law, governance explores the changing boundaries between public, private, and voluntary sectors. For many policy areas, these actors are interdependent, so decisions are a product of networks, their game-like interactions, rooted in trust and regulated by rules of the game negotiated and agreed by the participants. Such networks have significant degree of **autonomy** from the state; they are self-organizing, although the state can indirectly and imperfectly steer them. For clarity's sake, it is best if the word always has a qualifying adjective. So, network governance is a scalpel or diagnostic tool for exploring the extent to which governments work with and through networks and to which networks are self-organizing.

For lawyers, the term network governance provides an interpretive gloss to the reforms of the public sector described in constitutional and administrative law textbooks. It sees both the increased fragmentation caused by the market-inspired reforms of the 1980s and the whole-of-government approach of the 1990s, which sought to improve coordination between government departments and multifarious other organizations, as a challenge to the hierarchic Westminster model of responsible government. The core ideas of the Westminster model include the notions of **parliamentary sovereignty**, a strong executive, and ministerial **accountability** to **Parliament**. The governance narrative claims the Westminster model is no longer an acceptable account of how government works in Australia, Britain, and elsewhere. We have to tell a different story of the shift from government, with its narrative of the strong executive, to governance through networks. The boundary between public and private is opaque. Webs of organizations far removed from Parliament make policy. The executive is hollowed out from above (for example, by international interdependence); from below (by marketization and networks); and sideways (by agencies and the several species of parastatal bodies). Formal accountability disappears between the interstices of the webs of organizations that deliver ostensibly public services.

In short, governance explores the changing role of the state. In the Westminster context, where there is no state tradition comparable to the continental tradition of *rechtsstaat*, the literature on governance explores how the informal authority of networks supplements and supplants the formal authority of government. It explores the limits to the state and seeks to develop a more diverse view of state authority and its exercise.   ROD RHODES

AM Kjær, *Governance* (Cambridge: Polity, 2004)
RAW Rhodes, *Understanding Governance* (Buckingham: Open University Press, 1997)

governance and the rule of law in developing countries

The UN High Commissioner for **Human Rights** suggests:

Governance is the process whereby public institutions conduct public affairs, manage public resources and guarantee the realization of human rights. Good governance accomplishes this in a manner essentially free of abuse and corruption, and with due regard for the rule of law. The true test of "good" governance is the degree to which it delivers on the promise of human rights: civil, cultural, economic, political and social rights. The key question is: are the institutions of governance effectively guaranteeing the right to health, adequate housing, sufficient food, quality education, fair justice and personal security? (*http://www.unhchr.ch/development/governance-01.html*)

The **World Bank**, which defines 'good' **governance** as 'sound development management', also currently emphasizes the relief of poverty.

There is an obvious link between good governance, the **rule of law,** and **democracy**. While the essence of **colonialism** is the denial of democracy, its historical claim is that it brought the rule of law (and good governance) to the colonized. A current claim is that the absence of good governance and the rule of law are responsible for the underdevelopment of many countries. Some explain this at least partially as the post-colonial continuation of colonial policies. Colonial legality was undemocratic and authoritarian in essence, and involved wide discretionary powers and the use of vagrancy laws, arbitrary detention, and political offences to undermine the rule of law. On independence, ruling elites continued these authoritarian structures.

International Financial Institutions (IFIs) such as the IMF (*www.imf.org*) and World Bank (*www.worldbank.org*) emphasize 'good governance' and the rule of law as conditions of 'Structural Adjustment' assistance. For IFIs, good governance involves the efficient and incorrupt functioning of public institutions such as the executive, public services, legislature, and judiciary. In theory this does not mean support for multi-party democracy as IFIs are prevented by their Charters from being involved in politics. This restriction does not apply to donor governments which promote 'democratization' as an aspect of 'good government'. The rule of law is therefore seen as essential to 'good' governance or government and democratization.

Many development projects emphasize reform of the civil service, transparency and corruption prevention, training of **police**, **judges**, and lawyers, technological improvements in legal procedures, and improvements in public service and legal education. Corporate and commercial laws are reformed to ensure an efficient legal environment for the international and national commercial sector. Some attention is also given to access to **justice** for the poor. Donor governments support projects which promote multi-party democracy through appropriate constitutional and legislative changes, and training and support for Parliamentarians.

In theory, good governance, democratic government, and the rule of law combine to produce development, **human** rights, and social justice. However, a number of criticisms are levelled at these approaches. It is suggested that while some attention is given to human rights and access to justice for the poor, the effective aim of policies is to create a global neo-liberal legal framework to suit the needs of global corporations. While recent IFI policies, under the *Poverty Reduction Strategy Papers* ('PRSPs'), support local ownership and civil society participation, critics suggest that in practice, the World Bank sets the parameters for PRSPs, and Bank officials are closely involved in the minute details of a greater range of policies than previously. As a result, the IFIs have increased their influence on governance.

It is argued that good governance and the rule of law require control over the activities of global corporations whose practices contravene good governance and the rule of law. Attempts to make corporations socially responsible have had limited success. The OECD Anti-Bribery Convention 1997 and the UN Convention against **Corruption** 2005 are major steps forward but are not effectively implemented. The more directive draft UN Norms on Responsibilities of Corporations are resisted by the US. Other controls such as Codes of Practice or the Global Compact between the UN and Corporations emphasize voluntariness. Attempts to litigate against major corporate crimes, as with the Bhopal disaster, have not had much success.

A significant complaint is that global institutions such as the IFIs and European Union which attempt to promote good governance themselves have undemocratic governance structures weighted in favour of developed countries and set a poor example of democratic governance. A different contention challenges the link between democracy, the rule of law, and development. It is suggested that authoritarian Asian 'development states' have been able to achieve rapid economic development without the aid of democracy and the rule of law. In fact, a strong argument was made by Singapore's Lee KuanYew and others for 'Asian values' which placed emphasis on Confucian 'responsibilities' of citizens in contradistinction to supposedly 'Western' notions of rule of law, which emphasize human rights. The opposing argument is that development has been achieved *in spite of* rather than *because of* the absence of the rule of law and human rights, as indicated by strong economic development in the contrasting governance environments of China and India.

Putting aside the question of 'Asian' values, the underlying argument is not about whether good governance and the rule of law will promote human rights and social justice, but whether approaches which, while based in Western models of majority rule and individual rights, persist in global practice with top-down and unaccountable structures, will do so. Santos and others emphasize global coalitions of popular participatory movements for the rule of law, human rights, democracy, and social justice.

ABDUL PALIWALA

B Santos (ed), *Democratizing Democracy: Beyond the Liberal Democratic Canon* (London and New York: Verso, 2005)

World Bank Website *Governance and Anti-Corruption* (www.worldbank.org/wbi/governance accessed February 1 2007)

government departments   *see* **departments of state**

government lawyers Government lawyers are qualified lawyers (either barristers or solicitors) employed by the **Crown**, who act as lawyers for the government, and often for its executive agencies. Like other in-house lawyers they have relationships with clients similar to those of lawyers in private practice, and owe duties to their clients under their professions' ethical rules; they also have duties as civil servants under the **Civil Service** Code. They have no special duties towards the public interest beyond those which lawyers in private practice or other civil servants have, or any recognized special competence on issues of justice or fairness rather than legality, except to the extent that the law requires consideration of these issues. In particular, they may be asked to advise what is reasonably arguable rather than what, in their opinion, is the law.

Though from day-to-day they treat the administrators with whom they work as their clients, in the UK central government their actual clients are the relevant Departmental Ministers; they do not act for the government as a whole. Legal advice to the government has thus been described as 'departmentalized'. However, government lawyers in the Treasury Solicitor's Department ('TSol') provide litigation services for all government departments in domestic and EU courts, except in specific matters that arise within Her Majesty's Revenue and Customs and the Department of Trade and Industry; nevertheless the policies to be pursued in domestic litigation remain for Departments to decide. Lawyers in TSol also advise the Treasury and the Cabinet Office, as well as two other Whitehall Departments (Department for Children, Schools, and Families ('DCSF') and Department for Culture, Media and Sport ('DCMS')) and many other public bodies; but most legal advice is given by lawyers in Departments.

Though TSol is 'an Executive Agency acting under the remit of the Attorney-General', and the **Attorney-General** is the government's chief legal adviser, neither TSol nor any other departmental legal department is formally subordinate to the Attorney-General. Nevertheless where legal advice may be controversial, or it is unpalatable to Ministers or the subject of disagreement between Departments, it is likely to be referred to the Attorney-General for decision.

While lawyers may advise on very specific matters, their most significant role is in advice on the making of policy, whether in the making of decisions by or on behalf of Ministers, or in the steps leading up to the making of primary or secondary legislation. Here they play an important part in ensuring that **human rights** and **European law** are taken into consideration. They draft secondary legislation, give instructions to **Parliamentary Counsel** for the drafting of primary legislation, and more broadly act as intermediaries between Parliamentary Counsel and administrators. They also play a part in the parliamentary process, drafting speaking notes on the law for the use of Ministers, and along with Parliamentary Counsel reviewing amendments introduced at the Committee stages. Government lawyers do not have a monopoly on legal advice; standing Treasury Counsel (in private practice) play a significant part, and resort to other counsel in private practice is frequent. Privatizations were principally carried out by private firms of City solicitors.

Lawyers belonging to legal teams for most departments (not, however, including the Foreign and Commonwealth Office) and some agencies are members of the Government Legal Service, headed by the Treasury Solicitor, which provides training and career services to government lawyers, as well as a degree of coordination between Departments on some legal issues. It also seeks to spread 'legal awareness' amongst administrators through the publication *The Judge over your Shoulder* (most recent edition 2006).

Government lawyers in two of the devolved jurisdictions (Wales and Scotland) are also employed by the Crown. The lawyers in the Office of the Solicitor to the Scottish Executive differ from UK government lawyers in that they are not organized into separate departmental bodies, and owe their loyalties to the Scottish Executive generally, rather than to particular Ministers, as well to the **Lord Advocate** on matters of the competence of the Executive.

The Welsh Assembly was initially a single body corporate, to which its lawyers, like other Welsh civil servants, owed their loyalty. But an informal separation of legislature and executive left the large majority of civil servants, including the lawyers, working for the executive. The Government of Wales Act 2006 (of which the relevant provisions are not in force at the time of writing) gives proper recognition to Welsh Ministers and their staff.

Northern Ireland has its own civil service and lawyers, who owe their loyalties to local Ministers or to the relevant Ministers in Whitehall according to whether direct rule is in force or not.

PHILIP LEWIS

T Daintith and AC Page, *The executive in the Constitution: Structure, Autonomy, and Internal Control* (Oxford: Oxford University Press, 1999), chs 7–10
G Drewry, 'Lawyers in the UK Civil Service' (1981) 59 *Public Administration* 15

governmentality 'Governmentality' is a term invented by Michel Foucault in 1978, during a set of lectures dealing with the development of modern states and of liberal political economy. The lectures had been advertised under the title of '**Security, territory**, population', but, in the midst of one of them, Foucault commented that a better title would have been 'Lectures on governmmentality'. One of these lectures was translated into English, and it—together with accompanying articles by like-minded scholars—gave rise to further studies collectively known as 'the governmentality literature'.

These studies broke with structuralist habits of thought and with questions about 'who benefits' driving critical social science literature, asking instead about what and who is being governed—and

especially, how. Governmentality studies also put aside the distinction between state and non-state **governance**, breaking with Marxist paradigms. A key aim of the literature is to take seriously liberalism's promise to govern us through our very freedom by aligning governing objectives with our desire for **autonomy**. Governmentality writers thus provided a new take on the **neoliberalism** of the 1980s and 1990s, being more descriptive and less judgmental than Marxism, and focusing on techniques and practices of governance rather than on macro-level power relations.

In Foucault's work, 'governmentality', a modern and mainly liberal mode of governing, is specified by contrast with '**sovereignty**' and 'discipline'. Sovereign powers separate the legal from the illegal and the moral from the immoral, punishing those who break the rules in order to maintain authority over a territory and/or over a collection of **subjects**. Disciplinary authorities, in turn, aim at reforming, and, in Foucault's language, 'normalizing' individuals, body and soul. In contrast, 'governmentality' refers to innovations, roughly originating in late eighteenth century Europe, that target neither souls nor bodies but rather economic and social processes—especially those constituting that relatively new category, 'population'—without laying down prohibitory rules or individually disciplining deviants.

One example given in the 1978 lectures concerns the phenomenon of theft. The juridical code uses a sovereign logic to make a binary distinction between what is allowed and what is forbidden. Once an offender has been convicted by the juridical authorities, he/she passes into a system that from the mid-nineteenth century onwards is concerned not only to punish but also to train the prisoner through surveillance, diagnosis, and other 'correctional' tactics. By contrast with these two ways of governing theft, mechanisms of security (or governmentality) insert the phenomenon in a series of probable events. Thefts are counted and aggregated, statistics are produced, and statements are made about various populations' susceptibility to the phenomenon. Contemporary governmentality thus requires, as a precondition, that people be re-imagined as 'populations' measured by statistics.

In general, governmental power tends to work on people indirectly, by incentivizing and rewarding certain activities, and using expert or state knowledges to do so. Nevertheless, Foucault stresses that old-fashioned **punishment** and nineteenth-century discipline do not disappear with what he calls 'the governmentalization of the state'. Historic modes of governance continue to exist, and since the relation between them is not a zero-sum game, empirical investigation is always required.

MARIANA VALVERDE AND PAT O'MALLEY

government-in-exile   *see* **recognition of states and governments**

Great Britain   The implementation of the Treaty (or 'Act') of Union 1706 created Great Britain, the name for the new state established by the union between England (and Wales) and Scotland in 1707. The two kingdoms had shared the same **monarch** since 1603 when James VI of Scotland succeeded Elizabeth 1 of England and became James I of England in what is known as the 'union of the crowns'. The 1707 union did not lead to a traditional unitary state. There was a new Parliament of Great Britain which was located in the Westminster site of the former Parliament of England. However, Scotland's separate legal system was retained and the power of the new Parliament of Great Britain to legislate in relation to private rights in Scotland was on the condition of 'the evident utility of the subjects within Scotland' (**Act of Union,** Article 18). The continued existence of other Scottish institutions, such as the Presbyterian church and the educational system—in particular the universities—was guaranteed. The Treaty declared the Hanoverian succession to the throne, and made common arrangements for trade, weights and measures, and coinage. In respect of these separate Scottish issues, the new Parliament would pass legislation affecting only Scotland. Legislation on common matters would apply in England and Wales as well as in Scotland.

BRIAN THOMPSON

See also: **United Kingdom**

Greek law   'Greek Law' refers to the laws and judicial procedures of the many *polis* ('city-states') that flourished from around 1000 BCE until **Roman law**, and later Byzantine Law, gradually replaced it during the first millennium CE. Although each *polis* had its own laws, which sometimes differed significantly from one another, certain common features, especially procedural, justify treating Greek law as a whole.

Law originated in preliterate Greece as a procedure for settling disputes, as illustrated on Achilles' shield (Homer, *Iliad*, Book 18). Around 800 BCE the Greeks learned to write, and around 650 they began writing laws, mainly on stone. The earliest surviving law, from Dreros (in Crete) states that the *polis* has

decided that the city's highest official cannot serve more than one term every ten years. Many inscribed laws survive, often in fragments, from all over the Greek world, but one *polis*, Gortyn (also in Crete), stands out for its monumental Law Code—twelve columns with more than fifty lines each, inscribed around 450. The Code first requires citizens to go to trial rather than resort to force; then it addresses primarily property and inheritance matters: a man's estate is divided among all the children including daughters, who however receive only half as large a share as sons. Rape and adultery, divorce, adoption, mixed marriages (between slave and free), and sale are among the other subjects regulated.

Most of our evidence for law in Greece concerns Athens. The first Athenian law was Draco's homicide law, written in 621 BCE. It distinguishes between intentional and unintentional homicide, provides for trials, and regulates reconciliation between the victim's family and the killer. It also specifies details of procedures. Around 590, Solon wrote a new set of laws, keeping only Draco's homicide law. Solon's laws covered a wide range of subjects and were the basis of Athenian law for several centuries. Few laws now survive, but about 100 speeches, written ca. 420–320, reveal Athenian law in action. These were delivered by litigants in court, primarily before large juries (201–1501 members) composed of ordinary male citizens.

Athenian trials consisted of one or two speeches by each litigant, after which the jury voted without deliberation. A majority vote decided the verdict. The speeches were timed, the length varying according to the seriousness of the case, litigants had equal time, and no case took longer than a day. Litigants also presented evidence, such as witness depositions, contracts, and other documents. All evidence was submitted beforehand and then read out in court by a clerk. In most cases only male citizens could litigate, so that women, who could not own significant amounts of property in their own name, were represented in court by their husbands or other relative.

The speeches concern a wide range of issues, including homicide, assault, citizen status, slander, and embezzlement. Among the best represented are inheritance disputes, which are often complex and can continue for generations, maritime disputes concerning high-interest loans for transporting cargo, and political disputes, in which legal issues become the focal point for full-scale political debates. The most famous of these is the case 'On the Crown,' in which the proposer of a decree to honor Demosthenes with a crown was indicted by Demosthenes' political opponent Aeschines. Each litigant attacks the other's public career and defends himself; the technical issue—will the proposed crown be awarded at the right time and place?—is addressed only briefly. The verdict overwhelmingly favoured Demosthenes, and Aeschines was fined for receiving fewer than one-fifth of the votes.

Basic principles of Athenian law are that the people (*demos*) should control the law and that it should be open to all. Written laws were publicly displayed so that anyone could read them. Officials and clerks conducted trials, but no judge oversaw the jury, which decided all the issues, factual and legal, in one vote. There was no public prosecutor, so private individuals prosecuted almost all cases. Litigants pleaded their cases in court themselves without professional representation, but were sometimes assisted by one or more co-pleaders; and there were no jurists to deliver opinions or otherwise influence the system. Athenian law, like most Greek law, was run by amateurs; the only professionals were the logographers, who for a fee wrote speeches for litigants.

Greek law left no direct legacy, but some basic Greek ideas survive today: that everyone, including the highest official, is subject to the **rule of law** (*nomos*); that procedural **justice** (*dike*) is of highest importance; that ordinary citizen-jurors should decide cases; and that verdicts should be freely arrived at, not decided by automatic proofs (like ordeals) or formalistic procedures.

MICHAEL GAGARIN

Green Papers   *see* **White Papers**

grievances, workplace   The law imposes obligations on employers and employees in relation to workplace grievances.

Contract law, as it relates to **contracts of employment**, implies an obligation on employers to provide their employees with an effective procedure for resolving grievances (*WA Goold (Pearmark) Ltd v McConnell* (1995)). The law does not prescribe the procedure, but typically it should include a mechanism for raising, investigating, and determining grievances.

The *written* terms of an employment contract may include a process for handling workplace grievances, but in most cases grievance procedures are contained in an employee handbook, not the contract. The handbook will usually and effectively describe the procedure as non-binding on the employer. Therefore, any failure by the employer to follow the procedure will not be unlawful unless that failure amounts to a breach of the duty to maintain mutual trust and confidence or the duty, mentioned

above, to provide an effective process for resolving grievances. Workplace grievances are also regulated by **legislation**. In particular the statutory grievance procedure contained in Schedule 2 to the Employment Act 2002, sets out a compulsory process for dealing with most grievances. This involves three steps: (1) the employee must inform the employer of the grievance in writing; (2) the employer must arrange a meeting to discuss the grievance; and (3) the employer must hold an **appeal**, if requested to do so by the employee. If an employee wishes to use a grievance as the basis of a complaint to an employment **tribunal**, they must first complete step 1 of the statutory grievance procedure. Employment tribunals may adjust any award of **compensation** by between 10 and 50 per cent for failure by either party to follow the statutory procedure.

In 2007, the government announced its intention to revoke the statutory procedure and replace it with a voluntary procedure.

DAVID HOOD

See also: **mutual trust and confidence in employment law; staff handbooks and works rules**

group action   Over the past sixty years, the availability of products and services on a mass basis, coupled with increased emphasis on regulation of markets and on consumer protection, have meant that many people may have similar issues that they wish to raise through the courts. The courts have increasingly needed to put in place mechanisms under which similar claims can be managed through their processes efficiently.

In England and Wales, the main court mechanism is the Group Litigation Order ('GLO'), under which all claims that fall within the definition of a group will be managed together, in the same court and usually by the same judge. The GLO mechanism was formally introduced in 1999 and has operated successfully in a variety of situations, such as claims for product liability, holiday illness or quality, transport disasters, and abuse of children in care homes.

A court can make a GLO when there are a number of similar claims that give rise to common or related issues of fact or law. A judge will be appointed to manage the case, and will make directions as the procedure continues, usually at periodic case-management conferences. The GLO procedure provides that claimants can join a register, and can serve generic statements of their case, thus avoiding some formalities of starting individual claims. The court may appoint 'lead solicitors' to manage the claims, may control any advertising of the case, and may set a cut-off date for people to join the procedure.

Being included in a group can bring efficiency and lower costs. But in return claimants surrender some autonomy, as decisions need to be made on a group basis; and so as to make sure that the cases make effective progress through the courts, individuals are denied rights of veto. The funding of multiple cases, and arrangements over the sharing of costs and liability for costs, can be very complex in group cases. It is important that expert solicitors are instructed.

Group litigation can give access to justice for many who could not afford to bring an individual case, but the costs may outweigh the benefits where a case does not involve much money. Complex cases, such as those involving medicines where issues of causation are unclear or disputed, are notoriously difficult and expensive to bring. There is also some concern that mass cases can involve excessive litigation, and encourage a **compensation culture**.

In the USA there are two equivalent concepts. In a 'class action', a single person is a representative claimant on behalf of many others. When a court declares that a 'class' exists, every person who falls within its definition is included unless he or she 'opts-out', which can involve costly advertising and administration. The USA also has another mechanism called Multi-District Litigation, which operates differently, on an opt-in basis.

There are also collective mechanisms in UK under which approved consumer organisations can bring a representative claim on behalf of a group of consumers in specific circumstances involving breach of consumer protection or competition laws.

CHRIS HODGES

See also: **costs of complaining and claiming**

group taxation   *see* **corporation tax**

Guantanamo Naval Base   *see* **territory**

guarantees   This term has a number of different meanings. It may refer, for example, to a promise to repay another person's debt if that person fails to do so. In this entry, the concern is with consumer guarantees. Such a guarantee is an undertaking by a manufacturer or retailer ('the guarantor') to repair or replace goods which break down during a specific period after the date of purchase, usually as a result of poor workmanship or the use of defective parts. Guarantees are given free of charge. It is important to appreciate that there is no obligation on a manufacturer or retailer to offer a guarantee—they are entirely voluntary.

There are different reasons as to why a guarantee may be given. In the past, they were often intended to exclude the legal rights of a consumer under the legislation on the sale and supply of goods. This imposes legal responsibility for any defects which existed at the time the goods were supplied, even where these were not discovered until later, on the person who sold the goods to the consumer (usually a retailer). That person will be obliged to repair or replace a defective item, or to pay compensation. The law now prohibits any attempt to evade these rights, including attempts to make a consumer rely on a guarantee instead.

Guarantees may be used to suggest to a consumer that a product is of a certain level of quality—the more generous the guarantee, the better the quality. A five-year guarantee on a particular make of car might suggest that it is more durable than a car of a different make with a two-year guarantee. However, research shows that the link between guarantee and quality only exists in some instances. An alternative purpose of a guarantee is to make available to a consumer an additional mechanism for having defects rectified, but on terms set by the person offering the guarantee rather than by the law on the **sale of goods**. This might facilitate the speedy resolution of any problems with faulty goods, although it also creates the risk of undermining consumers' legal rights.

Guarantees are usually provided in a written document enclosed with the goods. This document needs to be written in plain and intelligible language. It has to include information about the guarantor, what the guarantee covers, and the steps that need to be taken in order to make a claim on the guarantee. There also has to be a clear statement that the legal rights of consumers are unaffected by the guarantee. Guarantees are legally binding as a type of contractual obligation, and the legislation on **unfair contract terms** applies to ensure that its terms and conditions are fair.

In addition to free guarantees, consumers are often given the opportunity of purchasing additional protection in case goods break down. This is known as an 'extended guarantee' or, more commonly, 'extended warranty'. Extended warranties on domestic electrical appliances are governed by separate rules, which require that a consumer is given a quotation before committing to purchasing a warranty, as well as a forty-five-day **cooling-off period**.

CHRISTIAN TWIGG-FLESNER

Christian Twigg-Flesner, *Consumer Product Guarantees* (Aldershot: Ashgate, 2003)

guardianship and children   There are three main areas in which the term 'guardian' might be used in relation to a **child**: upon the death of both parents; where a child is being educated in the UK and her parents live overseas; and where the natural parents are unable to care for the child.

Upon the death of a child's parents, the child may be cared for by a guardian provided the parents specified this is in a will prior to death. A child's legal guardian is the person responsible for the welfare and safe upbringing of a child until the age of eighteen. Guardianship of children in this context is governed by the Children's Act 1989. Only those with **parental responsibility** can appoint a guardian. Parental responsibility is defined by the Children Act 1989 as being 'All the rights, duties, powers, responsibilities and authority which by law a parent has in relation to a child and his property'.

Where a child is receiving full-time education in the UK and her parents are not resident in the UK, s/he must have a legally appointed guardian. The guardian has the power to make some decisions relating to the child's welfare (for example emergency medical treatment). The guardian would also usually provide the child with a home at weekends away from school and half terms, and attend parents' meetings.

Where the natural parents are unable to care for a child, a Special Guardianship Order ('SGO') may be made. A SGO is a legal arrangement made under the auspices of the Adoption and Children Act 2002 whereby the guardian is given parental responsibility for a child or children. Local authorities or an individual can apply to be a Special Guardian. SGOs are intended to be used where **adoption** is not appropriate, for example, in the case of older children who cannot live with their parents but do not wish to be adopted. A SGO might also be suitable for those for whom full adoption is unacceptable due to religious or cultural objections.

Under a SGO, the legal link between the child and her parents remains, and the parents retain parental responsibility. However, their ability to exercise parental responsibility is extremely limited. The Special Guardian will have responsibility for all day-to-day decisions concerning the care of the child and for other decisions about their upbringing (for example, where the child will live and choice of school). The Special Guardian has to consult with the child's parents about their decisions, but, in most cases, does not need the parents' consent.

Special Guardians have limits on their powers. For example, they cannot give their consent to change a child's surname, or live abroad for more than three months without the agreement of all those with parental responsibility, or leave of the **court**.

Special Guardianship Orders can be varied or discharged if there has been a significant change in circumstances. In general they will last until the child is eighteen. SARAH BERESFORD

guardianship and mental capacity A Guardian is appointed under the auspices of the Mental Health Act 2007 to make decisions on behalf of people (referred to in the legislation the patient), who do not have mental **capacity**. The Department of Health Code of Practice defines the purpose of guardianship as enabling 'patients to receive care in the **community** where it cannot be provided without the use of compulsory powers'.

Guardianship applies to people who are at least sixteen years old and who are medically assessed as suffering from a mental disorder. The Mental Health Act 2007 uses a single broad definition stating that mental disorder is defined as any disorder or disability of the mind, excluding drug or alcohol dependence, or learning disability (unless with abnormally aggressive or seriously irresponsible behaviour). A Guardianship order can only be made if it is deemed to be in the interests of the patient or for the protection of others. A Guardian can be a local authority or a named individual. The vast majority of Guardianship orders are conferred on local authorities.

A Guardianship order can only be made if two doctors and an approved mental health professional or nearest relative agree. The nearest relative is defined as follows in ascending order: husband/wife/civil partner; son/daughter; father/mother; brother/sister; grandparent/grandchild; aunt/uncle; nephew/niece; someone (not a relative) who the individual has been cohabiting with for at least five years.

The Guardian has no control over the patient's money or property, although they do have extensive powers over other areas of the patient's life. Their powers extend to the power to require the **person** to live at a specified place; to require the patient to attend specified places for medical treatment, occupation, education, or training; and to require that access be given to the patient by a doctor, approved social worker, or other specified person.

A Guardianship order lasts for up to six months but can be renewed for a further six months and annually after that. The patient has no right of **appeal** within the first six months of the order being made.

It is possible for the patient or the patient's nearest relative to object to a Guardianship order by applying to the Mental Health Review **Tribunal** ('MHRT'), to have the order discharged. There are usually three people on the MHRT—a lawyer, a psychiatrist, and a third (not medically qualified) person. The MHRT has discretionary powers to retain, discharge, or vary the order. However, the MHRT is under a legal duty to discharge the order if they consider the patient does not have mental illness or impairment, or psychopathic disorder, or, if it is apparent that the order is not necessary for the patient's welfare or the protection of others.

SARAH BERESFORD

See also: **health care proxy**

guest worker   *see* **migrant worker**

Gunpowder Plot The Gunpowder Plot was a failed Roman Catholic conspiracy that aimed, on the night of 4–5 November 1605, to blow up Parliament, killing King James I and the majority of the English ruling elite. At the same time, the plotters hoped to raise a rebellion of the Catholics in the Midlands, Wales, and the North of England to capture the infant Princess Elizabeth to be set up as a puppet Catholic monarch.

The plot was the brain-child of Robert Catesby, a Northamptonshire gentleman, who in 1604 gathered together like-minded conspirators including Thomas Winter, John and Christopher Wright, and Thomas Percy (a distant cousin of Henry Percy, the Earl of Northumberland). A number of Jesuit priests, including the superior Henry Garnett, knew of the plot in their role as confessors. The most historically infamous of the plotters was Guy Fawkes, a military engineer who had fought for the Spanish against the Protestant revolt in The Netherlands.

The plot failed when Fawkes was discovered with the gunpowder. Despite this, the plotters raised a rebellion in the Midlands. Catesby, Percy, and the Wright brothers were killed in battle at Holbeach House in Staffordshire. The surviving conspirators were imprisoned and, after long questioning, were charged with treason.

Fawkes was interrogated under torture, an act that was illegal without the **prerogative** consent of the King. The trial of the conspirators took place on 27 January 1606 in Westminster Hall. They were convicted and publicly hanged, drawn, and quartered on 31 January 1606.

ELLIOT VERNON

H

habeas corpus *Habeas corpus* is the **common law** remedy allowing anyone illegally imprisoned to petition the court for immediate release. The writ of *habeas corpus* ('have the body') commands the gaoler immediately to bring the prisoner before the court and to explain the reason for the imprisonment. If the judge finds the imprisonment to be unlawful, the prisoner is entitled to immediate release. *Habeas corpus* is a cornerstone of the **rule of law** and a fundamental common law constitutional guarantee to ensure the liberty of the subject.

The writ has deep roots in the common law tradition, and its origins can be traced to medieval court records. The modern form of the writ was established by the late sixteenth century when *habeas corpus* was used to challenge executive orders committing prisoners deemed to be enemies of the state. *Habeas corpus* played a significant role in the early seventeenth century in the constitutional struggle between the Stuart Kings and Parliament. The Petition of Right 1628 declared detentions 'by special command of the King' to be unlawful. The *Habeas Corpus* Act 1640 curtailed the power of the King to detain his enemies, abolished the Star Chamber, and gave anyone imprisoned by order of the King or **Privy Council** the right to be brought before the court without delay to have the cause of imprisonment shown and tested. The *Habeas Corpus* Act 1679 introduced several procedural reforms to guarantee a prompt response to applications for the writ and to ensure speedy trial for those accused of crime. The Act required gaolers to respond immediately to the writ and imposed fines on judges who unduly delayed dealing with applications. Prisoners facing criminal charges were given the right to be released on bail or to be tried without delay.

Habeas corpus can be used in a wide variety of situations to protect personal liberty. In *Sommersett's Case* (1772), *habeas corpus* was used to secure the release of a slave held on a ship. *Habeas corpus* is used frequently in immigration and **extradition** cases to protect the legal rights of detainees facing expulsion. *Habeas corpus* remains available in times of national crisis to challenge internment or executive detention orders, although this right has sometimes been effectively suspended by emergency legislation authorizing extraordinary powers of detention. An English court may issue the writ to secure the release of a prisoner held outside England in any dominion of the **Crown** where there is no local court to grant similar relief. *Habeas corpus* may be also used in civil cases to rescue a child from unlawful custody, or to release patients unlawfully committed to mental hospitals or other institutions.

Habeas corpus plays a residual role in modern criminal law. The writ is available to gain release from unlawful police detention. However, a prisoner who alleges wrongful conviction or improper sentence after trial must resort to the statutory right of appeal.

An application for *habeas corpus* enjoys precedence over all other court business to ensure speedy determination of the legality of the detention.

ROBERT SHARPE

habeus corpus and states of emergency The **prerogative writ** of *habeas corpus* offers a hallowed bulwark against incursions upon individual liberty by action of the **Crown** or a government Minister. Although relatively few cases have arisen, *habeas corpus* has been an important symbolic instrument of freedom ever since the seventeenth century, when it was strengthened by the Petition of Right 1628 and the Habeas Corpus Act 1679. It has advantages over internal appeal systems in that the process takes place before a senior **judge** and in public. It has advantages over **judicial review** in that the writ issues as of right, with expedition, without consideration of alternative remedies, and, since the liberty of the **subject** is at stake, with a degree of review which is often more searching as to the facts. Furthermore, the remedy is decisive—the detention is either upheld or quashed. There is an equivalent remedy in Northern Ireland but not in Scotland, where the High Court of Justiciary's *nobile officium* jurisdiction could provide an alternative.

When applying *habeas corpus* in emergency situations, the **courts** generally display considerable deference. They acknowledge that the state authority has to act quickly and decisively and that the state authority is privy to secret and sensitive information which cannot be revealed fully to the court. The high tide of obsequiousness was reached in *Liversidge v Anderson* (1942), where a majority of the **House of Lords** sustained that the Minister need say little more than that he was genuinely satisfied that the detainee was a threat to **security** during the Second World War. Lord Atkin bitterly accused his fellow judges of accepting 'arguments which might have been addressed acceptably to the Court of King's Bench in the time of Charles I'. Since that time, the judges have pronounced that Lord Atkin's approach is to be preferred and so will explore not only whether the Minister acted in good faith but also to some extent whether there are facts to justify the Minister's opinion. But the attitude of deference often resurfaces, as in *R v Secretary of State for the Home Department, ex p Cheblak* (1991), where, during the first Gulf War, the Court of Appeal accepted that the **Home Secretary** need not specify any factual reasons for a **deportation** on **national security** grounds of a Lebanese resident.

The *habeas corpus* **remedy** is now subject now to the **right to liberty** in Article 5 of the **European Convention on Human Rights**. The Convention may not provide as speedy a response as *habeas corpus* but offers a more wide-ranging and substantive inquiry, including, under Article 15, into the existence of the emergency which might be invoked as a justification to derogate from rights to liberty. However, the attitude of deference, encapsulated as a 'margin of appreciation' to be afforded to the national authorities, is again reflected in the jurisprudence of the **European Court of Human Rights**. Thus, in *A and others v Secretary of State for the Home Department* (2004), the House of Lords struck down the policy of **detention without trial** as discriminatory, but a majority accepted that there was an emergency threatening the nation because of al Qa'ida terrorism. Lord Bingham confirmed that in considering the existence of an emergency 'great weight should be given to the judgment of the Home Secretary, his colleagues and **Parliament**' on this question, because they were called on to exercise a pre-eminently political judgment' but a 'greater intensity of review' would apply to measures taken pursuant to an emergency (paragraphs 29, 44). CLIVE WALKER

ADR Zellick and R J Sharpe, *The Law of Habeas Corpus* (Clarendon Press: Oxford, 3rd edn, estimated publication date: September 2008)

AWB Simpson, *In the Highest Degree Odious* (Clarendon Press: Oxford, 1992)

habitual residence and social security benefits

A test of whether or not a person is 'habitually resident' in the **United Kingdom** was introduced in 1994 to prevent what ministers referred to as 'benefits tourism' (the idea that some non-UK citizens were attracted to the UK by the availability of welfare benefits). The test determines whether or not a benefit claimant is a 'person from abroad'. Generally, a 'person from abroad' will not be entitled to income support and other means-tested benefits such as income-based jobseeker's allowance, housing benefit, and council tax benefit. Persons from elsewhere in the **European Union** who enjoy a right to reside in the UK as migrant workers (not all do) must be treated as habitually resident.

The condition of being habitually resident is open to interpretation on the particular facts of the case. The core elements of the test are regarded as a person's intention to remain in the UK and a period of residence there lasting a reasonable length of time. Factors such as whether a person has come to the UK with a clear intention to remain, as evidenced by bringing their possessions and family with them, may be looked at, as may the existence of any long-term ties that they have in or with the country. The length of time the claimant needs to have been in the UK before a period of residence can become 'habitual' is uncertain. The onus of demonstrating that a person is not habitually resident falls on the state.

NEVILLE HARRIS

***Hadley v Baxendale* (1854)** In this much-cited decision an English appellate court deliberately laid down general principles for the assessment of compensation for breach of contract. If you are successfully sued because you owe money—say, the price of something you have bought, or repayment of a loan—you will be ordered to pay the sum due (plus interest). If you contracted to do something different—say to provide services—it is more difficult to see what compensation you should pay for breach.

Pickfords, the carriers, agreed, at a price just over £21, to take a miller's broken crank-shaft back to its makers to be used as a pattern in making a replacement. Delay took place and, having no other shaft, the mill was brought to a standstill, with losses put at £300. The court held that 'damages should be such as may . . . arise naturally or may be reasonably supposed to have been in the contemplation of parties at the time they made the contract', and ordered a new trial. Unless Pickfords had been told that this was the mill's only shaft, they could not have expected it to suffer so great a loss: in general carriers (of persons or goods) cannot know the particular loss that delay will cause to any one of their many customers. In **common law** countries the court's approach has been generalized to cover all cases where one party undertakes to do, or to refrain from, something. When you make a contract you know that the other party is relying on you but, unless they tell you in advance, you do not know what special loss they may sustain by your default. If so told, you can increase your price or insert some limit on damages.

The principle is widely assumed to be the work of English lawyers. In fact in the case itself, counsel and the judges were reading to each other from Theodore Sedgwick's *Treatise on the Measure of Damages* (New York, 1847), and the above quotation from the English judgment seems to have been borrowed (without attribution) from page 112 of the American book: 'where the contract is to do or refrain the party in default shall be held liable for all losses that may fairly be considered as having been in the contemplation of the parties at the time the agreement was entered into'. To support this, Sedgwick quotes the French Civil Code Articles 1149–1151 (described as 'the sensible rule' by Baron Parke during argument in the English case) and Robert Joseph Pothier's *Traité des Obligations* numbers160, 162 (1761). Pothier's main source is the first comprehensive textbook on damages, Jean Dumoulin's *De eo quod interest* numbers 49, 57 (1564), which roves back over centuries of civil law.

In applying the principle common law courts do not distinguish between a default caused by accident or negligence and one which is deliberate, or even malicious. This has made possible the theory of efficient breach, which encourages parties to contracts to commit a breach and pay damages if doing so would be economically more efficient than performance and denies that contracting parties have some sort of 'moral' obligation to perform.

BERNARD RUDDEN

Hague Peace Conferences of 1899 and 1907 *see* international dispute settlement

Hampden, John John Hampden was born in June 1595, the son of William Hampden, a Buckinghamshire gentlemen. Hampden was educated at Thame School, Magdalen College, Oxford, and the Inner Temple. In June 1619 he married Elizabeth Symeon of Pyrton, Oxfordshire. Hampden soon entered politics. In the 1621 Parliament he was returned as the MP for Grampound, Cornwall and served as

a Buckinghamshire JP in the 1620s. Hampden succeeded in restoring the Buckinghamshire borough of Wendover, which he sat as MP for in 1625 and 1626.

In 1627 Charles I tried to circumvent the laws forbidding the **monarch** to raise money without the consent of Parliament. Charles I tried to force a 'loan' on the nobility and gentry, with the consequence that a campaign to refuse to pay the 'forced loan' was mounted in the counties. Hampden was imprisoned until 1628 for refusal to pay, and his uncle, Sir Edmund Hampden, was one of the five knights who unsuccessfully applied for a writ of *habeas corpus* to secure their release.

Hampden began to believe that Charles I was attempting to subvert the English Protestant state towards an absolutist and Roman Catholic monarchy. He was presented with the opportunity challenge the King when Charles I chose Hampden as the defendant in the test case concerning Ship Money. English law did not provide the monarch with a mechanism for raising taxation for the navy; instead the King had to commandeer often-inappropriate local ships to be fitted out for military service. Charles I attempted to circumvent this by levying the English counties for money in lieu of ships. Hampden saw ship money as an illegal **prerogative** tax and part of the King's drive to get around the laws and parliament and push towards absolutism.

The case was heard in the Court of Exchequer Chamber in 1637–1638 before the Twelve Judges. Although Charles I succeeded against Hampden, the case was won by a slim margin. Lord Chief Justice Bramston and Lord Chief Baron Davenport gave dissenting judgments in favour of Hampden.

The King's victory was pyrrhic and refusal to pay ship money was one of the things that forced Charles to call the Short and Long Parliaments. Hampden was a leading figure of the early parliamentarian cause, maintaining the English alliance with the Scots and supporting the Root and Branch petition for the abolition of Episcopacy. He was a key figure in the executions of Thomas Wentworth, Earl of Strafford and Archbishop William Laud. That Charles considered Hampden one of his principal opponents is shown by Hampden's inclusion as one of the five members of the House Commons who were arrested in the Commons chamber by force on 4 January 1642.

When the First Civil War finally broke out in August 1642, Hampden took on the role of soldier as well as politician. Despite early successes, he was shot in action at the battle of Chalgrove Field on 18 June 1643, and died from his wounds on 24 June 1643.

ELLIOT VERNON

Hansard   'Hansard' is the usual name for the 'Offi-cial Report' of proceedings of Parliament (officially sanctioned by the Commons since 1878). It reports all that is said by members of either House in their chambers and committees (except select commit-tees). It is described as '...not strictly verbatim [but] substantially the verbatim report, with repetitions and redundancies omitted and with obvious mis-takes corrected...'. It also includes written answers to questions, written ministerial statements and other procedural material (though the authentic record of all decisions is that in the Journals of the Houses).

The two Houses' Hansards are published sepa-rately. Reports of the previous day's proceedings are published daily and subsequently reprinted in 'bound volumes' containing about a fortnight's debates, which may have been corrected. Commit-tee proceedings are printed in separate daily parts and are not corrected. All are available online.

The authority of Hansard as a true record is under siege from the availability of audiovisual archive material, but for the present stands. A 1993 judg-ment of the **House of Lords** (*Pepper v Hart*) finally overturned the doctrine that words used in debate could not be used by courts as an aid to statutory construction. The courts now regularly refer to Hansard where legislation is considered ambiguous or obscure or leads to an absurdity; where the mate-rial comprises ministerial statements (or the words of the promoter of a Bill); and where the statements relied upon are clear. This use of the parliamentary record remains an area of controversy.

PAUL EVANS

See also: **interpretation of legislation**

harassment   'Harassment' in the UK is primarily regulated by discrimination **legislation**, ie the **Sex** Discrimination Act 1975, **Race** Relations Act 1976, **Disability** Discrimination Act 1995, Employment **Equality** (Sexual Orientation) Regulations 2003, Employment Equality (**Religion** or Belief) Regula-tions 2003, and Employment Equality (Age) Regula-tions 2006. In this context harassment is defined as 'unwanted conduct which has the purpose or effect of (a) violating [another] **person**'s dignity, or (b) cre-ating an intimidating, hostile, degrading, humiliat-ing or offensive environment for him'. Harassment which also amounted to less favourable treatment on grounds of sex, race, or disability was implicitly reg-ulated by the relevant legislation, but it has only been relatively recently that amendments to the legislation have been made explicitly to regulate harassment.

The sexual orientation, religion or belief, and age legislation apply only in relation to employment and third level education but the Equality Act 2006 provides the basis for further regulations to apply a prohibition on harassment connected with sexual orientation beyond this context. Plans to regulate religious harassment outside the employment con-text were shelved because of concerns about freedom of speech.

The discrimination legislation is civil rather than criminal law and its breach results in civil rather than criminal liability. However, harassment may also breach criminal law prohibitions where it takes the form, for example, of physical or sexual assault and/or threats of violence. Specific criminal provisions also govern, for example, threats to kill and incitement to racial or religious hatred. In addition, the Protection from Harassment Act 1997 prohibits the pursuit of 'a course of conduct (a) which amounts to harassment of another, and (b) which he knows or ought to know amounts to harassment of the other', unless such con-duct 'was pursued for the purpose of preventing or detecting crime' or 'under any enactment or rule of law or to comply with any condition or requirement imposed by any person under any enactment', or otherwise was reasonable 'in the particular circum-stances'. The 1997 Act was intended to target stalking behaviour, but its provisions extend well beyond such behaviour and it is likely that, over time, the approach to harassment under the 1997 Act will reflect that developed under the recently amended discrimina-tion law provisions. In *Majrowski v Guy's and St Tho-mas' NHS Trust* (2006), the **House of Lords** applied the 1997 Act to a case of bullying at work.

Harassment under the 1997 Act can be dealt with as a civil matter (giving rise to a **compensation** claim) and/or as a criminal matter (which may result in imprisonment). There is no requirement under the 1997 Act that the conduct at issue relates to any particular characteristic (by contrast with the posi-tion under the discrimination provisions). It has also recently been confirmed that harassment in the form of bullying at work may give rise to liability in neg-ligence on the part of the employer where it results in injury to the employee (*Green v DB Group Serv-ices (UK) Ltd* (2006)). This form of liability, again, does not turn on any link between the harassment/ bullying and any particular characteristic of the complainant.

AILEEN McCOLGAN

See also: **dignity and discrimination; hate speech; sexual harassment**

Harmonization of laws in the EU   *see* **approxi-mation of laws in the EU**

Hart, Herbert Lionel Adolphus Herbert Lionel Adolphus Hart was born on the 18 July 1907 in the spa town of Harrogate where his family, which was Jewish, ran a furrier's business. Hart's was the first generation of the family to receive a university education: he was a Scholar at New College, Oxford, where he took an outstanding First Class degree in Greats (ancient history and philosophy) in 1929. He then qualified as a barrister, and enjoyed a successful practice at the Chancery Bar throughout the 1930s. In 1940, he became a civil servant working in military intelligence; in 1941 he married Jenifer Williams, a civil servant in the Home Office who was later herself to become an academic.

During the war, Hart's keen interest in philosophy was stimulated by regular conversations with Stuart Hampshire and Gilbert Ryle, who were working in a related department, and who introduced him to the new movements in linguistic philosophy. In 1945, after some hesitation, but encouraged by his close friend Isaiah Berlin, Hart accepted a fellowship in philosophy at New College. Despite his sixteen years outside the academy, he quickly established himself as a leading member of the influential group of analytic philosophers, including Ryle, JL Austin, GA Paul, and Friedrich Waissman, working in Oxford at the time. Such was his reputation that, notwithstanding having published very little, he was in 1952 elected Professor of Jurisprudence at University College, Oxford. During his tenure of the Chair, he revived what had become an intellectually sterile subject, bringing to jurisprudence the rigour of a philosophical method of which it had been deprived since the days of **Bentham** and John **Austin**, and introducing the fresh insights of Wittgenstein's and, primarily, JL Austin's philosophy of language. In short, he sought to provide, as RV Heuston memorably put it, 'a town planning scheme for the intellectual slum of English jurisprudence'.

Outside the UK, his reputation was especially strong in the United States, where he spent several periods, notably at Harvard in 1956–1957; and in Israel, which he first visited in 1964. He was elected President of the Aristotelian Society in 1959 and Fellow of the British Academy in 1962; he was for many years a delegate of Oxford University Press. In this last role he instituted and edited the Clarendon Law Series, which sought to provide readable and scholarly introductory texts suitable for students— an ambition of which his own *The Concept of Law* (1961; 2nd edn with a new 'Postscript' by Hart, eds PA Bulloch and J Raz, 1994), the book which consolidated his reputation and for which he remains best known, is exemplary. In 1968 he resigned from the Oxford Chair, taking up a Senior Research Fellowship at University College, Oxford, in order to devote himself to the systematic editing and analysis of the works of Bentham (Hart (ed), Jeremy Bentham *Of Laws in General* (1970); Hart and JH Burns (eds), Jeremy Bentham: *An Introduction to the Principles of Morals and Legislation* (1970, 2nd edn, 1996); Hart and JH Burns (ed), Jeremy Bentham, *A Comment on the Commentaries and a Fragment on Government,* (1977; paperback edition, 1982); Hart, *Essays on Bentham: Studies in Jurisprudence and Political Theory,* (1982)). From 1967–1973 he served as a member of the Monopolies Commission; he also chaired a committee which made important recommendations for the reform of Oxford's **governance** in the light of student unrest in the late 1960s (*Report of the Committee on Relations with Junior Members* Supplement to the *University Gazette* vol. Xcix (May 1969)). From 1973–1978 he was Principal of Brasenose College. Following his retirement he returned to University College as an honorary fellow, and continued for the rest of his life to write on legal and political philosophy. He died in Oxford on 19 December 1992.

Hart's intellectual contribution lies in two distinct but related fields. First, he revived the tradition of analytical jurisprudence, exploring both the concept of law in general and a number of specific concepts—**causation,** rights, obligation, **responsibility**, rules—which structure legal reasoning and doctrines. In this work (notably *The Concept of Law*), Hart emphasized JL Austin's assertion that one may use a 'sharpened awareness of words to sharpen our perception of phenomena'. He insisted, however, that the task was not one of simple definition: rather, the aim was to build a theory or elucidation of the relevant concepts by examining their operation within the practical contexts in which they are used, and paying heed to the 'open texture' of language, with its core meaning surrounded by an unsettled penumbra. Another outstanding example of these methodological commitments lies in Hart's and AM Honoré's monumental *Causation in the Law* (1959, 2nd edn, 1986), which sets its conceptual analysis of causation within the context of hundreds of legal cases, and which draws criteria for the identification of causes out of the common sense understandings which underlie everyday usage in the relevant contexts.

Hart's second contribution was in the fields of normative legal, moral, and political philosophy. Building out from his analytic conceptions, he made influential interventions in normative and policy debates about matters such as **capital punishment**,

abortion and the regulation of **homosexuality**, as well as advancing general theories of **punishment** and of criminal responsibility. His treatment of these issues was located within a tradition stretching back to Hobbes, Hume, Locke and, most obviously, JS Mill, to which Hart contributed, among other things, an elaboration of principles limiting the proper scope of state action (*Law, Liberty and Morality* (1963)); a novel account of the justification of punishment (*Punishment and Responsibility* (1968)); and an analysis of the relationship between utility and rights (*Essays on Jurisprudence and Philosophy* (1983)).   NICOLA LACEY

N Lacey, *A Life of H.L.A Hart: The Nightmare and the Noble Dream* (Oxford: Oxford University Press, 2004)
N MacCormick, *HLA Hart* (London: Edward Arnold, 1981)

See also: **legal positivism since 1970**; **legal positivism to 1970**

Hastings, Warren   Warren Hastings (1732–1818), governor-general of Bengal, was born in Oxfordshire. Hastings was employed for many years in the East India Company's Bengal service. His first stint in India lasted from September 1750 to January 1765, he returned in 1769, and in 1771 was appointed governor of Bengal. When the company's internal governance structure was overhauled by the East India Regulating Act in 1773 he became governor-general.

Hastings's administration was problematic in a number of ways. He was unable to increase the taxation revenue on which the company's financial health depended, and his handling of diplomatic relations with other Indian states was disastrous. Under Hastings's governorship the East India Company was drawn into a series of large-scale, enormously expensive wars. His reputation also suffered from accusations of personal corruption levied in 1775. These were political in origin. Hastings's conduct as governor-general had been consistently criticized by a cabal within the five-member supreme council created by the 1773 reforms, and his accuser, Nandakumar, was more than willing to assist the councillors who wanted the governor-general removed. It is also clear, however, that not all of Hastings's income derived from official sources.

By 1785 the British were convinced that the government of Bengal was in a state of crisis, and that responsibility for that crisis lay with Hastings. This view was actively promoted by Philip Francis, a councillor determined to replace Hastings as governor-general, but also in Parliament by Edmund Burke, who had no personal axe to grind

and genuinely believed that Hastings was guilty of gross mismanagement. Hastings's resignation in February of that year did not satisfy Burke, and the former governor-general was formally impeached on 10 May 1787 on charges of cruelty and personal and political corruption. His trial at Westminster Hall lasted for years. The prosecution closed its case in May 1791; Hastings's counsel took over two years to reply; Burke's nine-day concluding speech was delivered in 1794. Public interest in the trial was initially very high, with crowds packing the Hall to hear Burke, Sheridan, and Fox make the case for the prosecution. As interest waned sympathy for Hastings grew, and when the Lords finally rendered judgment in 1795 he was found not guilty on each of the counts. The impeachment itself no longer appears to have been justified.

Its inglorious conclusion notwithstanding, Hastings's governorship had significant consequences for the development of Indian law. While he believed that **Hindu law** and **Islamic law** should continue to operate, he also believed that the indigenous courts had been corrupted. British revenue officers were therefore given charge of local civil courts and British magistrates appointed to preside in new criminal courts, with appeal lying to British courts in Calcutta. Hindu civil law acquired a novel uniformity under the new system, and Islamic criminal law was amended in accordance with British prejudices: a decline in the punishment of mutilation was coupled with a significant increase in capital punishment. The legal reforms initiated by Hastings would ultimately lead to the emergence of a hybrid form of Anglo-Indian justice.   ALLYSON MAY

hate speech   Hate speech may be defined as expression which is likely to cause offence or distress to other individuals on the basis of their association with a particular group and/or incite hostility towards them. The most obvious example is the law on incitement to racial hatred in England and Wales (now contained in Part III of the Public Order Act 1986). This provides that it is an offence to use threatening or abusive words or behaviour with the intention of thereby stirring up racial hatred or where racial hatred is likely to be stirred up.

A form of this law has existed since 1965, but there have been remarkably few prosecutions under it. In recent years, there has been pressure to expand the range of protected groups. In 2005, a new offence of incitement to religious hatred was added on a somewhat narrower basis (unsurprisingly, Northern Ireland had had a similar provision for many years). Others have sought to argue that homophobic hate speech should be covered, and some feminists maintain that pornography is a form of hate speech against women.

The offences of incitement to racial and religious hatred have a number of unusual features. First, it is uncommon to have a crime of incitement where the matter incited is not itself a criminal offence (unlike, say, incitement to murder). It is not, of course, an offence to feel hatred for another race or religion. Secondly, there is no requirement to demonstrate any likelihood of violence as a result of the inciting speech. Defendants are therefore punished purely for the effect their expression has on the minds of other individuals. Neither successive governments nor the courts have set out a coherent justification for these laws. Presumably, the argument is that rabble-rousing racists make a limited contribution to the quality of public debate and people are entitled to be protected from expression which is related to fundamental aspects of their character such as their race or religion. To that extent then, the interests of **equality** trump the right to free speech. It is also true that many other democracies outlaw some form of hate speech.

This position is extremely difficult to sustain as a matter of principle. Matters of race and religion are at the core of political debate in most democracies, and the risk of a prison sentence of up to seven years must have the effect of inhibiting individuals from expressing themselves freely. This risk of self-censorship is especially great where the laws in question do not provide a clear definition of what is prohibited. For example, what does it mean to 'stir up' hatred and what counts as a religion in this context?

It is not sufficient to assert that people remain free to express their viewpoint in less extreme terms when speakers feel as strongly as they do about issues such as race and religion. It is also unclear what contribution such laws make to equality since we have other effective legal provisions which prevent social goods being denied to individuals on the grounds of their race or religion. The law on incitement to racial hatred has also proved to be counter-productive since prosecution brings vastly greater publicity to what is otherwise far from the mainstream. It is not surprising that Nick Griffen described his prosecution in 2006 as the best recruiting sergeant the British National Party ever had. In this respect, the United States Supreme Court follows a much more principled approach and has held that laws outlawing incitement to hatred are inconsistent with the protection of free speech enshrined in the First Amendment to the Constitution.   IVAN HARE

J Weinstein, *Hate Speech, Pornography, and the Radical Attack on Free Speech Doctrine* (Boulder: Westview Press, 1999)

I Hare, 'Crosses, Crescents and Sacred Cows: Criminalising Incitement to Religious Hatred' [2006] *Public Law* 521

See also: **freedom of expression; freedom of religion and belief**

Hayek, Friedrich von (1899–1992)   Born into a family of Viennese intellectuals and trained in law, political science, and economics at the University of Vienna, Friedrich Hayek spent much of his working life outside Austria at the London School of Economics and, later, in the Committee on Social Thought of the University of Chicago. A Nobel Prize winner in Economics in 1974, Hayek is best known for his fierce critique of socialism and state planning generally. First set out comprehensively in *The Road to Serfdom* (1944) and then refined in *The Constitution of Liberty* (1960), Hayek's libertarian economics attracted new supporters in the Anglo-American neo-conservative movement of the 1970s and 1980s (Hayek's ideas were influential in the Reagan and Thatcher administrations) and remain important today amongst conservative scholars. In later years, Hayek applied the arguments underlying his economic views to defend the classical **common law** legal tradition and the **rule of law** in *Law, Legislation, and Liberty, Vols I* (1970), *II* (1976), *& III* (1979).

Central to all of Hayek's work is the idea that **human** knowledge is limited. For Hayek, the fundamental objection to state planning and, more generally, to 'constructivist rationalism' is that no **person** or group can possess the knowledge necessary for such endeavours to succeed. Most human knowledge is dispersed amongst countless individuals or is 'tacit' knowledge, hidden within social norms and practices. The genius of the market, in Hayek's view, is that it can utilize dispersed knowledge. The market coordinates the desires and capacities—the 'knowledge'—of countless individuals through a signalling process that itself was not designed but evolved spontaneously. Market economies are successful because they both allow for, and are the product of, experimentation and emulation.

In his work on law, Hayek defended the (few) rules he considered necessary to provide the 'predictability of expectations' on which markets depend—basically Hume's 'three laws of nature' (the core rules of property law, contract, and tort)—and criticized schemes of 'social **justice**'. But perhaps of greater interest is Hayek's defence of the common law and the rule of law. For Hayek, the common law had two related virtues. First, like the market it is a spontaneous order: the common law was not designed but evolved, through trial and error, from countless decisions of individual **judges**. Secondly, the fundamental task of a common law judge (which Hayek equated to the rule of law) is not to create rules, but to affirm norms that spontaneously develop within society. The result, for Hayek, is that the common law utilizes the knowledge embedded in social norms.

Hayek's account of the common law remains influential, but it has been challenged on both historical and practical grounds. Hayek himself acknowledged that spontaneously developed norms may contain gaps, conflict, or, on occasion, be substantively inappropriate. But his suggestion that judges can and do solve such problems merely by 'universalizing' existing norms (a process he regarded as part of the rule of law) seems inadequate, while his theory of knowledge appears to preclude more concrete suggestions.   STEPHEN A SMITH

Health and Safety Executive   *see* **crime Investigation other than by police**

health and safety in the workplace   The United Kingdom has always addressed occupational health and **safety** by **legislation** with criminal sanctions. The radical Health and Safety at Work etc Act 1974 replaced many old laws. This remains the principal Act: amendments are by regulations. From the 1980s most new provisions have implemented European Directives. A review in 1999 concluded that the Act remained a satisfactory tool. Nevertheless, there are tensions between the European and UK systems.

The Act created general duties and established a system for their enforcement. Section 1(1) states its purpose as protecting both **persons** at work and people put at risk by work activities. Section 2 requires the employer to do what is reasonably practicable to ensure the health and safety of employees. Section 3 imposes an equally broad duty on the employer for the protection of persons other than employees. It protects workers, such as contractors' employees (eg *R v Swan Hunter Shipbuilders Ltd and Telemeter Installations Ltd* (1981)) and the general public (eg *R v Board of Trustees of the Science Museum* (1993)). Similar duties are put on controllers of premises and manufacturers of articles and substances. The employee has to take care for his own safety and that of others.

Case law established that the duty to do what is 'reasonably practicable' is tantamount to an absolute duty (eg *Austin Rover Group Ltd v HM Inspector of Factories* (1989)) but section 40 enables the accused to exonerate itself by showing that nothing more could have been done to comply with the duty. The enforcement agency has responsibility for policy as well as inspection and enforcement. Much inspection is delegated to local authorities. Inspectors may enter premises, investigate, and prosecute but they rely heavily on improvement and prohibition notices. Few cases are tried by **jury**. Most **prosecutions** are against employers and convictions result in **fines**. There is limited provision for imprisonment but this is valueless against corporate employers. **Directors** and senior managers are liable where an employer's offence can be attributed to them, but it is difficult to identify individual wrongdoers. The same difficulty existed when the **Crown Prosecution Service** brought a charge of manslaughter. The new Corporate Manslaughter and Corporate **Homicide** Act 2007 imposes liability on the 'organization'.

The Management of Health and Safety at Work Regulations 1999, implementing the EEC Framework Directive (89/391), Regulation 3, requires the employer to identify and address unlawful **risks**. It is questionable whether this is sufficiently stringent where UK law requires doing what is 'reasonably practicable' since the Directive's objective is 'the elimination of risk' (Article 1(2)).

The law is much concerned with the protection of health and many relevant UK regulations stem from EC directives, eg the Control of Substances Hazardous to Health Regulations 2002. There is no UK law expressly addressing psychiatric illness, but the HSE expects employers to consider **stress** in risk assessments.

UK law provides for employee involvement, but in practice such involvement is somewhat lacking.

BRENDA BARRETT

See also: **inspectors, workplace; workers' compensation**

health care proxy   From 2007, in England and Wales treatment decisions can be made on behalf of an incompetent individual by a proxy or surrogate, whether the proxy was appointed by the individual when still competent, or judicially appointed. The Mental Capacity Act 2005 ('MENCA') allows a competent **person** to appoint a donee of a lasting power of attorney ('LPAT') to make medical decisions on her behalf after the onset of incompetence. To be effective, the LPAT must meet certain formal requirements and be registered with the Public Guardian. Alternatively, a **court** may appoint a deputy to make medical decisions on behalf of an incompetent person who has not made an LPAT. Prior to this change in the law, the decision-maker for an incompetent person who had not made an anticipatory refusal was the person's physician, unless the court's intervention was sought. If no proxy has been appointed, the person's doctor will be the decision-maker under the general authority of the MENCA unless the jurisdiction of the Court of Protection is invoked. The Court of Protection is a new superior court to be set up to deal with matters relating to adults lacking **capacity**.

Regardless of the identity of the decision-maker, decisions on medical treatment for incompetent individuals are made using the **best interests test**, which involves weighing the benefit and detriment that will flow from the proposed procedure. The MENCA provides that the person making the determination of what is in the incompetent person's best interests must consider the person's past and present wishes and feelings, the beliefs and values that would be likely to influence his decision if he had capacity, the other factors that he would be likely to consider if he were able to do so, and the views of those close to the person.

In the case of a dispute about the person's best interests, the decision of the healthcare proxy, whether donee or deputy, prevails. However, a doctor who disagrees with that decision may seek a declaration from the court as to the person's best interests and in the interim may provide treatment necessary to sustain the person's life or prevent a serious deterioration in the person's condition.

In Scotland, the Adults with Incapacity (Scotland) Act 2000 ('AWIA') provides a similar, though not identical, structure. The AWIA allows a competent person to appoint a welfare attorney to make medical decisions on her behalf after the onset of incompetence. Alternatively, a court may appoint a guardian to make medical decisions on behalf of an incompetent person. A doctor will also have a general authority to do what is reasonable to safeguard or promote the incompetent person's physical or mental health. The best interests test has been replaced in Scotland by a set of principles which require that any intervention must benefit the incompetent person and that such benefit could not reasonably be achieved without the intervention, which must be the least restrictive option available. The person's past and present wishes and feelings must be taken into account as well as the views of those close to the person.

Unlike the situation in England and Wales, if the welfare attorney or guardian disagree with the doctor, the doctor may provide the treatment if a second medical opinion concurs that the treatment should be provided. The welfare attorney, guardian, or any person with an interest in the incompetent person's welfare may apply to the **Court of Session** for a determination as to whether the proposed treatment should be given or not. PENNEY LEWIS

See also: **guardianship and mental incapacity**

health care rationing Modern health care systems face increased demands from patients. The reasons are demographic (societies are growing older), technological (treatments are becoming more effective, but more expensive) and patient-led (encouraged by government, citizens are demanding more from health care providers). Rationing is endemic to any system in which demand for care exceeds the supply of resources. The following describes how rationing occurs in the UK. Rationing decisions take place at three levels: macro, meso, and micro.

First, responsibilities at the 'macro'-level are imposed on government. The **National Health Service** Acts impose on the Secretaries of State for England and Scotland and the Welsh Ministers a duty to 'continue the promotion of a comprehensive health service'. This leaves undefined the exact nature and extent of the care patients should receive, so the question of NHS priorities is within the lawful **discretion** of government and health authorities (see below).

Governments may use explicit national policies to guide health care resource allocation, for example, to tackle health inequalities, reduce hospital-acquired infections, or (in England and Wales) to fund treatments recommended by the National Institute for Health and Clinical Excellence ('NICE'). Government seldom says that treatment should *not* be provided.

England alone is also experimenting with 'market' mechanisms for managing health resources. Patients are viewed as **consumers**, with power to choose in which hospital to be treated. Hospitals must attract revenue from providing care by a process known as 'payment by results'. Failure to compete successfully for patients may lead to the closure of a clinical unit, or an entire hospital. The impact of market pressures on health care rationing is clear, but its affect is implicit. This experiment in health policy compares with the more managed systems that exist in Scotland and Wales.

Secondly, 'meso'-level duties are imposed on those responsible for allocating resources to local **communities**. The duty is imposed on primary care trusts (in England), health boards (in Scotland), and local health boards (in Wales) (now referred to as 'health authorities'). This is because the performance of the duty to promote a 'comprehensive health service' is delegated to health authorities, who are also duty-bound not to exceed their annual financial allocations. The way in which they commission (or purchase) care from hospitals and GPs is heavily influenced by government but much discretion remains. Rationing occurs because health authorities must decide how to purchase comprehensive health services without exceeding finite local budgets.

Patients may bring proceedings to challenge NHS rationing decisions by means of **judicial review**. The action is normally taken against the health authority. The **courts** impose strict procedural requirements as to how such decisions should be made. Following *R v NW Lancashire HA, ex p A, D & G* (1999), health authorities should bear in mind a number of considerations.

For rationing to be lawful, health authorities should: (a) adopt fair and reasonable resource allocation policies which treat patients equally and consistently; (b) assess the seriousness of the particular illness about which a decision is to be made and the effectiveness of treatments for it; and (c) estimate the cost of the treatment and its probable impact on other treatments in the health economy. If they fail to do this properly, or come to an unreasonable conclusion, the court cannot direct that the treatment is provided. Instead, the flawed decision is referred back to the health authority to be taken again in the light of the court's guidance.

Thirdly, at the 'micro'-level, the decision-maker is the doctor, or other clinician, exercising clinical judgment in relation to each patient. Generally, their judgments should be guided by their Hippocratic commitment; they should prescribe the treatments patients need. This does not mean that only the best and most expensive care should be provided. For many patients, less expensive care may be equally effective. However, for those for whom such care is not effective, clinicians should prescribe what is needed, notwithstanding its cost.

Inevitably, this may strain finite resources and adversely affect the care of others. Therefore, health authorities may limit the range of treatments available in hospital. Provided they have complied with the procedures described above, health authorities may normally refuse to purchase 'low priority' treatments: eg because of their cost; the limited evidence of their clinical efficacy; they provide insignificant additional benefit over existing, less expensive, treatments; or they are outside the responsibility of the NHS (eg some cosmetic surgery).

However, the courts have said that health authorities may not impose 'blanket bans' on treatments. Advised by competent clinicians, health authorities must have a system for hearing evidence (say, from the patient's doctor) that a 'low priority' treatment is of exceptional value to a particular patient so as to justify an exceptional response. Given the competing demands for health care resources, this will not guarantee the treatment is provided, but it demonstrates that the health authority has balanced the relevant considerations properly, including the patient's individual needs.

CHRISTOPHER NEWDICK

See also: **medical treatment, right to**

health service complaints   *see* **complaints procedures**

health service ombudsman   *see* **ombudsmen**

health, law, and development   Different ideologies and programmes of development have promoted distinctive relationships between 'law' and 'health'. Nineteenth-century colonial health policies were structured by then dominant European ideas of 'territoriality'. The imperial periphery was defined and feared as a reservoir of 'tropical' diseases. Colonial government aimed to protect settlers, armies and, indeed, the metropole itself from the spread of these diseases. Territorial segregation within the colony was crucial to this enterprise. Such Western concern as there was for the health of colonized peoples was realized through the medical missionaries of Christian denominations. Law was not prominent in that enterprise which fused the clinical and the charismatic. At inter-imperial level, an infectious disease control regime was maintained from 1851 through the International Sanitary Conferences. These allowed for limited health restrictions, balancing the protection of Europe with the demands of imperial trade.

After World War I a new phase of 'colonial developmentalism' opened up. This was marked, ostensibly, by a greater concern with the welfare of colonized peoples, including their health. Progressive, scientific, and beneficent, the spread of modern medicine justified imperial control, at least among the general public in Europe. It was distinguished sharply in this regard from the alleged backwardness of traditional medicine which marked the underdevelopment of the colonies and their need for tutelary guidance. Actual provision of health care always failed to match this promise. Where it was available, access

De Keyser's Royal Hotel at the east end of the Victoria embankment, *c.* 1875, (*Attorney General v de Keyser's Royal Hotel Ltd*).

Sign for the former Grand Junction Canal Company on the Leicester branch of the Grand Union Canal (*Dimes v Grand Junction Canal Co*).

The Gaumont Picture Theatre, Wednesbury, *c.* 1954 (*Associated Provincial Picture Houses v Wednesbury Corporation*).

The Four Courts, Dublin.

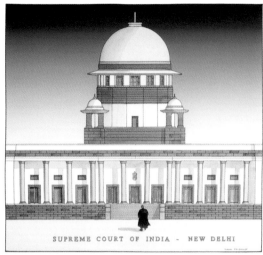

The Supreme Court of India.

The United States Supreme Court building. Designed by architect Cass Gilbert and completed in 1932.

The Royal Courts of Justice.

Fordwich Town Hall, built in 1544, the smallest town hall in England. It has a court room and jury room on the first floor, where criminal cases were tried until 1855.

The Peace Palace in the Hague, housing the International Court of Justice.

The first building to house the Court of Justice of the European Communities, the Villa Vauban was the seat of the Court from 1952 to 1959.

The European Court of Human Rights building in Strasbourg. Architect: Richard Rogers Partnership Ltd.

The New South African Constitutional Court in Pretoria.

'From the bar of the gin-shop to the bar of the Old Bailey it is but one step', etching from the *Drunkard's Children*, by George Cruickshank, 1905.

A Punjab court room, 1888. Watercolour by AFP Harcourt.

Hottentots trying a case *c.* 1805, from an unnamed travel book.

Left: Trial by ducking of a witch, woodcut, *c.* 1600.

Middle: The trial of Warren Hastings, 1788.

Bottom left: Portrait of Titus Oates, who invented the Popish Plot in 1677.

Bottom right: Portrait of Dr Hawley Crippen, 1910.

John Wilkes (1727–97), etching by William Hogarth, 1763.

Thomas Paine (1737–1809), 19th century engraving.

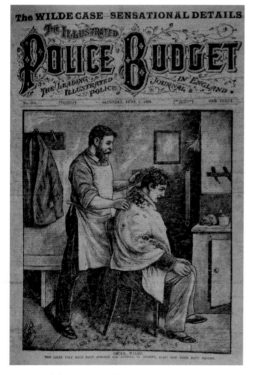

Oscar Wilde receiving a haircut in prison. Illustration entitled: 'The locks that fall have been admired and admired by society, alas! how they have fallen'. Image taken from *The Illustrated Police Budget*, 1895.

Portrait of Edward Carson on a cigarette card, 1926. Carson appeared as counsel in many famous trials including a libel action brought by Oscar Wilde against the Marquess of Queensberry, in which he represented the Marquess.

Demonstration in Paris calling for the pardon of Ethel and Julius Rosenberg, who were convicted of passing secrets to the USSR, and executed in 1953.

Two women outside a bookshop with copies of *Lady Chatterley's Lover*, after it was found that it was not obscene (*R v Penguin Books Ltd*).

Supporters of the under-ground magazine 'Oz' protest against the sentences passed on the magazine's editors under the Obscene Publications Act.

Helen Steel and Dave Morris protesting against McDonald's fast food chain, against whom they won their civil action, the longest in UK legal history (*McDonald's Corp. v Steel & Morris*).

The twenty-one defendants at the Nuremberg War Crimes Tribunal awaiting sentencing.

Crowd outside Wandsworth Prison watching the announcement of the execution of the fascist William Joyce ('Lord Haw Haw') for treason in 1946.

Adolf Eichmann on trial in Jerusalem, in 1961, inside a glass box for his own protection. He was found guilty of war crimes and executed in 1962.

Slobodan Milosevic before the War Crimes Tribunal in The Hague, in 2001, where he conducted his own defence. He died during the proceedings.

was usually determined on the basis of **race**. In truth, the increased agricultural and extractive activity promoted by colonial developmentalism had a considerably greater (negative) impact on the health of colonial **subjects**.

The independent states which emerged from decolonization after World War II pledged themselves to extend health care to the majority. Law was widely ignored in the pursuit of this objective. Mobilizations to promote environmental health and primary care relied more on political persuasion and coercion. Development aid for health was largely channelled through national ministries, reproducing typically Westphalian state–state relationships. Established in 1945, the World Health Organization ('WHO') shifted the focus of international health policy from infectious disease control to health promotion and access to care. This shift was due in part to the WHO's success in eliminating smallpox, and in part to the strength of the non-aligned, Third World bloc within the **United Nations**, especially in the 1970s.

Since the 1980s global **neo-liberalism**, constitutionally secured through the **World Trade Organization** ('WTO') and the Bretton Woods institutions, has radically curtailed the role of states in the provision and promotion of health. Structural adjustment programmes mandated the **privatization** of medical facilities and the introduction of user fees, with often severe consequences for the health of the majority, especially women. Consistent with a new emphasis on the **'rule of law'**, legal mechanisms gained in prominence. Increased private investment in health was to be secured by enforceable property rules; the rights of patient **consumers** would be protected through the law of contract and tort. Marketization of health care in the developing world has extended beyond service provision to drug testing and the **human** body itself. Outsourced clinical trials benefit from 'treatment naïve' subjects and weak ethical regulation. A thriving, though illegal trade in organs, tissue, and gametes similarly links wealthy patients and indigent donors across the global North-South divide.

The WTO's TRIPs Agreement (1995) and subsequent bilateral treaties have globalized pharmaceutical monopolies, just as the spread of **AIDS** poses the greatest health crisis for developing countries since the epidemics of the early colonial period. Campaigns for access to antiretroviral therapies have been driven by domestic and international **non-governmental organizations** ('NGOs'), sometimes in alliance with developing country governments, sometimes opposed. Like the corporations they criticize, health NGOs have profited from a post-Westphalian decline in the powers of the nation state. Pro-patient litigation and political struggles have revived the long-ignored right to health, protected by the **International Covenant on Economic, Social and Cultural Rights** and in national constitutions.

Recent WHO initiatives also contribute to post-Westphalian and neo-liberal arrangements in global health. Admittedly, the Organization's Framework Convention on Tobacco Control (2004) aims to protect developing country populations against tobacco multinationals seeking new markets beyond Europe and North America. But it has also promoted public–private partnerships in other areas such as drug and vaccine development. In line with neo-classical economic theory, the health needs of the poor are repackaged as 'global public goods', with the WHO, private philanthropists, and corporate actors seeking to make up for 'market failures'. The declining power of all states, except the most powerful, is further manifested in the new International Health Regulations (2005). These mandate a globalized disease surveillance network drawing information in real-time from state and non-state sources. As in the nineteenth century, a balance is sought between liberalized, cross-border trade and global health **security**. Given that the political and scientific core of this effort is concentrated in a few wealthy countries, some have questioned whether 'global health security' fully reflects the interests of developing nations.

JOHN HARRINGTON

DP Fidler, *SARS, Governance and the Globalization of Disease* (London: Palgrave, 2004)

NB King, 'Security, Disease, Commerce: Ideologies of Postcolonial Health' (2002) 32 *Social Studies of Science* 763–789

hearsay *see* **evidence (civil); evidence (criminal)**

hedge funds Hedge funds have recently emerged as a particular concern for financial market regulators internationally. But because hedge funds also provide an important source of market liquidity (they will often buy and sell in difficult market conditions where other investors will not), and facilitate risk transfer by other investors, there is considerable danger in over-regulation. Hedge funds are usually characterized as actively-managed investment funds the managers of which use a wide range of speculative investment strategies, including leverage (the use of loans to maximize investments and profits) and short-selling (involving the sale of a security that the fund does not own as a form of speculation on a security's price). Through speculative investments, a hedge fund aims to profit regardless of the overall direction of the market. Hedge funds have also gained a reputation as highly activist shareholders in the companies in which they invest; and this has generated some controversy.

Hedge funds have not been heavily regulated because marketing of investments to retail investors by hedge funds is usually prohibited. By contrast, the **caveat emptor** principle applies to sophisticated investors, although general rules prohibiting **insider dealing** and market manipulation will typically apply to the activities of hedge funds. Recently, regulators have become concerned about risks of market instability arising from the scale of hedge fund activities, risks of conflicts of interest, and indirect risks to retail investors that may arise when collective investment schemes and pension funds invest in hedge funds. Reforms are under development worldwide.   NIAMH MOLONEY

See also: **collective investment schemes; regulation; securities; shareholder power: dispersed ownership, small shareholders and institutional shareholders**

Hedley Byrne & Co Ltd v Heller & Partners Ltd (1964)

This case established liability in the tort of negligence for financial loss occurring through the making of a misstatement. In doing so, the **House of Lords** overruled its earlier and much-criticized decision in *Derry v Peek* (1889), which had restricted liability for misstatements to the tort of deceit, based upon the presence of fraud. A statement would ground liability in deceit only when made with a reckless disregard for its truth. But this position could not be sustained with the advent of the knowledge economy, characterized by increasing professionalization and reliance by all manner of decision-makers upon the supply of accurate advice and information by others.

The claimant in *Hedley Byrne* was an advertising agency, which incurred a large contractual liability when booking advertising space for its client. The claimant incurred this liability after relying on an inaccurate credit reference given by the defendant bank, but supplied in the first instance to the claimant's own bank. The House of Lords held that there could be no liability because of the presence of a disclaimer of liability, which indicated that the credit reference was for the use of the recipient bank only and that it was provided 'without responsibility'. But the breakthrough was the Court's acceptance that tortious liability could arise for a negligent misstatement which caused financial loss where a special relationship existed between the statement-maker and the recipient who relied upon it. This has proven to be of especial importance in three-party cases, like *Hedley Byrne*, where the statement-maker and recipient are not in contractual relations and deal with each other through an intermediary.

In opening up the possibility of tortious liability, the House of Lords cautiously crafted the conditions establishing a special relationship so as to approximate contractual responsibility—the major element of contract missing being the 'consideration' given in exchange for the undertaking of an obligation. The majority of the House of Lords required that there be some assumption or undertaking of responsibility in the making of the statement and that the claimant suffered loss through reasonable reliance upon it. Reliance would be reasonable where, for example, the statement-maker was possessed of a special skill and where the statement was made on a serious (eg business) occasion, rather than upon a social occasion.

Hedley Byrne remains important for its general discussion of the conditions of liability. However, the phrase 'assumption of responsibility' has been much criticized and the emphasis has shifted to an enquiry into whether a duty of care is owed with respect to statements upon an objective view of the links that exist between the parties, rather than upon the attitude of the statement-maker. The case can be seen as an early step in the regulation of professionals and others working in the knowledge economy. It compels those who make statements likely to be relied upon by others to take a minimum degree of care to ensure that the advice or information contained is accurate.   CHRISTIAN WITTING

See also: **contract law; fraud and misrepresentation; tort law**

Helsinki Final Act

On 1 August 1975, the Final Act of the Helsinki Conference on Security and Cooperation was adopted by thirty-five governments including all the major European states as well as Canada and the United States. The Helsinki Accords, as they are commonly known, contained three 'baskets' relating, respectively, to security in Europe, cooperation in the fields of economics, environment, technology and science, and cooperation in humanitarian and other fields. These baskets contain elaborations of and departures from some important existing norms of international law.

However, Helsinki is significant largely because of its political context, its foundational role in the **human rights** system, and its effect on understandings about law-making in the international community; and because it has spawned a large apparatus of institutions and organs (first as the CSCE (Conference on Security and Cooperation in Europe), and latterly as the OSCE (Organization on Security and Cooperation in Europe)). The Helsinki Process was initiated because the Soviet Union wanted recognition of the territorial gains it had made after World War II (in Eastern Europe and in the Baltic States). The Western powers, meanwhile, wished to extend and deepen the concepts of détente and co-existence that had marked recent Cold War relations. In a more adversarial posture, they saw Helsinki as a way of making diplomatic gains through the development of a European human rights order linked to security.

Basket One's inclusion of several human rights commitments may not have rendered these commitments legally binding (Helsinki is often referred to as an early example of **soft law**) but it did open up the Soviet bloc to human rights scrutiny. Much of the external scrutiny (by the Western states) may have been ideologically self-serving but internally the Helsinki Accords gave rise to a number of politically influential dissident movements, e.g. in Czechoslovakia (Charter 77) and in the Soviet Union (Helsinki Watch). GERRY SIMPSON

Henry II King Henry II (1154–1189) succeeded to the throne following the civil war of the reign of Stephen (1135–1154). During that strife there had been a marked diminution in royal control of **justice**. For example, we find less evidence of Stephen intervening in inheritance disputes involving the men of his lords than had been the case in the reign of his predecessor, Henry I (1100–1135). Henry II stated that his aim was to restore the rights that his grandfather, Henry I, had enjoyed. However, his efforts with regard to law and justice produced a rather different regime, exercising more routine control of the administration of justice and having considerably more contact with individual subjects in the localities.

Henry's reign saw major developments relating to crime, land law, and the administration of justice. The traditional method of individual accusation for an offence was, from 1166, supplemented by the '**jury** of presentment'. This consisted of a body of neighbours, twelve from each of the administrative units known as a hundred, and four from each village, to declare on oath 'whether there be in their hundred or village any man accused or notoriously suspect of being a robber or murderer or thief . . . '. Their indictments were to be heard by the eyre, that is, by justices travelling on circuit. Other reforms

concerned land cases. In particular various measures based on specific writs and involving enquiries by neighbours were established, offering speedier remedies for specific problems. Thus 'novel disseisin' dealt with recent and unjust dispossession, 'mort d'ancestor' with inheritance claims by close relatives. Such measures did not establish the ultimate right to land, and the defeated party could still use an 'action of right', for example to establish that although he had dispossessed the other party in an improper fashion, the disputed land really was his. Again, it was made possible to settle such cases not by the traditional method of trial by battle, but instead by the verdict of a body of twelve knights, the so-called 'grand assize'.

Henry II has been seen by some historians as the genius behind the creation of the **common law**, by others as having much more limited ends, for example simply trying to make the existing system of **courts** work according to its own terms. Whilst it is clear that Henry II was very aware of the importance of his position as a **judge**, it is less obvious how far he was personally involved in the creation of new legal measures and **remedies**. A balanced interpretation might be that Henry was assertive of royal power, without having any clear plan as to the legal outcome of the various measures taken in his reign. At the same time, he was surrounded by a body of advisers and administrators who encouraged the development of routine royal involvement in justice beyond that of his grandfather's reign. In practice reforms, particularly those concerning land-holding, proved very popular with those seeking justice, and had a profound effect on the development of the common law. JOHN HUDSON

hereditary peers Hereditary peerages are peerages that may be taken up by the best qualified heir upon the death of the current holder of the peerage. If no heir exists the peerage becomes extinct, or in some cases may become dormant or pass into abeyance for a period. A qualified heir must be a direct descendant of the original or first holder of the peerage. In the case of an ancient peerage this may be a distant relative of the most recent holder of the peerage. Hereditary peers may be peers of England, of **Great Britain**, of the **United Kingdom,** or of Scotland or Ireland.

Though in early times writs of summons to attend the **House of Lords** were not necessarily transferred through the generations, this gradually became normal; and the right to a writ became a means by which a hereditary peerage was established. Hereditary peerages could also be created by Letters Patent, and this became the usual method for conferment of a peerage.

Hereditary peers are divided into five ranks. The most senior are Dukes, followed by Marquesses, Earls, Viscounts, and Barons, the latter group being the most numerous. Several peerages may be held by the same individual, with heirs to high ranking peerages using one of the lesser peerages as a 'courtesy title'. Peerage law is complex, but few peerages can be held by women, and even where this is the case male heirs usually take precedence. Until 1963 women who held peerages in their own right were not allowed to take their seats in the House of Lords, but the Peerage Act removed this disability.

All the Lords Temporal were hereditary peers until the introduction of life peerages for law lords in 1876, followed in 1958 by the more general introduction of life peerages. Under the Act of Union 1707 provision was made for the 134 peers of Scotland to elect sixteen of their number for membership of the House of Lords during each Parliament. The number of peers who depended solely on their Scottish peerage decreased till in 1963 there were only thirty-one all told. In that year the Peerage Act provided for the admission of all peers of Scotland to the Lords. Under the Irish Act of Union 1801 Irish peers were given the right to elect twenty-two of their number for life to the UK House of Lords, but the machinery for holding such elections was abolished in 1922. The Irish peers then seated in the House of Lords remained; but as they died they were not replaced. The Peerage Act 1963 confirmed the exclusion of Irish peers.

Provision was made under the Peerage Act 1963 to allow hereditary peers to renounce their peerage for their lifetime. Previously those inheriting a peerage could not escape the disqualification this brought from membership of the **House of Commons**. Among those to take advantage of the provisions of this Act were several prominent MPs, but 'disclaiming' peerages never became widespread.

Under the House of Lords Act 1999 hereditary peers no longer sit as of right in the House of Lords, though an amendment made during the passage of that Act allowed for 10 per cent of hereditary peers (seventy-five) to be elected for continued membership of the House of Lords by their fellow peers in the same party group (forty-two Conservative, two Labour, three Liberal Democrat and twenty-eight Crossbench), and a further fifteen hereditary peers to be elected by the House as a whole, to remain members and fulfil roles as deputy speakers. Two further hereditary state office-holders were also given the right to remain members of the House of Lords, the Lord Great Chamberlain and the Earl Marshall. Though initially envisaged as providing continuity by enabling the House to draw on the considerable experience of some of its hereditary members, provision was made for by-elections to be held to fill vacancies caused by death. This has resulted in ninety-two hereditary peers remaining in the House until further legislation brings about their removal. The Clerk of the Parliaments maintains a list of hereditary peers who wish to take part in such elections.

The removal of hereditary peers from the House of Lords did not alter laws and customs relating to the peerage; for example the succession to peerages remains as in the past and any disputes can be resolved through the House of Lords Committee of Privileges.   DONALD SHELL

See also: **House of Lords; life peers**

heritage legislation Heritage **legislation** in the United Kingdom is made up of a complex set of international conventions, national Acts, and administrative guidelines and requirements at the sub-national and local levels. There are also a plethora of governmental, quasi-governmental, and private organizations which organize, manage, and monitor heritage initiatives. There is no one regime of heritage legislation. Because of this complexity, the best way to approach the available resources is by heritage area: archaeological, architectural, cultural, environmental, and natural sources and areas of heritage are each governed by discrete, if at times overlapping, legal regimes. Scotland and Wales may promulgate adaptations to the UK legislation regarding specific heritage issues. Broadly, therefore, at the international level, the UK acceded to the Convention concerning the Protection of the World Cultural and Natural Heritage (1972) but has not (yet) signed the 2003 Convention for the Safeguarding of the Intangible Cultural Heritage or the 2001 Convention on the Protection of the Underwater Cultural Heritage. On the national level, the Treasure Act 1996, the Dealing in Cultural Objects (Offences) Act 2003, the Human Tissue Act 2004, and the Commons Act 2006 protect aspects of the national heritage. A new Heritage Protection Bill is due to be published, and may lead to a Heritage Protection Act in the future. The Department of Culture, Media and Sport, and English Heritage, are responsible for the ongoing development of national initiatives and guidelines (see *Policy Planning Guidelines 15* and *16*, promulgated by English Heritage, and the White Paper on *Heritage Protection for the 21st Century*) in consultation with museums, professional organizations such as the Council for British Archaeology, and academic institutions. Finally, local **communities** and organizations generate zoning and other guidelines, and organize and fund public spaces, in order to protect area heritage. These legislative instruments reflect public debates regarding the definitions, meanings, and social and economic uses of 'heritage' in the UK. The law changes as perceptions of heritage change.

TATIANA FLESSAS

heritage markets There are two main markets for cultural artefacts: public museums and private collections. Public museums replaced the tradition of collecting classical sculptures on the Grand Tour for display in private houses. Archaeological objects were elevated to the status of high art as they were placed on display in institutions which housed collections of paintings and decorative arts. The $1 million paid by the Metropolitan Museum of Art in New York for the Athenian red-figured Euphronios krater placed the emphasis on the visual image and quality of painting: information about the archaeological context, almost certainly an Etruscan tomb in Tuscany, was considered to be incidental and irrelevant. In the UK, the guidelines issued by the Museums Association have helped to limit the acquisition of archaeological material which has newly surfaced on the market. The market confusingly talks in terms of provenance (or *provenience*) to chart the collections through which an object has passed. Chippindale and Gill ('Material consequences of contemporary classical collecting' *American Journal of Archaeology* 104 (2000) 463–511) have developed a set of codes to define the way that an object has appeared. History charts the route from the ground to the present collection; archaeology identifies the range of findspots cited, from secure contexts to the more vague 'said to be' locations.

Private collections are the second main market for heritage objects. Some of these private individuals have close links with institutions. Thus, the J Paul Getty Museum acquired the private collection of classical antiquities owned by Barbara and Lawrence Fleischman, and Barbara Fleischman served as a trustee of the Getty Museum until her resignation in 2006. Other collectors have been seen to be influential in the area of public policy on the movement of antiquities. For example, Shelby White, a New York collector, was part of the US President's Cultural Property Advisory Committee. In some cases antiquities reside with private collectors for only a matter of months before they are donated to a museum, raising suspicion that private ownership is one way that museums can avoid being seen acquiring from the dealers and galleries who are known to handle material which is likely to have been looted.

The markets of collectors and public institutions are supplied in the main by auction houses, specialized galleries, dealers, and their agents. The working practices of Sotheby's in London were revealed by the release of internal documents which demonstrated close links with dealers and agents in Switzerland who were acquiring antiquities from archaeological sites largely in Italy (see Watson, *Sotheby's, The Inside story* (1997)). Sotheby's decided to cease handling antiquities through its London base as a result, though it continues to auction such objects through New York; $216.3 million value of antiquities have been auctioned at Sotheby's alone for the period 1998–2007. Around 70 per cent of the Egyptian antiquities which were sold in this period surfaced for the first time after 1973 suggesting that the supply is being met not by the recycling of 'old collections' but rather by the recent looting of archaeological sites. Investigative journalism and **police** work have brought to light organizational diagrammes showing the networks of looters, dealers, and collectors (Watson and Todeschini, *The Medici conspiracy: The Illicit Journey of Looted Antiquities from Italy's Tomb Raiders to the World's Great Museums* (2006)). Trial evidence released during the Italian government's case against the curator of antiquities of a North American museum and an antiquities dealer revealed that several North American and European museums had acquired objects which came from these illicit sources. The effects are already being felt by the return of antiquities to Italy from several North American museums.

DAVID GILL

See also: **antiquities and looting**

N Brodie, J Doole, and C Renfrew (eds), *Trade in illicit antiquities: the destruction of the world's archaeological heritage* (Cambridge: McDonald Institute, 2001)
L Zimmerman, K D Vitelli, and J Hollowell-Zimmer (eds), *Ethical Issues in Archaeology* (Walnut Creek, CA; Oxford, UK: AltaMira; Society for American Archaeology, 2003)

heritage, anthropological issues *see* ecological heritage; heritage legislation; museums and galleries

heritage, international dimensions The notion of heritage and methods for its legal protection and preservation are defined in an international context through various international conventions and charters.

The Convention of the Protection of the **Architectural Heritage** of Europe (Council of Europe, 1985) sets out a series of articles on a number of issues including statutory protection measures, integrated conservation, finance and funding, and sanctions. The convention identifies three classifications for the component parts of this type, namely monuments, groups of buildings, and sites, which are in keeping with the definitions contained in the UNESCO Convention for the Protection of the World Cultural and Natural Heritage (1972) for designated World Heritage Sites. There is also a recognized relationship between the man-made and natural heritage, which may be identifiable through the notion of landscape via the European Landscape Convention (2000).

The European Convention on the Protection of the **Archaeological Heritage** (Council of Europe, 1992) revised an earlier convention (1969) by widening the scope of issues considered with particular reference to new threats concerning construction projects, by specifying the need to develop integrated conservation systems to reconcile requirements for archaeology and development. The convention also considers issues relating to definition, the use of inventories, designation measures and types, excavation, conservation and maintenance, public access, and enforcement measures. The UNESCO Convention on the Protection of the **Underwater Cultural Heritage** (2001) provided the basis for a global system of protection for the underwater archaeological heritage.

The European Convention on Offences relating to **Cultural Property** (Council of Europe, 1985) has never come into force but remains an important legal instrument and provides a comprehensive list of different categories of cultural property which may be deemed worthy of protection. Other legal instruments concerning the movable heritage include the UNESCO Convention on the Means of Prohibiting the Illicit Import, Export and Transfer of Ownership of Cultural Property (1970) and the UNIDROIT Convention on Stolen or illegally exported Cultural Objects (1995). There are also a number of European Directives concerning this issue.

Principles for the conservation and restoration of the architectural heritage were established through the International Charter for the Conservation and Restoration of Monuments and Sites in 1964 (the Venice Charter). A resolution to establish an International Council of Monuments and Sites (ICOMOS) was adopted in Venice at the same time as the Charter. A number of other Charters, Principles and other documents have subsequently been adopted by the General Assemblies of ICOMOS including

on Historic Gardens (1981), Conservation of Historic Towns and Urban Areas (1987), Protection and Management of the Archaeological Heritage (1990), Authenticity (1994), Recording of Monuments, Groups of Buildings and Sites (1996), Underwater Cultural Heritage (1996), Cultural Tourism (1999), the Built Vernacular Heritage (1999), Preservation of Historic Timber Structures (1999), Preservation and Conservation/Restoration of Wall Paintings (2003), the Analysis, Conservation and Structural Restoration of Architectural Heritage (2003), and the Conservation of the Setting of Heritage Structures, Sites and Areas (2005).

Further international conventions dealing with heritage issues include the Convention for the Protection of Cultural Property in the Event of Armed Conflict (UNESCO 1954, 1999), Convention for the Safeguarding of the Intangible Heritage (UNESCO, 2003), the Framework Convention on the Value of Cultural Heritage for Society (Council of Europe, 2005), and the European Convention for the Protection of the Audiovisual Heritage (Council of Europe, 2001) which came into force on 1 January 2008 and is the first binding international instrument in this field.   ROBERT PICKARD

R Pickard, *European Cultural Heritage (Volume II): A Review of Policies and Practice* (Strasbourg: Council of Europe Publishing, 2002)

heritage, protection during war Since the end of the Napoleonic era, states have developed a considerable body of **international law** for the protection of **cultural heritage** from destruction and plunder in war. Rules to this end are to be found today both in **customary international law** and, over and above this, in a range of **treaties**, most notably the Convention on the Protection of Cultural Property in the Event of Armed Conflict, adopted at The Hague in 1954, and its First and Second Protocols. By 'cultural heritage'—or, to use the language of these three main instruments, '**cultural property**'—is meant buildings and other monuments of historic, artistic, or architectural significance; archaeological sites; artworks, antiquities, manuscripts, books, and collections of the same; archives; and the like.

In accordance with these international rules, it is prohibited to attack cultural property unless it makes an effective contribution to military action and its destruction offers a definite military advantage. Since the likeliest way that cultural property might contribute to military action is through its use, its use for military purposes is prohibited too unless there is no other feasible way to obtain a similar military advantage. The demolition of cultural property under a party's own control is also forbidden unless military necessity imperatively requires it. In addition, it is illegal to attack a military objective, such as a tank, a military headquarters, or a munitions factory, if this cannot be done without inflicting on cultural property nearby damage out of proportion to the military advantage anticipated.

All forms of theft, pillage, misappropriation, confiscation, or vandalism of cultural property are unlawful. Parties to an armed conflict are required to prohibit, prevent and, if necessary, put a stop to all such acts. They are also forbidden to seize or requisition cultural property situated in the territory of an opposing party. Where a party is in **belligerent occupation** of the territory of an opposing party, it must prohibit and prevent any illicit export, other removal, or transfer of ownership of cultural property.

Individuals responsible for intentional attacks on cultural property can be punished for **war crimes**. The commanders who in 1991 ordered the bombardment of the Old Town of Dubrovnik were convicted by the International Criminal Tribunal for the former Yugoslavia. In fact, any deliberate destruction of cultural property not justified by military necessity constitutes a war crime. Persons were found guilty of such offences after World War II, and the Yugoslavia tribunal has convicted several people for the destruction of mosques and churches in the war in Bosnia-Herzegovina. Also considered a war crime is any form of plunder of cultural property, as Alfred Rosenberg, the organizer of the Nazis' seizure of artworks from occupied countries, found to his cost at Nuremberg. His trial and the trials of several participants in the Bosnian conflict further establish that widespread or systematic destruction and plunder of cultural property can qualify as crimes against humanity.

Where the 1954 Hague Convention and its Protocols apply, a handful of additional obligations arise, and special institutions and mechanisms for the enforcement of these obligations come into play.

ROGER O'KEEFE

R O'Keefe, *The Protection of Cultural Property in Armed Conflict* (Cambridge: Cambridge University Press, 2006)

See also: **cultural heritage; heritage, international dimensions; international humanitarian law**

Heydon's Case (1584) *Heydon's Case*, decided by the Barons (ie judges) of Exchequer, established the 'mischief rule' for the interpretation of statutes. According to Coke, the judges ruled that 'for the sure and true interpretation of all statutes' four things must be considered: 1. What was the common law before the statute was made? 2. What was the mischief and defect for which the **common law** did not provide? 3. What remedy has Parliament appointed to cure the disease of the commonwealth? 4. The true reason of the remedy. Then, they said, the office of all judges is to make such construction as will suppress the mischief and advance the remedy, to suppress subtle inventions for continuing the mischief, and to add force and life to the remedy, according to the true intention of the makers of the Act.

The case itself illustrates the rule. A religious college granted a copyhold estate in some of its land for two lives. While this estate still existed and just before the enactment of the Act for the Dissolution of Monasteries in 1539, the college made a lease to Heydon for eighty years. If the existing copyhold estate counted as 'an estate for life' the lease was void under a section of the Act designed to prevent religious houses from delaying the effect of dissolution by creating such overlapping interests. Anciently, copyhold estates were held at the will of the lord of a manor according to the custom of the manor, not under general rules of common law. That was still technically true in 1539. Anciently, a tenant wrongly evicted could complain only to the lord's court. But in the fifteenth century both the common law courts and the Chancellor began to protect copyhold tenants who were evicted contrary to the custom of their manor. By 1539, such estates were treated economically and socially as equivalent to a similar estate under common law. So, was a copyhold estate for life an 'estate for life' within the statute? Taking account of the mischief aimed at, the court held that it was.

Although not always dominant, the mischief rule has significantly influenced the interpretation of statutes from the time it was stated. It is the historical background to all general statutory rules requiring that courts take account of the point or purpose of a statutory provision in interpreting it.

JIM EVANS

See also: **equity as a system of law; interpretation of legislation**

High Court   *see* **courts**

Hindu law   Hindu law is not a territorial law, but basically a personal law system that originated in India thousands of years ago and migrated with Hindus all over the world. It is officially part of many legal systems (India, Bangladesh, Pakistan, Burma, Malaysia, Singapore, Trinidad, Fiji, Kenya) and operates as unofficial law among British Hindus, and in Europe and North America, raising many questions in today's multicultural courtrooms. About 80 per cent of India's population, c. 800 million people, apply Hindu personal law, mainly in family and property matters and religious issues. Indian Hindu law co-exists with other personal laws and with secular laws, and was reformed in four major statutes in 1955–1956. India's Constitution (1950) explicitly safeguards the continuation of different, now increasingly harmonized, personal laws within a Hindu-dominated secular system marked by **legal pluralism**, respect for diversity, and equidistance from all religions.

Since Hindu law applies to Hindus as religious communities and as individuals, the much-debated history of Hinduism is relevant for understanding contested interpretations of Hindu law. Practising Hindu lawyers view ancient Hindu texts as codes of law and often take rigid views of certain textual statements. In real life, to be a Hindu, it is not even necessary to hold a specific belief. In India, a Hindu is a person who is not a Muslim, Christian, Parsi, or Jew. Conversion to Hinduism is recognized as legally effective, provided the convert is accepted by the new social group.

Hindu law went through several phases of reconfiguration from Vedic times (c. 1500 BCE onwards) to the classical/formative periods (500 BCE to 500 CE), postclassical/medieval periods and Muslim domination (from c. eleventh century onwards). Exact chronology and authorship of the earliest texts remains impossible to determine. Two major 'schools' of Hindu law were created by scholars, and British colonial influence (1600–1947) produced Anglo-Hindu law as case law, while postcolonial Indian law developed into a largely codified legal system with a rich jurisprudence.

Currently popular understandings of Hindu law are influenced by a resurgence of religious identity ('hindutva' or Hinduness) and Hindu nationalism, often seeking to appropriate Hindu texts as binding legal rules. Many Hindus portray their legal system as 'Vedic', but Hindu law is at the same time ancient and new, a dynamic, extremely diverse, and constantly developing system. Nothing was ever set in stone, or just derived from ancient religious scriptures, which Hindus need not accept as a matter of belief. Consequently, the prominent basis of ancient scriptural texts remains debatable and Hindu law is in reality largely a common law constantly developed through customary practice, ancient recorded statements of elite Brahmins, and more recent state interventions, including a remarkably activist case law.

The ancient texts, written in the complex Sanskrit language, include collections of *smritis* ('remembered knowledge'), specifically *dharmasūtra* and *dharmaśāstra*, the 'science of righteousness', developed by a literate Brahmin elite, with important moral guidance on the idealized, highly sophisticated ethical roots of Hindu law. European interpretations created the misguided image of ancient Napoleonic lawmakers, leading to popular misrepresentation of the rich *Manusmriti* text, for example, as 'the laws of Manu'. To appreciate the enormous (and at the same time liberating and confusing) fluidity of basic Hindu law principles, one has to be aware of the key concept of duty or 'righteousness' (*dharma*), the obligation on every individual to do 'the right thing' at all times. This basic postulate constantly needs to be worked out in specific socio-cultural contexts; extremely dynamic, it leads to fine-tuned concepts of *varnāśramadharma*, a person's obligations (*dharma*) at any stage of life (*āśrama*) and depending on caste status (*varna*).

Acute awareness in Hindu law that fixed rules for all might cause injustice means that flexible situation-specificity is preferred to promote and measure appropriate behaviour. To outsiders, the whole system appears to make endless distinctions, discriminating on the basis of caste, gender, and age. But by treating every individual radically as a separate entity or microcosm, yet viewing all as interlinked through a common conceptual bond as part of a macrocosmic Order (*rita*) or secular Truth (*satya*), Hindu law overcomes the inherent contradictions between uniformity and difference, focusing on appropriate action (*dharma*) by any individual in a particular scenario, with a view to promoting the common good or public interest. Such concepts have, therefore, spawned ultra-modern perceptions of good governance and corporate responsibility, which Hindus claim to have known long before other people.

Today's Hindu law still largely respects the individual as ultimate agent of determining 'the law' in any particular situation and does not take the state alone as lawmaker. The results of such sophisticated methods of finding law appear often messy, unregulated and confusing. For example, Hindus in India marry according to customary rites and ceremonies (section 7 of the Hindu Marriage Act 1955); and no state registration is required for the legal validity of a marriage. Divorce, frowned upon as deviating from the ideal of permanent marriage (*samskāra*), was always permitted under custom and is now allowed through Hindu statute law on many grounds, though reluctantly. However, under Indian secular law, in a patriarchal system without state benefits, constitutional considerations imply that not only a Hindu wife under the *samskāra* principle, but any divorced Indian wife remains a 'wife' for social welfare purposes, so that women can rely on pre-existing rights to support and maintenance, putting men under obligations to share family resources. Modern efforts to grant Hindu daughters independent property rights from birth, found in the Hindu Succession (Amendment) Act of 2005, now co-exist with ancient Hindu concepts of joint family property, in which only male individuals used to hold a fluctuating share and take by survivorship rather than testate or intestate succession, while women were entitled to marriage expenses and maintenance out of joint family funds. The joint Hindu family system was abolished by statute in some parts of India, especially Kerala, but in social reality, concepts of interlinkedness, duty towards dependants, solidarity with close kin, and shared ownership continue to be strong.

Hindu law, not only in India, remains a vibrant legal system.   WERNER MENSKI

W Menski, *Hindu Law. Beyond Tradition and Modernity* (New Delhi: Oxford University Press, 2003)
VP Nanda and SP Sinha (eds), *Hindu Law and Legal Theory* (New York: New York University Press, 1996)

See also: **custom as a source of law**

hire-purchase Hire-purchase was a central method of selling goods on credit to middle and working class consumers during the twentieth century. It remains an important form of consumer credit in the UK notwithstanding the growth of credit cards and lines of credit. Hire-purchase is, however, a legal sham designed to protect the supplier and avoid regulation. It is in substance a grant of security over goods under which the seller relies on the goods sold as a guarantee of repayment. However, the **House of Lords** confirmed the legitimacy of this sham device in a test case in 1895. It held that because the transaction was a hire with the option to purchase, a person hiring goods could not pass a good title to a third party (such as a pawnbroker) and the owner could retake possession of the goods immediately on nonpayment. Since hire-purchase was not conceptualized as in substance a form of **mortgage of chattels** it also avoided the early consumer protection provisions associated with mortgages of goods in the Bills of Sale Acts 1878 and 1882, which are still in force.

Hire-purchase benefitted consumers by enabling individuals to purchase consumer goods that were often associated with social status and that they could not afford to purchase with cash. However, there was a dark side to hire-purchase. It was a costly form of credit; and it was often subject to unfair terms such as high depreciation payments if an individual returned hired goods and terms conferring a license on the owner to enter the hirer's property to repossess goods. Often no warranty was given concerning the quality of the goods. Finally, there was the 'snatch back.' This referred to the practices of certain companies that often repossessed goods on minor defaults even where an individual had almost paid for the goods. At **common law** there was no protection against this right of repossession. Although the snatch back had been noted in the late nineteenth century it was not regulated until 1938, when a private members Bill resulted in the Hire Purchase Act 1938. This required a court order for repossession when at least one-third of the purchase price had been paid, limited charges that could be made for returned goods, required owners to provide consumers with information about terms and a copy of the agreement, and avoided clauses that permitted lenders to go on to the purchaser's premises. Updated versions of these provisions now exist in the Consumer Credit Act 1974 which, notwithstanding other major changes it made to consumer credit law, retained the artificial concept of hire-purchase.

IAIN RAMSAY

historic rights   *see* **territory**

historical jurisprudence Historical jurisprudence was an influential school of jurisprudence in the nineteenth century, but one that currently has few adherents. It offered broad claims about the relationship of society, history, and law (in much the same way that certain forms of **Marxist legal theories** did). Historical jurisprudence asserts that communities go through predictable stages, and that the community's laws do or should reflect the community's stage of development. The two most prominent theorists associated with historical jurisprudence are Friedrich Carl von **Savigny** (1779–1861) and Henry **Maine** (1822–1888).

Henry Maine's historical approach to law was a sharp departure from the analytical approach that had been promoted by John Austin (1790–1859), and which had become prominent in England at the time Maine was writing. Maine offered a theory of legal evolution, under which law changes to reflect and facilitate social and cultural change. Based on historical work that ranged from ancient **Roman law** and **Irish law** to **Indian law** and modern **European law**, Maine argued that all legal systems go through certain set stages. His views on legal evolution were detailed in his best-known work, *Ancient Law* (1861). In that text, Maine famously wrote that 'we may say that the movement of the progressive societies has hitherto been a movement *from Status to Contract*'.

Savigny's work on historical jurisprudence was initially prompted by the 1814 proposal of a Heidelberg professor, Anton Friedrich Justus Thibaut (1772–1840), that German law be codified. Savigny argued in response that codification was only appropriate after the organic nature of a society's law is understood, along with the fundamental principles that reflect the 'common consciousness of the people' (*Volksgeist*). Savigny argued that law, like language, expresses the culture, spirit, customs, and history of a people. Savigny's work might be included with the ideas of Johann Gottfried von Herder (1744–1803) and some of the Romantic writers of the period, to be seen as a (German) nationalist response to (French) universalist thinking.

For Savigny, since law should, and usually does, reflect a community's stage of development, putting law into unchanging statutes runs the risk of stalling law into a prior stage of development that does not fit where the community currently is. The 1814 codification proposal for Germany was eventually rejected, and Savigny's arguments went on to be influential later in the century in the rejection, across the Atlantic, of an ambitious Civil Code for the State of New York.

Historical jurisprudence was analogous to the (often unarticulated) theories of the English **common law**: both approaches centring on the idea that legal norms were grounded and justified from below, from the people (their practices, customs, and culture), rather than from above (as the legal positivist command theorists, like Austin, argued), from the whim of the sovereign.

Some commentators have seen historical jurisprudence as a necessary third alternative to **natural law theory** (understood as connecting legal norms to universal and timeless moral truths) and **legal positivism** (understood as emphasizing the connection between law and political will); in this context, historical jurisprudence emphasizes the way that legal norms and institutions develop over time, and the way that different societies may require different norms and institutions.

The basic point of historical jurisprudence might be that history has normative force: that which has come before, and the way that we have dealt with circumstances before, matters. Reduced to this claim, one can see that the same animating principle permeates law—most obviously in the working of **precedent**. Law in general, and common law systems in particular, are grounded on the idea that something is justified, or even authoritative, to the extent it has been done before.

Historical jurisprudence, narrowly and conventionally understood, faded with the diminished faith, at least among theorists, in grand narratives in societal history (whether Marxist, Hegelian, Whig, or other). Additionally, though both legal sociologists and legal historians regularly claim to find connections between social conditions and a community's laws, and many theorists offer arguments about the connections between history and the development of certain, specific areas of law, there is little or no convincing work finding grand patterns that have held true across all societies and all periods of history. One can also find elements of historical jurisprudence (in particular, Maine's work) in aspects of modern legal anthropology.   BRIAN BIX

HJS Maine, *Ancient Law* (New York: Cosimo Classics, 2005) (first published, 1861)

FC von Savigny, *On the Vocation of Our Age for Legislation and Jurisprudence* (Abraham Hayward, trans, Lawbook Exchange, Ltd, 2002) (translation first published in 1831; original in 1814)

See also: **anthropology and law; codes and codification in national law; legal positivism since 1970; legal positivism to 1970**

historical research in law   Lawyers often resort to historical sources describing the origin of legal rules, in order to find persuasive authority within a system of **precedent** that dictates loyalty to past decisions. Historical research can thus advance professional objectives as lawyers strive to promote their clients' causes. However, in a modern system of precedent involving a unified pyramidical structure of **courts** topped by a legislature, historical inquiry in search of legal authority will be cut short once the most recent appellate judgment or statute is found. This is why **Maitland** quipped that lawyers want authority, as recent as possible, whilst legal historians will want evidence of the law, its sources, as old as possible. The easy likeness of professional-legal and historical-legal research is thus far more difficult than it seems, and it is not always obvious why modern lawyers need know any legal history. However, lawyers may have a genuine interest in the historical descent of rules for broader professional reasons. Where recent law does not speak clearly, or where the policy of the law seems obnoxious to modern needs and sensibilities, historical understanding of the evolution of rules may assist in attempts to understand and change the law and break away from old precedents. Historical consciousness is thus an essential part of the training of the lawyer who seeks to develop the law wisely as a system. This can help explain the remarkable dominance of **historical jurisprudence** in nineteenth century Germany, as Romanist and Germanist legal scholars vied in their researches to wrest control over the creation of a modern legal system, culminating in the promulgation of the German Civil Code in 1900 as a proud synthesis of doctrinal history. Likewise, some of the most formidable thinkers of the modern **common law** tradition, from **Maine** through **Holmes**, Maitland, **Pollock**, **Dicey** and Salmond to Atiyah and Birks, have been steeped in historical enquiry as they sought to shape legal doctrine along modern rational lines. This historical mentality amongst jurists has faded in the later twentieth century, however. Legal historical research has a much smaller part to play in the legal academy, and historical knowledge in the manner of Maitland, **Holdsworth**, Ames, or Holmes (for common lawyers) or **Savigny**, Jhering, or Gierke for German lawyers, is no longer a prerequisite for claiming authority or intellectual mastery of the law. Roman legal science has also faded across Europe, the US, and the UK, involving a loss of longer-term historical perspectives regarding legal structure and doctrine. Exceptional scholars such as Zimmermann continue to combine Roman and later legal history with modern doctrinal discourse, and mixed systems such as South Africa, Louisiana, and Scotland have also maintained a lively historical consciousness in their law schools. But a telling sign of the decline of legal history in the past three decades has been the eradication of historical material from leading texts in nearly every common law subject from contract and tort to **constitutional law**, company law, and **evidence**. Legal history, understood as lawyers studying the origins of their mental world and their rules and institutions, has become more a technical specialism than part of mainstream law.

Modern historical research into law maybe divided into two streams. A highly professionalized and sophisticated community of scholars in the common law world look to Maitland for inspiration in striving to penetrate the complex legal mentalities of the past. Maitland began his career by producing accurate editions of the vast trove of common law materials as an essential prelude to recreation of the legal past, and the Selden Society that Maitland helped found in 1887 plays a leading role in editing legal literatures from the earliest reports of the twelfth century onwards. Maitland's influence also rests on the aphoristic grace of his writing and his rare combination of imagination and accuracy in recovering the legal past, expressed most perfectly in his *History of English Law* (with Pollock, 1895). Maitland demonstrated the great rewards that legal-historical research could bring in reconstructing the medieval legal and social world and as a result he is still counted as one of England's greatest historians, a hero of professional scholars if little known to the reading public. Scholars such as Milsom, Thorne, Helmholz, Donahue, Baker, Ibbetson, Wormald, and Brand have carried the Maitland tradition of legal historical research forward into our times.

A second stream of historical research looks not to Maitland but to another great figure of the *fin de siecle*, Holmes, who published his own epochal work, *The Common Law* in 1881. Holmes was a pragmatic and policy-driven lawyer as well as an imaginative and questing scholar of legal doctrine, and it was his pragmatic message that prevailed. Scholars such as Pound and Hurst called for a more sociological historical scholarship, which turned away from scrutiny of the internal world of lawyers' debates and instead stressed the role of law in practical governance, addressing the hidden ideological meanings of the law. The breakthrough work in this new tradition was Horwitz's *Transformation of American Law 1780–1960* published in 1977, which borrowed from Weber and Marx to construct a thoroughly ideological 'external' account of American common law doctrine. Coming after the civil rights conflicts of the 1950s and 1960s, Horwitz's polemical message struck a deep chord in America and excited a new burst of historical research. Much of the new legal history focused on the role of law in articulating the interests and conflicts of business, of labour, and of interest groups in government and society, with a special interest in locating law within the themes of **slavery**, **race**, and **gender**. There were like movements away from 'internal' and towards 'external' legal history outside the US. **Commonwealth** scholars were particularly concerned with the legal form of colonial and post-colonial relations between native and settler peoples. A distinctive British Marxist school emerged studying the social history of crime and criminal law. More recently, some scholars have introduced economic methodologies and research agendas into their legal history to produce a new and fruitful subgenre. Yet another approach, pioneered by Simpson, is to write a detailed history of a famous case and show how the heat of historical contingency shaped the law.

Sometimes scholars practising the 'external' style of legal history deride the 'internal' school as antiquarian lawyers who do not practise a satisfying form of history addressing material, social and cultural development. The reverse criticism is sometimes voiced that 'external' historians have abandoned all interest in the internal qualities of law and have converted history into ideological rhetoric of no lasting value. Maitland's work needs only to be read carefully to see how the best historical research in the law manages to throw light on both law and the society within which that law operates. The most important message of historical research—that we better understand the nature of law and its role in society if we study its changing qualities over time—has not lost its potency, despite differences amongst its practitioners as to how best to carry on the business.

JOSHUA GETZLER

F Pollock and FW Maitland, *The History of English Law before the Time of Edward* I, 2 vols (1895, 2nd edn, Cambridge, 1898, reprinted 1968 with an introduction by SFC Milsom)
MJ Horwitz, *The Transformation of American Law 1780–1860* (Cambridge, Massachusetts, 1977)

HIV/AIDS The law represents both a source of protection and a challenge for people living with HIV and AIDS ('PLHA'). It is a protection because it is the most important means through which PLHA may assert the right to health (as articulated in various international **human rights** instruments), and to freedom from discrimination (through **disability** rights **legislation**). It is a challenge because it regulates the conduct and behaviour of PLHA (by imposing criminal liability on those who transmit HIV to others, and restrictions on liberty via **public health** legislation), makes it harder to take advantage of particular products and services (eg by allowing insurance companies to restrict access to life assurance), and may limit the availability and affordability of effective antiretroviral treatment (through the intellectual property rights that pharmaceutical companies have in the drugs they manufacture and distribute).

In 1987 AIDS became the first disease to be debated on the floor of the UN General Assembly. At that meeting it was recognized that an effective response to the HIV/AIDS pandemic would depend on the effective promotion and enforcement of human rights. Such rights are important, both in empowering PLHA and reducing the adverse physical and social impact of infection on them, and in reducing the vulnerability of those at risk of HIV infection. Human rights are of particular importance because the pattern of the epidemic is such that it has a disproportionate impact on those already economically, culturally, and politically marginalized, eg injection drug users, sex workers, **refugees** and displaced people, men who have sex with men, and—especially in the developing world—women. Although neither HIV nor AIDS are mentioned specifically in any of the principal international human rights treaties (AIDS was only identified in 1981), many of the rights they assert, such as the right to health, non-discrimination, and **equality**, respect for private life, to marry and found a family, liberty and **security** of the **person**, are of critical importance to PLHA. Of particular relevance are the *International Guidelines on HIV/AIDS and Human Rights*. These Guidelines are intended to provide a framework for a rights-based approach to HIV/AIDS that can be implemented at national level, and affirm *inter alia* the importance of a coordinated rights-based response (involving not only the state, but **community**-based organizations), community consultation, appropriate review, reform and deployment of public health and criminal laws, the need for effective anti-discrimination legislation, and for legislation facilitating the availability of prevention, treatment, care, and support products and services.

States and **courts** have responded in different ways and with varying degrees of commitment to the principles articulated in the Guidelines. In the UK, for example, the Disability Discrimination Act 1995 was amended in 2005 to protect people living with HIV from unfair treatment in the workplace, education, housing, and access to services from the point of diagnosis, rather than being limited to protecting those with symptomatic infection. As such, the legislation acknowledges the fact that simply being infected with HIV can result in discriminatory treatment. In stark contrast, the **European Court of Human Rights** held Sweden to be in breach of Article 5 of the **European Convention on Human Rights** (the right to liberty and security of the person) where its public health legislation allowed for the indeterminate detention of a person living with HIV so as to prevent him from transmitting the virus to others (*Enhorn v Sweden* (2005)).

Of the many human rights that PLHA need to be able to assert effectively, the right to health is arguably the most important. This right, expressed, eg in Article 25 of the Universal Declaration of Human Rights, is one that may come into conflict with the private sector's interest in reaping the rewards of investment in the development of antiretroviral drugs. Under the **World Trade Organization**'s ('WTO') Trade-Related Aspects of International Property Agreement ('TRIPs'), member states of the WTO are required to grant pharmaceutical companies twenty-year monopolies on their technological innovations. The concern of many states—especially in the developing world—was that TRIPs should be interpreted in such a way that it would be possible to deal effectively with the HIV/AIDS pandemic. As a result, the Doha Declaration of 2001 affirmed that TRIPs 'can and should be interpreted and implemented in a manner supportive of WTO members' right to protect public health and, in particular, to promote access to medicines for all'. This victory, which has been critically important in those resource-poor countries and regions most affected by HIV, does not, however, assist those unable to access treatment in countries where it is available because of their legal status. In the UK, for example, public concern about 'treatment tourism' resulted in an amendment to the NHS charging regulations so that those refused **asylum** or leave to remain, but not removed, have to pay for their HIV treatment and are thus denied it if they lack the means to pay.

One of the most morally complex and legally problematic areas of law impacting on PLHA is liability for the onward transmission of HIV, or for exposing others to the **risk** of transmission. In some jurisdictions, notably in some US states, PLHA have been charged with offences ranging from assault to attempted murder, in cases involving not only sexual activity but spitting, biting, and the selling of blood. In England and Wales there have been a number criminal cases in which people have been convicted under section 20 of the Offences against the Person Act 1861 for transmitting HIV to sexual partners. To establish liability for this offence the **prosecution** must prove that the defendant in fact transmitted HIV and was, at the time, reckless as to whether HIV would be transmitted (ie that he was aware of the risk of transmission). In *R v Dica* (2004), the English Court of Appeal determined that it was open to a defendant to argue that the complainant had consented to the risk of transmission. In so doing, it distinguished *R v Brown* (1993), a case in which the **House of Lords** had held that consent was held not to be available as a defence where bodily harm was deliberately inflicted in the context of consensual sado-masochistic sex. In *R v Konzani* (2005), the Court of Appeal elaborated on the decision in *R v Dica* and held that although an honest belief in consent would be a valid defence, it would be unlikely to succeed in the absence of prior disclosure of known HIV positive status by a defendant to the complainant. (In English law there is no positive duty of disclosure, unlike in Canada where the Supreme Court has held that there is such an obligation on a person who engages in sexual activity that carries a 'significant risk' of transmission (*R v Cuerrier* (1998).) Although consent will frequently be the defence that

defendants plead, it is also possible to avoid liability if there is no proof to the criminal standard (ie beyond reasonable doubt) that the defendant was the cause of the complainant's infection. In *R v Collins* (2006), the defendant was acquitted on the direction of the judge after an expert virologist testified that, in her opinion, it was impossible to determine on the basis of phylogenetic testing (which enables comparison of HIV sub-types from different people) whether the defendant was the source of the HIV in the complainant's body.

The concern of those who oppose liability for reckless transmission centres on the potentially adverse public health impact which it may have, whether because it may operate for some as a disincentive to testing (since only those who know their HIV positive status can be legally reckless), to accessing medical advice and treatment (since giving a true account of a sexual history may result in that account being used as evidence for the prosecution in a criminal case), or to disclosing to a partner after unsafe sex has taken place (since such an admission, which might enable that partner to access post-exposure prophylaxis and so prevent the virus from taking hold, could constitute a confession of culpable behaviour). For those in favour of liability where proof of fault exists, the transmission of HIV is no different from any other case of causing serious bodily harm, and arguments from a public health perspective that emphasize the importance of shared **responsibility** for preventing onward transmission are misplaced because they fail to acknowledge either the potential deterrent effects that the threat of criminal liability may have, or the morally defensible position that those who in fact know their status are best placed to minimize the risk of onward transmission and should thus bear responsibility if that takes place. MATTHEW WEAIT

International Guidelines on HIV/AIDS and Human Rights (consolidated version) (Geneva: UNHCR/UNAIDS, 2006)

Report of the WHO European Region Technical Consultation, in collaboration with the European AIDS Treatment Group (EATG) and AIDS Action Europe (AAE), on the criminalization of HIV and other sexually transmitted infections (Copenhagen: World Health Organization, 2006)

Holdsworth, Sir William Sir William Holdsworth (1871–1944) was the Vinerian Professor of Law in the University of Oxford from 1922 to his death in 1944. He is best remembered as a legal historian, author of the monumental *History of English Law* which was published in sixteen volumes, four of them posthumous.

Holdsworth was educated at Dulwich College and Oxford, where he was a friend and contemporary of FE Smith, the future **Lord Chancellor** Lord Birkenhead. He was called to the Bar in 1896, but by this time he was already gravitating towards an academic career and was elected a fellow of St John's College, Oxford one year later. It was here that his reputation was made. He was tipped as a strong candidate to succeed AV **Dicey** to the Vinerian Chair in 1910, though in the event the electors chose WM Geldart and Holdsworth had to wait until the next vacancy.

In the years around 1900 there was a perceived need for a new history of English law. Maitland had been invited to write one in the 1890s, but his magisterial work ended in 1272. Edward Jenks was approached, but in 1901 he declined the invitation and referred the publishers to Holdsworth. He was an ideal choice. As Tutor in Law at St John's, he was teaching right across the legal curriculum, and so had a wide knowledge of the whole of English law, and alongside this he was a sensitive historian. Although the publishers had in mind a one-volume survey, Holdsworth recognized that what was wanted was a more encyclopaedic treatment, using all of the historical sources in print and taking account of the secondary literature to which he had access. He began work immediately, bringing out the first volume, a history of the **courts**, only two years later.

It is all too easy to underestimate Holdsworth's achievement in pulling together the *History of English Law*. He did no archival research of the sort which Maitland had pioneered, and took no account of scholarship in languages other than English or French. Large sections of the work read like a *precis* of others' writings with relatively little original input from Holdsworth himself; and description predominates over analysis. But the value of the *History* as a major work of synthesis is immense (and it has still not been superseded, though its scholarship is now inevitably dated), and a good deal of very sound judgment lay behind the seemingly descriptive façade of the volumes.

Although concentrating on legal history, Holdsworth remained a versatile lawyer and was a willing public servant. He lectured on Equity and **Constitutional Law** at the **Inns of Court** School of Law, and his knighthood was awarded for his valuable political work in India in the late 1920s. As much for his work on governmental committees dealing with constitutional matters as for his writings on legal history, he was made a member of the Order of Merit in 1943.

As well as being a major academic lawyer in his own right, Holdsworth gave a good deal of time and encouragement to others. He was a generous critic of other scholars' work, was active in the Society of Public Teachers of Law, continued to teach undergraduates—unpaid—after his appointment to the Vinerian Chair, and was always willing to attend and speak at meetings of undergraduate law societies. The Birmingham law students' society was named the Holdsworth Club in his honour.

DAVID IBBETSON

holidays, recreational   When booking a holiday, a number of elements may be involved: accommodation; transport—air flights, train journeys, coach travel; activities, such as excursions; equipment, such as car or ski hire; and services, such as tour guides, skiing lessons, spa treatments. Domestic law may cover the contract, but holidays outside the UK can also involve foreign laws and conflict of laws issues.

If the holidaymaker books each element separately with the person or organization providing that element, there will be contracts with each supplier; and if subsequent problems arise over what is provided, the consumer may be able to claim compensation for breach of that contract. Under UK law, the supplier of accommodation and services is required to take reasonable care in providing them, and this can include such matters as the safety of hotel premises (eg swimming pools, glass doors, balconies), the meals and excursions (eg un-seaworthy boats, delays).

Regulations required by the **European Union** give additional protection for package holidays. For this purpose, a package holiday is pre-arranged, sold at an inclusive price, and combines at least two elements of accommodation, transport, and other tourist services, such as excursions, car hire. Further, to be a package holiday it must last for at least twenty four hours or involve overnight accommodation. Holiday organizers (tour operators) are liable for any misleading information in brochures (as are retailers—travel agents). Specified information must be provided in brochures and before contracting and departure. There are restrictions on price revisions and significant alterations to essential terms and cancellations. There are also withdrawal rights for consumers and protection when a significant proportion of the services contracted for are not provided.

An important provision makes the contracting party liable to the consumer for the proper performance of the contract requirements, both by themselves and by other suppliers, such as foreign hoteliers, train companies, etc. Compensation for failing to perform the contract and for improper performance can be claimed unless the failure was:

(a) attributable to conduct of the consumer (eg missing the train by over-sleeping) or some other person unconnected with the provision of the services; (b) unforeseeable or unavoidable (eg a bomb-warning at a station); (c) an unusual or unforeseeable circumstance beyond the party's control, unavoidable even if reasonable care had been taken (eg unexpected severe weather conditions); (d) an event not reasonably foreseeable or preventable (eg industrial action).

Tour operators are also required to provide evidence that deposits are secure and that consumers can be repatriated in the event of insolvency of the operator. This is done by setting up bonding schemes, by providing insurance, or by holding monies in trust.

If damages are awarded for breach of a holiday contract, this can include compensation for the fact that the holiday has been spoilt, as well as for any out-of-pocket expenses, actual harm done, etc. If a booking has been made by one person on behalf of several others, the other members of the group may be able to claim directly in contract for their losses, as identified third parties. Alternatively, compensation for disappointment may be claimed on their behalf by the person making the booking.

DEBORAH PARRY

holidays (workers)   Before the Working Time Regulations came into force in 1998, there was no general legal entitlement for workers to take either a period of annual leave or any of the public holidays—currently the customary holidays on Christmas Day and Good Friday plus the six bank holidays—as **time** off work. Until 2007, the Working Time Regulations gave all workers the right to four weeks' annual leave in each year and the eight public holidays could count towards this entitlement. In order to reflect the intention to provide a right to four weeks' paid holiday in addition to public holidays, in October 2007 the entitlement was increased by four days a year and it will increase by a further four days with effect from April 2009. However, while a worker can agree to receive pay in lieu of these additional days, the basic four weeks' annual leave must be taken as holiday and it must also be taken in the holiday year to which it relates. Only when a worker leaves a job can payment in lieu of any untaken part of this four weeks' entitlement be made. For this purpose, a worker's holiday entitlement is deemed to accrue *pro rata* over the course of the leave year, which begins either on the date stated in a collective or workforce agreement or, in the absence of such an agreement, the date on which the worker's employment began and each subsequent anniversary of that date. The **European Court of Justice** has ruled that workers must be paid their holiday pay at the time at which they take their holiday entitlement. Provisions for holiday pay to be 'rolled up' as part of each weekly or monthly pay packet do not, therefore, comply with the law.

BOB SIMPSON

See also: **hours of work**

Holmes, Oliver Wendell Jr   Oliver Wendell Holmes Jr (1841–1935) is doubtless the most celebrated jurist in US history. He began a life in the law with study at Harvard and private practice in Boston, followed by a short stint as a Harvard law professor; twenty years on the Massachusetts Supreme Judicial Court; and then nearly three decades as Associate Justice of the **US Supreme Court**. A thrice-wounded veteran of the American Civil War and the eponymous son of a nationally renowned essayist, Holmes was very much a legend in his own time and is carefully studied to this day, admired for the power and originality of his ideas and the uncommon eloquence with which he expressed them.

Known during his half century on the bench as 'the Great Dissenter', Holmes parted ways with his judicial contemporaries over some of the most contentious issues of the era, defending the right of workers to picket; the right of citizens to protest against governmental action; and the constitutional authority of legislatures to enact maximum-hours and other labour-protection statutes. In each case, his position eventually found its way into US law, and a passage from his dissent in the maximum-hours case—'[The Constitution] does not enact Mr Herbert Spencer's Social Statics', an oft'-quoted shot across the bow of a nineteenth-century British devotee of *laissez faire*—captures Holmes's characteristic wit and reveals an engagement with philosophy and political theory that was and still is decidedly unusual among American judges.

But Holmes was no 'liberal'. One of his best-known opinions upheld the forced sterilization of the mentally infirm ('Three generations of imbeciles are enough'), and legal historians have noted that he played a significant role in developing the body of speech-restricting law he came later to decry. His reputation as a judicial 'maverick' has likewise been called into question by scholars who have parsed the immense volume of his opinions and concluded that he was, with rare exception, a most prudent jurist who hewed closely to **precedent**, even when he disagreed with it or thought it badly outdated.

Indeed, the continuing scholarly fascination with Holmes is focused less on his complex judicial legacy than on his extra-judicial writings—most particularly *The Common Law* (1881), written while Holmes was still in practice and earning him his Harvard faculty appointment, and 'The Path of the Law' (1897), an essay the recent centenary of which was the occasion for numerous scholarly treatments. The former opened with a powerful challenge to formalism, then the reigning legal orthodoxy in the US, and the latter elaborated that challenge considerably, developing ideas which greatly influence American legal theory to this day.

Thus, Holmes famously argued that the 'life of the law is not logic' but rather 'experience'—that moral and political theory, conscious and unconscious policy choices, and even human prejudices 'have had a good deal more to do than the syllogism' in determining the outcome of judicial decisions—anticipating by several decades American **legal realism** and its critique of the supposedly sharp distinction between **legislation** (which is forthrightly based on moral and policy choices) and adjudication (which on the orthodox view means merely 'following' or 'applying' rules already laid down). Much of the ensuing history of American jurisprudence consists of the efforts of orthodoxy's heirs to put Humpty-Dumpty back together again—to identify some distinctively 'legal' form of reasoning that distinguishes the judicial task—while Holmes's realist heirs delight each time in having another go at the shell first cracked by Holmes.

Holmes is likewise the source of the idea that law is best understood as the 'prophecies of what **courts** will do' and the closely related notion of the hypothetical 'bad man', whose monomaniacal desire to avoid the material consequences of legal non-compliance offers a useful heuristic for such prophesying. Missing the point, some Anglo-American theorists have critiqued the 'bad man' theory as legal nihilism, but Holmes's nascent effort to explore 'law in action'—as opposed to merely 'law on the books'—finds lively current expression in American 'law and society' scholarship (which focuses not only on what courts do but also on the role of prosecutors, government agencies, corporations, and other actors in legal production) as well as an important echo in American **critical legal studies** (which brought Holmes full circle with the insight that what **judges** say is part of what they do and worthy of close examination as ideology and **legal consciousness**).

RICHARD MICHAEL FISCHL

GE White, *Justice Oliver Wendell Holmes: Law and the Inner Self* (Oxford: Oxford University Press, 1993)

SJ Burton (ed), *The Path of the Law and Its Influence: The Legacy of Oliver Wendell Holmes, Jr* (Cambridge: Cambridge University Press, 2000)

Holy See   *see* **states**

home schooling   *see* **school admissions**

Home Secretary   The Home Secretary is a senior **Cabinet** minister and political head of the Home Office, which has responsibility for those internal affairs in England and Wales not assigned to other departments. The focus of the Home Office is protecting the public and its key responsibilities include the administration of justice, **criminal justice policy** and criminal law reform, the criminal justice agencies (**police**, prisons, and probation), and the inspectorates and boards which operate across the criminal justice system. On all these matters, the Home Secretary is accountable to Parliament. However, accountability for the police is complicated by the tripartite arrangement which divides responsibility between the Home Secretary, chief constables, and local Police Authorities. Similarly, accountability for prisons and probation may be confused by the separation of policy, which is the Home Secretary's responsibility, and operations, which are the responsibility of the National Offenders Management Service.

Home Secretaries are also responsible for the Passport Agency, the Immigration and Nationality Directorate, and a myriad of other activities which do not fit into other departments (eg electoral arrangements, fire and civil defence services, some public safety matters, community relations). Additionally, they exercise some of the Queen's prerogative powers (most controversially the Royal Pardon) and have a range of statutory functions, including making the ultimate decision in **extradition** cases, famously including that concerning General Pinochet in December 1998. Reformers argue for a rationalization of the Home Secretary's responsibilities, including the separation of criminal justice policy and its enforcement.

DIANA WOODHOUSE

See also: **criminal justice system: England and Wales, Northern Ireland**; *Pinochet* **case**; **royal prerogative**

home, accidents in   *see* **tort system**

homelessness   Homelessness is a statutory concept, being defined in the Housing Act 1996, which draws on the framework originally enshrined in the Housing (Homeless Persons) Act 1977. A person who applies as, and is found to be, statutorily homeless by a local housing authority is entitled to the provision of suitable accommodation by that authority (unless they have a local connection with another authority, and none with the authority to which the application was made).

There is a common misconception that statutory homelessness is a broad concept and/or that it reflects a particularly acute housing need. In fact, it is neither. Some of the most needy—asylum seekers and other persons from abroad, who have no accommodation and no financial means—are excluded from consideration. They are 'ineligible'. Besides crossing this threshold, an applicant must be shown to be homeless, in priority need, and not intentionally homeless. These terms are defined loosely, allowing local housing authorities considerable discretion. However, that discretion has also been tempered by increasingly interventionist judicial oversight.

Although, colloquially, homelessness often refers to a state of rooflessness, it is clear that it extends beyond this in law. Originally, homelessness was defined as having no accommodation available for the occupation not only of the applicant but also their household; but, as Lord Brightman once observed, nobody would say that Diogenes (who, reputedly, lived in a barrel) had accommodation. The current statutory definition of homelessness requires that the household has no accommodation available for their occupation 'which it would be reasonable for them to continue to occupy'. Continued occupation is deemed not reasonable if it is probable that this will lead to domestic or other violence against the applicant.

An applicant is in priority need if they fall into one or more of the categories in the legislation. This includes those with dependent children or who are pregnant, those who are vulnerable (which means less able to fend for themselves than an average homeless person in finding and keeping accommodation) as a result, for instance, of fleeing violence, or being a minor, or having been made homeless by an emergency.

An applicant will be intentionally homeless if they deliberately do, or fail to do, something in consequence of which they lose their accommodation, which was available for their occupation and which it would have been reasonable for them to continue to occupy.

Perhaps unsurprisingly, homelessness is a particularly contested area. Local authorities have little accommodation and there is pressure on them to reduce homelessness. On the other hand, homelessness is a prevalent feature of cities and other areas. An unsuccessful applicant may request a review by the local authority in their case, with a right of appeal to a county court on a point of law. Strict time limits apply for both processes, although there is some discretion to accept late applications.

DAVID COWAN

A Arden, C Hunter, and L Johnson, *Homelessness and Allocations* (London: Legal Action, 2006)

D Cowan, S Halliday with C Hunter, P Maginn, and L Naylor, *The Appeal of Internal Review* (Oxford: Hart, 2003)

homicide   Homicide is the killing of another **person** in circumstances that the law would deem criminally blameworthy. England and Wales are relatively peaceful societies although killings have risen over recent decades, from 620 in 1980 to 755 in 2006–2007. This may be compared with the US where, in 2006, there were 17,034 murders and non-negligent homicides. Reliability of data varies but England and Wales have a homicide rate of approximately 1.62 per 100,000 of the population whereas, in the US, the rate is 5.9, in Russia 19.8, and, in South Africa, 39.5. A comparison of cities in 2001 showed that, in EU capital cities, the average number of homicides was 2.3 per 100,000 of the population, with the highest rates in Belfast (5.6), Amsterdam (3.1), Stockholm (2.8) and London (2.6). There were higher rates in American cities: Washington DC (42.9) or New York NY (8.7). Perhaps the safest city in the world is Canberra with a rate of 0.64.

Both the killer and the **victim** are likely to be young, male, and from the poorest neighbourhoods. However domestic murders are also very common with perhaps two women a week killed by their male partners in the UK. Yet, it is the **child** under one year old who remains most at risk—with fifty deaths per million, they are about four times more likely than average to be killed. **Stranger** killings are still the exception—the victim and the killer will be blood relatives, spouses, lovers, or other acquaintances in over 60 per cent of cases. The cause of the killing is usually a quarrel, revenge, or loss of temper, with many fewer incidents being in furtherance of gain.

In all offences of homicide, the prosecution must show that the accused caused the death. At *common law*, this involved the ' . . . .unlawfully killing [of] a reasonable person who is in being and under the King's Peace, the death following within a year and a day' (*Coke's Institutes* 1597). The 'year and a day' rule was abolished in 1996. But where the accused has caused the death, the common law still distinguishes between several offences of homicide: murder, voluntary manslaughter, involuntary manslaughter, and specific statutory homicide offences.

To establish murder, the **prosecution** must prove that the defendant caused death and possessed 'malice aforethought'. This ancient and rather misleading phrase means that the defendant must have intended to kill or at least to cause serious bodily harm.

With voluntary manslaughter, all the elements of murder are present—the defendant has killed with intent but either the defendant's mental condition (diminished **responsibility** under section 2 of the Homicide Act 1957) or the circumstances of the killing (provocation under section 3, or a suicide pact under section 4) are seen as reducing the defendant's culpability. In all these contexts, the offence may be reduced from murder to manslaughter.

Involuntary manslaughter encompasses situations where the defendant causes the death of the victim but there is *no* intent to kill or seriously injure. The defendant must be shown to have acted either with gross negligence or in the furtherance of another criminal act, for example, an 'accidental' killing which occurs during a minor assault. Finally, English law also has specific homicide offences: this may be for particular types of victim, such as section 5 of the **Domestic Violence**, Crime and Victims Act 2004 which created the offence of allowing the death of a child or vulnerable adult; for particular types of defendant, the Corporate Manslaughter and Corporate Homicide Act 2007 renders a company criminally liable where its activities are organized so as to cause a person's death, and to amount to a 'gross breach' of a duty of care owed to the deceased; or where the death is caused in a particular manner, such as causing death by dangerous driving under section 1 of the Road Traffic Act 1988.

The need for such differentiation comes from the penalties attached. Murder involves a mandatory life sentence whereas the penalty for manslaughter is at the discretion of the **judge,** with the possible maximum of life. Some offences attract less—causing death by dangerous driving has a maximum of fourteen years imprisonment.

The boundaries between homicide offences have led to difficult doctrinal borders especially between murder and manslaughter, as well as in the development of defences such as diminished responsibility and provocation. Should the factors affecting moral blame best be dealt with in **sentencing**? It has been argued that there should be single offence of culpable homicide (see, eg section 222 of the Canadian Criminal Code). Any distinction in the moral blame attaching to the death would then be taken account of at the sentencing stage. Certainly the stigma attached to the current labels does vary—it is argued that murder is seen as a peculiarly heinous offence and should be clearly seen as such. But using the mental state of the defendant is a relatively uncertain guide to distinguish moral guilt—the battered wife who kills, the doctor who kills the terminally ill patient or the disabled child soon after birth, often attract little blame or moral stigma. Yet they are liable to a mandatory life sentence. STEVE UGLOW

See also: **corporate criminal liability; crime and violence; fault-based criminal liability; justification, mitigation and excuse in criminal law**

homosexuality Whilst 'homosexual' is generally understood to refer to male and female **same-sex relations**, explicit criminal prohibitions and related legal reform work has predominantly focused on male homosexual sex. Whilst **lesbians** may well have benefited from a failure to fall within the reach of the criminal law, some critics have linked this to a more pervasive and damaging invisibility of lesbian subjectivity in law and more generally. The last two decades, however, have seen **equality** and reform initiatives broaden to encompass legal reform beyond decriminalization, and to be inclusive of Lesbian, Gay, Transgendered, and Bisexual ('LGTB') equality concerns and issues.

Legal attitudes to homosexuality have followed the social liberalization in evidence since the 1960s. The early 1950s saw the **police** actively enforcing criminal prohibitions against gay sex acts. This resulted in a number of high profile arrests and **prosecutions**. Legal liberalization arguably has its origins in public responses to these trials, in particular, in responses to the 1954 trial and conviction of Edward Montagu (3rd Baron Montagu of Beaulieu), Michael Pitt-Rivers, and Peter Wildeblood. Shortly after, the **Home Secretary** agreed to appoint a committee to examine the law governing homosexual offences, in August 1954 appointing a Departmental Committee of fifteen men and women to consider both **prostitution** and 'the law and practice relating to homosexual offences and the treatment of **persons** convicted of such offences by the courts'.

The Report of the Departmental Committee on Homosexual Offences and Prostitution—to become popularly known as the Wolfenden Report—was published on 3 September 1957. The Report recommended that 'homosexual behaviour between consenting adults in private should no longer be a criminal offence', arguing that 'homosexuality cannot legitimately be regarded as a disease, because in many cases it is the only symptom and is compatible with full mental health in other respects'. Institutional responses to the Report were mixed and, in May 1958, the Homosexual Law Reform Society was founded. The Society's main objective was to campaign for the implementation of the Wolfenden Committee's recommendations.

The **House of Lords** was the first chamber to see an attempt at a legislative response to the Wolfenden Report. In 1965, Lord Arran proposed the decriminalization of gay sex. The same Bill was introduced in the **House of Commons** in 1967. Almost a decade after Wolfenden, this Bill was to become the Sexual Offences Act 1967, joining a raft of liberalizing **legislation** which was to help to define the decade. The Act partially decriminalized gay sex. Such sex was no longer illegal if it occurred in private between two consenting adults (in this instance the age of consent was set at twenty-one). The notion of 'private' was interpreted narrowly by the **courts**; for instance, it was held not to include consensual sex taking place in a hotel room. Similarly, sex taking place in the bedroom of a house in which someone was occupying a different room was held to fall outside the scope of **privacy**. The Act was also partial in that it did not extend to Scotland, Northern Ireland, the Channel Islands, or the Isle of Man.

The 1967 legislation was left largely untouched until the 1990s. Whilst the 1980s saw decriminalization extended to Scotland (by virtue of the Criminal Justice (Scotland) Act 1980, section 80) and Northern Ireland (as a result of the ECtHR case of *Dudgeon v United Kingdom* (1982)), homosexual legal rights and LGTB rights more generally were restricted with the passing of the Local Government Act 1988, section 28 of which provided that a local authority 'shall not intentionally promote homosexuality or publish material with the intention of promoting homosexuality' or 'promote the teaching in any maintained school of the acceptability of homosexuality as a pretended family relationship'. The legislation led to confusion over its applicability and enforceability. Nevertheless, the fear of prosecution produced a degree of self-censorship and indeed some LGTB student support groups in schools and colleges were closed. No successful prosecution was ever brought under the section. The Act, which had the effect of galvanizing gay rights activists, was repealed in June 2000 in Scotland and November 2003 in the rest of the UK.

In February 1994, Conservative MP, Edwina Currie, tabled an amendment to the Criminal Justice and Public Order Bill to equalize the age of consent to sex to sixteen (as it was for heterosexual relations). Whilst the amendment garnered cross-party support it was defeated. However, an amendment to lower the age of consent to eighteen was passed

by 427 votes to 162. A final attempt in the House of Lords to equalize the age of consent at sixteen was rejected. On 1 July 1997 the **European Commission of Human Rights** found that the differential age of consent violated Articles 8 and 14 of the **European Convention on Human Rights**. It was held that there was no objective and reasonable justification for the higher minimum age for male homosexual sex. In June of the following year the Crime and Disorder Bill was put before Parliament. Amendments to the Act proposed equalization of the age of consent. The Commons accepted the provisions with a majority of 207, although the Lords subsequently rejected the amendment with a majority of 168. The Bill was reintroduced in December 1998 and was met with the same acceptance and rejection in the two chambers. Reintroducing the Bill for a third time in 1999, the Government announced its intention to use the **Parliament Act** to realize the change in law regardless of the wishes of the Lords. The Lords again rejected the Bill. On the 30 November 2000, the Parliament Act was invoked and the Sexual Offences (Amendment) Act 2000 received Royal Assent a few hours later.

Further reform of the law followed the equalization of the age of consent. Equality campaigns and legal responses widened the focus beyond sex. November 2004 saw the enactment of the **Civil Partnership** Act allowing same-sex couples to enter into a civil union with all of the rights of a **marriage**. The Act remains controversial both in excluding heterosexual couples from the benefits of civil partnership and excluding same-sex couples from marriage. Some critics also contend that the failure of the legislation to recognize differences between homosexual and heterosexual relationships creates a hierarchy which distinguishes 'good' homosexuals (those who civilly partner) from those who chose not to do so. Whilst there remains discrimination in the legal recognition of same-sex relationships there have been moves to challenge discrimination in other arenas. Perhaps most notably, April 2007 was marked by the coming into force of the Sexual Orientation Regulations outlawing discrimination in the provision of goods and services on the grounds of sexual orientation. This follows previous legislation in 2003 prohibiting sexual orientation discrimination in relation to employment.　　　　　MICHAEL THOMSON

See also: **privacy; queer politics**

homosexuality and education　*see* **secular curriculum in schools**

honour killings Honour killings involve the murder or attempted murder of a woman by close relatives for having brought dishonour on the family and are one of many manifestations of male notions of proprietary ownership over the female body, possessiveness, and sexual jealousy which contributes to the global problem of violence against women. Shameful conduct can include talking to a male, having a pre-marital relationship, or dressing provocatively. Both the Jordanian (Articles 340 and 98) and Pakistani (section 306; 302(c); 338-F; and 300 (1)) Penal Codes contain provisions which allow for anything up to a complete reduction in penalty where the killing is motivated by perceived transgressions of honour. Within the British context, honour killings are viewed as an 'ethnic' problem, and have recently received much media attention, and the Metropolitan **Police** are now reviewing up to 100 cases from the last ten years to learn more about the nature and scale of the problem.

However, there is a major disparity in the **courts'** treatment of perpetrators of honour killings and perpetrators of crimes of passion (where white men kill their partners/former partners). In the former, sentences range from fourteen to sixteen years, whereas in the latter, sentences can be as low as three-and-a-half years. This incongruity in treatment can be attributed to a number of factors—the presence of 'culture' versus 'non-culture'; perceptions of remorse; the relationship between **victim** and killer—in crimes of passion, the victim is often a former/current sexual partner, whereas in honour killings, the victim is often a daughter, sister, or cousin and so the act is viewed with greater abhorrence. It is suggested that underlying all of these factors is a culturally imperialistic and racist stance which views honour killings as barbaric acts representative of the whole, and crimes of passion as aberrant instances perpetrated by random individuals. Ultimately, both can be seen as acts of femicide or, in the words of Jill Russell, 'womanslaughter'.

SONYA FERNANDEZ

horizontal agreement   A horizontal agreement (which is to be distinguished from a **vertical agreement**) is one between firms operating at the same level of the market or economy. Normally, this is taken to mean an agreement between competitors, whether actual or potential competitors. **Competition law** prohibits such agreements that have the object or effect of restricting **competition**. An anticompetitive object can be shown by reference to the clauses or terms of the agreement. An anti-competitive effect, on the other hand, requires detailed assessment of the impact of the agreement on competition. A horizontal anti-competitive agreement

may be the backbone of a **cartel**. A horizontal agreement may be concluded orally or in writing and may be formal, informal, or merely a gentlemen's agreement. When seeking to show the existence of an anti-competitive agreement, competition authorities usually look for the existence of 'concurrence of wills' or 'meeting of minds' on the part of two or more firms.

It is important to note, however, that not every horizontal agreement is harmful to competition and consumers. In fact some horizontal agreements can be very beneficial—for instance where the purpose behind the agreement is that the competitors should engage in joint research and development activities which they would not be able to conduct individually.

MAHER DABBAH

horizontal application of human rights   Human rights protections usually ensure that rights are not breached by the state—for example local authorities, immigration officials, and the **police**. The horizontal application of **human rights** occurs when private institutions and individuals are required to protect human rights. There are two main ways in which rights can have horizontal application. First, human rights may have direct horizontal application. This means that an individual can rely upon a human right itself before the **court**, arguing that the action of a private individual harmed her right. Secondly, human rights may have indirect horizontal application. This occurs when other provisions of the law are used to protect human rights. Imagine that a newspaper printed a story about Sophie's extra-marital affair. If human rights had direct horizontal application, Sophie would be able to protect her right to privacy as the law would impose an obligation upon the newspaper not to print stories that breached her right to privacy. If human rights had indirect horizontal application, Sophie would have to find another provision of the law to protect her right to **privacy**. If, for example, the newspaper had obtained the story from Sophie's counsellor, the newspaper may have breached its obligation in tort not to print information that it obtained through a breach of confidentiality. The court would interpret this obligation broadly so as to protect Sophie's right to privacy.

The direct horizontal application of human rights appears attractive. Human rights are fundamental rights that could be harmed by other individuals as well as by the state. Surely an individual should be able to protect their human rights from all possible invasions. This argument is particularly strong where private individuals perform activities that are similar to those performed by the state. It is for this reason that section 6 of the **Human Rights Act 1998** provides a broad definition of the state, requiring all those performing a public service to ensure that their fulfilment of the public service does not breach human rights protections.

However, there are arguments against the direct horizontal application of rights. An indirect horizontal application of rights may suffice given the breadth of statutory and **common law** obligations imposed upon individuals which indirectly protect human rights. This is particularly the case given section 3(1) of the Human Rights Act 1998, which requires courts, where possible, to interpret statutes in a manner compatible with the **European Convention of Human Rights**. Secondly, a direct horizontal application of some human rights may impose unclear and onerous burdens on individuals, as human rights come into conflict with one another. In our example, Sophie's protection of her right to privacy conflicts with the newspaper's right to **freedom of expression**. To protect her right to privacy may require the newspaper to limit its right to freedom of expression. Also, Sophie's right to privacy could be interpreted so as to respect the newspaper's right to freedom of expression and vice-versa; from which we can see how the direct horizontal application of rights may impose unclear obligations.

ALISON YOUNG

horizontal equity in taxation   *see* **tax, ability to pay**

hospital complaints   About 2 per cent of patients admitted to acute care hospitals suffer harm that is serious, avoidable, and caused by healthcare; some (but not all) of these (or their families) will complain. Hospitals may also receive various complaints from patients who have not been harmed, from visitors, and from other people. Inadequate communication is often a cause of complaint and open disclosure should be part of any hospital's policy for responding to adverse events.

Complaints are important for improving the quality of healthcare, and should be encouraged. Willingness to complain is influenced by culture, and seems to be increasing in many countries. Reasons for complaining include: concern with standards of care (and a desire to prevent future incidents); the need for an explanation; an expectation of **compensation**; and a desire for **accountability**. These reasons may justify taking complaints beyond the hospital (eg to disciplinary bodies or the civil **courts**), but if complaints can be dealt with

satisfactorily by the hospital, this will usually be less expensive, less traumatic, and quicker for everyone.

All hospitals today should have formal processes for dealing with complaints. Patients and staff should be informed about these. Health professionals should receive training in dealing with complaints. Complaints should be recorded, and when appropriate, other processes for responding to adverse events (such as root cause analysis and sentinel event reporting) should be initiated.

The aim should be to resolve complaints locally and promptly. Staff involved in a complaint should consult their hospital's complaints officer and a lawyer (who should be independent of the hospital, in case interests conflict; such consultation may be a requirement of medical indemnity organizations). A meeting between the involved staff member(s) and the complainant (with family or other supporters) should then be held as soon as possible. A senior clinician not directly involved with the complaint should also attend. Preferably, lawyers should not. The fact that the complainant feels aggrieved should be acknowledged empathically. If the cause of the complaint is clear (eg the patient has been injured) then an apology should be given. This does not imply admission of liability, which should only occur with legal advice.

Notes should be taken, and a letter prepared in liaison with the complaints department and the consulted lawyer. It should summarize the discussion, outline a plan to resolve the complaint, and explain the complainant's options for taking matters further if he or she wishes to do so.   ALAN F MERRY

B Runciman, A Merry and M Walton, *Safety and Ethics in Healthcare: A Guide to Getting it Right* (Aldershot: Ashgate Publishing Limited, 2007)

hostile witnesses   *see* **evidence (criminal)**

hot pursuit   *see* **law of the sea**

hours of work   Legal regulation of the working time of at least some workers goes back to the beginning of the nineteenth century, but for almost 200 years it applied only to particular types of work and some of the **legislation** only imposed limits on the hours of work of **women** and young persons. Virtually all these provisions have now ceased to apply and the hours of work of most workers in Great Britain are subject to some degree of regulation by the Working Time Regulations 1998, which implement European Community directives. Similar provision is made in the separate regulations which apply in Northern Ireland. The best known and most controversial of

these regulations limits a worker's working time to forty-eight hours per week, averaged over seventeen weeks or any longer period of up to fifty-two weeks where this is agreed in a **collective agreement** with a **trade union** or workforce agreement with representatives of the workers concerned. Workers can 'opt out' of this right by written agreement with their employer, which can be terminated by an agreed period of written notice of at least seven days but not more than three months. 'Night work', a specified period of at least seven hours including the period from midnight to 5.00 am is limited to eight hours a day, averaged over seventeen weeks. For young workers under eighteen the maximum hours of work are eight a day and forty a week, with no night work permitted. In addition to the possibility of opting out of the maximum weekly hours, neither these rights nor the 'entitlements' referred to below apply to workers such as managing executives or 'other **persons** with autonomous decision making powers' whose working time is not measured or can be determined by the worker himself or herself.

As well as these 'rights', the Working Time Regulations provide a number of 'entitlements' for workers. All workers are entitled to a 'daily rest' period of eleven hours—twelve for young workers—in each twenty-four hour period. A 'weekly rest' entitlement of twenty-four hours in each seven days, or forty-eight hours in each fourteen days, must be given. Where daily working time exceeds six hours, workers have an entitlement to a rest break which must be either in accordance with a collective agreement or workforce agreement, or an interrupted period of at least twenty minutes. For young workers the entitlement is to a break of at least thirty minutes after four and a half hours work. These 'entitlements' are enforceable by actions in employment tribunals. While the Working Time Regulations are a 'health and safety' measure and the Health and Safety Executive is responsible for enforcing many of their requirements, it has been held that a worker has a right under his or her **contract of employment** to enforce the forty-eight hour week in the civil **courts**.   BOB SIMPSON

See also: **health and safety in the workplace; holidays (workers)**

House of Commons   The House of Commons is the directly elected House of the UK Parliament. It has currently 646 Members who each represent a single constituency, with the candidate being elected who obtains the largest number of votes in the constituency. General Elections to the Commons must

be held every five years, but in practice they are held within that period.

The House normally sits in plenary session in its own Chamber and also, since 1999, in 'Westminster Hall'; however, a substantial amount of parliamentary business is conducted away from the Chambers, in committee.

Constitutionally, the House has three principal roles. The first relates to legislation: the consideration and approval of **legislation**, principally primary but to an extent secondary legislation, and also the consideration of proposed EU policies and draft legislation. **Public Bills** are considered in the House, with detailed consideration normally in committee; **Private Bills** are largely considered in committee. The scrutiny and consideration of secondary legislation and of EU policy and draft legislation are also mainly undertaken in committee.

The second role, in which the Commons is the predominant House, concerns public finance: authorizing taxation, authorizing money from public funds for government policies and administration ('supply'), and scrutinizing government expenditure. Other than the scrutiny of expenditure, usually in the first instance by the Comptroller and Auditor General and the Public Accounts Committee, much of this has become rather formal in modern times.

The third function is the scrutiny of government policy and administration. This is done by parliamentary question and debate, and since 1979, has been underpinned by the work of departmentally-related select committees. Members also use questions and various forms of debate to pursue grievances of individual constituents.

The efficacy of the Commons in performing these roles is affected by the degree of independence that it can reasonably maintain both from the government of the day and also from external influences. As the government normally commands a majority in the Commons, it is usually in a position to control Commons procedure and deliberations, although there are political limits to exercising such control.

To allow Parliament to carry out its functions and to protect its members in doing so, and not without a degree of conflict with the courts, both Houses have historically claimed and enforced certain privileges and immunities for its members (some of which are now statutory), and also the exclusive right to regulate their own internal proceedings. Today the most significant of the privileges is freedom of speech, based on the Bill of Rights 1689, Article 9, which protects Members and others from any criminal or civil liability for anything said or done in respect of proceedings in Parliament. As part of regulating its own proceedings, each House may also punish both those who breach its privileges or otherwise commit a contempt of the House, and also those who breach its own rules. The latter includes failure of Members to register and declare their financial and other interests.   J BATES

See also: **House of Lords; parliamentary privilege; parliaments**

House of Lords The House of Lords is the second chamber of the **United Kingdom** Parliament. It is composed of Lords Spiritual and Lords Temporal, as it has been since it became a separate chamber from the **House of Commons** some 700 years ago. The Lords Spiritual are now the two Archbishops (of Canterbury and York), the Bishops of London, Durham, and Winchester, and the twenty-one other most senior diocesan bishops in the **Church of England**, with seniority measured from the date of an individual bishop's first appointment to any diocesan see. The Lords Temporal consist of three groups of peers. First are the ninety-two **hereditary peers** who continue to sit under provisions made in the House of Lords Act 1999, a number greatly reduced from the 750 hereditary peers who sat prior to that Act. Second are Life Peers created under the Life Peerages Act 1958; in October 2007 these totalled 605. Third are Life Peers created under the Appellate Jurisdiction Act 1876 ('Lords of Appeal in Ordinary'); these totalled twenty-five in 2007. Lords Spiritual cease to be members of the House when they retire (unless as individuals they are awarded life peerages). All other members have hitherto been members for life, but under the Constitutional Reform Act 2005, serving law lords (Lords of Appeal in Ordinary) will cease to be members of the House when the new Supreme Court is established, though those who have already retired will retain their life peerages. In 2007 the total membership of the House was around 750.

In political terms the House contains three roughly equal groups, Labour, Conservative, and Crossbench, with around 200 members each. There are some seventy-five Liberal Democrat peers. Not only does no party have a majority, but the governing party only has some 30 per cent of the total membership. The large group of Crossbench peers is unusual if not unique in any parliamentary chamber. Though the participation of Crossbench peers in divisions is lower than the participation rate for party peers, many Crossbench peers are active in the work of the House.

Though clearly the junior parliamentary chamber in political terms, the House of Lords makes a significant contribution to the work of Parliament. It is often referred to as a 'revising chamber' because it provides a parliamentary forum for discussing and amending the detail of legislation. Over half the time of the House is spent on this activity, mostly revising Bills brought up from the Commons, but also examining Bills first introduced into the Lords. The government is frequently defeated in the division lobby in the House, and though peers accept the deletion by the Commons of many of the changes they make to Bills, the work of the House of Lords does also result in many adjustments being made to government Bills. The House also engages in the classic scrutiny of government roles, with members having opportunities to ask questions and take part in non-legislative debate. The government is represented by some twenty to twenty-five who hold government office as ministers or whips, and other parties have their front-bench spokesmen in the House.

The scrutiny role of the House has been extended and deepened over the last thirty years through select committee work. In 1974 the House established a European Communities Committee to scrutinize EU matters including draft legislation, and this became for a time the major parliamentary means of providing such scrutiny, with up to 100 peers involved in a range of sub-committees. Subsequently sessional Select Committees on Science and Technology, Economic Affairs, and the Constitution have all been established. The House has also set up Select committees to improve the scrutiny of **delegated legislation**, notably the Delegated Powers and Regulatory Reform Committee and the Merits of Statutory Instruments Committee. *Ad hoc* Select Committees have been frequently used to examine topics or Bills, and in recent years more joint select committees have been set up to examine draft legislation.

The powers of the House in relation to taxation and public spending were constrained by Standing Orders passed by the Commons in the sixteenth century. These gave explicit expression to Commons financial privilege, which had been implicit in the emergence of separate Houses in the fouteenth century. The Parliament Act 1911 replaced the absolute veto the Lords had over legislation with a suspensory veto, initially of two years (one month for 'money bills'), but reduced to one year by the Parliament Act 1949. Since 1911 the Lords has not shown any desire seriously to contest the power of the Commons. Though the Labour Party for many years adopted a unicameralist stance, discussion about reform of the House has generally eclipsed debate about its possible abolition. The hereditary nature of the House was diluted by the arrival of life peers from 1958 onwards.

The Labour government elected in 1997 decided on a two-stage approach to reform of the House, first removing hereditary peers, then at a later date introducing a different basis for membership. In the event, the removal of hereditary peers was left incomplete, and no second stage of reform has yet taken place. Recent debate has focused around the possibility of a 'hybrid' House, with a proportion elected and a proportion appointed. In 2007 a government White Paper supported a House half-elected and half appointed, but the House of Commons then voted for an all-elected House, while the House of Lords voted for an all-appointed House. Ironically the post-1999 House, shorn of most of its hereditary members and thereby of its Conservative party preponderance, has become more confident and assertive than it was hitherto. The conventions which have constrained the role of the House have been placed under strain. If the membership of the House is reformed, and if the House is thereby perceived to possess greater legitimacy, then some attention may also have to be given to more precise definition of its powers.   DONALD SHELL

See also: **House of Lords reform; Parliament Acts**

House of Lords reform   The curious composition of the **House of Lords** has long made it a target for reformers. By the twentieth century it was one of just two parliamentary second chambers in advanced democracies to have no elected members—the other being the Canadian Senate. Despite numerous reform schemes being proposed, wholesale change has always proved elusive. Nonetheless, the chamber has developed gradually through a series of piecemeal steps.

Each reform to date has been seen as insufficient and temporary, intended as a stopgap until more comprehensive measures can be agreed. In 1911 the Parliament Act, which removed the Lords' power to veto legislation and replaced it with a delaying power, made no change to the chamber's membership. But its preamble stated the intention to create 'a Second Chamber constituted on a popular instead of hereditary basis'. No further action followed until the Parliament Act 1949, which again merely cut the chamber's power—despite Labour's official policy being abolition of the Lords, and the party having a large Commons majority. The Life Peerages Act 1958, introduced by the Conservatives as another temporary fix, implemented a proposal, which had been discussed for at least a century, to create a category of non-hereditary members of the House. The chamber was continually seen as 'unreformed', though these changes affected its role, culture, and behaviour in major ways.

The most notable reform failure was in 1968, when Harold Wilson's Labour government presented a complex Bill, which would have divided peers into voting and non-voting members and further cut the chamber's power. Such was the opposition on all sides of the Commons—with some wanting more radical reform and others seeking to defend the status quo—that the Bill was withdrawn. This episode serves as a cautionary tale for governments.

More recent reform has followed the established pattern. In 1999 Labour finally evicted the great majority of hereditary peers, although ninety-two remained as a result of a compromise amendment. A non-statutory Appointments Commission was established to vet prime ministerial nominations and select individuals to serve as non-party peers. But the promised further reform, despite establishment of a Royal Commission, did not follow. The Commission proposed a mixed elected-appointed chamber, but a government **White Paper** based on this model was rubbished by supporters of both election and appointment. In 2003 the Commons voted on seven alternate composition options, plus Lords abolition, and all were rejected.

The main barrier to reform is lack of agreement about the second chamber's role. The left was traditionally hostile to the Lords, which acted as a conservative force. But abolition proved too radical, and would have reduced Parliament's legislative capacity, while introducing elections would enhance the chamber's legitimacy to challenge government (and upset its established ethos). The issue splits both main parties, which have found many more pressing legislative priorities.

Although still seen as 'unreformed', the Lords today is very different from what it was a century ago, whilst the full impact of the 1999 change remains to be felt. A growing realization of this reform's significance, perhaps alongside further piecemeal reform, seems the likeliest future outcome.   MEG RUSSELL

See also: **Parliament Acts**

housing law   The origins of housing law can be traced back to concerns over poor sanitation in the early nineteenth century and to the cholera epidemics it produced. Early legal interventions were concerned with public health but gradually focused on the quality and fitness of accommodation. In the early twentieth century, two developments were particularly important. First, as a result of concerns over the free market for private rented accommodation, in particular during the world wars, the state intervened in the relationship between landlord and tenant creating security of tenure for occupiers combined with control of rents. Security of tenure meant that tenants could only be evicted as a result of a court order granted on limited grounds. Rent control was state control over rent increases; that was altered in the 1960s to rent **regulation**; and, in 1988, to rents being set on a market basis. Secondly, the state gradually developed its own housing stock through local councils from the late nineteenth century, a process that was kick-started between the end of World War I and the 1960s. This development provided a new focus of concern, particularly as that stock began to fall into disrepair and resources dwindled.

Housing law can only really claim to have emerged as a specialist area, as distinct from say the law of landlord and tenant, in the late twentieth century. It is because of this late discovery, perhaps, that its boundaries are as yet uncertain. Some scholars come to it from public law, where the concerns are with social housing (provided by councils and charities). Others come at the subject from a more contractual basis of landlord and tenant; while yet others see the subject as one which is primarily concerned with social policy and economics, and only indirectly with law. These different starting points reflect the divisions in the subject, the textbooks, and the methodological approaches of the authors. Those in the first two categories are more likely to focus on legal relationships, being concerned primarily with the rights of the parties to housing relationships. Their difference lies in the sectoral concern, public lawyers focusing on social housing and contract lawyers focusing on private housing. The focus of the second group is also likely to be on landlord and tenant relations. Those in the third category are more interested in going behind the formal law, and are sociological or socio-legal in orientation.

Broadly, although this is contested, the subject of housing law covers the four main housing 'tenures' (understood in a non-technical sense). These tenures are owner-occupation; public sector tenancy; tenancy in the charitable, not-for-profit sector (comprised of housing associations, now termed Registered Social Landlords); and tenancy in the private rented sector. These divisions are necessary because of the fundamental distinctions not only in the nature of the providers and funders of each tenure, but also because there are important legal differences between them. These differences can be summarized in terms of a triptych of inter-connecting issues: the regulation of housing relationships; access to housing; and, finally, rights and responsibilities.

Regulation refers not just to the relationships between the provider and occupier, but primarily to the various ways in which the state seeks, and has sought, to influence the ways in which we hold our accommodation. Primarily, the tools are economic in form, but they are also social. At the turn of the twentieth century, approximately 90 per cent of households rented their accommodation, whereas at the turn of the twenty-first century, approximately 70 per cent of households were owner-occupiers. In order to achieve this very substantial shift in housing tenure, a number of different regulatory techniques were used.

'Access to housing' refers to the ways in which households access their accommodation. In particular, consideration is given to the availability of mortgage finance and personal subsidies (such as housing benefit), as well as routes into social housing. This latter area has been the subject of significant legal intervention over the past thrity years in tune with the development of **administrative law** more generally. Since the 1960s, there have been concerns over equal access to social housing, particularly by black and minority ethnic households.

Finally, housing law is concerned with the balance between the rights and responsibilities of both housing providers and occupiers. The notion of housing rights here refers to the rights of occupiers against their housing providers and mortgage lenders. There are differences between the strength of these rights across all tenures, security of tenure being strongest in parts of the rented sector, especially the social sector. The notion of responsibilities refers to the responsibilities of occupiers not only to their housing providers and mortgage lenders, but also to a broader and more nebulous category of community or neighbourhood. The extent of these responsibilities, and what can be done to deal with issues in relation to them, is a particularly contested issue. It links housing law closely with a crime control agenda which focuses on low level deviance often described as **anti-social behaviour**. Social housing agencies have been recruited into the crime control process, and are entitled to obtain orders or **injunctions** against their own occupiers and others. Private landlords have also been recruited into the process through licensing arrangements in parts of the private rented sector.   DAVID COWAN

A Arden and C Hunter, *Manual of Housing Law* (London: Sweet & Maxwell, 2005)

A Arden and M Partington, *Housing Law* (London: Sweet & Maxwell, 2006)

housing ombudsman   *see* **ombudsmen**

human   *see* **humanity and humanism**

human (migrant) smuggling   Until the late 1990s academics and policymakers used the terms 'smuggling' and 'trafficking' interchangeably to refer to the illegal movement of people across borders. Two UN Protocols in 2000 established a legal distinction: The UN Protocol against the Smuggling of Migrants by Land, Sea, and Air defined migrant smuggling as: 'The procurement, in order to obtain, directly or indirectly a financial or other material benefit, of the illegal entry of a person into a state Party of which the person is not a national or a permanent resident'. A separate UN Protocol to Prevent, Suppress, and Punish Trafficking in Persons defined trafficking as: 'The recruitment, transportation, transfer, harbouring or receipt of persons, by means of the threat, or use of force or other forms of coercion, of abduction, of fraud, of deception, of the abuse of power or of a position of vulnerability or of the giving or receiving of payments or benefits to achieve the consent of a person having control over another person, for the purpose of exploitation'. As a result two distinct terms are currently in use—migrant smuggling and **human trafficking**.

In reality this distinction can become blurred. For the individuals involved, for example, smuggling can effectively degrade into trafficking. Thus a migrant may pay a proportion of a fee for what is understood to be a migration service, only to be forced into an exploitative situation upon arrival in the destination country in order to pay back the balance due.

A range of migrant types appears to be smuggled, although it may be hard to distinguish between them. These include voluntary as well as forced migrants, **asylum** seekers as well as economic migrants. As a result of their interaction with smugglers, they are often also labelled illegal migrants. The majority of policy documents and academic literature still focuses on trafficking—especially of women and children—even though it is likely that migrant smuggling takes place on a greater scale globally than human trafficking.

Significant problems arise in trying to gauge the scale of migrant smuggling (or human trafficking). By their nature these movements are informal, they often involve crossing borders clandestinely and working illegally in destination countries, and thus defy normal modes of measurement. There are conceptual problems too, particularly regarding how to discern trafficked from smuggled migrants, and how to distinguish other illegal migrants from either.

Most estimates of migrant smuggling are on a national basis. These are normally based on apprehensions of smuggled migrants, and thus cover only a proportion of the true total. Even less is known about the number of migrants in transit to their final destination. Nevertheless, most commentators are of the opinion that the overall scale of migrant smuggling worldwide has increased significantly.

Migrant smuggling is a growing global phenomenon, yet detailed knowledge about smuggling routes relies on small-scale and local studies. In North America the predominant focus has been on smuggling across the US–Mexico border. For Europe the principal destinations appear to be in Western Europe. The principal origins appear to vary largely according to the location of conflict, thus until the end of the 1990s Afghanistan was an important source for smuggled migrants. Central and Eastern Europe, Turkey, and Russia are important transit countries.

Even less is known about the organization of migrant smuggling. The scale of operations varies significantly from individuals or family- and community-based groups to large-scale transnational businesses. The services they are reported to provide range from assisting people to leave the country of origin to smuggling people into their destination countries, as well as arranging travel between the two. Methods employed range from the provision of false documentation to moving people clandestinely across borders. In addition smugglers in particular are often reported to be the source of detailed information on immigration and asylum policy and practice in destination countries.

Different case studies also reveal different details about costs and payment arrangements. Journeys from various Asian countries to Europe have been reported to cost between $1,500 and $10,000; estimates for the longer journey to North America range from $15,000 to $30,000. Globally it has been estimated that migrant smuggling attracts an income of between $5 and $7 billion per year.

One reason for the growth in migrant smuggling is that while the demand to move to richer countries remains buoyant, legal means of entry have reduced significantly. Many migrants have few alternatives but to move informally or illegally, and they cannot do so without the assistance of smugglers. There are also indications that migrant smuggling has evolved into a migration business, where different operators compete for trade. One implication is that smugglers no longer simply respond to demand, but actively recruit migrants in countries of origin and transit.

Given the apparent scale of migrant smuggling, it is perceived to pose challenges to the ability of states to control their borders. Limited evidence also highlights negative consequences for the migrants themselves. No-one knows how many do not leave their country of origin because they cannot afford the fee, even if they face persecution there. Neither is anything known about conditions for migrants in transit, where a proportion certainly perishes or becomes stranded. The majority of attention has focused on conditions after arrival—but most attention has been paid to the **victims** of trafficking rather than smuggled migrants.

There have been four principal policy initiatives to combat smuggling. One is the stricter penalization of smugglers. The second is to intercept smuggled migrants at borders, in transit countries, and at sea. The third policy target is to return smuggled migrants. The final current policy approach is to disseminate information in countries of origin to warn against the pitfalls of migrating with smugglers.

KHALID KOSER

D Kyle and R Koslowski (eds), *Human Smuggling: A Global Perspective* (Baltimore: John Hopkins, 2001)

J Salt and J Hogarth, *Migrant Trafficking in Europe* (Geneva: IOM, 2000)

human dignity In some legal systems, most famously the German, it is a matter of high constitutional principle that human dignity should not be compromised. Similar injunctions are found, too, in a wide range of modern European and international instruments.

Although respect for human dignity might be an important **common law** value, English law rarely refers to it explicitly. However, the implicit claim underlying challenges to the incremental licensing of **embryo research** and embryo screening is precisely that human dignity should not be compromised; and the same might be said about the majority ruling in *R v Brown* (1993) that consent is no defence to assaults and wounding inflicted during sado-masochistic encounters. Moreover, where European **legislation** (such as that relating to the patenting of biotechnological inventions) draws on notions of human dignity, this necessarily sets the tone for its English implementation.

According to Beyleveld and Brownsword, where the jurisprudence of respect for human dignity is developed, it reflects two quite different conceptions. Whereas the conception of 'human dignity as empowerment' emphasizes the importance of individual **autonomy** and personal choice, the rival conception of 'human dignity as constraint' not only sets dignity-respecting limits to personal choice, it insists that human life, from its conception through

to its natural cessation, has a dignity that demands protection.

The tension between these two conceptions is highlighted by competing perspectives on such matters as **stem cell** research, **abortion**, and **euthanasia**; and it is well illustrated by such legal landmarks as the German *Peep-Show* Decision (1981), the French 'dwarf-throwing' case (1995) and, most recently, the *Omega* case at the **European Court of Justice** (2004)—in each of which, the conception of human dignity as constraint prevailed to restrain the choices of adult spectators, participants, and players at different leisure facilities as well as the options of the performers.

ROGER BROWNSWORD

D Beyleveld and R Brownsword, *Human Dignity in Bioethics and Biolaw* (Oxford: Oxford University Press, 2001)

Human Fertilization and Embryology Authority

The establishment of the Human Fertilization and Embryology Authority ('HFEA') was the regulatory response to the birth in 1978 of Louise Brown, the first IVF baby. Her birth, the result of the pioneering work of Dr Robert Edwards and Dr Patrick Steptoe, was accompanied by widespread fears about **embryo research**, its morality and direction. Professional self-regulation started shortly afterwards: a Voluntary Licensing Authority including lay persons, a Code of Practice, and a clinic licensing system. Arguably, regulation of clinics and research would not have been seen as the solution if the NHS had provided IVF, but treatments are largely carried out privately and NHS treatment is available only to a minority. In 1982 the Committee of Inquiry into Human Fertilization and Embryology was established under the chairmanship of Dame Mary Warnock. Its terms of reference were 'to consider recent and potential developments in medicine and science related to human fertilisation and embryology; to consider what policies and safeguards should be applied, including consideration of the social, ethical and legal implications of these developments; and to make recommendation'.

The Warnock Report (Cmnd 9314, 1984) considered all the current techniques, namely donor insemination, IVF, donation, **surrogacy**, storage, and research, and made sixty-three recommendations. It proposed a statutory licensing authority to regulate the research and treatment, with lay **representation** and a lay chairman; that all practitioners and premises should be licensed; that embryo research and the creation of embryos for research should be permitted; and that embryos could be kept outside the body for fourteen days. Donor anonymity and payment of donors were to be allowed, and a limit of ten children from any one male donor set. Storage periods for embryos, counselling, and the collection of statistics on treatment were recommended. Criminal sanctions were recommended for unauthorized use of embryos and certain other practices; the legal status of the IVF **child** was considered; and surrogacy disapproved except in the most limited circumstances. The subsequent Bill faced a slow and contentious passage in both Houses of Parliament, but the time taken served to enhance public understanding of the benefits of IVF and research, and produced successful and flexible **legislation**. The structure of the Act has proved sound and has been a model for similar legislation in Canada, Japan, California, and France. It is based on informed consent.

The HFEA started work in its London offices in 1991 with the following statutory responsibilities: to license and regulate clinics carrying out IVF, the donation and storage of gametes and embryos, and human embryo research; to maintain a Code of Practice giving guidance on the proper conduct of the licensed activities; to maintain a register of licensed treatments given, and of the children born as a result; to give advice and information to licensed clinics, to prospective patients, and to the public; to keep the field under review; and to give advice, when asked, to the Secretary of State for Health. Gamete intrafallopian transfer, ovulation induction, and intra-uterine insemination are not licensable, except where donated gametes are involved.

The most significant achievement of the HFEA followed from the birth of Dolly, the first cloned mammal, in 1997. Together with the Human Genetics Committee it recommended in *Cloning Issues in Reproduction, Science and Medicine* (December 1998) the extension of the existing permitted categories of embryo research, which were limited to fertility related purposes, to research on serious disease and the use where necessary of embryos created by cell nuclear replacement. The Human Fertilization and Embryology (Research Purposes) Regulations 2001 added these categories. The HFEA facilitated **stem cell** research by proving that embryo research could be undertaken under strictly controlled conditions and by providing a base on which to establish specific stem cell regulation. On its recommendation, the Human Reproductive Cloning Act 2001 prohibited the placing in a woman of any embryo created otherwise than by fertilization.

The provisions of the Act have been tested in four cases raising new issues. First, posthumous conception, where the court affirmed the need for written consent to the removal of gametes, but called on the HFEA to give due consideration to the principles of European Treaty law in considering Diane Blood's request to export sperm obtained illegally from her dead husband for fertility treatment abroad (*R v Human Fertilisation & Embryology Authority ex parte Diane Blood* (1997)). In *R v Secretary of State for Health, ex p Quintavalle* (2003), the **House of Lords** held that the statutory definition of an embryo extended to those created by cell nuclear replacement, confirming the remit of HFEA over this research. In *Evans v Amicus Healthcare* (2004), the Court of Appeal confirmed the right of an ex-partner to withhold his consent to the use of stored embryos, and the **European Court of Human Rights** subsequently agreed with this. Then in 2005 the House of Lords gave a purposive interpretation to the meaning of 'treatment' under the Act to permit the selection of healthy and matching tissue typed embryos to provide a sibling who could assist in curing an older child with a genetic disease.

In its first fifteen years, the Authority established a comprehensive Code of Practice, designed a national regulatory system and a database, consulted with the public, and cooperated with professional organizations in the field. Amongst its decisions are the banning of **sex selection** for social reasons; permitting egg sharing and the payment of limited expenses to gamete donors; the publication of IVF clinics' success rates; the licensing of intracytoplasmic sperm injection, preimplantation genetic diagnosis, the use of frozen eggs and the limitation of the number of embryos allowed in any one treatment to two, in order to reduce multiple births. Many of the decisions are controversial and statutory regulation has the effect of giving them a high profile. Legal constraints, the media, political pressures, and the cost of litigation play their part in the process as well as ethical considerations.

There are twenty-one Authority members, composed of a mix of scientists, clinicians, medically-related professionals, and lay persons. They are appointed for three-year renewable terms. Dame Mary Donaldson chaired the Voluntary Licensing Authority; Sir Colin Campbell was the founding chair of the HFEA (1990–1994), followed by Baroness Deech (1994–2002), and Dame Suzi Leather (2002–2006). Neither the Chair nor the Deputy may be medically or scientifically qualified.

The Authority meets nine times a year to discuss and determine policy and practice and minutes of the meetings are published (*www.hfea.gov.uk*). Its committees are Ethics and Law, Scientific and Clinical Advances, License, Regulation, Audit, and Information Management Programme Board.

Legal regulation has helped to inform and support public debate on embryo research. It has created an attractive working environment for scientists and contributed to the UK's leading position in embryo research. Despite its strengths, the Act will not remain the last word, and it is likely that its requirements for confidentiality and that the clinician consider before treatment the welfare of the child and its need for a father will be relaxed. It has proved a catalyst for informed debate and a unique arena for public involvement with scientific decisions and merits its independent position.   RUTH DEECH

Human Genome, the   Whereas issues of ethics and regulation surrounding genetics have had a long history, the Human Genome Project and the transition to genomics marked an important change. The decision to map and sequence the Human Genome, the first draft of which was completed in 2001, had several consequences. First, it became clear that the human genome contains far fewer genes than had been predicted, only about 24,000. This was taken by some as evidence against genetic determinism, as such a small number of genes surely could not explain human complexity and variation. Interest in those parts of the genome previously described as 'junk' DNA, and those concerned with regulation, increased. The move to genome level research also led to the recognition of the importance of not only genes but also of genetic factors such as single base pairs on the genome (single nucleotide polymorphisms, or 'SNPs'), and variation in the number of copies of a genetic factor that an individual might have (copy number variants, or 'CNVs'). A change in the focus of discussion, from testing and screening for single gene disorders towards population wide association studies to establish the links between genetic factors for susceptibility to common diseases (eg cancer and heart disease) took place, along with research on the links between genetic factors and responses to substances such as drugs (pharmacogenomics) and foodstuffs (nutrigenomics).

The thesis of genetic exceptionalism holds that there is something special about genetics which makes traditional approaches to ethics problematic—for example, the fact that genetic information is independent of time, predictive, and has implications for blood relatives led to the suggestion that ethical and regulatory approaches may have to reconsider the individual-centred approach. For example, as genetic information about an individual potentially also has relevance to others, issues concerning **privacy** and confidentiality are at least more complicated. Although genetic exceptionalism

has been criticized on the grounds that it is not only in genetics that interests of third parties may be at stake, there has been increasing recognition that the issues surrounding population level research, which may involve contributing samples to biobanks for long-term storage, raise specific additional issues about informed consent and feedback of results, as well as the possible implications of identifying differences between population groups which may be used for discriminatory purposes. Discussion continues about the potential benefits of genomics research, how they should be shared, and how safeguards against possible **risks** can be put in place.
                                          RUTH CHADWICK

human nature   *see* **humanity and humanism**

human rights   The term 'human rights' contains a multitude of meanings that cross many academic disciplines. To the philosopher it is about the essential qualities of the human that lead us to an understanding of our duties towards others; to the specialist in international relations, it connotes a force in the management of relations between states; while to the political scientist, human rights are a tool in the construction of a liberal community. Law's approach to human rights is both simpler and more question-begging than any of these. At one level, law derives the meaning it ascribes to the term from the basic documentation available to it, the international, regional, and national instruments that set out codes of human rights. But the loose ends left by the superficial clarity of this approach leave many questions unanswered, thereby forcing law back into other disciplines in search of a set of truly adequate responses. This is why human rights is an inherently inter-disciplinary subject: law's grasp of the subject may be coherent but its reliance on authoritative documents renders its coverage inevitably incomplete.

The fount of much that follows in the field is the **Universal Declaration of Human Rights**, agreed by the **United Nations** in 1948. This (unenforceable) document sets out a range of human rights of such variety and depth as to amount (in the language of modern business) to 'a mission statement for humanity'. Later agreements, on economic, social, and cultural rights and on **civil and political rights** respectively, both agreed by the United Nations in 1966, serve to flesh out the insights of this 1948 declaration while providing a modest degree of enforcement. Later conventions on such matters as discrimination against women and the rights of the child have followed, some with mechanisms for the oversight of state practice that are more political than legal. After a pause of some years there are signs that the content of human rights law is beginning to expand once again with recent agreement at the UN on the rights of persons with disabilities and with further rights-oriented declarations on behalf of indigenous peoples.

With the exception of an optional protocol process in relation to civil and political rights, the chief characteristic of a legal discourse—namely adjudication by a judicial/quasi-judicial body of an allegation of a breach–is noticeably absent from this branch of **international law**. In particular, there is no world court of human rights, nor any likelihood of one in the near future. Study of **international human rights law** texts begs questions that inevitably take the subject outside law: what drives the decision to include an aspiration as a human right? Why the long gap between the 1948 declaration and the 1966 covenants, and why are there two? Why is it that enforcement of international human rights is so slip-shod? Can the moral imperative of halting human rights abuses justify military action?

The articulation of a law of human rights at regional and national levels more resembles the framework of ordinary law, with more or less direct enforcement by a court of sets of rights that are integrated into the legal systems of which they form a part. Thus both the **European Court of Human Rights** and the **European Court of Justice** enjoy rights jurisdictions that reach into the law of the states subject to their remit, and the rights to be found in, for example, the South African constitution have a not dissimilar role to play as proper law. In general the closer to (a national) home the term 'human rights' seems, then the more tangibly legal (ie justiciable and enforceable) will it appear to the lawyer.   CONOR GEARTY

See also: **Convention for the Elimination of all Forms of Discrimination against Women; Convention for Elimination of Racial Discrimination; Convention on the Rights of the Child; economic and social rights; International Covenant on Civil and Political Rights; International Covenant on Economic, Social and Cultural Rights; South African Bill of Rights**

Human Rights Act 1998 In the UK, basic rights and liberties have been mainly protected through political means. From the 17th century on, campaigns by activists, pressure groups, politicians, and **trade unions** have ensured respect for certain civil liberties, such as **freedom of expression** and freedom of association. Parliamentary **legislation** has also protected rights and liberties, often by imposing restraints upon the powers of the **police**

and other public authorities. The **courts** have developed the **common law** in a manner that has often extended basic rights. However, until the passing of the Human Rights Act 1998, individuals were not able to bring an action in court directly alleging a breach of their fundamental rights. **Remedies** for rights' violations had usually to be sought via political routes, not through the courts.

In contrast, most countries over the last century have copied the US constitutional system and introduced a form of judicial 'rights review', whereby courts are given the power to review whether decisions by governments, public authorities, and legislatures respect basic rights. Under the **European Convention on Human Rights** ('ECHR'), which the UK ratified in 1951, the **European Court of Human Rights** in Strasbourg is given a similar role. The Convention protects basic '**civil and political rights**' such as the **right to life**, the right to privacy, and the right to freedom of expression. Individuals who allege their rights under the Convention have been violated, and who cannot obtain a remedy within their own national legal systems, can apply to the European Court of Human Rights for relief.

Over time, the ECHR case law had a considerable influence on UK law: individuals bringing their cases to Strasbourg began to obtain remedies which they could not get within the UK legal system. This resulted in pressure building up for the UK to introduce some form of national system of judicial rights review. Finally, as part of the new Labour Government's constitutional reform package, the Human Rights Act 1998 ('HRA') was passed by **Parliament**, coming into force in 2000. The Labour Government described the HRA as 'bringing rights back home', on the basis that the ECHR, which had been partially written by British lawyers, is largely incorporated by the HRA into UK law. This means that most of the Convention rights become part of UK law and can be relied upon by individuals in seeking remedies before the UK courts.

The HRA has been described as a 'model of intelligent design'. Section 6 of the Act permits the courts to grant remedies to individual **victims**, where their Convention rights have been violated by public authorities. This means that courts can now strike down decisions by public authorities (including the Scottish Parliament and the Welsh and Northern Irish devolved assemblies) which violate the Convention, and grant **injunctions, damages**, or other forms of remedy where necessary. Only Acts of Parliament (and acts by public authorities which are directly authorized by Acts of Parliament) cannot be overturned by the courts. Unlike the USA, Germany, and other countries who give their courts the final say in deciding when basic rights have been violated, the HRA ensures that the UK Parliament retains the ultimate authority to make decisions about **human rights** matters.

However, under Section 3 of the Act, the courts are under an obligation to interpret parliamentary legislation 'as far as possible' so as to avoid violating Convention rights. In other words, if a court can interpret legislation in a way that ensures that no Convention right is breached, then it is required to adopt this interpretation. If legislation cannot be interpreted in this manner without unacceptably distorting its provisions, then the courts under section 4 of the HRA can make a 'declaration of incompatibility'. This is a non-legally binding declaration by the courts that the legislation in question appears to violate Convention rights. The Act provides for a special fast-track parliamentary procedure which permits legislation that is declared to be incompatible to be rapidly altered, if Parliament wishes to do so. Nevertheless, if Parliament chooses not to alter the legislation, the UK courts have no power under the HRA to intervene. However, although an individual would still be able to go to Strasbourg and challenge the legislation in question before the European Court of Human Rights. Also, to encourage Parliament to consider whether legislation affects human rights, ministers introducing a Bill into Parliament under section 19 of the HRA are obliged to state whether they believe the proposed legislation complies with the ECHR.

Some controversy exists as to when the courts should use their power of interpretation under section 3 HRA, and when they should issue declarations of incompatibility under section 4 instead. Uncertainty also surrounds section 6 of the HRA, which only applies to 'core' public authorities, such as central government ministries, and to bodies performing 'functions of a public nature'. This test has generated difficulties, as it will at times be unclear what bodies are subject to the Act. Also, the courts have given a narrow interpretation to this provision, thereby limiting its scope. Private individuals or private bodies which are not subject to the Act cannot be directly sued for breaching rights: however, the Act may have 'indirect horizontal effect', in that it may influence how courts develop and interpret private law.

Since its coming into force, the HRA has attracted a mixture of praise and controversy. Reviews by government departments and parliamentary committees have commented favourably upon the additional protection it provides for human rights and the sensible application of the HRA by the courts. However, the Act has also been subject to media attacks for allegedly weakening **national security** and encouraging an excessive emphasis upon individual rights at the expense of the collective good. The Conservative Party has proposed repealing the HRA and replacing it with a 'British Bill of Rights', while the Labour party has proposed supplementing the HRA with a similar new 'home-grown' Bill of Rights. However, the HRA has already had a considerable impact on UK law and, unless repealed, will continue to be a significant element of the UK constitutional system.   COLM O'CINNEIDE

human rights and civil liberties The terms 'civil liberties' and '**human rights**' enjoy a sibling-style relationship, usually complementing each other perfectly, but occasionally quarrelling over issues of mutual interest. 'Civil liberties' is an old phrase meaning different things. At one level it stands for the proposition that we are all free to do what we want and that the governmental authority, which inevitably must control us to some extent, is not the less unwelcome for being in this way necessary. This is the libertarian trend in civil liberties, one captured in the traditional English law position that one is free to do whatever is not prohibited by law. It is also to be found in human rights charters, both in the general commitment to freedom upon which these depend and in the practical expression of this perspective in such concretized guarantees as the rights to liberty and to **privacy**. Many of the controversies that civil liberties and human rights get themselves into—the refusal to accept any CCTV cameras on motorways; the claim to a right of access to any kind of pornography; the objection to controls on hunting with dogs—flow out of the anti-governmental strand that each shares. But in neither subject is this the dominant discourse: most human rights permit exceptions, and other non-libertarian versions of civil liberties take the subject in entirely different directions.

One of these is found in the practical concern that civil liberties show for the protection of personal liberty through the imposition of controls on police powers. Here human rights and civil liberties are once again closely aligned, the main theoretical difference between the two in this context being the emphasis civil liberties places on remedies for wrongs done (damages available through a successful civil action in tort) rather than redress for specific rights breached (the more traditional human rights approach). A similar commonality of purpose is also clear in the arena of civil and political rights; these rights can easily be recast in civil libertarian terms as the freedoms of assembly, expression, and association which, together with the right to vote, make democratic governance possible. Neither of these strands of civil liberties/human rights is wedded to libertarianism/unfettered freedom: the first works to make state power accountable, the second seeks to create the right conditions for the legitimate exercise of that power.

The difference between the two subjects becomes apparent when the language of human rights moves out of the civil and political arena into more social and economic spheres. Here the subject of civil liberties is largely left behind, having nothing similarly expansive to say about the quality of life. The term civil liberties is revealed as a narrower one, more focused on the political than the ethical health of a community. On some accounts the commitment to democracy that civil liberties manifests when taking its political shape leads it to be antagonistic to the language of human rights whenever it expands beyond the civil and political to incorporate policy matters that this kind of civil libertarian says properly belong to the political, not the legal.

CONOR GEARTY

See also: **civil and political rights; economic and social rights; freedom of assembly; freedom of association; freedom of expression; liberty, right to**

human rights and development   Human rights and development are central and defining preoccupations of the post World War II international order. Attention to individual rights and economic growth and **security** was seen by those rebuilding the international institutions as crucial to establishing and maintaining a just and peaceful world. Yet despite their common origins, they developed as fundamentally separate enterprises, and remained so for much of the post-war era. Development was consigned to economists and specialists concerned with economic and social issues and fell under the purview of the **World Bank** and certain specialized agencies of the **United Nations**. **Human rights**, by contrast, became the province of lawyers and fell to designated **human** rights organs such as the Human Rights Commission who largely concentrated on **civil and political rights**. Nonetheless, there has always been overlap in the subject matter of the fields, something that became particularly evident with the emergence of the 'right to development', a central part of call for a New International Economic Order by the newly decolonized states in the 1960s and 1970s. There have also been ongoing debates about the relationship and relative importance of the two fields, for example

whether human rights follows from development or vice versa.

The end of the Cold War marked an important shift in the relationship between human rights and development. The 1993 Vienna Declaration on Human Rights held that all human rights were universal, indivisible, interdependent, and interrelated; at the same time, human rights, markets, and **democracy** began to be represented as interlinked elements of a single project. By the mid-1990s, human rights had also emerged as the universal language of social **justice**. Activists and **social movements,** especially those wishing to reach an international audience, routinely framed a wide range of political, economic, and cultural issues as matters of human rights. This included criticism of development projects and policies: the adverse effects of infrastructure projects and structural adjustment policies of the World Bank and the International Monetary Fund, for example, were sometimes styled as violations of indigenous and **women'**s rights.

Since the fiftieth anniversary of the Universal Declaration of Human Rights in 1998 and calls to 'mainstream' human rights into the concerns and activities of all international institutions, it has become common to describe human rights and development as complementary rather than separate or opposing objectives. Amartya Sen's influential *Development as Freedom* identified human freedoms as both instrumental to the promotion of economic development and part of the very definition of development. Development institutions such as the World Bank now promote 'basic' human rights that are consistent with a market-centred approach to development, while maintaining that the realization of human rights is impossible without development.

Despite this apparent convergence, the relationship between human rights norms and development remains contested. Development policies that emphasize efficient and competitive markets, limited redistribution by the state, and an enhanced role for the private sector in the delivery of services remain subject to criticism due to their effects on a range of human rights and social objectives, from **gender equality** and respect for rights at work, to economic security and access to health and education. In response, some argue for giving normative priority to human rights through a 'rights-based' approach to development.

Reflecting their importance in development and the global economy, there is a new spotlight on the actions of corporations and private actors and their role in both violating and promoting respect for human rights. Pressure by **non-governmental**

organizations, civil society organizations, and social movements has led some corporations and industries to modify their activities and adopt codes of conduct grounded in human rights norms. For the most part, these efforts remain voluntary and are still inadequately monitored.

Activists and scholars in the Third World continue to raise concerns about the extent to which current human rights priorities and development projects reflect Eurocentric values as well as assumptions about the superiority of Western forms of political and economic organization. At the same time, they offer alternative conceptions of both human rights and development rooted in attention to power, distributive justice, and cultural diversity.   KERRY RITTICH

human rights and family law   Traditionally, family lawyers have been somewhat wary of **human rights**. There is a fear that human rights will impact on the wide **discretion** that the **courts** have traditionally enjoyed in family matters. Further once human rights are recognized there is a concern that these could too easily lead to arguments that the rights of parents or others require courts to make orders which did not promote a child's welfare. That would infringe one of the central principles of family law, that the interests of children should be paramount. Despite these misgivings, the **Human Rights Act 1998** has required the courts to at least refer to the rights of parties in family law cases.

The impact of the Human Rights Act 1998 in family law has been limited. A central reason for this is the assertion by the courts that an approach based on the **European Convention on Human Rights** ('ECHR') does not differ in effect from one based on the principle that children's welfare must be paramount. Any claim that a parent may have to respect for their private or family life under Article 8 can be interfered with, if necessary in the interests of children. The ECHR will, therefore, never require an order to be made which is contrary to the interests of children. Although this is an argument which has not convinced most academics, it has been adopted consistently by the courts.

There have, however, been some areas of family law in which the Human Rights Act 1998 has had a significant impact. One is the area of **child protection** where the courts have used the notion of proportionality in interpreting the ECHR. This requires the courts to make the order which least interferes in family life, while still protecting children from the **risk** of abuse. The rights of children to protection from abuse also impose a **positive obligation** on the

state and local authorities to ensure that children are not subject to inhuman or degrading treatment.

The notion of **children's rights** has not been greatly developed in English law. Some recent cases have made reference to the United Nations Conventions on the Rights of the Child. The Children's Commissioner in Wales is required to have regard to the rights protected there, although the English Commissioner need only be guided by the ECHR. The Commissioner for Children and Young People in Scotland is required to safeguard and promote the rights of children. The rights of children have already been used by the courts to restrict the availability of the defence of lawful chastisement in relation to the corporal punishment of children and to require more effective **representation** of children and their views in court cases. Time will tell whether the notions of children's rights will play in important role in family law in the future. Many academics feel that children's human rights are not yet adequately protected by the law.   JONATHAN HERRING

J Fortin, *Children's Rights and the Developing Law* (Cambridge: Cambridge University Press, 2003)

human rights and health   A right to health may appear to be a fundamental **human right**, and medical law has been characterized as a sub-set of human rights law. However, a right to health is rarely explicitly articulated in international human rights documents, which historically have focused on the protection of **civil and political rights**, rather than **economic and social rights** (such as health) which impose **positive obligations** on the state. Nevertheless, various rights protected under the **European Convention on Human Rights** (ECHR) are indirectly concerned with health. The **right to life**, which is protected under Article 2, the prohibition on **torture** and inhuman and degrading treatment (Article 3), the right to **privacy** and **family life** (Article 8), the right to marry and found a family (Article 12) have all been invoked by those asserting health rights. Since October 2000, it has been possible to rely on these provisions in domestic **courts**, so that practically the ECHR is the most important human rights document applicable to the UK. Rights guaranteed by the ECHR can be invoked against public authorities (which would include NHS Trusts, NHS research ethics committees, and health care-related quangos, such as the **Human Fertilization and Embryology Authority** and the Human Tissue Authority). In line with decisions of the **European Court of Human Rights**, UK courts have generally been disinclined to interpret Articles 2, 3 and 8 in such a way as to impose positive obligations on public authorities. However, commentators have suggested that Article 2 could be invoked in cases where potentially life-saving treatment was refused. Moreover, a decision of the Grand Chamber of the European Court of Human Rights held that UK law which denied the wife of a life prisoner access to assisted insemination breached Article 8, because this procedure represented the couple's only realistic opportunity to have a genetically-related **child** together. Article 8 was held to impose a positive obligation on the state to vindicate the rights guaranteed under it, and a majority of the Court decided that the policy of the **Home Secretary** did not strike a fair balance between the competing public and private interests involved (*Dickson v UK* (2007)). Thus, it appears that rights which traditionally have been interpreted negatively—as simply requiring the state to refrain from interfering in the lives of its citizens—may now impose direct obligations on the state. The *Dickson* case also demonstrates how the content of health rights may vary considerably. More generally the cultural shift effected by the Human Rights Act has prompted a greater rights awareness on the part of **judges**, and a concomitant willingness to scrutinize decisions by public authorities which impact on the rights and health of citizens.

Although not directly enforceable in domestic courts, other international documents do contain express commitments to health rights. Thus, the Universal Declaration of Human Rights states that '[e]veryone has the right to a standard of living adequate for the health and well-being of himself and of his family, including food, clothing, housing and medical care and necessary social services' (Article 25). Similarly, the Council of Europe's European Social Charter 1996 addresses social and economic matters, containing guarantees of accessible, effective health care facilities for the entire population, a healthy environment, and protection of **maternity rights**. However, while they remain pitched at this level of abstraction, such statements really amount to aspirations rather than rights.   MARIE FOX

human rights and property   Any argument that property deserves to be treated as a human right plainly depends on one's ideas of property and of **human rights**. Hence, it is not surprising that there are many different arguments for and against such treatment. For example, liberal theorists often argue that property defines an area of personal autonomy that is necessary for the enjoyment of a meaningful life. Against this, some would argue that property is a type of socio-economic right; and hence that treating it as an enforceable human right would give it

a status it does not warrant. In legal terms, treating property as a human right elevates private property to a special status, where there is some further check on the power of the state to take and regulate property that is not part of 'ordinary' law. It commits the state both to use its power to maintain a system of property (thereby protecting existing entitlements from other persons) and to refrain from modifying or taking those entitlements except under certain conditions.

The primary source of a justiciable human right to property in the **United Kingdom** is Article 1 of the First Protocol to the **European Convention on Human Rights**. It states that 'every natural or legal person is entitled to the peaceful enjoyment of his possessions'. It requires an interference with property to be lawful and for a legitimate purpose. In addition, in the landmark case *Sporrong and Lönnroth v Sweden* (1982), the **European Court of Human Rights** decided that an interference with property must strike a 'fair balance' between community and private interests. This often reduces to a question of compensation: is the owner entitled to compensation for the taking or **regulation** of property? And if so, how much must be paid?

Whether the right to property should go further is controversial. In particular, it has been argued that human rights law should guarantee access to the material resources that make life worth living. This could include, for example, a right to the resources needed for basic subsistence; to access to objects that are central to religious practices or to personal or cultural identity; and even to entry to the physical or virtual locations of political debate. While some recognition of a human right to property has been accorded where the claim is against resources held by the state, claims to resources legally held by other private persons are more problematic. Lawyers often assume that, rather than facilitating claims against private property, a human right to property restricts them. Accordingly, claims that human rights require some kind of access to private property are expressed more often in aspirational terms or '**soft law**'. Where these are implemented as enforceable rights to resources or to property held by others, it is usually through social legislation rather than human rights litigation.   THOMAS ALLEN

T Allen, *Property and the Human Rights Act 1998* (Oxford: Hart Publishing, 2005)

human rights in EU law   In the original European Economic Community ('EEC') of 1957, the protection of fundamental rights was not on the EEC's radar; by the late 1960s the Court had recognized the protection of fundamental rights as a general principle of law (*Stauder* (1969)) the source of those rights being both the 'constitutional traditions common to the Member States' (*Internationale Handelsgesellschaft* (1970) and international **Treaties** on human rights (*Nold* (1974)), most notably the **European Convention on Human Rights** ('ECHR'). The Court's approach is now confirmed by Article 6(2) TEU (and Article 6(3) TEU after the Lisbon Treaty amendments). Some argue that the ECJ began to recognize human rights for reasons of pure self-interest: the German courts threatened not to give supremacy to Community law because they considered the Community standards on human rights inferior to those in Germany. To avoid such a constitutional crisis, the ECJ rapidly developed a case law on fundamental **human rights**.

Whatever the original reasons, respect for human rights is now a central tenet of the ECJ's case law and forms a key pillar of **citizenship of the EU**. Like other general principles of law, human rights can be invoked when the ECJ reviews the legality of Community measures. For example, in *Netherlands v Council* (Biotechnology Directive) (2001), the Dutch government argued that Directive 98/44 on the legal protection of technological inventions was invalid because it undermined human **dignity** by allowing for isolated parts of the **human** body to be patented. The Court, while recognizing the fundamental right to human dignity and integrity, found no breach of the principle on the facts. The ECJ has also said that when Member States are acting within the sphere of **European Community law**, their actions must be compatible with fundamental rights. This means that the ECJ must review the compatibility of national measures with fundamental rights when implementing Community rules (*Wachauf* (1989)) and when derogating from a fundamental Treaty provision (*ERT* (1991)).

Political endorsement of the ECJ's approach to human rights came with the 'proclamation' of the **Charter of Fundamental Rights** 2000, adopted to make rights more visible. The Charter is grouped around six fundamental values shared by the 'peoples' (not just the citizens) of Europe: dignity (Articles 1 to 5); freedoms (Articles 6 to 19); **equality** (Articles 20 to 26); solidarity (Articles 27 to 38); citizens' rights (Articles 39 to 46); and **justice** (Articles 47 to 50). Thus, remarkably, civil and political rights and **economic and social rights** have been brought together in a single text.

At present the Charter is not legally binding, described instead by the Heads of State as a 'Solemn Proclamation'. However, the ECJ, the Court of First Instance ('CFI') and various Advocates General have referred to the Charter in their opinions to help shape their interpretation of Community provisions. The Constitutional Treaty, signed at Rome in October 2004, incorporated the Charter into Part II of the Treaty. Following the rejection of this Treaty by the French and Dutch voters, the Lisbon Treaty was negotiated. New Article 6(1) TEU gives legal effect to the Charter of 2000, making clear that the Charter is to have 'the same legal values of the Treaties', without extending in 'any way the competences of the Union'. However, the Charter is no longer part of the Lisbon Treaty but 'annexed' to it. Article 6(2) TEU now gives the EU the power to accede to the ECHR while Article 6(3) makes clear that fundamental rights are general principles of law.

The most striking aspect of the Lisbon Treaty is that a Protocol (whose content is unclear) gives the UK and Poland a so-called 'opt-out' from the Charter. To be precise, the Protocol prevents the ECJ and national **courts** from finding national rules incompatible with the Charter.   CATHERINE BARNARD

human rights in the workplace Human rights traditionally have been divided into two categories: **civil and political rights** on the one hand and **economic and social rights** on the other. The former are protected by measures such as the **European Convention on Human Rights** ('ECHR'), while the latter are protected by measures such as the Council of Europe's Social Charter of 1961, both of which have been ratified by the United Kingdom. It is the latter which is perhaps most obviously relevant to the workplace, with its provisions relating to the **right to work**, the right to just conditions of work, the right to safe and healthy working conditions, the right to a fair remuneration, the right to organize, and the right to bargain collectively (including the right to **strike**). In recent years, however, civil and political rights of the kind contained in the ECHR have assumed growing prominence, for a host of reasons. These include the changing nature of the global economy, leading to an increase in **human trafficking** and the use of gangmasters to recruit and supply labour from less developed countries to work in the United Kingdom. The death of twenty-three cockle-pickers in Morecambe Bay in 2004 revealed the dangerous conditions and squalid circumstances in which many of these workers labour and live. Although incidents such as this raise the spectre of *de facto* forced labour, they tend to be classified as immigration rackets and health and safety problems, sanitizing the nature of the abuse. The abuse of workers' **human rights** are evident in a number of other countries, relevant here because these countries produce goods for British markets and **consumers**, not least in the clothing industry where the suppliers of several well-known British retailers have been accused of exploiting **child labour** in Asia to satisfy domestic demands.

Other areas where employer conduct may come into conflict with human rights standards contained in instruments such as the ECHR have little to do with globalization, but with diverse factors such as new technology, **multiculturalism**, and rising expectations that people should be treated with dignity and respect, and ought not to be expected to leave their human rights at the workplace door, to be picked up again on the way home. These other areas are covered by the wide rubric of Articles 8–11 of the ECHR, covering matters such as the right to **privacy**, freedom of conscience and **religion, freedom of expression**, and **freedom of assembly** and association. Specific issues relate to drug testing, email monitoring, and other forms of surveillance, and the searching of employees and their property as they leave the employer's premises. Workplace disputes have also arisen in connection with the sexuality and sexual conduct of employees, in the case of the latter even where the conduct in question has taken place in the employee's private life at times when he or she was not on duty. Discrimination in the armed forces was brought to an end only after the intervention of the **European Court of Human Rights** in *Lustig-Prean v United Kingdom* (2000). Other human rights issues concern the employee's practice of his or her religion, with problems arising where the worker's desire to respect holy days (such as Fridays, Saturdays, or Sundays in the case of different faiths) conflicts with the obligations of his or her **contract of employment** or the standard business practice in some firms of rolling shifts over a twenty-four-hour period, seven days a week. Human rights issues may arise further where the worker expresses views that conflict with the business interests of his or her employer, or publishes information about the business which causes it harm, or communicates with fellow employees about issues or in a way that the employer dislikes.

There is also the problem of the worker who engages in political activity that attracts the disapproval of the employer, particularly where the worker is associated with a political party or political cause seen to be on the fringes of political life, which in the past might have included membership of the Communist Party. In some cases, indeed, workers are prohibited from having a public political profile (even with mainstream parties) in order not to undermine public confidence in the political

neutrality of public servants such as senior civil servants, some local government staff, and **police** officers. Although some human rights restraints of workers have been challenged successfully in the European Court of Human Rights, the problem for workers under the Human Rights Act 1998 is that the Act generally does not apply to regulate relationships between private parties (such as employers and workers governed by a contract of employment under private law). True, the Human Rights Act applies to the private relationships of public authorities, though this is a term narrowly defined by the courts. Nevertheless, a worker employed by a public authority could in principle seek a **remedy** against the employer under the Human Rights Act, though there is not a lot of evidence of this being done in practice. It is also true that, under the Human Rights Act, **legislation** must be interpreted consistently with Convention rights. So a worker dismissed for refusing to work in breach of his or her Convention rights could therefore bring an action for **unfair dismissal**, a statutory right that the **tribunals** and courts would have to interpret in a way that was consistent with his or her human rights. But although there have been a number of such cases, the Court of Appeal has been reluctant to encourage an over-reliance on Convention rights in unfair dismissal proceedings, and there is a sense that human rights arguments typically little to the weight of these claims.

Apart from the protection of human rights at work under the generic Human Rights Act, workers in some circumstances may be able to rely on specific legislation targeting particular human rights concerns. Under the **Abortion** Act 1967, medical and nursing staff may claim an exemption on grounds of conscience from taking part in abortions, while the Public Interest Disclosure Act 1998 deals in a limited way with **whistle-blowing** (though, in a different way, so does the Official Secrets Act 1989). In addition, the Data Protection Act 1998 regulates the use and misuse of personal data by employers; the Regulation of Investigatory Powers Act 2000 deals with the use of surveillance (such as tapping workplace phones) by employers; and the Employment **Equality** (Religion or Belief) Regulations 2003 address problems of religious discrimination at work, while the Employment Equality (Sexual Orientation) Regulations 2003 confronts discrimination on grounds of sexual orientation at work. Other important human rights protections are to be found in the **Sex** Discrimination Act 1975 and the **Race** Relations Act 1976 (both of which have been heavily amended as a result of EU law), as well as in the **Disability** Discrimination Act

1995. There are, however, many gaps in the coverage of this patchwork of statutory human rights protection, both in terms of the breadth and depth of the coverage. There is, for example, no specific protection against political discrimination, a curious oversight in a **democracy**. There are also human rights conflicts which have had to be addressed, reminding us that as a matter of positive law there is no such thing as an unqualified or unequivocal human right. Freedom of religion in particular controversially has been given a preferred status—albeit to a limited extent—in the Human Rights Act and in the Employment Equality (Sexual Orientation) Regulations 2003.

The equivocal nature of human rights law is illustrated further by the right to **freedom of association**, including the right to form and join **trade unions**, which at least in its latter aspect appears unusually in treaties dealing with civil and political rights as well as treaties dealing with economic and social rights. It is also recognized in domestic law, in the first instance as a right workers enjoy against their employers, in the sense that they ought not to be discriminated against or dismissed because of their membership or non-membership of a trade union, or their participation in trade union activities at an appropriate time. There are sometimes exceptions to this right, most famously when in 1983 the then Conservative government removed trade union rights at Government Communications' Headquarters. This was held not to breach either the ECHR or the Social Charter of 1961, although it was found by the ILO supervisory bodies to breach ILO Convention 87. British law unusually extends the right to freedom of association as a right of the worker against the union (as well as a right of the worker against the employer), in the sense that workers have a right not to be excluded or expelled from the union, except for reasons prescribed in statute. This extension of the worker's right to freedom of association may be said to conflict with the union's right to choose with whom it wishes to associate. The issue was brought into sharp relief in *ASLEF v United Kingdom* (2007), where the trade union was found to have acted unlawfully for expelling someone because of his membership of the British National Party in accordance with the policy of the union but contrary to an Act of **Parliament**. The **European Court of Human Rights** found that the union's right to freedom of association in these circumstances should prevail over the corresponding right of the worker, save for exceptional circumstances. This is the logical corollary of a right that has both positive and negative dimensions.   KEITH EWING

human rights scepticism Human rights law is currently very popular, with **human rights** protected by a battery of international **treaties** and domestic laws. Some, however, see human rights as a secular **religion** with the same irrational impulses that inform even more spiritual faiths. Just as spiritual religion has attracted its sceptics, so there is also a sense of a human rights delusion, to borrow from the title of Professor Dawkins provocative study (*The God Delusion*, 2007). There is, however, no organized or coordinated movement of sceptics, and the ranks of those sceptical about this new form of theism include those sceptical of the very *idea* of human rights at one end of the spectrum, through to those who are sceptical about the *politics* of the human rights movement, to those who are sceptical about the *means* adopted to protect human rights at the other end. It is admittedly also the case, however, that although the human rights movement now enjoys a dominant voice in the law schools, it too does not speak with one voice, with its Evangelical, Fundamentalist, and Liberation wings.

So far as the idea of human rights is concerned, this is something that can be traced back to the writings of the young Karl Marx who, in a critique of the late eighteenth-century French and American revolutionary texts, poured scorn on the idea of the so-called rights of man. Marx distinguished between the rights of the citizen (political rights designed to promote participation in the life of the **community**), and the rights of man (the rights of man separated from other men and from the community in which they live). The latter—including **property rights**—are seen by Marx as an instrument for subordinating the former and for limiting the power of the community and the rights of political participation. This is done to serve the ends of 'egoistic man', said to be 'an individual withdrawn into himself, his private interest and his private desires'. In other words, the so-called rights of man are about limiting the right of men and women to govern themselves, by subordinating the interests of all of the people to the interests of a few of the people.

It is true that not all human rights instruments include protection for the right to private property. It is also true, however, that that propertied groups are adept at using these instruments for protecting their commercial interests. The best example of this is in the United States where the First Amendment's guarantee of free speech enjoys cult status, while also helping to cement the political influence of economic power. In *Buckley v Valeo* (1976), the **US Supreme Court** ruled that Congress could not put spending limits on candidates for political office on the ground that 'money is speech'. According to the Supreme Court, 'the idea that government may restrict the speech of some elements of our society in order to enhance the relative voice of others is wholly foreign to the First Amendment'. This decision has been important in helping to create what has become probably the greatest elected plutocracy in the world. In 2004, federal candidates alone spent more than $4 billion, about the same as the GDP of Zimbabwe in the same year.

So far as scepticism of the political agenda of the human rights movement is concerned, this is a concern closely related to scepticism about the very idea of human rights. The principal concern is that the human rights movement appears to be heavily impregnated by the soft liberal centre. Although human rights treaties cover both **civil and political rights** (with a commitment to personal liberty) *and* **economic and social rights** (embracing a commitment to **equality**), the main concern of the human rights movement is with the former rather than the latter, which are sometimes barely acknowledged and usually treated as second class citizens. So while civil and political rights may be enforced by way of a complaint to a court (the **European Court of Human Rights**) for adjudication, at least in the case of the United Kingdom social and economic rights are supervised by a process of regular government reports to the Social Rights Committee of the Council of Europe. Some countries allow complaints to be made to the Committee, but it has limited authority.

This different treatment of the two categories of rights reflects a priority of liberty over equality, despite the claims in the Revised Social Charter of 1996 (signed but not ratified by the United Kingdom) that the two categories of rights are 'indivisible'. Scepticism about the political agenda of the human rights movement is reinforced by the extent of the failure to comply with social and economic rights, as reflected in the regular reports of the Social Rights Committee. In an investigation in 2007, the Committee examined the UK's compliance with twenty-three obligations under the Social Charter and reported that there were only thirteen cases of conformity, with seven cases of non-conformity, and three cases where there was insufficient information on which to reach a conclusion. In some cases (the right to organize and bargain collectively), there are multiple breaches of the relevant obligations (three and five respectively). But although reports of this nature are a regular occurrence, they make little impression on the mainstream human rights movement.

Turning to the means adopted to protect human rights, here the sceptical concern is with the role of human rights instruments in domestic law. While this brand of scepticism may accept some commitment to human rights, it questions the legitimacy and/or the effectiveness of courts in upholding these human rights. So far as legitimacy is concerned, some scholars point to the contradiction of judicial protection of human rights if this means that unelected, unaccountable, and irremovable **judges** are to second guess decisions made by elected and representative politicians with an electoral mandate. While this brand of scepticism does not diminish the importance of human rights, it would challenge the autonomy of the discipline and the attempt to insulate it through the legal process from political control. Sceptics of this hue may argue for greater parliamentary controls over the Executive, and may also argue for a more holistic vision of human rights which embraces both civil and political rights along with social and economic rights.

The other concern with this last sect of sceptics is that the human rights movement, with its emphasis on the need for judicial protection of human rights, underestimates the role of **Parliament** in the protection of human rights. Historically, the great human rights advances in the UK were made by Parliament (sometimes to reverse the rules of the **common law** made by judges). Notable examples include the legalization of **abortion**, the decriminalization of **homosexual** conduct, and the abolition of **capital punishment**. It was also Parliament that introduced **legislation** prohibiting discrimination on the grounds of **race**, **sex**, and now a much wider range of grounds as well. And it was Parliament that removed (and reinstated) common law rules restricting the ability of workers to form and join **trade unions** or to take industrial action in defence of trade union interests. Some sceptics also claim that **judicial review** is not always effective and that the judges tend to support the government, especially when human rights are challenged in times of crisis.   KEITH EWING

human rights, theories of   Human rights have gained such an important place in international, regional, supra-national, and national law that concentrating on theories of rights can be open to question. Why worry about a theory of rights when they are so ever present in law and practice? Surely our focus should be on their practical interpretation and application and not on their origins or theoretical basis? These are fair points; it is welcome that we can largely concentrate today on the practical realization of rights rather than the historical struggles for their **recognition**. However, it remains helpful to have an understanding of the different theories of rights that have emerged in history. When someone argues that an individual has a right by virtue of her **humanity**, but that right cannot be found in law, how are we to assess the argument? When an argument is made for a new right, or that the interpretation of a legal right does not reflect the moral right which underpins it, again how should we respond? How do rights relate to other values? Do groups have rights? What should we do when there is a conflict of rights? Which institutions are best placed to unearth the meaning of particular rights? How should rights relate to **community** interests and wider societal concerns? These questions invite us to reflect not just on the practical existence of rights but on their nature and the reasons why they exist. It is helpful to be clear on what precisely it means to talk about a 'right' in law and Wesley Hohfeld's analysis remains useful in identifying the particular right being discussed and what correlates to it (*Fundamental Legal Conceptions as Applied in Judicial Reasoning* (1919)).

Reference to **human rights** can be located in all major world traditions; they are not simply a reflection of secular values and ideals. However, in modern times, their development can be traced to the constitutional revolutions of the seventeenth and eighteenth centuries. In this context the doctrine of 'natural rights'—developed by liberal theorists such as John Locke—was used to justify radical and revolutionary movements seeking to challenge the existing order, the basic idea being that everyone had certain natural rights which it was the role of government and the state to protect. In other words, that a justification for the modern state could be found in the defence of certain natural rights which were inherent in the **person** and in the overarching idea of a 'social contract'. Natural rights were used to justify the English **revolutions** of 1642–1649 and 1688, and in particular the American and French revolutions. The doctrine of inalienable rights is explicitly acknowledged in the US Declaration of Independence 1776 and, in France, the Declaration of the Rights of Man and the Citizen 1789. The Bill of Rights in England 1689 talks of 'ancient . . . [and] undoubted rights and liberties', the US Declaration of Independence notes 'certain unalienable rights; that among these are life, liberty, and the pursuit of happiness . . . [t]hat to secure these rights, governments are instituted among men', the French Declaration of 1789 mentions the 'natural, inalienable, and sacred rights of man'. The underpinning assumption in all such documents was that government is based on a form of social contract and natural rights are there to be upheld and secured by government. These measures tended to stress the **civil and political rights** of the person. In the nineteenth and twentieth centuries, with the development of industrialization, the spread of **democracy**, and the emergence of socialism as a popular political ideology, an increased emphasis was placed on **social and economic rights**. Much of the early development of the idea of rights was at the national level. However, following the events of the 1930s and 1940s in Europe, it was recognized that rights had to find a more secure home within an international system of protection—rights needed a firmer basis beyond the state. Since 1945, the world has witnessed an explosion of standards at the international level. The influence of natural rights thinking is still evident with, for example, the Universal Declaration of Human Rights 1948, Article 1 providing that: 'All human beings are born free and equal in dignity and rights' and the preamble recognizing 'the inherent dignity and . . . the equal and inalienable rights of all members of the human family . . .'.

The idea that there are such things as 'natural rights' has been questioned. Jeremy **Bentham**, for example, argued against the notion of natural rights as nonsensical, the position being that rights must have a basis in a pre-existing political theory and they could only find useful meaning in positive law. The argument is not against human rights, but is one that seeks clarity on underlying political assumptions and demonstrates suspicion about simple assertion of what counts as a right.

Sceptical approaches to human rights are evident in criticisms that have come from conservative, Marxist/socialist perspectives as well as from **Critical Legal Studies** and feminist legal theorists. There is a concern about the individualist nature of rights talk, with the worry that this will fuel an atomistic society where communal values and aspirations are ignored or downplayed. These sceptical perspectives have resulted in questioning of the utility of human rights talk, as well as attempts to highlight the relational nature of rights and their social basis.

There will continue to be discussion about the substantive meaning of particular rights, whether moral and/or legal. Perhaps the most intriguing modern debates are those between positions which are rights-based, but which draw very different practical and institutional conclusions. This is illustrated in the contrasting approaches of Jeremy Waldron (*Law and Disagreement*, 1999) and Ronald Dworkin (*Taking Rights Seriously*, 1977) where there is ongoing debate on the role of legislatures and **courts** in taking rights seriously. Both scholars start from a rights-based theory but reach different conclusions of what this means in practice. The debate maps onto current arguments around the relationship between the executive, legislature, and judiciary. Is there a risk of overplaying the judicial role in certain theories of rights?   COLIN HARVEY

Human Tissue (Act)   The Human Tissue Act 2004, which came into full effect in September 2006, was the product of a series of scandals in UK hospitals at the turn of the millennium relating to **organ retention**. Its remit however extends not only to tissue taken from deceased persons for research, but the storage and use of 'relevant material' (consisting of or including human cells) of any volume (extending from whole corpses to tissue blocks or slides) from living and dead individuals for a range of scheduled, principally medical, purposes (*removal* of tissue from living persons remains governed by the general common law). It is applicable to England and Wales, and for the most part Northern Ireland. Apart from in one or two respects the statute does not extend to Scotland, where its counterpart, the Human Tissue (Scotland) Act 2006 now governs the field.

The central principle of the legislation is consent (although some limited exceptions exist). Appropriate consent is required for most scheduled purposes, including transplantation, research, public display, post-mortem examination, obtaining scientific or medical information relating to another person, establishing the efficacy of any drug or treatment post-mortem, and anatomical examination. In Scotland, the 2006 Act employs the analogous concept of 'authorization'. The statute stipulates *who* should provide 'appropriate consent' but is silent as to the information which needs to be provided to the person consenting (although **Codes of Practice** supplement the statute in this regard (see below)) or as to the *form* of the consent (although written consent is required for either public display or anatomical examination). As regards living persons, consent should be sought from the tissue source, which includes minors who possess *Gillick* competence, or in the case of minors without such competence or who do not wish to decide, a person with **parental responsibility**. With respect to deceased persons, the decision of such a person made when alive is afforded priority. If no such decision was made, then a decision should be sought from any person nominated as a representative by the deceased, and in lieu of such a person, from *a* person in the highest class of 'qualifying relatives' set out in the Act. Relatives may be discounted if unwilling or unable to make a decision, or if they cannot be contacted in time.

Significantly the Act also establishes, for the first time, a comprehensive regulatory framework under the control of the Human Tissue Authority, replacing the Inspectorate of Anatomy and the Unrelated Live Transplants Regulatory Authority. It has a wide remit to oversee aspects of the storage, use, import/export and disposal of human tissue, and licences tissue banks, considers approval (having regard to the validity of the consent and the absence of any commercial dealing) for all living donor organ transplants (also on behalf of the Scottish Executive for Scotland), and issues Codes of Practice (six to date). It is shortly (2008/9) to be merged with the Human Fertilization and Embryology Authority to form the Regulatory Authority for Tissue and Embryos ('RATE').   DAVID PRICE

D Price, 'The Human Tissue Act 2004' [2005] 68 *Modern Law Review* 798
M Brazier and S Fovargue, 'A Brief Guide to the Human Tissue Act 2004' [2006] 1 *Clinical Ethics* 26

human trafficking   Human trafficking involves the movement of persons for the purpose of exploitation. The interpretation provided in Article 3 of the United Nations Protocol to Prevent, Suppress, and Punish Trafficking in Persons, Especially Women and Children, Supplementing the United Nations Convention against Transnational Organized Crime 2003 (as of 2007 signed by 117 and ratified by 112 states) is rapidly becoming the dominant legal definition. It states as follows:

"Trafficking in persons" shall mean the recruitment, transportation, transfer, harboring or receipt of persons, by means of the threat or use of force or other forms of coercion, of abduction, of fraud, of deception, of the abuse of power or of a position of vulnerability or of the giving or receiving of payments or benefits to achieve the consent of a person having control over another person, for the purpose of exploitation. Exploitation shall include, at a minimum, the exploitation of the prostitution of others or other forms of sexual exploitation, forced labor or services, **slavery** or practices similar to slavery, servitude or the removal of organs.

If the **person** concerned is subject to the means described in the definition, consent is irrelevant; if the person is a **minor** (under eighteen years of age), then the means are also irrelevant. Trafficking does not require traversal of an international border, although cross-border movement typically elicits greater attention from the international community because of its implications for **sovereignty** and border control.

The tactics that constitute trafficking can include physical coercion, or deception regarding the destination or consequences in store. For example, one may consent to work as a dancer, only to be forced into domestic service. Or, one might consent to work in domestic service for certain wages and working conditions, but then be compelled to work excessive hours for little or no money.

The status of sex work within the trafficking definition is ambiguous. Some take the position that all prostitution is inherently exploitative, whether or not the person consents to engage in it. Others regard it as a form of work, which may or may not be exploitative, depending on wages, working conditions, and physical security. The international trafficking definition is sufficiently vague to accommodate both interpretations.   AUDREY MACKLIN

humanitarian intervention   *see* **intervention, prohibition of; use of force**

humanity and humanism   One of the noblest claims of modern law is that rights exist for the sake of humanity. **Human rights** in particular, as a combined term, draws both from the moral and political tradition of (legal) humanism and from the institutional and conceptual empire of law. If, according to a standard approach, human rights are a category of rights given to people on account of their humanity and not of any other attributes, the history, the (contested) concept, and the definition of humanity are important normative sources for contemporary law.

The meaning of 'humanity' differed widely across the ages. Slaves have been excluded from humanity, throughout history. On the other hand, pigs, rats, leeches, and insects were regularly and formally indicted and tried in law **courts** in the Middle Ages. **Companies** and other non-human entities were recognized in early modernity as legal **persons**. A strong movement argues today that animals as well as trees, parks, and other natural objects should be given rights.

Let us start with a brief history of humanity. Premodern societies did not develop a comprehensive idea of the human species. Free men were Athenians or Spartans, Romans or Carthaginians, Greeks or barbarians but not members of humanity. According to classical philosophy, a teleologically determined human nature distributes people across social hierarchies and roles and endows them with differentiated characteristics. The word *humanitas* appeared for the first time in the Roman Republic as a translation of the Greek word *paideia*. It was defined as *eruditio et institutio in bonas artes* (the closest modern equivalent is the German word *Bildung*). The Romans inherited the concept from Stoicism and used it to distinguish between the *homo humanus,* the educated Roman who was conversant

with Greek culture and philosophy and was subjected to the *jus civile*, and the *homines barbari,* who included the majority of the non-Roman inhabitants of the Empire. Humanity enters the Western lexicon as an attribute of the *humanus* and a term of distinction. **Cicero** believed that only those who conform to certain standards are really men in the full sense, and merit the adjective 'human' or the attribute 'humanity'.

A different conception of *humanitas* emerged in Christian theology, captured in the Pauline statement, that there is no Greek or Jew, free man or slave. All men are equally part of humanity because they can all be saved through God's plan of salvation. For classical humanism, man is a *zoon logon echon* or *animal rationale*; for Christian metaphysics, the body is the vehicle and prison of the soul. The idea of universal **equality**, unknown to the Greeks, enters Western metaphysics as a spiritual not political state. The Pope, feudal lords, the King, the representatives of God on earth, held power in Western Christianity. Their subjects, the *sub-jecti* or *sub-diti*, took their law from their political superiors.

The religious grounding of humanity was undermined by the liberal political philosophies of the seventeenth and eighteenth centuries. Early modern natural law, influenced by stoicism and Christian **universalism**, amended the classical differentiated ontology and developed the idea of species existence, of a common human nature that unites all people, irrespective of their individual characteristics and cultural or social determinations. For Hobbes or Locke, Descartes or Voltaire, men share a common humanity even though its contents differ for each philosopher. The foundation of humanity was transferred from God to (human) nature, initially conceived in deistic, and today in scientific, terms. By the end of the eighteenth century, 'man' had become the absolute value and individuality the centre of the socio-economic and political arrangements of modernity. Humanity entered the historical stage as a peculiar combination of classical and Christian metaphysics.

Humanism posits a universal human essence which is then attributed to every empirical **person.** As species existence, 'man' appears without differentiation or distinction in his nakedness and simplicity, united with all others in a nature deprived of substantive characteristics, except for free will, reason, and soul—the universal elements of human essence. This is the 'man' of the 'rights of man' of the American and French **revolutions** and declarations: an abstraction of little concrete humanity, since he lacks those characteristics (history, needs,

desires, **gender**, **race**, sexuality, etc) that build concrete **identities**. The minimum of humanity allows
'man' to claim **autonomy**, moral **responsibility**, and
legal subjectivity. If the epochal principle of modern
metaphysics is subjectivity, it is driven and exemplified by legal personality and the rights of 'man'.

Humanism marks the concern of modernity to
escape cosmological or theological determinations,
to release humanity from the bonds of prejudice and
ignorance, and to discover its worth exclusively in
itself. By believing in universal essences and accepting one interpretation of humanity as absolute and
eternal truth, humanism enthrones the subject as
master of the world. At the same time, it often mistakes a Eurocentric, epochal, and partial view of
human nature as eternal, absolute, and stable. The
universal man of human rights appears an unencumbered human being. But the empirical persons
who have enjoyed the 'rights of man' have been historically men, all too men — well-off, white, heterosexual, urban males — who condense in their person
the abstract dignity of humanity and the real prerogatives of belonging to the community of the powerful. The metaphysical closure is accompanied often
by the exclusion of those who do not meet fully the
requirements of the putative human essence. One
could write the history of human rights as the ongoing and failing struggle to close the gap between the
abstract man and the concrete citizen; to add flesh,
blood, and sex to the pale outline of the 'human'.

Legal humanism followed closely its philosophical progenitor and adopted the Cartesian and Kantian attitudes towards **subject** and nature. For legal
humanism, 'man' is the principle and end of everything, the author and end of law. The legal subject,
seen as an isolated monad with solitary consciousness and faced with a disenchanted, threatening but
also malleable world, turns to the self to discover the
principles of legislation and become autonomous.
For the legal mentality, the essence of humanity is
present in the free, willing, and solitary legal subject.
These subjective characteristics become the basis
for positing the objective legal universe. Rights, the
building blocks of modern law, are the tools through
which human beings, redefined as creatures of will
and desire, pursue their life plans. The legal person is
the humanist subject armed with rights.

The jurisprudence of rights is the necessary and
inevitable companion of legal positivism. Every posited rule presupposes an author, a legislative subject.
The Sovereign too is presented in the guise of a super-
individual entity with desires, rights, and powers.
Reason and will, the two facets of legal humanism
as well as rationalism and voluntarism, their two
deformations, are perfectly encapsulated in the perennial conundrum of British constitutionalism, the
contradiction between the rule of law and **parliamentary sovereignty** or human rights and national
sovereignty.

There can be no positivized law without the
humanist legal subject, the bearer of rights and duties;
there can be no conception of rights without a positive set of laws and institutions that bring the subject
into existence and endow it with the patrimony of
rights. Positive rule, subject, and right come together
and presuppose one another. The subject of law, as
the double genitive indicates, both legislates the law
and is subjected to it. The constitution of modernity
started with the humanist premise of supporting the
natural freedom of the individual but has now been
covered by a hyper-inflation of norms. The proliferation of rules and the obsession with **regulation** and
governance is a logical end of the humanist paradox,
according to which an external constraint supports
freedom. In an extreme form, this could lead to all
human relations turning into legal rights. But in
such a development some of the noblest traditions of
(legal) humanism will have been lost.

COSTAS DOUZINAS

M Heidegger, 'Letter on Humanism' in DF Krell (ed),
Basic Writings (San Francisco: Harper, 1977)
C Douzinas, *The End of Human Rights* (Oxford: Hart,
2000)

Hunt, Joseph   *see* Thurtell, John and Hunt, Joseph

I

ICTY   *see* **Milosevic, Slobodan**

identity   Identity is often used in relation to personal identity, namely, the distinct personality or characteristics of an individual. Identity, in this sense, is used to explore issues of sense of self and its persistence. However, identity has other philosophical meanings, including exact sameness, in the sense of identical. Identity may be qualitative (things share properties) and numerical (absolute or total qualitative identity: the thing and itself).

Personal identity involves a **person**'s individual sense of him or her self as a discrete and separate entity. It may involve self image and a sense of the characteristics that make a person unique. Social identity involves an individual identification as part of a collective or group, such as belonging to a nation, class, **ethnicity**, **religion**, or other subgroup. Cultural identity is similarly used to denote a person's self of affiliation with a particular cultural group.

Identity has been a central organizing feature in identity politics, which refers to a range of political theorizing and activism organized around shared experiences of discrimination or subordination of members of a social group. Often seen as having its first articulation in the 1977 statement of the Combahee River Collective, a black feminist group, identity politics seeks to empower a disadvantaged group through a consciousness-raising process of sharing common experiences of oppression. Through this process, members of the group will come to a shared and more authentic sense of self. Both the process and the resultant knowledge form the basis of political action. Identity politics is often associated with a standpoint epistemology which emphasizes the production of knowledge from the perspective of the situated and disadvantaged knower as a corrective to the dominant ways of knowing.

Identity politics has been the subject of considerable controversy and critique. Many argued that identity politics for its underlying essentialism, that is, its belief that a person has certain innate qualities. The idea that a particular social group was characterized by certain innate characteristics was seen as erasing the multiple differences within such groups, as well as imposing a kind of disciplinary function on the self-understanding of members of those groups. For example, within feminism, identity politics initially emphasized **women**'s shared experience of oppression. However, this emphasis on shared experience and identity became the subject of critique for its failure to appreciate the multiple differences between women, such as **race**, class, and other intersecting axes of power. Similar critiques occurred with race studies, with scholars rejecting the essentializing and naturalizing of racial categories. Yet other critiques of identity politics focused on the emphasis in identity politics on experience as a claim to truth, arguing that experience is itself mediated and social constructed, and requires a broader theoretical framework to give it meaning.

Struggles over sexual identity have played a particularly significant role in the gay and **lesbian** rights movement. Gay and lesbian activists initially mobilized around the idea of a shared and innate sexual identity. Others, following Foucault's groundbreaking work *History of Sexuality*, Volume I, argued that homosexuality was a genealogically constructed identity, took issue with the idea of an essentialist and biologically-based identity. Building on this approach, **queer** theory of the 1990s rejected this identity-based politics, arguing that the very identities of gay and lesbian are produced through the binary of homosexuality and heterosexuality, a binary that produces the normalcy of the former and the deviancy of the later. Queer theory, in advocating the deconstruction of this binary, was radically anti-identitarian in its orientation.

Another use of identity can be found in the concept of **gender** identity, which generally refers to a person's sense of gender identification, that is, whether a person identities as male or female. It was originally used as a medical term in relation to sex reassignment procedures, to explain the disjunction between a person's psychological sense of gender and their physical gender. This condition is referred to in the Diagnostic and Statistical Manual of Mental Disorders ('DSM') as gender identity disorder. In recent years, the idea of gender identity and gender identity disorder has been used in theory and activism around transgendered people. A similar debate has emerged within transgender theory and activism has occurred within earlier feminist, race, and sexual orientation debates around identity politics. Some argue that gender identity is innate—a person is born with it—and may require sexual realignment surgery if that identity is not consistent with one's physiological gender. Others have argued that this view of gender identity is unduly essentialist, and posited on a binary of gender that seeks to disciplines unruly bodies into compliance. Like queer theory, this view seeks to open up the range of possible gender identities beyond the male/female binary.

BRENDA COSSMAN

L Alcoff (ed), *Identity Politics Reconsidered* (New York: Palgrave Macmillan, 2006)

P Hill Collins, *Black Feminist Thought: Knowledge, Consciousness and the Politics of Empowerment* (New York: Routledge, 1991)

See also: **transsexual**

illegal migration The concept 'illegal' migration is commonly used to describe a variety of phenomena involving people who enter or remain in a country of which they are not a citizen in breach of national laws. These include migrants who enter or remain in a country without authorization, those who are smuggled or trafficked across an international border, unsuccessful **asylum** seekers who fail to observe a **deportation** order, and people who circumvent immigration controls, for example through the arrangement of bogus **marriages** or fake **adoptions**.

The use of the term 'illegal' in this context has attracted considerable criticism, and increasingly the term 'irregular' is used instead. One reason is the connotation with criminality. Most illegal migrants are not criminals; rather they are in breach of administrative rules. Secondly, defining **persons** as 'illegal' is also regarded by some as denying their **humanity**—a human being cannot be illegal. A third reason is the specific possibility that labelling as 'illegal' asylum seekers who find themselves in an irregular situation may jeopardize their claim on asylum.

The two other terms that are often used in this context are 'undocumented' and 'unauthorized'. The problem with the former is that it is ambiguous.

It is sometimes used to denote migrants who have not been documented (or recorded), and sometimes to describe migrants without documents (**passports** and so on). Neither situation applies to all illegal migrants. Similarly, not all illegal migrants necessarily enter a country without authority—they may become illegal at a later stage.

There are important regional differences in the way that the concept of illegal migration is applied. In Europe, for example, where the entry of people from outside the European Union is closely controlled, it is relatively easy to define and identify illegal migrants. That is not the case in many parts of Africa, in contrast, where borders are porous, ethnic and linguistic groups straddle state borders, some people belong to nomadic **communities**, and many people do not have proof of their place of birth or **citizenship**.

Another conceptual complexity arises because a migrant's status can change—often rapidly. For example a migrant can enter a country illegally, but then regularize their status by applying for asylum or entering a regularization programme. Conversely, a migrant can enter legally then become illegal by working without a work permit or overstaying a visa.

The analysis of irregular migration is further hampered by a serious lack of accurate data, making it difficult to identify trends or to compare the scale of the phenomenon in different parts of the world. One reason is conceptual—the term covers a range of people who can be illegal migrants for different reasons and whose status can change quickly. Another reason is methodological. People without regular status are likely to avoid speaking to the authorities for fear of detection, and thus go unrecorded. There is, nevertheless, a broad consensus that, as the number of international migrants has increased so too has the global scale of irregular migration. Most estimates of irregular migration are at the national level. It is thought, for example, that there are over 10 million illegal migrants in the USA and that, despite increased efforts at border control, about 500,000 additional migrants enter the USA without authorization each year. It is also estimated that there are between 3.5 and 5 million illegal migrants in the Russian Federation, originating mainly in countries of the Commonwealth of Independent States and South-East Asia. Up to 20 million illegal migrants are thought to live in India today.

Other estimates are provided on a regional or global scale. It is estimated by the Organization for Economic Cooperation and Development that between 10 and 15 per cent of Europe's 56 million migrants are illegal and that each year around half a million undocumented migrants arrive in the EU. Perhaps half of all migrants in both Africa and Latin America are also thought to be illegal. Overall, an estimated 2.5 to 4 million migrants cross all international borders without authorization each year.

People who move in an illegal fashion leave their countries for exactly the same reasons as any other migrants. The causes of all international migration are increasingly embedded in the wider process of globalization. Put simply these are a combination of increasing incentives to migrate, increasing awareness of opportunities elsewhere, and increasing access to the means to move and enter another country, even without authority. The reason that growing numbers of migrants move in an illegal rather than legal way is because of increasing restrictions on legal movements, mainly in destination countries. More people than ever before want to move, but there are proportionately fewer legal opportunities for them to do so.

Illegal migration undermines the exercise of state **sovereignty**. States have a sovereign right to control who crosses their borders and remains on their territory which is by definition challenged by illegal migration. Where it involves **corruption** and organized crime, illegal migration can also become a threat to public **security**. When it results in competition for scarce jobs, illegal migration can also generate xenophobic sentiments within host populations. Importantly, these sentiments are often directed not only at illegal migrants, but also at established migrants, **refugees,** and ethnic **minorities**. In certain circumstances illegal migration can also be associated with specific health **risks**, largely because illegal migrants rarely access **public health** services. Especially when it takes place on a significant scale, and when it receives a great deal of media attention, illegal migration can also undermine public confidence in the integrity and effectiveness of a state's migration and asylum policies.

Equally, however, illegal migration can undermine the human security of the migrants themselves. It can endanger their lives. A large number of people die trying to cross land and sea borders without being detected by the authorities—annually an estimated 2,000 trying to cross the Mediterranean from Africa to Europe and 400 trying to cross the Mexico–US border.

Smugglers may extract a high price from migrants and human traffickers exploit them. Some commentators have described **human trafficking** as a contemporary form of **slavery**. More generally, people who enter or remain in a country without authorization are often at risk of exploitation by employers and landlords. And because of their illegal status, migrants are usually unable to make full use of their skills and experience once they have arrived in a country of destination.

Women constitute a substantial proportion of illegal migrants. Because they are confronted with **gender**-based discrimination, illegal female migrants are often obliged to accept the most menial informal sector jobs. The majority of migrant domestic workers and migrants employed in the sex industry are women and are at particular risk of abuse. The latter in particular also face specific health-related risks, including exposure to **HIV/AIDS**.

Illegal migrants are often also unwilling to seek redress from authorities because they fear **arrest** and deportation. As a result, they do not always make use of public services to which they are entitled, for example emergency health care. In most countries, they are also barred from using the full range of services available to citizens and migrants with regular status. In such situations, already hard-pressed **NGOs,** religious bodies, and other civil society institutions are obliged to provide assistance to illegal migrants, at times compromising their own legitimacy.

Policies targeting illegal migration can be distinguished in two ways. First, there is a distinction between policies targeted on reducing the arrival of irregular migrants and those concerned with dealing with irregular migrants who have already entered. The former include more border controls, biometric tests, and extended **visa** regimes. The latter mainly concern either return or regularization.

A second distinction is between short-term policies aimed at trying to stem irregular migration and longer-term policies concerned to reduce incentives to move in an illegal manner in the first place. The latter include achieving development targets to increase security and livelihoods in origin countries, as well as increasing the opportunities to move legally.

There is growing consensus that while such policies may reduce the scale of irregular migration, it will nevertheless continue for the foreseeable future. One reason is that the forces that determine the scale of international migration are powerful and the ability to modify them is limited.   KHALID KOSER

B Jordan and F Duvell, *Irregular Migration: The Dilemmas of Transnational Mobility* (London: Edward Elgar, 2003)

K Koser, 'Irregular migration', in B Marshall (ed), *The Politics of Migration* (London: Routledge, 2006) 44–57

images, law and   *see* **visual arts, law and**

immigrant   *see* **immigration and emigration**

immigration and emigration At their most basic, immigration refers to people entering a country and emigration refers to those leaving. Usually, however, immigration refers to those who enter a country with the intent to live there on an on-going basis. Tourists and those staying for a defined time, such as students and temporary workers, generally are not considered to be immigrants. The law pays far more attention to immigration than to emigration.

Despite the international nature of immigration and emigration, **international law** pays little attention to these topics. International **human rights** instruments do establish that people have the right to leave their country of origin or nationality, but this right has not attracted much attention in the courts. Near the beginning of the twentieth century there were some attempts to establish international rules about immigration. These negotiations ultimately failed. As a result, there are really only two internationally-agreed rules about who can cross national borders. The first is that nations will allow their own citizens (or nationals) to enter. The second is that refugees will not be returned to places where they are in danger. Both of these rules are important, but neither is unproblematic for international law.

Given the almost complete absence of international law about immigration, this matter is governed by domestic law, that is, laws of nation states. Each country is free to determine who will be admitted to live there and under what conditions. In many countries, lawful immigration is a precursor to obtaining **citizenship**.

While people have immigrated and emigrated for centuries, the legal regime that is familiar to us today is comparatively recent. It is only since the early years of the twentieth century that the world has been fully and firmly controlled through a system of **passports** and **visas** that facilitates regulation of immigration, and could be adapted to regulate emigration. The great waves of immigration that marked the dramatic population growth of 'New World' settler nations, such as the United States, Canada, and Australia, in the nineteenth century took place largely outside any legal framework.

Those countries with fully articulated immigration programmes generally admit migrants in either three or four categories. The first three categories are economic migrants, family migrants, and humanitarian migrants. Sometimes a fourth category is also included, that of migrants with a common heritage or identity.

Economic migrants are admitted because the government of the day believes that they will assist the national economy in some way. Over time, and in different places, this can be articulated quite differently, but it has been a common theme since the inception of immigration regulation. Canada and Australia led the way in the 1970s in establishing 'points systems' as a method of determining which economic category of migrants to admit. The **United Kingdom** is poised to move to a similar system early in the twenty-first century.

Family migrants are admitted because of their kinship with people who are already citizens or **permanent resident**s of the country that is admitting them. This type of migration reflects a commitment to family as a core societal value. Some contentious issues that arise here. First, regulating family migration requires defining family membership. Life partners and children, the Western 'nuclear' family, are typically within the definition, but beyond this, definitions vary widely. As migration contexts span diverse cultures, variations and challenges to family definition are myriad. A second area of contention is that family migration intersects with international human rights commitments protecting **family life**. Human rights protections for the family have been put forward as a basis for permitting immigration that states wants to prevent. Such arguments have often failed, but are gaining some ground now under the **European Convention on Human Rights** and the **Convention on the Rights of the Child**. Family migration makes up by far the largest category of permanent, regular migration to the United States.

Humanitarian migrants are those who are admitted to the nation because of a belief that it is a good and just thing to do. This category of admissions casts the nation as generous and benevolent. A significant part of this category is comprised of **refugees**. While **asylum** seekers do have rights at international law, these rights are constrained in such a way that humanitarian considerations play a significant part of the admission system. In addition, humanitarian migration includes a variety of migrants who do not fit precisely into a legal category, but whom the nation nonetheless considers it valuable to admit. These people include individuals in situations similar to those of refugees and family members, but who are somehow outside the letter of the law. In Britain, the device of 'exceptional leave to remain' was a well established admission route for many years.

The most well-known examples of identity-based migration are those of Germany and Israel. Germany has long had an immigration policy allowing entry for ethnic Germans. While this was originally considered to be distinct from immigration, in recent years, ethnic German immigration has been subject to quotas which have reduced its significance and brought it much closer to the logic of other categories of immigration. Israel's Law of Return allows Jews a right to enter and live in Israel.

While policy discussions of immigration tend to focus on reasons for admitting people, the law of immigration is heavily weighted towards exclusions. Since about the 1980s, most Western states have developed increasingly strict exclusionary regimes. The main categories of exclusion are health and criminality. An important subset of criminality since 2001 has been exclusion based on potential threats to **security**. In general, immigration exclusions are forward-looking, so that individuals may be barred from entry on the basis of a threat they may pose in the future, rather than simply because of a criminal record in the past. Race-based exclusions were commonplace in migration laws of the first half of the twentieth century, but are now gone from the migration laws of Western nations.

CATHERINE DAUVERGNE

immigration security screening Excluding those who threaten the **security** of the United Kingdom has long been an important objective of immigration law. First, entry clearance or leave to enter the UK *must* be refused if the Secretary of State personally directs that it would be conducive to the public good (Immigration Rules, paragraph 320(6)). Immigration Officers also *may* refuse entry clearance or leave to enter, or cancel an existing clearance or leave, if it is conducive to the public good, for example where entry is undesirable because of the person's character, conduct, or associations (Immigration Rules, paragraphs 320(19), 321A(4)–(5), 321(iii)).

Determining what is in the 'public good' clearly involves policy judgments and decision-makers enjoy a considerable **discretion**, subject to public law and **human rights** constraints. Some decisions have been controversial, as when the American leader of the Nation of Islam, Louis Farrakhan, was prevented from entering the UK in 2002 because the Secretary of State feared that Farrakhan's incendiary views about Jews would create public disorder. While the **courts** upheld the decision, it suggests how the power may affect **freedoms of expression**, association, and movement, and raises questions about how deferential the courts should be towards executive opinions—not least due to the risk of political abuse.

Secondly, entry clearance or leave to enter should normally be refused if a person has been convicted in any country of an offence which, if committed in the UK, is punishable by twelve months or more imprisonment (Immigration Rules, paragraph 320(18)), unless admission is justified for strong compassionate reasons. In practice, the power has been applied inconsistently, since only nationals who required entry clearance prior to arrival had to declare convictions. While only ten to twenty people are refused entry each year, the power has been controversial, as when the Secretary of State discretionarily admitted the boxer, Mike Tyson, despite a **rape** conviction in the United States. If a person already possesses an entry clearance, leave to enter may be refused because of their criminal record (Immigration Rules, paragraph 321(iii)).

The Secretary of State has a discretion to deport a person if it is conducive to the public good for being in the interests of **national security**, UK foreign relations or the public interest (**Nationality**, Immigration, and **Asylum** Act 2002, section 97(2)). The power facilitates the removal of, for example, suspected foreign terrorists or war criminals and **appeals** may be heard by a Special Immigration Appeals Commission, which can protect security-sensitive information. In addition, travel bans imposed by the UN Security Council or the European Union, as on suspected war criminals or serious human rights violators, can be implemented by Orders of the Secretary of State (Immigration and Asylum Act 1999). Asylum seekers are subject to additional rules on exclusion and expulsion under **refugee** law.

Immigration officials routinely cooperate with law enforcement, intelligence, and customs services in screening security **risks**. Practical measures to improve security screening include **visa** regimes, posting immigration officers abroad, sharing passenger information and intelligence across jurisdictions, and biometric technology to reduce identity fraud. Special powers also exist to stop, detain, search, and question any person at a port of entry to determine if the person is involved in **terrorism** (Terrorism Act 2000).   BEN SAUL

immunity, diplomatic and state A court, in adjudicating a claim in accordance with the law, exercises jurisdiction. Immunity is a bar limiting the judge from exercising such jurisdiction against a certain class of persons or subject matter. Its purpose is not to defeat liability but to direct the claim to another method of settlement. Thus, in national law, parliamentary immunity bars legal proceedings against a MP while Parliament is in session.

In international law immunity secures respect for the equality and independence of states and for the settlement of disputes by consent rather than the diktat of one state. It does so by barring a national court from exercising jurisdiction against a foreign state, its head of state or of government, or a diplomat while carrying out official functions. Thus, 'to guarantee the proper functioning of the network of mutual inter-State relations, which is of paramount importance for a well-ordered and harmonious international system', ambassadors, and other members of a foreign mission, are granted immunity (in accordance with the 1961 Vienna Convention on Diplomatic Relations) from criminal and civil proceedings in the courts of the host state, save in respect of claims relating to land or to a business which they carry on for their own private purposes. **International customary law** confers similar immunities on heads of state and of government. In the *Arrest Warrant* case (2006) the **International Court of Justice** ruled that a serving Minister for Foreign Affairs was immune from criminal proceedings brought in a Belgian court for inciting the commission of an international crime.

Activities of governments and their departments were once accorded immunity by the courts of other states, even though the conduct complained of might arise from business. However, disputes relating to contract and trade are essentially matters to be determined by a court of law; and with increasing engagement of states in commercial activities, state practice, as reflected in the European Convention on State Immunity, and American and UK legislation, came to recognize that the immunities afforded to the state and its agents by international law for acts done in exercise of sovereign or governmental authority need not be extended to commercial transactions, into which the state entered in a manner similar to a private person. Thus states may now be sued in national courts for non-payment of debts and breach of contract. The 2004 UN Convention on State Immunity (not yet in force) sets out such rules of international law.

This development caused people to ask why, if national courts have jurisdiction under international law to adjudicate private commercial claims brought against states, international law should not equally permit national courts to exercise jurisdiction and disregard immunity where the defendant state commits a breach of 'established rules of international law of fundamental importance'. Questioners pointed to the development of **international human rights law**

and to the possibility of prosecuting international crimes of government officials, including heads of state, before the **International Criminal Court**. In plain terms, the question is: why should a claim, that a state or its official tortured an individual or caused loss of life or property in the course of armed conflict in breach of international law, be barred by a claim of immunity from adjudication in the national court of another state? In the **Pinochet case**, such an argument was successful to the extent that immunity was held not to bar criminal proceedings against a former head of state relating to commission, while in office, of the international crime of state torture.

Subsequently national courts have given conflicting rulings in respect of civil claims. English and German courts support immunity from civil jurisdiction in proceedings against states and their officials for reparation for international crimes, while Greek and Italian courts reject immunity in respect of claims for reparation for war damage caused by foreign states. The **European Court of Human Rights** has held that a UK court properly barred a claim for damages for torture against Kuwait on the ground that 'the grant of sovereign immunity to a State in civil proceedings pursues the legitimate aim of complying with international law to promote comity and good relations between States through the respect of another State's sovereignty'. State immunity from civil jurisdiction for acts in exercise of sovereign authority remains the present rule.

HAZEL FOX

impeachment   Impeachment was the method by which, in pre-democratic times, the British Parliament was able to hold Ministers of the **Crown** to account. The process was for such officers to be impeached by the **House of Commons** for the treason, high crimes, and misdemeanours for which they were allegedly responsible and for the matter then to be determined by the **House of Lords**. As responsible and then democratic government gradually became the norm, the use of impeachment declined in the **United Kingdom**, with the last instance of its deployment being the impeachment of Lord Melville in 1806, for alleged corruption. Nowadays British ministers face political rather than legal pressure to withdraw from ministerial life where they are found to have been implicated in serious wrongdoing, a sanction backed by the threat of a dismissal or a forced resignation. The one minister for whom this form of accountability does not arise is the Prime Minister, and it was on this basis that an effort was made in 2004 to have the then Prime Minister Tony Blair impeached for having allegedly mislead the

House of Commons over the circumstances justifying the invasion of Iraq the year before. Proponents of the move were undoubtedly alerted to its potential by the not-infrequent recourse to the motion of impeachment in the United States where—protected by that country's written constitution—it has continued to operate. In 1998–1999 President Clinton was impeached by the US House of Representatives but acquitted by the US Senate, while in 1974 President Nixon resigned rather than face such proceedings. CONOR GEARTY

implied repeal *see* **parliamentary sovereignty**

implied terms *see* **contract law; quality of products; quality of services**

imprisonment for debt *see* **enforcement of court orders**

imprisonment without trial *see* **detention without trial**

incapacitation theory There is room for argument about how far **punishment** deters crime, and even more room for argument about whether and how it can reform or rehabilitate offenders. However, one thing that some modes of punishment can certainly do is incapacitate those on whom they are imposed from committing further crimes. Apart from execution (which does incapacitate absolutely, but is objectionable on other grounds), imprisonment can incapacitate most prisoners from committing many (though not all) kinds of crime on anyone other than **prison** officials or fellow prisoners. Impressed by this fact, and by the fact that a very high proportion of crimes are committed by a relatively small minority of multiple offenders, some theorists argue that we should use imprisonment as an efficient mode of incapacitation. We should identify that relatively small group of multiple offenders, and subject them to extended terms of detention in order to prevent the many crimes that they would otherwise probably commit. (Previous crimes are a key indicator of future crime; such measures should therefore be imposed only on actual offenders.)

Such theories face two kinds of objection. One focuses on the problems of prediction. We cannot hope accurately to identify all and only those who would commit serious crimes if not detained: so we either use indicators that we know will produce a high proportion of 'false negatives'—people identified as low **risk** who will in fact re-offend; or use indicators that we know will produce a high proportion of 'false positives'—people identified as high risk who would not in fact have re-offended. In the former case, the practice will be ineffective; in the latter case, it will perpetrate serious injustices, by subjecting to lengthy detention people who do not deserve it and who are not in fact a danger to others.

Another objection focuses on the treatment of those who are *correctly* identified as being 'dangerous', ie as being very likely to commit further serious offences if left free. They will already have committed serious crimes, for which they deserve relatively severe punishment: but even if we allow that an offender with a serious prior criminal record deserves a longer period of imprisonment for his current offence than does one without such a record (which is itself controversial), incapacitative sentences far exceed what could be plausibly thought to be deserved, and are therefore unjust as punishments. We might instead portray them as non-punitive measures of preventive detention: but the objection would then be that they fail to treat those subjected to them as responsible citizens who must be left free to determine their own actions, and who can legitimately be coerced only in response to their voluntary criminal actions. Such purely incapacitative detention could be justified only if serious and persistent offenders forfeited their status as responsible citizens: but we should be very reluctant to take that view of them. ANTONY DUFF

A von Hirsch, AJ Ashworth, and J Roberts (eds), *Principled Sentencing* (Oxford: Hart Publishing, 3rd edn, 2008), ch 3

incapacity *see* **capacity**

incapacity for work The **social security system** operates rules governing incapacity for work to determine who is entitled to certain benefits (such as incapacity benefit and the employment and support allowance). Incapacity means the loss of capacity to earn an income through working which arises because of a person's disability. The relevant rules have changed over the years, principally because successive governments have sought to make the qualifying criteria for such benefits more restrictive. The definition of incapacity for work is an important boundary which reflects and reinforces values about the nature and extent of the social obligation to work.

Initially claimants are assessed by their ability to do their normal job, but after a period of time they are judged according to their capacity to do any type of work. Typically claimants undergo a medical examination designed to test their ability to carry out certain specified physical activities (eg walking, sitting, standing, reaching, etc), and to identify any mental health issues; points are assigned for each function according to the extent of the functional problem. If the aggregate of these scores reaches the defined level, a claimant is adjudged to be incapable of work for benefit purposes. This process is known as a Personal Capability Assessment ('PECA'). Traditionally, unemployed claimants who have been found to be incapable of work have been paid a higher rate of benefit than the able-bodied jobless. Decisions on incapacity for work form a significant proportion of appeals to **tribunals** in the social security system.

NICK WIKELEY

income tax   Income tax was first introduced in **Great Britain** in 1799. Income tax is a tax on income. Not everything that 'comes in' is necessarily treated as taxable income. Income is sometimes contrasted with capital. This raises problems with the treatment of capital gains. Should they be treated as income? In some systems they are. The UK did not have a **capital gains tax** until the 1960s, but now has a separate system of capital gains taxation. This raises further problems of categorization. Adam Smith's illustration of a tree as capital and the fruit as income is often referred to in the case law, but does not deal with difficulties such as whether a stalk is fruit or tree. It is often vital where, as in the UK, the effective rates of income tax and capital gains tax differ and the taxable amount may differ according to whether it is income or capital.

As in the UK, a list approach is often adopted to defining what income from what sources is to be taxed. Until recently this was done by 'Schedules', which were originally schedules to the Income Tax Act. Under the list approach (sometimes called the 'source doctrine'), only income from sources on the list is taxable. Governments may seek to overcome problems associated with this approach by including a provision making 'any other income' taxable. Sources that produce taxable income include employment, trade, interest, dividends, and annuities. Not everything liable to income tax would be income to an accountant. For example, employment termination payments can be liable to income tax but would often be capital for accounts purposes.

The problem of income measurement also arises. Should any expenses be allowed in computing the amount of taxable income? If so what expenses? Should an accounting approach be used? There was no real accountancy profession in Great Britain when income tax was introduced. Accordingly, an accountancy base for income measurement was not adopted. The UK has been moving more towards an accounting base recently, but only in certain respects. A trader's accounts still require adjustment for tax purposes. For example depreciation is not allowed but capital allowances may be available.

The next issue is what rate or rates of tax should be used. Originally income tax in the UK was a flat rate tax. All sources of income were taxed at the same rate. Whether higher income should attract higher rates of tax became an issue in the late nineteenth century. A progressive rate system was then introduced and remains today. Rates have varied considerably, the top rate having reached a high of 98 per cent under the Labour government of the 1970s. This was a marginal rate as the UK has a system of reliefs and allowances used in computing taxable income.

Another question concerns what connecting factors bring a person into the income tax net of a country. In the UK these are UK residence or having a UK income source. Other countries (eg the USA) use citizenship as a connecting factor.

In most systems there are many anti-avoidance provisions intended to stop the use of offshore entities and other techniques to avoid or reduce liability to income tax.

ADRIAN SHIPWRIGHT

incorporation   Incorporation refers to the process of forming a **company**. The word derives originally from Latin meaning to 'form into a body'. There are three different types of UK companies that can be incorporated; chartered, statutory, and registered. Chartered companies are rare and were formed by a charter from the **Crown.** They were usually accompanied by a **patent** grant conferring monopoly rights over an invention or trade route. The most famous chartered company was the East India Trading Company which was formed in 1600 by Elizabeth I. The formation charter was accompanied by a monopoly right to exploit trade in the East Indies. Statutory corporations are also relatively rare. Historically as the UK **Parliament** became more important the process of incorporation was largely taken over from the Crown by Parliament. Consequently the formation of a statutory company needed a combination of public interest venture and powerful lobby group. Great Western Railways ('GWR') for example was formed as a statutory company in 1835 to link the port of Bristol to London. The combination of a public infrastructure project and the lobbying of the Bristol merchants proved sufficient for Parliament to pass an Act forming the company. Registered companies were introduced in 1844 and are very different in character from statutory and charter companies as they can be formed by anyone filing the correct documents and paying a small fee. As such, incorporation became available to the masses rather than the privilege of the few. Most companies encountered today are registered companies.   ALAN DIGNAM

indecency *see* **obscenity**

independent directors 'Negligence and profusion', wrote Adam Smith in *The Wealth of Nations*, 'must always prevail, more or less, in the management of joint stock [public] **companies**'. For Smith, this was an inevitable consequence of their separation of ownership and management. The problems of directorial self-dealing, malpractice, and **accountability** have worsened since Smith's time as corporations have grown in size and power and as corporate shareholders have become ever more dispersed and *rentier* in nature. In recent decades, they have become particularly acute as post-war ideas about 'socially responsible corporations' (in which it was expected that **directors** would to some extent balance the conflicting interests of shareholders and other corporate constituencies) have waned and the principle of shareholder primacy has been vigorously reasserted. The problem of **corporate governance** has increasingly come to be defined as a straightforward 'agency problem': how can we ensure that corporate directors do not abuse their power and act in the interests of shareholder-owners? The problem is that many of the proposed solutions—lifting the barriers to take-overs to foster the development of the 'market for corporate control', realigning the interests of directors and shareholders through such things as **share** options—have created problems of their own as directors have sought artificially to inflate share prices. The rise of a 'greed is good' corporate culture has also contributed to the problem, as has the idea that no ceiling should be imposed on **executive pay**.

It is in this context that the non-executive director ('NED') with alleged independence from executives and management has been thrust forward as a solution to managerial self-dealing and incompetence. NEDs were originally largely ornamental, but from the 1950s they began to be employed in specialist, strategic roles. In the 1970s, however, they began to be touted not as strategic advisors but as monitors, prompting a search for 'independent' NEDS who could supervise the supervisors. The report of the Cadbury Committee (1992), set up following a series of corporate scandals, emphasized their monitoring role. Independent, non-executive directors, it is argued, can provide a solution to corporate managerial malpractice and incompetence. Moreover, they can do so within a non-legislative framework of voluntary self-regulation and without disturbing the unitary board. The monitoring role of NEDs was examined again by the Higgs Committee (2003) and although its recommendations met with substantial City opposition, they were incorporated, albeit much diluted, into the **Combined Code on Corporate Governance**. Higgs sought among other things to offer guidance on the meaning of 'independent' (suggesting, for example, that after ten years NEDs must automatically lose their quality of independence, a rule which was relaxed when incorporated into the Combined Code) and demanded that in larger companies independent NEDs should constitute half of the members of the board. Sitting on specialized committees (especially audit and remuneration), it is now expected that the strong and independent non-executive will perform crucial monitoring functions, ensuring that corporate executives do not behave in a self-serving manner and act in the interests of shareholders.

Serious questions remain, however, not only about the training and competence of non-executives (Lord Young of Graffham, one of Mrs Thatcher's favourite Ministers, thought they should be abolished) but about their appointment and independence. The independence of NEDs is still for the corporate boards they are meant to be monitoring to determine, and research suggests that the pool of NEDs is very narrow indeed, consisting largely of executive directors (or former executive directors) of other companies sitting as non-executives on other companies' boards. This has led to calls to expand the 'gene pool' from which NEDs are drawn. Nor is it clear how NEDs can balance their strategic and monitoring roles. It is, perhaps, not insignificant that on paper, Enron's board was, in this respect, state-of-the-art.

                                    PADDY IRELAND

Independent Police Complaints Commission *see* **complaints procedures; ombudsmen**

independent schools Independent schools are often also referred to as 'private schools' or 'public schools'. They are usually run by private organizations, such as limited **companies** or registered **charities**, or by individuals. Such an organization or individual is often referred to as the 'proprietor' of the school.

Generally, an independent school can be distinguished from a maintained school (often also referred to as a 'state school') by the fact that it is not funded by a local education authority. This means that a school may still be an independent school despite the fact that it is funded with public money from other sources (such as an academy, for example). Whilst it is often the case that the proprietor of an independent school will charge a fee for the attendance of a pupil at the school, the fact that no such fee is charged does not of itself affect a school's status as an independent school.

An independent school is unlikely to have any legal personality which is separate from that of its proprietor. Accordingly, the legal rights and obligations of an independent school are generally more properly characterized as the rights and obligations of its proprietor. For example, teachers and other staff employed at an independent school will normally be employed by its proprietor and, where they are acting in the course of their duties or the proprietor has authorized them to act in a particular respect, the proprietor will usually be liable for their actions.

If a parent wishes his or her **child** to attend an independent school, he or she will normally have to enter into a contract with the proprietor of the school. Such a contract will usually govern most aspects of the relationship between the parent and the proprietor, including such matters as the fees to be paid and the circumstances in which the proprietor may expel the child from the school. As the relationship between the parent and the proprietor will usually be governed by this contract, an act of the proprietor (or an individual acting on the proprietor's behalf) will normally only be susceptible to a challenge by a parent if the act amounts to a breach of the contract. This means that, for example, a parent will usually only be able to challenge the expulsion of his or her child if the expulsion constitutes a breach of contract. In this context, however, the express terms of the contract may not define the limits of the proprietor's duties. For example, there may be an implicit obligation on the proprietor to act fairly when deciding whether or not to expel a child.

It is unusual for a pupil at an independent school to be a party to the contract between his or her parent and the proprietor or for him or her to have his or her own contract with the proprietor. As a result, it is rare for a pupil at an independent school to have any contractual rights against a proprietor or, therefore, to have the ability to challenge any acts of the proprietor (or acts of individuals acting on the proprietor's behalf). However, a proprietor may have liabilities in tort towards a pupil. For example, it will often be the case that the proprietor of an independent school will owe a pupil a duty of care not to act negligently towards him or her.

Although the relationships between the proprietors of independent schools, parents, and pupils are primarily governed by contract and the law of tort, anti-discrimination **legislation** prohibits certain acts of discrimination against pupils or prospective pupils on grounds of **sex**, **race**, or **disability**. Legislation places additional duties on the proprietors of independent boarding schools, such as, for example, duties to safeguard and promote the welfare of boarding pupils. Because the proprietors of most independent schools are private bodies, it is unlikely that their decisions will be susceptible to **judicial review** by the **courts**.

Independent schools are subject to a measure of regulation. All independent schools have to be registered and it is a criminal offence to conduct an independent school which is not registered. The registration regime involves the inspection of independent schools and an assessment of whether they meet various standards. Where the relevant registration authority is not satisfied that the requisite standards are being met by an independent school, it may take various steps to address the situation, such as serving a notice requiring remedial action to be taken or removing the school from the register.

JONATHAN MOFFETT

independent taxation of husband and wife   *see* **family taxation**

indian law   *see* **commonwealth law; hindu law**

indictment   An indictment is the formal written accusation upon which a person is tried under the traditional, heavy form of criminal procedure known as 'trial on indictment' in England and in Northern Ireland, or 'solemn procedure' in Scotland; a procedure under which, where the accused pleads 'not guilty', the issue of guilt or innocence is then normally decided by a **jury**. In England (though not in Scotland) the indictment was originally 'preferred' (ie put forward) by a Grand Jury, which carried out a preliminary investigation as a result of which it 'found a true bill': a procedure which disappeared from English law in 1933, but in some other **common law** jurisdictions still survives. In early English law, indictments were simple, informal documents, but later they became subject to a number of highly technical rules, the neglect of any one of which could invalidate the resulting trial, irrespective of the merits: to the point where, as JF Stephen said in his *History of the Criminal Law of England* (1883) it was 'much as if some small proportion of the prisoners convicted had been allowed to toss up for their liberty'. From the mid-nineteenth century onwards, a series of reforms have both reduced the technical requirements, and limited the legal consequences of failing to comply with them. The style and content of indictments differ as between Scots and English law, a Scottish indictment being more narrative in style, and issuing in the name of the **Lord Advocate**, whereas in England and in Northern Ireland they issue in the name of the Queen. The formalities as the shape and contents of indictments in England are now contained in the Indictments Act 1915 and related secondary **legislation** (now forming part of the consolidated Criminal Procedure Rules); in Northern Ireland, virtually identical formalities are prescribed under the Indictments Act (NI) 1945. For Scotland, the formalities are prescribed by the Criminal Procedure (Scotland) Act 1995, Schedule 2 of which helpfully creates a set of templates, the contents of which, with period charm, reflect the age in which they were originally composed ('A B, you are indicted at the instance of A F R (name of Lord Advocate), and the charge against you is that on [X date], in a shop in George Street, Edinburgh, occupied by John Cruikshank, draper, you did steal a shawl and boa . . . ').   JOHN SPENCER

indigenous law Understanding the essence of 'Indigenous Law' requires, as an initial step, to identify the meaning of the term 'indigenous', for it sets the scope and context of this framework. The word 'indigenous' is frequently used to describe things native to a place in the sense of growing naturally in a region. Thus, corn is indigenous to North America while kangaroos are indigenous to Australia. From the perspective of botany, indigenous things are those that are not imported or alien to a place; yet they may also not be endemic as existing solely in that area and found naturally nowhere else.

Indigenous law in this sense would signify the legal rules, principles, and structures created by the peoples of a particular territory whether or not it was the first legal system to exist in that locale. Thus, one can speak of the common law of the United Kingdom as being indigenous to the UK even though civil law also exists in Scotland and both legal systems were developed long after earlier bodies of law flourished as the local customs and Roman civil law's dominance had disappeared. With this framework in mind, one could regard any new statute or municipal by-law originating in a place, rather than being imported, as indigenous law. This does not, however, reflect the way the term indigenous law is used in recent decades around the world.

Although there are no globally accepted definitions for minorities and indigenous peoples, minorities are inevitably described in contrast to the majority population within a specific country or region. They are usually characterized by their ethnicity, nationality, language, or religion. Indigenous peoples, however, have been identified by the United Nations Subcommission on Prevention of Discrimination and Protection of Minorities *(Study of the Problem of Discrimination against Indigenous Populations*, UN Doc. E/CN.4/Sub.2/1986/7/Add. 4, paragraph 379 (1986)) as:

. . . those which, having a historical continuity with preinvasion and pre-colonial societies that developed on their territories, consider themselves distinct from other sectors of the societies now prevailing in those territories, or parts of them. They form at present non-dominant sectors of society and are determined to preserve, develop and transmit to future generations their ancestral territories, and their ethnic identity, as the basis of their continued existence as peoples, in accordance with their own cultural patterns, social institutions and legal systems.

Even this description is imperfect as Indigenous peoples in some locales are the majority population (eg Bolivia and Nunavut) whereas in others they are the dominant political force (eg Fiji). No official definition has been adopted by the UN (even by its Permanent Forum on Indigenous Issues) or in any international legal instruments (eg the International Labour Organization ('ILO') Convention 169 of 1989 Concerning Indigenous and Tribal Peoples in Independent Countries or in the Declaration on the Rights of Indigenous Peoples ('DRIP') adopted by the General Assembly on 13 September 2007). Some nations have developed their own internal definitions with domestic legal status (eg Australia and Canada), while a number of countries refer to Indigenous peoples by some name within their national constitutions (eg Brazil, Canada, Columbia, and the USA). What is clear, is that there are at least 370 million recognized Indigenous peoples spread through seventy nations worldwide, and potentially far more depending how this concept evolves over time.

Similarly, there is no official definition for the term 'indigenous law', even though it has official status within DRIP as the Declaration acknowledges indigenous laws and 'legal systems', although it more frequently refers to 'traditions' and 'customs' in a manner suggesting they possess an equivalent legal significance. ILO Convention 169 uses the expressions 'customs' and 'customary laws' as alternative but older ways of capturing the same idea.

The lack of definition in part reflects the very nature of its origins, as indigenous law flows from the 'practices, traditions, and customs' of the people (as described by the Supreme Court of Canada in *Delgamuukw v British Columbia* (1997)). The context in which indigenous law is understood can also be affected by validly enacted domestic legislation. The Australian High Court in *Western Australia v Ward* (2002) has stated that the phrase 'traditional laws and customs' previously used in the landmark decision recognizing native title in Australia at common law for the first time in *Mabo (No. 2)* (1992), was now to be interpreted as modified by the federal Native Title Act 1993 ('NTA'), as amended. Thus, indigenous laws were to be viewed as a required element of proving the 'native title rights and interests protected by the NTA' as 'rights in relation to land or waters where, among other things, the peoples concerned, by traditional laws and customs, have a connection with the land or waters' (at 131).

Anthropologists generally avoid developing a uniform definition as the content of indigenous law varies among societies reflecting the rules that people live by on a daily basis as well as spiritual and cultural values since the law is backed by religious sanctions. Therefore, indigenous traditional law is comprised of the blend of relationships between people and the land, with each other and with their supreme god or deities. In other words, it consists of relationships affected by religion, social organization, and the natural environment in which the society lives.

Indigenous law is not limited to the customs, traditions, or legal rules prevailing at any moment in time, unless the imported legal system seeks to freeze it as of a critical juncture (such as, when a colonizing power declared ultimate sovereignty over the territory or a treaty was signed) for domestic legal purposes. Instead, it naturally has the capacity to evolve in reaction to changing circumstances.

All Indigenous peoples possess a right of self-determination at international law, which has now been recognized in aspirational terms by the UN through DRIP. Those who currently govern their own affairs to some degree have the capacity to codify or change traditional laws and to supplement those laws through new ones that address issues never previously arising, such as taxation, telecommunications, or corporations. At the very least, indigenous laws will inevitably include principles determining leadership and systems of government, dispute resolution, criminal conduct, marriage, land use and stewardship, allocating natural resources, personal property, inheritance, child welfare, civil wrongs, and enforceable promises (contracts). Some peoples possess more extensive traditional and modern legal regimes through state-recognized residual sovereignty or self-government treaties. For all Indigenous peoples, however, their law is central to their survival as distinct peoples possessing unique cultures.

BRADFORD W. MORSE

indigenous peoples Though there is no one universally accepted definition of the term 'indigenous peoples,' it has generally been understood to refer to the descendants of the people who inhabited a territory prior to colonization and who have maintained some or all of their social, cultural, political, and linguistic characteristics. They are or consider themselves to be distinct from the dominant societies that have developed around them. Indigenous peoples have suffered from historic injustices resulting from the deprivation of their right to **self-determination** and the dispossession of their lands, territories, and resources. To this day, they continue to face serious threats to their basic existence, and are still being discriminated against and denied their **human rights**.

Despite centuries of attempts by many states to forcibly assimilate indigenous peoples and create homogeneous nation states, indigenous peoples have to a large extent managed to preserve their traditional organizations. Originally associated with the decolonization movement, in recent years the right to self-determination has been at the forefront of indigenous rights discourse. The right to self-determination is recognized, in the United Nations Declaration on the Rights of Indigenous Peoples (2007), as the right of an indigenous peoples to 'freely determine their political status and freely pursue their economic, social and cultural development'. For indigenous peoples, effective self-determination includes the right to the lands they have traditionally used and occupied, and the right to maintain their autonomy and internal decision-making structures. However, self-determination does not necessarily imply the right to establish independent states, as it is sometimes misrepresented. Perhaps the central demand of the indigenous rights movement is the right to secure their lands and resources, as the relationship of indigenous peoples to their traditional territories forms a core part of their identity and culture, though indigenous peoples share other common concerns such as advancing rights to equality and non-discrimination, autonomy, participation, and culture.

A discrete body of **international human rights law** recognizing and protecting the collective rights of indigenous groups has emerged over the past couple of decades and continues to develop. The most notable examples of international instruments protecting these rights are the United Nations Declaration on the Rights of Indigenous Peoples and the International Labour Organization Convention Concerning Indigenous and Tribal Peoples in Independent Countries (1989). Several other international human rights treaties have been authoritatively interpreted to require states to respect the rights of indigenous peoples, including the **International Covenant on Civil and Political Rights**, the International Convention on the Elimination of All Forms of Racial Discrimination (1965), and the American Convention on Human Rights (1969). In addition, there is a growing practice of states to incorporate and protect indigenous rights in their domestic legal frameworks through constitutional amendments or the adoption of new laws. However, in many cases these protections of indigenous peoples' rights have yet to be translated effectively into practice at the domestic level.

Long before the emergence of the contemporary international human rights system, the British **common law** protected the rights of indigenous groups to their traditional lands and resources. Under the common law, any rights that indigenous peoples had under the laws of a territory at the time of British acquisition of sovereignty continued thereafter and became enforceable in common law courts. These rights have been interpreted to give rise to a legal entitlement to exclusive ownership, referred to as 'native' or 'aboriginal' title. Apart from such native title in its fullest sense, aboriginal rights may take the form of freestanding rights to fish, hunt, gather, or otherwise use resources or have access to lands. While there are variations in the test for aboriginal title across common law jurisdictions, all involve proof of a longstanding and continuous occupation of lands by an indigenous people in accordance with native **customary law**. In recognizing native title in the landmark case of ***Mabo v State of Queensland***, the Australian High Court rejected the theory of terra nullius ('empty land') as racially discriminatory. Previously, this theory had been used to justify the settlement of lands inhabited by indigenous peoples, who were assumed to have no valid laws or systems of property ownership.

All of these advancements contribute to the development of **customary international law** and general principles of international law recognizing and respecting the rights of indigenous peoples, which are among the principal sources of international law and are binding upon states.

MAIA CAMPBELL

See also: **colonialism; indigenous peoples and property; native title**

indigenous peoples, status of   The legal status of indigenous peoples is chronically unsettled and a persistent challenge to the sovereignty of the nation state that would purport to contain them. This sovereignty is supposed to provide an ultimate and singular source of authority. The historical establishing of this straitened sovereignty for any nation state inevitably involved a violence of exclusion; but this violence is usually softened, even forgotten, in myths of national origin and in the religiose elevation of the nation as a figure of encompassing unity. This convenient settlement of the national question is radically disrupted by indigenous peoples.

The key issue was starkly set in a case before the **United States Supreme Court** in the early nineteenth century: *Johnson v M'Intosh* (1823). For the status of indigenous peoples, it remains a leading case in the legal systems derived from, or substantially influenced by, the British system. It is mostly cited for the opinion of Chief Justice Marshall. The case held that Indian peoples did not have effective title to their lands. Marshall struggled to find justification for this outcome but, after discounting such colonial claims as those based on 'discovery', and after noting that 'some excuse, if not justification' could be derived from 'the character and habits of the people whose rights have been wrested from them', Marshall concluded that there was no justification at all. In the end, the decision was simply a pragmatic matter of not disturbing the way the country had been settled by the colonists, no matter how much that outcome 'may be opposed to natural right and to the usages of civilized nations'—and no matter how much, Marshall failed to add, the decision stood in stark opposition to a recently adopted constitutional Bill of Rights strongly protective of property.

In these enlightened days something less direct is needed. It is now widely recognized, largely because of effective legal and political action on the part of indigenous peoples themselves, that there has been an historical injustice, one quite incompatible with current values. A plethora of remedial cases and legislation has ensued. This has remained a sedulously limited exercise however. If indigenous rights were, to use the decreed terminology, 'recognized' fully, the sovereign assumption of the original colonial appropriation would be shattered. Minimally, full recognition would involve the opening out of sovereignty to an apposite space of the indigenous, embroil it in a plurality, and disintegrate it. It is little wonder, then, that national courts when confronted with this terminus, which is also a confrontation with the ground of their own authority, now refuse to enquire into the origins of the settler state's sovereignty. An influential example of this can be found in the Australian case of *Mabo v The State of Queensland (No 2)* (1992). Such a terminal encounter is avoided by the courts freezing the rights recognized within a distinctly neo-colonial frame—a frame which comprehensively subordinates the rights to the national society and the national legal system. Furthermore, the colonial constitution of these rights, and of the identities formed by them, is reproduced. That is, these identities and rights are legally tied to an invariant, or to a marginally varying, 'custom' or 'culture'. Should these talismans change, they disappear along with the rights and identities made dependent on them.

The reason for confining indigenous peoples in this condition of stasis is revealingly offered by Chief Justice Lamer in a leading Canadian case of *R v van der Peet* (1996), where he cautions, with emphasis, that the recognized rights 'are *aboriginal*', and that this 'aboriginality' means that 'the rights cannot . . . be defined on the basis of the philosophical precepts of the liberal enlightenment', on the basis of their being 'general and universal'. In other words, such rights could not adaptively and 'universally' extend to the infinitely changing future condition of indigenous society but had to remain the same, or much the same, as they supposedly ever were. Indigenous peoples are thence expected to stay the same, or to disappear.

That dismal conclusion is constantly challenged these days by the burgeoning success of indigenous peoples in resisting their relegation in such terms. A significant marker of that success has been the approval by the General Assembly of the United Nations on 13 September 2007 of the Declaration on the Rights of Indigenous Peoples, with four states voting against: Australia, Canada, New Zealand, and the United States.   PETER FITZPATRICK

C Perrin, 'Approaching Anxiety: The Insistence of the Postcolonial in the Declaration on the Rights of Indigenous Peoples' in E Darian-Smith and P Fitzpatrick (eds), *Laws of the Postcolonial* (Ann Arbor: The University of Michigan Press, 1999) 19–38

P Keal, *European Conquest and the Rights of Indigenous Peoples: The Moral Backwardness of International Society* (Cambridge: Cambridge University Press, 2003)

indirect discrimination Prohibiting unfair discrimination that is based directly upon particular personal characteristics, such as a person's **race**, ethnic origin, **gender**, **disability**, age, or sexual orientation, makes many unjust and oppressive forms of behaviour illegal. For example, it prevents an employer discriminating against a **woman** just because she is a woman. However, merely prohibiting **direct discrimination** in this way will not make illegal many forms of behaviour that can result in unfair consequences for many disadvantaged groups. For example, an employer might avoid promoting employees that have primary responsibility for the care of small children. This does not involve direct discrimination against women on the basis of their gender. However, it would particularly disadvantage many female employees, as in current social circumstances they often bear most of the burden of caring for small children. To take another example, a requirement that **police** officers be of a minimum height might particularly disadvantage women and members of some ethnic minorities: they would be less likely than others to be able to satisfy a height requirement due to their smaller average height.

In such situations, the employer is using a method of distinguishing between different **persons** which does not involve direct discrimination: no one is subjected to less favourable treatment on the ground that they are black or female. Nevertheless, the use of these methods can unfairly cause serious disadvantage to members of particular disadvantaged groups. Therefore, the prohibition of direct discrimination needs to be reinforced by legal controls on *indirect* forms of discrimination, ie where apparently neutral criteria are being used to distinguish between individuals but which in fact have an adverse impact on particular groups. In the legal terminology used in the United States, such situations are described as involving 'disparate impact'.

Not every situation where disparate impact exists will give rise to a successful claim for indirect discrimination. First, an individual can only bring a claim if she or he is a member of a group which has suffered *particular* disadvantage when compared to other groups: just being exposed to a disadvantage is not enough. Indirect discrimination is largely concerned with the protection of *groups* against disadvantage.

Secondly, anti-discrimination **legislation** will usually only protect groups of individuals that are defined in some way by sharing a common ethnic origin, gender, age, sexual orientation, or other 'protected characteristic'. A requirement that job applicants have a university degree or a similar third-level qualification may disadvantage poorer groups in society who are less likely to have such qualifications. However, in Britain, anti-discrimination legislation only prohibits indirect discrimination that adversely affects groups defined by gender, race, ethnic and national origin, age, sexual orientation, and **religion** or belief. (UK law does not as yet permit indirect discrimination claims in relation to disability.) The **Human Rights Act 1998** may permit other groups to challenge certain practices and behaviour by public authorities that subject them to disparate impact: however, considerable uncertainty remains in this area of the law.

Thirdly, even where a group sharing a common 'protected characteristic' is subject to adverse impact, the use of the requirements or differentiating factors in question might actually be fair, legitimate, or necessary. If an employer requires applicants for a job to have a university degree, this might particularly disadvantage older people or some ethnic minorities, who may be less likely than others to have obtained such a qualification. Therefore this requirement would have a disparate impact upon these groups. However, an employer might be able to show that having such a third-level qualification was necessary to perform the job in question. In the circumstances, it might be unrealistic or unfair to prohibit the employer applying this requirement.

Therefore, anti-discrimination law only prohibits the use of job requirements and other criteria used to differentiate between individuals that have a disparate impact upon disadvantaged groups, if their use is unfair, unnecessary, or *unjustified* in the circumstances. This is important: many social practices may have an adverse impact upon one or more disadvantaged groups, but if their use can be justified, then their use will be completely legal. However, whoever is applying the requirement or criteria in question will usually have to demonstrate that its use is justified. In other words, it will be up to the defendant to demonstrate justification.

The need for controls on indirect forms of discrimination was first recognized by the **US Supreme Court** in the case of *Griggs v Duke Power Co* (1971). This case remains a classic example of disparate impact analysis. Most of the defendant's employees were required to have successfully completed high school and to have achieved satisfactory results in certain aptitude tests. These apparently neutral and harmless requirements actually had the effect of predominantly excluding black applicants, who were much less likely to have passed their school diplomas and to perform well in the tests due to the legacy of segregation. The US Supreme Court held that the US Civil Rights Act 1964 should be read as prohibiting both direct discrimination and also 'practices that are fair in form but discriminatory in operation . . . if an employment practice which operates to exclude [black people] cannot be shown to be related to job performance, the practice is prohibited...'. The defendant **company** then failed to show that its job requirements were justified as necessary for effective performance of the jobs in question.

The *Griggs* decision had a direct impact on the UK, as it influenced the then **Home Secretary**, Roy Jenkins MP, to insert a prohibition on indirect discrimination in the race and **sex** discrimination legislation introduced in the mid-1970s. The UK legislation initially defined indirect discrimination in a highly complex and technical manner. This was compounded by the narrow interpretation was given by the English **courts** to some elements of this definition. However, decisions by the **European Court of Justice** from the 1980s on gave greater clarity and coherence to the law on indirect sex discrimination. This in turn has resulted in a gradual clarification and strengthening of UK indirect discrimination provisions.

The first step in establishing whether a claim for indirect discrimination exists is to identify any relevant practice, requirement, provision, or differentiating factor that may have an adverse impact on some groups. Secondly, it is necessary to establish that a particular group defined by an **equality** ground such as its gender, race, age, etc. is subject to a 'particular disadvantage'. (Picking the right groups or 'pools' to compare can often be a difficult and complex business.) In deciding whether a group has suffered particular disadvantage, courts and **tribunals** can take statistical evidence into account, as well as common sense assumptions. If it can be shown that a particular group suffers from a persistent and relatively constant disadvantage, then that can be enough.

If adverse impact can be shown to exist, then the person applying the practice, policy, or differentiating factor that is causing the problem will have to try to show that its use is justified. The case law of the European Court of Justice has established that this defence can only succeed if it can be shown that the use of the criteria in question is 'objectively justified', in other words that it was necessary to use the practice or policy in question to achieve a pressing and legitimate aim. Also, a justification defence cannot be based upon reasoning that is itself discriminatory. For example, an employer cannot justify a refusal to pay equal hourly rates to **part-time workers** on the basis that he wishes to discourage female employees who have extensive family responsibilities, or that part-time work has always been paid less, as this would involve reliance upon a history of discrimination to justify adverse impact.

The development of the law on indirect discrimination has had a considerable social impact. Examples of policies and practices that may have an adverse impact on women include refusals to allow flexible working or time off for family reasons, rigid seniority policies, lower rates for part-time work, and using established pay scales to continue to fix wages. Examples of practices that may have an adverse impact on ethnic and/or religious groups include imposing standard and inflexible uniform requirements, banning the wearing of religious symbols, and fixing minimum residence requirements for access to training or benefits. Particular hiring and promotion practices, age limits, seniority requirements, and other reliance on 'old boys networks' can give rise to adverse impact issues across all of the equality grounds. The requirement that adverse impact be justified means that many of these often exclusionary practices have had to be modified or ended since the 1970s. However, the scope of indirect discrimination is inevitably limited by the complexity of the law. As can be seen from the conclusions of the Macpherson Report into the death of Stephen Lawrence, patterns of **institutional discrimination** often remain untouched by the prohibition on indirect discrimination. Positive steps may be required to break down these structural and deeply embedded forms of discrimination, and to complement and build upon the legislative ban on indirect discrimination.   COLM O'CINNEIDE

individual autonomy   *see* **autonomy**

individual rights   At its simplest, this concept means basic rights claimed by individuals. As such, it may broadly be contrasted with the modern notion of 'group', 'collective', or **'third generation' rights**, which involve claims by distinct groups within society, or claims that can only be vindicated collectively. An example of the former would be a claim to the use of a particular language: while an individual might demand the right personally to use any particular language, the group demand for language rights requires the state to recognize and facilitate the language of the group, though its use in official documents, street signs, and in the delivery of public services. Moreover, the purpose of the claim is not so much the vindication of the freedom of individuals, as ensuring the survival and flourishing of the language of the particular group to which they belong, as an essential aspect of its **identity** and culture. An example of the latter kind would be the right

of workers to bargain collectively with employers over wages and conditions, and to the recognition of **trade unions**. While the individual right to **freedom of association** protects the freedom to join any existing trade union, laws requiring employers and others to recognize trade unions, and rights given to workers within a union, including, crucially, the right to **strike**, are plainly collective in nature.

In this context, group rights, designed to better the position of a particular section of society, can collide head-on with individual rights: the **'closed shop'**, in which individuals in particular industries were required to join a union as a condition of employment, plainly conflicted with the individual right of free association. The result, in UK law, has been the triumph of the individual's rights, with the abolition of the closed shop. In other instances, the two march alongside each other: rights given to **women** over **maternity** are aimed both at protecting the rights of individual women, and at securing and promoting the interests of women collectively, as a historically disadvantaged group.

Strictly speaking, the notion of individual rights could be used to denote any basic claim made by the individual against the state: thus it could be thought to include 'second-generation' rights to health care, social security, and housing, since all these amenities can be enjoyed by the individual in isolation. But as a matter of legal parlance, it is generally used to denote those rights which protect the essential *freedoms* of the individual: 'second generation' rights in contrast are more generally concerned with ensuring people's *welfare*. Thus claims of individual rights are most closely associated with what are known as **civil and political rights**, such as those enumerated in Articles 1–21 of the Universal Declaration of Human Rights and the **International Covenant of Civil and Political Rights**. These include the following: freedom of speech, thought, conscience, and belief; freedom from **slavery** or forced labour; **freedom of assembly**, and association, the right to vote, to personal liberty, to **privacy**, fair trial rights; the **right to life**, and to be free from **torture** and inhuman or degrading treatment.

Courts are historically seen as having a particularly important role in protecting the rights of individuals, while the legislature's premier responsibility is to advance the welfare of the population as a whole. In this sense, courts can represent the anti-majoritarian principle, in seeking to preserve and uphold a protective carapace around the individual which, in many countries, even laws passed by democratic procedures cannot infringe—a concept known as **entrenched rights**.

A final issue is whether **companies** and **non-governmental organizations** can claim individual rights: the answers given vary not only from jurisdiction to jurisdiction, but also in relation to the particular right claimed. Some claims by companies—for example, not to be subject to torture—would be nonsensical on their face. On the other hand, the **European Court of Human Rights** ('ECtHR') has allowed newspaper companies to complain of breaches of the right to **freedom of expression**, as in the famous *Spycatcher* litigation. The question of whether companies can claim a right to privacy is particularly controversial: some contend that since the foundation of the right is **human dignity** and **autonomy**, it would be a fundamental mistake to allow companies (as opposed to persons employed by them) to claim the right to privacy. But the ECtHR has allowed claims by companies of violations of the right to respect for private life in relation to unreasonable searches of company premises.   GAVIN PHILLIPSON

inducing breach of contract   *see* **economic torts**

industrial action   *see* **strikes; trade unions**

industrial designs   *see* **designs**

industrial injuries   The British system of providing **compensation** for work-related injuries has developed through case law. It dates from *Priestley v Fowler* (1837) which held that the master (ie the employer) was 'bound to provide for the safety of his servant (ie employee) in the course of his employment'. However, a caveat that the employer was not liable where the injury was caused by another servant in 'common employment' with the victim overshadowed subsequent developments.

Smith v Baker (1891) is considered the origin of the principle that there is an implied duty in every contract of employment requiring the employer to take reasonable care for the safety of the employee. The case also laid down that an employee is not to be assumed to accept a risk of injury merely because he or she works knowing the employer does not operate a safe system.

Following the development of protective health and safety legislation, *Groves v Wimborne* (1898) established the concept of civil liability for breach of statutory duty: ie the granting of compensation to a worker injured because the employer has failed to comply with relevant criminal law, for example by failing to guard machinery.

The impact of these late nineteenth-century cases is unclear because the Workmen's Compensation Act 1897 made the employer strictly liable to compensate a worker who suffered 'personal injury by accident arising out of and in the course of employment'. The scheme was subsequently extended to cover 'prescribed' industrial diseases but it was of limited success. It covered only some employees; the employer might not honour its liability; only modest income maintenance was provided and the worker who claimed workmen's compensation had to forego suing for the substantial **damages** available in a **common law** claim. There was little incentive to sacrifice the statutory entitlement and undertake the difficult and expensive task of claiming damages in the courts.

Lord Atkin's pronouncement in **Donoghue v Stevenson** (1932) that a person must take reasonable care not to injure a 'neighbour' formulated the tort of negligence and influenced employer's liability. Possibly it inspired the judges in *Wilsons & Clyde Coal Company v English* (1938), which laid the foundation of modern employer's liability by stating that the employer owed a personal duty to provide 'a competent staff of men, adequate material, and a proper system and effective supervision'. Nevertheless the doctrine of common employment was not abolished until the Law Reform (Personal Injuries) Act 1948.

When the **welfare state** was introduced after the end of World War II the workmen's compensation scheme was replaced by the National Insurance (Industrial Injuries) Act 1946 providing for injured employees a preferential state scheme of income maintenance funded jointly by employers and employees. The claimant no longer had to choose between claiming income maintenance and suing for damages. When this scheme was largely replaced by a statutory sick pay scheme the 'industrial preference' was lost apart from a pension for long-term disability, which is available to those injured at work but not to those injured in other ways. While payments made under the social security scheme are small compared to damages available at common law, they are paid irrespective of whether anyone has been at fault and without costly litigation. The scheme is therefore the first resort and principal provider for those suffering work-related incapacity.

Historically employer's common law liability focused on the employer's responsibility for its 'employees' as defined by the courts and the Employers' Liability (Compulsory Insurance) Act 1969 only requires an employer to insure against liability to employees; other workers and the general public will not be covered unless the organization has elected to take out cover for 'public liability'.

However, the tort of negligence has developed so that there is little difference between the duty of care owed by an employer to its own employees and that owed to other persons. In personal injury cases today the emphasis is less on whether the defendant has a duty to take care than on whether the duty was broken and whether the breach caused the damage claimed. Nevertheless an employer is more likely to have to take care in selection, training, supervising, disciplining, and monitoring performance of an employee.

In cases where the injury suffered by the employee is a disease or illness rather than an accident, the causal link between breach and damage can be difficult to prove; but the courts are inclined to find for a claimant if work may have caused the illness or disease. In cases of mesothelioma caused by asbestos where the employee has worked for a number of employers, the problem of identifying which employer's negligence caused the disease has proved problematic. The Compensation Act 2006 provides that any of the defendant employers may be held liable in such circumstances.

Claims for breach of statutory duty remain important. The principal statute is now the Health and Safety at Work, etc. Act 1974. It includes general duties which impose near absolute criminal liability on employers who fail to operate safe systems of work. While damage claims may not be made for breach of these duties, claims may normally be brought for breach of regulations made under the Act.

While it has become much easier for a claimant to obtain damages, the award may still be reduced either because of the claimant's contributory negligence or because the injury was made more severe due to something, for which the employer was not responsible, that happened after the injury occurred. Additionally the defendant must refund to the state a proportion of the social security payments it has made; thus further reducing the amount received by the claimant.

The reduction in heavy industry has reduced the toll of work-related accidents, but certain industries, particularly construction and agriculture, remain dangerous; and there are still over 200 work-related fatalities every year. The most common recorded reasons for work-related incapacity today are musculoskeletal injuries (often caused by lifting operations) and stressful work. Since *Walker v Northumberland County Council* (1995) held that an employer could be liable for psychiatric injury caused by work there has been much litigation, the main causes of such injury being overwork and bullying.   BRENDA BARRETT

See also: **causation; statutory duty, civil liability for breach of; strict civil liability; tort law**

infanticide   *see* **mental incapacity and crime**

information complaints commissioner   *see* **ombudsmen**

information disclosure   Generally, there is no obligation to disclose information in English **contract law**. If I sell my neighbour my lawnmower, which he thinks is in good condition, but I know is not, and I make no comment about its condition, he cannot later complain if the lawnmower breaks down. I have not breached any duty towards him. Only if I represent that it is in good working order or warrant (or 'give an assurance about') its condition will I be liable. This highly individualistic approach does not, however, apply to all contracts. Certain specific types of contract require information disclosure, for example, contracts of utmost good faith such as insurance contracts, fiduciary contracts, contracts of guarantee and, to a very limited extent, contracts for the sale of land. Custom and statute may also impose duties. Nevertheless, the general rule may be stated as '*caveat emptor*' (buyer beware).

There are, however, particular circumstances where a person may be found liable for non-disclosure. Under the law of misrepresentation, while silence does not generally give rise to liability, a statement of fact which is half-true (and so misleading) or which, while true initially, becomes false and is not corrected prior to contract, may render the representor liable. Equally, the court may infer a (false) statement of fact from the defendant's conduct, which will result in liability unless it is corrected. If one person assumes responsibility towards the other, for example to keep them fully informed, this may also give rise to liability in the tort of negligence.

A term requiring disclosure may also be implied into a contract, giving rise to damages if it is breached. For example, section 14(2) of the Sale of Goods Act 1979 provides that where the seller sells goods in the course of a business, there is an implied term that they are of satisfactory quality *unless* any defect is specifically drawn to the buyer's attention before the contract is made. The seller thus has an incentive to provide full information about his or her goods to avoid any claims under the Act. It is noticeable that a number of European Community Directives, which the **United Kingdom** must implement in domestic law, use implied terms as a means of protecting consumers by ensuring that they receive a basic level of information disclosure. For instance, the Package

Travel, Package Holidays and Package Tours Regulations 1992 (implementing a 1990 Directive) use civil and criminal law to require a minimum level of disclosure to ensure that consumers are fully informed of their rights under the contract.

Thus it cannot be said that there is *never* an obligation to disclose information in English law, but much will depend on the nature of the contract and the precise circumstances of the case. English law continues to resist arguments in favour of a general principle of good faith, under which duties to disclose would arise as a matter of course.　　　　PAULA GILIKER

See also: **fraud and misrepresentation; holidays, recreational; insurance contracts/policies; tort law**

information technologies While there appears to be no legal definition of information technologies, a useful description is 'the systems, equipment, components, and software required to ensure the retrieval, processing, and storage of information in all centres of human activity (home, office, factories, etc) the application of which generally requires the use of electronics or similar technology'. Although not synonymous with computers, lawyers frequently use the term when referring to the relationship between law and computer technologies, and in particular networked computers.

Legal regulation of information technologies encompasses the computer (the hardware), the software, and the information processed using the technology. Also covered are the uses to which information technologies are put. Many of these uses are legitimate, such as communication and e-commerce; but others are not, such as fraudulent activity or to disseminate child pornography. Legal **regulation** consists of a matrix of initiatives designed specifically to regulate information technologies, adaptation of existing measures, the **common law**, and more informal self-regulatory or self-help measures.

Hardware: The hardware (the computer, the peripherals) may be protected by **patent**, registered **design,** or a combination of the two. If the hardware (or part of the hardware) is new, involves an inventive step, and is capable of industrial application, a patent may be granted. Registered design protects the appearance of the hardware where it is new and has individual character. Features solely dictated by technical function are un-protectable. Other parts of the hardware, such as **integrated circuits**, may be protected differently.

Software: Software will be protected by **copyright** if it meets the test of being the author's own intellectual creation. Protection extends to literal copying of the software, but not to non-textual copying (sometimes referred to as the 'business logic'). Computer software as such cannot be protected by a patent except where it is a software-related invention of a technical character and produces a technical effect.

Information: The information processed by information technologies may take many forms including personal information, sound, video, text, and data. In response to the worry that the use of information technologies to process personal information could have negative impacts on the privacy of the subject (echoed in the Human Rights Act 1998) regulation was consolidated in the Data Protection Act 1998 (based on a **European Union** initiative). This Act requires data users to register with a supervisory body (the Information Commissioner) and to process data in accordance with eight principles (eg data must be processed fairly and lawfully). Individuals have a right to know what information is held about them, and to have inaccuracies rectified.

Using information technologies

Creative content: Creative works protected by copyright (such as music, computer software, films) can be copied and disseminated using information technologies. This makes enforcement difficult for the rights holder, a phenomenon exacerbated by the growth of peer-to-peer networks. Two copyright treaties, the **World Intellectual Property Organization ('WIPO')** Copyright Treaty (1996) and the WIPO Performances and Phonograms Treaty (1996), set increased standards of protection which have been translated into domestic law. Key provisions include the introduction of a right of communication to the public, and anti-circumvention measures, which make unlawful the circumvention of technical protection measures used to control dissemination of works.

Commerce: In the field of **e-commerce**, initiatives have been directed towards the use of information technologies to facilitate domestic and cross-border trade through the creation of orderly markets and provisions to increase consumer confidence. Measures (which originate in Europe) include the Electronic Commerce Directive, the Privacy and Electronic Communications Directive, the Distance Selling Directive, and the Digital Signatures Directive. Amongst other things, these provide basic rules for the formation of contracts; recognize digital signatures; detail information that must be given by sellers to buyers; provide a system for controlling unsolicited email through the creation of an opt-in framework, and encourage the establishment of alternative forms of dispute resolution.

Crime: Information technologies can be used to circulate information on, and be used for, criminal and other unlawful activity. The term 'cyber-crime' refers to crimes that cannot be carried out except with a computer, such as spamming (often associated with viruses or fraudulent activity). Information technology can also be used to commit the crime (such as child pornography, fraud, incitement of religious hatred), or may be the target of the crime (such as virus attacks).

Law enforcement agencies could gather information by intercepting communications. In response to fears from civil libertarians about the risk of a surveillance society, a framework has been developed (Regulation of Investigatory Powers Act 2000) which permits **interception of communications** on public and private systems and grants powers for the acquisition and disclosure of data and information. Any permissible interception must take place according to pre-defined conditions and is subject to judicial oversight. Evidence thus gathered can be used in court.

In addition to the **common law** and existing legislation, criminal measures have been designed specifically for information technologies. The following are examples of criminal activities which can be committed using information technologies: gaining unauthorized access to programs or data held on a computer (hacking) and the modification of information (viruses); publication of obscene material and possession of child pornography; sexual grooming; certain acts of terrorism; and incitement to religious or racial hatred.

Challenges

While much legal regulation in the field of information technologies is initiated at International and European level, as information technologies are increasingly deployed on an international scale, the legal processes needed to facilitate and support expansion, penetration, and use will need to become still better coordinated and sophisticated. For instance, increasing convergence of media including information, broadcasting, and telecommunications technologies (convergence of technologies) to provide a platform though which a varying types of interactive communication can take place (convergence of the use of information technologies) suggests legal regulation also needs to converge. Escalating levels of cybercrime points towards the need to foster ever greater levels of international cooperation. Progress to date include the European Cybercrime Convention and International Convention on Cybercrime.

Developments will inevitably be accompanied by lively debate from all sectors of society made possible by the very information technologies under scrutiny.   CHARLOTTE WAELDE

See also: **personal information, access to**

informed consent   *see* **consent to treatment**

inheritance   *see* **death in the family**

inheritance tax   The United Kingdom Inheritance Tax ('IHT'), introduced in 1986, is the principal tax charged when property passes on death. There is no **capital gains tax** charge on assets passing on death. IHT is also charged on certain transfers during life, which can have a knock-on effect on the amount of tax on death. It is commonly portrayed as a tax on those who die at the wrong time or who do not like their children. In recent years the rise in house prices has made many people potentially liable to IHT. As with so much of tax, this area has an extensive history; IHT was preceded by the originally much more stringent Capital Transfer Tax 1974–1986, which was preceded by Estate Duty (1894–1974).

Despite its name IHT is a tax charged on—and generally by reference to the circumstances of—the donor not the donee. Properly so-called inheritance taxes are in force in many other European countries; these charge the donee and have different rates of tax according to the degree of consanguinity.

On death IHT applies to all property belonging to D and forming part of D's estate immediately before the death. The threshold—or zero-rate band—for IHT is £300,000 in 2007–2008; once the estate passes this figure, IHT applies at 40 per cent, so an estate of £360,000 will, assuming there are no relevant lifetime transfers to be taken into account, pay no tax on the first £300,000 but will then pay at 40 per cent on the remaining £60,000, making total tax of £24,000. Exemptions on death include transfers to a surviving spouse or civil partner. There are also important exemptions or reductions for business assets, farms, and for gifts to charity.

To prevent very obvious avoidance, IHT reaches back to charge certain gifts made by D within the last seven years of life. So if a person makes such a gift of £100,000 and then dies next year leaving an estate of £260,000, the gift is taken into account on death; hence the £300,000 threshold will be used in part against the gift (£100,000) and partly against the £260,000 estate, leaving £60,000 of the estate to be taxed at 40 per cent. It follows from this rule that qualifying gifts which are made *more than seven years* before the death are fully exempt from IHT, a consequence which encourages people to give away assets in their lifetime in the hope of surviving seven years. These qualifying lifetime gifts are called 'potentially exempt transfers' ('PETs'); the precise definition of when a gift is a PET is technical but ordinary absolute gifts are usually PETs.

If a lifetime gift is not a PET, as is the case with certain transfers to trusts, it is chargeable at once. The donor can use the £300,000 threshold and so will pay no tax until that total has been passed. In deciding whether the total has been passed, account must be take of any other chargeable transfers made by the donor within the previous seven years before the gift. So whether any tax is due will depend on how many transfers of value D has made in the seven years before the gift, whether D has exceeded the threshold, and whether D can claim an exemption. Although the threshold is the same as for death, the rate of tax is only 20 per cent. In practice, the principal exemption is for normal and reasonable gifts out of income. D can also claim 'de minimis' exemptions of £3,000 per year and of £250 per donee.

Finally a word on trusts. IHT has two principal techniques for taxing trusts once they are established. The first has long applied where a person (A) has a beneficial interest in possession in the trust property. This technique treats A as entitled to the underlying assets. So, where A is entitled to a life interest in £1m, the whole £1m is treated as part of A's estate. The other technique is to impose a periodic charge on the trust assets every ten years, a rule which imposes the burden of valuing the assets. The current maximum rate of this ten-year charge is 6 per cent. Changes made in 2006 moved many interest-in-possession trusts from the first category into the second category. These changes applied to existing trusts but with transitional arrangements.

JOHN TILEY

CT Sandford, JRM Willis and DJ Ironside, *An Accessions Tax* (Institute for Fiscal Studies Publication No 7, September 1973)

DG Duff, ' The Abolition of Wealth Transfer Taxation: Lessons from Canada Australia and New Zealand' (2005) 3 *Pittsburgh Tax Review* 1

initiative as a means of instigating legislation
Initiative refers to a process in which citizens propose laws by presenting a petition containing a specified number of signatures to the relevant state official. Initiatives can be divided into two categories. The first is 'direct initiative' in which a proposal backed with a petition is put to the electorate for a popular vote. Under this procedure, a title and summary of the proposal is placed on the ballot and the proposal will become law if it is approved at the election. In the second category, 'indirect initiative', the proposed law is first put to the legislature to consider enacting.

The process is used in a small number of jurisdictions including some US states and Switzerland. Initiatives are distinct from referendums, in allowing the citizen to propose the law, whereas referendums allow citizens to vote on existing laws or proposals that will normally have been drafted by the legislature.

The number of signatures on the petition required to trigger this procedure varies according to jurisdiction. For example, in the US, North Dakota requires the signatures of only 2 per cent of the voting population in the case of a statutory initiative, whereas Wyoming requires 15 per cent of the number of votes cast in the previous election. A higher number of signatures may be required for proposed constitutional amendments than for proposed legislation.

While often associated with direct democracy, initiative procedures often work alongside representative democracy. The benefits of such procedures are contested. Critics argue that individuals often lack the time, resources, and expertise to assess the proposal and may lend their signature to support an initiative without fully understanding the proposal. Consequently, critics argue that far from empowering citizens, initiatives can often be used to advance the proposals of special interest groups that have the resources to collect the necessary signatures and run a high profile campaign.

JACOB ROWBOTTOM

injunction An injunction is a court order that requires a person to do or not to do some act in fulfillment of a legal obligation. Examples include an order not to pass across the claimant's land (prohibitory injunction), and an order to tear down a wall that encroaches on the claimant's land (mandatory injunction). Orders to pay money are not considered injunctions. The term is also not applied to orders to perform contractual obligations; such orders are called decrees of **specific performance.** The terminology is different in Scotland: there a mandatory order is called specific implement, while a prohibitory order is called an interdict. Injunctions, specific performance, specific implement, and interdict are traditionally understood as discretionary remedies: claimants do not have an absolute right to them, but rather they are granted in the discretion of the court. In English (but not Scots law, they are only supposed to be granted where money **damages** would be inadequate. Injunctions may be obtained against public bodies as well as private parties.

There are 'final' and 'interim' injunctions. A final injunction is made as part of the resolution of litigation, whereas an interim injunction is made while the litigation is still under way. Imagine that a person is building on land. The claimant alleges that this is unlawful, but the builder refuses to stop and litigation follows. It may be many months before the claim goes to trial. The claimant might seek an interim injunction, asking the court to order the building work to stop until the trial. Not yet knowing who is in the right, the court must balance the interests of the parties in deciding whether to issue an interim injunction. If the interim injunction is granted, but the claimant's claim ultimately fails, the claimant will be required to compensate the successful defendant.   LIONEL SMITH

injunctions (labour)   An employer which is faced with the threat of industrial action by workers may seek a labour **injunction** to halt the action. Labour injunctions (which are 'interim' in nature) can be applied for very quickly if necessary, usually on the basis of written evidence but sometimes even over the telephone. Statute provides that injunctions cannot be used to force individual workers to work. However, the practical effect of a labour injunction may not be very different. The injunction will bind the **trade union** and/or individual organizing the industrial action, who by engaging in such activity will almost always commit a **common law** tort, such as inducing participants to breach their **contract of employment**. A **court** order restraining this activity, or requiring instructions to take industrial action to be withdrawn, prevents concerted action taking place. As with other injunctions, non-compliance constitutes **contempt of court**.

An interim injunction is designed to preserve the *status quo* until the merits of the case can be considered at full trial, which may be months or even years away. In the context of industrial action, however, the interim stage effectively decides the issue; the dispute is likely to have been settled long before the case can come to trial and generally the parties will have dropped the proceedings by that time. The criteria used by the courts to decide whether an interim injunction should be granted are, therefore, crucial. The court must first decide whether there is a 'serious question to be tried'. Employers are unlikely to find this a difficult test to satisfy: the facts may be complex or disputed; respondents may be alleged to have committed a range of torts, not all of which are

well-defined; and where the court does not have sufficient evidence before it to decide a disputed matter this, alone, may lead it to conclude that there is a serious question. Once this test is passed, the court then considers whether the 'balance of convenience' lies in granting or refusing the injunction, that is whether **damages** would be an adequate **remedy** for either side if their position were vindicated at the trial. In industrial action cases this test tends to favour the employer; traditionally the courts have been more sympathetic to arguments from employers that they would suffer irrecoverable losses if the action went ahead than to those of unions that the interests of their members would be prejudiced if it did not. The damage that industrial action may cause to the 'public interest'—a concept which is undefined—may also be a factor in the court's decision. Where dispute organizers claim to have acted 'in contemplation or furtherance of a trade dispute' the court is required by **legislation** to have regard to the likelihood of the industrial action being protected by the immunities given by statute against liability in specified torts (such as inducing breach of contract) but the application of these immunities is often contentious and ill-suited for determination at the interim stage.   GILLIAN MORRIS

See also: **economic torts**

injunctions against businesses   *see* **enforcement orders**

innocent passage   *see* **law of the sea**

Inns of Court   The *hospitii curiae* or Inns of Court are obscure in origin but date back at least to the late fourteenth century. The Inns seem to have been at first mere arrangements of convenience and included two Sergeant's Inns, numerous Chancery Inns for clerks and attorneys, as well as the four Inns of Court where noble apprentices to the courts of judicature would stay. There are four Inns of Court or *hospitia majora*: the Inner Temple and the Middle Temple, dating to a grant of Edward III, and Grey's Inn and Lincoln's Inn which emerged somewhat later. The two Temple Inns took their title from the Knights' Templar and, as the name suggests, they had a fairly well evidenced religious root and atmosphere, such that by one account they were not corporations but 'convents of men' (Waterhouse, 1663).

From modest beginnings, the Inns rapidly grew in status and purpose. Chief Justice Fortescue, writing in the middle of the fifteenth century, depicts the Inns as places of worship as well as of learning and training. They were an elite gymnasium or college of morals and manners as well as a being a *studium* or site of serious legal study. In their heyday, prior to the ravages of the Civil war, the Inns were collectively termed the Third or Juridical University where the children of the nobility went, after learning logic and rhetoric, as well as some **Roman law**, Latin, and law French, at one of the Universities. At the Inns of Court the students would train through conversation with and observation of their seniors as well as through more formal readings and moots. Training would often take place over meals, and the sense of shared community and common opinion was frequently forged through feasts and revels (Raffield, 2004).

The crowning emblem of a dual profession, the Inns of Court have survived to the present day as the exclusive mode of entry to the status of barrister. While solicitors can now appear as advocates, it remains the case that the Inns of Court still train and govern the vast majority of advocates. Formal training has for some time been delegated to the Council of Legal Education but membership of an Inn is still a mandatory requirement for qualifying as a barrister. The Inns also still require the eating of dinners as a species of social qualification and although this criterion was revised in 1998, attendance at Education dinners, Domus dinners, and Social Dinners remain key qualifying criteria for call to the Bar.

PETER GOODRICH

JH Baker, *The Third University of England: The Inns of Court and the Common Law Tradition* (London: Selden Society, 1990)

P Raffield, *Images and the Culture of Law in Early Modern England* (Cambridge: Cambridge University Press, 2004)

inquest   *see* **coroners**

inquiries   Inquiries are a tool of government used to gather information which may then be used for decision-making on a project, or to uncover the causes of a serious accident or to deal with an episode which has political ramifications. An inquiry may also be held as part of an appeal against the refusal of planning permission by the local planning authority, although the inquiry procedure is used in less that 10 per cent of planning appeals.

Where an inquiry is used in relation to a project, it is usually because there are objectors whose property rights are directly affected by the project. Such projects may include development or regeneration of an area; provision of infrastructure, including transport; and construction of power stations.

Implementation of such proposals will often require acquisition of land and if the owners do not wish to sell, **compulsory purchase**. Objections to proposals and contested compulsory purchase orders are considered at an inquiry, which is conducted by an inspector (reporter in Scotland). Participants at the inquiry may include the promoters of the project, acquiring authorities, objectors, and permitted third parties, ie parties whose legal rights are not affected but who have an interest in the project, such as an amenity society. Participants may give evidence and may be subject to cross-examination by other participants. Third parties are usually not permitted to conduct cross-examination. The inspector prepares a report and recommendations for the minister who has the power to confirm, reject or vary the project. The inspector's report and recommendations are sent to the participants along with the minister's decision letter.

Adoption of this procedure followed recommendations of the 1957 Franks Report; and it main features—especially that the decision should be based on the evidence presented at the inquiry—were modelled on court procedures. Procedural rules for inquiries are contained in regulations which, in addition to setting out notification requirements and providing for pre-inquiry meetings, the setting of a timetable and inspection of the site of the project, regulate the giving of statements of evidence (and summaries of them) to the inspector conducting the inquiry and to other specified parties. The inspector has a general discretion over procedure at the inquiry and may refuse to allow cross-examination or the presentation of evidence that is considered to be irrelevant or repetitious. An inquiry may usually be re-opened if the minister is minded to disagree with the inspector's recommendation on the basis of new evidence, thus allowing those who participated and were entitled to appear at the inquiry an opportunity to comment upon this new material. In some circumstances such comments may be made in writing rather orally at a reconvened inquiry.

In the past, inquiries into accidents and other matters giving rise to public concern could be established in three ways: (1) under subject-specific legislation—eg the inquiry into train protection systems the Health and Safety at Work Act 1974; (2) under the Tribunals of Inquiry (Evidence) Act 1921—eg the inquiry into the shooting at Dunblane Primary School; and (3) on a non-statutory basis—eg the inquiry into the murder of young girls at Soham. All of these inquiries were held in public, but inquiries may be held in private, eg the inquiry under the National Health Service Act 1977 into the treatment of organs following post-mortem examinations at the Royal Liverpool Children's Hospital; and the Review of Intelligence on Weapons of Mass Destruction.

The Inquiries Act 2005 has established a new framework for creating inquiries both within and across all of the UK's jurisdictions. Ministers (at Westminster and in Edinburgh, Cardiff, and Belfast) are vested with the power to create inquiries, to appoint the chairman and other members and assessors if required, to set their terms of reference and their powers to obtain evidence and to conduct proceedings, including the power, if any, to restrict public access. The Act requires that a setting-up date be stipulated, before which the appointments must be made and the terms of reference published, and after which the inquiry may begin to take evidence. Ministers have a duty to inform the relevant Parliament/Assembly as soon as is reasonably practicable of the establishment of an inquiry, providing details about the chairman and any other members and the terms of reference. The terms of reference must include the matters to which the inquiry relates and any matters on which the inquiry is to determine facts; they must state whether recommendations are to be made and any other matters about the inquiry's scope which the minister may specify.

The Act makes it clear that the inquiry will not determine civil or criminal liability of any person. The chairman is to be consulted about the terms of reference and their amendment, and the appointment of any other members or assessors. Appointees must be suitable having regard to their expertise and any possible conflict of interest. If it is sought to appoint a judge, then there must be consultation with the senior judge in the relevant jurisdiction who cannot, however, veto a judicial appointment. In conducting the inquiry the chairman is required to act fairly and may take evidence on oath. The minister must arrange for publication of the inquiry report either personally or by delegation to the inquiry chairman. The report is to be published in full unless there are reasons to exclude material such as harm or damage to national security, international interests, the economic interests of the UK or any part of the UK, and commercial sensitivity. Such factors may also provide reasons to restrict public access to the inquiry.   BRIAN THOMPSON

inquisitorial system This term refers to the division of functions between the court and the parties in civil, criminal, and administrative proceedings in **civil law systems**. It is usually contrasted with the **adversary system** (or 'adversarial system') prevailing in **common law** jurisdictions. Under the inquisitorial system the court plays an active, authoritative, and interventionist role at all stages of the proceedings, whilst the parties have only a minor, tentative, and supportive function. In an inquisitorial system *par excellence* the court acts solely in the public interest in order to discover 'the truth'. As a result, it has the power, or even the duty, to initiate the proceedings, to determine what issues or questions are in dispute, to investigate and gather evidence of its own motion, to appoint court experts, to interview the parties, to examine or cross-examine the witnesses, to call witnesses whom neither party desires to call, to promote a settlement or compromise between the parties, to know the applicable law and carry out its own legal research, and to ensure that no party takes unfair advantage of any weaknesses or mistakes of its opponent. The epitome of the inquisitorial system is the French *juge d'instruction*, a judicial officer who, in the preliminary stages of a criminal trial, gathers evidence, questions the witnesses in private, interrogates the suspect, and records their statements in writing. This file forms the basis of the case against the defendant at the final trial.

The focus on the investigating judge has led many Anglo-American writers erroneously to assume a link between the inquisitorial model and other features of the administration of justice prevailing in civil law systems, such as the predominantly written character and alleged 'secrecy' of the proceedings, the absence of a jury, and the civil service background of a career judiciary. The term 'inquisitorial system' has therefore always carried a pejorative connotation, conjuring up images of torture, secrecy, papal oppression, and the police state. Consequently, continental procedure has been contrasted unfavourably with what were said to be the fundamentally different social, cultural, and political values underpinning the British understanding of what procedure is about: the British mentality of independence, freedom, and fair play would be reflected in the orality and the publicity of British court proceedings which, together with the existence of the jury trial and the non-étatist fabric of the British judiciary, are taken to be safeguards for the parties' rights.

The reality of civil law systems is far removed from the 'inquisitorial system' imagined by many common lawyers. The enormous differences between their procedural laws cannot be captured by a single model. All legal systems, including English and Scottish law, combine inquisitorial and adversarial elements. English civil procedure in particular has recently placed a much stronger emphasis on 'court control'. The term 'inquisitorial system' retains its value as an ideal-typical model constructed for explanatory purposes. But it makes far more sense to speak of particular aspects of procedure which are more or less adversarial or inquisitorial, instead of invoking the rigid inquisitorial-adversarial dichotomy. STEFAN VOGENAUER

insanity *see* **mental incapacity and crime**

insider dealing Insider dealing occurs when a person with access to information that is precise and not generally available improperly discloses that information or uses it to deal to his advantage in financial **securities** in a public market. Such conduct is both a criminal offence under the Criminal Justice Act 1993 and a regulatory contravention under the **Financial Services and Markets Act 2000**. The rationale for the legal prohibition is that inside information distorts the operation of the market and thereby reduces confidence in the operation of the market. The distortion arises by comparison with an idealized world in which the market prices securities by reference to information which comes into the public domain as a result of disclosure of financial information to the entire world simultaneously. While the extent to which that model accurately describes securities markets is disputed, it is widely recognized that the presence of inside information distorts the market and leads to insiders (with access to inside information) gaining a trading advantage at the expense of outsiders (without access to inside information). The long-term consequence of such a bias in favour of insiders is that investors may lose confidence in the operation of securities markets, with the result that a source of new capital may be lost for the corporate sector as well as the benefits of liquidity that markets provide for investors. The prohibition is therefore intended to protect the integrity of securities markets and ensure that they remain attractive to issuers (companies) and investors.

Legal **regulation** of insider dealing has a relatively short history in the UK and an even shorter history in some other Member States of the EU, particularly by comparison with the United States, which introduced legislation in 1934. The EC Directive on Insider Dealing was introduced in 1989 and superseded by the Market Abuse Directive in 2004. The UK first legislated to outlaw insider dealing in 1980. Unlike the United States, the **common law** in the UK did not develop so as to regulate insider dealing prior to the introduction of statutory controls.

The initial focus in the UK was on criminalizing insider dealing. However, few prosecutions were brought as evidence was difficult to obtain and to corroborate so as to meet the requirement that a case be proven beyond reasonable doubt. The failure to secure prosecutions, taken together with a widespread perception that insider dealing was widespread, led to a change of tack. The Financial Services and Markets Act 2000 introduced a 'market abuse' regime which incorporates a prohibition on insider dealing but makes it punishable under the disciplinary procedures of the **Financial Services Authority** ('FSA'), which are civil in character and therefore do not protect the accused to the same extent as criminal procedure. It is a defence to show that a person believed that his conduct was not 'market abuse' or that all reasonable precautions were taken to avoid it—in that sense there is no strict liability. The FSA is able to impose fines for insider dealing and has published a policy statement as part of its Handbook. It is also able to take action in appropriate cases to require **restitution** of profits by insiders to outsiders or compensation for loss suffered by outsiders.

IAIN MACNEIL

insolvency of an employer A **company** becomes insolvent at law when it has gone beyond mere financial troubles (or distress) and has arrived at the point when it is no longer able to pay its debts. During this progression in corporate decline, a number of possible procedures may be followed. Certain actions are often taken before the point of formal insolvency. Thus the company will often seek to turn its affairs around through reconstruction or its main banker will insist that certain rescue steps are taken. These may involve the negotiation of new terms with creditors, and the construction of financial packages that will sustain turnaround. Assistance with such operations can be gained from a growing band of rescue professionals (often referred to as 'company doctors', 'turnaround specialists', or by a host of other labels).

When informal rescues do not succeed, formal processes have to be resorted to. Such processes can be entered into voluntarily or at the instigation of a creditor. The Enterprise Act 2002 made significant changes here by largely abolishing the regime of administrative receivership and reforming the administration procedure. Under the old administrative receivership system, the major bank creditor who held a floating charge (over substantially all of the company's assets) could unilaterally impose steps to recover its debt. After the 2002 Act, the administration procedure became the normal preferred option. It involves the appointment of an independent insolvency practitioner and its primary objective is to rescue the company as a going concern. If this cannot be done, the aim is to make the best arrangement (short of a **winding up**) for creditors as a whole. If these two purposes cannot reasonably be achieved, the task is to distribute assets to secured or preferential creditors.

The rights of employees who are involved in reorganizations and rescues would be at risk without legal protections. Therefore, in 1981, the Transfer of Undertakings (Protection of Employment) Regulations ('TUPE Regulations') were introduced to ensure that employees do not lose their jobs or have their contracts varied when businesses are transferred or sold. The Regulations were replaced in updated form but under the same title in 2006. The broad strategy of the TUPE Regulations is to carry over to the transferee company the transferring company's employee liabilities. A dismissal will be unfair unless it is for a valid 'economic, technical or organizational' reason. The law applies such protections to employees who are dismissed in anticipation of a transfer. These protections, moreover, cover transfers made in order to continue trading, but not those made with the aim of liquidating the assets of the company. The new TUPE Regulations do, however, allow 'permitted variations' of contractual terms provided these are agreed with employee representatives in the course of a transfer that is effected by insolvency proceedings that are designed to preserve the business as a going concern.

When rescue efforts fail the company will have to go into liquidation and parties will be paid according to a pre-determined priority. Creditors with fixed charges have first call on the designated assets on which their charges are fixed. The next items to be paid from residual funds are the expenses and fees of the insolvency professionals who act as administrators or liquidators. Preferential creditors are then paid followed by the holders of floating charges (ie charges over the generality of corporate assets). Debts owed to unsecured creditors (often trade creditors and consumers) are then paid out *pro rata*.

The employees of the company constitute preferential creditors for such purposes and they are entitled to remuneration for up to four months prior to the winding up order or resolution for voluntary liquidation. The maximum for such payment is currently set at £800. Employees are also entitled to any holiday pay entitlement accrued before the above order or resolution and for any sum loaned and used for paying employees. Further protections

for employees are provided by a separate statutory scheme under which certain payments are made to them out of the National Insurance Fund (under the Employment Rights Act 1996). In order to qualify as an employee under the above rules a person must be employed under a contract of service rather than constitute merely an independent contractor with the company.   VANESSA FINCH

See also: **transfer of business**

insolvency, corporate   Where a **company** *owes* more than it *owns* it can be said to be insolvent. It is open to the company's shareholders to resolve that it should be liquidated (or 'wound up'), and where the company is insolvent this process is termed a creditors' voluntary liquidation ('CVL'). Creditors may petition the **court** for a **winding up** order to be made against the company, and the court may make such an order where the company is unable to pay its debts (Insolvency Act 1986, section 122(1)(f): see also section 123(1)(e) and section 123(2) for circumstances where a company will be *deemed* to be unable to pay its debts). The winding up process involves the appointment of a **liquidator**, who must be a qualified insolvency practitioner (Insolvency Act 1986, section 389(1)).

Whether the winding up is voluntary or compulsory, the liquidator's basic function is to collect in and realize the company's assets and, after paying the costs and expenses of the winding up, to distribute the proceeds to the company's creditors on a *pro rata* basis (see *Ayerst v C & K (Construction) Ltd* (1976), Insolvency Act 1986 section 107, and Insolvency Rules 1986, rule 4.181). Creditors who have taken security against the company's assets have a priority claim against those assets or their proceeds.

SANDRA FRISBY

See also: **corporate debt and registration of charges; debt finance**

R Goode, *Principles of Corporate Insolvency Law* (London: Sweet & Maxwell, 3rd edn, 2005), ch 5

insolvency, individual   Individuals who experience financial difficulties may go through a number of procedures be they consumers or traders. In the first instance, informal arrangements may be utilized, money advisors consulted, and debt counselling services resorted to. Informal schemes, however, depend on the consent of all of the creditors, each of whom is under no obligation to accept the proposals on offer.

In the case of debts under £5,000, though, a debtor can apply for a County Court Administration

Order to protect them during repayments. Where the debtor is unable to pay debts owed, or satisfy a judgment made against him, such an Order can provide for payment by instalment or otherwise, and offers protection from the bringing of bankruptcy petitions or the issuing of execution orders. This procedure is cheaper and easier than filing for bankruptcy.

Another course of action short of bankruptcy was provided for by the Insolvency Act 1986. This is the Individual Voluntary Arrangement ('IVA'), an increasingly popular process that can be instituted whether the individual is bankrupt or not. It allows the debtor to obtain an interim moratorium to stay debt enforcement proceedings pending the formulation of a plan to put to creditors. The IVA is supervised by an Insolvency Practitioner ('ISOP') and has to be approved by 75 per cent of creditors by value. Since 2004 there have been fast track IVA processes that apply after a formal bankruptcy regime has been commenced. These allow the bankruptcy order to be annulled if the Official Receiver believes it will result in increased or speedier returns for creditors.

Currently under consideration in Parliament is a further procedure short of bankruptcy: the proposed Debt Relief Order ('DRO') regime. This is a fast track procedure that offers a remedy to individuals with low levels of debts and assets and little surplus income. It would be cheaper and less complex than bankruptcy and involves the making of a DRO that offers discharge after a year. The regime would be administered by the Official Receiver rather than by the courts. It is proposed that the debtor would pay a fee in advance for such a service and that the voluntary sector would be involved in relevant debt advice work.

Bankruptcy, in contrast, is a system administered by the courts following the presentation of a bankruptcy petition. Many petitions are presented by creditors on the basis of non-satisfaction of a statutory demand of over £750. Debtors, however, may present their own petitions where they are unable to pay their debts. When a bankruptcy order is made, the bankruptcy estate vests in the trustee in bankruptcy (or Official Receiver). This includes, in many instances, the family home. After the Enterprise Act 2002 ('EA'), however, there is a limit of three years during which this interest has to be dealt with. If it is not, the (un-mortgaged) interest in the home reverts to the bankrupt.

The post-2004 regime, instituted by the EA, provides for the automatic discharge of most bankrupts after a maximum period of twelve months, but earlier discharge may be allowed where a bankrupt has fully cooperated with the Official Receiver and/or trustee, where creditors have not raised the issue of the bankrupt's conduct and where the Official Receiver has notified the court that there is no need for further investigation.

The EA draws a distinction between culpable and non-culpable bankrupts. In the case of the former, protection for third parties is provided for through 'Bankruptcy Restriction Orders' ('BROs'). These place restrictions on those bankrupts who have been deemed reckless, culpable, or irresponsible in their conduct and it prevents them from obtaining credit for two to fifteen years. The regime also introduced 'income payment agreements' as a way to repay debts out of the bankrupt's income. Income Payment Orders ('IPOs') can also be issued to last for three years.

Personal bankruptcy continues to raise contentious issues. In 2006, levels of personal debt had become so high that the **Financial Services Authority** issued a warning. There are signs that the stigma of bankruptcy is declining, but there are increasing worries that bankruptcy laws are open to 'tactical' use in a way that increases overall credit costs, causes unfairness to conscientious borrowers, and creates systemic threats to the credit regime.

VANESSA FINCH

inspection of schools *see* **school standards and inspection of schools and LEAs**

inspectors, workplace There is no inspectorate in any of the United Kingdom jurisdictions with general responsibility for monitoring and enforcing compliance with employment rights and obligations. Workplace inspection is, however, carried out as part of the machinery for enforcing observance of the law on **health and safety at work** and **minimum wage** legislation. The work of inspectors appointed under the Health and Safety at Work Act 1974 with rights to enter premises, carry out examinations and investigations, require answers to questions and production of documents, is the principal means by which the standards laid down by that Act, or in regulations made under it, are enforced. The inspectors' powers include the issuing of 'improvement notices' and, where activities involve a risk of serious personal injury, 'prohibition notices'. Appeals against these notices can be made to employment **tribunals**. An inspector who has reasonable cause to believe that an article or substance is a cause of imminent danger may 'seize it and cause it to be rendered harmless'.

The National Minimum Wage Act 1998 provides for the appointment of officers with powers to require employers to produce their pay records as the primary method of ensuring that all workers who qualify are paid being paid at least the appropriate minimum wage rate. Separate Agricultural Wages Inspectorates exist in England and Wales, Scotland, and Northern Ireland with powers to require compliance with pay rates set by Agricultural Wages Boards for agricultural workers in each of these jurisdictions.   BOB SIMPSON

institutional discrimination Certain types of discrimination take clear, obvious, and overt forms. Examples include hostile or intimidating behaviour directed against ethnic **minorities** and other disadvantaged groups, abusive language, and explicit or barely-concealed forms of segregation and **stereotyping**. When people refer to 'racism' or 'sexism', it is often these types of overt prejudice that they have in mind. However, other forms of discriminatory behaviour may take less immediately obvious forms, but can be just as corrosive and damaging. Often, those discriminating may not intend to cause harm or be consciously prejudiced. However, their assumptions or stereotypes about particular groups may result in damaging consequences. For example, a career guidance teacher might not bother giving black students information on particular professional careers, on the assumption that they would not be interested in pursuing this line of work. There might be no active hostility or prejudice at play here, but the black students may still be treated unequally as a consequence of the automatic application of a stereotype.

Both **direct discrimination** and **indirect discrimination** are generally banned in the UK, even if there is no evidence of active hostility or ill will on the part of the discriminator. However, anti-discrimination law is complex and highly technical: it only applies to certain situations and individuals who suffer discrimination may often be reluctant to bring a case. Assumptions, stereotypes, and preconceptions about particular groups can often be deeply rooted and difficult to change. This can have particularly negative consequences when such forms of conscious or unconscious prejudice have a major influence in how organizations or institutions treat disadvantaged groups. Public authorities, private **companies,** and other institutions often adopt policies and practices that can have a negative impact upon particular social groups. This can occur not just through the deliberate actions of a few bigoted members of an institution's staff, but through a more systematic set of institution-wide assumptions and practices. Black activists in the US in the late 1960s coined the term 'institutional racism' to describe the attitudes and practices of many US institutions, and in particular **police** forces, towards black **communities**. The concept has been taken up and used in other contexts to describe institutional practices that discriminate against **women**, **persons** with **disabilities**, **homosexuals,** and other disadvantaged groups.

This idea of 'institutional discrimination' generates controversy. When discrimination occurs in how an institution treats members of a disadvantaged group, it is often viewed as just stemming from the behaviour of a few individuals within it, who are considered to be 'rotten apples' within a generally sound institutional structure. However, the concept of 'institutional discrimination' emphasizes that discrimination can also be the result of underlying and often unconscious assumptions and stereotypes that permeate how members of disadvantaged groups are treated by an institution in general. This idea triggers some resistance. Many still consider that widespread overt hostility or discriminatory behaviour by staff is required before it can be said that an institution 'discriminates'.

This controversy became the focus of national debate in 1999 with the publication of the Macpherson Report into the death of Stephen Lawrence, a black teenager from South London who was killed in a racist attack. The London Metropolitan Police badly mishandled the investigation, assuming initially that the killing had been the result of gang **violence** among the black community, and disregarding evidence from black witnesses and the Lawrence family, who were treated in a very cavalier manner. Following the ensuing political controversy, an **inquiry** was established which was chaired by Lord Macpherson of Cluny, a High Court **judge**. The report of the inquiry concluded that the Metropolitan Police had been 'institutionally racist' in how it had handled the investigation. Stereotypical attitudes towards black youths and the black community at large had been at the heart of the errors that had been made.

While accepting that the phrase 'institutional racism' was the subject of debate and controversy, the Macpherson Report recognized that '[u]nwitting racism can arise because of lack of understanding, ignorance or mistaken beliefs. It can arise from well intentioned but patronizing words or actions. It can arise from unfamiliarity with the behaviour or cultural traditions of people or families from minority ethnic communities. It can arise from racist stereotyping of black people as potential criminals or troublemakers'.

The Report went on to define institutional racism as 'the collective failure of an organization to provide an appropriate and professional service to people because of their colour, culture, or ethnic origin. It can be seen or detected in processes, attitudes and behaviour which amount to discrimination through unwitting prejudice, ignorance, thoughtlessness and racist stereotyping which disadvantage minority ethnic people'. The Report concluded that institutional racism persists because of the failure of organizations to recognize openly and adequately its existence and causes. Clear internal policies, leadership, and guidance were required to address this 'corrosive disease', along with the development of partnerships with affected groups and external support from central government and other institutions.

These conclusions generated considerable controversy. Some newspapers and politicians attacked what they considered to be an unwarranted labelling of the entire Metropolitan police force as 'racist'. Some academics argued that the use of the 'unclear' concept of institutional racism was unhelpful. Nevertheless, in the wake of the Macpherson Report, there has been a wide acceptance that institutional discrimination in the public sector is a problem and that positive steps are required to tackle it. Positive **equality** duties requiring public authorities to assess the 'equality impact' of their policies and practices and to promote equality of opportunity on the grounds of **race**, **gender**, and disability have been progressively introduced in **legislation** since 2000. These have been supplemented by a series of government initiatives designed to encourage public authorities to reassess how their activities impact upon disadvantaged groups. There has been less focus on this problem in the private sector, but for now, institutional discrimination is increasingly accepted as a problem that requires a positive and vigorous response.   COLM O'CINNEIDE

The Stephen Lawrence Inquiry: Report of An Inquiry By Sir William Macpherson Of Cluny (February 1999) Cm 4262-I

institutional investor activism Institutional investors are shareholders in **companies** who invest on behalf of others. Examples are **pension** funds, unit **trusts,** and investment trusts: each provides a form of pooled investment under professional management for their participants. Institutional investment grew rapidly in the second half of the twentieth century as it provided better risk diversification, lower transaction costs, and tax advantages by comparison with direct investment in companies by individuals. Institutional investors now account for a large majority of shareholdings in public listed companies in the UK. In contrast, the proportion of **shares** held by private individuals has declined significantly over the same time period.

Activism refers to the extent to which shareholders become involved in monitoring and supervising companies in which they are invested. It is open to shareholders to exercise control over companies by initiating and voting on resolutions at company meetings. One measure of activism is the extent to which shareholders vote on resolutions, but there are also informal ways in which shareholders can exert pressure through dialogue with the **Board of Directors**. The historical passiveness of institutional investors in the UK has been explained by reference to two main factors. First, there is a disincentive to engage in costly monitoring in a country such as the UK, where shareholdings are widely dispersed. UK Institutional investors rarely hold a controlling shareholding in listed companies and therefore any benefits resulting from activism have to be shared with other shareholders who have not taken an active stance. Secondly, the relatively short-term contracts under which institutional funds are managed by professional fund managers provide a disincentive to incurring monitoring costs that do not yield an immediate benefit.

However, there are some signs that activism is moving to the fore. The development of **corporate governance** standards for listed companies during the 1990s (in reaction to a number of high-profile corporate failures) and increasing public scrutiny of executive remuneration acted as a catalyst for activism. Both the **Combined Code of Corporate Governance** for listed companies and the Guidelines adopted by the Institutional Shareholders' Committee recommend that institutional investors adopt an activist stance by making considered use of their voting rights. Neither instrument has the force of law, but each represents an important source of good practice for institutional investors.

Another factor that has brought activism to the fore is that a passive stance opens institutional investors to the charge that they are not acting in the best interests of the indirect investors whose funds they invest. In many cases there is a **fiduciary** relationship between institutional investors and their clients and therefore a legal duty to act in their best interests. It is possible for the legal duty to be discharged by considering a resolution and deciding to abstain from voting but it is doubtful if such a strategy can be regarded as discharging the duty if it becomes a standard pattern over the long-term.

A policy of activism provides a general response to this concern.   IAIN MACNEIL

insurance and investment Certain types of insurance are often rightly regarded as more of a form of investment than simple insurance. In general terms, insurance divides into types that compensate someone against the loss of some property or against a legal liability—under which they will receive only sufficient to compensate them for their loss or liability, and insurances of someone's life or against bodily injury, under which the insured will receive an agreed fixed amount of money or an amount of money determined by an agreed formula in the event of death or injury. Within the latter type, life insurance is often these days not simply an insurance that will pay out when the life insured dies, but is also a means of saving.

By itself, life insurance that does simply pay a fixed sum of money on death is normally used in order to provide money to be put towards the payment of inheritance tax. Sometimes, this type of simple life insurance may last for a fixed number of years and pay out only if the person whose life is insured dies within that period. It is more usual, though, for life insurance to be used simply as an element of a broader arrangement, or combined with a promise to pay money at a fixed date unless the person whose life is insured dies before that date, in which case the insured sum is payable. A common example is what is called 'endowment insurance'. Typically this will provide that the insurer will pay out £x if the person whose life is insured dies before they reach the age of, say, sixty; but that otherwise, when they reach sixty, they will receive the value of their 'investment', that is the value of the money that they have paid by way of premiums over the years, as invested by the company. In this type of case, the life insurance element can be more or less than the value of the money invested, which will depend on the skill of the company's managers and such things as the value of the property (for example, stocks and shares) in which the money has been invested. The normal expectation is that the value of the investment will be greater than the amount to be paid in the event of death before the agreed age. One case involved a contract under which the life insurance element was £1.1 million, whereas the potential investment value was the total of the gross national product of the UK for 460,000 years, but this was no doubt an exceptional case.

There are no limits on the type of arrangements that can be offered that combine investment with insurance; but only companies that are authorized by the **Financial Services Authority,** or companies based in another EU Member State that are authorized by their home country, can legally offer such arrangements.   JOHN BIRDS

insurance companies, claims against *see* **defence of claims; ombudsmen**

insurance contracts/policies An insurance contract can be described as a contract under which, in return for a payment, normally described as a premium, an insurer agrees to pay money or provide a service in the event of something happening to the person insured (often called the policyholder) that is adverse to them or their property. It must be uncertain as to whether or when the 'event' will occur. The contract is normally contained in a 'policy', although other documents, particularly the proposal form often used as the initial application for insurance, may also be incorporated into the contract, so that it is possible that the 'insurance contract' is more than simply the 'policy'.

An insurance contract is formed according to the general rules applying to all contracts and the law requires very few formalities. One notable qualification to this is that all insurance contracts must contain some basic information about the insurer and, in the case of life insurance, must contain a notice of the right to cancel the contract within fourteen days of receipt of the notice. Similarly the legal principles applying to contract generally apply to insurance contracts, subject to some important special principles as explained below.

The most important of these principles is that the insurance contract is a contract that requires both parties to display the utmost good faith in their dealings with each other. This means, in particular, that a person applying for insurance, or renewing an existing contract of insurance (which the law regards as the entry into a new contract) is under a duty of disclosure. In addition to not mis-stating facts when they answer questions put to them, primarily on a proposal form, they must disclose facts that a reasonable insurer would regard as 'material' and which the particular insurer can show it would have wanted to be told about. If the person applying for insurance fails to do so, whether they were aware of this duty or not, the insurer will have the right to avoid the contract in its entirety and refuse to pay any claim. Material facts will include core details of the property or life to be insured, but also matters relevant to the character of the insured, such as their claims record and details of certain criminal convictions. In some respects the duty of good faith has a continuing effect, and so it can apply to an insurer in the sense that it may be required to act in good faith when seeking to rely on its legal right to avoid a contract.

As well as containing the core terms that describe the risks covered and those that are not covered by it, an insurance contract will contain provisions imposing obligations on the insured. Failure to comply with these may give the insurer the right to refuse to pay a claim. A simple example is a failure to tell the insurer about a loss within the time specified in the contract. If this is a 'condition precedent' to the insurer's liability, then a breach will give the insurer the right to repudiate the claim. More fundamentally, a provision that is peculiar to insurance contracts is one that requires the policyholder to take specified steps to reduce the likelihood of a loss, for example a term requiring them to install and operate a burglar alarm or keep a car in a garage. This sort of term may be what is called a 'warranty' and, as a matter of strict law, the insurer is not liable on the contract if there is a breach of warranty, even if that has no relationship with a claim made by the policyholder.

Insurances of property of any sort are a species of what are called contracts of indemnity. This has several consequences. It means first of all that the policyholder can only recover sufficient to compensate them for their loss. So, for example, someone claiming for damage to their car cannot recover and keep both money from their insurer and money recovered from the person who caused the damage. In addition, when an insurer satisfies a claim, it will have the right to recover that, in the name of the policyholder, from the person responsible for the loss under what is called the doctrine of **subrogation**.

JOHN BIRDS

See also: **contract law**

insurance ombudsman   *see* **ombudsmen**

insurance, liability   *see* **liability insurance**

insurgency   *see* **war and armed conflict**

integrated circuits   An integrated circuit ('INC') is an electronic device made from semiconductor material in which the INC is embedded. There are two aspects to INCs: a functional aspect which dictates the operations it performs, and the design or physical aspect that determines the layout of the components. INCs are found in modern electrical devices such as computers, cars, and mobile phones. An INC processes information (eg tracking the keys used on a computer). To make an INC, a high energy light is shone through a mask onto a piece of silicon. The light only hits those parts not covered by the mask. These are processed so that their electrical properties change. Further layers are added. A final mask detailing the layout of the wires connecting the parts of the INC is placed on top. A complex web of protection exists for INCs by way of European Community and national registered design right and Community unregistered design right. In addition there is a *sui generis* unregistered design right under section 213(2) of the Copyright Designs and Patents Act 1988. Protection under this latter measure is given against copying of the pattern fixed on a layer of semiconductor product. To qualify, the design must be original and not commonplace. Private reproduction for non-commercial purposes is permitted as is some reverse engineering. It has been held that the design of even a single layer of a whole chip is a design within the meaning of the 1988 Act.

CHARLOTTE WAELDE

See also: **designs**

integrated pollution prevention and control   In both the United Kingdom and many other jurisdictions, **pollution** laws have tended to develop historically in a fragmented fashion, dealing with emissions to water, air, and the land under separate laws and often enforced by distinct governmental bodies. In 1976, the Royal Commission on Environmental Pollution considered such arrangements sub-optimal from an environmental perspective, and called for a more integrated approach to the regulation of emissions from industrial premises that would allow the environmental impact of a process to be considered and regulated as a whole system.

The first formal system of integrated pollution control ('IPC') was introduced in Britain under Part I of the Environmental Protection Act 1990 which applied a single permitting system for emissions for some 2,000 industrial prescribed processes. One of the core requirements of the **legislation** was that where there were emissions to more than one environmental medium, conditions should be imposed to reflect the best practicable environmental option, implying to need to evaluate trade-offs between different abatement strategies.

Within the European Union, the move towards more integrated permitting was reflected in the Integrated Pollution Prevention and Control Directive 1996 ('IPPC'), which applied to new installations falling within prescribed categories from 1999, and allowed for a further eight years for its gradual application to existing installations. Although the Directive reflected many of the underlying core concepts in the British integrated pollution control system, it went wider, in terms of both the numbers of processes covered and the range of environmental impacts to be encompassed, with noise and energy efficiency being included. As a result, the IPC regime under the Environmental Protection Act has been subsumed by new regulatory requirements implementing the EC Directive, know as Pollution Prevention and Control ('PPC').

A core requirement of the European legislation is that permit conditions must achieve a high level of protection for the environment as a whole by means of protection of the air, water, and land. Emission limit values and other technical measures contained in conditions must be based on the 'best available techniques'. The concept of 'availability' as defined in the Directive encompasses techniques that are reasonably accessible to the operator and take in consideration costs and advantages. The determination of permit conditions rests at national level, but under the Directive the **European Commission** is obliged to exchange information on 'best available techniques' amongst Member States. In practice it does so through an IPPC Information Exchange Forum which produces technical guidance known as BREF Notes for the various categories of processes falling within the scope of the Directive.

These legal developments in both the UK and the European Union towards a more integrated approach towards pollution control have tended to focus on the environmental impact of emissions from industrial processes, and as such represent a fairly narrow sub-set of wider concepts of integrated pollution control. An OECD Recommendation in 1991 adopted a much broader definition of integrated pollution control which encompassed the assessment of the whole commercial and environmental life cycles of substances. Such broader concepts have yet to be fully reflected in legal structures.

RICHARD MACRORY

integration   Integration is often claimed to be the antithesis of **assimilation**. Where assimilation demands sameness and the obliteration of difference, integration professes not only **recognition** of, but a respect for differences. Will Kymlicka and Wayne Norman suggest that notions of assimilation and integration in fact, share ideological grounds in their common insistence upon a shared overarching **identity** premised upon national identity and **citizenship**. The point at which the two ideas seemingly diverge is when

faced with the issue (or problem) of cultural identity. Where assimilation is premised upon the 'when in Rome' school of thought which seeks to divest **minorities** of all vestiges of their cultural identity certainly within the public sphere, integration instead suggests that it is possible to facilitate ethnic and cultural diversity to enable minority **communities** to retain cultural traditions and practices whilst still subscribing to a shared civic identity which transcends ethnic, racial, religious, and cultural boundaries.

More recently, the language of integration has been deployed as an indictment of minority communities and their perceived self-segregation into cultural and religious 'ghettos' and their unwillingness to integrate into dominant society. Tellingly, the failure to integrate, not at the level of culture or lifestyle, but at the level of *values*, has been blamed for the perpetration of the 7/7 bombings by British nationals. In a 2006 speech entitled 'The Duty to Integrate: Shared British Values', Tony Blair outlined six ways for policy to effect integration—the use of grants to promote the integration of community cultural, religious, and racial groups; a firm commitment to **equality** for all and clear policies which effect this, notably, in tackling issues of **gender** inequality; a demand for allegiance to the **rule of law**; more careful scrutiny of foreign nationals entering the UK as visiting preachers; the teaching of citizenship as part of the national curriculum; and finally, an emphasis upon English as the common language.   SONYA FERNANDEZ

intellectual property rights, european harmonization of   *see* **European harmonization of intellectual property rights**

intellectual property rights, international harmonization of   *see* **international harmonization of intellectual property rights**

intellectual property, commercial exploitation of   *see* **commercial exploitation of intellectual property**

intention   *see* **fault-based criminal liability; fault-based civil liability**

interception of communications   US Secretary of State Henry L Stimson famously remarked that 'Gentlemen do not read each other's mail'; but his advice has seldom been followed across the Atlantic. In England, the authorities have been intercepting mail since at least the reign of Elizabeth I. Indeed, an ordinance of 1657 proclaimed that a regular state post office was 'the best means to discover and prevent any dangerous designs against the Commonwealth'. The practice has, understandably, remained somewhat obscure, although periodically scandals have drawn public attention to it, as when a parliamentary committee investigated the interference with the mail of the Italian exile Mazzini in 1844. As technology has added new means of communication, first the telephone and then telegraphs, faxes, electronic mail, and text messages, so interception has extended to them.

The Birkett Committee, which reported in 1957 following a later scandal (the Marrinan affair), first confirmed that both 'phone tapping' and mail opening were conducted on the authority of a warrant issued by a Secretary of State. Although the origins of these warrants is obscure, the government relied on the **prerogative** as legal authority for this practice until it was challenged before the **European Court of Human Rights** in 1984. Following that decision, a statutory scheme for interceptions was enacted—currently contained in the Regulation of Investigatory Powers Act 2000. This permits warrants (still issued by a Minister, rather than a judge) for the prevention or detection of serious crime, in the interest of national security or for safeguarding the country's economic well-being. The system is overseen by a judicial Commissioner who reports annually.

Unlike many other countries, in the UK material obtained from interception is not admissible as evidence in legal proceedings. This has the effect of maintaining a degree of secrecy, and it also insulates the practice from effective legal challenges. Moreover, it is an offence under the Official Secrets Act 1989 to disclose details of interception.   IAN LEIGH

interest groups Democratic political systems do not merely permit the free association and open organization of private rights and interests outside the boundaries and control of the state. They also rely on these processes to align and aggregate political interests and to fuel the democratic state's functions of law-making, public policymaking and even routine administration of established public services. This 'civil society' constantly claims and complains through organized interest groups, and the government responds by allocating both tangible and symbolic benefits; the electorate judges the results at the next election.

Debate on the general value or dangers of organized interest groups should recognize them as providing the actual structure of accountable democratic government (together with free political parties and the mass media). Without them (eg as in Russia or much of Africa) governments lack practical contact with the public, even if they wish to implement the popular will.

This pluralist democratic theory of organized groups interests assumes that all social or economic personal interests can be (or even are) automatically able to be effectively organized. The country's banks or wealthy landowners and its least educated citizens or unskilled immigrant workers can all form interest groups (although enjoying hugely different practical resources) because they are equally legitimate. The alternative 'elite' explanation stresses the power of economic and social elites to prevail over their weaker rivals (eg big farmers over immigrant farm workers) not only using their much greater wealth and personal skills but also employing their 'structural' power in society, including state institutions such as the government and courts. The big firms and principal professional bodies are essential parts of the structure of state and society whereas even large numbers of individuals in community groups, political associations, or trade unions are often not. This 'elite' theory of organized groups is essentially leftist, or even Marxist, whereas the pluralist view is liberal or (in restricted form) social democratic.

Organized interest groups differ from political parties in having only limited, perhaps 'single issue' political goals and in wanting to influence governments, not become one. The popular term 'pressure group' should not replace 'organized interest group' because it is badly misleading. All groups claim to represent an interest. Membership groups (associations of firms, trade unions of employees, institutes of professionals, or other specialists) mainly protect their members' established representation. They are nearly all accepted, legitimated 'insider' groups continually negotiating, even daily, with government officials on current and prospective legislation and its supporting rules and practices. Resort to public 'pressure' (and certainly to 'protest') would be a defeat for their insider status.

Promotional groups claim to represent both a policy idea and those supporters who have joined it for that reason—usually with no personal gain in mind (in contrast to joining a trade union or association of firms). Promoting an idea—womens' rights, nature conservation, vegetarianism—requires political attention-seeking among the mass media, political parties, and government, which the established protective groups hope to avoid. But even this need not involve overt 'pressure' rather than offering information and persuasion, hoping to make these ideas into party election promises and government action.

ANTHONY BARKER

See also: **lobbyists**

inter-generational equity The principle of inter-generational equity defines the rights and obligations of present and future generations with respect to the use and enjoyment of natural and cultural resources, inherited by the present generation and to be passed on to future generations in no worse condition than received. While some authors have identified the principle as an integral element of the broader concept of sustainable development, the legal status and contours of the principle are controversial, and it has been questioned whether, in the concept exerts any normative terms, it is anything more than a chimera pull.

The interests of future generations have been recognized in non-binding 'soft law' declarations (eg the 1992 Rio Declaration on Environment and Development; and the 1997 UNESCO Declaration on the Responsibilities of the Present Generation Towards Future Generations), in the preamble to a number of environmental **treaties** (eg the 1946 International Convention on the Regulation of Whaling and the 1992 Biodiversity Convention) and, in a few instances, in the text of a treaty (eg the 1992 Climate Change Convention and the 1972 World Heritage Convention). However, no rights of future generations arise under these treaty texts and considerable doubt exists as to whether a particular treaty creates rights and obligations enforceable by individuals. Nor is there evidence that it has passed into **customary international law** through the practice of states. While states have yet to accept the principle as a binding international obligation, there is some evidence of the application of the principle by domestic courts as a basis for recognizing the interests of future generations.

CATHERINE REDGWELL

L Gündling, 'Agora: What Obligation Does Our Generation Owe to the Next? An Approach to Global Environmental Responsibility' (1990) 84 *American Journal of International Law* 190

EB Weiss, *In Fairness to Future Generations* (Dobbs Ferry: Transnational Publishers, 1989)

interlocutory proceedings Interlocutory proceedings concern issues brought before the court in civil proceedings the disposal of which does not result in a final determination of the case. In addition to routine case management matters, they often involve interim judgments, orders, **injunctions,** and **remedies** of crucial importance to a just outcome.

Under the **Civil Procedure Rules** 1998 interim remedies which the court may grant include: an interim injunction; an interim declaration; orders for the detention, custody, or preservation of relevant property; an order authorizing a person to enter any land or building in the possession of a party for the purposes of carrying out orders; a 'freezing injunction' restraining a party from removing assets from the jurisdiction; an order directing a party to provide information about the location of relevant assets; a 'search order' requiring a party to admit another party to premises for the purpose of preserving evidence; an order for interim payment by a defendant on account of any **damages**, debt, or other sum (except costs) which the court may hold the defendant liable to pay; an order in intellectual property proceedings making the continuation of an alleged infringement subject to the lodging of guarantees.

These measures can prevent either party frustrating the ability of the court to deal justly with the case. They can also protect from the outset, albeit on a provisional basis, the party who is ultimately found to have been wronged. This often involves trying to maintain the status quo until final judgment.

JOHN FITZPATRICK

internal market   *see* **single market**

internal restrictions The concept of an 'internal restriction' arises in legal and political theory of **multiculturalism**, and particularly of **liberal multiculturalism**. The latter idea allows that the state should grant rights to certain groups, such as exemptions from laws that generally apply, rights to group **representation** in government, and rights of legal and political **self-determination**. For a liberal proponent of self-government rights or language rights (such as Will Kymlicka, who has done the most to develop and clarify this position), these rights are justified in that they allow members of a group to pursue a way of life, culture, or **religion** on an equal footing with the rest of society. So (to take a further example) a **minority** language group may claim that equality of educational opportunity requires that this language be used as a medium of instruction in schools.

From the perspective of a liberal approach to multiculturalism, a difficulty arises when the group right demanded entails a significant restriction on the liberty of members of the group. This may arise as an unavoidable by-product of the right in question. For example, if a province (such as Wales or Quebec) is granted the right to impose its own language policy, in order to protect the language of that province, this can entail restricting the range of options for members of that group. In order to protect French in Quebec, for example, the right to public education in English is barred to the children of Francophone parents. It is only through such internal restriction, the argument in their support runs, that the minority language can be protected against English.

Another important area of controversy has concerned the treatment of formerly colonized and indigenous peoples. For example, there has been concern that Indian women in Canada and the United States might be subject to sex discrimination if the terms for self-government for those groups are not subject to constitutional requirements of **equality**. On the other side, supporters of a less qualified right of indigenous self-determination argue that this fear reflects prejudice and stereotype, or perhaps in a more radical vein that the language of sexual equality and internal restrictions are constructs that should be treated suspiciously as part of an effort to reject **colonialism** and reclaim an indigenous way of life. Where the worry about internal restrictions is not dismissed in this way, there are hotly contested questions about who is entitled to act and how: should a liberal state enforce the full panoply of anti-discrimination **legislation** or merely some minimal standards? Is the colonizing state entitled to intervene or should it cede powers of surveillance and enforcement to regional or international organizations?

There is another question in the background here, which concerns the extent to which (or sense in which) membership of a group is voluntary. Some libertarians (notably Chandran Kukathas) argue that we should view such groups as voluntary associations which members are able to leave as they please. Provided that there exists a **right of exit**, for this perspective, such associations should be permitted to treat members as they see fit, and it amounts to an illegitimate breach of the individual **right to association** for the state to worry about internal restrictions.   MATTHEW FESTENSTEIN

See also: **external protections**

internally displaced persons *see* **displaced persons**

International Center for Settlement of Investment Disputes (ICSID) *see* **investment protection**

International claims *see* **state claims**

International Committee of the Red Cross (ICRC) *see* **international humanitarian law**

International Court of Justice (ICJ) *see* **international courts and tribunals**

international courts and tribunals International courts and tribunals are established by states at the global or regional level. The term encompasses international or regional courts that are established by states on a permanent basis (such as the International Court of Justice or the **European Court of Human Rights**); and courts that are established for a limited period for a specific mandate (such as the International Criminal Tribunals for the Former Yugoslavia ('**ICTY**') and for Rwanda). The term can also encompass international arbitral tribunals established to decide a specific dispute. Such arbitral tribunals are addressed briefly at the end of this entry, which focuses principally on standing international courts and tribunals.

Standing international courts and tribunals are composed of independent judges, and their proceedings are conducted in accordance with pre-existing procedural rules. Thus, the parties to the dispute do not generally control the composition of the bench or the procedure to be followed. International courts decide disputes on the basis of **international law**, and they render judgments that are legally binding upon the parties.

The establishment of standing or permanent international courts is a relatively new phenomenon. The first, albeit short-lived, regional court was established in Central America in 1907. In 1920, states created the Permanent Court of International Justice ('PCIJ'), which was replaced, in effect, by the International Court of Justice ('ICJ'), the principal judicial organ of the **United Nations** ('UN'), after World War II. The 1950s saw the establishment of the **European Court of Justice** ('ECJ') and the European Court of Human Rights ('ECtHR'), but it was the period after 1990 that witnessed a rapid expansion of international courts and tribunals at the global and regional level. Many such bodies have been established within the framework of broader international or regional cooperation arrangements—as organs, or under the auspices, of intergovernmental organizations. It is worth noting that, in addition to the standing international courts and tribunals discussed here, many other types of quasi-judicial and other dispute settlement bodies also exist at the international level.

There are now around twenty standing international or regional courts, established to address different types of disputes. For example, they may be established: to decide disputes (or certain types of disputes) arising between states; to interpret provisions of regional economic cooperation or integration agreements; to provide a forum for individuals or groups to bring **human rights** complaints against states; and to try individuals charged with the commission of crimes against humanity, **genocide,** or other serious crimes. For the most part, in contrast to a domestic judicial system, no formal links or hierarchy exist between the various international and regional courts.

Some international courts and tribunals deal only, or primarily, with disputes between states. The ICJ, International Tribunal for the Law of the Sea ('ITLOS'), and the **World Trade Organization ('WTO')** Appellate Body fall within this category.

In addition to the ECJ, courts have been established in respect of regional economic cooperation arrangements in, for example, West Africa, Southern and Eastern Africa, the Caribbean, the Andean region, and Central America. The precise jurisdiction of the different regional economic courts varies, but they are established principally to deal with four categories of cases: first, questions from national courts of member states of the economic community in question regarding the interpretation of community law; secondly, cases brought by an organ or organs of the community against a member state for non-compliance with obligations (eg in the ECJ, cases brought by the **European Commission** against Member States); thirdly, cases reviewing acts of organs of the community in question; and fourthly, disputes between member states regarding the interpretation and application of their obligations under community rules.

Regional human rights courts address complaints, brought by or in respect of individuals, that a state party to a regional human rights treaty has violated its obligations. Such courts have now been established in Europe, the Americas and, most recently, Africa. In Europe, such complaints may be submitted directly to the ECtHR. In the Inter-American Court of Human Rights, complaints are first submitted to a commission, which determines whether the matter should be referred to the Court.

The adoption of the Rome Statute of the **International Criminal Court** in 1998 paved the way for the establishment of the first permanent tribunal to try individuals charged with crimes against humanity and other serious crimes. It builds upon experience of previous **war crimes tribunals**, including the Nuremburg and Tokyo Tribunals, and that of the two International Criminal Tribunals established in the 1990s for the former Yugoslavia and Rwanda.

International courts and tribunals are generally established by an international agreement. For example, the ICJ was established under the UN Charter; and ITLOS was created under the 1982 UN Convention on the Law of the Sea. By contrast, the International Criminal Tribunals for the Former Yugoslavia ('ICTY') and Rwanda ('ICTR') were established by resolutions of the UN Security Council.

The constitutive instrument of a court or tribunal (often termed its 'Statute') sets out its jurisdiction and powers, as well as other matters such as how many judges will compose the court and how they will be selected, and how the costs of the court will be met. It sets out certain procedural rules (generally elaborated subsequently in more detailed rules of procedure), and identifies the substantive law that the court will apply in deciding cases.

The power of an international court or tribunal to hear and decide a particular case (or its 'jurisdiction') may be defined or limited in a number of ways. First, jurisdiction may be defined in terms of subject matter (jurisdiction *ratione materiae*). For instance, the ICJ has general subject matter jurisdiction; this means that in principle, it can deal with disputes involving any aspect of international law. Its judgments have addressed a diverse range of substantive issues, including the delimitation of land and maritime boundaries, the use of force, fisheries, genocide, consular protection, and international watercourses. Other international courts and tribunals have more limited subject matter jurisdiction; for instance, addressing human rights questions, the **law of the sea**, trade or other economic disputes, or determining individual criminal responsibility.

Secondly, jurisdiction may also be defined in terms of parties (jurisdiction *ratione personae*). While only states may be parties to contentious cases in some international courts and tribunals (eg ICJ and the WTO Appellate Body), in others, individuals may be parties to proceedings. In the ECtHR, for example, individuals may bring cases directly against states; and in the ICC, individuals may be tried for serious crimes. In regional economic courts, parties to cases may be member states of the regional organization, organs of that organization (eg the European Commission, in the case of the ECJ), or, in specified circumstances, other entities (eg individuals or corporations).

Thirdly, jurisdiction may be defined by time (jurisdiction *ratione temporis*). In some cases there are temporal restrictions that limit the cases that the court is empowered to hear.

As well as deciding contentious cases (ie disputes), some international courts and tribunals also have so-called advisory jurisdiction. That is, they are empowered to give advisory opinions on legal questions falling within their remit. The entities permitted to request such opinions are generally organs or agencies of the international organizations of which the court forms a part (for example, the UN General

Assembly may request an advisory opinion from the ICJ on any legal question).

In some courts, the number of judges is the same as the number of states parties to the agreement establishing the court. This is the case, for example, in relation to the ECtHR (presently forty-seven judges) and the ECJ (presently twenty-seven judges). In many international courts, however, this is not the case. For example, the ICJ has fifteen judges, ITLOS has twenty-one, and the ICC has eighteen. In such circumstances, it is usually provided that there should be fair representation of different geographic regions and legal systems, and the judges are generally elected by a political body from amongst candidates nominated by states.

International arbitral tribunals may be established by two states, or by a state and another entity, to decide a specific case or category of cases. They differ from standing international courts in important respects. Most significantly, the members of the arbitral tribunal are chosen by the parties to the dispute themselves. Arbitral tribunals generally have three or five members, each of the parties to the dispute appointing one or two arbitrators, and the presiding arbitrator being selected jointly. The parties also have more control over the arbitral process than over process in a court or tribunal: they decide what procedural rules will apply (although they may select a pre-existing set of arbitration rules), and what substantive law the arbitrators will apply in deciding the dispute. As in international courts, the decision of an arbitral tribunal is binding upon the parties.

Arbitration may involve two states (inter-state arbitration) or it may be 'mixed', addressing a dispute between a state party on the one hand, and another entity (eg an individual or a corporation) on the other. Various mechanisms exist to facilitate arbitration by providing for example, administrative support and sets of rules for the institution and conduct of arbitral proceedings. These include the Permanent Court of Arbitration and, for foreign investment disputes, the **International Centre for Settlement of Investment Disputes**.

RUTH MACKENZIE

P Sands, R Mackenzie and Y Shany (eds), *Manual on International Courts and Tribunals* (London: Butterworths, 1999)

D Terris, CPR Romano, and L Swigart, *The International Judge: an introduction to the men and women who decide the world's cases* (Oxford: Oxford University Press, 2007)

International Covenant on Civil and Political Rights ('ICCPR')   The ICCPR was adopted by the United Nations General Assembly on 19 December 1966 at the same time as the **International Covenant on Economic, Social, and Cultural Rights.** It came into force ten years later, after thirty-five states had ratified it. In January 2007, the ICCPR had 160 parties.

The ICCPR gives binding treaty status to many of the rights contained in the **Universal Declaration of Human Rights** ('UDHR') of 1948. Although the drafters of the UDHR had contemplated that the Declaration would be translated into a single human rights treaty, the tensions of the Cold War led to the separation of civil and political rights from economic, social, and cultural rights. Western countries tended to support the former and Soviet-bloc countries the latter. The ICCPR protects rights ranging from the rights to life (Article 7) and to liberty and security of the person (Article 9), to the rights to privacy (Article 17), and nondiscrimination (Article 26), and the right of minorities to enjoy their own culture, religion, and language (Article 27).

A party to the ICCPR commits to ensuring the designated rights to all individuals within its jurisdiction (Article 2). Implementation is monitored by a system of periodic state reports to an eighteen-member expert group, the Human Rights Committee. An Optional Protocol to the ICCPR allows individuals to make complaints about breaches of the ICCPR to the Human Rights Committee.

The ICCPR has significantly influenced the drafting of a number of modern bills of rights, for example the Canadian Charter of Rights and Freedoms of 1982 and the New Zealand Bill of Rights Act of 1990.

HILARY CHARLESWORTH

International Covenant on Economic, Social, and Cultural Rights   The **United Nations** General Assembly voted to adopt the International Covenant on Economic, Social, and Cultural Rights ('ICESCR') on 19 December 1966, together with the **International Covenant on Civil and Political Rights** ('ICCPR'). The two Covenants gave treaty force to the catalogue of rights contained in the Universal Declaration of Human Rights ('UDHR') of 1948. The ICESCR came into force on 3 January 1976 after thirty-five states became parties to it. By March 2007, the treaty had 155 parties.

The ICESCR includes the **rights to work**, to form **trade unions**, to social security, to an adequate standard of living, to health care, and to education. The language of the ICESCR differs from that of the ICCPR: rights tend to be expressed in a more complex manner and the obligation to implement the treaty (Article 2) is more qualified. This difference derives from the belief that economic, social, and cultural rights are qualitatively distinct from **civil and political rights** because the former require **positive action** and expenditure by governments while the latter call simply for restraint; for this reason there has been considerable debate about whether courts could properly make decisions about ICESCR rights. Some scholars have challenged the asserted distinction between the two 'generations' of rights, pointing out that the protection of all **human rights** requires active governmental support.

The eighteen member Committee on Economic, Social, and Cultural Rights, established by a resolution of the UN's Economic and Social Council in 1985, rather than by the **treaty** itself, monitors the implementation of the ICESCR through a system of state reporting. Unlike the ICCPR, the ICESCR as yet has no mechanism to allow individual complaints, although this is being considered.

The ICSECR has influenced in particular the drafting of the South African Constitution, which protects a number of economic, social, and cultural rights. Decisions of the South African **Constitutional Court** have illustrated the scope of the rights to housing and health, for example.

HILARY CHARLESWORTH

International Criminal Court (ICC)   *see* **international criminal law**

international criminal law   International criminal law is the law which governs international crimes, ie crimes committed in breach of international law. It has been defined as being 'where the penal aspects of international law, including that body of law protecting victims of armed conflict known as international humanitarian law, and the international aspects of national criminal law, converge' (K Kittichaisaree, *International Criminal Law* (Oxford: Oxford University Press, 2001)). The Rome Statute of the **International Criminal Court** ('ICC') is evidence of the core crimes which are part of general international law: genocide, crimes against humanity, war crimes, and the crime of aggression (but the definition of the latter for the purposes of the Statute and the conditions under which the ICC will exercise jurisdiction over it have yet to be agreed). Article 5(1) of the Statute describes these as 'the most serious crimes of concern to the international community as a whole'. Other crimes under international law, such as aircraft hijacking and drug trafficking, are the subject of multilateral treaties. A distinction can also be drawn between offences against international order and security and transnational offences which threaten the interests of more than one State (eg organized crime, such as the smuggling of migrants and trafficking in persons).

International crimes engage the criminal responsibility of the perpetrators and not just the responsibility of states. The principle of individual responsibility was enshrined in the Nuremberg Charter under which the major Nazi war criminals were prosecuted after World War II. Like domestic criminal law, international criminal law involves a material element (*actus reus*) and a mental element (*mens rea*). The latter is reflected in the use of words like 'intentionally', 'wilfully' and 'wantonly'. The Rome Statute contains detailed provisions on the mental element of crimes within the ICC's jurisdiction. Some crimes require specific intent. Thus, the mental element for genocide is the 'intent to destroy, in whole or in part, a national, ethnical, racial or religious group, as such' (Article 6). The existence of intent and knowledge may be inferred from relevant facts and circumstances. Further assistance in interpreting and applying the Statute's provisions is provided by a supplementary text on the 'Elements of Crimes'. The jurisprudence of the International Criminal Tribunal for the Former Yugoslavia ('**ICTY**'), the International Criminal Tribunal for Rwanda ('ICTR') and other similar tribunals is another important source of guidance.

Jurisdiction to try persons accused of committing international crimes, and thus to enforce international criminal law, may be exercised by national courts as well as by international tribunals. Indeed, Article 1 of the Rome Statute provides that the ICC shall be complementary to national criminal jurisdictions. This means that even where the Court has jurisdiction, it cannot act if the case is being, or has been, investigated or prosecuted by a state with jurisdiction, unless the state concerned is, or was, unwilling or unable genuinely to investigate or prosecute. In other words, the ICC can act only if states do not do so or if they do not do so properly. Whilst a state's criminal jurisdiction is generally territorial or based on nationality, some international crimes—especially those involving attacks upon international order, such as piracy, slavery and war crimes—attract universal jurisdiction, which means that a state may apply its laws even if the act occurred outside its territory, was perpetrated by a non-national and did not harm its nationals. The right to exercise jurisdiction under the universality principle can derive from a treaty or from general international law. In 2005, an Afghan warlord was convicted of torture under section 134 of the UK Criminal Justice Act 1988, which gave effect to the UK's obligations under the UN Torture Convention 1984 by making acts of 'official' torture, wherever they are committed and whatever the offender's nationality, an extra-territorial offence in the UK. The defendant was not a British subject, the victims were not British and the acts were committed in Afghanistan.

As that case shows, whether a crime which exists under international law also exists in domestic law depends upon the law of the state concerned. Thus, the crime of aggression exists in customary international law but in the absence of statutory authority it is not yet a crime in English law. By virtue of the UK International Criminal Court Act 2001, however, genocide, crimes against humanity, and war crimes as defined in the Rome Statute are all criminal offences and triable in the UK. In addition, jurisdiction in respect of 'grave breaches' of the **Geneva Conventions I–IV 1949** or Additional Protocol I 1977 exists under the Geneva Conventions Act 1957 as amended.

Although the principle of sovereign immunity prevents a serving head of state or government who is suspected of having committed an international crime (even a crime against humanity) from being prosecuted before the courts of another state, it does not prevent his or her prosecution before an international court or tribunal. Article 7 of the Nuremberg Charter provided: 'The official position of defendants, whether as Heads of State or responsible officials in Government Departments, shall not be considered as freeing them from responsibility or punishment'. Similar provisions can be found today in the Statutes of the ICC, ICTY, ICTR, and other international tribunals. Former heads of state or government are immune from foreign criminal jurisdiction only in respect of acts performed in the exercise of their official functions. In the *Pinochet case* certain members of the House of Lords held that acts of torture could not be acts performed in the exercise of the functions of a head of state or governmental or official acts.

NICK GRIEF

A Cassese, *International Criminal Law* (Oxford: Oxford University Press, 2nd edn, 2008)

WA Schabas, *The UN International Criminal Tribunals* (Cambridge: Cambridge University Press, 2006)

international dispute settlement It is not necessary to settle every dispute: some persist for centuries without either side abandoning its position. The dispute between Spain and the UK over Gibraltar is an example. In such cases the main aim is to manage the dispute and prevent it from escalating, rather than to settle it. But generally disputes are an impediment to smooth and efficient diplomatic relations, and some attempt is made to settle them. Most disputes that arise in the context of international relations, as in all other social contexts, are managed and in many cases settled by negotiation. But because international relations are conducted by officials and representatives of bureaucracies, whose instinct is to record every significant act or omission and the reaction to it, the development and management of international disputes inevitably takes on a formal character.

States may settle disputes that arise between them by any peaceful means that they choose. Article 33 of the **United Nations** Charter lists the main procedures: negotiation, enquiry, mediation, conciliation, arbitration, judicial settlement, and resort to regional agencies or arrangements. There is also the possibility of referring the dispute to an international organization, such as the UN; or, in the case of disputes that have a particular technical character, one of the UN's specialized agencies or an independent organization such as the **World Trade Organization** ('WTO').

Negotiation is usually conducted through established diplomatic procedures, with subtle distinctions drawn between vehicles of communication such as *notes verbales, aides-mémoires,* letters, protest notes, and the like. Agreements are commonly recorded in the form of exchanges of notes and treaties. In cases where the dispute arises from a question of fact, states may establish an inquiry. An early example was the 1904 Dogger Bank incident, when an international commission of inquiry reported on the circumstances in which the Russian fleet in the North Sea fired on British trawlers during the Russo-Japanese war. The report defused the crisis, which had threatened to bring Britain into war on the side of Japan.

Sometimes relations between states are so bad that meaningful negotiations are not practicable. In such situations resort may be had to the good offices of a third party (typically the UN Secretary General or his nominee, or a retired statesman who commands the confidence of both sides) as a mediator. Mediation by the Pope brought a successful settlement of the boundary dispute between Argentina and Chile in 1984. Mediation by various parties in the Israel-Palestine dispute has so far failed to produce a settlement, though it has produced significant moves in that direction. Mediators traditionally have a broadly passive role, listening to each party and carrying its message to the other, highlighting areas of possible agreement. Conciliation is a similar procedure but involves more active third-party participation. The conciliator, having listened to both sides, will propose the terms of a settlement and try to negotiate it with the parties. Treaties providing for conciliation commissions enjoyed something of a vogue in the early twentieth century, and they are occasionally still employed. The conciliation commission established by Iceland and Norway to report on the dispute over the maritime zones around Jan Mayen in 1981 is an example.

The procedures described thus far leave the question, and the terms, of any settlement in the hands of the parties to the dispute. Arbitration is different. It makes the shift to a judicial process in which an international tribunal applies legal procedures and rules and makes a decision in the dispute that is legally binding upon the parties. The first major international arbitration was the *Alabama Claims* case in 1872, in which the USA successfully claimed against Great Britain for the damage caused by the Confederate warship *Alabama,* which had been supplied by Britain in breach of its duties of neutrality during the US Civil War. Encouraged by the success of that arbitration the international community negotiated the 1899 Hague Convention for the Pacific Settlement of International Disputes at The Hague Peace Conference. That Convention, revised in 1907, set out a framework for the conduct of mediation, commissions of inquiry, and international arbitration, defining the last as 'the settlement of differences between States by judges of their own choice, and on the basis of respect for law'. The Hague Conventions established the Permanent Court of Arbitration ('PCA'), which is not a court but a list of potential arbitrators nominated by states together with a permanent Secretariat, which can administer tribunals established by states. Long dormant, in recent years the PCA has been used as a venue for arbitral tribunals established under treaties such as the 1982 UN Convention on the **Law of the Sea**, or on an *ad hoc* basis. Its renaissance coincides with a revival in the popularity of *ad hoc* arbitration between states, itself a development influenced by the increasingly heavy workload of the International Court of Justice ('ICJ').

Enthusiasm for the peaceful settlement of international disputes rose after the carnage of World War I, and in 1920 the Statute of the Permanent Court of Justice ('PCIJ')—the predecessor of the ICJ—was established as part of the negotiations for the post-war peace treaties and for the establishment of the League of Nations. The PCIJ existed from 1921–1945, although its work practically ceased with the onset of World War II.

In 1945 the ICJ was established as part of the United Nations Organization. It is the principal judicial organ of the UN, and is generally regarded as the highest of international tribunals, although there is no formal hierarchy among international tribunals. The ICJ has jurisdiction only over disputes between states, although it is also empowered to give Advisory Opinions to designated UN bodies (as it did, for example, in the *Israeli Wall* case). The inter-state jurisdiction is, however, wider than it might at first appear. International law regards the mistreatment of a state's nationals in violation of international standards of treatment as a violation of the state's own rights. When a state takes up a claim in respect of one of its nationals, it is said to be exercising 'diplomatic protection'. While it is in principle a matter for each state to determine who its nationals are, the ICJ has set out principles of international law that govern the validity of claims to nationality in the context of diplomatic protection.

Again as a matter of principle, before a state may exercise diplomatic protection in respect of one of its nationals the national must exhaust local remedies, ie the national must seek a remedy from the courts of the allegedly wrongdoing state, by means of an appeal to higher courts if necessary. This process gives the state the opportunity to rectify any wrongs that may have been committed by its agents, so that not every alleged mistreatment of a foreigner (or 'alien', as they are known in **international law**) may immediately be presented to an international tribunal. The actual standard of treatment of aliens required by international law is not high. Though it was argued in the early twentieth century that it was sufficient if a state treated aliens as well as it treated its own nationals, it has long been established that there is an international minimum standard of treatment to which aliens are entitled, even if a state treats its own nationals in a more execrable manner. That international minimum standard requires that aliens not be arbitrarily punished or detained or suffer a 'denial of justice'—that is, discriminatory treatment or some other failure to observe basic provisions of due process or to deliver a final decision from courts within a reasonable period of time.

The exercise of diplomatic protection is now less common than it was in the first half of the twentieth century, because of a major innovation in international dispute settlement which permitted individuals and corporations to bring claims in their own names against states in international tribunals. This procedure assisted claimants by avoiding the need to persuade the national state to espouse and pursue the international claims, and assisted states by freeing them from the burden of handling international claims on behalf of their nationals and of the complications to their international relations that such claims could bring. The first major developments occurred in the field of **human rights**, where treaty regimes such as the **European Convention on Human Rights** opened up the possibility of individual actions against states. A second major development was the adoption of the Convention on the Settlement of Investment Disputes between States and Nationals of Other States (the 'CSID Convention') in 1965. Large numbers of claims are now brought by individuals and corporations in the fields of international human rights law and international investment law. This model is utilized in other contexts too: for example, the Iran-US Claims Tribunal, established in the wake of the crisis arising from the detention of US diplomatic and consular staff in the US embassy in Tehran in 1979–1981, provided for claims by nationals of each state to be made directly against the government of the other.

There are many specialized dispute settlement procedures in particular areas of international activity. The most prominent is the sophisticated and much-used dispute settlement procedure of the **World Trade Organization**. Other systems include the procedures for bringing disputes before the International Tribunal for the Law of the Sea ('ITLOS') and the dispute settlement systems established under regional economic agreements, among which those within the **European Union** and North America Free Trade Agreement ('NAFTA') are the most active.   VAUGHAN LOWE

See also: **international courts and tribunals**

international economic law   International economic law ('IEL') cannot neatly be characterized as a distinct system of law, but is rather one of the many branches of **international law**. This defining feature of IEL has two important consequences: first, the sources of IEL are the same as those of international law; and, secondly, the inter-governmental institutions of IEL are international organizations that operate under, and are governed by, international law.

The sources of international law are generally recognized as being law-making conventions, **customary international law**, general principles of law, and, to a considerably lesser extent, the writings of jurists.

The relationship between IEL and international law has the consequence that organizations operating in the area of IEL will often be required to consider and apply international law when making decisions. For example, when interpreting the provisions of its constituent treaty or other relevant agreements, an IEL organization will have to consider the relevant rules of treaty interpretation.

A number of international organizations that operate in the area of IEL are among the most influential and important organizations at both the global and regional levels. They include, for example, at the global level the **World Trade Organization ('WTO')**, the International Monetary Fund ('IMF;), and the World Bank ('WB') (including the closely associated International Centre for the Settlement of Investment Disputes (ICSID) which resolves disputes between states and investors); and at the regional level, for example, the European Communities Development Bank and the Inter-American Development Bank. Their activities focus on the three main subject areas of IEL—international trade, international monetary issues, and, to a lesser extent, debt reduction. But they also include related issues such as dispute resolution between states (in the case of the WTO) and between states and foreign-owned corporations (in the case of ICSID and under the dispute settlement provisions of Chapter 11 of the North American Free Trade Agreement ('NAFTA')).

These three subject areas of IEL—international trade, international monetary issues, and debt reduction—are all directed towards achieving the animating purpose of IEL: the promotion of global economic growth and prosperity. International trade has traditionally been seen as a key driver for global economic growth and prosperity, but also considered important is the stability of the international exchange rate system, which is the key facilitator of international trade transactions. Since the debt crises of the 1980s, IEL and its institutions have sought to address the paralysing debt burden of numbers of developing states who found it very difficult to focus on promoting economic growth and development when a considerable proportion of their gross domestic product and foreign exchange had to go towards the payment of the capital and significant interest on their sizeable and long-standing loans.

The inextricable link between investment, exchange rates, and trade has been long recognized, and it was the basis for the establishment in 1945 after World War II of the so-called Bretton Woods Institutions: the WB, the IMF, and the **General Agreement of Tariffs and Trade ('GATT')**.

The WB was originally intended to provide a source of investment loans for war-torn economies, and has over time evolved to provide loans to developing countries with the stated objectives of reducing global poverty and the improvement of living standards.

The IMF was originally intended to maintain stability in the global financial system by maintaining a fixed exchange rate system, but this system collapsed in the early 1970s. Since then the IMF has monitored exchange rates, but has largely redefined its objective to become a major source of loans for developing states. More recently, with the WB, the IMF has sought to address the debt levels of developing countries through its Heavily Indebted Poor Countries Initiative ('HIPC'). The IMF imposes an extensive set of economic 'conditions' on states who borrow from its resources, and these have been a source of considerable criticism of the organization. This IMF 'conditionality' has seen states increasingly turning away from the IMF towards the international money markets to obtain loans.

The GATT was intended to provide an agreed set of rules and tariff levels to promote trade. Since 1994 the GATT has been replaced by the WTO which includes not only a series of Agreements obliging States to maintain liberal trade in various areas, but also notably an additional organizational component designed to ensure that states comply with their obligations under the various WTO Agreements.

IEL and its institutions have traditionally sought to increase global economic prosperity and growth but they have not sought to redistribute wealth between developed and developing states. An important exception was the concerted attempt by developing states in the 1960s and 1970s to establish a 'New Economic Order' particularly through the **United Nations** General Assembly. The General Assembly adopted three main resolutions which sought to increase the share of developing countries in global wealth by seeking, *inter alia*, to improve their terms of trade and to establish international rules that would favour their position (such as one allowing states to nationalize or expropriate foreign-owned corporations on their territory and to pay a (lower) level of compensation calculated according to national and not international law). The opposition to these resolutions by developed states and the commercial reality that developing states needed to attract foreign investment meant that this scheme petered out. A source of constant criticism levelled at IEL is that it should be more concerned with achieving global justice through wealth redistribution rather than simply focusing on wealth creation.

The actual content of IEL is relatively sparse, and in practice IEL principles developed and applied by IEL organizations are more important. Consider, for example, the **Most Favoured Nation Treatment** and National Treatment principles. These principles are very widely used in the area of trade and foreign investment, are contained in, for example, the WTO Agreements and thousands of Bilateral Investment Treaties ('BIT') between states, and have been given content and applied in numerous cases before the WTO Dispute Settlement System and in numerous arbitration tribunal decisions. Despite this long-standing and impressive state practice, these principles cannot be said to constitute customary international law since the source of obligation for states to comply with these principles is always the specific treaty (the relevant WTO Agreement or BIT in question) rather than a perceived requirement to do so under a recognized customary rule.

While IEL is largely the creation of states, it is invoked in aid by a far broader range of actors including corporations and individuals. This is unsurprising given that a large number of IEL agreements, although being concluded between states, confer rights on corporations and a correlative duty on states. For example, BITs often require states party to the treaty to afford specified levels of protection to foreign investors and also often provide for a dispute settlement mechanism in the form of arbitration to resolve investor–state disputes.   DAN SAROOSHI

international environmental law   International environmental law is one of the more recent areas of development in **international law**. It is an area of law marked by the application of principles which have evolved in the environmental law context, such as the precautionary principle and the no-harm principle; but it also forms part of, and draws on, the general body of international law dealing with such issues as the sources of international law, state jurisdiction and state responsibility. It is thus part and parcel of international law and not an entirely separate, self-contained discipline. In this sense it is analogous to **international human rights law**, the **law of the sea** and **international economic law**. Institutionally it is less well-developed than these fields: there is no global environmental organization with competence over environmental matters analogous to the **World Trade Organization** ('**WTO**'), nor a dispute settlement body analogous to the WTO's Dispute Settlement Body or the Law of the Sea Convention's International Tribunal for the Law of the Sea. Nonetheless, there has been a steady development of customary law principles and an explosion of treaty-making in the environmental field in the last few decades. Today the vast bulk of environmental law is contained in treaty texts which are given dynamic force in part because they usually provide an institutional mechanism for their implementation, generally consisting of regular meetings of all states parties to the treaty assisted by a specialist scientific or technical body and a secretariat.

While there has been significant growth in the body of general and particularized rules governing state conduct in respect of the environment, there has not yet emerged a general customary or treaty law obligation on states to protect and preserve the environment *per se*. To be sure there is a relevant negative obligation found in **customary international law**—the no-harm principle, which establishes the obligation imposed on states not to allow their territory to be used in a such a manner as to cause harm to the territory of other states or to the global commons. This may be traced back to the seminal *Trail Smelter Arbitration* (1938/1941), which arose out of the emission of sulphur fumes from a Canadian smelter that caused damage in the US state of Washington. Positive obligations, however, remain largely sectoral or regional in focus, the most outstanding examples being the general obligation in Article 192 of the 1982 Law of the Sea Convention to protect and preserve the marine environment and the obligation, in Article 2 of the 1991 Protocol on Environmental Protection to the 1959 Antarctic Treaty, comprehensively to protect the Antarctic environment and dependent and related ecosystems.

The absence of a generally recognized obligation to protect the global environment is partly explained by the piecemeal development of the subject. Although the origins of international environmental regulation may be traced to the nineteenth century, the modern development of the subject dates from the post-Second World War era, a turning point undoubtedly being the first United Nations-sponsored conference on the environment, the 1972 Stockholm Conference on the Human Environment. Indeed, it is common to divide the development of international environmental law into several stages, with the pre-Stockholm era characterized by piecemeal and reactive responses to particular problems of resources use and exploitation (eg the 1946 International Convention for the Regulation of Whaling), including shared resources (eg the 1909 Treaty between the United States and Great Britain Respecting Boundary Waters Between the United States and Canada). Initial developments were largely limited to addressing the trans-boundary consequences of environmental harm, often in a strictly bilateral context (eg *Trail Smelter* arbitration). There were also early attempts at conservation of species and habitat, though often for anthropocentric purposes (eg the 1902 Convention to Protect Birds Useful to Agriculture; and the 1893 *Behring Fur Seal* arbitration).

Today, however, the increasingly large-scale nature of problems such as global warming, ozone depletion, and pollution of the oceans, has dictated a global and collective response to problems incapable of solution by any one state alone. The need to conserve biological diversity for future generations, to preserve species from extinction through trade, and to transmit outstanding natural and cultural heritage to future generations, has likewise engendered a collective, international response. It has become common to date the evolution of this contemporary international environmental law from the 1972 Stockholm Conference.

Certainly the run-up to and conclusion of the Stockholm Conference stimulated a great deal of regional and global treaty-making activity, much of it directed towards protection of the marine environment. The 1972 London (Dumping) Convention dates from this period, as does the regional seas programme of the UN Environment Programme which, from 1976 onwards, has led to the conclusion of a number of regional seas agreements that include environmental protection provisions. The terrestrial environment was also the focus of attention, with the conclusion of major **treaties** regarding the natural and cultural heritage (the 1972 UNESCO Convention Concerning the Protection of the World Cultural and Natural Heritage), and species and habitat protection (eg the 1971 Ramsar Convention on Wetlands of International Importance Especially as Waterfowl Habitat and the 1973 Convention on International Trade in Endangered Species). With one or two exceptions—such as the novel ecosystem approach of the 1980 Convention on the Conservation of Antarctic Marine Living Resources—this period of international legislative activity is characterized by a sectoral and fragmented approach to achieving environmental protection.

However, in the past two decades there have emerged new instruments adopting a holistic approach to environmental protection. They seek to marry such protection with economic development under the banner of sustainable development. This was the theme of the 1992 Rio Conference on Environment and Development which, in addition to producing a Declaration of Principles and a programme of action for the twenty-first century—Agenda 21—saw the conclusion of two major treaties under UN auspices, the 1992 Framework Convention on Climate Change and the 1992 Convention on Biological Diversity. This marked a new phase in international environmental regulation with the acknowledgement in each that the conservation of biological diversity and preventing further adverse changes in the earth's climate are the common concern of humankind. However, proposals further to develop the institutional framework of international environmental law to reflect these common and inter-generational concerns have not yet made any significant headway. Suggestions for revamping the UN Trusteeship Council to address global commons matters have become linked with broader and more vexed questions of UN institutional reform. The ten-year follow-up to the Rio Conference, the 2002 Johannesburg World Summit on Sustainable Development, neither achieved environmental institutional reform nor resulted in significant multilateral law-making, despite making a significant contribution, *inter alia*, to developments within the Southern African region.

While the vast majority of the rights and obligations of states with respect to the environment derive from voluntarily assumed treaty obligations, it would be misleading to suggest that no customary international law norms govern state conduct. State practice has given rise to a number of customary law principles. Of these the most significant is the 'good neighbour' or 'no-harm' principle, mentioned above, which has been enunciated in judicial decisions and reiterated in soft law declarations. State practice further supports the customary law obligation to consult about and to notify of potential trans-boundary harm. Other relevant principles of customary international law include the polluter-pays principle, the principle of preventive action, and equitable utilization of shared resources. More controversial is the customary law status of the precautionary principle, and of the principle of sustainable development and its buttressing principles (eg sustainable use, **inter-generational equity**, integration of the environment into economic and development projects, and common but differentiated responsibility).

The past decades have witnessed an evolution in law-making focus from environmental regulation incidental to some other primary focus, such as economic regulation of a resource, to an holistic approach to environmental protection within and beyond state borders. However, these stages are not necessarily sequential, current international law rules reflecting each of these stages of evolution. This overlap is particularly evident in the tension between, the traditional concept of states' permanent sovereignty over their own natural resources

on the one hand and, on the other, the recognition that the conservation of biological diversity and the protection of the global climate are the common concern of humankind as a whole on the other. Undoubtedly one of the remaining challenges facing international environmental law is the effective implementation and enforcement of existing rules and standards within, as well as between and beyond, states. Increasingly attention has shifted from a focus on the generation of new substantive rules of environmental regulation to the effective implementation of existing obligations through innovative treaty mechanisms such as non-compliance procedures (eg the 1997 Kyoto Protocol) and the further development of liability and compensation regimes. The increasing role of non-state actors (eg corporations, **non-governmental organizations**) in the environmental law-making and implementation process, albeit often in an informal capacity, and attempts to articulate binding international rules for corporate environmental accountability, are areas of further development in contemporary international environmental law.

CATHERINE REDGWELL

P and C Redywell AE Boyle and C Redywell, *International Law and the Environment* (Oxford: Oxford University Press, 3rd edn, 2008)

D Bodansky, E Brunnee and E Hey (eds), *The Oxford Handbook of International Environmental Law* (Oxford: Oxford University Press, 2007)

See also: **common but differentiated responsibility, principle of**

international financial institutions and development   Development is a concept which indicates both a process and a goal. It has come to dominate how we think about questions of global economic distribution both between and within nation-states since the end of World War II. Typically, development is associated with programmes directed toward the alleviation of poverty through economic growth. Recent debates have centred on whether development should be defined in more 'human' terms, focusing less on GDP and more on **human rights**, social capital, **democracy**, and **security** as a way of measuring development. However critical perspectives argue that development addresses the question of global inequality by positing some societies as having achieved a near ideal state toward which other states are now striving. This presents those 'developing' as being in a constant state of lack vis-à-vis the 'developed' world.

An enormous institutional machinery exists directed at effecting development. This includes the

'International Financial Institutions', typically referring to the World Bank, the International Monetary Fund and the increasingly important regional development banks, including the Asian, African, and Inter-American Development Banks. The Bank and the Fund, collectively known as the 'Bretton Woods Institutions' ('BWIs'), were established by international agreement after a conference in 1944. Legally they are 'specialized agencies' of the **United Nations** and were set up to prevent a repeat of the impoverishing economic policies of the inter-war period.

The World Bank initially comprised only the International Bank for Reconstruction and Development ('IBRD') with the original purpose of financing the post-war reconstruction of Europe. However, it was quickly overtaken by events and the American 'Marshall Plan' to reconstruct Europe stepped in to fulfil the Bank's original function. With 'reconstruction' off the agenda, it reoriented itself toward the 'development' of particular regions, a project then closely aligned with American Cold War strategy. Between 1956 and 1988, four other agencies were created to form a World Bank 'Group', including the two principal development agencies, the IBRD and the International Development Association ('IDA') established in 1960, as well as the International Finance Corporation ('IFC'), the Multilateral Investment Guarantee Agency ('MIGA'), and the International Centre for the Settlement of Investment Disputes ('ICSID'). The IBRD makes development loans, provides guarantees, offers advisory services, and is considered the world's leading knowledge producer on development. It sells bonds in private markets and makes near-market interest loans to 'creditworthy' developing countries. The IDA is known as the 'soft lending window' and gives loans to countries that are usually not considered 'creditworthy' in international financial markets. IDA loans carry no interest but a 0.75 per cent administration charge is made annually.

The International Monetary Fund ('IMF') was originally established to ensure an orderly system of payments between the industrialized nations, providing ready access to a pool of money for states to manage short-term balance of payments problems. When the system of fixed exchange rates collapsed in the late 1960s, it was thought the Fund would fall into irrelevance. However, during the oil crisis of the 1970s, the Fund was drawn in to lending to the 'Third World' through extended facilities to help states cope with rising oil prices. That position was consolidated during the Mexican Debt Crisis. Its influence relies on its ability to make loans with rafts

of conditions, known as 'conditionality'. In recent decades, that influence has stretched well beyond its capacity to lend its own limited funds through its *de facto* position as gatekeeper to international finance for the Third World.

The World Bank also attaches conditions to its loans through various lending vehicles, including 'Structural Adjustment Programmes' and more recently, the 'Poverty Strategy Reduction Papers' ('PRSPs') jointly with the IMF. In order to be a member of the Bank, a state must also be a member of the IMF. Unlike most UN institutions which operate according to a one-state one-vote principle, both the Bank and the Fund have weighted voting systems based on contributions, allowing the United States an effective veto. Both institutions have Boards of Governors constituted by Ministers (often finance) of member states. The Boards of Governors of the IMF and the Bank have jointly held annual meetings once a year, in recent years accompanied by broad civil society protest. Boards of Governors delegate their authority to Executive Directors based in Washington and charged with the management of the organizations. By convention, the Fund's Managing Director is always European, the Bank President always American.

Both the Bank and the Fund have been subject to intense criticism from several quarters since the end of the 1970s and the realization that these agencies were not delivering the benefits of development. In some cases, countries were quantifiably worse off than they had been before international financial institution ('IFI') intervention, a series of high profile disasters for each of them through the 1980s and 1990s radically reducing their legitimacy. Examples include Bank projects in Brazil and India and Fund action during the Asian Debt Crisis. Criticisms of the BWIs usually take four forms; that their quota-based voting system renders them undemocratic in their constitution; they are unaccountable for their prescriptions; their policies exacerbate the problems they are meant to fix; and they re-allocate **risk** away from the rich towards the poor. Those states who can afford to are increasingly rejecting Fund lending and the conditions that go with it. Regional development banks already exist and moves are afoot to establish at least one regional monetary fund. These and other developments will certainly alter the sphere of influence of the BWIs in the not too distant future.

SUNDHYA PAHUJA

international harmonization of intellectual property rights Generally speaking, intellectual property rights are national rights which are created by national laws and the decisions of national judges. This is an inconvenience to those involved in international trade as those traders may have to contend with a variety of laws affecting the sale of individual products. They are obliged to seek intellectual property rights in each of the countries in which they currently trade and may trade in the future, as well as in countries which might be the source of infringing products. This is a costly, as well as a complicated and time-consuming process. Since the first international intellectual property convention—the Paris Convention for the Protection of Industrial Property of 1883—attempts have been made to introduce some uniformity into nations' intellectual property laws. The approach taken in the Paris Convention and in the contemporaneous **Berne Convention for the Protection of Literary and Artistic Works** 1886 was for basic norms to be prescribed with which countries should comply in the drafting of their national legislation.

A logical solution to the problem of diverse national intellectual property laws is, of course, international legislation having direct effect in each country. However, for a variety of reasons this has not been pursued. Among these reasons are the differences between national legal traditions and national intellectual property establishments which have a vested interest in their own survival. By way of example, the countries of the **European Union** have been involved in a protracted negotiation to establish a regional patent, regulated by a European patent court, but the political obstacles to this goal appear almost insurmountable.

The most practical alternative to uniform legislation is the international harmonization of national intellectual property rights. The principal facilitator of this harmonization is the **World Intellectual Property Organization ('WIPO')**.

The precursor organization to WIPO was the Bureaux internationaux réunis pour la protection de la propriété intellectuelle ('BIRPI'), which was established in Berne, by the Swiss Federal Government to administer the Paris and Berne Unions. BIRPI also assumed responsibility for the various special treaties which were promulgated under those conventions. By a Convention of 14 July 1967, BIRPI was replaced by WIPO, which was established as a specialized agency of the **United Nations** Organization.

The agreement between the United Nations and WIPO was expressed to be 'subject to the competence and responsibilities of the United Nations and other specialised agencies'. This was to take into account the fact that at least three other specialized agencies at that time were concerned with aspects of intellectual property. The United Nations Educational Scientific and Cultural Organization ('UNESCO'), was responsible for the administration of the Universal Copyright Convention ('UCC'), the International Convention for the Protection of New Varieties of Plants ('UPOV') was responsible for the administration of an international convention on this subject and the **United Nations Conference on Trade and Development ('UNCTAD')** was concerned with the role of intellectual property in the transfer of technology to developing countries.

The creation of the **World Trade Organization ('WTO')** in 1994 and the correlative obligation of Member States to accede to the **World Trade Organization Agreement on Trade Related Aspects of Intellectual Property Rights ('TRIPs')** added another inter-governmental organization to the international intellectual property landscape. In December 1995 the Director General of WIPO and the Director General of WTO signed an agreement which provides for the mutual exchange of the laws and regulations of both organizations. The TRIPs Council has agreed that both organizations should use a uniform system for notification by members of their intellectual property laws and that this system should be administered by WIPO. The TRIPs Council has also agreed that assistance will be provided by WIPO to members in drafting TRIPs-compliant legislation.

The intellectual property harmonization which has been undertaken by WIPO, involves the harmonization of procedural as well as substantive aspects of intellectual property laws. An example of the former are the special treaties which have established international classification procedures for **patents**, **trade marks**, and industrial **designs**, and treaties to streamline the filing of multi-country patent trade mark and industrial design applications. Additionally, since 1883, there have been a number of international agreements dealing with aspects of substantive **copyright**, patents, trade marks, **geographical indications**, and integrated circuits, as well as the TRIPs Agreement which covers all of these subjects. The periodic meetings of the various unions established by the treaties administered by WIPO and by the TRIPs Council ensure the ongoing progress of harmonization.

MICHAEL BLAKENEY

international human rights law International human rights law is the term applied to the body of international legal rules binding upon states that aims to guarantee the freedom of the individual from arbitrary state action in a democratic society (civil and political rights), as well as requiring states to ensure that conditions are provided to secure a basic standard of living in terms of needs such as food, shelter, and health care (economic, social, and cultural rights).

The rules create obligations as between states themselves and from state to individual. The idea that the state has obligations towards individuals and that human beings have rights against the state by virtue of the fact that they are human beings was developed particularly during the period of the Enlightenment, which gave birth to significant domestic constitutional instruments such as the French Declaration on the Rights of Man and of the Citizen (1789) and the US Bill of Rights (1791). During this period, however, rights were conceived as pertaining to the relationship between a state and its citizens, rather than being a matter of international concern *between* states. Thus, prior to 1945, how states treated their nationals was viewed as an internal matter into which other states should not intrude. Following World War I, a series of inter-state treaties in Central and Eastern Europe did protect some of the minority groups that were created as a result of changes in state borders, but there was otherwise no concerted attempt to protect the human rights of individuals. It was the universal condemnation of the Holocaust and other atrocities that took place during World War II that led to the inclusion of human rights as one of the purposes and principles of the United Nations. Thus, Article 1(3) of the UN Charter (1945) requires states to achieve international cooperation in promoting and encouraging respect for human rights and fundamental freedoms.

On 10 December 1948, the General Assembly of the **United Nations** adopted the **Universal Declaration of Human Rights**. This Declaration set out a list of civil and political, and economic, social, and cultural rights and provided a starting point for the elaboration of those standards that now form the body of international human rights law. Unlike a treaty (such as the UN Charter itself) the Declaration is not a legally binding instrument; however, certain of the rights and obligations do create legal obligations by virtue of the fact that they are now recognized as part of **customary international law**. These are rules that bind because states have recognized through their practice that the rules are obligatory. The right not to be tortured, for example, is so fundamental that it belongs to a special body of legal rules (termed *jus cogens*) forming part of customary international law, by which states are bound, whether they wish to be or not.

Following the Declaration, the United Nations worked to produce treaties embodying and further elaborating the **human rights** set out. Ideological differences between West and East resulted in separate treaties, the **International Covenants on Civil and Political Rights ('ICCPR')**, and the **International Covenant on Economic, Social, and Cultural Rights ('ICESCR')**, which together are commonly known as the International Bill of Rights. These instruments have been ratified by most states and create legally binding obligations between the signatories. Treaties protecting human rights have also been created by regional bodies, including the **European Convention on Human Rights** ('ECHR') promulgated by the Council of Europe, the American Convention on Human Rights by the Organization of American states, and the **African Charter on Human and Peoples' Rights** by the Organization of African Unity (now African Union). All these instruments form part of international human rights law and the various bodies that are charged under these instruments with supervising state obligations contribute to the interpretation, elaboration, and development of the rights set out in the treaties.

The primary aim of international human rights law is that states should act to ensure that those within their borders (who may not be citizens of the state, because many rights extend to non citizens) enjoy the protected rights through domestic laws and legal and other processes. For instance, cases of maltreatment of prisoners should be addressed through legal rules that ensure accountability and, where appropriate, compensation through domestic courts and other regulatory mechanisms. However, where a state fails to fulfil its obligations at domestic level, the aggrieved individual may ultimately pursue a complaint against the state using the machinery established by the relevant treaty for that purpose. In the case of the ECHR, for example, a person may take their complaint to the **European Court of Human Rights**. However, it is a fundamental principle that a person should exhaust his remedies in his own state before resorting to such action. The case law and decisions or determinations (many human rights instruments do not establish a court, but do have provision for supervision by, and complaints to, a Committee of Experts) made by supervisory bodies under the various human rights treaties also contribute to the development of international human rights law.

Reference has been made to the distinction between civil and political rights on the one hand, and economic, social, and cultural rights on the other. The former are broadly those rights that guarantee liberty, physical safety, and the right to participate in a democratic society, such as freedom from arbitrary arrest, the right to a fair trial, freedom of expression and association, rights to vote and stand for office. The latter are those rights that secure sustenance, shelter, education, and health. Civil and political rights are sometimes seen as creating negative obligations of non interference while economic, social, and cultural rights create positive obligations that require disbursement of state resources for their fulfilment. The division is not watertight: civil and political rights require states to invest in due process for example and the ECHR (broadly speaking embodying civil and political rights) includes the right to education.

However, the two categories of rights have been treated differently in terms of realization and enforcement: the ICCPR creates immediate, binding obligations to achieve minimum standards, while the ICESCR imposes an obligation on states to take steps to the maximum of available resources to progressively realize the rights set out. The ICCPR also provides for the possibility of petition to the Human Rights Committee, where a state has violated the rights set out. There is no individual complaints procedure under the ICESCR. Western states took the view that economic, social, and cultural rights did not constitute justiciable rights, while those in the Eastern bloc and elsewhere argued that these rights should take priority over civil and political rights. Following the break up of the Soviet Union and the end of the Cold War, however, all human rights have been recognized as 'universal, indivisible, interdependent and interrelated', to be treated in a 'fair and equal manner' and 'with the same emphasis' (Vienna Declaration and Programme of Action (1993)). However, the differences in machinery for enforcement of treaty obligations remain.

Although human rights treaties create obligations between states, instances of formal complaint between states are rare. Under the ECHR, cases have been brought between Cyprus and Turkey with regard to the treatment of the Cypriot community in Turkish-occupied Northern Cyprus, and Ireland took proceedings against the **United Kingdom** in relation to the British policy of internment, but these are rare examples. There are no examples of the inter-state procedure being used under the ICCPR.

The effective enjoyment of human rights requires states to act to control the actions not only of governmental agencies (the police force, the courts, health and education authorities), but also non-state actors. For example, in the case of the human right to private life (**privacy**), interference may occur as a result of intrusive reporting of personal information by a non-governmental body, such as the popular press. It is therefore incumbent upon the state to ensure that it has laws to protect citizens from interference by such non-state actors. The increasing trend in some states to contract out government functions (for example, the privatization of prisons) requires that the private body should be obliged to act compatibly with human rights obligations. The state cannot escape from its obligations under international human rights law by devolving governmental functions and responsibilities to other non-state bodies. If such bodies do violate human rights, it is the state which will be answerable before the treaty body.   JANE WRIGHT

international humanitarian law International humanitarian law is the part of **international law** which regulates the conduct of armed conflicts and provides for the protection of those not taking part in fighting during such conflicts. It is also known as the law of armed conflict or the law of war, although the latter term is now becoming rarer.

Humanitarian law is based upon two, not always consistent, principles. The first, humanity, reflects the idea that in armed conflicts, people should still be protected from its effects as much as possible. The countervailing principle is military necessity, which dictates that although the law in the area is intended to protect people, it cannot, and ought not to, prevent actions which are strictly militarily necessary. If it did, it would be ignored. Humanitarian law is thus fundamentally practical and accepts the context in which it operates, whilst seeking to regulate that context. Similarly, the law applies equally to all parties to a conflict, irrespective of the lawfulness or justice of their cause.

One outcropping of the interplay of these two principles is the principle of distinction. This is that the only legitimate deliberate target of attack is (broadly speaking) the war machine of the other party. Those who are not taking a direct part in hostilities are not legitimate targets. So civilians, prisoners of war, and those who are wounded and sick are protected, so far as possible, from the effects of conflict. The principle of distinction has recently, although not uncontroversially, also been said to include protection of the environment. Other disagreements remain about what amounts to taking a direct part in hostilities. Humanitarian law also reflects some of its historical origins in chivalric law, which provided for specific protections for, amongst others, women and children, as well as the prohibition of certain weapons and practices.

Rules akin to humanitarian law can be found throughout history and in all major cultural traditions. For example, the Mahabharata contains description of rules of warfare, as does Sun Tzu's *The Art of War*. In the Middle Ages chivalric codes in Europe provided detailed rules of applicable to armed conflict, although they were not always effective. **Islamic law** also provides for the humane regulation of conflict. The modern history of international humanitarian law, though, began in the mid nineteenth century.

In 1859 Henri Dunant, a Swiss businessman, happened upon the aftermath of the Battle of Solferino, where the injured and dying had been left unassisted. Having arranged for *ad hoc* help, Dunant then advocated the creation of an organization to assist war victims and a treaty requiring such assistance. This led to the creation in 1863 of the International Committee of the Red Cross ('ICRC'), which remains the pre-eminent organization dedicated to humanitarian law to this day, and the 1864 Geneva Convention on assistance for soldiers wounded in armed conflicts.

The next major development was the Russian decision to convene the St Petersburg Conference in 1868 to ban exploding anti-personnel bullets. The preamble of that conference's declaration remains an important aspect of humanitarian law, which evidences the interplay of military necessity and humanity: unnecessary suffering ought not to be caused by weaponry. The precise ambit of this stricture, outside of the specific treaties banning particular weapons, however, is contested. Major codifications of the law occurred in the late nineteenth and early twentieth century. The most important of these codifications was Hague Convention IV of 1907, which contained a set of regulations which contained much of this area of law for conflicts on land until after World War II.

Much of modern humanitarian law can be found in the four Geneva Conventions of 12 August 1949 which regulate the treatment of the wounded, sick, and shipwrecked, Prisoners of War, and civilians. The conventions were updated in 1977 by two Additional Protocols ('AP'), one of which (API) dealt with international armed conflicts, the other (APII) being the first treaty to deal entirely with non-international armed conflicts. 1980 saw the creation of a treaty limiting the use of certain weapons. In addition to treaty-based humanitarian law, there is a considerable body of **customary international law** on point. This latter part of the law was the subject of a decade-long study by the ICRC, which reported in 2005 that large parts of the treaties were, in fact, also reflective of customary law, and thus binding on all states. Not all states agree with the report, though.

There is a fundamental distinction which affects humanitarian law between international armed conflicts (to which the majority of humanitarian law applies) and non-international armed conflicts, ie civil wars (to which an attenuated version of the law is applicable). This is because states are more willing to accept limitations on inter-state conflicts than on those involving rebels in their own country. There are suggestions that the 'war on terror' is a non-international armed conflict, separate from the particular conflicts in, for example, Afghanistan; but these suggestions have not been generally accepted.

Common Article 3 of the Geneva Conventions is a distillation of the four Geneva Conventions of 1949, and is now considered applicable to all armed conflicts. It reads (in part):

[E]ach Party to the conflict shall be bound to apply, as a minimum, the following provisions:

(1) Persons taking no active part in the hostilities, including members of armed forces who have laid down their arms and those placed hors de combat by sickness, wounds, detention, or any other cause, shall in all circumstances be treated humanely, without any adverse distinction founded on race, colour, religion or faith, sex, birth or wealth, or any other similar criteria. To this end, the following acts are and shall remain prohibited at any time and in any place whatsoever with respect to the above-mentioned persons:
   (a) violence to life and person, in particular murder of all kinds, mutilation, cruel treatment and torture;
   (b) taking of hostages;
   (c) outrages upon personal dignity, in particular humiliating and degrading treatment;
   (d) the passing of sentences and the carrying out of executions without previous judgment pronounced by a regularly constituted court, affording all the judicial guarantees which are recognized as indispensable by civilized peoples. The wounded and sick shall be collected and cared for. An impartial humanitarian body, such as the International Committee of the Red Cross, may offer its services to the Parties to the conflict.

Exactly what some of the terms in Common Article 3 mean is the subject of dispute, although the Conventions often provide additional assistance, as, when relevant, do Article 75 of API and/or Article 4 of APII. The former provision is generally considered customary, and as such provides a base-line for the treatment of people in all international conflicts, and has also been used to interpret common Article 3. Article 4 of APII is an uncontroversial interpretation of that provision.

Humanitarian law also contains various limits on the means and methods of war, such as the prohibition of poisoned, chemical, and biological weapons. The status of nuclear weapons in humanitarian law remains contested, and the **International Court of Justice** in 1996 was unable to determine definitively if any possible use of nuclear weapons would be lawful or not. Humanitarian law also limits the use of weapons such as booby traps, incendiary devices, and landmines (the last of which are the subject, for many states, of a complete ban). Direct attacks on civilians, as well as indiscriminate attacks on them are forbidden, both by treaty-based and customary law. The prohibition on indiscriminate attacks also covers attacks which cause excessive collateral damage. This refers to damage to civilian objects occurring as an incidental but undesired result of attacks on military targets. What is excessive is not always agreed, and there remain disagreements about what is, or is not, a military target. Humanitarian law also sets out the rights and duties of military occupiers. The main duties on occupying powers are to provide for the needs of the occupied territories and not to alter existing laws more than necessary.

Humanitarian law has a number of methods of enforcement, for example, in very limited circumstances, reprisals may be resorted to. Serious violations of humanitarian law are also **war crimes**. On occasion international tribunals, such as the Nuremberg Tribunal, the International Criminal Tribunal for former Yugoslavia ('**ICTY**'), and the **International Criminal Court** have prosecuted such offences, although domestic courts are the primary enforcers of humanitarian law. Still, prevention is better than cure, and the Geneva Conventions and APs require that states provide for training, advice, and education in humanitarian law. One of the most effective methods of enforcement is service-members' viewing compliance as being good soldiering.

Although the law in the area is not perfect, it provides for a basic standard of conduct even in difficult wartime circumstances, complements human rights law, and is now a staple of public debate about armed conflicts.   ROBERT CRYER

D Fleck, *Manual of Humanitarian Law* (Oxford: Oxford University Press, 2nd edn, 2007)
A Roberts and R Guellf, *Documents on the Laws of War* (Oxford: Oxford University Press, 3rd edn, 2000)

international labour law   *see* **international Labour Organization and international labour law**

International Labour Organization ('ILO') and international labour law   The ILO was founded in 1919 as part of the Treaty of Versailles. In 1946, it became the first UN specialized agency. Its role is to set, monitor, and enforce international labour standards. It currently has 179 member states.

The ILO's main decision-making body is the International Labour Conference, which meets once a year. Each member state sends four delegates to the Conference: two from the government, one from trade unions, and one from employers' associations. The delegates from each state may vote independently of each other. The Conference approves new international labour standards, adopts the ILO's budget, and elects the Governing Body. The Governing Body meets three times a year. It consists of twenty-eight government representatives, fourteen worker representatives, and fourteen employer representatives. Its role is to set the ILO's policy direction. The day-to-day running of the ILO is the responsibility of the International Labour Office in Geneva. The Office is headed by the Director-General who is elected by the Governing Body for five-year renewable terms. One of the ILO's unique features is its tripartite structure: unlike most international organizations, it incorporates non-governmental bodies into its governance arrangements. However, in recent years, concerns have been raised by some commentators about the ILO's ability to address the needs of non-unionized workers.

The ILO is responsible for what is often referred to as the international labour code, a body of detailed labour law consisting of Conventions and Recommendations. Conventions have the legal status of international treaties. Once they have been agreed by the International Labour Conference, ILO member states must consider whether or not to ratify them. Ratification means that a state is bound in **international law** to comply. Recommendations are not legally binding. They usually set out guidelines for the interpretation of Conventions. Since its establishment, the ILO has enacted over 180 Conventions covering every aspect of labour law, though some have been 'shelved' or redrafted.

States which have ratified a Convention must submit regular reports to the ILO explaining their efforts to comply. States' reports are scrutinized by the Committee of Experts on the Application of Conventions and Recommendations. This body consists of twenty independent legal experts appointed for three-year terms. It produces an annual report containing 'observations' regarding member states' compliance with their obligations. This report is considered by the Conference Committee on the Application of Standards. This Committee may invite recalcitrant states to explain themselves and may publish its recommendations.

The ILO also has mechanisms for hearing complaints against states which fail to comply with the Conventions they have ratified. These rely heavily on adverse publicity as a means of 'shaming' recalcitrant states. Under the 'representations' procedure, a trade union or employers' association may make a representation to the Governing Body when it considers that a state is in breach of a Convention it has ratified. The Governing Body may establish a tripartite sub-committee to examine the representation and the government's response, and to make recommendations. Where the government's response is unsatisfactory, the Governing Body may publish the representation and response. Under the 'complaints' procedure, a member state, a Conference delegate, or the Governing Body itself may bring a complaint against a state for breaching a Convention it has ratified. The Governing Body may set up a three-member independent Commission of Inquiry to investigate and to make recommendations. This procedure is reserved for serious cases and has only been used eleven times in the ILO's history. If a state fails to comply with the recommendations of the Commission of Inquiry, the Governing Body may 'recommend to the Conference such action as it may deem wise and expedient to secure compliance' under Article 33 of the ILO Constitution. This provision has been used only once, in relation to the problem of forced labour in Burma/Myanmar.

A separate procedure exists to deal with concerns regarding freedom of association. Because the ILO has long regarded protecting freedom of association as one of its main aims, this procedure applies to all member states regardless of whether or not they have ratified the relevant Conventions. A trade union or an employers' association may make a complaint to the Committee on Freedom of Association ('CFASS'), a tripartite sub-committee of the Governing Body. The CFASS investigates the complaint and makes recommendations to the government concerned via the Governing Body. The CFASS has produced an important body of jurisprudence on trade union matters.

Another important ILO role is the provision of technical assistance to member states. The ILO's many and varied projects include providing training to government labour inspectors, helping employer and union representatives to develop skills in dispute resolution, and providing information to disadvantaged workers about their rights. Technical assistance is of particular importance in tackling the problem of child labour. The ILO's International Programme on the Elimination of Child Labour helps governments to develop comprehensive policies on child labour which not only strengthen

legislation and enforcement mechanisms but also provide educational opportunities for the children affected and support for their families.

For many years, the ILO has been criticized for its inability to enforce the international labour code effectively. Some governments turned their attention to the **World Trade Organization** and sought to include a 'social clause' in the **General Agreement on Tariffs and Trade** to permit the use of trade sanctions to enforce labour rights. However, this did not succeed, largely due to opposition from developing countries. In the meantime, the ILO tried to re-focus its efforts on the task of seeking compliance with a small group of fundamental labour rights. At the heart of this process is the 1998 Declaration on Fundamental Principles and Rights at Work. The Declaration identifies four rights as 'core rights': freedom of association and collective bargaining, freedom from forced labour, freedom from child labour, and freedom from discrimination. It provides that all ILO member states are bound to respect these rights by virtue of their membership of the organization, regardless of whether they have ratified the relevant Conventions. The ILO reports on the global situation with regard to each of the rights once every four years. The Declaration has succeeded in increasing ratifications of the Conventions relating to the core rights, and giving fresh impetus to the ILO's technical assistance programme.

Nowadays, it is no longer appropriate to regard the ILO as the only 'enforcer' of international labour law. Many other actors are involved. International financial institutions, such as the **World Bank**, may take account of the impact their activities have on states' compliance with **human rights**, including labour rights. National governments and regional bodies may seek to enforce labour rights through their external trade agreements. For example, the EU offers enhanced tariff preferences to states which demonstrate compliance with core labour rights. Many multinational enterprises have codes of conduct which require their suppliers to observe core labour rights. Some of these actors make use of the ILO Declaration to define the core labour rights they seek to implement. Some commentators have expressed concerns that the international labour code is becoming increasingly fragmented, while others have acknowledged the value of using multiple methods to enforce core labour rights.

ANNE DAVIES

HG Bartolomei de la Cruz, G von Potobsky, and L Swepston, *The International Labour Organisation: The International Standards System and Basic Human Rights* (Boulder, CO: Westview, 1996)

international law   There are two species of international law: public and private. Public international law is the body of rules that governs the rights and duties of states and their organs and agencies and of international organizations in their international dealings with one another and with individuals, corporations, and other legal persons. Private international law (also known as the '**conflict of laws**') determines the scope of the jurisdiction of national courts over cases that have a foreign element and the law or laws (whether national or foreign) that are applicable to their decision. Public international law is in principle global, although there may be slight regional variations in certain fields, such as the regional rules formerly applicable within the British **Commonwealth** and the Soviet bloc. Private international law is a branch of the domestic law of each state or jurisdiction (such as English Law and Scots Law), although many of its principles are common to all the major legal systems.

The scope and content of public international law have grown rapidly in the past century. Several specialized areas, such as **international human rights law**, **international economic law**, **international environmental law**, and **international criminal law** have appeared; and there is some concern that increasing specialization among international lawyers, and international courts and tribunals whose jurisdiction is limited to certain kinds of dispute, is leading to a fragmentation of international law, with rules and procedures in different fields diverging from one another.

Rules of public international law emerge as rules of **customary international law**, or are laid down in international **treaties**, or are inferred from those general principles of law that are recognized by civilized nations and are apposite for application in the field of international law. Certain texts, such as some resolutions of the **United Nations** and other international organizations and declarations made by states, while not in themselves legally binding, may exercise a strong influence on state behaviour. Such texts are sometimes referred to as sources of 'soft law'.

VAUGHAN LOWE

See also: **Commonwealth law**

international law and municipal law   In the eyes of **international law**, municipal law is merely fact, not law as such. As far as international law is concerned, municipal legislation and case law represent no more than practice on the part of a state, on a par with any other governmental conduct. In this light,

an international tribunal is not barred from determining whether a municipal statute or judicial ruling is in conformity with international law; and as to the merits of such conformity, it is axiomatic that a state may not invoke provisions of, or insufficiencies in, its municipal law, including its constitution, as an excuse for failure to perform its international obligations.

Conversely, the status of international law in the three bodies of municipal law within the **United Kingdom**—English law, Scots law, and the law of Northern Ireland—varies according to whether the rule in question has its source in treaty or **customary international law**. **Treaties** cannot affect private rights and obligations in the UK unless Parliament enacts legislation to give effect to them. The explanation for this lies in the constitutional doctrine of the **separation of powers**. In the **Westminster system**, treaty-making is a **royal prerogative**, exercised by the executive. If a treaty concluded by the executive were directly to affect private rights and obligations, this would represent a usurpation of the legislative function of Parliament.

A corollary of the rule that a treaty forms no part of English, Scots, or Northern Irish law unless given legislative effect is the general rule that courts in the UK have no jurisdiction to interpret or otherwise have regard to a treaty not given such effect. So-called 'unincorporated' treaties, including treaties between third states, are generally non-justiciable, the exceptions being where it is necessary to refer to the treaty to determine rights and obligations under municipal law.

Where an Act of Parliament is intended to give effect to a treaty to which the UK is party, any ambiguous provisions of the Act are to be construed by reference to the treaty. If more than one meaning can reasonably be ascribed to a provision, the one consonant with the treaty is to be preferred. The principle is actually of wider application, since there exists a general presumption that Parliament does not intend to legislate in a manner contrary to the UK's existing international obligations. It may be that an Act is not intended to incorporate a treaty but merely regulates a sphere of domestic activity that is also, perhaps coincidentally, within the material scope of a treaty. In short, the Act and treaty may deal with the same things. In such cases, provided the treaty obligation predates the statute, and regardless of whether the treaty is incorporated, Parliament's presumed intention to act in conformity with the treaty obligation will apply, with the consequence that if the Act is ambiguous, and capable of an interpretation consonant with international law, the courts must construe it that way. (This is a situation where an unincorporated treaty can be justiciable.) But in either case, if the Act is unambiguous, the court has no choice but to give effect to it, even if this places the UK in breach of its treaty obligations. The constitutional doctrine of **parliamentary supremacy** prevails.

When it comes to customary international law, the situation is quite different. In what is referred to as the doctrine of 'incorporation', customary international law forms part of the **common law** of England and Wales, of Scotland, and of Northern Ireland respectively without the need for legislative enactment. Moreover, if a rule of customary international law changes with the result that municipal **precedent** ceases to reflect it, a court is free to disregard the outdated decision and to apply the new rule of customary international law. But the doctrine of incorporation is subject always to countervailing constitutional principle, with at least two practical consequences. First, since Parliament is supreme, an unambiguous Act of Parliament is applied over a common law rule derived from customary international law, even if this places the UK in breach of its international obligations. Secondly, when it comes to crimes embodied in customary international law, the doctrine of incorporation is trumped by the constitutional principle that it is up to Parliament to create new crimes: in the absence of legislation, crimes under customary international law are not crimes under English, Scots, or Northern Irish law.

If a court in the UK is called upon to apply an alleged rule of customary international law where customary international law is inconclusive, the court must, as with any alleged rule of common law, ascertain whether the rule exists. In these and all cases involving international law in the various UK courts, customary international law—in contradistinction to foreign law—is pleaded as law, not fact. Expert evidence as to its state may not be led. In cases involving a jury, it is a matter for the judge.

To date, the only successful reliance on the doctrine of incorporation in courts in the UK has been by defendants, and only then to claim the various forms of immunity accorded foreign states and their representatives by customary international law. It is unlikely that the doctrine could ever be relied on by a claimant to ground a cause of action. Leaving aside the rules of **international criminal law** binding on individuals and rules binding on **international organizations**, international obligations direct the conduct of states, and **states in international law** are treated as legal persons wholly distinct from the governments, **government departments** and government officials which constitute their reality. Put simply, only the fictive 'state', and not any one of its governmental organs or officers, is bound by international law. But a state, be it the UK or (at least in this context) a foreign state, can never be a defendant to a claim under the common law of England and Wales, Scotland, or Northern Ireland in an English, Scottish, or Northern Irish court. Rather, claims in the municipal courts are directed towards the conduct of precisely those governmental organs and officers incapable, in their own right, of breaching international law. As for international criminal prohibitions, which bind individuals as such, there is no reason why a crime under customary international law would give rise to a common law action for **damages**: as seen above, such crimes are not common law crimes, and, even if they were, they would not for that reason alone also constitute torts.

Leaving aside the doctrine of incorporation, customary international law considered as international law can play an equivalent role in statutory construction to that played by unincorporated treaties.

ROGER O'KEEFE

International Law Commission (ILC)   *see* **customary international law**

international lawyers   At the beginning of *The Concept of Law* HLA **Hart** notes the striking fact that even among specialists, there is uncertainty about the meaning of the word 'law'. This certainly extends to the meaning of '**international law**' as well. Is it 'rules' or 'processes', values or facts? Cutting the Gordian knot, it may be suggested that whatever international law is, at least it is what international lawyers do and think. This is what Hart himself, too, seems to suggest: law is what legal officials recognize as such. This response has particular power in the international world. For international law has always been much more dependent on the profession that practices it than, say, **contract law** or **administrative law** that are firmly embedded in the domestic social world and thus have a certain distance from the thinking and acting of their respective specialists. Without international lawyers, there would have been no international law. From Hugo Grotius to the **International Criminal Court**, international law has been a *project* carried out by international lawyers. It has been sometimes a religious, sometimes a secular humanitarian project, a project for order, civilization, peace, security, development, rule of law, and so on. Most of the time it has been a project by which European or European-born lawyers or intellectuals have advanced their universalist ideals so as to substitute new rules and institutions for the present political or diplomatic world.

But international lawyers have never been a fully homogeneous group. They have also disagreed on how the world ought to be and, thus, just what direction their project should take. Such disagreements have reflected political preferences, cultural backgrounds, as well as professional experiences and ambitions. In most periods, mainstream views and assumptions have been juxtaposed with typical challenges: right of sovereignty versus the interests of an 'international community'; international security versus cosmopolitan justice; self-determination and national autonomy versus international rules on human rights, development, and environment. Reform has proceeded through critique of earlier generations as either excessively utopian or then ignorant of the realities of an inter-sovereign world. A shared internationalist language has allowed wide divergence in local approaches. To be an international lawyer in India has not been the same thing as being an international lawyer in Sweden or the United States. In each period and location, there have been both a series of orthodox understandings of the field as well as more or less well-established challenges.

Early Lawyers

A professional vocabulary of international legality, distinct from theology, philosophy, and the *raison d'état*, emerged in late sixteenth and early seventeenth centuries together with European expansion and the consolidation of early modern statehood, laying the ground rules for European diplomacy and warfare. But even as they were pleading international cases and writing treatises on the laws of war and diplomacy, neither the Italian Alberico **Gentili** nor the Dutchman Hugo Grotius saw themselves as 'international lawyers'. Gentili was a Professor of Civil Law in Oxford, mixing the outlook of the Italian school with historical borrowings; Grotius a diplomat who regarded his religious writings as his most important work. It was not until the end of the seventeenth century and the early eighteenth century that lawyers such as Samuel Pufendorf, a professor and writer of dynastic histories, as well as the Huguenot activist Jean Barbeyrac, articulated a project of 'law of nature and of nations' (*jus naturae et gentium*) as the Grotian heritage to succeeding generations. This remained a wide project for a universal jurisprudence until the Swiss essayist and lawyer Emmerich de Vattel in 1758 dressed it in a coherent inter-sovereign structure of diplomacy, treaty-making, and war in the sense we recognize as

'modern'. By the end of the eighteenth century, diplomatic academies provided instruction in European treaty-making and inter-sovereign relations, conceptualized as *Droit public de l'Europe*, and academic lawyers began to publish manuals and treaty collections for diplomats and lawyers with international clients.

The Profession Emerges: 1873 to the League of Nations

The developments since the Congress of Vienna (1814–1815) gave concreteness to writings on the law of nations and pushed natural law to the background. The collection of international treaties by the Göttingen academic, later diplomat, GF von Martens was widely distributed in European capitals and universities. His textbook was published in many languages through the early years of the nineteenth century, laying the paradigm for the historically oriented work of the period. But it was only in connection with the liberal ascendancy in Europe in the last third of the century that lawyers with an international interest, academics as well as practitioners, began to meet and discuss matters of domestic and international reform from a shared point of view. As a result, the first international law journal (*Revue de droit international et de législation comparée*) was published in 1869 and the first two professional associations (*Institut de droit international*, and the *Association for the Reform and Codification of International*, later *International Law Association*) were set up in 1873.

The first university chairs in international law proper, distinguished from natural law, were established in the same period. Large international conferences such as those held in Brussels in 1874 and Berlin in 1885, as well as the Hague Peace Conferences of 1899 and 1907, prompted foreign ministries to employ lawyers, such as Louis Renault in France or Sir Travers Twiss in Britain, who had specific competence in treaties and doctrine, to give regular advise on international law matters. As the peace movement turned to advocating arbitration and pacific settlement, legal experts were increasingly found also in its ranks. Progress in international law was understood as closely related to Europe's 'civilizing mission'.

During the inter-war era the League of Nations provided a principal platform for organized international legal activity. An *esprit de corps* developed at places of coordinated training such as The Hague Academy of International Law, which began its work in 1922. Delegations at international conferences were accompanied by international lawyers, and the subject was included in the curriculum of European and US law schools where it was treated sometimes as an independent subject, sometimes (as in Germany) as part of public law or (as in Italy) together with private international law ('**conflict of laws**'). A common law approach stressed the importance of custom and the work of international tribunals such as the Permanent Court of International Justice, while civil lawyers focused on codification and relations with domestic law. New collections of international case law and accumulating commentary devoted to international law strengthened the sense of international lawyers as a distinct specialization, and provided a platform for advancing international reform. Sophisticated analyses by scholars such as Hersch Lauterpacht in Cambridge and Georges Scelle in Paris put a critique of sovereign statehood and an emphasis on international organizations at the heart of their writings—provoking thereby the standard suspicion about the profession's inherent 'utopianism'.

The United Nations

After 1945, international lawyers made a commitment to pragmatic work at the **United Nations**, their ambition limited by the Cold War but strengthened by decolonization, which brought new countries within their compass. International lawyers saw themselves as speaking across both the East–West divide and the ever sharpening North–South confrontation by focusing on practical cooperation in such fields as economic and technological development, uses of the oceans and outer space, protection of **human rights,** and the environment. Oscar Schachter, a member of the UN legal staff and later Professor at the Columbia University, referred to the emergence of an 'invisible college of international lawyers', the humanitarian and welfarist legalism of which appeared to cut across political divisions.

But homogeneity at the United Nations concealed important distinctions between three groups of international professionals. Foreign office legal advisers were accustomed to working with diplomats and often shared a political realist critique of the activities of international advocacy groups. Academic lawyers at European universities pursued the anti-sovereignty rhetoric of the inter-war generation while putting forward proposals for constitutional reform of intergovernmental organizations. US lawyers were divided between doing exactly the same (seeking methodological renewal from political science) and enlisting themselves as supporters of US foreign policy. In the 1970s lawyers from developing countries sought to protect the autonomy of their often-fragile states while seeking a wholesale reform of the international economic system. The possibilities of legal codification and 'progressive development' at the UN were largely conditioned by the North–South conflict. The development of more intensive human rights or economic integration regimes was directed into regional channels.

Diffusion

In the last three decades, the profession has been marked by functional specialization and political controversy. The emergence of new institutional regimes reflecting new priorities has been accompanied by the consolidation of distinct forms of expertise in 'human rights law', '**international trade law**', '**international environmental law**', '**international criminal law**', and so on. As a result, intra-professional division no longer takes place so much by formal position (legal advisor, academic expert, activist) as commitment to a particular specialization. Among themselves 'human rights lawyers' or 'trade lawyers' tend to think and act in relatively homogeneous ways (with more or less significant minorities challenging the mainstream) while the objectives of such regimes may often be different, even contradictory. When environmental and trade preferences, for example, conflict (as they often do), lawyers are pushed into increasingly antagonistic positions. Likewise, the 'fight against terrorism' has created a gap between human rights and security institutions that is often reflected in tensions between the corresponding legal experts. The profession's traditional commitment to the United Nations and third world development may have recently weakened as new alliances are made with private and public lawyers. The fragmentation of the international social world has led to a clutch of new and often interdisciplinary approaches that may have accentuated the divisions between groups of international lawyers.

MARTTI KOSKENNIEMI

M Koskenniemi, *The Gentle Civilizer of Nations. The Rise and Fall of International law 1870–1960* (Cambridge: Cambridge University Press, 2001)

O Schachter, 'The Invisible College of International Lawyers,' (1977) 72 *Northwestern Univ L Rev* 217

international military tribunals   *see* **war crimes**

international monetary fund (IMF)   *see* **international economic law**

international monetary law   International monetary law is a somewhat esoteric subject. Yet debates about international monetary law have become a matter of public interest over the last decade. This entry will deal with two of the main episodes, namely, the introduction of the euro and the dispute between the USA and China over the valuation of the latter's currency. First of all, however, it is necessary to outline precisely why such an apparently remote subject should have assumed such importance. The answer lies in the occasional tension between national sovereignty and **international law**.

The expression 'national sovereignty' encompasses a range of detailed legal principles. In its essence, however, sovereignty connotes the ability of a state to manage its own domestic affairs, free from interference by other countries. In the modern world, of course, matters are not quite so straightforward. International law limits a state's freedom of action. The rights of one state may be inconsistent with those of another, and conflicts between sovereign claims will inevitably arise. Equally, a state may voluntarily limit its future freedom of action by entering into treaty obligations. These general principles find expression in the narrow field of monetary law. The Permanent Court of International Justice long ago held that all states enjoy the right to issue and regulate a currency. This includes the right to fix interest rates or to impose exchange controls. But it is quite open to a state to restrict its monetary sovereignty by agreement with other states. Treaties of this kind have been at the heart of recent controversies in this field.

The adoption of the euro by the eleven original eurozone Member States on 1 January 1999 was one of history's foremost monetary events. The euro was to be the *single* currency of the entire euro area. Accordingly, by signing up to the Maastricht Treaty, which led to the birth of the new unit, the relevant Member States had agreed to forego their national monetary sovereignty or (perhaps more accurately) they had agreed to *transfer* that sovereignty to the **European Community**. In any event, the right to issue an individual, national currency would be lost.

It was the outright and irrevocable transfer of national monetary sovereignty which cased such angst in the debates over the **United Kingdom**'s prospective membership of the eurozone. Yet in practice, monetary sovereignty is not simply *lost* when a monetary zone is created. Rather, sovereignty is *pooled* because the new institutions charged with the conduct of monetary policy are composed of representatives of the various national central banks. In other words, if each state *loses* a portion of its own sovereignty then it correspondingly *gains* a portion of the monetary sovereignty of the other states within the zone.

In view of those considerations, and despite the occasionally fierce political debate, abstract arguments about the loss or transfer of sovereignty seem to be of limited value. States frequently enter into treaties which restrict their freedom of action; it may be in their interests to do so if other states also agree to be bound by corresponding restrictions. It is, therefore, more pertinent to ask whether the sovereign right to determine a monetary policy is best exercised over a very large area (such as the eurozone) whose regions may suffer different economic problems at different times, or whether a more fragmented approach allows for a more locally appropriate monetary policy. Nevertheless, the political debate in the UK was heavily influenced by 'monetary sovereignty' issues. These were principally responsible for the UK's well-known 'opt out' from the single currency process.

China has pegged its currency to the US dollar for a number of years. However, China's domestic economy has grown massively during that period, and this has led to suggestions that the currency is significantly undervalued. This, it is said, provides Chinese businesses with an advantage when competing in foreign markets.

China has occasionally responded that the management of its currency falls within the scope of its domestic jurisdiction. This is undoubtedly true, but its sovereignty in this sphere is limited by treaty obligations. In particular, the Articles of Agreement of the International Monetary Fund prohibit the manipulation of exchange rates with a view to preventing effective balance of payments adjustments or to gain an unfair competitive advantage. This dispute will almost certainly be resolved by diplomatic means, rather than through recourse to formal proceedings. Nevertheless, the dispute provides a clear illustration of a clash between national sovereignty and international monetary law.

CHARLES PROCTOR

international organizations   International organizations ('IGOs') have been a major feature of the international legal environment since the nineteenth century. IGOs are created by states for carrying out specified tasks for their mutual benefit. Early IGOs included the International Postal Union (1875) and the Union for the Protection of Industrial Property (1883). In 1919 the creation of the League of Nations and **International Labour Organization** ('**ILO**') demonstrated a commitment to multilateralism and international legal **regulation**. Despite the failure of the League to prevent World War II this commitment was reaffirmed in the creation of the **United Nations** Organization ('UN') in 1945.

The UN is based upon principles of sovereign equality, collective security, and peaceful settlement of disputes. Although originally membership was confined to 'peace loving' states, today the principle of universal membership prevails, and there are 192 member states.

There are now over 400 IGOs. Differences in their size, function, and operation are enormous. While the UN has nearly universal membership, others have very few members (the Czech-Slovak Customs Union has two) and may not be open to all states. IGOs may have broad functions within specified areas such as the ILO (labour), the World Health Organization ('WHO') (health), or United Nations' Children's Fund ('UNICEF') (children). Others may be functionally more limited such as collective defence organizations like the North Atlantic Treaty Organization ('NATO'). Regional IGOs have been created for political and social affairs, including the promotion of human rights (eg the Council of Europe, Organization of American States, African Union, Association of South East Asian Nations ('ASEAN'), the Arab League), for economic integration (eg the **European Union**, the Economic Community of West African States) and for financial affairs and development (the International Financial Institutions). Other IGOs are formed around diverse interests such as common belief systems (eg Organization of the Islamic Conference), commodities (eg the Organization of Petroleum Exporting Countries ('OPEC')) or shared histories (the **Commonwealth of Nations**). Although IGOs are all different, there are certain commonalities.

IGOs are created by states, generally through the adoption of a multilateral treaty, although some have been created by resolution of another organization (for example the UN Industrial Development Organization was created by General Assembly resolution). The founding instrument becomes the constitutional basis of the organization. In the *Legality of the Use by a State of Nuclear Weapons in Armed Conflict* case (1996) the **International Court of Justice** ('ICJ') stated the function of the constitutive treaty to be the creation of 'new subjects of law endowed with a certain autonomy, to which the parties entrust the task of realising common goals'. The treaty is thus both conventional and institutional. It specifies such matters as organs, membership, voting rights, mandate, rules, powers, and financial arrangements. IGOs may also be disbanded by member states, as occurred to the Southeast Asia Treaty Organization in 1977 and to a number of commodities organizations.

The law applicable to IGOs is **international law**. IGOs are political bodies, subjects of international law and may have international legal personality. This was clarified with respect to the UN in the *Reparation for Injuries Suffered in the Service of the United Nations* case (1949). The ICJ held that an IGO has legal personality when states intended to create an entity separate from themselves and the IGO in fact operates autonomously. In the case of the UN, the ICJ found it 'was exercising and enjoying functions and rights which can only be explained on the basis of the possession of a large measure of international personality and the capacity to operate on an international plane'. The constitutive treaty may specify whether the states parties intended the organization to have separate international legal personality. For example the Rome Statute of the **International Criminal Court**, Article 4(1) states that the Court shall have international legal personality. In contrast the European Union does not (although the **European Community** and Euratom do).

Since IGOs have different functions and powers, they also have differing levels of international personality. Each IGO has the capacity to carry out its functions. Competencies may include the capacity to enter into and be bound by treaties, to be sued or sue in the organization's own name for harms committed by or against it, to own property, and to be accorded immunity in national courts. These competencies may be effective against non-member states. IGOs have only limited competence and can act only within the powers delegated to them by states. This is true even of the Security Council, which is 'subjected to certain constitutional limitations, however broad its powers under the constitution may be'. An example of an IGO seeking to act outside its powers is the *Legality of the Use by a State of Nuclear Weapons in Armed Conflict* case. UN specialized agencies may seek an advisory opinion from the ICJ 'on legal questions arising within the scope of their activities'. The Court declined to give an advisory opinion in response to the request by the WHO on the basis that the question of the legality of nuclear weapons is not pertinent to the health mandate of the WHO.

The ICJ has recognized that an IGO cannot function effectively if its powers are limited to those expressly bestowed, and has accepted the need for implied powers that may be extended according to changing needs and conditions. Implied powers are those that can be read into the express powers attributed to the organization by its constitutive instrument. For example, in pursuance of its primary responsibility for the maintenance of international peace and security the Security Council has been accorded broad powers under UN Charter Articles 41 and 42. However they do not stipulate the right to create judicial tribunals such as the *ad hoc* criminal tribunals for Former Yugoslavia ('**ICTY**') and Rwanda ('**ICTR**'). The ICTY affirmed the power of the Security Council to do this. Another example is the UN's exercise of territorial administration as part of its peacekeeping functions (eg in East Timor 1999–2002 and Kosovo since 1999) although the Charter bestows no express powers to so. An organization may also develop customary powers through its practice. Express powers may be allocated between different organs of the organization, but actions taken by another organ will not be deemed *ultra vires* ('beyond the power') of the organization, provided they are appropriate for fulfillment of its overall purposes.

IGOs require an institutional structure and at least one organ independent of member states. Typically an IGO comprises a secretariat, an assembly, and a governing body responsible for management. Some IGOs have a judicial body such as the European Court of Justice or the WTO panels and appellate body. Through their secretariats IGOs develop technical and specialist expertise that is available to member states. IGOs make decisions binding upon states parties, 'perhaps even when not all of the members have favoured the decision concerned'. IGOs may participate in international standard setting through providing the forum for inter-governmental meetings, expert background preparation and administrative assistance. Agendas and priorities may be determined within the institutional setting. International institutions also make international law directly, for example by entering into treaties and memoranda of understanding with other international actors and amending existing treaties through institutional decisions or practice. Indeed states constantly devolve more and diverse functions onto IGOs, mandating regulatory powers, for example formal law-making through institutional treaty amendment processes and supervisory duties such as fact-finding and monitoring compliance.

CHRISTINE CHINKIN

P Sands and P Klein (eds), *Bowett's Law of International Institutions* (London: Sweet & Maxwell, 2001)
HG Schermers and NM Blokker, *International Institutional Law : Unity within Diversity* (Dordrecht: M. Nijhoff, 1995)

international prize court   *see* **war and armed conflict**

international rivers   *see* **international waterways and watercourses**

international sea-bed area   *see* **law of the sea**

international tax   Since tax is imposed by individual states (or occasionally by associations of states, as with customs duties in the European Union) it may be questioned whether international tax exists as a topic. The expression is normally used to denote first, domestic tax provisions dealing with international situations, for example, controlled foreign company provisions under which profits of a foreign subsidiary in a low tax country are taxable in the hands of the parent company; and secondly, provisions governing international tax relations, such as tax treaties, and now increasingly EU law.

The **United Kingdom** taxes first, the worldwide income of a resident of the UK (in fact UK tax law makes additional distinctions in taxing based on ordinary residence and domicile), and secondly, the income of a non-resident arising in the UK (which may be charged by deduction at source—'withholding tax', or by assessment as for example taxing the profits of a branch). This jurisdiction accordingly requires definitions of residence in domestic law for all taxable persons, including individuals, companies, and other bodies such as trustees, and also definitions of when income arises in the UK. If another country taxes income with a source there (eg it taxes the profits of a branch of a UK resident company situated in its country), the UK taxes the worldwide profits of the taxpayer, including therefore the branch profits, but gives a credit for the foreign tax by setting it against the UK tax (up to the amount of the UK tax on the branch profits). This results in capital export neutrality (profits are taxed in a state in the same way whether they are earned in the UK or abroad) so long as the foreign tax does not exceed the UK tax. The competing system is capital import neutrality (profits are taxed in a state in the same way whether earned by a resident or non-resident) which requires the state of residence to exempt profits taxed in another state, rather than giving credit for the tax imposed in the other state, as does the UK. The exemption system is found in many, but not all, European countries. Such countries typically give credit in some situations, such as withholding tax on dividends, interest and royalties, and exemption in others, such as profits of a foreign branch. The UK never uses exemption.

Apart from taxes in both source and residence states, problems of overlapping jurisdiction to tax are additionally caused by states taking a different view about whether the taxpayer is resident in its state by applying different tests of residence, such as one state treating companies as resident if they are incorporated in the state, and the other state if they are managed in the state; or taking a different view about whether the source of income is in the state. Such problems are normally solved by bilateral tax treaties between states based on a Model with accompanying commentary produced by the Organization for Economic Cooperation and Development ('OECD') and continuously updated, which is adapted to the particular circumstances of the two states. Tax treaties were developed from the 1920s starting with Models produced by the League of Nations, which was succeeded in this respect by the OECD (and a UN Model treaty exists for developing countries, but now most developments are by the OECD, which also recognizes the interests of non-member countries). The UK has a network of over 100 tax treaties. In general, imposition of tax is a matter of domestic law, and treaties merely relieve from tax.

A tax treaty will typically first determine which is the state of residence, so that if the person is a resident of both states under different domestic law definitions, treaty provisions will resolve the dual residence into a single residence for treaty purposes. For individuals, this is determined by a series of tests generally called the tie-breaker, and for companies it is generally where the place of effective management is situated. Secondly, the tax treaty will reduce or eliminate the tax in the source state by (a) exempting profits from tax in a state, such as taxation of business profits if the presence in the source state does not amount to a permanent establishment (effectively a branch), an expression that will be defined in the treaty; (b) exempting shipping and aircraft profits in states other than the state of effective management (sometimes residence) of the enterprise; (c) exempting governmental income in states other than the paying state; (d) exempting source taxation of capital gains on securities; and (e) exempting source taxation of pensions paid to non-residents.

Alternatively the tax treaty may limit taxation in some way, such as where a permanent establishment exists, to the profits of the permanent establishment computed on an arm's length basis, the method of determining which is the subject of much controversy; and in other cases by reducing or eliminating the amount of withholding tax normally on dividends, interest, and royalties. In yet other cases, such as income from immovable property, the domestic law charge in the state where the land is situated is left to apply. The tax treaty will also provide that each state must give credit for foreign tax permitted by

the treaty or, as the case may be, exempt from tax the income permitted by the treaty to be taxed by the other state. In addition, there will be administrative provisions, such as those preventing discriminatory taxation, normally limited to specific situations in relation to inbound business investments, and discrimination on the ground of nationality (although nationality discrimination is unusual in practice because taxation is usually based on residence—but the US does tax on the basis of citizenship). There are provisions dealing with settlement by mutual agreement of disputes between the two states; increasingly arbitration is being discussed, but few treaties have so far included this. The OECD commentary is useful as an aid to interpretation of treaty provisions based on the Model; the courts in most countries now consider it but without being bound by it.

Some international tax problems are not adequately solved by tax treaties and have to rely on domestic law provisions. These include provisions (referred to as controlled foreign company provisions) dealing with the case where a parent company located in a high-tax country establishes a subsidiary (taxed as a separate legal person) resident in a low-tax country so that profits of the subsidiary cannot in principle be taxed in the parent company's country. Such provisions generally tax the profits of the subsidiary in the parent company's country where there is no genuine business reason for the subsidiary in the low tax country. Another example is where the parent company establishes a subsidiary in a high-tax country and lends it an excessive amount of debt (referred to as thin capitalization) on which interest is deductible in computing the profits of the high-tax subsidiary's country (often with a reduced or nil rate of withholding tax on the interest in accordance with a tax treaty). Thin capitalization provisions limit the deduction for interest to interest on a debt of an arm's length amount that an independent bank might be prepared to lend.

Increasingly EU provisions relating to fundamental freedoms are being invoked in direct tax in cases brought before the **European Court of Justice**. Because such provisions were not designed with direct tax in mind, they generally produce answers different from those developed in tax treaties and international tax practice, such as thin capitalization provisions based on a fixed ratio of debt to equity being prohibited. They also apply more widely than tax treaty non-discrimination provisions, including outbound investment, and are interpreted to extend to covert discrimination, such as discrimination against non-residents which, while not on the grounds of nationality, is likely to affect non-nationals. They also extend to situations where there is a restriction on the exercise of the fundamental freedom—such as an exit charge to **capital gains tax** on ceasing to be resident—since logically, a restriction may prevent the person from being in a position where discrimination is an issue.

It now seems clear that EU law does not require most favoured nation treatment. This is a fast-moving topic in which the limits of the rules are being developed. In a few situations directives dealing with direct tax apply, including preventing withholding tax in the EU on dividends, interest, and royalties paid within a group of companies. There is also an arbitration convention between EU states, deliberately not a directive, providing ultimately for eliminating double taxation in transfer pricing cases (disputes about the determination of an arm's length price for international transactions between related entities or between different parts of the same legal entity) through an arbitration procedure.

Indirect taxes, particularly VAT, do not give rise to international tax problems as they are designed to be charged on international transactions in one state only, typically the destination state; but there are proposals to move to an origin state basis for VAT in the EU. Since the basis for VAT in the EU is governed by directives it generates fewer uncertainties in international situations than direct tax.

JOHN AVERY JONES

International Tribunal for the Law of the Sea (ITLOS) *see* **international courts and tribunals; law of the sea**

international waterways and watercourses The uses of international waterways and watercourses are governed by international law. While it is often a private person or company who actually uses the water, rather than the government of the country in which the use is made, the country itself is responsible for observing its international legal obligations toward other countries sharing the watercourse. However, this does not exclude the possibility of redress on the private level, through domestic courts applying national law. An example of such a lawsuit is one brought in the mid-1970s, by a Dutch nursery gardening business and an organization for the protection of the water quality of the Rhine, against a French potash mine. The Dutch plaintiffs complained to a court in Rotterdam that chlorides discharged into the Rhine by the French mine caused damage downstream in The Netherlands. The parties ultimately reached a monetary settlement on

the basis of a judgment of the Dutch Supreme Court finding the French mine liable. While private suits of this kind may be possible in some circumstances, the focus here will be upon the rules of **international law** governing international waterways and watercourses. Thus in this example, the question would be whether France had breached obligations owed to The Netherlands.

A word concerning terminology is appropriate at the outset. The term 'waterway' is generally used in reference to a navigable river or lake. Thus the law of international waterways principally concerns navigation on such internationally shared surface waters. The term 'watercourse' is a more general expression and is understood in a broad sense, encompassing both surface water and groundwater that is shared by two or more states. It is understood to refer chiefly to the water contained in the river or lake bed or groundwater aquifer, rather than—as the suffix 'course' might suggest—simply to the solid matter that contains the water. A waterway or watercourse is considered to be 'international' if parts of it are situated in more than one country. This would thus include rivers that form or cross international borders, border-straddling lakes and aquifers, and even aquifers that are located in one country but are hydrologically connected to surface water that is itself international. Finally, the term 'riparian' will be used here for convenience to refer to a state through or along whose territory a watercourse flows.

The rules of international law applicable to these shared waters have developed along two lines: one concerning navigation and the other concerning non-navigational uses. These two aspects of the law will be addressed separately.

Navigation has long been an important use of international rivers. The major peace treaties, beginning with the Peace of Westphalia in 1648 and extending through the Versailles Treaty ending World War I, all contain provisions on navigation. The Final Act of the 1815 Congress of Vienna, concluded following the Napoleonic Wars, provided for freedom of commercial navigation on navigable rivers that separated or crossed the states parties. This principle was followed in a number of treaties over more than a century. While the Congress did not confine this right to riparians, later treaties—notably the 1921 Barcelona Convention and Statute—tended to restrict freedom of navigation to parties or riparian states. The principle of freedom of navigation applies chiefly to commercial vessels, rather than public ships, and is subject to policing regulations of the territorial state. It is probably applicable today throughout Europe, even without the aid of treaty. In the rest of the world its application is more likely to depend on treaties.

Societies have also used watercourses for non-navigational purposes since time immemorial; but rules of international law governing the use of international watercourses for irrigation and other non-navigational purposes were rather slow to develop. In 1994 the UN **International Law Commission** ('ILC') completed a comprehensive set of draft articles on the subject after twenty years' work. Negotiations held in the **United Nations** ('UN') on the basis of the ILC's draft resulted in the 1997 UN Convention on the Law of the Non-Navigational Uses of International Watercourses. This treaty sets forth the basic rules governing the subject—rules that in large measure are applicable whether or not a state is bound by the treaty. Foremost among these are the following three obligations: to utilize an international watercourse in a manner that is equitable and reasonable vis-à-vis other riparian states; to prevent the causing of significant harm to those states; and to notify other riparian states of planned measures that may adversely affect them.

STEPHEN MCCAFFREY

internet regulation   The internet is a complex, global network which is regulated at three levels: the communications infrastructure, internet intermediaries, and the content/services available online.

Internet infrastructure: Internet communications are carried by telecommunications networks, which are regulated by national **telecommunications regulation** and, cross-border, via the International Telecommunications Union. Those communications need to comply with non-binding technical standards for inter-operation and communication, such as Transmission Control Protocol/Internet Protocol ('TCP/IP'), which are set by a number of global bodies whose legal status is unclear, primarily the Internet Engineering Task Force.

To access an internet resource, its address is needed. At the machine level numerical IP addresses are used, allocated by five regional registries. These IP addresses are mapped to domain names via database lookup. **Domain names** are obtained from domain name registries and are of two types. Top-level domains, such as '.com' and '.org', are regulated by the Internet Corporation for Assigned Names and Numbers, a US not-for-profit corporation, which grants to registries the right to issue domain names. Country-level domains, such as '.uk', are controlled by national bodies (Nominet for the UK).

Registration of a domain name is normally under a contract with the registry, though some national domains and '.eu' are regulated by the general law .

A **trade mark** holder may be able to obtain transfer of a domain name which is confusingly similar if the name was registered in bad faith. The Uniform Domain Name Dispute Resolution Policy, which is contractually binding on top-level domain name holders and registries, regulates such disputes, which are resolved by online arbitration. Disputes between legitimate claimants to a domain name can only be resolved by negotiation or litigation. Similar dispute resolution schemes operate for most country-level domains.

The use of a domain name (as opposed to its mere registration) may infringe a trade mark. If so, this is a matter for the national trade mark law of the place(s) where the name is used.

Intermediaries: Intermediaries such as Internet Service Providers ('ISPs') carry internet communications, and some host resources such as websites. Attempts have been made to require ISPs to police the third party content they host and carry, either through imposing direct legal obligations—eg the US Communications Decency Act 1996 and the Australian Broadcasting Services Amendment Act 1999, both of which failed—or through licensing ISPs and including policing obligations in those licence condition, as in Singapore and China, for instance.

The more common approach is now to grant ISPs immunity from liability for their activities of transmission, caching, and hosting. For the UK, these immunities derive from the EU Electronic Commerce Directive 2000, under which the hosting immunity is lost once the hosted content is known to be unlawful. There is no international consensus whether linking to third party content should also attract immunity.

Content and services: The non-binding technical standards for communicating content, such as HTML, are regulated by global bodies such as the World-Wide Web Consortium and the Internet Society. The actual content and services themselves are regulated, if at all, by the national laws of the countries which have jurisdiction over the content or service provider's activities.

Content is often regulated by **defamation** or **indecency** laws, or may be regulated as **advertising**. Content will always be regulated by the country where it is hosted, but is also likely to be subject to the laws of the country where it is viewed or downloaded. This creates compliance difficulties as these types of law define very different standards because of their varying historical and cultural origins. For example, in *LICRA v Yahoo!* (2001) a French court issued an order in 2000 requiring Yahoo!'s US auction site not to make pro-Nazi material available to French residents. In response, Yahoo! obtained a declaration from a Californian court in 2001 that the French judgment could not be enforced in the US because of the US Constitution's free speech protections.

Regulation of services is also potentially regulated both in the service provider's country and where the customer is located, depending on the activities which are regulated. For example, online provision of banking and investment services usually requires the bank to be authorized in each customer's country.

This problem of multiple, overlapping **regulation** is solved within the **European Union** via the country of origin regime of the Electronic Commerce Directive 2000. This provides that for most online activities, authorization and conduct of business is to be regulated only by the country in which the provider is established. In most cases, the only area which the recipient's country still regulates is contracts with consumers from that country.   CHRIS REED

internment in international law   *see* **international humanitarian law**

internment without trial   This term refers to the holding of someone in restricted areas or in state custody without charging that person with any criminal offence and without there being any medical or welfare reason for the denial of liberty. It is sometimes resorted to when states are at war or facing internal emergencies resulting from a violent insurgency. The UK government used statutory powers to intern many 'enemy aliens' during World Wars I and II. In *Liversidge v Anderson* (1942) the **House of Lords** held that the courts could not interfere with the Home Secretary's statutory discretion to detain people whom he had 'reasonable cause to believe' had hostile origins or associations. There may also be a prerogative power to intern in English law. By Presidential Executive Order the US government severely restricted the movements of Japanese-Americans living on the US West Coast during World War II; and by six votes to three the Supreme Court upheld the constitutionality of this practice in *Korematsu v United States* (1944). On 9 August 1971 the government of Northern Ireland authorized the use of internment, and 342 men were immediately detained. The practice continued for four years, affecting the nationalist community much more than the unionist and alienating many against the state. It was eventually scrapped in 1975, but the provision conferring ministerial power to order its recommencement was not repealed until 1998.

The Irish Republic practised internment during the IRA's 'border campaign' in the 1950s, leading to the first ever decision by the **European Court of Human Rights**: in *Lawless v Ireland* (1960) the Court held that the internment was lawful because the Irish government had, in accordance with Article 15 of the **European Convention on Human Rights**, properly derogated (ie excused itself) from complying with the Article 5 obligation not to deprive people of their liberty. The derogation was valid because there was an 'emergency threatening the life of the nation'. Following the events of 9/11 in the USA, the UK enacted the Anti-terrorism, Crime and Security Act 2001, section 23 of which permitted indefinite detention without trial of non-British nationals suspected of involvement in international terrorism. However in 2004, by 8 votes to 1, the House of Lords declared section 23 to be incompatible with the right to liberty guaranteed by the European Convention because the measures taken were disproportionate and discriminatory (*A v Home Secretary* (2005)). The government responded by enacting the Prevention of Terrorism Act 2005, which allows 'control orders' to be issued to restrict the activities of suspected international terrorists. In 2006 the Court of Appeal ruled that some of these control orders, in so far as they required people to spend long periods within their own homes, were also incompatible with Article 5. Contrary to all international legal standards, the US has detained hundreds of people it designates as 'unlawful combatants in the war against terror' at Guantánamo Bay in Cuba.   BRICE DICKSON

internship   *see* **vocational legal education**

interpretation, law as   Nobody doubts that interpretation of legal texts forms an important part of what lawyers and **judges** do in their everyday professional activities. The law is not always sufficiently clear to determine a particular result, and interpretation may be required to determine what the law means in a particular context. 'Law *as* interpretation', however, is a much more ambitious and general thesis about the nature of law, propounded by the philosopher Ronald Dworkin (in *Law's Empire* (London: Fontana Press,1986)) and subsequently endorsed by others. On this view, interpretation is what lawyers and judges always do; there is no other way in which they can figure out what the law is. Interpretation is not an exceptional activity, required only when the law is not entirely clear; instead, every understanding of what the law prescribes must be a result of interpretation.

Why does it matter? For one thing, there is a debate here about the nature of language and what it takes to grasp the meaning of a linguistic expression, whether or not the expression is legal: is it always an interpretative process, or is interpretation only an exception to the standard understanding of what expressions mean? With respect to the nature of law, however, there is more at stake. According to a very influential tradition in legal theory, called 'legal positivism', a clear separation exists between what the law *is*, and what the law *ought to be*. Legal positivism maintains that moral and other evaluative considerations do not necessarily have a bearing on what the law is. If Dworkin is correct about the necessarily interpretative nature of law, however, the legal positivist tradition in jurisprudence may have got it quite wrong here. That is so because interpretation, by its very nature, is difficult to separate from various evaluative considerations. Thus, Dworkin's general argument is basically the following:

(1) Each and every conclusion about what the law is in a given case is a result of interpretation.
(2) Interpretation is essentially an attempt to present its object in the best possible light.
(3) Therefore, interpretation necessarily involves evaluative considerations.
(4) And therefore, every conclusion about what the law is necessarily involves evaluative (moral) considerations.

Because the relevant evaluative considerations in the legal case are bound to be moral or political in nature, given law's essential function of regulating human activities, Dworkin's argument, if sound, would show that morality and law cannot be separated. They are necessarily entangled by the interpretative nature of understanding law.

Critics of 'law as interpretation', however, have raised questions. Some doubt Dworkin's theory that interpretation necessarily strives to present its object, the relevant text, as it were, in its best possible light. Mostly, however, critics question the soundness of the argument's first premise. For those who regard interpretation only as an exception to standard understandings of what legal or other expressions mean, the argument cannot show that law and morality are inextricably linked; law might sometimes depend on moral considerations, perhaps when interpretation is called for, but this would not always be the case. The debate here partly concerns the nature of language and what it takes to grasp the

meaning of an expression, and partly the nature of law, and whether there is anything special about the law that would require an interpretative understanding of it in all cases.   ANDREI MARMOR

A Marmor, *Interpretation and Legal Theory* (Oxford: Hart Publishing, rev 2nd edn, 2005)
A Marmor (ed), *Law and Interpretation: Essays in Legal Philosophy* (Oxford: Oxford University Press, 1995)

See also: **legal positivism since 1970; legal positivism to 1970**

interpreting constitutions   The interpretation of any legal text is complicated by the indeterminacy of language and the inability of its authors to foresee and make provision for all the circumstances to which it will be applied. Constitutional interpretation is complicated further by the distinctive characteristics of **constitutions** themselves. The terms in which a constitution is written typically are less specific and more open-textured than those of ordinary legislation. Constitutions may be designed to reflect and protect important values, on which the solidarity and cohesion of society may depend. Most constitutions are based on premises that are not fully articulated. Most also are intended to last for a long period of time and some do so; in extreme cases for a century or more. Typically, constitutions are more difficult to change than ordinary laws. Some are effectively resistant to change because of the difficulty of the alteration procedure. Parts of others cannot be changed as a matter of law, either because the text so provides, as in Germany, or because the courts have so held, as in India.

Any person who applies or is knowingly affected by a provision of a Constitution must engage in interpretation in order to make a decision about what the provision means. A Constitution thus has many interpreters, bringing different perspectives to bear. Nevertheless, in most constitutional systems the task of finally resolving disputes about constitutional meaning falls either to a specialist Constitutional Court or to the highest appellate court, exercising constitutional jurisdiction. The decision of such a court sets the meaning of the Constitution in a way that can be changed only by alteration of the Constitution or a change of heart by the court itself. It thus has continuing implications for the authority of the elected branches of government, representing current majorities, and for the rights of individuals within the community as a whole.

The sensitive nature of constitutional review requires a court to tread a fine line between giving the Constitution appropriate effect and confining its own role within limits that are accepted as legitimate. Its approach to constitutional interpretation is critical for this purpose. Interpretative method embraces a range of practices and techniques, including the attitude of the court to the authority of its own previous decisions; its willingness to take international law or the jurisprudence of other constitutional systems into account; the existence of presumptions that favour the constitutionality of the challenged action, whether through a doctrine of deference or otherwise; and the significance attached to the availability of a factual setting for the interpretative process. At the core of the interpretative method of a court, however, lies a broader, philosophical view of what constitutional interpretation requires, which in turn may reflect understanding of the nature of the Constitution itself.

Philosophical approaches to constitutional interpretation can be ranged along a spectrum. Towards one end are approaches that, to a greater or lesser degree, treat the Constitution as an instrument made at a particular point in historical time and interpret it accordingly. These approaches place relatively greater weight on the text of the Constitution, often elucidated by traditional legal considerations of structure and context. They attach relatively greater significance to contemporary understanding at the time the Constitution was made, which may draw on the subjective intention of those by whom the instrument was framed, but need not do so. Towards the other end of the spectrum are approaches to interpretation that accept the need for a Constitution to evolve in a way that responds to changing conditions over time. These approaches are more likely to interpret the Constitution by reference to purpose, to conceive purpose in terms of constitutional values and to accept that values should be understood by reference to standards at the time the problem of interpretation is raised.

Approaches to constitutional interpretation vary between states, for reasons that relate to history, legal tradition, the age of the Constitution, the significance of its role in the political community, and the perception of the function of the court. The differences should not be exaggerated, however: all courts acknowledge that the character of a Constitution calls for a distinctive interpretative approach and all accept that there are limitations imposed by constitutional text, previous judicial decisions, and considerations of judicial legitimacy. Approaches to constitutional interpretation may also vary within a state, in response to different challenges presented by different parts of a Constitution, or over time. No court is entirely consistent in its interpretative

approach; there is an inescapable element of pragmatism in constitutional interpretation.

CHERYL SAUNDERS

See also: **entrenchment of constitutions and legislation; interpreting legislation**

interpreting legislation Legislation differs from general principles of law or **precedent** because it contains a specific formulation of a legal rule. The task of the lawyer is to apply the rule to specific circumstances. The process of interpretation has three elements: compiling, construing, and applying. In many cases, the interpreter will have to bring together fragments of the law from different sources. A statute may amend another statute, or may be expanded by **delegated legislation**, so the current text of a provision may not be gathered in one place. The lawyer will have to examine all these texts and compile from them the definitive text of the rule to be interpreted. Then the lawyer has to determine the meaning of the words used in the rule. Some terms will be defined specifically within the statute, others (such as '**marriage**') will be left to common knowledge.

The typical approach to reading the words of a statute or other legislation is to adopt the grammatical or literal meaning of the words in ordinary or legal language. If the law is to be followed by citizens (with appropriate legal advice) they will expect to be guided clearly by the legislator. The text cannot be taken in isolation, but will have to be read in the overall context of the specific enactment and of the law in the field. The law is presumed to be coherent and consistent, so that the preferable interpretation is one that makes sense of the specific legislative text as part of a systematic whole. Such a systematic approach is often contrasted with a purposive or teleological approach. A teleological approach seeks to give effect to the objective of the specific statute or of the law in general. Unlike the literal approach, it is less tied to the ordinary meaning of rules in order to ensure that the overall objective is achieved. The literal approach is rarely used in relation to multi-lingual laws or treaties, but is frequently adopted for the interpretation of criminal or tax laws, which impose penalties or burdens. Because the legislature is not able to foresee all eventualities and is often unable to find time to amend legislation, the courts adopt a teleological approach, especially in relation to supranational legislation, eg from the **European Union**.

In undertaking interpretation, the courts frequently appeal to 'the intention of the legislature'. This is a construct that identifies the overall purpose of the legislation. In discerning such an intention attention is not typically limited to the context in which the text was originally enacted, but can frequently involve reference to more recent events so as to produce an intention that relates to all cognate provisions of the law currently in force. When lawyers interpret legislation they frequently have recourse to deliberations that preceded the enactment of a text as recorded in committee papers, parliamentary debates and so on. Legal systems differ about the weight to be attached to these. The extent to which courts can adopt a teleological approach, update the intention of Parliament, and rely on sources outside the text will depend on the contemporary role of the judges in law-making.   JOHN BELL

intersectional discrimination   *see* **multiple discrimination**

intersectionality   Intersectionality is a concept developed within black feminist theory to capture multiple and overlapping axis of subordination, particularly in relation to **race**, **gender**, and class. As a term, 'intersectionality' was first coined by legal theorist, Kimberle Crenshaw, to capture the ways in which race and gender interact to shape Black women's experiences. Intersectionality was distinguished from the idea of additive discrimination. Black women did not simply experience gender discrimination plus racial discrimination as two distinct systems of oppression. Rather, the idea underlying intersectionality was that the particular ways in which race, gender, and other forms of subordination intersect and overlap are mutually constitutive, creating unique experiences and locations of subordination. Crenshaw did not offer the concept of intersectionality as an overarching theory of **identity**, but instead, as a concept that could help to account for the multiple grounds of identity. In her work on **violence** against women, she further elaborated on different categories of intersectionality, including structural, political, and representational.

The idea of intersectionality built on previous black feminist theory, which was highly critical of both feminist theory and race theory for their insular focus on gender and race respectively. It was linked to the ideas of simultaneity developed in the 1970s by the Combahee River Collective, as well as other black feminist writers like bell hooks who were critical of the exclusive focus on gender within feminist theory, and its implicit privileging of the experiences of white **women**. The concept was used to theorize the ways in which the location of Black women at the intersection of multiple systems of subordination produced unique interests and identities. Patricia Collins Hill, for example, developed the concept of intersectionality in relation to the matrix of domination, that is, the overall organization of power in society. Black women were located at particular points of intersection of systems of race, class, gender, as well as sexuality, **ethnicity**, nation, and age within this matrix.

The concept of intersectionality has been extended beyond its roots in black feminist thought to examine the ways in which other disadvantaged groups are similarly located at points of multiple and overlapping axes of subordination. It has been used to explore, for example, the ways in which the study of sexuality **minorities** similarly requires attention to these intersecting vectors of subordination, such as race, gender, and class. Others have used the concept to challenge the black/white paradigm that has dominated race theory, particularly in the United States, in order to better capture the multiple identities and locations of Asian Americans and Latinos/as. At its most general, intersectionality has been expanded to encompass the relationship between multiple modalities of social relations and **subject** positions.

The concept has also been subject of debate and critique. While sympathetic to the project of developing more complex and robust analyses of subordination, some critics have noted that intersectionality is susceptible to the problem of infinite regress. As the categories of identity multiply, individual subjects risk becoming infinitely distinguishable from each other. Others have pointed to the problems of categories and identity politics that have plagued the concept of intersectionality, suggesting that it has focused too much attention on question of identity and difference, rather than more systemic analyses of the operation of power.

More recently, some scholars have gestured towards the development of post-intersectionality approaches that loosen their conceptual attachment to categories of identity. Concepts such as cosynthesis and symbiosis have emerged as possible replacements to intersectionality, as a way of capturing the ways in which the very categories themselves are not fixed and stable, but mutually producing and shifting over time and place.

At the same time, the concept of intersectionality continues to enjoy considerable analytic traction in a number of fields of study and debate. The idea of attending to the ways in which two or more forms of discrimination intersect has become the subject of discussion in forums ranging from **human rights** policy to international women's rights. As a legal and policy concept, intersectionality continues to structure discussions about **multiple discrimination** in human rights claims. Similarly, the concept of intersectionality continues to be deployed in concrete analyses of a range of public and social policies, from black women in politics, to HIV-infected women, to **rape** in war, and genocide. Despite the theoretical criticisms, the concept is contained in these studies by trying carefully to delineate the focus of the analysis to several or more axes of power.

BRENDA COSSMAN

K Crenshaw, 'Demarginalizing the Intersection of Race and Sex: A Black Feminist Critique of Antidiscrimination Doctrine, Feminist Theory and Antiracist Politics' (1989) *University of Chicago Legal Forum* 139

P Hill Collins, *Black Feminist Though: Knowledge, Consciousness and the Politics of Empowerment* (New York: Routledge, 1990)

inter-temporal law   The principle of the inter-temporal law in international law says that a juridical fact must be appreciated in the light of the law contemporary with it, and not the law in force at the time when the dispute in regard to it arises or is settled.

The doctrine is an essential element in the international law of title to territory, the function of which is to protect the stability of title. Suppose that title to some territory was obtained by military acts of conquest in the nineteenth century, when this was a lawful means of gaining title. If a dispute about title to the territory arose today, later changes in the law, which would deny legal effect to attempts to gain title in this way, would not destroy the title. However, developments in the law of self-determination have meant that the principle is no longer applied to full effect.

The principle of inter-temporal law is also an aspect of the interpretation of treaties. It serves to protect the sovereignty of states by focusing on the conditions when their consent to the treaty was given. Recently though, the principle is yielding to a combination of the effectiveness principle and the principle that treaties ought to be interpreted in the light of their (present) international legal context. This approach has been developed in the interpretation of the basic instruments of international organisations and of human rights treaties. It reflects the view that the objects of certain kinds of treaties are better achieved by a contextual interpretation, which may include taking account of changes in social practices, technical knowledge, and economic relations, as well as changes in the law itself.

COLIN WARBRICK

PC Jessup, 'The Palmas Island Arbitration' (1928) 22 *American Journal of International Law* 735

DW Greig, *Intertemporality and the Law of Treaties* (London: British Institute of International and Comparative Law, 2001)

intervention, prohibition of   The prohibition of intervention is based on the sovereignty and equality of states. Each state is free to choose its own economic, political, and social system and to determine its own foreign policy; it must not be subject to coercion in these regards. The **International Court of Justice** made an authoritative statement of the law in this area in *Military and Paramilitary Activities in and against Nicaragua (Nicaragua v USA)* (1986). In this case Nicaragua accused the USA of unlawful intervention through its support for the opposition forces whose aim was forcibly to overthrow the Nicaraguan government. The Court held that the USA, through its training, arming, equipping, financing, supplying, and otherwise encouraging, supporting, aiding, and directing military and paramilitary actions in and against Nicaragua, had violated **international law**. It found that the principle of non-intervention was part of **customary international law** as set out in the Friendly Relations Declaration (1970). This principle involves the right of every state to conduct its affairs and to choose its own form of government without outside interference. Every state has the duty to refrain from organizing acts of civil strife in another state and the duty not to foment, incite, or tolerate subversive, terrorist, or armed activities directed towards the violent overthrow of the regime of another state. States in practice have not expressly claimed such a right to overthrow a foreign government. The International Court of Justice recently confirmed this statement of the law in the case concerning *Armed Activities on the Territory of the Congo (DRC v Uganda)* (2005).

The International Court of Justice deliberately left open the controversial question of the right of a state to intervene to assist a national liberation movement. During the decolonization process a clear division was drawn between states on this issue. Former colonies and developing states generally supported the right of peoples subject to colonial or alien domination to use force against the colonial government and to seek forcible assistance from third states in pursuit of self-determination; colonial powers resisted such a right to use force. This debate is now of mainly historical interest except in cases such as that of the Palestinians.

The Court drew a fundamental distinction between unlawful assistance to an opposition to help it forcibly overthrow a government, and assistance to a government, which is generally lawful. Although intervention to overthrow a government was common during the Cold War it was generally covert. States in practice did not openly assert such a right to intervene. And today most states still regard forcible 'regime change' as unlawful. It is also doubtful whether humanitarian intervention is an exception to the prohibition of intervention. Even assistance to a government may be problematic in the absence of express Security Council authorization; during the Cold War there were frequent disagreements as to which body actually constituted the legitimate government. The traditional rule is that it is forbidden to intervene in a civil war even to assist the government, but third states have circumvented this prohibition by claiming that a particular conflict does not amount to a civil war and that their intervention is simply to help to maintain order. More recently the USA has claimed the right to intervene to assist foreign governments in a 'war on drugs' or the 'war on terror'. States are very reluctant to admit the existence of a civil war on their territory. However, once there has been a prior foreign intervention against the government, it is accepted that assistance to a government may be permissible in response.

CHRISTINE GRAY

See also: **use of force**

interviewing   *see* **lawyering skills**

intestacy   *see* **death in the family**

intimidation   *see* **economic torts**

investment diversification   A key principle of efficient investment is that the risks of investments should be diversified across different corporate sectors, geographic sectors, asset sectors (such as equities, bonds, fund investments, property) and so on. The risks of a particular company's investment in securities can be diversified across investments in different industry sectors, while the risks of an overall domestic market can be diversified through a portfolio of **securities** issued by international issuers or companies. The benefits of risk management by international diversification, particularly for large institutional investors such as pension funds, are regarded as a key potential benefit of the integrated EU financial market sought by the new regulatory framework for financial markets adopted under the EU's Financial Services Action Plan, which has had major implications for UK financial markets.

Financial market regulators often seek to promote diversification and to educate investors (especially retail investors) about the benefits of diversification. **Collective investment schemes**, in particular, are favourably regarded as allowing investors to achieve diversification efficiently and to benefit from the fund's economies of scale. The major regulated collective investment scheme marketed in the UK and across the EU, the UCITS (Undertaking for Collective Investment in Transferable Securities), is subject to specific regulation which addresses the type and proportion of assets in which a UCITS fund can invest and which is designed to promote diversification.

NIAMH MOLONEY

See also: **European Union influence on financial markets**

investment firm licensing   In order to provide investment services in the UK, investment firms need to be licensed—or to use the technical term—'authorized'. This requirement was first imposed on all investment firms in the UK by the Financial Services Act 1986 and is now contained in the **Financial Services and Markets Act 2000**. All Member States of the EU have been obliged to have a licensing system for those investment firms based in their territories since the Investment Services Directive of 1993 was adopted (replaced by 'MiFID': the Markets in Financial Instruments Directive 2004). A so-called 'single market' in financial services operates in the EU so that once a firm obtains a licence (or authorization) to undertake that activity in its 'home' EU state, it may provide that service anywhere in the EU after merely notifying the licensing authority of the 'host' EU state. The firm is said to have the 'EU single passport' in that a licence from its home state dispenses with the need to obtain a licence elsewhere in the EU. Underpinning this system are uniform licensing requirements imposed by EU legislation; and these are given effect in the UK by the Financial Services and Markets Act 2000. The UK authority responsible for licensing UK investment firms (and also banks and insurance companies) is the **Financial Services Authority** (the 'FSA').

Licensing is essentially a vetting process and achieves two main objectives. First it controls who may undertake the activity; it regulates who may enter the market as service provider. Secondly, it provides a means to control how the licensee operates, most obviously by the threat of revoking the licence. Investment activity is regarded as needing such control for a number of reasons. The first reason is investor protection. Investment firms, whether they promote or sell investment products, provide investment advice, or manage investments, have plenty of opportunities to make money at their clients' expense. This is especially the case with retail clients who have little choice but to rely on the probity and expertise of investment firms. There have been many instances when clients have lost money through the fraud or incompetence of their investment dealers, advisers, or managers. The second reason for controlling investment firms is the so-called 'systemic risk' they pose. This is well recognized in the banking sector where the collapse of one bank may affect the whole financial system. However, it is also a problem in the case of investment firms whose failure may have a contagion effect.

The conditions that an investment firm must satisfy in order to become and remain authorized are essentially threefold: probity, competence, and adequate financial resources. The first condition is particularly important in a sector that deals with large amounts of other people's money. The need for competence is also obvious, as is the need to ensure that investment firms remain solvent, the latter being secured through the financial resources requirement. The FSA undertakes a rigorous vetting process in deciding which firms to authorize. It requires applicants to submit an application pack with detailed information about those intending to run the business and with a business plan and details as to financial resources. The authorization is tailored to the applicant and so is limited in scope to specified investment activities and is often subject to 'requirements' which further circumscribe the nature of the activities the firm may undertake. The FSA keeps a register, open to public inspection, of those it authorizes.

Obtaining authorization brings with it regulatory control by the FSA. The FSA has issued a detailed 'Handbook' which contains the rules that authorized persons must comply with. These rules reflect the twin objectives of investor protection and the avoidance of systemic risk. There are rules on how investment business is to be conducted and what financial resources the investment firm must maintain to ensure its solvency. The FSA also monitors whether authorized firms comply with the rules by requiring them periodically to notify it of relevant information and by having the power to undertake its own investigations. The FSA also has disciplinary powers over those it authorizes: it can publicly reprimand, impose unlimited financial 'penalties' and ultimately limit or revoke the licence to operate. Investment firms that wish to challenge the FSA in the exercise of these powers may take the matter to the Financial Services and Markets Tribunal which can decide the issue anew. An appeal on issues of law which arise may be brought to the ordinary courts.

As well as having the assurance that an authorized investment firm is subject to regulatory oversight, some clients of an authorized investment firm are able to resort to the Financial Services Compensation Scheme if the firm nevertheless becomes insolvent. Authorized investment firms are also required to be members of the Financial Ombudsman Scheme which provides a swift and informal mechanism, as an alternative to court proceedings, to deal with disputes that clients have with investment firms.

The requirement for authorization is underpinned by a number of sanctions. First, an investment firm that undertakes investment business without becoming authorized commits a criminal offence. Secondly, a non-authorized firm cannot enforce any agreements it makes and clients may choose to undo any agreements entered into. In addition, if an authorized firm makes agreements as a result of referrals from a non-authorized firm, those agreements are also unenforceable and in this way authorized firms have an incentive to check that those who refer clients to them are also duly authorized. Thirdly, the FSA is given the power to apply to court on behalf of investors for compensation orders if clients of a non-authorized firm have lost money and for 'disgorgement of profits' orders if the firm has made profits. However, clients of non-authorized firms have no recourse either to the Financial Services Compensation Scheme or to the Financial Ombudsman Scheme.   EVA LOMNICKA

See also: **bank runs and capital adequacy; conduct of business regulation; European Union influence of on financial markets; financial regulation; investor compensation schemes; mis-selling of investment products; ombudsmen**

investment protection   The protection of investment is a long-standing concern in international law. It is closely linked to the process of decolonization. The first disputes arose in the nineteenth century in the context of injuries to aliens and their property in the newly independent states of Latin America, resulting in diplomatic claims by the national state of the investor and, at times, forcible intervention. Such cases led to the development, by the major Western powers, of international minimum standards of treatment under **customary international law**. These aimed to establish binding rules of protection for aliens' rights to property and for the observance of contracts by host countries. They were backed up by rights to compensation and **international dispute settlement**.

Such international rules were opposed by the Latin American countries, which argued that foreign investors were entitled to no more than the same treatment as national investors, and to remedies before local courts and tribunals only. This was known as the Calvo Doctrine, after the Argentine jurist Carlos Calvo, who is seen as its progenitor. Similar concerns were expressed in later times by other countries. Thus, in the early twentieth century, following the socialist revolutions in Mexico and Russia, mass nationalizations of foreign owned property occurred in defiance of the Western powers' international standards of treatment. Again, after World War II, the mass decolonization movement in Asia and Africa was accompanied, by the early 1970s, with calls for a New International Economic Order ('NIEO') which sought, among other things, to enshrine a state's right to regulate its natural wealth and resources and to control multinational corporations that invested upon its territory.

In respect of the latter the United Nations established a Commission on Transnational Corporations ('TNCs') which was tasked with the development of a binding Code of Conduct for TNCs when investing in host countries. These demands for economic self-determination, as an aspect of wider political self-determination, were opposed by the major Western powers, which saw them as an unwarranted intervention by the state into private commercial activities. They acted to prevent the adoption of the UN Code of Conduct, offering an alternative code in the Organization of Economic Cooperation and Development ('OECD') Guidelines on Multinational Enterprises. In addition, investment protection was furthered by the conclusion of bilateral investment treaties ('BITs') between capital exporting and capital importing countries. Such treaties contain general standards of protection, including non-discrimination and fair and equitable treatment, and specific standards such as controls over expropriation and guarantees of full protection and security of investments and the free transfer of funds. A further important feature is the inclusion of investor-state dispute resolution procedures, which allow the investor to select international arbitration in cases where an amicable settlement of a dispute has failed. In such cases the most significant choice is for investor-state arbitration before the World Bank Centre for Settlement of Investment Disputes ('ICSID'). There are now around 3,000 BITs. They are complemented by Free Trade Agreements and Regional Economic Integration Agreements that contain investment protection provisions.   PETER MUCHLINSKI

PT Muchlinski, *Multinational Enterprises and the Law* (Oxford: Oxford University Press, 2nd edn, 2007) Pt IV
United Nations Conference on Trade and Development (UNCTAD) *International Investment Agreements: Key Issues* (New York and Geneva, United Nations, 2004, 3 Volumes). Available at www.unctad.org/iia.

investment tax   *see* **savings taxes**

investor compensation schemes   Investor compensation schemes pay compensation to investors when an investment firm fails without fulfilling its obligations to its clients. Their primary purpose is to increase investor confidence in the investment services market. The existence of such schemes encourages investors to use the services of an investment firm, safe in the knowledge that they are protected if the firm becomes insolvent. In the banking context, the analogous deposit-protection schemes also contribute to systemic stability in reducing the likelihood of customers rushing to withdraw funds. Such potential contagion, although less of a problem in the investment firm sector, also provides further justification for investor compensation schemes in that they ensure an orderly resolution of investors' claims. Such schemes are generally funded by the investment firms, usually by way of direct levy.

There are a number of arguments against investor compensation schemes, all based on their anti-competitive effect. One is that they distort **competition** in protecting customers of all firms to the same extent and in requiring prudent and solvent firms to pay for those firms that fail. Another (the so-called '**moral hazard**' problem) is that the existence of such schemes provides no incentive to investors to choose carefully the firms they use. Hence, it is argued, reckless firms promising unrealistic returns thrive at the expense of the more prudent who, if the reckless fail, then have to underwrite their losses. In partial response to these concerns, most compensation schemes only pay compensation in relation to a proportion (typically 90 per cent) of the claim.

Historically, individual compensation schemes were established in the UK in the various sectors of the financial services industry. The initiative for the first scheme, the London Stock Exchange's Compensation Fund, came from the sector itself, with the aim of instilling investor confidence in that market. However, when the individual regulatory regimes relating to insurance, banking, and investment business were placed on a statutory footing, compensation schemes became part of those statutory regimes. Those schemes have now been amalgamated into one 'Financial Services Compensation Scheme' ('FSCS'), which provides compensation to certain customers of most financial firms authorised by **Financial Services Authority** ('FSA'). Meanwhile, as part of the establishment of the EU 'single market' in financial services, Member States became obliged to operate compensation schemes in the banking and investment business sectors.

Although there is now just one FSCS in the UK, in its funding and amounts payable, it is essentially sub-divided into the main sectors it covers: banking, insurance, and investment business. To avoid cross-subsidy between the various sectors, levies from firms in each sector fund claims in that sector. Moreover, the maximum amounts payable vary and reflect the historic position before the FSCS was established (a maximum of £31,700 for bank deposits, £48,000 for investment business, and an unlimited amount for insurance business), with a cap of 90 per cent of the amount claimed. EVA LOMNICKA

See also: **banking and investment services industry; bank runs and capital adequacy; deposit protection; European Union influence of on financial markets; investment firm licensing**

investor protection in securities markets
Securities markets enable investors to deal in various **securities**, typically company **shares**, bonds, and more sophisticated 'instruments'. Companies issue securities in order to raise capital for the business they undertake. Investors part with their money in acquiring these securities in the hope that their capital will appreciate and/or will produce income. The markets therefore facilitate both the initial issuing of the securities (the primary market) to investors and the subsequent dealing by investors in those securities (the secondary market). Investor confidence in securities markets is accordingly essential to the successful raising of capital in this manner. However, investor confidence can be undermined in a number of ways, and hence securities markets are characterized by special investor protection measures which seek to maintain investor confidence.

Investors in securities merely acquire intangible rights and therefore their position is very different from that of investors in tangible property, who at least acquire a physical asset they can value and take care of. The value, present and future, of intangible rights is dependant entirely on the status and future performance of the issuer of those rights, and accurate information about these factors is crucial to investment decisions. Investor confidence will be threatened if the information on which the price of securities is based is incomplete or inaccurate.

Redressing the 'information asymmetry' which exists between the investor and issuer is a key feature of investor protection in securities markets. For this reason, issuers wishing to be admitted to a securities market are invariably obliged to comply with mandatory disclosure requirements, both at the time of the issue of the securities and on an on-going basis. Not only does such mandatory disclosure enhance investor confidence that the true financial position of the issuer is revealed, but it also promotes the efficient allocation of capital to those issuers that are genuinely more successful. However, some argue that mandatory disclosure is not enough and that there should also be a degree of so-called 'merit' **regulation** where further control is exercised over the offer process or even the nature of the issuer. However, securities markets in developed economies limit their investor protection to requiring issuers to disclose specified information at specified times. On the other hand, intermediaries who deal in or manage securities are subject to more interventionist regulation, which ensures that they are 'fit and proper' and operate in accordance with conduct of business rules.

Whilst, in a free market, the price of all commodities is determined by the forces of supply and demand, the securities markets are particularly vulnerable to interference in this price-forming process, for example by the dissemination of false information or the undertaking of artificial transactions. Attempts to protect investors from such **market manipulation** activities by penalizing those engaging in them is a feature of most securities markets. The prohibition of **insider dealing** is also sometimes justified on the basis of investor protection: ensuring that all investors have access to the same information and hence that the markets are 'fair'. EVA LOMNICKA

See also: **conduct of business regulation; disclosure in financial markets; financial regulation; investment firm licensing; stock exchange**

Iran-US Claims Tribunal   *see* **international courts and tribunals**

***IRC v Duke of Westminster* (1936)** This case once defined the approach of the **United Kingdom** courts in tax cases, viz. that they were confined to applying the words of the statute literally, whether for or against a taxpayer, and took a rather blinkered view of the facts. This meant that they would decide a case in favour of a taxpayer even though the facts presented a carefully crafted and, in some sense, quite artificial scheme created solely for the purpose of avoiding tax. This is no longer the correct approach to **tax avoidance**, as the **House of Lords** explained most recently in 2004. However the case is also authority for the more general proposition that when the courts interpret legal rules based on legal rights, courts are bound by those rights and not by some underlying 'substance'. This is, in broad terms, still good law; but the modern approach is to point out that this leaves the court with the task of deciding what the true legal rights are, and that courts are free to take a broader view of the facts. In other jurisdictions (the United States, for instance), the judicial balance between form and substance is struck differently.

The problem: an employer (D, the Duke) pays E, his employee, £15 a week. D makes a legally binding promise to pay E £5 a week for a period of seven years, whether or not E remains in D's service. D explains to E that while E is still legally entitled to the full £15 a week by way of wages in addition to the promised £5, he is expected to take only the balance of £10 by way of wages, so that E's total receipts remain unchanged (£15).

How should the £5 payment to E be classified for income tax purposes? The Inland Revenue argued that the payment of £5 per week should be treated as employment income. D argued that the income was an annual payment and so, under rules no longer in force, D could deduct the payment in computing total income. D emphasized that his 'advice' to E not to claim his full wage in addition to the payment was not legally binding. Moreover, E was entitled to the £5 per week even if he left D's employment. Four members of the House agreed with D. This decision led to the 'Westminster approach' of benevolent neutrality to tax avoidance, famously summarized by Lord Tomlin: 'Every man is entitled if he can to arrange his affairs so that the tax attaching under the appropriate Acts is less than it otherwise would be'.

One judge, Lord Atkin, rejected D's analysis of the legal rights, holding that E was not entitled to the £5 in addition to the wage of £15 and so the whole weekly payment of £15 was employment income. Today, many people, including many judges, prefer Lord Atkin's decision, but largely because they would agree with his analysis of the legal rights.

JOHN TILEY

Lord Robert Walker, 'Ramsay 25 Years On' (2004) 120 Law Quarterly Review 412–427

A Likhovski, 'The Duke and the Lady: Helvering v. Gregory and the History of Tax Avoidance Adjudication' (2004) 25 Cardozo Law Review 953–1018

See also: **income tax**

Irish law Prior to the arrival of the Anglo-Normans in the twelfth century, Ireland had its own indigenous system of law. **Brehon law**, as it is referred to, was developed from custom and existed in oral tradition until it was written down in Irish law tracts in the seveneth and eighth centuries. Shortly after the Anglo-Norman invasion of 1169, led by Strongbow, King Henry II held a Council in Waterford in which he declared that 'that laws of England were by all freely received and confirmed'. Despite numerous attempts to affirm the supremacy of English laws, it was not until the seventeenth century that such laws began to dominate in the greater part of Ireland. This supremacy was further consolidated by Oliver Cromwell's military campaign (1649–52), the Penal Laws of the late seventeenth and eighteenth centuries which facilitated the legal establishment of a Protestant Ascendancy, and the Act of Union of 1800 which dissolved the Irish Parliament and established the **Westminster Parliament** in London as the sole legislative body of the **United Kingdom** and Ireland.

Following the War of Independence (January 1919–July 1921), a truce was declared between the British forces and Irish nationalists. This led to the Anglo-Irish Treaty of 1921 which was signed on the 6 December by British and Irish plenipotentiaries. It provided for the establishment of an Irish Free State (Saorstát Eireann)—eventually comprising twenty-six of the thirty-two counties of the island of Ireland—which would have dominion status within the British **Commonwealth**. The Treaty was approved by the Dáil (the lower house of the Oireachtas, the Irish Parliament) in January 1922 by sixty-four votes to fifty-seven. The Free State Constitution was adopted on 11 October 1922 but was subject to the provisions of the Treaty. Gradually, however, all links with the **Crown** were removed and in 1937 a new Constitution (Bunreacht na hÉireann) was introduced after it had been put to a plebiscite (685,105 in favour to 526,945 against). It declared that Ireland (Éire) was a '[s]overeign independent and democratic state'. In April 1949 Ireland was declared a republic and ceased to be a member of the Commonwealth.

Ireland's modern legal system is comprised of a number of sources. First it is derived from the English **common law** tradition. Indeed Ireland is often described as 'the first adventure of the common law'.

Law-making power is also conferred on a bicam-eral legislature, the Oireachtas, by Article 15.2.1° of the Constitution. Ordinarily a Bill is signed into law by the Irish President between five and seven days of its being passed by the Oireachtas. The Act is then promulgated by the publication of a notice that it has become law in Iris Oifigiúil (the Irish Gazette). In certain circumstances, however, the President may, having consulted with the Council of State, refuse to sign a Bill that has been presented for signature. The Bill is then either referred to the Supreme Court for a decision on its constitutionality, or, if it involves a proposal of 'national importance', the will of the people is sought.

The 1937 Constitution (Bunreacht na hÉireann) provides a source of law superior to both common law and legislation. It can be divided into two compo-nents: those articles which describe the institutions of State (the President, the Oireachtas, the Executive, and the Courts) and those which describe the funda-mental rights of persons. In addition to these rights, Article 40.3 has, since the 1960s, proved a source of additional unenumerated rights including the right to bodily integrity, the right to travel, the right to procreate, and the right to marital privacy. The Constitution can only be altered by a referendum in which every citizen in Ireland aged eighteen or over is entitled to vote.

Ireland, along with the UK and Denmark, became a member of the European Economic Community (as it then was) on the 1 January 1973, following a ref-erendum in which 83 per cent of Irish citizens voted in favour of membership. No provision of the Con-stitution can invalidate laws enacted, acts done or measures adopted by the state necessitated by mem-bership of the **European Union**. A commitment to the principles of **international law** is also enshrined in the Constitution, though a dualist approach is adopted in that any international agreement must be specifically enacted into domestic law by the Oire-achtas. For example, although the **European Con-vention on Human Rights** entered into force in Ireland in 1953, it did not form part of domestic law until the Oireachtas adopted legislation in 2003 to give it further effect.

SHANE KILCOMMINS

R Byrne and JP McCutcheon, *The Irish Legal System* (Dublin: Lexis Nexis, 4th edn, 2001)

G Hogan and G Whyte, *Kelly's Irish Constitution* (Dublin: Butterworths, 4th edn, 2003)

Irving v Penguin Books and Deborah Lipstadt

This **libel** action, fought in the High Court from 11 January to 11 April 2000, centred on allegations made by the American historian Deborah Lipstadt in her book *Denying the Holocaust: the Growing Assault on Truth and Memory*, published in the USA in 1993 and in the UK by Penguin Books the follow-ing year. Lipstadt alleged that a growing number of individuals and organizations denied that the Ger-man Nazis had killed some 6 million European Jews during the Second World War, and that they claimed that there had been no gas chambers and no central order from Hitler, the German leader, to kill the Jews. Lipstadt declared that the deniers falsified the evi-dence in order to reach their perverse and erroneous conclusions and that they were motivated mainly by anti-Semitism. Amongst the deniers she numbered David Irving, a freelance writer who had written a number of books on Hitler and the German conduct of the Second World War.

Irving issued a writ for defamation in September 1996. Irving waited for publication in the UK not only because he was a British citizen but also because English libel law was more favourable to the claim-ant than its American counterpart, which requires proof of malice and allows a defendant to claim 'fair comment' where the allegations were made against a 'public figure' (a very broadly defined term that would certainly have included Irving).

The defence was undertaken by the solicitors Anthony Julius and James Libson, of the London partnership Mishcon de Reya. In view of the fact that Irving's reputation and income were undoubtedly damaged by Lipstadt's allegations, they opted for the defence of 'justification'; ie they undertook to prove that Lipstadt's allegations were true, an absolute defence in English law. Expert academic witnesses were engaged to present the evidence Irving was alleged to have falsified, and to examine his work, comparing it with the sources on which he claimed to base it, in order to test the veracity of Lipstadt's allegations. Irving agreed that in view of the tech-nicalities involved, including the close examination of texts in the German language, the trial should be held without a jury. He conducted his own case as a litigant in person. The defence was led by Mr Richard Rampton QC. In an extensive cross-examination of Irving he effectively forced him to admit numerous instances of falsification and Holocaust denial in his work. In his cross-examination of the expert wit-nesses, Irving failed to cast doubt on their detailed demonstration of the truth of Lipstadt's central allegations.

Mr Justice Gray concluded that Irving was a Holo-caust denier who doctored the historical evidence to make it conform to his pro-Nazi, anti-Semitic prejudices. He found in favour of the defendants and awarded them costs, which came to over £2 million. Irving refused to pay and was declared bankrupt. His application for leave to appeal was rejected by the Court of Appeal. The case aroused worldwide media attention and resulted in the final and complete discrediting of Irving as a historian and of Holocaust denial in general. RICHARD EVANS

R J Evans, *Telling Lies About Hitler: The Holocaust, History, and the David Irving Trial* (London: Verso, 2002)

D E Lipstadt, *History on Trial. My Day in Court with David Irving* (HarperCollins: New York, 2005)

Islamic law Islamic law is one of the most important non-Western laws in the world today. It continues to be applied to hundreds of millions of Muslims in many countries and recently there has been a resurgence of interest in its application to areas such as commerce and estate planning. Islamic law is not a single, monolithic, or unified system but is made up of a number of traditions each of which is considered valid.

In Arabic, Islamic law is known as 'the Shari'a', meaning 'path' or a 'guide'. This name refers to the all-encompassing nature of Islamic law, which purports to provide a set of principles for living a good Muslim life that, if followed, will ensure the Muslim adherent everlasting life in Paradise. Thus the Shari'a contains rules concerning moral and religious behaviour; these are considered to be just as much part of the law as rules on matters such as marriage and inheritance. Islamic law classifies conduct according to a five fold system: prohibited actions, actions detested but not prohibited, recommended actions, mandatory actions, and actions about which Islamic law is indifferent.

Islamic law is a divine law in the sense that Islamic legal scholars consider the two main formal sources of the law—the Qur'an and the Sunna—to have been divinely inspired through the agency of the Prophet Muhammad, who lived in what is now Saudi Arabia from c570–632 CE. The Qur'an is the single most important original written source of Islamic law. It is considered to be the actual word of Allah as revealed to Muhammad. Strictly the whole of the Qur'an is law in the Islamic sense of a set of beliefs and precedents for the ideal conduct required of individuals by Allah. Thus, the Qur'an contains many specific provisions on prayer, fasting, giving alms, Hajj and other similar religious duties. The Qur'an is more a religious and historical than a legal text. Hence it contains few of what a Western lawyer would recognize as legal rules providing clear guidelines and definitions. The legal rules in the Qur'an pertain mainly to family matters (succession, marriage, and divorce), but there are also some rules on criminal law (such as the crimes of adultery, slander, and wine drinking), evidence (the acceptance of witnesses), and a few commercial matters (the importance of written contracts and the prohibition of riba, translated variously as 'unjust gain', 'interest', or 'usury'). Of 6,000 verses in the Qur'an perhaps no more than 600 have a legal content in the Islamic sense; and perhaps only 100 have such content in a Western sense.

The second major source of Islamic law is the Sunna, which means 'practice' or 'tradition' and refers to collections of stories ('hadith') about the sayings and doings of the Prophet Muhammad. The Prophet's actions were considered to be divinely inspired by Allah, and he became an example of what it is to live the good Muslim life. The stories were at first transmitted orally and were not written down until about a century after the Prophet's death. A number of different collections of hadith exist, varying very considerably in size and content. Over time, however, certain texts gained acceptance as being authoritative. This is a much bigger source of law than the Qur'an, but like the Qur'an it lacks organizing elements or general principles.

What we now call the principles of Islamic law were developed by religious jurists called 'fuqaha'. In the eighth and ninth centuries CE each major urban centre of the newly expanding Islamic world developed its own school of Islamic law (mathhab) centred around an Islamic scholar who sought to develop workable legal rules by applying the Qur'an and Sunna to particular circumstances (ijtihad) by the methods of analogy (qiyas) and consensus (ijma). These became accepted as supplementary sources of Islamic law. Over time, some of the schools merged while others failed, and by the eleventh century CE four main schools of Islamic law existed: the Hanafi, the Maliki, the Shafi'i, and the Hanbali, each named after and based upon the teachings and inspiration of a particular Islamic jurist, and associated with a geographical and urban centre. As the religion of Islam spread so did the schools of Islamic law. Hanafi law is applied on the Indian sub-continent, Shafi'i law in South East Asia and Indonesia; Maliki law predominates in sub-Saharan Africa.

The Islamic jurists were religious men and academics who gave opinions (fatawa—plural of 'fatwa')

which could be referred to in an Islamic court. From the earliest times, Islamic law was applied in Islamic courts by judges called 'qadis'. They were quasi-governmental officials and religious leaders who had learnt Islamic law at one of the recognized religious centres in the Islamic world such as the University of Al-Azhar in Cairo, founded in 975 CE. However, Islamic law permitted the operation of other religious courts, such as Christian and Jewish courts applying Christian and Jewish law respectively. Islamic rulers also created courts to hear complaints against the administration ('mathalim' courts) and minor criminal matters ('shurta' courts).

From the beginning of the nineteenth century the history of the Islamic world is one of increasing Western colonial domination and reduced application of Islamic law. The decline of Islamic law was partly forced—as where the colonial power simply replaced Islamic law in certain areas by Western laws and courts (as was done, for example, by France and Great Britain in the Levant), and partly voluntary—for example the Ottoman Empire adopted a number of Western-style laws in order to be able to join the Club of Europe. The Ottoman Empire was also responsible for the first attempt to codify parts of Islamic law in a Civil Code (Mejelle) of 1876 and the Ottoman Law of Family Rights of 1917. These incursions into traditional Islamic law were highly controversial at the time and engendered a debate—which continues to this day–about the role and place of Islamic law in the modern state.

In recent times, a number of Muslim states, such as Tunisia and Egypt, have abolished separate Islamic courts even though their legal systems continue to be partly based on Islamic law. The Constitutions of almost all modern Muslim states give Islamic law a major role in the legal system, and many Muslim states have codified the areas of Islamic law which are still applicable. However, in Saudi Arabia substantive Islamic law is still uncodified, although the King has laid down by decree rules for the jurisdiction and procedure of the Shari'a courts which are more in accordance with modern standards.

The foregoing account is based on the Sunni tradition of Islamic legal theory, which was historically and still is the dominant tradition of Islamic law. The Shia sect, to which approximately 10 per cent of Muslims belong, resulted from a political rift which dates back to the very beginnings of Islam. The Shia descend from a group that attributed sole religious and secular authority to descendants of the Prophet. This doctrine was anathema to the mainstream group (now known as Sunnis) who chose leaders on the basis of merit and support within the Islamic community. Shia legal theory—which is sometimes called the fifth school of Islamic law—is based on the doctrine of the Imamate, which reveres the writings of certain descendants of the Prophet. The major school of Shia law (the Ithna Ashari or Twelvers) reveres the first twelve descendants of the Prophet Muhammad (known as Imams). Thus, Shia law permits the family of the Prophet in the present day (such as the Aga Khan for the Ismaili sect) and agents on behalf of the twelfth Imam (such as the Grand Ayatollah of Iran) to act as interpreters of the law. As a result, Shia law can be altered more easily than Sunni law to accord with changing social norms.

In the contemporary world, both Islamic and non-Islamic, the application of Islamic law has become a much-debated topic. On one side are those who seek to apply some version of Islamic law to the exclusion of all other laws; and on the other are those who seek to develop Islamic law in line with social and moral changes in society either by some form of re-interpretation of the original sources or more radically by hybridization with Western law or even replacement by Western law. The non-Islamic world is as much concerned with this as the Islamic world as increasing numbers of Muslim immigrants to Western countries seek to harmonize their Islamic religious and legal obligations with the duties required of them by secular or quasi-Christian states. Some issues—such as wearing of the veil—are more cultural than legal or religious, but the rise of new forms of Islamic finance and banking is one example of how Western and Islamic ideas can be merged to the advantage of both systems. More controversial is the suggestion that Shari'a courts applying Islamic law to Muslims should be set up and recognized by Western states. Even if this is a purely voluntary jurisdiction—for instance, for arbitration of family disputes prior to divorce—many people oppose the creation of avowedly religious tribunals.   IAN EDGE

NJ Coulson, *A History of Islamic Law* (Edinburgh: Edinburgh University Press, 1964)

J Schacht, *An Introduction to Islamic Law* (Oxford: Clarendon Press, 1964)

Israeli law   *see* **mixed jurisdictions**

Israeli Wall Case   In December 2003 the Tenth Emergency Session of the **United Nations** General Assembly adopted resolution ES-10/14, in which it asked the International Court of Justice to give an Advisory Opinion on the question of the legal consequences of the construction of a wall by Israel in the Occupied Palestinian Territory, including in and around East Jerusalem. The General Assembly was able to seek the Opinion because the Security Council, which has primary responsibility under the UN Charter for the maintenance of international peace and security, had failed to exercise that responsibility as the result of a series of vetoes cast by the United States. The 'Uniting for Peace' resolution, 377A (v), adopted by the General Assembly in 1950 affirms the right of the General Assembly to act in such circumstances.

Forty-eight states and international organizations made written submissions to the Court; and fourteen states and international organizations, and Palestine, made oral submissions to the Court, relying heavily upon factual data drawn from UN and Israelis sources. Israel did not appear before the Court.

The Court's judgment affirmed the status of the territory to the east of the 1949 Armistice line (the Green Line) occupied by Israel in the 1967 Arab-Israel conflict, including East Jerusalem, as Palestinian territory under military occupation by Israel. The Court held that Israeli settlements in the West Bank had been established in breach of **international law**, and that the Wall (or 'security barrier', as Israel called it) erected by Israel created a *fait accompli* which could become permanent and amount to *de facto* annexation of Palestinian territory. The judgment also affirmed that **international humanitarian law**, the law of war, and **international human rights law** apply cumulatively in the Occupied Territory under conditions of military occupation. The right of self-defence under Article 51 of the UN Charter, possessed by Israel, did not override Israel's legal obligations as an occupying power.

The Court found that the Wall, and the legal regime imposed with it, violated international law and the provisions of several international **human rights** instruments, and that Israel was under a duty to dismantle the Wall and to make reparation for the damage arising from its unlawful conduct. The case concerned only those parts of the Wall constructed on Palestinian territory: Palestine and others specifically acknowledged the right of Israel to build a 'security barrier' on Israel's own territory.

VAUGHAN LOWE

IT in legal education Information and Communications Technologies ('IT') are transforming both the world of law and legal education through a wide range of equipment from personal computers to mobile MP3s, software ranging from word processors to simulations and internet-based systems. The law has to cope increasingly with issues such as electronic commerce, intellectual property, fraud, and **pornography**. Lawyers use complex technology in drafting documents and litigation. The internet has changed the way people interact—for example IT enables new kinds of cooperative interaction such as *myspace (www.myspace.com)*, *wikipedia (www.wikipedia.org)*, *Second Life* (www.secondlife.com), and *free and open software* (www.fsf.org, www.opensource.org).

Today's law student learns mainly through lectures and textbooks and writes exams on paper. And yet, information technology has become ubiquitous to student learning as legal education adapts to change. Law courses increasingly involve dealing with technology issues. The nature of education itself is changing through *eLearning*, which involves the use of computer and mobile devices and a wide range of learning techniques.

First, students can access online texts of laws, case reports, and law journals, using either dedicated services such as LEXIS (*www.lexis.com*) or Google and Wikipedia as starting points. Course teachers provide lecture notes, presentations, illustrations, links to online reference material and, occasionally, audio or video 'webcasts' of lectures accessible anywhere at any time. Secondly, 'courseware' such as IOLIS (*http://www.law.warwick.ac.uk/lcc/iolis*) involves multimedia interactive exercises solving hypothetical legal problems or complex series of questions, answers, and feedback. Thirdly, the classroom also becomes transformed as course teachers use *powerpoint* slides and the internet to illustrate their talks with text, audio, and video. Students may have access to internet on their laptops in the classroom as aids to classroom discussion and exercises. Electronic Whiteboards enable the lecturer or student to project computer images on a whiteboard while writing and drawing on the board with electronic pens. Fourthly, advanced learning systems enable the students to work in virtual groups. For example, the Glasgow Graduate School's Transactional Learning Environment (*http://technologies.law.strath.ac.uk/simple*) enables student teams to work as lawyers in litigating hypothetical cases in Ardcalloch virtual town. Alternatively, students can collaborate to develop a legal website.

This gradual electronic transformation of learning has several implications. First, emphasis shifts from lecturers to independently learning students who, individually or collaboratively, explore the knowledge world under lecturers' expert guidance.

Secondly, IT can manage the simulated and even live delivery of the actual experience of lawyering to large numbers of students. Thirdly, learning becomes global as students can access law of any country and communicate with law students anywhere. Fourthly, IT enables the rise of multi-campus and virtual law schools. Fifthly, most law schools don't abandon traditional teaching but blend the old with IT. Sixthly, fear of plagiarism means that systems of exam-based assessment have hardly changed, in spite of the great potential of electronic forms of assessment such as e-portfolios and computer assisted assessment.

In conclusion, virtue is gradually being recognized in the virtual, but not by abandoning the real.

ABDUL PALIWALA

P Maharg and A Paliwala, 'Negotiating the Learning Process with Electronic Resources' in R Burridge et al (eds), *Effective Teaching and Learning in Law* (London: Kogan Page, 2002)

UK Centre for Legal Education Website, *ELearning http://www.ukcle.ac.uk/resources/ict/index.html* (accessed 1 February 2007)

IT skills   *see* **IT in legal education**

IVF treatment   *see* **assisted conception**

J

Japanese law Japan has a well-established legal system that is institutionally and functionally similar to those of the industrial democracies of Western Europe. Formal legal processes are profoundly influenced, however, by deeply embedded communitarian values and orientations. Japanese law reflects several influences. These include patterns of law and governance affected initially by Chinese conceptions of law and a millennium of administrative control by a warrior class. Beginning in the late nineteenth century European-based codes and institutions were introduced and effectively adapted in a process of transforming institutional reform. By the turn of the twentieth century the five basic codes—the civil, criminal, commercial, and two procedural codes—had been enacted, and the basic structure of Japan's contemporary legal system formed. The 1889 Constitution provided the framework, introducing the principle of representative government and an independent judiciary. Since 1945 the influence of the United States as well as the **European Union** has produced a hybrid of approaches. The mix is especially notable in constitutional, regulatory, and commercial law. These changes also tended to reinforce adherence to the **rule of law**, redefined to emphasize American notions of judicial protection and enforcement of more absolute constitutional protections.

The current Constitution, in force since 1947, was adopted under the Allied Occupation as an amendment to the 1889 Constitution. It describes the Emperor of Japan as the 'symbol' of the nation and expressly grants the Emperor responsibility for the exercise of functions performed by most heads of state. It provides for a bicameral Parliament, the Diet (Kokkai), with a politically accountable cabinet of ministers, headed by a prime minister. The composition of the two houses of the Diet, the ministries and the electoral system are determined by statute. At present (2007) the House of Representatives (*Shūgi-in*) has 500 seats, 200 of which are elected on a proportional representation basis from eleven regional blocks. The remaining 300 seats are elected from single seat constituencies. The upper House of Councillors (*Sangi-in*) has 252 seats. One-half are elected every three years to serve fixed six-years terms, with seventy-six members elected from the forty-seven prefectures as multi-member districts and fifty elected by party vote from a single nationwide list. As reorganized in 2001, the government comprises ten ministries and a number of separate administrative organs under the Cabinet or Cabinet Office.

The Constitution also contains a long list of political, economic, and social rights including a broad explicit guarantee of all fundamental human rights as 'eternal and inviolate' subject, however, to the caveat that the exercise of such rights shall not be abused and are subject to the public welfare. Litigation over these constitutional guarantees has been frequent, and despite a tendency by the courts toward conservative caution, the rare instances of blatant infringement have been emphatically condemned.

The most controversial provisions of the Constitution are the renunciation of war and prohibition of military establishment clauses. Although lower courts have held Japan's self-defence forces to be unconstitutional, the Japanese Supreme Court (*Saikō saibansho*) has avoided a decision on the merits. As a result, the issues have been resolved by the political branches, giving the Cabinet Legislation Bureau (*hōkika*) a decisive interpretative role.

Below the Supreme Court are eight high courts (*kōtō saibansho*) as the primary courts of first appeal, fifty district courts (*chihō saibansho*) and fifty family courts (*katei saibansho*), each with 203 branches as the primary courts of first instance, and 438 summary courts (kan'i saibansho) for relatively small claims and minor offences.

The Supreme Count comprises fifteen justices. In practice, the majority of justices are career judges. Their pattern of appointment has been remarkably consistent. Partisan political considerations have not played any apparent role. The process of judicial appointments instead reflects recommendations emanating from the Japanese legal establishment—senior judges, senior prosecutors, and the leaders of the organized bar. The justices thus tend to share the intrinsic conservatism of Japan's legal elites, especially the senior judges who control the administration of the judiciary.

The Supreme Court is subtly constrained in other respects. First, its caseload is heavy. Although civil procedure reforms in the late 1990s have eased the problem by allowing routine dismissal of many appeals, the Court decides several thousand cases each year. Compounding the caseload is turnover. Few justices ever spend more than eight or nine years on the Court. The mandatory retirement age is seventy and nearly all justices are at least sixty years of age when appointed. Most are in their mid-sixties. These factors contribute to a cautiously conservative adherence to precedent and past practice and the justices perceptions of community consensus—the sense of society (*ippan shakai no gannen*).

Predictability and consistency are widely held judicial values, reinforced by the size and structure of Japan's career judiciary. The number of judges is small—less than 3,000. They are reassigned and transferred nationwide to different courts, at different levels, at three-year intervals for most of their careers. In common with nearly all medium to large private and public organizations and agencies, a central personnel office is responsible for hiring, assignments, and promotions. Located in the general secretariat in Tokyo, it is staffed by senior career judges, who carefully monitor the progress of individual judges. District, regional, and national judicial conferences are also held regularly, enabling judges to air solutions to common issues and set common standards that enable consistent outcomes among disparate courts.

Judges play a very active role in the development of legal norms and the process of social change through law. There is no dearth of litigation. The civil caseloads of all Japanese courts are extraordinarily heavy. As judges at all levels have managed to reduce delay, the number of cases continues to rise. Civil and administrative litigation is critical in the interpretation of codes and statutes, and the adaptation of legal principles to satisfy new social and economic needs. Although grounded in nineteenth-century European—especially German—jurisprudence, Japan's civil and criminal codes have been adapted to contemporary contexts by means of judicial interpretation and application.

German influence remains quite strong. German legal theory is especially robust in much of Japanese administrative, contract, criminal and procedural jurisprudence. Even areas of law that have no ostensible German or European roots, such as Japanese competition law, are often interpreted or revised in light of European law and practice. Consequently, Japan remains quite firmly within the Civil Law tradition.   JOHN O HALEY

See also: **civil law systems; codes and codification in national law**

Jewish law   Jewish law is the religious law of Jews, not the law of a state. While its origins may go back to the Hebrew Bible, it is not identified with the law of the ancient Israelite state. For most of its history, it has developed in diaspora Jewish communities, where its relationship to state law has naturally arisen. Jewish law recognizes the validity of state law in civil (as opposed to religious) matters. However, the borderline between the 'civil' and 'religious' may be differently defined by the two communities, and Jewish law does not recognize the capacity of state law to override religious obligations.

The history of Jewish law is conventionally divided into the following periods: (1) the Hebrew Bible; (2) the later second Jewish Commonwealth (from the Maccabees to the destruction of the Temple in 70 AD); (3) the early rabbinic period (culminating in the Babylonian Talmud, in the sixth century); (4) the period of the Geonim (Heads of the Babylonian Academies up to the eleventh century); (5) that of the Rishonim (until the 'codification' of Joseph Karo in the sixteenth century); and (6) that of the Aharonim (subsequent authorities). This chronology is relevant to questions of authority. Although the Hebrew Bible (the 'written law') is in theory supreme, it is viewed by Jewish tradition through the eyes of rabbinic interpretation (the 'oral law'), and in this the highest authority is that of the Talmud. Many issues, however, are not addressed at all in the Hebrew Bible, and this lack had to be supplied by rabbinic tradition, with little or no support from the biblical text. The Talmud itself is a literary record of debate in the rabbinic academies, written in a concise style which itself often poses questions of interpretation. While later authorities are in theory entitled to overrule the views of their (post-talmudic) predecessors, there is in practice considerable reluctance to do so.

Jewish Law was not always synonymous with the rabbinic tradition: the diversity of the Second Commonwealth period is reflected in the Dead Sea Scrolls and the origins of Christianity. A somewhat comparable pluralism has re-emerged in modern times, as secular knowledge has penetrated the Jewish community from the eighteenth century. Nowadays, the principal Jewish religious denominations—*Haredi* (ultra-orthodox), Modern

Orthodox, Conservative (*Masorti*) and Progressive ('Reform' and 'Liberal')—differ in their attitudes to the authority of Jewish law.

The very term 'Jewish law' is of modern vintage, and reflects the use of models of modern secular legal systems to describe what the Jewish tradition calls *Torah* (instruction) or *Halakhah* (the way [of life]). In the latter, the 'law' is just one part of divine revelation, albeit the part which that revelation seeks to have enforced, in varying degrees, by human agencies. Whereas Jewish law may seek to analyse the law in terms of authoritative sources and institutions, the tradition itself understands the issues in terms of different forms of revelation (eg prophecy, charismatic authority), and the strength claimed for them in different historical periods.

The attempt to analyse Jewish law in positivistic terms, based on authoritative sources, is best exemplified in modern times by the four-volume *magnum opus* of the former Deputy President of the Israel Supreme Court, Professor Menachem Elon (*Jewish law, History, Sources, Principles* (Philadelphia: Jewish Publication Society, 1994)), who distinguishes between the historical, literary, and legal sources of Jewish law, and identifies the latter as Legislation, Custom, *Ma'aseh* and Precedent, and Legal Reasoning. However, the dispersal of the Jewish people throughout most of the history of Jewish law has meant that these institutions have lacked the unified, centralizing characteristics they possess in modern state systems. There has been no central legislature for Jewish law since the demise of the Second Commonwealth Sanhedrin. Although attempts have been made from time to time to 'codify' Jewish law (notably by Maimonides in the twelfth century and Karo in the sixteenth century), such documents do not possess 'legislative' authority, but are treated rather as influential statements of legal doctrine. Custom has sometimes differed significantly in different Jewish communities, reflecting in part the differing cultural contexts within which they lived.

Strictly speaking, Jewish law has no doctrine of **precedent**, certainly in the strong, **common law** sense. Indeed, there is no systematic tradition of law reporting in Jewish law; the published 'case law' consists rather in the opinions sought by the court from leading contemporary authorities (described as 'responsa' reflecting, not inappropriately, the Roman *responsa prudentium*). This is linked by Elon with *Ma'aseh*, which refers to the 'practice' of respected rabbinic figures, not necessarily in judicial contexts. In post-talmudic times, *responsa* are the principal medium for the transmission of 'legal reasoning', which includes biblical and talmudic interpretation,

assessment of the views of earlier authorities (often making fine distinctions in order to distinguish between them) and argument on the basis of the underlying policy and values of the *Halakhah*.

The range of Jewish law is far greater than that of secular legal systems, since it includes the whole of the ritual law (even though the latter is largely left to divine enforcement). While there are some conceptual differences between 'ritual' and 'civil' law, for most purposes the two are treated as a unified whole, and arguments by analogy may be made from one sphere to the other. As for 'civil' (here including criminal) law, Jewish law is comparable in extent to any other system of private law. Thus, there is a Jewish **contract law**, **tort law**, commercial law, **succession** law, and family law. Succession and family law, however, are regarded as having important religious connotations, and Orthodox Jews seek to regulate both their marriages and wills in ways compatible with both Jewish law and the secular law of the host country.

Jewish law is not the law of the land in the State of Israel, although it has some influence in both Knesset legislation and the jurisprudence of the courts. A major exception, however, consists in the exclusive jurisdiction of the rabbinical courts over the marriages and divorces of Jews.

BERNARD JACKSON

M Elon, *The Principles of Jewish law* (Jerusalem: Encyclopaedia Judaica, 1975)

NS Hecht, BS Jackson, *et al*, *An Introduction to the History and Sources of Jewish Law* (Oxford: Oxford University Press, 1996)

Joint Intelligence Committee *see* national security

joint liability Joint liability arises where two or more persons are civilly liable to an injured claimant for the **causation** of the 'same damage'. The 'same damage' is damage that is indivisible, that is which cannot sensibly be attributed to one only of the wrongdoers.

Joint liability might arise as between wrongdoers who are responsible for a breach of contract and the commission of a tort, or as between those responsible for the commission of a number of torts. With respect to joint torts, damage might be sustained through: the commission of related acts, a common design amongst the wrongdoers, unrelated acts which combine to cause damage (such as a crash between two cars causing a pedestrian injury), or the mere fact of a legal relationship between wrongdoers (especially the relationship of employment). In an age dominated by the tort of negligence and by the **vicarious liability** of the employer for the acts of employees, joint liability often involves actions being brought against a negligent employee and the responsible employer.

Joint liability offers considerable practical advantages for the claimant contemplating litigation because he or she has the ability to bring an action against one only of the wrongdoers who have injured him or her and can obtain judgment (or force a settlement) for **compensation** representing the entire amount of the damage from that wrongdoer—even if that wrongdoer only caused a small proportion of the damage. This is advantageous where one or more of the wrongdoers has died (or, in the case of a **company**, has been dissolved), cannot be located, or is impecunious. The wrongdoer bears the risk of one of these problems affecting the ability to sue other wrongdoers. (Where these problems do not arise, **courts** usually expect all wrongdoers to be sued at once and discourage successive actions against wrongdoers because of the burdens that these place upon the administration of **justice**.)

Joint liability is accompanied by a right of 'contribution' under the Civil Liability (Contribution) Act 1978, section 3. This means that one wrongdoer held liable to the claimant is able to bring an action for contribution against other wrongdoers liable for the same damage by requiring that they be sued in the action to which the first wrongdoer is a party or in a separate suit (especially relevant where the other wrongdoers are only located after the initial suit by the claimant has been determined but without full compensation being paid for damage). Liability will be divided between wrongdoers on the basis of what is 'just and equitable'. This, usually, is determined on the basis of the degree of wrongdoing of each party and the extent to which the wrong of each was significant in causing the damage (the court assessing the impact of each wrongdoer's conduct upon the claimant).

Joint liability does not arise in cases where wrongdoers cause distinct lots of (or 'divisible') damage. In such cases, the claimant must proceed against each wrongdoer separately. Also, courts have departed from the principle of joint liability in cases concerning exposure to asbestos and disease when scientific evidence does not permit accurate findings of causation. In such cases, courts are required to limit liability to the proportionate responsibility of each wrongdoer, which might be done on the basis of length and intensity of exposure to the harmful agent. In these cases, the risks of death, company dissolution, difficulty of locating a wrongdoer, and impecuniousness lie upon the claimant.

CHRISTIAN WITTING

See also: **negligence in civil law; tort law**

joint venture   A joint venture ('JV') is an arrangement whereby two or more parties combine to carry out some form of commercial activity. As this broad explanation suggests JVs may take many forms, and may perform many different activities. The extent to which **competition law** will be applicable to any JV will depend on the nature of the activity carried out, and the approach may depend on the form of the JV.

For the purposes of competition law JVs are defined as either cooperative or concentrative. Cooperative JVs are those arranged by agreement (contract) between the parties, and do not typically involve either party in the acquisition of assets or resources of the other or of a third party. Concentrative JVs involve the acquisition of 'joint control' by at least two undertakings, of an entity that functions on a lasting basis. Cooperative JVs are analysed within the framework set out in EC and UK competition law for the analysis of agreements. Concentrative JVs in the EC are analysed as part of the law of **merger control**.

Some specific provision is made in competition law to deal with the most common types of JVs (research and development, specialization, etc), but others will fall to be dealt with on a case-by-case basis. Broadly, the greater the extent to which the JV limits competition between the parties to it, the more likely it is to be condemned, and the more substantial the benefits flowing from its operation the more likely it is to be lawful.

MARK FURSE

journalistic privilege   In domestic law, journalists enjoy a statutory privilege not to disclose the identity of their sources under section 10 of the Contempt of Court Act 1981. However, this privilege is limited, being subject to four exceptions, namely where a court is satisfied that the disclosure of a source is 'necessary in the interests of justice or **national security** or for the prevention of disorder or crime'. Additionally, other statutory provisions give the state further powers to demand information on specific issues. Thus, journalists may find themselves asked to divulge information in respect of investigations into serious fraud, indictable offences, espionage, and terrorism.

The protection of journalists' sources is valued for reasons that are connected with the Convention right to **freedom of expression** and more broadly, democratic self-governance. A presumption against disclosure allows journalists to engage in investigative journalism and bring into the public domain information, from persons who wish to remain anonymous, on matters of public interest that may either contradict an existing official account or simply bring a hitherto neglected matter under public scrutiny. Sometimes, as has occurred in the case of persons willing to speak to the media about the alleged involvement of **security services** in Northern Ireland with sectarian murders, an informant may have insisted upon non-identification as a pre-condition of any interview. Any subsequent court order to disclose identity will entail the breach a professional commitment and may, in certain contexts, put journalists and/or their sources in physical danger. Beyond this, disclosure orders will inevitably staunch the flow of facts and information into the public domain to enable informed discussion. The ready grant of disclosure orders in criminal cases may even suggest that media organizations have been annexed as an ancillary investigative arm of the police and prosecuting authorities.

At the same time, an undue weighting of freedom of expression interests might mean that the pursuit of vital societal interests (such as those in respect of the detection and prevention of crime) could be seriously hampered. Of course, aside from assisting the effective prosecution of criminal activity, orders may serve other legitimate state interests (such as national security) as well as more obviously private interests (in the case of commercially sensitive information relating to business organizations). In respect of the latter, opportunities for would-be informants to raise matters of genuine public interest directly to a wider audience, without fear of subsequent victimization or dismissal, have been created by the Public Interest Disclosure Act 1998.

Naturally, it has fallen to the courts to decide when disclosure has been shown to be 'necessary' in the interests of one of the enumerated exceptional categories. The resulting jurisprudence straddles two periods: before 1998, when the **European Convention on Human Rights** was incorporated into domestic law, and afterwards.

Initial indications suggested that the English courts were prone to undermine the flow of information into the public domain by readily acceding to applications for disclosure. Thus, in *AG v Morgan Grampian* (1991) the **House of Lords** decided to order disclosure after a journalist, William Goodwin, was sent details of a company's confidential financial restructuring package. Publication of the package had already been prevented by an **injunction** granted previously. The 'interests of justice' were interpreted broadly here to include the ability of an employer to exercise legal rights or to avert legal wrongs. This might include rights under contract law to dismiss/discipline an employee found to have breached a duty of confidentiality, which is implied into the contract of employment. Clearly, on the facts, the plaintiffs could point an impairment of their ability to exercise their legal right to dismiss/discipline the leaker unless the documents which would identify the leaker were disclosed to them. Goodwin contested the order successfully in the **European Court of Human Rights**. The injunction already issued to prevent publication of the confidential financial information meant that the additional measure of a disclosure order was unnecessary and a disproportionate interference with Goodwin's Convention rights.

In the **Human Rights** Act era, UK judges have on the whole been less inclined to order disclosure. This fact is attributable to (i) an insistence on being satisfied that alternative means of discovering the source have been tried and failed; and (ii) the express weighting now given to the constitutional importance of freedom of expression as a vital factor in any balancing exercise that is conducted.

IAN CRAM

See also: **confidential information**

Joyce, William   William Joyce (1906–1946), better known as Lord Haw-Haw, was tried for treason in 1945, and was the last man to be executed for this crime in the United Kingdom. His trial, one of a number of trials for treason which followed the end of the World War II, was notable because it raised an important point about the scope of the law of treason.

Joyce was prominent in the British fascist movement in the 1930s, and with the outbreak of war in 1939 he travelled to Germany, where he began broadcasting Nazi propaganda for Germany's main English-language radio station. His distinctive accent and style led to notoriety in Britain, reflected in his nickname, Lord Haw-Haw. At the end of the war Joyce was captured by British soldiers as he attempted to escape to Sweden, and was returned to London where he was charged with treason. What was expected to be a routine trial was complicated when Joyce revealed that he had never legitimately held a British **passport**, and therefore claimed that he owed no allegiance to the British sovereign. He had falsely obtained a British passport in 1933 by claiming that he had been born in Ireland (he was in fact born in the US), before taking German **nationality** in 1940.

His trial took place at the **Old Bailey** on 17–19 September 1945. The prosecution argued that at the time he held a British passport, even if fraudulently obtained, he was under the protection of the **Crown** and owed allegiance in return. This view of the law was upheld by the trial judge, Mr Justice Tucker, and Joyce was found guilty. The point was appealed to the Court of Criminal Appeal, and then **the House of Lords** which upheld the conviction by a majority. Joyce was executed on 3 January 1946.

LINDSAY FARMER

See also: **capital punishment; treason, sedition and public order**

judges Judges are holders of public office. The role of a judge is largely determined by the court in which he or she sits. These functions may include hearing trials in the civil legal process and the criminal process, hearing appeals from determinations of lower courts, and adjudicating on constitutional questions. Outside the courtroom, judges may be called upon by government to chair public or **judicial inquiries** into disasters, scandals, and other controversial events—a task that some critics suggest risks undermining public confidence in the judiciary.

Judicial appointments take place in a wide range of ways in different legal systems. In some (especially those of continental Europe) there is a career judiciary, with selection by examination leading to appointment at a relatively young age. In **common law** systems, such as the three legal systems of **United Kingdom**, judges are recruited from among members of the legal profession who have acquired several years of practical experience.

The principle of **judicial independence** provides safeguards against unwarranted interference in the work of judges from other state institutions (especially the executive and legislative branches of government). When appointed, judges in almost court systems are required to take an oath of office by which they pledge to uphold the law and to be impartial.

Views about judges in the UK are mixed. Empirical research has found that two-thirds of people— irrespective of social background and experience of the courts—hold the negative view that 'most judges are out of touch with ordinary people's lives' (H Genn, *Paths to Justice: What People Do and Think About Going to Law* (Oxford: Hart, 1999), 239). The wearing of wigs and gowns by judges in the higher courts was perceived as accentuating the age, distance, and 'degree of menace' of judges. The same study also revealed a widespread 'depth of ignorance about the legal system'. The Government's view— and one widely shared by lawyers—is that at 'all levels of our justice system, we are fortunate to have a strong, independent judiciary respected nationally and internationally' (Department for Constitutional Affairs, *Consultation Paper on Constitutional reform: a new way of appointing judges*, July 2003). And in surveys of public confidence in various professions, judges feature as among the most trusted in the UK.

About one fact there is general agreement: that the professional judiciary throughout the UK lacks diversity in terms of the proportion of women judges and those from ethnic minorities. Judges are overwhelmingly white males. There is broad consensus that the continuing lack of diversity risks undermining public confidence. Research commissioned by the Department for Constitutional Affairs in 2006 found that whereas women make up 51 per cent of the population, only 26 per cent of judges were female (and most of those were in the junior levels). The first woman appointed as a Lord of Appeal in Ordinary (a 'Law Lord') was Baroness Hale of Richmond as late as 2004. Although ethnic minorities are 8 per cent of the population, only 5 per cent of judges are from those minorities (again mostly in the lower courts). The judicial appointments commissions in England and Wales, Scotland, and Northern Ireland have as one of their tasks a duty to widen the pool of lawyers eligible for appointment to the bench.

The term 'judge' might be thought to imply a legally-qualified person, but some judicial functions are carried out by non-lawyers. In England and Wales, the vast majority of less serious criminal trials are heard by Justices of the Peace (or 'lay magistrates') who sit as a bench of three, advised by a legally qualified clerk. There is also a significant lay involvement in more serious criminal cases where juries of twelve (in Scotland, fifteen) randomly selected members of the public sit as the 'judge of fact'. Legal proceedings in **tribunals** are typically heard by a legally qualified tribunal judge (or chairman) sitting with two non-lawyers.

The judiciary of England and Wales The most senior judge is the **Lord Chief Justice** of England and Wales, who under the Constitutional Reform Act 2005 is 'Head of the Judiciary' and 'President of the Courts of England and Wales' and is entitled to sit in any court (though in practice sits mostly in the Court of Appeal Criminal Division). Next in order of seniority is the **Master of the Rolls**, who presides over the Civil Division of the Court of Appeal. Then there are the heads of the various divisions of the High Court and judges with strategic responsibilities: the President of the Queen's Bench Division, the Head of Criminal Justice, the President of Family Division, the Head of Family Justice, and the Chancellor of the High Court (heading the Chancery Division). Other judges are set out in the following table.

Type of Judge	Title	Main court	Number in 2006
Lord Justice of Appeal	Lord/Lady Justice Bloggs ('My Lord/Lady' in court)	Court of Appeal	37
Justice of the High Court ('puisne judge')	Mr/Mrs/Miss Justice Bloggs ('My Lord/Lady' in court)	High Court and serious criminal trials in the Crown Court	108
Circuit Judge	His Honour Judge Bloggs ('Your Honour' in court)	County courts, the Crown Court and a small number in specialist parts of the High Court	600
District Judge	Mr/Mrs/Miss Bloggs ('Sir'/'Madam' in court)	County courts, magistrates' courts and a small number in the Family Division of the High Court	434

High Court Justices 'go on circuit', meaning that for several weeks a year they may be required to leave the Royal Courts of Justice in London to conduct the most serious criminal trials in the Crown Court around the country. Circuit judges in England and Wales are appointed to one of six regions (called 'circuits').

The judiciary of Scotland

Scotland's senior judges all sit in the highest civil court (the **Court of Session**) and the highest criminal court (the High Court of Justiciary). The head of the judiciary holds two titles—Lord President of the Court of Session and Lord Justice General. The second most senior judge has the title Lord Justice Clerk. The other thirty-four judges who sit in these two courts are known collectively as the 'Senators of the College of Justice' and take the courtesy title of 'Lord'/'Lady'.

Sheriffs Principal and Sheriffs, numbering about 140, sit in the Sheriffs Courts dealing with criminal offences and civil claims. Lay people sit in the Justice of the Peace Courts, introduced in 2007, to deal with the most minor criminal offences.

The judiciary in Northern Ireland

There are many similarities between the judicial ranks of Northern Ireland and those used in England and Wales. The head of the judiciary is the Lord Chief Justice of Northern Ireland. Lord Justices of Appeal serve in the Court of Appeal; Justices of the High Court in the High Court of Northern Ireland; and judges are appointed to sit in the county courts and magistrates' court.

The Law Lords/Justices of the United Kingdom Supreme Court

Twelve full-time judges, formally titled Lords of Appeal in Ordinary, form the United Kingdom's top-level courts—the Appellate Committee of the **House of Lords** and (in relation to 'devolution issues') the Judicial Committee of the **Privy Council**. In October 2009, those judges become the first judges of the new UK Supreme Court. By convention two of the twelve have a background in Scots law and a practice has developed of appointing one with experience of Northern Ireland. Appointees in recent years have, without exception, been judges from the appeal courts of the three legal systems.

ANDREW LE SUEUR

J Bell, *Judiciaries within Europe: A Comparative Review* (Cambridge: Cambridge University Press, 2006)

See also: **courts; judges, distinguished; judicial appointments; judicial law-making; judiciary in developing countries**

judges, distinguished Distinction, among **judges**, is almost always a product of the assumptions, expectations, and appraisal of the legal profession. This group includes fellow judges, practitioners, law reformers, and academic commentators from within the jurisdictions of the UK and, sometimes, those legal professionals in other **common law** jurisdictions such as Australia and New Zealand. The question of what factors are salient in the legal profession's assessment of judicial distinction has no easy answer. One factor not considered here is the personal influence (or charismatic authority) of particular judges upon the legal profession. In the UK jurisdictions little serious empirical research exists about the extent to which a judge's personal influence determines her standing amongst the profession, although some hints emerge from Alan Paterson's *The Law Lords* (1982) and the task has been started in the USA (see, eg Posner, *Cardozo: A Study in Reputation* (1990)). The relative scarcity of such research ensures that this aspect of judicial distinction is a swamp of anecdotal speculation. Are there any more reliable indicators of 'distinction'? Consider four plausible candidates.

First, those judges regarded as most distinguished by their legal professional peers have usually had a long career, most often (but not necessarily) in the highest appellate **courts**. (In England and Wales these are the Court of Appeal (Civil and Criminal Divisions) and the **House of Lords**; in Scotland they are the Inner House of the **Court of Session** and the House of Lords (civil law) and the High Court of Justiciary (criminal law); in Northern Ireland, the Court of Appeal in Belfast and the House of Lords.) It seems, however, unnecessary that in order to be distinguished a judge's career or life must have ended. That distinction is rarely conferred upon judges quickly—the notion of the judicial prodigy is virtually unknown to the profession—is not just an indicator of lawyers' professional conservatism. Rather, it also shows that both judging and legal learning, success in which usually triggers claims of distinction, often take time to develop.

Secondly, the legal learning of judges is a near universal indicator of their distinction. Most judges regarded as distinguished in the common law world are taken to be so in part because of their undoubted and respected expertise in the law, either in general or in particular areas of law. In these jurisdictions, other judges, practitioners, and academics are often in agreement that a particular judge's judgments in a specific area of law are excellent, displaying a superb grasp of the law and the highest standards of intellectual rigour. In the High Court of Australia, Chief Justice Owen Dixon's private law judgments were almost always highly regarded, as were Lord Edmund-Davies's decisions in criminal law cases in the House of Lords in England; in the Inner House of the Court of Session the judgments of Lord Cooper were usually accepted by the profession as of the highest quality. Thirdly, many judges are distinguished by their mastery of what, for lack of a better term, can be called 'judge-craft'. Alongside the intellectual rigour and respectability of their judgments, distinguished judges judge well, always alert to the pertinent issues and difficulties in a case, open to the arguments offered by counsel on both sides and aware of the consequences of their judgments both within and beyond the legal world. Good judge-craft is thus a matter of engagement and openness: engagement with the law and the consequences of one's decision as well as receptivity to the arguments presented. Distinguished judges are almost always good judges in this sense. In recent history it seems that the Scottish Lord of Appeal in Ordinary, Lord Reid, was noteworthy for combining this quality

with the desire to get the law right, even when that meant changing the law (see Paterson, pp 76–78, 91 and 170–189).

Fourthly, alongside a commitment to intellectual rigour and good judge-craft, distinguished judges also grapple well with a constant tension that most appellate court judges face. The careers of distinguished judges as a whole, and thus many of their particular judgments, are marked by a tension between intellectual rigour—their desire to get the law 'right' on a particular issue and to clarify the ambiguities and difficulties that have generated the particular legal dispute they are called upon to decide—and their duty of fidelity to the law. They are not, as a result, judges who always make expected, entirely predictable judgments, although this is not to imply that their decisions are completely unpredictable. The parameters within which judges must decide cases are conservative, emphasizing the importance of the law being as stable and predictable as possible. Change for the sake of change is thus never an option. Yet distinguished judges are often willing and able to change or develop the law in circumstances when doing so will make it 'better'. And making the law better can mean making it morally better (see, eg Lord Atkin's judgment in **Donoghue v Stevenson** (1932) or practically better (*Williams v Roffey* (1991)). In addition, distinguished judges are sometimes content to affirm that the law embodies obvious principles of justice and morality (*A (FC) and others (FC) v Secretary of State for the Home Department* (2004)), while on other occasions they will change the law so that its results are not blatantly contrary to common sense. What makes some judges more distinguished than others is how well they negotiate, in their judgments, their commitment to follow and apply the existing law while also ensuring that that law is in their view either right, or respectable, or both. There is, of course, no guarantee that this will be possible in each and every case that comes before a judge.

If the degree of success with which judges mediate this tension marks out the distinguished from the non-distinguished, it also highlights a consequence of judicial distinction. For it seems that distinguished judges often leave more 'focal-point' judicial decisions in the course of their careers than their non-distinguished brethren. These may be majority or unanimous judgments that the profession (or a subgroup thereof, such as the commercial or criminal bar) accepts as correct, but not just in relation to the *ratio decidendi* of the particular case. Such decisions are also regarded as correct or important or good in the broader sense of illuminating the general nature and history of the area of law in question and its various problems. Equally, such focal-point decisions might be minority dissenting judgments which cannot be formally accepted as correct, but which nevertheless have a great influence upon the legal profession's thinking on the particular issue in question. The decision might remain a point against which every subsequent discussion of the issue, either in court or in the textbooks, law journals, and reports of law reform bodies, must react (like Lord **Mansfield's contract law** decisions on consideration). Alternatively, such judgments might be 'rehabilitated' in the sense of, although dissents at the time they were made, becoming accepted at some later time as a better statement of the law than the majority decision (see the dissent in *Candler v Crane, Christmas & Co* (1951) and *Hedley Byrne & Co Ltd v Heller and Partners Ltd* (1964)). If this is indeed a genuine by-product of judicial distinction, then it implies that distinguished judges must sometimes be bold in their decision-making, having the fortitude to run contrary to the views of their peers.

In a long career any permutation of these four considerations could well lead to a particular judge being regarded as distinguished. Furthermore, it is surely the case that not all four considerations are equally necessary for a judge to be distinguished, although the presence of all surely makes that more likely. Might other factors be in play in the determination of judicial distinction? Some of the most distinguished judges in the common law world have turned their intellectual rigour, and their interest in getting the law right, to purposes beyond the courtroom and have had a presence in the academic and public world of law. In the former context, distinguished judges are sometimes found writing in the most important legal journals and publishing scholarly books (Lord Goff and G Jones, *The Law of Restitution* (2002); Lord **Devlin**, *The Enforcement of Morals* (1968) and *The Judge* (1979)). Some recent judges in the UK jurisdictions even combine, or at some point have combined, a career in legal practice or on the Bench with a career in academe. In the wider public world of law, distinguished judges sometimes have a presence because of their involvement in discussion about particular legal developments. These developments are sometimes of great public interest (the incorporation of a **Bill of Rights** into English law, or the decriminalization of homosexuality), sometimes of less interest to the public, although deeply interesting to lawyers (like reform of the civil justice system). Judicial involvement in these discussions also sometimes leads to publication and involvement in the academic world of law. Yet since almost any judge can play a role in both the academic and wider public life of law, and since not all who do so do so with distinction, it seems unlikely that such involvement is a reliable indicator of distinction. It may well be that the contributions of distinguished judges to these discussions are accorded most weight; if that is so, then we must return to the four considerations just adumbrated in order to determine which judges are distinguished and which are not.

WILLIAM LUCY

judicial appointments   In each of the UK's three legal systems—England and Wales, Scotland, and Northern Ireland—responsibility for judicial appointments is shared between independent bodies (which advertise for and select candidates and make recommendations), government Ministers (who have limited rights to veto recommended candidates), and the Queen (who has an entirely formal role of making the appointment). Parliament has no direct role in the appointments process.

In England and Wales the Judicial Appointments Commission ('JAC') (created by the Constitutional Reform Act 2005) is chaired by a non-lawyer and has fourteen other members: five **judges** of varying seniority; five non-lawyers; a solicitor and a barrister; a person involved in tribunals; and a lay magistrate. Appointment to the JAC is for a five-year term, renewable once. The JAC works by advertising judicial vacancies, and it identifies suitable candidates using a competence-based set of criteria relating to qualities and abilities. A single preferred candidate for each vacancy is recommended to the **Lord Chancellor**, who in the vast majority of cases is expected to accept the recommendation. The Lord Chancellor does however retain a reserve power to reject a nomination (but must give the JAC reasons for doing so). For the most senior appointments—judges of the Court of Appeal, heads of the Divisions of the High Court, and the **Lord Chief Justice**—a special four-person selection panel is convened, including two senior judges who are not members of the JAC.

In Scotland, the ten-person Judicial Appointments Board (a non-statutory body with an even balance of legal and non-legal members) provides the First Minister with a list of candidates for each vacancy. The Northern Ireland Judicial Appointments Commission (established by the Justice (Northern Ireland) Acts 2002 and 2004) has thirteen members—a mix of judges, legal professionals, and lay members—and is chaired by the Lord Chief Justice of Northern Ireland. A single name is nominated to the Lord Chancellor who, as in England and Wales, has a limited power of veto.

Vacancies for the new UK Supreme Court will be filled on recommendations from a selection commission of two senior members of the Court and a member of each of the three judicial appointments bodies described above, at least one of whom must be a lay member. The name of the preferred candidate will be given to the Lord Chancellor. The Lord Chancellor has limited power to request that the commission re-consider its nomination or reject it.

The arrangements are relatively new in each jurisdiction, and it remains to be seen how successful they will be in meeting the goals of increasing the diversity of the pool of eligible candidates (so that more women and ethnic minority lawyers, who are currently under-represented, are appointed as judges), maintaining 'merit' as the sole criterion for appointment, and providing insulation from party political influences. The new systems are certainly more transparent than those which existed previously, under which the Lord Chancellor (in England and Wales and Northern Ireland) and the Secretary of State for Scotland (in Scotland, relying on the advice of the **Lord Advocate**) made appointments based on 'secret soundings' of senior judges and practitioners, and vacancies were filled by a 'tap on the shoulder' rather than open competition. The government took the view that while these arrangements had 'worked in practice, this system no longer commands public confidence, and is increasingly hard to reconcile with the demands of the Human Rights Act'. (Department for Constitutional Affairs, *Consultation Paper on Constitutional reform: a new way of appointing judges*, July 2003).

ANDREW LE SUEUR

Department for Constitutional Affairs, *Consultation Paper on Constitutional reform: a new way of appointing judges* (July 2003)

K Malleson and P Russell (eds), *Appointing Judges in an Age of Judicial Power: Critical Perspectives from Around the World* (Toronto: University of Toronto Press, 2006)

See also: **courts**

judicial discretion   *see* **discretion; legal positivism since 1970; legal positivism to 1970**

judicial independence   The independence of the judiciary is a principle recognized (if not always fully respected) in all constitutional democracies. It seeks to ensure that cases are decided according to the law as interpreted by the judges, and that judges are insulated from improper extraneous influences. The principle operates at two levels: it protects individual judges, and it calls for the collective protection of the institution of the judiciary.

In many legal systems around the world the greatest threats to judicial independence are financial and political corruption. In the UK, the main threats are of a different character: populist tabloid newspapers, which delight in personalized attacks on judges oblivious to the risks of undermining public confidence in the administration of justice and **the rule of law**; and the tendency, since the 1990s, for some government ministers to disparage judges and judgments which are regarded as politically inconvenient.

In the UK, the Constitutional Reform Act 2005 has brought about important reforms to some aspects of judicial independence:

- There is a clearer division of responsibility between the role of the government minister responsible for judiciary-related matters (the **Lord Chancellor**) and the senior judiciary. The Lord Chancellor is no longer a judge or head of the judiciary. The Lord Chancellor does, however, have an express statutory duty to 'defend the independence of the judiciary' and all other ministers and those involved in the administration of justice must 'uphold' that independence. The chief judges of each legal system (the **Lord Chief Justice** of England and Wales, the Lord Chief Justice of Northern Ireland, and the Lord President of the Court of Session) also have important leadership roles to play in defending and promoting judicial independence. They have power under the Constitutional Reform Act to make written representations to Parliament, a power that appears as if it will be used only in exceptional circumstances.
- The new systems for **judicial appointments**, operating at arms' length from ministers, also promote independence.
- The creation of a new top-level court, the UK Supreme Court, physically and procedurally separate from Parliament, will also enhance perceptions of judicial independence.

Judges are protected from dismissal by the Act of Settlement 1701. Senior judges may be removed from office only following an address to the Crown from both Houses of Parliament, something that has not happened in modern times. Judges of the lower courts may be dismissed for misbehaviour by the Lord Chancellor. Judicial salaries may not be reduced except by Act of Parliament. In practice, judicial salaries fall under the auspices of the Senior Salaries Review Body, which makes recommendations to the Prime Minister.

Judges enjoy a high degree of immunity from civil actions (for example for the torts of negligence and **defamation**) that might otherwise arise from things said or done during the trial process. For their part, judges in the UK are expected to refrain from involvement in party politics. They should also avoid making comments on matters of political controversy outside the courtroom.   ANDREW LE SEUER

AW Bradley, 'A Threat to Judicial Independence' (2003) *Public Law* 403

G Canivet *et al* (eds), *Independence, Accountability, and the Judiciary* (London: British Institute of International and Comparative Law, 2006)

judicial inquiries   *see* **judges**

judicial law-making   In the traditional doctrine of **separation of powers**, the legislature is supposed to make the law, and the judge merely to apply it. Various attempts to enforce this strict division of functions have been tried and failed. No legal system can work without a creative, law-making role for the judiciary. So the real question is what kind of law-making do judges undertake?

Most of the work of judges involves the resolution of disputes that turn on the careful analysis of fact situations. The judge will be applying an uncontroversial rule to the facts. Judicial law-making occurs in the small number of cases that require a statement of the rules of law that govern a generality of cases. This occurs in at least three situations. First, the applicable rule may be expressed in very general terms and require further precision for application to particular classes of situation. For example, homicide may be defined as the killing of a 'person'; but the question may arise whether a foetus counts as a person, in circumstances where a doctor or an attacker has caused it to die. Secondly, the applicable rule may need updating. For example, a rule on the formation of contracts by post will have to be adapted to deal with electronic communication. Thirdly, a new set of issues may arise, for example because of the creation of the internet. In all such cases, policy choices have to be made about the direction in which the law is to be applied or developed by analogy.

Judicial law-making in such circumstances differs from some kinds of legislation. Judges cannot remake the whole of an area of law. They proceed incrementally, using analogy with existing rules and values within the law, and making very specific adjustments to rules of law. All the same, and over time, the effect of such incremental changes can be very significant. In addition, judges have to justify their law-making differently from the legislature. The legislature can introduce radically distinct principles, such as changing the kinds of tax that are imposed on businesses and introducing new forms of taxation. It justifies it decisions on the basis that it is elected and can change the direction of state policy radically. Judges have to justify their law-making by showing that the new solution is broadly consistent with the rules and principles of law that remain untouched by the law-making and that the values underlying the reform are consistent with the values underlying the rest of this branch of law. Because judges do not have a broad mandate for law reform and they have a greater obligation to justify what they are proposing.

The acceptability of judicial law-making varies over time. Where the legislature is overburdened or inactive in a particular area, judges may see it as appropriate that they undertake more law-making than in situations where the legislature is more active. Equally, judges will typically avoid topics which are politically sensitive, even if they are prepared to make decisions in areas that are socially sensitive.   JOHN BELL

judicial review   As understood in the UK, judicial review is the process by which the High Court (the **Court of Session** in Scotland) can review decisions taken by public bodies to ensure that such bodies have acted in accordance with the law and have not exceeded or abused their powers. Judicial review is based on **common law** principles that have been developed by the courts over several centuries. The law has developed greatly since the 1960s and especially during the past decade. This period has witnessed an increase in the range of decisions that are subject to review, an extension of the grounds on which judges can review decisions, and an improvement in the procedures and remedies available to claimants.

The constitutional importance of judicial review is twofold. It provides a means, rooted in the common law, by which individuals and groups can challenge the exercise of public power on legal grounds. It is also gives practical effect to the fundamental principle that public bodies, including government ministers, must have legal authority for their actions and must act within that legal authority. If public bodies exceed or abuse their powers then their actions have no legal effect. This principle, sometimes referred to as the principle of legality, is a key component in the prevention of arbitrary governmental power and as such a vital element in our **liberal democracy**.

Despite its constitutional importance, public bodies do not relish having their decisions challenged in the courts, still less do they relish having them struck down on the ground that they constitute an excess or abuse of power. Following decisions in which judges have struck down decisions in sensitive areas such as terrorism and asylum, government ministers and others have complained that unelected judges are over-stepping their authority and trespassing into issues of policy that should fall within the exclusive remit of the elected government. There is no single answer as to how activist or interventionist our judiciary should be, and disagreements exist even amongst the judges. However, when assessing the claim that judges are becoming too powerful it is necessary to understand the constitutional importance of judicial review and its limits. Its importance has just been emphasized, but two limits in particular must be mentioned.

The first is that judicial review is essentially concerned with the process by which decisions are reached rather than with the merits of the decisions themselves. In the typical judicial review the key question is whether in reaching its decision the authority has properly applied the law, followed the correct procedures, and taken proper account of relevant factors such as the claimant's **human rights**. The court is not concerned with whether the decision is right or wrong, good or bad; and judges cannot overturn a decision of a public body solely because they don't like it and would have reached a different one. In this respect judicial review may be contrasted with appeal procedures established by statute which may permit an appellate tribunal or court to overturn decisions that are considered to be factually or legally wrong. Judges in judicial review are not concerned with the merits of governmental decisions or policies but only with whether these decisions or policies are lawful and have been lawfully taken.

The second limitation is constitutionally very important. One implication of the principle of **parliamentary supremacy** is that the effects of court decisions can be reversed by an Act of Parliament. Another implication is that judges do not have the general power to review and strike down **Acts of Parliament** on the grounds that they are unlawful or unconstitutional (although they can decide that an Act of Parliament is non applicable to the extent that it conflicts with European Community law or that an Act of Parliament is incompatible with human rights under the provisions of the Human Rights Act 1998). In this respect judicial review in the UK contrasts with the system of judicial review, or constitutional review, that exists elsewhere, including in the USA. This means that the last word on the law ultimately resides with Parliament and not with the judges. While judicial review is of growing constitutional and practical importance, concerns that judges now

have too much power in our system should not be exaggerated. Judicial review can be used to: ensure that public bodies follow appropriate legal processes; strike down particular decisions; force government to rethink its approach; and to provide guidance on the applicable law. It can act as a significant irritant to government and other public bodies, cause delay, attract publicity, and absorb resources; but it cannot, and most would say that it should not, prevent a government that has the support of Parliament from ultimately achieving its policy aims.

When placed against the millions of decisions taken annually by public bodies, the scale of judicial review, although it has grown substantially in the past few decades, remains very small indeed. In 2005, for example, in England and Wales there were 5,381 applications for permission to seek judicial review. A high proportion of these cases concerned immigration, asylum, and housing and smaller numbers involved a spectrum of topics such as land use planning, prisons, licensing, education, and community care. The number of public authorities regularly challenged is also very small. Most local authorities in England and Wales, for example, are unlikely to experience more than two or three challenges a year. Some authorities, most notably some London Boroughs, by contrast, are regularly challenged and experience judicial review on a daily basis.

These comments concern challenges that are taken to courts, but the numbers of cases actually dealt with by judges is far lower than the number of challenges. Except in Scotland, those seeking judicial review must obtain the permission of the High Court in order to do so. The requirement that permission be obtained from judges in order to commence proceedings is unique to the judicial review process and is imposed in order to protect public authorities from unwarranted litigation and to save court and judge time. Permission will only be granted if: the case is arguable; the claimant has a 'sufficient interest' or standing to bring the proceedings; the matter is brought within strict time limits (the claim must be brought promptly and in any case within three months of the date of the decision that is being challenged); and, all other available procedures have been exhausted. In 2005 according to the official statistics only 14 per cent challenges were granted permission to proceed. In that year there were 281 judicial reviews fully dealt with by the judges.

Several reasons may account for the relatively low overall use of judicial review including that judicial review can only be used as a last resort; difficulties in obtaining appropriate legal assistance; the costs of litigating; and the sheer energy levels required to pursue judicial review, especially given the need to exhaust other procedures. Another factor is that although judicial review can provide successful claimants with a range of useful remedies, including **injunction**s and orders that quash unlawful decisions or which force public authorities to act, the process is not generally suitable for those who seek financial compensation.

Judicial review is a constitutionally important process whose role is circumscribed by limits that are fundamentally concerned to achieve an appropriate balance between legal and political responsibility for the exercise of public power in the UK.

MAURICE SUNKIN

See also: **administrative law**

judiciaries in developing countries   Judiciaries in developing countries have long struggled to establish their independence and secure adequate public resources to maintain their court systems. In developing countries, despite their great diversity, judiciaries have routinely faced interference by political actors and powerful private interests, irrespective of whether government is democratic or authoritarian. Some of the most important battles between judiciaries and other branches of government have been over the control of **judicial appointments** and promotion and in relation to chronic under-funding and understaffing. In addition, in many regions of the world, judicial bodies compete with or sit alongside non-state bodies such as village councils, Islamic shari courts, or political bosses. Particularly but certainly not only in rural areas, such non-state bodies apply a variety of legal norms to resolve property and contract disputes, address family conflicts, and provide **restitution** or punishment for what are seen as violations of **community** norms. The extent and nature of this 'legal pluralism' varies greatly across developing countries, according to the strength of government presence and/or agreement of bounded autonomy made with ethno-linguistic or religious **minority** groups.

However, profound changes are sweeping through the world's judiciaries. There has been a significant expansion in the role and importance of the judiciary in many developing countries, visible both in the rapid growth in (non-criminal) cases and in the prominent role of judges in resolving political disputes between parts of government and between other political actors. In many, but not all, countries, these changes reflect a combination of greater state presence across national **territory** and in more areas of social life, the expansion of citizens' rights, and ability to access the courts that has accompanied

transitions to democratic rule started over a quarter century ago, as well as demographic shifts that come with greater urbanization and higher levels of education.

There has been a democratization of the profile of litigants before the courts, and a tremendous expansion in the volume of cases and in the areas of social life covered. Judiciaries used to adjudicating elite claims involving property and contracts, alongside a limited number of criminal matters, have become involved in adjudicating constitutional issues through **judicial review** and in resolving disputes of a strictly political nature. They now face the middle class, and in some contexts the poor, in court, as non-elites make claims on each other, on businesses, and on government through the judicial system. Alongside cases involving property and contracts, there are now cases involving abuse of public authority, violations of **consumer** rights, and denial of government entitlements. One of the noteworthy trends in countries as different as Brazil and the Philippines is the rapid increase in women bringing family disputes to the judiciary.

The growing demand on the courts, along with sustained international pressure, has led to a cycle of large-scale judicial reforms seeking to speed up the wheels of **justice** and strengthen **judicial independence**. One set of reforms has established, as a part of, or sometimes alongside, the judiciary a variety of court systems to handle specific types of cases. Most countries have a system of labour court specializing in employment disputes, a range of administrative courts for citizen-government agency disputes, and some form of **small claims** courts to settle disputes in which the monetary value at stake is low. Generally these specialized courts have less onerous procedures and are friendlier and more accessible to the general population. They also represent a substantial expansion in access to justice as well as in the state's role in resolving social conflict.

In the belief that strict enforcement of contracts and property rights are a prerequisite to direct foreign investment and economic growth, international actors have encouraged and financed judicial reforms aimed at strengthening 'the **rule of law**.' On the one hand, international actors such as the World Bank, regional development banks, and bilateral agencies such as USAID, have sought to accelerate case clearance time with substantial investments in upgrading and expanding the administrative structure of judiciaries and in introducing information technologies. They have also supported legal reforms to strengthen judicial independence. On the other hand, these international actors have sought to reduce the demand on judiciaries, by sponsoring the creation of **alternative dispute resolution** mechanisms or the coupling of customary, non-government adjudication bodies with the formal courts, to reduce the volume of cases reaching those courts. This coupling is an alternative to expanding the judiciary's own capacity to process cases. In a growing number of developing countries, people must first attempt to resolve disputes (non-criminal matters) in customary or alternative dispute resolution forums, accessing the courts only when these fail. For many people this makes customary bodies the primary locus of dispute resolution or protection.

There is no clear evidence whether such coupling with customary or other non-government adjudicating bodies reduces the demand on the courts, but two difficulties have been documented. One is potential conflict between the principles that govern the two types of justice bodies. While judiciaries apply liberal norms placing great value on individual rights and legal **equality** (however well achieved in practice), customary bodies often apply norms that focus on community harmony and collective interests. Women's organizations and feminist legal scholars in particular have been critical of the role given to customary legal bodies, fearing they repress legal demand and reproduce local communities' longstanding biases against women. The second difficulty is regulating to ensure that non-government bodies do not trespass into matters reserved for the formal judicial system, and, in particular, in criminal matters such as **rape** and murder.

PETER P HOUTZAGER

See also: **customary law**

juridification   Where social and economic activities come increasingly to be governed by legal rules at the expense of the values and principles that develop within those social and economic spheres themselves, academic lawyers sometimes refer to this as juridification. In the United States the related term of legalization is sometimes used. Processes of juridification involve an overall sense of a shift towards law as the basis for **governance** of an activity. Such a shift may involve a number of different aspects. The most obvious sign of juridification is the growth of litigation in an area where previously there was little. The growth of **judicial review** of administrative action in England and Wales since the late 1960s, a process by which actions of government officials are challenged in litigation, may be characterized as juridification of public administration. Underlying such litigation

processes may be other, less visible changes. Lawyers may become more involved in advising on what actions to take or what processes to use, where previously officials acted without legal advice. Thus law may have a greater role in framing the way decisions are taken, as a by-product of its increased role in resolving disputes. A related aspect is a perception that **judges** are growing in power in areas where they previously had less involvement. The development of the domestic jurisdiction over **human rights** in the **Human Rights Act 1998** has been particularly significant in accentuating the sense of judges deploying power in new areas.   COLIN SCOTT

juries   The jury is an ancient and venerated institution with origins dating back almost a thousand years. Jury trial has been transplanted from England to over fifty countries throughout the world, and juries of some kind now exist in the United States, in **Commonwealth** countries, Africa, Asia and even in some of the civil law countries of Europe (including Russia), Central and South America. Trial by jury is often described as the cornerstone of the adversarial trial system. Jurors are frequently reluctant conscripts and their engagement with the criminal courts is only temporary. But the importance of their decisions should never be underestimated since they have a critical bearing upon individual liberty.

In England and Wales and in Northern Ireland (as in most other countries), juries consist of twelve people. Scotland is very unusual with fifteen-member juries (twelve in civil trials). Jurors are chosen at random from the electoral register and, since the general trend in recent years has been towards universal jury eligibility, the number of persons and groups exempted or excused from jury service has accordingly shrunk. Unease about the under-representation of ethnic minority groups nonetheless continues to be voiced.

Jury service normally lasts for two weeks although some trials—complex fraud is the example always given—may run for several months. Jurors are not paid and receive only limited compensation for loss of earnings and payments for travel and subsistence expenses. They are required to decide whether or not accused persons are guilty of a criminal act or, in civil cases, which party's case to uphold. (Jury trial in civil cases is, however, now an extremely rare occurrence in the UK.) In addition to certain grave criminal offences which must be tried by jury if they go to trial, in England and Wales, and in Northern Ireland, there is a range of offences of intermediate gravity in relation to which defendants have a right to elect trial by jury. In Scotland, this right of election has never existed, and it is for the prosecution to determine whether cases will be tried by jury.

The available literature indicates that public confidence in jury trial is very high and attacks on the jury as a rule provoke fierce controversy. This confidence appears to be shared within the judiciary and the legal profession. Despite frequent complaints about the disproportionate costs of jury trial in minor cases, few people have ever called for the abolition of juries. Indeed, the jury tends to elicit praise from commentators to an extent unparalleled by other legal institutions, and its critics are greatly outnumbered by supporters. The political and constitutional role of the jury is especially prized. Citizens' participation in the administration of justice through jury service is said to promote public confidence in the courts and, by injecting democratic or community values into decision-making, to enhance the legitimacy of the criminal process too. It is often claimed that the jury system provides protection for individuals against political oppression, and Lord Devlin's celebrated statement, written half a century ago, is commonly cited:

The first object of any tyrant in Whitehall would be to make Parliament utterly subservient to his will; and the next to overthrow or diminish trial by jury, for no tyrant could afford to leave a subject's freedom in the hands of twelve of his countrymen. So that trial by jury is more than an instrument of justice and more than one wheel of the Constitution: it is the lamp that shows that freedom lives.

Despite the eulogies, trial by jury is in sharp decline throughout the UK. This decline is particularly marked in Northern Ireland where jury trial was actually suspended between 1973 until 2007 for terrorist offences because of fears that jurors might be intimidated, these cases being heard instead by judges sitting alone in the so-called Diplock courts. (The Justice and Security (Northern Ireland) Act 2007, which came into force in August 2007, has effectively restored jury trial in the province although section 1 of the Act continues to make provision for Diplock trials in exceptional circumstances.) But it is important to note that, throughout the UK, very few criminal cases—only about 1 per cent of prosecuted crimes in England and Wales and a smaller proportion still in Scotland and Ireland—are tried by jury. The vast majority of cases are dealt with as guilty pleas in the lower courts. Considerable efforts continue to be made, however, to reduce this tiny proportion still further, especially by restricting defendants' right to opt for jury trial in less serious criminal cases, increasing sentencing powers in the lower courts or making adjustments to the categories of case that can be tried by jury.

The main justification for jury trial lies in the jury's independence: juries can resist all pressures from government, judges, or anyone else to reach a particular verdict. But the independence of the jury cannot be viewed as an unqualified benefit, and what many writers take to be the jury's greatest strength is seen by others as its most serious defect. For some, independence is the jury's *raison d'étre* since verdicts can be tempered by commonsense and innate sense of fairness, if need be in defiance of the law, the evidence and indeed the jury's own oath. Others consider this to be an unacceptable affront to the rule of law, giving juries license to behave in arbitrary and unpredictable ways. While verdicts based solely on a cold, clinical application of the law and of the evidence might not always be desirable, there is certainly a danger that, if juries are given free rein in reaching verdicts, ignorance and prejudice will so distort verdicts that the integrity of the criminal justice system will be undermined.

Jury trial has always prompted considerable controversy and two other questions have been much debated:

- Should the prosecution and defence be able to challenge individuals in the jury pool to influence the composition of a jury? The possibilities of challenge are now much more limited in the UK since challenges are said to conflict with the principle of random jury selection. The defence right to 'peremptory' challenge (where no reason is given) has been abandoned in England and Wales and in Scotland, though retained in Northern Ireland. Challenges 'for cause' are allowed in the UK but used infrequently.
- Should verdicts be unanimous? Allowing 'majority verdicts' can prevent the intimidation and bribing of jurors but weakens the requirement that the prosecution establish proof beyond reasonable doubt. While unanimous verdicts remain the norm in most countries, majority verdicts are permissible in England and Wales and in Northern Ireland—and are quite common—although there can be no more than two dissenting jurors, otherwise the jury is 'hung'. The situation in Scotland is more anomalous. A bare numerical majority is all that is required—eight–seven is quite sufficient. 'Hung' juries are not possible in Scotland but juries can return 'not proven' verdicts and apparently often do so. This option does not exist elsewhere in the UK.

We know little about how juries reach their decisions. Conducting research on juries is problematic in the UK because jurors are prohibited by law from revealing the secrets of the jury room. The Contempt of Court Act 1981 makes it a contempt of court for jurors to disclose details of what happened in jury deliberations, and all efforts made by researchers to have this prohibition relaxed have so far fallen on deaf ears. Despite the difficulties, numerous empirical studies of jury decision-making have been undertaken, especially by basing them on re-enactments of trials heard by 'simulated' juries. The available research, though limited, supports the following tentative (and largely reassuring) conclusions about jury trial:

- jurors take the task extremely seriously;
- jury verdicts are on the whole consistent with the evidence that is presented in court; few are based on sympathy or prejudice towards defendants;
- most jurors are able to understand and absorb evidence presented in court. The same applies to legal language, terminology, and judicial instructions. Insofar as problems arise, these relate less to the capacity of jurors to follow what is happening than to unsatisfactory presentation;
- however, a significant proportion of verdicts are regarded by judges and other participants in trials as at least questionable;
- jurors are more likely to convict when they know about a defendant's criminal record;
- the 'inscrutability' of verdicts makes appeal against perverse verdicts extremely difficult.

It might be thought curious that we expect twelve randomly selected, untrained, lay people with no experience of law, legal procedure, or the courts, to reach sensible verdicts in the most serious criminal cases. They are obliged to base their verdicts on what is frequently complex and confusing evidence. They deliberate in secret and give no justifications for their decisions, no matter how foolish they might appear. Some people have suggested that, if we wish to retain public confidence in jury trial, we are better off remaining in ignorance of how decisions are reached. Perhaps the observation made by one commentator is about right: he said, paraphrasing Winston Churchill's view of democracy, that trial by jury is 'the worst mechanism for trying cases except for any alternative'.   JOHN BALDWIN

See also: **adversary system; jury, origins and development**

jurisdiction and social discourse   At their broadest questions of jurisdiction engage with the fact that there is law, and with the power and authority to speak in the name of the law. Such questions encompass the authorization of law as such, as well as determinations of authority and the administration of **justice** within an institutional order.

Jurisdictional thinking—and thinking about questions of authority in general—operates on a number of different levels. At one level, it is concerned with the technical management of the business of **courts** and tribunals. At another level, questions of jurisdiction address political–legal and social ordering through the delimitation of the authority to judge and to act. Typically in Western legal orders jurisdictional authority has been ordered and exercised in terms of the procedural organization of **persons** (both **human** and artificial), places (such as land-based **territories**, ports, or market) and activities or events (such as trades but also **genocides** and crimes against humanity). Questions of jurisdiction also address the conceptual ordering of authority as part of what structures or authorizes law and social existence. Modern social and critical thinking on authority has phrased these issues in terms of the sovereign and the **subject**. If located as a question of action and event, questions of jurisdiction are linked to those of sovereign power and of ordered—often territorial—space. If considered as a part of a discourse of moral authority, jurisdiction takes its place as an embodiment of the moral authority of institutional and social life.

The language of jurisdiction also offers an important reminder that questions of authority need to be approached in terms of their institutional organization and practice. At the centre of jurisdictional arrangements are the various devices, techniques, and procedures that make the enunciation of the law and social life practicable. Questions of jurisdiction were as central to the accounts of the protocols of government of imperial Rome as to the mediaeval ordering of the spiritual and temporal relations of church and state and to the rise of the modern nation state. Contemporary social concerns with **multiculturalism** and globalization too contend with the same issues of authority and jurisdiction. In a less obvious manner the legal and social work of categorization is also jurisdictional. The classification of relations in terms of rights and wrongs or in terms of obligations and property relations delimits a life subject to legal authority. Whether closely tied to a legal institution or not, a claim of authority, if responsible, brings with it an account of jurisdiction.

SHAUN MCVEIGH

jurisprudence   *see* **theory in legal research**

jury, origins and development In his *Commentaries on the Laws of England*, William **Blackstone** called trial by jury 'the grand bulwark' of every Englishman's liberties, both 'for the settling of civil property', and to guard against 'the violence and partiality of judges appointed by the **Crown**'. This mode of trial spread throughout the British Empire and is still regarded as an invaluable protection, especially in criminal cases.

Two types of juries became established in England in the medieval era, the grand jury and the petit (trial) jury. Initially the grand jury was charged as a 'jury of presentment', to survey and report criminal behaviour within the community. This role decreased when the accusatory function passed to public servants, and the grand jury was left to decide whether bills of indictment were justified in particular cases. This function continues to be performed by grand juries in the US, though critics contend that indictment procedures favour the prosecutor so strongly that the grand jury is no longer a meaningful protection for the accused. The grand jury was abolished in England in 1933.

The English trial jury of the medieval era has been described as 'self-informing', since jurors came from the neighbourhood and were expected to know something about the matter being tried. By the 1500s, however, a different concept of the trial jury was taking shape—that the jurors should have no particular knowledge of the case but should base their verdict entirely on evidence produced in court. This model continues to the present day.

A persistent refrain about jury trial is that the defendant is entitled to a 'jury of peers', an expression that has been linked (inaccurately) to the Magna Carta. The expression suggests that a defendant is entitled to jurors who will have some identification with him or her, perhaps through race, gender, culture, or socio-economic status. This, however, has almost never been possible. The closest approximation, historically, was the jury *de medietate linguae* ('of the half tongue'), which entitled a foreign defendant to have foreigners fill half the jury. But until well into the twentieth century, large segments of the population were excluded from jury service. Women could serve only on 'juries of matrons' for the special purpose of deciding whether a convicted female defendant was 'quick with child'. Racial and ethnic minorities were regularly excluded, as were those who fell below statutory property qualifications. These barriers have all been removed, and in the US jurors in federal courts are required to be chosen from a jury pool that represents a 'reasonable cross-section' of the community from which the jurors are drawn. This makes it impossible to form juries with special expertise, such as the special juries of merchants that were common in both England and America in the eighteenth and nineteenth centuries.

Traditionally each trial jury was required to have twelve members and the verdict was required to be unanimous. These requirements are no longer universal. Since 1974 in England, for example, a verdict by a jury of eleven or twelve requires a vote of at least ten. Historically in England and the US, prospective jurors could be challenged for cause and a number of peremptory challenges were allowed. These procedures survive in the US, but in England peremptory challenges were abolished in 1988 and challenges for cause have become extremely rare.

Despite its rich history and public veneration, the civil jury has largely disappeared in England. Only in actions for **libel**, **slander**, malicious prosecution, false imprisonment, or fraud can a jury be requested in a suit for damages. In the US the right to a jury in civil cases is preserved by the Constitution; nevertheless, the number of jury trials actually conducted in civil cases decreased sharply during the late twentieth century. Juries in criminal cases are also preserved by the Constitution, but the number of jury trials has plummeted, primarily because of the spread of plea-bargaining. A similar reduction has occurred in England for serious (indictable) offences due largely to the fact that in all but the most serious types of cases defendants are allowed to waive the right to a jury, and increasingly they do so.

The traditional understanding is that the jury decides questions of fact; the judge, questions of law. There have been times when juries have insisted on deciding the law as well as the facts. Well-known instances occurred in the seventeenth and eighteenth-century era of 'the Bloody Code' in England when even relatively minor offences were punishable by death. Juries often refused to convict despite the most damning evidence. Similarly, juries in England and America refused to bring in guilty verdicts in seditious libel cases when the juries thought the publications justified or harmless, even though the law (until Fox's Libel Act of 1792) assigned the question of seditious content to the judge. This behaviour has been termed 'jury nullification', and popular support for the power of the jury to act in this way persists.

Jury trial remains an important part of Anglo-American jurisprudence despite the drop in caseload. Indeed, in one form or another, the procedure is used in countries worldwide, having even been adopted in Russia in the 1990s.   JAMES OLDHAM

WR Cornish, *The Jury* (London: Allen Lane, The Penguin Press, 1968)

N Vidmar (ed), *World Jury Systems* (Oxford: Oxford University Press 2000)

jus cogens *Jus cogens*, or 'peremptory law', is the body of international norms that protect the fundamental interests of the international community as a whole, not reducible to individual interests of states, and hence that constitute the public order (public policy) of the international community.

The link to the community interest and public order makes the norms of *jus cogens* non-derogable through the acts and transactions of international legal persons. Examples of peremptory law include the prohibition of the **use of force**, prohibition of genocide, war crimes and crimes against humanity, basic rights of the individual, such as the prohibition of torture or arbitrary deprivation of life, and humanitarian norms protecting the individual in armed conflicts.

The principal characteristic of peremptory law is its primacy over other international norms; and this results in the nullity of the conflicting norms, titles, and transactions. This is illustrated by Articles 53, 64 and 71 of the 1969 Vienna Convention on the Law of Treaties, which govern the invalidity of treaties conflicting with *jus cogens*. Other, and consequent, effects of peremptory law include the duty of non-recognition of acts, titles, and situations produced through the breach of peremptory norms; the establishment of universal jurisdiction over the breaches of *jus cogens*; and the deprivation of the entitlement to state immunity with regard to such breaches. Peremptory law also imposes limits on the treaty-based competence of international organizations, and can be invoked in international judicial proceedings by the state that has no individual interest in the matter (*actio popularis*).   ALEXANDER ORAKHELASHVILI

See also: **international criminal law; international humanitarian law**

justice Justice is complex moral concept relating to human relationships generally, but closely associated with the operation of legal institutions. Justice concerns both the correct or fair distribution of benefits and burdens as between groups or classes of persons (social justice), and treating individuals properly or fairly (individual justice). More specifically, justice can be about the proper basis for agreements or exchanges (commutative justice) or about putting right past wrongs or injustices (corrective justice). In all these spheres, justice may be focused on defining the proper outcomes of social relationships (substantive or material justice) or on the processes or procedures that ought to be followed in reaching these outcomes (formal or procedural justice). Procedures may be considered formally just insofar as they result in a substantively just outcome, but, in cases of 'pure procedural justice', where the desired outcome is not known or in dispute, procedures may considered just or unjust independent of their results, if, for instance, they are thought to be fair and impartial. In courtroom settings, this is referred to as 'due process' or 'natural justice'.

It is disputed whether there is a necessary connection between law and justice. Legal positivists hold that a law is a law however unjust it may be. Most natural law theorists hold that seriously unjust 'laws' are not laws at all and should not be enforced by courts. A compromise position is that court decisions that fail to meet certain standards of procedural justice are unacceptable and should be overturned on appeal, but questions about the substantive justice of the content of a law are for political, not legal, decision-making. It is a matter of controversy how far courts, through the development of the **common law**, the **interpretation of legislation**, and the use of **judicial review** to override legislation on human rights grounds, should seek to render laws and legal process more just in other than a procedural sense.

The idea of justice is as central to the domain of politics as it is to law, the two spheres being intimately connected through the concept of the **rule of law**, according to which government ought to be conducted through the enactment and impartial enforcement of general rules and in accordance with the constitution of the jurisdiction in question. The rule of law implements Aristotle's view that equals should be treated equally and unequals unequally. A narrow conception of the rule of law focuses on achieving this through the strict application of general rules which state the category of person and type of conduct to be allocated certain benefit and burdens. This is 'formal justice', as its application does not require any judgment as to the justice of the rules themselves. Perhaps formal justice has no value in itself, but strong feelings of resentment are aroused when an authorized rule is not applied in the same manner to all persons who are similarly situated. Moreover, formal justice may be necessary for the attainment of substantive justice.

Formal or procedural justice requires ascertaining what is the relevant rule (a question of law) and determining whether its terms apply to the case in question (often a question of fact). Since both elements may be disputed, formal justice requires that there be appropriate procedures in place regulating how authoritative decisions on these matters are reached in individual cases. For instance, there must be charges or pleas expressed in terms of recognized rules, evidence must be presented with respect to facts relevant to these rules, and the opportunity must be given to those involved to counter this evidence, call and cross-examine witnesses, and present their case. The justice of the procedures adopted depends both on giving those who are liable to adverse outcomes the opportunity to understand and refute the case against them, and on their reliability as a means for ascertaining the truth about the events in question and settling disputes about the relevance and interpretation of the rules that are to be applied. In criminal cases procedural justice involves giving the benefit of the doubt to accused persons.

Substantive justice concerns who are to be considered equals and unequals for the purposes of the distribution of benefits and burdens in a society. Thus, such distributions could be in accordance with (1) merit or desert; (2) need or relative poverty; (3) contribution to the general wellbeing; or (4) fundamental rights. The first, meritorian, conception, according to which morally good conduct should be rewarded and morally bad conduct penalized, is deeply entrenched in the discourse of justice, but its assumptions are fiercely disputed by those who believe that what we do is not within our control or think that we are seldom in a position to make an accurate assessment of moral culpability. The second, egalitarian, conception of substantive justice focuses on bringing about a more equal distribution benefits and burdens in the belief that the happiness and wellbeing of every person is of equal importance. It may concentrate on relieving basic needs or bringing about total equality. The third, 'utilitarian' (or 'consequentialist'), conception sees the distribution of benefits and burdens as an instrument for maximizing human welfare generally, the assumption being that providing the necessary incentives to socially useful conduct will bring the greatest good to the greatest number in a calculus that assumes everyone's pleasures and pains to be of equal importance. The fourth conception of substantive justice, that distribution be in accordance with fundamental rights, assumes that there are rights which exist independently of any laws made by human beings. Thus John Locke holds that everyone has a 'natural right' to life, liberty, and property. Building on these natural rights, Robert Nozick argues that justice is not about distributing benefits and burdens at all, and requires only that people do not violate the rights of others and, as a matter of corrective justice, rectify any such violations as do occur. More expansive

sets of rights are included by those who see justice as respecting human rights.

John Rawls (in *A Theory of Justice* (Oxford: Oxford University Press, 1971) combines all except the first conception of substantive justice outlined above in a theory based on the Enlightenment idea that the institutions of a just society are those that would be endorsed in a social contract in which everyone involved would have an equal say. He constructs a hypothetical 'original position' in which individuals, under a 'veil of ignorance' regarding their particular talents and future position in society, agree on certain basic rights that will be guaranteed to them all, and adopt the 'maximin' principle for the distribution of benefits and burdens according to which no inequalities are allowed that do not benefit the worst off group in a society. Rawls checks this against his 'intuitions' as to what social arrangements are just, and, reaches an 'equilibrium' view that turns out to embody the beliefs of 'liberal' intellectuals in the United States at that time.

Rawls's approach includes everything that he regards as of 'overriding' importance for the evaluation of basic social institutions, including law. Others take a narrower conception of justice, such as the meritorian position that justice is fundamentally about desert, but without holding that (meritorian) justice ought to be an overriding consideration. A compromise position, of particular relevance to law, involves developing the formal analysis of justice to take in a more substantive conception of 'legality'. Thus Lon **Fuller**, in *The Morality of Law* (New Haven: Yale University Press, 1969) includes under 'rule governance' the requirement that law is a moral ideal which consists of general rules that are clear, consistent, practicable, prospective, known, stable, and consistent. Meeting these conditions manifests 'a commitment to the view that man is, or can become, a responsible agent, capable of understanding, following rules and answerable for his defaults' (p162). This has affinities with the meritorian conceptions of moral responsibility and includes those civil and political rights that concern 'natural justice' in the sense of due process, together with liberty as freedom from 'arbitrary'(ie non-rule-governed) restrictions.

Other conceptions of legality include more rights, such as non-discrimination, freedom of speech, freedom of movement, and a decent standard of living, roughly along the lines of Rawls's basic rights. The rationale for adopting such extended conceptions of the rule of law, which blur the distinction between formal and substantive justice, is often the promotion of the type of constitutional democracy that empowers courts to override legislation that they deem incompatible with a constitutionally entrenched bill or covenant of rights. This may be contrasted with less rights-based and more socially oriented conceptions of justice whereby a commitment to self-determination and wellbeing is given expression in democratic institutions that are designed to promote social justice. Courts then have the duty of securing formal justice and the wider community has the duty of promoting substantive justice through legislation. This approach acknowledges the significant moral disagreement that exists both with respect to what constitutes justice and in relation to how these conflicting ideas may be best put into practice.   TOM CAMPBELL

T Campbell, *Justice* (London: Palgrave, 2001)

JUSTICE (British section of the International Commission of Jurists)   JUSTICE is an all-party lawyers' organization dedicated to the use of law reform to advance access to justice, **human rights,** and the **rule of law**. It has around 1500 members and is governed by a council.

JUSTICE was formed in 1957 to keep under observation treason trials in South Africa and their equivalent in Hungary. It subsequently developed more of a domestic focus, leaving developments outside the UK to the International Commission of Jurists, of which it became the British section. For its first forty years, it was probably best known for its casework in relation to **miscarriages of justice**. However, it ceased this work in the late 1990s on the establishment of the **Criminal Cases Review Commission**.

JUSTICE has been influential in the development of many areas of legal policy. It published early papers supporting the establishment of **ombudsmen** and the concept of 'spent' convictions. It has been engaged on all recent bills with major implications for human rights, particularly anti-terrorism measures. It has intervened in a number of key cases concerning the scope of operation within the UK of the Human Rights Act 1998 and its effect on events occurring abroad. JUSTICE is interested in how the 1998 Act is changing the relationship between the judiciary, executive, and legislature. Other concerns include the development of legal cooperation in criminal matters within the EU; **equality**; criminal justice; and **legal aid**.   ROGER SMITH

Justices of the Peace   In England and Wales, reliance upon the lay people appointed as Justices of the Peace (also known as 'JPs' or, more commonly, lay justices or lay magistrates) is without parallel in the world. JPs have been in existence for some 600 years in England and Wales, and about 28,000 now sit in the lower **courts**. They are unpaid volunteers entitled to claim no more than a loss of earnings allowance and expenses. They have no legal qualifications and the vast majority have, on appointment, no experience of the courts either. Justices of the Peace also exist in Scotland although they are far fewer in number, deal only with minor criminal cases and have much more limited sentencing powers than JPs in England and Wales. In Northern Ireland, the lay magistracy is still in its early infancy, a campaign to recruit volunteers having only begun in 2004 and the first few appointments made in 2005. The focus here is therefore upon the role played by Justices of the Peace in England and Wales.

Lay justices can impose sentences of imprisonment of up to six months (or twelve months if there are consecutive sentences) as well as financial penalties exceeding £5,000. Sitting in benches of three, supported by a qualified court clerk, they conduct the great bulk of the work of the lower courts. They have indeed been described as the backbone of the **criminal justice system** in England and Wales. In addition to exercising a limited civil and family jurisdiction, the magistrates' courts handle about 96 per cent of all criminal cases. While a substantial proportion of the latter are minor summary cases, about five out of six of 'indictable' cases (ones that might be tried before a **jury**) are heard in the magistrates' courts. Lay magistrates are assisted in this work by about 300 professional District Judges who sit alone (full-time or part-time) in magistrates' courts, although they are found in only the large city courts.

It is quite extraordinary that work on this scale and of such seriousness should be entrusted to lay volunteers. It is even more remarkable when one considers the sacrifices that those appointed as JPs are required to make. As a minimum, they must spend half a day every fortnight sitting in court in addition to attending compulsory training courses, bench meetings, committees, social gatherings, etc. Not surprisingly, it has always proved difficult to find enough people of the right calibre prepared to make these huge personal sacrifices.

The appointment of JPs is on merit although **Lord Chancellors** have insisted that they be recruited from a broad spectrum of society and form a balanced cross-section of local **communities**. The local bodies responsible for making nominations to the Lord Chancellor 'need to ensure that the composition of the bench broadly reflects the community which it serves in terms of gender, ethnic origin, geographical spread, occupation and . . . political affiliation', a very tall order. The theory is that people from different walks of life will have a breadth of knowledge and experience of the life of a particular local community that no professional lawyer could equal. But there is no doubt that this insistence on socio-economic balance makes the task of recruiting lay magistrates much more difficult. For obvious reasons, it is much easier to recruit magistrates from certain social and occupational groups than from others. Since having time and money to spare is a great help, the composition of many benches is disproportionately middle class and middle aged and, whatever the theory, it is fair to note that the lay magistracy has always been an unrepresentative body. Despite national recruitment campaigns, only limited success has been achieved in changing this picture.

The standard of **justice** dispensed in magistrates' courts has been subjected to considerable public criticism over the years, and many have viewed the appointment of large numbers of unpaid volunteers as merely a convenient way of cutting the cost of running the criminal courts. Yet the fact that lay people are so deeply involved in the administration of justice is in itself impressive. Lord Chancellors have always expressed great confidence in lay magistrates and a firm commitment to their continuance. A former **Lord Chief Justice**, Lord Bingham, has described the lay magistracy as 'a democratic jewel beyond price'. A lay judiciary, with roots embedded in the local community, demonstrates at least that the justice system is not a closed shop or one that is dominated by lawyers and other professionals.

JOHN BALDWIN

justification, excuse, and mitigation in criminal law 'He was trying to strangle me and I had to protect myself.' 'He had been winding me up all afternoon and I finally lost my temper.' 'My new medicine had a strange effect on me so I had no idea what I was doing.' All of these are answers that people might give to the accusatory question: 'Why did you hit him?' They are answers that do not involve denying the accusation. 'You're right, I hit him,' the answer goes, 'but let me explain.' Lawyers call such answers 'defences'.

The three defences just listed are of different types. 'I had to protect myself' is an attempt to *justify* what one did. It is an attempt to explain why hitting was, all told, the right thing to do in the circumstances. 'I finally lost my temper', by contrast, is an attempt at an *excuse*. Although hitting was not the right thing to do, it was a perfectly understandable human reaction. 'I had no idea what I was

doing,' finally, is an attempt to *deny responsibility for one's actions*. When one is not responsible for one's actions, one has no need to justify or excuse oneself.

Although criminal law tends to be sparing in which defences it recognizes, most systems of criminal law recognize defences of all three types. In criminal law, the main justifications are self-defence, prevention of crime, and consent. The main excuses are duress and provocation. The main responsibility-eliminators are infancy and insanity. Different defences may, of course, be available in respect of different crimes. In English Law, for example, duress has (for most of its history) not been available as a defence to murder. Consent has likewise not been available as a defence to crimes involving physical injury.

Some defences are hard to classify in this tripartite scheme. Suppose a fire engine goes through a red light on its way to a fire, and causes a serious accident. When the driver is prosecuted for dangerous driving, is his defence of necessity to be thought of as a justification (like prevention of crime) or an excuse (like duress)? Should we say that he acted rightly given the emergency or merely acted understandably under pressure? Different legal systems might think differently about the case. Indeed the same legal system may think differently about it depending on the details of what happened (how fast he was going, and so on).

In criminal law there is also a fourth class of *procedural* defences. These defences include diplomatic immunity and double jeopardy (the defence that one has already been tried for the same crime and found not guilty). In some legal systems, passage of time since the crime is also a procedural defence. It is in connection with these defences that onlookers are most likely to say that an accused person was 'let off on a technicality'. That is because procedural defences have no equivalent in ordinary life outside the law, whereas the other three types of defences mentioned above figure equally in personal relationships, political debate, and so on.

The result of mounting a succesful defence in a criminal court is that one is not convicted (found guilty) of the crime for which one is being tried. Since the result of mounting a successful defence is always the same, why bother to classify defences into different types? In many legal systems, there is no official classification of defences. The classification of defences is a task undertaken by legal commentators and theorists. Some argue that the classification is important because it can have secondary legal implications (for example, one might be justified in defending oneself against an excused

assault, but not against a justified one). But mainly the classification matters for moral reasons. To develop the law intelligently, and to treat those who appear before them appropriately, **courts** need to be able to understand and explain not only what counts as a defence but also why it counts as a defence. So they need to know how the defence is supposed to function: whether it justifies the crime, or excuses it, or eliminates the accused person's responsibility for her actions, or whether it is merely a procedural defence.

Some commentators resist the tripartite classification of non-procedural defences. A common alternative classification is bipartite. On this view, there are only justifications and excuses. Denials of responsibility are simply a sub-type of excuses. Admittedly the word 'excuse' can be used loosely to cover denials of responsibility as well. But this loose sense of the word conceals an important distinction. The importance of this distinction is brought out by thinking about the defences available to those who are driven by repeated abuse to kill their abusive spouses or partners. Such people sometimes argue that they were acting in necessary self-defence (justification). They sometimes argue that the abuser provoked them to do it (excuse). And they sometimes argue that the abuse had finally made them mentally ill (denial of responsibility). The second defence is like the third (and unlike the first) in that it does not claim that killing the abuser was the right thing to do. It admits that it was a mistake. But it is also like the first (and unlike the third) in that it claims that the reaction to the abuse was a reasonable one, even if reasonably mistaken.

Someone charged with murder in this situation may well prefer to plead provocation rather than relying on their mental illness, even if relying on mental illness would be a more efficient way to avoid conviction. It is natural for **human** beings to want to stand up for their own reasonableness and to be judged accordingly. This is part of preserving one's self-respect. So here is another moral reason to care about the classification of defences. Justifications and excuses allow one to hold one's head up high in a way that denials of responsibility do not.

Some defences in the criminal law (eg provocation and diminished responsibility) have come to be known as 'partial' defences. But strictly speaking they are not partial defences. They are complete defences to one crime (eg murder) that are not defences to a lesser crime (eg manslaughter), of which one can accordingly be convicted instead. Strictly speaking there can be no partial defences in the criminal law because there is no such thing as a partial conviction for a crime. Regarding any crime, one is either convicted or one is not.

Yet the **punishment** for the crime may, of course, be a matter of degree. So an unsuccessful defence (one that did not prevent one's conviction for the crime) may still be offered again as what lawyers call a *mitigating factor*: a reason for reducing the punishment. Mitigating factors may include (among other things) justificatory factors, excusatory factors, and factors bearing on the offender's responsibility for her actions. The criminal law is typically much more relaxed about mitigating factors than it is about defences; while the list of possible defences is heavily regulated, the list of possible mitigating factors is almost a free-for-all. Outside the law, however, mitigating factors are not distinct from defences, because being guilty of a wrong outside the law is not an all-or-nothing affair. In everyday life there are degrees of justification and excuse (and perhaps—although this is trickier—degrees of responsibility for one's actions).

JOHN GARDNER

Justinian The Emperor Justinian (AD 527–65) is generally reckoned the last Roman and the first Byzantine emperor. He recovered for the Empire, and for orthodox (as opposed to heretical Arian) Christianity, Northern Africa from the Vandals, and Rome and Italy from the Ostrogoths. Justinian's ecclesiastical interests still have their monument in the great church of Hagia Sophia in Istanbul, as well as, remotely, in the continuing discords between Catholic and Orthodox Christianity. However, his enduring memorial is in the field of law: as well as issuing new laws, he 'codified' existing law.

Justinian was born around AD 483 in Thrace, a native Latin-speaker. He could identify with the old western Roman culture; he saw himself as the new Augustus, re-founder of the Empire. He says in the opening sentence of his *Institutes*: 'Imperial majesty should be not only enhanced by arms but also armed by laws, so that, whether in time of war or peace, there can be right government. Let the Roman Emperor, not only victorious in war with the enemy but also banishing the crimes of evildoers through the machinery of law, be as solicitous of justice as he is triumphant over defeated foes'. The **rule of law** was thus for him an integral part of government, which is why he preserved, and transmitted to us, the bulk of what we have of the law of Rome, in the compilation later known as the *Corpus Iuris Civilis* (the *Body of the Civil Law*). It is fourfold: the *Institutes*, explicitly an elementary textbook for law students; the *Digest*, an edited collection of jurists' writings, from the very late Republic to the mid-third century; the *Code*, a collection of imperial enactments from the Emperor Hadrian (117–38) on; and the *Novels*, never officially collected, Justinian's own legislation after the publication in 533–34 of the other three parts.

Of Justinian's own legislation, his few changes to the law of property were mostly minor, or confirmed the existing state of affairs. In the field of obligations there was even less that was new. However, in family law and succession he was a radical. The agnatic family, the family traced strictly through the male line, had since the earliest Republic been the dominant legal institution of Roman society, the source of the authority of the *paterfamilias*, the explanation for many rules about succession, all of which had of their nature been biased toward male dominance. Justinian effectively abolished the agnatic family in Novel 118 of AD 543, and put men and women on terms of legal equality in their family rights, although not, of course, altering the inferior social and political status of women.

Justinian set out to make more user-friendly the great mass of statute and jurisprudence that went back to the time of the Twelve Tables in the mid-fifth century BC, nearly a thousand years before. He must have been contemplating whole-scale legal reforms before his succession, for in February 528 he ordered the compilation of a new Code, making use of earlier codes. His compilers, legal experts, both academics and practitioners, led by Tribonian, were to bring his Code up-to-date, removing superfluities, correcting inconsistencies, and fusing separate enactments where appropriate. This was published in 529, but a revised Code–the version that survives–replaced it in 534. Then, in 530, Justinian told his compilers to edit a collection of juristic writings, ascribing each text to its author, and again amending as necessary. This, the *Digest*, is roughly one and a half times the length of the Bible; we are told that it is approximately 5 per cent of what the compilers read. Since the Humanists in the sixteenth century, scholars have been concerned with the extent of these amendments, known as interpolations, but the dogmatic importance of the *Corpus* has been relatively little affected.

The *Corpus Iuris Civilis* is the foundation of law in Europe, and its colonies. The continuing usefulness of the *Corpus*, particularly the *Digest*, as a source of law, lies not only in its great store of ideas but also in its displaying argument, showing law as something dynamic, not mere rules. From its rediscovery as a written text in the eleventh century until the era of codification, it was the fundamental study wherever there was a law faculty. Even in countries where **Roman law** was barely received, or lawyers were not educated at universities, the style of legal argument, the vocabulary of legal thought, is indebted to Justinian's work.   OLIVIA F ROBINSON

K

Kahn-Freund, Sir Otto Sir Otto Kahn-Freud QC, FBA (1900–1979) was one of the most influential legal scholars in Britain in the twentieth century. He published seminal works in comparative law, conflict of laws, family law, and labour law. His great influence lay as much in the socio-legal approach he brought to legal studies as in the particular ideas he expressed. He grew up in Germany and studied law at Frankfurt, where, during his doctoral work, he learned to approach the study of law in its social, economic, and political context under the direct influence of his teacher, Hugo Sinzheimer, and the broader intellectual influences of Marx, Ehrlich, von Gierke, and Weber. He became a judge in a Berlin labour court, but his social democratic views, his Jewish background, and his judgments upholding the rights of workers against fascist oppression, led to his illegal dismissal by the Nazis and his flight to England in 1933. Starting his life again, with his characteristic optimism and humility, he became a LLM student and then lecturer at the London School of Economics, where he discovered new influences such as Harold Laski and Henry Phelps Brown. Joining English progressive academic lawyers at the LSE, such as Chorley and Gower, together with fellow refugee, Wolfgang Friedmann, he quickly became involved and influential in the development of the distinctive and novel approach to legal scholarship in the *Modern Law Review*, which had been founded in 1937. In the Review and elsewhere, Kahn-Freund began to publish essays that explored more deeply than had anyone before in England the relation between law and its social context. His 'Introduction' to a translation of Karl Renner's *The Institutions of Private Law and Their Social Functions* (1949) revealed his general perspective in which it was necessary to understand the social and economic effects of laws, and how the function of laws could become distorted in new social contexts. In labour law, his favourite subject, to which he gave this nomenclature as opposed to the law of master and servant, these insights, combined with his knowledge of other legal systems, permitted him to present a compelling analysis of the strengths and weaknesses of the British system, by using his concept of 'collective laissez-faire' in an essay in Ginsberg's *Law and Opinion in England in the 20th Century* (1959). He became an influential member of the Donovan Royal Commission on Trade Unions and Employers' Associations (1965–1968), for which he drafted the later chapters on proposed legal reforms such as the introduction of the law of **unfair dismissal**. His own definitive statement of the subject appeared in his Hamlyn Lectures, *Labour and the Law* (1972). The lectures are replete with memorable phrases; best remembered perhaps is his remark about the relation between employer and employee: 'In its inception it is an act of submission, in its operation it is a condition of subordination, however much the submission and subordination may be concealed by that indispensable figment of the legal mind known as the "contract of employment".' At the age of sixty-four, he became professor of comparative law at Oxford, retiring in 1971. As well as the Hamlyn Lectures, this septuagenarian then produced the Hague Lectures on *General Problems of Private International Law* (1976) and the British Academy lectures, *Labour Relations: Heritage and Adjustment* (1979). In Britain, Kahn-Freund was one of the pioneers of socio-legal approaches to legal scholarship, thereby rejecting the existing tradition of examining solely strictly legal materials in legal education and publications. As well as inspiring generations of law teachers and students, his work greatly influenced the development of the law relating to employment and **trade unions** during his lifetime.   HUGH COLLINS

Keech v Sandford (1726) This case established the modern rule that no profit may be derived from a position of trust. The rule is particularly concerned with situations where property is held on trust for a beneficiary by a trustee who then 'self-deals' or uses that property to make a personal profit. The rule also binds fiduciaries who do not necessarily own property on behalf of another but who are duty-bound to manage that other person's affairs solely in that person's interest. So fiduciaries may not exploit commercial opportunity or information coming to them by virtue of their fiduciary position; they are disabled from pursuing private interest, even if the interests of their beneficiaries are unharmed or even promoted by such self-enriching activity.

Keech v Sandford itself concerned a trustee who took a lease over market rights at Rumford that he had previously held on behalf of an infant beneficiary. The trustee argued that the benefit (the lease) could never have been won directly for the infant because the owner of the market had refused to renew it for the use of an infant, and that no harm had therefore been done to the infant's interests. Precedent favoured the trustee, but the court nonetheless decreed that a constructive trust of the lease should be imposed in order to give the infant all the benefits of the lease. The court may have been swayed by the contemporary custom of 'tenant right', amounting to a legitimate expectation that leases would generally be renewed unless the tenant had behaved badly. Lord Chancellor King stated that that if trustees thought they might exercise a tenant's right for themselves, they would rig events to ensure that leases held for their beneficiaries were never renewed. King was careful not to accuse the trustee in *Keech* of fraud, but the pleadings did allege that the trustee had conspired to block the lease renewal, and had then embezzled trust funds to buy the lease. By upholding a broad policy of prohibiting all profit to trustees without full consent, it was possible to cleanse fiduciary relationships without having to go into precise evidence of fraud and wrongdoing. King acknowledged that it might seem hard to forbid trustees to profit in all situations, but it was crucial for the law to shield trustees from venal temptation; the rule was thus deterrent in design.

The brief and cryptic decision in *Keech v Sandford* was not taken at the time to be any kind of leading case. King was a common lawyer placed at the head of the Court of Chancery in 1725 in order to combat corruption and abuses that had crept in under his predecessors. The Chancery's own officials had taken litigants' money paid into court as part of the litigation process, and had invested and lost those funds during the South Sea Bubble and ensuing financial collapse of 1720. King disciplined his own officials and prohibited them from using other people's money. Building on this experience, King may have been concerned generally to prevent all fiduciary powers being exploited for personal gain: hence the uncompromising stance taken in *Keech*. By the early nineteenth century the case had emerged as the foundation of the fiduciary rules governing not

only trustees but also partners, agents, and directors. Occasionally today the breadth of the rule is criticized for banning profit not obviously connected to trust business or harmful to beneficiaries; but courts continue to apply the *Keech v Sandford* doctrine as a fundamental principle of equity.

JOSHUA GETZLER

J Getzler, 'Rumford Market and the Genesis of Fiduciary Obligations' in A Burrows and A Rodger (eds), *Mapping the Law: Essays in Memory of Peter Birks* (Oxford University Press: Oxford, 2006) 577–98

See also: **equity as a system of law**; **trusts**

Kent, Constance Constance Kent (1844–1944) was tried for the murder of her younger brother, Savill, in July 1865. The crime, which came to be known as the Road murder after the name of the village, was one of the most notorious crimes of the period both because of its subject matter, and the confusion which surrounded the investigation and identification of the perpetrator.

The boy, aged four, went missing on the night of 29 June 1860, and his body was discovered a few hours later in a disused privy in the grounds of the family home. Constance was initially suspected of the murder by the police, who believed that she had been motivated by feelings of jealousy of the boy. She was arrested and brought before local magistrates in Devizes, but she remained silent, and no evidence was adduced of her guilt. She was subsequently discharged.

Some years later she underwent a religious conversion, under the influence of the Revd Arthur Wagner, and resolved to make a public confession of her guilt. This she did at Bow Street Magistrates' Court in April 1865. Wagner gave some details from the confession, but declined to make others public, claiming the privilege of the confessional—although it was later affirmed by the Lord Chancellor that no such privilege existed. She was brought to trial at Wiltshire Assizes on 21 July 1865, where she pleaded guilty to the murder and was sentenced to death. Because of strong doubts about her actual guilt arising from discrepancies between the confession and the evidence, the capital sentence was commuted to penal servitude for life. She was released from prison in 1885 and subsequently emigrated to Australia, where she died in 1944.   LINDSAY FARMER

kitemarks The kitemark is the symbol of the British Standards Institute ('BSI'). It can be seen on a very wide range of products and services.

British standards go back to the early part of the twentieth century. BSI develops standards for products and services, which ensure they are of high quality. These standards are generally of a performance nature, but a few are more comprehensive, laying down methods of manufacture. Each standard is given a number (eg BS5678). More recently, European ('EN') and International ('ISO') standards have been produced.

Anybody can display on their product, or associate with their product, a British Standard number. The display of the kitemark is, however, limited to manufacturers who are licensed by the BSI. The Institute carries out an initial series of tests to ensure that the product or service does meet the required standard. It also checks the quality control system employed by the manufacturer. If the BSI considers the product meets the requirements it will issue a licence. There are over 2,500 licences currently in force. The BSI will periodically buy the product (often anonymously) and test it to ensure that standards continue to be met. The display of the kitemark is regarded as a guarantee that the product meets the required standard.

The Trade Descriptions Act 1968 makes it an offence to display a BS number or a kitemark unless the product does in fact comply with the relevant standard, and there have been a number of such prosecutions over the years.   RICHARD BRAGG

knowledge and belief   *see* **fault-based criminal liability**

L

L'Estrange v Graucob Ltd (1934) Miss L'Estrange, who ran a café in Great Ormes Road, Llandudno (then a well-known holiday resort), ordered a cigarette vending machine from Graucob Ltd. She was given a long brown form, which she signed, having 'no clear idea of what it was'. The machine proved disastrous: she rejected it and sued for her money back.

The contract contained a clause 'Any condition or warranty, expressed or implied, by statute or by common law, is hereby excluded'. In English law a 'condition' means an important promise in a contract, a 'warranty' a lesser promise. So it could be said that Graucob Ltd had effectively excluded any liability for what had happened.

At the time the general test for whether a term was incorporated into a contract was to ask whether reasonable notice had been given of it. The Llandudno county court judge found that it had not. But the document had been signed, and for lawyers the case still stands for the proposition laid down by the Court of Appeal that where a document is signed the signer is bound by it whatever it says, unless there is fraud or its contents have been misrepresented.

Counsel for Graucob was AT **Denning**, a young barrister who later became Lord Denning, one of the great twentieth- century judges. In lectures (and one of his books) he used to say that the reporters did not report the case, his clients had the judgment privately printed, and that he went round county courts winning cases on the strength of it. The relevant period must however have been short as the case was reported in the Official Reports later in the same year. It was condemned by PA Landon, an Oxford academic, in the *Law Quarterly Review* ((1935) 51 *LQR* 272) as 'a menace to the community—not to the commercial community, but to the great majority of us who are buyers rather than sellers'.

The case also performed a second and looser function in drawing attention to the need for restraining the operation of wide exclusions of contract liability. It provided a stimulus to the doctrine of fundamental breach of contract, which helped to control such clauses in the 1950s and was associated with Lord Denning. That doctrine was eventually discarded because of difficulties of definition and of juristic basis; but it was succeeded by statutory control in the Unfair Contract Terms Act of 1977, adopted at a time when such problems were regarded all over Europe as requiring attention.

Mr Graucob was Danish, but lived in England from 1922, founding his cigarette machine business in 1925. In 1943 he bought the Nu-Swift Engineering Co, which made fire extinguishers. Retiring to Jersey in 1975, he died in 1978. He sometimes wrote letters to *The Times*, including one in 1929 complaining about the standard terms of the Southern Railway, which he had obviously not omitted to study.

FRANCIS REYNOLDS

See also: **unfair contract terms**

labour law and trade union law in developing countries Basic principles of labour law grow out of the employment relationship. The employment relationship is primarily governed by the **contract of employment**. However, the peculiar position of the employee as the weaker party in the employment contract has led to efforts to strengthen this position. Workers' efforts to consolidate their position usually lead to the establishment of **trade unions** while the corresponding effort of the state to protect workers is demonstrated in the enactment of labour laws. In developing countries where employees often have very low bargaining power, statutory provisions serve to create a floor of rights which operate as minimum terms and conditions of employment. With the Declaration on Fundamental Principles and Rights at Work by the **International Labour Organization** ('ILO') in 1998, four core rights have emerged as basic standards that should be met by domestic labour law. These core principles are the right to **freedom of association**, the abolition of forced labour, the abolition of **child labour,** and freedom from discrimination.

In many developing countries with a **common law** origin, especially in Africa and Asia, contemporary labour law has evolved from old master and servant ordinances. With the growth of wage employment and Western forms of government introduced by colonial governments, a distinct labour law framework for workers in the public service became a feature of many post-colonial labour systems. Thus, it is common to find a dual system of labour regulation in many developing countries, with one set of laws applicable to public service employees and another applying to workers in the private sector. Labour statutes in such contexts typically provide for basic employment contracts, terms and conditions of employment, **collective bargaining**, termination of employment, apprenticeship contracts, occupational health and safety, and social security. This interplay of influences from colonial labour law legacies, international labour law **governance,** and domestic labour situations largely defines the nature and character of labour law systems in many developing countries.

Developing countries are faced with severe challenges to their labour law systems, some of which are local, while others are linked to the effect of globalization and commercialization. These challenges include the increasing trend of casualization and informalization of labour as enterprises restructure. This trend has resulted in the creation of categories of workers whose employment status is not adequately protected by traditional labour law. Another challenge is the increased incidence of migration from developing countries to developed countries or to other developing countries perceived as more prosperous. Some of this migration occurs between neighbouring countries while others occur across and between continents. There is also the problem of lack of infrastructural capacity in labour institutions for monitoring employment establishments in order to secure compliance with labour law provisions. Other problems include extreme income disparities among the employed as well as the absence of social protection for a vast number of workers, especially those in informal forms of employment. Perhaps the most urgent challenges are those of growing levels of unemployment, the informal sector, and the impact of diseases such as **HIV/AIDS** on the working population.

Domestic attempts to address some of these challenges have led to labour law reform in a number of developing countries. In Southern Africa for example, there has been a spate of new labour **legislation** and bills as well as regional collaboration in the training of labour officers in the 2000s. Labour law reform in this region addresses various issues, including the entrenchment of the core labour rights in domestic laws, the creation of a floor of rights at the workplace, the establishment of **alternative dispute resolution** methods, the management of HIV and AIDS in employment systems, the restructuring of **social security systems,** and the strengthening of labour institutions.

Beyond core rights, the ILO has gone further to redefine the goals of labour systems to be the creation of decent work. The concept of decent work is articulated around four pillars, which are freedom of association, employment creation, social protection, and participation. The decent work agenda ('DWA') is also a key factor driving labour law reform in many developing countries, promoting a broader agenda of integrated development.

Related to and deriving from labour law is trade union law. Trade union law emerged primarily to give expression to employees' rights and freedom of association. Workers' entitlements and expectations from employment invariably converge to bring workers together in trade unions. Trade unions are therefore a platform for the collective promotion of the labour rights of workers. Trade unions work to secure the observance of protective provisions of domestic labour law, while negotiating improved working conditions for workers. They also participate in the broader effort to create a conducive workplace environment for compliance with international labour standards. Trade union law is therefore not only useful, but imperative for the purpose of creating a structure for the activities of organized labour.

Beyond the workplace, trade union movements have been highly instrumental in achieving democratic reforms and monitoring transition to democratic governance in many developing countries. Over the years, trade union law has emerged as a distinct branch of law in many countries, but in some jurisdictions, it is still subsumed under labour law. Trade union law usually provides for the registration, organization, and structure of trade unions. Most countries recognize employees' associations as well as employers' associations as trade unions. However, in some countries, only a registered trade union is legally recognized, while in others, all associations of workers are allowed to operate as trade unions under existing labour law or under broad constitutional provisions guaranteeing the freedom of association. In many developing countries, trade union roles are steadily expanding to address issues that have to do with the impact of globalization on workers, in addition to domestic issues such as **poverty reduction** and employment creation. Trade union law in developing countries will need to adjust, where necessary, to these changes.

EVANCE KALULA AND ADA ORDOR

ILO, *Decent Work*: Report of the Director-General International Labour Conference 87th Session 1999 (Geneva: International Labour Office, 1999)

C Fenwick, E Kalula, and I Landau, *Labour Law: A Southern African Perspective* (Geneva: ILO, 2007)

labour market conditions *see* **voluntary unemployment**

Labour Relations Agency *see* **ACAS**

Lady Chatterley's Lover The trial of Penguin books for publishing DH Lawrence's novel *Lady Chatterley's Lover* took place at the Old Bailey in 1960. Parliament, in passing the Obscene Publications Act 1959, had tried to make a workable distinction between 'literature' (which it wanted to protect) and 'pornography', which it wanted to suppress. The book's acquittal prematurely suggested that this legislative purpose had been achieved, if only in respect of serious works. It took the trial of *Oz* magazine in 1971 to achieve freedom for bad literature, while today it is accepted (even by judges) that run of the mill pornography does not 'deprave and corrupt' adult readers or viewers.

That would have come as a great shock to Mervyn Griffith-Jones, the old Etonian Treasury counsel whose sarcastic but unscholarly bombast lost the case for the **Crown**. His rhetorical question to the jury—'Is it a book that you would even wish your wife or your servant to read?' came to epitomize, for an imminent Beatles generation, the class-ridden sexist prudery against which they could happily rebel. An immaculate performance for the defence by Gerald Gardiner QC (later a reforming Labour Lord Chancellor) punctured the pomposity of the prosecution and deflected the hostility of the judge.

The 1959 Act had made three notable reforms in the **common law** *Hicklin* test for obscenity. It required that the work 'deprave and corrupt' a *significant* number of *likely* readers, instead of any hypothetical reader (14-year-old schoolgirls were the class previously used by prosecutors to secure convictions). It required the work to be judged 'as a whole' and not by reading only its 'purple passages', and it set up a special public good defence under which experts were allowed to testify that notwithstanding a book's tendency to deprave, its publication would be in the interests of literature, art, and 'other objects of general concern'. This defence was relentlessly exploited by Penguin books, which called thirty-four experts—professors of literature, authors, teachers, prelates, and moral philosophers—who exaggerated the literary merits and ethical benefits of Lawrence's rather dull novel. The prosecution, for reasons of arrogance or laziness or both, did not call experts in rebuttal.

Mr Justice Byrne created a lasting precedent when he declared that 'deprave' meant 'to make morally bad' and told the jury that 'the mere fact that you are shocked or disgusted, the mere fact that you hate the sight of the book when you have read it, does not solve the question as to whether you are satisfied beyond reasonable doubt that the tendency of the book is to deprave and corrupt'. This distinction was crucial to obtain acquittals for works that shocked but could not be proved to cause harm. It was endorsed by the Court of Appeal in quashing the obscenity convictions of *Last Exit to Brooklyn* and *Oz Magazine* and remains important for the defence of satirical art and explicit photography, which can produce aversion but not necessarily perversion.

There were 3 million paperback copies of *Lady Chatterley's Lover* sold (at 3/6d) in the three months following the acquittal—an early example of what was later termed *The Spycatcher* effect, whereby an attempt to suppress a book through an unsuccessful prosecution served only to promote massive sales. The novel was recently read on the BBC as a 'book at bedtime', providing a nostalgic reminder of an era when youthful sexual curiosity was sated by surreptitious reading of banned literature rather than by internet downloadings from hardcore porn sites.

GEOFFREY ROBERTSON

land mines *see* **arms control; international humanitarian law**

land reform in developing countries Land reform has a long history and a variety of meanings. This contribution will be confined to considering land reform programmes which have taken place since 1945 as within this period of sixty years, virtually every variant of land reform has been attempted in developing countries.

Six distinct approaches to land reform exist:

- abolishing private ownership of land and substituting state ownership, with citizens allowed a long lease or usufructuary right or reduced to being a licensee on land, liable to be moved at any time by the government; this was the position with respect to Africans in most of colonial Africa, retained at independence in many cases and was also the *de facto* position in communist countries such as China and Vietnam;
- redistributing interests in land; undertaken in the Middle East, Japan, Latin America, India, and South Africa where land reform consists of

restitution and redistribution of land from land-owners to persons who have no or very little land;

- reallocating interests in land between landlords and tenants where the balance between the two parties is grossly unequal; this has been a feature of land reform in the Indian sub-continent, the Middle East, Japan, and Latin America;
- converting interests in land from one system of land law, eg communal customary tenure as it exists in most countries in Africa, the South Pacific, and in Indonesia to an individualized statutory system based on some Western model of land law;
- demarcating, adjudicating, and registering who owns what interest in what land; the purpose of land reform programmes in some small islands in the Caribbean in the 1950s and 1960s and the focus of land reform programmes now in many countries in Africa;
- privatizing collective and state-owned land as occurred in Russia and transitional countries in Eastern Europe such as Albania on the collapse of communism, and is taking place in China and Vietnam.

Land reform programmes are often presented as technical programmes designed to bring about greater efficiency in land management; in reality, they are the driving force of fundamental social and economic change. This was most overt in communist countries where private ownership of land was either abolished or curtailed both in terms of how much land any landowner could own and in terms of what one could do with one's land, but underlying social concerns are present in other programmes as well. The land reform programmes developed by the US Alliance for Progress in the 1960s in Latin America were a reaction to the land reforms instituted in Cuba by the **revolution** and were aimed to some extent at changing the existing power structure in agriculture rather than just bringing about more efficient land management. Similarly, the 'profound agrarian revolution' of land reform instituted by the USA in Japan after 1945 was a key part of the programme of democratizing Japan and 'cutting the political ground from under the feet of the Communists' (Ladejinsky (1963)).

More recent programmes of land reform throughout the developing world have been externally driven by the World Bank and the donor community and directed at privatizing, individualizing, and registering title to land in the interests of creating efficient land markets. In the 1980s and 1990s, such programmes were quite explicitly designed to replace communal land tenure governed by **customary law** in countries in Africa, the South Pacific, and in Indonesia, with individualized land tenure governed by 'Western' law in the belief that communal land tenure and customary law did not provide for secure title, sustainable land use and management, or promote investment in land. Similarly in Mexico, the government was persuaded to move from the communal 'ejido' system of land tenure back towards individualized land tenure for the same reasons.

At the commencement of the twenty-first century, three contradictory positions on land reform can be discerned. First, the 'globalized land market' approach remains dominant in aid circles: land reform should be designed to assist the development and management of land markets and foreign direct investment which involves individualized land titles, a national land law which is based on 'Western', preferably Anglo-American, models, title registration and minimal restrictions on land transactions. This approach emphasizes the importance of improving the rights of **women** to access and own land and stresses a connection between land reform and **democracy**.

Secondly, the 'national land management' approach is beginning to emerge in many countries in Africa and may be discerned too in China and Indonesia: land reform should build on and not replace existing systems of land tenure; customary tenure is accepted as having great strengths and, carefully managed and reformed, can provide for adequate rural livelihoods and sustainable land use. This approach controls foreign investment in land especially with respect to land ownership and is less committed to advancing women's rights to land, seeing that to some extent as an alien attempt to subvert local customs. Both the globalized and the national approach emphasize the central role of law in land reform.

The third approach is populist; the people themselves are taking over land and redistributing it without regard to legal niceties. Examples can be pointed to in every continent with Brazil and Mexico in Latin America, South Africa and Zimbabwe in Africa (the latter state-sponsored and legally provided for), and some states in India being the best examples. This approach emphasizes the democratic input into land reform.   PATRICK MCAUSLAN

WI Ladejinsky, 'Land Reform in Japan: A Comment' in KH Parsons, RJ Penn, and PM Raup (eds) *Land Tenure* (Madison: The University of Wisconsin Press, 1963), 225

landfill tax   *see* **environmental taxes**

landless peoples' movements Over the last twenty years a wave of groups has emerged to campaign for the rights of landless people. This diverse and growing body, described broadly as Landless Peoples' Movements ('LPMs'), includes organizations ranging from Brazil's *Movimento dos Trabalhadores Rurais Sem Terra* (Landless Workers' Movement (1985)), and *Kilusang Magbubukid ng Pilipinas* (Peasant Movement of the Philippines (1985)), to South Africa's Landless People's Movement (2001). While the struggle for the landless has also been highlighted by other groups with wider agendas, like Zapatistas in Mexico, and Zimbabwe's National Liberation War Veterans Association, LPMs are making their own distinctive contribution.

Historically speaking there is nothing new about the occupation of idle rural lands by landless workers. However the process of coordinating, sustaining, and expanding their actions—maintaining an effective mass political organization—has proved extremely difficult. The Diggers movement of mid-seventeenth-century England which campaigned against the progressive establishment of individual **property rights** for large landowners, the abolition of customary land rights, and mass expulsion of poor peasantry from the land, was quickly suppressed. By contrast, LPMs, which have faced similar pressures (including criminalization by the **courts**), have established a durable and growing presence, with hundreds of thousands of members.

Landlessness itself depends upon multiple factors. People move into and out of the condition all the time. Like peasants, landless workers may have multiple occupations. Competing ideas about the significance of these social relations means that universal yardsticks of landlessness (eg a precise number) are hard to develop. The breadth of the term—it can include tenant farmers, sharecroppers, agricultural labourers and, more controversially, even former agricultural workers living and working in urban areas—reflects the desire to embrace these realities. Unlike conservative analysts, many LPMs believe that it is essential to include certain categories of urban workers within their ranks and to mobilize them.

Factors exacerbating landlessness include the legacy of **colonialism** (to which current mobilizations in southern Africa are a notable response), and population pressure (since finite land cannot endlessly be divided among expanding generations of a family). The most marked factor, however, is the absence of employment opportunities for hitherto rural populations—patterns most closely associated with capitalist accumulation in Asia, Latin America,

and Africa. Within these contexts, land—and land reform discourses (of which LPMs form a part)—reacquire their political significance. Far from being anachronistic, therefore, LPMs offer political responses and survival strategies to contemporary problems. The dramatic replication of these problems in former communist states, notably China and Vietnam, partly under pressure from so-called multilateral organizations, indicates their global and enduring nature. The absence of LPMs in these countries, despite the presence of numerous structural stimuli, including mass expulsions from land, merely underlines the fact that such movements have always been contingent upon local conditions. For the time being, the policy of containment by Communist Parties and justice systems has succeeded against thousands of fragmented land protests.

Tension and ambiguity invariably characterize LPM relationships to law, politics, and the state. The state (and conservative judges through policies of criminalization) cannot eliminate these movements, but equally LPMs are incapable of imposing their will upon the state—even when, as in the case of Brazil, the president happens to be a sympathizer. While autonomy from political parties has allowed LPMs to mobilize quickly and effectively, thereby forcing land issues to the top of the political agenda and recasting key aspects of the debate, this necessarily remains a limited form of politics. The radical content and methods of LPMs, including mass land occupations and other forms of direct action, need to be placed alongside elements of tactical and strategic pragmatism. Attitudes to law are one example. Most movements do not engage in so-called 'land grabs', but occupy land in order to pressure the state into fulfilling its constitutionally mandated legal obligations. Despite all these tensions, LPMs are here to stay. They offer significant sources of political leverage to formally powerless social classes.

GEORGE MESZAROS

language and law Every profession has an argot or lexicon of its own. Whether esoteric or popular, be it law, poetry, or medicine, its practice will depend to some extent upon its own technical vocabulary and customary forms of diction. In rhetorical terminology, each genre of discourse has its own distinct topics and terms, as well as modes of dress, sites of appearance, and proper manners of elocution or delivery. Nowhere is this more evident than in law, which has historically been most strikingly distinct as a guild or community by virtue of using foreign languages of record and of reporting well into the modern era—law reports were in English after 1704 but Latin and law French abounded in pleadings, writs, and judgments. Even now the student of law must come to terms with innumerable Latinate maxims and forms, and with a prolixity of expression that is a result of the plurality of national languages from which **common law** is derived. Common legal phrases such as 'null, void, and of no further force and effect' (from the Latin *nullius* and *effectus*, the French *vide* and *force*) simply state the same idea in words derived from the different languages of common law. The resulting repetition does little more in practice than add an air of authority to an exercise in prolixity.

The discipline of common law is founded upon a linguistic and substantive importation of **Roman law** and its accompanying Latin. The importation was complicated by a French (Norman) invasion and the result was a common law supposedly buried in a native time immemorial but expressed in Latin, Law French, and middle English. While the plurality of legal subjects were not always keen on a foreign language of **governance**, the ends of the legal profession were jealously preserved and closely guarded in what were explicitly called hieroglyphic modes of expression. Latin, according to **Bacon**, is the proper language in which to convey the maxims or truths of law, because Latin has the appropriate majesty and authority. Sir Edward **Coke** was in accord, believing that law was an artistic vocabulary with a grammar peculiarly its own. He advocated the continued use of Latin on the basis that it had the necessary dignity and honour as well as the appropriate precision in which to distinguish the infinite particularities of common law cases. The permanence of law required a language that would reflect its longevity and superiority to everyday speech. Lawyers and law dictionaries proliferated, with the first attempt at systematic translation of terms coming in 1527 with the law printer John Rastell's discursive dictionary of terms. Let the layman loose on law, however, and the sages of law, the *iuris periti*, were all agreed that he would rapidly run to ruin and end in penury.

The foreign dialects of legal rule have always been contested both by popular resentment and scholarly critics. The first Act of **Parliament** legislating English as the only and proper language of common law dates back to the Statute of Pleadings of 1362. It was itself paradoxically written in French, stipulated that legal records be in Latin, and allowed that where it was more convenient, 'ancient terms and forms' in Latin and French could still be used. The Act was ignored by the profession. Subsequent **legislation** from the interregnum had a similarly nugatory effect in practice and was quickly repealed with the

Restoration. The Statute of Pleadings of 1731 required English for all law but was so unpopular at the Bar that it was amended significantly even before it was to take effect. In the contemporary era, the demand for 'plain English' in statutes and in legal standard forms has sounded throughout the last half century and has slowly had the effect of translating those legal documents that the public is most likely to encounter directly into a somewhat more comprehensible jargon. It remains the case, however, that legislation, judgment, and the other transactional forms of law remain encoded in a professional lexicon that is at best opaque and at worst formidably incomprehensible to those not trained in the linguistics of law. The vocabulary is polyglot and distinctively archaic, the grammar is both objectivizing and generally passive, meaning that motivation appears logical and that authorship is thus secondary to what the law desires, stipulates, and dictates. Even where expressions are apparently self-evident, express rules and tacit conventions of **interpretation** can rapidly dispel the apparent simplicity of the surface.

PETER GOODRICH

P Goodrich, *Languages of Law* (Cambridge: Cambridge University Press, 1990)

D Mellinkoff, *The Language of the Law* (Boston: Little Brown, 1963)

Latin American law   'Is there any?' is a frequent response students and scholars receive when informing others that they work on law in Latin America. On closer examination, the common perceptions of Latin America as a lawless region governed only by rent-seeking, corruption, impunity, and self-help, give way to a spectacularly rich, complex, and woefully under-studied discipline that has both practical and academic import. Indeed, Latin American law, as found in the constituent countries of the region, now governs the lives and legal affairs of over 500 million people, and affects countless others through trade, tourism, and family ties throughout the world.

There is a lot of law in Latin America, but it must be considered in its particular context. Challenges to the **rule of law** in Latin America are rife; difficulties with implementation, impediments to enforcement, lack of governmental support, and well-accepted societal practices weave a fabric of resistance to pervasive legality and compliance with legal rules. Nonetheless, industry produces raw materials and finished goods and steers its activities though corporations, contracts, investment financing agreements, and banks. Workers are paid, and grievances with employers are settled. People die and their property is distributed to their family members; others buy and sell houses. Legal disputes are brought before courts and other dispute-settling bodies. In Latin America, it is perhaps better to think of pockets of legality in which the rule of law functions well, and pockets where the penetration of law and legal culture is lacking.

In pockets where there is little compliance with the written law, one often thinks of a 'gap' between the 'law as written' and the 'law as practised'. Although the gap occurs in all legal systems, the breadth of this gap in Latin America is seen as a particularly important attribute of Latin American law and legal practice. The gap has been historically and especially wide in the area of criminal law and the protection of constitutional rights of criminal defendants and government opponents. Assertions of a gap are frequently used to justify both domestic and international law reform projects in the region.

Latin American law today is a product of its historical development. Indigenous legal systems were, for the most part, wiped out by the colonizing powers, who imported a Roman, civil law system of law from the Continent to the colonies. The intellectual foundation of Latin American law is the law of the medieval and early modern law faculties of Europe, above all of Spain. Colonial law assisted the colonization process in many ways. Trade, the establishment of new cities and towns, and the new realities of colonial society incorporating substantial slave and indigenous populations, are reflected in the colonial law. The metropole jealously guarded its power through law and ensured many aspects of daily life and economic activity were funnelled through the administrative centres of Seville and later Cadíz.

Independence from European powers brought significant changes in law. On the political level, the new condition of independence led to written constitutions delineating the structure of government without a monarch. Profoundly influenced by thought from France and the United States, the newly independent states of Latin America restructured their governments and abolished slavery, titles of nobility, special privileges called *fueros*, entailed estates, and other legal institutions that were inconsistent with new republican notions of citizenship and meritocracy.

The political moment of independence brought these immediate changes in **constitutions** and public law. Changes in the substantive rules of private law took somewhat longer. For the first fifty years or so after independence, most Latin American countries continued to rely on the colonial law for most commercial transactions, land disputes, marriage laws, procedural rules in courts, inheritance, and other aspects of daily life. While reformers called for codification, or the placing of laws into codes following the European models, various obstacles prevented such projects. These obstacles included political instability within the new republics, a paucity of legal talent dedicated to law reform, and a lack of state funds to finance such projects.

By the mid-nineteenth century, however, Latin American countries entered the age of codification by both shunning Spanish colonial sources and incorporating them in the new provisions of modern codes. The code as a central source of Latin American law continues. Indeed, the major codes addressing civil law, commercial law, criminal law, and procedural law form the foundational texts for law in Latin America today. These are supplemented by numerous other codes on many topics such as taxation, labour law, consumer protection, and **competition law**.

The colonial legacy of extreme discrepancies in the distribution of wealth led to land reform programs in the twentieth century. In its modern variant, land reform came about as countries sought to counter a perceived threat from international socialism in the 1960s. Responding to the Cuban Revolution and with the encouragement of the United States, many countries of the region undertook land reform projects that could be easily justified under the social limitations placed on private property found in many of their constitutions. Since the mid-twentieth century, land reform has been frequently used to political ends. The shift away from land reform seemed to have been complete in the 1990s. Nonetheless, in the first decade of the twenty-first century, leftist and populist presidents have one again initiated land reform programs for both political and ideological reasons.

Challenging the centrality of codes as the core of Latin American legal systems in recent years are constitutions and constitutional law. Constitutions and constitutional law in Latin America have suffered from being too closely related to political change and legitimation. Indeed, extra-constitutional political change in Latin America, including *coups d'état*, are often justified by calling a new constitutional assembly to write a new constitution to legitimize the *de facto* government. Despite prevalent constitutional language conferring on citizens many rights, most countries in the region lack an entrenchment of constitutional protections that would parallel those in Europe and North America. Nonetheless, under recent constitutions several countries have created either constitutional courts or divisions of their supreme courts dedicated to the enforcement of constitutional norms. The activities of these courts tend to challenge the traditional function of judges and courts in civil law countries by issuing opinions that may go far beyond the scope of the individual dispute. They also use methods of judicial decision-making that implicitly recognize the law-making function of the judiciary, particularly as constitutional decisions shape societal practices and political rights. Thus, fostering the independence of the judiciary for constitutional security, as well as economic prosperity, has been an important theme in Latin American law reform projects in recent decades.

In addition to the rise of modern constitutional thought and remedies, there are many other important recent legal developments. Most developments can be centred around efforts to increase the rule of law in the region. Two sometimes-overlapping concerns inform rule of law projects: economic development and **human rights**; and international actors are often involved in their financing and operation. Thus, projects have addressed the selection, education, and independence of the judiciary, the functions and efficiency of courts, the status and protection of **indigenous peoples** and property, and methods of decreasing impunity and corruption in criminal law. These topics give a flavour of the dynamism and challenges Latin American legal systems face today as they attempt to balance a host of interests including economic development, foreign investment and international trade, protecting workers and indigenous peoples, bettering the legal and economic status of women, and ensuring transparent governments operating under the rule of law.

MATTHEW MIROW

MC Mirow, *Latin American Law: A History of Private Law and Institutions in Spanish America* (Austin: University of Texas Press, 2004)

AR Oquendo, *Latin American Law* (New York: Foundation Press, 2006)

See also: **civil law systems; codes and codification in national law; colonialism**

law and aesthetics   Much of the practice and study of law proceeds by way of texts—law reports, wills, **constitutions**, writs, and so on. These are written texts, but the activity of understanding law is also an art of speaking and a practice of looking. Testimony in court is oral; **justice** has an architectural style and an iconography (blindfolded statues; judges robed and bewigged). Law is a distinct, albeit plural, textual enterprise?

The dominant trend has been to deny the textual medium of law. Yet law tells its stories in different voices; it is transmitted in historically and socially differentiated idioms. Trials, as much as legal studies, have been physical and spiritual exercises. The **common law** is regarded as an oral practice, the teachings of which are handed down and received by the spoken word. But the problem with bodily signs and the spoken word is that their meanings are ambiguous and their effects indeterminate. While the reason of the common law is unwritten, the law of the modern state is nothing if not written. If there is a social problem, throw a statute book at it. The **subject** of law relates to the state through **standard form contracts**, while police file **anti-social behaviour** orders. This would be the apotheosis of the **rule of law**, with its promised certainty of meaning and effect: the writing of law and social existence would come to coincide. And in court, not only do we increasingly find closed circuit television, but the will of the people has always been formed through the visual cues of law. One thread of law and aesthetics has been to remark the often unremarked textual medium of law—its corporeal, oral, written, and visual dimensions.

Another thread has a more august lineage. It initially takes its cue from literature. Literature has a long history of using the language of law, as well as reflecting on the themes, institutions, and *dramatis personae* of justice. In the 1970s, however, a movement of judges and jurists focused research on the relations between **literature and law**. Since then, relations have expanded: law is now analysed with the aid of popular culture, television, film, architecture, painting, and sculpture. And the methods of analysis have similarly diversified: encompassing not only literary criticism and cultural studies, but also linguistics, film theory, visual studies, anthropology, and psychoanalysis. In this shift from 'law and literature' to 'law and aesthetics', the analysis begins to account for the sensorium of the body: its tastes and moods, its demeanour and dress; the hand that writes and touches as much as the eye that sees and believes the law.

All this has given new life to legal analysis. The initial gesture of the law and literature movement was to turn to the classics in order to return the question of meaning and value to the largely analytical and scientific traditions of modern scholarship. While this was an expansive brief, it was limited. A number of limits can be noted.

First, law and literature are regarded as disjunctive endeavours which could nevertheless be bridged analogically (law *like* literature) or collapsed into an identity (law *as* literature). Much has been written on this; it inherits the ancient quarrel between philosophy and poetry (Plato banished the poets from the lawful city, and reduced the community of law to the certitudes of writing). The reception of law becomes framed by the coordinates of substance, formalism, transparency, *mimesis*, and *logos*; while the literary inheritance is framed as matters of style, *poesis*, *pathos*, and rhetoric.

Secondly, a quite specific understanding of literature is privileged. Shakespeare sometimes gets a look in, as does Sophocles, but the favoured texts are the novels of the English nineteenth century (think Dickens, rather than Baudelaire). Arguably, however, other genres are at least as important to the understanding of law: tragedy, romance, melodrama, the funeral oration, and the lyric come to mind (although the teachings of these genres might not be so edifying for a legal audience).

A third limit is more significant. When the coupling of law and literature turns to law, the problem of judgment emerges at the intersection not only of law and aesthetics, but also of ethics. The character of the judge is marked by the activity of judgment, and no more so than when what is at stake is a vision of the good.

Consider this. If the dominant image of law gives us a rule-bound universe, then the central character in the legal story becomes the legislator and the regulator. The *dramatis persona* of the judge is downplayed. Against this, an interpretive turn emphasizes that the authority and meaning of the legal text is derived not from the rules of logic but from the moral knowledge and ethical values of the interpretive community. This is a question of character. Literature (as much as the visual arts) holds out the promise of a more compassionate, more humane, judge. Its pedagogy edifies the legal institution by returning sensibility to the sense-making practices of law.

Yet the literary turn and its vision of good judgment is not uncontested. It evinces a desire to constrain the potentials of institutional enunciation; it wants to stabilize the meaning and effect of legal judgment. In contrast, a rhetorical analysis has gone in search of that which interrupts and opens law to its others. Here, the community of law is not so much interpretive as affective—unstable, corporeal, imagistic, and gendered (Aristodemou, Young). The affective community cannot be consciously represented but is expressed in the figures of speech, slips of the tongue, and sleights of hand through which the judgments of law are handed down, passed on and received by those constituted as fit to receive it (Goodrich). Law is a mystery—to its adherents, its enforcers and to itself—and its *aesthesis* remains as

a shadow or stain on the reason of law. When all is said and done, there remains a style and a taste to the anaesthesiology of law.   PETER RUSH

P Goodrich, *Languages of Law: from logics of memory to nomadic masks* (London: Weidenfeld & Nicolson, 1990)

A Young, *Judging the Image: Art, Value, Law* (London: Routledge, 2005)

See also: **film and law; language and law; narrative and law; visual arts, law and**

law and development movement Broadly conceived, law and development concerns the relationship between legal rules and institutions and economic development or 'modernization'. Study of the relationship between law and economic development dates back to at least the nineteenth century; intellectual forebears include Adam Smith and David Ricardo through to Marx, Weber, and Coase. Although there are significant continuities with earlier efforts by colonial powers to codify and 'modernize' traditional or **customary law**, the law and development movement itself is a phenomenon of the post-World War II era. During this time, there have been different moments or 'waves' informed by quite distinct ideas about the role of the state in promoting economic growth.

Law surfaced as a policy concern during the 1960s when development was understood to occur through state-led policies of import substitution. Law and development studies were initially an outgrowth of development assistance funded by the USAID and private institutions such as the Ford Foundation. Drawing on expertise in the fields of **comparative law**, area studies, legal anthropology, and social theory, law and development scholars promoted reforms to legal education, including the export of the American case method, in hopes of effecting broader change in the legal cultures of developing states that would prove conducive to economic growth. Their efforts were almost immediately subject to criticism by English and other *Commonwealth* scholars; by the 1970s, as described by Trubek and Galanter in 'Scholars in Self-Estrangement', even the initial proponents of the movement had become disenchanted, questioning the extent to which their work advanced values such as freedom, **equality,** and **democracy**.

During the 1990s a significantly transformed law and development movement re-emerged with different theoretical underpinnings and policy objectives and enhanced institutional power. The key movers in the second wave were the international financial institutions, the **World Bank,** and the IMF, who by the 1980s, had decisively rejected state-led development in favour of export-led, market-centred economic growth. After advocating far-reaching structural reforms in developing countries, often referred to as the 'Washington Consensus' or **neoliberalism**, including the **privatization** of publicly-held assets, 'deregulation' of economic activities, and the liberalization of trade and investment in conjunction with debt relief, by the 1990s they had identified **corruption**, lack of transparency and **accountability**, and other '**governance failures**', including inadequate legal structures, as barriers to economic growth.

Legal reform initially came to occupy a central place in development assistance in the context of the states in transition from plan to market economies. There is now a general claim that respect for the **rule of law** and implementing a defined set of legal rules and institutions are required to encourage investment and facilitate transactions, thereby fostering economic growth and alleviating poverty. The orthodox view is that development requires respect for **property rights** and the enforcement of contracts as well as the elimination of regulations that are impediments to the efficient operation of competitive markets. The World Bank has funded hundreds of rule of law projects across the world and sponsored numerous related projects including training for the judiciary. Land titling projects and intellectual property rights have been among the most high profile areas of reform in recent years.

Two additional trends are visible in the law and development movement at the current time. The first is an increased emphasis on empirical research documenting the role of **regulation** in economic growth through the monitoring and evaluation of selected economic and regulatory 'benchmarks'; see for example the World Bank's *Doing Business* series. The second, a response to the fierce critiques of neoliberal reforms by a wide range of **social movements** in the development world, is greater focus on the social dimension of economic development. 'Second generation' development proposals now typically include reference to basic **human rights** and **gender** equality; following Amartya Sen's widely-celebrated *Development as Freedom*, good governance and the rule of law are now often described as among the ends of development itself.

Despite these reforms and responses, the law and development movement seems destined to remains a site of controversy. There are persistent concerns about the extent to which governance norms and legal reform initiatives advanced in the name of development trench upon sovereign prerogatives and unduly restrict democratic political choices.

Legal scholars with a grounding in **international law**, human rights, and colonial history have argued that the preoccupation with corruption, particularly in Sub-Saharan Africa, reflects lingering perceptions about the inherent 'backwardness' of many non-Western states and fails to reflect the significant role of external forces and institutions in the success or failure of development initiatives. Although the World Bank has officially rejected the 'one size fits all' approach to law and development that prevailed in the 1990s, it has yet to endorse a truly plural approach to development, one that would encompass more wide-ranging variation and experimentation in regulatory and institutional design.

There are also recurring criticisms of the theoretical and empirical premises on which the current law and development agenda is founded. For example, scholars of **comparative law** have observed as a historical matter that many different legal regimes can be associated with economic growth. Legal scholars have also pointed out the unreliability of many causal claims, due to the complexity of linking particular legal rules with economic outcomes and the wide range of variables other than law that inevitably affect the path of economic growth.

Despite the greater attention to the social dimension of development since 1999, there are ongoing concerns about the impact of legal and economic reforms on social objectives and human rights and, by extension, fundamental debates over how to conceptualize development itself. Some activists and scholars have proposed adoption of a 'rights-based' approach to development which would subordinate development initiatives to international law and international human rights norms; however, the conflict between economic objectives and other normative concerns remains a live issue. Recent studies such as Branko Milanovic's *Worlds Apart*, documenting a growing divide between the developing and industrialized worlds during the era of neoliberal economic reforms, have raised further questions about development, equality, and **human** welfare.

KERRY RITTICH

See also: **gender and development; human rights and development; international financial institutions and development**

law and economics   *see* **economic analysis of law; Coase, Ronald**

law and order debates   The term 'law and order' is of long standing and traditionally seen as the basic requirement of and for good government. 'Law' and 'order' are conventionally taken to be complementary, though some have stressed the potential for conflict, as in the contrast of law *versus* order, or that between 'due process' and 'crime control' models of law enforcement. In general, crime control and criminal justice have been seen as the preserve of the judiciary and allied practitioners, with **legislation** emanating from the **Home Office** and the **Lord Chancellor**, informed by legal and academic expertise, and insulated from populist pressures by the professional civil service.

Over the past few decades, the political salience of 'law and order' has been transformed from a broadly apolitical discourse to a highly contested set of partisan issues. The change began in the USA in the 1964 presidential election; in the UK in the 1970, and pivotally the 1979, general elections; and even in The Netherlands, long associated with a minimal resort to custody, in the mid-1980s. The transition has been strongly characterized by the embrace of the politics of 'populist punitiveness' or 'penal populism' (Pratt 2007), heavily driven by electoral advantage. It is associated with steeply rising **prison** populations and, in the case of the USA, with mass imprisonment. Societies that have so far resisted the change, such as Canada, the Scandinavian countries, France, and Germany, have maintained lower and more stable levels of imprisonment.

The phrase 'governing through crime' (Simon 2007) captures the climate in which crime control becomes a template for partisan claims to legitimacy, setting the agenda for legislative strategies to outsmart the opposition. Blair's much quoted agenda for Labour to be 'tough on crime, tough on the causes of crime' in 1993 stimulated the Conservative government's 'Prison Works' U-turn, a reversal of the previous bipartisan policy of reducing the prison population, which doubled in size over the next fifteen years, from 43,000 in 1992 to some 80,000 in 2007. That in turn was inspired by the success of Clinton in rebranding the Democratic Party as tough-on-crime following the debacle of their defeat by George Bush in 1988. In the 1990s, the US prison population rose from one to two million, entailing felon disenfranchisement on a scale which proved pivotal in the fraught presidential election of George W Bush in 2000.

Much debate hinges on how far the 'new' politics of crime control result from what Garland describes as the 'culture of control' inherent in late modernity (David Garland, *The Culture of Control* (2001)), the product of the seemingly endless rise in crime rates of the post-World War II period. This culture moves away from 'penal-welfarism' and rehabilitative ideals to stress '**zero tolerance**' in policing; the reinvention of the prison (with a new, super-maximum security core); curbs on civil liberties; and a 'perpetual sense of crisis' engendered by the 'war on crime'. The mass media fuel the fear of crime by a 'breaking news' approach to high-profile crimes as a breakdown in 'law and order'. Against that view, it is contended that many societies have resisted this trend; that political economy variables, such as commitment to egalitarian welfare, are a bulwark against penal populism; and that contrasting democratic traditions account for the growing divide between the USA and Europe in the resort to 'harsh **justice**'. As things stand, however, no society to embrace the new politics of law and order has been able to relinquish it. While there is no way back to the era of 'elitist' policymaking that ignores populist pressures, ways have been suggested, such as deliberative polling, to counteract the most contentious media portrayals of the crime problem, and how to control it, by more informed democratic means.

DAVID DOWNES

J Pratt, *Penal Populism* (London: Routledge, 2007)
J Simon, *Governing Through Crime* (New York: Oxford University Press, 2007)

See also: **social control and crime**

Law Commission   The Law Commission of England and Wales was set up by the Law Commissions Act 1965, which simultaneously created the Scottish Law Commission. The statutory remit of the Law Commission is broad and reflects the modernizing optimism of the Labour government whose idea it was; it is charged with reviewing all of the law of the jurisdiction, 'with a view to its systematic development and reform, including in particular the codification of such law, the elimination of anomalies, the repeal of obsolete and unnecessary enactments, the reduction of the number of separate enactments and generally the simplification and modernisation of the law'.

The Chairman of the Law Commission has by tradition always been a High Court Judge. The Law Commission Act has now been amended to make this a statutory requirement, thus ensuring the Commission's reputation and independence. The four other Commissioners—who are required by the statute to be full-time appointees—are drawn either from the judiciary or from practice, or are university teachers of law. The first Chairman of the Law Commission, Lord Scarman, established its working methods of producing consultation papers to which responses are invited from academics, practitioners, and the public, before final reports are written taking account of the views expressed. The implementation of law reform recommendations takes place either through primary legislation (bills are drafted by the Commission's own team of Parliamentary drafters), through regulatory reform orders, or through judicial decisions.

The Chairman of the Law Commission at the time of writing, Sir Terence Etherton, stated in a lecture in November 2007 given to the Bar Law Reform Committee that, 'About 90 Acts of Parliament enacted since 1965 have contained Law Commission recommendations'. Those statutes include in the area of civil law, the Defective Premises Act 1972, the Matrimonial Causes Act 1973, the Inheritance (Provision for Family and Dependants) Act 1975, the Unfair Contract Terms Act 1977, the Civil Liability (Contribution) Act 1978, the Sale and Supply of Goods Act 1994, the Family Law Act 1996, the Law of Property (Miscellaneous Provision) Act 1989, and the Land Registration Act 2002. In criminal law, recent legislation derived in whole or in part from Law Commission work includes the Criminal Justice Act 2003, the Domestic Violence, Crimes, and Victims Act 2004, the Fraud Act 2006, and the Serious Crime Act 2007. Despite this however, the Law Commission frequently faces difficulties in getting its work implemented, and has something of a reputation for producing reports that sit on a shelf in a government department, gathering dust. Times—and politics—have changed from the 1960s: Parliament is more dominated by the Executive, which is dedicated to enacting manifesto commitments, and parliamentary time has become extremely precious. Sir Terence indicated that he would like to reformulate the vision of the 1960s. In response to the government green paper on citizenship, the Law Commission has proposed legislation to enshrine the fundamental right of the citizen to 'accessible, intelligible and modern law'. This it believes would ensure that appropriate priority would be given to its work.

HELEN CARR

Law in Context movement In the world of academic law a 'movement' is vaguer than a 'school' but more specific than a 'trend'. 'The Law in Context Movement' is a convenient retrospective label for quite varied approaches to broadening the study of law that developed in the UK from the mid-1960s. In 1966 Professor Abraham Goldstein of the Yale Law School reported after a visit that English law teaching and the conception of law that animated it had yet to experience 'its legal realist revolution'. By this he meant that English law teaching and legal scholarship were dominated by a quite narrow orthodoxy

that focused almost exclusively on expounding and analysing legal rules, whereas in the United States this kind of approach had been undermined by the American Realist movement of the 1920s and 1930s. This was broadly accurate, but by then another 'revolt against formalism' had already begun in the UK. Between 1965 and 1975 many manifestations of broader approaches to law teaching and legal scholarship emerged; there were clarion calls for a break with tradition; new law schools claimed to be developing fresh approaches ('broadening the law from within' at Warwick, multidisciplinary perspectives at Kent); some established law schools, notably the London School of Economics and the Queen's University, Belfast, broadened their curricula; three series of books entitled 'Law in Context', 'Law in Society', and 'Law and Society' were launched; *The British Journal of Law and Society* (later the *Journal of Law and Society*) began in 1974, and the Socio-Legal Studies Association emerged in the early 1970s. The Institute of Judicial Administration in Birmingham (1968) and the Oxford Centre for Socio-Legal Studies (1972) joined the Cambridge Institute of Criminology (1959) as significant centres of empirical research.

The Law in Context movement was similar to the American Realist movement in being centred on university law schools, in mainly involving a fresh generation of younger law teachers, and in claiming to be in reaction against a dominant orthodoxy. As in America, there were a few individual scholars who had earlier advocated broader approaches to academic law, including Wolfgang Friedmann, JL Montrose, LCB Gower, Julius Stone, and RM Jackson. However, in the UK in the 1960s the context and the intellectual climate were quite different from those in the US: the post World War II welfare state, the end of Empire, the rapid expansion of universities, a tradition of professional training outside the universities, an academic milieu hospitable to socialist and Marxist ideas, and many other factors made up a contrasting background. Some of the advocates of broader approaches had studied in American law schools, but others had returned from teaching in newly independent countries, where they had needed to confront problems of adapting or replacing English law in radically different political, economic, and social conditions. It was natural for such returnees to emphasize 'context'.

Intellectually, there were also some significant differences between American Legal Realism and British contextual approaches. Both largely defined themselves in terms of a revolt against a caricatured '**formalism**': in America the prevailing orthodoxy

('Langdellism') had been charged with two main weaknesses: a deluded emphasis on deductive logic and a lack of empirical concern with the realities of the law in action. This resulted in a split between those who wished to develop more sceptical, policy-oriented approaches to case method teaching and those who wished to develop the study of law as an empirical social science—two very different enterprises. The English version of formalism was also criticized for being out of touch with the 'law in action' (both professional legal practice and the operation of law in society); it was also castigated for being narrowly focused, educationally illiberal, and politically conservative. On one interpretation, in the UK different diagnoses prompted varied prescriptions: a more humanistic pedagogy, inter-disciplinary cooperation, empirical research, progressive law reform, and radical social-theoretical critique.

The idea of 'law in context' is not rooted in a particular or distinctive general theory of or about law. It accommodates positivists and non-positivists, proponents of **legal pluralism**, advocates of liberal legal education and of enlightened vocational training. It can accommodate a wide range of political views, although it has a 'progressive' tendency. It is not an 'ism'. 'Context' is vague, but not entirely meaningless. 'Contexere' (Latin: 'to weave') suggests inter-disciplinary perspectives. Such an approach favours thinking in terms of total pictures and total processes. For example, the first book in the *Law in Context* series, Patrick Atiyah's *Accidents, Compensation and the Law* (London: Weidenfeld & Nicolson, 1970) critically analysed the common law action for negligence in the context of a total picture of accidents in society and an overview of different kinds of compensation system; students of civil and criminal procedure set the detailed study of contested trials and appeals in the context of a total process model, emphasizing the interrelationship between different stages in the process of litigation, the relative rarity of contested trials and successful appeals, and the importance of settlement out of court and plea bargaining.

It is a commonplace of both realist and contextual approaches that 'the study of rules alone is not enough'. In order to interpret rules and to understand their operation in practice they need to be studied 'in context'. A recent formulation states that '[a] rule is part of and a sign to a social setting comprised of understandings and conventions, interests and values, whose origins and force derive from experience and practice. Each rule has its own little social world of which it is only part, and only by entering that world can we assess a rule's significance and obtain

a full understanding of what is required or permitted, condoned or condemned' (D J Galligan, *Law in Modern Society* (Oxford: Oxford University Press, 2007) at 54). A great deal of recent sociology of law has focused on the immediate social setting of formal rules and how informal rules and 'soft law' influence their invocation, interpretation, application, modification, and enforcement.

A leading American sociologist of law, writing in a British journal summed up some of the central ideas as follows:

In law-and-society theory, the phrase "law in context" points to the many ways legal norms and institutions are conditioned by culture and social organization. We see how legal rules and concepts, such as those affecting property, contract, and conceptions of justice, are animated and transformed by intellectual history; how much authority and self-confidence of legal institutions depend on underlying realities of class and power; how legal rules fit into broader contexts of custom and morality. In short, we see law in and of society, adapting its contours, giving direction to change. We learn that legal order is far less autonomous, far less self-regulating and self-sufficient, than often portrayed by its leaders and apologists. This perspective encourages us to accept blurred boundaries between law and morality, law and tradition, law and economics, law and politics, law and culture. Accepting the reality of blurred boundaries leads to much puzzlement and controversy. Law loses some of its special dignity, and some jurisprudential questions cannot be avoided. (P Selznick, (2003) 30 *Journal of Law and Society*, 177–178)

Not all who are sympathetic with the general approach will agree with Selznick's specific formulation. The idea of 'law in context' overlaps with, but is broader and even vaguer than 'socio-legal studies', 'sociology of law', 'law and society', and '**critical legal studies**'. During the past forty years 'law in context' has been largely absorbed into the mainstream of academic law in the UK and most other **common law** countries. It has become respectable. Today the most visible signs are in academic legal literature: in 2007 the *Law in Context* series, now published by Cambridge University Press, had over fifty volumes in print; the *Journal of Law and Society* is well-established and has been joined by *Law in Context* (Australia) and The *International Journal of Law in Context* (London). 'Context' regularly appears in the titles of books and articles. Just because of its widespread acceptance, the central ideas are open to many different interpretations.

WILLIAM TWINING

DJ Galligan (ed), (1995) 'Socio-legal Studies in Context: The Oxford Centre Past and Present' (Symposium) (1995) 22 *Journal of Law and Society* 1–154

W Twining, *Law in Context: Enlarging a Discipline* (Oxford: Oxford University Press, 1997)

See also: **legal education and liberal education; legal
positivism since 1970; legal positivism to 1970; legal
realism; sociological jurisprudence**

law lords   see house of lords; courts; judges

law of the sea   The law of the sea is that branch of
public **international law** dealing with the rights and
duties of states at sea. Much of this law is codified in
the UN Convention on the Law of the Sea, which was
adopted in 1982 and came into force in 1994. By the
end of 2006 the Convention had been ratified, and so
was binding on, some 150 states (including the UK)
and the European Community. Even for those forty or
more states (including the USA) that have not ratified
it, large parts of the Convention are binding because
they represent **customary international law**.

The Convention has frequently been described
as a 'Constitution for the Oceans', which indicates
both its comprehensive nature and its status as the
basic treaty regulating marine activities. The Convention aims to establish a legal order that will
facilitate international communication, promote
the peaceful, equitable, and efficient exploitation of
the sea's resources, and protect the marine environment. One of the principal means by which the Convention establishes such an order is by dividing the
sea into various zones, each with its own distinctive
legal nature.

Starting from land, the first maritime zone is the
territorial sea, which extends up to twelve nautical
miles from the coast. Within this zone the coastal
state (ie the state having sovereignty over the adjacent land) has the exclusive right to regulate and
exploit the zone's natural resources (such as fish and
seabed minerals) and to regulate foreign shipping,
for example by prescribing safety and anti-pollution
measures. Foreign ships have the right of 'innocent
passage' through the territorial sea, which means
that they may pass through the territorial sea provided that they refrain from engaging in certain
listed activities, including the use or threat of force,
smuggling, fishing, and scientific research. In straits
used for international navigation that consist entirely of the territorial seas of the states bordering the
strait (such as the Straits of Dover), foreign ships
have a right of transit passage rather than innocent passage, and thus are subject to fewer restrictions. A similar right exists through the sea lanes
of archipelagos, such as Bahamas and Indonesia.
Beyond its territorial sea, a coastal state may, but is
not obliged to, establish a contiguous zone twelve
nautical miles in breadth, within which it may arrest
ships that it suspects are going to violate customs,
fiscal, immigration, or health regulations within its
territory or territorial sea or that it believes to have
already done so. The UK is among many states that
have not (yet) established a contiguous zone.

Further seawards a coastal state may establish
an exclusive economic zone ('EEZ'), the outer limit
of which is 200 nautical miles from its coast. Most
states (although not the UK) have done so: the UK
has instead claimed a 200-mile fishing zone. Within the EEZ, a coastal state has the exclusive right to
regulate and exploit fisheries; construct artificial
islands and installations; use the zone for other economic purposes (such as the generation of energy
from wind and waves); regulate scientific research;
and, to a limited degree, regulate pollution from
foreign ships. Subject to these rights, the ships (and
aircraft) of other states have the right to pass freely
through (and over) the zone, as well as to lay cables
and pipelines.

A coastal state also has the exclusive right to regulate and exploit the natural resources of the seabed
beyond its territorial sea (notably oil and gas) up to
200 nautical miles from its coast or to the outer edge
of the continental margin, whichever is further, subject to an overall limit of 350 nautical miles from the
coast or 100 nautical miles beyond the 2,500-metre
isobath. Legally, this zone is known as the continental shelf.

Where the maritime zones of neighbouring states
overlap, the states concerned must try to agree on a
boundary. Usually this is done as a result of direct
negotiations, but in some cases the states concerned
may ask an international court to delimit the boundary, as the UK and France did in the 1970s. Around
half of all overlapping maritime zones have now
been delimited by agreed boundaries, most of which
are equidistance lines.

Beyond coastal states' maritime zones lie the high
seas, which may be used by all states for fishing, navigation, the laying of cables and pipelines, scientific
research, the construction of artificial islands, and
any other activity not prohibited by international law. Apart from a limited number of exceptions,
ships on the high seas are subject to the jurisdiction
only of the state whose flag they fly. The exceptions
include piracy and hot pursuit. The latter refers to a
situation where a coastal state pursues on to the high
seas and arrests a ship suspected of having violated
its laws in one of its maritime zones. Furthermore,
a warship may board a foreign ship on the high seas
if it suspects that the ship does not have a nationality (because, for example, it is not flying a flag or has
blacked out its name) or if the flag state of the ship
gives its consent to the boarding.

These powers form the legal basis for the interception of ships on the high seas suspected of carrying weapons of mass destruction ('WMD'), their delivery systems or related materials to non-state actors or states of 'proliferation concern' under the Proliferation Security Initiative. The latter, set up by the USA in 2003 and involving over sixty states, is a loose framework for international cooperation aimed at preventing the proliferation of WMD. States are urged to use their existing legal powers not only to intercept ships on the high seas but also to stop and search ships in their ports, territorial seas, and contiguous zones, as well as to prevent trafficking in WMD by land and air.

The seabed beyond the continental shelf and underlying the high seas is the International Seabed Area. The exploitation of the mineral resources of the Area is regulated by the International Seabed Authority, an organization established by the 1982 Convention. If and when mining of these resources begins on a commercial scale, part of the profits will be distributed to developing states in accordance with the principle that the Area is the common heritage of mankind.

The 1982 Convention is unusual among treaties in providing for the compulsory settlement of disputes relating to its interpretation and application. Disputes that cannot be settled by agreement may be referred unilaterally by either party to the **International Court of Justice**, the International Tribunal for the Law of the Sea or arbitration for a legally-binding decision.

Although the 1982 Convention is described as a constitution for the oceans, it does not contain the whole of international law relating to the sea. It is supplemented by a network of other treaties that provide detailed regulations dealing with the safety of shipping, the well-being of seafarers, the management of fisheries, and the protection of the marine environment.   ROBIN CHURCHILL

Law Officers *see* **Attorney-General; Lord Advocate; Solicitor-General**

law reform commissions Law reform means legal change of a non-incremental nature usually effected by statute. It normally connotes improvement, although some reforms misfire. Law reform was essentially a part-time activity until 1965, when the English and Scottish Law Commissions were established as permanent, full-time, independent bodies to keep the law under review and to make authoritative recommendations with something approximating doctrinal status. This basic model was followed later in most **Commonwealth** countries.

Law reform commissions ('LRCs') are normally set up by statute, chaired by judges, and include legal practitioners and academic lawyers. The experience of using non-lawyers as commissioners has been limited, although law reform benefits from interdisciplinary research. LRCs produce consultation or discussion papers which are followed by reports. The reports usually recommend legislative reform. Some of the legislative reform includes consolidation and codification. The early enthusiasm of the English Law Commission for codification waned after a decade of ineffective attempts to codify the law of contract. The Commission has also hesitated over radical reforms such as adoption of a Personal Property Securities Act along Canadian lines. It had more success with family law, where significant reforms were preceded by a social survey of attitudes towards family property. Out of about 300 reports, a substantial number has been implemented by legislative reform and it is now revisiting earlier reforms.

The Australian Law Reform Commission has had mixed success in spite of the first brilliant chairmanship of Justice Michael Kirby. Justice Kirby was a very energetic law reformer and a great publicist for reform ideas. However, the Commission had to contend with the innate conservatism of Australian federalism. Canada, after initial enthusiasm, has had doubts about the use of LRCs. New Zealand has been more successful, starting with strong leadership by Sir Owen Woodhouse as the first President, and has had a good track record. The recent appointment of Sir Geoffrey Palmer, former Attorney-General and Prime Minister, will no doubt restore its more radical reforming zeal.

A distinction is sometimes drawn between technical, 'lawyers' law' reform and other reform. It is, however, difficult to sustain this distinction as matters which are regarded as technical have social implications. It is, however, the trend of most Commonwealth jurisdictions to appoint a Royal Commission which includes some non-lawyers for matters that are more controversial. Where Royal Commissions consist of only one person there have sometimes been problems, as with the inquiries into the Mount Erebus crash and the Canadian Pipeline inquiry.

LRCs sometimes commission empirical research but their ability to do so depends on funding. Good empirical research is expensive. In practice, not enough research is done on the efficacy and efficiency of law or into law as a method of changing social attitudes. Some reform is referred to specialist bodies rather than LRCs, and in recent times there has been a tendency to bring some matters back into the government departments. Increasingly, LRCs work in collaboration with government agencies while seeking to retain their independence.

A successful technique developed by the Australian Law Reform Commission is the use of public forums as a way of taking reform proposals to the people for consultation. Information technology and the internet are revolutionizing consultation with the public and allowing greater informal interaction. If done properly, this improves the process and increases the legitimacy of law reform.

Nineteenth-century law reforms were influenced by Jeremy **Bentham** and the Utilitarians. This led to reforms of the courts and to a number of codes. This ideology lingered on into the twentieth century but became part of larger debates about social welfare. Added to this was the increasing interest in **human rights** in the post-1945 world, and then the impact of the United Kingdom's membership of the **European Union** from 1973 which has greatly complicated the process of law reform in areas covered by the relevant treaties. This has broadened the approach to reform on the one hand and limited the utility of **United Kingdom** reforms for the Commonwealth countries on the other. The essential unity of the **common law** is now under threat.

LRCs are predicated on a theory of modernization and increasingly fit uneasily into a post-modern world characterized by diffusion of power, the rise of the media, and scepticism about the capacity of law and the legal system to deliver **justice** at moderate cost in both criminal and civil matters. Added to this has been the tendency of government in recent years to make neo-liberal cost/benefit assessments and adjustments to the machinery and pattern of law reform. This has led in Canada to sunset clauses for some law reform bodies. In future, the study of LRCs must take into consideration the complex way in which they consult with the public and interact with interest groups, the media, and government in modern society.   JOHN FARRAR

See also: **codes and codification in national law**

law reform movements The history of the **common law** has seen two different kinds of law reform movements. The first approach is associated with the early seventeenth-century **Lord Chancellor**, Sir Francis Bacon. Writing in an era when there was widespread agreement that the law needed reform, Bacon recommended 'pruning and grafting the law', rather than ploughing it up and starting again. His

reformism remained influential for the next two centuries. The mid-seventeenth-century judge Sir Matthew Hale, who also favoured 'due husbandry', noted that while some amendment could be left to the judges, parliamentary intervention was required where the fabric of laws were rotten. This approach to law reform, which sought to leave the body of the common law intact, but modified by judges and updated by legislation, was taken up in the eighteenth century by judges such as Sir William **Blackstone** and in the nineteenth century by politicians such as Sir Robert Peel.

A second, more radical, approach was that associated with the popular Leveller movement of the 1640s. They demanded a simplified code of law, written in English, administered in local courts with a simple procedure, so that every man could be his own lawyer. They saw the **common law** as a snare for the poor. The demand for a new code of English law was taken up after 1770 by Jeremy **Bentham**. For Bentham, the common law, made by judges deciding cases after the event, was hopeless as a guide for conduct, and should be replaced by a new code. He thought he could write a complete code, which could be adapted to the needs of any nation. Unlike the Levellers, his programme failed to attract popular support, but his disciples continued to argue for codification. Several unsuccessful attempts were made in the mid-nineteenth century to codify the criminal law. But codification in general was resisted by English judges and politicians who defended the incremental and organic development of the common law against codes which (they felt) would set in stone the ideas of one generation and limit judging to statutory interpretation. Despite this hostility, codes of law were drafted by nineteenth-century English jurists for India, while English law relating to particular areas (such as bills of exchange or marine insurance) was also put into codes.

For the most part, reform of the common law occurred in a manner which was hesitant and piecemeal. Many of the reforms which were regarded as necessary in the mid-seventeenth century were not effected until the nineteenth or twentieth centuries. One of the most ambitious official blueprints for reform was drawn up in 1652, by a commission chaired by Hale. This commission proposed a reform of the superior courts and its procedure, as well as the creation of small claims courts and registries of deeds. It prepared bills to reform criminal law, land law, matrimonial, probate, and mercantile law; but by the time the Rump Parliament was dissolved, nothing had been done. The movement for law reform waned after the Restoration, and remained muted throughout the eighteenth century, which saw a sharp decline in the number of people seeking to litigate.

Political pressure to reform the institutions, procedures, and substance of the law only revived in the early nineteenth century, when litigation trends once more increased. A set of Royal Commissions appointed in 1828 looked into reform of land law and the practice of the superior courts. The establishment in 1843 of a Law Amendment Society provided a pressure group devoted to law reform. As a result of pressure from the legal profession, the mid-nineteenth century saw important reforms in the structure of the Court of Chancery and in the procedure and practice of the common law courts, which paved the way for the union of judicatures in 1875. Matrimonial and probate jurisdiction was transferred from the **ecclesiastical courts** to new courts established in 1857. The later nineteenth century also saw reforms in the law of married women's property, debt recovery, and bankruptcy, and the long anticipated reform of land law was eventually achieved in 1925.

Where law reform in the nineteenth century was the product of uncoordinated parliamentary inquiries resulting from professional pressure, by the twentieth century, law reform resulted more frequently from official initiatives. After the 1880s, the Lord Chancellor's Office became a *de facto* ministry of justice, able to act as a crucial liaison between ministers, the legal profession, and the judiciary. Its work was assisted after 1934 by a Law Revision Committee, and by the Law Commission set up in 1965. These new bodies refined the old methods of law reform rather than revolutionizing them. In many ways, Lord Woolf's report on *Access to Justice*, prepared in the 1990s for the Lord Chancellor, rehearsed many of the concerns about delays and costs which had troubled reformers since the era of Hale.

MICHAEL LOBBAN

D Veall, *The Popular Movement for Law Reform 1640–1660* (Oxford: Oxford University Press, 1970)

M Lobban, '"Old Wine in New Bottles": the Concept and Practice of Law Reform, 1780–1830' in J Innes and A Burns (eds), *Rethinking the Age of Reform* (Cambridge: Cambridge University Press, 2003)

See also: **law reform commissions**

law reports   The law French word *reporter* means to bring back, to carry back, to recollect. It was used on occasion not only to refer to the earliest written reports of arguments in cases, the Year Books, but also refers to oral narratives of cases, to readings in the Inns of Court, and even to registers of writs. The root meaning of the word is a useful reminder of the fact that **common law**, technically *ius non scriptum*, meaning that it is an uncodified system of law, was in origin simply the custom of the royal court. It was recollected and reported in manifold forms, as the common memory or opinion of the bar, as oral tradition, in early treatises and plea rolls, as well as in express records of cases and their later collection in abridgments.

The earliest tradition of express reports refers to the Year Books, which provided somewhat haphazard records of arguments in cases and were probably written as didactic texts for the benefit of legal apprentices at the Inns of Court. Although common law had long adhered to the Roman principle *procedere ad similia*, meaning decide by analogy, by similarity, the practice had not been governed by any more concrete criterion than selection of a principle drawn from an earlier record or memory that appealed to the judge as being most apposite in the circumstances. Plowden, one of the earliest named reporters simply remarks *semblable reason semblable ley* ('if it seems reasonable it seems it is law') and this notwithstanding judgments that determined in contrary manner.

The advent of the printing press increased the availability of the earlier reports and although reporting was often highly unreliable, two principal characteristics are incontestable. First, law became a matter of record. By the time that Sir Edward Coke was writing, the records of common law, the infinite particulars of the case law reported in Littleton, as well as other Year Book sources provided what **Coke**, borrowing from **Cicero**, terms the testament of time and the witness of memory. They were vestiges of antiquity and truth. By the same token, in *Entick* v *Carrington*, decided over a century later (1765), Lord Campbell remarks simply: 'if it be law, it be found in our books. If it is not to be found there, it is not law'. The books, meaning primarily the Year Books and Plea Rolls, had grown in visibility and in authority and three sets of reports, Plowden's *Commentaries*, Coke's *Reports*, and Bulstrode's *Reports* of the King's Bench, inaugurated a tradition of rigorous and detailed reporting with commentary and explanation. What mattered was the accuracy of the doctrine rather than the decision, and it was only later that a more consistent method of reporting allowed for a more clearly articulated system of **precedent**.

The modern system of reporting is a nineteenth century phenomenon and grew up in conjunction with the development of the **House of Lords** as a court of final appeal, with only professional law lords sitting. The emergence of a rigid and systematized hierarchy of courts coincided with the standardization of law reporting and the first semi-official series of reports. These have now multiplied and commercial reporting series now include decisions of numerous specialized courts and **tribunals**. Online reporting by LEXIS and WESTLAW now means that the availability of reports has grown exponentially even if the authority of the decisions so reported has thereby declined.   PETER GOODRICH

JH Baker, *Judicial Records, Law Reports, and the Growth of Case Law* (Berlin: Duncker & Humblot, 1989)

law schools   *see* legal academics

***Law, Liberty and Morality* (by HLA Hart)**   *Law, Liberty and Morality* (Oxford: Oxford University Press, 1963) argues, as against Patrick Devlin and James Fitzjames **Stephen**, that democratic states are not entitled to enforce moral standards for their own sake. With the exception of certain cases where paternalistic legislation can be justified, the state should respect individual freedom, intervening only to prevent or punish the commission of tangible harms.

The book attacks Devlin's analogy (first drawn in a lecture in 1958) between the criminal enforcement of morality and the criminalization of treason (*The Enforcement of Morals*, Oxford: Oxford University Press,1965), using it to illustrate the difference between J.S. Mill's liberal position (***On Liberty*** (New York: Legal Classic Library, 1992; first published in 1859), that coercion should only be used to prevent harm to others, and the conservative view that a society which fails to criminalize immorality—that to which the 'man on the Clapham omnibus' would react with 'intolerance, indignation and disgust'—risks disintegration. In the absence of any empirical evidence that a failure to enforce morality leads to social collapse, Devlin's argument amounted to the proposition that any widely held prejudice justified criminalization, and that any change in common morality constituted, conceptually, a 'disintegration' of the social order. This argument overplayed the power of law as a socially stabilizing and educative force. What good, Hart asked, can outweigh the cost in human misery of enforcing morality, and in particular sexual morality? Social moralities can be multiple and mutually tolerant: their value is to secure happiness for individuals, and it is voluntary rather than coerced compliance which is valuable.

Devlin's argument belonged to an era which celebrated conformity through fear; the gratifying of hatred through retributive punishments; moral conservatism. In its place Hart advocated a liberal vision of tolerance, a concern with human suffering, and a respect for human freedom, tempered only by limited paternalism. Written with a passionate intensity which stands out among Hart's oeuvre, *Law, Liberty and Morality* remains the resounding late twentieth-century statement of principled liberal social policy.   NICOLA LACEY

lawyer–client relations   The lawyer–client relationship is characterized by an imbalance of knowledge and power. Like other professional–lay client relationships it has undergone considerable change in recent years. Lawyers are no longer set on a pedestal, unchallengeable in their opinions and actions. A large number of complaints are made to the Legal Complaints Service (18,434 new complaints in 2006–2007) relating to the work of solicitors and a large machinery of complaints handling involves the Solicitors' Regulation Authority, the Legal Services Complaints Commissioner, and the Legal Services Ombudsman.

Most complaints made about legal professionals concern their inability to communicate properly, the costs they charge, and delays in their work. Although both delay and cost may not be the fault entirely of the lawyers concerned, poor communication about such issues often leaves clients very unsatisfied.

Some early researchers considered who was in control of the lawyer–client relationship and one suggested that lawyers were 'conceptive ideologists' who 'translate' their clients' needs into the terminology and operations of legal practice. Early empirical work also showed that there were major deficiencies in the abilities of new professionals to carry out the role of interviewer and counsellor. Considerable attention has subsequently been paid to training in client care since the inception of the Legal Practice Course as a qualifying examination for solicitors in the early 1990s.

Rules governing the conduct of lawyers also reflect a more caring attitude. Solicitors have some discretion in accepting new clients whilst barristers, at least in theory, have less. Solicitors are broadly free to decide whether to take on a particular client, provided they respect issues of equality and diversity, and have sufficient resources and competence. For barristers the 'cab rank rule' applies. They may not refuse work in any area of their practice because they find the nature of the case objectionable or the conduct, opinions, or beliefs of the prospective client unacceptable; or on any grounds relating to a proper source of funding. Barristers are not obliged to conduct work for less than a proper fee, or to work under **conditional fee arrangements**.

Solicitors are required to 'act in the best interest of each client' and barristers to 'promote and protect fearlessly . . . . . . the lay client's best interest'. Whilst barristers are usually instructed by the solicitor, it is to the lay client they owe their primary duty, subject only to their overriding duty to the court. Both codes refer to the interests of the client rather than their expressed wishes, a paternalistic model of the relationship in which lawyers make decisions based on their clients' broader instructions and goals. Lawyers in England and Wales have a greater duty to the court than to their clients, unlike the 'zealous advocacy' expected of lawyers in the United States. Perhaps these issues also lead to some sense of dissatisfaction and therefore to complaints against lawyers.

An important characteristic of the lawyer–client relationship is the privilege afforded to it in law. **Legal professional privilege** attaches to all communications between a legal adviser and the client whether written or oral, provided that it was made for the purposes of giving legal advice. While the leading case on the question of whether a communication qualifies for privilege provides a wide interpretation of what constitutes legal advice, it leaves open the question of which employees of a client company are to be considered the lawyer's client for these purposes. The privilege also applies to communications with a third party where the communication is solely for the purposes of litigation. Communications in these situations are protected from disclosure unless the client waives the privilege. This privilege vests in the client and applies to both criminal and civil proceedings. The lawyer–client relationship is the only one recognized in this way (although the journalist–source relationship is also subject to a more limited form of protection).

From a Durkheimian view, lawyers serve their clients and society as a whole. Weberians see lawyers as being more self-serving in their approach (see R Abel, *The Legal Profession in England and Wales* (Oxford: Blackwell, 1998), 3–31). Rules of conduct often seem to operate closer to the latter model. The Legal Services Act 2007 creates a regime of regulatory oversight of the work of the legal professions and their attention to complaints. It also allows for new forms of ownership of legal practice. It remains to be seen whether such changes will make a difference to the lawyer–client relationship.

AVROM SHERR AND MARC MASON

A Sherr, *Client Care for Lawyers* (London: Sweet & Maxwell, 2nd edn, 1999)

D Nicholson and J Webb, *Professional Legal Ethics* (Oxford: Oxford University Press, 1999)

See also: **journalistic privilege; legal profession, governance, structure and organization of; legal profession: social background, entry and training**

lawyering skills   The term 'lawyering skills' originated in the USA. It represents an approach to becoming and being a lawyer which focuses on the whole package of what being a lawyer means. It encompasses the more traditional, academic approach to learning legal skills, which seeks to develop knowledge and understanding of legal rules and principles and their application to legal problems. However, it also stresses the ethics and social **responsibility** of lawyers as well as their personal qualities as key contributors to their professional competence. Many of the lawyering skills programmes emphasize the importance of continually learning from experience throughout an individual's career.

The notion of lawyering relocates the study of law as the study of problems in the abstract to the centrality of the human interaction: ie real people with real problems with real consequences following from the advice and actions of their lawyers. It may be helpful to look at lawyering skills from three perspectives: (1) the core professional skills; (2) the core lawyering skills; and (3) the skills necessary for continuing professional development.

With regard to professional skills, professionals are there to help people identify and deal with problems which the professionals have the expertise to solve. These problems are often complex, with uncertain boundaries, and the consequences of any course of action may be unpredictable. This implies a set of skills and values: the ability to define the problem; detailing what can or cannot be done; explaining the consequences of various courses of action. At the same time, professional practitioners have to remain aware of both their responsibility to act in the client's best interests and to behave with professional integrity. In all interactions with clients and other professionals they need to be able to master the detail of the situation, whilst continuing to see the bigger picture. Moreover, the ability to listen, question for information, check understanding, and empathize are critical interpersonal skills. Recent changes in the way legal work is organized— for example, the growth of specialist areas of law, the demand from clients for better quality and efficiency—have led to changes in the way lawyers work. In a number of situations they work in teams, either with others from the same profession, or in multi-disciplinary teams. Consequently, the ability to understand how groups operate, how to work to the strengths of other team members, and an awareness of their own team member contribution are valuable skills.

Professionals have heavy workloads. This means that all professionals operate under pressures of time. So that this does not become stressful, and consequently unhealthy, professionals need to be able to manage their workload appropriately. They need to understand how long it takes to carry out routine activities, how to make time to plan work, how to say 'no', what is required to have a healthy work-life balance, and what strategies to adopt to avoid falling foul of burnout.

In addition to professional skills are key skills required to be a lawyer. These are based on the specific knowledge and functions associated with the legal professions. It goes without saying that lawyers are expected to have mastered legal knowledge, both substantive—the rules and principles which define our rights and obligations; and procedural—the rules and instructions which need to be followed in order to achieve the outcome the client wants. They must be able to analyse complex material, which involves reading, understanding, and interpreting **legislation**, regulations, legal judgments, contracts, and other legal documents. They have to be confident in using the method of reasoning their academic tutors have taught them—to identify legal issues from a set of facts and predict how a **court** might decide the matter. They have to develop competence in oral skills and writing, dealing both with lay people and other professionals.

Consequently, the core skills of being a lawyer are:

- Interviewing: used in a variety of contexts both to elicit facts and provide information.
- Fact handling and legal analysis: this involves eliciting facts from clients, documents, witnesses, experts; identifying the legal issues that arise from the facts in order to build a case or resolve a problem.
- Legal research: to find or verify the law applicable to the case.
- Writing: to clients to keep them informed, to other parties in the case to give or receive information, to keep accurate records of transactions. The ability to write clearly and comprehensibly to many different types of reader is a key skill of a lawyer.
- Drafting legal documents such as business contracts, wills, conveyances. Lawyers also need to be able to draft 'statements of case' for court hearings, which set out the material facts of a case. There are formal rules and conventions that prescribe the form and content of these documents.

- Negotiation: interacting with representatives of the other side to resolve a dispute and so avoid going to court; making agreements on behalf of business concerns.
- Advocacy: speaking on someone's behalf in a court or **tribunal**; questioning and cross-questioning witnesses. Advocates must have a full working knowledge of court procedures, rules of evidence, and etiquette. This translates into a set of skills about how to question, what is fair or unfair to ask, how to address participants in the hearing, how to present a summary of a case, how to explain the law in lay terms.

The distinctions between the barrister and solicitor branches of the profession are becoming increasingly blurred. However there are still some key differences, which are reflected in the separate vocational training routes. On the whole, with some notable exceptions, most of the above core lawyering skills are not developed in legal education until the vocational stage. For would-be solicitors this is the Legal Practice Course ('LPC') and for those aspiring to the Bar, the Bar Vocational Course ('BVC').

In Scotland the two branches do not diverge until the later period of 'on the job' training. Would-be solicitors or advocates undertake the same course of vocational training, the Diploma in Legal Practice. Trainee solicitors then go on to a training contract with a firm of solicitors whilst aspiring advocates take up pupillage (known as 'devilling') with an advocate.

In addition to developing their core skills at the vocational stage of training, each branch of the profession focuses on those which help develop competent practitioners in their respective branch. Would-be barristers are required to focus on the skills of advocacy and a specialized form of drafting known as 'opinion-writing'. This is a specialist's statement on an aspect of law and its application. Opinions are usually responses to requests from solicitors. Solicitors' training emphasizes the skills involved in client care. Core skills are developed within the contexts of business law and practice and property law and practice.

Finally, lawyers must acquire and maintain the skills necessary to continuing professional development. Law is a complex and ever-changing field of study and practice. Moreover, the roles and structures of the profession are also changing and public expectations of what the legal profession will provide for them are expanding. This means that practitioners need to be constantly updating themselves on substantive and procedural law, but, just as important, on maintaining and developing their skills to satisfy changing markets. This process is usually known as 'continuing professional development' ('CPD'). It requires of the practitioner a set of 'metaskills'. These are skills which enable learning and development. They include an ability to develop a responsiveness to events, the ability to identify opportunities for learning and development, to set objectives and targets for learning, and through reflection, to continually develop and modify a repertoire of professional behaviours.

The late Donald Schön in *Educating the Reflective Practitioner* (1987) was concerned about the way university professional schools had developed a system of 'technical rationality'. By this he meant a cycle of research into professional practice, the development of theories and the applications of those theories to professional problems, and the teaching of those theories and applications to aspiring professionals. He referred to this kind of professional education as learning on the 'high ground'. In effect, this saw professional education as a closed system, sealed off from some of the messier, unpredictable, and multidimensional situations that professionals are faced with in day-to-day practice. He characterized everyday professional life as taking place in 'the swamp'. For him, professional competence was more than technical expertise. It involves an integration of professional and personal experience, values, and ethics. It requires the development of confidence from the ability to understand, reflect on, and learn from our professional interactions. The 'lawyering skills' approach attempts to move professional learning down from the high ground and into the swamp.

CAROLINE MAUGHAN

See also: legal professional ethics and values; vocational legal education

lawyers, complaints against   *see* ombudsmen

lawyers, remuneration and funding of   The ways in which lawyers are paid is controversial for a number of reasons. The traditional and still dominant model of charging is sometimes called the 'time and line' or 'hourly rate' model. Under this model, lawyers charge their clients for all work reasonably done at an hourly rate appropriate to their experience. Ordinarily, lawyers should advise their clients of the relevant hourly rates charged by them and their team and, where possible, give an overall indication of the likely amount of work on the case. Lawyers are particularly reluctant to estimate costs and they are even more reluctant to provide quotes. Under the time and line method, whatever the job requires the

consumer is required to pay. There are some controls (notably through the courts and professional bodies) to restrain overcharging, but conventional economic wisdom suggests that these are largely ineffective ways of restraining increases in lawyer costs. Generally consumers of legal services, even sophisticated repeat players, do not have either the skills or knowledge necessary to judge whether a lawyer reasonably did all the work they claim for.

Where an area of work is particularly competitive, lawyers are more likely to be willing to quote a fixed fee for a job. This is typically likely to occur in relation to **conveyancing** and internet-based legal services such as handling divorces and wills. Similarly, certain types of cases under the UK's **legal aid** schemes (such as routine criminal defences in magistrates' courts) are paid on a fixed fee basis, and the Civil Justice Council has led initiatives to introduce fixed fees into some areas of civil litigation, such as simple personal injury cases arising from road traffic accidents. Fixed fees provide a far greater level of control over costs for the consumer and provide consumers with the opportunity to shop around for legal services in the same way as they might purchase insurance or a holiday. Similarly, fixed fees make costs more predictable. To consumers uncertain whether to take a case to a lawyer, a fixed fee may overcome the fear that they have opened up a bottomless pit in their own finances. To third party funders, such as legal expenses insurers and legal aid administrators, fixed fees enable them to control their budgets better and, potentially, offer legal services to more people. There is, however, also a concern that fixed fees can diminish the quality of legal services where they are set at inappropriately low levels.

An increasingly important method of remuneration of lawyers in England and Wales are **no-win, no-fee arrangements** called Conditional Fee Agreements ('CFAs'). Under these arrangements, lawyers are paid no fee by the client if they lose the case. If they win the case, they are paid a fee by the client, which the client can ordinarily recover from their opponent. The fee itself is also increased by a percentage sum (the 'uplift') to reflect the level of risk to the lawyer in taking on the case. This has led to concerns that lawyers have an interest in winning the case which compromises them ethically by (for instance) making them willing to bolster the evidence of weak cases. Conversely, because the added incentives for winning a case are relatively modest, this may lead lawyers to settle the case for an unreasonably small amount of compensation as soon as they have done most of the basic preparatory work, leaving clients with lower settlements than they would have had under other payment arrangements. Neither criticism has been conclusively proven. A more substantial concern is that because law firms have to be reasonably sure that they will win their cases, and because they bear the costs of losing cases, they are reluctant to take any but the strongest cases and to take cases which may take a long time to settle or cost a lot to investigate. Although advertising for CFAs, and insurer complaints about the increased costs of such cases, have fuelled complaints that there is a **compensation culture** driven by self-interested lawyers, the evidence suggests that under CFAs the number of personal injury claims has either steadied or declined.

There are other ways of remunerating lawyers. It is common in commercial practice for some clients to pay a retainer for general advice (a kind of annual fixed fee for general legal services). Increasingly certain sorts of jobs are put out to competitive tender: firms tender on the basis of quality and price and allow the client to choose whomever they think most appropriate.   RICHARD MOORHEAD

lay participation in criminal justice system   *see* **juries; Justices of the Peace**

League of Nations   *see* **international organizations; United Nations**

learning outcomes of legal education   The intended learning outcome ('ILOC') of any process of education is a statement of what a student who successfully completes that process will know, understand, and be able to do. As in education at large, legal educators have, in recent years, been asked to think in terms of ILOCs. This represents a significant change in educational philosophy. Traditionally, providers of legal education offered programmes defined in terms of a curriculum, describing what would be taught. Thinking in terms of ILOCs moves the focus of attention in two ways: from teacher to student; and from teaching to learning. In particular it recognizes that being taught is only one way in which students learn. As educators come to embrace this new thinking, ILOCs become important reference points in critically evaluating existing provision and developing new programmes.

Closely related to this change in approach is the increasing importance of skills in Higher education. While for most academics, it is the subject which is of primary importance, for most for students it is what they learn *through* that subject that will matter most, namely the skills, both subject-based and general transferable. Explicitly spelling out ILOCs is valuable not only for educators, but also important for students themselves and for the other stakeholders such as parents, funding agencies like the Quality Assurance Agency ('QAA'), the governments higher education watchdog, and potential employers. Students, particularly with the advent of variable fees, want to know what they will get for their money, as do employers, in the form of knowing what a qualification, such as a law degree, means in terms of what someone with one will be able to do. The concern to make clear what a particular qualification will enable student to do finds direct expression in the QAA of Benchmark Statements.

The Law benchmark statement, first published in 2000, identifies the minimum abilities of a student at the bottom of third class honours. These are of three types: first, subject-specific abilities, including knowledge of the main features of the legal system studied, the ability to apply this knowledge to problem situations, and the ability to conduct legal research; secondly, general transferable skills, including the ability critically to identify flaws in an argument and to learn independently; thirdly, key skills such as oral and writing skills, ITC skills, and group working skills. While the statement prescribes where a law graduate must get to, it makes clear it is for each institution to decide how to get there and how that might be evidenced. Similarly, the UK legal professions have produced ILOCs of qualifying Law degrees. However, apart from requiring students to demonstrate knowledge of particular areas of law, these statements add little to the QAA benchmarks. For more detail one has to look to each institution's programmes specifications. These specifications, originally recommended by the Dearing Report, must now be available in a publicly accessible form. Often expressed in opaque 'QA speak', and varying between institutions, they commonly emphasize legal problem-solving and analytical skills while giving more or less emphasis to studying law in context (socio-economic, historical, philosophical, etc) and to acquiring the capacity critically to evaluate law and laws. For most, thinking like a lawyer, understood in terms of the capacity for clear and precise thought and for reading and interpreting text with exactness, is seen as a key learning objective.

Although generally viewed as contributing to the enhancement of education, ILOCs have their critics. For some they are too prescriptive, denying an idea of education as an open-ended process of intellectual discovery. For others, especially when in the form of national benchmark statements, ILOCs create the danger of standardization and stagnation.

                                        ALAN THOMSON

leasehold enfranchisement This term refers to the tenant's statutory right to acquire compulsorily the freehold interest of the landlord. After a long period of controversy, the right was granted to qualifying private sector residential tenants in the Leasehold Reform Act 1967. It enables them to buy out the landlord's interest on fair terms. The 1967 Act was unsuccessfully challenged by a major landlord in *James v United Kingdom* (1986). The **European Court of Human Rights** found that it did not result in a deprivation of possessions contravening Article 1 of the First Protocol of the **European Convention on Human Rights**. As an alternative to buying the freehold, tenants can claim an extended lease.

These rights originally applied only to houses but, by the Leasehold Reform, Housing and Urban Development Act 1993 and the Commonhold and Leasehold Reform Act 2002, they have been extended to flats. The qualifying conditions are complex but include a general requirement, applicable to houses and flats, that the lease was granted for a term exceeding twenty-one years. In the case of houses, the tenant has an individual right to acquire the freehold, but in the case of flats a group of tenants (representing not less than 50 per cent of the flats in the building) have to buy the freehold of the whole building together ('collective enfranchisement') and then act as their own landlords. Where an extended lease is claimed instead of the freehold, it adds fifty years (or ninety in the case of flats) to the unexpired term of the current lease.   LETITIA CRABB

A Radevsky and D Greenish, *Hague on Leasehold Enfranchisement* (London: Sweet & Maxwell, 4th edn, 2003 and First Supplement 2005)

leasehold estate In everyday language, a lease gives a right to use land for a period, usually in return for the payment of rent. A leasehold estate is a more precise legal term and indicates that this right is proprietary and capable of being enforced against third parties so that, for example, even if the property is sold to a new owner the tenant can continue to use the land.

For a leasehold estate to exist there must be (1) an intention to create legal relations; (2) exclusive possession; and (3) a grant for a term certain. An intention to create legal relations shows that the parties intend to be legally bound, and it can usually be assumed from the promise to pay rent. Exclusive possession is the tenant's legal right to exclude others: the tenant can keep out strangers and keep out the landlord unless the landlord is exercising limited rights reserved to him by the tenancy agreement

to enter and view and repair. A term certain means that at the start of the lease it must be possible to know the date the lease begins, how long it will last, and when it will come to an end. An unpredictable end-date, such as 'until you find somewhere else to live', will prevent the agreement being a leasehold estate. Provided it is certain it can be of any duration; and a 'periodic' tenancy counts, as each discrete period is of known maximum duration.

SUSAN BRIGHT

legal academics The legal academic staff who work in universities and colleges in the UK perform a number of different roles. Traditionally, they teach students, carry out research into aspects of the law and the legal profession, and also participate in the administration of their workplace by sitting on committees. In different institutions, they may carry out different proportions of these tasks, with some being more focused on teaching, and some on research.

Since studying law as an undergraduate in higher education does not lead directly to qualification as a practising lawyer, the majority of legal academics are not training lawyers, and many of them are not themselves qualified to practise law, although a minority do so alongside their academic appointment. Some legal academics may also hold judicial office, for instance as **tribunal** chairs. In a small number of higher education institutions, training courses for entry to the legal profession are offered, in which case some academics do become involved in training lawyers. However, the majority of them focus solely on their academic tasks.

Law has long been seen as a masculine discipline; this is particularly reflected in the small numbers of women present at senior levels. Research suggests that taking higher education as a whole, only about 15 per cent of law professors are female, while nearly 50 per cent of law lecturers are female. There is some evidence that women face a particular 'credibility gap' in establishing themselves as legal academics, because of the association of law with values such as rationality, neutrality, and objectivity. The small number of ethnic minority law lecturers and those who are openly gay or **lesbian** reinforces the view that it may be more difficult for those other than the stereotypical white heterosexual male to take their rightful place in the law school.

Although in some respects legal academics do not reflect the diversity found in contemporary society, in other respects the profession attracts a very diverse group of people. This is because it is increasingly the case that scholars from around the world are being appointed to UK law schools, with the result that many departments are composed of legal academics from a great variety of countries, which enriches not only the legal scholarship produced, but also the learning experience of law students.

A common question put to legal academics is 'Why don't you want to be a practising lawyer?'. Given the pay differentials between the legal profession and academia (which are much greater than the differentials in some other disciplines), the implication is that only those who 'can't make it' in the legal profession would end up in academia. However, there is sufficient evidence of academics moving successfully into legal practice or developing a judicial career (often at very high levels) after they have worked in academia for some time, to suggest that this view is simplistic and largely inaccurate. Recent research reveals that legal academics make their choice of profession for reasons other than monetary reward. The thing they value most is the freedom to organize their own working lives in a way which is impossible in practice. In relation to the research they choose to do, the content of their teaching, and the organization of their working time, legal academics, like others who work in universities, have considerable amounts of personal choice about the way in which they carry out their job. This is true even for junior lecturers, and, to the extent that institutions of higher education remain collegial organizations, they are often able to have more influence on their department than junior members of the legal profession can have on their working environment. While a hierarchy exists in academia, it is often less rigid than that in legal practice, although there are many variations between institutions, and those working in 'new' universities may experience a greater degree of managerial control than those working in 'old' universities. Other aspects of the academic job which are highly valued include the variety of tasks involved in being an academic—particularly the opportunity to do *both* research *and* teaching, which are very different tasks—the first often involving considerable amounts of time spent alone, developing ideas and writing, while the second calls for the exercise of interpersonal skills and involves considerable interaction with large numbers of very different types of people. Legal academics also value the opportunity to do something 'worthwhile', both in terms of contributing to the intellectual life of society and in terms of the contribution to the education of (over the length of a career) thousands of students. The work of a legal academic is profoundly different to that of a practising lawyer, and it is not surprising, once this is understood, that for some people, it is a positive career choice.

The difference between being a legal academic and being a practising lawyer is increasingly reflected in the different training which is necessary to pursue these different careers. While practising lawyers follow a vocational course which focuses on skills such as advocacy, drafting, negotiation, and so on, the requirement for those wishing to become a legal academic is generally that they should possess a PhD. As far as legal academia is concerned, this is a relatively recent development. It used to be the case that qualification as a practising lawyer was regarded as a desirable attribute for a legal academic. However, as law has found its feet as an independent academic discipline, attention has focused on academic skills, and skills used in the legal profession have become increasingly irrelevant. Institutions are now demanding a high level of academic qualification, so that a majority of early-career legal academics do not possess any qualifications as practising lawyers, but hold PhDs (and have often published articles in scholarly journals before obtaining their first academic appointment).

FIONA COWNIE

F Cownie, *Legal Academics: Culture and Identities* (Oxford: Hart Publishing, 2004)

legal advice and assistance   While there is some disagreement over what, exactly, constitutes legal advice, it is generally taken to involve more than the simple provision of information about the law and/or legal process. Advice must involve a degree of enquiry into, and analysis of, specific circumstances and, then, the application of information to them. The products of advice are tailored information, options, and recommendations. Legal assistance goes beyond advice and involves practical help in bringing about desired outcomes within a legal framework. Assistance can take many forms, ranging from the preparation of paperwork, through to the conduct of negotiation and representation in **courts** and **tribunals**.

Legal advice and assistance may be obtained by both individuals and organizations and can relate to any aspect of law. The huge growth of law over recent decades—including significant extensions in the reach of criminal law, the establishment of a broad range of civil law rights and obligations, and the accumulation of laws regulating the conduct of business—has contributed to substantial growth in the numbers of people and organizations providing legal advice and assistance, in a market now worth many billions of pounds each year.

Certain forms of advice and assistance can be provided only by those who are appropriately authorized. Across the United Kingdom, these include the provision of advice about immigration matters, the conduct of **conveyancing**, the administration of deceased people's estates, and advocacy in the courts. Most recently, since 2007 many claims management services in England and Wales (notably, claims assessors and claims management companies, which act as intermediaries in compensation claims) have required authorization from the Secretary of State for Constitutional Affairs. Where no authorization is required, any person or organization can provide advice and assistance.

Any person arrested by the police in connection with a crime is entitled to be advised by a lawyer. Assistance is provided through solicitors' firms or, occasionally, a **public defender** office. Where a person does not wish to see a particular solicitor (or solicitor's representative), then a 'duty' solicitor can be called upon.

It might be thought that all people offered advice following arrest would accept the offer, but research suggests this is not the case. In England and Wales, it has been estimated that only around half the people offered (free) advice at a police station take it up. However, this is a greater proportion than the 25 per cent estimated to have been exercising the statutory right to advice which was introduced by the Police and Criminal Evidence Act 1984. Additional legal advice and assistance is also available to people once charged (or facing being charged) with criminal offences. Again, this is provided through solicitors' firms or public defender offices.

The number of civil (in the sense of non-criminal) law problems and issues that people encounter each year runs to many times the number of criminal arrests and, most likely, well into eight figures. Recent surveys of the incidence of 'difficult to solve' civil legal problems suggest that at least 8½ million such problems are faced each year across the **United Kingdom**. The most common concern consumer transactions, neighbours, housing, personal finance, employment, relationship breakdown, and injuries. To these can be added many less serious problems that people face, along with problems of a variety not included within the surveys, and non-contentious legal issues. For example, more than one million house sales are concluded each year.

When faced with a civil law problem or issue, it is up to people to find their own advice and assistance. Reflecting the broad range of civil law rights, responsibilities, and processes that now exist, people seek advice from a wide variety of types of adviser. As well as the more than 10,000 solicitors' firms in the United Kingdom (which represent the most frequent source of advice and assistance for non-trivial matters)

people also frequently seek advice from sources such as advice agencies, local authorities, their employers, **trade unions**, insurance companies, and the **police**. Less frequently, people seek advice from sources such as politicians, social workers, the media, banks, charities, and court staff.

There are thousands of independent advice agencies across the UK, mostly represented by the Advice Services Alliance. These include organizations as varied as Law Centres (of which there are around seventy across the United Kingdom), **Citizens Advice Bureaux**, single-issue charities (such as Shelter), and small volunteer services. The number of Citizens Advice Bureaux, alone, now stands at over 900 (834 in England and Wales, 76 in Scotland and 28 in Northern Ireland). Indeed, citizen advice organizations have reported that, in 2005–2006, they provided advice in relation to almost 6 million issues, often through volunteer advisers.

When people obtain advice from insurance companies, this is usually through dedicated legal help lines. More generally, such help lines are being increasingly used as a means of providing inexpensive basic legal advice to the broader public. In recent years there has been a substantial increase in the capacity and promotion of public legal help lines such as CLS Direct, Consumer Direct, National Debtline, and the National Domestic Violence Helpline, along with the development of many commercial help lines. To give an idea of the rate of growth, Consumer Direct, introduced on a regional basis in 2004, handled more than 1 million calls on a national basis by 2005–2006. The English and Welsh Civil and Social Justice Survey indicates that, for civil law problems people find difficult to solve, the telephone is now used for the majority of initial advice enquiries and is the exclusive means of obtaining advice around one-quarter of the time. Where the telephone is not used to obtain substantive advice, it is frequently used as a means for referral though Accident Line, for instance.

Internet and email advice services are also becoming increasingly available, though they have yet to make the impression of telephone services.

While people buying or selling a house will invariably obtain advice and assistance, from either a solicitor or licensed conveyancer, people encountering many civil law problems or issues will not. Only around half the people who face civil law problems that are difficult to solve will obtain advice, of one form or another. A somewhat lower percentage will obtain explicitly legal advice.

In general, people become less likely to seek advice as problems become less serious. Linked to this, the rate at which people seek advice varies by problem type. So, people facing problems concerning consumer transactions seek advice less often than people facing a divorce or problems concerning their employment or home. Some people also appear less likely to seek advice than others. For example, there is evidence that young people, people in some minority ethnic groups, and men are less likely than others to seek advice.

Across many problem types, poor understanding of sources of advice is a significant obstacle to advice. Not only can it prevent people from seeking advice, it is also the main reason why around 10 per cent of people who seek advice fail to obtain any. Other obstacles include problems accessing advisers over the telephone, long waits to see some advisers in person, the cost of advice, and physical accessibility. While the last two obstacles have only a small impact on initial general advice, there is evidence that they present greater obstacles to more specialist assistance (such as from solicitors or barristers). This is because many initial advice services are offered at no cost, or included within more general insurance products. For specialist assistance, costs can be considerable, although **legal aid** is available to help people on low income to access such services. Various *pro bono* schemes also operate to assist people who might otherwise be unable to afford help. Frequently, people who do not obtain advice about problems express regret at not having done so.

Different problem types are also associated with different sources of advice. For example, whereas people typically seek advice about family problems from solicitors, they are more likely to seek advice about housing problems from advice agencies or local councils. This can impact on the form of advice and assistance provided. Solicitors, for example, will more often propose an overtly legal problem-resolution strategy than advice agencies. They will also provide greater active assistance—such as preparation of paperwork and conduct of negotiations—than many agencies, which often emphasize the role of advice in empowering people to resolve problems themselves.

As well as private individuals, government, charitable, and commercial organizations can have need for legal advice and assistance. Almost 2,000 lawyers within the Government Legal Service ('GLS') provide the main source of legal advice and assistance within government. In addition, UK organizations outside government employ more than 20,000 in-house lawyers. Organizations also frequently obtain legal advice and assistance from the wider advice sector; in particular from solicitors' firms. These generate a substantial proportion of their income from organizations. For the largest solicitors firms, only a minority of income is generated from individual private clients. Even mid-size firms, with thirteen to forty solicitors, generate around one-third of their income from organizations.

PASCOE PLEASENCE

H Genn and A Paterson, Paths to Justice Scotland: What People in Scotland Do and Think About Going to Law (Oxford: Hart Publishng, 2001)

P Pleasence, *Civil Law and Social Justice* (Norwich: TSO, 2006)

See also: **complaints: internet information; duty solicitor scheme; government lawyers; legal help and representation; legal profession, private and voluntary sector of; legal profession, public and employed sector of;** *pro bono* **legal services**

legal adviser (court clerk)   *see* **courts**

legal aid   Legal aid is the means by which people who cannot afford to employ their own lawyers are sometimes enabled to have access to legal services. It is available in relation to civil and criminal matters. In England and Wales, legal aid is overseen by the Legal Services Commission, which has overall responsibility for the Community Legal Service (which is concerned with civil matters) and the Criminal Defence Service (which is concerned with persons facing criminal charges).

In England and Wales, publicly-funded legal services can be provided only by those lawyers who hold contracts with the Legal Services Commission. This enables the Commission to use its contracting power to exercise control over expenditure, and to concentrate its funds in priority areas. It also exercises quality control and ensures that proper standards of service are maintained. The financing of legal aid is an almost constant source of concern, as costs can rapidly spiral. Various measures have been introduced to control expenditure, but there are accompanying concerns that if insufficient funds are allocated to the legal aid budget, many people will be denied access to justice.

In relation to civil matters, legal aid falls under the auspices of the Community Legal Service, whose purpose is to promote the availability of a range of legal services. Precisely which services are available depends on the nature of the client's case and the terms of the provider's contract with the Legal Services Commission. Community Legal Service funding is not available for certain types of work, including **conveyancing**, boundary disputes, the making of wills, matters of company and partnership law, and asylum decisions. Areas which are covered include family, housing, debt, immigration, employment, contact and consumer law, clinical negligence, and actions against the police.

In order to be eligible for Community Legal Service funding, an individual must satisfy both a means test and a merits test. The means test is set at a low level; those with very low incomes and little capital will be entitled to full Community Legal Service assistance, while those who are slightly better-off may be required to pay a contribution towards certain services. Others will be financially ineligible for funding. Factors to be considered in relation to the merits test include the potential benefit to the client of providing the service in question and the likely cost to the Community Legal Service of funding it, the prospects of any legal action being successful, and the public interest. If a legally-aided person is successful in winning monetary compensation, they are generally required to pay back the financial assistance they have received. A common misconception is that legal aid is always in the nature of a gift; often, it is a loan.

The Criminal Defence Service administers criminal legal aid. All solicitors providing publicly-funded criminal legal services in England and Wales must hold a General Criminal Contract and a Specialist Quality Mark. All the services provided are subject to some form of merits test, though many of them are not means-tested. In addition, the Criminal Defence Service is responsible for organizing **duty solicitor schemes** in police stations and magistrates' courts. These schemes provide free help, offering telephone advice in connection with less serious offences, and face-to-face assistance with more serious matters. To a limited extent, the Criminal Defence Service is also able to provide legal services through lawyers it employs itself. This is known as the **Public Defender** Service. It is only available in certain cities in England and Wales.

The Northern Ireland Legal Services Commission has responsibility for the provision of publicly funded legal services in Northern Ireland, while the Scottish Legal Aid Board is responsible for managing legal aid in Scotland. The three systems are broadly similar in relation to criminal legal aid, though there are an increasing number of differences in relation to civil legal aid. The system of provision of legal services through practitioners holding contracts with the Legal Services Commission is unique to England and Wales. In the other parts of the UK the system of contracting does not exist, so any lawyer who wishes may undertake legal aid work. In Scotland and Northern Ireland, the scope

of matters for which civil legal aid is available is wider than in England and Wales, although cost is a constant problem. In Northern Ireland, for instance, the Legal Services Commission is under a statutory obligation to demonstrate value for money in all its expenditure on publicly funded legal services.

FIONA COWNIE

legal basis of EU law   *see* **European Community powers**

legal clinics   *see* **clinical legal education**

legal consciousness   The concept legal consciousness is used to name analytically the understandings and meanings of law circulating in social relations. Legal consciousness refers to what people do as well as say about law. It is understood to be part of a reciprocal process in which the meanings given by individuals to their world become patterned, stabilized, and objectified. These meanings, once institutionalized, become part of the material and discursive systems that limit and constrain future meaning-making. Consciousness is not an individual trait nor solely ideational; legal consciousness is a type of social practice reflecting and forming social structures.

The study of legal consciousness documents the forms of participation and interpretation through which actors sustain, reproduce, or amend the circulating (contested or hegemonic) structures of meanings concerning law. Although researchers collect signs of legal consciousness by observing people thinking, doing, talking, telling stories, lumping grievances, working, playing, marrying, divorcing, suing a neighbour, refusing to call the **police**, or joining a **social movement**, legal consciousness, as participation in the production of legal meanings, cannot be understood independent of its role in the collective construction of legality, or the **rule of law**.

As a theoretical concept and topic of empirical research, legal consciousness developed among socio-legal scholars to explain how law sustains its institutional power across wide spans of time, space, and variable performance. Researchers theorize that law is a durable and powerful human invention because a good part of legality invisibly suffuses everyday life so much so that, where there is a rule of law, legal authority is normally uncontested, or challenged primarily within the legally provided channels for dispute. This legal hegemony derives from long habituation to routinized forms of legal authority that are fused into the material, as well as social organization of ordinary life, for example, in traffic lanes, parking rules, ticket stubs, and sales receipts. Law's mediations of social transactions have been sedimented throughout the habits of daily living, helping to make things move around in more or less expected ways, without having to invoke, display, or wield its elaborate and intricate procedures, especially its ultimate physical force. Of course, this sedimentation and normative regulation is never complete. People do not always stay within the boundaries of legally sanctioned expectations and the reach of law is always disputed. However, visible legal battles, eg trials, are the outliers of the law's more routine, habituated activities. Ironically, it is the outliers that end up constituting the textual body of legal doctrine, especially in **common law** regimes.

Thus, the study of legal consciousness traces the ways in which law is experienced and interpreted by specific individuals as they engage, avoid, or resist the law and legal meanings. The research seeks to connect theoretically all these pieces: to show how the lived experiences of ordinary people produce simultaneously open, malleable yet stable systems of practice and signification; to demonstrate how the law remains rich with variation and possibility; and to explore how in representative **democracies** governed through law, the people might be simultaneously both the authors and victims of their history.

SUSAN SILBEY

P Ewick and S Silbey, *The Common Place of Law: Stories From Everyday Life* (Chicago: University of Chicago Press, 1998)

legal education *see* **assessment in legal education; benchmarking in legal education; clinical legal education; gender issues in legal education; IT in legal education; legal academics; legal education and liberal education; problem-based education; vocational legal; education**

legal education and liberal education Historically legal education in universities in the United Kingdom has been closely tied to the legal professions with university law schools largely being seen, by themselves and by others, as being a training ground for these professions. For this reason law schools were intellectually and not infrequently geographically separated from their parent universities who saw themselves as having a wider role in relationship to both scholarship and education. However, from the 1960s onwards, the nature of legal scholarship in law schools broadened. Research in law schools, which had been focused on providing explanations of legal rules for barristers and solicitors, began to consider a greater range of issues to do

with the nature, operation, efficiency, and morality of law. At the same time, it became clear that law students were frequently not entering the legal professions after graduation. As a consequence, legal academics began to reassess their task and consider the value of a liberal education in law. Rather than a legal education simply being a vocational matter, equipping students with the technical knowledge that they needed in order to work as a legal professional, it was argued that a legal education should enable a student to develop as a person, giving them the intellectual tools to make a wider range of choices as a citizen and an individual as well as a worker and to be conscious of their own ethical responsibilities in making those choices. Traditionally the curriculum had concentrated on those aspects of law that were of greatest interest to solicitors and barristers and, because of this, had often concerned itself with commercial matters. New subjects began to look at other areas of law. A liberal education in law means that students must be aware of the way that law permeates all of society. Civil liberties are thus as important as **company** law. More than this, rather than simply being able to explain the content of law, students have to be capable of critically examining its impact. New tools for examining the law thus become essential. Feminist analysis is as important as doctrinal reasoning. The pursuit of a liberal education in law also changes the research agenda of the law school. Knowledge is studied for its own sake rather than for any utility that the knowledge might have. A liberal educational approach therefore means that legal academics have to examine law in all its manifestations; that which can be known about law should be known. The audience for legal research becomes not just those in the legal profession or **judges** but policymakers, politicians, and those who are simply curious about legal phenomena. More importantly, the conception of law changes once a liberal educational approach is taken. State law, which is of paramount importance to legal professionals, is now seen as just one form of law with other non-state legal systems such as those that arise within a religious community taking on equal significance.

ANTHONY BRADNEY

A Bradney, *Conversations, Chances and Choices: The Liberal Law School in the Twenty-First Century* (Oxford: Hart Publishing, 2003)

legal education, research on The rapid increase in the scale and scope of legal education in the second half of the twentieth century has led to a growing recognition of the need to treat legal education itself as a subject for research.

Legal education research has tended to fit into one of four broad categories. First, there is a substantial body of descriptive, quantitative, research that has sought to chart the basic changes affecting law schools, such as the numbers of students and staff, their **gender** and **ethnicity**, the range of modules and courses offered, and the kinds of learning environments and resources available. Such data has been usefully deployed in studies examining changes in legal education policy and their consequences.

Secondly, researchers have also looked at law schools as institutions which are shaped by and help to shape the social and legal systems. Law schools matter in sociological terms because they act as gatekeepers, controlling initial access to the legal professions. They both possess an institutional culture of their own and constitute a stage in professional **identity** formation, and, as such, are part of the process whereby social elites and hierarchies are constructed, perpetuated, and perhaps even transformed. Researchers in this context have explored issues of access and recruitment to legal education, the social experience of law school for different student groups, and students' perceptions of the transition from education to the workplace, as well as investigating the attitudes and (professional) values held by law students and, to a lesser extent, academics.

Thirdly, a growing body of conceptual research is exploring the influences of the wider political economy of both law and higher education in shaping the direction of legal education policy and practice. Research exploring these complex trends has tended to rely largely on historical and documentary analysis techniques.

Lastly, research also explores the nature and consequences of specific teaching and learning experiences. This is commonly called pedagogic research. It employs a range of empirical approaches. It may be quantitative or qualitative. It can be longitudinal— looking at changes in the learning experience of a group of students over time—or it may be simply a snapshot analysis of a specific process or intervention. It may focus on the experience of a single class or cohort, or be comparative, looking at experiences across a range of institutions, disciplines, or countries.

Much of the pedagogic research produced so far has involved small scale, often module- or course-specific, case studies. While this includes some useful and methodologically sophisticated work, much has been relatively unsophisticated, and of limited explanatory power. These problems are not unique to pedagogic research in law. Identifying what works (better) and why is often difficult in educational research, reflecting the complexity of learning processes as well as some specific ethical and practical problems of research design. Nevertheless these issues are exacerbated, in the UK at least, by a shortage of social science and educational research training for law teachers, a relative lack of funding for larger scale studies of legal education, and an associated failure to use multi-disciplinary research teams.

JULIAN WEBB

legal expenses insurance   *see* **costs of complaining and claiming; legal aid**

legal help and representation   *see* **legal advice and assistance; legal aid**

legal philosophy   *see* **theory in legal research**

legal pluralism   In the last thirty years of the twentieth century a scarcely qualified view of law as state law gave way to much more expansive formulations, as the social world became conventionally conceptualized as constituted by multiple, interpenetrating 'legalities'. Beyond state law now lies 'a great variety of legal orders circulating in society' (B de Sousa Santos, *Toward a New Common Sense: Law, Science and Politics in Paradigmatic Transition* (1995), 429). Law has somehow come to be seen as 'everywhere', even as co-extensive with the social and thus present in social aggregations from the simplest to the most complex. Much of this transition has taken place under the self-consciously adopted banner of 'legal pluralism', advanced in the 1970s and 1980s as an explicit critique of 'legal centralism'. So we have to think of legal pluralism both as identifying a pivotal movement in late twentieth-century legal scholarship and as a way of conceptualizing social space.

Before we begin to examine legal pluralism, there is the preliminary question of how we should conceptualize heterogeneity generally in the social world. Scholars have talked about 'pluralism' and the 'local' in very different ways: as fields, arenas, domains, regions, discourses, systems, and orders. Each of these terms has a particular resonance for one or more strands of modern social theory, now complicated by the uncertain currents of post-modernism. Within this contemporary scene, legal pluralism has been widely recognized as a key concept for post-modern views of law.

A determination to conceptualize law as going beyond state law can be traced back a long way in twentieth-century legal scholarship. Eugen Ehrlich's *Grundlegung der Soziologie des Rechts*, published in

1913, lamented 'the tragic fate of juristic science' in being devoted exclusively to 'state law' (*Fundamental Principles of the Sociology of Law,* trans Walter Moll (1936), 13) and went on to identify law with associations in the social world at all levels, including the factory and the family.

The label 'legal pluralism' seems to appear first in Franz von Benda-Beckmann's *Rechtspluralismus in Malawi* (1970) and rapidly came into common use. This use signalled legal scholars' growing interest in the governmental arrangements developed at a local level in former colonial territories across Africa, Asia, the Caribbean, and the Pacific during and immediately following the colonial period. Colonial legal orders, in many cases involving specific provision for the qualified survival of local normative orders as 'native law', were self-consciously plural in nature. Only later did attention turn to the trans-national field occupied by multi-national corporations, non-governmental organizations, and moving populations. This shift of focus resulted in now familiar conceptualizations of 'trans-national', 'global', and 'cosmopolitan' law.

A first, general point about the provenance of the legal pluralist movement needs to be underlined. Legal pluralism is not just the shorthand for some theoretical and empirical problems brought about by **colonialism**, by the internal fragmentation of the old West, or the growth of commercial activity at supra-national level. It is specifically the banner coopted by a contemporary intellectual movement in the law schools, seen to be an emancipated way of looking at law and contrasted by its adherents with traditional 'legal centralism' which just aspired to keep the law of the nation state under observation. Its claim to legitimacy was quickly registered through the formation of an international professional association, *The Commission on Folk Law and Legal Pluralism.* The journal *African Law Studies* re-emerged as the *Journal of Legal Pluralism and Unofficial Law*; a conference was held at Bellagio in 1981, providing an imprimatur for the new field, around which a considerable literature has now developed. So we need to register the imperial nature of this venture. 'Legal pluralism' has been a term by which lawyers label their own activities, marking out a new sub-discipline of academic law, and identifying a wider area of the social world for their professional operations.

'Legal' pluralism presupposes a distinctive way of thinking about norms and about social space as being made up of a number of co-existing, more-or-less discrete compartments. Adopting this conceptualization, two questions are immediately posed:

how can we best view the relationship between these different orders; and where should the new boundary of 'the legal' be fixed? The questions are the same whether we are contemplating the rapidly developing 'global legal order', adjacent fields within the metropolis, or the relationship between the 'secretariat' and the localities in the colonial context.

A number of shots have been made at characterizing the relationship between adjacent normative fields. There is general agreement about the naiveté of a vertical, top-down, command view under which national law inundates and supersedes existing local regimes, permitting the latter limited, licensed survival. Leopold Pospisil, in *Kapauku Papuans and their Law* (1958), rejected this extreme positivism. For him 'law' should rather be seen as located at different points in the social world, wherever 'authorities' can be found imposing normatively-based decisions. Accordingly, whether you look at the metropolis, or at colonized territories, 'law' should be seen as residing at a number of hierarchically ranged, more or less discrete, 'legal levels'. Sally Falk Moore proposed a more flexible formulation in her seminal essay, 'Law and Change: the Semi-Autonomous Social Field as an Appropriate Area of Study' ((1973) *Law and Society Review* 719). There she substitutes the concept of 'social field' for that of 'legal level', and represents normative orders, including national legal systems, as partially discrete, but nevertheless overlapping and interpenetrating social fields.

With a move away from a conception of law as state law, marking the boundary of legal orders has proved problematic. Latterly the argument has been between what Brian Tamanaha (see below) has characterized as 'essentialist' and 'conventionalist' positions, as agonized efforts have been made to specify the boundaries of an authentic legal domain. A forceful statement of the essentialist position has been made by Gunther Teubner in attempting to clarify the relationship between law and other social practices. In *Global Law without a State* (1997), Teubner openly recognizes that the idea of law at global level is problematic and needs to be argued for. He nonetheless claims to observe the 'the emergence of genuinely legal forms', and that 'a theory of legal pluralism is capable of identifying authentic legal phenomena operating on a global level'. Teubner specifies carefully how we should go about identifying law in this expanded field, pointing to the line which the discursive practice of law draws between itself and its environment. For the key to this self-proclaimed boundary, Teubner looks to the code in which legal communications are expressed, the binary code 'legal/illegal'.

For some purposes one would not wish to fault Teubner's preoccupation with the boundaries law draws for itself; these are important features of a particular scene. But the apparently differentiated character of national legal orders in the contemporary West and, indeed, state law's 'native' claim to systemic qualities, reflect quite parochial and, perhaps, transitory characteristics of a particular cultural assemblage, making it questionable whether these distinctive features can carry the analytic weight that Teubner demands of them for comparative purposes.

Responding directly to Teubner in *A General Jurisprudence of Law and Society* (2001), Tamanaha rejects what he identifies as the dominant 'essentialist' approach to legal pluralism, which he sees Teubner's work as exemplifying. This approach: '…assumes that law consists of a singular phenomenon which can be defined, and … gives rise to unresolvable analytical and instrumental difficulties that inhibit the development of the idea of legal pluralism'. Tamanaha proposes instead what he identifies as a 'conventionalist' approach under which: 'Law is whatever people in a social arena conventionally recognize as law through their social practices'. At first sight, Tamanaha's approach seems to get away from the interminable definitional problems encountered by the 'essentialists'. But he raises other difficulties in apparently elevating local, 'native' understandings to a position in which they shape the field and govern the analysis.

This recovery and respectful recognition of previously marginalized normative orders is obviously welcome. It is the mode of recognition that is problematic, namely hegemonic recovery of such orders within the discourse of *law* in a manner that carries an unselfconscious tendency to privilege the folk categories of Western law. Inaugurating an explicit pluralism, lawyers have done more than register their interest in a particular field of study: they have marked some rather varied forms with a distinctive imprint. State law's commentators have long been garrulous about its attributes; now, graciously embracing others in this discourse, lawyers are seeking to tell those others what *they* are.

We need to recognize this openly, and be cautious about it for a number of reasons. First, legal rules are so unlike most norms that we risk getting into immediate difficulties if we treat them as the paradigm case. The codified, differentiated form of legal rules, in particular, contrasts sharply with most social norms. The understandings utilized by lay persons about how to behave are not generally like this. They are implicit, and picked up—largely

unconsciously—as everyday life goes on. They constitute a largely implicit, loosely constructed, undifferentiated repertoire, rather than plural sets of formulated rules which actors move between in a conscious way. Again, the negotiated orders above state level have a very different character from state law; and understanding of both can be diminished if we aggregate them together.   SIMON ROBERTS

J Griffiths, 'What is Legal Pluralism?' (1986) 24 *Journal of Legal Pluralism* 1

S Merry, 'Legal Pluralism' (1988) 22 *Law and Society Review* 869

See also: **anthropology and law; colonial administration and law; cosmopolitanism; global civil society; globalization and law; indigenous law; sociological jurisprudence**

legal positivism to 1970   From the late eighteenth to the mid-nineteenth centuries, the utilitarian philosophers Jeremy **Bentham** and John Austin developed an influential theory of law which is known as 'legal positivism'. Rejecting the idea that law derives its authority from God, or from some metaphysical conception of nature or reason—so-called 'natural law'—Bentham and Austin argued that law is essentially man-made: it is a command issued by a political superior or sovereign, to whom the populace is in a habit of obedience.

This early positivist conception of law did not develop significantly for some time after Austin's death. In the early decades of the twentieth century, such legal theory as was taught in Britain tended to consist in either **historical jurisprudence** or a dry offshoot of technical legal analysis, informed by no attempt either to link conceptual analysis to any broader idea of the nature of law, or to consider how technical legal concepts assisted law to serve its various social functions. Prescriptive questions about what purposes law *ought* to pursue were left to the attention of moral and political philosophy—the latter itself a field which was relatively stagnant at this time.

This extended period of stagnation was brought to an abrupt end by HLA Hart's election in 1952 to the Oxford Chair of Jurisprudence. Hart's approach to legal philosophy was at once disarmingly simple and breathtakingly ambitious. His first single-authored book, *The Concept of Law* (Oxford: Clarendon Press, 1961; 2nd edn, 1994) claimed to provide a general, descriptive theory of law which was at once a contribution to 'analytical jurisprudence' and to 'descriptive sociology': to elucidate a concept of law which would be of relevance to all forms of law, wherever or whenever they arose. In pursuing this project, Hart returned to the insights of Austin and Bentham, but combined their methods with those of the new linguistic philosophy represented by the work of JL Austin and Ludwig Wittgenstein.

The nub of Hart's theory was the simple idea that law is a system of rules structurally similar to the rules of games such as chess or cricket. The rules are of different kinds, with complementary functions. Some—'primary rules'—directly govern behaviour; others—'secondary rules'—provide for the identification, interpretation, and alteration of the former. The most obvious example of primary rules would be criminal laws; examples of secondary rules range from constitutional laws to laws governing the creation of contracts, marriages or wills.

Hart's positivism insisted that although legal rules generate genuine obligations, they are not straightforwardly moral rules. Their authority derives not from their content but from their source, which lies in a distinctively institutionalized system of social recognition. For example, the rule that we should drive on the left is authoritative not because there is any intrinsic value to driving on the left. Rather, its authority derives from the fact that the rule can be identified in accordance with an agreed set of criteria for recognition, such as parliamentary enactment or judicial precedent. Precisely the same is true of legal rules which overlap with moral standards: the legal prohibition on murder is not the same as, and derives its validity in a different way from, the moral injunction against killing.

Hart's account of how legal rules are recognized as valid, and hence as generating obligations, served, conversely, to distinguish law from a mere system of force, or 'orders backed by threats'. For legal rules have not only an external but also an internal aspect: we know that a rule is in existence not only because it is regularly observed, but also because those subject to it use it as a reason or standard for behaviour, criticizing themselves or others for breaches of the rules. It was in this aspect of Hart's theory that linguistic philosophy became important: for example, he explored the distinction between habitual behaviour (going to the pub on Sunday lunch time) and rule-governed behaviour (going to church on Sunday morning); between being obliged to do something (handing over money because someone threatens to kill you if you do not) and having an obligation to do it (paying your taxes).

By moving from the early 'positivist' notion of law as a sovereign command to the notion of law as a system of rules, Hart produced a theory which better fitted the impersonal idea of authority embedded in modern democracies: his theory of law encapsulated a modern understanding of the ideal of 'the **rule of law** and not of men'. It provided a powerful and remarkably widely-applicable rationalization of the nature of legal authority in a secular and pluralistic world. The starting point for virtually every positivist contribution to what has become a veritable industry of analytical jurisprudence since 1961, Hart's position has come under particular scrutiny from the neo-**natural law theory** of Ronald Dworkin, whose publications from the late 1960s onwards (see in particular 'Is Law a System of Rules?' (1967) 35 *University of Chicago Law Review* 14) launched a fundamental attack on Hart's convention-based conception of law as a system of social rules; and from socio-legal accounts which criticize Hartian positivism as a version of arid formalism which tears law from its socio-political context and is blind to its own evaluative assumptions (Peter Fitzpatrick, *The Mythology of Modern Law* (London: Routledge, 1992)).

NICOLA LACEY

PMS Hacker and J Raz, *Law, Morality and Society: Essays in Honour of HLA Hart* (Oxford: Oxford University Press, 1977)
AWB Simpson (ed), *Oxford Essays in Jurisprudence: Second Series* (Oxford: Clarendon Press, 1973)

legal positivism since 1970   Two disputes about the relation between law and morality have dominated recent discussion of positivism, both deriving from issues raised in Hart's *The Concept of Law* (Oxford: Clarendon Press, 1961). According to Hart, the law is a social institution which, through the operation of its system of rules, provides guidance to both officials and citizens. It is a kind of social instrument, or technology, and as such may be used for good or evil; the fact that the Nazi legal system promoted many wicked ends did not mean it was any less a legal system. That a law is valid in an existing legal system does not ensure that it has any moral merit. Indeed, it might be regarded as the single most significant claim of positivism that legal validity, per se, does not entail moral validity; to put it another way, whether a law is valid or not does not depend on its being morally good. This does not, however, mean that there are no necessary connections between law and morality. Both the law and morality are normative, ie set standards for behaviour, and they employ much of the same vocabulary, such as 'rule', 'right', and 'duty'. The broad scope of what the law regulates will of necessity involve it with moral matters—for example wrongs such as murder or theft; and in consequence, the law is always capable of being judged according to moral standards.

The first dispute focuses on the way in which judges decide cases where the law is in dispute. According to Hart, where the law is unsettled (where, for instance, the cases do not clearly indicate one answer, or where a governing statute is badly drafted), judges have a duty to decide a case according to their best judgment. This will require attention to be paid to various considerations such as reaching a just result, developing the law coherently, and so on. If the court is sufficiently senior, the new ruling itself will be treated as law. Thus judges can make new law. Ronald Dworkin strenuously disagrees. According to him, there is always a pre-existing, correct, legal answer to any dispute, and lawyers and judges reflect this understanding when they argue and decide. On this view, in any particular case the applicable law is that rule which best coheres with the existing rules and which best accords with moral principles, such as justice and equality. On Dworkin's view, then, the validity of the law turns on its moral validity. Sometimes, the dispute is framed in terms of judicial **discretion**: Hart claims that judges sometimes have discretion to make new laws; Dworkin denies that they ever have this power. 'Soft' positivists have taken a middle course, holding that conventional legal sources, such as statutes, can incorporate moral criteria into criteria for legal validity. For example, a statute may require judges to give a remedy which is 'just and reasonable in all the circumstances'. In such a case, a judge must act justly (a moral requirement) in order to act legally. 'Hard' positivists such as Joseph Raz deny the incorporationist thesis. The problem they see is that, for the law to be a working social technology of behaviour guidance, it must be able to give people more or less straightforward directives. Given that what morality requires is controversial, instructing citizens or judges to act 'justly' is not telling them how to act, but rather sending them off on a research project. If this line of thought is right, then whenever a statute instructs a judge to give a 'just' remedy, it requires him to exercise discretion to give substance to the idea of a 'just remedy' by giving a precise answer. When doing this, the judge makes new law.

The second large dispute concerns the methodology of legal philosophy. On the one side are those who might be called 'descriptivists' and on the other, those who might be called 'normativists'. The former believe that theorists of the law can make true statements about it, describing the kind of social instrument it is; the latter contend that any description of a normative, morally-connected phenomenon like the law will be shaped by the theorist's view of the law's moral value (if any).

The normativists' argument is somewhat obscure. While theorizing is 'value-laden', the values in play are 'epistemic' values such as relevance or theoretical power, not moral values. The theorist's moral values, in particular but not only as expressed in the theorist's moral appraisal of the object of study, are not germane to his or her ability to uncover the truth.

JAMES PENNER

legal practice, styles and skills of Although it is common to think of all lawyers as performing the same tasks—examining witnesses and making arguments at trials, interviewing and counseling clients, preparing wills, and drafting contracts, **deeds** and other legal documents—in fact there are many different kinds of lawyers who generally specialize in doing only a few of the tasks commonly associated with lawyering. And lawyers do things for various reasons, with various motivations and goals, which may determine the style or approach with which they practice their profession.

The sorts of tasks lawyers perform depend to some extent on the type of legal system in which they practise. In an **adversary system** (generally associated with **common law** systems)—where parties in court proceedings are expected to present their own evidence and arguments to a neutral third party, such as a judge or arbitrator who makes a decision on the basis of the cases presented—lawyers will be engaged in writing briefs, making arguments to courts in support of their clients and urging interpretations of the law—both legislation and judge-made case law—on behalf of their clients. Typically in common law systems, **judges** are either appointed or elected from amongst the ranks of practising lawyers.

By contrast, in an **inquisitorial** system (generally associated with **civil law systems**) judges are typically more active in investigating the case and seeking evidence, thus reducing the role of the parties and their lawyers: instead of listening to the parties at a set-piece trial, judges themselves gather evidence, investigate and examine witnesses, and create dossiers over a period of time and then issue an order, which is normally much briefer than a judgment of a court in a common law system. Decisions of courts in civil law systems generally do not create law, and judging is generally a career path separate from that of practising law.

However, a growing convergence of these two systems has been noted, so that lawyers are likely to be doing relatively similar tasks in both systems. And, regardless of legal system, lawyers working for similar kinds of clients (large corporations, government agencies, public interest organizations, injured individuals, labour unions, refugees, parties seeking divorce or child custody, and so on) are likely to be doing similar tasks for their clients. Although the practice of law is still mostly regulated at national level, increasingly the practice of law is becoming 'globalized' so that lawyers practice their craft across borders, but with increasing specialization in particular subject areas or in working for specific types of clients.

In the UK and some other countries, a distinction is still observed between 'barristers' (or 'advocates') and 'solicitors'. Historically, barristers alone had the right to appear in court (the so-called 'right of audience'); and they still may wear special clothing (wigs and robes) to connote their status. Traditionally, solicitors could only advise clients outside of the courtroom; but increasingly, rights of audience have been extended to them as well. In England, barristers and solicitors have different training requirements. Barristers are members of law offices called 'chambers' in which they have a 'tenancy'. Barristers are members of the **Inns of Court**. In many countries the legal profession is not formally divided in this way; but informally, there is much specialization in the practice of law.

'Trial lawyers' such as barristers specialize in the legal work associated with non-criminal ('civil') disputes and litigation (such as may arise out of torts and breaches of contract), and with criminal trials. In systems where the legal profession is not divided, trial lawyers investigate facts, collect and analyse evidence (or hire investigators to do so), interview witnesses, take photographs, and so on. They may also hire experts to advise and testify about complex scientific or medical issues such as **causation**, or economic issues such as the appropriate amount of damages. In the UK, much preparatory work of this sort is done by solicitors, while barristers concentrate on preparing and presenting cases in court.

Trial lawyers are the type of legal practitioner most commonly depicted in popular culture, from the lawyers in the long-running **Chancery Court** case of *Jarndyce v Jarndyce* in Charles Dickens' *Bleak House*, to John Mortimer's *Rumpole of the Bailey* (a criminal lawyer), the noble and inspiring Atticus Finch in Harper Lee's novel *To Kill a Mockingbird*, and the many lawyers that populate John Grisham's novels such as *The Firm* and *The Pelican Brief*, and films such as *Erin Brokovich* and *A Civil Action*. The courtroom drama is a standard literary and dramatic genre.

In reality, however, very few civil or criminal cases actually come to a formal hearing before a court or other tribunal. It is much more likely that lawyers will negotiate some kind of settlement of the case in order to avoid the expense and uncertainty of trial. In civil cases such settlements culminate in the making of a contract between the parties. Most criminal prosecutions that result in a conviction involve a simple plea of guilty on the part of the accused; and many offenders are not prosecuted at all but may be dealt with in other ways, such as by being cautioned. In negotiating a settlement, lawyers and litigants may seek the assistance of a mediator, a third party neutral who facilitates communication and may suggest possible solutions to disputing parties. Increasingly, lawyers (and retired judges) are choosing to do this kind of **alternative dispute resolution** work instead of or in addition to the more traditional lawyering jobs.

The vast majority of lawyers never appear in court at all. Rather they advise governments, businesses, and individuals about the law—what it allows them to do, requires them to do, and prohibits them from doing. Such lawyers undertake legal research (identifying the law—both legislation and court decisions) relevant to the client's circumstances), draft documents (such as letters of advice, contracts, deeds, **trusts**, conveyances, and a wide variety of commercial instruments), and attend meetings and conferences with other parties and their lawyers. They increasingly work in large law firms, with as many as a thousand or more lawyers, that have offices all over the world ('global law firms') and are managed like big businesses. Others ('in-house' lawyers) are employed by and work solely for, a single corporation. Yet other lawyers work for governments, or for **non-governmental organizations** representing 'causes' rather than individual clients.

All of these forms of lawyering require a certain core set of skills—the ability to undertake legal research, to write well, to interpret legal language and construct good written and oral arguments. In addition, lawyers must develop various other skills—questioning (both for client interviewing and witness examination), counselling (which involves listening, advising, and speaking), investigating and analysing facts, negotiating, persuading, communicating, and problem solving. Such skills are taught in university law schools, in specialized courses or clinics with real clients to practice on, and in courses undertaken between the end of academic study of law and its formal practice. Some jurisdictions, such as the UK, still require a period of apprenticeship (as an 'articled clerk', for instance) under the supervision of a qualified lawyer as a condition of becoming fully qualified. In other jurisdictions (such as the US) it is sufficient to pass a written bar examination.

In performing these various tasks lawyers may adopt different approaches and styles. Though sometimes exaggerated, it is now common to hear talk of 'tough barracudas' or 'hired guns' who are particularly aggressive, skilled, and domineering in their representation of parties in courts or in power struggles associated with corporate mergers and acquisitions. Opposed to this aggressive form of practice, other lawyers prefer to think of themselves as legal 'problem-solvers', seeking solutions that will meet the needs of the various parties to a dispute or transaction. Such lawyers will seek the best outcome, which may not necessarily be a 'win' for their own client. In the US a new breed of lawyers describe their ethos as 'collaborative'; they seek to resolve clients' problems through negotiation and mediation and will refuse to go to court and litigate if parties fail to settle their differences peacefully. Other lawyers think of themselves as cultivating good judgment, and as 'wise counsellors' who advise governments, businesses, family members, workers, and so on, how best to accomplish their life-goals. Such lawyers would describe themselves as seeking justice, as well as peace, when 'winning is not everything'. Finally, for many lawyers, participation in the making of legal rules, whether as legislators, litigators, regulators, or private advisors, is important.

CARRIE MENKEL MEADOW

C Menkel-Meadow, 'When Winning Isn't Everything: The Lawyer as Problem Solver' (2000) 28 *Hofstra Law Review* 905

R Abel, *English Lawyers: Between Market and State* (Oxford: Oxford University Press, 2003)

See also: **cause lawyering; globalization and large law firms; government lawyers; legal profession, governance, structure and organization of; legal profession, public and employed sector of**

legal profession, definition and special characteristics of

In the first decade of the twenty-first century the legal profession is undergoing radical transformation, but an account of its traditional characteristics is essential to understand its contemporary form. In the UK it has comprised two branches: solicitors, and barristers or counsel (in England and Wales) and advocates (in Scotland). Solicitors, epitomizing the professional ideal of the autonomous master craftsman, practised on their own or in partnerships located throughout the country: the (family-like) High Street general practice was the paradigmatic organizational form of the profession. Although responsible for all legal work undertaken in their practice, much was (and still is) delegated to non-qualified staff and legal executives

who have their own governing body. Barristers have been sole practitioners but tend to operate in a collegiate structure from sets of chambers located in major cities, their high status indicated through ritualized etiquette, distinctive dress, and the fact that the higher judiciary was drawn from their ranks. A significant element of the training of both solicitors and barristers was undertaken through apprenticeship with the profession, reinforcing professional homogeneity.

If we define the profession in terms of its functions, at the mundane level solicitors acted directly for the client, offered advice, guidance, and low-level representation, generally on a range of matters (traditionally property, family, contract, and crime). Barristers were more likely to specialize, offer opinion on complicated areas of law, draft pleadings, and act as advocates with a monopoly in the superior courts. In societal terms, the profession's functions centre on the enactment of the **rule of law** through the instantiation of the normative structure of society.

The profession adheres to a 'trait' definition of its qualifying characteristics, namely lengthy training, specialist expertise, and a value-base deriving from an ethic of disinterested service and independence from special interests. These characteristics were held to justify the self-**regulation** until recently enjoyed by both solicitors and barristers. An alternative approach identifies lawyers as having achieved a form of state-sponsored monopoly over specific occupational activities which enables them to control the price of the services they deliver ('market control theory'). These two approaches have a synchronic dimension, in that they are concerned with who may or may not be a legal professional at any point in time. However market control theory also posits the profession as historically contingent and dynamic; from this perspective, it is the product of the struggle for occupational control, status, and financial reward. This process of transformation of lower middle class occupations into a (white) 'gentleman's profession' was primarily enacted throughout the nineteenth and into the twentieth centuries.

The dynamic nature of professionalism is evident if we focus on the functional definition. The accelerating juridification of everyday life and expansion of citizenship especially characteristic of the second half of the twentieth century produced increased demand for and accessibility of legal services, whilst the development of the welfare state encompassed the establishment of legal aid and these developments helped maintain the profitability of the High Street general practice. However they also fuelled a process of diversification in terms of both organizational forms (law centres, niche practices, radical practices), and social origins of lawyers, and a parallel process of erosion of professional status.

This process of diversification is associated with economic change resulting from the articulation of national financial and legal systems into a rationalizing globalized economy, producing supra-national legal orders As a result, the UK profession has become explicitly commercialized and its traditional configuration challenged: whilst the corporate sector has grown in size and influence, state intervention to end lawyer monopolies and cap the legal aid budget has created downward pressure on costs, weakening the High Street generalist practice, particularly in rural areas. White men continue to dominate the diminishing number of equity partnerships despite the ongoing increase in the participation of women (over 50 per cent of new entrants in many jurisdictions since the mid-1990s) and of other groups, who have met the growing demand for salaried specialists both in large law firms and as in-house lawyers in the rest of the private and public sectors. These changes are mirrored in many other jurisdictions.

Most recently, in the UK the strains on the state's tolerance of occupational closure have caused it to turn to cheaper forms of dispute resolution and advisers, to end barristers' monopoly of the higher courts, qualify the right of self-regulation for both branches, and allow new forms of business organization. These developments are eroding the unity and traditional hallmarks of the profession.

HILARY SOMMERLAD

M Blacksell, K Economides, and C Watkins, *Justice Outside the City* (Harlow: Longman, 1991)

G Hanlon, *Lawyers, the State and the Market* (London: Macmillan, 1995)

legal profession, geography of The spatial context of access to justice has become increasingly apparent over the past thiorty-five years ever since K Foster made the first study of the location of solicitors' offices based on the 1971 Law List ('The Location of Solicitors' (1973) 36 *Modern Law Review* 153). This showed significant variation in the distribution of law firms that displayed high correlations with the distribution of retail distribution outlets. A further study by K Economides and M Blacksell ('Access to Justice in Rural Britain: Final Report' (1987) 16 *Anglo-American Law Review* 353) based on data for 1985 confirmed the presence of significant spatial inequality in the distribution of legal services, reflecting solicitors' perceptions of their local markets, but noted a far less disturbing picture at district, rather than county, level. Solicitors were in fact disproportionately well

represented in rural communities, apparently basing the location of their practices on lifestyle choices rather than simple profit maximization. Yet they remained underrepresented in the hinterlands and immediate fringes of major population centres. However, despite maintaining a physical presence in rural locations, not all areas of law were well covered, much of the slack here being taken up by **para-legals** and lawyers working in the public sector. Increasing sensitivity to market pressure, local legal cultures, and government policy on **legal aid** was also noted by M Blacksell and C Fussell in their study of the barristers' branch of the legal profession ('Barristers and the Growth of Local Justice in England and Wales' (1994) *Transactions of the British Institute of Geographers* NS 482).

Today, large international law firms, many based in the United States with branches overseas, have emerged which transcend jurisdictional boundaries and offer legal and other interdisciplinary services to corporate clients on a truly global stage. According to B Warf the US, with 4 per cent of the world's population, has over half of its lawyers (940,000 in 1996) ('Global Dimensions of US Legal Services' (2001) 53 *The Professional Geographer* 398). At the other end of the spectrum, sole practitioners and small provincial law firms are in many countries increasingly under threat and face difficult decisions as to whether they should close, merge, or withdraw altogether from the provision of legal aid, thus shrinking supply points to legal service provision and giving rise to what have become known as 'advice deserts', which in turn raises fundamental concerns for and about the **rule of law**. It remains to be seen whether developments in technology, **cause lawyering**, para-legal and public legal services guided by policy emanating from government, the professional bodies, and the voluntary sector—all working in concert—can ever overcome the barrier of physical distance in order to grant citizens effective access to legal services.

KIM ECONOMIDES

M Blacksell, K Economides, and C Watkins, *Justice Outside the City: Access to Legal Services in Rural Britain* (Harlow: Longman, 1991)

legal profession—governance, structure and organization of Apocryphally not the oldest profession in the world (whatever its critics may say) law—along with the religious ministry and the military—is one of the three ancient professions or vocations. Functionally, lawyers have since time immemorial been involved in the performance of (or in assisting others in the performance of) three core law jobs: the making of the law, the determination and application of the law in the event of disputes, and the interpretation and application of the law in everyday life. Although the legal profession in many modern countries is formally divided into different sectors, curiously it is rare for the divisions to map exactly onto the three core tasks. Assisting in the making of the law is a function shared between a relatively small number of legislative drafters and a rather larger number of judges (who in English speaking jurisdictions and some continental countries are former lawyers). Determining and applying the law (and sometimes ascertaining the facts) in disputes that reach an adjudicative forum is left to judges, arbiters, and tribunal members, usually advised or assisted by, lawyers. However, most disputes (civil and criminal) which are recognized by the legal system will be resolved by negotiations between lawyers for the opposing parties or by an unopposed application from a lawyer for one of the parties. In the UK and some of the Commonwealth countries, court lawyers fall into two or three categories—barristers (known as advocates in Scotland), solicitors, and solicitor advocates (solicitors with rights of audience in the higher courts). In many other jurisdictions, court lawyers form a distinct and specialized sector of the profession. Finally, the application and interpretation of the law to smooth the handling of a myriad of ordinary commercial and private transactions—including the drafting of binding agreements, contracts, leases, property transfers, powers of attorney, wills, and trusts—has long been a major function of solicitors in the UK and of notaries and chamber lawyers in other jurisdictions.

The imperfect fit between the core law jobs and the division of labour within the legal profession reflects the messiness of history. Barristers and advocates in the UK attained a monopoly of rights of audience in the higher courts several centuries ago, as did their court lawyer counterparts in Europe. Around the same time, notaries in Europe also gained control of the authentication of deeds, but gradually lost ground to and merged with the solicitors' branch of the profession in the UK. Solicitors in the UK, for long the less prestigious branch of the profession, did not attain their limited monopolies on **conveyancing** and probate work for gain, until the nineteenth century. Yet in other countries, such as the US, where the profession is formally undivided but actually specialized into corporate-client and private-client sectors, the legal profession's monopoly extends much further, to the giving of any legal advice. Armed with these monopolies and other constraints on competition, such as bans on advertising and on price competition, the UK legal profession entered what has come to be seen as the traditional era of professionalism

reaching unbroken for fifty years from the 1930s. During this period, what it meant to be a lawyer—adherence to the core values of independence, integrity, diligence, competence, loyalty, disclosure, confidentiality, and a commitment to the rule of law—was perceived to justify high social status, reasonable financial rewards, professional autonomy, and widespread anti-competitive practices. By the 1980s, however, the forces of change could no longer be resisted. The tacit bargain with the state began to unravel with the growth of a new consumerism, which demanded that the balance between the public interest and the profession's interest should be re-negotiated—and not just by the lawyers. The reduction of entry barriers stimulated by the baby-boom generation led to a doubling in size of the profession and the start of a gender revolution. Deregulation produced a dismantling of the monopolies, the removal of the ban on advertising, price competition, and the replacement of self-regulation by co-regulation. All this may have emanated from the English-speaking world but today the movement is global.

How different is the professional world of today from that of only a century ago! Even the 15,500 barristers and advocates practising in the UK (who have been least affected by the changes) are increasingly working as employees (15 per cent), taking instructions direct from public institutions and bodies, and facing the threat of partnership with solicitors and other barristers. Even the status of senior counsel ('silk') is under scrutiny by the competition authorities. For solicitors the pace of change has been dramatic. There are still sole practitioners (8 per cent), but they are no longer a homogenous grouping, since like the rest of the profession many of them have succumbed to the need to specialize. Over 20 per cent of the 115,000 or so solicitors in the UK now work in the employed sector and over 40 per cent of those in private practice work in the top 1 per cent of firms by size. These firms (and their American counterparts) have begun to dominate global legal markets. Little wonder that observers question whether the core values and common training, which once were thought to unite the profession, now mask a deeply fractured profession. Yet those who suggest that we now have not one profession but many (based on specialism) are only re-discovering history. In former times solicitors co-existed with proctors, attorneys, procurators, notaries, law agents, and scriveners. Turf wars for legal business waged against non-lawyers and quasi-lawyers were as common in earlier centuries as skirmishes with accountants, banks, licensed conveyancers, claims companies, legal executives, and paralegals are now.

As might be expected the governance and regulation of today's legal profession is proving increasingly problematic. The new consumerism of the 1990s challenged the complacency of self–regulation, which to outsiders all too often seemed more self-serving than in the public interest. *Ad hoc*, unconnected co-regulators began to emerge: the Department of Trade and Industry, the Department for Constitutional Affairs (now the Ministry of Justice), the **Office of Fair Trading**, the Legal Services Commission, the **Financial Services Authority**, the Legal Services Ombudsman, the Immigration Services Commissioner and more, producing the regulatory maze described in the Clementi Review of the Regulatory Framework for Legal Services in England and Wales (2004). In sharp contradistinction to the profession, other providers of legal services in the UK are less regulated than lawyers, sometimes to a very considerable degree. This raises difficult questions (of paternalism, client choice, and competition policy) about the extent to which there should be a level playing field in the regulation of all providers of legal services and the extent to which clients should be able to contract out of public protection measures. Clementi declined to be drawn into this quagmire, settling instead for separating the representative functions of the professional bodies from their regulatory functions, eg admission and training, standard setting, business structures, and complaint handling. Ultimately, Clementi and the Ministry of Justice opted for an overarching, independent regulatory body whilst leaving the professional bodies as front line regulators. In Scotland an independent complaints commission is being established, but other aspects of regulation have been left untouched. Whilst the boldness of these reforms may ultimately prove to be justified, the route the government and the Scottish Executive have chosen is undoubtedly more complex and more expensive than if they had replaced ineffective co-regulation with effective co-regulation through an ombudsman with extensive powers of scrutiny, intervention, and review such as exists in the Australian state of New South Wales.

Today's lawyers live in challenging times. However, the tide of reform has far from run its course. The UK competition authorities, like their Australian counterparts, have begun to press for reforms which some fear may destroy the profession itself. Noting that the professional rules frequently ban lawyers from sharing their fees or entering into partnerships with non–lawyers, they have begun to push for the introduction of multi-disciplinary partnerships, for non-lawyers to be able to invest in law firms, and for institutions such as banks, insurance companies, or supermarket chains to deliver legal services to their clients through the use of lawyers employed by the institutions. Whilst many within the consumer movement regard this as a natural and timely development, some lawyers who hold true to the core values of the profession see it as the tipping point that may ultimately consign lawyers to the role of specialized businesses with few remaining pretensions to professionalism.   ALAN PATERSON

R Abel, *English Lawyers between Market and State* (Oxford: Oxford University Press, 2003)

Alan Paterson, 'Professionalism and the Legal Services Market' (1996) 3 *International Journal of the Legal Profession* 137.

legal profession, history of Barristers and solicitors form the two branches of the modern legal profession in England and Wales. Pushing back in time only slightly a wider array of legal professions is found: serjeants-at-law, attorneys, advocates, and proctors, amongst others. The boundaries can be unclear in that anyone who represents another before tribunals, records agreements in writing, aids in dispute-resolution, or acts as agent for another's business performs lawyer-like functions.

The origins of a legal 'profession' in England and Wales are murky. Prior to the twelfth century there was little in the nature of a professional caste dedicated to representing litigants in the Royal Courts or attending to procedural matters. Professional agents or 'attorneys' (from the French, 'attorner') emerged during the twelfth century, and professional pleaders, known as serjeants (from 'serviens'), had become established by the early thirteenth century. A functional separation, presaging the later division between barristers and solicitors, had taken root by the second half of the thirteenth century. A third group, 'apprentices of the Common Bench', had emerged by the 1280s. Initially literally apprentices to attorneys or serjeants, they quickly came to enjoy an independent right of audience before most courts. The apprentices over time founded four 'Inns of Court' and laid the foundation from which the barristers' profession ('Bar') would emerge. Edward I's 1292 ordinance *de Attornatis et Apprenticiis* gave recognition to both professions, putting them under the control of the Judges. Many consider this to mark the origins of the legal professions.

Over time, this functional division between general legal agents and specialists in advocacy became an important distinguishing feature of the English legal profession. The origins of the modern barristers' profession lie in four professional guilds that formed the focal points of legal life in London.

Lincoln's Inn, Grey's Inn, Inner Temple, and Middle Temple, at first merely properties on the outskirts of the City of London, became gathering places for lawyers. From these beginnings, guilds and, much later, modern professional organizations emerged. The oldest records of Lincoln's Inn date to 1422, but associational life amongst lawyers certainly existed before this. The early Inns provided a professional home for solicitors (who worked as agents in the **Chancery Court**), attorneys (who played a parallel role in the courts of **common law**), and barristers (who enjoyed exclusive rights of advocacy in the Royal Courts). Professional distinctions congealed over time and solicitors and attorneys (the 'lower' branches of the or profession) were excluded from the Inns in the sixteenth century. The exclusion was honoured in the breach until well into the eighteenth century. In 1590 the Bar's monopoly of pleading in the superior courts was formally entrenched.

Some ten 'Inns of Chancery' developed by the late fifteenth century, each close-by the **Inns of Court**. These first provided a way-station en route to joining an Inn of Court, eventually evolving into professional associations for attorneys and solicitors. Attorneys' or solicitors' work was, however, never as tightly tied to the Royal Courts as barristers and local professional associations (often denoted as 'law societies') emerged. One, the Society of Gentlemen Practisers in the Courts of Law and Equity, founded in London in 1737, subsequently gave rise to the London Law Institution in 1823, in turn rebranded in 1825 as a body with national pretensions designated as 'The Society of Attorneys, Solicitors, Proctors and others not being Barristers, practicing in the Courts of Law and Equity of the United Kingdom'. Granted a Royal Charter in 1831 and another in 1845, this 'Law Society' took on increasingly important roles in professional life for the 'lower' branches of the legal profession. It was officially renamed 'The Law Society' in 1903. Meanwhile, the Inns of Chancery had fallen fell into desuetude and all were wound up before 1900.

For their part the Inns of Court admitted barristers, provided the primary locus for social interaction within that profession, served as centres of legal education and, occasionally, took on regulatory functions. There is no straight-line history to be found and their effectiveness in any of these roles varied from time to time. The Inns provided a more—or less—rigorous educational experience for aspiring barristers at various times, just as they were more—or less—effective in their other roles. By the mid-nineteenth century they failed more or less entirely, at least in middle class opinion. Some

regulatory functions were carried out by itinerant dining societies known as 'Circuit Messes' organized by barristers while 'on circuit'. The understandings of the bar, understood as matters of 'etiquette', lacked an enforcement mechanism other than peer pressure. Indeed, some barristers considered it unconstitutional for the Inns to so intrude on their professional work.

Matters came to a head during the nineteenth century as a reform-minded middle class increasingly viewed the customs, practices, and notions of etiquette accreted over previous centuries with suspicion. Intra-professional conflict threatened to destabilize the division of labour between solicitors or attorneys (the two had become practically indistinguishable by the nineteenth century) on the one hand and barristers on the other. In an age of business, solicitors expanded their services, gained rights of audience in the new County Courts, and adopted a less differential attitude toward the Bar. Meanwhile, the expanding jurisdiction of the County Courts shrunk the area of legal work within the scope of the bar's exclusive monopoly. Growing railway networks disrupted the pace and intimacy of Circuit messes and growing numbers of barristers sought to establish permanent places of work in the provinces. The influence of the Inns waned.

At one point these forces threatened to break down entirely the distinctiveness of the two professions. Work in the new County Courts sustained a new class of solicitor-advocates, who enthusiastically launched into areas previously the preserve of the Bar. Conversely, members of the Bar sought to bring 'free trade' principles to the profession. Barristers set up permanently in the provinces, sought out work in the lower criminal courts in London, took instructions directly from clients (without the mediation of a solicitor, as 'etiquette' required), undertook work on contingency fee arrangements, and held themselves out as qualified to do any of the work solicitors considered their own. The spirit of the age seemed to align powerfully in favour of a functional merger of the two legal professions, just as had happened in the USA.

Significant transformations in the regulation of legal work were required to retain a divided profession. The courts ruled that barristers could not sue for their fees, while the Inns of Court for the first time created themselves as disciplinary bodies able and willing to act coercively against individual barristers who breached etiquette. Etiquette became more sharply defined, transmogrifying from gentlemanly understandings into enforceable rules, and a central 'Bar Council' emerged in 1894 to ensure consistency of approach. The result was to prevent barristers from competing directly in key areas of solicitors' work, while rendering them dependent on solicitors to bring them clients. A symbiosis emerged in lieu of inter-professional competition. Largely mollified, the solicitors' branch did not aggressively assault the Bar's remaining privileges.

From the nineteenth century onwards the two legal professions worked in overlapping but separate and mutually supportive roles, more or less on the basis of this accommodation. In the late twentieth and early twenty-first centuries a new spirit of 'free trade' combined with European integration, the growing influence of US models of professionalism, and a heightened sense that privilege should be publicly, not privately, regulated. Such forces have produced further pressure on traditional arrangements around legal services. All of this has provoked changes in the work and regulation of both branches of the legal profession, and led to proposals for new regulatory arrangements, such as proposals to create a Legal Services Commissioner. These processes continue today.   WESLEY PUE

P Brand, *The Origins of the English Legal Profession* (Oxford: Blackwell, 1992)

WW Pue, 'Moral Panic at the English Bar: Paternal vs. Commercial Ideologies of Legal Practice in the 1860's' (1990) 15 *Law and Social Inquiry* 49–118

legal profession, impact of information technology on
Information technology ('IT') has had considerable impact on the legal profession and is likely to have an increasing influence in coming years. Initially, IT served to streamline, improve and speed up the working practices of lawyers. Recently, more powerful technologies, especially in the field of communications, have begun to challenge and change the way that the legal profession operates. The first serious and sustained investigations into the use of IT in support of legal research and legal decision-making can be traced to the early 1960s. Since then, the impact of IT has extended to practising lawyers, judges, legal academics, and clients of the legal profession.

For practising lawyers in advanced legal systems, there has been a steady and growing investment in IT since the 1970s. This has affected lawyers in law firms and private practice, advocates who specialize in court work, and legal advisers who are employed within businesses and governments. The early uses of IT by these lawyers were largely in the back-office—for accounting, word processing, and general administrative purposes. It was later recognized, in the 1980s, that information systems could be used

to capture and share the collective know-how and experience of a legal team, so that databases of legal opinions and standard form documents were developed and made easily accessible to lawyers from their desktops. At that time, these internal knowledge systems complemented the emergence of a range of subscription-based electronic legal research services, such as Lexis, which enabled dial-up access to primary legal sources.

The coming of the internet led to IT becoming a mainstream tool for practising lawyers. Since the late 1990s, email has become the dominant way in which lawyers communicate with one another and with their clients, while hand-held machines are used extensively to maintain contact while out of the office. The worldwide web and Google have transformed the information seeking habits of many lawyers, by making legal resources and information about organizations and markets more readily available. The next step in the evolution of legal technology is likely to be online systems that actually perform legal tasks, such as offering legal updates, drafting documents, providing advice, and solving legal problems. The most widely used of these so far are automatic document drafting systems.

In most advanced jurisdictions, judges are also using IT. Email and word processing by judges are now firmly established applications. Many judges use a wide variety of online research resources, while some are benefiting from judicial intranets and online discussion forums as mechanisms for sharing information with one another. Where the courts are suitably equipped, judges may also have access to case management systems, which enable them to monitor and progress the cases before them. Courtrooms are increasingly equipped with IT, including systems for the display of documents and exhibits, large monitors and wall screens, computer assisted real-time transcription, video-linking for remote evidence, wireless networks with internet access, and tools (from computer graphics to virtual reality) for the presentation of evidence. More ambitious is the concept of online dispute resolution (known as 'ODR')—some lawyers, technologists, and commentators are challenging the assumption that court work requires parties to congregate in one physical space; and they are developing systems to allow litigants to present arguments and evidence through online systems. Today, these online submissions are adjudicated upon, remotely, by human beings, but artificial intelligence specialists envisage the day that computers will replace some judicial functions.

Academic lawyers, involved in legal education and research, are also being significantly affected by IT. Law students now have a wealth of primary materials (legislation and case law) and secondary materials (articles and books) at their disposal on the worldwide web, while the emergence of multi-media e-learning systems (from web-casts through to virtual legal environments) are complementing traditional teaching and sometimes replacing methods of the past. Students can attend and replay online lectures and tutorials at their convenience. Legal scholarship is also undergoing substantial change. Aside from unprecedented access to legal sources, legal academics also enjoy easy access to fellow scholars around the world. While conventional conferences and symposia remain important for personal contact and human networking, ongoing dialogue by email is now pervasive and, increasingly, social networking systems will underpin online communities of interest.

If IT enables lawyers to be more efficient and responsive, to reduce their costs, or to work to a higher standard, then their clients should also benefit. Another related trend is being noted and studied. Whereas, in the past, citizens generally had to consult human lawyers if they sought advice on most legal problems, today these non-lawyers can secure legal help on a wide range of legal issues from websites developed and maintained, amongst others, by government agencies, consumer bodies, and trade associations. While the counsel provided by these sites may be less tailored, detailed, and rigorous than that offered by traditional lawyers, they can provide useful briefings for people before they seek formal legal advice. And where it is not feasible for citizens to obtain lawyers' help directly, these websites are generally far more useful than having no legal guidance at all.

As IT advances, further applications for lawyers, clients, and citizens will emerge. New technologies that take hold across society tend, in due course, to exert impact on the legal profession, even if their relevance is not immediately apparent. Most lawyers could no more see the applicability of email and the worldwide web in the mid 1990s than they can of social networking and wiki technologies in 2007.

In most legal systems, historically, the potential of IT has not been fully realized, in part because of under-investment by the public and private sectors, and also because, generally, lawyers are relatively slow to adopt new technologies. With sufficient investment and careful planning, research suggests that IT can greatly enhance the efficiency of lawyers and significantly increase access to justice. This can be achieved not simply by automating traditional working methods but by using IT to change the way the legal profession functions.

RICHARD SUSSKIND

ME Katsh, *Law in a Digital World* (New York: Oxford University Press, 1995)
RE Susskind, *The End of Lawyers?* (Oxford: Oxford University Press, 2008)

legal profession: international comparisons and trends   All countries have legal professions (although some are relatively recent and revolutionary regimes have temporarily abolished them as expensive, exploitative, or alienating). Rapid, and accelerating, increases in the division of labour over the last two centuries compel reliance on knowledge specialists—including lawyers. Yet people everywhere continue to lawyer for themselves: negotiating agreements (employment contracts, leases), drafting documents (conveyances), making claims, and representing themselves in **small claims** courts and administrative **tribunals**. Para-professionals also perform a variety of legal services: processing claims for injury victims, help in filing tax returns, divorce mediation. As the cost of legal services continues to increase there will be more pressure for DIY and para-professionals.

Countries define legal professions differently. All new lawyers today have university degrees; but these are not always in law; and in some countries most law graduates do not become lawyers. Most countries (but not some American states) require an examination (set by profession or state). Most countries (but not the US) also require an apprenticeship (until recently the exclusive preparation of many lawyers). Some countries consider everyone who has passed these hurdles to be a lawyer; others limit that category (and its perquisites) to privately practising advocates. As lawyers' functions and practice settings further diversify, it will become harder to require common training, which will be supplemented by specialization. Countries define the lawyers' monopoly differently: only in the US does it include legal advice; everywhere but Finland it includes courtroom advocacy.

Legal professions are divided internally. Most historically distinguished between courtroom advocates and transactional lawyers (who advise, draft, negotiate, and prepare litigation). The former was the profession's core; but its relative importance has diminished in terms of the amount of work and remuneration (if not prestige). Most professions distinguished between independent practitioners and employed lawyers (French *conseils juridiques*,

German *syndici*), often forbidding the latter to appear in court; but employed lawyers enjoy increasing status and competence. The **Crown Prosecution Service** has largely supplanted the private Bar; American house counsel hire, supervise, and set the fees of large firm lawyers. And *conseils juridiques* have merged with *avocats*. The **common law** adversarial systems of the English-speaking world assign more responsibility to private practitioners; inquisitorial **civil law systems** (continental Europe and its former colonies) make greater use of **government lawyers** (judges and prosecutors combined in the magistracy). In the common law world, therefore, private practitioners greatly outnumber judges and lawyers employed by companies and the state; in the civil law world private practitioners and government and privately employed lawyers are roughly equal in number.

In most countries, lawyers began by representing individuals (aristocrats or bourgeoisie). But everywhere today there is a growing divide between lawyers representing individuals and those representing companies, with the latter growing in number, income, and prestige. Although historically all lawyers were solo practitioners, the proportion of the profession is declining as (predominately Anglo-American) law firms become national and even global agglomerations of thousands. Just as legal professions emerged as a form of specialized knowledge and function, so they are subdividing by: substantive speciality (eg divorce, company law), function (litigation, negotiation), employment (public or private, independent practice), practice structure (firm size), and forum (specialized courts, administrative agencies). Their professional associations reflect these shifts, changing from local to national and from comprehensive to pluralistic.

All legal professions have been growing rapidly, for varied reasons. Higher education has expanded since World War II, often dramatically. Women, who were virtually excluded, now equal or outnumber men; other excluded groups (racial minorities, immigrants) also are entering. Whereas traditional legal professions sought prestige through exclusivity, today they seek to be representative of the larger society. The demand for legal services is stimulated by: economic growth; the fall of communism and the spread of neo-liberalism in the Third World; state **regulation** (now also regional and international), the shift from the production of goods to services; and the growth of new forms of intellectual property. But the growing number of lawyers produces a backlash, in which they are blamed for an alleged litigation explosion and over-legalization.

Just as the profession lost its control over numbers (through apprenticeships, examination pass rates, and limited initial positions), so its restrictive practices have been challenged by internal and external competition and state action. Lawyers can no longer fix prices or prohibit advertising (although they still restrict solicitation of business). Non-lawyers seek to compete (eg to advise injury victims or divorcing couples) or to employ lawyers and offer vertical integration (conveyancing by mortgage lenders, estate agents, or insurers). Multi-disciplinary partnerships (dominated by accountants) threaten to take business from large law firms. Internal divisions crumble under **competition** between branches: solicitors demanding higher court audience rights, barristers seeking direct access to clients.

Historically, all lawyers services were purchased from private practitioners. Although fragmentary **legal aid** emerged in the nineteenth century, postwar **welfare state**s greatly expanded those programmes. In most of the advanced industrialized world governments reimburse private lawyers. In the US, legal aid offices employ lawyers in both civil cases and criminal (**public defender**s). But today many countries are using salaried lawyers, while the US resorts to private practitioners. As welfare programmes everywhere shrink under fiscal pressure and ideological hostility, legal aid excludes subject matters (relegating personal injury cases to conditional fees), restricts eligibility (to the poor), and lowers reimbursement levels. Partly in response, large firms expand pro bono activities, and philanthropies support public interest practice.

Self-regulation is the hallmark of all professions. But lawyers' dismal performance (delay, tolerance of misconduct) has led to state takeover of regulatory responsibility, more damage claims for malpractice and misconduct, and a heightened role for insurers (by setting premiums).

Legal professions assumed distinctive national forms by the late nineteenth and early twentieth centuries. The dramatic changes of recent years—feminism, globalization, the fall of communism, technological change—are effecting transformations whose outcome remains unclear.

RICK ABEL

RL Abel and PSC Lewis (eds), *Lawyers in Society* (4 vols) (Berkeley: University of California Press, 1988–89, 1995; reprinted, Washington, DC: Beard Books, 2006)

RL Abel, *English Lawyers between Market and State: The Politics of Professionalism* (Oxford: Oxford University Press, 2003)

See also: **legal profession: competition, consumer protection and regulation; legal profession, private and** voluntary sector of; legal profession, public and employed sector of; paralegals; *pro bono* legal services

legal profession, private and voluntary sectors of

The legal profession, comprising solicitors and barristers, covers broad sectors of work. Over 75 per cent of some 90,000 solicitors with practising certificates in England and Wales are in private practice in just over 9,000 firms. The remainder are employed in a number of sectors, including commerce and industry, local government, and the **Crown Prosecution Service**.

Traditionally, solicitors' firms were small, with very few reaching anything near the legal partnership limit of twenty. Although, currently, around 80 per cent of solicitors' firms have four partners or fewer, the last fifteen-year period has seen a move towards larger and medium-sized firms. Since the partnership limit was removed in 1985 a sector comprising large corporate and commercial law firms has come to dominate the legal landscape. Firms with twenty-five or more partners employ over a third of all solicitors. They command high fees, pay high wages, and provide most training places. They tend to have over 500 employees and the largest employ thousands, often in offices around the world. In the **United Kingdom**, these firms are concentrated in the City of London, which is also host to many firms based in other countries, particularly in Europe and the USA. In the UK, large City firms account for 4.4 per cent of total overseas earnings from business services exports. The past fifteen years have also seen the relative decline of 'high street firms', generalist practices serving local communities. Since the 1980s, such firms have suffered reduction of income from **conveyancing**, because of market slumps and competition, and from **legal aid**, which has been reined in by government.

The tilting of legal services towards corporate clients and commercial work has occurred at a time when access to legal services has become a political issue. A linked problem is the geographical distribution of legal services. Since private practice firms tend to be located where there is plentiful and profitable business, the cities and conurbations tend to be well served by the legal profession. For example, nearly 4,000 solicitors' firms are in London and the South East, 43 per cent of firms in England and Wales. There are only 298 in the North East, 632 in the South West, and 475 in the whole of Wales. London solicitors' firms employ well over a third of private practitioners. Similarly, the Bar in England is largely focused on the Inns of Court in London, although provincial cities in England often have a few barristers' chambers serving regional courts.

In sparsely populated areas, people may have to travel long distances to see lawyers or find difficulty locating someone with suitable expertise. Many solicitors maintaining profitable practices in rural locations are not particularly interested in cases involving welfare law or legal aid generally. These problems may yet get worse. Firms in some rural areas have an ageing population of solicitors. They find it difficult to offer trainees the range of work required, or to match the supervision obligations imposed, by the Law Society, and difficult to compete with metropolitan salaries in attracting young lawyers.

Another problem of access to legal services is cost, which may deter many wishing to claim legal rights. The legal profession has a long tradition of voluntary legal work, or *pro bono publico*, usually called 'pro bono work'. It has been argued that such work is a social obligation, part of the price of the profession's monopoly of legal work. One of the best-known examples was the Poor Persons' Procedure for divorce, which operated between the World Wars and led to the creation of the legal aid scheme. The growth and increasing professionalism of the **Citizens' Advice Bureaux** ('CABx') after World War II provided another avenue for lawyers offering voluntary services. By the 1960s some advice centres were supervised by solicitors full-time, with solicitor and barrister practitioners offering voluntary services. In 1972 a group of Bar students established the Free Representation Unit ('FRU') to represent welfare benefit claimants. With the decline of legal aid in the 1990s, the legal profession came under pressure from New Labour, first in opposition and then in government, to offer more free services. In 1996, a Law Society working party report on solicitors' *pro bono* concluded that legal professionals had an obligation to provide free services, but that such services could never fill the gap left by legal aid cuts.

The ambivalent conclusions of the Law Society's Pro Bono Working Party led to the formation of the Solicitors' *Pro bono* Group ('SPBG'), sponsored by large firms. It built relations with organizations in the voluntary advice field, such as CABx and Law Centres, with a view to establishing a nationwide referral system. Changing its name to Law Works, it supported a number of initiatives and projects, including a partnership with the Law Centres Federation to match lawyers with advice centres. In 2001 it had 500 volunteers, mainly from large firms, and by 2006 it had set up fifty-five free clinics in CABx and council buildings, helping 26,000 people a year in areas such as bankruptcy, which are not supported by legal aid.

In 1996 the Bar Pro Bono Unit ('BPBU') was established as an independent charity to complement existing schemes, especially the regional schemes run on the Northern Circuit, Western Circuit, and Wales and Chester Circuit, and the schemes run by subject area Bar Associations. Barristers were asked to donate two or three days a year. In 2002 the BPBU set up a solicitors' panel of eleven firms to investigate and prepare cases for barristers. In 2000 the bar sponsored and launched 'Bar in the Community' to recruit barristers to the management committees of voluntary organizations.

In 2002 the Attorney-General's Pro Bono Co-ordinating Committee encouraged the various professional interest groups to initiate and promote National Pro Bono Week, an annual event intended to build support for voluntary legal work. In 1998 the Young Solicitors' Group established an annual competition making up to a dozen awards to members with an unusually high commitment. A wide range of work is covered, from helping in advice agencies, through advising charities on legal matters, to working on the appeals of prisoners on death row overseas.

Government has been keen to address the uneven distribution of legal services, and in 1999 launched the Community Legal Service ('CLES'), under the Access to Justice Act (1999). This was a scheme to join up the patchwork of assistance provided by advice agencies and law centres. Some agencies were awarded franchises that enabled them to represent clients on legal aid, and there is evidence that the advice given is at least as good as that given by private practitioners. Although the government was initially uncertain about the involvement of lawyers in the CLES, 153 of approximately 300 advice agencies employ solicitors to assist or supervise advice-giving and representation, many firms act as referral points from agencies, and many lawyers work as voluntary advisers in these centres.

It is almost impossible to verify the volume or value of *pro bono publico* legal services provided annually. The BPBU produces records of cases handled and processed, but lawyers also work without payment outside established structures. This is particularly true of solicitors, who often claim that free work is part of their everyday activities. There is, however, no agreement of what constitutes *pro bono publico* and, in the early days of the SPBG, some firms argued that general charitable work should be included. The Law Society's Working Party clouded the issue by suggesting a name change to 'voluntary legal services',

to include work done at reduced cost. Attempts to collect data as part of their annual statistical report was undermined by similar lack of clarity. It is, nevertheless, undoubtedly true that there have been many notable and significant victories in substantial court cases brought by lawyers working *pro bono publico* in recent years. These cases have secured benefits, such as pension payments, or established rights for many beyond the clients assisted free of charge. Therefore, while solicitors and barristers routinely involved in providing legal services that are unambiguously *pro bono publico* represent a relatively small proportion of the total, probably well under 10 per cent of each branch, the work is a valuable social contribution.

ANDY BOON

A Boon and J Levin, *The Ethics and Conduct of Lawyers in England and Wales* (Oxford: Hart Publishing, 2001)
The Solicitors' Pro Bono Group, *A Guide to Law Firm Pro Bono Programmes in England and Wales* (London: Solicitors Pro Bono Group, 2004)

See also: **legal profession, geography of;** *pro bono* **legal services**

legal profession, public, and employed sector   The archetypal legal professional is a barrister in chambers or a partner in a law firm. Both own their own businesses: one as a self-employed practitioner renting space and support in chambers; the other as part of a, sometimes very sizeable, partnership structure. Nevertheless, the paradigm is in fact a misrepresentation. Over 60 per cent of all solicitors with practising certificates are in fact employees within their firms; and it is increasingly reported that the 'ultimate prize' of partnership is no longer the goal of a substantial proportion of this salaried sector. The solicitors' profession is, thus, substantially an employed sector, albeit employed by its certain members of the sector.

Outside those employed in solicitors firms, it is harder to get a precise idea of how many solicitors and barristers work in the private or public sector. Law Society data tends to concentrate on those with practising certificates, and those working in the employed sector do not generally need to have practising certificates. We do know, from the Law Society's Annual Statistical Reports, that about seventy government departments employ solicitors and barristers. These members of the Government Legal Service provide legal advice on government policy, as well as conducting litigation. Local government lawyers similarly advise on a range of legal issues (from land acquisitions, to public law questions, employment disputes, child care cases, and housing cases) in about 500 local authorities. The Court Service, too, employs lawyers in over 150 locations. Magistrates' court clerks are the obvious example—they work in magistrates' courts to advise the magistrates on legal matters arising during the course of their work. Many other governmental agencies—such as the Legal Services Commission and the Health and Safety Executive—employ lawyers in advisory and litigation capacities. The Treasury Solicitor's Office probably has the most concentrated body of central government lawyers, employing about 350 solicitors and barristers. It deals with a large number and vast range of cases including personal injury, **judicial review**, **inquest**s, planning, charities, and vexatious litigants. Its biggest clients are the Prison Service, the Immigration and Nationality Directorate, and the Ministry of Defence.

A second area where there are a large number of publicly-employed lawyers is the **Crown Prosecution Service** ('CPS'). The CPS is principally responsible for prosecuting criminal cases in England and Wales. Although the police investigate cases, it is the CPS that prosecutes; and it increasingly advises the police on the charges to be brought against suspects at the outset of a case. It deals with the vast majority of day-to-day prosecutions from mundane driving offences to serious crime. Other **regulatory agencies** also employ lawyers to conduct prosecutions. For instance, Her Majesty's Revenue and Customs deal with sometimes-serious tax matters; and the Serious Fraud Office deals with the exceptionally serious fraud and corruption enquiries. Established to provide a high quality prosecution authority independent of the police, the CPS had difficult early years when lack of resources and morale problems contributed to the view that they did not provide such a service. Complaints about delay in the criminal justice process continue to be laid, in part, at the door of overworked prosecutors dealing with inappropriately large caseloads. Controversially, the CPS has moved to employing non-lawyer caseworkers increasingly in advocacy positions to deal with cases more quickly and cheaply than qualified staff.

Outside of these agencies, public sector lawyers are a rarer breed. In the United States and Canada there are extensive public defender programmes of state salaried lawyers employed to defend their clients. In the UK, swayed for a long time by the reputation of some US public defenders for very poor quality defence, such programmes have only recently been introduced. In Canada, where public defenders are well established and resourced, they have been shown to provide a decent level of service, dealing with cases more quickly and cheaply, but also getting their client better sentence discounts for

pleading guilty without making them more likely to be convicted. This experience persuaded UK administrations to give public defenders a closer look. An experiment was commenced in Scotland in 1998, but it produced more mixed results: cases were dealt with more quickly, but clients were marginally more likely to be convicted as a result and were not getting a sentence discount (probably because the trade-offs for guilty pleas common in other systems were not so common in Scotland). Nor was the service cheaper, because it failed to attract the large volume of clients necessary to reduce its unit cost. Having started out as one office, there are now three. Public Defenders have also been piloted in England and Wales, with six offices being opened initially, and further small branch offices following on from that. At the time of writing, the results of that pilot have not been made public; but published information shows that the English and Welsh offices have generally struggled initially to attract sufficient volumes of work to keep case costs down.

The voluntary and charitable sector is also an area where solicitors and barristers are employed to provide legal services, usually to members of the public. The most established network of advice agencies are the **Citizens Advice Bureaux** ('CABx'). CABx, whilst having a corporate identity and common systems of training, information, and support are in fact largely independent of each other. Staffed significantly by volunteers, they increasingly employ some solicitors and barristers as specialist caseworkers. Law Centres are another high profile arm of the employed sector. Built on a belief that lawyers could and should link with and empower communities, Law Centres set out to pioneer a political model of lawyering which sought to challenge local authorities and bring test cases on behalf of the disempowered groups. Whereas CABx emphasize non-lawyer and voluntary caseworkers, Law Centres tend to have a higher proportion of qualified lawyers working within their walls. There are a variety of other advice agencies that employ lawyers either as part of a campaign arm or, more often, as part of a casework function. Shelter has been particularly successful in developing its housing advice functions; Help the Aged takes a significant interest in legal matters; and there are a whole host of money advice, debt, and welfare benefits organizations where occasionally solicitors and barristers may be found. Funding sources for these organizations are diverse and often precarious. The Legal Services Commission, which administers the **legal aid** fund, often contracts with CABx, Law Centres, and specialist advice agencies for the provision of legal aid services to the public; local authorities are also a key funder of these services. However, variations in local political conditions and interests mean that local authority commitments to fund legal advice services is patchy and inconsistent. Some charities and businesses also fund these centres.

A final, quite different, but important group of employed lawyers are in-house lawyers. Most large, and may medium-sized, companies employ in-house lawyers. This reflects two features of the modern corporate world. First, many corporations generate considerable routine legal work relating to contracts, property transactions, and employment, pensions, and tax issues; and they take the view that these would be more efficiently provided in-house by salaried employees. Secondly, there is a view that in-house lawyers can be used to improve the way companies choose and manage outside lawyers. The theory is that in-house lawyers can use their knowledge of law and legal practice to ensure that their company chooses the best lawyers, and can manage the outside lawyers sufficiently to secure better quality service and lower bills.

A final comment on employed and in-house lawyers is that these careers, shielded as they are somewhat from the billing pressures of private practice, seem to recruit more women than does private practice. The typical explanation is that they provide more flexible, and family friendly, environments within which to work. Practitioners within the sector also report a more varied role within organizations which stretches beyond the purely legal towards strategic and policy functions and ultimately provides more attractive careers.   RICHARD MOORHEAD

See also: **government lawyers**

legal profession, theories about The study of the professions emerged as one of the early interests of modern sociology, having a place in the work of many of the subject's founders, including Karl Marx (1818–1883), Emile Durkheim (1858–1917), Max Weber (1864–1920), and Talcott Parsons (1902–1979). Each of these in their different ways saw the professions as occupying a critical role in the development of Western industrial society, and their work has continued to influence scholarship to this day.

The earliest 'sociological' work specifically on the legal profession dates back to the 1930s to 1950s. This work, which has continued to be influential, focused on defining professions (and hence also the notion of professionalism) by reference to their distinctive characteristics or 'traits'. Thus, the legal profession could be characterized as a profession by virtue of, among other things, its expectation of high educational attainment and relatively lengthy training; its deployment of specialized knowledge on behalf of its clients; its practice of self-regulation through a professional association; and its commitment to public service, latterly reflected in a formal code of ethics.

The obvious problem with trait theory is that is quite narrowly descriptive, and tends to take the claims of the professions largely at face value. It thus risks reproducing the ideology and self-description of the profession, and consequently provides us with a rather narrow and possibly a-historical vision of professionalism. This is not to say that such groundwork has been useless, or that trait theory is not influential. The identification of such traits has been significant in shaping social understanding of what a profession is. Moreover, useful academic work has subsequently been able to focus on one or more of these core traits, and explore their role in professional formation in greater depth, and often with a conceptual sophistication that the original trait scholarship lacked.

Today, however, we can say that theories of the profession are broadly derived from one (or more) of three perspectives. No one of these necessarily represents a 'right approach' or a privileged position from which to view the profession. Rather, each of them, and their derivatives, offers a different focus on the profession and its role in society.

First, there is what is often called the 'functionalist', or 'structural-functional', perspective. Functionalists focus on a society or part of society as a whole unit or entity. A functionalist approach thus requires us first to identify the basis on which we can define the group as a distinctive group, and then ask questions such as, what purpose does this group perform in society? How does this group or unit fit with other parts of that society? For Parsons, one of the founders of functionalism, lawyers were an important social group, contributing significantly to operations of social control and consensus building. Lawyers' work, in his view, placed the profession in an uneasy but dynamic relationship with the state, since legal work had the potential both to redefine political authority, and to transform clients' (citizens') relationship with political society.

During the late 1960s and the1970s the functionalist perspective started to go out of fashion. Its emphasis on social control, and on 'society', as a set of interacting systems, was seen to be rather narrow and rigid. It came to be challenged by two very different theoretical approaches. The first of these is called the 'interactionist' approach, and is the complete opposite of the 'big picture' perspective taken by those who adopt a functional-structural approach. It focuses, as the name suggests, on individual relationships and activities—it is much more a sociology of what lawyers do, than of the profession as a social institution; and this has been both its strength and its weakness. Interactionists thus tend to focus on the minutiae of legal practice, on everyday social relations, most often amongst the lawyers themselves, but also between lawyers and their clients and other social actors. For example, they explore the ways in which legal training and work relationships socialize lawyers and construct professionalism as an expression of individual and group identity. They will look at how 'meaning' is constructed and negotiated in individual lawyer–client relationships. Interactionism also provides insights into the distance between the reality of daily practice and the ideology which professions claim to embody. It has thus opened the way to a rather different image of the profession and professional work, stressing diversity, complexity, and conflict in professional work, and in the professionalization process itself.

Our third approach, called 'market control theory', is one that came to dominate scholarship in the 1980s and has remained influential ever since. It has focused on the power of the profession and its relationship with the development of the market economy and the modern state. It has been primarily influenced by the works of Marx and Weber.

In a sense, market control theory takes seriously George Bernard Shaw's famous charge that professions act as 'a conspiracy against the laity'. It shows how many of the professional traits (eg lengthy training, self-regulation, monopoly over certain restricted areas of work) also operate (as the name suggests) to hand control over their markets to the profession. It suggests that, even if this is not always the deliberate intent of the profession, professionalism actually operates as a set of strategies for restricting the supply of lawyers, for dampening competition between lawyers, and for restricting access by non-lawyers to the market for legal services. Obviously this perspective stands in direct contrast to the public interest arguments for professionalism most often advanced by the profession itself.

The significant transformations shaping the relationship between the English legal profession and the state since the 1980s, culminating, for now, in the creation of a new independent and market-based regulator by the Legal Services Act 2007, have provided an important test-bed for market control theory. Critics of the theory, who mostly see it as having some explanatory force, have nevertheless questioned how well it stands up as a general theory in

the light of this far more interventionist approach by the state. Market control theorists, such as Richard Abel, have responded by arguing that the loss of market control since the 1980s is in fact indicative of a quite fundamental social transformation: a massive decline in professionalism, as we traditionally understand it, and in the power and status of the legal profession. This conclusion too has been contested by those who argue that the market control thesis is too absolute, and too ready to declare the end of professionalism. Instead, they argue that market control theory does not pay enough attention to the normative and ideological dimensions of professionalism, nor to the extent to which the configuration of professionalism has been, and still is, subject to continuing renegotiation.

In recent years attempts have also been made to bridge some of the gaps between interactionist, structuralist, and market control perspectives, to develop a more sophisticated understanding of the ways in which power and status both shape and reflect the construction of the profession. This work has been strongly influenced by French sociologist Pierre Bourdieu's (1930–2002) analysis of 'capital' (despite the fact that very little of his own work focused on lawyers).

Bourdieu uses the concept of 'capital' in quite a specialized way. It describes not just economic capital as we normally understand it, but the value attached to a whole variety of social assets and credentials. Thus, a lawyer's stock of 'social capital' is seen as constructed out of their family ties and other personal and professional support networks. They will also derive 'cultural capital' (best understood as a 'feel for the game' of legal practice) from their knowledge and skills, the status attached to their education, their shared tastes and values with other lawyers and clients, and the extent of their tacit understanding of how to relate to clients and colleagues. The basic point of this analysis seems an obvious one: status and power in the legal field will reflect the way in which capital in all its forms is distributed—unevenly—through the profession. But what makes the work of Bourdieu and his followers valuable is its capacity to move beyond the either/or focus of earlier theories—whereby our attention was drawn either to the individual actors or to the market—to consider *how* actors, and institutions together, function to reproduce economic and social practices.

JULIAN WEBB

legal profession: competition, consumer protection and regulation   Traditionally, legal professions in all **common law** countries, including those of the **United Kingdom**, regulated themselves in ways that restricted competition and largely ignored consumer service issues, with the justification that this was the best way to establish and maintain high professional standards. Despite a range of reforms since the 1980s, self-regulation still plays an important part in the structure and regulation of UK solicitors and barristers, with more market and consumer-oriented reforms layered over the top of it.

At the height of legal professional self-**regulation** in the first half of the twentieth century, legislation entrenched barristers' and solicitors' monopolies over various areas of legal work including the conduct of litigation, the right to represent people in court, and the provision of **conveyancing**, immigration, and probate services. The professional associations for barristers and solicitors decided what qualifications potential lawyers needed in order to be allowed to practise in these areas, and set and enforced the conditions for that practice. They established professional ethical conduct standards, and received, investigated, and prosecuted complaints about the breach of those standards. The tribunals and courts that heard these prosecutions were also predominantly made up of lawyers and judges (who are former lawyers). The professional associations prohibited most forms of **competition** between lawyers, including any form of **advertising** or price competition. They also prosecuted any non-lawyers who performed legal work in breach of the legal professions' monopolies.

Self-regulation restricted competition from outside the legal profession in the market for legal services on the basis that lawyers' knowledge and skills are so complex that it is beyond the ability of lay people to ever be able to choose for themselves a legal service provider to provide good quality service at an appropriate price. Consumers must therefore be protected from making the wrong choice, by regulation that makes sure that only people who have met the professional hurdles of educational qualifications and good character provide legal services in the first place. This regulation must be self-regulation since it is only legal professionals who have the knowledge and experience to know what skills and character are necessary to be a good lawyer. According to this rather circular argument, the public has little choice but to grant the profession a monopoly on legal services and then trust them to regulate themselves appropriately, subject to the implicit threat that they might lose their monopoly if they failed to do so. Many lawyers also argue that the state can have no role in regulating the legal profession, since lawyers need to remain completely independent of government so that they can defend individuals against the state (for example in criminal defence work) without fear of reprisal.

Self-regulation also restricted competition within the profession on the basis that lawyers needed to be free from the sort of competitive pressures that face ordinary businesses so that they could concentrate on fulfilling their ethical obligations to clients, the courts, the law, and justice. For example, market pressures might encourage lawyers to cut prices and cut corners if standard fees were not fixed. More significantly, the lack of competition within the profession was supposed to leave lawyers free to fulfil the profession's higher public service of ensuring fairness and justice in the legal system by making sure they were always honest to the court, and advised clients to comply with the law, even where clients might be willing to pay lawyers handsomely to assist dishonesty, unfairness, or illegality. Lack of competition within the profession also gave lawyers more scope to improve access to justice by voluntarily providing free or low cost legal services to the needy.

Once lawyers had entered the profession, ongoing self-regulation did little to make sure that they maintained high standards of competence and client service. Instead the self-regulatory professional associations focused almost exclusively on investigating and prosecuting misconduct that reflected dishonesty or poor character on the part of lawyers, such as deliberately misleading a court or tribunal, falsifying a document, or breaching trust account rules (including lawyer misappropriation of client funds) and other fiduciary duties (particularly conflicts of interests).

Until recently, the professional associations did very little to resolve or redress complaints about poor or incompetent consumer service by lawyers, or to identify problematic practices in the profession and raise overall standards. Only in the case of 'gross negligence' could a lawyer be sanctioned for lack of care and competence. Overcharging was generally only disciplined where it was extreme or dishonest. This was despite the fact that the vast majority of complaints clients make about lawyers concern poor service—delay, incompetence, over-charging, discourtesy, and failure to communicate. Indeed the professional associations simply dismissed many of those client complaints that related to consumer issues without investigation or attempted resolution. The Law Society of England and Wales, in particular, was repeatedly criticized for handling complaints from customers in a way that was slow, cumbersome and often oriented towards defending the conduct of the solicitor rather than identifying and resolving problems.

Since the 1980s a series of incremental reforms to the self-regulation of the legal professions have removed many restrictive practices, made complaints-handling more transparent, efficient, and consumer-oriented, and introduced independent oversight of the self-regulating legal professional associations. Yet many aspects of self-regulation remain in place. The result is a system in which consumer and market-oriented regulation, similar to that applied to other businesses, has been layered over the top of the distinctive self-regulatory controls that have traditionally been seen as appropriate for professions.

The traditional professional monopolies on legal work are largely untouched, with the same strict requirements set by the profession for entry into the profession. The legal professional associations have, however, been forced to abolish many of their most restrictive practices, including the setting of standard fees and the prohibition on advertising. Licensed conveyancers now compete with solicitors for conveyancing work. Previously, lawyers could only operate in solo practice or through partnerships with other lawyers, a restriction that was criticized for stifling innovation and external investment in the market for legal services. Now lawyers can work together with non-lawyers to offer legal services and other services through the same business entity.

In Scotland the professional associations, the Law Society of Scotland and the Faculty of Advocates, continue to receive and investigate all complaints about lawyers, subject to oversight by the independent Scottish Legal Services Ombudsman. In England and Wales, an independent agency, the Office of the Legal Services Complaints Commissioner, now receives and resolves all those complaints about legal professionals that can be classified as 'consumer complaints'. But the professional associations still continue to set standards and investigate and prosecute conduct complaints against lawyers. A separate, independent agency in England and Wales, the Legal Services Board, now regulates the legal professional associations' self-regulation by setting performance standards and targets for their self-regulatory functions. There is also an increasing emphasis on requiring legal practices to implement their own in-house customer complaints systems, and to inform their clients of these mechanisms. But much more could be done to force lawyers to educate and inform their clients about the nature and quality of the services they should expect, particularly, the costs of legal services.

Overall it is not clear to what extent the goals of the newer independent, consumer-oriented regulatory agencies are likely to be in tension with the emphasis of traditional professional self-regulation on the character of lawyers, which continues to underlie the system. A more proactive, regulatory approach may be needed to address public concerns about consumer service quality and the administration of justice.   CHRISTINE PARKER

legal profession, social background, entry, and training Qualification for entry to the legal profession in England and Wales consists of three stages: the academic stage, the vocational stage, and a period of practice-based training. The academic stage requires either a Qualifying Law Degree, or alternatively a degree in another subject followed by either the Common Professional Exam ('CPE') or Graduate Diploma in Law ('GDL;). All of these courses cover, as a minimum, the seven foundation subjects of: Contract, Tort, Criminal Law, Equity and **Trusts**, **European Union** Law, Property Law, and Public Law. This requirement is common to both branches of the profession.

The vocational stage consists of the Legal Practice Course ('LPC') (for solicitors) and the Bar Vocational Course ('BVC') (for barristers), both generally lasting one year full time. Those completing the BVC are 'called to the bar' at this stage. The final stage is either a two-year training contract for solicitors, or a one-year pupillage for barristers. Both of these are periods of practice-based training under the supervision of experienced practitioners. During this stage solicitors must complete the Professional Skills Course and they can then be 'admitted to the roll'. Both branches of the profession require qualified practitioners to undergo Continuing Professional Development. There are also mechanisms for transfer between the branches and admission of foreign lawyers under the Qualified Lawyers Transfer Test.

A small number of would-be solicitors qualify first as Members or Fellows of the Institute of Legal Executives, and are then exempt from parts of the academic stage. Fellows are exempt from the training contract, although both must still complete the LPC and the Professional Skills Course. Justices' Clerks assistants are also exempt from the Training Contract in certain circumstances.

Both the Law Society and the Bar Council have recognized that the demographic profile of their members does not conform to modern ideas of diversity. In 1919 Parliament overturned a judicially sanctioned ban on female entry to the profession, but it took fifty years for women to exceed 10 per cent of new entrants. Female entrants now slightly exceed male entrants in number at all stages of entry, for both branches. Women represented 42.5 per cent of practising solicitors in 2006. The Bar fares worse, with women representing only 33.4 per cent of practising barristers. At the higher echelons of the professions the picture remains poor with less than 10 per cent of QCs, 23 per cent of partners in solicitors' firms, and 18 per cent of the judiciary being female.

The position of ethnic minorities is similar. Some 9.1 per cent of practising solicitors, and 11.2 per cent of barristers, are from an ethnic minority background (compared to 7.9 per cent of the general UK population in 2001). However researchers have reported a bias against applicants from ethnic minority groups in terms of both admissions to the LPC and availability of training contracts. Only 4 per cent of QCs and 3 per cent of the judiciary are from an ethnic minority, and only 21.5 per cent of ethnic minority solicitors are partners, compared to 31.8 per cent of white European solicitors.

Neither professional body publishes data on the socio-economic class background of their members. Historically, particularly at the Bar, surveys based on education or parental occupation, have shown that the less advantaged form only a small minority of entrants. According to Nicolson (2005) this still appears to be 'the greatest obstacle to entry and progress'. Previous studies had found that those studying law were predominantly drawn from professional and managerial classes. In 2004 researchers found that 68 per cent of barristers at the leading eight commercial chambers attended fee-paying schools, and 82 per cent studied at Oxbridge Colleges. The figures for judges of the High Court and above was 75 per cent and 81 per cent respectively; and for partners at 'Magic Circle' firms the figures were 55 per cent and 53 per cent.

The cost of a legal education would appear to be one source of this imbalance. Fees for the LPC currently range from £5,200 to £9,000, and the BVC from £8,500 to £12,700. A survey in 1994 indicated that over 50 per cent of those law students choosing not to apply for the BVC or LPC made this decision because they could not afford to fund themselves, and a similar proportion of those receiving offers for the LPC also turned them down for the same reason. The key role of work placements in selection of aspirant lawyers also makes it more unlikely that those under financial pressure to work during the summer will obtain a training contract. A reported bias in the allocation of training contracts towards those studying at Oxbridge or the College of Law, and those taking the CPE has the further effect of reducing the number of entrants from less privileged backgrounds and ethnic minorities who are under-represented in all these groups. Richard Abel (*English Lawyers Between Market and State* (Oxford: Oxford University Press, 2003)) also reminds us that criteria of educational institution attendance and academic performance both admit and sort, and represent transmission of human capital, thus being potential grounds for indirect discrimination. In this way over-reliance on academic performance, or preference for particular universities can unintentionally lead to under-representation of some groups.

These demographics are not uniform throughout the professions. For example, many of the biases are found more strongly in City firms, and large provincial firms. This is particularly relevant given the higher salaries and the elite status often accredited to these firms, and the high proportion of training contracts which they provide.

The interaction between these groups and their path into the professions is also less than straightforward with, for example, the possibility that 'The entry of women . . . may have narrowed class recruitment both because it doubled competition for entry and because women, confronting sex discrimination, may have come from higher social classes than men' (Abel, 150). The interaction between socio-economic class and ethnicity is of a different kind: those from a minority ethnic group are more likely to come from a less privileged background leading to multiple disadvantage for this group.

Whilst entry to training for the professions is showing progress, this has not travelled to the higher levels of the professions, nor even to the progression from training to practice stages. Care should therefore be taken when looking at entry numbers or summary figures, which fail to reflect the nuanced patterns of employment, status, and progression.

AVROM SHERR

D Nicholson, 'Demography, discrimination and diversity: A new dawn for the British legal profession?' (2005) 12:2 *International Journal of the Legal Profession* 201–228

M Shiner, 'Young, Gifted and Blocked! Entry to the Solicitors' Profession' in P Thomas (ed), *Discriminating Lawyers* (London: Cavendish Publishing, 2000), 87–120

See also: **vocational legal education; women and gender in the legal profession**

legal professional ethics and values   Observing high ethical standards and upholding professional values in the practice of law is an important professional duty lawyers owe not only to their clients and consumers of legal services but also to the courts, fellow lawyers, and society at large. High standards of ethical practice may indirectly support the **rule**

of law; and in many countries lawyers are expected, both individually and collectively through their professional associations, to promote—and when necessary to defend—core civic and professional values connected with **justice** and due process of law.

These values, alongside principles of professional conduct and etiquette, are commonly expressed in the form of a formal written code of practice regularly updated and policed by professional associations, whose work is increasingly overseen by, if not subject to, independent external regulatory scrutiny. Codes that inform legal practice are also emerging at the European and global levels. Since no code can ever predict every ethical dilemma, the values and principles governing professional conduct are also embedded in the ethos and culture of institutional legal practice and communicated more informally through social ritual and more private storytelling. Furthermore, ethics are used by lawyers to justify their professional status, restrictive practices and higher fees—and thus help to differentiate them from **paralegals** and non-lawyers who may compete for work in the legal services industry.

Given the centrality of ethics in defining and maintaining the identity, practice standards, markets, and status of legal professionals, it is perhaps surprising that until recently professional ethics has received such scant attention from academic lawyers and researchers. Outside the United States, there have been few courses that aim to teach professional responsibility at the academic stage of legal education, though other common law jurisdictions such as New Zealand and Australia have recently followed suit by introducing mandatory courses in legal ethics at undergraduate level. A critical, philosophically-informed literature examining the nature and scope of professional duties in legal practice has only begun to emerge over the past decade, and it is now supported by a specialist journal serving the field, *Legal Ethics*.

At the vocational stage of legal education, courses exist in professional responsibility—in civil law jurisdictions such courses tend to be taught under the label 'Deontology'—but they have been taught uncritically and concentrate on communicating to future lawyers their privileges and the conduct to be followed if they wish to avoid disciplinary proceedings for egregious behaviour. Little attention is given, either in courses on legal ethics or in the codes themselves, to promoting positive duties or aspirational norms that may transcend the lawyer-client relationship. The overwhelming emphasis is on the immediate duties owed to the private client, which border on the absolute, rather than the wider duties owed to the court, the public interest or third parties. The key professional values taught tend to be connected with the duties of confidentiality and loyalty owed to clients; but increasingly there is recognition that something more needs to be done, by law schools as well as the professional bodies, to promote understanding of the public duties that also must form part of professional responsibility.

It is feared that increasing competition in the market for legal services may be driving down standards while at the same time inflating fees (eg through 'bill padding') as lawyers cut corners and costs in order to maximize their profits. Such practices pose a challenge to regulatory strategy and a risk to professional status but, interestingly, have also increased interest in the teaching of legal ethics, which may help lawyers internalize and strengthen their commitment to fundamental lawyering values. If regulation is of limited relevance for a profession that by definition is able to master (and hence evade) rules, including those rules designed to catch or curb lawyer defalcations, perhaps an education in ethics at a formative stage in the development of professional character offers more hope. The problem here is to know whether ethics and values can be taught meaningfully to lawyers and, if so, when and how. Several jurisdictions have concluded that far more emphasis needs to be given to the teaching of legal ethics and at all stages of the educational continuum and a number are currently experimenting with introducing ethics into the law curriculum. The most promising approach towards 'making lawyers good' would seem to lie in a combining educational and regulatory strategy so that the regulatory framework governing professional conduct seeks to educate both lawyers, as providers of legal services, and clients, as consumers of those services.

KIM ECONOMIDES

K Economides (ed), *Ethical Challenges to Legal Education and Conduct* (Oxford: Hart Publishing, 1998)
D Nicholson and J Webb, *Professional Legal Ethics: Critical Interrogations* (Oxford: Oxford University Press, 1999)

legal professional privilege   Parties to litigation are often subject to duties to disclose documents and to answer questions. Legal professional privilege is an exception to these duties; the litigant who invokes the 'privilege' is permitted to keep documents confidential and to refuse to answer questions. Other similar exceptions to these duties include the privilege against **self-incrimination**, the **journalistic privilege** (against being compelled to reveal the name of a source). and the 'without prejudice' privilege (against being compelled to disclose 'without prejudice' communications made in the course of an attempt to settle a dispute).

It is common to divide the material for which legal professional privilege can be claimed into two classes. The first class, covered by what is sometimes called 'legal advice privilege', consists of communications between client and lawyer in the course of seeking and receiving 'legal advice'. The second class, covered by what is sometimes called 'litigation privilege', consists of material generated for the purpose of being used in anticipated litigation, including communications between a lawyer and third parties. Clearly these two classes overlap. But, to highlight two key differences, 'legal advice privilege' covers advice about matters other than anticipated litigation (for instance, about the drafting of contracts, wills, and leases) whilst 'litigation privilege' covers material other than 'legal advice' (for instance, communications between a lawyer and a potential expert witness). The scope of both classes of material can be contentious; important precedents have helped to identify the line between 'legal advice' and 'general business advice', to determine how likely 'anticipated' litigation must be and to define the necessary strength of the link between the litigation and the generation of the material ('dominant purpose').

The most persuasive justification for 'legal advice privilege' is that it ensures that clients suffers no detriment through being open and forthcoming in discussions with their lawyers and, consequently, the privilege facilitates access to the best possible legal advice. Indeed, the association between the privilege and access to legal advice has led some lawyers to treat the privilege as an aspect of the right to a fair trial. 'Litigation privilege' is commonly justified by the argument that each party should be able to prepare its case without the potentially distorting effect of the other party's surveillance. In particular, no party should be able to sit back and rely on its opponent to identify all the useful documents and witnesses. In modern times, however, the force of the counter-argument that parties are more likely to be able to settle their dispute and save costs if each party is able to judge the force of its opponent's case has led to the development of exceptions to 'litigation privilege'.

RODERICK BAGSHAW

See also: **fair trial, right to**

legal realism   Legal realism refers to two separate, if parallel, movements in the United States and Scandinavia. The American realists were active during the 1920s, 1930s, and 1940s, and their work challenged ideas about legal reasoning and adjudication

dominant in judicial and legal academic writing at the time. The realists were strongly influenced by the work of Oliver Wendell **Holmes**, Jr (1841–1935), and the sociological jurisprudence that Roscoe Pound (1870–1964) wrote early in his career (later Pound was to become a critic of the realists), as well as theorists from the European 'Free Law' movement. Prominent figures in the American legal realist movement included Karl N Llewellyn (1893–1962) and Jerome Frank (1889–1957).

The American realists asserted that a proper understanding of judicial decision-making would show that it was fact-centred, and that judges' decisions were often based (consciously or unconsciously) on personal or political biases and constructed from hunches. They also argued that public policy and social sciences should play a larger role in judicial decisions. The realists argued that judicial decisions were strongly under-determined by legal rules, concepts and precedent (that is, that judges in many or most cases could, with equal warrant, have come out more than one way). Feeding into this central focus on adjudication was a critique of legal reasoning: a claim that beneath a veneer of scientific and deductive reasoning, legal rules and concepts were in fact often indeterminate and rarely as neutral as they were presented as being.

The form of legal analysis dominant at the time the realists were writing was criticized as 'formalistic'. 'Formalism' (also sometimes called 'conceptualism' and 'mechanical jurisprudence') was an extreme view about the autonomy of legal reasoning, and entailed judicial analysis that moved mechanically or automatically from category or concept to conclusion, without consideration of policy, morality, or practice. The argument against formalism was that the rushed move from category to legal conclusion was both unwarranted and unwise.

The American legal realists grounded their approach on an instrumental view of the law: that it was a tool meant to serve social purposes, and to whatever extent it did not serve those purposes, or did not serve them well, the law should be changed. This attitude was also reflected both in the law reform work that many American realists did for President Franklin D Roosevelt's 'New Deal' programmes, and in Karl Llewellyn's later efforts, as the primary author of and moving force behind Article 2 of the American **Uniform Commercial Code** ('UC Code'), a code regulating the sale of goods. UC Code Article 2 reflects a realist approach, in that its legal standards purport to reflect the customs and expectations of business people, rather than trying to impose legal technicalities upon them.

American legal realism can be seen as the fore-runner of more recent jurisprudential schools of thought—eg law and economics, critical legal studies, critical race theory, and feminist legal theory. By undermining confidence in the 'science' or autonomy of law and the ability to deduce unique correct answers from legal principles (as well as questioning the 'neutrality' of those legal principles), the American realists created a need for a new justification of legal rules and judicial actions. Also, they offered a set of arguments (eg arguments about the indeterminacy of law and challenges to a 'public'/'private' distinction in law) that later critical approaches would use to support claims of pervasive bias (against the poor, against women, and against minorities) in the legal system.

The Scandinavian legal realists wrote around the same time as the American legal realists, but they had significantly less long-term influence, and they are now only rarely read (even in their home countries). The movement's intellectual leader was the philosopher, Axel Hägerström (1868–1939); and its most prominent theorists were Alf Ross (1899–1979), Karl Olivecrona (1897–1980), and AV Lundstedt (1882–1955). Scandinavian legal realism was based on a skeptical approach to metaphysical claims in general, and metaphysical language in law in particular.

Much of the work by the Scandinavian legal realists attempts to translate references to 'rights', 'duties', 'property', etc to more empirical terms, rejecting any explanation that seemed to posit unworldly entities. Instead, these theorists sometimes offered psychological and anthropological explanations to fill the vacuum (eg that these terms referred to subjective feelings of empowerment or constraint, or were connected to ancient beliefs in magic). Other times, the normative terms were reduced to predictions of or authorizations for institutional sanctions.

BRIAN BIX

WW Fisher III, MJ Horwitz. and TA Reed (eds), *American Legal Realism* (Oxford: Oxford University Press, 1993)

K Olivecrona, *Law as Fact* (London: Stevens & Sons, 2nd edn, 1971)

See also: **economic analysis of law; feminist theories of law**

legal rules, types of A legal rule can be thought of as a precept that attaches a definite legal consequence to a definite detailed state of fact. Such rules, moreover, can be thought of as occurring in primary, secondary, and tertiary forms. Primary legislation is encountered in statutes, or **Acts of Parliament**.

Secondary legislation (often called 'delegated legislation') is the product of exercise of a power to legislate that is conferred by an Act of Parliament. The term 'tertiary rule' can be used to refer to the wide array of governmental rules that are not directly enforceable through criminal or civil proceedings, but which may, nevertheless, produce indirect legal effects. Examples of such tertiary rules include guidelines, circulars, codes of conduct, and administrative rules. Tertiary rules are often called 'soft law'

Secondary legislation can be produced by means of a variety of originating procedures. Thus, the following varieties of secondary rule are often seen in the law: Statutory Instruments; Orders in Council; Regulations, Directives, and Orders; Special Procedure Orders; Local Authority Orders; and By-Laws. Much work is still to be done to rationalize the terminology and procedures applicable to secondary legislation. What can be said, however, is that such rules are made under the authority of Parliament and that they carry the full force of law.

The common justifications for secondary legislation are that delegations of rule-making are necessary and useful because Parliament does not have the time or detailed knowledge to make specialist bodies of rules; that some subjects are too technical to justify parliamentary attention; that secondary rules are much more flexible and responsive than statutes; and that delegations of rule-making power allow adjustments and updating or amending exercises to be carried out efficiently.

Much modern legislation is carried out by means of 'framework' items of primary legislation, which do little more than confer on certain parties (usually ministers or agencies) powers to issue secondary legislation. This prompts the common criticism that parliamentary and democratic scrutiny is weakened by such heavy reliance on secondary legislation since such legislation does not involve the full parliamentary process and the debating stages that are associated with primary legislation. There is, indeed, widely seen to be some force in this point. Orders in Council and Statutory Instruments have to be issued in accordance with fixed statutory procedures (governing printing, publication, and so on) but, apart from local authority by-laws, there are no general provisions covering the production of other forms of subordinate legislation or tertiary rules.

A 'parent' statute that confers a rule-making power may, nevertheless, require that certain forms of 'laying' procedure be followed. These procedures include 'bare laying' (whereby the instrument is tabled in Parliament after being made); 'negative resolution procedure' (in which the instrument is tabled but can be annulled within a prescribed time by a vote); and 'affirmative resolution procedure', which requires that an instrument be tabled but cannot take effect until approved.

Tertiary rules present greater problems of identification and classification. Analysing them functionally, it is possible to point to at least eight types: *procedural rules* (laying down procedures to be followed in, for instance, making applications to public bodies); *interpretative guides* (offering explanations of how rules are to be applied or criteria are to be taken into account); *instructions to officials* (which are designed to encourage consistency of approach in decision-making); *prescriptive rules* (which offer guidance or encouragement on compliance issues); *evidential rules* (which advise courts on the meaning of other legal rules); *commendatory rules* (which recommend courses of behaviour); *voluntary codes* (which serve self-regulatory roles); and *rules of practice* (such as extra-statutory tax concessions, which lay down enforcement arrangements).

Such rules, codes, and guides are often very useful in informing the public how laws will be applied and discretions exercised. They also help to ensure that officials apply laws in consistent ways. They allow guidance to be offered to untrained or less expert public servants. They are more cheaply produced and flexible than statutes and can be framed in more accessible language. The legal force and status of such rules is, however, often unclear. They have no formal force, but have evidential value when used in courts; and they can create legally enforceable expectations (for instance, to the effect that when a body states that it will act according to certain rules or criteria for action, it will do so). A difficulty is that there are no set procedures for producing tertiary rules and, accordingly, their forms may be haphazard and the mechanisms of accountability associated with them may be weak. Critics argue that soft laws allow the executive to exercise too much power, that they involve no standardized consultation mechanisms, and that they can be used both to bypass parliamentary scrutiny and to manipulate judicial approaches to potentially contentious issues.

Similar points can be made concerning the varieties of legal or quasi-legal rule found at the European level of government—where the Treaties can be seen as the sources of primary rules; where Regulations, Directives, and Decisions can be deemed to make up the body of secondary rules; and tertiary rules appear in the form of such items as recommendations, opinions, resolutions, declarations, communiqués, deliberations, memoranda, and guidelines.

A final issue is whether the production of soft laws should be rationalized and put on a statutory footing by means of an Administrative Procedure Act (as encountered in the USA). Those sceptical of such an approach tend to argue that whether a given rule will be covered by such an Act will often give rise to expensive contention and that many rules will inevitably escape such controls. Critics are likely to add that such an Act would slow down rule-making, jeopardize the advantages of informality, and discourage the production of useful rules and guides. They would caution that this kind of reform would encourage the **juridification** of bureaucratic and regulatory processes. Soft laws may be untidy in appearance but, say their supporters, they are extremely useful and produce more desirable results than more formal alternatives.

ROBERT BALDWIN

See also: **codes of conduct in international law; codes of practice in consumer law; legislative drafting; legislative processes**

Legal Services Commission   *see* **legal aid**

Legal Services Ombudsman   *see* **ombudsmen**

legal services, demand and need for   Measurement of the 'unmet' need for legal services has been a contentious issue since the expansion of interest in the use of law for the poor in the 1960s. Activists, academics, and policymakers have grappled with difficult definitions and potentially subjective understandings of 'demand', 'need', 'unmet', and 'legal services'. Most recently, interest has focused around the quantifiable incidence of 'justiciable events' in a methodology which has now been replicated in a number of different jurisdictions.

In the UK, a number of studies in the early 1970s concluded that the poor lacked access to the legal services they required. An influential early example was undertaken by B Abel-Smith, M Zander, and R Brooke in 1973 (*Legal Problems and the Citizen: a Study of Three London Boroughs* (London: Heinemann, 1973)). A similar study of the use of lawyers was undertaken by B Curran in the United States and published in 1977 (*The Legal Needs of the Public* (Chicago: American Bar Foundation, 1977)). This was more ambitious than the UK study; it was based on a national sample and interviewed respondents about their experience of dealing with a range of specified problems during their lifetime.

Work in the US culminated in the American Bar Association's ('ABA') *Comprehensive Legal Needs Survey* published in 1994. This concentrated on the needs of low and moderate income households. It deployed a broad definition of legal need as relating to specific pre-defined situations that 'raised legal issues'. Unmet need was shown where such situations were either simply not brought to the justice system, or where the affected person did nothing, or was dissatisfied with their own or a third party's efforts. This indicated, for example, that somewhere between a half and three-quarters of the legal needs of low-income households were unmet. Those critical of the survey argued that its explicit inference, that unmet need equated with a need for the services of the ABA's members, was false. Even sceptics, however, had to acknowledge that it painted a formidable picture of the kind of problems faced by the poor.

A similar analysis was made of the work of Abel-Smith's team. It had argued that some problems (included housing disrepair, for instance) were 'inherently legal'. Critics countered that many of these might be seen differently, eg as political problems, which could be addressed by local councillors and local authorities.

The issue of unmet need was rather poorly dealt with by the Benson Royal Commission on Legal Services in England and Wales, which reported in 1980, but very much better by the Hughes Commission, which was its Scottish equivalent. The latter defined need for 'legal services' as need for 'services—facilities, advice, assistance, information or action—to enable a citizen with a problem to assert or protect his rights in law'. Need is unmet if the citizen remains ignorant of his rights or fails to exercise them, though he wishes to do so, because of 'want of adequate supply or quality'.

In a major study published in 1999 (*Paths to Justice: What People Do and Think about Going to Law* (Oxford: Hart Publishing, 1999)), Professor Hazel Genn sought to avoid some of the earlier definitional pitfalls. She dodged many of these by claiming to measure only the incidence of 'justiciable events' and what people did about them. A justiciable event was defined as a matter 'experienced by a respondent which raised legal issues, whether or not it was recognised by the respondent as being "legal" and whether or not any action taken by the respondent to deal with the event involved the use of the civil justice system'. She asked respondents about a specified set of problems, as had the earlier studies, and she sought additionally to screen out the trivial, less serious problems as well as those where the respondent accepted that they were personally to blame or that no-one was to blame. She classified respondents into three categories: 'lumpers', those who did nothing

to resolve their problem; 'self-helpers' who did what they could themselves; and those who got advice. In this way she was able to obtain results which showed variations in response for different problems.

The *Paths to Justice* survey introduced a further degree of methodological rigour into analysis of the need for legal advice. It proved attractive in other jurisdictions, too. Professor Genn herself participated in a replication of the approach in Scotland published in 2001. Even more interestingly, researchers overseas took up the methodology and generated broadly compatible data in countries such as The Netherlands and Canada. Furthermore, the methodology was developed further by the Legal Services Research Centre of the **Legal Services Commission** of England and Wales. It has been able to undertake and repeat national surveys that allow increasingly sophisticated analysis. It has begun to track, for example, the health consequences of certain types of justiciable problems. It has definitively established what many practitioners have long instinctively understood: that problems have a tendency to come in clusters around events such as loss of a job or illness and disability.

Thus, studies of unmet legal need have an increasingly long academic pedigree and have reached a considerable sophistication that allows cross-cultural analysis of such matters as why, for example, the Scots report fewer civil justice problems than the English. Behind these apparently neutral studies lies, however, an essentially political project. These studies were called in aid of the movement that gathered pace in the 1970s to argue that the poor had legal needs very similar to those of the rich, and merely lacked the knowledge to identify their need and the money to pay for lawyers. It is somewhat of a paradox that the Legal Services Commission in England and Wales is now funding research that traces with increasing accuracy the consequences of lack of legal assistance at crucial moments in the life of a person who cannot afford to pay for a lawyer, and is doing so just at the time when unprecedented cuts are being made to the Community Legal Service that provides exactly for such needs.

An excellent literature analysis of work in this area was undertaken by Tony Dignan for the Northern Ireland Legal Services Commission in 2004 (see below).   ROGER SMITH

T Dignan, *Legal Need in Northern Ireland: Literature Review* (Northern Ireland Legal Services Commission, 2004) (accessible at *http://www.nilsc.org.uk/uploads/research/documents/legalneedsfinal.pdf*)

legal theory   *see* **theory in legal research**

legal theory and legal history   The basic problem which has dogged, in some cases haunted, both would-be legal theorists and legal historians is in a sense the same: what is *legal* theory; what is *legal* history? To non-specialists these may seem like rather navel-gazing questions. But they do indicate the difficulty of disentangling 'law' from history, politics, and economics more broadly. The ambiguous status of legislation in this mix—is the Education Act or the Poor Law 'law' for these purposes?—intensifies the dilemma.

But there is a difference in the situation in which would-be legal theorists and historians have found themselves. With the secularization of philosophy in the nineteenth and twentieth centuries, it was possible for legal theorists to find a vocabulary and a set of problems which gave them something 'pure' and distinctive to do or to work on. Legal historians had noble influences, especially Maitland, but what were they to do? Emulate other historians and read the sources. But which ones? The choice of sources is everything.

Legal history for many years reproduced the narrowness of legal theory—the ghost of John **Austin**'s *Province of Jurisprudence Determined* (first published in 1832, republished with an introduction by HLA **Hart**, London: Weidenfeld & Nicolson, 1955) loomed large here. This narrowness should not be seen as some kind of intellectual defect but as a consequence of the pressure on legal historians to carve a niche of their own in a differentiating academic environment. FW **Maitland** could still range widely at the end of the nineteenth century. This became more difficult in the twentieth century and also, perhaps, as legal history in the UK became increasingly synonymous with the study of medieval legal sources. The downside of this approach—which secured the reputation of a number of scholars like TFT Plucknett and SFC Milsom—was the problem of relevance. Studies of medieval texts seemed, for the most part, to be study of the past for the past's sake. To non-lawyers and lawyers alike, this was boring and shed little light on contemporary concerns and preoccupations.

As legal history pursued this rather lonely furrow, legal theory developed in a way which largely ignored any lessons of history or the worthy products of legal historians. Legal theorists became centred on the question 'What is law?' but with a rather peculiar or particular emphasis. Not least because of the professionalization of philosophy, this question became increasingly an issue of the basis of law's validity and legitimacy. This is especially marked in HLA Hart's *The Concept of Law* (Oxford: Clarendon Press, 1961;

2nd edn with postscript, 1994) which entirely misleadingly claimed to present a sociological approach to the understanding of law. Since legal anthropology was in fairly poor shape by the time the first edition of Hart's book appeared, perhaps Hart's ignorance of how simple or 'acephalous' societies function is forgivable. But it was clear from the start that the main driver of this book was to articulate a distinction between force and obligation, and the question of the obligation to obey the law has remained a legal-theoretical theme ever since.

Another enduring theme has been the distinction between law and morality. Perhaps, looking at the field more broadly, Hart's most influential contribution was his *Law, Liberty and Morality*, in which he sought in effect to update JS Mill. This fed directly into the re-emerging tension between positivism and **natural law theory**. For a long time the death of God had seen off natural law; from the time of the **Nuremberg trials**, however, natural law has enjoyed a slow but steady revival. The terms of engagement have now changed: the issue now is posed in terms of a tension between universalism and particularism. A new fashionable term, retrieved from Kant, is cosmopolitanism.

This shifting climate made the UK (and Europe more generally) a fertile ground for an American like Ronald Dworkin, who succeeded Hart as Professor of Jurisprudence at the University of Oxford. This was an odd but highly influential move. It was odd because like many of his US predecessors (especially Karl Llewellyn, Roscoe Pound, and Lon Fuller) Dworkin over-inflated the role of judges. Hart's rule of recognition captured succinctly the cosiness of the then judicial world; Dworkin contributed strenuously to a new moralizing stridency.

In the UK, the European influence was, for a long time, rather muted. The Kantian Hans Kelsen was vaguely there in the background; but most authors were not available in the English language and it was largely due to a few writers of jurisprudence textbooks for students to distil and disseminate what they saw as the essence of the thought these of writers. As a result, their influence was minimal. Those in search of wider horizons turned increasingly to the US. The situation changed with the rather rapid arrival in translation of a number of European theorists who were not lawyers but whose work could suggest either content or methods to legal (and many other) academics. (Michel Foucault and Jacques Derrida have had the greatest impact.) In parallel with this, there has been the growing salience of Jurgen Habermas, and to a lesser extent, of Niklas Luhmann.

As legal theorists became preoccupied with these issues, any attempt to engage with legal history largely disappeared. Theory and history became entrenched as distinct intellectual activities. What opened up a potential for change was the arrival on the landscape of a new social history, spearheaded by EP Thompson and a strong army of followers. This was an attempt to produce history from below, often based on legal records. But it was also, if in a mild way, theoretically informed. The possibility of a renewed engagement between legal theory and legal history emerged on the back of this work. Historians needed theory to get to grips with what they were doing; theorists needed history to contextualise their concepts (the impact of Quentin Skinner cannot be underestimated here). But these were and are only possibilities; and increasing pressures towards specialization and an intensification of the moralization of political culture constitute obstacles in this path.

TIM MURPHY

See also: **anthropology and law; legal positivism since 1970; legal positivism to 1970; sociological jurisprudence**

legal treatises before 1800 Most surviving pre-nineteenth century legal literature is primarily concerned to state rather than to analyse or explain the law. The earliest medieval law books which have come down to us were utilitarian workaday tools, case-notes and formularies detailing the opinions and practices of the courts, written aids to memory which supplemented the profession's oral tradition. Few attempted or purported to provide a systematic overview of their subject. The outstanding early exception is *Bracton*, a thirteenth-century Latin account of 'the laws and customs of England' much influenced by **Roman law** learning. But despite its numerous extant manuscript copies, this text seems to have retained little influence once the Inns of Court and Chancery began to develop their own educational regime. Then in the mid-fifteenth century Thomas Littleton's law-French *Tenures* provided an authoritative, immediately successful introduction to real property law, the central core of English legal learning, henceforth serving as both preparative and complement to the Inns' learning exercises.

Copies and notes of those readings and moots continued to circulate, mainly if not exclusively in manuscript, down to and even after the collapse of that educational system in the later seventeenth century. But meanwhile Judge Littleton's book had become the first printed common law text, as well as one of the earliest books of any sort printed in England. More specialized expository works, such as

Christopher St German's *Doctor and Student* (1530), on the relationship between **common law**, equity, and **ecclesiastical law**, William Stanford's criminal law primer *Les Plees del Coron* (1557), and William Lambard's *Eirenarcha: or the Office of the Justices of Peace* (1581) appeared during the sixteenth century. Other contemporaneous offerings from the London bookseller-printers deal with the jurisdiction of the courts and procedural aspects of particular branches of law, or provide vocational manuals for practitioners, clerks, and students. But the staple law book stock comprised collections of statutes and case-notes or reports ancient and modern, together with abridgments, dictionaries, indices, formularies, and procedural handbooks. This huge mass of miscellaneous learning, organized at best on merely alphabetical or chronological lines, understandably daunted many of the students now flocking to the Elizabethan and early Stuart Inns of Court.

More than seventy editions and translations of Littleton's *Tenures* had appeared by 1628, when Sir Edward **Coke** published the first part of his *Institutes of the Laws of England,* better known as *Coke on Littleton,* a massive commentary with extensively rambling glosses on almost every word of Littleton's text. That so chaotic if erudite a compilation could remain the chief authority on English property law well into the nineteenth century, notwithstanding a thoughtful practitioner's claim that it was 'the confusion of a student', seems no less indicative of the condition of early modern legal literature than of Coke's own stellar professional standing. Yet serious attempts were now underway to 'methodize' or systematize the common law, like other bodies of knowledge, for pedagogical purposes. Henry Finch launched his ambitious project at Gray's Inn some time before 1586, applying Ramist concepts and techniques acquired as a Cambridge undergraduate; his law-French *Nomotechnia* ('Art of the Law') was published in 1613, with an earlier English version appearing posthumously as *Law or a Discourse thereof . . .* (1627). If Finch's treatises never enjoyed the acclaim of Coke's *Institutes* and *Reports,* they nevertheless continued to be copied, epitomized, paraphrased, reprinted, and translated long after his death, being still recommended to law students as late as 1822.

English legal literature further expanded and diversified during the later seventeenth and the eighteenth centuries. Nevertheless analytical treatises on specific branches of substantive law, as distinct from compilations of authorities or guides to procedure, remained a rarity, although the judges Matthew Hale (d. 1676) and Jeffrey Gilbert (d. 1726) both left works of that kind in manuscript, some being published posthumously. The real break-through came with William Blackstone's *Commentaries on the Laws of England* (1765–1769). For Blackstone's widely-acknowledged success in producing an accessible, accurate, coherent, and comprehensive overview of English law encouraged others to attempt more exhaustive accounts of specific topics which he had treated only in passing. Thus William Jones introduced his pioneering *Essay on the Law of Bailments* (1781) by observing that 'our excellent Blackstone ... comprised the whole discussion [of bailments] in three paragraphs, which, without affecting the merit of his incomparable work, we may safely pronounce the least satisfactory part of it'. Charles Fearne similarly deprecated the 'confined' or 'thrown together' manner in which the abstruse topics of his *Essay on the Learning of Contingent Remainders and Executory Devises* (1772) had been previously treated. His own well-ordered text, 'disposing the most material point of learning on this subject into one connected view' attracted sufficient professional readers for its initial 105 pages to expand into two volumes by the time a fourth edition was issued in the 1790s.   WILLIAM PREST

AWB Simpson, 'The Rise and Fall of the Legal Treatise: Legal Principles and the Forms of Legal Literature' (1981) 48 *University of Chicago Law Review*, 632–679

JH Baker, *An Introduction to English Legal History* (London: Lexis Nexis, 4th edn, 2002), ch 11

legislation   Legislation consists of written rules of law which are authoritatively ratified; it is an ancient form of law and examples are found in early Sumeria. In the modern state, legislation is commonly enacted or authorized by the **Parliament**, and takes precedence over conflicting rules or principles developed by the **courts**, but not over the written constitution of the state nor, in some cases, certain of its international legal obligations.

In the UK, statutes enacted by the UK Parliament are, in constitutional theory, the supreme source of domestic law. A principal classification is between primary legislation (such statutes) and secondary or delegated legislation (legal rules made by others on authority granted under a statute passed by Parliament, for example regulations made by a government minister under statutory authority). Virtually all delegated legislation is considered by Parliament; it cannot be amended by Parliament, but much of it may be annulled (although this is rare) and some requires formal parliamentary approval.

Both primary and secondary legislation may be authoritatively interpreted by the courts. UK courts cannot hold primary legislation to be legally incompetent, although they may be required to prefer EU law to conflicting domestic legislation, and certain courts have the statutory capacity to declare primary legislation to be incompatible with the **European Convention on Human Rights**. UK courts can, however, declare secondary legislation to be unlawful on the ground that it has been made in excess of the powers to make such legislation granted by primary legislation.

In the UK, government-promoted primary legislation is almost invariably drafted centrally by government lawyers who specialize in drafting, on instructions of the relevant government department. This institutional model is considered to facilitate consistency in drafting and has been adopted in many **Commonwealth** countries; in other states primary legislation is commonly drafted by lawyers within the promoting government department. The UK follows this latter decentralized institutional model in drafting secondary legislation made by government; it is usually drafted by lawyers within the relevant department.

A common criticism of legislation, in the UK and elsewhere, is that it is drafted in complex, often technical and sometimes archaic, language; and this makes it difficult to understand. At one level such criticism in unduly severe; in terms of comprehension, the language and structure of modern legislation compares favourably with much drafting of commercial legal documents. While by no means entirely unfounded, the criticism sometimes also fails to appreciate sufficiently the distinctive nature of legislation and the contexts in which it exists. First, as society becomes more complex, the legislation regulating it must also often be more complex. Secondly, as legislation regulates rights and duties it is important that the scope of that regulation is precisely defined. In achieving that precision, the drafter may have to resort to more complex language than would be required for more general description. Thirdly, legislation is commonly placed under greater stress than most texts. Those affected by legislation will seek to interpret in a manner which best serves their interests, even if that leads to a strained interpretation; this similarly tends towards more complex legislative language. Finally, governments are sometimes reluctant to cede much discretion to the courts to give authoritative interpretation to legislation it has promoted, and this also leads to the adoption of more complex language.

Certainly, judicial interpretation is a significant aspect of legislation as a source of law. In the

UK, interpretation of legislation is to some extent regulated by statute, although those statutory provisions are themselves susceptible to judicial interpretation. So, for example, the Human Rights Act 1998, section 3, requires the courts to construe and give effect to domestic legislation as far as possible in a way compatible with rights under the European Convention on Human Rights. Other legislation provides default rules for statutory construction and interpretation (for instance, the Interpretation Act 1978); and usually there are rules within legislation for its interpretation (for example, interpretation sections). Courts may also be constrained in the interpretation of specific legislation by **precedent**.

Beyond that, courts approach statutory interpretation by giving language its natural meaning (unless a technical meaning is evidently intended) within generally accepted grammatical rules, and construing provisions in accordance with their purpose and in the context of the legislation as a whole. In addition, the courts have developed a variety of interpretative presumptions, rebuttable by clear statutory language; an example is the presumption a legislative provision is not intended to have retrospective effect. T ST JOHN BATES

See also: **Acts of Parliament; interpreting legislation; legal rules, types of; parliamentary counsel; parliamentary sovereignty**

legislative and general committees Formerly, **House of Commons** procedure distinguished clearly between 'select' and 'standing' committees. Standing committees debated and **select committees** investigated. The creation of Public Bill Committees in 2006 eroded this distinction (responding to dissatisfaction with purely adversarial scrutiny of **legislation**) and the generic term 'general committee' replaced 'standing committee'.

General committees still proceed mostly by debate rather than inquiry; and they are principally involved in examination of legislation. Membership (appointed by the Committee of Selection) is divided between the parties in proportion to strengths in the House. There are four main groups.

Public Bill Committees undertake the committee stage of a particular public Bill, ceasing to exist thereafter. They generally have between eighteen and thirty members. Government public Bills are, currently, almost invariably subject to a programme motion, which specifies a date by which the committee must report. Within this limit the committee decides the number and timing of its sittings

and the parts of the bill considered at each. A Public Bill Committee has power to take evidence (like a select committee), and will determine at how many, if any, sittings evidence will be taken. At other sittings, it considers each clause of and schedule to the Bill. Amendments may be proposed, debated, withdrawn, negatived, or made, and it must decide if each separate clause or schedule is to be included in the Bill. New clauses and schedules may be added. Proceedings are overseen by the chairman, who has the power of 'selection', enabling them to decide which proposed amendments will be considered and voted on. The majority of amendments made will be proposed by the government.

Delegated Legislation Committees (with around sixteen members—any MP may participate) consider draft or already-made statutory instruments and other items of **delegated legislation** requiring approval, or in respect of which a motion to annul has been tabled. Their debates are generally limited to ninety minutes per instrument. No amendment of the text can be proposed. Debate takes place on a take-note motion: when the instrument has been reported a vote may be taken on it on the floor of the House without further debate.

European Standing Committees (with thirteen members) debate legislative proposals and other matters emanating from institutions of the **European Union**. Matters are referred to them by the European Scrutiny Committee (a select committee), and debated on the basis of a substantive and amendable motion. Debates last up to two-and-a-half hours, which may include up to ninety minutes questioning of a Minister. Once reported, the matter is voted on the floor of the House without debate and is deemed to have cleared the 'scrutiny reserve', freeing Ministers to vote upon it in the legislative bodies of the EU.

Grand Committees (in the Commons) comprise all MPs from constituencies in, respectively, Northern Ireland, Scotland, and Wales. They debate matters relating to those countries referred to them by the House.

The Lords does not use debate committees. Public Bills may be considered in a grand committee, to which all Members of the House automatically belong. PAUL EVANS

W McKay (ed), *Erskine May's Treatise on The Law, Privileges, Proceedings and Usage of Parliament* (London: Lexis Nexis Butterworth, 23rd edn, 2004)

See also: **legislative processes**

legislative drafting *see* **drafting of legislation**

legislative processes In the UK Parliament, there are two legislative processes—primary and secondary.

Proposals for primary legislation are introduced in either the **House of Commons** or the **House of Lords** as Bills. A public Bill introduced by a Minister is a government Bill: otherwise it is a private member's Bill. Public Bills, when enacted, are general law. Private Bills propose particular powers for legal individuals and are introduced by a 'promoter'.

The first reading of a public Bill is formal: there is no debate. The second reading debate is in plenary and invites consent to the principles of the Bill, not its detailed provisions. No amendment to the text can be made at this stage. In current practice, government Bills are almost invariably subject, in the House of Commons, to a programme motion which, following second reading, provides for the timetabling of all subsequent stages in that House. If given a second reading, the Bill goes to committee, where most detailed scrutiny takes place. This stage may be on the floor of the House (usual in the Lords, rare in the Commons) or in some other committee, or may be split between both. In committee, amendments may be proposed to any part of the text, and new clauses or schedules may be added. The process may take a few minutes or many sittings.

The Bill is reported back to the House, which then reconsiders it—the 'report stage'. Further amendments to the text may be made, though this stage is more concentrated than committee, and there is no requirement as in committee to adopt separately each clause or schedule. At third reading the House decides whether to accept the Bill in its revised form. If passed, it is sent to the other House, where it must pass through all these stages again. If the second House alters it, the two Houses seek to agree a single text through an exchange of messages. If consensus is achieved, it is sent for the royal assent and becomes an Act of Parliament. If not finalized by the end of the session in which it was introduced, a Bill is lost. However, mechanisms exist for carrying-over a Bill from one session to the next in the House of introduction.

There are complex rules relating to provisions in a Bill relating to taxation or public expenditure, which must be authorized by 'money' or 'ways and means' resolutions. Only the Commons may do this (its 'financial privilege').

Exceptions: The **Parliament Acts** create a mechanism by which, under certain conditions, the Commons alone can send a Bill for the royal assent if the Lords refuse to pass it in two successive sessions.

Section 1 of the Act defines a category of 'money bills', which the Lords cannot amend or delay.

Private Bills follow a procedure notionally similar to that described above, though largely invisibly. If a private Bill is opposed by those potentially adversely affected, the promoter must defend the Bill before a committee, which will hear those who petitioned against it.
PAUL EVANS

W McKay (ed), *Erskine May's Treatise on The Law, Privileges, Proceedings and Usage of Parliament* (London: Lexis Nexis Butterworths, 23rd edn, 2004)
P Evans, *Handbook of House of Commons Procedure* (London: Dod's Parliamentary Communications, 6th edn, 2007)

See also: **acts of parliament**

Leisure Accidents *see* **tort system**

lesbian Lesbians have been largely invisible in all UK jurisdictions. At the same time, socially, lesbians have been viewed with suspicion as falling outside the control of men. In contrast to **homosexual** acts between men, which were illegal between 1885 and 1967, lesbian sex has never been a criminal offence—the sole attempt to outlaw it failed in 1921—although it was grounds for dismissal from the armed forces until 2000. In earlier centuries a number of 'female husbands' were prosecuted for fraud. With the rise of psychological theories of sexual development, lesbianism came to be seen as a perversion, leading to the successful **prosecution** for **obscenity** of Radclyffe Hall's novel, *The Well of Loneliness* in 1928. A similar attitude denied lesbian mothers custody of their children for many years, and even today lesbians prosecuted for indecent assault tend to receive heavier sentences than heterosexual men. The current trend is for the law to treat lesbians and gay men as a group with identical interest notwithstanding the different social and material circumstances of **women** and men. There is a growing acceptance in law that discrimination on grounds of sexuality is no longer acceptable, demonstrated, for example, in the **Civil Partnership** Act 2004 which gives registered same-sex couples essentially the same rights and responsibilities as spouses. Although gender-neutral in its terms, in its first year the Act attracted twice as many male couples as female, suggesting that the legal regulation of lesbians' relationships is of less interest—or perceived to be of less benefit—than gay men's.
ROSEMARY AUCHMUTY

lex mercatoria *see* **international dispute settlement**

liability insurance Like other forms of insurance, liability insurance is a way of protecting oneself financially against the **risk** of some adverse event taking place. Specifically, it confers protection from the risk of being held legally liable to pay **damages** to some third party (neither the insurer nor the insured himself)—hence the alternative name, 'third party insurance'. Insurance is commonly carried against potential civil liability in **tort law**. Indeed, it is required by law before undertaking certain risky activities.

Insuring against liability was at one time thought to be very dubious, so much so that it was deemed 'contrary to **public policy**' and legally invalid. To the extent that civil liability is intended to punish the defendant, this was obvious enough—allowing insurance against punishment removes its sting, since the insurer and not the defendant will bear the cost. Such attitudes seem to have changed by the end of the nineteenth century, however, when liability insurance became readily available in England. This reflected a shift in the law's perceived reason for imposing civil liability: away from punishing defendants, and towards the **compensation** of claimants (which liability insurance, as will be seen, positively facilitates). However, even today one may not insure against the risk of being held guilty of a crime—it would be against public policy for insurance to blunt the penalty handed down upon conviction. And with regard to tort liability insurance, insurers recognize that there is a problem of 'moral hazard'—that is to say, someone insured against liability will have reduced incentives to avoid such liability. With regard to the tort of **negligence** in particular, the fear is that those insured will be less careful than those who would have to pay the damages themselves. To a limited extent, insurers try to counteract this tendency with devices such as variable premiums based on the risk rating of the insured (such as the driver's 'no claims bonus').

As well as undermining tort law's deterrent effects, it has been argued that insurance contradicts the principle of 'corrective justice', that when one person damages another by his wrong, he ought to compensate the other (or the loss should be shifted from the victim to the wrongdoer). The concern is that when the defendant is insured, the loss is shifted not to him, but to the insurer (and ultimately to all payers of insurance premiums). Taken together, the critique is that insurance undermines individual **responsibility**. And yet liability insurance has been current in England for over a century, and seems to be universally accepted in legal systems around the world (a notable exception at one time was the USSR, which interestingly treated liability insurance as inconsistent with socialist values; post 1990 Russia has fallen into line with the West). Why the dramatic, and pervasive, reversal of legal attitudes?

While insuring against liability might appear to be for the benefit of the person paying the premium (the potential defendant), in reality it benefits the potential victims of his torts equally, if not more. If insurance were not allowed, then in most cases of serious injury caused by a tort, it is unlikely that the victim/claimant would receive much or perhaps any of the damages awarded to him. Simply, large lumps sums of damages are beyond the means of most defendants. English law therefore requires that drivers must have insurance against their liability to fellow road users, and employers to their employees, for example. The relevant **legislation** is clearly intended to protect the financial position of potential victims, and not potential tortfeasors. Hence one of the principal concerns of the Road Traffic Act is to make sure that issues between the insurer and tortfeasor insured, concerning the validity of the liability insurance policy, do not defeat the victim's claim for damages.

About 90 per cent of tort claims are brought against insured defendants: in practice, there is little point in bringing a claim against an uninsured individual (although large public and commercial organizations may 'self insure'—pay the damages themselves). The insurer takes over the defence of such claims. Therefore, insurers' practice has a decisive impact on tort law in action—not least because the vast majority of claims are settled before coming anywhere near a **court**, or indeed any qualified legal advisor. The decisions about which cases are litigated though the court system will typically be driven by the insurance industry's desire to have a point settled (or indeed, changed), rather than by the interests of the individual defendant.

Some have argued that because tort defendants are in practice always insured (or if not, 'deep pocketed'), the courts have consistently tended to develop tort law in a way favourable to claimants. By expanding liability, accident victims can be compensated, without bankrupting individual defendants. A possible example might be the imposition of a very stringent, objective standard of care in motor negligence cases. Some **judges** (especially Lord **Denning**) have candidly admitted moving the law in this direction. However, the influence is rarely acknowledged openly, and some have argued that it does not exist at all. Undoubtedly, it remains true that whether an accident victim can obtain compensation through the liability insurance 'system' depends upon him showing that he was injured through the fault of another. This requirement makes no sense from the vantage point of pure compensation, which would consider only the victim's needs (and not how the injuries came about).

To sum up, liability insurance has made tort better at compensating accident victims. Indeed, without it, tort would long since have become obsolete given that individuals could not afford to pay personally. But the compensation 'system' that results is an odd one, determined by defendants' fault, not victims' needs. Moreover, it seems to undermine core principles of tort law. Therefore there have been calls to replace tort by a state no-fault compensation scheme (as in New Zealand), but there is currently little sign of the political will necessary to bring this momentous change about. Tort and liability insurance are set to continue their uneasy, symbiotic relationship.

JONATHAN MORGAN

See also: **civil liability, theories of; fault-based civil liability**

libel   Libel is the form of civil action for defamation when allegations are published in writing or other permanent form; it may also amount to an offence (**criminal libel**). Since the overwhelming majority of defamation actions are brought against the media, libel has become more important than **slander,** actionable when allegations are published orally. Defamation actions are brought to protect the reputation of a claimant, generally an individual, but sometimes a corporation. But public authorities are not entitled to sue in libel, as that would be inimical to the right to **freedom of expression** about political matters.

The allegations must be defamatory, not merely abusive; that means they must tend to bring the claimant into hatred, ridicule, or contempt, or to lower him in the estimation of right-minded members of society. So it would not be defamatory to write that someone has retired from work or has been indisposed for a week. It would not now be regarded as defamatory to allege that the claimant is gay, but it might be if the imputation were coupled with the suggestion that he had misrepresented his sexuality, so implying hypocrisy. The precise meaning of the words is crucial; in practice this is a more important issue than the question whether they are defamatory. The allegations should be considered in their context, and it should be assumed that readers will look at the whole of an article rather than merely glance at a headline or photograph.

The claimant must show that reasonable people would understand the allegations to refer to him or her. It has been regarded as immaterial whether they were intentional or negligent. So a writer may be liable for disparaging remarks about a character in a novel if readers believe that they refer to a real person of whose existence the writer was unaware. But this strict liability may now be regarded as incompatible with the right to freedom of expression. Another controversial aspect of libel law is the presumption of falsity: it is for the defendant to show the allegations are true. Truth is almost always a complete defence to a libel action. But it may be difficult for the writer to prove the truth of a factual allegation where, for instance, key witnesses have disappeared.

If the allegations express an opinion, the publisher can argue that they amount to fair comment on a matter of public interest. The comment must be honest, but need not be objectively reasonable, so the views of a prejudiced person can be freely expressed. It may not always be easy to decide whether statements are allegations of fact or the expression of an opinion. To write simply that a politician is 'corrupt' is an allegation of fact, but if a politician is described as 'corrupt' because he or she used public money to entertain friends, that is a comment on the stated facts. The writer must prove the truth of the facts on which his comment was based.

Another important defence is privilege. On occasions when freedom of expression is particularly important, the makers of defamatory allegations enjoy *absolute privilege* from defamation actions. The best known of these immunities is that conferred by the Bill of Rights 1689 on Members of Parliament in respect of allegations made during parliamentary proceedings. Reports of these proceedings in **Hansard**, statements made in the course of legal proceedings, and accurate reports of legal proceedings also enjoy absolute privilege. References to prospective employers and the reports of many types of public meeting enjoy *qualified privilege*, a defence which, in contrast to absolute privilege, may be defeated if the claimant proves express malice: that the allegations were made knowing that they were untrue, out of spite or for other improper motive.

In *Reynolds v Times Newspapers* (2001) the House of Lords extended the qualified privilege defence to cover the publication of untrue defamatory allegations which the media believe on good grounds to be accurate, provided they are incorporated in a story of public interest and have been properly investigated. But *Reynolds* privilege does not go as far as the constitutional privilege recognized under the First Amendment in the USA: see **freedom of expression.** The position of the media in libel actions has also improved as a result of a reform in the Defamation Act 1996, which provides for the publication of an apology and correction, and the payment of reduced compensation, when allegations are published inadvertently.

The majority of libel actions have been tried by a jury, rather than judge alone. Juries have often awarded large sums of money to successful claimants, perhaps because they consider that celebrities—typical libel claimants—can only be compensated lavishly. Moreover, owing to the presumption of damages in libel (as opposed to slander) the claimant does not have to show that he or she suffered any loss as a result of the publication but may be awarded a significant sum to vindicate reputation as well as for injured feelings. The courts have tried to impose limits on large awards, but they are still made from time-to-time. Procedural reforms have recently encouraged judges to determine libel actions without a jury where the case does not present serious issues; the judge may then make a low maximum award, trivial compared with the sums given by juries.

The libel actions brought by celebrities such as Elton John, Jeffrey Archer, and Mohamed Fayed have brought enormous entertainment to the public. But there is a dark side to this area of law; it has often been used by claimants, notably Robert Maxwell, to protect a reputation they did not deserve and to deter freedom of expression. The costs of bringing or defending an action are high. It is widely regarded as an unsatisfactory area of law which would benefit from further reform to allow the media more freedom to publish stories of public interest, free from the fear of a libel action, while enabling, if possible, deserving claimants to protect their reputation.

ERIC BARENDT

E Barendt, L Lustgarten, K Norrie, and H Stephenson, *Libel Law and the Media: the Chilling Effect* (Oxford: Oxford University Press, 1997)

D Hooper, *Reputations under Fire* (London: Little Brown & Co, 2000)

libel trials *see Irving v Penguin Books; McDonald's Corporation v Steel & Morris*

liberal democracy **Democracy** is a form of self-government that embodies and secures the political equality of citizens. When all citizens have the vote and are eligible to stand for public office there is the greatest prospect that laws will be enacted, and policies adopted, that meet with popular approval and consent. Self-government also requires **freedom of speech**, enabling people to express their political opinions and seek to persuade others to support their favoured causes. The freedom to participate in government and politics is not, however, the only feature of a decent society, which ought to serve a wide range of fundamental human interests. Political equality does not guarantee **justice**, unless one thinks that justice is simply whatever the majority approves or desires. A liberal believes that such fundamental rights as those of speech, conscience, association, and **privacy** are necessary to human well-being: they have a special value beyond any contribution they make to democratic decision-making. Certain basic individual rights should therefore be protected from political interference. If democracy means government by a majority of citizens, or a majority of elected representatives on their behalf, there is always the danger that individual freedom will be sacrificed to the popular political ends of the moment, and that the legitimate interests of minorities will be unfairly overridden.

In his famous work, *Democracy in America* (two volumes: 1835 and 1840), Alexis de Tocqueville warned that the principle of popular sovereignty had given rise in the North American republics to a 'tyranny of the majority', which threatened personal freedom. His fears about democracy were echoed by John Stuart Mill, who sought to preserve an inviolable sphere of individual freedom or independence, immune from legal interference or even the moral coercion of public opinion. The state could properly restrict a person's activities only when they threatened harm to others; over matters concerning only his own welfare, he was his own 'sovereign' (*On Liberty*, 1859). Liberalism celebrates the right of the individual to live according to his or her own ideas about the pursuits and purposes that make life valuable, even when the majority disapproves.

In a liberal democracy, political power is moderated by the **rule of law**: the individual is subject to coercion only in accordance with law, previously announced and fairly administered by independent and impartial judges. Government officials, accordingly, must observe legal limits on their powers even when they are seeking to give effect to the popular will, or the will of a parliamentary majority. In many countries, basic freedoms (such as freedoms of speech and conscience) are secured by a written constitution binding on all governmental institutions, including the legislature. In the **United Kingdom**, **parliamentary sovereignty** is tempered by a constitutional tradition of respect for individual freedom. The courts are not empowered to reject **Acts of Parliament** for breach of individual rights or fundamental law, but they are expected to interpret them, as far as possible, on the assumption that Members of Parliament intended the basic rights of the individual to be preserved.

TREVOR ALLAN

J S Mill, *On Liberty* (various editions; originally published in 1859)

FA Hayek, *The Constitution of Liberty* (London: Routledge & Kegan Paul, 1960)

liberal education *see* **legal education and liberal education**

liberal multiculturalism The term 'multiculturalism' is sometimes used synonymously with 'cultural diversity', as a term to characterize a society with a variety of cultures, **religions**, and ways of life. However, when it comes to law and politics, it normally refers to a doctrine, set of policies, or social ideal which prescribes how to accommodate this variety. In particular, multiculturalism is the thought that it is only through some form of legal and political **recognition**, expressed in rights granted to particular groups, that cultural **minorities** can be treated justly. This has become one of the most fertile and contentious areas in legal and political theory.

Now there are ways of granting rights to groups that are plainly incompatible with liberalism, eg the so-called 'millet system' of the Ottoman Empire, which granted a form of **self-government** to minority Christian and Jewish **communities**, but without permitting freedoms of speech, thought, and conscience, so that members of those groups could not question or renounce the tenets of their faith. Advocates of liberal multiculturalism argue that certain group rights are not only compatible with liberal political principles but may be required by them. At the core of this argument, which has been advanced by Will Kymlicka, Charles Taylor, and others, is the claim that cultural minorities may suffer an unjustifiable disadvantage in the absence of such rights. To gain a sense of what this claim involve, let us briefly note five of the more celebrated and notorious types of claim.

First, groups sometimes claim exemptions from laws that otherwise, they argue, would hinder their freedom of religion. For instance, in the United Kingdom, Sikhs successfully gained an exemption from laws governing the wearing of crash helmets, in order to accommodate the turbans required by their religion, and, in Canada, this has famously extended to an exemption from the traditional Stetson in the uniform of the Royal Canadian Mounted Police. Jews and Muslims in many states have won exemption from Sunday-closing **legislation** affecting shops and other businesses. Secondly, where exemption rights permit members of a designated group not to fulfil requirements obligatory to others, assistance rights are claimed in order to support activities that the majority, or otherwise privileged group, can do unimpeded. The most famous examples of this sort of right are embodied in affirmative action programmes and quotas that are implemented in a range of private and public organizations, particularly affecting the spheres of employment and education. But they also include language rights, including multilingual ballot papers and legal proceedings, bilingual or minority language educational programmes, and a bi- or multilingual civil service or health service. The third category of claims is for rights to the **representation** of a group within the political processes of a state, for example, through consociational power-sharing in the executive or through guaranteed seats in a legislature. The fourth category is probably the most incendiary of cultural claims, for self-government. Groups seek to establish a political unit in which they are dominant, and demand that borders should be drawn and political powers reconfigured in order to establish this. This may take the form of a demand for a sovereign state, for a federal or confederal relationship, or for enhanced rights within such a relationship. Fifth, there is the claim for the recognition or enforcement of a traditional legal code, again in the name of freedom of worship. Cultural groups seek to have their members bound by traditional communal laws, at least with respect to some areas of life, rather than the general laws of the political community. For examples, some Muslims have sought legal standing for *sharia* law in family law and in civil law. Unsurprisingly, family law, and particularly **divorce** law, have generated some of the fiercest debates.

On the other side, there are liberals (such as Brian Barry) who vehemently oppose liberal multiculturalism. For this species of liberal, multicultural rights violate fundamental precepts of liberty and **equality**. What is valuable in the liberal multicultural argument is wholly captured by liberal conceptions of non-discrimination and **freedom of association**, rather than by the idea that groups ought to be granted rights: granting rights to groups opens up the possibility of illiberal control of some members on the part of others. For their part, the liberal multiculturalists argue that these rights are justified on the grounds that they eliminate injustice to individuals and that they do not necessarily imply granting to groups worrying levels of power over their own members. How deep the differences run between these two sorts of liberal attitude toward multiculturalism remains a matter of some controversy.

MATTHEW FESTENSTEIN

liberation movements *see* **peoples**

liberty (National Council of Civil Liberties)   Liberty (formerly the National Council of Civil Liberties) is a UK-based organization that campaigns on issues of civil liberties and human rights. It was founded in 1934 by Ronald Kidd, who had become concerned with police incitements to violence during the 1932 hunger marches. More recently, Liberty has been at the forefront of campaigning for, and educating the public on, the Human Rights Act 1998, which came into force in October 2000. Alongside the Human Rights Act, Liberty's current concerns include the 'war on terror', **torture, terrorism, privacy, asylum, equality**, free speech and protest, anti-social behaviour orders ('**ASBOs**'), and the rights of young people.

Liberty runs a **human rights** advice line for members of the public. It also operates 'second-tier' advice lines providing specialist advice on human rights law to lawyers and non-governmental organizations. The legal team takes on cases that have a likelihood of establishing important human rights principles, and it also intervenes in relevant cases to provide expertise to the courts. Recent cases have addressed bans against peaceful protesting near to the Houses of Parliament, deaths in police custody, the ability of UK courts to hear evidence obtained through torture, the denial of a pension to a **transsexual** woman at age sixty, and a ban on asylum seekers receiving benefits.

Despite its high media profile, Liberty operates with a small number of employed staff, and a large number of volunteers, from modest premises in South London. The staff consists of human rights lawyers, campaigners, parliamentary and media experts, and fund-raisers. Liberty is run largely on public donations and grants from charitable bodies. Membership of Liberty is open to members of the public.

EMILY GRABHAM

liberty, right to   *see* **right to liberty**

licences relating to land   In 1673, it was said of a licence relating to the use of land that it 'passes no interest nor alters or transfers property in anything, but merely makes an action lawful, without which it would have been unlawful'. This statement still captures the essence of licences: they are personal rights based on the permission of another landowner.

Two main issues arise. The first is the respective positions of the licensor and the licensee; the second is whether a purchaser of the licensor's land will have to give effect to the licence. In considering this, one must consider the two main types of licence which can arise.

Licences can be gratuitous, as where I give a general permission to the children next door to enter my garden to collect balls knocked over the fence. Such licences can always be revoked, the only question being the amount of time which must be given for the licensee to leave. These licences will never affect a purchaser: if I sell my house, the buyer will not be compelled to extend the same generosity to the neighbours' children as I had done previously.

Where the licence is contractual the position is less clear. An example of a contractual licence is when a person buys a ticket to enter a cinema. Originally the position was that such licences could always be revoked. In one case a person attending Doncaster races, having bought a ticket, was evicted with no more force than was necessary. An action for assault failed because it was always open to the licensor to insist that the licensee vacate the land. Gradually this position changed. It was recognized that whether or not a contractual licence could be revoked depended upon the proper construction of the particular contract; and that some contracts, such as building contracts, would not allow revocation. A striking example of this was when the National Front had contracted to hire a local authority's hall in which to hold a conference. After the political complexion of the council changed, it was sought to renege on the contract and pay damages. The Court of Appeal made an order forcing the council to allow the Front to use the hall.

As between the parties to the contract, then, a contractual licence may be irrevocable. But will such an irrevocable licence be enforceable against a purchaser from the licensee? Originally, the **House of Lords** was emphatic that it could not be. In a series of cases, however, Lord **Denning** sought to establish the contrary position, but this attempt did not survive his retirement. The position is now clear. A contractual licence does not bind a purchaser of the land. So, if I have a season ticket at a football club, and that club is sold, my ticket will not be valid against the new owner. Unless the purchaser chooses to honour it, my only remedy is for damages against the seller of the club.

MARK P THOMPSON

licensing as consumer protection   One method of protecting consumers against traders or the suppliers of professional services is to require that the traders or professionals be licensed before they can lawfully supply in the market. To acquire the licence, the individual must satisfy certain conditions, notably relating to training, competence, 'good character' (or at least the absence of a criminal record) and, in some cases, financial viability. The applications are normally processed by a specialist agency which, in the case of professional services, may be wholly or partly a self-regulatory agency. The licence is renewable on a periodical basis and in cases of serious default may be suspended or revoked.

Although it is a criminal offence to engage, without a licence, in the activity which is subjected to a licensing regime, defining the scope of that unlawful activity is not always easy. Take the giving of legal advice or the supply of health care. Obviously, it would be impossible and inappropriate to prohibit these activities being undertaken by lay persons; and legislation must, therefore, limit the prohibition to the undertaking of more specific tasks, such as preparation of certain legal documents, or engaging in the general activity for financial reward.

Subject to this qualification, all the liberal professions are governed by licensing regimes. The extent to which the supply of services by other professions and traders is so regulated varies enormously across jurisdictions and legal cultures. In Britain the list of regulated businesses includes taxis, gambling establishments, the sale of alcohol for on-premises consumption, pet shops, consumer credit, and residential care homes. Consumer products may also be subjected to licensing regimes, but beyond the familiar example of pharmaceutical products, the technique is not frequently used in this context.

Legally, licensing is sharply to be distinguished from what is generally known as 'certification', a scheme under which service or product providers receive accreditation if they satisfy the prescribed conditions. However, it is not unlawful for uncertified individuals to supply in the market and the system therefore operates as a signal to consumers, rather than as a constraint. Nevertheless the market demand for non-certified services may be so small as to render the activity unprofitable; in that case a certification has *de facto* the same effect as a licensing regime.

In comparison with other regulatory instruments, licensing has significant disadvantages. In the first place, because licensing limits entry to the market, it can inhibit technological development and the system can be exploited by existing licence-holders to generate increased profits, particularly if the agency granting the licenses is a self-regulatory agency. Secondly, it is obviously very costly for an agency to scrutinize the quality of all those intending to supply in the market, as well as to police the marketplace to ensure that unlicensed supply does not take place. The cheaper alternative is to impose no *ex ante* (prior) control but to subject supply to quality standards, with sample monitoring and enforcement only *ex post*.

There are, nevertheless, benefits to be weighed against these disadvantages. The *ex post* (retrospective) approach operates on a deterrence basis, significantly different from prevention, which is the basis of licensing. A desire to prevent detrimental outcomes may, therefore, help to explain why some activities, which can potentially cause large amounts of harm to consumers, are governed by licensing regimes. A second advantage is to be found in enforcement. The suspension or loss of the ability lawfully to supply in the market is a severe sanction which might be more effective in inducing compliance with quality and safety standards than the imposition of a financial penalty, the typical consequence of non-compliance in ex-post regimes. However, by means of so-called 'negative licensing' it is possible to combine the licensing sanction with an *ex post* regime: *ex ante* licensing may not be required, but those found guilty of particularly serious defaults on service standards may be deprived of the ability lawfully to continue to supply the market in the future. In Britain, this sanction can be imposed on defaulting estate agents.

A final small, but not insignificant, feature of licensing regimes should be noted. The exaction of a licensing fee means that it is possible to internalize to an industry the administrative costs of regulating it. On the other hand, it is not unknown for the level of fees to exceed those costs, thus generating surplus revenue for governments. The experience of some developing countries shows that this may be a less painful way of securing revenue than more conventional taxation methods.   ANTHONY OGUS

G Williams 'Control by Licensing' [1967] *Current Legal Problems* 81
A Ogus and Q Zhang, 'Licensing East and West' (2005) 25 *International Review of Law and Economics* 124

See also: **regulation**

licensing of intellectual property rights   *see* **commercial exploitation of intellectual property**

licensing of medicines   It was the tragic association of phocomelia in children with thalidomide in 1962 which led to a global appreciation of the need for regulation of medicines on a much firmer scale than ever before. The realization that self-regulation was insufficient culminated in the enactment of the Medicines Act 1968, which provides a framework for the **regulation** and control of all dealings with medicinal products, including manufacture and wholesaling. The key feature of the **legislation** is the system of licensing new medicinal products by reference to considerations of **safety**, quality, and efficacy. The main types of licence which are granted are product licences, manufacturer's licences, and wholesale dealer's licences, for which applications are made to the Licensing Authority, a body consisting of the health and agriculture ministers, which is responsible for the grant, renewal, variation, suspension, and revocation of licences. The Commission on Human Medicines is also established under the Medicines Act to give advice to the Licensing Authority in making its decisions, and the Commission appoints expert groups to advise on safety, quality, and efficacy of medicinal products.

The greatest achievement in EU licensing of medicinal products has been the establishment of two approval systems for marketing authorizations: a centralized system, in which a single marketing authorization valid throughout the Union is granted by the **European Commission**, on advice from the European Agency for the Evaluation of Medicinal Products ('EMEA'), and a decentralized system, based on mutual recognition of marketing authorizations valid only for individual Member States.

RICHARD GOLDBERG

life peers   Life peers hold peerages granted for their lifetime only. When life peers die their peerages become extinct. Life peers are created by the **Crown** and there is no provision for life peers to disclaim their peerages. Life peers may, however, be temporarily disqualified from sitting in the **House of Lords** by reason of bankruptcy or imprisonment, and they may, like other peers, apply for leave of absence from the House, or they may simply cease to attend on account of old age, infirmity, or disinclination.

The modern House of Lords has been dominated by life peers. But until 1958 the only life peers were a strictly limited number created as 'Lords of Appeal in Ordinary' under the Appellate Jurisdiction Act 1876, initially two, but raised by stages to twelve in 1994. When the new **Supreme Court (UK)** is established serving law lords will no longer be members of the House.

The object of the Life Peerages Act 1958 was to increase the working strength of the House, and in particular to provide for those who objected in principle to hereditary peers becoming members of the House. Though initially new hereditary peerages continued to be created alongside life peerages, when the Labour Government of 1964 came to power it was made clear that only life peerages would in future be awarded, a position that prevailed until the 1980s when Mrs Thatcher as **Prime Minister** recommended a small number of hereditary peerages.

The Life Peerages Act provided for women as well as men to become life peers. This brought the first females into the House. The number of new peerages created increased greatly with the advent of life peerages. By 2007 over 1,100 peerages had been created under the 1958 Act, with Mr Blair the most prolific averaging some thirty-five new peerages per year throughout his ten year tenure. Almost 200 women have been created life peers, and of the 605 extant life peers in late 2007, 141 were women.

In 2001 a non-statutory House of Lords Appointments Commission was created, and this took particular responsibility for making non-party nominations to the House. It also took on the role of the former Political Honours Scrutiny Committee. The early work of the Commission was criticized because it seemed to nominate for membership of the House exactly the same sort of people as had previously been given peerages. Public confidence in the integrity of the process by which nominations have been made has weakened. Calls have been made for the Appointments Commission to be re-established on a statutory basis, a step likely to be made in the context of any further reform of the House.

The largest single group of people who have received life peerages have been former MPs. Almost all cabinet ministers take a peerage upon retirement from the Commons, as do many other senior MPs. But life peers have also been drawn from a wide range of professions, as well as from the worlds of business, finance, and academia.

All life peers have been created at the rank of baron, and it seems unlikely that life peers could be created at higher ranks within the peerage.

DONALD SHELL

See also: **hereditary peers**

life, right to   *see* **right to life**

Lilburne, John   Lilburne was born in 1615 and received a grammar school education and apprenticeship as a London cloth merchant. By 1636 he had become involved with the puritans John Bastwick, Henry Burton, and William Prynne. In December 1637 Lilburne was arrested for distributing Bastwick's anti-episcopal *A Letany* and stood trial in **Star Chamber** in early 1638. Lilburne was convicted after refusing to take the oath, and was sentenced to be whipped and pilloried and then imprisoned.

Lilburne was released on 13 November 1640 after Oliver Cromwell's intercession in Parliament. With the coming of civil war, he enlisted as a captain in the Parliamentarian army. By 1644 he had attained the rank of Lieutenant-Colonel; however, his military career ended in 1645 as he refused to subscribe to the Solemn League and Covenant.

Lilburne returned to London, joining with radicals who sought to win constitutional reform from Parliament. He fell out with Bastwick and Prynne, who, in 1645, were instrumental in having him committed to prison for **slander** and printing seditious books. In prison, Lilburne read works of constitutional and legal theory and developed the argument that the **House of Commons**, as the elected representative of the people, was the supreme authority in England above the King and Lords. For Lilburne, the Commons' supremacy was subject to legal and constitutional restraints to prevent tyranny and to ensure the well-being of the people. In legal proceedings, he championed the doctrine of due process as a guarantor of judicial propriety.

This theme would arise in Lilburne's own trials. He was called to the **House of Lords** on 11 June 1646 to answer charges of **libel** and scandal but refused to plead on the basis that the Lords had no jurisdiction over him. The consequence of Lilburne's challenge to the Lords' authority was a long period of imprisonment: first, in Newgate and later in the Tower. Here he wrote works calling for law reform and for the abolition of the prerogative and arbitrary powers of public officials.

In late 1647 and early 1648, whilst released on bail, Lilburne rejoined army and civilian radicals (called 'the Levellers') in calling for a written constitution entitled the 'Agreement of the People' to be the basis for the constitutional settlement of England. As a result of his association with these radicals Lilburne was returned to prison, only to be released on 2 August 1648 by Presbyterians hoping to use him against his old friend Oliver Cromwell.

Lilburne was an opponent of the Republic established after the execution of Charles I in 1649, considering it little more than a military junta, and was arrested for treason in March 1649 for writing a work critical of the new regime. He refused to be silenced, and was tried and acquitted twice for treason, the first time in October 1649 the second time in summer 1653. Despite his acquittal, Cromwell's Council of State refused to release Lilburne, and he was imprisoned in Jersey and Dover until his death on 28 August 1657.   ELLIOT VERNON

limitation of actions   The rules of limitation are the statutory time limits for bringing civil (non-criminal) legal proceedings. After the limitation period has expired, a claimant can in theory no longer enforce the legal right (it is 'time barred'), although this will only occur in practice if the opponent spots the issue and pleads limitation as a defence. Limitation rules seek to strike a balance between protecting defendants from having to defend stale claims and giving claimants sufficient opportunity to enforce their rights.

Different limitation periods apply to different sorts of claims. So someone suing for **defamation** or under the Human Rights Act 1998 must commence proceedings within one year; actions for **damages** for personal injury must be brought within a three-year period whereas claims for breach of contract or to enforce debts must be made within a six-year period. The period is not arbitrary but reflects the context of the claim. So **judicial review** proceedings to challenge a public authority's decision must be brought within three months, the short period being designed to prevent the review unnecessarily hampering political life. By contrast, the time limit for an action by a landowner to recover land from a trespasser is twelve years, on the basis that a shorter period would make title to land unnecessarily vulnerable and give undue protection to 'squatters' rights'.

'Time starts to run (ie the limitation period begins) on the first date on which the claimant's 'cause of action accrued', meaning the date on which everything had occurred which must occur in order to trigger a right to bring that particular claim. For example, a cause of action for negligence requires not just negligent conduct, but also that this negligence caused the claimant damage. Negligent conduct and damage typically occur at much the same time. But imagine that a worker is wrongfully exposed to **asbestos** fibres; his lungs may suffer 'latent', undetectable changes some years before symptoms of an asbestos-related condition occur, which may in turn not be diagnosed as asbestos-related until later still. When does legally relevant 'damage' occur, starting the limitation clock ticking?

The asbestosis example shows that simple limitation periods alone can be unjust. The worker may not be able to discover the illness and its link to the employment until the principal limitation period (three years from the date damage occurs, in the case of personal injury claims) has expired. This is why— at least in relation to claims of which damage is an essential element—legislation creates a secondary limitation period, which does not commence until the date on which the claimant ought reasonably to have discovered various facts (such as the occurrence of damage), knowledge of which would have made it reasonable to commence proceedings (even if this date is later than when the damage occurs). Such 'discoverability' provisions are problematic, particularly because they also state that 'knowledge that any acts or omissions did, or did not, as a matter of law, involve negligence is irrelevant'. This causes difficulty, for example, in claims against solicitors for negligent legal advice. Moreover, judges have no discretion (other than in personal injury litigation) to allow claims outside the limitation period.

Special rules prevent time running against minors (so that the limitation period does not begin until the age of majority); while in cases of fraud or deliberate concealment by defendants of facts relevant to the cause of action, time does not start to run until the claimant discovered or ought reasonably to have discovered the truth. JANET O'SULLIVAN

limited liability Limited liability refers to a key advantage of operating a business through a registered **company**, that is, the liability of the shareholders is limited to the amount they have agreed to pay for their shares. As a result the personal assets of the shareholders are not at **risk** beyond what they choose to invest in the company.

Corporate personality and limited liability are intricately related. The creation of a corporation prior to the registered company meant that simply by being a legal **person** from the shareholders, the debts of the company belonged to the company not the shareholders. The Joint Stock Companies Act 1844 provided for incorporation but held shareholders liable for the company's debts because of a concern that widespread avoidance of liability was immoral. It was not until the Limited Liability Act 1855 that 'limited liability' was provided. Thus, whenever anyone deals with a limited company in the UK they are met with the warning 'Ltd' or 'PLC' attached to the company's name to signify that the shareholders of this company have limited liability. In other words they are not liable for the debts of the company—so be careful.

The impact of the registered company with limited liability is said to have facilitated the second industrial revolution in late nineteenth-century Britain. Limited liability obviously encourages investment as the shareholder's risk is minimized. This in turn facilitated the development of large scale **stock exchanges**. It also encourages risk taking on the part of management who know that the shareholders will not lose everything. Companies have also been allowed by the judiciary in the UK to form other companies, in effect allows a company itself to achieve limited liability by being a shareholder. As a result,

group structures where one company (referred to as the parent company) forms a number of other companies through which it runs its business (referred to as subsidiary companies) are a common way of enhancing the limitation of liability in running a business. Creditors have also been forced to monitor and protect against risk more effectively than in an unlimited liability world. However, not all creditors can mitigate their risk when dealing with a limited liability company. Those physically injured or killed by a subsidiary company's activities cannot easily protect themselves from the effects of limited liability when seeking redress. In 1984, a subsidiary of the US company, Union Carbide (now owned by Dow Chemical Company), was responsible for possibly the world's worst corporate disaster when approx 18,000 people died from the effects of 40 tonnes of poisonous gas released in the city of Bhopal, India. While Union Carbide and Dow Chemicals have been unable to shake off moral **responsibility** for the disaster, the fact that they operated in Bhopal through a subsidiary company with limited liability meant that they could and can largely avoid any legal **responsibility** for the disaster. ALAN DIGNAM

H Hansmann and R Kraakman, 'Toward Unlimited Shareholder Liability for Corporate Torts' (1991) 100 *Yale Law Journal* 1879

See also: **corporate criminal liability**

limited liability partnerships Limited liability partnerships were introduced by the Limited Liability Partnerships Act 2000 which was passed following extensive lobbying by the accounting industry. Although this type of entity is called a **partnership** it bears little resemblance to partnerships described above. A **limited liability** partnership ('LLP') is a separate legal **person**, a body corporate, with unlimited capacity to engage in any endeavour (section 1(2) and (3) of the Limited Liability Partnerships Act 2000). In order to form an LLP, *two* or more persons must register the LLP with the Companies Registrar. The owners of the LLP are not partners, rather members of the LLP. The members are not liable for the debts of the LLP, they are only liable for their agreed contribution. Accordingly, this business form is more akin to a **company** than a partnership. Indeed, several sections of the Companies Acts 1985 and 2006 apply to LLPs, for example, the provisions requiring the filing of accounts with Companies House (see section 3 of the Limited Liability Partnerships Regulations 2001). The Act states that the law relating to partnerships does not apply to LLPs unless specifically stated otherwise by the Act (section 1(5) of the Limited Liability Partnership Act 2000). However, there are some aspects of the LLP which resemble a partnership. Most importantly from the perspective of anyone thinking about using the LLP form, it is treated as a partnership for tax purposes. One might ask why anyone would choose to use the partnership form instead of an LLP. Perhaps, the most important disadvantage of the LLP is the requirement to publicly disclose certain information about the LLP such as accounting information that would not be made publicly available if the traditional partnership form is used.

DAVID KERSHAW

linguistic minorities   *see* **minorities**

liquidator   When a **company** enters liquidation (or **winding up** as it is often called), a person who is known as a liquidator must be appointed to wind up its affairs. The liquidator will be appointed by the members of the company if the company is entering liquidation voluntarily, whereas if a **court** orders the liquidation of a company, the official receiver (an office provided for under statute and usually occupied by former civil servants) will become the liquidator initially, and he or she might be replaced as liquidator by a private practitioner if the creditors and members so determine at requisitioned meetings.

Most liquidators are practising accountants, who must be qualified insolvency practitioners. When a liquidator is appointed, the powers of the **directors** of the company cease, and the liquidator takes over the management of the company's affairs. A liquidator acts as the **agent** of the company and is empowered to do all that is necessary to wind up the company's affairs. This will involve ascertaining what assets the company has, collecting and preserving them, selling the assets for the best price possible, and then distributing the proceeds to the creditors who have established that they are owed money by the company. If the company is solvent, that is, it can pay its debts, the funds which remain after the payment of creditors will be distributed amongst the members, according to the constitution of the company. Importantly, liquidators are duty bound to investigate the company's affairs and, where the company is insolvent, ascertain the reasons for the company's collapse and whether anyone involved with the company acted improperly.

Liquidators are subject to strict duties in the carrying out of their functions. They are to act impartially at all times and to ensure that they do not place themselves in a position where their interests conflict with the interests of the creditors and members of the company, for whom the liquidator is to act. They are not to demonstrate bias or to benefit from their role except for receiving a fair amount of remuneration. In discharging their functions, liquidators are expected to exercise professional skill and a high standard of care and diligence.

While there are alternative methods provided in **legislation** for determining the remuneration of a liquidator, the practice is—and favoured by the courts—to fix it on a percentage basis calculated upon the value of the assets sold and distributed.

Creditors or members of the company may seek to have a liquidator removed from office at a meeting convened for that purpose, or they are able to apply to the court for a removal order, if they can establish that there is sufficient cause. Applications may also be made to the courts for a review of decisions of the liquidator.

The final act of a liquidator is to procure the dissolution of the company, effectively its death.

ANDREW KEAY

A Keay, *McPherson's Law of Company Liquidation* (London: Sweet & Maxwell, 2001)

P Loose and M Griffiths, *Loose on Liquidators* (Bristol: Jordans, 5th edn, 2005)

See also: **distribution of assets; insolvency, corporate; winding up**

listed companies   *see* **prospectus; public offer**

listing   A public company may decide to list its **securities** on a formal securities exchange to raise capital from the public. An important benefit of listing on a securities exchange is that it increases liquidity of the securities, enabling investors to convert their shares into cash easily and efficiently. Another benefit of listing is that it provides access to currently quoted prices for securities. When a company becomes listed on a securities exchange or bourse (such as, for example, the London Stock Exchange, the NYSE Euronext, Nasdaq, Deutsche Börse AG, or the Australian Securities Exchange) its securities will become 'quoted', or admitted to the official list, and can then be traded on the market operated by the exchange. Many securities exchanges throughout the world are today themselves listed **public companies**.

Some exchanges operate a two-tier system which will include a market for mature companies, and a secondary market, with more relaxed listing requirements, for smaller developing companies, including venture capital start-up companies. Many companies that initially list on the secondary market will later convert to listing on the main securities exchange.

Before a company can be admitted to the official list, it must satisfy certain eligibility preconditions. The listing authority may impose requirements concerning, for example, the minimum market capitalization and spread of shares for listing, and the company's governance structure. The listing authority may also oblige the company to prepare a prospectus for any new securities which are to be issued to the public, as a precondition of admission to the official list.

Listing may affect the capital structure of companies. In general, companies possess considerable discretion concerning the terms on which **shares** are issued and the rights attached to shares. Companies also generally have the power to issue different classes of shares. Listing, however, will sometimes constrain this freedom, since the listing rules may provide for minimum voting rights, prohibiting dual class shares and other control enhancing mechanisms.

Certain provisions under the relevant companies legislation will lay down additional rules for listed, or 'quoted', companies. Also, once a company is admitted to the official list, it will be required to comply on a continuing basis with the security exchange's own listing rules. These listing rules create another layer of regulation for public listed companies beyond the basic requirements of the companies legislation. The listing rules often provide for stringent **regulation** on a range of matters including, for example, disclosure of financial information and transactions between the company and related parties. Failure to comply with the listing rules may result in the listing authority suspending, or cancelling, the company's listing.

Many listing authorities have become increasingly involved in **corporate governance** in recent times, particularly after the series of international corporate collapses epitomised by **Enron**. In some jurisdictions, the listing rules establish mandatory corporate governance rules, relating to matters such as the proportion of independent directors on boards and board committees. Other jurisdictions, including the UK, have preferred to avoid a prescriptive approach, adopting instead a principles-based approach to corporate governance. Under the latter style of regulation, listed companies must disclose in their annual reports or accounts whether or not they comply with the listing authority's governance principles, and if not, provide an explanation for that deviation. Although the governance principles are limited in their operation to listed companies, they

will inevitably influence the governance practices of unlisted companies.

Companies may choose to list on more than one securities exchange, in order to raise finance in different capital markets. This practice, known as cross-listing, has been viewed by some commentators as a form of regulatory competition, which would inevitably result in further harmonization of governance practices across different jurisdictions. Nonetheless, the conspicuous trend in favour of cross-listing on US securities exchanges, appears to have been reversed in recent times, following the introduction of more stringent regulation adopted in the wake of Enron and other corporate scandals.

JENNIFER HILL

See also: **stock exchange**

literature and law 'A lawyer without . . . literature is a mechanic, a mere working mason; if he possesses some knowledge of th(is), he may venture to call himself an architect.' With this line from *Guy Mannering*, Sir Walter Scott expressly linked two discourses, subsequently ironized as the 'happy couple' or more soberly characterized as 'self and other': namely, law and literature. Textuality, narrativity, discourse: each of these terms have been adduced by subsequent law-and-*litterateurs* as the reason for law's 'value-added' turn to the 'the literary', the synonymous nature of which point to law's and literature's shared linguistic, or word-oriented basis. In short, *both tell stories*. Biography, as well, may play a role here in this linking of the legal and the literary, especially given how many 'men (*and women*) of letters' either studied law (Robert Louis Stevenson, Henry James, Harper Lee), had some legal training (Charles Dickens), qualified as (Andrew 'Banjo' Patterson of 'Waltzing Matilda' fame) or were practising/professorial lawyers: Wall Street chronicler, Louis Auchincloss; McGill law dean and poet, FR Scott; Scottish medico-legal scholar and mystery writer, Alexander McCall Smith; Australian Indigenous activist/academic and novelist, Larissa Behrendt. Not to mention a phalanx of lawyers writing *about* the law: the UK's John Mortimer (*Rumpole*), the USA's John Jay Osborn (*The Paper Chase*) and Australia's Chris Nyst (*Crook as Rockwood*). With this sort of interdisciplinary crossover, no wonder world literature is so replete with tales of 'crime and punishment' and that **common law** legal judgments bristle with vivid metaphors (Brennan CJ's 'bare bones of the common law' in the Australian *Mabo* decision), memorable phrases (Oliver Wendell **Holmes**' 'clear and present danger' in *Schenk v US* (1919)) and scene-setting narrative techniques (Lord Denning's celebrated opening in *Hinz v Berry* (1970): 'It was bluebell time in Kent.').

As an academic movement—that is, *studying* rather than enacting the law in literature or literature in the law—'Law and Literature' has a distinguished scholarly pedigree, dating back to the nineteenth century, and to jurists who set the terms of debate that are still with us today. Critical of literature's (*mis*)representation of the law is the UK's great codifier, Fitzjames **Stephen**, while in the US, evidence scholar John Henry Wigmore and jurist Benjamin **Cardozo** tout literature's mitigating qualities for law: that is, novel-reading as 'improving' the lawyer, making him or her a better person—and, perforce, lawyer. Literature's 'civilizing mission' for law is clearly in evidence in the book that marks the beginning of the modern movement, James Boyd White's elegant and abiding classic, *The Legal Imagination* (1973). The timing of this text was crucial; for one of its key messages—highlighting the significance of, and the need for explicatory techniques addressing law's formal, literary properties—resonated with a generation of lawyers, judges, and legal academics who witnessed, throughout the 1970s and 1980s, the dramatic move centre-stage of law's *textualism* in the *interpretive* debates over the Constitution in American political life. Assisted by various others, Boyd White put Law and Literature on the map—of, at least, the American legal academy where toeholds were established in several leading universities, and out of which a journal sprung: *Cardozo Studies in Law and Literature* (now simply *Law and Literature*). This movement, however, was not the work solely of legal scholars; literary criticism, as well, played its part in the development of Law and Literature in the US, drawing attention generally to the 'cross-examinations' each field made of the other, and making good on UK literary critic Ian Watt's '50s insight that 'the rise of the novel' was coincident with the origins of modern legality.

A critique of Law and Literature, however, was mounted by Law and Economics jurist, Richard Posner; he questioned the relevance of the movement, arguing that law *in* literature was a mere prop of the *mise-en-scene*, and that literature *in* law was entirely misplaced, out-of-joint with legal judgment. Law and Literature fought back in the form, *inter alia*, of Robin West's spirited defence of the movement. But further developments—largely in the form of contemporary *theory*—had overtaken Posner's critique (and West's defence). For the law-and-*litterateurs* of the late 1980s and 1990s resituated the discipline, embedding it in notions of '**representation**', at once

discursive *and* descriptive, sublating and superseding issues of form and content. In America, avant-garde literary critics analysed, respectively, the panopticism of the **police**, the dynamics of witnessing, and the role of confessions in law and literature. But by now, the real centre of gravity of the Law and Literature movement had shifted to the United Kingdom, where a group of critical legal scholars, based largely at Birkbeck College London, were radically remaking the field, restoring strong, semiotized notions of classical rhetoric and philosophy to the law. Aided and abetted by feminists critics and a legal aesthetics scholar, the Law and Literature movement took, most decidedly, the 'postmodern turn' in Britain, drawing upon notions of the sign, gender difference, the unconscious, and the sublime; and finding outlets in conferences (the British Critical Legal Conference) and journals (*Law & Critique*). This dissemination of Law and Literature extended to Australia where, throughout the 1990s and 2000s, a vibrant Law and Literature Association hosted conferences and special journal issues (eg *Law, Text, Culture*).

An American commentator has recently questioned whether Law and Literature has had its day, promoting 'culture' instead of 'literature' as the new word *du jour*: that is, as *the* 'sign of the times' to come, with *Law, Culture & the Humanities* impresario and editor, Austin Sarat, and the 'Amherst school' of cultural legal studies in the ascendant, as Law and Literature fractures and fragments into explorations of, variously: the Gothic, stalking narratives, Russian curial *causes celebre*, adventure novels, slavery as ownership, show trials, literary and legal obscenity, the racialized 'madwoman in the attic', bushrangers, sexual assault as poetic archetype, Indigenous jurisprudence, children's literature, and monstrous bodies. Alternatively, this diversity—generic, thematic, national, linguistic—can be seen as a sign of the movement's vitality, as a symptom of its continuing significance *for* and its ongoing relevance *to* the law *in* and *as* literature.

WILLIAM MACNEIL

litigants in person   *see* **self-representation**

Liversidge v Anderson **(1942)**   In *Liversidge v Anderson* (1942), the **House of Lords** had to decide the appropriate stance for judges to adopt when reviewing government decisions made on grounds of **national security** during a wartime emergency. In issue was a regulation which permitted the Secretary of State to detain individuals whom he had 'reasonable cause to believe' were security risks. The only protection detainees had was that they could make representations to an ineffectual advisory commit-tee. The court had to decide whether it could require particulars to be given about the grounds for mak-ing a detention order so that the validity of the order could be tested. The majority held it could not despite the fact that the phrase 'reasonable cause' had been substituted for the more subjective sounding 'if sat-isfied that' of the original regulation in order to head off a revolt in Parliament. In the majority's view, if the minister produced an authenticated detention order, the detainee had the onus of establishing that the order was invalid or defective, basically by show-ing that the minister had not acted in good faith. The effect of this ruling was that in the situation of war-time emergency 'reasonable cause to believe' means 'if satisfied that'.

In a lone dissent, Lord **Atkin** went to great lengths to show that a requirement of 'reasonable cause' has only one meaning in both statute and **common law**, namely that judges are entitled to review a deci-sion to ensure that it was in fact made reasonably. His speech, in which he accused his fellow judges of being 'more executive minded than the executive', is widely regarded as setting out the approach which would inform the reasoning of any court today, par-ticularly in an era of **human rights** and constitu-tionalism. However, in national security cases after the Second World War English courts adopted the stance of the majority in *Liversidge*, even when there was no allegation that the nation faced an emergency. And in the first House of Lords decision on national security after 9/11, three years after the enactment of the Human Rights Act 1998, Lord Hoffmann articu-lated a view of the **separation of powers** which again affirmed that stance. The judicial record thus seems uniformly one of extreme deference to the executive on matters of national security, even outside of an emergency context.

One might suppose that this problem arises because judges lose their nerve in the face of execu-tive claims about national security. However, a second problem is that not only do the ordinary courts seem ill-suited to review determinations of national security, but also the kinds of information on which the security services rely is often sensitive, and so cannot be properly tested by a lawyer acting on the advice of a client. Given the secrecy and dupli-city of the secret services and the judicial inability to go beyond their claims about the need to protect their information from scrutiny, the kinds of reasons and explanations for their actions that they are likely to proffer, and with which judges will have to content themselves, will not allow for any genuine testing of their decisions. It might thus appear that dissents,

such as Lord Atkin's, in truth pay only lip-service to the **rule of law** and represent attempts to shore up the judges' sense of their constitutional role in the face of the reality of necessarily uncontrolled executive discretion.

The first problem (loss of judicial nerve) might thus be explained by the second (lack of informa-tion). That is, one might claim that the judicial record of deference is a result not of judicial loss of nerve but of the special character of national secur-ity decisions. *Liversidge* both supports and under-mines that claim and remains relevant to debates in the wake of 9/11 about the rule of law and national security. In this regard, it is important to be aware of a commonly overlooked area of agreement between Lord Atkin and Viscount Maugham, who gave the leading speech for the majority. Viscount Maugham reasoned, from the fact that information and sources would often have to be confidential, that it would be futile to try to impose a general requirement that the Secretary of State justify detention orders to a court. He also said that if an appeal against the Secretary of State's decision 'had been thought proper, it would have been to a special tribunal with power to inquire privately into all the reasons for the Secretary's action, but without any obligation to communicate them to the person detained'.

The area of agreement between Maugham and Atkin is that both judges think it possible that such detentions be reviewed. They differ, however, in that Lord Atkin will go as far as he can to implement review, while Viscount Maugham holds that effect-ive review requires that the legislature establish a special tribunal with authority to inquire into confi-dential material. Once one takes seriously Viscount Maugham's idea, it can be seen to prove the power of Lord Atkin's dissent. If rule-of-law controls are appropriate, but difficult to impose given the struc-ture put in place by legislation, judges should try in so far as they can to impose such controls, and not only to deal with cases of bad faith or the like (as *Liversidge* was), but also to tell the legislature to put its house in order. That judges are only able partial-ly to enforce the rule of law is hardly a reason not to enforce it. Rather, they should go as far as they can, both because that is their duty to the individuals who would otherwise be subject to executive whim and because they should send a message to the legislature about the need for it to cooperate better in maintain-ing the rule of law.

The risk here is that this approach might pro-duce only a thin veneer of legality, rather than the substance of the rule of law. However, this risk is unavoidable in a society genuinely committed to the rule of law, as can be seen in the wake of *A v Secretary of State for the Home Department* (2004), where the majority of the House of Lords, against the historical trend, followed the spirit of Lord Atkin's dissent.   DAVID DYZENHAUS

living wills   *see* **advance directives**

lobbyists   Generally, anyone seeking to influence another is nowadays said to be lobbying. In political life, 'lobby' has changed in Britain from a noun to a verb, following America. The central lobby of the **House of Commons** now occasionally sees ritualized mass public 'lobbying' of MPs, although real lobbyists and their targets are now mainly located in private talks in Whitehall and among journalists. In America, too, the term 'lobbyist' was first applied to paid persuaders meeting federal or state legislators in open lobbies. But for at least fifty years such lobbyists have been involved in the private influencing of political heads (ministers), senior officials, advisers, journalists, and editors—as well as legislators. As government power has grown, the value of lobbying legislators (even powerful American legislators) has declined. In almost powerless chambers such as the Commons, it has been marginal to the work of influencing the government.

Britain has moved steadily, though undramatically, towards US practice since about 1970, developing 'public affairs consultants' (political lobbyists) alongside a much broader 'public relations' industry—itself grown out of the general advertising business. Basic (and lucrative) 'PR' advice, to client firms and organizations able to pay, is that 'good relations' (the chosen name of one successful agency) must be promoted generally and continuously, not only with government and MPs but also firms' customers, users, shareholders, staff—as well as the news media. Sudden 'fire brigade' efforts to offset troubles will not work, nor will *ad hoc*, unprepared demands on government. Good PR is always 'helpful' (informative, cooperative) to its target.

Following this more general PR style, the public affairs consultants claim to offer their (usually commercial) clients expert access to Whitehall officials or even ministers, with access to MPs and House of Lords members (peers) as a side salad. Their claims to expertise in gaining access usually rest on employing ex-ministers, ex-officials, or ex-journalists with presumed knowledge about whom to contact. Such claims, when made by still-young former aides to ministers, for example, are particularly thin. As current ministers and officials cannot, in principle, discuss the government's business with even ex-insiders, this much-vaunted 'access' has severe limitations.

Internationally, lobbyists are readily seen as corrupting the politicians and government officials whom they seek to influence, whether by routine, mostly petty, bribery (gifts, hospitality, trips), or by cash or shares. In America, the politicians' appetite for ever-larger re-election funds is dominant. In Germany, lavish government grants to political parties were expected to obviate secret, possibly corrupt, gifts from business; but some politicians proved to need both. Experience in Italy has been broadly similar.

In Britain, civil servants' instincts (including to protect their personal reputations) are sufficient defence. The less important Commons and Lords fronts are protected by a compulsory public register of all favours received beyond official salary and allowances. This register's trivia receive media attention, helping the public to ignore the secret lobbying of actual decision-makers. But the willing acceptance of a lobbyist's influence is undetectable. No inducement is needed if lobbyists representing established organized **interest groups** can help officials and ministers to clear paths to technical policymaking or regulation. 'Insider group' lobbyists usually enter through open official doors to exchange information (at least on matters of detail within an official policy) and cooperation (which governments need) for influence (which the lobbyists need their clients to see them achieving).

ANTHONY BARKER

local government ombudsman   *see* **ombudsmen**

local government in England and Wales   In England and Wales local government, although centuries old, enjoys no constitutionally protected status. This accounts for the ease and regularity with which it has been reorganized, its functions added to or deleted, and its financial powers amended. Despite these changes some enduring defining characteristics can be identified: local authorities are elected, administrative in nature, and have limited legal and fiscal powers. Local government exists—apart from the practical necessity of delivering and administering local public services—to allow public participation in local affairs and a degree of political pluralism. The possibility, however, that a council may be under different political control to central government has in the past (especially during the 1970s and 1980s) given rise to repeated challenges in the courts to decisions of local authorities.

Local government based upon parishes, boroughs, and **Justices of the Peace** existed for hundreds of years before the idea of democratically elected authorities emerged in the nineteenth century. The Poor Law Amendment Act 1834 created the first elected local bodies—local boards of guardians—but on a considerably restricted franchise. It was followed shortly by the Municipal Corporations Act 1835, which provided for councils elected by burgesses (subject to a property qualification) in the towns. Elected county councils did not follow until the Local Government Act 1888, with elected rural district councils introduced in the Local Government Act 1894.

The changes since then have been not so much to the democratic character of local government as a regular process of adjusting its structures. The most prominent were the reforms of the Local Government Act 1972, establishing a two-tier system of elected counties and districts over much of the country. Much of this was reversed by a further reorganization in 1992–1996 which left most of England and all of Wales with a single tier of elected local authorities. In places these are district, borough, or city councils and in others county councils. In some parts of rural England, however, the two tiers of counties and districts introduced in 1972 survive, with functions divided between them. In its 2006 **White Paper** *Strong and Prosperous Communities*, the government has signalled a preference for unitary authorities by proposals to make it easier for councils to seek this status by agreement. In London a strategic level authority was reintroduced in 2000: the Greater London Authority and the Mayor of London exist alongside elected borough councils (formerly the Greater London Council had existed between 1963 and 1986).

The history of local government is one of a movement from single function local Boards in the nineteenth century towards the multi-functional authorities of today. Local government is now responsible for a range of important services affecting the lives of individuals and the well-being of communities. These include education, social services, libraries, highways, planning, and refuse collection and disposal. In practice, however, the degree of discretion to govern according to local choices is limited by detailed legislation, central direction, and financial constraints. Since the introduction of rate capping in the 1980s the raising of local taxation (currently through the property-based council tax) has been carefully circumscribed, with the threat of central government intervention against spendthrift local authorities. Although local authorities no longer have to market-test their services through compulsory competitive tendering (a process introduced in the 1980s), the legacy has been a more flexible approach, with many local authorities continuing to contract-out delivery of services such as cleaning, refuse collection, and road maintenance. Overall there has been a steady shift since the 1970s towards seeing the role of councils as being to provide the focal point of their communities through coordinating the public, private, and voluntary sectors, rather to exercise direct responsibility and delivering all public services.

Local authorities are statutory corporations, with the legal powers of the corporation vested in the elected members (councillors). Until recently there was a contradiction between the legal form—which made all councillors legally responsible—and the political reality of one-party dominance of most councils. The Local Government Act 2000 addressed this accountability gap by providing for a split of executive and scrutiny functions among elected members. The 2000 Act also introduced the possibility of elected mayors (a development common in many countries but previously unknown in England and Wales). Apart from the high-profile Mayor of London, however, in practice relatively few areas have opted for an elected mayor.

The elected nature of local authorities inevitably introduces party political conflict (although it is still common to find independent councillors). It also creates the possibility of conflict with central government, with each layer claiming their own electoral mandate. From a long-term perspective, however, local democracy appears to be in steady decline due to electoral apathy. Local elections have rarely produced turnouts of more than 40 per cent for decades, unless coinciding with a General Election. But when, during the 1990s, voting dropped to around 10 per cent in some parts of the country the legitimacy of local democracy was seriously called into question. Reforms introduced since 2000, intended to reverse this decline and to stimulate voter interest, have so far failed to make a major impact.

The issues of constitutional subordination to central government and declining democratic legitimacy are linked to the attitude of the courts. No doctrine of judicial deference to local government as an elected layer exists. As 'creatures of statute' local councils are subject to the *ultra vires* principle (ie the principle of **administrative law** that decisions beyond the powers of the decision-maker are illegal), which in their case is strictly applied. Councils have not, for example, been permitted to use popular endorsement of their local manifesto policies through electoral success as justification for otherwise unlawful decisions. Incidental or ancillary powers of councils have been narrowly construed by the courts (if broadly construed, such powers may significantly expand the range of lawful activity open to local authorities). Attempts to mitigate the harshness of this legal regime by statutory reform (for example, a power of community initiative introduced under the Local Government Act 2000) have taken the form of small-scale incremental changes, in contrast to the approach in a number of other countries of recognizing the general competence of elected local bodies.

IAN LEIGH

See also: local government, Northern Ireland; local government, Scotland

local government, Northern Ireland   The local government system currently operating in Northern Ireland was established in 1973 under the Local Government (NI) Act 1972. Twenty-six councils—city, borough, and district—replaced a plethora of urban and rural and county councils and corporations. The changes were the result of recommendations made in 1970 in the McCrory Report on the administration of local government in Northern Ireland. This followed a period of social unrest and civil rights protest, partly in response to discrimination practised by councillors.

As a consequence local government in Northern Ireland was stripped of many of its functions. Since 1973 councils have been mainly concerned with refuse collection, cemeteries, and leisure services, their work often derided as being 'births, bins, and burials'. Latterly, waste management has become a significant task as councils strive to meet EU environmental requirements. Councillors also represent local government, alongside nominees from other sectors, on public bodies concerned with housing, education and libraries, health and social services, and other matters.

The twenty-six local councils comprise 582 councillors covering a population of approximately 1.7 million people. Northern Ireland's councillor/citizen ratio is 3,000, comparing favourably with that in Scotland (4,100) but less well with that in Wales (2,300) and England (2,500). However, councils are insufficiently representative of their local communities; for example, less than 22 per cent of councillors are women, and women senior officers fall well below the number in Britain.

Councillors are elected for a four-year term, under a single transferable vote proportional representation system. Councils elect a mayor (city or borough councils) or chair annually; and are encouraged—although not all agree—to exercise a system of rotational power-sharing of key posts among political parties in recognition of the need to build an inclusive political culture and leave behind a system that gave rise to discrimination and violent conflict. City and Borough councils may bestow the ceremonial title of Alderman on up to a quarter of their councillors.

Councils are legally required to strike the district rates by 15 February each year. In addition to their rates income, Councils' incomes come from government grants, fees, and charges for services. Their combined expenditure was estimated to be £584.2 million for 2007–2008.

Local government is facing its most significant reform since the early 1970s. In 2005 the Secretary of State for Northern Ireland began to modernize public administration and proposed to reduce the number of councils to seven but increase their functions and powers. Progress slowed when devolution returned in 2007 after cross party agreement on issues of governance, with the Northern Ireland Executive reviewing proposals in the context of a fully-functioning regional Assembly and Executive.

As minister responsible for local government, the Minister for the Department of the Environment in Northern Ireland leads the Executive review that focuses on a shared vision for local government, the number of councils, and the range of enhanced functions. There is also attention to new community planning responsibilities and a power to promote economic, social, and environmental well-being within the area, offering councillors the opportunity to demonstrate greater civic leadership and become respected advocates. Despite work undertaken already by the Local Government Boundaries Commissioner, proposals made by direct rule ministers will be scaled down in response on the one hand to councillors' demands for a greater number of councils, and on the other to Executive Ministers' interests in retaining regional control over a number of functions previously marked for transfer to local government.

Given its history and the necessity to adapt to modernization, local government will be circumscribed with appropriate checks and balances to guarantee equitable political participation, fair decision-making, collective responsibility, higher standards of behaviour and performance, and effective accountability, all underpinned by an enforcement regime that assures results. These will be included to a greater or lesser degree in legislation, supplemented by council constitutions, rules of procedure and codes of conduct, and by protocols governing inter-agency relationships. External oversight mechanisms will augment councils' own internal enforcement methods.

At the time of writing, the Minister for the Environment had reported the results of the review to the Northern Ireland Executive and Assembly, and further consultations with departments and stakeholders were in progress. The Executive was expected to announce its decisions in the course of 2008.

Change will impact across all partners in the local government sector which includes: the Northern Ireland Local Government Association, potentially the strategic leader of the sector; the Local Government Staff Commission with its focus on equality, capacity-building, and human resources; the National Association of Councillors representing councillors; and SOLAS, the body representing chief executives and senior officers employed in the sector.

BRONAGH HINDS

local government, Scotland   Local government has existed in Scotland in various forms since the twelfth century when Scottish burghs emerged as local administrative units. Nowadays, the constitutional position of local government rests firmly on statute. Local authorities have been created and reorganized by Acts of the UK Parliament and derive virtually all their powers from statute. They are subordinate bodies and have no constitutional guarantee of continued existence. Nevertheless, local government is truly a form of government, as opposed to local administration, as councillors are directly elected and councils have tax-raising powers.

The current structure was established by the Local Government etc (Scotland) Act 1994, an Act of the UK Parliament. Following the creation of the Scottish Parliament in 1999 by the Scotland Act 1998, responsibility for most aspects of local government was devolved to the **Scottish Parliament**, with the exceptions of the right to vote at local elections and various functions, such as weights and measures and the administration of housing benefit, which are reserved to the UK Parliament.

The current structure of local government in Scotland is single tier, the previous two-tier system of regions and districts having been abolished in 1996. There are thirty-two local authorities, twenty-nine on the mainland and three islands authorities. They may be described as 'most-purpose' rather than 'all-purpose' as some of the councils are too small in terms of population and geographical area to be able to perform some functions efficiently, such as policing, fire-fighting, property valuation, and

strategic planning. These are carried out either by joint boards or joint committees formed from members of two or more councils.

Councillors are elected by the local government electors of the local authority area. Until 2007, Scotland was divided into 1,222 wards with populations ranging from 6,000 in the large cities to less than 1,000 in the islands, and a single councillor was elected in each ward by the first-past-the-post electoral system. For the election in 2007, pursuant to the Local Governance (Scotland) Act 2004, the existing 1,222 wards were grouped together to form three or four-member wards and the electoral system was changed to the single transferable vote, a form of proportional representation. This system will continue for the foreseeable future. **Elections** are held every four years and currently coincide with the general elections to the Scottish Parliament (though this is a matter of some controversy, and the elections may be decoupled).

Most adults aged 18 or over and resident in Scotland are entitled to vote in local government elections and are also entitled to stand for election, provided their names are on the local election register. In addition, candidates for election must have some local connection with the local government area in which they wish to stand.

The councillor who is appointed to chair the meetings of a council is generally known as the Convener, though the term Provost may also be used. In the cities of Aberdeen, Dundee, Edinburgh, and Glasgow only the term Lord Provost must be used.

As creatures of statute, local authorities are subject to the well-established *ultra vires* rule (see **administrative law**) and their actions are thus subject to **judicial review** by the **Court of Session**. The rule was relaxed to some extent by the Local Government in Scotland Act 2003 which gives local authorities the power to do anything considered likely to promote or improve the well-being of the area and persons within it. The 2003 Act also imposed on local authorities the duty to secure best value and continuous improvement in the performance of their functions, and the duty of community planning, which involves working in partnership with other bodies in the public sector and with local community bodies.

Local government expenditure accounts for about one-third of public spending in Scotland. Grants from the Scottish Executive account for around 80 per cent of local government's net revenue funding and about 20 per cent is contributed from council tax-payers, fees, and charges. Capital expenditure is generally financed by borrowing, capital receipts, reserves, and grants from various bodies such as the

National Lottery and European Funds. Some schemes are financed by public-private partnerships.

The Accounts Commission for Scotland is responsible for securing the audit of Scottish local authorities and also has a role in enforcing the duty to secure best value.

In addition, the Scottish Public Services Ombudsman has power to investigate complaints made by members of the public that they have suffered injustice or hardship as a result of **maladministration** by local authorities.

Councillors are required to abide by a statutory Code of Conduct. Enforcement of the Code of Conduct is the responsibility of the Standards Commission for Scotland, which has the power to censure, suspend, or disqualify for up to five years any councillor who has been found to have contravened the Code.   JEAN MCFADDEN

local remedies, exhaustion of   *see* **international dispute settlement**

Lockerbie trial (*HMA v Abdelbaset Ali Mohamed Al Megrahi and Al Amin Khalifa Fhimah*)   On 21 December 1988, Pan Am flight 103 exploded in the air above the Scottish town of Lockerbie killing all 259 passengers and crew and eleven residents. The resulting trial is famous for a number of reasons. It is the largest mass murder trial in Scottish legal history involving 270 victims; it marked the first time that a Scottish Court sat abroad; and it is the first modern murder case where a trial has proceeded before three judges, in the absence of a jury.

Following an investigation involving domestic and international law enforcement agents, a warrant for the arrest of the two accused was issued in 1991. This and the indictment issued in 1999 narrated three charges against the two accused acting in concert together and with unnamed others. The charges were (1) conspiracy to destroy a civil aircraft and murder its occupants; (2) murder of the 270 victims; and (3) contravention of section 2(1) and (5) of the Aviation Security Act 1982. In defiance of three UN Resolutions, the Libyan government refused to hand over the suspects for trial and sanctions were extended and tightened. On 24 August 1998, the UK and US governments proposed that the trial be held in the Netherlands before three Scottish judges and with no jury. This offer was accepted by Libya, and on 5 April 1999 the two accused surrendered for trial in the Netherlands. In anticipation of this, a former US military base at Camp Zeist had been declared part of Scottish jurisdiction to allow the High Court to sit there. The two accused were taken to Camp Zeist

and 'extradited' to Scottish jurisdiction by the Dutch authorities.

The trial began on 3 May 2000. The prosecution alleged that the first accused (Al Megrahi) had, with the assistance of his co-accused, introduced a suitcase containing the bomb to a flight from Malta to Frankfurt and that the said suitcase was tagged to travel via London Heathrow to New York JFK on Pan Am 103. In the absence of eyewitnesses, the prosecution case was circumstantial. Great importance was attached by the trial judges and the media to the evidence of the Maltese shopkeeper who sold the clothes contained in the suitcase with the explosives, and the owner of a company, MEBO Ltd, which was alleged to have produced the timing device used to detonate the explosives. Following an unsuccessful submission of 'no case to answer' (ie that the prosecution had failed to prove a case against him), the second accused (Fhimah) led no witnesses in his defence. His co-accused, Al Megrahi, led three witnesses and the defence case closed on 8 January 2001. On Wednesday 31 January Al Megrahi was convicted of murder and Fhimah was acquitted. Al Megrahi subsequently appealed his conviction. The appeal was refused on 14 March 2002. Al Megrahi successfully applied to the Scottish Criminal Cases Review Commission and a further appeal will be heard in 2008.

CLARE CONNELLY

Lord Advocate   The Lord Advocate is Scotland's senior Law Officer. The office has a long history. There is evidence from the fifteenth century of the **Crown** being represented in civil legal proceedings by advocates. But it was more in relation to criminal matters that an office of King's Advocate, later known as Lord Advocate, became recognized. In 1587 the Scottish Parliament granted the Lord Advocate powers to prosecute crimes. Prior to this, prosecutions were private matters between victim and offender, though the Lord Advocate often joined the proceedings to represent the King's interest. Ever since, the Lord Advocate has been in charge of criminal prosecutions in Scotland. The Lord Advocate is now assisted by the Solicitor General, though in practice prosecutions are usually conducted by Advocates Depute.

Additionally, the Lord Advocate has always been the senior advisor to the Crown on Scots law matters. Prior to 1707 he was a member of the Scottish Parliament *ex officio*. After 1707, the Lord Advocate was a member of the UK government. Following devolution, however, advice to the UK government on Scots law is provided by the Advocate General for Scotland. The Lord Advocate is now senior legal advisor to, and a Minister of, the Scottish Executive. The Lord Advocate is appointed by the Queen on the advice of Scotland's First Minister, though the First Minister may not make a recommendation without the agreement of the **Scottish Parliament**. The Lord Advocate at the time of writing (2007) was Elish Angiolini, the first woman to have been appointed to the office.   SIMON HALLIDAY

Lord Chancellor   The office of Lord Chancellor is nearly as old as the monarchy and older than Parliament. Early Lord Chancellors were clerics who assumed the position of royal chaplain and acted as secretary to the King and custodian of the royal seal. These responsibilities, together with the development of a judicial role, put them at the centre of religious, legal, and political life such that, during Tudor times, Cardinal Wolsey was second only to Henry VIII. While the religious function lapsed, the mix of executive and judicial functions remained. Twentieth-century Lord Chancellors were therefore not only senior members of the **Cabinet** with their own government department, they also acted as Speaker in the legislative **House of Lords** and President of its judicial bench (the Appellate Committee). They were, in addition, responsible for most judicial appointments and assumed the position of head of the judiciary and defender of judicial independence.

The Constitutional Reform Act 2005 changed the position. In response to increasing concerns about the appropriateness of a minister exercising major judicial functions, it removed the Lord Chancellor's judicial role, transferred the function of head of the judiciary to the **Lord Chief Justice,** and established a Judicial Appointments Commission. It also ended the Lord Chancellor's role as Speaker; and while holders of the office retain responsibility for defending judicial independence (which is, for the first time, is a statutory responsibility) they are no longer confined to the House of Lords but can be elected politicians sitting in the **House of Commons**.
                                DIANA WOODHOUSE

See also: **judicial appointments**

Lord Chief Justice   The Lord Chief Justice of England and Wales is President of the courts and head of the judiciary of England and Wales. The courts comprise the Court of Appeal, the High Court, the Crown Court, the county courts, and the magistrates' courts.

The office evolved from that of Chief Justice of the King's/Queen's Bench, which had been established

by 1268 and continued (save for a temporary name-change between 1649 and 1660) until establishment of the Supreme Court in 1875. The Chief Justice of the King's/Queen's Bench then became an *ex officio* member of the Court of Appeal and President of the King's/Queen's Bench Division, assuming the title of Lord Chief Justice of England. All holders of that office save for the first (Sir Alexander Cockburn) have been peers. In 1881 the residual functions of the Lord Chief Justice of the Common Pleas and the Lord Chief Baron of the Exchequer were transferred to him. The words 'and Wales' were informally added to the title in 1998, a change formalized in the Constitutional Reform Act 2005. The most recent office-holders have largely sat in the Criminal and Civil Divisions of the Court of Appeal and the Queen's Bench Divisional Court.

Under the 2005 Act, the Lord Chief Justice is, or may appoint another person to be, the Head of Criminal Justice. In addition to judicial duties he has very extensive administrative, representational, and disciplinary responsibilities.

There is a Lord Chief Justice of Northern Ireland, an office created in 1921 when that of Lord Chancellor of Ireland was abolished.   TOM BINGHAM

Louisiana law   *see* **mixed jurisdictions**

loyalty, employer   Although the modern employment relationship is based on the idea of contract rather than status, it remains a relationship in a meaningful sense in a way that goes much further than that between parties involved in, for example, the contractual purchase of a newspaper from a newsagent's. One way this manifests itself is in the duty of fidelity owed by the employee to the employer. Sometimes, this expressly appears in the agreement made by the parties and is inserted into the employee's written statement (often referred to as the **contract of employment**), but sometimes the duty has to be implied by law. Nevertheless, it is fundamental and is based on the requirement of honesty, such as the duty to account for all money and property received during the course of employment. However, it does not extend to a duty to disclose the employee's own misdeeds, although there is a duty to disclose those of fellow employees. (There are signs that the courts are now moving away from this general idea.) Other manifestations of the requirements of loyalty are the employee's duty not to set up in **competition** with his employer and the duty, after leaving employment, not to use the employer's resources or confidential information to enable him to set up in competition. An obvious way this could be done is by listing the employer's customers and then attempting to poach their custom. Nevertheless, such activities may additionally be prohibited expressly by restrictive covenants made between the parties.

SIMON HONEYBALL

See also: **confidentiality, work; whistle-blowing**

Lumley v Gye   *see Lumley v Wagner*

Lumley v Wagner   The background of this case, decided in 1852, was a fierce rivalry between two London theatres, Her Majesty's Theatre, Haymarket, managed by Benjamin Lumley, and the fairly new Royal Italian Opera, Covent Garden, managed by Frederick Gye. Both opera houses sought to secure the services of the famous German singer, Johanna Wagner. She was first in contact with Gye, but in November 1851 she entered into an agreement with Lumley for the season of 1852. By February, Wagner was regretting her bargain, having formed the view that she could have obtained a better price for her services, and that Covent Garden was the better theatre. In March 1852, Gye approached Wagner with a very attractive offer, which Wagner accepted, thinking, wrongly as it turned out, that she was legally entitled to terminate her contract with Lumley.

Wagner arrived in London, and her debut was announced for April 24 at Covent Garden. But Gye's victory was short-lived. On April 23 Lumley obtained an order (**injunction**) from the **Chancery Court** to restrain her from appearing. An appeal was dismissed by the **Lord Chancellor** (Lord St Leonards) on May 26. Just as Gye's victory was short-lived, so also was Lumley's, for in the end Wagner did not sing at either theatre, and the 1852 season was a disaster for Lumley, and for Her Majesty's Theatre, which closed from 1853 to 1855, Lumley attributing the closure largely to Johanna Wagner's defection.

In 1852 there were two separate systems of courts, namely, the **common law courts**, which had power to award damages, but not to give injunctions, and the Chancery Court, which alone had the power to issue injunctions. An injunction, an order to do or not to do some specific thing, is a coercive remedy that takes immediate effect, as in this case, forcing the cancellation of an opera on the eve of its opening performance: the order requires instant obedience on pain of imprisonment for contempt of court.

It was conceded that the Chancery Court would not actually make an order requiring Wagner to sing for Lumley; the debatable question was whether the court might nevertheless make an order requiring her *not* to sing for Gye. The Lord Chancellor held that such an order could be made. His chief reasons were that, in the circumstances, **damages** at **common law** (ie damages awarded by a common law court) against Wagner would not be an adequate remedy, and that the prospect of having to pay such damages was insufficient to deter breach of contract in other similar cases. *Lumley v Wagner* has not generally been applied to ordinary employees performing routine work, but it has been followed in later cases of 'star' performers, such as film actors in one era, and sports stars in another.

Lumley also brought an action against Gye for damages at common law, and, though the action eventually failed on its facts, the case (*Lumley v Gye* (1853)) in effect created a new wrong of inducing breach of contract, and remains an important precedent.

STEPHEN WADDAMS

See also: **economic torts**

lunatic   *see* **capacity**

M

M v Home Office (1993)   In this case the **House of Lords** rejected the proposition that the courts have no power to enforce the law by **injunction** or proceedings for **contempt of court** against a **Minister of the Crown** in his official capacity. Anything else, said Lord Templeman, would mean that the executive obeyed the law only 'as a matter of grace and not as a matter of necessity'. The case is thus of fundamental importance in subjecting the executive to the **rule of law**.

What had happened was that M, a failed asylum seeker, was about to be removed to Zaire when he made an application to court for leave to apply for **judicial review** of the decision to remove him. The judge thought that he had received an undertaking from counsel for the Home Office that M would not be removed pending his decision. However, M was removed as planned. Learning of this the judge made an interim injunction against the **Home Secretary** requiring him forthwith to procure M's return to the UK. On legal advice, the Home Secretary did not comply with this order. Instead he applied, successfully, to the court to set it aside on the ground that the court had no power to make an injunction against a Minister.

Thus M was not returned and his fate is lost to history. His counsel now moved the court to commit the Home Secretary for contempt of court. But the Home Secretary argued that just as no injunction could be made against a minister, so he was not subject to contempt proceedings. The crucial conceptual confusion that underlay these propositions was the conflation of Ministers of the Crown with the **Crown** itself. The Crown is immune from proceedings in its own courts, so an injunction cannot be issued nor can a finding of contempt be made against the Crown. But the vast majority of statutory powers and duties are conferred upon designated ministers not upon the Crown; and Ministers have, or should have, no immunity. But several cases, relying upon superficial readings of section 21(2) of the Crown Proceedings Act 1947 (which said injunctions could not be issued against officers of the Crown if the effect would be to grant such relief against the Crown), allowed Ministers to shelter under the Crown's immunity and created the problem that came to a head in *M*.

Lord Woolf's judgment is a tour de force through the technicalities of Crown immunity. Vitally it restricts section 21(2) to its proper role and recognizes the importance for the rule of law of the distinction between Ministers of the Crown and the Crown. The injunction requiring the return of M had been properly made and it was a contempt of court for the Home Secretary not to procure his return. As Sir William Wade remarked *M* 'put the rule of law back on the rails' (*The Times* 17 August 1993). But it was made clear that in the absence of personal wrongdoing Ministers would not be punished for contempt: 'The very fact of making such a finding [of contempt] would vindicate the requirements of justice' said Lord Woolf.

CHRISTOPHER FORSYTH

M'Naghten's Case (1843)   In January 1843 Daniel M'Naghten shot and killed Edward Drummond, who was the Private Secretary of the then Prime Minister, Sir Robert Peel. In doing so M'Naghten thought he was killing the **Prime Minister**; but little did he know that his deed would make English legal history. After the shooting M'Naghten was immediately arrested. Shortly afterwards he made a statement saying that that the Tories had compelled him to do it, having persecuted him wherever he went. He was brought for trial at the **Old Bailey** some thirteen days after the shooting and eight days after Drummond's death. However his lawyer Alexander Cockburn QC—later to become **Lord Chief Justice**—was able to delay the trial in order that evidence as to the accused's state of mind could be sought.

At his trial M'Naghten relied on the defence of insanity. The prosecution tried to undermine this by stressing the normality of the accused's behaviour together with the fact that he understood what he was doing and that it was wrong. In order to counter this Cockburn called eight medical witnesses who painted a very different picture of M'Naghten. In doing so it was argued that at the time of the killing M'Naghten had acted under an insane delusion which had deprived him of all self control. The essence of the defence was summed up by Cockburn as follows: 'The question is whether under that delusion of mind he did an act which he would not have done ... save under the impulse of the delusion which he could not control and out of which delusion alone the act itself arose'. In summing up to the jury Lord Chief Justice Tindal stated that if they considered that the accused was able to distinguish right from wrong then he should be convicted but emphasized that the medical evidence all pointed one way. The jury immediately returned a verdict of 'not guilty by reason of insanity'. M'Naghten was taken to Bethlem Hospital and later to Broadmoor.

The verdict created a public outcry. There was much comment in the press and the topic was raised in Parliament. As a result the government was pressurized to clarify the law. In order to do this Lord Lyndhurst, the Lord Chancellor, invited the judges themselves to answer five questions dealing with the defence of insanity. The answers to these questions, pronounced some three months later in Parliament, have become known as the M'Naghten Rules. They hold a special place in English legal history for without doubt they represent the current criminal law in England (and many other countries) in respect of the defence of insanity. However, they have never been incorporated into law by an Act of Parliament nor are they part of judge-made law. In that sense they are unique as a form of law-making. More importantly, the Rules are markedly different from the law outlined in the M'Naghten trial itself—so much so that ironically it seems most unlikely that Daniel M'Naghten would have been found 'not guilty by reason of insanity' had the Rules which bear his name been applied to his case.   RONNIE MACKEY

See also: **mental incapacity and crime**

Mabo v State of Queensland (1992)

One of the most politicized decisions in the history of the High Court of Australia, *Mabo & Ors v State of Queensland (No 2)* (1992) has, by some, been acclaimed as a legal triumph, laying to rest the 'legal fiction' that Australia was, at settlement, *terra nullius* and recognizing the prior ownership of Indigenous people. Others have attacked it as judicial legislation, undermining settled understandings of tenure and crippling development.

Like the US Supreme Court decision in *Brown v Board of Education* (1954) it was both a decision which was almost inevitable, and one which,

arguably, has been far more potent in its symbolism than in positive outcomes for Indigenous people. Critical Race scholar Derrick Bell, *And We Are Not Saved: The Elusive Quest for Racial Justice* ((New York: Basic Books, 1987), pp 187–188) has argued 'that the Supreme Court's decision in *Brown v Board of Education* should be seen as furthering the nation's foreign and domestic interests far more than it helped black people gain the critically important citizenship right to equal educational opportunity'. Similarly, the symbolic freight embedded in *Mabo*, both within the Indigenous community and among those Australians caricatured by some current political figures as the 'chattering classes', is immense. In the political climate of its time, it clearly furthered Australia's interests. Its positive outcomes for Indigenous people, whether in substantive improvements to their health, education, and economic status or to their level of self-determination, are far less substantive than proponents hoped.

More disturbingly, the understanding of native title which underpinned the decision was profoundly flawed. The legal test reified Indigenous culture and law, treating it as frozen in time. According to the leading judgment, that of Brennan J:

'when the tide of history has washed away any real acknowledgment of traditional law and any real observance of traditional customs, the foundation of native title has disappeared . . . Australian law can protect the interests of members of an indigenous clan or group, whether communally or individually, only in conformity with the traditional laws and customs of the people to whom the clan or group belongs and only where members of the clan or group acknowledge those laws and observe those customs (so far as it is practicable to do so).'

So saying, the High Court established a dichotomy, taking with the one hand what it gave with the other. While **native title** was acknowledged, potential claimants must have maintained their connection with the land and continue to practice their traditional customs and laws. Urbanized Indigenous people and those whose cultural and legal practices have adapted to the circumstances in which they found themselves, including the circumstance of colonisation, were seemingly excluded. This treats Indigenous culture as an artefact, rather than a living (and evolving) organism, making it more, rather than less, difficult to sustain Indigenous identity and participate in the economic, cultural, and social milieus of contemporary Australia.

SANDRA BERNS

MacPherson Report   *see* **indirect discrimination; institutional discrimination**

magistrates *see* **courts; judges; Justices of the Peace**

magistrates courts *see* **courts**

Magna Carta The charter issued by King John to his realm at Runnymede on 15 June 1215, and known as Magna Carta, was the direct product of the political failures of his reign, but also reflected the practices of twelfth-century kingship and lordship. John had been notably unsuccessful in his rule, losing a large part of his continental possessions, including Normandy and Anjou, to the French king. His regime, driven in part by his need to raise money for his efforts to regain his lost possessions, was harsh and he also developed personal quarrels with leading men. The result in 1215 was baronial rebellion, and Magna Carta formed part of the attempted peace settlement for that rebellion.

Magna Carta dealt with many matters relating to law and justice. Some clauses took the form of general statements of principle: 'to no-one will we sell, to no one will we deny or delay right or justice'. Others sought to make access to justice easier: 'common pleas shall not follow our court, but shall be held in some specific place'. There were also measures relating to criminal law: 'a free man shall not be amerced [that is, incur a monetary penalty] for a trivial offence, except in accordance with the degree of the offence'. There were also provisions concerning lordship and land-holding, notably on matters of inheritance: 'if any of our earls or barons or others holding of us in chief [that is, directly from the King rather than as a sub-tenant] by knight service shall die, and at his death his heir be of full age and owe relief [the payment to take up an inheritance], he shall have his inheritance on payment of the ancient relief, namely the heir or heirs of an earl £100 for a whole earl's barony, the heir or heirs of a baron £100 for a whole barony, the heir or heirs of a knight 100s. at most for a whole knight's fee'. The ability to exact an arbitrary relief, as John and his predecessors had sometimes done, was thus removed. Indeed one of the purposes of Magna Carta was to establish control over royal arbitrary lordship, corresponding to the control that royally-enforced law increasingly exercised over possible arbitrary lordship by others.

Whereas some continental rulers made grants of liberties to their leading men, Magna Carta was a grant to all free men of England. This characteristic helped to establish its central position in English law and English political thinking. Although King John had the charter annulled by the Pope soon after its issue, it was then reissued in slightly modified forms by his successors, as a promise of good kingship. It appeared as the first statute in English statute books as they started to be put together in the later middle ages. Then, in the political struggles of the seventeenth century, Magna Carta had an extremely prominent position in the constitutional debates of the period, notably through the work of the lawyer Sir Edward **Coke**. Sir William **Blackstone** published an edition in the mid-eighteenth century. Use of Magna Carta for political and rhetorical purposes continues to the present day. In her famous Bruges speech of 1988, concerning the contemporary political development of Europe, Prime Minister Margaret Thatcher stated that 'We in Britain are rightly proud of the way in which, since Magna Carta in 1215, we have pioneered and developed representative institutions to stand as bastions of freedom'. Meanwhile, clauses 1, 9 and 29 of the 1225 version of Magna Carta remained on the statue book into the twenty-first century.

JOHN HUDSON

mail order Mail order is the label used for consumer purchases made away from retail premises without any face-to-face contact between consumer and trader. It includes orders made by post or telephone based on catalogues or advertisements, as well as online shopping (electronic commerce) and telephone selling. Mail order purchases involve risks which consumers do not face when purchasing goods in the High Street: in particular, goods cannot be inspected in advance and may not be suitable. Moreover, pre-payment for goods or services is often required at the time of ordering, but goods may not be delivered. The relevant legislation on mail order is contained in the Consumer Protection (Distance Selling) Regulations 2000 (based on EU Directive 97/7).

The Regulations cover consumer contracts for goods or services which are concluded exclusively at a distance, provided that the trader usually sells goods or services at a distance. The Regulations do not apply where a trader takes the occasional telephone order, or where consumer and trader meet face-to-face at some stage during the conclusion of the contract.

If a contract is subject to the Regulations, a trader is required to make available to the consumer certain items of information before a contract is concluded: (i) identity and address of supplier; (ii) main characteristics of the goods or services; (iii) prices including all taxes; (iv) delivery costs; (v) arrangements for payment, delivery, or performance; (vi) the existence of the **cooling-off period**; (vii) the cost of the method of distance communication used to place the order, if that is higher than the basic rate; (viii) the period for which an offer or price remains valid; and (ix) if relevant, the minimum duration of the contract. Such information must be given in a clear and comprehensible manner. Once an order has been placed and a contract concluded, much of this information has to be confirmed in writing, together with additional details about complaints procedures, after-sales support, and conditions for cancelling a contract which is not limited to a fixed term.

If all the required information has been given, the consumer is given a cooling-off period of seven working days after receiving the goods; if not, the start of the cooling-off period can be delayed by up to three months. If the consumer elects to cancel the contract, he is entitled to a full refund, although he may be required to cover the cost of returning the goods to the trader if this was made clear at the outset.

The trader must send the goods within thirty days, and if unable to do so, must refund any prepayments, although goods of equivalent value may be substituted if that was mentioned before the contract was made. Additionally, several codes of practice are applicable, including those of the Direct Marketing Association ('DMA') and the Mail Order Traders' Association ('MOTA'). The latter offers a fourteen-day cooling-off period, for example.

CHRISTIAN TWIGG-FLESNER

Maine, Henry J S Sir Henry Maine (1822–1888) wrote about law and social change in ways which broke with the traditions of English lawyers. He saw law as a social creation which was best understood through being placed in its historical context and this led him to look far beyond England and the law reports. For him, law and legal systems developed over time, and they should be understood by reference to international examples taken from other cultures in India, continental Europe, and elsewhere.

In his early years, Maine had a successful academic career at Cambridge and when he was twenty-five he became Regius Professor of Civil Law. Within a few years his restless mind was exploring legal practice as a barrister and writing for both the popular press and informed journals such as the *Saturday Review*. He moved to London and became a Reader in Jurisprudence at the **Inns of Court**. There is some evidence to suggest that it was here, in the 1850s, that he began to prepare drafts for what was to become his most famous book, *Ancient Law* (1861). In this book he used information from a wide range of societies. He was interested in the ideas of contemporary geologists and early writers on **Roman law**. He began to develop a fascination with India and its numerous systems of law and the nature of caste. In places he would relate his analysis to current events such as the collapse of financial institutions or arguments about **slavery** in the USA. His interests were both historical and contemporary and this combination helps to explain his attraction to the general reader and the public success of *Ancient Law*.

Maine wrote well and succeeded in integrating this mix of sources into succinct generalizations. In part, he looked at ancient systems in which law went through phases of being controlled and shaped by different groups such as aristocracies. Later in time there might be progressive change through the successive use of fictions, equity, and **legislation**. In his famous phrase, this was where there was the possibility of a movement from 'status to contract'. Slaves had their status determined for them. Free individuals could contract their way through life, making changes which assisted them and, through liberating their energies, enhance the prospects of others. This enthusiasm for progress did not mean that he had found a full explanation for change; it could be seen and identified but what produced progress was as yet unexplained.

His reflections on social change led him to look with scepticism on much that lawyers did. In his view 'social necessities and social opinion are always more or less in advance of law'. But this did not make him an enthusiastic reformer. His experience of working in India between 1862 and 1869 on projects for new statutes led him to balance the merits of novel and clear laws against the need for historical judgment and political caution. His relationship between his thought and that of other English writers on the nature of law and legal change could be subtle in its details, but there was truth in the public perception that his historical and comparative arguments put his ideas in sharp contrast with other theorists. He had little respect for the views of professional lawyers and what he saw as their invented beliefs about continuity in the **common law**. He distrusted utilitarian theorists if, like Jeremy **Bentham**, they placed confidence in the possibilities of law as an instrument of social engineering. The capacity of John **Austin** to analyse concepts of '**sovereignty**' or 'command' might have the value of clarity but was of limited merit without reference to changing social contexts over time.

Maine's later works such as *Village Communities* (1871), *Lectures on the Early History of Institutions* (1875), *Dissertations on Early Law and Custom* (1883), and *Popular Government* (1885) were as broad in their range of subject as his first book, but his work was increasingly subject to criticism. He came to be associated with grand generalizations rather than patient scholarship, and his reputation was in many respects eclipsed in English universities by the start of the twentieth century. Many years later, towards the end of the century, this began to change with an increasing interest in socio-legal studies and respect for writers on law who did not attempt perfectly consistent analysis of all aspects of law so much as reveal its colourful diversity in everyday life.

RCJ COCKS

mainstreaming 'Mainstreaming' refers to the policy of incorporating an emphasis on **equality** into 'into all policies and programmes, so that, before decisions are taken, an analysis is made of the effects on protected groups'. **Gender** mainstreaming was adopted in the 'platform for action' by the Fourth UN World Conference on Women in September 1995 (the Beijing conference), strongly backed by the EU delegation to the Conference. Mainstreaming has subsequently been incorporated into European thinking, Article 3 of the Treaty Establishing the European Community, as amended by the Treaty of Amsterdam, states that 'In all the activities [of the Community], the Community shall aim to eliminate inequalities, and to promote equality, between men and women'.

The first significant legislative example of equality 'mainstreaming' in the UK took the form of section 75 of the Northern Ireland Act 1998 which imposes upon 'public authorities' an obligation 'in carrying out [their] functions relating to Northern Ireland' to have 'due regard to the need to promote equality of opportunity—

(a) between persons of different religious belief, political opinion, racial group, age, marital status or sexual orientation;
(b) between men and women generally;
(c) between persons with a disability and
(d) between persons with dependants and persons without.'

Section 75(2) provides that, without prejudice to the obligations imposed by section 75(1), public authorities shall also have regard to the desirability of promoting good relations between persons of different religious belief, political opinion, or racial group.

Section 75 had its roots in the Policy Appraisal and Fair Treatment ('PAFT') guidelines, first issued in Northern Ireland in December 1993, which in turn drew upon the British guidelines launched in the 1980s by the Ministerial Group on Women's Issues, which encouraged Whitehall Departments to develop basic guidance with a view to producing tailored guidelines on 'equality proofing'. According to the Northern Ireland Government's Central Community Relations Unit, PAFT was intended to:

'ensure that, in practice, issues of equality and equity condition policy-making and action in all spheres and at all levels of government activity, whether in regulatory and administrative functions or in the delivery of services to the public. The guidelines identify a number of areas where there is potential for discrimination or unequal treatment to occur and outline steps which those responsible for the development of policy and the delivery of services should take to ensure that, in drawing up new policies or reviewing existing policies, they do not unjustifiably or unnecessarily discriminate against specified sections of the community.'

The operation of PAFT was heavily criticized, the guidelines not having been made public and, it seems, being largely ignored by decision-makers. Section 75 of the Northern Ireland Act, however, gave mainstreaming legislative force. It provided a model for the introduction of mainstreaming obligations in the **Race** Relations Act 1976 (which happened in 2001), the **Disability** Discrimination Act 1995 (amended to this effect in 2006), and the **Sex** Discrimination Act 1975 (amended from 2007). Although the precise details vary between the Acts, all three impose obligations on public authorities to pay 'due regard' to the need to eliminate unlawful discrimination and promote equality of opportunity.

AILEEN MCCOLGAN

maintenance The financial arrangements made at **divorce** continue to give rise to difficulty for the families concerned, and to exercise both legal policymakers and practitioners. The variety of personal circumstances and the lack of clear statutory principles can be seen as making for either problematic uncertainty or helpful flexibility. Spousal maintenance refers in practice to women with children, although **child support** is dealt with separately by the Child Support Agency.

Until 1984, section 25 of the Matrimonial Causes Act 1973 ('MCA') directed the **courts** to 'place the parties so far as is practicable and having regard to their conduct, just to do so, in the position they would have been had the marriage not broken down'. In 1984, this requirement was removed but nothing was put in its place. Instead by amending the MCA (section 25A91) the court is to look for a clean break between the couple (though not their children) wherever possible, and under section 25(1) of the MCA to give 'first consideration . . . to the welfare while a **minor** of any **child** of the family'.

Men and women who divorce may lack resources, in which case if there is a family home it will have little equity so that, although the man may be willing to leave it in the hands of the woman and children, he is unlikely to pay the kind of spousal maintenance which would enable her to run it. The most likely outcome will be a small lump sum and a child support requirement under the Child Support Agency. If the couple are of average means there may be a struggle to try to maintain a standard of living for both comparable to that which they enjoyed while together. This is especially difficult when both parents seek staying access for the children and need suitable housing. Solicitors are skilled in income packaging and making best use of available assets. But the likely outcome will be sale of the home, smaller properties for each, and perhaps some transitional spousal maintenance in addition to child support. In rare cases, there may be a great deal of wealth and argument about its distribution, and for this situation the courts have developed their own principles. In *White v White* (2001) the House of Lords moved on from the 'reasonable requirements' approach to give Mrs White an award which accepted that financial and homemaking contributions to a **marriage** are of equal value, thus removing the ceiling which had developed in practice for housewives. This was an unusual case involving agricultural land, and there were no children. But the yardstick of **equality** approach has trickled down to lower value cases, and may have had a detrimental effect on wives who need more than a 50/50 division of the value of the house to recompense them for years out of the labour market. Finally, in 2006, we have the case of Mrs McFarlane (*Miller v Miller, McFarlane v McFarlane* (2006)), which addressed the issue that in some big money cases equality did not seem to be fair. Mrs McFarlane had given up a well-paid city job to bring up the three children of the marriage, and, on divorce, had been given maintenance for only five years. The **House of Lords** made the award open-ended, Baroness Hale in her judgment highlighting the scale of the loss related to being out of the labour market and drawing attention to the particular need for **compensation** for the homemaker. The result then is a move away from clarity of principle and back to flexibility and the use of discretion to support the weaker party.

MAVIS MACLEAN

See also: **property, family**

Maitland, Frederic William Frederic Maitland (1850–1906) was the foremost English legal historian of the first half of the twentieth century, and occupies a dominant place in the historiography of the subject. Born in London, he was educated at Eton and Cambridge. He took the Moral Sciences Tripos, having found that neither Classics nor Mathematics was wholly congenial to him. From here he drifted towards a career at the Bar, to which he was called in 1876. He had already fallen under the influence of **Frederick Pollock,** but the turning point in his life came in 1880, when he met the Russian scholar, Paul Vinogradoff. Inspired—or needled—by Vinogradoff's knowledge of the sources of English legal history, Maitland turned to the subject himself. Having been turned down by Oxford, he was elected to the newly-created Readership in English Law at Cambridge in 1884, and to the Downing Professorship in 1888; he remained in Cambridge for the rest of his life.

The main thrust of Maitland's early work was the edition of medieval texts, and this was always to be a significant part of his work. He began with the Crown pleas of the Eyre of Gloucester of 1221, moved on to the three-volume *Bracton's Note Book*, and then turned his attention to the Year Books of Edward II. His editorial scholarship was exacting, both in the collation of Year Book manuscripts and the linking of reported cases to formal entries in the Plea Rolls. Much of his work was channelled through the Selden Society, which he had played a principal part in founding in 1887 and of which he was the Literary Director from 1895.

Alongside this editorial work, Maitland was a prolific writer on legal history. From essays in the 1880s, he moved to more substantial books in the 1890s. The most important of these by far was the two-volume *History of English Law before the Time of Edward I*, which first appeared in 1895. Though nominally co-authored by Frederick Pollock, Maitland was in practice responsible for all but the section on Anglo-Saxon law. Three major features distinguish this work from what had been written previously: it was not narrowly insular, but set against the background of contemporary European (especially German) scholarship; it made substantial use of the thirteenth-century records remaining in manuscript at the Public Records Office; and it was shot through with sharp analysis and sound judgment. Its arguments have not gone unchallenged, of course; in particular, scholars of the late twentieth century have argued that Maitland read the legal ideas of the thirteenth century back into the twelfth, consequently underestimating the changes which had occurred between 1150 and 1300. Nonetheless, the *History of English Law* remains the fundamental study on the subject more than a century later.

Perhaps the most influential of Maitland's works other than the *History of English Law* was his Rede Lecture of 1901, *English Law and the Renaissance*. In this he asked why it was that England experienced no reception of **Roman law** in the sixteenth century, a question he went on to answer with an impressive ballast of evidentiary material in its footnotes. Later scholars have concluded that Maitland overestimated the **risk** of a Roman reception, but the broad outlines of his explanation—in terms of the depth of learning of the Common lawyers in the **Inns of Court**—have remained widely accepted.

Maitland was a brilliant expositor. His written style retains the flow of his oral delivery, and his points are made with simplicity and precision. As a result, it is not only his works on legal history which have continued to be read after a century. Especially important are his *Constitutional History of England*, a set of lectures of which he was not especially proud, and his *Lectures on Equity*, which are still used by some teachers to lay out the framework of the subject and which were translated into Japanese in 1991.

In his inaugural lecture as Downing Professor, *Why the History of English Law is not Written*, Maitland suggested that a legal historian had to be a true lawyer and a true historian. His success owes a great deal to his having been both. The author of the *Lectures on Equity*, a work of pure legal doctrine, was in 1902 offered the Regius Chair in History in the University of Cambridge. Though he turned down the office, he is still claimed by historians as one of their own: his memorial stone in Westminster Abbey reads simply 'F W Maitland, 1850–1906, historian'.

DAVID IBBETSON

majority rule principle and collective shareholder rights   Where a wrong is committed against a **company**, the company, as a distinct legal entity, is the proper plaintiff to instigate proceedings to remedy it. As a general rule, a shareholder will be precluded from commencing an action in the company's name unless he has the support of a vote of the majority of the membership. The 'majority rule principle' is embodied in the rule taken from the judgment of Wigram VC in the case of *Foss v Harbottle* ((1843). The rule is prohibitive of the availability of minority actions, because as the judgment makes clear, every individual shareholder must realize that on becoming a member of a company, majority rule will prevail, as in all other walks of society. However, by way of an exception, in circumstances prescribed by section 260 of the Companies Act 2006, a shareholder may be afforded the **capacity** to pursue a derivative action. Nevertheless, the **courts**

are reluctant to overturn the majority rule principle and will only do so where the wrong in question is of a serious nature. The motive for pursuing a derivative action must be one that seeks to benefit the company as a distinct commercial entity, as opposed to a motive which seeks to benefit the personal interests of a shareholder(s). Prior to the Companies Act 2006, the derivative action was regulated by the **common law** and a shareholder was obliged to establish that the wrong constituted a 'a fraud on the company'. Although case law established that fraud was not defined in a literal sense to require a dishonest intent or deception, there were very few case examples of successful derivative actions. The justice of a particular case could not, in itself, be regarded as a standard exception (*Prudential Assurance Co Ltd v Newman Industries (No 2)* (1982)). Where 'fraud' was established, ratification of the alleged wrong would be ineffective other than where, for example, an independent **board of directors** or a majority of the independent part of the minority (those not involved in the wrongdoing) resolved to rescind from proceeding with an action.

Following the Companies Act 2006, the derivative action is now regulated by statute, the statutory derivative action attempting to provide a shareholder with a more accessible method of challenging corporate wrongdoing (the action is regulated by sections 260–264 of the Companies Act 2006). The statutory derivative action may be commenced in respect of a cause of action arising from an actual or proposed act or omission involving negligence, default, breach of duty, or breach of **trust**. The cause of action may be against a **director** or another person (or both) and it is immaterial that the cause of action arose before or after the person seeking to bring or continue the derivative claim became a member of the company (section 260(4)). In deciding whether a derivative action should proceed, the court must refuse the application if it is satisfied that the wrongful act had been authorized by the company and approved by its membership or that the action was not in the best interest of the company. However, even if those conditions do not prevent proceedings from continuing, the court may still refuse to allow the continuance of the action. Here the court must take into account matters that seek to determine whether the applicant was acting in good faith in seeking to continue the claim, the likelihood that the wrongful act would be ratified by the membership, whether the company had decided not to pursue the claim, and whether the wrongful act could be pursued by the applicant in his own right rather than on behalf of the company.

In deciding whether to allow a derivative action to proceed, the ratification of the wrongful act by ordinary resolution (a majority of the membership who vote on the matter) will not be effective where the ratification is or would be dependent on the votes of those who were responsible for the wrongful act (to include persons connected to the wrongdoers) (section 239). Further, in determining whether to allow the action to proceed the court must have particular regard to the views of the independent members of the company, ie those members who have no personal interest in the matter.

STEVE GRIFFIN

maladministration   The concept of maladministration exists to deal with administrative actions taken primarily by government departments and agencies, local government, the health services, and some other public bodies which, whilst not illegal, are unfair, improper, or fall short of the standards of service the public expect and have resulted in injustice. The Parliamentary Commissioner Act 1967, which established the Parliamentary Ombudsman and set out the procedures for making a complaint, provides no definition of maladministration and none was given in subsequent legislation. The concept has instead developed from the description provided in the **House of Commons** by Richard Crossman, the minister responsible for the 1967 Act. He stated that it included 'bias, neglect, inattention, delay, incompetence, ineptitude, perversity, turpitude, arbitrariness.'

This has been translated and augmented by **ombudsmen** to include individual errors, oppressive behaviour, failure to apply the rules or take account of legal advice, breaches of confidentiality, a denial of **natural justice**, bias because of race, sex, or any other grounds, faulty procedures, neglecting to inform individuals of their rights of entitlement or appeal, and knowingly giving advice which is wrong or misleading. There is, therefore, a close affinity between the expectations of the ombudsmen and the **courts** regarding the administrative process, which are based on considerations of equity, fairness, **justice**, reasonableness, and adherence to **human rights**. However the standard applied by the ombudsmen goes beyond that upheld as law by the **judges**, for instance, requiring a level of behaviour which is considerate and polite and which provides mitigation when the application of a statute produces an unjust result in an individual case or when things have gone wrong. The most common instances of maladministration are those concerning unreasonable delay, or a failure in communication or the provision of information. Like **judicial review**, maladministration is not concerned with the merits of a decision; nor is it concerned with issues of policy, although given the thinness of the line between policy and its operation, it may, at times, be difficult to separate them.

Ombudsmen have no power to impose their findings. They therefore rely for their implementation on the cooperation of those they are investigating. This is not always forthcoming; for example, in March 2006 the Department of Work and Pensions rejected the parliamentary ombudsman's findings that official information on the security of final salary pension schemes had been misleading. A further weakness of the parliamentary ombudsman is that in most instances individuals have to channel their grievances through a Member of Parliament rather than approaching the ombudsman directly.

The concept of maladministration, as supported by ombudsmen, has extended beyond the public sector to some service industries including, for instance, banks and insurance companies.

DIANA WOODHOUSE

malicious falsehood   An action for malicious falsehood, sometimes known as 'injurious falsehood', may be brought in respect of a false statement to a person other than the claimant, which is made maliciously and which causes damage to the claimant. In contrast to **libel** and **slander** actions, the claimant must prove that the statement was false and that it was made maliciously, ie that the defendant knew it was untrue or made it recklessly, not caring whether it was true or false. The claimant must also prove special (ie material) damage unless the statement was written and likely to cause damage; or, though oral, statement was likely to damage the claimant in work or business. But the claimant does not have to prove that the statement was defamatory of him. An action for malicious falsehood can, therefore, be brought, for instance, if it is falsely and maliciously stated that the claimant's business has closed or that the claimant's goods, through no fault of the claimant, are of inferior quality; in these circumstances it is very doubtful that an action for libel or slander could be brought. A malicious falsehood claim was upheld when a newspaper published a fictitious interview with a television actor while he was in hospital, falsely claiming he had consented to the interview and depriving him of the opportunity to sell another interview for profit. In these circumstances the tort acted as a surrogate for a **privacy** or breach of confidence action.

ERIC BARENDT

See also: **confidential information**

mandates and trusteeship   *see* states

mandatory sentencing   Mandatory sentencing measures cover a range of statutory **sentencing** provisions that can restrict, and in some cases completely control, sentencing **discretion**. A fixed penalty (where the **court** has no discretion, such as a mandatory death penalty) and a minimum penalty provision (where nothing less than the minimum can be imposed) are mandatory sentences. The mandatory death penalty and penalty provisions in which **Parliament** sets both a minimum and a maximum sentence were common in the first half of nineteenth-century Britain, but were gradually repealed. For much of the twentieth century it was widely accepted that sentencing should be a matter of broad judicial discretion; accordingly, legislative provisions provided upper limits only. The mandatory penalties for murder—death and later life imprisonment—stood out as exceptions to this general picture. However, in the last decades of the twentieth century mandatory prison sentencing provisions became popular in the US along with new forms of mandatory penalties such as 'three strikes' **legislation**, which requires three convictions to trigger the mandatory sentence. This trend spread to Britain, Canada, and Australia. In England and Wales, 'three strikes' provisions were introduced in 1997 for repeat burglars and drug traffickers; there are 'automatic' life sentences for an offender convicted for a second time for a 'serious offence' (such as manslaughter or **rape**) and five-year minimum sentences of imprisonment for firearms offences. Scotland and Northern Ireland have similar mandatory minimum sentences for firearms offences (Criminal Justice Act 2003 (UK), sections 287 and 292) and Scotland has three strike provisions for drug traffickers (Criminal Procedure (Scotland) Act 1995, section 205B). Mandatory sentences can also apply to other sentencing options and obligatory licence disqualification is common for drink driving offences. While lawyers are uncomfortable with mandatory sentences in general because of their potential to offend against principles of parsimony, proportionality, and individualized **justice**, it is mandatory **prison** sentences that are the most controversial. Advocates of mandatory prison sentences argue that they eliminate inconsistency, ensure harsher sentences, promote public confidence, and enhance deterrence. In addition, their supporters argue that mandatory sentencing laws targeting repeat offenders make society safer. However, their opponents contend that they redistribute sentencing discretion from the judiciary to the **police** and prosecuting authorities, escalate sentences, and swell prison populations and, by restricting sentencing discretion, lead to injustice in individual cases. It is also claimed that international experience demonstrates that mandatory sentences are discriminatory in impact—they disproportionally affect certain groups, usually the young, the disadvantaged, and **minorities**. Some commentators claim mandatory sentences fail to deter for reasons such as low detection rates and a lack of public awareness of mandatory penalties and that they can lead to greater inconsistency when some **judges** and prosecutors circumvent the application of the mandatory penalty to avoid injustice. It seems that politicians largely ignore these instrumental and normative objections to mandatory penalties because of the perception that tougher penalties appeal to the general public and increase public confidence in the **criminal justice system**.

KATE WARNER

mandatory share buy-backs   Under the Companies Act 2006, sections 979–982, a person who has made a **takeover** offer to acquire all the **shares** in a **company**, or all the shares of a particular class in the company, can, in certain circumstances, compulsorily buy out the remaining **minority shareholders** in the company. These provisions are triggered where the offer has been accepted within the preceding four months by the holders of at least 90 per cent of the value of the shares to which the offer relates (rather than 90 per cent of the voting rights). Shares which are the subject matter of the offer go into this calculation, but not shares already acquired (or contracted to be acquired) by the maker of the offer or his associates.

Once the provisions are triggered, the offeror can, within the following two months, make a statutory declaration, serve notice on the holder of any remaining shares to which the offer relates, and acquire those shares compulsorily. Provision is made for the determination and payment of the consideration for the shares. These provisions mean that small minority shareholders cannot block, or extract a disproportionate price for, the completion of a takeover. Dissatisfied shareholders can apply to court for relief under the Companies Act 2006, section 986.

Under the Companies Act 2006, sections 983–985, the minority shareholders can require the offeror to buy their shares, so they are not locked into the company.

RICHARD C NOLAN

Mansfield, William Murray   Described by Sir William **Holdsworth** as 'the greatest lawyer of the century', William Murray, first Earl of Mansfield, was born in 1705 at Scone Palace near Perth, Scotland. At age fourteen he removed to London to enter Westminster School, later prompting Dr Johnson's famous quip, 'Much can be made of a Scot if caught young'. Able and ambitious, young Murray advanced from Westminster School to Christ Church, Oxford, graduating as a BA in 1727; then proceeding to Lincoln's Inn, London. He was called to the bar in November 1730.

Murray established himself in his profession as counsel in a number of Scottish appeals in the **House of Lords** and in colonial disputes heard by the Commissioners of Trade and Plantations. He developed an active practice in the Court of **Chancery** in the late 1730s, undoubtedly contributing to a later judicial inclination to find equitable solutions to many **common law** cases (for which he was famously attacked in the *Junius* letters).

Under the patronage of the Duke of Newcastle, Murray was appointed **Solicitor General** in 1744 and entered the **House of Commons** as MP for Boroughbridge. He worked closely with **Attorney General,** Sir Dudley Ryder, until 1754 when Ryder was appointed **Chief Justice** of King's Bench and Murray became Attorney-General. Ryder died two years later, and Murray was his natural successor, both by tradition and ability. He demanded a peerage, which George II grudgingly granted, creating Murray Baron Mansfield.

Mansfield understood that in his own time England had entered a vigorous mercantile era of trade and manufacture, and he seized every opportunity to adapt the common law to the burgeoning commercial activity. In the interest of stability and predictability, he sought to articulate sensible common law principles that corresponded to established mercantile custom.

Through the cases that came before him, for example, he virtually 'wrote' the law of marine insurance. He has been justly called the founder of English commercial law.

In politics, Mansfield was invariably supportive of the **Crown**, as in his denunciation of the American **Revolution**. He also regularly upheld seditious **libel** prosecutions, insisting that it was the job of the **judge** and not the **jury** to decide whether a publication was seditious. This doctrine, though dating from the time of Queen Anne, drew rancorous opposition during the 1760s and afterwards from followers of Wilkes and advocates of freedom of the press.

In other areas, Mansfield was strongly supportive of individual rights. He became famous for the *Somerset* case of 1772, in which a former slave was brought before the court by a writ of *habeas corpus* obtained by abolitionist, Granville Sharp, and was set free. Mansfield also believed in religious toleration, prompting him and his fellow judges to interpret statutes restricting religious freedom so narrowly that the statutes were rendered impotent. An unfortunate consequence was that Mansfield's house in Bloomsbury Square, including his splendid library, was sacked and burnt by the anti-Catholic mob that pillaged London in the Gordon riots of 1780.

Mansfield and his wife Elizabeth, whom he had married in 1737, shared an evidently happy, childless life together until she died in 1784. In 1786, Mansfield's health faltered, though he did not resign until 1788. Thereafter, he lived in comfortable retirement at his country home, Kenwood, until his death on 20 March 1793.   JAMES OLDHAM

J Oldham, *English Common Law in the Age of Mansfield* (Chapel Hill and London: University of North Carolina Press, 2004)

CHS Fifoot, *Lord Mansfield* (Oxford: Clarendon Press, 1936)

manslaughter   *see* **crime and violence; homicide**

Manx law   The nature and sources of the law of the Isle of Man are best understood by an appreciation of its constitutional status. The history of the Isle of Man, originally a kingdom, is of Celtic and Viking origins, and includes periods when it was under the suzerainty of Norway, and then at various times a possession of both the Scots and English Crowns. It was effectively reacquired by the the UK **Crown** from the Atholl family by the Isle of Man Purchase Act 1765. It has always maintained a degree of constitutional autonomy.

It is a dependency of the Crown, retaining domestic autonomy within the constitutional convention that the Crown maintains responsibility for its defence and external affairs and 'ulimately the good government of the island'. The Isle of Man also has a limited legal relationship with the European Union (which is governed by Protocol 3 of the Act of Accession annexed to the (UK) Treaty of Accession 1972). From its complex history, Manx law has some traces of **Brehon law** and Udal law but apparently none of Scots law. However, it has been, and continues to be, significantly influenced by English law.

Legislation is the most important source of Manx domestic law. Tynwald, the Parliament of the Isle of Man, enacts both primary and secondary legislation for the Island. The Parliament reputedly dates from 979 and its legislative competence, asserted to be unlimited in respect of the Island, is at least coeval with that of Westminster. Acts of Tynwald require Royal Assent, which is now commonly granted, under delegated powers, by the Queen's representative, the Lieutenant Governor of the Isle of Man.

However, the Crown had asserted, even prior to the 1765 Act, the capacity to legislate for the Island by Act of Parliament. **Acts of Parliament** relating to areas for which the Crown is conventionally responsible (for example, nationality and extradition) extend to the Island. Other Acts commonly expressly provide for their extension to the Island by **Order in Council**; however, the modern convention is that such Orders would not be made without consultation with the Manx government, which usually, but not invariably, elects to introduce parallel legislation in Tynwald. It has also been held that Acts of Parliament may apply to the Island by necessary implication. Some UK legislation is applied directly by Manx legislation, as with much social security legislation; and, in many other areas, Manx legislation commonly adopts UK statutory provisions with appropriate insular amendment.

Together with customary law, English common law principles also provide the basis of Manx **common law**. The Isle of Man has its own courts, although the final court of appeal is the Judicial Committee of the **Privy Council**. However, being a small jurisdiction, the Isle of Man generates a correspondingly limited volume of case law (although there is a commercial series of *Manx Law Reports*). The doctrine of **precedent** applies within the Manx court system, but outside its operation the decisions of English appellate courts are particularly persuasive. In *Frankland v R* (1978) the Privy Council observed: 'Decisions of English **courts**, particularly decisions of the **House of Lords** and the Court of Appeal in England, are not binding on Manx courts, but they are of high persuasive authority . . . Such decisions should generally be followed unless either there is some provision to the contrary in a Manx statute or there is some clear decision of a Manx court to the contrary, or, exceptionally, there is some local condition which would give good reason for not following the particular English decision'.

As might be expected from the foregoing, many areas of Manx substantive law are broadly similar to English law; for instance, contract, tort, **trusts**, family, employment, and social security law. The same is true of criminal law; it was codified in the nineteenth century; and although elements of the code are still in force, it was not maintained and much modern criminal law is now found in individual legislation. Land law has some distinctive features.

It is in areas relating to the operation of its finance sector that modern Manx law differs more significantly from English law. These include direct taxation (which, for instance, provides, with some exceptions, for 'zero-rate' company tax), company law (which has distinctive forms of company structure), and financial supervision, which is somewhat more rigorous and comprehensive than in the UK (there are, for instance, statutory Manx licensing and supervision regimes for both trust and corporate service providers).   T ST JOHN BATES

Marbury v Madison (1803)

Marbury v Madison was the first **United States Supreme Court** decision holding a federal statute unconstitutional. Thomas Jefferson defeated John Adams in the presidential election of 1800, and his party gained a majority in Congress as well. Retaining control of the national government for several months after the election, Adams's Federalist party enacted several statutes whose effect was to entrench their appointees in the national judiciary. Seeing the national courts as partisan, the new majority soon repealed the most important of those statutes. Among the statutes the Federalists enacted was a minor one creating positions for justices of the peace in the national capital. When Adams left office, the document formally naming William Marbury a justice of the peace remained undelivered, although Adams had signed it. Without seeking relief from any lower court, Marbury asked the Supreme Court to issue a writ of mandamus (a mandatory order) directing Jefferson, through his Secretary of State James Madison, to deliver the commission.

Chief Justice John Marshall, appointed by Adams to his position after the 1800 election, knew that Jefferson would refuse to comply with such an order. His opinion criticized Jefferson's failure to deliver the commission, saying that the rule of law required that remedies be available for violations of vested rights. Marshall strained to read the statute setting out the Court's jurisdiction as giving the Court the power to issue the writ Marbury requested, then strained to read the Constitution as defining the Court's jurisdiction in a way that barred Congress from enacting that statute. The opinion thus held that the Court lacked the power to issue the writ.

Marbury's enduring significance lay in this final step. By 1803 the theory of constitutional review was uncontroversial; many lower courts had already articulated the theory and some had actually applied it to invalidate legislation. In *Stuart v Laird* (1803), decided a week after *Marbury*, the Court upheld the constitutionality of the more important Jeffersonian responses to the Federalists' legislation dealing with the national courts, thereby averting a deeper constitutional crisis.

Marbury failed to address the most substantial arguments about review of legislation for constitutionality. That a statute cannot be enforced if it is inconsistent with the constitution is uncontroversial. The real difficulty, concealed only slightly by Marshall's strained readings of the applicable statutory and constitutional provisions, arises when the courts disagree with a reasonable constitutional interpretation fairly attributable to the legislature. Should the judges enforce their independent judgment, or defer to the legislature's different albeit reasonable interpretation? *Marbury* chooses the first option without defending the choice.

The Supreme Court did not invalidate another national statute until 1857, in *Dred Scott v Sandford* (1857), striking down Congress's attempt to limit the spread of slavery into the western territories. *Marbury* was rediscovered in the twentieth century, when it became celebrated as a building block of American constitutionalism.   MARK TUSHNET

maritime law   *see* **admiralty law**

market investigation references   A market investigation reference may be made by the Office of Fair Trading ('OFT') under the powers granted to it by the Enterprise Act 2002. The market investigation system is a development from the monopoly investigation provisions found in the Fair Trading Act 1973. The reference procedure is the first stage in the market investigation process, which is designed to allow the UK **competition** authorities to investigate markets in which they believe there are competition problems. Market investigations complement the OFT's powers under the Competition Act 1998.

Under section 5 of the Enterprise Act 2002 the OFT has the function of acquiring information to allow it to undertake its tasks. It may gather information of it own accord, it may receive complaints from interested parties, or 'super-complaints' from consumer bodies. After undertaking an investigation into the operation of a market, the OFT may decide to make a market investigation reference to the Competition Commission. The OFT has investigatory powers to allow it to decide whether to make a reference. The OFT has the power to require parties to attend and give evidence, to require the production of documents, and to require the supply of specified information.

Following its own investigation the OFT may make a reference to the Competition Commission, for a fuller investigation, where it has reasonable grounds for suspecting that any feature, or combination of features, of a UK market prevents, restricts, or distorts competition. The OFT has a discretion whether or not to make a reference. The OFT must identify the market, and the features of that market, to which the reference relates. A 'feature' includes the structure of the market or the conduct of one or more parties supplying or acquiring goods or services on that market. The OFT is required to consult any person on whose interests the reference is likely to have substantial impact. The OFT may decide not to make a reference to the Competition Commission where a binding undertaking has been accepted in lieu of a reference. An undertaking in this regard would include commitments from one or more parties involved to alter their future conduct in a manner which would address the competition problems identified by the OFT. As a full investigation by the Competition Commission can be lengthy and costly to business in a market there may be commercial benefits in negotiating an undertaking with the OFT.

Market investigation references are likely to be very useful when the OFT is investigating oligopolistic markets in which a small number of large undertakings control production or supply. The prohibitions in the Competition Act 1998 are not well suited to dealing with such markets, and it is believed that a fuller investigation of the structure and operation of such markets through a market investigation reference may be more appropriate to deal with the competition problems they create.

ANGUS MACCULLOCH

market manipulation   'Market manipulation' refers to interference in the normal working of securities markets for the purpose of creating a misleading impression as to the supply of, or demand for, or the price of securities, or to secure the price at an abnormal or artificial level. The objective of a person engaging in market manipulation is to benefit from the distortion in the market which results from the manipulation. For example, manipulation in the form of buy and sell transactions in which there is no change in real ownership may give a false impression that there is an active market in a security, thereby attracting buyers. The rationale for a prohibition of such activity is to safeguard the integrity of securities markets and maintain investor confidence in their orderly operation. Without a prohibition, investors may be deterred from trading in securities and the development of a capital market may be limited.

The prohibition of market manipulation forms part of the 'market abuse' regime contained in the **Financial Services and Markets Act 2000**. The prohibition is formulated so as to apply to behaviour that (a) is not accepted market practice; (b) is a manipulative device; or (c) would be regarded by a regular user as distorting the relevant market. The prohibition also extends to action which requires or encourages another person to engage in manipulation: the effect in many cases will be to make a firm liable as well as an individual. While in a dynamic and evolving marketplace the line between behaviour that is or is not manipulation may be a fine one, it is not possible to engage accidentally in market manipulation as the Act provides a defence that a person believed on reasonable grounds that his behaviour was not manipulation or that he took all reasonable precautions to avoid behaving in that way. That defence may also provide a basis for a firm to avoid liability when a 'rogue' employee engages in manipulation on his own initiative.

The **Financial Services Authority**'s Code of Market Conduct provides detailed guidance on manipulative behaviour, with illustrative examples of manipulation and reference to factors which are relevant in establishing whether or not a particular transaction amounts to manipulation. Two factors in particular are indicative of legitimate behaviour: first, the existence of a legal or regulatory obligation owed to a third party to carry out the transaction (eg an obligation to deal at an agreed price or point in time); and second, compliance with the rules of the relevant market as to how transactions are to be executed (eg as regards trading process and trade publication). The FSA is able to impose the same sanctions for market manipulation as it can for **insider dealing**.

Market manipulation is also a criminal offence. This offence is formulated in simpler terms than its counterpart in the market abuse regime (above). It differs also in the sense that it must be prosecuted through the criminal courts (with the appropriate safeguards for the defence) rather than through the Financial Services Authority's disciplinary procedures.   IAIN MACNEIL

market stability and the financial system

In the **United Kingdom** the stability of the financial system as a whole and of individual service providers (banks, building societies, insurance companies, and investment service providers) is especially important because London is arguably the world's leading financial centre and the financial services sector is an extremely important part of the UK economy.

A Memorandum of Understanding between HM Treasury, the **Bank of England,** and the **Financial Services Authority** sets out the framework for cooperation between these bodies to promote financial stability in the UK's financial system.

The Bank of England, in its role as the central bank of the United Kingdom, has responsibility for the overall stability of the UK financial system and is able to undertake financial support operations where necessary to prevent risk spreading throughout the financial system. With regard to the banking sector, the central bank also acts as lender of last resort to provide emergency lending to banks which are suffering from liquidity problems. This facility is meant to be a temporary solution for banks which have a cash flow problem, and such financial assistance is not available to other types of financial services providers, which are not thought to pose systemic risk. The Bank of England is an independent body which also has responsibility for setting interest rate levels. The responsibility for regulation and supervision of the providers of financial services rests with the Financial Services Authority.

ANDREW CAMPBELL

See also: **bank runs and capital adequacy**

marketing   *see* **unfair commercial practices**

marriage   Despite the prevalence of **divorce**, marriage is still an important social institution in the UK: the majority of couples who make a life together are married, and the majority of marriages are ended by **death** rather than by divorce. Marriage is also an important legal institution: although some rights have been conferred on cohabiting couples, the rights and responsibilities conferred on spouses are far more extensive. One practical reason for conferring rights on married couples is that it is usually clear whether a couple are married, both entry to and exit from marriage being regulated by law.

Eligibility to enter into marriage depends on the intending parties having attained adulthood (in England and Wales, although not in Scotland, parental consent is required if either is aged sixteen or seventeen), and not being of the same sex, already married or in a civil partnership, or closely related. A person who has undergone legally-recognized gender reassignment may marry in their reassigned sex.

A valid marriage may be contracted in various ways, but all of the prescribed routes involve the same three elements: preliminaries designed to publicize the intended marriage; a ceremony; and registration. In England and Wales the majority of marriages are celebrated in a civil ceremony. Such a ceremony may take place either in a register office or in a venue (such as a hotel) that has been approved for the celebration of civil marriage. Couples will usually supplement the bare legal formalities with their choice of readings and music. The ceremony may not include readings from religious texts or the singing of hymns, although poems and songs containing incidental religious references are permitted.

Unlike in many Continental countries, couples are not obliged to marry in a civil ceremony. The complexity of the law relating to religious marriages reflects historical distinctions between different religions and sects. An Anglican marriage may be preceded either by civil preliminaries, or by preliminaries particular to the **Church of England** (that is, banns, licence, or a special licence granted by the Archbishop of Canterbury). Those marrying according to the rites of other religions must comply with the civil preliminaries. For those marrying according to Quaker or Jewish rites, there are no further legal prescriptions: the time and place of the marriage is a matter for their religious authorities. By contrast, couples marrying according to other recognized religions may only do so in a place of worship that is licensed for marriage. The law further requires that the celebrant must be authorized.

Whatever form the ceremony takes, the **legislation** does not spell out the precise moment at which the parties become married. On the rare occasions when it has proved necessary to determine the issue, the **courts** have decided that the exchange of consent is the point of no return. For this reason, a failure to register the marriage cannot affect its validity: the parties are already married by this stage and cannot be 'unmarried' by a failure to record what has taken place.

The position in Scotland differs in certain details. There are uniform civil preliminaries for all marriages, and a religious wedding may take place anywhere provided that the celebrant is authorized. A civil wedding must take place in a registrar's office or other approved venue, although it is possible for temporary approval—for example of one's home—to be obtained. In the past, one key difference between Scots law and that of England and Wales was the possibility of a marriage arising without any formalities: if a couple lived together and were reputed to be married a court could deem them to be married 'by cohabitation and repute'. This possibility was, however, abolished in 2006.

The rules on the recognition of marriages celebrated overseas are complex. In broad terms, the parties must comply with the formalities prescribed by local law, while their **capacity** to marry will be determined by the laws of the country where they reside. If a couple travels from their UK home to a country that permits **polygamy** and there enter into a polygamous marriage, the marriage will not be recognized in the UK. By contrast, a polygamous marriage entered into while the parties were living in a country that permits polygamy will be recognized. A different rule applies to same-sex marriages (which at present can be celebrated only in The Netherlands, Belgium, Spain, and Canada): statute prescribes that such unions have the status of a **civil partnership** in the UK.

REBECCA PROBERT

marriage and divorce, history of The history of **marriage** and **divorce** is intertwined with the history of religion, and the distinctions embedded in the modern law owe much to its piecemeal development. It was the Church which, in the twelfth century, decided that the essence of marriage lay in the exchange of consent and which prescribed the formalities by which consent should be expressed. The Catholic concept of marriage as an indissoluble union meant that divorce was not available. Church courts decided on the validity of disputed unions, and were able to grant an annulment if certain impediments to the marriage existed. An annulment was, and remains, distinct from a divorce in the modern sense: a divorce is a means of bringing a marriage to an end, while an annulment is a mechanism for declaring that it never existed. This remained the basic approach for many centuries. After the Reformation, divorce was available in Scotland on the basis of adultery or desertion, but not in England or Wales (Henry VIII's 'divorces' were in fact annulments). It was not until the late seventeenth century that the forerunner of the modern divorce appeared: a small number of aristocrats succeeded in obtaining private **Acts of Parliament** dissolving their marriages and permitting them to remarry. Throughout the eighteenth century there was a trickle of such divorces, though barely one per year.

The second half of the seventeenth century also witnessed changes to marriage. During the English Commonwealth, a new civil procedure for marriage was introduced but proved short-lived. It has been assumed that the requirements of the Church were resented and ignored even prior to this, but the fact that under the Commonwealth some couples chose to marry before a clergyman even when such a ceremony had no legal effect calls into question that assumption. The new civil procedure, though rescinded in 1660, left its legacy in the willingness of couples to marry in ways other than those set out by Church and state. The Restoration saw an increase in 'clandestine' marriages (legitimate marriages celebrated before a clergyman though not according to Church requirements). Attempts to check this irregular practice by imposing fines enjoyed some success, but such initiatives merely shifted the problem: clergymen imprisoned for debt had little to fear from sanctions, and in London's debtors' prisons (including, most famously, the Fleet) such men conducted clandestine marriages in ever-increasing numbers. By the 1740s, an estimated one half of London's marriages took place within the Rules of the Fleet. It is often claimed that it was possible to marry at the time simply by exchanging consent, though the popularity of such Fleet marriages is strong evidence that this modern belief is mistaken. An informal exchange of consent to marry did bind the parties (though supporting evidence was needed in case of dispute), but this was not in itself regarded as a complete marriage. Couples who had merely exchanged consent to marry would be ordered to solemnize their marriage in church and could be punished for 'anticipating the wedding'. The best analogy is the two-stage process of purchasing a property: the parties are bound to proceed with the sale once the contract has been signed, but it is only upon completion that the buyer is entitled to take possession of the house. The vast majority of couples in the period either married regularly in church or clandestinely before a clergyman rather than by exchanging consent.

Even so, the number of clandestine marriages—with their associated problems of fraud, forgery, and bigamy—clearly indicated that reform was required, and in 1753 the Clandestine Marriages Act was passed. This gave statutory force to the requirements of the **canon law**, stipulating that a marriage that was not preceded either by banns or licence, and which was not celebrated in church, would be void. It also required parental consent for the marriages of minors, although this requirement was not absolute and could be evaded by an elopement to Scotland (notably to Gretna Green) where the Act did not apply. Jews and Quakers were exempted from compliance with the Act, as were members of the Royal family. However, Catholics were required to go through an Anglican ceremony of marriage if they desired a valid marriage. Most did so, although most went through an additional ceremony according to their own rites. After 1753 the church courts could no longer enforce an informal exchange of consent, although until 1970 the **common law courts** could

still grant damages for breach of promise if one party later changed his or her mind.

Over time, changes in religious allegiance meant that the obligation of an Anglican ceremony for all but Jews and Quakers became increasingly unwelcome. In 1836 the option of civil marriage was introduced, as was marriage according to the rites of other religious groups, although distinctions between different types of religious marriages remained. A new chapter in the history of marriage and divorce began in 1857, when the role formerly played by the church courts was transferred to a new civil court. This new court was also able to grant divorces, and from that time the law has had to grapple with the consequences of divorce on an increasingly large scale. Scottish marriage law was not modernized until the twentieth century: until 1939 it was possible to be married by exchanging consent or by having sexual intercourse after promising marriage.

REBECCA PROBERT

See also: **divorce, history of**

Marshall Hall, Sir Edward Sir Edward Marshall Hall (1858–1927) was one of the leading criminal barristers of the Edwardian period. His enduring fame rested on his skill as a defence counsel, with a reputation for being able to secure acquittals in even the most hopeless of cases. He was a flamboyant and theatrical advocate, whose behaviour gave rise to large numbers of anecdotes about how witnesses had collapsed under cross-examination or how unsympathetic juries had been won over.

After graduating from Cambridge in 1883, he was called to the bar and took silk in 1888. Although his early career was successful and generated a comfortable income, his fame rested on his appearance in a string of cases after 1907. He acted for the defence in a number of the most sensational murder trials of the early twentieth century, such as the cases of Robert Wood (1907), Frederick Henry Seddon (1912), George Joseph **Smith** (1915), and others—even if in several of these cases his presence was unable to prevent the jury from finding the accused guilty.

His reputation and standing were based primarily on his skills as an advocate rather than his knowledge of the law. He had a good understanding of forensic science and was able to use this to challenge expert witnesses. He was also a formidable presence in court and was liked by juries and the public more generally. He continued to practice until shortly before his death in February 1927.

LINDSAY FARMER

martial law   *see* **military law**

Marxist legal theories   Theories about law from a Marxist perspective have evolved in line with developments in Marxism as a whole. Early writers, including Marx and Engels in the *Communist Manifesto* 1848, and later Lenin in *The State and Revolution* 1917, stressed the function of law in capitalist societies as an instrument of class oppression. In the nineteenth century, Marxists could point convincingly to many instances of law, such as the laws of theft, commerce, and labour law, which served to protect the interests of owners of property and capital against the interests of workers and the poor. The legal system could be described as a superstructure, which supported and consolidated the underlying economic infrastructure of a capitalist society. This legal system was controlled by powerful interests who manipulated the rules and its operations in order to protect and enhance their position.

Yet Marxist writers were conscious that this fairly simple formula that law is an instrument of class oppression could not be easily applied to all aspects of legal systems, such as those protecting individual civil liberties or laws that enable freedom of contract to be realized. These laws appeared to function in a neutral way between classes or, indeed, in some instances, to protect weaker persons and workers against oppression and exploitation. Indeed, the emerging powerful ideas of the **rule of law**, **judicial independence,** and the protection of individual human rights, posed a major challenge to the Marxist theory of law.

A part of the answer offered by Marxists was the explanation that ideologies such as the rule of law and the protection of civil liberties, though apparently neutral, were at bottom connected to a broader set of beliefs described as the ideology of the ruling class. Although these beliefs and views about the world might appear to be no more than common sense or essential moral standards, Marxists argued that ultimately these ideas were shaped by the interests of the ruling class. The idea that stealing was always wrong, for instance, though widely respected as a moral, religious, and a legal principle, ultimately favoured the interests of the bourgeoisie against the workers and the poor. By articulating in detail these values and ideas, the legal system might appear to embody moral principles and common sense values; but when subject to critical analysis, which Marxists would supply, the neutrality and fairness of these values would be demystified and exposed as ideologies that served the interests of the ruling class. As Anatole France quipped, the law forbids equally both the rich and poor from sleeping under the bridges over the Seine.

After 1945 Marxists in Western Europe had to confront the problem that Communist regimes in the Soviet Union and elsewhere used totalitarian systems of government, which, in the name of Marxism, paid scant attention to values such as the rule of law and individual liberties. Was this lawlessness a correct interpretation of Marxism? It could be supported as an interpretation of Marxism because it seemed to follow, as Lenin had pointed out, that once a class-based society had been abolished and replaced by a Communist society, there would not longer be any need for instruments of class oppression such as the law. Communist governments themselves rejected that interpretation and insisted rather that they had developed a model of socialist legality. Western intellectuals found this notion of socialist legality implausible, and instead tried to draw a distinction between, on the one hand, laws that could be used to protect the interests of the working class, such as the right to freedom of association and to join a trade union; and on the other hand, laws that reinforced social structures of exploitation. Yet it always proves extremely difficult to apply this distinction. In the case of the protection of human rights, for instance, do these laws significantly protect the interests of workers or do they rather serve, by virtue of their false neutrality, individualism, and appeals to equality, to mystify the underlying reality of the system of class exploitation? The confusion among Marxists about how to incorporate ideas of legality and liberty in their theory, whilst at the same time continuing to criticize the mystifications of the ideology of the rule of law and human rights, perhaps helps to explain the declining interest in Marxist theories of Law in recent decades.

HUGH COLLINS

Master of the Rolls   The Master of the Rolls is the president of the civil division of the Court of Appeal of England and Wales and ranks second in precedence to the **Lord Chief Justice** among judges in that jurisdiction. The office-holder has a dominant influence on the administration of civil justice.

Originating before—perhaps well before—1286, the office was known in early days as Keeper of the Rolls of Chancery, a title which described its function for some centuries. The office developed gradually into a judicial office, many holders in early days being churchmen and canon lawyers. In due course the Master of the Rolls became a judge of the Court of Chancery, until 1831 the only such judge other than the **Lord Chancellor**.

When the Supreme Court of Judicature was created in 1875, the Master of the Rolls became a member of both the Court of Appeal and the Chancery Division of the High Court, but from 1881 he ceased to be a judge of the High Court and sat exclusively in the Court of Appeal. This change reflected the unusual eminence of Sir George Jessel, from whom (it was judged) no one was thought worthy to hear appeals. The most recent holders of the office have been common or commercial lawyers and not chancery lawyers.

Until 1958 the Master of the Rolls was nominally the Keeper of Public Records. He remains responsible for the records of the Chancery of England and manorial records, and retains an advisory role in relation to public records more generally. He has long-standing responsibilities for the regulation, conduct, and discipline of solicitors.

TOM BINGHAM

match fixing This is the corrupt practise of manipulating the scores, statistics, or final results of a sporting match, race, or other event. Americans refer to it as 'tanking' a match. The typical purpose of match fixing is usually financial gain through cheating at gambling on scores, statistics, or final results that are pre-determined through the 'fix'. But in some cases the purpose of match fixing is a sporting one, ie to gain an advantage or progress in a competition. For example, where a specific score or result in a football match is required in order for one or both teams to avoid relegation or to be promoted, those teams may conspire to achieve that score or result.

One of the most famous examples of 'match fixing' occurred in the 1919 baseball World Series. Eight players from the Chicago White Sox (later nicknamed the Black Sox) were accused of throwing the Series for gambling purposes and were subsequently banned for life. Other match fixing scandals include: the lifetime bans imposed on international cricketers Hansie Cronje, Mohammed Azaruddin, Ajay Jadeja, Ajay Sharma, and Salim Malik in 2000 and 2001; football referees exposed for fixing matches in Germany and Brazil in 2005; and the Italian football scandal when four leading clubs, AC Milan, Juventus, Fiorentina, and Lazio were implicated in 2006. The UK Gambling Act 2005 criminalizes match fixing.

URVASI NAIDOO

S Wilde, *Caught: Hansie Cronje and Cricket's Match Fixing Scandal* (London: Aurum Press, 2001)

maternity Our commonsense understanding of maternity is widely understood as a status which derives from giving birth to a **child** or children. The term is publicly displayed in hospitals—'Maternity Unit' to signpost the place where new mothers and their babies temporarily reside. Traditionally, the word 'maternity' is used to denote a biological and genetic connection between a particular **woman** and her child and it is the act of giving birth to a child which establishes a woman's maternity. Once maternity is established through the birth of the child certain state entitlements derive from it such as paid maternity leave and visits from health care professionals. However, it is important, especially in legal terms, to differentiate between 'maternity' and **motherhood**. Maternity is almost exclusively concerned with the biological or genetic connection between a child and her or his mother. Motherhood may be understood very differently. In order to demonstrate the distinction between maternity and motherhood one might draw upon the example of **surrogacy**.

Surrogacy poses a challenge to this common sense understanding of maternity. In surrogacy the law has to choose who should be treated as a child's mother. This is due to the fact that two or three women might be involved in the creation of a child. There is firstly the woman who *carries or gestates* the child at the behest of another person or couple who are unable to have their own child naturally. The woman who gives birth to the child may have no genetic connection to the child due to the fact that a *donor* egg or the *commissioning* woman's egg has been used. However, she will have a biological connection whilst she carries the **foetus** which arises through the foetus's dependency on her for survival. In law, the woman who carries the child is treated as the mother of the child regardless of her lack of genetic relationship to the child through section 27(1) of the Human Fertilization and Embryology Act 1990. She will find herself in the maternity unit along with others who have given birth in the more usual way. After the birth of the child, the commissioning couple will apply through various orders to acquire full responsibilities for the child. The commissioning woman or mother would assume the responsibilities which normally arise from the establishment of maternity through birth. It is not true to say therefore, that motherhood *necessarily* follows maternity.

JULIE WALLBANK

maternity rights Employment law provides a number of rights specifically in connection with maternity, these being in addition to parental leave rights and the right not to be subject to **sex** discrimination. It is worth noting that discrimination on grounds of pregnancy will always be regarded, at least in an employment and related context, as sex discrimination (Sex Discrimination Act 1975, section 6A). In addition, women employees are entitled to a period of leave in connection with pregnancy and birth. This is currently a total of 26 weeks' 'ordinary maternity leave' to which all pregnant employees are entitled, followed by a further 26 weeks' 'additional maternity leave'.

During ordinary maternity leave employees are entitled, broadly, to enjoy all the terms of their employment contract except those relating to pay (maternity pay is pegged at 90 per cent of salary for six weeks followed by a fixed rate for a period which is currently 33 weeks). During additional maternity leave, rights are more restricted. On return from ordinary maternity leave, a woman is entitled to exactly the same job, while, if she chooses to take additional maternity leave, her right is to return to the same job or, if that is not reasonably practicable, to return to a job which is both suitable for her and appropriate for her to do in the circumstances. Having said this, if a woman is disadvantaged for a reason related to her absence on maternity leave, this is likely to be unlawful sex discrimination.

Rights to adoptive leave are similar but can be taken by either adoptive parent.

AILEEN MCCOLGAN

Maybrick, Florence The trial and conviction of Florence Maybrick (1862–1941) for the murder of her husband by poisoning in Liverpool in July 1889 was a notable miscarriage of justice, and contributed to the building of public pressure for the establishment of Court of Criminal Appeal in England.

James Maybrick was a successful cotton broker in Liverpool, and married Florence in 1881. The marriage was not a success. James maintained several mistresses, and Florence also had an affair with a local businessman. The couple fought when James learned about this, and shortly afterwards he died under mysterious circumstances. After death his body was found to contain significant, but not necessarily fatal, quantities of arsenic. Florence was charged with murder, and was tried at Liverpool Assizes before Sir James Fitzjames **Stephen**, the eminent criminal lawyer and historian.

The key legal issues in the trial were the questions of whether James Maybrick had in fact died of poisoning by arsenic, and whether Florence had administered arsenic with intent to kill. The prosecution relied on evidence that Florence had purchased fly papers containing arsenic and had steeped them in water to remove the poison. Arsenic was also discovered in a bottle of meat juice for administration to her husband, which she was proved to

have tampered with. The defence laid great stress on the contradictory medical evidence and the failure by the prosecution to fix a cause of death. There was clear evidence that James Maybrick had self-administered poisons, including strychnine and arsenic, either in the belief that they had aphrodisiac properties or possibly to suppress a venereal infection. The post-mortem, moreover, revealed that while there was arsenic in his liver, intestines and kidney, there was none in his heart or bloodstream, which would be normal where arsenic was the cause of death. There was also evidence that he had taken a variety of other medicines, some of them poisons, during his final illness, the combined effect of which could have caused his death. It was also maintained that Florence had obtained and used the arsenic for cosmetic purposes, as was common at the time, and she testified that she had prepared the dose of arsenic for her husband at his own request. Stephen's summing up lasted two full days but was muddled and contradictory. He was also significantly prejudiced against Florence because she had committed adultery, which was taken as evidence of both motive and a criminal nature. She was convicted and sentenced to death.

The public outcry which followed led to the evidence being reviewed by the Home Secretary and **Lord Chancellor** who reached the conclusion that while there was evidence that Maybrick had administered poison to her husband with intent to murder, there was doubt that this poison had been the cause of his death, but that there was no need for a retrial. The death sentence was then commuted to life imprisonment. Stephen was censured for his remarks, and left the bench shortly afterwards, but there was no possibility of judicial appeal. Although campaigners continued to petition for her release, this was refused by successive Home Secretaries. Maybrick was finally released from prison in 1904.

LINDSAY FARMER

McDonald's Corporation v Steel & Morris Proceedings in the 'McLibel' case arose from the distribution of a six page leaflet entitled 'What's wrong with McDonald's?' as part of a campaign organized by Greenpeace against the international fast-food corporation in the late 1980s. The company issued a writ for libel against two Greenpeace members, Helen Steel and David Morris, in 1990. After much preliminary litigation, the trial proceeded without the jury that is normal in defamation actions, because the issues were considered too complicated. Although the judge's decision in favour of McDonald's was upheld by the Court of Appeal, the defendants eventually achieved success at the **European Court of Human Rights** ('ECtHR').

Politically, the case became a focus for opposition to the economic practices of multinational companies. It also showed that the public relations impact of libel litigation may be negative; and, although McDonald's won their action in the UK, they decided not to enforce the damages award against the protesters. Legally, the case showed the extent to which English libel law is weighted in favour of the financially powerful, since **legal aid** is not available. Steel and Morris were only able to defend the claim because they attracted public donations and considerable support from lawyers sympathetic to their plight.

The substance of the action involved a range of sweeping allegations. Examples that the judge found to be untrue were that McDonald's had been to blame for starvation in the Third World, had bought tracts of land in the Third World and evicted small farmers from it, were guilty of destruction of rainforest, knew that their food was unhealthy but did not make it clear, offered low wages for bad working conditions, and used promotional gimmicks to cover up the true quality of their food. He found that it was true to say that McDonald's exploited children's susceptibility to advertising and that, overall, they were culpably responsible for cruel practices in the rearing and slaughter of some of the animals used to produce their food. Overall, the judge concluded that McDonald's reputation had been materially damaged and he awarded compensation, which on appeal was only slightly reduced to £48,000.

However, the ECtHR decided in 2005 (*Steel and Morris v The United Kingdom* (2005)) that the free speech rights of Steel and Morris had been breached because they had been unfairly disadvantaged in defending the UK action. The lack of legal aid had left them with the choice of withdrawing the offending leaflet and apologizing to McDonald's or themselves bearing the burden of proving the truth of the complex allegations contained in it. Whilst the ECtHR emphasized that untrue statements will not normally attract protection, it held that the interest in the free circulation of information and ideas about the activities of powerful commercial entities outweighed McDonald's rights and reputation. Steel and Morris were awarded €35,000 for the stress and anxiety suffered, together with a contribution to their costs.   TOM GIBBONS

'McLibel' Case   *see McDonald's Corp v Steel & Morris*

means-tested benefits Means-tested benefits are targeted at people whose income and capital are insufficient to enable them to maintain a minimum standard of living as defined by the state. They provide or ensure a basic income, help with some housing costs, and assistance with rent and council tax liability. For basic income maintenance, the principal means-tested benefits are income support and state pension credit. However, the basic means-tested benefit for those who are of working age and expected to maintain an engagement with the labour market is income-based jobseeker's allowance. Other major means-tested benefits are council tax benefit, and housing benefit, which will meet all or a proportion of the claimant's 'eligible' rent (namely the rent for which he or she is responsible, up to a particular level). Some social security benefits are partially means-tested. For example, if an incapacity benefit claimant receives an occupational pension above a prescribed rate, his or her incapacity benefit entitlement will be reduced.

In some cases a claimant may be entitled to means-tested benefits even though in receipt of other benefits, although these other benefits may be taken into account in assessing the claimant's income, possibly reducing the means-tested benefit. Examples of benefits taken into account in this way include contribution-based jobseeker's allowance and the state retirement pension. In other cases, such as where the claimant receives disability living allowance, none of the benefit will count as income for the purposes of their means-tested benefit. Entitlement to a means-tested benefit may be a passport to other forms of state welfare support, for example, grants or loans from the social fund, or free school meals for children.

Means-tested benefits are the most complex element of the social security system and the most costly to administer. As they are targeted on needs and the needy, the law has to identify the kinds of costs that the state regards as appropriate for the benefit to cover, the persons who are in the greatest need, and a level of support that is considered appropriate in the particular circumstances. Sometimes this is done fairly crudely, as in the case of age bands in income support (so that a person aged 25 automatically receives more than someone aged 24 or below) or, in the case of housing benefit, where eligible rent is related to a local limit regardless of the actual rent payable by the claimant. In other cases, the rules may make fine distinctions—for example, between payments received by the claimant that qualify as 'income' and those that qualify as 'capital'. The effect of capital limits for means-tested benefits is that savings or other capital above a prescribed limit will reduce or preclude entitlement.

NEVILLE HARRIS

media concentration The media industry is particularly prone to concentration because some aspects of media production and delivery make exploitation of economies of scale and scope desirable. Normally, **competition law** will be used to prevent concentration or to minimize the impact of a concentrated industry. However, media concentration presents additional concerns. The fewer the number of media controllers or companies within the market, the greater is the risk that diversity of information and opinion may be stifled. In liberal democracies, the media are regarded as essential to a properly functioning democracy and an informed citizenry, because they provide access to information, views, and ideas, and an arena for public debate. The tools of competition law are not well suited to address concerns about the 'market for ideas'. Thus, it has been common for countries that value informed debate to impose specific rules on the media industry to promote diversity. This form of **regulation** is not seen as detracting from, but as promoting, freedom of expression, and so can be found even in jurisdictions which have express free speech guarantees such as the **United Kingdom** and the United States.

A number of regulatory approaches can assist in promoting diversity, but the main approach has been to limit the extent of ownership and control of media companies to ensure that the industry is not dominated by only a few individuals or companies. Ownership and control rules apply mainly to broadcasting, but they can also affect newspapers. They are generally complex in their design and are usually drafted to catch orthodox means of control, such as shareholdings, and more practical means, such as ability to influence the operations of the media company. Ownership and control rules might include limits on the accumulation of interests within media of a certain type. Thus, for example, there might be a limit on the number of television broadcasting licences which can be controlled by one person or company within a designated area, or a limit on the share of the market (measured, for example, by audience share) controlled. Also important are cross-media restrictions. These limit interests held across different types of media. Here it is usual for rules to prohibit or restrict cross-interests in television, radio, and newspapers.

Although ownership and control rules have a long history in jurisdictions such as the UK and the US, there has frequently been pressure for their removal.

In recent years this pressure has intensified with the media industry arguing that new forms of content delivery and the internet provide sufficient diversity, making such rules redundant. Such arguments are questionable because, whilst there may be new forms of content delivery, it is less clear how much new content is being developed. Relaxation of such rules also generates considerable public concern. In 2003, the UK relaxed its ownership and control rules substantially, and other jurisdictions have been following this example. However, to date, governments have not been willing to remove such rules altogether.

LESLEY HITCHENS

media reporting of courts and tribunals, restrictions on UK **courts** have frequently warned against 'trial by media', particularly in criminal proceedings before lay juries, reflecting a concern that sensational or selective reporting may prevent defendants receiving a fair trial. Where this is found to have happened, proprietors, editors, and journalists respectively face a range of penalties that theoretically includes imprisonment, although in practice it is usual for transgressors to be given substantial fines. In addition to penalties for prejudicial publication, UK law has a formidable array of restrictions that prevent the reporting and publication of selected matters in order to safeguard the administration of justice as well as the privacy and safety of some defendants, victims, and witnesses.

Despite all the domestic restrictions that inhibit media reporting of court proceedings and related matters, UK law remains committed in principle at least to the ideal of 'open justice'. The notion that the courts ought, as far as possible, to conduct their business in front of both ordinary members of the public and media representatives has several complementary rationales. Openness of judicial proceedings, and the wider scrutiny of judicial processes which it entails, serves to make the courts and judges more accountable to the community on whose behalf they act. Publicity offers one means of ensuring a competent judicial performance. Protection from incompetent or even biased conduct on the part of court officials also benefits defendants. Open justice further enhances the prospects of an informed public debate about legal issues generally. Moreover, where justice is seen to be administered fairly, there is a further and important benefit of enhanced levels of public confidence.

Court reporters clearly play a vital role in opening up the administration of justice to public scrutiny and comment, although the commercial realities behind (mainly tabloid) media reporting of court cases mean that court coverage tends to concentrate on cases involving extreme violence, such as murder or sexual offences, and those concerning well-known persons or with bizarre facts.

A major limit on media freedom to report and comment upon specific legal proceedings is known as the *sub judice* rule. Under the Contempt of Court Act 1981, this rule applies whenever proceedings are 'active'. In the case of criminal proceedings this is defined to mean the period commencing, for example, with the arrest of a suspect or the issue of a warrant for the suspect's arrest. Proceedings only cease to be active where they are discontinued, or upon the acquittal or sentencing of the defendant, or when any other verdict puts an end to the proceedings. In a prosecution under the Act, the **Attorney-General** need not show that the publisher or journalist *intended* to cause a risk of interference with particular proceedings. It is sufficient to establish that, judged at the time of publication, the relevant risk was created. This is known as the *strict liability* rule, which has the effect of making it easier to secure a conviction against media organizations. The standard of liability set by the 1981 Act is that a publication creates a 'substantial risk' of 'serious prejudice' to the course of justice in particular proceedings. The prejudice in question may be caused to the defence or prosecution. A 'substantial risk' has been defined by the **House of Lords** as including any risk which is more than remote. Examples of matters that are capable of meeting the standard include the publication of an accused person's previous convictions or their photograph (when the identity of the suspect is a live issue). Sometimes, in the context of trial reporting, it is the addition of material in a published article that has not been put before the jury that causes difficulties for media organizations.

Liability must be assessed according to conditions prevailing at the time of publication. In assessing whether a publication meets the 'substantial risk of serious prejudice' standard, factors that are important include whether publication occurs in an area from which jurors are likely to be drawn, the number of copies of the offending publication which are circulated (or the number of listeners/viewers in the case of broadcast material) and the residual impact of the publication on a notional juror at the time of trial. On this latter point, relevant criteria include: (i) the length of time between publication and likely trial date; (ii) the likely focusing effect of listening over a prolonged period to evidence in the case; and (iii) the likely effect of the judge's directions to the jury. Thus, a nine-month delay between the publication of prejudicial material and likely start of any criminal trial might serve to blunt the prejudicial impact of a publication that reveals a defendant's criminal past. However, if the words are spoken by well-known television personalities on prime time television, the extent of any 'fade' factor will be diminished. In the case of prejudicial publicity that occurs once trial proceedings have started, there is little or no scope for the fading of prejudicial materials. However, not all speech which causes a substantial risk of serious prejudice to active proceedings results in criminal liability. Discussion of matters that have some connection to legal proceedings is lawful provided that it touches only incidentally upon those legal proceedings.

In addition to limits imposed by the strict liability rule, media organizations wishing to report court proceedings are subject to a panoply of constraints that curtail (in some cases severely) what may be published. Two main types of restriction can be identified: prior restraints and automatic restraints. The former comprise orders made in exercise of judicial discretion (sometimes itself conferred by statute) and operate prior to publication to restrain the publication of certain matters. Automatic restrictions, on the other hand, apply without the need for a formal court order. Both may be considered problematic—the former because (as a US court put it in 1975) a 'free society prefers to punish the few that abuse rights of speech *after* they break the law than to throttle them and all others beforehand'. Automatic reporting restrictions have tended to emerge from parliamentary debates characterized by the absence of a principled concern for freedom of expression.

IAN CRAM

media, regulation and freedom of Freedom of the press and the other media is essential in a liberal democracy, because it is through the media that citizens acquire information about politics and subjects of social concern. The media also provide a platform for discussion of these topics by citizens, as well as themselves influencing this discussion by, for example, highlighting issues for extensive treatment. Press freedom is closely linked to **freedom of expression**. On one view, the freedom of newspaper editors and journalists is the same as their freedom of expression to publish what they like. From another perspective, freedom of the media not only contains these individual freedoms of expression, but also confers separate institutional rights designed to ensure that newspaper publishers and broadcasting corporations are independent of the state. For instance, it would be incompatible with press freedom to require a licence to publish a newspaper or magazine, or to impose discriminatory taxation on them. There would be no broadcasting freedom if government officials determined the programme schedules or decided who should be allowed to appear on radio and television.

But the treatment of the different mass media is inconsistent. There is little **regulation** of the press in modern democracies. The licensing and censorship of newspapers is incompatible with freedom of expression and press freedom. Newspapers must comply only with the general laws concerning **libel, privacy, contempt of court**, official secrets, and other restrictions on free expression. In some countries press laws provide for a legally enforceable right of reply where an individual considers that an inaccurate statement has been made about him. That does not exist in the **United Kingdom**. Instead, a complaint may be made to the **Press Complaints Commission** that a newspaper has published a significant inaccuracy, has infringed privacy, intruded into grief or shock, or in some other way broken the published code of press ethics. But the Commission cannot impose any financial sanction when it finds a breach of the code, let alone stop the publication of a story which clearly infringes privacy.

The broadcasting media are more heavily regulated. That has been the case since the inception of broadcasting in the 1920s, when it was usually the monopoly of a public company such as the **British Broadcasting Corporation** ('BBC'). It is illegal to broadcast without a permit from a regulatory authority. That authority generally has power under statute to formulate and enforce programme standards which go beyond the restrictions imposed by the criminal and civil law. Characteristic of these standards are requirements on broadcasters to treat controversial questions impartially and to ensure that programmes do not contain scenes unsuitable for children. Public service channels, such as the BBC and the principal commercial channels, have to provide news bulletins, which must be accurate as well as impartial. These channels may also be required to transmit documentaries, original drama and music, religious and children's programmes, and other programmes which attract fewer viewers and are therefore less well supported by advertising income. Further, there are limits on both the content and the quantity of advertising. In the UK the government has retained its controversial power to direct that some matters are not broadcast. With its power to appoint the members of broadcasting authorities and to determine the licence fee by which the BBC is financed, the government's influence poses some danger to broadcasting freedom. Certainly, it is more circumscribed than press freedom.

It is not easy to explain these differences in the legal regimes governing the mass media. It used to be argued that broadcasting frequencies were scarce, so that those fortunate enough to be awarded a licence should hold it as a trustee for the public; it was reasonable not to allow them to show whatever programmes they liked. That makes little sense now. Digital broadcasting enables greater use to be made of these frequencies, while the scarcity argument hardly applies to cable and satellite channels. A better explanation is that television is a particularly powerful medium, with its combination of pictures, sound, and music; but that argument is unpersuasive for radio, which is indeed subject to less regulation. A third argument is that hitherto many people have acquired particular expectations of the broadcasting media, which they do not have of the press. Because the former have been subject to impartiality and other rules, listeners and viewers rely on them for objective news and other quality programmes. These expectations may currently be changing with the proliferation of channels, most of them devoted to films and popular entertainment.

The advent of the electronic media raises new regulatory problems. The internet provides a revolutionary means of communication by which individuals can communicate their ideas instantaneously around the world. Given the amount of traffic, it is difficult, perhaps impossible, to regulate it in the same way as the broadcasting media have been regulated. Yet it can create great harm by the immediate distribution worldwide of child pornography, other sexually explicit images, racist speech, and libellous messages. Governments in liberal democracies, unlike authoritarian regimes, have not attempted to licence either use of the internet or the internet service providers ('ISPs') that provide the means for electronic communication. Even television services provided on the internet fall outside the control of the broadcasting authorities, an immunity which is hard to justify in principle. Courts in the US have held incompatible with media freedom attempts to impose special restrictions on the communication of indecent material on the internet in the interests of children, emphasizing that their protection is primarily a matter for parents. In the UK there is a system of voluntary regulation, operated by agreement between the ISPs.

What is unclear is whether the internet will take the place of the traditional mass media, in particular public service broadcasting, in providing an effective platform for public debate. Unless it is clear that it will discharge that role, it would be misguided to jettison public service broadcasting standards, which at least ensure that there is something on television worth talking about.

ERIC BARENDT

T Gibbons, *Regulating the Media* (London: Sweet & Maxwell, 2nd edn, 1998)

mediation   One of the most striking developments in justice systems of the West across the last years of the twentieth century has been the progressive re-emergence of mediation. With the increasing dominance of the **courts** in an evolving public sphere as the nation state consolidated, and the parallel ascendancy of lawyers as a specialist service profession, mediation had receded into the background. While it was always 'there', an irreducible potential of any situation in which more than two agents were involved, this ancient mode of intervention was scarcely institutionalized outside the fields of international relations and labour disputes. Yet, over a few short years, as part of a wider shift towards participatory modes of decision-making, public disputing has been transformed with the appearance of professional mediators and the parallel, growing readiness of the courts themselves to sponsor 'settlement'.

The mediator receives quite limited attention in classical social theory, but a defining analysis was provided early in the twentieth century by the German sociologist Georg Simmel in his great *Soziologie* (1908). There, Simmel pointed to the fact that the mediator, in the shape of the 'third' person, is always present in the social world even though not named as such and even though the role is left unexamined; the constellation yielding the mediator is a structural feature, generally observable across cultures. Simmel identifies two core features for mediation: first, it is an intervention carried out from a non-aligned standpoint—mediators are not partisans; secondly, it is an intervention supportive of other people's decision-making—the mediator has no determinative authority. Although Simmel thus fixes the mediator firmly in a non-aligned, non-determinative role—and so marks a contrast with the lawyer on the one hand and the arbitrator on the other—mediation still represents an elusive, fugitive label, claimed by interveners of widely differing rank and ambition. It may be attempted by anyone from the hesitant neighbour to the dominant political superior; and the help provided may range from minimal assistance with communications to an extensive and expert guiding role.

Under the contemporary re-institutionalization of mediation, two contrasting prototypes of the disinterested professional intervener have emerged. One attempts a self-consciously limited intervention, confined to responsibility for *process*, thus enabling disputing parties to reach decisions on the *substance* of issues that divide them. For the purposes of this model, mediation is conceptualized as an intervention facilitating other people's negotiations: so without first imagining negotiation, we cannot imagine mediation. The other stereotype contemplates a much more active intervention, the exercise of a role akin to expert consultancy, requiring skills of information retrieval, diagnosis, and prescription. In much of the literature on mediation, these differences are treated lightly as simply involving variant 'facilitatory' and 'evaluative' strands of a single professional activity. But this inclusive approach seems to paper over an important analytic divide between mediation and primarily advisory interventions.

While a revival of mediation during the last two decades has been visible across a wide range of social fields, progress towards the emergence of a unified profession has been limited. Training, provision, and regulation of mediators in the commercial, community, family, international, labour, and restorative justice (criminal) fields evolved with little theoretical exchange or institutional cooperation. However, mediators working in these fields participated, with the Law Society, in a government-sponsored project to create 'occupational standards' for mediation, leading to a mediation qualification as part of a larger governmental scheme to devise National Vocational Qualifications ('NVQs'). Subsequently, mediation organizations in the commercial, community, and family fields came together in a Joint Mediation Forum to draft a common Model Code of Conduct for mediators. The Forum proved short-lived, but mediation providers in the civil and commercial fields have formed a Civil Mediation Council with a potential role in quality assurance. Only in the area of family mediation has an embryonic professional association, The UK College of Family Mediators, so far emerged.

Two complicating factors have inhibited the evolution of mediation as an autonomous profession. One of these has been the growing aspiration of adjacent professions to dominate this field, reflected in the determination of the Law Society to treat mediation as part of 'legal practice' and the move by the Chartered Institute of Arbitrators to claim overall control of mediation. Both aspirations seem problematic: the partisan advisory and representative role traditionally occupied by the lawyer and the determinative role of the arbitrator are equally at odds with the non-aligned facilitation attempted by the mediator. A second complicating factor has been the hostility of mediation provider bodies towards the emergence of regulatory regimes essential for professional development.

SIMON ROBERTS

PH Gulliver, *Disputes and Negotiations: A Cross Cultural Perspective* (London & New York: Academic Press, 1979)

M Roberts, *Developing the Craft of Mediation: Reflections on Theory and Practice* (London: Jessica Kingsley Publishers, 2007)

See also: **alternative dispute resolution; settlement of claims**

mediation of civil disputes   *see* **alternative dispute resolution**

mediation of international disputes   *see* **international dispute settlement**

mediation, criminal   *see* **mediation**

mediation, family   *see* **mediation**

medical accidents   *see* **medical negligence**

medical confidentiality   Confidentiality requires that certain information is kept secret. It is a crucial aspect of relationships such as priest and penitent, solicitor and client, and accountant and client. It is also one of the cornerstones of health care law since, without assurances that information would be kept confidential patients would be reluctant to disclose sensitive information relevant to their medical diagnosis and treatment.

To be protected by the **common law** information must hold the necessary quality of confidence and must be imparted in circumstances that import an obligation to maintain confidence. A legal breach of confidence will occur under the common law when such information is disclosed in an unauthorized manner which is detrimental to the person who originally communicated the information. A breach committed by a professional person will generally be regarded as professional negligence.

Confidentiality is also protected by several statutes and Conventions. Key amongst these is Article 8 of the **European Convention of Human Rights** (along with the domestic **Human Rights Act 1998**) which confers a right to respect for the **privacy** of **family life**, home, and correspondence. This provision pertains as against any interference with that right by public authorities such as health care institutions and newspapers.

The Data Protection Act 1998 includes eight principles of data protection which aim to ensure that all data (information) are protected. The overarching principle is that data are processed fairly and lawfully according to the subject's rights. Data handlers (anybody who collects, collates, stores, or transfers data relevant to the Act) must ensure that data are only obtained and processed for specified purposes, are relevant to that purpose, securely stored, but for no longer than is necessary, and adequately protected when transferred. This Act also enables patients to gain access to information contained in their own **medical records**, unless disclosure is likely to cause harm to the patient or others. The Access to Medical Reports Act 1988 is similar in that it permits patients access to information in medical reports prepared by their doctor for their employers, potential employers, or insurers.

The duty of confidence is not absolute however and there are numerous situations where information may be legitimately disclosed. For example, in specified circumstances confidential information may be passed on either with the consent of the person concerned, or when disclosure is required by law or is necessary in the public interest. It is in the public interest that confidences are preserved unless there is another, more weighty countervailing interest favouring disclosure. An obvious example is where disclosure of information is relevant to purposes related to preventing harm to others, for example for the detection or prevention of crime. In these circumstances confidential information, including health information such as DNA, can be accessed under the Police and Criminal Evidence Act 1984 ('PACE').

Also, based on the utilitarian principle of securing the greatest good for the greatest number, confidential health information may also be legitimately disclosed for the purposes of teaching, audit, or **medical research** under the Health and Social Care Act 2001, section 60.

HAZEL BIGGS

See also: **negligence in civil law; personal information, access to**

medical ethics   Medical ethics is the collective name for the principles and values which bind doctors and help safeguard patients' trust in them. Professionals caring for sick people are expected to abide by particularly high standards and not take unfair advantage of their privileged access to patients' bodies and their secrets. Respect for patients' dignity and confidentiality feature strongly in medical ethics. Since Hippocrates, such principles have dominated ethical codes which, recognizing the power imbalance between doctors and patients, require doctors to compensate by acting selflessly in patients' best interests.

Traditionally, medical ethics was a set of quasi-commandments developed by medical authorities. In the 1960s, it became less associated with codes of behaviour and more concerned with using critical analysis to resolve individual dilemmas. Lawyers, philosophers, and patients became involved in defining the moral parameters and the main emphasis switched from well-intentioned medical paternalism to patient **autonomy**. Fundamental core duties remain, including doctors' obligation to minimize harm and maximize benefit but interpretations of what constitutes 'harm' and 'benefit' have changed. In the context of individual cases, what is judged beneficial and ethically acceptable for some patients may be deemed harmful and unethical for others with different priorities and values. Modern medical ethics provides analytical tools for weighing conflicting claims and making ethically appropriate decisions in situations where no single 'right' answer may be possible.

Modern medical ethics encourages partnership and dialogue between doctors and patients. It emphasizes patient rights, mirroring **human rights legislation** which impacts significantly on it. **Courts** play a key role in defining what is 'ethical' in medicine. In the late twentieth century, the UK went from a relative paucity of medical case law to a situation where the courts regularly arbitrate in cases of moral uncertainty, such as when life-prolonging treatment can be refused or withdrawn. In practice, law and ethics work together to provide acceptable answers to moral dilemmas, especially those posed by new technology. Statute and case law set the framework within which ethical choices can be made. Ethical analysis provides the reasoning to justify prioritizing some interests over others. Acceptance of **abortion** or **euthanasia** within well-defined legal parameters in some jurisdictions and their prohibition in others indicate how each society's views and laws influence perceptions of what is ethically acceptable in medicine. Also, as health care has become a multidisciplinary activity, medical ethics has transmuted into 'bioethics' and 'healthcare ethics', applying similar standards across professional boundaries.

ANN SOMMERVILLE

See also: **withdrawing/withholding life-sustaining treatment**

medical malpractice   *see* **medical negligence**

medical negligence   Doctors are under a legal duty to take care in the diagnosis, the provision of information about treatment, and the treatment of their patient. A patient who is harmed as a consequence of the carelessness of their doctor will be compensated for that harm as long as the components of a **negligence** action—duty of care, breach of duty, and causal link with the harm—are established.

This legal duty arises from the doctor/patient relationship which exists once the doctor assumes responsibility to care for the patient. The requisite relationship exists once the doctor/patient consultation commences or the patient is examined in the accident and emergency department. A doctor who goes to the assistance of another, for example, in the street would come under a duty to that person although the standard of care they would be expected to provide would be dependent upon the circumstances. Unusually in English law, the doctor/patient relationship creates a positive duty on the doctor who can thus be liable for failure to treat a patient.

The duty owed by a doctor is an individual duty to the patient who is receiving treatment and not to, for example, relatives such as the parents of a **child** patient. In a small number of cases, doctors have been held to owe a duty for causing **psychiatric damage** to mothers of children who have died or suffered serious injuries as a consequence of negligent medical treatment, although not to parents who suffered as a result of careless investigation of suspicions that they had harmed their children.

What the law requires of doctors in acting carefully was established in the case of *Bolam v Friern Hospital* (1957). According to the 'Bolam test', a doctor will not be found to have been negligent if the care provided—the diagnosis, information, or treatment—was the same as would have been provided by other competent doctors. The courts are not placed to choose between different bodies of professional opinion: as long as the doctor acted in accordance with a competent body of professional opinion, they will not be held negligent just because there is another body of opinion—only if there is no competent body of professional opinion which would have acted in the same way. The practice of the doctor must be an acceptable practice. The courts reserve the right to find the common practice to be unreasonable, irrational, or without a logical basis. The courts have thus undertaken to review common practice, although it is rarely found wanting.

Doctors hold themselves out as having special skills and are required to meet the standards of the ordinary professional with that special skill: to this extent, the standard varies according to the speciality of the medical practitioner. Standards are not varied due to inexperience in that post. When you receive medical treatment you want to be able to trust that the doctor caring for you has a minimum level of competence and not that any lesser care is permissible because it is their first day on the job! It is accepted that doctors must learn part of their practice on the wards and if they do not have the experience to achieve a minimum level of competence they must be supervised.

Medical negligence may also take the form of failure to inform the patient about the inevitable risks inherent within a procedure. The 'Bolam test' also applies to determine whether doctors have fulfilled their duty to provide information about the risks inherent within treatment. The patient should be informed of significant risks which will affect the judgment of the reasonable patient. In deciding which risks about which to inform the patient, all the circumstances should be considered including the physical condition and mental well-being of the patient and the ability of the patient to understand the information.

It is also necessary to establish that the carelessness of the medical practitioner caused the patient to suffer harm. This is complicated by uncertainties about the development of the disease, illness, or injury for which the patient consulted the doctor. Particularly difficult issues of **causation** are raised by failure to inform cases as the patient has to establish that, had they been properly informed, they would not have consented to the procedure at that time.

The focus of a negligence claim is the individual doctor whose act can be considered to have caused harm to the patient. Doctors fear being sued for negligence, taking it to be a slight upon their professional capabilities. Medical negligence actions are handled on behalf of hospital doctors and their employers, NHS Trusts, by the National Health Service Litigation Authority. In an attempt to reduce the costs and to address the culture of blame and cover up which surrounds medical negligence cases and to support the move to learning from 'adverse events', the NHS Redress Act 2006 gives the Secretary of State the power to establish a redress scheme for those harmed in hospital treatment. If established, the scheme must provide for **compensation** for waiving the right to bring civil proceedings, an explanation, apology, and details of how reoccurrence will be prevented. It may provide for a care package or financial compensation to be made. Settlement under the scheme will involve waiving the right to bring civil proceedings. This redress scheme is, however, only aimed at cases of minor harm with low levels of monetary compensation. It would not extend to the small number of medical negligence cases which amount

to the greatest financial cost to the NHS and enormous personal cost to families; that is, where a child sustains brain damage due to carelessness in the care provided immediately prior to, or during, birth.

JO BRIDGEMAN

See also: **consent to treatment**

medical records Information about personal medical matters concerning identifiable individuals is covered by very strict tests of confidentiality at **common law** and personal privacy under the Human Rights Act 1998, whether it concerns a record or other item of information (*Campbell v MGN Ltd* (2004)). The provisions of the Data Protection Act 1998 ('DPA') apply to medical records covered by that Act as part of an 'accessible record'. These are records to which access was allowed prior to the DPA, and include both paper and computerized records. The DPA applies to both public and private medical organizations. A health record is defined as a record consisting of information about the physical or mental health or condition of an identifiable individual made by or on behalf of a health professional in connection with the care of that individual.

Under the DPA, access may be denied where, in the opinion of a 'health professional', disclosure would be likely to cause serious harm to the physical or mental health or condition of the 'data subject' or another. Special provision is made to prevent disclosure, in certain cases, of information about children to those with parental responsibility, and of information about a person incapable of managing their own affairs to a person claiming access on their behalf. Access to records relating to a deceased person is dealt with by the Access to Health Records Act 1990. The Access to Medical Reports Act 1988 provides a right of access, for employment or insurance purposes, to reports about oneself made by a medical practitioner. The government proposes to computerize NHS records on one national database leading to public concern about security of records.

PATRICK BIRKINSHAW

medical research Research involving human participants is vital for medical progress. The most obvious form of such research is the clinical trial of new therapeutic pharmaceutical products and preparations. However, medical research is much broader in scope. It also encompasses the testing of innovative therapeutic interventions and diagnostic techniques such as x-ray imaging, the use of tissues and data in research, and the study of the provision of medical care more generally. Some experiments can be performed on animals to provide basic data on the safety and tolerance of new drugs but this does not remove the need for testing on human beings.

Law regulates the protection of research participants and the conduct of researchers. It takes the form of both statute and **common law** and is based upon long established ethical codes of conduct concerning experimentation involving human beings. These insist that research subjects should participate voluntarily, with fully informed consent and that their dignity, rights, safety, and welfare are adequately protected. The law relating to consent and confidentiality plays a major role in this regard and failure to observe proper standards may make a researcher liable for negligence.

Clinical trials involving medicinal products are governed by the Medicines for Human Use (Clinical Trials) Regulations 2004, which requires all such trials to be conducted according to the ethical principles established in the Declaration of Helsinki and to be consistent with international requirements on Good Clinical Practice. These regulations incorporate the European Directive 2001/20 on clinical trials of medicinal products into UK law and require that research involving people must be scrutinized by an ethics committee. Under this law, researchers who fail to comply with the regulations face criminal penalties.

Participants harmed as a result of medical research may be entitled to **compensation** hence researchers are required to hold professional indemnity.

HAZEL BIGGS

medical treatment, right to   The National Health Service Act 2006 imposes a duty on the Secretary of State for Health to promote a comprehensive health service. Under section 3 she is required to provide 'to such extent as he considers necessary to meet all reasonable requirements' services including, hospital accommodation, medical, dental, ophthalmic, and nursing provision, and 'such other services or facilities as are required for the diagnosis and treatment of illness'. The vagueness and breath of this statutory duty has given rise to the question of whether patients have any meaningful right to medical treatment. In practice, since politicians and medics operate within the constraints of finite resources coupled with an almost infinite demand for various kinds of medical treatment, any 'right' to treatment is necessarily relative, as vindication of such rights will impact on the medical treatment of others. In recognition of this, **judges** historically have been reluctant to intervene in NHS resource decisions challenged by way of **judicial review**, citing their inability to

judge resource allocation decisions reached by public bodies, and their lack of knowledge about other patients who could be more advantageously treated. It is thus difficult to demonstrate that decisions have been reached unlawfully, unreasonably, or irrationally, and equally hard to prove that the Secretary of State has breached her statutory duty under section 3. Nevertheless, in line with a general trend towards imposing **accountability** on health professionals and public bodies, recent judgments have sought to hold health authorities to standards of fairness and transparency in reaching resource allocation decisions and to impose obligations to provide explanations and to consider cases on their merits. Beyond such procedural rights, however, any judicial role in framing a right to medical treatment is necessarily heavily circumscribed.

MARIE FOX

medical treatment, right to refuse   *see* **consent to treatment**

medicines, access to   The phrase 'access to medicines' is a campaign slogan that is used by international non-governmental organizations, such as *Médecins Sans Frontières* and Oxfam, to draw attention to the fact that most poor people in developing countries are unable to afford the price of essential medicines.

Problems of access to medicines have gained prominence because of a complex series of events and processes that starts with the HIV/AIDS pandemic. HIV infections began to occur in many countries during the 1980s. By the 1990s HIV/AIDS had reached explosive proportions in some countries, especially in Africa. During the 1990s HIV/AIDS began to be treated successfully using a class of drugs (referred to as antiretrovirals ('ARVs')) that reduced the amount of the virus in an infected person. The cost of treatment was in the range of US$10,000 to $15,000 per person per year. At the end of the 1990s the cost of ARVs went down to about a dollar a day per person. This decline in cost was the product of a complex interaction between **patent** law and trade law. Many of the ARVs being used in the 1990s had not been patented in India because India's patent law did not allow for the patenting of pharmaceutical products. Indian generic companies could thus make ARVs at a price that for the first time made it possible to think about treating millions of poor people.

However, India was one of the members of the **World Trade Organization** ('WTO') when it came into operation on 1 January 1995. All members of the WTO have to comply with the **World Trade Organization Agreement on Trade-Related Aspects** of Intellectual Property Rights ('TRIPs'). TRIPs requires all members to recognize patents on pharmaceutical products. Using TRIPs rules, India took maximum advantage of a transition period and introduced this change to its patent law on 1 January 2005. Multinational pharmaceutical companies can now register patents on products such as ARVs in India.

Some people predict that as a result of this change it will be hard for India to remain a source of high quality, cheap, generic drugs. There are few countries in the world capable of exporting generic drugs on a large scale. China is one such country, but like India it has recognized patents on pharmaceutical products. Generic producers in these countries can wait for the patent to expire, but a patent on a pharmaceutical product may remain in place for up to twenty-five years. Another option is for governments or generic companies to use the pharmaceutical invention without the permission of the patent owner. TRIPs allows for this (known as a compulsory licence), but requires that the patent owner be compensated. In 2001 WTO Members agreed to a Declaration on TRIPs and Public Health that recognized the right of states to protect public health and 'promote access to medicines for all'.

The spread of the patentability of pharmaceutical products by means of free trade agreements has given rise to an international policy debate about the relationship between patents, price, and access to medicines, as well as deeper questions about how the costs of research and development should be met and which countries should bear the brunt. Patents remain at the core of this debate because bringing down the price of an essential medicine is the first necessary step in making the medicine available.

PETER DRAHOS

membership boundaries Membership boundaries define who falls inside and who falls outside a group. Historically, **citizenship** laws have played this demarcating role for modern nation states. Citizenship laws define who is entitled to claim membership in a political **community**. With the emergence of the nation state, criteria were adopted to specify the conditions for acquiring and maintaining citizenship. In the context of multicultural arrangements, and claims to group-differentiated rights, membership boundaries take on a different but equally crucial role. Those who fall within a group may be subject to distinct sets of laws or may qualify for dedicated state supports.

Proponents of group differentiated rights highlight the role that group affiliation plays in human development and flourishing. Membership boundaries seek to preserve the distinct *nomoi* of a group and are often hotly contested.

The criteria used by groups to demarcate boundaries may draw on biological descent or cultural affiliation criteria. Some groups define themselves exclusively in linguistic or religious terms. Groups defined by biological descent often have strict membership transmission procedures. Groups may also draw on a mixture of biological descent criteria and cultural or religious affiliation criteria.

For groups applying biological descent criteria, family law plays a key role in constructing group **identity** and in asserting and preserving difference (Schachar (1998)). Family laws may define who is eligible for group membership through **marriage** and who is not. Strict lineage rules define how membership is transmitted by birth. Within Jewish traditions, for example, membership is transmitted along matrilineal lines. Other religious traditions provide that membership is transmitted along patrilineal lines. In this way, rules demarcating membership boundaries often mirror citizenship laws and underlying principles of *jus sanguinus* (right of blood) or *jus soli* (right of soil).

SIOBHAN MULLALLY

A Schachar 'The Paradox of Multicultural Vulnerability: Individual Rights, Identity Groups and the State' in C Joppke and S Lukes (eds), *Multicultural Questions* (Oxford: Oxford University Press, 1998)

memorandum and articles of association Until 2006 the memorandum and articles of association formed what was called the constitution of the **company**. The memorandum of association is an outward-looking document informing the general public of the company name, its share capital, the address of its registered office, the objects of the company (in essence what it is going to do), and a statement that the liability of its members is limited. The articles of association are an inward-looking set of rules governing the running of the company. The articles form the core of the organizational structure of the company: the **board of directors** (the management committee) and the general meeting (the shareholders' committee), and generally allocate the powers of each committee. A model set of articles called Table A is provided as a default for those setting up a company. Table A is generally adopted with some slight amendments. In order to form a company the memorandum and articles are submitted along with the registration forms and are available for inspection by the general public. Over time, problems with the objects clause and the enforcement of the articles has led to a complete reform of the constitutional documents of the registered company. The Companies Act 2006 requires only the articles of association to be registered as the constitution of the company. Under this new regime the memorandum is no longer needed and unless a company wishes to do so it will not be required to have an objects clause.

ALAN DIGNAM

See also: **shareholder meetings**

A Dignam and J Lowry, *Company Law* (Oxford: Oxford University Press, 2006), ch 8

memory and law   The paradigmatic intersection between memory and law takes the form of personal testimony offered in a trial. Anglo-American bars on hearsay testimony generally restrict testimony to a recitation of the lived memories of the individual witness. These memories may be challenged and contested by pitting the memory of one witness against another.

While the trial generally involves a contestation over the accuracy or veracity of personal memory, it may also serve as a site for the creation of collective memory. Coined by the sociologist, Maurice Halbwachs, 'collective memory' denotes forms of group or societal remembrance constructed through collective acts of ritual or display. Collective memory is distinct from the aggregate memories of individuals; it can be shared, passed on, and constructed through rituals of commemoration (such as national holidays) or structures of memorialization (such as public monuments and war memorials). Legal documents such as **constitutions**, declarations of independence, and **common law decisions** may also serve as repositories of collective memory.

Trials staged in the wake of historical traumas may also serve as sites for the construction of collective memory. In the **Eichmann** trial, for example, the **prosecution** used an accumulation of survivor testimony to rehabilitate the collective image of the **genocide** victim. Challenging the received image of the passive **victim** who went as sheep to the slaughter, the trial used testimony to construct a memory of the victim as heroic resister. This image became embedded in Israeli public consciousness through the retransmission of accounts and images of the trial. This example reminds us that the construction of collective memory through the trial is thus didactic and normative, as lessons are teased from the past to support present political commitments. The construction of collective memory is thus closely associated with the trial's use as a political tool.

The utility of the law as a tool for constructing collective memory must be seen as distinct from its role as a tool of clarifying contested history inasmuch as collective memory need not be faithful to the historical record *per se*. As is the case with all memory, collective memory is necessarily selective, and trials staged by successor regimes may aim to define the terms of collective memory through acts of erasure. Quasi-legal forums, such as **truth and reconciliation** commissions, may also be viewed as instruments through which the aggregate testimonies of individual witnesses are used to define terms of collective or national remembrance.

The use of trials and other forums as instruments of collective memory has contributed to new scholarly and juridical understandings of the intersections between memory and law that invert the conventional view of testimony as simply a form of evidence to be weighed by a deliberative body. In this new conception, the trial serves as a vehicle by which anguished memory can be honoured, recorded, and sacralized in a public space. **Justice** comes to be understood as the law's means of fulfilling a debt to the past.

LAWRENCE DOUGLAS

WJ Booth, *Communities of Memory: On Witness, Identity, and Justice* (Ithaca: Cornell University Press, 2006)
L Douglas, *The Memory of Judgment: Making Law and History in the Trials of the Holocaust* (New Haven: Yale University Press, 2001)

See also: **political trials**

mental capacity   *see* **capacity**

mental disorder, treatment of   Mental disorder is extremely broadly defined in international diagnostic manuals such as the Diagnostic and Statistical Manual of the American Psychiatric Association ('DSM-IV') or the World Health Organization's International Classification of Diseases ('ICD-10'). Mental disorder includes mental illnesses, learning **disability** (what used to be called mental handicap), personality disorders (including antisocial personality disorder, psychopathic disorder, and sexual fetishisms), and substance addiction. With mental disorder there is much greater reliance on the clinician's observations rather than scientific tests. Hence there is greater scope for subjective judgment in the diagnostic process.

Mental illness includes conditions such as depression, psychotic illnesses such as bipolar illness and schizophrenia which are characterized by delusions and hallucinations, eating disorders such as anorexia nervosa, and mental illnesses of old age such as Alzheimer's and dementia. Mental illnesses are generally treated by medication. Depression is generally treated with anti-depressant drugs, but where these have not proved effective or where the situation is so urgent that there is no time to wait for such drugs to take effect, Electro-Convulsive Therapy may be used as a treatment of last resort for depression. Bipolar illness is treated by mood stabilizing drugs. Antipsychotic drugs are used to suppress the delusions and hallucinations which accompany schizophrenia, and specialized drugs (cholinesterase inhibitors) temporarily to arrest the decline in mental functioning which accompanies the mental illnesses of old age. Mental illness also includes anxiety states such as post traumatic stress disorder and obsessive compulsive disorder. These are treated by anxiolytic drugs. Occasionally, in extreme cases, obsessive compulsive disorder may be treated by psychosurgery. Attention deficit hyperactivity disorder is primarily diagnosed in children although sometimes adults are treated for it too. The standard treatments are medications such as Ritalin.

Learning disability (formerly mental handicap) was characterized for much of the twentieth century as a medical problem, and many people with learning disabilities were routinely sedated with psychiatric drugs. Learning disability, as the name suggests, is now seen as a developmental disorder to be addressed by training, education, and psychological treatments rather than medical interventions. There has been a move away from medical models of treatment in hospitals towards an emphasis on small residential units, integrated into the **community**, where the skills of residents can be developed and their individuality can be better respected. Drugs may still be used, most often to address sporadic episodes of disturbed behaviour.

Personality disorder is controversial, since it is here that the boundary between mental disorder and deviant conduct can become blurred, and the scope for exercise of subjective clinical judgment is most pronounced. Broadly speaking, personality disorder is a persistent pattern of inner experience and behaviour that deviates markedly from the individual's culture and has manifested itself since childhood. It adversely affects sufferers' perception of themselves, other people, and events, the intensity and appropriateness of their responses to events, their impulse control, and their interpersonal functioning. Some personality disorders may induce a compulsion to self-harm, whilst others may cause an individual to behave aggressively or to harm others. The main treatments for personality disorder are psychotherapeutic interventions, primarily cognitive behaviour therapy where sufferers, through counselling, are taught different ways of interpreting and responding to life events.

Another group of mental disorders which excites controversy is fetishistic disorder or paraphilia, which includes paedophilia. These may be treated by psychotherapies such as cognitive behaviour therapy, or possibly by injections of libidinal suppressant drugs such as cyproterone acetate.

PHILLIP FENNELL

See also: **compulsory treatment of patients with mental disorders; mental health law**

mental harm   *see* **psychiatric damage**

mental health law   Mental ill health strikes at the rights of **self-determination** and **citizenship** to a degree that physical ill health rarely does. Given the prevalence of mental disorder, mental health law potentially affects everyone or someone they love. It is important at the outset to distinguish between mental health law and mental health **legislation**.

Mental health legislation is national law which provides express authority to interfere with the **right to liberty** and physical integrity. Its principal role has been to provide a framework of powers to detain and treat mentally disordered people without their consent. Latterly, inspired by **international human rights law**, a body of procedures and safeguards has developed offering mental health patients the opportunity to seek review of decisions to detain or treat without consent. Mental health legislation represents an exception to the general rule that medical interventions must be based on the patient's informed consent. The justification for depriving mentally disordered people of their right to **autonomy** and self-determination has been that they may pose a risk to their own health or safety or the safety of others, and may refuse treatment for reasons connected with their mental disorder. Mentally disordered people, in contrast to physically disordered people, may be forced against their will to take medication deemed necessary for their health or safety or for the protection of others, medication which can have toxic side effects.

Mental health law is the body of law, including international **human rights** law, governing the rights of mentally disordered people to challenge detention and compulsory treatment. Mental health law also governs service users' entitlement to provision of services to ensure that necessary treatment is delivered in a setting which imposes the least restrictions on their liberty. Special criminal justice procedures exist to provide for mentally disordered offenders to be sentenced to therapeutic rather than penal disposals where their mental disorder renders them unable to participate in their trial (where they are unfit to plead), where mental disorder stops them understanding the nature of their criminal acts or understanding that they are wrong, or where it substantially impairs their **responsibility** for those acts. Mental health law also confers positive entitlements on service users and their carers to community support, and to the protection of laws protecting against **disability** discrimination.

The nineteenth-century approach to mental disorder was to provide care under detention in asylums or licensed madhouses, following 'certification' under Lunacy legislation as a lunatic or person of unsound mind. Lunacy legislation provided basic procedural safeguards against wrongful detention. A patient could only be detained in a public asylum or private licensed madhouse, all of which were visited, inspected, and regulated by the Lunacy Commission, the body established to protect patients against mistreatment. The early twentieth century saw the development of specialized mental deficiency legislation, distinguishing 'mental defectives' (people with learning disabilities) from 'lunatics and persons of unsound mind', and placing them in specialist institutions for mental defectives. This project was inspired in large measure by the eugenics movement and their concerns to limit the opportunities of 'the unfit' to procreate. In many countries the policy of compulsory sterilization of mental defectives was aggressively pursued.

Whilst nineteenth and early twentieth century approaches to mental health law laid emphasis on certification prior to admission as the principal judicial safeguard against wrongful psychiatric detention, the entry into force of international human rights instruments such as the **European Convention on Human Rights** 1950 and the **International Convention on Civil and Political Rights** 1966 have reinforced the legal safeguards for patients. Article 5 of the European Convention on Human Rights protects against arbitrary detention. Article 5(1)(e) provides that a **person** may be deprived of liberty on grounds of unsoundness of mind only if detention is carried out in accordance with a procedure prescribed by law, and case law has established that such detention requires objective medical evidence of a true mental disorder to be presented to a competent authority, which must review the need for continued detention at periodic intervals. The case law also establishes that detention must be a proportionate response to the risk to the patient or to others. Article 5(4) entitles everyone deprived of liberty, including those subject to psychiatric detention, to seek review of the lawfulness of that detention before a **court** or **tribunal** which must have the power to order their discharge.

At the same time as increasing patients' legal safeguards, Article 5(1)(e) contributes to the stigma associated with mental disorder by listing unsoundness of mind alongside vagrancy, drug or alcohol addiction, and prevention of the spread of infectious diseases as grounds on which a person may be lawfully detained even though they have committed no crime. In 1980, the **European Court of Human Rights** referred to the Article 5(1)(e) group as 'socially maladjusted' people, who may be deprived of their liberty either because 'they have to be considered as occasionally dangerous for public safety', or because 'their own interests may necessitate their detention', or both (*Guzzardi v Italy* (1980), paragraph 98). Such statements foster an association of mental disorder with dangerousness which is at odds with modern philosophies of non-discrimination, **equality**, and social inclusion, and are offensive to sufferers from mental disorder. Mental health legislation creates problems from the civil liberties perspective in that it creates the possibility of preventive detention of those who are deemed to present a risk to themselves or others, provided they are diagnosed as having a mental disorder of a kind or degree warranting confinement.

Since the 1980s there has been increasing recognition of mentally disordered people's entitlements, not just to procedural safeguards against interferences with liberty and physical integrity, but also to the provision of services in a way which represents the least invasion of their rights through treatment in the **community** rather than under detention in institutions. This approach has been variously described as a 'new legalism', and ideology of entitlement, supplementing the focus on procedural safeguards towards positive obligations on the state to provide reciprocal services to those forced against their will to accept psychiatric treatment. Over the past thirty years, inspired by the disability rights movement, psychiatric service users have increasingly demanded protection against discrimination on grounds of mental ill health, to be protected against social exclusion, and now, under the United Nations Convention on the Rights of Persons with Disabilities 2007, to independent living in the community. Often people with mental health problems require support from family 'carers' in order to enable them to be cared for in the community without the need for in-patient treatment, and the rights of carers as well as service users to support services are squarely within the purview of mental health law.

Modern mental health law includes but goes much wider than specialist mental health legislation which seeks to enable management of the risk posed by mentally disordered people to themselves or to others and to provide specialized safeguards for patient's individual rights. Many common jurisdictions, including England, Wales, and Scotland currently have two-track legislation authorizing hospitalization and treatment without consent: mental health legislation, where intervention is based on the presence of mental disorder and risk to self or to others; and mental **capacity** or adult **guardianship** legislation where intervention is based on mental incapacity and must be in the patient's own best interests. Current debates concern the possibility of dispensing altogether with specialist mental health legislation on the grounds that it is discriminatory and stigmatizing and should be replaced by legislation where the power to override a patients refusal of treatment or admission to hospital is based on decision-making incapacity rather than risk. This ideal, whilst attractive in principle, has proved difficult to realize in practice. The signs are that this is the inevitable direction of travel of enlightened mental health law. Mental health law is now part of disability rights law, and disability rights law is now firmly established as part of anti-discrimination law.

PHILLIP FENNELL

P Fennell, *Mental Health: The New Law* (Bristol: Jordans, 2007)

See also: **compulsory treatment of patients with mental disorder; mental disorder, treatment of**

mental health review tribunals   *see* **tribunals**

mental incapacity and crime   The mental capacity of an accused (D) is a prerequisite for criminal responsibility and punishment. With this in mind, a complex body of judge-made and statute law has developed a range of defences to reflect the basic premise that those who lack mental **capacity** are not culpable and should be excused from criminal liability in whole or in part.

Insanity and Automatism

The insanity defence is based on the M'Naghten Rules which resulted from the impact of *M'Naghten's case*. The Rules require D to prove that at the time of the offence he 'was labouring under such a defect of reason, from disease of the mind, as not to know the nature and quality of the act he was doing, or, if he did know it, that he did not know he was doing what was wrong'. This means that D will have a defence if he proves that, because of a 'disease of the mind' from which he suffered, he did not know either what he was doing (eg D believed he was putting a log on the fire when, in fact, it was a baby), or that it was against the law (eg D thought the law entitled him to extract the devil from his child by killing him). In either case, a successful insanity defence results in a special verdict of 'not guilty by reason of insanity' ('NGRI') which must not be confused with an ordinary acquittal as the former ensures that the court may, if medically appropriate, send D to hospital for treatment or require that s/he is supervised in the community. These disposal options reflect a need for public protection which at the same time has resulted in some difficulty over the scope of insanity, a term which is deeply stigmatic. For example, should D, who offended whilst sleepwalking and so did not know what he was doing, be found NGRI or simply not guilty? This problem has taxed the **courts** and stems from judicial interpretation of the phrase 'disease of the mind' and its relationship with the defence of *automatism*. The latter reflects the fact that unless the **prosecution** can prove that D's acts were conscious and voluntary then s/he should not be convicted. Thus, if D was hit on the head whilst playing rugby and, as a result of being concussed, punched the referee s/he would be acquitted of assault. In such a case, provided D is otherwise mentally normal, there is no risk to the public in such an acquittal, commonly known as 'sane automatism'. But the same cannot be said of other mental conditions which result in automatism. In consequence, the courts have created another form of automatism, the 'insane' variety, which is the result of their wide interpretation of the 'disease of the mind' requirement. What this means is that if D's automatism is caused primarily by an 'internal' mental condition then it is likely to be interpreted as having stemmed from a 'disease of the mind' and classified as 'insane'. Thus, D will not be acquitted but will rather be found NGRI and subject to a disposal option. So, if D, an epileptic, suffered a seizure and involuntarily hit his child he would be found NGRI. Although such a result favours public protection, at the same time it labels epilepsy as a form of 'insanity'. Further, to return to the question posed above about sleepwalking, the courts have again opted in favour of public safety and have likewise classified this form of automatism as 'insane'. This is because D's mental condition, resulting from a sleep disorder, is primarily 'internal' as opposed to the concussed D whose automatism is caused by an 'external factor', the blow to his head.

Such a distinction, namely between 'internal' and 'external' factors, as a basis upon which to classify D's condition as a 'disease of the mind' is at best problematical: take diabetes, a common condition

Gerard Conlon, first of the Guildford Four to be released in 1989 after their convictions for pub bombings in 1974 were quashed.

Timothy Evans was hanged in 1950 for murdering his baby daughter. He was granted a posthumous pardon in 1966.

Stefan Kiszko following his acquittal of the murder of 10 year old Lesley Molseed. He served fifteen years and died shortly after his release in 1992.

The Birmingham six on their release from prison in 1991 after their convictions for pub bombings in 1974 were quashed.

Demonstration in Copenhagen Fields, London, 21 April 1834, protesting against the deportation of the Tolpuddle Martyrs.

Strikers at the Bryant and May's factory in London, 1888.

Traffic passing the Law Courts during the General Strike, 1926.

Pickets and police outside the Grunwick photo-processing factory in Willesden, London, 1977.

Left: Police carry bedding to prepare for a long fight during the coal strike in Tonypandy, 1910.

Below left: Police surround a miner following disturbances at the Taff Merthyr Colliery during the strike, 1935.

Below right: Miners picketing outside Battersea Power Station, during the miners' strike, 1974.

Bottom: Police line during the confrontation with miners at Orgreave during the 1984 miners' strike.

Above left: Women MPs after visiting the House of Commons with a petition of 80,000 signatures. Left to right: Irene Ward, Barbara Castle, and Dr Edith Summerskill, 1954.

Above right: Members of the National Association of Women Civil Servants, the National Union of Women Teachers, and the St Joan Alliance protesting against the government's refusal to grant women equal pay in public services, 1955.

Left: Equal Pay for Equal Work demonstration in Trafalgar Square, three women bus conductors, 1968.

Below left: Women picketers outside the Trico factory in London during an equal pay for women dispute, 1976.

Above left: Around 10,000 children were born with severe deformities in the 50s and 60s, allegedly as a result of their mothers having taken the drug thalidomide in pregnancy.

Above right: The oil tanker Torrey Canyon broken in two off the coast of Cornwall in 1967. This was the first major oil spill at sea, with huge environmental consequences.

Left: Thousands of people were stricken by a poisonous gas leak from the Union Carbide chemical plant in Bhopal, India in 1984.

Below left: 31 people died when two trains collided at Paddington in 1999. Network Rail was fined £2m.

Slave being flogged, 1839.

A group of slaves being led to the West African coast by traders. French, 1814.

Children in the stocks, Hong Kong, 1908, postcard.

Eddie Mabo (*Mabo v the Commonwealth*).

Margaret Thatcher burying White Supremacy (Ian Smith, ex PM of Rhodesia) in the coffin as Zimbabwe was inaugurated, cartoon by Gibbard, *The Guardian*, 30 July 1979.

"There's no need for all that—I'm a scientist and a lawyer and I say he's dead. So there."

'Imperial Federation', map of the world showing the extent of the British Empire in 1886, the insert shows a smaller map of the world showing the extent of the British Territories in 1786.

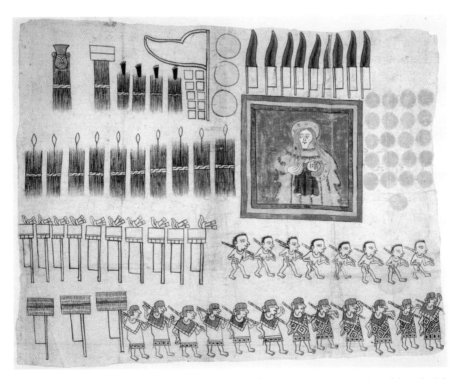

The Huexotzinco Codex is part of the testimony in a legal case against representatives of the colonial government in Mexico, which was won by the Nahua Indian peoples in 1538.

Above left: Immigrants from Jamaica arrive on the Empire Windrush, 1948.

Above right: Asian immigrants arrive at Stansted Airport, 1968.

Left: Immigrants queue for a registration ceremony in Golders Green, London, September 1939.

Below left: Vietnamese boat people arrive in Britain, 1979.

relating to imbalance in blood sugar levels. No right-thinking person would equate such a condition with 'insanity'. And yet the law has achieved just such a result by classifying diabetes as an 'internal' condition which, if it results in automatism, is to be regarded in law as a 'disease of the mind' and automatism of the 'insane' variety; unless, that is, D's condition can be shown to have resulted from an 'external' factor such as an insulin injection. This in turn means that the diabetic runs the risk of being labelled 'insane' if the diabetes alone was the cause of the automatism. Small wonder then that there may be reluctance amongst those who suffer from conditions which are essentially physical, like diabetes, to use automatism as a defence through fear of being labelled 'insane'. In short, it is not just the major mental illnesses, such as schizophrenia, which are categorized as falling within 'disease of the mind' but any mental condition which is 'internal' to D, be it epilepsy, sleep-walking, or diabetes.

Further, the insanity defence under the M'Naghten Rules is narrow. It only applies to those whose conditions lead to a cognitive defect, ie D did not 'know' either what he was doing or that it was legally 'wrong'. Thus, it does not include those, like M'Naghten himself, who knew it was against the law to shoot the **victim** but believed it was morally right to do so. Nor will the defence apply to those who 'know' what they are doing and that it is against the law, such as the kleptomaniac who steals not for gain but rather because s/he cannot control their behaviour by reason of mental disorder. As a result of such restrictions **Parliament** decided to create the wider defence of diminished responsibility.

Diminished Responsibility

Unlike insanity, which is available as a defence to any crime, diminished responsibility can only be pleaded where D is charged with murder. If successful, D will be convicted of manslaughter, a less serious offence. In essence this defence, much like provocation, is used by defendants as a vehicle to avoid the mandatory penalty of life imprisonment which results from a murder conviction.

To plead diminished responsibility successfully, D must satisfy the requirements of section 2 of the **Homicide** Act 1957: D must prove that at the time s/he killed the victim s/he was suffering from 'an abnormality of mind' which 'substantially impaired his mental responsibility'. The 'abnormality of mind' must be the result of one or more of the causes specified in section 2, namely 'arrested or retarded development of mind or any inherent causes or induced by disease or injury'. These causes were interpreted widely in the leading case of *R v Byrne* (1960) to include those, such as the psychopathically disordered, who lack the ability to control their physical acts. As a result, 'abnormality of mind' includes a wider range of mental conditions than fall within the insanity defence. In addition, the diminished responsibility plea has been used liberally to ensure that some 'mercy killers' are not convicted of murder. For example, where D is driven to kill his terminally ill spouse in order to put her 'out of her misery', a plea of diminished responsibility is often looked upon favourably by the court, provided there is psychiatric evidence, perhaps of depression, supporting 'abnormality of mind'.

As a result, diminished responsibility is viewed as a more flexible defence than insanity. It enables D to plead guilty to the less serious offence of manslaughter. In addition, if all the psychiatric evidence supports the plea then it is unlikely to be contested by the **prosecution** so D's guilty plea will be accepted without the need for a full **jury** trial. This is cost-effective and ensures that those mentally ill defendants who need treatment can be dealt with quickly and efficiently without subjecting them to the stress of a trial. Further, this latter point illustrates another advantage of this plea, namely that a conviction for diminished responsibility manslaughter gives the **judge** sentencing flexibility. If in need of psychiatric treatment, D may be sent to hospital; if dangerous he may be imprisoned; if a 'mercy killer', he may be given **probation**.

Infanticide

The Infanticide Act 1938 only applies to mothers who purposely kill their own child under the age of twelve months but at the time of the killing 'the balance of her mind was disturbed by reason of her not having fully recovered from the effect of her giving birth or by reason of the effect of lactation' following the birth of the child. While somewhat analogous to diminished responsibility in that it similarly permits D to avoid a murder conviction by pleading guilty to this lesser offence, it also has the advantage of being an offence in its own right which may itself be charged by the prosecution. As a result, if all the evidence supports infanticide, the prosecution need not charge D with murder. Rather D is charged with infanticide to which she pleads guilty.

Although infanticide is limited to biological mothers who kill their own child under the age of twelve months it has been viewed as a legitimate way to deal with what are essentially tragic cases. As a result, the courts have consistently sentenced such women in a lenient manner by using probation orders rather than imprisonment.

Intoxication

Although not a defence in its own right, the criminal law recognizes that those who are intoxicated may, in rare cases, have lacked the mental element (*mens rea*) required for the commission of the offence. Thus, for example, if D's soft drinks were spiked prior to his committing an offence for which the prosecution failed to prove *mens rea*, then, in principle, D should be acquitted as he bears no culpability for the crime. But compare the much more common example of D voluntarily drinking alcohol and/or taking drugs in such quantities that once more the prosecution cannot prove the *mens rea* of the crime D committed whilst so intoxicated. Here D is culpable in the sense that his condition is 'self-induced'. As a result, the criminal law adopts a different approach to such cases, regarding them as 'voluntary intoxication' with the result that D, if charged with an offence which can only be committed 'intentionally' like murder, s/he will be acquitted of this more serious crime but will still be convicted of the less serious crime of manslaughter.

Unfitness to Plead

Although not a defence, unfitness to plead plays a crucial role in relation to mental incapacity and crime. It does so by ensuring that those who are charged with crimes should not be tried in the normal way if they lack the mental capacity to understand and follow the trial process. To do otherwise would be unfair to D and would bring the law into disrepute.

In essence, D will be found unfit to plead if the court, without a jury, is satisfied that s/he cannot understand the charge s/he faces, cannot instruct a lawyer, or is unable to follow the trial process. Following such a finding, the prosecution must prove to a jury's satisfaction that D 'did the act' which forms the basis of the charge against him. This is known as the 'trial of the facts' and was introduced to protect innocent but mentally unfit defendants. Consequently, if the jury is not so satisfied then D will be acquitted and rightly so. But if the jury is satisfied that the unfit D committed the 'act', then a finding to that effect, which is not a conviction, is made and s/he is then subject to the same range of disposals as can be given to those who successfully plead insanity. This means that such unfit defendants can be sent to hospital for treatment if medically appropriate or, alternatively, can be supervised in the community. In this way, mentally vulnerable defendants are protected from the stresses and strains of the trial process and are dealt with therapeutically rather than punitively.

RD MACKAY

See also: **mental health law**

MEP   *see* **European Parliament**

mercenaries   *see* **combatants**

merchandising and licensing in sport   Merchandising in sport is the commercial exploitation of the name, badge, logo, or other **trade mark** associated with a particular sporting property (eg a team, individual, league, or event) in order to sell goods or services. Licensing is the contractual relationship which underpins merchandising. Rights owners will often grant a licence of their intellectual property rights to third parties who produce merchandising bearing some or all of that intellectual property for distribution to the public. Distribution is usually by way of sale, but can sometimes be by promotional giveaway (known as premiums). Common sporting merchandise includes replica shirts, team scarves, and other clothing and items bearing individual or team logos and images.

Rights owners' normally enter into a contract with specialist manufacturers to produce the merchandising in return for payment. The contract should set out the rights licensed, the duration of those rights, territorial restrictions, the goods in respect of which those rights are licensed, quality control requirements, and detailed payment provisions. Ownership of the rights and the associated intellectual property remains with the person granting the licence, but the licensee is granted the right to use the intellectual property rights for the duration of and subject to the terms of the licence. Licences can be either exclusive or non-exclusive, and are often divided on a territorial basis. The payment terms commonly involve an initial fee plus a royalty based either on units sold or revenue generated by sales of the merchandising. The merchandising companies also benefit from sales revenues and often (as seen in replica shirts) have rights to include their own logo on the merchandise (a form of sponsorship).

The grant of merchandising rights is often exclusive for the goods which the merchandiser manufacturers, which enhances the value of those rights. Properly licensed goods are often referred to as 'official merchandise'. Rights owners will usually have a number of merchandisers and licensees in their merchandising programme, each producing a different type of good or service, often with different licensees in different territories.

The longstanding problem of counterfeit merchandising can devalue the status of official merchandise. The counterfeit merchandise is often of a sub-standard quality and will, therefore, diminish the value of the rights owner's brand.

WARREN PHELOPS

See also: **sports image rights**

merger control A merger is a combination of firms by which two or more enterprises cease to be distinct entities. This may occur in various ways. First, two companies may create a new company which holds the assets of the two together and is managed by a board of directors composed of members of the two original companies. Secondly, one company may acquire all (or a majority of) the shares in another. Acquisitions may be voluntary (where the target company helps the acquirer to obtain the shares) or hostile (where the acquirer obtains control against the wishes of the directors of the target). Thirdly, two firms may create a joint venture that holds assets of both parent companies and operates independently of them. Merger control refers to the review of such transactions under the **competition** laws. Typically, merger control is carried out by national competition authorities: once a merger is announced, the companies submit the proposal to the relevant competition authorities whose role is to examine whether the merger should be allowed because it has no adverse effect on competition, blocked because it causes a substantial lessening of competition, or allowed only subject to modifications (eg asking the merging parties to divest certain assets, or license some of their technology).

The UK's first formal merger control system was established by the Monopolies and Mergers Act 1965. The current regime is in the Enterprise Act 2002. The new law replaces a politicized merger regime with one based on economics. First, the old law gave the Secretary of State for Trade and Industry the final say in merger cases, while the current law restricts this power to exceptional public interest mergers; the competition authorities play a central role. Secondly, the old public interest test is replaced by a standard which considers whether the merger will cause a substantial lessening of competition. Merger control is a two-stage process. Stage one is carried out by the **Office of Fair Trading**: it may clear the merger unless it takes the view that the merger may substantially lessen competition, in which case a reference is made to the **Competition Commission** for a second stage of assessment.

Mergers are reviewed only if they involve significant players: either the merger involves enterprises that control more than 25 per cent of the share of the supply of goods involved, or the enterprises have a turnover of more than £70 million. Mergers that take place in the UK may require scrutiny by competition authorities in other places where the parties conduct activities. However, mergers involving parties that have turnovers of more than 2.5 billion euros, and significant turnover in several Member States, have an EC dimension and are reviewed solely by the **European Commission**; they do not fall under the jurisdiction of national authorities in the EC unless a national authority can make a special case on grounds that the merger has particular and distinct effects in that Member State or that it affects a legitimate national interest of that State (eg national security or media pluralism). When mergers are reviewed by two or more competition authorities (eg the UK and France or the EC and the US), cooperation mechanisms are in place, but each authority remains independent, so each has a veto over the merger. International cooperation by competition authorities is gradually aligning criteria for merger control.

Merger control involves predicting whether the merger will have anti-competitive effects. The most significant anti-competitive risks occur when the merger is horizontal (that is, between firms that are competitors). First, the merged entity might have market power to raise prices and harm consumer welfare. Secondly, the merged entity may collude with remaining competitors, a risk which is particularly prominent in **oligopoly** markets. A merger is vertical when the firms are active in two stages of a production process (eg a steel maker merging with a car manufacturer), and conglomerate when the firms are active in two different but complementary activities (eg a brewer merging with a firm that makes soft drinks). Vertical and conglomerate mergers are likely to be efficient because cost savings can be achieved by combining complementary businesses; but competition authorities consider the likelihood that the merged entity may use its market power to harm or eliminate competitors.

GIORGIO MONTI

Mesopotamian law *see* **ancient Middle Eastern law**

method in legal theory In scholarly terms, a 'method' or 'methodology' is a process through which knowledge is generated. If knowledge or truth is the objective of scholarship, the 'method' is the means of reaching that outcome. In contemporary scholarship, 'knowledge' is often regarded as constructed within a social, political, cultural, and linguistic environment: it therefore changes over time and according to context. However, even where the end-point of scholarship is not an absolute or universal truth, the idea of method is important to indicate the type of knowledge being generated and to ensure its intellectual coherence. For instance, the use of a feminist method will lead to a different knowledge outcome from the use of Marxist method (though the two may also be combined). In this way, it is not possible to distinguish absolutely between a particular method and the object of knowledge produced by that method.

All legal theory adopts one or more methods, whether explicitly or implicitly, and there has been wide-ranging discussion about the nature of the different approaches to understanding law. Legal theory does not have one particular or even one dominant method: contemporary legal theory employs a wide variety of methods and as a field of scholarship, it is truly 'methodologically diverse'. Although some of these methods have developed within legal theory, many are derived from disciplines in the humanities or social sciences, or are associated with broadly based political movements such as feminism or anti-racism.

While it is impossible to provide a watertight classification of methods in legal theory, three broad methodological types cover most scholarship: the conceptual, the empirical, and the critical. These are not mutually exclusive approaches: many legal theorists make use of elements within more than one of these broad clusters. Some key methodological questions intersect with all of these approaches. For instance, should legal theory be purely descriptive or should it also engage in the evaluation of law? Perhaps most crucially, what *is* the law which is the object of legal theory?

First then, some legal theory is conceptual, meaning that its central insights are derived from analysis of the necessary structure of law, rather than from how law operates within a particular society. For instance, Hans Kelsen presented his methodology as 'a "pure" theory of law, because it only describes the law and attempts to eliminate from the object of this description everything that is not strictly law': *Pure Theory of Law* (Berkeley: University of California Press, 1967, 1). Thus Kelsen excluded sociological, historical, and political approaches from legal theory. Kelsen's theory was 'positivist' in the sense that it claimed that law was not *necessarily* connected to morality. Much **natural law theory** is also conceptual because it is based upon an intuitive and non-empirical approach to human nature and an alleged universal moral order.

Secondly, legal theory may be informed to a greater or lesser degree by its empirical context. Most legal theory, including that labelled 'analytical', falls into this category. The positivism of legal theorist such as **Hart** is positivist in the same sense as Kelsen's theory. Unlike Kelsen, however, Hart adopts a positivist methodology in the sociological and scientific

sense, because his theory is based at least partly on observation and experience of law. His methodology is also 'analytical' in the broad sense of attempting to achieve a high degree of precision in the analysis and classification of legal theoretical concepts. However, Anglo-American positivism is not necessarily analytical in the narrow philosophical sense, where analytical truth is strictly non-empirical. Other forms of empirically-informed legal theory include **sociological jurisprudence, economic analysis of law, legal realism,** and **legal pluralism**.

Thirdly, a great deal of contemporary legal theory is 'critical'. Conceptual and empirically-informed legal theories emphasize law as an object of cognition or fact in the world. By contrast, critical theory rejects the view that objective knowledge of law is possible, arguing instead that both objects and subjects (holders) of knowledge are interconnected. This does not mean that critical theory is subjective or that it rejects analysis of the 'real' legal world. Rather, it situates such analysis in a complex network of cultural, social, and political influences. The aim of critical legal theory is to reveal the basic assumptions and values of legal theory. Much critical legal theory has, for example, argued that law is inherently political since it reproduces social distributions of power. The apparent neutrality of law masks its fundamentally political nature. Such an argument is found in feminist legal theory, postcolonial and race-based approaches to law, and postmodern legal thought.

MARGARET DAVIES

See also: **critical legal studies; philosophical analysis of legal concepts; positivism since 1970; positivism to 1970; postmodern jurisprudence**

migrant worker   A migrant worker is someone employed in a country other than his or her own, although international legal definitions of 'migrant worker' also include persons who are still in their own country but are travelling to work in another country or those who have completed their employment abroad and have since returned home. This extended legal definition is important because migrant workers may be entitled to certain rights before taking up employment in the destination country (eg by virtue of a work contract signed in their country of origin which ensures that their travel expenses are paid by the employer), and after they have completed employment (such as entitlements to outstanding wages or social security). A migrant worker includes a person who is working illegally in a country, whether this is someone who has entered without authorization or in a clandestine manner, or a person entering lawfully as a tourist or student but who then works in contravention of the conditions relating to their admission.

The specific laws adopted in respect of migrant workers at international, regional, and national level are principally concerned with their protection, and especially from discrimination. While highly skilled migrant workers are in demand in many countries and generally constitute a well protected and privileged category of persons under the laws of these countries, most migrant workers are employed in medium to low skilled jobs and are consequently more vulnerable to abuse and exploitation in the workplace. They are also more likely to experience restrictions regarding access to important social rights, such as education, health, and social welfare. This vulnerability is often exacerbated where migrant workers are in an irregular situation or if they are women. Approximately 50 per cent of the world's migrant workers are women who tend to work in gender-specific jobs or jobs in sectors where women predominate at both ends of the skills spectrum (eg nurses, domestic, and care workers).

While national labour legislation and general human rights standards apply in principle to all persons regardless of their nationality or legal status, and thus should be equally applicable to migrant workers and members of their families, vulnerable groups of migrant workers remain relatively poorly protected in practice. Specific safeguards have therefore been developed at the international and regional levels to address this gap in protection; although to date such standards have not been widely accepted. There appears to be reluctance among many governments, particularly in those countries in which migrants work, to explicitly recognize the rights of migrant workers and particularly the rights of those working without authorization.

The protection of persons working in countries other than their own, however, is usually enhanced if their country is part of a wider project to strengthen political, economic, and social integration among states at the regional level and where the free movement of workers for the purpose of employment is viewed as an important component of such a project. For example, within the **European Union**, nationals of Member States can move freely to other Member States to take up employment, establish themselves there, and provide services, and are also entitled to a generous set of social rights.

RYSZARD CHOLEWINSKI

N Baruah and R Cholewinski, *Handbook on Establishing Effective Labour Migration Policies in Countries of Origin and Destination* (Vienna: Organization for Cooperation and Security in Europe ('OCSE'), International Organization for Migration ('IOM'), International Labour Organization ('ILO'), 2006) http://www.osce.org/item/19187.html

R Cholewinski, *Migrant Workers in International Human Rights Law: Their Protection in Countries of Employment* (Oxford: Clarendon Press, 1997).

military law Military law is the term applied to the statutory code of military discipline to which members of the British Army, its reservists and Territorials are subject. The term is also, perhaps inaccurately, applied to members of the other British armed services. However as a result of the enactment of the Armed Forces Act 2006, there is now a uniform and tripartite code of law applicable across all services which replaces the separate service discipline codes formerly contained in the Army Act 1955, the Air Force Act 1955, and the Naval Discipline Act 1957.

Military law is particularly concerned with prescribing military offences such as mutiny, desertion, going absent without leave, insubordination and conduct to the prejudice of good order, and military discipline. However, service personnel are also made subject under military law to the ordinary rules of English criminal law wherever they serve. As a result, if a member of the services commits an offence such as theft or assault abroad during, say, a training exercise or a tour of duty (and assuming that a 'status of forces agreement' exists between the United Kingdom and a host nation), they may be tried before a service court for such offence rather than being made subject to the jurisdiction of the courts of the host nation.

Under the International Criminal Court Act 2001 service personnel may also be tried for and convicted of war crimes before courts martial. The first such conviction occurred in early 2007 when a defendant soldier pleaded guilty at a court martial at Bulford, near Salisbury, to abusing a detainee in Iraq. A very serious civilian offence committed by a member of the services in the **United Kingdom**, such as rape, murder, or manslaughter, can only be tried before a civilian criminal court. For a lesser civilian offence committed by a member of the services in the UK, the civilian courts have primacy, though this is frequently waived, allowing service discipline law to be enforced.

Under certain circumstances, civilians abroad, such as families of service personnel or civilian staff on overseas barracks, are made subject to military law. Thus commission of offences such as breaches of a commanding officer's standing orders restricting speed limits on barracks, or offences such as theft and assault, may render such civilians subject to military discipline. The forum for the civilian defendant may be summary dealing before the commanding officer ('CO'), a Service (formerly Standing) Civilian Court in Germany or at the Sovereign Base Area in Cyprus, or even a court martial.

The term 'military law' is also applied to what may be described as service 'administrative' law, covering such issues as enlistment, discharge, redress of grievances, equal opportunities and treatment, pay and pensions, health and safety, billeting and so on. Some of these matters are dealt with in the armed forces legislation but others by measures (such as the Commissioning Regulations or the Pay and Pensions Warrants) made under the **royal prerogative**. Queen's Regulations may make detailed provision relating to some of these matters, such as the procedures for the administrative discharge of service personnel or regulations as to what actions are or are not permitted in areas such as dealings by service personnel with the media and engagement in political activity. Breaches of Queen's Regulations do not, per se, lead to disciplinary proceedings but any breach may provide evidence to support charges under the service discipline statute.

A further, lower, level of military regulation is to be found in 'Administrative Instructions' for each of the three services—eg the Army General Administrative Instructions ('AGAI'). Amongst other things, these lay down detailed in-house procedures for dealing with disciplinary, administrative, and employment issues such as anti-discrimination policies, procedures for dealing with complaints up the chain of command, and procedures (including legal aid provisions) in respect of formal disciplinary proceedings (though detailed provisions are also contained in Queen's Regulations and in the Armed Forces Act 2006 itself). In 2005 the Army introduced within AGAI a system of low-level swift disciplinary procedures as a result of which minor punishments, following a relatively informal hearing, can be imposed even by the most junior of commanders such as a lance-corporal.

The most formal disciplinary forum in military law is the court martial. Under the 2006 Act there is now a tripartite (joint service) standing court martial instead of separate ad hoc courts martial for each service. Though some military trappings remain, the procedure at a hearing is similar to that at a crown court. Serious offences are tried before at least five officers (effectively the jury), which may include a warrant officer. For lesser offences tried by court martial there are at least three officers or warrant officers. No member of the court will be in the same chain of command as the accused. Punishment may include imprisonment, detention at the Military Corrective Training Centre, Colchester, dismissal from the service, fines, compensation orders, reduction in rank, and so on.

In the mid 1990s in *Findlay v United Kingdom* (1997) the **European Court of Human Rights** ('ECtHR') ruled that the composition, structure, and procedures of British Army courts martial breached the right to fair trial by an independent and impartial tribunal as guaranteed by Article 6 of the **European Convention on Human Rights** ('ECHR'). In the wake of this decision, various changes were made by the Armed Forces Act 1996. A civilian, legally-trained, 'judge advocate' now fulfils a judicial and not merely an advisory role at courts martial. The Act abolished the anomalous situation that the convenor of a court martial was the complainant CO's own superior (the brigade or divisional commander). In order to remove the taint of command influence, courts martial are now convened by an administrative body, the Military Courts Service, composed mainly of retired officers, which is separate from the chain of command.

Complaints about less serious offences may be investigated either by the service police or by the battalion's regimental police. Interviews, identification parades, fingerprinting, taking of intimate samples, and so on are all governed by service equivalents of the Codes made under the Police and Criminal Evidence Act 1984 ('**PACE**'). The police may identify possible charges and submit a report to the CO, who will 'investigate the charge(s)'. If the matter falls within the CO's jurisdiction, the CO may dismiss the charge(s), stay the proceedings (in which case the matter may possibly be passed to the civilian authorities), or deal with the matter summarily in person.

Summary dealing is an informal system of trial where no legal representation is available to the accused and the rules of evidence do not apply. The accused may elect for trial by court martial instead. Schedule 1 to the 2006 Act contains a list of offences triable summarily. Most formal disciplinary proceedings are conducted in this way. In 2000, a Summary Appeal Court was created to enhance the compatibility of the summary procedure with the ECHR.

COs have no power to deal personally with (and possibly to dismiss without a court martial) very serious charges listed in Schedule 2 to the 2006 Act. Allegations relating to such offences, which include mutiny, desertion, as well as the civilian offences of murder, manslaughter, and certain sexual offences (where these are committed abroad), must be reported to the service police. The police will prepare a file for the Director of Service Prosecutions ('DSP'). The latter makes the ultimate decision whether or not to court martial the suspect, that is, whether to 'direct the charge'. The DSP also decides whether a court martial should be held in respect of offences not listed in Schedule 2 but which have been referred to him by a CO unwilling or lacking the legal power to try the offence summarily. The service authority under the DSP, which may consider the 'service interest' and the chances of a conviction in deciding whether to prosecute, is independent of the chain of command and separate from the military lawyers who offer legal advice to commanders on the ground. It is answerable to the (civilian) **Attorney-General**, not to the (military) Adjutant-General. This system for dealing with serious cases was introduced by the 2006 Act following a decision by a CO after the Iraq war to dismiss a complaint of homicide made against one of his tank commanders. The Attorney-General took over the (subsequently abortive) prosecution of the trooper for murder at the Old Bailey.

In the view of some, acquittals of service personnel charged with serious offences allegedly committed in Iraq following the Iraq War have cast serious doubt on the efficacy of courts martial and of the military justice system as a whole to deal effectively with, and to punish, grave wrongdoing (though civilian prosecuting counsel were, unusually, employed in one of the trials). One hearing, in particular, revealed widespread regimental amnesia, and perhaps suggested that other defendants should have been on trial. For others, the conditions in Iraq surrounding the collection of forensic and other evidence were far from ideal. In the meantime, while both stronger civilian oversight of courts martial and more 'civilianization' of their processes and procedures are noticeable, courts martial, for the moment at least, remain a feature of British military law.   GR RUBIN

Millet system The term '*Millet*' is derived from the Arabic word *Millah* and connotes 'nation' or 'community'. *Millet* system refers to a scheme deployed by the Ottoman rulers for granting autonomy to certain religious **communities** within the Ottoman Empire (1301–1922). The idea behind this system stems from the *Sharia's* (**Islamic law**) treatment of those **religions** regarded as *Ahal-il-Kitab* (People of the Book). The *Ahal-il-Kitab* are followers of religions who believe in the presence of the Al-mighty though follow Prophets other than Prophet Mohammad, the Prophet of Islam. Under the *Sharia*, *Ahal-il-Kitab* could be granted the political status of *Dhimmis* (whereby they entered into a pact *Dhimma*—with

the Muslim ruler to accept subjugation to Islam and payment of special capitulation tax, *Jizya*, in return for peaceful co-existence).

The Ottomans reshaped the Islamic ideal of *Dhimma* to establish the *Millet* system. Each *Millet* represented an autonomous and self-governing community and was led by its religious leaders and governed by its own religious laws. The main *Millets* were the majority Muslims, the Greek Orthodox, the Catholic, Jewish, and Armenian *Millet*. The leader of each religious community (for example Patriarch, Chief Rabbi, Ethnarch) was obliged to undertake responsibility for the actions of his community and was directly answerable to the government. Autonomy was granted on the basis of religious affiliation and not on regional or territorial basis. Thus, members of a religious community established a single *Millet* regardless of the place of residence of these community members. In practice, this scheme allowed for the establishment of separate legal **courts** applying the **personal laws** of each *Millet*. Each *Millet* was granted autonomy to set its own laws, and to collect and distribute its own taxes. Within this system, each *Millet* was responsible for its own educational arrangements and was allowed to use its personal laws in the regulation of such areas as **marriage**, **divorce,** and inheritance. Notwithstanding its innovative nature, the *Millet* system provided a system which allowed various religious **minorities** to enjoy a generous measure of autonomy, in social, civil, and religious affairs. Such exceptional case of religious autonomy and independence provides a striking contrast to the overall global picture, where religious minorities were consistently harassed and persecuted. The granting of autonomy through the *Millet* system has been applauded by various Western scholars and jurists. According to Professor Vernon Van Dyke, the *Millet* system 'was an application of the right of **self-determination** in advance of Woodrow Wilson'. Similarly, John Packer makes the observation that 'while the [Millet] system was hardly based on any recognition of "**human rights**", its application is most compatible with the philosophy of human rights'.

Despite this granting of autonomy and self-governance, religious minorities were considerably disadvantaged when compared to the members of majority Muslims. In conflicts between a Muslim and non-Muslim, the law of the former prevailed. Non-Muslims could not, for example, marry Muslim women and strict laws of apostasy were applied to conversions from Islam. Towards the end of the nineteenth century, the Ottoman Empire was considerably weakened. It was pressured into recognizing the tutelage of European Powers in the protection of religious minorities through capitulations. Thus, the French adopted the role of formal protectors of Roman Catholics, the British were protectors of Jews, and the Russians claim protection of the Jewish minorities of the Empire.   JAVAID REHMAN

Milosevic, Slobodan Slobodan Milosevic was born in Pozarevac, Yugoslavia, on 21 August 1941. He studied law in Belgrade and became an international banker before entering politics. From 1989 to 1997 Milosevic served as the President of Serbia, and from 1997 to 2000 as the President of the Federal Republic of Yugoslavia. During the NATO air war of 1999 against the Yugoslav Republic, Milosevic was indicted by the International Criminal Tribunal for the Former Yugoslavia (ICTY) for war crimes and crimes against humanity perpetrated in Kosovo. Ousted from power after an electoral defeat in 2000, Milosevic was arrested by the Yugoslav government in 2001 and delivered to the ICTY to stand trial.

Shortly after Milosevic's arrival in the Hague in July 2001, a second indictment charged the former president with war crimes and crimes against humanity allegedly perpetrated in Croatia after the breakaway state declared its independence in 1991. A third indictment was added in November 2001, which included crimes allegedly committed in Bosnia and Herzegovina between 1992 and 1995. These included crimes against humanity, war crimes, and genocide, the most serious charge levelled against Milosevic.

The trial, the first ever of a former head of state before an international court, started in February 2002 but was plagued by delays. Milosevic's myriad health problems slowed the proceeding, but crucial missteps by the court and prosecution also contributed to the length and unwieldiness of trial.

Early on, the court acceded to Milosevic's petition to present his own defence. Although the court appointed two counsel as *amici curiae* (friends of the court) to assist him, Milosevic never cooperated with his appointed counsel, relying instead on help from lawyers and researchers in Serbia. From the outset, Milosevic disputed the legitimacy of the Tribunal and the charges brought against him. Deriding the proceeding as a **political trial**, Milosevic dismissed the ICTY as an instrument of NATO and frequently sparred with prosecution witnesses such as Croatian President Stipe Mesic. These displays permitted Milosevic to cast himself as a fierce nationalist standing up to the West, a picture that played well to a domestic Serb audience that closely followed the trial on television.

Problems also arose as a result of the prosecution's broad indictment. The Appeals Chamber of the ICTY permitted the prosecution to bring forward all the charges in a single trial, but insisted that the prosecution start with Kosovo, the subject of the original indictment. The Kosovo charges involved crimes allegedly committed in 1999, however; the court's decision thus frustrated the prosecution's plan to mount its case chronologically, and contributed to an unfocused presentation of evidence. This played into Milosevic's argument that history was too complicated to be digested in a courtroom. Still, the prosecution succeeded in building a powerful case against Milosevic for crimes against humanity and war crimes, if not genocide.

On 11 March 2006, Milosevic died in his prison cell in the Schveningen detention centre as his trial, after four years of court time, was nearing conclusion.   LAWRENCE DOUGLAS

C Stephen, *Judgement Day: The Trial of Slobodan Milosevic* (New York: Atlantic Monthly Press, 2005)

minimum harmonization in EU law   *see* **approximation of laws in the EU**

minimum wage   Most workers in the United Kingdom have had a legal right to be paid at least the rate of the national minimum wage ('NMW') since April 1999 when the National Minimum Wage Act 1998 came into force. Earlier **legislation** in force from 1909 to 1993 had provided for tripartite 'wages councils' to fix minimum pay rates in particular industries, and separate minimum pay rates for agricultural workers are still fixed by the three Agricultural Wages Boards in England and Wales, Scotland, and Northern Ireland; these cannot be lower than the NMW. The NMW rates are set by the government, in practice after the tripartite Low Pay Commission, which was established by the 1998 Act, has made recommendations in a report on the reference of this and possibly other issues by the government. The NMW is expressed as an hourly rate of pay. In 1999, the main rate was £3.60 per hour; by 2008, this had been increased by stages to £5.73. A lower so-called 'development' rate is payable to workers aged 18–21 inclusive; from October 2008 this was £4.77. A third rate for 16 and 17 year olds was introduced in 2004 and increased to £3.53 in October 2008.

Since not all workers are paid by the hour, provision is made for calculating a worker's NMW entitlement for each 'pay reference period' which is one month or any shorter period by reference to which a worker is paid (e.g. a week). Calculating the NMW entitlement of workers whose pay is determined by reference to some measure of their output, such as a piece rate, requires employers to carry out a satisfactory test, or make a satisfactory estimate, to determine the 'mean hourly output' of these workers. They are then taken to have worked 120 per cent of the number of hours that a worker producing this 'mean hourly output' would have worked in the pay reference period. Most sums distributed through the payroll count towards a worker's NMW entitlement (including tips that are shared out among workers in this way) but premium payments for overtime or shift working or allowances for working in London or any other identified area are excluded. The only benefit in kind that can be taken into account is the provision of accommodation by the employer which counts towards the worker's NMW entitlement as a payment of, from October 2008, £4.46 for each day in the pay reference period for which accommodation is provided.

While workers have the right to enforce their NMW entitlement by claims in employment **tribunals** or the County Courts, the main responsibility for enforcing the law lies with designated 'officers', currently part of HM Revenue and Customs. They have power to inspect employers' pay records, issue 'enforcement notices' requiring employers to make good specific failures to pay workers their NMW entitlement, and 'penalty notices' which in effect impose fines on employers who fail to comply with enforcement notices. The Revenue's NMW unit is accessible to members of the public through a telephone hotline.   BOB SIMPSON

Ministerial Code   Guidance on how **Ministers of the Crown** should conduct themselves in office was formerly issued by successive Prime Ministers as a confidential internal memorandum. It was first published in 1992 as 'Questions of Procedure for Ministers' and revised versions of what is now entitled the Ministerial Code have since been published at intervals (most recently in July 2007). Although lacking the force of law it provides a focus for accountability to Parliament and the public and a set of benchmarks for Ministers in carrying out their duties.

The Code declares that Ministers must observe the 'Seven Principles of Public Life': selflessness, integrity, objectivity, accountability, openness, honesty, and leadership. It requires Ministers to 'give accurate and truthful information to Parliament', to 'uphold the political impartiality of the Civil Service' and not to use government resources for party political purposes. It includes specific rules on, for instance, acceptance of gifts and avoidance of conflicts between Ministers' public duties and their private interests.

Although much of the Code is carried over from previous administrations and parts have been included following recommendations from outside bodies such as parliamentary committees, the **Prime Minister** is the 'author' of the Code and the ultimate judge of ministerial behaviour and the consequences of any breach of the Code's provisions. An independent adviser is appointed to advise Ministers on observance of the Code and, if requested by the Prime Minister, to investigate alleged breaches. The Adviser's Annual Report is laid before Parliament to enable it to scrutinize ministerial conduct.

COLIN TURPIN

See also: **ministerial responsibility; sleaze; standards in public life**

ministerial responsibility   Ministers of the Crown in former times owed their duty or responsibility exclusively to the **monarch**, who appointed and could dismiss them. In the constitution as it developed after the Glorious Revolution of 1688, while ministers by stages achieved an authority independent of royal favour, Parliament established an ascendancy over the ministers, who were able to exercise governing power only while they enjoyed the support of a majority in the elected House of Commons. 'Responsible government'—the dependence of government upon the support of the Commons—became embedded as a firm and abiding principle of the constitution.

The maintenance and enforcement of the principle of responsible government depends not on law but on **conventions of the constitution**. The constitution consists both of laws and established constitutional practices or 'conventions', which are not legally enforceable but are generally observed because they support the democratic principles on which the constitution rests. They are not fixed for all time but rather can be seen to change—informally and usually by degrees—to accommodate changes in society or the political system.

The conventions that support the principle of responsible government are those which, taken together, we speak of as 'ministerial responsibility'. They are broadly distinguished as the 'collective' (or 'joint') and 'individual' responsibility of ministers. Each of these is a responsibility owed—at least primarily—to Parliament, although by reason of Parliament's representative character there is also reflected in them an idea of responsibility to the people.

Collective ministerial responsibility

By this is meant that all ministers (not only those in the **Cabinet**) are jointly responsible to Parliament for all the policies and decisions of the government. They owe this responsibility whether or not they took part in the making of a particular policy or decision. A decision may have been taken by the whole Cabinet, or by one of its committees, or by a single minister heading a government department, but every minister, when speaking in Parliament or indeed outside, is bound by this convention to support the decision so taken. This is to say that the responsibility is owed by ministers as well to their colleagues as to Parliament, and it obliges ministers to suppress their own reservations or differences about a policy once it has been adopted. A minister who decides to make public his or her disagreement with government policy will be expected to resign from office. Robin Cook acted in accordance with the convention when he resigned from the ministerial posts of Lord President of the Council and Leader of the **House of Commons** in March 2003 because he was unable to support the Cabinet's decision to take military action against Iraq without specific **United Nations** authorization.

It is in the power of Parliament to enforce the collective responsibility of ministers to itself by dismissing the government from office. This remedy of last resort is effected by the House of Commons in passing a motion of no-confidence in the government, which can avert dismissal only by appeal to the people in a general election. In practice such dismissals are rare, for normally the government will be rescued by the votes of loyal backbenchers on its side of the House. The last instance of government defeat on a confidence vote was in 1979.

Individual ministerial responsibility

Each minister in charge of a department is held responsible to Parliament for his or her own official conduct and for all the actions and decisions of the department. This responsibility includes an obligation to 'give account'—answering Questions in the House and providing information to parliamentary **select committees**, being excused from responding only on recognized public interest grounds, such as **national security**. In addition, for any significant failure of policy or defective administration in the department the minister much 'accept responsibility', taking any necessary corrective action and, in an extreme case, resigning from office. Resignation is, however, a somewhat rare and unpredictable outcome, depending essentially on political circumstances such as the minister's record and standing, and support, or lack of it, from the **Prime Minister**,

ministerial colleagues, and backbenchers on the government's side of the House. Resignation is unlikely if the departmental failure cannot be attributed to the minister's own errors or lack of leadership.

The absence of any firm convention of resignation does not drain ministerial responsibility of its substance, as is sometimes suggested. The principle conditions the whole relationship between ministers and Parliament and legitimizes Parliament's primary function of the critical scrutiny of government.

COLIN TURPIN

Ministers of State   *see* **Ministers of the Crown**

Ministers of the Crown   The highest-ranking Ministers of the Crown are political heads of **departments of state** who normally have seats in the **Cabinet**. They are either Secretaries of State or holders of other senior offices, some of which are of great antiquity. The office of Lord Chancellor may be traced back to the reign of Edward the Confessor, that of Lord Privy Seal to the fourteenth century and that of Lord President of the Council to the fifteenth century. The term 'Secretary of State' was used as far back as Tudor times. In 2006 there were fourteen Secretaries of State in charge of the various departments of state. There is an informal hierarchy amongst Secretaries of State. The First Secretary of State is commonly appointed to the office of Deputy Prime Minister. The Foreign Secretary, Home Secretary, Secretary of State for Defence, the Chancellor of the Exchequer, and the Lord Chancellor are recognized as senior members of the Cabinet.

Also usually designated as Ministers of the **Crown** are junior ministers who are attached to departments and are charged with particular departmental responsibilities by the Minister of the Crown heading their department. They are not normally members of the Cabinet. Junior ministers are either Ministers of State, ranking immediately below the ministerial head of the department or, at a lower level, Parliamentary Secretaries (or Parliamentary Under-Secretaries of State).

In principle, many of the powers and responsibilities allocated by statute to a Secretary of State can be performed by any official holding that office. In practice, however, a power will normally be exercised by the Secretary of State for the department that performs the functions to which the power relates.

All Secretaries and Ministers are appointed in the name of the Crown in exercise of the **royal prerogative** on the advice of the Prime Minister, and hold office at the pleasure of the Prime Minister. The conduct of all Ministers of the Crown is regulated by **conventions of the constitution** and the **Ministerial Code**.   JOHN MCELDOWNEY

minor In England and Wales the word 'minor' is now used synonymously with **child**. The period of minority is, therefore, the period which reflects childhood. It runs from birth (and not conception) until the age of 18 years. The major significance of minority—or childhood—is that it affects the **capacity** of a **person** to perform legal acts and to have legal obligations. During minority a person's legal capacity is limited. Although she is a person entitled to the ordinary rights of people (both legal and fundamental), she is only able to assert those rights or have rights asserted against her in limited ways. She is also able to claim some special, **children's rights**. Throughout minority most of the limitations on capacity can be made good with the assistance of others (historically, a guardian or curator, usually a parent).

Traditional conceptions of childhood (especially in the civil law tradition, followed most closely in the UK in Scotland) divided it into phases in each of which a different set of limitations on capacity operated. As *infants* children had no capacity at all, but as *pupils* they acquired greater capacity which, while greater than their *infant* legal capacity, still did not reflect the capacity of *minors* or adults (majors). But in the modern era minority has become the whole of childhood and its effects on capacity have become much more flexible. Although its basic parameters are determined by age, the limitations it imposes on capacity vary greatly during this period. Sometimes capacity is simply age-determined. However, often personality and personal maturity play as important a role on the determination of capacity.

Perhaps the best illustration of the variable legal capacities of minority arises in relation to decisions about the medical treatment of children. As a general rule, minors do not have the capacity to make medical decisions for themselves; those with **parental responsibility** must do so for them. However, in England and Wales legislation empowers children at sixteen to consent to their own medical treatment. The courts have also allowed children under sixteen to consent to their own treatment if they demonstrate a sufficient maturity to do so. In the case of both these enhancements of capacity to consent, minority remains relevant. Those with parental responsibility retain their own independent capacity to consent to the medical treatment of the children in question, even in the face of their disagreement.

Other areas of law in which minority has a significant impact, from the perspective of legal capacity, include the commercial activities of children (ranging from the opening of bank accounts, through general contractual capacity, to employment), their criminal activities (the capacity to commit crime and the consequences of their commission are affected by the minority of the perpetrator), their **citizenship** (obtaining **passports** and voting), their status in the family (**marriage** capacity, their status in care proceedings, rights to support), and their sexual relations.   CRAIG LIND

See also: **children and medical treatment; guardianship and children**

minorities Minorities, as collective entities, exist in varied forms and sizes. There are ethnic, linguistic, cultural, racial, religious, sociological, political, and sexual minorities in every state of the world. State practices have been inconsistent and incoherent in so far as protection of **minority rights** is concerned. Some states have adopted generous policies in not only recognizing the existence of minorities but also protecting their **identity**. However, there have been other states where **genocide** and physical extermination of minority groups has taken place. In their practices, many states continue to refuse to recognize that minorities physically exist, or have used forcible mechanism of **assimilation**. With the establishment of the League of Nations in 1919, an elaborate regime on minorities was set up. However, the mechanisms adopted were limited in nature and collapsed well before the start of World War II. With the establishment of the **United Nations**, emphasis shifted to individual **human rights** and the United Nations Charter (1945) contains several references to human rights. The Universal Declaration of Human Rights ('UDHR', 1948) is committed to promoting individual rights and non-discrimination. There is no reference to minorities in either the UN Charter or the UDHR. The now defunct Human Rights Commission established a Sub-Commission in 1947, whose specific mandate included the promotion and protection of minority rights. After the establishment of the Sub-Commission, efforts were made to project the **subject** of minority rights in the international arena. However, such efforts stalled far too frequently not only because of divisions over substantive claims put forward by minorities, but also because defining and identifying the subject of protection proved an intractable problem.

'Minority' is an ambiguous term, potentially definable through an endless combination of interacting variables, like **religion**, language, **ethnicity**,

race, culture, **gender**, sexuality, physical characteristics, and a variety of other traits. In the light of
these diversities, it is hardly surprising that the issue
of definition has been a problematic one. In 1966,
Special Rapporteur, Franceso Capotorti, an Italian
jurist, was assigned by the UN to prepare a definition
of minorities. The scope of Professor Capotorti's
mandate was strictly limited to the **International
Covenant on Civil and Political Rights** ('ICCPR',
1966) which contains an article referring to the rights
of '**persons** belonging to [ethnic, religious or linguis-
tic] minorities' (Article 27). In producing a detailed
examination of the rights of persons belonging to
ethnic, religious, and linguistic minorities, Capotorti formulated the following definition: A 'minority' is a 'group numerically inferior to the rest of the
population of a state, in a non-dominant position,
whose members—being nationals of the state—possess ethnic, religious, or linguistic characteristics
differing from those of the rest of the population and
show, if only implicitly, a sense of solidarity, directed
towards preserving their culture, traditions, religion, or language'.

Although generally regarded as authoritative,
this definition has been criticized for a number of
reasons. These include an emphasis on 'numerical' inferiority, exclusion of non-nationals, and difficulties in establishing the meaning of 'ethnicity',
'language', or religion'. Such definitional difficulties have been a major contributing factor in the
UN's inability to formulate binding international
standards on minority rights. In the absence of a
universally binding treaty, a range of international
instruments have been used to promote and protect
minorities. The Convention on the Prevention and
Punishment of the Crime of Genocide (1948) protects the physical existence of minorities. Although,
this Convention does not mention the term 'minorities', its provision and historical context confirms
that the primary beneficiaries are minorities, such
as European Jews targeted and brutalized during
World War II. According to Article II of the Convention, genocide consists of:

any of the following acts committed with intent to destroy
in whole or part a national, ethnical, racial or religious
group...

(a) Killing members of the group;
(b) Causing serious bodily or mental harm to members
of the group;
(c) Deliberately inflicting on the group conditions of life
calculated to bring about its physical destruction in
whole or in part;
(d) Imposing measures intended to prevent births with in
the group;

(e) Forcibly transferring children of the group to another
group.

Despite the coming into operation of the Genocide
Convention, there have been several instances where
minority groups have faced death and destruction
and a number of cases have highlighted weaknesses
both in substance as well as implementation. The protected groups in the Convention are 'national, ethnical, racial or religious . . . '. The Convention makes
no reference to political and 'other' groups. Several
cases reveal that political opponents have been a
primary target of destruction and this omission is
unfortunate. The Convention does not criminalize
the destruction of a culture, language, or religion.
Thus, individuals may be deprived of their culture or
symbols of identity, upbringing, language, or faith
and yet those responsible cannot be held accountable
under this Convention. There is no definition of the
meaning of 'national' or 'ethnical' 'racial' or 'religious' group as used in Article II.

A more disturbing feature has been weaknesses
in implementation. Article VI allows for trails to
be conducted either in the territory where genocide
was committed or through an international criminal **tribunal**. Genocide, as an activity associated
with governments (or by powerful elements within
governments) has gone on almost unchallenged. The
International Criminal Court (established in 2002)
allows for the **prosecution** of individuals charged
with crimes of genocide and crimes against humanity. The Court proceedings may eventually lead to
successful prosecutions of individuals indicted for
genocide, though thus far, successful prosecution
have only been achieved through the establishment
of *ad hoc* tribunals such as the International Crimi-
anl Tribunal for Former Yugoslavia ('ICTY') and
the International Criminal Tribunal for Rwanda
('ICTR') or in domestic tribunals (eg the trial court
for the former Iraqi dictator, Saddam Hussein).

It is well established that the rights of minorities
are built upon the existing framework of **international human rights laws**, which insists on a regime
of **equality** and non-discrimination for all individuals without regard to race, religion, ethnicity,
gender, or sexual orientation. The focus on equality and non-discrimination is evident in the provisions of the UN UDHR, ICCPR, **International
Covenant on Economic and Social Rights** (1966),
and in the regional human rights treaties of Council of Europe's **European Convention on Human
Rights** (1950), the **African Charter on Human and
People's Rights** (1981), and the American Convention on Human Rights (1969). An international

treaty, which prohibits discrimination based on race, colour, descent, or national or ethnic origin was adopted by the United Nations in 1965. The **Convention on the Elimination of all forms of Racial Discrimination** carries a special value for minority groups since it not only authorizes and encourages affirmative action policies for racial or ethnic group (Articles 1(4) and 2(2)), it also allows (on an optional basis) individuals or groups to petition complaints for racial discrimination to the independent Committee on Racial Discrimination. The UN has also formulated specialized non-discriminatory standards for those sections of the **community** whose rights are consistently undermined and can in the wider sense be regarded as minorities: these include **women (Convention on the Elimination of all forms of Discrimination against Women**, 1979); children (**Convention on the Rights of the Child**, 1989); **migrant workers** (International Convention on the Protection of the Rights of All Migrant Workers and Members of their Families, 1990); **refugees** (Convention Relating to the Status of Refugees, 1951); and the disabled (The International Convention on the Protection and Promotion of the Rights and Dignity of Persons with **Disabilities**, 2006).

Minorities also claim to have the right to autonomy and in some instance a right to **self-government**. Religious, linguistic, and/or cultural autonomy is not a novel concept for minorities. It can be traced to the *Millet* **system** granted during the Ottoman Empire or through the minority treaties as established in the aftermath of World War I. With its emphasis on equality and non-discrimination for all individuals, the UN human rights regime has not had a particular focus on minority claims of autonomy. Article 27 of the ICCPR is the only article in international binding instruments that provides direct protection to members of ethnic, linguistic, and religious minorities. Article 27 provides as follows '[i]n those States in which ethnic, religious or linguistic minorities exist, persons belonging to such minorities shall not be denied the right, in community with other members of their group, to enjoy their own culture, to profess and practice their own religion, or to use their own language'. The attenuated nature and limited scope of this article however does not provide a basis for claiming a right to autonomy within **international law**.

More recent international instruments such as the UN Declaration on the Rights of Persons Belonging to National or Ethnic, Religious and Linguistic Minorities (1992), and the Council of Europe's Framework European Convention for the Protection of National Minorities 1994 and European Charter for Regional or Minority Languages (1992), are positive initiatives and may eventually lead to the established of a universally binding treaty on minorities which would also contain a specific right to autonomy. It is encouraging to note that the recently adopted UN Declaration on the Rights of the **Indigenous Peoples** (2007) explicitly provides for the right to autonomy for indigenous peoples. Freedom of religion, and cultural, linguistic, and political autonomy for minorities is often related to notions of **self-determination** and possibly independent statehood. This latter claim of political self-determination leading to secession and independence poses a major threat to the existing world order states and governments are thus very sceptical of encouraging such claims.   JAVAID REHMAN

minority rights   Minority rights provide protection and at times **empowerment** for groups that are inferior in numbers to the majority in a multicultural society and at risk of discrimination, persecution, or repression due to cultural, ethnic, racial, religious, linguistic, or social differences. Special protection and empowerment of **minorities** is considered necessary either because of violations of their dignity in the past or the fact that there are well-founded reasons to believe that such violations will happen in the future. Minority rights are thus applied both to keep the peace and to prevent conflict.

However, the presence of two objectives render minority rights confusing both in application and understanding. First, minority rights can be applied both as negative and positive rights depending on the objective. An example of a negative minority right is **Article 14** of the **European Convention on Human Rights** (1950) aimed at preventing discrimination, whereas positive minority rights, sometimes called affirmative action, seek to enable members of minorities and are found mainly in statutes regulating education and employment. Secondly, there is confusion as to whether minority rights are individual or collective. Typical individual minority rights are non-discrimination rights. Examples of collective minority rights are self-administration or **self-government** rights, such as the **devolution** Acts establishing the governments and **Parliaments** of Wales, Northern Ireland, and Scotland (1998).

In **international human rights law**, minority rights are codified as individual human rather than collective. For instance, Article 27 of the **International Covenant of Civil and Political Right**s (1966), the Declaration on the Rights of Persons Belonging to National or Ethnic, Religious, and Linguistic Minorities (1992), and the European Framework

Convention for the Protection of National Minorities (1995) refer to individual minority rights. However, the need to denote the collective notion of minority rights is achieved according to a pragmatic method. Thus, **human rights**, such as rights to assembly and association, existence, **freedom of expression,** family, linguistic freedom, freedom of religion, and to culture are understood as collective minority rights. The reason why collective rights are not applied directly is that there is no agreed definition of a minority in international human rights law and hence, no collective group upon which to confer these rights.

Thirdly, minority rights tend to clash with the principle of **equality** which holds that all people should be treated equally. Since minority rights allow for special treatment of certain minorities, minority rights appear to violate this principle, albeit often in the name of promoting equality. Reconciling equality and diversity is one of the enduring problems of minority rights application.

The dilemma of diversity as a key to understanding minority rights has been pointed out by J Jackson Preece who argues that minority questions speak to an inherent tension in **human** relationships between competing desires for freedom and belonging, mostly in terms of **religion**, **race**, language, and **ethnicity**. Indeed, we find the oldest minority rights as freedom of religion guarantees in the Edict of Nantes (1598) and in the *Millet* **system** of the Ottoman Empire. Later national affiliation and language became issues of minority rights in the Minority Treaties imposed on the defeated powers subsequent to the Paris Peace Conference (1919). Increased immigration later in the twentieth century brought ethnicity to the fore of minority rights. The Canadian philosopher, Will Kymlicka, in his book *Multicultural Citizenship* speaks of **poly-ethnic rights** aimed at integrating ethnic groups in multicultural societies. The ethnic cleansing in the Balkans in the 1990s and the events of 11 September 2001 have fused religion and ethnicity as aspects of minority rights in need of attention in the twenty-first century.

TOVE MALLOY

J Jackson Preece, *Minority Rights. Between Diversity and Community* (Cambridge: Polity, 2005)

P Thornberry, *International Law and the Rights of Minorities* (Oxford: Clarendon, 1991)

See also: **liberal multiculturalism; multiculturalism**

minority shareholders   A minority shareholder may petition the **court** under section 994 of the Companies Act 2006 in circumstances where the **company's** affairs have been conducted in a manner which is unfairly prejudicial to the shareholder's membership interest. A successful petition may result in the court invoking an order whereby the court may grant relief as it sees fit. Frequently, the type of order sought will be to provide the petitioner with an exit route from the company by providing that the **shares** of the aggrieved shareholder be purchased by those responsible for the instigation of the unfairly prejudicial conduct, namely the majority shareholder(s)/**director(s)** of the company. The section 994 provision subjects the legal rights of the membership to equitable constraints and to this end a membership interest is founded on a petitioner's relationship, as a shareholder, with the other members of the company, a relationship based on mutual trust and understanding. This type of personal relationship may be apt to describe the internal workings of a private company but is misplaced in the context of a public company. Accordingly, the section 994 provision will almost exclusively be confined to the protection of shareholder interests in the context of a private company.

The court employs an objective test to determine whether a particular type of conduct is of an unfairly prejudicial nature. Prejudicial conduct relates to damaging conduct of a commercial nature to the extent that if conduct is to be construed as 'prejudicial' it must depreciate or fetter the financial worth of a member's shareholding interest. To justify the operation of section 994, the prejudicial conduct must also be unfair. Here, a petitioner will often rely on establishing an intentional act of discrimination or an intentional and improper exercise of the company's powers. It is doubtful whether an act of corporate misjudgment, for example, a poor investment decision, will ever amount to unfair conduct in so far as section 994 does not seek to penalize gambles of a commercial nature. However, a ridiculous and unreasonable commercial folly may be deemed unfair, especially in circumstances where the conduct equates to a breach of a duty of care or where the conduct results in a disproportionate and unreasonable financial gain for the controlling shareholders.

To substantiate a finding of unfairly prejudicial conduct, the petitioner must show that the conduct of the company's affairs resulted in more than a trivial assault on the substance of his/her membership. The alleged unfairly prejudicial conduct must affect a membership interest or there must be evidence to establish the likelihood of a threatened act. A shareholder's interest in a company is not subject to expectations founded on a general concept of fairness (ie expectations unrelated to the legal rights of membership (*O'Neill v Phillips* (1999))). However, a minority shareholder may have grounds to complain of an act of unfairly prejudicial conduct in circumstances where there has been a breach of the legal rules which governed the manner in which the affairs of the company should be conducted, or alternatively, but more exceptionally, where equitable considerations make it necessary to abandon the application of strict legal rights with an objective of preventing unfairness.

Where a petitioner succeeds under section 994, the court may make an order under section 996 of the Companies Act 2006. Here the court is afforded a wide **discretion** in the nature of the relief to be granted with an ability to make 'an order as it thinks fit'. The most common type of order sought is purchase of the petitioner's shares. This **remedy** provides the petitioner with an exit route from the company. However, it is possible for the court to order that the minority shareholder purchase the majority's holding.

A minority shareholder may also seek relief under section 122(1)(g) of the Insolvency Act 1986. Here, a company may be wound up on the premise that its liquidation would provide a just and equitable remedy (*Ebrahimi v Westbourne Galleries* (1973)). Unfairly prejudicial conduct and conduct justifying a **winding up** order under section 121(1)(g) of the Insolvency Act 1986 will often be indistinguishable. In common with section 994, a petition under section 122(1)(g) of the Insolvency Act 1986 must be based on an interest which is linked to a legal right of membership; the choice of provision will often be dependent upon the anticipated remedy. Nevertheless, in some cases there will be a subtle difference in the application of the two provisions. For example, a course of conduct may not justify a classification as unfairly prejudicial conduct, but that same conduct could, in a quasi-**partnership** type of company, result in a breakdown of mutual confidence and trust, thereby justifying a petition under section122(1)(g) of the Insolvency Act 1986.

However, it will be rare for a petitioner to be granted a winding up order on the just and equitable ground in circumstances where there is an alternative remedy under section 994. Further, section 125(2) of the Insolvency Act 1986 provides that a winding up order may be struck out if the court considers that it was unreasonable for the petitioner not to have pursued an alternative course of action. Nevertheless, section 122(1)(g) of the Insolvency Act may, in ending the existence of the company, afford the most equitable remedy, for example, in a situation where a petitioner contends that a company's conduct and formation was directed at defrauding minority shareholders and the investing public, or where the petitioner would gain a greater financial benefit in having the company wound up, rather than seeking a remedy under section 994.

STEVE GRIFFIN

Miranda v Arizona (1966)   The Fifth Amendment to the US Constitution creates a privilege against compelled self-incrimination, enforced in the national courts by excluding evidence from trial evidence. By the 1960s the Supreme Court had interpreted the Fourteenth Amendment to make the same privilege available in criminal prosecutions in state courts. For several decades the Supreme Court struggled to identify the circumstances under which the tactics police officers used in questioning suspects compelled the suspect to provide incriminating answers, engaging in seemingly psychological inquiries into how individual suspects responded to interrogation tactics. These decisions failed to provide adequate guidance to lower courts or to police officers.

The *Miranda* decision shifted focus from suspects to police practices. Chief Justice Earl Warren's majority opinion argued that the coercion inherent in custodial interrogations could be dispelled by informing suspects of their rights to silence and the assistance of counsel. The decision required that police officers questioning a suspect in their custody first inform him that he had a right not to answer, that any answers could be used against him, and that he had a right to the assistance of counsel, provided if necessary by the government. These 'Miranda warnings' were modelled on, but were somewhat more protective than, the existing practice of the Federal Bureau of Investigation, and resembled the cautions used by British police except that, in the United States unlike Great Britain, prosecutors cannot argue in a criminal trial that the jury should consider the suspect's failure to respond to questions in determining guilt.

The *Miranda* warnings shifted judicial inquiry from coercion to whether the suspect was 'in custody,' and, more importantly, to whether the suspect had knowingly relinquished his right to silence by responding to questions. The decision was controversial from the moment it was announced, eliciting a strong dissent from four justices and a critical response from Congress, which in 1968 enacted a statute purporting to require the admission into evidence of any statement made voluntarily by a suspect, without regard to whether the *Miranda* warnings had been given. Justices appointed to the Supreme Court after *Miranda* tended to be unsympathetic to the decision's thrust, and the Court generally interpreted the decision narrowly, defining 'custody' restrictively, finding waivers of the right to silence relatively easily, and allowing the use of statements taken before the warnings were given to attack the credibility of a defendant's direct testimony.

After an initial period of hostility, police agencies adapted relatively easily to *Miranda*. The warnings became familiar to the public in the US and elsewhere through depictions in films and television dramas. Believing the 1968 statute to be unconstitutional, federal law enforcement officials refused to introduce statements taken in violation of the *Miranda* requirements in federal prosecutions. In *Dickerson v United States* (2000) the Supreme Court held the statute unconstitutional, emphasizing that *Miranda* had become embedded in the culture of law enforcement both by police agencies and by the public.   MARK TUSHNET

miscarriages of justice   Whilst the phrase 'miscarriage of justice' could be applied to errors which occur in any part of the legal system, or even be extended to cover every and any failure to achieve justice whether in the legal system or beyond, it is usually applied, both within the legal system and outside, to refer to wrongful convictions following trial in the criminal courts. But beneath this consensus lurks disagreement as to what constitutes a wrongful conviction, a disagreement that has considerable implications for the legal system and its relationship to politics, the media, and other sections of society.

Outside the legal system, a miscarriage of justice is generally understood to involve conviction of someone who did not commit the crime for which they were convicted, whether because they did not carry out the actions that constituted that crime, or lacked the necessary criminal intention in so doing. As such, the possibility of a miscarriage of justice arises whenever there is any reason to believe that a person convicted of an offence did not in fact commit that offence.

However, inside the legal system, most particularly within the criminal appeal courts, matters are less straightforward. Those responsible for correcting miscarriages of justice have to take account of the methods and procedures by which their particular legal system comes to the conclusion that the convicted person is guilty in the first place. Facts do not simply announce themselves, but have to be established through the various procedures that make up a criminal trial. These procedures are justified not only by reference to their ability to establish the factual truth of a person's guilt, but also by

reference to ideas of fairness and due process, and ultimately the **rule of law**. Such ideas operate as a restraint on the pursuit of truth, on the basis that some ways of establishing whether an individual is in fact guilty of a crime would be unfair, or contrary to their human rights (as with the classic example of evidence obtained through the use of torture). But they also operate to justify the conviction and punishment of individuals even though one can never be totally sure of their guilt. If individuals are convicted in accordance with a legal system's normal criminal trial procedures, then they are routinely considered to be factually guilty.

The need to construct guilt routinely through the use of legal procedures that are imperfect (because, for instance, unlike clinical trials that involve multiple testing, the criminal trial can test the evidence only once) points to the need for bodies that have responsibility for correcting miscarriages of justice. The main bodies with such responsibility currently operating in the English legal system are the Court of Appeal, Criminal Division, set up in 1907, and the **Criminal Cases Review Commission**, set up in 1995. But what, in this context, constitutes an imperfect legal procedure? If the benchmark for imperfection is the normal trial (the routine, less than perfect operation of criminal justice) then bodies such as appeal courts will have little difficulty in identifying miscarriages; but the ones which they identify may not coincide with expectations outside the legal system. Especially when no order is made for a retrial, quashing a conviction on the basis that there was an error of procedure may be interpreted as the release of a guilty individual on a 'legal technicality'. Similarly, where an individual is widely believed (as a result of media publicity and public campaigns) to be innocent of a crime, refusing to quash a conviction because there is nothing in their trial, or procedures pre-trial, which falls short of the normal processes, can lead to accusations that criminal appeal bodies are failing in their responsibility to remedy miscarriages of justice.

This dilemma is well illustrated in the two sets of litigation that followed the conviction of Mullen (illegally deported from Zimbabwe with the assistance of UK security forces in order to stand trial in the UK for terrorism). His conviction was quashed when his illegal deportation came to light after he had served many years in prison, on the basis that limiting miscarriages of justice solely to the question of factual guilt threatens due process and the rule of law. But his application for compensation for wrongful conviction was denied, and this decision was upheld by the **House of Lords**, on the basis that a miscarriage of justice (for these purposes) **could** be limited to questions of factual guilt.

RICHARD NOBLES AND DAVID SCHIFF

R Nobles and D Schiff, *Understanding Miscarriages of Justice: Law, the Media, and the Inevitability of Crisis* (Oxford: Oxford University Press, 2000)

C Walker and K Starmer (eds), *Miscarriages of Justice: a Review of Justice in Error* (London: Blackstone Press, 1999)

misleading prices   *see* **price marks**

misleading product descriptions   'Nothing but the truth' said *The Economist* on the enactment of the Trade Descriptions Act 1968. Notwithstanding the hyberbole of this statement, the Trade Descriptions Act, which introduced criminal prohibitions of false and misleading product and service descriptions and of misleading pricing claims, was a watershed in UK **consumer** protection. It imposed a duty to enforce the Act on local Weights and Measures Officers (now Trading Standards Officers), ushering in a new era of public regulation of misleading sales statements. Forty years later the main provisions of the Act as they affect consumers have been repealed by the Consumer Protection from Unfair Trading Regulations 2008, implementing the EU Unfair Commercial Practices Directive.

The Trade Descriptions Act probably contributed to higher standards of candour in some markets such as used car sales, a primary area of prosecutions in the 1970s and 1980s; and it may have resulted in improvements in pricing claims. The Act did not indicate clearly when a product description was misleading—did it have to mislead a reasonable or credulous person? The courts in general looked at the effects of descriptions on a reasonable consumer, treating the issue as a question of fact and rarely engaging in sophisticated normative analysis of the implications of the choice of standard. The Act, with its criminal liability baggage, never reached the subtle persuasions of image advertising, which constitute the bulk of modern advertising and which are regulated by the Advertising Standards Authority, a form of 'mandated **self-regulation**' which is now embedded within the overall structure of government **regulation**. The Trade Descriptions Act also contained anachronistic terminology—it was a modernization of the nineteenth-century Merchandise Marks Acts—and was under-inclusive in its regulation of misleading marketing practices. While some may regret its demise and consequent disappearance from popular lore—'Have you checked that with Trade Descriptions?'—the 2008 regulations provide a more comprehensive regulation of false and misleading commercial practices.

IAIN RAMSAY

misrepresentation   *see* **fraud and misrepresentation; unfair commercial practices**

mis-selling of investment products   Investment products take many forms; but in essence they are devised by investment firms to enable members of the public to participate in a wider range of investment opportunities than they would otherwise be able to. As the capital value of savings diminishes with inflation, investing in assets that at least keep pace with inflation is an attractive alternative. However, whilst the characteristics of saving are generally understood by most members of the public, the characteristics of investment products are generally not.

Collective investment schemes, such as unit trusts, are prime examples of investment products. Here investors with limited resources obtain the benefits of contributing to a large fund (with consequent possibilities of spreading risk through diversification of investment and of economies of scale) that is expertly invested and managed. But whichever form the investment product takes, when a member of the public buys such a product they only obtain intangible rights against the investment-product provider. The greater potential for mis-selling investment products, in comparison to tangible investments, is clear. An investor can readily value tangible investments and understands how that value may change. That is why the well-known principle **caveat emptor** operates in that context. On the other hand, the value—especially the future value—of intangible rights depends on a number of factors which are all far more difficult for an investor (at least a private investor) to understand and assess. The principle of *caveat emptor* is therefore modified as the investor inevitably must rely on the integrity and expertise of those who sell the product. The law, including the regulatory regime to which investment advisers are subject, reflects this by imposing greater obligations on sellers of investment products. If those sellers do not adequately explain, or if they misrepresent, the features of the investment product then the product will have been 'mis-sold'. In addition, if an investment adviser is to choose a product to suit the investor's investment objectives and appetite for risk, then again a product will have been mis-sold if it does not fulfil those criteria.

In recent times, there has been a series of wide-spread instances of the mis-selling of investment products. A common theme—some would say the reason why the practice continues to be problematic—is that the investment-product sellers are often rewarded by a commission from the investment-product provider and thus have a clear incentive to sell particular products. Moreover, insofar as the amount of commission varies between products, there is also an incentive to sell the product generating the greatest commission rather than one which really suits the client. In the UK, paying a fee for impartial investment advice is a practice generally only adopted by the affluent. Hence most investors buy investment products through agents on commission, whose focus is likely to be maximizing their income through sales rather than ensuring that the investment products are not mis-sold.

A major recent investment product mis-selling episode followed the introduction of personal **pensions** in 1988. Many employees were already members of occupational pension schemes but these schemes were regarded as inflexible and inhibitory of the movement of labour. The personal pension was promoted by the government as a means whereby individuals could take responsibility for their own pension provision. In addition, such a 'portable' pension would not tie an employee to any one employer. New legislation provided that employees could no longer be obliged to join occupational pension schemes. Moreover, transferring out of such schemes was made easier. However, whilst personal pensions were clearly suitable for many, they were not always suitable for those with the alternative of an occupational pension scheme. These schemes, especially those for non-mobile, public sector employees, provided more generous benefits than most personal pensions. Nevertheless, a large number of such employees were sold personal pensions by commission-driven salespersons. Many were encouraged to transfer out of their occupational pension schemes and pay the lump sum thus realized into a personal pension scheme or to buy a personal pension scheme instead of joining an occupational one.

By the mid-1990s it became clear that large-scale mis-selling of personal pensions had occurred, primarily to those who had forgone the more suitable alternative of an occupational pension scheme. Rather than rely on individuals to take the initiative and check if they had been mis-sold personal pensions, the regulators ordered the investment advisers to review all past sales to check if mis-selling had occurred. When mis-selling was discovered, the regulators then both disciplined the advisers (imposing large financial penalties, totalling nearly £10m, on the most culpable) and required compensation (totalling £11.5bn) to be paid. Similarly, so-called Free Standing Additional Voluntary Contributions ('FSAVC') were also mis-sold to a large number of employees in circumstances where they would have been better off making further contributions to their occupational pension schemes. Again the regulators took action to require compensation to be paid and imposed penalties.

A further high-profile incident of investment-product mis-selling involved so-called 'home income' or 'equity release' schemes. These enable homeowners who have little or no borrowing secured on their homes, to release the capital in their homes. The schemes involve the homeowner taking out a mortgage on their home and using the lump sum borrowed to invest in a scheme which promises them income. Many (often elderly) homeowners who where sold such schemes were not told that the performance of their investment would depend on interest rates and how the stock market performed. In the early 1990s, when interest rates (and hence the cost of the mortgage) rose and the stock market (and hence the investment income) and house prices fell, many homeowners who had purchased these products found themselves in financial difficulties, and some even lost their homes. Again, the imposition of penalties and payment of compensation followed.

The incidence of investment product mis-selling has not diminished over the years, and is likely to continue as long as the public relies on 'advisers' who are really salespersons on commission.

EVA LOMNICKA

See also: **conduct of business regulation; financial regulation; investment diversification**

mitigation, criminal   *see* **justification, excuse and mitigation in criminal law**

mixed jurisdictions   Despite the name, a mixed jurisdiction is not merely one in which the law is 'mixed' in the sense of being drawn from disparate sources, as indeed law usually is. Rather, the label implies something as to the content of the mixture. It can be traced back to the early days of the science of comparative law. At the beginning of the twentieth century it was fashionable to divide the legal systems of the world into two main groupings according to which type of law was said to apply—whether this was the civil law, which was prevalent in continental Europe and derived ultimately from **Roman law**, or the **common law**, which had developed in England through centuries of judicial decision-making and was later exported throughout the British Empire. Not all countries, however, could be made to fit this rather simplistic division, and mixed jurisdictions were those jurisdictions which, combining significant elements of both common law and civil law, could not properly be assigned to either camp.

The jurisdictions which are usually regarded as mixed in this special sense are Scotland, Quebec, Louisiana, Sri Lanka, Puerto Rico, the Philippines, Israel, and the states of southern Africa: South Africa, Zimbabwe, Lesotho, Swaziland, Botswana, and Namibia. In addition, a claim can be made for certain others such as Malta, Cyprus, and Jersey and Guernsey in the Channel Islands. The grouping is hardly a homogeneous one, and the jurisdictions display striking diversity as to location, constitutional status, and social and economic development.

They also differ as to the reason for their mixed character. The most common explanation is a change in colonial power. Quebec was a colony of France until it fell to the British at the end of the Seven Years War in 1763. By the beginning of the following century the British had taken the Cape Colony and Sri Lanka from the Dutch. Louisiana was successively a French, a Spanish, and then again a French colony before being sold to the United States in 1803. The Philippines and Puerto Rico were Spanish colonies which fell to the US at the end of the Spanish-American War in 1898. Out of this highly varied experience there emerged a broadly similar pattern of legal development. Under the original colonial masters, the law which was introduced was civil law, because France, Spain, and The Netherlands were all civil law jurisdictions; and while that law survived their loss of colonial control, over time it came to be affected, and partly replaced, by the common law espoused by their British and American successors.

The experience of other jurisdictions was different. In entering into a union with England in 1707, Scotland chose to expose its predominantly civil law tradition to the common law of its larger and more powerful neighbour, with predictable results. In the new state of Israel, the common law of what had been previously a UK-mandated territory was subjected to the robust influence of a group of immigrants who had received their legal training in continental Europe.

With the exception of Israel, the common law always followed the civil law and, on one view, threatened its integrity, so that is hardly surprising that, in those jurisdictions where nationalism was a political or cultural factor, the preservation of the civil law was often adopted as one of its objectives. The result, in a number of jurisdictions, was to check the common law's further advance, although only in South Africa, in the years after 1948, was its

influence actually reduced. Today, however, the balance between civil law and common law is generally both stable and accepted, and the status of mixed jurisdiction is seen, not as a temporary misfortune, but as something which is respectable or even advantageous.

For a long time mixed jurisdictions were of little interest to comparative lawyers or even to one another. However, since the 1990s—building on the pioneering work of the Scottish comparatist, T B Smith, some 40 years earlier—they have been subjected to serious comparative study. Although much work remains to be done, it is already possible to suggest some tentative conclusions. On the one hand, it is plain that mixed jurisdictions display significant differences. Thus a mixed jurisdiction is sometimes an independent state and sometimes a constituent part of another state in which the law of the other parts is common law. The dominant influence may be either civil law or common law, and there may be other influences at work such as customary law. The civil law element may be Dutch in origin, or French or Spanish or, as in the case of Louisiana, both, while the common law element may be English or American. The law of a mixed jurisdiction may be codified in the continental fashion, or un-codified. But the similarities are more important still. In a mixed jurisdiction the legal methodology and institutional structure are largely common law in inspiration while the content of the law is mixed: as a general rule, public law follows a common law orientation whereas private law is strongly influenced by civil law. Property law is always the most civilian part of private law, and yet room is found for the trust, that most characteristic product of English law. A detailed study of private law in Scotland and South Africa has shown that, at the level of specific rules, the law in the two jurisdictions is quite often similar or even the same.

It is too early to say what use will be made of this comparative endeavour. If there is to be further harmonization of private law within the **European Union**, then the experience of the mixed jurisdictions will be of value, both as demonstrating the possibility of an accommodation between the main European legal traditions and also as showing how in practice such an accommodation might be achieved. Furthermore, it is evident that the mixed jurisdictions themselves have much to learn from a study of their sister systems, for there is no surer guide to development than the experience of a sibling.

KENNETH REID

VV Palmer, *Mixed Jurisdictions Worldwide: the Third Legal Family* (Cambridge: Cambridge University Press, 2001)

First Worldwide Congress on Mixed Jurisdictions—Salience and Unity in the Mixed Jurisdiction Experience: Traits, Patterns, Culture, Commonalites (2003) 78 *Tulane LR* 1–501

See also: **civil law systems; common law of Europe**

Model Penal Code While each of the American states has its own criminal code, more than two-thirds of those codes are based upon the Model Penal Code of the American Law Institute. The Institute, a prestigious national academy of law, usually produces 'restatements' of the law; but when it took up the subject of criminal law in 1951, American criminal law was in such a sorry state that it decided to produce a model code instead. After more than a decade of work by judges, lawyers, and professors, the Model Penal Code official text was promulgated in 1962 and joined later by six volumes of Official Commentaries.

The clarity of the drafting and the rationality of the underlying reasoning set the Model Penal Code as the template for criminal code reform throughout the United States during the 1960s and 1970s. Because it has been influential even in jurisdictions that have never enacted comprehensive codes, the Model Code's position is usually, but not always, the majority view among American states.

The Code's greatest hallmark is its comprehensiveness, containing essentially all the substantive criminal law rules required for the adjudication of a criminal case. Unlike some other well-developed criminal codes, such as the German code, it does not rely upon an external scholarly literature to give meaning to its central concepts. Perhaps because of this self-sufficiency, it has been an influential model in criminal code reform efforts around the world.

Foremost among the substantive changes that the Code contributed are the use of a conceptually organized Special Part of the code, which defines offences in a way that minimizes overlap between them, and a robust General Part, which sets out general principles of criminal liability applicable to all offences defined in the Special Part, including such general principles as the definition of offence culpability requirements, general inchoate offences, justification and excuse defences, the requirements for complicity liability, and the liability of non-human legal entities. A third part of the Code, concerning the sentencing, treatment, and correction of offenders, has never been influential, perhaps because it was highly dependent upon the sentencing philosophy of the 1950s, which has been replaced several times over by other philosophies.

The rationales espoused in the Official Commentaries are unabashedly utilitarian, with primary focus on distributing liability and punishment in a way that will reduce future crime. Even though notions of how best to do this have changed significantly since its drafting in the 1950s, the Code's provisions remain influential. The Code's definitions of wrongdoing and liability rules appear to be useful under a wide range of different punishment theories and programmes.

Views on some sorts of wrongdoing have changed since 1962—domestic violence, drunk driving, sexual offences, terrorism-related offences, and newly invented forms of fraud, to name a few. In these areas the Model Code appears increasingly dated; yet the Institute has resisted calls for a revised Model Penal Code. If the Model Code does not change with the times its influence is likely to diminish, but it will never lose its place in history as having brought comprehensive and coherent codification to the United States and to many other countries in the world.

PAUL ROBINSON

See also: **criminal law; restatements of the law (USA); Uniform Commercial Code**

Mogul Steamship Co v McGregor, Gow & Co **(1892)** This case is one of a trilogy of cases decided by the **House of Lords** towards the end of the nineteenth century which held that the existence of an intention to cause damage to another was not in itself enough to found a claim in the law of tort (the other two cases were *Bradford Corporation v Pickles* (1895)-; and *Allen v Flood* (1898)). Something more was required.

The facts of *Mogul* are intriguing in that they arise out of an activity that at one and the same time encapsulates the competitive spirit of around-the-world sailing and of unbridled nineteenth-century capitalism. That activity was the tea trade which, by the middle of the century, had been freed from its former monopolies and had become the centre of attraction for intense commercial competition. This competition in turn fuelled major technological developments in cargo-carrying sailing ships, famously resulting in what became known as the 'tea clippers' whose speed was more than double that of the older galleons and whose commercial races across the oceans, so as to be the first to deliver the new tea harvest, generated much excitement and even wagering amongst some sections of the English population. The plaintiffs were a shipping company trying to break into this tea trade and the defendants were a combination (a 'conference') of other ship-owners which had tried to exclude them from the trade by lowering their own rates (through rebates) and shadowing the newcomer's ships. The aim was to put the plaintiffs out of business.

The plaintiffs had recourse to the courts. Having tried unsuccessfully to obtain an **injunction** against the conference members, that is to say an order prohibiting the defendants from 'boycotting' the plaintiffs, they subsequently brought an action for damages. The action failed in front of Lord Coleridge, and an appeal to the Court of Appeal was rejected by a majority. A further appeal by the plaintiffs to the House of Lords also failed.

As Lord Bramwell in the House of Lords noted, 'the plaintiffs in this case do not complain of any trespass, violence, force, fraud, or breach of contract, nor of any direct tort or violation of any right of the plaintiffs, like the case of firing to frighten birds from a decoy; nor of any act, the ultimate object of which was to injure the plaintiffs, having its origin in malice or ill-will to them'. In other words the facts could not be fitted within any existing 'cause of action' precedent and thus they did not disclose any tort. Moreover, he went on to say, a person is entitled to sell goods and services at any price he wishes and it is not for the courts to declare such behavior as fair or unfair, reasonable or unreasonable.

All this may seem dated today given the apparent strict regulation of competition in Europe by legislation. Yet *Mogul* remains of importance in as much as it is probably still true to say that English case law refuses to recognize a doctrine of abuse of rights (that is exercising a right maliciously) or, indeed, a doctrine of *concurrence déloyale*. Moreover, at the social level, within the facts and judgments of *Mogul* are to be found the spirit of the times and of capitalism: 'Victorian values', as some might say to their children when visiting what is left of the *Cutty Sark*.

GEOFFREY SAMUEL

monarch Under the United Kingdom's constitutional arrangements the hereditary monarch (King or Queen) is head of state. In formal legal terms many of the powers of the executive branch of government (ie the **Prime Minister, Ministers of State,** and **Departments of State)** are vested in 'the **Crown'.** Central government and the state are often described in terms of 'the Crown', and many historic immunities and practices associated with the monarchy have been carried over to the executive government. There are government agencies called 'Her Majesty's **Treasury**' and 'Her Majesty's Revenue and Customs'. Ministers hold office 'under the Crown' and judicial appointments are made in the name of the Crown ('Her Majesty's judges').

The Monarchy is financed partly from the Civil List (for expenditure incurred in exercising the monarch's official duties as head of state) and partly by income received by the Queen in her personal capacity. Since 1993 the Queen has voluntarily paid tax on her private income. Prince Charles, the Prince of Wales, as heir to the throne, also voluntarily pays tax on income derived from the Duchy of Cornwall.

It is impossible to list all the functions and duties of the monarch. There is a published list of public occasions when official and ceremonial functions are performed. State occasions provide an opportunity to welcome foreign heads of state, and the State Opening of Parliament provides a formal setting for the start of the parliamentary term. The Queen also performs largely symbolic functions as Head of the Commonwealth, for example. Behind the scenes, and away from the glare of media attention, the monarch receives all major cabinet papers and regular reports from the Prime Minister and Foreign Secretary on the activities of the government. The monarch may offer them advice but they are not bound to take it.

In performing formal constitutional functions as head of state, the monarch is generally bound to act 'on the advice of' the Prime Minister or senior member of the Cabinet. The monarch is required to give formal consent to various Crown appointments and her signature is required for many official documents. The monarch has a Private Secretary who has an important role in communicating with ministers and who may advise the monarch on decisions that need to be taken. The monarch's powers may appear to have diminished in modern times. However, in appointing a Prime Minister, the monarch's role may be decisive in determining who is in the best position to command the support of the majority of MPs in the House of Commons. This role may not have much significance where there is a strong majority in favour of one party. It would becomes more significant if there were a minority government or a hung parliament.

The monarch may, at the request of the Prime Minister, dissolve Parliament, resulting in a general election. Serious constitutional questions would arise if the monarch were to refuse to accede to such a request made by a serving Prime Minister with a parliamentary majority. Equally serious issues would arise if the monarch refused to accept the advice of ministers including the Prime Minister. Refusal by the monarch to assent to a Bill already passed by Parliament would create a major constitutional crisis.

The monarch's role and importance lies beyond the symbolic, as the monarch provides the continuity of tradition that has survived many centuries of change. The monarch's role, while subservient to the government of the day, provides an important public image for the United Kingdom's constitutional arrangements.   JOHN MCELDOWNEY

See also: **acts of parliament; conventions of the constitution**

Money Claim Online   Since 2002, claimants in England and Wales have been able to progress money claims through Money Claim Online, a virtual adjunct of Northampton County Court. Online claims are limited to fixed amounts of less than £100,000, involving no more than two defendants. Claimants and defendants must have addresses in England and Wales. Claimants must also be at least eighteen years of age and able to set out details of their claim in no more than twenty-four lines or 1,080 characters of text. In general, provided a claim is not disputed, it can be concluded online, through to judgment and enforcement. In 2005–2006, over 70,000 claims were issued through Money Claim Online, more than through any local court.

Similarly, since May 2006 claimants in Northern Ireland have been able to progress money claims for fixed or estimated sums up to £2,000 through Small Claims Online, a service managed through the Small Claims Central Processing Office in Belfast. Again, unless there is a dispute, Small Claims Online enables claimants of at least eighteen years of age, who are able to set out details of their claim in no more than 2,000 characters of text, to conclude claims entirely online; though online enforcement is not possible. Currently, 200 claims per month issue through Small Claims Online.

Online money claims are not yet possible in Scotland. However, a 2004 consultation on the use of IT in the Sheriff Courts recommended that there should be a 'centralized virtual court' for small claims and summary causes.   PASCOE PLEASENCE

monuments and listed buildings   *see* **English Heritage**

moral hazard   This term generally refers to a situation where a person who is exposed to a risk of whatever nature has no incentive to avoid the materialization of the risk because its effects have been transferred to or taken over by someone else. This transfer can be realized through a contract, an insurance contract being the most obvious illustration. The transfer of risk can also be the consequence of government provision of social security and health care, for instance. Moral hazard will induce a person who is immunized from the (financial) effects of the occurrence of a risk to behave in a

less careful way then if he or she were more exposed to it.

In the area of **financial regulation**, moral hazard is most commonly identified in the field of **deposit protection**: in order to maintain confidence in the banking system, depositors of a failed bank will be compensated for their losses out of a fund principally financed by the industry. Provision of excessive compensation is likely to generate moral hazard in the behaviour of financial institutions, which can adopt more risky strategies without having to fear advere reactions from customers. Conversely, customers will be less attentive to the risks of their financial decisions knowing that these are covered by the compensation scheme. Under European directives on deposit guarantee and **investor compensation schemes**, the moral hazard issue is addressed mainly by putting a cap on the amount of compensation per depositor or investor of 20,000 EUR, although Member States may provide for a higher threshold.

MICHEL TISON

moral rights   Moral rights (the term is derived from the French *droit moral*) generally protect the author's non-economic interests in a **copyright** work. Unlike economic interests, which comprise the exclusive rights granted to the copyright holder under copyright law, moral rights are enjoyed by the author of the copyright work, irrespective of whether the author is also the owner of the copyright. Unlike copyright, moral rights cannot be transferred, although they may be waived.

Members of the **Berne Convention for the Protection of Literary and Artistic Works** are required to grant at least moral rights, which are the rights of paternity and integrity. Both of these rights are recognized by the UK Copyright Designs and Patents Act 1988 ('CDPA'). With some exceptions, they apply to the authors of literary, dramatic, musical, and artistic works, and films. They last for the duration of the copyright in the work. Two further types of so-called moral right are also recognized by the CDPA. These are the right to object to false attribution and the right to privacy in certain photographs and films. As will become evident, both these rights tend to strain the concept of moral rights as being authors' rights.

The right of paternity or attribution is, however, clearly an author's right. In relation to certain copyright works, this is the right to be known as the author of the work. In order to be enforced the right must be asserted in writing by the author. The situations in which the right may be exercised vary depending on the type of work in question. The right of paternity is subject to a number of exceptions, some of which reflect copyright exceptions, such as fair dealing for the purpose of reporting the news, incidental inclusion, and use for the purposes of public administration.

The right of integrity gives the author of certain copyright works the right to object to a treatment of the work that amounts to a distortion or mutilation or is otherwise prejudicial to the honour or reputation of the author. However, the right only operates where the derogatory treatment is made available to the public, and it does not necessarily prevent physical destruction of a work. The exceptions to this right are generally narrower than those applying in relation to the right of paternity.

The right against false attribution attaches itself to a person other rather than the author of a copyright work. Lasting for twenty years from the death of the person asserting the right, it permits a person to object to the publication or exhibition of material that falsely attributes authorship to that person.

Like the right against false attribution, the right to privacy in certain photographs and films is not an author's right. Rather, it confers a right on persons commissioning photographs and films for personal and domestic purposes to object to their publication. This right, which is subject to a range of copyright-type exceptions, lasts for the duration of the copyright in the photograph or film.

FIONA MACMILLAN

More, Sir Thomas In early Tudor England a legal career was a common route to advancement. A baker's son, John More was determined that his eldest son Thomas (born in 1477 or 1478) should follow the path that had served him well. Thomas duly entered Lincoln's Inn in 1496, but was attracted to a life of contemplation among the monks at London's Charterhouse and also to the world of humanist scholarship. Although More did not display the single-mindedness that his father expected, by 1505 he had chosen **marriage** and a legal career. In *Utopia* (1516) More satirized the common lawyer's social conservatism and pedantic pleading; the profession was barred from More's half-ironic fantasy island. Yet More's own career prospered; his eloquence also drew him to the attention of the **Crown**. In 1517, with feigned reluctance, More entered Henry VIII's council, foregoing his lucrative legal career. Henry valued More for his fame as a humanist, avant-garde learning, and ready wit rather than for his legal skills.

Nevertheless, in 1529, More was unexpectedly appointed **Lord Chancellor** in succession to the disgraced Cardinal Wolsey. As chancellor, More presided over the **Courts of Chancery** and the **Star Chamber**. Unencumbered by the rules of **evidence** and **pleading** binding **courts** of record, and basing their decisions on equity, these courts proved popular with litigants, whilst business in the King's Bench and Common Pleas slumped. Constitutional proprieties prohibiting these courts from determining titles and reviewing decisions at **common law** were circumvented. Wolsey's highhandedness had exacerbated tensions with common lawyers; despite his training as a common lawyer, More did not resile from his predecessor's practices. Indeed, he was stricter than Wolsey had been on those who disobeyed the courts' decrees, and he prosecuted heresy more rigorously. This notwithstanding, More's reputation for incorruptibility would endure in Protestant England. His diligent application to the judicial responsibilities of the chancellorship, however, reflected his estrangement from the direction of royal policy.

Unable to secure papal annulment of his **marriage**, Henry VIII assailed the Church's jurisdictional independence, which provoked More to resign the chancellorship in 1532. Careful to avoid appearing overtly to oppose the King's actions, More made his dissent obvious and gave discreet encouragement to the like-minded. He refused to take the oath recognizing the King's **divorce** and remarriage. In 1535, More was charged under the new Treason Act with denying royal supremacy over the Church. Convicted on the basis of a private and uncorroborated conversation, More delivered his celebrated motion in arrest of judgment: an Act of Parliament 'directly repugnant to the laws of God and His Holy Church' was 'insufficient to charge any Christian man'. In principle, everyone accepted that man-made laws which contravened divine laws were void; in practice, More's motion was unheard of—common lawyers increasingly seeing **Parliament's** legislative power as untrammelled. His motion therefore failed, and he was beheaded. He did not die championing individual conscience against the state: unlike Henry VIII and the Protestants whom More persecuted, More believed that the individual should conform his conscience to the consensus of Christendom.

PAUL R CAVILL

JA Guy, *The Public Career of Sir Thomas More* (Brighton: The Harvester Press, 1980)

JDM Derrett, 'The Trial of Sir Thomas More' (1964) 79 *English Historical Review* 449–77; reprinted with addenda in RS Sylvester and GP Marc'hadour (eds), *Essential Articles for the Study of Thomas More* (Hamden, CT: The Shoe String Press, 1977), 55–78

mortgage advice and regulation A mortgage is an interest in property which is created as security for a loan. In most jurisdictions, mortgages are the most common way for housing to be purchased without having to find the full amount in advance. The main types of mortgage in the UK are repayment mortgages and interest-only mortgages. Under a repayment mortgage, monthly repayments go towards reducing the amount owed as well as paying the interest charged by the lender. Under an interest-only mortgage, the monthly payment pays only the interest on the loan. The borrower has to find another way of repaying the loan at the end of the mortgage term, for example by taking out some form of savings or investment product.

Since 31 October 2004 the **Financial Services Authority** ('FSA') has regulated most mortgage sales in the UK. Regulation takes a number of different forms, but is largely focused upon ensuring that consumers are appropriately informed about a mortgage before sale by requiring that specific documentation be provided at specified times. This is designed to help consumers to shop around and make informed comparisons between lenders, and also to ensure that they understand the characteristics of the mortgages they take out. Two of the main documents required are the Initial Disclosure Document ('IDD') and the Key Facts Illustration ('KFI').

The IDD sets out key information in a standard form in numbered sections. These sections state: that the FSA regulates financial services and that firms are required to provide the document; whose mortgages the firm offers; which service the firm will provide; what the consumer has to pay for the service; and whether the firm will refund a fee in any circumstances. Research for the FSA found that while most consumers found the document useful and accessible, more than half the IDDs examined contained five or more errors. The KFI is designed to help consumers to compare a particular mortgage with rival products by presenting information about its most important features in a standard way. It contains thirteen or fourteen sections which explain important points about the mortgage on offer, such as the overall cost of the mortgage, what fees must be paid, and what happens if the consumer wants to make overpayments. A common criticism of KFIs is that firms make them longer and more complex than they need to be.

The FSA draws a distinction between information and advice, but this distinction may not always be clear. Some firms offer mortgages from the whole market, some from a limited number of suppliers, and some from only a single lender. In many cases, the consumer will be dealing with a lender directly, which will usually sell only its own mortgages. The IDD will make it clear which service is being provided. Where a consumer buys with advice, the FSA's rules apply, and they can expect providers to recommend only products and services that are suitable.

PETER CARTWRIGHT

mortgages of chattels A mortgage is the transfer of ownership of property as security for a loan. The borrower has an equity of redemption—ie a right to the property back free from the encumbrance represented by the mortgage once the loan has been repaid. The borrower retains possession, but 'ownership' is transferred to the lender during the loan period.

In technical terms, there is a narrow distinction between a mortgage and a charge. A charge involves no transfer of ownership, but the lender has a right of recourse against the charged property if the loan is not repaid. The lender's rights in the property could be classed as a form of ownership, and judges have often used the terms 'mortgage' and 'charge' interchangeably. Statute sometimes does the same or refers to a 'charge' as also including a 'mortgage'. The charge was originally developed by courts of equity.

It is not possible to mortgage property not yet owned by the borrower, but it is possible to create a charge over property not yet owned. Borrowing by companies is commonly secured by a charge that extends to both existing and future property.

Mortgages or charges over chattels executed by individuals come within the Bills of Sale Acts and must be in a particular statutory form to be effective. Using this form is quite cumbersome and lenders are loath to do so. **Hire purchase** agreements are therefore much more common.

GERARD MCCORMACK

mortgages of land A mortgage charges a loan on property belonging to the borrower (or 'mortgagor') as security for repayment, thus protecting the lender (or 'mortgagee') against the borrower's insolvency. Since repayment is secured the cost of borrowing will be cheaper than in the case of an unsecured personal loan. Land is especially suitable as security because it is immovable; but practically any kind of property can be mortgaged. Historically it was usual to transfer the land being mortgaged to the lender or to grant the lender a long lease (a 'mortgage by demise'); but today the usual form is a legal charge, which leaves the ownership of the land with the borrower and merely earmarks the land for repayment. This has the advantage that the borrower can act as owner of the land subject to the mortgage and could, for example, remortgage it. A mortgage will not be apparent to a potential buyer who inspects the land; and so, to ensure that the land is not sold until the loan has been repaid, it is necessary to register a mortgage. A lender will usually insist upon a 'legal mortgage'–a charge which is entered on the charges register of the title being mortgaged—since this gives the best remedies to a lender. Short-term borrowing, such as a bank overdraft, may be secured by an 'equitable mortgage', created less formally and merely noted on the register, saving registration fees but possibly reducing the remedies available to the lender. In the past, mortgages of land title to which was unregistered were protected by the deposit of the title deeds with the lender; but now, when unregistered land is mortgaged, title to the land must generally be registered.

A mortgage generally secures a loan, called the principal, as well as interest and costs. Most domestic (non-commercial) mortgages provide for payment by instalments, which may include capital and interest or may be 'interest only', and in the last case generally coupled with an endowment policy intended to build up a fund to repay the principal. Interest rates are usually variable, but it is possible to fix the rate for a set period, usually at the price of a redemption penalty (if the loan is repaid before the expiry of the period).

If the borrower defaults, a lender has the right to possession of the mortgaged property—though owners of dwellings are protected against repossession for minor defaults. After repossession the lender will be able to effect a sale out of court. From the proceeds the lender may deduct costs and the amount outstanding, with any other lenders standing in a queue behind. What is left after all lenders are satisfied is called the 'equity', more properly the 'equity of redemption', the unmortgaged value remaining to the borrower. If property prices fall, the borrower may owe more than the land is worth, a trap called 'negative equity'. Foreclosure is a judicial remedy by which the lender can bar the borrower's right of redemption—the borrower's ownership is extinguished in favour of the lender—but this is now extremely rare, though the term 'foreclosure' is often misused colloquially.

Mortgages are redeemable (ie the property can be got back by repaying the loan): 'in equity, the estate is no more than a pledge or security for the debt'. The contractual redemption date was once insisted on, as in *The Merchant of Venice*; and so frequently was the pledge forfeited because of late redemption that it was thought to be dead, hence the name 'mortgage' (dead pledge). Today this redemption date, conventionally six months hence, has little function except to set the earliest possible date for sale of the property by the lender. The redemption date has lost its terror because the harsh treatment meted out to borrowers (at common law) has been superseded by (equitable) rules which compel a lender to accept interest for a delay in repayment and prevent demands for exorbitant or unfair interest.

Property to be mortgaged must be valued, given the prevalence of frauds involving misrepresentation of the value of a security, and a proper loan to value ratio imposed. The creditworthiness of the borrower must also be checked. If the purpose of the mortgage is to guarantee business debts of someone other than the mortgagor (a spouse, for instance), or if for some other reason the mortgagor secures no benefit from the mortgage, the lender must take steps to make sure that the consent to the mortgagor is genuine and not obtained by undue influence, the usual method being to insist upon the provision of independent legal advice.   PETER SPARKES

See also: **mortgages of chattels; registration of title**

Moses v Macferlan (1760)   This is the founding case of the modern law of **restitution**, or unjust enrichment. Its fame rests more on Lord Mansfield's observations than his ruling, which many of his successors thought was wrong. Moses owned four promissory notes signed by one Jacob. He sold them to Macferlan. The technical law of notes would have made Moses, and not merely Jacob, liable to Macferlan; and so Moses obtained from Macferlan a collateral written agreement that Macferlan would look only to Jacob for payment. Despite his promise, Macferlan sued Moses on the notes in the Court of Conscience (a small claims tribunal). That court held it could take no account of the collateral agreement, and gave judgment against Moses. Moses, having paid up, responded by suing Macferlan in the Court of King's Bench, not for breach of the collateral agreement, as perhaps he ought, but in an action to recover moneys unfairly obtained. This choice of action was upheld.

Mansfield's life of learning and of practice in both **Roman law** and **common law** systems (including in the latter, the law of equity) left him uniquely placed to weave from them a generalized duty to account for moneys unfairly obtained, or retained. Although there were already English precedents for most of what this duty encompassed (particularly in the judgments of Holt CJ, 1689–1710), the Roman sources predominated in the resulting synthesis: 'If the defendant be under an obligation from the ties of natural justice to refund, the law implies a debt, and gives this action, founded in the equity of the plaintiff's case, as [if] it were upon a contract ("quasi ex contractu," as the Roman law expresses it)'.

Broad though this formulation was, Mansfield enumerated the principal instances of the right to recover as involving: money (not owed) that has been paid by mistake; money obtained by imposition, extortion, or oppression, or by taking undue advantage of the plaintiff's situation contrary to laws made for the protection of persons under those circumstances; and conditional payments where the conditions were not met. Further structure was added by his explaining that the plaintiff could not recover where (mistakenly or not) he had paid money he did not owe in law but did 'in point of honor and honesty' (eg by paying time-barred debts; by paying, as adult, debts incurred in infancy; and by honouring gambling debts).

To those aspects of the claim, Mansfield added that there could be defences; indeed, just as the claim was open-ended, so too a defendant could 'defend himself by every thing which shows that the plaintiff, ex aequo et bono [in equity and fairness], is not intitled to the whole of his demand, or to any part of it'. Mansfield's subsequent judgments established the principal defence as one allowing a worthy defendant to plead that, owing to events occurring after the payment, her position, if restitution were ordered, would be worse than if she had never received it (the 'change of position' defence).

PETER WATTS

PBH Birks, 'English and Roman Learning in *Moses v Macferlan*' [1984] *Current Legal Problems* 1

W Swain, '*Moses v Macferlan* (1760)' in C and P Mitchell (eds), *Landmark Cases in the Law of Restitution* (Oxford: Hart Publishing, 2006)

See also: **equity as a system of law**

most-favoured-nation treatment   Most-favoured-nation ('MFN') treatment is a standard of conduct, normally found in international agreements, particularly of an economic character. According to the standard, a country undertakes, either conditionally or unconditionally, to give its best or 'most favoured' treatment, in its relations with a country or countries, to all other countries within a specified group. In other words the country undertakes not to discriminate as between countries within a group. This prohibition of discrimination as between countries is to be distinguished from the discrimination that is prohibited as a consequence of the application of the national treatment principle. Under the national treatment principle the country undertakes not to discriminate as between its nationals and foreigners.

An example of the operation of the MFN standard is to be found in international trade amongst members of the **World Trade Organization ('WTO')**. Thus, members of the WTO have undertaken not to discriminate, in relation to the import and export of goods and services, between like products and services originating from the territory of other members, or destined for the territory of different members. This prohibition of discrimination involves the extending of any benefit, with respect to imports or exports granted to one member, to all other members. For example, Australia may not impose a customs duty on the imports of cars from Korea alone whilst all other members enjoy the benefit of not being the subject of such a duty.

ASIF QURESHI

motherhood   Motherhood is a term with layers of meaning. Culturally or ideologically, motherhood entails nurture and care and assumes moral, emotional, and physical bonds with and **responsibilities** to care for a **child**. Perhaps incorporating some of this understanding, legal motherhood gives a woman automatic **parental responsibility** for a child. However, while determining who, in law, is a mother was a simple matter historically, with the advent of technology and 'new' family forms, that determination is now not always straightforward. A child can have potentially five different mothers: a genetic mother, a gestational mother, a commissioning mother in a **surrogacy** situation, an adoptive mother, and an 'other mother' who is her **lesbian** partner. While motherhood as a cultural or moral concept may attribute bonds between the child and any one or more of these women, legally, priority is given to biology, with law reserving for itself the **discretion** to make orders otherwise (such as **adoption** orders). Before the advent of IVF, the genetic and the gestational mother would be the same **person** and this 'biological mother' remains the legal mother where the child's conception was not assisted by technology. In cases of IVF, however, where a choice must be made between genetic and gestational connections, the **woman** who carries and gives birth to the child is the legal mother (Human Fertilization and Embryology Act 1990). However it is understood, the status of motherhood confers upon women myriad moral, emotional, social, and economic consequences which may or may not be acknowledged by law.

ALISON DIDUCK

multicultural citizenship Globalization and the rise in the number of settled **communities** of colour within Western states as a result of increases in transnational migration have led many to question about whether an allegiance to democratic ideals necessitates a demand for multicultural citizenship. Such an ideal of **citizenship** is premised upon the state's need for interested, loyal citizens committed to its values and principles. Thus, it is suggested that a theory of citizenship which incorporates **multiculturalism** and accommodates and respects **minority** rights would facilitate this sense of cohesion and belonging and so ensure the continued commitment and survival of modern liberal **democracy**.

Will Kymlicka, the most famous exponent of multicultural citizenship premises his argument upon a demand for group-differentiated rights for cultural, racial, ethnic, and national minorities. Kymlicka proposes three distinct forms of group rights—**self-government** rights, **polyethnic rights**, and special **representation** rights. Self-government rights are premised upon the right of national groups to **self-determination** as guaranteed by the **United Nations** Charter. Kymlicka locates this idea of self-government within the context of a federal system, arguing for the devolution of political power to members of the national minority group. To facilitate the rights of immigrant groups, Kymlicka proposes a concept of polyethnic rights centred on 'group-specific measures' such as legal exemptions and public funding for cultural practices, designed to promote 'cultural particularity and pride without . . . hampering their success in the economic and political institutions of the dominant society'. Kymlicka's third proposal looks upon special representation rights to facilitate the reduction of barriers to the entry of minorities into political representation, the adoption of group representation rights via the reservation of a certain number of parliamentary/legislative seats for each group, or alternatively, the adoption of a form of proportional representation.

The practical realities of multicultural citizenship have however been subject to much criticism. Within the United Kingdom, there has been much discussion of the perceived failures of multiculturalism and its over-emphasis upon difference which has thus resulted in a loss of shared national **identity**. There now appears within British social and political discourse to be a crisis of identity brought about by the over-enthusiastic privileging of difference at the expense of common British values. Thus, what is being witnessed within political rhetoric is a retreat back towards national identity and citizenship and

a away from distinct cultural identities. Efforts to promote 'Britishness' include endless debates on British values and what it means to be British—debates which have thus far proved fruitless, a citizenship test based upon specifically 'English' questions which has been likened to Norman Tebbit's infamous 'cricket test', and an emphasis upon citizenship within the national curriculum. In reality then, the ideological underpinnings of multicultural citizenship as a means of strengthening citizen loyalty through the accommodation and facilitation of cultural identity appears to have backfired, and instead has resulted in a loss of the commonality which it was originally intended to promote.

SONYA FERNANDEZ

multiculturalism The term 'multiculturalism' can be used either prescriptively or descriptively. Multiculturalism as description refers simply to the existence of plural cultures within a given state. Multiculturalism as prescription implies the need to effectively manage the existence of these culturally plural groups. Most countries can be accurately described as 'multicultural'; however, not all states have adopted necessarily coherent policies of **governance** in response to the diverse **communities** in existence.

The need for a more coherent approach to the management of multiculturalism arose from the increasing number of settled communities of colour within predominantly Western countries following decolonization and the surge in transnational mobility and migration. This increase in diaspora communities heralded a need for a shift in approaches to managing cultural diversity within the host nations. The discontent with policies of Anglo-conformity signified a need for an evolution in thought and strategies, a need which was met with a move towards multiculturalism as both theory and practice. Whilst many states began to adopt what can broadly be described as multicultural policies from the 1960s onwards, it was not until the early 1990s that multicultural theorizing in its current form began truly to take off. Multicultural theorizing rejects the notion of sameness implicit within assimilationist ideas and instead, to coin Charles Taylor's phrasing, seeks to argue for a 'politics of difference' which affords rights of **recognition** predicated upon conceptualizations of group **identity** and belonging. The central underlying premise of multiculturalism as prescription is that cultural groups should be afforded respect and recognition for their practices and traditions, with the general admonition that this recognition is contingent upon a respect for liberal values, in particular, gender **equality**, individual freedom, consent, and choice. One criticism of liberal theories of multiculturalism (which most heavily influence practice) is that they are premised upon a distinction between liberal and illiberal groups which implicitly assumes the superiority of liberal values and culture. This assumption to some extent negates the value of such theorizing.

The 'multiculturalness' of Britain is such that in 2001 chicken tikka masala was proclaimed the national dish, whilst nine boroughs in London (including Newham, Hackney, Tower Hamlets, and Ealing) have ethnic **minority** populations of over 50 per cent. Yet, in spite of this, it is questionable whether the drive towards coherent multicultural policies is actually facilitative of a truly diverse society, or whether claims as to the diversity of British society simply act as a veil over a racism inherent in liberal norms. Since the Bradford, Burnley, and Oldham riots in the summer of 2001, and the events of 9/11 and later, 7/7, there has been a marked shift in the narrative of multiculturalism, from the celebration of different and distinct cultural identities to an emphasis upon community cohesion predicated upon an acceptance and incorporation of a common core of liberal values. Governance of Britain's uneasy multiculturalism has shifted towards the institutionalization, management, and reification of an acceptable form and level of cultural diversity. According to the official narrative of multiculturalism, law acts as a key means by which difference and diversity are effectively managed. So viewed, the problem posed by a multicultural society is one of governance—how to manage and/or govern the diverse cultural groups coexisting within a given society. Multicultural policies such as legal exemptions, funding for arts, and education have often been proffered as the solution to these problems of management to which diversity gives rise. In practice, multiculturalism has proved to be something of a double-edged sword within Britain. In the drive to manage cultural diversity through the recognition of difference and diversity, common values appear to have become lost and British society is now faced with a crisis of identity which has created something of a backlash against multiculturalism manifest in attributions of blame to multiculturalism for the July 7 bombings and for the segregation and isolation of minority communities. Multiculturalism it seems is single-handedly responsible for cultural enclaves which breed fanaticism, extremism, and **terrorism**. Indeed, multiculturalism has come under fire so much that Trevor Phillips, former chairman of the Commission for Racial Equality and current chair of the **Equality and Human Rights Commission** has even called for its eradication, arguing that the term suggested separateness. It seems then that there is some disillusion with multiculturalism. What was seen as the answer to problems of cultural diversity is now being blamed as the cause of those self-same problems. It remains to be seen whether multiculturalism as prescription can be positively resurrected, or whether it is simply an outdated failure of a concept which instead, needs to be replaced with **integration** and community cohesion.

SONYA FERNANDEZ

See also: **Assimilation; liberal multiculturalism; multicultural citizenship; segregation and desegregation**

multinational corporations Also referred to as Multinational Enterprises ('MNEs') or Transnational Corporations ('TNCs'), Multinational Corporations ('MNCs') are enterprises that finance, manage, and control productive assets in more than one country. Thereby, they create a transnational network of production, or, increasingly, services provision, which crosses national borders. They may be of private, state, or mixed ownership. The MNC is usually headed by a parent **company** incorporated in the home country. It owns and controls regional and/or national holding and subsidiary companies (and/or unincorporated branches) in one or more host countries, thereby creating a cross-border group of affiliated entities. It is not necessary for a multinational economic enterprise to be a corporate entity. It is possible for a MNE to exist through a network of interlocking contractual relationships that establish an integrated transnational production chain. In addition, a MNE may take the form of a strategic alliance of otherwise independent enterprises linked by a partnership expressed through, for example, a consortium agreement or a joint venture company. Thus the term MNE is an inclusive description that captures more fully the true nature of the underlying economic entity than does the company law centred concept of the MNC. The term TNC is, by contrast, a term of art found mainly in **United Nations** ('UN') practice. It arises out of the debates on the adoption by the UN of a Code of Conduct for TNCs in the 1970s and 1980s. However, there is little practical difference between the MNC and TNC. They describe the same kind of corporate entity.

A MNC may be little more than a small- or medium-sized enterprise that owns and controls an affiliate in another country, or it may be a vast undertaking that operates across many countries. In legal or economic terms, it is not size that is definitive. That said, the operations of the world's largest MNCs have given rise to significant concerns over their effects on national economies. This is especially the case in developing countries where the process of economic development may be highly dependent on attracting and benefiting from Foreign Direct Investment ('FDI'), the main type of investment carried out by MNCs. FDI consists of investment involving not only finance but also management of productive assets in the host country. This may be contrasted with portfolio investment which provides finance without direct managerial control. As providers of long-term FDI, major MNCs are therefore central to the development process. Specifically, this has raised concerns as to the effects of the economic power of MNCs on market structure, with the risk that large foreign investors might 'crowd out' less efficient local producers and cause concentration in the host country's economy. In addition, by reason of their international production network, MNCs might be able to shift their profits across borders to low tax jurisdictions thereby depriving developing host countries of much needed revenue. They may also control access to world markets for locally produced commodities by reason of their integrated distribution chains. Apart from market effects based on firm size and organization, MNCs may also create problems of group liability. As illustrated by the Bhopal case in the United States (*In Re Union Carbide Gas Plant Disaster in Bhopal India* (1986) affirmed as modified 1987)) or *Adams v Cape Industries* (1990) in England it may be possible for the parent company to avoid liability for the harmful activities of its foreign subsidiary by reason of the corporate separation between them. Such effects have given rise to calls for the development of international corporate responsibility on the part of the parent for the acts of its group as a whole. However, law reform of this kind still awaits implementation.

PETER MUCHLINSKI

PT Muchlinski, *Multinational Enterprises and the Law* (Oxford: Oxford University Press, 2nd edn, 2007)

C Day Wallace, *The Multinational Enterprise and Legal Control: Host State Sovereignty in an Era of Economic Globalization* (The Hague: Martinus Nijhoff, 2002)

multi-party action   *see* **group action**

multiple discrimination   The term 'multiple discrimination' refers to the way in which discrimination may be based on more than one ground simultaneously. Experiences of multiple discrimination include that of an Asian woman who is refused a job on the assumption that she will be submissive to men and will not therefore be an effective worker, or a black man who is persistently targeted by **police** because they assume he is a drug dealer.

Multiple discrimination may be either *additive* or *intersectional*. *Additive* discrimination occurs where a **person** is subject to discrimination on a number of separate but cumulative grounds. This would be the case, for example, where an employer would choose to recruit men rather than women and practising Christians rather than others. An Atheist or Jewish woman would find herself doubly disadvantaged if she applied for a job with that employer. A practising Christian woman and a Jewish man would also be disadvantaged by comparison with a practising Christian man, but their disadvantage would be less: if, for example, only three suitably qualified practising Christian men applied for five vacancies, the employer might well recruit the practising Christian woman and the Jewish man, but is unlikely to offer the Jewish woman a position.

Additive discrimination can be challenged under the current framework of domestic discrimination law. The unsuccessful Jewish woman applicant may be able to point to evidence of anti-woman and pro-Christian bias, although proving this may be difficult if the employer has, as in the example above, had to recruit in a way which is inconsistent with his prejudices.

Intersectional discrimination gives rise to more difficulties. This occurs where, for example, an employer does not generally discriminate against men, or against African-Caribbeans, or against Muslims, but where s/he refuses to recruit a man of African-Caribbean background who is a convert to Islam. The employer may act in this way because s/he regards persons in this category (but no others) as carrying an increased likelihood of involvement in **terrorism**. The prospective employee in this case is the subject of intersectional discrimination, but he will have great difficulty in pursuing a claim under domestic law.

We are all of us the product of intersecting factors of **sex**, **race**, **religion,** etc, together with many other characteristics not 'protected' by discrimination **legislation**. However, the relationship between multiple discrimination and intersecting characteristics cannot be understood without reference to the background 'norm' which, in the UK, is 'white', male, 'mainstream', Christian or irreligious, heterosexual, and not apparently disabled. It is, of course, not the case that men are more numerous than **women**. Nevertheless, given the power disparities between men and women, women are typically identified as being 'different from' or 'other than' male (male being taken as the unspoken 'norm' and women being defined by their departure from this norm) in much the same way as 'white', 'mainstream' Christian or irreligious, and heterosexual are taken as 'norms' from which those who do not share these characteristics are defined by their departure(s). Whiteness, maleness, etc are rendered invisible by their 'normal' quality and 'difference' is located not in the *relationship* between (for example) 'white' and 'black', but in the quality of being black.

The invisibility of characteristics corresponding to the 'norm' has the effect that discrimination against white women *as white women* tends to be recognized as sex discrimination, whereas discrimination against black women *as black women* tends to be seen as something other than 'ordinary' sex discrimination. The same is true of discrimination against disabled women *as disabled women* or against Muslim women *as Muslim women*. This makes it very difficult for people who are discriminated against because of their intersecting (protected) characteristics to prove that they have been discriminated against contrary to domestic law. In *Bahl v Law Society* (2004), for example, the Court of Appeal ruled that an employment tribunal had been wrong to accept that the claimant, an Asian woman, had been discriminated against *as a black woman*. The Court of Appeal ruled that the tribunal had failed 'to identify what evidence goes to support a finding of race discrimination and what evidence goes to support a finding of sex discrimination'.

Had the claimant in *Bahl* been either white or male (and otherwise 'norm-conforming'), the first instance decision would have been immune from interference: a **tribunal** is entitled to draw an inference of unlawful discrimination from a finding of less favourable treatment and a difference in sex or (but not, it appears, *and*) race. As it was, Dr Bahl would have had to make separate claims under the Race Relations Act 1976 by reference to the treatment of real or hypothetical white women, and under the Sex Discrimination Act 1975 by reference to black men. If the discriminatory treatment which she alleged was intersectional, that is, specifically connected with her **identity** as a black woman, the race and sex claims could each readily be defeated by evidence relating to the employer's non-discriminatory treatment of black men and white women respectively.

The other difficulty that arises in cases of intersectional discrimination occurs where one of the (intersecting) reasons for the discrimination is not a protected ground. In *Canada v Mossop* (1993), for example, Canada's Supreme Court rejected a claim

under Canada's anti-discrimination statute by a gay man who argued that he had been discriminated against on grounds of his family status (undefined by the Act) by being denied leave in connection with the death of his partner's father. A majority of the Supreme Court deduced from the fact that the claimant was gay that the discrimination of which he complained could only be understood as discrimination on grounds of sexual orientation, which at the time was not covered by the relevant legislation.

A similar effect is evident in the decision of the **House of Lords** in *Pearce v Governing Body of Mayfield School* (2003) in which their Lordships ruled that a **lesbian** subject to gender-specific abuse had been subject only to discrimination on grounds of her sexual orientation, which was not at the time subject to regulation, rather than her sex. And yet further examples of this problem can be found in the US cases dealing with sex discrimination claims by 'effeminate' men and 'butch' women. The **US Supreme Court** has recognized (in *Oncale v Sundowner Offshore Servs Inc* (1996)) that same sex **sexual harassment** can amount to sex discrimination as long as the harassment is motivated by **gender**. It has also accepted (in *Price Waterhouse v Hopkins* (1989)) that discrimination on the grounds of failure to conform to gender stereotypes can amount to sex discrimination. Most US jurisdictions have accepted that the requirement for proof that same sex **harassment** be motivated by gender can be satisfied by evidence that the plaintiff was targeted for a failure to comply with gender-based stereotypes. But it remains virtually impossible for a gay man or a lesbian (or even someone suspected of being either) to convince a court that workplace harassment was because of their *sex* rather than (or as well as) their sexual orientation.

Yet a further legal difficulty to which intersectional discrimination gives rise concerns **indirect discrimination**. To take an example, a black woman claiming indirect sex discrimination must show that she has had applied to her 'a provision, criterion or practice which [was] applie[s] or would apply equally to a man, but . . . which puts or would put women at a particular disadvantage when compared with men'. It is not sufficient for the claimant to show that women of her racial group are put at a particular disadvantage by the employer's practice (the same is true when it comes to establishing indirect discrimination on grounds of sexual orientation, religion or belief, or age). A woman of Bangladeshi origin who wishes to challenge discrimination against homeworkers may, in a particular workplace or sector, be unable to establish a sufficiently disparate impact on women (taken together) to satisfy the requirements for indirect sex discrimination, in circumstances such that virtually all the women affected were also of Bangladeshi origin and the practice has a clearly disparate impact on women of Bangladeshi origin. She may equally be unable to establish indirect race discrimination if the number of Bangladeshi women engaged as homeworkers is relatively small by comparison to the overall number of men (or men and women) of Bangladeshi origin employed in the particular workplace or sector. Other practices may impact disproportionately on older women (but not older men or younger women), on gay men (but not straight men or lesbian women), on Orthodox Jewish women (but not Orthodox Jewish men or on other women). These will not be capable of challenge under the current approach to indirect discrimination unless claimants are allowed to combine in law those factors which in fact combine to their disadvantage.

AILEEN MCCOLGAN

See also: **intersectionality**

multi-speed Europe   see **closer cooperation in the EU**

Munchausen Syndrome by Proxy   Munchausen Syndrome by Proxy achieved public notoriety in the UK through the case of Beverley Allitt, a nurse who killed four children in her care and injured another eleven in 1993. It was first described by the paediatrician, Sir Roy Meadow, in 1977 and was initially regarded as a form of **child** abuse perpetrated by mothers who either falsely reported illness in their children, or deliberately induced them to become unwell. The motivation for this behaviour is believed to be attention-seeking to fulfil an emotional need. More recently, it has been recognized that the syndrome is not unique to mothers and it is now accepted as a form of pathological abuse where carers induce or fabricate illness in those for whom they care. Today it is known as fabricated or induced illness ('FII').

A great deal of controversy has been attached to the condition in recent years, particularly following the case of Sally Clark, who was convicted of murdering her two infant sons in November 1999. The death of her first son eleven weeks after his birth was originally regarded as due to cot death or sudden infant death syndrome, but the death of her second, eight-week-old, son a year later resulted in a **police** investigation leading to her **arrest**. At her trial, **evidence** was given by Sir Roy Meadow that the chances of two cot deaths occurring in the same,

affluent, non-smoking family of a mother aged over twenty-six were vanishingly small; 73 million to one, to be precise. However, following Sally Clark's conviction for the murder of her children the statistical evidence given in **court** was discredited. In addition, at a subsequent appeal, new evidence was presented suggesting that the death of her first son may have been the result of a bacterial infection. Her appeal was upheld.

The case called into question the status of **expert evidence** and its impact on jurors in criminal court proceedings. The presentation of authoritative testimony and misleading statistics has the potential to subvert **justice**, perhaps even to reverse the criminal law presumption of innocence until proven guilty. Two other women, Angela Cannings and Trupti Patel, were also accused and convicted of killing their children, largely on the basis of expert evidence that relied on what was sometimes known as 'Meadow's Law' that one cot death is a tragedy, two is suspicious, and three is murder. The evidence in their cases was reviewed after Sally Clark was exonerated and both were subsequently released. After Sally Clark, Angela Cannings, and Trupti Patel were freed, the **Attorney-General** ordered a review of nearly 300 cases in which similar evidence was implicated.

Expert evidence of this type has also been influential in the Family Courts where **child protection** is of paramount importance. Proceedings operate differently in the Family court. Cases involving children are reported anonymously and evidence is weighed *on the balance of probabilities*, rather than the criminal court standard of *beyond a reasonable doubt*. In cases where there is evidence suggesting that children are at risk of harm they can be removed from their family and taken into care or even adopted in order to avoid a perceived threat to their **safety**. Following concerns about the efficacy of evidence in suspected instances of Munchausen Syndrome by Proxy, there have recently been calls for more openness to help ensure that child welfare decisions are safe.

HAZEL BIGGS

murder   see **crime and violence; homicide**

museums and galleries, management of   Museums and galleries are institutions that collect, preserve, and make accessible to the public artefacts, works of art, and specimens. There are approximately 2,500 private and public museums and galleries in the UK that hold some 200 million artefacts.

Museums and galleries can be either publicly or privately managed. The government, through the Department for Culture, Media, and Sport ('DCMS'), manages twenty-two museums and galleries (eg the British Museum, Tate Gallery, and National Gallery). Each of these institutions has its own board of trustees whose members are appointed by the **Prime Minister** or the Secretary of State, and its own contractual relationship with the DCMS. They are directly sponsored by the DCMS and all have been freely accessible to the public since 2001 (although they can charge an entry fee for temporary exhibitions). Other departments support museums through different councils. For instance, the Department for Education supports university museums, and the Department for Defence supports war museums. The government can also associate itself with public bodies to manage museums. English Heritage, for example, runs historic sites and is partly funded by the DCMS and partly by fees and commercial activities.

Local authorities were permitted to manage museums and galleries by the Public Libraries and Museums Act 1964. They can charge entry fees and are sponsored by the DCMS through the Museum, Library, and Archive Council and its nine regional branches. Most of the revenue distributed by the DCMS comes from Lottery fund.

Private institutions and **charities** such as the National Trust are independent of the DCMS and rely for income on entry and membership fees, donations and legacies, and revenue raised from commercial activities (shops, souvenirs). Their legal status is the same as a **company** or **trust**/charity depending on their form.

So as to bring some order to the disparate activities and concerns, various institutions independent of government and the DCMS coordinate their actions. Depending on their size and status, they may join the Museum Association, the Association of Independent Museums, the National Museum Directors' Conference, or the Museums and Galleries commission.

National and local authority museums can add to their collection by purchases, gifts, exchanges, or loans. They can buy items for their collection if they have the funds available and if the item(s) fit within their existing display. They can receive gifts (to which the donor can attach conditions) and, by arrangement with the Commissioners of Inland Revenue, receive objects in lieu of **inheritance tax**. The exchange of items between the institutions directly managed by the DCMS was facilitated by the Museums and Galleries Act 1992 on the basis that exchange does not impoverish the national collection. Most museums (except otherwise stipulated

in a gift) can loan part of their collection for temporary exhibitions but have to apply for an export license for cultural goods if the collection travels abroad. In order to facilitate loans and exhibitions at a national or international level, the Government Indemnity Scheme is an insurance scheme that carries the risk of damage to the item(s) while in transit from the lending venue to the display and back.

Because national institutions hold their displays in trust for the population of the UK, their powers of disposal are limited. According to the Museum and Galleries Act 1992, a national museum may dispose of an item only if it holds a duplicate, if the item is printed matter made after 1850 and the institution holds a photograph of it, if the object has become unfit to be retained in the collection and can be disposed of without detriment to the interests of students or members of the public, or if the object has become useless because of its physical deterioration. However, if the display was given as a gift, the trustee must comply with any condition imposed by the donor, including one that forbids its disposal. For example, the 'Wallace Collection' was bequeathed to the British nation on condition that it is kept together and unmixed with other objects; so the trustees can neither add to nor dispose of any item in the collection.

A special allowance was made for human remains by section 47 of the **Human Tissue** Act 2004. Nine museums were allowed to transfer from their collections any remains of a person who died less than one thousand years ago if it seemed appropriate to do so (the process is called de-accession). The party claiming the remains must prove a continuous link with them: ie that the remains are of a genealogical ancestor or a member of the claimant's original cultural community.   SOPHIE VIGNERON

museums and galleries, regulation of   Museums in the UK fall broadly into three categories: national museums, such as the National Gallery and the Victoria and Albert Museum; local authority museums, funded by local authorities under enabling powers first given in 1845; and independent museums, which constitute by far the largest sector numerically and the vast majority of which are constituted as charities. Larger independent museums also have corporate status or have set up subsidiary companies for trading purposes. Except in the case of national museums, there is no legislative framework for the regulation and administration of museums.

Museum trusts are usually formed for the benefit of the public at large and collections are held on their behalf. This can cause difficulties for institutions wishing to raise funds by selling pieces from their collection (known as de-accessioning in the US and disposal in the UK). Disposal is a controversial process that requires careful management and which can be extremely difficult for national museums to implement at all.

Museums and galleries are subject to the normal requirements of trust, employment, copyright, and health and safety law (to name but a few): these will not be considered here. This entry focuses on two of issues of particular interest.

Illicit Trade

An effort to curb illicit trade was first instigated by the United Nations Educational Scientific and Cultural Organization ('UNESCO') when in 1970 it adopted the *Convention on the Means of Prohibiting and Preventing the Illicit Import, Export and Transfer of Cultural Property*. The Convention prohibits signatories from importing or exhibiting objects which have been stolen or illegally exported. Although this convention was not ratified by the UK until 2002, its inception promoted a concerted stand against dealings in illicit goods. In 1998, the British Museum published a statement outlining a policy not to acquire antiquities that had appeared on the market after 1970 and which could not be provenanced. The Department for Culture, Media and Sport ('DCMS') published guidelines in 2005 offering guidance to institutions on the acquisition of goods where provenance is uncertain. The International Council of Museums ('ICOM') and in the UK, the Museums Association ('MA'), have both issued a code of ethics for their members outlining minimum standards for acquisition activity.

Prior to 2003, looters and dishonest dealers were typically prosecuted under the Theft Act 1968. In 2003, the Dealing in Cultural Objects (Offences) Act 2003 created a new offence of dealing in tainted cultural objects. 'Cultural object' is broadly defined to include any object of 'historical, architectural or archaeological interest'. An object is tainted if a person removes the object from a building or structure of historical, architectural, or archaeological interest and the object had at any time formed part of that building or structure; or, if the object is removed from a monument of such interest (including caves and building remains); or, if the object is excavated and the removal or excavation constitutes an offence. 'Dealing' includes acquiring, disposing of, importing or exporting, or an agreement to do any of those things.

An exceptional example of illicit trading is the looting, and subsequent trading, of objects stolen by the Nazis between 1933 and 1945. Some such items have ended up in UK institutions. There has recently been a movement to redress the wrongs that were committed during this era. In the UK, the National Museum Directors' Conference set up a working group in 1998 to consider issues surrounding the spoliation of art during the Nazi era. The Spoliation Advisory Panel was appointed by the Secretary of State in 2000 and provides advice to claimants, institutions, and the government on possible claims.

Exportation

Under the Exports of Cultural Interests (Control) Order 2003, a licence is required for the export of any object of cultural interest from the UK where that object was manufactured or produced more than 50 years before the date of exportation (subject to limited exceptions, eg stamps, personal papers, and objects exported by their maker or his/her spouse, widow, or widower). The Secretary of State may issue an individual export licence following the recommendation of the Independent Reviewing Committee and an Independent Expert Adviser (usually a Director, Keeper, or Curator of a national museum or gallery).

The committee must consider the 'Waverley' criteria: is the object so closely connected with our history and national life that its departure would be a misfortune? Is it of outstanding aesthetic importance? Is it of outstanding significance for the study of some particular branch of art, learning, or history? If one or more of these criteria are satisfied, the Expert Adviser may object to the granting of an export licence and in turn the Secretary of State may defer the issue of a licence to the applicant in order to give a UK institution time to indicate an intention to acquire it. Such 'export stops' are usually given for a specific and limited period, usually a few months, which may be extended if there is a serious intention to purchase. If the intention to acquire is successful, an export licence will be refused.

Museums and galleries that regularly lend objects to or exchange objects with other institutions may be able to take advantage of 'Open Licences' which may be granted by the Secretary of State. There are two types of open licence: an open general export licence, which is available to any exporter, permits the export of some 'common' items, below certain values, for periods of three months or less; and an open individual export licence can be granted to named individuals, companies, or institutions permitting them to export specified objects.

LUDOVIC DE WALDEN

mutual recognition   *see* **approximation of laws
in the EU**

**mutual trust and confidence in employment
law** The law generally requires employers and
employees not to act in a way that is either calculated, or is likely, to destroy, or seriously to damage, the
relationship of confidence and trust between them.
This duty was first formulated by **judges** in the late
1970s. However, it was only some twenty years later
that it was put on a firm legal footing by the **House
of Lords** endorsing its creation. This happened in
a case about whether the failed Bank of Credit and
Commerce International had breached its employment obligations by acting dishonestly (*Mahmud v
BCCI* (1998)).

It is important, first, that the duty is judge-made
and, secondly, that it is classified legally as a contractual term. The judges' rationale for implying the duty
of mutual trust and confidence into **contracts of
employment** was that it was a 'necessary legal incident'. This implied that employment contracts would
be dysfunctional without the obligations included
in the duty of mutual trust and confidence. So the
law presumes that it is contained *in every contract of
employment*. However, the contractual nature of the
duty also matters. The law generally (although not
always) allows people to contract as they wish. It follows that, at least in theory, employers and employees could agree to exclude the implied duty of mutual
trust and confidence.

It is not clear how often workplace obligations
of trust and confidence are in fact written out of
employment contracts. Realistically, this depends
on whether employers want to take this step, since
they frequently dictate the content of employment
contracts. But an employer may not want to be seen
unilaterally to be exonerating themselves from significant obligations, and would certainly not want to
absolve employees. Beyond this, it is perfectly possible that the **courts** will some day decide that the duty
of mutual trust and confidence cannot be dispensed
with by agreement.

Recognition of the duty of mutual trust and confidence is one of the most significant developments
in modern employment law. The precise demands
that it places on employers and employees have been
worked out in a vast range of cases. This has led to
standards of workplace behaviour being enshrined
in law, while also contributing to wider debate, in
workplaces and beyond, about what those standards
should be.

It should be remembered, nonetheless, that there
are work situations in which employers, in particular, are not bound by duties of trust and confidence.
The most important is dismissal. It can be very difficult, however, to work out when the duty ceases to
apply, for example where dismissal is the last in a
complex chain of events.

Another contentious issue is the role of the duty in
relation to precarious or novel work arrangements.
For example, where an employee works intermit-
tently or through an agency, their work status may be
extremely difficult to work out. If they are not legally
classified as employees, the duty of mutual trust and
confidence might not apply, or might apply only in
modified form.   LIZZIE BARMES

N

narrative and law Narrative is a polymorphously perverse term. It can refer to anything from a grand theory on the creation of the universe to a type of speech style. In its basic sense of recounting events in a structured sequence, that is, telling a story that involves chronology as well as causation and typically including characters, motive, and a temporalization of events, it is both ubiquitous and primordial. As Aristotle suggested, **humans** slip into the practice of narration from the moment we acquire language: narrative, as 'the imitation of an action', is a basic human instinct. For Aristotle himself the purest and highest form of narrative was tragedy, which should consist of 'a beginning, a middle, and an end', and through its evocation of the emotions of fear and pity, have a cathartic effect on the audience.

Whether tragic, cathartic, or otherwise, narratives serve a more general purpose: with narratives human beings aim to impose order on an unknowable past, understand a seemingly chaotic present, and counteract their fear of an unpredictable future. Narratives are therefore found and function on a variety of levels from the individual, to groups, to **communities**, to nations, to global systems. Such entities use and abuse narrative to make sense of their histories by suggesting answers to perennial questions like 'why, when, how, who, who with, who against, for who'.

Legal systems are also not immune from reliance on narrative to tell and retell the story of their conception and continuing existence. What if, however, the origin of the system is, as is more often than not, unknown, traumatic, and/or violent? In such cases, narrative, and the repetition of narrative, serves to supplant the gaps in our knowledge and to smooth over unacceptable or unspeakable facts in our individual or collective histories. In particular, the drive for a unifying and coherent narrative which is faithful to Aristotle's formula, is oblivious to the fact that gaps are endemic to every social, including legal, system and to every human being, and therefore irremediable.

In Western liberal **democracies**, the narrative of the **rule of law** has achieved the status of a narrative of narratives, (a 'meta-narrative') that, in the hands of legal theorists such as Ronald Dworkin and historians such as Fukuyama, is hailed as the narrative to end all narratives. However, like myths, grand narratives, whether of liberalism, communism, or any other ism, usually arise in response to persistent and conflicting interests and forces. In such cases, narratives can obfuscate irreconcilable differences, not by overcoming them, which is impossible, but by ignoring and thus repressing unavoidable deadlocks.

From a psychoanalytic perspective, our relentless repetition of the same narratives suggests that the traumas these narratives try to explain are never entirely dissipated, always threatening to return and haunt their tellers. Indeed what lies at the centre of repeated narratives is not what is said but what is missing, that is, the gaps the teller circulates around and avoids touching. Narratives, in other words, function as fantasies, effacing the inconsistencies in our individual and collective histories, and shielding us from the anxiety of encountering the reality of trauma. As fantasies, narratives are static, monotonous, and therefore difficult to dislodge.

This may explain why narratives can be the object of both idealization and reproach: exalted and advocated on the one hand as instruments of **revolution**, demonized on the other hand as tools of conservative reaction and affirmation of the *status quo*. For the critical legal scholar, the task is not to repeat, embellish, or solidify the legal system's inherited narratives, but to excavate, dismantle and, ideally, overcome them.

One branch of the **Critical Legal Studies** movement saw its role as exposing and demystifying the hierarchical and often oppressive ordering of some narratives over others. Their attack on grand narratives was accompanied by the exaltation of 'micro' narratives, focusing on the struggles of individuals and groups whose stories had been silenced by the master discourses. Such narratives, sometimes referred to as 'victim narratives' in their focus on stories of subordination by marginalized groups, highlight the close association between **story-telling and law**.

Despite the recent proliferation of such micro-narratives, the question remains whether either truth or **justice** is a necessary property of narrative. What is beyond doubt is the normative, that is, the law-making dimension of narratives, large or small, in law and in other disciplines. Since legal narratives have the potential of wielding power over life and death, our continuing examination and interrogation of their function and power is essential.

MARIA ARISTODEMOU

National Audit Office   *see* **Auditor-General**

National Consumer Council   The National Consumer Council ('NCC') was established in 1975, and there are separate committees for Scotland and Wales. There is a separate General Consumer Council for Northern Ireland, which runs along similar lines. The Council has nine members at present, appointed by the government, with business, public service, consumer, social, or voluntary work backgrounds, and full time staff. It is mainly funded by government. Until 2007 it was non-statutory in form but it is now a statutory body and has absorbed the functions of the gas and electricity consumers council and the consumer council for postal services.

The NCC has no executive powers and does not deal directly with individual consumer problems (except a consumer facing disconnection of energy supply). Rather its role is to advise and campaign on more general issues and in particular to represent the consumer interest as an advocate in dealings with government, regulators, the European Commission, and other bodies. It may research consumer matters and can disseminate advice and information to consumers generally. The statute under which it operates requires the NCC to give special attention to the needs of vulnerable consumers when exercising its functions. It is also required to enter into cooperative arrangements with other bodies such as the **Office of Fair Trading**.

A highlight of the work of the NCC over the last thirty years has been to take the initiative in areas where other consumer groups have not campaigned actively—especially the provision of public services. For example, it has produced reports and campaigned on financial services regulation, the provision of legal services, the **regulation** systems that operate in health care, telecommunications, energy, water, and media policy, and **freedom of information**. It conducts 'consumer concerns' surveys on a regular basis looking, for example, at the quality of public services.

ROSS CRANSTON

National Council of Civil Liberties (NCCL)
see **Liberty (formerly National Council of Civil Liberties)**

national curriculum   *see* **secular curriculum in schools**

National Health Service   The National Health Service ('NHS') is the UK's public healthcare system. It was founded in 1948. Its guiding principle is that healthcare should be funded through general taxation and should (for the most part) be provided free of charge to those who use it. The organizational structure of the NHS is slightly different for each of the four nations of the UK.

In England, the Secretary of State for Health has overall responsibility for the running of the NHS. Primary Care Trusts ('PCATs') are responsible for the provision of care in the local community, such as community hospitals, district nursing, dentistry, and general practitioner ('GP') services. GPs are patients' first point of contact with the NHS. They play an important role as 'gatekeepers' with responsibility for referring patients to specialized services. Most GPs provide their services to the NHS as independent contractors. In a process known as 'commissioning', PCATs arrange and pay for acute or secondary care services for their local population. Some of these services are provided by private firms or voluntary sector organizations, but the vast majority are provided within the NHS by NHS 'Trusts' (a term which is not used in its technical legal sense in this context). Strategic Health Authorities monitor the performance of PCATs and NHS Trusts. NHS Trusts may apply for 'Foundation' status, which gives them greater independence from this type of scrutiny. The Healthcare Commission monitors the quality of NHS services.

In Wales, health is a devolved matter so responsibility for NHS Wales lies with the Minister for Health and Social Care in the Welsh Assembly Government. Local Health Boards are responsible for the provision of primary care services and the commissioning of secondary care services. Secondary care is provided primarily by NHS Trusts. Oversight is provided by three Regional Offices of NHS Wales.

In Northern Ireland, there is greater integration of health and social services. Health is a devolved matter and falls within the remit of the NI Department of Health, Social Services, and Public Safety. There are four Health Boards with responsibility for commissioning health and social services. NHS Trusts have responsibility for provision and there are separate acute and community Trusts in most areas. GPs work more independently than in England and are not integrated into community Trusts.

In Scotland, health is the responsibility of the Scottish Executive Health and Social Care Department. The NHS in Scotland is often described as 'single system' in that it does not draw sharp organizational boundaries between primary and secondary care. There are fifteen NHS Health Boards in Scotland. Each board is responsible for the provision of primary and secondary care in its region. In primary care, there is a move to develop Community Health Partnerships that would bring together NHS and local authority responsibilities for the provision of care within local communities.

The National Institute for Health and Clinical Excellence ('NICE') has responsibility for evaluating new treatments and issuing guidelines for their use in the NHS. These guidelines are influential throughout the UK. ANNE DAVIES

R Klein, *The New Politics of the NHS: From Creation to Reinvention* (Oxford: Radcliffe, 5th edn, 2006)

C Newdick, 'The Organisation of Health Care', in A Grubb (ed), *Principles of Medical Law* (Oxford: Oxford University Press, 2nd edn, 2004)

national insurance The national insurance system is part of the wider **social security system**. The concept of national (or social) insurance, with employers, employees, and the state making contributions to a fund from which benefits are paid to contributors, was first developed in Bismarck's Germany in the 1880s. In the United Kingdom the first national insurance benefits to be introduced were sickness benefit and unemployment insurance in 1911. Beveridge's 1942 report on *Social Insurance and Allied Services* led to the National Insurance Act 1946, which sought to provide the framework for a 'cradle to grave' welfare state based on the contributory principle.

National insurance differs from private insurance for similar risks in at least two respects. First, membership of the national insurance scheme is compulsory, allowing for the pooling of risks. Secondly, national insurance is not governed by the law of contract, so the state can either extend or narrow the scope of cover provided as it sees fit. The main national insurance benefit is the state retirement pension; other national insurance benefits include bereavement benefits, contribution-based jobseeker's allowance and employment support allowance. Typically national insurance benefits are not means-tested (although employment support allowance may be reduced where an occupational pension is being received). Entitlement to national insurance benefits depends on the claimant (or their spouse or civil partner) having paid sufficient national insurance conditions in the past. For long-term benefits, such as the retirement pension, the contributions test is based on the individual's working life. For short-term benefits, such as contribution-based jobseeker's allowance and incapacity benefit, the test requires the payment of contributions in the previous two tax years. Contributions are divided into different classes according to status. Employers and employees pay Class 1 contributions, self-employed people pay Class 2 and Class 4 contributions, and voluntary contributors may pay Class 3 contributions. Employees who are members of an occupational pension scheme (and their employers) pay a lower contracted-out rate of contribution. People who are unemployed or carers may be credited with contributions for the purpose of protecting their national insurance record.

Each individual contributor is allocated a national insurance number ('NINo') to which their contributions are attributed. All contributions, together with a Treasury payment, are paid into the National Insurance Fund, from which national insurance benefits are paid. However, there is no direct or actuarial link between individuals' payment of contributions and their entitlement to benefit, which means that governments are free to modify the eligibility criteria for national insurance benefits at any time, subject to human rights considerations. To this extent the contributory principle is something of a political fiction, and in recent years the rules governing liability for national insurance contributions have been increasingly aligned with the income tax system.

NICK WIKELEY

See also: **welfare state**

national minority *see* **minorities**

national security National security is perhaps *the* overriding public interest recognized in law. It dates back to Cicero's maxim *salus populi suprema lex est* ('the safety of the people is the highest law'). In modern usage national security encompasses more than protecting the state's territorial integrity and extends to military and strategic secrets, and protection from terrorism and protection of essential infrastructure from sabotage. More controversially, since the Cold War national security has been claimed to embrace threats to the constitutional order (for example, from 'subversion') and to international relations with key military or intelligence allies.

National security manifests itself either in the recognition of special legal powers of state agencies or in the creation of exceptions from otherwise applicable legal rights. In the first category obviously falls the legal recognition of the security and intelligence agencies (in the UK these have had statutory mandates since 1989 and 1994 respectively). More generally, national security may, for example, be a reason for intercepting a person's communications under warrant, for deporting or refusing entry to a non-citizen, or for the appropriation of property or internment without trial during wartime. The second category includes, for example, exceptions to **freedom of information**, **privacy** and anti-discrimination legislation, the overriding of **journalistic privilege**, and the suppression of evidence in the public interest (**public interest immunity**).

For the courts, national security poses a challenge to the **rule of law**. Lord Parker of Waddington famously voiced this concern in a case decided during the First World War. 'Those who are responsible for the national security must be the sole judge of what national security requires. It would obviously be undesirable that such matters be made the subject of evidence in a court of law or otherwise discussed in public' (*The Zamora* (1916)). On closer analysis there are two related but separable difficulties here, one constitutional and the other evidential and practical.

Concerning constitutional difficulties, the courts have consistently recognized that decisions based on national security are for the government and that they have neither the necessary information nor the competence to assess the issues involved. This principle has been followed both in wartime and in peacetime. It still applies in the modern era of human rights. Where, however, the government advances arguments that are contradictory or has chosen to act in a way that interferes more than necessary with individual rights, the courts may intervene—as is shown by the **House of Lords'** landmark decision in the *Belmarsh* detainees case (*A v Secretary of State for the Home Department* (2004)).

So far as practical and evidential difficulties of handling secret material in court are concerned, attitudes are now more sceptical. The **European Court of Human Rights** has insisted that the right to a fair trial (**European Convention on Human Rights**, Article 6) requires courts to accommodate some form of adversarial challenge to intelligence material even if normal trial procedures, such as full cross-examination, cannot apply. This has led in recent years to procedural innovations such as the introduction of the Special Immigration Appeals Commission and, more widely, of Special Advocates who are security-cleared.   IAN LEIGH

national treatment principle   *see* **most-favoured-nation treatment**

National Trust   *see* **architectural conservation**

nationalized industries   Although the number and role of nationalized industries has been severely reduced since 1980 by the process of privatization, important examples remain, such as the Post Office. The main legal structure adopted for nationalized industries was that of the public corporation, with its own distinct legal identity separate from that of the government. The public corporation was run by a board appointed by a minister, but in theory operating at 'arm's length', at least in its day-to-day operations. This was the model adopted, for example, by the post-war Atlee government for coal, rail, gas, and electricity nationalization. In practice, it posed serious difficulties. Ministers were reluctant to intervene publicly in the industries, but exercised considerable informal influence. The confusion of responsibilities between minister and board limited accountability, and this was made worse by the weakness of the consumer councils, created to protect the customers of nationalized industries. Attempts to clarify relations by, for example, the setting of financial targets for the industries, consistently failed; and this was one of the reasons for their privatization.

Another model was that of government owning shares in what was, in legal form, a private limited company. This has been the favoured solution for the remaining nationalized industries, and shareholdings in twenty-seven wholly or partly government owned companies are now managed by the Government's Shareholder Executive. These include the Post Office, which is regulated by an independent Postal Services Commission like that set up for the major privatized companies.   TONY PROSSER

See also: **privatization**

nationalism   Nationalism is an ideology that supports a direct relationship between political state and ethnic group. It is also dependent upon limiting the prerogatives of non-nationals (as compared to citizens) within the nation state. Nationalism is built upon the **identity** of national groups, who come to view themselves as deserving of the status of a nation state in the world order. The boundaries of nations and nation states are rarely identical, but the belief that they should be has served as the basis of nationalism. Through nationalism, some groups have dominated at the expense of others, and some **minorities** have been constructed as 'outsiders' to the nation state.

The nation is a social construction that emerged at a particular historical moment in Western consciousness. The idea of national **sovereignty** was dependent upon a conception of borders as finite and limitable (and therefore capable of being mapped) and on the determination of membership in national collectivities (through, for example, the census). Both the map and the census, which often serve as tools of nationalism, emerged during the sixteenth century.

In understanding nationalism, it is important to recognize its historical trajectory. In the thirteenth century, 'nation' was first used in the English language to connote a racial or religious group, thus creating the relationship between **ethnicity** and nation. A second meaning emerged in the eighteenth century, when nation was increasingly employed to define smaller groups, each constituting a separate people, which became defined as constituting fundamental **human** divisions. A third meaning is associated with the idea of political nationalism, in which the nation is a product of political agreement between individuals, rather than being coterminous with a racially defined people. Despite its redefinition as an agreement between members who are its citizens, nationalism has remained a primary ideology of racism. It continues to resonate with the belief in a common blood bond shared by its members. Through the connections between race and nation, a biologically- and culturally-based nationalism is reinforced.

It is sometimes argued that nationalism may be altering in the face of economic and cultural globalization. However, while globalization may undermine the power of the nation state, nationalism remains an important force, as exemplified by the current focus on tightened border controls. In fact, nationalism is frequently deployed by elites within politically weakened nation states as a means of resisting globalization, and in order to bolster their own support.

Nationalism has been closely connected, not only to **race**, but also to **gender** and sexuality within the West. Feminists have argued, for example, that nationalism has been a masculinist and heterosexist ideology, dependent upon the subordination of **women** who are relegated to the private sphere.

Nationalism has also been used ideologically by **social movements** seeking legal change. An example is the Black Nationalist movement in the United States, which existed parallel to the Civil Rights movement during the 1960s. Similarly, nationalism has been a valuable tool in struggles against **colonialism** in large parts of the world.   CARL STYCHIN

B Anderson, *Imagined Communities* (London: Verso, rev edn, 1991)

P Fitzpatrick (ed), *Nationalism, Racism and the Rule of Law* (Aldershot: Dartmouth, 1995)

nationality   Nationality is the legal link between an individual and a state. Although used interchangeably with 'citizenship' the concepts can be distinguished. 'Nationality' stresses the international framework for thinking about membership in law and 'citizenship' highlights the national domestic context.

International law places significance on the legal status of nationality. Indeed it is the way that an individual relates to the international legal system, for nationality secures rights for the individual by linking her to the state. This is shown through the concept that nationality makes one state's interference with a national of another a violation of the other state's sovereignty; and it highlights the important principle allowing a state to exercise diplomatic protection on behalf of its nationals when they have been wronged by the actions of another state.

Courts have grappled with the question whether diplomatic protection is a right enjoyed by the state or an individual right. The position established in *Barcelona Traction, Light and Power Company, Limited* (*Belgium v Spain*) (1970) is that a state has no duty or obligation to protect its nationals but that the right to do so belongs to the state. This is becoming more contentious and the 2006 report of the International Law Association conference on Diplomatic Protection of Persons and Property has challenged the traditional notion. It argues that the state should assert the right of the individual affected by a wrong and that public law remedies of judicial review should be applied to a state that determines not to assert diplomatic protection.

The **Universal Declaration of Human Rights** recognizes that each person enjoys a right to a nationality. Although the conferral of nationality is primarily a matter of domestic law, Article 1 of the 1938 Convention on Certain Questions Relating to the Conflict of Nationality Laws states: 'It is for each State to determine under its own law . . . [who are] its nationals. This law shall be recognised by other States in so far as it is consistent with international conventions, international custom, and the principles of law generally recognised with regard to nationality'. Integral to the modern concept of nationality is the principle espoused in *Nottebohm (Liechtenstein v Guatemala)* (1955) that the basis of the right of a state to have its conferral of nationality recognized internationally is 'the individual's genuine connection with the State'.

This involves 'a social fact of attachment, a genuine connection of existence, interests and sentiments, together with the existence of reciprocal rights and duties'.

A survey of legislation on the acquisition of nationality reveals a broad consensus in the principles for granting nationality. The two widely in use are *jus sanguinis*, conferred through descent, and *jus soli*, based on birth in the state's territory. Whether these are indicative of general patterns of state usage or whether they have yet been incorporated as norms in **international customary law** is an open question. The granting of nationality to non-citizens as a formal act initiated by the applicant is also recognized almost universally. The loss of nationality is not provided for under international law but the Universal Declaration of Human Rights states no one shall be arbitrarily deprived of her nationality.

KIM RUBENSTEIN

P Weis, *Nationality and Statelessness in International Law* (London: Stevens & Sons, 1956)

Committee on Feminism and International Law, International Law Association, 'Final Report on Women's Equality and Nationality in International Law' in *Report of the Sixty Ninth Conference of the International Law Association* (London, International Law Association: 2000)

native title   This term is used to describe what is more widely known as the doctrine of **common law** aboriginal title. Building upon an American jurisprudence dating from the mid-nineteenth century, courts in Canada (1973), New Zealand (1986 and 2003), Australia (1993 and 1996), Malaysia (1998 and 2002), and South Africa (2003) articulated the doctrine in response to claims by the indigenous tribal polities to legal validation of their customary land rights. Until these 'breakthrough' judgments of those years the prevailing belief had been that subsisting traditional land-rights were non-justiciable. They had been seen as morally binding on the **Crown** (the state) as holder of the legal title to the land but otherwise incapable of recognition at law, a position summed up most notoriously in the *terra nullius* fiction applied in Australia. In keeping with the wider trend then evident in public law at large, the courts extended the common law notion of justiciability to include tribes' customary property rights, holding that the Crown's assumption of *imperium* (sovereignty) did not give it an unqualified *dominium* (ownership of land). That feudal principle applied to settlers' land titles, which had to derive from a Crown grant, but the Crown's title to its ungranted land was characterized as burdened by any aboriginal property-interest, which, thenceforth, was cognisable at law. Further, the courts held that the Crown was subject to a special fiduciary duty in its management of such land. This common-law jurisprudence has been the most elaborated in Australia and Canada.

These court judgments sparked considerable national controversy and meant that economic exploitation of regions such as the Australian interior, Canadian Arctic, and New Zealand coastline had to take formal account of tribal proprietary interests. The judicial validation of native title necessitated governmental negotiation with the tribes. That, in turn, led to major settlements in all jurisdictions and the development of contemporary institutionalized processes, often fraught and slow-moving, for the resolution of such claims. The Australian (Commonwealth) and New Zealand Parliaments passed statutes to encompass the inchoate aboriginal proprietary rights and facilitate third-party access to land subject to native title. Canada's capacity to legislate for native title was qualified by section 35 of the Constitution Act 1982 protecting 'existing aboriginal and treaty rights' and by a common law requirement of appropriate official prioritization, including consultation, of aboriginal titleholders.

A common law native title exists along a spectrum ranging from the claim to full ownership (called 'territorial title' in New Zealand, 'aboriginal title' in Canada) to a bundle of itemized rights down to single stand-alone site-specific rights ('non-territorial title' in New Zealand, 'aboriginal rights' in Canada). The difference between a territorial and non-territorial title lies in the courts' recognition that the former carries the right to exclude.

The courts have established tests for proof of native title. The Australian 'bundle of rights' test stresses the basis of the title in the actual continuity of customary law. The Canadian 'aboriginal title' test emphasizes factual use and presence whilst the much-criticized test for 'aboriginal rights' requires proof that the right is integral to the distinctive aboriginal culture since European contact (so constraining the commercial potential of the right).

Having been proven, the courts will ask if the title-right is of a character that the common law can recognize. A claim to exclusive ownership of the foreshore and seabed, for example, cannot be recognized since it is incompatible with the nature of Crown sovereignty over that space. If the title-right is proven and capable of recognition, courts will then ask if the right has been extinguished. Proof is a question of *fact* requiring production of the appropriate evidence of **customary law** alongside historical identity and presence of the claimant group. Extinguishment is a question of *law* by which customary rights, or elements of them, though subsisting in fact are extinguished at law. National courts are still articulating the principles of extinguishment. It can occur through legislation or executive act (such as issue of a Crown grant or other interest entailing exclusive possession). In Canada extinguishment is also constrained by section 35 of the Constitution Act.

As part of this formal process of vesting of title assets in indigenous groups, governments have insisted upon their having suitable legal vehicles for the management of those restored assets and their membership. As a consequence a new and intensifying—and, in some eyes, disordered—legalism began engulfing indigenous groups in the 1990s, concerned with rights-management (governance) and rights-integration (squaring the group right with other rights-bearers in the legal system). This legalism is the downstream consequence of the initial judicial recognition of native title, which fundamentally changed the position of indigenous groups in the national legal systems.   PAUL MCHUGH

natural justice In everyday usage, to say that someone has been 'denied natural justice' means, more or less, that the person has been treated unfairly. As might be expected, the legal meaning of 'natural justice' is rather more complex than this. It is also considerably narrower. There are two so-called 'rules of natural justice': the 'no-bias' rule and the 'fair-hearing' rule. The no-bias rule has an associated Latin tag: *nemo judex in sua causa* or *nemo debet esse judex in propria causa*, meaning (quite literally) that a person ought not to be judge in their own cause. The word 'natural' suggests that these rules are considered to be more than mere legal technicalities; and the right to a fair hearing before an independent and impartial tribunal is enshrined (for instance) in Article 6 of the European Convention on Human Rights. The 'justice' we are concerned with here is 'procedural', as opposed to 'substantive'. A substantively fair decision may be understood as one that correctly applies whatever rules are applicable to the case. The distinction between procedure and substance implies that fair procedures do not guarantee fair outcomes. No doubt, it is reasonable to assume that fair procedures are more conducive to fair outcomes than unfair procedures. However, procedural fairness is valued not only for its 'instrumental' relationship to fair decisions but also because it expresses respect for the individual whose interests are at stake in the decision-making process. Related is the idea that the point of the rules of natural justice

is not (only) that justice should be done but (also) that it should be seen to be done. So, for instance, it is important not only that decision-makers be unbiased but also that they appear unbiased. People are less likely to accept even fair decisions that adversely affect their interests if they feel that they have not had a 'fair crack of the whip'. Natural justice thus plays an important part in establishing the legitimacy of decision-makers.

The rules of natural justice (unlike **due process rights**) are typically treated as being part of **administrative law**. As such, they are applicable to public decision-making (about social security benefits and immigration, for instance) and not normally to dealings between citizens. The rule against bias is designed to obviate conflicts of interest that may arise when, for example, a decision-maker has a significant financial or personal interest in the outcome. Government officials may often seem to have political or ideological motivations for deciding one way or the other; but this is unlikely to offend the rule against bias unless there is some reason to think that the official has prejudged the issue and there is no possibility of independent review of the decision. The basic model of a fair hearing is the sort of procedure followed in **courts**. However, it is recognized that oral hearings, cross-examination of witnesses, the involvement of lawyers, and other characteristics of courts, may not be appropriate in all contexts. This insight is expressed by insisting that the demands of procedural 'fairness' are context-specific.

PETER CANE

See also: **due process rights; tribunals**

natural law theory Broadly speaking, theories within the natural law tradition emphasize an essential conceptual connection between law and morals. In response to the core jurisprudential question, 'What is law?', such theories elaborate a conceptual view that necessarily links (and subsumes) legal reason to moral reason, legal obligation to moral obligation, legal validity to moral validity, and so on. In some versions, the link is procedural, moral notions of fair dealing shaping legal doctrines of due process; in others, the link is substantive, moral principles setting the standard for the content of legal rules. In some versions, the grounding is secular; in others, it is religious (most famously perhaps in the schematic thought of Thomas **Aquinas**). However, the common denominator in all versions of natural law theory is that the 'separation thesis' of legal positivism—the thesis that, while the existence of law is one thing, its moral merit or demerit is quite another matter—is contested. Or, to put this another way, if we follow natural law theory, we will reject the idea that law is an entirely autonomous, discrete body of rules and principles; law might not be identical to morality, but there is a sense in which they are necessarily related and integrated.

In practice, it is not always clear whether judges view themselves as legal positivists or as natural lawyers. Some, such as Coleridge LJ in *R v Instan* (1893), see a close relationship between law and morals:

'It would not be correct to say that every moral obligation involves a legal duty; but every legal duty is founded on a moral obligation. A legal common law duty is nothing else than the enforcing by law of that which is a moral obligation without legal enforcement.'

Thus, in *Instan*, the defendant, having omitted to feed or procure medical assistance for the elderly aunt with whom she lived, was judged to be in breach of a moral obligation and, quite rightly, to have been convicted of the crime of manslaughter. Other judges, however, sounding more like legal positivists, insist that they are sitting in courts of law rather than courts of morals, apparently signalling that the determination of legal rights and obligations operates at some distance from morality. What should we make of this?

Quite plausibly, we might reason that, since some judges seemingly side with natural law theory, while other judges go out of their way to reject it, the next step is to consider which is the better view. How should we do this? In *The Concept of Law* (Oxford: Clarendon Press, 1961), HLA Hart helpfully suggests that the case in favour of a particular concept of law (whether positivist or natural law) must rest on either its desirable practical effect or its theoretical superiority to rival views.

Positivists, such as Hart, tend to assume that practical considerations tell strongly against viewing public regulation in the way that natural law theory proposes. Most significantly, opponents claim that a natural law mind-set is an invitation to more than one kind of extremism. At one extreme, critics contend that a natural law view encourages citizens to adopt a revolutionary attitude to established public authority (justifying the rejection of regulatory decrees as 'law' on the ground of their perceived immorality). At the other extreme, critics maintain that natural law encourages the citizenry to adopt an attitude of uncritical compliance (the claimed 'legal validity' of a regulatory decree being taken as indicative of its moral authority). While claims of this kind might have some plausibility in some settings (Jeremy **Bentham**, for example, famously feared the extremist expressions of natural law and natural

rights in revolutionary France), it is clear that such tendencies are both highly speculative and context-specific. Against such claims, it seems more plausible to think that our actions tend to be driven by our prudential (self-interested) and moral calculations rather than by our conceptual view of law. That is to say, the fact that we resist the de facto rulers, or that we succumb to their rule, depends much more on whether we judge that their requirements are in line with our moral standards or our self-interest than whether we view their edicts as 'law'. If so, while the practical arguments against natural law theory are weak, any such practical counter-arguments equally count little in its favour.

If the practical implications of adopting natural law theory do not settle the matter, how might it be argued that such a view is to be preferred on theoretical grounds? Unless we assume that law is unproblematically 'out there' and that we simply need some conceptual apparatus that corresponds with or represents the actuality, the argument must be about the internal coherence and consistency of our conceptual thinking. But, where would such an argument start?

In *The Morality of Law* (New Haven: Yale University Press, 1969), where Lon Fuller argues for a procedural version of natural law, it is treated as common ground that the jurisprudential debate focuses on 'the enterprise of subjecting human conduct to the governance of rules'. In other words, the protagonists are not simply talking past one another: it is not as though natural law theory is looking at some quite different part of the social world. Rather, just like legal positivism, natural law theory is concerned with how we should view public regulation: the making and enforcing of rules, the settlement of disputes in the light of those rules, and so on. What natural law theory must assert, if it is to make its case on theoretical grounds, is that our view of the regulatory enterprise will be distorted if we do not see the paradigm (of rule-making, rule-adjudication, and the like) as an articulation of moral reason. If this is where the argument starts, how does it proceed?

Briefly, the argument runs on the following lines. In modern nation states, the regulatory enterprise is designed to present us with a range of general prescriptions and specific decisions all of which we are urged to respect as 'the law'. The law does not simply command that certain acts are required or prohibited; the law presents itself as a set of prescriptions that commands attention and respect. So it is that 'the law', like 'morality' and 'self-interest', presents us with a reason for action—in other words, legal reason, like prudential reasoning and moral reasoning, must be viewed as a dimension of our practical reasoning (reasoning about what to do and how to behave). In this light, the crux of the matter becomes how we understand the relationship between these dimensions of practical reason. Are these independent dimensions of practical thought, sometimes converging and intersecting, but essentially unrelated: or are these dimensions that fit together in an organized way with moral reason as the cornerstone? For natural law theory to represent the better view (simply on theoretical grounds), there must be some inconsistency in thinking that we can engage in legal reasoning without also necessarily engaging in moral reasoning.

Sceptics will take some persuading that any such inconsistency can be demonstrated. Even if we do not invoke the hypothetical amoralist, who resolutely refuses to give favourable consideration to the interests of others, sceptics will see no reason why engaging in legal reasoning necessarily involves moral reasoning. After all, we can make perfectly coherent detached, or 'at a distance', statements about the legal position relative to the rules of a particular regime without, at the same time, making any moral commitment to the regime or its rules. During the apartheid years, for instance, a comparative lawyer might have reported on the legal position in South Africa without, in any sense, endorsing the legislation that expressed the State's racially discriminatory policies. Even if the regime is viewed by its sponsors as morally authorized, we need not affirm the moral authorization when we report on the legal position. However, this is no reason to give up on natural law theory. Quite simply, such detached reports beg the critical question of whether the rules whose implications we draw out in a disinterested way are 'law' in the first place. If, with our concept of law properly in focus, we should not treat such rules as 'law', then the position on which we report should not be characterized as 'legal'—all that we have is a regime that *de facto* rules, the rules laid down by that regime, and the implications of such rules.

In sum, as John Finnis—one of the leading modern exponents of a natural law approach—recognizes, the fundamental question is whether the only coherent larger picture is one that makes the moral viewpoint central to practical reason. If this is so, if moral reason is necessarily the organizing focus within practical reason, then on good theoretical grounds, we should use this template to conceptualize law; and it follows that, scepticism notwithstanding, natural law theory is on the right conceptual track.

ROGER BROWNSWORD

J Finnis, *Natural Law and Natural Rights* (Oxford: Clarendon Press, 1980)

See also: **legal positivism since 1970; legal positivism to 1970**

natural monopoly An industry is characterized by natural monopoly when the number of inputs required to produce a good or service (and therefore the cost of production) is lower for a single provider than if the good or service were provided by a number of suppliers, and the single firm can satisfy all of the market's demand. This is generally so when production benefits from economies of scale and economies of scope. Economies of scale exist if the long-run average cost of production falls as the quantity of goods or services produced increases. They may exist when production requires a large fixed cost that is spread over the increasing units of output increases.

Local telephone service and natural gas supply are often given as examples of natural monopolies because of the large initial investment required. The cost per user of the cable and pipe networks are smaller the greater the number of users the service providers can attract. Economies of scope exist when it is cheaper to produce two or more products together than it is to produce them separately. Savings arise because production requires shareable or common inputs, and the cost of providing the inputs jointly is less than providing them separately. As an example, a farmer with sheep that produces mutton and wool has a lower cost of production than the combined costs of a farmer with sheep that produces mutton and a farmer with sheep that produces wool.

Though production by a single firm minimizes cost in natural monopoly industries, monopolists may act to the detriment of consumers. Natural monopoly thus provides one of the clearest cases for government intervention in the market. Intervention either involves nationalizing the industry so that government provides the service, or government **regulation** of the industry.

OKEOGHENE ODUDU

natural resources The UK is endowed with a variety of natural resources. The most important being crude oil, gas, coal, water resources, and land suitable for agriculture and related activities. Almost all these resources are at the base or otherwise related to economic activity in the country. For example, energy resources (coal, oil, and gas, and their derivatives) contribute 10 per cent of the gross national income.

Historically, coal has been the dominant natural resource in the UK especially in the last two centuries. It provided the energy that powered the industrial revolution in the eighteenth century and subsequently. Production peaked at over 145 million metric tonnes in 1970. Since then production has declined steadily for a number of reasons including competition from less expensive sources and concerns about the environmental implication of coal mining and usage. In 1995–1996, the UK produced more than 50 Mt of coal from 83 deep and 122 surface mines. Currently, production is at approximately 20Mt annually from both deep and surface mines. With the oil price surge in the last couple of years and concerns about security of supply and encouraged by advances in cleaner technologies, interest in coal production has seen a bit of a resurgence. Hitherto abandoned mines at Hatfield and Aberpergwm have been re-opened. It is estimated that the UK has 400Mt of recoverable coal reserves. The coal produced is used predominantly to fire power stations. The main locations for coal are in the midlands, Manchester, Merseyside, Yorkshire, Newcastle, and South Wales. On average 35 per cent of electricity is generated from coal. In the winter of 2005–2006, half of electricity was generated from coal stations.

Crude oil was first discovered in Derbyshire in 1919. Production peaked at 1,700 gallons a week, followed by rapid depletion. More important discovery was made in the UK Continental shelf in the North Sea in the 1960s. Production is about 2 million barrels per day. This meets the domestic demand for oil with a small surplus for exports. Proven reserves of oil are about 4.5 billion bbl but production is said to have peaked in 1999. In another ten years the UK will be net importer of crude oil. The same goes for natural gas. Current production of natural gas from the North Sea is about 102 billion cu m with estimated reserves of 628 billion cu m. The gas is used mainly for electricity generation and for domestic purposes. In 2004 the UK became a net importer of gas with Norway and The Netherlands as the main source using the Bacton-Zee-Brugge inter-connector. Soon Russia will be another source of gas imports.

The law relating to natural resources can be divided into two—upstream and downstream—based on the stage of resource activity, that is, production and distribution. Access to and production of coal, oil, and gas is based on a license system administered by the Secretary of State for the Department of Business, Enterprise, and Regulatory Reform ('DBERR'). Gold and silver were excepted from the **common law** principle of land ownership and its extension to all things to the centre of the earth. The 1934 Petroleum Production Act and the 1938 Coal Act (later the 1946 Coal Nationalization Act) (as subsequently amended) vested all oil, gas, and coal in their natural state in the **Crown**.

To rationalize the exploitation of these resources, the government, through the Secretary of State for the DBERR, demarcates blocks and invites bids by interested **companies** for exploration of oil and gas in the Continental Shelf in the North Sea. Based on qualifications such as technical expertise, financial capability, and satisfactory bid, the fields are allocated for exploration. The methods of allocation are therefore discretionary, variable cash tender and discretion with a fixed premium. Although no blocks of coal reserves are pre-determined for exploration, licence must be obtained from the DBERR for the exploration and production of coal. The downstream activities of carriage and distribution are also regulated mainly with the view to fostering competition, fiscal responsibility, provision for safety, and environmental protection. The current overarching **legislation** on coal, oil, and gas, particularly on downstream activity, is the Energy Act 2004.

FRANCIS N BOTCHWAY

naturalization Naturalization is a legal term for making a non-citizen (**alien**) a citizen of a state. Some countries no longer use the term in their citizenship **legislation**, referring to the process as **citizenship** by conferral or grant. Naturalization is still the term used in the British Nationality Act 1981.

Under the **common law**, a **person's** place of birth created permanent allegiance to the sovereign of the land. Individuals could not revoke their allegiance and take up another **nationality** of their own accord. Naturalization under the common law could occur, but only through the acquisition of new **territory** by conquest or cession. Otherwise naturalization required legislation to override the common law.

The first recorded examples of 'naturalization' date from thirteenth century England and were more correctly 'endenization'—an exercise of **royal prerogative** through letters patent. But, until the mid-nineteenth century, 'private' Acts of **Parliament** naturalizing individuals and 'letters of denization' from the sovereign were normally the only means of acquiring the status of British **subject**.

The first modern naturalization Acts were passed in 1844, 1847, and 1870. The 1844 Act took the important step of authorizing naturalization by government officials, removing the need for personal legislation. The 1847 Act confirmed that colonial legislatures could naturalize aliens within their own jurisdiction. The 1870 Act established the principle that aliens should live in Britain before being accepted as subjects, specifying five years residence or the same period 'in the service of the **Crown**'.

Historically, 'naturalized' subjects lacked the full rights and privileges of their 'natural-born' counterparts. In the UK, they could not be granted Crown land or become a Privy Councillor or Member of Parliament, and their children born overseas were not considered British nationals. While the Naturalization Act 1870 removed most of these restrictions for the UK, the various British Dominions continued to discriminate between different classes of British subjects. Some remnants remain today—naturalized Australians, for example, cannot run for Parliament unless they renounce their original nationality.

The most important disadvantage faced by naturalized subjects, however, is the legislature's ability to deprive them of their adopted nationality. An Australian High Court Justice noted in 1988 that 'the power to legislate with respect to naturalization . . . seems necessarily to carry with it a power to revoke the grant of naturalization'. After the formation of the Commonwealth of Australia in 1901, federal authorities cancelled colonial naturalization certificates issued to Chinese migrants. In World Wars I and II, substantial numbers of Australians 'of enemy origin' had their naturalization taken away as a prelude to **deportation**.

As these examples illustrate, naturalization laws—along with immigration restrictions—have been central to controlling membership of the nation. At times, this has been done on a racial basis. The colony of Queensland, for example, passed a law in 1861 restricting the naturalization of any 'African or Asiatic alien'. In 1896, New Zealand prohibited the naturalization of Chinese settlers. Shortly after federation Australia excluded 'aboriginal natives of Asia, Africa, or the Islands of the Pacific' from naturalization.

The desire of the self-governing British Dominions to retain discriminatory naturalization (and immigration) measures presented an obstacle to uniform naturalization laws in the former British Empire. The sole nationality throughout the Empire was 'British subject'. However, while colonial Parliaments could naturalize foreigners, the effect of their legislation was limited to their own territory. As a prominent commentator noted in 1902, this meant that:

'A man may be a British subject in one part of the empire, and an alien in another part. In New Zealand he may be an Englishman, and in England a Frenchman. In Victoria he may owe permanent allegiance to the British Crown, and on crossing the border into New South Wales he may find himself an alien'.

A common naturalization code was proposed to rectify this problem. Lengthy negotiations occurred between 1901 and 1914, covering a number of Imperial Conferences, with the main struggle over uniformity of racial treatment. The proposal only moved forward after the UK assured the self-governing Dominions (Canada, New Zealand, Australia, South Africa, and Newfoundland) that royal assent would not be withheld for naturalization measures conflicting with this principle.

The intervention of two world wars largely sidelined the Imperial naturalization code, which was never simultaneously in force throughout the countries of the British Empire. It was replaced from 1946 by a new scheme of local citizenship, introduced first by Canada, followed shortly afterwards by the UK itself, Australia, and other members of the **Commonwealth**. People naturalized in Commonwealth countries became citizens of the particular country as well as British subjects. In later decades, the citizens of these countries lost their dual status as British subjects.

Some of the requirements for naturalization in current legislative schemes include a period of residence in the country, good character, and sufficient knowledge of the new country of citizenship, the language, and the responsibilities and privileges of citizenship.   KIM RUBENSTEIN

C Parry, *Nationality and Citizenship Laws of the Commonwealth and Republic of Ireland* (London: Stevens & Sons, 1957)

EB Sargant, 'Naturalisation in the British Dominions, with Special Reference to the British Nationality and Status of Aliens Bill' (1914) 14 *J Soc Comp Legis* 327–336

nature conservation   Nature conservation law is the field of law relating to the protection and conservation of wild animals, plants, and natural habitats. Four main legal tools are used.

The first is conserving important habitats by designating and safeguarding key sites, habitat loss having the greatest impact on nature conservation. The law here either seeks to facilitate favourable management if the land is owned by a nature conservation agency or sympathetic landowner, or strike a balance between the nature conservation interests and those of private landowners. The main laws are Part II of the Wildlife and Countryside Act 1981 (which was significantly amended by the Countryside and Rights of Way Act 2000; for Scotland, broadly similar controls are in the Nature Conservation (Scotland) Act 2004), and laws implementing EC Directives on Wild Birds (79/409) and on Natural Habitats and of Wild Fauna and Flora (92/43) ('the Habitats Directive').

Before amendment, the 1981 Act took a voluntaristic approach. On designated sites of special scientific interest ('SSSIs'), the law prevented damaging development for a short period during which the Nature Conservancy or its successors could try to negotiate a management agreement with the landowner, a regime described as 'toothless' (*Southern Water Authority v Nature Conservancy Council* (1992) per Lord Mustill). Management agreements included payments to compensate landowners for profits lost by not developing their land in ways harmful to wildlife, and did not necessarily provide money to encourage sympathetic land management. Now, a more regulatory and proactive approach is taken; permission for damaging operations can be refused indefinitely, and harmful activities can only be carried out with consent, or if carried out under a management agreement or management scheme (the latter being a legal power to control damage by neglect). Payments are only made for positive conservation works. However, planning permission still 'trumps' these controls, so much depends on what conditions planning authorities impose on developers. Current policy guidance is ambiguous as to whether nature conservation interests must be mitigated and compensated for (eg by providing alternative habitat), or can be traded against economic development.

EC laws on habitat conservation are aimed at designating a coherent EC-wide network of sites, known as 'Natura 2000', and non-ecological factors (such as economic development) cannot be taken into account when selecting sites. For less endangered habitat types, and habitats of less endangered species, there must be proactive management, and deterioration and damage must be avoided. Plans or projects likely to have a significant effect on the site must be assessed, and damaging activities can only be consented to if they will not adversely affect the site's ecological integrity. Some major development, such as port expansion at Dibden Bay on the Solent, has failed this test and been blocked. If there is no alternative, development may be carried out only if there are 'imperative reasons of overriding public interest, including those of a social or economic nature'. But the Member State must provide ecological compensation to ensure the overall coherence of Natura 2000. For the most threatened habitats, the approval of the **European Commission** is required, but this tends to be given where major economic development is at stake.

The second method used is protecting listed species, regardless of their location, through criminal offences (eg disturbing a breeding site, or egg collecting). The law is in Part I of the 1981 Act (for Scotland, see the 2004 Act), and the Wild Birds and Habitats Directives. In the 1981 Act, cruelty and wildlife considerations intermingle, and offences usually require intentional or reckless behaviour. EC conservation laws are not welfare-oriented, and liability is generally stricter. Offences will not be committed where the damage was necessary (eg to control pests), but generally a licence is required and, unlike under the 1981 Act, EC law requires that no satisfactory alternative existed and the conservation status of the species is not prejudiced. Inadequate **sentencing** powers and enforcement levels have been a long-standing criticism; some improvements have been made, eg specialist wildlife crime officers; and prison sentences may now be imposed. Another criticism is that protection is piecemeal and larger and more charismatic species tend to be listed.

A third approach relies on private property law. At **common law**, wild creatures have no rights of their own, and qualified **property rights** can be acquired in them if they are lawfully taken from the wild. Wild plants are part of the land itself. Without **regulation**, this gives landowners great power over wildlife, which is at odds with the wider public interest in conserving nature. But property rights can protect wildlife, since anyone other than the landowner who kills or injures a wild animal or picks a wild plant will commit a tort and an **injunction** could be obtained. Significant tracts of land are owned by sympathetic wildlife organizations such as the Royal Society for the Protection of Birds ('RSPB').

A fourth approach, increasingly used, integrates nature conservation concerns into other areas. Institutionally, nature conservation is now linked to landscape management in each UK country, and—in line with an obligation in the 1992 Biodiversity Convention—there are integrative **biodiversity** action plans for a wide range of species and habitats. Financing under agri-environment schemes has been rising significantly; farming subsidies are conditional on compliance with conservation laws; and the EC Common Agriculture Policy has now decoupled subsidies from productivity (which encouraged overgrazing and intensification). Increasingly, if only at the margins, farmers are paid to produce landscapes and habitats, rather than to maximize the agricultural productivity of their land.

A striking feature of nature conservation law is the paucity of proscriptive regulation. Partly this is because safeguarding most species and habitats requires active land management, especially when trying to conserve dynamically active populations in protected areas. But, also, nature conservation laws conflict with the idea that landowners enjoy a near absolute right to determine the use of their property, though scholars are increasingly emphasizing the environmental **responsibilities** that flow from land ownership.

Until recently, the marine environment has been neglected, partly because of the absence of land rights; the conservation interests have been relatively poorly understood; and because the law has been more concerned with matters like navigation and fishing. In the UK there are ongoing proposals for a Marine Bill which would address nature conservation alongside competing interests such as fisheries and energy generation.

At international level, specimens of species, and their habitats, either fall within national state **sovereignty** or, as with species on the high seas, are common resources exploitable by all. A number of **treaties** seek to control the exploitation of species either directly (eg the 1946 Whaling Convention) or indirectly via trade controls (eg the 1973 Convention on the International Trade in Endangered Species ('CITES')). The 1992 Biodiversity Convention recognizes the 'intrinsic value' of biological diversity but does not challenge state sovereignty, and what conserving biodiversity actually entails is contested: is it about conserving the most species; or higher taxonomic categories; or the breadth of these categories; or the evolutionary distance between species? There is no real consensus.

For the future, the greatest challenge will be to meet the increasing effects of **climate change**. This will require something altogether different from conserving the best of what we have where it currently is. It is a challenge that is beyond the reach of the law as it now stands, and will require a more strategic approach.   DONALD MCGILLIVRAY

C Reid, *Nature Conservation Law* (Edinburgh: W Green, 2nd edn, 2002)

S Bell and D McGillivray, *Environmental Law* (Oxford: Oxford University Press, 7th edn, 2008), chs 19 and 20

necessity   *see* **justification, excuse and mitigation in criminal Law**

negative rights   This term is used in two senses: in the first sense, it is used to encapsulate the position of civil liberties (often called '**civil and political rights**') in a national **constitution** without a Bill of Rights, such as the United Kingdom before the **Human Rights Act** 1998 ('HRA'), or contemporary Australia. Since the UK adopted the HRA, negative rights have now largely been replaced by rights positively guaranteed by the **European Convention on Human Rights**, domestically implemented by the HRA. Strictly speaking, the term used should be 'negative liberties', since the notion of a 'right' is often used in the sense argued for by the legal theorist, Hohfeld, as a positive claim on the state, generating a corresponding duty. The term 'negative right' in the sense discussed here means a negative liberty: that is, simply a **human** activity which is currently not prohibited by the state, and which is thereby not unlawful, on the presumption that the everything is permitted which is not specifically proscribed by law. Negative liberties are thus described as 'interstitial'; they exist only in the gaps between laws. They are of course always vulnerable to encroachment by more and more restrictive laws.

Thus, prior to the HRA, it was widely thought that there was a 'right' to protest, or to peaceful assembly in the UK. In fact, this was simply a negative freedom. There was a negative liberty to protest only in the sense that: (a) there was no general law forbidding political or other protest, as would be found in totalitarian states; (b) there was no general **police** practice of harassing or violently breaking up protests; (c) therefore peaceful protest was a lawful and tenable activity, but only provided that protestors complied with relevant law, such as the Public Order Act 1986, and lawful directions given to them by police officers under it, and also did not infringe numerous other laws on obstruction of the highway, **trespass**, aggravated trespass, **nuisance**, **breach of the peace**, and so on. In the same way, the 'right' to **freedom of expression** simply meant that one could lawfully write or say whatever one wanted, provided that one did not infringe the criminal law of **obscenity**, indecency, **contempt of court**, racial hatred, **blasphemy**, official secrecy, and that one bore in mind potential civil liability for defamation, breach of confidence, **copyright** and so on.

In the second sense of the word, the term is used to suggest those rights which represent a claim to be *free from* something (eg arbitrary detention, **torture**) as opposed to a claim to be *given* something (a fair trial, shelter, education). Thus used, the term captures the notion of a basic area of freedom into which the state may not trespass—a right to be let alone by the state, and by others. However, the strict boundary between positive and negative rights can break down: it is often not possible to classify a given right as solely negative in character. For example, the right to peaceful protest sounds, at first blush, like a negative right: the citizen is (in effect) saying to the state, do not interfere with my protest. But **courts** have held that it can include a positive claim to be protected by the police from hostile counter-demonstrators, so far as is practically possible. Similarly, the right not to be subject to inhuman or degrading treatment—which even in its formulation sounds like a classic, negative right—has been held to require the state to provide a minimum level of support such that the individual is not left utterly destitute and at **risk** from cold and hunger.

Generally speaking, what are termed 'civil and political' rights—speech, assembly, liberty, and so on—are thought of as 'negative rights', in that they merely require the state not to interfere with the individual. Conversely, **economic and social rights**—to healthcare, shelter, and education—are generally seen as 'positive rights', in that they require often very substantial action by the state—such as the provision of the National Health Service—to vindicate the right in question. However, this is not always the case: the right to vote is a classical 'political' right, but requires major investment by the state in organizing and guaranteeing free and fair **elections**; similarly, the **right to a fair trial**—a classic civil right—requires the maintenance by the state of a vast and complex system of civil and criminal justice, including some provision for **legal aid**.

GAVIN PHILLIPSON

negligence in civil law   For present purposes, civil law is contrasted with criminal law. In civil law, the term 'negligence' is used in two main senses. One sense, specific to **tort law**, refers to the 'tort of negligence'. The other sense refers to conduct of a certain quality—ie 'negligent conduct'.

Negligence as a tort

Saying that negligence is 'a tort' means that it provides a basis on which a person can make a 'tort claim' against another and on which the other can be held liable 'in tort'. Understood in this way, a tort is a set of rules and principles that specify when a person can be held legally liable and, conversely, how a person must behave in order to avoid being held legally liable. The main rules or principles in such a set are sometimes referred to as the 'elements' of the tort. The tort of negligence is said to have three such elements: in order for a defendant (D) to be liable to a claimant (C) 'in (the tort of) negligence' D must have 'owed a duty of care' (or, alternatively, a duty 'to take care') to C; D must have breached that duty; and as a result of the breach, C must have suffered harm that is not too 'remote'. This third element can be further unpacked. First, the requirement of harm can be alternatively expressed by saying that harm is 'the gist' of the tort of negligence. Secondly, the

requirement that the injury result from the breach can be stated in terms that there must be a 'causal connection' or a 'relationship of **causation**' between the breach and the harm. Thirdly, the concept of '**remoteness (of damage)**' expresses the idea that even if the harm was caused by the breach, there may be good reason why D should not be legally liable for it—for instance, if the harm was highly unusual or the result of a bizarre coincidence.

The tort of negligence was created in 1932 in the famous case of *Donoghue v Stevenson*. Negligent conduct as such was well established as a ground of liability in tort by the mid-nineteenth century. (Concerning the earlier history of liability for negligence see **trespass, case and negligence**.) For instance, doctors could be held liable in negligence to their patients, vehicle drivers to pedestrians, occupiers of land to visitors, and so on. In *Donoghue v Stevenson* Lord **Atkin** drew together these various 'categories' of negligence by enunciating the famous 'neighbour principle': you owe a duty to take care not to injure your 'neighbour' who, in legal terms, is any person whom you ought to foresee might be harmed by lack of care ('negligence') on your part. You will owe a duty of care to another even if you did not actually foresee harm to them, provided you ought to have foreseen that possibility; or, in other words, provided harm to the other was 'reasonably foreseeable'. Harm will be reasonably foreseeable if the '**reasonable person**' would have foreseen it. The reasonable person is a product of the judicial imagination (or, as it was once put, 'the legal personification of fairness'); and provides the 'objective' model against which the behaviour of real people is judged to be negligent or not.

As the law has been developed since 1932, foreseeability of injury to another is a necessary condition, but may not be a sufficient condition, of the existence of a duty of care to that person. Foreseeability is normally a sufficient condition of the existence of a duty to take care not to harm another's body or physical property (cars, houses, and so on); but it may not be sufficient in relation to mental harm or financial loss. This is partly because it is considered not as important for the law to protect people from mental harm and financial loss as from bodily injury and property damage. Nor may foreseeability be sufficient for a duty to *prevent* (rather than inflict) harm. So there will normally be no duty to rescue a complete **stranger**, even from physical danger. The law does not expect people to be good Samaritans. Also, if a person has an 'immunity' from liability, they will owe no duty of care to anyone. For instance, **judges** owe no duty to take care not to cause harm by negligent judging. In this sense, judges as such have no legal 'neighbours'.

The 'scope of the tort of negligence' (we may say) is defined by the rules about when a duty of care is owed. There is constant pressure to extend the reach of liability for negligence; and duty of care is one of the most contentious and difficult topics in tort law. This is partly because of disagreement about the extent to which people should be expected to take care of themselves, and to what extent they should be entitled to expect others to protect them. For instance, should landowners be required to warn visitors of *obvious* dangers—perhaps that the depth of water in a river or lake may be variable and difficult for a diver to judge?

In practical terms, the tort of negligence is the most important of all torts. The vast majority of tort claims made each year are claims for **damages** for personal (ie bodily or mental) injury suffered in road, work, or recreational accidents, or in the course of medical treatment; and nearly all personal injury claims (including most high profile **group actions**) are based on the tort of negligence. The tort of negligence is also the basis of the majority of claims for damage to property—most commonly, perhaps, damage to vehicles involved in road accidents. In addition, the tort can also be used to make claims against lawyers, surveyors, accountants, builders, and other professionals for financial loss. In recent decades, too, public authorities have become increasingly popular targets for negligence claims arising out of the provision of welfare and educational services.

Negligence as conduct

The second element of the tort of negligence is breach of a duty to take care. This is equivalent to negligence in the second sense in which it is used in civil law, referring to conduct of a certain quality. Negligent conduct may consist of **acts and omissions**—misfeasance or nonfeasance in legal jargon. Negligence in this sense is formally defined as failure to take reasonable precautions, against foreseeable risks of harm to another, either by doing something that the reasonable person would not do (such as driving under the influence of alcohol), or by omitting to do something that the reasonable person would do (such as stopping at a red light). Failure to take reasonable precautions against foreseeable risks of harm to oneself may amount to **contributory negligence**. If a person suffers harm partly as a result of their own negligence a partly as a result of the negligence of another (sometimes called 'actionable' negligence), any damages payable to the harmed person may be reduced to take account of their contributory negligence.

Whereas foreseeability that a particular person may be harmed is relevant to the existence of a duty of care to that person, foreseeability of particular risks of harm is part of the legal definition of negligent conduct. The law does not require precautions to be taken against unforeseeable risks of harm to C even if some other harm to C is foreseeable. Negligence is failure to take *reasonable* precautions against foreseeable risks. Reasonable precautions are the precautions the reasonable person would take. Whether any particular precaution is reasonable depends on various factors. One is the likely seriousness of the harm. For instance, it is more likely to be unreasonable not to guard against loss of the good eye of a one-eyed person than the loss of one eye of a two-eyed person. Another is the magnitude of the **risk**: it is more likely to be unreasonable not to guard against a 1 in 10 risk than a 1 in 100 risk. On the other hand, the more expensive the precautions required to guard against the risk, the less likely it will be unreasonable not to take them. Precautions that it would be reasonable to take to guard against a serious, 1 in 100 risk may not be reasonable to guard against a less serious, 1 in 1,000 risk. Also relevant is the value of the risk-creating activity. For instance, it may be reasonable for the driver of an emergency vehicle to take risks that it would be unreasonable for a recreational driver to take. However, the greater the risk, the greater would be the required precautions (such as sounding a siren).

Negligence understood in this way is not only an element of the tort of negligence. For instance, contracts often impose duties to take care on the contracting parties. Furthermore, even if a contract for the provision of services—for instance, a contract between solicitor and client or a doctor and patient— does not explicitly say so, a provision, requiring the service-provider to exercise reasonable care in performing the services, will be 'implied into' the contract. Some of the obligations of **fiduciaries** are duties of care. Indeed, obligations to take reasonable care are pervasive in all areas of civil law.

PETER CANE

See also: **criminal liability without fault; fault-based civil liability; fault-based criminal liability; medical negligence; public bodies, liability of; strict civil liability; tort system**

negligence in criminal law   *see* **fault-based criminal liability**

negotiable instruments   The huge increase in the use of debit and credit cards in recent years has led to a decrease in the use of negotiable instruments as a method of payment. This is mainly because payments by cheque have become far less common.

In the UK the forms of negotiable instrument in use include cheques, bills of exchange, bank drafts, and bank notes. Most of us will never see a bill of exchange, other than a cheque, as they tend to be used as specialist instruments for financing trade transactions, especially for international trade. A cheque is a 'bill of exchange payable on demand' and, therefore, a negotiable instrument (but see below). This entry concentrates on cheques.

Cheques, and other types of bill of exchange, became popular because they have the attribute of being negotiable. Negotiability, in English law, is more than transferability. Where a person gives value and acts in good faith that person will get a perfect title free of any defects which the title of the person transferring the document may have been subject to. The general common law rule has always been that you cannot give a better title than you yourself have. For example, if I take a cheque (which is uncrossed—see below) in payment for something and it turns out to have been stolen, I will have good title to the cheque provided I paid for it and acted in good faith. (There are some other requirements such as that the document must have been properly completed and be in a deliverable state).

In the modern world the use of cheques has declined greatly in recent years; and even where cheques are now used they are issued as a payment instrument and not as a negotiable instrument. The law relating to cheques changed in 1992 and the position now is that not only are most cheques not negotiable—they are also not transferable. The reason for this is that cheques are now routinely issued to bank customers with what is called a crossing already printed on the front of the cheque. This usually takes the form of the words 'A/C PAYEE' printed between two parallel lines. Such a cheque cannot be transferred to another person but must be paid into an account in the name of the person to whom the cheque is payable. This change in the law was introduced to reduce the amount of cheque fraud; but it should be appreciated that customers are entitled to remove the crossing and issue the cheque as a fully negotiable instrument. In practice bank customers are extremely unlikely to do this.

While it is perfectly acceptable to most people to issue and receive cheques which contain the 'A/C PAYEE' crossing, it does create a problem for someone who does not have a bank account and while most of the adult population in the UK will have a bank account there is a small percentage of the population who for various reasons, do not.

ANDREW CAMPBELL

negotiation *see* **lawyering skills**

neighbouring rights Probably the most important rights 'neighbouring' on, or related to, **copyright** are those available to performers. It was not until the early twentieth century that calls for protection of performers were made, triggered by technological advances which enabled performances to be fixed, reproduced, played, and broadcast to wider audiences than those present at the live event. Attempts to protect performances under copyright law were unsuccessful, at both domestic and international levels, because performers were seen as lacking creative authorship, offering merely creative interpretation of existing works.

Protection to performers was introduced in the UK as early as 1925. However, this protection was limited to criminal sanctions against unlawful fixation of performances and did not include civil remedies. At an international level, it was not until 1961 that the **Rome Convention (International Convention for the Protection of Performers, Producers of Phonograms and Broadcasting Organizations)** was signed, requiring contracting states to provide performers with the possibility of preventing: the broadcasting and communication to the public, without their consent, of their performance; the fixation without their consent of their unfixed performance; and the reproduction, without their consent, of a fixation of their performance, for a term of at least twenty years from when the performance took place or was fixed in a phonogram. Subsequent international treaties, in particular the **World Intellectual Property Organization ('WIPO') Performances and Phonograms Treaty 1996 ('WPPT')**, have extended protection for performers by requiring that performers have property rights in their performances, along with moral rights, and increasing the length of protection to fifty years.

The UK Copyright Designs and Patents Act 1988 ('CDPA') improved the protection available to performers because it introduced civil remedies for unlawful fixations, reproductions of fixations, and broadcasts of performances (known as 'non-property' rights). However, it was not until **European Union** law intervened in this field, in the form of the EC Rental and Lending Rights Directive of 19 November 1992, that protection for performers was truly bolstered, requiring the UK had to amend the CDPA to introduce property rights for performers in respect of performances. As a result, UK law also complies with the WPPT provisions on property rights.

Part II of the CDPA confers rights on individuals in respect of their live performances, provided they are dramatic or musical performances, or involve the reading or recitation of literary works or performances of variety acts. This is typically restricted to where the individual is a UK citizen or resident, or a citizen or resident of a Member State of the **European Community** ('EC') or where the performance takes place in the UK or a Member State of the EC. The two major sets of rights that are granted are non-property rights and property rights.

A performer's non-property rights are infringed if, without their consent, a person: makes a recording of the whole or substantial part of a performance directly from the live performance; broadcasts live the performance; makes a recording of the performance directly from a broadcast of the live performance; or shows or plays in public or communicates to the public the performance by means of a recording which was made without the performers' consent where that person knows or has reason to believe was made without the performer's consent. Infringement occurs where the above acts are done in relation to the whole or substantial part of the performance. Importing or commercially dealing in illicit recordings, where there is knowledge or reason to believe they are illicit recordings, is also an infringement.

A performer's property rights are infringed if, without their consent, a person: makes a copy of a recording of a performance; distributes, rents, or lends to the public copies of a recording of a performance; or makes available to the public a recording of the performance, such as via the internet. Infringement occurs where the above acts are done in relation to the whole or substantial part of the performance.

There are exceptions to infringement, such as fair dealing with a performance for the purpose of reporting current events or for the purpose of criticism or review, and those favouring educational establishments and not-for-profit organizations.

The above rights are owned by the performer and endure for fifty years from when the performance takes place or from when a recording of the performance is released. Only property rights may be transferred (ie assigned) or licensed (either exclusively or non-exclusively) to third parties. By contrast, non-property rights are only transmissible on death, as part of the performer's estate.

Importantly, a performer has a right to equitable remuneration from owners of sound recordings where a commercially published sound recording which includes the whole or substantial part of their performance is played in public or communicated to the public. The amount payable is as agreed between the performer and owner or, where they cannot agree, is decided by the Copyright Tribunal.

This right cannot be assigned, except to a collecting society, which will exercise the right on behalf of the performer.

Most recently, the CDPA has been amended to introduce **moral rights** for performers. Performers are granted the right to be identified as performer (attribution right) and the right to object to any distortion, mutilation, or other modification of their performance that would be prejudicial to their reputation (integrity right). The attribution right is only triggered if asserted by the performer and applies where a performance is given in public or is broadcast live, or where a sound recording of a performance is communicated to the public or copies of such a sound recording are distributed to the public. The integrity right does not require assertion and applies where the performance is broadcast live or the performance is played in public or communicated to the public by means of a sound recording. Moral rights are non-economic in nature; therefore, it is not possible to transfer them. However, it is possible for performers to waive their moral rights. The rights endure for fifty years. With the introduction of performers' moral rights, it is now possible for the UK to ratify the WPPT.

TANYA APLIN

neo-liberalism Neo-liberalism is an economic and political theory which argues that **human** well-being is best advanced through the extension of free market exchange. Although its intellectual roots can be traced back to the liberal political economy of the eighteenth and nineteenth centuries, its contemporary origins lie in the confluence of two rather different (and contradictory) bodies of thought: Austrian economics, with its emphasis on individual liberty; and neo-classical economics, with its emphasis on the efficiency of the market. Having fallen from favour for much of the twentieth century, liberal political economic ideas underwent an intellectual revival in the 1940s and 1950s, and began to find policy expression in the personified forms of **Thatcherism** and Reaganomics in the 1970s and 1980s. By the 1990s, these ideas, by now dubbed 'neo-liberalism', had in policy terms become mainstream, underpinning the so-called 'Washington Consensus' reform packages promoted by the International Monetary Fund ('IMF') and the World Bank, and the imposition of free trade on the developing world.

Neo-liberalism is premised on the belief that there exists a universal, market-based, purely 'economic' rationality, rooted in human nature, which, if allowed to function without impediment, will serve to maximize freedom, efficiency, wealth, and welfare. Neo-liberal policy agendas thus typically entail 'rolling back the state', the transformation of as many things as possible into private property capable of being transacted in markets (**privatization**), and the 'deregulation' of markets so as to allow the unfettered forces of supply and demand to regulate economic activity. In that the extension of the scope of 'free' markets is assumed to increase individual freedoms, neo-liberal policies are seen as freedom (as well as efficiency) enhancing.

Within neo-liberal theory, this autonomous economic rationality—that of 'the market'—is considered to be politically neutral and the 'economic' is treated as a spatially separate sphere from the political (and legal), hence the idea that states (spatially separate powers) 'intervene in' and 'regulate' markets (spatially separate economic spheres): from a neo-liberal perspective, '**regulation**' (political interferences in the self-regulating market) should be confined to instances of 'market failure'. Indeed, a key neo-liberal goal is the 'depoliticization' of the economic sphere and the promotion of the view that economic affairs involve technical, rather than political, issues. As a result, although neo-liberal economic ideas are frequently supplemented at the political level by a commitment to **democracy**, the marriage of (neo) liberalism with democracy (as in liberal democracy), rather than representing a harmonious unification of compatible ideals, is in reality fraught with tension. Indeed, from a neo-liberal perspective, there are few more potentially serious threats to the economic rationality of the market than those posed by 'unlimited democracy'. For neo-liberals, democracy must be contained, and rights (especially those to private property) protected, ideally by (quasi) constitutional means, hence the idea, popularized by international political economists such as Stephen Gill, of the 'New Constitutionalism'. Much neo-liberal policy is thus concerned with insulating 'economic' policy (and private property rights in particular) from 'political' interference and control. Indeed, like the Spencerian liberalism of the late nineteenth century, neo-liberal thinking is markedly economically determinist and Darwinian in character. Paralleling the biological evolution of the species, it suggests, there is at work a process of natural selection among productive units and among the practices, institutions and rules of different societies, in which only the most efficient survive and prosper, hence the idea that liberal capitalism represents 'the end of history' and that 'there is no alternative' ('TINA'). Within the legal academy, neo-liberal ideas of this sort are particularly prominent in the work of the law and economics movement.

The beliefs underpinning neoliberal ideas have been much criticized, not least by lawyers noting the socially (politically and legally) constructed nature of private property and exchange rights. Drawing on the work of Wesley Hohfeld, for example, Robert Lee Hale, a legal critic of early twentieth-century *laissez-faire*, observed that as property and exchange rights were to a significant extent legally constructed, there was no such thing as an 'unregulated' market operating according to a purely 'economic' rationality. Like private **property rights**, markets could be (and were) legally and politically constituted in many different ways, generating different rationalities and different distributional outcomes. From this perspective, markets are as much the products of regulation as they are the subjects of it. This, some argue, accounts in part for why neo-liberal policies have not generally resulted in smaller states despite the anti-state rhetoric that accompanies them.

Markets are also, Hale argued, not only realms in which people exercise their freedoms, but realms of coercion, in the sense that market participants, backed by the state, are able to use their rights (especially those to private property) to exercise coercive power over one another: they are 'structures of mutual coercion'. Views similar to Hale's find contemporary expression in the work of the economist, Ha-Joon Chang, a leading critic of modern neo-liberalism, who emphasizes the highly political nature of the property rights and other legal entitlements that neo-liberalism takes as given.

Recognition of the legally and politically constructed nature of property and markets has led some, like David Harvey, to argue that neo-liberalism is best seen as a political project to restore the power and wealth of capital and (financial) property-owning elites. This has been achieved, in significant part, by reconstructing market relations, by effecting radical changes to prevailing structures of legal rights so as to enhance the coercive market power of owners of capital and their institutional representatives. Thus, these critics argue, while the overall economic record of neo-liberalism may be poor, the widespread adoption of neo-liberal policy programmes has generated major increases in income and wealth inequality, both within and between nation states.

PADDY IRELAND

D Harvey, *A Brief History of Neoliberalism* (New York: Oxford University Press, 2005)

nervous shock   *see* **psychiatric damage**

neutrality   The law of neutrality concerns the rights and duties of states that do not participate in an international armed conflict. It exists to limit the conduct of hostilities; to regulate belligerents' conduct towards non-participating states; and to preserve the freedom of non-participating states to conduct their commercial activities during armed conflict. Temporary neutrality endures for the duration of armed conflict or until the neutral enters the conflict. A permanently neutral state must not enter into the conflict and must not compromise its neutral status during peacetime.

Rights and duties associated with neutrality come into effect if a non-participating state declares, or otherwise indicates, a decision to assume a status of neutrality. The neutral state is under a primary obligation of complete abstention from the conflict: it must not furnish belligerents with materials valuable to the prosecution of hostilities. The neutral state must prevent, by means at its disposal, belligerent conduct on its neutral territory. For example, it must prevent its neutral territory, ports, and territorial waters from being used as a base of belligerent operations, and must not permit the recruitment and raising of troops on its territory. It must intern all belligerent forces (except escaped prisoners of war) who enter its territory. It has the correlative right of inviolability from belligerent incursion into, or damage to, its neutral territory, airspace, or territorial waters. The neutral state is obliged to acquiesce in the exercise of belligerent rights: outside neutral territorial waters, a belligerent may intercept and search neutral merchant vessels for contraband, or may blockade an enemy state. The neutral state has an obligation to discharge its duties towards belligerents in an impartial manner.

While neutral states are required to take action to preserve the neutral character of the state and to behave impartially towards both belligerents, under traditional law they were not required to prevent the export and transit of war materials by private persons. With increasing state controls over arms production and export, the distinction between neutral states and neutral individuals in this area is no longer tenable. **Customary international law** suggests the development of a duty on the neutral state to prevent all export of war materials to belligerents.

The body of rules comprising the law of neutrality is contained in a variety of sources. The modern form of neutrality developed in customary international law in response to changes in the concept of just war, and reached its most detailed elaboration during the eighteenth and nineteenth centuries. In earlier centuries, a specific legal status of neutrality did not exist and non-participation in hostilities was governed largely by bilateral treaties. The customary rules of neutrality have been partially codified in numerous conventions: in the Paris Declaration

Respecting Maritime Law of 1856; in the Hague Conventions of 1907; in the Geneva Conventions of 1949; and in the first Additional Protocol to the Geneva Conventions of 1977.

The application of the law of neutrality in contemporary **international law** is uncertain due to the profound changes in the legal framework governing the recourse to armed force. The law of neutrality was traditionally applicable upon the existence of a state of war. Some writers suggest that this threshold of application endures in contemporary international law and that neutrality has no application to an international armed conflict that is not 'war' in either a formal or material sense. Others argue that the prohibition on the threat or use of force in contemporary international law destroys the basis for the law of neutrality and renders it inapplicable to any conflict. Customary international law, however, suggests that neutrality may apply in situations of protracted armed conflict not amounting to a formal or material state of war. Because the law of neutrality is not automatically applied but voluntarily assumed, current debate surrounds the legal status of states which choose not to participate directly in hostilities but decide not to assume neutral status, and whether belligerent rights are exercisable against them.

While neutrality is not abolished under the UN Charter, it is modified in situations where the UN Security Council takes binding enforcement measures under Chapter VII of the UN Charter. To the extent that a neutral state is required to discriminate between belligerents by a binding decision of the UN Security Council and therefore to depart from the duty of impartiality, neutrality may be said to be 'qualified.' However, a neutral state is under no duty to offer assistance to states acting in collective self-defence, or to modify its status of neutrality when the UN Security Council fails to take binding action.

JAMES UPCHER

S Neff, *The Rights and Duties of Neutrals* (Manchester: Manchester University Press, 2000)

See also: **international humanitarian law; sanctions in international law; war and armed conflict**

neutralization   *see* **neutrality**

New International Economic Order   *see* **international economic law**

new property   *see* **welfare rights**

New Zealand Accident Compensation Scheme   *see* **compensation; tort system**

New Zealand law *see* **Commonwealth Law**

Next Steps Agencies These agencies were established in the wake of the 1988 Efficiency Unit Report: *Improving Management in Government: the Next Steps* (the 'Ibbs Report'). The intention was to improve governmental efficiency by hiving off service-delivery functions from ministerial departments and giving them to agencies, leaving the department to focus on policy formulation. By the end of the millennium there were more than 100 Next Steps Agencies employing more than three-quarters of civil servants. This development is commonly included within the notions of the 'new public management' and the 'contractualization' of government.

The central thrust of the Ibbs Report was that agencies should perform executive functions of government within a policy and resources framework set by a department. It was anticipated that Ministers would be responsible for overall policy but that agency Chief Executives would have managerial autonomy and answer for delivery of services. Under the Next Steps arrangements (which were instituted without legislation) Ministers answer to Parliament for setting the policy framework for agencies by issuing Framework Documents. Departments maintain their traditional role in providing policy support to Ministers but also fulfil new roles in establishing and managing a policy and resources framework for agencies. Departments no longer offer those services designated for agency delivery 'at arms-length' from the Department. Agency Chief Executives are responsible for execution of the policies and delivery of the services outlined in the relevant Framework Documents and annual performance targets. They are accountable to Ministers (and appear before Select Committees) but make their own managerial decisions within a regime that is contractually-rather than command-based.

It has been said that this 'agencification' of government improved many managerial and service-delivery systems. But it has also raised a number of contentious issues, notably concerning: lines of accountability and responsibility for decisions that relate to both policy and service-delivery; the feasibility of separating out policy from delivery; and the potential inefficiencies, uncertainties, and confusions that can result from departmental and ministerial interference in agency activities.

ROBERT BALDWIN

NHS Litigation Authority Although the NHS Litigation Authority ('NHSLA') is not technically an insurer, its main function is to handle legal claims against NHS hospitals and primary-care providers, and to meet successful claims out of a fund to which all NHS bodies make contributions assessed actuarially to reflect the liability **risk** presented by each. The NHSLA was established in 1995, before which NHS bodies handled their own claims. In 2006–2007 more than 60 per cent of the 8,719 claims received by the NHSLA related to medical treatment, while the rest concerned various 'non-clinical' matters such as injuries suffered by NHS employees and members of the public in accidents on NHS premises. In 2006–2007, the NHSLA paid out about £579 million to meet clinical claims, and about £34 million to meet non-clinical claims. In addition to handling the legal liabilities of NHS bodies, the NHSLA also, in effect, provides them with insurance against other types of loss, such as damage to their property. In 2006–2007 about £4 million was paid out on this account. In that year the NHSLA estimated that the potential total cost (spread over many years) of claims already made or in the pipeline was around £9 billion. Besides its insurance-like functions, the NHSLA sets and monitors compliance with risk-management standards for NHS activities, provides NHS bodies with advice on **equal pay** claims and the impact on their activities of the **Human Rights Act 1998**, and runs the Family Health Services Appeal Unit, the main function of which is to resolve disputes between Primary Care Trusts (such as GPs) and their existing and would-be service-providers (such as hospitals).

PETER CANE

See also: **medical negligence; tort system**

Nicaragua case In 1984 Nicaragua filed an application with the International Court of Justice asking the Court to declare that the United States of America was unlawfully encouraging, assisting, and directing military and paramilitary activities against Nicaragua, chiefly through its support for the 'contras' who sought to overthrow the Sandinista Government in Nicaragua. The case was brought on the basis of a dispute settlement clause in a 1956 bilateral Nicaragua-US treaty and of Article 36(2) of the Court's Statute. The United States contested the Court's jurisdiction in the 1984 jurisdiction phase of the case. The United States had amended its Declaration accepting the Court's jurisdiction under Article 36(2) very shortly before Nicaragua filed its application, so as to exclude the Court's jurisdiction over disputes with Central American States. The Court held, however, that the amendment would take effect only after the six-month period of notice that was specified in the Declaration. Accordingly, the amendment did not exclude the case from the Court's jurisdiction. The United States did not participate in the 1986 phase of the case in which the merits of Nicaragua's claim were addressed.

The Court's judgment on the merits contained a detailed analysis of the legal responsibility of States for acts of assistance to armed groups acting against other States and found that the United States had unlawfully used force against Nicaragua and violated its sovereignty. In particular, it clarified the degree of direction and control necessary to render acts imputable to a State, finding that alleged violations of **international humanitarian law** by the contras were not imputable to the US. The Court, did, however, find that the US had unlawfully used force against Nicaragua by training, equipping, and financing the contras and supporting military and paramilitary activities against Nicaragua. It rejected US claims to be acting in collective self defence against attacks by Nicaragua because, though unlawful, alleged supplies by Nicaragua to armed groups in other states did not amount to 'armed attacks', against which a right of self defence would exist. While those other states were entitled themselves to take proportionate counter-measures against any such unlawful Nicaraguan activity, the Court held that there is no right to take collective counter-measures akin to the right of collective self defence: action may be taken only by the victim. It is not altogether clear that these delicate distinctions will survive in the rough environment of state practice.

While the Court's judgment was not accepted by the United States' government, it proved an important element in the focusing and strengthening of opposition to the US Congress to US involvement in Nicaragua.   VAUGHAN LOWE

See also: **responsibility, state**

non-aligned movement   *see* **United Nations**

non-contributory benefits   These are a range of benefits in the **social security system**, eligibility for which is in no way dependent upon paying any contributions into the National Insurance Fund. The level of one's insurance record, or the lack of one at all, is quite simply immaterial. Some non-contributory benefits are payable regardless of means. Others are means-tested in that they will not be payable to those with more than a certain amount of income each week or those with capital above a certain amount. One example of the non-means tested category is child benefit, payable to a

person responsible for a child. Another example is disability benefits.

Non-contributory benefits were introduced to cover a group which did not really figure in Beveridge's predictions or system, and provide assistance to a group many of whom never get a chance of a job and of contributing to the insurance system. Incapacity benefit (replacing severe disablement allowance) is payable without a contribution record to those incapacitated in youth (below 20 and, sometimes, 25). Disability living allowance is a benefit payable to disabled people to give some help with the extra costs that disability brings; it has a care component and a mobility component. Its predecessors were attendance allowance and mobility allowance. Industrial injuries benefits (worker's compensation) are also non-contributory. In the means-tested category of non-contributory benefits come income support, state pension credit, jobseeker's allowance, and payments under the Social Fund. Tax Credits for those in low-paid work are also in this category.

DAVID BONNER

See also: **national insurance**

non-governmental organizations   Non-governmental organizations ('NGOs') are a manifestation of the broader concept of civil society. They are defined primarily by what they are not: they are not established by a government or by inter-governmental agreement and their resources should come primarily from voluntary contributions. They are generally private bodies, established under the domestic law of a state, and have an internal mandate. Their members are private individuals or corporate bodies. They may operate solely or primarily in a single state (national NGOs) or across a number of states (international NGOs). Such general criteria provide a broad umbrella for a range of institutional arrangements the interests, strategies, target audiences, and objectives of which do not necessarily coincide.

NGOs alone among civil society actors are given international legal status by the **United Nations** ('UN') Charter. Article 71 provides that the Economic and Social Council 'may make arrangements for consultation with non-governmental organisations which are concerned with matters within its competence'. Consultative status allows NGOs to contribute to the work of the UN in various ways including providing technical expertise, accessing UN meetings and, under specified circumstances, making interventions. Since 1945 the number of international NGOs has expanded exponentially, and there are over 2,700 NGOs with consultative status. Their mandates vary enormously. Although the term is often used to describe organizations with humanitarian or social justice 'public' objectives, such as those relating to the promotion of human rights (eg Amnesty International and Human Rights Watch) and environmental standards (eg Greenpeace), development (eg Oxfam) and disarmament (eg Lawyers and Physicians against Nuclear Arms), it also covers such diverse associations as those representing commercial interests (eg the International Chamber of Commerce), academic interests, religious affiliations (eg the World Muslim Congress), women's groups and professional interests.

International NGOs use their consultative status to influence international standard-setting through lobbying and advocacy at the national level and accessing the law-making activities of international institutions. Networking and coalition building are facilitated by electronic communications and the internet, allowing participation by members who cannot attend meetings. NGOs have been widely credited with the adoption of international treaties, such as the Convention on the Rights of the Child (1989), the Rome Statute of the International Criminal Court (1998), and the Landmines Convention (1997). They also participated in large numbers in the global summit meetings that were prominent throughout the 1990s such as those on the environment (1992), human rights (1993), population and development (1994), and women (1995). Accredited NGOs held parallel forums with workshops, lectures, demonstrations, and numerous other activities, and sought to influence the wording of the Declarations and Programmes of Action, adopted by states. NGOs are also credited with stopping the negotiation of certain treaties, such as the proposed Multilateral Agreement on Investment in 1998. The internet provided an organizing tool and a site for mobilizing sufficient antagonism to the Agreement to make it politically unacceptable.

Consultative status was the first formal step into the UN for NGOs and the starting point for their much greater influence today. The language of consultative status has since shifted to that of partnership at the conceptual, operational, and economic levels. The UN General Assembly in its 2005 consideration of UN reform stressed the importance of continued engagement between governments, NGOs, the private sector, and other civil society bodies.

CHRISTINE CHINKIN

S Charnovitz, 'Non-Governmental Organizations and International Law' (2006) 100 *American Journal of International Law* 348

P Willetts (ed), 'The Conscience of the World' The Influence of Non-Governmental Organisations in the UN System (London: Hurst, 1996)

non-proliferation treaty   *see* **arms control**

non-recognition in international law   *see* **recognition of states and governments**

nonsense on stilts?   *see* **human rights scepticism**

North American Free Trade Area (NAFTA)
   see **international economic law**

Northern Ireland Assembly   The Northern Ireland Assembly was established under the terms of the Northern Ireland Act 1998, which was 'An Act to make new provision for the government of Northern Ireland for the purpose of implementing the agreement reached at multi-party talks on Northern Ireland set out in Command Paper 3883'. Precursors to the current Assembly were the devolved Parliament which operated in Northern Ireland from 1921–1972, the abortive 'Sunningdale' power-sharing assembly (1973–1974) and 'rolling devolution' assembly (1982–1986).

The powers and remit of the Northern Ireland Assembly and the model of devolution are similar to that of the other regional assemblies. However, the Assembly and the Northern Ireland Act 1998, unlike their counterparts in Scotland and Wales, were not simply a product of a UK-wide move to devolution, but must also be understood in the context of the Northern Irish peace process and the Belfast or **Good Friday Agreement** in which the Assembly's make-up and powers were negotiated. As a result, the Northern Ireland Assembly has some distinctive features. In particular it has a shared 'Office of the First and Deputy First Minister'; proportional representation in the electoral system; a power-sharing executive made up of the major parties according to their proportion of the vote; and a cross-community voting mechanism for 'key decisions' that require the support of a majority of both unionists and nationalists (all politicians must specify themselves as 'unionist', 'nationalist', or 'other'), in addition to an overall majority of Assembly members. In addition, there were further human rights safeguards provided for, including a Human Rights Commission. These mechanisms are described by political scientists as 'consociational', and are often used in some form in situations of ethnic division. A second set of distinctive features reflects the bi-national nature of the agreement. In particular, the executive must form North–South Ministerial Councils with the Republic of Ireland government, and there is provision for a British-Irish Council and British-Irish Intergovernmental Conference. The operation of the power-sharing Assembly and the cross-border bodies are linked (neither can operate on its own) in what has been termed 'a mutually assured destruction clause'.

The first Assembly elections were held in June 1998. However, the initial Executive formation was delayed until November 1999, and then was controversially suspended in February 2000, again for ten days in August and around a month in September 2001, and from October 2002 until May 2007. New negotiations between the governments and the parties saw legislative changes to the Assembly's functioning, with new elections to the Assembly taking place in March 2007, and the restoration of devolved power and the Assembly itself on 8 May 2007.

CHRISTINE BELL

C McCrudden , 'Northern Ireland, the Belfast Agreement, and the British Constitution' in J Jowell and D Oliver (eds), *The Changing Constitution* (Oxford: Oxford University Press, 5th edn, 2004)

C Bell, *Peace Agreements and Human Rights* (Oxford: Oxford University Press, 2000), 134–143

See also: **devolution; Scottish Parliament; Welsh Assembly**

Northern Ireland law Northern Ireland law is similar but not identical to that of England and Wales. When the Act of Union created the **United Kingdom** of Great Britain and Ireland in 1801 there were already some differences between the laws applicable in the two islands; and throughout the nineteenth century not all laws passed at Westminster applied uniformly across the land. The Government of Ireland Act 1920 partitioned Ireland, the southern part becoming the Irish Free State (and, in 1949, the completely independent Republic of Ireland) and the Northern part remaining a constituent part of the United Kingdom. The Act gave Northern Ireland its own government, subordinate bicameral Parliament and court system.

The powers of the Parliament in Belfast were limited to the 'peace, order and good government' of Northern Ireland. Other legislative powers stayed with Westminster. Until 1972, when it was suspended and then prorogued because of serious civil unrest, the Northern Ireland Parliament passed much primary and secondary legislation which mirrored legislation passed a few years earlier at Westminster. In some areas of law, however, especially land law and family law, the English model was not followed. The Law of

Property Act 1925, for instance, was never mirrored in Northern Ireland

From 1972 to 1999 nearly all of Northern Ireland's legislation was approved by Parliament at Westminster in the form of Orders in Council. Again, most of these Orders were Northern Ireland equivalents to Acts, or parts of Acts, already passed for England and Wales (eg the Companies (NI) Order 1986 and the Children (NI) Order 1995). After the **Good Friday Agreement** of 1998 a new **Northern Ireland Assembly** and Executive were created in 1999, but due to difficulties with the peace process both institutions were at times suspended, in particular from October 2002. Following further talks they were eventually restored in May 2007 and a period of legislative stability looked to be on the cards. The Secretary of State for Northern Ireland retains responsibility for non-devolved matters at Westminster, which include criminal justice and policing.

Northern Ireland is a more conservative and less diverse society than England and Wales. It has usually been relatively slow to accept liberal reforms: divorce became possible only in 1939, homosexuality was not decriminalized until 1982 (following the judgment of the **European Court of Human Rights** in *Dudgeon v UK*), race discrimination became unlawful only in 1997, gay and lesbian couples still cannot adopt children, and abortion is permitted only where it is necessary to save the life of the mother or where continuation of the pregnancy would involve risk of serious injury to her physical or mental health. But many laws have been passed to deal with the specific problems of Northern Ireland. There has been extensive 'emergency' law in place ever since the partition of Ireland (the Civil Authorities (Special Powers) Acts 1922–1932 were notoriously draconian), but most of this has recently been replaced by UK-wide anti-**terrorism** legislation. Juryless 'Diplock' courts were used to try terrorist suspects between 1973 and 2007. Legislation has existed since 1976 to deal with discrimination on grounds of religious or political belief in the workplace (except in the appointment of teachers) and, since 1989, in access to services; and positive discrimination measures are in place to allow more Catholics to be appointed as police officers. All elections in Northern Ireland, except for seats at Westminster, are based on single transferable vote ('STV') proportional representation, while the so-called d'Hondt system ensures that ministerial portfolios are distributed on a power-sharing basis.

The substance of Northern Ireland's criminal law, **contract law**, **tort law**, consumer law, commercial law, employment law, welfare law, and succession law is almost completely identical to that of England and

Wales. In family law and property law there are more significant differences: eg the 'quickie' divorce system has not yet been introduced, and reforms to the way in which land can be held and transferred have not been implemented. There are also some procedural differences when cases are taken to court. Northern Ireland has its own Police Ombudsman (with more extensive powers than virtually any other police complaints office in the world), an Equality Commission, and a Human Rights Commission, and various bodies dealing with peculiar problems in Northern Ireland, such as the Parades Commission, the Community Relations Council and the Independent Monitoring Commission (to report on activities of unlawful paramilitary organizations). The Police Service of Northern Ireland replaced the Royal Ulster Constabulary in 2001 following a series of recommendations in the report of the Independent Commission on Policing (the Patten Report). However there is still no environmental protection agency for Northern Ireland. There are still rates, as opposed to a **council tax**.

The court system of Northern Ireland displays a few minor differences from that of England and Wales. Magistrates' courts are staffed by salaried qualified lawyers called 'Resident Magistrates', with supplementary 'lay magistrates' being used mainly in criminal cases involving young people. In criminal cases, appeals lie from magistrates to county courts, not—as in England and Wales—to the Divisional Court of the Queen's Bench Division. Appeals lie to the **House of Lords** in the same circumstances as in England and Wales, there being three or four such appeals each year. The head of Northern Ireland's legal system is the Lord Chief Justice of Northern Ireland, who is now customarily appointed in due course as a Lord of Appeal in London. There is no **Master of the Rolls**.

Cases can be referred from **courts** and **tribunals** in Northern Ireland to the **European Court of Justice** in the same way as in England and Wales, and the Human Rights Act 1998 applies in Northern Ireland exactly as it does elsewhere in the United Kingdom. Northern Ireland's tribunal system is partly home grown (in the fields of employment and social security) and partly integrated with systems used in the rest of the UK (eg in the fields of taxation and immigration). Coroners operate under slightly different rules, as does the Ombudsman.

BRICE DICKSON

See also: **devolution**

Notable British Trials series   The *Notable British Trials* series was a phenomenally successful collection of books on famous trials published by Edinburgh publishers, William Hodge, between 1905 and 1959. In all a total of eighty-three volumes were published in the series (including volumes on the **Nuremberg Trials**), some of which went through several editions. They are an important, if neglected, form of legal literature.

The structure of each volume mimicked the distinction between fact and opinion in law, presenting the reader with the facts and evidence in the case to allow them to make their own judgment. Each volume contained the complete transcript of the trial, including a record of cross-examination, the evidence of all witnesses, and speeches by counsel and the trial judge—and often such bonuses as the police photograph of the murder weapon and detailed plans of the scene of the crime. In the case of many of the older trials, which may have been rather short, there would often be included appendices containing contemporary pamphlets or other ephemera. Each trial was preceded by a lengthy introduction from the editor setting out a narrative account of both the crime and its detection, as well as providing a guide to the evidence, legal argument, and social context. Many of the introductions attained a classic status, being published and republished in a series of Penguin books on notable trials, itself running to ten volumes. The format spawned many imitators before the publication of trials eventually began to decline in the latter half of the twentieth century.

LINDSAY FARMER

notice of termination of employment   Where an employer wishes to dismiss an employee on notice, the first question is what the **contract of employment** says about this. Contracts of employment used often to be made orally. This is now less common, especially because employers are required to give written particulars of the main terms and conditions of employment, or of any changes. Even still, ascertaining exactly what the contract permits or requires in any given situation can be complicated. For example, a working relationship might have changed over **time**, or its terms may be contained in a wide variety of documents like **collective agreements** or works handbooks.

In the typical case, nevertheless, it is usual to find that both employer and employee have an express contractual power to terminate on notice. Even if not expressed, such a power will frequently be implied by the **courts**. Great care should be exercised, however, to determine if there are steps an employer (particularly) is contractually required to take before the notice power can lawfully be invoked. For example, it is not unusual to find an express disciplinary procedure that employers must observe before giving notice. Even absent an express contractual procedure, there may be implied contractual obligations of either a procedural or substantive nature. Particular caution is needed where dismissal would have deleterious consequences on an employee's access to health or other benefits. Finally, employers should be mindful of the statutory minimum notice periods that apply whatever a notice clause says about duration.

There are situations, however, where, even though this has not been expressly agreed, dismissal without notice, known as summary dismissal, will not breach the contract. Where an employee has committed a fundamental, or repudiatory, breach, the employer has a **common law** right to treat the contract as immediately at an end. It cannot be stressed enough, however, that it has become risky for employers to rely on this aspect of the common law. For example, modern employment contracts often spell out when employees will be liable to summary dismissal. Paradoxically, this can circumscribe employers' common law entitlement to treat contracts as summarily terminated.

Three important closing points should be made. Even if a dismissal on notice is not a breach of contract, the employee may have one or more statutory claims, including for **unfair dismissal**. Secondly, it is not uncommon for employers to dismiss on notice but not then to require the employee actually to work. Arrangements are sometimes made for this *ad hoc*, or the contract might have catered for this situation. Finally, an employment contract without an express or implied notice term will typically be for a fixed term. Such contracts can be immensely valuable to employees. This is because an employer who terminates prematurely will be liable to pay wages for the unexpired contract term subject to the employee's duty to mitigate their loss. This explains why this kind of contract tends to be encountered in high status, insecure work contexts.

LIZZIE BARMES

no-win, no-fee arrangements No-win, no-fee arrangements have become an important part of the litigation landscape in England and Wales over the last decade. In essence, they are arrangements between a solicitor and a client which stipulate that the lawyer will receive no fee for services if the litigation fails. In other words, the lawyer takes a financial stake in the outcome of the litigation, and therefore bears a financial risk from losing the case. Normally, therefore, some 'reward' is required on winning cases to induce the lawyer to take on this risk.

To understand the background to the emergence of the no-win, no-fee arrangement as the dominant source of funding for civil proceedings in England and Wales, and to understand the problems it has introduced into the legal services market, it is necessary to go back to the 1980s, at which time such arrangements were actually unenforceable (as a consequence of legislation dating back to the reign of Edward I). At the end of the 1980s, the financial risk of litigation was borne by the client, who may or may not have been entitled to **legal aid**. In the face of ever increasing legal aid costs, and against a political emphasis on privatization and market liberalization, successive governments were at that time looking to alternative ways of funding legal actions. In 1989, the Lord Chancellor's Department published a series of Green Papers on legal reform, one of which specifically looked into the possibilities of legalizing US style 'contingency fees' in England and Wales. These are no-win, no-fee arrangements where the lawyer's reward is directly related to the outcome of the litigation—that is, where the lawyer stipulates a percentage of the damages won as the fee prior to agreeing to represent the client. The Green Paper considered this option for the England and Wales, but in the face of significant objections based on arguments that they would produce excessive fees and excessive litigation, recommended instead a hybrid type of no-win, no-fee arrangement, in which the lawyer would receive an agreed percentage mark-up on the usual hourly fee if the case was won, and no fee if the case was lost. This hybrid fee type was termed a 'conditional fee agreement' ('CFA').

CFAs were subsequently introduced by the Courts and Legal Services Act 1990, which made provision for agreements specified by Order by the Lord Chancellor in which it was explicit that part or all of the legal representative's fees were payable only in the event of a successful outcome, subject to a maximum percentage by which normal fees may be increased (the 'success fee'). The first such Order was brought into force on 5 July 1995 and was subsequently extended in 1998 to all civil proceedings, other than family cases. The Law Society produced guidance for solicitors about the use of CFAs and a model agreement for use between clients and solicitors. It advised solicitors to apply a voluntary limit of 25 per cent on the proportion of damages which a success fee should represent. It is important to recognize that the success fee was at the time not recoverable from the defendant, and this limit was therefore introduced to prevent clients from seeing the majority of their damages lost to legal fees.

Moreover, while a CFA removed the client's risk of having to pay their own legal representative when a case was lost, it did not remove the obligation under English law to pay the other side's legal costs. Consequently an insurance product emerged, known as an 'after the event' ('ATE') legal costs policy, which was typically bought from an insurer on behalf of the client by the solicitor. In spite of this development, and the limit on the success fee as a proportion of damages, the take-up of CFAs was not seen as being sufficient to deliver the objective of allowing legal aid to be completely withdrawn from personal injury litigation, and pressure was brought to make both the success fee and the ATE insurance premium recoverable from the defendant.

The Access to Justice Act 1999 made the winning party's success fee and ATE insurance premium potentially recoverable from the other side when the claim was successful. These apparently innocuous changes, which were introduced almost simultaneously with major reforms to civil procedure, have had large (and perhaps unanticipated) consequences for the way in which legal costs are agreed between parties following a claim for damages in England and Wales. To begin with, the changes introduced by the 1999 Act explicitly shifted the litigation cost risk (ie the cost consequences of losing a case) from the claimant to the defendant, or more typically to a liability insurer acting on the defendant's behalf. This meant that, for the first time, liability insurers were directly involved in decisions by lawyers that affected the litigation cost risk, in that they were being asked to pay sums of money that were based, not on actual amounts spent, but on an assessment of the risk of failure and the expected costs of that failure.

In addition, the growth in the ATE insurance market following the introduction of recoverable CFAs saw the emergence of so-called 'accident intermediaries' such as Claims Direct and The Accident Group ('TAG'), whose business models involved a combination of loans to clients and ATE premiums which incorporated an element of advertising and profits. As a consequence of these developments, liability insurers recognized a need to strengthen the monitoring process by which costs were negotiated; and indeed, many of them appointed so-called 'cost negotiators' to review, not only the actual costs and disbursements, but also the success fees and ATE premiums being claimed. In many cases, it began to emerge that the size of the success fees and ATE premiums were being disputed, and a period of litigation over costs ('satellite litigation') ensued. The situation became critical, both for the accident intermediaries

(several of which went out of business), and for those claimant solicitors who were faced with substantial delays over the settlement of costs. Eventually the Civil Justice Council (the body set up to oversee the civil justice reforms referred to earlier) was forced to intervene and attempt to obtain a mediated agreement over what would be an acceptable (and proportionate) level of costs for the large volume category of low value road traffic accident ('RTA') cases in order to introduce a degree of predictability into what had suddenly become somewhat unpredictable.

Despite the turbulence in the market, it is now true that the majority of personal injury claims in England and Wales are funded via CFAs. Recent research (P Fenn, A Gray, N Rickman and Y Mansur, *The funding of personal injury litigation: comparisons over time and across jurisdictions* (London: Department of Constitutional Affairs Research Series, January, 2006)) found that 91 per cent of personal injury claims opened between 1 October 2002 and 30 September 2003 were funded by some form of CFA. The CFA market was dominated by bulk purchasers of legal services: 26 per cent of new CFA claims were referred through accident intermediaries, 25 per cent through **trades unions**, and 8 per cent through legal expenses insurers.

These developments have attracted some negative commentary. A report from Citizens Advice (P Sandbach, *No win, no fee, no chance—Access to personal injury compensation and the problem of a largely unregulated market for handling personal injury cases* (London: Citizens Advice, 2004)) was critical of the complexity of CFAs and ATE insurance, the poor advice received from accident intermediaries, and the increasing costs of claiming. In spite of the emergent importance of this type of funding arrangement, very little empirical work had been undertaken on the impact of CFAs on litigation behaviour. Yarrow (S Yarrow, *The Price of Success: Lawyers, Clients and Conditional Fees* (London: Policy Studies Institute, 1997) and Yarrow and Abrams (S Yarrow and P Abrams, *Nothing to lose? Clients' experience of conditional fees* (London: University of Westminster, 1998)) used survey data to explore the claimant's experience of CFAs, while two studies for the Department of Constitutional Affairs collected quantitative data from solicitors on CFA claims both before and after the Access to Justice Act 1999 (Fenn *et al*, above and P Fenn, A Gray, N Rickman and H Carrier, *The Impact of Conditional Fees on the Selection, Handling and Outcomes of Personal Injury Cases* (London: Lord Chancellor's Department Research Series, London, July, 2002)). In these studies no evidence was found to show that CFAs were encouraging 'weaker' claims to be made by comparison with other types of funding.

It has been suggested that the fall in the number of personal injury claims made in recent years could be linked to the switch from legal aid funding to CFAs. In fact, the evidence for this is weak: in general accident claims have been falling for some time due to a decline in the underlying risks. As far as the apparent upwards trend in legal costs associated with claiming is concerned, this would indeed appear to be partly due to the new funding arrangements and the accident intermediaries which have emerged in their wake. However, it is important to bear in mind that some increase in cost would be inevitable as a consequence of the removal of legal aid, and the need to induce lawyers to accept the risk and supply the market. Finally, it is also important to recognize that the new funding arrangements have been introduced simultaneously alongside major reforms to the operation of civil justice procedure, and care is needed to ensure that the consequences of one are not attributed to the other.

PAUL FENN

HM Kritzer, *Risks, Reputations, and Rewards: Contingency Fee Legal Practice in the United States* (Stanford, CA: Stanford Law and Politics, 2004)

See also: **costs of complaining and claiming; lawyers, remuneration and funding of**

Nuclear Tests case   In May 1973 Australia and New Zealand brought claims against France before the International Court of Justice, relying on the jurisdictional provisions in the 1927 General Act for the Pacific Settlement of International Disputes and Article 36 of the Court's Statute. They sought a declaration from the Court that the carrying out of atmospheric nuclear weapons tests in the South Pacific Ocean is not consistent with **international law**. France did not participate in the proceedings or file any formal written pleadings in the case.

After the filing of the claim, and after the hearing of the case in 1974, the President, the Minister of Foreign Affairs, and the Minister of Defence of France all made public statements in which they indicated that the atmospheric weapons tests then taking place were the last, and that future tests would be carried out underground. These statements were treated by the International Court as unilateral declarations, legally binding upon France because they were made publicly and with the intention that France should be bound by them. The Court stated that nothing in the nature of a *quid pro quo*, nor any subsequent acceptance of the declaration, nor even any reply or reaction from other states, was necessary for the declaration

to take effect. Accordingly, the declarations having been made, the Court declared the applications by Australia and New Zealand to be moot, and declined to rule upon them.

The decisions were much criticized because the Court adduced no evidence to support either the rule of law concerning unilateral regulations on which it purported to rely, or its finding that France had intended to enter into binding legal obligations by making the statements. The decisions were widely regarded as a device by which the Court avoided having to rule against an absent respondent state which was not expected to submit to the legal force of any ruling the Court might make. The passage in the judgments concerning the legal effects of unilateral acts was distinguished practically out of existence by another decision of the Court in 1986.

VAUGHAN LOWE

nuclear weapons   *see* **arms control**

nuisance   The term 'nuisance', as a legal expression, primarily connotes a tort the function of which is to protect those legally entitled to occupy land from interference inhibiting them from making full use of their land for all normal purposes. The interference may take the form of physical damage, such as the undermining of buildings by encroaching tree roots, or inconvenience or discomfort caused by such factors as noise or smell. The interferer will usually be the occupier of the neighbouring land from which the nuisance emanates. In addition to its primary usage, commonly referred to as 'private' nuisance, the term is also used to denote the two related concepts of 'public' and 'statutory' nuisance. The former, which is a crime as well as a tort, may be either a private nuisance on a particularly large scale, affecting many neighbouring occupiers, or an interference with the safety and convenience of the public in another context such as use of the highway. 'Statutory' nuisances are situations, most of which will also involve private nuisances, in which a summary remedy is available to deal with the more common types of interference.

In assessing for the purposes of private nuisance whether inconvenience or discomfort suffered by the claimant is actionable, a balance must be struck between the interests of the claimant and the interferer taking into account factors such as locality and any abnormal sensitivity of the claimant. The defence that the interference was authorized by statute may be available in certain cases; but the interferer cannot argue in defence that the claimant 'came to the nuisance' by choosing to occupy land adjacent to that of the interferer with knowledge of the latter's activities. Moreover, activities embarked upon with the deliberate intention of annoying the claimant may amount to a nuisance, particularly in cases involving noise, even though the same level of interference might have had to be tolerated in other circumstances.

The remedies available in private nuisance cases include **injunction**s, to restrain the interferer from continuing to interfere with the claimant's enjoyment of the property, damages, and abatement. The latter is a form of self-help, permitted in straightforward cases where the victim of the nuisance is able to bring it to an end by simple measures, such as cutting branches from a neighbour's overhanging trees.

In cases where compensation is sought for actual damage to property, often as a result of flooding or land erosion, uncertainty has sometimes arisen as to whether *fault* on the interferer's part is necessary for liability. This uncertainty has now largely been resolved in favour of applying the concept of foreseeability (was the damage foreseeable?), from the tort of negligence, in preference to older notions of strict liability. The influence of negligence has also limited significantly the scope of the nineteenth-century 'rule in **Rylands v Fletcher**', which had its origins in the law of nuisance. This rule may nevertheless still enable claimants, unable to prove negligence, to recover compensation when dangerous substances escape from another's land and cause damage to their property.   RICHARD BUCKLEY

See also: **negligence in civil law; strict civil liability**

Nuremberg trials In the wake of Germany's unconditional surrender on 8 May 1945, the four victorious powers of World War II—the United States, the Soviet Union, the **United Kingdom**, and France—staged the first international war crimes trial in human history in Nuremberg, Germany. In the Moscow Declaration of January 1945, the Allies resolved to return Nazi criminals to the countries 'in which their abominable deeds were done', but also to conduct an international trial of the major Nazi war criminals whose offences had 'no particular geographical localization'. Nuremberg was chosen for reasons both practical and symbolic. The Palace of Justice, Nuremberg's massive municipal courthouse, was one of the few structures of its kind to survive Allied bombing of German cities, and the city had played host to the gigantic Nazi party rallies immortalized in Leni Riefenstahl's propaganda film, *Triumph of the Will*.

The idea of trying leading Nazis was not uncontroversial. The British originally favoured a 'political solution'—the summary execution of two-dozen leading members of the Nazi apparatus. The British proposal enjoyed early Soviet support. Among the Americans, Henry Morgenthau, the Secretary of the Treasury, also prominently recommended that major war criminals be summarily executed, an idea originally accepted by President Roosevelt. The insistence upon, and design for, a trial came largely from Americans within the Department of War. Henry Stimson, the Secretary of War, insisted that a trial would apply, extend, and enforce principles of international law. The trial was also intended as collective pedagogy, instructing the citizens of both Germany and the Allied nations about the atrocities perpetrated by the Nazi state.

The trial of the major Nazi war criminals before the International Military Tribunal ('IMT') ran from 20 November 1945 until 1 October 1946. The legal basis of the trial was supplied by the London Charter of 8 August 1945, which established that each of the four Allied powers would be represented by a team of prosecutors responsible for handling an aspect of the case; the four Allies were likewise equally represented in the eight-member panel of judges. Sir Geoffrey Lawrence, a British Lord Justice of Appeal, served as the tribunal's president.

The trial was enormously complex, both as a logistical and legal matter. The sixty-five-page indictment charged twenty-two defendants with a spectacular range of offences, committed over the course of a decade and spread over the space of a continent. The twenty-one men in the dock—Martin Bormann was tried in absentia—included many of the leading functionaries of the defeated Nazi state. Although Hitler, SS chief Heinrich Himmler, and Propaganda Minister Joseph Goebbels had committed suicide, present were Hermann Goering, the former Reichmarschall and designated Hitler-successor; Joachin Rippentropp, the foreign minister; Wilhelm Frick, the Reich's Minister of the Interior; Wilhelm Keitel, Chief of the German High Command; Ernst Kaltenbrunner, the Nazi's leading security officer; and Albert Speer, Hitler's architect and the Reich's minister for armaments and war production.

The defendants were charged with three substantive international crimes: first, crimes against peace, that is, waging a war of aggression in violation of international treaties; second, war crimes, which included the murder and ill-treatment of prisoners of war and other violations of the laws and customs of war; and third, crimes against humanity, which embraced extermination, enslavement, and other inhuman acts committed against civilian populations. The indictment also accused the defendants of engaging in a 'common plan or conspiracy' to perpetrate these substantive offences. Also adding to the complexity of the case, the prosecution sought to have six groups, including the entire SS and Gestapo, declared 'criminal organizations'. While such a declaration carried no punishment in the case of the major war criminals, it was intended to expedite the subsequent trials of thousands of other suspected offenders detained by the Allies.

The prosecution pursued a trial by document. Concerned that allegations of Nazi atrocity might be dismissed as propaganda, Chief Allied Prosecutor Robert H Jackson tactically structured the prosecution's case around captured documentary evidence, material considered 'harder' and more reliable than eyewitness testimony. The trial by document included thousands of captured written documents and still photographs, as well as film and other artifacts. This approach built solid cases against the defendants, nineteen of whom were convicted and twelve sentenced to death; it also established an archival trove that has proved invaluable to historians. The documentary approach disappointed many contemporaneous observers, however. Rebecca West, who covered the IMT for London's *Daily Telegraph,* famously called the trial a 'citadel of boredom'.

The IMT represented a radical innovation in the law's response to crimes of war. The trial marked the first time that waging aggressive war and committing crimes against humanity were formally recognized as crimes in international law. The novelty of these incriminations gave rise, though, to charges of 'victors' justice'. Of equal significance, the IMT revolutionized the international community's treatment of the question of responsibility, as it assigned 'individual responsibility' for the violations of international law under its purview. By rejecting an 'acts of state' plea, the IMT pierced a traditional shield of sovereignty, transforming international law into a tool capable of challenging the impunity of reprobate statesmen. Among its other accomplishments, the IMT offered a substantial, if imperfect, history of the Nazis' most extreme crime, the extermination of the Jewish population of Europe.

An *ad hoc* court, the IMT disbanded after the end of the trial. A plan to conduct a second trial of major war criminals was abandoned amid escalating cold war tensions. The Allies did, however, independently conduct smaller trials of lesser Nazi criminals before military courts in their respective occupation zones. The Americans, who controlled southern Germany, conducted a series of follow-up trials—twelve in total—in Nuremberg, the so-called Nuremberg Military Tribunals ('NMT'). These twelve proceedings included trials of former members of the Nazi justice, industrial, and medical establishment, as well as members of the Einsatzgruppen, the mobile extermination units responsible for the murder of over a million eastern European Jews.

LAWRENCE DOUGLAS

T Taylor, *The Anatomy of the Nuremberg Trials* (New York: Alfred A Knopf, 1992)

See also: **international criminal law; international humanitarian law; war and armed conflict; war crimes tribunals**

O

Oates, Titus Titus Oates (1649–1705) was born in 1649, the son of Samuel Oates, a baptist preacher who conformed to the restored Anglican Church at the Restoration. Titus was born physically ugly and his poor relationship with his father left him with an attention seeking personality. Oates was educated and later expelled from Merchant Taylor's School, London and then studied at Cambridge, but left without taking his degree; a fact that did not prevent him from misrepresenting to the Bishop of London that he was qualified to be ordained.

Oates' career as a clergyman began with his appointment as vicar at Bobbing, Kent in 1673. He was soon dismissed and took up the curacy of his father's parish of All Saints, Hastings. In 1675 Oates, whose reputation as a homosexual would follow him throughout his life, accused the schoolmaster William Parker of sodomizing a pupil. Oates calculated that this lie would allow him to take Parker's position and income. Oates was rewarded with a charge of perjury and fled to London, joining the Navy as a chaplain to avoid trial.

Oates was expelled from the Navy in 1676 for homosexuality and was arrested to face his perjury trial. He again escaped and was employed as chaplain to the Protestant staff of the Earl of Norwich. By March 1677 Oates had converted to Catholicism, although this conversion seems prompted by a greater opportunity for pecuniary advantage amongst Catholics rather than religious conviction. In April 1677 Oates attended the Jesuit College in Valladolid, Spain, but was soon expelled. Oates returned to England boasting a 'doctorate' from the University of Salamanca and found a position at the seminary at St Omer in December 1677. Oates was expelled in June 1678 and returned to London by July.

In London, Oates met the anti-Catholic polemicist Israel Tonge, to whom he gave depositions concerning a Catholic plot to kill Charles II and to turn England into a Papal puppet state. Oates was soon before the Privy Council and the House of Commons giving evidence. The aftermath of Oates' tall tale was the so-called 'Popish Plot' of 1678–1681, a ruse that led to thirty-five Catholics, including the Viscount Stafford, to be tried and executed for treason. Oates basked in his fame, declaring himself 'the Saviour of England'.

Oates' story was full of contradictions and fantasy and it was the then-prevalent fear of Catholic intrigue that allowed so many Catholics to be sentenced to death. The Popish Plot began to unravel when Oates lost a number of libel trials brought by some he had accused of involvement in the plot. He further discredited himself when he accused bastions of the Protestant establishment such as Lord Chief Justice Scroggs. In May 1685 he was tried and convicted of perjury, and was sentenced by Judge Jeffries to be whipped and pilloried, and to serve a life sentence.

With the coming of William III and the Glorious Revolution in 1688, Oates was released and given a modest pension; he died in 1706.

ELLIOT VERNON

See also: **Popish Plot**

obscenity The definition of what is 'obscene' under English law has its origins in *R v Hicklin* (1868), which adopted a test based on a 'tendency to deprave and corrupt'. A modified version of this test is currently used in relation to publications (including films, DVDs, internet publications) by virtue of the Obscene Publications Act 1959, and plays, by virtue of the Theatres Act 1968. According to the definition, a publication will be obscene if:

'its effect . . . is, if taken as a whole, such as to tend to deprave and corrupt persons who are likely, having regard to all relevant circumstances, to read, see or hear the matter contained or embodied in it.'

There is no requirement that the article was *intended* to deprave and corrupt—'obscenity depends on the article not the author'.

There are two main problems with this definition. First, who exactly has to be depraved and corrupted? Secondly, what is meant by 'deprave and corrupt'? As regards the first question, since it is 'likely' readers that must be considered, the context of publication may be important. If children are unlikely to see the material, its effect on them need not be considered. It has at times been held necessary that a 'significant proportion' of likely readers are likely to be affected, but the most recent ruling suggests that in a straightforward case it may not be necessary to consider this issue at all.

As regards the meaning of 'deprave and corrupt', case law on the Act shows that it means more than 'lead morally astray'. The required effect can be on the mind of the reader regardless of any change in behaviour. The effect can come from material dealing with violence, or drugs, as well as publications with a sexual content. Material which simply shocks and disgusts, however, will not tend to deprave and corrupt. All this leads to a very nebulous concept which it is hard to pin down. As a result, in practice, prosecutors no longer take action against the written word, and the focus is almost entirely on sexually explicit pictorial material, in the form of photographs, magazines, films, or websites. Material involving children, and/or violence, in a sexual context is particularly targeted. It is difficult to imagine that magistrates or a jury presented with such material spend long considering whether it tends to deprave and corrupt; an approach based on whether it goes beyond the limits of acceptable publication is much more likely to drive the conclusion as to whether it is or is not 'obscene'.

Both the Obscene Publications Act 1959 and the Theatres Act 1968 provide for a defence of 'public good'. This requires the defendant to prove that the work has artistic, literary, or scientific merit by virtue of which its publication will be for the public good. The existence of this defence is another reason why the focus of prosecutions tends to be on material which can have little claim to artistic or other merit, but is produced explicitly to excite the viewer. Any work which is produced with a more serious purpose is likely to be able to benefit from the public good defence.

The Obscene Publications Act 1959 does not apply in Scotland, but a similar control of obscene material is to be found in section 51 of the Civic Government (Scotland) Act 1982. The 'deprave and corrupt' definition is not in the section, but a similar approach has in practice been adopted. The **common law** offence of 'shameless indecency' has also been used in this context. RICHARD STONE

See also: **pornography**

obscenity trials *see* **Lady Chatterley's Lover; Oz trial**

occupation, belligerent Belligerent occupation occurs when one state invades foreign territory and exercises control over it through the deployment of its armed forces. Annexation of occupied territory before the formal conclusion of a conflict is unlawful, even if the entire territory of the adversary has been occupied.

The start of an occupation is essentially a question of fact. Article 42 of the Regulations annexed to the 1907 Hague Convention IV respecting the Laws and Customs of War on Land (which also have the status of **customary international law**) provides that 'territory is considered occupied when it is actually placed under the authority of the hostile army. The occupation extends only to the territory where such authority has been established and can be exercised'. In a 1949 decision, the US Military Tribunal ruled that 'an occupation indicates the exercise of governmental authority to the exclusion of the established government. This presupposes the destruction of organised resistance and the establishment of an administration to preserve law and order'. Nevertheless, in one case the **International Court of Justice** ruled that (Ugandan) occupation of (Congolese) territory would be established if its forces 'had substituted their own authority for that of the Congolese Government', and it would be irrelevant 'whether or not Uganda had established a structured military administration of the territory occupied'.

A belligerent occupant does not gain sovereignty over the territory it occupies, but simply exercises administrative control as a substitute for the displaced sovereign. Article 43 of the Hague Regulations provides that 'the authority of the legitimate power having in fact passed into the hands of the occupant, the latter shall take all the measures in his power to restore, and ensure, as far as possible, public order and safety, while respecting, unless absolutely prevented, the laws in force in the country'. This is the general basis for the occupant's duties towards the inhabitants of the territory which, apart from ensuring good governance, include ensuring food and medical supplies and maintaining hospitals and public health. Its powers to promulgate legislation for the territory are circumscribed and, in principle, should only comprehend laws and regulations which are necessary for reasons of military security.

As the occupant is only a temporary administrator, it must not exploit the territory to benefit its home economy or further its war aims. Thus private property may not be confiscated, although moveable property belonging to the state may be seized. By contrast, the occupant can only act as the administrator of public immoveable property, such as real estate and natural resource deposits. The aim of these rules is to remove economic incentives for armed conflict and to avoid the prolongation of occupation once hostilities have ceased.   IAIN SCOBBIE

E Benvenisti, *The International Law of Occupation* (Princeton, NJ: Princeton University Press, 1993)

G von Glahn, *The Occupation of Enemy Territory: A Commentary on the Law and Practice of Belligerent Occupation* (Minneapolis: University of Minnesota Press, 1957)

occupational pensions   *see* **pensions**

occupiers' liability   In broad terms, 'occupiers' liability' refers to the law governing the civil liability of an occupier in respect of the physical state of his property, or other activities that he carries on or permits to take place there. More specifically (and for the purpose of what follows) it means the area of civil law governing the liability of an occupier of premises for injury or damage suffered by those who enter them. The basis of occupiers' liability in this sense is fault: the occupier is liable in tort (or in Scotland, delict) if the damage or injury resulted from his negligence—or *a fortiori*, was caused by him recklessly or intentionally—but not otherwise. The basic principles are virtually the same as those that now govern liability for negligently inflicted injuries in general. However, this particular area of liability grew up before English law had come to accept that there is a general principle of liability for negligence, and in consequence the vocabulary and legal thought processes are slightly different. The status of occupiers' liability as something related to, but distinct from ordinary liability in negligence has been reinforced by the fact that, in all three jurisdictions, the rules governing liability have now been codified by statute: in England with the Occupiers' Liability Acts 1957 and 1984, in Northern Ireland with the Occupiers' Liability Act (Northern Ireland) 1957 and the Occupiers' Liability (Northern Ireland) Order 1987, and in Scotland with the Occupiers' Liability (Scotland) Act 1960. The major respect in which the rules governing occupiers' liability formerly differed from the rules of 'normal' liability in negligence involved liability towards trespassers. According to the **House of Lords** in *Addie v Dumbreck* (1929), an occupier was liable to a trespasser only if he injured him intentionally or recklessly—and towards trespassers he incurred no liability for negligence, however gross. Thus, where an occupier installed a haulage system operated by an endless cable passing at the far end around a wheel that was unfenced, and controlled from a point where the operator could not see if anyone was on or near it, the occupier was not liable when a trespassing **child** who was playing on the wheel got crushed when it was started. This rule

was thought to be unduly harsh, and was reversed by statute, first in Scotland in 1960, then in England in 1984, and finally in Northern Ireland in 1987. More recently, a major issue in occupiers' liability has been the liability (if any) of an occupier towards those who, with or without his permission, make use of his property for some obviously dangerous purpose, such as climbing trees, or diving into shallow water. In *Tomlinson v Congleton Borough Council* (2003), the House of Lords, reversing the Court of Appeal, held that there is no liability in such a case where the danger in question is obvious, and the visitor knew what he was doing: a decision which is reckoned to have struck a blow against the '**compensation culture**'.   J R SPENCER

See also: **civil liability, theories of; fault-based civil-liability; negligence in civil law**

OFCOM   *see* **communications regulation**

offences against property   *see* **criminal regulation of property relations**

offensive speech and behaviour   The legal regulation of speech and behaviour presents the law with one of its most enduring and difficult tasks of boundary setting. Lines must be drawn between rights to **freedom of expression** and speech (which would include behaviour constituting symbolic expression) on the one hand, and the rights of others to go about their lawful business without being unwillingly and unduly exposed to language and behaviour that they find objectionable. Underlying the tensions to which such conflicts give rise are various considerations that have to be taken into account. Concern for the preservation of public order frequently underlies attempts by the law to constrain the exercise of free speech, particularly where there are racial and religious dimensions. Free speech that is enormously provocative may give rise to outbreaks of public violence by those whose views are vilified and held up to contempt. Without legal protection or redress, those antagonized might resort to vigilantism to right perceived wrongs. But tolerance of the different views of others is integral to the proper functioning of a democratic society. In the words of Sedley LJ: 'Free speech includes not only the inoffensive but the irritating, the contentious, the eccentric, the heretical, the unwelcome and the provocative provided it does not tend to provoke violence. Freedom only to speak inoffensively is not worth having'.

The enactment of the **Human Rights Act 1998**, incorporating the right to freedom of expression in Article 10 of the **European Convention on**

Human Rights ('ECHR'), has altered the mechanism through which the **police** and the British **courts** must now mediate in disputed cases. In the past, the courts tended to defer to the judgment of the police on the spot as to the seriousness of the risky situation by which they were confronted. They were also inclined to employ a somewhat crude 'balancing' metaphor when free speech and public order were in conflict. Both the courts and the police are now obliged by ECHR jurisprudence to treat any exercise of freedom of expression as presumptively protected, subject to certain identified exceptions, which must be narrowly construed and which must meet the additional tests of proportionality and legal certainty. In a further departure from pre-Human Rights Act law, they must now, as part of that exercise, take into account the objectives and purposes of those engaging in the impugned behaviour. A person whose speech or behaviour was an exercise in unthinking or mindless rowdyism could not expect that the police (or the courts) would be particularly solicitous to protect such activity if it did in fact cause serious and needless offence. By way of contrast, the fact that the actors were actually seeking to engage in discussion (even very robust expressions of view that could easily be characterized as offensive) as part of the democratic exercise of the right of freedom of speech would be a strong factor in favour of treating the speech as being lawful until the contrary is proven.   ATH SMITH

Office for Judicial Complaints The Office for Judicial Complaints ('OJC') was established in April 2006 to support the **Lord Chancellor** and the **Lord Chief Justice** in their joint responsibility for the system of judicial complaints and discipline following the implementation of the Constitutional Reform Act 2005 and the Judicial Discipline (Prescribed Procedures) Regulations 2006. It is an associated office of the Ministry of Justice (formerly the Department for Constitutional Affairs). Its purpose is 'fairly, consistently, and efficiently' to consider and determine complaints about the personal conduct—for example the use of insulting, racist, or sexist language—of all judicial office holders in England and Wales and some judicial office holders who sit in **tribunals** in Scotland and Northern Ireland. Complaints relating to a judicial decision or a judge's management of particular case—the length or type of sentence imposed, appropriateness of evidence, and so on—fall outside the Office for Judicial Complaints' remit. Complaints must be made within twelve months of the conduct complained about. The actual complaint procedure differs slightly for each judicial

office. However, in all cases, if the Lord Chancellor and Lord Chief Justice—after consultation with the judge in question and reviewing the appropriate evidence (tape recordings, witness interviews, and so on)—agree to uphold the complaint they have the power to advise, warn, or remove a judge for misconduct and, in exceptional cases only, award an *ex gratia* compensatory payment to the complainant.

ERIKA RACKLEY

Office of Fair Trading The Office of Director or General of Fair Trading was created by the Fair Trading Act 1973. The Act reorganized the institutional structure of **competition** policy, giving the Office the primary role in monitoring **competition** regulation. It also gave the Office rule-making and oversight responsibilities in relation to **consumer** protection along with limited enforcement powers where traders persisted in unfair trading conduct. Bringing together competition and consumer law responsibilities in one agency underlined the legislative objective of making markets work better for consumers.

The creation of the Office was intended to provide continuity and expertise in the monitoring and **regulation** of consumer markets, taking these issues out of the political process. The intellectual inspirations for its creation included the US New Deal model of the administrative agency whose legitimacy and authority are based on technical expertise, and the Swedish Consumer Ombudsman. However, significant political control of merger references remained under the 1973 Act, and it was only in 2002 that the Enterprise Act substantially reduced the possibility of political intervention in **merger control** decisions. To replace the Office, the Enterprise Act also formally created the Office of Fair Trading ('OFT'), a non-ministerial government department, which is now governed by a board rather than a single Director General.

Like many agencies, the Office/OFT has gone through more and less active periods since its creation, often related to changes in government, political ideology, and assumptions about the optimal role of regulation. During the 1970s the Office was active in rule-making initiatives and the promotion of industry codes of practice to protect consumers. In the 1980s it focused on harnessing market incentives, lifting barriers to competition and adopting economic market failure analysis as a guide to policymaking. European initiatives in consumer policy during the 1990s resulted in new powers for the Office, including the enforcement of regulation of unfair terms in consumer contracts. The election of the New Labour government in 1997 with a commitment to the consumer interest and a crusade against 'rip off' Britain resulted in a substantial increase in resources for the Office in the early twenty-first century. The ascendancy of national competitiveness as an international goal, and consequent changes in the UK competition regime in 2002—which increased sanctions for anti-competitive activity as well as the powers of the OFT—mean that **competition law** and policy are central aspects of the contemporary work of the OFT.

Although the Office originally had limited enforcement powers in consumer law it now has a variety of administrative sanctions in addition to its broad licensing powers under the Consumer Credit Act 1974. Under the Enterprise Act 2002 it may bring actions for **injunctions** in other EU countries against businesses which contravene EU consumer protection directives and harm the collective interests of consumers. The OFT is also part of European and international networks of consumer enforcement agencies. The OFT is therefore a central actor in a web of national, regional, and international regulation of consumer markets.   IAIN RAMSAY

Office of Independent Adjudicator   *see* **universities and higher education**

official secrets   The origins of legislation making it a criminal offence to disclose official information lie in the failure during the nineteenth century to deal with a growing trend of leaking of official documents to newspapers by public servants. The Official Secrets Act 1889 made it an offence for Crown servants to disclose information, to a person to whom it should not have been communicated, to the detriment of the public. This legislation was little used but, during the Agadir crisis, with spy fever running high, Parliament replaced it with the notorious Official Secrets Act 1911. That Act proved altogether more useful to the authorities and more enduring (it remained in force until partially replaced with the current legislation in 1989). Similar legislation existed in Canada, India, Ireland, and New Zealand.

The 1911 Act created the offence of espionage, for which a number of infamous spies, such as George Blake (sentenced in 1961 for forty-two years for passing secrets to the Soviet Union) have been prosecuted. The Act also introduced a much broader offence of communicating official information (regardless of whether doing so was harmful). Such was the vague scope of the relevant provision (which included a sentence running to more than 300 words) that the Franks Committee remarked in 1972 that it created

no fewer than 2,134 different offences. The Act was increasingly criticized for over-breadth and for granting excessive protection to the executive, enabling the covering-up of politically embarrassing mistakes. It came to be seen as unworkable after a jury acquitted the Ministry of Defence official, Clive Ponting, in 1985 following his leaking of documents on the sinking of the Belgrano during the Falklands War. When the government attempted to suppress the book *Spycatcher*, written by a former MI5 Assistant Director, Peter Wright, it turned (unsuccessfully) to the civil law of breach of confidence instead, and reform of official secrets became inevitable.

The offences concerning unauthorized disclosure have been substantially narrowed and sharpened. The Official Secrets Act 1989 applies to all disclosures by officials working for the security and intelligence agencies, and to damaging disclosures by **Crown** servants and contractors concerning defence, foreign relations, and law enforcement. It also applies to people to whom such information is passed, including journalists. There are wide associated powers of **arrest** and search. Unlike earlier legislation, the Act contains no defence that disclosure was in the public interest. Uncertainty over the availability of the defence of duress of circumstances has, however, led to suggestions that it should be revised.

Concern over the sensitivity of material disclosed in court during an official secrets prosecution has led to unusual procedural protections. Prosecutions require the consent of the **Attorney-General**. Trials may be held *in camera*, with only the sentence being passed in open court. Moreover, during the 1970s and 1980s details emerged of the controversial practice of jury vetting conducted in official secrets' and terrorism trials. This takes the form of an 'Authorised Check' under Attorney-General's Guidelines. The purpose is to guard against the possibility of a biased juror in cases of exceptional public importance, and vetting may result in the prosecution objecting to a particular juror during jury selection (a practice known as 'Stand By for the Crown').   IAN LEIGH

See also: **freedom of information; national security; public interest immunity**

Ofsted inspection   *see* **school standards and the inspection of schools and LEAs**

Old Bailey   London's principal criminal court, originally located just outside the western wall of the City and next to Newgate Prison, was named after a fortification, or 'bailey'. The first courthouse was built in 1539. Destroyed in the Great Fire of 1666, it was rebuilt with one wall open to the elements to prevent the spread of typhus brought in by prisoners, though the courtroom was enclosed in 1737. The courthouse was subsequently rebuilt in 1774 and 1834, and the current building, which now extends to cover the former site of Newgate Prison, dates from 1907 (with an extension completed in 1972).

The court's original jurisdiction covered serious crimes committed in the City of London and Middlesex, with lesser crimes tried by the **courts** of quarter sessions. In 1834, when it was renamed the Central Criminal Court, its jurisdiction was extended to metropolitan Essex, Kent, and Surrey, and to include crimes committed on the high seas or abroad which had previously been tried by the Admiralty sessions. In 1856 its jurisdiction was further extended to include cases from elsewhere in England and Wales when it was deemed necessary to move the trial to avoid delay or ensure a fair trial. With the growth of London, court business increased significantly and additional courtrooms were added. In 1972 the court became part of the Crown Court, and its jurisdiction was no longer geographically constricted. Since 1981 it is part of the **Supreme Court**. The most serious cases are tried by High Court **judges**, with lesser cases tried by circuit judges, including the Recorder and Common Serjeant of the City. Some special privileges remain, including traditional ceremonies and robes (such as the Lord Mayor's role opening sessions) and the fact that when the Crown Court is held at the Old Bailey it is still known as the Central Criminal Court.

Popular awareness of the court expanded dramatically in the late seventeenth century with the publication of summary accounts of trials in the *Proceedings of the Old Bailey* (also known as the 'Sessions Papers'), following each sessions of the court. This remarkable periodical, licensed by the City, was initially targeted at a popular audience but as its content and size grew and City regulation increased, readership declined until it was largely confined to lawyers and court officials, who used it as an unofficial court record, and publication was subsidized by the City. First published in 1674, publication continued until 1913, when funding ceased. The 200,000 published trial accounts, available online at www.oldbaileyon line.org, document the changing nature of the **criminal trial**, from the brief, direct altercations between the victim and the defendant of the pre-industrial period to the lengthy, lawyer-dominated trials of modern times, and the transformation of the penal regime from one based on corporal and **capital punishment** to one based almost entirely on imprisonment. Famous trials include those of William Penn (1670), Jack Sheppard (1724), Oscar **Wilde** (1895),

William Joyce, 'Lord Haw Haw' (1945), and Peter Sutcliffe, the 'Yorkshire Ripper' (1981).

ROBERT SHOEMAKER

J Langbein, *The Origins of Adversary Criminal Trial* (Oxford: Oxford University Press, 2003)

Old Bailey Sessions Papers   Old Bailey Session Papers ('OBSP'), alternatively known as *Proceedings on the King's Commissions of the Peace, Oyer and Terminer, and Gaol Delivery . . . in the Old Bailey*, are pamphlet accounts of trials held at London's premier criminal court. The series began in 1674 as a commercial enterprise and was originally aimed at the general public; but in the eighteenth century the OBSP developed into genuine law reports with semi-official status. By the late 1770s the City of London had effectively assumed control of their publication; and the shorthand writers employed were required to provide a record that would both assist the authorities in determining which convicts should be spared the gallows and persuade the public of the justice of the system.

The OBSP have been widely used by social historians investigating the lives of the labouring poor and legal historians interested in the development of the criminal trial. The late eighteenth-century reports, for example, reveal the growing participation of counsel. The nineteenth-century publications are less useful in this regard, as the City authorities decided in 1805 to expunge arguments of counsel from the reports: it did not want their 'ingenious addresses' to form part of the record.

When the Old Bailey changed its name to the Central Criminal Court in 1834 the series title was altered to reflect the change; publication finally ceased in April 1913. Proceedings for the period 1674–November 1834 are now available online at *www.oldbaileyonline.org* and digitizing of the remaining trials is currently underway.   ALLYSON MAY

oligopoly   Oligopoly describes a market structure composed of a small number of firms selling competing goods (eg three cement manufacturers). There are two related terms: duopoly (two competitors in the market) and oligopsony (a market structure with a small number of firms purchasing certain goods). The discussion that follows also applies to these two market structures.

Economists disagree about when oligopoly markets reduce economic efficiency. For some, inefficiencies only arise when the firms meet in secret to create a **cartel**, agreeing to raise prices (express collusion). While express collusion may occur in markets that are not oligopolistic, most instances cartels have been unearthed in highly concentrated markets with a relatively small number of competitors: it is easier to establish and monitor a cartel when there are few firms. Other economists suggest that cartel-like conduct can also arise without express collusion, as each firm realizes that it is in its interests to cooperate with other firms in the oligopoly (tacit collusion). For example if one of three cement manufacturers raises its prices, the other two find it profitable to follow the price increase, because then all three set the same high price for a product that has no readily available substitutes, and buyers have to accept the higher price. Economic studies of tacit collusion draw upon game theory to model the behaviour of oligopoly markets and predict that under certain conditions, tacit collusion is likely; for example homogeneous goods and market transparency, which allow each firm to monitor how competitors behave. Tacit collusion is controversial because the difficulties that firms face when setting up a cartel by express collusion (to agree prices and monitor that everyone follows them) seem impossible to surmount tacitly.

Oligopoly markets are monitored by the competition authorities (the **Office of Fair Trading** ('OFT') and the **Competition Commission**). The OFT has powers to investigate and prohibit express collusion under the Chapter I prohibition in the Competition Act 1998, which prohibits anti-competitive agreements. Fines or criminal sanctions (including imprisonment) may be imposed upon cartel members. To address tacit collusion, the merger rules in the Enterprise Act 2002 allow the Competition Commission to block a merger in an oligopoly market when tacit collusion is more likely after a merger (for example, in an oligopoly of four firms, where one is a 'maverick' that regularly instigates price cuts, the acquisition of the maverick firm by one of the other three may stabilize the oligopoly and make tacit collusion more likely among the remaining three).

Merger control facilitates prevention of tacit collusion; less clear is what may be done to stop tacit collusion when it is already taking place. The Chapter I prohibition is inapplicable because there is no agreement. Two approaches are possible. The first is to treat the firms in the oligopoly as holding a position of collective dominance and to find that they have abused it by tacit collusion. This allows the application of the Chapter II prohibition in the Competition Act that prohibits **abuse of a dominant position** by one or more firms. However, this approach is laden with difficulties, not least in determining what penalty to impose: the normal remedy (a fine) is unlikely to deter the parties because tacit collusion occurs when the firms naturally discover the advantages

of following each other's behaviour—a fine cannot prevent normal market behaviour. Secondly, the Competition Commission could apply the market investigation procedures in the Enterprise Act. These allow the Commission to carry out a general investigation of markets where competition appears to be distorted. The Commission has a wide range of remedial powers if it finds that the market is not competitive, which seem to be ideal for remedying tacit collusion. For example price controls, or breaking up the oligopoly by ordering assets to be divested, thereby increasing the number of competitors, making tacit collusion less likely. However neither statute has been deployed by the competition authorities, in part because intervention restricts the natural play of market forces and may have unforeseen adverse effects.   GIORGIO MONTI

Olympic Games   The governing instrument of the Olympic Games is the Olympic Charter (the current version of which came into effect on 1 September 2004), written in French and English. In homage to Baron de Coubertin, founder of the modern Olympics, the French text prevails in the event of discrepancy. The International Olympic Committee ('IOC') is an international non-governmental not-for-profit organization with legal personality recognized by Swiss Federal Law. Supreme power is vested in the IOC executive board, whose rulings on all matters within the scope of the Charter are expressed to be final with one significant exception, namely that 'any dispute arising on the occasion of or in connection with the Olympic Games shall be submitted to the **Court of Arbitration for Sport** in accordance with the Code of Sports related arbitration'.

Since the Atlanta Summer Olympic Games of 1996, and at every Winter and Summer Games thereafter, the Court of Arbitration for Sport has provided an international twelve-person *ad hoc* panel of arbitrators, who (sitting in groups of three) have determined a range of issues ranging from eligibility to compete, through doping, to commercial issues such as the size of logos on athletes' vests or the expulsion of athletes from the Olympic village. On occasion the IOC has itself been party to the proceedings and the object of coercive orders; medals it has awarded have been reallocated. In the Charter, fundamental principles, five chapters and sixty-one rules are supported by a substructure of by-laws, and deal with the Olympic movement, the respective roles and competences of the IOC, of the International Federations for various sports and of the National Olympic Committees. The also deal with the Games themselves, including the designated sports, media coverage, publications, propaganda, and protocols. Prime among the matters covered are the procedures for the selection of host cities, the regulations governing which are complex and wide-ranging, and the subject of a separate volume designed, amongst other matters, to eliminate the possibility of corruption.

An essential bid requirement is that a candidate city guarantees adequate legislative protection for the Olympic marks, symbol, flag, anthem, identification, designations, emblems, flames, and torches, the commercial value of which is substantial. In the last two decades countries have met this requirement by enacting temporary legislation to prohibit ambush marketing for a specified period before, during, and after the Games. The **World Intellectual Property Organization** has registered the five-ring symbol internationally and some countries (including the UK) have enacted permanent legislation for its protection.

However, to stage a modern Olympic Games more is demanded of a host city than symbol protection. For the 2012 London Olympics, legislation establishes an Olympic Delivery Authority ('ODA') with the function of preparing for the Games, including the acquisition and disposal of land, and includes specific provisions to deal with transport, advertising, and trading as well as updating and enhancing mark protection. As a Statutory Corporation, the ODA is a public authority amenable to **judicial review**.

MICHAEL BELOFF

ombudsmen Ombudsmen resolve complaints against institutions, either public or private, in an informal and flexible manner, usually at no cost to the complainant and without necessarily applying the strict letter of the law. The first Parliamentary Ombudsman was appointed in England in 1967, based on an idea derived from Scandinavian and New Zealand experience. The office has been developed since then and there has been a proliferation of ombudsmen in the UK with the beneficial result of enhancing access to justice.

The Parliamentary Ombudsman decides whether complaints raise matters of maladministration by public officials associated with central government, although certain categories of decision may not be investigated (eg court proceedings, commercial transactions, personnel matters). Maladministration extends beyond matters that can give rise to a legal claim to include neglect, inattention, delay, incompetence, mistake, and inequity. If a complainant could reasonably be expected to proceed by making a claim in a tribunal or court, the Parliamentary Ombudsman need not take up the complaint. More controversially, the Parliamentary Ombudsman cannot investigate unless there has been a referral from an MP. If it is decided that injustice has been caused through maladministration, the matter can be reported to Parliament if it is not remedied by the body responsible. There is moral pressure on government to accept the Ombudsman's decision, including any recommendation as to payment of compensation.

Since the Parliamentary Ombudsman was established in 1957, the number of ombudsmen has greatly increased. The Parliamentary Ombudsman is now the Parliamentary and Health Service Ombudsman, since services provided by the NHS in England are also covered. Complaints of maladministration in other parts of the public sector are dealt with by various bodies, such as the Local Government Ombudsman, the Independent Police Complaints Commission, the Information Complaints Commissioner, and the Prisons and Probation Ombudsman. Just as significant for access to justice are the considerable number of ombudsmen concerned with the private sector. While some, like the Legal Services Ombudsman, the Housing Ombudsman Service, and the Pensions Ombudsman, have a statutory basis, others have been set up by the relevant industry itself, no doubt in some cases to forestall legislative action. Among the private sector ombudsmen are the Estate Agents Ombudsman and the Telecommunications Ombudsmen. The Financial Ombudsman Service, established by statute in 2000, absorbed some eight private ombudsman schemes including the Banking Ombudsman, the Building Societies Ombudsman, and the Investment Ombudsman.

In one case a judge said that the purpose of ombudsmen was that of 'delivering rapid, unlegalistic justice, without cutting too many legal corners'. Those complaining need not pay. Nor need they compile the amount of evidence necessary for proceedings in a court or tribunal. Often a letter is all that is necessary, and the Ombudsman then uses an inquisitorial process to investigate and decide on the complaint. In the great bulk of cases there will be no oral hearing, so as to keep costs low. Dissatisfied complainants are not bound by the ombudsman's decision (although the organization may be) and so can later pursue their case in the courts if they wish. Few choose to do that.

The volume of complaints dealt with by ombudsmen is considerable, and far greater than the number of trials and small claims hearings in the courts. The high volume of complaints to ombudsmen partly reflects ease of access: there is no fee and typically, apart from having to have a complaint first considered by the relevant organization, no other condition of access. The limited evidence available suggests that complainants to some ombudsmen may come disproportionately from higher socio-economic groups, although this may simply reflect the subject matter they handle.

The ombudsman system has two broad functions. The first, and obvious, function is to handle individual grievances. Generally speaking people must exhaust an organization's internal **complaints procedures**, but having done that can have a matter taken up by the relevant ombudsman. In this sense ombudsmen are an alternative to the courts, although in an important respect their jurisdiction is broader in that they may decide a matter on other than legal grounds. For example a complaint may be determined by reference to what is, in the opinion of the ombudsman, fair and reasonable in all the circumstances of the case. However, not all complaints about a particular body may fall within the terms of reference of the ombudsman covering the relevant sector or industry. Moreover, some private sector ombudsmen have surprisingly limited coverage extending, for example, to only some of the bodies in their business sector.

The second function of ombudsmen is to establish benchmarks of good practice within a sector and to raise its standards. Thus an ombudsman may produce guidance indicating how particular issues should to be dealt with by entities in its sector. Courts are not generally adept in doing this, even if they wanted to: they tend to have general, rather than a specialized, jurisdiction and do not always have a sufficient caseload to acquire a detailed knowledge of, or to monitor, changing practice within a particular sector. An ombudsman can not only give guidance to a sector, but can also liaise with relevant regulators when there appears to be a systematic problem, in addition providing input to government in relation to new law.

The British and Irish Ombudsman Association has identified four key criteria to be met before it will grant an ombudsman formal recognition: independence, effectiveness, fairness, and public accountability. Independence turns primarily on whether the ombudsman is independent of those subject to investigation; thus, their representatives should constitute no more than a minority of the membership of the body which appoints the ombudsman and to which he or she reports. Effectiveness depends firstly on coverage. In due course it is expected that all, or virtually all, organizations in a sector should participate in the relevant ombudsman scheme. Secondly, the office must be adequately staffed and funded. Accessibility is the third aspect: the right to complain should be adequately publicized by those subject to

the scheme; those subject to complaint must have proper internal complaints procedures; the ombudsman's office should be directly accessible to complainants unless specified by statute; the ombudsman's procedures should be straightforward for complainants to understand and use; and those complaining should be entitled to do so free of charge. Fourthly, the criteria require that the ombudsman be entitled to investigate a complaint without the prior consent of those against whom it has been made. Finally, the ombudsman's decisions should be legally binding or there should be at least a reasonable expectation that they will be complied with. In cases where they are not, the ombudsman should have the power to require publication of the fact of non-compliance.

Fairness, according to the criteria, depends on proceeding in accordance with the principles of **natural justice**; making reasoned decisions; explaining to the complainant, when a particular case is not taken up for investigation, the reason why; and notifying the decision and the reasons for it in writing. Finally, there is public accountability, crucial to the rule of law. Under the criteria this depends on publication both of the jurisdiction, powers and method of appointment of an ombudsman and of his or her annual report including, if the ombudsman decides, anonymous reports of investigations. The latter enable bargaining in 'the shadow of the ombudsman', and would seem essential when, unlike the courts, decisions are not made public.

Among suggestions for reform of the ombudsman system are that annual reports should reveal the identity of any body persistently guilty of maladministration. Not only might this act as a deterrent but it could also enhance the independence of an ombudsman in the eyes of the public. To further accountability it has been said that there should be an independent commission, with majority public-interest and consumer representation, to monitor the various ombudsman schemes. Specific proposals include removing the MP filter to the Parliamentary and Health Service Ombudsman. In practice this is not an obstacle, although it sits strangely with the notion of furthering access to justice. There does not appear to be great enthusiasm in official circles for a general consumer ombudsman mainly because (it is said) in an overcrowded ombudsman market it would be confusing. Empirical work is needed to determine whether, at present, complainants are being properly referred to the appropriate specialist ombudsman or whether the creation of a general consumer ombudsman would significantly improve access to justice.   ROSS CRANSTON

See also: **inquisitorial system**

omissions *see* **acts and omissions**

***On Liberty* (by John Stuart Mill)** *On Liberty* is probably the most famous and enduring work by the leading English political philosopher of the nineteenth century, John Stuart Mill. For Mill, the importance of liberty is its tendency to encourage the evolution of knowledge and of valuable forms of life. Mill is sceptical of both state power and social criticism as methods of restraining the free flow of ideas and unconventional ways of life. This led Mill to insist on restrictions on both the imposition of legal sanctions and the expression of negative public opinion as forms of punishment. The former, Mill thinks, is limited by the harm principle, perhaps the idea that has retained the most influence from this work. The principle is that harm to others is the only legitimate grounds for interfering with liberty through legal sanctions. The relevant harm, for Mill, is restricted to setting back the interests of others, constituting an interference with their rights. Hence, not all setting back of another's interests constitutes harm; for example setting back a person's interests by succeeding in fair competition with them would not constitute harm. If a person's conduct is merely hurtful to others, but does not constitute interference with their rights, Mill thinks that it may be legitimate to punish them through public opinion, but not through the law.

The ideas developed in *On Liberty* have been enormously influential on the development of public policy and legal rules, particularly in the area of sexual relations, as well as on liberal academic thought. Mill's central claims have been defended and developed by HLA Hart in *Law, Liberty and Morality* (Oxford: Oxford University Press, 1963), Joseph Raz in *The Morality of Freedom* (Oxford: Oxford University Press, 1986), and in Joel Feinberg's four volume series *The Moral Limits of the Criminal Law* (New York: Oxford University Press, 1984–1990).

VICTOR TADROS

See also: *Law, Liberty and Morality* (by HLA Hart)

open access This term does not have a legal definition but refers to two principles: first, that products of scholarly research should be available online free of charge at the point of use; and secondly, that outputs should be re-usable for legitimate scholarly purposes. Three major public definitions of open access are contained in the Budapest (2002), Bethesda (2003), and Berlin (2003) Declarations. While the first open access source of information was made available in 1966, the movement gained momentum early in the twenty-first century. The spiralling costs to research institutions of subscribing to academic outputs, the promises digital dissemination heralded for accessibility of scholarly writings, and the complexities of working within the boundaries of **copyright** law, combined to galvanize support for the movement. The result has been a plethora of initiatives, both regulatory and institutional, to facilitate access to, and re-use of, scholarly outputs. In 2004 the **House of Commons** Science and Technology Select Committee advocated that higher education institutions should establish institutional repositories in which published output could be stored and read free online. In 2005 Research Councils UK indicated it would make future funding grants conditional on a copy of all outputs being deposited in a repository and available free online, subject to copyright or licensing arrangements. There has been opposition, most notably from the academic publishing sector. One, as yet unresolved, issue is how open access publishing is to be financed. A related question is whether the model is sustainable over the longer term.

CHARLOTTE WAELDE

open government *see* **freedom of information**

open method of coordination *see* **approximation of laws in the EU**

opt outs *see* **closer cooperation in the EU**

Orders in Council *see* **legal rules, types of**

organ donation and transplantation Since the first successful kidney transplant between twins in 1954 and the first heart transplant in 1967, organ transplants have become an established treatment option for those whose own organs have failed. Kidneys are the most common organ transplanted in the UK, but other body parts can be transplanted including lungs, heart valves, corneas, skin, and bone. There is a significant gap between the demand for and supply of organs. In the UK, approximately 2,700 people receive a transplant each year, but over 6,500 are on the waiting list. The number of organs available for transplantation urgently needs to be increased, and people can record their wish to donate by joining the NHS Organ Donor Register.

The central idea behind the law in the UK is 'appropriate consent' or 'authorization'. The **Human Tissue** Act 2004 applies to England, Wales, and Northern Ireland, and the Human Tissue (Scotland) Act 2006 to Scotland. Removing, storing, or using human tissue for transplantation without consent or authorization is illegal, as is storing or using human tissue donated for transplantation for another purpose. With some exceptions, buying or selling human material for transplantation is illegal (commercial trafficking). Minimum steps may be taken to preserve the organs of a deceased person whilst attempts are made to determine the deceased's wishes or consent or authorization is sought from the relevant person. The 2006 Act includes a specific duty on Scottish Ministers to promote, support, and develop transplantation programmes, and promote awareness and information on donating for transplantation.

Under the 2004 Act, consent is required for organs or tissues to be removed, stored, and used from a deceased person for transplantation. If the deceased was a competent adult over eighteen, her consent prior to death is needed. If this does not exist, her nominated representative or, if no representative, someone in a 'qualifying relationship' with her immediately before she died can consent. There is a list of relatives who must be approached in order and if two people in the same category disagree, consent is only needed from one. In Scotland, competent adults over sixteen and competent children over twelve can authorize the removal and use of their **body parts** for transplantation, in writing for the latter. If no authorization exists for an adult, there is a list of 'nearest relatives' to be consulted in order, or the person with parental rights and responsibilities for a **child** over twelve will be asked to consider authorizing donation, based on what they believe the deceased's wishes would have been. Across the UK if it is believed to be in the best interests of an adult without the **capacity** to consent to the storage or use of her organs or tissues for transplantation, then she is 'deemed to have consented' to it. With a sufficiently mature and intelligent deceased child under eighteen, her prior consent is needed. If she is not mature then it can be provided by someone with **parental responsibility** for her. In Scotland, authorization must come from a person with parental rights and responsibilities for a deceased child under twelve.

Appropriate consent is also required for organs or tissues to be stored and used from living donors, but the removal continues to be regulated by the **common law**. For a competent adult over eighteen and a mature **minor**, her consent to storage and use is required. If the child is not a mature minor or is competent but unwilling to make a decision, consent can be provided by a person with parental responsibility for her. Transplants from a living adult without capacity will be rare and require approval from the Human Tissue Authority and, for some types of

transplant, the **courts**. In Scotland, a living donor must authorize the removal of organs or tissues and there must be no coercion or reward involved. Only regenerative tissue or an organ, or part of an organ, for a domino transplant can be removed from children under sixteen and adults without capacity. *All living donations in the UK must be authorized by the Human Tissue Authority.*

The wishes of the deceased will now take precedence over the wishes of relatives but will health care professionals act against families' requests, regardless of consent or authorization from the deceased? Just because it is lawful to remove organs with the required consent or authorization does not mean it is obligatory to do so. Indeed, health care professionals are likely to make such decisions on a case-by-case basis. It is good practice to consult relatives and, to support best practice, the Human Tissue Authority has published Codes of Practice on consent and donation.   SARA FOVARGUE

organ retention   Controversy arose across the UK in the late 1990s as evidence came to light that institutions and clinicians remained in possession of, sometimes very large, quantities of human organs, tissues, and even stillborn children and foetuses (54,000 items since 1970 according to the Chief Medical Officer's audit), often even after initial burial or cremation. They were typically taken and stored, or least retained, for research following (generally **coroners**') post-mortem examinations. This precipitated various **Inquiries**, including: in England, the Bristol Royal Infirmary (Interim Report), Alder Hey, and Isaacs Inquiries; in Scotland the Independent Review Group on Retention of Organs at Post-Mortem; and in Northern Ireland, the Human Organs Inquiry.

Neither human material (used and intended as a generic neutral term for present purposes) taken from hospital post-mortems, nor from post-mortems conducted under the auspices of the coroner for forensic purposes, were able to be legitimately retained for research (nor most other) purposes under the (then) Human Tissue Act 1961 unless either the deceased requested this or there was no evidence of any objection from the deceased or any surviving relatives. It was nevertheless revealed that in very many instances, relatives, very often parents of dead children, had either not been asked if they objected, had objections ignored, or misunderstood the intentions of the clinicians (many failed to realize for instance that 'tissue' might be taken to apply to all parts of the corpse, even whole organs such as hearts or brains).

The furore generated by such revelations led the then Health Secretary, Alan Milburn MP, to utter the strident words 'Never again', intimating the government's commitment to law reform and to the specific recommendations in the Advice of the Chief Medical Officer. The central theme was the endorsement of consent being required before such removal, and storage and use, would be permissible. The notion of consent as opposed to the 'non-objection' terminology of the 1961 Act was described by Gage J in *AB v Leeds Teaching NHS Hospital Trust* (2004) as a 'less passive' process. In the interim, a special health authority, the Retained Organs Commission was established to liaise with Health Trusts regarding enquiries about retained tissue and, where appropriate its return or disposal, and to hold meetings to permit the airing of public views and grievances. Legal actions were also commenced by aggrieved parents who formed Action Groups, including the *AB* case above, the Nationwide Organ Group Litigation. Two separate settlements were reached, one with the Alder Hey parents and the other with relatives elsewhere. In addition, following widespread public and professional consultation, and some very significant alterations during its passage through Parliament, the **Human Tissue Act 2004** was passed.

The organ retention controversy brought to the fore tensions between the desire of clinicians for advancement of human knowledge and a wish to avoid unnecessary additional suffering of relatives at a time of extreme grief, and relatives' and the public's assumption that permission was essential prior to any retention and use of human material for research or other non-diagnostic purposes. The relatives themselves invariably conceded that they would have consented had such permission been explicitly solicited. Moreover, there was consternation that a considerable volume of material retained had no realistic prospect of being used for research in any event. A dichotomy may also have been revealed regarding the meaning attached to tissue emanating from, or forming part of, corpses. The dissociation of dead tissue from the 'person' or 'self' and a tendency toward a utilitarian perspective may have been manifest in the attitude of many clinicians but was at odds with the perspective of the public in general and especially the parents of deceased children. The tension between public and private interests remains, but the 2004 Act henceforward sets up 'consent' as the ordinary default position for permitting the storage and use of human tissue in England, Wales, and Northern Ireland, albeit subject to some (sometimes significant) exceptions (as, analogously, does the Human Tissue (Scotland) Act 2006 by means of the concept of 'authorization' in that jurisdiction).   DAVID PRICE

M Brazier, 'Law and Regulation of Retained Organs: The Legal Issues' [2002] 22 *Legal Studies* 550

D Price, 'From Cosmos and Damien to Van Velzen: The Human Tissue Saga Continues' [2003] 11 *Medical Law Review* 1

Orton, Arthur   The case of Arthur Orton (1834–1898), the 'Tichborne claimant', was a major 'cause célèbre' of Victorian England, giving rise to two lengthy trials, one civil and the other criminal, and even popular political unrest. At the heart of the case lay the question of the true identity of the man claiming to be Sir Roger Tichborne, heir to the Tichborne estate.

Sir Roger Tichborne had left England in 1852, and his ship had been presumed lost at sea in April 1854, with all on board declared dead. Sir Roger's mother refused to accept that he had died and, after advertisements were placed in various newspapers around the world, in 1865 a man called Tomas Castro, from Wagga Wagga, Australia, claiming to be Sir Roger. He stated that he had survived the shipwreck, and had been rescued by a ship heading for Australia, where he had made a new life for himself. Although the physical resemblances with Sir Roger were slight, Lady Tichborne recognized him as her son. The rest of her family refused to do so, citing evidence that he was in fact Arthur Orton, originally from Wapping, London.

On Lady Tichborne's death in 1868 the claimant brought an action of ejectment against the Tichborne trustees before a judge and special jury in the Court of Common Pleas. The trial lasted for 102 days (May 1871–March 1872) but the claimant was proved to be ignorant of many facts which Sir Roger must have known, and the jury found for the defendants. Following this the claimant was charged with perjury, giving rise to a second, criminal, trial which lasted for 188 days, and ended with the claimant being found guilty and sentenced to two periods of seven years imprisonment, to run concurrently. On his release from prison in 1884 the claimant scraped a living from his notoriety, before dying in poverty in London in 1898.   LINDSAY FARMER

Other, the   The concept of 'Other' has been deployed in a range of academic fields, including law, most prominently in relation to critiques of racial and cultural differences. The Other is sometimes used interchangeably with 'alterity', with both terms used to connote a difference from another thing, entity, or being. Whilst the concept of Other retains a central position in various academic disciplines, it is difficult to pin down a precise understanding of what it encompasses. It is often employed with little explanation on the assumption that its meaning can be known from the context in which it is employed.

Charting the origins of otherness is difficult, although it can perhaps be traced to the early Greek writings of Plato and Aristotle as a reference to that in opposition to the Self. The etymology of the word indicates that it was originally used as a means of distinguishing one item in a pair from another in a manner reminiscent of its later use as a binary construction of difference. Gradually, its meaning was broadened to include reference to one out of three, or four. In lay usage, 'Other' is simply a means of connoting difference or opposition—the difference or opposition of one entity from/to another—for there can never be One without the Other.

Some have argued that the idea of otherness is predicated upon a Western preoccupation with binary constructions—West/East, us/them, first world/third world. Whilst there may be some merit to this argument, it ignores dualisms existent within non-Western cultures and, in doing so, negates the range and complexity of ideologies of otherness. If one looks to Chinese philosophy for instance, one finds an emphasis upon the notion of *yin* and *yang*, the male and female essence which together bring harmony and balance. In contrast, Christian theology centres on the idea of the Holy Trinity, thus displacing to some degree, the easy categorization of binaries as purely Western.

The meaning/understanding of Other has been highly unsettled, and perhaps nowhere has the concept been more hotly contested than in phenomenology, where its **identity** varies from a positive to a negative attribute. For Jean-Paul Sartre, the existence and meaning of the Other is dependent upon the existence and meaning of the Self. An understanding of one is impossible without an understanding of the other. The relationship then becomes one of dominant and dominated, an understanding reminiscent of that adopted by many feminists and post-colonial theorists. In contrast, Emmanuel Levinas' discussion of the Other centres around the possibilities for ethics of the Other's relationship with the **subject**. In challenging the complacency of the I, the Other offers a means of attaining a conception of ethics which goes beyond settled parameters. Levinas' preoccupation with otherness has been criticized by Alain Badiou who argues that this preoccupation acts as a diversion from that which really matters. For Badiou at least, the notion of Other is obsolete, for in discussing otherness, and respect for

the Other, what is really respected is the Self. This understanding dominates liberal conceptions of the Other.

Within legal thinking, the concept of the Other has been most frequently invoked to explain relations of dominance and difference by feminists, critical race, and post-colonial (legal) theorists. For example, within **feminist theories of law**, Catharine Mackinnon's work on 'Difference and Dominance' expands upon the work of Simone de Beauvoir to explore the ways in which law casts women in opposition to men, with men as the norm, and women as inferior, subordinate, and other. Similarly, in the context of **critical race theory**, Angela Harris' work on essentialism interrogates the ways in which legal discourse posits women of colour as Other to white women in a manner which presents whiteness as the legal norm. This is a critique much utilized by post-colonial legal scholars such as Ratna Kapur and Sherene Razack, who use otherness as an analytical tool by which to highlight hidden assumptions of **racism** within legal thought.

Some commentators argue that theorists subscribing to the terminology and ideology of otherness are simply perpetuating and maintaining the hierarchical structures of dominance at play, rather than inverting them; by deploying the Other as a discursive tool such theorists remain within Western-dominated frameworks of analysis. Furthermore, a return to the idea of the 'Other' as that which is not 'I', is in itself, counterproductive and meaningless, because all persons, things, and entities are, by their very nature, always Other, so negating the return to the I.

Moreover, even if the concept of the Other is accepted as unproblematic, the question of 'what now?' must also be raised. Whilst the theme of otherness is useful as a means of critiquing the ways in which the dominant group marginalizes and oppresses 'inferior' or **minority** groups, once such critique has been achieved, it could be contended that the utility of Other as a means of analysis has been fulfilled. Furthermore, with the advent of postmodernism and its preoccupation, or obsession, with the Other, otherness can be found everywhere, so rendering it useless as a category. The issue here is whether the concept of the Other precludes investigation of the complexity, diversity, and intersectionality of 'that which is not I'. As all oppressed people in their very different circumstances of oppression are 'other', can there be a future for the Other as an analytical and discursive tool?

Whilst there is some validity to these criticisms, it could be also argued that the value of the Other lies in its ability to draw attention to hegemonic hierarchies within discourse. The very nature of the Other implies an opposition—and it is suggested that the very existence of this opposition imbues the concept of otherness with theoretical significance. Devaluing the Other as a discursive tool simply aids in the perpetuation of dominance and hierarchy by facilitating an epistemological ignorance as regards these discursive power structures. Ignoring these structures of dominance fails to afford a means of disrupting them. Accordingly, reclaiming the Other carves out a path for exposing norms of gender and race-based superiority and dominance, so creating the possibility for subverting them.

Finally, whilst the notion of otherness has been deployed in a multitude of contexts, so much so that everything and everyone is Other, the very banality of the Other in certain invocations lends strength to its use in more 'serious' contexts. For example, positing smokers or fox-hunters as oppressed 'Others' arguably serves to lend more credibility to the notion of people of colour as really Other. Situating everybody as oppressed, enables a fuller comprehension of those who are *really* oppressed.

SONYA FERNANDEZ

outsourcing   *see* **contracting out; transfer of business**

overpayment of benefits and tax credits   There are strict rules governing the recovery of overpaid social security benefits and **tax credits**. In general, the Department for Work and Pensions ('DWP') may recover overpaid benefits if it can show that a person either failed to disclose, or misrepresented, a material fact and that this caused the overpayment. The underlying decision on entitlement must also be changed. This is a civil process; the individual's mistake may have been entirely innocent. If it was fraudulent, then the DWP may consider prosecuting the person concerned. Recovery is usually sought against the claimant, but the DWP may recover an overpayment from anyone who failed to disclose or made a misrepresentation (for example an appointee acting for an incapacitated claimant). Recovery can also be sought from a deceased claimant's estate. The DWP's decision on whether an overpayment is recoverable can be appealed to a tribunal. Different rules apply to housing benefit and council tax benefit; local authorities may usually recover overpayments of these benefits in all cases unless the overpayment was caused by an official error. The rules governing tax credits are stricter still; in principle all tax credit overpayments are recoverable, including those caused by official error. There is also no right of appeal to a tribunal against a decision to recover an overpayment of tax credits, although there is a right of appeal against the prior decision about the level of entitlement to credits. There are no time limits governing the recovery of overpayments of benefits and tax credits.

NICK WIKELEY

overstayer   An 'overstayer' is a person who has remained in a state beyond the expiry date of his or her **visa** for temporary entry, or, if that person did not require a visa, beyond the period for which leave to remain in the country was authorized.

The term encompasses people who overstay for a few days, as well as those who overstay for many years. Governments often refer to such people as 'illegal migrants', because although they lawfully *entered* the country on a valid visa, remaining in the country beyond the authorized period renders their status unlawful in domestic law. Governments are concerned that overstayers compromise the immigration system by bypassing stringent visa application processes and working illegally, although some commentators have observed the reliance of many Western economies on this 'black market' labour force.

There are three main outcomes for overstayers: regularization of status through the grant of a new visa (not possible in all states); voluntary departure; or removal by the state. Under Australian law, people who have overstayed their visa by twenty-eight days or more are precluded from obtaining a temporary visa to Australia for the next three years, regardless of whether or not they ultimately departed voluntarily. Furthermore, they will not be granted a visa unless they have repaid any debt owed to the Australian government, such as for the costs of immigration detention and removal.

Since October 2000, visa overstayers in the United Kingdom have been liable to administrative removal rather than **deportation**. This has expedited the removal process and reduced **appeal** rights, but has also lifted the three year ban on reapplying for entry to the country. A person issued with an administrative removal notice (detailing his or her immigration status) may be detained, or subjected to an order restricting freedom in relation to residence, employment, or occupation and requiring regular **police** reporting. A subsequent decision determines whether or not that person will be removed, and removal directions may be set. Since July 2007, if a person has overstayed for twenty-eight days or more, regularization of status will automatically be refused. Administrative removal decisions can only be appealed in the UK if an overstayer lodges an **asylum** or **human rights** claim (on the basis that removal would contravene the UK's treaty obligations), or, if the overstayer is a national of the European Economic Area, the decision could breach his or her rights to enter or reside in the UK under the Treaty establishing the European Community.

A number of countries are now seeking to use biometric data collected on entry to 'count people in and out' of their territories (such as the United States and the UK). Some states also conduct immigration compliance checks through a network of officers in the community (such as Australia and New Zealand).

JANE MCADAM

***Oz* trial**   The London version of the underground magazine *Oz* was founded in 1967. Satirical and antiestablishment, it covered the controversial issues of the time. The 1970 School Kids Issue, No 28, was edited by Richard Neville, Jim Anderson and Felix Dennis, assisted by school children—although it was not directed at their age group. It contained topical content relating to drugs, sex, homosexuality, and alternative lifestyles, and it was illustrated with typically exciting, but very explicit, pictures and cartoons, including a Rupert Bear parody.

The editors and magazine were prosecuted for conspiring to corrupt public morals, for breaches of the Obscene Publications Act 1959 (publishing an obscene article and possessing such articles for gain), and for sending indecent material through the post. The trial attracted much media attention and became a rallying point for dissenting opinion, both in general and specifically about moral **censorship** and Judge Argyle's evident antipathy to the defendants. They were acquitted of the corruption offence but convicted on the other charges. In an outrageous symbolic act, even before receiving prison sentences of nine to fifteen months, all three had their heads shaved whilst on remand. However, they were freed on appeal, the **obscenity** convictions being quashed (*R v Anderson* (1972)). The judge had wrongly directed that 'obscene' should be applied in its common meaning of 'indecent' rather than its statutory meaning of 'depraving and corrupting'. He had also failed to allow an 'aversion' defence, that the articles might actually cause revulsion from disgusting activity.

TOM GIBBONS

P

PACE The Police and Criminal Evidence Act 1984, or 'PACE' as it is usually called, although substantially amended by other Acts over the ensuing years, remains one of the most important statutes concerned with criminal law. The Act covers two broad areas: laws relating to **police** powers and duties; and laws relating to **evidence** in criminal **courts**.

The gestation of the Act was long. It was based on the 1981 report of the Phillips **Royal Commission** on Criminal Procedure which had been set up in 1977 by a Labour government. A Police and Criminal Evidence Bill was introduced in 1982 by the Conservative government but failed to get on to the statute book because a General **Election** interceded in May 1983. A further Bill was introduced by the new Conservative government; this formed the basis of the Act passed in October 1984. In the words of Baron Stevens of Kirkwhelpington, the former Commissioner of Police for the Metropolis, the introduction of the Act 'fundamentally altered the approach and working practices of all those involved in the operation of the **criminal justice system** [and] at a stroke . . . swept away old practices and systems that had been the mainstay of criminal lawyers and police officers for many years . . .'.

The PACE Codes of Conduct

The importance of the Act is greatly enhanced by the Codes of Practice issued under it, which provide rules and guidance on police functions. They apply not only to police officers but in addition, to **persons** 'charged with the investigation of offences or charging offenders' (eg officers of the Serious Fraud Office performing that function) who are required to have regard to them. Amendments made by the Police Reform Act 2002 place the same duty on persons who are not police constables but are given certain police functions by a police authority (ie the local body responsible for the police force in that area).

A failure by any police officer, or any such person, to comply with the provisions of the Codes will not of itself give rise to criminal or civil liability but can be used as evidence in criminal or civil proceedings.

In practice, breach of the Codes by a police officer can be a highly significant factor in both criminal and civil proceedings. It can lead to the exclusion of evidence in criminal proceedings or assist in proving unlawful conduct on the part of the police in a civil action brought against the police.

There are now eight Codes of Conduct which cover the following: police **stop and search powers** (Code A); police search of premises and seizure of property found on persons and premises (Code B); detention, treatment, and questioning by police (Code C); police procedures for the identification of persons (Code D); audio recording of police interviews with suspects (Code E); visual recording with sound of police interviews with suspects (Code F); statutory power of **arrest** by police (Code G); detention, treatment, and questioning by police in **terrorism** cases (Code H). The Codes are from time-to-time updated. They may be found on the Home Office website.

Part I of the Act: Powers to Stop and Search

Part I provides police officers with powers to stop and search persons and vehicles for stolen or prohibited articles without first exercising their powers of arrest. Code A, which expands and explains the provisions in Part I, emphasizes that the powers must be used 'fairly, responsibly, with respect for people being searched and without unlawful discrimination'. Accordingly, the Act also provides safeguards (section 2) and imposes duties (section 3) upon those using those powers. Sections 4 and 5 of Part I set out similar powers and duties governing road checks.

Part II of the Act: Powers of Entry, Search and Seizure

The powers and duties covered by this Part are (i) search warrants and access to material (sections 8–16); (ii) entry for particular purposes, including arrest; and entry and search after arrest (section 18); and (iii) general provisions relating to seizure, retention, and rights and duties with respect to seized things (sections 19–22).

With regard to (i), the Act gives power to issue search warrants both to magistrates (section 8) and **judges** (the 'special procedure' under section 9 and Schedule 1), reserving to the latter the more complex and sensitive applications. It separates the two by creating special categories of material (sections 11–14) which are used to describe the type of items which can only be obtained by an application to a judge. Under the special procedure, an alternative to a search warrant is provided by Schedule 1, paragraph 4, which provides a procedure for compelling a person, by a notice, to provide access to material. Legally privileged material (section 10) cannot be obtained by any application. Section 15 provides safeguards as to the form of the application and the form of the warrant. Section 16 sets out the requirements and procedure for the execution of warrants. Extensive guidance is contained in Code B.

Part III: Arrest

This Part covers: arrest without warrant by constables (section 24) and other persons (section 24A); requirement for offenders to attend for fingerprinting and arrest in default (section 27); information to be given on arrest (section 28); powers and procedures with respect to persons arrested elsewhere than at police station (section 30); the **bail** of persons arrested elsewhere than at police station ('street bail') (sections 30A, 30B, and 30C); the arrest of persons at police stations, attending voluntarily (section 29) or by arrest for further offence (section 31); search of persons and search and entry of premises upon arrest at a place other than a police station (section 32).

Part IV: Detention

Part IV of the Act sets out: the conditions under which a person can be held in police detention and when they must be released; the role and responsibilities of the custody officer; and the timetable within which decisions relating to detention and charge must be made. Code of Practice C applies to this Part and contains important provisions to safeguard a detainee's rights.

Part V: Questioning and Treatment of Persons

Part V encompasses disparate but important provisions relating to: the rights and treatment of detainees; interviews; and identification. Sections 53–55 allow for the detainee to be searched both to ascertain what items the person searched is in possession of and to assist in identifying the detained person. Code D is the Code applicable to identification procedures and a failure to abide by the provisions of that Code has frequently resulted in the exclusion of evidence. Sections 56–59 provide detainees with important rights; notably the right to have someone informed of their arrest and the right to legal advice. These rights are expanded upon in Code C of the Codes of Practice which sets out minimum standards for the conditions in which a person is held in police detention. Sections 60 and 60A provide for police interviews to be tape-recorded, whether on audio or audio-visual tape. Although only 2 sections of the Act relate to interviews, substantial detail can be found in Codes E and F. Sections 61–64 provide the police with the power to take fingerprints, impressions of footwear, intimate and other samples, and photographs; and to test the detainee for the presence of Class A drugs. Juveniles and other vulnerable detainees, referred to in the Code as 'special groups' have additional rights and safeguards applicable to their detention.

Parts VII and VIII: Documentary Evidence & Evidence Generally in Criminal Proceedings

Part VII is now virtually obsolete. Section 69, which dealt with evidence derived from computer records, has been repealed; and provisions relating to the admissibility of documentary evidence (originally found in section 68 of the Act) are now to be found in the Criminal Justice Act 2003. The only remaining section in Part VII relates to proving the contents of a document by the production of a microfilm copy.

Part VIII, by contrast, retains enormous importance. Sections 76–77 (confessions) and 78 (exclusion of unfair evidence) are among the most significant of the entire Act providing a tribunal of law with the power to regulate proceedings by excluding evidence that has been unfairly or improperly obtained (whether through a breach of the provisions of the Act and Codes, or otherwise). Other sections deal with proof of previous convictions and acquittals (sections 73–75), provisions that deal with the competence and compellability of the accused's spouse (section 80–80A), and the necessity to give advance notice of expert evidence.

The remaining Parts

Part VI concerns the status of the Codes of Practice. Parts VIII and XI contain miscellaneous and supplementary provisions. Part IX originally contained provisions relating to Police Complaints and Discipline. They are now to be found in the Police Act 1996 and the Police Reform Act 2002. Part X contains a number of general provisions relating to the police.

PAUL OZIN AND HEATHER NORTON

See also: **search and seizure**

package tours   *see* **holidays, recreational**

pacta sunt servanda   *see* **treaties**

pain and suffering   In an action for personal injury, damages for the claimant's non-pecuniary losses are awarded under the heading pain and suffering and loss of amenity ('PSLA'). Strictly speaking, pain and suffering should be distinguished from loss of amenity, though it is common to find the first term referring to both. In the **United Kingdom**, pain and suffering properly refers to the claimant's own feelings of pain and actual suffering. The concept is subjective, and damages for pain and suffering cannot be awarded where the claimant has wholly and permanently lost consciousness (eg in a coma). By contrast, loss of amenity is assessed objectively, and the damages compensate for the fact of disability even where an unconscious claimant is unaware of the loss. The distinction is often blurred in practice, however, as the courts award a single global sum for PSLA rather than separating the two elements. Except in Scotland, where jury assessment of personal injury damages remains possible, the award is determined judicially, usually by reference to the tariff of indicative amounts in official Guidelines issued by the Judicial Studies Board. Damages for non-pecuniary loss are not susceptible of accurate calculation; all that can be done is to ensure fairness and consistency.

Other legal systems adopt substantially different strategies for their award, with some adopting a 'functional' approach concentrating on the claimant's needs—and therefore making no award at all for non-pecuniary loss in cases of permanent unconsciousness. More radically, some question whether non-pecuniary loss is sufficiently important to warrant compensation at all. In practice, non-pecuniary loss accounts for more than 50 per cent of the average personal injury compensation payment, and an even higher percentage of small awards.

KEN OLIPHANT

Law Commission, *Damages for Personal Injury: Non-Pecuniary Loss* (Law Com No 257 (1999))
Judicial Studies Board, *Guidelines for the Assessment of General Damages in Personal Injury Cases* (Oxford: Oxford University Press, 8th edn, 2006)

Paine, Thomas (1737–1809)   Born to a family of moderate means in Norfolk, Paine emigrated to America in 1774 after his business and marriage failed. Two years later his *Common Sense* (1776), which denounced the despotisms of Europe, pilloried hereditary monarchy, presented America as the natural home for freedom, and demonstrated the inevitability of independence, made him the most influential pamphleteer of the American revolution. In 1787 he returned to Europe, becoming caught up in the French revolution and its reverberations in Britain. His *Rights of Man* (1791), written to rebut Burke's *Reflections on the Revolution in France*, combined a narrative of events with a trenchant attack, based on natural rights, on Burke, the Revolution Settlement of 1688, and the fiction of a British Constitution. Its second part (1792) drew on his American experience to advocate the principles of a commercial society coupled with representative, republican government, founded on a periodically renewable covenant. In the final chapter he sketched proposals for a welfare system for the poor and indigent in society. *Agrarian Justice* (1796) extended these proposals, advocating an inheritance tax to provide a capital grant to all at twenty-one and an annual pension for those above fifty. His most controversial work, *Age of Reason* (1794) challenged the authority of the Bible while affirming a deist understanding of the divine order of the universe. He was outlawed in Britain in 1792, narrowly escaped execution in France in 1794, and was shunned when he returned to America in 1803.

MARK PHILP

Palmer, Dr William   Dr William Palmer (1824–1856) was tried and convicted for the murder of John Parsons Cook in May 1856. He became notorious as the 'Rugeley poisoner' for although he was convicted of a single murder, suspicion had long circulated that he had poisoned members of his family.

After qualifying as a medical doctor, Palmer had left his medical practice in 1852 to devote himself to the breeding of racehorses. He owed large sums of money to various moneylenders, and raised money by forging bills, using the name of his mother as acceptor. He also took out insurance policies on various family members, including his wife and brother, who died in suspicious circumstances in 1854 and 1855, and the insurers became suspicious and refused to pay out on the latter policy. Shortly afterwards he attended Shrewsbury races with Cook, who won a large sum of money. Cook, who returned to Rugeley with Palmer, was then taken ill and died after five days of vomiting. A post-mortem on the body found no evidence of strychnine in the stomach, but suspicions had been raised by Palmer's behaviour in purchasing strychnine and attempting to bribe the Coroner, and by the disappearance of Cook's betting book. Palmer was subsequently arrested and charged with murder.

Palmer was tried at the Central Criminal Court in London because concern over the prejudicial impact of pre-trial publicity led to the enactment of a special Act of Parliament allowing the Court of Queen's Bench to order the trial, at the Central Criminal Court, of indictments found elsewhere. Although there was no clear evidence that Cook had died of strychnine poisoning, Palmer was nonetheless found guilty on the basis of extensive circumstantial evidence, primarily the similarity between Cook's death and that of other known strychnine victims. He was executed outside Stafford gaol in June 1856.

LINDSAY FARMER

paralegals Paralegals are perhaps best described as legal assistants that work in law firms to support the work of solicitors; although the definition of 'paralegal' is rather more complicated than that description would suggest. Paralegals have been described as support workers who have some legal knowledge and/or experience but who do not have the requisite qualifications to be members of the solicitors' or barristers' profession; whereas others consider that many paralegals are would-be trainee solicitors who have the legal credentials to become solicitors or barristers but who have yet to find a vocational training place as a trainee solicitor or a pupil barrister. Yet others consider that paralegals make up a separate branch of the legal profession, similar to but not accredited in the same way as legal executives, solicitors, or barristers. A final approach would include legal executives within the term paralegal, but distinguish legal executives as the professionalized subset of paralegals. This is because legal executives are accredited and regulated by the Institute of Legal Executives after undertaking legal study and examinations similar in scope to undergraduate legal studies. Other terms are also used to describe paralegal activity, some of which have been borrowed from the barristers' profession— 'outdoor clerks' and 'general clerks' are terms used in barristers' chambers to describe legal assistants who provide legal support services to barristers and barristers' clerks. These may all be considered to be paralegals, although more usually the term is used in the context of legal support workers in firms of solicitors.

The difference in opinion over the nature and role of paralegals is in part due to the fact that their duties vary widely, there is no single professional association or body that represents paralegals, and the term 'paralegal', unlike 'legal executive', 'solicitor' and 'barrister', is not legally defined. Consequently, the term paralegal may be best described as an umbrella term that covers all forms of legal support workers that are not professional administrative support employees such as legal secretaries and executive assistants, nor traditional legal professionals, nor expert consultants drawn from academia or other disciplines and professions.

Paralegals undertake a wide variety of work. Paralegals are most frequently found in large law firms such as those in the City of London and large provincial centres, providing services in relation to large corporate or commercial transactions; although they may work in any size of firm, in the public sector, advice agencies, and in commerce, and may undertake work on any type of legal matter including criminal law matters. What they do depends on the needs of the firm, their level of legal knowledge and experience, and their competence. Duties may range from legal clerical work, to legal research, the preparation of documentation for court and for client meetings, to the provision of legal advice to clients. Legal assistance by a paralegal would be provided under the supervision of a solicitor rather than in isolation. Paralegals may be employed on a full-time or part-time continuing basis, or they may be employed for the duration of a particular transaction. In 1997 Sidaway and Punt estimated that there were approximately 25,000 paralegals working in legal practice in England and Wales. The National Association of Licensed Paralegals believes the figure today to be over 150,000, of which 6,500 are legal executives.

Paralegals have a long history in law firms. The 1990s saw a marked increase in the number of paralegals being employed in the legal profession. Some have argued that this was because law firms were using paralegals as a way to retain law graduates to undertake duties akin to those of trainee solicitors without the need to commit to a two-year training contract and the Law Society's minimum training salary requirement. Others explain the rise in numbers in terms of a business efficiency model under which routine legal tasks are carried out by paralegals, permitting solicitors to concentrate on more complex legal issues. The disparity between the individuals employed as paralegals has made it difficult for a paralegal professional identity to develop.

Many paralegals have undertaken some legal study, and some may have attended training programmes that are aimed at paralegals, either in-house at their law firm or organized more generally by training providers. Attempts have been made to professionalize paralegals through paralegal training leading to assessments and qualifications. The National Association of Licensed Paralegals and the

Institute of Paralegals both have accreditation procedures as well as paralegal qualifications, but it is believed that their members account for only a small proportion of those employed in this capacity.

Concerns have been expressed that paralegals are increasingly being used to provide legal services to those on limited financial means or receiving legal aid funding, as low cost alternatives to solicitors. This charge has been levelled at law firms and also at companies that provide legal services to the public—insurers, for example—which may make use of legally qualified staff, who are not fully professionally qualified as solicitors, in order to keep salary costs to a minimum and so retain a competitive edge. Some commentators suggest that the Clementi review of the regulation of legal services augments the drive towards paralegal advice services in preference to the traditional solicitor-client relationship. The extent to which this is a true reflection of how legal practice is being organized in some quarters is difficult to judge, as the role of paralegals remains a relatively under-researched area of the legal profession, in part due to the definitional difficulties associated with paralegal work.   LISA WEBLEY

J Sidaway and T Punt, *Paralegal Staff in Solicitors' Firms* The Law Society Research and Policy Planning Unit, Research Study No. 23 (London: The Law Society, 1997)
Johnstone and Flood, 'Paralegals in English and American Law Offices' (1982) 2 *Windsor Yearbook of Access to Justice* 152

parallel imports   Parallel imports, also known as grey market goods, are goods protected by intellectual property rights (**patents**, **copyright**, **trade marks** and allied rights) that have been placed on the market by, or with the consent of, the right holder in one jurisdiction, but subsequently imported without the consent of the right holder into another jurisdiction. Although parallel imports are genuine goods, right holders often seek to exploit the territoriality of intellectual property rights to prevent parallel trade. For example, the holder of parallel trade marks in the United Kingdom and Australia, who has placed goods on the market in Australia, may seek to rely on its UK trade mark to prevent import of those goods into the UK. The essence of the right holder's argument is that the Australian and UK trade marks are legally independent. Therefore, unauthorized importation of goods bearing the Australian trade mark constitutes infringement of the right holder's UK trade mark, even if the marks are substantially identical.

Incentives for parallel trade arise whenever the same goods are available in different jurisdictions at significantly different prices. This may occur for a variety of reasons, including price discrimination, oversupply, and fluctuations in exchange rates. Right holders generally oppose parallel trade because it undermines their investments in intellectual property. For example, parallel importers are often able to undercut authorized distributors by 'free-riding' on the costs of advertising and other promotional expenditure. In contrast, consumer groups tend to favour parallel imports because they make genuine goods available to consumers at lower prices. However, where there are material differences between goods marketed in different jurisdictions, parallel imports may also generate consumer confusion.

The legality of parallel imports depends on the doctrine of exhaustion of intellectual property rights applied by the importing jurisdiction. In jurisdictions applying national exhaustion, rights are exhausted by first sale within the national territory, but not by any sale outside that territory. Right holders may therefore rely on their intellectual property rights to prevent unauthorized importation of goods into the national territory. In contrast, jurisdictions applying international exhaustion treat the first sale in any territory where the right holder has parallel intellectual property rights as sufficient to exhaust all parallel rights. Therefore, under international exhaustion, right holders cannot generally prevent parallel imports. There is currently no international consensus on the exhaustion of intellectual property rights. States are therefore free to adopt whatever doctrine of exhaustion best suits their needs.

Member States of the European Community have adopted a concept of regional exhaustion, consistent with the Community's single market objectives. Once goods have been placed on the market in any Member State by or with the consent of the right holder, parallel importers enjoy a significant degree of freedom in distributing those goods to other Member States, including limited rights to re-label or re-package goods where necessary to gain effective market access. In contrast, goods first placed on the market outside the Community may not be imported into a Member State without the right holder's consent.   ANDREW CLARK

pardons   From time immemorial, the rulers of peoples have exercised a power not only to punish those who break the law, but also to show mercy or clemency towards them. Today, most national governments continue to exercise this traditional power, subjecting it to varying degrees of regulation. We may conceive of clemency as an order made by a designated governmental officer (most commonly, the head of state), which suspends, reduces, or removes entirely the punitive consequences of criminal behaviour.

A pardon is a particular form of clemency by which an individual offender (or, by way of a type of pardon known as an **amnesty**, a class of offenders) is conditionally or unconditionally absolved from the legal consequences of their offence. Pardons may be granted any time after the commission of an offence. Although they are usually granted following conviction, occasionally they are offered prior to the offender even being charged or convicted. As a result of being pardoned, an offender may avoid trial, conviction, or sentence and may be relieved of any legal disabilities which might attach to conviction (such as exclusion from holding public office).

Notwithstanding its tension with both the **rule of law** and **separation of powers** doctrines (according to which, **courts**, not the executive, are charged with the conviction and **punishment** of criminal offenders), the pardons power is often justified as offering an important extra-judicial safeguard should the judicial system fail or otherwise operate in a manner inconsistent with the public interest or public standards of **justice**. ANTHONY J CONNOLLY

parental choice of school *see* **school admissions**

parental leave The right to parental leave is the right to take time off in order to care for a young **child**. It differs from **paternity** and **maternity** leave in that it is available to both parents. It serves several aims: *inter alia* it promotes an equal division of unpaid work between parents; it seeks to facilitate gender **equality**; it encourages fathers to play a role in their children's lives. As such, parental leave is an important component of the policy and **legislation** aiming at reconciling work and family life. Parental leave is now provided by the majority of European countries. Research, however, has shown that in order to be effective and to encourage a high take-up by fathers, a statutory entitlement to parental leave is simply not enough. First, the right must be constructed as an individual right rather than a family entitlement. In fact, where conceived as a family right, it is mainly used by mothers. Secondly, parental leave must be flexible: parents should be able to use it in blocks or on a part-time basis so as to suit their needs and those of their family. Research has shown that flexibility would encourage greater take-up by fathers. Thirdly, if parental leave is unpaid, it is likely to be an empty provision as not many employees can afford to take the unpaid time. If unpaid, parental leave is most commonly used by mothers.

Indeed, as fathers are often the main source of financial support within the family, it is likely that they may feel unable to take unpaid leave. Accordingly, women continue to work and earn less thus reinforcing **gender** segregation, the gender pay gap, and the stereotype that the caring role is primarily a female one. Finally, parental leave should be reasonably long. A couple of weeks a year are not enough to care for a young child.

Therefore, depending on its implementation, the right to take parental leave can be either an asset to the policy and legislation on reconciling work and family life or a measure that being *de facto* addressed to mothers rather than parents, merely entrenches stereotypes and gender roles.

Examples of these extremes can be found in the UK and Scandinavian countries. In the UK, the right to parental leave is constructed in a very minimalist fashion. Although the scheme is constructed as an individual right, it remains inflexible as exemplified in *Rodway v South West Trains* (2005), very short and, crucially, unpaid. In practice, far from being a measure promoting a new concept of parenting, parental leave in the UK remains very low down in the hierarchy of the family-friendly rights and this is confirmed by its low take-up. By contrast, in the Scandinavian countries the right is not only an individual right but is also extremely flexible, can be taken in blocks of days, part-time or full-time, can last up to two years, and is paid at a very high proportion of the salary.

EUGENIA CARACCIOLO DI TORELLA

G Bruning and J Plantega, 'Parental Leave and Equal Opportunities: Experiences in Eight European Countries' (1999) 9 *Journal of European Social Policy* 195

parental responsibility Parental responsibility is defined in section 3 of the Children Act 1989 as 'all the rights, duties, powers, responsibilities and authority which by law a parent of a child has in relation to the child and his property'. Essentially, parental responsibility means decision-making power, so that a person with parental responsibility for a **child** is authorized to make a wide range of decisions about that child, for example, which school the child is going to attend or even whether the child should have a haircut. However, the **courts** have also stressed that there is a symbolic dimension to parental responsibility.

Parental responsibility is a relatively recent legal concept, only introduced into the law in 1989, replacing the previous concept of parental rights, because the **Law Commission** felt that the concept of parental responsibility better reflected the fact that parental powers existed for the benefit of the child not the parent. However, parental rights have re-entered the picture alongside parental responsibility since the **Human Rights Act 1998**, particularly Article 8, which provides that everyone has the right to respect for his or her **family life**.

All mothers have parental responsibility; contrary to popular belief, not all fathers do. Fathers who are married to the mother have parental responsibility and, like mothers, they never lose it unless the child is adopted. This means that parental responsibility is retained if the parents **divorce**, on the grounds that parenthood is for life. It is also retained if the child is taken into local authority care. Fathers who are not married to the mother may acquire parental responsibility in a number of ways outlined below; however, unlike fathers who are married to the mother (and all mothers), unmarried fathers' parental responsibility is contingent: it can be removed by a court order.

Since late 2003, fathers who are not married to the mother have had parental responsibility if they have signed the child's birth certificate jointly with the mother. They may also acquire parental responsibility by obtaining a residence order (see below), by making a formal agreement with the mother, or by applying to the court for an order giving them parental responsibility. The judge will make a parental responsibility order if he or she considers it to be in the child's best interests, and, in deciding that question, will take into account three factors, namely, the degree of commitment which the father has shown to the child, the degree of attachment between the father and the child, and the father's reasons for making the application. In the overwhelming majority of cases, fathers' applications for parental responsibility are successful: courts only refuse to make parental responsibility orders in extreme cases, for example, if the father has been violent to the mother or child.

People other than the mother or father may also acquire contingent parental responsibility. If a court grants anyone an emergency protection order then that person will acquire limited parental responsibility for the duration of the emergency protection order. If a court makes a care order then the local authority responsible for the child will acquire parental responsibility for the duration of the care order. If a court makes a residence order in favour of anyone who does not already have parental responsibility then that person will acquire parental responsibility for the duration of the residence order (unless this person is the father, in which case he will be granted a parental responsibility order, which will be retained

unless and until it is revoked). Since late 2005, a step-parent has also been able to acquire parental responsibility by agreement with those parents who have parental responsibility or by court order. However, a step-parent is defined as someone who is married to or has entered a **civil partnership** with a parent, so this method does not allow the large proportion of new partners who are living with a parent to acquire parental responsibility. One way round this is for the court to make a joint residence order in favour of the parent and the parent's new partner, or even the parents and the parents' new partners.

It is apparent that a large number of people may all have parental responsibility for the same child. Two provisions in section 2 of the Children Act 1989 aim to deal with the consequences of this. First of all, no one may exercise parental responsibility inconsistently with a court order; so, for example, if a child has been taken into care, the mother is not allowed to remove the child from the foster parents' home. Secondly, each person with parental responsibility may act alone and without the others in meeting his or her parental responsibility.

However, there are some exceptions to this second provision. Section 13 of the Children Act 1989 states that if there is a residence order in relation to a child, no one may take the child out of the United Kingdom for more than a month or cause the child to be known by a new surname unless they have the written agreement of everyone with parental responsibility or the consent of the court. Also, the courts have developed a group of what they regard as important decisions that may only be taken with the agreement of everyone with parental responsibility; if agreement is not forthcoming then these decisions have to be taken by a judge. These important decisions include changing the child's surname, circumcising the child, and inoculating the child. The courts have also stressed on several occasions that parents should consult each other on major decisions such as which school a child will attend.

This is the theoretical position. In practice, many decisions about children are taken by people who do not know or care whether they have parental responsibility but who simply know that they care about (or for) the child. Many parents consult or agree when they are not legally obliged to and many others do not consult or agree when they are legally supposed to. Of course, such decisions tend to be scrutinized only when there is a legal dispute.   HELEN REECE

H Reece, 'From Parental Responsibility to Parenting Responsibly' in M Freeman, *Law and Sociology: Current Legal Issues Vol 8* (Oxford: Oxford University Press, 2006)

S Sheldon, 'Unmarried Fathers and Parental Responsibility: A Case for Reform?' (2001) 9 *Feminist Legal Studies* 93

See also: **residence in family law**

parenthood   English law divides the legal aspects of parenthood into two categories: parentage—who is the child's parent; and **parental responsibility**—what rights and duties a parent has.

Parentage

The blood tie is generally used as the link establishing legal parentage, but, given the limitations of medical science until the late twentieth century, it was necessary to rely on legal presumptions or the best proof available to try to ascertain such a link. With the development of assisted reproduction techniques, permitting gamete or embryo donation, the blood tie has now been superseded in certain circumstances, outlined below.

Mothers

At **common law**, it is presumed that the **woman** who gives birth to the **child** is the child's mother. Under the **Human Fertilization and Embryology Act** 1990 (to be replaced by a new Act in 2008), in the case of egg or embryo donation, the woman who carries the child is regarded as the legal mother of the child, displacing the donor of the egg and overriding the blood tie. Under the 2008 **legislation**, the same-sex partner of such a woman may be regarded as the other parent of the child.

Fathers

The common law presumes (the so-called 'marital presumption') that the husband of the woman giving birth is the child's father. The presumption may be rebutted by evidence showing that the husband cannot be the genetic parent. DNA testing is now usually conducted to establish this. Where sperm has been donated, the husband of the woman receiving treatment is regarded as the child's father, again displacing the donor, unless he proves that he did not consent to her treatment and he rebuts the marital presumption. Where donated sperm is used for a man and woman who are not married, the man will be regarded as the legal father, provided treatment is provided at a licensed clinic.

If a single woman uses donated sperm to conceive, the sperm donor will be regarded as the legal father of the child, unless the woman was treated at a licensed clinic, in which case, the child will have no 'legal father'. Following the Diane Blood case (where Mrs Blood used sperm taken from her dead husband to conceive two children), the 1990 Act was amended to provide that where a man gave his consent to the use of his sperm posthumously, he may be registered on the child's birth certificate as the father. Children born as a result of donations of eggs or sperm provided in licensed clinics after 1 April 2005 will be able to discover the identity of the donor once they reach the age of eighteen.

A couple (including a same-sex couple) who use a 'surrogate mother' to carry the child may acquire legal parentage of the child, either through a 'parental order' under the Human Fertilization and Embryology Act, or by adopting the child.

Establishing parentage

Under the Family Law Reform Act 1969 a court may direct that a scientific (ie DNA) test be carried out where parentage is in dispute. The court will make such a direction unless satisfied that it would be against the child's interests to do so. The usual approach of the courts is to consider it better for the child to 'know the truth' about his or her parentage and to direct a test. An adult cannot be required to undergo a test, but the court may (and will) draw adverse inferences from a refusal to do so, even to the extent of overriding the marital presumption. The court may order that the test be carried out on a child against the wishes of the child's carer, provided that it considers it in the best interests of the child to do so.

Birth registration

Under the Births and Deaths Registration Act 1953 the married parents of a child must register the birth within forty-two days. Where the parents are unmarried, the obligation falls on the mother. The father has no right to be registered on the birth certificate unless she agrees or he has a parental responsibility order or agreement or a court order requiring him to make financial provision for the child. Where the child is registered with no father's name given, it may be re-registered showing his name subject, again, to the mother's agreement or an appropriate court order. Married fathers have automatic parental responsibility by virtue of their marital status. Unmarried fathers have such responsibility if registered on the birth certificate (or by court order or agreement with the mother).   GILLIAN DOUGLAS

See also: **motherhood; fatherhood**

parents, unmarried   *see* **unmarried parents**

Paris Convention for the Protection of Industrial Property   The origins of proposals for an international convention on the protection of industrial property have been traced, to a suggestion of Prince Albert, the Consort of Queen Victoria, made at the time of the Great Exhibition of 1851, that there should be some form of international protection for inventions. The first international conference, which addressed the possibility of an international industrial property regime, was a conference on patent law, which was convened on the occasion of the 1873 Vienna International Exposition. At the time that plans for the Vienna Exposition were announced, US inventors and manufacturers had threatened a boycott of the event unless the Austrian Patent Law could be improved to provide more satisfactory protection to foreign inventors. These discussions were taken further in 1876, on the occasion of the Paris Universal Exposition and in a diplomatic conference in Paris in 1880. The Conference proposed the establishment of a 'Union for the Protection of Industrial Property'. The term 'Industrial Property' was defined broadly to include not only to the products of industry, but also agricultural products. A proposed convention was finally adopted by a second diplomatic conference convened in March 1883.

The Paris Convention prescribed some basic rules for the protection of inventions by **patents** and for the protection of **trade marks** and industrial **designs**. The Convention established the principle of national treatment for the protection of industrial property by which nations were obliged to treat foreigners the same way as they treated their nationals. It also created grace periods by which the owners of national registered industrial property rights within which they had the exclusive right to seek similar protection in Paris Union countries.

The Convention provided for its periodic revision in special treaties between Paris Union members. Thus subsequent treaties dealt with the subjects of unfair competition, designations of origin, industrial designs, patents, and trade marks.

The administration of the Paris Union and also of the Berne Union had been combined by the Swiss Government in an administrative Bureau of the Swiss Government, the Bureaux Internationaux Réunis pour la Protection de la Propriété Intellectuelle ('BIRPI'). From 1952, BIRPI began to assume a greater administrative independence and to move in the direction of becoming a specialized agency of the **United Nations**. This evolutionary process was consummated at the Stockholm Revision conference, which on 14 July 1967, adopted a Convention which established the **World Intellectual Property Organization** to administer the Paris Convention and its various specialized treaties, as well as the **Berne Convention for the Protection of Literary and Artistic Works** and other copyright conventions.

The principal provisions of the Paris Convention were adopted by the **World Trade Organization Agreement on Trade Related Aspects of Intellectual Property Rights ('TRIPs')** in 1994. That Agreement also adopted the national treatment principle and amplified some of the basic rules in relation to patents and trade marks and geographical indications which had been set out in the Paris Convention.

MICHAEL BLAKENEY

Parliament Acts The Parliament Act 1911 resolved the conflict over power to legislate in the **United Kingdom** between the (Liberal) **House of Commons** and the **House of Lords**, which then had a permanent Tory majority of hereditary peers. After the election of the Liberal government in 1906, the Lords rejected many reforms approved by the Commons, including the Finance Bill that gave effect to Lloyd George's budget of 1909. The 1911 Act turned the power of the Lords to veto bills approved by the Commons into a delaying power (sometimes called a suspensive veto).

The key points in the Act (as amended in 1949) were: (1) Money Bills could become law without any delay imposed by the Lords; (2) most other public bills could be enacted without Lords' approval when they had been sent from the Commons to the Lords in two (in 1911, three) successive sessions of Parliament, and one year (in 1911, two years) had elapsed between a bill's second reading in the Commons in session 1 and its third reading in the Commons in session 3; (3) bills to extend the life of Parliament beyond what became in 1911 a period of five years, were exempted from the operation of (2).

The 1911 Act passed through the Lords only when, after two general elections in 1910, George V agreed to create enough new peers to give the Liberal government a majority in the Lords. The preamble to the Act stated that it was intended to substitute for the Lords 'a Second Chamber constituted on a popular basis' but that this could not be done immediately. The 1949 Act reduced the delaying power from two years to one year.

Few Acts have been enacted under the provisions of Parliament Acts, the general practice of the Lords since 1945 being not to reject measures in the manifesto of the victorious party at the previous general election. The validity of the Parliament Act 1949 was upheld by the House of Lords in *R (Jackson) v Attorney-General* (2005), when a challenge was made to the Hunting Act 2004, enacted under the Parliament Acts.

ANTHONY BRADLEY

See also: **Acts of Parliament**

parliamentary counsel These are a group of lawyers, part of the Cabinet Office, who specialize in the drafting of government Bills and certain other legislation. They also review secondary legislation which amends primary legislation. Their product aims at certainty, and may require concentration to understand. Though this has been a ground for criticism of their monopoly in these tasks, experiments in bringing in others have shown no improvement in quality and considerable increases in cost. For the most part, Parliamentary Counsel are recruited directly from lawyers in private practice.

Drafting is carried out in teams of two and occasionally three, in response to a government-approved timetable and according to instructions received from departmental lawyers. Parliamentary Counsel usually subject these instructions to penetrating analysis to ensure that the policy behind them is clear and can lead to workable legislation. The anticipation and effects of this scrutiny in turn cause departmental lawyers to review instructions coming from administrators in a similar spirit, and thus Parliamentary Counsel exercise an effect on the making of legislative policy which is disproportionate to their numbers. They also have a special function of review in relation to matters of 'legal policy' such as the retrospectivity of legislation, and provide expert advice to the government about parliamentary procedures such as the application of the **Parliament Acts**.

Scotland and Northern Ireland (but not yet Wales) have their own parliamentary draftsmen, who draft legislation within their jurisdiction and contribute clauses on local matters or law to Westminster Bills.

PENNEY LEWIS

G Engle, ' "Bills are made to pass as razors are made to sell"': practical constraints in the preparation of legislation' (1983) 4 *Statute Law Review* 7

T Daintith and AC Page, *The Executive in the Constitution: Structure, Autonomy, and Internal Control* (Oxford: Oxford University Press, 1999), 251–256

Parliamentary Ombudsman *see* ombudsmen

parliamentary privilege Parliamentary privilege in the **United Kingdom** 'consists of the rights and immunities which the two Houses of Parliament and their members and officers possess to enable them to carry out their parliamentary functions effectively' (the Nicholls Report, Joint Committee on Parliamentary Privilege, 1999, paragraph 3). It is an historic part of the 'law and custom of Parliament', and it has never been the subject of comprehensive legislation.

The practical significance of parliamentary privilege has changed over centuries. The most important privilege of the **House of Commons** today is **freedom of speech**. By article 9 of the **Bill of Rights 1689**, 'the freedom of speech and debates or proceedings in Parliament ought not to be impeached or questioned in any court or place out of Parliament'. Members are not subject to criminal or civil liability for words spoken in Parliament. However, the House has power to control its own proceedings and may exercise its disciplinary jurisdiction if an MP abuses the freedom of speech, for example by making scurrilous allegations against individuals during debate. When civil or criminal proceedings are pending in the courts, the House enforces the *sub judice* rule to avoid statements in debate that would prejudice the fair conduct of the proceedings. Freedom of speech extends to evidence by witnesses to parliamentary committees. It applies to statements by members during all parliamentary proceedings, not solely in debate, but it does not extend to defamatory statements made outside the House. Members formerly enjoyed freedom from civil arrest while Parliament was sitting, but this privilege is unimportant today. Unlike legislators in many countries, they enjoy no privilege from arrest or prosecution under the criminal law. For historical reasons, the House of Commons enjoys certain privileges as against the Lords in respect of financial legislation. Each House controls its own proceedings and regulates its internal affairs without interference by the courts. Even if certain conduct is not a breach of privilege, it may be a contempt of the House.

Disputes over election results have long been decided by election courts, but the House retains the right to expel or suspend a member for serious breach of privilege or contempt. It has limited power to impose penalties on non-members: power to detain wrongdoers has not been exercised since the nineteenth century. Today the House makes a restrained use of its powers when a minor breach or contempt is committed by a non-member. Complaints of breach of privilege are raised initially with the Speaker and may be referred to the Committee on Standards and Privileges for investigation and report to the House so that a decision may be made by the House, on a vote which by custom is not subject to the party whips.

In many countries (such as the US), the written constitution grants privileges, powers, and immunities to the legislature and its members and officers. In some countries, particularly in the **Commonwealth**, the legislature's privileges are derived from the Westminster model. The authoritative account of that model is found in successive editions of Erskine

May, *Parliamentary Practice (The Law, Privileges, Proceedings and Usage of Parliament)*.

ANTHONY BRADLEY

parliamentary sovereignty In the **United Kingdom**, the sovereignty (or legislative supremacy) of Parliament refers to a fundamental doctrine that has long governed the relationship between Parliament and the courts. The nineteenth-century jurist, AV Dicey, defined Parliament for this purpose as comprising the **monarch**, the **House of Lords,** and the **House of Commons**, acting together in the legislative process: 'Parliament thus defined has under the English constitution the right to make or unmake any law whatever; and, further, . . . no person or body is recognised by the law of England as having a right to override or set aside the legislation of Parliament' (AV Dicey, *Law of the Constitution* (London: Macmillan, 8th edn,1915), 38–39). The doctrine has generally been considered as preventing Parliament from legislating so as to bind a future Parliament, for the reason that, if this were possible, a future Parliament would not be sovereign.

In many countries today, the written constitution both confers powers on the legislature and imposes limitations upon it, for example by declaring fundamental rights that the legislature must respect. Frequently, a supreme or constitutional court has power to determine whether these limits have been observed and, if necessary, to set aside legislation as unconstitutional where it exceeds those limits. This function of judicial review of legislation derives from the US Supreme Court's decision in *Marbury v Madison* (1803).

By contrast, the doctrine of parliamentary sovereignty excludes judicial review of legislation, and indeed the possibility of there being legally enforceable limits upon the subject matter of legislation. The historical origins of the doctrine are a matter for debate. One common explanation is that the doctrine resulted from the Settlement in 1688–89 (reflected in the Bill of Rights 1689) of the conflicts between Parliament and the monarchy, when the courts (it has been said) transferred their ultimate allegiance from the **monarch** to Parliament. But this transfer of allegiance did not require Parliament to be endowed with legislative omnipotence. Certainly, the doctrine could not have survived unless there had been radical changes in the political reality of the legislative process, with the House of Commons becoming more democratic during the nineteenth and twentieth centuries, the powers of the monarch coming to be exercised solely on the advice of ministers, and with the loss in 1911 by the House of Lords of

its veto over legislation under the **Parliament Acts**. But the sovereignty of Parliament is not, and cannot be regarded as, the sovereignty of the government or the House of Commons.

Nor must parliamentary sovereignty be confused with national sovereignty. The members of the **United Nations** may all be sovereign states, but many of them have written constitutions that to a greater or lesser extent impose limits on the national legislature. It is not obvious today that the legislature of any state should possess absolute power that would enable it (for instance) to authorize indefinite detention without trial, the infliction of torture, or in any way lead inexorably to the denial of fundamental rights.

Many jurists still defend the doctrine of parliamentary sovereignty in absolute terms, and so do many politicians. But in 2005 Lord Hope, a senior judge, said: 'Our constitution is dominated by the sovereignty of Parliament. But parliamentary sovereignty is no longer, if it ever was, absolute' (*R (Jackson) v Attorney-General* (2005), paragraph 104). There are several reasons for this view. States that are members of the **European Union** (including the United Kingdom) are obliged to give direct effect to EU law in their legal systems. Their legislatures may not make laws that conflict with EU law; and if they do so, the legislation may be disapplied by national courts and compensation may be payable to those whose rights under EU law are infringed. Moreover, it is incompatible with obligations accepted by the United Kingdom through ratifying international instruments concerning **human rights** to claim that the Westminster Parliament may authorize **torture**, **genocide**, racial discrimination, and the like. The Human Rights Act 1998 was intended to go as far as parliamentary sovereignty permits in enabling United Kingdom courts to review primary legislation that is claimed to be inconsistent with the **European Convention on Human Rights**. The scheme of the Act allows for the possibility of Parliament legislating in breach of European human rights. However, the Act also allows judicial review of **Acts of Parliament** on Convention grounds; it stops short only of enabling the courts to strike down such legislation, entrusting them only with the lesser, but significant, power of declaring the legislation incompatible with the Convention. A further reason for doubting whether the sovereignty of Parliament is absolute arises from the constitutional status of Scotland within the United Kingdom. The **Treaty of Union** in 1707 gave guarantees for certain Scottish institutions, including the church and the Scottish legal system, which on their face are incompatible with an English claim of absolute parliamentary sovereignty.   ANTHONY BRADLEY

J Goldsworthy, *The Sovereignty of Parliament: History and Philosophy* (Oxford: Oxford University Press, 1999)

See also: **Factortame** case (*R v Secretary of State for Transport, ex p Factortame Ltd*)

parliamentary supremacy   *see* **parliamentary sovereignty**

parliaments   As the name suggests, a parliament was, in its original conception, a deliberative assembly, commonly of the elite, to give authoritative advice on customary law to those with direct executive power. This sometimes extended to advice on contemporary legislative matters, and sometimes to advice on, or a share in, executive matters. Such assemblies existed in many ancient civilizations. Over time, some of these entities formed the institutional origins of more representative assemblies; this was, for instance in part the development of the *Curia Regis* (royal council) in England, from which emerged the English Parliament, amongst other state institutions.

Other early deliberative assemblies were developed as institutions of freemen with both law-making and executive competences. Some of the later developments in the ancient Greek city-states may be seen in this light. Certainly it was an element of Viking culture in which the *ting* was apparently such an assembly. It became an important element of the evolution of modern parliaments in Scandinavia and elsewhere. It was, for instance, the forerunner of the Parliament of Iceland, the Althingi, and of the Isle of Man, Tynwald, which are the oldest of modern parliaments.

The composition, structure, role, and functions of modern parliaments depend on the constitutional context in which they operate. There are supranational parliaments created by treaties that determine many of these matters. So, for instance, the **European Parliament** has significant legislative, financial, and scrutiny competences; the (African Union) Pan-African Parliament presently has scrutiny, advisory, and consultative functions, and is due to acquire legislative competence in 2009; while, by contrast, the Latin American Parliament and the Central American Parliament both essentially have the function of furthering integration in their respective regions.

In states with written constitutions, the constitution is commonly the instrument that both legally creates the national parliament, and also determines its competence and many of its attributes; importantly, as it is the creature of the constitution, such a parliament cannot legislate in violation of the constitution. The constitution also often provides for the relationship between the parliament and other institutions of the state. In states—a small minority—without a written constitution, such matters are established over time. In the UK, for example, this has been true of the legislative competence of Parliament—which in formal constitutional theory is largely unlimited—and of the constitutional relationships between Parliament and other institutions of the state.

Finally, there are sub-national parliaments. These will often be parliaments of the legal entities that form a federal state, but they may be parliaments of regions of a unitary state or parliaments of entities that have some form of dependency relationship with a state. Where the state has a written constitution, for the first two of these categories at least, the constitution will commonly provide for at least the division of legislative competence between the national parliament and the subnational parliaments. In states without a written constitution, matters are determined otherwise. In the UK, the creation, competence, and composition of the legislatures for Scotland, Wales, and Northern Ireland (but not those of the **Crown** dependencies) are provided by legislation of the UK Parliament, although some of the mechanics of the relationships between the subnational parliaments and the UK parliament are actually regulated by mutual agreement or **conventions of the constitution**.

Notwithstanding the constitutional context, the structure and composition of parliaments display significant variation. Most parliaments are either unicameral or bicameral, but they can be tricameral (for instance, Tynwald, the Parliament of the Isle of Man) and there are past examples of tetracameral legislatures (for example the Finnish Parliament until 1906). In bicameral legislatures, the second chamber, whether or not it has powers and functions broadly parallel with the first chamber, is often perceived in the public and political mind as a chamber which provides an opportunity to reconsider policy initiatives and revise legislation adopted by the other chamber. Unicameral parliaments tend to compensate for this by having a more extensive legislative process and more elaborate scrutiny procedures. In some states, the second chamber is also the one which directly represents interests different from those represented in the first chamber. The interests directly represented are commonly the units forming the federal state (as in the United States), but they may be economic and related interests of the state (as in Ireland), or they may reflect linguistic communities in the state (as in Belgium).

Parliamentary **elections** display similar diversity. Commonly they will have either a geographic focus, where a member is elected to parliament to represent a particular area (such as a constituency or a unit of a federal state); or a political focus, where members are elected from political party lists depending on the relative success of each party at an election. Sometimes members are elected on the basis of a combination of these two (as in, for instance, the Scottish Parliament and the National Assembly for Wales). However, elections may have an economic and structural focus (where members are elected to parliament to represent an industry or educational institutions) or a linguistic focus (where members are elected by specific linguistic groups within the state). In some cases, members are not elected but nominated, either as the normal procedure (for instance, in the Canadian Senate) or as an exceptional procedure (for instance, in the US Senate).

Aside from their diversity, most modern parliaments usually have three broad functions: considering and passing of legislation; scrutinizing Executive policy and administration of the Executive; authorizing the transfer of public monies to the Executive to carry out its policies and existing responsibilities, ensuring that such monies have been properly spent and (certainly in the case of national parliaments) authorizing the raising of public money by taxation. A common dilemma which parliaments face is to balance the performance of these functions in a manner sufficiently independent of the Executive of the day to make them meaningful, while allowing Executive government to be conducted reasonably and efficiently.   T ST JOHN BATES

See also: **House of Commons; House of Lords; Northern Ireland Assembly; Scottish Parliament; Welsh Assembly**

parole Parole is a mechanism which allows for the discretionary release of offenders who are serving custodial sentences for their crimes. **Discretion** is vested in a Parole Board, appointments to which are made by ministers. Prisoners who are granted parole spend a shorter proportion of their sentence in custody than they would have done had they not been granted parole and a longer period in the **community** under the supervision of an offender manager. Parolees are released subject to conditions which are included in a 'licence'. Should they breach these conditions, they may be returned to custody.

Release decisions are based on the **risk** that returning an offender to the community would pose to the **safety** of the public balanced against any benefits that might accrue from releasing the prisoner early. If the risk to public safety is judged unacceptable, parole should be denied. Assessing risk accurately is notoriously difficult. The process can, however, be improved by clear, well-structured criteria and by requiring decision-makers to pay attention to statistically-calculated actuarial 'risk of reconviction' scores. The value of using these scores—which provide a 'base expectancy' probability of a prisoner being reconvicted following release from custody— was reinforced by a recent study of parole decision-making in England and Wales published by Roger Hood and Stephen Shute (2002) which found that Parole Board members were, on aggregate, making decisions at that time on the basis of unduly pessimistic estimates of risk as compared with objectively-determined risk of reconviction data.

STEPHEN SHUTE

R Hood and S Shute, *The Parole System at Work* (Home Office Research Study No 202, 2002)

partnership law A partnership is defined in the Partnership Act 1890 as 'the relation which subsists between persons carrying on a business in common with a view to profit' (section 1(1) of the Partnership Act 1890). This definition tells us what a partnership is and sets out preconditions to a partnership coming into existence. Whilst we may talk generally about partnerships as if they existed in their own right, in fact in English law the partnership is not an entity or a legal **person** in the sense that a company is a legal person (although in Scotland a partnership *is* a legal person); rather it is 'a relation' between two or more persons. This means that partnership property is not owned by the partnership itself but is held by the partners together (as tenants in common). Contracts are entered into by the partners who are **agents** of the partnership and the other partners. This means that the contracts will bind the other partners provided that the contracting party was acting within his or her authority in entering into the contract. As the partnership is not a legal entity, one might expect that the partnership could not sue or be sued in the name of the partnership. For a long time this was the case. However, as this led to considerable complexity and difficulties, changes were made in the civil procedure rules to allow a partnership to sue and be sued in its own name.

The preconditions to forming a partnership are: first, that two or more persons carry on a business 'in common', that is, together for the benefit of them both; and second, that this business is carried on with a view to profit, that is, generating a net gain from the activities of the business. It is possible, therefore, for two persons to enter into a partnership inadvertently if they enter into a business venture together aiming to make a net gain. This is important because the effect of being a partnership is that the terms of the 1890 Act will apply to this venture. It is not always easy to determine whether an arrangement is a partnership. To help with this, the 1890 Act provides a list of factors to which a court should have regard in determining whether an arrangement is a partnership. Of particular importance is the sharing by the involved persons of the profits of the business (section 2(3) of the Partnership Act 1890). Prior to 2002 there was a prohibition on having more than twenty partners in a business partnership. This was removed by a regulatory reform order and there is no longer any limitation on the number of partners.

Any business arrangement that is a partnership, whether by design or unintentionally, is subject to the provisions of the 1890 Act. Amongst others, the Act provides a set of rules that regulate the interests and conduct of the partners in relation to the partnership unless the partners expressly, or by implication, disapply those rules (section 24 of the Partnership Act 1890). Typically, where it is intended to set up a partnership, these rules will be varied by a written partnership agreement. Where there is no partnership agreement these rules will apply unless impliedly varied, for example, through a repeated course of conduct by the parties. The rules cover a variety of areas, for example: they provide for an equal share in the capital and profits of the business; that all partners may participate in the management of the partnership and that matters will be decided by majority vote, although a change in the nature of the business must be decided by unanimous approval of all partners. It is also usual for a partnership agreement to provide for the duration of the partnership, for example a fixed period of years. However, if there is no express or implied agreement as to fixed term, the partnership is a partnership at will, terminable at any time on notice by one partner to the other partners (section 26(1) of the Partnership Act 1890).

As the partnership is not a separate legal person, the partners, *whose relations are the partnership*, are personally liable for the debts of the partnership, that is, the debts that all partners incur in the course of carrying out the business. This renders the partnership an unattractive **form of business organization** for those persons who wish to shield their personal assets from the debts of their business ventures. An alternative option for such persons would be to form a company with limited liability. However, in addition to the company option, the Limited Partnerships Act 1907 provides for the registration of limited partnerships which must have a minimum of one general partner, whose liability is not limited and may participate in the management of the partnership, and one limited partner whose liability is limited to the agreed capital contribution but may not participate in the management of the partnership. If a limited partner does involve herself in the management of the partnership, the shield of limited liability is lost (section 6(1) of the Limited Partnerships Act 1907). Following a joint report of the Scottish and English Law Commissions on partnership law (Law Com No 283 and Scot Law Com No 192), the government has agreed to take forward the Commissions' recommendations on Limited Partnership Law which are expected to be effected by regulatory reform order when parliamentary time allows. In this regard, the reforms will, amongst others, set forth a set of partnership activities which do not contravene the limited partner management prohibition.

DAVID KERSHAW

partnership law, sources of   In contrast to UK **company** law which does not have separate company law statutes for different types of company, UK **partnership law** provides such statutory categorization. Partnerships are subject to the Partnership Act 1890, limited partnerships are subject to Limited Partnership Act 1907, and limited liability partnerships are subject to the Limited Liability Partnership Act 2000. A substantial body of case law supplements the 1890 and 1907 Acts. Unless otherwise stated in the 2000 Act, the law, including any case law, applicable to partnerships does not apply to Limited Liability Partnerships.

In addition to statute and case law, an important element of the rules that govern the operation of a partnership are set forth in the partnership's partnership agreement, where the partners have entered into such an agreement.   DAVID KERSHAW

partnership taxation   In many jurisdictions **partnership**s, unlike corporations, are not treated as separate legal personalities but as a group of persons carrying on business. This creates the problem for the tax system of how the profits from such a partnership should be taxed. Should the partnership as an entity be taxed or the partners individually? At present in the UK, partners are taxed individually on their share of the profit of the partnership.

Problems can also arise when a company is a partner in a partnership because companies and individuals may be taxed on different bases. In the UK there are special rules about the taxation of corporations in this type of case.

Dealings with partnership assets and the interests of the partners in a partnership can also cause difficulties for a tax system. A partner does not necessarily own an interest in the underlying assets of a partnership, sometimes called 'partnership assets'. A partner has a right, to a share of the proceeds of the capital of the partnership, net of debts, and other expenses, as part of what is sometimes called a 'partnership share'. The UK legislation seeking to deal with this is somewhat obscure and a Statement of Practice has been issued which usually forms the basis of taxation. Essentially, dealings with partnership assets are treated as dealings by the partners individually, and are taxed accordingly.

Special complex rules often apply to Limited Partnerships and **Limited Liability Partnership**s. In the UK these are broadly intended to equate the taxation of such entities with that of other partnerships but to limit their use for tax-avoidance (eg by imposing restrictions on the use of losses). Limited Partnerships are sometimes accorded special tax treatment for investment purposes (eg land investment and venture capital in the UK).

Different rules apply to partnerships in relation to value added tax ('VAT'). In the UK the members of a partnership are allowed to register for VAT under one name. Difficulties can arise, where a partner makes a supply to a partnership, as to whether the supply was made by the partner acting as such (no VAT) or as a third party (potentially subject to VAT).

There are complex rules for partnerships in relation to **Stamp Duty Land Tax**. These are intended to tax the land element of dealings with and by partnerships and partners and prevent 'abuse', but not catch 'normal' dealings by partnerships concerning the premises which they own and from which they operate.   ADRIAN SHIPWRIGHT

partnership, civil   *see* **civil Partnership**

part-time worker   Part-time is the most popular form of atypical work. A worker on a part-time contract is someone who works fewer hours than a worker on a full-time contract. Although there is not a specific number of hours that qualify a worker as full or part-time, a full-time worker normally works thirty-five hours or more a week. There are several reasons for choosing to work part-time: these can range from the need to balance work and personal commitments, such as caring responsibilities, to simply wanting to have a different work–life balance. Research has shown that part-time work is more likely to be provided by the public sector and is mainly undertaken by women.

Part-time work was often associated with low-skilled and poorly-paid jobs and, as a result, part-time workers were in a disadvantaged position. In order to avoid this situation, many legal systems now require that this type of contract is regulated by law. Part-time workers must have the same statutory employment rights, such as rates of pay, **pension** opportunities, contractual benefits, training and career development, holiday entitlements, opportunities for career breaks, sick pay, **maternity**, **adoption**, **paternity,** and parental benefits, as an 'equivalent' full time-employee where equivalent is defined as a worker performing a similar job on the same type of contract. These benefits must normally be given on a *pro rata* basis. Furthermore, being part-time cannot be used as a reason for transfer or **redundancy**, or refusing a promotion. Part-time workers can only be treated less favorably than a full-time worker when there is an objective justification for doing so. This means that the employer has to show that the reason is justifiable, and the right way to meet a genuine aim of the business.

EUGENIA CARACCIOLO DI TORELLA

party walls   At **common law** (ie apart from statute) the expression 'party wall' has no precise meaning, but generally signifies a wall separating structures belonging to different owners. It could apply (1) to a wall owned by both owners in common; (2) to a wall divided into longitudinal halves in separate ownership; (3) to a wall belonging entirely to one owner subject to **easements** in favour of the other to have the wall maintained in position; or (4) to a wall as in (2) subject to cross-easements of support. Following abolition of tenancy in common by the Law of Property Act 1925 section 38, walls in category (1) were effectively transferred to category (4).

There is no common law obligation to repair the party structure to make it weatherproof. But removal by one owner of his building, leading to the wall suffering damage from water or loss of support, may give rise to liability in tort for **nuisance** or negligence.

Under the Party Wall etc Act 1996 'party wall' means '(a) a wall which forms part of a building and stands on lands of different owners to a greater extent than the projection of any artificially formed support on which the wall rests; and (b) so much of a wall not being a wall within paragraph (a) above as separates buildings belonging to different owners'.

The Act defines 'party fence wall' 'as a wall (not being part of a building) which stands on lands of different owners and is used or constructed to be used for separating such adjoining lands, but does not include a wall constructed on the land of one owner the artificially formed support of which projects into the land of another owner'.

The 1996 Act does not alter the ownership of party walls but allows one owner to carry out works to a party wall or party fence wall going beyond his rights at common law. The exercise of these rights is conditional on service of the appropriate notice to the other owner. Disputes about any aspect of the work to be done are resolved by surveyors appointed in accordance with the Act. An appeal lies to the County Court against the surveyors' decisions ('award').

STEPHEN BICKFORD-SMITH

passing off   The **common law** tort of passing off provides a remedy against the deceptive invasion of a person's property interest in the goodwill of a business, which is likely to be injured by a misrepresentation on the part of another that the other's goods or services are that person's goods or services. The modern formulation of the tort may be reduced to three essential elements: the claimant trader must establish first, that their business possesses sufficient goodwill; secondly, that the defendant trader made a misrepresentation in the course of trade, to customers, or prospective customers, about the goods or services concerned, which is likely to deceive them into believing that the goods or services the defendant offers are those of the claimant; and thirdly, that the misrepresentation caused actual damage to the claimant's business or goodwill or will probably do so.

Goodwill is defined as the good name and reputation of a business; it is the 'thing' that attracts consumers to a particular business, product, or service. The claimant must prove that the goodwill existed at the date of commencement of the conduct complained of.

The claimant must prove that a relevant misrepresentation was made in express words or was implied in the use or imitation of a trade mark, trade name or get-up. While evidence of actual consumer confusion is relevant, the courts have historically also required the presence of deception, rejecting claims for passing off where the misappropriation of goodwill was not deceptive. Proof of intentional or deliberate deception is not necessary. Nor are the parties required to share a common field of business activity. Where a false suggestion by the defendant that the parties' businesses are connected is likely to damage the claimant's goodwill, an action for passing off will lie.

The claimant must show that as a result of the misrepresentation the goodwill of the business has been damaged or is likely to suffer damage. Damages may be assessed in the form of lost sales or lost income. If the wrong consists in dilution of the claimant's goodwill (ie in lessening the capacity of a sign or mark on which it depends to identify and distinguish the claimant's goods or services), damages will be assessed according to the loss of value of the goodwill as a result of the injurious association with the defendant's business.

The action for passing off has traditionally been the means used for defending unregistered **trade marks** against unauthorized use. Passing off is also commonly invoked as an alternative action in claims for infringement of a registered trade mark. More recently, courts in the United Kingdom have extended passing off to protect well known geographical indications from deception as to source or quality (eg by use of the name 'Elderflower Champagne', which has been found damaging to the distinctiveness of 'Champagne' as the name for sparkling wine from the Champagne district of France); to provide protection from the use of **domain names** incorporating **well-known trade marks** (eg domain names confusingly similar to 'Marks and Spencer'); and to protect personality in situations involving the endorsement of goods and services (eg false suggestions that a celebrity has positively endorsed an advertised product).   GAIL EVANS

See also: **character merchandizing**

passport   A passport is a basic **identity** document accepted as valid for crossing international borders. Passports are generally considered to provide conclusive evidence of a person's **citizenship**. Passports are linked to the right of a state to provide diplomatic protection to the passport holder and to the right of nationals to enter their own country of **nationality**. Passports can be denied to nationals in some circumstances as they are not an unassailable right of citizenship.

Passports have been in use for centuries. The first passports were often sealed letters from the sovereign identifying the bearer and seeking his safe passage. Moves to standardize passports worldwide date to the early decades of the twentieth century, at the same time as migration controls became commonplace.

Passports contain the citizen's name, place, and date of birth, photograph, signature, and other identifying information. Some wealthy countries are moving towards using biometric indicators such as fingerprints, hand measurements, or facial feature measurements. Such details are typically embedded in a chip in the passport, and specialized machinery is necessary to 'read' this information which is not yet widely available. Biometric data make it more difficult for passports to be produced fraudulently. Most passports are now machine-readable, relying on a system that is managed by the International Civil Aviation Organization (established in 1946 pursuant to the Chicago Convention on Civil Aviation of 1944) which sets standards for passports.

In addition to the ordinary passports carried by most travellers, states also issue diplomatic passports, official passports, and temporary passports. Diplomatic passports identify those whom a state believes are likely entitled to diplomatic courtesies and protections. Official passports may be used by travellers on official business who are not likely entitled to diplomatic protection. Temporary passports may be issued in circumstances when a government has not been able to fully verify all underlying identity documents, such as when a **child** citizen is born overseas or when someone has lost their passport.

Recently Members States of the European Union have moved to having a standardized passport format. While individual Member States retain their authority over matters of citizenship and the issuing of passports, the common format for European Union passports is a convenience reflecting the border-crossing privileges of European Union citizenship.   CATHERINE DAUVERGNE

patent agent   A patent agent is a person with recognized expertise in the field of intellectual property generally and **patents** specifically. In the UK patent agents form an elite professional community, membership of which is denoted by inclusion on the Register of Patent Agents. The Register exists under statute and is maintained by The Chartered Institute of Patent Attorneys ('CIPA'), a body empowered by royal charter of which most patent agents are also members.

To register as a patent agent a person must pass certain examinations and complete two or more years' supervised practice, or four or more years' unsupervised practice, in a field of intellectual property, including a substantial component in patent agency work. While registration is not required to advise on patent matters or appear as a representative before the UK Patent Office, it is a clear indicator of professional competency, including competency in the technical skill of preparing a patent application.

Referring to oneself as a patent agent without being registered to do so is a criminal offence.

With one exception the term 'patent agent' is synonymous with 'patent attorney'. The exception relates to solicitors, who may refer to themselves as patent attorneys without being registered as patent agents. A patent agent or attorney who is also a member of CIPA may also use the titles Chartered Patent Agent and/or Chartered Patent Attorney. Patent agents and attorneys are frequently also European Patent Agents and Attorneys, for whom a separate Register exists maintained by the European Patent Office under the European Patent Convention.

JUSTINE PILA

Patent Cooperation Treaty   The Patent Cooperation Treaty ('PCT') is an international treaty concluded in 1970 as a special agreement under the 1883 **Paris Convention for the Protection of Industrial Property**. It establishes an international system for the filing and examination of patent applications and the conduct of 'prior art' (technical literature) searches that is administered by a network of national and regional patent offices acting as Receiving Offices, International Searching Authorities, and/or International Preliminary Examining Authorities. Its specific purpose is to help inventors obtain a patent for the same invention in two or more PCT countries by allowing them to assert their claim internationally and have it subjected to preliminary assessment before committing to one or more local applications. It thus reduces the risk of wasted expenditure by enabling an applicant to postpone the decision to pursue an application to grant until confident of its success. By creating a series of pre-grant procedures with recognized validity in each of the PCT's nearly 140 countries, it also provides a basis for the harmonization of patentability standards and facilitates the move toward the creation of an international patent.

The network of offices that administers the PCT system includes the Patent Offices of many PCT countries and the International Bureau of the **World Intellectual Property Organization**, under whose predecessor the PCT was formed. The UK and European Patent Offices are both Receiving Offices for PCT purposes, and the European Patent Office an International Searching Authority and Preliminary Examining Authority as well.

The PCT system can be used by anyone seeking a patent in one or more PCT country or associated region. It requires that an otherwise local application be commenced as an international application by (among other things) being filed with a Receiving

Office and designating the countries or regions in which a patent is sought. Once filed, an international application is forwarded to an International Searching Authority, which searches for evidence that the invention was known or technically obvious at its filing or other priority date. The results of the search are incorporated into two documents which the Authority prepares: a search report, produced for the public and made available with the application eighteen months after the priority date or as soon as possible thereafter; and an opinion on the invention's patentability, produced for the applicant as a non-binding assessment of the likely success of the application.

Following publication, an applicant has a limited period within which to pursue an application by entering it into the 'national phase' in each of the designated countries and regions from which a patent is sought. In the UK and many other PCT countries that period is thirty-one months from the priority date. Before entering the national phase an applicant may amend the application to address any weaknesses revealed by the search report, and may also request its examination by an International Preliminary Examining Authority in order to obtain a more detailed report on its strength and thus a more accurate assessment of its likelihood of success.

JUSTINE PILA

patents   The term 'patent' is an abbreviation of 'letters patent', the open form of document historically issued by the **Crown** for the purpose of conferring a right or privilege or otherwise communicating the royal will. In contemporary law it denotes the species of intellectual property that is granted as an inducement for the creation and disclosure of novel, inventive, and industrially applicable inventions. In the UK that property is conferred under the Patents Act 1977 or, with similar effect, the European Patent Convention ('EPC'), and it comprises the exclusive right to use and sell a protected invention for up to twenty years.

A protected invention may be any subject matter having technical character; a definition derived from the Act's express exclusion from patentability of (among other things) discoveries, scientific theories, business methods, and computer programs 'as such'. Also excluded are surgical, therapeutic, and diagnostic methods (for lack of industrial applicability), and inventions the commercial exploitation of which would be contrary to public policy or morality. In these and other respects the Patents Act follows the EPC, which it was the explicit purpose of that Act to implement.

Patents are territorial, and are thus only valid and can only be infringed in their country of issue. A UK inventor who wishes to obtain protection outside the UK must obtain a patent from that country, either directly by applying under its laws, or if it is a party to the EPC or other intergovernmental agreement, indirectly by applying under that agreement. Inventors seeking protection for an invention in more than one country will often do so by means of the **Patent Cooperation Treaty**.

In the UK, patents are granted by the UK Patent Office or the European Patent Office after compliance with the application process set down in the Patents Act or EPC. The grant of a patent by either body is however no assurance of its legal validity, which can always be challenged before the courts.

The central requirement of the application process is that an applicant provide a written specification, including a statement and description of the invention sufficient to enable any appropriately skilled person to use it. Provision of the specification is the *quid pro quo* for which the patent is granted, and accounts for the conception of patents as involving a contract between the state and public on one hand and the inventor on the other. Under that contract, the state grants a patent in exchange for the disclosure of a new and inventive idea of industrial utility. While the effect of the grant is to prevent the public from making unauthorized use of the idea in the short-term, by first requiring its disclosure, the patent system also ensures its availability to the public in the long-term. Hence the importance of the specification, which constitutes the public record of the invention as well as of the scope of the patentee's monopoly. Drafting patent specifications is an important technical skill of a **patent agent**.

Origins of the patent

The practice of granting patents for inventions has its origins in the English feudal custom of conferring exclusive privileges of manufacture and trade on the early merchant and craft guilds. In the fourteenth century a weak economy convinced the Crown of the need to compromise the guild monopolies in order to encourage the development of local industry and exploitation of local resources. The Crown's original preferred method was to lure foreign workers with the promise of special trade privileges, including exemption from the rules of the guilds, in exchange for a commitment to practice and train local apprentices in their trades and crafts.

The early letters of privilege tended to offer expedients other than monopolies. By the fifteenth century, however, the use of monopolies to encourage innovation was becoming common in the city-states of Italy; an oft-cited example being the 1421 grant to Brunelleschi of a three-year monopoly over the manufacture and use of a new device for transporting heavy loads over the Arno and other rivers. In 1474 the first general patent statute was enacted, in Venice.

Knowledge of the Italian practice of rewarding inventions with monopolies spread to England in the early sixteenth century, reportedly by letter from a Venetian silk maker to the King's Principal Secretary, Thomas Cromwell, in 1537. In 1561 it was embraced by Elizabeth I as a means of encouraging the introduction of new trades and devices in the hope of making her realm industrially and economically self-sufficient.

The patent policy of Elizabeth I was vulnerable to abuse, and it was not long before a practice developed of rewarding the Crown's favoured courtiers with extended monopolies over the manufacture of known devices and the practice of established trades, including the manufacture and sale of such basic and locally produced commodities as starch, salt and vinegar. These so-called 'odious monopolies' were devastating for trade and the public, and provoked intense political opposition, leading in 1601 to a debate between the **House of Commons** and the Crown over the scope of the **royal prerogative** that ended with a royal promise to revoke the worst of the monopolies and recognize the future jurisdiction of the **common law courts** to determine their legality. That jurisdiction was first tested in the *Case of Monopolies* (1602), in which the Court of King's Bench established the general proposition that by reducing employment and encouraging manufacturers to raise their prices and lower their manufacturing standards, monopolies were contrary to the public interest and thus to the common law. However, the King's Bench also recognized a limited exception covering patents for new and useful trades and engines, which it reportedly justified with reference to the 'charge or industry' or 'wit or invention' which their introduction to the realm required.

Despite this decision, the grant of odious monopolies continued under James I, prompting further intervention by the Parliament and, finally, the introduction of the Statute of Monopolies 1623. By that Act monopolies were declared 'contrary to the law' and 'utterly void and of none effect', with a limited exception for patents and grants for 'the sole working or making of any manner of new manufactures . . . not contrary to the law, nor mischievous to the state, by raising prices of commodities at home, or hurt of trade, or generally inconvenient'. Drafted by Lord **Coke** as a codification of the common law principles reported (by him) to have been expressed in the *Case of Monopolies*, it is this exception on which the modern patent systems of the common law world are built. Indeed, the current Patents Acts of Australia and New Zealand refer explicitly to the Statute of Monopolies, as did the UK Patents Act before its amendment in 1977 to incorporate the EPC.

Contemporary patent issues

Patents are typically justified as an inducement to innovation without which research and development would lag and research-intensive industries (like the biotechnology industry) would collapse. For every patent enthusiast, however, there is a patent sceptic ready to challenge the basic and largely unproven economic assumptions on which the patent system rests, particularly as it extends into new and emergent fields of technology with ever-widening implications for international trade and development.

Still, patent scepticism is not reserved to those who would abolish patents altogether as an unjustified exception to the general prohibition against monopolies. Indeed, the more commonly held view is that while justified in theory, the patent system is and has always been problematic in practice. One of the reasons for this view is the liberal patent-granting practices of patent offices and the difficulties of challenging and regulating the patents they grant. Thus, patent offices have long been criticized for failing properly to apply the statutory standards of patentability when considering applications, and for issuing patents of excessive breadth or doubtful validity. Such patents have been particularly controversial since the advent of recombinant, digital and (other forms of) information technology, which many believe to be unsuited for, if not statutorily excluded from, patent protection. At the least, those technologies have raised the question of the role and impact of patents and the patent system in the post-mechanical age; a question further complicated by the impacts of globalization and international trade agreements like the **World Trade Organization Agreement on Trade Related Aspects of Intellectual Property Rights ('TRIPs')**, and by the establishment of the EPC system, the Patent Office and legal boards of which have supported different and at times conflicting approaches to patent law and administration than those of their national counterparts.

Add to this the difficulties created by the technical and often complex nature of the subject matter for which patents are sought, and the pressures on patent offices of providing an efficient service to inventors, and one can see how matters of patent policy and the wider public interest become obscured in the day-to-day operation of the system. Such issues are among those identified in The Gowers Review of Intellectual Property—the comprehensive study of the UK intellectual property system that was published in December 2006.   JUSTINE PILA

patents and copyright in developing countries The weight of economic activity, particularly in the developed countries, has increasingly shifted towards knowledge-based products and services, giving rise to what is often characterized as the 'knowledge economy'. Consequently, there has been an increasing emphasis, in the last two decades, on the protection of knowledge, through the medium of **intellectual property rights**, the main types of which are, **patents** and **copyright** (hereafter referred to, collectively, as 'IPRs'). The adoption of the **World Trade Organization Agreement on Trade Related Aspects of Intellectual Property Rights ('TRIPs')** at the conclusion of the Uruguay Round of the General Agreement on Tariffs and Trade ('GATT') negotiations in 1994, ushered a comprehensive regime requiring both developed and developing countries to legislate minimum standards for the protection of IPRs.

The practical reality however, is that developing countries are, almost invariably, net users of IPRs, in comparison to the developed countries, which are, on average, net producers and holders of such rights. Developing countries have, historically, argued that the IPR regime places them at a disadvantage in terms of access to technology and is, therefore, a handicap to their own development. On the other hand, developed countries, whose industries hold the bulk of IPRs, argue that, they provide necessary incentives for innovation. Consequently, IPRs have, generally, been at the centre of political, economic, and legal conflicts between developed and developing countries.

A key area of contention is the impact of patents on access to medicines and other basic needs for citizens of the developing countries. Developing countries argue that patents for essential medicines give holders monopolies, which enable them to set prices, which are often beyond the reach of the majority of their citizens, who have limited economic capacity. Yet, the pharmaceutical industry in the developed countries argues that research into medicinal drugs is expensive and patents enable them to recoup their costs, while the profits provide incentives for further research and development. It has been difficult to reconcile these arguments, demonstrating the conflicts between developing countries' efforts to meet the social needs of their citizens and the developed countries' desire to meet their industries' interests to earn a profit from their investments.

A further, critical issue is, whether or not, and, if so, the extent to which IPRs provide sufficient protection to all forms of knowledge. Some researchers and developing country activists argue that the nature of IPRs is such that they are tailored towards the protection of Western-oriented knowledge systems, as opposed to traditional knowledge systems, which tend to be held, mainly, by **communities** in developing countries. There have been accusations of, for example, bio-piracy, the practice by which the traditional knowledge and biological resources existing in developing countries are appropriated and used by the pharmaceutical industry in drugs research, without acknowledgement or compensation to the communities. Similar problems arise in relation to traditional forms of art, designs, symbols, artefacts, and names that may be used commercially, without recognizing the legal rights of the communities that have historically created or held them.

The trouble is that even if IPRs could sufficiently protect such traditional forms of knowledge, communities in developing countries face additional practical impediments resulting from their economic incapacity to participate and compete effectively with large multinational **companies** in obtaining IPRs, let alone maintaining the necessary vigilance to fight against infringements of those rights.

Overall, serious debate continues in relation to the benefits, if any, to developing countries, of the expansion of the IPRs regime. There is a real risk of increasing costs on countries already suffering under the weight of poverty. The dangers of limiting **access to medicines**, books, and seeds threaten efforts to alleviate poverty. It appears inevitable that the contests over the expansion of IPRs between developed and developing countries will persist. Whether or not IPRs actually benefit developing countries in the long run remains to be seen.   ALEX MAGAISA

paternity Legal paternity refers to the status of being a child's father, entitling a man to be registered as such (sections 2, 10, and 10A of the Births and Deaths Registration Act 1953). Law recognizes only one man as having this status at any given time. To have paternity is very different from having **parental responsibility**. Paternity is a status, while parental responsibility gives a **person** legal power to act as a parent. Only married fathers have automatic parental responsibility.

With sexual reproduction, paternity is firmly grounded in genetics, unless **adoption** occurs.

This reflects the traditional **common law** position, which vested paternity in the genitor, despite the fact that genetic fatherhood could not be positively determined. **Marriage**, therefore, was the regulator of paternity and genetic fatherhood was assumed by virtue of being married to the child's mother. The advent of donor insemination further highlighted how firmly paternity was grounded in genetics. Until 1987, the semen donor was considered the legal father, even if the **child** was born to a married couple. Secrecy surrounding the procedure, however, typically resulted in the woman's husband being surreptitiously registered as the child's legal father, despite this being an offence under the Perjury Act 1911.

Recent statutory law regulating **assisted conception** has changed this legal position. Now, in the context of assisted conception, paternity can also be grounded on a man's relationship with a child's mother and/or his intent to create a child. The Family Law Reform Act 1987 allowed a married man to be vested with paternity in donor insemination cases. Section 28 of the **Human Fertilization and Embryology Act** 1990 extended this principle to other assisted conception techniques. Furthermore, section 28 allows a man who has neither a genetic connection to a child, nor a legal connection to its mother to be vested with paternity, provided he and the mother have received fertility treatment 'together'. Finally, the Human Fertilization and Embryology (Dead Fathers) Act 2003 amends the 1990 Act to allow men whose semen is used after their death to be considered a child's legal father, on the condition that his consent has been obtained before his death.

JULIE MCCANDLESS

paternity leave   *see* **parental leave**

patronage   The basic idea of one high-status patron authorizing the appointment to some public position of a lower-status beneficiary is as old and universal as government (of a tribe, court, nation, church) itself. Modern, developed nations may claim that their meritocratic education systems and objective examinations for **public appointments** have long since wholly expunged old, corrupt traditions of personal patronage appointments. Beyond 'civil service' structures—notably in political parties and the media—personal patronage based on subjectively assessed talent still counts.

  In developing countries patronage often dominates, with strong 'moral' pressure on public officials to find jobs or favours for their extended family and tribal kinsmen. This 'corrupt' patronage system in modern Africa and elsewhere was exactly presented

in (for example) British plays and novels of 150–300 years ago in which mendicants pleaded with their rich or well-connected kinsmen to get them public positions, military commissions, or government pensions based wholly on their personal link, not qualification or suitability. This tradition was defended against the rise of competitive examinations. (*The Times* protested that appointing junior officers by ability rather than patronage based on payment for commissions would ruin the army.)

Unfettered church patronage has much declined as formal qualifications and procedures to become a priest or minister now determine entry. But subsequent appointments to particular churches and, of course (as in other professions), promotions require patronage. The legal establishment of the **Church of England** entails the **Prime Minister** having an ecclesiastical appointments secretary for some priests' and all bishops' appointments.

Elected politicians (MPs and local councillors) in Britain live entirely by patronage particularly when theirs is the governing party. Their leaders control all promotions to ministerial jobs, **House of Commons** committee chairs and memberships, and similar moves on local councils. At Westminster, the government's senior party manager (chief whip) used also to be called the patronage secretary because he advised on every ministerial appointment.

Modern governments' patronage has extended massively as numberless semi-official bodies have arisen to link the state more closely with civil society, usually for the regulation of commercial business or work with charitable (not-for-profit) or professional bodies. Many thousands of appointments give these private citizens public status in exchange for their usually unpaid advice and knowledge, perhaps regulating anything from the standards of advertising to those of zoos. In Britain, these 'quangos' (quasi-nongovernment organizations) or government 'task forces' are the home of modern mass government patronage. But government domination cannot be assumed. If ministers want to take advantage of these many bodies' effort and representative legitimacy, they must respect their semi-independence or risk failing to recruit the best people to them.

ANTHONY BARKER

pay   *see* **wages and deductions; minimum wage**

PAYE   *see* **employment tax**

peacekeeping   Peacekeeping is the term used to describe a particular kind of military operation conducted under the auspices of the **United Nations**

('UN'). Peacekeeping, however, does not appear in the UN Charter as one of the grounds upon which recourse to force may be authorized, nor is peacekeeping included as one of the functions of the UN. Peacekeeping operations were created through the practices of the UN and its members. While the UN had installed observer missions involving military personnel in Palestine in 1948 and in India and Pakistan in 1949, the first force-level peacekeeping mission to be deployed was United Nations Emergency Force I ('UNEF I'), created in response to the 'Suez crisis' of 1956. This mission, together with later models and guidelines prepared by the UN, established the key principles of peacekeeping—consent of the parties to the deployment of military personnel, impartiality, and the use of force only in self-defence. As UNEF I illustrates, peacekeeping emerged alongside the process of decolonization. Peacekeeping offered a means of responding to the challenges that decolonization posed—to the peoples of newly independent states, to the integrity of the fledgling UN, and its international legal regime for governing peace and security, and to the protection of foreign investment.

Since the end of the Cold War, peacekeeping operations have proliferated and become increasingly complex. Where once their mandates tended to be limited to monitoring ceasefires or restoring peace and security, post-Cold War objectives include delivering humanitarian assistance and exercising legal and administrative authority. The legitimacy of peacekeeping operations remains controversial. For some, peacekeeping is one of many legal innovations which have allowed the UN to remain relevant in a changing world. For others, the lack of a firm legal foundation for peacekeeping means the practice is open to abuse by powerful states.

ANNE ORFORD

Pearson Royal Commission   *see* **tort system**

pensions   Pensions are regular payments of income to those retired from work because of age or disability. State pensions are payable to those over pensionable age. Occupational pensions are payable to many retired employees. Individuals can also arrange private pensions. Widows and other surviving partners and dependents are often entitled to pensions payable in respect of those who have died.

Retirement pensions

Retirement pensions used more accurately to be called 'old age pensions'. There are three kinds, dependent on age, retirement, or both. They are:

- State pensions for those over state pensionable age. This is currently 60 for women and 65 for men.
- Occupational pensions for employees who have been members of pension schemes run by their employers and are now retired and over the retirement age for the pension scheme. This is usually between 60 and 65. It must be the same for women and men.
- Personal pensions purchased by or for individuals, including the self-employed. They are usually payable in full when the individual reaches an agreed age not less than 50.

Although these pensions are called retirement pensions, most do not require pensioners to retire and stop all work. The state pension is not payable until pensionable age is reached but can be postponed for up to five years. Postponed pensions are paid at a higher weekly rate to reflect the late start to entitlement. Pension rights may be lost by failure to claim. State pensionable age for women rises after 2010 from sixty and becomes sixty-five in 2020. It is likely to be further increased for everyone after that as people live longer.

Occupational pensions are usually paid only when the employee stops working for, and receiving earnings from, the employer. Traditionally that happens between sixty and sixty-five. Many schemes with retirement ages below sixty-five are now increasing them. **European Union** law requires that the same age is set for men and women. Pensions may be payable below usual retirement age if the employer agrees to the employee taking early retirement. Pensions payable early are usually reduced by an actuarial discount. This reflects how much longer the employee is likely to receive the pension because of early retirement. Employers seeking to reduce staff sometimes offer enhanced pensions to those retiring early.

The age at which personal pensions are paid is agreed between the contributor and the pension scheme. In practice, pensions are rarely paid to individuals below fifty. This is because tax rules set that minimum age. Some may be fully paid only at seventy.

State retirement pensions

Entitlement to British state retirement pensions depends on the claimant being over state pensionable age and a claim having been made. They have four elements:

- basic retirement pension;
- additional pension—also called SERPS or state second pension;

- graduated retirement benefit;
- state pension credit.

All bar state pension credit depend on a **National Insurance** ('NIns') contributions record; to claim state pension credit the claimant must live in Britain.

Basic state retirement pension is a fixed weekly amount for an individual pensioner (more for a couple). To receive the full amount NIns contributions must have been paid at a minimum level for most of a person's working life from sixteen to pensionable age. The Customs and Revenue's NIns Contributions Office keeps contribution records. Contributions are paid by all employees earning over a weekly minimum level, and by most self-employed individuals. Contributions are credited to those incapacitated from work. They are not payable by those claiming home responsibility protection ('HRP'). This is a relief from contributions that can be claimed by those not working while they look after children or other dependents. Voluntary contributions may be paid to make up a defective pension record. HRP and contribution records can be checked through the DWP Pension Service.

Additional or second pension is paid to former employees whose employment did not involve membership of an occupation pension scheme, or whose occupational scheme pays less than the guaranteed minimum pension for that person. It is not paid to anyone in respect of years for which the pensioner is receiving a full occupational pension. The amount of additional pension depends entirely on the total of NIns contributions paid as an employee since 1975. Graduated retirement benefit is paid for contributions made by employees before then. Both are claimed from the Pension Service.

State pension credit is payable on claim to anyone over sixty living in Britain with no other income, or whose pension is below a weekly minimum level for the claimant (or couple). It does not depend on any contribution or tax record. It is income-based, and so is payable only to make up total income to a set weekly level. It also takes into account all savings held by anyone claiming. In practice most people receiving basic state pension but no other pensions, and who have only small savings, will be entitled to state pension credit. Those getting state pension credit are usually also entitled to council tax benefit and, if paying rent, housing benefit.

Example

Mervyn is sixty-five in November 2009. He entered the NIns scheme in November 1955 when he was sixteen. To receive full basic retirement pension at sixty-five he must have paid or been credited with NIns contributions to cover forty-four of the forty-nine years between 1955 and 2008. Provided he claimed them (or claimed benefit), he should have credits for any gaps caused by staying on at school until eighteen or for illness or unemployment. If he worked in another European Union state, contributions paid there will also count. Mervyn can claim graduated retirement benefit for graduated contributions made before 1975 as an employee. He can claim additional pension if employed and paying NIns contributions from 1975 but not in an occupational pension scheme. If he only gets a small pension and has no other income, he can claim state pension credit.

Occupational pensions

Employers are not currently required to provide pension schemes for employees. Where employers provide pensions, they usually replace the state additional or second pension.

Designs and values of occupational pensions vary widely. Specific rules for each scheme must be set out formally. The pension fund must be run by a trust separate from the employer. It depends on fund rules whether the fund is invested in the employer's business or entirely separately. Where pension funds are invested in the employer's business there is a risk that employees lose both their jobs and their future pensions if the employer becomes insolvent. There is a limited public scheme to protect employees caught in this way.

There are two types of occupational pension: defined benefit (final salary-based) schemes and defined contribution (contribution-based) scheme. Final salary schemes pay pensions based on earnings of employees when retiring. Pensions from contribution-based schemes depend entirely on total contributions paid by or for individual members. Final salary schemes guarantee set pension levels on retirement—often half the final earnings for those who have worked long enough. But many companies are shutting these schemes down as too expensive. Pensions from contributions-based schemes are not guaranteed. They depend on the value at retirement of investments made from total contributions paid.

Normally both employees and employers contribute to occupational pensions at fixed percentages of earnings. This has tax advantages. Employees do not pay income tax on earnings used for contributions and pay a lower rate of NIns contributions. They also benefit because the employer's contribution is ignored when calculating their total income for income tax purposes. Further, income and any capital gains earned by contributions held in the pension fund are not income of employees for their income tax purposes. So there is a tax exemption both for income used for contributions and the fund income from contributions. Occupational pensions are taxed in the same way as earnings.

Other pensions

Individuals may buy personal pensions by regular contributions or by investing capital sums. Properly funded personal pension schemes also receive income tax advantages like those for occupational pensions up to maximum annual limits. These include tax exemptions to help the self-employed buy their own pensions.

The state pension system provides some help to a widow, widower, or civil partner after the death of a contributor. Occupational pension schemes often also provide pensions for survivors. In practice, all employees have to pay towards this whether or not they have partners. Contributions may be refunded to the estates of those who die without partners.

Occupational pensions are usually payable from retirement to those forced to retire early through ill-health. Private pensions can be purchased to protect against early retirement being forced in this way. Pensions from final salary schemes often assume the person worked to retirement.   DAVID WILLIAMS

pensions ombudsman   *see* **ombudsmen**

pensions taxation   *see* **savings taxes**

peoples   The definition of the term 'peoples' is contentious. Anthropologists, archaeologists, political and social scientists, and many others, have different ways of defining who are 'peoples'. In law, the main focus of the discussion about this term has been in international law, especially in relation to the rights of peoples and the possible consequences of peoples exercising these rights. For example, during the break-up of the former Yugoslavia, there was much debate about which groups within that region were 'peoples' and whether they could exercise their rights by becoming independent countries.

In international law 'all peoples' have a right of self-determination. This has been established as meaning that, by virtue of that right, peoples can freely determine their political status, freely pursue their economic, social, and cultural development, and freely dispose of their natural wealth and resources. The exercise of the right of self-determination by peoples may include securing independence, or some form of autonomy within a country, or power over decisions

in areas such as language and culture. However, it is clear that this right does not automatically mean that the people may legally secede from an existing country. The right is also limited in its exercise by the rights of others (including the right of other peoples to self-determination) and the general interests of the communities affected by the exercise of the right, including interests in peace and security.

There have been many attempts to clarify what is meant by 'peoples' for the purposes of international law. These attempts have either sought a subjective definition, according to which the group is considered to be a people if it has a clear consciousness of being a people; or an objective definition, based on recognition by an external body (such as a country) of a group as a people because they have certain defined characteristics, such as common racial or ethnic identity separate from that of those governing them, long-term territorial connection and economic strength. None of these definitions has been of great assistance. The realities of political and economic power often stand in the way of objective recognition of a group as a people. A group's consciousness of themselves as a people may be affected by oppression and the application to them of national processes such as particular discriminatory laws; and it can change over time.

Despite this uncertainty over the definition, it is universally agreed that the term 'peoples' applies to those who live in colonies, such as the many African colonies in the 1960s and 1970s. Indeed, exercise of the right to self-determination has been closely linked to the legal justifications for decolonization. Yet it is now generally accepted that the term also applies to some non-colonial peoples, such as the Bangladeshis (when they were seeking independence from Pakistan), the Germans (on unification of the two Germanys), and the Palestinians. It also applies within many countries, such as to the Scots in the **United Kingdom** and the Catalans in Spain. Some groups, such as the Eritreans, fought long armed conflicts to assert their right of self-determination as a distinct people. Indigenous populations, minorities, and oppressed regions have also asserted that they are peoples with a right of self-determination. While there is no complete agreement as to who is included and who is excluded from the term 'peoples', it is clear that there are potentially different 'peoples' in every country in the world. One result of this is that the concept of a single 'nation state' is no longer sustainable.

The consequences for a group of being considered to be, or not to be, a 'people' may be significant. As a result, in some instances a group may be able, or unable, to negotiate for a separate state or for significant autonomy of decision-making in one region of an existing country (or across more than one country). In other instances, a group may be able, or unable, to seek powers over particular aspects of life that are important to their group as a group, such as language, access to water and land, and cultural activities. At the same time, if a government or a number of governments refuses to acknowledge that a group is a people with certain distinct characteristics, this can lead to long-term conflict, both social and armed. A flexible definition of 'peoples', which enables both the representatives of the group and the government to discuss how core aspects of the group's identity can be exercised while taking into account the legitimate interests of the communities involved, would seem to be a way forward.

ROBERT MCCORQUODALE

J Crawford (ed), *The Rights of Peoples* (Oxford: Oxford University Press, 1988)
P Alston (ed), *Peoples' Rights* (Oxford: Oxford University Press, 2001)

***Pepper v Hart* (1993)** When interpreting legislation, the courts claim to look for 'the intention of Parliament'. One might have assumed that when the meaning of legislation was in doubt, courts could freely consult parliamentary materials, such as debates, standing committee proceedings, and reports commissioned by government preparatory to legislating, in order to elucidate Parliament's intention. Before the House of Lords' decision in *Pepper v Hart*, however, the courts' right to use such materials was tightly circumscribed. As recently as 1975 a majority of the House of Lords had held that a command paper presented to Parliament shortly before the passing of the Act the court had to construe, which incorporated a draft Bill substantially adopted in the eventual legislation, might only be consulted to determine the mischief at which the Act was directed and the state of the law, as then understood; otherwise, no matter how pertinent, a court had to ignore the committee's recommendations and its comments on its own draft Bill.

Parliament rarely has a single, defined intention when enacting legislation: it proceeds by majority vote, rather than by consensus. Parliamentary materials are diffuse and not always readily accessible. The **rule of law** demands that any aids to statutory interpretation should be predictable, identifiable, and publicly accessible. Therefore, it is often asserted that the courts' proper task is to seek the true meaning of the words used in the legislation itself, and at all costs to avoid confusing the intention of parliamentarians—or, worse still, of the executive—with the 'intention of Parliament'.

In *Pepper v Hart* a seven-strong **House of Lords** appellate committee, by a majority, made 'a limited modification to the existing rule' of statutory construction. Henceforth, if legislation was ambiguous, obscure, or led to absurdity, *and* if there existed one or more clear statements by a minister or other promoter of the relevant Bill, a court might have regard to them together with any other Parliamentary material needed to understand such statements and their effect. In *Pepper v Hart* itself, the minister responsible for steering a Finance Bill through Parliament had delivered a clear assurance before the standing committee on the meaning of the very clause, concerning teachers' taxable benefits, which fell to be construed. In these particular circumstances, the executive was effectively estopped from resiling from the undertaking the minister had given before Parliament.

Counsel regularly invoke *Pepper v Hart* in argument, and once in a while a court will find parliamentary materials illuminating. Whilst some judges are prepared to extend the principles of *Pepper v Hart* to the governmental Explanatory Notes that since 1998 accompany public Bills through Parliament, courts continue stoutly to refuse to treat the intentions of government, as generally revealed in debates, as reflecting the will of Parliament. More generally, lawyers view with increasing scepticism the very notion that one isolated ministerial pronouncement should be taken to embody the collective will of Parliament at all. Lord Mackay of Clashfern, LC, dissented in *Pepper v Hart*, anticipating that his colleagues' modest innovation would render litigation more costly. His Lordship's reservations are now widely thought to have been justified. RODERICK MUNDAY

See also: **interpreting legislation**

performers' rights *see* **neighbouring rights**

periodical payments *see* **structured settlements**

Permanent Court of Arbitration *see* **international courts and tribunals**

Permanent Court of International Justice (PCIJ) *see* **international courts and tribunals**

permanent resident A permanent resident is a foreign citizen who has acquired the right to live in another country indefinitely. Permanent residents are distinguishable from temporary residents, who have a legal right to remain for some defined period of time.

Temporary residents are most often admitted to work or study. Permission to remain is conditional on the temporary resident remaining in the job or educational institution which provides the basis for their permission to enter. A change in enrolment or employment typically necessitates a change in visa status. Like temporary residents, visitors are allowed to remain for a limited period, but they are not permitted to work or study. Permanent residents are often considered to be immigrants because of the enduring nature of their status. If they chose, they need never return to the country of their **nationality**.

Permanent residents have most of the rights of citizens in Western **democracies**. They are allowed to enter and exit the country as often as they wish. They can change jobs, collect welfare state benefits for which they are eligible, and study. In many countries, the children of permanent residents acquire **citizenship** of the state of residency at birth. The principal distinctions in rights of permanent residents as compared to citizens are typically that permanent residents cannot vote, cannot hold some civil service positions, and can more easily be stripped of their status than citizens.

In the early years of the twenty-first century, there is a global trend towards making permanent residency more precarious. While **deportations** of permanent residents were previously rare, most states have now made their rules regarding criminality more stringent. As such, even permanent residents who have lived virtually all their lives in their country of residency are vulnerable to deportation if they run foul of the law.

In the European Union, the progressive development of European citizenship has resulted in a relative downgrading of permanent residency status. This occurs because as European integration progresses, citizenship in a European Union Member State increases in value. This in turn creates a greater distinction between persons with citizenship in a European Union Member State and those with permanent residency status there. As European citizenship is derivative, gaining citizenship in a Member State provides rights throughout the Union. The rights which attach to permanent residency, however, are limited to the one state that grants this status. Accordingly, the near equivalency of status between citizens and permanent residents has been significantly altered in Europe since the Treaty of Amsterdam. European Member States set their own criteria for admission to permanent residency.

While migration analysts and government policymakers are accustomed to the categories of permanent and temporary residents, the contemporary reality of migration does not fit neatly into these categories. Many people who have the status of permanent residents, and thus a right to remain indefinitely, return to their country of nationality, or move to another country. Similarly, many people who have a temporary immigration status become permanently established immigrants over a period of time. In the United States, temporary status, later converted to permanent status, is the most common route for economic category immigrants.

CATHERINE DAUVERGNE

See also: **citizenship of the European Union; working holiday**

persistent vegetative state   'Persistent vegetative state' ('PVS'), which results from severe injury to the cerebral cortex, has been described as a state of 'chronic wakefulness without awareness'. It is distinct from 'brain death', 'irreversible coma', 'locked-in syndrome', and 'terminal illness' in that a PVS patient is, respectively, clearly alive, breathing unaided; has sleep/wake cycles; is thought completely unaware; and can live for many years, subject to the provision of food and fluids, antibiotics, and nursing. Misdiagnosis is not uncommon. Emergence from PVS is possible, albeit often with brain damage. Reports in 2006 of a PVS patient who recovered consciousness after being given a sleeping pill and of another whose brain patterns showed she responded to speech illustrate the limits to current knowledge about this syndrome.

British Medical Association guidelines recommend that a diagnosis of PVS should not be considered confirmed until the patient has been insentient for a year and allow withdrawal of tube-feeding thereafter, subject to **court** approval. In *Airedale NHS Trust v Bland* (1993) the **House of Lords** unanimously upheld a declaration that a doctor could lawfully discontinue tube-feeding a patient in PVS because it was, at least in the opinion of a responsible body of medical opinion, a futile medical treatment since it could not lead to the patient's recovery. A majority of their Lordships so held even though they took the doctor's intention to be to kill the patient. The case has proved controversial, not least for leaving the law, in the words of Lord Mustill, in a 'morally and intellectually misshapen' state: prohibiting the intentional killing of patients by an act but permitting the intentional killing of patients by omission. Court approval is required for withdrawal of tube-feeding in England and Wales (*Bland*) unless the patient has made an advance decision refusing tube-feeding or has granted another a Lasting Power of Attorney to do so (Mental Capacity Act 2005). In

Scotland, court approval is required only to ensure immunity from prosecution (*Law Hospital v Lord Advocate* (1996)).   JOHN KEOWN

See also: **withdrawing/withholding life-sustaining treatment**

B Jennett, *The Vegetative State. Medical Facts, Ethical and Legal Dilemmas* (Cambridge: Cambridge University Press, 2002)

J Keown, 'Restoring Moral and Intellectual Shape to the Law after *Bland*' (1997) 113 *Law Quarterly Review* 481–503

person 'Person' is a fundamental term for lawyers. It is typically defined as a being, entity, or unit which can bear legal rights and duties and so possesses what is called a legal personality: the ability to act in law. To most lawyers, the person is a formal legal abstraction and only that. It is only as rights holders or duty bearers that legal persons exist and relate to one another. Rights and duties are therefore the building blocks of legal relations and the sole constituent parts of legal persons.

In this strict account, legal personality is in essence a set of abilities or capacities to participate in legal relations and the legal person is the being or entity which possesses those capacities and comes into legal being through their possession. Nevertheless, the terms person and personality are often used interchangeably and as synonyms.

The significance of legal personality is not confined to explicit references to 'persons' in any given law. Every time a right is recognized or denied, legal personality is implicitly brought into issue. For the creation of a legal right, and its corresponding legal duty, necessarily means that the two parties to this legal relation are constituted as legal persons. They are then capable of acting in law. The legal recognition of a right and a duty therefore creates two legal persons: one with the right and the other with the duty. If someone or something is incapable of assuming a single legal right or duty, they do not carry the status of persons in law and so they have no personality.

The legal person can possess one or many rights and/or duties. Rights and duties, which effectively make the person, therefore can come in thick and thin bundles. The rational adult possesses the biggest bundle. It follows that personality can be analysed in much the same way as the concept of property, from which it is typically distinguished. (It is often said that that which is person is not property and the converse is also said to apply, although the corporation puts pay to this stark distinction as it is both person and property: it can buy and be bought.) Bundles of rights and duties are said to make up the idea of property; so too bundles of rights and duties make up the idea of the legal person. Both personality and property may also be viewed as cluster concepts. They entail the possession of transient clusters of rights and duties arising in shifting legal relations.

Legal personality is to be distinguished from the idea of legal competence (sometimes also, confusingly, called **capacity**) which is the ability of legal persons to enter into legal relations without the assistance of a third party such as a parent or guardian. Thus children and the intellectually disabled are both types of legal person, in that they are able to bear rights, but they are usually not competent to enter into legal relations, such as contracts, personally, on their own behalf. By contrast animals, it is generally said, are unable to assume any legal rights: they have neither the capacity for rights nor the competence to enter personally into legal relations (which can only be had by persons).

Legal personality is also to be distinguished from legal standing (or *locus standi*) which is the right of a legal person to challenge an administrative decision in a court of law because it is detrimental to their **common law** rights to life, liberty, or property (and which is determined by the sufficiency of their interests in the matter).

Legal personality is further to be distinguished from legal status which can be regarded as the legal character of any entity. Thus, we can say that the legal status of an animal is that of property and the legal status of a **human** is that of a person. Although perhaps to complicate matters a little further, legal status can sometimes also refer to the ability of a legal person to engage in certain legal relations. Thus, it is said that the legal status of **children** (who are legal persons) is that of a minor and therefore certain legal actions are disallowed. For example, children cannot vote and, if young, cannot work. Adults and children have different legal statuses but both are persons.

The concept of the legal person has played a critical role as gatekeeper, both permitting and excluding people from the legal community. Until the American Civil War, in many respects slaves were not 'persons' but were rather a form of property. Well into the twentieth century, women could not run for certain public offices open only to 'persons' because the **courts** declared that they did not count as persons for these statutory purposes. And in virtually all ways, animals continue to be excluded from the category of person. There is no question of them being protected by the offences against 'the person'. It is impossible to murder the family pet because it is not, in this respect, a 'person'. It is possible, however, to cause damage to someone's property by the same act.

The most interesting jurisprudential conundrum concerning law's person is whether it is connected to or reliant upon popular and philosophical definitions of the person. To strict legalists, the legal person should not be confused with real flesh-and-blood people. Rather legal personality exists essentially and only as an abstract capacity to function in law. The construct of the legal person and her legal personality, in this view, is purely a matter of legal expedience. To other jurists, the legal person has an important moral dimension. To some it connotes a human being with a rational will who is capable of engaging with and acting according to law, which is close to the philosopher's idea of the person. (It follows that corporations should not be persons, in this view.) To others, law's person, when in human form, refers to a being with inherent or sacred value. Such debates have a direct bearing on the legal status of the **foetus** (which is currently not a person) and those who are permanently comatose but legally alive (who currently are persons).

NGAIRE NAFFINE

R Tur, 'The "Person" in Law' in A Peacocke and G Gillett (eds), *Persons and Personality: A Contemporary Inquiry* (Oxford: Basil Blackwell, 1987), 121

N Naffine 'Who are Law's Persons? From Cheshire Cats to Responsible Subjects' (2003) 66/3 *Modern Law Review* 346

See also: **animals, rights of**

personal information, access to Common law and the Human Rights Act 1998 may be important for access to personal information but the most important provision is the Data Protection Act 1998 ('DPA'). The DPA implemented an EC Directive and repealed the Data Protection Act 1984. The DPA covers holders of personal data (data controllers ('DC')) on data subjects ('DS') in both the public and private sectors. It should be noted that not all personal data is protected by the DPA. It only applies to personal data as defined in the Act. Basically this includes data held electronically, data contained in a relevant filing system or 'structured files', and 'accessible records'. The Court of Appeal has defined 'structured files' and 'personal data' under the DPA in a restricted manner so that the former basically covers files that could be operated by a temporary clerical replacement, ie they are virtually automated with detailed cross references. It should be noted that the Freedom of Information Act 2000 ('FOIA') added a new category of data covered by the DPA where that data is held by a public authority ('PA'). This category may be referred to as 'unstructured files', eg loose papers held separately or in a folder or in policy papers. However in order to gain access to such data, a requester has to provide specific information including a description of the data. The PA does not have to comply with the request for access to unstructured data, or inform the DS that it is processing information on the DS, if the cost of compliance exceeds the FOIA limit (£600 or £450: see **freedom of information**).

DCs have to comply with the requirements of the Act and in particular with the Data Protection Principles ('DPPR'). These state that data must be processed (eg held, used, disclosed, etc) 'fairly and lawfully' and in accordance with a stipulated condition, ie that the DS has *consented* to processing, or processing is *necessary* for one of several purposes. The eight DPPRs specify the purposes for which data are obtained; they deal with their quality, content, and accuracy; they require that information be held only for as long as necessary for particular purposes and that it be processed subject to the rights of the DS; and they deal with transfer of information outside the European Economic Area. Statutory guidance on interpreting the DPPRs is contained in the DPA. Special provisions apply to 'sensitive data' and 'special purposes'. The latter relate to the press and publishing, and seek to provide **freedom of speech** protection for the use of data. DCs must notify the Information Commissioner ('IC') that they are processing data and provide specified particulars. The IC maintains a register of notifications which is publicly available. Processing without notification is a criminal offence as is failure to keep the notification particulars up-to-date. There may be exemptions from registration.

'Processing' must take place subject to the rights of the DS. The basic rights are a right of access to and a copy of the data for a fee, although the DC does not have to comply with such a request unless supplied with such information as may reasonably be required to satisfy the DC of the requester's identity and to locate the data. The DPA also provides for the protection of the identity of third parties who may be identified from the data. Further rights include the right to specified information, the right to be notified of various matters, the right to stop certain kinds of processing, and to have data rectified. Breaches of the DPA may lead to compensation and rectification. The rights of the DS may be subject to exemptions and modification.

The IC has wide powers of investigation and enforcement, but he is not a general ombudsman for data protection complaints.

PATRICK BIRKINSHAW

R Jay, *Data Protection Law and Practice* (London: Sweet & Maxwell, 2nd edn, 2003)

See also: **medical records**

personal information, disclosure of The notion that the individual has a right to control their own personal information is seen by many scholars as lying at the heart of the right to personal **privacy**, although it is true that privacy is also closely bound up with the notion of home, family life, and property. Referred to as the right to 'informational autonomy', under this view it is an essential aspect of individual dignity to be free to decide to what extent, when, and to whom, disclosures about oneself shall take place. This is seen not only as an inherent individual right but also as a necessary condition of various aspects of human development and flourishing. In particular, the ability to form intimate relationships with others is dependent, in very large part, upon the fact that in such relationships highly sensitive information, feelings, and thoughts can be confided while being withheld from the rest of the world. Moreover, informational autonomy, as many scholars have pointed out, protects individuals' ability to make substantive choices about their private lives. Particularly where the formation of certain human relations (including sexual relationships), and certain modes of development may be controversial in what has been termed 'the judgment of the mob', privacy allows for the exercise of individual liberty and for what one scholar has termed 'experiments in living'. Whilst control over private property provides the physical space in which such 'experiments' can occur, if there were no ability to withhold information about them from the disapproving majority, not only would such exercises of individual choice be penalized by the reaction of others, but many would likely be deterred by the anticipation of such disapproval.

Furthermore, the ability to share information and ideas in private, with perhaps one or two trusted friends, is seen as vital for the formation of the individual's personality and her cultural, political, and moral views: few are ready to express their ideas in public until they have explored them thoroughly in private. Privacy is thus linked with the fundamental rights of **freedom of expression** and freedom of thought, conscience and belief.

There are currently two primary sources of concern about the unauthorized disclosure of personal data in the UK (and, to an extent, in other countries). The first is that there exists a vast industry devoted to the dissemination of personal information, often without the subject's consent, for the purposes of entertainment. That industry is the media, or more narrowly, the tabloid newspapers and similar 'gossip' magazines, which use a range of unscrupulous and intrusive measures to obtain personal data, including of course, the notorious telephoto lens.

The second concern is the ever-increasing amount of personal information held by government about individuals, the use to which that information is put and its security. Recent illustrations of this trend include the Identity Cards Act 2006 and the new **National Health Service** database, a centralized system upon which the medical data of most of the population will be stored.

At the same time, there has been a very marked increase in privacy protection in UK law in the last ten years or so. The **Human Rights Act 1998** introduced Article 8 of the **European Convention on Human Rights** into domestic law. It confers a right to respect for private life and for correspondence, subject only to such exceptions as are 'necessary in a democratic society', in the interests of a wide variety of social goals, such as **national security** and the prevention of crime, or to protect 'the rights of others'. Article 8 requires strict controls over intrusions into private life such as telephone tapping, and careful protection of medical data. Recently the **European Court of Human Rights** has held in a landmark decision (*Von Hannover v Germany* (2004)) that Article 8 requires the state to provide protection for the individual against the attentions of the mass media in obtaining and disseminating personal information, particularly in the form of photographs, without their consent. Moreover, the Court made it clear that, in general, reportage of stories relating to an individual's private life will gain little protection under the right to **freedom of expression** particularly where, as in the *Von Hannover* case itself, the individual has no official functions.

English courts have recently developed the action for breach of confidence, which traditionally provided protection against unauthorized disclosure of confidential information obtained in the context of a confidential relationship (such as doctor-patient, or husband-wife) or under a confidentiality agreement between the parties. The more recent developments provide protection for personal information even where neither of these situations obtains. Thus in the seminal case of *Campbell v Mirror Group Newspapers* (2004), the **House of Lords** found that Naomi Campbell was entitled to a remedy against the *Daily Mirror* when it published information about her treatment for drug addiction at Narcotics Anonymous ('NA'), including a picture of her, taken surreptitiously and without consent, outside NA after a meeting. The fact that the House of Lords imposed liability in respect of the photograph, taken by a journalist who had no relationship with Campbell and in the absence of a confidentiality agreement, was of critical importance for the protection of privacy against the media.

It showed that nothing was required to create an obligation not to use private information obtained without consent other than its personal nature—in this case, the fact that it related to therapeutic treatment for drug addiction. The decision thus opened the way for recovery against the press when journalists obtain personal information about an individual simply by recording it without consent through the use of telephoto lenses or listening devices.

The second major advance in the protection of personal information has come about through the Data Protection Act 1998 ('DPA'). The DPA defines 'personal data' very broadly, and binds 'data controllers', that is, persons who determine the purpose for, and manner in which personal data will be processed. Particular safeguards apply to what the DPA terms 'sensitive personal data', which includes information about a person's sexual life, physical and mental health, religious beliefs, and racial or ethnic origin. Importantly, the Act applies both to public authorities and to private bodies holding data about individuals, such as commercial enterprises, credit reference agencies, and newspapers.

The DPA sets out a number of key principles applying to the processing of personal data. The first principle is that 'Personal data shall be processed fairly and lawfully'. In particular, it shall not be processed unless one of a number of specific conditions is met. These include: consent by the data subject; that the processing is necessary for the performance of or for entering into a contract, or is required to comply with any other legal obligation; that the processing is necessary in order to protect the vital interests of the data subject, or is necessary in order for the administration of justice or the performance of any other statutory or public function; or that the processing 'is necessary for the purposes of legitimate interests pursued by the data controller' or by the disclosees of the the data 'except where the processing is unwarranted . . . by reason of prejudice to the rights and freedoms or legitimate interests of the data subject'. In relation to 'sensitive personal data', the conditions are much stricter, and include explicit consent, public function, protection of the vital interests of the data subject, and so on.

The remainder of the Data Protection Principles are as follows:

- personal data shall be obtained only for one or more specified and lawful purposes, and shall not be further processed in any manner incompatible with that purpose or those purposes;
- personal data shall be adequate, relevant and not excessive in relation to the purpose or purposes for which they are processed;
- personal data shall be accurate and, where necessary, kept up-to-date;
- personal data processed for any purpose or purposes shall not be kept for longer than is necessary for that purpose or those purposes;
- personal data shall be processed in accordance with the rights of data subjects under this Act.

Two final principles require practical protection against improper processing or loss of data, including a bar on transferring it outside Europe without proper safeguards.

Data subjects—that is, those whose data are held by data controllers—have a number of specific rights under the DPA, including: the right to view the data about them held by the data controller; the right to request that inaccurate data be altered—enforceable by the remedy of court-ordered correction or destruction; the right to a remedy if improper processing causes damage or, in some cases, distress; the right to prevent processing likely to cause substantial and unwarranted damage or distress.

There are a number of broad exemptions from the provisions of the DPA, including where processing is carried out of the purposes of the safeguarding of **national security**, the prevention of crime, the collection of taxes, and the carrying out of research. Importantly in relation to the pursuit of journalistic, literary, or artistic purposes, there is an exemption where the data controller reasonably believes that publication would be in the public interest. It has been held that this exemption covers not only the processing by newspapers of personal data but actual publication of articles containing personal data. The DPA thus creates a broad exemption for journalism reasonably thought to be carried out in the public interest.   GAVIN PHILLIPSON

See also: **confidential information; data protection; personal information, access to**

personal laws   In Western liberal theory, citizens agree that their public activities will be regulated by their state; in exchange the state will not interfere with the private aspects of their lives. The public relationship between the citizen and the state is regulated through laws. Citizens are free to practice their **religion** or follow their own social customs as long as these do not break the laws of the state but these practices are not recognized as laws by the state. In practice, the distinction between public and private aspects of life is not so clear-cut. States do have laws which regulate **family life**, for instance to protect children from danger or **women** from **violence**.

The concept of personal laws is a product of **colonialism**. The colonial rulers created laws based on their own legal understandings to govern commerce and law and order which were intended to replace the laws of the indigenous communities. British colonialists in particular did not seek to interfere too much with the laws relating to family and religious life: those aspects of local, customary, and religious rules which covered family relations such as marriage, divorce, custody of children, property distribution, and inheritance were recognized as personal laws. In India, for instance, the British moulded diverse local rules and practices into four personal law codes: Hindu, Muslim, Parsee, and Christian. In sub-Saharan African countries, unwritten customary practices relating to the family relations of the various clans and **communities** were generally codified and recognized. These laws were then applied by courts. On independence the new states adopted **constitutions** which recognized both the former colonial general laws and the personal laws. There are therefore state recognized plural legal systems in many post-colonial societies.

Mass migration, often based on former colonial relationships, has led to the establishment of **minority** communities in most industrialized societies. Communities continue to follow their own social, religious, and family practices which they may regard as laws given that they were recognized as such in the countries of origin. For example, in Britain, many south Asian couples will marry twice: one civil and one religious ceremony. The religious **marriage** alone has no legal validity. While legal pluralism exists as a social reality, it is not recognized within the UK legal system.

Personal laws raise difficult issues relating to the rights of minority communities and to women. Where personal laws are recognized, there may be great resistance by local communities to state intervention. In India, the Muslim community fears that a move to a uniform civil code (which would replace the four codes and apply to all Indian citizens) would undermine their position. In South Africa (and other Sub-saharan countries), there are tensions between constitution guarantees relating to sex **equality** and the recognition of **customary laws**. Some members of minority communities in the UK argue for **recognition** of personal laws while others consider that these laws are not commensurate with **gender** equality. ANN STEWART

personal loan Personal loans, which may be secured or unsecured, are usually for a fixed sum, over a fixed period, at a fixed rate of interest. The principal tool used to calculate the cost of the loan is the annual percentage rate ('APR'). This has been developed to help consumers to compare the cost of different loans. It takes account of a variety of factors including the interest rate, the length and timing of repayments, any fees associated with the loan, and the cost of any compulsory insurance premiums (such as compulsory payment protection insurance).

Most personal loans are governed by the Consumer Credit Act 1974. This contains provisions relating to factors such as the form that agreements must take, and the information that must be provided to consumers. The Act also requires businesses which lend to consumers to be licensed by the **Office of Fair Trading** ('OFT'). The Act was substantially amended by the Consumer Credit Act 2006. Among the 2006 Act's most significant changes are the abolition of the rule that credit agreements above £25,000 are not regulated by the Act (only specifically exempt agreements will not be covered), the extension of the Financial Ombudsman Scheme to consumer credit complaints, and the replacement of the much-criticized extortionate credit bargains provisions with provisions that allow consumers to ask a court to reopen an agreement on the basis of unfairness.

PETER CARTWRIGHT

See also: **consumer protection in retail banking**

personal work contracts *see* **contract of employment**

personality *see* **person**

personhood *see* **person**

philosophical analysis of legal concepts Legal concepts do not appear to be particularly puzzling. Most laymen seem to have a sufficient grasp of the concepts of 'right' and 'duty', 'contract' and 'murder', sufficient at least for them to understand what lawyers say, or what papers report about court cases or business before Parliament. Lawyers are, of course, in an even better position in this respect, using them regularly as the conceptual 'tools' of their trade. It is important, therefore, to grasp that the philosophical analysis of legal concepts is not, at least in the first instance, motivated by an urge to reform or improve the operation of legal discourse, or legal reasoning. Rather, it is to address the philosophical puzzles or issues to which legal concepts, or their use, give rise.

In the case of law, the philosophical puzzles tend to arise because, compared to other concepts, legal concepts can appear mysterious, or at least hard to pin down. Think of rights. You say that you have a right to life. But if I ask you what you mean, you can't point to anything, in the way you can if I ask you what a tree or a chair is. You can't even draw me a picture of a right. The explanation you will have to give will be more complicated, perhaps much more complicated. And your troubles will only get worse if I start asking 'philosophical' questions like, 'are rights *real*?', or perhaps, 'when does a right *exist*?'. A fancy way of putting this sort of issue is, 'what is the ontological status of rights?' In other words, on what basis do they exist, if they do? One doesn't have to be a sceptic about rights to ask these sorts of questions. They are the sort of question anyone interested in rights must eventually ask if they are to understand what rights are. Not 'understand' in the sense of being able to use the word 'right', and understand what it means when someone claims their rights have been violated, or that they have the right to freedom of speech. But 'understand' in the sense of having a sort of overview of our use of the concept of right which makes it explicable in relation to our use of other kinds of concept, and our use of words in other realms of human discourse, such as the realm of natural science.

Whether you are a philosopher or not, you understand that you wouldn't go to a physicist to tell you whether you had a right to have an abortion. You know this, as it were, implicitly. One of the tasks of the philosopher of legal concepts is to explain how you know, and what it is for you to know, something this obvious. Certain philosophers of law, the Scandinavian Realists in particular, took the view that unless words had some sort of experiential referent, the way that 'tree' refers to trees, they were essentially meaningless. Thus words like 'rights', referring to nothing one could point to, were essentially meaningless; or rather, whatever meaning they had was misleading and flawed. Thus a claim that you have a right to free speech is to be reframed as an expression of your psychological desire to be allowed to express yourself freely. This way with legal concepts has not been regarded as successful, for the simple reason that claims of right do have meaning (otherwise they wouldn't figure so prominently in working legal practices), and they are not synonymous with expressions of desire. Clearly, the error here lay in thinking that the only things concepts could represent were objects that could be experienced by our senses.

In a similar way, HLA **Hart**'s early flirtation with the view that the significance of legal concepts lies in the way they are used is now regarded as largely wrong-headed. Hart argued, for example, that legal concepts predominantly figure in 'performative' utterances, where the uttering of words *does* something—when for example, a priest says 'I now pronounce you husband and wife' or a judge finds,

in expressing his judgment, that a person is liable to pay damages, or sentences someone to prison. In these cases, it is by the very uttering of the words, or in issuing the written form of the judgment or order, that a change in a person's legal position is brought about. This view, however, is unsatisfactory, for the use of legal concepts is made in all kinds of utterances, from simple declarative sentences, 'This contract is valid', to interrogatives, 'Is this contract valid?' and so on. The point here is that while certain *utterances* within legal discourse have performative effects (as they do elsewhere, for example when an umpire says 'you're out!'), the use of legal concepts is not restricted to such utterances.

What *has* been found fruitful as a way into understanding legal concepts is the realization, and exploration, of the fact that legal concepts are typically 'normative'. That is, legal concepts, like moral concepts, typically concern standards of behaviour with which people are expected to comply. If someone has a right to be paid £10 under a contract, then the other contracting party has a duty to pay that amount, and in having that duty, that party *ought* to pay it. This recognition of the normativity of legal concepts, following on largely from the work of Hans Kelsen and Hart, is now recognized as essential for understanding the nature of law and legal concepts.

The sustained work of both Joseph Raz and Ronald Dworkin has done most to frame the current issues. For Raz, normative concepts like 'right' and 'rule' are essentially connected with practical reason, the assessing of the various reasons upon which we decide to act. In the case of normal, everyday decisions, we decide what to do having weighed the reasons for and against. Whether I decide to pop out for a sandwich will turn on whether I am hungry, whether I have the time, whether I am trying to lose weight, whether I might run into a colleague I'm trying to avoid, and so on. The importance of rights, duties, and rules lies in the way they make me depart from this normal way of deciding on the balance of reasons. If I promised you that I wouldn't eat lunch today, so as to have a good appetite for dinner, then, if I take promises seriously, I take having made the promise as the reason for acting as I do (not going out for a sandwich), rather than deciding as I normally would on the balance of reasons. Similarly, when I stop at a red light, I treat the legal rule that I must do so as excluding my deciding whether to stop for all the other reasons which I would take into account in deciding what to do when coming to a junction without a red light, such as whether the traffic was heavy, whether I could see well, etc. Thus Raz explains normative concepts like 'rule' or 'duty' by showing how they work to alter the way we practically reason when we are subject to one of them, and furthermore shows how using these 'devices of communal practical reason' can be useful.

Perhaps the simplest example is the way in which rules can solve coordination problems. Traffic flows more smoothly and safely when, for example, the law lays down the rule that one must drive on the right, rather than leaving it up to individual drivers to decide for themselves on the balance of reasons as they understood them. While certain aspects of Raz's work remain controversial, it is widely recognized that the way he links normativity to reasons for action is a significant advance. Dworkin's foray into the nature of legal concepts, on the other hand, while productive of much discussion, has generated much more in the way of opposition. Dworkin claims that legal concepts are 'interpretative', and 'essentially contested'. By this he means that what a concept such as '**justice**' represents will be a matter of unending controversy amongst the people who possess the concept. This ongoing argument about the nature of justice is 'interpretative', looking back to past practices, such as the practice of the courts; and it is the essence of our idea of justice, on this understanding, that we will continue to dispute what justice really amounts to. Indeed, were we all to agree on what justice 'really is', we would have lost a true sense of justice; ie we would no longer have a true grasp of the concept. Only a 'Herculean' jurist/philosopher, to employ Dworkin's metaphor, could come to certain knowledge of what justice amounts to; the rest of us mere mortals accept that dealing with justice will always involve trying to persuade others, with the best reasons at our command, that in a particular case our resolution is more just than any proffered alternative. JAMES PENNER

physical abuse   *see* **abuse, civil liability for**

physical damage   In law, 'damage' has been defined as 'loss or harm occurring in fact'. It involves interference with a claimant's protected right or interest (*Crofter Hand Woven Harris Tweed Co v Veitch* (1942)). Different torts protect different interests, just as different insurance provisions might 'cover' damage to different interests. Historically, the **trespass** torts such as battery and assault protected physical interests in the body, land, and personal property. They offered a high degree of protection, no substantial damage being required. Later in time, this was augmented by protection in the tort of negligence. Damage is said to be the 'gist' of the action in negligence—thus warranting the discussion in this article. Negligence is highly protective of physical interests and less protective of non-physical interests, such as intangible wealth.

'Physical damage' usually involves an interference amounting to more than temporary loss of use of a bodily function or of tangible property. It involves deleterious changes in the physical state or structure of the body or property, such as to impair functionality. Examples of impaired functionality include a broken arm and a damaged car windscreen. Ordinarily, physical damage is manifest to the eye, but recovery is available for the causation of diseases which disrupt the internal functioning of persons, animals, or plants. In negligence, the claimant must have suffered a *non-trivial amount* of physical damage, encapsulated in the maxim *de minimis non curat lex*. Such damage might subsist, for example, in 'excess mucus with associated bouts of expectoration' or in excessive amounts of dust 'trodden into the carpet'.

Traditionally, the **common law** has distinguished between claims for bodily injury and claims for **psychiatric damage**. As a matter of medical understanding, this might be indefensible. However, it is consistent with the general approach of the **courts** regarding *how* physical damage arises. Ordinarily, physical damage is caused by the operation of an *external force* upon the person or thing, such as a collision. Where illness is caused without such force, through the medium of the mind, the claimant's case is considered to fall into a different duty of care category, which is subject to its own (restrictive) set of rules. However, there are exceptions in the physical damage cases to the requirement that there have been an external force impacting upon the body or tangible property. In negligence, it is possible for either a misstatement which causes a person to do something, or a complete failure to act despite an obligation to do so (an 'omission') to result in recognized physical damage. This might be the case, for example, with respect to a claim of medical negligence, a doctor having failed properly to treat an injury, disease, or ailment and this failure having caused the claimant's disablement.

Undoubtedly, courts have been expanding the protection offered in negligence to physical interests. They have recognized claims for bodily injury with respect to '**wrongful conception**'. In such cases, a mother gives birth to an 'unplanned' **child** as a result of a failure in treatment or of the provision of inaccurate advice by a doctor. She is able to recover for the physical pain, suffering, and inconvenience involved in the carrying of the **foetus** and subsequent labour and birth (*McFarlane v Tayside Health Board* (2000)). This kind of claim involves 'unwanted changes' in the body of the mother and a considerable loss of personal **autonomy** but no damage to organic functioning.

And courts have recognized claims for physical damage in cases of contamination of property, for example by low levels of radiation carrying a minimal risk of injury to persons using it. Whether or not a claim of contamination rises to the level of physical damage is a matter of fact and degree, relevant considerations including the need for work and the expenditure of money to restore the property to its former condition. In *Blue Circle Industries Plc v Ministry of Defence* (1999), **damages** were awarded under the Nuclear Installations Act 1965 for low-level nuclear contamination because 'the addition of plutonium to the topsoil rendered the chemical characteristics of the marshland different' and reduced the sale value of land.

But in other instances, courts have drawn the line against recovery for physical damage. In contrast to cases of externally-inflicted disease, birth with a genetic disorder is not regarded as physical damage. There can be no award of damages at **common law** against a negligent doctor in a '**wrongful life**' claim for the birth of a child with a naturally-occurring genetic disorder because the child could never have been born free from the disorder. In such circumstances, the courts consider that there is no measurable damage to the claimant (*McKay v Essex AHA* (1982)). **Legislation** in England and Wales mandates a similar result (Congenital Disabilities (Civil Liability) Act 1976). Following the same logic, the negligent construction of a building or other structure with latent defects, the functional characteristics of which deteriorate after the claimant has purchased it, is not regarded as a case of physical damage *to* property. This is regarded, instead, as a mere 'quality claim' and is not compensable.

CHRISTIAN WITTING

See also: **acts and omissions; negligence in civil law; tort law**

physiotherapy and personal training　Physiotherapy is a healthcare profession concerned with human function and movement and maximizing physical potential. All physiotherapists and physical therapists working within the **National Health Service** ('NHS') are registered with the independent regulatory body for healthcare professionals, the Health Professions Council ('HPC'), and only practitioners registered with the HPC are entitled to use these titles when practising.

There is no mandatory professional registration requirement for personal trainers. However, a system of self-regulation has been established by the Register of Exercise Professionals ('REP') to protect the interests of people who are using the services of exercise professionals. The REP requires its members to achieve and maintain a certain level of qualification and to work within a Code of Ethical Practice.

As is the case with medical practitioners, physiotherapists and personal trainers owe a duty of care to their patients to exercise a reasonable degree of skill and knowledge in their assessment and treatment/training. The standard of care required of each is that of the ordinary skilled practitioner exercising and professing to have the special skill in question. In assessing whether the standard was met in a particular case, the courts will have regard to the codes of practice adopted by each profession, such as the Core Standards of Physiotherapy Practice published by the Chartered Society of Physiotherapy and the Code of Ethical Practice set down by the REP. A breach of this duty of care, with resulting damage to the patient, may give rise to liability in negligence.

CATHERINE BELOFF

picketing　Picketing is a practice long associated with (but not confined to) trade disputes. It involves a group of workers and/or trade union officials being stationed outside a workplace, usually for one (or more) of three purposes. The first is to persuade other workers employed by the employer in the dispute not to go to work; the second is to persuade workers employed by suppliers not to deliver to the employer in the dispute; and the third is to persuade potential customers not to do business with the employer in the dispute. In the past, striking workers may have extended their dispute by picketing other employers. This was called secondary picketing, and would be undertaken (a) to persuade workers employed by a customer or supplier of the employer in the dispute; and (b) to support the strikers perhaps by refusing to handle goods for or from the employer in the dispute. By these means the pickets aim to bring the dispute to a conclusion, by putting economic pressure on their employer.

The current **legislation** permitting peaceful picketing has its origins in the Trade Disputes Act 1906. The latter provided that it was lawful—in contemplation or furtherance of a trade dispute—to attend at or near someone's house or place of work (or a place where a person happened to be), for the purpose of peacefully persuading him or her to work or abstain from working. However, this did not provide a blanket protection for those who picketed in large numbers or in a boisterous manner, though it did provide protection for peaceful secondary picketing. Nor did it prevent the **police** from taking whatever steps they thought were necessary to prevent a **breach of the peace**. Some major industrial disputes in the 1920s and the 1970s in particular were attended by picketing on a large and sometimes violent scale, with allegations of excessive force being used by the police, most notably during the miners' lock-out in 1926 and the miners' strike in 1984–1985.

The position is now governed by the Trade Union and Labour Relations (Consolidation) Act 1992, which provides that—in contemplation or furtherance of a trade dispute—workers (along with their union officials) may attend at or near their own place of work to peacefully communicate information, or peacefully persuade people to work or not to work. The picketing must be conducted in accordance with a government Code of Practice, which recommends that no more than six people should picket any particular entrance to a workplace. Pickets have no right to stop vehicles, and there is no duty on the part of anyone to listen to what the pickets have to say. If the police feel it is necessary—in order to keep the peace—that fewer than six pickets should attend any entrance, then the judgment of the police will override the recommendations of the Code of Practice. In practice, larger assemblies may take place some distance away from entrances to the workplace.

KEITH EWING

pillars of the European Union   Under the Treaty of European Union ('TEU') three areas of European Union ('EU') activity were established, each of which forms a separate pillar of the EU: the European Community (Community), the Common Foreign and Security Policy ('CFSP'), and cooperation on Justice and Home Affairs ('JHA'). These three pillars are linked by common institutions (the **European Commission**, **European Council**, **European Parliament**, and **European Court of Justice**) and shared values, notably respect for fundamental rights and the principle of **subsidiarity**.

According to the TEU, 'the Union shall be founded upon the European Communities, supplemented by the policies and forms of cooperation established by this Treaty' (Article 1). The central pillar is thus the first, the Community pillar, which includes the original European Economic, Euratom, and European Coal and Steel Communities, and technically it is to this pillar and its provisions and law that references to 'European Community' and '**European Community law**' now relate. Under the TEU, the European Economic Community was renamed the

European Community, dropping the 'economic' to more accurately reflect its development to include non-economic spheres of policy, including environmental and social policies. The Community pillar is characterized by supra-nationality in its decision-making, and this contrasts with the second and third pillars which employ more classic methods of inter-governmental cooperation. Furthermore, it is only the Community pillar which has legal personality, and thus the capacity to enter into agreements with third states. The EU itself does not have legal personality (including in relation to the CFSP) notwithstanding that it is through the CFSP that the EU is to assert its international identity.

This is indeed the objective of the second pillar, the CFSP. To this end the Member States, acting in Council, can adopt common positions or joint actions. In adopting a Common Position, the EU sets out its approach to a particular matter and the Member States must then act in accordance with the Common Position, similarly Member States are committed to Joint Actions, examples of which include the EU's action in Yugoslavia in the 1990s. Significantly, although the second pillar is inter-governmental in character, joint actions and common positions are adopted by qualified majority rather than unanimity. However, if a Member State indicates that it will oppose a decision the Council can refer the matter for decision of the European Council by unanimity.

The third pillar, Justice and Home Affairs, originally included cooperation relating to **asylum**, immigration, and third country nationals as well as **police** and judicial cooperation on criminal matters (including, for example, the establishment of the European Police Office ('Europol')). Again the Council had the key role—having the power to adopt joint positions and draw up agreements acting by unanimity. In this context the Commission could, however, make proposals.

The balance of power between the institutions, and the respective roles of the institutions varied in each of the pillars (and indeed has changed following the amendments of the **European Treaties** of Amsterdam and Nice). From the outset it could be said that the European Council was the only institution which meaningfully operated in relation to all three pillars. The European Parliament's role in the second and third pillars was restricted to being kept informed, and the ability to ask questions and make recommendations which should be taken into consideration. The European Commission had a greater (albeit still limited) role in relation to JHA than the CFSP.

Under the Treaty of Amsterdam a significant body of material (concerning **visas**, **asylum**, immigration, and other policies relating to the free movement of persons) was moved from the third pillar (JHA) to the first (Community) pillar. On the face of it this could be a fairly straightforward transfer from inter-governmental cooperation to the supra-nationalist approach of the European Community ('EC'), and consequently could reflect a clear expansion of EC activity. However, the new Community provisions are the subject of opt-outs for the UK, Denmark, and Ireland. Furthermore, the Court's jurisdiction in respect of these provisions was limited in comparison with that regarding other areas of the EC Treaty and the role of Parliament was originally limited to consultation at most. In light of this, it would be simplistic to suggest that this area of cooperation was the subject of a straightforward move from inter-governmental cooperation to the institutional processes of the EC Treaty.

Conversely, there has also been some traffic in the opposite direction—notably the extension of the Court of Justice's jurisdiction to the third pillar and the enhanced (consultative) role of Parliament, again in relation to the third pillar.

The relatively straightforward structure established in the TEU was thus rather blurred through subsequent amendments and indeed under the proposed Constitution for the European Union the three pillar structure would have been replaced by a single institutional framework. (This should not, however, imply a single decision making process—as exemplified by the free movement of persons provisions following the Treaty of Amsterdam, different procedures can be applied to different areas within a single framework.) While the Constitution has not come into effect, it does serve to give some indication of the will of Member States, and therefore, perhaps, an indication of the potential direction of any future change.

The development of the three pillar structure allowed for the formalization of activity in fields in which the Member States had previously cooperated on an *ad hoc* basis under the auspices of the European Council, and also subsequently as European Political Cooperation under the Single European Act. However, the three pillar structure allowed different means of action to be developed for each of the areas of activity, allowing the level of cooperation in the second and third pillars to be distinguished from that of the central Community pillar. Crucially, in political terms, it also emphasized that distinction: the second and third pillar methods of cooperation left control of that cooperation firmly with the Member States—unlike under the first pillar there could be no autonomous (supra-national) policy development.   EMILY REID

See also: **Constitution of Europe; person**

Pinochet case (R v Bow Street Metropolitan Stipendiary Magistrate, ex p Pinochet Ugarte) (No 3) (2000)

In 1973, General Augusto Pinochet, commander of the Chilean army, led a coup against the government of Chile, which had been elected in 1970. Pinochet consolidated his seizure of power by a variety of violent measures against those members of the opposition suspected of resistance to the new regime. Deaths, torture, disappearances, and other violations of human rights were carried out on Pinochet's direct orders as systematic state policy, not just in Chile but abroad, in pursuit of those Pinochet deemed to be his enemies. Although widely condemned internationally, Pinochet made good his position domestically. He became President in 1974, a position he held until 1990. Before he resigned, he secured the passage of an impunity law which prevented proceedings against him in Chile for the excesses of his administration.

On a visit to London in 1998, Pinochet was arrested on an extradition warrant, issued by an examining judge in Spain, who was investigating Pinochet's actions in Chile, some of which amounted to torture under the United Nations Convention against Torture ('UNCT'). Pinochet resisted the proceedings on the ground that any acts were committed in the discharge of his official functions as head of state, for which he enjoyed a continuing immunity *ratione materiae* (since he could no longer rely on any personal immunity as head of state). Immunity *ratione materiae* may be asserted by the state for official acts of public servants or its agents. The government of Chile supported Pinochet and demanded that he be returned to Chile where, it said, investigations were going on into acts committed during Pinochet's tenure.

An initial decision of a five-judge panel of the **House of Lords** (*R v Bow Street Stipendiary Magistrate, ex p Pinochet Ugarte (Amnesty International and others intervening)* (2000)) held (3–2) that Pinochet was not entitled to immunity. However, the judgment was challenged on the ground that one of the majority, Lord Hoffmann, had links with Amnesty International, which, unusually, had been allowed to intervene in a criminal proceeding. Uniquely, the House of Lords reconvened with a wholly new panel of seven judges which confirmed that, by reason of his association with one of the parties in the case,

Hoffmann ought not to have sat because the connection gave rise to an appearance of bias (*R v Bow Street Stipendiary Magistrate, ex p Pinochet Ugarte (No 2)* (2000)). Another seven-judge court in the House of Lords then held that Pinochet was not immune in relation to certain allegations of torture committed after the UK, Spain, and Chile had all become parties to the UNCT (*R v Bow Street Stipendiary Magistrate, ex p Pinochet Ugarte (No 3)* (2000)). The obligation under the UNCT to make torture (as there defined) a crime in UK law had been performed by the enactment of section 134 of the Criminal Justice Act 1988 (CJA).

The holding in *Pinochet (No 3)* is very narrow, namely that there is no immunity *ratione materiae* for an ex-head of state for torture within the meaning of section 134 of the CJA (and Article 1 UNCT) because to allow an immunity would undermine the purpose of the UNCT, which is to provide a regime for the prosecution of those charged with torture under the UNCT, which is an offence that can be committed only by officials. The restriction of immunity applies only to officials of parties to the UNCT for acts of torture done after the treaty came into force for their state and the UK. This narrow reading has been confirmed by more recent torture cases and more broadly where officials have claimed various kinds of immunities from criminal process for other offences. In these cases, either there is a treaty basis for overcoming the immunity or the state entitled to the immunity has waived it. The *Pinochet* judgment has an iconic status in the fight against impunity. It was widely held out as deciding that there are no immunities where a case involves prosecution for conduct which constitutes a crime against international law. This interpretation raises expectations which will not be realized. Progress will be incremental through the drafting of the appropriate treaties or by waiver of immunity in particular cases.

Although investigations had been undertaken against him in Chile on various matters and he had been arrested on several occasions, Pinochet died in 2006 without having faced a criminal trial on any indictment.   COLIN WARBRICK

R van Albeck, 'The *Pinochet* case: International Human Rights Law on Trial' (2000) 71 *British Yearbook of International Law* 29

N Roht-Arriaza, *The Pinochet Effect: Transnational Justice in an Age of Human Rights* (Philadelphia: University of Pennsylvania Press, 2005)

piracy   In **international law**, piracy is any illegal act of violence, detention, or depredation committed for private ends by the crew or passengers of a private ship against another ship, or by a mutinous crew or passengers against their own ship, on the high seas or in any other place outside the territorial jurisdiction of any state. Piracy includes similar acts against, or on board, private aircraft. Piratical acts committed within the territory of a state, its ports or territorial sea, are not considered piracy but 'armed robbery against ships' and fall under the coastal state's exclusive jurisdiction. Warships and government ships are assimilated to private ships if their crew has mutinied and taken control; otherwise the 'official' nature of actions by such ships precludes their classification as piracy. Privateers (private ships furnished by the state in times of war with a commission to carry out hostile acts against enemy shipping) are not pirates so long as they operate within their commission.

For centuries, pirates have been considered *hostis humani generis*—an enemy of humankind. Piracy is an international crime and all states have universal jurisdiction to punish acts of piracy and to seize pirate ships outside the territorial jurisdiction of other states. The **customary international law** on piracy is now codified in the 1982 **United Nations** Convention on the **Law of the Sea.**

The term '(product) piracy' is also employed to describe the illegal reproduction of **copyright**ed material.   STEFAN TALMON

AP Rubin, *The Law of Piracy* (Irvington-on-Hudson, NY: Transnational Publishers, 2nd edn, 1989)

piracy (intellectual property)   *see* **border control of intellectual property; copyright**

place   Place is a highly contested concept, both theoretically and as a context for social life. Critics of conventional notions of place have pointed out that place is not simply a container, a set of boundaries. Place is a socially constructed concept of the surroundings in which people conduct their lives. People constitute their surroundings, *placing* themselves and others as well as the physical objects, meanings, and actions which, taken all together, make up a place that is shared, negotiated, and contested. Recent studies of territoriality emphasize the connections between concepts of place as territorially bounded, and therefore subject to formal legal definition, and concepts of place as an expression of **identity** tied to shared notions of **community, ethnicity**, or nation.

Some theorists have emphasized the 'sense of place' according to which people interpret landscapes, give meaning, and develop attachments to specific places such as home, workplace, or nation. Such definitions tend to invoke romantic notions, or to present highly personal interpretations, because they do not take account of the interactive and often conflicting ways in which places are mediated. Others view the construction of place discursively, as the negotiation of meaning within a web of social processes that include **race**, class, **gender**, and other forms of identity, both ascribed and affective. As social constructions, places are valued not only by the meanings attached to them by individuals or groups, but also by economic and political factors that range from the real estate market to legal definitions of public and private, and by both legal and normative definitions of the activities that are appropriate for particular places.

The meaning of place shifts according to many factors. Places are constellations of resources that include people as well as things: houses, roads, and other infrastructure, aesthetic qualities, all understood qualitatively and in terms of their relative lack or abundance. Places are separated or connected by systems of transportation, communication, physical boundaries, or by the judgments through which people relate one place to another. Recent studies in transnational **citizenship**, for example, show that by living between two places people change the meanings of those places, and deploy those meanings strategically to meet a range of economic, political, and cultural needs.

The concept of place is also deployed at different scales, from that of the nation state to the region, the city, and the home. At each scale, the negotiation of place involves differential power over the ways in which places are inhabited, controlled, and regulated. At each scale occur practices of inclusion and exclusion, normative regulation of human behavior, and varied expressions of attachment. The politics of place can be mobilized progressively as a basis for groups to improve their surroundings; for example, to overcome conditions of poverty or environmental degradation. But the politics of place may also be the basis for oppression, warfare, and other forms of aggressive **nationalism**. At any scale, place is a basis for the regulation of daily life and the political struggles, large and small, through which people define, and are defined by, their material lives.

AUDREY KOBAYASHI

J Agnew, *Place and Politics: The Geographical Mediation of State and Society* (Boston: Allen and Unwin, 1987)

T Cresswell, *In Place/Out of Place* (Minneapolis, MN: University of Minnesota Press, 1996)

planning permission *see* town and country planning

players of sports The most fundamental legal changes concerning the players of sports in recent

years are derived from the historic *Bosman* ruling delivered by the **European Court of Justice** ('ECJ') in December 2005. This has required all European Sporting Associations (notably but not exclusively professional football) that operate a transfer system to ensure their rules permit out-of-contract players to move to another club. Apart from young players, it is no longer permissible for a club to retain a player under a new contract, so that the player cannot move, unless another club is prepared to pay a transfer fee.

Moreover, a threatened legal challenge to any form of transfer system, mounted by the **European Commission** under EU **competition law**, led to FIFA, in July 2001, instituting a new transfer system regulating international transfers. Under this system, players over the age of twenty-three are permitted to jump a contract outside that contract's protected period. This is defined as a period of three entire seasons in the case of all contracts concluded prior to the twenty-eighth birthday of the player, and two seasons in the case of contracts concluded after the player's twenty-eighth birthday. Once the protected period has expired a player is able to join a new club in breach of contract provided appropriate compensation is paid to his club. Moreover, a player is also permitted to terminate his contract for sporting just cause. For example, if a player is not being selected for first-team football he may be able to leave, even though his club has not itself committed any breach of contract.

Whilst the European Commission gave its approval to this new system, it cannot be concluded for certain that it is fully compatible with **European Union** ('EU') law. Most significantly, the Premier and Football Leagues in Britain have not adopted the FIFA system with respect to transfers between domestic clubs. Therefore, it is a distinct possibility that a player under contract with a British club, who wishes to move to another domestic club in breach of that contract, will succeed in the challenging the domestic transfer system under EU law.

The other major change instigated by the *Bosman* ruling is with respect to rules limiting the number of foreign players that can be available for team selection. Such quota restrictions can no longer be applied to players who are EU nationals or nationals of the European Economic Area states of Liechtenstein, Iceland, and Norway. Whilst, as can be seen from clubs such as Arsenal and Chelsea, this has again been of particular significance for football, it has also been important for other sports—notably basketball.

Indeed, in the case of *Kolpak*, the ECJ extended this aspect of *Bosman* to a Slovakian goalkeeper who played for a German handball club. At that time, Slovakia was outside of the EU but was a 'third country' with which the EU had a trading agreement. Other such third countries, still outside the EU, whose nationals benefit from *Kolpak* include Algeria, Bulgaria, Croatia, and Turkey.   ROGER WELCH

plea bargaining   Unlike some jurisdictions, criminal process in the United Kingdom recognizes guilty pleas. Rather than contesting guilt at a trial, the defendant can plead guilty and the case will proceed straight to **sentencing**. The vast majority of defendants do in fact plead guilty. Often the guilty plea—which means that the defendant foregoes any chance of being acquitted—will come about because the defendant expects to gain some advantage from it. This situation, where a defendant pleads guilty not simply because he acknowledges guilt but because he hopes to gain something from it, can be referred to as 'plea bargaining'. However, it should be said straight away that plea bargaining in the UK is for the most part a much less formal process of negotiated justice than that which exists in the United States. There, prosecutors have considerable power because they can make recommendations to the judge about sentence. This enables **prosecution** and defence to agree on a sentence before trial, and this agreement will usually bind the judge. A defendant may therefore agree to plead guilty in exchange for a reduced sentence.

What forms of plea bargaining exist in the UK—what advantages may defendants expect to get from a plea of guilty? By avoiding contested trials, guilty pleas save considerable resources; thus the criminal process has an interest in maintaining the high rate of guilty pleas by offering incentives to plead guilty. The most significant incentive is the sentence discount: defendants should receive a lighter sentence if they plead guilty. In England and Wales, the discount is set at a quarter to a third, with the full discount awarded to those who plead guilty at the earliest opportunity. Connected to this, English law has also come to recognize the legitimacy of sentence canvassing, whereby a defendant can enquire of a judge or magistrate as to the sentence he would get on a plea of guilty at a particular point in time, a practice which may signal that a guilty plea could mean the difference between a custodial and non-custodial disposal. Another form of plea bargaining is charge-bargaining: prosecutors in the UK can indirectly affect sentence in some cases by agreeing to a particular level of charge. Thus, a defendant may

agree to plead guilty if a charge of **rape** is changed to sexual assault, or a charge of causing grievous bodily harm to causing actual bodily harm. This form of plea bargaining appears to be quite common; another, probably rarer, occurrence, is 'fact-bargaining', where a defendant pleads guilty on the understanding that the prosecutor will present the facts to the court in a certain way. Plea bargaining is controversial for several reasons: by offering, in some cases, a strong incentive to plead guilty, it may encourage the innocent to plead guilty. Charge-bargaining and fact-bargaining, in particular, can disappoint **victims**, who may feel that 'their' offence has been downgraded in the pursuit of efficiency. The sentence discount also appears to distort sentencing principles: sentencing is used as a way of managing resources within the system, rather than as a way of expressing the seriousness of an offence.

MIKE REDMAYNE

A Ashworth and M Redmayne, *The Criminal Process* (Oxford: Oxford University Press, 2005), ch 10

M McConville and CL Mirsky, *Jury Trials and Plea Bargaining: A True History* (Oxford: Hart Publishing, 2005)

pleadings   The pleadings are the written statements exchanged by the parties in civil proceedings which set out the cause of action, the facts relied upon, the remedy sought, the grounds of defence, any counter-claim, and any further statements expanding, qualifying, amending, particularizing, etc those statements.

As it was pithily put by Lord Justice Saville in a case before the Court of Appeal in 1994: 'The basic purpose of pleadings is to enable the opposing party to know what case is being made in sufficient detail to enable that party properly to prepare to answer it', as Lord Hope cited this statement with approval in a **House of Lords** decision in 2001, but also said that 'a balance must be struck between the need for fair notice to be given on the one hand and excessive demands for detail on the other . . . as a general rule, the more serious the allegation of misconduct, the greater is the need for particulars to be given which explain the basis for the allegation'.

In Scotland rules of civil procedure in the Court of Session are formulated by a 'Rules Council' and passed as Acts of Sederunt by the Court; and in the Sheriff Courts they are formulated by the 'Sheriff Courts Rules Council' and passed as Acts of Sederunt by the Court of Session. In England and Wales such matters are now governed by the **Civil Procedure Rules** 1998.

Although the terms 'pleadings' is still used in its generic sense, it has given way within the Rules to the somewhat inelegant formulation 'statements of case' (which also lacks the Anglo-Norman colour of the traditional term). A 'statement of case' means a claim form, particulars of claim where these are not included in a claim form, defence, counterclaim, additional claim, or reply to defence; and includes any further information given in relation to these statements either voluntarily or by court order requiring clarification of, or further information about, any matter in dispute. Many statements of case, including the claim form, particulars of claim, and defence are required to be verified by an accompanying 'statement of truth' from the party submitting them.

Pleadings are formal documents in the proceedings and those of each party are expected to be internally consistent. The letter of claim or letter before claim (formerly 'letter before action'), is not considered to be part of the pleadings.

The pleadings are expected to: contain a concise statement of the nature of the claim and a concise statement of the facts on which the claimant relies; specify the remedy which is sought (eg **damages**, an **injunction**, an order for possession); state the amount of any specific sum of money claimed and any interest accrued on that sum; and in the defence, state which allegations are admitted and which are denied, with reasons.

Much of this information is required not only by the other party but also by the court in order that it can administer the case and deal with it justly.

JOHN FITZPATRICK

W Rose, *Pleading Without Tears* (Oxford: Oxford University Press, 2002)

pleas For most criminal defendants, the high principles of the criminal trial—the presumption of innocence, an onus on the **prosecution** to prove its case beyond reasonable doubt, and the right to a fair and public hearing—have very little relevance. Well over 90 per cent of all defendants plead guilty in the criminal **courts**. Where there is a guilty plea, the prosecution's evidence tends to be dealt with perfunctorily by the court and, instead of cases taking hours or even days to resolve, they are disposed of in minutes. There is no trial, no testing of evidence, no calling of witnesses, and no public adjudication. Although it is commonly assumed in legal texts that defendants will plead not guilty and even be tried by **jury**, this is in practice a rare exception. Only about 1 per cent of defendants are tried by jury and the vast majority of cases are heard in the lower courts.

The fact that such high proportions of defendants plead guilty in court is remarkable yet, until recently, it scarcely merited a mention in most textbooks. It is

on the surface astonishing that so many defendants forego their right to put the prosecution to proof by pleading guilty. There are, however, powerful institutional incentives and pressures which induce them to do so. The most potent pressure is the so-called discount principle in **sentencing**. This principle is well established, bolstered by a long line of Court of **Appeal** decisions, and is even enshrined in statute in England and Wales. It ensures that those who plead guilty are rewarded by receiving a considerable reduction in their sentence. This reduction is often as much as one-third and can sometimes even make the difference between **prison** and a non-custodial sentence.

The **criminal justice system** is, then, an efficient mechanism for generating a very high level of guilty pleas, and recent years have seen an intensification of the pressures on defendants to plead guilty. It is often assumed that, if hefty reductions in sentence were not offered in return for guilty pleas, the criminal courts would be unworkable because they would be quickly overwhelmed with contested trials. This assumption is, however, questionable. Although a discount principle of some kind has been adopted in most **common law** countries (and in many civil law countries too), it has always been resisted in Scotland. Yet Scottish criminal courts do not appear to be submerged by cases as a consequence.

Anxieties continue to be voiced about the excessive pressures brought to bear on defendants, innocent and guilty alike, to plead guilty. We know enough about **miscarriages of justice** to understand how innocent defendants might be persuaded to plead guilty. Although high guilty plea rates produce massive savings in costs and other benefits for the court system, lawyers, and defendants, there is great unease that the sentencing discount principle reflects a preoccupation with cost and administrative convenience, not **justice**, and serves to encourage the development of unsavoury practices like **plea bargaining**. JOHN BALDWIN

police Who and what are police officers? Historically a constable was the holder of an unpaid and independent **Crown** office, recognized by the **common law**, with powers to enforce the criminal law. Nowadays the new constable still makes a declaration in front of a justice of the peace, reflecting that independent office; but the officer will also be an employee of a police force under the command of a chief constable. There are over 140,000 full-time police officers in England and Wales, not including community support officers, traffic wardens, and special constables. There is no single national force directly under a government department: the police are organized into forty-three local forces, organized geographically either on the basis of urban conurbations (the Metropolitan force for London) or on counties (such as Lancashire) or groups of counties (such as Devon and Cornwall). Alongside these forces are others such as the British Transport Police, the UK Atomic Energy Constabulary, and the Port of Dover police. The forty-three geographic forces are financed by a combination of local and national government with a budget of over £16bn, which is derived from three main sources: the police grant from the Home Office, revenue support or non-domestic rates from the Department of the Environment, and the council tax from local government.

Despite government funding, police forces remain autonomous legal entities which determine their own operational strategies and are independent of political control. The local forces have their own identities, often associated with a particular policing strategy such as community or geographic policing, problem-oriented policing, or intelligence-led policing. Day-to-day operational management is in the hands of the Chief Constable (or Commissioner in the Metropolitan Police) who, under the Police Act 1996, has the legal power to direct and control the force and to ensure that officers undertake the tasks and activities that the senior management consider appropriate. Failing to obey such instructions would be a disciplinary offence, and the individual constable has only limited independence. On patrol, however, an officer operates independently of direct control and exercises significant low visibility discretion. Above street level, there is a tight and hierarchical chain of command and there can be a military quality to policing which is seen at its extreme in the control of public disorder, when the officer works as part of a squad, directly responding to an officer's commands.

What are the basic functions of the police? These have never been defined in statute. Peel, in his General Instructions to the force in 1829, spoke of the prevention rather than the detection of crime '…the object to be attained is the prevention of crime. To this great end every effort of the police is to be directed'. More recent statutes have also not defined the boundaries of police activity, a position which reflects the traditional image of the constable as simply a private citizen in uniform who may do anything which is not prohibited by law. The primary function of police is the enforcement of the criminal law—their coercive statutory powers such as **arrest** and detention are based on the commission of an offence. Beyond the crime-fighting role, the public are accustomed to

the police playing a wide community role, whether it is naming and shaming kerb crawlers or running community schemes for young offenders. They provide 24/7 emergency cover and respond to a wide range of community problems. Many phone calls to the police are about problems such as noise, disputes between neighbours, missing persons, or lost property. The force operates as a focus for and provides information about many other assistance agencies—accommodation for the homeless, women's refuges, or drug and detoxification centres.

Locally the Chief Constable is accountable to a Police Authority. This body consists of local councillors, magistrates, and independent members. It is independent of the local council and has the statutory duty to maintain an 'efficient and effective force'. This involves appointing senior officers, supervising finances, and keeping a watching brief over the quality of local policing. The Authority has no power to influence police operational decisions. But, under the Crime and Disorder Act 1998 and the Police Act 1996, both local and national government publish plans and objectives for the police. Currently there are three national aims, namely to promote safety and reduce disorder, to reduce crime and fear of crime, and to contribute to delivering justice in a way which secures and maintains public confidence in the rule of law. Police authorities publish area plans and local authorities produce a three-year community safety plan, identifying crime and disorder problems and strategies for dealing with them.

Nationally, the Home Secretary has no power to instruct a Chief Constable to carry out or to refrain from a particular policy but has a statutory duty to promote efficiency and effectiveness. This is done through setting national objectives and performance targets as well as publishing a national policing plan. Furthermore, the Home Office influences forces by a system of circulars which advise chief officers on all aspects of running a force, be that financial management, best practice on operational matters, or criminal justice strategy. Because government provides 75 per cent of police funding, the Home Secretary is in a position to make such interventions count. A minister can now require police authorities to take specific remedial action. The Home Office monitors the quality of policing through the Inspectorate of Constabulary and the National Policing Improvement Agency, introduced in 2007.

The police are subject to regulation by the courts, through criminal prosecution and civil actions for damages. The police are subject to **judicial review**, but in several High Court decisions the scope for judicial intervention in the exercise of the Chief Constable's discretion was held to be limited. A decision of the **House of Lords** in 1999 involving control of protestors at a port, suggested a more robust approach to judicial review of police action. The House held that police must strike a reasonable balance between the right to trade lawfully and the right to protest lawfully, and that a fundamental freedom should not be restricted any more than is necessary.

The most straightforward system of accountability will always be the individual complaint to an officer's superiors about the officer's behaviour. Anyone aggrieved by the behaviour of a police officer would anticipate a simple mechanism for complaining and would expect an explanation, apology, and perhaps some form of reprimand or disciplinary action. After decades of internal systems of inquiry under which the police themselves dealt with complaints, the machinery for investigation of complaints is now regulated by the Police Reform Act 2002, which set up the Independent Police Complaints Commission.

STEVE UGLOW

Police and Criminal Evidence Act 1984   *see* **PACE**

police detention and questioning   *see* **PACE**

police powers   *see* **PACE**

political broadcasting   *see* **reporting politics**

political fund   *see* **strikes**

political honours   *see* **patronage**

political participation   Broadly defined, political participation refers to actions of citizens that aim to influence or exercise power over collective decisions. The term refers to a wide range of activities including voting, campaigning, debating political issues, and forming and joining **political parties** and **interest groups**.

If **democracy** means government by the people, it entails some degree of participation by citizens in making collective decisions. Such participation played a central role in Athenian democracy in which each citizen was entitled to attend and vote in the Assembly, and public offices to be held for a limited period were allocated to citizens randomly by lot. Given the size and complexity of government activities, as well as the number of citizens, the Athenian model of democracy is generally thought not to be feasible in the modern state. Consequently, much political participation tends to be focused on the selection and accountability of representatives. While low turnouts at elections and declining party membership are often lamented in the **United Kingdom**, there is considerable disagreement among democratic theorists about the role of political participation by citizens in the process of collective decision-making.

At one end of the spectrum, some social choice theorists suggest a minimal role for political participation. According to this school of thought, most citizens have little incentive to incur the costs of participation, given the limited impact that one citizen can have. Consequently, such a theory sees mass political participation as little more than voting in periodic elections and the formal protection of civil liberties from state interference. Under this view, most political decisions are made or influenced by an elite of representatives, bureaucrats, opinion formers, and those with sufficient incentive to incur the costs of participation. Such theories do not see mass participation as a desirable part of a democracy, distrusting citizen involvement as leading to instability, tyranny of the majority and, potentially, totalitarianism. Under this school of thought, political participation has a minimal role in providing a check on the power of the public officeholders by removing them from office in the event of an abuse of power.

At the other end of the spectrum are theories of democracy that place political participation at the heart of collective decision-making. Such theories do not attempt to replicate the institutions of the Athenian model, but seek to broaden the citizen's input beyond electing representatives. The 'participatory' theorists of democracy focus on making the institutions of representative government more accessible and responsive to citizens. Furthermore such theorists seek to provide greater opportunity for direct citizen input, by emphasizing local level decision-making and proposing to decentralize certain decisions. Such calls are distinct from modern-day proposals for direct democracy, in which collective decisions are made through **referendums** and initiatives. Instead, the participatory theorist conceives of the citizen's role as more than just expressing a view on an outcome, and seeks to involve the citizen in earlier stages of the process such as deliberation with other citizens.

Within this spectrum of minimal and maximal participation there exist many competing and varied theories. The point made here is that modern democratic theories differ dramatically about the level of political participation that should take place and is realistic to expect.

A further area of difficulty concerns the conditions that are necessary to enable citizens to participate. Most models of democracy will require the protection of political rights, such as the right to vote, to form political parties, and **freedom of speech**. However, even where such rights are protected from state interference, there may be other barriers preventing citizens from participating, such as lack of time, resources, and expertise. This raises the question of whether more than just an absence of state interference is necessary and whether citizens should be provided with the resources to participate. Such resources may range from education to a level permitting the comprehension and analysis of political issues, to the money needed to publicize political views. If such resources are necessary to ensure participation, then further disagreement arises as to how those resources should be distributed. On some views a basic threshold of political resources is sufficient to ensure that every citizen has some chance to participate, whereas more demanding accounts suggest that some political resources should be distributed equally among citizens.

JACOB ROWBOTTOM

See also: **initiative as a means of instigating legislation**

political parties Political parties are key actors in major constitutional events such as the formation of government and the conduct of elections. They also conduct discreet but invaluable tasks in the selection and training of candidates and enable citizens to play a role in policy formation. That many of these functions are regulated by constitutional convention and political fact accounts in part for the lack of legal attention parties have received. Similarly, the evolution from fluid political associations during the Glorious Revolution, to loosely organized parliamentary factions in the nineteenth century, to disciplined, mass member and finally 'catch all' parties in the era of universal suffrage took place without apparent legal influence.

The prominent role played by political parties in our system of government is often taken for granted by constitutional lawyers. The work of notable exceptions such as Sir Ivor Jennings has been coolly received, it being said of his three volume study that it 'was a mistake to complete and publish *Party Politics* [which] will remain unread'. Leading textbooks typically pay parties scant attention, arguing that until recently the law has played little part in regulating political parties. Whilst it is certainly the case that legal regulation has increased since 1997, it is not the case that political parties were previously unknown

to the law. Unknown to many constitutional lawyers perhaps, but not to the law.

Reference is commonly made to the Ministers of the Crown Act 1937 (which defined and granted a salary to the Leader of the Opposition) as the first legal acknowledgement of the existence of political parties. The story certainly starts earlier, not least since the Labour Party was substantially forged in legal disputes concerning its financial relationship with trade unions. More recently the same party lost a challenge to its attempt to adopt 'all women shortlists' for parliamentary candidate selections. On both occasions the decisions were reversed by primary legislation. The intervention of the state has also augmented the capacities of parties, with successive broadcasting regulatory regimes requiring licensed broadcasters to allocate a certain quantity of 'party election/political broadcasts' free of charge to parties. The BBC, whilst not subject to this regime, has agreed to parallel rules of allocation.

The most significant process of subjecting political parties to legal regulation commenced with New Labour's assumption of power in 1997, which sought *inter alia* to respond to the corruption allegations that dogged the previous Conservative administration. A voluntary scheme of party registration was introduced by the Registration of Political Parties Act 1998 for the purpose of protecting parties' identities, which was quickly subsumed into the wide-ranging Political Parties Elections and Referendums Act 2000 which made registration compulsory. More importantly, it introduced a complex and comprehensive regulatory scheme for party political funding including the establishment of an Electoral Commission with extensive monitoring, investigatory, reporting, and reforming powers.

Political parties fulfil vital and varied constitutional functions, based on their ability to act as proxies for democratic opinion. Yet in the face of apparently unceasing funding scandals and declining memberships—a feature common to almost all Western democracies—their legitimacy, and therefore prospects, are under strain.

NAVRAJ SINGH GHALEIGH

I Jennings, *Party Politics* (Cambridge: Cambridge University Press, 3 volumes, 1960–2)

M Ostrogorski, *Democracy and the Organisation of Political Parties* (London: Transaction Books, 1982)

political party funding   *see* **political parties**

political science and law The study of politics goes back more than two millennia to the time of Aristotle (384–322 BCE) and beyond. But political *science*, as a branch of the social sciences, is a modern academic discipline, and an eclectic one. It draws inspiration from many intellectual traditions, including history, philosophy, economics, sociology—and law. Law is inextricably bound up with the world of politics—and hence, with the academic study of that world.

Constitutions and rules of public law supply the ground rules of political practice and are key mechanisms for limiting the exercise of governmental power. International relations—the study of which is a major sub-discipline of political science—are conducted within an extensive framework of international law. The judicial function is one of the three 'powers' (the others being executive and legislative functions), whose 'separation' was advocated by the eighteenth-century French philosopher and jurist, Montesquieu and later adopted by the founding fathers of the US Constitution. Courts are arenas for pressure group activity. The appointment of judges to the courts in which such contests take place is a matter of recurrent interest both to politicians and to political scientists—the academic and media attention given to the ratification hearings by the US Senate of presidential nominations to the **United State Supreme Court** provides a particularly high profile instance of this.

Law-making is a manifestation of state power. Laws are the devices by which policy is translated into action. Legislatures are not only law-making bodies, they are also democratically elected arenas in which politicians operate—and in many countries a high proportion of legislators (not to mention the bureaucrats who advise them) have legal backgrounds. Many of the concepts that are central to the study of political science—separation of powers, legitimacy, authority, sovereignty, justice, etc—are also important elements of legal theory. Authors of key works on the reading lists of political science students—**Bentham**, Mill, Marx, Hegel, Weber, Rawls, Foucault, and many others—will also feature in the reading lists of students studying theoretical jurisprudence.

Notwithstanding the many links between political science and law, we find that British political science was, until quite recently, slow to engage with the 'legal' dimensions of the discipline. American students of political science would at least, and as a matter of course, learn about the role of their Supreme Court and be taught that the justices of that court are significant political actors. But, until the last quarter of the twentieth century, it was unlikely that a student studying political science in any UK university would have much exposure to law or legal sources,

and textbooks on British government made hardly any mention of law, judges, and courts.

In part this reflects the direction in which modern political science has developed. In American universities in the 1950s and 1960s, and in the UK a little later, there was something of a rebellion (a 'behavioural revolution') against the dry formalism of traditional constitutional approaches to the study of government and politics. The quest to make the study of politics more 'scientific' encouraged a preference for quantitative and comparative methods, focusing on political behaviour rather than rules and institutions. In any case, the main purpose of the academic study of law is to train would-be practising lawyers rather than to engage in the more theoretical and speculative debates that are central to political science.

But the neglect by British political scientists of the legal dimensions of their discipline also owed much to the peculiarities of the British system. Unlike the USA, the UK lacks a codified constitution, and has no counterpart of the US Supreme Court. Administrative law has (perhaps owing to the late nineteenth-century legacy of AV **Dicey**) been much slower to develop than elsewhere in Europe. The British courts were not places where big constitutional issues were addressed or where the legality of government action was regularly challenged. As the courts had such a low political profile, political scientists tended to pay little attention to them and were little interested in the ideological propensities of the judges and how they were appointed.

All this began to change in the 1970s, and the pace of change has quickened. In 1977, JAG Griffith (a lawyer, not a political scientist) broke an old taboo against questioning the ideological predispositions of the judges, in his book, *The Politics of the Judiciary* (London: Fontana, 1977). Around the same time, the procedures for obtaining **judicial review**—enabling citizens to challenge the legality and fairness of the actions of public bodies and officials (including ministers)—were streamlined and made more user-friendly. Judicial review became a major growth-area; the judges began to divest themselves of their former reticence about upholding challenges to state power. This process has been taken a step further by the enactment of the Human Rights Act 1998, giving effect to the **European Convention on Human Rights** ('ECHR') in UK law. Since October 2000, England has had an Administrative Court, specializing in the ever-increasing volume of judicial review and other administrative law proceedings. And in 2009, the appellate jurisdiction of the **House of Lords** is to be transferred to a new **Supreme Court**

(UK) (albeit without the constitutional function of its US namesake).

Meanwhile, in 1973, the **United Kingdom** joined the **European Communities** (now broadened in to the **European Union**), and the **European Treaties**, enforced by the **European Court of Justice** in Luxembourg, have become a kind of 'external constitution', constraining the unfettered sovereignty of government and Parliament. The perspectives of lawyers and politicians acquired a substantial 'European' dimension.

The cumulative effects of these changes have been substantial. The political impact of judicial decisions has grown (the various challenges to the government anti-terrorism actions in the wake of the 9/11 atrocities are a case in point). Courts and judges have been increasingly recognized as worthwhile targets of political science research. No textbook on UK government and politics would be complete without at least a substantial section on legal aspects of the subject. There is still some way to go, but law has at last come to be recognized as a vital spanner in any self-respecting UK political scientist's tool kit.

GAVIN DREWRY

JAG Griffith, *The Politics of the Judiciary* (London: Fontana, 5th edn, 1997)

political strikes   *see* **strikes**

political trials   The term 'political trial' may strike some as an oxymoron, others as a tautology. From the perspective of strict legal formalism, trials must be conducted according to prospective, predictable, and generalizable norms of fairness that distinguish the legal process from the tumult of politics. From the perspective of critical jurisprudence, all trials have an ineradicably political element that can be masked only on the level of ideology.

More usefully, the term 'political trial' applies to those proceedings designed to advance specific political goals by using the trial as a tool for suppressing political dissent or opposition. Still, confusion may arise as the term 'political trial' is used at times as a pejoration; at others, as a description. Also, while political trials commonly take the form of criminal prosecutions, they may also appear as **slander** or **libel** suits, in which a group or party seeks to suppress the critical views of an opposition group through the use of the law of defamation.

As a species of criminal prosecution, the political trial finds its extreme form in the **show trials** of the Stalinist purges. Here the trial functions as an instrument of state terror: trumped-up charges,

bogus evidence, and public confessions are deployed to eliminate political opponents.

A second type of criminal prosecution serving as a political trial includes prosecutions for sedition, treason, **terrorism**, aggressive war, and the like. Descriptively, such incriminations are necessarily connected to politics. As a normative matter, trials for such crimes may be conducted in a fair manner, though such incriminations, if not defined and applied narrowly and precisely, may turn into all-purpose tools for suppressing the voice of political dissent.

A third type involves prosecutions in which the charge is non-political, but the motive to prosecute is political. This is commonly the case in selective prosecutions, in which, for example, the state brings tax evasion charges only against vocal critics of the current political administration. Individual trials may be deemed fair, but not the ulterior motive to use the criminal law to suppress or punish the expression of legitimate political dissent.

A fourth type of political trial includes prosecutions staged by successor regimes. These may include trials of former state functionaries or collaborators—persons accused of lending assistance or support to a reprobate regime or occupying force. In the wake of World War II, thousands of collaborator trials were staged across Europe. These trials differ from sedition trials in that the effort is less to protect and consolidate existing state power, than to use the trial as a tool of lustration—a means of doing away with the past to make possible a new politics of the future. Political trials of this variety remind us of the intersections between **memory and law**, as collaborator trials often serve as didactic tools for defining collective memory. They construct—and at times erase—connections between a nation's fraught past and its political present, teasing lessons from memory to support new political commitments.

A fifth type includes prosecutions conducted by international tribunals, such as the **Nuremberg trials**, or the trials of the International Criminal Tribunal for the Former Yugoslavia ('**ICTY**'). These differ from both the sedition and the collaborator trials in that they are exercises of extra-state power rather than of state power. These trials serve a broad political agenda; didactic in scope, they attempt to contribute to the creation of democratic institutions and a politics of accountability in societies accustomed to authoritarian practices. Such trials, however, have also been castigated as political in the pejorative sense of the term. Some observers have disparaged trials by successor regimes and international criminal courts as exercises in 'victor's justice'—in which defendants are condemned for conduct that either was lauded at the time of its commission or was fundamentally of a kind with conduct engaged in by the accuser. The charge of victor's justice often takes the form of a *tuo quoque* (you, too) argument. As used by advocates such as Jacques Verges in his defense of Klaus **Barbie** and by Slobodan **Milosevic** in his trial before the ICTY, the *tuo quoque* argument insists that if the defendant's actions were criminal, then so too were those of many others, including the prosecuting authority. This argument is not a defence per se as much it is an accusation of partisan or selective prosecution.   LAWRENCE DOUGLAS

J Shklar, *Legalism: Law, Morals and Political Trials* (Cambridge, MA: Harvard University Press, 1964)

O Kirchheimer, *Political Justice: The Use of Legal Procedure for Political Ends* (Princeton: Princeton University Press, 1961)

politician-lawyers The pursuit of a career at the Bar has long been an effective vehicle for political ambition. The personal independence of the barrister/advocate, the hours of attendance in court, the qualities and skills required of the successful practitioner, have fitted more happily with the demands of a political career than have the duties and constraints of almost any other employment or profession. While the rise of a class of political apparatchiks, who have known no other employment but politics, has significantly changed the complexion of the contemporary **Parliament**, the importance of lawyers is demonstrated by the fact that until the 1992 general election, barristers formed the largest single professional group in the **House of Commons** (9.1 per cent). Even today, barristers and solicitors together make up 11.7 per cent of the House, led only by business people (19.2 per cent), political professionals (14 per cent), and other white collar workers (12.7 per cent). The two most prominent political leaders of recent years, Margaret Thatcher and Tony Blair, each chose the English Bar as their route into politics.

An obvious objective for the politician-lawyer is appointment to those Ministerial offices which carry professional legal responsibilities: the Law Officers. Holders of these posts are politically responsible members of the United Kingdom government (or in the case of the **Lord Advocate** and Scottish **Solicitor General** since the Scotland Act 1998, of the Scottish Executive) and ideally will be drawn from among parliamentarians with high legal qualifications. Often that ideal has not been realizable, and the **Prime Minister** has chosen legal distinction over answerability to the House of Commons, as with the appointment of Lord Williams, already a Minister in

the **House of Lords**, as **Attorney-General** in 1999, and even over political experience, as when Lord Goldsmith was appointed to the post, and to the peerage, straight from private practice in 2001. In Scotland, with relatively few constituencies and a substantial imbalance between the parties, political experience has recently been the exception rather than the rule: only one of the last eight Lords Advocate (Lord Fraser of Carmylie, 1989–1992) had previously been a member of the House of Commons.

Until the passing of the Constitutional Reform Act 2005, the highest legal office within the government, that of **Lord Chancellor**, combined the headship of the judiciary, Ministerial responsibility for the management of the judicial system, and the speakership of the House of Lords. Here too the ideal combination of legal distinction and political experience and commitment has not always been available: a recent Lord Chancellor with little political background was Lord Mackay (1987–1997), a former Lord Advocate appointed to that post with no previous parliamentary experience.

The persistence over centuries of the Lord Chancellor's remarkable combination of executive, judicial, and legislative functions, like the principle of the political responsibility of the government's Law Officers, reflects a rejection by our **constitution** of the notion that political commitment is necessarily incompatible with legal objectivity. The fact that a lawyer has pursued an active political career has not traditionally been seen as a disqualification from high judicial office—if anything, the contrary was true until the early years of the last century, when lawyer-MPs might still be appointed straight to the High Court Bench. Part-time judicial office can still be combined with membership of the House of Commons. For a while, in England, the Attorney-General was understood to have first refusal of any vacancy in the office of **Lord Chief Justice**, but this understanding did not survive the rigorously non-political appointments practice of Lord Jowitt as Lord Chancellor (1945–1951). In Scotland, however, the understanding that the Lord Advocate had a claim on any vacancy in the **Court of Session** has persisted longer, with four of the last eight Lords Advocate moving directly to the Court of Session bench on resignation from the office, and a fifth taking a seat after a short period as an Opposition spokesman in the House of Lords following loss of office at a general election.

Another evidence of a British tradition of closeness, not separation, between judicial and other state functions is the governmental practice of calling upon senior **judges** to undertake *ad hoc* **inquiries** into difficult and controversial situations and events.

Examples from recent years include Lord Hutton's inquiry into the death of government scientist, David Kelly (2004), and Lord Justice Scott's inquiry into the sale of arms to Iraq (1996). Although these inquiries expose the judges who conduct them to press controversy, and subject them to government-controlled terms of reference, the senior judiciary appears to accept this sort of task as an informal extension of their judicial function, and one which offers no threat to judicial independence.

There is however reason to think that this tradition is on the wane and that we shall in future see a more stringent separation between law and politics and the consequent decline of the politician-lawyer. Politics is increasingly acquiring the characteristics of a professional career; so too is judging. While the notion of judging as a lifetime career remains alien to us, a strong element of career progression has developed in recent years, with many judges moving up the hierarchy from part-time to full-time and from junior to senior judicial appointments. The creation in 2005 of an apolitical **Judicial Appointments** Commission can only reinforce this process. Since 2002, the Scottish First Minister makes his recommendations to the Queen for Scottish judicial appointments on the basis of a shortlist drawn up by an independent Judicial Appointments Board. The chances that senior judges will have held executive office, or even have had significant political experience, seem likely to diminish rapidly, while the proportion of successful politicians having a legal background also seems set to decline, perhaps more gradually. One result of the recent constitutional reforms is that the most senior judges will no longer be eligible to sit and vote in the upper house of Parliament as they have done hitherto, though distinguished lawyers who have **not** gone on to the judicial bench will doubtless continue to be appointed to the House.   TERENCE DAINTITH

politics   In contrast to politics which is often regarded as partisan and heated, law is generally seen as impartial, neutral, and objective, with judicial decisions the outcome of a measured, reasoned, and apolitical process. Such qualities are thought to make lawyers and **judges** wise and unbiased mediators in disputes between citizens, and between individuals and the state. However, critics argue that law and politics are in fact closely entwined, and that law's impartiality is a shibboleth.

At one level, law is clearly political. The '**rule of law**' is generally seen as a restraint on the arbitrary and capricious 'rule of man'. Indeed, the 'rule of law' is widely regarded as the main means by which society constrains the exercise of power and position.

This view of law sees it as one of the main bulwarks of liberal (if not democratic) society. However, history provides a number of examples which throw law's affinity with liberalism into doubt. Authoritarian regimes have used law, lawyers, and legal systems to oppress entire populations and abuse **human rights**. Both fascist and communist regimes have claimed that they are 'ruled by law', thereby lending their policies the legitimacy of law.

The existence of an independent judiciary makes manipulation of the legal system by a political regime more difficult. **Judicial independence** requires, at a minimum, a system of appointment not amenable to political manipulation (so that **judicial appointments** are independent of the executive), non-interference in judicial decisions, and security of tenure. The latter means that judges who rule against a government cannot easily be dismissed, enabling them to make their decisions without fear of the consequences.

An independent judiciary should, then, be free to act as a check on political power. However, clashes can occur between the executive and the judiciary where one challenges the power of the other. There have been instances around the world where governments have dismissed all of the nation's top judges; others have found themselves imprisoned for refusing to support the laws of a particular regime. Where a political system lacks checks and balances, or where the 'loyal opposition' is too weak to hold the government to account, an independent judiciary may become the main check on state power. On the other hand, as members of the 'Establishment', judges may uphold (or decline to challenge) the status quo. If, as some argue, courts protect powerful economic and social interests by taking controversial issues out of politics and off the table, judges may become an unaccountable 'juristocracy'. A question then arises as to whether, where judges are not democratically elected, they should be able to make important decisions without being accountable to society as a whole.

Where a political system lacks channels through which citizens might air their grievances, courts of law can become as important a site as the streets for challenging the state. **Judicial review** has also brought opportunities for citizens to bring government officials to account for abuse of power. However, how far citizens can use the courts depends heavily on their having the time, money, confidence, and legal skills. Not everyone has ready access to these, making equal access to justice itself a political issue. Government departments and large corporations are, for example, more likely than the ordinary citizen to possess such resources. They are also more likely to have prior experience of the legal system, enabling them to use it more effectively to defend their interests against individual complainants. Whatever the 'truth' or justice of the matter, this inequality of resources means that the 'haves' are more likely to win in court than the 'have nots'.

The law also has an inbuilt tendency to de-politicize issues. It does this in a number of ways. Judges, for example, generally present their decisions as if they are derived purely from legal principles, even when they are driven by policy. Where the judiciary is drawn from a relatively narrow social background, it may also adopt an unrepresentative approach to social issues with which its members lack familiarity.

The supposed neutrality of law and claims that it treats all people equally have also been criticized as gender-biased and/or tilted in favour of the (male) status quo. For example, where the law holds that the state should not intervene in disputes within the home or between married couples, this produces judicial silence on matters such as marital **rape** and **domestic violence**. In delivering decisions which are supposed to take no account of **race**, class, or **gender**, the (predominantly male) judiciary is apparently blind to the fact that the law's silence disadvantages these sections of the population. Changing the idea that the law was 'unbiased' and 'gender-blind' itself became a political issue for feminist lawyers in the 1980s.

Law also takes the politics out of injustice on a more day-to-day basis. When a person goes to see a lawyer, the lawyer generally sifts through their story to identify the *legal* issues, arriving at a view as to what the law is in this *individual* case. For example, a worker who suffers an injury at work is unlikely to find their lawyer advising them about the inequities of capitalism or fighting for better rights for **company** workers. In some situations, the lawyer might advise that multiple clients can mount a common case (a **class action**) but the court will still consider these claims on an individual rather than a collective basis. Moreover, most civil cases settle out of court, so that the general public (and other workers) seldom come to know what the dangerous practice was which caused the accident, how widespread it is in the industry, or what needs to be done to prevent it recurring. Some argue that by taking the politics out of the matter, law disguises the socio-economic forces at work. They argue that lawyers should be prepared to advise clients of other, political, options, such as taking collective action, forming a **trade union**, or lobbying the government for structural change. A decision in a court case may benefit the individual but, in the long run, it does not alter the underlying forces which produced the problem in the first place.

Thus, even when it claims to be apolitical law may be deeply political, obscuring the play of wealth, power, and position, accepting things as they are instead of saying what they should be. The exception to this is, perhaps, **constitutional law**. **Constitutions** frequently set out a 'blueprint' for living, making clear the powers of the executive, judiciary, and legislature as well as the rights of citizens. Controversy readily arises here, especially as to how such an obviously political document should be interpreted and who has the power to perform that interpretation. Generally, this power falls to judges and courts of law. Their experience in such matters perhaps makes it no surprise, then, that around the world lawyers have often become politically active, if not political leaders.

CAROL JONES

politics in the school curriculum   *see* **secular curriculum in schools**

politics of crime control   Until 1970, crime and its control was not a significant concern for the major political parties. However, the Conservative Party's general **election** manifesto changed this position when it discussed the rise in crime that had allegedly occurred under the then Labour government. This concern intensified throughout the 1970s so that by the 1979 election, law and order had moved to the centre of political and popular debate with vociferous demands to punish offenders. Why did the bipartisan approach change from a post-war crime control model based on a discourse of **rehabilitation** (although how often rehabilitation was put into practice is a matter of debate) to one based on **punishment**?

In 1975 Margaret Thatcher was elected leader of the Conservative Party. Thatcher's rise to the leadership was built on challenging the post-war, bipartisan consensus and what she and her fellow New Right Conservatives regarded as the fatal compromises that previous Conservative governments had made not only with their traditional opponents in the Labour Party but also with traditional interest groups such as civil servants, **trade unions**, and the law and order establishment. In their 1979 Manifesto, the Conservatives argued that the then Labour government had done little to challenge the lawlessness and disorder which appeared to be engulfing the country. In short, crime appeared to be out of control.

For the Thatcherite bloc, the rise in crime became a powerful metaphor for the broader economic, political, and cultural decline of the United Kingdom. Conversely, the lack of crime control indicated the misguided faith of both major parties in the post-war settlement whose politicians had shaken hands with the devil of compromise and bent with the political wind. They argued that the declining respect for the traditional institutions of authority, the subversion of the nuclear family, the challenge to the government by trade unions, and the broader economic decline of the country were symbolically represented in the rise in crime in general and the crime of mugging in particular. The moral panic around this crime, amplified by the mass media, was the defining moment when the politics of crime control shifted to the centre stage of British politics symbolizing as it did the uncertainties and insecurities felt by the wider population in a society experiencing economic stagnation and declining political influence.

With the election of the Conservatives in May 1979, crime control became a central concern for the major political parties. Increasingly, the discourse through which it was articulated was overwhelmingly authoritarian and uncompromising. The first Thatcher government employed more **police**, built more **prisons,** and introduced tougher sentences, all of which was underpinned by a broader philosophical view that crime was a matter of individual choice and **responsibility** while crime control needed to be built on individual and collective deterrence. Throughout the 1980s, while there were tensions and contradictions between liberal and hard line members of Mrs Thatcher's different Cabinets, the thrust and direction of crime control policy was authoritarian and retributive. This was to have a significant hegemonic impact particularly on the Labour Party.

In the early 1990s, three significant events reinforced the authoritarian crime control agenda. First, in February 1993, two-year-old James Bulger was murdered by two ten-year-old boys. This was a profound moment for both parties (and the wider society) as it appeared to exemplify the continuing downward spiral of lawlessness and disorder gripping the society's youth in particular. Despite the fact that many more **children** continued to be killed by individuals who knew them, rather than by **strangers**, the moral panic around the Bulger murder consolidated the law and order drive. Secondly, Tony Blair became Shadow Home Secretary in the summer of 1992. In January 1993, he famously indicated that New Labour would be 'tough on crime, tough on the causes of crime'. This pronouncement was to lock Blair, and the New Labour hierarchy, into an intensified spiral of policy and counter-policy innovations with the Conservative Party as they sought to outflank each other in matters of crime control. Thirdly, Michael Howard's appointment as Home Secretary in May 1993 intensified the drive towards more law and order particularly after Howard's conference speech in October 1993 where he outlined a twenty-seven point law and order plan underpinned by the slogan 'prison works'.

These events were crucial in laying the foundation for a politics of crime control based on a retributive, authoritarian, and disciplinary response to offenders. Driven forward by an often rabid popular press whose reporting and editorializing targeted particular groups seemingly out of control—young people, single parents (especially **women**), the homeless, scroungers, drug takers, illegal immigrants, and the conventional criminal—politicians became so alarmed by being seen to be 'soft on crime' that they proactively became part of the clampdown and the ongoing drive away from a welfare-orientated, rehabilitative, inclusive view of crime control (however idealized that might have been) to a model based on discipline, punishment, and **retribution**, at least for the powerless. The illegal activities of the powerful—income tax evasion, fraud, **health and safety at work** violations, environmental degradation—effectively remained outside the crime control network where conventional state servants such as the police were being vigorously reinforced by private security personnel and a massive increase in surveillance technologies such as CCTV cameras. In combination, the old and the new constituted a formidable presence in the landscape of crime control, a hybrid whose target population however had not changed; the powerless continued to be the objects of intrusive punishment while the powerful remained subjects of unobtrusive regulation.

These trends continued with New Labour's election in May 1997. Blair's slogan, 'tough on crime, tough on the cause of crime' remained heavily weighted towards the first part of the slogan with the second dimension lagging behind the frenzied political and popular calls to take drastic action against those groups, especially the young, overwhelmingly concentrated on the economic and political margins of the society, who were regarded as undermining its good order and discipline. Thus **Anti Social Behaviour** Orders emerged as a central tool in the government's drive to curb crime. Additionally, the **Prime Minister** insisted that crime control should concentrate on the small minority of disreputable individuals who committed a disproportionate number of crimes. Blair's speeches constantly juxtaposed the small minority of law-breakers with the vast majority of law-abiding, decent citizens. However, many of these 'decent' citizens were themselves engaged in criminal activity. In 2002, the annual cost of crime was £35 billion. Embezzlement accounted for 40 per cent of this figure. Recorded white-collar crime increased by 500 per cent during the year, while there was a 7 per cent drop in burglary and robbery. In 2005, it was estimated that corporate fraud was costing UK businesses £72 billion each year. The Public and Commercial Services Union ('PSU') noted that VAT fraud was also costing £5 billion annually. And while police numbers continued their inexorable rise, reinforced by the growing presence of the private security industry with their relentless focus on conventional crime, the PSU noted that the numbers employed to police such fraud were being cut back.

Additionally, the intensification in more authoritarian crime control measures since the 1970s has been legitimated by the idea that **victims** of crime have been marginalized in the **criminal justice system**. However, even here the argument is contentious because when politicians and media commentators talk about victims, the focus is on those whose lives have been devastated through the violent loss of a relative or friend and who call for vengeance against the perpetrator. And yet there are other voices in this debate which have not resorted to the clamour for vengeance, but whose hurt, pain, and sense of loss is no less acute. In July 2005, Anthony Walker's mother provided one example of dignified forgiveness in the midst of unimaginable grief after her son's brutal, racist murder. While politicians condemned Anthony's murder as an act of racist barbarism, they were much less forthcoming with respect to his mother's plea for forgiveness. Why? Arguably her sentiments did not chime with the retributive crime control philosophy that has dominated political and media circles since the 1970s.

Similarly, those who have been victims of corporate criminality are not considered by politicians (and the majority of those working in the mass media) as 'real' victims in need of empathy and **justice**. Their needs remain on the political and criminal justice margins, subjugated in the drive to create an image of respectable victimization that is then used to legitimate a further increase in the authoritarian powers of the state. The contrast between the introduction of victim impact statements which give a voice to victims in **court**, and the struggle to have corporate manslaughter recognized as a criminal offence, provides a striking indication of where the sympathies of most politicians and media personnel lie.

The final dimension to the politics of crime control is the 'war on terror'. For a number of critics this situation has allowed New Labour (in the same way as political violence in Northern Ireland in the 1970s allowed their predecessors in government) to push forward with their authoritarian agenda. Thus, the government has elided the issue of **terrorism**, with populist concerns around community **safety** and public protection, with bogus **asylum** seekers and crime, with animalistic youths, and with single parents. Supported by a feral, tabloid press, this nightmare scenario has worked its way into public consciousness whose concerns, however exaggerated, further legitimate crime control policies that are then used not only to 'round up the usual suspects' but also to clamp down on democratic dissent as the exceptional and repressive powers claimed by the state increasingly become normalized.

JOE SIM

See also: **corporate criminal liability; law and order debates; Thatcherism**

politics of identity   see **identity**

poll tax   see **council tax; tax, ability to pay**

Pollock, Sir Frederick Frederick Pollock (1845–1937) was one of the few English jurists that **judges** and barristers embraced as one of their own; though, considering that he was the poorest of conversationalists, it is difficult to imagine many striking up a rapport with the man. He was educated at Eton and Trinity College, Cambridge, and he belonged to a family of legal luminaries (his grandfather, Jonathan Frederick Pollock, and his cousin, Ernest Murray Pollock, were both senior judges). In 1871, when Pollock entered Lincoln's Inn, his legal career promised much. It would deliver much, too, but not conventionally so. Pollock lived, and worked, into his nineties, and for all his professional life was closely connected to the **Inns of Court**. He was, however, neither a practising barrister nor a judge (he was appointed to the **Admiralty Court**, but never called on to adjudicate) but a prolific and influential jurist. From 1883 to 1903 he was a professor of jurisprudence at Oxford. While holding that post, he continued to work mainly from Lincoln's Inn and, though he wrote a good introductory jurisprudence book, his most significant and enduring works—*Principles of Contract* (1876) and (especially) *The Law of Torts* (1887)—set out the principles underpinning core areas of the **common law**. For four decades he was responsible for selecting and editing the judicial decisions to be published in the official **Law Reports**

of England and Wales, and for nearly thirty-five years he was the editor one of the major British law journals, the *Law Quarterly Review*.

NEIL DUXBURY

N Duxbury, *Frederick Pollock and the English Juristic Tradition* (Oxford: Oxford University Press, 2004)

polluter pays principle   *see* **international environmental law**

pollution   Pollution has long been a core concern of what is now termed environmental law. Before the industrial revolution, legal protection against pollution was largely focused on the rights of individual property owners to protect their interests through private **nuisance** actions, leaving it to the judiciary to determine on a case-by-case basis environmental standards and the extent of pollution that was deemed legally acceptable. Private legal rights continue to play a significant role but have severe limitations in providing truly effective controls over pollution. Aside from the costs of bring an action, the claimant must be able to prove who caused the pollution, action is generally possible only after damage has occurred, and those parts of the environment which are unowned (such as wildlife or the atmosphere) will fall outside the remit of such actions.

In the United Kingdom, the nineteenth century saw the gradual development of regulatory controls designed to provide a more comprehensive and preventative system of protection. Many of the core legal approaches adopted over 100 years ago remain in contemporary legal systems and for industrial processes are typically based on the requirement to operate in accordance with a permit or licence granted and supervised by a public authority. Conditions imposed by the authority essentially reflect the extent of pollution deemed legal and acceptable to society. Until the mid-1970s, the preferred policy approach in the UK was to leave as much flexibility in the **legislation** as possible, with laws concentrating on the requirements and procedures for permits, but avoiding specifying precise environmental standards beyond the use of broad qualitative phrases such as 'wholesome water' and 'best practicable means'. Public demands for greater legal transparency, the new regulatory frameworks that followed **privatization** of key industrial sectors, and, above all, the need to transpose an increasing number of **European Community law** directives concerning pollution saw a transformation of traditional legal approaches. Modern pollution legislation contains a proliferation of different forms of pollution standards, such as minimum emission limits, environmental quality standards, product standards, and, in some cases, overall national loads for specific pollutants.

A number of important strands can be identified in recent developments in pollution law. Pollution is essentially concerned with the impact of sources on receptors, and law must identify which sources require control, which receptors require protection, and what level of impact is considered permissible. Part I of the Environmental Protection Act 1990, for example, defines 'pollution of the environment' to mean pollution of the environment due to the release into any environmental medium from any process of substances capable of causing harm to man or any other living organism supported to the environment. 'Harm to man' is further defined to include property damage, and offences caused to human senses (such as smell) as well as damage to human health.

Scientific expertise clearly plays a key role in identifying pathways and likely levels of impact but increasingly it is recognized that the determination of pollution standards as contained in legislation and reflecting society's choice of acceptable levels of pollution is a transcientific question, and ultimately a political decision, involving economic, technical, and ethical choices. The UK long advocated a policy approach which recognized that the physical environment had a considerable capacity to absorb and disperse pollutants, but in doing so came into conflict with more sceptical perceptions from other members of the European Community, especially in the context of the release of potentially dangerous substances into water. An increasing awareness of the level of scientific uncertainties concerning the impact of pollutants has seen the development of more preventative approaches, and the use of the **precautionary principle** to justify regulatory action despite the absence of firm scientific evidence of cause and effect.

Another contemporary theme has been a far broader acknowledgement of the rights of the general public in pollution regulation. UK pollution law was long based on what was essentially a closed relationship between the regulator and the regulated industry, and a perception that rights of public access would threaten industrial trace secrets. The **Royal Commission** on Environmental Pollution consistently challenged these assumptions, and from the mid 1970s most UK pollution laws have now introduced rights of public participation in licence application procedures, and extensive rights to information concerning both the details of consents and licences, and the results of monitoring. These rights of the public to environmental participation and information are now reflected internationally in the

1998 UN/ECE **Aarhus Convention** which has been ratified by almost forty European Countries including the UK, as well as the European Community.

New regulatory approaches beyond the familiar licence and consent systems are being developed. In particular, emissions trading regimes are advocated as a more efficient means of reducing overall pollution loads, in that they incentivize industries to reduce emissions below legal minimum standards and to sell surplus rights to those less able to achieve reductions. Pollutants with significant local impacts where the public are unlikely to find it acceptable that an local industry can 'buy the right' to pollute at higher levels are likely still to require more traditional legal controls, but an emission trading regime for carbon dioxide and other greenhouse gases was introduced across the European Union in 2005. In the US, emission trading regimes have been used as a component of air pollution control at both federal and regional for over thirty years.

Pollution laws have tended to develop in a fragmented fashion, dealing with water, air, and land in separate laws and often with distinct enforcement bodies. It has been increasingly recognized that it is preferable to consider impacts on the environment as a whole, and a contemporary trend has been to establish **integrated pollution prevention and control** regimes for industrial processes, where the total emissions from a process are regulated under a single regime. Such a system was first introduced in UK law in 1990 and at European Community level in 1996. At the same time, the UK as well as many other jurisdictions has seen the development of integrated environment agencies, responsible for regulating pollution across the different environmental media.

Enforcement of pollution laws remains largely the responsibility of public agencies, such as the Environment Agency in England and Wales and the Scottish Environment Protection Agency in Scotland. UK agencies possess considerable **discretion** in how to respond to a legal breach, and various techniques to ensure compliance are employed including the issuing of warning letters and the service of notices. But the core sanction for most pollution laws has long been a criminal **prosecution,** with most pollution offences drafted in strict terms meaning that the prosecution need not prove intention or recklessness on the part of the offender. In the future, a more extensive range of sanctions are likely to be made available, including the greater use of administrative **fines**, similar to those used by economic regulators in the UK, and by environment agencies in many other countries, including the United States.

At the same time, regulators are moving to a more **risk**-based approach towards enforcement, concentrating resources on those areas and industries posing greater environmental risk.

Pollution law has largely been concerned with reducing the polluting effects of processes and products, and contemporary regimes have clearly developed more preventative and integrated approaches. Yet there still remain considerable challenges in the design of effective systems. Linkages between pollution control regimes and areas such as land use and transport planning, and energy consumption that deal with fundamental sources of pollution loads remain problematical. The principle of **sustainable development** and the more radical concept of sustainable consumption are likely to underpin future legal developments in this area.

RICHARD MACRORY

poly-ethnic rights Poly-ethnic rights is a term used by Canadian political theorist, Will Kymlicka. He uses the term to refer to group-specific claims made by **minority** ethnic and religious groups. These claims may include calls to be exempt from generally applicable family laws, official **dress codes**, school dress codes, or Sunday trading laws. They may also include claims to public funding and support for cultural activities, events, or museums.

The objective of poly-ethnic rights claims is to safeguard group-based differences and to preserve distinct religious or cultural **identities**, without disadvantaging group members. Proponents of poly-ethnic rights (also referred to as group-differentiated rights) argue that states have a duty to safeguard such rights, to ensure that minority groups are not disadvantaged (the **equality** argument), or to ensure the survival of distinct group-based identities (the diversity argument). Historical arguments (linked, for example, to the terms of **treaties** negotiated between first nation peoples in North America, and colonizing states), may also be drawn upon to justify poly-ethnic rights.

Critics of poly-ethnic/group differentiated rights express concern that **recognition** of such rights can lead to state support for discriminatory practices within groups, where, for example, religion-based family laws discriminate against **women**. Critics also highlight the failure to recognize intra-cultural differences within groups, the potential to elide differences, and to presume that cultures or **religions** are monolithic entities. Others note the potential for fragmentation, division, and conflict that may come with group-differentiated rights (the so-called 'Balkanization' effect). In response to such concerns, we see an increasing emphasis on social cohesion and **integration** in government policies.

SIOBHAN MULLALLY

polygamy Polygamy is commonly used to refer to the practice of having more than one **marriage** partner at a time. There is a common misconception that polygamy refers to men with multiple wives when in fact, *polygyny* refers to having more than one wife, whilst *polyandry* is that of having more than one husband. However, the Kiyorangs of Tibet are perhaps the only truly polyandrous society, whereas, the practice of polygyny is significantly more widespread and is most prevalent amongst Mormon followers of the Fundamentalist Church of Jesus Christ of Latter Day Saints; Muslims, who are permitted to have up to four wives under *Surah an Nisa* 4:3 of the *Qu'ran* which states 'And if you fear that you cannot act equitably towards orphans, then marry such women as seem good to you, two, three and four, but if you fear that you may not do **justice** to them, then (marry) only one'; and in a number of African societies, most notably, Nigeria, Senegal, and Ghana, where the practice of polygamy is culturally, rather than religiously situated.

A number of justifications are proffered for the practice, with the common theme being that a woman's social survival and status was/is dependent upon her marital status. For example, the *Quranic* injunction was issued at a time when war was prevalent, and the female to male ratio was much higher than normal; whereas, in those African societies which practice polygamy, it is believed that reproduction of the male line is paramount, the status of a man being dependent upon the number of children (particularly, sons) that he has and so the more wives, the more opportunity for a surviving male line.

Such justifications in turn raise a number of objections to the practice, most notably from feminist thinkers, who argue that polygamy is fundamentally and inextricably linked to gender inequality, and the oppression and subordination of women. Polygamy is viewed as premised upon the unacceptable notion that female status is dependent upon male patronage through the bonds of marriage and serves only to reproduce patriarchal notions of ownership and control over the female body. Many proponents of polygynous marriage argue that such criticisms are based upon a Western bias, and ignore the prevalence of extra-marital relationships which occur in the West. Polygamous marriages, they argue, are infinitely more preferable as the status of being married offers women and their offspring legal and social protections that they would not otherwise

have. Others argue that the notion of the monogamous nuclear family is a western construct, and to impose that on other societies is a form of cultural imperialism. Many Muslim proponents also argue that under **Islamic law**, polygamous marriages can only occur with the **consent** of *all* parties, and so empower women, rather than disempower them. In reality, there is some question as to the truth of this. Many polygamous marriages occur without the consent and/or knowledge of all the parties involved.

From a legal perspective, very few countries actually explicitly permit polygamy. Of those countries with a large Muslim population, only Tunisia explicitly prohibits polygamy, although there is also no corresponding provision to invalidate polygamous marriages. Syria, Iraq, and Pakistan all allow polygamous marriages with the permission of the Court/Arbitration Council, and subject to certain criteria, for example, there being some lawful benefit, or financial competence; and Article 31 of the Moroccan Code of Personal Status allows a wife to stipulate in a pre-marital contract that her husband cannot take a co-wife. Nigerian law incorporates three forms of marriage—monogamous marriage under the 1915 Marriage Ordinance; customary marriage which is potentially polygamous, governed by **customary law**, and has no prescribed limit on the number of wives; and in the Northern States, marriage as governed by Islamic law, wherein a man may legally marry up to four wives. In India, polygamy is recognized for Muslims under sharia law, although the Hindu Marriage Act 1955 prohibits polygamy for non-Muslims. Under English law the Matrimonial Causes Act 1973 renders void marriages contracted where one of the parties is already married, where one of the parties to a polygamous marriage was domiciled in England and Wales. Perhaps the most pertinent issue is that whilst many countries prohibit polygamous marriages under state law, this does not preclude those marriages which occur unofficially or under customary law.

SONYA FERNANDEZ

Ponting, Clive Clive Ponting was tried and acquitted at the Central Criminal Court in 1985 for breach of section 2 of the Official Secrets Act 1911. He was a civil servant in the Ministry of Defence who disclosed Ministry of Defence documents to an MP, Tam Dalyell, who was pressing the government to provide a full explanation of the circumstances surrounding the sinking of the Argentine warship, the General Belgrano, in 1982—the event which precipitated the Falklands conflict.

Ponting conceded that he had passed on the relevant documents, but claimed that he had acted in good faith and in the public interest because of his belief that Parliament was being misled by the government. Although the judge clearly directed the jury that they should convict, the jury returned a verdict of 'not guilty'. The Conservative government later reacted by reforming the law on official secrets (Official Secrets Act 1989) to remove the 'public interest' defence.

The trial is chiefly notable as a modern example of jury nullification. This is understood as the power possessed by juries to return a verdict of not guilty even where this might conflict with the judge's direction on the law, on how the law applies to the facts of the case, or on the evidence in the case. The power has its origins in *Bushel's Case* (1670) in which the imprisonment of jury members, who refused to convict Quakers for the unlawful assembly, was declared illegal. The power is often defended as a vital popular safeguard against oppressive laws, though it might also allow juries to return perverse verdicts in other cases.   LINDSAY FARMER

poor law   The Poor Law provided the framework for the relief of poverty before the modern **welfare state**. The origins of the Poor Law lie in fourteenth-century statutes that sought to control begging and vagrancy. Tudor legislation providing for a system of poor relief administered by parishes was consolidated in the Poor Relief Act 1601, the basis for the Old (or Elizabethan) Poor Law. The concept of 'settlement' was central to this scheme, as it attributed responsibility for the relief of a pauper to the parish in which that person was linked through birth, marriage, or employment. Poor relief was provided either in kind, by accommodating paupers in workhouses, or through 'outdoor relief' (cash payments to paupers living in the community).

The system came under great pressure in the late eighteenth and early nineteenth centuries in the wake of economic and social change. Malthus, Ricardo and others criticized the system of outdoor relief for encouraging dependency on the Poor Law and creating perverse incentives for the poor to have children they could not afford. The New Poor Law of 1834, enacted in the wake of a critical Royal Commission report, led to the rationalization of the many parishes into a smaller number of unions. The 1834 Act also sought to impose the principle of 'less eligibility', by reducing the availability of outdoor relief and making the workhouse regime so unattractive that only the desperate would apply for relief. As a result of local opposition, the full rigour of the New Poor Law was not implemented across the whole of England and Wales. Thus the Poor Law was not a uniform statutory scheme; it was also based on the custom and practice of individual parishes and unions.

The Royal Commission on the Poor Laws of 1909 could not agree on a unanimous approach to further reform, and in the early twentieth century the Poor Law was gradually marginalized by the development of the modern **social security system**. Although the Poor Law itself was formally abolished in 1948, there are aspects of today's means-tested benefits schemes which can trace their origins back to the system of poor relief. For example, social security legislation today requires spouses to support each other. In the event of default, the Department for Work and Pensions ('DWP') has the power to seek recovery of benefits paid to dependants from the so-called liable relative (in relation to children, this function has now been subsumed within the **child support** scheme). This right of recovery is the direct descendant of a provision in the Poor Relief Act 1601.

The history of the Poor Law in other parts of the British Isles was different; in Scotland the Church played a central role, in the absence of effective local government, at least until the Poor Law (Scotland) Act 1845, while the Irish Poor Law Act 1838 imposed a regime that was harsher still than that embodied in the 1834 statute in England and Wales.

                                    NICK WIKELEY

Popish Plot   The 'Popish Plot' of 1678–1681 was the invention of Titus Oates (1649–1705). **Oates**, who had been expelled from a number of Jesuit seminaries, informed Israel Tonge, a vehemently anti-Catholic, that Roman Catholic agents had conspired and plotted to assassinate Charles II and replace him with either James, Duke or York, or a puppet ruler appointed by the Pope.

In August 1678, Tonge attempted to convince Charles II and the Earl of Danby of the plot. Danby apparently was unconvinced and Tonge arranged to have Oates give evidence before the magistrate Sir Edmund Berry Godfrey. As a result Tonge and Oates were summoned to attend before the Privy Council in September 1678. The **Privy Council** chose to believe the veracity of Oates' ever more spectacular and contradictory revelations. The mysterious death of Edmund Berry Godfrey in October gave fuel to Oates' story and the **House of Commons** intervened to have the 'plot' investigated. Papers found in the possession of Edward Coleman, the Duchess of York's secretary, appeared to confirm the conspiracy.

Protestant England had long feared the invasion and conspiracy of Catholics. Oates' evidence ignited this deeply ingrained national fear into hysteria. As a result thirty-five men, including Jesuit priests and Viscount Stafford, were tried and executed between 1678 and 1681. The plot collapsed under the burden of Oates' contradictions and his desire to implicate any person who crossed him including Lord Chief Justice Scroggs. Oates himself was imprisoned for perjury, but was released after the Glorious Revolution.

ELLIOT VERNON

pornography The legal regulation of pornography engenders intense debate about **human rights**, free speech, the role of the criminal law, feminism, and sexuality. Adult pornography has traditionally being governed by **obscenity** laws which focus on the potential harm of pornography to its consumers; obscenity being defined in moral terms as that which may 'deprave and corrupt' the viewer. Obscenity laws have been broadly supported by conservative thinkers who see pornography as a threat to the moral order of society. The dominant challenge to obscenity regulation has traditionally come from liberals, with philosophers such as Ronald Dworkin emphasizing the value of **freedom of expression** and the harm of **censorship**.

In the 1980s, a significant challenge was made to this conservative/liberal paradigm, when radical feminists, most particularly US feminists Catharine MacKinnon and Andrea Dworkin, advocated the legal regulation of pornography on the basis of the harm caused to women. MacKinnon and Dworkin defined pornography as the 'sexually explicit subordination of women in words or pictures' in scenarios of degradation, exploitation, objectification, and abuse. They advocated reform of the civil law to provide a remedy to those establishing harm resulting from pornography, on the basis that this constituted a violation of principles of **sex equality**.

While these proposed reforms failed to win legislative approval, either in the US or in the UK, they have had a lasting impact on pornography debates, with it no longer being possible to ignore a feminist perspective or the impact of pornography on women.

This feminist legacy is evident in recent media and policy debates which have placed the legal regulation of pornography back at the forefront of debate. New measures are being discussed, possibly due to the widespread availability of pornography on the internet, which has rendered controls via obscenity **legislation** largely moribund. New proposals include a criminal offence of possessing (including downloading) 'extreme' pornography, defined as pornographic images of bestiality, necrophilia, and serious **violence**. There is a broad consensus of conservative

and feminist approval of these measures, with resistance coming largely from 'sexual freedom' organizations which fear repression of alternative sexualities and practices.

The proposals to criminalize possession of material echoes the regulation of images of **child** abuse (often called 'child pornography'), the distribution, creation, and possession of which are criminalized via the Protection of Children Act 1978 (England and Wales, with similar provisions in the rest of the UK). There is a broad consensus that such measures are necessary in view of the fact that images of child abuse constitute an actual record of abuse, there being no debate regarding consent as there is in relation to adult pornography. Current prohibitions include photographic and filmic images, as well as pseudo-images. The UK Government is currently consulting on extending the law to cover cartoon images of **child abuse**.

CLARE MCGLYNN

C MacKinnon and A Dworkin, *In Harm's Way* (Cambridge, MA.: Harvard University Press, 1997)

N Strossen, *Defending Pornography* (New York: New York University Press, 2000)

positive action The law prohibiting discrimination in the United Kingdom does not require that everybody is treated the same as everybody else in every walk of life. It is limited to preventing discrimination on particular grounds (**sex**, **race**, **disability,** and others) in particular areas, principally but not exclusively, employment, education, and access to goods and services. It is almost entirely based upon a requirement that people be treated the same. Thus, the prohibition against discrimination on the ground of a person's sex means that a woman must be treated the same as a man in similar circumstances. Likewise, the prohibition against discrimination on grounds of sexuality means that gay men and **lesbians** must be treated the same as straight men and women. This means that, for example, treating lesbians and gay men differently in order to improve their position is generally prohibited, because it might result in people of heterosexual orientation being treated comparatively worse and result in their being discriminated against on the ground of their sexual orientation.

There are, however, some important exceptions to this rule. Common to all the discrimination **legislation** except disability is the concept of 'genuine occupational qualification' ('GOQ'). This permits employers to select candidates for posts from a particular grouping, for example, women only, where something about the nature of the job or its location makes that necessary. Because this is an exception to the general rule, the circumstances in which it can be relied on are tightly drawn by the relevant legislation and restrictively interpreted by the **courts**. In certain circumstances, the operation of the concept is entirely uncontroversial, for example the requirement that the attendant in a public convenience for women be female. In others, however, it is less so. There is, for example, a law permitting women-only short lists for political parties and other elected bodies, and the sexual orientation regulations permit employment for the purposes of organized religion to be confined to people of heterosexual orientation. Both of these provisions have provoked considerable debate.

Although there is no GOQ provision in the Disability Discrimination Act 1995 ('DDA'), there is, uniquely, a positive duty upon employers of, and providers of goods and services to, people with disabilities. This is the duty to make adjustments to prevent any physical feature of a building, or any policy or procedure, putting a disabled person at a substantial disadvantage. In the context of employment, even the requirement that a person be physically fit enough to undertake a job (for example street sweeping) is a criterion which triggers the duty when a person develops a disabling condition rendering them unable to meet that requirement. Depending upon the circumstances, this duty may require anything from a minor alteration to a building to a major overhaul of an employer's sick pay procedure or finding alternative employment for the disabled person. It is important to note, however, that the requirement is only to do what is reasonable.

All the anti-discrimination legislation allows limited permission to provide training for particular employment specifically aimed at disadvantaged groups and to encourage members of those groups to take advantage of such employment. In the more recent legislation covering sexual orientation, **religion**, and age, these provisions are specifically referred to as 'exceptions for positive action'. They permit, for example, an employer to include reference to the under-representation of a particular group in the advertisement for a post and to encourage applications from candidates in a particular group or groups, say, from ethnic **minorities** or people with disabilities. It is important to observe, however, that there is no requirement that bodies take advantage of these exceptions and an employer failing to frame its job advertisements in the manner described above, for example, breaches no law.

That is not the case, however, in the case of the positive equality duties placed by some of the legislation upon public bodies. In general, these amount to a duty on public authorities to carry out their functions having regard to the need to eliminate discrimination on the particular ground covered by that legislation and to promote equality. Individual pieces of legislation also identify specific extra duties. For example, the Disability Discrimination (Public Authorities) (Statutory Duties) Regulations 2005 require the named public bodies each to publish a Disability Equality Scheme demonstrating how they will comply with the general requirement to eliminate disability discrimination in the carrying out of their functions (imposed by section 49A of the DDA) and similar specific duties are imposed by regulations made under the Race Relations Act 1976 and the Sex Discrimination Act 1975. Compliance with these duties is monitored and enforced by the relevant statutory bodies such as the Commission for Racial Equality (soon all to be amalgamated into an overarching Equalities Commission).

Uniquely Northern Ireland has the Equality Commission for Northern Ireland whose duty is to enforce the legislation seeking to end discrimination between Protestants and Catholics. Not only does the Equality Commission for Northern Ireland have equivalent duties to monitor performance by public bodies, but it also oversees the compliance by employers with a range of positive duties placed on them. These duties require employers to register with the Commission, provide annual returns about the composition of their workforce, and to carry out regular reviews of their policies and practices to ensure that members of each **community** are enjoying 'fair participation in employment in the concern' (Article 55 of the Fair Employment and Treatment (Northern Ireland) Order 1998). The fair employment regime provides by far the most extensive example of positive action in UK legislation and is best explained by the particular history and consequences of the divide between the two main religious communities in Northern Ireland.

Finally, it is worth mentioning the existence of a number of specific provisions which might be regarded as permitting or requiring positive action in favour of a potentially disadvantaged group. Women, in particular, benefit from a range of such measures in relation to pregnancy and **maternity**. These include a duty upon employers to carry out a Health and Safety risk assessment for all pregnant employees, and to make specific provision for maternity leave and pay. There are also state benefits payable only on the grounds of pregnancy or maternity. Similarly, the state has designated benefits for people with disability specifically to recognize their extra needs (perhaps unfortunately, the definitions of disability adopted for entitlement to these benefits differ from the definition in the DDA). Other minor exceptions to the general rules permit **charities** to confer benefits on a single-sex, racial grouping, or group of disabled persons and allow for the existence of single-sex schools. Similarly, the general prohibition in England and Wales against discrimination on religious grounds by providers of further education is lifted in favour of certain designated (almost all Roman Catholic) faith-based sixth form colleges allowing them to show positive preference for applicants of that faith.

Overall, because of the particular approach taken to the prevention of discrimination in the UK, with its emphasis on **formal equality**, the scope for taking action to benefit disadvantaged groups is very limited. Only the weaker versions of '**positive discrimination**', known as 'positive action' policies, outlined above, are lawful in the UK. Moreover, since the legislation emanating from the European Union leaves broad discretion to its Member States in this respect (see Directive 2000/78, Article 7; Directive 2000/43, Article 5), there is very little incentive for change. The significant problem with the UK's current approach is that, with the exception of the public duties described above, enforcement of formal equality rests with individuals. This may result in an individual sufferer of discrimination being compensated; it may even result in a cultural change in the guilty body. It cannot, however, by its nature, have the effect of significantly improving the lot of the members of the disadvantaged groups as a whole or of addressing the broader structures which create the disadvantage in the first place. In recognition of this phenomenon, some other jurisdictions have adopted stronger 'positive discrimination' policies, for instance, where individuals in the disadvantaged group are given positive rights, such as quotas of jobs or places on public bodies being reserved for them.

TAMARA HERVEY AND PHILIP ROSTANT

positive discrimination A particular group of people may have suffered centuries of exclusion from representation in public life, education, or the labour market (as was for instance the case for Black Americans). In order to achieve **equality**, it will be insufficient merely to formally open public democratic institutions and places of employment or education to members of that excluded group. Simply treating like persons alike in a formal libertarian sense ignores the various historical, social, and structural differences between the experiences, opportunities, and social roles of different groups of people. Positive discrimination (sometimes known as 'affirmative action', particularly in the USA) responds to

that realization and aims to ensure substantive, as opposed to merely formal, equality.

Positive discrimination policies are often highly controversial. They may be opposed by members of the majority, who feel unfairly treated where criteria other than merit are applied in situations in which individuals are chosen for some benefit (be that a job, a place in a school, college, or University, or a political position). They may equally be opposed by members of the **minority**, who do not wish to be stereotyped as someone in need of 'special treatment', or who see positive discrimination as tokenism. There may be scepticism about whether positive discrimination works in practice. There is some evidence that such policies help only the more powerful or wealthy members of the minority group. Finally, because they involve different treatment of people on a 'forbidden ground' (in particular, **sex**, **race**, colour, ethnicity, religion, language, sexuality, disability, political or other opinion, property, birth, or social status), positive discrimination policies are vulnerable to legal challenge in societies based on libertarian concepts of equality.

In UK law, positive discrimination is conceptualized as an exception to the general principle of non-discrimination, rather than a means for achieving it. This is unusual. It has resulted in the position that only the 'softer' version of positive discrimination—'**positive action**'—is lawful in the UK. Other jurisdictions have taken a different approach.

The **US Supreme Court** departed from a **formal equality** approach during the 1970s and 1980s. This led to its acceptance of positive or affirmative action programmes instituted by employers (eg *Johnson v Transportation Agency of Santa Clara County* (1987)). However, the judges on the Supreme Court have adopted a range of different approaches in their judgments. More recently, the Supreme Court's overall approach has been shifting. In the context of programmes where a city (*City of Richmond v Croson* (1989)) and the federal government (*Adarand Constructors v Peña* (1995)) set aside a certain percentage of government contracts for businesses owned by members of racial minorities, the Supreme Court has used a **strict scrutiny** standard to overturn such positive discrimination measures. In educational contexts, positive discrimination admissions policies have been highly controversial and have not always been supported by the courts (compare *Regents of the University of California v Bakke* (1978); *Grutter v Bollinger* (2003); and *Gratz v Bollinger* (2003)).

The **Canadian Charter of Fundamental Rights and Freedoms** includes a specific section (15(2)), providing that the Charter's equality guarantee (section

15(1)) 'does not preclude any law, program or activity that has as its object the amelioration of conditions of disadvantaged individuals or groups…'. The Canadian Employment Equity Act 1995 obliges employers to institute 'positive policies and practices' and to make 'reasonable accommodations' to ensure that women, Aboriginal peoples, persons with disabilities, and members of visible minorities are represented in the workforce in appropriate proportions by reference to the population as a whole. Canada also has a multicultural education policy, which promotes positive discrimination in educational settings.

South Africa also has an Employment Equity Act 1998, whose positive discrimination provisions apply to employers with fifty or more employees. The Act requires employers to take action to ensure that suitably qualified black people, women, and people with disabilities are equitably represented in all jobs and levels of the workforce. Such positive discrimination may include preferential treatment for members of disadvantaged groups, and numerical goals, but not numerical quotas. In 1994, the African National Congress adopted quotas for women on political party lists in the country's first democratic elections. Argentina, Rwanda, and Costa Rica have taken similar steps.

The Indian Constitution allows for the reservation of a certain proportion of government jobs, publicly funded places in educational establishments, and electoral constituencies for 'backward classes of citizens', which essentially means those who have been historically disadvantaged through the caste system. Although these are constitutional provisions, their enforcement is problematic (for instance, Universities have not filled their quota places). Overall, the Indian positive discrimination system has been only partially successful.

Closer to home, European Union law permits (although does not mandate) positive discrimination. The EU's longest-standing provisions on the matter concern equality for women in the employment sphere. EU law permits national measures providing for specific advantages in order to make it easier for women to pursue employment or to prevent, remove, or compensate for disadvantages that women face in their professional careers. These measures are seen in EU law as promoting 'equal opportunity' for men and women. Similar provisions of EU law apply to discrimination on grounds of race (Directive 2000/43, Article 5), **religion** or belief, age, disability, or sexual orientation (Directive 2000/78, Article 7). These are seen as having the aim of ensuring 'full equality in practice'. Thus EU law at least attempts to escape from the formal libertarian notion of equality on which UK law is based.

In spite of these permissive provisions of EU law, men falling foul of German and Swedish positive discrimination programmes involving quotas for women in public employment, such as in schools and Universities, have brought legal challenges on the grounds that the programmes were inconsistent with EU law. However, the **European Court of Justice** has held that, so long as they are not rigidly applied, positive discrimination measures such as quota systems are permitted in EU law (*Marschall* (1997)). TAMARA HERVEY AND PHILIP ROSTANT

See also: **substantive equality**

positive obligations This phrase acts as shorthand for the following concept: obligations upon a state to act in such a way as to vindicate an individual right or prevent its breach. The notion may be contrasted with the situation in which the state is merely under a duty *not* to do something (the correlative of a '**negative right**'). The notion of a state having positive obligations to protect or secure the enjoyment of **human rights** is most obviously seen in relation to the class of rights classified as '**economic and social rights**': rights to education, housing, or health care plainly require positive and very extensive action by the state in order to provide sufficient facilities to vindicate the right in question; such rights also involve potentially massive expenditure by a given state. For this reason, economic and social rights treaties, such as the **International Covenant on Economic, Social, and Cultural Rights**, typically impose obligations on states to realize the goals they set out progressively, depending upon available resources.

The notion of positive obligations has two further fields of operation: first, it is not confined to economic and social rights: classic '**civil and political' rights** may of necessity place considerable positive obligations upon states: for example, the **right to a fair trial**—a classic civil right—requires the establishment and running by the state of a complex system of civil and criminal justice, which has major resource implications, including **legal aid**. Moreover, rights that on their face seem to call simply for the state *not* to do something, such as the right to be free from **torture** or inhuman treatment, can and have been interpreted by **courts** as requiring states to provide a minimal level of subsistence to the destitute, so that they are not at risk of acute suffering from hunger or cold.

Finally, the term 'positive obligations' is used in a way that differs from both the above. In this third sense it is used to describe the notion that a state may be required not only *itself* to act or refrain from acting in a particular way: it may also be under an obligation to intervene between *private parties* in order to ensure that one person's rights are not effectively curtailed or destroyed by another, or by a **company** or other **non-governmental organization**, such as a church or **trade union**. This sense of positive obligations corresponds to the notion of the 'horizontal effect' of human rights guarantees: the notion that interests such as **privacy**, or **freedom of assembly**, should be protected not only against the state but against powerful non-state actors also. Thus the **European Court of Human Rights** has held that states must ensure that the personal privacy of individuals, guaranteed by Article 8 of the **European Convention of Human Rights**, is protected against the intrusive attentions of newspapers. Similarly, it has found that the laws of the state must guarantee effective protection for children who suffer excessive physical discipline inflicted by their parents.

GAVIN PHILLIPSON

See also: **horizontal application of human rights**

possessory security   Possessory security is taken by a creditor as assurance for the performance of an obligation, usually a monetary obligation, by the debtor. Its advantage over non-possessory security for the creditor is that it gives the creditor physical control over the property by restricting the debtor's ability to deal with it in a way that is adverse to the creditor's interests. The disadvantage is that it may involve storage and maintenance costs, more or less, that will add to the sum that the creditor seeks to recover from the debtor.

Possessory security is created either consensually or by operation of law over goods or documents of title to goods. If it is created consensually, it is called a pledge, an expression often used for the property that is the subject of the security. Pledge (or *pignus*) was known to **Roman law** and was one of the four so-called real contracts. A pledge lasts so long as the creditor, the pledgee, retains possession of it. Unlike modern **civil law systems**, the **common law** has not extended pledge to embrace non-possessory security, but it is flexible enough to accommodate the continuance of the pledge where the property is released to the pledgor for a limited purpose or period. This is a common feature of export sales where a bill of lading representing a cargo is released by a bank extending finance to the buyer, so that the buyer may take delivery of the cargo from the carrier at the discharge port. At common law, pledge is a type of **bailment**. The pledgee has a special property in the pledge with a power of sale upon default by the pledgee, but must account to the pledgor for any surplus achieved and so may not exercise rights of foreclosure.

The business of making short-term advances against precious items and usually for consumer purposes is called pawnbroking and is regulated by consumer credit legislation. Pawn is pledge under another name.

Non-consensual security is referred to as lien and, at common law, is limited to possessory security, though equity accommodates non-possessory lien, chiefly in the case of land and the unpaid vendor. At common law, a lien is conferred on a finite list of service providers and professionals. That list includes carriers and innkeepers, in respect of goods in their possession or control, and solicitors and accountants, holding the papers of their clients. A lien of this sort amounts to a passive right of retention, though there are legislative exceptions that confer a power of sale and it is common for contract to grant a power of sale. Special rights by way of lien can also be created by statute.

Possessory liens are called general liens when either at law or under the contract they can be claimed in respect of all moneys owed. They are called special liens when limited to moneys owed under the transaction giving rise to the lien. The lien is lost when possession is surrendered by the person exercising the lien.

MICHAEL BRIDGE

post-colonial law   The 'post-colonial' refers to a genre of literature, a historical epoch, and a social and legal order which has departed from its colonial antecedents. Post-colonial law thus immediately invokes a temporal dimension. The 'post-colonial' seemingly denotes the law *after* colonialism. But what makes a colony a *post-colony*? When does colonial law make the transition to post-colonial law—and what are the conditions for such a transition? Attention to the '**time**' or 'event' of post-coloniality can itself be misleading. A literature, movement, or order that challenges, mimics, adjusts, and reverses colonial norms and conventions may already be in existence prior to any formal constitutional transition—and, to that extent, post-coloniality is a hybrid and liminal space/time of law, literature, language, and social norms.

An indicative example will probably best illustrate the complexity of post-colonial law. Australia is a Constitutional **Monarchy** which has legislative independence from its erstwhile colonial master, the United Kingdom (Canada and New Zealand are other white settler colonies that fall into the same category). But this 'independence' is itself the product of **legislation** passed by the British **Parliament** to gradually bring about political, and then later, legislative and judicial autonomy. There has been no unequivocal constitutional or political event that marks a transition to a post-colonial order. Judges of the Australian High Court have been deeply ambiguous about when Australia emerged as a sovereign nation state (see *NSW v Commonwealth* (1975) (*The Seas and Submerged Lands* case)). Indeed, many indigenous Australians regard themselves as living under conditions of colonial occupation—a 'conquest' of their territory that the Australian High Court has steadfastly refused to acknowledge, preferring the spurious 'settled colony' doctrine. On this account, the Australian courts labour under the 'extravagant pretention' (to borrow words from Chief Justice Marshall in *Johnson v M'Intosh* (1823)) that the foundation of law is explained by the reception of English law which was brought to a vacant land by colonial settlers and administrations. A conquered **territory** continues to be treated *as if* it was discovered. While the High Court of Australia attempted to adjust the concomitants of colonial law and **sovereignty** in *Mabo v Queensland (No 2)* (1992) by recognizing a *sui generis* species of indigenous title to land called '**native title**', the foundation of Australian law and society in a colonial usurpation of land and sovereignty was preserved. This is typical of the hybrid and liminal character of post-colonial law. Colonial sovereignty and law is preserved and disavowed at the same time. The 'renewed' legal order purports to recognize pre-existing indigenous forms of **customary law**. But a hierarchy is maintained whereby the colonial legal order would disallow any custom it regards as repugnant. Colonial sovereignty and legal institutions are thus preserved while adjustments are made to recognize post-colonial demands for justice, such as land rights. Since the foundation of the legal system in colonial **violence** is preserved, post-colonial law is not a pure and complete departure from the colonial order.

Post-colonial law is often regarded as a feature of **transitional justice**. For instance, the post-**apartheid** Constitution of South Africa contributed to other processes, such as the **Truth and Reconciliation** Commission, which attempted to eliminate and transform a racially divided society. Again the liminal character of the post-colonial event is central. **Reconciliation** itself connotes a passage, bridge, or movement between the past and future. Coming to terms with the violent excesses of the past is central to the possibility of previous antagonists having a future together. But there is no clear departure as the post-apartheid legal order also seeks to preserve the property and wealth that was acquired during the colonial and later apartheid era economic and legal orders. The present social and economic order

thus stubbornly retains continuities of apartheid era divisions and disparities. Post-colonial law essentially manifests a preservation and disavowal of the colonial past. STEWART MOTHA

E Darian-Smith and P Fitzpatrick (eds), *Laws of the Post-colonial* (Ann Arbor: University of Michigan Press, 1999)
Archille Mbembe, *On the Postcolony* (Berkeley: University of California Press, 2001)

post-conflict reconstruction This phrase refers in general terms to the need to reconstruct not just the physical infrastructure of a country after war, but also the political and legal infrastructure and often its economy as well. At first, it was used with particular reference to conflicts occurring primarily within state boundaries, but has more recently also been used with respect to reconstruction after inter-state use of force in Bosnia, Afghanistan, Kosovo, and Iraq. These conflicts have been tied up with prior or subsequent internal conflict.

The term 'post-conflict' is often inaccurate and can be viewed as contentious. The period described as 'post-conflict' is the period after the signing of a peace agreement or accord that purports to establish a ceasefire and an agenda for developing new political and legal institutions in what is, essentially, a form of constitution. However, this period is seldom post-conflict: often violence re-emerges in the same or in new forms; and even when it does not, the peace agreement may at best translate the conflict into the new political and legal institutions. So the term 'post-agreement reconstruction' might be preferred. Sometimes the term 'state-building' is used, where there is no effective state infrastructure to 'reconstruct'. Nevertheless, the term 'post-conflict reconstruction' will be used in this entry as a term of convenience.

Post-conflict reconstruction typically includes some or all of the following elements: stabilizing the ceasefire by steps including demobilization of armed forces, demilitarization and reintegration of armed forces into civilian life (often called 'DDR'); holding elections; establishing new political institutions; establishing new legal institutions; returning refugees and internally displaced persons, and reallocating land; repairing war-torn infrastructure; establishing mechanisms to deal with past atrocities, and establishing the rule of law. In addition, measures may also be imposed by financial institutions, aimed at market-based economic reform.

A range of international organizations play a wide variety of roles in post-conflict reconstruction. International organizations, regional organizations, *ad hoc* regional groupings, international non-governmental organizations, and third party states, often all play a role. The types of activities they are involved with can range from monitoring the cease-fire or elections to training police and judiciary, establishing international courts and providing international judges for 'hybrid' international and domestic courts. In some cases, international actors will undertake the country's entire administration for periods of time ('international territorial administration'), as happened in Bosnia, Kosovo, East Timor, and (even more contentiously because it was not UN-led) Iraq.

Post-conflict reconstruction poses a number of legal dilemmas. First, the post-conflict environment raises questions of authority and appropriate legal regime. International involvement in post-conflict reconstruction has grown rapidly, with an ever-increasing range of tasks being undertaken by international actors. Neither transitional periods nor the forms of international involvement square easily with international law's traditional conception of distinct domestic and international spheres that delimits legally the role of international actors. Fluctuations in levels of violence, the giving of consent to international organizations and its withdrawal, and changes in the locus of state sovereignty, mean that the appropriate legal regime is often in question. It may be unclear whether the international presence is to be viewed as consensual or force-based, for peacekeeping or peace-enforcement, or amounting to 'occupation'. Often the nature of the international involvement will have to change as events change. In addition, the more that international actors take on governance roles, the more questions will arise as to their own accountability, for example, under human rights standards. International legal instruments such as human rights conventions do not automatically apply to these actors, whose relationship to the state does not easily fit one of 'agency', and whose direct accountability is not dealt with by human rights conventions.

These dilemmas of legality link to the more practical difficulty: namely, that post-conflict reconstruction in the wake of a tentative ceasefire is extremely difficult. Even if early challenges such as demobilization are overcome, longer-term projects such as building the rule of law may remain elusive. Here international actors face the dilemma that the longer they retain primary responsibility for these tasks, the more it undermines local political responsibility and calls into question the legitimacy of international actors themselves. As a result, post-conflict reconstruction is recognized as raising some of the deepest questions around what the scope of international involvement should properly be. In particular, questions have been raised as to whether post-conflict reconstruction amounts to an inappropriate form of liberal peace-building, and even neo-colonialism or trusteeship, or whether it is justified as a pragmatic attempt to assist war-torn societies. These debates have gained new impetus after the US-led use of force in Iraq, which has raised more sharply questions of authority, the law of occupation, and the permissible scope of post-conflict reconstruction. It has been argued that the practices of post-conflict reconstruction constitute a new *lex pacificatoria* (law of the peacemakers) that is changing the remit of international law, and that the post-conflict period requires a new *ius post bellum* (law post-conflict) to supplement existing *ius ad bellum* (laws of war) and *ius in bellum* (laws in war). CHRISTINE BELL

C Stahn, '"Jus ad bellum", "jus in bello"… "jus post bellum"? Rethinking the Conception of the Law of Armed Force' (2007) 17 *European Journal of International Law* 921–943

R Paris, *At War's End: Building Peace after Civil Conflict* (Cambridge: Cambridge University Press, 2004)

postmodern jurisprudence Postmodern jurisprudence is a reaction against the descriptive inadequacies and moral impoverishment of dominant (positivist and normative) jurisprudence and an attempt to account for the postmodern condition in law. It is motivated by a widely-felt sense that **justice** has miscarried in law. **Miscarriages of justice** and denials of access to justice, racial and gender discrimination, institutional violence and racism, dogmatism, and formalism indicate that the insulation of law from morality has undermined the legitimacy of law.

For positivism, the legal system is a closed set of norms or rules; jurisprudence the discourse of truth about norms. Using a strict distinction between facts and values, positivism tries to exclude or minimize the influence of morality, ideology, or politics. Legal statements follow a process of subsumption of inferior to superior norms and, at the top of the pyramid, a presupposed 'ground' (or 'basic') norm guarantees the consistency of the system. Normative jurisprudence disagrees and turns its attention to values, principles, and rights. For the (mainly American) jurisprudence of rights, the law follows principles and is a valuable source of meaning. The technical rules of legal reasoning can be replaced by the protocols of interpretation, hermeneutical criteria, and the study of rhetorical tropes. This literary and hermeneutical turn gave legal theory a new lease of life and a long-lost sense of excitement. But there is a catch. According to Ronald Dworkin, the law embodies and follows moral values and principles. Judges are asked to construct the 'right answer' to legal problems by developing political and moral theories which would present the law in the best possible light and create an image of the 'community as integrity'.

This presentation of law as a unified and coherent body of norms or of values is rooted in the metaphysics of truth rather than the ethics of justice. Law is the form of power, and power should be exercised in the form of law. Power is legitimate if it follows law (*nomos*) and if the law follows reason (*logos*). Postmodern jurisprudence sets the task of deconstructing *logonomocentrism* in the operations of law. This involves (a) an understanding of the role of force and power in legal operations; (b) deconstruction of the claims to coherence, systematicity, and closure of law; and (c) a return to ethics and justice appropriate for the postmodern world of pluralism and diversity.

(a) In postmodernity, power relations have proliferated and penetrate deep into the social. In a complementary process, areas of private activity are increasingly legalized, while public services and utilities are released from their re-distributive aims and given over to the stricter disciplines of private profit and the market. The legal system abandons the unrealistic claim that it forms a consistent system of norms. Postmodern law is constituted through a myriad of rules and regulations, statutes, decrees, administrative legislation and adjudication, formal judgments, and informal interventions and disciplines. Legal language games have proliferated and cannot be presented as the embodiment of the public good, the general will, the wishes of the sovereign people, of parliament, or some other coherent system of principle.

Rights promised protection against domination and subjection but they came into existence and were supported by the disciplinary technologies, which acted as the dark side of the pronouncements of freedom, **equality,** and the **rule of law**. In postmodern societies of control, rights protect people; but they are also instruments of power used to discipline, exclude, and dominate. Social orders establish and perpetuate themselves by rejecting, silencing, and banning certain 'others' as mad, foreign, criminal, inhuman. People are excluded because their existence is inimical to the systematic nature and political claims of dominant powers or because they are cognitively unthinkable: ie it is beyond the ability of current knowledge to comprehend their difference.

The condition of postmodernity has irreversibly removed the aspiration of unity in law, always an impossible hope. Everything that successfully attaches the term 'law' to its operations and mobilizes the coercive force of the state becomes law. In this sense, the 'law' cannot be constituted theoretically but only intuitively and politically. The law does not have an essence but only operations.

(b) Postmodern jurisprudence shows how legal concepts, doctrinal lines, and claims to systematicity fail because of the contradictions and heterogeneities that litter the law. Various textual strategies are used in this effort. A first involves a close reading of key concepts of jurisprudence and judicial decisions. American critical legal scholars homed in on the conceptual bipolarities—such as the public/private, fact/value, rule/policy, and universalism/relativism divides—that organize legal texts. These are presented as markers of two distinct and antagonistic forms of legal reasoning but they are not external to each other. No concept can be properly constituted without a trace of its opposite inhabiting and undermining its purity. If legal concepts are non-identical at their core, the dream of legal unity, totality, and order is seriously undermined.

Another type of openness results from the intertextual character of law. Legal texts are interwoven with elements, citations, and grafts from other texts and contexts, thus acquiring great richness, but also discrepancies and inconsistencies. Law is not constructed and evaluated against some 'hard' external reality. The major and minor premises of the legal syllogism (the interpretation of the law and the evidence offered in trials) follow narrative frameworks drawn from specialist and common knowledge. The potential for multiple formulations of facts and law, and the continuous dialogue of legal texts with non-legal contexts, creates a fertile ground for alternative readings. These discursive dependencies and discrepancies do not amount to formal contradictions and cannot be weeded out by simple legal reasoning.

Despite their contradictory, paradoxical, and conflicting meanings, however, legal texts are kept together. One interpretation is authorized over possible others and gives them the power to order the world. After a period of textual and aesthetic deconstruction, postmodern jurisprudence turned towards ethics and justice, the missing link of positivism, or the ever-present dream of normative jurisprudence.

(c) Emmanuel Levinas's ethics of alterity and Jacques Derrida's deconstruction have been the most important philosophical influences of postmodern jurisprudence. Levinas starts with **the Other** and challenges the ways in which the Other has been reduced to the same. The Other is the condition of existence of language, of self, and of the law. (S)he cannot be turned into the instance of a concept or the application of a rule. The source of ethics is the concrete historical and empirical encounter with the Other. It is the Other's situated and unique demand which assigns me to morality and makes me a bound and ethical subject. But while the Other's appeal is direct, concrete, and personal, the law must also introduce the demands of the third party. Because the third is always present in my encounter with the Other, the law is implicated in every attempt to act morally. The law limits our infinite **responsibility** for the Other and introduces the element of calculation, synchronization, and thematization. It makes the conflicting demands contemporaneous and comparable. The law must bracket difference and otherness and, in this sense, it cannot escape injustice. Every community is therefore double: an ethical encounter of unequals where I am responsible to respond to the Other's demand. But it is also the commonality of law, the calculation of equality, and the symmetry of rights. A politics of law disturbs the totalizing tendency of the legal system if it allows the Other to reappear both as the point of exteriority that precludes the closure of law and as the excluded and un-representable of jurisprudence. This principle of immanent transcendence leads to the postmodern '*aporia* of justice': to act justly you must treat the Other both as equal and entitled to the symmetrical treatment of norms and, as a totally unique person who commands the response of ethical asymmetry.

COSTAS DOUZINAS

See also: **critical legal studies; legal positivism since 1970; legal positivism to 1970; natural law theory; Other, the**

poverty reduction Poverty has a profound impact on people's physical, social, and emotional welfare. In its extreme forms, it can undermine their **human dignity** and deprive them of the fundamental human **right to life**. Poverty reduction is a major political challenge both for the international community and within most states in the world community. For example, at the international level, the **United Nations** has mobilized all the world's governments behind the Millennium Development Goals which range from halving extreme poverty to halting the spread of **HIV/AIDS** and providing universal primary education, by the target date of 2015. Most countries have also adopted **legislation** that regulates a broad range of areas relevant to poverty

reduction such as social security, housing, health care, and education.

Human rights law has the potential to redress poverty by enabling people to exercise their civil and political freedoms to advocate for economic and social policies that help achieve this goal. In most democratic societies, people can also expect the courts to protect basic civil liberties such as the right to **freedom of expression**, **freedom of association**, fair trial rights, and the prohibition of discrimination on grounds such as **race**, **sex**, and **religion**.

Economic, social, and cultural rights are directly relevant to the reduction of poverty. They seek to protect people's existing access to economic resources and social services, and also place **positive obligations** on the state to expand access to these social goods, particularly to vulnerable and disadvantaged groups. These rights have been an integral part of international human law since the adoption of the Universal Declaration of Human Rights in 1948, and today they are protected in a number of international and regional human rights treaties. The major international treaty protecting this group of rights is the **International Covenant on Economic, Social, and Cultural Rights** (1966). The **European Convention on Human Rights** (1950) protects mainly **civil and political rights**, a notable exception being the right to education protected in Article 2, Protocol 1. **Economic and social rights** are protected in a separate treaty, namely the European Social Charter (1961, revised in 1996), but the rights in this Charter are not enforceable in a court unlike the rights in the European Convention on Human Rights. Other regional human rights treaties integrate both civil and political rights as well as economic, social, and cultural rights in a single instrument, most notably the **African Charter on Human and Peoples' Rights** (1981). The African Charter also recognizes rights that have generally not been recognized within the classical liberal framework of rights. These include, for example, the right of peoples freely to dispose of their wealth and national resources (Article 21), the right to development (Article 22), the right to national and international peace and **security** (Article 23), and environmental rights (Article 23).

There are a number of obstacles that prevent economic and social rights from fulfilling their potential in reducing poverty. One of the major obstacles is that the mechanisms that exist for their enforcement are generally weak. For example, the Covenant does not contain a mechanism providing individuals with redress for violations of the rights protected therein. Many national **constitutions** either fail to recognize these rights at all, or recognize them in the weak form of directive principles of state policy which are not directly enforceable in the **courts** (for example, Article 45 of the Irish Constitution). Another reason is that many governments prefer to view economic and social rights as a set of political aspirations, rather than rights which impose binding legal obligations on them to adopt policies and legislation that reduce poverty, and to refrain from conduct which increases hunger, **homelessness**, and economic marginalization. According to classical liberal conceptions, the function of human rights guarantees is to serve as a shield against the power of the state to intervene in 'private' institutions such as the family and marketplace. Economic and social rights challenge this conception in that they place duties on the state to take proactive measures to redress conditions of material deprivation. Finally, courts are often reluctant to enforce social and economic rights as they are perceived to undermine the doctrine of separation of powers in that they require the judiciary to make decisions which have budgetary and policy implications. The latter areas are perceived to be the exclusive preserve of the executive and legislative branches of government according to an interpretation of the **separation of powers** doctrine which posits watertight divisions between the role and functions of the three spheres of government. However, academics have pointed out that most **civil and political rights**, such as fair trial rights, the right to vote and **equality** rights, also have budgetary and policy implications. Moreover, the function of the separation of powers doctrine is to prevent a concentration of power in any one branch of government, and to provide a system of checks and balances between the three branches. On this more flexible conception, the judiciary is entitled to make decisions which have resource and social policy implications where this is necessary to protect people's rights.

Unless these obstacles are addressed and overcome, economic and social rights will not fulfil their potential to provide effective mechanisms of redress for groups experiencing poverty and social deprivation. International and national legal systems will be deprived of important tools for reducing poverty in the world.   SANDRA LIEBENBERG

A Eide, C Krause, and A Rosas (eds) *Economic, Social and Cultural Rights: A Textbook* (Leiden: Martinus Nijhoff Publishers, 2001)

power of attorney   *see* **capacity**

practical legal education   *see* **vocational legal education; legal professional ethics and values**

precautionary principle   The precautionary principle is a legal principle concerned with how power is exercised in relation to taking environmental and public health protection measures in circumstances of scientific uncertainty. The principle primarily applies to the exercise of power by a public body whether in regulating health and environmental risks within a jurisdiction or in the exercise of their international obligations. The principle applies to the way in which discretion is exercised in relation to the assessment and management of environmental and health risks and, in particular, to the process of decision-making and how information is assessed in that process. The principle means that 'no evidence of harm' does not mean that there is 'no harm', and requires decision-makers to act cautiously in such circumstances although the principle does not dictate a particular outcome. While the principle originated in relation to environmental regulation it has also been widely understood to apply in the context of regulating public health risks as well. This is particularly the case in the **European Union**.

The nature and meaning of the principle varies from jurisdiction to jurisdiction; but a generally accepted statement is Principle 15 of the **United Nations** Declaration on Environment and Development which states: 'Where there are threats of serious or irreversible damage, lack of full scientific certainty shall not be used as a reason for postponing cost-effective measures to prevent environmental degradation'. Some interpretations of the principle understand it as a principle which enables the exercise of flexible discretion while other interpretations understand it more narrowly as a 'shifting of the burden of proof' onto the proponent of an action.

While historical antecedents of the principle can be identified, the principle in its present form originated in West Germany in the 1970s as the principle of *Vorsorgeprinzip*. From the later 1980s onwards the principle was included in a significant number of international environmental law documents. At the international level there have been academic debates over whether the principle simply expresses an 'approach' or is part of **customary international law**. The principle has also been implemented in numerous different jurisdictions including Canada, France, Australia, and the **European Union**. The result is that the principle has been included in an array of legislation and other legal texts including the Constitution in France. The principle has given rise to a substantial body of case law particularly in Australia.

The precautionary principle has been highly controversial and has given rise to debates over the appropriate role of the state in relation to environmental and public health regulation. Proponents of the principle argue that the principle is important because it requires decision-makers to take the problem of scientific uncertainty seriously, a problem which has been historically ignored in environmental and health regulation with disastrous consequences. Critics argue that the principle promotes arbitrary action, is used to justify inappropriate decisions, and is impossible to apply.

ELIZABETH FISHER

P Harremoës *et al* (eds), *Late Lessons from Early Warnings: The Precautionary Principle 1896–2000* (Copenhagen: European Environment Agency, Environmental Issue Report No 22, 2002).

precedent Precedent is a method of making decisions in individual cases in the light of legal principle exemplified in previous judicial decisions. The authority given to those previous decisions varies according to the rules and practice of different legal communities and periods of time.

At one extreme, *stare decisis* is a *rule* giving binding legal authority to the previous decisions of higher courts or even previous decisions of the same court. A subsequent court is required to follow the ruling laid down in such a previous decision. At the other extreme, lawyers may simply adopt a good practice of consulting previous decisions and according them weight in their deliberations. In most jurisdictions, judicial decisions are not a formal source that creates the law, but only interpretations of the constitution, treaties, legislation, and custom. But previous decisions have authority because judges are expected, as a matter of professional duty, to respect previous decisions of the courts. Lawyers are expected to discover previous cases and consider them in coming to decisions. The strength of this good practice is shown by the way in which many supreme courts will convene in a more solemn assembly to deliberate on departures from established case law.

Not everything said by a judge in a previous case counts as a precedent. A precedent is a ruling on a point of law that is laid down within a judicial decision as the justification for the outcome which is reached in that case. Common lawyers usefully distinguish the essential reason for the decision (the *ratio decidendi*) from other statements (*obiter dicta*). Only the former could be a binding or strongly authoritative statement of the law. There are thus four elements that make a *ratio decidendi*: (i) a ruling on a point of law; (ii) expressly or impliedly given by a judge; (iii) related to an issue raised within the case; and (iv) which is necessary as a justification for the decision reached. Any statement of the rule will include a description of the essential facts to which it applies. For example, a rule that a transporter owes a passenger a contractual duty to get her safe and sound to her destination will need to specify that the passenger is in the transporter's vehicle. As a result, the rule laid down in a case is often a rational reconstruction of what was said, rather than simply a quotation of the words used by the judge. Other statements of law made by a judge may nevertheless be persuasive, particularly if it is laid down by a judge who has an eminent reputation.

Where a judge does not wish to follow a precedent, he or she will seek to 'distinguish' the precedent, to show why it does not apply. In doing so, the judge may restate the rule in the precedent case so as to narrow its scope. For example, the rules about the transporter's duty may be restated to specify that duty does not arise where the transporter provides someone with the means of transporting themselves: for instance by hiring out a horse.

JOHN BELL

pre-implantation genetic diagnosis Pre-implantation genetic diagnosis ('PGD') is a technique developed in the mid-1990s by which the genetic constitution of an embryo can be determined prior to implantation during *in vitro* fertilization ('IVF') procedures. From an embryo created by IVF, one cell is at the 8–16 cell stage and tested for chromosomal abnormalities or for some specific genetic disorder or condition. It is currently technically impossible to test for many genes at the same time, due to the limited genetic material in one cell, but it is likely to become possible in the future.

PGD is currently used for three different purposes, ie to select embryos for transplantation that: (1) are free from a specific genetic disorder known to be present in the family (eg cystic fibrosis); (2) do not have chromosomal abnormalities, partly to avoid the birth of children with Down's syndrome and rarer chromosome abnormalities, partly to increase the efficiency of IVF by avoiding the implantation of embryos with abnormalities that lead to early spontaneous **abortion;** and (3) are tissue type compatible with an already living person needing a bone marrow transplant (so-called '**saviour siblings**').

Like IVF in general, the use of PGD in the UK is regulated by the **Human Fertilization and Embryology Authority** ('HFEA') established by the **Human Fertilization and Embryology Act 1990**. The Act states in section 3(1) that: 'No person shall—(a) bring about the creation of an embryo, or (b) keep or use an embryo, except in pursuance of a licence'. The revision of the Act going through Parliament at the time of writing (January 2008) will not change the regulatory role of the HFEA with regard to PGD.

The HFEA has taken this to apply to all uses of PGD and has required specific licensing of every new genetic diagnosis for which a clinic wants to offer testing. PGD itself is controversial because it involves the selection of 'healthy' embryos and the destruction of other embryos. The use of PGD for tissue typing is even more controversial since it involves creating and using one person, the 'saviour sibling' as a means to the treatment of another person.

No legal challenges have been raised against the HFEA decisions concerning PGD, except PGD for tissue typing. The HFEA allowed use of PGD for tissue typing in 2002 in cases where the disease to be treated by bone marrow transplant in the sibling was genetic and where the embryos to be tested where therefore at risk of developing the same disease, and extended this in 2004 to cases where the disease was non-genetic (eg leukaemia). The right of the HFEA to allow this use was challenged by Josephine Quintavalle on behalf of the interest group Comment on Reproductive Ethics ('CORE') in a case for **judicial review**. The claimants argued that the HFEA was not authorized to license this use of PGD because it is not related to the purposes enumerated in Schedule 2, section 1(1)(d) of the HFE Act: 'practices designed to secure that embryos are in a suitable condition to be placed in a woman or to determine whether embryos are suitable for that purpose'. The case was won by CORE in the High Court in 2003, lost in the Court of Appeal in 2004, and finally lost on appeal to the **House of Lords** in 2005 (*Quintavalle (on behalf of Comment on Reproductive Ethics) v Human Fertilisation and Embryology Authority* (2005)).

The use of PGD for sex selection is also controversial. PGD is used when a disease is linked to the X chromosome and therefore only occurs in boys, but where there is no specific genetic test. The sex of the embryos is determined and all male embryos are discarded. However, PGD can also be used for non-disease related **sex** selection. This use is currently not licensed by the HFEA. This decision was confirmed in 2005 after extensive public consultation, but through so-called '**reproductive tourism**', UK couples may access this outside the UK, eg in the USA.

The use of PGD is also very controversial in other jurisdictions where similar debates have taken place. Germany has a total ban on PGD and many jurisdictions only allow PGD for serious conditions or chromosomal abnormalities and do not allow PGD for sex selection.   SØREN HOLM

preliminary offences   *see* **attempts, conspiracy and incitement**

preliminary reference   The system provided in Article 234 of the EC Treaty enables national **courts** and **tribunals** in the European Union to make a reference to the **European Court of Justice** when a question on the interpretation or the validity of **European Community law** arises in a case pending before them and a decision on the question is necessary to enable them to give judgment. For a body to be considered a national 'court or tribunal' for the purposes of making a reference it must be established by law, have a permanent existence, exercise binding jurisdiction, be bound by rules of adversary procedure, and apply the rule of law. Article 234 EC distinguishes between national courts that have **discretion** to make a reference and national courts that have an obligation to refer. *Any* national court in the European Union, however low in the judicial hierarchy, *may* make a reference to the European Court of Justice. In recent years, however, the European Court has emphasized that referring national courts must fulfil certain requirements for their request for a preliminary ruling to be declared admissible. Thus, national courts must ensure that the parties before them are engaged in a genuine dispute and are not simply contriving proceedings in order to obtain a ruling from the European Court on a point of Community law. Furthermore, they must provide adequate factual and legal information on the case to the European Court. Finally, the question referred must be relevant to the outcome of the case pending before them. Courts of *last resort* are *obliged* to make a reference if a question of Community law arises before them and on which a decision is necessary to enable them to give judgment. The European Court has held that a court of last resort for the purposes of Article 234 EC is the highest court competent to hear a particular case—ie one from whose decisions there is no appeal. The case law has determined that there are three exceptions to the duty to refer imposed on national courts of last instance: first, where the European Court has previously ruled on the same question; secondly, if the question referred is irrelevant; and thirdly, where the correct interpretation of Community law may be so obvious as to leave no scope for any reasonable doubt as to the manner in which the question raised is to be resolved. This last exception is otherwise known as the *acte clair* doctrine and its application is subject to certain rigorous conditions laid down on the judgment of the European Court in *CILFIT* (1982). In terms of the subject matter of preliminary references, there are two main types of references: references on the interpretation of Community law and references on the validity of Community law. National courts and tribunals can put questions to the European Court on the interpretation of EC Treaty provisions, Acts of the institutions of the Community and the European Central Bank, and statutes of bodies established by an Act of the Council, where those statutes so provide. By contrast, they can only refer to the European Court questions on the validity of acts of the Community institutions and of the European Central Bank.

ALBERTINA ALBORS-LLORENS

prenatal testing Prenatal testing involves testing or screening a **foetus** in the womb. Prenatal tests can identify treatable health problems, the foetus' condition (such as its position in the womb), and a number of congenital, genetic, or chromosomal abnormalities. Some prenatal tests only indicate whether there is a possibility of a particular trait or condition (known as prenatal screening), whereas others are designed fairly accurately to diagnose particular traits or conditions from which the foetus is thought to be at particular risk (known as prenatal diagnosis). There are a number of prenatal tests. Ultrasound, which seeks to obtain a visual image of the foetus in the womb, is usually used as a form of prenatal screening. Chorionic villus sampling ('CVS') and amniocentesis are forms of prenatal diagnosis. CVS involves the removal of a sample of the placenta from the womb by either a catheter (a thin tube) or a needle, usually between 8–12 weeks gestation. Amniocentesis involves removing a sample of amniotic fluid by inserting a thin needle through the abdomen into the womb, usually performed at or after 15 weeks gestation.

Any invasive prenatal test requires the consent of the pregnant **woman**, or other lawful justification, if the doctor is to avoid committing a crime or civil wrong.

The woman might wish to abort a foetus that is discovered to have an undesired trait. The Abortion Act 1967 (as amended by the **Human Fertilization and Embryology Act 1990**) provides that **abortion** is not unlawful if certain conditions are satisfied. It must be performed by a registered doctor in circumstances where two doctors are of the opinion, formed in good faith, that grounds specified in the Act are met (section 1(1)). Also, the abortion must take place in an approved place (section 1(3)) and the Chief Medical Officer must be notified within the time, and in the form, prescribed by regulations (section 2).

One of the grounds under which abortion is lawful under the Abortion Act is the foetal abnormality ground. This provides that abortion is lawful where the doctors believe that there is a 'substantial risk' that the **child** would be born 'seriously handicapped' (section 1(1)(d)). Only about 1 per cent of abortions performed in England and Wales are performed under this provision. The key phrases—'substantial risk' and 'seriously handicapped'—are not defined. Professional bodies such as the Royal College of Obstetricians and Gynaecologists have provided guidance, but this is not legally binding.

SHAUN PATTINSON

SD Pattinson, *Medical Law and Ethics* (London: Sweet & Maxwell, 2006), ch 7

prerogative Prerogative powers are the special powers that remain from the time before the establishment of the modern parliamentary system in the late seventeenth century and which are now exercised on behalf of the **Crown** either by the **Monarch** or by government ministers. No new prerogative powers can be established and existing prerogatives can be abolished or placed on a statutory footing.

The formal powers exercised by the monarch include the granting of the royal assent to Bills, the summoning, prorogation, and dissolution of Parliament, and the appointment of the Prime Minister and other ministers. While these powers are of the utmost constitutional importance and may conceivably involve the monarch in exercising personal judgments, in practice the Monarch will follow established conventions and act on advice. No Monarch, for example, has refused to grant royal assent to a Bill passed by Parliament since 1708, and it would be virtually inconceivable that the Monarch would now do so.

Other prerogatives, however, do permit the exercise of significant real power. For example, the decisions to declare war and to enter into treaty obligations, and decisions in relation to the organization and deployment of the armed forces, are all exercised by government ministers by virtue of the prerogative.

The executive will be generally accountable to Parliament for decisions taken using prerogative powers. Such decisions may also be subject to **judicial review**, provided the courts consider the subject matter appropriate for judicial determination. Nonetheless lower levels of political and legal **accountability** are possible in relation to the exercise of prerogative powers as compared to the exercise of powers conferred on the executive by **Act of Parliament**. In particular, prerogative powers are not delineated by Parliament and generally Parliament is only involved in their exercise when and to the extent that the executive chooses. For instance while there are few political decisions more important than the deployment of the armed forces, parliamentary approval is not required for the deployment of forces abroad: although as occurred in relation to the government's decision to invade Iraq, MPs may be given a chance to vote.

The government has now accepted 'that in general prerogative powers should be put onto a statutory basis and brought under stronger parliamentary scrutiny and control': *The Governance of Britain* (July 2007). Accordingly it has suggested various reforms that should increase parliamentary involvement and improve levels of political accountability. However, given that many prerogatives relate to areas that fall within core areas of executive responsibility, such as national defence, some will doubt that these changes will substantially alter the way prerogative decisions are taken or their substance.   MAURICE SUNKIN

prerogative orders   The prerogative orders are the main remedies available in the application for **judicial review**. This type of case can be brought by those who have been affected by a public authority's unlawful acts.

There are three orders: the quashing order (formerly known as *certiorari*) which quashes a public authority's unlawful decision, the mandatory order (formerly *mandamus*) which orders a public authority to perform its duty, and the prohibiting order (formerly prohibition), which forbids an authority to carry out an unlawful act. The quashing order renders the authority's decision void: it will be treated as if it never had legal effect. When the court decides to quash a decision, it may either substitute its judgment for that of the original decision-maker or remit the matter to the original decision-maker to decide afresh. In addition to the prerogative orders, the remedies of **injunction** and declaration are also available in an application for judicial review.

Historically, the prerogative orders could only be sought using a procedure which suffered from significant defects. The claimant could not seek any other remedies (such as a declaration) in the same action, and there was no power to order discovery of documents. Although claimants could overcome evidential problems by seeking a declaration instead, this was a less powerful remedy.

In 1976, the Law Commission proposed the creation of a new procedure, the application for judicial review. This proposal was implemented by amendment to the Rules of Court and was subsequently confirmed in the Supreme Court Act 1981. The application for judicial review has simplified the claimant's

task considerably because any combination of public law remedies—the prerogative orders, declaration, or injunction—can be sought in a single application. The procedure also gives the courts improved fact-finding powers, including discovery, though in practice these are rarely invoked.

Prior to these reforms, the prerogative orders each had their own 'standing' rules to determine whether or not the applicant was entitled to seek the remedy. In *Inland Revenue Commissioners v National Federation of Self-Employed and Small Businesses* (1982), the **House of Lords** confirmed that the 'sufficient interest' test in section 31 of the Supreme Court Act 1981 lays down a single standing test regardless of the remedy being sought.

The remedies available in judicial review, including the prerogative orders, are discretionary. Even if the applicant establishes that the public authority has acted unlawfully, the court may choose not to grant a remedy. Thus, the court may refuse a quashing order where it would cause considerable disruption to the administration and where the authority's errors were procedural in nature. A remedy may also be denied where the claimant failed to draw the problem to the authority's attention at the earliest possible opportunity. It is generally thought that the discretion to refuse a remedy should be used sparingly. There is a danger that it may signal to public authorities that compliance with public law rules is unimportant.

ANNE DAVIES

prescribed diseases   The industrial injuries scheme, the part of the **social security system** which replaced workers' compensation in 1948, pays benefits to employees (but not the self-employed) who are injured at work. Injured workers may qualify in one of two ways: either because they have suffered an accident 'arising out of or in the course of their employment' or because they have contracted a 'prescribed disease'. Official regulations contain a list (or Schedule) of prescribed diseases. Formally, the Secretary of State for Work and Pensions makes the decision to prescribe a disease on the basis of advice from the Industrial Injuries Advisory Council ('IIAC'). Under statute two tests must be satisfied before a disease can be prescribed. First, the condition must be a risk of a particular occupation, rather than a common risk. Secondly, the link with particular employments must be established or presumed with reasonable certainty. So injured workers must establish both that they have a particular prescribed disease and that they worked in the relevant prescribed occupation. For example, occupational deafness is a prescribed disease, but only for those working in certain carefully defined noisy occupations. The process of prescription can be very slow, as the Council requires a convincing body of epidemiological evidence to satisfy the statutory tests for prescription. Thus lung cancer was not prescribed in relation to asbestos workers until 1985, some thirty years after the first evidence of the association between asbestos exposure and lung cancer appeared.

NICK WIKELEY

N Wikeley, *Compensation for Industrial Disease* (Aldershot: Dartmouth, 1993)

Press Complaints Commission Established in 1991, following the Calcutt Report, the Press Complaints Commission ('PCC') is a self-regulatory body that deals with the conduct and standard of reporting in UK newspapers and magazines, whether in paper or online formats. It examines complaints about breaches of its code of conduct relating to accuracy, privacy, and harassment, reporting about children and vulnerable people, the use of subterfuge and surveillance, discrimination, conflicts of interest in financial journalism, and payments to criminals and to witnesses. The requirements of the Code are subject to public interest exceptions relating to the detection or exposure of crime or serious impropriety, the protection of public health and safety, and preventing the public from being misled, together with freedom of expression itself. The PCC initially seeks to resolve the complaint informally, and proceeds to a more formal investigation if that fails. If it finds for the complainant, it expects the adjudication to be published with due prominence by the offending newspaper or magazine.

Although the PCC cannot impose sanctions on the press, it maintains that its conciliatory approach does secure effective compliance. Although it is funded by the industry and its code is drafted by a committee of editors, it maintains that its independence is secured by the fact that its chair and the majority of its members have no media affiliations. Self regulation reflects the industry's claim that it can voluntarily encourage high standards of professional conduct and integrity without resorting to legislative intervention which might unduly interfere with freedom of expression.   TOM GIBBONS

Home Office (Chair: Sir David Calcutt), Report of the Committee on Privacy and Related Matters (1990, Cmnd 1102)

press freedom   *see* **freedom of expression**

Press, the   *see* **freedom of the press; media, regulation and freedom of**

pressure groups   *see* **interest groups**

Pretty, Diane   Diane Pretty and her husband, Brian, found themselves in the public eye in Britain at the beginning of the twenty-first century because of her tragic medical condition and the unsympathetic state of the law. She suffered from motor neurone disease and by 2001 was almost wholly paralysed. She wished to terminate her own life to avoid the indignity and suffering associated with the terminal stages of the disease and she needed and wanted her loving and devoted husband to assist. This brought the couple into potential conflict with the criminal law, **assisted suicide** being an offence. It appears that the couple prioritized **autonomy** over **sanctity of life** but also prioritized compliance with law over autonomy. Through their solicitor, they asked the **Director of Public Prosecutions** ('DPP') to undertake not to prosecute. He responded that he could not address a hypothetical question in advance.

The couple sought the assistance of the **courts**. Eight **judges** (in the Divisional Court, and the **House of Lords**) agreed that the DPP has no power to give an undertaking not to prosecute a **person** before an offence has been committed and that section 2(1) of the Suicide Act 1961 is not incompatible with the **European Convention on Human Rights** (*R (on the application of Pretty) v the DPP* (2001)). Like everyone who had read about or had seen Diane Pretty these judges were desperately sorry for her, but even in such a 'sad case' this conclusion was 'inescapable'. Seven more judges in the **European Court of Human Rights** also agreed that section 2(1) is not incompatible with the ECHR and that even if Article 8 (the right to **privacy** and **family life**) was engaged, any interference was necessary and proportionate in pursuit of legitimate social policy (*Pretty v UK* (2002)). This last point is open to question. How many slow and painful deaths can be justified as a price worth paying to protect the lives of the vulnerable and of the weak? Morally, society should not impose excessive burdens on individuals. Taking **human rights** seriously entails that individuals will not be sacrificed to the social good, at least not without overwhelming or compelling justification, arguably lacking here.

Diane Pretty died in 2002 in exactly the circumstances that she and her husband had been most anxious to avoid, that is, in terrible agony and robbed of every shred of **dignity**. She lives on however as an icon and inspiration for legal reform.

RICHARD TUR

Dame B Hale, 'A Pretty Pass: When is There a Right to Die?' (2003) 3 *Clinical Medicine* 142–148

D Calvert-Smith and S O'Doherty, 'Legislative Technique and Human Rights: a Response' (2003) *Criminal Law Review* 384–390

price marking   Price marking is governed by the Prices Act 1974 and the Price Marking Order 2004 made under it. This order implements an EU Directive. The order requires traders to mark a price for each individual item offered for sale. Either the price must be marked on goods themselves or displayed adjacent to the goods. A shelf marker is acceptable. The price must be marked in an unambiguous way, easily identifiable, and clearly legible. The rule does not cover advertisements for goods, unless the advertisement is for goods for sale by mail order—in which case, not only the price of the goods must be stated, but also any additional charges for packing and postage.

Where goods are being sold in bulk and not pre-packaged, a price per quantity must be shown. The quantity used must be a metric unit (kilogram, millilitre, etc). So vegetables, for example, must be priced per kilogram. There is, however, no prohibition on showing an additional price per imperial unit, so the same vegetables may be priced per pound as well. The only main exception to this is draught beer which may be sold and priced by the pint (although the EU may remove this concession in the near future). Weights and measures legislation requires any calculation to be accurate.

Under the Price Marking (Food and Drink Services) Order 2005 restaurants, public houses, etc are required to display a price list, usually in the form of a menu. This must state any compulsory additional general charges such as a service charge.

The price displayed must be in pounds sterling. However, a trader is entitled to state that he accepts other currencies (eg Euro), but must then clearly state the exchange rate to be applied. This may be by a general notice, but it must be clear and easily seen. Bureaux de Change are required by a separate order to display a list of representative exchange rates and a note of all charges to be made. There is a general exception to the display rule for small retail outlets, where the nature of the premises makes individual pricing difficult. There is also an exception in respect of jewellery priced in excess of £3,000.

The Price Marking Order has no application to damaged goods (seconds) or packages of goods (a combination of different items). It permits the display of reduced prices and comparative prices, but these are separately governed by the Consumer Protection Act 1987 and the Code of Practice for Traders on Price Indications. The essential requirement is that the price stated must be the accurate selling price and any comparison must not be misleading. Under this legislation prices are ordinarily required to be VAT inclusive. A separate Order deals with the situation where a trader will charge a higher price if payment is made with a credit card. In such a case the trader is required to display a notice to this effect and inform the customer at the point of sale, before the sale is completed.

Breach of any of these requirements is a criminal offence.

RICHARD BRAGG

primary markets   *see* **secondary markets**

Prime Minister   The first holder of this office was Robert Walpole, who served as Prime Minister and First Lord of the Treasury from 1721–1742. The Prime Minister is the senior minister of the government and, as head of the executive branch, is the minister for the Civil Service and makes all appointments to ministerial office. The Prime Minister's appointments to the **Cabinet** shape the direction and style of the government. As Minister for the Civil Service, the Prime Minister exerts control and influence over the machinery of government and may decide how government departments are administered and organized.

The Prime Minister's powers are considerable, but there is no definitive list and in reality, the Prime Minister has considerable flexibility in deciding how to govern. The leadership style and approach of Prime Ministers vary and may reflect personal character, party politics and the size of the government's majority. Style and personality affect the influence and power of a Prime Minister. The Prime Minister is often described as being *primus inter pares,* first among equals. But as the dominant and most senior minister of the government, modern Prime Ministers tend increasingly towards a presidential style. This may be as a result of media hype or because the Prime Minister is in a key position to communicate with and through the media. The trend towards a presidential style of Prime Minister is most noticeable in the past decade or so, and is unlikely to be reversed.

The Prime Minister may call a general election and advise the monarch to dissolve Parliament at any time within its five-year fixed-term duration. This gives the Prime Minister considerable control over the conduct of the government and its relationship with its political party. There is an important party-political dimension to the role of the Prime Minister. The Prime Minister is the leader of the political party that holds the majority of seats in Parliament. After losing a general election, the Prime Minister resigns and the party may choose a new leader.

The Prime Minister chairs cabinet meetings. According to the doctrine of collective **ministerial responsibility**, once the Cabinet reaches a decision, it is binding on all Cabinet members even though there may have been reservations or disagreements. In modern times, there has been a Deputy Prime Minister appointed to stand in for the Prime Minister when abroad or absent. The Prime Minister answers questions in the House of Commons on Wednesdays. This is an opportunity to defend government policy or make policy announcements. At other times, the Prime Minister is free to respond in debates and contribute to debates in the Commons at a time of his choosing.   JOHN MCELDOWNEY

See also: **departments of state; ministers of state**

prior convictions   *see* **evidence (criminal)**

prior restraint   *see* **freedom of expression**

prisoners of war   *see* **international humanitarian law**

prisoners' rights   The subject of prisoners' rights has proven controversial since the implementation of the Human Rights Act 1998. Notable decisions include, in particular, that of the **House of Lords** in *Anderson v Secretary of State for the Home Department* (2003), in which the House ruled that exercise by the **Home Secretary** of the decision whether or not to release on licence mandatory life prisoners (those sentenced for murder) breached that Act (specifically by infringing the right of a convicted person under Article 6 of the **European Convention on Human Rights** to have a sentence imposed by an independent and impartial tribunal). The relevant legislation was amended accordingly and the decision is now one for the Parole Board to make on the basis of dangerousness once the original tariff set by the judge for punishment purposes has been served.

Anderson gave rise to unfavourable comment (notably by the then Home Secretary, David Blunkett) about judicial 'interference' under the Human Rights Act. But what has been notable over recent decades is a much broader activism on the part of the courts in defence of prisoners who constitute, with asylum seekers, perhaps the most disparaged and vulnerable group in society. The **European Court of Human Rights** has made a large number of decisions on matters such as prisoners' conditions and deaths in custody. It ruled against the UK in *Price v*

UK (2002), in which it found that detention of a four-limb-deficient woman in a police cell without adequate heat, toilet facilities, or medical attention breached Article 3 of the Convention, which prohibits inhuman and degrading treatment. In *Edwards v United Kingdom* (2002) prison authorities were found to have breached Article 2 of the Convention (the right to life) by taking inadequate steps to prevent the suicide of a prisoner. Domestically, in *Napier v Scottish Ministers* (2005) Scotland's **Court of Session** found a breach of Article 3 where a remand prisoner was held in a cell without a toilet, and confined in a cell for very long periods with inadequate lighting, space, and ventilation. Even before the Human Rights Act 1998, the domestic courts had made a number of decisions under the **common law** in which they had adopted a robust approach, in particular, to prisoners' rights of access to courts, interpreting this (in *R v Secretary of State for the Home Department, ex p Leech* (1993)) to protect prisoners' correspondence with lawyers and (in *R v Secretary of State for the Home Department, ex p Simms* (2000)) to prevent the prison authorities from blocking prisoners' access to journalists.

Such decisions are often unpopular with the general public and with politicians but perhaps serve to illustrate the efficacy of legal rights in the protection of some unpopular minority groups.

AILEEN MCCOLGAN

prisons   In December 2007, prisons in England and Wales are housing over 82,000 men, women, and children and operating at unprecedented levels of overcrowding. When the numbers from Northern Ireland and Scotland are added in, the total confined population rises to nearly 90,000. Within prisons, industrial relations are poor, inmate **suicides** are up, and more than two-thirds of prisoners re-offend within two years of release. Prisons, it seems, are in crisis, yet, despite all the problems they encounter, their place within the **criminal justice system** is secure.

For the most part, those behind bars are white and male, although Black and ethnic minority prisoners are statistically over-represented. The majority of inmates suffer from mental health problems and, often co-existing, drug addiction. Most were unemployed before their incarceration, and their levels of literacy are low, with prisoners typically reading at or below the level of an 11-year-old.

If we break the prison population down by **gender**, we can see that **women** make up about 6 per cent of the total population. Partly reflecting their smaller numbers to begin with, however, the female incarcerated population has expanded at a rate that has far outstripped that of men since the 1990s, increasing by 173 per cent between 1994–2004. Many are serving short sentences, most commonly for theft or handling stolen goods. In addition to the general social deprivation they have in common with male prisoners, at least 50 per cent of women behind bars report being **victims** of childhood abuse or **domestic violence**. The majority of them are mothers, often leaving their children without a primary caregiver when they are taken into custody.

Although **communities** have always employed some method of **punishment**, the prison as we conceive of it today—ie as a mechanism of punishment in its own right central to the operation of the criminal justice system—emerged during the nineteenth century. Modern penal confinement, in this view, is characterized by a series of initiatives that include: architectural design, systems of classification, reasonably consistent **sentencing** practices, centralized administration, and the related goals of deterrence, reform, and **rehabilitation**. Before such developments, institutions known as prisons did exist. However, they were usually utilized merely as receptacles to hold offenders prior to their 'real' punishment, or to house debtors. Punishment was almost always physical, and included whipping, branding, and the death penalty. Offenders could also be fined and publicly humiliated by being placed in the stocks.

By the end of the eighteenth century, such practices were coming under growing criticism, from figures such as John Howard, Cesare Beccaria, and Jeremy Bentham. Yet, it was not until the nineteenth century that large-scale legislative reform occurred. From 1815, for example, jailers were prevented from charging prisoners for room and board, while the Gaols Act 1823 prohibited the use of manacles and irons and, in response to the influential work of Quaker, Elizabeth Fry, required women matrons to guard women prisoners. Finally, the 1878 Prison Act formally established the parameters of a national prison system, complete with salaried guards hired by merit.

For most of the twentieth century British punishment was shaped by the welfare ideals of rehabilitation and reform. Crime was considered to be an illness or a result of socio-economic deprivation, and prison was its cure. 'The purpose of the training and treatment of convicted prisoners' Prison Rule 3 of the Prison Act 1952 made clear 'shall be to encourage and assist them to lead a good and useful life'. From 1968, prisons and inmates were subject to a detailed classification scheme designed equally to safeguard **security** as to facilitate training and

reform. Despite ongoing rhetorical commitment to 'positive custody', however, it soon became apparent, not only that prisons were failing to reform but also that conditions within them were poor.

Crime rates and prison disturbances rose throughout the 1970s and 1980s, while staff morale dropped. The growth of the prison population, which soon outpaced the capacity of the prison service, undermined the capacity of institutions to address offenders' needs, while the Victorian prisons in most cities fell into squalid disrepair. Double-bunking, 'slopping out', and staff brutality became widespread. All together, such factors undermined commitments to welfare ideals, which, though they remain in place to some extent (Prison Rule 3 still allegedly guides penal practice after all), have been radically reshaped.

In many respects the nature of twenty-first century British prison dates to events of the final decade of the twentieth century. First, the 1991 Woolf Report, published in response to the April 1990 riot in Manchester Prison (commonly referred to as Strangeways), blamed the disturbance largely on prisoner dissatisfaction with unaccountable and unfair processes and practices in the prison system. In response to the high-profile report and to accompanying public and political censure, the prison service instituted a number of key administrative reforms. As in other periods, they vowed to increase time out of cells and meaningful activity. More significantly, perhaps, they embraced a new managerialist style of governance and a new administrative structure. Hived off, at least in part, from the Home Office, in 1993, when it was made into a semi-autonomous Agency, the Prison Service of England and Wales initially increased the autonomy of governors within the restrictions of such administrative measures as 'Key Performance Indicators' and 'Strategic Planning' in order better to compete with the emerging private sector prisons. The first private prison contract in England was awarded to GSL in 1991, the same year as the Woolf Report, to open Wolds Prison in 1992. By the end of the decade, private companies ran 10 per cent of the prison estate in England and Wales. Nearly a decade on from this period, Northern Ireland has no private prisons at all, and Scotland has opened only one.

By the mid-1990s, the reformism initiated under Woolf in England and Wales was waning. Two sets of high-profile escapes from high-security prisons and the suicide of alleged serial killer, Fred West, while in custody, lead to two critical reports in 1994 and 1995, which called for a new emphasis on security and custody. In many ways, such tensions between **justice** and security have never fully been resolved. Thus the punitive sentiment of most media accounts of crime and punishment, as well as the legislative activity under New Labour that has led to an ever-expanding prison population, exists uneasily alongside the English Prison Service's commitment to the 'Decency Agenda', the Northern Ireland's evolving 'Integrated Standards Programme', and the Scottish Prison Service's 'Vision for Correctional Excellence'.

In 2006, Baroness Jean Corston urged the government to disband the national web of women's prisons and replace them with small, local, secure housing. Such a system, she alleges, as others have before her, would enable women to maintain contact with their children, and help them to access drug treatment and other counselling services which, at present, are unevenly available to them. Organizations like the Howard League for Penal Reform and the Penal Reform Trust, along with numerous academics have, similarly called for a reduction in prison numbers and a rethinking of penal policy to reduce the numbers in custody.

Despite the problems facing the current prison service, however, the British government announced in December 2007, in response to the findings of the Carter Report, that it would fund an additional 10,000 places in prison. Such a decision speaks to the pervasive hold the prison retains on the imagination of most policy-makers and those who confer sentence. Thus, despite the apparent failure of prison to reform or deter, and notwithstanding the pressures facing most institutions in dealing with a diverse and vulnerable population, the British penal state seems set only to grow.   MARY BOSWORTH

Pritchard, Dr William Dr William Pritchard (1825—1865) was with Dr William **Palmer** one of the most notorious poisoners of the nineteenth century. He was convicted of the murder of both his wife and mother-in-law, though much of his notoriety derives from his expressions of piety and implacable assertions of his innocence throughout the process.

After an early career as a naval surgeon, Pritchard married and eventually settled in Glasgow with his wife. Here he established a reputable practice in the centre of the city. His private life was less ordered, however, as he carried on a series of relationships with female servants, for at least one of whom he procured an abortion. In late 1864 his wife became ill and her mother, Mrs Taylor, came to Glasgow to nurse her. Mrs Taylor died suddenly on 25 February 1865 after eating a tapioca pudding. Pritchard's wife died three weeks later, on 17 March. In both cases Pritchard signed death certificates. The Procurator Fiscal later received an anonymous letter accusing Pritchard of murder and began an investigation. The

bodies were exhumed and large quantities of antimony were found in both. Pritchard was then charged with the murder of both by poisoning.

The trial took place at the High Court of Justiciary in Edinburgh in July 1865 and lasted for five days. Though Pritchard protested his innocence, the medical evidence for the Crown was largely uncontested, and it was established that Pritchard had purchased quantities of poison throughout the period of his wife's illness. Though he tried to throw the blame onto a servant whom he had seduced, there was little evidence to support this and he was duly found guilty and sentenced to death.

Pritchard confessed to the murders before his execution on Glasgow Green on 28 July 1865. 100,000 people were reputed to have attended this, the last public execution in Scotland.   LINDSAY FARMER

privacy It has frequently been asserted to be a central feature of liberal thinking that there should be a distinction between public and private arenas of social living. Within this framework, the law has been viewed as a crucial mechanism through which to ensure that the state is not permitted to overreach its influence into the private sphere. While the exact boundaries of what counts as public and as private have been debated and disputed over time, the general claim that there should remain a realm of private existence that is *prima facie* protected against state/third party intervention has enjoyed considerable support amongst legislators, policymakers and the public alike.

This is reflected most clearly perhaps in the right, enshrined in Article 8 of the **European Convention on Human Rights**, to respect for private and family life. Jurisprudence in this area has yielded a number of different articulations of the concept of privacy and of the nature of the protection to be afforded by the law thereto. However, Lord Mustill's statement in *R v Broadcasting Standards Commission, ex p BBC (Liberty Intervening)* (2000) seems most apt. He asserts that 'the privacy of a human being denotes at the same time the personal "space" in which the individual is free to be itself, and also the carapace, or shell, or umbrella, or whatever other metaphor is preferred, which protects that space from intrusion'. This contribution is particularly valuable since it highlights the dual nature of the legal right to respect for private life, as a result of which it entails not only a non-interventionist approach, but also a positive commitment from the state to ensure the means through which individuals can craft relevant relationships and interests. It is clear, therefore, that respect for private life protects not only the right to be removed from others but also the right to be involved with them. Thus, in *Botta v Italy* (1998), the **European Court of Human Rights** ('ECtHR') made it clear that Article 8 required respect for both physical and psychological integrity, and was 'intended to ensure the development, without outside interference, of the personality of each individual in his relation with other human beings'.

At the same time, however, it is important to bear in mind that the right to respect for private life established under Article 8 is not an absolute right. Indeed, the requirement under Article 8(2) that 'there shall be no interference by a public authority' in the exercise of this right is subject to the exception that interference will be justified and appropriate where this is established to be 'necessary in a democratic society' (eg in order to protect the rights of others or to maintain public order). Article 8 provides a right not to private life, but to *respect for* private life; and establishing what this respect requires involves striking a fair balance between the general interest and the interest of the individual.

But despite this potential for intervention, it has often been argued that the *prima facie* protection afforded by the law to the private has generated a reluctance on the part of state officials to lift the veil in order to uncover the incidents of harm that occur in this sphere. Feminist commentators in particular have suggested that the division between public and private has insulated the injustices that arise in the latter sphere from scrutiny or reform, and has problematized the implications of this in a context in which those injustices are predominantly visited upon women or children. These feminists have emphasized that the threshold between what counts as public and what counts as private is a contested and constructed one. Through the use of their slogan that 'the personal is political', they have campaigned to shift those boundaries in ways that will better protect victims of domestic violence or intra-familial dominance.

Where the Article 8 right to respect for private life is breached and this cannot be justified on the grounds of being necessary and proportionate in order to protect others, to preserve public order, or in any other relevant way to maintain democratic society, a remedy must be made available under domestic private law. In the UK context, there are a number of means through which domestic law strives to protect this personal privacy, but it has stopped short of creating a specific tort of privacy as such. Provisions of the Protection from Harassment Act 1997 may be invoked, for example, to claim a civil or criminal remedy where a person's conduct causes another distress in such a way as to show disrespect for a person's privacy. In addition, the Data Protection Act 1998 was passed with a specific aim of protecting rights to personal privacy by prohibiting and providing remedies against the wrongful processing of personal data by various organizations.

In the UK, however, the right to privacy has received most sustained consideration in the context of a number of high-profile breach of confidence cases. At issue in these cases has been the question of whether the publication of sensitive (but truthful) information against the wishes of the person concerned can be seen to be a legal wrong. Traditionally, the law of confidence required not only that the information in question was 'confidential', but also that the information was secured in circumstances which imposed an obligation on the receiving party to deal with it confidentially and that the receiving party had gone on, without authorization, to disclose or use the information. But more recent case law has supported a less restrictive approach, according to which an obligation of confidence arises where a person can establish that the information is 'private' in nature. This suggests a fusing together of the ideas of confidentiality and privacy, and this is an approach that the UK courts have largely welcomed. In *Douglas & Others v Hello! Ltd* (2001), for example, Keene LJ noted that whether any remedy given is said to be 'for breach of confidence or for breach of a right to privacy may be little more than deciding what label is to be attached to the cause of action'. Similarly, in *Campbell v MGN Ltd* (2004), Lord Hoffmann accepted that there had 'been a shift in the centre of gravity of the action for breach of confidence' and Lord Nicholls noted that 'the essence of the tort is better encapsulated now as misuse of private information'. But to the extent that this is so, it is important to bear in mind that this does not give rise to an absolute right to privacy. On the contrary, a defence to liability for breach of confidence will arise where it can be shown that the confider consented to the publication or that disclosure was in the public interest. As with Article 8, this is subject to a test of proportionality, such that the more intimate the aspect of private life at issue, the more compelling the reason for interference will need to be in order to render the intrusion legitimate.

The ideal of a society in which citizens can create and preserve a realm of private life that is protected from state, or other third party, intrusion is one that animates contemporary liberal legalism. While this is cemented in law in the form of an actionable right to respect for private life, it is clear that this right is neither absolute nor unconditional. On the contrary, it is dependent on countervailing evaluations of harm and public interest. To the extent that this is so, it seems, therefore, that the power to define what is permissibly private remains, ultimately, beyond the exclusive reach of the individuals immediately involved. VANESSA MUNRO

See also: **personal information, access to**

Private Bills Private Bills are Bills promoted by organizations outside Parliament (such as local authorities, companies, and academic institutions) which, if enacted, would alter the general law as it relates to a particular area, or specifically place the promoters in a legal position different from that they would have under the general law. Procedures under the Transport and Works Act 1992 and the Scotland Act 1998 have reduced the volume of Private Bills.

Private Bills follow the same stages as Public Bills (ie Bills promoted by the government or by individual Members of Parliament) but are subject to a more investigative and quasi-judicial procedure.

On a strict annual timetable, the promoters must petition Parliament for the Bill, publicly advertise its promotion, directly notify those likely to be particularly affected by it, and publicly display related documents. Those 'directly and specially' affected by it may petition Parliament against the Bill. Promoting and opposing petitions must comply with the standing orders of each House.

The committee stage in each House is the most significant for a Private Bill. A committee considering an 'opposed' Bill (ie one against which there are petitions) normally hears counsel for both the promoters and opponents. The task of a Private Bill committee is to determine whether the Bill is 'proved' (ie whether the purpose of the Bill declared in its preamble has been established as proper and desirable). Where a committee finds the Bill is not proved, that is tantamount to a total rejection of the Bill. Where it is found proved, the committee may propose amendments to the Bill. T ST JOHN BATES

See also: **Acts of Parliament; Private Members' Bills**

private companies Most **companies** registered in the UK are private companies. The Companies Act defines a private company as any company that is not a **public company**. Unlike public companies, private companies cannot apply to have their **securities** (**shares** or bonds) listed on the **stock exchange** and cannot offer their securities for purchase by the general public. However, private companies can re-register as public companies should they wish to access the capital markets.

Private companies can be incorporated in one of three forms: (i) unlimited; (ii) limited by guarantee; or (iii) limited by shares. Most private companies are limited by shares as this is the most suitable medium for commercial enterprise. Accordingly, references hereafter to private companies are to private companies limited by shares.

Private companies can raise working capital by issuing shares or taking out loans. They provide their members with the benefits of **corporate personality** and **limited liability**. The name of a private company must end with 'limited' or 'ltd' (or, in the case of a Welsh private limited company, 'cyfyngedig' or 'cyf') to indicate that the members have limited liability.

Private companies are straightforward and cheap to establish. They can be formed from scratch by filing prescribed documents with the Registrar of Companies or can be purchased ready incorporated 'off the shelf' from a company formation agent. It is permissible to form a private company with only one member. There are no minimum capital requirements meaning that the founders need only subscribe nominal sums (as little as £1 or £2) for their initial shares. One consequence in recent years is an increased tendency for businesses based in and trading exclusively from other European jurisdictions (notably Germany) to incorporate in the UK rather than in their home country in order to avoid the costs associated with home country minimum capital requirements. This practice has been supported by decisions of the **European Court of Justice** invoking the principle of freedom of establishment.

The distinction between public and private companies originated in the nineteenth century. Companies were originally designed to enable entrepreneurs to raise capital from a wide investor base. This was reflected in the Joint Stock Companies Act 1844 which required registered companies to have at least twenty members (reduced to seven in 1856). However, in the landmark case of *Salomon v A Salomon & Co Ltd* (1897), the **House of Lords** established that it was lawful for an individual trader to incorporate a business, combine the functions of ownership and management, and take advantage of the principles of corporate personality and limited liability to shelter his personal assets from claims by business creditors. *Salomon* led to the establishment of private companies capable of being formed by two members as a statutory concept in the Companies Act 1907 and gave the green light to the mass incorporation of owner-managed private companies that occurred during the twentieth century. As private companies cannot raise capital from the general public they are less regulated than public companies. ADRIAN WALTERS

private international law   *see* **transnational civil litigation**

Private Members' Bills   Private Members' Bills are Public Bills introduced by individual members in either House, rather than by the government. To be enacted, these bills must pass through the same parliamentary stages in both Houses as government-promoted Public Bills. However, procedural constraints, particularly in the **House of Commons**, result in few Private Members' Bills being enacted. In the ten years to 2006, less than 8 per cent of such bills introduced in Parliament became law; and those enacted were around 10 per cent of all Public Bills enacted over that period.

Standing Orders provide three procedures for introducing Private Members' Bills in the Commons: through a ballot procedure, introduction under the ten minute rule, and by giving formal notice. Bills are commonly introduced under the latter two procedures to publicize an issue rather than with any realistic hope of enactment, although some do become law. The majority of the Private Members' Bills that are enacted are introduced by the first seven or so MPs whose names are drawn at the beginning of each parliamentary session in a ballot of backbenchers for precedence to introduce bills on thirteen Friday sittings which the Commons largely devotes to Private Members' Bills.

Procedural constraints effectively ensure that Private Members' Bills only become law if they attract broad parliamentary approval; though sometimes, where the government approves its objectives, it may facilitate the Bill's enactment by providing additional parliamentary time, or other assistance to the promoter.   T ST JOHN BATES

See also: **Acts of Parliament; Private Bills**

private wrongs and human rights   Human rights have been traditionally conceptualized as being enforceable only as against the state: that is, as safeguarding fundamental rights and freedoms against interference by the state. To a degree this approach is reflected in the **Human Rights Act 1998**, which domesticates certain provisions of the **European Convention on Human Rights**. The European Convention is binding only on states which are party to it, and only states can be sued in the **European Court of Human Rights**. Similarly, the Human Rights Act provides for direct legal actions only against 'public authorities', although these are defined to include private actors carrying out public functions, in their carrying out of those functions. An example might be the conduct of a private security company running a **prison** which would be covered by the Act in relation to its custodial functions (although not in relation to 'private' functions such as employing catering assistants or ordering stationery).

Despite the restricted operation of the European Convention, the European Court has provided some protection against private conduct which would, if it were carried out by the agents of the state, breach one or more Convention rights. The Court has imposed **positive obligations** on state parties to prevent or to provide a **remedy** for such conduct. Cases in which such duties have been recognized include those in which protestors asserted a right to freedom from interference by counter-demonstrators (*Plattform Artze für das Leben v Austria* (1988)) and in which children won claims that the UK government had breached their right to be free from inhuman and degrading treatment by failing to remove them from an abusive parent (*Z & Ors v United Kingdom* (2002)). State parties will not be held responsible for all 'quasi breaches' by private actors, but will be so liable where their preventative action falls far short of what might reasonably have been expected, or where the legal system fails to provide a deterrent to such action (*A v United Kingdom* (1999)), in which a breach of Article 3 was found because the claimant's step-father had available to him a defence of reasonable chastisement to a criminal **prosecution** in respect of his physical ill-treatment of the claimant).

Under the Human Rights Act 1998 an additional form of 'horizontal' application (that is, enforcement of rights against private bodies) is through section 3 and the definition of **courts** as 'public authorities' by the Act (section 6). Section 3 requires that all **legislation** is interpreted compatibly with the domesticated provisions of the Convention 'so far as possible'. This will apply whether the parties are public or private. And section 6 of the Act binds courts and **tribunals**, as public authorities, to act compatibly with the Convention unless bound by (generally) primary legislation to do otherwise. Courts should develop the **common law** compatibly with the domestic Convention Articles but not (*Wainwright & Anor v Home Office* (2003)) create new causes of action to give effect to those rights.   AILEEN MCCOLGAN

See also: **horizontal application of human rights**

privateering   *see* **piracy**

privatization   It is important to understand that privatization refers to a number of different activities through which the private sector undertakes tasks which were previously in the public sector. This entry will cover the sale of the major public enterprises, but other privatization has involved **contracting-out** of public services or **public procurement** through the private finance initiative.

The largest and most celebrated examples of privatization have been the sales of the large public utilities through a public offering of shares. This was the model adopted to sell, for example, British Telecom (1984), British Gas (1986), the British Airports Authority and British Airways (1987), the water authorities (1989), the electricity industry (1990–1991), and Railtrack (1996). The legal process for the sales was a straightforward one. A limited company was established with share capital wholly owned by the minister. An Act of Parliament for each privatization then transferred the business of the nationalized industry and its assets to the new company. The minister and his advisers then offered the shares to the public, sometimes in several phased sales, in other cases all at once. In some cases, including the largest of all, the sale of British Petroleum, no legislation was necessary as the enterprise already had the form of a public limited company in which the government owned shares.

In many other cases, enterprises were sold directly, without a public offer of shares, through 'trade sales' to a single purchaser, as in the case of the coal industry in 1994. This form of privatization has continued under Labour governments, for example with the sale of a majority stake in National Air Traffic Services and of QinetiQ, a defence research and development company. Such direct sales have also frequently been used where an enterprise was split up and subsidiaries sold individually, as with the National Bus Company. The most important example of the splitting up of an enterprise before sale was that of British Rail, which was divided into over a hundred different companies; as well as the sale of Railtrack, the running of trains was passed to a number of different train operating companies under franchises, a form of contract.

Some limited means were used briefly to retain governmental influence over privatized companies. Experiments with retaining government directors and minority government shareholdings were short-lived; but in addition 'golden shares' were used in several cases to give government a veto over takeovers and some other important decisions of the company. However, **European Union** law has imposed restrictions on the use of such shares, and they have only been retained in a small number of enterprises where defence or major public interest considerations apply, for example the defence contractor BAE Systems and National Air Traffic Services. In the major public utilities, such as energy and water, the public interest is protected by independent **regulation**.

TONY PROSSER

Privy Council   The Privy Council has ancient historical origins. Its formal role is to advise the **monarch** as Head of State. Over the centuries, it has adapted to meet changing conditions. Cabinet Ministers are Privy Councillors, as are various members of the Royal Family, certain senior judges, the Archbishops of the Church of England, and the leaders of the main opposition political parties. Currently there are about 500 members.

The ministerial head of the Privy Council Office (the Council's secretariat) is the Lord President of the Council. The Privy Council meets at least nine times a year, and more frequently when the need arises. Meetings are usually chaired by the Lord President. The main work of the Privy Council relates to the 400 or so institutions that are incorporated by Royal Charter. In addition, the Privy Council has various regulatory functions relating, for instance, to universities. Orders in Council are an important form of subordinate legislation. Issues of significant constitutional importance (relating, for instance, to national security) may be referred to the Privy Council for its opinion.

The Privy Council also has a judicial role. Since 1833, its Judicial Committee has been the final court of appeal for UK colonies, territories, and dependencies, and for certain (but increasingly fewer) Commonwealth countries. The Judicial Committee is also the final court of appeal on devolution matters relating to Scotland, Wales, and Northern Ireland. It hears around sixty appeals annually.

JOHN MCELDOWNEY

See also: **legal rules, types of**

prize competitions   *see* **advertising; unfair commercial practices**

prize law   *see* **war and armed conflict**

***pro bono* legal services**   The term '*pro bono*' has come into recent use from the United States, though there is a long tradition of lawyers in the UK giving their services free. Lord Goldsmith, first as chairman of the Bar and then as **Attorney-General**, particularly encouraged its growth. He established a committee to promote the idea and an envoy to advance it. England and Wales now has an annual *pro bono* week.

Both branches of the legal profession have organizations that encourage *pro bono* work. The oldest is the Free Representation Unit, formed in 1972 by bar students who wanted to provide representation in venues, such as **tribunals**, that were traditionally not the preserve of barristers. In 1996, Lord Goldsmith was instrumental in setting up the Bar *Pro Bono* Unit. Meanwhile, solicitors set up the Solicitors *Pro Bono* Group in 1997, renamed LawWorks in 2006. All three work in essentially the same way, as brokers putting potential clients in touch with potential providers of services.

The Bar *Pro Bono* Unit and the Solicitors *Pro Bono* Group defined *pro bono* in a 2005 protocol that was widely signed by participating lawyers as:

'legal advice or representation provided by lawyers to individuals and community groups who cannot afford to pay for that advice or representation and where public funding is not available.'

In practice, however, *pro bono* legal services are usually defined rather more widely and include all work undertaken by lawyers without fee, including provision of services to national organizations and activities other than advice and representation, such as lectures and teaching.

The commitment to *pro bono* is such that most barristers' chambers and solicitors' firms have members who provide considerable amounts of free assistance. The major commercial firms give some indication on their website of the kind of work in which they are participating—though sometimes under the heading of 'corporate social responsibility'.

One reason for the slow growth of *pro bono* in the United Kingdom relative to the United States has been the relatively high level of public funding available for legal aid. At no time, however, was the level of public funding completely sufficient to cover all needs, and this is particularly the case as legal aid coverage has been reduced. The institutional providers of *pro bono* have been aware of the danger of undermining free provision and the protocol mentioned earlier noted that 'Pro Bono Legal Work is always only an adjunct to, and not a substitute for, a proper system of publicly funded legal services'.

A recent trend has been the establishment of *pro bono* provision within educational institutions. This move was led by the College of Law and then widely followed. This points to an important conjunction between *pro bono* legal services and **clinical legal education**. The undertaking of *pro bono* work can have an important educational function for the provider as well as giving a service to the client.

ROGER SMITH

See also: **legal profession, private and voluntary sector of**

proactive policing,   *see* **entrapment**

probation   The origins of probation are attributed to John Augustus, a boot maker in Boston, Massachusetts, who in 1841 persuaded a judge to release a drunkenness offender on **bail** under his personal supervision instead of imposing the normal **prison** sentence. Subsequently, Augustus became a regular figure at the courts, working voluntarily and unofficially, speaking on behalf of offenders and encouraging their supervised release on bail. In England and Wales, the Probation of Offenders Act 1907 introduced the probation system, providing both for the supervision of offenders by means of a probation order and for the appointment of probation officers. In this original guise, the probation order represented a withholding of **criminal conviction** and punishment while a defendant was released under cognizance to come up for judgment at a future date, when his/her behaviour would be reviewed. During this period, the defendant was required to maintain contact with a probation officer, to be of good behaviour, and to lead an industrious life. Successful completion of the period of supervision entailed that no further action would be taken in respect of the original offence. Additional requirements could be added according to individual need, for example to reside for a period in a hostel. Standing in lieu of conviction and punishment in this way, the imposition of a probation order required the defendant's consent. Moreover, it was available to **courts** to impose in respect of any offence for which the sentence was not mandatory: for example, women convicted of **infanticide** while mentally ill might be placed on probation and required to receive psychiatric treatment. Failure to abide by the conditions of probation or commission of a further offence during the period of probation led either to the imposition of a fine for the breach of the conditions of probation or to the revocation of the order with a new sentence imposed for the original offence.

The introduction of probation was hailed with considerable optimism, reflecting the contemporary confidence in the effectiveness of **rehabilitation**. Initially administered by Police Court Missionaries, probation supervision was formally recognized in the 1960s as an area of professional social work. After the collapse of faith in rehabilitation during the 1970s, numbers of offenders placed on probation declined, reaching a nadir in 1981. During the 1980s, however, the probation service began to experiment with more intensive supervision in order to compete for potentially prison-bound offenders. Additional requirements in probation orders began to be used more frequently for the specific purpose of addressing offending behaviour and associated problems such as alcohol and drug misuse. The Criminal Justice Act 1982 made formal provision for such requirements, including a requirement of attendance at a day centre for an intensive programme of offence-focused intervention.

The Criminal Justice Act 1991 re-created the probation order as a sentence, placed it on the tariff of punishments and expanded the range of additional requirements. Subsequent **legislation** has removed the requirement to gain the defendant's consent (1993), changed the name 'probation order' to Community Rehabilitation Order in England and Wales (2000) and further re-titled it to Community Order (2006), in which a variety of previously separate community penalties are integrated into a single disposal. The confusion created, nationally and internationally, by these changes in the name of the order, while the term 'probation' is retained in Scotland, Northern Ireland, and the rest of the world has to date generally been resolved by ignoring the new nomenclature. JUDITH RUMGAY

problem-based legal education Legal education is strongly *problem-focused*. This is because much learning occurs through the study of fact patterns or 'problem questions' which require students to analyse and explain how the law applies to that situation. Conventionally, problems are worked through as exemplars in lectures and as practical exercises in small group classes. Such exercises are usually attempted after students have been introduced to the general principles of the relevant area of law in lectures.

Genuine *problem-based* learning ('PBL'), however, differs somewhat from this approach. PBL is a learning method rather than a teaching method, since it places the onus primarily on the student to manage their learning. PBL puts the problem first in the learning process. Problems are not presented in the context of prior teaching on that topic, precisely because a real problem is, by definition, unfamiliar. The student thus learns both the rules and principles of law, and, even more importantly, skills of knowledge acquisition and problem analysis by working through the problem and reflecting on that experience. PBL, it is said, makes learning a more personalized process, and enables students to experience more realistic problems and respond creatively to them. On the other hand, there are concerns that PBL tends to leave bigger gaps in substantive legal knowledge than more traditional approaches. While PBL can deliver greater depth of understanding of specific problems, students may lack the breadth of knowledge provided by more traditional approaches, and may find it harder to organize that knowledge into a coherent system. JULIAN WEBB

procedural justice *see* **due process rights; fair trial, right to**

processions and demonstrations The British have throughout history taken to the streets in protest (and celebration), but the law regulating such activities is unstructured. It is to be found in legislation and judicial decisions, in regulations and in by-laws. Special places such as Parliament, and national monuments such as Stonehenge and Trafalgar Square, have been accorded special legal protections. Before the enactment of the **Human Rights Act 1998**, the police were regarded as having an overriding duty to preserve the peace but were not perceived to have a corresponding duty to protect assemblies. Arguably, Article 11 of the **European Convention on Human Rights**, which guarantees **freedom of assembly**, changes that position so that there is at least a presumption in favour of the lawfulness of such activity.

So far as processions on public highways are concerned, until 1986 the law was contained in an array of local legislation whose scope differed considerably in detail from one part of the country to the next. As a result of the reorganization of local government effected in 1972, much of that legislation was due to lapse, and the opportunity was taken in the Public Order Act 1986 to introduce a national regime for the regulation of processions (and, to a lesser extent, meetings). That legislation requires notice to be given to the **police** of the intention to hold a procession. This is not an application for a permit to march; the legislation tacitly acknowledges that there is a right to hold a procession. However, if the police take the view that certain public order considerations are satisfied, they can give directions as to the conduct of the march. If they (reasonably) take the view that the imposition of conditions will be insufficient to prevent serious public disorder, they may apply to the relevant local authority for a ban on all processions in the area for a period of up to three months, and that ban must be approved by the **Home Secretary**. This tripartite arrangement means that there are very few bans imposed upon marches.

Public meetings are controlled under a slightly different regime. No advance notice is required for holding a public meeting. But if the meeting is to be held in a public place, the locale will almost certainly be subject to police (or possibly private) control through local legislation or by-laws. If the gathering or demonstration takes the form of a static meeting on the highway, it is in all likelihood a **trespass** to the highway, in which case the police have a power to require demonstrators to move on. There is no power to ban demonstrations comparable to that available for marches. But since the enactment of the Anti-Social Behaviour Act of 2003 there has been a power to impose conditions on an assembly of two or more persons, and the existence of such a power might very well give rise to a disguised power to ban particular gatherings. But because of the existence of Article 11, one would expect the courts to give strenuous scrutiny to any attempt to use the powers in the context of a demonstration held for political purposes.

ATH SMITH

Procurator Fiscal   *see* **criminal justice system: Scotland**

product defects   A number of legal questions arise out of the supply by producers of defective products. Where the defect causes no harm other than affecting the utility and value of the product itself, then consumers will generally only have rights against the person who sold them the product, although for some products it may be possible also to rely on a manufacturers' warranty directly against the producer (discussed more extensively in the entry on **product quality).**

The law on defective products more generally focuses on the legal consequences of a consumer being physically harmed by a defective product. One of the most famous cases in English and Scottish law, *Donoghue v Stevenson* (1932) involved a claim by a woman that she had been harmed by the act of consuming ginger beer from a bottle in which the remains of decomposed snail were found. The woman was unable to claim against the café owner who had sold the ginger beer because it had been bought for her by a friend, with the result that the claimant had no contract (or other legal relationship) with the café owner. Consequently the claimant sued the manufacturer claiming that the manufacturer was liable for the tort of negligence. It was critical to her success in the case that the ginger beer bottle was opaque, with the result that neither the café owner nor the friend could detect the alien object in the bottle. The **House of Lords** determined that a producer owes a duty of care to the ultimate consumer where first, it is foreseeable that the failure to take care could harm the consumer, and where the nature of the product affords no reasonable opportunity for inspection between the product leaving the producer and being

used by the consumer. The claimant succeeded and the general proposition remains true.

Even where a consumer is physically harmed by a product it is not always straightforward to prove that the producer failed to take appropriate care. Where products are assembled of parts produced by a number of manufacturers (cars, for example), or products are supplied partially assembled and then completed by a retailer (as with bicycles), then it may be difficult to apportion responsibility. This will be particularly true where the nature of the problem involves a defect in manufacturing, as opposed to a defect in design (the latter being more readily attributable to the actions of those involved in the design stage). In some instances consumers may be the authors of their own misfortunes, for example when they use products for purposes for which they were not designed, and/or contrary to warnings supplied with the product. The provision of a warning on a product may be sufficient to protect a producer from claims, to which would otherwise be vulnerable, that they had been negligent. The **common law** position was supplemented by legislative reform in the Consumer Protection Act 1987, Part I (which implemented an EC Directive on Product Liability), the main impact of which was to substantially remove the requirement that the claimant prove that the producer failed to take care (ie was negligent).

Consumers seeking to claim damages whether in negligence, or under the strict liability regime (that is to say a regime in which it is no longer necessary to prove fault) are required to prove that the harm they suffered was caused by the defective product. In many instances proving that the defective product caused the harm will be straightforward. But with more complex products, such as drugs, this may be more challenging and can create a significant obstacle to securing compensation.

Whilst the civil law relating to defective products is generally triggered only by actual harm to consumers, the criminal laws governing the safety of products enable administrative authorities to enforce the law, seeking the removal of unsafe products from the market and fines for their producers, as preventive steps and not just in response to harm. These proactive regulatory measures are further discussion in the entry on **safety standards**.   COLIN SCOTT

product liability   'Product liability' is not a legal term of art with a precise meaning. Although it is generally used only to refer to liability imposed on commercial suppliers of products, it may be used in other ways as well. The widest sense of 'product liability' refers to any ground on which such a supplier may be held legally responsible to a claimant on the basis of the condition of the product when the supplier supplied it. Used in this sense 'product liability' would include, for example, the liability incurred by a car retailer as a result of selling a car with brakes that cannot function in wet weather. Such a sale breaches the retailer's contractual obligation to the buyer to supply a car of satisfactory quality: a car with brakes that cannot function in wet weather does not fulfill this obligation of quality.

In its intermediate sense 'product liability' refers only to that subset of liabilities incurred by the supplier when the condition of the product when supplied was historically involved in—ie was a 'cause' of—physical damage to the claimant or the claimant's property. For example, suppose that, in the earlier example, the reason the brakes were not functional was that the manufacturer had inadvertently and carelessly disconnected one of their components. Suppose further that the buyer does not discover the problem with the brakes until driving the car away from the garage forecourt in the rain, and that she is unable to halt at a red light whereupon she runs over a pedestrian, breaking his leg. The car manufacturer is liable to the pedestrian for its breach of obligation of care, and this liability falls within the subset of liabilities referred to by the intermediate sense of 'product liability'.

In its narrowest sense, 'product liability' refers only to liability incurred by product suppliers under a specific rule of **tort law**. This rule was first formulated by courts in the United States in the mid-twentieth century. In the **European Union** it was adopted in a 1985 Directive, which was domestically implemented in the UK in Part 1 of the Consumer Protection Act 1987. Liability is incurred under this rule if, at the time the supplier supplied the product, it was in a defective condition, and the defect was a cause of physical damage to the claimant or the claimant's property. One important advantage of this rule for claimants is that if the product was defective when the defendant supplied it, the claimant need not show she had a contract with the defendant or that the defendant had been careless. Thus, in the example in the previous paragraph, the pedestrian who suffers a broken leg could sue the retailer (as well as the manufacturer) under this rule.

Two features of this special rule of product liability have generated particular controversy. First, it is not yet clear how courts will judge defectiveness. How strong should a chair be to escape the judgment that it is defectively designed? How strong and 'crashworthy' should the side panels of a vehicle be? Of what relevance is the price of a product to the notion of defectiveness? How should the defectiveness of prescription drugs be judged given that they will typically be unavoidably toxic in some sense and that certain deleterious side-effects will only be discoverable after mass usage by the public?

The second controversy surrounds the uncertain width of an important defence, which is available to the supplier under the special tort rule when 'the state of scientific and technical knowledge at the time when he put the product into circulation was not such as to enable the existence of the defect to be discovered'. Critics point out that scientific understanding evolves over time from immature hypothesis to the sort of scientific consensus that might qualify as 'scientific knowledge'. At what moment is the defence lost? Certain consumer groups argue the defence is very narrow and that once someone, somewhere has the idea that would allow the defect to be discovered the defence becomes unavailable. Product suppliers argue that the only coherent way to interpret the defence is by applying a standard of reasonable discoverability.

This uncertainty tracks an underlying division of opinion about what was intended when the law reform process crystallized in the adoption of the Directive in 1985. It is generally agreed that this process had been triggered by the disaster associated with Thalidomide, a drug used by pregnant women in the late 1950s, which was later found to be associated with grave birth defects. The deformed Thalidomide children were unable to establish any legal right to damages because they were unable to show that the supplier of the drug had acted unreasonably, as was necessary under the then-existing liability rules. In advocating a narrow interpretation of the defence in the context of the special tort rule, consumer groups argue that this is crucial if the Directive is to achieve an improvement in the legal position of consumers such as children deformed by drugs taken by their mothers while pregnant. In contrast, product suppliers argue that the defence was included precisely to protect innovation in sectors such as the pharmaceutical industry by allowing the supplier to prove positively that it had exercised reasonable care to discover dangerous conditions in its products.

Interestingly, although formally there is no equivalent of this defence in the special product liability rule developed by US courts, there are virtually no US cases in which liability has been imposed under that rule on a pharmaceutical manufacturer that was able to show that it had acted with due care.

Another interesting contrast is that in the United States, claims against product suppliers represent a greater proportion of claims relating to physical loss than in the non-US **common law** world. This is largely because the vast majority of US employees are prevented from suing their employers for injuries suffered at work: statutory workers' compensation statutes provide the sole remedy for the employee against the employer. Since benefits under such legislation are much lower than the **damages** likely to be awarded in a successful tort claim, it is extremely common for US employees to sue the suppliers of products with which the employees have been required to work, and which they claim have caused them personal injuries. Typical examples include unfenced machinery, asbestos, lead-based paint, and vehicles.   JANE STAPLETON

See also: **causation; industrial injuries; product safety; sale of goods**

product safety   Products must be safe for people to use. There are various direct controls that are intended to ensure that an adequate level of **safety** is maintained. The concept of 'safety' is, however, not absolute. Many products have some intrinsically dangerous characteristics, which are tolerated since, without them, the product would not be useful. An obvious example is a sharp kitchen knife: it will be safe if it is not used, but since people want to use knives to cut hard objects, whether the knife is used safely or not is the responsibility of the user. More complex examples are where the braking and steering systems on cars or lawnmowers must be designed and manufactured so that they function safely as intended. Also, the use of therapeutic medicines may inevitably give rise to undesirable side effects. Thus, proper information must be presented to users so that they can be aware of the potential **risks**.

The key concepts are *hazard, risk*, and *benefit*. Almost all substances and engineered products present a mixture of risks and benefits. The test is that the benefits of the product must outweigh its risks. Applying this test in individual situations can be difficult. In some cases, one errs on the side of caution, through applying 'the **precautionary principle**'. Making decisions on what is an acceptable level of safety can be difficult, and involve an understanding of highly technical and often incomplete scientific data. The complexities inherent in this situation can be difficult for non-experts to understand, and there is widespread misunderstanding that all products are 'absolutely safe', which could never be true.

Essential safety information is primarily known only to the manufacturer, others involved in the supply chain, and public regulatory authorities. Legal obligations are, therefore, imposed on manufacturers, distributors, retailers, and authorities so as to ensure that **consumers** and users are sufficiently protected and have the information necessary to enable them to use products safely.

Extensive and sophisticated product regulatory systems have been constructed over the past fifty years. Product regulatory systems are the same throughout Europe. There are 'families' of systems covering medicines, many engineered products, cosmetics, biocides, motor vehicles, food, and general consumer products. In some cases, notably medicines, the systems are similar in all developed countries, allowing global collaboration on safety issues.

The systems all adopt some of the following regulatory techniques: pre-market approval (whether by a public authority or the manufacturer), and control of the processes of design, manufacture, labelling (information supplied with the product, and use of standard symbols), packaging, storage, and distribution. These techniques are usually based on the manufacturer and distributor(s) operating quality systems, which apply best standard practice and record all steps and decisions that are taken. The operation of the quality systems are approved and regularly audited by independent expert bodies. Official standards and guidelines are also widely used.

Responsibilities also extend after a product has been sold, at which stage companies must operate post-marketing vigilance procedures, which record and review complaints and safety information, and recall systems. Important safety data must be reported to the public authorities: for medicines and medical devices, periodic safety overview reports may also be required. Employers are also subject to duties to provide safe products in the workplace environment, under health and safety **legislation**.

The public authorities themselves have duties to oversee the safety of products, especially through operating market surveillance systems (including testing sample products and reviewing safety reports) and taking enforcement action when the rules are broken. The authorities have extensive powers to investigate, inspect, test, prohibit further marketing or product supply, and prosecute. These obligations are backed up by obligations on manufacturers and others to pay **compensation** to those who are hurt (**product liability**).

The above systems are reviewed periodically, and subject to constant evolution. Since the 1990s, for example, there has been increasing emphasis on improving post-marketing systems and techniques. However, there is an inevitable tension between improving safety regimes and imposing excessive cost on **companies** and public authorities, such that funding may not be available for new and useful products, and jobs or shareholders and **pension** funds.

Policy on product safety is the responsibility of government departments. Executive and enforcement functions for the safety of consumer products generally are the responsibility of local councils' **Trading Standards** Departments. For some more complex products, executive functions are exercised by independent agencies, such as the Medicines and Healthcare Products Regulatory Agency, or the Vehicle and Operator Services Agency, which draw on medical or technical experts both in-house and as external consultants.   CHRISTOPHER HODGES

See also: **product defects**

professional service lawyers   *see* **para legals**

professional services   *see* **quality of services**

profits *à prendre*   A profit *à prendre* is a right which allows the right holder access to land owned by another in order to remove produce from the soil of that land, or animals existing on it. Examples of profits *à prendre* include fishing and shooting rights over land (including rights to take game from the land), the right to fell wood on land, rights of pasture, or to remove turf or vegetables. These rights can either be appurtenant (attached) to the land of the right holder or they can exist as a right independent of land ownership of the right holder. In the latter case these rights are called 'profits *à prendre* in gross'.

Profits *à prendre* can be created by express grant of the parties, by statute, or by long use (known as a right acquired by 'prescription'). In their acquisition, nature, and extent, profits *à prendre* are similar to **easements**; but, unlike easements, profits allow the right holder to bring an action in **trespass** if the right is infringed. Additionally easements cannot exist in 'gross'. This is a significant distinction because rights existing in gross, such as profits *à prendre*, can be sold or assigned separately due to the fact that they are independent of land. Consequently, profits *à prendre* in gross are important forms of property in themselves and, since the Land Registration Act 2002, they can be registered with the English Land Registry as a separate title in their own right.

ALISON DUNN

See also: **registration of title**

programme standards and complaints   Audiovisual programming is subject to the general law

relating to, for example, **obscenity**, **defamation**, **privacy,** and **contempt of court**. However the powerful impact of television and radio is said to justify the imposition of additional standards on them. A distinction is made between basic requirements, which apply to all services, and public service expectations, which apply in varying degrees to free-to-air television channels provided by the BBC, ITV, Channel 4, S4C, and Five.

Under the Communications Act 2003, Ofcom's Broadcasting Code makes detailed provision for the following basic 'standards objectives': children under eighteen must be protected; material likely to encourage or to incite the commission of crime or to lead to disorder must not be included in programmes; a proper degree of responsibility must be exercised in relation to religious programming; generally accepted standards must be applied to provide adequate protection for the public from offensive and harmful material; advertising must be excluded if it is political, misleading, offensive, or harmful; and subliminal programming is prohibited. The Code also makes provision for the protection of privacy and for fair reporting. All these requirements apply to the BBC as well as to commercial providers. However, in two areas, the BBC has independent responsibility although its editorial guidelines are similar to Ofcom's: news must be presented with due accuracy and, together with matters of political or industrial controversy and public policy, must be presented with due impartiality; and special attention must be given to the fair reflection of political parties' campaigns during elections.

Ofcom also regulates sponsorship (paying to promote a company or its products by associating it with a programme). It requires that the arrangements are transparent, that the producer's editorial control is preserved (for example, product placement is prohibited), and that sponsorship is clearly separate from the programme and from advertising.

The regulation of **advertising** (any publicity by advertisers in breaks during or between programmes) is now sub-contracted to the Advertising Standards Authority under a co-regulatory scheme. Its code requires advertisements to be 'legal, decent, honest and truthful' and not to mislead or cause harm or serious offence. Advertising is prohibited of products and services that include breathalysers, betting, tobacco products, private investigation agencies, guns, pornography, and the occult. In respect of other products (especially medicines), there are detailed rules intended to ensure that claims about their benefits are justified and to prevent exploitation of the audience by taking advantage of vulnerabilities such as children's credibility, superstitions, religious beliefs, or the use of alcohol.

Ofcom hears complaints and publishes its findings about breaches of its Broadcast Code, including the provisions which apply to the BBC. It also considers complaints about its sponsorship rules. Grievances about advertising are entertained by the Advertising Standards Authority. In cases of deliberate, serious, or repeated breaches of any kind, Ofcom has the power to impose sanctions, such as a fine or even the revocation of a commercial provider's licence.

TOM GIBBONS

See also: **fairness in broadcasting**

progressive taxation   *see* **tax, ability to pay**

proliferation security initiative   *see* **arms control; law of the sea terrorism**

proof   *see* **evidence, civil; evidence, criminal**

proof, early modes of   Early medieval dispute settlement across north-western Europe, including Anglo-Saxon England, was characterized by two features in tension with one another. On the one hand, courts were lay assemblies. This made practical dispute settlement as much political as 'legal'. On the other, early medieval European societies were in the cultural shadow of the later Roman empire, including its imperial codes and the idea of a ruler as a lawgiver. This led to the production of royal law-codes, to a greater or lesser extent influenced by the clergy. The tension was equally present in modes of proof of disputed claims.

The law-codes showed an effort to achieve certainty and give religious backing to judicial decisions. Parties were to swear to the truth of their cases; their oaths were to be buttressed by the support of oath-helpers who swore the same oath along with them (compurgation, or in the language of the later **common law** 'wager of law'). A step further was to support the party's oath by his submission to an ordeal, presided over by a priest. There were various ordeals: the best attested in England are the ordeals of hot iron and of cold water. In the first, the party taking the ordeal was required to carry a red-hot bar of iron, blessed by a priest, over a set distance; his hand was then bound up; if it healed cleanly, he had succeeded in the ordeal and his oath was valid, if it festered it failed. In the ordeal of cold water, the party was tied up and thrown in a blessed pond; if he sank, his oath was valid, if he floated, it failed. A similar idea of preventing perjury through the immediate intervention of God's providence is found in legislation of the Carolingian emperor Louis the Pious (814–840): where there were witnesses on each side of a lawsuit, they were required to fight each other with spiked clubs, the losers being convicted of perjury. This idea of 'trial by battle' did not catch on in Anglo-Saxon England, but it was introduced by the Normans after 1066.

The judicial practice was very different. A law-suit was a disorganized altercation between the parties and the members of the lay court, in which arguments from custom and from royal laws were mixed inextricably with presentation of a variety of forms of evidence not wholly distinct from one another: party confessions, witnesses, documents and their makers or attesting witnesses, presumptive and circumstantial evidence, the testimony of local officials or members of local courts, and groups of neighbours from the location of the alleged events summoned by the court. Compurgation was commonly used to reinforce a decision already reached; the ordeals were used only in cases of exceptional difficulty.

On the continent, this regime was gradually replaced from the twelfth century by a systematic professionalized law of proof, developed, mainly by canon lawyers, from Roman materials. England took a different path. As the professionalized common law began to develop in the reign of Henry II, legislation, and later the emerging legal doctrine following in its footsteps, allocated different proofs to different sorts of dispute. In public prosecutions for capital crimes, if reasonable suspicion was established by the oath of groups of locals, the defendant was forced to take the ordeal of water; in private prosecutions for these crimes, the appeal of felony—trial by battle between prosecutor and defendant—became normal. Battle, this time between witnesses, was also the default form of proof in the **writ** of right for the recovery of land. Legislation prescribed the use of the oath of groups of locals in the 'petty assizes' (Novel Disseisin, Mort d'Ancestor, Utrum). Legislation brought in the use of a special form of oath of a group of locals, the 'grand assize', as an alternative to trial by battle in the writ of right at the election of the defendant.

The treatise *Glanvill* tells us that the 'general mode of proof' in the King's court is by documents or by battle; and that witnesses to prove a debt must be willing offer battle. However, if these ideas were ever used in practice, they went out of use. It came to be possible to prove debts in the royal courts by producing 'suit', supporters of the claimant's claim; the defendant could then disprove the claim by waging his law.

In 1215 the Lateran Council prohibited clergy participation in the ordeals. As a result, in England the use of the oath of locals—the jury—was substituted for the ordeals in public prosecution of capital crime. Exceptions to the use of battle in private prosecution, with juries being substituted, had also begun to emerge. In addition, juries were used in the new writs of entry to recover land. Battle was gradually restricted to the case of the 'approver', a man accused of crime who 'turned king's evidence' by confessing and undertook to convict his fellow-criminals by appealing them. However, jury trial did not become a *general* mode of trial until the early modern period.

The later medieval period saw further development of specific forms of proof attached to specific issues of fact, and of legal boundaries between them. For example, claims in covenant came to require a sealed document, a deed, to be produced. The death of a relevant person in the county where the facts of the claimant's claim were laid could be proved by jury; but death outside that county would be proved 'per proves', probably by individual witnesses. Where a trespass against the King's peace was alleged, compurgation was not available and trial by jury was required.

In the early modern period, the medieval law of actions was displaced by the use of trespass variants for almost all purposes, carrying with them more or less universal trial by jury. The old modes of proof, apart from proof by documents in the actions of debt on a bond and covenant, disappeared with the old forms of action from practice: the chief landmark being *Slade's Case* (1602) which (as reported by Coke) disapproved of wager of law. But trial by battle and wager of law remained *theoretically* available until they were finally abolished, the first in 1819 and the second in 1833. The medieval rules of proof by documents in the actions of debt and covenant technically disappeared with the abolition of the forms of action in 1852, but have left various shadows behind in the modern law.   MRT MACNAIR

W Davies and P Fouracre (eds), *The Settlement of Disputes in Early Medieval Europe* (Cambridge: Cambridge University Press, 1986)

R Bartlett, *Trial by Fire and Water* (Oxford: Clarendon Press, 1986)

property and human rights Any argument that property deserves to be treated as a **human right** plainly depends on one's ideas of property and of human rights. Hence, it is not surprising that there are many different arguments for and against such treatment. For example, liberal theorists often argue that property defines an area of personal **autonomy** that is necessary for the enjoyment of a meaningful life. Against this, some would argue that property is a type of socio-economic right and hence that treating it as an enforceable human right would give it a status it does not warrant. In legal terms, treating property as a human right elevates private property to a special status, where there is some further check on the power of the state to take and regulate property that is not part of 'ordinary' law. It commits the state both to use its power to maintain a system of property (thereby protecting existing entitlements from other persons) and to refrain from modifying or taking those entitlements except under certain conditions.

The primary source of a justiciable human right to property in the United Kingdom is Article 1 of the First Protocol to the **European Convention on Human Rights**. It states that 'every natural or legal person is entitled to the peaceful enjoyment of his possessions'. It requires an interference with property to be lawful and for a legitimate purpose. In addition, in the landmark case, *Sporrong and Lönnroth v Sweden* (1982), the **European Court of Human Rights** decided that an interference with property must strike a 'fair balance' between community and private interests. This often reduces to a question of **compensation**: is the owner entitled to compensation for the taking or regulation of property? And if so, how much must be paid?

Whether the right to property should go further is controversial. In particular, it has been argued that human rights law should guarantee access to the material resources that make life worth living. This could include, for example, a right to the resources needed for basic subsistence, or to access to objects that are central to religious practices or to personal or cultural **identity**, or even to entry to the physical or virtual locations of political debate. While some recognition has been available where the claim is against resources held by the state, claims to resources legally held by other private persons are more problematic. Lawyers often assume that, rather than facilitating claims against private property, a human right to property restricts them. Accordingly, claims that human rights require some kind of access to private property are expressed more often in aspirational terms or 'soft law'. Where these are implemented as enforceable rights to resources or to property held by others, it is usually through social **legislation** rather than human rights litigation.

                    TOM ALLEN

T Allen, *Property and the Human Rights Act 1998* (Oxford: Hart Publishing, 2005)

property and privacy There is plainly a strong link between these two concepts, but it primarily relates to the concept of property as home rather than to the notion of *ownership* of land. Thus a tenant would regard intrusion into her flat by the **police** as just as much of a violation of her privacy as if she owned the property. One conception of **privacy** is that it describes a condition of being *inaccessible* to others, except by choice. While this can be protected through safeguarding the use of one's personal information, it is also importantly protected by the ability to retreat into a physical space in which one is unobserved by the world. Hence, US law recognizes two distinct privacy torts: publication of private facts and intrusion into solitude, the second of which does not require that any information be obtained or published as a result of the intrusion.

England has no comparable pure 'intrusion' tort: however, where information or photographs are obtained through intruding onto someone's property, the case will be treated differently and more seriously than, for instance, where a photograph of a person taken is in a public or semi-public place; moreover liability is more easily established. Privacy torts in New Zealand and the US draw this distinction much more starkly. In the US it is virtually impossible to win a case in which the claimant was in a public or semi-public place when photographed, even if the photograph reveals highly sensitive information such as the fact that a woman was walking from an abortion clinic into a taxi. Similarly, in New Zealand the courts have said that only exceptionally will a claimant be able to recover for a picture taken in public.

The importance of being able to enjoy one's privacy in the home is also reflected in the high importance given in democracies to tight control over the circumstances in which the **police** or other agents of the state may enter the home for the purposes of **arrest** or **search and seizure**. The United States Bill of Rights provides that citizens shall 'be secure in their persons, houses, papers, and effects, against unreasonable searches and seizures...'. In the **United Kingdom**, in the famous case of *Entick v Carrington* (1765), servants of the Secretary of State entered Entick's home and seized some of his papers. In his action for trespass it was found that any intrusion onto private property was a trespass requiring legal authorization, that the servants' plea of executive privilege was unknown to the law, and that the search was therefore unlawful. Camden LJ said, '...every invasion of private property, be it ever so minute, is a trespass [and] liable to an action...'. Crucially, this rule applied to the state as much as it did to any individual. The basic principle still survives today, although there are now numerous statutory grounds upon which agents of the state can enter the home. But there are strict statutory guidelines governing the procedure and grounds for search and seizure.

GAVIN PHILLIPSON

See also: **personal information, disclosure of**

property misdescriptions There are a number of claims which can arise from misdescriptions of property. A false statement of fact, or even of opinion, by a person with superior knowledge or expertise (eg the property owner or salesperson) which materially induces a person to purchase the property can give rise to a claim for misrepresentation. The consequences will differ according to the degree of turpitude, but fraudulent and negligent misrepresentation give the claimant a right to damages (discretionary for innocent) and, subject to various legal bars, the option to set the contract aside.

If the misdescription relates to a term of the contract, an action may be brought for compensation for breach. If the misdescription is substantial, the purchaser may terminate the contract, or, alternatively, seek **specific performance** of a contract for the sale of land with a reduction of the purchase price to compensate for the misdescription.

The Property Misdescriptions Act 1991 deals specifically with the problem of false or misleading statements about property matters in the course of estate agency or property development business. Section 1 makes it an offence, punishable by fine, to make 'a false or misleading statement about a prescribed matter'. The Act does not, however, render any contract void or unenforceable or give any right of action in civil proceedings for any resulting loss. The prescribed matters include location, aspect, view, proximity to any services, places, or amenities, tenure, or estate. It is, however, a defence to show that all reasonable steps were taken and all due diligence was exercised to avoid committing the offence.

PAULA GILIKER

See also: **fraud and misrepresentation**

property offences   *see* **criminal regulation of property relations**

property relations, criminal regulation of   *see* **criminal regulation of property relations**

property, family Unlike many continental jurisdictions where community of property regimes operate to determine the control of property held during **marriage**, the division of assets at the end of marriage and the division of debts, marriage and civil partnership have only a very limited effect on the ownership or use of property in English law. Since the Married Women's Property Act 1882, the basic rule has been that each spouse or civil partner has separate property. Ownership is determined according to the general law; a person who pays for an item, even the matrimonial home, will own it unless he or she gives it to the other. Similarly, each partner can dispose of his or her own property. Neither is liable for the other's debts unless they have acted as guarantor. Even where the couple operates a joint bank account, each spouse will generally retain individual ownership of any item he or she buys using money from the account. Only if the purchase is clearly a joint one will the property be co-owned. For this reason, furniture and other contents of the family home are often not jointly owned. If a couple chooses to hold property jointly, they do so as any other two persons would do.

Joint ownership of the family home is now very common. The high cost of housing, the need to take account of both spouses' income when taking a mortgage, and the practices of building societies and other lenders means that the legal title of the home is put in the names of both spouses, unless one of them acquired it before marriage. Joint ownership of the legal title does not necessarily mean that spouses own equal shares in the value of the property. It is also possible the value to be co-owned even though only one person holds the legal title. Where any land is co-owned, English law imposes a trust to protect the rights of the owners and facilitate transactions. Unless a different arrangement is specified in a trust deed, the shares each person has in the property value will be in proportion to the contribution he or she has made. There is an exception to this where a husband buys property which is put in his wife's name. Unless he can prove otherwise, he is presumed to have made a gift to the wife. This 'presumption of advancement' is now much weaker than it was when a wife was seen as her husband's dependent, and does not operate where a wife puts property in the husband's name.

Separate ownership, of household contents, particularly, is out of step with the notion that marriage and civil partnership is a joint enterprise of equals. In Scotland, the Family Law (Scotland) Act 1985 provides for **co-ownership** of household goods, but not for cars or caravans. In 1988, the **Law Commission** proposed a similar law for England so that that couples would jointly own property bought for their joint use unless the person who paid for it intended otherwise. Any wider form of automatic co-ownership was considered to be too complex and too controversial for wide public support. However, English law was not reformed.

Despite the general rule of separate property there are some limited statutory exceptions which apply to specific property held by a married person. First, under the Matrimonial Property Act 1964, 'savings from any allowance provided by the husband for the expenses of the matrimonial home' are treated as belonging to both spouses in equal shares unless they have made another agreement. Secondly, where a spouse or civil partner makes a contribution which improves property owned by their partner, the Matrimonial Proceedings and Property Act 1970, section 37 provides that the contributor will increase their share in proportion to the increase in value of the property. Thirdly, a spouse or civil partner who owns no share of the matrimonial home was given 'occupation rights' by the Matrimonial Homes Act 1967, these are now found in the Family Law Act 1996. These rights prevent one partner evicting the other from the matrimonial home without a court order, and allow a spouse who is out of occupation to obtain a court order so that he or she can live there. Theoretically, these rights can be enforced against third parties, but this is the case only if the right is registered before other rights come into existence. So rights registered when a relationship fails will not prevent a mortgagee realizing the security created earlier. Only limited protection is provided for the family home against a trustee in bankruptcy; a year after the bankruptcy, the trustee can apply for possession of the property and this can only be refused in exceptional circumstances.

The lack of a concept of family property does not mean that marriage has no effect on property rights. When a marriage is ended by **divorce** or a nullity decree, or a civil partnership is dissolved, the **courts** have wide powers to adjust the ownership of the parties' assets. No similar provision yet exists for cohabitants. The court's powers extend to all property owned by either party, there is no special class of **family property**. The court makes orders for ancillary relief. In contrast in Scotland, the court's powers are restricted to distributing 'matrimonial property' which means the matrimonial home and any property acquired by either party during the marriage and before the separation, other than as a gift from a third party. Under the Inheritance (Provision for Family and Dependents) Act 1975, the courts also have wide powers to redistribute property on the death if a will or intestacy does not make adequate provision for family members. A widow or widower can claim reasonable provision and awards are more generous than for former spouses, cohabitants, other dependants, and children. Tenancies in social housing can also be transferred to certain family members when a tenant dies and the courts can also transfer them on divorce or even where an unmarried couple's relationship breaks down.

JUDITH MASSON

JG Miller, *Family Property and Financial Provision* (Croydon: Tolley, 1993)

See also: **family property**

property, feminist perspectives on   Two key issues are recurring themes in feminist analyses of property: women's access to ownership of property and women 'as' property. These two themes are linked by histories which, in most jurisdictions, consolidated property ownership in the hands of men through the institution of marriage, and inheritance practices which favoured sons over daughters. In countries in which the most important form of property is capital in land, being able to accumulate sufficient wealth to buy land and the legal right, as women, to own it, bring together women's access to paid employment with their domestic roles, especially as wives, as well as with civic rights. In England, until the Married Women's Property Act of 1882, married women could not own freehold land at **common law** (although it was possible for land to be 'held for their benefit' using **trusts**), and their earnings (if any) were deemed the property of their husbands. Under such circumstance, women could not gain full civic status, which importantly brought with it the ability to enter into contracts and the right to vote, and which was, at that time, tied to property ownership.

Drawing on such histories, many feminist scholars (particularly those influenced by Hegel's insistence on a sharp distinction between subject and object) trace women's struggle, from being objects 'owned' by men, to become legal 'persons' with the ability to own property themselves. However, holding sharply to a distinction between object and subject is very obviously challenged when, for instance, ideas of ownership and property become mapped onto 'the body', a significant issue in contemporary scholarship. Destabilizing key aspects of classical property theory is increasingly an aspect of feminist work, which asks such questions as whether extending the idea of 'ownership' is really a good vector for carrying values associated with feminism and for meeting the needs of women; and, indeed, whether 'property theory' rather than the actuality of 'property practices' is the best place to begin.

Meanwhile, and illustrating the argument that it is in the 'messiness' of our everyday lives that we need to begin, such issues as ownership of the family home, especially for those who cohabit outside of marriage and without access to family law, remain crucial. England remains one of the few jurisdictions which has not yet amended the law to extend statutory protection to cohabitants, and it is generally argued that cohabiting women suffer from rules which still tend to look to monetary contributions to the home, rather than taking into account other factors, in disputes on separation. Factors such as the impact of childcare on employment prospects, and the continued patterns of women's domestic labour in caring for families, still constrain women's access to property ownership. Perhaps, some argue, contrary to classical property theory, we should be focusing on rights of 'use', rather than rights arising from 'ownership'.   ANNE BOTTOMLEY

M Davies and N Naffine, *Are Persons Property?* (Aldershot: Ashgate, 2001)

M Radin, *Contested Commodities* (Cambridge, MA: Harvard University Press, 1996)

property, theories of   If property is an institution devised to regulate the use and allocation of things, theories of property are general accounts exploring its many possible forms and actual features. They can be divided into two basic categories: first, justificatory theories that seek to defend a particular model of property; and secondly, theories that analyse its nature and functions.

In contemporary industrialized societies, the dominant model among justificatory theories is private property. It has the support of many philosophers. One of the most enduring is the labour theory of John Locke who concluded that whenever a person 'mixed' their labour with an object, a property right is generated over it. A different defence of private property appears in the utilitarianism of Jeremy Bentham, for whom property is a guarantee of the greatest happiness for the greatest number because it will generate the maximum abundance of wealth by fully rewarding, and thereby encouraging, individual effort. A further set of arguments, Aristotelian and Kantian in origin, recommend private property because of its freedom-maximizing qualities, essential to personal autonomy.

A contrary stream of theorizing is critical of private property and seeks to justify instead collectively-owned, public, and common property. Rousseau is an early exponent, who saw the act of appropriation lauded by Locke as an infringement of the natural rights of other members of society, and the very origin of social inequality. Likewise, for Proudhon private property is 'theft' from the community; while for Marx, private property is a tool for the capitalist class to exploit the proletariat by extracting the surplus value of their labour.

A final group of justificatory theories sits between these extremes. They propose an institutional balance of private and public property in society. So, John Stuart Mill argued that excessive accumulation in the hands of a few is socially harmful and advocated limits on the aggregation of property. Veblen, Tawney, and Rawls recommended even more extensive wealth redistribution.

The second class of property theories focuses on how property affects individuals, groups, and societies. They parallel the range of justificatory theories in their accounts of how private property's function has historically been alternatively beneficial, or destructive, or a blend of both. So, a liberal view of private property, such as that of Hardin, seeks to demonstrate how the rise of private property represents a break with the 'tragedy of the commons' where collective ownership inevitably leads to over-exploitation and ensuing loss for all. Similarly, the 'law and economics' movement explains how the rise of private ownership historically benefits all citizens. Against this position stand accounts, such as Karl Renner's Marxist approach, that see the rise of private property as pernicious in its effects, generating unacceptable inequalities of wealth and power. A compromise position is advanced by Reich and Macpherson who see the rise of the regulatory/welfare state as posing threats to individual autonomy and well-being because of the economic dependency they generate. Accordingly, governments should be legally restrained in the discretion to cut off their largesse; but they should also be obliged to dispense more of it, and redistribute wealth from the more advantaged, in the pursuit of greater equality.

BRENDAN EDGEWORTH

proportionality in EU law   EU law provides for a set of general principles to protect individuals. Amongst these principles, is that of proportionality. This principle restricts authorities in the exercise of their powers by requiring a balance to be struck between the means used and the intended aim. It is used to assess the legality of an exercise of power where a legitimate aim is pursued but at the same time other objectives deserving protection are damaged. Although not expressly mentioned in any provisions, Article 5(3) EC captures the concept by stating that '[a]ny action by the Community shall not go behind what is necessary to achieve the objectives of the Treaty'. The principle has been further developed by the case law of the **European Court of Justice**. The Court uses a two-stage test: first whether the measure is suitable for securing the achievement of the objective; secondly, whether the measure goes beyond what is necessary to achieve it.

The Court applies the principle of proportionality to both Acts of EU institutions and Member States. In the context of the Acts of EU institutions a good example is *R* v *Secretary of State, ex p British American Tobacco* (2002) where the applicants brought an action before the Court alleging that in choosing the legal base of a specific directive the principle of proportionality was violated. In the case of Member States' actions, the Court has used the proportionality test to decide whether measures derogating from EU law to protect legitimate national interests are justifiable.

EUGENIA CARACCIOLO DI TORELLA

G Bermann, 'Proportionality and Subsidiarity' in C Barnard and J Scott (eds), *The Law of the Single European Market* (Oxford: Hart Publishing, 2002)

P Birkinshaw, *European Public Law* (London: Butterworths, 2003)

proportionality in human rights law   In law, few **human rights** are absolute. There will be circumstances when the lawful interference with a right will be permissible, and intriguing questions are raised around who is best placed to make the assessment and the tests that should be adopted. The principle of proportionality is central to the **European Convention on Human Rights**, and therefore the application of the **Human Rights Act 1998** in UK law. In the European Convention system, the key phrase in triggering the principle is 'necessary in a democratic society'. For example, Article 8(1) guarantees the right to private and **family life** but Article 8(2) outlines when an interference with the right may be justified, including the 'necessary in a democratic society' test. In addressing this, the questions to be asked are: Does the interference relate to a pressing social need? Is it proportionate to the legitimate aim pursued? Are the reasons provided relevant and sufficient?

In the Strasbourg system, the 'margin of appreciation' doctrine is particularly important in this context, with the Court often stressing the supervisory nature of its international role, the primacy of national systems, and the significance of acknowledging the direct experience of state authorities. In UK law, reference is made to a 'discretionary area of judgement' when dealing with the actions of public authorities in the different and distinct context of the domestic interpretation and application of Convention rights under the Human Rights Act 1998.

A notion of deference is at work in both instances with **judges** sometimes displaying a marked awareness of the limits of their role. However, as those charged with the interpretation of the law, judges have a clear constitutional mandate for defining the relevant tests, as well as applying them in particular cases.

The assessment will tend to remain context-dependent. However, there are four questions which will inform the application of the principle of proportionality. First, is the legislative objective sufficiently important to justify limiting the right? Secondly, are the measures designed to meet the legislative objective rationally connected to it? Thirdly, are the means used to impair the right or freedom no more than necessary to accomplish the objective? And finally, is a fair balance being struck between the right of the individual and the interests of the community? (*Huang v Secretary of State for the Home Department*; *Kashmiri v Secretary of State for the Home Department* (2007); *de Freitas v Permanent Secretary of Ministry of Agriculture, Fisheries, Lands and Housing* (1999)).

COLIN HARVEY

See also: **derogations in human rights law**

proprietary remedies   Legal **remedies** are generally provided by the enforcement of existing rights or the award of a monetary sum. In certain circumstances, however, a claimant may obtain a proprietary remedy—a new property right over particular assets held by the defendant.

Proprietary remedies take the form of new rights arising in the form of implied **trusts** (trusts imposed by law rather than voluntarily created) and equitable liens or through the transmission of existing legal or equitable rights through the processes of **subrogation** and tracing. All these terms demand further explanation. Implied trusts are characterized as either 'resulting' or 'constructive'. The beneficial interest in property 'results' back to the transferor leaving the transferee with a bare legal title (essentially the obligation to manage the assets for the benefit of the transferor) where title was transferred gratuitously and there is no evidence that the transferee was intended to enjoy the beneficial interest in the property. A constructive trust, in contrast, arises in a variety of contexts where it would be unconscionable for legal owners to enjoy property for their own benefit. Equitable liens (essentially charges over specific assets to secure the payment of personal obligations) arise in a variety of circumstances, often in context of the transitional stages of transfers of property. The process of subrogation allows a claimant to assume and exercise another party's rights, and in some circumstances allows someone who enabled a debtor to pay off a secured debt to enforce the creditor's rights of security against the debtor. The process of tracing, in contrast, provides for owners whose property has been exchanged without their consent to 'trace' their rights in the proceeds of the exchange.

Proprietary remedies offer a number of advantages. Most importantly, they allow a claimant, as the holder of a proprietary right, to have recourse to the relevant assets ahead of the defendant's unsecured creditors—effectively assuring that a claimant has priority in the event of the defendant's being insolvent. Additional benefits include the right to sue third parties who have received the assets in question from an initial recipient, the right to claim any appreciation in value of the assets or to utilize tracing to take advantage of the fact that the proceeds of those assets might be worth more than the original assets, and the right to claim compound rather than simple interest.

There is little agreement as to the principles and policies determining the availability of proprietary remedies. An example of the confusion found in this area is provided by the question as to when, if ever, a transfer motivated by a mistake should result in a proprietary remedy. Generally, judicial analysis has paid too much attention to considerations relating to the defendant's state of mind and not enough to the matter which is typically at stake: the contest between the claimant and the defendant's general creditors.

CRAIG ROTHERHAM

A Burrows, *The Law of Restitution* (London: Butterworths, 2002)

C Rotherham, *Proprietary Remedies in Context* (Oxford: Hart Publishing, 2002)

propriety   The term 'propriety' has been used by theorists of property law to refer to the extended social and political meanings of property ownership. 'Propriety' reflects the relationship of property to the proper social ordering of a **community**. As Carol Rose explains, the purpose of 'property as propriety' is 'to accord to each **person** or entity what is "proper" or "appropriate" to him or her'. Property is seen to be an essential part of good political order, an order which includes the political status and authority of individual **persons**.

In the context of law, the idea that property is a significant determinant of political order can be best illustrated by reference to legal history. In feudal society the political and social order was strongly associated with a hierarchical system of land-holding. Political authority was explicitly connected with a person's status as a land-holder and inequality between people was assumed to be a natural and defensible element of social order. Even after the decline of feudalism, for several centuries property was still regarded as important to a person's ability to participate in political life. Property restrictions on suffrage lasted until the late nineteenth century in Britain and it is only recently that the link between the **House of Lords** and inherited status has been challenged. The system which viewed 'property as propriety' therefore excluded many men from political life, while women's place completely outside the proper political order was enforced both by restrictions on women's ability to own property and by exclusion from suffrage.

An alternative to the set of meanings which connects property to political order and propriety is that property ownership can be seen simply as 'wealth' or as 'commodity' ownership. In the modern context, a person's status is not formally determined by his or her status as an owner of land or other significant resources. In insisting upon the principle of **equality**, liberal political theory distinguishes between the public ordering of the political sphere, and the private system of individual ownership. Public status is differentiated from private status, meaning that in law all people are equal regardless of what they own.

Despite this modern liberal view, the connection between property and propriety still resonates in moral, legal, and political theory. The institution of property is often regarded as essential to individual **autonomy** and the good functioning of a democratic society. In a practical sense, pursuit of legal rights as well as participation in the political sphere can be dependent on a person's socio-economic status. Owners, especially large corporate owners, sometimes exercise a disproportionate level of political influence. In a metaphorical sense, cultural standards of propriety in behaviour can be linked to perceptions of who is deserving of **recognition** as a citizen, and how citizenship rights are distributed. Although formally the system of property as propriety has been dismantled, there are still many cultural and practical reminders of the idea that property is linked to political status and good political order.

MARGARET DAVIES

G Alexander, Commodity and Propriety: Competing Visions of Property in American Legal Thought, 1776–1970 (Chicago: University of Chicago Press, 1999)

C Rose, Property and Persuasion: Essays on the History, Theory, and Rhetoric of Ownership (Boulder: Westview Press, 1994)

prosecution Before the establishment of **police** forces in the mid-nineteenth century in England and Wales, most prosecutions, if they took place at all, were done by **victims**. Only serious public order and political matters were prosecuted by government. Victims had little, if any, help or financial assistance, so gradually the police gradually took over prosecutions although they were not given formal prosecuting powers. Thus the right of victims—indeed, all citizens—to prosecute the majority of offences remains to this day.

Towards the end of the nineteenth century, a professional prosecuting agency was established for England and Wales: the office of the **Director of Public Prosecutions** ('DPP'). This remained responsible for a tiny number of the most serious crimes, for the next 100 years. Thus, for most of the nineteenth and twentieth centuries, the police were solely responsible in most cases for: initial prosecution decisions (whether or not to take no further action ('NFA'), to caution, or to prosecute); what particular charge(s), if any, there would be; and whether, faced with not guilty pleas, to continue cases, drop them, or negotiate **plea bargains**. Although the police were increasingly provided with prosecuting solicitors departments and/or used solicitors and barristers in private practice (the latter were essential for Crown Court cases), the preparatory work, the key decisions, and much of the magistrate court prosecuting was done by the police.

The **Crown Prosecution Service** ('CPS') was created in the 1980s, with the DPP at its head, to curtail police dominance. The aim of the CPS was to prosecute fewer weak and cautionable cases than hitherto, prosecute strong cases more successfully (and help the police to strengthen cases that would otherwise be weak), and make prosecution decision-making more consistent. To these ends, the CPS has gradually been given more of the prosecution powers exercised by the police. Also every case has to satisfy two tests before being prosecuted. The first is evidential: there must be a realistic prospect of conviction. Secondly, prosecution must be in the 'public interest', ie not be suitable for **cautioning**, and not be too minor to be worth the resources involved.

Criminal justice in Scotland was at one time very different to that of the rest of the UK. The Procurator Fiscal Service has for many years handled prosecutions. Its powers are similar to those the CPS has now, and so the systems have converged over time. Similarly, Northern Ireland now has an office of the DPP very much like the CPS. But although all the UK prosecuting authorities now have a relatively central role, they still lack the power and independence of those of many Continental jurisdictions. This is primarily because UK **criminal justice systems** are adversarial, as distinct from inquisitorial systems such as in France. Adversarialism means that each side puts its side of the case as best it can, without trying to get an overview of 'the truth'. UK prosecutors do not get information from defence witnesses. Thus UK prosecutors are, despite protestations to the contrary, police prosecutors.

Not all prosecutions come via the police. There are private prosecutions, which can, however, be taken over by the CPS (or equivalent) and then (when it wishes) dropped. Also, a huge range of offences are enforced by bodies such as the Health and Safety Executive, HM Customs and Revenue, and **environmental agencies**. Unlike the police and CPS (and their equivalents in Northern Ireland and Scotland), these agencies prosecute very rarely, instead employing a range of alternatives aimed at securing compliance with the law, as distinct from being punitive *per se*. English prosecutors could, but do not, adopt this approach: most cases are prosecuted, as distinct from being cautioned. The pattern of prosecutions in England and Wales in the twenty plus years since the CPS was created is unchanged.

The only non-police bodies that behave like the police and CPS are those dealing with social security fraud and TV licence evasion. It cannot be a coincidence that these agencies' offenders, like most of those with whom the police deal, are largely poor and socially marginal. The prosecution system deals most harshly with those who life has treated most harshly—despite the same evidential and public interest tests applying to all law enforcement and prosecution bodies. Similarly, 'political'(eg **Official Secrets** Act) cases and prosecutions of police and **prison** officers seem to be based more on expediency than consistency—not surprising when, in the former case, the government's own **Attorney-General** makes the decisions. One searches in vain for the application of the **rule of law** in relation to prosecutions.   ANDREW SANDERS

K Hawkins, *Law as Last Resort* (Oxford: Oxford University Press, 2002)

A Sanders and R Young, *Criminal Justice* (Oxford: Oxford University Press, 3rd edn, 2007), ch 7

See also: **adversary system; inquisitorial system**

prosecution time limits   *see* **prosecution**

prospective overruling   A court 'overrules' the decision of an earlier court when it decides that a rule laid down in the earlier case should no longer be the law. In general, a change in the law effected by overruling applies 'retrospectively' to the case in which the overruling takes place as well as to

all future cases to which it is relevant. 'Prospective overruling' refers to a situation where the change in the law effected by overruling is not applied to the case in which the overruling takes place but only to future cases to which it is relevant. Changes in the law effected by legislation (as opposed to judicial decisions) generally take effect only prospectively and not retrospectively.

Prospective overruling has a long and controversial history, originating in the decision of the **United States Supreme Court** in *Great Northern Railway Co v Sunburst Oil and Refining Co* (1932), in which Justice Cardozo concluded that there are no insuperable jurisprudential or constitutional obstacles to its adoption. It has been celebrated by some as an innovative technique which allows **judges** to develop the law without disappointing legitimate expectations, but condemned by others, notably Justice Scalia in *Harper v Virginia Dept of Taxation* (1993) as 'the handmaid of judicial activism . . . formulated in the heyday of **legal realism**'. It has also been perceived as offending against the principle of the equal protection of the laws and therefore as constitutionally suspect in its homeland.

However it has been adopted in other jurisdictions, including India, Canada, and New Zealand, and by the **European Court of Justice**. It has not been enthusiastically accepted in England, despite an argument that it would greatly assist in orderly judicial development of the law, perhaps because an unavowed alternative ('not following' a decision as opposed to overruling it with prospective effect) achieves much the same temporal outcome.

In *In re Spectrum Plus Ltd (in liquidation)* (2005) **the House of Lords** accepted that there could be a place for prospective overruling although not in that case itself because the legal profession well understood that the precedent overruled had been regarded with suspicion for some time. Therefore there was no unfairness in adopting the standard practice of overruling retrospectively as well as prospectively.

RICHARD TUR

M Arden, 'Prospective Overruling' (2004) 120 *Law Quarterly Review* 7

RHS Tur, 'Time and Law' (2002) 22 *Oxford Journal of Legal Studies* 463

prospectus   Public companies can raise finance by issuing **securities**, such as **shares** and debentures. The law regulates this process through disclosure. A prospectus is the traditional disclosure document released by a company that issues securities to potential investors. Fundraising provisions generally require the company to prepare a prospectus (or other type of disclosure document) and lodge it with the relevant corporate regulatory authority before making any offer of its securities. Sometimes fundraising provisions go further, by requiring the regulatory authority to examine and formally approve the prospectus or the investment on its merits.

A prospectus will be required when a company makes an offer of its securities to the public or when securities are admitted to trading on a regulated market. Prospectuses perform an investor protection function. Their purpose is to ensure that the company provides all material information that would enable a person acquiring its securities to make a rational and informed investment decision. Some exemptions from disclosure will inevitably exist in situations where the cost and regulatory burden imposed by a prospectus requirement cannot be justified, or where the need for investor protection is less acute. Typical exemptions from the prospectus disclosure requirement include relatively small-scale offerings, or offers to sophisticated or professional investors.

A critical element of any fundraising provisions will be prospectus content. There are different regulatory approaches to the issue of what information must be contained in a prospectus. Some fundraising regimes sometimes adopt a prescriptive 'checklist' approach, specifying in precise detail the information to be included. Other regimes use a general disclosure standard to the effect that a prospectus must contain all information that investors and their professional advisers would reasonably require to be make an informed assessment of the company's financial position and the securities offered. Where circumstances change or there is a material mistake or omission in a prospectus, it will be necessary to submit a supplementary prospectus. If the securities are quoted on a securities exchange, the prospectus must also comply with the exchange's listing rules.

Administrative, civil or criminal sanctions and liability may apply in relation to misleading or deceptive statements or material omissions in a prospectus, and an investor who has suffered loss in reliance on a defective prospectus may be entitled to compensation. Depending on the scope of the relevant prospectus liability regime, a range of persons, including the company, its directors, underwriters, advisers, and experts, may potentially be liable for misstatements and omissions in the prospectus.

Some prospectus liability regimes are fault-based; others are not. Thus, some fundraising regimes impose strict liability for defective disclosure in prospectuses. Other regimes, however, include liability protection, such as 'due diligence' and 'reasonable reliance' defences. A 'due diligence' defence, for example, will exempt persons involved in the preparation and issue of the prospectus from liability, provided they made all reasonable inquiries and were unaware of the defect in the prospectus. The regulatory authority will have a range of powers to ensure compliance with the fundraising provisions.

JENNIFER HILL

See also: **disclosure in financial markets**

prostitution   Prostitution involves one **person** selling sexual services to another. Although the selling of **sex** is not itself a criminal offence under English law, conduct facilitating or flowing from prostitution—such as brothel-keeping (Sexual Offences Act 1956), kerb-crawling (Sexual Offences Act 1985), or causing/controlling prostitution for gain (Sexual Offences Act 2003)—is criminalized; and prostitutes—particularly those working on streets in residential areas—are often penalized for soliciting or loitering (Street Offences Act 1959) or for breach of **anti-social behaviour** orders.

Prostitution can take place in both street and off-street locations, but the lack of visibility of off-street sex markets, together with the wide variety of its forms (strip clubs, massage parlours, brothels, private flats, escort services), mean that more tends to be known about its street counterpart. Links have been suggested between street prostitution and poverty, social exclusion, drug addiction, or domestic abuse. The majority of prostitutes are female and most clients are heterosexual men. However, increasing numbers of men also sell sexual services—usually to other men, although there is also evidence of women paying for sex, particularly from male 'escorts'. In recognition of this, the Sexual Offences Act 2003 has amended previous **legislation** which restricted the definition of 'prostitute' to women. In recent times, there has also been acute concern about the involvement of **minors** and trafficked women in prostitution. Reliable estimates on the scale of these problems are lacking, but new laws designed to curb it in England and Wales were introduced in the Sexual Offences Act 2003.

The question of how best to respond to prostitution has incited heated debate. Some argue that prostitution is an inherently exploitative act in which vulnerable parties are compelled (if not by direct coercion than by dire circumstance) to trade their sex for cash. This is often linked to a claim that prostitution is a form of gender **violence**. It is suggested that commodification of sex is inherently degrading for those involved, and has broader consequences in terms of the objectification of women. At the same time, others insist that the harms associated with prostitution are attributable to the conditions under which sexual exchanges often take place. Many women, it is argued, choose to work as prostitutes and any vulnerability they experience would be significantly reduced by proper regulation of the sex industry, as well as by the development of a less judgmental social response. Each side of this debate draws on regimes elsewhere in Europe in defence of its position. In Sweden, where the purchase of sexual services has been criminalized, commentators argue that there has been a significant reduction in prostitution but critics suggest that this regime has simply 'driven prostitutes underground', placing them at increased risk. By contrast, in The Netherlands, where prostitution is legalized, commentators argue that conditions in the sex industry have improved markedly but critics suggest that this has created a two-tier system in which unregulated establishments still prosper. In a recent consultation paper on prostitution in 2004 (*Paying the Price*), the Home Office offered both models as possible new directions for prostitution regulation in the UK, but ultimately rejected them in preference for minor reform to the status quo, coupled with the development of stronger multi-agency networks designed to support people in leaving prostitution.   VANESSA MUNRO

protected grounds   A key issue within any system of discrimination law will be identifying the 'protected grounds'; in other words, what kinds of discrimination are (or should be) prohibited by law? The first issue to consider is whether law should seek to enumerate an exhaustive list of protected grounds. The second issue concerns the interpretation of the scope of grounds. Providing a legal definition for terms such as 'race' or 'disability' has proven highly contentious.

Three main options can be identified in terms of how law approaches the delineation of prohibited grounds. At one end of the spectrum, there is the 'open-ended' approach, where discrimination is forbidden, but no specific grounds are mentioned in the relevant legal provisions. This is typically found within constitutional documents that speak in broad terms, such as 'everyone is equal before the law'. Within such a framework, any distinction is potentially unlawful, be it between **women** and men, rich and poor, or even tall people and short people. Given that the law's reach will capture all sorts of distinctions, it will be necessary to provide flexibility for **courts** to determine when a difference in treatment may be justified. For example, the taxation systems of most European countries are founded on

distinctions based on level of earnings and these would be commonly regarded as legitimate choices of government.

A variation on the open-ended approach described above is to adopt a 'non-exhaustive' list of protected grounds. Certain grounds will therefore be expressly mentioned in the relevant legal provisions, but this list of grounds will not exclude the possibility that other, unmentioned grounds of discrimination should also enjoy protection. A good illustration is the right to non-discrimination in **Article 14** of the **European Convention on Human Rights** ('ECHR'). This contains a lengthy list of prohibited grounds (such as **sex**, race, **religion**) but concludes with the phrase 'or other status'. This approach combines certainty with adaptability. On the one hand, the lawmakers have identified in advance certain grounds where discrimination is 'suspect', ie particularly deserving of judicial scrutiny. On the other hand, the door has not been closed on the courts recognizing other grounds as also giving rise to unlawful discrimination. This flexibility has been valuable in the application over time of Article 14 ECHR. The courts have been able to reflect social change through acknowledging that distinctions previously viewed as permissible are now regarded as discrimination. Most notably, sexual orientation is not mentioned in Article 14, but it is now well-established in the case law of the **European Court of Human Rights** that distinctions based on sexual orientation may constitute unlawful discrimination.

A 'closed list' approach means that the law exhaustively lists all the protected grounds. Any ground not expressly mentioned will not be a prohibited form of discrimination. The principal advantages of this model are certainty and precision. It is clear to all actors which are the protected grounds. Moreover, knowing the exact list of protected grounds permits the legislature to define in greater detail the circumstances where distinctions based on those grounds are justified. This is the model which has been followed with UK anti-discrimination **legislation**. Discrimination is primarily forbidden on grounds of sex, race, disability, religion or belief, sexual orientation, and age.

Underlying the choice between open and closed list approaches is the assumption that some grounds of discrimination are more deserving of protection than others. Most people would accept that a system of taxation that required higher contributions according to **ethnicity** is more objectionable than a system where the rate of contribution is linked to level of income. 'Race' is typically viewed by courts and legislators as a more suspect classification than income level. Various factors influence whether a ground is treated as particularly suspect (and hence deserving of protection). Immutability is commonly cited as a key ingredient of protected grounds; this is simply the notion that individuals should not suffer discrimination because of characteristics over which they have no control. Sex and ethnicity are relatively immutable, although even these are not absolutely fixed. Another key variable is a history of disadvantage. Where it is evident that a particular group of persons has been socially and economically disadvantaged as a result of shared characteristic, this can propel legislative intervention. The disadvantage experienced by disabled persons in many areas of life was undoubtedly an important influence on the UK **Parliament's** adoption of the Disability Discrimination Act 1995.

Factors such as those described above contribute to explaining why certain grounds have been selected for protection in law whilst others remain unprotected. Yet, the appropriate balance is difficult to strike. Some characteristics that are not normally viewed as suspect might be in a specific situation. As discussed above, distinctions based on income level are not viewed as suspect in the context of taxation, but they would be if eligibility to vote was contingent on income level. Therefore, many legal systems combine general constitutional principles of **equality**, based on an open or non-exhaustive list, with more detailed anti-discrimination legislation, which is restricted to a closed list of grounds. In recent years, there has been a trend to expand the number of grounds found within the closed list.

The second main theme in this area is the definition of the protected grounds. This is pivotal within closed list approaches and it often leads to litigation seeking to stretch the meaning of the protected grounds. As many of the grounds are terms used in everyday speech, it is tempting to assume that their meaning is obvious. Yet, even the ground of 'sex' has given risen to protracted litigation. Anti-discrimination legislation in the UK mostly provides a legal definition of the relevant ground; however, this has not been given in respect of age. This suggests that age is regarded as 'natural' and that a definition would be superfluous.

Beginning with 'sex', this ground principally covers discrimination between women and men. The Sex Discrimination Act 1975 identified marital status as a closely related ground, often used to conceal sex discrimination. Consequently, discrimination *against* married persons is forbidden under the Sex Discrimination Act, although there is no corresponding protection if discrimination occurs

because someone is not married. Sex discrimination also encompasses less favourable treatment related to pregnancy, given that only women can become pregnant. Furthermore, discrimination related to gender reassignment is treated as sex discrimination. In contrast, British courts have rejected the argument that sex discrimination includes discrimination on grounds of sexual orientation. Instead, specific legislative protection has been introduced by both the EU and the UK to forbid discrimination on grounds of sexual orientation.

The Race Relations Act 1976 prohibits discrimination on 'racial grounds', which is defined in section 3(1) as 'colour, race, **nationality** or ethnic or national origins'. Of these grounds, ethnic origin has given rise to the greatest debate. In particular, the courts have recognized that some groups which share a common religious **identity** are simultaneously ethnic groups. In *Mandla v Dowell Lee* (1983), the **House of Lords** decided that Sikhs constituted an ethnic group. Whilst the **judges** differed on the precise way to define an ethnic group, two key factors were evidence of a long-shared history and a distinct cultural tradition. This resulted in uneven protection of religious **communities** depending on their cultural cohesiveness and historical roots. Therefore, Jews have been treated as an ethnic group, but not Rastafarians or Jehovah's Witnesses. These difficulties have been alleviated in recent years as anti-discrimination legislation has introduced specific protection from discrimination on grounds of religion or belief.

Finally, the definition of disability has also proven complex. Section 1(1) of the Disability Discrimination Act 1995 states 'a person has a disability for the purposes of this Act if he has a physical or mental impairment which has a substantial and long-term adverse effect on his ability to carry out normal day-to-day activities'. As a result of this definition, the first hurdle for many litigants is to demonstrate that they have an impairment of sufficient severity to fall within the scope of the Act. Temporary impairments, such as a sprained wrist, will not normally constitute a protected disability. Difficulties have arisen around the interpretation of terms such as 'substantial' adverse effect. For instance, persons who are **HIV** positive, yet presently asymptomatic, were unable to demonstrate that they had an impairment which currently had a substantial adverse effect. Whilst Parliament legislated in 2005 to extend protection to persons who are HIV positive, the underlying problem remains the medical model of disability, focusing on the individual's level of impairment. Therefore, a person who experiences discrimination because their employer wrongly perceives them to be disabled will not be protected under the Act.

MARK BELL

J Gerards, 'Discrimination Grounds' in M Bell, D Schiek, and L Waddington (eds), *Cases, Materials and Text on National, Supranational and International Non-Discrimination Law* (Oxford: Hart Publishing, 2007)

A McColgan, *Discrimination Law—Text, Cases and Materials* (Oxford: Hart Publishing, 2nd edn, 2005)

protest   *see* **civil disobedience; processions and demonstrations; social movements**

Provocation   *see* **justification, excuse and mitigation in criminal law**

psychiatric damage Where personal injury caused by negligence is not physical (eg a broken leg) but is solely psychiatric in nature (eg a depressive illness), special rules and limitations apply which govern the right to **damages**. Liability for what was once called 'nervous shock' has long engendered debate, divided opinion, and been seen by some as controversial. **Courts** once declined to award damages for psychiatric injury in the absence of 'impact' in the form of some kind of contemporaneous physical injury—damage of a type thought to guarantee the genuineness of the claim for something unverifiable by the naked eye. Initially claims for 'mental' damage were greeted with considerable scepticism. Ignorance of the medicine involved, concerns that courts would be deluged with claims and limitless liability, the ramifications for the insurance industry, the potential for feigned claims, inherent difficulties in establishing a causal connection between the alleged negligence and the onset of illness, and perceived administrative and practical difficulties associated with assessing damages combined to produce an entrenched reticence to provide legal redress for disruption to psychiatric health. **Compensation** for actual physical harm was considered a far greater priority for the **common law** than the perceived trivialities of 'hysterical stress'.

This is no longer the position. The common law developed over the years with an increasing knowledge and appreciation of the effect on the human psyche of strong emotion. The ambit of recovery has expanded very slowly however. It remains the case in the United Kingdom that there are significant restrictions on liability for the negligent infliction of psychiatric injury which do not apply to suits for injuries which are purely physical in nature. That those restrictions remain despite better understanding concerning the onset and effect of psychiatric illness continues to evoke criticism. They have been abandoned elsewhere. It is, speaking generally, now easier in some countries such as Australia to obtain damages for psychiatric damage caused through negligence.

What is meant by 'psychiatric damage'? Confusingly, this label has been used interchangeably with 'psychological injury', 'mental harm', and 'emotional distress' as well as the dated expression 'nervous shock'. 'Nervous shock' is an unsuitable description because it does not describe the harm for which compensation may be had. Transient shock does not attract damages. It is the mental and physical consequences which flow from it which may be compensable. In order to succeed, a claimant must suffer legally recognized harm—ie some recognizable psychiatric injury or illness resulting from the infliction of traumatic shock rather than mere mental or emotional distress such as grief, anxiety, fear, or anger. In the UK there can be no recovery for emotions which, however debilitating, fall short of this level of harm. In some jurisdictions, most notably in the United States, the damage threshold is lower. The physical symptoms resulting from shock (eg miscarriages or strokes), although compensable, are treated as conceptually distinct from damage to the psyche.

In the earlier cases which repudiated the 'impact' rule and granted recovery, liability was based on the principle that in order to give rise to a cause of action the 'shock' had to arise from 'a fear of immediate personal injury to oneself'. It was necessary for the claimant to be within the 'zone of danger' and therefore likely to suffer harm through physical impact. Within twenty-five years, the courts were persuaded to remove this restriction.

Dominating this area of the common law are cases where the claimant, safely outside the zone of possible impact, sustains psychiatric injury through the fear or anxiety that another person has been or may be killed, injured, or placed in peril. For many years the primary factors limiting the scope of liability were that the claimant be present at the scene of the accident or event and that he or she sustain psychiatric injury by experiencing it through his or her own 'unaided senses'. Injury suffered in this way was regarded as distinct from injury consequent on being informed of what had occurred by another which injury did not give rise to liability. In most cases the claimant was a close relative, usually a parent or spouse, of the 'primary' **victim** of the defendant's negligence. The relationship between the two was an important factor in the determination of the fundamental inquiry whether the psychiatric damage sustained was reasonably foreseeable to the defendant.

Controversially, some **judges** contemplated recovery where a close relationship of this type was absent and by 'mere' 'bystanders'.

The early 1980s saw important decisions of the highest courts in the UK and Australia. *McLoughlin v O'Brian* (1983) and *Jaensch v Coffey* (1984) eased further restrictions on liability. Earlier cases had affirmed that the determinant of liability was foreseeability of injury through shock. Psychiatric injury was foreseeable (at least to close relatives) even where the relative was absent from the scene of the accident or event but arrived there shortly afterwards—usually as a consequence of having been told of the situation—and saw the 'aftermath'. The **House of Lords** and the High Court of Australia ratified the 'aftermath' doctrine and extended it to cover cases where the claimant never arrived at the scene but saw the relative or loved one injured at hospital a short time later. The heightened emphasis on the role of foreseeability was accompanied by a stance that it was insufficient in itself to ground a duty of care and that policy played a part in the determination of that inquiry.

With these developments came shifts in the balance between factors considered material. Presence at the scene, at one time essential, began to assume less importance. That knowledge of an accident or event came through communication with others was no longer regarded as inevitably fatal. The role of one factor was elevated—the relationship to the injured or endangered person became critical. English courts imposed artificial limits on recovery, confining it in the main to parents and spouses. The position of non-relatives, even where events unfolded before them, became more uncertain.

In the last twenty years or so courts of different jurisdictions have charted different courses. Mass disasters in the UK, most notably Hillsborough in 1989, spawned a series of cases in which the courts here moved to prevent further expansion of liability. During the FA Cup semi-final of that year, ninety-five fans were crushed to death and several hundred injured due to negligence of **police** in allowing overcrowding in a section of the terraces divided from others by a high wire fence. Sixteen claimants, including brothers, fathers, other relatives, and a fiancée, claimed to have sustained psychiatric damage. Some were present in other parts of the ground. Some searched for loved ones at local hospitals and a temporary morgue. Some watched live TV broadcasts or heard news on TV or radio. No claimant succeeded. In *Alcock v Chief Constable of South Yorkshire Police* (1992) the House of Lords ruled that the police did not owe a duty of care to any of the relatives, either on the ground of a lack of a sufficiently close relationship of love and affection or because they had not come within the limits of the 'aftermath' doctrine. Direct perception of trauma and sudden shock were seen as essential. In *White v Chief Constable of South Yorkshire Police* (1999), their Lordships rejected the claims of six police officers who alleged they had been injured psychiatrically as a result of their involvement in the tragedy.

The Hillsborough litigation led to extensive review of the law by the English **Law Commission**. Their 1998 report recommended a statutory scheme removing most of the impediments to recovery affirmed by the House of Lords where there are close ties between the 'primary' accident victim and the claimant. No scheme has been implemented.

The restrictive stance adopted by courts in the UK over the last two decades stands in contrast to the dismantling by Australian courts of artificial barriers to recovery. The landmark decision of the High Court of Australia in *Tame v New South Wales* (2002) decides that the duty question in psychiatric injury cases is to be determined essentially by asking whether such injury was reasonably foreseeable (supported by general policy notions inherent in the concept) and that direct perception, sudden shock, and ordinary fortitude, although relevant to that determination, are not separate prerequisites to liability. The current responses of English and Australian law to secondary victim cases are very different. There is discernible, however, in the last few years a shift in the response of lower court judges in the UK in the direction of the Australian common law model. Recent decisions reflect a more flexible application of the 'aftermath' principle, particularly in **medical negligence**. This is encouraging. Hard cases have produced bad law which can take decades to cure. With the publication in the fifteen years since *Alcock* of a number of significant decisions of lower courts in the UK and of courts elsewhere and the thorough examination by the Law Commission, it is appropriate that the House of Lords revisit this topic. The perfect timing may be following the decision of the Supreme Court of Canada in the first case of this type to come before it scheduled to be argued in 2008 (*Mustapha v Culligan of Canada Ltd*).

NICHOLAS MULLANY

P Handford, *Mullany and Handford's Tort Liability for Psychiatric Damage* (Sydney: Lawbook Co, 2nd edn, 2006)

The Law Commission, *Liability for Psychiatric Illness*, Consultation Paper, No 137 (HMSO, 28 February 1995); *Liability for Psychiatric Illness*, Final Report, Law Com. No 249 (HMSO, 10 March 1998)

See also: **negligence in civil law; tort law**

psychiatry and law The disciplines of psychiatry and law have a long-standing association which has two very distinct dimensions: criminal law and civil law. In the former it is the relationship between law and forensic psychiatry which is familiar to most people. During various stages of criminal proceedings law looks to psychiatric experts for advice on a person's state of mind. For example, in a criminal investigation psychiatrists can advise the police on matters such as profiling of offenders, especially in relation to serious crimes involving sexual or physical violence and serial offending. Prior to trial psychiatrists can advise lawyers on a defendant's mental competence to plead, and the availability of any criminal defences such as whether the defendant may be criminally insane or suffering from diminished responsibility so that she or he cannot be held fully liable in law for their actions. After conviction psychiatrists may be asked for advice in regard to sentencing and the availability of suitable treatment for offenders.

In civil cases one aspect of the psychiatry–law association occurs when lawyers instruct psychiatrists to interview clients to prepare background reports in contemplation of litigation, and subsequently to appear as expert witnesses. This might be done, for example, in relation to tort claims for negligence to demonstrate the existence and effects of psychiatric injury following an accident, or of trauma caused by long-term exposure to harm or stress in the workplace. The entitlement to recover damages for '**nervous shock**' or other forms of psychiatric injury has strict limits in law. Such cases often involve multiple and complex technical issues only one of which is the onus on the claimant to show that a recognized psychiatric illness was caused by the behaviour of the defendant.

Society has an interest in the relationship between psychiatry and law not least because certain psychiatric diagnoses can result in a person's loss of liberty through their compulsory detention in a unit where psychiatric care is delivered. This may not necessarily be as a result of a criminal conviction. Mental health legislation provides for the involuntary detention of persons in other circumstances. Thus, a person may be detained if they are so mentally impaired as to be unable to look after themselves, such that they present an imminent risk of harm to others.

There is an ongoing controversy in relation to persons who have been diagnosed with a psychiatric illness that makes it likely they will cause harm to others even if they have not yet done so, especially where the illness is of a type that will not respond to treatment. Psychiatrists explain that persons diagnosed with severe personality disorders (sometimes described as psychopaths) have non-treatable illnesses. They argue that the mental health regime should not be used to lock up people who cannot benefit from treatment. The government's position is that it has a duty to protect people with serious mental health problems from harming themselves or others, and that in some cases this should extend to their detention even if they have not actually been convicted of a crime. The debate reflects a continuing tension between the appropriate role of psychiatrists within the mental health regime, ie care and treatment, and the expectations the criminal justice system tries to place upon them of a preventive role in identifying and detaining potential offenders.

As noted, psychiatry also plays an important role in non-criminal proceedings where issues concerning autonomy, consent, and capacity feature large in the mental health framework. In addition to psychiatrists' expertise in civil litigation, they are central to decision-making in the care of the elderly mentally infirm and younger persons who suffer from such severe mental impairment that they require institutional care to avoid harm to themselves or others. A key dilemma in these cases is that the mental impairment will almost certainly prevent that person having the capacity to consent to admission to care or to treatment.

There are obvious **human rights** considerations relating to the decision to detain, the conditions of detention, the availability of treatment, and the scope for rehabilitation. This can create questions of the lawfulness of admission and detention. While the principal responsibility for the continuous review of the need for detention lies with the treating psychiatrist, in all cases it is clear that the law requires there to be adequate procedural safeguards for review of clinical decisions by a mental health tribunal or a court.

FIONA RAITT

public appointments The politically advanced democracies are expected to appoint only the best available professionally and ethically suitable persons to salaried posts in the public service, at any level. By contrast, their governments are free to exercise **patronage** in favour of supporting politicians to be ministers in charge of government departments or in favour of other supporters to be political heads of agencies, state-owned industries, and so on; or advisers and members of commissions or policy reviews. Short of glaring conflicts of interest or corrupt links, most countries allow governments to make such patronage appointments on the basis of subjective (political) suitability. Unlike the public service itself, they are not objectively professionalized.

Public service objectivity and rationality—in both appointments and conduct in office—developed in late nineteenth-century Europe to replace historic patronage and to resist corrupt links, notably with the new large capitalist firms. The sociologist Max Weber characterized these values as requiring recruitment (at least to senior, policy-making, posts) without bias and only from the best candidates at public examinations who had gained suitable university degrees. Only ability and potential quality should count. Adequate salary and pension must ensure full-time commitment to a professionalized ethic of rational, impartial, and fair-minded work, whether on policymaking, organizational duties, or public case-loads. All (Germany, Sweden) or some (France, America) of these senior officials may rotate in and out of policymaking posts as governments change, or they may remain in place, serving each elected government impartially (Britain)—but unbiased appointments and ethical professional service are essential.

Low-level public service recruitment has been treated either similarly (Britain) or more politically subjectively (in Italy local political party patronage is exercised at this level and in the American federal government service there is a national policy bias favouring ethnic minorities).

Senior recruitment on Western principles has commonly been pursued by national public service commissions, applying as much true independence from ministerial interference as each country can manage. Creating a senior cadre of properly recruited and ethically committed officials is essential to good governance. But it may inhibit adding new 'outside' senior talent as modern needs develop (eg for financial, semi-commercial, computing, or science-based management tasks). Young officials with such backgrounds may be recruited normally but senior experts must be 'parachuted' in by informal, non-competitive selection. Critics (including offended existing officials) may see the public service ethic suffering from a business ethic, and the state's identity and legitimacy weakened. Partisan or nepotistic bias may also be charged while ministers may claim that they seek only flexibility and necessary public service 'reform'.

The Western democracies constantly urge Weberian principles of public appointment and service upon developing countries where family or tribal obligations produce nepotism (and absenteeism) among officials at all levels. The public service ethic (eg in Britain or Scandinavia) has weakened as state, economy, and civil society have interacted ever more closely. As governance (politics, public policymaking) and commerce each lose some of their distinctive identity, the objective rationality of public service ethics and appointments standards is increasingly vulnerable to the pressures of political rationality.   ANTHONY BARKER

See also: **civil service**

public authorities and recreation   A broad range of public authorities make provision for recreational facilities and opportunities. Local education authorities have particular duties to provide recreational facilities for persons in education. Local authorities have powers to provide for indoor and outdoor facilities for all manner of sports, recreations, and premises for the use of clubs or societies with athletic, social, or recreational objects. Local authorities also have the power to acquire and maintain 'open spaces' being any land, whether enclosed or not, on which there are no buildings or of which not more than one-twentieth part is covered with buildings, and the whole or the remainder of which is laid out as a garden or is used for purposes of recreation, or lies waste and unoccupied.

A local planning authority, as respects any open country in their area, have the power to acquire land compulsorily if they consider that it is requisite and expedient that the public should have access to that land for open-air recreation and that access thereto should be secured by the acquisition of that land. The Secretary of State has similar powers in respect of open country in a national park. A public right of access for recreation can only exist by virtue of a statute giving such a right, or where the owner of open country land enters into an 'access agreement' with the local planning authority. This may be contrasted with the customary rights of inhabitants of an area to use common land for lawful sports and pastimes. There is no common law right to stray over open space or to remain on that space.

The needs of the public to enjoy the open air and recreation are met by various bodies that have been set up for that purpose. The National Trust was incorporated by private Act of Parliament and, although independent of government, its purposes include promoting the permanent preservation for the benefit of the nation of lands and buildings of beauty or historic interest. It also has the power to acquire lands and buildings and to manage them as open spaces or places and buildings for purposes of public recreation, resort, or instruction. The Countryside Commission and the Countryside Council for Wales exercise functions in England and Wales, respectively, for the purposes of encouraging the provision and improvement of facilities for the enjoyment of national parks and the opportunities for open-air recreation therein. The Broads Authority has responsibilities which include the conservation and enhancement of the natural beauty of the Broads and the promotion of their public enjoyment.

The Countryside Commission, and the Countryside Council for Wales, have the duty, in relation to England and Wales respectively, to designate extensive tracts of country as national parks. These are areas which, by reason of their natural beauty and the opportunity they afford for open-air recreation, require measures to ensure the preservation or the conservation and enhancement of such natural beauty, wildlife, and cultural heritage and to promote opportunities for the understanding and enjoyment of their special qualities by the public.

DAMIAN FALKOWSKI

See also: **common land; rambling; rights to roam; village greens**

public bodies, liability of　The issue of liability of public bodies can be addressed by way of an answer to the question of how far public bodies (within which term it is appropriate to include 'public officials') are subject to the same legal liabilities as private bodies and individuals. Any attempt to provide an answer will be complicated, however, by the wide range of public bodies that exist and the range of different types of liability (criminal, civil, statutory, etc) recognized by law. To make the task manageable this entry will concentrate on liability for torts and breaches of contract. It has sometimes been argued that the liability of public bodies should not depend on a finding that a tort and/or breach of contract has occurred; instead public bodies should be liable for all harm which they inflict without legal authority, or all harm caused by their unlawful actions. So far, however, English law has not recognized legal liabilities of this scope.

A first distinction should be drawn between 'public bodies' and the individual **human** beings who perform acts as 'public officials'. With the exception of the **monarch** herself, it is a fundamental of English **constitutional law** that human beings who are 'public officials' are in general subject to the same legal liabilities as other persons *unless and until* they are able to demonstrate a special legal power to behave in a way which would otherwise give rise to liability (or a special immunity). Thus a minister who orders soldiers to enter into another person's property will be liable for the **trespass**, and so will the soldiers, unless he or she can establish that the law has recognized a power to enter the other's property in such circumstances: merely appealing to 'expediency', 'public interest', or 'state security' will not be sufficient.

Although it is generally true that 'public officials' are subject to the same legal liabilities as other persons there are some important exceptions. First, some doctrines exist, most notably the special tort of misfeasance in public office and the availability of exemplary **damages** for arbitrary and oppressive tortious behaviour by a public official, which have imposed additional liabilities as a way of disciplining the behaviour of public officials. Secondly, some fragments of special immunity from ordinary liability exist, such as the rule that a public official who purports to bind a public body to a contract but has no actual or ostensible authority to do so is nonetheless not liable for breach of a warranty of authority.

In order to describe the liability of 'public bodies', as opposed to 'public officials', it is useful to draw a second distinction, between the **Crown** (a term which includes the departments of central government) and the other corporate entities which carry out governmental functions (for instance, executive agencies and local authorities). The latter entities are generally corporations created by statute and are, like 'public officials', generally subject to the same legal liabilities as other persons *unless and until* they are able to demonstrate a special legal power to behave in a way which would otherwise give rise to liability (or a special immunity). By contrast, with regard to tort liability, until the Crown Proceedings Act 1947 the Crown continued to benefit from the proposition that 'the King can do no wrong.' The 1947 Act extended most forms of tort liability to the Crown as if it were 'a private **person** of full age and **capacity**' and also made it possible straightforwardly to bring claims for breach of contract against the Crown. It remains the case, however, that certain **remedies**, particularly **injunctions** and orders for specific performance of contracts, are not available against the Crown in civil proceedings.

The proposition that public bodies are subject to the same tort liabilities as other persons is useful up to a point, that is so far as the public body concerned is performing some task commonly undertaken by private persons, such as driving vehicles, occupying buildings, or designing systems of work for its employees. But where the public body is performing some task which is not commonly undertaken by private persons, such as seeking to regulate the financial services industry, inspecting buildings under construction for by-law compliance, or carrying out the functions of the modern police force, it has proved necessary for the **courts** to consider how far it is appropriate for the law of torts to create private law entitlements with regard to the performance of such tasks. The courts' answers to these questions permit two generalizations. First, it is generally easier to find a private law entitlement that a public body will not act incompetently and inflict additional harm on a claimant than an entitlement that a public body will intervene so as to save a claimant from harm or confer a benefit. Secondly, it is generally easier to find an entitlement to competent performance of a basic task or professional service than an entitlement to a desired standard of political decision-making.

Turning to contractual liability, the proposition that public bodies are subject to the same liability for breach of contract as private persons is generally valid, but subject to two important qualifications. First, contractual liability necessarily presupposes a valid contract, and whilst the Crown has a general power to make contracts some other public bodies only have a limited power. Where a public body, with a limited power to contract, purports to make a contract beyond these limits, then it will be void unless statute prescribes otherwise. Secondly, although the scope of this doctrine is controversial, it is widely believed that public bodies cannot make contracts which restrict their capacity to serve the public interest to too great an extent, and that consequently they may disregard contractual promises without incurring liability where the public interest demands this. In practice, the examples of this doctrine tend to involve contractual promises which might have limited the capacity of the public body concerned to pursue its war aims. RODERICK BAGSHAW

See also: **contract law; negligence in civil law; tort law**

public bodies, status of The term 'public body' might loosely be used to denote a body subject to the rules of public law. However, this statement is fraught with ambiguity. There are a number of different contexts in which the question of a body's 'publicness' might arise and each has its own separate tests to determine a body's status.

The decisions of a public body are potentially susceptible to **judicial review**. Some bodies are clearly public for this purpose. One indication that a body is public is that it is created by statute, though this is not conclusive. Central government departments are rarely statutory and they are clearly public bodies for the purposes of judicial review. Non-statutory bodies can be subject to judicial review where they are performing public functions. The leading authority on this point is the *Datafin* case (1987), in which the City Takeover Panel was held to be susceptible

to judicial review even though it was an industry body with no statutory powers. Private firms may be subject to judicial review in respect of public functions they perform, for example, where they are in a contractual relationship with a public body such that their activities are 'enmeshed' with the public body's performance of its statutory duties. However, it would not be a normal use of language to refer to these bodies as 'public bodies' just because some of their activities are open to judicial review.

Even where a body is clearly public—it is a central government department or a local authority, for example—not all of its decisions will be subject to judicial review. For example, most employment decisions made by public bodies will be regarded as a matter for the ordinary private rules of employment law so public sector employees will not usually be able to bring successful applications for judicial review.

It should also be noted that the susceptibility of a decision to judicial review is, itself, an ambiguous concept. Judicial review is, of course, a procedure. In the well-known case of *O'Reilly v Mackman* (1983), it was held that 'public law' cases ought to be brought as applications for judicial review unless the public law issue was a minor element in an otherwise private law action. Nowadays, this strict rule has been relaxed very considerably so that the **courts** will hear public law cases brought in the ordinary way unless there is a good procedural reason for insisting that the application for judicial review should be used. Thus, the susceptibility of a decision to judicial review should be taken to denote its susceptibility to review using the principles of public law, which may be applied outside the procedural framework of judicial review.

Public bodies are also susceptible to the application of the **Human Rights Act 1998**. Like judicial review, the Act clearly applies to central government departments, local authorities, and statutory bodies. Unlike judicial review, the Act applies to all the activities of these bodies. Thus, public bodies must respect **human rights** in their decisions on contractual and employment matters as well as when exercising their main statutory functions. The Act also applies to bodies 'certain of whose functions are functions of a public nature'. Some commentators have used the term 'hybrid' public body to refer to bodies in this category. However, it may not be helpful to think of such bodies as having public status: a private firm that performs some public functions is still a private firm, but it is subject to the Act when it is performing public functions. The courts have interpreted the concept of a public function relatively restrictively for these purposes, requiring a clear 'governmental' element to the body's activities even where it is acting on behalf of a public authority.

Status as a public body is also important for purposes of EU law. For example, if certain conditions are met, an EU directive can be relied upon in litigation against public bodies but not against private parties. Directives are said to be 'vertically', but not 'horizontally', directly effective. For these purposes a body is public where it has special powers or duties beyond those granted to ordinary citizens. This is a broad definition which has been used to give 'public' status to private firms with special powers, such as utility companies. Similarly, a broad definition of the state is used in connection with Article 28 EC, on free movement of goods. The behaviour of bodies which are supported by the state (such as trade associations or self-regulatory bodies) may be scrutinized for its impact on the free movement of goods.

In addition to the three main areas of judicial review, human rights, and **European Community law**, a body's status as a public body is important for a variety of other purposes. Given the difficulty of defining a public body, some statutes simply list the public bodies to which they apply. This is true of the Parliamentary Commissioner Act 1967 and the Freedom of Information Act 2000. In both cases, the Secretary of State is given a power to add bodies to the list provided that they meet certain broad criteria of 'publicness'.

Finally, it is important to note that a body's status as a public body may affect ordinary civil litigation in various ways. For example, the statutory context in which a public body must act may be taken into account when determining the scope of its duty of care in tort. It is unusual for a duty of care to exist where the public body is acting under statutory powers, rather than statutory duties. The delicate nature of some tasks carried out by public bodies may also influence the courts' view of the duties of care, or the standard of care, that they owe. Actions brought against the **Crown** are subject to the special rules of the Crown Proceedings Act 1947.   ACL DAVIES

public companies   Companies can be classified in a number of different ways. One way is on a public/private axis. There are regulatory consequences to this classification. Public companies are permitted to raise finance by issuing their **securities** to the investing public; private (or proprietary) companies are not. Public companies will also be subject to more intensive **regulation** and more stringent financial reporting requirements than **private companies**.

Although private companies vastly outnumber public companies, the size and market capitalization of public companies are far greater, and most major industrial and commercial businesses adopt the public company form.

Public companies can be either unlisted or listed. Listed public companies are **companies** that are admitted to the official list of a securities exchange, which will enable their securities to be publicly traded on the market operated by the exchange.

A traditional feature of public companies is the division between ownership and control. This means that shareholding is dispersed, with managerial control vested in a cadre of professional corporate managers and the **board of directors**. This contrasts with many private companies, where the shareholders also manage the business. Nonetheless, the managerial structures of public and private companies can be blurred in practice.

International capital markets have in recent years experienced massive growth of private equity. While some commentators have forecast the eclipse of the public company, it is unlikely that such dire predictions will be fulfilled, and the rise of private equity appears to be merely a cyclical development.

JENNIFER HILL

See also: **listing**

public defender   *see* **legal advice and assistance**

public domain   Even though the concept of the public domain in intellectual space has become an integral part of the language governing intellectual property law its precise meaning remains open to debate. Some commentators take the view that material subject to enforceable intellectual property rights, which is nevertheless available to the public, resides in the public domain. However, the more usual understanding of the public domain refers to that part of intellectual space in which either no intellectual property rights are owned or intellectual property rights cannot be enforced. The conception of the public domain employed in this entry reflects this approach.

The idea of the public domain in intellectual space appears to have been derived from **Roman law** concepts relating to physical space. As in Roman law, the importance of the public domain is said to lie in its ability to preserve a zone of relative freedom in which creative and synergistic interactions may take place. The two Roman law concepts most frequently analogized to the concept of the public domain in intellectual space are *res communes* and *res publicae*.

The former refers to things incapable by their nature of being exclusively owned; while the latter refers to things open to use by the public by operation of law despite being subject to ownership rights. In intellectual space, these concepts tend to merge since the identity of those things by their nature incapable of being owned is largely determined by intellectual property law, as is the identity of things open to the public despite the existence of intellectual property rights.

Despite recent imperialistic trends in intellectual property protection, there is a range of things in intellectual space that have been identified by intellectual property law as incapable of being owned. Patent law, for example, rejects the concept of ownership over a range of innovations, including discoveries, scientific theories, and business methods. **Copyright** law rejects the ownership of ideas; and, creative acts falling outside the definition of a copyright work remain in the public domain.

Where intellectual space is subject to intellectual property rights, the public access is generally promoted by three mechanisms: disclosure requirements, limits on duration, and exceptions to the exercise of the exclusive rights of the intellectual property holder. With respect to the first two mechanisms, the provisions of the law automatically defend the public domain, whereas in relation to the last those seeking to use the exceptions must make a case. Despite the existence of these mechanisms, concerns are frequently expressed about the shrinkage of the public domain.

Intellectual property law alone may not be adequate to protect the public domain. However, other laws also regulate activity in intellectual space. These include **censorship**, **obscenity** and **blasphemy** laws, **defamation**, laws governing **national security**, and laws protecting **human rights**, including the right to free speech. Some of these laws have the effect of altering the boundary between the public domain and the propertized zone so that the former is increased at the expense of the latter.

FIONA MACMILLAN

H MacQueen and C Waelde (eds), *Intellectual Property: The Many Faces of the Public Domain* (Cheltenham: Edward Elgar, 2007)

See also: **freedom of speech; patents**

public finances The term 'public finance' refers to an annual process of parliamentary oversight of public revenue and expenditure. It is premised on the constitutional principle that the government cannot raise or spend money without the express authority of Parliament. The annual process gives Parliament control over the government's plans to tax and spend. The **Treasury** has the responsibility of ensuring that the expenditure and taxation plans of the government are coordinated and meet the requirements of statutory authority and parliamentary approval. There are complex and technical procedures for checking that there is legal authority for raising money through taxation and that public money once received is properly managed and receipted. There are also procedures for ensuring that the expenditure of public money is correctly undertaken and that there are properly certified accounts audited by the National Audit Office.

Administration of both direct and indirect taxation is undertaken by Her Majesty's Revenue and Customs under the direction, control, and authority of the Treasury. Revenue derived from all forms of taxation is paid into a central fund known as the Consolidated Fund. In the case of borrowing and lending there is a separate fund known as the National Loans Fund. Both funds are managed by the **Bank of England**.

Public expenditure is organized on an annual basis. The control of public expenditure is one of the most important aspects of public finances. The planning of public expenditure is based on the government's fiscal rules, including the *Code for Fiscal Stability*, and the principle that government borrowing should only be undertaken as a means of investing. The Treasury has the pivotal role, both in terms of authorizing expenditure and also in supervising, prioritizing, and implementing good-value-for-money strategies. One economic device used by the Treasury is the New Control Total ('NCT'), which is used to set limits on departmental programme expenditure. Planning is undertaken on a three-year cycle and the NCT is monitored over each annual cycle of expenditure. Treasury control is exercised through the appointment of an Accounting Officer, usually the permanent secretary, in each department. As well as signing accounts, the Accounting Officer is responsible for appearing before the Public Accounts Committee, Parliament's influential public spending watchdog, which is chaired by a senior opposition MP. There are strict rules and procedures to be observed by Accounting Officers in discharging their responsibilities. The aim is to achieve financial propriety, and also prudent and economical administration that is efficient and effective. The Accounting Officer is also responsible for agencies set up within the departmental portfolio. In the case of an agency that operates at 'arms length' from the department, an Accounting Officer will be appointed within the agency.

Control of public expenditure rests on the principle of parliamentary authority and supervision. The Comptroller and **Auditor General** ('CAG') is an independent officer of the Parliament appointed to ensure that public money is used for the purposes intended. The CAG is head of the National Audit Office, set up in 1983 to oversee central government public spending. The National Audit Office also undertakes value for money examinations to ensure that a department's spending achieves efficiency through economy and effectiveness.

Government accounting practices have been subject to intense scrutiny in recent years and this has led to major changes. The Government Resources and Accounts Act 2000 introduced the concept of resource accounting. This replaced the cash-based system and requires all government departments to produce a balance sheet that includes assets and liabilities alongside an analysis of expenditure aims and objectives. The new system is intended to improve the quality and amount of information available to Parliament. Another innovation in accounting is the concept of 'whole government accounts'. This means that public sector accounts should be modelled on the private sector idea of balance sheets showing profit and loss accounts. The aim of this innovation is further to improve accountability.

Public finances and the 'power of the purse' lie at the heart of government decision-making. Managing the economy involves a balance between taxation and expenditure. The Treasury is responsible for making available appropriate economic data to inform the key economic decisions of the government of the day. The Treasury operates a computer model of the United Kingdom economy, which is regularly used to forecast economic activity. Economic measurements and key performance data provided regularly by the Treasury play an essential role in the development of economic strategy in relation to public finances.   JOHN MCELDOWNEY

public health   Public health medicine has changed since the nineteenth century as infectious diseases such as cholera have been checked or eradicated via state-led initiatives such as improved sanitation and vaccination. Consequent changes in patterns of causes of death, types of ill-health, and understandings of disease have all altered the focus of public health **regulation**. Increases in life expectancy, aspirations in keeping with the WHO definition of health as 'a state of complete physical, mental and social well being and not merely the absence of disease or infirmity', and the high proportion of the population dying from incompletely understood chronic complaints like cancer and cardio-vascular conditions have together led to today's focus on lifestyle and environmental factors in public health policy.

Under Article 11 of the European Social Charter, the United Kingdom must take steps to remove the causes of ill-health, prevent disease, and advise citizens on how to look after their health. This raises issues of how far public health concerns justify state involvement in citizens' private lives, definitions and causes of health and ill health, and the allocation of resources and responsibility for maintaining citizens' health. The stress on individual **responsibility** characterizing governments in the UK, taken together with the impact of chronic conditions on scarce resources, means that citizens are increasingly exhorted to conduct their lives in ways which maximize health or risk losing access to healthcare. Yet epidemiological studies reveal that socio-economic factors such as poverty and poor housing may have more of a detrimental affect on health than the lifestyle practices currently targeted.

Agencies seeking to protect the health of citizens by ensuring clean air, water, and **pollution** control are usually overseen by local authorities or specialist agencies rather than health authorities. Health professionals, however, have powers to control what people may do in order to advance public health conferred by the National Assistance Acts of 1948 and 1951 and by the Public Health (Control of Diseases) Act 1984. Local authorities have statutory responsibility for infectious disease control but will usually appoint health authority employees to carry out associated duties. Under the Public Health Act 1984, doctors should recognize and inform local authority officials of an increasing number of notifiable diseases or suffer criminal penalties. Drastic powers of entry and investigation, compulsory medical examination, and powers to remove, isolate, and detain unwilling **persons** suffering from notifiable diseases are all in place. Those who are not suffering from such a disease may also be compulsorily removed and disinfected.

How far public health powers should override **human rights**, especially in relation to anti-terrorist measures, is a contentious issue. While protection of public health is accepted as a limitation on many of the freedoms in the **European Convention on Human Rights**, much public health **legislation** predates human rights obligations being enshrined in the law. For example, under the AIDS (Control) Act 1987, health authorities and NHS trusts are obliged to provide statistics on AIDS sufferers and services provided for them. The powers under the Act include compulsory examination, removal to hospital, detention in hospital, and the removal and isolation of dead bodies. Nonetheless, more recent legislation also provides powers which take precedence over human rights, such as provisions in the **Human Tissue** Act 2005 allowing tissue samples from the dead or the living to be obtained without consent in extreme public health emergencies. How far such coercion may be justified in relation to protecting the public's health is difficult to specify in policy or legislation. Hence procedures to challenge and limit public health powers on human rights grounds are vital, but are not always part of public health law in the UK.   ROBIN MACKENZIE

public illegality   Public illegality has no formal meaning in law but is a topic in the name of which a variety of research has been conducted which focuses on what has been termed 'governmental excess', the illegal or unlawful **acts or omissions** of those with governing functions. What ties this research together are concerns about the moral and political dimensions of law, as well as the relationship between space and **community**. Thus, this area overlaps with understandings about the relationship between law and geography.

Such acts or omissions do not necessarily have repercussions in law. Public illegality may refer to the opinion held by a certain section of the public that an illegal act has been committed. Often, then, research conducted in the name of public illegality is controversial. Two illustrations may assist. Depending on one's view, Tony Blair committed an act of public illegality by allowing the UK to take part in what many perceive to be an unlawful invasion of Iraq. Although attempts were made to fit such an act within legal rules, they were unsuccessful. The head teacher of a school in Hackney who refused discounted tickets to a ballet of Romeo and Juliet, for reasons which were represented as the heterosexual nature of the work, was not subject to legal disciplinary processes, although law operated to structure relations between the school and the local education authority.

Sometimes, though, law and legal process are at the heart of the grievance. For example, one of the most prominent acts of public illegality during the 1980s and 1990s—the sale by Conservative-led Westminster City Council of its properties in key marginal wards on the basis that owner-occupiers were more likely to vote Conservative (inaccurately referred to as 'gerrymandering')—did result in a finding by the **House of Lords** that the council's leader and deputy had engaged in an unlawful policy (*Porter v Magill* (2002)). What this case also demonstrated was that

the line between public and private illegality can be narrow. The council's leader, Dame Shirley Porter, had a high profile and her view that owner-occupiers were more likely to vote conservative was personally held, although one which is commonly believed to be the case. She, together with her deputy, was fined personally (£26.5 million). Other examples of public illegality, which have been reversed by the **courts,** include the decision of Leicester City Council not to allow a local rugby team to use a council sports ground because members of the team had played in **apartheid** South Africa (*Wheeler v Leicester CC* (1985)); and the decision of Somerset County Council to ban hunting on part of its land (*R v Somerset CC, ex p Fewings* (1995)). As has been observed, such decisions would have been unimpeachable if made privately, but because moral and political concerns were improperly included within those decisions made by public bodies, they were found to be unlawful.

DAVID COWAN

D Cooper, *Governing out of Order: Space, Law and the Politics of Belonging* (London/New York: Rivers Oram, 1998)
N Blomley, D Delaney and R Ford, *The Legal Geographies Reader* (Oxford: Blackwell, 2001)

public inquiries   *see* inquiries

public interest immunity   The due administration of justice requires that litigants have access to relevant documents held by the other party. This is known as disclosure and inspection. Rules of court procedure allow a claim (or 'plea') to withhold documents from disclosure or inspection on grounds of the public interest. These rules maintain the **common law** principle of public interest immunity ('PII'). It is not confined to cases involving **Crown** or public bodies, though it almost invariably will involve such bodies.

The rationale for the rule allowing non-disclosure in the public interest is the overriding need to protect certain kinds of information from dissemination, even in litigation. The claim to withhold will be successful where serious injury would be caused to the processes of government and public service by disclosure, to protect the identity of informers or to ensure the supply of reliable information. Confidentiality alone is not a sufficient basis for allowing non-disclosure, but it may be 'a very material consideration to bear in mind' when the immunity is claimed. In cases where the documents in question are held by central government, a claim for public interest immunity is made in what is called a PII 'certificate', issued in the name of a government minister, to the effect that the conditions for granting of immunity are satisfied in the particular case.

Until the aftermath of the notorious events surrounding the *Matrix Churchill* episode, which was controversial partly because of the use of PII certificates in a criminal trial, PII claims could be made on the basis of the specific contents of documents—a 'contents claim'—or on the basis that the documents belonged to a class of documents which ought not, in the public interest, to be disclosed—a 'class claim'. In the latter case, the class to which the documents belonged had to be specified. In December 1996, the government announced that as far as it was concerned, class claims would no longer be made. Claims to immunity from disclosure would be based only on the contents of documents. This announcement did not apply to the police or local authorities; but it did apply to prosecuting authorities, which are Crown bodies. In *R v Chief Constable of the West Midlands Police, ex p Wiley* (1995) the **House of Lords** held that written statements made in the course of investigations of complaints against the police could no longer be protected from disclosure on a class basis, but only on a contents basis. However, it was subsequently held that the investigating officer's report and papers could be protected as a class.

A plea for public interest immunity should only be made if the public interest in non-disclosure of the documents outweighs the public interest in securing justice—which will normally be served by disclosure. The court has to balance those interests. Once it is established that there are justifiable grounds for making a claim for immunity, the burden rests on the party seeking disclosure to convince the court that the balance of considerations favours disclosure. Where a judge entertains doubts about the bona fides, plausibility or clarity of the reasons given in support of a claim for immunity, the judge may inspect the documents.

The widespread use of PII certificates in criminal trials was seen as endangering the fairness of the trial from a defendant's perspective. The House of Lords, moved by the jurisprudence of the **European Court of Human Rights**, has ruled that in a criminal trial, the 'golden rule' is that full disclosure should be made to the defence of any material held by the prosecution which weakens its case or strengthens that of the defendant. Where this golden rule cannot be adhered to fully, or at all, because of an overriding public interest and risk of serious injury to that interest, some derogation may be justified; but only to the minimum extent necessary to protect the public interest and 'never to imperil the overall fairness of the trial'. Under the Criminal Procedure and Investigations Act 1996 and a code of practice, a new framework of rules governs the release of information to the defence by prosecutors.

In cases where **national security** is in issue before the Special Immigration Appeals Commission, 'special counsel' may be appointed. Their use has been extended to non terrorist cases. These may be given closed material which is not shown to their 'client'. The Prevention of Terrorism Act 2005 makes provision for rules of court to deal with 'control order' procedures and non-disclosure of material.

PATRICK BIRKINSHAW

public interest litigation in developing countries   The conventional rubric 'public interest litigation' ('PIL') requires vigilance because while labels can be borrowed, histories cannot. Typically North American in its origins, the rubric misleads comparative analyses. In developing societies ('DSs'), democratizing judicial access is a part of a wider social and political process and movement rather than an affair of technical or 'lawyer's' law reform. The agenda, actors, resources, processes, and outcomes of this movement vary greatly from the comparable Euro-American experience. The politics of naming requires a more adequate historical grasp of the developmental dynamic. I have minted the notion of 'social action litigation' ('SAL') for India and other DSs societies, which enables a differentiation of the DSs SAL experience from PIL developments elsewhere.

The Indian SAL itinerary begins with epistolary jurisdiction, a process in which individual citizens write letters to justices of the Supreme Court of India ('SCI') and the High Courts ('HC') and argue before them as petitioners-in-person for the vindication of human and constitutional rights of the worst-off co-citizens and persons. The SCI relaxes *locus standi* (ie the rules governing the right to approach the court) dramatically; and via the device of socio-legal commissions of enquiry into the processes of fact-finding and monitoring manages to ascertain the truth about state lawlessness and governmental deviance. Typically, SAL stands presented not so much as adverersial contention but as acts of executive-judicial partnership summoning best forms of social cooperation between the state and the active citizenry. SAL thus remains an act of profound political and civic conversation across governance institutions. The SCI actually creates new judicially-enunciated human rights not previously textualized or scripted in the Indian Constitution (such as a right to due process of law, privacy, information, speedy trial, bail, health, shelter, environmental integrity, livelihood, literacy, and so on.) Circumspectly, it also invokes the power to punish for **contempt of court**, or its threat, in aid of its constitutional jurisdiction to 'do complete justice'. The Indian SAL remarkably thrives on a fiduciary conception of adjudicative power which legitimates the exercise of apex judicial power as a public trust on behalf of the worst-off peoples. Slowly but surely the Supreme Court *of* India converts itself into a Supreme Court *for* India's worst-off peoples. This inaugural charismatic SAL moment dissipates somewhat with the routinization of SAL, a process of administrative judicial coping with the judicial overload thus created, especially by farming out cases to the HC and related national human rights institutions.

SAL has fostered a different kind of judicial globalization, a form in which the DSs apex courts have begun to take human suffering seriously as a way of taking human rights seriously. In South Asia (barring Burma) SAL has been institutionalized creatively and variously. The mood, message, and method of the Indian SAL have also spread across many Anglophone African societies, notably, for example, South Africa, Tanzania, Botswana, and Nigeria. And SAL now thrives also in Eastern and Central Europe, too. COCOS (comparative constitutional studies) traditions need to engage with different achievements of semi-autonomous DSs fields of judicial activism. Although it is generally felt that authoritarian political closure curbs resilient judicial activism, the stirrings of SAL in People's Republic of China and its persistence in Pakistan suggest otherwise.

Outcries of judicial governance and, even, usurpation have greeted the DSs SAL experience. These, in part, derive 'legitimacy' from the North philosophic cottage industry, which proselytizes a universal theory of judicial process, power, and role under which the apex justices ought not transgress the thresholds of governance. Unfortunately colonial/neo-colonial teaching and research traditions often counteract the gains of postcolonial judicial activism. However, DSs SAL activist justices continue to innovate the doctrine of fiduciary powers of judicial review, refusing to mime any mechanical understanding of the separation of powers doctrine.

The disorders of governance desires often lead to outcries encoding inane, and often insidious, protests against 'judicial governance' to which SAL jurisdiction responds in the first place in therapeutic modes! A vigorous neo-liberal effort now under way seeks the structural adjustment of SAL habitats of judicial activism. Perforce, when most DSs SAL justices now pursue a hands-off policy of restraint in matters of macroeconomic policy, they still manage to retain the activist power to interrogate, and often arrest, microeconomic impacts on human rights. This displacement has often led to activist disenchantment with specific SAL processes and outcomes; yet human rights and social movement folks resiliently continue to offer SAL docket explosion suggesting the triumph of normative expectations that continue to survive existential disappointments.

Unlike the PIL genre, the DSs SAL continues to pursue struggles to re-democratize governance and to offer in full plenitude a reconfiguration of the old notions of the **rule of law,** thus entailing Sisyphean labours incrementally to make the state more *ethical*, governance more *just*, and power of the corrupt sovereign, in all its hiding places, increasingly more *accountable*. Even so, the spectres of neo-liberalization and the two 'terror' wars—the war *of* and *on* 'terror'—continue to haunt DSs SAL.

UPENDRA BAXI

public offer Efficient capital markets are increasingly important in a globalized economy. **Public companies** may engage in fundraising by offering their securities to the investing public. They may decide to raise equity finance by issuing **shares**, including ordinary and preference shares. They can also issue debt **securities**, such as debentures, or various kinds of hybrid security, which share features of both debt and equity.

Companies will often operate as private companies until the need to raise capital in financial markets arises. An initial public offering ('IPOFF') refers to the first time that a company raises capital through a public share issue. Private companies are prohibited from offering their securities to the public. In view of this restriction, a private company would first need to convert to public company status before it could make a public offer of its securities.

A public company that wishes to raise funds through a public offer may decide to list on a formal securities exchange, which will increase the liquidity of the securities for the benefit of investors. When a company's securities are admitted to the official list and become quoted, they can then be traded on the market operated by the exchange.

Although the decision to raise funds from the public is a business decision, it has important legal ramifications. The law regulates public offers of securities by requiring a company to make extensive disclosure to potential investors via a **prospectus**. Prospectus-based disclosure, which serves an investor protection function, will involve significant compliance costs for the company. The relevant fundraising regime will carve out some exceptions to the general prospectus requirement for public offers of securities. Exemptions often exist, for instance, in relation to small-scale offerings, where the regulatory burden of requiring a prospectus may be disproportionate, or offers made to sophisticated or professional investors, who are regarded as less in need of protection.

A company may also seek to raise finance by making an offer of shares to existing shareholders through a rights issue. Under a rights issue, the company will offer its shares to its own members on a *pro rata* basis at a discounted price relative to market value. A rights issue may be renounceable or non-renounceable. Where the company is listed on a securities exchange, trading in the rights will usually occur. Whether a rights issue requires the company to prepare a prospectus will depend upon the scope of the disclosure obligation, and its exemptions, under the relevant fundraising regime.

When a company makes a public offer of its securities, it may require advice from a range of professionals, including investment bankers, lawyers, and accountants; and this will result in significant expense. The company may also choose to engage an underwriter, to guard against the danger that the public offer of securities will be undersubscribed. Underwriting protects the company, by typically requiring the underwriter to take up any shortfall in shares. There will be significant additional fees where the company engages an underwriter in relation to a public offer of securities.

JENNIFER HILL

public order, criminal regulation of　*see* **criminal regulation of public order**

public policy　The legal concept of 'public policy' identifies a set of fundamental values that qualify or override the specific rules of statute or **precedent**. Negatively, as Article 6 of the French Civil Code makes clear, all specific rights and duties established by law are subject to the qualification that they do not infringe public policy. Positively, public policy offers a justification for action, typically by public authorities, in circumstances that are not specifically defined in legal texts. Public policy offers a conceptual framework through which the law is able to reconcile its specific provisions with the fundamental rights of other people or the need to protect social institutions. For example, individuals are free to agree to contracts, but the law will not enforce contracts that interfere with fundamental rights, such as a contract to become a slave. Likewise, a person can freely stipulate conditions for gifts made by her

will, but could not insist that the beneficiary purchase a peerage, since this is unlawful. Even where there is no express provision, public authorities will be allowed to use their powers to protect fundamental social institutions. The content of 'public policy' is not defined specifically and varies from time-to-time. This concept thus provides a significant margin of appreciation to decision-makers. The values that have to be balanced are often complex. This indeterminacy has led to frequent arguments that this is an inappropriate basis for judicial decisions and judges are encouraged to use the argument with caution.

JOHN BELL

public procurement　Public procurement is the process by which government enters into contracts for the supply of assets, goods, and services. Unlike many continental European countries, the UK does not have a special law of government contracts. They are governed by the ordinary **common law** principles as amended by statute. Central government has a common law power to make contracts supplemented by statutory powers; local government powers are purely statutory. This means that, whilst local government contracting is subject to legal control through **judicial review**, the same does not necessarily apply to contracting by central government unless there is some special public law element such as the use of the contract to implement a public policy rather than simply for commercial purposes, or a statutory basis for the contracting.

The most important controls on public procurement come from **European Union** law. A Directive sets out a number of procedural requirements for the award of different types of public contracts above a specified value, including advertising in the EU Official Journal. A number of different procedures are available for the selection of those who will bid for a contract; in most cases the 'open' or 'restricted' procedures will apply, where the public body chooses between all or a selection of bidders. In limited circumstances the 'competitive dialogue' or 'negotiated' procedures may be used; these permit negotiation with preferred bidders to agree contractual terms. The Directive also limits the grounds on which decisions as to the award of the contract can be based; contracts must be awarded on the basis of the lowest price or the 'most economically advantageous' offer (best value for money); the UK Government adopts the latter. There is some scope for incorporating into the process environmental or social criteria (such as meeting the needs of disadvantaged groups). The Directive is incorporated into UK law by regulations, and the High Court can award damages for their breach. In addition to these requirements, the UK Office of Government Commerce publishes detailed rules on the procurement process applying to all government departments. As well as the EU rules, the **World Trade Organization** Government Procurement Agreement may require non-discrimination between signatory states in the public procurement of some goods and services.

In the past, procurement was used a means of implementing important aspects of public policy, including a non-statutory prices and incomes policy and preferential treatment for workshops employing the disabled. This use of contract is now much less important. A more recent type of procurement is through the use of the private finance initiative ('PFI'), where government contracts with a private company to build and run facilities such as schools and hospitals, with payment either from government during the life of the asset or directly by users through charges. The essence of the initiative is to transfer risk from the public to the private sector, though this has not always been fully achieved in practice.   TONY PROSSER

public rights of passage over land and water   In England, Wales, and Scotland, no one may enter land belonging to another for the purpose of recreation or passage without a right or permission. Permission may be express or implied but can be withdrawn. It is, nonetheless, important because a great deal of land held by public and quasi-public bodies is subject to permissive access.

The following are the principal public rights of passage. In England and Wales the Countryside and Rights of Way Act 2000 confers on the public a right to enter on foot and remain on 'access land' for the purposes of open-air recreation. 'Access land' refers principally to land shown on conclusive maps as 'open country' or registered common land and land above 600 metres where no map has been published. In addition, England and Wales are well endowed with public rights of way, which the public may use for passage. Most such ways arise through deemed dedication under the Highways Act 1980. Local authorities are required to prepare and maintain a 'definitive map' of these routes. Unless already included in a conclusive map under the 2000 Act, the public have a right of access for air and recreation to 'urban commons' (as defined in the Law of Property Act 1925). Registered town and village greens are also subject to a right of access by the inhabitants for certain recreational purposes. Statutory powers continue to be available to provide, by agreement or order, for linear or area access to the countryside by the public but

these powers are little used in practice. The public also have a right of passage on navigable rivers; and access is customarily permitted to the foreshore, the area of land between the high and low water marks, where it still belongs to the Crown.

Public rights of passage over land and water in Scotland differ in important respects from those in England and Wales. The principal right is to be found in Part 1 of the Land Reform (Scotland) Act 2003 which confers a public right of non-motorized access, subject to certain exceptions, to all land and inland water for recreational purposes and for passage. The right is not confined to a linear form. The advent of this right is likely to reduce the importance of other public rights of passage in Scotland but they are mentioned below for completeness. If a linear route across land satisfies certain requirements, it may be recognized as a public right of way. There is, however, no definitive map in Scotland and it can be difficult to determine the status of a route. This right is to be distinguished from a private or servitude way which, in certain cases, may be exercised by a defined community but not by the public at large. The public also have a right of passage on navigable rivers and, where it belongs to the Crown, a right of access along the foreshore.   JEREMY ROWAN ROBINSON

public service broadcasting   The **United Kingdom** is unusual in that it has a dual system of public service broadcasting ('PSB'). It has in the British Broadcasting Corporation ('BBC') the world's most celebrated PSB institution; but it has also required the main commercial broadcasters to commit themselves to PSB requirements. This is for reasons of competitive quality: high quality programming is more likely to be produced where there is no single monopoly provider. Although the PSB provision in different **European Union** countries varies hugely, there is also a limited attempt to provide harmonization of basic standards through the EU 'Television Without Frontiers' Directive which, for example, contains provisions for protection of children and limitations on advertising, and for a quota for European productions. A new version of the Directive was agreed in 2007.

The BBC derives its powers from a Royal Charter rather than from statute; this is supplemented by an Agreement between the Minister and the BBC which sets out the main PSB requirements. A new Charter and Agreement came into effect at the beginning of 2007. The Charter sets out the 'public purposes' of the BBC, which include sustaining citizenship and civil society, promoting education and learning, and stimulating creativity and cultural excellence.

They are to be promoted through output consisting of 'information, education and entertainment'. The Charter also states that the BBC is to be independent from the government; the latter has limited powers to require announcements to be broadcast and to ban programmes, though these have rarely been used. The Agreement sets out more fully how the public purposes are to be achieved and the detailed regulatory obligations on such matters as accuracy and impartiality, and on fairness and content standards (such as portrayal of explicit and violent content) where the BBC is subject to the same obligations as the commercial public service broadcasters. There is a complex system of quotas to ensure that the BBC provides a large proportion of original productions (rather than programmes bought in ready-made), shows regional programmes and commissions independently-made productions. As the BBC offers extensive commercial services, the Agreement also requires there to be fair trading policies to avoid unfair competition with the private sector.

The BBC is funded by a licence fee payable by the users of television sets and radios; it carries no advertising. A new formula for annual increases in the licence fee was set by the Government in 2007.

Under the new arrangements put in place in 2007, the BBC is governed by a BBC Trust, appointed by the Queen on government advice; it is not a trust in the technical legal sense but is both the 'sovereign body' within the BBC and the supervisor of its management and programmes. The Trust is responsible for setting the overall direction of the BBC, approving high-level strategy and budgets, and assessing its performance. Management is by a separate Executive Board, accountable to the Trust. In some of its activities, for example aspects of fair competition, the BBC is subject to regulation by the Office of Communications (see below) but otherwise there is no independent regulator, the Trust performing this function instead. As regards accountability, one of the functions of the Trust is to represent the interests of licence fee payers, and it is required to establish Audience Councils to provide input from the viewers and listeners. The BBC is subject to the Freedom of Information Act 2005 except in relation to information held for the purposes of journalism, art, or literature. Judicial review may also be sought to enforce the requirements in the licence and agreement.

In addition to the role of the BBC, the Communications Act 2003 established a new broadcasting regulator, the Office of Communications ('Ofcom'), covering the commercial broadcasters. It must report periodically on the extent to which all broadcasters have met the public service remit set out in the Act; this includes providing programmes which deal with a wide range of subject matters, which meet the needs and satisfy the interests of as many different audiences as possible, which are properly balanced, and which maintain high general standards of quality. The Act also sets public service remits for three of the commercial broadcasters; ITV, Channel 4, and Channel 5. For ITV and Channel 5 the remit is 'the provision of a range of high quality and diverse programming'; for Channel 4 the programmes must additionally demonstrate innovation, appeal to the tastes and interests of a culturally diverse society, and exhibit a distinctive character. Enforcement of these remits is through a combination of self-regulation by the broadcasters and, if this fails, action by Ofcom. The licences under which these commercial public service broadcasters operate also contain detailed public service requirements, such as those for original productions; these are enforced by Ofcom. Ofcom also enforces the basic rules on fairness and programme standards in relation to all commercial broadcasters; it has responsibility for broadcast advertising although matters of advertising content are delegated to the Advertising Standards Authority. Finance for PSB obligations of commercial broadcasters is from advertising; they do not receive any of the licence fee.

The system of public service broadcasting is currently under some strain. The future of the BBC has been made secure for at least the next ten years under the new Charter and Agreement. However, commercial broadcasters have argued that their public service requirements are becoming unsustainable due to the proliferation of new digital channels. This removes a traditional justification for the requirements, namely the broadcasters' access, to a scarce resource. Channel proliferation also divides up advertising revenues thus causing the broadcasters financial difficulties in meeting their PSB remits. In its first review of PSB, in 2003–4, Ofcom concluded that PSB provision is still necessary on democratic and citizenship grounds, but will be difficult to sustain in its present form in the new digital age. It proposed the public funding of a new public service publisher to preserve some plurality of PSB provision by commissioning public service programmes which would then be shown on a variety of channels.

TONY PROSSER

See also: **European broadcasting obligations**

public sphere   The separation between public and private spheres of life is a notable characteristic of liberal democratic societies. The public sphere is conventionally associated with affairs of government; the private sphere with the family and intimate relations, but the distinction between them is ambiguous and complex. This is because of the existence of two further significant areas of activity that are neither wholly public nor wholly private. These hybrid areas are civil society and the market, both of which are domains of freedom.

Within civil society, or the social public, individuals are free to associate, litigate, travel, worship, and participate in education. Within the market, individuals are free to contract and engage in entrepreneurialism and private sector employment. While private benefits accrue from all these activities, they are supported by government and may be subject to legal **regulation**, although the degree to which they should be regulated is a matter of ongoing contestation.

The private sphere in the sense of family was historically thought to be a realm beyond law altogether, for there, as Lord Atkin famously expressed it, 'the King's writ does not seek to run' (*Balfour v Balfour* (1919)). Instead of the law of the state, the 'law of the father' prevailed, a position that was trenchantly critiqued by feminist activists in the late twentieth century. As a result, government now intervenes selectively in the private sphere in matters such as **domestic violence** but continues to uphold the notion of separate spheres. Even in the case of **sex** discrimination **legislation**, which involves measures designed to effect **equality** between men and women, legal regulation is diffident about addressing inequalities that derive from the private sphere, such as the disproportionate responsibility for caring that is assigned to women.

Equality, like freedom, has come to be viewed as a hallmark of the public sphere and has similarly acquired a masculine hue, because only men could formerly participate in public life as equals. By dint of association, the characterization of the public sphere as the domain of law and **justice** has also marked it as a realm of rationality and universality. The private sphere *qua* family came to be associated with inequality and un-freedom because of domination by a master. As a site of reproduction, care, and affectivity, the private sphere has also been marked as feminine.

The public/private configurations are not set in stone but constantly shifting because of their susceptibility to prevailing socio-political values. The emergence of the **welfare state** resulted in an expansion of the public sphere and government regulation in the early twentieth century, but the **privatization** of public goods and the privileging of the market by the century's end shifted the balance in favour of the private. Nevertheless, it is the public sphere that has facilitated and promoted the market; there is no invisible hand at work here. Rather than representing two analytically distinct spheres, the public/private dichotomy might more properly be thought of as an ideological tool; private being invoked when the state espouses non-intervention and public to the contrary.

MARGARET THORNTON

MR Thornton (ed), *Public and Private: Feminist Legal Debates* (Melbourne: Oxford University Press, 1995)
J Weintraub and K Kumar (eds), *Public and Private in Thought and Practice: Perspectives on a Grand Dichotomy* (Chicago: Chicago University Press, 1997)

punishment, history of Punishment practices shifted significantly during the eighteenth and nineteenth centuries. In the early modern period, punishment was commonly inflicted in public on the body of the offender. From the eighteenth century corporal punishment declined; **capital punishment** declined from the early nineteenth century and, increasingly, **prison** became the key institution for dealing with offenders. The difficulty lies in explaining these changes. Was it the result of a growing humanitarianism? Or was it the manifestation of a society increasingly concerned with discipline, surveillance, and categorization by experts?

At the beginning of the eighteenth century, the punishment for felony was death. Judicial **discretion**, royal clemency, and practices such as benefit of clergy, by which a degree of literacy enabled an offender to escape the gallows, limited the numbers executed. Nevertheless, **judges** and politicians were keen to develop a major secondary punishment for serious offenders. The answer was found in transportation and, following **legislation** of 1718, for the next 140 years convicts were sent first to the American colonies and then, from 1787, to Australia. Various forms of mutilation—branding, cutting off ears, and slitting noses—declined in the early eighteenth century, and judges increasingly began to limit sentences of whipping.

Gaols were used for holding accused before trial and for punishing petty offenders with sentences that rarely amounted to more than a year. By the close of the eighteenth century, however, there were significant and increasing calls for an improved system of prisons in which offenders might be punished by the deprivation of their liberty, but also encouraged to recognize their errors and learn the virtues of hard work. In England the first national convict prison (Millbank) was opened in 1816 and the first national penitentiary (Pentonville) in 1842. A prison inspectorate was created to establish uniformity and good practice across the patchwork of provincial gaols in 1835, and in 1877 all prisons were brought under central government control.

Legislative reforms in the second quarter of the nineteenth century reduced the number of capital statutes so that, by the 1840s, little more than murder and **treason** were punishable by death. The last public execution was carried out in 1868. Unlike its contemporaries in continental Europe and in much of America, the British legislature clung to corporal punishment. It disappeared as a judicial sentence only in 1948 and remained as an option for punishing disruptive and violent male prisoners for another fifteen years.

There were periodic swings of opinion as to whether prison should principally punish or rehabilitate offenders. From the end of the Victorian period, however, **rehabilitation** became more prominent. In addition, there were attempts to keep many petty and first-time offenders out of prison with the development of **probation** and training institutions for juveniles. These practices continued in the inter-war years with restrictions on the imprisonment of **fine** defaulters, the closure of many local prisons and the establishment of the first open prison. In the last quarter of the twentieth century, however, faced with soaring crime rates and with penal policy becoming high on the political agenda, there was an expansion of the numbers incarcerated and a new prison-building programme. CLIVE EMSLEY

See also: **law and order debates; politics of crime control**

punishment, theories of Theories of punishment are theories of how (if at all) systems of criminal punishment can be justified. They have traditionally been categorized into backward-looking, or retributivist, theories, which find punishment's justification in its character as an appropriate response to the crime for which it is imposed; and forward-looking, or consequentialist, theories, which find punishment's justification in its beneficial consequences.

Retributivists focus on the idea of desert. Those who culpably commit crimes 'deserve to suffer'— to suffer something burdensome, whose severity is proportional to the seriousness of their crime; the purpose of punishment is to impose that deserved burden. The challenge for retributivists is to make morally plausible sense of this intuitively forceful but obscure idea of desert, as the justifying relationship between crime and punishment: what is it about crime that makes punishment an appropriate response? Various accounts have been offered: some talk of punishment as annulling the crime, others of restoring a balance that crime disturbs, others of negating the message that the crime sends out. Critics argue that such metaphors obscure more than they clarify, and that what really underpins retributivist theories is either the less attractive face of revenge, or an implicit appeal to some beneficial consequences of punishment.

Consequentialists hold that punishment is justified if and only if it is an efficient means to some further social good which outweighs the harms that punishment certainly causes. The most obvious such good is the reduction of crime, which punishment can help to achieve by deterring, incapacitating, or perhaps reforming or rehabilitating potential offenders (for whilst punishment is supposed to be imposed on actual offenders, its benefits lie in the effects that it, or its threat, will have on those who might otherwise commit future offences). Consequentialists face difficult empirical questions about the extent to which punishment, or particular systems or modes of punishment, can be cost-effective means to such social goods. They also face moral questions about whether such ends, beneficial as they certainly are, can justify such means. One such question concerns the punishment of the innocent: such ends as deterrence might sometimes be efficiently served by framing someone known (by those who frame him) to be innocent, so long as he is publicly thought to be guilty; consequentialists are then accused of being willing to sanction the injustice of deliberately punishing the innocent.

That charge might be met by a 'mixed' theory of punishment that combines retributivist and consequentialist ideas. Punishment is still, on such a view, justified as an efficient means to suitable social goods: but our pursuit of those goods is constrained by the requirements of **justice**, in particular the demand that we should punish only those who deserve punishment because they committed crimes (and should punish them no more harshly than they deserve). The retributivist idea of desert is thus given a role, not as setting punishment's positive aim, but as setting limits on what we may do in pursuit of the ends set by consequentialist theories. Such mixed theories will not justify the deliberate punishment of the innocent: but they face moral questions about the punishment of the guilty. For, critics argue, if we use punishment simply as a threat to deter potential offenders; or if we punish people in order to incapacitate them, or deter others, from crime: we treat those who are either punished or threatened with punishment not as responsible citizens, but rather as amoral beings who must be controlled or coerced—which is not how a liberal state should treat its citizens. (Central to this objection is the claim that we do not forfeit our standing as citizens when we break the law.)

Some try to meet this problem by emphasizing punishment's communicative dimension. Punishment does not merely impose burdens. It communicates a message, to the offender and to others: a message that condemns the crime for which it is imposed and censures the person who committed it. Punishment thus addresses offenders as responsible citizens, who deserve such censure for their wrongdoing. The key challenge for such theorists is to explain why we should communicate this message by the imposition of materially burdensome punishments, rather than by verbal declarations or by purely symbolic punishments. Some then appeal to a qualified form of deterrence: the material burdens of punishment provide a further, prudential incentive to obedience for those who are insufficiently moved by censure's moral message. Others argue that appropriate materially burdensome punishments can themselves serve the ends of communication: they can help to drive the message of punishment home, and to bring offenders to confront their wrongdoing more adequately. Both kinds of view give punishment a forward-looking aim—dissuading offenders from re-offending; but, they argue, what makes punishment the appropriate way to pursue that aim is precisely its retributive character as a deserved, condemnatory response to the crimes for which it is imposed.

Finally, we must not forget that the question is not *how* punishment can be justified, but *whether* it can be justified. 'Abolitionist' theorists argue that it cannot be: that our responses to crime should seek not the coercive imposition of punitive pain (which is neither productive nor humane), but constructive ways of repairing the harm that was done and of restoring the relationships that were damaged. Some advocate 'restorative' (rather than retributive) justice, which is achieved not by formal trials and punishments, but by informal **mediation** between offenders, **victims,** and other interested parties, resulting in some agreed reparation that serves to reconcile those who were in conflict. One question about such proposals is whether they could be plausibly applied to more serious crimes, or only to relatively minor offences. A related question is whether they take the idea of wrongdoing seriously enough: advocates of punishment will argue that at least the more serious kinds of

crime require a response that formally condemns the wrongdoing that they involve—ie that they require punishment.   ANTONY DUFF

RA Duff, 'Punishment', in LaFollette (ed), *Oxford Handbook of Practical Ethics* (Oxford: Oxford University Press, 2003)

See also: **incapacitation theory; rehabilitation; restorative justice; retribution**

pupillage *see* **vocational legal education**

pyramid schemes Pyramid selling offers a potential investor the possibility of high returns based on recruiting other individuals into the pyramid. The vice of a pyramid scheme is that it must ultimately collapse, and the great majority of individuals who are at the bottom of the pyramid when this occurs will lose money, although a small minority at the top of the pyramid will have made a return on their investment. Because a small minority do profit, it is possible to develop initial enthusiasm for the pyramid. Pyramid selling is a variation on the classic Ponzi swindle, and will usually have the following characteristics: payments to participants based on the recruitment of other participants; commissions to participants based on sales by their recruits and on the initial investment by a recruit (such as a training course). A pyramid selling structure does not expand because of the retail sale of any product but by recruitment of further participants into the pyramid.

Pyramids and Ponzis proliferated during the 1990s partly through the growth of the internet. A scheme entitled 'Hearts of Women Empowering Women' arrived in the UK in 2000 and attracted about 150,000 participants. This traded on the concept that individuals provided other members with 'emotional support'. The scheme involved an initial investment of £3,000 that purchased a 'heart' and you progressed up the pyramid by recruiting others. Like a Ponzi, the initial members did benefit and so spread good news about the scheme that was bound to fail with the majority losing their investment.

Pyramid selling is not easy to regulate because, like many trade practices, it is difficult to distinguish from legitimate forms of selling such as direct or multi-level marketing. Detailed regulation invites the Holmesian 'bad man' to exploit any loophole. The law often uses a 'badges of fraud' approach striking down schemes that have particular characteristics such as head-hunting fees. This is the approach in English law. The EU Unfair Commercial Practices Directive that will be implemented in the UK in 2008 defines a pyramid scheme as an arrangement in which a consumer 'gives consideration for the opportunity to receive compensation that is derived primarily from the introduction of other consumers into the scheme rather than from the sale or consumption of products'. Although direct marketing schemes may be distinguished from pyramids, they have also often been criticized for holding out unrealistic promises of earnings; and the law requires the warning 'Do not be misled by claims that high earnings are easily achieved' in advertisements for direct marketing.   IAIN RAMSAY

M Zuckoff, *Ponzi's Scheme: The True Story of a Financial Legend* (New York: Random House, 2005)

Q

qualifying periods *see* **unfair dismissal**

quality of products Traditionally consumers of products have been able to assess for themselves the quality of what they are buying. Economic, social, and technological changes in the twentieth century, associated with mass production and the rise of the consumer society, greatly increased the diversity and complexity of products available in the consumer market place. The underpinning of legal rights and duties associated with consumer products has accordingly become more important. Legal guarantees of quality are important not only for consumers but also for producers. Where consumers are unable to ascertain the quality, in the absence of legal protections, they may be less willing to buy, or only willing to pay a lower price. For producers it is claimed that the absence of quality guarantees creates incentives to pass off lower quality goods as higher quality goods. This in turn tends to undermine markets completely, which is in no-one's interests. Thus, the arguments go, legal guarantees of quality are good for all.

The main basis for such legal guarantees of quality is the contract between buyers and sellers. The Sale of Goods Act 1979 implies into every such contract conditions for the sale of goods. These include requirements that goods are of satisfactory quality, that they correspond to their description (for example in the case of packaged goods), and that they correspond to a sample (for example where the buyer sees a sample of flooring rather than the actual flooring to be supplied). Additionally where a particular purpose is made known by the buyer to the seller prior to conclusion of the contract, the goods should be fit for that purpose. Where businesses sell to consumers these conditions apply even if the business purports to exclude them (for example with a sign stating 'no refunds'). Breach of these quality conditions entitles the buyer to **damages** (compensation) reflecting the difference in price between the goods contracted for and the goods as provided, or to repair or a replacement, or to reject the goods and get a full refund. Which of these remedies is available in the particular case depends upon a number of circumstances concerning the transaction. The legal rules relating to goods supplied as part of a wider contract under which services are supplied also (as with installations, repairs, and so on) are distinct but create similar rights for consumers.

The strict legal position concerning what the standards are and who is responsible is, in many cases, overridden by the voluntary conduct of businesses. First, larger retailers frequently offer refunds to consumers who simply change their minds, even if the goods are not faulty. Secondly, many manufacturers offer product guarantees direct to consumers even though their legal responsibilities would otherwise only be owed to the distributors or retailers to whom they sold the products. These manufacturers' guarantees are the source of widespread confusion. The existence of a manufacturer's guarantee does not reduce or eliminate the responsibility of the retailer; but in practice it may be more straightforward to rely on such a guarantee for replacement or repair of a defective product. The only exception to the general proposition that a manufacturer who does not offer a guarantee does not owe duties to ultimate consumers—because they are not in a contract with them—arises where defective products cause damage to people or to other things.

COLIN SCOTT

See also: **product defects**

quality of services The legal rules governing the provision of services generally are rooted in the contract between consumer and service provider. Service providers commonly use what is called a 'standard form contract' to set down the various terms and conditions relating to the provision of the service. In the absence of written or oral terms the law implies certain terms into such contracts, for example that the service will be provided within a reasonable time and at a reasonable charge, and to a workmanlike standard. The provisions as to the charge or price only have effect where no price is agreed beforehand,

and would commonly come into play where goods such as cars are left for repair and the scope of the required repairs is uncertain at the outset. Where services are not delivered properly then consumers are entitled to compensation (**damages**). In some instances it may be possible for a consumer who has not yet paid the full price for the service to pay a lesser amount, thus effectively retaining their compensation rather than having to claim it. This would be equally true for a poor quality restaurant meal as for poor quality building work.

The widespread use of standard form contracts by businesses—a necessity in the age of mass contracting heralded by mass transit by trains in the nineteenth century—created concern that unfair terms were being imposed on consumers. A particular area of difficulty relates to things going wrong in the contract. What if the film handed in for processing is lost, or the consumer fails to make payment on their mobile phone contract? A number of legislative measures are designed to address some of the most common **unfair contract terms** and have the effect of making them unenforceable.

Many areas of service provision are too complicated to rely on general contractual rules and are subject to more specific rules contained in legislation. This is true of the provision of many financial services such as insurance, banking, and consumer credit, and for other important areas of service provision such as holidays. Extra statutory protection is given to those who buy package holidays (defined as pre-arranged combinations of two or more of transport, accommodation, or other significant tourist services). In particular, the legislation fixes on the tour operators responsibility for providing compensation when things go wrong.

Some areas of service provision are governed almost exclusively by special legislation and consequently fall outside of the general contractual rules. This used to be the case for utility services such as water, energy, and telecommunications, though the privatization and liberalization of these services has increasingly put them within contractual arrangements. A key area where services are provided under a statutory regime is health. Thus treatment by a doctor or in a hospital within the **National Health Service** is typically not governed by contractual rules (but the position is different where private healthcare is paid for directly or by an insurer). A central consequence of this is that the patient who receives poor service has no contractual remedy, but if they are harmed they may seek compensation within the rules of **tort law**.   COLIN SCOTT

See also: **holidays, recreational**

quangos   *see* **public bodies, status of**

quasi-public land   'Quasi-public' land is the term used to denote land or space which serves a public function but which is privately owned. The archetypal example of quasi-public land is the modern town-centre shopping complex, but the term is not confined solely to these. The notion of the 'quasi-public' suggests the phenomenon of the increasing privatization of urban space. There is a growing tension, in such quasi-public spaces, between the public interest in access to sites of civic, social, and economic importance and the traditional **common law** power of exclusion from land possessed by private landowners. In some jurisdictions, such as United States, Canada, and Australia, the courts have recognized that owners of quasi-public land should only be able to exclude members of the public on reasonable grounds; but in England and Wales, the traditional law of **trespass** still broadly applies, with the result that members of the public can be excluded from land on more arbitrary grounds. Tension has grown more acute in recent years as increasing amounts of land are sold to private developers. At the heart of the notion of 'quasi-public' land is a crucial opposition between inclusory and exclusory conceptualizations of civic society. The question ultimately invoked by the notion of 'quasi-public' land is the question of what kind of society we want to build, and what kind of controls we should place on the power of the private landowner to control the vital public spaces in which we exercise important social, economic, and civil freedoms.   ANNA GREAR

Quebec law   *see* **mixed jurisdictions**

Queen Caroline   Caroline of Brunswick (1768–1821) was the estranged wife of George IV. She is best known for the failed divorce proceedings brought against her in 1820. Caroline married the Prince of Wales in April 1795, but they soon separated. Thereafter, and especially during the period 1814–1820 when she lived abroad, Caroline was rumoured to have had several romantic affairs. The government sponsored inquiries into her conduct in 1806 and 1818. The latter contained serious allegations, but the actual divorce proceedings were prompted by her decision to return to England and assert her rights as Queen.

It was possible in 1820 to end a marriage by statute, if the wife had committed adultery. The husband had first to obtain a separation in an **ecclesiastical court**, and then a judgment in a **common law court** for the injury he had suffered. Regardless of Caroline's guilt, such a course was impossible in her case. An ecclesiastical court would not separate a couple on the grounds of a wife's adultery if her husband had committed the same offence. Moreover, a husband was not recognized as suffering an injury if his wife committed adultery while they were living separately. Ministers, therefore, turned to a wholly parliamentary mechanism. Adultery by a Queen was addressed in the Treason Act 1351, but the circumstance of Caroline's alleged adultery meant that the statute did not apply. Parliament, however, could pass legislation to criminalize conduct retrospectively. Very serious conduct could be criminalized by a Bill of attainder, and less serious by a Bill of pains and penalties. At the second reading of such a Bill, the process could assume a judicial character. Counsel could be heard and witnesses called, while peers and MPs could participate in cross-examination. This 'trial' could determine whether the Bill succeeded.

On 5 July the government introduced a Bill of pains and penalties in the **House of Lords** depriving Caroline of her royal status and dissolving her marriage on the grounds of adultery. The 'trial' of the second reading lasted from 17 August until 6 November, and was far from straightforward. Complicated legal questions were raised, but the greater difficulties resulted from the unusual nature of the process, with which neither the peers nor the lawyers were familiar. The case also had a significant political dimension, as some Opposition politicians supported Caroline to embarrass the King and the government.

The second reading was approved, as was the proposal to retain the divorce clause. However, some peers supported the clause because they believed it would render the Bill more objectionable in the Commons. When the vote on the third reading was taken, the majority fell to nine. Anticipating failure in the **House of Commons**, the government moved to delay consideration for six months. Effectively, the Bill was defeated. The immediate aftermath was public adulation for Caroline, but in the subsequent months both her popularity and her value as a political weapon faded. She died on 5 August 1821, less than a month after her husband's coronation.

ROSE MELIKAN

queer 'Queer' is a contested term often used to describe people who do not identify as heterosexual and monogamous, including **lesbians**, gay men, bisexual women and men, and those who practice polyamory. 'Queer' sexuality is often opposed to 'straight' sexuality. While it was once a term of abuse and was considered highly offensive, 'queer' was reclaimed in the late 1980s and early 1990s by activist groups such as Queer Nation and ACT UP. These groups brought together different sexual **minorities** and adopted deliberately provocative tactics in an effort to disrupt sexual 'normality' in politics and cultural life. The term 'queer' is now used in a positive way, but is still regarded as offensive when used derisively.

Not all lesbian, gay, and bisexual people accept the term 'queer'. There are various reasons for this. Lesbians have argued that the word 'queer' traditionally refers to homosexual men and erases lesbian **identity**. 'Queer' has also been associated with a more radical political agenda than the movement for lesbian and gay rights. Legal reforms welcomed by many in **same-sex relationships**, such as the recognition of all sexual relationships in forms which replicate **marriage**, are often regarded with suspicion by radical queer theorists or activists because they reinforce heterosexual norms. 'Queer' has also been said to carry too many negative connotations: the adoption of the term can be seen as an internalization of these negative meanings, rather than a positive affirmation of alternative sexualities.

At the same time, in its broad popular usage 'queer' means 'non-heterosexual' and does not refer to a **person's** sex- or gender-identity. Thus, people with either **transsexual** identities or intersex conditions, especially those who identify as heterosexual, have also often objected to being referred to as 'queer'.

Despite such criticisms, in the practical context of 'queer' communities, the term can be conveniently inclusive and retains a strong presence as both a general term to refer to different identities and a marker of radically disruptive politics and theory.

In the more theoretical context 'queer' refers to practices or ideas which challenge or deliberately transgress fixed **gender** identities or sexualities. **Queer theory** combines postmodernism's anti-universalist thinking with gay and lesbian studies. It is based on the insight that 'normal' identity types are the product of social and political influences, and are not natural or universal categories. According to Judith Butler, for instance, **sex** and gender are constantly being created and recreated by *performances* in a social domain: sexual identities are inherently unstable and fluid constructs which become stable and often oppressive through conformity to fixed social expectations. In order to challenge oppression based on sex and sexuality, it is necessary to find ways of disrupting 'normal' categories, by highlighting the ambiguous and dynamic potential of identity. In legal thought, queer theory has been used to challenge some of the accepted categories of law, such as relationships, the family, and property. It has also been used to highlight and subvert law's institutional power to create social concepts of normal and marginal sexuality.   MARGARET DAVIES

J Butler, *Gender Trouble: Feminism and the Subversion of Identity* (New York: Routledge, 1990)

D Halperin, *Saint Foucault: Towards a Gay Hagiography* (New York: Oxford University Press, 1995)

queer politics   Queer politics refers to an activist approach adopted by some **lesbians**, gay men, and other sexual dissidents. It emerged in the United States, and its provocative ideas and methods proved popular with those who felt unrepresented by mainstream sexuality politics. Queer politics traces its origins to 1990, when a group labelled themselves 'Queer Nation', and appropriated a derogatory term of abuse for political ends. The methods associated with queer politics include demonstrations, **civil disobedience**, and public performance, often in unlikely places including shopping malls and corporate headquarters. The sometimes militant and radical tone of queer politics must be situated within the broader conservative politics of the period, particularly as regards attitudes towards **HIV/AIDS**. Targets of queer politics included corporate culture, churches, the military, and politicians. One of the more controversial tactics of queer politics was the 'outing' of well-known, closeted lesbians and gay men. Queer politics was organizationally diffuse, which contrasted to the increasingly disciplined and corporatist politics found elsewhere within the lesbian and gay movement.

Queer politics is a deliberately ambiguous term, and both its aims and 'membership' were deliberately different from more liberal, mainstream politics. The term queer is sometimes used as a synonym for lesbian, gay, and bisexual. However, it was also intended to have a more inclusive meaning, embracing all those who identified as being outside of the dominant norms of respectable heterosexuality. This might include, for example, sadomasochists, fetishists, and 'swingers'. Not surprisingly, queer politics was unappealing for those lesbians and gay men who identified more closely with mainstream society or who rejected this sexual politics. Thus, like queer theory, queer politics had the potential to challenge rigid sexual **identity** categories, but it could also prove exclusionary and divisive.

The strategy and tactics of queer politics are sometimes distinguished from the 'assimilationist' lesbian and gay movements in the United States and, to a lesser extent, the United Kingdom. Although gay politics of the late 1960s and early 1970s was often revolutionary and liberationist in its aspirations, it became increasingly focused on the achievement of legal rights to **equality** through the **courts**. These claims were often made on the basis of the normalcy, sameness, immutability, and the respectability of lesbians and gay men. By contrast, queer politics emphasized shock value, outrageous behaviour, cultural spectacle, and a rejection both of mainstream 'family values' and the coherence and stability of sexual identity. However, such crude distinctions fail to capture the complexity and richness of sexual politics. Aspects of queer politics, for example, have centred on rights, and lesbian feminist politics has been wary of legal strategies for social change in favour of cultural transformation.

In recent years, queer political activist groups in the United States have disbanded, but queer politics continues under different names. Many of the ideas articulated through queer politics remain important, particularly for those who are sceptical of the strategic importance of same-sex **marriage** in gay politics, and who are disappointed by the centrality of consumerism in some quarters of the gay community.   CARL STYCHIN

M Warner (ed), *Fear of a Queer Planet: Queer Politics and Social Theory* (Minneapolis: University of Minnesota Press, 1993)

EK Sedgwick, *Tendencies* (Durham: Duke University Press, 1993)

queer theory   Queer theory is a diverse body of scholarship that emerged primarily within North American and British universities beginning in the late 1980s. Originating within humanities departments, queer theory subsequently proved valuable for academics within other fields. Queer theory is eclectic, and it draws insights from psychoanalysis, Marxism, deconstruction, feminism, semiotics, and poststructuralism. At times, queer theory has been criticized for being inaccessible and reliant upon jargon. However, queer theory can be understood simply as the analysis of texts in order to render problematic the rigid hetero/homosexual binary, and to demonstrate that the coherence of heterosexuality is dependent upon homosexuality as its 'other'. Queer theorists seek to demonstrate that it is through the maintenance of rigid sexual **identity** categories that sexual dissidents have been labelled, regulated, and repudiated.

Given this academic project, the label 'queer theory' is unsurprising. Unlike terms such as '**lesbian**' or 'gay', queer has a more ambiguous and broad meaning, and queer theory seeks to use this (usually) derogatory term as a way of troubling sexual identity categories. It is argued that the construction of rigid sexual identities, including 'lesbian' or 'gay', provides the framework within which a system of compulsory heterosexuality can flourish. The destabilization of the categories thus becomes both a theoretical as well as a political project (the latter is often referred to as 'queer politics'). Sexuality has been described by queer theorists (particularly Judith Butler) as 'performative', rather than as 'natural'. Consequently, practices such as drag and sadomasochism have assumed an important role given their emphasis on performance and artifice.

A more fluid conception of sexual identity also has been advocated within queer theory as a means of responding to exclusions within lesbian and gay politics and theory. For example, queer theory has paid particular attention to the role of bisexual and transgendered people.

Queer theory has provided important insights for the analysis of legal texts. Queer legal theorists problematize the legal **regulation** of identity categories. They also critically analyse political strategies and expose the limitations of claims for **equality**, 'sameness', and 'normalcy'. Rather than advocating the social incorporation of a **minority** group, queer legal theorists have critically interrogated the coherence of the legal category of 'homosexuality' which, it is argued, has been necessary for the creation of 'heterosexuality' as the dominant background norm. The distinguishing of sexual practices such as sodomy or buggery from the identity of homosexuality has been another central concern.

Despite its importance in the history of sexuality studies, queer theory has also been criticized on several fronts. Some have argued that it is overly abstract and divorced from everyday political struggles. Relatedly, it has been claimed that queer theorists privilege cultural texts over material conditions and that they fail to recognize the importance of identity-based politics as a strategy for social change. Still others have expressed concern that queer theory is itself exclusionary and that it is specific to Western cultures. Nevertheless, queer theory has provided many important and useful insights.

CARL STYCHIN

J Butler, *Excitable Speech: A Politics of the Performative* (New York: Routledge, 1997)

K Thomas, 'Corpus Juris (Hetero) Sexualis: Doctrine, Discourse, and Desire in *Bowers v Hardwick*' (1993) 1 *GLQ: A Journal of Lesbian and Gay Studies* 33

questioning of criminal suspects *see* PACE

R

R v R (1992) The absence of woman as a legal **subject** was only too evident in the common law rule that a husband could not be guilty of raping his wife. Until 1991, a wife's lack of consent to intercourse was legally irrelevant in English law. The historical development of the law had effectively silenced any protest of sexual abuse by married women: implied consent to sexual relations was built into the structure of **marriage** itself.

Since 1949, the courts had developed increasingly important exceptions to this rigid rule but it was not until 1991 that the **House of Lords** in *R v R* confirmed that **rape** by a husband of his wife is always a criminal offence. The case arose out of an incident when R attempted to have sexual intercourse with his wife against her will. The couple had been separated for three weeks and both were considering a divorce. The wife had returned to live with her parents but R had forced his way into the house and attacked his wife. R pleaded guilty to attempted rape.

R appealed against his conviction on the basis that a husband could not be found guilty of raping his wife. His appeal was unanimously dismissed by the Court of Appeal, which swept aside the marital exemption from rape, as it 'no longer even remotely represents what is the true position of a wife in present-day society'. The House of Lords upheld the judgment of the Court of Appeal.

One aspect of the decision raised an important constitutional issue. It is for Parliament and not the **judges** to legislate in the field of criminal law, however outdated the judiciary may perceive a rule to be. Section 1 of the Sexual Offences (Amendment) Act 1976 defines rape as 'unlawful' non-consensual sexual intercourse. Submissions had been made that this meant that the **common law** marital exemption had been enacted into legislation by Parliament and it was therefore outside the power of the courts to abolish it. Not one appellate court judge accepted the argument that the use of the word 'unlawful' was a legislative device for excluding intercourse within marriage from the definition of rape, thus requiring a change in the law by Parliament rather than through the courts. They concluded that there was nothing to inhibit them from 'removing a common law fiction which had become anachronistic and offensive'.

R petitioned the **European Court of Human Rights** ('ECtHR') arguing that his conviction constituted retrospective punishment in breach of Article 7 of the **European Convention on Human Rights**. He complained that at the time the 'rape' was committed, the common law marital exemption from rape—subject to certain limitations—was still effective. The ECtHR rejected this argument and endorsed the appellate English courts' conclusion that 'a rapist remains a rapist subject to the criminal law, irrespective of his relationship with his victim'. Importantly, the ECtHR acknowledged that this change in the common law was in accordance with the fundamental objectives of the ECHR, the very essence of which is respect for human dignity and human freedom.

The affirmation of the human dignity of women marks this case as significant in European human rights jurisprudence. The law represents the formal expression of the values and aspirations of society, and the abolition of the marital rape exemption was a positive, if overdue, development.

STEPHANIE PALMER

race Race reveals a sharp contradiction in law, a contradiction that is integral to law itself. On one side, law can be seen as compatible with racism, even as identified with it. So, there have been slave societies based on a legally constituted racial status. With racially based colonialisms, law was placed in the forefront of their 'civilizing mission'. In the very emergence of modern law in the West, law was identified as civilized and progressive in constituent contrast to 'backward savages'. Even in societies set against division in racial terms, such as liberal societies so-called, racism has been shown to inhabit the law intimately.

There is, however, another side to the relation between law and racism, a side which would seem to be quite contrary to that dismal picture. Here law is revealed as profoundly resistant to racism. So we find law at the forefront in resisting and overturning systems of ascribed status such as those based on race. Law played a significant, if insufficiently recognized, part in the various liberation movements of colonized peoples. And law continues to be at the forefront of struggles for restorative justice on the part of **indigenous peoples**. Furthermore, law has proved to be effective in countering racial oppression in modern Western societies, the civil rights movement in the United States providing a conspicuous example.

Recent history offers us a dramatic instance of this deeply divided law in the life and writing of Nelson Mandela. In his autobiography, *Long Walk to Freedom* (London: Abacus, 1995), Mandela also provides an explanation for this legal duality. South Africa was, of course, a country comprehensively and oppressively structured in racial terms, and these terms were set by law. Mandela was particularly acute in his criticism of this law, especially of its instrumental subordination to 'the ruling class' (p 309). The law's oppressions were brought pointedly to bear on Mandela himself, both in his legal career, and, more conspicuously, as a political prisoner—one who narrowly avoided legally decreed execution. Yet this same law was also exalted by Mandela. In the very midst of a devastating critique of such law, he lauds the court system as 'perhaps the only place in South Africa where an African could possibly receive a fair hearing and where the rule of law might still apply' (p 308). And when he was being tried in the courts he used the openness of the legal hearing to draw a wider community into a resistant participation in the law (pp 384–395, 428–431). It is the openness of the law which accounts for Mandela's remarkable adherence to it. As a condition and means of society's continued existence, law has to be adaptively open to change. So, no matter how oppressive the existing law may be, law is always capable of being otherwise. This capability extends, as the South African experience illustrates, to the inclusion of those once racially excluded.

Manifestly, law is not simply resistant to racial oppression. Its very openness makes it susceptible to appropriation by dominant powers including a dominant racial group. Such appropriation can extend to the very idea of law itself. A unique and proprietary relation to law, especially as the rule of law, is characteristically claimed as an achievement of Western European civilization. Such an encapsulated law is seen as evolving in tandem with the development of this civilization. From its European location, that law is supposedly spreading to the less enlightened parts of the globe, a continuation of the civilizing mission. Law of this kind can carry with it

a racial bias which contradicts the efforts it makes at times to counteract racial 'discrimination'. We find this whole Euro-centric scenario countered, however, by scholarship revealing the very formation of that supposedly Western law to have come not just from a self-elevating West but also from 'the East' and Africa. Such scholarship as Monateri's reveals law to be not the product of some racially-oriented evolution, but rather the product of a large and protean diversity of peoples—a variegated process, and not an evolutionary straight line. That perception of law accords with its openness, and with its resulting ability to resist racial oppression.

PETER FITZPATRICK

PG Monateri, 'Black Gaius: A Quest for the Multicultural Origins of the "Western Legal Tradition"' [2000] 51 *Hastings Law Journal* 479

P Fitzpatrick, *The Mythology of Modern Law* (London: Routledge, 1992)

See also: **ethnicity; protected grounds**

race and crime   It can be argued that **'race'** functions as a social construction emphasizing and maintaining supposedly inherent (biologically determined) behavioural characteristics between different ethnic categories. For example, immigrant populations have historically been constructed as 'trouble', and Afro-Caribbeans in particular, have been constructed as being more 'prone' to criminal behaviour than other groups. Thus, young, black men were constructed as 'muggers' during the 1970s in the UK, despite the fact that street crime has a long history involving all types of populations. Research has demonstrated that such preconceived ideas—known as the **'racialization'** of **minority** populations—has led to the over-policing of minority ethnic groups, and Home Office statistics indicate that black people are consistently over-represented within every aspect of the **criminal justice system**. For example, young black men are five to eight times more likely to be stopped and searched than young white men. They are five times more likely to be arrested despite the fact they are no more likely than whites to be subsequently charged with an offence. The imprisonment rate for black people is 934 per 100,000, more than eight times higher than for whites (114 per 100,000). In 1999–2002, the total **prison** population increased by 12 per cent but the number of black prisoners increased by 51 per cent. Since 1990, eight **deaths in custody** (**police** and prison) have resulted in 'unlawful killing' verdicts. Seven of these concerned black men, the eighth being Irish.

The over-policing of ethnic communities, together with the over-representation of black people within the criminal justice system, has led to severe tension in the relationships between minority ethnic cultures and the police, who, as guardians of established white culture, increasingly have come to be associated with discrimination against and exclusion of black culture. In turn, this tension played a key role in initiating the various civil disturbances during the 1980s and 1990s.

The publication of the Macpherson Report in 1999 signalled a turning-point in the relationship between black people and the police, because following an inquiry into the murder of the teenager, Stephen Lawrence, in a racist attack in 1993, the presence of institutional racism within the Metropolitan police force was officially recognized for the first time.

Since the attack on the twin towers in New York in 2001, evidence suggests that members of the Muslim community has become the most recent target of racialization through the demonization of 'Islamic terrorists', the **stereotyping** of Asian people as religious extremists, and their perceived 'failure' to integrate into British culture by maintaining key features of their ethnic origins. The growth in 'Islamophobia' as a result of the war on terror is supported by the **Director of Public Prosecutions** who warned in 2005 that the increase in both racial hatred crime and the number of young Asian men being stopped by police may lead to serious alienation of Muslim **communities** within the UK. Since the introduction of racial hatred laws in 1999, racially aggravated offences have increased by 2,500. In the year between April 2003 and March 2004, 4,728 racially aggravated cases were reported to the **Crown Prosecution Service**. Of these 3,616 were prosecuted. Meanwhile, religiously aggravated crimes more than doubled during 2004, with Muslims being identified as the **victims** in half of all such cases. Thus, while there is some evidence to suggest that black people have developed increased confidence in the police since the publication of the Macpherson Report, for example, by reporting a higher proportion of racial abuse and attacks, other evidence suggests that new divisions are being created within ethnic communities which will present a new challenge to race relations, particularly in terms of avoiding the alienation and exclusion of Muslim communities from mainstream culture and social life within Britain.

ANETTE BALLINGER

See also: **crime and social differentiation; racial and ethnic minorities in the criminal justice system**

race discrimination   *see* **protected grounds**

race to the bottom   *see* **Social Chapter**

racial and ethnic minorities in the criminal justice system   In pursuance of a duty created by section 95 of the Criminal Justice Act 1991, the Home Office regularly produces statistical information on **race** and the **criminal justice system**. The data reveal that people from Black and **Minority** Ethnic ('BME') groups are over-represented at each stage of the process: they are more likely than white persons to be stopped, searched, arrested, prosecuted, convicted of serious crimes, and imprisoned. A particularly striking fact is that, for British nationals, the proportion of black prisoners relative to the population is five times higher than for white people.

However, it is not easy to reach firm conclusions about the causes of these disproportionalities. They could result from discrimination, either direct or indirect, although other explanations have also been suggested: that socio-demographic differences or **police** practices when recording crime are a factor; that people from BME groups are more likely than white people to be out on the streets; and that offences committed by people from BME groups are more likely to be detected than offences committed by white people, because a larger proportion of the BME population is known to the police. There is, however, no evidence to suggest that the disparities arise because people from BME groups are more likely than white people to commit crime.

To date, only one major study has examined whether adults from BME groups are treated in a discriminatory way by the criminal **courts** (Roger Hood, *Race and Sentencing* (1992)). Based on 1989 data taken from five Crown Court centres in the West Midlands, Hood's study found that the probability of African-Caribbean male defendants being sentenced to custody was between 5 and 8 per cent higher than would have been expected on the basis of their characteristics. However, until a new study is commissioned, it is impossible to say whether similar disparities would be found today.

Whether defendants from BME groups *believe* they are treated fairly by the criminal courts was assessed in a large-scale empirical study carried out by Stephen Shute, Roger Hood, and Florence Seemungal (*A Fair Hearing?* (2005)). The authors found that one in five black defendants in the Crown Court and one in ten in magistrates' courts believed that there had been racial bias in their case, as did one in eight Asian defendants in both types of court. Significant though these findings are, the proportions are lower than many commentators had assumed.

Efforts have been made over the years—and especially since the 1999 enquiry by Sir William Macpherson into the killing of Stephen Lawrence—to improve race equality in the criminal justice system. These include better training, improving the available statistical information, and establishing a Criminal Justice Race Unit within the Home Office. Ethnic monitoring has also improved. From April 2003, ethnicity began to be recorded using a standardized system based on sixteen categories created for the 2001 National Census. These categories are sub-divisions of five larger ethnic groupings: white, mixed, Asian, black, or 'other'. Individuals self-classify by selecting the category that they feel describes them best. STEPHEN SHUTE

racialization The idea of racialization connotes the determination of political, social, and economic ordering according to racial difference. Whilst the organization of racial hierarchies differs across the world, in most Western developed regions, European races have dominated their African, Asian, and Latin- American counterparts.

Legal systems have an unsettled relation with the complex processes of racialization; at times creating and endorsing racial difference, at other times outlawing it in a variety of settings. Protection against racial discrimination is most developed within the employment context and in relation to the provision of public services.

The institution of **slavery** provides an early example of the encounter between law and racial ordering. Here, the legal category of contract was deployed to regulate the sale of slaves. US **Critical Race Theory** has been instrumental in revealing the tensions in **contract law** caused by the commercial appropriate of human freedom and dignity. *The Alchemy of Race and Rights: Diary of a Law Professor* (1991) by Harvard scholar, Patricia Williams, is a classic example of work of this kind. An early UK example of the legal endorsement of the trade in slaves was the decision of the court of Kings Bench in *Butts v Penny* (1677), which defined slaves as 'goods' or 'merchandise', subject to an action in 'trover'—an early contractual cause of action.

Whilst slavery deprived mainly African people of liberty, various **international law** doctrines deprived Native American Indians and **indigenous people** in Australia, Canada, and New Zealand of land rights. Towards the end of the eighteenth century the jurist, Vattel, developed the *terra nullius* doctrine, which declared that lands inhabited by tribes deemed primitive would be treated as if they were occupied by no-one and therefore open to settlement by European explorers. Indigenous tribes (often referred to as First Nations) have made many legal claims for recovery of land rights. A case allowing limited recovery of land seized is the Australian Supreme Court decision, *Mabo v Queensland* (1992).

The legacies of slavery and colonization have haunted the settlement of ethnic minority groups in Western states. Immigration laws of these states often appear to privilege white settlement. An example of this privileging in UK immigration law is the now defunct 'primary purpose' rule which posed difficulties for Asian people seeking to settle in the UK on the basis of arranged **marriages.** In the context of **refugee** protection it has been argued that the grounds for claiming **asylum** under the Convention relating to the Status of Refugees (1951) do not encompass refugee producing phenomena experienced by individuals seeking asylum from developing countries.

Spurred on by the process of decolonization, civil rights movements, and the reception of a broader **human rights** ideology, legal systems in the latter half of the twentieth century have adopted an antithetical stance toward racism and racial ordering. Most states have anti-discrimination laws that place racial discrimination at the forefront. In the UK, anti-racist laws were first enacted in 1968, extended in the Race Relations Act 1976 and most recently amended by the Race Relations (Amendment) Act 2002, which places greater obligations on public authorities to address racial disadvantage. Despite these measures, concern over institutional racism remains. Following the racist murder of a young black man, Stephen Lawrence, an **inquiry** was set up under the chairmanship of Lord Macpherson (1999), which concluded, among other things, that a deeply embedded culture of racist attitudes existed in the police force. An emerging body of work from critical race and post-colonial scholars highlights the ways in which racial oppression and discrimination have survived into the post-civil rights era.

PATRICIA TUITT

Rainbow Warrior case The Rainbow Warrior, a Greenpeace ship registered in the UK, was sunk in Auckland harbour on 10 July 1985 by agents of the French external security service. Two of the French agents involved were arrested by the New Zealand authorities and sentenced to ten years' imprisonment for manslaughter and wilful damage.

France admitted its responsibility for the attack and sought the return of the agents on the basis that they had been acting under orders. France was willing to make an apology and compensate New Zealand for damage suffered, acknowledging that the act was in violation of New Zealand sovereignty and accordingly of **international law**. Negotiations failed to resolve all aspects of the dispute, and it was agreed in 1986 to refer the matter to the **United Nations** Secretary-General ('UNSG'), Perez de Cuellar, for a binding ruling. He ruled, *inter alia*, that France should make an apology to New Zealand, and pay New Zealand US$7 million in compensation for all damage suffered; and that the French agents should be transferred to a French military facility at Hao in French Polynesia for a period of three years, during which they should not be permitted to leave without the mutual consent of France and New Zealand. A dispute over the implementation of this ruling was submitted to arbitration in 1989 after the two agents were repatriated to France early on medical grounds, without New Zealand's consent. The arbitral tribunal found that France had committed breaches of its obligations under the agreements implementing the UNSG's ruling.

France also paid compensation to the family of a Dutch national killed in the attack; and, in separate arbitral proceedings, was ordered to pay compensation to Greenpeace.   RUTH MacKENZIE

M Pugh, 'Legal Aspects of the Rainbow Warrior Affair' (1987) 36 *International and Comparative Law Quarterly* 655

JS Davidson, 'The *Rainbow Warrior* Arbitration Concerning the Treatment of the French Agents Mafart and Prieur' (1991) 40 *International and Comparative Law Quarterly* 446

Ralegh, Sir Walter   Sir Walter Ralegh (1554–1618) was born at Hayes in Devon. Ralegh's star rose as a courtier under Elizabeth I, charming her with his poems and theatricality. He was knighted on 6 January 1585 and became Captain of the Guard in 1591.

Ralegh was MP for Devon in the 1580s and spent most of the decade attempting the colonization of America, including sending out expeditions for the unsuccessful Roanoke project in modern day North Carolina. His illicit marriage to Elizabeth Throckmorton in 1591 led to his disgrace at Court and imprisonment in the Tower of London. After his release Ralegh became pre-occupied with finding the fabled city of El Dorado, which he believed to be far up the Orinoco River.

With the accession of James I in 1603, Ralegh found himself under suspicion. He was tried and convicted of treason in November for involvement in the Main Plot. James I gave Ralegh clemency but not pardon, and he remained a prisoner for thirteen years, where he wrote his famous *History of the World*. Upon his release in 1616 Ralegh conducted another expedition to find El Dorado, attacking the Spanish outpost of San Thomé in the process. This attack compromised the peace between Spain and England and on 10 August 1618 Ralegh was again confined to the Tower. James I wanted Ralegh executed and despite a spirited defence the Privy Council confirmed the death sentence of 1603. He was executed on 29 October 1618.   ELLIOT VERNON

rambling   The rambler, in pursuing the activity of walking for pleasure, may face legal obstacles as well as fences and stiles. The most vexed issue relates to access. The starting point is that it is a **trespass** to enter another's land without authority; the fact that one enters for the purposes of recreation provides no defence.

A public right of way, such as a footpath or bridleway, may provide the necessary authority. And recent statutory intervention has improved the rambler's lot. In England and Wales, the Countryside and Rights of Way Act 2000 gives authority for any person to walk across 'access land'. Registered common land and land consisting wholly or predominantly of mountain, moor, heath, or down are all included. Maps showing access land are available online. The Act gives the rambler authority to enter and walk across access land; it does not prevent the owner from developing his land in a way which interferes with access.

The Act, said to give a 'right to roam', does not yet extend to the coastline or beaches, and is certainly less extensive than the Land Reform (Scotland) Act 2003. That Act gives a *prima facie* authority to enter any land in Scotland, subject of course to exceptions. It does permit access to coasts and beaches and even, controversially, over golf courses. Unlike its English equivalent, it also allows access for camping and canoeing. However, neither Act permits access for hunting, shooting, or fishing.   BEN McFARLANE

See also: **public rights of passage over land and water**

rape   The offence of rape has presented, and continues to present, difficulties to the **criminal justice system**. It is a notoriously under-reported offence. There are a number of explanations for this ranging from the **victim**'s failure to recognize the experience as criminal, or fear of the perpetrator, to concerns about the treatment s/he is likely to receive at the hands of **police**, prosecutors, and the **courts**. Contrary to the image of rape often presented to the public, it is an offence that most often involves intimate partners or acquaintances, tends to occur in private, and does not always involve **violence** (at least not of a sort that will produce physical injury). In addition, while men can be, and are, raped, it is significantly more likely to involve a female victim.

While it is widely accepted that the treatment afforded to rape complainants in the past (in the UK and elsewhere) has left a great deal to be desired, there has been a concerted effort at improvement in recent decades. For example, dedicated sexual assault referral centres have been established, police officers and prosecutors have received specialist training, and sexual history **evidence** has been restricted wherever its prejudicial effect outweighs its probative value in the courtroom. Yet, research suggests that the practical impact of these reforms has often been limited. The 'culture of disbelief' that surrounds rape has proven resilient and continues to be reflected in high rates of attrition. What's more, evidence about the complainant's sexual history, or her character more generally, is routinely introduced by defence barristers in rape cases, and appears to have a detrimental impact upon assessments of her credibility.

Conviction rates in rape cases have remained in steady decline. This has precipitated a renewed vigour for rape law reform, reflected—amongst other things—in the passing of the Sexual Offences Act 2003 in England and Wales. In contrast to Scotland, where, until the decision in *Lord Advocate's Reference (No 1 of 2001)*, securing a rape conviction required evidence that force—be it actual or constructive—had been used by the defendant to overbear the complainant's will, English law has long insisted that the *actus reus* component of rape is satisfied simply by an absence of consent to intercourse. In addition, it was made clear that there is a difference between consent and mere submission, and that it is for the **jury** to determine—applying their common sense to the facts of each case—whether consent was present. Building on this, the Sexual Offences Act 2003 now stipulates that rape occurs where there is penile penetration (of the vagina, anus or mouth) in circumstances in which the complainant does not consent, and the defendant either knows that there is no consent or holds a belief in consent that is not reasonable in all the circumstances.

For the first time, in English law, this Act provides a definition of consent—a person consents when she agrees by choice and has the freedom and **capacity** to make that choice—and gives an exhaustive list of circumstances under which such consent will be presumed, on either a rebuttable (section 75) or conclusive (section 76) basis, to have been absent. To the extent that this provides a clearer framework for guiding jury deliberation, it is hoped that it will improve the consistency and predictability of decision-making in rape cases. Its attempt to encourage a more 'communicative' model of sexual relations, grounded in agreement about intercourse *between* the parties rather than on the presumption of male proposition, has also been welcomed by many commentators. At the same time, however, critics have challenged the wisdom of setting up a hierarchy of rape, of the sort implied in the three-pronged approach to sexual consent. Concerns have also been expressed about the content of these exhaustive lists, and about the low threshold for rebuttal under section 75. In addition, critics have questioned whether defining consent in terms of such complex and contested notions as freedom and capacity will provide any meaningful assistance to the court, and more specifically to the jury, in real cases.

While the Act's shift from a standard of honest to reasonable belief in consent has been more positively welcomed, it too has generated disquiet. On the one hand, some commentators have argued that this departure from normal standards of objectivity in the assessment of criminal responsibility is unjustifiable. Meanwhile, others have accepted that there may be legitimate grounds for holding defendants to a higher level of **accountability** in rape cases, but remain unconvinced that the **legislation** will be able to achieve this goal. In a context in which less than two decades ago, English law deemed it impossible for a husband to be guilty of raping his wife, traces of a social history in which women are seen as the (sexual) property of men—either 'their' men or men in general—remains. It is evidenced by popular acceptance of 'rape myths' according to which women who fail to conform to feminine roles—by going out alone, drinking alcohol, dressing provocatively, initiating intimacy, etc—will be viewed as less credible rape complainants by third party observers. These behaviours are often viewed as signalling a level of sexual interest which cannot then be easily revoked by the complainant. Critics points out, therefore, that any assessment of the defendant's belief will be made in a context in which it is 'reasonable' for him to construe these behaviours as constitutive of consent and to treat with suspicion any subsequent assertions of reluctance that he encounters.

Ultimately, then, while there have been a raft of changes to the legal understanding of, and response to, rape in recent decades, and while many of these have had some positive impact, the area where reform is now perhaps most needed is not in the law but in social attitudes. Proposals currently under consideration in England and Wales to dislodge popular but questionable beliefs about rape by educating jurors on the realities of this offence seem to recognize this new direction.

VANESSA MUNRO

See also: **crime and sexual integrity**

rape trauma syndrome   *see* **syndrome evidence**

rational markets and regulation   Securities **regulation** worldwide to a large extent relies on the assumption that financial markets are rational. This assumption is commonly known as the Efficient Capital Market Hypothesis ('ECMH'). This theory basically contends that stock prices fully reflect all available information in the market, which implies that investors cannot consistently generate profits out of a set of information once it is available in the market. The development of the ECMH is generally attributed to Eugene Fama.

From a regulatory point of view, the information disclosure regimes applicable to issuers of financial instruments (**prospectus** regulation) and listed companies (ongoing information disclosure obligations) are related to the ECMH: by ensuring that financial or any other information that can influence the behaviour of a rational investor is made public in a specified way, thus providing equal access to that information by the various market actors (market analysts, financial institutions, investors and so on), the regulatory disclosure regime enables markets to absorb the information so that it will be reflected in prices. Likewise, the obligation for listed companies to disclose price-sensitive 'inside information' should prevent insiders from taking advantage of information that has not (yet) been reflected in the market prices.

In cases of deficient information disclosure, the ECMH will facilitate claims by investors to recover **damages** from those who have negligently omitted to disclose relevant information, or who have disclosed false or misleading information: the ECMH assumes that every single investor relies on the information that is available in the market in making its investment decision. Thus, an aggrieved investor will generally be presumed to have relied upon the deficient, false, or misleading information without having to demonstrate that it actually possessed that information and effectively used it. The price correction after disclosure of the true information will quantify the losses incurred by the aggrieved investor. This is known as the 'fraud-on-the-market-theory'. US courts have consistently applied this theory in **securities** fraud cases. Under UK law, this theory is reflected in section 90 of the Financial Services and Markets Act 2000 regarding prospectus liability: any person who acquires securities for which a prospectus has to be published may sue the issuer for losses suffered as a result of any untrue or misleading statement in the prospectus or any omission from it without having to demonstrate the reliance on that information.

In recent years, the theory of rational markets and the ECMH have come under increased criticism in academia, notably with the emergence of research in the field of behavioural finance. Proponents of behavioural finance challenge the axiom of rationality of financial agents and attempt to integrate elements of psychology into economic research with a view to explaining observed inefficiencies in the markets (such as under-reaction or over-reaction to information).   MICHEL TISON

E Fama 'Efficient Capital Markets: A Review of Theory and Empirical Work' (1970) 25 *Journal of Finance* 383

See also: **disclosure in financial markets; insider dealing**

reasonable accommodation   The requirement to provide a reasonable accommodation—or, to use the terminology of the UK Disability Discrimination Act 1995, a reasonable adjustment—is an element of modern (**disability**) non-discrimination law. However, the reasonable accommodation requirement differs from the standard requirements found in non-discrimination law not to directly or indirectly discriminate. This is because non-discrimination law is traditionally underpinned by the idea that the protected characteristic, such as **race** or **gender**, is rarely relevant to the (employment) decision, and only in exceptional circumstances allows for unequal treatment. The protected characteristic should therefore be ignored. In the case of employment, the race or gender of an applicant should play no part, positive or negative, in the decision whether to award the individual the job or not. This is the general position of UK non-discrimination law.

However, in some cases ignoring a characteristic can result in denying an individual equal opportunities. The reasonable accommodation or adjustment requirement therefore recognizes that, on occasions, the interaction between an individual's inherent characteristics, such as impairment, **sex**, **religion**, or belief, and the physical or social environment, can result in the inability to perform a particular function or job in the conventional manner, or in the inability to use a good or service in the standard way. As an example, the absence of a lift in a building (the physical environment) will result in a person who uses a wheelchair being unable to reach the upper floors of the building and therefore being unable to work or visit others there. The characteristic is relevant in that it can lead to an individual being faced with a barrier that prevents him or her from benefiting from an opportunity that is open to others who do not share that characteristic. The resulting disadvantage is a restricted set of employment opportunities, or limited access to the benefits enjoyed by people without that characteristic.

The reasonable accommodation requirement therefore requires a covered party, such as an employer or service provider, to consider what steps it can take to remove the barrier which hampers the full enjoyment of the benefit by the individual, and where possible, requires the party to actually take those steps. In the employment context a reasonable accommodation requirement prohibits an employer from denying an individual with a disability or other relevant characteristic an employment opportunity by failing to take account of the characteristic, when taking account of it—in terms of changing tasks or the physical environment of the workplace—would enable the individual to do the work. Employers are required to recognize the characteristic and to consider what changes they could make to the work environment to allow an individual to carry out the work to the required standard. This obligation applies at all stages of employment, including pre-employment (eg recruitment and interview procedure) and post-employment (eg occupational **pensions** and benefits given to ex-employees). In principle, employers remain able to appoint and promote on merit—but the reasonable accommodation requirement ensures that individuals are considered for positions based on their abilities.

The need for accommodations is most obvious with regard to disabled people, and indeed UK law only explicitly provides for a reasonable accommodation requirement for this group. The Disability Discrimination Act 1995 imposes an obligation on a variety of parties, including employers, providers of (public) services, and educational institutions, to provide reasonable adjustments for individuals with a disability. An unjustified failure to provide an adjustment (ie a failure which cannot be justified by the existence of a disproportionate burden) amounts to discrimination.

Accommodations can take a wide variety of forms—ranging from a one-off instalment of a ramp to allow wheelchair users access to a building to the ongoing employment of an assistant to work with a disabled employee or disabled customers. In the example given above, the accommodation might involve the installation of a lift—although a less radical step would be to allocate the individual an office on the ground floor, or hold meetings in a location that is accessible. The accommodation requirement can also oblige the covered party to adapt its standard procedures in order to remove a barrier experienced by a disabled individual. For example, in *Archibald v Fife Council* (2004) the **House of Lords** held that

the requirement could oblige a Council to relax its standard redeployment policy which required that an employee who wished to move to a higher status job had to undergo a competitive interview and be selected on the basis of merit. A reasonable accommodation in this case could involve the redeployment of an employee, who had developed a disability and could no longer carry out her previous manual job, to a low-grade office job for which she was qualified, without the need for her to succeed in a competitive interview.

Nevertheless, the obligation to make an accommodation or adjustment is not unlimited. Covered parties are not obliged to make an accommodation if this would result in a disproportionate burden. A burden may be disproportionate if it results in significant costs that it would be difficult for the enterprise to bear. The burden could also be disproportionate if it would result in significant disruption. In determining whether an accommodation results in a disproportionate burden, consideration will be given as to what can be expected of any particular enterprise. In general, more can be expected of a large, wealthy undertaking—in terms of costs and flexibility—than a small, cash-strapped firm. Assessing whether a disproportionate burden exists involves an individualized analysis, and **legislation** cannot set out exactly what is expected of any covered party in terms of acceptable costs. Such an individualized approach is also required with regard to identifying appropriate accommodations.

In addition to disabled people, other groups, such as individuals whose religion requires them to follow a certain dress code or worship at certain times, could also potentially benefit from reasonable accommodations. This requirement is explicitly recognized in, for example, US and Canadian law with regard to employment, but not, thus far, in UK or EC law.

LISA WADDINGTON

See also: **dress codes in employment**

reasonable person The reasonable person is one of the most important and variable tools of the **common law**. It plays a role in many areas including **tort law**, criminal law, and **administrative law**. The reasonable person has recently undergone a transformation—for most of his 150-year existence, he was the reasonable *man*. **Courts** most often use the reasonable person as a test for blameworthiness, asking whether the litigant acted as a reasonable person would have in the circumstances. If the answer is yes, then the conduct is legally blameless and does not attract liability. However, if the litigant fails to do what the court believes the reasonable person would have done, then the conduct is considered legally at fault or culpable.

A famous early example of this use of the reasonable man is found in *Vaughan v Menlove* (1837). Mr Menlove set up a dangerous hay rick which caught fire and destroyed his neighbour's cottages. He said he was blameless because he was not 'of the highest order of intelligence'. The court pointed out that he had been warned repeatedly and had insured his own property. It described the standard as objective not subjective and held Menlove liable on the basis that he was bound to act as a reasonable man, which he had manifestly failed to do. Since *Vaughan* the reasonable person has been the major tool that courts use to determine whether a defendant was negligent, that is culpably careless, towards another. Accordingly, the reasonable person is a cornerstone of the most important modern ground of civil liability—negligence. In the law of negligence the reasonable person is also vital to evaluating the plaintiff's attentiveness to his or her own security. So, to the extent that a plaintiff failed to act like a reasonable person in the circumstances, any **damages** will be reduced because they are attributable in part to the plaintiff's own carelessness.

Although the reasonable person is most prominent in the tort of negligence, it also makes other important appearances in private law. One significant role it plays is in the assessment of consent in intentional torts such as assault and battery. Thus, in medical cases where there is no actual consent, courts ask whether a reasonable person would have consented in order to determine when they can impute consent. If so, no battery will have occurred. Similarly, in the doctrine of mitigation in contact law the plaintiff's conduct is compared to that of the reasonable person to assess whether the damages should be reduced because the plaintiff failed to be sufficiently active in protecting her own interests.

In addition to its pivotal role in private law, the reasonable person is critical to criminal law. Indeed, apart from the law of negligence, the most important and debated uses of the reasonable person are found in self-defence and provocation. Both of these defences to a charge of culpable **homicide** rely on a reasonable or ordinary person test in order to assess the accused's response to a threatening or provocative situation. To the extent that the accused responded as a reasonable or ordinary person would have, his or her criminal culpability is diminished. The use of the reasonable person has also been much debated, including in the academic literature, in the American law of **sexual harassment** where it is used to determine whether particular conduct creates a hostile work environment. In that context, many feminists have argued that when courts evaluate whether conduct amounted to harassment they should use the reasonable woman as a point of reference rather than the reasonable person. While some American courts have been tempted by this idea, the **United States Supreme Court** instead invoked the reasonable person.

As the common law's most enduring legal fiction, the reasonable person has always attracted notice. In part, this is because despite its critical role, the actual workings of the reasonable person are remarkably unclear. Its appeal seems to be found in its ability to combine fixed or objective elements with some of the subjective qualities of the litigant in question. Yet, it offers little guidance on the vital question of exactly which qualities of the reasonable person are objective and hence fixed and which vary to mirror the litigant. Critics have long suggested that this makes the application of the standard highly discretionary. But the worry is not just that the test is unpredictable. Indeed, some **equality** critics have worried that the **discretion** inherent in the test tends to be used in ways that are all too predictable: the reasonable person often seems to bear a suspicious similarity to the judge—typically male, white, and privileged. This enduring equality concern about the reasonable person was articulated, perhaps unintentionally, as early as 1935 in AE Herbert's classic *The Uncommon Law*. There the court in the fictional *Fardell v Potts* puzzles over how to judge a woman's behaviour when the law makes no mention of a reasonable woman.

In recent decades, equality worries about the reasonable person have become much more pressing, fuelled by feminist and other critical movements within the law as well as by the increasing diversity of common law jurisdictions like the UK, Canada, and Australia. Early critiques focused on the fact that all litigants were judged by the standard of the reasonable *man*. The response was a gradual shift to the reasonable *person*. But the egalitarian critics were not persuaded, arguing that the test remained highly discretionary and that its use reinforced stereotypical ideas of normal behaviour. The criminal law uses of the test in particular, they said, showed that the reasonable person reflected the perspective of the privileged white men who dominate the judiciary. The result was that its application disadvantaged women, gays and **lesbians**, and other marginalized or racialized groups. For instance, they pointed out how deeply gendered uses of the provocation defence functioned to excuse male **violence** in the face of female infidelity. Critics across common law jurisdictions also noted how provocation excused deadly force even as a response to non-violent **homosexual** advances. And at the same time, because the reasonable person reinforced gendered conceptions of normal reactions to threatening situations, self-defence and provocation were routinely rejected as defences in the case of women who killed their abusive male partners.

Courts across common law jurisdictions have attempted to respond to these difficulties with the reasonable person in a number of ways. In self-defence, for instance, courts have allowed the introduction of evidence to provide a more subtle understanding of violent relationships. Similarly, the critiques of the reasonable or ordinary person in provocation have led many to suggest that the defence should be abolished altogether. Although the critiques have not been so pointed in other areas such as negligence and public law, the fact that the reasonable person is widely seen as both unhelpful and controversial has spurred a move away from detailed reliance on the test. Instead, courts tend to try to understand the normative import of the behaviour. The reasonable person, if he appears at all, is increasingly only a way of stating a legal conclusion, rather than a tool to arrive at one.   MAYO MORAN

See also: **justification, excuse, and mitigation in criminal law; negligence in civil law**

reasonable pluralism   Reasonable pluralism is a term coined by John Rawls in his later works on political liberalism. Rawls uses the term to denote the fact of a plurality of reasonable, though irreconcilable, moral, religious, or philosophical doctrines.

Pluralism is an enduring feature of modern liberal societies. For Rawls, it is both inevitable and desirable. Pluralism is the inevitable consequence of democratic societies' commitment to the principle of liberty. Diversity in religious or moral practices is presumed to be the consequence of the exercise of reason by autonomous individuals, protected by the safeguards of liberal democratic states.

This plurality of doctrines and beliefs is not eroded through dialogue or cooperation. There may not be any convergence on fundamental conceptions of the good life. A key question, then, for political theory and for legal systems is how to achieve stability, given the fact of reasonable pluralism. Despite the absence of convergence on conceptions of the good life, liberals such as Rawls argue that it is possible to arrive at an 'overlapping consensus', to agree on a set of institutional arrangements that will secure **justice** and harmoniously regulate relations between adherents of diverse moral or religious doctrines.

Reasonable pluralism presumes the possibility of a reasonably harmonious and stable pluralist society. Illiberal doctrines, that deny a political commitment to the equal moral worth of all **persons**, cannot meet the requirements of reasonable pluralism. The requirement of reasonableness applies both to the comprehensive doctrine itself, and to the individual adherents of such doctrines.

SIOBHAN MULLALLY

received law   Law is 'received' when the law-makers in a society, wishing to amend or develop radically their existing law, adopt a body of law which is already in force in another society. This process has also been called 'transplantation of law'. Some commentators have written of 'imposed law'. Another term, currently gaining usage, is 'diffusion of law'.

Many legal receptions in modern history have been effected by Western colonial powers, which created new legal systems in colonized **territories** and required them to apply their law. Thus British colonies received English law—although, curiously, not Scottish law. That received law continues to be applied today in the independent states which have succeeded colonial rule. Amendments have been made to the received laws but there has been a tendency to adopt patterns of legal development in the countries of origin of that law. Another instance in modern history was the reception by a number of European countries of the law of the Roman Empire, a process which was the foundation of modern civil law systems. New legal receptions are currently occurring in states which, until recently, were economically underdeveloped, or had state-socialist economies. They sometimes now receive law from states with liberal economies with a view to developing such economies themselves.

Received law is necessarily more than a set of rules. Other elements of a legal culture, such as the techniques employed in the interpretation and application of precedent, **legislation**, and other legal texts, are needed if law is to be used to direct society and decide disputes. Thus, a reception requires an enculturation of the legal professions. However, even if this is achieved it cannot be assumed that received law will convert a society fundamentally different from that of the territory of origin into one which is very similar.   GORDON WOODMAN

W Twining, 'Diffusion of Law: a Global Perspective' (2004) 49 *Journal of Legal Pluralism* 1

A Watson, *Legal Transplants* (Georgia: University of Georgia Press, 2nd edn, 1993)

recidivism   Recidivism rates are widely used to judge the effectiveness of various interventions to either deter or reform offenders and to calculate **risk** assessments for the release of prisoners. It is somewhat surprising, then, that a concept that is so central to understanding crime and the **criminal justice system**, is so difficult to define (or at least measure).

Recidivism is the tendency for those who have been convicted once to re-offend. The difficulty becomes how this should be measured. Researchers have operationalized recidivism by collecting measures as diverse as re-arrest, re-conviction, **probation** violation, and re-institutionalization. All of these measures utilize official statistics, however, and so are likely to involve substantial under-reporting of actual re-offending. Alternative measures, utilizing self-reports, on the other hand, require individuals to honestly report their offending, which may be less likely in cases of serious crimes like **child abuse**. For this reason, other researchers have measured recidivism by relying upon the reports of significant others (eg the self-reports of partners in studies of **domestic violence**).

The duration period of the follow-up window is also crucial. Because research suggests that most individuals will re-offend in the first twelve months after release, the recidivism window is often set at two years. In the United Kingdom, 57.6 per cent of prisoners released in both 2003 and 2000 were re-convicted within two years of their release although these rates differ by the age group of the individual. Young people, aged eighteen to twenty, re-offended at a rate close to 70 per cent, compared to around 40 per cent for those over thirty-five. Recidivism also differs by offence type. Individuals convicted of theft from vehicles had a reconviction rate of nearly 85 per cent, whereas child sex offenders were reconvicted in only 15 per cent of cases. Reducing recidivism rates for all offenders has become a central priority of the National Offender Management Service in the UK.

SHADD MARUNA

C Lloyd, G Mair, and M Hough, *Explaining Re-offending Rates: a Critical Analysis*, Home Office Research Study 136 (London: Home Office, 1994)
A Shepherd and E Whiting, *Re-offending of Adults: Results from the 2003 Cohort* (London: Home Office, 2006)

recklessness   *see* **fault-based criminal liability**

recognition   To recognize someone is to acknowledge them in some way, etymologically speaking, it is to 're-know' them. Within social and political theory, recognition is a concept closely associated with notions of self, **identity**, and difference. Recognition expresses the idea that 'self' and 'other' are inter-constitutively inter-related or, to put it in plain terms, that our sense of who we are (self) is crucially related to recognition (or lack thereof) by others. Recognition of and by others is a formative aspect of the creation of the self-conscious, thinking subject, of identity formation. For this reason, recognition is an indispensable element of any conception of social justice. A socially just society must be one which facilitates recognition in ways which nurture and enhance rather than ignore and repress identity and selfhood. Similarly, if law is to promote social justice, it must take account of the importance of recognition.

Traditionally, progressive approaches to law have tended to focus on economic inequality, drawing on Marxist-derived analyses of the role of law in maintaining and reinforcing capitalist social relations. Within this framework, critical legal scholars have emphasized law's *distributive* role, the way in which, for example, through the protection of private property rights, law produces unequal and class-based distributive results. Such scholars have also speculated about how law might be deployed more progressively to *redistribute* wealth and resources in more egalitarian ways.

In contrast to such a 'political of redistribution', the 'politics of recognition' emphasizes the importance within a social justice framework of acknowledging diversity of identity and tackling identity-based forms of disadvantage. This is the politics from which stems, for example, demands by gays and **lesbians** for an end to sexuality-based discrimination and for formal recognition of **same-sex relationships**. This is also the politics of religious groups who argue for exemptions from laws which violate their religious norms or **reasonable accommodation** of their religious beliefs in the workplace or in other social contexts. Thus, within law, recognition is closely aligned with struggles for individual and group rights which tackle identity-based disadvantage (whether based on **sex**, **race**, or other identity grounds). By contrast, redistributive politics tends to translate in legal terms into debates about workers' rights, the role of trade unions, the desirability of the welfare state, the scope of state-based economic entitlements, and the normative bases for taxation.

Within the context of progressive legal politics, issues of recognition and redistribution often seem to be in tension with one another. Thus, for example, some people might argue that recognizing the right of gays to marry is less important than tackling child poverty. In this kind of argument, redistribution and recognition are posited as in conflict. A more nuanced approach would be to argue that any gay rights agenda which does not take on board issues of redistribution is likely to fail in its objectives. This is because issues of redistribution and recognition are deeply intertwined. Similarly, a politics of redistribution which does not take account of the role of identity in effecting particular distributive outcomes is not going to get to grips with, for example, child poverty or any other manifestation of economic inequality. In this sense, the tension between recognition and redistribution may in some ways be mediated by the idea of **intersectionality**, that is, the idea that inequalities are the result of multiple, cross-cutting forms of disadvantage which are, in turn, closely associated with and shaped by social perceptions of identity and difference. JOANNE CONAGHAN

D Cooper, *Challenging Diversity: Rethinking Equality and the Value of Difference* (Cambridge: Cambridge University Press, 2004)

N Fraser and A Honneth, *Redistribution or Recognition: A Political-Philosophical Exchange* (London: Verso, 2003)

recognition and execution of foreign judgments and arbitral awards *see* **transnational civil litigation**

recognition of states and governments The term 'recognition', when used in the context of recognition of states and governments, may have several different meanings. It may indicate the recognizing state's willingness to enter into official relations with a new state or government, or manifest its opinion on the legal status of a new entity or authority, or both. The subject has been further complicated by the introduction of several variants of the term. Distinctions between '*de facto* recognition', 'diplomatic recognition', and '*de jure* recognition' may be traced back to the secession of the Spanish provinces in South America in the early nineteenth century. Like 'recognition', these terms can be given meaning only by establishing the intention of the authority using them within the factual and legal context of each case. Recognition is a unilateral act performed by the recognizing state's government. There is probably no other subject in the field of **international law** in which law and politics are more closely interwoven. Recognition of states must be distinguished from recognition of governments, each form having its own theories and practices.

The question of the legal effect of recognition of new entities calling themselves 'states' has been characterized for over a century by the 'great debate' between 'constitutive' and 'declaratory' schools of thought. While the former contends that a state only becomes a state by virtue of recognition, the latter (which is now widely accepted) argues that a state is a state because it is a state, that is, because it meets all the international legal criteria for statehood. In the first case recognition is status-creating, in the latter it is merely status-confirming. **International lawyers** and states do not always distinguish clearly between the requirements for recognition of an entity *as* a state (the criteria for statehood) and the requirements for recognition *of* a state—that is, the preconditions for entering into optional or discretionary relations with the entity (the conditions for recognition). While the former are prescribed by international law, the latter may vary from state to state.

When a state recognizes a new 'government' of an existing state, it usually acknowledges a person or group of persons as competent to act as the organ of the state and to represent it in its international relations. The only criterion in international law for the recognition of an authority as the government of a state is its exercise of effective control over the state's territory. States may, however, continue to recognize a government-in-exile if an incumbent government is forced into exile by foreign occupation or the *de facto* government *in situ* has been created in violation of international law. Despite a trend in the literature to the contrary, there is still no rule of general or regional **customary international law** that a government of a state, to be government in the sense of international law, must be democratically elected. Attempts to introduce such a requirement either by treaty or as a matter of national policy have failed.

States may be roughly divided into three groups according to their recognition policy: states (such as the **United Kingdom** before 1980) that formally recognize governments; states (such as the US) that generally do not formally recognize governments but do so in exceptional circumstances for political reasons; and states (such as the UK since 1980) that formally recognize only states, not governments. The last group has not abolished the recognition of governments, only the making of official statements of recognition. The British Government (for instance) still has to decide whether a group of persons qualifies as the government of another state, especially if there is more than one claimant to governmental status. Its opinion on the legal status of a claimant may be determined on the basis of the nature of the dealings (non-existent, limited, or government-to-government dealings) which it has with a claimant.

The legal consequences of recognition differ depending on the forum. While in international and continental European courts recognition has only probative value, in English and American courts recognition by the forum government is conclusive evidence as to the legal status of a foreign authority or entity and determines access to the courts, issues of privilege and immunity, the right to recover state property and the judicial cognizance of foreign laws.

The non-recognition of a *de facto* existing state or government may be motivated by political reasons, as in the case of US non-recognition of the Chinese Communist Government (1949–1979). It may also be used as a sanction in response to a violation of a fundamental norm of international law, especially when applied collectively, as in the case of the State of Rhodesia (1965–1980).   STEFAN TALMON

S Talmon, 'The Constitutive Versus the Declaratory Theory of Recognition: *Tertium Non Datur?* (2004) 75 *British Year Book of International Law* 101

S Talmon, *Recognition of Governments in International Law: With Particular Reference to Governments in Exile* (Oxford: Clarendon Press, 1998)

recognition of trades unions   *see* collective bargaining; trades unions

reconciliation The concept of reconciliation has grown in resonance in the last two decades, emerging as a key term of political discourse. In turn, the processes of reconciliation have implicated the law in functions that one, perhaps, does not ordinarily associate with it—like helping emergent societies deal with traumatic pasts—or that sit somewhat uncomfortably with the ideal of the '**rule of law**'—like engineering and effecting political transitions. For societies emerging from pasts of colonization, **violence**, structural discrimination, and oppression, from South America, to Africa to eastern Europe, the demand that reconciliation places on law is, paradoxically, both that of recalling past injustice and of putting it aside in the name of **democracy, community,** or the nation. In what has been described as our 'age of atonement', law is thus implicated in the immensely complex task of bringing to mutual accommodation the demands of **justice** and reconciliation.

This articulation forces us to rethink some of our assumptions about the relationship of law as a limit to and corrective of politics. The use of law internationally to bring about political objectives of a certain kind has been widespread. It has been used amongst others: to engineer the transition in South Africa and to guarantee a new constitutional dispensation for a reconciled nation; to renounce Australia's racist *terra nullius* doctrine and acknowledge (within strict limits) the aboriginal title to land in *Mabo*; to frame the **Good Friday Agreement** in Ireland and provide for the release of 'political' prisoners;

to furnish responses to **genocide** in Rwanda, Australia, and Armenia; to set up **tribunals** and truth commissions throughout Africa and the Americas with the purpose of establishing a record of the past by circumventing the official criminal **prosecutions** route; to introduce flexibility in the prosecution of state officials of the former Warsaw pact, and in the treatment of political prisoners of the RAF in Germany. The examples are numerous and there is always a danger that in moving from historical contingencies and jurisdictional particularities to generalizable premises and conclusions one might miss what is specific and salient in each case. Nonetheless, it is important to look at the lessons that can be drawn from the legal-institutional function in these cases, and nowhere more prominently that in the case of the **Truth and Reconciliation** Commission ('TRC') in South Africa. Key among the **transitional justice** institutions that have been entrusted with managing precarious transitions, the TRC is widely held up as a model, the most advanced of its kind, a way of negotiating a 'third way' between **punishment** and impunity in coming to terms with the past and upholding processes of corrective justice and social reconstruction. From the point of view of law's involvement in political reconciliation, the TRC is interesting because in every aspect of its working, it is steeped in law. It engaged in legal interpretations of key notions: 'just ends, just means' and '**crime against humanity**'; 'victim'; 'severe ill-treatment'; 'political context, political motivation'; '**accountability**'. It enjoyed significant procedural powers, amongst them the power to issue subpoenas and force people before it, to compel witnesses' testimony. It decided on the admissibility of evidence; it authorized **searches and seizures**; it could subpoena documents. Most significantly it had the power to grant **amnesties**. At the same time, it was seen to have a specific function beyond the ordinary norms and procedures of crime and punishment and the 'narrow business', as its architects put it, of determining guilt or innocence. To perform its 'august role', the criterion of 'beyond reasonable doubt' was replaced by the test of a 'balance of probabilities', and many findings were accepted on untested premises. It is noteworthy that both of these compromises were justified on grounds of the Commission's unique mandate: reconciliation, not **retribution**.

One way to bring out the complexity of law's task in bringing about reconciliation is to look at the challenges it faces in the process and the problems and objections that such a specific orientation encounters. In this respect, one might identify five broad areas of tension.

First, because of the increasing demand that the past be dealt with for the sake of shared and peaceable futures, and due to the inability of conventional notions of justice to succeed in this context, law is forced to incorporate a structural and symbolic element of *mercy*. This results in a new demand being placed on law, on an unprecedentedly grand scale, to be merciful rather than just in the conventional sense, involving law in a huge, explicitly symbolic effort of a type it ordinarily shuns. It is here that one manifestation appears of a paradox that has been the focus of theological and philosophical discussion for centuries. Briefly stated the paradox is this: either mercy—as stipulating conditions under which certain departures from formal requirements of justice are legitimate—is itself an element of justice, and thus not an independent value, or in requiring a departure from justice it is unjust.

A related issue involves the difficult simultaneous accommodation of the demands of justice, understood in a traditional, retributive, sense, and as restorative. In coming to terms with the past, conventional criminal notions of punishment based in retribution have been disrupted and seen variously to be inefficacious, impossible, or undesirable. As such, different sets of demands are placed on legal systems as the stakes are tied not to individual retribution or the restoration of value, but instead to demands for truth, reconciliation, and national unity in the face of a divided past. In South Africa, it was argued in the constitutional case of *Azapo* (levelled against the constitutionality of the amnesty provisions) that impunity for those who propped up the **apartheid** regime flew in the face of the new South Africa's commitment to upholding human rights. While the case was not successful, its claim that circumventing the requirements of justice in the name of reconciliation is unconstitutional is variably present in all objections to putting the exigencies of reconciliation ahead of those of justice.

Thirdly, reconciliation, it is sometimes claimed, places too high a demand on law in requiring resolution of conflicts that may be best understood as unresolvable, or solvable only through political means. Fourthly, reconciliation invites 'quietism', a burden on the victims of history to 'forgive and forget' in contradiction to the attribution of **responsibility,** collective or individual.

Finally, it is argued that the function of law and reconciliation are not compatible and thus to use the former as an instrument of the latter introduces an impossible tension. That is because the function of law is to stabilize expectations in society according to pre-given (past) standards, whereas reconciliation involves breaking with the past, is future-oriented, and for the most part requires *ad hoc* decision-making.

The various problems, tensions, and objections that surround the ideal, including the increasingly pertinent question: 'under what conditions reconciliation?' have turned reconciliation into a contested concept when read in certain political contexts and against certain socio-political backgrounds. The tension is amplified with the involvement of law in the processes. On the one hand, of course, law is the means through which a society can act to determine the terms of living together and thus also of the conditions of reconciliation; on the other hand, law appears sometimes inert and sometimes (as above) even unaccommodating of the political burden placed on it. The demands placed on the theory and practice of law by the exigencies of reconciliation require an attentiveness to these complexities in place of the too often rather uncritical call for a 'blanket' reconciliation at all costs.

EMILIOS CHRISTODOULIDIS

See also: **restorative justice**

Red Cross *see* **international humanitarian law**

redemption of shares The Companies Act 2006, section 684 gives **companies** with a **share** capital the power to issue redeemable shares—shares which are to be redeemed or are liable to be redeemed at the option of the company or the shareholder. This allows companies flexibility in raising finance. Redeemable shares can only be issued if the company already has some non-redeemable shares in issue.

Redeemable shares have to be issued as fully paid shares. Also, the terms of redemption have to be fixed by the articles of the company issuing the shares, or by the company's directors pursuant to its articles, and in either case before the shares are issued.

There are strict rules as to how the redemption of shares may be financed. These rules flow from the need to ensure that a company's capital is not returned to its shareholders to the prejudice of its creditors, whose claims on the company's funds generally rank in priority to those of the shareholders. Consequently, the redeemable shares of **public companies** may only be redeemed out of profits available for distribution (within the meaning of the companies legislation), or out of the proceeds of a fresh issue of shares made for the purposes of the redemption. A **private company** may redeem shares in these ways and, in addition, redeem shares out of capital funds subject to strict procedural and accounting constraints designed to protect the interests of the company's creditors.   RC NOLAN

redundancy The notion of redundancy is one which is encountered especially, though not uniquely, in the employment law of the United Kingdom, in which it is used to denote the idea of a worker losing his or her job 'through no fault of their own' but rather because their job has disappeared, or their work has ceased to be 'needed' by the enterprise in which they are employed. Other systems of employment relations and employment law tend to use different terminolgies, perhaps even somewhat different concepts to encapsulate the same general idea; in North America the language of 'lay-off' tends to be used, while in Continental European systems the idea of 'collective dismissals' tends to be invoked for this definitional purpose. The heyday of this concept occurred during the 1960s and 1970s, when it was deployed in employment law to identify a notion of entitlement to **compensation** for loss of one's job as the result of the technological advance of industry and the automation of many human functions in manufacturing processes; it would subsequently be strongly linked to the rapid advance of computerized information technology and to the globalization of production of and commerce in both goods and services. The concept came to be the subject of contradictory instrumentalities when, as well as being the condition of entitlement to compensation for workers, it also became, under systems of **unfair dismissal** law such as that of the UK, a justification for dismissal; employees would argue for a wide view of 'redundancy' for the former purpose, but a narrow view of it for the latter purpose. In the legal definition or exposition of the concept of redundancy, there are typically two alternative elements, one being the closure of the undertaking or distinct part of the undertaking in which the worker in question is employed (without its transfer to another employing enterprise); the other, even more elusive, alternative element is the cessation of the demand for the job in which the worker in question is employed (despite the continuation in existence of the employing undertaking). Because of the strong tendency of English law to mediate the concepts of employment law through the **contract of employment** there has been a continuing issue under that employment law system as to whether or how far to elaborate the concept of redundancy, particularly in the latter form of cessation of demand for the job, through the contract of employment, thus testing the flexibility of particular contracts of employment in the way that they specify the occupational and geographical mobility which can be expected of the employees in question. A contrasting approach defines redundancy more empirically by considering the work or function which the worker is normally asked to do, rather than the adaptations which the worker could contractually be called upon to accept. On either approach, this issue could be regarded as an aspect of **good faith performance in employment law**.   MARK FREEDLAND

referendaire   see **European Court of Justice**

referendums A referendum is a process in which an existing or proposed law (normally drafted by the legislature) is referred to the electorate. Its use varies according to jurisdiction. In the **United Kingdom** the legislature decides when a referendum should be held, generally where the proposed law is of constitutional importance and requires some degree of popular approval to secure legitimacy. In some other jurisdictions a referendum may be constitutionally required where the law or proposal deals with a particular issue. Alternatively, some jurisdictions permit referendums on existing laws or proposals to be initiated by citizens presenting a petition to the relevant official within a specified period of time. The phrasing of the question to be put to the electorate is of crucial importance and can impact on the result of the vote. In the UK, the phrasing will normally be stated in the legislation proposing the referendum, although the independent Electoral Commission has an advisory role on the intelligibility of the question.

In many jurisdictions, the result of a referendum is binding and determines whether the measure becomes or remains law. By contrast, in the UK referendums are only advisory and the legislature is legally free to follow or ignore the result (although there will generally be political pressure to follow it).

While advocates of referendums argue that the process permits greater citizen involvement in democratic decisions, the procedure has been subject to a number of criticisms. One criticism is that most citizens lack the time, resources, or expertise to make an informed assessment of the issues. Another sceptical view is that politicians employ the procedure to avoid a difficult decision and 'pass the buck' to citizens on a particularly divisive issue. The process also limits the role of the citizen to giving a 'yes' or 'no' answer to a law or proposal that has been drafted by the legislature.   JACOB ROWBOTTOM

See also: **initiative as a means of instigating legislation**

refugees Although refugee movements have occurred since time immemorial, only in the nineteenth and early twentieth centuries did they become a subject for law and regulation. The emerging practice of inter-state extradition based on treaty increasingly accepted the appropriateness of making an exception for the 'political offender' (see, eg the Extradition Act 1870), and the Aliens Act 1905 expressly accepted that refusal of entry for want of means should not apply in the case of those 'seeking to avoid prosecution or punishment on religious or political grounds or for an offence of a political character, or persecution involving danger of imprisonment or danger to life or limb on account of religious belief'.

Later developments in **United Kingdom** law have tended to take account of international law and practice, which effectively began with the appointment by the League of Nations of the first High Commissioner for Refugees in 1921. Refugees were initially defined or described by the League as persons who no longer enjoyed the protection of their government and who had not acquired another nationality. Following the experiences of the 1930s and 1940s, states recognized in the 1948 **Universal Declaration of Human Rights** that everyone had the right to seek **asylum** from persecution, and thereafter agreed on a definition of the refugee as someone who was outside their country of origin, and unable or unwilling to return there because of a well-founded fear of persecution for reasons of race, religion, **nationality**, membership of a particular social group, or political opinion; this now forms the central focus of the 1951 Convention relating to the Status of Refugees, which provides also for the 'exclusion' from refugee status of war criminals, serious common criminals, and those who pose a serious risk to security. At the time, states were only prepared to accept international obligations towards refugees 'as a result of events occurring before 1 January 1951'; and some limited their commitment still further, to refugees from events in Europe. These limitations have now been removed by the 1967 Protocol to the 1951 Convention, to either or both of which the UK and 146 other states are now party.

The UK played an active role in the work of the International Refugee Organization, set up under the **United Nations** to deal with the population displacement problems of World War II, in the establishment of its successor, the Office of the United Nations High Commissioner for Refugees ('UNHCR'), and in the drafting of the 1951 Convention. At the international level, the UNHCR's responsibility is to provide protection to refugees and, together with governments, to seek lasting solutions to the problem of refugees. This includes promoting international cooperation and support for voluntary repatriation when conditions permit, and local asylum or resettlement in other countries where appropriate. The UNHCR also oversees the application of the 1951 Convention/1967 Protocol, and tries to ensure protection for refugees and asylum seekers through access to national procedures for the determination of status and protection against return to risk of persecution or torture.

Until the enactment of the Immigration Act 1971, the 'protection' of refugees and the grant of asylum in the UK were decided by the Home Office, in the exercise of essentially unreviewable discretionary powers to determine who should be allowed to enter and remain. **Commonwealth** citizens, who were not subject to immigration control at the time, were thus outside the asylum field, which was firmly located in the context of decisions on admission and deportation or removal. Following the recommendations of the 1966 Wilson Committee on immigration appeals and the enactment of the Immigration Appeal Act 1969, a person has been able to challenge the refusal to grant asylum, where eligibility to enter or remain is conditional in the first place upon the individual satisfying the refugee criteria described above. Appeals from initial Home Office decisions lay first to Immigration Adjudicators, and thereafter to the Immigration Appeal Tribunal ('IAT'); following recent reforms, the Adjudicator is now styled an 'Immigration Judge' and the IAT has been reconstituted as a court of record—the Asylum and Immigration Tribunal. The Wilson Committee also recommended that in any appeal in which a person is or claims to be a refugee, the UNHCR Representative in the UK should be entitled to become a party. This practice has been maintained in the Rules of Procedure, and the UNHCR has also successfully sought permission to intervene in various cases involving refugees or the interpretation and application of the relevant treaties.

The Convention and Protocol have not been expressly incorporated in UK law, but the effect of successive legislative references and the content of the rules adopted for implementation of immigration and asylum law have led the courts to conclude that, to all intents and purposes, they are indeed now part of domestic law. Section 2 of the Asylum and Immigration Appeals Act 1993, for example, is entitled 'Primacy of the Convention'; it provides that, 'Nothing in the immigration rules . . . shall lay down any practice which would be contrary to the Convention'.

Although it has been the practice of the UK, in common with most other states in the developed world, to grant asylum to refugees, no duty to do so is recognized as a matter of law. What is generally accepted, however, as a matter of both treaty and customary international law, is a duty not to send a refugee back to a country in which he or she would be at risk of persecution or torture (the principle of *non-refoulement*). UK law in fact expressly defines an asylum application as an objection to removal or refusal of admission.

UK courts have made some notable contributions to the international jurisprudence on interpretation of the refugee definition and other aspects of the 1951 Convention. In other instances, however, they have not always recognized the full implications of the **human rights** dimensions to refugee identity and protection.

Various lacunae in the international system of refugee protection and solutions—for example, acceptance of *non-refoulement*, but not of an obligation to grant asylum; no clear demarcation of which state should deal with an asylum application or of the responsibilities of 'transit' states; no mechanisms for equitable sharing in solutions; lack of effective protection in first countries of asylum—together with the blending of refugee and migration flows and the problems of differentiating between them, have led many states, including the UK, to try to prevent or deter asylum applicants from arriving in their territory. Such policies have included visa requirements, sanctions on airlines and other carriers which transport passengers with inadequate or false documentation, detention, denial of social support, refusal of the right to work, accelerated procedures, and expedited removals.

Since the entry into force of the Treaty of Amsterdam in 1999, the **European Union** has also moved in the direction of a common European asylum policy, with emphasis first on the harmonization of approaches at the national level. For example, the Dublin Regulation (following on an earlier treaty) aims to establish a mechanism to determine which EU state is responsible for deciding an asylum claim lodged in one state following entry in or transit through one or more other Member States. A series of directives also seek to lay down common procedural standards (though at a minimum level), common standards of interpretation of refugee status and exclusion criteria, as well as common approaches to temporary protection (for example, in the case of mass movements such as occurred as a result of the break-up of Yugoslavia), reception of asylum seekers, and family reunion. The EU's Qualification Directive also takes account of European (and international) human rights obligations, making provision for the grant of 'subsidiary protection' to some

individuals who, while not satisfying the criteria for Convention refugee status, may nevertheless face certain types of serious harm if required to return to their country of origin. The Nationality, Immigration and Asylum Act 2002 expressly mentions Article 3 of the **European Convention on Human Rights** (prohibiting torture) as a ground for an asylum application and as the basis of an obligation not to return or refuse admission to certain categories of asylum seekers.   GUY S GOODWIN-GILL

refusal of treatment   *see* **consent**

Regicides, the   Parliament's victory over Charles I, who remained ungracious and dishonest in defeat, in 1645 failed to lead to any lasting political settlement. It became apparent to the Army and their supporters in Parliament that Charles had to be dethroned; and on 6 January 1649 the purged **House of Commons** named 135 commissioners to try Charles I for treason. The Commons specified that the trial could proceed with a quorum of twenty commissioners and well over half of those named attended in some capacity to try the King.

Charles I's trial began on 20 January 1649 with John Bradshaw chosen as its presiding judge. The barrister John Cook was chosen as Charles' prosecutor. Charles I was uncooperative and refused to plead, arguing that as the **monarch** by divine right the Court had no power to try him. He was convicted and sentenced to death. Fifty-nine of the commissioners signed the death warrant on 29 January 1649 and he was beheaded on 30 January outside the Banqueting House in Whitehall, London.

With the Restoration of the monarchy in 1660, many of the forty-one or so surviving Regicides were tried and convicted under Treason Act of 1352. In all thirteen men were executed; most who pleaded guilty had their sentences commuted to imprisonment and other Regicides escaped to Holland, Switzerland, or America.

The main protagonists in the Regicide: Oliver Cromwell, Henry Ireton, John Bradshaw, and Thomas Pride had already died. As symbolic punishment Parliament ordered their bodies to be exhumed, hanged, and beheaded.   ELLIOT VERNON

regional assemblies   *see* **Northern Ireland Assembly; Scottish Parliament; Welsh Assembly**

regional development agencies   The creation of regional development agencies in England was promised in the Labour Party's election manifesto of

1997, a promise fulfilled in the Regional Development Agencies Act 1999. This Act sets out the five basic purposes of the agencies: (1) to further economic development and regeneration; (2) to promote business efficiency, investment, and competitiveness; (3) to promote employment; (4) to enhance development and application of skill relevant to employment; and (5) to contribute to sustainable development. Each agency pursues these aims in relation to its own region. There are nine such regions: West Midlands, East Midlands, North West, North East, South East, South West, Yorkshire, East of England, and London.

Regional development agencies are Non-Departmental Public Bodies ('NDPBs'). With the exception of the London Development Agency, they are accountable to the Secretary of State for Trade and Industry. The London Development Agency is accountable to the London Assembly. Each agency has a board responsible for ensuring that the agency fulfills its statutory purposes. Boards comprise between eight and fifteen members. Board members are appointed by the Secretary of State.

Equivalent development agencies exist in other parts of the **United Kingdom** and have longer histories. Scotland has Scottish Enterprise and Highland and Islands Enterprise. Northern Ireland has Invest Northern Ireland. In both cases, these agencies are accountable to devolved government. In Wales, the functions of the Welsh Development Agency were subsumed into the Assembly Government's Department of Enterprise, Innovation, and Networks.

SIMON HALLIDAY

registration of title The phrase refers to a system of recording and guaranteeing rights in relation to land, designed to facilitate speedy and reliable transactions with land. Legal (as opposed to equitable) fees simple (see **fee simple estate**) and leases (see **leasehold estate**) exceeding seven years may be registered, whereupon the registered title is guaranteed. Although the system is often described as land registration (the title of the legislation), estates in the land are registered rather than the land itself. There may thus be two registered titles (fee simple and lease) for the same plot of land. However, the land plays a crucial role in that the registration is by reference to a plan showing the extent of the land.

Registration of title was first introduced on a voluntary basis in 1862. It became compulsory on sales in specified areas in 1899 and since 1990 has been compulsory on sale (and certain other transactions with the legal title) without geographical limit. As of 2007, approximately 90 per cent of titles were registered.

The Land Registry encourages landowners to register on a voluntary basis and has expressed the hope that 100 per cent registration may be reached by 2012. The current governing legislation is the Land Registration Act 2002. Introduced following a number of reviews by the Law Commission, it introduced numerous changes to the scheme which had operated largely unchanged since 1925.

The holder of a registered title, the proprietor, may enter into the same dispositions as in the case of unregistered land. However, certain dealings must comply with registration requirements before they are effective to create legal (as opposed to equitable) interests. These dealings include transfers, leases exceeding seven years, **easements**. and **mortgages of land**. Once this procedure is completed, the purchaser (or other disponee) takes free from any right to the land which affects the seller but which is not 'protected'.

As well as the registrable dispositions mentioned above, virtually all proprietary rights to the land (including, for example, estate contracts and restrictive covenants) should be protected by entry on the register. In most cases this will be by entry of a notice. This means that a purchaser will be bound by the interest, though the interest is not guaranteed either against any flaw in its creation or as regards its priority prior to its protection. If the interest is not protected, then it will not bind a purchaser, even if the purchaser is in bad faith. It remains possible that the conduct of a purchaser who is aware of an unprotected interest may give rise to the tort of interference with contract or an equitable duty (a **constructive trust** based on unconscionable receipt).

Overriding interests are also treated as protected. These are interests which affect purchasers even though they are not entered on the register. The most important categories are legal (as opposed to equitable) leases not exceeding seven years, rights of persons in actual occupation of the land, and legal easements. Actual occupation has provoked much debate and litigation. It means that those who have failed to place an entry on the register will still be protected if in actual occupation. The onus is on those dealing with proprietors to inspect the land as well as the register. The present legislation attempts to minimize the scope of overriding interests so that, as far as possible, those dealing with the proprietor can rely on what the register reveals. One example is that actual occupation operates as an overriding interest only if the occupation is obvious on a reasonably careful inspection of the land.

Entry of a restriction on the register limits the circumstances in which transfers and other dispositions will be registered. The most common example of a restriction is where there is a trust of land. For a disposition to operate free from interests of trust beneficiaries (so that they are overreached), the proceeds of sale must be paid to at least two trustees. For registered land, this requirement of two trustees can be implemented by entry of a restriction requiring there to be two trustees before a disposition is registered. The restriction is so effective for trusts of land that entry of a notice is not allowed.

If a mistake is made on the register, it may be corrected by alteration. If this adversely affects the proprietor, it is called rectification Unless at fault, the proprietor in possession is protected against rectification save where the court considers that it would be unjust not to rectify. If loss is caused, whether by rectification, a mistake, or some administrative error, the Land Registry pays indemnity to the losing party. These rules further illustrate the guarantee provided by the registration of title.

The system described above is that applicable to England and Wales. The Land Registration (Scotland) Act 1979 establishes a system of registration of title in Scotland. ROGER J SMITH

regressive taxation *see* **tax, ability to pay**

regulation Regulation refers to legal rules which seek to steer the behaviour of mainly private citizens and **companies** but also of central and local government as well as public agencies. Regulation scholarship inquires into whether and how law can fulfil regulatory functions. It is a newer area of legal practice and analysis having developed in connection with late nineteenth- and twentieth-century **welfare states**' attempts to shape the behaviour of private and public actors. Regulation in a narrow sense (the 'regulatory state thesis') denotes new forms of legal regulation arising from the reform and streamlining of contemporary welfare states. It involves departure from 'old regulation', such as public ownership, planning, and central administration.

Classic definitions of regulation focus on state regulation of private activity. Recent scholarship also includes regulation between private actors, self-regulation, and the regulation of public powers by the state itself or private actors. Public powers can be regulated through 'new public management' which involves the transfer of private sector management ethos and techniques to the central government civil service and local government. 'New public management' should enhance effectiveness and efficiency in the delivery of public services and regulatory functions. It can involve deregulation, contracting out, **privatization** (techniques strongly associated with **Thatcherism**) as well as the creation of autonomous agencies and audit approaches, measuring and assessing the exercise of public powers through performance indicators and customer satisfaction, for instance, through citizens' charters. Recent initiatives inspired by 'Third Way', New Labour politics—both in the UK and the European Union—focus on 'better regulation'. They still seek to cut 'burdens on business' and limit public expenditure but do not perceive deregulation as the only option (eg the Legislative and Regulatory Reform Act 2006 in the UK and the European Union Inter-institutional Agreement on Better Law-Making signed by the **European Parliament**, the Council of the EU, and the **European Commission**). 'Better regulation' initiatives aim to improve enforcement of existing regulations. They also seek to avoid unchecked proliferation of legal regulation by requiring legislators to carry out 'regulatory impact assessments'. These assess the costs and benefits of proposed new regulation. This 'meta-regulation' regulates the regulators.

Given these wide definitions of regulation it is clear that it does not just involve traditional constitutional and administrative law. It draws on a number of specific areas of law and is thus a cross-cutting field of legal practice and research. Contract, tort, property, labour, and criminal law all involve regulation through law. The key distinction between economic and social regulation helps further to clarify what regulation is. Economic regulation seeks to ensure fair prices and product/service quality through maintaining **competition** between economic actors. In the absence of competitive market forces, as in the case of monopoly operators, legal regulation—often in the form of specific statutory obligations—directly regulates pricing, access, and quality standards. It is particularly significant in areas of monopoly operators, such as utilities, supplying telecommunications, electricity, gas, water, and transport services. By contrast, social regulation involves more than maintaining competitive markets or compensating for their absence. It seeks to realize wider objectives by preventing harm or conferring benefits on citizens generally. It includes regulation for social inclusion, environmental, **consumer**, and health and safety protection.

Regulation can also be considered in terms of the question of *how* legal rules steer the behaviour of private and public actors. Regulators employ various instruments. Through traditional 'command and control' administrative regulation the state requires specific behaviour from corporations. This regulation is often implemented by independent regulatory agencies, operating at arms' length from the state, such as the **Environment Agencies** in the United Kingdom. For instance, conditions in a factory's licence may stipulate that it can only emit a limited amount of pollutants into the air. Failure to comply with '**command and control' regulation** is often sanctioned by criminal or regulatory penalties. 'Hard command and control' regulation is sometimes contrasted with 'soft' regulation. The latter relies on incentives, often financial, such as taxes, subsidies, or trading in environmental emissions. It can also involve regulation simply through information, for instance, when companies are required to disclose information about their products and services to consumers. 'Responsive', 'reflexive', or 'co-regulatory' regulation avoids abstract choices of either 'hard' or 'soft' regulation. Instead regulators develop standards and enforcement strategies by working with the regulated. Regulation responds here to the characteristics and motivations of the particular regulated organization.

Regulation, however, is not just concerned with the mechanics of different regulatory instruments. In fact whether state law—regardless of choice of regulatory tool—can really shape the behaviour of private and public actors is questionable. Implementation studies show that legal regulation often fails to achieve its stated policy aims. Indeed, some, such as Gunther Teubner, perceive a 'crisis in regulation'. Doctrinal legal analysis, but also theoretical and empirical inquiry into law and society relationships is necessary to understand whether and how law can regulate. Regulation also benefits from political science, economics, sociological, and criminological perspectives. Political science highlights the importance of institutions and networks in the design and delivery of regulation. It address questions such as how to make regulation more democratic through participation of and deliberation among citizens and corporate actors, transforming initial fixed preferences, and perceptions of individual interests. Democratic **accountability** and transparency are salient given that, not just interest group politics, but also scientific expert knowledges increasingly inform the regulation of technological and social **risks**.

Economists have contributed their own theories of why and how law should regulate. For instance, **pollution**, work-related injuries, and defective consumer goods are considered as 'externalities' of private economic activity. When companies fail to account for and remedy these internally, they pass on the costs of these risks to their customers, workers, or the wider public. Efficient, rational resource allocation and production, however, require the internalization of such costs, for instance, through financial incentives or tort or **property rights**. Hence, regulation works to reallocate these costs to companies.

Criminologists advance understanding of the failure and successes of legal regulation through theories of corporate crime and **governance**. Sociologists also contribute further insight into regulation, for instance, through analysis of governments' tactics and strategies of social control. Research on the 'art of government' or '**governmentality**' in advanced liberal **democracies** suggests that regulation does not just arise from formal state activity but occurs in a range of social locations, including the family and various administrative regimes, such as social security, medical care, and housing. Regulation encompasses here a wide range of small scale techniques of control, discipline, and surveillance. It can also include internal regulation, such as one's control of the self.

To summarize, regulation is more than simply specific legal instruments and approaches deployed for the control of private and public power. Regulation is at the heart of wider social theoretical debates about the relationship between a public and a private sphere, states and markets, state and civil society. These relationships are changing as the state becomes 'decentred'. Private actors increasingly matter, for instance in various forms of voluntary regulation. These include self-regulation, legally non-binding agreements between regulators and regulated, as well as standard-setting by private actors. For instance, companies may regulate themselves through compliance with voluntary industry codes of conduct, such as environmental management standards. For public lawyers the key issue here is how established principles of administrative and **constitutional law**—such as procedural fairness, legitimacy, accountability and transparency—can still be applied to innovative, informal, negotiated, and privatized regulation.

Finally, globalization and regional integration projects, such as the European Union, further decentre the nation state in transnational regulation. Transnational regulation often involves networks of both private and public actors. State regulation may be combined with merchants' private regulation, such as *lex mercatoria* developed in international contract chains. The European Union's new supranational legal order and its integrated market also curb Member States' powers to regulate through national law. But this does not simply amount to deregulation. It often involves reregulation through EU law. EU regulation of national economic activity ranges from macro-economic policies of the

Stability and Growth Pact, to competition, utilities, consumer, and environmental law as well as legislation on the supply of services (see the proposed Directive of the European Parliament and Council on services in the internal market COM (2006) 160 final). Transnational regulation can also result from legal regulation transplants from countries of the North-West to post-colonial societies of the South and North-East, sometimes imposed by international organizations, rather than locally developed.

To conclude, regulation is a constantly evolving, dynamic field of law and scholarship, driven also by competing perspectives of social justice in the prevention and distribution of risks. Political debates about the merits of social democracy and **neo-liberalism** shape how legal regulation affects citizens' lives in practice. Increasing resort to a language of economics runs the danger of sidelining ethical considerations in discussions over whether and how to regulate.   BETTINA LANGE

J Braithwaite, 'The New Regulatory State and the Transformation of Criminology' (2000) 40 *British Journal of Criminology* 222–238

R Baldwin, C Scott, and C Hood, *A Reader on Regulation, Oxford Readings in Socio-Legal Studies* (Oxford: Oxford University Press, 1998)

regulations (EU)   *see* **community legal instruments**

regulations, orders and bye-laws   *see* **legal rules, types of**

regulatory agencies   This term refers to a range of organizations which shape and direct social behaviour so as to contribute to the attainment of whatever goals a society wishes to achieve. A regulatory agency is a kind of 'social engineer'. Its task is to monitor and oversee the conduct of designated social activities to ensure that they are carried out in the desired manner. In its most familiar form, a regulatory agency is a representative of the state, responsible for implementing and enforcing prescriptive controls over particular kinds of social and economic activities, if necessary through the application of sanctions.

In Britain, the number of such agencies grew substantially following the industrial revolution, but state intervention in economic social activity to promote collective goals can be traced back to the Tudor and Stuart periods. Although the flourishing of large scale industrial activity throughout the nineteenth century was generally welcomed because of its contribution to general economic growth and prosperity, it had unwelcome side-effects, such as polluting the environment and jeopardizing the health and safety of workers through injury and illness. Accordingly, the state intervened through the regulation of industrial activity to prevent, or at least reduce, the undesirable effects of otherwise valuable enterprise. For example, a factory inspection system was established in England in the early nineteenth century (considered the first of its kind and subsequently imitated in other countries). The Alkali Inspectorate was established later that century to limit the quantity of certain emissions into the atmosphere.

Regulatory agencies can be established within the departmental structure of central government (for example, the first Factory Inspectorate was set up within central government as part of the Home Office). But so-called 'independent' regulatory agencies, operating at arm's length from government rather than subject to direct control by government ministers but nevertheless as representatives of the state, have gained increasing popularity in many Western industrialized countries (including Britain) since the 1960s. Their popularity is often explained by their capacity to combining professionalism, operational autonomy, political insulation, flexibility to adapt to changing circumstances, and policy expertise in highly complex spheres of activity. Further impetus for the growth of such agencies emerged during the 1980s and 1990s as successive governments shifted the responsibility for delivering so-called 'public services' into the private and non-governmental sector, whilst seeking to retain power to oversee and guide overall service provision. The independent regulatory agency was considered a useful vehicle for carrying out this oversight and monitoring function. The resulting shift in state involvement in economic and social activity has been aptly described as one of 'steering rather than rowing', as the state turns from direct service provision to non-governmental service provision combined with regulatory oversight.

Although the 'independent' regulatory agency has become a well-established organizational form, the term 'regulatory agency' may encompass a wide array of institutional arrangements, displaying considerable variation along several dimensions, including their relationship with the state. Not only have such agencies flowered at the state level, but regulatory agencies and other similar bodies have also proliferated *within* the state to oversee the provision of services provided by other state providers. Examples in the UK include the Office for Standards in Education (which is responsible for the inspection and oversight of schools in England) and HM Inspectorate of Prisons (which regulates prisons in England and Wales). Others operate above and beyond the state within trans-national governance regimes, such as the **World Trade Organization** and those bodies responsible for regulatory oversight established within the **European Union**, such as the **European Central Bank**. A number of regulatory agencies also operate without direct state involvement, and this form of oversight is often referred to 'self-regulation'. Such bodies are often found in professional service industries (medical, legal, engineering, and so forth). Thus, the degree of state involvement in any agency may vary considerably, from its complete absence (in the case of self-regulation) through to complete state control (in the case of regulatory bodies overseeing public service provision) with some form of mixed or 'hybrid' regime involving both public and private sector involvement (sometimes described as 'co-regulation') lying between these two extremes.

Considerable variation exists in the legal powers and policy instruments of regulatory agencies. The most familiar technique, frequently called 'command and control', involves establishing legal standards for the conduct of the regulated activity, which the agency may enforce by the application of legal sanctions against those who violate those standards. Regulatory agencies may, however, seek to encourage the desired behaviour in other ways, such as the provision of economic incentives, promotional publicity aimed at encouraging the desired behaviour, agreeing with members of the regulated community to forbear from some kind of intrusive action in return for their commitment to undertake desired activities, and so forth. Although the technique adopted by an agency will be the product of many factors, chief among them will be the legal framework within which they operate; and this varies considerably between sectors and, indeed, jurisdictions. Partly as a result of this variation, the notion of 'regulatory law' it is not yet a well-established category in UK law, unlike criminal law, **tort law, contract law,** and so forth, although the term is sometimes used in legal writing.

Regulatory agencies are the focus of study in law and a range of social scientific disciplines, including politics, economics, management studies, and criminology. Scholars of public law and politics often emphasize the need for agencies to be accountable for the exercise of their regulatory power. A recurring concern has been their perceived lack of democratic legitimacy (the so-called 'democratic deficit'). Because such agencies often make decisions that have a differential impact upon group interests, in which some gain more than others, their decisions have a political dimension. Yet their insulation from direct government intervention often generates claims that

agencies lack a democratic mandate for their decisions. Various strategies are adopted in response to such claims, such as providing scope for public participation in agency decisions (especially standard-setting), requiring the agency to give reasons for their decisions and to report to the legislature on a regular basis, and providing for **judicial review** or appeal against agency decisions.   KAREN YEUNG

regulatory offences   A distinction is commonly made between 'conventional' or 'proper' crimes, such as murder or assault, and 'regulatory ' offences. The former are regarded as *mala in se* (wrong in themselves) and the latter as *mala prohibita* (wrong because the law deems this to be the case, not because any moral turpitude is involved). ' Regulatory' offences are often referred to as 'technical' breaches even though, in formal terms, they involve full scale criminal liabilities and potential sanctions. In the health and safety field, for instance, it has more than once been said that regulatory offences are not 'real crimes' and the Robens Committee Report that laid the foundations for the British health and safety regime stated that the traditional concepts of the criminal law were not readily applicable to the majority of infringements in that area. Such attitudes to regulatory offences have been said to create problems when magistrates and **judges** tend to impose mild sanctions in reflection of society's moral ambivalence concerning these infringements. Regulators frequently complain that these approaches to **sentencing** lead to massive under-deterrence and to inefficiency in regulatory regimes.

The majority of regulatory offences involve strict liability and prosecutors are able to secure convictions without proof of *mens rea* (guilty mind or fault). A criticism of strict liability regulatory offences is that, because there is no need to show the presence of negligence, recklessness, or intention, such offences can involve punishing 'innocent' parties—persons or firms that are not blameworthy but have caused a prohibited result (eg they have unwittingly stored a particular substance on site without notifying the regulator as required by the relevant regulations).

Proponents of strict liability regulatory offences tend, however, to justify resort to such offences by arguing that the lack of any underpinning moral turpitude means that convictions for such offences do not carry the stigma that is normally associated with the criminal law. 'Innocent' parties, as a result, may have to pay **fines** or suffer other sanctions but are not subjected to social condemnation. Strict liability can also be justified on the grounds that dispensing with the need to prove fault brings dramatic efficiency gains to the enforcement process; that proof of *mens rea* is often disproportionately difficult and expensive (especially when large numbers of individually non-serious offences are involved) and that using the criminal law in association with strict liability provides a very useful (and often essential) tool of control in relation to such matters as traffic **safety** or environmental health.

A further argument in defence of regulatory offences is that 'punishing the innocent' rarely happens in practice. Inspectorates, it is said, are usually so thinly resourced and reluctant to prosecute that they will only proceed to law in relation to the most serious cases of non-compliance, which almost invariably involve a party who has evidenced some fault in the form of at least gross negligence or recklessness.

The imposition of regulatory offences raises a set of issues concerning strategies used in enforcement. These strategies can range from: strict 'deterrence' approaches (in which breaches are met with **prosecution** and emphasis is placed on deterrence); to 'compliance' procedures (which rely on persuasive and negotiation-based approaches to compliance-seeking); to 'responsive **regulation**' strategies in which the regulator commences operations with negotiatory contacts but escalates in punitiveness if 'softer' approaches do not produce the desired levels of compliance.

Regulating through the imposition of offences has been dubbed '**command and control' regulation** and this broad approach has often been condemned as excessively restrictive and productive of 'red-tape'. Critics also urge that 'command' regimes tend to prove inflexible and vulnerable to 'capture' (so that regulation favours the interests of the controlled firms rather than the public interest). Further complaints are that command systems are restrictive of managers, expensive to administer, and chilling of enterprise. Such attacks have produced a movement in the last twenty-five years in favour of 'less-restrictive' or 'incentive-based' regulatory methods such as reliance on self-regulation, control through tax incentives or subsidies, resort to **competition** laws, disclosure strategies, and reliance on civil **remedies** or the insurance markets.

A final matter for consideration with respect to regulatory offences is the extent to which punitive or deterrence approaches are limited in effectiveness. Research work in a number of countries and sectors has revealed that most corporations are quite poorly informed regarding their potential criminal liabilities for regulatory offences. Even when corporations are reasonably well informed of the regulatory rules, moreover, their behaviour may be driven by concerns other than fears about potential penalties. They may, indeed, not always see compliance with the law as the obvious response to a potential liability and may, for example, seek a scapegoat or shift the **risk** of liability by out-sourcing the risky activity. In the case of hard-pressed companies, these may lack the resources necessary to experience the appropriate level of deterrence (as where they cannot pay the kind of fine that would reflect their capacity to damage other parties or the environment). Their attention, moreover, is liable to be focused on economic survival rather than the chances of incurring a regulatory fine. In such instances there is a strong case for using controls other than liabilities for regulatory offences—such as compulsory insurance requirements or licensing mechanisms that involve the screening of entry to an industry or activity.

ROB BALDWIN

See also: **criminal liability without fault; corporate criminal liability; enforcement; strict criminal liability**

rehabilitation   Central to rehabilitation is faith in the ability of penal measures to reform offenders. Rehabilitation claims to change those aspects of the offender's personality, traits, views, lifestyle, and life chances that predispose them to crime and to develop such qualities, skills, and opportunities as might enable them to desist from offending. It relies heavily on the expertise of members of the psy-professions, social workers, and educationalists who diagnose the causes of offending behaviour, and prescribe and implement reformative programmes in response. It is characterized by considerable **discretion** both at the **sentencing** stage and, more particularly, in the implementation of penal measures.

Rehabilitation or welfarism remained prominent for much of the first half of the twentieth century and arguably reached its zenith in the 1960s in programmes of training, treatment, counselling, psychotherapy, drug, and even shock treatment. It was particularly influential in respect of juvenile offenders who, unlike their adult counterparts, were considered in need of moral education and particularly susceptible to its teachings. A now infamous article by Martinson, that began with the question 'what works?' and concluded dramatically that 'nothing works', sparked a decline of penal optimism in the 1970s. Martinson's refutation of rehabilitation has since been challenged by studies that suggest that some forms of treatment, adapted to the specific needs of certain types of offender, do work. The rise, collapse, and rekindling of faith in the rehabilitative ideal would seem to have more to do with changing political climate, therefore, than any conclusive evidence of its failure or success.

Rehabilitation is based upon a series of premises which when subject to critical scrutiny look decidedly questionable. It assumes that delinquency always has causes which are discoverable and open to treatment; that if offenders are not treated they will get worse; and that treatment, even if coerced, is not punitive since it is doing the offender good. It overlooks the fact that much offending is opportunistic. It ignores evidence that, amongst juveniles especially, offending may represent no more than a passing phase, out of which the majority will grow unaided. It fails to recognize that crime is not necessarily the product of pathology but may represent perfectly rational behaviour in the constrained circumstances in which the offender is placed. Despite claims of 'doing good', rehabilitation is often experienced by offenders as painful and unwelcome. Women, in particular, are liable to be subject to intensive treatment for relatively minor offences, particularly if they are considered to be at risk to themselves or their dependents. The treatment dictated by rehabilitation may be considerably more intrusive and painful than that dictated by conventional **punishment**. Rehabilitation is justified by its power to reform offenders. Yet it is difficult to fix criteria by which they can be considered reformed. Reconviction rates provide information only about those who have been successfully prosecuted and tell nothing of those who have evaded detection. Moreover, if the only criterion of success for rehabilitation is preventing reoffending, then incapacitation or diversionary tactics might equally succeed. LUCIA ZEDNER

R Martinson, 'What Works? Questions and Answers about Prison Reform' (Spring 1974) *Public Interest* 22–54

J McGuire (ed), *What Works: Reducing Reoffending* (Chichester: Wiley, 1995)

See also: **diversionary programmes; incapacitation theory**

Reid, James Scott Cumberland, Baron Reid of Drem Born in 1890, Reid was called to the Scottish bar in 1914, having studied law at Cambridge and Edinburgh Universities. Active service during World War I preceded a legal and political career in Scotland, becoming a Conservative MP 1931–1935 and 1937–1948 and successively holding the offices of **Solicitor General** for Scotland and **Lord Advocate** from 1936–1945. Elected Dean of the Faculty of Advocates in 1945, he had never held judicial office before, in 1948, he was appointed to the **House of Lords**. By the mid-1950s, he had become the dominant force in the House and led it in active development of English law for over twenty-five years. There were a number of important decisions on fundamental questions in criminal law, while liability in tort and contract was considerably extended. **Judicial review** of administrative action became a much more significant brake on governmental power than hitherto. Reid was also active in establishing from 1966 and then defining the Law Lords' power to overrule their own **precedents**. His speeches were notable for their combination of principle, pragmatism, and clarity. However, his contribution to Scottish law was less notable, perhaps through lack of opportunity with ever fewer appeals from the **Court of Session** in his time. He rejected as a 'fairy tale' the constitutional theory that the judges do not make law, and was an early proponent of the value to the higher judiciary of academic writing. Lord Reid died on 29 March 1975, less than three months after his retirement from the bench.

HECTOR L MACQUEEN

TB Smith, 'Reid, James Scott Cumberland, Baron Reid (1890–1975)', rev, *Oxford Dictionary of National Biography* (Oxford: Oxford University Press, 2004)

A Paterson, *The Law Lords* (London: The Macmillan Press Ltd, 1982)

reinstatement *see* **unfair dismissal**

reintegration *see* **shaming and stigmatization of offenders**

rejection of goods When goods are purchased under a sale of goods contract, if a major term of the contract (a condition) has been broken, one possible remedy for the buyer is 'rejection' of the goods.

Rejection involves informing the seller of the breach and, usually, returning the goods to the seller who refunds the purchase price to the buyer. If the goods have been delivered to the buyer, they need not, unless previously agreed, be physically returned following rejection, but may be retained for the seller to collect. Partial rejection may be possible if some goods are unaffected by the breach.

The buyer can usually choose whether to reject the goods or, instead, keep them and claim **damages** for breach of contract. There are, however, two restrictions on the right to reject. First, where the buyer is dealing as a business, not a 'consumer', and the breach is so slight that it would be unreasonable to reject the goods, the buyer can only claim damages. Secondly, if the buyer (whether non-consumer or consumer) has 'accepted' the goods, then the right to reject is lost.

The Sale of Goods Act 1979 specifies three situations when acceptance occurs. The first is where the buyer informs the seller that he is accepting the goods. If a delivery note, indicating that goods are satisfactory, is signed by the buyer, this might amount to acceptance. However, where goods have not previously been examined, the buyer must have a reasonable opportunity to examine them to check conformity with the contract before acceptance occurs. In the case of a buyer who is a consumer, this right cannot be removed by any agreement. Thus, signing a delivery note prior to examination would not be acceptance by a consumer buyer.

Secondly, acceptance occurs if, having received goods, the buyer does something to them indicating that they are no longer the property of the seller, for example using eggs to make an omelette. Two actions, which might otherwise appear to come within this description, are specifically excluded by statute. One is a request by the buyer for or the buyer's agreement to a repair by, or with the consent of, the seller. This could, however, be treated as acceptance if the buyer goes directly to the manufacturer for a repair. The other action, not treated as acceptance in itself, is sale of the goods by the buyer to a third party.

Thirdly, goods are 'accepted' when the buyer has kept them for a 'reasonable period of time' without informing the seller he is rejecting them. Precise definition of 'reasonable' time is not possible. One consideration is whether the buyer had a reasonable opportunity to check the goods for conformity with the contract. Clearly, the more complex the goods, the longer the time needed. The courts have held that sometimes about four weeks is appropriate, on other occasions five or six months may be permitted. In the case of hidden defects, it is quite possible for goods to have been 'accepted' due to lapse of time before the buyer discovers the defect.   DEBORAH PARRY

religion   The extent to which the law in the **United Kingdom** protects religious interests is a function of a complex set of laws and arrangements. Prominent among these are the established status of the **Church of England**; the protections for religion contained in the Human Rights Act 1998 (the 'HRA'); new laws covering religious discrimination (previously covered only in Northern Ireland); and restrictions on anti-religious speech.

The establishment of the Church of England involves significant links between the Church and the state. The Monarch is the supreme governor of the Church; parliamentary approval is required for church legislation; the monarch appoints the senior clergy; and the **House of Lords** contains a number of Lords Spiritual who sit as representatives of the Church. Although the **Church of Scotland** is recognized by law as the official church of Scotland, it is not established in the same sense: it is free of state interference and it is not represented in the United Kingdom Parliament. There is no established church in Wales and Northern Ireland.

Does state endorsement of a particular religion diminish religious liberty? Some argue that it does not, provided that those who do not adhere to the official religion are free to practise their own religion. Others, however, argue that religious tolerance is not enough for full religious liberty. They claim that the centrality of Anglican (ie Church of England) Christianity in the UK sends a symbolic message to non-Anglicans that they are outsiders and exerts a subtle form of coercion on them. Believing that a state church is anomalous in the religiously plural context of the UK, they support a stricter separation between church and state.

Although it appears that the privileged position of the Church of England does not breach the HRA, in other ways the HRA is very protective of religious diversity, marking a shift from a regime of tolerance to one which regards religious liberty as a fundamental right. The HRA guarantees freedom of thought, conscience, and religion. It confers an absolute right to hold (or not to hold) a religion and to change one's religion, and a qualified right to practise one's religion or beliefs. The latter right can be restricted for reasons such as the protection of public safety, public order, and the rights of others. The HRA also provides a guarantee against religious discrimination. Furthermore, subject to certain reservations, such as the need to avoid unreasonable expenditure, it recognizes the right of parents to have their religious convictions respected in their children's education. Finally, it specifically mentions the rights of religious organizations, in response to fears that the HRA would restrict their autonomy—for instance, by forcing the Church of England to marry divorced people.

The courts have confronted several controversial religious freedom cases under the HRA. In one case, the House of Lords ruled in favour of a school that had a dress code which respected 'mainstream' Muslim beliefs but did not allow the wearing of a jilbab. The Court found that the school's policy did not breach the right to freedom of religion. Another difficult question concerns exemptions: can believers demand exemptions from laws with a legitimate secular objective which incidentally burden their religious interests? On the one hand, the value of equal treatment suggests that everyone should be subject to the same rules. If the objective of the law is legitimate, it is difficult to see why an exemption should be granted. On the other hand, the belief that individuals suffer unique hardship when they are prevented from acting on their religious beliefs suggests that the law should, where possible, accommodate religious difference. The House of Lords rejected a claim for accommodation in a recent case. Teachers and parents at independent schools argued that they should have been exempted from a ban on corporal punishment in schools because they believe in a religious duty to impose corporal punishment on children. The Court held that Parliament was entitled to protect children by imposing a universal ban.

The right against religious discrimination contained in the HRA is limited. It does not directly apply to the acts of private individuals and corporations and it does not cover all forms of religious discrimination. It merely prevents the state from discriminating when it exercises power in a way which affects the enjoyment of other **human rights**. A law may not, for instance, impose discriminatory restrictions on the right to marry. Legislation aimed at preventing sham marriages—which required individuals subject to immigration control to apply for a certificate of approval to marry but excluded Anglican marriages—was successfully challenged on this basis.

Recent measures supplement the HRA's protection by outlawing religious discrimination in areas such as employment, the provision of goods and services, housing, and education. They also, however, create certain exceptions to this prohibition—for instance, where adherence to a religion is required to perform a particular job. Furthermore, exceptions in other laws permit religious groups to discriminate on grounds such as **sex** and sexual orientation. Such exceptions raise questions about the circumstances in which religious autonomy should trump anti-discrimination norms.

At **common law**, **blasphemy** is an offence but it covers attacks on Christianity only—in its Anglican form—and it has not been successfully prosecuted since *Gay News* published a blasphemous poem in 1976. In response to the law's preferential treatment of Christianity, some commentators believe that the offence should be extended to other religions, while others argue for its abolition. Recent legislation has chosen to protect all religious sensibilities by creating a new offence of incitement to religious hatred—a law which some commentators fear may chill debate and artistic expression.

There is a common theme underlying all the issues discussed here: how should the law respond to issues of religious identity and difference? These issues have become increasingly salient as religion has enjoyed a resurgence and the United Kingdom has become more religiously diverse. Whether the law has struck the right balance—between the competing values of secularism and state solicitude towards religion, universally applicable standards and special treatment for minority groups, anti-discrimination norms and religious autonomy, and free speech and the prevention of offence to believers—will be a matter of continuing debate.   DENISE MEYERSON

R Ahdar and I Leigh, *Religious Freedom in the Liberal State* (Oxford: Oxford University Press, 2005)
PW Edge, *Religion and Law: An Introduction* (Aldershot: Ashgate, 2006)

See also: **freedom of religion and belief; sexual orientation discrimination**

religion in the media   A hotchpotch of legal provisions constrains the portrayal of religion in the media. A number of provisions relate to the regulation of the visual media, while others impose criminal liability in certain circumstances for offending against religious sensibilities or arousing hatred on religious grounds.

The visual media are regulated by a self-regulatory body, the British Board of Film Classification ('BBFC'), and a statutory body, the Office of Communications (Ofcom), for broadcasting. The BBFC does not expressly censor or classify film content with a view to avoiding offence to religious sensibilities. But local authorities have the power to disregard the BBFC decisions, and certain films have been banned by some local authorities on the ground of their impact on religious sensibilities. They include *The Life of Brian* and *The Last Temptation of Christ*. The criminal law is taken into account; the BBFC decided in 1989 to refuse a certificate to the short, explicit video film, *Visions of Ecstasy* since it was concerned that if it issued a certificate its own members might have been prosecuted for **blasphemy.**

Ofcom is required to set standards for the protection of religious sensibilities and to regulate the content of religious programmes. An indication of the stance that Ofcom is currently taking was given when, in 2005, Ofcom cleared the BBC of offending against religious sensibilities by screening *Jerry Springer–the Opera*. This was a very important and telling decision in free speech terms, bearing in mind the subject matter.

The criminal law, in the form of the ancient offence of blasphemy and the brand new offence of incitement to religious hatred, also has some impact on the portrayal of religion in the media. The elements of the offence of blasphemy were re-determined in *R v Lemon* (1979), a prosecution for blasphemy in relation to a poem expressing religious sentiment in describing a homosexual's conversion to Christianity. All that needed to be shown, it was found, was that the material in question, which was published with the defendant's knowledge, had crossed the borderline between moderate criticism on the one hand and immoderate or offensive treatment of matter sacred to Christians on the other.

For various reasons, the impact of these aspects of criminal law is marginal and peripheral in relation to all media except the internet. Criminal prosecutions for blasphemy are very unlikely, partly because the law is so unclear as to be almost unusable. Secondly, the visual media are regulated in relation to religion in a way that makes prosecution of those media under the criminal law unlikely. Third, religious hatred law is aimed more at extremists who march, put up posters, or hand out leaflets. However, religious hatred law could be used against, for example, extremist anti-Muslim sites on the internet.

Blasphemy law is clearly highly problematic in free speech terms; it is also discriminatory since it only protects Christiantiy. The Racial and Religious Hatred Act 2006 outlaws incitement to religious hatred. Under section 29B a person who uses threatening words or behaviour is guilty of an offence if he intends thereby to stir up religious hatred, and subsequent sections apply this offence to the media. Thus the 2005 Act is non-discriminatory—especially of significance in relation to Muslims—and aimed at a far narrower area of speech. It is therefore anomalous that blasphemy law was not abolished by the 2005 Act.   HELEN FENWICK

religious affiliation and school dress Rules establishing school uniform derive their legitimacy from the head teacher's powers and duties in respect of the conduct of the school, behaviour, and discipline. Traditionally, education law has approached potential conflict over religious convictions by giving parents the right to remove their child from Religious Education class and from acts of worship. There is no such right in respect of school uniform requirements, but there are two routes by which this apparently unfettered discretion may be challenged. One is **equality**-based and the other is **human rights**-based.

In *Mandla v Dowell Lee* (1983), the Race Relations Act 1976 was used to challenge a ban on wearing the turban in school as indirect **race** discrimination. This was possible because Sikhism, primarily a religious grouping, met the definition of 'ethnic origin' in the Act. The use of race **legislation** to deal with religious discrimination is however far from satisfactory as not all religions meet the requirement of

ethnicity. Judaism, for example, satisfies this definition but Christianity and Islam do not. Section 43 of the Equality Act 2006 now prohibits direct and **indirect discrimination** in schools on religious grounds, providing a clearer basis for challenging uniform policy. However, indirect discrimination has a justification defence and, as such, not all disadvantage caused by dress codes will be caught by the Act. The protection is also incomplete as some of the provisions do not apply to voluntary and foundation schools that have a recognized religious ethos.

The human rights route was explored in *Begum v Headteacher and Governors of Denbigh High School* (2007), where a pupil sought **judicial review** of a decision to send her home from school for wearing the jilbab (a long, loose fitting garment covering from head to toe). The **House of Lords** found that this was not a breach of her right to manifest her religious belief under Article 9 of the **European Convention of Human Rights** and hence there was no breach of the **Human Rights Act 1998**. Three of the five judges felt that the pupil's Article 9 right was unaffected as she could have changed schools. The other two judges felt her right had been affected, but that this was justified within the terms of the Convention. The school had consulted its religious **communities** and the uniform satisfied the requirement of modesty for the great majority of pupils from Muslim, Hindu, and Sikh faiths, contributing to cohesion within the school. The House also considered whether the pupil's treatment amounted to exclusion from school and whether this denied her the right to education under Article 2 of the First Protocol to the European Convention. The House decided that this was not exclusion—the school wanted her to attend, but only in the correct uniform. This aspect of the decision can be criticized for not taking into account departmental guidance that pupils should not be excluded solely for breaches of school uniform policy and for undermining **legislation** designed to ensure that informal exclusions do not deprive parents of appeal rights.   ANN BLAIR

See also: **education and human rights**

religious discrimination *see* **protected grounds**

religious education and worship in schools Religion has had a profound influence on Britain's educational system. Church schools have long educated a significant proportion of the nation's youth, and will almost certainly continue to do so in view of the government's plans to increase the number of faith schools. Today **religion** plays an important role in

Britain's schools, and its influence is particularly obvious in two areas: collective worship and religious education.

Collective Worship

The law relating to school worship differs according to the various regions of the United Kingdom. For example, in Scotland, there is no statutory requirement for a daily act of worship, whereas in Northern Ireland all grant-aided schools are under a legal obligation (subject to the parental right of withdrawal) to provide collective worship. In England and Wales, where school worship is regulated by the School Standards and Framework Act 1998, a daily act of worship must be held in all schools maintained by local authorities. The format of the worship depends on the nature of a particular school. For example, in schools that are specifically of a religious character, the act of worship may reflect that particular denomination. Yet, by way of contrast, in 'community' (ie ordinary state) schools, as well as private schools that are not of a religious character, collective worship must be 'wholly or mainly of a broadly Christian character'. The 1998 Act stipulates that school worship satisfies these criteria if it 'reflects the broad traditions of Christian belief without being distinctive of any particular Christian nomination'. It is noteworthy that not *every* act of collective worship need comply with this rule, 'provided that taking any school term as a whole, most such acts which take place in the school do comply'. Individual parents retain the right to withdraw their **children** from school worship, while schools that are not of a religious character and have a significant number of non-Christian pupils, can apply to their local Standing Advisory Councils for Religious Education (a body comprised of teachers, local councillors, and representatives of faith groups) to hold their own acts of worship. These may be 'distinctive of any particular faith' but must not be reflective of a single branch of any religion. Thus, 'alternative' worship may, for example, be held for Muslims as a whole, but not for pupils from every branch of Islam (eg the Shia and Sunni traditions) at the school.

Religious Education

In Scotland and Northern Ireland, education authorities and state schools are under a legal obligation to provide Religious Education ('RE'), and parents in both regions retain the right to withdraw their children from RE classes. This 'parental veto' is also found in operation in England and Wales where RE, although not part of the national curriculum, is compulsory in all maintained schools. The way in which RE is taught depends on the nature of each school. For example, 'community' schools, which are not affiliated to a particular religious faith, are required to make use of the local authority 'agreed syllabus'. The content of this syllabus is determined by representatives of the Local Education Authority, faith groups, and teachers. Each local syllabus must 'reflect the fact that the religious traditions in Great Britain are in the main Christian' and must take 'account of the teaching and practices of the other principal religions represented in Great Britain'. Schools that are of a particular religious ethos (sometimes called 'confessional' schools) may also use the local authority 'agreed syllabus' or alternatively may rely on one that reflects their own faith tradition. Irrespective of school, the aim of RE is to 'educate' rather than to 'indoctrinate', with the latter being contrary to UK law and Britain's international **human rights** obligations.

Reforming Collective Worship and Religious Education

A duty was first imposed on state schools to provide 'religious instruction' and to hold a daily act of non-denominational worship under the Education Act 1944. Just over sixty years ago this reform was relatively uncontroversial but today, in an increasingly secular albeit religiously diverse nation, this is no longer the case. As a consequence, a number of arguments have been put forward for the abolition of school worship and RE.

First, opponents of collective worship and RE insist that the obvious correlation between faith and **identity** can foster division in the schoolroom, and that this risks crystallizing underlying racial and cultural differences between pupils from different backgrounds. Secondly, some maintain that it is the duty of parents and religious leaders, rather than teachers, to instruct children in a particular faith or to lead acts of worship. And thirdly, given that Her Majesty's Inspectorate ('HMI') reports reveal that many schools fail to comply with the law relating to collective worship, and that RE is often poorly taught, one could argue that fundamental reform of the law in this area is long overdue.

In spite of these considerations, advocates of RE and school worship can also make a good case for maintaining the status quo. To begin with, RE (and to a lesser extent collective worship) provides schoolchildren with useful information about religion, which gives them a better understanding of the sectarian dimension to long running conflicts in the UK (eg Northern Ireland) and overseas (eg the Middle East). Moreover, it can be argued that RE and school worship encourages young people, in a materialistic age, to consider matters spiritual rather than those that are merely temporal. And finally, in practice, religious leaders, from a broad cross-section of faiths, would almost certainly object strongly to any attempt by the British government to adopt a US-style policy, whereby religion is kept out of the classroom in public schools. Given the considerable influence of religious organizations in the field of education (if not within society generally), calls for the abolition of school worship or RE thus seem unlikely to be heeded in the foreseeable future.

PETER CUMPER

religious laws   *see* **customary and religious laws**

religious minorities   *see* **minorities**

religious programming   *see* **religion in the media**

remand in custody   Defendants may be remanded in custody whilst awaiting trial or after conviction whilst awaiting sentence. Most defendants who are remanded in custody are legally innocent. Defendants are remanded in custody when the presumption of **bail** has been rebutted and bail has been refused. This occurs when the risks associated with releasing defendants are perceived to be too high. There are three main grounds on which bail is refused, namely, that defendants' may abscond, commit further offences, or interfere with witnesses. In practice, defendants charged with serious offences and/or who are persistent offenders who have allegedly committed offences on bail are the most likely groups to be remanded in custody. Defendants who are remanded in custody are held in **prison** where, as remand prisoners, they are supposed to have certain rights including daily visits and to be kept in separate and better conditions than convicted prisoners. In practice, remand prisoners are housed in some of the worst and most overcrowded prisons. Approximately 15 per cent of defendants are remanded in custody which equates to around 12,000 remand prisoners in prison at any one time.

When **courts** refuse bail initially, defendants are remanded in custody for seven days after which, defendants have the right to apply for bail on one further occasion. If bail is refused again, defendants are remanded in custody for up to twenty-eight days. Thereafter, defendants are remanded in custody for up to twenty-eight days or the earliest day on which the case can progress. No further application for bail may be made to the court unless different circumstances arise. Limiting the number of bail applications to two as of right was introduced in order to increase efficiency and stop courts hearing bail applications on the same grounds as they had heard previously but this is arguably at the expense of defendants' rights. Defendants may also apply for bail to Judge in Chambers once bail has been refused. The consistency and fairness of remand decision-making is questionable as custodial remand rates vary between courts and between different groups of defendants.

Custodial remands should be kept to a minimum as they have consequences for defendants. Subsequent decisions taken by both the court and defendants are affected. Defendants who are remanded in custody are more likely to plead guilty, less likely to be acquitted, and more likely to have custodial sentences imposed. Potentially, custodial remands can be used as bargaining tools to exert pressure on defendants to plead guilty. Custodial remands may have long-term effects on both defendants and their families. Defendants may lose their jobs and home and their future employment prospects may be jeopardized. Financial and emotional problems may also arise.

A significant minority of defendants who are remanded in custody are later acquitted or receive non-custodial sentences. This suggests that some custodial remands are unnecessary although it is possible that some defendants receive non-custodial sentences because they have served time in prison on remand. No **compensation** is available to defendants who are remanded in custody but are later acquitted.

ANTHEA HUCKLESBY

remedies   The word 'remedy' is used in different ways in law. At one level, a remedy is any solution to a legal problem. For example, if a defendant is in possession of the claimant's bicycle, the claimant can simply re-take possession, as long as this can be done without a **breach of the peace**. This is called 'recaption' and would be within a wide sense of 'remedy'. Usually 'remedy' is used more narrowly, to describe legal solutions that issue from courts of law. Recaption would not be a remedy in this sense; but a court order that required a defendant to pay **damages** for harm he had negligently caused would be. Some writers refer to 'judicial remedies' to isolate this sense of the word.

Most judicial remedies are orders to pay money. Even this basic remedy has a wide variety of configurations, which essentially reflect different remedial goals. The actual amount that the defendant will be ordered to pay will depend on the goal of the order. Assume that the defendant misappropriated the claimant's car and made use of it without authorization. If the car was damaged or destroyed, or the claimant suffered a lost opportunity by its absence, the claimant can seek 'compensation' for the losses. This is the most common situation. In addition, the claimant might ask for 'punitive' damages, sometimes called 'exemplary' damages; these go beyond compensation, and are used to punish defendants who have acted in flagrant disregard of the claimant's rights. Such awards are usually assessed by a judge in the UK, and they are modest by comparison with the practice in the United States, where they may be assessed by a jury.

It is possible that the claimant suffered no loss at all; for example, the car might be returned in pristine condition, and perhaps the claimant never noticed its absence. In such a case, it is possible to seek 'nominal damages', where a nominal sum (perhaps £10) is awarded as a symbolic vindication of the claimant's rights. The courts may also make substantial awards even where the claimant suffered no loss. The award may be seen as a money substitution for the violated right. Alternatively, the award may be aimed at taking away a profit that the defendant made by his wrong; perhaps by avoiding the cost of hiring a car lawfully, or by using the claimant's car in a profitable business. In such a case the claimant may ask for 'disgorgement' of the defendant's gain, sometimes (though perhaps imprecisely) called 'restitution'. Disgorgement may in some contexts be described as an 'account of profits'.

Similar possibilities can arise in a contractual context. Assume that the claimant makes a contract with the defendant for the sale of the defendant's house to the claimant, but the defendant refuses to perform. The claimant could seek compensation for losses he has suffered by the defendant's failure to perform. In extraordinary cases, he may be able to seek disgorgement of a gain made by the defendant through his breach. Punitive damages are traditionally not available for breaches of contract, but nominal damages could be. Contracts may also give rise to claims in debt; that is, an obligation to pay an ascertained sum of money. A landlord might claim rent owing; a lender claims for money lent, with interest; an employee claims her wages; a seller of goods or land claims for the agreed price. In this kind of case, the claim is simply that there is a debt arising under an agreement, and if the claim succeeds, the court will order the defendant to pay the amount he promised to pay. Debts can also arise by operation of law. If a claimant owes the defendant £100, but mistakenly

pays £150 due to an accounting error, the defendant comes under a debt to repay £50. This is a claim for restitution of an **unjust enrichment** and the court will make a money order against the defendant.

Non-money remedies include **specific performance**, **injunction**, and 'subrogation'—the last of these referring to a situation where one person takes over rights formerly held by another person. On some views, certain **constructive trusts** and 'equitable charges' are also remedies. Courts can grant 'declarations' of legal rights, where a claimant is not seeking a coercive award but merely wishes to clarify the legal position. Another non-money remedy is 'rectification', in which a legal document (like a contract or a will) is judicially corrected to remove discrepancies between what was intended and what was recorded. A claimant who has entered into a contract or other legal act through mistake or duress can seek 'rescission' of the contract, by which the contract will be set aside. Sometimes rescission can be effected without going to court.

In many situations, a judge may have some discretion as to which remedy shall be granted to the claimant. The scope of this discretion is somewhat controversial in legal theory; some writers have argued that such remedial discretion is inconsistent with the ideals of clarity in law and the **rule of law**, and that it should be minimized or eliminated.

LIONEL SMITH

remoteness (of damage)   *see* **causation; scope of liability**

rendition   *see* **extradition**

repairs   Repairs occur in two main situations: where an existing possession breaks down and a person is employed to repair it, and where a new product is faulty and a repair is sought as a remedy from the supplier.

If a business repairs a broken item, there are three main statutory obligations contained in the contract of repair. If no price has previously been agreed, then a 'reasonable' price can be charged for the work. If no time has been fixed for doing the work, it must be done within a 'reasonable' time. Finally, the work must be performed with 'reasonable care and skill', at a standard in keeping with that expected from an equivalent tradesperson. In other words, the work must not be done negligently. Failure to comply with any of these obligations can lead to a contractual claim for damages.

When defective goods have been sold by a trader to a consumer, one remedy available is to seek to have the goods repaired by the seller. The repair must be done within a reasonable time and without significant inconvenience to the consumer. The supplier has to bear the costs involved, including labour, materials, and postage. It is not, however, possible to demand a repair if :(1) it is impossible to repair the goods; (2) the repair costs are disproportionate to the cost of replacing the goods; or (3) the repair costs are disproportionate to the cost of giving a partial or complete refund of the purchase price.

DEBORAH PARRY

reparation and other remedies in international law When a state commits an act that is wrongful according to **international law**, a duty is imposed on the state to make full reparation for any injury, whether material or moral, caused by such act (as codified in Articles 31 and 34–39 of the International Law Commission's Articles on State Responsibility). The objective of reparation was defined in *Chorzów Factory (Germany v Poland)* judgment (1928) as being to 'wipe out all the consequences of the illegal act and re-establish the situation which would, in all probability, have existed if that act had not been committed'.

Reparation may take different forms including 'restitution', 'compensation', and 'satisfaction'. Full reparation for the injury caused by the wrongful act may be achieved through the award of any of these forms of reparation either singly or in combination. Moreover, contribution to the injury by negligent action or omission of the injured state or any person in relation to whom reparation is sought may be taken into account in determining the form and amount of reparation.

'Restitution' refers to the responsibility of the offending state to re-establish the situation which existed before the wrongful act was committed. However, this obligation only extends to situations in which restitution is not materially impossible, and does not impose a burden disproportionate to the benefit to be derived from awarding restitution instead of compensation. Restitution may involve such measures as return of property wrongly seized, release of persons wrongly detained, or revocation of a legislative provision enacted in violation of international law.

Where the loss resulting from the wrongful act cannot be made good by restitution alone, the state responsible for the act is under an obligation to compensate for the consequential damage. 'Compensation' refers to monetary recompense for any resulting economically assessable damage. The types of compensable damage and the standards of valuation

may vary depending on the content of the particular obligation, the nature of the conduct of the parties, as well as the interest protected by the international obligation. 'Punitive damages' (a remedy used in **common law** systems to punish the wrongdoer or deter them from pursuing a course of action such as that which damaged the victim) seem to be unavailable under international law.

'Satisfaction' is available when neither restitution nor compensation can rectify the damage resulting from the wrongful act. This form of reparation may consist in an acknowledgement of the breach, an expression of regret, a formal apology, or another appropriate modality. However, satisfaction must be proportionate to the injury and must not be humiliating to the offending state.

International courts and tribunals may also have power to order that provisional measures (or interim measures) be taken to mitigate the effects of the delays involved in the settlement of an international dispute. These measures may take the form of both positive and negative orders.

FEDERICO ORTINO

reporting politics It was Edmund Burke, the eighteenth-century parliamentarian, who reputedly observed: 'there were three Estates in Parliament, but in the Reporters Gallery yonder, there sat a fourth Estate more important than they all'. His point remains apposite some two centuries later: free and open reporting of issues touching on the nation's political life is one of the cornerstones of the United Kingdom's constitutional framework and an essential part of the institutions of representative democracy. In recognition of this fact, the UK's legal system has long adopted a largely *laissez faire* attitude towards public discussion of political matters. Today, Article 10 of the European Convention on Human Rights ('ECHR'), given effect in UK law by the Human Rights Act 1998, underscores this traditional approach by expressly recognizing a general right to freedom of expression. The European Court of Human Rights has emphasized repeatedly that this right applies with greater force to topics of 'public concern'. Furthermore, in the case of *The Observer and the Guardian v United Kingdom* (1992), the Court noted that freedom of expression is 'of particular importance as far as the press is concerned', due to 'its vital role of "public watchdog"'.

Nevertheless, even though the UK's legal framework generally permits the free reporting of political matters, a variety of restrictions apply to some types of discussion. Article 10(2) of the ECHR permits such limits in certain circumstances, provided they are 'prescribed by law' and 'necessary in a democratic society'. In so doing, the ECHR recognizes that the need to protect other important values may at times outweigh the benefits that accrue from having a free marketplace in political reporting.

One set of restrictions reflects the importance of protecting individuals' public reputation and private lives. Consequently, the general civil law of **defamation** and breach of confidence applies to statements about political figures and their behaviour, although the defences of fair comment and qualified privilege have a greater scope where matters of public interest are implicated. Furthermore, the Bill of Rights 1688, article 9, protects all persons involved in parliamentary proceedings from being sued or charged for anything said during those proceedings. The truthful and accurate reporting of such proceedings is likewise protected.

Secondly, legal constraints exist to prevent the reporting of political issues directly leading to public disorder or violence. The various offences contained in the Public Order Act 1986 apply even to speech that is political in content. Furthermore, it remains an offence at **common law** to utter or publish words with a 'seditious intention', while the Treason Act 1848 technically makes it an offence to advocate the overthrow of the monarchy. However, as Lord Scott of Foscote noted in *R. v Attorney General, ex p Rusbridger* (2004), 'It is plain as a pike staff . . . that no one who advocates the peaceful abolition of the monarchy and its replacement by a republican form of government is at any risk of prosecution'.

Thirdly, regulations attempt to ensure there will be balance and fairness in reporting of political issues by the broadcast media. Direct access to the broadcast media for political purposes may only take place through the system of Party Election Broadcasts. The Communications Act 2003 and the OfCom Broadcasting Code govern the broadcast media's general activities, and impose a variety of duties of fairness and impartiality on broadcasters. However, no such controls apply to the print media: the **Press Complaints Commission**'s voluntary Code of Practice does not require any 'impartiality' on the part of newspapers.

Fourthly, in order to maintain something of a 'level playing field' between electoral contestants, limits are placed on their election expenditures. The Political Parties, Elections and Referendums Act 2000 not only restricts how much political parties and candidates can spend on campaigning, it also covers 'third parties' wishing to spend money on promoting or opposing a political party or candidate. Consequently, any individual or group intending to expend more than £10,000 on such communications in England (or £5,000 in Scotland, Wales, or Northern Ireland) must register with the Electoral Commission, disclose the sources of any donations received and abide by a variety of spending limits.

Finally, preserving **national security** requires some restrictions on political discussion. It is thus a criminal offence to report a matter known to be covered by the Official Secrets Act 1989. A system of Defence Advisory Notices ('DA Notices') also provides advice and guidance to the media about defence and counter-terrorist information, the publication of which would be damaging to national security.   ANDREW GEDDIS

See also: **fair reporting by media**

repossession of goods English **common law**, unlike continental systems, historically favoured self-help by creditors seeking return of their goods. Where credit agreements created security in a debtor's goods for repayment of a debt, as in a **hire-purchase** contract or conditional sale, creditors could repossess goods without the necessity of a court order. This right to repossess was based on ownership rights or on a term in the lending contract. The only limitation on this power was that repossession should be by peaceable entry and not provoke a **breach of the peace**. The meaning of 'peaceable entry' remains vague and while physical violence is prohibited, entries through open windows or unlocked doors may be permitted. The arcane nature of this law, which has changed little since **Blackstone** wrote about it at the end of the eighteenth century, is partly accounted for by the inability or unwillingness of individuals subject to these procedures to challenge seizures through litigation. As a consequence, there has been little discussion of this topic and academic lawyers in the UK have demonstrated little interest in the law of creditor–debtor relations.

The powerful self-help remedy of repossession could be abused. An example was the 'snatch back' in hire-purchase transactions where a creditor could take back goods for minor defaults in repayment even where an individual had almost paid the full price of the goods. Moreover it was not necessary for those seizing goods to be court officers or licensed, and there was evidence of the use of 'bruisers' to repossess goods. There are still only modest regulatory controls on the licensing of bailiffs. The government reviewed bailiff law as part of the recent Tribunals Courts and Enforcement Act 2007, which has modernized parts of enforcement law, requiring all bailiffs, henceforth known as enforcement agents, to be certified.

The law has tempered self-help in consumer credit transactions. Thus in conditional sales and hire-purchase a court order is necessary to repossess goods where one-third of the purchase price has been paid, and a creditor or his agent may not enter a debtor's premises without a court order. Debtors must be given notice that they are in default and that repossession may take place if an individual does not respond to the notice. These controls on private power reflect the spirit of **human rights** values of due process and protection of **privacy** and the family home.

IAIN RAMSAY

representation   The word 'representation' in a legal context is used and understood in a number of ways, falling into four distinct yet related categories. First, often accompanied by a prefix such as electoral, judicial, or legal, 'representation' is typically understood by the lay person as the noun to the verb 'represent'. The politician, lawyer, judge, for example, literally stands for; assumes the role of; or denotes the individual, or group of individuals—the constituent, the defendant, and so on—they represent within civil society.

This understanding of representation is usually coupled with a more functional meaning of the word grounded in the belief that representatives should be—or at least should be seen to be—representative of those they represent. Hence, for example, increasing efforts to ensure a judiciary, Parliament, or legal profession which better reflects a wide variety of backgrounds, cultures, opinions, styles, perspectives, values, and beliefs through the increased participation of women, individuals from **minority** ethnic, religious, or social groups, those with **disabilities**, and so on. Accordingly, 'representation' sits at the intersection of law, politics, and civil society, its success or failure dependent upon effective identification and interaction between the representer and represented.

A third understanding of representation focuses on the extent to which political and legal practice re-presents the social or non-legal. It focuses on the way in which law produces and constitutes that with which it comes into contact. Put another way, it is concerned with the representation of a particular action, word, or event in and by law. Consider, for example, the way law translates a social dispute into a legal one: a 'senseless' killing is represented as a potential murder; an unwanted kiss as founding a possible action in the tort of battery; developing world debt as a contractual disagreement between world banks and states. Similarly, words or actions—negligence, recklessness, even representation itself—have legal

meanings and ensuing consequences which differ from their everyday usage. Thus, for example, a statement of belief or opinion made by one party to another as they enter into a contract once identified as a 'representation' and found to be untrue gives rise to an action under the Misrepresentation Act 1967.

Finally, representation can also be understood in terms of the representation *of* law. This involves an exploration of the portrayal or representation of law and the legal system in literature, film, music, art, theatre, and so on. So understood, works and artists as diverse as Lewis Carroll's *Through the Looking Glass,* Harper Lee's *To Kill a Mockingbird,* JK Rowling's *Harry Potter,* Mozart, Bob Dylan, Turner's *The Slave Ship,* and Shakespeare's *The Merchant of Venice* and the representation of law therein have all been utilized as a means of developing understandings of law, its systems and players and, ultimately, its role with society.

ERIKA RACKLEY

See also: **literature and law; visual arts, law and**

representation, legal   Legal representation is generally taken to mean representation of a party by a barrister or solicitor who appears before and addresses a court or tribunal and may also call and examine witnesses. At one time there was a third category of legal representative known as 'serjeants', from the ranks of whom senior **common law** judges were chosen; but after 1875 no more serjeants were appointed. These days, legal representation also includes representation by people with specialist legal training who are neither solicitors nor barristers. The right to represent another person before a court or tribunal is generally known as the 'right of audience'.

Until relatively recently barristers practising at the independent bar (ie self-employed practitioners) had the exclusive right to act as advocates in civil matters before the higher courts. Except for certain procedural applications, and some cases in bankruptcy, solicitors could not appear before the higher **courts**. However, solicitors have long been able to appear in civil matters before the lower courts. Barristers and solicitors have always been able to appear as advocates in tribunals and other similar bodies in England and Wales. With few exceptions, such bodies have never followed the practice in some jurisdictions of preventing lawyers from appearing before them as advocates. However, in practice, legal representation before such bodies has not been common for financial reasons. As for criminal matters, until 1836 no one could represent those accused of serious offences, except to argue points of law. Subsequently barristers at the independent bar had exclusive rights of audience in criminal trials to represent those accused of such offences. Traditionally the right of solicitors to appear as legal representatives of parties in criminal matters (as in civil matters) was confined to the lower courts. In practice, the absence of a barrister sometimes led to solicitors being permitted to conduct a client's case.

To foster access to justice, and to promote greater competition in the provision of legal representation, legislation in 1990 began to break down the restrictions on rights of audience. As a result, employed barristers are entitled to full rights of audience in all courts provided they have undergone the sort of training required of barristers in practice at the independent bar. Moreover, solicitors in private practice (as opposed to employed solicitors) can now obtain rights of audience in the higher courts ('higher rights of audience') by undertaking training in advocacy. Although a considerable number of solicitors have obtained the requisite qualification, there has not been the major incursion onto the barrister's territory that some were expecting. However, solicitor-advocates can be found employed by some of the largest law firms and appearing in important civil cases in the High Court, as well as acting for accused persons before the Crown Court. Employed solicitors have only limited rights of audience in the higher courts. This means that solicitors working for the **Crown Prosecution Service** cannot appear as advocates in the higher courts unless they are 'led' by a barrister or a solicitor in private practice.

There has been growth as well in representation by those with legal knowledge and training but who do not appear as barristers and solicitors (called here 'specialist representatives'). Sometimes these specialist representatives will have a law degree but will not have the professional qualifications required to be admitted to practise as a barrister or solicitor. Generally there have been no restrictions, as there are in some jurisdictions, on specialist representatives appearing for clients before **tribunals**. For example trade union officials have long argued members' cases before employment tribunals. Specialist representatives from advice agencies and law centres regularly represent clients before tribunals in housing and welfare matters. The empirical evidence is that they are often as effective as, and in some cases more effective than, barristers and solicitors because of the expertise they have in these areas and their familiarity with relevant procedures.

In relation to appearance before courts, the position of specialist representatives was changed in 1990. Legislation eroded the monopoly which barristers and solicitors had hitherto enjoyed. Specialist representatives are now able to represent clients in small claims proceedings in the county court. Moreover, bodies with suitable rules, ethics, discipline, complaints handling procedures, and so on can now obtain rights of audience for their members before the courts. The organization representing legal executives is one such body. Its members can appear, for example, in open court in the county court in all civil matters and family proceedings, and in the Crown Court on appeal from the magistrates' courts in criminal matters. Similarly, patent attorneys have rights of audience in the Patents County Court and (on appeal from the Patent Office) in the Patents Court, part of the High Court.

Specialist representation is not always uncontroversial. A public scandal over unscrupulous immigration advisers led to the establishment of the Office of the Immigration Services Commissioner ('OISC'), which regulates those who are not fully qualified lawyers with respect to competence and behaviour. Importantly, however, in specialist areas like employment and welfare the competent and ethical specialist representative can provide service of as high a quality as a barrister or solicitor. That does not mean that barristers and solicitors will become redundant. In these areas financial support is not available for the use of barristers and solicitors. Elsewhere, if clients can fund them—from their own or public sources—they will typically use them.

ROSS CRANSTON

See also: **government lawyers; lawyers, remuneration and funding of; legal profession, private and voluntary sector of; legal profession, public and employed sector of; para-legals**

reprisals A reprisal is conduct which would breach **international law** but is rendered lawful because it is a response to a prior violation of the law by those against whom the conduct is aimed. Reprisals are a form of self-help remedy which the international legal system, as a system that does not have a comprehensive and centralized system of adjudication and enforcement, has traditionally accepted. Reprisals are nonetheless a risky, *ersatz* form of law enforcement, containing within themselves the risk of both abuse and a 'race to the bottom' between states claiming the right to engage in reprisals against each other, against a background of disputed facts and tense relations.

Accepting the potentially dangerous nature of reprisals, international law subjects them to tight limitations. The most important limitation is that reprisals involving the use of force are banned.

Under the now more common title 'countermeasures', the International Law Commission's Articles on State Responsibility, which probably reflect **customary international law**, provide standards to which reprisals must conform. These include that they must be a response to a prior breach of international law by the affected party, proportionate to that breach, and intended to bring that party back into compliance with international law. They also must not breach certain fundamental norms, such as those relating to **human rights**. During armed conflicts **international humanitarian law** severely restricts the rights of belligerents to engage in reprisals.   ROBERT CRYER

J Crawford, *The International Law Commission's Articles on State Responsibility* (Cambridge: Cambridge University Press, 2002)

reproductive autonomy 'Reproductive **autonomy**' is often associated with or used as a synonym for terms such as 'reproductive choice', 'planned parenthood', 'right to choose', procreative liberty/freedom', or general notions of 'bodily integrity', 'individual/personal autonomy' in the reproductive context. The invocation of 'reproductive autonomy' in bioethical, feminist, and legal literature illustrates a significant variance as to its precise meaning, and the extent of commitment towards **self-determination**/ authorship in reproduction. At its most general level, the concept refers to the freedom to have children or to avoid having them. However, given advances in reproductive medicine, the question of whether to become a parent is now far more complex. Although increasingly dependent upon clinical expertise, and, for many, the availability of public funding, individuals can potentially exercise their reproductive autonomy in numerous ways, utilizing techniques such as vasectomy/sterilization, artificial insemination and *in vitro* fertilization, and screening technologies (eg prenatal and **pre-implantation genetic diagnosis**). Nor does scientific development sit still; the creation of Dolly, a sheep cloned from an adult mammary cell in 1997, illustrates controversial possibilities for our reproductive futures. Such developments not only excite ethical debate, raising questions around the limits of reproductive autonomy, but the law has correspondingly gained greater prominence as reflected by **common law**, statute, and other regulatory forms in governing the fast moving terrain of **human** reproduction.

As originally conceptualized, the core concern expressed by notions of procreative/reproductive autonomy was with women's **equality**. Traditional roles accorded to **women**, child-bearing,

motherhood, and domesticity, have constituted significant barriers to women's freedom and entry into public life; therefore, key to fostering equality has been the need to realize an **identity** for women *untied* to procreation. The ability to decide, *when*, if ever, to have children, remains one of the most critical freedoms captured by the notion of reproductive autonomy. Yet, in this sense, 'reproductive autonomy' and its expression in law arguably continue to express a political aspiration rather than a reality. While the women's movement fought for greater reproductive *control,* including demanding safe and legal access to contraception and **abortion**, abortion remains a *prima facie* criminal offence (the Abortion Act 1967 contains a set of defences to the offence of procuring a miscarriage, under the Offences Against the Person Act 1861) and access to abortion services continue to be subject to restrictive medical control (see the Abortion Act 1967 which applies to England, Scotland, and Wales, but not Northern Ireland where the law is as it was in Britain prior to 1967).

However, while women's reproductive autonomy in this context is restricted, a woman's sexual partner has no right to prevent her from obtaining an abortion; in abortion decision-making, a woman's right to respect for her private life prevails over that of the putative father (see *Paton v Trustees of the British Pregnancy Advisory Service* (1979); *Paton v United Kingdom* (1980)).

As is clear from the abortion context, the law's recognition of reproductive autonomy is limited, in often controversial ways. For example, the **Human Fertilization and Embryology Act 1990** ('HFEA'), which, alongside the **Human Fertilization and Embryology Authority**, regulates the provision of **assisted conception** services, contains a clause insisting that clinicians must not provide treatment services to a woman unless they have considered the welfare of the **child** that would result, *including the need of that child for a father* (section 13(5)). This clause, though exhibiting apparent respect for the reproductive autonomy of some, regards others (eg single women or **lesbians**) as less deserving of the opportunity of **parenthood**. Furthermore, while women with 'healthy/normal' pregnancies seeking abortion are subject to an upper gestational time limit of twenty-four weeks, a woman may terminate up to term on grounds of foetal abnormality (see the Abortion Act 1967 as amended by section 37 of the 1990 Act) providing further room for suspicion as to those occasions when the law will or will not respect reproductive autonomy.

Although the notion of reproductive autonomy can be seen to loosely underpin older judgments regarding reproduction, including a vindication of the right of a pregnant woman to refuse medical treatment which would save the life of her viable **foetus** (*St George's Healthcare NHS Trust v S* (1998)), the concept is a relatively new addition to judicial vocabulary. Its deployment in case law, increasingly framed in terms of 'rights', is undoubtedly assisted by the **Human Rights Act 1998**, in particular, Articles 8 and 12 of the **European Convention of Human Rights:** the rights to **privacy** and to found a family. In the context of **wrongful conception** cases, the concept underpinned the creation of a **remedy** ('conventional award') designed to recognize the loss of autonomy entailed in the setback of individuals' reproductive lives following the birth of a child born as a result of negligence in family planning procedures (see *Rees v Darlington Memorial Hospital* (2003)). However, while the concept of reproductive autonomy is traditionally concerned with protecting women's reproductive decision-making, in limited circumstances Article 8 claims can also be successfully advanced in support of men's reproductive autonomy (against women's reproductive autonomy), illustrating the increasingly contested/complex nature of the concept in an era of technological advance (see the case of *Evans v Amicus Healthcare Ltd and Others* (2004); *Evans v UK* (2006), turning on the provisions of the HFEA; this case involved a legal dispute between former sexual partners over the fate of stored embryos created by artificial methods).

NICKY PRIAULX

E Jackson, *Regulating Reproduction: Law, Technology and Autonomy* (Oxford: Hart Publishing, 2001)
S Sheldon, *Beyond Control: Medical Power and Abortion Law* (London: Pluto Press, 1997)

reproductive cloning   We are all the product of fertilization. Our parent's gametes joined together and became the embryo from which we developed. Occasionally, embryos split into two, producing identical twins, which are naturally occurring clones. A *clone* in this context is someone who is genetically identical, or almost genetically identical, to another. 'Reproductive cloning' involves cloning for the purposes of reproduction; in other words, the creation of a cloned human **child**.

A cloned child could be created in a number of ways. One way is to artificially split an embryo to create two or more genetically identical embryos, which could then be implanted and develop into identical twins. The birth of Dolly, the most famous sheep in history, opened up another possibility. Most of the genetic material in our cells is in the cell nucleus. (If you imagine a cell as a chicken egg, the

nucleus would be the yolk.) Dolly was created by removing the nucleus from a body cell and putting it into an ovum (egg) from which the nucleus had been removed. Dolly was therefore (almost) genetically identical to the sheep from which the body cell had been taken. If this technique was successfully used to create a human child, that child would be clone of the person who donated the body cell. The Dolly technique might therefore be used to clone an existing **human** being. The results of experiments on animals have not, however, been particularly encouraging. Animal clones are usually lost before implantation or birth and few survive to term. Some of those born alive die prematurely or are euthanized to prevent suffering. Even if the Dolly technique becomes a safe and efficient method of human reproduction, some will continue to object to it as a matter of ethical principle.

When Dolly was created the licensing authority set up by the **Human Fertilization and Embryology Act 1990** ('HFEA') declared that, depending on the method used, cloning was either prohibited or subject to a licensing requirement. The HFEA explicitly prohibited the creation of a clone by replacing the nucleus of an embryo (section 3(3)(a)). It also required a licence for the creation and use of an embryo outside the body (sections 3(1) and 1(2)) and, therefore, embryo splitting was regulated. The creation of a clone using the Dolly technique was not as clearly regulated. The HFEA defined 'embryo' in section 1(1) to mean 'a live human embryo where fertilisation is complete', including 'an egg in the process of fertilisation'. After a court decision holding that the Dolly technique did not fall within the HFEA, **Parliament** passed the Human Reproductive Cloning Act 2001 ('2001 Act'). Section 1(1) of the 2001 Act declares that it is a criminal offence to place 'in a woman a human embryo which has been created otherwise than by fertilisation'. Subsequently, the above-mentioned court decision was overturned. The **House of Lords** in *R (Bruno Quintavalle) v Secretary of State for Health* (2003)) ruled that although the Dolly technique did not involve an act of fertilization, the application of the technique to humans fell within the HFEA. The HFEA was to be interpreted purposively and its purpose was to regulate live human embryos created outside the body. Thus, all forms of reproductive cloning are now regulated in the UK, either by prohibition under the 2001 Act or by licence under the HFEA. The licensing authority has declared that it will not (for the time being at least) issue a licence for embryo splitting or, by implication, any other form of reproductive cloning falling within its remit.

SHAUN PATTINSON

SD Pattinson, *Medical Law and Ethics* (London: Sweet & Maxwell, 2006), ch 10

See also: **embryo research**

reproductive tourism   There are two principal reasons why people might travel abroad to access reproductive treatment services: either the treatment which they seek is unavailable in their home country, or it is prohibitively expensive. Of course, healthcare tourism is by no means confined to reproductive treatment services: UK citizens have travelled abroad for organ transplants, cosmetic surgery, and even **assisted suicide**. Nevertheless, it is undoubtedly true that the expense of IVF in the UK, as well as restrictions on access to certain treatments, means that patients are increasingly willing to travel to other countries for **assisted conception** services.

Given that the UK has a liberal regulatory regime, why might some treatments be unavailable? There are two possible scenarios. The first, best illustrated by the case of Diane Blood, is that the treatment which the patient seeks might not be lawful in the UK. Sperm was harvested from Diane Blood's husband after he had lapsed into a coma, just before he died. Under the Human Fertilization and Embryology Act 1990, consent to the use of one's gametes in treatment must be in writing. Although Mrs Blood claimed that the couple had discussed the posthumous use of his sperm, Mr Blood had not consented in writing to the use of his sperm, and, without such consent, it would have been unlawful for Mrs Blood to use the sperm samples for treatment in the UK. Mrs Blood applied to export the sperm to Belgium, and while the **Human Fertilization and Embryology Authority** ('HFEA') initially refused, the Court of Appeal decided that they had not taken adequate account of Mrs Blood's right, under European law, to receive treatment in another Member State. Subsequently, export was permitted, and Diane Blood has had two children using her deceased husband's sperm. Another example of treatment which is now unlawful in the UK is treatment with anonymously donated sperm or eggs. Since the removal of donor anonymity in the UK in 2005, patients who would prefer to use gametes from an anonymous donor might travel to another country, such as Denmark or the US, where anonymity is still the norm.

Secondly, the treatment which the patient seeks may not be available because of a shortage of, for example, sperm or egg donors. Travelling to other countries where donated gametes are more plentiful, perhaps because the donors are paid, allows people to avoid long waiting lists in the UK.

It is also possible that people will travel to poorer countries where IVF is much cheaper than it is in the UK, and perhaps less well regulated. For example, in some countries, there are no restrictions on the number of embryos which can be transferred to a woman's womb. Patients may then have treatment abroad and return to the UK pregnant with higher order multiples, such as triplets or quads. Because of the massively increased health risks of higher order multiple births, the costs this imposes on the NHS are considerable.   EMILY JACKSON

See also: **gamete donation**

rescue, duty to   *see* **acts and omissions; negligence in civil law**

research assessment exercise   *see* **legal academics**

residence in family law   The residence order was introduced into family law by section 8 of the Children Act 1989. It did not replace any strictly comparable order but, rather, aimed to reduce parental conflict on separation and **divorce**. Before 1989, the divorce court would make custody and access orders, to specify with whom the **child** would live and have contact. Crucially, only the custody order also gave parental rights. Under the new legal framework, neither parent loses **parental responsibility** (itself a new legal concept to replace parental rights): the residence order simply specifies with whom the child is to live. Further, orders are no longer routinely made on divorce: parents are expected to agree residence.

Non-parents, including grandparents and foster parents, may also apply for a residence order (subject to certain conditions) which automatically gives them parental responsibility. Further, a child can apply if the court is satisfied he or she has sufficient understanding. Whoever has a residence order in their favour can change the child's surname and remove the child from the jurisdiction only with the consent of all those with parental responsibility or by order of the court.

Where the child's residence is contested, case law currently suggests that the **courts** give weight to various factors deemed important for the child's welfare including continuity of care, schooling and social networks, and the views of older children. Joint or shared residence orders may be awarded but there is little consensus as to their merits.

CHRISTINE PIPER

See also: **children and divorce; co-parenting**

residence principle of taxation   *see* **international tax**

resident   *see* **permanent resident**

responsibility   Responsibility is a multi-faceted concept, the many surfaces of which can barely be scratched in this entry. It is helpful to distinguish between forward-looking, 'prospective' responsibility and backward-looking, 'historic' responsibility. The former is in play when we say, for instance, that it is Robin's responsibility to lock the shop at the end of each business day; and the latter when we say, for instance, that Robin was responsible for the fact that the shop was not locked on Tuesday. Prospective responsibility is a matter of creating and allocating duties and obligations, whereas historic responsibility is a matter of accounting and being held to account for the past (non-)performance of allocated duties and obligations. Prospective responsibility and historic responsibility are two sides of the one coin. Law is centrally concerned with both types of responsibility. It is one of the most important sources of our duties and obligations to others. Morality is another. Although popular images of law tend to focus on holding people to account through criminal prosecutions and civil claims, the prime significance of law for most people most of the time is that it tells them how to behave towards others and how, consequently, to avoid being prosecuted or sued. No legal system could survive if this were not so. On the other hand, some of the most noticeable differences between law and morality as 'responsibility systems' are found in the ways in which they each hold people to account rather than in the obligations and duties each creates and allocates. Legal processes and methods of accountability—operated by police, regulatory agencies, courts and so on—are, on the whole, much more institutionalized, formal, and coercive than their moral analogues, such as social criticism, mild forms of parental discipline, and so on.

Concerning accountability, it is important to distinguish between responsibility and liability. To hold a person liable is to say that some sanction ought to be imposed on them—shaming, perhaps, or ostracism; physical punishment, or an obligation to repair harm. (Historic) responsibility for some conduct or state of affairs is the most common justification for imposing liability both within and outside the law; but responsibility is not necessary for liability. For example, an innocent recipient of a mistaken payment (from a bank, for instance) may have to return it—even if the payee was in no sense responsible for the making of the payment—simply because the payment is an unjust enrichment. Nor is responsibility always sufficient for liability. For instance, judges cannot be sued for harm caused by negligent judging, not because of lack of responsibility for the harm but because it is thought that allowing individual judges to be sued might cause undesirable damage to the legal system more generally.

Law reflects our reluctance to hold responsible people who lack a certain minimum of physical and mental capacity. But once this threshold has been crossed, the fact that some people are more competent than others tends to be ignored in allocating responsibility. A legal exception is the defence of diminished responsibility; but this can be pleaded only in answer to a prosecution for murder, not for other crimes; and if the plea is successful, it justifies a conviction for the less serious crime of manslaughter, not an acquittal. Degrees of responsibility can also be taken into account in sentencing criminal offenders. In civil law, by contrast, the harm-doer's obligation to compensate is measured by the harm done, not by the harm-doer's culpability.

This difference is one aspect of an important distinction between a civil-law model and a criminal-law model of responsibility: whereas the latter finds the prime justification for imposing liability in the conduct and culpability of the agent, the former also puts considerable emphasis on the adverse consequences of the agent's conduct. The weight given to adverse consequences helps to explain why **strict civil liability** (ie civil liability without culpability) is less controversial than strict criminal liability, and why liability for negligently (as opposed to intentionally or recklessly) causing harm is more common in civil law than in criminal law. Indeed, some people think that there can be no moral responsibility without culpability, and that moral responsibility should be a pre-condition of criminal liability in law. Some also think that criminal liability should depend solely on what a person does, regardless of consequences—so, for example, that attempted crimes should be punished as severely as completed crimes.

Some people think of 'moral' responsibility primarily in terms of the accountability of individual human beings for their own conduct. By contrast, states and corporations, as well as individuals, can be legally liable; and in law, vicarious liability can be imposed on employers for the conduct of employees.
                                                        PETER CANE

P Cane, *Responsibility in Law and Morality* (Oxford: Hart Publishing, 2002)

See also: **attempts, conspiracy and incitement; criminal liability without fault; fault-based civil liability; fault-based criminal liability**

responsibility, state   When a state breaches an international obligation, it is—not surprisingly—responsible for that breach. In particular the breach of an international obligation gives rise to obligations to cease the breach (if it is continuing) and to make reparation. The **international law** of state responsibility determines when there has been a breach of an obligation, which other states or entities have standing to complain of the breach by seeking cessation and reparation, and what is the form and amount of reparation due. Within the framework of remedies for a breach, it also covers countermeasures taken by the injured state.

What amounts to a breach of international law by a state depends on the content of that state's international obligations, which vary from one state to the next. Many obligations derive from multilateral or bilateral treaties with different participating states. There is no such thing as a uniform code of international law. But the underlying concepts of state responsibility—attribution, breach, excuses, invocation, reparation—are general in character. These have been set out in the International Law Commission's (ILC's) Articles on Responsibility of States for Internationally Wrongful Acts (2001). The ILC Articles provide a structure within which issues of state responsibility can be treated.

Unlike many national legal systems, in international law there are no distinct subcategories of responsibility, thus no distinction between public and private law or between tort and contract (or treaty). The general rules of state responsibility are presumed to apply whatever the character or origin of the obligation breached.

For there to be a breach of international law by a state, the conduct in question (whether it is an act or a failure to act, or some combination of the two) must be *attributable* to the state. The mere fact that conduct occurs on the territory of a state does not mean the state is automatically responsible for it. Generally speaking the state is not responsible for the conduct of private parties, although it may be responsible if it failed to fulfil some obligation of prevention—which is normally an obligation of due diligence, not a guarantee. For example there is an obligation to protect embassies and diplomats. Private individuals may invade embassy premises or seize diplomatic personnel; if it did not order or control their conduct the state is not responsible for it but it may well be responsible for not taking necessary measures to evict the occupiers and to release their hostages. Likewise for protection of the ozone layer the state has the obligation to prevent CFC emissions by private producers. Analogous considerations apply in terms of the responsibility of states for the actions of other states. Unless joint organs exist acting on behalf of participating states, they are each responsible for their own conduct—an increasingly important consideration in an era of 'coalitions of the willing'.

As to invocation, where the obligation is bilateral in character (eg under a bilateral treaty) only the other state party can complain. Like other aspects of the law of state responsibility, this is subject to any special arrangement that may be made (eg allowing affected individuals or companies to bring proceedings in their own name, as has become the norm under bilateral investment treaties). On the other hand many international obligations are established by multilateral treaties or through the medium of international organizations established multilaterally. States individually injured by a breach may invoke responsibility in such cases—but so too may other states if the obligation is established for the protection of a collective interest, eg in preservation of the environment or freedom of navigation.

Apart from diplomatic contacts (protests, negotiation, reference to a competent international organization), there is no automatically available third-party process in disputes concerning responsibility. The jurisdiction of **international courts and tribunals** depends on consent—though this is often given in advance under specific treaties, eg in the field of international trade, the **law of the sea** or **human rights**. In the last resort a state injured by a breach may take countermeasures (in earlier times known as **reprisals**), but as these will often exacerbate the dispute they are rather exceptional.

Modern international law developed as a dominantly inter-state system. But these days, international action is frequently taken by or mediated through international organizations; and a major international actor, the **European Union**, is not a state but a regional organization with separate personality. Arrangements for responsibility of international organizations are currently embryonic. As with Kosovo and Iraq, states resist being held responsible for collective action and the result in practice may be that no-one is held legally accountable.

There are also embryonic ('soft-law') developments in the direction of the accountability of private sector entities such as so-called 'transnational corporations' and even individuals. But so far international law—while allowing for individuals to invoke responsibility of states through bodies such as the **European Court of Human Rights** and the Inter-American Court of Human Rights—has not established rules or arrangements for individual or corporate responsibility. The exception is the sphere of **international criminal law**, and it is limited and applicable only to individuals. Generally it remains the case that states have a monopoly of responsibility on the international plane.   JAMES CRAWFORD

See also: **international dispute settlement**

responsible government   *see* **ministerial responsibility**

Restatements of the law (USA)   Restatements of the law are compendiums of legal doctrines on subjects such as torts, property, or foreign relations. The Restatements are authored by the American Law Institute ('ALI'), which was formed in 1923. The self-declared purpose of the ALI is to clarify and simplify law in the United States, and to eliminate unnecessary complexities, while also promoting those changes that allow law to adapt to social needs. Law professors, including such notables as Hohfeld, Corbin, Gilmore, and Beale, and The Association of American Law Schools, played a prominent role in the formation of the ALI. The ALI itself is composed of members of the bar, the judiciary, and law schools in good standing. Some members are clearly prominent within their profession.

The ALI has a fairly elaborate internal structure for the promulgation of its Restatements. The process of Restatement publication begins with the designation of a legal scholar as Reporter. The Reporter does basic research and prepares the initial draft of the material. The Reporter then submits the initial draft for suggestions and revision to a group of Advisers with special knowledge of the subject. Next, the revised draft is submitted for further consideration to a group of sixty judges, lawyers, and law professors (Council of the Institute). Once the Council approves the draft, the draft (having been further revised) is presented as a 'Tentative Daft' to an annual meeting of the ALI membership. After the production of a series of tentative drafts in this manner, a proposed final draft may be submitted to the Council and the membership. Once both approve the Proposed Final Draft, the ALI prepares the text for publication.

Restatement provisions mediate between the ALI's view of what the law is and its view of what the law should be. Some sections seem to be almost trivial summaries of widely agreed-upon doctrine. Other sections, by contrast, have clear reformist ambitions. Restatements constitute secondary authority: a Restatement provision is not binding on a court unless officially adopted as the law by that jurisdiction's highest court.

While ALI Restatements are generally held in moderate to high esteem among legal academics and judges, the ALI project is not without its critics. Adherents of the old **common law** analogical approach fault the ALI for its doctrine-oriented representation of law—a representation that ostensibly lacks subtlety and violates the common law architecture. Similarly, legal thinkers at elite legal institutions often view the Restatements with a certain amount of disdain—viewing the ALI's doctrinal project as ad hoc and insufficiently theorized.

PIERRE SCHLAG AND KIMBERLY C DIEGO

See also: **precedent**

restitution   Restitution means giving back. Most claims in private law aim at **compensation** of a loss suffered by the claimant, as where the defendant has wrongly caused injury to the claimant. A claim for restitution, however, is a claim to recover something that has passed from the claimant to the defendant. Such claims usually arise in private law, although in criminal convictions for **theft**, the judge has the power to make a 'restitution order'. This is an order to give back the property stolen, or, in some cases, its value in money.

Private law restitution claims can arise in different ways. A person might innocently pick up the claimant's umbrella when leaving a party. The umbrella (or its value in money) must be returned, and this is a kind of restitution. It is founded on the claimant's ownership of the umbrella. Most legal discussions of restitution, however, look to slightly more complicated situations. A typical case is a mistaken transfer of funds. Assume that the claimant is filling out the bank form for a funds transfer. He mistakenly writes the wrong destination account number on the form, and hands it across the counter at the bank with a £100 note. As a result, the defendant finds £100 in a bank account that should not be there. This is more complicated because the claimant no longer owns the £100 note; it belongs to the bank. The defendant 'owns' the increased bank balance, which is, in law, a claim against his own bank. Taking notice of the mistake, however, the law grants to the claimant a right of recovery against the defendant. This is a core case of restitution for what the law calls an unjust enrichment. This case demonstrates the autonomy of unjust enrichment as a source of legal obligations. The main sources of private law obligations are agreements (including contracts), and wrongful acts; but neither one helps us here. The defendant is obliged to pay £100, but this obligation arises not from any contractual promise, nor from any wrongful or unconscionable action by the defendant. We might say that non-payment by the defendant of the £100 would be wrongful or unconscionable (just as the breach of any duty is wrongful); but that does not tell us what created the duty to repay £100. For these reasons, the law recognizes unjust enrichment is an independent source of legal rights and obligations.

A study of the law of unjust enrichment involves several inquiries. First it must be asked whether the defendant was enriched. In the case of the £100, this is straightforward. But consider this case: the claimant makes an agreement to paint the outside of a house for £1,000; he mixes up the numbers of the houses, and paints the wrong house. Although he has made an honest mistake, just as in the funds transfer case, it is not at all clear he will have a claim for £1,000. The owner of the mistakenly painted house may feel that so far from being enriched, he preferred his house the way it was before. So there can be difficult questions when enrichments are in the form of services, or improvements, or property other than money.

If the defendant has been enriched, and the enrichment has come at the expense of the claimant, there is the crucial question whether the law requires it to be reversed or not; in other words, whether the law considers it to be an unjust or unjustified enrichment. Enrichments conferred by mistake are considered unjust; the same is true where enrichments are conferred under illegitimate forms of pressure, such as threats of violence. Enrichments conferred under undue influence are also considered unjust. There is a very important category of case in which the enrichment is perfectly justified at the time it is conferred, but it is conferred subject to a mutual understanding about the future; if that mutual understanding turns out to be false, then the enrichment may be unjust. For example, the claimant agrees to hire out the defendant's music hall on a particular evening for £1,000, and pays in advance. There is no mistake or compulsion or other problem; the enrichment is valid and indeed the claimant is obliged to confer it. But imagine that the music hall burns down before the night in question. This is a 'frustration' of the contract, and the defendant is no longer obliged to provide the hall. The defendant is, however, obliged to make restitution of the £1,000, even though there is no contractual obligation to do so. Because the money was paid to obtain a counter-performance, and the defendant is no longer obliged to provide that counter-performance, what was a valid enrichment becomes an unjustified enrichment.

Restitution is usually made by way of a money order. A claimant might, however, seek restitution of specific property, and this may be possible by way of a **constructive trust**. In some cases, courts will impose other remedies such as subrogation or an equitable charge. Another important part of the field is defences; the most important one in unjust enrichment is called 'change of position'. It applies where the defendant, acting in good faith, has so changed his situation that it would now be unjust to order restitution. If the defendant received a mistaken payment of £100, and, thinking it was his to keep, immediately gave it to his favourite charity, he would be protected by the defence. Unjust enrichment can require people to return things they should never have got, but because it does not arise out of wrongdoing by defendants, it does not allow defendants to be made worse off. The defence of change of position ensures that this does not happen.

Sometimes when defendants commit wrongful acts, such as torts or breaches of contract, they may derive a profit from the wrong. In many situations, the courts will require such defendants to 'disgorge' the profit to the victim of the wrong. This is not restitution in the sense of giving back; rather, it is a case giving up. Most writers are of the view that such claims do not arise out of unjust enrichment, but rather out of the wrongful act. There are various controversies as to the terminology, however; some writers say that these cases can be understood within a wide sense of unjust enrichment, and some writers take the view that the word 'restitution' should be used both for giving back and for giving up. Sometimes the word 'restitution' is used even more loosely. In trust law, it is often said that trustees who cause a loss to their trust fund are liable in a 'restitutionary' measure. This only means that they must restore the fund to its proper size, and it would be better called compensation.   LIONEL SMITH

See also: **remedies**

restitution in international law   *see* **reparations and other remedies in international law**

restorative justice   Restorative justice is a term usually used to refer to processes that encourage wrongdoers to take responsibility for the harm they have caused and to make amends to their **victims**. Its main sphere of influence is the **sentencing** stage of criminal proceedings. Face-to-face meetings between offenders and victims, facilitated by a third party, are the most well-known manifestation of the concept. The focus of the meetings is on the material and psychological harm caused by the offence rather than the character or life circumstances of the offender. The exposure of the various harms caused by the offence often prompts an apology from the offender. Many victims are satisfied with the apology alone, although others ask for **compensation** or the performance of some practical reparative task.

Where either offenders or victims decline to meet each other directly, diluted forms of restorative justice (such as the delivery of a letter of apology) can be attempted. Where victims decline any participation in restorative processes, offenders may nonetheless be encouraged to make reparation in some other way, such as paying money into a victim compensation fund. Standard punishments can be used for those unwilling to make amends although, here, adherents of restorative justice would prefer compensation orders to **fines**, and community service orders to therapeutic measures. In practice, however, restorative justice options have often simply been added to an incoherent mix of penal ideas and practices.

In the 1990s, there was a surge of enthusiasm for restorative justice across many jurisdictions, resulting in various experiments and, in some cases, the transformation of routine criminal justice procedures. For example, the youth justice system of New Zealand is based on restorative justice in all but the gravest cases, while youths in England and Wales convicted at court for the first time are usually dealt with by a Youth Offending Panel which adopts a mixture of rehabilitative and restorative approaches. These examples might suggest that restorative justice is 'just for kids' and cannot cater for crimes such as **rape** or murder. It is known, however, that the families of murder victims often have a profound need or desire to meet the offender and can benefit greatly from restorative processes. Restorative justice has also been used to tackle ongoing intra-family **violence** and abuse; independent evaluations have reported positive results here too.

Restorative justice does not always have a more beneficial impact on re-offending rates than other approaches; sometimes it makes things worse. There is also the argument that punishment should be administered in the public interest and one component of this is to ensure **equality** of treatment of similarly situated offenders. However well meaning those operating restorative justice may be, restorative justice involves punishment, and it is wrong that punishment should be shaped by the preferences of particular victims. Another criticism is that restorative justice places excessive emphasis on the individual **responsibility** of offenders, downplaying those aspects of social structure (such as poverty) that are implicated in the kind of offending on which the **criminal justice system** tends to focus.

RICHARD YOUNG

See also: **young offenders**

restraint of trade An employer may require its employees to agree that if their employment ends they will not enter or conduct a competing business within a specified geographical area for a specified period thereafter. Such terms are particularly common in fields in which employees have a personal relationship with clients of the business; financial services or hairdressing, for example. Such agreements may be struck down under the doctrine of restraint of trade, under which a term that purports to restrict **competition** is void unless it is judged to be 'reasonable'. Ex-employees who conduct competing activities may invoke this doctrine as a defence if their ex-employer seeks an **injunction** to restrain their activities and/or **damages** for breach of contract.

An employer cannot lawfully restrain ex-employees from acting as competitors merely because they would be using general skills and knowledge acquired during the period of employment. Rather, the employer must point to a specific 'proprietary interest' that the restriction is designed to protect, such as **confidential information** (secret designs or recipes, for example), or the protection of its existing customer base or possibly (such as in the case of an employment agency) its workforce. In addition, the duration and geographical scope of the restraint must not be greater than necessary for protecting the employer's legitimate interest. What is reasonable here will depend upon the geographical area, and part of the business, in which the ex-employee had previously worked; his or her position within it; and the nature of the employer's business.

GILLIAN MORRIS

See also: **confidentiality (work)**

retail banking services *see* **consumer protection in retail banking; deposit accounts, financial Services Authority; personal loan**

retirement The law relating to retirement is a significant tool used by government in the management of two of the most important social issues of our time, namely the **pensions** crisis and **unemployment** control. However, these pull in opposite directions and the law of retirement reflects that. Additional complicating factors include moral considerations such as **equality** of treatment. So, although **age discrimination** is now outlawed in principle, several exceptions remain in law insofar as retirement is concerned. For example, an employer may dismiss employees once they reach age sixty-five or some other specified higher age, or if they have a normal retiring age of below sixty-five and that is objectively justified. Employees over retiring age may now claim **unfair dismissal** and **redundancy** payments but only if this is not occasioned by reaching that age. Furthermore, **sex** discrimination law does not apply to provisions made in relation to retirement.

The main area of law relevant to retirement is pensions law. This is highly complex and, for private pensions, is built upon the law of **trusts** rather than being a separate body of law in its own right. The basis is thus **common law** but this is supplemented by statute, and particularly subordinate **legislation** made by ministers to fill in the detailed rules. The pension funds are owned by trustees who must administer them with the financial interests of all the beneficiaries in mind. In addition there are public sector pension schemes, but private sector schemes are the most important. SIMON HONEYBALL

retorsion *see* **reparations and other remedies in international law; reprisals**

retribution In ordinary parlance retribution has had the connotation of severe **punishment**. In legal-philosophical discourse, however, it refers to deserved sanctions: a conception of punishment is retributive, to the extent that the penalty should be based on the blameworthiness of the conduct.

Traditional retributive theories emphasized that the penalty should 'requite' the wrongdoing. That approach has, however, attracted little modern penological support. In the decades since the 1970s, another retributive perspective has become influential: the communicative view of penal desert. This rests, not on notions of requital, but on the idea of punishment as a blaming institution. Criminal sanctions involve *censure* of the actor for his criminal conduct. This censuring feature explains, in substantive criminal law, why fault (eg intention or negligence) should be required for liability. It also, in **sentencing** doctrine, calls for an emphasis on the degree of seriousness of the criminal conduct. The severity of the punishment (and thereby its degree of implied censure) should comport with the blameworthiness (that is, degree of seriousness) of the conduct.

This communicative perspective does not require talionic punishments—of imposing suffering as severe as the victim's. Instead, punishments should be *proportionate* to the conduct's seriousness. Proportionate punishments may be imposed without increasing (indeed, while substantially decreasing) overall sentence-severity levels, so long as penalties are graded according to crimes' gravity, and comparably reprehensible criminal acts are penalized with approximate parity. Contemporary desert theorists have thus favoured an overall scaling-down of penalty levels.

Modern desert theory has had considerable impact on sentencing policies. Since the mid-1970s, a number of European and American jurisdictions have adopted proportionality-orientated sentencing schemes, including Sweden, Finland, Minnesota, Oregon, and (albeit now, with significant dilutions) England. Other jurisdictions (Canada and New Zealand) have enacted declarations that proportionality should be of primary concern in sentencing. The desert perspective also remains influential among academic criminologists and legal scholars writing on sentencing theory and policy.

Communicative desert theories take a variety of forms. These differ, for example, on the permissible scope of variation in sentences for comparably-serious offences, and on whether the sentence may be designed as penances. However, there has been a shared interest in specifying sentencing criteria more fully. Desert theorists thus have, for example, developed doctrines concerning the role of previous convictions in determining sentence: these give prior offending a relatively limited role.

Sentencing theory today offers differing perspectives: economic models emphasizing of deterrence or incapacitation; rehabilitatively-oriented approaches; **restorative justice**; and desert-based conceptions. None of these dominate the discussion, in the way the rehabilitative ideal did in the 1950s and 1960s; and vigorous debate continues among them. The communicative desert model thus should be viewed as an option among these competing views, but one that remains important and influential.

ANDREW VON HIRSCH

RA Duff, *Punishment, Communication and Community* (Oxford: Oxford University Press, 2001)
A von Hirsch and A Ashworth, *Proportionate Sentencing: Exploring the Principles* (Oxford: Oxford University Press, 2005)

See also: **rehabilitation**

revision *see* **social security appeals**

revolution Revolutions involve radically overturning some kind of establishment, occasioning rupture or discontinuity. Political revolutions overthrow established forms of government, for example replacing a monarchy with a republic. Revolutions often involve violence and popular unrest.

The legal analysis of the concept 'revolution' looks to the question of legal continuity and how disruptions occur therein. The most influential analysis has been that of Hans Kelsen. His analysis applies to that form of relatively centralized legal order which belongs to, or (more accurately, in Kelsen's view) constitutes, a state. States have constitutions established at some point in history or by some human acts (perhaps only acts constituting a custom) expressive of a will concerning the order of governance of a territory. Legal systems are dynamic in that they regulate their own creation and amendment. A constitution may be amended by use of its own clauses concerning amendment, and the laws made under the constitution may change from time to time through acts of legislation or of judicial interpretation of legislation or of the constitution itself. The element of legal continuity is tested solely by applying this test: for any given change in the constitution or law, was this change authorized by the constitution as it stood prior to that change? Constitutionally unauthorized changes are in themselves instances of revolution, once they take effect and are maintained in force.

All constitutions originate from some originally revolutionary act, that of the 'founders' of a given state. Yet for the law to be normative, there must be some presupposition that the founders had authority to do as they did. This presupposition Kelsen calls a 'basic norm' or *Grundnorm*. Hence the test for the occurrence of a legal revolution can be cast in terms of discontinuity in the *Grundnorm*. The thesis about constitutional continuity is not dependent on the basic norm theory, however. Adoption of De Gaulle's proposed constitution established the French Fifth Republic in 1958. It did so in a way not authorized by the Fourth Republic's constitution. Thus there had to be presupposed a new basis of authority for the adoption of the new constitution. This was a legal revolution, but the events that brought it about forestalled possible widespread violence, sparing the French people the anguish of a full-scale political revolution. Legal revolution facilitated political stability and was achieved without substantial violence.

The adequacy of this approach to explaining legal revolutions and legal continuity has been tested from time to time in contexts such as decolonization. An example was the Unilateral Declaration of Independence by the white minority government of Southern Rhodesia (now Zimbabwe) in 1965. To what extent courts in the **United Kingdom** could or should recognize acts of the 'independent' government in this case of illegal seizure of power came into controversy. The idea that necessity might give authority to an illegal regime, though itself questionable, received some support from the **House of Lords**. Certainly, societal continuity can be uninterrupted

by legal discontinuity. Legal 'revolution' is a rather technical concept.   NEIL MACCORMICK

JM Eekelaar, 'Principles of Revolutionary Legality' in AWB Simpson (ed), *Oxford Essays in Jurisprudence, Second Series* (Oxford: Oxford University Press, 1973)
J Finnis, 'Revolutions and the Continuity of Law' ibid

***Ridge v Baldwin* (1964)**   This case laid the foundations of the modern English law of **natural justice**. Lord Reid remarked, on his retirement after twenty-six years in the **House of Lords**, that it was the decision that he remembered with 'greatest satisfaction'.

Ridge, the Chief Constable of Brighton, had been tried and acquitted of a charge of conspiring to obstruct the course of justice. Two other police officers tried with him were convicted, and the trial judge commented adversely on the chief constable's leadership. The Brighton Watch Committee, which had statutory power to dismiss any constable 'whom they think negligent in the discharge of his duty, or otherwise unfit for the same', unanimously dismissed Ridge without giving him notice or offering him a hearing. The Committee did allow Ridge's solicitor to appear before a later meeting. But, after hearing him, the Committee confirmed their decision (but no longer unanimously). The Chief Constable exercised his statutory right of appeal to the Home Secretary, but his appeal was dismissed.

Today it would seem obvious that a constable should be heard before dismissal, but that was not the case in 1964. The view had taken hold in English law in several decisions since the 1930s that the rules of natural justice were not applicable unless the power could be classified as 'judicial or quasi-judicial'. If the power were only 'administrative' no hearing at all was required. Moreover, it was not enough that the power should determine the rights of individuals. There had to be 'a superadded duty to act judicially', some further indication that the power was to be exercised as a judge would (ie after a hearing).

Lord Reid's speech contains a *tour de force* journey through the classic nineteenth-century decisions on natural justice and shows that this classification approach was an aberration. The rules of natural justice applied to administrative as well as quasi-judicial decisions. All that was required was that the power determined the rights of individuals. Lord Hodson in the same case put the point clearly. It was not a question of whether '… the giver of the decision is acting in an executive or administrative capacity as if that were the antithesis of a judicial capacity. The cases … show that persons acting in a capacity which is not … . judicial but … administrative have been held by the courts to be subject to the principles of natural justice'. Thus Ridge should have been heard and his dismissal was declared void (Lord Evershed dissenting). The opportunity afforded to his solicitor was not sufficient and his appeal to the Home Secretary did not prevent a challenge to the Committee's decision.

Although not realized by all commentators at the time, *Ridge v Baldwin* was of fundamental importance to the development of the modern law of natural justice. Lord Reid's satisfaction was well founded.

CHRISTOPHER F FORSYTH

right of abode   Right of abode is the centerpiece of British immigration law. It is the most secure status aside from **citizenship** itself. Those with a right of abode in Britain are permitted to live and work in Britain without restriction and to enter as often as they choose without immigration screening. Right of abode is an incidence of British citizenship and is also accorded to some **Commonwealth** citizens who were born before 1983. Those with a right of abode can apply for British citizenship, if they do not already have it, after a period of residency in the United Kingdom. Right of abode is a status between citizenship and permanent residency that was used as a means of drawing distinctions between citizens of the UK and colonies when that status existed between 1948 and 1982. It is not ordinarily accorded to those with forms of permanent residency in the UK (such as indefinite leave to remain). Right of abode is evidenced by a British **passport** or by a certificate of entitlement, typically stamped in a passport. Right of abode is a peculiarity of British law which directly reflects its imperial era. It was hotly contested during the round of 1980s law reform which led to the tripartite structure of British citizenship. Some argue that this round of reform was directly at restricting the rights of former colonies by restricting right of abode. This controversy was again important during the negotiations preceding the end of British rule in Hong Kong.   CATHERINE DAUVERGNE

See also: **immigration and emigration; immigration security screening; permanent resident**

right of exit   The significance of cultural belonging for individual wellbeing is increasingly acknowledged by liberal theorists. To protect distinct cultural **identities** and to safeguard cultural membership, group rights may be granted by states. Such rights might include claims to be exempt from generally applicable laws within a state.

For liberal theorists, the right of exit defines the limits of group rights. All individuals must have a right to exit and disassociate from a group. The claims of **community,** the ties that bind, can be given only limited state protection.

The right of exit reflects the fundamental liberal commitment to the priority of individual **autonomy**. Group membership and, with it, commitment to a distinct way of life, must remain optional. For proponents of group-differentiated rights, the right of exit is a solution, a remedy to the problem of 'illiberal' **minorities**.

For liberal multicultural states, problems arise when groups impose internal restrictions on their members, when repressive practices form part of a group's way of life. Such practices might include discrimination in rules regulating ownership and transfer of land or property, in family law, or in school curricula. The right of exit sets the minimum threshold that must be met to avoid state intervention in a group's way of life. What may generally be considered to be unjust by a state may be permitted if the possibility of opting out, of exiting from the group, is protected.

Exit may bring with it a loss of privileges associated with group membership. In some jurisdictions, such loss may be subject to legal regulation, prohibiting **sex** discrimination for example. Without such regulation, we end up with the kind of discrimination evident in cases such as *Santa Clara Pueblo v Martinez* (1978), where a Santa Clara court upheld an ordinance granting member status to the children of men marrying outside of the pueblo, while excluding the children of women who did so.

Many commentators question whether a right of exit is a genuine safeguard against repressive practices within a group. The possession of a right, it is argued, is not enough; exit must be a meaningful option for group members. For vulnerable members of a group, subjected to ongoing discrimination, the possibility of exit may be illusory. The liberal appeal to choice and autonomy, it is argued, ignores the limited range of options that may be available to women or girls who have had limited access to education or paid employment.

For others, the liberal appeal to the right of exit gives only limited recognition of the significance of cultural belonging. Exiting means choosing between different parts of one's identity. To paraphrase Ayelet Schachar, it means choosing between 'your culture and your rights'.   SIOBHAN MULLALLY

A Schachar, 'Group Identity and Women's Rights in Family Law: The Perils of Multicultural Accommodation'(1998) 6/3 *Journal of Political Philosophy* 285–305

See also: **liberal multiculturalism**

right of reply   *see* **fair reporting by media**

right to buy   This phrase refers to the right of secure tenants of housing provided by a local authority or Housing Action Trust to purchase the property they are occupying. The right was introduced in the Housing Act 1980, one of the earliest interventions of the Thatcher government in housing policy. It had been one of the central commitments in the 1979 Conservative election manifesto. Although the right to buy was politically controversial for some time, it seems to have become an acceptable facet (if, for some, a poor relation) of government housing policy across the parties. Between 1980 and 2006, approximately 1.6 million households have exercised their right to buy. The right to buy should not be confused with the similar, but more limited, scheme which applies to occupiers of registered social landlords, known as the right to acquire.

There had always been a power of sale attached to council housing and, when it was first developed in the late nineteenth/early twentieth century, councils often built housing for the purpose of immediate or delayed sale. However, the 1980 Act not only gave secure tenants the right to buy for the first time, but also imposed a concomitant obligation on local authorities to sell. The 1980 Act, as amended, set out a procedure and timetable governing the right, as well as a series of discounts given to occupiers depending on how long they had occupied the property. The discounts differed depending on whether the property was a house or a flat (the latter, being less desirable, were offered at a more substantial discount). Difficult questions of legislative interpretation have arisen in relation to the timetable where the local authority has sought a possession order against the secure tenant at around the time they decide to exercise their right to buy. From 1999, there has been legislative intervention designed to restrict the right, reducing discounts in certain areas for example.

The effect of the right to buy differed depending on the local authority concerned, as the desirability of purchasing property depended on the quality of the housing stock as well as the rent–mortgage differential. One result was that generally the better quality stock was sold off to households which were better able to afford the mortgage. The consequences of this for the local authority housing sector have been significant; the terms most often used by researchers being residualization and marginalization. The former refers to the fundamental shift in local authority housing away from being a mass tenure to being one that provides housing for marginal groups. The latter refers to the nature of the population remaining in the local authority sector (although a more modern term is, perhaps, social exclusion). Residualization was, in retrospect, an inevitable consequence of such an intervention; however, marginalization was already occurring in the local authority sector prior to 1980 and the right to buy hastened this trend further.   DAVID COWAN

I Cole and R Furbey, *The Eclipse of Council Housing* (London: Routledge, 1994)

R Forrest and A Murie, *Selling the Welfare State* (London: Routledge, 1990)

right to liberty   At an abstract level, the right to liberty connotes the freedom that each of us enjoys in view of our **humanity**. This notion has had an important role to play in forging the democratic idea. It was by speculating upon the kind of natural rights that the **person** would enjoy in a world without any external authority that innovative thinkers of the seventeenth and eighteenth centuries were able to characterize government as something that free individuals would have turned to in order better to secure the ends that they willed but which the uncertain nature of their free but vulnerable lives had made quite impossible in the absence of authority. In the insight that state power could be the servant of men and women and not an alien oppression imposed by a king or a church lay the seeds of what was to grow over time into the democratic system of government.

This pre-law character of the right to liberty is evident in the old **common law** assumption that one is free to do whatever is not prohibited by law. Writing in the nineteenth century, the influential jurist Albert Venn **Dicey** saw in Britain's commitment to this kind of residual freedom a stronger guarantee of liberty than he thought could be accommodated within a more rights-based framework. The infringement of freedom which occurred without specific statute or common law-based authority left the violator open to being proceeded against in the ordinary **courts**, for **damages** or for some other appropriate remedy, with the fact that this occurred even where the violator was an agent of the state demonstrating for Dicey the even-handedness, and therefore the superiority, of the common law model. This approach has however not survived both the plethora of laws that have narrowed the zone of residual freedom almost to zero in recent years, and the shift to the language of rights that has been one of the worldwide legal phenomena of recent times.

In the context of **human rights** instruments, the right to liberty is understood in the narrower sense of involving freedom from arbitrary **arrest** or detention. Echoed in early constitutional documents like the **Magna Carta** (1215), the fifth amendment to the US constitution (1791) and Article 7 of the French Declaration of the Rights of Man and of the Citizen (1789), in its modern **international law** form, the right appears in Article 9 of the Universal Declaration of Human Rights (1948), Article 9(1) of the **International Covenant on Civil and Political Rights** (1966), and Article 5 of the **European Convention on Human Rights and Fundamental Freedoms** (1950).

As a general rule, the more justiciable the right is, the greater the range of exceptions that it permits. Thus the guarantee in the European Convention is heavily circumscribed and has been further attenuated by interpretation, both by the **European Court of Human Rights** and by national judicial bodies. A more general override is also permitted by the Convention where the authorities form the view that there exists a public emergency threatening the life of the nation—it was the invariable existence of clauses such as this in national **constitutions** that had led Dicey to his sceptical view of the capacity of rights' instruments truly to protect freedom. However the right to liberty can be asserted even against such large **security** claims, where for example the courts are prepared to rule that there is no rational and/or proportionate basis for the assertion that the interests of the state demand such departures from fundamental rights. This is what occurred in the well-known Belmarsh detention case in December 2004, when the **House of Lords** found the **detention without trial** of international (but not 'home-grown') suspected terrorists to be unwarranted by the emergency the existence of which was nevertheless not denied by a majority of their lordships.

While not of course blindly guaranteeing freedom to all those who place reliance upon it, the concept of a right to liberty has functioned as a useful corrective to the exercise of over-broad state power in areas of public policy of such low visibility that victims have hitherto found great difficulty in drawing attention to their plight. It is as a back door to improved procedural fairness for vulnerable persons whose freedom has been or is about to be truncated that the right to liberty in its legal form has done much valuable work in democratic society, in the field of **prisoners' rights** for example and also in relation to persons whose mental ill-health might otherwise produce an incarceration that, being quickly forgotten, would in the absence of such procedural guarantees have become in practice indefinite.

CONOR GEARTY

right to life   The right to life is the most fundamental guarantee in **human rights** law. All other human rights are dependent on it. It has gained widespread recognition in **international law** and is a non-derogable human right. The Universal Declaration of Human Rights 1948, Article 3 provides that 'everyone has the right to life, liberty and security of the person'. It is also reflected in the **International Covenant on Civil and Political Rights** 1966, Article 3, the **European Convention on Human Rights** 1950, Article 2, the American Convention on Human Rights 1969, Article 4, and the **African Charter on Human and Peoples' Rights** 1981, Article 4. The fact that this is a right guaranteed in law is not in doubt; debates continue on the scope of the right, particularly at the beginning and end of life.

The straightforward implication is that the state should refrain from taking life. This simple proposition is complicated by the fact that the right to life is not absolute. For example, Article 2(1) of the European Convention on Human Rights envisages the use of the death penalty for convicted criminals. This position has been addressed through Protocols to the Convention (Protocols 6 and 13) which seek the abolition of the death penalty. Article 2(2) provides that deprivation of life will be held not to violate the right to life where it involves the use of force which is no more than absolutely necessary: in defence of a person from unlawful **violence**; to effect a lawful **arrest** or prevent someone who is lawfully detained from escaping; and action taken lawfully to quell a riot or insurrection. Given the significance of the right, the limitations are interpreted narrowly and absolute necessity is linked to a strict proportionality test.

This is an area of human rights law where there are also **positive obligations**. Article 2 of the European Convention contains a duty on the state to investigate suspicious deaths. When an individual is killed through, for example, the use of lethal force by the security forces, Article 2 requires an effective official investigation. The European Court has provided useful clarity on what precisely this requires in a series of cases from Northern Ireland (eg *Jordan v UK* (2001)). For example, the investigation must be conducted by someone who is fully independent of those being investigated, and it must be capable of leading to a determination of whether the force used was justified, as well as the identification and punishment of those identified. These are only some of the main requirements laid down by the Court. The obligation to deliver an effective official investigation will apply in other instances where the Article 2 right is engaged. The principal aim of the Court is to ensure that domestic laws which protect the right to life are effectively implemented.

There is also a positive obligation on the state to demonstrate the steps it is taking to protect the lives of those within its jurisdiction. This can extend quite broadly to any activity in which the right to life may be at stake. For example, it can arise in the prison context where there is a **suicide** risk or where there is a possibility of serious harm from other prisoners. Where there is dangerous but lawful activity taking place the duty on the state is to ensure that a proper system of regulation is in existence.

The European Convention does not define when life starts (unlike the American Convention on Human Rights 1969 which defines it as beginning from the moment of conception) and it does not define 'every-one'. The European Commission suggested that the term 'everyone' did not apply to the unborn **child**. The Court has acknowledged the lack of consensus on the nature and status of the embryo and/or **foetus** at European level and has largely avoided answering the question of whether the unborn child is a person within the meaning of the Convention. However, what appears clear is that the foetus does not have an absolute right to life for Convention purposes because of the intrinsic connection to the well-being and life of the mother.

The issue of **euthanasia** is subject to ongoing debate in Europe. The European Court of Human Rights, however, has made clear that Article 2 does not include a 'right to die' (*Pretty v UK* (2002)).

COLIN HARVEY

See also: **derogations in human rights law; proportionality in human rights law; sanctity of human life**

right to treatment *see* **medical treatment, right to**

right to work The right to work has been much articulated, both nationally and internationally, extending great promise and potential to workers. Despite this guise of weightiness, its content and enforceability remain doubtful and controversial. Indeed, the content of the right to work varies according to the politics of those who assert it and its definition remains notoriously imprecise.

The principle of the 'right to work' originated in the French Revolutions of 1789 and 1848 as a desire to exact jobs from the state for the relief of the poor. The right to work has since been articulated in various communist regimes to justify the obligation to labour. This mode of reasoning can also be found in UK law in the Independent Labour Party's creation of the Unemployed Workmen Act 1905 which made provision for the creation of workshops for the unemployed and destitute to receive poor

remuneration for state-created work. The socialist understanding of the right to work as imposing a duty upon states to regulate the labour market to ensure employment for all has not been enforceable in England but gained political strength in the era of the Great Depression and in Keynesian economic theory. Natural rights theorists and liberals construed the right to work as a valuable **human right** to employment. Right-wing theorists have used the right to work to justify non-union membership and strike-combating action.

Many international and European instruments express their belief in and respect for a right to work. Most notably, the right to work figures in the **Council of Europe**'s European Social Charter of 1961 (Article 1, Part II) and in the **United Nations**' Universal Declaration of Human Rights of 1948 (Article 23). Although the right, a settled definition of which remains elusive, is unenforceable, it has generally been interpreted as giving rise to guarantees of **equality** between individuals in the labour market and prohibiting discrimination in their access to, and maintenance of employment.

In current law, there are some limited **common law** expressions of the right to work derived from judicial concern to prevent capricious exclusions from employment (see *Nagle v Feilden* (1966)). By way of exception, there also exists a tightly circumscribed common law right to be provided with work by the employer (see *William Hill Organisation v Tucker* (1999)).

REBECCA GREENLAND

See also: **unemployment**

rights and duties A right is an entitlement authorizing a person to do or to have something. The entitlement overrides other normative considerations, such as whether or not the person doing or having that thing is for some other reason considered to be right or wrong. Rights are therefore valued possessions since having a right means having a strong normative power which others ought to respect. Similarly, duties are characteristically unwelcome, mandatory requirements that must be carried out, even against the wishes and opinions of those involved.

According to legal positivists, rights are desirable acts or things to which (existing or 'positive') social rules entitle us, and duties are undesirable things that such social rules require of us. Both may be said, routinely, but not always, to 'trump' or 'exclude' other considerations. This is most evident when the rules are part of a legal system, where there are formal institutions for making and enforcing rules; but it also applies where the rules are customary or conventional and their implementation informal. On this view, talk of 'moral' rights and duties may then be taken as referring to either: (1) the rights and duties people have in relation to existing customary (as distinct from legal) rules; or (2) the rights and duties people would obtain in a morally desirable system of social or legal rules. Natural law theorists, on the other hand, hold that there are 'natural' rights and duties which exist over and above positive rights and duties. These are rights and duties that are based on a religious or rational, or 'natural' system of norms, of which we can have knowledge through revelation, reason, or empirical experience, independently of their social or legal recognition.

Analysing rights and duties in terms of rules enables us, adapting Wesley Hohfeld (*Fundamental Legal Conceptions as Applied in Legal Reasoning*, New Haven: Yale University Press, 1919), to formulate a typology of rights and duties. Thus a pure 'liberty right' (or 'privilege') exists when there is no rule requiring the rights holder to do, or not do, something. This liberty is 'pure' in that no-one else is required to allow or enable me to smoke. Such liberties are important in a society where a person is assumed to be free to do that which is not forbidden.

In contrast, 'claim rights' exist when there is a rule requiring others not to prevent (in the case of a negative claim right) or actually to assist (in the case of a positive as distinct from a negative claim right) the rights holder in doing or having that which she has a right to do or have. All claim rights have 'correlative duties', in that for A to have a claim right there must be another person B with a duty to A relating to A's right. Thus I have a claim right to smoke when others have a duty to allow (or enable) me to smoke. Some of these correlative duties require third parties (particularly governments) to protect and promote rights by making sure that the correlative duties of others are performed, thus securing the interests identified by the right.

Another category of rights is the capacity or 'power' to alter the rights and duties of others, as when we enter into contracts or vote in an election. These power (or 'facilitative') rights correlate with the 'liabilities' of others, in that A's right is to change B's rights and duties, to their potential detriment or benefit. Some power rights involve the capacity to require or excuse the fulfilment of a duty that is correlative to a claim right. Thus, if A owes B money, B has not only a claim right against A, but also a power right to release A from that duty. Some hold that all claim rights involve this power of waiver.

A fourth type of right exists when there is a rule that gives the rights holder immunity from the power rights of others. With an 'immunity right' the rights holder is not liable to have her rights or duties changed through the exercise of the power rights of others. Thus claim rights may be protected through the existence of an immunity right that prevents them being taken away or overruled by other considerations.

Not all duties correlate with someone's rights. Those duties which do correlate with rights are said to be 'owed to' someone. 'Will' theorists interpret this to mean that A's duty is 'owed to' B if B has the normative power to require or waive that duty. This approach usually goes with the view that rights exist for the promotion of choice and empowerment, particularly, following Immanuel Kant, enabling human beings to be responsible moral agents.

In contrast, the 'interest theory' of rights contends a duty is 'owed to' B (the rights holder) when the justification for the existence of A's duty is the interests of B. This explains why a rights holder is normally entitled to waive his right. The interest theory, but not the will theory, allows us to think of small children, who do not have the capacity to waive a duty or exercise moral choice, as possibly having rights, because they have interests.

Neither theory assumes that rights are generally conditional on their holders performing their duties, or more specifically, on performing those duties that correlate with the same rights of others (so that A's right to life is conditional on A not violating another's right to life), although it may be that some rights depend on the rights holder fulfilling such a duty.

Within this conceptual scheme, we may define 'basic' rights and duties as those that are necessary for living or maintaining a minimally acceptable human life and therefore being in a position to benefit from less basic rights. 'Fundamental' rights and their correlative duties we may define as those that are given high priority or special protection and emphasis, sometimes through constitutional recognition. '**Human rights**' are those fundamental rights that morally ought to be secured for all human beings.

TOM CAMPBELL

R Dworkin, *Taking Rights Seriously* (London: Duckworth, 1978)

T Campbell, *Rights: A Critical Introduction* (London: Routledge, 2006)

See also: **natural law theory**

rights of way   *see* **easements**

rights to roam   The argument that there are historic 'rights to roam' is based on some notion of lost ancient rights. The argument has suffered from a lack of legal precision, largely because it has been advanced in terms which have been more political or philosophical than legal. It has foundered on the right of owners to the exclusive use of land and the courts have resisted suggestions that ownership could be qualified by some right amounting in England to a *ius spatiendi* and in Scotland to a servitude of public recreation.

Attempts during the twentieth century to confer greater rights of access to areas through statutory agreements met with only limited success. Eventually, the incoming Labour Government in 1997 responded to the continuing pressure for reform. In England and Wales the Countryside and Rights of Way Act 2000 now confers on the public a right to enter on foot and remain on 'access land' for the purpose of open-air recreation. 'Access land' refers principally to land shown on conclusive maps as 'open country' and land above 600 metres. This confers qualified rights to roam in identified areas.

In Scotland, more serious deficiencies in secure access led to more radical reforms. The Land Reform (Scotland) Act 2003 confers on the public a non-motorized right of responsible access, subject to certain exceptions, to all land and inland water for passage and recreation. This comes close to conferring rights to roam.   JEREMY ROWAN ROBINSON

C Willmore, 'The "Right to Roam"–An Empty Dream?' in P Jackson and DC Wells (eds), *Property Law: Current Issues and Debates* (Aldershot : Ashgate/Dartmouth, 1999)

See also: **public rights of passage over land and water; rambling**

rights, limitations on   Most rights, including fundamental **human rights**, are subject to varying limitations. The **right to life**, the most basic of all human rights, is subject to express limitations under the **European Convention on Human Rights** ('ECHR'). Reflecting the era in which it was drafted, the ECHR permits judicial **capital punishment**. However, during the subsequent half century, European penal policy has evolved to disapprove of the death penalty and amending Protocols (additional texts) have been adopted by Member States to prohibit capital punishment. Other limitations on the right to life, under the ECHR, include the use of 'absolutely necessary' lethal force to defend a person from unlawful **violence** by another and in quelling a riot. The **European Court of Human Rights** ('ECtHR') requires any use of lethal force by **agents** of the state to be strictly proportionate. So, for example, the use of firearms during the purported **arrest** of unarmed and non-violent suspects which resulted in their deaths was found to be unjustified and a breach of the right to life.

The **right to liberty** also has a number of specified limitations, under the ECHR, which enable states to lawfully detain persons. These include: to arrest persons reasonably suspected of having committed criminal offences, to imprison those convicted of offences, and to detain persons who pose a danger to themselves or others (eg because they have a serious mental illness). The ECtHR prohibits governments from using these limitations for improper purposes. For example, the limitation enabling states to detain mentally ill persons can only be invoked where medical evidence justifies such a draconian measure. Thus, European states bound by the ECHR cannot use the pretext of mental illness as a justification for detaining persons who simply oppose the prevailing ideology of the government (as occurred in the former Soviet Union to political dissidents).

Some rights have a very broad social ambit. The rights to respect for private/**family life** and one's home have been held to encompass, *inter alia*, a person's sexual **identity**/life, changing names, discovering one's **paternity**, securing legal recognition of maternal relationships, and protection of one's home from serious environmental pollution. Therefore, it is understandable that states subjected these rights to extensive limitations under the ECHR. Interferences with these qualified rights can be justified for specified legitimate aims including: **national security**, the economic wellbeing of the country, and for the protection of morals. However, states which seek to justify interfering with these rights will have to show that they have a 'pressing social need' to act and that their response is a proportional measure. Frequently, alleged violations of these rights involve complex issues of social and economic policy, such as the extent to which governments should be required to recognize the new identity of post-operative **transsexuals** or limit the noise from aircraft using major airports. The ECtHR has developed the doctrine of the 'margin of appreciation' to accord states **discretion** to make these difficult decisions. The extent of the margin of appreciation will vary according to a matrix of factors including the importance of the right at stake (eg a person's sexual orientation is accorded a high level of protection), the aim of the limitation (historically, states have been given great leeway to determine their national security needs), and whether there is a European consensus on the issue (if there is, then the margin of appreciation will be narrowed).

The right to **freedom of expression** is subject to similar limitations under the ECHR. However, the ECtHR has distinguished different forms of expression. Expression, both by the media and politicians, about matters of politics (including issues of public concern, such as **police** behaviour) is accorded great protection by the ECtHR, because of the importance of the free flow of information and comment about these subjects to help sustain vibrant **democracies**. Whereas the ECtHR has been much more willing—some critics say it has gone too far—in upholding states placing limits on artistic and commercial expression (ie concerned with the economic activity of businesses), due to differing views on these topics across Europe.

A rare example of a fundamental right that is not subject to any limitations is the prohibition of **torture** under the ECHR. States are not permitted to subject persons to this form of cruel maltreatment (or 'lesser' inhuman/degrading treatment) in any circumstances. Therefore, irrespective of how great a danger a person may pose to a state (eg as a suspected terrorist), he/she cannot be subjected to such maltreatment. This strict prohibition reflects the willingness of democratic states to reject forms of maltreatment that are incompatible with civilized behaviour and respect for **human dignity**.

ALASTAIR MOWBRAY

A Mowbray, *Cases and Materials on the ECHR* (Oxford: Oxford University Press, 2nd edn, 2007)

risk The idea of risk is not new to law. **Contract law** and **tort law** have operated as risk-allocating techniques for more than two centuries. The doctrines of 'reasonable foreseeability' and 'negligence', for example, impose legal duties on individuals to calculate the risks created by their actions. From the late nineteenth century, common sense calculation of risk increasingly was challenged by statistical probability—the two techniques often respectively being referred to as 'uncertainty' and 'risk'. The rise of **workers' compensation** insurance schemes was an early instance, displacing much tort law from the workplace, while other social insurance schemes were used to govern **unemployment**, health, and accidental harms. Indeed, insurance has been widely advocated as a more effective alternative to tort law, delivering more certain **compensation** with lower transaction costs. In contract law, these changes were paralleled by increased market **regulation**, as probabilistic economic and social expertise was deployed to improve the efficiency of markets. The influence of such risk management ideas has ebbed

recently as neo-liberal politics promote individual **responsibility**, risk-taking, and enterprise. Disputes over allocating responsibility for risk management to individuals and markets versus the state and technical expertise remain central to contemporary law and **governance**. However, in some high risk fields—such as **product liability**—compulsory insurance is rarely challenged.

In criminal justice statistical calculation of risk has gained prominence in the past two decades, partly reflecting an increasing focus on **victims**. In 'actuarial justice', sentencing based on the statistical risk of re-offending rather than the seriousness of the current offence has challenged the traditional proportionality of offence and **punishment**. In practice, partly due to effective judicial resistance, greater advances have occurred in post-sentencing risk techniques. Statistical risk calculation is now widely used in **parole** and **probation** release decisions. In risk-needs analysis, it determines which programmes are administered to prisoners, and is deployed in post-release community notification programmes ('Megan's Laws') where the public is informed of the risks specific offenders represent. Policing has also been strongly affected by risk-based approaches in this period. Crime prevention, formerly a minor field, has become the subject of major government initiatives and is a core activity of most **police** services. Programmes such as Neighbourhood Watch have become commonplace, and risk-based 'designing-out crime' techniques influence architecture and urban planning. Increasingly, much public police work is organized around the gathering, processing, and distribution of risk-based **security** information, while the expansion of private security is also linked to risk concerns.

Two major theoretical approaches have been used to understand these changes in the past thirty years. '**Governmentality**' has stressed analysis of the diversity of risk techniques, and explores their nexus with different rationales of governance. One key focus has been on individual 'responsibilization' for risks and its relationship to **neo-liberalism**. The 'risk society' thesis, on the other hand stresses the rise of new catastrophic risks, such as global warming and **terrorism**, and their impact on law and government. The spread of the **precautionary principle**, prohibiting technological development in high risk fields, is seen as a major index of this.   PAT O'MALLEY

D Lupton, *Risk* (London: Routledge, 1999)
P O'Malley, *Risk and Uncertainty in Government* (London: Cavendish, 2004)

risk and criminal justice policy   Risk is the probability of contingent harm, assessed in terms of the frequency of occurrence and severity of loss. Criminal justice organizations are dedicated to crime **risk** assessment and management that will prevent harm and provide **security**.

A key focus of criminal justice policy is identifying people who pose risks of criminality. This identification may be based not only on past criminal behaviour, but also on other risk characteristics, such as a person's physical or biological make-up, psychological profile, family background, peer networks, lifestyle, and behavioural record in school, workplace, and other institutional contexts. An assessment of risk characteristics may be used for various screening purposes, for example profiling who should be subject to **police** surveillance, denying access to certain spaces (airports, commercial properties, football grounds, residential complexes), or placing in training programmes that will provide opportunities for legitimate rather than criminal careers. For those convicted of criminal offences, such risk characteristics may be used to determine sentences, and the specific conditions of **probation**, imprisonment, and **parole**. In all of these contexts of 'actuarial justice', risk assessments are used to decide both who should be subject to greater surveillance and control, and what programmes will most benefit the individual and encourage desistance from crime.

Actuarial justice is fraught with problems. People are often subject to surveillance, control, and exclusion, more for who they are than for what they have done. This undermines legal principles such as due process of law, and **punishment** in proportion to the seriousness of a known offence and **responsibility** in committing it. There are also limitations in risk assessment systems which clash with legal standards of **justice**. In particular, all risk assessment systems result in some false positives (wrongly identifying a **person** as harmful and controlling that person unnecessarily) and some false negatives (failing to identify a person as harmful and therefore failing to act in ways that would reduce their harmfulness). Aggregate data that profile risky populations can never be used precisely to indicate whether the individual under scrutiny is an actual source of harm. Probabilities offer only possibilities, and risk assessments inevitably involve other forms of knowledge that are intuitive, emotional, aesthetic, moral, and speculative.

Criminal justice policymakers increasingly acknowledge their limited capacity in risk assessment and management. As a result, criminal justice policy is becoming more focused on uncertainty and the fears associated with it. This focus leads to a precautionary logic that stresses the need for pre-emption of any possible harm through extreme security measures. The security measures include new laws that criminalize not only those who actually cause harm, but also those merely suspected of being harmful, as well as authorities who are deemed responsible for security failures. Traditional principles, standards, and procedures of criminal law are being eroded or eliminated altogether, and civil and administrative law, with their lower evidentiary standards, are becoming more salient in processes of criminalization. There is a parallel expansion of surveillance technologies and networks: CCTV, smart cards, data matching, data mining, and private policing all facilitate criminalization of the merely suspicious and security failures. Security trumps justice, and uncertainty proves itself.

RICHARD V ERICSON

R Ericson, *Crime in an Insecure World* (Cambridge: Polity, 2006)
A Dershowitz, *Preemption: A Knife that Cuts Both Ways* (New York: Norton, 2006)

risk and return   Financial market theory finds a relationship between the degree of risk carried by an investment and the rate of return (the capital appreciation/depreciation and the dividend, interest, or other income generated) from that investment. Higher-risk investments generate higher returns to compensate for the increased risk.

The risk/return relationship has been used to justify **regulation** and the imposition of mandatory disclosure requirements on issuers of securities. Where an investor does not benefit from investor protection rules, including information requirements, and carries increased risk as a result, theory suggests that the investor will demand a higher return for the investment. This increases the cost of capital for issuers in the form, for example, of higher interest rates on a bond. Regulation, however, can reduce the cost of capital by providing investors with protection and lowering the risk burden.

Conduct of business regulation, including the rules imposed by the **Financial Services Authority** under the **Financial Services and Markets Act 2000**, requires investment advisors to disclose risks associated with investments so that investors can assess the degree of risk involved. Derivative investments are subject to particular risk-disclosure requirements. The split capital investment trust scandal over 2001–2002 led the FSA to investigate the sale of these investments to the public as it subsequently suspected that the risks of the product had not been made sufficiently clear to the investing public.

NIAMH MOLONEY

See also: **disclosure in financial markets**

liability insurance; road accidents   *see* **tort system**

road tax   *see* **environmental taxes**

Rodney King trials   The decision of a white, suburban Los Angeles jury to acquit three white police officers (the jury failed to reach a verdict concerning a fourth officer) following a 1992 state trial for the beating of Rodney King, an African-American motorist, set off a wave of riots in predominately black central Los Angeles that resulted in fifty-four deaths, over 7,000 arrests, and hundreds of millions of dollars of property damage. The following year, two of the four officers, Sergeant Stacey Koon and Officer Laurence Powell, were convicted on federal charges of violating King's civil rights.

On the night of 2 March 1991, highway patrol officers spotted King speeding on a freeway. Following a high-speed chase, officers stopped King's car and ordered him out of the car. When King began behaving erratically, Sergeant Koon ordered him to lie on the ground. Claiming later that he resisted arrest and appeared dangerous, Los Angeles police officers twice shocked King with an electric stun gun. When he still did not remain motionless, four officers approached King and struck him over fifty times with metal batons. The sequence was captured on videotape by a George Halliday from his nearby apartment. The videotape received extensive airplay in the press and convinced most Americans that King had been the victim of a brutal police beating.

At the 1992 trial of four officers in Simi Valley, California, the defence argued that King made the clubbing necessary by resisting arrest and that the officers stopped the violence as soon as King submitted to arrest. The prosecution, on the other hand, presented testimony from observers, including the highway patrol officer who spotted King's speeding vehicle, that there 'was no reason' for the beating. The prosecution also introduced evidence suggesting that the beating might have been racially motivated and provided the jury with the text of a message typed by one of the officers on the night of King's arrest: 'I haven't beaten anyone this bad in a long time'. The videotape itself became a key piece of evidence in the trial, with the defence playing the tape in slow motion and identifying movements by King that they claimed demonstrated the physical threat he presented to officers.

On the day after the jury's decision was announced, President George H Bush declared that the verdict 'has left us all with a deep sense of personal frustration'. As the riots in Los Angeles continued, President Bush promised, in a televised address to the nation, a federal prosecution of the officers involved in the King beating. The prosecution in the 1993 federal trial benefited from a racially mixed Los Angeles jury and avoided use of witnesses whose testimony backfired in the earlier state trial. The two officers convicted in the federal trial received sentences of thirty months. Both officers were released from prison in 1995. King, meanwhile, won a $3.8 million dollar civil verdict from the City of Los Angeles for his injuries.

DOUG LINDER

Roe v Wade **(1973)**   In 1973 the **United States Supreme Court** for the first time applied the right to **privacy**, developed in cases protecting parental control of children and access to birth control, to protect a woman's choice to have an abortion. The decision invalidated restrictive state anti-abortion laws and limited state power to regulate abortion by specifying that the decision to abort or carry a pregnancy to term be left to the woman and her physician 'up to the points where important state interests provide compelling justifications for intervention'. The 6–3 decision specified that during the first trimester of pregnancy, when the mortality rate in abortions is less than the mortality rate in normal childbirth, the state could require that only licensed physicians be allowed to perform abortion; but beyond that, that the state should not interfere with the decisions and medical judgment of the woman and her physician. From and after the end of the first trimester, the state's legitimate interest in preserving and protecting the health of pregnant women becomes 'compelling' and the state should be allowed to regulate the abortion procedure in ways reasonably related to preservation and protection of maternal health. The state's distinct, legitimate interest in the protection of potential human life first becomes 'compelling' when the fetus becomes 'viable', at the beginning of the third trimester of pregnancy. From and after the point at which the fetus becomes viable, the state may 'if it chooses, regulate and even prescribe, abortion except where it is necessary, in appropriate medical judgment, for the preservation of the life or health' of the pregnant woman.

Roe v Wade rejected the claim that a fetus was a 'person' under the Fourteenth Amendment entitled to equal protection of the law and refused to extend constitutional protection to the unborn. The Court also refused to rule that women have a right to control their bodies or that the abortion right was 'absolute' and not subject to state regulations of any kind. In this sense, it tried to carve out a middle ground and can be understood as a compromise. This compromise has been rejected by a small but dedicated alliance of religious and political opponents who have spent decades trying to amend the Constitution, limiting and undermining the decision, and packing the Court with appointees opposed to abortion. Largely as a result of these efforts, for the first time in the history of the United States, the Supreme Court now has a majority of Justices who are Catholic—the only major religion that maintains an absolute, uncompromising doctrinal opposition to abortion (and birth control).

Critics from the opposite side argue that abortion restrictions are based on and reinforce women's subordination and that access to abortion should be protected under the rubric of sex equality. The opinion's dependence on privacy is said to obscure or depoliticize the sexual politics of reproductive choice and to reinforce the public-private distinction that was so severely criticized by feminists at the end of the twentieth century.   FRANCES OLSEN

RB Ginsberg, 'Some Thoughts on Autonomy and Equality in Relation to *Roe v Wade*' (1985) 62 *North Carolina Law Review* 375

F Olsen, 'The Supreme Court—Comment: Unraveling Compromise' (1989) 104 *Harvard Law Review* 105

Roman law   Most of the world has taken its law from the West. The Western legal tradition began with the Romans. Roman law began in much the same way as that of many Germanic peoples. One party would formally confront the other and state his claim using a set form of words. That party would then swear an oath that his claim was true, and the other party that it was false. What happened then is not clear. Presumably, the claim was settled by some mechanical procedure that left little to human judgment such as oaths or ordeal. By the early Republic, the mechanical procedure was gone. The outcome was determined by referring the claim to a *iudex* or judge who was a lay person who held no public office. The judge heard evidence and listened to the arguments of advocates (*oratores*) with a freedom in sharp contrast to the formality with which claims were presented and denied. Once the judge had decided the case, there was no appeal. If the complaining party prevailed, he could seize the debtor's person or property with the state's authorization, and subject to its regulation, but without its active assistance. In the late Republic, a new procedure was developed in which written pleadings replaced the formal preliminary claim. The complaining party submitted a *formula* summarizing his complaint, which would be allowed or disallowed by an official called the *praetor* after consultation with the defending party. The *praetor* would then instruct the *iudex* to decide the case according to the *formula*. This procedure lasted until late into the Empire.

Neither the *praetor*, nor the *iudex*, nor the advocates who argued the cases, had any specialized legal training. They were advised by people who did. These people were the jurists, the *iurisconsulti*. Initially, knowledge of the law and its set formulas for bringing claims was confined to priests who belonged to the college of pontiffs. They remained its exclusive interpreters long after the law was made public on Twelve Tables displayed in the forum (451–450 BC), supposedly in response to the demands of the plebeians. In the second half of the Republic, however, the law was decisively shaped by a learned class of jurists who were neither priests nor holders of public office and whose authority rested on their own reputation. The work of the Republican jurists was perfected by those of the classical period of Roman law, often dated from the foundation of the Empire by Augustus (27 BC) to its authoritarian reorganization by Diocletian (284 AD). The Roman law that influenced the West was in large part the creation of the classical jurists. Their writings composed the largest part of the sixth century compilation of the Emperor Justinian that later became known as the *Corpus iuris civilis*.

Their deepest influence was on private law, the law governing the relations of private people to each other. Some of it governed institutions which have passed away, such as those parts of the law of persons which governed the property of offspring during the lifetime of the head of their family, or the dealings of slaves, who were legally both persons and property. Some of it, such as the law of marriage and divorce, was later reworked beyond recognition since it governed institutions which came to be thought of quite differently. It is extraordinary, however, how much of modern private law a Roman jurist would recognize.

Roman property law drew a series of distinctions which passed into the civil law of continental European countries and eventually and selectively into the English **common law**. Possession was protected as well as ownership. Various ways of becoming an owner were recognized: one might find treasure, capture fish or animals, appropriate abandoned property, sever crops from land, mingle another's property with one's own, create a new thing out of another's materials, or, under some circumstances, take delivery from an owner. Interests that different people might have in the same land were distinguished: for example servitudes, which were created by the will of the landowners but then passed as property rights to their successors.

The Roman law of tort or delict, like modern law, distinguished among harms done intentionally, those done negligently, and those for which one was liable even if caused without fault. The Romans discussed such questions as the liability of the insane, of those who lose control of mules through inexperience, of those who kill in self-defence, of those who kill in a boxing match, of those who kill a person who is already dying, and of those whose combined activity causes death.

Roman contract law was a law of particular contracts, each with its particular rules, rather than a law with general rules applicable to all contracts. Nevertheless, many modern legal systems have taken their general rules, such as those governing mistake, fraud, and duress, from observations that the Roman jurists made in particular contexts. Their treatment of particular contracts was sophisticated and rich. Contracts such as sale, lease, and partnership required each party to perform whatever unstated obligations were required as a matter of good faith. In many countries, the modern law of sales, leases, and partnership is a restatement of what the Roman jurists believed these obligations to be.

The Romans did not approach these problems theoretically. They developed fundamental legal concepts of ownership, negligence, sale, and the like—concepts which have endured. But they did not try to derive them from higher principles concerning human nature or **justice**, or to define them abstractly. Greek philosophers such as Plato and Aristotle had discussed the justification of private property, the basis for human **responsibility**, and the form of justice exemplified in a sale. They reasoned by framing definitions and exploring their implications. While the Roman jurists were familiar with their work, their own references to higher principles were occasional and unsystematic. They fixed the meaning of their concepts by examples. A person owned the treasure he found or the fish he captured. A person was negligent if he made a fire on a windy day without watching it, or cut a branch off a tree over a public way without calling out. A person could sell wood he owned but had not yet cut, but could also sell whatever he might catch with the next cast of his net. Much of Justinian's *Corpus iuris civilis* is a petrified forest of these particulars in which the work of the classical jurists was preserved long after their age had ended. Before modern codes replaced the *Corpus iuris civilis*, much of the effort of modern jurists was spent systematizing and explaining these particulars. The texts of modern codes were themselves a product of this effort.

The classical jurists had much less to say about public law. That is not surprising given the epoch in which they wrote. The fundamental question of where power resided had been settled by Augustus. It resided with the Emperor who could do what he wished without the limits of his power being scrutinized by courts or jurists. The Empire eventually developed a bureaucracy, but never an **administrative law**. Nevertheless, the image of public power found in Justinian's *Corpus iuris civilis* reshaped Western legal thought. Legitimate authority belonged to a sovereign who either exercised power directly or delegated it to those who did so on his behalf. Some medieval lawyers claimed this authority was still possessed by the Holy Roman Emperor; others said that each king had the power of an emperor within his own kingdom. In either case, the image was more like our own of the power of a sovereign state, than like a feudal image of power that was limited and divided. The question then became one which the Roman jurists had not confronted: how law could limit the authority that law itself recognized as sovereign. But that question, too, was addressed by people whose thinking about law had been shaped by the legacy of the Romans.

JOSHUA GETZLER

See also: **civil law systems; glossators and post-glossators; Roman law, reception in Europe**

Roman law reception in Europe   Roman law, in this context the rules contained in the Emperor Justinian's *Corpus Iuris Civilis* dating from the sixth century—was partially integrated into legal systems in Europe in the distinct waves: around 1100; around 1500; and around 1700. Traditionally this integration has been referred to as the 'reception of Roman law', though modern historians prefer to avoid the term on the grounds that it is insufficiently nuanced.

In northern Italy round 1100 the Digest, the most important part of Justinian's *Corpus Iuris Civilis*, was rediscovered. This coincided with (or perhaps triggered) a revival of the scientific study of legal texts, which soon came to be centred on the University of Bologna. From here it spread rapidly through France and northern Spain, reaching England perhaps by 1160, and formed the basis of legal study in all medieval universities. In northern Europe its influence was largely confined to the universities and to the church; but in Italy, southern France, and northern Spain it infiltrated into legal practice. It did not completely displace customary law, but local rules were understood through the prism of Roman law and were applied within a procedure derived from the Roman law texts.

The second wave of integration occurred around 1500, and took place across much of the rest of continental Europe apart from Scandinavia. England and Ireland were largely immune from it, though Scotland was not. It took several different forms. In the German Empire, for example, a supreme court, the *Reichskammergericht*, was set up in 1495, and it was explicitly provided that it should be staffed predominantly by university-trained lawyers who would apply the *ius commune*, that is the Roman law as it had been developed by the scholars in the medieval universities. In France and The Netherlands, by contrast, there was no such express imposition of Roman law; but a common requirement that lawyers should be examined in Roman law before they were allowed to practise, and the formal reduction of local customs to written form, meant that the *ius commune* was increasingly dominant in forensic arguments. In Hungary and Poland, there were attempts to write down local laws according to a template borrowed from Roman law. In Scotland, the *ius commune*—perhaps here primarily the **Canon law**—provided the source of the legal procedure adopted by the newly created **Court of Session**, and gradually came to shape or supplant the Scots customary law which had previously existed.

These rather different phenomena were held together by two common features. First, they represent the intellectualization of the law. Law was no longer seen as custom known (in some sense) to the wiser, more experienced, or politically more powerful members of the community; it was something that could be learned. Moreover, the identification of legal rules in situations where there was disagreement was no longer something which depended on an apparent act of memory, but something which was achieved by a process of reason from generally accepted legal texts. In principle, any legal question had a single right answer which could be found by the lawyers. The second feature, which flowed from this, was that throughout Europe (excluding England and Scandinavia) Roman law, in the form of the contemporary *ius commune*, came to play the dominant part in legal reasoning. This had the consequence that by the end of the sixteenth century almost the whole of Europe fell under a unitary legal system; a unitary legal system with substantial local variants, it is true, but one derived from substantially the same legal texts, with a common mass of scholarly literature, and in which decisions reached in one place were regarded as 'authorities' everywhere else. Unsurprisingly,

this system collapsed. It was impossible to keep up with the sheer mass of literature, and the belief that the application of thought would generate demonstrably right answers to legal questions slipped into a reality that the application of thought simply produced reasons for practically any conclusion one wanted to reach. A common core of law, transparently based on Roman law, remained, but in the seventeenth century it was a relatively slim core whose content was rather general, leaving the detailed rules to be determined by each national legal system for itself.

The third wave occurred around 1700. In formal terms it involved not a 'reception' of Roman law as such, but the general acceptance across Europe (now including England) of a set of basic moral principles identified as rules of 'natural law'. Most influential in this context were the *De Iure Belli ac Pacis* of Hugo Grotius and especially the *De Iure Naturae et Gentium* of Samuel Pufendorf. Although purportedly based on pure moral reasoning, both Grotius' and Pufendorf's work depended very heavily indeed on the basic principles of Roman law. Their influence was twofold. They provided a mechanism for the injection of rules derived from Roman law into systems which had previously been reluctant to accept them, dressing them up as objective moral principles of general applicability. Secondly, they provided a skeletal framework for the rules of individual systems, a framework owing a good deal to Roman law. In continental Europe natural-law writers played an important part in shaping the codes of the eighteenth and early nineteenth centuries, locking in place their Roman law characteristics. In England and Scotland, where there was no substantial codification, they brought about a reorientation of legal thinking; the modern tort of negligence, and much of the modern law of contract, were shaped in the later eighteenth century by the adoption of a model rooted in Roman law but borrowed directly from the natural lawyers.

DAVID IBBETSON

Roman–Dutch law   This term signifies a variant of pre-codification continental European law, which consisted of a set of similar (but regionally varying) amalgams of **Roman law** and the indigenous laws of the peoples of Europe. (The Dutch rendition of this term, '*Rooms-Hollandse recht*', strictly speaking, refers only to the law of the province of Holland in the United Netherlands. However, although it is used in this sense in certain contexts, it is usually taken to refer to the law of The Netherlands as a whole at that time (Holland having been the leading region.)

The high period of Roman–Dutch law was in the seventeenth and eighteenth centuries, and in its developed form it is essentially a product of the Enlightenment. Roman–Dutch law is of interest to scholars of the interaction between **common law** and **civil law systems** because, in several countries that had been successively colonized by The Netherlands and Britain, it was merged with English law to form so-called 'mixed legal systems' in the wake of incomplete Anglicization processes in countries such as South Africa, Sri Lanka, Lesotho, and Zimbabwe. During the colonial period the **Privy Council** was on several occasions called upon to decide matters on the basis of Roman–Dutch law.

The treatises of the main exponents of Roman–Dutch law (the equivalent of the works of the Institutional writers of Scots law) remain authoritative in modern South African law when there is no legislation or judicial precedent on a particular point. Several have been translated into English. The most significant of these are: Hugo Grotius, *Introduction to the Jurisprudence of Holland* (1631, translated by RW Lee in 1926) and Johannes Voet *Commentary on the Pandects* (originally published in two folio volumes in 1698 and 1709 and translated by Percival Gane in 1955). Grotius's central influence on the development of the law in The Netherlands during the pre-codification period (and in South Africa) rests in the first place on his intellectual authority and mirrors his wider impact as a natural lawyer, mainly through his seminal work on **international law** *De Iure Belli ac Pacis*, 1625 (*On the Law of War and Peace*). The authority of Voet's *Commentary*, though not as great as that of Grotius's work, was nevertheless considerable during his own time, especially in practice—as it has been in South Africa. (The *Commentary* also had considerable influence in other European countries before codification as a result of it having been published in a large number of foreign editions.) Also important is a Frisian author, Ulrich Huber (*The Jurisprudence of my Time*—the 5th edition of which (1768) was translated by Percival Gane in 1939). The most recent translation of a work on Roman–Dutch law in English is Jacobus Voorda's *Lectures on the Contemporary Law* (1744–1760, Ms Leeuwarden P.B.E., Hof 33), edited and translated by Margaret Hewett in 2006. These works provide a useful point of entry for English speakers who would like to gain first-hand knowledge of the state of the *ius commune* in the two centuries preceding the codification of European law.

The South African Law Reports encapsulate the 'second life the Roman–Dutch law', and they contain a large number of citations and applications of Roman–Dutch sources. The direct citation of Roman–Dutch sources has tapered off in recent times, partly because the original sources have to a large extent been incorporated into the body of South African law through the cases, partly because of the decline in the number of people able to read Latin and Dutch, and partly because the focal point of the development of private law of late has been the Constitution of the Republic of South Africa, 1996 (which, in section 8, decrees that constitutional values are also to be applied to disputes between private individuals). The liberal values embedded in the Roman–Dutch rootstock of South African law made the constitutionalization of South African private law (which had shaken off the encrustations of apartheid in 1994) much easier than it might otherwise have been.

During the second half of the twentieth century, South Africa experienced a (partly politically inspired) *bellum juridicum* between those who wanted to unmake the 'mixedness' of South African law is. On the one side the so-called 'purists' wanted to rid South African law of its English-law components, while on the other the 'pollutionists' strove to complete the Anglicization of South African law—and in the middle were the 'pragmatists', who held the mix of English and Roman–Dutch law to be appropriate, with both sources having made a positive contribution to the modern law. This last group in the end carried the day.

The **law reports** of Sri Lanka also make it clear that Roman–Dutch law, directly and through the citation of South African cases, continues to have a modern application in that country.   DANIEL VISSER

E Kahn, *The South Legal System and its Background* (Cape Town: Juta & Co, 1973), chs 15–17

MHJ van den Horst, *The Roman-Dutch Law in Sri Lanka* (Arnhem: Gouda Quint, 1985)

See also: **mixed jurisdictions**

Rome Convention (International Convention for the Protection of Performers, Producers of Phonograms and Broadcasting Organizations)   The International Convention for the Protection of Performers, Producers of Phonograms and Broadcasting Organizations was concluded in Rome in 1961 and came into force in 1964. Its genesis lies in discussion at the 1948 Brussels Revision Conference of the **Berne Convention for the Protection of Literary and Artistic Works**. Like the Berne Convention, it is now administered by the **World Intellectual Property Organization ('WIPO')**. However, three international organizations collaborated in its drafting: WIPO's forerunner, the United International

Bureaux for the Protection of Intellectual Property ('BIRPI'); the **International Labour Organization** (ILO), which was concerned with the issue of performers' rights; and the United Nations Educational, Scientific and Cultural Organization ('UNESCO').

The Rome Convention is concerned with rights said to be neighbouring on **copyright**. Article 1 of the Convention, however, makes it clear that it does not affect or prejudice the protection of copyright in literary and artistic works. Unlike the Berne Convention, which aimed to reflect existing copyright laws, the Rome Convention led the development of law in this area. This may be one of the reasons why it has not commanded the range of adherents enjoyed by the Berne Convention, despite its associated subject matter. However, the Rome Convention has enjoyed recent significant growth in its membership, which reflects widespread acceptance of the protection of neighbouring rights.

The founding principle of the Rome Convention is that of national treatment. Consequently, contracting states are required to offer the same protection to nationals of other contracting states as they offer to their own nationals. This protection is subject to the minimum protection that the Convention requires each contracting state to provide. In relation to performers, this minimum protection must confer 'the possibility of preventing' the following acts if done without the performer's consent: communication to the public of a live performance; recording an unfixed performance; and, reproducing an unauthorized fixation of a performance. It is open to contracting states to satisfy this obligation through criminal sanctions. The minimum protection for producers of phonograms (sound recordings) is the right to authorize or prohibit reproductions of their phonograms. Broadcasting organizations must have the right to authorize or prohibit: simultaneous rebroadcasting; fixation of broadcasts; reproduction of unauthorized fixations; and, communication of broadcasts in places accessible to the public against payment. The Convention also lays down the minimum duration of protection, which is twenty years, and a range of discretionary exclusions and limitations to the rights conferred by the Convention.

A number of other international agreements build on the Rome Convention. Of recent importance in this respect are the **World Trade Organization Agreement on Trade-Related Aspects of Intellectual Property Rights ('TRIPs')** and the WIPO Performances and Phonograms Treaty ('WPPT'). The TRIPs Agreement, which came into force in 1995, contains its own provision on neighbouring rights protection, but allows 'conditions, limitations,

exceptions and reservations to the extent permitted by the Rome Convention'. The WPPT, which was concluded in 1996 and came into force in 2002, addresses issues arising in the context of digitization and developments in communications technology.

FIONA MACMILLAN

A Ilardi and M Blakeney, *International Encyclopaedia of Intellectual Property Treaties* (Oxford: Oxford University Press, 2004)

Rosenbergs Julius Rosenberg (1918–1953) and Ethel Rosenberg (1915–1953) were convicted on espionage charges in 1951 and executed at Sing-Sing Prison in New York two years later. The controversial trial and harsh sentence led to large public demonstrations in support of the Rosenbergs. The release of deciphered Soviet cables in the 1990s, however, removed most doubts that Julius, if not his wife, had been the head of a Soviet spy ring in the United States.

The FBI arrested Julius Rosenberg in July 1950 after following a trail of leads that began with the arrest of British physicist Klaus Fuchs who, in February of that year, confessed to disclosing to the Soviets information about the Manhattan Project, the top secret project based in Los Alamos, New Mexico that led to construction of the first atomic bomb. Fuchs told authorities of meetings with a Soviet spy (Harry Gold) who, in turn, admitted to receiving secret information from a machinist working on the Manhattan Project. The machinist proved to be David Greenglass, the brother-in-law of Julius Rosenberg, who then told authorities that his espionage activities were directed by Julius and that Ethel was present at meetings when spy activities were discussed.

The government, in the 1951 trial, relied heavily on the testimony of Greenglass and Gold. The defence suggested that Greenglass lied to authorities concerning Rosenberg's role in an effort to gain a reduced sentence and to save his wife from prosecution, but the jury believed otherwise.

DOUG LINDER

Roughead, William   William Roughead (1870–1952) was a Writer to the Signet in Edinburgh who became a leading commentator on criminal trials, elevating the disreputable genre of 'true crime' to new levels of intellectual and social respectability. He was also the editor of the ten volumes in the **Notable British Trials** series, and had a significant impact on the style and presentation of these volumes.

Roughead claimed to have attended most of the significant murder trials in Edinburgh between 1889 and 1949, earning the distinctive privilege of his own seat in the well of the court. He wrote extensively on both contemporary and historical trials. Most of his essays on matters 'criminous' were published in the *Juridical Review*, before being republished in volumes of collected essays which attracted admirers as diverse as Henry James, John Buchan, and FD Roosevelt. He also played a significant role in the exoneration of Oscar **Slater**. He attended the original trial in 1909, and first published a volume on the trial in 1910, in which he was critical of the police investigation and the use of identification evidence. He published three later editions of that work as new evidence came to light, and was instrumental in the campaign to free Slater. He finally gave evidence at the hearing before the newly established Scottish court of criminal appeal in 1928.   LINDSAY FARMER

royal commissions Royal commissions are or have been national committees of inquiry into policy issues or events, created by some **Commonwealth** governments (notably Britain, Australia, and Canada) but formally appointed by and reporting to the **monarch** (or governor-general).

Quite frequently established in Britain before 1914, their apparently special status as inquiries lent weight to their reports, but also encouraged delay. The joke that royal commissions 'take minutes and waste years' was revived by two critical prime ministers (Harold Wilson and Margaret Thatcher—she created none). Governments wishing to delay controversy can set up an inquiry or review and royal commissions have sometimes served this purpose in Britain. Following decline since about 1920 (and much more so since about 1975) the royal commission is now almost extinct in Britain but continues in Australia in particular, examining both policy issues and events, including 'scandals'. Britain has seen only one (on the future of the **House of Lords**, established by Blair's Labour government) since the 1970s.

Royal commissions in Britain were usually reactive inquiries rather than sponsors of new research. Memberships were carefully balanced with rival opinions, requiring heavily compromised recommendations if a highly self-damaging split into majority and minority reports was to be avoided. This often admirably thorough, fair, and rational tradition of generating potential public policy from a civil society source outside the government has long since proved too slow for modern (and impatient) British ministers. The British royal commission's final potential redoubt is probably constitutional reform issues such as the Lords, voting reform, further devolution from Westminster or (conceivably) some formal legal changes to the monarchy.
          ANTHONY BARKER

royal prerogative The term 'royal prerogative' refers to many or all non-statutory powers of the **Crown**, whether exercised directly or by Order in Council. For **Blackstone**, the prerogative was 'singular and eccentrical', covering 'those rights and capacities which the king enjoys alone, in contradistinction to others, and not . . . those which he enjoys in common with any of his subjects' (*Commentaries on the Law of England*, 16th edn, 1825, vol I, 239). However, **Dicey** adopted a wider view, including within the term *all* common law powers of the Crown: 'Every act which the executive government can lawfully do without the authority of [an] Act of Parliament' (*Introduction to the Study of the Law of the Constitution* (London: Macmillan, 10th edn, 1959), p 425). Whichever definition is preferred, nearly all prerogative powers are nowadays exercised by ministers in the monarch's name, exceptions being the appointment of the **Prime Minister** and the dissolution of Parliament. Constitutional conventions govern the operation of most prerogative powers, including the last-mentioned, and the exercise of any such power is in principle open to parliamentary scrutiny (although current parliamentary practice excludes certain areas).

Where a statute regulates matter previously governed by the prerogative, the relevant prerogative power falls into abeyance. In *R. v Secretary of State for the Home Department, ex p Fire Brigades Union* (1995), the **House of Lords** applied this principle with such rigour that the existence of statutory provisions which had not been brought into force was held to preclude the use of the prerogative in an inconsistent fashion. Furthermore, no new prerogatives may be recognized by the courts. Nonetheless, there is sometimes uncertainty about whether a prerogative power has in fact been displaced by, or merely sits alongside, a statutory provision.

Until *Council of Civil Service Unions v Minister for the Civil Service* (1985), it was thought that courts could determine the existence and extent of prerogative powers, but could not judicially review their exercise. The House of Lords held that **judicial review** was now permissible, although Lord Roskill suggested that the exercise of certain 'excluded' prerogatives—concerning treaty-making, defence of the realm, granting pardons or honours, dissolving Parliament, and appointing and dismissing ministers (including the Prime Minister)—should remain immune since their subject matter made them unsuitable for judicial scrutiny. It is frequently argued that this policy of exclusion has been weakened or abandoned in some later cases. There is controversy about how far the prerogative overlaps, in

Left: 'Imperial Welcome', cartoon by David Low, *Evening Standard*, 7 September 1943, (*Constantine v Imperial Hotel Ltd*).

Below left: Children in the landmark civil rights case *Brown v Board of Education* which challenged segregation in schools, 1953.

Below right: 'No coloured' signs on for-rent notices were common in London, 1967.

Bottom: The Memphis sanitation workers' strike lasted from February to April 1968, and was supported by Martin Luther King who was assassinated just before it ended.

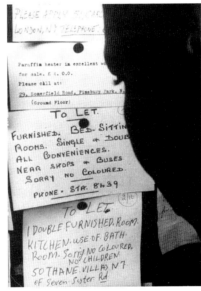

Signing the Anglo-Irish
Treaty, 6 December 1921.
Seated from left: Arthur
Griffith, Eamon Duggan,
Michael Collins, Robert
Barton, standing from left:
Erskine Childers, George
Gavan Duffy, John Chartres.

British paratroopers take away
civil rights demonstrators on
Bloody Sunday, when paras
opened fire on a civil rights
march, killing 14 civilians.

Coffins of the 13 civilians
killed on Bloody Sunday
(the 14th died later).

Above left: Protest in sympathy with IRA hunger strikers, 1981.

Above right: The Home Secretary, Roy Jenkins, leaving the wreckage of the Horse and Groom public house in Guildford, two days after an IRA bomb exploded killing five and injuring 65, 7 October 1974.

Left: Ian Paisley and Martin McGuinness after being sworn in as First Minister and Deputy First Minister of the Northern Ireland Assembly at Stormont, Belfast, 8 May 2007.

Below left: Stormont.

Sharpeville massacre, 1960. Police opened fire on a peaceful demonstration against the pass laws in Sharpeville, near Johannesburg, killing 69 people.

Nelson Mandela outside the court in Pretoria, during the treason trial in 1958.

Mandela with his wife Winnie on his release after 27 years imprisonment, 11 February 1990.

'There, I think that'll hold him', Judge, speaking to Verwoerd, holding copy of the Mandela judgment, following Mandela's life sentence for sabotage in 1964, cartoon by Leslie Illingworth, *Daily Mail*, 15 June 1964.

Nelson Mandela, President of South Africa, in 1995.

Nelson Mandela receives the final report of the Truth and Reconciliation Commission from Archbishop Desmond Tutu in 1998.

Albie Sachs is sworn in as a judge at the South African Constitutional Court's opening ceremony. Sachs lost his arm in a bomb attack while in exile in Mozambique.

Yvonne Mokgoro is sworn in as a judge at the South African Constitutional Court's opening ceremony. She is the first black woman to be appointed a judge in South Africa.

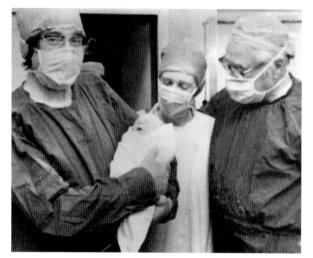

Above left: Doctors hold Louise Brown, the first baby to be born by in vitro fertilisation, in 1978.

Above right: Demonstrators outside the US Supreme Court supporting the State of Oregon's physician-assisted suicide law, which was upheld by the Court in 2006.

Left: Demonstration in favour of abortion rights and the protection of *Roe v Wade*.

Below left: Diane Pretty and her husband after the European Court of Human Rights' decision to deny her 'right to die' petition.

Above left: Henry Fonda in *12 Angry Men*, directed by Sidney Lumet, 1957.

Above right: Gregory Peck as Atticus Finch in *To Kill a Mockingbird*, directed by Robert Mulligan, 1962.

Left: Spencer Tracy and Frederic March in *Inherit the Wind*: a fictional account of the Scopes 'Monkey trial', directed by Stanley Kramer, 1960.

Below left: Julia Roberts as Brockovich and Albert Finney as Aaron Eckhart in *Erin Brockovich*, directed by Steven Soderbergh, 2000.

LONDON LAUGHS: Lawyers' Offices
"Could I interest you gentlemen in a modern filing system!"

Above left: Cartoon by Austin, *The Guardian*, 15 July 1997.

Above right: 'London Laughs: Lawyers' Offices', cartoon by Joseph Lee, *The Evening News*, 21 August 1936.

Left: 'The New Compensation Act', postcard from an original by Tom Browne (1870–1910), illustrating the Workmen's Compensation Act 1906.

Below left: The first mobile Citizens' Advice Bureau, 1941.

foreign affairs, with the concept of act of state. Acts of state are non-justiciable, but the ambit of the plea of act of state is unclear.

Parliamentary scrutiny may of course be possible in the absence of judicial review, demonstrating that prerogative powers provide an important test case for debate about the appropriate ambits of 'political' and 'legal' **accountability** within the constitution. This needs to be kept in mind when considering whether some or all prerogative powers should be placed on a statutory footing.

The areas regulated by some of the key prerogative powers are of such great constitutional importance that it might be thought desirable, in order to promote clarity and accountability, to convert those prerogatives into statutory form. For example, while constitutional convention dictates that the monarch, after a general election, should invite the leader of the party with the largest number of **House of Commons** seats to form a government, and should use the prerogative to appoint that person Prime Minister, it is unclear when that power should be used following an inconclusive election. Prerogative power is also used to declare war or to commit troops to serve overseas, without—in contrast to most constitutional democracies—any formal need for parliamentary approval. On a broader basis, the constitutional concept of legal certainty might be felt to demand that all prerogatives be converted into statutory form. However, the most obvious controversy (drafting difficulties aside) associated with such an exercise is the possibility that it might encourage judicial review—not least, in the case of the most constitutionally important prerogatives—of very sensitive political decisions. This is suggested by the probable qualification, to date, of Lord Roskill's list of 'excluded' prerogatives, together with judicial reluctance to interpret statutory provisions which exclude judicial review or other judicial scrutiny save in the narrowest possible fashion. NICHOLAS BAMFORTH

PP Craig, 'Prerogative, Precedent and Power', in C Forsyth and I Hare (eds), *The Golden Metwand and the Crooked Cord: Essays on Public Law in Honour of Sir William Wade* (Oxford: Oxford University Press, 1998)

HWR Wade, 'Procedure and Prerogative in Public Law' (1985) 101 *Law Quarterly Review* 180, 190–199

See also: **conventions of the constitution**

rule of law The rule of law is an ideal to which every legal system aspires, and against which it must be judged. It expresses the value of legality, which is closely linked to the equally important values of **justice** and freedom. Neither justice nor freedom can survive without scrupulous adherence to the rule of law, which affords the citizen protection from arbitrary power—power exercised, whether by government officials or private individuals or corporations, in a manner that pays no regard to the citizen's legitimate interests or concerns. The law should constitute a barrier against whim or caprice, as well as against unfair treatment that betrays contempt for the citizen, or a minority group. It should be a safeguard against tyranny, whether the tyrant be a powerful fellow citizen, an overbearing official, or a ruthless political faction seeking the support of an elected majority in Parliament. The law can only perform that role, however, when it meets certain standards of law-making that acknowledge the citizen's dignity, as a recipient of intelligible laws which he can understand and obey in recognition of their contribution to justice and the common good.

Statutes that impose duties on the citizen must be published, and their content made clear and consistent, so that their requirements are made accessible to those they affect. The precept *nulla poena sine lege* is fundamental to the rule of law: no-one should be punished in the absence of law, stipulating the prohibited conduct in advance of his actions. A retrospective penal law is an arbitrary invasion of personal liberty; and laws that punish conduct committed without any intentional wrongdoing are usually condemned on the same ground. Arbitrariness is avoided only when the laws are framed in a manner that enables the citizen to conform to their demands, and when such laws are faithfully applied by judges and other officials according to their true meaning. If citizens and officials were not equally bound by the law, there would be no security against oppression. However draconian the content of the laws, as regards their consequences for the lives and liberties of the citizen, freedom is served by their just and impartial application; for at least the citizen is free to act without fear in relation to matters or activities left unregulated.

The need for the law to be faithfully applied to particular cases shows the importance of fair judicial procedure. The facts of a case must be fairly and accurately ascertained, giving the person affected an opportunity to address the court or tribunal, which must be open-minded and unbiased. He must be able to challenge the details of the case presented against him, as well as offer evidence or argument in favour of his own position; and these requirements are of special importance in the case of criminal proceedings. The defendant's right to a fair criminal trial, based on public testimony in open court before an impartial judge, or judge and jury, may be considered a prime ingredient of the rule of law.

We can also say that **separation of powers** between legislature, executive government (ministers and officials), and judiciary is a natural and necessary ally of the rule of law. The citizen is shielded from arbitrary state power only if those officials who may employ coercive force are constrained by rules of law they cannot themselves remove. Parliament may confer discretionary power on ministers or officials, but such power must be used for its proper purpose in furtherance of the public good; and the appropriate limits and conditions can be determined and enforced by independent judges. In the absence of a legally recognized power to act, an official is as much bound by the ordinary laws of the realm as the private citizen. English common law, at any rate, acknowledges no general governmental discretion to commit trespasses or other wrongs for reasons of 'state necessity': see *Entick v Carrington* (1765).

Laws, properly so called, are general in form, applicable to all persons whose activities provoke a need for legal **regulation**. Such generality helps to ensure that the law furthers a genuine common good, rather than discriminating unfairly against particular groups or identifiable persons. A 'bill of attainder', prescribing punishment for a specific person or persons, violates the rule of law by depriving its victims of the basic safeguard of a judicial trial for alleged breach of a general rule. It is a 'law' only in the most formal and empty sense of the term, mocking the value of legality it pretends to honour. We must concede, of course, that all laws distinguish between persons for various purposes, and they may also confer discretionary powers which enable officials to discriminate between persons for reasons of public policy; but such reasons and purposes should be open to question and scrutiny. The rule of law is infringed when the state cannot justify differences in the treatment of persons or groups, consistently with accepted political values. If, for example, we recognize individual rights to **freedom of speech** or freedom of conscience or **freedom of association**, we must apply them fairly to all; for such freedoms are of equal value to all and their denial to anyone flouts his dignity as a citizen, equal in status to other citizens, whatever may be his political allegiances or economic or social standing.

Even a 'sovereign' Parliament may be regarded as subject to the rule of law in the sense that only its enactments are binding on the citizen, rather than the expectations or intentions of those (usually government officials) who promoted or supported the bill. It is the duty of an independent judiciary to construe the words of a statute, so far as possible, in accordance with settled principles of the general law.

Even a majority of elected representatives should govern in the interest of all; if their purposes are benign their enactments will make no arbitrary distinctions between different groups of citizens.

TREVOR ALLAN

BZ Tamanaha, *On the Rule of Law: History, Politics, Theory* (Cambridge: Cambridge University Press, 2004)
TS Allan, *Constitutional Justice: A Liberal Theory of the Rule of Law* (Oxford: Oxford University Press, 2001)

See also: **parliamentary sovereignty**

Russian law   The term 'Russian' in connection with law has been understood narrowly to mean the law of Kievan Rus (c ninth to eleventh centuries), the entire territory that came to be the Grand Dukedom of Muscovy (eleventh to sixteenth centuries), the Russian Empire (sixteenth century to 1917), the former Soviet Union (1917–1991), and officially the Russian Federation from 1991 to the present. With reference to law in force on these territories 'Russian Law' embraces the legislation issued by the ruler or assemblies in power and a vast group of subsystems, amongst them the customary law of hundreds of ethnic minorities, the canon law of the Russian Orthodox, Islamic, Jewish, and other faiths, and legislation of principalities, khanates, kingdoms, tribes, and other entities absorbed by Russian expansion (Baltic provinces, Caucasus, Central Asia, Siberia, and others).

The influence of neighbouring legal traditions on Russia is undoubted, although its precise nature is debated. From the earliest surviving legal monuments (peace treaties between Byzantium and Kievan Rus dating from 907 onwards; canon law texts, the surviving versions of the Russian mediaeval law text *Pravda Russkaia*, and princely charters) to recent codifications of the Russian Federation (Part IV of the Civil Code on intellectual property, in force from 1 January 2008) foreign legal experience from outside the Empire has been imposed or absorbed by conquest, precept, or adaptation. All surviving major legal documents up to the *Sobornoe ulozhenie* (1649), whether canon or secular, contain evidence of foreign legal terminology. The subjugation of Russia by the Tatar invasions left an enduring legacy in Russian administrative terminology and, some would argue, in Russian administrative style. Peter the Great (1672–1725) assertively drew upon European legal systems in his naval, military, administrative, fiscal, and other legislation and directed the translation into Russian of leading European doctrinal writers. Jeremy **Bentham,** through his writings translated into Russian and personal contacts, influenced Russian approaches to codification, as did the leading German and French schools. Throughout the nineteenth and early twentieth centuries Russian doctrinal writings followed European experience closely.

The emergence of the Union of Soviet Socialist Republics ('USSR'), which incorporated the Russian Soviet Federated Socialist Republic ('RSFSR') as a constituent entity, witnessed the first attempt by Russia to assertively export a legal model to countries within its sphere of power and to other countries by way of a model in the form of **socialist law**. With the dissolution of the Soviet Union in December 1991, many public law and administrative elements of the model disappeared, but others have endured side by side with market legal institutions to such an extent that many regard Russian Law today as a 'transitional' legal system which may or may not advance beyond that level. In a world of hostility, rivalry, competition, and aggrandizement during the twentieth century, the Soviet legal system, in its capacity as a model, induced in other legal models an adjustment to legal values that might not otherwise have transpired. Nonetheless, although ideologically disposed otherwise, Soviet jurists followed foreign legal experience and drew upon it when advisable.

WILLIAM BUTLER

HJ Berman, *Justice in the USSR* (Cambridge, Mass.: Harvard University Press, rev edn, 1963)

WE Butler, *Russian Law* (Oxford: Oxford University Press, 2nd edn, 2003)

***Rylands v Fletcher* (1868)** Thomas Fletcher operated a coal mine in Lancashire. Nearby was the Ainsworth Mill, owned by John Rylands, the largest employer of labour in Victorian Britain. He employed a contractor to excavate a reservoir to service the mill. Under the site were old coal workings; the water in the reservoir escaped into them and flooded Fletcher's mine. Fletcher sued Rylands and his manager: at this time it was not established that they would have been answerable for any negligence by the contractor. The reason the contractor was not sued was perhaps that he was unable to satisfy any judgment; his identity is not known.

The action was originally based on allegations of negligence. But after it was commenced there occurred, in 1864, the gravest dam failure ever to occur in Britain, the collapse of the Dale Dyke dam, built by the Sheffield Waterworks Company. This caused widespread devastation and loss of life. By the terms of the statute-based scheme under which it was constructed the company was liable to pay compensation whether there was negligence or not, and a huge sum was paid out. This statutory scheme did not however apply to Ryland's reservoir, so any liability had to be based solely on the judge-made **common law**. In the course of the litigation the nature of the claim was changed, raising the question whether proof of any negligence was essential to success or whether there would be liability even without such proof.

The ruling by the **House of Lords**, to which an appeal was taken, was that liability for the escape of the water was 'strict', that is it did not depend on proof of any negligence in the construction, or in the selection of the contractor. At this time the general idea that liability in civil claims for wrongs or torts should turn on proof of negligence, or fault, was gaining ground in the law. Negligence was taken to mean failure to take the care that a reasonable person would have taken in the circumstances. The decision in the case seemed at odds with this tendency. It may have been influenced by the context in which the case was decided, in which strict liability had been imposed by Parliament on those who operated reservoirs constructed under statutory powers. Since then courts in the common law world have adopted different views as to when liability should be strict, and when it should depend on negligence. The two principles of liability in effect compete in tort law, some courts favouring the extension of strict liability and others favouring its restriction. The common law system has never wholly adopted one or the other. The reservoir still exists near Bolton in Lancashire, and is still leaking water into what remains of Fletcher's coal mine, now long disused. Fishing tickets can be obtained from the Ainsworth Fishing Club.

AW BRIAN SIMPSON

AWB Simpson, *Leading Cases in the Common Law* (Oxford: Oxford University Press, 1995), ch 8

See also: **negligence in civil law; strict civil liability**

S

safety Safety is a pervasive theme in law. Statutory terms such as 'public safety 'and '**community** safety' highlight its significance in relation to criminal law and criminal justice. Its use in relation to children (**child** safety) and the mentally ill (hospitals as places of safety) draws attention to the way it is associated with particular (in current parlance 'vulnerable') people. Football safety **legislation** and cinema safety regulations illustrate its association with particular locations. '**Health and safety in the workplace'** conjoins safety in a particular location (the workplace) with safety as an attribute of various social practices, social relations, and technologies. Laws related to a various modes of transport put safety at the heart of regulation of movement: road safety, maritime safety, railway safety. 'Fire safety' is an example of its use in relation to a particular danger. '**Consumer** safety', '**food safety**', and 'motor vehicle safety' highlight its significance in relation to consumption in general and particular types of consumer goods. Far from being exhaustive, this list is just the tip of the legislative safety iceberg.

Safety is defined in everyday language in various ways: as freedom from danger and without danger. These two definitions highlight some key points about the nature of 'safety'. First, it tends to be defined by way of its opposite, 'danger'. Secondly, safety is defined in the negative, as the absence of something. 'Danger' is a term that can be endlessly elaborated upon and illustrated while 'safety' in itself appears to be a term almost without substance. Safety is also defined as the condition of being secure. So what is **security**? Security is commonly associated with the plethora of techniques and technologies used to produce safety, with the construction and maintenance of defences, boundaries, and borders. Safety is the effect of security.

With this in mind it is perhaps hardly surprising that while 'safety' is a ubiquitous category in law, a search for legal definitions of the term is unrewarding Sometimes 'safety' is associated with a particular place—a hospital, a care home—but the nature of safety associated with that particular place remains undefined. A more common approach of safety laws, that avoids the need for definition, is to set in place complex regulatory mechanisms. These mechanisms have several features in common. They establish a set of '**safety standards**'. For example, in the context of consumer safety, they prescribe the composition or contents of the product, its design, construction, finish, packaging, and so on. Authorization, by way of a system of licensing or certification, is a technique used to promote compliance. Surveillance, disclosure, and auditing provide for ongoing monitoring. Compliance is further secured by way of powers of investigation and enforcement. Through this regime, safety does not need to be defined. It is nothing more than the (expected) outcome.

While the ubiquity of safety legislation suggests that the modern state has a key role to play in producing individual and collective safety such a conclusion has to be treated with caution. First, as scholars working in the field of criminal justice have noted, safety is no longer delivered solely by way of the institutions or mechanisms of the sovereign state. Safety is produced through a multi-agency approach. Secondly, individuals have a key role to play in the generation of safety. Failure to perform according to standards and expectations may lead to punishment or the denial of access to those state and multi-agency services associated with the delivery of safety.

While safety may seem to be a universally approved objective, it is not without problems; in particular, in the process of achieving it, many positive values, freedoms, and liberties may be destroyed. The best contemporary example of this is legal responses to the 'war on terror' which have the objective of securing our collective safety. In the process of realizing safety, basic **human rights** and respect for **human** dignity are under threat. Another problem is that not all have equal access to safety. For example, women, **lesbians** and gay men, racial and ethnic minorities, and **refugees** have all experienced difficulties accessing the safety that the state purports to offer to those within its borders. Safety is often associated with social and political elites. LES MORAN

safety in sport Under the Occupiers' Liability Act 1957 playing arenas must be reasonably safe for the purpose for which people have been invited onto the premises. This duty applies equally to players and spectators. Facility owners and event organizers must ensure that the playing area is suitable for the particular activity taking place and safely maintained for those taking part. Organizers should not make do with using a sports hall with an inappropriate floor covering—eg one that has been waxed and prepared for ballroom dancing when a less slippery surface is required for a PE lesson. Further, they should ensure that once the activity has begun, the playing area is safely and appropriately maintained—eg by raking a long jump pit after every jump, not at the end of every round of jumps.

Where provided, event organizers should ensure that they have complied with any safety guidelines provided by the sport's governing authorities; where none are available, common or accepted best practice should be followed. Failure to follow such guidelines or practices will almost always result in liability being imposed for any injuries that are caused. A failure by a governing authority to create the necessary safety environment in its sport could lead to the national governing body or the international federation of the sport being liable in negligence for any injuries caused.

All those who play a role in respect of player safety must ensure that they are fulfilling their role by taking all reasonable steps to ensure that the playing environment is reasonably safe for those for whom they are responsible. This duty of care is imposed on coaches, referees, and governing bodies.

Coaches must ensure that they have trained players to play the game in a safe manner and taught them how to use any necessary equipment. For example, allowing swimmers to dive from racing blocks into the shallow end of a pool, without having taught them how to perform a racing dive is a clear case of negligent coaching. Opposition coaches also owe a duty of care to ensure that their players are not trained in a manner that is likely to cause injury to their opponents. Hard physical play is allowed, but play designed to cause injury or which is overly aggressive, may be considered to be a result of negligent training where injury is caused.

By analogy to the duties owed by coaches, mountain guides and other organizers of adventure sports owe a duty of care to less experienced members of their party. If common sense if used, the duty is easily discharged by following established mountaineering practice.

Once the game is underway, referees must ensure that they are applying the safety rules of the sport when officiating. In one case, the referee in a rugby game had failed to apply safety rules applicable to the engagement of scrums. The court held that the safety of the players was one of the paramount concerns of the referee and that his failure to run the scrums safely was a breach of the duty of care that he owed to the players under his control.

The governing bodies of sport must also ensure that their playing rules and safety and medical advice are reviewed regularly and updated where necessary. In one case, the national governing body and international federation responsible for motor racing in the UK were exonerated for following best practise in respect of track inspection and licensing procedures. In contrast, in another case the governing body was found negligent for failing to follow best practice in the provision of ringside medical treatment.

Although participants run the risk of injury from the inherent dangers associated with the playing of their chosen sport, they do not consent to the negligence of others. Just because a scrum collapses and a player is injured does not mean that the referee has been negligent. Only where the referee has allowed a dangerous situation to develop and has taken inadequate steps to abate it will the referee be guilty of negligence. Further to this, under the Unfair Contract Terms Act 1977, where sport is being conducted as a business, waiver clauses exempting defendants from liability for causing them injury by negligence are ineffective. A player can be warned of the risks of injury but cannot exclude liability for negligence.

MARK JAMES

See also: **spectators at sporting events**

safety standards Private law rules which entitle consumers injured by defective products (see **product defects**) were found to be insufficient to ensure a high degree of protection for consumers against unsafe products. From the 1960s onwards legislation has provided for standards relating to particular products and general safety standards applicable to all products, which are enforced proactively by local authority regulatory services officers (see **trading standards**). Enforcement officers have powers to prosecute businesses which put unsafe products on the market and to seek their compulsory withdrawal from the market. In practice, where risks associated with particular products are detected by enforcement officials, these powers are often used to reach negotiated solutions.

Many products are marketed across many countries, and in response to this the **European Union** has a system for the Rapid Exchange ('RAPEX') of product safety information, which frequently triggers simultaneous enforcement action in two or more Member States. Recent enhancements to EC legislation require businesses that detect defects in their products which render them unsafe to notify this to the **Office of Fair Trading** ('OFT'). The OFT has powers to require producers to recall unsafe products so as to remove them from sale and have unsafe products already sold returned by consumers to the producer for modification or destruction. In practice most businesses will organize a recall of products when defects making them dangerous are discovered, though there have been high profile incidents in which producers with strong market reputations have damaged themselves through failing to organize a rapid recall in these circumstances.

Standards governing the safety of products range between the privately developed 'BS' standards of the British Standards Institute ('BSI'), through the statutory standards relating to particular products (such as bunk-beds, children's clothes, aerosols, cosmetics, bicycles, pushchairs, and toys) to statutory general safety standards under which products must be as safe as it is reasonable to expect. This general statutory safety standard represents the default position for consumer products which are not subject to more specific statutory or non-statutory rules (such as the BS standards). Thus, the primary obligation of businesses is to comply with the detailed standards for particular products, and the general safety requirement only applies where detailed standards do not exist or in respect of such matters as are not covered by the detailed standards. COLIN SCOTT

sale of goods Sale of goods is a body of law dealing with contract and the passing of property (ownership) from the seller to the buyer. The original Sale of Goods Act 1893, adopted in most British colonies and dominions, was also the model for the American Uniform Sales Act 1906. The 1893 Act was consolidated in 1979 with various intervening changes in the law. Important statutory changes were also made in the 1990s.

A sale of goods occurs where one party agrees to buy goods from another for a money consideration called the price. This definition excludes barter transactions, sales of shares, transfers of bills of exchange, money-lending, hire purchase agreements, and equipment leases. Goods may be specific, identified at the contract date, or they may be unascertained, requiring the seller later to acquire,

manufacture, or identify them so as to apply them to the contract. Unascertained goods must first be identified before the seller can transfer the property in them, though sometimes a buyer may acquire instead an undivided share of a larger bulk identified in the contract or at a later date. Subject to this, English law treats the intention of the parties as paramount when determining whether property has passed. It therefore recognizes reservation of title clauses by which the seller reserves ownership after delivery until payment is made by the buyer. If no such clause is present in the contract, it will be assumed that property passes when the goods are physically delivered to the buyer.

The fact that sale involves the transfer of property in goods is also witnessed by the statutory obligations regarding the strength of the seller's title that must be transferred to the buyer, the seller's guarantee of the buyer's 'quiet possession' of the goods once property has passed, and the seller's guarantee that no third party has intellectual property rights preventing the buyer from using the goods.

The passing of property is significant for insolvency purposes because goods still owned by the seller are not distributed to the buyer's creditors. It also determines whether an unpaid seller may sue the buyer for the price. Although the risk of loss is presumed by the Sale of Goods Act to pass to the buyer at the same time as the property in the goods, this rule is largely excluded where goods are sold to overseas buyers. The unpaid seller will usually reserve title until payment takes place, often some time after shipment. It makes commercial sense, however, for the buyer to pay to insure the goods from the moment of shipment and thus to bear the risk from that time.

The old rule that the buyer has to put up with defective goods unless the seller gives an express warranty of their quality (caveat emptor) survives in the statutory provision that the buyer may not invoke implied terms concerning the quality or fitness of the goods apart from those laid out in the statute. These terms, however, give extensive protection to the buyer. They include the seller's duty to supply goods that correspond to the contractual description; in modern times, description has come to mean the identity or essential attributes of the goods. The seller must also supply goods that are of satisfactory quality (formerly, merchantable quality), a variable standard that refers to the fitness for purpose of the goods, the price paid for them and the way they are generally described in the contract. The more specific implied term of reasonable fitness for purpose in practice almost completely overlaps satisfactory quality. The seller's liability is strict. In a chain of sales transactions, a buyer will often sue a retail seller; the retail seller will then sue the wholesale seller; and the wholesale seller will sue the importer or manufacturer. The buyer will not usually sue the manufacturer directly.

For a breach of the implied terms, the buyer, apart from claiming damages, is entitled to terminate the contract, except that commercial buyers may not terminate the contract for technical breaches. The same restriction applies in the case of the seller's obligation to deliver the right quantity. Apart from statute, implied conditions of the contract are recognized at **common law** in respect of the time of performance and the quality of documents that a seller is required to tender. There is no statutory limitation on the exercise of these rights. English law is generous in the grant of termination rights for breach of the contract of sale, but a buyer's right to terminate is heavily circumscribed in practice by the requirement that the buyer reject the goods within a short period or else be treated as having affirmed the contract.

Apart from strict liability, the most important feature of damages for breach of the sale of goods contract is the way that presumptively (but not invariably) damages are calculated by reference to the market price prevailing at the due date of delivery, whether for a seller delivering defective goods, or delivering late, or not delivering the goods at all. The same applies to a seller's claim against the buyer for non-acceptance of the goods. In referring to the market, English law shows a general preference for simple rules of damages calculation, even if they do not precisely quantify the claimant's loss.

MICHAEL BRIDGE

See also: **contract law; strict civil liability**

sale of organs   see **organ donation and transplantation**

Salem witchcraft trials   The Salem witch-craze of 1692 is the most famous episode in the history of colonial witchcraft, indeed in the entire history of early modern witch-trials. The play it inspired—Arthur Miller's *The Crucible*—has made the tragedy a byword for political paranoia, intolerance, and oppression. But as an example of a witch-hunt, particularly in America, Salem was unique. Almost 150 people were charged and many others implicated. Previously the largest witch-trial in New England—at Hartford in 1662—had involved just eleven accusations.

The witch-hunt began in Salem Village, a small agricultural community, and quickly spread throughout Essex County. Half the accused lived in

Salem or in nearby Andover, but some twenty-four towns had been drawn in by the time the trials were halted in October 1692. Nineteen people were hanged, and one pressed to death for refusing to plead. Up to this point most accusations never came to trial, and few which did ended in executions. Other anomalies of Salem include the nature of the accusations and accusers. As in old England, before 1692 most alleged crimes had been acts of physical harm, prosecuted by male householders. But at Salem the accusations were given momentum by young women and girls who suffered fits and claimed that spectral visions of the suspected witches haunted and tormented them. Among them were the daughter and niece of Salem minister Samuel Parris, who forced the girls to name their oppressors. These included the family slave, a West Indian woman called Tituba.

Tituba's confession in February sparked a major crisis. By mid-April fourteen people had been charged, and a month later, when the new governor of Massachusetts William Phips appointed a special court, this had risen to nearly fifty. Many confessed to consorting with Satan and named their accomplices. In a cruel twist, only those who refused to confess were executed; others, who in effect perjured themselves, were spared. Almost immediately, judgments based on spectral evidence generated bitter controversy among jurists and clergy alike. Could these visions not, in fact, be satanic illusions conjured up to divide Christians?

The causes of Salem were extremely complex, combining social, economic, religious, political, and cultural factors. There was competition between godly but declining Salem Village and the more worldly and prosperous town and port. The political vacuum that existed prior to Phips's arrival allowed suspicions to proliferate, and aggravated a perceived threat to colonial independence from the government at Westminster. Anxiety was further exacerbated by savage Indian wars along the northern frontier in the 1670s and 1680s. Many of the inhabitants of Salem Village—men like Samuel Parris—felt isolated and embattled, a sensation which in a seventeenth-century context was readily interpreted as all-out assault by Satan. But the spirit of the age was against them, the legal policies of 1692 were reversed the following year, and within a short time the names of those accused, tried, and executed had been cleared. In this way Salem helped to undermine colonial witch-trials and the belief in witchcraft itself.

MALCOLM GASKILL

P Boyer and S Nissenbaum, *Salem Possessed: the Social Origins of Witchcraft* (Cambridge MA: Harvard University Press, 1974)

Mary Beth Norton, *In the Devil's Snare: the Salem Witch-craft Crisis of 1692* (New York: Alfred A Knopf, 2002)

sales promotion   *see* **advertising; unfair commercial practices**

Salomon v A Salomon & Co Ltd (1897)

Salomon's case marks a turning-point in the history of company law, and remains its most important decision.

Legislation establishing the limited liability company in 1844 and 1855 had declared the company's fundamental characteristics: first, that it is a species of 'corporation'—an entity separate from the persons who are its members, capable itself of enjoying legal rights, and correspondingly subject to legal duties; and secondly, that its members are not liable to contribute towards its debts beyond the limit fixed by the terms of their shares. The question in *Salomon's* case was inherent in the word 'company' itself: in the mid-nineteenth century the company was invariably seen as an incorporated group: an association of co-venturers or investors joining together with a view to making a common profit, and usually intending to raise further funds on the share market. Initially, the statute set a minimum of twenty-five members, later reduced to seven.

Salomon had for years run a successful leather and boot-making business in Whitechapel. In 1892 he formed a company to take over this business, in which he and his wife and adult children were shareholders: he with 20,000 shares, the other six with one share each. This was not a novel arrangement: similar small companies had become fairly common. Salomon was also managing director and held a secured loan of £10,000 giving him a charge over the firm's assets. Times turned bad, and the company collapsed with many debts; but Salomon as secured creditor claimed priority. The issue for the court was simple: was there any 'association' here, in reality? It was still essentially a one-man show. Was this a legitimate use of the companies legislation? Was it proper for the owner of a business to avoid personal liability for its debts by interposing the corporate form between himself and its creditors? Worse, to become its senior-ranking creditor himself?

Legal opinion, as expressed in the judgments of the trial judge and the Court of Appeal and in contemporary journals, with one voice answered: 'No'. But the **House of Lords**, unanimously and emphatically, took a contrary view: Salomon had observed all the statutory requirements and so the company was entitled to full recognition as a legal entity, distinct from Salomon and competent to contract with him. Legislation shortly after the case confirmed this

recognition of the private company; but that is not the real legacy of *Salomon*. Except in rare cases where there has been fraud or sharp practice, the courts ever since (both in England and generally throughout the **common law** world) have strictly respected the principle that a duly incorporated company is legally a separate entity from its members. This has made possible the use of the company in an infinite variety of situations: by corporate groups in structuring control systems and the management of risk, and by individuals in inheritance and tax planning, in the confident knowledge that no judge will strike down such an arrangement by denying the company's legitimacy.   LEN SEALY

GR Rubin, 'Aron Salomon and his Circle', in J Adams (ed), *Essays for Clive Schmitthoff* (Abingdon: Professional Books, 1983)

LS Sealy, 'Perception and Policy in Company Law Reform', in D Feldman and F Meisel (eds), *Corporate and Commercial Law: Modern Developments* (London: Lloyd's of London Press, 1996)

same-sex relationships   Same-sex relationships are increasingly being recognized as marriage-like in the laws of many jurisdictions. In 1989, Denmark became the first country to create a comprehensive, marriage-like status for same-sex relationships, called a registered partnership. This was largely the same as **marriage**, though with a few exceptions, and was not available to heterosexual couples; it was a provision for 'gay marriage'. Several other jurisdictions, particularly in Northern Europe, followed Denmark's lead in creating a separate system of relationship recognition for same-sex couples that paralleled marriage. In 2001 The Netherlands became the first nation to open up marriage to same-sex couples followed by a handful of other jurisdictions, including Canada. In 2004, the United Kingdom followed the Danish model of creating a parallel but legally equivalent status for same-sex couples, called a **civil partnership**.

Under the Civil Partnership Act, a British same-sex couple who marries or registers their relationship abroad will automatically have a civil partnership when they return to the UK in the same way as a heterosexual couple who marries abroad will be married in the UK under the rules of private **international law**. In 2006, a British lesbian couple who had married in Canada petitioned the High Court to recognize their Canadian marriage as a marriage rather than a civil partnership (*Wilkinson v Kitzinger and Attorney General* (2006)). They argued that the symbolic status of the name marriage was as important as its legal status and, as such, civil partnership was a lesser provision, even though it conferred the same legal rights and obligations as marriage. Their claim was rejected by the High Court in a judgment that referred to marriage as being *by definition* between a man and a woman and primarily for the purpose of procreating. The court emphasized that this did not mean that same-sex relationships are inferior to heterosexual ones, merely different.

The issue of the extent to which same-sex and heterosexual relationships are the same is a contentious one. Recent legal judgments prior to the *Wilkinson* case had begun to emphasize the similarities between them and acknowledge (as *Wilkinson* also does) that same-sex relationships can be as loving, committed, and monogamous as heterosexual relationships. This is also emphasized by gay rights organizations, such as Stonewall, who lobbied for the Civil Partnership Act. Some gay and **lesbian** scholars, however, have found evidence that same-sex relationships do differ in significant ways from that assumed by the (heterosexual) marriage model. In particular, they found that friendship networks (referred to as chosen families) played an important part in the lives of many lesbians and gay men, and that monogamy, while often evident in same-sex relationships, was more often negotiated than assumed. As the legal recognition of same-sex relationships does not take these (and other) differences into account, such provisions are sometimes criticized as assimilationist to the extent that they expect same-sex relationships to conform to a heterosexual norm.

NICOLE BARKER

R Wintemute and M Andenaes (eds), *Legal Recognition of Same-Sex Partnerships: A Study of National, European and International Law* (Oxford: Hart Publishing, 2001)
J Weeks, B Heaphy, and C Donovan, *Same-Sex Intimacies: Families of Choice and Other Life Experiments* (London: Routledge, 2001)

sanctions in international law   The lack of enforcement of **international law** is sometimes perceived as its greatest failure. This view neglects the myriad of enforcement possibilities though countermeasures and sanctions. A countermeasure is any legal reaction by a single state to a previous violation of an international obligation owed to that state. Sanctions, on the other hand, are multilateral reactions to a violation of an obligation owed to the international community as a whole or as help for the injured state. In common parlance, unilateral countermeasures are increasingly, but inaccurately, referred to as sanctions.

International organizations, especially the **United Nations**, often adopt sanctions. However, other general and specific collaborations of states have occurred for the purposes of adopting sanctions or making them more efficient. The main legal requirement is that sanctions, just like countermeasures, have to be proportionate to the illegal act. As such, depending on the circumstances, it may be disproportionate to sanction a treaty violation with the complete suspension of diplomatic relations with that country.

The UN administers most sanctions today. Historically, only exclusion from the UN for the violation of Charter principles and suspension of voting rights could properly be considered sanctions. By contrast, it was not clear if other enforcement measures (taken under Chapter VII of the UN Charter) were sanctions, ie reactions to wrongful acts, or whether they could be adopted if the Security Council considered a situation to constitute a threat to peace and security without any violation of an international obligation. Regardless of how this debate is decided (and many commentators would probably not insist that the Security Council would have to identify the specific breach of an obligation in order to adopt Chapter VII measures) these measures are commonly known as sanctions.

Sanctions in general can take many forms—diplomatic, economic, or even military. The most common are economic sanctions. For example, the UN Security Council may adopt a weapons or even a trade embargo against a state that endangers peace and security. Countries may also suspend cooperation with a third country or cease development aid as a form of economic sanction. The **World Trade Organization ('WTO')** has a specific mechanism for trade sanctions. These can only be authorized after the dispute settlement procedure has been followed and the WTO member which ultimately lost its case has failed to implement the decision. Such trade sanctions, called 'suspension of concessions', are often adopted as punitive tariffs or even import bans.

Diplomatic sanctions are usually enacted as declarations against *personae non gratae*, ie persons declared not welcome to enter the territory of another state. They can also take the form of expulsion from the territory, or even the cutting of consular or diplomatic ties and suspension of official visits and conferences. Official boycotts of sport and cultural events also fall in this category. The legal use of such measures has long been established in **customary international law** and more recently in the Vienna Convention on Diplomatic Relations. Even the full suspension of diplomatic or consular relations does not mean that the legal relationship established through a treaty ceases to exist, unless such relations are necessary for the application of the Treaty.

There is also a range of military sanctions, from weapons embargoes, ie declarations that certain goods or weapons cannot be sold to certain countries, to suspension of military cooperation. Finally, even military intervention authorized by the Security Council can be seen as a form of military sanction.

Recently a new category of sanctions has been created. So-called 'smart sanctions' attempt to target the actors responsible for breaches of obligations rather than the general population, which often suffers from the imposition of sanctions, or neighbouring countries, which are often indirectly affected by economic sanctions. As such, flight and travel bans, individual restrictions of entry and, especially, financial sanctions have become more common. In response to the development of such targeted sanctions, it may be possible (through the UN regime on the financing of terrorism) for private persons who find their names and other details on a list of individuals or organizations suspected of financing terrorism, legally to challenge sanctions on the ground that they have been wrongly identified as contributing financially or otherwise to terrorism.

MARKUS GEHRING

sancity of human life   Sanctity of life is a principle with roots in the Judaeo-Christian **religion**, which treats life as sacred because it is given by God and can therefore only be taken away by him. It is found in other religions too. It is endorsed by the Hippocratic Oath (which proscribes **euthanasia**) and the Declaration of Geneva, but in both these documents the emphasis is not on providing treatment at all times but on doing no harm. It has support also in secular approaches (eg Ronald Dworkin) which emphasize the intrinsic value of life (and it is also an aspect of the **right to life** in Article 2 of the **European Convention of Human Rights**). The doctrine of the sanctity of life is said to respect 'the integrity of the human body'.

UK law does not regard the sanctity of life as an absolute value. If it did it would have to prioritize health care services over everything else. There would be no cars or cigarettes, and certainly no waiting lists.

Sanctity of life is qualified in a number of ways. First, acts which terminate life (eg a lethal injection) are distinguished from omissions. Life-prolonging treatment can thus be withheld and also withdrawn. Artificial nutrition and hydration are regarded as 'treatment', not care, and can thus be removed by doctors from someone in a **persistent vegetative state**.

Secondly, the law adopts a distinction, found in Catholic theology as the **doctrine of double effect**, between medical treatment which is intended to kill and treatment where death is foreseen and may be accelerated, but is not intended (for example, the administration of a drug to relieve pain).

Thirdly, competent adults can refuse treatment even if this leads to their death. As Lord Goff put it (in *Airedale NHS Trust v Bland* (1993)) 'the principle of the sanctity of human life must yield to the principle of **self-determination**'. Competent children—that is those who satisfy the test of *Gillick* competence—may have their refusal to accept medical treatment gainsaid by parents or by a court, acting in their best interests.

Fourthly, where patients are incompetent, **courts** use the **'best interests' principle** to justify withholding and withdrawing treatment. This is strikingly exemplified by cases involving seriously handicapped premature babies where the quality of life to be expected is very low, so that the burdens outweigh the benefits. These decisions can be controversial particularly where parents and doctors disagree—parents wanting treatment to continue which doctors assess as futile. The brain-dead **child** and the child in a persistent vegetative state pose least problems. More difficult are cases where the child can survive with treatment, but impairment is such that it is unreasonable to expect him/her to bear it. What is intolerable is not constant through time (once Down's syndrome was thought to be), and is inevitably dependent on values although those with religious beliefs may expect greater fortitude.

MICHAEL FREEMAN

See also: acts and omissions; capacity; consent to treatment; withdrawing or withholding life-prolonging treatment

satellite TV   *see* **digital television and radio regulation**

satisfaction   *see* **reparations and other remedies in international law**

satisfactory quality   *see* **sale of goods; quality of products**

Savigny, Friedrich Karl von   Friedrich karl von Savigny (1779–1861), professor at Landshut and then at Berlin, may have influenced the study of private law more than any jurist of his age. Although his work on **Roman law** in the Middle Ages became a classic (*Geschichte des Römischen Rechts im Mittelalter*, 1815–1831), he is best known for developing a unique approach to law. It was philosophical but did not subordinate the study of law to that of philosophy; it was national but rejected national codification; and, while claiming to be historical, it pioneered the conceptualist method characteristic of the *Pandektenschule* which dominated nineteenth-century German legal thought. Law, as Kant had said, secures personal freedom, but its content, according to Savigny, was determined, not by an abstract concept of freedom, but by the mind or spirit of each particular people, its *Volksgeist*. As the *Volksgeist* was the true source of law, codified law was arbitrary. It lacked inner unity and could only be interpreted arbitrarily (*Vom Beruf unserer Zeit für Gesetzgebung und Rechtswissenschaft*, 1814). Savigny claimed, paradoxically, that German *Volksgeist* was expressed in the Roman legal texts that had been accepted in Germany for centuries. The task of the jurist was to elucidate the system of thought that lay behind those texts, identifying and defining the concepts underlying them. He pursued this programme in doctrinal works that became models for later jurists. (*Recht des Besitzes*, 1803; *System des heutigen Römischen Rechts*, 1840–1849; *Das Obligationenrecht*, 1851–1853).

JAMES GORDLEY

Saville Inquiry   *see* **Bloody Sunday inquiries**

savings taxes   Under a comprehensive **income tax**, all forms of real accretion to wealth, for example, labour income, returns on savings, and accrued capital gains, would be taxed each year as income. However, no real-world tax jurisdiction operates a pure system and it is especially in the taxation of returns on savings that mongrel features are found. The position is affected by two main factors. First, most tax systems operate a slightly artificial distinction between returns on savings in the form of *income* and those in the form of *capital*. Income returns are usually taxed at the full nominal amount of the return, which can result in a heavy tax burden: for example, the taxation of interest with no relief for inflation can result in a negative real return on the investment. In contrast, capital gains are often either not taxed at all, or are subject to a separate tax and given relief based on inflation or on the length of time of ownership. They may also be eligible for an annual exemption in addition to any exemption given to taxable income. The second factor which creates deviations from a pure tax system are deliberate incentives introduced by governments to encourage saving: eg tax relief on

particular types of investments (mortgage relief for house purchase, relief on insurance contributions, pensions), or relief on particular types of returns (tax-free gain on homes, special savings vehicles providing tax free income).

There are two main methods of deliberately limiting the impact of taxes on savings. The first gives a tax deduction on the act of saving itself, deferring the tax charge until the point at which the savings, and the return on these savings, are spent. This form of taxing savings is termed an 'expenditure tax'. It has gained the support of many economists, although it has never successfully been implemented in practice. However, examples of expenditure tax treatment can be found in corners of many tax systems. Private pension provision is usually taxed along these lines: pension contributions are normally deductible for tax purposes, there is no taxation on the pension provider, but when the pension is paid to the member, it is treated as the member's taxable income. In fact, the tax-free lump sum on retirement makes the UK's treatment of pension saving particularly attractive.

The second method protecting returns on savings from tax is the mirror image of the first: instead of providing the tax relief on the act of saving (with the result that savings are made out of *taxed* income), under this method there is no tax on the *return* on the savings or when the savings are spent. A UK example is the individual savings account ('ISAC'). The same effect is achieved in relation to assets which do not provide income but grow in capital value instead, where relief from tax on any capital gains is given. Another UK example here is the taxation of gains from homes, where the return is usually in the form of a tax-free capital gain.

The extent to which tax incentives to save (or to save in a particular form) are successful is open to debate. Occupational pension provision particularly flourished in the UK as a result of union pressure during the period of government wage restraints in the 1960s, not as a result of tax reliefs, which had been around since 1921. And whilst considerable funds are now invested in ISACs in the UK, it is doubtful whether these vehicles have increased saving or simply encouraged shifting of portfolios.   SARAH EDEN

See also: **capital gains tax**

saviour siblings   In 1969, when a Kentucky court authorized the removal of a kidney from Jerry Strunk (a mentally incompetent twenty-seven-year-old) and its transplantation to his elder brother, Jerry was, so to speak, cast in the role of a 'saviour sibling'. However, it is only with recent developments in the procedures for screening embryos—in particular, pre-implantation genetic diagnosis (PGD) and HLA (Human Leuko-cyte Antigen) tissue-typing—that the term 'saviour sibling' has entered the legal lexicon. Specifically, the term signifies the employment of such procedures to select an embryo (for implantation) that has the right profile to serve as a donor (of cord blood, or bone marrow, or even whole organs) for the life-saving benefit of a sibling. If the non-consensual procedure in the Strunk case was controversial, the selection of embryonic saviour siblings is even more so.

In England, the attempts of the Hashmis and the Whitakers to produce saviour siblings have been much publicized. Responding to the application for the Hashmis, the **Human Fertilization and Embryology Authority** ('HFEA') announced that, exceptionally, it would license HLA tissue-typing of embryos but only where PGD was already being licensed for a serious genetic disorder. This created problems for the Whitakers, whose son suffered from a disease for which there are no genetic markers, and who thus sought a licence for freestanding HLA tissue-typing. However, the announcement was wel-come news for the Hashmis, who needed PGD to test for thalassemia as well as HLA tissue-typing.

While the Whitakers went to the United States for the treatment they required, the Hashmis began their treatment under the authorization of an HFEA licence. However, their project was put on hold when legal proceedings were brought to challenge the power of the HFEA to grant such a licence (see *R (Quintavalle on behalf of Comment on Reproduct-ive Ethics) v Human Fertilisation and Embryology Authority* (2002) (2003) (2005)).

The legal issues were far from straightforward, the framework **legislation**, the **Human Fertiliza-tion and Embryology Act 1990**, not making express provision for PGD, let alone HLA tissue-typing. In the absence of clear legislative guidance, three inter-pretations were canvassed, namely that embryonic screening is permitted: (i) to ensure that a woman can carry her **child** successfully to full term; (ii) as in (i) but also to eliminate gene and chromosome defects such as may affect that child; or (iii) in order to provide information about the characteristics of the embryo which is relevant to the woman's decision whether or not to carry the child. At first instance, where the first interpretation was adopted, the chal-lenge succeeded. However, this decision was reversed on **appeal**, first by the Court of Appeal (unanimous-ly favouring the second interpretation) and then by a unanimous **House of Lords** where the third, and most expansive interpretation, was adopted.

The implications of the case are yet to be fully worked through, Lord Hoffmann acknowledging that 'once one allowed the mother's choice to be a legitimate ground for selection, one could not stop short of allowing it to be based upon such frivolous reasons as eye or hair colour as well as more sinis-ter eugenic practices'. If the **courts** are not to draw the line against unacceptable reproductive projects, the legal future will rest with the HFEA (who have already amended their position to permit free-standing HLA testing) and the politicians once they have completed their review of the 1990 Act.

ROGER BROWNSWORD

Scandinavian law Scandinavian (or better 'Nor-dic') law can be divided into two subgroups. From the seventeenth century, Denmark, Norway, and Ice-land had a common legal history that ended when, in 1814, the more than 400-year-old union between Norway and Denmark was dissolved (Iceland con-tinued as a colony, later in a union with Denmark, until 1944). Sweden and Finland, on the other hand, were one country until Russian conquest of Finland in 1809; and even after that time Finnish law was still based on their common law book dating from 1736. Differences between the two subgroups can still be seen, however.

In many fields, close collaboration in legislation between the Nordic countries, which started in 1870 in the field of commercial law and was later extended to the law of obligations and family law, has led to such a high degree of harmonization that it is pos-sible to speak of a specific Nordic legal family with its own style. It should especially be pointed out that the influence of **Roman law** has been considerably less important than the influence of **Canon law** in the Middle Ages. Even so, the Nordic countries may be considered an area where no reception of Roman law occurred. Roman law, as a method and a means of studying law, has been known in the Nordic coun-tries for a long time; but apart from a few examples from Swedish legal history, Roman law was not quot-ed as a source before Nordic law courts.

Another feature to be stressed is the late devel-opment of a legal profession. In the Middle Ages students from the Nordic countries went to Italian Universities and later also to French, Dutch, and German Universities; but most who studied law were clerics. The Lutheran Reformation in all Nor-dic countries changed academic life. Most Danish students abroad were either noblemen on the Grand Tour or future ministers of the church who studied theology. Nordic Universities were founded in Upp-sala in Sweden in 1477 and in Copenhagen in 1479, both with law faculties. However the University of Uppsala declined shortly after its foundation and the University of Copenhagen was reformed after 1536. In Denmark it was only in 1736 that a professional legal education was introduced in the University. Common to the Nordic countries, therefore, was a long tradition of lay judges and a non-professionalized law in the vernacular. Only in the eighteenth and the nineteenth centuries did a national approach, based on the law of the respective Nordic countries, come into being.

Common to the Nordic countries is a tradition and continuity in law that stems back to written legislation from the twelfth and thirteenth centuries. The oldest laws were in Norway. In Denmark the most famous of the so-called 'provincial laws' is the law of Jutland, dating from 1241 and given by King Valdemar. The Swedish law of Uppland dates from 1296. Iceland had its own laws, Grágás, which was replaced by the Jónsbók in 1281 when the Icelandic free-state came under Norwegian rule.

After the Lutheran Reformation in the sixteenth century, royal legislation had a greater impact. Gradually in the seventeenth century the power balance between the Nordic countries was reversed. Denmark, which had been the leader in the Kalmarunion of 1397, lost dominion of the Baltic Sea. In 1658, Denmark lost huge territories to Sweden. A consequence was the introduction in Denmark of absolutism that found its legal expression in the *lex Regia* of 1665. Absolutism in Denmark lasted till 1848. Sweden had absolutist rulers for shorter periods. The Swedish Estates, which were rooted in the Middle Ages, functioned until 1866. As a result of all this, the development of public law, both constitutional law and administrative organization and law, have developed differently in each of the Nordic countries and still function in different ways. Denmark gained a constitution in 1849 that was amended in 1866, 1915, and 1953. The Danish constitution of 1953 abolished the two-chamber system and introduced the institution of the ombudsman, which had been known in a somewhat different form in Sweden since 1809. From 1948 the Faroe Islands enjoyed some autonomy within the Danish state. (Greenland gained similar autonomy in 1978.) Sweden underwent constitutional reform in 1809 and again in 1866 and in 1975. In 1814 Norway acquired the Eidsvoll constitution, the oldest constitution in Europe still in force.

In private law, a Danish code from 1683 was a result of absolutism. For its time, this code was a considerable achievement. However it was a mainly collection of articles from older legislation systematized in six books on procedure, ecclesiastical matters, estate

and family law, law of the sea, property, and torts and crime. As a result of de-codification since the end of the seventeenth century, the code is now not in force except for from a few basic principles of ecclesiastical law, vicarious liability, and certain kinds of torts. The Danish code was copied and issued as a Norwegian code in 1687 with the exclusion of large parts of older Norwegian law. Since that time Denmark and Norway have had a common approach to law, and only one law school—at the University of Copenhagen. In Sweden a code was issued 1736 that still forms the basis of Swedish and Finnish law.

In the nineteenth century the Nordic countries entered a period in which old antagonism was replaced by cooperation. Dreams of a political union were never fulfilled; but in the field of law, after 1900 cooperation led to common legislation on sale of goods, contracts, and family law. Insurance and the law of bonds are other important field in which legislation, in the absence of a code, has the force of general principles of private law.

Today Nordic cooperation is affected by the influence of **European Union** law. Denmark was the first Nordic country to enter European Economic Community in 1973, later followed by Sweden and Finland. However, Norway and the Faroe Islands (which became independent in 1944) are not members.

Seen from a European point of view, Nordic legal thought and terminology are closer to continental **civil law systems** than to **common law**. However, as in other countries, Americanization has taken place; although the fact that English is the leading foreign language has opened Nordic law to influences from other English-speaking countries. We may conclude that as a result of their history and their shared basic principles of private law, the Nordic countries can be treated as separate legal family related to civil law systems.

DITLEV TAMM

Scandinavian legal realism   *see* legal realism

Schengen agreement The Schengen acquis is concerned with establishing a legal framework for the abolition of internal border controls between participating member states. In order to achieve this aim, a number of other 'flanking' measures are necessary and have been established.

Initially cooperation took place on an inter-governmental basis outside the framework of **European Community law** because of disagreement on the extent to which Third Country Nationals could be permitted freedom of movement across borders. The original Agreement was signed in Schengen (a small town in Luxembourg) in 1985 by France,

Germany, Belgium, The Netherlands, and Luxembourg. A further Implementing Convention was signed in 1990 but did not come into effect to lift border controls until 1995. The Treaty of Amsterdam provided for the incorporation of the existing Schengen aquis into the legal framework of the EU. Provisions had to be allocated to the First or Third Pillars. A list of measures making up the 'Schengen acquis' and allocating each to a legal basis in the EC Treaty or the TEU was adopted and published in 1999. Criticisms concerning lack of transparency, accountability, access to justice, and judicial control have not been entirely eliminated by this move. The pattern of inter-governmental cooperation between some signatories outside the EU framework is being pursued separately again under the 2005 Treaty of Prum.

Membership has gradually extended to include almost all EU Member States although incorporation in the EU legal framework required some exceptions. Ireland and the UK only participate in some parts of the acquis (notably excluding border controls), and Denmark, although signatory to the initial Agreement and Convention, maintains particular arrangements regarding new measures. Because of the Nordic Passport Union, Norway and Iceland also participate as associates and Switzerland has also decided to participate in a similar manner. New EU Member States are required to accept the Schengen aquis in full, although full implementation and abolition of border controls may be delayed until the state is ready to do so. Because of the positions of Denmark and the UK, the categories of Schengen measures and measures building on Schengen aquis retain some relevance.

Internal border checks are removed—but identity checks can be and are still carried out within the **territory** of states and, exceptionally, Member States may temporarily reinstate border controls. Common rules on short-term **visas** for Third Country Nationals exist and such a Schengen visa is valid for short-term travel throughout the Schengen area. A long-term residence permit and travel document also allows such short-term travel. Measures also deal with coordination of administrations on border surveillance, carrier liability, and separation of travellers internal and external to the Schengen area at airports and seaports.

In policing and criminal law, measures cover rights of surveillance and hot pursuit across borders for **police** forces, **extradition**, and exchange of information on implementation of criminal judgments. Extradition is now governed by the Framework Decision on the European Arrest Warrant in 2002.

The Schengen Information System ('SIS') has also been set up to exchange information on individual non-EU Member State nationals (including in particular those wanted for **arrest** or to be refused entry) or on vehicles or lost or stolen objects. A new-generation SIS-II is under development, as is a Visa Information System.   HELEN TONER

See also: **European treaties; pillars of the European Union**

school admissions   School admissions are at the centre of controversy within the school system in England and Wales and have been used by successive governments as a vehicle for pursuing key goals of educational reform, notably the enhancement of parental choice of school and subjection of education to market forces. Parental choice has been recognized as a factor within the statutory system of schooling since the Education Act 1944, which provided in section 76 that the Secretary of State and local education authorities ('LEAs') should have regard to the general principle that pupils should be educated in accordance with their parents' wishes, so far as compatible with efficient instruction and training and avoidance of unreasonable public expenditure. This provision is now found in section 9 of the Education Act 1996, and reflected in the second sentence of Article 2 of the First Protocol to the ECHR, by which states are required to respect parents' religious and philosophical convictions in the provision of education. These provisions do not, however, impose a clearly enforceable duty on public authorities to comply with parental wishes. They do however underpin parental choice of school, which may be based on a range of academic, religious, geographic, social, linguistic, and other considerations. While the statutory provisions recognize parental preferences, they do not give the **child's** preferences as to choice of school explicit support, despite the fact that this is an area where there is potential for conflict between parents and children.

The Conservative government elected in 1979 introduced the first significant statutory regulation of the process of allocating school places in the Education Act 1980. This Act imposed on LEAs a duty to arrange for parents to express a reasoned preference as to the school at which they wished their child to be educated, and created a qualified duty upon the LEA or the governing body concerned to comply. It also established a new appeal mechanism for parents dissatisfied with their allocation. LEAs were initially permitted to impose artificially low limits on the number of pupils who could be admitted to particular schools, in order to enable them to plan admissions across the area as a whole and to protect less popular schools from drastic decline in pupil numbers. This was changed by the Education Reform Act 1988, which introduced 'open enrolment,' under which schools were required to admit pupils up to their 'standard number', which effectively meant their maximum physical capacity. Parental choice was considerably enhanced by open enrolment, and the capacity of LEAs for strategic planning of school provision was correspondingly diminished. The combination of enhancement of parental choice and basing the funding of schools primarily on the number of pupils on the school's roll went a considerable distance towards introduction of market forces into the provision of schools, a key element in the Conservative government's drive to improve educational standards in the 1980s and 1990s.

The Labour government elected in 1997 continued many of the reforms introduced by its predecessor in relation to choice of school. It re-enacted the provisions of the 1980 Act with some amendments in the School Standards and Framework Act 1998, followed by further amendments in the Education Act 2002. These are now the main statutes governing school admissions, read together with Codes of Practice on School Admissions and School Admissions Appeals issued by the Department for Children, Schools, and Families.

LEAs are required to set up an admission forum to advise them in relation to the admissions process, and LEAs are required to coordinate the admissions process in their area. School admissions authorities (either the LEA or the governing body, depending on the type of school) are required, following consultation, to promulgate their admissions arrangements, including the criteria to be applied in the event of over-subscription, and their planned admissions number. These arrangements may be challenged before the Schools Adjudicator by other admissions authorities or, in some cases, by parents. Other information is required to be issued relating to the school, including its performance in test results, in order to inform parental choice. Under section 86(1) of the School Standards and Framework Act, parents are permitted to express their reasoned preference as to which school their child should attend, but this does not guarantee that their preference will be met. The LEA or governing body is permitted to deny parental preference in certain situations, the most important being where the school is over-subscribed—where compliance would prejudice the provision of efficient education or the efficient use of resources. Such prejudice may (but does not necessarily) arise where the school's admissions number has been reached. In the case of admissions to infants' classes in primary schools, such prejudice may arise where the school is required to take measures to ensure compliance with the class size limit of thirty pupils. Parental preference may also be denied where admission of the pupil would be incompatible with selection on the basis of ability or aptitude, where permitted at the school; or in the case of a pupil who has been permanently excluded from two or more schools, where the last exclusion took place within the past two years. In practice, schools which are over-subscribed apply a range of criteria to distinguish between competing applicants, including residence, catchment areas, the presence of a sibling at the school, social, psychological, or medical considerations, or, in the case of faith schools, commitment to the relevant faith. They are not, however, permitted to give priority to children living within the LEA area. Parents may appeal to an independent appeal panel against allocation decisions. Appeal panels have the difficult task of distinguishing between competing claimants for a very limited number of places. Where the pupil has been denied a place on the ground of prejudice to efficient education or use of resources, the panel must first consider whether such prejudice genuinely exists, and if so, then consider whether the prejudice is outweighed by particular considerations raised by the parents. In appeals concerning infants' classes, the considerations taken into account by the panel are more restrictive.   PAUL MEREDITH

school discipline and the exclusion of pupils Traditionally, teachers derived disciplinary authority from the principle of *in loco parentis*, namely, that they stood 'in place of the parent'. They also gained protection from the acceptance by **common law** that 'reasonable chastisement' of a **child** constituted a defence in tort to **trespass** to the person. Other disciplinary sanctions, such as detention and confiscation, were also governed by general principles of law. **Legislation** in England and Wales in 1986 gave head teachers express power to exclude pupils, define acceptable standards of conduct, and impose disciplinary rules and sanctions. School governing bodies were also given oversight and some policy control over these matters. A right of appeal against a permanent exclusion from school was introduced. In Scotland, the equivalent right applies to all forms of exclusion. Corporal punishment was in effect banned in the case of pupils educated at the state's expense, by removing the reasonable chastisement defence. In 1998 (and 2000 in Scotland) this ban was extended to cover all pupils in private schools. In a 2005 judgment, the **House of Lords** held that parents cannot authorize the use of corporal punishment by any school, even on religious grounds (*R v Secretary of State for Education and Employment, exp Williamson*).

In England and Wales disciplinary powers and the procedures for their use are today legislatively based. Teachers are permitted to use 'reasonable force' (but not as punishment) where there is a risk to pupil **safety**, or of damage to property, or to prevent behaviour prejudicial to the maintenance of good order and discipline. Among the conditions for the imposition of detention are that it must be expressly included within the school's disciplinary measures, have been publicized to pupils and parents as a possible sanction, and, in the individual case, that the requisite twenty-four hours' or more written notice has been given to parents. Exclusion from school may be imposed on a pupil only on a permanent basis or for a fixed period or periods totalling not more than forty-five school days in any school year. There is also official guidance governing exclusion, to which schools and the appeal panel must have regard. When a pupil is permanently excluded it remains the statutory duty of the local authority to make suitable provision for his or her education. If it upholds an appeal, the independent appeal panel may order the pupil's reinstatement at the school. In Scotland, the appeal committee can annul the decision to exclude.

The Education and Inspections Act 2006 has brought common principles to bear on each of the above 'disciplinary penalties' (as the Act calls them) in England and Wales. For example, the imposition of any penalty must be consistent with the statute and reasonable in the circumstances, having regard to prescribed factors. Confiscation of property is now covered by a statutory power. The circumstances in which parenting contracts and parenting orders may be made in cases of a pupil's indiscipline are being extended. Parents have a duty to ensure that their child is not in a public place during school hours in the first five school days of their exclusion from school.   NEVILLE HARRIS

school governance, structure, and organization

Maintained schools are today governed in accordance with the Education Act 2002, in particular sections 19–40 and Schedule 1. More detailed provisions are found in regulations. The governing body is a body corporate comprising elected and appointed governors, including elected parent and staff governors and members appointed by the local education authority ('LEA'). There are generally also community governors, and foundation schools also have appointed foundation governors. The number within each category of governors varies in accordance with the nature and size of the school. The governing bodies of two or more schools may form a federation of schools under a single governing body.

The governing body has responsibility for the conduct of the school, in conjunction with the head teacher who has day-to-day responsibility. The governors are required to conduct the school with a view to promoting high standards of educational achievement. Governing bodies have extensive financial responsibilities, the majority of the schools budget being delegated from the LEA to the governing body. In practice, the most critical responsibility is generally in relation to staffing, but the governing body has many other responsibilities, including formulation of school policies in respect of discipline and sex education.

The current structure of maintained schools may be traced back to the Education Act 1944, but is today based largely on the School Standards and Framework Act 1998. This Act provided for a re-categorization of schools: the previous categories of county, voluntary controlled, voluntary aided, special agreement, special, and grant-maintained schools were reallocated to new categories as community, voluntary controlled, voluntary aided, foundation, community special, and foundation special schools. The largest category—community schools—are wholly funded by their LEA, and their staff are employed by the LEA. Voluntary controlled and voluntary aided schools are mainly denominational schools, with some differences in terms of funding, staffing, and governance. Foundation schools were first established under the 1998 Act: schools which had previously been categorized as grant-maintained were given this new status, unless they had had aided status before becoming grant-maintained, in which case they were re-categorized as voluntary aided schools. Other categories of schools within the maintained sector include special schools, nursery schools, and pupil referral units.

Current government policy strongly promotes specialist schools: schools may apply for specialist status within a designated subject area or areas, having obtained a limited amount of private sponsorship. Such schools obtain additional government funding. Private sector sponsorship and specialization are also evident in the establishment of academies under the Education Act 2002 as independent schools focusing on particular specialisms, a category of school which the government is currently seeking to expand considerably. Under the Education and Inspections Act 2006, the government is also currently seeking to promote 'trust' schools outside LEA control: these will be foundation schools with trusts under a **charity** as their foundation, with significant freedoms including freedom to set their own admissions arrangements.

PAUL MEREDITH

school standards and the inspection of schools and LEAs Responsibility for school standards is shared primarily between individual schools and local education authorities ('LEAs'), although, in the case of independent (private) schools, it rests with the proprietor. LEAs must ensure that their functions concerning education in schools are exercised with a view to promoting high standards. Under a parallel duty, the Secretary of State (for Children, Schools, and Families) must exercise his or her powers in connection with schools with a view to, among other things, improving standards. Governing bodies of state schools have a duty to set annual targets for their school concerning the performance of pupils in public examinations and National Curriculum assessments. Similarly, since 2005, the Secretary of State has had a power to require LEAs to set annual targets in respect of the educational performance of pupils at schools they maintain. Under the Education and Inspections Act 2006 ('the 2006 Act') LEAs must appoint for each school maintained by them a 'school improvement partner' whose role is to provide advice to the school's governing body and head teacher 'with a view to improving standards at the school'.

In its White Paper *Excellence in Schools* published in 1997 shortly after being returned to power, the Labour government argued that 'standards matter more than structures'. The government steered the School Standards and Framework Act 1998 through **Parliament** and, in addition to containing an earlier version of the above duty on LEAs to promote high standards, it restricted the size of classes for five-, six-, and seven-year-olds to a maximum of thirty pupils. It also extended the powers of intervention by LEAs and the Secretary of State in cases where schools are under-performing and especially where they are adjudged to be failing to provide an acceptable standard of education or to be in danger of doing so. These powers, now contained in an amended form in the 2006 Act, include the suspension of the school's right to a delegated budget, the direct appointment of alternative governors, and, ultimately, the closure of the school.

In England, the standards being maintained by individual schools and schools collectively are monitored by the Office for Standards in Education, Children's Services, and Skills (Ofsted), a statutory body which exercises various functions on behalf of the Chief Inspector of Education, Children's Services, and Schools in England. The Chief Inspector, who is appointed by the Queen, has a general duty to keep the Secretary of State informed about various matters concerning schools and other services within his or her remit, including the quality of their provision, the standards in them, and the extent to which they are 'user-focused' and use their resources effectively and efficiently. The Chief Inspector must report annually to the Secretary of State, who must lay a copy of the Chief Inspector's report before both Houses of Parliament.

Inspections of individual establishments are carried out, at prescribed intervals, in the name of the Chief Inspector. They are conducted in some cases by Her Majesty's Inspectors of Education, Children's Services, and Skills ('HMIs'), who are appointed by the Queen by Order in Council, and in others by arrangement with 'additional' inspectors or via 'inspection service providers'. All schools are to be inspected, including nursery schools. The views of the head teacher, other staff, registered pupils, and parents, and certain others, expressed in the course of the inspection, must be taken into account. A framework for school inspections published by Ofsted guides the process. There are separate arrangements for the inspection of denominational education and collective worship in voluntary and foundation schools designated as having a religious character. The Chief Inspector may also investigate a complaint about a school made by a parent.

If the statutory inspection of a school and the comments made lead the Chief Inspector to conclude *either* that a school requires significant improvement *or* that it is failing to provide an acceptable standard of education and the persons in charge of the school are not demonstrating the capacity to secure the necessary improvement, the Chief Inspector must take certain steps. The first is to send the draft inspection report to the governing body or proprietor of the school and consider their comments on it. If, in the light of those comments, the Chief Inspector still considers that the school meets either of the above criteria he or she must then give a written notice of this conclusion to the Secretary of State and the LEA (and the proprietor in the case of an independent school). If remedial action, including action taken by the school's governing body, does not rectify the problems, intervention action may be taken, as noted above. A copy of an inspection report must be sent to all interested parties, including the head teacher and the governing body or LEA. Parents must be provided with a copy of the report.

Regulations prescribe standards relating to education at independent schools. The schools must in any event meet registration requirements. Among the matters covered by the standards regulations are teaching (for example, it must 'involve well planned lessons, effective teaching methods, suitable activities and wise management of class time'), the welfare, heath, and safety of pupils, and the suitability of staff and premises. Inspection of independent schools is now carried out at the instigation of the registration authority under the aegis of Ofsted by HMIs or by another inspector as arranged by the Chief Inspector. An independent school's failure to meet the required standards of educational provision could lead to its removal from the register immediately if there is a risk of serious harm to pupils, or to a requirement that the proprietor carries out remedial work identified by the registration authority, failing which there could be removal from the register. Other orders that could be made include a direction to close off part of the school's premises or not admit new pupils (there is an offence of non-compliance). There is a similar power to remove a school from the register if there is an unsuitable person as proprietor, teacher, or other worker. The proprietor has a right of appeal in such a case.

In Wales, responsibility for school inspections rests with 'Estyn', which performs a similar function to Ofsted in England. The inspection regime parallels that in England. However, the inspections are carried out in Wales either by Her Majesty's Inspectors of Education and Training or by persons registered as inspectors in the register maintained by the Chief Inspector of Education and Training in Wales. In Wales the Chief Inspector has broadly the same functions as his or her counterpart in England, including those of reporting (to the National Assembly for Wales) on various matters relating to the quality of education in schools, making arrangements for the regular inspections, and arranging for the publication of inspection reports. In Scotland school inspection is the responsibility of Her Majesty's Inspectorate of Education ('HMIe'), but inspections may also be conducted by other persons appointed by the Scottish Ministers for that purpose. Where necessary improvements identified by HMIe have not been carried out by the school, the institution may be referred to the Scottish Ministers, who have enforcement powers. Inspections in Northern Ireland are the responsibility of the Education and Training Inspectorate, led by a Chief Inspector, within the Northern Ireland Department of Education ('DENI').

A regime for the inspection of LEAs in England and Wales was established in 1997. The responsibility for such inspections rests with the Chief Inspector in each jurisdiction. An inspection will be carried out by one of Her Majesty's Inspectors of Schools (or Her Majesty's Inspectors of Education and Training in Wales) or an additional inspector. Reports of LEA inspections must be published. The LEA must prepare a written statement of the action it proposes to take in the light of the inspection report. If and when LEA functions in England are subsumed within local authority functions, as appears to be planned, local authorities' education functions will be subject to inspection under these statutory arrangements (in the 2006 Act).

Both the Secretary of State, in England, and the Assembly, in Wales, possess a reserve power to secure the proper performance by an LEA of its functions. The power can be exercised, on complaint or otherwise, where an LEA is failing to perform any particular function or is not performing it adequately. A direction may be given to any officer of the LEA concerning the performance of the function. It can provide that the function should be carried out by the Secretary of State or his or her nominee, thus someone outside the authority. LEAs with underperforming schools can also be directed to enter into a contract for the provision of advisory services to them by a specified person. Scottish education authorities are also subject to statutory inspection, under the aegis of HMIe.   NEVILLE HARRIS

schools adjudicators   *see* **school admissions**

scope of liability   Not all the consequences of a breach of obligation fall within the appropriate scope of liability for that breach. For example, suppose that by careless driving a motorist breaks a pedestrian's leg. On the way to hospital the pedestrian's ambulance is coincidentally struck by lightning, and the pedestrian is severely burnt. Suppose further that once the pedestrian eventually reaches hospital he is intentionally poisoned by a mentally disturbed nurse, and is blinded. The motorist's breach of obligation to the pedestrian was historically involved in, and so was a 'cause' of, the broken leg, the burns, and the blinding: but-for the motorist's breach of obligation, these events would not have occurred. But the law must draw a line somewhere down the stream of consequences of which the breach was a cause. This is because that stream is infinite and, for reasons of fairness and practicality, there must be some finite limit to the consequences for which a person in breach of an obligation can be held liable.

The rules that govern the appropriate scope of liability for the consequences of a breach are legal rules—ie they are chosen by courts weighing considerations of **justice** or policy. Such rules of law therefore tend to vary over time, between jurisdictions, and in relation to the type of legal norm that has been breached.

For example, suppose that as a result of breach of an obligation of care (ie negligence), a log falls from a crane into the hold of a ship. Suppose further that fumes that had unforeseeably accumulated in the hold are ignited by the impact of the log on the floor of the hold, causing the ship to explode. It can be said that the explosion was a direct, albeit unforeseeable, consequence of the breach. In England in the early twentieth century a consequence would not fall within the scope of liability for negligence unless it was a 'direct' consequence of the breach: under this legal rule the person in breach would have had to pay for the damage resulting from the explosion. By the end of the twentieth century English courts had changed the rule to a requirement that the consequence was 'foreseeable': under this rule the person in breach would not have to pay for the damage resulting from the explosion.

Another question courts must address is what scope rule to adopt in relation to consequences of a breach, such as the pedestrian's burns in the above example, that are 'coincidental' in the sense that though the breach was a cause of the consequence in the instant case, the type of conduct constituting the breach—careless driving in our example—does not generally increase the likelihood of the type of consequence—lightning burns in our example.

Yet another question that arises in the scope area is whether the intervention of a third party should be taken to truncate responsibility for later consequences of a breach of obligation, such as the blinding of the pedestrian in the earlier example.

Most scope rules can be formulated and explained in simple general terms. For example, in cases where the obligation can be breached by inadvertent conduct, such as in the speeding example, most jurisdictions exclude from the scope of liability for the breach consequences that are coincidental. The explanation for this exclusion is that imposing liability for coincidental results can have no direct effect on the avoidance of such injuries in the future.

In one area courts have so far been unable to formulate a clear non-arbitrary norm. Suppose that in breach of obligation a prison carelessly allows an habitual thief to escape. It is foreseeable that the escapee will steal during his escape, and most jurisdictions would hold that losses resulting from any such theft were within the appropriate scope of the prison's liability for the consequences of its breach.

But it is also foreseeable that the escapee will continue to steal unless and until recaptured. For reasons of fairness and practicality, the law must specify some point after which the prison will not be liable for the escapee's thefts. So far, however, no court has been able to formulate a clear non-arbitrary scope rule to achieve this result.

Finally, it should be noted that many courts, when confronted by the various and complex issues in the area of the appropriate scope of liability for consequences of breach, obscure their normative reasoning behind bald assertions that a particular consequence was 'too remote' or that the breach was not 'the proximate cause', 'the cause', or 'the common sense cause' of the consequence.

JANE STAPLETON

See also: **causation; negligence in civil law; negligence in criminal law**

Scott (otherwise Morgan) v Scott (1913)

This is a remarkable case for two reasons, the one social and the other constitutional. Like many others it began in a mundane way. It was decided in the early years of the last century. The Scotts had been married for more than ten years. Eventually, Annie Scott petitioned for a decree of nullity. She was still a virgin. The marriage had not been consummated. An order was made directing 'that this cause be heard in camera' (ie in private). Despite this, Annie Scott obtained the transcript and gave copies to the father and sister of the respondent (Mr Scott) and to one other person. She did this, as the court accepted, to 'vindicate her character against false reports to her prejudice, which led to her separation from the respondent'. This was a fighting Edwardian wife.

The High Court held that Annie had committed **contempt of court**. The Court of Appeal got distracted by the issue of whether the alleged contempt was criminal—in which case there was, at that time, no appeal. The **House of Lords** had no such problems and discharged the order holding Annie in contempt. Husbands could not use rumour to damage their wives. The emancipation of women took a further step.

The speeches in the House of Lords are marked by unusual passion and, on occasion, by very English xenophobia. Subject to a few exceptions, the case lays down that justice must be administered in public. It was said to be 'an almost priceless inheritance'. In *Three Rivers Council v Bank of England (Application for Judgment in Private)* (2005), Rix LJ described it as still the 'leading authority'. The principle, that justice should be administered in public, can conflict with other values, for example, decorum, candour, privacy, expediency, or even perhaps now especially, efficiency. However, the basis of the exceptions to the principle is not any of these, but rather that the principle must yield only where publicity would destroy the subject matter of the action. The House emphasized in particular that the courts 'who are the guardians of public liberties, ought to be doubly vigilant against encroachments by themselves'. As Lord Loreburn said 'The right of this lady to tell the truth and to furnish the best evidence of the truth in defence of her own character and reputation is inalienable, and cannot lawfully be taken away by any judge'. JOSEPH JACOB

J Jaconelli, *Open Justice: A Critique of the Public Trial* (Oxford, Oxford University Press, 2002)

J Jacob, *Civil Justice in the Age of Human Rights* (Aldershot: Ashgate, 2007)

Scottish Law, 1000–1500 Although elements of the earlier order survived down to the fifteenth century and later, the mainstream history of Scottish law begins in the twelfth century. Two major influences thereafter shaped the legal system.

First was the emergence under the authority of the kings of Scots of a customary system of law and courts, which, despite its essentially localized administration in sheriff, burgh, and justiciary courts, was sufficiently mature by the thirteenth century to have both internal and external recognition as a system of law common to the whole kingdom. Although contemporaries clearly distinguished their law from that of other countries and in particular England, a leading characteristic of its development was selective and critical borrowing, mainly occurring before 1300, from the burgeoning English **common law**. This had its main substantive impact in the feudal land law and in certain aspects of civil procedure such as the use of initiating writs (brieves) issued by the king's chapel for different types of dispute, and the deployment of the assize (or jury) to decide the resultant litigation. Although an important part of the medieval law was thus built around 'forms of action' recognizably English in origin, only a select few, such as the brieves of right, mortancestry, and novel dissasine—all actions for the recovery of land—came north, and they were never quite the same as their English counterparts. Nor was there the vast elaboration of writs found in England: there were only a half-dozen or so major forms of 'pleadable brieve' for contentious litigation, plus others of a more administrative nature used to determine such matters as entitlement to inherit land. Institutionally, the offices of sheriff and justiciar were also transplanted to Scotland from England, and the courts which they held remain today in the form of the sheriff court and the High Court of Justiciary. Scotland also developed its own parliament which legislated actively, producing statutes some of which still form part of contemporary law.

The second major influence on legal development in medieval Scotland arose from the kingdom's full and generally loyal membership of the medieval church. In consequence, many areas of social life fell to the **canon law** and ecclesiastical jurisdiction, to the exclusion of secular authority. If there can be said to have been a legal profession in Scotland before 1450, its ranks were almost entirely formed by the clergy. A degree of integration between the ecclesiastical and the secular existed: for example, the secular rules on succession to land were dependent upon the church's laws of **marriage** and legitimacy. Ecclesiastical sanctuary afforded protection from unlawful harms to those accused of certain secular crimes, but was often territorially supplemented by royal grants. Thus the secular distinction between homicide by 'fore-thocht' (premeditation) and on 'suddenty' (in hot blood), with only the latter entitling the perpetrator to sanctuary, sprang ultimately from the law of the church.

There were more subtle influences on the substance of the law: for example, a sharp distinction between ownership and possession, despite the analytical problems posed by the dependent nature of feudal tenure in which A held land of B as a return for some service to him rather than outright, must have been influenced by the law of the church. Procedure in the secular courts was much affected by the church court model, and direct reference by court pleaders to the canon law and to its near relation (in medieval terms), the Roman or civil law, was certainly not uncommon. Indeed, in the fifteenth century the belief, that more knowledge of and skill in the civil law could be of benefit to the kingdom and its people in the administration of lay justice, in part underlay the foundations of universities with some law teaching at St Andrews (1411), Glasgow (1451), and Aberdeen (1495). No doubt that belief also encouraged the steady flow of Scots churchmen to the great universities of continental Europe (notably Paris and Orléans) to study canon and civil law. Finally, Parliament sometimes relied on civil law concepts in the drafting of legislation; for example, in statutes on prescription and tutory.

The principal text of medieval Scots law is known from its opening words as *Regiam Majestatem*. Composed in the fourteenth century, it begins as a heavily edited version of the English treatise *Glanvill*, has an extensive Romano-canonical secretion on pacts and arbitration, continues as a lightly edited *Glanvill*, (the editing being mostly by omission), and concludes with a miscellany of purely native laws from the twelfth and thirteenth centuries. At some stage it was divided into four books, apparently on the model of **Justinian**'s *Institutes*; from whence also, via *Glanvill*, its proemium and the title of the work. The mixture of influences thus apparent in *Regiam* characterizes medieval Scottish law as a whole.

HECTOR L MACQUEEN

HL MacQueen, *Common Law and Feudal Society in Medieval Scotland* (Edinburgh: Edinburgh University Press, 1993)

J W Cairns, 'Historical Introduction', in K Reid and R Zimmermann, *A History of Private Law in Scotland* (Oxford: Oxford University Press, 2000) vol 1, 14–184

Scottish Law, 1500–1900   After 1500, a more organized legal profession started to develop in Scotland among those who practised before the new central court, reconstituted in 1532 as the College of Justice or **Court of Session**. The advocates and judges were commonly graduates in **Roman law** and **Canon law** of a continental university, and the Court adopted a version of Romano-Canonical procedure, in which legal argument became increasingly reduced to writing. Process on brieves vanished other than for limited purposes. By 1700, advocates (now incorporated as a Faculty) were exclusively admitted by examination in Latin on Roman law in a procedure copied from examination for a university degree in law. After 1707, judges also had to have undergone such an examination.

Groups of procurators before provincial courts also developed into local legal professions, though they tended to train by apprenticeship. Over the same period, men practising as writers and notaries developed the styles and forms used in initiating litigation and recording transactions, particularly in land. Under the influence of Canon law a system of probative writs developed, and recording of deeds in court books and registers became common. Of particular importance was the creation by statute of the Register of Sasines in 1617, helping the development of a secure system of land tenure, with publicity of encumbrances.

Until the Union with England in 1707, Scots tended to emphasize the statutory nature of their 'proper' law, as distinct from Romano-Canonical 'common' law. From before 1500 to the 1690s there were regular projects to 'codify' Scots law; none of these came to fruition, though they did stimulate editing and printing of statutory and other material. A perceived lack of statute led some authors even to describe the Roman law as Scots 'proper' written law. This meant

that, though collections had been made of decisions of the Court of Session from the beginning, they were only valued as possibly indicating a line of custom. The literature of the Roman and Canon laws was given much greater weight. This affected even criminal practice before the (High) Court of Justiciary, reconstructed in 1672. This meant that by 1707 certain areas of Scots law had become thoroughly Romanized.

For a century after Union with England in 1707, Scots law was neglected by the new British Parliament, except in moments of political crisis. With the decline of direct influence from Roman law, Scots lawyers, influenced by versions of the moral-sense philosophy taught in the universities, came by stages to view their law as based on **precedent** and as developing according to its own logic. This contributed to a reform of the Court of Session and its procedure that led to clearer precedents. Between 1808 and 1830, the Court was restructured into a first instance Outer House and second instance Inner House. Reporting of the decisions of the Session became increasingly successful, while certain classic works of the seventeenth and eighteenth centuries came to be regarded as foundational and especially authoritative. Other courts were amalgamated into the Court of Session and the Sheriff Courts, which developed an increasingly important local civil and criminal jurisdiction.

In the first decades of the nineteenth century, the legal profession tripled in size, increasing a demand for university instruction in Scots law and conveyancing for the apprentices of writers and procurators. Many bodies of writers, law agents, solicitors, and procurators (all names are found) sought incorporation through royal charter, to make clear their right to privileges of audience (ie to appear before a court to represent a litigant) and to hold property. Many such bodies now started to collect libraries, as the Faculty of Advocates in Edinburgh had already done. Parliament now regulated the training and education of procurators and other law agents, while the Faculty of Advocates reformed its own admission requirements, demanding that those admitted possess university degrees in both arts and law or pass examinations of equivalent standard.

The nineteenth century was marked by the tremendous development of Scots law both by the Court of Session and **House of Lords** and by statute. These reforms created the modern property law (though land law retained a feudal foundation) and commercial law necessary for what was now a highly urbanized commercial and industrial society. The modern law of obligations was also created, though still based on Roman roots, emphasizing individual rights and responsibilities. While the period saw a measure of assimilation to English law, particularly in mercantile affairs, Scots law remained distinctive. The later nineteenth century in particular saw a flourishing legal literature and culture. In 1885 a Secretary for Scotland was created, from 1892 a member of the **Cabinet**. From this date a separate Scottish administration developed, with obvious implications for the future of the law, which the new discipline of comparative law recognized as 'mixed'.

JOHN W CAIRNS

JW Cairns, 'Historical Introduction', in K Reid and R Zimmermann (eds), *A History of Private Law in Scotland* (Oxford: Oxford University Press, 2000), vol 1, 14–184

See also: **mixed jurisdictions**

Scottish law after 1900   Even as late as 1900, law in Scotland remained predominately unenacted in character, or in other words based more on court decisions and the writings of certain eminent jurists than on **Acts of Parliament**. The twentieth century, however, was marked by the passing of legislation on an unprecedented scale. Some of this legislation was novel, making provision for subjects for which, in 1900, there was no law at all: for example, town and country planning, immigration, road traffic, food standards, and discrimination on grounds of race, gender, and age. Rather more of it elaborated on areas on which there had been previous but often meagre statute or case law: for example, taxation, the environment, education, health, and so on.

Much statute law was public law (ie law concerned with the relationship between state and citizen), and its growth tracked the growth in the role of the state itself, leading in turn to a new and vigorous branch of law in which decisions of public officials were reviewed by the courts. But increasingly statute intruded even into private law (ie the law concerned with relations between citizens), where, typically, it was a response—sometimes grudging and often late in the day—to social and economic change. So for example, under legislation passed in 1939 it finally became possible to marry in a registry office; after 1964 more of the property of a person who died without a will was inherited by that person's spouse and a great deal less by the eldest son; divorce on grounds other than the fault of one of the parties first became available in 1976 and was extended in 2006; the legal disadvantages of illegitimacy were dismantled beginning in the 1960s and the status itself was abolished in 2006; and a whole series of measures protected consumers in relation to the purchase of goods and

services. Legislation passed in 1998 to incorporate the **European Convention on Human Rights** led to a reappraisal or even a reinterpretation of existing law in the light of such Convention principles as the right to life, to liberty and security, to a fair trial, and to respect for private and family life.

Unexpectedly, one area of law remained largely affected by this legislative flood. In many other countries, including England, parts of criminal law have been reduced to legislation or, more ambitiously, re-expressed in the form of a complete code which is intended to be accessible to ordinary citizens. In Scotland, however, the principal crimes continue to derive from a long tract of court decisions, comprehensible only to the expert.

In 1900 and for much of the century which followed, all legislation which applied to Scotland derived from the **United Kingdom** Parliament in Westminster. But when the UK joined the European Community in 1973 it became subject to Community legislation, which prevails over the legislation of Member States. And in 1999, after a false start twenty years before, a legislature was restored to Scotland for the first time since the **Act of Union** of 1707. Admittedly, the powers of the new Scottish Parliament are far more modest than those of its predecessor, which was the legislature of a sovereign state. Nonetheless, the Scottish Parliament has law-making powers over private law (excluding certain commercial topics) and passes around fifteen Acts a year, some of them substantial and dealing with matters of considerable importance—for example, the abolition of feudal tenure (2000), the conferral of a public right to roam over open land (2003), and the banning of smoking in public places (2005). Despite devolution to Edinburgh, the UK Parliament continues to legislate for Scotland although, by convention, it does not do so in respect of devolved topics except with the agreement of the Scottish Parliament.

The growth of 'primary' legislation (ie Acts of Parliament) in the twentieth century was accompanied by an explosion of 'secondary' legislation (ie legislation made by ministers under powers conferred by primary legislation), and there was an increasing tendency for primary legislation to contain only framework provisions, leaving the details to be decided later by ministerial order, largely unchecked by parliamentary scrutiny. In 2005 alone, 661 statutory instruments were issued by the devolved Scottish Executive, covering topics ranging from bird flu to mental health to the wearing of uniforms by traffic wardens in South Lanarkshire.

The growing complexity of law, and the difficulty of tracking it down, contributed to increasing specialization within the legal profession. By the closing decades of the twentieth century, the familiar small law firm, staffed by solicitors willing to offer advice on practically anything, was beginning to give way to large or very large firms, concentrated in the cities, and organized on the basis of narrow specialisms. The number of lawyers grew too, reflecting soaring crime rates, but also rising levels of commercial activity and greater personal wealth. Between 1900 and 2005 the number of practising solicitors increased more than threefold, to 9,637, while the number of practising advocates more than doubled to 450. By 2005 there was one solicitor to every 525 citizens compared with one to 1,490 in 1900; and 42 per cent of all solicitors were female, a striking change from earlier times. Following legislation in 1990, advocates lost their exclusive rights of audience before the supreme courts but, in the face of competition from the new breed of solicitor advocates, clung all the more tenaciously to their traditional dress of wig and gown. Unlike in England, admission to the legal profession was almost always by law degree, at first studied part-time in conjunction with work in a law office but full-time from 1960. A pass in the postgraduate Diploma in Legal Practice was made an additional requirement in 1980.

Over the twentieth century there was a large increase in litigation, matched by a corresponding increase in the number of judges, who, after 2002, were appointed by a judicial appointments board with a majority of lay members and not, as previously, at the behest of the **Lord Advocate**. A new appellate court for decisions in jury trials, the Court of Criminal Appeal, was set up in 1926 following a much-publicized case of miscarriage of justice, while in 1968 most offences committed by children under sixteen were taken out of the criminal justice system and dealt with by lay tribunals under the children's hearings system. For impecunious litigants, a system of **legal aid** was introduced in 1949 for civil matters and in 1964 for criminal matters, replacing the longstanding practice of litigation under the Poor's Roll.

In the middle decades of the century considerable attention was paid to the question of whether Scots law could, or perhaps even should, survive as a system independent from that of England. After all, much of the new statute law applied throughout the UK, while legislation passed specially for Scotland was often modelled on an English counterpart. And even within the heartland of private law—traditionally the area of greatest distinctiveness—there had been considerable movement in the direction of English law after the Union and in particular from the middle of the nineteenth century onwards. Given its robust institutional structure, there was perhaps never any serious danger that Scots law would actually disappear, but it seemed likely to face a future of slow assimilation, coupled with bouts of often ill-considered borrowing from the well-stocked law south of the border. By the end of the twentieth century, however, it had become apparent that this fate would be avoided. A key reason was the expansion of law teaching in the universities, which provided both the personnel to carry out much-needed research as well, in due course, as lawyers in sufficient numbers to supply a market for its products. In the decades after 1960 scholarly books were published in criminal law and in virtually all the main areas of private law, to add to the rather meagre material from earlier in the century. Periodical literature flourished as well. A notable feature of this new work was the uncovering, sometimes self-consciously or even programmatically, of the Roman-civilian (or at least non-English) roots of much of the modern law.

Other factors tended in the same direction. These included the founding of a professional law reform body in 1965, the Scottish Law Commission, which was a source both of research and of carefully considered legislation; the growing importance of the **European Union**—most of whose Member States had legal systems based on Roman-civil law—and of projects aimed at the harmonization of European private law; and close contact with other legal systems which contain a mixture of civil law and English law, most notably South Africa. By the end of the century the establishment of the Scottish Parliament put a seal on the survival of Scots law, even if there were no particular grounds for supposing that the legislators in Edinburgh would be more attentive than their counterparts in London to that law's spirit and traditions.   KENNETH REID

HL MacQueen (ed), *Scots Law into the 21st Century: Essays in Honour of W A Wilson* (Edinburgh: W Green/Sweet & Maxwell, 1996)

DM Walker, *A Legal History of Scotland*, vol VII: *The Twentieth Century* (Lexis Nexis UK, 2004)

See also: **civil law systems; mixed jurisdictions; Roman law**

Scottish Parliament   Nearly 300 years after abolition of its predecessor, a Scottish Parliament was re-established in 1999. Under the Scotland Act 1998, it has a general power of law-making in respect of Scotland ('The Scottish Parliament may make laws, to be known as Acts of the Scottish Parliament') except in areas that are expressly reserved to Westminster. In effect, its legislative powers extend over nearly the whole of private law in Scotland, the criminal law with a few exceptions such as abortion, drugs, and treason, and such matters of public law as are not of common concern to the whole **United Kingdom**. Reserved matters include succession to the throne, foreign and defence affairs, and customs and excise. General taxation and macro-economic policy are reserved, though the Parliament has a power to vary the standard rate of income tax up or down by 3 per cent. Otherwise, the devolved administration is financed by an annual grant from the UK Treasury calculated according to a formula.

The Parliament's powers are subject to review, exercisable either in the ordinary course of litigation or by special reference to the Judicial Committee of the **Privy Council**. Under the Constitutional Reform Act 2005, power over devolution issues is transferred to the United Kingdom Supreme Court. The Parliament is elected for a fixed four-year term by the 'additional member system' of proportional representation. The First Minister, and the other Ministers of the Scottish Executive, are elected by the Scottish Parliament after a General Election. Coalition government tends to prevail.

NEIL MACCORMICK

J McFadden and M Lazarowicz, *The Scottish Parliament: an Introduction* (Edinburgh: T & T Clark, 2nd edn, 2000)

search and seizure Searches and seizures of property by officials are useful tools for investigating crime, but interfere with both property rights and **privacy**-related rights. It has therefore long been recognized that searches and seizures can be legitimate, but require special legal justification in order to prevent arbitrary and oppressive action. At **common law** it was possible to search private premises for suspected felons. By the seventeenth century, search for stolen goods was also permitted with a search warrant issued by a justice of the peace. Statutes allowed searches for other prohibited or regulated articles or for evidence of crime, usually on the basis of a warrant but sometimes without warrant; but where neither common law nor statutory authority existed a search would be unlawful: *Entick v Carrington* (1765).

The fundamental importance of freedom from arbitrary searches has been widely recognized, and has received constitutional status in a number of countries. The first example was the Fourth Amendment to the Constitution of the United States of America in 1791, which protects the people's right to be 'secure . . . against unreasonable searches and seizures', and provides that no warrant is to issue except 'upon probable cause, supported by Oath or

affirmation, and particularly describing the place to be searched, and the persons or things to be seized'. This sums up the widely accepted requirements for legitimate searches and seizures.

The freedom has also been included expressly or by implication in a number of international human rights instruments, including the **European Convention on Human Rights** ('ECHR'), Article 8 and the **International Covenant on Civil and Political Rights**, Article 17. Where the protection is founded on privacy as well as property, it can have a wide scope, covering (for example) searches in more or less public places where people nevertheless have a reasonable expectation of privacy as under the Fourth Amendment and the ECHR Article 8, such as cars on roads.

Yet there has been a growing tendency for legislatures to enact ever more intrusive powers of search and seizure. One wide power of warrantless search in customs cases is of long standing: in England and Wales a writ of assistance issued out of the office of the Queen's Remembrancer (the senior Queen's Bench Master *ex officio*) allows Customs officers to enter and search any place where there is reasonable cause to believe that there are goods liable to forfeiture under the Customs and Excise Acts. Wide statutory powers have been extended to other fields in response to enhanced threats from organized crime and terrorism. In England and Wales a warrant under the Serious Organized Crime and Police Act 2005 can authorize search of a number of premises which need not be identified in the warrant, and searches on a number of occasions. It remains to be seen whether these extraordinary measures will become long-term features of legal systems.

DAVID FELDMAN

secession Secession can be defined as a process leading to the creation of a new state upon territory previously forming part of an existing state, the latter often referred to as the 'host' state. This process is usually initiated by the proclamation of the existence of a new state by the representatives of a territorial community within the host state. In some, but not all, cases in which independence is so proclaimed, other states formally recognize its independence. When a sufficient degree of recognition has been achieved the proclaimed state becomes, at that time, a state in reality. At this point the process of secession is complete.

There are different *types* of secession depending upon the circumstances in which the new state arises. *Unilateral* secession occurs where, notwithstanding the continued opposition of the host state, part of that state becomes a new state and the host state continues its existence. *Devolutionary* secession occurs where, irrespective of whether or not it initially opposed the creation of a new state, the host state consents to its creation at the time the new state is created and the host state continues its existence. *Consensual* secession occurs where the demand for the creation of a new state leads to the host state being dissolved by consent, leading to the creation of new states. *Dissolving* secession occurs where the demand for the creation of a new state leads to the factual dissolution of the host state, leading to the creation of new states.

This definition of secession is not universally accepted. For some scholars, a necessary element of the definition of secession is the continued opposition of the host state to the creation of the new state or what has been referred to above as unilateral secession. The question of whether the creation of new states as a result of decolonization is within the scope of secession is also contested by scholars.

Whatever definition of secession one adopts, what is here defined as unilateral secession raises the most important questions from the perspective of the legal regulation of secession. The legality of secession can be addressed from the perspectives of **international law** and the host state's **constitutional law**. Judicial decisions in the United States, Canada, and the former Yugoslavia all confirm that unilateral secession is illegal from a constitutional law perspective and that the only way a part of a state can legally secede is by amending the host state's constitution. This would apply even if the host state's constitution stipulates, as many do, that the state is indissoluble. The requirement of a constitutional amendment means that the consent of the host state is necessary for lawful secession to occur. From the perspective of international law, a qualified right of secession arguably arises pursuant to paragraph 7 of Principle V of the United Nations Declaration of Principles of International Law Concerning Friendly Relations and Co-operation Among States in Accordance with the Charter of the United Nations of 1970, which deals with the principle of **self-determination**. The right arises when a group within a state is discriminated against by a state and thus denied its right to internal self-determination. Such discrimination transforms the right of internal self-determination into a right of external self-determination or secession. In international law, it is the fact of discrimination against a group that allows that group to secede unilaterally. However, in domestic constitutional law, no requirement of discrimination exists—a territorial community can secede simply because it wants to, provided

it can get the agreement of the host state to an appropriate constitutional amendment.

JAVAID REHMAN

D Raič, *Statehood and the Law of Self-Determination* (The Hague: Kluwer Law International, 2002)

A Pavković and P Radan, *Creating New States: Theory and Practice of Secession* (Aldershot: Ashgate Publishing Co, 2007)

P Radan, 'Secession: A Word in Search of Meaning' in A Pavkovic and P Radan (eds) On the Way to Statehood, Secession and Globalisation (Aldershot: Ashgate Publishing Co, 2008) pp 17–32

secondary action   *see* **strikes; picketing**

secondary markets   A 'secondary market' is not a physical market. The term refers to markets in which **securities** are traded between investors after their sale by the issuer in a **primary market**. Primary markets are dwarfed by secondary markets, in which the vast majority of transactions take place.

Primary markets are associated with the raising of finance by issuing securities. Secondary markets provide a venue where investors generate and realize capital appreciation (or suffer losses) on those securities. Secondary markets remain important for issuers because the strength of an issuer's securities can help an issuer raise finance again in a primary market. Ongoing and periodic disclosure of the issuer's subsequent performance dominates secondary market **regulation**. Transparency rules, which require disclosure of a security's price, are also a feature of secondary market regulation, as are insider dealing and market manipulation rules.

Secondary markets include **stock exchange**s, **alternative trading system**s ('ATSs') and the 'over-the-counter' ('OTC') markets in which professional investors enter into bilateral agreements, often concerning complex securities. The degree of regulation reflects the nature of the market. Stock exchanges are typically subject to the highest degree of regulation given their central role in financial markets and the participation of retail investors. It also reflects the nature of the security and the investor base. Bonds are typically traded on ATSs while derivatives are often traded in the OTC markets, both of which are dominated by professional investors and less heavily regulated than stock exchanges.

NIAMH MOLONEY

See also: **transparency of securities trades**

Secretaries of State   *see* **Cabinet; Ministers of State; Ministers of the Crown**

secular curriculum in schools   Under the Education Act 1944, determination of the contents of the secular curriculum was a matter for local education authorities ('LEAs'), subject to a broad duty imposed on the Secretary of State to promote the education of the people. In practice, LEAs generally regarded curricular content as a matter for teachers' professional expertise. In the 1970s and 1980s, however, there was a growing perception that educational standards in schools were declining, that there were unacceptably wide variations in curricular provision within schools, and in some cases that these problems were being exacerbated by radical movements within the teaching profession. The Conservative government under Margaret Thatcher felt that local determination of the curriculum was no longer acceptable and, in the Education Reform Act 1988, established a statutory framework for the creation of a national curriculum for maintained schools in England and Wales. England and Wales moved in the years that followed from having one of the least prescriptive to one of the most heavily prescriptive school curricula in Europe.

The main statutory provisions governing the school curriculum are now to be found in the Education Act 2002. Section 78(1) requires that the curriculum for a maintained school shall be balanced and broadly based and that it shall promote the spiritual, moral, mental, and physical development of pupils and of society, and prepare pupils for the opportunities, responsibilities, and experiences of later life. Section 80 sets out a 'basic curriculum' for every maintained school, comprising religious education for all registered pupils (subject to a parental right of withdrawal), sex education for all registered pupils in the case of secondary schools (also subject to a parental right of withdrawal), and a national curriculum for all registered pupils from three to sixteen years. The national curriculum covers the foundation stage from the age of three, through each of four key stages covering the ages six to seven, eight to eleven, twelve to fourteen, and fifteen to sixteen years. The Secretary of State is charged under section 87 with the establishment and revision of a national curriculum applicable to each of these stages, specifying by order attainment targets, programmes of study, and assessment arrangements for each stage (in the case of the foundation stage, 'early learning goals' and 'educational programmes' replace attainment targets and programmes of study). The orders themselves refer to documents which contain the detailed requirements. The process of formulating and promulgating the orders is laid down in section 96 and includes consultation by the Qualifications and Curriculum Authority with associations representing LEAs, school governing bodies, and teachers. The curriculum for the key stages (following the foundation stage) comprises the core subjects of mathematics, English, and Science (and Welsh in the case of Welsh medium schools in Wales) throughout each stage, and a range of 'other foundation' subjects, depending on the key stage concerned. These include design and technology, information and communication technology, physical education, history, geography, art and design, and music. **Citizenship** is compulsory as a foundation subject at key stages three and four, as is a modern foreign language at key stage three. At key stage four there is a greater element of flexibility: in addition to the core subjects and the foundation subjects of information and communication technology, physical education, and citizenship, key stage four includes prescribed elements which include work-related learning and may also include arts, design and technology, humanities, and a modern foreign language.

Many subjects within the curriculum, particularly history and citizenship, may involve consideration of conflicting political opinions: teachers must exercise professional judgment in the presentation of such issues in the classroom, but there are also legal constraints in this context. Section 407 of the Education Act 1996 provides that the LEA, governing body, and head teacher shall take 'such steps as are reasonably practicable' to secure that, where political issues arise, the pupils are 'offered a balanced presentation of opposing views.' Furthermore, Article 2 of the First Protocol to the ECHR, which requires public authorities to respect parents' religious and philosophical convictions in the provision of education, has been interpreted by the **European Court of Human Rights** as importing an obligation avoid indoctrination and to present issues in an objective, critical, and pluralistic manner (*Kjeldsen, Busk Madsen and Pedersen v Denmark* (1979–80)).

The sensitive subject of sex education is included as part of the 'basic curriculum' for secondary schools, but is not part of the national curriculum. It may also be provided in primary schools, depending on the governors' policy. Wherever provided, it is subject to an unconditional parental right of withdrawal under section 405 of the Education Act 1996, a right which may conflict with the rights of the **child**. The content of sex education, unlike the national curriculum, is determined at the level of the individual school: the governing body is required under section 404 of the Education Act 1996, to formulate a written statement of their policy on sex education. LEAs, governors, and head teachers must, however, have regard to guidance issued by the Secretary of State on sex education: this guidance itself must be designed to secure that pupils 'learn the nature of **marriage** and its importance for **family life** and the bringing up of children', and that pupils are protected from inappropriate teaching and materials, having regard to their age and religious and cultural background. Governors and head teachers are also required by section 403 to take reasonable steps to secure that sex education is given in such a manner as to encourage pupils to have due regard to 'moral considerations and the value of family life'. The requirement in Article 2 of the First Protocol to the ECHR that states respect parents' religious and philosophical convictions, and the emphasis placed by the European Court of Human Rights in the *Kjeldsen* case (above) on the importance of adopting an objective, critical, and pluralistic approach to the provision of education, is of particular importance in the context of sex education, where religious and cultural sensitivities are of central concern.   PAUL MEREDITH

See also: **education and human rights; religious education and worship in schools**

secularism The word 'secular' comes from the Latin, *saecularis*, which was used to describe clergy who lived within medieval society rather than in seclusion in a monastery. It then became used to distinguish between the worldly and the spiritual but also to be used in a negative way to mean 'godlessness'. Later, in Dr Johnson's Dictionary (1755), secularism was defined as 'worldliness—attention to things of the present life'. Its modern political usage developed in the nineteenth century in the context of concerns expressed within the positivist movement of the need to move away from the idea that laws were derived from God and asserting the view that politics should be free from religion. Figures such as George J Holyoake and Charles Bradlaugh presented secularism as a new kind of morality which, they believed, should be concerned with the wellbeing of **human** beings in the present life based on tenets of rationality rather than religion. Religion was not to be done away with altogether but relegated to the sphere of private worship.

In modern politics, secularism is generally invoked to denote the theoretical idea of the separation of religion (church) from the key branches of the state: the executive, judiciary, and legislature. Accordingly, those governing the country should not be religious authorities such as the Church; nor should the state govern on the basis of religious principles or rules. The state should be neutral concerning religion. This does not prevent people, including politicians, from holding a religious belief; it just means that their religious beliefs should not influence state affairs. Secularism can exist in varying forms depending on the level of influence of religion and religious beliefs in government policies, politics, law, and public life.

In some countries, such as France, there is a complete separation of religion from state affairs (a form of secularism known as *Laïcité*). This means, amongst other things, that the wearing of conspicuous religious symbols in public government institutions such as schools is restricted. This does not affect people's right to **freedom of religion and belief**, including the freedom to exercise or manifest religious beliefs in private life.

Whilst the UK is not governed according to Christian religious dogma, Christianity does have a role in the political life and establishment of the nation. For example, Bishops sit in the House of Lords and The Queen (Head of State) is the Head of the **Church of England**. Religion also has a role in areas of public life such as education where worship and religious studies classes are part of school life. The number of Faith Schools funded by the state is also growing.

Despite these examples of religion existing within political and public life, the UK is generally perceived to be secular because people within British society have become less religious and fewer people go to church (although this does not take account of whether people from **minority** religions such as Hinduism and Islam are becoming increasingly secular or, indeed, are more active in their religious practices). Freedom of religion is often a feature of secular states and an important part of *Laïcité*. However, whilst secular states tend to guarantee a freedom to have a belief in religion (or not) they can restrict people from practising their religion in public as has been the case in the UK with the wearing of Muslim religious dress in schools.   SUHRAIYA JIVRAJ

See also: **religious affiliation and school dress; religious education and worship in schools**

securities Securities are financial instruments issued by entities for the purpose of raising finance through the markets. Securities support market finance, as opposed to finance raised through bank loans (bank finance) or through the issuer's internal cash flow and profits. Market finance is raised through the purchase price which is paid by investors to the issuer for the securities. The initial financing transaction between the issuer and the investor occurs in what is called a **primary market**. Securities are subsequently traded between investors in a **secondary market**.

In terms of financial market regulation, **regulation** of the issuance of securities is strongly directed towards disclosure and ensuring that investors have sufficient information about the issuer and the securities to make an informed investment decision. With respect to issuers which are companies, company law requirements also apply internally within the company and restrict the extent to which, and conditions (typically involving shareholder approval) under which, a company can issue securities, particularly new shares.

The major categories of securities include equities (shares), debt (bonds), and derivatives.

Equities are **shares**. Companies can access market finance by issuing shares to raise cash (eg for an acquisition). Equity investments give investors an ownership share in the issuer or company. Dividends and capital gains will accrue to the investor if the financial position of the company remains healthy, if the share price rises, and if the company decides to issue dividends—it may not. Holders of equity securities also carry residual risk. They are the last to be paid out in the event of the company's insolvency. Bondholders, by contrast, will be repaid the capital amount they have loaned the company (assuming there are sufficient funds) before shareholders can recover.

Bonds are securities in the form of a debt owed by the issuing entity to the holder of the debt (the bondholder). The issuer raises finance by raising a loan from the bondholders and promising to repay the loan (the principal) within a defined term (when the bond is 'redeemed') and to pay an interest rate. Bonds represent, in effect, a very large loan split among the bondholders. A bond issue for £100 million, for example, might have hundreds of investors. Unlike a share, a bond does not give an ownership stake in the issuing company—bonds, or debt securities, are a form of credit. Also unlike shares, bonds can be issued by a wide range of entities including companies, governments, and public authorities. Bond investors are typically institutional investors, although bonds are popular with retail investors in continental Europe. Bonds became the subject of close regulatory attention following the US WorldCom and European Parmalat scandals, following which retail investors, in particular, sustained losses on bonds when these companies became insolvent.

Derivatives are not used to raise finance, but they provide a key risk-management device in the finance-raising process. At its most basic, a derivative security sets out the obligation of the issuer of the derivative to deliver, and the right of the holder or investor to receive assets at some point in the future. The obligation to deliver/right to receive, and the security's value, 'derive' from the possible occurrence of future events specified in the derivative contract. These events and assets 'underlying' the derivative have become almost infinite in variety as derivatives have become ever more complex. The

more common events are changes in the price of a security or commodity, exchange and interest rate movements, the weather, and the performance of loans. Credit derivatives, for example, are based on the likelihood of a default on a loan, and are currently extremely popular and a cause of some concern to regulators. They are used to manage credit risk. A bank concerned that a loan might not be repaid may enter into a credit derivative with another party who agrees to bear the loss of the loan, if the borrower defaults, for payment of a fee by the bank. Risks to market stability arise, however, where regulators are not aware who is carrying credit risk, and whether these parties are sufficiently robust, or if too much risk is being carried through derivatives. Similarly, risk related to interest and exchange rates can be managed using derivatives. 'Swaps' are often used by companies to limit their interest rate/currency exposure when borrowing. Typical derivatives also include futures (an obligation to buy or sell in the future) and options—options to buy (call options) and options to sell (put options).

NIAMH MOLONEY

See also: **insolvency, corporate**

security   The term 'security' derives from the Latin *securus* (without care) and *securitas* (freedom from anxiety or fear). It is now deployed in a variety of circumstances to refer both to a state of mind (a feeling of wellbeing or assurance, or its reverse, a feeling of *insecurity*) and to a range of activities, including the use of physical security measures, the protection against victimization afforded by the activities of both public policing and private security agencies, and those activities undertaken in the name of protecting the nation state and its citizens from 'external threats'.

Security is a slippery concept. At its most abstract it may be taken to refer to either a negative or a positive presence—something that we have and value, or something that we lack and desire. The politicization of crime and its control in recent decades have been accompanied by apparently increasing concern about **safety** and security. In turn, a market in security has developed, comprising a range of commodities, as well as 'manned security' in the form of a variety of private security operatives from guards to nightclub bouncers.

The growing visibility of privatized security arrangements and personnel is argued to be a distinguishing feature of our late modern social environment. A number of influential authors have argued that policing is being transformed and restructured in the modern world. A developing literature has focused on different elements in this process of change, including: the emergence and spread of transnational policing bodies; changes in the organization and goals of **police** work; the rise of a proactive, **risk**-oriented mentality; and the emergence of a more complex policing division of labour.

One of the consequences of these processes is that the state is increasingly seen as being only one of a number of 'auspices' of policing alongside private governments and citizens. This is so substantial a shift away from the traditional state-centred view of policing that a number of authors have argued that we should now be talking about the '**governance** of security' rather than of policing.

This literature challenges the existing scholarly preoccupation with the police at the expense of other sources of private sector security provision. However, it has yet to devote much attention to those forms of governance that are involved in the security of the state itself whether this is done by security agencies or law enforcement bodies. Growing concerns about **national security** since the September 2001 attacks in the US and subsequently in Madrid, London, and elsewhere, have begun to change this.

The end of the Cold War and the rise of international **terrorism** have led to the emergence of what some observers now refer to as the 'new security agenda'. Concerns about the new terrorism have begun to reshape the governance of domestic security generally and policing more particularly. These changes may lead to something of a blurring of the roles of the police, the military, and the security agencies, as well as the boundaries between international security and domestic concerns of order maintenance.

TIM NEWBURN

DH Bayley and C Shearing, *The New Structure of Policing: Description, Conceptualization and Research Agenda* (Washington DC: National Institute of Justice, 2001)

L Zedner, 'The Concept of Security: an Agenda for Comparative Analysis' (2003) 23 *Legal Studies* 153–176

security services   *see* **national security**

security vetting of teachers   *see* **teacher training and employment**

segregation and desegregation   Segregation and desegregation define two different processes in which polices, practices, and law actively divide society along racial, ethnic, religious, and other 'primal' lines or alternatively work towards the breakdown of these same divisions. However, popular ideology and law often presume that segregation is the result of a natural sorting based on private preferences. Thus the concepts of segregation and desegregation require repeated clarification. These naturalizing assumptions are evident in popular culture, which assumes and reinforces the notion that 'birds of a feather flock together'; and they are incorporated into the constitutional law of the United States, which defines segregation as being either *de jure* or *de facto*. This distinction presents the fact of segregation as either the product of formal laws and practices—which have been declared unconstitutional since **Brown v Board of Education** (1954)—or of unofficial and private forms of social separation that are presented as 'natural' or even 'normal' consequences of pre-existing and even 'primal' distinctions, and thus beyond the scope of legitimate government action.

By contrast, desegregation is viewed as a form of state intervention and a disruption of the natural order of things. In contrast to policies of segregation which have long been endorsed by laws and official practice, attempts to achieve desegregation have been simply marginalized or repeatedly challenged as violating the assumed race neutral guarantees of the United States Constitution or presented as a form of reverse discrimination when affirmative action or quotas are used to desegregate educational institutions, public services, or workplaces. Compared to the very limited policies of affirmative action in the United States, post-colonial states such as India, Malaysia, and now South Africa have adopted much more explicit policies aimed at desegregating public and private institutions. While there is consistent resistance to desegregation in all these societies, there have been much more concerted efforts to break down societal discrimination in post-colonial societies in which the community that was formerly discriminated against is now the democratic majority. However, desegregation remains a major challenge in most societies where there has been an increasing confluence of these particularistic societal divisions with class with the result that segregation of specific communities is now ascribed to poverty rather than to the historic legacy of segregation.

History is essential to any understanding of segregation and desegregation. While it is often assumed that these social distinctions are the products of long historical realities or conflicts, a careful review of the historical record often demonstrates how these divisions have been socially constructed or manipulated in particular contexts. On the one hand, it is not surprising that particular immigrant groups, often following family, language, or other bonds, might cluster together in a foreign land, at least through the first generation. On the other hand, it is well demonstrated that the segregation of particular communities is less the product of affinity than the active intervention of political and social forces which mobilize these social distinctions to their own purpose (as in the case of anti-semitism in Europe), or in defence of pre-existing social institutions (as in the case of slavery and racial discrimination in the United States), or for the purpose of maintaining a racist minority in power (as in the case of apartheid South Africa). The achievement of segregation in these contexts often relies explicitly on violence, such as lynching and 'race riots' in the United States, but also on informal practices of discrimination that become 'culturally embedded' as well as on official policies and law.

The struggle for desegregation remains an important part of the political landscape in the United States and post-apartheid South Africa. However, it is only beginning in parts of Europe where the influx of former colonial subjects and citizens has produced a new mix of exclusion and segregation along lines of race, culture, religion, immigration status, and class. Civil wars in the Balkans and some former Soviet Republics have also produced new forms of ethnic exclusion and segregation that have entwined issues of cultural survival, minority protection, and security for the foreseeable future. In the United States the inability of African Americans to participate effectively in the political system—despite the fourteenth and fifteenth Amendments of the US Constitution, which guarantee equality and the right to vote—led to the formation of the National Association for the Advancement of Colored Peoples ('NAACP') in 1909 and the turn to the courts as the only institutional spaces within which to challenge segregation. Despite early victories before the **United States Supreme Court**—such as the striking down of a Louisville residential segregation ordinance in 1917 and individual victories for applicants challenging exclusion from institutions of higher education from 1938 to1950—it was only in the context of the Cold War, and after the Supreme Court declared in *Brown* that 'separate but equal' was not constitutional in the context of public education, that the struggle for desegregation managed to gain some headway in the US. Inspired by these victories the civil rights movement blossomed in the 1960s and produced significant opportunities for many individual African Americans; yet the problem of segregation has remained evident in the ghettos of the inner cities and in the failure of law and policy to truly desegregate society. As Professor Patricia Williams has argued, the 'attempt to split bias from violence' in which overt racist violence is condemned but 'private' attitudes of discrimination are insulated from public or official condemnation, is 'this society's most enduring and fatal rationalization' (PJ Williams, *The Alchemy of Race and Rights: Diary of a Law Professor* (Cambridge, MA: Harvard University Press, 1991), 61).

Law has always played a central role in practices of segregation and desegregation. Despite collective amnesia and denial, laws prohibiting interracial sex and marriage as well as the policies and practices of the Federal Housing Authority and local school boards in the US have long perpetuated the patterns of exclusion and segregation that began with slavery. In Nazi Germany and South Africa what began as 'legal' segregation soon begat policies of extermination and national oppression. While the Holocaust was brought to an end by the defeat of Nazi Germany in 1945, the policy of apartheid formalized segregation in South Africa after the Afrikaner Nationalist victory in racially constituted elections in 1948, creating a system of cradle-to-grave regulations in which the lives of all South Africans were defined by their placement in racial categories assigned by law. Nelson Mandela's election as President may have ended apartheid in South Africa but the legacies of racial segregation, based on geography and wealth, will remain a challenge for the foreseeable future. As in the US, claims of reverse discrimination and arguments that the state must not use racial categories in policy formulation or implementation have arisen to challenge efforts to use the law to achieve effective desegregation. While the South African Constitution and other post-colonial constitutions provide for the use of affirmative action and other race-conscious polices to achieve equality, the US Supreme Court has taken an increasingly sceptical view of the use of race-conscious policies and only narrowly upheld the use of race as one factor in the admission of students to institutions of higher education after the Court, in *Grutter v Bollinger* (2003), was bombarded with *amici* briefs from business and military leaders arguing that these policies were essential to ensure an integrated and competitive workforce so that the United States can function effectively in the global economy. HEINZ KLUG

ML Dudziak, 'Desegregation as a Cold War Imperative' (1988) 41 *Stanford Law Review* 61

DS Massey and NA Denton, *American Apartheid: Segregation and the Making of the Underclass* (Cambridge, MA: Harvard University Press, 2003)

select committees Select committees are the investigative organs of Parliament. The Commons has appointed them since the time of its earliest records, originally mostly to draft bills—which function had atrophied by 1700. Subsequently they were appointed regularly but unsystematically: **royal commissions** superseded them to an extent. They underwent a renaissance with the establishment of the **House of Commons** departmental select committee system in 1979. Historically the **House of Lords** rarely used select committees. Its European Union Committee (established in 1974) which, through several subcommittees, examines matters emanating from the institutions of the **European Union**, is now an institution, and other more or less permanent committees have since been established. This entry describes select committees of the Commons.

Select committees are generally small (around a dozen MPs chosen in proportion to party strengths in the House, usually appointed for a whole Parliament). Typically, they are supported by a Clerk and a team of between three and a dozen permanent staff: they also appoint part-time experts to advise them.

Committees do not debate but deliberate in private. They have power to 'send for persons, papers, and records' ('PPR') which, in theory, equals or exceeds that enjoyed by courts to compel the submission of evidence and the attendance of witnesses. In practice the power is respected but circumscribed, and would rely for ultimate enforcement on securing an order of the House. Select committees have power to report 'from time to time', which is their key function. They have freedom to conduct formal proceedings away from Westminster. Typically, a select committee inquiry will pass through the following stages: determination and publication of terms of reference; call for the submission of written evidence ('memoranda'); public oral examination of witnesses; preparation of draft report on behalf of chair; informal and formal consideration and amendment of draft report; publication of report with written and oral evidence.

The main body of permanent committees are the eighteen departmentally-related committees. One 'marks' each government department, charged with examining its 'expenditure, administration, and policy' and that of its 'associated public bodies'. Committees interpret this remit widely and variously. By convention the government will respond to recommendations in reports within sixty days: around a quarter of reports published are debated, in one way or another, in the House.

There are many other committees concerned with both external and internal matters: the select committee is an extremely flexible procedural tool. They include the Public Accounts Committee which, with the Comptroller and **Auditor General**, has statutory duties to ensure that public money is spent by central government in accordance with the authorization of the Commons; the European Scrutiny Committee which examines legislative and other proposals emanating from the institutions of the EU; and the Standards and Privileges Committee which polices the conduct of MPs and guards the privileges of the House against abuses or contempts.

The two Houses may appoint select committees to work together: these are called joint committees. These are regularly appointed to examine draft bills.

PAUL EVANS

R Blackburn and A Kennon, *Griffith and Ryle on Parliament: Functions, Practice and Procedures* (London: Sweet & Maxwell, 2nd edn, 2003)

P Evans, *Handbook of House of Commons Procedure* (London: Dod's Parliamentary Communications, 6th edn, 2007)

See also: **legislative and general committees**

selective schools   *see* **school admissions**

self   *see* **subject**

self regulation   *see* **regulation**

self-defence   *see* **justification, excuse and mitigation in criminal law**

self-defence in international law   The right of self-defence is the main exception to the prohibition on the use of force in Article 2(4) of the **United Nations** Charter. It is regulated by Article 51 which provides: 'Nothing in the present Charter shall impair the inherent right of individual or collective self-defence if an armed attack occurs against a Member of the United Nations, until the Security Council has taken measures necessary to maintain international peace and security. Measures taken by Members in the exercise of this right of self-defence shall be immediately reported to the Security Council and shall not in any way affect the authority and responsibility of the Security Council under the present Charter to take at any time such action as it deems necessary in order to maintain or restore international peace and security'.

The law on self-defence is very controversial. There are long-standing and apparently irreconcilable divisions between states as to whether self-defence is a wide or a narrow right; and in particular as to whether self-defence is limited to a response to an armed attack. States agree on the central core of self-defence: the right to use necessary and proportionate force against an armed attack. But even on this relatively unproblematic core right there are difficult questions. The definition of armed attack is crucial. In the **Nicaragua case** the International Court of Justice turned to the *Definition of Aggression* (1974) to establish that an armed attack does not have to be carried out by a regular army; it may be by armed bands provided that they are sent by or on behalf of a state. The Court also held that an armed attack must be of a certain gravity and not a mere frontier incident; the supply of arms and money does not amount to an armed attack. The Court affirmed that any use of force in self-defence must be necessary and proportionate. In further developing the law on self-defence in later cases the Court has taken a generally restrictive view while avoiding decisions on some of the more controversial issues.

Some developed states argue that there is a wider inherent right of self-defence under **customary international law**. Thus the US, Israel, and the **United Kingdom** assert a wide right extending to cover anticipatory self-defence and the protection of nationals abroad. Some commentators still invoke the exchange of diplomatic notes between the UK and the US after the 1837 *Caroline* incident as authority for the existence of a wide inherent right, but this seems unconvincing, given that the incident took place before the development of the legal concept of self-defence.

The terrorist attacks of 9/11 have led some states and commentators to call for a reappraisal of the law of self-defence. The UN Security Council affirmed the right of individual and collective self-defence after the attacks, but it did so in general terms, which left many questions unanswered. It is still controversial how far there can be self-defence against non-state actors such as terrorists. Does the 'global war on terror' proclaimed by the US give the right to use force against terrorists in a third state which was not involved in the terrorist attacks? President George W Bush proclaimed a right of pre-emptive self-defence, but it is not clear what will trigger the right, or how the restrictions of necessity and proportionality could apply to such a right. Other states have not followed the US in claiming such a wide unilateral right.

Article 51 also provides for collective self-defence. The *Nicaragua* case gave an authoritative statement of the law on this issue: it is necessary that the victim state declare that it is the victim of an armed attack and request help from the third state. But collective self-defence has been relatively rare in practice. It provided the original legal basis for the North Atlantic Treaty Organization ('NATO'), which invoked the right for the first time after the terrorist attacks of 9/11.

Article 51 gives the Security Council a central role in regard to self-defence. States must report their use of force to the Security Council; and, since the *Nicaragua* case, they have generally been scrupulous about making such reports. That case held that the absence of a report may be one of the factors indicating whether the state in question was itself convinced that it was acting in self-defence. Also, the right to self-defence is temporary in the sense that it only continues until the Security Council has 'taken measures necessary to maintain international peace and security'.   CHRISTINE GRAY

self-determination Self-determination for all peoples is an antiquated and historic ideal. In its modern incarnation, self-determination was visualized through the experiences of the American, French, and Bolshevik **Revolutions** with its emphasis on popular **sovereignty**. At the end of World War I, the former United States President, Woodrow Wilson, advocated claims based on self-determination, although the final settlements, as well as the Covenant of League of Nations (1919), ignored the validity of any such claims. During the inter-war period (1919–1939), self-determination was widely deployed by European leaders and politicians as an instrument to galvanize nationalistic feelings. The concept however failed to be appropriated by the vocabulary of **international law** until the establishment of the **United Nations** (1945). Articles 1 and 55 of the United Nations Charter (1945) provide for self-determination, although the Universal Declaration of Human Rights (1948) avoids any reference to a right of self-determination. The **European Convention on Human Rights** 1950 ('ECHR') also does not provide for a right to self-determination. The first explicit recognition of an established right to self-determination within international treaty law is contained in common Article 1 of the **International Covenant on Civil and Political Rights** 1996 ('ICCPR') and the **International Covenant on Economic, Social, and Cultural Rights** 1966 ('ICESCR'). Article 1 provides that:

(1) All peoples have the right of self-determination. By virtue of that right they freely determine their political status and freely pursue their economic, social and cultural development.
(2) All peoples may, for their own ends, freely dispose of their natural wealth and resources without prejudice to any obligations arising out of international economic co-operation, based upon the principle of mutual benefit, and **international law**. In no case may a people be deprived of its own means of subsistence.
(3) The States Parties to the present Covenant, including those having responsibility for the administration of

Non-Self-Governing and Trust **Territories**, shall promote the realization of the right of self-determination, and shall respect that right, in conformity with the provisions of the Charter of the United Nations.'

The right to self-determination is reinforced by a range of international instruments including the **African Charter on Human and Peoples' Rights** (1981, Article 20(1)), the Helsinki Final Act of the OSCE (Article VIII), the Convention Concerning Indigenous and Tribal Peoples in Independent Countries (ILO) No 169, and the United Nations Declaration on the Rights of **Indigenous Peoples** (2007, Preamble, Articles 3, 4). Customary international law affirms the legally binding nature of the right to self-determination. Right to self-determination is affirmed by two of the most highly authoritative UN General Assembly Resolutions, the Declaration on the Granting of Independence to Colonial Territories and Peoples (GA Res 1514, 1960) and the Declaration of the Principle of International Law Concerning Friendly Relations and Co-Operation Amongst States in Accordance with the Charter of the United Nations (1970, GA Res 2625, XXV). Dicta from the case law of the International Court of Justice affirms that the right to self-determination has the character of rights *erga omnes* (*Barcelona Traction, Light and Power Company, Limited Case Belgium v Spain* (1970)).

Notwithstanding such an elevated stature, self-determination is a difficult right to define and there remains a significant amount of controversy as to its exact parameters in the post-colonial context. The beneficiaries of this right are described as 'Peoples' though blurring in the definition of 'Peoples' has meant that **minority** groups as well as indigenous peoples have made substantial claims to self-government, autonomy, and independent statehood based on the right to self-determination. At the level of implementation, state practice has varied significantly. International law appears to dispense this right into a two-dimensional fashion: the 'external aspect' of self-determination allows for the establishment of a sovereign and independent state, free association and integration with independent states (1970, GA Res 2625, XXV), whereas the 'internal' aspects emphasizes the right to **democracy** and the right to participation in public affairs of the state (Article 25, ICCPR; Protocol 1, Article 3 ECHR). In practice, self-determination claims have inevitably provoked controversy and conflict. The reunification of Germany and the splitting of the Czechoslovakia into the Czech Republic and Slovakia provide rare exceptions to the otherwise bloody conflicts that have raged around the right to self-determination.

Many states are particularly concerned that minority groups and indigenous peoples within independent states may use this right as a basis of their claims to **secession**.   JAVAID REHMAN

self-employment   *see* **contract of employment**

self-government   Self-government is an ambiguous and abstract concept which is applicable to a variety of circumstances and institutions. Within the context of **international** law and **constitutional laws**, self-government is akin to self-governance or **autonomy**. For **minorities** and **indigenous peoples**, self-government claims could result in independent statehood or autonomous existence within existing state structures. In the aftermath of World War II, the concept of self-government was enshrined in the **United Nations** Charter (1945). Chapter XI of the Charter, in its Article 73, requires those member states with responsibilities for **territories** whose people had not attained a full measure of self-government to ensure *inter alia* their cultural development, political, economic, social, and educational advancement and to develop self-government of these peoples. After 1945, within the United Nations, the issue of self-government became almost synonymous with independence to former European colonies. Once independent statehood was attained all claims of self-governance and **self-determination** were exhausted. Such a focus meant not only a neglect of indigenous peoples or minorities without a territorial base, but also a disregard of those aspects of self-government which emphasize internal self-determination through **constitutionalism**, autonomy, and democratic governance. This has unfortunately been the history of many of the new states of Africa and Asia which gained their independence during the 1950s and 1960s.

In the current political and legal environment, self-government has attained considerable significance for indigenous peoples and ethnic, linguistic, and religious minorities. International and national instruments place an increasing amount of reliance upon the various facets of self-government, through institutions of autonomy or democratic governance. Self-government is nevertheless not an established right, with considerable ambiguity surrounding its implementation. Attempts to incorporate a right to self-government were unsuccessful in the United Nations Declaration on the Rights of Persons Belonging to National or Ethnic, Religious, and Linguistic Minorities (1992). Although the United Nations Declaration on the Rights of Indigenous Peoples (2007) establishes this right (Article 4) the practical implementation of the Declaration, as well as the substantive value of provisions on self-government, remain a matter of conjecture.

JAVAID REHMAN

selfhood   *see* **subject**

self-incrimination   *see* **evidence (criminal)**

self-representation   It is an ancient principle of **common law** that we, as citizens, have access to the courts. In the absence of state funding, and where litigants are unable or unwilling to pay for their own representation, parties must represent themselves or abandon their rights. There is an increasingly alarmist view that the courts are about to be swamped by these 'litigants in person'. Outside of the Court of Appeal, claims that the numbers of litigants in person are increasing are probably overstated or wrong, but such litigants do pose problems.

A related assumption is that litigants in person are difficult, obsessive, or even vexatious. Such litigants are in fact far from common, but a small number of litigants either make very far-fetched claims or repeatedly litigate the same case in as many different ways against all possible parties (and increasingly against all the relevant legal participants, such as the lawyers and the courts). They pose significant resource issues disproportionate to their number and challenge the skills of judges and staff. The **courts** have developed a range of powers to prevent such litigants bringing their cases and stop them harassing their opponents and the officials involved in their cases.

Although 'difficult' or 'vexatious' litigants are rare, unrepresented parties in cases are reasonably common in first instance courts and appeal courts, and they are the norm in small claims hearings. Their lack of legal knowledge and experience poses significant problems for a court system which struggles to adapt to their needs. As a result, many unrepresented parties do not participate in their cases (even where the consequences of non-participation can be severe, such as the loss of their house) and others participate only very transiently. Such parties are typically defendants being sued for housing or other debts. Whilst, from the defendant's perspective, this disengagement may be for rational reasons such as having a weak case or seeking to evade any judgment, disengagement for reasons of fear, inability to secure representation, or as a strategy of avoiding enforcement, weakens the legitimacy of the court process.

Litigants go unrepresented for a number of reasons. A common reason is cost, the litigant being unable or unwilling to pay for a lawyer's services; but other reasons challenge the view that clients would necessarily consider it desirable for a lawyer to represent them. Sometimes respondents are advised to represent themselves (either because the value of the case is less than the lawyer's fees would be, or because the lawyer forms the view that the client's case is a 'waste of time' but thinks that the client should have their day in court if they wish). Some litigants in person think they have a better understanding of the facts and can present cases better than (sometimes junior) lawyers, either because they 'know their case inside out' or because they have significant experience of taking cases through the courts themselves. Sometimes a decision by a commercial organization to self-represent is prompted by a desire that relations with the other side should be re-established quickly after the litigation: lawyers may be perceived as threatening to such attempts to reestablish relations.

Self-representing litigants are not necessarily proceeding without legal advice; but the evidence suggests that the help they do receive is often *ad hoc*: litigants might have lawyer friends whom they would ask about cases, or they may have picked up some help from a **Citizens Advice Bureau** ('CAB'), or perhaps from a brief telephone call or free interview with a solicitor. There is little evidence of systematic, coherent support for such litigants by way, for instance, of lay representation by a non-lawyer who acts as an advocate on the litigant's behalf with the permission of the judge, or of assistance by a so-called 'McKenzie friend'—ie a non-lawyer who advises the litigant quietly during the course of the hearing. Although the case law encourages judges to permit such assistance, judges have different views on when they will permit such representation.

There are a number of factors which point to the vulnerability of self-representing litigants. Usually they face a represented opponent who can be expected to have a greater familiarity with the law, the court, and the best way of dealing with the case. Litigants in person are thus almost always victims of an imbalance of expertise. Such an imbalance can also cause ethical problems for opposing lawyers negotiating with a weak opponent. Unrepresented litigants in family cases often show further levels of vulnerability such as being victims of violence, depression, alcoholism/drug use, or mental illness, or being extremely young parents.

The imbalance in expertise shows itself in other ways. Self-representing litigants are less likely to use the usual tactics and procedures of the court, and are thus likely to fail to exploit their own cases to the maximum. They are less likely to file formal defences; they are more likely to make minor and serious errors in the documents they file; and they are less likely to attend and participate in hearings. The last is a critical problem. Self-represented litigants who fail to attend court hearings can crucially damage their cases. There are two reasons for this: judges do not have relevant and useful facts put before them; and sometimes, judges interpret non-attendance as a lack of respect or an indication of culpability or a weak case. Similarly, complexity, jargon, and lack of time all render courts (and court offices) unsympathetic to litigants in person. All of these factors, alongside the tendency of some litigants in person to have weaker cases, combine so that litigants in person get significantly poorer results than represented litigants.

In summary, litigants in person pose many challenges to court staff who are under pressure to hit administrative targets and lack the training and knowledge to help litigants; to judges who have to adapt traditional styles of judging to a new set of situations; to opponents who have to negotiate with inexpert adversaries; and to the litigants themselves, who struggle with an alien process, alien language and a machinery (usually) being used against them by their opponent.   RICHARD MOORHEAD

R Moorhead and M Sefton , *Litigants in Person: Unrepresented Litigants in First Instance Proceedings* (London: Department of Constitutional Affairs Research Unit, 2005)

See also: **representation, legal**

sell-by date   *see* **food safety**

semiotics and law   Legal semiotics—from the Greek *semeion,* a sign, a trace; even an omen—analyses law's language, power, and effects. The modern study of semiotics developed in linguistics with the work of Ferdinand de Saussure (1857–1913) and, in a remarkable example of parallel intellectual evolution, in the writings of the logician CS Peirce (1839–1914). Each in their own way attempted to examine language not in terms of the meaning of words but the structures—linguistic, mental, and social—which make that meaning possible. A word is an arbitrary sign that points us to a referent; but it has meaning for us only because grammar has given us our assumptions about cause and effect, time and space, subjects and objects; and semantics

has organized sounds for us, allowing us to recognize the difference between 'dog', for example, and 'God'. A word's meaning lies not in its relationship to a 'thing', but rather in its relationship to other words and to the whole system of language through which we think and experience the world. Semiotics is, as Ronald Barthes (1915–1980) put it, 'a science of forms, signification apart from content'; it is the study of how systems of *signs* are organized in particular cultures. Law is one such culture and one might identify four modes of studying it.

(1) Path-breaking work by Bernard Jackson and AJ Greimas reflected this structuralist heritage, analysing the internal coherence of parts to wholes, the taxonomy and organizational relationships which allow law to function. Their project, analytic and descriptive by and large, attempted to understand law as a specialized, distinct, and largely autonomous language. Yet they certainly recognized that the legal system's intricate structure, with its mobile army of binary distinctions (subjects and objects, fact and law, chattel and fixture, civil and criminal, public sphere and private life, making and interpreting law) govern our apprehension of the world.

(2) One trajectory would therefore be to further develop a critique of the social and political implications of legal structure. Peter Goodrich takes just such a turn, rejuvenating the ancient tradition of the study of rhetoric in Aristotle, in Roman law, and in the early common law. Property and rights, for example, come to have very specific meanings in law—property must be exclusive, for example, and rights belong to individuals—that have political effects on what and how things can be talked about in law. Indeed, there are important social effects to legal rhetoric itself: its studied detachment and high level of abstraction; its obsession with hierarchies and the past; its passive voice, obscure Latinisms, and long-winded, opaque, and sometimes incomprehensible reasoning.

(3) An alternative avenue, however, would be to look for law's signs in radically different contexts. A map forms part of a semiotic system too, since it shows us the way; so does a fingerprint that reveals the trace of a burglar, or a lightning bolt that warns us to expect thunder: a trace is a present sign that reminds us of the past, while an omen is a present sign that warns us of the future. These are different kinds of signs, but no less important. Scholars working here (eg Roberta Kevelson, Costas Douzinas and Lynda Nead, and Anne Wagner) have sought to discern the *traces* of law well beyond written and spoken language, on the one hand, and well

outside self-consciously 'legal' documents such as Acts or cases, on the other. This also draws on a long tradition (Alciatus, 1531) of the constitution of symbolic meaning through visual and aesthetic phenomena. Recent work has looked at the architecture of law libraries and law courts; at the interpretation of road signs; at the depiction of law and state in art, monuments, and even in the naming of streets; at the relationship between urban planning and how we construct individuals' relations to each other and their environment. Thus if (as some people believe) our legal order divides the public sphere from the private, naturalizes the nuclear family, and constructs a world populated by autonomous individual actors, then we find in suburban fences, roads, and shopping malls the physical traces of legal structure: and each semiotic system reinforces the other.

(4) Semiotics is not interested in the intention of these signs but their effects; it is as interested in the unconscious representations of law in society as in the conscious productions of formal 'law'. This has even led some (such as Peter Goodrich and Pierre Legendre) from the semiotics to the psychoanalysis of law. In what ways does law's language and metaphors, its concerns and obsessions, its organization and its silences, deliver us not a story about where we come from, but a warning about where we are heading? Now the 'signs of the times' are indeed *omens*; and the semiotician hunting for them resembles a therapist hunting for symptoms. From such an approach we can learn quite a lot, about ourselves and our society, to which conventional analyses of law remain blind. We might even find ways of addressing the problems that law only attempts to repress. But perhaps this is just a dream.

DESMOND MANDERSON

R Kevelson (ed), *Law and Semiotics*, Volumes 1–3 (New York: Plenum, 1987–9)

P Goodrich, *Legal Discourse: Studies in Linguistics, Rhetoric and Legal Analysis* (London: Macmillan and New York: St Martin's Press, 1987)

senior Law Lord The title of senior Law Lord is used to describe the most senior of those holding office as Lords of Appeal in Ordinary under the Appellate Jurisdiction Act 1876. It was not, for about seventy years after 1876, a significant role, since the **Lord Chancellor** ordinarily presided at judicial hearings in the **House of Lords** and the Judicial Committee of the **Privy Council** and the more important administrative decisions (such as composing the bench to hear particular cases) were made by him.

As the significance of the Lord Chancellor's judicial role diminished after 1945, that of the senior Law Lord (an office held by such major figures as Lord **Reid** and Lord Wilberforce) grew. Under changes announced in May 1969 by Lord Gardiner, precedence in presiding (in the absence of the Lord Chancellor) was to depend on date of appointment and not (as before) on previous service as Lord Chancellor or rank in the peerage.

In June 1984 Lord Hailsham of St Marylebone, the Lord Chancellor, announced that in future the senior and second senior Law Lords would be appointed as such by the Queen, on advice, like other senior judges. In practice, a second senior Law Lord was not always appointed, and until 2000 appointment as senior Law Lord always went (save for a three-month period beginning in September 1985) to the next senior serving Law Lord in order of appointment. In 2000 the pattern was broken when Lord Bingham of Cornhill, Lord Chief Justice of England and Wales but not a Lord of Appeal in Ordinary, was appointed to succeed Lord Browne-Wilkinson on his retirement. By this time decisions on such matters as listing and allocation were made by the two senior Law Lords without reference to the Lord Chancellor.

Under the Constitutional Reform Act 2005, the person who, immediately before establishment of the Supreme Court of the UK, is the senior Lord of Appeal in Ordinary will become the President of that Court, and the title of senior Law Lord will cease to be used.

TOM BINGHAM

sentence discount see pleas

sentencing—types of sentence For many people the word '**punishment**' brings to mind images of imprisonment. However, **courts** have a wide range of sentences available to them and the most common form of punishment in the United Kingdom is the **fine** rather than a custodial sentence. Although fines are paid to the state, not to the **victim,** another sentencing option is the **compensation** order, which involves money paid to the victim of a crime or to their family. In many cases a compensation order is made in addition to a fine or some other sentence, but in cases where the defendant has limited financial resources, it may be the only sentence awarded. Financial penalties are not the lowest level of punishment available to a court: in some cases a defendant will be given an absolute discharge, in which case there is no punishment at all following the finding of guilt. Somewhat more serious than this is the conditional discharge, under which the defendant is not immediately punished. However, if he commits a further offence within a specified period, he will be subject to punishment for the original offence as well as the new one.

The sentences described so far do not restrict the offender's liberty in any significant way. A more serious sentencing option is the **community** sentence, which may take one of several forms. The offender may be asked to undertake unpaid work, to undergo drug or alcohol treatment, or attend some other rehabilitative programme, or to undergo supervision by the **probation** service. The offender may also be subject to a **curfew** or be excluded from a certain place. More than one of these requirements may be combined. More serious than a community sentence is imprisonment. The offender may be sentenced to immediate custody, but a suspended sentence of imprisonment is also possible, under which an offender will only be imprisoned if he breaks the terms of a community sentence. A further possibility is intermittent custody, where the period of imprisonment is broken up by periods of release on licence, for example so that an offender can continue in employment while spending weekends in **prison.**

These various sentencing options give courts a fairly wide choice of punishment, but the choice may be restricted in various ways. The lower courts have limited sentencing powers, and many offences have maximum sentences specified by statute, which create a ceiling beyond which courts may not go. Where a defendant has been convicted of murder, the only sentence available is life imprisonment. Where a defendant is convicted of burglary or a serious drugs offence and has two previous convictions for such an offence, **legislation** specifies a mandatory minimum sentence. Apart from such situations, a court will have to choose the exact amount of punishment to inflict. The general principle is that the length of custodial sentence should be proportionate to the seriousness of the offence. The level of a fine should reflect both the seriousness of the offence and the offender's ability to pay.   MIKE REDMAYNE

A Ashworth, *Sentencing and Criminal Justice* (Cambridge: Cambridge University Press, 2005)

separation of powers   The separation of powers is an important principle of liberal constitutionalism. In its classic formulation by Montesquieu in *L'Esprit des Lois* (1748), it asserts that there are three different functions of government, which should be discharged by distinct institutions; the principle requires a separation of *functions* and a separation of *persons* discharging them. The point of the latter is easy to grasp: it would be dangerous for the

legislative and executive powers to be controlled by the same body, for it might enforce its own laws tyrannically. Judicial separation, or independence, from the other powers is crucial; otherwise courts might discriminate when they apply laws—to the advantage of the government and against its opponents. A *pure* separation of powers is observed in France, where ministers may not sit in the National Assembly and the ordinary courts may not interfere with decisions of the executive or declare laws invalid. A different approach has been taken in the United States. Under the *partial* separation principle the three branches of the government—Congress, President, and courts—are controlled by different people, but they participate in the work of the others. For example, the President may veto legislation and the Supreme Court can invalidate unconstitutional legislation. Under this approach the principle provides checks and balances to stop the concentration of power.

Although Montesquieu based his doctrine on the British constitution, the separation of powers has not really been observed in the **United Kingdom**. Indeed, Walter Bagehot, writing in 1867, described the secret of the Constitution as 'the close union, the nearly complete fusion, of the executive and legislative powers'. The government is formed from Members of Parliament, so there is no separation of *persons*; Ministers exercise legislative powers delegated by Parliament, so there is no clear separation of *functions*. (However, the **Crown**, now the government, has not been able to enact general laws without delegation since the *Case of Proclamations* (1611).) The separation principle has not even been strictly followed with regard to judicial power. The **Lord Chancellor**, a member of the **Cabinet** and Speaker of the **House of Lords**, could sit in the Appellate Committee of the House as a judge. Equally, the Law Lords could vote as legislators in the House, although many thought it wrong to do this. On the other hand, a full-time judge could not sit in the **House of Commons**. As a result of the Constitutional Reform Act 2005, the Lord Chancellor is no longer entitled to sit as a judge, while the judges in the new **Supreme Court (UK)** will not be members of the House. The separation of *persons* is, therefore, now observed in the judicial context. But it is unclear whether UK courts would invalidate a law convicting identified people of a particular offence (an 'act of attainder'), though it would certainly infringe the strict separation of legislative and judicial *functions*. Though judges sometimes claim the UK constitution is based on the separation of powers, these remarks should not be taken too seriously.   ERIC BARENDT

MJC Vile, *Constitutionalism and the Separation of Powers* (Indianapolis: Liberty Fund, 2nd edn, 1998)

E Barendt, 'Separation of Powers and Constitutional Government' (1995) *Public Law* 599

Serious Fraud Office   *see* **crime investigation other than by police**

service marks   A service mark is any sign, such as a personal name or logo, used by a business to distinguish its services from those of other businesses. A service mark, such as McDonald's for restaurant services, constitutes a trade mark, except that it identifies and distinguishes the source of a service rather than a product. Traditionally, service marks were protected exclusively by laws regulating **competition** and by the tort of **passing off**. Now, however, the system for registration of **trade marks** has been extended to include marks used in relation to services. The Nice Agreement on the *International Classification of Goods and Services for the Purposes of the Registration of Marks* (1957 as revised) has been amended to include numerous classes of services, including online advertising and retail services. It is also possible to register collective and certification service marks. The former distinguish services held by members of an Association; the latter certify that services meet specific standards of quality. Only those service marks that are distinctive, that is capable of acting as indicators of origin, are eligible for registration. Once issued, registration is valid for ten years, then renewable for further periods of ten years indefinitely, provided the trade mark remains in use. Registration by means of either a national or a community trade mark confers the exclusive right to prevent unauthorized third parties from marketing identical or similar services under an identical or a confusingly similar mark.   GAIL EVANS

service of documents   'Service' is defined in the **Civil Procedure Rules** 1998 ('CPR') to mean 'Steps required by rules of court to bring documents used in court proceedings to a person's attention'.

CPR Part 6 provides that all parties are required to provide an address for service, including a full postcode, within the jurisdiction (England and Wales) being either their residence or business address, or the address of their solicitor. Service, personal and otherwise, must be made to a party's solicitor who provides written notification of authorization to accept service. The court can employ alternative methods of service, and can dispense with service. There are special rules for service outside the jurisdiction, and for the service of foreign process within the jurisdiction.

Service of a document can be made (a) by leaving it with an individual party or with a senior person in a company, in which case service is deemed to occur on that day, or on the next business day if left after 5pm ('personal service'); (b) by first class post to an address for service, in which case service is deemed to occur on the second day after it was posted; (c) by leaving the document at an address for service, in which case service is deemed to occur on the day after it was left; (d) through a document exchange, in which case service is deemed to occur on the second day after it was left at the document exchange; or (e) by fax, in which case service is deemed to occur on the day it was transmitted if before 4pm, and on the next business day if transmitted later in the day; or other means of electronic communication, in which case service is deemed to occur on the second day after the day on which it is transmitted.

JOHN FITZPATRICK

services of general economic interest   The services represented by this phrase may include telecommunications and postal services, the supply of water, electricity, and gas. These are economic services that every citizen is entitled to receive on a regular basis at reasonable prices. Public services that are not provided on commercial terms (eg policing) are not included. The phrase has its origins in Article 86(2) of the EC Treaty. This Article was inserted to accommodate the interests of some Member States (eg France) whose constitutional traditions provide that the state has a duty to provide, or ensure the provision of, public services. Article 86(2) provides that a Member State's obligations under the EC Treaty (eg to develop competitive markets and to allow the free movement of goods and services) can be suspended when these would obstruct the provision of services of general economic interest. In **European Community law**, the significance of this derogation has grown as more economic sectors have been liberalized with the risk that the provision, of services of general economic interest to vulnerable groups, may be eroded. The **European Court of Justice** has relaxed its interpretation of Article 86(2) to make it easier for Member States to justify restrictions of **competition**. Article 16 was added to the EC Treaty in 1997, imposing a shared obligation on the Community and Member States to safeguard the provision of these services.

In the UK similar rules apply under the Competition Act 1998. The Act provides that its two prohibitions (forbidding anti-competitive agreements and abuse of a dominant position) do not apply if two conditions are met: first if firms have been entrusted with a service of general economic interest (by central or local government); and secondly, if the competition rules would obstruct the delivery of the services in question. For instance, a local authority that licenses three bus companies and demands that each company offer regular, affordable services to remote towns, has entrusted the three bus operators with a service of general economic interest. The three might agree to divide the bus routes to remote towns among themselves to discharge their duties. This agreement restricts competition (as there is only one bus provider for each remote route) but the bus companies may argue that the agreement is necessary for them to discharge their obligations given the high costs of each providing services on all three routes. The **Office of Fair Trading** has indicated that services of general economic interest are best protected by effective competition, and in the light of the extent of deregulation and liberalization of UK industries, it is unlikely that it will accept pleas to exclude the application of **competition law**: public services are provided effectively through competitive markets. Accordingly, it would prefer to see the three firms compete along all routes, thereby driving prices down. The market ethos of UK competition authorities is in contrast with the position in other Member States that see competition as likely to harm the provision of these services.   GIORGIO MONTI

settlement of claims A small fraction of legal claims lead to formal legal proceedings, and a small fraction of claims involving legal proceedings result in a decision by a judge or tribunal. Most claims are settled by negotiation between the parties, either with or without legal representation. In claims involving injuries to persons or property, an insurer usually negotiates on behalf of the party alleged to be responsible for the injury.

Settlement of claims can involve both monetary and non-monetary elements. The analysis of settlement depends on whether the claim can be considered entirely monetary or involves non-monetary elements.

When a claim is exclusively monetary, the best understanding of the process involves the consideration of a set of economic elements: the likely value of the claim as determined by a successful trial, the likelihood of claimant success at a trial, the costs of trial, and the parties' risk preferences. Central to this analysis is the 'expected value' of a claim, which is equal to the product of the value of the claim at trial and the likelihood of success at trial. For example, a

claim that would yield £10,000 at trial with a probability of success of 0.7 has an expected value of £7,000. If two risk-neutral parties agreed on the value and the likelihood of success, and if there was no cost associated with going to trial, the parties would be expected to settle for £7,000.

Of course, going to trial does impose costs, and this modifies the calculation above. Under the traditional English system of costs, the plaintiff would expect to recover a significant portion of her costs if she wins at trial, and to have to pay her own costs plus a significant portion of the other side's costs if she loses. The same applies to the defendant. The calculations involved should tend to lower the claimant's valuation and raise the defendant's valuation. The result, assuming the two sides agree about what would be the value of the award at a successful trial and about the probability of the claimant winning at trial, will be that the defendant should be willing to pay more than the minimum the claimant is willing to accept; that is, rather than there being a settlement *point* there is a settlement *zone*.

A further complication in this analysis is that some parties will be risk averse and some will be risk neutral. As noted by Marc Galanter ('Why the "Haves" Come Out Ahead: Speculations on the Limits of Legal Change' (1974) 9 *Law & Society Review* 95), 'one shot players' are likely to be risk averse, meaning that they will be willing to accept a discount at settlement to avoid the risk of losing at trial. In contrast, 'repeat players' tend to be risk neutral in that they are more interested in what happens over the long run than in what happens in a single case. Of course, in practice, even repeat players may be risk averse at times, either due to the amount at stake or because of concerns beyond the instant case (such as reputation, precedent and so on).

The combination of costs and differences in risk preferences results in situations where there is a settlement zone even if the claimant is substantially more optimistic than the defendant (in the sense of thinking that a trial will yield a larger award and/or that success at trial is more likely).

Changes in recent years have substantially modified some elements of the settlement of monetary claims in England. The introduction of conditional fees (whereby a solicitor agrees to a no-win, no-pay fee arrangement in exchange for an increased fee if a recovery is obtained), after-the-event insurance (which protects the plaintiff from the risk of having to pay the defendant's costs in the event of losing at trial), the recoverability of the higher conditional fee and the after-the-event insurance premium from the defendant, and the prominent role played by claims companies (which solicit cases through advertising and either settle them directly or refer them to solicitors) together change the specifics of the calculations outlined above. While claimants are still likely to be risk averse, they no longer have to worry about having to pay either their lawyer or the opposing side's costs if the case is a loser. Defendants now have to pay higher costs and this increases the value of the claim. Moreover, defendants in the form of insurance companies have raised significant challenges concerning what is reasonable for them to pay in after-the-event insurance premiums and success fees. All of this has left the contemporary situation in a great deal of flux.

A further element in the English system is what is historically known as 'payment into court'. This is a mechanism whereby a defendant can make a formalized settlement offer (and deposit the settlement with the court). The effect of this is to shift some additional risk onto the claimant because if the claimant declines the offer and then fails to achieve a better result at trial, the claimant cannot recover costs incurred after the date of the offer and the defendant is entitled to recover its costs from the claimant. Under the same rules that allow for payment into court, the claimant can also make a formal offer to settle; if the defendant declines the offer and the claimant does better at trial than the offer, the claimant is entitled to greater than the usual costs.

Claims involving some significant non-monetary elements create opportunities for settlement that go beyond the economic calculations described above. Specifically, one side or the other may be willing to give up something in terms of money to achieve other goals. Moreover, what is offered in terms of non-monetary elements can be highly creative even when they involve real monetary costs. For example, in a consumer complaint, the defendant might offer to replace the defective product with a more expensive item; the claimant would look at this in terms of the retail cost while the defendant would see it in terms of its marginal wholesale cost.

HERBERT M KRITZER

P Fenn and N Rickman, 'Four Offers and a Trial: The Economics of Out-of-Court Settlement,' in K Hawkins (ed), *The Human Face of Law: Essays in Honour of Donald Harris* (Oxford: Clarendon Press, 1995)

H Genn, *Hard Bargaining: Out of Court Settlement in Personal Injury Actions* (Oxford: Oxford University Press, 1988)

sex This entry uses a glossary, or lexicon, of law on sex: in total, it provides four sub-entries on 'sex'.

To discriminate based on 'sex'

Today this form of discrimination is often (though not always) unlawful. However, it took until well into the twentieth century before law was used in any consistent way to promote and protect **equality** between **women** and men. Indeed, prior to that point, women—especially married women—were legally subordinate to men in a whole range of ways.

Law's shift from explicit subordination of women to promotion of equality can be divided into stages. In the first stage, a range of formal legal barriers were removed, including the exclusion of married women from **property rights** and rights over their children, and the exclusion of all women from the suffrage. In the second stage, discrimination on the grounds of sex in employment, education, and services was made unlawful. The third and most recent stage introduced a positive duty to promote equality, thereby supplementing the stage two prohibition on discrimination.

The courts have had to address the meaning of 'to discriminate based on sex'. So, for example, they have been asked: does the prohibition on sex discrimination cover discrimination against *transsexuals*? Their answer: 'yes'. They were also asked: does pregnancy fall within the scope of sex discrimination law? This may seem an odd question. Its origins can be traced to the argument that equality mandates treating likes alike. But a pregnant woman is not 'like' a man: there is no male **comparator** and no issue of consistency or similar treatment. One way around this would be to use an indirect comparator, comparing the treatment received by pregnant woman with that of a man who is ill. This approach was used at one point by the courts. Thereafter, however, they moved beyond the idea of equality as consistency and thus beyond the need for a male comparator, acknowledging that discrimination on the grounds of pregnancy does fall within the prohibition on sex discrimination precisely because it is a sex-specific condition for which there is no male equivalent.

To 'sex'

At the point of birth, the question 'Is it a girl or a boy?' is commonplace. But what if the wrong answer is given? What happens if, upon reaching adulthood, an individual requests a change to the sex (male/female) that appears on their birth certificate? Putting it another way: are transsexuals recognized by the law? The answer is yes. Two examples: **legislation** allows for female to male transsexuals to be recognized as fathers in some circumstances, and the law of **rape** provides that surgically reconstructed penises can penetrate and surgically reconstructed vaginas can be penetrated.

'To sex' has a different meaning within feminist legal scholarship, namely 'to sex the law' or, more narrowly, 'to sex the **subject** of law'. For the most part, though, feminist legal scholars—including many who describe their work as being about *sexing* the law—have been more concerned with **gender** and less with sex. In other words, as in feminist scholarship more generally, sex has tended to be seen as a matter of biology and gender as a set of socially defined characteristics, and the primary focus has been on showing how gender is not bound to biology but is a product of social structures, including law and legal practice. One consequence of this is that, until recently, there was little discussion of the extent to which beliefs about gender may also be fundamental to what we tend to think of as 'natural' facts concerning sex or biological difference.

To reproduce/procreate

Sex can be reproductive or non-reproductive, and reproduction can be assisted or natural. Medically assisted reproduction is heavily regulated by law. There are, for example, rules on access to treatment, **gamete donation**, the creation, use, and storage of embryos, and the storage and use of gametes (sperm and ova), and the parentage of **children**. These rules also include a range of absolute prohibitions, including a ban on human **reproductive cloning**. Using a surrogate to assist reproduction is also regulated by law.

To commit a 'sexual' offence

The law relating to sexual offences was the subject of an extensive overhaul in 2003. The new statute—the Sexual Offences Act 2003—aims to rid the law of the incoherence that had built up as a result of development via incremental change. In addition, it aims to update the law on sexual offences so that it reflects contemporary attitudes and practices. Priority is given to removing discriminatory elements of the previous law and also to providing adequate protection for the vulnerable. Another notable feature of the new law is its use of language. So, for example, the statute emphasizes the need for proof of 'sexual' activity, rather than proof of 'indecent' activity. It also creates offences based on 'touching'; under the old law, the emphasis centred on acts involving 'assault'. Finally, the new Act endorses gender-neutrality by framing more laws so that offenders and **victims** can be of either sex. The offence of rape is an exception to this trend: it is a sexual offence that only men can commit (but whose victim can be male or female). Complete gender-neutrality was rejected on the grounds that the offence needed to resonate with the general public understanding of 'rape' as an act involving penile penetration.   THERESE MURPHY

sex discrimination   *see* **protected grounds**

sex education   *see* **secular curriculum in schools**

sex offenders, treatment of   The applicability and efficacy of the treatment of sex offenders has become a focus of government, professional, and public attention in recent decades. Amongst both professionals and the public, views on the treatment of sex offenders range widely, encompassing the 'nothing works' view at one extreme as well as a variety of more positive if cautious perspectives on treatment. The diversity of these views is connected to the conceptual binary—prisoner/patient, evil/ill—on which sex offenders are positioned. The effect of this binary is that the boundary between treatment and containment or management of sex offenders has become blurred. Whether treated in institutional or **community** settings, sex offenders may be engaged in one of a range of psychological and/or pharmacological treatment programmes, which focus on both managing and treating sex offenders. These programmes may involve individual counselling, group therapy and, if an offender is being treated in the community, a residential programme. In recent years, cognitive-behavioural treatment, which aims to modify patterns of thinking and reduce the likelihood of **recidivism**, has risen to prominence as a therapeutic paradigm. Positive results have been recorded in a number of studies, although the utility of this type of treatment remains contested. Since the passage of the Sexual Offenders Act 1997, individuals living in the community who have been convicted of or cautioned in relation to certain sex offences have been required to register their name and current address with the police. The length of time for which a registration requirement exists varies but it is a lifelong requirement for any individual who received a custodial sentence of thirty months or longer.   ARLIE LOUGHNAN

sex selection   There are a variety of different ways in which parents might try to control the **sex** of their offspring. First, there are a number of ineffectual folk remedies, such as having sex at a particular time during the woman's menstrual cycle, or in a particular position. Secondly, preconception sex selection might be accomplished by sperm sorting, which involves separating X and Y sperm, and artificially inseminating the **woman** with the separated sperm. Sperm sorting is not always successful, but it does significantly increase the chance of getting a **child** of the desired sex. Thirdly, and more successful, is pre-implantation sex selection, using **pre-implantation genetic diagnosis** ('PGD'). Fourthly, women can undergo prenatal sex diagnosis during pregnancy, and abort the **foetus** if it is the 'wrong' sex. This would be lawful only if it could be established that the pregnant woman's mental or physical health was endangered by carrying the pregnancy to term. It seems unlikely that a doctor would knowingly authorize an **abortion** requested purely on the grounds of the foetus's sex, but it is of course possible that a woman might discover her foetus's sex, and be prompted to seek an abortion ostensibly for other reasons. Finally, **infanticide** has been used in the past in some countries when a woman gives birth to a child of the 'wrong' sex.

In the UK, pre-implantation sex selection is lawful only if it is carried out in order to prevent the transfer of male embryos where there is a risk that the parents will pass on an X-linked disease, such as haemophilia or muscular dystrophy. The Human Fertilization and Embryology Authority ('HFEA') carried out a public consultation on the question of sex selection in 2003, and found overwhelming public hostility to the prospect of sex selection for social reasons. When it acquired power to regulate sperm sorting as a result of the incorporation of an EU Directive, the HFEA decided that it should not be allowed for social reasons, for consistency's sake, and that it is not effective enough to be used for medical reasons. In reforming the Human Fertilization and Embryology Act 1990, the government have continued this prohibition on non-medical uses of sperm sorting and PGD.

So what are the arguments against allowing sex selection for social reasons? First, it is argued that sex selection embodies a consumerist attitude towards children. Instead of welcoming a child regardless of its **gender**, would-be parents who want to choose their child's sex are accused of seeking to ensure that their new baby meets their specifications. Secondly, it is thought that the use of sex selection for social reasons is sexist and discriminatory. Of course, a couple with four sons are not necessarily guilty of discriminating against boys when they hope that their next child will be a girl. But it is sometimes argued that even this sort of preference depends upon sexist preconceptions about a child's gender-specific behaviour. A couple with four boys only want a girl, some would argue, because they think that she will be different from their sons.

The principal argument in favour of allowing sex selection for social reasons is the protection of reproductive liberty. In the absence of demonstrable harm to others, the default position in a liberal **democracy** should be freedom of choice. Some would argue that it is not the purpose of law to translate disapproval of a person's idiosyncratic preferences into prohibition.

A different argument in favour of *limited* access to sex selection for social reasons is that it facilitates 'family balancing'. On this view, where there is an uneven number of children of each sex in a family, sex selection might be legitimate. Although it is undoubtedly true that many parents do hope to have children of both sexes, it is not absolutely clear why the preference for one son and one daughter should be any more deserving of respect than a preference for two daughters.   EMILY JACKSON

sexual abuse, civil liability for see abuse, **civil liability for**

sexual harassment   According to the 1988 *General Survey* of the ILO's Committee of Experts sexual harassment can take the form of:

'insults, remarks, jokes, insinuations and inappropriate comments on a person's dress, physique, age, family situation, and a condescending or paternalistic attitude undermining dignity, unwelcome invitations or requests that are implicit or explicit whether or not accompanied by threats, lascivious looks or other gestures associated with sexuality, unnecessary physical contact such as touching, caresses, pinching or assault.'

Sexual **harassment** may serve to maintain the homogeneity of male jobs or workplaces by discouraging 'outsiders' from entry. It is no coincidence that sexual harassment tends to be particularly prevalent in traditionally male sectors such as fire-fighting, **police** jobs, the military, etc where the entrance of women into very masculinized environments can be seen as a threat to cohesion and morale.

Sexual harassment has been regarded as a species of discrimination and as actionable as such, for almost thirty years in the United States, at least half that long in parts of the European Union. The term 'sexual harassment' was coined in the United States in the 1960s. The phenomenon was generally considered at this time to be connected with questions of sexual attraction and pursuit, but feminists argued that sexual harassment was about power rather than about sex; activists/theorists, including Catherine MacKinnon and Susan Brownmiller, categorizing sexual harassment as a species of **sex** discrimination which operated to keep women in their traditional place, rather than of 'normal', if misguided, male-female interactions. In 1975, sexual harassment did not feature in most analyses of women at work. However, sexual harassment had begun even then to be challenged in the US by feminists and, in the 1970s, racial harassment was recognized by the US courts as a form of unlawful discrimination.

Because 'discrimination' is frequently regarded as a relative concept (that is, one which requires some form of comparison to establish *less favourable treatment* on grounds of sex or **race**, etc), the regulation of sexual harassment as a form of discrimination has resulted in gaps in legal protection where (for example) the harasser claims that he would have subjected a man to the same unwanted sexual advances to which the woman complainant was subjected. In the UK, discrimination law only protected against harassment when the claimant established that harassing behaviour was either motivated by his or her sex, or was qualitatively different and less favourable than the type of treatment to which a person of the other sex would have received. In *Strathclyde Regional Council v Porcelli* (1986), which was for many years the leading case on harassment, Scotland's **appeal** court recognized that sexual harassment could amount to sex discrimination contrary to the Sex Discrimination Act even where there was no 'sex-related motive or objective' to the objectionable treatment, where the harassers used 'a particular kind of weapon, based upon the sex of the victim [there an indecent assault] which ... would not have been used against an equally disliked man'. In *Pearce v Governing Body of Mayfield School* (2003), however, the **House of Lords** suggested that the decision in *Porcelli* was wrong and that even a sexual assault on a woman would not necessarily amount to actionable sex discrimination in the absence of evidence that the treatment was less favourable than that to which a man was or would have been subjected.

The fit between **direct discrimination** defined as 'less favourable treatment' and 'harassment' was never complete, but discrimination law was used in an attempt to provide a **remedy** for behaviour which would frequently have otherwise gone unchecked in the absence of explicit regulation of sexual harassment. More recently, the amendment of the Sex Discrimination Act 1975 in 2005 has the effect that sexual harassment is regulated regardless of any comparison. Thus the Act now prohibits unwanted conduct which is *either* 'on the ground of' the complainant's sex or which is 'verbal, non-verbal or physical conduct of a sexual nature', where that conduct 'has the purpose or effect of violating [the complainant's] dignity, or of creating an intimidating, hostile, degrading, humiliating or offensive environment for her'. (It goes on to state that 'conduct shall be regarded as having the effect [of violating the complainant's dignity, or of creating an intimidating, hostile, degrading, humiliating, or offensive environment for her] only if, having regard to all the circumstances, including in particular the perception of the woman, it should reasonably be considered as having that effect'.)

Unwanted conduct which violates dignity or creates an 'intimidating, hostile, degrading, humiliating or offensive environment' is generally referred to as 'hostile environment' sexual harassment. Such sexual harassment might be explicitly sexual or not: it could, for example, consist simply in bad treatment of an apparently sex-neutral variety which is in fact motivated by hostility towards persons of the claimant's sex, or (more commonly) to persons of that sex in the particular job or workplace. So, for example, women who enter very predominantly male jobs as police officers or fire-fighters frequently find themselves subject not only to explicit sexual taunting, sexual overtures, and, not infrequently, sexual assault; but also to non-'sexual' bullying, physical abuse and, for example, being undermined by persistently being required to engage in trivial, low status, or particularly demanding tasks.

The Sex Discrimination Act also prohibits the less favourable treatment of a sexually harassed person 'on the ground of her rejection of or submission to unwanted conduct' of one of the varieties outlined. This form of sexual harassment is generally referred to as *quid pro quo* sexual harassment which will almost invariably be of a sexual nature, concerned as it is with sexual contact as a job condition.

AILEEN MCCOLGAN

See also: **comparators**

sexual orientation discrimination   *see* **protected grounds**

shaming and stigmatization of offenders   The concepts of shaming and stigmatization play a prominent role in thinking about how society should respond to crime. At the core of these concepts is the notion that an offence is not just the breaking of a rule but is also abhorrent because it violates moral standards. Having been convicted, the offender suffers the social stigma of being disgraced, a status that is imposed or reinforced to varying degrees by society or its institutions through expressions of social disapproval.

Attitudes towards the stigmatization of offenders have varied over time and are still the subject of ongoing debate. In some historical periods, particularly the seventeenth and eighteenth centuries, extreme forms of stigmatization often characterized punishments handed down by courts in various European countries. Practices such as branding of prisoners, public forms of punishment such as the stocks and pillory, public torture, and execution, were widely used as degradation ceremonies. Punishment was constituted in part by these public forms of shaming, that were designed to humiliate offenders, to mark them as offenders (sometimes physically), and outcast them from society. From the late eighteenth century acceptance of such punishments diminished to the extent that states actively sought to protect offenders from unnecessary public exposure. Explicit shaming of crimes was largely replaced by sentencing regimes that sought to emphasize unemotional and rational punishment.

This is not to say that stigmatization is absent in contemporary criminal justice, as it still represents one justification for punishment: a function of sentencing can be to denounce the offence and reaffirm the values that have been violated. Moreover, denunciation of an offender may be expressed through the court process, publication of convictions, and the recording of criminal records. Labelling theorists have drawn attention to the fact that conviction and punishment mark offenders as deviant, whether or not explicit forms of shaming occur. They argue that the social and psychological effects of explicit, or even implicit, shaming are counterproductive because labelling an individual as deviant undermines the potential for their reintegration. While this perspective has influenced some criminal justice practices, it is not universally accepted, and 'shaming penalties', such as carrying placards that announce one's crimes, have been used by courts in some parts of the world (eg United States).

In the discussion so far shaming and stigmatization are understood as social processes that are strongly coupled: shaming is a social process that leaves offenders with a stigma. Reintegrative shaming theory has recently challenged this assumption by pointing to circumstances, such as discipline in families, where disapproval or denunciation of an act can occur without labelling or outcasting of the person. Applying this to criminal justice, the theory argues that reintegrative shaming reduces offending though its moralizing qualities and the emotion of shame, without suffering from the disadvantages of stigmatization. The recent advent of **restorative justice** as an alternative to traditional forms of criminal justice can be seen as a application of this ideal.

NATHAN HARRIS

J Braithwaite, *Crime, Shame and Reintegration* (Cambridge: Cambridge University Press, 1989)

N Walker, *Punishment, Danger and Stigma: The Morality of Criminal Justice* (Oxford: Basil Blackwell, 1980)

See also: **punishment, history of**

shareholder democracy and voting   There are three central questions that must be answered to understand any regime of shareholder **democracy**

and voting: first, who can vote; secondly, how much voting power do those shareholders who are entitled to vote have; and thirdly, how do they vote? UK **company** law provides considerable flexibility to adjust these arrangements to company circumstances.

Typically the ordinary **shares** of a company will entitle the shareholder to a residual economic interest in the company equating to one vote per share. However, it is possible to issue shares with no votes at all or with multiple votes for each share. Companies may issue different classes of share with different voting rights attached to shares. In some instances this allows shareholders who have a minority economic interest in a company to have voting control of the company.

At a shareholder meeting, shareholders may exercise their votes in person or by proxy. A shareholder who is unable to attend a meeting may vote by appointing a proxy who may vote that shareholder's shares on her behalf at the meeting. At the meeting, the votes may be cast by poll or by a show of hands. Where there is a show of hands vote it means that, as each person only has one voting hand, no matter how many shares she holds she only has one vote. Accordingly, a show of hands vote is only likely to used where the issue in question is non-contentious. On a poll each shareholder may exercise the number of votes attached to her shares.

At the meeting, different issues on which the shareholders vote will require different majorities depending on the nature of the issue. The two most common majorities are simple majority (ordinary resolution) and 75 per cent majority (special resolution) of those voting *at the meeting*.

DAVID KERSHAW

shareholder meetings   Shareholders typically exercise their voting power at a meeting of the shareholders known as a *general meeting*. In private companies the constitution may, however, provide for the **company** to vote by written resolution. There are two types of general meeting, an Annual General Meeting ('AGM') and interim meetings between consecutive AGMs, known as extraordinary general meetings ('EGM').

An AGM, as the label suggests, must be held at least once a calendar year (see the Companies Act 2006 in relation to AGMs of **public companies**). It will address several important annually recurring governance matters for any company. This includes, for example, the appointment of directors and auditors, the approval of accounts for the previous financial year, the approval of any dividend recommended by the directors, and approval of the directors' remuneration report. The meeting may also address non-recurring matters, for example, amending the company's constitutional documents or granting authority to issue additional shares.

Under the Companies Act 1985 **private companies** could elect not to hold AGMs if all the shareholders entitled to vote agreed to waive this requirement. Under the new Companies Act 2006 private companies are not required to hold an AGM, although their constitution may provide that they must do so.

Companies may require shareholders to consider a particular issue or make a decision more than once a year and shareholders themselves may wish to meet and take action if they are concerned or unhappy about the way the company is being run. Accordingly, it must be possible, but it is not necessary, to have a shareholder meeting more than once a year. Currently, the articles of most companies provide directors with the power to call an EGM. The 2006 Act gives statutory effect to this power. With regard to the shareholders, the Companies Acts of both 1985 and 2006 provide that regardless of what the articles say a shareholder or shareholders holding 10 per cent of the voting shares may require the board of directors to call an EGM. If the directors fail to convene the requested meeting, the shareholders can convene a meeting and will be reimbursed by the company for their reasonable costs.   DAVID KERSHAW

See also: **shareholder power**

shareholder power   To understand the distribution of power between the managers of the **company**, the **board of directors** of the company, and the shareholder body, one must distinguish between the formal distribution of power and the reality of the distribution of power in practice.

In UK company law, the formal source of the power of the company's board of directors and its management is the shareholder body. The shareholder body can determine what powers the board may exercise and when it must ask the shareholders for their approval. The extent to which shareholders transfer power to the board of directors and enable the board to transfer power to senior management such as a Chief Executive Officer ('CEO') will be set forth in provisions of the company's **articles of association**. Currently Article 70 of Table A Articles provides that 'the business of the company shall be managed by the **directors** who may exercise all the powers of the company'. However, this transfer of authority is made subject any other provisions set forth in the articles and subject to any instruction given by the shareholders provided that 75 per cent of

the shareholders who vote at the shareholder meeting vote in favour of the instruction. Remember, however, that this article in Table A may be amended as the original shareholders of a company so chose or as the shareholders (by a 75 per cent majority) agree at a later date. For example, the article transferring power could reserve a right to instruct the board to take action by a simple majority or reserve certain powers to the shareholders, for example, the power to enter into contracts worth an amount above a specified value. If the company is a listed company then the Listing Rules issued by the UK's Listing Authority will require certain major decisions to be subject to shareholder approval regardless of what the articles provide (**Listing** Rule 10).

In addition to the distribution of power which we find in the company's constitution, of central importance to the formal distribution of power between the board and the shareholder body is the law regulating the **appointment and removal of the directors**. The Companies Acts of 1985 and 2006 have little to say about appointment which is typically dealt with in the company's constitution. Table A provides for the retirement and appointment of a third of the board each year. However, more importantly, the Companies Act of 1985 and 2006 provide that directors may be removed from office at any time and without the need to provide any reason to remove a director if a simple majority of the shareholders voting at a **shareholder meeting** vote in favour of removal (section 168 of the Companies Act 2006). The provision cannot be amended by any provision in the company's constitution. This means that should the shareholders become dissatisfied with the performance of the board they can vote to remove them. This provision above all ensures that the *formal* balance of power in a company is with the shareholder body. Of course, in order to be able to vote to remove them, the shareholders need to pass a resolution to that effect. English company law ensures that shareholders can act to remove the board by providing rights to force the board of directors to call a meeting.

This formal balance of power in favour of the shareholder body may not, depending on the type of company, be mirrored in practice. In small **private companies** where there only a handful of shareholders it will relatively straightforward for a small group of shareholders to coordinate to exercise their authority where they are unhappy with the board of directors. In large listed **public companies** whose shares are held by many hundreds if not thousands of shareholders, who each own only a very small percentage of the shares in the company, it may not be in the economic interests of these shareholders to invest their time and money in monitoring the company's activities to determine whether the board is doing a good job, and then to attempt to coordinate enough shareholders to be able to exercise shareholder power. With only a small percentage shareholding, the costs of monitoring and coordinating shareholders is likely to exceed the fractional return that a shareholder will benefit from as a result of monitoring and acting. For these types of companies although the shareholders formally have the balance of power, in practice power is rarely exercised.

In recent years, large amounts of UK listed company shares have come to be held by what are called institutional shareholders, for example, **pension** funds and insurance companies. Although these investors typically hold low single digit **shares** in listed companies it is easier to coordinate the activity of several of these shareholders. For some observers of company law, this development holds out the hope that, in practice, even in large companies the shareholder body can exercise or at least threaten to exercise its formal power and hold the board of directors and management more accountable.

DAVID KERSHAW

See also: **shareholder democracy and voting**

shareholder risks and residual claims The term 'shareholder' refers to a person holding a defined **share** in the capital of a **company**. Capital is paid into companies by shareholders for an indefinite period, in the sense that there is no date for repayment because a company has an indefinite lifespan. Nor is any return guaranteed to shareholders on their capital. Company law restricts but does not entirely prohibit the subsequent return of capital to the shareholders. The most obvious risk for shareholders is loss or erosion of their capital as a result of a company recording trading losses. That risk may arise from general economic conditions or circumstances specific to the business or company. A second risk is that a shareholder may find that a company is not run in the way that she wishes, because companies make decisions according to the principle of majority rule. A third risk is that a shareholder may become 'locked in' to a company. While transfer of shares to another person provides shareholders in principle with a mechanism to withdraw from a company, it may not be possible to do that if a buyer cannot be found. A counterbalance to risk is the power given to shareholders to control a company through voting on resolutions at company meetings. If a company becomes insolvent all the creditors must be paid before any remaining capital (the residue) can be returned to members. In that sense, the shareholders have a residual claim to what remains when a company is wound up.

IAIN MACNEIL

shares A share in a **company** is an item of personal property (Companies Act 1985, section 182, continued by Companies Act 2006, section 541). While statute defines a share as personal property, it does not define what rights are conferred by the share. That is because the rights conferred by a share in a company are essentially defined by the company's constitution (or by subordinate documentation made under the authority of the company's constitution, such as a resolution of the company's board). These rights are supplemented and modified by various provisions of law. So, statute defines the status of a share as property for the purposes of other rules of law, such as those which concern dealings with property; but the company's own constitution is the key to defining what the contents of that **property right** actually are. Thus, shares are in principle transferable, as objects of property usually are, but that general principle is subject to modification by the company's constitution (Companies Act 1985, section 182(1)(b), continued by Companies Act 2006, section 544(1)).

The company's constitution (its **memorandum and articles of association**) operates as a contract between the members of the company and the company (Companies Act 1985, section 14, continued by Companies Act 2006, section 33). Acquisition of a share will entitle the shareholder to be placed on the register of members (Companies Act 1985, section 22, continued by Companies Act 2006, section 112) and thus to become party to the company's constitution, and to the rights and obligations contained in it.

Thus, a share is a participatory interest in a company. That means the holder of the share will have the rights to vote, and to receive dividends and distributions of capital, in accordance with the constitution of the company. Those rights may vary from company to company, and may even be abrogated entirely. For example, it is possible to create voting or non-voting shares; shares which carry fixed, or variable, or even no rights to **dividends,** or no rights to capital. So far as the company's constitution does not make provision, there are various default rights attached to shares: for example, the right to vote (Companies Act 1985, section 370, continued by Companies Act 2006, section 284) and the right to equality of treatment as to dividends and return of capital (*Birch v Cropper* (1889)).

A company's constitution may divide its share capital up into different classes with different rights. This may be done when the company is first created, through its constitution, or it may be done afterwards (Companies Act 1985, section 121, continued by Companies Act 2006, section 617). If there are different classes of share, the rights of the class can only be varied if the class consents (Companies Act 1985, Part V Chapter II, continued by Companies Act 2006, Part 17 Chapter 9).

As a participatory interest in the company itself, a share does not confer any proprietary right to the underlying fund of assets which in law are said to be the company's property. Of course, a share may entitle its holder to receive property from the company under certain circumstances, whether by way of dividend, return of capital, or when the company is wound up.

Shares must be issued for a fixed nominal value (Companies Act 1985, section 2(5), continued by Companies Act 2006, section 542) and may be issued for a premium beyond that. The holder of a share must pay these sums, but if the liability of the company's members is stated to be limited (which it almost universally is), then the shareholder is not liable to contribute any further to the company in respect of his shares (Insolvency Act 1986, section 74(2)(d)). So, as well as creating an interest in a company, a share defines the extent of the shareholder's liability in respect of the company's debts.

In summary, a share is (a) a species of intangible personal property in its own right, which may be dealt with as such, save as restricted by its own particular terms; (b) a measure of the holder's interest in the company as an association and the basis of his right to become a member and enjoy the advantages of membership; and (c) a fraction of capital, denoting and defining the holder's proportionate financial stake in the company (see *Borland's Trustee v. Steel Bros & Co Ltd* (1901)).   R C NOLAN

sharia law   *see* **islamic; law personal laws**

ship-money case   *see Bate's case*; **Hampden, John**

shipping law   *see* **admiralty law**

ships   There is no generally applicable definition of what constitutes a 'ship' in **international law** or domestic law. In the Merchant Shipping Act 1995 (UK) '"ship" includes every description of vessel used in navigation'. Previously, the Merchant Shipping Act 1894 (UK) had excluded vessels 'propelled by oars' from the definition of 'ship'. The terms 'ship' and 'vessel' are often used interchangeably and their precise meaning will depend on the circumstances and context of the particular case. Courts have found the term 'ship' to include rowing boats, rafts, floating storage units, and even personal water crafts such as jet skis, water scooters, and surfboards.

Every state and some international organizations have the right to sail ships under their flag on the high seas. Each state must fix the conditions for the grant of its nationality to ships, for the registration of ships in its territory, and for the right to fly its flag. Ships have the nationality of the state whose flag they are entitled to fly. There must exist a genuine link between the state and the ship; in particular, the state must effectively exercise its jurisdiction and control in administrative, technical, and social matters over ships flying its flag. Ships which sail under the flags of two or more states may not claim any of the nationalities in question and may be treated as a ship without nationality which may be boarded by any warship outside the territorial jurisdiction of any state.   STEFAN TALMON

H Meijers, *The Nationality of Ships* (The Hague: Martinus Nijhoff, 1967)

show trials   The term 'show trial' denotes criminal prosecutions, often involving allegations of treason, in which the guilt of the accused has been predetermined and the possibility of acquittal does not exist. In their public character, show trials differ from other instances of legal proceedings rigged by the state. In regimes of both an authoritarian and democratic character, travesties of justice may be conducted in secret, concealed from the public eye. Show trials, by contrast, are generally practised only by authoritarian states and are defined by the logic of display. Most powerfully associated with the Stalinist trials of prominent political figures such as Grigory Zinoviev and Lev Kamenev during the Great Purge (1936–1938), show trials often rely on the coerced confessions of defendants repeated in 'open' court. With a predetermined outcome based on bogus evidence and coerced confession, the show trial is an instrument of state terror, a device designed to eliminate perceived enemies of the state through a spectacle of humiliation. As a tool designed to consolidate political power and make an example of the enemies of a regime, the show trial is an extreme form of the **political trial**.

More recently, some scholars have used the term 'show trial' in a non-pejorative sense to denote the didactic dimension of proceedings such as the **Nuremberg trials** and the trial of Adolf **Eichmann**: proceedings deliberately staged to serve pedagogic ends by 'showing' the history of extreme crimes to a national and international audience.

                LAWRENCE DOUGLAS

M Koskenniemi 'Between Impunity and Show Trials' (2002) 6 *Max Planck Yearbook of United Nations Law* 1

sic utere tuo ut alienum non laedas   *see* international environmental law

sick pay   The employment contracts of most workers make provision for their entitlement to be paid during absence due to sickness. Provision for a maximum amount of time on full pay, part pay, or payment under a special sick pay scheme is common. Where no such provision is made it may be possible to imply a term into a worker's **contract of employment** concerning entitlement to sick pay on the basis of what actually happens in practice when workers are off sick. This may give rise to an implied term that there is no entitlement to any pay under the terms of the employment while a worker is off sick. Under the social security legislation, employees who are off sick are entitled to be paid 'statutory sick pay' ('SSP') by their employer for period of up to twenty-eight weeks starting with the fourth day of absence due to '**incapacity for work**'. Periods of absence which are separated by less than eight weeks can be combined so that it is not necessary for an employee to have a further three unpaid days off sick before becoming entitled to SSP where he or she had been off sick within the preceding eight weeks. SSP is paid at a flat rate which is increased annually. For the year beginning in April 2007 it was £72.55 per week. Where the amount of SSP paid exceeds 13 per cent of their liability for social security contributions in any tax month, employers can recover the excess from the Revenue. Where workers are entitled to sick pay under their contracts, this is normally higher than, and is expressed to include, their SSP entitlement.

BOB SIMPSON

Sidney, Algernon   Algernon Sidney (1623–1684) was born in London, the second son of Robert Sidney, Earl of Leicester and Dorothy Percy, daughter of the Earl of Northumberland. Sidney grew up in Penshurst Place, Kent and accompanied his father in the 1630s on embassies to Denmark and France. Sidney served as a parliamentarian captain in Ireland in the period 1641–1643 and as a cavalry colonel in the Eastern Association in England. He was seriously injured fighting at the battle of Marston Moor and became governor of Chichester in May 1645. Sidney was elected MP for Cardiff in December 1645 and allied himself with Viscount Saye and Sele's 'Independent' faction. In 1648 Sidney was appointed as the governor of Dover castle. He opposed the **Regicide**s, but not so much out of love for Charles I but

out of fear of a military dictatorship. He was elected to the English Republic's Council of State in 1652 and together with Sir Henry Vane focused on building the navy.

In May 1659 Sidney was appointed an ambassador to Sweden and used the military confidence of the Interregnum regime to broker a peace between Sweden and Denmark. His overt republicanism meant that he could not return to England after the restoration of Charles II, instead he travelled through Europe visiting Rome, Switzerland, France, and Holland avoiding numerous assassination attempts of Royalist agents. Sidney returned to England in 1677 to care for his dying father. He became embroiled in a Chancery action against his brother to secure his inheritance, and soon found himself involved in Whig and Republican intrigue, standing for election in the Parliaments of the Exclusion Crisis. His experiences of the Exclusion Crisis formed the basis of his *Discourses Concerning Government*, a manuscript that, like Locke's *Two Treatises on Government*, argued for the right of rebellion against an oppressive regime.

In 1683 Sidney became involved in planning a rebellion with the leading surviving Whigs to overthrow Charles II. In June 1683 Sidney was arrested for his alleged part in the Rye House Plot. However, the government lacked the requisite two witnesses to testify to Sidney's treason and he was confined to the Tower whilst the government sought to build its case. With Sidney's application for *habeas corpus* the government was forced to bring its prosecution. Lord Chief Justice George Jeffreys ruled that Sidney's manuscript of his *Discourses* was sufficient evidence to convict; a legal innovation in the law of treason. Sidney was tried on 21 November 1683. The outcome of his trial was never in question, and Sidney used the court process to attack the legitimacy and independence of the Stuart legal system in general and Jeffreys in particular. He was beheaded at Tower Hill on 7 December 1683.   ELLIOT VERNON

signature   *see* **standard form contracts**

Simpson, OJ   Celebrity sports star and announcer OJ Simpson was acquitted of murdering two people, including his former wife, in a closely followed 1995 trial. The verdict in the *Simpson* trial surprised many trial observers, who found the DNA evidence linking Simpson to the two victims to be compelling. In general, reaction to the verdict in the United States divided along racial lines, with a solid majority of African-Americans believing the jury's decision to be correct and a clear majority of whites believing

Simpson to have been guilty. The trial is also cited as an example of what can happen when a judge fails to exercise firm control in the courtroom: a trial that went on too long with too many sideshows.

Nicole Brown Simpson and a twenty-five-year-old acquaintance, Ronald Goldman, were brutally stabbed to death on the night of 12 June 1994 near the front gate of Brown Simpson's Los Angeles condominium. Simpson's whereabouts at the time of the murder was disputed, but later that night he boarded a plane for a previously scheduled flight to Chicago. He returned the next day to Los Angeles, where he was questioned by police about the murders. Several days after the killings, an arrest warrant was issued for Simpson's arrest. Simpson broke an agreement to turn himself in and instead set off in a white sports utility vehicle with a false beard and mustache, a loaded gun, and his passport. Simpson was identified on a highway by a motorist who notified police, setting in motion a long, slow-motion chase that captivated millions watching the event live on television.

Prosecutors chose to file the *Simpson* case in the downtown Los Angeles district, a move that ensured a mostly non-white jury and probably contributed to his ultimate acquittal. The trial began on 24 January 1995 in the courtroom of Judge Lance Ito. Lead prosecutor Marcia Clark presented seventy-two prosecution witnesses. The witnesses included a dispatcher who testified as to an emergency phone call received from Nicole Brown Simpson describing an ongoing assault by Simpson, a limousine driver who testified that Simpson did not answer his door at his estate about the time prosecutors said he was out committing murder, and DNA experts who testified that blood found at the crime scene matched Simpson's.

The defence suggested through its witnesses that Simpson was the victim of a police frame-up. The defence effort was aided by Los Angeles police officer and prosecution witness Mark Fuhrman, who had been captured in the past on audio tape making racial slurs—slurs he had denied making in his testimony. In his closing argument, defence attorney Johnnie Cochran compared Fuhrman to Adolf Hitler and urged jurors to send a message that the community no longer tolerated racist police officers. The jury verdict of 'not guilty' was announced on 3 October 1995.

In a subsequent civil suit, a jury found Simpson responsible for the murders and ordered him to pay $33.5 million in damages to the families of the victims.   DOUG LINDER

Single European Act   *see* **European treaties**

single market   The Single Market, also referred to as the internal or common market, is defined by Article 14 of the European Community Treaty as an 'area without internal frontiers in which the free movement of goods, persons, services and capital is ensured'. Thus, the European market should resemble, as much as possible, an 'internal market' where to move goods, services, labour, and capital between two Member States is no different than doing so within a single Member State. However, since the Member States have different regulatory traditions and standards, the achievement of the single market is dependent upon a complex interaction between the Community and Member States' regulatory frameworks.

In certain areas, such as the common customs area and the common commercial policy, the Community has acquired exclusive regulatory competence. As a result, a single Community regulatory regime applies to all Member States. However, in most areas, the Community regime co-exists with national regulatory regimes, and the competence to regulate is shared between Member States and the Community. In these areas, the single market is achieved through a mix of positive and negative integration. The former arises when the Community uses its competence to approximate the **legislation** of the Member States so as to provide a common regulatory framework. The latter arises when, lacking harmonizing legislation, the regulatory competence of Member States is preserved but the application of national legislation to foreign goods/persons/capital might be restricted by the Treaty free movement provisions (Article 28, 29, 39, 43, 49, and 56 of the European Community Treaty). Those provisions expressly prohibit Member States from discriminating on grounds of **nationality** of the **person** or origin of the goods. Moreover, the **European Court of Justice** has made clear that, in the case of goods, Member States must, as a matter of principle and exception given for the possibility of relying on imperative grounds of public interest, allow goods lawfully produced and marketed in another Member State to be sold in their market *Cassis de Dijon* (1979)). Similarly, rules which restrict the movement of persons, services, and capital by creating barriers to market access can be imposed upon a foreign economic actor only to the extent to which to do so is justified on imperative grounds of public interest, and is necessary and proportionate. The broad interpretation given by the Court to the free movement rules has, from time-to-time, come under attack because of its pervasive effects on national regulatory autonomy. However, it is fair to say, that given the very slow pace in the adoption of Community rules, the Court's interpretation has been crucial in ensuring the achievement of the Single Market.

Finally, the Single Market is also dependent upon the existence of a level playing field where **competition** is not distorted. For this reason, the Treaty imposes constraints both on anti-competitive behaviour carried out by private actors, and on the state's ability to distort competition by granting subsidies to its own industries and undertakings.

ELEANOR SPAVENTA

See also: **European treaties; free movement in the EU**

situational crime prevention Crime is prevented when the inclination to offend is reduced. This is difficult to bring about, either in respect of people in general or officially processed offenders. It can be regarded as largely the preserve of state agencies. Fortunately, crime prevention may be more readily achieved when the obstacles to its commission are increased or the benefits from its commission are reduced. These obstacles and benefits may be real or perceived. This route to crime reduction is termed situational crime prevention, since it manipulates the situation which a potential offender faces or thinks he or she faces. Most of what individuals and organizations do to protect themselves against crime can be deemed situational prevention, from locks on homes to passwords on computers, to security printing, to the auditing of company accounts.

Much situational prevention is common sense. It can also be quite subtle. For example, cards in hotel rooms sometimes state that dressing gowns like the one provided can be purchased from reception. These cards remove excuses for theft by telling guests that the garment should not simply be taken.

The most frequently voiced objection to situational prevention is that specific crimes prevented are merely moved to another place, time, or offence. This problem, known as displacement, appears to be far from universal. Indeed, in a large number of studies, crime prevention in one locale is associated with a crime decrease in contiguous areas. This extension of effects beyond their operational compass is known as the diffusion of benefits. KEN PEASE

See also: **early intervention; risk and criminal justice policy**

slander An action for slander is one of the two forms of civil action for defamation in English law, the other being the action for **libel**. The distinction does not exist in Scots law, but obtains in many other **common law** jurisdictions. It is a slander when defamatory allegations are communicated orally or in some other transient form, such as a gesture; an allegation communicated in a written or other permanent form is a libel. But oral allegations made in the course of a film, on the stage, or during a broadcast are treated as libel, not as slander. The principal consequences of the distinction are first, that slander is only a tort, while the publication of a libel is a crime as well as a tort; and secondly, that the presumption of damage for libel does not normally apply to slander. However, a slander claimant does not have to prove damage in four types of case: when the words charge the claimant with the commission of a serious offence; impute to the claimant certain contagious diseases; disparage the claimant in respect of their work or business; or impute unchastity or adultery to a woman claimant. (The last exception was made by the Slander of Women Act 1891, and highlights the archaic character of this area of law.) There are very few slander actions now. There seems no good reason for preserving the distinction between slander and libel; the rules governing the latter should apply to both torts. ERIC BARENDT

Slater, Oscar The case of Oscar Slater (1872–1948) was one of the most notorious miscarriages of justice in modern Scottish legal history. Slater, a German Jew living in Glasgow, was convicted in 1909 of the murder of Mrs Marion Gilchrist. Initially sentenced to death, his sentence was commuted to life imprisonment, and he served seventeen years before being released in 1927.

Mrs Marion Gilchrist was beaten to death in her home on 21 December 1908. Her maid, who had been out on an errand, returned in time to disturb the murderer, who fled the scene. Slater was suspected because he had attempted to sell a pawn ticket for a brooch resembling one taken from Mrs Gilchrist, and had also left the city for the US shortly after the murder. Police detectives travelled to New York to interview Slater and apply for extradition, and though this was unlikely to have been successful given the paucity of evidence, Slater none the less volunteered to return to Scotland to clear his name. He was tried at the High Court of Justiciary in Edinburgh in May 1909.

The prosecution case was built around three main points: first, the supposed identification of Slater as a man who was disturbed in the flat, by a servant girl and a neighbour, immediately after the crime was committed, and of passers-by who saw a man fleeing the scene of the crime; secondly, the circumstances of Slater's 'flight from justice', leaving Glasgow for New York at around the time that it became public that the police were looking for him; and thirdly, evidence of Slater's character, as it became clear that he was a professional gambler and dealer in jewellery, who may also have lived off the earnings of prostitution. Although this evidence was seriously flawed, Slater was convicted on a majority verdict (9:6).

Public criticism of the verdict was given a boost by the publication of William **Roughead**'s book on the trial in the **Notable British Trials** series in 1910. Later books by the Glasgow detective who investigated the case and Sir Arthur Conan Doyle, who also coordinated a campaign in the press and Parliament, kept the case in the public eye. On his release on licence in 1927, Slater petitioned the Scottish Secretary to remit the case to the newly established Appeal Court. It is a measure of the enduring public dissatisfaction with the verdict that a special bill was presented to Parliament to allow this. In 1928 the Appeal Court quashed Slater's conviction on the ground that the trial judge had failed to direct the jury on the irrelevance of Slater's bad character. Slater, who liked to describe himself as the 'Scottish **Dreyfus**', received £6,000 compensation from the government for his ordeal.

The case was notable in a number of respects. It demonstrates the unreliability of identification evidence and the need for safeguards in this area. It remains a leading case in Scots law on the presumption of innocence and the irrelevance of bad character. But above all it demonstrates how prejudice can distort the legal process.   LINDSAY FARMER

slavery   Slavery is the ownership of one human being by another. The master has power over the life, labour, and liberty of the slave. People may become slaves in various ways: capture of enemies in war; kidnapping or slave raiding; punishment for criminal acts; payment for debt; or the transfer of ownership from one master to another. Although the origins of slavery are unknown, slavery existed at least as early as the Shang dynasty in China (eighteenth to the twelfth centuries BC). The Chinese practised self-sale into slavery and the sale of the relatives of executed criminals. Kidnapping also figured prominently in the creation of slaves.

A society where slaves constitute at least 20–30 per cent of the total population is generally considered a slave society. Athens is the first known major slave society; one-third of the population of classical Athens were slaves. In 594 BC, Solon abolished citizen slavery. At that point, Athens acquired slaves both through Aegean trade and through wars with the Persians. Philip II ended the Athenian slave society with the freeing of many slaves at the battle of Chaeronea in 338 BC.

In 1619, the first African slaves in North America arrived in the colony of Virginia. African slaves replaced English indentured labourers. Although slavery had not existed in England for many centuries, the chronic shortage of labour in the colonies and the presence of hostile indigenous populations spurred the reliance on slavery. By 1681, 2,000 slaves existed in Virginia. After the invention of the cotton gin in 1793, cotton plantations became prevalent and by the mid-nineteenth century, America's slave population exceeded 4,000,000. Moral condemnation of slavery in the United States began to spread during the eighteenth century. The Vermont Constitution, for instance, abolished slavery in 1777. As for Britain, Parliament abolished the slave trade with the colonies in 1807. In 1833, slavery was made illegal by the Slavery Abolition Act.

In the US, most Northern states abolished slavery by 1804. In 1863, during the American Civil War, President Abraham Lincoln issued the Emancipation Proclamation—an executive order proclaiming the freedom of all slaves in those states then in rebellion against the government of the United States. Because the proclamation only applied by its terms to territory remaining under control of the Confederate government, it did not have the effect of immediately freeing any slaves. On 18 December 1865, the Thirteenth Amendment to the United States Constitution ('Neither slavery nor involuntary servitude . . . shall exist within the United States or any place subject to their jurisdiction') became effective and abolished slavery in the US. While the Thirteenth Amendment abolished slavery, the social and economic conditions of the newly free slaves did not change radically. The Fourteenth Amendment, designed to provide equal status to the freed slaves, and the Fifteenth Amendment, designed to protect their right to vote, were largely neutralized by the Supreme Court and other government actions. 'Jim Crow' laws were enacted to deprive freed slaves of their civil rights. In combination with lynchings, violence, racist ideology, and caste behavior, these laws established an enduring system of racial subordination and segregation lasting well into the twentieth century. The lasting harms of slavery— the destruction of family, culture, language, and community—have never been redressed. Reparations have never been made.

Worldwide, slavery still remains. There are an estimated 27 million enslaved persons today. Among the modern practices identified by the **United Nations** as constituting slavery or slavery-like practices are: children sold into prostitution, women forced into sexual slavery, and migrant workers whose passports are confiscated by their employers.

PIERRE SCHLAG AND KIMBERLY C DIEGO

sleaze The term 'sleaze' began to be widely used in the 1990s as the generic description for disreputable and seedy behaviour on the part of Conservative politicians. It referred to standards in both private and public life, and its association with the Major government helped to defeat that government in the general election of 1997.

Since that time the term has been generalized to include every kind of questionable behaviour on the part of all parties and politicians, including the allegation in 2006, that peerages had been traded for party donations, which prompted a police investigation. It has become a term of general political abuse, much used by the media and for impugning the integrity of political opponents.

It was as a response to the prevailing climate of sleaze that John Major established the Committee on Standards in Public Life in 1994 as a standing body. It was initially referred to as the 'Nolan Committee', after its first chairman, and has been described as an ethical workshop. In a series of reports, on matters ranging from the regulation of the conduct of Members of Parliament to the funding of political parties, the Committee has made recommendations which have invariably been translated into new machinery and legislation.

However this has not had the effect of banishing the language of sleaze, although it has mutated into the issue of 'trust'. Because sleaze is inherently ill-defined, lacking any legal precision and covering matters which have nothing to do with law, this makes it both useful and infuriating as a term of political description. TONY WRIGHT

See also: **standards in public life**

slippery slope arguments The slippery slope argument is commonly used in ethical and legal thinking to object to a proposed change. Thus, if we allow a **wrongful life** action when a **child** is born with **disabilities**, we will be asked to recognize it for birth out of wedlock; if we recognize **civil partnerships**, there will be a demand to legalize gay **marriage** and then **polygamy** or marriage between pets. The argument is found most often in bio-ethical discussion. It is often used loosely, referring to little more than a dangerous precedent. There are two types of slippery slope argument. One objects to what is at the bottom of the slope, the other to the fact that there is a slope. As far as the first type is concerned, we should object to experiments on pre-embryos because, by a succession of stages, we will find ourselves experimenting on developed embryos, even on children. The second type of argument relies on the concern that once one has got on a slope, any discrimination will be arbitrary. So, if fertility treatment is only available to married couples, a straightforward line can be drawn. Permit the unmarried access to it and line-drawing becomes different and arbitrary: What about single women, **lesbian** couples, etc? The slippery slope is also sometimes invoked where it is not the real objection. Thus those (conservatives, Catholics) who say if we allow **abortion** we will end by accepting that **infanticide** is legitimate are really saying they object to the killing of an innocent **human** being. But someone invoking the slippery slope argument is saying in effect that there is a progression from abortion (or even contraception or **embryo research**) to infanticide. Discussions of the slippery slope distinguish a logical form of the argument from a causal one. The logical form hypothesizes that once we accept *a* we are committed to accepting *b, c, d,* and ultimately *n*. The causal form predicts that the acceptance of *a* will lead onwards and eventually to *n,* and certainly to acts of the type *a* being done more often. MICHAEL FREEMAN

small claims A main problem confronting the civil courts is how disputes which involve relatively small sums of money can be resolved without litigants incurring costs that exceed the sums at stake. It is widely accepted that those involved in legal disputes should have reasonable access to the courts, regardless of their means and the monetary value of their claims. However, nothing inhibits access to the courts more than the fear of running up a huge legal bill. This is why special simplified procedures have been developed in dealing with small claims. These procedures have been specifically devised to enable unrepresented litigants to take relatively straightforward claims to the civil courts and, no less important, to give them a fighting chance of succeeding when they do so.

It is obviously not possible—and probably not desirable either—to provide refined judicial procedures for resolving all legal disputes, however minor they might be. Traditional civil court processes are much too cumbersome, expensive, and protracted to provide a realistic means of resolving disputes involving relatively small sums of money. For small claims procedures to work effectively, lay people need to be able to present cases themselves in court. In the case of small claims, therefore, the preoccupation is inevitably with cost and expedition, not procedural refinement.

Small claims are heard in the county courts in England and Wales and in Northern Ireland; in the sheriff courts in Scotland. Proceeding with a claim is quite simple: claimants complete a short form, pay a modest court fee and, if the matter is defended, attend a court hearing. Clearly written and informative leaflets (which are now available online) guide prospective litigants through the procedure. Claims up to a prescribed maximum financial limit—a figure set at the time of writing at £5,000 in England and Wales, £2,000 in Northern Ireland and £750 in Scotland—are designated as small claims, and specially modified judicial procedures are adopted when dealing with them.

What is special about these small claims hearings? Although there are variations from country to country—and indeed from judge to judge—there are a few basic characteristics:

- hearings are more straightforward, relaxed and informal than is customary in the civil courts; the aim is to make procedures comprehensible to lay people;
- the emphasis is upon the parties presenting their own cases and legal representation is discouraged;
- judges play a proactive or 'interventionist' role at hearings, seeking to ensure that the relevant evidence is elicited from the parties and freely offering assistance to them (especially when unrepresented) in presenting their cases and in putting questions to the other side;
- strict evidential and procedural rules are relaxed: judges have enormous latitude in conducting hearings and can adopt the method of proceeding that they consider will fairly resolve the dispute in question;
- the parties pay their own costs, whether the judgment is in their favour or not. In civil proceedings, the losing party is as a rule expected to pay the winner's costs, but this rule is abandoned in small claims where a 'no costs' rule applies.

Small claims procedures are, then, intended to provide a cheap, simple, and risk-free mechanism which will enable people, unfamiliar with the law and the courts, to bring disputes to the civil courts. Expanding the scope of small claims has been one of the main ways that governments have sought in recent years to facilitate access to the courts and to ease the problems that beset the civil justice system. The small claims regime has come to occupy a position of unprecedented importance in civil justice administration, the great majority of defended civil claims now being dealt with under small claims procedures.

But serious questions can be raised about small claims procedures. First, one might express scepticism about whether lay people, even with a helping hand from the judge, are able to perform adequately in a judicial hearing where the law and legal procedures are unfamiliar to them. Can they be expected to know how to prepare a compelling case in law and decide what is relevant and what is not? Secondly, doubts might be expressed about whether the emphasis on cheap and expeditious disposition is appropriate in claims which (in England and Wales) might involve as much as £5,000. Are the unrefined methods that judges inevitably adopt, the inspired guesswork in which they frequently have to engage, even their occasional disregard of the law, acceptable at this level? Finally, ambiguities surrounding the role that lawyers play at hearings remain unresolved: these proceedings have after all been adapted to meet the needs of lay litigants who have chosen to dispense with representation. What, then, is the appropriate role for legal representatives? Does their presence create undue formality and thus defeat the object of the exercise?

Despite these difficulties, the available research indicates that litigants are rarely perturbed by the adoption of informal and unrefined judicial approaches in small claims. They seem generally to relish the opportunity of speaking directly to the judge rather than through a lawyer. They do not, it seems, set great store by legal and procedural rectitude and are in general content with the judge's decision as long as he or she is seen as acting in an independent and fair-minded manner. Even in claims that involve larger sums, the research suggests that the small claims regime continues to operate to the satisfaction of most litigants.

JOHN BALDWIN

Smith, FE, 1st Earl of Birkenhead FE Smith, 1st Earl of Birkenhead (1872–1930), was a celebrated lawyer and politician who was Lord Chancellor between 1918 and 1922, undertaking a series of important legal reforms. He was known for his wit and quickness of mind, with many anecdotes about his courtroom behaviour passing into legal folklore.

After graduating from Oxford in 1895, Smith embarked on his twin careers in law and politics. He was called to the Bar in 1899, initially practising on the northern Circuit. He moved to the London bar following his election as conservative Member of Parliament for Walton in 1906, where he quickly established himself (with **Carson**, and **Marshall Hall**) as a leading criminal barrister. He had a thriving political career as a vocal opponent of the Liberal reforms of the House of Lords and Irish Home Rule. He took the posts of Solicitor-General and then Attorney-General in the coalition government of 1915–1918, leading the prosecution of Sir Roger **Casement** in 1916. He then became Lord Chancellor in Lloyd George's government of 1918–1922. As Lord Chancellor he undertook a number of substantial and lasting reforms of law and legal procedure, reforming the law of property, extending the jurisdiction of the county courts, and speeding up divorce proceedings. He was also instrumental in securing domestic and Sinn Fein support for the creation of the Irish Free State in 1921. He returned to government in 1924 as Secretary of State for India, though he had little impact in this post. He left government in 1928 and died in September 1930.   LINDSAY FARMER

Smith, George Joseph   George Joseph Smith (1872–1915), the 'brides in the bath' murderer, was convicted in one of the most notorious murder cases of the early twentieth century. He was a serial bigamist preying on vulnerable women, 'marrying' at least seven times and committing three murders before being convicted and executed for the murder of Bessy Mundy in 1915.

In 1910 Smith, using a false name, married Bessy Mundy who had inherited some money on the death of her father. In July 1912 they executed wills in favour of each other. He then took her to the doctor, claiming that she had suffered a fit, and the following morning she was found dead in her bath. The coroner concluded that she had suffered an epileptic fit and drowned, and Smith inherited the money. The other two murders, of Alice Burnham (1913) and Margaret Lofty (1914), followed a similar pattern, each woman being found dead in their bath a short time after the wedding. In each case Smith (using a false name) had taken out small insurance policies on their lives. The police were alerted when the father of Alice Burnham and the son of their landlady saw a report of the *Lofty* inquest in the national press and remarked on the similarities in the facts. Smith was soon arrested and charged with the murder of Bessy Mundy.

The trial took place at the Central Criminal Court in June 1915, and Smith was defended by Sir Edward **Marshall Hall**. Although Smith was charged only with the murder of Mundy, the prosecution relied on evidence that Smith's previous two wives had died in a similar manner to establish 'system'—that is, not to prove that he did the acts charged, but that if he committed them he must have done so intentionally. The case remains an authority on the use of similar fact evidence.   LINDSAY FARMER

See also: **evidence, criminal**

Smith, Madeleine   Madeleine Smith (1835–1928) was the accused in one of the most notorious poisoning trials of the nineteenth century. She was charged with murdering her secret fiancé and lover, Emile L'Angelier, in 1857. The nation was scandalized by her sexual freedom revealed in the content of her love letters, which were read out in court in the course of the trial, and her deception of her father. Notwithstanding this the jury returned a verdict of 'Not Proven'.

Smith was the daughter of a wealthy Glasgow architect. In late 1854 or 1855 she met L'Angelier, who was of a lower social class than her but who had ambitions of raising his social status through marriage. They conducted a clandestine correspondence throughout 1855, and became secretly engaged, subsequently becoming lovers in May 1856—though Smith's father had refused his consent to the union. Later that year she became engaged to a respectable neighbour and sought to break off the relationship. L'Angelier threatened to show the letters to her father. In March 1857 she acquired arsenic from various chemists, on the pretext of killing vermin and for use as a cosmetic face wash. She invited L'Angelier to her house on 21 March, and on 23 March he died. His body was later found to contain eighty-eight grains of arsenic.

The trial took place at the High Court of Justiciary in Edinburgh over nine days in June and July 1857. The prosecution contended that she had poisoned him in order to prevent exposure and to escape from the relationship. She was defended by John (later Lord) Inglis who contended that she had no motive to kill so long as the letters remained undiscovered, and that L'Angelier could have committed suicide in despair at the ending of the relationship. While his speech to the jury came to be regarded as a model piece of advocacy, his success in getting the court to hold that L'Angelier's diaries were inadmissible as evidence was probably of greater importance to the outcome of the case, as the Crown were unable to prove that he had met Smith. Although the presiding judge, Lord Justice-Clerk Hope, was strongly disapproving of Smith's sexual character and actions, he directed the jury that, notwithstanding the strong presumption of guilt created by Crown, there were important gaps in the evidence, particularly relating to proof of their meetings on the nights when the poison was supposed to have been administered. The jury returned a verdict of not proven, the third or 'Scotch' verdict, which is usually understood to indicate a belief in guilt where it has not been proved beyond reasonable doubt.   LINDSAY FARMER

Social Chapter   There was next to no social policy in the original EEC Treaty whose purpose was primarily to facilitate free movement (of goods, persons, services, and capital). The view was that since economic integration would, in time, ensure the optimum rate of economic growth and thus an optimum social system there was little need for the EEC to have a proper social dimension. Nevertheless, the EEC Treaty did contain a 'Title on Social Policy' but its name was misleading: it made no provision for the central core of social policy: social insurance, public assistance, health and welfare services, education, and **housing** policy. Instead, the 'Title' contained, on the one hand, Articles 117 and 118 EEC (now 137 and 140 EC) aspiring to improve working conditions and cooperation between states and, on the other, the more substantive Article 119 (new 141) on **equal pay** and Article 120 (now 142) on paid holiday schemes. These provisions were introduced to protect French industry. Broadly speaking, France was a country with relatively high labour standards. With the creation of the common market France feared that (1) capital would flee from France to states which did not have high labour standards (so-called social dumping); and (2) the competitiveness of French industry would be undermined by goods produced in states with low labour standards which were then imported into France. In other words, France was worried that such social dumping would force it into a race-to-the-bottom: in order to protect French industry, France would have to reduce its labour standards; other states would respond by cutting theirs; France would then have to cut hers still further. This process would continue until the 'bottom' was reached. The French thought that the only way that this downward spiral could be prevented was by the inclusion of Articles 141 and 142 into the EEC Treaty requiring all states to respect the (high) French standards.

This analysis of the French situation suggests that the so-called social provisions in the EEC Treaty had in fact an economic purpose, a market-making function: it was about creating a 'European-wide labour market', by removing obstacles to the mobility of workers (see, for example, Article 39 EC considered under **freedom of movement in the EU**) and also about removing distortions to competition by seeking to harmonize costs on firms and by preventing social dumping by firms and a race-to-the-bottom by states. It therefore stood in stark contrast to social policy at national level which has traditionally served a 'market-correcting' function, correcting the operation of the market in line with political standards of social justice.

However, in the ECJ's hands the dichotomy between market-making and market-correcting has become less stark. In *Defrenne (No 2)* (1976), the Court while recognizing the market-making function of social policy said that Article 141 formed part of the 'social' objectives of the Community. Since that landmark decision the ECJ has played an important role in fleshing out the meaning of the social policy provisions and giving them a rights-based perspective, especially in the field of **equality** law.

The process started by the ECJ of reorienting the social provisions away from a purely economic function culminated in the adoption of the Community Charter of Fundamental Social Rights 1989 (the 'Social Charter'), by all the Member States except Britain (which did subsequently opt into the Charter in 1997). This 'solemn proclamation of fundamental social rights' listed certain social rights but lacked legal effect (albeit it has been invoked by the **European Court of Justice** as an interpretative tool). However, it was followed up by an Action Programme which led to the adoption of some important measures including the Working Time Directive.

The process of giving the EU a more truly social face was due to have continued at Maastricht. The drafters of the Maastricht Treaty proposed that Articles 117–122 EEC be amended to expand the EC's social competence (powers) to include more genuinely 'social' matters. However this idea was met by stubborn resistance from the UK and, in order to secure the UK's agreement to the TEU as a whole, the proposed changes were removed from the main body of the Treaty and placed in a separate Protocol and Agreement (the Social Policy Agreement ('SPA') and the Social Policy Protocol), together referred to as the 'Social Chapter' (not to be confused with the Social Charter discussed above) which would not apply to the UK.

The Social Chapter is significant for two reasons. First, it broadens the scope of Community competence in the social field and it increases the areas in which measures could be taken by qualified majority vote. Thus, measures concerning, for example, working conditions, information and **consultation of workers**, and equality between men and women could be adopted by qualified majority vote. In addition, measures in more controversial areas such as social security and social protection of workers, protection of workers on termination of their contracts, representation and collective defence of the interests of workers and employers, could be adopted by unanimous vote. Thus, contrary to popular (mis) conception, the Social Chapter is not a charter of social rights. Rather, it gives the Community greater powers to adopt **legislation** in the social field should it choose to do so. However, Article 2(6) (new Article 137(5)) expressly said that the Community did not have competence in the most sensitive areas of all: pay, the right of association, the right to strike, and the right to impose lock-outs.

The second reason for the Social Chapter's significance lies in the greater role it envisages for the 'Social Partners' (representatives of management and labour): they can, if they choose, negotiate **collective agreements** which can be extended to all workers by a Council Directive. Thus, for the first time in the social field private actors (management and unions at EU level) can actually make legislation.

A change of government in the UK in 1997 meant that the UK opted back into the Social Chapter at the Amsterdam summit. The chapter on social policy, incorporating both Articles 117–121 of the EC Treaty and the SPA, was included in the EC Treaty. The Social Chapter is now binding on the UK. However, the pace of legislative activity in this field has diminished considerably since the early 1990s and the heyday of the Social Charter.   CATHERINE BARNARD

See also: **European Community powers**

Social Charter   *see* **Social Chapter**

social control and crime   Social control processes constrain individual behaviour and facilitate social order. In *Control: Sociology's Central Notion* (1989), JP Gibbs attempts to make control the unifying theory of sociology. More narrowly, criminologists identify the social control mechanisms that prevent deviance. Some take conformity as a baseline and explain deviance as a break-down in social control. Others take deviance as a baseline and then explain conformity as the product of social control. For example, Travis Hirschi's *Causes of Delinquency* (1969) claims that social bonds with conforming individuals help to prevent juvenile delinquency.

Several mechanisms of social control cause individuals to comply with criminal law. The most obvious example is state **punishment**, which works through deterrence, incapacitation, or **rehabilitation**. Economic empiricism suggests that the practice of punishment causes individuals to modify their behaviour to avoid future punishment. Sociological and psychological research questions the claim. Incapacitation is discussed primarily in the context of **prison**, where it is physically difficult for the prisoner to commit offences against those outside the prison, although crime within prisons is common. Rehabilitation may occur if the form of punishment instils a renewed sense of guilt or shame

about offending or gives the individual better non-criminal opportunities (eg by treating addictions). Aside from formal sanctions, certain state processes operate like informal sanctions; being arrested or having one's home searched, for example, may be experienced as negatively as a criminal **fine**. By threatening **arrest** or other such interactions, **police** and other state agents may exercise social control.

Non-state mechanisms of social control work via ideology. Individuals internalize norms regarding specific behaviours or the general obligation to obey law. When such individuals violate the norm, even in private, they feel guilt and/or a loss of **identity**. Individuals may care about the approval of others with whom they share social bonds and expect to damage the bond or to incur shame if their norm violation is detected. Individuals may also internalize broad social roles and use the beliefs of others as evidence of whether they have satisfied their role's obligations in a concrete case.

Formal and informal mechanisms of social control interact. First, for the formal law to be recognized as such, its constituent actors—police, prosecutors, judges, jailers, etc—must themselves be subject to social control. Secondly, some forms of social control, such as violent revenge, violate formal law. Thirdly, different mechanisms may reinforce each other. Some contend that the criminal law will enjoy 'moral credibility' that allows it to control behaviour more effectively if it reflects popular understandings of justice (P Robinson and J Darley, *Justice, Liability and Blame: Community Views and the Criminal Law* (1997)). Law may strengthen weak social norms by direct enforcement and also because, in a democratic society, the law's existence supplies evidence to an individual of what the **community** expects or desires of him, which, if he values approval, may work to control his behaviour.

From a normative perspective, some criticize social control as a coercive means for repressive ends, furthering the interests of the powerful at the expense of the weak. Others emphasize a functional account, by which society prevents normatively undesirable behaviour.   RICHARD H MCADAMS

See also: **incapacitation theory; shaming and stigmatizing of offenders**

social dumping   *see* **Social Chapter**

social exclusion and education   There is no universally agreed definition of 'social exclusion', but the concept derives from the idea that some people are unable to participate fully in society because of particular forms of disadvantage. Poverty is the main cause of social disadvantage, but other problems associated with social exclusion include illness/ **disability**, teenage pregnancy, drug addiction, and family breakdown. Education has a dual relationship with social exclusion among individuals. On the one hand, problems such as poor educational achievement, truancy, and exclusion from school, which are disproportionately experienced by some ethnic groups, compound social exclusion; indeed, reference has been made to a 'spiral of disadvantage' affecting the socially excluded. On the other hand, education can play a key role in combating the disadvantage that leads to social exclusion in the first place. The term 'social exclusion' has been adopted by the government post-1997 in its policy goal of improving social **justice**. The targets set centrally for improving levels of attainment in English and mathematics, reducing truancy and school exclusion, and increasing the number of young people continuing in education beyond the age of sixteen or entering higher education, particularly those from under-represented social groups, are part of this wider policy. Legislative reforms have included the introduction of a new separate offence where truancy occurs with parental knowledge and new provisions on sex education. The government established a Social Exclusion Unit in 1997 which has focused on education. Its first report was on *Truancy and School Exclusion* (1998); another was *A Better Education for Children in Care* (2003).   NEVILLE HARRIS

N Harris, *Education, Law and Diversity* (Oxford: Hart Publishing, 2006)

social fund Helping people to meet exceptional needs has been a continuing problem in social security provision. In the 1980s, policy had veered from a discretionary approach to providing legal entitlements. The present scheme, a 'discretionary' fund intended to respond flexibly to such exceptional needs and a 'regulated' fund to cover maternity, funeral, winter fuel, and heating expenses, was implemented in 1987–1988.

The introduction of the discretionary scheme, subject to budgetary control, was accompanied by controversy. There are three payments: 'budgeting loans' to meet intermittent needs (more automatic and less discretionary since 1998); 'crisis loans' for emergency situations; and 'community care grants' to help vulnerable people live independently rather than enter care institutions (part of a wider strategy to promote care in the community and link 'cash' and 'care' provision). The merits of each application must be considered taking into account: the nature of the need; the existence of available resources; the

possibility there is a more suitable provider; and the budgetary allocation.

The complaints procedure differs from regular appeal arrangements. Social fund inspectors, managed by a Social Fund Commissioner appointed by the Minister, undertake reviews applying both a merits and **judicial review** test. The details of the discretionary social fund are set out in 'directions', an unusual form of secondary legislation, and fully annotated in TG Buck, *The Social Fund: Law and Practice* (London: Sweet & Maxwell, 3rd edn, 2008) a work which also refers to an extensive research literature on the social fund.

The 'regulated' social fund, by contrast, is not cash-limited but based on legal entitlement and the regular appeal arrangements apply.

                    TREVOR BUCK

K Legge, Y Hartfree, B Stafford, M Magadi, J Beckhelling, L Predelli and S Middleton, *The Social Fund: Current Role and Future Direction* (York: Joseph Rowntree Foundation, 2006)

National Audit Office, *Helping Those in Financial Hardship: the Running of the Social Fund*, HC 179 (London: The Stationery Office, 2005)

social insurance   *see* **compensation; social security system; tort system**

social movements Social movements have proliferated in modern societies where social and economic developments have provided ever larger numbers of people with the resources for and aspiration to participation, and where political conditions have permitted it. Indeed, so widespread has the habit of participation in forms of collective action not simply contained by established political institutional arrangements become that some observers have described modern liberal **democracies** as 'social movement societies'.

The scale of social movement mobilizations ranges from the local to the transnational, although a truly global social movement remains an aspiration rather than accomplished fact. The range of issues they address is vast; since World War II, they have included the civil rights of ethnic **minorities**, peace and nuclear disarmament, the personal liberation of **women** and sexual minorities, and, most persistently, the environment. The demographics of the people so mobilized have varied—from the oppressed themselves, through students, to the socially privileged—but participation in social movements has, like participation in conventional politics, been increasingly skewed toward an over-representation of the highly educated middle classes, especially those employed in education and the creative or caring professions.

Social movements are untidy phenomena. They are not neatly bounded and there is no consensus about how they should be defined or theorized. Almost any statement about social movements is likely to be contested, and much about them is paradoxical.

Social movements are most generally conceived as loose, informal, un-institutionalized or semi-institutionalized mobilizations of substantial numbers of people that are critical of established regimes. Mobilization must persist for some time, and some degree of organization is required. Although social movements are not coterminous with a single organization, in some cases a single organization may be predominant. Nor are social movements usually identical with a single campaign or campaign coalition, although campaigns, coalitions, and movement organizations are typically the most visible features of social movements.

Characterized as phenomena of civil society in order to emphasize their autonomy from the state, social movements, more often than not, address the state. Indeed, they are largely symbiotic with the state; social movements flourish where the state is strong but only moderately repressive, but not where it is weak or severely repressive. The present weakness of global institutions—and the corresponding under-development of a global polity—goes far to explain the limited development of transnational movements.

In an heroic attempt to articulate a 'consensual' definition of social movements, Mario Diani, in 1992, defined them as networks of informal interaction among people and organizations engaged in political or cultural conflict based upon a shared collective identity. There is, however, contention about every element of that definition. How much networking is required? Of what kind? How extensive or frequent does interaction need to be? How much 'identity' needs to be shared? Is evidence of shared concern sufficient? How explicit and/or fundamental does their conflict with and critique of existing social and political arrangements need to be? How institutionalized may collective action be before it ceases to be a social movement? Some, such as Eyerman and Jamison, identify social movements with the 'liminal moment' in which societies are in greatest flux; from this perspective, the 'institutionalization' of a social movement is a contradiction in terms. Yet environmental movements, in particular, have become at least semi-institutionalized whilst preserving their capacity to mobilize disruptive protests.

Many commentators have identified social movements with protest, but disagree about whether protest is an essential characteristic. Most social movements, explicitly or implicitly, protest against or propose alternatives to established regimes or more powerful, and usually more institutionalized, actors, but how explicit and radical must their protest be? Direct action, considered essential by some, is only one of many forms of action practised within social movements. Further to complicate matters, some movements are 'positive', being expressly mobilized *for* rather than against policies or established regimes, and some—'counter-movements'—are mobilized against other social movements.

Social movements have often been regarded as forms of collective action associated with emancipation. That, however, is arbitrarily to exclude movements such as fascism and Nazism, and nationalist, ethno-nationalist, and racialist movements. Although such mobilizations can only tortuously be represented as emancipatory, they can nevertheless be analysed and explained using the same conceptual and theoretical apparatus as has been developed to explain other social movements.

Although social movements are not new phenomena, systematic social scientific investigation and theorizing of them was slight before the explosion of social movements in the second half of the 1960s. Historically, American and European perspectives on social movements were different. American theorists took an essentially nominalist and pluralist approach, whereas Europeans more often adopted an essentialist position according to which there could be only one social movement for each historical epoch. Thus, with the demise of the labour movement, Europeans began the search for *the* new social movement that would replace it. However, by the 1980s, Europeans mostly spoke comfortably of the 'new social movements' in the plural. The conceptual and analytical toolkit of modern social movement theory mostly originated in North America, but it has been elaborated, applied, and refined in the course of a long transatlantic conversation, and has been successfully employed to illuminate social movements far beyond the North and West.

The relationship to social movements of particular laws, or, indeed, of law in general, is problematic. Social movements may secure social change by increasing the pressure for passage of **legislation**, but typically the changes demanded are more general, and the legislation passed in response to social movement demands is generally only a token of more extensive social changes. Sometimes, however, social movements are mobilized in response to the actual or threatened passage of legislation, especially legislation perceived to impose new burdens or disabilities upon citizens. Occasionally, legislation makes social movements possible, as when prohibitions upon democratic political activity are removed or ameliorated.

As societies have become more participatory, so the distinctiveness of social movements, and the differences between them and interest groups, have been eroded. Movements that were once seen as threats to established political order—or, viewed differently, as holding the promise of transcendence of existing social and political arrangements—are increasingly viewed as simply part of the expanded portfolio of forms of collective action by which, in liberal democratic states, political claims may legitimately be made. In response, scholarly language has changed, with 'contentious politics' now contending as the more inclusive term to designate the phenomena previously rather indiscriminately labelled 'social movements'.   CHRISTOPHER ROOTES

D della Porta and M Diani, *Social Movements: an Introduction* (Malden, MA and Oxford: Blackwell, 2nd edn, 2006)

R Eyerman and A Jamison, *Social Movements: a Cognitive Approach* (Oxford: Polity, 1991)

social security appeals   Decisions on entitlement to most social security benefits are taken by staff in the Department for Work and Pensions ('DWP') known as decision-makers. Such decisions can only be changed through formal legal procedures. A decision cannot simply be altered by an office manager. Decision-makers themselves can change a decision by either of two processes: revision and supersession. Revision changes an initial decision that was wrong, with effect from the date of that original decision. Supersession involves substituting a new decision with effect from some later date, eg because of a change in circumstances.

Most decisions on social security claims can be appealed, whether or not there has been an application for a revision or supersession. Claimants may opt for an oral hearing of their appeal, which they may attend, or a 'paper hearing'. The appeal **tribunals** are independent of the DWP and consist of one, two, or three members, depending on the matter in issue. Appeals about disability benefits are heard by three-member tribunals comprising a lawyer, a doctor, and a carer or disabled person. Two-member tribunals (a lawyer and a doctor) deal with incapacity for work appeals while one-member tribunals (a lawyer alone) decide most other social security appeals. The tribunal's task is to consider the facts and the law

afresh and reach its own decision either to confirm or reverse that of the decision-maker below. Tribunals are not subject to the strict rules of evidence and their proceedings are relatively informal. Appellants may bring along a representative or friend to help, but legal aid is not available. The DWP may send a representative to the hearing (a 'presenting officer') but this is not common. The tribunal's decision is usually announced at the end of the hearing.

The appellant and the DWP each have the right of appeal against the tribunal's decision, subject to two conditions. First, any appeal must relate to a point of law, not an issue of fact. Secondly, the party wishing to appeal must apply for permission (or 'leave') to appeal. Appeals from tribunals are dealt with by specialist judges formerly known as the Social Security, Child Support and Pensions Appeal Commissioners, who are now Judges of the Upper Tribunal. The Commissioners deal with most appeals on paper, on the basis of the parties' written submissions, although they also hold oral hearings. Nearly all appeals are decided by a single Commissioner, although cases involving especially difficult questions of law may be heard by a Tribunal of three Commissioners. These may include 'test cases' brought by welfare rights groups, designed to challenge the DWP's interpretation of a point of social security law, where the outcome will affect many other cases. The Commissioners' decisions form a body of case law precedent which appeal tribunals and decision-makers must apply when deciding like cases. There is a further right of appeal from the Commissioner to the Court of Appeal (or in Scotland to the Court of Session), but again only on a point of law and only with permission.   NICK WIKELEY

J Baldwin, N Wikeley, and R Young, *Judging Social Security* (Oxford: Clarendon Press, 1992)

T Buck, D Bonner, and R Sainsbury, *Making Social Security Law* (Aldershot: Ashgate, 2005)

social security system   The origins of the modern social security system lie in the **Poor Law**; and the main aim of social security is often assumed to be the relief of poverty. Means-tested benefits, the first category of benefits in the modern system, are supposed to provide a basic subsistence income to ensure that no-one falls below the 'poverty line'. However, the **national insurance** scheme, the second main part of the social security system, takes a different approach. These benefits, which are not usually means-tested, provide a form of income maintenance or replacement where contributors to the national insurance scheme suffer an interruption or loss of earnings though unemployment, incapacity for work, bereavement, or retirement and so on. The third principal category of social security benefits, non-contributory benefits, depend neither on a means-test nor the prior payment of contributions. Rather, they are principally designed to provide support for meeting specific costs, such as those associated with raising children (child benefit) or with disability (disability living allowance).

The common theme across all three categories is that each involves the state setting eligibility criteria authorizing income transfers in the form of cash benefits. Social security is therefore one means of delivering welfare, but is not synonymous with welfare. Welfare objectives may be achieved through fiscal welfare (eg **income tax** allowances) and occupational welfare (eg occupational **pensions**). Social security must also be distinguished from the provision of social services, which are concerned with the delivery of welfare in kind (eg through community care services). Moreover, in the **United Kingdom** (but not in continental Europe) the health care system is regarded as separate from the social security system.

In addition to relieving poverty, providing income maintenance, and meeting special needs, the social security system is also used to deliver other policy objectives, such as the redistribution of resources within society, either vertically (from rich to poor) or horizontally (eg from people without children to **families**). Similarly, means-tested benefits payable to those in low-paid work (such as family credit) have been transformed into tax credits in order to emphasize the rewards of work over welfare. The social security system is also used by government to seek to modify people's behaviour (eg the abolition of one parent benefit was designed in part to discourage lone **parenthood** and the imposition of local limits on the payment of housing benefit was intended to check increases in private sector rent levels).

There are in fact two social security systems within the UK. Uniform legislation covers the social security system of England, Wales, and Scotland while a parallel but legally separate system operates in Northern Ireland. Within **Great Britain**, both policy and operational responsibility for the social security system is shared between the Department for Work and Pensions ('DWP'), HM Revenue and Customs ('HMRC') and the Treasury. The DWP administers most social security benefits through its various agencies (eg Jobcentre Plus and the Pensions Service) through a network of both central and local offices, although housing benefit and council tax benefit are dealt with by local authorities, subject to policy oversight from DWP, and employers administer benefits such as statutory maternity pay and statutory sick pay. HMRC has responsibility for collecting national insurance contributions and administering the child benefit and tax credits schemes. The Treasury inevitably has a strong influence on the development of social security policy, not least as the cost of both means-tested and non-contributory benefits are met from general taxation. National insurance benefits are paid out of the National Insurance Fund, to which contributions are made by individuals, employers, and the Treasury.

Social security law governing both the conditions of entitlement to benefits and liability to pay national insurance contributions is notoriously complex. It is primarily contained in legislation (the main exception being the discretionary parts of the **social fund**, which are subject to Directions issued by the Secretary of State, with no direct parliamentary oversight). Typically, social security statutes establish the overall framework for the rules, but grant extensive powers to ministers to make subordinate (or secondary) legislation in the form of regulations. Most of the detailed provisions governing benefit entitlement and liability for contributions are contained in these regulations, which are subject to frequent and complicated amendments. Social security provision is also influenced by international conventions, and especially by **European Union** law (in particular in relation to migrant workers and the principle of equal treatment for men and women) and by the **European Convention on Human Rights**. A further source of social security law is case law, which interprets and applies the provisions in the primary and secondary legislation.

Decisions on social security claims are made in the first instance by decision makers in the DWP or by HMRC officials. In most cases there is a right of appeal on matters of fact or law to an independent tribunal. Tribunal decisions do not carry any precedent value; rather, social security case law is to be found in the authoritative decisions of the Commissioners (now the Upper Tribunal) and the higher courts. Thus an individual appellant, the DWP and the HMRC each has the right to appeal a tribunal decision to the Upper Tribunal, but only on a point of law and with permission. There is then a further right of appeal to the Court of Appeal (in Scotland to the Court of Session) and the House of Lords.

NICK WIKELEY

N Wikeley and A Ogus, *The Law of Social Security* (London: Butterworths, 5th edn, 2002)

N Harris (ed), *Social Security Law in Context* (Oxford: Oxford University Press, 2001)

Socialist Law   This term is associated with the former Soviet Union, principally from the period

1936 to 1991, and eventually the 'socialist legal systems' and 'legal systems of a socialist orientation' that were (Mongolia, Czechoslovakia, Poland, German Democratic Republic, Romania, Hungary, Bulgaria, Yugoslavia, Albania) or are (China, Vietnam, North Korea, Cuba) linked with the so-called 'socialist camp' or attracted by it (Ethiopia, Somalia, Yemen, Afghanistan, and other developing economies). Classical Marxism regarded 'socialist law' as a contradiction in terms. Karl Marx had spoken briefly of a transition period between a capitalist society and a communist system when the former would transmute into the latter; the state would be the 'revolutionary dictatorship of the proletariat'. VI Lenin pursued the notion in *State and Revolution* (1917), suggesting that the transitional proletarian state would be essential to crush the bourgeoisie but would nonetheless commence to die out immediately. Law, in other words, was an attribute of a state, and under communism there would be no state and no law. The classics of Marxism were explicit with respect to state and law of the old order: it was to be smashed; the power base of the old order was to be dismantled with all the legal institutions that supported it. Much of Soviet Marxian legal theory thereafter was devoted to the relationship between those contradictory processes and the relative weight to be accorded to each.

The 1936 USSR Constitution declared that the Soviet Union had become a socialist society, would set about the completion of the building of socialism, and would then address the building of communism. A socialist society would perforce have a socialist state and law during the transition era. Antagonistic classes had been eliminated; the state under socialism would not die away rapidly; but for the state ultimately to disappear, Stalin said, it must pass through the dialectically contradictory stage of becoming stronger. A definition of Soviet Law, which here meant essentially socialist law, was endorsed at a Conference in 1938: '…law is the aggregate of rules of conduct established in a legislative procedure by the power of the working people expressing their will and the application of which is ensured by the entire coercive power of the socialist State for the purpose of the defence, consolidation, and development of relations and procedures advantageous and suitable for the working people, the full and final destruction of capitalism and its survivals in the economy, domestic life, and consciousness of people, and the building of a communist society'. This definition dominated socialist legal thought throughout the Soviet era in all socialist legal systems, although it was criticized for various inadequacies in the post-Stalin era.

The Khrushchev era brought attempts to actually implement certain ideological tenets of Marxism-Leninism. The socialist Soviet state was declared to be an all-people's state. Efforts were made to make the Soviet administrative system more participatory and responsive, and quasi-legal institutions were introduced to assume responsibilities traditionally associated with the state (comrades' courts, people's guards). The linkage between stages of societal development and socialist law led to investigation of the minimum threshold for a social system completing the transition from a people's democracy to a socialist legal system, leading comparative lawyers to ask: 'What makes a socialist legal system "socialist"?'. Firm criteria were never developed. Soviet experience suggested the termination of class struggle, the introduction of comprehensive state economic planning, the abolition of 'private law' and reliance entirely upon public law, the dominant role of a vanguard communist party, state ownership of the instruments and means of production, collectivization of agriculture, a state monopoly of foreign trade, and an emphasis upon the collective or social interest over that of the individual. Some countries in the socialist camp regarded themselves as having satisfied these tests (Czechoslovakia, Hungary, Romania); others were more restrained (Bulgaria, China, Mongolia, Poland).

Although a formal commitment to socialist law has been abandoned in most of the former socialist legal systems (China, Cuba, North Korea, and Vietnam retaining some commitment), many of the values of socialist law remain embedded in positive law and legal theory. The 1993 Russian Constitution provides, *inter alia*, that Russia is a 'social' state, and much of the debate in Russian legal doctrine as to precisely what that term means revolves around values previously associated with socialism. And while socialist law theories are now discredited, no new legal theory has emerged in Russia to assist the legislator in pursuing democratic reforms. The Russian legal system remains a theory-minded system in search of a theory.   WILLIAM BUTLER

W E Butler, *Russian Law* (Oxford: Oxford University Press, 2nd edn, 2003)

JN Hazard, *Communists and Their Law* (Chicago: University of Chicago Press, 1969)

See also: **Marxist legal theories**

Society of Legal Scholars   *see* **legal academics**

socio-economic rights   *see* **economic and social rights**

socio-legal research A number of definitions have been offered for socio-legal research. They range from describing socio-legal studies as an approach to law and legal studies and as a methodology for legal studies to viewing it as an entirely new discipline. Pre-occupation with this question has subsided in recent years and this might be connected with the rise in popularity of socio-legal studies as a vehicle for producing research that is original, highly innovative, and sometimes policy-relevant. The criteria for legal research in the Research Assessment Exercises for 1996, 2001 and 2008 expressly refer to socio-legal research as coming within the definition of material recognized as legal research for the purposes of the exercise. This has considerably enhanced the reputation of socio-legal research within the discipline of law. **Common law** jurisdictions such as the UK, Canada, and Australia all have at least two academic journals that are dedicated to socio-legal research. In the thirty years or so since socio-legal research became a recognizable feature of legal research in its own right it has come to the forefront of law schools both in quality and quantity terms. Where it has been less successful is in attracting as practitioners a constituency wider than legal or legally trained academics. With a few notable exceptions participants in the tradition are to be found in law schools and not in sociology, political science, or other social science or arts departments.

Socio-legal research differs from doctrinal research in law in that it situates legal phenomena in a broader context. Two traditions have emerged within socio-legal research that speak to this broader context. In the early years of socio-legal research the context was often seen as the empirical reality of the operation of law and legal structures—colloquially referred to as 'law in action' or the 'law in action versus the law the books'. The early work of the ESRC-funded Oxford Centre for Socio-Legal Studies is sometimes described as falling into this category. (The ESRC is the Economic and Social Research Council which distributes funding for research, much like the Australian Research Council in Australia and the National Science Foundation in the US.) The definitional paucity of this description can be seen from a simple examination of some of that work. The Compensation Study that the Centre undertook was a huge national survey with research instruments designed by sociologists and with input from psychologists and economists as well as lawyers. Its conclusion that the system by which victims recovered **damages** for loss and injuries suffered in accidents revolutionized the way in which lawyers understood that part of the legal system.

'Law in action' (it seems) describes socio-legal work which does not expressly use the ideas of another discipline to interrogate law and legal phenomena, whilst using social research methods to conduct its inquiries. In the early years of socio-legal research it was work of this type that dominated. Now that is not the case. It is hard to identify precisely the reasons for this beyond changing intellectual fashions. It is worth noting however that law-in-action research often requires external funding to pursue its particular questions and this, until recently, did not sit very comfortably with the traditional model of legal research, which was that of the lone scholar working on desk-based research. Until 1990 the ESRC funded a dedicated Centre for Socio-Legal Research in Oxford. This was an interdisciplinary centre which provided a considerable amount of law-in-action research.

This type of socio-legal work is open to the criticisms—in particular from the critical legal studies tradition—that by its adoption of the labels and categories of doctrinal law it facilitates the continuance of the very law and legal structures that it has demonstrated to be inaccurate; and that it creates a policy nexus with government that prevents radical findings and impact. Neither of these charges is wholly inaccurate. Socio-legal research that adopts the law-in-action model still operates against law in the books as an oppositional discourse. It has not created a new structure or structures, but it has provided the tools from which a powerful critique can be mounted. Government departments in the UK, in particular, commission this type of research from socio-legal academics with briefs of varying specificity. Work in the areas of family law, family proceedings, **legal aid**, legal process (eg court-ordered **mediation**, stipendiary magistrates) has been particularly popular. The UK **Law Commission** has begun to make use of socio-legal work and socio-legal researchers in preparing its recommendations on law reform for government. The findings of this research often have a direct policy transfer effect. Whether the policy nexus that this involves is desirable or not is part of a much larger argument about the function of universities within society.

In 2006 a report funded by the Nuffield Foundation titled the *Nuffield Inquiry into Empirical Legal Research in the UK* identified a lack of capacity to undertake socio-legal work in the law-in-action tradition. Some of the reasons it identified for this lack of capacity are cited above—namely the lack of a mass of empirical research experience within law schools as opposed to specialist research units with limited funding, and a lack of appreciation within law schools of the multi-disciplinary teams required to produce work of quality. Other reasons point to the nature of the undergraduate legal curriculum which fails to introduce students, other than in a passing moment, to the intellectual or methodological contribution of law-in-action research and to the fact that researchers steeped in this tradition are an ageing cohort. Recent changes in the funding regime for universities and a linking of the bodies that award research money on a national basis may help to address some of these concerns.

Besides law-in-action research, a second tradition of socio-legal research examines legal phenomena and legal institutions through the lens of a different discipline in both substantive and methodological inquiry. The list of disciplines used to interrogate law includes sociology, social theory, political theory, feminist theory, philosophy, and economics. This is by no means an exhaustive list but it does highlight the most popular interfaces. From this tradition a significant body of socio-legal theory has emerged and has found itself incorporated into the undergraduate legal curriculum. However this incorporation is often into specialist modules—such as law and gender, **governance** and **regulation**, and medical law—rather than into core components. Socio-legal research done in this way has created or considerably advanced fields of study that were hitherto underdeveloped or did not exist at all. Examples of this would be work in the areas of social, political, and economic regulation and governance and of work in the field of **gender** and sexuality. These fields are now established within the socio-legal canon. New fields of study can be seen in the interfaces of law and technology, law and bioethics, and law and geography. Socio-legal research has sparked off a collapse in the traditional boundaries of law as a discipline. Undoubtedly this expansive theoretical engagement with the discourses of other disciplines has been fostered by the spirit of post-modernity that seems to have had more impact amongst legal scholars than those of other disciplines.

Socio-legal research has moved in a relatively short space of time from a rather niche interest to one which is now considered in its theoretical, rather than its empirical, incarnation to occupy the mainstream of legal scholarship.   SALLY WHEELER

S Picciotto and D Campbell (eds) *New Directions in Regulatory Theory* (Oxford: Blackwell, 2002)

D Cowan and M McDermot, *Regulating Social Housing: Governing Decline* (London: Glasshouse, 2006)

sociological jurisprudence In the English-speaking world, the term sociological jurisprudence is most often associated with the legal philosophy of the American jurist Roscoe Pound, which emphasizes the need to understand law—especially as developed by **common law** judges—in terms of its social functions of balancing interests (individual, social, and public) and promoting social welfare. Otherwise 'sociological jurisprudence' refers to a variety of legal philosophies, mainly developed in Europe and North America in the first half of the twentieth century, that have either called on the social sciences for juristic inspiration or have advocated that lawyers' thought and practice should be guided by careful study of changing social conditions.

Today the term has a markedly obsolescent ring, its projects having been displaced by others that have seemed more fruitful. Since Pound first set out his programme for a sociological jurisprudence early in the twentieth century, social scientific studies of legal phenomena have flourished. The relations of law and the social sciences are now extensively explored, with a great proliferation of empirical and theoretical studies, especially in the United States (where extensive funding for this kind of research has long been available) but also in most other Western nations since the mid-twentieth century. This rich research area is labelled variously sociology of law, socio-legal studies, 'law and society' research, or 'law and social theory'. The term sociological jurisprudence is now rarely used. For most socio-legal scholars today it indicates a pioneer, pre-scientific phase of social studies of law, in which lawyers proposed drawing on the emerging discipline of sociology to improve law or legal thinking. Since it gave rise neither to enduringly significant social theories of law nor to substantial empirical research, sociological jurisprudence is usually seen as having contributed little to modern socio-legal studies. Equally, since its priorities were set by lawyers and geared towards juristic issues and legal reforms it fitted poorly with the ambitions of legal sociologists wishing to establish their own scientific priorities and aims in studying law as a social phenomenon.

Legal philosophers usually associate the term with Pound's philosophy of law built especially on the ideas of Rudolf von Jhering and Josef Kohler, or with early modern writings in sociology of law, such as those of the Austrian jurist Eugen Ehrlich. For a time Ehrlich's work (promoted in the United States by Pound) had much juristic influence, especially through its claims about the creative significance of judicial law-making and its implication that legal processes could be revitalized by studying state law's relations with other powerful social norms. But Ehrlich and other pioneers of legal sociology were mainly seen as offering insights about law's social impact and effectiveness, rather than legal philosophy as such. Pound's work stressed the functions of law in balancing competing interests to avoid social friction, the importance of research on law's effects in society, and the need for social scientific input in determining legislative policy. As such it was widely regarded in the first three decades of the twentieth century as progressive, realistic, and enlightened, and was influential with reform-minded jurists, such as Benjamin Cardozo, later one of the most celebrated justices of the **United States Supreme Court**.

From the 1930s, however, Pound's sociological jurisprudence was increasingly seen as a programme that had failed to deliver. It was considered, on the one hand, not to offer a theory of law with the power and rigour to compete seriously in legal philosophical debates. Thus, its claims about law's functions could easily be treated as either truisms or unsubstantiated assertions, and its valuable revival of the idea, that law consists not only of rules but also of fundamental non-rule standards of many kinds, was more rigorously pursued by other scholars such as John Dickinson and Ronald Dworkin. On the other hand, its claims to link legal thought to the social sciences were revealed as largely rhetorical. Despite Pound's legendary erudition and exhaustive citation of literature in many languages on legal theory, his lack of engagement with developing sociological literature and his apparently declining interest in the social sciences over time contributed to a strong sense of unfulfilled promise.

It seemed that by the 1930s, legal philosophy had left sociological jurisprudence behind. In the United States it had been largely superseded by **legal realism**, a movement that took the critical, behavioural study of legal phenomena (especially adjudication) far more seriously and, in some of its forms, actively promoted empirical socio-legal research. In Britain, dominated by a positivist analytical jurisprudence focusing on conceptual rather than functional analysis of law, sociological jurisprudence had minimal direct influence. Outside the United States, Pound's most enthusiastic supporter was the Australian jurist Julius Stone.

Pound's aims and approach are still of interest, however, in considering the prospects for a renewed sociological jurisprudence today. From some of his earliest writings he emphasized the importance of fundamental legal values, or what he called the ideal element in law, as a concern for sociological jurisprudence. He claimed that the social sciences, unlike the natural sciences, must be concerned with how (social and legal) conditions ought to be, and not merely with how they are. He distanced himself from all conceptions of sociology as a purely observational, behavioural study that refused to make value judgments. Since law and legal processes necessarily evaluate and judge social life, sociological jurisprudence must be centrally concerned with the purposes and ideals of law and the means of making them an effective guide for legal and adjudicative practices.

Pound correctly saw that if social scientific ideas are to be able to reshape juristic thought and practice they must be made to engage directly with law as a system of normative ideas. Just as he refused to accept positivist claims that law and morals must be analytically separated and always saw moral ideas as infusing law and legal processes, so he recognized that it would not be possible for sociology to engage with juristic understandings of law if it, too, considered society only in terms of value-neutral behavioural observation and did not see the structures of social life as framed by values that required interpretation. If only vaguely, Pound sensed preconditions for a genuine engagement between the worlds of the jurist and of the sociologist.

Unlike, for example, Ronald Dworkin, who has similarly (but in a far more sophisticated philosophical framework) emphasized the importance of values, principles, and other standards in law and their very diffuse sources in social life, Pound held, at least in his early work, to the idea that sociological insight was necessary for lawyers to appreciate the nature, significance, sources, and development of these standards. In this way he pointed to, though never exploited, an important route to the development of a sociological jurisprudence that could have engaged directly with juristic assumptions by drawing on the best available resources of social science and social theory. But, as Pound's interest in sociology waned, so he avoided efforts to understand how basic legal values acquired their meaning and changed with historical conditions, and with social and cultural experience. Increasingly, he came to see them as absolutes, as fundamental underpinnings of civilization and law, not requiring empirical study; a kind of historically-validated natural law. In this way the promise of sociological jurisprudence evaporated. It became, as most of Pound's critics clearly recognized, a conservative defence of assumed truths of common law and of the traditional wisdom of common law **judges**.

As originally proposed, sociological jurisprudence stood in opposition to untrammelled individualism. It rejected 'mechanical jurisprudence' (the application of legal rules without concern for their social purposes or consequences) and stressed the significance of policy analysis and judicial discretion in developing law in the courts. It reflected an optimism that, with the aid of social science, judicial law-making (with legislation in support) could produce adequate social regulation. In an age when regulatory problems in most advanced societies were expanding, juristic appeals to sociology for the purposes of legal reform were widespread in Germany, France, and elsewhere, as well as in the United States.

Today, socio-legal studies of many kinds have undertaken the tasks that the sociological jurists proposed for practical improvement of law through policy analysis and empirical study of law's social effects. What remains still largely unfulfilled is the need for a serious engagement of sociology and social theory with legal philosophy, and the development of a practical, sociologically informed juristic theory. Social theories of law have often, at least by implication, revealed the barrenness of some typical questions and debates in legal philosophy. But the promise of sociological jurisprudence to reshape and enrich juristic thought sociologically has not yet been fulfilled. Current social change is so rapid and extensive that the challenge of developing law in new forms and contexts makes the fulfilment of this promise necessary and, it may be suggested, ultimately inevitable.   ROGER COTTERRELL

soft law   *see* **legal rules, types of**

Solicitor-General   In England and Wales, Her Majesty's Solicitor General is one of the Law Officers and the deputy to the **Attorney-General**. Under the Law Officers Act 1997, the Solicitor-General may exercise any function of the Attorney-General. Like the Attorney-General, the Solicitor-General is a political appointment of the **Prime Minister**, made from among the legal qualified members of his party in the **House of Commons** or **House of Lords**. The legal qualification may that of either a barrister or solicitor.

HM Solicitor-General also acts as a deputy for the Law Officers, created following devolution in the UK, who are responsible for advising the UK government on legal issues relating to Northern Ireland and Scotland. They are the Advocate General for Northern Ireland and the Advocate General for Scotland.

The Solicitor General for Scotland is an entirely separate post, the role of which is to act as a deputy for the **Lord Advocate**, the senior law officer of the Scottish Executive.

Many English-speaking legal systems outside the UK also have an office called the Solicitor-General.

As in the UK, the title is often used to identify the deputy to the principal legal adviser to the government.
ANDREW LE SUEUR

Somerset v Stewart   Slavery in England was not outlawed by Parliament until 1833–1834, although the slave trade was legislatively prohibited in 1807. These enactments were the culmination of a campaign for abolition that developed in the mid-eighteenth century. Early episodes in the abolition story involved applications for the writ of **habeas corpus** in English courts. The pivotal case was that of a slave named James Somerset, decided in 1772 by the Court of King's Bench, Lord **Mansfield** presiding.

In November 1771, James Somerset was confined in irons aboard the ship *Ann and Mary* lying in the Thames, bound for Jamaica. Word of his plight reached Granville Sharp, a committed, fiercely energetic abolitionist, who immediately applied for a writ of *habeas corpus* seeking Somerset's release. The writ was returned by the ship's captain, John Knowles, who claimed that Somerset was the slave of Charles Stewart, and that Stewart had delivered Somerset to Knowles to be transported to Jamaica and sold.

Prior to *Somerset*, the question of the legality of slavery in England had not been squarely decided by the courts. In 1765, William **Blackstone** in the first volume of his *Commentaries on the Laws of England* declared that the 'spirit of liberty is so deeply implanted in our constitution, and rooted even in our very soil, that a slave or a negro, the moment he lands in England, falls under the protection of the laws, and with regard to all natural rights becomes *eo instante* a freeman'. This declaration was, however, contradicted by a later passage in the *Commentaries*, and by the presence in England of an estimated 15,000–16,000 domestic slaves.

Lord Mansfield tried repeatedly to get the parties to settle Somerset's claim for the writ of *habeas corpus*, but both Granville Sharp, for Somerset, and the West India merchants, for Knowles and Stewart, insisted that the case be resolved by the court. After a delay of six months, the court acceded and issued its opinion, concluding that Somerset must be set free. Mansfield declared that the state of slavery 'is so odious that it must be construed strictly', that it could only derive 'from positive law', and that 'no authority can be found for it in the laws of this country'.

The *Somerset* case was celebrated by the community of free blacks in London, and news of the decision quickly travelled to America and to the Caribbean islands. In popular culture, the idea took hold that the case had ended slavery in England. Strictly speaking, however, the legal effect of the decision was quite narrow—as Mansfield himself later insisted, *Somerset* and prior cases 'go no further than that the master cannot by force compel him to go out of the kingdom'. Nevertheless, Mansfield and his fellow judges had issued, albeit reluctantly, a powerful message against slavery, a message that gave slaves in England and elsewhere the immediate opportunity to assert their freedom. In the years that followed, *Somerset* was a potent catalyst in the march toward abolition.   JAMES OLDHAM

J Oldham, 'New Light on Mansfield and Slavery' (1988) 27 *Journal of British Studies* 45

R Paley, 'After *Somerset*: Mansfield, Slavery and the Law in England, 1772–1830' in N Landau (ed), *Law, Crime and English Society 1660–1830* (Cambridge: Cambridge University Press, 2002)

South African Bill of Rights   An integral part of the South African **Constitution** is the justiciable Bill of Rights which is contained in Chapter Two. It is an emphatic manifestation of the South African nation's determination to make a complete break with a past in which fundamental rights had often been disregarded with impunity. Now, any **person** whose rights have been infringed may approach a competent court for redress, and the court may make an order that is just and equitable.

Section 2 of the Constitution proclaims the supremacy of the Constitution and prescribes that all law or conduct that is inconsistent with the Constitution or the Bill of Rights is invalid and must be struck down by the court that makes that finding. The Bill of Rights contains wide-ranging provisions to protect civil, political, socio-economic, and group rights. Thus the rights protected range from **equality**, dignity, life, and freedom, and **security** of the person, to rights to culture, and the right to a clean environment. All three generations of rights are therefore protected and justiciable. It also binds private and juristic persons to the extent that the rights are applicable to them. Rights are however subject to limitation, in terms of section 36 of the Constitution which requires that such limitation be permitted only if it is effected in terms of a law of general application and that the limiting provision must be such that it is reasonable and justifiable in an open and democratic society based on **human dignity**, equality, and freedom.   PIUS LANGA

See also: **Constitutional Court, South Africa**

South African law   *see* **Roman-Dutch law; mixed jurisdictions**

South African Truth and Reconciliation Commission   *see* **reconciliation**

sovereign immunity   *see* **immunity, diplomatic and state**

sovereignty   Sovereignty is regularly asserted to be an indivisible monistic power that stands above other powers. With this capacity it is often regarded as the source of laws. Historically, such monistic sovereignty has been attributed to God, Monarch, Prince—and in modern democracies—to 'the people', Parliament, or constituent assembly. Sovereignty is generally regarded as the secularization of a theological concept. Does such a monistic sovereignty with a plenitude of power actually exist? Instead, is sovereignty divisible, justiciable, capable of being shared, questioned, or limited? The viability of **international humanitarian law**, the **European Union**, or the **International Criminal Court** rests on such divisibility and justiciability of sovereign power. To sharpen the question, what is the relationship between sovereignty and law?

Jean Bodin, the French jurist writing in the sixteenth century, explained the indispensability of sovereignty in accounting for law. Since Bodin's *On Sovereignty: Four Chapters from The Six Books of the Commonwealth* (1576), it has been a regular dictum that sovereignty is 'that which gives the law'. As Bodin put it, 'the first prerogative (*marque*) of a sovereign prince is to give law to all in general and each in particular'; to which he adds, 'without the consent of any other, whether greater, equal or below him', with the exception of God. The right to declare war and make peace are elements of this first prerogative of the sovereign to 'give law', recognizing that by the decision on war the sovereign determines 'the ruin or preservation of a state'. However, the sovereign is not, for Bodin, entirely beyond the limits of law. Not only must the acts of the sovereign conform with divine law, but he must also have 'just cause' to deprive a person of private property or levy taxes. What is evident from Bodin's account is that even in this early modern account sovereignty is not regarded as an absolute power beyond law.

The early theorists of sovereignty such as Jean Bodin, Thomas Hobbes, and Jean Jacques Rousseau have been criticized for developing an authoritarian or absolutist notion of sovereignty and thus making the 'gift of totalitarianism' to modern political communities. It is true that the imperative for the early modern thinkers of sovereignty was to provide an account of the 'authority of a mortal God', to put it in Hobbesian terms. However, this did not rule out legal limits on the sovereign. These early theorists did envision the right, power, or capacity to resist the sovereign in certain circumstances. The ambivalence about the monism and absolutism of sovereignty is readily apparent in Hobbes's *Leviathan* (1651). There is indeed a 'Common Power' or 'one Will' that Hobbes regards as essential to ensure that the 'Covenant' to submit to one will is lasting, to defend the Commonwealth from invasion of foreigners, and the injuries that the covenanting parties can cause to each other. But Hobbes provided for certain limits to the sovereign's power. If the sovereign commanded a man to 'kill, wound, or mayme himself; or not to resist those that assault him' he was allowed the liberty to disobey. Nor is a man bound to confess a crime, or be obliged to accuse himself. Although a sovereign can punish the refusal of a soldier to fight with the penalty of death, the man can nonetheless refuse 'without injustice'.

Rousseau provided an account of sovereignty as a 'general will' in *The Social Contract* (1762). The ideal-type of republic is conveyed through the anatomic metaphor of a 'whole body and its parts', where the will of the sovereign is the 'general will' of a body composed of parts, the citizenry. There is an 'at-oneness' asserted between the sovereignty of the general will and the multiplicity of individual wills of which the One sovereign body is composed. However, for Rousseau sovereign power must be general: 'The sovereign power, absolute, sacred, and inviolable as it is, does not and cannot exceed the limits of general conventions, and that every man may dispose at will of such goods and liberty as these conventions leave him; so that the sovereign never has a right to lay more charges on one subject than on another, because in that case, the question becomes particular, and ceases to be within its competency' (Book II, Ch. IV).

The German jurist Carl Schmitt in *Political Theology: Four Chapters on Sovereignty* (1922) famously defined sovereignty as the 'decision on the exception'—and thus deepened the focus on the limit that separates sovereignty and law. For Schmitt, the sovereign is the person who decides when a state of exception or emergency is present and suspends the normal legal order. Schmitt explained that modern constitutional systems have struggled to define and regulate this sovereign intervention even though the established order relies on this sovereign intervention for its own preservation. Indeed, this is so obviously the case that the law might in fact willingly withdraw in the face of the sovereign exception. An example of this is the notorious refusal of US courts to extend constitutional rights to those in detention in Guantánamo Bay. While the sovereign exception might suspend the normal legal order, Schmitt insisted that it remained a juristic event, and not chaos.

The attention of juridical theorists and political philosophers was on accounting for the juridical limits of a centralised sovereign power. Foucault suggested that we should abandon this preoccupation with the centrality of the sovereign—and famously asked why we have not yet cut off the head of the King. What is needed, he suggested, was a focus on power at its extremities. In his lectures at the *Collège de France* (1975–1976), published later as *Society Must be Defended* (2003), he argued that the individual is a 'power effect', a 'relay for power': 'power passes through the individuals it has constituted'. A type of power that Foucault termed 'non-sovereign power' or 'disciplinary power', can be exercised, circulates, and forms networks. Rather than the attention given to determining the juridical limits of sovereignty, or the relationship between sovereignty and law, Foucault suggested that we explore how power penetrates bodies, how it acts to normalize and regularize behaviour.

But the capacities of a totalizing sovereign power have not vanished. The most influential contemporary accounts of sovereignty have observed that sovereign authority is constituted through the abandonment of a life that would ordinarily be subject to legal protection. Giorgio Agamben in *Homo Sacer: Sovereign Power and Bare Life* (1998) has elaborated how the 'camp' is the paradigm of modern sovereignty. In the camp, the hollowness of the sacredness of life associated with the elevation of the 'human' above the 'animal' is exposed. Life is rendered 'bare'—subject to sovereign calculations and beyond legal protections. Others have argued that life in the 'camp', from Abu Ghraib in Iraq, to the detention of 'asylum seekers' in Port Hedland, Australia, is mediated by juridical authority. These camps are the product of governmental practices which have surrendered the security of states, the management of prisons, and the conduct of interrogations to private contractors. These practices of detention reveal much more about the diffuse nature of power, and suggest that the medieval preoccupation with a sovereign figure might distract us from attending to the most invidious forms of normalisation of power and **violence**.　　　　　　　　　　STEWART MOTHA

G Agamben, *Homo Sacer: Sovereign Power and Bare Life*, Trans. D Heller-Roazen (Stanford: Stanford University Press, 1998)

M Foucault, *Society Must be Defended: Lectures at the Collège de France: 1975–1976*, Trans. David Macey (New York: Picador, 2003)

sovereignty and the European Union A claim of sovereignty asserts that there exists a supreme power within a particular political community. Such an assertion involves two basic propositions: first, that the supreme power has the function of maintaining the political community and its identity *vis-à-vis* other such communities; and, secondly, that supreme power is the source of legal authority within the political community. We might think of the first of these propositions as referring to the 'international' dimension of sovereignty, and the second to the 'national' dimension.

When countries sign multilateral international treaties, this involves exercising international exercise of powers that constitute the national sovereignty of each country. This is often a reaction to the realization that the forces affecting states in the modern world cross territorial boundaries and can only be addressed by coordinated action effective beyond such boundaries. Such treaties often create an international organization for the supervision and exercise of such powers on the international level. This can affect the traditional international dimension of state sovereignty, since that organization's international action may bind a number of states collectively, rather than allowing each to pursue its own approach on the international plane. Further, the rules created by, or adopted under, such treaties may have an effect within the national legal systems of each signatory state. Where this is so, those rules may affect the ability of the national sovereign power to adopt rules for its own national political community.

The European Community ('EC') Treaty is perhaps the quintessential example of such 'pooling' of national sovereignty by individual states, allowing the exercise of state powers by the EC on the international level. In two cases decided as early as 1963 and 1964, the **European Court of Justice** ('ECJ') stated that the Member States had granted powers to the European Community 'stemming from a limitation of sovereignty', which meant that 'the Member States [had] limited their sovereign rights', although only within those fields covered by the EC Treaty. This interpretation of the EC Treaty formed the basis for the recognition of the highly significant EC legal doctrines of the 'supremacy' and 'direct effect' of **European Community law**. These doctrines have the consequence that certain (directly effective) rules of EC law have the effect within the national legal systems of the EC's Member States of applying even where national legal rules conflict with them.

EC law purports to be the source of legal authority of such directly effective rules. Yet, from the national perspective of most Member States, such a power to create rules that have legal effect within national territory may only be exercised consistently with the rules and principles governing exercise of sovereign power at the national level. Typically, these rules and principles will be contained in the national Constitution. This means that a State may enter into an international treaty which provides for the use of national powers by an international organization only where it has the authority under the national Constitution to grant such power to the international organization. Thus, from that national perspective we can trace the authority of EC law within the national legal system back to the national constitutional provisions that give EC law that effect (in the **United Kingdom**, this is the European Communities Act 1972). Equally, a state cannot grant powers to the EC that the state itself does not possess under its national constitutional arrangements.

Where the direct effect of EC law is consistent with the national Constitution, then no conflict arises between EC law's claim to sovereignty and the national sovereignty expressed in the national Constitution. Yet the ECJ has held that directly effective EC law is supreme within the legal systems of Member States even in the face of conflicting provisions of national constitutional law. In such cases, national courts have been faced with what might be described as conflicting claims to sovereignty (in the sense of supreme legal authority) made by these competing legal rules. In most Member States, it seems that the claim that directly effective EC law is supreme has been respected by national courts, albeit typically on the basis that that relevant rules of national constitutional law allow for this. However, at the same time these national courts have specifically referred to restrictions placed by national constitutional requirements on the supremacy of EC law. This highlights that the sovereignty expressed in the national constitutional rules continues to be defended and upheld by national courts. In particular, national guarantees of fundamental rights, national constitutional restrictions upon the powers of the state, and other express national constitutional protections (such as the Polish constitutional prohibition upon the extradition of any Polish national) have all been held capable of defeating the claims of EC law to supremacy when applied in the national legal system.

In the United Kingdom, the courts will presume that Parliament does not intend to act in a manner contrary to directly effective EC law rules. This preserves the power of Parliament expressly to pass legislation which conflicts with EC law; and it is assumed that were Parliament ever to do so, the courts would uphold the will of Parliament over the requirements of the conflicting EC law rule. In this way, the core of the sovereignty of Parliament (in the 'national dimension' sense of its legislative supremacy) is said to be preserved.

Ultimately, the final expression of the sovereignty of any individual Member State of the **European**

Union would be a decision to renounce membership and to leave the Union. While there has been debate in some circles as to whether this would be legally possible (given that the current treaties contain no express 'exit clause'), it is inconceivable that such an exercise of sovereignty by a Member State would not in practice be effective. Of course, the negotiation of the practical implications of such a decision would be fraught, extremely complicated, and no doubt protracted.   ANGUS JOHNSTON

See also: **European treaties**

space law   see **air and space law**

space/spatiality   Spatiality is socially produced space. Scholars of spatiality reject the Kantian division between space and society. Spatiality is not simply an outcome of social forces but is itself constitutive of society and politics. Such arguments challenge the modernist tendency to treat **time** and history as the privileged vector of enquiry, the effect of which was to treat space as inert or passive.

While there are some exceptions, such as **comparative law**, legal scholarship has until recently been disinterested in space and spatiality. If space was a focus of enquiry, it tended to be regarded as an independent variable. Whether law was explained by reference to space, or space was seen as produced by law, the tendency was to impose separations on law, space, and society. Either way, space was circumscribed as an analytic variable. Even scholarship hostile to the legal mainstream, such as **critical legal studies**, relied upon the historical imagination, sidelining space as a result.

However, this has changed over the last two decades, in line with the 'spatial turn' in social theory. Drawing broadly, though not exclusively, from poststructuralist concerns with interpretation and the production of social meaning, spatiality has been identified as crucial to legal analysis.

In brief, it is argued that law and space are both socially produced and socially productive. Spatiality is in turn productive of law, as well as produced, in part, by law; law produces spaces (such as the legal boundary, or the sovereign state) yet is itself produced and interpreted in relation to space (for example, being interpreted within local settings). Legal geographies are also seen as deeply implicated with power relations, given the particular importance of law and space to resistance and domination.

A category like public space, for example, is simultaneously a legal and a geographic category. Legal institutions and practices, such as **courts** and by-law enforcement, help constitute public spaces in particular and politically important ways. Yet the spatial dimensions of the public sphere are not simply an outcome of law. They may also help sustain or complicate legal orderings. The effect of a legal category such as jurisdiction upon social and political **identities** derives, in large part, from its spatiality. Reliant upon **territory** as a technology of definition and identification, jurisdiction can also make resultant oppressive identities and relationships appear natural, by virtue of its spatial ordering. Spatiality, precisely because it appears inert and apolitical, can hide power and naturalize injustice.

This scholarship is remarkably diverse and lively, engaging with topics such as nature, jurisdiction, landscape, state practice, **nationalism**, property, and boundaries. Scholars draw from a range of theoretical sources, including **queer theory**, urban political economy, actor-network theory, and cultural studies.   NICHOLAS BLOMLEY

J Holder and C Harrison, *Law and Geography* (Oxford: Oxford University Press, 2003)
A Sarat, L Douglas, and M Umphrey, *The Place of Law* (Ann Arbor: University of Michigan Press, 2003)

Speaker, House of Commons   The office of Speaker, under that title, dates from 1377, although the functions were performed by Members for more than a century earlier. The Speaker is an MP elected after each General Election by the **House of Commons** to represent it in communications with the **Monarch** and the **House of Lords**, and on other formal occasions; to preside over sittings of the House; to maintain order in the Chamber (and exercise sanctions to do so); and to apply and interpret the procedural rules of the House ('Standing Orders'). The Speaker also has administrative duties. As an aspect of representing the House, the Speaker, on election, claims on behalf of the Commons 'all their ancient and undoubted rights and privileges'.

An important routine role of the Speaker is to choose ('call') Members to speak in proceedings, and the order in which they do so. In exercising this function, and others, the Speaker accepts a particular role of protecting minority opinion in the House. The Speaker acts in an overtly apolitical and impartial manner. One aspect of this is that the Speaker does not vote in divisions except, where a vote is tied, to exercise a casting vote to allow debate to continue on the matter or, if that is not possible, to maintain the *status quo*.

The Speaker has three deputies, one of whom—the Chairman of Ways and Means—presides when the

House is sitting as a committee and when it is considering certain financial motions.

                                    T St JOHN BATES

special educational needs   Following the Warnock Report of 1978, the system of Special Educational Needs ('SEN') in England and Wales was established to meet the needs of pupils with learning difficulties. Similar systems exist in Scotland and Northern Ireland ('NI') and are discussed below. At the centre of each system is an assessment procedure which can result in the drawing up of a formal statement of the learning difficulty, the needs arising therefrom, and the provision required to meet those needs. **Legislation** is accompanied by statutory guidance (with separate guidance for Wales) which emphasizes that SEN should be identified early and steps taken to address learning difficulties before needs become serious or complex enough to merit a formal statement of SEN. The guidance promotes a sliding scale of interventions involving other professionals as needs become more acute, with a formal assessment and statement necessary only where other intervention cannot address the learning difficulties.

The Education Act 1996 as amended by the Special Educational Needs and **Disability** Act 2001 ('SENDA') establishes that a **child** has a learning difficulty where he or she:'

(a) has a significantly greater difficulty in learning than the majority of children of the same age; or
(b) has a disability which either prevents or hinders the child from making use of educational facilities of a kind provided for children of the same age in schools within the area of the LEA'

This definition covers conditions including specific learning difficulties (such as dyslexia and dyspraxia), emotional and behavioural difficulties, and sensory and physical impairments. Schools are required to use their best endeavours to ensure that any child attending the school receives the special educational provision for which their learning difficulty calls. Education authorities are under a duty to identify pupils with learning difficulties who need or probably need a formal statement of SEN. Once such a pupil has been identified, the authority is under a duty to consider whether a formal assessment is necessary. If such assessment indicates that authority provision is needed to meet the learning difficulty, the authority must make the statement and arrange, monitor, and review the provision within it. Education authorities are under a duty to ensure that the provision necessary to meet the educational needs specified in the statement is made. Authorities are, however, at liberty

to meet the need in the most cost-effective manner—leaving room for disagreement about what exactly is needed and whether need has been met.

Differences may also arise over whether needs should be met in mainstream or special schools, and whether the need should be met in the maintained or the independent sector. SENDA introduced a presumption that a child should be educated in a mainstream school where this is compatible with the wishes of the parent and with the provision of efficient education for other pupils. As with other **school admissions**, parents are entitled to express a preference for a particular school and where an education authority makes a statement they must name the parent's preferred school unless:

(a) the school is unsuitable to the child's age, ability, or aptitude or to his special educational needs; or
(b) the attendance of the child at the school would be incompatible with the provision of efficient education for the children with whom he would be educated or the efficient use of resources.

This is significant as the governors of a maintained school must admit a child if their school is named in the statement.

Regulations set out strict time limits for each stage of the formal assessment procedure. Regulations also set out the details of rights to appeal to the Special Educational Needs and Disability **Tribunal** ('SENDIST') or in Wales the SEN Tribunal for Wales. The tribunal can substitute its own view of what should be included in a statement, giving the child the right to these resources. However the appeal system does not provide appeal to SENDIST where the resources specified in the statement are not provided. Here judicial review may provide a remedy, but an alternative may be a complaint to the Local Government Ombudsman ('LGO'). Recourse to the LGO can be particularly effective where time limits have not been met and the child has been unjustly deprived of the educational benefits they are entitled to because of the delay.

Almost identical provisions apply in NI through the Education (NI) Order 1996 as amended. These provisions include the duty to educate pupils with SEN in mainstream schools. The Scottish system adopts a slightly different framework and terminology. The system, which was reformed in 2004, is phrased in terms of 'Additional Support Needs' ('ASN'). The Education (Additional Support for Learning)(Scotland) Act 2004 defines ASN in terms of a child or young person being unable or likely to be unable to benefit from school education, where school education is defined in terms of it being 'directed to the development of the personality, talents and mental and physical abilities of the child or young person to their fullest potential'. ASN gives rise to duties that are broadly equivalent to those in the English legislation. In particular, education authorities are responsible for making adequate and efficient provision for such additional support as is required, and for making appropriate arrangements for keeping a child's ASN and the adequacy of the additional support provided under consideration. It used to be that the concept of a statement of SEN was matched in Scotland by the 'Record of Needs' but this has been replaced by the 'Co-ordinated Support Plan' for children with enduring complex or multiple barriers to learning who need a range of different support from different services. A complex factor is defined as one that has or is likely to have a significant adverse effect on the school education of the child or young person. One difference between the Scottish and other systems is that although there is a presumption of education in mainstream schools in the Standards in Scotland's Schools etc Act 2000, the exception to this is defined in terms of exceptional circumstances rather than parental wishes and the impact on other pupils. ANN BLAIR

Special Educational Needs and Disability Tribunal   *see* **special educational needs; tribunals**

specialist schools   *see* **school admissions**

specific performance   A decree of specific performance is a court order that requires a person to carry out a contractual or other consensual obligation. In Scots law it is called specific implement, and extends to obligations imposed by law. Imagine that the claimant made a contract with the defendant to buy the defendant's house, but the defendant now refuses to go ahead with the deal. The claimant might seek money compensation for the breach of contract, but might instead ask for specific performance; that is, an order requiring the defendant to convey the house to the claimant. An order to perform an obligation to pay money (for example, to repay a loan of £100) is not considered to be a decree of specific performance.

Specific performance is traditionally understood as a discretionary remedy; claimants do not have an absolute right to specific performance, but rather it is granted in the discretion of the court. In principle, English courts will not order specific performance if the claimant's loss is readily compensable in money (although in Scots law, specific implement is not subject to this restriction). This means that specific performance is readily granted where there is a contract to sell a unique thing, including an interest in land. Courts are reluctant to make orders that would require constant supervision by the court (for example, a contract to carry on a business). Also, courts will usually not order specific performance of contracts involving personal service, like most employment contracts, on the ground that they do not want to force people into a kind of involuntary servitude. Furthermore, in some cases specific performance is not possible; in the example above, this would be the case if the defendant has already sold the house to another party who was unaware of the first sale. LIONEL SMITH

See also: **remedies**

spectators at sporting events   The law usually becomes involved with incidents relating to spectators at sporting events when someone has been injured by the fabric of the stadium or by the activity taking place in it, or because s/he has been involved in disorder, or hooliganism, of some kind. Actions for injuries caused by the collapse of all or part of the stadium will be brought under the Occupiers' Liability Act 1957 (in England and the equivalent (1960) statutory provision in Scotland). This provides that the premises must be reasonably safe for the purpose for which they are being used.

Where appropriate, reasonable protection must be provided to prevent objects, such as ice hockey pucks, from entering spectator areas as this carries a significant risk of serious injury. However, it is assumed that those present at the game will be aware of its inherent dangers. Thus, in contrast to ice hockey, a cricket spectator would be expected to take evasive action when the ball is hit into the crowd for six as this is an integral part of the playing of the game.

A less onerous duty is owed to trespassers. Where a spectator is injured having entered a restricted part of the arena, for example by running onto the course at a race track, the occupier will escape liability where the risk of injury has been brought to the attention of the spectator by adequate signage.

Sports participants owe a limited duty of care towards spectators to avoid causing them injury whilst they are competing. In *Wooldridge v Sumner* (1963), it was held that a competitor need not pay attention to spectators' safety when going flat out to win. Only when they are acting with a reckless disregard for the safety of the spectator will the competitor breach their duty of care. MARK JAMES

See also: **players of sports; sport and public order**

spectrum regulation   The radio spectrum constitutes the environment within which all forms

of wireless electronic communications operate. In common with other forms of natural commodities, the resource is finite. With the worldwide growth in electronic communications, issues of how and to whom elements of the spectrum are allocated assumes increasing importance, as epitomized by the massive sums bid by mobile telephone companies in the **United Kingdom** seeking a share of the spectrum made available for 3G mobile telephony.

Spectrum regulation takes place at a number of levels. Use of the spectrum is coordinated at the global level by the International Telecommunications Union ('ITU'). Now a specialized agency of the **United Nations**, the ITU is the world's oldest international agency. Operating through world radiocommunications conferences held every two or three years, the ITU allocates elements of the spectrum both for specific uses and to specific countries. The nature of the allocation changes over time, reflecting political considerations and changes in technology that create additional demands in some areas and reduce demand in others. An example can be seen in the switch from analogue to digital television in the United Kingdom, which will free up significant elements of the spectrum for other uses.

Spectrum allocation has featured in the **European Union**'s telecommunications policy. Member States are obliged to develop and publish frequency allocation policies and establish an EU Committee to monitor activities and ensure that policies are applied in a fair and non-discriminatory manner. Within the UK, this task is carried out by the Office of Communications ('Ofcom'). The Communications Act 2003 lays down the basis for spectrum management and provides that, save in cases where activities pose no serious risk of causing interference with other users, use of the spectrum for transmission purposes will be an offence.   IAN LLOYD

sponsorship in sport   Sponsorship is a commercial arrangement where a sponsor enters into an agreement with a rights owner under which the sponsor usually agrees to pay a sponsorship fee (or sometimes provide services or other support) to the rights owner in return for the right to promote its brand or product in association with an event, team, organization, individual, and so on.

Individual athletes/players, teams, clubs, tournaments, leagues, stadiums, sporting events, and sporting broadcasts all attract sponsorship. The key reasons for a sponsor associating its brand with such 'property' (as they are referred to in the marketplace) are to raise its profile in alignment with brand and corporate values, and sometimes to drive sales and revenues through association with the sponsored 'property'. Sponsors may also be granted ancillary rights such as hospitality, tickets, and other promotional rights.

Sponsors will often enter into a myriad of legal agreements to obtain rights to exploit and activate their sponsorship, as a number of different rights owners may own rights which the sponsor wishes to use, or wishes to prevent others from using (such as rights to player images, team crests, official event logos, and so on).

Sponsorship is principally founded on **contract law** and intellectual property law. The sponsorship contract itself should deal with the grant of the rights and the exploitation of those rights by the sponsor. It will also impose certain obligations on and reserve certain rights for the rights owner. It is not uncommon for payments to be structured to include bonuses as well as rights fees to reward positive exposure, while allowing termination or withholding of bonuses for negative publicity.

Sponsors and rights owners often have to rely on **trade mark** infringement or **passing off** to enable them to prevent non-sponsors from associating themselves with the sponsored property. Unauthorized association in this context is commonly referred to as 'ambush marketing'.

In some circumstances, sponsorship is supported by legislation which creates statutory rights to prevent unauthorized association. For example, in England and Wales the London Olympic Games and Paralympic Games Act 2006 created a 'London Olympics Association Right' and makes it an offence to create an unauthorized association with the London 2012 Olympic or Paralympic Games.

WARREN PHELOPS

sport and central government   The relationship between sport and central government operates at a number of different levels. Most obviously, government is involved through the work of the Department of Media, Culture, and Sport and of UK Sport, which was established by Royal Charter in 1996 and is the UK's High Performance sports agency. In addition, various aspects of the business of sport are regulated by law including the protection of intellectual property rights in sport and the prohibition of anticompetitive aspects of this business. In this respect professional sport in the United Kingdom has been deeply affected by the impact of European Community law. The manner in which sports governing bodies exercise their functions, including their disciplinary codes in respect of players, is subject to challenge in the courts. Finally, where behaviour on the field of play by players and referees, or the organization of a sporting event, or the manner in which sports safety rules are operated by governing bodies cause harm either intentionally or negligently, this can generate both criminal and/or civil liability.

NEVILLE COX

sport and competition law   Sport and **competition law** have an uneasy relationship. Sport is big business and is dominated by a small number of large organizations. It is thus an obvious target for the **European Commission** and national competition authorities, who are concerned with anti-competitive market behaviour and the existence of monopolies. Conversely, sport is largely self-regulating and does not fit neatly within traditional market ideas.

Sport is subject to the competition law rules insofar as it constitutes an economic activity. The rules can therefore apply to federations; clubs; and individual participants receiving remuneration, even if classed as amateurs.

There are however, many aspects of sport that are separate from the business side of the industry. As such, the law attempts to distinguish between economic matters and matters of 'purely sporting interest'. The latter are not subject to the rules. The obvious 'purely sporting' matters are the basic rules of a particular sport. Thus recent modifications to the offside rule in football, the changes to the length of table tennis games, and the alterations to the number of points awarded at the end of Formula 1 races are all outside of the scope of the competition rules. Nonetheless, the distinction can be difficult to draw. Rules on player eligibility, for example, have an obvious economic effect on those who are excluded.

Competition law issues arise in many sporting contents. There are three main sporting markets: the market for the production of the actual sporting contest; the market for the exploitation of secondary features of the performance, such as broadcasting rights and merchandising; and the market for the buying and selling of players. Within these markets, typical areas of interest have been ticket sales, television rights, multiple club ownership, club relocation, player transfer rules, and the monopoly position of sporting federations such as UEFA.

As in many sectors, competition law is encroaching further upon sport and the distinction between economic and 'purely sporting' matters is being blurred. In 2006, the ECJ ruled that, as the International Olympic Committee's anti-doping rules, seen as essential to the fair conduct of athletics, permitted the exclusion of athletes from sporting participation (with obvious economic consequences), the rules

could be contrary to competition law. It was ultimately held that the rules were acceptable, but only because they were 'limited to what was necessary to ensure the proper conduct of competitive sport'. As the reach of competition law increases, structural changes at the heart of sport seem more and more likely.

MARIE DEMETRIOU

A Egger and C Stix-Hackl, 'Sports and Competition Law: a Never- Ending Story?' (2002) 23(1) *European Competition Law Review* 81

See also: **merchandising and licensing in sport; players of sports; sport, broadcasting of**

sport and criminal law   The criminal law can become involved with sporting contests in four very different ways. First, it can be a means of controlling players' conduct. The Court of Appeal has held that a prosecution for a criminal assault will only rarely be in the public interest if it arises from the playing of sport. Only those assaults that are so violent as to be deemed unconnected with the playing of the game should be considered to be criminal. In an unusual case in Scotland, a professional footballer was convicted of assault having kicked the ball with excessive force into the crowd (so treatment could be administered to a teammate), injuring a young girl sitting near the front of the stand.

Secondly, criminal law can be used to control spectator disorder. In particular, the Public Order Act 1986 and the Football Offences Act 1991 are used to prosecute suspected 'hooligans' whilst Football Banning Orders can be imposed following the procedures in the Football Spectators Act 1989.

Thirdly, in recent years the criminal law has been used to investigate incidents of corruption and match-fixing in sports like horse racing and cricket. The most likely charge in such a situation is conspiracy to defraud, where those defrauded are the gamblers who have lost money because of a jockey's deliberate failure to try to win the race or where confidential information about team selection has been used to improve specific gamblers' chances of winning. Charges may now also be brought under a provision of the Gambling Act 2005 dealing with cheating at gambling, and a provision of the Fraud Act 2006 dealing with fraud by the making of a false representation (where, again, the fraud would be the jockey's failure to try).

Finally, the criminal law can be used to outlaw activities that have been considered previously to be lawful sports. The Firearms (Amendment) Act 1997, although intended to reduce the incidence of gun crime, criminalizes the ownership of many categories of small calibre pistols that are used for

Olympic-type target sports. This Act makes it illegal to practise those disciplines which use the now illegal weapons in the UK. A more controversial example of the banning of a sport by legislation was the Hunting Act 2004, which outlawed the hunting of wild mammals with dogs and hare coursing.

MARK JAMES

See also: **blood sports**; **combat sports**; **players of sports**; **sport and public order**

sport and discrimination   Sport is a field which is partly covered by, and partly exempted from, the reach of the anti-discrimination statutes and regulations. In general, discrimination law will apply to sport as to other activities. So, for example, to discriminate against a tennis agent because he is black, or to decline to employ a football coach because she is a woman, or to refuse teach a child to swim because she is a Muslim and wishes to wear an adapted swimming costume, will all be unlawful because of the general provisions relating to discrimination on grounds of race, sex, and religion in the fields of agency, employment, and education. However, there are a few exceptions.

Section 44 of the Sex Discrimination Act 1975 exempts, from both the employment and non-employment provisions of the Act, any act related to the participation of a person as a competitor in any sport, game, or other activity of a competitive nature where the physical strength, stamina, or physique of the average woman puts her at a disadvantage in comparison with the average man, and where the events involving that activity are confined to competitors of one sex. The case law shows that this exception applies to children no less than adults.

Whilst the Gender Recognition Act 2004 generally requires someone with a re-assigned gender to have that new gender recognized, it provides that a body responsible for regulating the participation of competitors in a 'gender-affected' sport may prohibit or restrict the participation of a person in a competition in their re-assigned gender if the prohibition or restriction is necessary to secure fair competition or the safety of competitors.

Section 39 of the Race Relations Act 1976 exempts, from both the employment and non-employment provisions of the Act, any act whereby a person discriminates against another on the basis of that other's nationality, or place of birth, or on the basis of length of residence in a particular area or place if the discriminatory act is done in selecting one or more people to represent a country, place, or area or any related association in any sport or game, or in pursuance of the rules of any competition so far as they relate to eligibility to compete in any sport or game.

Age discrimination legislation only applies in the field of employment. Consequently, to divide juvenile competitors by age is not unlawful, and may even be required by health and safety law.

HELEN MOUNTFIELD

sport and human rights   Human rights and sport may seem strange bedfellows but that has not stopped sports lawyers citing human rights arguments in the period since the Human Rights Act 1998 ('HRA') came into force on 2 October 2000.

Initially there was lots of debate about whether sporting bodies would be considered to be public authorities and hence amenable to the HRA. As it transpired, however, it did not matter whether they were or not. The courts are public authorities, and are obliged to consider the human rights of parties before them, whether public or private. This, together with the courts' willingness to take a supervisory view of the decisions of sporting bodies, means that there is no bar to human rights points being raised in sports proceedings.

Article 6 of the **European Convention on Human Rights** ('ECHR'), conferring the right to a fair trial, has been something of a favourite. In one case a question arose as to whether a football agent had voluntarily waived his full Article 6 rights in relation to a dispute about disciplinary proceedings under the Football Association's arbitration rule. The Court of Appeal concluded that the agent's rights had been freely waived. In any event, the arbitration proceedings were fair, as the arbitrators were obliged to act fairly and impartially under the Arbitration Act 1996.

Article 10, conferring the right to freedom of expression, pops up less frequently. Football players and managers have occasionally claimed that their rights to free speech have been violated by virtue of their being disciplined for talking to the press. In a different connection, a magazine publisher alleged that the refusal of press accreditation for the Australian Grand Prix was a breach of his Article 10 rights. (Unfortunately, since the 1998 Act does not have extraterritorial effect, there was some difficulty in bringing this claim against the FIA (Federation Internationale de L'Automobile)—based in France.)

As for the right to property under Article 1 of the First Protocol to the Convention, it has been determined that the prevention of enjoyment of a sport or hobby is not a deprivation of a possession.

JANE MULCAHY

sport and public order   Discussion of public order in sport usually focuses on football hooliganism.

Although such disorder can constitute any number of criminal offences under the Offences Against the Person Act 1861 or the Criminal Damage Act 1971, the most commonly charged crimes are found in the Public Order Act 1986 and the Football Offences Act 1991. The police have found that the most effective means of securing convictions in these situations is to charge those involved with either affray, or causing harassment, alarm, or distress to another under the Public Order Act. These offences are relatively easy to prove where large groups of fans are acting in a disorderly or intimidatory manner. The Football Offences Act contains three specific crimes that can only be committed at football matches: throwing objects at the playing area or other spectators; engaging in indecent or racial chanting; and going on to the playing area without lawful excuse.

The most high-profile weapon in the anti-hooligan armoury is the Football Banning Order. If convicted of a football-related offence, an Order can be imposed under the Football Spectators Act for a period of six to ten years depending on the offence committed and the defendant's degree of involvement in the incident and its organization. Where a spectator is suspected of being involved in football-related disorder, though not having been convicted of an offence, the chief officer of police for the area where the suspect lives can apply for an Order to be imposed for two to three years where he considers it necessary to prevent future football-related disorder. Either type of order prevents a banned person from entering, or going within a specified distance of, every professional football ground in the country, including Football Conference and League of Wales grounds, when a match is taking place. These orders can also prevent a person from travelling abroad to watch their chosen club, or the England and Wales national teams, by requiring them surrender their passports to their local police station five days prior to the game's kick off. These powers are extended to Scotland by the Police, Public Order and Criminal Justice (Scotland) Act 2006. The breach of the terms of these Orders is a criminal offence.

To prevent breakdown of the segregation of rival fans at football matches, the unauthorized selling of tickets to all professional football games is illegal. Ticket touting at all other sporting events, apart from the London 2012 Olympics, is not a criminal offence but merely a matter of breach of contract. All unauthorized sales, including the reselling, of tickets to Olympic events are illegal under the London Olympic Games and Paralympic Games Act 2006.

Finally, sports participants can be bound over to keep the peace if their actions are likely to incite the crowd to violence or disorder. This has been a particular concern in Scotland where footballers have been prevented from crossing themselves or mimicking playing the pipes to antagonize opposition fans of Protestant or Catholic backgrounds respectively.

MARK JAMES

sport and taxation There is no overriding exemption from UK tax for income arising from sporting activities and the tax system potentially applies to participation in sport in many different ways. For example, **income tax** can apply to earnings of sports people in the form of salaries and wages as well as appearance and sponsorship fees. **Corporation tax** may be payable by clubs and their league and governing bodies on profits from trading and investment income, the sale of capital assets and fund-raising activities (although it may be possible to claim tax benefits if charitable status can be obtained or if a local amateur sports club can be registered as Community Amateur Sports Club under the Finance Act 2002). The possible application of **value added tax** ('VAT') must also be considered on all transactions.

The significant investment in the sports industry (particularly in the form of the construction of new sporting venues) has highlighted that tax is important not just for those who are directly involved in sport but also for those, such as the investors and financiers, who are involved indirectly.

Whilst the UK has a number of double tax treaties with overseas countries which have the aim of preventing double taxation, sports people are usually unable to take advantage of these treaties and are exposed to tax in both the country of their residence and the country in which the income is earned. However, credit will normally be given in the country of residence for any overseas tax which has been paid on the same income. WARREN PHELOPS

sport, broadcasting of Broadcasting has played a key role in sport's increasing commercialization. English law does not, however, recognize a named 'broadcasting right'. Rather, the right to broadcast sporting events arises in one of two main ways. The first is through an associated real property right: a licence. A venue's owners grant a broadcaster a licence to enter the venue to make a recording. The second is through an associated intellectual property right: a company owns the copyright in the recordings it makes of sporting events. This **copyright** can then be sold or licensed to broadcasters.

The legal extent of broadcasting rights is still being worked out. For example, the Football Association Premier League ('FAPL') licenses domestic and international broadcasters to show matches in their respective countries. Recently, however, certain companies have begun selling satellite 'SMART' cards from overseas to pubs in the UK, enabling them to broadcast Premier League matches that would otherwise be unavailable. FAPL has alleged that this violates its intellectual property rights. Criminal prosecutions have been brought against pub landlords, and, though the issue is as yet unsettled, it is likely that civil actions will follow against the sellers.

The control of broadcasting rights has also become a significant legal issue: in particular, whether the law should guarantee that certain events are broadcast by a free-to-air broadcaster (such as the BBC); or whether one broadcaster should be entitled to acquire exclusive rights to show certain sporting events.

At **European Union** level, the Television without Frontiers Directive lays down a framework guaranteeing the public free access to broadcasts of important events. This is given effect by UK legislation under which the Secretary of State creates a list of important events. 'Group A' events must be shown live by a free-to-air broadcaster, and secondary coverage of 'Group B' events (such as highlights) must also be provided. 'Group A' events include the Olympic Games, the FA Cup Final, and the Rugby World Cup Final; 'Group B' events include domestic England cricket test matches, and all other Rugby World Cup matches.

Competition authorities have been concerned that the granting of exclusive rights to broadcasters is anti-competitive. In the UK the 'stranglehold' of BSkyB over the rights to screen Premier League football matches has been the subject of action by the **European Commission** and the **Office of Fair Trading**. The grant of broadcasting rights must not distort **competition** in the market for the broadcasting of sporting events. Thus, in future, broadcast rights packages will necessarily run for shorter periods of time, with tiered 'packages' available, allowing bids by a greater number of broadcasters. Ultimately, BSkyB may be required by the competition authorities to sub-license some of its matches to rival broadcasters.

The collective selling of broadcast rights has also been viewed as anti-competitive. FAPL sells the rights to all Premier League matches, rather than allowing each individual club to sell the rights to its own games. This may hinder competition and prevent new broadcasters from entering the market. However, collective selling has been permitted as being for 'the good of the game': the greater

money generated is distributed between all football clubs, supporting the weaker clubs and preventing the escalation of the gap between football's rich and poor.   MARIE DEMETRIOU

S Clover 'Confused Signals—Satellite Broadcasting and Premiership Football' (2007) *Entertainment Law Review* 126

D McAuly, 'Exclusively for All and Collectively for None: Refereeing Broadcasting Rights between the Premier League, European Commission and BSkyB' (2004) 25(6) *European Competition Law Review* 370

See also: **sport and competition law**

sports governing bodies   In the **United Kingdom**, the government traditionally takes a non-interventionist stance to the sports sector. It is private sports governing bodies ('SGBs') (such as The Football Association, the Lawn Tennis Association, and the Rugby Football Union) that take responsibility for governing, nurturing, and championing the many facets of their respective sports as a healthy pastime for the massed ranks of amateurs, as a consumer product and an opportunity for riches for the professional elite, and as a platform for both volunteering and employment at all levels.

Through membership of the relevant international federation (such as the International Cricket Council in cricket, FIFA in football, and the UCI in cycling), SGBs exercise sole authority over their respective sports within their domestic jurisdictions within of a global regulatory framework. A strong SGB is crucial: sport is a collective enterprise that depends on substantial cooperation and coordination between its various participants to preserve the competitive balance that is the key to the one feature (uncertainty of outcome) that makes sport unique.

Like a mini-sovereign state, each SGB has a more or less well-defined legislative function (issuing sporting rules and regulations through councils or general assemblies), executive function (administering and policing the rules through its directors and officers), and judicial function (enforcing the rules through disciplinary bodies). Crucially, however, an SGB's authority is not sovereign, but instead depends entirely upon the consent of its members, expressed through continued participation in officially sanctioned events. In short, the rulebook constitutes a contract between the SGB and the sporting participants that creates the SGB's authority over the collective.

That explains why, when tensions arise (often, but not always, between the professional and amateur ranks of the sport), the usual threat is to 'break away', and competition law is often the weapon of choice used to combat the alleged 'abuse of regulatory authority' and 'cartel-like behaviour' of the incumbent SGB. It also explains why challenges in the courts to the actions of SGBs are private law rather than public law claims.

However, courts exercise only a supervisory jurisdiction over the actions of an SGB: in deference to the SGB's assumed specialist expertise, courts are often reluctant to intervene when an SGB's actions are challenged; and so the private law standards applied upon such challenge have become indistinguishable from public law standards applicable upon **judicial review** of the actions of public bodies.

SGBs are destined, however, to remain frequent visitors to the courts, and not only because commercialization has raised the stakes so high. They are seen as custodians of public assets (football, for example, is considered 'the national game'), and are charged with protecting sporting integrity from a host of enemies (including doping, match-fixing, and rampant commercialism). At the same time, however, SGBs have to reconcile their various stakeholders' oft-competing demands as well as satisfy government agencies that want to use sport to advance their public policy agendas. Consequently, modern SGBs are being forced to emerge from their amateur origins to become mature, professional, and accountable organizations.

JONATHAN TAYLOR

A Lewis and J Taylor (eds), *Sport: Law & Practice* (London: Tolleys, 2nd edn, 2008)

See also: **sports regulation**

sports image rights Sport is big business: worth 3 per cent of world trade; and 2 per cent of the combined gross national product ('GNP') of the twenty-seven Member States of the **European Union**. Sport is now a commodity and sports persons are also treated in the same way: as 'properties' to be commercialized. The image rights of famous players such as Tiger Woods and David Beckham are worth millions of dollars. But how can they legally control and protect them? This varies from country to country and even the nomenclature is different. In the **United Kingdom**, these rights are known as 'rights of privacy'; in the rest of Europe, 'rights of personality'; and in the United States, 'rights of publicity'. Even in the US, the legal protection varies from one state to another. And, in the UK, there is no image right *per se*. A personality can only take legal action 'if the reproduction or use of [his/her] likeness results in the infringement of some recognised legal right which [he/she] does own' (Laddie J in *Elvis Presley Trade Marks* (1997)). Thus, a personality has to rely

on a 'rag bag' of laws, such as the statutory law of **trade marks** and **copyright**, and the **common law** of **passing off**. However, for UK tax purposes, image rights are considered to be 'capital assets' and recognized as such.

In Continental Europe, rights of personality are generally protected by specific provisions in the constitutions of the countries concerned. In Spain, for example, the Constitution guarantees the right to honour, to personal and family privacy, and to self-image. And these rights, including the right to control one's image, belong to everyone—whether famous or not!

In Germany, the right of personality is protected by the Constitution; and, in a landmark decision rendered by the Hamburg District Court on 25 April 2003, the Court held that the general personality right of the famous German goalkeeper, Oliver Khan, had been infringed when his pictorial representation and name had been used for commercial purposes without his consent in a computer game entitled 'FIFA World Championship 2002'. However, generally speaking, rights of personality in continental Europe are subject to the rights of **freedom of information** and **freedom of expression** also the subject of constitutional guarantees. Thus, there will be no infringement of the right of personality where the image of the personality concerned that has been reproduced has been taken in a public place. In other words, a public interest right may override a private right of personality, especially where the personality concerned is well-known to the general public.

In the US, certain states, for example, California, also recognize so-called *post-mortem* rights of publicity, which protect the exploitation of the name and likeness of the personality after their death.

IAN BLACKSHAW

IS Blackshaw and RCR Siekmann, *Sports Image Rights in Europe* (The Hague: TMC Asser Press, 2005)

sports law No-one disputes that sport is an area of human activity increasingly subject to legal constraints as it develops from recreation to business. There is, however, a continuing debate about whether there is an identifiable body of sports law, ie special rules, principles, procedures, and institutions which govern sport as distinct from an aggregation of rules for sport culled from separate substantive legal areas. Similar debates surround other areas, for example, environmental law or computer law.

Sports law is certainly adopting the apparel of a recognized legal discipline: there are various books dedicated to the subject; degrees in sports law; and **tribunals** which adjudicate solely on sports-related issues. Furthermore many countries (such as Malaysia and France) either have legislation that is sports-specific or vest regulatory authority and substantial promotion of sports in a government ministry or commission. In the UK by contrast the autonomy of **sports governing bodies** is generally respected.

The drive towards to creation of a globalized '*lex sportiva*' is promoted by the Court of Arbitration for Sport ('CAS'), based in Lausanne, to whose jurisdiction most major international sports subscribe, track and field and football being the most recent adherents, cricket and Formula 2 motor racing the most conspicuous outsiders. CAS was recently described by the Swiss Federal Tribunal as a 'true supreme court of world sport'.

The principles developed by CAS reflect the fundamental requirements of sport itself—fair competition, speed and certainty of result, player participation, and spectator enjoyment. They include: the autonomy of the official (subject to bad faith or corruption); the reticence of courts to interfere with the decisions of sports regulators when these depend upon the exercise of discretion; emphasis on adherence to time limits, whether related to eligibility to compete or duration of competition; and a bias towards allowing players to compete if possible and not to be impeded by arbitrary or discriminatory rules.

MICHAEL BELOFF

sports regulation   In general, sport is regulated by **sports governing bodies** ('SGBs') at the national, regional, and international levels. Football, for example, is governed by national football associations; at the European level by UEFA (Union of European Football Associations); and globally, by FIFA (International Federation of Football Associations). These bodies regulate their sports both on and off the field of play; and increasingly, as sport is big business, they also control the commercial aspects, including sponsorship, merchandising, and broadcasting rights. The right to televize football matches is particularly lucrative—the English Premier League has recently sold these rights for three seasons beginning in 2007 for £1.7 billion!

SGBs are private associations and particularly active in safeguarding the integrity of their sports by exercising disciplinary control over those who compete in and practise them—especially the use of performance-enhancing drugs. They are also responsible for maintaining safety standards for participants and spectators.

These SGBs are very powerful and jealously guard their autonomy. Self-regulation is the name of the game. And, generally speaking, they are not subject to outside control. In England, there is a long tradition that courts do not normally intervene in sports disputes. They tend to leave matters to be settled by the sports bodies themselves considering them, in the words of former Vice-Chancellor Megarry, 'far better fitted to judge than the courts'. Lord **Denning**, a former **Master of the Rolls**, put the matter thus: '…justice can often be done in domestic tribunals by a good layman than by a bad lawyer'. However, English courts will intervene where there has been a breach of the rules of **natural justice** and in restraint of trade cases, where livelihoods are at stake. Elsewhere in Europe, the courts do not intervene in cases concerning the 'rules of the game'.

In the US, sports disputes are considered private matters and courts only intervene in cases involving breach of **due process rights**, breach of contract, and breach of sports rules. Even then, their involvement is limited to correcting breaches of the rules. In one case, the judge in an eligibility dispute remarked:

…there can be few less suitable bodies than federal courts for determining eligibility, or the procedure for determining the eligibility of athletes…'. In Canada, a judge refused to order the Canadian Yachting Association to hold a second regatta for selecting the 'mistral class' team to compete in the 1996 Olympics remarking: 'The appeals bodies determined that the selection criteria had been met … [and] *as persons knowledgeable in the sport … I would be reluctant to substitute my opinion for those who know the sport and knew the nature of the problem* (emphasis added).

In the **European Union**, the **European Commission** and the **European Court of Justice** ('ECJ') only intervene in so far as '…. the practice of sport . . . . constitutes an economic activity . . . .'.

The ECJ case of *Dona v Mantero* (1976) concerned nationality rules in Italian football. The Italian Football Federation heavily restricted non-Italian footballers from playing professional football in Italy. An Italian football agent, who had attempted to recruit players from abroad, challenged these rules in the Italian courts, which referred the issue to the ECJ to determine whether these nationality requirements were compatible with EU law. The Court said:

Rules or a national practice, even adopted by a sporting organisation, which limit the right to take part in football matches as professional or semi-professional players solely to the nationals of the state in question, are incompatible with … the Treaty, unless such rules or practice exclude foreign players from participation in certain matches for reasons which are not of an economic nature, which relate to the particular nature and context of such matters and are thus of sporting interest only.

Thus, in its evolving legal policy on sport, the EU has drawn a distinction between the regulation of sport *qua* sport—the so-called 'rules of the game'—which, broadly speaking, are not subject to EU law generally or the EU Competition Rules in particular, and regulations which have an economic effect.

In practice, it is often difficult to draw this distinction. For example, the football transfer rules are 'rules of the game' of football, but also have significant economic effects, witness the famous 1995 *Bosman* ruling of the European Court of Justice (*Union Royale Belge des Sociétiés de Football ASBL v Bosman*), and the resulting Commission investigation into the FIFA football transfer rules, 'settled' on 5 March 2001. In another case in 2006 the ECJ held that, although doping rules are sporting rules, as they also have economic effects, a review of them under the EU Competition Rules is not *per se* excluded.

The 'Nice Declaration on Sport' was agreed in December 2000 by the EU Heads of State. Comprising more than 1,000 words, its underlying principle is that EU bodies are required to '*listen to Sports Associations when important questions affecting sport are in issue*'. It is not legally binding, but of persuasive authority only. At the Community level, the Declaration calls for 'the application of the Treaty's competition rules to the sporting sector [to] take account of the specific characteristics of sport, especially the interdependence between sporting activity and the economic activity that it generates, the principle of equal opportunities and the uncertainty of results'. At the Member States' level, the Declaration states that national authorities 'need to clarify the legal rules in order to safeguard the current structures in the social function of sport . . . [and] that each Member State should give legal recognition to governing bodies of each sport'. At the level of the sports federations, the Declaration points out that 'the basic freedoms guaranteed by the Treaty do not generally conflict with the regulatory measures of sports associations, provided that these measures are objectively justified, non-discriminatory, necessary and proportional'.

Regarding the commercial activities of the Sports Federations, the Declaration states that 'operations within economic dimensions should be founded on the principles of transparency and balanced access to the market, effective and proven redistribution and clarification of contracts, while prominence is given to the "specific nature of sport"'.

In the summer of 2006, the EU established the European Independent Sport Law Review with the following terms of reference: 'To produce a report, independent of the Football Authorities, but commissioned by UEFA, on how the European football authorities, EU institutions and member states can best implement the Nice Declaration on European and national levels'. The following year, the European Commission published its long-awaited White Paper on Sport, which confirms the approach taken in the Nice Declaration. Both the Review and the White Paper are currently the subject of comments from the major international sports bodies and the sporting world generally. In its evolving sports policy, the EU keeps a 'legal eye' on the activities of SGBs, whose economic power and influence, as already mentioned, are not insignificant and who are seeking more autonomy, if not a general exemption of sport from EU law, which is not likely to be granted.

Finally, SGBs are also subject to the **European Convention on Human Rights**, and in particular, when dealing with disciplinary matters, to Article 6, which guarantees a fair trial.   IAN BLACKSHAW

S Gardiner *et al*, *Sports Law* (London: Cavendish Publishing, 3rd edn, 2006)

RCR Siekmann and J Soek, *The European Union and Sport: Legal and Policy Documents* (The Hague: TMC Asser Press, 2005)

See also: **sports governing bodies**

Stability and Growth Pact The Stability and Growth Pact is at the heart of the economic union aspect of **Economic and Monetary Union** ('EMU') in the EU. It is a development of the excessive deficits procedure laid down in the EC Treaty, the basic elements of which also form one of the convergence criteria to be fulfilled by those joining EMU. This criterion relates to the sustainability of the government financial position: government deficit must not exceed 3 per cent of Gross Domestic Product ('GDP'), and government debt must not exceed 60 per cent of GDP, although these criteria are not absolute. A Member State will not be regarded as having an excessive government deficit if the ratio has declined 'substantially and continuously' and reached a level that comes close to the reference value, or, alternatively, the excess over the reference value is only 'exceptional and temporary' and the ratio remains close to the reference value. Furthermore, a higher ratio of government debt will not be regarded as excessive if the ratio is 'sufficiently diminishing' and approaching the reference value 'at a satisfactory pace'. During the transition to EMU, Member States were merely under the obligation to 'endeavour' to avoid excessive government deficits, and this remains the situation for the United Kingdom under its Protocol.

The excessive deficits procedure establishes machinery for determining whether there is an excessive deficit, which applies to all Member States, and sets out its own enforcement machinery which, however, only applies to participant Member States. A common thread running through this enforcement machinery is that it is discretionary—it states what the Council 'may' do, but does not require it to take any action. The feeling that EMU needed to rest on something firmer led to the adoption in June 1997 of a group of measures compendiously known as the Stability and Growth Pact, which introduced an element of automaticity into the process. The Stability and Growth Pact consists of a European Council Resolution on the Stability and Growth Pact, together with a Council Regulation on the strengthening of the surveillance of budgetary positions and of economic policies, and a Council Regulation on speeding up and clarifying the implementation of the excessive deficit procedure.

The Resolution sets out a clear political commitment to use the sanctions machinery, which is reflected and supplemented in the legally binding obligations introduced by the original version of the Council Regulation on speeding up and clarifying the implementation of the excessive deficit procedure, in particular with regard to the imposition of sanctions.. However, the fundamental problem with the original version of the Regulation was that an excessive deficit could only be regarded as 'exceptional' if there was an annual fall in real GDP of at least 2 per cent. In effect, therefore, short of economic disaster, no deficit could be regarded as 'exceptional', and it may be suggested that this is part of the background to the failure of the Council to follow Commission recommendations that France and Germany should be required to take specific measures to deal with their continuing deficits in 2003–2004. Rather, the Council failed to achieve the necessary majority to follow these recommendations, but instead adopted 'conclusions' which held the excessive deficits procedures against France and Germany in abeyance. The Commission took the matter to the **European Court of Justice**, which accepted that the procedure might *de facto* be held in abeyance if there was not a majority in the Council to take the matter forward; but it held that there was no legal power formally to decide to hold the matter in abeyance. The Court therefore annulled the Council's conclusions even if the lack of a majority meant it could take no further action.

Following this judgment, the Stability and Growth Pact was revised in 2005. The relevant Regulation now provides that an excess resulting from a severe economic downturn may be regarded as 'exceptional' if it results from a negative annual GDP volume growth rate (rather than minus 2 per cent) or 'from an accumulated loss of output during a protracted period of very low annual GDP volume growth relative to its potential'. It may be suggested that this is a totally different concept from the original version. Furthermore, under new provisions, in all budgetary assessments in the framework of the excessive deficits procedure, the Commission and the Council are required to give due consideration to the implementation of **pension** reforms. Again, it would appear that pension policy was a factor in the French and German deficits. Following these reforms, the system appears to have functioned relatively smoothly.

JOHN A USHER

See also: **European treaties**

staff handbooks and works rules Employers commonly issue their staff with handbooks that cover a range of matters relating to their employment. There are no set rules as to what these handbooks should contain. They generally include provisions governing conduct at work, such as dress codes, health and safety procedures, and policies on alcohol consumption; they may also cover staff benefits such as sickness and **disability** schemes; and may be the place where disciplinary and grievance procedures are located.

The **courts** sometimes need to decide whether provisions contained in staff handbooks or works rules constitute contractual terms—in which case they can be altered only by mutual agreement between employer and worker—or whether they are simply a codified set of instructions from the employer which can be altered unilaterally under the employer's managerial prerogative. This is not always an easy question to determine. The court or **tribunal** will need to decide, first, whether such provisions have been incorporated into the contract, either by an express or implied term or by custom and practice. At one time, the mere fact that the employer had posted a notice on a board could be sufficient to give its contents contractual effect, even if the employee had never seen the notice. These days the statutory requirement for employers to issue employees with a written statement setting out the main terms of their employment means that this is less likely to happen; if that statement makes no reference to the contents of the notice and the notice dealt with a matter required by statute to be included in the statement, such as **sick pay**, it would be for the employer to show that the contents of the notice nevertheless had contractual force.

Even if some works rules or provisions of a staff handbook are regarded as contractual, others may not be; this will depend upon their context and their wording. Rules relating to hours of work or discipline are generally seen as too precise to be subject to unilateral variation unless they are specifically stated to be non-contractual. By contrast, provisions in an employer's code of practice on staff sickness which specified the number of days' absence to trigger a management review were not regarded as contractually binding.

The status of works rules is important when considering whether 'working to rule'—a form of industrial action that involves applying all rules to the letter—constitutes a breach of contract. If these rules are merely emanations of the managerial prerogative, as the courts have sometimes found, then their literal application will constitute a breach of the implied contractual 'duty of cooperation' which employees owe to their employer.

GILLIAN MORRIS

See also: **contract of employment**

Stair, James Dalrymple James Dalrymple of Stair, a descendant of an old Ayrshire family of that name, was born in 1619. He graduated in Arts from Glasgow University in 1637 and was a regent in philosophy there from 1641 to 1647, when he resigned to join the Faculty of Advocates, the professional body of pleaders before the **Court of Session** in Edinburgh. Dalrymple was called to the bar in 1648, but seems to have had no formal education in law. The basis of his considerable legal learning was probably laid through private study during his Glasgow regency. Protestantism was also a key part of his intellectual make-up, and would have a significant role in the more controversial aspects of his later public career.

In 1657, during the Cromwellian period, Dalrymple was appointed as a commissioner for the administration of **justice**, that is, as one of the **judges** who had replaced the Court of Session at this period. An objective of the commissioners was to bring **Scottish law** into closer alignment with English law. Nonetheless, after the restoration of King Charles II in 1660, he was named as one of the Lords of the also restored Session in 1661, and it is from this period that he began to be known as Lord Stair. To judge from the surviving manuscripts, *Institutions of the Laws of Scotland*, the work for which Stair was to become best known, had mostly been written and had gone into circulation amongst the legal profession by the mid-1660s. Heavily influenced by **natural law theory** and the writings of Grotius, the book drew upon native Scottish sources to compare them systematically—and generally favourably—with the 'equity' exemplified

by the civil and **canon laws**. While Stair's scheme thus depended upon both learned and indigenous material, he used the idea of law as a system of individual rights to move beyond his sources and push Scottish law in new directions.

In 1670, Stair was a member of a parliamentary commission considering the possibility of an Anglo-Scottish union. The following year he became Lord President of the Session, in which office he and his fellow judges were to become embroiled in dispute with the Faculty of Advocates in 1674. The issue was the possibility of **appeal** to **Parliament** from decisions of the Session. Further controversy arose in 1681, when Stair was compelled to resign as President after declining to take the 'Test', an oath required by statute, the effect of which was to assert royal supremacy over the church. The *Institutions* were finally published at this difficult time, but the hostile political climate meant that in 1682 Stair had to depart Scotland for Leiden in The Netherlands, where he spent most of the next seven years. While at Leiden, Stair published *Physiologia Nova Experimentalis* (1685), a work on natural philosophy or physics rather than law, as well as his *Decisions of the Lords of Session* (1683 and 1687), the first printed law reports in Scotland.

Stair returned to Scotland following the Glorious Revolution of 1689 and was reappointed Lord President in the same year following the assassination of his successor from 1681. He remained the subject of political controversy and in 1690, the year in which he became Viscount Stair, he published *An Apology for Sir James Dalrymple of Stair, President of the Session, by himself*, refuting the criticisms to which his public career had certainly left him open. A second edition of the *Institutions* appeared in 1693, and, in 1695, there was published a further, theological, work attributed to him, *A Vindication of the Divine Perfections, illustrating the Glory of God in them by Reason and Revelation, methodically digested into several meditations by a Person of Honour*.

Stair died in Edinburgh on 25 November 1695 and is buried in the Kirk of St Giles in the city. Over the next hundred years, his *Institutions* were to achieve the status of a formal source of Scottish law, authoritative unless contradicted by later statute or binding precedent. In the nineteenth and twentieth centuries he became the avatar of Scots law and its independent identity: biographies and public monuments appeared; a legal history society was named after him in 1934; and the tercentenary of the publication of the *Institutions* saw the launch of a twenty-six-volume encyclopaedia of Scottish law (now completed and progressing in a second edition) also named for

Stair. His contribution to the philosophy as well as the substance of law has also attracted increasing international scholarly interest.

HECTOR L MACQUEEN

JD Ford, 'Dalrymple, James, first Viscount Stair (1619–1695)', *Oxford Dictionary of National Biography* (Oxford: Oxford University Press, 2004)

DM Walker (ed), *Stair Tercentenary Studies* (Edinburgh: Stair Society, vol 33, 1981)

stakeholders Stakeholders are those persons with an interest in the structure and operation of organizations. The term has come to the fore in the context of business organizations in recent years as attention has focused in particular on whether, and if so how, interests other than those of shareholders should be recognized by **companies**. The emergence of the term is linked with the political movement known as the 'third way', which was championed by the Blair government in the late 1990s as an alternative to liberal capitalism or democratic socialism.

A number of different stakeholders in companies can be identified. Employees have an interest in the success of a company because their jobs are dependent on it. They often make a significant investment in acquiring relevant skills and therefore it is argued that their interest should be represented in companies which use those skills. Company law in the UK provides for only an indirect **representation** of their interest, through a requirement that **directors** are to have regard to the interests of the employees. However, only the company (to whom directors owe their duties) is able to enforce this duty.

Creditors are also stakeholders. Their interest in the success of a company lies in its link with the repayment of the credit they have provided. There is no specific legal duty owed to creditors so long as a company is a going concern, because in those circumstances the law takes the view that there is no risk posed to creditors as regards repayment. Moreover, creditors can, depending on their bargaining power, agree contractual terms which provide some protection against default. However, company law does require that, when it appears likely that a company will become insolvent, the interests of creditors must be prioritized over those of shareholders.

It is also argued that the community or society at large is a stakeholder in companies on the basis of a public interest in the operation of companies. This interest extends to matters such as the environment, employment practices, health and safety issues, and **takeovers** and mergers. It reflects the importance that the company, as the dominant form of business organization, exerts over everyday life.

The 'stakeholder' debate focuses primarily on whether and how these interests should be given effect in company law. In the main, UK company law has prioritized the interests of shareholders. That has not meant, however, that stakeholders' interests have been ignored: they have instead been given effect through discrete systems of **regulation** such as environmental law and health and safety law. For proponents of stakeholder rights, that response is not sufficient because it does not integrate stakeholders' interests into the organizational structure of companies and therefore means that companies remain unduly focused on the interests of shareholders. The appointment of a Company Law Review Group by the government in 1998 raised hopes that stakeholders' interests would be strengthened but it soon became clear that this would not in fact be the case, with reform being limited to more technical matters.

IAIN MACNEIL

stamp duty *see* **stamp taxes**

stamp duty land tax *see* **stamp taxes**

stamp duty reserve tax *see* **stamp taxes**

stamp taxes Stamp taxes comprise three distinct taxes: stamp duties, stamp duty reserve tax, and stamp duty land tax. These taxes are charged throughout the UK (the UK for this purpose consisting of England and Wales, Scotland, and Northern Ireland ending at the low water mark but not the Channel Islands or the Isle of Man) although the jurisdictional basis of each tax differs from one another as noted below.

Stamp duties have been charged since 1694; but following the introduction of the Stamp Duty Land Tax Act 2003 now apply only to documents relating to **shares** and **securities**, bearer instruments, and the transfer of interests in **partnership**s owning shares and securities. Stamp duties are in general charged on the document effecting the transaction rather than the persons carrying out the transaction, and thus are not directly enforceable. The payment of stamp duty is encouraged by the inadmissibility of the relevant document for registration or enforcement unless the payment of the correct amount of duty has been evidenced by stamps to the required amount embossed on the document. There are also interest and penalties for late stamping (generally more than thirty days after execution). The rates of duty vary from a fixed duty of £5 to *ad valorem* duties of between 0.5 per cent for shares and securities to 4 per cent generally. Stamp duties are charged on a worldwide basis, although in practice only transactions which require registration or enforcement in the UK require the payment of the tax.

Despite its name, stamp duty reserve tax ('SDRT') is the principal transfer tax charge on the sale of shares and securities. It applies where a person agrees with another person to transfer chargeable securities (basically shares in UK entities) for consideration. The tax charge is directly enforceable against the purchaser, but is cancelled if stamp duty is paid on the transfer document and is repaid if the stamp duty is paid after the tax has been paid, in each case within six years of the sale agreement. The tax is normally collected by the relevant share exchange or professional intermediary where one is involved. There are five types of SDRT being the principal charge (0.5 per cent on shares and securities), the entry charge on clearance services, and the entry charge on depositary receipts at up to 1.5 per cent, the optional regime for clearance services, and the charge on dealings in unit trusts.

Stamp duty land tax replaced stamp duty on land in the UK from 1 December 2006 in order to accommodate the eventual introduction of online conveyancing and to make avoidance of the tax more difficult. Stamp duty land tax is charged on 'land transactions' whether or not there is a document and regardless of whether or not any party is present or resident in the UK. A 'land transaction' is any acquisition of a 'chargeable interest' which is defined widely as an estate, interest, right or power in or over UK land, and associated rights. Certain things such as licences, mortgages, and tenancies at will are exempt. The tax is charged as a percentage of the consideration given depending upon whether the land is residential or non-residential. For residential land the tax is charged at 1 per cent above £125,000, 3 per cent above £250,000, and 4 per cent above £500,000. For non-residential land the tax is charged at 1 per cent above £150,000, 3 per cent above £250,000, and 4 per cent above £500,000. In both cases the relevant percentage applies to all the consideration and not just the slice above the threshold. There are extensive anti-avoidance provisions.   PATRICK CANNON

standard form contracts   A standard form contract is a contract whose terms have not been agreed through negotiations between the parties, but were drafted in advance by one of the parties (sometimes with modifications made to individual terms). This has the advantage of saving time, particularly for transactions which are repeated frequently, such as consumer contracts, where individual negotiation would be inefficient. They are also important for international commerce. Standard form contracts can be drafted by individual businesses, as well as

trade associations and international organizations (eg the International Chamber of Commerce).

There is a risk that a standard form contract may be one-sided by favouring the party that drafted it; but exclusion clauses and **unfair contract terms** can be controlled by courts and other bodies.

Where a set of standard terms forms the basis for a transaction, they need to be 'incorporated into the contract' between the parties. This may be done by referring in the contract to the standard terms, and provided that both parties put their signature to the contract document, the standard terms will apply, even if the terms have not been read by the parties.

Standard form contracts are often drafted by a business for use in dealings with its customers. There may be a conflict between competing standard terms where businesses are seeking to contract with each other on their respective standard form contracts (the so-called 'battle of the forms'). A careful examination of the exchanges between the parties will be necessary to determine which standard form contract applies.   CHRISTIAN TWIGG-FLESNER

standard of care   *see* **care, standard of**

standard of proof   *see* **evidence, civil; evidence, criminal**

standards in public life   Standards of conduct in public life in Britain are established and regulated in a number of different ways. There is legislation, such as the Public Bodies Corrupt Practices Act 1889; there is the **common law**, such as the offence of bribery; and there are a variety of codes of practice, such as the **Ministerial Code**. There are also international obligations.

Concern about standards, at a time when there were scandals about 'cash for questions' and other matters, prompted the establishment of the Committee on Standards in Public Life in 1994. In its first report, in 1995, it identified the Seven Principles of Public Life; and its subsequent reports have produced new regulation in many areas of public life, including the appointment process for public bodies and the funding of political parties. The task of the Committee is to keep standards under continuous review and to respond to new issues as they arise.

In some areas this has involved legislation; in others codes of conduct. Parliament has remained an arena of self-regulation, but this has been strengthened in recent years by the appointment of a Parliamentary Commissioner for Standards, a Committee on Standards and Privileges, new rules on the registration of interests, and the adoption of a code of conduct. These measures have been in place since 1995.

There has been much discussion in the past thirty years about the need to reform and consolidate the law on corruption. A Draft Corruption Bill, building on a Law Commission report, was introduced in 2003 with the purpose of 'raising standards in both public and private life'; but it was not possible to find agreement on its contents, and this remains unfinished constitutional business.   TONY WRIGHT

See also: **sleaze**

standing committees   *see* **legislative and general committees**

Star Chamber   In the centuries since the English Parliament abolished the Star Chamber in 1641, the court has become a byword for injustice, brutality, and the arbitrary use of judicial power commonly associated with police states. This image is largely a myth, one that owes more to matters of politics than law; but like most myths it contains grains of truth that prevent it from being altogether dismissed.

The Star Chamber began life as a location rather than an institution, a room with a ceiling of gold stars on a sky blue background in a complex on the east side of Westminster palace yard. From the foureenth century members of the king's council met in 'the starred chamber' to conduct all manner of executive, administrative, and judicial business. The Court of Star Chamber emerged from the council in the gradual separation and demarcation of that body's different functions that began in the later fifteenth century. Cardinal Wolsey, during his tenure as Henry VIII's **Lord Chancellor**, enlarged and reorganized the court and its procedures, and its popularity with litigants grew dramatically in the later sixteenth and early seventeenth centuries.

To a large extent the Star Chamber's procedure mirrored the 'English bill' procedure of the **Chancery Court**, with written pleadings, interrogatories and depositions, and defendants sworn on oath. Its jurisdiction was expansive, drawing on the broad judicial authority of the king's council from which it sprung. In theory its focus was on criminal matters relating to the preservation of public order, but in practice it heard cases involving a range of subjects, from testamentary matters to disputes over title to land. Litigants filled their pleadings with allegations of riot, 'force of arms', and unlawful assembly, but most of these were legal fictions included to facilitate entry into the court. Throughout its existence the bulk of Star Chamber litigation was civil, not criminal; and for many litigants it was a bastion against political corruption and misuses of power and authority, the antithesis of its later mythical *persona*. What made the court so popular was its flexibility, especially in the Elizabethan and Jacobean periods when population levels rose and market relations and transactions became more complex and more numerous. Lawyers and their clients sought remedies in Star Chamber that were unavailable in the larger Courts of King's Bench and Common Pleas, and innovations in the court in areas such as defamation and commercial transactions became models for later developments at **common law**.

In short, the Star Chamber was an innovative, efficient, and highly professional court that provided impartial legal remedies to thousands of litigants. How then did it secure a place in history as the definitive English symbol of injustice and oppression? The answer to this puzzle lies in the tiny proportion of the court's proceedings that was initiated by the **Crown**. Tudor monarchs used the Star Chamber to prosecute instances of conspiracy, perjury, jury-rigging, and other offences that threatened order and good government. James I and Charles I continued this practice, but extended it to enforcing royal proclamations, a move that some read as an attempt to rule without Parliament. They also used it to prosecute outspoken critics such as William Prynne, who was sentenced in the Star Chamber to have his ears cut off in public and the letters 'S' and 'L' branded on his forehead to denote 'seditious libeller'. In the tumultuous years leading up to civil war and revolution, authors of parliamentary propaganda increasingly singled out the Star Chamber as a visible embodiment of unfettered royal power.

Punishments like the ones William Prynne endured also shaped the court's reputation: barred by medieval statutes from prosecuting crimes that attracted the death penalty, the court's judges drew upon alternatives (many of them statutory) that subsequent critics have found shocking. These ranged from ordering someone convicted in 1549 'to be in the king's galleys forever as a slave' to physical mutilations including boring holes through offenders' ears and cutting off the hands of forgers. The abolition of the court and the loss of the order and decree books detailing its decisions acted to stifle counter voices, allowing the myth of the tyrannical Star Chamber to prosper in the hands of later Whiggish commentators and historians bent on glorifying **parliamentary sovereignty**.   TIM STRETTON

See also: **common law courts**

state aid (in EC law)   One important aspect of European Community competition rules, distinct in both substance and procedure, is control of public subvention of industry and service providers, or 'aids granted by states'. That rules are necessary is self-evident: any support granted an economic operator (in EC terms, an 'undertaking'), public or private, distorts the level playing field the Community is meant to safeguard by giving it a comparative (unfair) advantage over its competitors.

A state aid is (a) 'any aid granted by a Member State or through State resources in any form whatsoever' which (b) 'favours' the assisted undertaking(s), (c) distorts (or threatens to distort) **competition**, and (d) affects (or might affect) trade between Member States. It embraces not only subsidies but 'interventions which, in various forms, mitigate the charges which are normally included in the budget of an undertaking and which, without, therefore, being subsidies in the strict meaning of the word, are similar in character and have the same effect' (*Gezamenlijke Steenkolenmijnen in Limburg v High Authority* (1961)). Investment in publicly-owned undertakings is not aid unless it exceeds that which would be secured under normal market conditions (the 'market investor principle'). State funding of an undertaking, publicly or privately owned, in order that it can discharge a public service obligation is not a state aid, but mere 'compensation' for the service, if various conditions (the '*Altmark* criteria'; from *Altmark Trans v Nahverkehrsgesellschaft Altmark* (2003)) are satisfied.

If the four cumulative elements are present the subvention is a state aid and is, in principle, prohibited. However the EC Treaty lists by way of exception various categories of state aids which are, and which may be, permitted. Authority to approve aids falls exclusively to the **European Commission**. It is required to keep under constant review all existing state aids, and may direct those it finds objectionable to be abolished or altered. Any new aid must be notified to the Commission, which has two months to object, unless it initiates a 'formal investigation procedure' and thereafter, within a period of eighteen months, approves the payment, with or without conditions, or prohibits it. It has set out various criteria it will consider and has adopted a number of sectoral notices providing informal guidance; but because it requires examination and appraisal of economic facts and circumstances, which may be complex and liable to rapid change, the Commission necessarily enjoys a wide latitude. It also discharges its task by means of 'group exemption regulations' ('GERs'), declaring state aids to be permitted without need of notification if they meet the criteria set out. All existing GERs are likely to be regrouped into a single GER

in 2007/8. Any new aid that is unauthorized—or *a fortiori* unnotified (unless falling within a GER)—is, irrespective of its merits, 'unlawful', and the Commission, or a national court, may order its suspension and recovery.

Significant reform is in train in light of the Commission's 'State Aid Action Plan' adopted in 2005 and setting out its policy for the period 2005–2009 with a view to 'less and better targeted' state aids and a more economic approach to them.

ROBERT LANE

state claims This is a compendious category which includes all ways in which a state presents to another state a formal claim for reparation for a breach of **international law**. This may be done directly, one state to the other, or it may be done by bringing an application before a body, such as a tribunal, with the competence and jurisdiction to reach a conclusion, binding or otherwise, about the claim.

'State claims' is used in this entry in a restricted way to refer to those situations in which a claim is made against a state where the direct victim is an individual or corporation, injured by an act of a state official or because the state has failed to provide redress for injury caused by another private person—a 'denial of justice'. Usually, there are two conditions for the admissibility of a claim at the international level. First, the local remedies rule must be satisfied. This means that the injured party must have tried all potentially effective remedies in the injuring state's legal system. Secondly, the applicant state must show that the person injured falls within the confines of the nationality of claims rule, which requires that, at all relevant times, the person injured was its national. Excluded from this entry are claims based on the direct infringement of one state's rights by the act or omission of another state.

At the international level, the claim is the claim of the state. The state-to-state institution of diplomatic protection may provide satisfaction; but, if it does not, the state might seek a remedy before a tribunal, if it can find one with jurisdiction. In the early part of the twentieth century, many thousands of cases were brought to special 'claims tribunals', established under treaties to adjudicate this kind of claim. To all intents and purposes, these were 'individual claims' but the formality was preserved because the applicant state brought the claim and administered any award. Later, large numbers of claims which followed wide-scale expropriation of property led to states reaching 'lump-sum settlements', which were then distributed to claimants by their own state through mechanisms set up in their national laws.

Major deprivations of property, such as the entire operations of primary extractive industries like oil, were sometimes pursued by the companies themselves through 'mixed arbitrations', though these are hardly 'state claims' in the sense used here. These possibilities have been enhanced by the conclusion of many Investment Promotion and Protection treaties, which allow individuals to bring their own claims to international tribunals.

In addition, *ad hoc* arrangements have been set up for the settlement of large numbers of claims, sometimes including both claims where individuals have suffered damage and ones where the injured part is a state, such as those between Iran and the US in 1981 and the United Nations Compensation Commission to settle claims against Iraq following the invasion of Kuwait in 1991. Although such arrangements vary, they give individuals and companies a greater role in the pursuit of redress for the injuries they have suffered. These developments represent a trend towards acknowledging the real nature of the claims—that they are to secure the interests of individuals, interests which are identified by reference to international law.

It should not be thought that the institution of diplomatic protection has been made obsolescent, particularly in individual instances and where matters can be settled between the governments involved. Any institutional and procedural deviations from the traditional arrangements require the consent of states.   COLIN WARBRICK

R Lillich and B Weston, *International Claims: Their Settlement by Lump-sum Agreements* (Charlottesville: University of Virginia Press, 1975)

Permanent Court of Arbitration, *Redressing Injustices through Mass Claims Processes: Innovative Responses to a Unique Challenge* (Oxford: Oxford University Press, 2006)

state liability in domestic law   *see* **public bodies, liability of**

state liability in EU law   The principle established by the **European Court of Justice** in its seminal decision in *Francovich and Bonifaci v Italy* (1991) states that a Member State of the European Union may be liable for damages to an injured party for breach of **European Community law**. The Court understood that, despite the silence of the EC Treaty on this point, state liability was a natural corollary of the individual rights granted to private parties by Community law. In *Francovich*, the breach of Community law attributable to the Italian State was its failure to implement a Community directive. Later case law extended the principle to cases where the national legislature enacted **legislation** incompatible with Community law, where Member States incorrectly transposed Community directives, and where an administrative authority acted in breach of Community law. Furthermore, recent case law has laid down that national **courts** can also be made liable in **damages** under this principle. The following conditions must be fulfilled in order for state liability to arise. First, the rule of law infringed must be intended to confer rights to individuals. This condition will be satisfied by directly effective provisions of Community law but can also be satisfied in some cases by non-directly effective provisions. Secondly, the breach of Community law must be sufficiently serious. Thirdly, there must be a direct causal link between the breach of the obligation resting on the state and the damage suffered by the injured party.

The European Court has decided that it will be for national courts to decide the link of causation and the *quantum* of damages in accordance with national law. The extent of the liability falling on the state will depend on the second condition. In general terms, the Court has interpreted this as meaning that a sufficiently serious breach of Community law will exist where the state has manifestly and gravely disregarded the limits of its **discretion**. A failure to implement a directive will, in itself, be a sufficiently serious breach because while Member States generally enjoy discretion as to *how* to implement a directive, they do not have discretion as to *whether or not to implement* a Community directive. Equally, if an administrative authority acts in circumstances where it has limited or no discretion at all, the mere infringement of Community law may be sufficient to establish liability. However, where the state acts in a legislative capacity and enjoys the ample discretion associated with the legislative function—and which is essential for the implementation of policies—it will have to be proved that the national legislature manifestly and gravely disregarded the limits of its discretion. The Court has provided criteria that could help national courts in deciding whether an infringement reaches the required threshold of seriousness to create liability. These include the clarity and precision of the rule breached, whether the infringement and the damage caused was intentional or involuntary, whether any error of law was excusable or inexcusable and the fact that the position taken by a Community institution may have contributed to the omission.

The principle of state liability fulfils three main functions in Community law. It constitutes a sanction against Member States that fail to comply with their Treaty obligations. Furthermore, it constitutes a mechanism to render Community law more effective. Finally, it protects the rights of private parties by allowing them to sue the state in damages in certain cases when a Community directive has not been implemented or has been incorrectly implemented. This last function is particularly important considering the consistent refusal of the European Court to recognize horizontal direct effect to Community directives. ALBERTINA ALBORS LLORENS

M Dougan, *National Remedies before the Court of Justice* (Oxford: Hart Publishing, 2004)

state responsibility in international law
see **responsibility, state**

State Trials *State Trials* was a series of cases that was published in different editions between the early eighteenth and late nineteenth centuries. Although it mainly covered trials for treason and other political offences since 1163, the scope of the series was wider, including cases of murder or even sexual scandal where there was some wider political significance. The series was for many years the main source of information about the history of criminal procedure and evidence. It also played an important role in the political education. In the eighteenth century it was conceived as a manual of how to defend liberty against state oppression. To the Victorians it was a record of liberties achieved in the areas of trial by jury and parliamentary democracy.

The first edition, edited by Thomas Salmon, was published anonymously in 1719 in four volumes, with a preface that stated the explicit aim of showing how life, honour, and innocence were to be defended. A second edition, in six volumes, appeared in 1730 under the editorship of Sollom Emlyn (1697–1754). This edition contained a lengthy preface critically surveying the condition of English law at the time. Further volumes were added in 1742 and 1766 before the third edition was published between 1776 and 1781. The definitive series, known as *Cobbett's Complete Collection of State Trials*, was published between 1809 and 1826 and is a remarkable achievement. This edition is in thirty-three volumes; twenty-one of them, giving the more important state trials down to 1781, were edited by Thomas B Howell, and the remaining volumes, bringing the trials down to 1820, by his son Thomas J Howell. This collection is an invaluable record of constitutional history and the development of criminal procedure.

A new series, under the direction of a parliamentary committee, was projected in 1885, with the object of bringing the trials down to a later date. Eight volumes were published in 1888–1898, bringing the work down to 1858. The first three of these were edited by Sir John Macdonell, the remaining five by John E P Wallis.

There was also a market for abridged selections from the original edition which popularized the cases. These largely eschewed the illustration of constitutional history in favour of a more dramatic narrative form, which stressed crimes and personalities. LINDSAY FARMER

state, concept of 'State' is a notion that has never found a firm footing in British political discourse and is effectively absent from our domestic law. In most other countries, it functions as a conveniently monolithic abstraction referring to the diverse institutions and persons holding public power under the constitution. As such it serves to add legitimacy to their actions and interests. It also permits a shorthand distinction, important in political and social theory, between the official institutions of a country's government on the one hand, and its social institutions and the private lives and interests of its inhabitants ('society') on the other. Its key legal application is in **international law**, for which it is the state as a whole, and not its component parts or institutions, that enjoys rights and is subject to duties. While **United Kingdom** law recognizes this external face of the state, notably through the doctrine of act of state, it eschews any use of the concept for internal purposes. Instead the monarchy continues to supply the law with its unifying metaphors for the institutions holding power in all branches of national government: hence '**Crown**' as the collective legal term for the central institutions of executive government, 'Crown-in-Parliament' for the legislature, 'Her Majesty's judges' to describe the judiciary. Whether it is safer for the extensive powers of public authorities today to be disguised under the obviously fictitious and anachronistic abstraction of the Crown, or the more plausible one of the state, remains a matter for argument. TERENCE DAINTITH

K Dyson, *The State Tradition in Western Europe: a Study of an Idea and Institution* (Oxford: Martin Robertson, 1980)

stateless persons *see* **refugees**

statements of special educational needs
see **special educational needs**

states in international law states constitute the basis of the international legal system and the primary subjects of public **international law**. states consist of a defined territorial entity seen as externally sovereign, exercising internal sovereignty in accordance with domestic considerations but subject to relevant international legal rules.

The creation of sstatehood imports both factual and legal criteria and is a topic of some complexity. Since there are few areas of the world open to acquisition by states and few colonies that may become independent, the birth of a new state can only be accomplished as a result of the diminution or disappearance of existing states. This explains the need for careful regulation, as may be seen from events such as the break-up of the Soviet Union, Yugoslavia, and Czechoslovakia. Article 1 of the Montevideo Convention on Rights and Duties of States 1933 lays down the most widely accepted formulation of the criteria of statehood in international law. It notes that the state as an international person should possess the following qualifications: (a) a permanent population; (b) a defined territory; (c) government; and (d) capacity to enter into relations with other states. However, other factors may be relevant, including the principle of self-determination and recognition by the international community. The relevant framework will revolve in the first place around territorial effectiveness.

While the existence of a permanent population is clearly required, there is no specification of a minimum number of inhabitants, as examples such as Nauru and Tuvalu demonstrate. The need for a defined territory focuses upon the requirement for a particular territorial base under the undisputable control of the authority of the claimed state, but there is no necessity for defined and settled boundaries, as the examples of Albania prior to 1914 and Israel since 1948 demonstrate. It is also possible for the territory of a state to be divided into distinct parts, separated by the territory of another state, such as Pakistan prior to the Bangladesh secession of 1971. The third criterion is that of government, which essentially relates to the need for a central body exercising effective control over the core of territory claimed. Such control need not be exercized over the whole territory of the state, as the examples of Croatia and Bosnia in the early 1990s demonstrate, both of which were recognized as independent by states and admitted to United Nations' membership at a time when the authorities clearly did not control all of the territory of the states concerned. The fourth criterion is the capacity to enter into relations with other states, which focuses upon independence and constitutes a formal statement that the state is subject to no other sovereignty. Also relevant as an additional criterion of statehood may be the principle of **self-determination**, which would require that the state in question conform with the rules of equality and non-discrimination of peoples. The European Community Guidelines on Recognition of New States in Eastern Europe and the Soviet Union adopted on 16 December 1991, for example, referred specifically to the principle of self-determination and called for guarantees for the rights of **minorities**.

Of particular importance to the creation of states is the approach adopted by other states to the new entity. One view is that formal recognition is a condition of statehood (the constitutive principle); however the more accepted approach today is that recognition of an asserted state constitutes not a determinative step, but rather powerful evidence of the existence of the entity as a new state (the declaratory principle). A new state may arise in the absence of recognition by members of the international community as a matter of principle, but in practice this is likely to be extremely rare, not least because of the difficulties inherent in maintaining international relations. In addition, existing states may formally decide as a matter of policy not to recognize a new entity as a state. Where this takes place by binding **United Nations** Security Council resolution—for example, as happened with regard to the claimed 'Turkish Republic of Northern Cyprus' in 1983 or the so-called South African 'Bantustans' in the late 1970s and early 1980s—the invalidity of the claim to statehood cannot be contradicted.

Statehood may be extinguished as a consequence of merger, absorption. or the dismemberment of an existing state. It is relatively uncommon and will not happen, for example, as a result of the illegal use of force, as the Kuwait crisis of August 1990 shows. Recent examples include the merger of North and South Yemen (22 May 1990); the reunification of Germany as a result of the constitutional accession of the *Länder* of the German Democratic Republic to the Federal Republic of Germany (3 October 1990); and the dismemberment of the USSR in 1991 and the coming to independence of fourteen new or, in the case of the Baltic States, newly revived states and the acceptance of Russia as continuing the international personality of the USSR. It was not until 2000 that it was accepted by all states that the Former Yugoslavia had been dismembered and five new states created (Slovenia, Croatia, Bosnia, Macedonia, and Serbia). In 2006, Montenegro seceded from Serbia and became an independent state.

States are recognized in international law as possessing a series of fundamental rights. Perhaps the outstanding characteristic of a state is its independence or **sovereignty**. This was defined in the Draft Declaration on the Rights and Duties of States, 1949, as the capacity of a state to provide for its own well-being and development free from the domination of other states, providing it does not impair or violate their legitimate rights. Independence is a formal legal concept and is unaffected by any political or economic dependence that may in reality exist, so long as the state is not formally subject to the authority of another state.

The starting point for the consideration of the rights and obligations of states within the international legal system remains that international law permits freedom of action for states, unless there is a rule constraining this. However such freedom exists within and not outside the international legal system; and it is, therefore, international law which dictates the scope and content of the independence of states and not the states themselves individually and unilaterally.

The notion of independence in international law implies a number of rights and duties: for example, the right of a state to exercise jurisdiction over persons situated, and events occurring within, its territory and in certain situations nationals wherever situated, or the right to engage upon an act of self-defence in certain situations. It implies also the duty not to intervene in the internal affairs of other sovereign states in the absence of the consent of the latter. The **International Court of Justice** has pointed out that 'between independent States, respect for territorial sovereignty is an essential foundation of international relations' (*Corfu Channel* case, 1949). However, precisely what constitutes the internal affairs of a state is open to dispute and is in any event a constantly changing standard. Today it is clear that issues related to human rights and racial oppression do not now fall within the closed category of domestic jurisdiction.

The principles surrounding sovereignty, such as non-intervention, are essential in the maintenance of a reasonably stable system of competing states. By setting limits on the powers of states vis-à-vis other states, it contributes to some extent to a degree of stability within the legal order. By a similar token a state cannot purport to enforce its laws in the territory of another state without the consent of the state concerned, so that, for example, the presence of foreign troops on the territory of a sovereign state requires the consent of that state.

One other crucial principle is the legal equality of states. This principle established equality of legal rights and duties, and does not, of course, mean that states are equal in political or economic terms. States irrespective of size or power have the same juridical capacities and functions, and are equal members of the international community. The doctrine of the legal equality of states is an umbrella category comprising within its scope the recognized rights and obligations that attach to all states. These include, for example, the inviolability of the territorial integrity and political independence of the state; the right of each state freely to choose and develop its political, social, economic, and cultural systems; and the duty of each state to comply fully and in good faith with its international obligations and to live in peace with other states.   MALCOLM SHAW

See also: **territory**

statutory audit   A statutory audit is a legally required examination of a **company's annual accounts** and financial records. The examination enables the auditor to form an opinion as to whether the accounts and financial records comply with the law. The audit is like a business 'MOT', first, to protect the **company** itself from the consequences of undetected errors or, possibly, wrongdoing and, secondly, to provide shareholders with reliable intelligence for the purpose of enabling them to scrutinize the conduct of the company's affairs and to exercise their collective powers to reward or control or remove those to whom that conduct has been confided. The stewardship role of the audit assists shareholders in monitoring the performance of the **directors**.

The auditor must be independent of the company and a member of a recognized supervisory body. Acting in accordance with professional standards, the auditor provides in an audit report his or her opinion on whether or not the accounts show a 'true and fair view' of the company's financial position. The auditor may give a qualified opinion signifying that either the scope of the auditor's work is limited or the auditor disagrees with the treatment or disclosure of a matter in the accounts. An adverse opinion means that the auditor disagrees with the accounts and considers that they do not give a 'true and fair view'. UK auditors are directly accountable and hence owe a duty of care to the company's existing shareholders as a body.   CHARLOTTE VILLIERS

See also: **auditors' liability**

statutory duty, civil liability for breach of   Broadly understood 'breach of statutory duty' describes any breach of a tortious duty created by statute. Some statutes, for example the Occupiers' Liability Act 1957 and Part I of the Consumer Protection Act 1987, specifically create a duty actionable by an individual in private law. Liability arises according to the provisions of the statute detailing the standard of conduct required, the applicability of any defences and the appropriate remedy.

Traditionally, however, breach of statutory duty refers to the 'tort of breach of statutory duty'. This is a separate and conceptually distinct tort from the general tort of negligence, which enables a claimant in certain circumstances to recover **compensation** for losses caused by the defendant's failure to comply with a statutory obligation. The classic example is an employee who has been injured at work as a result of their employer's failure to follow health and safety **legislation**. Unlike the statutory duties described above, in an action for the tort of breach of statutory duty the duty created by the statute is a public law, typically criminal, duty which gives rise to a civil law action indirectly, either as a matter of judicial construction or because the statute so provides. However, the existence of a private law action for **damages** following the defendant's breach of their statutory obligations is not inferred automatically. Clearly, where a statute explicitly states whether or not a breach of its provisions gives rise to a **remedy** in tort as, for example, in the Sex Discrimination Act 1975, section 66 or the Health and Safety at Work Act 1974, section 47(1), there is no problem.

Difficulties arise when the statute imposes a duty but is silent as to whether it intended there to be a civil action for its breach or some other remedy. Crucially, it does not follow that because **Parliament** has not included such a provision, no remedy exists. After all, it is arguably more politically astute to place responsibility for the absence of a civil law remedy following a public body's failure to perform its statutory duty at the feet of the judiciary rather than to explicitly state it in the statute itself. Factors the **courts** take into account in considering whether a statute gives rise to civil liability include: whether the duty was imposed for the protection of a limited class of the public; the provision of other remedies for its breach by the statute; the extent to which the statute's scope is limited and specific or general and administrative; as well as various, ubiquitous policy considerations. However, while the articulation of these factors is relatively straightforward, their application in any particular case is somewhat less so: 'the dividing line between the pro-cases and the contra-cases is so blurred that you may as well toss a coin to decide it' (Denning MR (as was) *Ex Parte Island Records Ltd* (1978)). Once it is established that a statute does allows for an action for breach of statutory duty, in order for their claim to be successful the claimant must also show that the duty has in fact been breached, that the harm suffered falls within the scope of the duty as well as establishing **causation** and the inapplicability of any relevant defences.

All this works significantly to limit the scope of the action for breach of statutory duty. In recent years its use has declined to such an extent that it plays a minor role in the law of tort beyond providing compensation for **industrial injuries** which fall outside the remit of the tort of negligence. In fact, its existence as a separate and distinct nominate tort—largely the result of a historical need in the late nineteenth century to eschew the harshness of the **common law** in relation to employer's liability—is increasingly difficult to justify. In most American jurisdictions and also in Canada, breach of statutory duty has been subsumed within the tort of negligence either as negligence *per se* or as evidence of negligence where the common law already imposes as general duty of care. Nevertheless, despite ongoing criticism, the possibility of replacing breach of statutory duty with a concept of 'statutory negligence' in either form, at present, seems somewhat unlikely in the UK.

ERIKA RACKLEY

RA Buckley 'Liability in Tort for Breach of Statutory Duty' (1984) 100 *Law Quarterly Review* 204
KM Stanton 'New Forms of the Tort of Breach of Statutory Duty' (2004) 120 *Law Quarterly Review* 324

See also: **negligence; tort law**

statutory instruments   *see* **legal rules, types of**

statutory interpretation   Law is a hierarchy. This means not only that **common law** courts are bound to a system of authority which requires that lower courts obey the determinations of higher courts but also that the judiciary obey the sovereign. The term hierarchy derives from the Greek 'hieros' meaning sacred and refers, at least legally, to the priority and authority of the word of God. The sovereign is classically subject to God and law, *sub Deo et lege*; but as the English sovereign was from early on supreme head of both Church and state the maxim did not imply any great degree of external control over sovereign will. The pinnacle of legal authority in modern common law is the legislature which speaks not in oracles but **Acts of Parliament**. The divine roots of this sovereign speech subsist in the preamble to the Act which manifests Royal Assent in the words: 'Be it enacted by the Queen's most Excellent Majesty, by and with the advice and consent of the Lords Spiritual and Temporal, and Commons, in the present Parliament…'. This invocation of the Christian and monarchical roots of the primary source of law, the references to majesty and spirituality also help explain the rhetoric of deference proffered by those who interpret the legislation. An Act of Parliament is traditionally a decision of the highest court of appeal in the land and it must be followed literally, to the letter.

The concept of **parliamentary sovereignty** lies at the basis of a number of rules that govern construction of statutes. The initial rule is exegetical, meaning that the function of interpretation is in the first instance supposed to be strictly expository. It requires that the text of the statute be applied literally, each word, every syllable even, ideally dictating direct and submissive application. To this can be added further rules of construction that resolve ambiguities and achieve legally desirable results in actual cases by attending to the enactment as a whole, the context of the rule, and the purpose sought to be achieved through legislation. The judges in point of practice are the final arbiters of meaning and treat the words according to their own sense of proper legal interpretation: if a statute prior to 1925 used the word 'person', for example, that meant man and excluded women; and inversely, if a statute post-2004 uses the word spouse, that now must be taken to include same-sex cohabitants. Such meanings were evident and embedded in the common opinion of lawyers rather than expressly enacted or present in the legislative text.

The modern judiciary is realistic, pragmatic, and pretty much explicit in devising means of interpretation that draw upon a wide variety of aids to construction that will help determine the application of statutory provisions in accord with the contemporary contexts of their imposition. A striking recent example of this process in action can be taken from the interpretation of the Rent Act 1977 as amended by the Housing Act 1988. The question that came before the court was whether same-sex couples were 'spouses' for the purpose of the Act. The Act itself defined the word spouse as 'a person living with [another tenant] as his or her wife or husband'. The majority of the **House of Lords** decided that this included same-sex couples. Although the ordinary meaning of the word spouse was a heterosexual partner, the purpose of the legislator, viewed in the context of the Human Rights Act 1998, required a different outcome. While, as a dissenting judge put it, calling a homosexual cohabitant a spouse was 'to read "black" as meaning "white"', and so could not feasibly be done, the majority relied on European doctrine supported by philological and literary techniques of emendation of corrupt texts, to determine that the purpose of the statute was best served by extending the meaning of the word to same sex couples (*Ghaidan v Godin-Mendoza* (2004)).

This example indicates a general tension between statute and interpretation. This can be formulated in terms of the legal paradox that the letter of the law determines—it must be obeyed—but the letter is dead and has to be given life through interpretation. The judges have always sought the intention of the legislator, the *mens legislatoris* or reason of enactment, through the text as much as in it. The words of the enactment, of course, provide one clue to the intention of the legislator; but classical authority is consistent and insistent in the belief that the meaning of the words is simply the avenue to the spirit or reason, *anima* or force of the utterance. Sir Edward Coke can stand as emblematic in his borrowing from the Roman jurist Celsus to declare '*in lectione non verba sed veritas est amanda* [in reading it is not the words but the truth that is to be loved]' (Coke, *Reports*, 1777 edn). 'Thus it is not possible', Plowden remarked even earlier and specifically with reference to statutory meaning, 'for a man to delay on the letter alone…' [*Et issint home ne poet targer sur le letter solement . . .*]' (S Thorne (ed), *A Discourse upon the exposicion and understanding of statutes, with Sir Thomas Egerton's additions* (San Marino, 1942)). If the letter of the legislation conflicts with the reason or spirit of the law, as divined by the judges, then as *Dr Bonham's Case* (1610) evinces, it is the reason and not the letter of the law that will prevail.

Judicial overruling of a legislative provision is rare in England and takes the form of purposive statutory interpretation, creative semantics, or judicial vandalism, depending upon one's point of view. The general principle of submitting statutory meaning to the reason of common law—to what was historically termed 'the equity of the statute'—continues resolutely in the form of the practices of judicial interpretation that decreasingly view the principle of the supremacy of Parliament as sacrosanct. The art of construing statutes thus involves recourse both to the prior context and the potential effect of interpretation. The decision of Parliament is placed side-by-side with the exigency of the current case and the determination of the meaning in its present context will take account of a wide variety of factors. These range from etymology to moral sense, and will where necessary include a broad accounting of the legislative purpose of enactment as well changes in mores and circumstance since the Act received the Royal Assent.   PETER GOODRICH

F Bennion, *Statutory Interpretation* (London: Butterworths, 1992)

P Goodrich, *Reading the Law A Critical Introduction to Legal Method and Techniques* (Oxford: Blackwell, 1986)

See also: **interpreting legislation**

stem cells Following the announcement by the Wisconsin-based biologist, James Thomson, that his research group had successfully isolated **human** embryonic stem cells ('hES cells'), the opening decade of the twenty-first century has seen a worldwide interest in the therapeutic and drug development potential of stem cells. For some years, so-called 'adult' stem cells have been used in clinical practice in the form of bone marrow transplantations. However, it is the potential of hES cells and their derivatives that has prompted the current explosion of interest; for hES cells, still being in a pluripotent state, have the potential to develop into any one of the many human cell types. If researchers fully understood how to isolate and purify hES cells, to direct their development to the required cell type, and to deliver compatible cells to patients, we might be on the cusp of a medical revolution. However, before researchers could lawfully undertake such work, the regulatory environment would need to be set up in a relatively permissive way; and, at minimum, this would entail permitting the use of human embryos for research.

In the United Kingdom, the regulatory framework for research using human embryos is laid out in the **Human Fertilization and Embryology Act 1990**. Having identified five approved research purposes, largely relating to reproductive matters, the Act also provides that research may be licensed 'for such other purposes as may be specified in regulations'. However, this enabling provision is limited: the said 'other purposes' must be designed to 'increase knowledge about the creation and development of embryos, or about disease, or enable such knowledge to be applied'. Following a period of consultation, the government decided to rely on this enabling clause in order to open the way for hES cell research to deliver on its apparent potential.

Thus, the new Regulations, the Human Fertilization and Embryology (Research Purposes) Regulations 2001, add the following three new purposes to the original five:

(a) increasing knowledge about the development of embryos;
(b) increasing knowledge about serious disease; or
(c) enabling any such knowledge to be applied in developing treatments for serious disease.

Coming to these Regulations without any explanation, one would be unlikely to appreciate that they were designed to facilitate stem cell research and **therapeutic cloning.** However, Parliamentarians were fully apprised as to the significance of these Regulations and there were lengthy debates in both Houses before the Regulations were approved subject to a House of Lords' **Select Committee** being set up to consider their implications. When the Select Committee reported about a year later, it endorsed the spirit and intent of the new purposes. Almost at once the **Human Fertilization and Embryology Authority** began to issue licences under the new purposes; funding bodies announced that money for hES cell research would be released; and, in due course, a national stem cell bank was established with the first stem cell lines being deposited in 2004.

In the larger European and international picture the regulatory position struck in the United Kingdom is relatively permissive. Elsewhere, the concern that **human dignity** should not be compromised has led to a far more restrictive approach. In some legal systems, the use of human embryos for research purposes is prohibited; in other legal regimes, it is unlawful to *create* human embryos for research and it is only those embryos that are surplus to IVF requirements (so-called 'supernumerary embryos') that are available to stem cell researchers; and, notoriously, in the United States the restrictions on Federal funding for stem cell research co-exist with a degree of regulatory permissiveness in many states.

Even if the law does not impede research on hES cells, the regulatory environment is not adequate for researchers unless it also facilitates their work. Crucially, this means that inventive research and development in the field needs to be patentable. However, although the policy of the United Kingdom **Patent** Office is supportive of hES cell work, the position of the European Patent Office (which sets the regional standard) is much less clear—again reflecting the dignitarian values of much of Continental Europe.

Globally, then, stem cell research and development is subject to a patchwork of regulation, the upshot of which is that research on hES cells is being carried out in those zones where the regulatory environment least impedes such work.

ROGER BROWNSWORD

See also: **embryo research**

Stephen, Sir James Fitzjames   Sir James Fitzjames Stephen, first baronet (1829–1894); Victorian England's foremost jurist on criminal law and criminal justice, Stephen was a great legal historian and legal thinker. Self-confident and self-opinionated, he was a larger-than-life character, possessed of formidable energy, a rigorous rationality, and a strong belief in self-reliance. He belonged to an upper-middle class family of considerable distinction at the heart of England's 'intellectual aristocracy'. Through his writings and force of character, Stephen had a lasting impact on legal thought and practice in England, India, Canada, and the USA, giving direction to the development of legal systems throughout the British Empire. He contributed to opinion-forming debates on politics, society, **religion**, and the arts.

Throughout most of his life he was engaged in two professions, the Bar and 'higher journalism'. He wrote hundreds of articles on contemporary issues for leading periodicals and it was his journalism that first brought him to the attention of a wider public.

Stephen's *A General View of the Criminal Law* (1863) is an original attempt to demonstrate that the study of the criminal law could be an 'art founded on [social] science'. He set about improving the exposition and systematization of the criminal law, the elucidation of its underlying principles and its interrelationship with morality and politics. He sought to demonstrate the significance of a regime 'by which men rightfully, deliberately, and in cold blood, kill, enslave, or otherwise torment their fellow creatures'. In advance of its times, it heralded the renaissance of legal scholarship and academic law in late Victorian and Edwardian England.

Serving as a legal member of the Governor-General's Council in India during 1869–1872, Stephen demonstrated prodigious industry in the drafting, preparation, revision, and piloting of a host of **legislation**, all shaped by European (especially Benthamite), as distinct from indigenous, notions of law and society. Like his father, Stephen adopted a view of **colonialism** that stressed the superiority and the responsibilities of the mother country.

His reputation as a foremost legislative draftsman and codifier assured, on returning home in 1872 Stephen undertook the codification of the law of **evidence** (1872), a **Homicide** Law Amendment Bill (1872 and 1874) and, most notably, the restructuring and reform of the English criminal law as a criminal code (1877–1880). He also published digests on evidence (1876) and criminal law (1877) to provide a foundation for legislative codification and further enhance his reputation as a draftsman. While legislative success eluded him at home, largely because of changes in government and judicial opposition (Lord Chief Justice Cockburn was especially hostile), his schemes and writings were a seminal influence on the reform of the criminal justice elsewhere in the English-speaking world.

During this period he sought election as Liberal MP for Dundee, but came last in the polls. In the same year (1873), he published *Liberty, Fraternity and Equality,* the first sustained attack on **Mill's** *On Liberty.* A penetrating defence of conservative values, the work reflected his dark view of human nature, his increasing disquiet about the emerging **democracy**, and his belief, in contrast to Mill, that law was the principal expression of, and sanction for, morality. Stephen's book was an immediate bestseller, making a significant contribution to the political thought of the period and to conservative liberalism more generally. In the twentieth century, his arguments were championed by the judge, **Patrick Devlin**, in his celebrated debate with the Oxford legal philosopher, **HLA Hart**, and in this form are still read by many students in law, politics, and sociology.

Stephen was appointed a High Court judge in 1879. Having finally secured the recognition and financial stability that he craved, Stephen set about completing his three-volume, *History of the Criminal Law* (1883). Despite its idiosyncratic organization and overly-linear narrative, it remains a major reference work in the field. Stephen's period on the bench was undistinguished and he was forced to resign in 1891 as a result of physical and mental decline. *The Times* obituarist described him as 'this sturdy spokesman of plain truths, the last of the Benthamites'.

DAVID SUGARMAN

KJM Smith, *James Fitzjames Stephen* (Cambridge: Cambridge University Press, 1988)
S Collini, *Public Moralists* (Oxford: Clarendon Press, 1991)

stereotyping Stereotyping commonly refers to the assumption that a **person** possesses a particular (usually negative) characteristic due to her membership of a particular social group. For example, in the immediate aftermath of the discovery of **HIV/AIDS** in the 1980s, there was a prevailing stereotype that gay men were more promiscuous than heterosexuals or lesbians. Stereotyping was first used to describe the social dynamics of discrimination by the columnist, Walter Lippmann, in the 1920s. The metaphor of the 'stereotype' originally recalled printing and typography, evoking the image of high speed press runs and pages that were locked into position, ready for swift reproduction. This reflects the categorization and fixed patterns of thought which contribute to many forms of discrimination. The term has been widely used in the social sciences, particularly in social psychology and media studies, although it has more recently been replaced by a focus on concepts of the '**Other**', the '**stranger**', and of marginal social positions.

In law, stereotyping has been used to describe discrimination by individuals or organizations on the basis of misconceptions about a person's abilities or **identity**. It is arguably a very narrow term, with limited capacity to express the complexities of social, structural, and institutional dynamics through which inequalities emerge and are reproduced. Without further elaboration, stereotyping does not express very clearly or subtly the social and personal impact of inequalities. Nevertheless, the concept is commonly used in **equality** law in particular. Its legal applications in this area fall into four different types: legal guidance; decisions of statutory bodies charged with upholding equality; **consultations by government** and public debate around proposed changes in the law; and decisions of the **courts**.

The concept of stereotyping can be found throughout the legal guidance on equality law. For example, in its statutory guidance on the **Race** Relations Act 1976, the Commission for Racial Equality ('CRE', now incorporated into the **Commission for Equality and Human Rights** ('CEHR')) recommended that employers 'make sure all staff understand that it is against the law to discriminate on racial grounds . . . . and that stereotypes and generalizations about racial groups can affect the way they treat people from these groups' (Code of Practice on Racial Equality in Employment, November 2005 at 5.16(c)). The CRE also conducted an inquiry into the National Bus Company, which found that Asian bus conductors were being passed over for promotion because of stereotypes that they were 'passive' and 'too weak' for the bus conductor job. Stereotypes about race were also the concern of the campaigning group, Southall Black Sisters ('SBS'), in 2006 when they responded to a government consultation on a proposed law to criminalize **forced marriage**. Pragna Patel, Chair of SBS, stated in the *Independent* (7 June 2006) 'We don't see the need for criminalization of forced marriage, which is yet another way of stereotyping and criminalizing entire **communities** at a time when there is heightened racism in this country'.

The UK courts have decided a number of stereotyping cases relating to **gender** and **dress codes in the workplace** (*Schmidt v Austicks Book Shop* (1977)). They have also tackled assumptions about gender roles in the family as in *Horsey v Dyfed CC* (1982) which concerned the assumption by a recruitment panel that although a wife would follow her husband if he was offered a new job in another part of the country, the same would not be true for the husband if a wife (in this case, the job applicant) was offered a job away from where her husband was employed. More recently, with widespread popular panic about groups of youths in inner cities, **anti-social behaviour** orders ('ASBOs') have been used by the **police** to disperse young people in shopping areas, a technique that is likely to draw on stereotyped assumptions about which individuals pose a threat. In the case of *Marc Bucknell v DPP* (2006), a young man, who had been part of a group of Black and Asian

youths dispersed from a shopping centre in Wimbledon, South London, with no evidence that he or his friends were acting in an intimidating manner, successfully challenged in the High Court his conviction under the Anti-Social Behaviour Act 2003. Stereotyped assumptions about race were also the subject of a very different case in 2004: the popularly termed '*Prague Airport*' case, which concerned the posting of UK immigration officers in Prague airport to prevent Roma people boarding planes to the UK, preventing them from travelling to, and in some cases seeking **asylum** in, the UK (*R (European Roma Rights Centre and Others) v Immigration Officer at Prague Airport and Another (United Nations High Commissioner for Refugees intervening)* (2005)). Examining the UK government's policy of allowing immigration officials to question Roma people more intrusively and require more proof of matters that were taken on trust from non-Roma people on the assumption that they were more likely to make a false application for entry into the UK, the **House of Lords** decided that this was a clear case of discrimination. Referring to an analogous case of a supplier refusing goods to a person on the basis of her race, Baroness Hale stated: 'The whole point of the law is to require suppliers to treat each person as an individual, not as a member of a group. The individual should not be assumed to hold the characteristics which the supplier associates with the group, whether or not most members of the group do indeed have such characteristics, a process sometimes referred to as stereotyping' (at paragraph 74). In this way, whilst stereotyping has not been used specifically as a legal term, the adoption of concepts from the social sciences into law has meant that stereotyping continues to exert conceptual force in legal decision-making and in popular debates about the law.

EMILY GRABHAM

C Palmer et al, *Discrimination Law Handbook* (London: Legal Action Group, 2002)
M Pickering, *Stereotyping: The Politics of Representation* (New York: Palgrave, 2001)

sting operations *see* **entrapment**

stock exchange Until recently, stock exchanges occupied a quasi-monopoly position in financial markets by providing a range of essential services. Exchanges provide trading (or execution) services by centralizing trades in **securities** admitted to the exchange and by providing venues, systems, and rules under which buyers and sellers of securities can securely interact and finalise trades. They also impose trade transparency requirements under which security prices are disclosed to market participants. As a result, they provide an important price-setting function. Although this role is decreasing, they may also fulfil a quasi-regulatory role by admitting securities and, in particular, by listing securities and imposing disclosure, corporate governance, and other requirements on issuers and securities which seek admission to the exchange.

Exchanges typically operate a series of markets, often termed 'first tier' and 'second tier', with less stringent rules applied to the second tier. This is usually reserved for younger companies which lack the longer financial record of the more established companies admitted to the first tier and which may be perceived as riskier investments. The London Stock Exchange, for example, operates a Main Market and an Alternative Investment Market. Second tier markets worldwide became highly prominent during the 'dotcom' boom.

Regulation of stock exchanges is usually directed to the overall stability and integrity of the market rather than to investor protection, which is more strongly associated with regulation of investment firms. For example, the International Organization of Securities Commissions (the umbrella body for market regulators) recommends that exchange regulation address: oversight of the exchange; integrity of trading; transparency of trading; prevention of market manipulation; and proper risk management. The regulation of exchanges has traditionally reflected a 'public service' model of the exchange, and one in which the exchange is owned its members—typically investment firms. It frequently relied heavily on self-regulation mechanisms, subject to backstop government oversight and licensing of the exchange.

The nature of exchange regulation has, however, changed following the emergence of competition and changes to the traditional role of the exchange. Competition has strengthened following the arrival of **alternative trading systems**. Many stock exchanges, including the London Stock Exchange, have also changed their member-based ownership structures and de-mutualized, becoming public companies accountable to profit-driven shareholders. The risk of conflicts of interest has therefore arisen where exchanges fulfil quasi-regulatory roles but are subject to commercial and competitive pressures.

Following its de-mutualization, and reflecting requirements imposed under the EU's rules for offering securities to the public and listing securities on a regulated market (or exchange) under the Prospectus Directive 2003, the London Stock Exchange no longer 'lists' securities by imposing initial

disclosure requirements in the form of a prospectus and ongoing corporate governance and board structure requirements. This function is now carried out by the **UK Listing Authority**, which forms part of the **Financial Services Authority**. The London Stock Exchange does, however, retain responsibility for admitting securities to its markets and imposes rules for its Main Market and Alternative Investment Market.   NIAMH MOLONEY

***Stockdale v Hansard* (1839)**   This case concerned the relationship between ordinary law and the special internal laws and customs of the two Houses of Parliament. Stockdale was a publisher with a reputation for producing lewd books and a penchant for litigation. The Hansard family were the printers to the **House of Commons**. Stockdale had published what he described as a 'physiological and anatomical book written by a learned physician on the generative system'. The Inspectors of Prisons, however, having found a copy in the possession of a prisoner in Newgate Gaol in 1836, described it in their report as 'disgusting', with 'indecent and obscene plates'. The Secretary of State laid the report before both Houses of Parliament.

On 13 August 1835, the House of Commons had for the first time resolved that parliamentary papers and reports printed for the use of the House should be made available for sale to the public. On 18 March 1836 the House had ordered Messrs Hansard to undertake the printing and sale. Subsequently the House of Commons ordered the Inspectors' Report and some further material relating to Stockdale's book to be printed and offered for sale to the public. When the material was published Stockdale sued the printers for **libel**, claiming that the Inspectors' description of the book had injured his reputation. The printers pleaded the orders of the House of Commons as a defence. The **Attorney-General** argued for the defendants that the publication was protected by **parliamentary privilege**; the ordinary **courts** were inferior to the High Court of Parliament and had no jurisdiction to decide whether the privilege existed.

The **judges** unanimously rejected this claim. Parliament could not give itself privileges merely by deciding that it had them: such a power would be arbitrary and irresponsible. The mere fact that one of the Houses has authorized a thing to be done cannot make it lawful if it would otherwise be unlawful. The court accepted that each House had power to regulate its own proceedings and internal procedures without regard to the ordinary law, but that did not entail allowing the Houses to regulate the legal effect of libels published outside Parliament without an

Act of Parliament, or allowing one House unilaterally to infringe people's legal rights outside Parliament by extending its privileges.

Parliament responded by enacting the Parliamentary Papers Act 1840 to reverse the effect of the decision and extended absolute privilege to papers published by order or under the authority of either House. Subsequent legislation provides a qualified privilege for people who make fair and accurate reports of proceedings in Parliament, although this privilege is lost if the publication is actuated by malice. However, the case remains important as authority for the propositions that Parliament is not a court superior to the ordinary courts, and ordinary courts are competent to settle the scope of parliamentary privileges which affect people's legal rights out of Parliament, absent an Act of Parliament.

DAVID FELDMAN

stop and search powers   Stop and search powers authorize police to detain people (and vehicles) briefly in order to search them for various types of articles which are specified by statute. Beyond this bland definition lie controversy and complexity concerning the relationship between law and policing practice.

Stop and search has long been a source of tension between police and some minority communities. This was acknowledged in two defining reports on modern policing, Lord Scarman's inquiry into the Brixton Disorders of 1981 and Lord Macpherson's inquiry into Stephen Lawrence's murder. While Scarman found that intensive stop-and-search operations had severely exacerbated problems in police-community relations, Macpherson commented that 'If there was one area of complaint which was universal it was the issue of "stop and search"'). How stop and search is done is vital for police legitimacy, which in turn is a pre-condition of police effectiveness in crime control and order maintenance.

The authorities' response has been consistent, with a general strategy of authorization and regulation becoming dominance in the 1980s. Police practices which were deemed necessary for criminal investigation, but which either lacked legal authority or relied on uncertain **common law** or narrow, often local, provisions, were authorized, consolidated, and extended in national legislation. Such authorization was accompanied by legal and bureaucratic means of regulation. For example in England and Wales, the Police and Criminal Evidence Act 1984 ('**PACE**') provided police with authority to stop and search people for stolen or prohibited articles. This power was subject to the requirement of reasonable suspicion, which was explained in a code of practice

that also required officers to record stop and search events and to provide a copy of the record to the person searched.

Research on the operation of PACE has demonstrated the limitations of the authorize-and-regulate strategy. First, police officers could simply evade its restrictions by purporting to stop and search not by using legal authority, but by relying on the suspect's 'consent'. The free-willed, empowered citizen of legal mythology rarely figures in encounters between police and suspects on the street. When it is asked by an officer, the question 'Can I have a look in your bag?' invites only one answer. Moreover, a simple demand on the street, 'Open your bag', could subsequently be represented as a question in the rare circumstance of complaint being made. By its very nature, the interaction between officer and suspect on the street is difficult to supervise. Unless every exchange between police and people is to be electronically recorded, what was said will be open to dispute. The authorities' response to abuse of 'consent' was to direct officers that they should only stop and search using statutory powers. This suggests excessive faith in the authorize-and-regulate strategy.

The strategy conceives of stop and search as a preliminary stage of a linear criminal investigation-and-justice process punctuated by decisions about individuals: a police officer decides whether he or she has the appropriate level of suspicion about an individual's possession of certain items. However, this is a misleadingly narrow view of stop and search both in terms of its general functions and the way it is used in specific encounters. Officers stop people not just to search them for specified articles, but also to obtain information, to impose authority on individuals, groups, and areas, and to disrupt activities such as drug markets. In dealing with individuals, an officer's suspicion may be prompted by the kind of specific indicator contemplated by legislators (eg slipping a packet into a bag), but it is more likely to be a complex mixture of pre-conceptions about what is normal in a particular place at a particular time, stereotypes, and assumptions about types of people. Specific encounters are to be understood not as characterized by discrete legalistic decision-making, but rather as a process of interaction between officer and citizen in which suspicion is constructed (or dispelled).

The authorize-and-regulate strategy is further challenged by fundamental shifts underway in contemporary criminal justice. Increasingly, police are authorized to counter **terrorism** and other emergencies by stopping and searching without reasonable suspicion. More generally, enthusiasm for policing strategies, which target groups rather than individuals, prioritize pre-emption rather than criminal process, and seek to identify risk rather than guilt, provides stop and search with new priorities.

DAVID DIXON

D Clark, *The Investigation of Crime* (London: Lexis Nexis, 2004), ch 3

A Sanders and R Young, *Criminal Justice* (Oxford: Oxford University Press, 2007), ch 2

stop-now orders *see* **enforcement orders**

storytelling and law The distrust with which grand theories in law and other disciplines has been greeted in our post-modern era, has been accompanied with an emphasis on storytelling as an alternative means with which to relate, and perhaps change, our legal experiences. 'Stories from the bottom' or, as is sometimes termed, 'oppositional storytelling' is a growing feature in legal scholarship, used by marginalized groups to challenge the assumptions of the legal academy.

The claim by some feminists, critical race theorists, and advocates of the law and literature movement amongst others, is that their 'different voice' has been ignored by mainstream legal discourse, and that for that difference to be heard we need a different mode of communicating. Storytelling is allegedly more suited to the political task of transmitting the experiences of the oppressed than abstract legal analysis. By favouring the particular over the universal, storytelling may infuse empathy and compassion into a cold and disembodied legal system. Such qualities, it is claimed, have long been banished from the teaching and practice of law due to the insistence of **legal positivism** on the separation between law and morality.

However, claims about the importance, novelty, and political potential of storytelling are by no means obvious. Storytelling, whether acknowledged or not, has always been central to law-making and law-enforcing, with law telling stories not only about its **subjects**, but also about itself. Moreover, as Robert Cover famously put it, law operates in the realm of 'pain and death': every time it tells a story, whether or not it convinces rhetorically, it carries material conviction, that is, someone is at risk of losing her property, liberty, or even life.

Furthermore, whether we refer to stories told by the law or by its subjects, neither truth nor **justice** are inevitable properties of storytelling. 'We may swear', as Lacan puts it, 'to tell the truth, the whole truth, and nothing but the truth, and that is precisely what will not be said'. Lacan's point is that stories told by subjects about themselves are invariably suspect: there is no subject who doesn't lie because the subject comes into being at the moment it starts manipulating language. What we should focus on, therefore, is not what the subject tells, but what the subject consciously or unconsciously 'forgets' to tell.

'Law and storytelling' advocates also assume that listeners will identify with their tales. Sadly, whether we listen to legal, literary, or other stories, we invariably listen narcissistically, that is, by importing our own presuppositions into the scene. Storytelling cannot therefore be said to be any more privileged than other forms of communication regarding truth or justice.

'Forgetting', we must remember, is inherent to our being as **humans**. There is no human being without forgetting or without repression, which is why the truth can never be fully told, and the stories we tell can never be final or total. While storytellers can consciously or unconsciously hide the truth, and listeners can consciously or unconsciously hear part of the truth, only the elusive unconscious, to quote Lacan, 'doesn't bullshit'.

MARIA ARISTODEMOU

See also: **critical race theory; literature and law; narrative and law**

stranger Who is a stranger? For some, it is the person never before met, for others, the one who seems unrecognizably different. Early twentieth-century European and American sociologists defined the stranger as the outsider who entered a **community** to stay. Their work focused on Jewish and Black migrants; but that image of the stranger is also captured in the popular culture of American Western movies–the outsider whose entry through the dusty saloon bar dramatically unsettles the norms, values, and secrets of an insular community.

More recently, sociological work has suggested that in Western urban metropolises we are all strangers. In cities with diverse, ever-changing populations, no single kind of **person** can constitute an insider or, conversely, an outsider. Yet, despite such heterogeneity, governments continue to talk about strangers, emphasizing their danger and **risk**. Law also relies upon the idea of the stranger. But who are strangers for governments and law? In countries, such as Britain, the injunction to beware of the stranger, taught particularly to children, focuses, on the surface, on unknown people deemed, because they are unknown, to be inherently risky. Yet, underlying this injunction is the suggestion that certain kinds of people are dangerous—newcomers, transient, or homeless people, those who seem unfamiliar because they least resemble governmental and media depictions of the local population.

In law, the stranger is a different kind of person or, rather, relationship. The stranger represents the default position when a more formal legal relationship is denied and to whom fewer obligations are therefore owed. Thus who gets treated as a stranger is an intensely political matter. The struggle for same-sex relationship recognition has been largely aimed at changing couples' status so they are no longer seen by law as strangers to each other, turning them instead into kin as relationships of interdependence, intimacy, and **cohabitation** become recognized as legitimate bases for allocating rights of decision-making, parenting, inheritance, and financial support. In other areas of law too people's status changes as new obligations evolve. Thus, extending the duty of care in **tort** law converts people, previously seen as legal strangers, into neighbours—as relationships of connection and proximity are recognized and forged.

Yet, while one political strategy is to challenge legal relationships defined as between strangers, another is to question the assumptions upon which the concept of stranger depends. Feminists have argued extensively that risks of **violence** and sexual abuse in the West do not come mainly from unknown outsiders but from family members and acquaintances. They challenge the focus of law and policing which sidelines violence between intimates, focusing instead on stranger attacks. Elsewhere in law, people have sought to generate legal obligations towards strangers, for instance, by requiring the imposition of a duty to rescue which extends to strangers. This can be seen as part of a more general humanitarian, environmental, and political ethic to hold nations, corporations, and individuals responsible for the effects of their actions *and omissions* with respect to distant others.

While international legal action in this respect is uneven, changing how we think about strangers in law, culture, and politics has a knock-on effect on how we think about the familiar. What is interesting is the contribution that re-evaluating the stranger offers in adopting a more critical stance towards ties of family, kin, and community.

DAVINA COOPER

See also: **alien; Other, the**

strategic environmental assessment Assessing the potential environmental impact of major development projects has now been well established in UK environmental law for nearly two decades.

Environmental Impact Assessment (or 'EIA') was established formally in the UK in 1988, after implementation of the 1985 EIA Directive (85/337). However, assessing and preventing or mitigating the potential impact of individual developments like housing schemes, roads, and industrial development can only really limit the environmental consequences rather late in the day. Many significant impacts are actually determined by earlier more strategic decisions made by government and local authorities through strategic plans and programmes, which dictate where and how individual development projects are brought forward.

To anticipate and prevent such impacts, Strategic Environmental Assessment ('SEA') has been introduced, governed by the SEA Directive (2001/42). The SEA Directive requires that the likely significant effects on the environment of a formal plan or programme prepared by a public authority are identified and assessed and presented in an Environmental Report ('ER'), and consulted upon publicly before a decision to adopt or approve the plan or programme is taken. EU Member States were required to implement these requirements by July 2004. The UK has done this in a number of ways, which differ somewhat among the various devolved administrations, but particularly between Scotland and England. However, through the Environmental Assessment (Scotland) Act 2005 the Scottish Executive extended the application of SEA not just for formal plans and programmes, but potentially to all plans, programmes, and strategies produced by public agencies.

The government in England, with regard to land use and spatial planning, had already decided to introduce Sustainability Appraisal ('SA')—which seeks to assess plans and programmes for their likely impacts on sustainability (ie impacts on environment, social, *and* economic factors)—prior to the SEA Directive being implemented. Consequently, England has incorporated the requirements of the SEA Directive into SA for land use and spatial planning through the Planning and Compulsory Purchase Act 2004. Local development plans, regional spatial and economic strategies must now all undergo SA incorporating SEA. The challenge for local authorities over the last two years has been to introduce SA/SEA at the same time as implementing the new planning system introduced by the 2004 Act. In other sectors, however, SEA alone is required, eg for local transport plans. SEA is also now being applied in the agriculture, forestry, offshore energy, and water sectors. It is, however, still early days as the criteria for deciding which plans and programmes require SEA under the Directive, and just how much information must be presented in an ER have still yet to be tested properly through the courts.

WILLIAM SHEATE

stress   There are two central questions about the legal response to stress. First, can **compensation** be claimed for the wrongful infliction of 'mere' stress? Secondly, how does the law determine the stress to which employees may lawfully be exposed?

On the first question, the starting point is that feelings of stress on their own do not attract **damages**. Consequently a person who experiences stress because of a wrongful act will not normally be compensated for these feelings alone. Distress might, however, indirectly affect the damages awarded. An example is where stress induced by the circumstances of a wrongful act worsens its physical effects. More commonly, feelings of stress are part of a recognized psychiatric illness, like Post Traumatic Stress Disorder, which does attract damages. There are also exceptions to the general rule. When **Parliament** created certain wrongs by statute, like the different kinds of unlawful discrimination, it spelled out that compensation would be payable, not only for the usual losses and expenses, but also for 'injury to feelings'.

On the second question, there are many statutory rules about working life that limit the pressure under which an employee may lawfully be placed. Obvious examples are rules that regulate working time, for example by providing for daily and weekly breaks and by specifying a maximum working week. Also, subjecting an employee to excessive stress will sometimes result in an employer being liable for a statutory wrong like **unfair dismissal**, even though that wrong is, on the face of it, not about stress. In this case the link comes from the law normally viewing conduct which unreasonably pushes an employee into leaving work as tantamount to unfair dismissal.

Most significant of all is the duty on employers to take reasonable care to avoid causing illness or injury to their employees. This is a specific example of the general **common law** prohibition on negligence. Employers' duties are typically broken down into requirements to provide, first, competent fellow workers, secondly, a proper system of work and, thirdly, a safe place of work. It is important that the duty arises only in respect of injuries that are reasonably foreseeable.

There has been a proliferation of decisions applying these general principles to claims about stress at work. The Court of Appeal recently laid down general guidelines, which were subsequently approved by the **House of Lords** in *Barber v Somerset County Council* (2004). The guidelines stress that foreseeability depends on what the employer knows, or ought reasonably to know, about the individual employee. In order for the duty to take preventive steps to be triggered, the indications of impending harm to health must be sufficiently plain for any reasonable employer to realize he should do something. In addition, the size and scope of the employer's operation, its resources, and the demands it faces (including considering the interests of, and the need to be fair to, other employees) are all relevant to what is reasonable.

LIZZIE BARMES

See also: **negligence in civil law; psychiatric damage**

strict civil liability   Civil liability is contrasted with criminal liability; and strict liability is contrasted with fault-based liability. Although not uncommon, strict criminal liability is much more controversial than strict civil liability. Some think that it is wrong to punish people for conduct that may have been faultless. Others say that stigmatizing faultless conduct may reduce the social utility and force of the criminal law. By contrast, civil law is primarily concerned with reparation for harm, not with **punishment**; and this shift of focus from the doer to the sufferer of harm may be thought to weaken, if not eliminate, objections to strict liability.

Strict liability is liability regardless of fault, not liability in the absence of fault; liability without proof of fault, not liability without fault. A person may be held strictly liable even though they were, in fact, at fault. Indeed, research has shown that some strict liability criminal offences are typically prosecuted only in cases where the offender was actually at fault. In civil law, there are two main reasons for creating liability regardless of fault. One is to overcome potential problems of proving fault—not primarily to catch the faultless, but to make is easier to catch the faulty. The other is to shift the balance of **responsibility** as between doers and sufferers of harm. When liability requires proof of fault on the part of the harm-doer, the sufferer ends up bearing harms that are not proved to be the doer's fault; but not when it is strict.

Strict liability may be liability for breach of a strict obligation. Unlike an obligation of care, which requires a person to take care to behave or to avoid behaving in a certain way, a strict obligation requires the person to behave or to avoid behaving in that way, full stop. Many contractual obligations are strict, as are some obligations of **fiduciaries** and trustees, and some obligations breach of which can give rise to tort liability. On the other hand, a person may be strictly liable to repair harm even if the harm did not result from breach of an obligation on their part. **Vicarious liability** in tort law and the law of **restitution** provide important examples.

Despite the apparent simplicity of the contrast between strict liability and fault, strictness is a matter of degree. For instance, even if a harm-sufferer need not prove that the harm-doer was at fault, the doer's liability may be reduced if the harm was partly the result of **contributory negligence** of the sufferer. Even if the harm-sufferer need not prove that the harm-doer failed to take reasonable care, the doer may be liable only for such of the harm caused as was foreseeable. And so on.

Despite being common in law, many consider strict liability to be 'immoral'. Careful analysis of concepts of 'moral responsibility' suggests that this conclusion results partly from an unbalanced focus on criminal law at the expense of civil law, and partly from a contestable belief that moral responsibility is independent of social practices of holding people responsible.   PETER CANE

See also: **fault-based civil liability; fault-based criminal liability**

strict criminal liability see **criminal liability without fault**

strict liability trading offences see **due diligence defence; trading standards**

strict scrutiny Strict scrutiny is a concept of the **constitutional law** of the United States of America. The US Constitution includes the '**Equal Protection Clause**' of the Fourteenth Amendment' which provides that 'No State shall . . . deny to any person within its jurisdiction the equal protection of the laws'. But, of course, when states make laws, they frequently distinguish between different groups of persons—for instance, in setting the age for lawful consumption of alcohol in public bars, or granting welfare entitlements to war veterans. The **US Supreme Court** has recognized that such distinctions are a legitimate element of law-making. In general, so long as the state articulates a rational basis for such a distinction, it will be lawful.

However, some distinctions are inherently suspect. Where state activity distinguishes on such a basis, it will be subject to 'strict scrutiny' by the courts. The best-known 'suspect classification' is **race**. National origin, **religion**, and alienage have also been so recognized. (There is also an 'intermediate' category, in which distinctions based on **gender** and illegitimacy fall.)

Strict scrutiny implies two strands of analysis. The racial classification 'must serve a compelling governmental interest'. Further, it 'must be narrowly tailored to further that interest' (*Adarand v Peña* (1995)). Because of the strictness of these two requirements (the interest must be *compelling*; there must be an extremely close fit between the racial classification and the furthering of that interest), application of the 'strict scrutiny' standard usually means that the state's law, policy, programme, or other activity is set aside by the reviewing court.

However, in a very few well-known cases, the Supreme Court has upheld public policies or activities that discriminate on the grounds of race. In *Korematsu v United States* (1944), the Supreme Court upheld a compulsory relocation programme applicable to Japanese Americans resident in the West Coast area of the USA during World War II. Justice Black confirmed that 'all legal restrictions which curtail the civil rights of a single racial group are immediately suspect'. However, he found that 'pressing public necessity may sometimes justify the existence of such restrictions…'. By a narrow majority (5:4), the Supreme Court has also accepted the admissions programme of the University of Michigan Law School, which used race as part of its admissions criteria (*Grutter v Bollinger* (2003)). The policy was designed to create a more diverse student body, through recruiting a critical mass of **minority** students.

TAMARA HERVEY AND PHILIP ROSTANT

See also: **positive discrimination**

strikes It was established at an early stage in the history of British trade unionism that the organizing of strike action was a criminal offence, with offences being created by **legislation** and the **common law**. The gradual removal of most statutory restrictions and the introduction by statute in 1875 of an immunity from criminal liability gave way to the emergence of judge-made liabilities in civil law for those individuals (such as trade union officials) who organized industrial action. This development was confirmed by three leading decisions of the House of Lords between 1901 and 1905, including the famous *Taff Vale* case in 1901, where it was held for the first time that **trade unions** had a quasi-corporate status and that as such they could be sued in **damages** for the tortious acts of their members and officials. This major blow to trade union freedom created long-term distrust between organized labour and the **judges**, and, more immediately, led to trade union demands for parliamentary **representation** to reverse the decision, and the foundation of the Labour Representation Committee for this purpose. The Labour Representation Committee changed its name to the Labour Party in 1906, and political pressure to reverse the *Taff Vale* decision led to the Trade Disputes Act 1906. This gave trade unions and their officials immunities from various heads of civil liability, and protected trade union funds by providing that a court was not to entertain an action in tort brought against a trade union.

The Trade Disputes Act 1906 was repealed by the Conservative government's Industrial Relations Act 1971, when a new (and highly restrictive) legal framework was introduced to deal with industrial disputes. But the immunities were soon restored by the next Labour government, by means of legislation passed in 1974 and amended in 1976. Although the 1974 and 1976 Acts strengthened the immunities for trade union officials who organized industrial action, the restored immunities for trade union funds did not go as far as the blanket immunity of the 1906 Act. Nevertheless, the new legislation set the trade unions on a collision course with the Court of Appeal under the leadership of Lord **Denning** who saw it as a threat to constitutional principle (in this case the **rule of law**). In a handful of important cases, the court proceeded narrowly to construe the immunities, in a way designed to limit the purposes for which industrial action could be taken, and restrict the circumstances in which secondary or solidarity action could be pursued. This controversy led in turn to conflict between the Court of Appeal and the **House of Lords**, the latter taking the view that the former was in danger of compromising another constitutional principle, namely the **separation of powers**, by trespassing on the power of **Parliament**. The approach of the Court of Appeal was to succeed in the long term, however, as the Conservative government of Mrs Thatcher elected in 1979 set about again to dismantle the statutory immunities.

The position is now governed by the Trade Union and Labour Relations (Consolidation) Act 1992, with the settlement contained therein being largely accepted by the Labour governments since 1997, with only slight modifications having been made. However, the restrictions on lawful action have been criticized repeatedly by several international agencies as violating **human rights treaties** to which the United Kingdom is a party, most notably ILO Convention 87 and the European Social Charter of 1961. There is thus no right to strike, but a now heavily curtailed immunity from certain specified torts

for acts done in contemplation or furtherance of a 'trade dispute'. For these purposes, a 'trade dispute' is narrowly defined so as to exclude various forms of political strikes (such as strikes directed against the government, or strikes directed against the policies of a foreign government). It is also the case that the immunity does not apply to all forms of industrial action, being withdrawn from secondary action, which would otherwise be protected as being done in 'furtherance' of trade dispute. Secondary action would cover the situation where (a) the workers on strike, (b) ask workers employed by a supplier to or customer of their employer, (c) to refuse to handle any material to be supplied to or which has been delivered from the employer in the dispute. This is sometimes referred to as a secondary boycott, and had been protected under the legislation of 1974–1976.

Even if covered by the immunity, industrial action will be lawful only if the union has given due notice to the employer and only if the action is supported by a ballot. If the action is unlawful for any reason (because it falls outside the definition of a trade dispute, constitutes unlawful secondary action, or fails to comply with the detailed notice and balloting requirements), the employer can seek a remedy against the union, usually in the form of an **injunction** to have the action stopped. An employer may also seek damages, though there is a statutory ceiling on the amount that may be recovered, based on the size of the union. Workers who take part in a strike are also vulnerable to dismissal, as participation in industrial action will generally be considered to be a breach of contract at common law, and may authorize dismissal without notice. Under statutory **unfair dismissal** laws, however, it is now unfair to dismiss an employee for taking part in industrial action covered by the immunity. The protection applies for the first twelve weeks of the action, and may be extended thereafter depending on the conduct of the parties. Employees unfairly dismissed in these circumstances are entitled to **compensation**, but they are unlikely in practice to be reinstated in their employment. A Trade Union Freedom Bill drafted with the support of the TUC in 2006 to commemorate the Trade Disputes Act 1906 would have modified some of the restraints on the right to strike, but was not supported by the government, despite significant endorsement by Labour MPs.   KEITH EWING

See also: **economic torts; Thatcherism**

structured settlements   A structured settlement is a financial arrangement used to compensate a claim for damages for personal injury. Traditionally,

damages were paid only by means of a once-and-for-all lump sum. By contrast, a 'structure' involves paying all or part of the compensation by means of periodical payments, thus imposing a continuing liability upon a defendant.

Following their widespread use in North America, structures were imported into the UK in the 1980s. They are generally only considered in cases involving substantial damages for the cost of future care or for the loss of future earnings. Although there is no minimum threshold, usually they are confined to claims exceeding £250,000. Even in such cases lump sums continue to predominate.

The periodical payments continue for as long as the loss is expected to last, and usually this means that they are guaranteed for the rest of claimant's life. The regular payments offer greater security and peace of mind compared to the uncertain returns from a lump sum which, for a variety of reasons, may be dissipated before death. Payments can be protected against inflation by linking them to the Retail Prices Index. Unlike the income that arises on investment of a lump sum, the payments are free of tax and can preserve entitlement to means-tested benefits. As against these advantages, the arrangement denies the claimant access to the capital that otherwise would be received. This limits the ability to make alternative provision should unforeseen circumstances arise requiring, for example, greater care. The payments end on the death of the claimant even if this is premature, although further payments then may be provided for dependants.

The liability to make continuing payment can be met in one of two ways. In most cases the real defendant is a liability insurance company and it usually purchases an annuity from a life insurer. Alternatively a defendant may choose to self-fund the payments and thus make cash flow savings by avoiding the immediate payment of a large capital sum. This approach is commonly adopted by **National Health Service** trusts in settling clinical negligence claims.

Until 2005 periodical payments could not be obtained if either party objected. However, courts now have the power to impose such an arrangement even if both parties object. They can only avoid this possibility by settling out of court. If a case involving future financial loss comes before a judge, a periodical payments order must be considered. Whether such an order is made depends upon the claimant's needs and the expert financial advice obtained, but the resulting capital cost of the annual payments is not a relevant factor. This is a major change in assessing damages.

A periodical payments order can be varied to take account of future developments, but only if changes are foreseen and provision made in the original court order. In essence the damages award thus continues to involve a once-and-for-all assessment, although now a defendant can be required to make continuing payment.   RICHARD LEWIS

student visa   *see* **visa**

subaltern   see **Other, the**

subcultures and law   At a minimum, a subculture can be thought of as a set of ongoing social affiliations, a relatively distinct grouping of people organized around some shared interest or problem. Often, the shared interests and activities that set the subculture apart also push it past the margins of mainstream social life; in this sense a group of people can indeed come to exist as a *sub*-culture, developing a collective, secretive way of life that survives beneath, or perhaps beyond, the perception of those not involved in it. At the same time, though, subcultures regularly develop distinctive styles of dress, language, and comportment in the interest of maintaining subcultural boundaries and affirming subcultural **identity**, and so intertwine private rituals with public displays of cultural difference. As Dick Hebdige argues in *Subculture: The Meaning of Style* (1979), contemporary subcultures in this way not only 'hide in the light' of encoded public display; they present a significant if stylized challenge to everyday social practices and cultural assumptions, a public presence that interrupts the taken-for-granted course of daily life.

It is this contested cultural context that often defines the dynamic between subcultures and law. While some legal regulation aims to control the illicit association of subcultural members, or to minimize threats to person or property posed by subcultural practices, other laws focus on the styles, performances, and public displays—even the simple public presence—of subcultures and their members. Further, the policing of subcultures increasingly involves stylistic surveillance, with policing agencies 'reading' subcultural displays for indications of conflict, expansion, or threat. From zoot suiters, mods, rockers, and punks of past years to contemporary hip hop performers and graffiti writers, subcultures—and especially the youth subcultures prominent in the decades since World War II—have been the target of countless laws designed to police subcultural style and so symbolically to restore the order of everyday life. A particularly notable case in this regard is Britain's 1994 Criminal Justice and Public Order Act, which criminalized open air gatherings, 'a succession of repetitive beats', and other activities associated with the rave subculture.

Aimed at particular subcultural practices, such laws themselves often emerge from yet another set of cultural practices. As Stanley Cohen documented in *Folk Devils and Moral Panics* (1972), and as countless criminological studies have since confirmed, subcultural legal regulation regularly develops from a context of 'moral panic' over the supposed threat posed by the subculture and its public practices. Inflamed by sensationalist media coverage, stoked by the overheated rhetoric of political authorities, public perception comes to characterize the subculture as an embodiment of social disorder, or a harbinger of social decay—and so aggressive legal regulation is proposed, supported, and passed. This harsh legal response, though, often sets up one final dynamic between subcultures and law: an amplification of the subcultural 'threat', a consolidation of commitment amongst subcultural members, and so a trajectory from subculture to counterculture.

JEFF FERRELL

subject What is the difference between a legal subject and legal **person**? Sometimes the two terms are used synonymously so the 'legal subject' simply refers to anyone who is subject to the laws within the country in which he or she lives. However, the term 'subject' has some connotations that are not shared by the term 'person'. The layperson would usually associate the use of the term subject with the idea of being subject to the **Crown** compared with a citizen of a Republic. In this context, reference to a subject implies the existence of a monarch to whom the subject is subordinate.

The arguments around the meaning of the term 'subject' can be understood by looking at its philosophical history. Within philosophy, a subject is usually the counterpart to an object. This is reflected in common parlance when we refer to the 'subject' and 'object' of a sentence. The subject is viewed as active and the object as passive. As subjects we use objects. This is illustrated by the fact that feminists have argued that men have treated them as sexual objects (as things) when they should be treated as subjects, whose own intentions and desires matter. Given that here subjectivity denotes the ability to be active, this usage sits uneasily with the idea of someone who is the (passive) subject of a monarch.

A further distinction between the meaning of 'legal subject' and 'legal person' derives from the meaning of personhood itself. This is usually

employed as a political and moral concept, as in the works of the philosopher, Immanuel Kant. To be a person, for Kant, is linked with Enlightenment ideals. It connotes the ability to be autonomous, to be able to think for oneself. For Kant, this involved having the ability to employ reason, which was closely associated with morality. We use reason in order to obey moral laws. It was therefore linked with the **capacity** to be a citizen. However, in purely legal terms, to be a person simply meant that you the right to sue and be sued in the courts. Historically, whilst companies were able to act as legal persons, this was denied to women.

In his discussion of legal subjectivity, the twentieth-century pragmatist philosopher, John Dewey, considers the ways in which the law employs philosophical concepts, sometimes unconsciously importing their assorted baggage. He points out that in Germany there was an attempt to explain the meaning of the 'legal subject' by asking, 'what is the essence of the subject?'. This was taken to be an analysis of what it was to be a human being, which they then tried to apply to the term 'legal subject'. So, for example, to decide if a **company** could be treated as a legal subject, legal theorists compared the characteristics of a company with these essential qualities. However, Dewey points out that **courts** can (and do) continue their work without worrying about the meanings of such terms. He argues that the question: 'what is the legal subject?' could be replaced by a different mode of questioning by asking: 'what is the effect of describing someone or thing as a legal subject?'. This shifts the analysis to the question of how law works in practice. So, to classify companies as subjects has certain social effects that have nothing to do with definitions of human subjectivity.

Some areas of current legal theory, like other areas of the humanities in the UK, have been influenced by contemporary continental philosophy, within which there is also suspicion of the idea that it is possible to define 'who we are' in terms of anything that is fixed. The idea that there is some fixed, underlying 'essence' of a thing—a view that has been attributed to Aristotle—has again been questioned. Feminist philosophers have argued that theories about what it is to be a 'subject' or a 'person' have taken men as the (supposedly) neutral universal term. Similarly, feminist legal theorists have been concerned to show that the legal subject is viewed as 'male'. In some circumstances this may make no difference. However, there may be scenarios in which men and women differ, for example, at certain times men have viewed some behaviour as a joke that women experienced as **sexual harassment**. In a culture in which there are these differences, legal judgments as to what constitutes 'reasonable behaviour' for a legal subject will differ depending upon the perception of the subject.

There could be as many different views of the legal subject as there are views about what it is to be a subject. One example will be used to illustrate a currently influential and controversial strand of thought, drawing upon the work of philosopher Michel Foucault.

Michel Foucault discusses what he calls 'subjectification'. This describes the way in which someone *becomes* a subject. So, legal academics employing Foucault's work analyse law's role in shaping us as subjects. Foucault details different 'disciplinary techniques' (for example, the bell telling prisoners/ school children/workers when to perform certain acts and thus inculcating habit, the ways in which we are examined and graded both medically and educationally, and compared with others statistically as a case file). These disciplinary techniques become employed in different areas of life so that, for example, the prisons, schools, and factories come to resemble each other. The most famous disciplinary technique is the panopticon, an idea for a model prison suggested by Bentham, in which the architecture is such that prisoners do not know at any given time whether or not they are being observed. They are therefore encouraged to police themselves. Foucault argues that this approach is repeated in the factories, schools, and hospitals. Critics have argued that Foucault describes a dystopia, in which we become 'who we are' as a result of disciplinary techniques from which there is no escape. In response, he argues that such techniques rely upon the view that subjects are free to act otherwise. In both civil and criminal law, the treatment of subjects is predicated upon this idea that the subject is free and hence responsible for his or her actions.   JANICE RICHARDSON

subjectivity   *see* **subject**

subjects of international law   *see* **international law**

subrogation   Subrogation is most easily explained by example. If someone's car is damaged in a road accident by negligent driver, the owner will usually take the simplest course of action and claim against the insurer. Perhaps surprisingly, the insurer will then be entitled to sue the negligent driver. This is so, even though the insurer was not the victim of the accident and had no contractual or other legal relationship with the negligent driver. What the insurer does is 'stand in the shoes of the insured' and exercise

any rights the owner may have which could diminish the loss insured against.

This idea of 'standing in another's shoes' is subrogation. Subrogation effectively transfers the insured's rights to the insurer, allowing the insurer to sue the wrongdoer. This happens by operation of law, without the need for any assignment by, or assent from, the insured, even though it is these rights that are being transferred to the insurer. The mechanism is commonly seen in insurance contracts, as in the example just described, but it occurs in a wide variety of very different circumstances.

Subrogation is therefore concerned with three-party situations. A has rights against B, but C is entitled (for some reason, such as because of the insurance contract between A and C) to stand in A's shoes and sue B. It follows from this that C's claim will suffer from all the advantages and disadvantages of A's claim against B. For example, suppose A had been the negligent driver, not B. A would then have no claim in negligence against B. The insurer (standing in A's shoes) would then also have no claim against B. It would be irrelevant that the insurer had paid out to A under the insurance contract.

SARAH WORTHINGTON

subsidiarity   The principle of subsidiarity addresses the question: which is the most appropriate level at which public powers should be located and exercised? Historically, it rests upon the assumption that public power is most appropriately allocated to, and exercised at, the lowest possible tier of government which can exercise such powers effectively.

It first entered the EU and EC Treaties as a general principle in 1993, after the Treaty of Maastricht. In the Treaty of European Union ('TEU'), subsidiarity amounts to a statement of the general political value that 'decisions are taken . . . as closely as possible to the citizen' (Article 1(2) TEU).

In the EC Treaty (see its Article 5), however, subsidiarity exists to require the EC's legislative institutions to consider whether a particular goal could be 'sufficiently achieved' by the Member States. If so, then the achievement of that goal should be left to Member States. If, however, it can be shown 'by reason of the scale or effects' of the proposed measure that the goal can be 'better achieved' by the EC, then EC legislation may be adopted to pursue that goal. The principle does not apply to areas of power (or competence) held by the EC which are *exclusive* to the EC and are no longer held by Member States: thus, subsidiarity applies to areas where competence is *shared* by the EC and its Member States, where either EC or Member State action to achieve a particular goal is possible.

The key question is when and how it can be shown that the goal in question cannot be sufficiently achieved by the Member States and can instead be better achieved by the EC. Qualitative and (where possible) quantitative indicators must be used to show: transnational aspects with which Member States could not deal; or clear benefits flowing from EC-level action that Member State action would not create. These considerations show that it will be the EC's *political* institutions which will have responsibility for the day-to-day operation of the subsidiarity principle: ie the Commission (in proposing legislation), the Council, and the **European Parliament** (in debating and agreeing the terms of definitive) legislative texts. When combined with the principle of **proportionality in EU law**, it may be that the most enduring significance of subsidiarity will be to: require more carefully reasoned decisions explaining the need for EC action; and influence the content of EC legislation so that it does not at the EC level go further than necessary to achieve the relevant goals.

Subsidiarity is a *legal* principle laid down in the EC Treaty, and it can be relied upon before the European Courts to argue that EC legislation has not been adopted properly. Procedurally, the principle requires that clear reasons are provided in support of adoption of legislation at EC level, demonstrating that such EC rules are compatible with subsidiarity. As to the substance of those reasons, the **European Court of Justice** has allowed the political institutions a wide **discretion** in deciding upon whether action should be taken at the EC level.

ANGUS JOHNSTON

See also: **European treaties**

substantial lessening of competition When a merger is scrutinized under the Enterprise Act 2002, first by the **Office of Fair Trading** and second, if a more in-depth study is required, by the **Competition Commission**, the two agencies consider whether the transaction may cause a substantial lessening of **competition** in the market; and if so the transaction is prohibited. The substantial lessening of competition standard is recognized worldwide as the best way to assess mergers because it allows competition authorities to apply the law in an economically sound manner.

A lessening of competition occurs in one of two ways. First, the merger may result in a firm with increased market power, which can increase prices unilaterally or have less incentive to innovate. Secondly, a merger in an **oligopoly** market may make collusion among the merged entity and its competitors more likely, which also harms consumers by raising prices. The merger must cause a substantial harm to competition; so where an already dominant firm (eg with a market share of 60 per cent) that has the power to harm consumers acquires a small, weak competitor (eg with a market share of 1 per cent), the merger is unlikely to be blocked because the additional harm to competition caused by the merger is insignificant.

The substantial lessening of competition standard replaces the one applied in the earlier law (the Fair Trading Act 1973) by which a merger was judged according to whether it was contrary to the public interest, a standard which drew criticism for being open to political manipulation. GIORGIO MONTI

substantive equality Equality is a complex ideal, and the law contains many different approaches to achieving it. One approach is '**formal equality**', which aims to treat everyone alike. Briefly put, the problem with following 'formal equality' in law is that it does not allow us to work out why people are treated differently and it does not allow us to address less visible, more institutional or systemic forms of inequality.

Many of the **equality** laws that came into force in the UK during the 1970s are based on a formal equality model. However, in recent years, the concept of substantive equality has been more and more influential in UK, EU, Canadian, and South African equality laws (to name but a few examples), as well as in many international **human rights** instruments. Substantive equality goes beyond treating likes alike and attempts to address the reasons for, and effects of, complex discrimination. This entails allowing, and promoting, **legislation** that targets the inequalities that particular groups experience, something that under a formal equality model would either be classed as unlawful discrimination or allowed as a narrowly defined exception. For example, an employer might wish to increase the number of **women** working in a particular sector and it might use a range of different methods to achieve this, ranging from positive encouragement, through outreach and training targeted at women, to recruitment policies that give priority to women (see *Badeck v Landesanwalt beim Staatsgerichthof des Landes Hessen* (2000)).

Apart from endorsing, and even requiring wide-ranging '**positive action**' or 'ameliorative action' measures, substantive equality has a number of further implications. Recognizing that apparently neutral or non-interventionist state policies have disproportionate effects on certain groups of people, a substantive equality approach challenges the concept and ideal of state neutrality, instead focusing on how the state inevitably distributes resources through decision-making. This has led to an approach in equality law that moves away from a narrow 'civil liberties' model of rights to demands for **economic and social rights**, which ensure minimum living standards. Post-**apartheid** South Africa is one jurisdiction that takes such socio-economic rights extremely seriously, including in its Bill of Rights specific positive rights to housing, healthcare, food and water, social security, and education (Chapter Two, Constitution of the Republic of South Africa, 1996), although there has been wide-ranging criticism of the South African government's record in putting these rights into effect.

A further implication of a substantive equality approach is a move away from individualism. With its emphasis on systems of inequality and institutional dynamics, substantive equality looks at the connections between individuals' experiences of discrimination and wider social and historical circumstances. This requires a broader concept of how inequalities arise, become embedded, and how they affect people based on their class, **gender, race, disability,** or sexual orientation. In turn, it affects what we expect the law to do about subtle and entrenched inequalities. Following a substantive equality approach, the argument is that responsibility for discrimination does not lie with individual discriminators, but with organizations (employers, for example, or service providers) and the state. Instead of requiring individuals to undertake costly and risky legal action to establish a person or organization's liability for discrimination, organizations are put under positive obligations to ensure that certain groups are not discriminated against. Using methods such as monitoring of recruitment, promotion, and retention and drafting equality plans can assist with this. In addition, legal **remedies** for discrimination are not targeted to individual litigants but to groups of affected people and may go beyond financial **compensation** to target an organization's wider practices.

Substantive equality varies widely from jurisdiction to jurisdiction, depending on whether a country has a Bill of Rights or similar domestic human rights instrument, and depending on the prevailing rights culture: how lawyers, activists, and other people conceptualize the way that law can contribute to equality. The language of substantive equality has been current in Canadian **constitutional law** since the debates around the drafting of the **Canadian Charter of Rights and Freedoms** in the early 1980s, whilst conceptualizations of equality as 'equal treatment' have given way to positive duties, obligations on public authorities, and equality action plans

in the UK over the past ten years. In spite of these contextual differences, different jurisdictions' concepts of substantive equality share a number of core themes: a move away from securing rights through individual litigation, a broad-based commitment to social **justice**, a focus on the effects of discrimination rather than whether discrimination was intended, and future-oriented equality measures.

EMILY GRABHAM

succession The law of succession deals with the transfer of a person's property on death, particularly by means of disposition by will (testate succession) and on intestacy (ie where the deceased never made a valid will, or the will does not dispose of all the deceased's property). In some jurisdictions, for example, Scotland, protected rights of inheritance are recognized. These guarantee certain relatives a given share in the deceased's property, and cannot be varied by the will or rules of intestacy. The law of succession is inextricably linked with estate planning during a person's lifetime, in order to minimize the effects of inheritance tax on a person's estate (property) on death.

Any person who has mental capacity and is over the age of eighteen can make a will. The person making the will (the testator) sets out how he or she wishes their property to be disposed of after death, and appoints persons (executors) who will deal with the estate. The executors may be the same persons who are benefiting under the will (the beneficiaries). There is no restriction on the number of persons who may be appointed as executors. A person nominated as executor is not bound to accept the executorship and may renounce the office, provided they have not intermeddled with the estate. A will may be revoked at any time before the testator dies. Until the testator's death it is nothing more than a declaration of the testator's wishes, and the beneficiary has only a 'mere hope of inheriting' (*spes successionis*).

The formalities for creating a will must be strictly complied with, except in the case of wills made by soldiers, sailors, and airmen on active service, for whom informal directions are sufficient. The will must be in writing; signed by the testator, or some person in the testator's presence and by the testator's direction; the testator must intend the signature to give effect to the will; the testator's signature must be made or (if unable to sign) acknowledged in the presence of two witnesses present at the same time; and, the witnesses must either sign and attest the will or acknowledge their signatures in the presence of the testator (but not necessarily in the presence of the other witness). Any person may be a witness provided he or she understands what is going on. A will that does not comply with these requirements is void. However, a witness who is also a beneficiary, or a husband, wife, or civil partner of such a person, will lose the beneficial entitlement, but will remain a valid witness. Additionally, a will is not valid where it is induced by force, fear, fraud, or undue influence.

In England and Wales, a testator may theoretically dispose of property in any way the testator wishes, and may even direct that his or her spouse or children be deprived of any benefit from the estate. However, under the Inheritance (Provision for Family and Dependents) Act 1975, it is possible for the terms of the will (or the rules of intestacy) to be varied by a court after the testator's death to make provision for a surviving spouse, civil partner, former spouse or civil partner, child, dependant, or cohabitee.

Where a person dies intestate in England and Wales someone must apply to be appointed administrator to deal with the deceased's estate. The modern law of intestacy is contained in the Administration of Estates Act 1925. On a person's intestacy, the estate is held by the administrators, who will pay the deceased's debts and distribute the remainder of the estate according to the order of entitlement in the Act. The surviving spouse or civil partner has the primary right to succession. Where a spouse or civil partner and issue (ie children and grandchildren) survive the deceased the spouse or civil partner is entitled to a fixed sum of £125,000, the deceased's personal chattels, and a life interest in half of the residuary or remaining estate. The issue are entitled to the other half of the residuary estate and the surviving spouse's or civil partner's life interest once he has died. Where the deceased is survived by a spouse or civil partner but no issue or specified relatives, the spouse or civil partner takes the whole of the estate. If the deceased is survived by a spouse or civil partner and a specified relative but no issue, then the surviving spouse or civil partner takes a fixed sum of £200,000, the deceased's personal chattels, and one half of the balance of the estate. The relative takes the remaining balance of the estate. If the deceased is survived by issue only, but no surviving spouse or civil partner, the issue take the whole estate. If the deceased leaves no issue and no surviving spouse or civil partner, the estate will pass to certain relatives. Where there are no such relatives the property passes to the **Crown**.   MERYL THOMAS

A Borkowski, *Textbook on Succession* (Oxford: Oxford University Press, 2nd edn, 2002)

R Kerridge, *Parry and Clark, The Law of Succession* (London: Sweet & Maxwell, 11th edn, 2002)

suicide   The word suicide has many definitions, depending on one's particular interest (eg religious, sociological, legal, ethical, or medical). In simple terms, however, to commit suicide means to kill oneself intentionally and non-instrumentally, ie where the only objective is to die. In this sense, it is debatable whether or not Captain Oates' altruistic self-sacrifice on the Scott expedition would qualify.

Previously regarded as the felony of self-murder, suicide was decriminalized in England and Wales (having never been a crime in Scotland) in the Suicide Act 1961, when it became clear that, following changes in social attitudes, criminal (and religious) sanctions were inappropriate, did not act as a deterrent, and added to the pain and distress of bereaved families. This reflected a shift away from the Dark and Middle Age condemnation of suicide as a crime and a sin (although it is not unequivocally forbidden in the Bible) towards some kind of tolerance—more fully expressed in Greek and Roman times and by some subsequent warrior races—of suicide as being rational and right in some circumstances.

Because the Suicide Act also created the offence of 'aiding, abetting, counselling or procuring suicide', the medico-legal aspects of suicide have been raised in the context of (i) positively assisting a terminally ill patient to die (*R (on the Application of Pretty) v DPP* (2002); and *Pretty v UK* (2002)); (ii) refusal of life-sustaining treatment by a competent patient (*Re Ms B v NHS Hospital Trust* (2002)); and (iii) disconnecting life support mechanisms which keep patients alive (*Airedale NHS Trust v Bland* (1993)). Interpreted as omissions (thus raising the question whether suicide can be committed by omission) the latter two events have been held to be non-suicidal.

GLENYS WILLIAMS

See also: **acts and omissions; Bland, Tony; Pretty, Diane**

summary dismissal   *see* **wrongful dismissal**

summons   *see* **indictment**

supersession   *see* **social security appeals**

supremacy of EC law   The principle that EC law is supreme over any conflicting national law establishes a hierarchy of legal rules which national and European courts must respect and enforce. This means that Member States may not plead that national legal or political restrictions are a justification for their failure to comply with EC law obligations, such as the duty to implement a Directive within the prescribed time limit or the requirement to respect directly effective provisions of the EC Treaty. Where such matters are raised before an international court, this position is well established as a matter of **international law**: when a state signs a treaty, it is bound to respect its requirements as a matter of international law, and international courts will rule upon any breach of such obligations in the same way.

However, what is far-reaching about the principle of the supremacy of EC law becomes clear when it is considered in conjunction with the principle of direct effect. National **courts** are also obliged to respect the supremacy of directly effective EC law when adjudicating upon cases brought before them. This requires the national court to disapply any national law rule (even a rule which is part of the national **constitution**) which is inconsistent with a directly effective EC law rule that applies to the situation in question: instead, it must apply the EC law rule. The **European Court of Justice** has explained this effect by saying that Member States, when they signed the EC Treaty, created an EC legal system which became an 'integral part' of their national legal systems and established a 'body of law which binds both their nationals and themselves'. This is supported by Article 10 of the EC Treaty, which requires Member States to take 'all appropriate measures . . . to ensure fulfilment of the obligations' under the Treaty or legislation passed according to the EC Treaty's rules: this obligation also applies to national courts when dealing with directly effective EC law rules.

At the same time, this focus upon the supremacy of directly effective principles of EC law provides a limitation upon the scope of that supremacy. The principle of supremacy of EC law in national courts only applies to EC law rules which are directly effective. Thus, any provisions which do not meet the criteria for direct effect will not require the disapplication of inconsistent national law.

The day-to-day practice of most national courts seems to have accommodated the supremacy of EC law within the national legal system. However, some national (constitutional) courts have reserved the right to apply national law if the EC rules exhibit a consistent and ongoing disregard for constitutional principles (such as fundamental rights). The reasoning behind this stance is: first, the EC only has the

powers granted to it by Member States, and those states only have the powers which they are granted by their national constitutional frameworks; and, second, that so long as the European Court of Justice provides a level of protection for fundamental rights which is broadly similar to that protected in national law, there is no ground to challenge the supremacy of EC law.   ANGUS JOHNSTON

See also: **direct applicability of EU law; European Community law; European Community legal instruments; European Community powers**

Supreme Court (UK)   The Supreme Court of the **United Kingdom** was established by Part 3 of the Constitutional Reform Act 2005 and is expected to begin operation in October 2009 when refurbished premises in Parliament Square are ready. When this happens, the centuries-old link between the top-level court and Parliament will be severed as members of the Supreme Court will be barred from taking part in parliamentary business (such as chairing committees and occasionally speaking on the floor of the **House of Lords**).

It replaces the Appellate Committee of the House of Lords as the highest court for civil and criminal appeals from the courts in England and Wales and Northern Ireland and for civil (but not criminal) appeals from Scotland. The new court will also hear appeals on 'devolution issues' (disputes about the power of the devolved executive and legislative bodies in Scotland, Wales, and Northern Ireland) in place of the Judicial Committee of the **Privy Council**. The creation of the new court was controversial. Proponents of reform argued that, in an era of **human rights** and greater judicial involvement in adjudication on government policy and compliance of legislation with rights in the **European Convention of Human Rights**, it was increasingly anomalous for the UK's highest court to have the formal status of a committee of the legislature. Opponents rejected the notion that any constitutional principle of **separation of powers** applied and argued that the existing arrangements enjoyed a high reputation at a modest cost.

The senior judge is the President of the Supreme Court and there are eleven other permanent members of the court known as Justices of the Supreme Court. The initial members of the new court will be the existing Lords of Appeal in Ordinary ('the law lords'). Senior judges from courts of England and Wales, Northern Ireland, and Scotland and retired Supreme Court judges may also sit as 'acting judges'.

Hearings will take place before a panel of five justice or occasionally more.

The function of the Supreme Court is to determine appeals on questions of law that have general public importance. Like its predecessors, the Court is expected to receive several hundred petitions for leave to appeal each year, but to select only fifty to seventy for full hearing. The selection is not primarily concerned with whether there has been an error or injustice by the court below but with the strategic development of the **common law** and issues of **statutory interpretation**. The Court may hear appeals across the whole spectrum of legal disputes, including public, family, crime, commercial, and **tort law**. The powers of the new Court are essentially the same as its predecessors in the House of Lords and Privy Council. It has no power to strike down legislation as unconstitutional (as the **United States Supreme Court** does), though some have expressed concerns that the new court may become increasingly 'activist'. This is mere conjecture. It is equally plausible to suggest that in its early years the new Court will be anxious to establish its legitimacy by avoiding to be seen as having any agenda other than to decide appeals according to legal principle.

ANDREW LE SUEUR

A Le Sueur (ed), *Building the UK's New Supreme Court: National and Comparative Perspectives* (Oxford: Oxford University Press, 2003)

D Morgan (ed), *Constitutional Innovation: the Creation of a Supreme Court for the United Kingdom; Domestic, Comparative and International Reflections* (Special Issue of the journal *Legal Studies*, 2004)

See also: **judicial appointments**

surrogacy   Surrogacy has been defined as 'the practice whereby one **woman** carries a **child** for another with the intention that the child should be handed over after birth' (Warnock Committee, Report of the Committee of Inquiry into Human Fertilisation and Embryology (1984) Cmnd 9314 paragraph 8.1). The woman who gives birth to the child is referred to as the 'surrogate mother' and the persons for whom the child is intended are known as the 'commissioning couple'. It is unusual for single persons to engage a surrogate.

There are two main ways in which surrogacy can be arranged. In the case of 'full' or 'gestational' surrogacy, an embryo, created *in vitro* from the sperm and egg of the commissioning couple, is implanted into the surrogate mother's uterus. 'Partial' surrogacy involves the insemination of the surrogate mother with the sperm of the commissioning father. Because self-insemination is relatively simple, this usually takes place in private and without medical intervention. Although it is governed by the Surrogacy Arrangements Act 1985, partial surrogacy is virtually unregulated. Gestational surrogacy arrangements, however, fall within the purview of the **Human Fertilization and Embryology Authority**, which licenses treatment centres, as well as the Human Fertilization and Embryology Act 1990.

The Surrogacy Arrangements Act reflects an ambivalent attitude towards surrogacy. Surrogacy is not unlawful but no surrogacy arrangement is enforceable (section 1A). Payment to the surrogate mother is not unlawful but commercial surrogacy arrangements, which are perceived to be associated with exploitation and baby-selling, are. The Act makes it an offence for anyone, except for a prospective surrogate or prospective commissioning parent, to set up a surrogacy arrangement on a commercial basis, or to offer to do so (section 2). It is also an offence to publish advertisements relating to surrogacy arrangements (section 3). The effect of this is that couples have to find a surrogate mother themselves, although there are non-profit organizations which put prospective surrogate mothers and commissioning parents in touch with one another.

When the child is born, the commissioning couple do not have parental status. This is because the law designates the birth mother, and so the surrogate mother, as the legal mother (section 27 of the Human Fertilization and Embryology Act 1990 ('HFEA')). This applies even in the case of full surrogacy, where the birth mother has no genetic link with the child. As far as legal fatherhood is concerned, this varies. There is a **common law** presumption that the father of a child borne by a married woman is her husband and this would include the husband of a surrogate mother. There is also a presumption that the man registered on the birth certificate, who could be the surrogate's husband or partner, is the father. Both presumptions can be rebutted. However section 28(2) of the HFEA provides that the husband of the surrogate mother, and no-one else (section 28(4)), must be treated as the father unless he has not consented to the procedure. And if the surrogate mother is not married, her partner is treated as the father if the two of them were treated together (section 28(3)). In the more likely event that she and her partner are not considered to have been receiving treatment together, or indeed if a surrogate mother's husband does not consent to her treatment or if she is single, the child will have no legal father at all.

The HFEA does not apply if conception is the result of sexual intercourse between the surrogate mother and the commissioning father. The legal father in such a case is the commissioning father but he will not have **parental responsibility** unless he is registered as the father or obtains parental responsibility by means of an agreement or a court order.

The only way a couple subject to the HFEA can gain the status of parenthood is through adopting the child under **adoption** legislation or by obtaining a parental order under section 30 of the HFEA. Adoption is a complicated and lengthy process and it is simpler to get a section 30 order. However section 30 can be used only by married couples. Unmarried couples have to apply for adoption. In addition, section 30 cannot be used unless at least one of the applicants is a genetic parent. Also, the child must not have been conceived as a result of natural intercourse; the application must be made within six months of the birth; the child must be living with the applicants; and the surrogate mother and any legal father must consent. Finally, the court must be satisfied that no money or other benefit, other than for reasonable expenses, has changed hands, although the court can retrospectively authorize the payment. In deciding whether to make an order, the court must give priority to the welfare of the child (Parental Orders (Human Fertilization and Embryology) Regulations 1994, Schedule 1(1)(a)). Since it is normally in the child's best interests to remain with his or her carers, the court will usually make a parental order in favour of the commissioning couple and will authorize expenses even if these are in reality covert payments.

Assisted reproduction at a licensed treatment centre is closely regulated. For example, the HFEA Code of Practice (6th edn) states that before a woman is given treatment, consideration must be given to the welfare of the child who might be born, and, in particular, to the child's need for a father (section 13 (5) of the HFEA). In contrast, where self-insemination is used, there is no legal regulation of the process apart from the ban on commercial surrogacy. This may be attributable to misgivings about surrogacy, to a wish to discourage it and a reluctance to afford it the legitimacy that regulation might confer.

It is said that wealthier women might use the services of a surrogate in order to avoid the inconvenience of pregnancy. There is the potential for the commodification of women's reproductive capacity, the risk of exploitation, and the degradation of being used as a means to an end. There are concerns for the surrogate mother's own children who see their mother abandoning 'her' baby. It could be damaging for the children born of the process to know that they were relinquished in exchange for money. There is consternation at the risk of the commodification and trafficking of children.

These arguments have been criticized. To say that a person should not be a means to an end could preclude practices like **organ donation**. There is no evidence that children suffer psychological harm and, in any event, we do not restrict procreation to parents who can show that their children will be well-adjusted. That the surrogate mother might be exploited is also speculative; bearing a child for another person might be preferable to other forms of employment for some women. To say that choices made in such circumstances cannot be real is to suggest that women cannot make rational decisions. It embodies an essentialist assumption that pregnancy creates an indissoluble bond between the woman and the **foetus**. It also ignores the fact that the boundaries between altruism and commerce can be blurred.

While some countries have outlawed surrogacy, the UK has opted to recognize it, but it is seen as a last resort and perhaps as unnatural. It appears that the legislators and policymakers, by stressing the need for **marriage**, father, and genetic link, were attempting to ensure that the family created should replicate as closely as possible the traditional nuclear family. The regulatory measures that exist and the gaps in the law testify to the unease that surrogacy engenders, raising questions of **autonomy**, of what is natural, what is ethical and what is dangerous.

FELICITY KAGANAS

M Brazier, A Campbell, and S Golombok, *Surrogacy: Review for Health Ministers of Current Arrangements for Payments and Regulation* (Cm 4068, 1998)

See also: **welfare principle**

surveillance in the workplace *see* **human rights in the workplace**

surveillance, surreptitious Surveillance takes many forms; and dramatic advances in technology in recent decades have tended to leave legal protection against improper surveillance lagging behind. Devices that need to be physically located on the premises, such as bugging devices, to enable clandestine listening or watching are now somewhat dated. Other surveillance methods involve the use 'stand off' devices that can interpret sound waves, for instance, on a pane of glass. Moreover, the widespread use of computers connected to the internet presents possibilities for turning the computers into remote surveillance devices, as well as for the surreptitious installation of software to monitor activities of the computer itself ('spy-ware'). Advances in camera and audio technology and the ubiquitous CCTV systems have also diminished the opportunities for maintaining **privacy** in public or semi-public spaces. Mobile phones and their associated messaging systems are not only vulnerable to unauthorized interference but can also be used to track the user's whereabouts. These techniques are widely available not just to state officials but also private individuals, such as journalists.

Faced with this range of possibilities, the law's traditional approach of protecting privacy as a by-product of protecting property from interference through the civil law of trespass is now completely outmoded. Equally, where police surveillance is concerned, the courts have been consistently reluctant to exclude evidence that has been obtained by either illegal or dubious means of surveillance. These shortcomings in legal control mean that attention has focused increasingly on the development of a right of privacy. The common law in England does not contain a right of privacy; but Article 8 of the **European Convention on Human Rights** (which establishes a right to respect for private life, home and correspondence) has had an important impact on the regulation of surreptitious surveillance.

The need to demonstrate a clear legal basis for state surveillance in order to comply with the Article 8 obligation led to the introduction of an umbrella regime for covert surveillance by the police and other public bodies in the Regulation of Investigatory Powers Act 2000. The Act provides for authorization of 'intrusive surveillance' (of a person in private premises or a private vehicle) in the case of suspected serious offences. Authorization is by the relevant Chief Constable and the grant of authorization is overseen by judicial Surveillance Commissioners. The legislation also covers 'directed surveillance' and the use of 'covert human intelligence sources' (ie informants) to obtain private information about an individual, although in these instances the criteria for authorization and the level of control are less stringent. **Interception of communications** is regulated by a system of ministerial warrants.   IAN LEIGH

suspects   *see* **crime investigation by police; PACE**

sustainable development   Sustainable development has been widely adopted as a policy objective by institutions, governments, businesses, voluntary bodies, and others; but its exact meaning remains unclear. The most common definition, 'development that meets the needs of the present without compromising the ability of future generations to meet their own needs' (World Commission on Environment and Development, *Our Common Future (The Brundtland Report)* (Oxford University Press, 1987) ('the Brundtland definition')), brings together different and conflicting interests, but is vague and imprecise. Most interpretations work within the Brundtland formula but vary in three respects. First, different emphases are given to the three components of sustainable development: economy, environment, and society. Strong sustainable development defines certain environmental assets critical to our well-being as irreplaceable, while weaker interpretations focus more on development and are indifferent to the form in which capital stock is passed on. Secondly, disparities exist about the nature of human needs and technology's role in meeting those needs. Finally, views differ over the importance of fairness and inter-generational equity.

The definitions have evolved over time. In the early 1990s sustainable development was often described as a trade-off between the environment and economic development. Later interpretations consider the three components of economy, environment, and society as interdependent and mutually reinforcing pillars. Recent definitions favour sustainable growth over high economic growth and include references to human rights and good governance.

When differing values combine with these different definitions sustainable development can be construed as legitimizing 'business as usual' patterns of economic growth or, at the other extreme, requiring a fundamental reworking of the global socio-economic order. From a legal perspective, sustainable development is a social, political, economic, and moral objective which may have certain normative consequences. Opinions vary on the extent of that normative influence in any given legal regime.

Sustainable development has been included in many binding and non-binding global and regional texts. Most references do not attempt a definition but simply (either explicitly or implicitly) state sustainable development as a purpose either in the preamble or in an early substantive article. Certain procedural requirements linked to sustainable development have also been introduced. Historically, the UK's approach to sustainable development has been non-legislative. Since 1995, however, sustainable development has become more commonplace in UK and Scottish statutes either as a duty on an agency, an objective for a regime or agency or, increasingly, as a procedural requirement such as a report or strategy. None of the statutes attempts a definition.

While generally, sustainable development provides insufficient normative certainty to impose an enforceable primary obligation, the legal provisions are making an impact. First, they have symbolic benefits—acting to heighten awareness. Secondly, although many laws do not require development to be sustainable, at both national and international levels, they may require development to be the outcome of a process which promotes sustainable development. Thirdly, the term has received judicial recognition both internationally and by the UK courts. Finally, there is evidence that sustainable development may be emerging as a mechanism for balancing conflicting objectives and providing a framework for decision-making.

ANDREA ROSS-ROBERTSON

SW v UK *see R v R*

syndrome evidence   The term syndrome means 'a group of concurrent symptoms of a disease' (Concise Oxford Dictionary, 9th edition) and is generally of a medical or psychological nature. When used to describe a medical condition, such as Down's Syndrome, or Acquired Immune Deficiency Syndrome ('AIDS'), its use in law is usually uncontroversial. However, the last two decades have witnessed increasing efforts to use expert witnesses in the courtroom to give evidence about psychological syndromes which have proven to be much more controversial. In particular, syndrome explanations are becoming a common way of accounting for the actions of **women** in cases where they are accused of criminal offences, as in Battered Woman Syndrome, or, where they accuse others of crimes against them, as in **Rape** Trauma Syndrome. Typically, though not exclusively, it is women who are characterized as suffering from these types of syndromes.

It is much easier for syndrome evidence to be admitted in the **courts** if it has been officially recognized as a syndrome through inclusion in the DSM-IV-TR (the American Psychiatric Association's Diagnostic and Statistical Manual of Mental Disorders, Fourth Edition, Text Revision), and/

or the ICD 10 (the World Health Organization's International Statistical Classification of Diseases and Related Health Problems, 10th Revision). The process of inclusion of a syndrome can be complex and protracted as a high level of consensus must be achieved within the mental health community. As a compromise, syndromes are sometimes not included under their familiar names but as a sub-set of a recognized disorder. Battered Woman Syndrome is an example of this as it is classed as a form of Post-traumatic Stress Disorder ('PTSD').

Diagnosis with a syndrome listed in these manuals amounts to diagnosis of a psychiatric disorder. This has generated considerable controversy in several areas. For example, experts often disagree that a particular set of symptoms amounts to a syndrome. In some instances, definitions tend to be cast very broadly to capture a large range of behaviours, many of which may seem quite ordinary, normal, or innocuous. Matters may be further complicated when symptoms which some characterize as of a largely psychological nature also produce biological and physical effects. In such circumstances, those who experience particular symptoms may resist the notion that they suffer from a psychiatric disorder, ie they do not wish to label themselves as mentally ill. For although the inclusion of a syndrome in the DSM as a 'disorder' may serve some useful purposes, eg allowing a defendant to found a claim of **diminished responsibility** if facing criminal charges, it may have unforeseen and unwanted consequences such as calling into question a person's suitability as a mother or as an employee. Separately, persons who have undergone severe trauma as in violent sexual assault or in armed combat, and then understandably experience serious emotional disturbance, may not want the generalizing effects of being classified as suffering from, respectively, Rape Trauma Syndrome or Gulf War Syndrome. Both of these syndromes are regarded as anxiety disorders in the DSM and a subset of PTSD.

While the appearance of newly emerging syndromes has most frequently started life in the US courts, it has only been a matter of time before they made their way to these shores. This occurred with Battered Woman Syndrome, Rape Trauma Syndrome, and False Memory Syndrome, where complainants in sexual assaults alleged to have occurred some time ago are said to be suffering from false **memories**, perhaps induced by therapy. An emerging trend in the use of syndrome evidence is its expansion from the criminal courts into the civil courts. Thus we have recently seen an employer sued for a breach of the duty of care owed to an employee who claimed her PTSD-induced depression was caused by **sexual harassment** from another employee. In the family courts, suggestions that a parent (almost always a mother) is suffering from Parental Alienation Syndrome are frequently made by estranged fathers to explain why their children are unwilling to have contact. Although Parental Alienation Syndrome is not yet included in the DSM, as with many other syndromes it has many adherents who seek to have it included. As the impetus builds to permit more of this type of evidence into the UK courts, it is reasonable to consider whether it has a wholly beneficial effect, especially given the controversial aspects described here. FIONA RAITT

See also: **expert evidence**

systems theory Systems theory, as developed by Niklas Luhmann (1927–1998), is a theory about society. Society, within this theory, consists of its communications. The theory leads to novel conclusions about the nature of law, which include: that law cannot be reduced to politics, or be steered by politics, or vice versa; that the principles and values associated with legal decisions (including **justice**) are generated internally within the legal system itself; that only the law can determine what is legal as opposed to illegal (so that legal validity amounts to nothing more than an endless process of coding and applying this distinction).

Within systems theory what distinguishes modern from earlier societies is the differentiation of its communications into sub-systems: law, politics, economics, media, and so on. The central claim of this theory is that in modern society both society as a whole, and its sub-systems, are autopoietic. This term is taken from biology, where it refers to the manner in which cells replicate themselves from their own elements. Adapted to a theory of society as communications, it refers to the fact that meaningful communications can only be formed through their relationship to other communications. One may communicate about things other than communications, but one can only actually make communications by linking new communications to existing ones. The physical world can be communicated about, but its processes are not themselves communications and, as such, remain outside of society. Similarly, and more controversially, whilst the consciousness of human beings might generate communications, consciousness itself is not a communication; and so this too remains outside of society (only the communication which results from consciousness is social, not the consciousness that stimulated it). Communications

remain closed to both the physical world and human consciousness, both of which can stimulate communications, but are not themselves communications. There is no straightforward one-for-one correspondence between any event in the real world, or any particular state of consciousness, and specific communications.

The radical conclusions which follow from this theory arise from the claim that sub-systems are also autopoietic. This duplicates the insights which result from an understanding of society as a meaning system that is closed to both consciousness and the physical world. It is common to describe law in terms of political, moral, and economic inputs, or to talk of law having a political, moral, or economic content. But if legal communications can only form legal meanings through their relationship to other legal communications, then the communications of other systems of communication cannot themselves become legal communications. Even if law utilizes communications that have exactly the same form as political or moral communications, they will take their legal meaning from their relationship to other legal communications and, as such, will not duplicate the meaning that they had when used within a different sub-system. In place of common meanings, one finds mis-readings, whereby common syntax is given different meanings within different systems. Where such mis-readings are regularly reproduced within each system, one has a situation described within the theory as 'structural coupling'. Each system is able to coordinate its own communications, with their separate meanings, around common terms. For example, the meaning of 'miscarriage of justice' is not the same within the legal system and within the media. This is because 'conviction' in the legal system refers to legal guilt constructed in accordance with legal procedures, whereas in the media it is usually taken to establish the fact that a particular individual committed a particular crime. Nevertheless, the media utilizes its own meaning of conviction routinely to generate news stories. Another common example of structural coupling would be 'contract' (in law a basis for determining questions of legality and of rights and duties, in economics a basis for staging payments, and in production a source of resources).

Whilst most legal theories seek to establish the identity of the legal system by reference to fundamental structures, such as **constitutions**, systems theory argues that identity is the unintended consequence of a distinction: the system's binary code. In the case of law the code is legal/illegal; in economics it is payment/non-payment; in politics government/opposition; in science true/false. These binary codes have no inherent meaning; but law, alongside every other sub-system, develops complex conditional programmes ('if' clauses) for the application of its code. These programmes evolve, and may, at particular historical moments, include structures that have such an important relationship to so many communications that they are understood, within the system, as foundational. In accounting for system identity as the application of a system's code, rather than by reference to the communications which currently structure its coding, systems theory avoids the imperialism of much legal theory, whereby structures which have evolved only under relatively recent conditions are claimed to represent a universally fundamental feature of the system. Take, for example, constitutions. Systems theory would not see national constitutions as an essential feature of legal systems. Instead, national constitutions represent an evolution of law's conditional programmes whose absence, in areas such as international commercial law, has not prevented the continuing application of law's binary code.

Systems theory does not deny that a particular system is affected by the communications of another system. But, all that systems can do in response is to continue communicating, which requires them to continue to identify, by reference to their existing communication, further communications that belong to themselves. This is the basis of the claim that systems exhibit operational closure, whilst remaining cognitively open. Systems can only respond to outside stimuli through internal variations. This makes it impossible for one system to control, in any direct manner, the operations of another. So, for example, though politics may have evolved a stable relationship with the legal system through the processes of enacting legislation, the consequences of legislation within the legal system are not dictated by the political system. This is not simply a consequence of differences between the terms of statutes and the behaviour of its addressees (the so-called gap between law in the books and law in action). Rather, the political system, at best, can only anticipate the meanings likely to be given to statutes within the legal system. Once enacted, statutes begin a process of interpretation (by reference to other legal communications—litigation, other statutes, precedents, legal principles) whose outcomes cannot be controlled. This lack of control is regarded, within the theory, as productive (in terms of the complexity

that systems can develop). Indeed, law's general failure to alter in response to events (facts do not automatically alter norms—only legal communications alter norms) means that a by-product of its coding is the maintenance of normative expectations in the face of counter-factual examples (disappointment). In this way, the law remains immune to factors that would generate altered communications in the systems that surround it. But this allows it to provide a normative framework (structural coupling with the operations of other systems) that these systems could not produce for themselves.

Communications retain their identity through the application of a common code, but they build conditioning programmes for the application of their codes through further communications that 'observe' on applications of the code. Law observes on its own decisions (where it has applied the code legal/illegal) by reference to the requirement to 'treat like cases alike'. These observations generate doctrines including, at a high level of abstraction, concepts like **parliamentary sovereignty**, the **separation of powers**, and the **rule of law**. Justice, within this process, is not outside the system, but something that the system produces through its own operations. Whether existing structures are followed, or new ones develop, the observations required to maintain or alter conditioning programmes must take the form 'treat like cases alike'. This formula is an internal critique of law's programmes, as well as the means by which they are constructed. This generates a legal idea of justice that reproduces existing legal structures whilst also offering the potential to transcend them. As such, justice is never fully represented by law's existing structures, since it is both the law, and its potential to be different.

As a theory of society, systems theory provides a basis for the observation of all systems: law, politics, economics, science, media, and so on, and the manner in which systems alter their internal elements, including their most important structures, in response to each other. As such, it offers a methodology for much of what is covered by 'interdisciplinary' studies. However, there is a strong caveat. According to the theory, there is no possibility of a meta-language into which systems can translate their respective meanings. And whilst human beings obviously enjoy membership of many different systems (involving multiple structural coupling between their consciousness and each of the systems in which they communicate) there is no reason to believe that human agents can control the production or coordination of communications in multiple systems, even if they develop expertise in systems theory. According to the theory, any observation, including observation using systems theory, can only occur within a system of communication, and cannot reproduce the meanings of the communications which it manages to observe.

RICHARD NOBLES AND DAVID SCHIFF

N Luhmann, *Law as a Social System* (Oxford: Oxford University Press, 2004)

G Teubner, *Law as an Autopoietic System* (Oxford: Blackwell, 1993)

T

**Taff Vale Railway Co v Amalgamated Society of
Railway Servants (1901)** The decision in this case
is one of the most important in the legal history of
trades unions. It concerned their legal capacity and
whether, even though they were not corporations,
unions could be sued in their own name. The Court
of Appeal had answered this question in the negative
on the basis that, if Parliament had intended unions
to be able to take legal action in their own names, this
would have been expressly provided for or provision
would have been made for their incorporation. The
House of Lords rejected this analysis and restored
the judgment of Farwell J, who had found for the
employers, and treated a union as a quasi corporation which could indeed be sued in its own name:
'The proper rule of construction of statutes such as
these is that in the absence of express contrary intention the Legislature intends that the creature of the
statute shall have the same duties and that its funds
shall be subject to the same liabilities as the general
law would impose on a private individual doing the
same thing. It would require very clear and express
words of enactment to induce me to hold that the
Legislature had in fact legalised the existence of such
irresponsible bodies with such wide capacity for
evil'.

The decision was a surprising one which conflicted with the received wisdom. Frederic Harrison,
who some thirty years previously had done so much
to devise the existing legal framework commented,
in the *Positivist Review*, that 'It is not too much to say
that these judgments have practically made new law;
law which might prevent trade unions from doing
things that for twenty five years, they have believed
they had a right to do; and which exposes the whole
of their funds to legal liabilities to which till now
they have been thought to be exempt'. As Harrison
recognized, the decision exposed union funds to
the possibility of extensive claims in damages for
infringements of the **economic torts** should trade
disputes take place. The decision was to lead to the
enactment of the Trade Disputes Act 1906, the issue
having come to the fore in the course of the 1906
general election. Section 4 of that Act restored the
position which had existed prior to *Taff Vale*.

DOUGLAS BRODIE

takeovers A takeover occurs where a financial
or industrial company makes a successful offer (or
'bid') to purchase the entire **share** capital of another
company ('the target'). The bid is addressed directly to the shareholders of the target company; if the
target's board does not recommend the bid to shareholders, it is termed 'hostile'. The bidder offers cash
(which may be borrowed, in which case the takeover is said to be 'leveraged') or shares in itself, or
a combination of both, in return for the shares. The
price paid for each share normally exceeds the current market price for the shares in question; this is
referred to as the takeover premium.

If the bid is accepted by 90 per cent of the target company's shareholders, the bidder can use the
provisions of the Companies Act to 'squeeze out'
any **minority shareholders** who did not accept the
bid, but, broadly speaking, must pay them the same
price that the majority accepted. Once the bidder has
obtained control of the company, it can appoint new
directors. The new directors must then integrate
the target's business with the bidder's business or,
in the case of a leveraged takeover, ensure that sufficient revenues are generated to service the debt that
funded the takeover.

The procedure by which takeovers of **public companies** occurs is, for the most part, not regulated by
statute, but by the City Code on Takeovers and Mergers. The City Code is a self-regulatory measure put
in place by financial institutions in the City of London and administered by the Takeover Panel, which
advises on whether proposed actions are compatible
with the Code and imposes sanctions on wrongdoers. The key provisions of the City Code prevent the
board of directors of the target from taking any
action that is likely to frustrate the bid, and require
any shareholder whose holding passes a 30 per cent
threshold to make a mandatory bid for the remaining share capital of the company. Given that many

shareholders in public companies do not bother to vote, 30 per cent is assumed to confer control. The mandatory bid ensures that the bidder must pay a control premium.

Views on the merits or otherwise of takeovers tend to be strongly polarized. Orthodox economics insists that the operation of a market for corporate control is good for the economy as it puts pressure on corporate managers to maximize shareholder value by raising the company's share price, failing which they may be confronted with a hostile takeover and risk removal from the board in its aftermath. Dissenters from this position contend that takeovers effect a wealth transfer from **stakeholders** in the company, such as employees, to shareholders, that bidders tend to overpay for their acquisitions (and so prejudice their own shareholders), and that the pressure on managers to maximize the share price that results from a market for corporate control leads to short-termism in the way companies are managed. Concerns have also been expressed recently about the viability of companies burdened with large amounts of debt following leveraged takeovers.

ANDREW JOHNSTON

taper relief   *see* **capital gains tax**

tax adjudicators   *see* **ombudsmen**

tax administrative and compliance costs   Tax systems, or particular taxes, can impose three sorts of burden. First, there are the taxes themselves. Secondly, there are the efficiency costs that can arise when tax causes the behaviour of individuals or corporations to change. And finally there are the operating costs of the tax system: the public sector costs to the government (ultimately borne by taxpayers) of administering and collecting the taxes (usually referred to as 'administrative costs'), and the private sector costs expended by taxpayers in complying (or sometimes not complying) with their tax obligations (usually referred to as 'compliance costs').

At first blush, it may appear to be relatively simple to identify administrative costs and compliance costs relating to taxation. But first impressions can be misleading, and the literature reveals that there is some degree of uncertainty about the precise definitions of these terms, and the manner in which they are expressed for comparative purposes. Tax administrative costs typically include the costs of running the revenue authority, which can range between 0.5 per cent and 2 per cent of the tax revenue collected, depending on the type of tax involved. In the UK, for example, it is estimated that it costs about 13 pence

to collect each hundred pounds of income tax and about 7 pence to collect the same amount of corporation tax. Overall it costs the UK tax office about 11 pence to collect each hundred pounds of tax. But such estimates are very imprecise and often do not include various capital costs incurred by revenue authorities (such as on offices and buildings), or the costs of developing tax legislation or of tax dispute litigation and resolution.

Tax compliance costs are usually taken to comprise three main elements. First there is the value of the time that taxpayers actually spend on complying with their tax obligations, whether it is the business person keeping books and records for tax purposes or an individual preparing and submitting an annual tax return. Secondly there are the monetary costs that taxpayers incur when they obtain professional advice on tax compliance and planning from accountants and lawyers. And thirdly there are various incidental expenses incurred in completion of tax activities, including computer software, postage, travel, and so on.

In addition to this generally accepted hard-core of compliance costs, there are a number of other costs that need to be considered. For example, taxpayers suffer stress, anxiety, and frustration as a result of attempting to comply with their taxation obligations. Unfortunately, no studies have yet managed to successfully quantify these psychological costs.

There is also contention over other aspects of the precise boundaries of compliance costs. Compliance costs are sometimes divided into computational (unavoidable) and tax planning (avoidable) costs; or into commencement (or once-only) and recurrent (or regular) costs; and there is almost certainly some overlap between business or accounting costs and tax compliance costs.

Three major themes emerge from the literature that has flourished in recent years: compliance costs are high and they are significant (typically between 2 per cent and 10 per cent of the revenue yield from those taxes; and usually a multiple of between two and six times administrative costs); compliance costs are regressive (in that they fall disproportionately on lower income and smaller business taxpayers); and compliance costs are not reducing over time largely because tax systems are becoming ever more complex.

CHRIS EVANS

C Evans, 'Studying the Studies: An Overview of Recent Research into Taxation Operating Costs' (2003) 1(1) *e-Journal of Tax Research* 64

C Sandford, M Godwin, and P Hardwick, *Administrative and Compliance Costs of Taxation* (Bath: Fiscal Publications, 1989)

tax avoidance   Today's tax lawyers distinguish tax avoidance from tax mitigation and tax evasion. Tax avoidance is an industry, as readers of the Sunday newspapers know. However, it is a lawful activity and it means so arranging one's affairs as to avoid the maximum incidence of taxation. As shown by the case of *IRC v Duke of Westminster* (1936), the effectiveness of the tax system depends in part on the attitude of the judges when interpreting and applying the legislation. There, a blinkered view of the facts meant that the taxpayer (Duke) was entitled to his tax deduction. Today's judges will be much more sceptical than the judges of 1936. The intellectual turning point for this was the decision of the House of Lords in *Ramsay (WT) Ltd v IRC* (1982) where the House took a series of transactions and treated it as one single transaction rather than taking each step separately. The result that was that while one part of the transaction gave a large loss while another gave rise to a large and, the taxpayer hoped, non-chargeable gain, the House held that the two parts should be put together and so only a relatively tiny loss resulted. In the year following 1982 the limits and indeed the very basis of the *Ramsay* composite transaction principle were much litigated and the results often controversial. The current position (*Barclays Mercantile Business Finance Ltd v Mawson* (2005)) is that there is no 'rule' as such and so one does not have to worry about its 'limits'. Now everything is treated as a question of interpretation; the modern approach which applies to tax as much as to any other area of statute law is a purposive one which looks at Parliament's words in their context having regard to the purpose Parliament is taken to have had in mind. This makes for conceptual tidiness and constitutional propriety.

Tax avoidance causes governments problems since a judicial approach which favours the taxpayer means that governments will receive less money than they had hoped. Moreover, the fairness of the system is undermined if those who have access to (expensive) legal advice pay less by way of tax than others. In response, governments persuade legislatures to counteract tax avoidance with new rules. These may vary widely in type, but many make the 'avoidance of tax' the test for applying the counteracting legislation. This requires the court to interpret the term 'avoidance'; it is in this context that the courts have, since 1996, developed the concept of 'tax mitigation' in order to decide which schemes work from the taxpayer's point of view ('tax mitigation'), and which do not (tax avoidance). This is all a matter of what the judges think Parliament intended.

In this context therefore, tax mitigation and tax avoidance are mutually exclusive. Tax mitigation arises where the taxpayer takes advantage of a tax rule in the tax legislation, and genuinely suffers the economic consequences that Parliament intended to be suffered by those taking advantage of the rule. So if a person sells some shares subject to capital gains tax asset and buys them back again he will, subject to any special anti-avoidance rules, be held to have realized a gain or loss on the original assets. Tax avoidance arises where the taxpayer reduces a liability to tax without incurring the economic consequences that Parliament intended to be suffered by someone qualifying for the reduction. So, if the person sells the shares under circumstances where he is not actually at any risk from price movements between the sale and the acquisition, he will not be treated as having made any disposal of the shares. Some judges and other critics see the mitigation avoidance terminology as unhelpful and as simply stating a conclusion rather than enabling the courts to decide a particular case.

The third concept is tax evasion. This is not a lawful activity; it involves illegal circumvention of tax, eg by not reporting relevant facts or claiming deductions which are not allowable. Evasion may attract penalties under the tax legislation or prosecution under the criminal law, eg for the offence of cheating the public revenue or the offence of fraudulent evasion of income tax (introduced in 2000). Such behaviour is a part of what is sometimes called non-compliance, which is a wider expression covering both deliberate and accidental under-reporting.   JOHN TILEY

Lord Hoffmann, 'Tax Avoidance' (2005) *British Tax Review* 197–206
J Freedman, 'Defining Taxpayer Responsibility: In support of a General Anti Avoidance Principle' (2004) *British Tax Review* 332–357

tax, ability to pay   The ability-to-pay principle underpins modern tax law systems. In his seminal *Canons of Taxation*, the economist Adam Smith wrote that 'the subjects of every state ought to contribute towards the support of the government, as nearly as possible, in proportion to their respective abilities' (*The Nature & Causes of the Wealth of Nations*, Book V, Ch. 11, Part II, 1776).

As a theoretical basis for taxation, the ability-to-pay principle competes with the benefit principle under which the tax an individual pays should relate to the benefit received by the individual from the state. There are severe practical problems with the benefit principle, since it is impossible to measure the benefits the state provides or exclude those who do not, or cannot, pay for public goods.

This is not to suggest that the ability-to-pay principle is free from difficulty. Even Adam Smith's statement is ambiguous, as it is not clear whether it supports proportional taxation, under which the same proportion of each taxpayer's income is taken in taxation, or progressive taxation under which the proportion of income that is taken in taxation increases with income. Given that poor people will spend a higher proportion of their income on necessities than people of higher income, there is a justification for progressivity and it is a concept embedded into modern tax systems. This is sometimes referred to as the principle of vertical equity. A related principle is that of horizontal equity, which requires that taxpayers with equal income should pay the same amount in taxes. However, there are many problems in measuring ability to pay, and thus in applying both horizontal and vertical equity requirements. Issues include whether actual or potential income should be measured, and to what extent other matters such as wealth, human capital, and personal circumstances should be taken into account. Should the aim be to achieve equity within each annual period or over the lifetime of the taxpayer? The aim is one of 'equal sacrifice'; but in practice it will not be possible to devise a system which measures this precisely or delivers it with accuracy. Some taxes, such as consumption taxes (**value added tax**, for instance), are inherently regressive; that is they take a larger proportion of lower than of higher incomes. This does not necessarily mean such taxes have no value within the system however; it is possible to adjust for this through other elements of the tax system or through the **social security system**.

It is not essential for a progressive income tax system to have a large number of income tax rates, nor even very high ones. If there are at least two rates, of which one can be the nil rate applicable below a minimum threshold at which tax has to be paid (a personal or tax free allowance), the system has some progressivity. The idea of a flat tax—that is, a single flat rate percentage tax taken from all income—has been in vogue with some politicians and economists in recent years. Under the version proposed by its leading proponents, Hall and Rabushka, the flat tax would also be combined with other simplifications, such as the removal of special exemptions and reliefs to broaden the tax base. The main advantages claimed for a flat rate tax are that it would simplify the tax system, and improve incentives to work and invest and, consequently, economic growth as well. To the extent that there is any evidence for this it comes from recent experience in Eastern European countries; but there may be other explanations for these developments in those cases. The disadvantages claimed are a decrease in

progressivity, at least at the upper income end, and a drop in tax revenues. A flat rate tax could, however, retain some progressivity by being combined with a high personal allowance. The proponents of the flat tax argue that economic growth would pay for the tax cuts. The debate on the practicality of such a regime continues.

JUDITH FREEDMAN

RE Hall and A Rabushka, *The Flat Tax* (Stanford, CA: Hoover Institution Press, 3rd edn, 1995)

tax credits   There are two kinds of tax credit. Child tax credit ('CTC') is paid to 6,000,000 households with children. Working tax credit ('WTC') is for lower-paid workers. WTC includes assistance for working parents paying childcare bills for their children. Despite the name, they are not credits against tax. Rather, they are an amalgam of a social cash benefit and a state subsidy to working parents and lower-paid employees. CTC and WTC are administered by HM Revenue and Customs.

All UK residents responsible for children can claim CTC. Weekly entitlement depends on family size and on the income of those claiming. It can be claimed for all children below sixteen, and for young people at school or college until eighteen. CTC is paid to the person responsible for the child. Where responsibility is shared, it is paid only to the person with main responsibility. There is a maximum yearly rate of CTC, depending on family size, which is reduced to take account of income. Couples must make a joint claim and both incomes are taken into account. In broad terms, families with incomes below £50,000 get some CTC—currently at least £10 a week. Those with incomes under £15,000 receive much more. The precise amount is calculated by working out the maximum entitlement, then reducing it by 37 per cent of the amount by which family income exceeds that year's income threshold. The maximum rate includes an element for each child, and more for disabled children. In 2007, someone with three children gets a maximum of about £2,600. That is reduced by 37p for each £1 income over the threshold of about £14,000. This is additional to the WTC childcare credit below.

WTC can be claimed by four groups of workers: those working sixteen or more hours weekly and responsible for children; disabled workers working sixteen or more hours weekly and suffering disadvantage in the job market; those over fifty returning to work after a break and working sixteen or more hours weekly; and all those over twenty-five and working thirty or more hours a week but with low earnings. Anyone working for sixteen or more hours weekly and responsible for children can claim both WTC and CTC. WTC includes a childcare credit, worth 80 per cent of weekly childcare bills of up to £300 for two or more children. WTC and CTC together provide generous support to working parents. The family with three children can receive CTC and up to £240 a week for childcare. WTC is less generous to others. The actual amount paid depends on total incomes of claimants. But the income threshold is much lower than for CTC—about £5,000 in 2007.

Tax credits are calculated on an annual basis. A provisional award is made at the beginning of the year and is then checked at the end. If the award was too high, HM Revenue and Customs can demand back the overpayment.   DAVID WILLIAMS

tax evasion   *see* **tax avoidance**

tax harmonization   *see* **European Community taxation**

tax planning   *see* **tax avoidance**

taxable profit   *see* **business taxation**

taxation of trusts   The taxation of **trusts** might be thought to present no particular difficulty, given that any necessary adjustments to the regime for individuals could be expected to be no more complex than those involved in the taxation of, say, companies or partnerships. But matters have not proved straightforward, difficulty flowing from the need to consider **income tax**, **capital gains tax,** and **inheritance tax** (to take the principle relevant taxes) in the context of all or any of settlors, trustees, and beneficiaries. What follows can only be the barest outline of a complex subject, sufficient perhaps to hint at the many issues of policy and principle which may direct reform in future.

The Income Tax Act of 1842 contained no general provisions for the taxation of trustees and beneficiaries, whose treatment was accordingly largely invented from first principles by the courts, although now those principles are considerably overlaid by statutory provisions. Where income arises from a trust it continues to be taxed at two separate stages. First, trustees are chargeable because they receive the income; and, secondly, beneficiaries are taxed on any income received from the trust, their liability taking into account income tax already paid by the trustees. The precise treatment and rates differ where income is retained within the trust. Where a settlor retains any interest under the trust, further provisions deem

income as it arises to remain that of the settlor in a wide range of circumstances.

So far as capital gains tax is concerned, where a trustee holds property for a beneficiary who is absolutely entitled to it as against the trustees, the acts of the trustees are treated as acts of the beneficiaries and any gains or losses attributed directly to the beneficiaries. In the case of other kinds of settlement, gains or losses on the switching of the trust investments are those of the trustees. Consistent with this logic of charging trustees to tax on disposals of the underlying trust assets, disposals by beneficiaries of beneficial interests under the settlement do not generally give rise to a chargeable gain (unless the interest was acquired for consideration, or where offshore trustees are involved). On the creation of a settlement by a living settlor, there is a disposal by the settlor of the property settled (an 'entrance charge'); and there is a deemed disposal (an 'exit charge') when a beneficiary becomes absolutely entitled to settled property other than on the death of a previous beneficiary. If a settlor retains any interest under a settlement, the settlor, rather than the trustees, remains chargeable to gains made on subsequent switching of the trust investments.

The inheritance tax regime is founded upon a distinction between trust property in which someone has an interest in possession (such as a life interest), and that in which there is no interest in possession (as in the case of a discretionary trust). In the former case the person entitled to the interest in possession has been treated as beneficially entitled to the settled property itself (and so, subject to the provisions for potentially exempt transfers, there is the possibility of a charge on the settled property whenever the beneficial enjoyment of it ceases, for example on the death of a life tenant). In the latter case, apart from certain favoured trusts, the trust property has been subject to an automatic charge at 30 per cent of the usual lifetime rate of 20 per cent (ie 6 per cent) every ten years, and to an 'exit charge' where property ceases to be comprised in such a settlement. Since the Finance Act 2006 the former class of trusts has been narrowed, and so most trusts (apart from a now-smaller category of favoured trust, such as those for a disabled beneficiary) will now be subject to the ten-year charge. Property settled on trust on or after 22 March 2006 (unless within the favoured category, when such a transfer remains potentially exempt) is generally now subject to an immediate inheritance tax charge.   EDWIN SIMPSON

***Taylor v Caldwell* (1863)**   In 1861, Taylor and Lewis arranged to hire the Surrey Music Hall and Gardens, complete with various entertainments, from Caldwell and Bishop for four summer nights to hold promenade concerts. Before the first of these nights, and without the fault of either party, the Music Hall burnt down when workmen left a fire untended. Taylor and Lewis sued Caldwell and Bishop for their failure to provide the Music Hall; they sought the £58 they had incurred in preparatory expenditures.

At the time the action was brought English law did not excuse the contractual performance of a party on the ground that through some inevitable accident the performance the party had undertaken by contract had become radically changed or even impossible. Where there was a positive contract to do a lawful thing, which had not been breached by the other party, the contractor was obliged to do the thing or to pay damages. This absolute liability had been established in 1647, and the law admitted few exceptions to it. If parties wished to excuse their contractual performance on the occurrence of certain events, they needed to provide for these events in their contract.

In *Taylor v Caldwell*, Blackburn J, on his own initiative, introduced an incremental change to English **contract law**. He referred to Justinian's *Digest* and Pothier's *Treatise of Obligations* for underlying legal principles. His decision was, however, rooted in the **common law**. While Blackburn J affirmed the general rule of absolute liability, he then qualified it by stating that 'this rule is only applicable when the contract is positive and absolute, and not subject to any condition either express or implied'. The condition had to pertain to something essential for contractual performance. Where the parties clearly contemplated that the contract could not be fulfilled unless something existed, such that at the outset the continued existence of the thing formed the foundation of the contract, and where neither party had warranted that such a thing would exist, if it ceased to exist without the fault of the contractor (and before any breach) such that performance became impossible, the parties were excused from performance. Blackburn J then implied a term, on the ground that this was what the parties would have done, that in the event that the Music Hall was destroyed, the contract was discharged.

The decision is often regarded as establishing the doctrine of 'frustration': that where a supervening event occurs without the fault of either party which renders contractual performance impossible or radically different, and for which the contract makes no provision, the contract will be discharged where it would be unjust to hold the parties to it. Such a depiction is inaccurate because this was neither the intent nor the effect of the actual decision. It did, however, produce the change of thought, which allowed a gradual erosion of absolute liability in contract and the later accumulation of cases concerned with subsequent impossibility, failure of consideration, and frustration of the adventure cases to become the modern doctrine of frustration.

CATHERINE MACMILLAN

teacher training and employment   Industrial strife in the 1980s led to centralized control of teachers' pay and conditions in England and Wales through statutory **regulation**. During the same period, the conflict which emerged over 'traditional' and 'permissive' approaches to education was manifested in the centralization of control of teacher training. The Education Act 1994 removed control of teacher training from the training institutions and placed it in the hands of what is now the Training and Development Agency for Schools ('TDA'). Further centralization of control of the teaching profession continued into the 1990s as the Teaching and Higher Education Act 1998 established the General Teaching Council ('GTC') for England and equivalent regulations established the GTC for Wales.

In England and Wales, the TDA and the GTCs regulate entry to the teaching profession through the registration and qualification requirements for teachers and their training. The main functions of the GTC are to provide advice on teachers' roles, conduct, and training, combined with a power to produce a code of practice, and to maintain a register of qualified teachers. Registration may be refused or withdrawn where a teacher/applicant is guilty of unacceptable professional conduct or serious professional incompetence, or has been convicted (at any time) of one of a number of defined criminal offences. There are a series of sanctions that the GTC may use but removing a person from the register is quite rare. The GTC maintains the register but does not itself discipline or dismiss a teacher for incompetence or misconduct. The currency of the register is maintained by requiring employers of registered teachers to notify the GTC when a teacher is dismissed for incompetence or misconduct, or where a teacher resigns in circumstances that would have led to such disciplinary consequences. There are separate provisions which prohibit some persons from being employed in teaching. The GTC has a statutory role advising on the training of teachers, but responsibility for that training lies with the TDA. The TDA is the funding agency for the training institutions and determines the content of the curriculum. A further level of scrutiny is the inspection of the training institutions by Ofsted against standards set by the TDA, also introduced by the Education Act 1994.

In Scotland arrangements are governed by the Teaching Council (Scotland) Act 1965 as amended. The Scottish GTC reviews education standards, maintains a register of qualified teachers, and has disciplinary powers. Teachers are employed by local school boards. The Education (Northern Ireland) Order 1998 established a GTC in Northern Ireland ('NI') which maintains a registration certificate system. The same **legislation** places control of qualification to train as a teacher with the Department of Education. Teachers in state schools in NI are employed by the Education and Libraries Boards and in Maintained Catholic Schools employment is controlled by the Council for Catholic Maintained Schools.

The fitness of teachers for employment in the independent sector is regulated primarily through provisions relating to the registration of schools.

ANN BLAIR

teaching quality assessment   *see* **legal academics**

technology transfer   Technology may be defined as the information necessary to achieve a certain production outcome from a particular means of combining or processing selected inputs. Technologies may be particular production methods, layout of plant and production lines, training of staff, organizational structures, management techniques, access to finance, advertising and marketing methods, or various combinations of these.

Technology may be codified in patent specifications, formulas, blueprints, architectural drawings, or chemical formulae. It may also be uncodified in the sense that it is part of the know-how of individuals. The access to technology may occur through both codified and uncodified sources. For example, the technology disclosed in a patent specification will often require a certain amount of know-how to put that process into commercial production. Technology may also be classified as embodied or disembodied. Information may be embodied in the form of particular products. These may be analysed if they are chemical products; or they may be reverse-engineered to discover the underlying technology. It may be disembodied as know-how.

Technology transfer involves at least two actors—a provider and a receiver. A transfer may involve a one-time purchase of a technology or it may be a long-term relationship between the parties, such as a joint venture. A transaction may have

direct financial ramifications or obligations, such as the **sale of goods**, services, or intellectual property. It may also involve non-commercial exchanges such as at conferences, or through scholarly publishing.

Much technology transfer occurs between demanders and suppliers of technology which is traded in technology markets. Some technologies are transferred outside the market within corporate groups as inter-firm transfers or as joint ventures. Some technological information may be obtained from reverse engineering, or it may be available within the public domain, for example within patent documents or in scholarly publications.

The method adopted for technology transfer will be determined by a number of variables. If the technology is complex and the capacity of the acquirer is limited, then the mode of transfer may be a turnkey agreement, where a completed plant is handed over. This will be accompanied by consultancy and technical assistance agreements to deal with putting the plant into operation and the recruitment of staff, accounting services, and the marketing of completed products. Where the technological capacity of the acquirer is high the mode selected may be a simple licence agreement. Where a transferor wishes to retain some control over the technology, the mode of transfer may be a joint venture or a franchise. Where there is absolutely no technological capacity on the part of the acquirer, the transferor may decide to establish an affiliate to commercialize the technology.

The business decision of the transferor to transfer technology may be influenced by the desire to expand the technological base of the transferor, to secure access to new markets, to diversify the commercial operations of the transferor, and may be a means of transferring financial resources along with technology, particularly in the case of intra-enterprise transfers.

MICHAEL BLAKENEY

telecommunications regulation   For much of the twentieth century, between its nationalization in 1911 and the beginnings of privatization in 1984, the provision of telecommunications services was controlled through public ownership. Weaknesses in the public corporation model, identified by a number of official reports in the 1970s, and in particular its vulnerability to interventions based on political rather than economic grounds, created part of the case which underpinned the decision of the Conservative government of Margaret Thatcher to privatize the sector in 1984. The decision to privatize was accompanied by a policy of gradual liberalization, under which competition would be encouraged in the previously monopolistic sector, and the establishment of a regulatory agency charged both with promoting competition and protecting consumers. The Office of Telecommunications ('OFTEL'), established in 1984, was subsumed within the new Office of Communications ('Ofcom') in 2003. Ofcom combines responsibility for the regulation of telecommunications with the allocation of broadcasting spectrum and the regulation of broadcasting in the UK.

The promotion of **competition** has required the regulators to go beyond the enforcement of simple competition rules concerned with preventing **abuse of a dominant position**, and develop positive regulatory rules for tackling the dominance of the dominant incumbent British Telecom ('BT'). This has involved the regulators in enforcing rules relating to interconnection between the network owned and operated by BT and the networks of newer and smaller operators, and creating positive obligations in respect of matters which would otherwise prevent competition developing. These areas include obligations to permit customers to take their old phone number with them when they change service provider, and requiring BT to permit other firms to establish themselves in BT telephone exchanges (referred to as 'local loop unbundling').

General **competition law** is applied to the telecommunications sector by Ofcom jointly with the general competition authorities. In practice competition, supported by regulatory monitoring and enforcement, has taken a number of forms. In addition to the creation of competing telecommunications infrastructure, competition has come from cable TV companies offering telephone services as part of their bundle, and from firms using the networks of other companies to offer telephone services. The major themes in telecommunications regulation today relate to the effects of convergence between computing, telecommunications, and broadcasting. Traditional assumptions of telecommunications regulation are being rapidly undermined by the emergence of competition from Voice Over Internet Protocol ('VOIP'), which is provided to business networks and available to consumers through services such as Skype. The fact of competition from the outset in mobile telephony has greatly reduced the perceived need for regulation in that sector, although issues have arisen from time-to-time. A recent initiative from the **European Commission** is targeting excessive charges for roaming (where a mobile phone customer uses their phone on the network of an operator abroad).

At the time of privatization the protection of consumers from poor service and high prices was thought to be only a temporary requirement. In practice consumers, and in particular those who are vulnerable and or low users of telecommunications services, have required continuing protection in order to ensure access to appropriate services at reasonable prices. As competition has developed the regulators have increasingly aimed to provide better and more transparent information so that consumers can make informed choices about switching operators, and taking advantage of reduced rate services. Important regulatory issues remain in areas such as the pricing of premium rate services and the control of unwanted phone calls. Premium rate services are regulated by a self-regulatory body, the Independent Committee for the Supervision of Standards of the Telephone Information Services ('ICSTIS'). ICSTIS supervises the honesty of charging information and appropriateness of marketing of such services, and offers an adjudication services to deal with complaints. Commercial cold calling is regulated largely through registration by consumers with the Telephone Preference Service ('TPS'). Marketing organizations are not permitted to cold-call numbers registered to the TPS. Enforcement against companies in breach of the requirements is the responsibility of the Information Commissioner.

COLIN SCOTT

telephone tapping *see* **interception of communications**

television images of law Like film, television was quick to exploit the dramatic possibilities of the courtroom and attracted a number of lawyers as writers, directors, and producers: Canadian lawyer David Shore on *Due South* (Canada), British barrister Peter Moffat on *North Square* (UK), and that one man Law-and-TV cottage industry, the somewhat over-exposed American attorney David Kelley on, *inter alia, LA Law, Ally McBeal, The Practice, Boston Legal*, and so forth (US). Not surprisingly, given this sort of legal professional input, it is TV's imaging of the lawyer—his (or her) life and loves, career ups and downs—that has attracted the most public attention as well as journalistic and scholarly commentary. Nowhere more so than in America, and especially, in the programmes of Kelley: academics, journalists, and lawyers were dazzled (or disgusted) by his (and producer, Steve Bochco's) glamorized version of legal practice as portrayed in *LA Law*. Kelley's subsequent *Ally McBeal* provoked even more controversy; its caricatures, fantasy sequences, and general air of theatrical contrivance, were attacked for their unreal disconnection from the actualities of legal practice. Nevertheless, what Kelley and his various shows prove 'beyond a reasonable doubt' is that TV has an *impact*: that is, it effects, shapes, and alters public perceptions of the legal profession—a point made by many sociological studies of the media and the law. This sort of result is not, however, a recent phenomenon; think of that hoary old US chestnut, *Perry Mason*, and its lead lawyer who never lost a case. Nor is this phenomenon an exclusively American peculiarity: consider the UK's *Rumpole of the Bailey* whose courtroom antics dominated British screens in the 1970s; and Australia's *Rafferty's Rules*, one of that nation's most popular TV shows in the 1980s. TV's 'love affair' with the lawyer has not abated; in fact, it has intensified, extending now to screen representations of '**Other**' kinds of lawyers: not just middle-aged white males (still well represented in shows like Britain's *Kavanagh Q.C.*) but a range of race and gender identities. Women, for example, were showcased, not only in *Ally McBeal* above, but also in the UK's *This Life* (solicitor Jamilla, barrister Anna) and Australia's *Sea Change* ('Country Victoria' magistrate, Laura Gibson); African Americans, in *The Practice* (attorney Eugene); homosexuals in *Queer as Folk* (lesbian lawyer Mel); even 'Canadians, eh?' in the Toronto-based *Street Legal*.

As well as lawyers, different actors in the legal process have begun to appear in television programming: specifically, juries and judges—the latter especially, moving centre stage with the phenomenal success of US TV show *Judge Judy* and its mimicry of 'small claims' courtroom process as a form of all-too-real alternative dispute resolution. Mention of *Judge Judy*—and the emergence of, for example, the network Court TV: that is, the law as 'entertainment'—raises the problematic, adumbrated by trial expert Richard Sherwin about the 'vanishing' boundaries between law and popular culture and the pervasive role visual media have come to play in the US courtroom not only in terms of coverage (eg the televised trial of OJ Simpson) but process and outcome. Indeed, American curial use (and abuse) of video and film is one of the most pressing issues confronting lawyers today, and legal scholars have shown how judgments have been shaped, even determined by video-taped/filmed evidence exploiting televisual (and cinematic) techniques to 're-enact' the crime, selectively interview witnesses on screen, and so forth. The law, however, may be striking back at television: namely, in the form of tighter regulations on, and restriction of the putatively 'criminal' activities of 'reality TV' in the US and elsewhere (eg

the national debates in Australia over a would-be sexual assault on *Big Brother*).

But TV continues to fascinate lawyers, and, law, in turn, remains a perennial staple of television writers and producers. And one not necessarily restricted, generically, to 'courtroom drama'. Indeed, issues of law, legal process, and legal philosophy can be found in a host of genres, even 'teen horror. 'I am the Law', proclaims Buffy the Vampire Slayer in one the sharpest, smartest TV shows of the millennium. *Buffy's* focus on a 'higher law' ('Slay all vampires!') finds its 'sci-fi' equivalent in, for example, *Star Trek's* law of laws, the 'Prime Directive', a principle enabling the crew of Enterprise to boldly go where no other lawyer has gone before. Cartoon comedy, as well, has had 'a go' at, or has 'gone to law': character Lionel Hutz in *The Simpsons* was a walking barristerial send-up (under-prepared, alcoholic, venal), rethreading every known 'lawyer joke'. Lawyers and legal scholars have been quick to take up and examine representations of the law afforded by television; and commentaries can be found in a several excellent, edited collections/anthologies on law and popular culture and in the work of various individual scholars.   WILLIAM MACNEIL

television without frontiers   *see* **European broadcasting regulation**

temporality   *see* **time/temporality**

temporary workers   *see* **fixed-term workers**

terra nullius   With minor and often temporary exceptions such as the volcanic island that appeared off Iceland late in the twentieth century, land is permanently out of production. There is only so much of it and no more. This makes it the most prized commodity in the world. Across all cultures, those that possess land wield considerable status and comparative social and economic advantage over those that do not.

Similar comparative advantages persist among nation states in relation to the **territories** they control. This is also why, in the past, states began to explore new frontiers with the specific intention of extending their influence and authority across the world. This led to the development in **international law** of rules for the management of that enterprise, rules that have evolved over time and crystallized to establish an immutable doctrine on the acquisition of title to territory. The doctrine determines which territories states may lay claim to and which they may not. It also sets out the conditions that must first be fulfilled for any such claim to be valid.

Initially, states could acquire territory through several means, including conquest and annexation. This was possible during the early days when the waging of war against other states was still not illegal. This approach was later discarded because it clashed with notions of civility, **justice**, and peaceful co-existence among states.

States could also acquire territory through cession. Cession of state territory is the voluntary transfer of sovereign control by the owner-state to another state. Although it rarely happens nowadays, in theory it could still happen.

The enduring principle is that a state may still acquire title to new territory if it can demonstrate that until the arrival of its agents, that land was *terra nullius*—that is, vacant and belonging to no one else. Those first to arrive on vacant territory enjoy full ownership rights over that particular piece of land because they have no competing rights previous to theirs to observe. The principle sets a strict test, the determination of which is simple but decisive in the **equal protection** of the **human rights** of everyone regardless of their status—be they poor and weak or wealthy and powerful.

This principle supports the view that indigenous populations enjoy the perpetual right of ownership of their land regardless of whether they are rich and powerful enough to defend it or poor and unable to fend off invaders. It is consistent with the critical date theory, which requires that where there are competing claims to ownership of any territory, time between the contesting Parties should be stopped on that significant date to which they both point. Whatever were the Parties' respective positions and corresponding rights then should be enforced now.

If one of them had indigenous rights over the territory, they are deemed to have them now. Nothing that happens afterwards can operate to change their rights, as they then existed. Whatever the situation was, it is deemed in law still to exist; and the rights of the Parties are governed by it.   BEN CHIGARA

territorial sea   *see* **law of the sea; territory**

territory   The role of territory in **international law** is central, for without territory there can be no state, and without states there would be no international system as currently known. A state's territory comprises the physical space in which the domestic legal jurisdiction is manifested and the principles relating to territorial sovereignty lie at the heart of the system. Article 2(4) of the **United Nations** Charter, for example, forbids the threat or use of force against the territorial integrity of states, which is regarded as inviolable. Territorial sovereignty constitutes a collection of legal rights, powers, liabilities, and duties, depending upon the precise circumstances.

The territory of a state consists of the landspace comprised within the boundaries of the entity in question, together with the airspace above it and any territorial sea (a band of up to twelve nautical miles) around it. Almost all of the world's land area falls within the sovereignty of one state or another, the major exception being the continent of Antarctica, where the 1959 Treaty provides for the suspension of all state claims for the (undefined) life of the treaty. Two or more states may also act as joint sovereigns over a particular territory, such as the **United Kingdom** and France over the New Hebrides prior to its independence as Vanuatu in 1980. Territory may be leased from one state to another for either a specified or an unspecified period of time (for example, the lease of the New Territories of Hong Kong from China by the UK from 1898 to 1997 and of Guantanamo Bay by the United States from Cuba in 1903, reaffirmed in 1934).

The five classical methods of territorial acquisition under international law, based upon **Roman law**, were defined as occupation of *terra nullius* (land under the sovereignty of no other state or organized political or social entity); prescription (effective and undisputed control over a meaningful period); cession (handing over of territory from one state to another usually by formal treaty); accretion (the process by which land is added to a coastal state by natural means); and conquest (the forceful capture of territory from another entity, now illegal as a basis for title to territory).

However, this traditional classification is deficient, as relevant facts might give rise to more than one means of acquisition, particularly with regard to occupation and prescription as both essentially rely upon effective control. Accordingly, international tribunals have concentrated rather upon the existence of relevant treaties, effective sovereign acts by the parties, and recognition by other states as determinative. Attention is placed upon the relevant law of the period when the act in question took place (the principle of **intertemporal law**), so that a valid title to territory today may based upon conquest where this occurred at a time when it constituted a legitimate means of territorial acquisition. While the acquisition of territory is a state sovereign act, it may be accomplished by private parties (such as chartered companies in previous centuries in, for example, India) provided that such parties are acting on behalf of the sovereign of a state or such activities are subsequently adopted by the authorities of the state.

In territorial acquisition, boundary treaties are of particular significance. The situation created by such treaties will constitute an objective reality, so that the boundaries thus established will persist even though the treaty itself has come to an end, for reasons related to the need for the stability of boundaries. A boundary may also be established in a treaty by reference to an earlier document (which may or may not be binding in itself), including a map. This being so, many boundary disputes will in fact revolve around the question of treaty interpretation and the existence of any relevant subsequent practice. Where there is no relevant treaty, attention will be focused upon concrete manifestations of sovereignty by the parties (exercise of effective control or '*effectivités*') and upon the attitude adopted by other states (whether by formal recognition of or refusal to recognize the particular claim). A state which comes to independence will presumptively do so within the territorial limits of the unit that it had previously constituted (*uti possidetis*). Claims may be made to territory on the basis, for example, of historic rights or ethnic or economic ties, but these will constitute political assertions only and will not in themselves constitute a legal basis for a valid territorial title in the absence of the relevant factors as discussed above.

MALCOLM SHAW

See also: **states in international law**

terrorism   In contemporary parlance, 'terrorism' is a label most commonly applied to 'revolutionary' or sub-state violence for political ends which occurs when two pre-conditions prevail. First, the group's objectives cannot be attained by direct force because of the overwhelming strength of state forces. Secondly, the group cannot pursue constitutional means since it represents a minority viewpoint. In short, terrorism is said to be the weapon of the weak. Rather than military victory, the terrorists seek, through the 'propaganda of the deed', to raise public consciousness of their own cause and also to provoke their state opponents into over-reaction and public alienation. The most common proponents of revolutionary terrorism since 1945 have been nationalist groups, such as the Irish Republican Army in Northern Ireland; and it has also been deployed by political radicals such as the Red Army Faction (or Baader-Meinhof Group) in Germany. More recently, al Qa'ida, which perpetrated the attacks in America on 9/11, has been perceived as representing a clash of civilizations, with its rejection of the values of modernity, as well as 'Western' influence in the Middle East.

At the same time, 'terrorism' is often an opportunistic and pejorative ascription designed to denigrate an opponent rather than a simple description of a tactic. It also serves to bolster claims to the legitimacy of counter-force. The effect might be summed up in the common aphorism, 'one person's terrorist is another person's freedom fighter'. The careers of Menachim Begin in Israel and Nelson Mandela in South Africa bear witness to the fluidity of the tag, for they were, at various times during their lives, both condemned as terrorists and also hailed as great national leaders. Therefore, while the emphasis in politics and law is nowadays upon sub-state violence, it should be realized that state terrorism has been far more powerful and destructive in history. Indeed, the term, 'terrorism' was first coined to describe the excesses of French revolutionaries after 1789. Vastly more people died as a result of the terror tactics of Hitler and Stalin than in any sub-state campaign.

As far as national laws are concerned, the definition of terrorism is set out in the Terrorism Act 2000. Terrorism involves any from a list of possible actions: serious violence against a person or endangering another's life; serious damage to property; creating a serious risk to public health or safety; or seriously interfering with, or disrupting, an electronic system. These activities, used or threatened, should be designed to influence the government or an international governmental organization or to intimidate the public or a section of the public, and should be made for the purpose of advancing a political, religious, or ideological cause. Pursuant to that concept, a wide range of counter-measures are implemented. Some have the objective of bolstering the criminal justice system by augmenting policing powers, making court process more effective or sentences more severe. Several of the most controversial have provided for measures of control over suspected terrorists outside of the criminal justice system, on the basis that terrorism is too dangerous to require the compilation of proof on the basis of admissible evidence beyond reasonable doubt. Initiatives against terrorism in national laws have proliferated over time and are currently distributed amongst several legislative sources.

The Terrorism Act 2000 covers proscribed (banned) organizations; terrorist property; powers related to terrorist investigations; special offences (such as the possession of items useful to terrorism); and extra measures relating to criminal process and policing powers confined to Northern Ireland, including non-jury trials. It is intended to represent a permanent code whereas some of the later legislation is subject to annual renewal. It is supplemented by the Anti-terrorism, Crime and Security Act 2001, a response to the 9/11 attacks which includes further measures about terrorist property and cash, the regulation of mass destruction materials, and data mining. But, most controversial, Part IV provided for the detention without trial of foreign terrorist suspects. This policy ended after being condemned as discriminatory under human rights legislation by the **House of Lords in *A v Secretary of State for the Home Department* (2004)**. The Prevention of Terrorism Act 2005 replaced Part IV of the 2001 Act with a system of restrictions by way of control orders imposed by the Home Secretary. The orders can check movement, residence, contacts, activities, and communications.

The Terrorism Act 2006 was a reaction to the London bombings of July 2005 and contains some contentious offences against publications that amount to a direct or indirect encouragement (including 'glorification') of terrorism. Several other broad offences are promulgated, relating to preparation and training, and most are applied to activities throughout the world, without discernment as to the nature of the regime attacked. The police powers of detention after arrest are also extended to twenty-eight days. The government had sought a period of ninety days but was rebuffed by Parliament: an augmented period of pre-charge detention is being advocated again by a pending Counter-Terrorism Bill 2007–2008.

Many of these provisions are draconian, even by successive governments. They are therefore subject to an exceptional amount of scrutiny by Parliament (including by select committees) and by an independent reviewer. They also raise concerns about compliance with the Human Rights Act 1998.

There is a growing body of **international law** about terrorism which, to some extent, shapes domestic law, though there is no agreed global definition. Consequently, the international law approach is to concentrate upon the more egregious aspects of terrorism about which condemnation can be universal, no matter whose cause it serves. Examples include conventions about attacks on diplomats and against the taking of hostages, a range of **treaties** against the hijacking of aircraft or attacks on marine platforms, and some more wide-ranging measures against the financing of terrorism and the bombings of civilian targets. Following 9/11, the **United Nations** established the Counter-Terrorism Committee to oversee the implementation of such measures. At regional level within Europe, inter-governmental cooperation is evidenced by measures on data exchange, extradition without exception for political causes and Europe-wide arrest warrants.   CLIVE WALKER

C Walker, *The Anti-Terrorism Legislation* (Oxford: Oxford University Press, 2002)

P Wilkinson, *Terrorism versus Democracy* (London: Frank Cass, 2000)

terrorism, international measures against
see **terrorism**

test case   *see* **social security appeals**

text books after 1850   The legal text book, sometimes also termed a treatise, is a systematic exposition of a specific and discrete body of law. It is a didactic work aimed primarily at law students but also available to and ideally informative for practitioners and judges as well. The defining characteristic of the text book, as the singular form of the initial noun suggests, is that it reduces the disparate and often chaotic plurality of cases and statutes to a manageable and coherent set of principles. The aim of the classical text book was thus that of expounding the law of a given domain—as, for example, crime, contract, tort, property—as a singular, self-contained, and logically cohesive body of substantive rules.

The era of the text book dates back to the 1850s, although there are obviously earlier instances and inspirations, and most notably **Blackstone's** *Commentaries*, published between 1765 and 1769, an institutional work based on Roman principles, which provided, as Cairns observed, a systematic but 'elementary treatment of a whole system of law treated as a national law'. Blackstone's goals were multiple and explicit. First, outside the Chancery Inns, the 'juridical university', there was no university teaching of **common law**. He wanted to lay claim to a new university discipline, a science of common law. Secondly, he aimed to raise the rather dismal quality of common law literature so that it could match the scholarship of the civil law countries, and not least so that common law writings would not look paltry next to the relative profusion of institutional and monographic literature produced 'just to the North', in Scotland. Blackstone provided both legitimacy and motive for the subsequent and novel text book literature of the nascent English and American legal academies but the change was hardly swift.

The **Select Committee** on Legal Education that reported to the **House of Commons** in 1846 concluded that 'no legal education, worthy of the name of a public nature, is at this moment to be had' either in England or Ireland. The Committee went on to deplore the dearth of coherent student law texts, the absence of jurists, and the general lack of any legal science in England. As late as 1883, in a lecture delivered as the new Vinerian Professor of Law at Oxford University, **Dicey**, who was himself to become one of the principal authors of text books, resoundingly declared that: 'If the question whether English law can be taught at the Universities could be submitted in the form of a case to a body of eminent counsel, there is no doubt whatsoever as to what would be their answer. They would reply with unanimity and without hesitation that English law must be learned and cannot be taught'. Responding to the hostility of the profession, as well as to the strictures of the Committee, and drawing inspiration from Blackstone's apologetic and strongly didactic introduction to the first volume of his *Commentaries*, a tradition of text books emerged to remedy a glaring lacuna in the university curriculum.

Associated most closely in England with Anson on *Contracts*, **Pollock** on *Torts*, Dicey on the *Law of the Constitution* and also on the *Conflict of Laws*, the early text book tradition was pitched to achieve a double goal. Trained most usually at the Bar and through practice, the first fidelity of the new academics was to the profession and to the didactic presentation of the authorities of common law wrought as best they could into a logical frame and expounded as a full and complete body of rules derived from the case law and, as they used to be called, the 'decisions of Parliament'. The text book was thus primarily expository and descriptive, rather than critical or censorious. Pollock, for example, in his 1895 *Torts* text book notes that he does not deem it 'proper' in a practical law book to criticize an Act of **Parliament**, and a similar disposition amongst authors and editors generally precluded anything other than the most reverently formulated and intricately technical commentaries upon judicial decisions.

Established in the latter half of the nineteenth century, the text book tradition held venerable sway over the founding of the provincial university law schools in the first half of the twentieth century. As Glanville Williams, author of the most widely used modern preparative to the study of common law, published in 1945, puts it, the student of law has but one choice in terms of method of study: he can 'sit in the library reading case reports', or he can spend his time 'stewing over a textbook' in his own room. There could be no better image of the exegetical character of the common law curriculum than this depiction of the student either sitting or stewing over one of two unitary and self-contained expositions of the rules of law as found first hand in the reports and second hand, more mobile and manageable in the text book, the ambulant reporter. It was the bedrock of what is termed the 'black letter' tradition in which the function of the author is to work internally within doctrine and so constantly

to update the text as new cases come down and new **legislation** is passed.

The text book should cover all of the discipline, it should cite all current authority, and act as a resource for students and professionals, academics and judges alike. It was intended to influence both students and judges and it is fair to say that despite the imbalance of power, in which academics continue to suffer a sense of their status inferiority and financial impoverishment in comparison to the Bar and the bench, academics do have their say. The judges are clear that their task would be close to impossible without the work of the text book writers and other academic commentators. Critical exchanges with academic texts are common enough in the law reports and as Duxbury points out there has always been and continues to be a two-way street between Oxbridge colleges and the bench. It is also clearly the case that as legal scholarship has expanded and become increasingly interdisciplinary, the nature of the exchange has changed and become somewhat more complex and diffuse.

The text book tradition is alive and well as the bastion of traditional legal pedagogy and the repository of classical legal thought. It has also expanded in scope and diffused in content as law has come increasingly to be defined within the university as a social science and the professional aura and obsequiousness of the discipline has given way to a more humanistic academic endeavour. In Britain, the **'law in context' movement** that began in the 1970s produced a number of doctrinal studies that infused social scientific methods and a broader sense of juridical subject matter into the writing of student texts. Patrick Atiyah's *Accidents, Compensation and the Law* is a good early example of a sociologically and contextually-informed text book. Hugh Collins *Law of Contract* is a good later instance of a critically informed, and theoretically open analysis of a legal discipline in terms of market forces and political consequences that would likely make Anson chill in his Oxford sepulchre. Further still from the black-letter paradigm, critically oriented introductions to text book topics, feminist, socialist, and 'critical legal' monographs on the doctrinal disciplines have also emerged and have had their impact, though this has been primarily upon the student body rather than more directly influencing the bench or bar. The ambitious and critically motivated student of law can now enjoy a certain ferment in their room as they pick up critical text books—what Fitzpatrick has described as 'dangerous supplements'—on many of the core subjects or peruse critically acclaimed feminist introductions to the foundational subjects.

PETER GOODRICH

J Cairns, 'Blackstone, an English Institutist: Legal Literature and the Rise of the Nation State' (1984) 4 *Oxford Journal of Legal Studies* 318

D Sugarman, 'Legal Theory, the Common Law Mind, and the Making of the Textbook Tradition', in W Twining (ed), *Legal Theory and Common Law* (Oxford: Oxford University Press, 1986)

thalidomide   *see* **product liability**

Thatcherism   Usually attributed to the sociologist Stuart Hall, 'Thatcherism' is a term commonly used to describe the policies and philosophy of the Conservative governments of Margaret Thatcher, 1979–1990. A product of the growing economic difficulties faced by 1970s capitalism and influenced by thinkers such as Friedrich Hayek and Milton Friedman (and, more parochially, Keith Joseph and Enoch Powell), Thatcherism is generally associated with support for free markets and a reduction in the scope and size of the state (not least in relation to welfare), and with the privatization of state-owned industries, the curbing of trade union power, monetarist economic policies (aimed at securing low inflation), and the lowering of direct taxation. Along with 'Reaganomics', Thatcherism was at the forefront of the transformations in economic thought and management associated with the rise of neo-liberalism. It is also, however, associated with authoritarianism and growing state intrusion into social affairs. Indeed, some see this as its dominant strand—hence the view that Thatcherism attempted to combine, in an inherently unstable mix, market liberalism with social conservatism; a free economy with a strong state.

The originality, coherence, and achievements of Thatcherism are controversial, as is the source and extent of its political appeal. Some see it as a bold and broadly successful attempt to reverse decades of British economic decline, writing admiringly of the 'Thatcher miracle' despite the de-industrialization, growing centralization, and social and regional schisms it engendered. Others see it as a coherent and premeditated attempt to restore the power of capital through mass unemployment and a variety of legal changes aimed at diminishing Trade Union and working class power; still others see it as 'adventurist', as poorly thought out, lacking coherence and pursued with a limited grasp of consequences. Whatever its inconsistencies, however, and there were many, the Thatcher era undoubtedly marked the beginnings of the major upward redistribution of wealth seen in recent decades and fundamentally altered the economic and political landscape in the UK.

Neo-liberal economic policies have since been wholeheartedly embraced by her successors—Major, Blair, and Brown—hence Peter Mandelson's declaration that 'we are all Thatcherites now'. Indeed, if Thatcher's economic rhetoric outstripped her actions, New Labour has done its best to put things right, plunging in where even she feared to tread, stretching privatization and 'marketization' ever further, bringing private sector values and methods to the heart of the public sector (and to areas where outright privatization would be politically unpalatable), and championing public-private partnerships which many commentators, from across the political spectrum, see as having pawned the future. New Labour has also displayed both a deeply authoritarian streak, promoting the increasing state 'regulation' of all facets of social life, and a marked centralizing tendency. Hence the view that it represents Thatcherism without Thatcher.   PADDY IRELAND

the Other   *see* **Other, the**

theatre   Theatres are required to be licensed by a local authority. As regards the content of what is shown, however, the theatre has moved from being one of the most closely regulated areas, to one of the freest. Prior to 1968 all scripts for theatre productions had to be approved in advance by the Lord Chamberlain, who operated very strict rules. The Theatres Act 1968 removed this **censorship**, and made the theatre subject to the criminal law, at least as regards the presentation of plays (which would include operas) and ballets. There is no prior control over what can be performed, but if the production proves to be obscene, or to incite racial hatred, for example, then those responsible for it can be prosecuted. **Obscenity** here is defined in terms of a tendency to deprave and corrupt, but there is a defence of 'public good' for productions which can claim 'artistic merit'. Control of prosecutions is in the hands of the **Attorney-General**. To date the Attorney has only exercised the power to prosecute in one case: in 1971 a revue in Manchester was successfully prosecuted on the basis of its explicit sexual content.

In relation to performances which do not fall within the definition of a play or ballet, the **common law** offences or presenting an indecent exhibition or keeping a disorderly house, may be used. There are examples of these offences being used in relation to live sex shows involving 'exotic dancing' and similar activities.   RICHARD STONE

theft   *see* **criminal regulation of property relations; fraud, honesty, and markets**

theory in legal research   Broadly speaking, 'theory' refers to systematic and abstract knowledge.

Beyond this general definition, 'theory' can have several different meanings, two of which are especially significant. First, it is possible to speak of *a* theory, meaning a specific understanding of the underlying principles of an area of knowledge. Numerous scholars have formulated *a* theory of law in this sense. Usually, when we speak of a theory, we are using it in this first sense to mean an explicit and coherent statement of a set of principles about an object of knowledge. A second sense of theory (without the article) is more general, meaning a conceptual or abstract approach to analysis, evaluation, or critique of an object of knowledge.

Both senses of 'theory' can be located in legal research. In the fields of jurisprudence and legal philosophy, many scholars have developed specific theories about law as an object, a discipline, and a practice. These theories attempt to provide definitive answers to questions such as the following. What is law? How does law relate to other systems of rules and principles such as those associated with morality, **religion**, and politics? How should we understand judicial decision-making? What is the source of the obligation to obey the law? The most influential group of theories of law over the past two hundred years has been those categorized under the broad umbrella term of **legal positivism**. Positivism holds that law is created by human acts and social institutions formed especially for the purpose of making and applying law. According to legal positivism, moral principles, natural, divine or otherwise, are not a necessary foundation of valid law although moral values are often in practice used in setting the content of law. In fact, there is no single theory of legal positivism, but many different theories which converge around these broad claims. The legal theories of John **Austin**, Hans Kelsen, and HLA **Hart** are all variations of legal positivism. Similarly, specific areas of law are also the object of theories in this first sense. Legal scholars have participated in broad philosophical debates over, for instance, the nature and justification of property, but they have also articulated distinct theories of property *law*. Thus theory in legal research can take the form of an investigation into the conceptual foundations of a particular area of law. This indicates the general point that theory-construction in legal research is sometimes broadly interdisciplinary in its engagement with philosophy, political theory, and social theory, but that it can also be specifically focused on positive law.

The underlying theory in legal research is often unarticulated. There are theoretical presuppositions informing much legal research but which are not always explicitly stated as such or reflected upon

by researchers. For instance, much legal research is based upon the broad theoretical claims of legal positivism. It presumes that law is a social product rather than an element of the natural world or derived from natural reason. In keeping with positivist thought, **doctrinal legal research** often assumes the institutional and/or the conceptual separation of law from other spheres of social existence. The theory of legal positivism has the status of a paradigm of knowledge because, although it can be contested as a theory, it is assumed to be true by many practitioners and scholars of law. Thus, although much legal scholarship does not explicitly engage with any theoretical framework, it is nonetheless shaped by theory.

In the second sense of 'theory' mentioned above, 'theory in legal research' does not involve constructing a distinct theory or coherent explanation of law. Rather, it means taking a conceptual approach to the subject matter of law without the aim of identifying a system of explanatory principles. Towards the end of the twentieth century, the idea of theory in the first sense went into a sharp decline. Many researchers now no longer believe that it is possible to construct *a* theory of law, or of any other complex social phenomenon, in the way that it might be possible to construct a theory of the natural world. Law is simply too contingent, too complicated, and too internally contradictory for a single theory to encapsulate satisfactorily. Moreover, the very possibility of objective knowledge, which is formed independently of language, culture, and individual researchers, has been strongly questioned by critical and linguistic approaches to philosophy. However, this decline in the idea that it is possible to construct definitive and coherent theories about social phenomena has not meant the end of theory, but rather a reorientation for theoretical research. It has been accompanied by a move towards greater reflectiveness about the underlying theoretical presumptions of all research and by a broadening of the types of theory used in legal research. In particular, the inter-related areas of social theory, cultural theory, and continental philosophy have had a far greater impact on legal research in the past two decades than they did previously.

Many areas of law, as well as the philosophy of law itself, reflect these changes in the use of theory. Much recent feminist scholarship, for instance, rather than constructing a general theory of legal patriarchy, has taken the form of unmasking the gendered assumptions in established thought, including legal scholarship. These assumptions operate differently in different contexts, and cannot be generalized into a single form. Judicial decision-making and legislative actions have been criticized for failing to take into account the different material conditions of **women** and men. Rather than construct a unified theory of law and **gender** (though this has been attempted), feminist scholarship tends to critique the theories and theoretical assumptions of mainstream legal thought with a view to uncovering and correcting unequal distributions of social and political power. In so doing, feminist thought has made extensive use of theory originating in disciplines other than law, such as sociology, politics, and cultural studies.

Contemporary theoretical approaches to research in law are genuinely diverse. Legal theorists as well as researchers making use of some form of theory use a wide range of philosophical and theoretical methodologies and traditions. While much legal research is informed by theory developed within the specifically 'legal' traditions of jurisprudence and legal philosophy, much theory is now interdisciplinary.

MARGARET DAVIES

therapeutic cloning 'Therapeutic (non-reproductive) cloning' involves the removal of the nucleus of a **human** egg, its replacement with the nuclear content that is to be cloned, stimulation of the egg to form a CNR (cell nuclear replacement) embryo, and then harvesting the embryonic stem cells. In order to clear the way for this kind of procedure, bespoke Regulations were introduced in 2001. Notwithstanding this extension of the legal framework, there remained doubts about the status of a CNR-embryo.

Arguably, the Human Fertilization and Embryology Act 1990 ('HFEA'), is drafted on the dual assumption: (i) that a human embryo will be the product of a process of *fertilization*; and (ii) that cloning procedures will involve manipulation of an *embryo* (rather than manipulation of an *egg*). Accordingly, the HFEA provides that 'embryo means a live human embryo where fertilisation is complete', and that no licence may authorize 'replacing a nucleus of a cell of an embryo'. With the prospect of therapeutic cloning, these assumptions were undermined and the legal position was put to the test in the *Pro-Life Alliance* case (2001) (2002) (2003).

Eschewing literalism, the **appeal** courts ruled that CNR-embryos (albeit not the product of fertilization) fall within the scope of the HFEA; but, espousing literalism, they also ruled that the prohibition against nuclear replacement does not cover CNR in an *egg*. This ruling meant that the HFEA did not leave a loophole in relation to human reproductive cloning; that there was no legislative obstacle in the way of therapeutic cloning; and, that there was no need for **Parliament** to revisit the vexed issue of research using human embryos.

Beyond the United Kingdom, there is little agreement about the right regulatory approach to therapeutic cloning. The **United Nations** Declaration on Human Cloning (2005), prohibiting 'all forms of human cloning inasmuch as they are incompatible with **human dignity** and the protection of human life', is shot through with ambiguity. In particular, the notion of human dignity is open to a variety of readings, as is the reference to the protection of human life. So far as the UK is concerned, the Declaration prohibits reproductive but not therapeutic cloning.

Although, within the UK, the legal position has been clarified so that research into therapeutic cloning can be licensed, there is unfinished regulatory business—for instance, to regularize the incentives that may be offered to women who agree to supply eggs, to decide whether eggs from rabbits or cows might be used by researchers, and to determine whether an embryo resulting from the stimulation of an enucleated animal egg falls within the scope of the HFEA.

ROGER BROWNSWORD

See also: **stem cells**

third generation rights This term is sometimes used to describe **human rights** attributed to cultural groups, including minority language rights, the rights of **indigenous peoples**, and of cultural **minorities** in general. The most common usage, however, is in relation to so-called 'solidarity' rights or the rights of peoples, a category which builds upon but also goes beyond those rights considered to make up the first two generations of human rights. Based on historical generalizations, the first generation was said to consist of rights to be free from arbitrary state action as exemplified by the rights proclaimed in the French and American Declarations of 1789 and 1791 respectively. The second generation, exemplified by the rights recognized in the Mexican Constitution of 1917 (rights to education, food, health, etc) and reinforced by the claims which underpinned the Bolshevik or Socialist Revolution in Russia in the same year, were rights to positive assistance from the state. These two generations were then reflected in the **International Covenant on Civil and Political Rights** and the **International Covenant on Economic, Social, and Cultural Rights**, both adopted by the **United Nations** in 1966, and which today form the cornerstone of international human rights treaty law.

The proposition that there is a third generation emerged in the 1970s in response to two related movements. The first was the assertion by developing countries, many newly emerged as a result of

decolonization and others newly empowered as a result of the success of the OPEC oil cartel, that the human rights framework needed to accommodate the preoccupations and claims of the poorer states in relation to economic development. The second was a sense that human rights needed to be made more directly relevant to the major challenges confronting the international community as a whole, including development but also environmental wellbeing and peace.

The right to development was the first of these rights to be endorsed at the international level (by the UN Commission on Human Rights in 1977), followed by the right to peace (by the UN General Assembly in 1978). UNESCO, and especially its then Legal Adviser Karel Vasak, then extended and consolidated these rights into a new category or generation of solidarity rights. The range of rights included has varied over time but, in 1997, Vasak confined the list to five solidarity rights: the right to development, the right to peace, the right to a healthy and ecologically balanced environment, the right to share the common heritage of mankind, and the right to humanitarian assistance. Their distinguishing characteristic is said to be the extent to which their realization is dependent upon international cooperation in an increasingly interdependent world. They are also rights that are vested in peoples as well as individuals.

The concept has been criticized on various grounds: (1) the concept of generations suggests that one replaces another; (2) solidarity is just as important to the realization of many of the rights of the other two generations; (3) the collective or peoples' rights dimension is incompatible with the individual nature of human rights; and (4) the notion seeks to elevate the rights of states to the same level as those of individuals.

Third generation rights have received a mixed reception in **international law** and policy. Their most significant embrace came in the 1979 **African Charter of Human and Peoples' Rights** which recognizes, among other rights, peoples' rights to 'economic, social and cultural development', 'national and international peace and security', and 'a general satisfactory environment favourable to their development' (Articles 22–24). Some of the third generation rights have been the subject of extensive discussion. In particular the right to development was the subject of a UN Declaration in 1986 and has since been the focus of numerous activities of the UN Human Rights Council (and its predecessor, the Commission on Human Rights). The right to peace has been taken up from time to time by UNESCO, while the

right to share in the common heritage of mankind has so far had little resonance as a human rights concept. The right to a clean and healthy environment has been the subject of extensive elaboration, albeit rarely within the framework of a third generation or solidarity right. And while humanitarian assistance is systematically claimed and frequently provided, virtually all governments have gone out of their way to deny that it is being accorded as of right. In sum, much remains to be done if the concept of third generation rights is to occupy a significant place within the international law of human rights.

PHILIP ALSTON

P Alston, 'Peoples' Rights: Their Rise and Fall', in P Alston (ed), *Peoples' Rights* (Oxford: Oxford University Press, 2001), 259

SP Marks, 'Emerging Human Rights: A New Generation for the 1980s?' (1981) 33 *Rutgers Law Review* 435–452

Thompson, Edith   *see* **Bywater, Frederick and Thompson, Edith**

Thompson, Robert and Venables, Jon   Robert Thompson ('T') and Jon Venables ('V') achieved notoriety when, on 24 November 1993, they were convicted, at Preston Crown Court, of the murder, in Bootle, Liverpool on 12 February 1993, of James Bulger, who was then aged two. They themselves were aged ten at the time of the offence (just over the age of criminal responsibility, which was, and remains, ten, in England and Wales). At the trial they were both eleven.

They abducted James Bulger from a shopping centre, took him on a walk of over two miles and then killed him, primarily by hitting him with bricks, leaving him, unconscious, on a railway line where he was run over by a train. T and V were identified partly through a video from the shopping centre's security cameras, which showed a small child being led by the hand by an older child, with another older child walking slightly ahead. This video became iconic of the case and added a visual dimension which was heavily used in press and television reporting. Indeed, T and Vs' extreme youth, juxtaposed with the brutal nature of their crime, and the even greater youth of the victim, led to unprecedented levels of media coverage and spawned a debate on the nature of childhood which is, in some respects, still ongoing.

T and V were both sentenced to 'detention at Her Majesty's pleasure'. This is an indeterminate sentence prescribed by statute for persons aged under eighteen convicted of murder. The final decision on release was, in 1993, taken by the Home Secretary.

Under the law at that time, in all such cases, the Home Secretary set a 'tariff'—a period designed to represent retribution and deterrence—which had to be served before the child-offender could be considered for parole. The Home Secretary imposed a tariff of fifteen years on T and V. They, in turn, sought **judicial review** of this decision, ultimately by the **House of Lords**. They also, subsequently, took a case to the **European Court of Human Rights** and were successful in their claim that their right to a fair trial had been violated.

As a direct result of the case, decisions on tariff must now be made by the judiciary and the release of a child-murderer can only be deferred beyond the end of the tariff on grounds of dangerousness, a decision which is taken by the Parole Board. In order to ensure that the trial is fair, courts dealing with children must take measures to ensure their active participation.

In 2001, T and V were each granted wide-ranging **injunction**s ensuring their anonymity, and the protection of the new identities given to them on their release, for the rest of their lives.

CLAIRE MCDIARMAID

B Morrison, *As If* (London: Granta Books, 1997); D Haydon and P Scraton ' "Condemn A Little More, Understand A Little Less": The Political Context and Rights Implications of the Domestic and European Rulings in the Venables-Thompson Case' (2000) 27 *Journal of Law and Society* 416

Throckmorton, Sir Nicholas   Sir Nicholas Throckmorton (1515/16–1571) was born to an established Warwickshire family and was a relative of Katherine Parr, the last wife of Henry VIII. Throckmorton began his diplomatic career in the service of Henry VIII and the Parr family as well as serving as MP for various boroughs, including Maldon and Devizes. He was knighted by Edward VI for bringing news of Protector Somerset's defeat of the Scots at the battle of Pinkie and was awarded the position of Treasurer of the Mint.

Under Mary, Throckmorton supported Lady Jane Grey's attempt to become queen and remained a visibly staunch Protestant despite the suppression of evangelicals by Mary's regime. This inevitably led him into trouble and on 1 January 1554 he was bound over in the sum of £2,000 to be of good conduct. Throckmorton apparently ignored this bind-over for on 20 February 1554 he was committed to the Tower on a charge of treason for involvement in Sir Thomas Wyatt's rebellion. The charge on his indictment of 17 April 1554 read that he was the 'principal deviser, procurer and contriver of the late rebellion:

and that Wyatt was but his minister'. In his trial at Guildhall, Throckmorton rose to the occasion by advancing learned legal arguments to ridicule the basis of the prosecution case: his main defence was that as the Treason Acts of Henry VIII's reign had been repealed he would have to be convicted under the Treason Act 1351. As Throckmorton had not committed treason within the definition of the 1351 Act the jury acquitted him.

Despite his acquittal Throckmorton was imprisoned until January 1555. He was forced to flee to France in June 1556 as he was suspected of involvement in Henry Dudley's conspiracy. Throckmorton protested his innocence and in May 1557 Mary I accepted that he had no involvement in this plot and allowed him to return to England.

Under Elizabeth I, Throckmorton was appointed as ambassador to France. He attempted to support the struggles of the Protestant Huguenots and brokered a deal whereby the Huguenots were given the port of Le Havre in return for military aid. His reward for this deal was imprisonment by Catherine de Medici. Throckmorton's Machiavellian political style managed to alienate all French factions, especially the Guise, against him and, his embassy having failed, he returned to England in 1564.

Throckmorton was appointed Chamberlain of the Exchequer and Chief Butler of England in 1567 and was sent to Scotland to attempt to broker a compromise between Mary Queen of Scots and the Scottish lords. Once again Throckmorton only succeeded in alienating all against him. In 1569 he was accused of further entanglement with Mary, Queen of Scots and was imprisoned at Windsor before being placed under house arrest. He died in London on 12 February 1571 of pneumonia.

ELLIOT VERNON

Thurtell, John (1794–1824) and Hunt, Joseph (1797–1861)   Born into a respectable merchant family, Thurtell's own business ventures—as a bombazine manufacturer in Norwich and a publican in Long Acre, London—ended in failure and he was also a heavy and unsuccessful gambler. In 1823, resentful and in dire financial straits, he decided to murder William Weare, whom he believed to have cheated him of £300 at cards. On 24 October Weare left London in Thurtell's company. Their gig was followed by Thurtell's two accomplices, Joseph Hunt and William Probert. When they reached the lane to Probert's cottage near Radlett, in Hertfordshire, Thurtell shot Weare with a pistol, cut his throat, and rammed the pistol into his skull. The three men were soon arrested and the subsequent trial proved the most notorious of the 1820s. Probert turned King's

evidence to avoid trial and punishment (he was executed for horse theft in 1825); Thurtell and Hunt were
both convicted. Thurtell was hanged outside Hertford gaol on 9 January 1824 and his corpse was publicly dissected at St Bartholomew's Hospital. Hunt's
sentence was commuted to transportation to Botany
Bay in return for his disclosure of the location of
Weare's body.

Moralists seized on this murder as a demonstration
of the evils to which card-playing and prize-fighting
led (Thurtell had trained and backed pugilists); but
it was also immediately turned into a play (*The Gamblers*), and the novelists Bulwer-Lytton and Dickens,
among others, made later use of the story.

ALLYSON MAY

Tichborne Claimant   *see* **Orton, Arthur**

time/temporality   There is an intriguing match
between law and the qualities we associate with time.
We think of time as the present moment, yet we also
think of it as a past and a future into which the present is always disappearing. In shaping the present
we bring the past to bear on it and we also orient it
towards the future; likewise with law. Law offers or
prescribes positions that are like an enduring present. In doing so, law brings the past to bear and ori-
ents determinate positions towards the future. This is
what we expect it to do as the **rule of law**—to provide
us with some certainty of position. Yet we also expect
law to accommodate changing positions. If it failed
to do so, it would, even as a rule of law, cease to rule
situations inevitably changing around it. So whilst
there is a traditional emphasis in law on following
precedent, on applying the law as it is, and thereby providing some security of expectation, **judges**
increasingly emphasize law's adaptability to changes
in society, and the ever-growing volume of **legislation** attests to law's incessant transformations.

There is, however, a significant difference between
our personal experience of time and the law's relation to it. By and large, we accommodate the imperatives of time without taking much explicit account
of the past and the future, although on occasion
we are more deliberate about this. Law is different.
Although much of our collective being together, like
our individual being, accommodates time without
deliberate consideration, law is that element of our
being together where there is such consideration.
Law has explicitly to accommodate past and future
time and bring them to bear in the making of the
legal decision, whether the decision be that of the
legislator or judge, or whether it be that involved in
our own bringing of the law to bear.

In explicitly constituting the terms of our being
together, law's predominant regard is for the future.
Although considerable regard will be had to the
past, law is not ultimately bound in or by any past.
It can, and often does, jettison the most hallowed
precedents. It can make its own dictates retroactive
and, in so doing, it can create a past where none
had existed. An example would be where an action
is made criminal when it was not at the time it was
done. Some would see the **Nuremberg trials** in this
way. An even more spectacular example is where a
constitution is made in the name of a 'people' but the
people as an effective entity only comes into existence as a result of that same constitution. Examples
of law's presumptuous domination of time could be
multiplied, but perhaps the most telling is the type
of 'legal fiction' where the letter of the law stays the
same but the substance has been changed to accommodate changed social conditions. In this way law's
stability in time is seemingly affirmed whilst in time
it has changed utterly.   PETER FITZPATRICK

tobacco   *see* **diseases, liability for; group
    action; product liability**

tobacco duties   *see* **excise duties**

tolpuddle martyrs   The Tolpuddle martyrs is the
name given to six agricultural workers who were
convicted of offences under the Unlawful Oaths Act
1797 for forming a **trade union** of agricultural workers in the Dorset village of Tolpuddle in 1833. Their
conviction and sentence to seven years transportation to Tasmania caused widespread concern; and
after an extensive campaign including large demonstrations and petitions to the government and Parliament, they were granted free pardons. The case
of the Tolpuddle martyrs was an extreme reaction
against the freedom to combine granted to workers when the Combination Acts, which made the
mere fact of combination a criminal offence, were
repealed in 1824. The Combination Act 1825 re-enacted some criminal offences for acts of molestation
and obstruction, but the act for which the Tolpuddle martyrs were convicted was simply that of forming a trade union supported, as was common at the
time, by an oath of fidelity. Prosecution of workers
under the Unlawful Oaths Act 1797, an Act passed in
response to naval mutinies, undermined the repeal
of the Combination Acts. The conduct of the trial
of the Tolpuddle martyrs exacerbated the abuse of
the law in prosecuting workers for an activity that
Parliament had made lawful. The case has come to
symbolize the lack of sympathy, if not open hostility,

often displayed by the law towards trade unions and the determination which working people have had to show in order to assert their social right to act collectively.   BOB SIMPSON

tort law 'Tort law' is often treated as synonymous with 'accident law' although in fact this is misleading as tort addresses many situations which go beyond **compensation** for accidents. That said, it is the principal mechanism for the provision of compensation for personal injuries—through the tort of **negligence**—so it is in that context that people are most likely to encounter it.

Yet torts in the wider sense are all around us. They may take the form of scurrilous attacks on a person's reputation (defamation); deliberate physical harm (**trespass** to **person**); or calling a **strike** (inducing breach of contract). Some torts, such as trespass to person or negligence, are well established; others have only recently emerged or are still in the course of becoming (witness, for example, recent legal debate on the extent to which English law protects a right to **privacy**). Some torts have been abolished by statute. There used to be a cluster of torts around **family life** which protected the interests of the husband/father in relation to his wife/children. These 'domestic torts' included an action for loss of 'consortium' (understood in terms of a wife's services and companionship), the tort of 'seduction', and a claim for 'criminal conversation' (essentially a suit by a cuckolded husband against the adulterous couple). As these torts suggest, tort law takes much of it colour and form from its historical, social, and cultural context. Hence the emergence of new torts in recent years addressing newly recognized social problems such as **harassment**.

So what exactly is a tort? The standard legal answer, absorbed by generations of undergraduates, is 'a civil wrong', the word deriving from the Old French *tort*, meaning wrong or injury, in turn emanating from the Medieval Latin, *tortum*, meaning injustice (which, interestingly, provides the same etymological root for '**torture**'). A civil wrong is a breach of a civil obligation by one party entitling another party to sue. What constitutes a civil obligation and its breach is primarily a matter of **common law**, drawn from centuries of judicial decision-making, although, increasingly, tort law has been the subject of *legislation*, as, for example, in the statutory codification of occupiers' duties to visitors and trespassers (Occupiers' Liability Act 1957 and 1984). Moreover some civil claims which are entirely the creation of statute—for example discrimination claims—are so similar in form and character to tort claims as to be better understood as 'statutory torts' (although most tort text books still do not include their coverage). By contrast, there are other civil wrongs, most notably those deriving from **contract law** or **trusts**, which are regarded as quite distinct (although the lines between these various branches of civil law are often more theoretical than real).

As indicated, tort law spans a range of wrongs all with their own particular 'ingredients', evolving over years of judicial crafting and finessing. The evolutionary nature of their creation means that they are not necessary subject to any coherent classificatory scheme. Perhaps the best way to view tort schematically is in terms of the protection of different interests. Broadly speaking tort seeks to protect three types of interest: (1) interests in property; (2) interests in personal **security** and integrity; and (3) economic interests—in profit, capital investment, and economic expectation. In relation to property, the primary torts are private **nuisance** (the unreasonable interference with the use and enjoyment of **property rights**); trespass to land or goods; and negligence causing property damage for example to your car. A wide range of torts govern personal security and integrity. These include negligence causing personal injury, the torts comprising trespass to person (assault, battery, and false imprisonment), and the torts governing damage to reputation (**slander** and **libel**, comprising the law of defamation). As is evident from the above examples, the acts which comprise a tort may also, simultaneously, be criminal, although different rules apply to determine whether a crime, as opposed to a tort, has been committed. Thus, for example, while American football star, OJ Simpson, was held not guilty in criminal law in relation to the alleged killing of his wife and her boyfriend, he was later held liable in tort for their unlawful killing.

It is often said that tort law is better at protecting the *physical* integrity of the person than their emotional or psychological integrity and it is true that, in a negligence context in particular, tort law struggles to recognize and remedy emotional harm, particularly where no physical damage has occurred. That said, there are some torts, for example, in relation to reputation, which are wholly concerned with non-physical violations of personal integrity so it is not entirely accurate to say that tort is not concerned with non-physical injury as such. It is really a question of what has evolved as legally recognizable harm in the context of social, political, and cultural conditions. The courts had no difficulty in acknowledging the non-physical dimension to the 'harm' sustained by husbands/fathers in relation to the domestic torts, in their time. Likewise, in recent years, with changes in social and cultural attitudes, the courts have begun to view as potentially tortious harms which previously would have attracted no liability, for example, damage to educational opportunity (*Phelps v Hillingdon LBC* (2001)) or interference with the integrity of family life (*M v Newham BC* (1995)), a process of opening up the parameters of remediable harm, which has been assisted by the implementation of the **Human Rights Act** and a heightened **human rights** culture.

With regard to the protection of economic interests, tort law has developed a range of **economic torts**, mostly around industrial action, to proscribe and delimit the scope of legitimate conduct. These torts also apply in the context of harmful business practices; indeed one of the earliest economic torts, inducing breach of contract, emerged in the context of a theatre director's efforts to 'poach' a singer from a business competitor (**Lumley v Wagner** (1852)). And, of course, the tort of deceit, understood as a false statement of existing fact made with knowledge of its falsity and the intention that it should be acted upon to the detriment of the claimant, is also concerned primarily with economic harm. Indeed taken as a whole, these economic torts might be understood as basic rules governing business transactions, rules which incidentally, if unsurprisingly given their origins, also operate to contain the collective industrial strength of workers engaged in **strikes**.

Viewed historically, it is difficult to characterize tort law as a particular set of rules governing civil obligations which can be presented in any absolute or determinate way. Properly understood, tort law is a dynamic and evolutionary process, an open-ended dialogue within law about individual and social **responsibility**. This fluidity lends itself to instrumental deployment; and indeed tort is sometimes invoked not to remedy individual wrongs (although that is generally the form a claim will take) but to address broader social concerns, for example, the rights of **consumers**, the protection of the environment, and/or social and cultural inequalities. One might, for example, bring a claim in nuisance to limit the polluting emissions of a nearby factory; one might seek to bring a claim against the **police** for poor investigation of a racially motivated crime as a way of combating the perceived racism of police practices; one might sue a school for failing to address the educational needs of a dyslexic pupil as part of a broader campaign to promote the educational rights of the disabled. In all these instances, although individual rights have and, indeed, must be violated, tort law also poses an opportunity for wider political engagement about social issues and concerns. In this sense it is a potential tool in the armoury of activist organizations and campaign groups.

Some people disapprove of the idea of using tort as a tool or instrument for bringing about social change. Tort law, it is argued is about correcting injustices arising from the breach of obligations owed to a particular party or parties; it is not concerned with ensuring a more just or equitable distribution of losses and gains in wider society. The integrity of tort law, as an end in itself, is violated it is argued, by such instrumental, outward-seeking applications. That said, there is little to stop such instrumental deployments of tort; life does not adhere to the scholar's order and the complaints of traditionalists merely evidence the inevitable fact that the aims, functions, and operation of tort have changed over time and context, reflected in corresponding changes in the basis, scope, and operation of civil liability. What is important is tort law's continued relevance, vitality, and adaptability in the context of a world very different from the one in which it was first fashioned.

JOANNE CONAGHAN

J Conaghan and W Mansell, *The Wrongs of Tort* (London: Pluto Press, 2nd edn, 1999)
P Cane, *The Anatomy of Tort Law* (Oxford: Hart Publishing, 1997)

See also: **civil liability, theories of; tort system**

tort system   Tort law is the repository of a wide range of actions protecting diverse interests which include (to varying degrees) personal and physical autonomy, private property, integrity and reputation, and protection from economic loss. Although framed in terms of individual interests, it may also be deployed strategically in pursuit of wider social goals—for example, protecting consumers or the environment—and, increasingly, is being so deployed.

When we speak of the tort *system*, however, we tend to think of **tort law** in a narrower sense, that is, in terms of its role, largely through the tort of negligence, in compensating the victims of accidents. Moreover, viewed as a system, we may consider tort alongside other systems for compensating accidents—eg insurance (public and/or private, liability and/or first party) and state-based schemes (accident compensation schemes, social insurance/social security provision, **criminal injuries compensation schemes**)—and consider the relative effectiveness of tort in this broader context.

The emergence of a perspective on tort law as a system of accident **compensation** can be traced back to the 1960s and is attributable to a number of factors. First, there developed growing public policy concern about the incidence and social impact of certain kinds of accidents, particularly road traffic, product, and work-related accidents. Secondly, there was increased recognition that, notwithstanding the purported aims of tort to *shift* loss onto blameworthy perpetrators, the effect of **liability insurance** was to *spread* losses much more widely. Then there was the thalidomide tragedy and its aftermath: in the early 1960s, a number of mothers were prescribed anti-sickness pills during pregnancy, which caused them to give birth to children with severe disabilities. The difficulties encountered by the thalidomide claimants in suing the company that had marketed the drug in Britain brought into sharp public relief the severe limitations of the tort system in relation to mass product-related injuries. Around the same time, New Zealand introduced a state-based accident compensation scheme, dispensing with tort law in the context of most personal injuries. The New Zealand scheme, which excited a lot of interest among academics worldwide, was a no-fault system, ie there was no need for accident victims to show that their injuries resulted from another's fault in order to qualify for compensation. This generated substantial debate about the relative merits of fault versus no-fault schemes, and, within tort theory, between fault and strict liability as the preferred basis of a legal claim for **damages**. Finally, the late 1960s also saw the emergence in British legal scholarship of the '**law in context movement**' which emphasized the study of law within its broader social context. Among the pioneers of this approach was Patrick Atiyah, whose path-breaking text, *Accidents, Compensation and the Law* (1970), was largely devoted to the analysis of tort law as a system of accident compensation.

Driven by these developments, the (then Conservative) government set up a **Royal Commission** in the early 1970s, reporting in 1978 (*The Report of the Royal Commission on Civil Liability and Compensation for Accident Compensation* (known as the 'Pearson Report')). The Report concluded that compensation for personal injury was best served via the promotion of a 'mixed system' in which tort, social insurance, and private insurance all played a part. Interpreting its brief narrowly (eg to exclude from its remit any consideration of the merits or demerits of a general no-fault accident scheme such as New Zealand's) the Report broadly endorsed a fault-based approach to tort liability, favouring an extension of strict liability in a limited number of areas, eg in relation to product defects and vaccine damage. In sum, the Pearson Report did not pave the way for any radical shift away from tort as a primary means of compensating accident victims. However it did endorse a view of tort as a 'system among systems', to be considered alongside and in conjunction with the operation of other systems concerned with the needs and entitlements of people with injuries and/or disabilities.

The actual significance of Pearson lies not its recommendations but in the huge quantity of data it generated about how the tort system operates in practice. This data continues to exercise a significant influence on contemporary analyses of tort law and, although supplemented by later, generally smaller, studies (the results of which did not substantially depart from the Pearson findings), has not been displaced as the most comprehensive source of empirical data about how the tort system operates.

Among the findings generated by Pearson and subsequent studies (including a study by the Oxford Centre for Socio-Legal Studies: D Harris et al, *Compensation and Support for Illness and Injury* (1984) and the Civil Justice Review, *Report of the Review Body on Civil Justice* (1988)) are the following:

- only about 6.5 per cent of accident victims receive anything from the tort system;
- most claims are settled or abandoned before trial; only a very small percentage—according to Pearson, 1 per cent—reach the court;
- claimants commonly encounter a range of problems bringing claims including rising costs, inadequate representation, and long delays, all of which encourage them to abandon or settle claims, often to their disadvantage;
- some kinds of accidents make better tort claims than others. For example, you are more likely to secure compensation for a road accident or an accident at work than for an injury inflicted at home. Moreover, some kinds of claims are, by their nature, dependent on the availability and accessibility of complex technical evidence (eg medical injuries and/or product-related harm). This can exacerbate problems of delay and costs. There is then a 'lottery' aspect to tort law's ability to compensate accident victims. If you're 'lucky' you'll get injured at work and not in your back garden; by a careless driver and not by a negligent doctor;
- notwithstanding a perception that tort claims result in huge damages awards, most tort settlements produce low damages awards and it is only in very few tort claims (about 1 per cent) that damages exceed £40,000 (this figure is adjusted upward from the Pearson figure of £10,000, to take account of inflation).

Although it is widely alleged that Britain is in the grip of a 'compensation culture' and that the number of claims and level of damages has gone up extensively since the 1970s, the empirical evidence does not really support this (see in particular Lewis, Morris and Oliphant (2006)). At the same time, the legal landscape has changed significantly since Pearson and many of the changes effected are in response to the kinds of concerns which Pearson and subsequent studies raised.

For example, **conditional fee arrangements** ('CFAs', ie 'no-win no fee' arrangements) are now the dominant means by which personal injuries are financed. Moreover, as a result of the Woolf Report on *Access to Justice* (1996), there has been a radical overhaul of the civil justice process focusing, *inter alia*, on reducing delays by introducing a fast track system. That said, tort as a system of accident compensation remains the subject of considerable criticism. For some, the argument is not against tort liability as a *general* approach to accident compensation but against its application in some contexts, for example, in relation to medical negligence where success is frequently hampered by the technicality of the evidence and difficulties with accessing it. This has led to calls over the years for the introduction of no-fault scheme in a medical context. Although this has not in fact occurred, the government did legislate in 2006, introducing by means of the NHS Redress Act, facilitating the settlement of low damages claims without the need to resort to court proceedings. This is not about moving away from fault however but rather about reducing the costs of litigation by encouraging dispute resolution outside the courtroom.

Some scholars subject the tort system to a more general indictment. For example, Patrick Atiyah in *The Damages Lottery* (1997) argues for the substitution of tort with a private first party insurance scheme in relation to personal injuries. Atiyah's argument here is in large part driven by a perceived need to counter the 'blame culture' which he views tort as encouraging. However, Conaghan and Mansell, in *The Wrongs of Tort* (1999), argue that a private insurance scheme will produce gaps in coverage weighted inevitably against the poor and that the socially just response to accident and injury must be state-based (ie social insurance).

Whatever the merits of these competing positions it remains the case that as a 'system' of accident compensation, tort is both deeply flawed and severely limited.   JOANNE CONAGHAN

P Cane, *Atiyah's Accidents, Compensation and the Law* (Cambridge: Cambridge University Press, 7th edn, 2006)

R Lewis, A Morris, and K Oliphant, 'Tort Personal Injury Claims Statistics: is there a Compensation Culture in the UK' (2006) 2 *Journal of Personal Injury Law* 87–104

See also: **civil liability, theories of; negligence in civil law; strict civil liability**

torture   Torture is a gross violation of the dignity of the **person** and its prohibition has a longstanding basis in national and **international law**. The prohibition against torture has gained widespread recognition in international law, both in general **human rights** treaties and in those designed specifically to prevent torture. It is an example of an absolute protection in human rights law and abhorrence of the practice is also reflected in criminal law. The Universal Declaration of Human Rights 1948, Article 5, makes clear that no one should be subjected to torture and this was confirmed in the **International Covenant on Civil and Political Rights** 1966, Article 7. In order to underline this message the **United Nations** has adopted the Convention against Torture and other Cruel, Inhuman, or Degrading Treatment or Punishment 1984. There is a monitoring body (UN Committee against Torture) which examines compliance with the Convention. An Optional Protocol to further strengthen the prohibition and prevention of torture was concluded in 2002, and is now in force. The UN has also created the post of Special Rapporteur on Torture.

These universal mechanisms are supplemented and enhanced by regional human rights systems, such as the **European Convention on Human Rights,** Article 3 (absolute and non-derogable), the European Convention for the Prevention of Torture and Inhuman or Degrading Treatment or Punishment 1987, and the Inter-American Convention to Prevent and Punish Torture 1985. The focus of the European system is primarily on prevention and the **European Court of Human Rights** has developed an extensive jurisprudence on Article 3. For example, the Convention provides absolute protection to an individual from return to another state where there substantial grounds to believe that there is a real risk that he or she will be tortured.

General human rights instruments, such as the Universal Declaration of Human Rights, do not define 'torture'. However, a definition of 'torture' can be found in the UN Convention against Torture 1984. For the purposes of that Convention it means:

'any act by which severe pain or suffering, whether physical or mental, is intentionally inflicted on a person for such purposes as obtaining from him or a third person information or a confession, punishing him for an act he or a third party has committed or is suspected of having committed, or intimidating or coercing him or a third person, or for any reason based on discrimination of any kind, when such pain or suffering is inflicted by or at the instigation of or with the consent or acquiescence of a public official or other person acting in an official capacity. It does not include pain or suffering arising only from, inherent in or incidental to lawful sanction.'

Approaches are evolving as, for example, the European Court of Human Rights has demonstrated in its recent case law (*Nevmerzhitsky v Ukraine* (2005); *Selmouni v France* (1999)). The principal objective of the law remains to ensure the effective prohibition and prevention of torture.   COLIN HARVEY

tourist visa   see visa

town and country planning   The modern system of town and country planning is entirely a creation of statute and the basic structure was laid down by the Town and Country Planning Act 1947. The principal Act is now the Town and Country Planning Act 1990 as amended ('the 1990 Act'). There are three other Acts which are linked to the 1990 Act. The Planning (Listed Buildings and Conservation Areas) Act 1990 created special controls over our **architectural heritage**. The Planning (Hazardous Substances) Act 1990 similarly imposed a special system of **regulation** over the keeping of hazardous substances. These Acts apply only to England and Wales and there are separate systems for Scotland and Northern Ireland.

The central feature is the definition of development contained in section 55 of the 1990 Act. Although unauthorized development is not in itself a criminal offence (unlike the position with listed building and hazardous substances controls), it is unlawful and can result in enforcement action which eventually could lead to a criminal **prosecution** for non-compliance. The definition is very wide in scope as it covers both physical operations (building, engineering, mining, and other operations) and material changes of use to land and buildings. It therefore gives the local planning authority ('LPA') through the powers to determine whether to grant planning permission or take enforcement action, the ability to control societal change. Moreover, while the **courts** have given guidance as to the meaning of development, they have laid down that whether or not development has taken place is primarily a question of fact and degree and is not a matter of law. So the decision in a particular case whether a change in an activity is or is not development depends on the judgment of the local planning authority (who in most cases is a local authority) or, where there is an appeal, on the judgment of a government official.

The wide scope of the definition is then in turn qualified by the 1990 Act making clear that certain operations and material changes of use are deemed not to be development. In addition, the government is given the power by way of subordinate **legislation** to specify certain broad classes of uses (the Use Classes Order) with the consequence that changes that keep within those classes do not require planning permission and also to grant permission for certain prescribed types of development (the General Permitted Development Order).

Otherwise an application for planning permission must be made to the relevant LPA: where there are two local authorities for an area, development control is shared between the two authorities depending on the nature of the development but most applications are determined by the district authority. Where the LPA decide to grant permission they also have a wide power to impose conditions as to how the development will be carried out. Reasons must be given for refusing permission and the applicant has right to appeal to the Secretary of State. On appeal there is a right to a hearing but in most cases the appeal is decided by a planning inspector by way of written representations. There is no right of appeal against a grant of planning permission, though a summary of the reasons for granting must now be given and the legality of the decision can be challenged by **judicial review**.

In determining the planning application or an appeal the decision-maker is required by section 70 of the 1990 Act to have regard to any material policies in the development plan and to any other material considerations. Material considerations have been very widely interpreted by the courts to include social and economic considerations as well as the impact on the environment. However the application must be decided in accordance with the policies in the development plan unless material considerations indicate otherwise thus giving a presumption in favour of those policies. The Planning and Compulsory Purchase Act 2004 significantly changed the system of development plans and the development plan is now defined as the Regional Spatial Strategy (prepared by the Regional Planning Boards) and the Local Development Plan Documents (prepared by the LPAs).

Enforcement is normally effected by the issue of an enforcement notice. There is a right of appeal against such a notice both on the grounds that planning permission should be granted and that the LPA have erred in the way they issued and drafted the notice. Failure to comply with the notice within the specified time is a criminal offence.

While the LPAs have the primary responsibility for the operation of the planning system, central government has wide powers to supervise the way this is done and to ensure that the LPAs do not act in way contrary to government policy. In particular, through the power to call in applications and to determine appeals, the government can ensure that its planning policies are followed.   MIKE PURDUE

trade and the environment As a legal issue, the relationship between environmental protection and international trade essentially concerns potential conflicts between rules of national and **international environmental law** and rules of economic law aimed at the liberalization of trade. Such conflicts arise when environmental law seeks to further environmental policy objectives through measures which either directly regulate or indirectly affect trade in products. While environmental law relies on product regulations as an increasingly important policy instrument, economic law tends to view such regulations as 'technical barriers to trade' which are to be removed as far as possible.

The clash between environmental and trade policies became the subject of worldwide political attention in the early 1990s, as a result of a dispute between Mexico and the United States under the General Agreement on Tariffs and Trade ('GATT'), the precursor to the **World Trade Organization** ('WTO'). In this dispute, a GATT panel declared unlawful under the rules of the Agreement a law which banned the import into the United States of tuna and tuna products from Mexico because Mexican tuna fishing operations resulted in a high level of incidental mortality of dolphins. In order to protect dolphins, the United States prescribed the use of particular fishing methods by its own tuna fishermen and prohibited the import of tuna from any country which did not apply fishing regulations affording a comparable level of protection to dolphins. However, this import ban was considered to be a 'quantitative restriction' on trade prohibited by the GATT. This ruling, which equated national environmental legislation with unlawful protectionism, effectively launched a 'trade-versus-environment' controversy, which became even more acute as the multilateral trading system, originally established through the GATT, was consolidated and further expanded by the creation of the WTO, with its strengthened mechanisms for the settlement of trade disputes.

The rules of the WTO multilateral trading system have trade liberalization as their overriding objective. Their rationale is to ensure the fullest possible liberalization of international trade by the gradual reduction and removal of tariff barriers and other national fiscal and regulatory measures which may impede market access for imported products. As a result of globalization, the range of domestic policies that fall within the scope of WTO principles and are open to challenge under the rules of the multilateral trading system is continuously expanding. Environmental product policies which rely on such instruments as binding technical standards, labelling, or tax incentives are increasingly subject to scrutiny for compliance with WTO rules. Governments contemplating the introduction of new environmental standards are commonly faced with pressure from their trading partners and industry, arguing that such rules violate WTO law by creating 'unnecessary' obstacles to international trade.

A more recent dispute brought before the WTO may serve to illustrate the extremes to which such pressure can go. The most basic requirement to be observed by WTO members in laying down their environmental regulations is that of non-discrimination against imported products, or 'national treatment', as the principle is known. Under this rule, imported products are to be treated as favourably as 'like products of national origin'. It was argued by Canada that a French decree banning the sale and use of products containing asbestos violated the national treatment principle because asbestos fibres should be given the same regulatory treatment as any other fibres marketed for the same uses and it was not legitimate to discriminate them on the basis of their toxicity. A panel first ruled that asbestos fibres and other fibres used for similar purposes were indeed to be treated as 'like products' regardless of the toxicity of asbestos, but this decision was eventually reversed by the WTO Appellate Body.

A national regulatory measure that contravenes a basic rule of the multilateral trading system, such as the national treatment principle or the prohibition of quantitative restrictions on trade, may nevertheless be justified under certain conditions. Derogations are explicitly allowed, *inter alia*, for measures which can be shown to be 'necessary to protect human, animal or plant life or health' or 'related to the conservation of exhaustible natural resources'. While a country can invoke these grounds in support of certain environmental measures, it still has to demonstrate they are not applied in a way which constitutes 'arbitrary or unjustifiable discrimination' or a 'disguised restriction on international trade'. Similarly, the WTO Agreement on Technical Barriers to Trade explicitly recognizes environmental protection as a 'legitimate objective' but at the same time provides that national regulations pursuing it 'shall not be more trade-restrictive than necessary'. Thus, while in principle international trade law accepts the legitimacy of national environmental regulations, it does place a rather onerous burden on governments to prove the necessity, proportionality, and non-discriminatory nature of such regulations when challenged by other WTO members.

MARC PALLEMAERTS

G van Calster, *International and EC Trade Law—The Environmental Challenge* (London: Cameron May, 2000)

J Wiers, *Trade and Environment in the EC and the WTO* (Groningen: Europa Law Publishing, 2002)

trade law and development International trade law broadly consists of the various laws related to trade that crosses borders between sovereign states. Such laws include domestic and international laws, public and private laws, and customary standards and norms, concerning such diverse topics as sales of goods, transportation, and insurance services, and investment transactions such as joint ventures.

However, consideration of international trade law in relation to development usually focuses on the public **international law** and international institutions of trade. The most important multilateral trade rules developed after the collapse of the world trading system during the Great Depression and World War II. The post-war trading regime was founded in 1947 on the General Agreement on Tariffs and Trade ('GATT') concerning trade in goods, and reached new significance with the Uruguay Round of negotiations that established the **World Trade Organization** ('WTO') in 1994 and that expanded the depth of **regulation**, scope of coverage (services, intellectual property, investment), and procedural foundations of the multilateral trade regime. Since 1947, membership has expanded to over 150 states, including many developing countries. A range of bilateral treaties and regional trade arrangements—such as the European Union and the Mercosur—add further trade rules beyond WTO commitments.

The international trade regime is centrally concerned with regulating the use of sovereign measures that impede international trade. Such measures include border measures such as tariffs (border taxes and duties) and quantitative restrictions (border quotas). They also include internal barriers such as domestic taxes, internal regulations, and governmental subsidies that impede full **competition** among foreign and domestic goods and services. International trade law now also includes some positive harmonization of domestic laws, such as laws of intellectual property protection. Trade agreements establish procedures for dispute settlement,

although the resolution of disputes also turns on political negotiation and voluntary compliance.

The focus on regulating sovereign measures that impede trade serves a number of underlying purposes for trading societies. Basic theories of international trade, including theories of absolute advantage associated with Adam Smith and theories of comparative advantage associated with David Ricardo, focus on the cooperative benefits that societies potentially gain through specialization and open trade. As individuals can mutually gain from specialization and consensual trade, so can societies mutually benefit through increases in total production and consumption possibilities that result from specialization and trade based on the different economic attributes of different societies. Efficiency can be further enhanced as societies take advantage of economies of scale and innovations generated by focus on particular industries. Such mutual gains explain why states should and do trade; they also explain why sovereign states consent to limit their **sovereignty** through an international law regime.

Economic and social development is advanced as a derivative of the process of trade. By focusing production in sectors in which it has a comparative advantage and trading to increase its total consumption possibilities, a society makes available more resources for development. This theory is subject to a number of critiques from a development perspective. For example, the focus on specialization according to comparative advantage is criticized for ignoring the desire for economic production in particular sectors with particular developmental benefits, such as modernization or worker training. Such specialization also ignores the desire to ensure development of sectors important to **national security**, considered narrowly (as in military industries) or more broadly (as in access to domestic food supplies), as well as concerns for diversification of economic production. It is further argued that compliance with international trade rules can be particularly detrimental to developing country social concerns; this has been sharply demonstrated in the controversy surrounding the effect of WTO requirements related to intellectual property protection on access to affordable medicines to deal with the **HIV/AIDS** pandemic.

Other critiques from a development perspective note that comparative advantage can be constructed by factors such as governmental policies. Infant industry critiques argue that many sectors cannot be developed without various forms of assistance, especially where later-developing societies must overcome a head-start advantage. Such perspectives suggest that selective use of trade barriers as well as other trade-distorting tools such as subsidies might be important to development, especially in developing countries.

The contested relation of trade to development is reflected in international trade law. Few developing countries were parties to the GATT in 1947, but developing country concerns increased as **decolonization** proceeded. In 1964, additional provisions for developing countries were added as Part IV of the GATT. The concerns for development and needs of developing countries are identified in the preamble to the WTO Agreement and other key Uruguay Round agreements. The multilateral regime includes some provisions for special and differential treatment of developing countries. For example, there is greater latitude for developing countries to use trade-restrictive measures to address balance of payments problems, and extended periods for the implementation by developing countries of certain obligations. However, almost all of these provisions are limited by, and are in tension with, an overall push towards equal obligations for all WTO member states.

Through exceptions and waivers to the WTO rules on non-discrimination, many developing countries benefit from preferential access to the markets of certain developed economies, through programmes such as the Generalized System of Preferences. However, such programmes remain at the discretion of granting states and can be tools for bilateral pressure, as well as divisive favouritism, by granting countries.

In spite of the provisions for differential treatment and the granting of preferential market access, it remains contested whether existing trade law adequately serves the needs of developing countries. The concerns of developing countries are a focus of the current round of WTO negotiations, the Doha Development Round. The success of this round is uncertain. As the international trade regime remains an inter-sovereign arrangement, the need to find agreement and cooperative gains among states with varied policy priorities limits the responsiveness of the trade regime to development concerns.

ROBERT WAI

See also: **law and development**

trade mark agent   Trade mark agents play a key role in promoting enterprise by advising businesses about the selection, registration, and enforcement of **trade mark** rights. They assist in the creation of new marks, audit marketing material to identify marks that have not yet been registered and, where the applicant markets various different products or services, ensure that all of them are covered by claiming protection in the appropriate classes. They perform searches to determine that use of a mark will not infringe any existing trade mark rights. They advise in which countries to seek registration; and, depending on whether the applicant wishes to trade only in its own country or additionally in various countries abroad, they file applications with the national registry (in the UK the Intellectual Property Office), European Community registry (Office for the Harmonization of the Internal Market) and international registries. They manage any objections from registries or opposition from other businesses to the registration of the mark.

Once registration is obtained, a trade mark agent may advise on portfolio management, including the maintenance of registrations in force, renewals of registration, transfers of ownership, licences, and technology transfer agreements. Trade mark agents may also help to resolve disputes over alleged trade mark infringements by advising whether the right has been infringed in the first place, negotiating with infringers with a view to preventing further infringement, and negotiating licensing agreements with infringers. Potential conflicts are frequently resolved by means that include letters of consent, co-existence agreements, or undertakings as to future activities. In the event of litigation, trade mark agents work in conjunction with solicitors and barristers.

GAIL EVANS

trade marks   As symbols of the goodwill or reputation attaching to the source and quality of a product, trade marks constitute a key marketing tool for business and consumers alike. Trade marks such as NOKIA and MOTOROLA are signs that guarantee to consumers the origin of goods by enabling them to distinguish the goods of one manufacturer from other identical or similar products provided by competitors. A trade mark is therefore defined as any sign capable of being represented graphically which is capable of distinguishing the goods or services of one undertaking from those of other undertakings. Given the breadth of this definition, a trade mark may comprise any sign or combination of signs, including words, numerals, logos, colours, and sounds, as well as shapes of products or packaging.

Registration of a trade mark grants the proprietor of the mark a statutory monopoly in the mark, which means the right to sue for infringement when another person uses the same or a confusingly similar mark relating to the same or similar goods or services to those covered by the registration. Distinctiveness, or the mark's capacity to act as an indicator of the origin of the goods or services, is an essential requirement for registration. Only those marks that are either distinctive or capable of acquiring distinctiveness are eligible for registration. It is this capacity to distinguish goods or services from a particular source that differentiates trade marks from other trade *indicia*, such as domain names and trade or company names. The most easily registrable marks are those that are inherently distinctive. Such marks are otherwise meaningless, consisting of fanciful or coined words such as KODAK for film or STARBUCKS for coffee. Likewise, words that are arbitrary or suggestive in relation to the products or services with which the mark is used, such as AMAZON for an online book store or GREYHOUND for a bus service, will readily acquire the necessary 'secondary meaning' as indicators of source.

Signs that are descriptive of the kind or quality of the goods or services will not be registrable without proof of that they have acquired, through use, the distinctiveness or 'secondary meaning' that enables consumers to identify the source of the product. In the interests of a competitive marketplace, signs that are generic or customary in the trade will be also declined for registration. Thus, the generic term CHAIR to sell chairs, or the word HAMBURGER, a term that other traders need to use in order to compete, will be refused registration unless they are part of an otherwise distinctive device. Similarly, qualitative or laudatory terms, such as WHOPPER in respect of hamburgers, are likely to give rise to objections. Finally, marks that are contrary to public policy or to accepted principles of morality, or marks that contains flags, armorial bearings, official hallmarks, and emblems of states and international organizations, are excluded from registration. References to geographical origin will be treated as primarily descriptive in the absence of proof of acquired distinctiveness. For example WATERFORD can be registered for crystal glassware: its geographical designation has gained a new significance so is no longer descriptive but identifies the trade origins of the product and thus has acquired secondary meaning. There is an exception to the rule about geographical references in respect of what are called collective marks—such as the logo mark NOTTINGHAM LACE that distinguishes goods produced by members of the British Lace Federation; and certification marks—such as DARJEELING, certifying that that tea contains at least 60 per cent tea originating in the Darjeeling region of India.

Once registered, a mark must be used in commerce within five years of the date of registration. Marks that have not been used in that period are subject to withdrawal and revocation from the register with a resultant loss of rights. Once the registration certificate issues, it is valid for ten years, then renewable for further periods of ten years indefinitely, provided the trade mark remains in use.

Although a trade mark can be protected by means of an action for **passing off**, the statutory system of registered trade marks makes protection easier since it provides presumptive evidence of the validity of the mark. Registration gives the trade mark owner the exclusive right to use the mark in relation to the particular class of goods or services for which it is registered. The registered owner of a UK mark or a CTM (Community Trade Mark) has the right to prevent unauthorized third parties from marketing identical or similar products under an identical or a confusingly similar mark. **Well-known marks** receive additional 'anti-dilution' protection against unauthorized uses of the mark that are detrimental to its distinctive character or reputation and which lessen the capacity of the mark to distinguish the relevant goods or services.

Because of the availability of both national and CTM registrations, rights may be enforced not only within the territory of each individual Member State (of the **European Union**) in which the trade mark is registered, but also on a European-wide basis. Remedies for infringement of a registered mark can include injunctions and seizure of infringing merchandise, as well as damages and occasionally, in the case of counterfeiting or wilful infringement on a commercial scale, imprisonment.

The law provides certain defences or exceptions to claims for trade mark infringement. Honest use of personal or trade names, even though that name is used in the course of trade, does not constitute an infringement. The condition of honest use is an expression of a duty to act 'fairly in the legitimate interests of the trade mark owner'. Similarly, descriptive use is also a good defence. Thus, in one case, use by the defendant on the label of a jar of spread of the words 'Robertson's Toffee Treat' was found not be an infringement of the plaintiff's mark TREAT. Finally, a trade mark owner is not entitled to prevent a person from using the mark for the purpose of informing the public that he carries out the repair and maintenance of goods covered by the trade mark and put on the market with the trade mark owner's consent.

GAIL EVANS

See also: **European harmonization of intellectual property rights; geographical indications; service marks; trade mark agent**

trade secrets   *see* **confidential information**

trade union members Trade union members have a number of legal rights against both the union to which they belong and their employer. Whether or not an applicant for **trade union** membership is qualified to become a member depends primarily on the union's rules. While some 'general' unions have eligibility rules which are very widely drawn so that most workers are qualified to belong, most unions restrict their membership to people who work in particular occupations, specified areas (eg Scotland), or for named employers. A union's right to expel or discipline members is also determined in the first place, by provisions in its rules. The courts have held that members can only be lawfully disciplined or expelled from membership after a hearing at which members have the right to be heard in their own defence and the decision-making body is independent in the sense of not party to any of the allegations that are made against the member. In addition, **legislation** enacted in 1993 gives applicants for membership and members the right not to be excluded or expelled from membership except on one of four permitted grounds. These enable a union to confine its membership to people who work for particular employers or in a particular area, to exclude individuals on grounds of their conduct (which cannot include the bare fact of membership of a political party), and to define eligibility for membership in terms of possessing specified skills, qualifications, or experience, or working in a particular industry, profession, or occupation. Union members have several other statutory rights relating to the way in which their union is governed. A union's principal executive committee and, subject to some qualifications general secretary and president, must be selected by elections which comply with statutory standards and are held at least every five years. The elections must be conducted by postal ballot in which all costs are borne by the union and supervised by an independent scrutineer. While union rules may provide for disciplinary action to be taken against members for activities in breach of specified standards, it is not lawful for unions to discipline members for a wide range of reasons relating to 'strike-breaking' or opposing union-organized industrial action.

Job applicants have the right not to be discriminated against because they are members of an independent trade union. The dismissal of an employee because he or she is a member is automatically unfair under the law of **unfair dismissal**. So too is dismissal for taking part in union activities outside working hours (or inside working hours where the employer has agreed to this), for making use of union services, or for not accepting any inducement by the employer to exercise any of these union membership rights. Equivalent protection and redress by way of **compensation** is provided to workers who are trade union members and subjected to any detriment short of dismissal by an employer on any of these grounds.

BOB SIMPSON

trades unions A trade union is an organization of working people formed for purposes which include the regulation of relations between workers of the same description as its members and their employers. The legal definition of a trade union has always been defined in these functional terms so that some organizations that would not necessarily think of themselves as trade unions, for example, professional associations, may nevertheless fall within it. In Britain, trade unions can formally establish their trade union status by applying to be entered in the list of trade unions which is maintained by the Certification Officer. Entry in the list of trade unions is voluntary. Listed trade unions can apply to the Certification Officer for a 'certificate of independence', the condition for which is that the union is neither under, nor liable to interference tending towards, the domination or control of an employer. Independent trade unions and their members have the benefit of a number of legal rights and protections which do not apply to non-independent unions.

The legal definition reflects the fact that the principal function of most trade unions is to negotiate with employers over the terms and conditions of employment of workgroups which include their members. In Britain, 'recognition' of trade unions by employers for the purposes of collective bargaining has traditionally been achieved on a voluntary basis in the sense that there has been no legal right or procedure through which a trade union has been able to secure bargaining rights. Legal procedures for resolving disputed claims by trade unions were in force for short periods in the 1970s and a new procedure enacted in 1999 and inserted into the Trade Union and Labour Relations (Consolidation) Act 1992 ('TULRCA') as Schedule A1 enables independent trade unions to refer disputed claims for recognition to the Central Arbitration Committee ('CAC') for resolution. Through this procedure trade unions may secure the right to be recognized by an employer of at least twenty-one workers, but only for the purposes of **collective bargaining** over pay, hours, and holidays. The procedure is detailed and prescriptive; in broad terms it enables an independent trade union to obtain an order that it should be recognized by an employer (where this cannot be agreed) either on the basis of having a majority of workers in the 'bargaining unit' in membership or after a ballot in which both a majority of those voting and at least 40 per cent of the workers in the bargaining unit have supported recognition.

Independent trade unions which are recognized by employers for the purposes of collective bargaining also have the benefit of a number of rights relating to the provision of information by employers and consultation in relation to the matters to which the information relates. These unions can appoint safety representatives who have rights to receive certain information concerning **health and safety in the workplace** and who can require an employer to establish a safety committee. Independent recognized unions must be informed and consulted in advance of workers being made redundant where the number of intended **redundancies** is at least twenty within a period of ninety days. A similar right for a recognized independent union to be informed applies where the employer's 'undertaking' is going to be transferred to another employer, and, where such a transfer will involve measures affecting the employees concerned, the recognized union must be consulted about these.

While trade unions are popularly associated with **strikes** and other industrial action such as overtime bans or working to rule, they do not have the benefit of any legally protected 'right to strike' that does not apply generally. Where a union calls on its members to take any form of industrial action, it will usually be committing a tort or civil wrong which is actionable by the employer of the workers concerned and possibly also by other affected parties such as that employer's customers. It will, however, usually have the benefit of statutory defences against some of these liabilities where two conditions are satisfied. The first is that the industrial action is being taken 'in contemplation or furtherance of a trade dispute' which is defined as a dispute between workers and their employer relating to one or more of a range of matters affecting these workers' employment. The second condition is that the union members who the union intends to call on to strike or take other action have voted in favour of this action in a ballot which satisfies stringent statutory criteria. Where workers take part in industrial action which is lawful in the sense that these two conditions are satisfied, if they are dismissed by their employer within the first twelve weeks of the action, and possibly after this time, they will have a **remedy** against their employer for **unfair dismissal**.　　　　BOB SIMPSON

See also: **consultation with workers**

trading standards The term 'trading standards' refers to a wide range of regulatory legislation (dealing with matters including **weights and measures** and **safety standards**) governing the conduct of businesses in their dealings with consumers and enforced by local authorities. In many parts of the country the term 'trading standards' is no longer used and has been displaced with 'consumer protection', 'fair trading', or 'regulatory services'. The core legal requirements on businesses relate to accuracy in the way that goods and services are described, and the avoidance of misleading price indications. So, for example, claims about the properties of goods—what they are made of, how they perform, where they were made, and so on—must be accurate. Rules relating to price indications extend beyond simply requiring that the shelf price correspond to the price charged at the till to include principles governing pricing claims in winter and summer sales. These rules are targeted at businesses which seek to persuade consumers that they are getting more of a bargain than is in fact the case (for example because the item was never sold at the higher price). Furthermore, there are some positive requirements relating to prices, for example the obligation to display unit prices for many food items.

Most of the trading standards rules are contained within criminal legislation. A key legislative instrument is the Trade Descriptions Act 1968 which makes it an offence to give a false trade description in respect of goods or services, and the related Consumer Protection Act 1987 (Part III) which creates offences in respect of pricing. Consequently, breach of the rules makes businesses subject to fines and/or imprisonment of key staff or directors of a company. In practice much of the enforcement activity involves attempts to educate businesses to comply with the rules and the use of warnings, with few prosecutions; and consequences of convictions in all but the most persistent or blatant wrongdoing are restricted to fines. The informal approach to enforcement is deemed effective in most cases, and is consistent with government's 'Enforcement Concordat', which promotes a staged approach to enforcement, on the assumption that most businesses want to comply with the rules and will do so when advised they are in breach.

Whereas most of the responsibility for enforcement of trading standards rules lies with local authorities, many businesses operate on a national basis. This is particularly true of the retail chains selling such products as groceries, electrical products, and clothes. It has long been recognized that inconsistencies and inefficiency in enforcement might result from numerous local authorities taking a retailer to task over claims made in marketing or in-store material which is widely distributed around the country. The issue is addressed through the Local Authorities Coordinators of Regulatory Services ('LACORS'), established in the 1970s. LACORS operates the 'home authority principle' under which the local authority within which the head office of a company is located takes lead responsibility for advising the company on compliance with trading standards legislation and for enforcement of the law. Other local authorities have a responsibility to report problems with a company to the home authority so that a coherent approach to enforcement can be taken.

At the time of writing the British government is in the process of implementing a European Community Directive on Unfair Commercial Practices (2005) which will require substantial reform of UK legislation.   COLIN SCOTT

traditional cultural expressions   see traditional knowledge

traditional knowledge   This is the term used to describe the intellectual creativity of indigenous peoples and traditional communities. Since the mid 1980s, when the **World Intellectual Property Organization ('WIPO')** and the United Nations Economic Scientific and Cultural Organization ('UNESCO') had convened a Group of Experts on the Protection of Expressions of Folklore by Intellectual Property, there has been a lively debate about the terminology which should be used to describe the creations of a cultural community. In 1985 the relevant expression adopted in the *WIPO/UNESCO Model Provisions for National Laws for the Protection of Folklore Against Illicit Exploitation and Other Prejudicial Actions* was 'folklore':

'Folklore (in the broader sense, traditional and popular folk culture) is a group-oriented and tradition-based creation of groups or individuals reflecting the expectations of the community as an adequate expression of its cultural and social identity; its standards are transmitted orally, by imitation or by other means. Its forms include, among others, language, literature, music, dance, games, mythology, rituals, customs, handicrafts, architecture and other arts.'

This terminological approach persisted until the conclusion of the World Forum on the Protection of Folklore, convened by WIPO and UNESCO in Phuket in April 1997. At the Forum, a number of speakers referred to the negative connotations and Eurocentric definition of the term 'folklore', which tended to focus on artistic, literary, and performing works, whereas in Africa, for example, it was much more broad; encompassing all aspects of cultural

heritage and including scientific knowledge. Exception was taken to the use of 'folklore' as being too narrowly defined and implying an inferiority of the cultural and intellectual property of indigenous peoples to the dominant culture.

The expression 'traditional knowledge' accommodates the concerns of those observers who criticize the narrowness of 'folklore'. However, it significantly changes the discourse. Folklore was typically discussed in **copyright**, or copyright-plus terms. Traditional knowledge is broad enough to embrace traditional knowledge of plants and animals in medical treatment and as food. In this circumstance the discourse would shift from the environs of copyright to those of **patents** law and biodiversity rights. This shift is, in part, an explanation of the suggestions for *sui generis* solutions to the protection of traditional knowledge, outside the established categories of intellectual property law.

In the debate about the protection of traditional knowledge, the implied beneficiaries of this protection are traditional peoples. Invariably, these are referred to as '**indigenous peoples**'. A definitional issue related to the delineation of the content of traditional knowledge, is defining the groups or communities who can assert property rights over this knowledge.

The definition which appears to enjoy widest support, is that of Dr Martinez Cobo who describes indigenous communities, peoples and nations as 'those which, having historical continuity with pre-invasion and pre-colonial societies that developed on their territories, consider themselves distinct from other sectors of the society now prevailing in those territories or parts of them'. However, it should be acknowledged that a number of representatives of these groups have asserted that the diversity of the world's indigenous peoples renders problematic an all-embracing definition and that efforts by the international community to develop a binding, all-inclusive definition are a diversion of energies.

Dr Erica-Martin Daes identifies four factors which provide practical definitional guidance: priority in time with respect to the occupation and use of a specific territory; the voluntary perpetuation of cultural distinctiveness, which may include the aspects of language, social organization, religion and spiritual values, modes of production, laws, and institutions; self-identification, as well as self-recognition by other groups; and an experience of subjugation, marginalization, dispossession, exclusion, or discrimination, whether or not these conditions persist.

A perceived corollary to an acceptable definition of the concept 'indigenous peoples' is the expectation that as peoples they will be able to avail themselves of the protections conferred by international instruments such as the **United Nations** Charter, which in Article 1 refers to 'the principle of equal rights and self determination of peoples' and the **International Covenant on Civil and Political Rights ('ICCPR')** and the **International Covenant on Economic, Social and Cultural Rights ('ICESCR')** which similarly refer to the 'right of all peoples to self-determination'. However, as General Assembly Resolution 1514 (XV) on the Granting of Independence to Colonial Countries and Peoples, subsequently provided, the rights of peoples are subordinated to the sovereignty of states. This statist interpretation of the rights of peoples has been a barrier to the recognition of various political and property rights, including intellectual property rights, of indigenous peoples and traditional communities.

Alan Jabbour suggested a taxonomy of four 'inchoate' concerns or anxieties which have led to international proposals for the protection of folklore. First, a concern for the authentication of folklore in the face of the economic, psychological, and cultural threat from alien sources. Secondly the expropriation, not only of physical objects, but also the documentary and photographic record of traditional societies. Thirdly, the issue of compensation for appropriation and cultural harm. Fourthly, the issue of nurture, or cultural health.

A particular contemporary impetus for the formulation of an international position on the protection of traditional knowledge has been the current debate concerning the review of Article 27.3(b) of the plant variety provision of the **World Trade Organization Agreement on Trade Related Aspects of Intellectual Property ('TRIPs')**. In the Doha Declaration issued by the WTO Trade Ministers in November 2001, the Council for TRIPs was requested 'to examine, *inter alia* . . . the protection of traditional knowledge and folklore, and other relevant new developments raised by Members' pursuant to the periodic reviews of the Agreement. The Doha negotiating agenda was reaffirmed by the Trade Ministers in the Hong Kong Ministerial in December 2005.

In 2000 WIPO established an Intergovernmental Committee on Intellectual Property and Genetic Resources, Traditional Knowledge and Folklore. It has mainly addressed the question of the application of traditional knowledge in the access to genetic resources and the way in which benefits from the exploitation of those resources might be shared with traditional communities. MICHAEL BLAKENEY

A Jabbour, 'Folklore Protection and National Patrimony: Developments and Dilemmas in the Legal protection of folklore' (1982) XVII, No.1 *Copyright Bulletin* 10

See also: **genetic resources, access to**

traineeship see vocational legal education

transfer of business When a business is sold, what happens to the employees? The old owner may well declare them redundant. **Common law** principles indicate that, as the new owner is not their employer, it can choose whether to offer them jobs or not. Yet, apart from the change of ownership, the business may continue much as before.

TUPE—the Transfer of Undertakings (Protection of Employment) Regulations—fundamentally overrides the common law. This UK legislation was first introduced in 1981, to comply with the European Community's Acquired Rights Directive. Its mainspring is the principle that: '[i]t is necessary for the protection of employees in the event of a change of employer . . . to ensure that their rights are safeguarded'.

TUPE has the effect that the employees do *not* lose their jobs merely because the business changes hands. Instead they are transferred, automatically, into the employment of the new owner; and it inherits them on the same pay and other terms as applied before the transfer (save in relation to occupational **pensions**, for which separate regulations make specific provision). If the new owner refuses to accept the employees, *it* will be regarded as having dismissed them, and will be liable to meet their outstanding claims.

The 1980s and 1990s saw the growth of outsourcing of public services, such as refuse collection and hospital cleaning. Case law soon confirmed that TUPE can apply to such transactions, whether the work is being tendered to an outside contractor, re-tendered, or brought back in-house. This is because TUPE applies whenever there is an identifiable 'economic entity' before the transaction, which 'retains it identity' afterwards. But that test is often easier to state than to apply; and a string of court decisions did little to reduce the uncertainty as to when a particular change of provider would amount to a TUPE transfer.

In 2006 new Regulations were introduced (replacing TUPE 1981) which seek to address that problem. TUPE 2006 applies if there is a transfer of 'an economic entity which retains its identity', but also to what is called a 'service provision change'. This concept directly covers situations involving a change of provider of a particular service to a given client. Where a particular team (whether in-house or employed by a contractor) has been responsible for that service, their employment will transfer from one provider to the next.

After job security, what the workforce usually most wants in a transfer situation is information. TUPE addresses that concern by requiring that worker representatives be consulted, in the run-up to the transfer, about what measures are envisaged that may affect the employees. TUPE 2006 also plugs a gap in TUPE 1981, by requiring the old employer to provide essential information about the transferring employees, and their terms and conditions, directly to the new employer.

So the concept of a 'TUPE transfer' applies not just to business sales, but to a range of transactions, thus ensuring that employment, and employees' rights, are preserved, notwithstanding changes in the identity of the employer.   SIMON AUERBACH

J McMullen, 'An Analysis of the Transfer of Undertakings (Protection of Employment) Regulations 2006' (2006) 35 *Industrial Law Journal* 113

transfer of land   In England, the **conveyancing** process has three stages. A prospective buyer, first, has an offer accepted, 'subject to contract'. Some time later, contracts are exchanged and the buyer and seller are legally bound to complete the transaction. Some time after that, the conveyance occurs, the money is paid, and the buyer is registered as the new owner of the property at the Land Registry.

The 'subject to contract' stage is a fraught period. Either side can withdraw from the contract without penalty: the agreement is binding in honour only. There are two reasons for this procedure. First, the seller gives no warranty as to the physical condition of the property, and so the buyer must commission a survey. Secondly, the transaction in question is very commonly part of a chain. It is vitally important that the contracts for all the transactions in the chain are entered into at the same time. Failure to do so can lead to a person being committed to buying one house, without having sold his or her own: a position which can be financially disastrous. Achieving the necessary synchronization can entail the elapse of a considerable period between the formation of the 'subject to contract' agreement and the formation of a binding contract. During that period, the seller may accept a higher offer for the house from another party, pulling out of the original 'subject to contract' agreement. The first prospective buyer is then left out of pocket, having had to pay, amongst other things, for an unnecessary survey. This practice is termed 'gazumping'.

The government sought to alleviate the position of the disappointed buyer by provisions in the Housing Act 2004. Since 14 December 2007 the seller is required to produce a Home Information Pack. It was originally intended that the information to be provided in the Pack would include a home condition report. This, it was thought, would obviate the need for the purchaser to commission a survey so that if gazumping did occur, the purchaser would not be out of pocket. However, as a result of opposition from institutional lenders, this idea was dropped and the seller is not required to provide a home condition report.'

Assuming that nothing untoward happens, the parties exchange identical contract documents, each signed by the other, and the contract is then formed. Neither side can then withdraw from the sale. After exchange of contracts, the buyer conducts various legal searches and, if all is in order, the transaction is completed and the buyer is registered as the new owner at the Land Registry. When provisions of the Land Registration Act 2002 are brought into force, all the current documentation will be replaced and it will be compulsory to effect the transaction online.

In Scotland, there is a significant difference from the English procedure. There is no 'subject to contract' stage. Interested parties submit sealed bids and the most attractive offer is accepted. At that stage a binding contract is created. This negates the problem of gazumping but has other problems, most notably the difficulty of synchronizing transactions.

MARK P THOMPSON

transfer of personal property   People transfer all manner of property to others by gift, sale, and even barter. Whatever the type of transaction, intended recipients will be keen to know whether they have become new owners. Other parties, too, may be interested. The right to use and enjoy the property, the right to dividends or rentals, the liability to tax, the application of laws of **succession,** and laws of insolvency, may all depend upon a proper assessment of the effectiveness of the transfer.

Effective transfers of personal property are not always straightforward. Much depends upon the type of property. Transfers of tangible goods, such as apples and cars, are the simplest. Legal rules define the steps that are necessary for each type of transfer. These steps differ depending upon whether the property is tangible or intangible (eg a bicycle or a billion dollar debt), legal or equitable (eg legal ownership of a car, or an equitable interest in corporate securities held on trust), and whether the transfer is by gift or sale. And still more rules determine whether unsuccessful attempted transfers according to the **common law** rules might nevertheless be effective in equity. At the end of all this analysis, a new owner can be told whether he or she has a legal or equitable interest in the property, or nothing.

The basic rule which underpins all forms of transfers—whether by gift, sale, bailment, or security—is that a person cannot give what is not his or hers to give. This is summed up in the Latin maxim *nemo dat quod non habet*—or *nemo dat* for short. This rule is subject to several significant commercial exceptions set out in statutes, but the basic rule remains crucial. Notwithstanding the *nemo dat* rule, business would come to a halt if it were not possible to enter into binding arrangements to buy and sell property that the seller does not yet own. These contracts are effective and enforceable, although clearly there can be no property transfer until the seller comes into the property.

In addition to the restrictions imposed by the *nemo dat* rule, other restrictions can make it impossible to deal with certain forms of property. For example, statutes may impose restrictions on dealings with currency, or with cultural or intellectual property. The general law, too, prohibits assignments that are deemed contrary to public policy. Slavery, for example, is outlawed. Finally, there are procedural hurdles. Parties who wish to transfer assets between themselves are often obliged by statute to implement the transfer in writing, or at least to evidence it (either before or after the event) in writing. These writing requirements are generally intended to reduce the incidence of fraud. Because they afford tangible proof of a transaction, neither party will find it easy to deny the arrangement and the resulting changes in ownership. These statutes typically ensure compliance with their demands for writing by providing that non-compliance will render the underlying transaction either void or unenforceable or both.   SARAH WORTHINGTON

See also: **equity as a system of law**

transfer pricing   *see* **international tax**

transferable skills   *see* **learning outcomes of legal education**

transgender   *see* **transsexuals**

transgression   Transgression is the act of violating a law, command, or moral principle. Etymologically, it was defined as the process of crossing over, of passing over, or beyond. In contemporary social and political theory, the concept of transgression is used in relation to the idea of boundary-crossing. Michel Foucault in 'A Preface to Transgression' linked transgression to sexuality and the death of God. Building on the work of Nietzsche and Bataille, Foucault argued that transgression has become the

site of profanation in a world without God as the sacred. Since limits are no longer imposed from God, transgression now opens the vast vista of the limit, with transgression and limit replacing the sacred and the profane. Sexuality has a particularly central role in this world, as 'perhaps the only source of division now possible in a world emptied of objects, beings and spaces to desecrate' (Foucault, at 9). Transgression and limits go hand in hand; there is no transgression without limits. 'The play of limits and transgression seems to be regulated by a simple obstinacy: transgression incessantly crosses and recrosses a line which closes up behind it in a wave of extremely short duration, and thus it is made to return once more right to the horizon of the uncrossable' (33–34). Foucault insisted that the relationship between transgression and limits remains complex and always uncertain.

The idea of transgression as boundary-crossing and its association with sexuality has played an important role in **queer theory** and pro-sex feminism. Crossing the established limits of gay/straight or male/female was seen as a political and normative project towards the displacement of heteronormativity and its **gender** roles. Transgression is, in this context, often associated with ideas of inverting regulatory regimes and displacing authenticity, such as Judith Butler's 'subversive repetition' or Jonathon Dollimore's 'transgressive reinscription'. Sexual practices, such as sado-masochism, butch femme, and drag, are valorized for their transgressive potential. Some theorists have criticized a simplistic affirmation of the transgressive, arguing that it is always possible for the dominant culture to recuperate these representations. Others defend its political potential, while acknowledging that the effect of transgression or subversion is incalculable. These ideas of transgression as sexual boundary-crossing have been used by some legal scholars in analyses of **sex** and sexuality, including debates around **pornography** and feminism, transexuality, and gay/queer **identity**.   BRENDA COSSMAN

M Foucault, 'A Preface to Transgression', in DF Bouchard (ed), *Language, Counter-Memory, Practice: Selected Essays and Interviews* (DF Bouchard and S Simon trans) (Ithaca: Cornell University Press, 1977)

J Dollimore, *Sexual Dissidence: Augustine to Wilde, Freud to Foucault* (Oxford: Clarendon Press, 1991)

transit passage   *see* **law of the sea**

transitional justice   Transitional justice refers to the different styles of **justice** that take shape in societies emerging from violent conflict or dramatic political transformation. Since the early 1990s, the term has increasingly dominated debates on the intersection between democratization, **human rights** protections, and state reconstruction after conflict. As well as its historical associations with the post-war **tribunals** in Nuremberg and Tokyo, and the democratization of previously authoritarian regimes in Latin America and the former Soviet Union, the term is now regularly deployed with regard to the Balkans, Rwanda, Sierra Leone, South Africa, East Timor, Northern Ireland, and elsewhere. It has recently been defined by the **United Nations** as:

'compris[ing] the full range of processes and mechanisms associated with a society's attempts to come to terms with a legacy of large-scale past abuses, in order to ensure accountability, serve justice and achieve reconciliation. These may include both judicial and non-judicial mechanisms, with differing levels of international involvement (or none at all) and individual prosecutions, reparations, truth-seeking, institutional reform, vetting and dismissals, or a combination thereof.'

A distinguishable transitional justice template has emerged which seeks to deal with the legacies of a violent past and assist in post-conflict justice reconstruction. That template may include prosecutorial mechanisms such as bespoke international tribunals such as those established to deal with the crimes committed in Yugoslavia and Rwanda and the permanent International Criminal Court which was established in 2002. It may involve hybrid tribunals (made up of both international and local legal actors) such as have been established in places like Sierra Leone, East Timor, and Cambodia or local trials designed to prosecute key former human rights abusers.

In addition, many societies emerging from conflict (sometimes with international assistance) have established:

- different processes of truth recovery (including truth commissions) designed to determine and formally record past abuses;
- reparations programmes for **victims** (including **compensation**, **restitution**, rehabilitation and symbolic reparation);
- programmes designed to assist former combatants return to civilian life including numerous Demobilization, Disarmament, and Reintegration ('DDR') initiatives as well as **amnesties** for offences committed during a previous conflict;
- programmes of institutional reform which in some instances have included lustration initiatives (removing from office those tainted by abuses committed under the former regime) and\

or recruitment, professionalization, and human rights training programmes for **judges**, lawyers, **police**, and other justice professionals;
- programmes designed to identify and meet the needs of particular grouping which have been affected by previous conflict on the basis of **gender**, age (eg '**child** soldiers'), or indigenous status;
- initiatives designed to promote **reconciliation** between former enemies, or indeed between former combatants and the civilian populations who they may have harmed;
- different forms of memorials, museums, and other means of commemoration which are designed to acknowledge the hurts of the past and preserve the memory of those who may have been killed, injured, or disappeared in the past conflict.

Given that the **rule of law** is often either absent or hugely distorted in many conflicts, the self-evident need to create or reshape a justice system based on human rights principles has perhaps inevitably left transitional justice with a fairly 'statecentric' focus to much of its theory and practice. However, in a number of transitional contexts, increasing innovative efforts have evolved (sometimes drawing from indigenous or tribal legal traditions) which are designed to meet needs which formal 'top-down' styles of state justice may struggle to meet. Thus **community**, civil society, church, and other grass-roots efforts at truth recovery, memorialization, victim assistance, localized reconciliation, and ex-combatant resettlement in places like Guatemala, Northern Ireland, Rwanda, East Timor, Colombia, Uganda, and elsewhere have received increased international prominence. While some such instances operate in partnership with state or international community run programmes, elsewhere, they are largely stand alone. Thus an increased focus upon 'transitional justice from below' is arguably emerging in the area.

In sum, transitional justice is now an established field for consideration of the organization or reorganization of justice delivery in the aftermath of violent conflict or profound political change. From historically exceptionalist origins, it is now a framework which is increasingly normalized, institutionalized, and mainstreamed.　KIERAN MCEVOY

R Teitel, *Transitional Justice* (Oxford: Oxford University Press, 2000)

K McEvoy, H Mika, and K McConnachie, *Reconstructing Transitional Justice: Transforming Cultures of Violence 'From Below'* (Cambridge: Cambridge University Press, 2008)

transnational civil litigation　Transnational civil litigation is civil litigation that has an aspect that is not local to a single country. Historically, transnational civil litigation was uncommon compared with civil litigation which was entirely local to one country ('domestic civil litigation'). The increased availability of international communication and transport and the globalization of trade and commerce mean that many individuals and corporations are now involved in transnational activities, and consequently in potentially litigious transnational disputes.

Transnational activities include relationships between individuals and corporations from different countries—for example, a Frenchman marries an Englishwoman. They encompass transactions between two countries, sometimes affecting property in another country—for examples, a Scot purchases a book from, or securities in, a company in the USA; or purchases a house in Spain. When such activities give rise to disputes (the marriage breaks down, the book is never delivered, the company is insolvent, the house is in a state of disrepair), those disputes may become litigious. This entry relates only to civil disputes—disputes involving matters of private, rather than public, law. Transnational civil litigation may arise in any area of private law, including contract, family law, torts, property, intellectual property, **succession,** and company law.

In each country transnational civil litigation is conducted following procedures similar to those which apply in domestic litigation. In transnational litigation, legal problems with no counterpart in domestic disputes may arise. Each country has its own legal rules to resolve these problems. These rules reflect international law norms of territorial sovereignty and respect for the authority of other countries. Individual consent plays a significant role in transnational civil litigation. The area of law which regulates transnational litigation is called 'the conflict of laws', or 'private international law' (as opposed to 'public international law' about which see the entry on **international law**).

The fundamental distinction between transnational and domestic litigation is that more than one country is affected by transnational disputes. Therefore, two or more countries may attempt to resolve the same dispute. To minimize inefficient and ineffective duplication in litigation of the same dispute in different countries, there have been various political efforts to coordinate transnational civil litigation. This has been particularly effective within the **European Union**. Other international agencies coordinate the negotiation of multilateral agreements regulating transnational litigation. This has been successful in family law and enforcement of

international arbitral awards. Countries also negotiate bilateral treaties to cooperate in transnational litigation. This has been effective in the recognition of foreign judgments.

In the absence of political cooperation, courts attempt in an *ad hoc* fashion to ensure the relatively effective and efficient resolution of transnational disputes through deference to the jurisdiction of the courts of other countries, the recognition of foreign judgments, and the application of foreign law (each is discussed below). This is attempted through specific rules, which are intended to achieve the fundamental objective of transnational civil litigation, which is to require a close and substantial connection between the subject of the litigation and the country in which litigation is conducted, or the country whose rules are applied to resolve the dispute. This *ad hoc* approach is not always effective, because the main criterion used to legitimize regulation generally is territorial sovereignty. The nature of transnational disputes is such that there are always at least two countries with a territorial connection to the dispute. Resolving two or more countries' competing claims to regulate is the enduring problem of private international law. It cannot be achieved solely by reference to territorial sovereignty, which requires a territorial connection but does not stipulate which of several territorial links should dominate. Three distinct legal issues arise in transnational civil litigation. The first is whether the courts of the legal system to which the claimant has applied are competent and appropriate to determine the dispute. That legal system is 'the forum'. These questions are resolved by the forum's 'rules of jurisdiction'. The second issue is the effect of a foreign judgment within the forum. This issue largely depends on whether the forum court recognizes the jurisdictional competency of the foreign court. The third issue is identifying the legal rule which the forum court applies to resolve the actual issue at the centre of a transnational dispute. This is determined according to the forum's 'choice of law' rules.

The rules of jurisdiction determine, first, whether the forum court is competent to hear the dispute, and (in **common law** countries) if so, whether it is appropriate for that court to hear it. Competency requires a connection between the dispute and the forum. In most civil cases, competency is governed by the EC Regulation on Jurisdiction and the Recognition and Enforcement of Judgments in Civil and Commercial Matters ('the Regulation'). The Regulation treats a court as competent in transnational litigation if the parties have agreed to litigate in that court and provided the litigation and the forum are connected in one of several specified ways, including that the litigation concerns property within the forum; or that activities related to the litigation (such as a breach of contract) occurred in the forum; or that the defendant has a personal connection to the forum. Similar rules apply in litigation which is not governed by the Regulation. A separate EC Regulation governs jurisdiction in family litigation within the EC.

In common law countries, courts may decline to exercise jurisdiction even if they are competent, if the courts of another country are more appropriate. This discretion is unavailable in civil law countries. The civilian influence is manifest in the Regulation in that courts cannot decline to exercise jurisdiction because another court is more appropriate. Jurisdiction can be declined under the Regulation only if proceedings have already been commenced in another forum which is competent according to the Regulation. If so, the second court must decline jurisdiction in favour of the jurisdiction of the first court. In cases where the Regulation does not apply, a court may decline jurisdiction if the courts of another country are more appropriate; and a court will usually defer to litigation which has already been commenced in another country.

Rules of jurisdiction attempt to achieve the fundamental objective of transnational litigation—that there should be a close connection between the litigation and the forum. These rules determine the preliminary procedural issue of where the litigation is conducted. Choice of law rules resolve the substantive dispute between the parties (see below).

The second issue specific to transnational litigation is the effect that is given to foreign judgments. In transnational disputes one party may obtain a judgment from the courts of one country, but will often have to attempt to enforce the judgment in the courts of another country in which the other party has assets ('the forum court'). The effect of the foreign judgment depends on whether the forum court recognizes the jurisdictional competency of the foreign court. The primary purpose of the Regulation is to facilitate the recognition of judgments within the EC. The scheme of the Regulation is to specify acceptable grounds of jurisdiction. If a court within the EC has exercised jurisdiction in a case in which it was competent under the Regulation, the judgment of that court can readily be enforced in courts of countries within the EC.

Judgments of courts outside the EC can often be enforced in the UK. The UK has reciprocal arrangements with countries that are not members of the EC, under which foreign judgments can be registered in and enforced through UK courts. If there is no bilateral arrangement in place, a foreign judgment may be recognized and enforced if the foreign court is recognized as jurisdictionally competent.

Transnational civil disputes, particularly commercial disputes, are sometimes resolved by arbitration rather than litigation. Foreign arbitral awards are readily enforced in the UK. The New York Convention on the Recognition and Enforcement of Foreign Arbitral Awards facilitates the enforcement of foreign arbitral awards. In many countries including the UK, this Convention enables the enforcement of arbitral awards made under an arbitration agreement to which the Convention applies, between individuals who are subject to the jurisdiction of countries which are parties to the Convention.

The third issue peculiar to transnational civil litigation is choice of law. This refers to the problem of choosing between the potentially applicable legal rules of two or more countries which, if the dispute were domestic to either of those countries, would be applied to resolve the controversy between the parties. Choice of law rules identify the country with which the dispute is most relevantly and closely connected, and apply that country's law to resolve the dispute. Specific choice of law rules apply in each area of private law—contract, tort, family law, etc. Within the EC, contract choice of law rules are stipulated by an EC Convention. It states that international contract disputes are resolved by applying the contract law of the country chosen by the parties. If the parties have not chosen a country, then the contract law of the country with the closest connection to the contract is applied. Transnational tort disputes are usually resolved by the law of the country in which the tortious act or omission occurred. In international family disputes, the forum court usually applies its own law.   MARY KEYES

transparency of securities trades Disclosure of information about issuers and **securities** (and the disclosure of information by investment firms about the products and advice offered by the firm) forms a central plank of financial market **regulation**. But disclosure rules also apply to the securities trading process in the form of transparency requirements designed to protect investors and the integrity of price formation. Trading transparency rules are a key element of trading market regulation and apply, in varying degrees, to most trading venues from **stock exchange**s to **alternative trading system**s to investment firms which 'internalize' investor orders against their own securities books (or proprietary trading books).

Transparency requirements concern price and volume-trading information, which is continuously produced by trading markets. They address when and how quickly this information is made available to investors. The underlying principle is that all similarly-situated investors should have fair access to trading information such that they can assess prices in advance and verify transactions after the trade has completed. Transparency rules therefore promote investor protection because they enable investors to monitor the direction of trading and the quality of execution (eg whether their trades are being executed at the best price in the market and the nature of the commission charged). They are also important in supporting fair markets, exposing market manipulation, enhancing information efficiency and price formation, and, in particular, in supporting 'best execution'. Transparency rules allow brokers to assess and compare pricing and, in fulfilment of the best-execution obligation, to achieve the best price possible for the investor under the particular circumstances.

There are two elements to transparency regulation: pre-trade transparency, which concerns bids and offers (or buy and sell prices); and post-trade transparency, which concerns the price and volume of completed transactions.

Regulation in this area is controversial because not all market participants will freely provide this information. The difficulty reflects the distinction between order and dealer markets. In an order market (part of the London Stock Exchange, for example, operates as an order market), all orders are channelled to a central point or system where they interact and match, and a price is formed. Trading information is made available as soon as the central trading system automatically matches the orders. In a dealer market (such as the US NASDAQ) trades are not formed by central interaction; rather, offers are made by particular investment firms or 'dealers' who stand ready to make trades. Bid and offer quotes to buy and sell, and information on completed transactions, are accordingly competitive and commercially sensitive. Transparency regulation must therefore reflect the particular risks and structures of different trading markets as well as accommodate the particular structures of alternative trading systems and 'internalizing' investment firms. The UK regime is based on the EU Markets in Financial Instruments Directive 2004, this aspect of which generated very considerable controversy. It applies a graduated transparency regime to stock exchanges, alternative trading systems, and internalizing firms, which, to varying degrees, takes into account the particular risks of lack of transparency in each venue.   NIAMH MOLONEY

See also: **disclosure in financial markets; financial regulation**

transportation   see **punishment, history of**

transsexual   Transsexual people have presented a profound problem to the law, ever since the first **gender** reassignment surgeries took place in the 1930s. From the late 1960s a sprinkling of cases concerning transsexual people and their legal status, along with the legality of performing '**sex** change' operations, went before the **courts** in several countries. In 1970, the 'April Ashley' case (*Corbett v Corbett* (1970)) came before the English Family Court. Lord Justice Ormrod created a medical 'test' to determine the legal status of April Ashley and, by extension, all transsexual people. He then determined that transsexual people could not contract a legal **marriage** in their new gender, and further could not consummate that marriage using a new vagina (and therefore, a phalloplasty). Consequently most transsexual people hid their previous histories and attempted to 'disappear' into their new gender.

However, the 1980s saw the growth of advice groups which in the UK in 1992, led to an effective political lobbying group, Press for Change (*www.pfc.org.uk*). Press for Change sought protection in employment and access to goods and services, family **recognition**, protection from public and private **violence**, as well as birth certificate change and the right to marry. Its working methods have since been copied by groups of transsexual people throughout the world.

In 1996, the first 'successful' case was that of *P v S and Cornwall County Council*. The **European Court of Justice** ('ECJ') held that Article 5(1) of the Equal Treatment Directive (76/207) prohibits the dismissal of a transsexual person who is 'intending to undergo, undergoing or who has undergone gender reassignment'. Subsequently, the Sex Discrimination (Gender Reassignment) Regulations 1999 ('SDGRR') came into force, amending the Sex Discrimination Act 1975. The SDGRR provided a series of exemptions where there was a 'Genuine Occupational Qualification'. Most fell at the first hurdle as employment **tribunals** found the regulations unworkable in practice. In 2004, in *A v Chief Constable of West Yorkshire Police & another*, the **House of Lords** finally concluded that transsexual people are to be regarded as members of their acquired gender for the purposes of employment and vocational training.

A series of **human rights** applications then went from the UK to the **European Court of Human Rights** ('ECtHR'). Most failed, including the case of *X, Y & Z v UK* (1997) which concerned the right of a transsexual man to be named the father of his partner's donor inseminated children. The case demonstrated that the law had a complex relationship with the transsexual **person**, and that previous analyses were framed far too narrowly.

Finally, in *Goodwin & I v UK Government* (2002), the ECtHR held that there had been violations of Article 8 (the right to **privacy** and **family life**) and Article 12 (the right to marry) of the **European Convention on Human Rights**. As a consequence, the Gender Recognition Act 2004 came into force on the 1 April 2005. The Act affords transsexual people the right to apply for a gender recognition certificate which brings a new birth certificate to those born in the UK and legal recognition in the acquired gender for all purposes including the consequent right to marry in their acquired gender, along with strict privacy rights. Genital surgery is not a pre-requisite for legal recognition, successfully opening up the possibility for transsexual people who have not yet had surgery, or transgender people, to apply for recognition.

Further cases at the ECJ and ECtHR have confirmed this case law. Because of EC Directive 2004/113, in December 2007, some protection in goods, services, and facilities will be afforded to transsexual people. It has also been suggested by Jack Straw, as Minister for Justice, that consideration will be given to protection against 'incitement to hatred on the grounds of gender **identity** or gender presentation'.

STEPHEN WHITTLE

treason trials   *see* **Casement, Sir Roger**

treason, sedition, and public order   Legislation in 1351 settled the law of treason. Passed in reaction to attempts to extend the **common law**, it defined the crime as compassing or imagining the death of the king, queen or heir to the throne; violating the king's wife, his eldest unmarried daughter or his heir's wife; levying war against the king in his realm; and killing the chancellor, treasurer, or justices while performing their office. Any doubtful cases were to be referred to Parliament. The Act entrenched the notion that allegiance was due to the person of the king, rather than to a broader concept of the '**crown**', and settled the notion—elaborated in the reign of Edward I—that any rebellion against the king constituted treason.

The law of treason was greatly extended by draconian statutes under Henry VIII in the 1530s. His Tudor successors reconfirmed the older statute as the

basis of the law, though each of them passed legislation to protect the monarch from political attacks. The seventeenth century saw broad interpretations of treason, to protect the state, in the parliamentary impeachments of Charles I's advisers Strafford (1641) and Laud (1644), and in his own trial by a special High Court of Justice (1649). The 1351 statute was again reaffirmed as the basis of treason law after the restoration, but a further Treason Act was needed in 1696 to provide procedural safeguards, including the right to counsel.

Despite the narrow formulation of 1351 Act, its reach was extended from the later Middle Ages to include 'constructive treasons', such as attempts to depose the king, or make him yield forcibly to demands. The notion of constructive treason was dealt a blow in 1794 by Thomas Erskine's successful defence of the leaders of the London Corresponding Society. Their acquittal was followed in 1797 by a Treasonable Practices Act, which aimed to restore a broader interpretation of treason. It was unused however and was replaced in 1848 by a Treason Felon Act, which made certain 'constructive treasons' (such as using force to induce the crown to change its measures) into felonies. The law of treason continued to be used into the twentieth century, being applied in 1946 to acts done outside the realm by an alien, William Joyce.

By the early nineteenth century, the law of seditious libel, seditious conspiracy, and unlawful assembly was increasingly used against perceived enemies of the state. The law of seditious libel had grown after the ending of press licensing, being developed particularly by Holt CJ. Lord **Mansfield**'s era saw much controversy over the roles of judge and jury in determining whether a publication was seditious. This dilemma was resolved in 1792, when Fox's Libel Act gave juries control of the question. In the early nineteenth century, prosecutions were increasingly brought for seditious conspiracies, aimed at bringing the government or constitution into hatred or contempt. As the century wore on, sedition became increasingly linked with the notion of disorder, with courts focusing attention on the likelihood that the words or actions would incite violence.

MICHAEL LOBBAN

JG Bellamy, *The Law of Treason in England in the later Middle Ages* (Cambridge: Cambridge University Press, 1970)

J Barrell, *Imagining the King's Death: Figurative Treason, Fantasies of Regicide 1793–1796* (Oxford: Oxford University Press, 2000)

treasure   *see* **antiquities and looting; coroners**

Treasury Her Majesty's Treasury, despite being one of the smallest government departments in terms of personnel, is one of the most significant, exercising immense influence and control over the workings of other departments. Its existence may be traced back to 1714 when the ancient office of the Lord High Treasurer was placed under Commission. Today the Board of Commission is composed of the Prime Minister, the First Lord of the Treasury, the Chancellor of the Exchequer, and the Junior Lords of the Treasury. Other ministers associated with the Treasury are the Paymaster General, responsible for taxation, and the Financial Secretary to the Treasury, whose responsibilities include procurement policy. The Treasury has two main roles. First, it is the primary regulator of government expenditure. This function is exercised through the Accounting Officer in individual departments and agencies. Guidance provided through regular updates of *Government Accounting 2000* is taken very seriously and normally followed by departments and agencies. The Treasury's other main role is to ensure 'sound and prudent financial management' in the running of the economy and the funding of the public sector, the latter accounting for nearly 40 per cent of GDP. The Treasury sets the inflation target for the Monetary Policy Committee of the **Bank of England**. It also commissions reports into the working of the economy and the challenges that face policymakers. *The Stern Review on the Economics of Climate Change* (2006) considered major economic challenges facing the UK and the world community. *The Eddington Transport Study* (2006), conducted jointly by the Treasury and Department for Transport, examined long-term links between transport and economic productivity.

JOHN MCELDOWNEY

See also: **departments of state**

treaties A treaty is an agreement under **international law**, usually between states but also between other subjects of international law, in particular, **international organizations**. There are no specific requirements of form, though the Vienna Convention on the Law of Treaties of 1969—the accepted statement of the law—says that a treaty should be in writing. Exchanges of notes may constitute a treaty and the name given to the document is not decisive. How parties conclude treaties is also left for them to agree. Treaties may be binding on signature or may provide for subsequent ratification. It is normal for multilateral treaties to require ratification or, for non-signatories, accession. In such cases signature does not mean becoming a party. Thus the United States signed the Treaty of Versailles (1919) but failed to ratify it.

Treaties address a vast range of topics, from bilateral interstate relations to the regulation of world political and economic order. Most subjects of international concern are now regulated by multilateral treaty and the number of multilateral treaties has increased correspondingly. The Consolidated Treaty Series contains some 466 multilateral treaties from 1864 to 1919; the League of Nations Treaty Series and the **United Nations** Treaty Series include 3,462 multilateral treaties in force. But in certain areas bilateral treaties continue to be significant: eg boundaries and boundary rivers, investment protection, visiting forces. Some fields are governed by a mixture of multilateral and bilateral treaties: eg diplomatic relations, extradition, air navigation. Sometimes the major instruments are regional, as with economic integration agreements (the treaties creating the **European Union**, the North American Free Trade Agreement, and so on). In the field of **human rights** much standard setting is done by universal agreements, but the most important implementing mechanisms are regional (Europe (1950), the Americas (1969), Africa (1981)).

Multilateral treaties often have a law-making purpose and are not just mutual bargains. Examples include the United Nations Convention on the Law of the Sea (1982) and the four Geneva Conventions on the Laws of War (1949). There are 194 states which are parties to the Geneva Conventions, making them effectively universal. In order to achieve as wide a participation as possible, international law allows states when becoming party to make reservations to non-essential provisions—the reservation must be 'compatible with the object and purpose of the treaty' as the International Court said in the *Genocide Convention* opinion (1951). But many problems have been caused by apparently inconsistent reservations, and the more recent tendency is to stipulate that no reservations are permitted. This is the case with the **Law of the Sea** Convention and the 1994 package of treaties establishing the **World Trade Organization** ('**WTO**'). To the extent that such treaties are accepted by all or virtually all states, they will have a genuinely legislative—even a constitutional—role.

Nonetheless, treaties are agreements and they are only binding on the parties, even if the parties happen to be all the states there currently are in the world. If a state is not party to a treaty—for example, the United States is not a party to the Statute of the **International Criminal Court** (1998)—it cannot be held to the provisions of the treaty as such. But formulations in a treaty may be so generally accepted that they become part of **customary international law**. This is possible with general normative treaties but practically excluded for organizational treaties such as the ICC Statute.

There is a common assumption that it is easy to terminate a treaty, and this is true if the parties agree. But unless there is a withdrawal clause (as with the Nuclear Non-Proliferation Treaty) unilateral termination is legally difficult. JAMES CRAWFORD

Treaty of Amsterdam *see* **European treaties**

Treaty of Maastricht *see* **European treaties**

Treaty of Nice *see* **European treaties**

Treaty of Rome *see* **European treaties**

Treaty of Union **Great Britain** was founded as a 'united Kingdom' by the Treaty of Union agreed in 1706 by Commissioners representing the separate kingdoms of England and Scotland. The 1707 Acts of Union of the Scottish Parliament and then subsequently of the English Parliament implemented the Treaty for each country. In each case, the Treaty was made conditional on respect for annexed legislation that preserved the existing church establishment, Presbyterian in Scotland, Anglican in England, to continue in all time coming notwithstanding the Union. This was a foundational treaty, but there has been controversy whether or not it had continuing effect as 'fundamental law'. The issue is important, for the Treaty contains guarantees concerning the law and the **courts** and the system of local government in Scotland as well as that concerning the **Church of Scotland**. Most have been substantially respected over three centuries, though not without occasional glaring breaches.

A full legal, as distinct from merely dynastic, union had not come about through King James VI's succession (as 'James I') to Elizabeth in England in 1603 as the King desired. But dynastic union was not good for the smaller partner. The King's (or Queen's) Scottish ministers were committed to the same policy line as the English ones regardless of parliamentary or popular opinion in Scotland. After the Restoration, royal attempts to impose episcopacy alienated large sections of the Scottish population in a way that had no parallel in England. The great Scottish colonial adventure in Darien (1698–1700) collapsed as much through English enmity as through Spanish, King William having no will to alienate English opinion for the sake of Scottish venture capitalists.

The death of the future Queen Anne's last son provoked a crisis. In 1701, the English Parliament passed the Act of Settlement entailing the Crown to Sophia Electress of Hanover and the heirs of her body being Protestants. The Scots, not consulted about this, passed the Act of Security whereby the next succession to the Scottish Crown would be independently decided by the Scottish Parliament. England responded with the Aliens' Act, and in 1705 Lord Godolphin marched a menacing army toward the Scottish Border. Thus were union negotiations triggered. The English price was full union with complete suppression of the Scottish Parliament and separate Scottish Crown. There was to be a full customs union and equal taxation throughout. Beyond that, Scottish distinctiveness might be guaranteed. The Scots sought guarantees of full access to English markets including the North American colonies and demanded recognition of the continuance of Kirk and Courts and their own laws in matters concerning 'private right'.

The Union proposal was at first hugely unpopular in Scotland, multitudes rioted and petitions were delivered to Parliament. Nevertheless the pro-Union parliamentary majority held the day against their somewhat diverse opponents, led by the deeply unreliable Duke of Hamilton. The first sitting of the Parliament of Great Britain took place on 1 May 1707. Union with Ireland occurred in 1801.

NEIL MACCORMICK

N MacCormick, *Questioning Sovereignty* (Oxford: Oxford University Press, 1999), ch 4

C R Munro, *Studies in Constitutional Law* (London: Butterworths, 2nd edn, 1999), 23–7, 137–42

trees and hedges Because patterns of development shape the landscape, many landscape features are in effect protected by the general system of planning laws. But agriculture and forestry have always been given generous exemptions in the planning legislation. Moreover, negative restrictions are not very suitable management tools for plant species. With afforestation, for example, the main regulatory tool is incentive payments, and a similar technique is used to protect a range of landscape features, including trees and hedges, through the positive conservation payments made to farmers. However, some traditional legal tools are used.

Local planning authorities must make adequate provision for trees when granting planning permission. (A 'tree' is anything ordinarily called a tree.) This can involve attaching conditions relating to trees to the permission or, on amenity grounds, imposing a tree preservation order ('TPO'). A form of 'general TPO' applies in conservation areas. Separate rules apply in effect to woodland trees, for which a felling licence from the Forestry Commission is required. TPOs cannot be made for hedgerows. The Hedgerows Regulations 1997, which do not apply to domestic hedges, give local councils powers to retain 'important' hedgerows. 'Importance' is determined, amongst other things, by verifiable indicators of species they contain. This objective approach stresses legal certainty but only covers around 20 per cent of hedgerows of historic importance.

Part VIII of the Anti-Social Behaviour Act 2003 allows local authorities to reduce high evergreen hedges to a reasonable height. These provisions tackle neighbour disputes rather than wider aesthetic concerns, since they apply when the reasonable enjoyment of a neighbour's property is affected.

DONALD MCGILLIVRAY

C Mynors, *The Law of Trees, Forests and Hedgerows* (London: Sweet & Maxwell, 2002)

trespass Trespass to land is the act of unauthorized and unjustifiable entry upon land in another's possession. (An equivalent concept of trespass to goods covers any unlawful interference with another's chattels.) Trespass to land is actionable regardless of the extent of the incursion and without any necessary showing of injury or damage to the claimant. In the generality of cases the act of trespass on another's land is merely a civil wrong for which the remedy is, at most, monetary compensation or, in flagrant or repeated instances, the grant of an **injunction**. For many centuries the **common law** has also recognized that reasonable force may be employed to repel an unwanted intruder, although the modern trend is to discourage this form of self-help remedy (not least because the definition of 'reasonable' force is open to dispute). In certain circumstances trespass may also constitute a criminal offence and, indeed, in a more security-conscious age the criminalization of trespass has been significantly extended by recent legislation.

Subject to certain express statutory exceptions the person in possession of land has, in most cases, an unchallengeable discretion to grant or withhold rights of entry. In particular, the concept of the home as one's 'castle and fortress' has long served as a pillar of constitutional liberty. Only extremely reluctantly does the law acknowledge any defence of necessity or just cause for unconsented entry upon private premises. In some jurisdictions, however, there is now a wider recognition of the citizen's right of non-consensual access to certain kinds of '**quasi-public land**' and to certain kinds of wild or uncultivated landscape for the purpose of open-air recreation.

KEVIN GRAY

See also: **chattels and fixtures; public rights of passage over land and water; rambling; rights to roam**

trespass, case and negligence The root of the modern **tort law** can be traced to the thirteenth century, when a single undifferentiated action for wrongs separated into the (criminal) appeal of felony and the (civil) action of trespass. Although the word 'trespass' simply meant 'wrong', the writ of trespass, which initiated cases in the royal courts, was restricted to wrongs done 'against the king's peace'—meaning within his jurisdiction—and 'with force and arms' (*vi et armis*). The notion of a forcible wrong gave conceptual shape to the action. It identified **trespass** with wrongful physical interferences with person or property, and distinguished it from breaches of contract or **defamation** for which other legal **remedies** were available. It also served to control the volume of litigation which came to the king's court. But the threshold of force needed was low: provided the plaintiff's case was consistent with some level of force having been used, the courts would entertain it. This meant that courts heard (for example) trespass actions where blacksmiths had killed horses or carriers had delivered damaged goods. Such cases were often contractual disputes, brought by parties lacking the formal **deed** necessary to commence an action of covenant.

It was soon evident that some cases, such as those where innkeepers lost customers' goods, could not plausibly be described as forcible wrongs. In others, a focus on the allegation of force was thought likely to mislead **juries** as to the real issue in dispute. By the mid-fourteenth century, pleaders therefore sometimes dropped the allegation of force. Within twenty years a new distinct writ of 'trespass on the case' had emerged, alongside the older action of trespass *vi et armis*. This flexible action, specially adaptable to any wrong alleged, may have arisen simply because courts accepted that the allegation of force was fictional and unnecessary. Equally, it may have reflected a change in policy brought about in the wake of the Black Death, to make it easier to enforce obligations. Whatever its origin, 'case' was the form under which the law of tort expanded most dramatically. In the sixteenth century, it began to displace older legal remedies whose modes of procedure and proof were less attractive to litigants. New actions on the case for **nuisance**, conversion, and defamation developed in this era. Another offshoot—*assumpsit*—grew to become the principal action for informal contracts.

Before the nineteenth century, tort liability, both in trespass and case, was for the most part strict, save in cases of misfeasance against professionals. In cases of trespass for injuries to person or property, defendants were liable if they had caused the plaintiff's loss. Only if the harm had been an inevitable accident would the defendant win. Similarly, in nuisance and conversion, the central question was whether the defendant had caused the loss. Since the plaintiff's right to unhindered enjoyment of his property was protected, questions of fault were not entertained. Nor was the defendant's intention the focus of attention in cases of defamation. But a change in the intellectual underpinnings of the law of tort can be traced from the late eighteenth century. Following the example of natural law thinkers, judges and jurists now began to put greater emphasis on the notion of fault. The change can also be traced in the growing road accident litigation. These cases presented courts with a technical dilemma. It was unclear whether litigants should use the action of trespass, which was the standard form for 'direct' harms, and which focused on whether the defendant had 'caused' the accident, or case, which was the standard form for 'consequential' harms, and which focused attention on the driver's neglect. By the 1830s judges solved the dilemma by concentrating on negligence as the principle underpinning liability for all accidents.

Negligence was defined in terms of fault, as the failure to act in a way which a reasonable, ordinary person would act, and to avoid foreseeable harms. Mid-nineteenth century courts defined specific situations in which a duty to take care arose, and in so doing sought to limit the scope of negligence. But in the era of the abolition of the forms of action, jurists began to search for a broader single duty underpinning the tort of negligence. Their approach was endorsed in 1932 in *Donoghue v Stevenson,* when Lord Atkin identified a general duty to take reasonable care to avoid acts or omissions which one could foresee as likely to injure one's neighbour. Despite the search for principle, the law of tort remained fragmented in the twentieth century, with its contours still shaped by its past. Large areas of strict liability remained, and in many areas, legal doctrine centred on protecting historically defined interests rather than preventing blameworthy conduct. Furthermore, the rise of insurance in the twentieth century put in question the focus on moral fault which lay behind many nineteenth-century developments.

MICHAEL LOBBAN

DJ Ibbetson, *A Historical Introduction to the Law of Obligations* (Oxford: Oxford University Press, 1999)
SFC Milsom, *Historical Foundations of the Common Law* (London: Butterworths, 2nd edn, 1981)

See also: **fault-based civil liability; negligence in civil law; strict civil liability**

trials, civil   *see* **civil trials**

trials, criminal   *see* **criminal trials**

tribunal procedure   **see natural justice; tribunals**

tribunals   Tribunals have been with us for centuries. The oldest extant tribunal is said to be the General Commissioners of Income Tax, whose underlying structure and powers date from the early 1800s. Tribunals in the UK come in many different forms and possess few if any universally common features. They deal with matters as disparate as **patents**, immigration, and parking appeals. But, whatever the differences in their form and operation, tribunals are essentially mechanisms for determining disputes either between two individuals or, more commonly, between an individual and the state. Thus tribunals have a role very similar to that of the **courts** but, significantly, they are distinct from the court structure.

Tribunals are commonly more accessible and less formal than courts and many have evolved in areas of specialized legislation dealing with the relationship between state and citizen in such fields as immigration, welfare benefits, and taxation. The first half of the twentieth century saw a significant growth in the number of tribunals. The liberal reforms of the first two decades established the foundations of the modern tribunals system, while the welfare reforms introduced by the post-war Labour government in the late 1940s brought with them the need to provide additional mechanisms for the resolution of disputes relating to claims for benefit. The implications of this proliferation of tribunals were considered by the Franks Committee which reported in 1957. The Franks Report *(Report of the Committee on Administrative Tribunals and Inquiries* (London: HMSO, 1957, Cmnd 218) is still commonly regarded as one of the most significant points in the modern development of tribunals. The Report was unambiguous in its view that tribunals were not 'appendages of Government', and confirmed that 'tribunals should properly be regarded as machinery provided by Parliament for adjudication rather than as part of the machinery of administration'. Reinforcing this model of tribunals as part of the machinery of adjudication the Franks Report identified the three basic characteristics of openness, fairness, and impartiality, against which tribunals continue to be judged.

As stated above most tribunals resemble courts in that they determine disputes between parties; but they are designed to be more accessible and less formal than courts. They tend to be established to deal with disputes arising out of the application of specialist programmes of entitlement or **regulation**, such as social security or immigration, where the relevant law is typically detailed and specialized. But this feature alone is insufficient to explain the choice of a tribunal rather than a court to deal with disputes. In some cases the additional factor might be the low monetary value of the sums involved, as in social security; while in others the need to involve expertise beyond the law may be significant, as in Mental Health Review Tribunals or Employment Tribunals. In yet other cases there may be a desire to insulate the courts from sensitive, high-volume work, as in asylum and immigration. Originally many tribunals followed the classic model of a three-person panel, only one member of which might be a lawyer. The other members would represent other relevant experience or expertise. More recently greater use is being made of single person tribunals but the three-person model, including non-lawyers, remains common.

Although tribunals are distinct from courts, they are seen as part of the judicial branch of government. This brings with it the need for 'ostensible independence', that is the obvious and apparent independence from government and, in particular, from the government department whose decisions are under scrutiny. Until recently tribunals tended to be administered by their 'parent' government department, but now increasingly they are being given institutional independence. Since April 2006 the larger tribunals concerned with the decisions of central government have been transferred from their old parent departments, such as the Department of Work and Pensions and the Department of Health, to become the responsibility of the Tribunals Service, an executive agency of the Ministry of Justice. A Bill was presented to Parliament in 2007 to provide a statutory base for these new arrangements by creating a simplified statutory framework for tribunals and a new post, the Senior President of Tribunals, the judicial leader of the tribunal system. It is envisaged that gradually all central government tribunals which operate in England, Wales, and Scotland and some which operate in England and Wales only, will be included within this framework.

In terms of their procedures tribunals are intended to be less formal and legalistic than courts. Most tribunals derive their basic procedural rules from statute supplemented by more detailed rules typically found in secondary, or **delegated legislation**. While the nature of the procedural requirements deriving from these sources vary across the different tribunals, they are distinct from the rules of procedure and evidence which apply to ordinary courts and are, in many respects, less formal. Unfortunately it is not possible to provide a general description of the way tribunals work in practice. The range is far too great. Nonetheless, most tribunals do strive to create a less formal environment than that which is common within a court. The nature of the accommodation, the presence of non-lawyers on the panel, and the forms of address and language used, all help to create a more relaxed atmosphere. But research has shown that informality is not always achieved. In a study published in 2006 tribunal users were interviewed immediately following their hearings. Those who had found the hearing more formal than expected were significantly less likely to have felt comfortable during the hearing, and among those who felt uncomfortable by far the most common factors mentioned related to feeling under pressure, nervous, or intimidated (H Genn, B Lever, and L Gray, *Tribunals for Diverse Users* (London: Department for Constitutional Affairs, 2006)). Much, it seems, depends on the skill of the tribunal chair and the quality and availability of advice.

The question of advice and representation is crucial. Although tribunals are designed to be informal and accessible, there is evidence to suggest that applicants can be at a severe disadvantage if they lack advice and representation. However, many tribunal applicants do not have sufficient funds to pay for legal representation or advice, and publicly-funded legal assistance is not generally available at tribunals, proceedings before the Mental Health Review Tribunal and the Asylum and Immigration Tribunal being the most significant exceptions. Many applicants therefore have to rely on other sources of general or specialist advice, where it is available, or they have to appear on their own. In light of this and in the knowledge that additional funds are unlikely to be made available, the government has been keen to encourage tribunals to develop procedures designed to help applicants present their own cases as effectively as possible.

Traditionally even though tribunal procedures may be less formal than those adopted by courts, they have reflected the adversarial model common within UK courts: an impartial decision-maker listens to argument presented by the two sides to the dispute and reaches a conclusion on the argument and evidence presented. This adversarial model is thought to disadvantage unrepresented and inexperienced parties. Thus, in recent years there have been calls for a so-called 'enabling' approach, that is one which supports parties in such a way as both to give them the confidence to participate in the proceedings and to reassure them that the tribunal will endeavour to compensate for any party's lack of knowledge. In the absence of affordable and expert advice and representation it is essential that ways be found to assist inexperienced applicants.

Although tribunals are distinct from courts, their procedures and decisions are subject to court oversight. The precise nature of this oversight varies, however. In some tribunal jurisdictions specialized appellate tribunals have been established, such as the Employment Appeal Tribunal. Where no special provisions exist an appeal on point of law will lie from the first tier tribunal to the courts. There is also the possibility of **judicial review**, the mechanism through which the senior courts review the legality of the decisions of other public authorities, including tribunals. The 2007 legislation mentioned above attempts to simplify these procedures and establishes a single Upper Tribunal to hear appeals on point of law from the first tier tribunals. Appeal from the Upper Tribunal will lie to the Court of Appeal or to the **Court of Session**.

Finally the Council on Tribunals, established following the Franks Report, has a duty to keep under review the constitution and working of the tribunals under its remit, which in practice includes all the major tribunals in England, Wales, and Scotland. It therefore performs an oversight role which under the new Bill will be extended beyond tribunals to include the whole administrative justice system.

GENEVRA RICHARDSON

truancy *see* **social exclusion and education**

trusteeship in international law *see* **mandates and trusteeship**

trusts The trust is a legal mechanism by which English law recognizes and enforces a separation between the legal ownership of property and the right to enjoy the benefits of that property. When a trust has been created, the trustee holds legal title to the property but the beneficial entitlement to the property rests in the hands of the trust's beneficiaries. Trusts were originally recognized only in courts of equity, and not by **common law courts**, with the consequence that the beneficiaries' entitlement to the property is an equitable interest, whereas the trustee's ownership (which always was recognized by common law courts) is a legal title. All courts now have jurisdiction to enforce trusts, but the nomenclature has remained to reflect the different nature of the interests held by the trustee and the beneficiaries respectively.

Trusts are ordinarily created by the trust's creator (the settlor) entrusting property to a trustee who expressly or impliedly undertakes to hold the trust property for the benefit of the beneficiaries in accordance with the terms of the trust instrument. The undertaking may be also given by the settlor without any transfer of property to a third party. In either case, the person giving the undertaking becomes bound by the terms of the trust and becomes a trustee. Once the trust has been constituted, the settlor no longer has any enforceable rights in respect of the trust property unless the settlor reserved such rights at the outset (eg by making himself or herself one of the beneficiaries of the trust, or by including a right to revoke the trust as one of the terms of the trust). The beneficial rights to the trust property reside thereafter with the beneficiaries and are inversely correlated with the trustee's powers and duties in respect of that property. The beneficiaries have a right to exclude others from enjoying the benefit of the trust property otherwise than in accordance with the terms of the trust and the trustee's powers and duties.

The trust beneficiaries each have an enforceable right to compel proper administration of the trust by the trustee in accordance with the terms of the trust and the trustee's powers and duties. Trustees are normally given powers (eg to invest trust property) in order to permit them to deal with the trust property for the benefit of the beneficiaries. At the same time, trustees owe numerous duties which control their conduct as trustees, notably duties to act prudently and to act loyally. Most of the trustee's powers and duties are default rules of law which can be modified by agreement at the outset when the terms of the trust are settled. They cannot, however, be modified so as to remove the trustee's irreducible core duty to perform the trust honestly and in good faith for the benefit of the beneficiaries—if that duty is removed then there is no real trust. Once the trust has been created, the trustee's obligation to comply with the terms of the trust can subsequently be avoided only if all the beneficiaries are of majority age and sound mind, and are willing to consent to the trustee's conduct, or if the court provides its consent to the conduct—such consent effectively constitutes a variation (to whatever degree necessary) of the terms of the trust.

The trustee is capable of being one of the beneficiaries, should the settlor so wish; but the trustee cannot be the sole beneficiary: in the absence of any separation between the holder of legal title and the holder of the right to benefit from the property, equity refused to recognize any trust as one cannot sensibly owe duties to oneself alone. As the beneficial entitlement to trust property resides with the trust beneficiaries, and merely legal title with the trustee, the trust property is not vulnerable in the event of the trustee's insolvency. The trust property does not form part of the trustee's beneficial patrimony and so is not available to pay his or her general creditors in **bankruptcy**.

Although trusts are ordinarily created intentionally, courts also recognize a trust where it would be against good conscience for the owner of property to deny to someone else the right to the benefit of that property. In such trusts, which are generally referred to as constructive trusts, the courts are effectively imposing the trustee's undertaking. However, as a consequence of the fact that the undertaking is imposed, such trustees do not necessarily possess all of the normal trustee's powers and duties.

MATTHEW CONAGLEN

See also: **equity as a system of law; uses and trusts, history of**

trusts, taxation of   *see* **taxation of trusts**

truth and reconciliation   Until quite recently, societies which wanted to make a break with an unjust and authoritarian past tended to adopt one of two models to mark that break and to usher in a better, democratic future. They looked to a retributive or criminal accountability model using international criminal tribunals (most famously the Nuremberg Tribunal), or domestic tribunals, or some combination of the two. Alternatively, they looked to a model which marks the break by a formal declaration of amnesia—the society puts the past behind it, most notably through an amnesty for the perpetrators of injustice. In the last decade or so, a new model, the 'truth and reconciliation' model, has become a popular alternative, in large part inspired by the experience of South Africa's Truth and Reconciliation Commission ('TRC').

The elites who negotiated South Africa's transition decided not to rely on criminal trials as the main mechanism for dealing with the past of **apartheid**. Instead, perpetrators of gross **human rights** violations who testified before the TRC received both criminal and civil amnesty if the amnesty panels of the TRC were satisfied that the perpetrator had fully disclosed his role and that the violation was committed in pursuit of a political purpose. One can view this decision as born of necessity—the old regime retained enough muscle to sabotage the transition and the new regime lacked the resources to mount successful prosecutions. In these circumstances, justice was unlikely to be achieved, so it was traded for the truth that emerged from the hearings at which victims of violations, or their relatives, testified as well as the hearings at which perpetrators sought amnesty.

Alternatively, there is the claim made by the TRC itself that truth was not traded for justice. Rather, the way the TRC went about finding out the truth achieved a kind of justice different from criminal justice, namely '**restorative justice**'. Restorative justice, it is claimed, has something of the virtue of retributive justice in that it holds perpetrators accountable for their actions; but also, at least in a transitional context, many advantages over retributive justice. It promotes a process of truth finding in which a fuller picture of the truth emerges than would in a series of criminal trials. The testimony of victims of gross abuses of human rights has a role that goes well beyond serving as an instrument to achieve conviction of wrongdoers; and amnesty seekers have an interest in making full disclosure, which in turn implicates others who therefore will come forward to seek amnesty. In this process, victims might find not only that they can come to terms with the abuses but also that they are 'restored' to a relationship of equality with the perpetrators, so that they develop a sense of personal agency appropriate for participation in a democratic society. Even more generally, it is said, the supporters of the old regime are forced through the confessions of the perpetrators to acknowledge its nature; while those who suffered under that regime but were not victims of gross human rights violations, can—through the re-telling of the experiences of those victims—also come to terms with the past and develop a sense of personal agency appropriate for a democratic future.

There are stronger and weaker versions of restorative justice. The weaker, more convincing versions accept that something important is lost when one foregoes retributive justice; but also that, depending on the context, the moral sacrifice involved is outweighed by the moral gains for a society in a transition towards, one hopes, a better future.

DAVID DYZENHAUS

See also: **Nuremberg trials; reconciliation**

***Tulk v Moxhay* (1848)**   In 1808 Tulk, who, with his father, was ground landlord of three sides of Leicester Square, sold its central garden to Elms, who covenanted to maintain it and admit the Tulks and their tenants on payment of a small fee. After various intermediate transfers, by the 1840s the garden was 'ruinous'. Moxhay then bought it for building, despite knowing of the covenant. At **common law** such covenants did not bind successors, the neighbourhood's character had changed since 1808, and, after making sure he would not be liable to Elms's successors, he thought himself safe. Nevertheless, Lord Chancellor Cottenham asserted equitable jurisdiction over covenants independently of common law and restrained Moxhay from building.

Cottenham's decision soon became a 'leading case', for confirming, rather than inspiring, an innovation. Draftsmen since the 1780s had included similar covenants in conveyances and urban subdivisions. Equity judges had reacted guardedly, but generally without disapproval. The Real Property Commissioners had blessed the device cautiously in 1832; Sugden, authoritative text-writer on land sales, forthrightly in 1839. Only Lord Chancellor Brougham had demurred, in 1834, condemning these private covenants for allowing idiosyncratic obstacles to a free market in land. Now Cottenham settled it: binding knowing purchasers to prior equities prevented them scheming to frustrate their predecessors' economic calculations and undermining obligations beneficial to covenantees. For about thirty years equity judges endorsed this essentially moral view. But from the 1880s *Tulk v Moxhay* was reinterpreted, reined back, and transmuted from application of equitable principle to progenitor of a new species of servitude: the restrictive covenant, cornerstone of private control of urban development.

The covenant was inadequate to preserve what remained of Leicester Square's garden. Within days of his victory Tulk died, and Moxhay soon followed. Moxhay's mortgagees sold the garden to James Wyld, whom Tulk's family licensed to erect there for ten years his 'Great Globe' (60 feet high, admission 1 shilling) in return for an option to purchase the freehold. On exercising the option the Tulks regained their full inheritance, the covenant therefore lapsed, and they themselves looked to build. In 1868 statutory intervention against them failed, the Exchequer Chamber ruling that since the garden had never been dedicated to the public the Metropolitan Board of Works could not compulsorily buy it, despite acquisition of this very site being the motivation for the statute. But, it transpired, Tulk's 1808 covenant was not the genesis of the duty to maintain the central area as a garden. Former rights of common over the area had mutated into residents' privileged access to the garden; then in 1788 the **Chancery Court** had cast the duty of maintaining the garden upon the Tulks, in the selfsame partition decree that awarded them their three sides of the Square. In 1873, at the suit of a tenant on the fourth side, Jessel MR construed that as a trust 'for ever afterwards'. Its speculative value thus removed, the ground was acquired for public use a year later.   STUART ANDERSON

FHW Sheppard (gen ed), *Survey of London*, vol. 34, 416–40 (1966)

SI George, 'Tulk v. Moxhay restored—to its historical context' (1990) 12 *Liverpool Law Review* 173–93

See also: **equity as a system of law**

U

UK Listing Authority   *see* listing

UK Supreme Court   *see* **Supreme Court (UK)**

Ulpian   Ulpian (Domitius Ulpianus) was born about 170 and died about 223 AD A leading lawyer and office-holder of the Severan dynasty (193–235) he was a proud citizen of Tyre in Syria and a Roman by birth. In his thirties he was drafting replies to petitioners on points of law (rescripts) for the emperors, Septimius Severus and Caracalla. He taught law, often in public debates on points of law (disputations). He gave legal advice to a number of magistrates (praetors). He was attuned to the cosmopolitan outlook of the age, which saw the extension in 212 of Roman citizenship to all free people in the empire, whatever their sex or ethnic background. His large-scale restatement of **Roman law** in the years 213–217 can be interpreted as a response to this extension, which enormously increased the range of **persons** subject, at least in theory, to Roman law. A protégé of Julia Mammaea, who belonged to the Syrian family of Septimius' second wife, he became the chief minister (praetorian prefect) of her son, the young emperor Alexander Severus, in 222 but was murdered by rebellious troops, probably in 223.

In writing about the law Ulpian embraced the point of view that law is the true philosophy. He was much concerned to emphasize the social and moral reasons that underlie and justify the rules of Roman law. Lawyers have an ethical, religious, and practical function. By the law of nature, all people are born free and equal. Even slaves have a degree of dignity, which can be enforced on their behalf by the action for injury (*actio iniuriarum*). Ulpian's works cover civil, criminal, and public law and include discussions of particular statutes and branches of the law, such as adultery or appeals. He writes clearly and in plain language, freely citing the opinion of other lawyers, and often asking what the legal position would be if the facts were slightly different. When discussing the facts of a given situation he is adept at finding legally defensible arguments, often based on equity or utility, for reaching the conclusion that seems fairest in the circumstances. His style of reasoning is similar to that to be found in the arguments of many modern lawyers. Indeed, he is the easiest of the ancient jurists for a modern lawyer to understand and appreciate.

Ulpian's historical importance stems from the fact that in his sixth-century Digest **Justinian** made more use of his work than that of any other author. Excerpts from Ulpian come to over 40 per cent of that work; the next most favoured author's contribution comes to 17 per cent. Moreover three-fifths of the 432 titles (chapters) in the compilation begin with a text of his. The Digest was a main source of law in European legal education, jurisprudence and practice until 1800, so that Ulpian is probably the lawyer who has most influenced the Western legal tradition over its long history. Moreover the influence has been broadly healthy, and has helped to prepare the ground for developments such as the elaboration of **human rights**.   TONY HONORÉ

unconscionability   *see* **contract law**

undertakings in competition law   The **competition** provisions of the EC Treaty and the UK equivalent law are directed exclusively at 'undertakings' (in the original French, the term used was 'entreprise'). The concept of 'undertaking' is not defined in any relevant legislation, and does not have a ready equivalent in domestic law, leaving it to the **European Commission** and to the European courts to define the term in practice. A standard definition, often employed by the **European Court of Justice**, is that 'the concept of undertaking encompasses every entity engaged in economic activity, regardless of the legal status of the entity and the way in which it is financed'. In essence, the term undertaking is employed so as to direct **competition law** to the activities of those engaged in commerce, taking into account the realities, rather than the formal structure of the way in which that commerce is organized. Thus, for example, different legal companies which are part of the same wider corporate body—eg subsidiary companies of a single parent—may be held to be part of the same 'undertaking', even though for the purposes of company law they would be seen as discrete entities. A natural person may be an undertaking where they are operating as an 'entity engaged in economic activity' (eg a recording artist); and a charity may also be an undertaking where it is engaged in economic activity (eg a fee-paying school registered as a charity).   MARK FURSE

undue influence   Undue influence is a form of wrongdoing which concentrates upon the manner in which the intention to enter a contract is produced. It arises in circumstances where there is some form of superiority which has induced the victim to enter a transaction which that person otherwise would not freely and knowingly enter. The law will not permit such a transaction to stand.

Courts have tended to divide undue influence into two categories: 'actual' and 'presumed'. Establishing actual undue influence requires proof that the wrongdoer actually exerted undue influence on the complainant to enter into the transaction. The person claiming to be wronged must prove that the other party had the capacity to exert influence, that influence was exercised and was undue, and that this brought about the transaction. In order to establish presumed undue influence there must be a pre-existing relationship of trust and confidence between the parties of such a nature that it is fair, in the light of the transaction, to require the alleged wrongdoer to prove that the other party entered into the transaction freely. Certain formal relationships (eg doctor and patient and solicitor and client) automatically give rise to the irrebuttable presumption that such a tie of trust and confidence exists. There is, however, no presumption that wrongdoing has occurred. For that to be inferred there needs to be something about the transaction which calls for explanation. If so, the onus shifts to the alleged wrongdoer to adduce evidence to show that there was nothing undue about the influence exerted.   LARA MCMURTRY

UNESCO World Heritage Centre   World Heritage is the branch of UNESCO which encourages the identification, preservation, and protection of natural and **cultural heritage**. Its mission focuses on encouraging nations to sign the Convention for the Protection of the World Cultural and Natural Heritage (1972), in order to aid and encourage parties to that Convention to maintain their heritage sites. The World Heritage Centre and the Convention employ broad conceptions of 'heritage'.

'Cultural' heritage consists of monuments (including monumental sculpture, works of art, and cave paintings), archaeological sites, sites that combine built and natural elements, and groups of buildings that are of 'outstanding universal value' from the point of view of history, art, or science (Article 1). 'Natural' heritage consists of geological features and formations which are of 'outstanding universal value' from the point of view of science, aesthetics, conservation, or beauty (Article 2). The World Heritage Centre's programmes include educational, political, archaeological, legal, and economic initiatives to share and protect heritage. Although each Party to the Convention nominates its own sites, the Centre develops and maintains the international World Heritage List. Importantly, this list includes heritage in danger of destruction. The Centre provides emergency assistance, long-term planning, and technical assistance to all sites on the World Heritage List. The effects of being included in the list are considerable, bringing the heritage under the Centre's umbrella of programmes and, ideally, generating national protection, increased tourism, and world attention that may stop the incidents of destruction (through political action, economic development, looting, or decay) that otherwise threaten heritage resources. The Centre functions as a key player in international and national discussions of heritage management. With its global sphere of influence and focus on preservation, the centre is a major resource for heritage protection and studies.   TATIANA FLESSAS

unfair commercial practices   'Commercial practice' is a broad term which encompasses the range of steps which any trader might take in order to promote goods or services to consumers, and to encourage them to purchase these. This includes **advertising** and other marketing activities, as well as sales promotions and prize competitions. Generally, such practices are not objectionable; but where a particular practice has the effect of impeding a consumer's free and informed choice with regard to the acquisition of goods or services, the practice may be regarded as unfair.

Following the adoption of the EU Directive on Unfair Commercial Practices ('UCPD'), an EU-wide prohibition against such practices is in effect from December 2007. Prior to the adoption of this Directive, there were very different approaches to the control of unfair commercial practices in operation in the EU Member States, many of which had adopted a general obligation to trade fairly. In the UK, the approach has traditionally been to adopt legislation dealing with specific commercial practices rather than a general framework of wider application, reflecting the reluctance to adopt so-called general clauses, which are more difficult to apply and therefore less certain in their scope. Examples include the legislation on trade descriptions, misleading advertising, and misleading pricing.

Following the implementation of the UCPD, the landscape of UK consumer protection law will change, with one piece of legislation taking the place of more than twenty. This is possible because the UCPD introduces a general prohibition against all unfair commercial practices. This is of much wider application than existing legislation aimed at particular practices. A commercial practice will be unfair if a trader does not exercise reasonable skill and care in dealing with consumers by failing to act honestly and openly, where this would cause an average consumer to decide to purchase (or not purchase) goods or services which he would not otherwise have chosen (or would otherwise have chosen). In establishing unfairness, the focus is on the impact of the commercial practice on the average consumer. This is a benchmark derived from EU law and sets an objective standard. It is not a fixed threshold and may vary depending on social, cultural, or linguistic factors; moreover, where a commercial practice is aimed at a particular sub-group of consumers (such as children or other vulnerable consumers), then the benchmark will be an average consumer in that sub-group.

This general prohibition is expressed in very broad terms, and on its own, would be difficult to apply in a given situation. That is why there are additional prohibitions against misleading and aggressive commercial practices. A practice can be misleading either by action or omission. Thus, providing false or misleading information in respect of matters such as the main characteristics of a product, price, or the need to have a particular part or replacement, is also regarded as unfair. More importantly, if significant information which an average consumer needs to make a properly informed decision is not given, or only provided in an unclear, unintelligible, or ambiguous manner, then this will be a misleading omission and also unfair. Although expressed in terms of a prohibition against misleading commercial practices, the practical impact is that a trader will have to comply with a detailed disclosure obligation.

The prohibition against aggressive commercial practices covers circumstances where harassment, coercion, or physical force are used which would cause the average consumer to take a decision he would not have taken otherwise.

Some practices are regarded as inherently unfair, and should consequently be prohibited outright. The UCPD outlaws more than thirty practices, ranging from false claims that a code of practice is being followed, to false claims that a product or price will only be available for a short time, to refusal to leave a consumer's home when asked to do so.

The framework introduced by the UCPD is not intended to create rights for individual consumers, and the Directive provides that it is to have no effect on individual contracts. However, an unfair commercial practice could, at the same time, amount to a misrepresentation or duress, which would enable an individual consumer to take action against a trader in contract law. Enforcement of the law based on the UCPD is likely to follow the approach adopted in respect of **enforcement orders**. In addition, the criminal law may be utilized to combat unfair commercial practices. Finally, codes of practice may be used to deal with unfair commercial practices in particular sectors.   CHRISTIAN TWIGG-FLESNER

G Howells, H Micklitz, and T Wilhelmsson, *European Fair Trading Law—The Unfair Commercial Practices Directive* (Aldershot: Ashgate, 2006)

See also: **codes of practice in consumer law**

unfair contract terms   Every contract is made up of individual terms, setting out the rights and obligations of the parties to the contract. The classical model of **contract law** assumes that the parties to the contract freely negotiate the terms of the contract. However, modern day contracting largely revolves around **standard form contracts**, particularly where contracts with consumers are concerned. Such standard forms will be put forward by one party, who is likely to be in a stronger position than the other party with regard to its economic ability or knowledge about the transaction. This creates the risk that the terms may be disadvantageous to the other party.

Although the traditional view is that parties are bound by the terms which they have accepted, modern contract law displays a greater willingness to intervene where terms are potentially unfair. Such intervention is made possible by legislation such as that dealing with **exclusion clauses**. However, although exclusion clauses are an obvious type of unfair term, other terms may also be unfair because, for instance, they impose significant duties on one party without there being any obvious benefit. In the consumer context, these terms can be challenged under the Unfair Terms in Consumer Contracts Regulations 1999 ('UTCCR'), implementing an EU Directive.

Terms in contracts between businesses are not open to the same degree of challenge, although the Unfair Contract Terms Act 1977 permits challenges to a limited range of terms, such as exclusion and limitation clauses, including those which the parties have negotiated. The different approaches towards consumer and business contracts are often justified on the basis that the respective bargaining strength of the parties in a business context is likely to be similar, whereas a consumer is assumed to be in a much weaker position. However, there is a growing recognition that a small business dealing with larger one may face similar difficulties. Proposals have been put forward to control terms in business contracts where one party is a small business, but these are not yet law.

Most terms in consumer contracts can be examined for their fairness, although some are excluded. Significantly, terms which were individually negotiated are not covered. If a consumer is in a position to influence what a particular term says, then, arguably, the consumer's position is not as weak as it would be if the contract were a standard form contract. The focus of the law is therefore on pre-drafted standard form contracts. This does leave room for argument as to when a term may be individually negotiated and therefore not open to review. Also, those terms which simply state what the contract is for, and at what price, cannot be reviewed for their fairness.

If a term is found to be unfair, it will have no effect. The test for unfairness is a broad one, and one that has caused some anxiety for English lawyers. It is necessary to show that a term does not comply with the requirement of good faith, and that its effect is to create an imbalance between the parties' respective rights and obligations under the contract which is detrimental for the consumer. The notion of 'good faith' is common to many continental jurisdictions, but one that is not generally found in English law. Its scope and function are uncertain, although it has now been established that it reflects a requirement of open and fair dealing. In essence, this means that terms should not be confusing, and those that impose a burden on a consumer should be clearly identified. Moreover, the business should not seek to take advantage of the consumer. The test is inherently flexible, and it will be some time before a sufficient body of case law is established that will provide greater clarity about this test. It needs to be borne in mind that determining whether a term is unfair requires consideration of the circumstances in which the contract was made, and the purpose of the contract. This can make it difficult to draw on court decisions regarding the unfairness of a term in the context of a different contract.

In order to facilitate the application of the unfairness test, an indicative list of terms which might be unfair is provided as part of the legislation. Whilst of some use for the courts dealing with individual cases, it has proven to be of greater use in another context. One of the hallmarks of the law on unfair terms in consumer contracts is that it is not limited to circumstances where an individual consumer complains about a particular term. Various public bodies and organizations dealing with consumer protection have the power to challenge terms which are used by traders. As such challenges will be to the standard forms used by a trader and will not be based on the circumstances in which a particular contract was concluded, the indicative list of terms provides the main yardstick by which the unfairness of a term can be established. The lead body in this regard is the **Office of Fair Trading**, which has secured changes to numerous standard form consumer contracts through educating and negotiating with businesses. Ultimately, it is possible to apply to court for an **injunction**, or an enforcement order, to force a business to stop using unfair terms, but it has not been necessary to use this power frequently. Also, if an individual consumer dispute is before a court, that court has the power to consider the unfairness of a particular term, even if the consumer has not raised this.

The UTCCR have introduced a requirement that all contract terms are expressed in plain and intelligible language. If a term is ambiguous, then the benefit of the doubt should be given to the consumer.

The law in this area is set to undergo changes in the near future, following reform proposals from both the **Law Commission** and the **European Commission**.

CHRISTIAN TWIGG-FLESNER

unfair dismissal   A statutory right to claim unfair dismissal was first introduced by a Conservative government in 1971 as part of a package of reforms aimed at curbing industrial action and raising productivity. Since then it has become a central plank of UK employment law, supplementing and indeed to a substantial extent displacing the previously meagre protection from dismissal offered by the **common law** action for wrongful dismissal. Currently enshrined in the Employment Rights Act 1996 ('ERA') and associated case law, the right not to be unfairly dismissed can (broadly) be reduced to a series of key questions:

- Does the person claiming unfair dismissal ('the claimant') qualify to bring a claim?
- Has the claimant been dismissed?
- What was the reason for the dismissal?

- In light of the reason for the dismissal and the manner in which it was carried out, was the dismissal fair or unfair?
- What is the claimant's remedy?

Does the claimant qualify to claim?

In general, only a claimant employed by the defendant employer for a continuous period of one year or more is qualified to bring a claim of unfair dismissal. Protection against unfair dismissal does not therefore extend to the self-employed, sometimes called 'independent contractors'. In exceptional cases involving automatically unfair dismissals (see below), the qualifying period may not apply.

Has there been a dismissal?

To pursue a claim of unfair dismissal the claimant must show they have been dismissed. Section 95 of the ERA describes a dismissal as occurring in the following situations: (i) the employee's **contract of employment** is terminated by the employer (whether with or without notice); or (ii) the employee is employed under a contract for a limited term and that term expires without being renewed; or (iii) the employee terminates the contract in response to conduct by the employer that amounts to a fundamental or very serious breach of contract (including a breach of the duty to maintain mutual trust and confidence); or (iv) the employee is under notice of dismissal when they announce their resignation and the resignation is to take effect before the end of the notice period.

What was the reason for the dismissal?

There are a number of reasons for dismissal which the law designates as 'automatically unfair', for example, dismissals relating to pregnancy and family leave reasons or dismissal on grounds of **trade union** membership and/or activities. If a claimant wishes to rely on one of these automatically unfair reasons, then the burden falls on him or her to allege and demonstrate it. Otherwise, to successfully defend a claim of unfair dismissal an employer must convince an employment **tribunal** that the reason for the dismissal was one of the 'potentially fair reasons' listed in section 98(1)(b) and (2) of the ERA, namely (i) lack of capability or qualifications; (ii) misconduct; (iii) redundancy; (iv) contravention of a statute (eg dismissing a lorry driver who has been banned from driving for multiple speeding offences); (v) 'some other substantial reason'(this is broad enough to capture a variety of miscellaneous factors and behaviours, eg pressure from a customer, clash of personalities, etc). If the employer cannot show

that the reason for the dismissal falls within one of these five categories, the dismissal will be unfair.

Was the dismissal fair?

Where the reason for the dismissal is potentially fair, an employment tribunal will go on to consider whether the dismissal was *actually* fair. The essential question is whether in the circumstances (including the size and administrative resources of the employer's business) the employer acted *reasonably* when it dismissed the employee (section 98(4) of the ERA). It is possible to divide this enquiry into two broad questions, both of which must be answered in the affirmative in order to prove a fair dismissal: did the decision to dismiss fall with the 'range of reasonable responses' an employer might make (*Iceland Frozen Foods v Jones* (1983)) and, was the process followed in relation to the dismissal fair?

Because there may be a range of reasonable responses, many dismissals may be found to be fair despite the fact that a sizeable proportion of employers would not have chosen to dismiss in those circumstances. The range of reasonable responses to a situation of, say, fighting at work, could be from an informal 'don't do that again', to a formal warning, to dismissal. At the same time, it is frequently the case that a dismissal for a reason within the range of reasonable responses is nonetheless found to be unfair for lack of a fair procedure. The courts have refused to prescribe a fair procedure, although the **House of Lords** in *Polkey v AE Dayton Services Ltd* (1988) declared that it would normally include, amongst other things, giving employees an opportunity to hear and respond to the allegations against them before a decision is made. Also, the dismissal will usually be unfair if the employer fails to follow its own disciplinary procedure, whether that procedure is contractually binding or not.

In 2004, the Labour government introduced a minimum dismissal procedure which employers are obliged to follow or the dismissal will be automatically unfair (Employment Act 2002, Schedule 2). The procedure involves three steps: (i) the employer must set out in writing the issues which have caused the employer to contemplate taking disciplinary action, and send a copy of this statement to the employee inviting him to attend a meeting; (ii) the meeting should take place before action (eg dismissal) is taken; (iii) after the meeting the employer should inform the employee of the decision and notify him of his right of appeal. If the employee wishes to appeal, a further meeting should be arranged at which the parties should attend, and after which the employee should be notified of the outcome. It is important to recognize that adherence to the statutory procedure does not mean the tribunal will find that the dismissal is fair. Compliance with the statutory procedure simply avoids a finding of automatic unfairness for non-compliance. The tribunal must still consider whether the dismissal was in all the circumstances reasonable. The statutory procedure was introduced as part of a package of measures to facilitate employment dispute resolution without resort to law. However, a review of employment dispute resolution carried out in 2006 and 2007 ('The Gibbons review') found that the statutory procedure was costly and cumbersome and recommended its repeal. At the time of writing (December 2007), this proposal has been the subject of a government consultation and further changes are anticipated.

What is the claimant's remedy?

If the employment tribunal finds that a dismissal was unfair, it will then consider what, if any, remedy should be awarded to the claimant. Here the tribunal has a choice of any of three **remedies** (which may be requested by the employee) reinstatement, reengagement, or **compensation**. The first two involve the employee returning to work in the same position and on the same terms and conditions (reinstatement) or doing comparable work on comparable terms and conditions (re-engagement). These two remedies are rarely awarded, in large part because they are infrequently asked for by the claimant. Compensation is the most frequently awarded remedy, and may take the form of a basic award (calculated by reference to the claimant's age and length of service) and a compensatory award. The basic award cannot exceed (from February 2007) £9,300. The compensatory award is an amount to compensate the claimant for the financial loss they have suffered as a result of the dismissal. Here, the level is capped at £60,600. The employment tribunal may reduce the amount of compensation if it considers that the claimant's behaviour contributed to dismissal.

Within labour law it has often been debated whether unfair dismissal law is best viewed as an employment protection measure, protecting employees from arbitrary and unfair treatment, or an unnecessary 'burden on business'. In practice, the 'burden' is not very great; average awards run low (compared, for example, to discrimination claims) and many workers do not qualify as employees and therefore fall outside the scope of protection. As much as anything, unfair dismissal serves as a management tool which encourages employers to manage their 'human resources' effectively and efficiently. That said, it still

constitutes part of a 'floor of rights' without which British workers would be vulnerable indeed.

DAVID HOOD

See also: **discipline in the workplace; mutual trust and confidence in employment law**

Uniform Commercial Code   The Uniform Commercial Code ('UC Code')—a statute governing a wide variety of commercial transactions in every US state save one—is a singular feature of American **federalism**, and its drafting represents an important chapter in the longstanding struggle over the role of law in American commerce.

Federalism first. As much by convention as by constitutional design, US commercial law—the regulation of contracts, **negotiable instruments**, etc—is the province of individual states rather than the national government. Most states adopted the English **common law** as the starting point for such regulation, but by the end of the nineteenth century they had taken that tradition in diverse directions, and some had supplanted the common law altogether in favor of statutory governance.

Tensions between the increasing regulatory cacophony and a rapidly integrating national economy spurred harmonization and modernization efforts, including an abortive attempt in the 1930s to secure national legislation from Congress pursuant to its power to regulate interstate commerce. The solution that eventually emerged was the UC Code, an omnibus commercial statute designed for adoption at the state level and drafted under the sponsorship of two **non-governmental organizations**—the National Conference of Commissioners on Uniform State Laws ('NCCUSL'), whose membership comprises representatives appointed by each US state and territory, and the **American Law Institute** ('ALI'), a prestigious society of legal professionals. A protracted drafting process—more about which in a moment—finally bore fruit in 1958, and within a decade the UC Code had been enacted in every American jurisdiction except Louisiana, which adheres to a version of the French civil code. A permanent NCCUSL/ALI editorial board proposes occasional revisions in response to commercial and legal developments; the rise of the information economy, for example, prompted the drafting of new legislation governing transactions involving 'computer information' (software, databases, etc) and the modification of existing provisions to accommodate electronic contracting.

The protracted drafting of the original text was largely the product of deep divisions among American legal professionals over the proper functions of commercial law. The project's Chief Reporter was Karl Llewellyn, a leading exponent of American **legal realism**, and the early drafts he developed with other prominent legal academics bore a strong Realist imprint. Thus, many of their proposals were designed to eradicate the extreme **formalism** of existing law by eliminating common law 'technicalities' at odds with standard commercial practices. Other provisions were forthrightly regulatory, intended to level the commercial playing field by reducing advantages born of superior bargaining power and/or clever contracting.

As the drafting process continued, lawyers representing commercial interests embraced much of the technicality-eliminating agenda but saw to it that most of the regulatory proposals wound up on the cutting room floor. Some of the most controversial among the latter—including an innovative provision authorizing **product liability** suits by consumers against manufacturers—eventually found life elsewhere in American law, but resurgent formalist and anti-regulatory impulses ensure that the struggle over the UC Code's chastened Realist legacy continues to this day.   RICHARD MICHAEL FISCHL

AR Kamp, 'Downtown Code: A History of the Uniform Commercial Code 1949–1954' (2001) 49 *Buffalo Law Review* 359

ZB Wiseman, 'The Limits of Vision: Karl Llewellyn and the Merchant Rules' (1987) 100 *Harvard Law Review* 465

unincorporated associations   An unincorporated association is a group of individuals who voluntarily enter into an agreement to form a body or organization for a particular purpose. They are defined by their lack of corporate status and, therefore, separate legal personality. Unlike corporate bodies, which can sue and be sued in their own names and enter into contracts, unincorporated associations have no rights or duties separate from those of their individual members. In *Conservative and Unionist Central Office v Burrell* (1982), they were defined as existing where 'two or more persons are bound together for common purposes by mutual undertakings, each having mutual duties and obligations, in an organisation which has rules identifying in whom control of the organisation and its funds is vested, and which can be joined or left at will . . . .'.

Unincorporated associations are created for a wide range of purposes, some aimed at profit-making, some not. Unincorporated business associations are usually called **partnerships**. Unincorporated non-profit associations encompass everything from clubs and societies to small **charities**, community organizations, self-help groups, and campaigning organizations. It follows from this diversity of purpose that unincorporated associations vary greatly in nature, size, and structure. At one end of the scale they might be substantial associations with property, employees, and contractual obligations; at the other end, they might be small, informal, and temporary groupings of people brought together briefly for a very specific purpose.

The advantages of the unincorporated association are to be found in its flexibility, potential simplicity of formation and running, its independence, and freedom of action. The main disadvantages lie in its lack of separate legal personality, which creates a number of legal difficulties. It is often, for example, difficult to determine the precise legal basis upon which the association holds assets: property usually has to be held by the members jointly or by trustees. In the case of unincorporated business associations, such as partnerships, and charities, the lack of **limited liability** can also be a problem as it means that the members are personally liable if the association is sued or incurs liabilities.

The seemingly simple legal distinction between incorporated bodies and unincorporated associations is, however, greatly complicated by the fact that although unincorporated associations formally lack separate legal personality, some of them—partnerships and **trades unions** for example—are nevertheless in certain respects and for some purposes, treated by law as effectively separate entities. The law sometimes veers between an aggregate and an entity theory of the unincorporated association. Under the aggregate theory, the members of the association are considered not as merged into a composite unit but as so many individuals who acquire joint rights and incur joint obligations; under the entity theory, the members are considered to be merged into a composite unit which has a continuing identity and which acquires rights and obligations of its own. Different bodies of rules have been developed for application to different sorts of unincorporated associations. Some of these in effect permit corporate advantages to be obtained without incorporation.

PADDY IRELAND

EH Warren, *Corporate Advantages without Incorporation* (New York: Baker, Voorhis & Co, 1929)

SJ Stoljar, *Groups and Entities* (Canberra: ANU Press, 1973)

See also: **corporate personality; person**

unit trusts   *see* **collective investment schemes**

United Kingdom   The United Kingdom of Great Britain and Northern Ireland is the official name of the state sometimes known as **Great Britain** or Britain. The United Kingdom is an unusual state in that it is comprised of three separate legal systems, England and Wales, Scotland, and Northern Ireland. This reflects the history of relationships amongst these entities. When the United Kingdom came into being in 1801, it was not a traditional unitary state. While a head of state, government, and Parliament were all shared, when the new United Kingdom Parliament legislated for this new state it was not making United Kingdom or British law, but rather making common provisions which would apply in all of the three legal systems. This continues under the devolution arrangements which have been in place since 1999. There is no separate system of federal law in respect of those powers which have not been devolved from the **Westminster Parliament** to the **Scottish Parliament,** the **Welsh Assembly,** and the **Northern Ireland Assembly**.

The United Kingdom has no codified constitution. Its constitutional arrangements are derived from a range of sources including legislation (eg the Scotland Act 1998, the European Communities Act 1972, the Human Rights Act 1998), court decisions (eg *R (Jackson) v Attorney-General* (2006) dealing with the scope of **parliamentary sovereignty**), **conventions of the constitution** (non-legal rules and customs regulating matters such as **ministerial responsibility**), and the **royal prerogative,** which is the basis of powers such as the giving of the royal assent to legislation.   BRIAN THOMPSON

United Nations   The United Nations ('UN') was founded in 1945 after representatives of fifty states participated in the San Francisco UN Conference on International Organization, which adopted the UN Charter signed on 26 June 1945. The founding of the organization was inspired by the initiative of US President Roosevelt who had gathered support through the 'Declaration on United Nations' in the war against the Axis Powers. The UN Charter entered into force on 24 October 1945 after ratification by all permanent members of the Security Council ('SC') and the majority of other states.

Today the UN is arguably the most important international organization and is unique in several ways. The UN was established to address general political and other relations between states and has now reached close to universal membership—nearly all states are members of the UN. Membership is open to all peace-loving states which accept the obligations of the Charter and, in the view of the UN, are willing and able to carry out these obligations. Admission depends on a positive recommendation by the General Assembly and the Security Council.

For a long time, Switzerland was not a member of the UN because of its experience with the League of Nations, which was seen as ineffective in preventing World War II, and because membership was thought incompatible with its strict neutrality. Switzerland joined the UN in 2002.

In the early *Reparations for Injury* advisory opinion the **International Court of Justice** ('ICJ') held that the UN had international legal personality and did not merely represent its member states. It could therefore claim reparations for injury caused to one of its staff even from states that were not members of the organization. Legal uncertainty remains as to the exact rules applicable to **treaties** concluded by the UN itself and the responsibility that the UN can incur. Because of its special character, its important role in international law-making and its near-universal membership, the UN has been described as the nucleus of an international constitutional order.

The UN's main goal is to secure peace and security in the world. Its main purpose is to save future generations from the scourge of war, ensure fundamental **human rights,** and promote **justice,** the **rule of law,** and social progress in the world. The UN recognizes that international cooperation is the principal way to achieve these ends.

The UN was created as a successor to the League of Nations, but the UN Charter included important provisions aimed at avoiding what were perceived as the main reasons for the failure of the League. For example the five victorious states of World War II were given permanent seats on the Security Council and veto power.

The organizational structure is simple. The principle organs are: the General Assembly, The Security Council, the Economic and Social Council ('ECOSOC'), the ICJ and the Secretariat.

The General Assembly ('GA') is comprised of all members of the UN, who are usually represented by their Ambassadors to the UN in New York. (Heads of State or Foreign Ministers can also choose to represent their countries in the GA and it has become common for Heads of State to open each new session of the GA.) The GA meets in regular annual sessions (usually taking place from October to December) and special sessions. Every UN member has one vote and decisions are usually taken by majority. Decisions on important issues, such as recommendations for the maintenance of peace, election of non-permanent SC members, and the admission of new members or expulsion, have to be taken by two-thirds majority. The legal value of UN GA Resolutions is disputed. In the past, several GA Resolutions have had an important impact on the development of international law, such as the Friendly Relations Declaration. Some see GA Resolutions as a new form of **international law** because many receive overwhelming support from a large number of states; but most consider them to be **soft law**. However, GA Resolutions are not without legal value. The important element of *opinio juris* can accumulate around GA Resolutions, because the resolution constitutes either the expression of an opinion by individual states or an expression of the law itself, especially if it concerns customary rules about what states should refrain from doing.

The SC is, in legal and political terms, the highest organ of the organization. It has the power to take decisions which are binding upon all members, and as such it has been argued that it contributes to the creation of international law. Its main purpose is to maintain peace and security. Originally it was contemplated (in Chapter VII of the UN Charter) that all UN members would contribute troops to a UN armed force under the SC's mandate. In reality, such a force was never created because no country was willing to give up their command over their own troops to an international organ. Since the beginning of the 1990s, the SC has occasionally authorized the use of force by UN member states under Chapter VII. At an early stage, the UN developed the practice of peacekeeping missions, using the so-called 'blue helmet' forces, which did not have an express legal basis in the UN Charter. They were nevertheless found to be legal in the ICJ's *Certain Expenses of the United Nations* advisory opinion. They developed over time during the Cold War, when permanent members could not agree on Chapter VII measures but authorized peacekeeping missions invited by the parties to the dispute.

There is a growing debate as to whether the SC itself is bound by international law or simply makes political decisions. A middle line in this debate is probably advisable, whereby the SC as a whole is bound by international law but its members make political decisions. Following this line of argument the High Level Panel on the Reform of the UN recommended that permanent member states of the SC should refrain from using their veto powers in situations of large-scale human rights violations. The reform of the SC and the UN as a whole is still being debated and several states have expressed an interest in becoming permanent members, in order better to reflect the geographical distribution of its membership and financial contributions to the UN as an organization.

The head of the UN administration is the Secretary General, who oversees day-to-day administration of the UN and its affiliated organizations. The Secretary General is appointed by the GA, on the recommendation of the SC, for a five-year, renewable term. The UN has today about 7,000 staff from over 170 member states, and the whole UN family of organizations employs about 63,000 people. The UN headquarters are in New York City, Geneva, Vienna, and Nairobi.

Besides the ICJ, the ECOSOC and the now dormant Trusteeship Committee are the other principal organs of the UN. ECOSOC consists of fifty-four UN members and is responsible for a broad range of issues: employment, standard of living, social progress, health, culture, education, human rights, and fundamental freedoms. In other words, this is the organ where most political discussions on matters other than security recommendations to the GA are formulated and special international conferences are initiated. ECOSOC also consults with **non-governmental organizations** ('NGOs') and has established a process of granting NGOs observer status. ECOSOC has also created five regional commissions as well as the Commission on Sustainable Development and the Commission on the Status of Women.

The UN also has several subsidiary organs created by the principal organs. Subsidiary organs established by the GA include the International Law Commission, the UN Environment Programme, the UN Development Programme, the **UN High Commissioner for Refugees**, UNICEF, the new Human Rights Council, and the UN Administrative Tribunal. The SC has set up the peacekeeping missions such as the UN Peacebuilding Commission, UN SC Sanctions Committees, the Counterterrorism Committee, and **ICTY** (International Criminal Tribunal for former Yugoslavia) and ICTR (International Criminal Tribunal for Rwanda). The last two subsidiary organs are not without legal controversy since commentators have questioned the legal ability of the SC to create courts and have considered their founding to be *ultra vires* ('beyond power').

The UN Charter also refers to specialized agencies that operate in various technical fields. There are currently seventeen UN agencies such as the International Labour Organization, the Food and Agriculture Organization, UNESCO, the World Health Organization, the International Civil Aviation Organization, several sub-agencies of the World Bank, the International Monetary Fund, and the International Maritime Organization. The treaty secretariats of UN treaties are also considered part of the UN family and have close ties with UN organizations, even though they are legally only responsible to their conference of the parties, ie the assembly of nations that have ratified the treaty in question.

The UN has embarked on a series of reform discussions mainly focused on internal streamlining and management reform. The overall goal is to enable the organization to fulfil its mandate in the twenty-first century given that it has many more challenging tasks and a more diverse membership than at its founding.   MARKUS GEHRING

United Nations Commission on International Trade Law (UNCITRAL)   *see* international economic law

United Nations Conference on Trade and Development (UNCTAD)   *see* international economic law

United Nations High Commissioner for Refugees ('UNHCR')   As one of the world's leading humanitarian agencies, the Office of the **United Nations** High Commissioner for Refugees ('UNHCR') is a multilateral, intergovernmental organization, created by the UN General Assembly through resolution 319A(IV) of 3 December 1949, and provided with its Statute in resolution 428(V) of 14 December 1950. The UNHCR Statute is, however, not the only source of UNHCR's constitutional underpinning since it contains provisions which have allowed a further evolution of UNHCR's functions and activities. It is the General Assembly and, to some extent, the Economic and Social Council (ECOSOC) which can further develop the mandate, and this has occurred since the inception of UNHCR's work.

The Office is headed by the High Commissioner who is elected by the General Assembly with a five-year term. With its Headquarters in Geneva (Switzerland), UNHCR has about 6,300 staff working primarily in the field in some 250 offices in over 110 countries. The agency's budget, amounting annually to around US$1 billion, is mainly funded by voluntary contributions from governments. The organization is non-political, humanitarian, and social in character. UNHCR reports annually through ECOSOC to the General Assembly while its budget and operational activities are guided by a smaller intergovernmental body, the Executive Committee of the High Commissioner's Programme.

UNHCR's competence extends to the following categories of persons of concern: (i) **refugees** and **asylum**-seekers; (ii) returnees; (iii) stateless persons; (iv) internally **displaced persons**; (v) persons threatened with displacement or otherwise at risk. The latter two categories do, however, not fall under the general mandate of the Office. The term 'refugees of concern to UNHCR' departs from the idea of a single refugee concept, covering all persons outside their country of origin for reasons of feared persecution, generalized violence, or other circumstances which have seriously disturbed public order and who, as a result, require international protection. Returnees are refugees who have returned to their country of origin spontaneously or in an organized fashion but are yet to be fully integrated. With regard to stateless persons, UNHCR acts as the intermediary between stateless persons and states, *inter alia*, by providing special expertise in the area of **nationality** legislation or promoting accession to international statelessness instruments. While UNHCR does not have a general mandate for internally displaced people, it has been authorized by the General Assembly to be involved under certain circumstances in enhancing protection and providing humanitarian assistance to them as part of the UN collaborative approach. In this connection, UNHCR has assumed lead responsibility for those displaced internally by conflict in the area of protection (including return), camp coordination, and emergency shelter. Moreover, UNHCR has on occasions been involved with local residents, war-affected civilians, or besieged populations, especially in circumstances where it was neither feasible nor reasonable to treat them differently from other categories of concern.

UNHCR is primarily mandated to provide international protection and humanitarian assistance and to seek permanent solutions for persons within its competence. The functions of UNHCR have expanded considerably over time. Other mandated activities include preventive action and participation in those humanitarian endeavours of the UN for which the Office has particular expertise. Humanitarian functions would, for instance, include relief distribution, emergency preparedness, broader development work, and issuance of documentation for persons falling under its competence.

As regards the main function of international protection, it is not only a legal concept but also a highly operational function covering the gamut of activities through which the rights of refugees and others of concern are assured, including securing admission and **asylum**, respect for basic **human rights**, and an appropriate standard of treatment, as well as achieving a durable solution through restoration of national protection either in the country of origin, the host country, or another country. The ultimate goal of international protection is to achieve a satisfactory and durable solution for refugees and others of concern. This can only be achieved when the need for international protection ceases to be necessary and national protection—be it by the country of origin or by another country—is fully effective and sustainable. If the solution of voluntary repatriation, which is in fact preferred by the vast majority of refugees, is not feasible, the other durable solutions of local integration in the host country or resettlement in third countries are pursued. Until such time as a durable solution can in fact materialize, an environment allowing refugees in the meantime to become self-reliant has turned out to be an effective way of reducing the costs of hosting refugees, as well as of ensuring that refugees are able to get on with their lives and are better prepared for an eventual durable solution.

To exercise its international protection function vis-à-vis states, UNHCR relies on its Statute, including the development of its competence through subsequent General Assembly and ECOSOC resolutions, and on the whole body of universal and regional refugee law and standards, complemented by relevant international human rights and humanitarian law instruments, as well as relevant national legislation and key jurisprudence. This body of law and standards constitutes the international refugee protection regime at the core of which is the UNHCR Statute and the 1951 Convention/1967 Protocol relating to the Status of Refugees. Within the international refugee protection regime, there is no doubt about the centrality of the 1951 Convention/1967 Protocol. They set forth a universal refugee definition and incorporate the basic rights and obligations of refugees. The implementation of the international refugee protection regime, while firmly anchored in law, is based on different tools and methods of protection. These tools can be diplomatic, operational, and practical-material and be applied over the short term or a long time. In relation to international refugee instruments UNHCR also exercises a supervisory function which enables it to monitor state practice concerning the implementation of international obligations in the refugee protection and statelessness area. This specific legal foundation of UNHCR operations has given the Office its special and unique identity and considerable independence. In recognition of its work, UNHCR has twice won the Nobel Peace Prize.   VOLKER TÜRK

E Feller, V Türk, and F Nicholson (eds), *Refugee Protection in International Law* (Cambridge: Cambridge University Press, 2003)

GS Goodwin-Gill and J McAdam, *The Refugee in International Law* (Oxford: Oxford University Press, 3rd edn, 2007)

United States Bill of Rights   The Bill of Rights is the term given to the first ten amendments to the US Constitution which came into effect in 1791. They share relatively few similarities with modern bills of rights such as the **Canadian Charter of Rights and Freedoms** (1982) or South Africa's Constitution (1996), but do protect freedom of speech and assembly, the right not to be subjected to unreasonable **search and seizure,** or to cruel and unusual punishment, due process, and fair trial rights (these as well as the right to bear arms). In *Marbury v Madison* (1803) the **US Supreme Court** ruled that a federal legal provision was unconstitutional: this was the first occasion on which the Court had assumed the power to declare acts of Congress, and, by implication, acts of the President, unconstitutional if in the view of that Court they went beyond the powers granted to the relevant body or office by the Constitution.

Because of the relative age of the US Bill of Rights and the difficulty of amending the US Constitution, rights have been read into the document over time. Some Constitutional scholars however favour the theory of original intent: the Constitution means what its original framers intended it to mean, and nothing more. Such theorists disapprove of the decision in *Roe v Wade* (1973) in which the Supreme Court read a right to **abortion** into a right to **privacy** which in turn was located in the 'penumbra' of other protected rights. Others point out that the Constitution became law only as a result of its ratification by hundreds of delegates in thirteen state conventions, and question the possibility of determining 'intent' in such circumstances.   AILEEN MCCOLGAN

See also: **South African Bill of Rights**

United States of America, law of   America is as much an idea as a place. Moreover, the idea of America as it relates to law has always been more powerful than the reality of law itself. This may not appear self-evident to a British reader, especially due to the unpleasantness associated with the thirteen North American colonies declaring their independence from **Great Britain** and then proceeding to justify it with a bill of particulars, the Declaration of Independence (1776). Together with the United States Constitution (1787) and its first ten amendments, the Bill of Rights (1791), these documents early stated the ideal in law and government and have been influential in other countries' own nation-building.

Commentators such as Alexis de Tocqueville in *Democracy in America* (1835) and the Scotsman, James Bryce in *The American Commonwealth* (1888), recognized many peculiarities in United States law, legal institutions, and legal culture, which remain in the twenty-first century as American exceptionalism.

Four elements of the founding fathers' vision seem especially significant for the evolution of the US legal system and legal culture: liberty, distrust of government, tolerance, and optimism. The Declaration of Independence best states the desire for liberty. 'We hold these truths to be self-evident, that all men are created equal, that they are endowed by their Creator with certain unalienable Rights, that among these are Life, Liberty and the pursuit of Happiness. That to secure these rights, Governments are instituted among Men, deriving their just powers from the consent of the governed.' Although this liberty was initially intended only for white adult males, the history of the nineteenth and twentieth centuries was about the gradual extension of liberty and certain legal rights to former slaves, women, native Americans, and even resident foreigners. This process of greater inclusion was validated by the outcome of the Civil War, which abolished slavery and established the equality principle in the Constitution's Fourteenth Amendment (1868).

The natural right of liberty was to the pursuit of happiness; it was not a guarantee of happiness. The American experiment did not emphasize **communitarianism** and did not sow the seeds for socialism. It rejected the confessional state; there would be no Church of America, but rather a free market for religious belief and membership. An individual had the liberty to contract to improve his welfare, the liberty to travel wherever, the liberty to speak his mind, the liberty to do nothing. The physical environment of North America facilitated the exercise of this right. It was a spacious continent, much less densely inhabited than Great Britain. It invited mobility, independence, and enterprise. Liberty realized breeds optimism. Americans felt that they had a personal stake in the future; they were inclined to experiment, to gamble, to waste. Whatever promised to increase wealth people considered good. The negative side of liberty, however, led to vast environmental despoliation and tragic human exploitation. This is a preoccupation of the twenty-first century.

The signers of the Declaration of Independence did not believe all government was bad, since 'to secure these rights, Governments are instituted among Men'. Some government was necessary to secure liberty. Nevertheless, government had to be watched, as the Declaration implied: 'whenever any Form of Government becomes destructive of these ends, it is the Right of the People to alter or to abolish it, and to institute new Government'. One mechanism early favoured to moderate the tension between the need for government and its potential for tyranny was the **rule of law**. The Constitution's Fifth Amendment

guarantees that no person shall 'be deprived of life, liberty, or property, without due process of law'. The US Constitution itself is an intricate design to secure a government of laws and not of men. Its details make clear that the framers distrusted government. Government actions, in the framers' reading of history, were as likely to bring human misery as to promote human happiness. It was better to design an inefficient governmental machine to unite the thirteen states. The trick was to increase the power of national government, after the failure of the Articles of Confederation (1777), but to avoid creating a centralized authority so effective that it threatened a return to tyranny, a matter much discussed during the 'war on terror' following the 2001 attack on New York City and Washington DC.

First, the Constitution only creates the national government, which is limited to certain enumerated powers. The federal structure of government divided legal authority between a national government of restricted powers and thirteen original states (now fifty states, the capitol district, and affiliated territories such as Puerto Rico), each with its own constitution and divided powers. Each state has a full set of legal institutions: a governor and executive agencies and staff, a legislature, and a complete hierarchy of ordinary courts with the power to adjudicate state law questions and even to hear most federal cases. States have further indulged in political decentralization by creating smaller governmental units, such as counties, cities, and districts—for water, fire protection, schools, and other special concerns— some with their own taxing and regulatory power and even their own police force. Today there are an astounding 87,500 governmental units in the United States, which employ 21.5 million persons. State and local government employs 87 per cent of these workers. The states within this federal structure are like fifty huge social laboratories with plenary authority over their own administrative and tax law, as well as over property, contracts, torts, families, inheritance, and most commercial matters. States and cities create and enforce thousands of mundane rules that affect the daily life of average citizens and businesses. States are in competition with each other. A state's legal policies, along with its climate, economic situation, and other factors, attract or repel citizens who are free to stay or to leave.

Second, the Constitution separates national government into three branches, each with a primary function: legislation, administration, or adjudication. No one person can participate in more than one branch, unlike the parliamentary system where the prime minister is at once head of the executive and of the majority party in the legislature. Moreover, the Constitution is a written document—not unwritten as in England—and it is difficult to amend formally.

Third, the Constitution sets out an elaborate framework of checks and balances among and within the three branches of national government. Within the Congress, for instance, there exist two chambers: one to satisfy small states that wanted equal representation (the Senate), and the other to accommodate the populous states with membership based on population (the House of Representatives). Federal district courts are checked in their power by the process of appeal to the **United States Supreme Court** and by Congress for its budget. In general, no new governmental action can proceed without the assent of at least two branches. A bill only becomes law if both the Senate and the House of Representatives pass it by majority vote and the President does not veto it. Congress can control or terminate executive programs by denial of funds, as it debated in 2007 regarding the Iraq War. The President may make a treaty, but only if two-thirds of the Senate provides its advice and consent. The President appoints Justices to the Supreme Court, but a majority of the Senate must confirm them. Other checks were implied, such as judicial review to invalidate legislative or executive acts based on constitutional supremacy.

Americans in the first century of the republic were ambivalent about law. The wild West was associated with the task of taming a frontier. Today many remain ambivalent. On one hand, the Constitution is the supreme law. Along with the flag, it stands for national unity. America has no royal family, no timeless heritage, no national church. Since the federal judiciary emerged as the ultimate arbiter of what the Constitution means, for much of the past 200 years the judiciary and especially the Supreme Court has been America's most respected legal institution. It is surely the contemporary world's most powerful judiciary, as evidenced by its decision deciding the 2000 presidential election. On the other hand, Americans are notoriously lawless; their attitude towards authority and rules is in general disrespectful, since they often see these as a threat to liberty. The number of adults in jail or prison, or on probation or parole, expanded from 1.8 million in 1980 to about 7.0 million in 2004, which represents an increase from 1 to 3 per cent of the total adult population. People also realize that government officials have not always respected the framers' vision for the Constitution. However, the ambivalence to law goes deeper. Rules represent tradition, the past. This is the New World; action is what matters most. Any problems this attitude generates one can sort out later. Perhaps that

is why there are more than one million lawyers and judges—about one third of the world's total—in the United States today.

The European settlers of the thirteen colonies that formed the new republic came from many lands under different circumstances. Nevertheless, one common element characterized their situation: they were dissenters and nonconformists. Either they could not get along with the political or religious authorities in their homeland or their social or economic condition was sufficiently unacceptable that they packed their bags and made the long voyage across the Atlantic. They dissented with their feet. The United States itself was born of dissent, as the complaints against King George III made clear. The right of religious conscience and the freedom to express an opinion were enshrined in the capstone amendment to the Constitution, the First Amendment. The right of dissent in a political community requires tolerance of dissenters. Tolerance, in turn, promotes assimilation.

Americans were restless in a way that linked dissent to optimism. Pioneers who pulled up stakes and rode to the frontier were dissenting from the past while at the same time expressing their confidence in an unknown future. Liberty was their right. Government would not stand in the way. Europeans lived in the past, bound by the remnants of feudalism and nurtured by cultural nationalism. Those who emigrated to America escaped this past and marvelled at the bounty of natural resources. The right to pursue happiness led not to just the philosophical idea of progress, but to the experience of progress: the conversion of wilderness into farms, the growth of villages into cities, and the emergence of America as a world power.   DAVID CLARK

DS Clark and T Ansay (eds), *Introduction to the Law of the United States* (The Hague: Kluwer Law International, 2nd edn, 2002)

DS Clark et al (eds), *The Oxford Companion to American Law* (Oxford: Oxford University Press, 2002)

United States Supreme Court   Created in 1791, the United States Supreme Court is the oldest and arguably the most important constitutional court in the world. Designers of modern constitutions have generally rejected most of the details of the US Supreme Court's design, but they have almost universally concluded that they should create a constitutional court with the power to invalidate, if only provisionally, legislation inconsistent with constitutional limitations or requirements. That conclusion rests on designers' evaluation of the performance of the US Supreme Court over two centuries.

Structure

The Constitution of 1789 provided that the 'judicial Power of the United States shall be vested in one supreme Court', thereby requiring that the national legislature create a Supreme Court. In addition, the Constitution provided that the judges of the Supreme Court, today called Justices, would hold their offices 'during good Behaviour', which has been understood since the beginning as giving them tenure in the position for life (or until they choose to leave voluntarily). To protect them further against legislative retaliation based on disagreement with their decisions, the Constitution guaranteed that judges' salaries could 'not be diminished during their Continuance in Office'. Neither the Constitution nor later implementing legislation specifies any other qualifications for service on the Supreme Court, not even that a Justice be a lawyer (although all who have served have had legal training). Justices can be removed from office only through impeachment, by a majority vote in the nation's lower house and a two-thirds vote in the upper house. An early failed effort to impeach and remove Justice Samuel Chase because of strong disagreement with his judicial rulings created an unwritten constitutional convention that Justices cannot be impeached for their rulings. There is no formal mechanism for removing Justices who have become debilitated by age or illness, although an ailing Justice's colleagues frequently place strong pressure on the Justice to resign.

Initially consisting of one Chief Justice and four Associate Justices, the Supreme Court grew during the nineteenth century to accommodate demands from the nation's regions that each have some representation on the Court. The size peaked at ten, then stabilized at nine. Occasional efforts to manipulate the Court's size to achieve political goals ended in 1937. Frustrated by the Court's invalidation of important statutes and fearing even more drastic decisions, President Franklin D Roosevelt proposed a 'Court packing' plan that would have expanded the Court's membership from nine to fifteen. The plan failed of enactment, and there now appears to be agreement that the Court should remain permanently at its present size, with a Chief Justice and eight Associate Justices.

The President nominates Justices, who take office if the Senate confirms the appointment by simple majority vote. The characteristics of the appointment and confirmation process have varied with changes in the structure of legislative politics. For long periods, Supreme Court appointments were matters of patronage politics, with presidents nominating their friends and political allies and the Senate responding by determining whether it agreed with the allocation of patronage. Alternatively, appointments were matters of interest group politics, with presidents calculating that particular nominations would find favour with groups important to the president's political standing. In the late twentieth century, the nomination and confirmation process became more focused on the perceived judicial ideologies of nominees, and on predictions about how they would rule on particularly contentious constitutional issues, primarily abortion and the rights of criminal defendants.

Jurisdiction

The US Supreme Court is a generalist high court, with authority to interpret national legislation and rule on the constitutionality of national, state, and local legislation. In recent years the Court's decisions have been divided roughly evenly between statutory and constitutional rulings. The Court has almost no authority to determine the content of the general law of contract, torts, or property. The Court gained control over its docket in the twentieth century. The Court must await cases presented to it in actual disputes, and may not render advisory opinions. Otherwise the Court has almost complete discretion to choose the cases that it will give full consideration. Congress has occasionally, though rarely, created a procedure for expedited review in the Supreme Court of constitutional challenges to particularly important statutes.

History

In its early years, the Supreme Court was not an important participant in American government. One early Chief Justice resigned to become Governor of New York. John Marshall's appointment as Chief Justice in 1803 began a gradual process of enhancing the Court's power. The Marshall Court invalidated only one national statute, but indicated its willingness to exercise that power more extensively, and it invalidated numerous state laws, sometimes producing political controversy which, when resolved in favor of the Court's decisions, contributed to the Court's growing power. The Court became a focal point for political controversy in the late nineteenth century, and remained one through the twentieth century . Beginning in 1895 the Court occasionally invalidated progressive legislation regulating employees' wages and hours. These holdings became the basis for the Court's more substantial interventions against Depression-era New Deal legislation. Franklin D Roosevelt was able to appoint five Justices to the Supreme Court within a few years of the Court-packing plan's defeat, and the Court retreated from its efforts to impose constitutional limitations on legislative power in economic matters.

The Court turned its attention to **human rights**, developing a vigorous jurisprudence of freedom of expression and equality in the 1950s and the 1960s, when Earl **Warren** was Chief Justice. The public approved of much of that jurisprudence, but the Warren Court's rulings expanding the rights of criminal defendants became deeply controversial in an era of increasing crime. New appointments to the Supreme Court moved in a more conservative direction, but the jurisprudence of individual rights retained real force in cases involving **abortion**, homosexual rights, and free expression. By the turn of the twenty-first century the Supreme Court excluded from its purview a wide range of important issues, such as those dealing with economic growth and war-making, but within the domain of individual rights the Supreme Court was the nation's most important institution.

MARK TUSHNET

Universal Declaration of Human Rights
see **international human rights law**

universalism Universalism, the principle positing the equal moral worth of all **persons**, finds its roots in Enlightenment philosophies of the seventeenth and eighteenth centuries. Central to the principle of universalism is the belief that all human beings, simply by virtue of their **humanity**, are entitled to equal moral respect. The requirement of equal moral respect entails certain minimum entitlements to **human rights**, entitlements that arise, regardless of one's particular religious, cultural, or socio-economic background.

The commitment to universalism presumes the equal worth of all persons and the equal entitlement to human rights. It is this commitment that underpins the international human rights movement. Human rights norms are presumed to be universally valid, applicable to diverse religious or cultural contexts. Universalism meets with opposition from cultural relativists, feminists, communitarians, and others, who appeal instead to the local, the particular, and to the significance of difference. The possibility or even the desirability of identifying universal human rights norms is questioned. This questioning suggests that claims to universality, in fact, mask the particular values and standards (often 'Western') that underpin them. This criticism suggests, however, that the problem is not necessarily universalism *per se*, but rather eurocentrism masquerading as universalism.

Since the Enlightenment, philosophers have been debating the normative basis for universalism and for human rights claims. The content and scope of such claims is also disputed. Perhaps the most well-known attempt to justify the principle of universalism is to be found in Immanuel Kant's categorical imperative, of which the best known version runs: *Act only on that maxim through which you can at the same time will that it should become a universal law.* Kant claims to show that all imperatives of duty can be derived from this one imperative as their principle. No reference is made to individual particulars and neither is the principle dependent on contingent factors such as happiness or desires, consent or agreement.

It is this abstraction from particulars, this emphasis on sameness that has attracted much criticism. Postmodernists, communitarians, feminists, and others have expressed concern that the denial of the particular leads also to a denial of the significance of difference. Universalism is criticized as bringing with it a totalizing movement, an assimilationist and homogenizing impulse. Iris Marion Young notes, the 'totalizing movement always leaves a remainder'. Feminist sceptics have questioned whether 'women's full inclusion in the universal register may indeed be an impossibility'.

A concern with difference has led to continuing questioning of the normative basis of universalism. The possibility of justifying universal claims or agreeing on the foundations for universalism is contested. Responding to criticisms, defenders of universalism have increasingly sought to portray universalism as sensitive to difference, and, indeed, as a precursor to the flourishing of difference. Jürgen Habermas has called for a *nonlevelling* and *nonappropriating* universalism, noting that 'Equal respect for *everyone* is not limited to those who are like us; it extends to the person of the other in his or her otherness . . . those who are strangers to one another and want to remain strangers'. Critiques of universalism are often premised on a belief that the misuse of universalism exhausts its limits, that universal norms can only represent a false universality, an imaginary common humanity. Certainly, human rights discourse has not yet fulfilled its promise of universalism, and human rights law and practice continues to be deeply flawed. However, the potential and the promise of universalism remain.

SIOBHAN MULLALLY

M Nussbaum, *Sex and Social Justice* (Oxford: Oxford University Press, 1999)
J Habermas, *The Inclusion of the Other: Studies in Political Theory* (Cambridge, MA: MIT Press, 1998).

See also: **cultural relativism; human rights, theories of**

universities and higher education The law of higher education is concerned with how law impacts on the complex organization that is the modern university (or higher education institution—'HEI' hereafter). Generally that impact is the same for the HEI as for any other legal entity, but seven specific areas need to be considered.

The legal status of HEIs

HEIs are private corporations, either statutory (the 'new' or 'ex-poly' universities) or chartered (the 'old' institutions). They are also **charities**. They are not public sector entities controlled by government (as in the case of US State HEIs or most mainland European HEIs). Sovereign autonomous power lies with the lay-dominated Board of Governors or Council, but the collective of academics/faculty remain influential via the Academic Board/Senate; and there is considerable debate about the balance of managerialism/corporatism versus collegiality/shared-values in their governance and management.

HEIs and government/agencies, including fair access to higher education

Government finances HEIs as private autonomous entities and monitors their use of taxpayers' money via various agencies: the funding councils (see *R v Universities Funding Council, ex p Institute of Dental Surgery* (1994)), the research councils, and the National Audit Office. Also HEIs voluntarily follow a HEFCE (Higher Education Funding Council for England) Code of Governance, and submit to academic audit by the Quality Assurance Agency. This dependence by HEIs (albeit lessening) on public money is used by government to oblige them to have, in the name of social equity, widening-participation plans monitored by OFFA (Office for Fair Access created by section 31 of the Higher Education Act 2004 ('HEA')).

The visitorial jurisdiction

The chartered HEIs are subject to the visitatorial jurisdiction, rooted in medieval **canon law** and the means by which the Founder of an eleemosynary corporation ensured the entity fulfilled its objectives over the centuries and used its permanent endowment appropriately. The Visitor's role in relation to members of the HEI, whether as academic staff and more recently students, has been removed by **legislation**, but a residual role remains as the interpreter of the HEI's Domestic Legislation and the arbiter of faculty/student disputes that do not relate to the academic **contract of employment** or to the student.

Academic freedom and academic tenure

A credible university requires institutional autonomy and independence (*Sweezy v New Hampshire* (1957)) and 'the four essential freedoms of a university': the HEI alone decides, purely on academic grounds, who can teach what and how to whom, and within the HEI academics are protected by the dual linked concepts of academic freedom and academic tenure (job security) whereby they can 'speak truth to power' for the greater benefit of society (providing they do so in an intellectually rigorous and responsible way: *Rigg v University of Waikato* (1984)). The only formal protection, given the absence in the UK of a written **constitution** and the effective abolition of academic tenure by Part IV of the Education Reform Act 1988, is section 202(2)(a) of the same Act which creates a duty on HEIs 'to ensure that academic staff have freedom within the law to question and test received wisdom, and to put forward new ideas and controversial or unpopular opinions, without placing themselves in jeopardy of losing their jobs or privileges that they may have at their institutions'. A related issue is campus free speech for student political societies and their speakers, balanced against campus **security** and **safety**.

The academic's intellectual property

HEIs increasingly exploit their intellectual property (via patenting, licensing, and spin-out companies). The academic's contract of employment will determine the ownership of such IP and the terms for sharing the proceeds of its exploitation. The HEI typically does not, however, lay claim to an academic's **copyright** in books/articles, nor to his/her lecture notes. The HEI's desire to exploit IP, the commercial interest of the external sponsor of research, and the academic's concern for academic freedom can clash.

The contract to educate and judicial deference

The student–HEI legal relationship is essentially contractual (*Moran v University College, Salford (No 2)* (1994)), but with elements of public law in the statutory HEIs and a residual role for the Visitor in respect of the student's 'membership' of the chartered HEI. The contract to educate is a **consumer** service contract, with an implied term that the HEI will operate fair academic appeal and social discipline procedures, and with section 13 of the Sale of Goods and Services Act 1982 applicable (ie requiring the delivery of teaching/examining 'with reasonable care and skill'). That said, there is judicial deference to the exercise of expert academic judgment and, short of procedural defects, courts will not second-guess the HEI award of exam marks (*Clark v University of Lincolnshire and Humberside*

(2002)): such deference or academic immunity operates in most legal jurisdictions, although, since the decision of the **House of Lords** in *Phelps v Hillingdon LBC* (2000), there is theoretical scope to sue for academic negligence/educational malpractice (as notably in *Young v Bella* (2006) a recent Canadian HE case, in which **damages** of c$840K were awarded); there is no such tortious claim recognized (yet) in US law. There may be scope for mental distress/disappointment damages arising from any breach of the contract to educate, as perhaps one of the few types of contract where such **compensation** is available. The HEI also clearly has a tortious duty of care in organizing field trips and study abroad (*Tuttle v Edinburgh University* (1984)); and for laboratory/premises safety (*Lewis v University of Bristol* (1999)).

Office of the Independent Adjudicator ('OIA')

The OIA was created by section 12 of the HEA to handle complaints voluntarily referred by students, but not complaints concerning the HEI's decision on admissions or in relation to academic judgment (marking and degree classification, unless procedurally defective) and not before all internal HEI appeal procedures have been exhausted. The OIA, if it finds the complaint is justified, can recommend the HEI should pay compensation (including for any distress and disappointment suffered by the student): neither the HEI nor the student is bound by the OIA's determination, and hence the complaint can still proceed to litigation. The OIA is subject to **judicial review** (see *Siborurema v OIA* (2007); see also the OIA Annual Reports at *www.oiahe.org.uk*).

DAVID PALFREYMAN

D Farrington and D Palfreyman, *The Law of Higher Education* (Oxford: Oxford University Press, 2006), updated online and supported by a 'Law Casebook' at *www.oxcheps.new.ox.ac.uk*

WA Kaplin and BA Lee, *The Law of Higher Education* (San Francisco: Jossey-Bass, 4th edn, 2006)

unjust enrichment *see* **restitution**

unlawful combatants *see* **combatants**

unlawful eviction It is a criminal offence unlawfully to evict, or attempt to evict, an occupier of residential premises. Although the offence is primarily intended to cover landlords who wrongfully evict their tenants, it can be committed by any person and against any occupier. It could, for example, cover an owner-occupier evicted by a mortgage lender, or the eviction of a 'licensee' merely living in property with the owner's permission. The occupier must have some legal right to occupy the premises, however, or the eviction would not be 'unlawful'. The offence is punishable by a fine or up to two years' imprisonment or both.

Unlawful eviction can also create civil liability towards the occupier. The civil wrong can be committed only by landlords or persons acting on their behalf. It is framed so as to include not only eviction as such but also acts of harassment which lead to the occupier ceasing to occupy the premises: a kind of constructive eviction. There is no liability unless the occupier has finally moved out, so that reinstatement of the occupier in the premises (whether by the landlord or by the courts) is a defence to the suit. This is because of the way **damages** are calculated. These represent the difference between the value to the landlord of the premises with the occupier in place and their value unoccupied, the aim being to deprive the landlord of any profit resulting from the eviction.

RE THORNTON

unmarried parents Parental responsibility is an important concept for unmarried parents. All mothers automatically have **parental responsibility** but not unmarried fathers, who only have parental responsibility if they have a relevant court order, have a parental responsibility agreement with the mother, or, since either December 2003, or in Scotland, May 2006, are registered on the child's birth certificate. Having parental responsibility gives parents certain rights, for example the right to decide on their child's education or **consent to medical treatment**. Whether or not parents are living together, fathers must be consulted over these crucial areas in a child's life. If parents are in disagreement the matter must be resolved by a court.

Fathers are automatically entitled to apply to court for orders in relation to their **child**. If applying for parental responsibility, it will normally be granted, only being refused if it is clearly contrary to the child's welfare. The most usual orders sought are those for residence (custody) and contact (access). In deciding whether to grant either order, the court will decide on the basis of what is in the best interests of the child. A shared residence order can be made but is unusual. Contact is presumed to be beneficial to the child. Therefore, unless it is shown to be contrary to the child's welfare, the order will be granted. Contact can be either face-to-face or indirect, such as telephone calls and letters. In Scotland, parents have both a responsibility and a right to maintain personal relations and direct contact with their children, although the right can only be exercised if in the child's interest to do so.

Provided there is no court order prohibiting it, a child can lawfully be removed from the UK to live elsewhere. However, if a father objects, application can be made under the Hague Convention on Abduction for the swift return of the child. But, if the father does not have parental responsibility for the child, he may find that he does not have 'rights of custody', even although the child has been living with him. If he does not possess such rights then any removal from the UK by the mother is not 'wrongful' and the Hague Convention does not apply.

On separation, mothers may wish to change the surname of their child. If aware that the father is likely to object, a mother is not entitled to change a child's name, whether or not the father has parental responsibility. Either parent has to get a court order to permit a change.

Fathers must make **child support** payments for their child regardless of whether or not they have any contact with the child or have parental responsibility.

Parents with parental responsibility can appoint a guardian in the event of death. However, if there is a surviving parent with parental responsibility the appointment will only come into effect after the death of both parties. In Scotland, the appointment comes into effect straight away, so parent and guardian share responsibility.   CATHY WILLIAMS

See also: **contact, family; guardianship and children; residence in family law; welfare principle**

use of force   After the World War II the founding member states of the **United Nations** decided to create a new regime to regulate the use of force. They outlawed the use of force by states except in self-defence. Article 2(4) of the UN Charter provides that 'All Members shall refrain from the threat or use of force against the territorial integrity or political independence of any State, or in any other manner inconsistent with the Purposes of the United Nations'. Thus the Charter does not merely prohibit 'war', as earlier treaties such as the Covenant of the League of Nations had done. The term 'war' was generally regarded as a narrow, technical term which left unregulated lesser uses of force not amounting to war. The Charter prohibits the 'use of force', a wider term. This prohibition is now accepted as **customary** international law, and even as a peremptory norm of **international law** of higher status than normal rules.

The UN Charter also created a collective security system. The plan was that the UN would respond to any use of force which amounted to a threat to the peace, breach of the peace or act of aggression. The UN Security Council is given primary responsibility for the maintenance of international peace and security under Article 24 of the UN Charter. It may take decisions binding on member states under Article 25. But its decision-making is subject to the veto of the five permanent members' China, France, Russia (which succeeded to the place of the USSR), the UK, and the US. During the Cold War it was the US and the USSR which made frequent use of the veto to protect their own international interests; since the end of the Cold War the veto power has most often been used by the US to prevent any condemnation of Israel.

Under Chapter VII of the Charter the Security Council may determine that there is a threat to the peace, breach of the peace, or act of aggression. It may then make recommendations or decide non-forcible measures under Article 41 or forcible measures under Article 42. It can also take provisional measures under Article 40. The Security Council has found threats to the peace in a wide range of situations, including civil wars and the breakdown of law and order. It has determined the existence of breaches of the peace in cases of inter-state use of force such as the 1980–1988 Iran/Iraq war. It has very rarely determined the existence of an act of aggression, the most serious type of use of force. The definition of aggression has proved problematic. The General Assembly worked on this for many years and eventually produced the *Definition of Aggression* (1974); this provides a general definition and a list of specific acts which constitute aggression by states.

During the Cold War the Security Council was able to impose economic sanctions under Article 41 only on Southern Rhodesia and South Africa. Since the end of the Cold War it has been much more active in this regard, imposing arms embargoes in response to civil conflicts, and taking measures against those parties which do not cooperate with UN peacekeeping forces or with a UN-brokered peace process. After the difficult experience of the comprehensive sanctions regime imposed on Iraq under Resolution 687 (1991) the UN has been working to develop smart or targeted sanctions against those directly responsible for challenges to its decisions.

If the Security Council considers that the measures provided for under Article 41 would be or have proved inadequate then it also has the power to take forcible action under Article 42 to maintain or restore international peace and security. The original plan was that the UN would have its own standing armed force available to respond to the threat or use of force by states. However, it proved impossible to establish such a force during the Cold War, and the

Security Council has never expressly taken action under Article 42. The UN Charter scheme has thus not been implemented as originally planned, but it has proved sufficiently flexible to allow the Security Council to act with regard to the use of force.

During the Cold War the Security Council did not rely on Article 42, but it did authorize the use of force against North Korea in response to its invasion of South Korea in 1950 and also to implement the economic embargo on Southern Rhodesia. Subsequently it has authorized the use of force by member states as 'coalitions of the willing', first under Security Council Resolution 678 (1990) against Iraq after its invasion of Kuwait. Acting under Chapter VII, it authorized the use of 'all necessary means' by member states. This resolution marked a new start for the Security Council; it was followed by many later resolutions authorizing force in the former Yugoslavia, Somalia, the Democratic Republic of the Congo, Liberia, and elsewhere, for a range of purposes, to secure the delivery of humanitarian aid, the implementation of economic sanctions, to assist a UN peacekeeping force, and to restore peace and security. These member state operations range from small short-term forces to massive long-term interventions such as those in Kosovo and East Timor. The US and the UK controversially claimed this justification as the basis for their use of force in *Operation Iraqi Freedom* in 2003: they said that the authorization of force by member states against Iraq under Resolution 678 (1990) had been revived by later resolutions because of Iraq's material breach of the terms of the cease-fire with regard to the development of weapons of mass destruction. China and Russia rejected this argument and even NATO members, such as France and Germany, said that the use of force was not authorized by the UN, but was designed to secure an unlawful regime change in Iraq.

The UN also created the institution of peacekeeping even though there is no express provision for this in the UN Charter. The first major operations were established in the Middle East and in Congo (DRC). The principles governing such peacekeeping operations were that they should be impartial, be established with the consent of the host-state, and that they should not use force except in self-defence. Since the end of the Cold War the Security Council has also created more robust forces under Chapter VII of the Charter.

The prohibition of the use of force in Article 2(4) creates a presumption that the unilateral use of force by states is illegal. However, there have been controversies about the proper interpretation of this provision. First, it refers to the threat or use of 'force'; developing states have argued that this is wide enough to cover not just armed force but also economic coercion. Developed states have resisted this claim. Even if Article 2(4) does not itself contain such a prohibition, economic coercion is unlawful under other instruments such as the Declaration on Friendly Relations (1970).

Secondly, what is the meaning of 'threat of force'? The ICJ in the **Nicaragua case** and in its Advisory Opinion on the *Legality of Threat or Use of Nuclear Weapons* (1996) took the narrow view that a threat of force would be unlawful where the force threatened would itself be unlawful. Thirdly, Article 2(4) refers to the use of force in 'international relations'. In practice civil conflicts have been by far the most common type of conflict since World War II, often with outside intervention as in the Cold War proxy conflicts or more recently in the complex conflict in the DRC (1998–2003).

The most controversial issue about Article 2(4) is whether it should be interpreted as a wide or a narrow prohibition. Some commentators argue that the unilateral use of force is lawful if it is for a beneficial purpose such as humanitarian intervention to prevent or terminate massive humanitarian catastrophe in cases where the territorial state is not willing or able to act. They claim that such a use of force does not harm the territorial integrity or political independence of a state and is not contrary to the purposes of the UN. The experience of the genocide in Rwanda (1994) led some to argue not just for more effective UN action but for a unilateral right of humanitarian intervention. The question arose with regard to the NATO operation in Kosovo (1999); a few member states used humanitarian intervention as the justification for the bombing campaign. But the doctrine is still extremely controversial. The UK is a strong supporter and has attempted to develop a legal framework to govern its scope. The 2005 UN World Summit accepted the existence of a responsibility to protect in cases of humanitarian disaster, but left unclear whether Security Council authorization was necessary for the use of force. The 116-member Non-Aligned Movement strongly reject any unilateral right of humanitarian intervention.

CHRISTINE GRAY

uses and trusts, history of   Trusts developed in the context of the English distinction between courts of **common law** and courts of equity. The common law courts arose first. Complaints to the king of injustice in their operation then gave rise to courts of equity, including, in particular, the **Chancery Court**. Trusts depended upon this jurisdictional distinction. If A (settlor) transferred property to B (trustee), on the understanding that B would hold it for the benefit of C (beneficiary), the common law courts saw B as the owner and went no further; but the courts of equity, building upon B's common law ownership, would order him to exercise it for C's benefit.

C's equitable entitlement might have operated only as against B. But regular enforcement of trusts against both trustees and strangers, beneficiaries' ability to transfer their interests to third parties, and protection of the beneficial interest against external claims (eg by the trustee's creditors), gradually gave a strong proprietary aspect to the beneficial interest: in many ways C could be regarded as the owner against the world.

While famously flexible and versatile, trusts have tended to be concentrated in particular contexts: the handling of family wealth, finance and commerce, and charity. Their historical development falls into three parts: the period before the Statute of Uses 1536; the following period in which the statute's effects were worked out, and the groundwork of the modern law laid; and the period from the earlier nineteenth century, in which trusts law was adapted to a new economic and social climate.

Trusts have their roots in medieval 'uses', land being transferred from a settlor ('feoffor to uses') to trustees ('feoffees to uses'), to the use of (ie for the benefit of) a beneficiary—either the feoffor or another. Following legislation in 1290 land became more freely transferable, and during the fourteenth century uses began to be common, in particular to direct the devolution of family land across generations, and to allow payment of debts from landed wealth; the common law prohibited wills of freehold land, but their effect could be achieved by transferring land to feoffees to uses, to hold to uses declared in the settlor's will.

In the fourteenth century judicial interpretation and enforcement of uses became available in some church courts. By the early fifteenth century the court of Chancery had a settled jurisdiction over uses, and began to develop rules: for example, if the feoffees transferred the property to a third party, he was bound by the uses unless he took the land for value without notice of them. Uses could arise by implication. For example a 'resulting' use would arise in favour of the transferor if land was transferred for no value without a use being expressed. The beneficiary came to be seen as having a kind of ownership, but conscience remained significant: corporations, lacking a conscience and so unable to be trusted, could not yet be feoffees to uses.

An important consequence of uses was financial loss to the king. In certain circumstances feudal lordship gave him income from land when its owner died (eg during the owner's heir's infancy), but only where it passed to the heir directly. No revenue accrued if land had been transferred to feoffees before the owner died to hold to the uses declared in his will. The Statute of Marlborough 1267 gave some protection for the king's revenue against uses, and legislation began again in the later fifteenth century, leading to the Statute of Uses 1536, which followed a decision by the common law judges in 1535 (under royal pressure) that uses could not be employed to achieve the effect of a will of land.

The Statute of Uses 'executed' uses, transferring common law ownership from the feoffees to uses to the beneficiary, thus ending the use. Wills of land by means of uses now seemed impossible, though the Statute of Wills 1540 permitted wills of defined proportions of a testator's land while reserving the king's revenue over the rest. Thereafter this statute was the main protection for the king's revenue. The Statute of Uses did not apply to all uses; the exceptions founded modern trusts. Unexecuted uses (commonly called trusts) included cases where the trustees had active duties; trusts of leases; trusts of property other than land; and trusts taking the form of a use upon a use (which could arise either expressly or by implication). The Statute of Wills 1540 had removed the will-making role of uses, but trusts remained common after 1536, including trusts for charitable purposes; for the payment of debts; to provide for the incapable; to give married women independent control of property; and in the settlement of family estates.

The court of Chancery likewise continued to enforce trusts, drawing upon rules developed for uses. Lord Chancellor Nottingham (1673–1682) was significant in giving substance to trust beneficiaries' interests, and in setting out the framework of the law, including that applying to resulting trusts and trusts constructed by the court (eg to prevent a trustee benefiting from the trust). Also in Nottingham's time legislation required that expressly created trusts be evidenced in writing. Nottingham's work was developed and refined in the eighteenth century, in particular under Lord Chancellor Hardwicke (1737–1756). In the first half of the nineteenth century the development of trusts law was largely completed, and an abstract conception of trusts appeared in the possibility of declaring oneself a trustee. As investment opportunities widened dramatically, trusts expanded beyond the landed gentry and aristocracy, becoming increasingly centred upon management of interchangeable funds. In consequence the rights and duties of trustees were re-evaluated.

The abolition of separate courts of common law and equity in the 1870s left trusts unscathed, though in modern debate over 'fusion' of law and equity even trusts are not universally regarded as incapable of practical integration. But the flexibility of trusts, re-emphasized in the twentieth century as they have adapted to modern taxation regimes, unit trusts, family breakdown, and occupational pension provision, may owe much to their conceptual complexity and ambiguity, rendering fusion a challenging undertaking.   NEIL JONES

JH Baker, *An Introduction to English Legal History* (London: Butterworths, 4th edn, 2002), ch 14 and pp. 290–297

AWB Simpson, *A History of the Land Law* (Oxford: Oxford University Press, 2nd edn, 1986), ch 8

See also: **equity as a system of law**

usury   Usury may refer to three phenomena: lending money at interest, lending at an interest rate higher than permitted by law, and lending money at an excessive interest rate. This entry focuses on the latter two practices since they represent the understanding of usury in many parts of the world—but merely taking interest is still prohibited by **Islamic law**. **Regulation** of usury has a long history. It is perhaps the oldest form of market regulation and is a live contemporary issue. Many countries, such as France, South Africa, and Japan, have usury laws—ie laws limiting the permissible rate of interest. These laws are often justified as a method of protecting lower income consumers from high credit prices on the basis that it is unfair that the poor should have to pay a high price for credit that is often needed for the purchase of necessities and that high-cost credit undercuts any progressive effects of redistribution of wealth. However, while it is widely agreed to be unfair that the poor should have to pay high prices for credit, many also doubt that usury laws are the most effective method of achieving affordable credit.

Jeremy **Bentham** was a trenchant critic of usury laws and policymakers in the United Kingdom remain influenced by the propositions he put forward in his 'Defence of Usury' written in 1787. Bentham outlined several arguments that were made in favour of legal limitations on the rate of interest: the prevention of 'prodigality'; protection of the poor against extortion and against being taken advantage of; and discouragement of excessive risk-taking. Bentham argued that usury laws would not achieve these objectives because they would backfire or be ineffective. Thus, assuming a workably competitive market, usury laws would exclude the poor from the legitimate credit market and force them to pay a higher price in the more dangerous illegal market. The prodigal would evade a ceiling on the interest charged for borrowing money by purchasing goods on credit terms. Bentham's ideas triumphed in 1854 and since that date the UK has not had usury laws, although from 1909 until 1974 there was a presumption that a loan by a moneylender was usurious if the interest rate exceeded 48 per cent. In 1971 the Crowther Committee on Consumer Credit concluded that individuals should not have to borrow at interest rates of over 100 per cent and that their needs should be met by the **welfare state**. However, the Consumer Credit Act 1974 did not include interest-rate ceilings, but rather an extortionate credit-bargain provision that was of marginal significance as a form of credit-price control.

Concerns about over-indebtedness and the high price of credit in lower-income credit markets resulted in pressure for the introduction of interest-rate ceilings in the 2006 amendments to the Consumer Credit Act. However the government rejected this option partly on the basis of an analysis that suggested that interest-rate ceilings in Germany and France had resulted in some consumers being excluded from the credit market or in the substitution of higher-cost forms of supply where the cost of credit is buried in the price charged. But the argument over interest-rate ceilings continues, and reflects a concern about the legitimacy of the credit system in a society of high inequality where the poor continue to pay more for credit.   IAIN RAMSAY

V

vaccine damage *see* **tort system**

value added tax Value added tax ('VAT') is typically a type of consumption tax charged on sales and other transfers for consideration at every stage of production. Every producer (or supplier) of goods or services is required to charge VAT (sometimes referred to as 'output tax') on the price at which it sells its goods or services, but the supplier is entitled to a credit for the VAT it has been charged on all its purchases from other suppliers ('input tax'). The supplier pays the difference between the amounts of output tax and input tax to the tax authority. The result of this is that the same amount of tax is paid to the tax authority as if the tax were charged on the value that the supplier added to the cost of its inputs, and from this comes the name of the tax.

The first national VAT was introduced in France in the 1950s. Since then it has become very widespread. It was introduced throughout the European Economic Community (now the **European Union**) in 1970, and is now used by countries on every continent of the globe. In some countries (notably Australia, Canada, and New Zealand) the tax is called GST ('goods and services tax' or 'general sales tax').

VATs are generally intended to be consumption taxes. Strictly speaking a VAT will only be a tax on consumption if it gives a full deduction for the cost of capital goods (which ensures that it is not charged on savings) and is charged on imports with a full deduction for exports (known as the 'destination basis', this ensures that it is charged only on goods and services consumed domestically).

In the EU every country is required to set a standard rate of VAT, which must be at least 15 per cent. Most countries also impose reduced rates of VAT on certain goods and services, typically ones regarded as essentials. This is true of all European Union countries. Some countries also impose higher rates on certain luxuries, but this is not permitted in the EU. The rate differences are seen as a response to the argument that VAT is a regressive tax, imposing a greater burden on those who are less well off and who must therefore devote a greater proportion of their incomes to consumption. However, New Zealand introduced its GST with a single rate to get the full benefit of VAT as a consumption tax. The lowest possible rate is a rate of zero (used extensively in the UK, Ireland, and Canada), in which case the supplier charges no VAT, but is still entitled to a credit for the tax on inputs.

There are a number of reasons for the widespread popularity of VAT. The structure of VAT as a multistage tax with credit for input tax makes it easy to impose on a very wide range of goods and services without distorting the structure of business. This means that VATs can generate large amounts of revenue for the government even when imposed at relatively low rates. In addition, the multistage nature of the tax means that, although VAT is normally structured as a tax on consumption, it is collected early in the productive process, improving government cash flow. Furthermore the failure of some small suppliers to pay the tax they owe has only a limited impact on government revenues, since each supplier is only liable to pay the proportion of the tax referable to the value it adds. This helps to keep the overall cost of collection for the government low. These features give VAT an advantage over retail sales taxes, commonly used by US states and Canadian provinces. Its multistage nature also makes a VAT easier to charge on services than a retail sales tax.

Under VAT a supplier is typically required to demonstrate its entitlement to a credit for input tax by producing an invoice for the purchase it has made. This means that there is in principle a record both of the charging of the VAT on the purchase and of the claim for a credit, which is described as making VAT 'self enforcing'. However, this also makes invoices for inputs valuable and can be a source of fraud.

Despite the popularity of VATs, they have a number of problems. When services are provided across borders, it can be difficult to determine which country has the right to charge VAT, and this may even give opportunities for avoiding any charge to VAT. There are also difficulties in imposing VAT on financial transactions and transactions in real estate without creating distortions or loss of revenue. The system currently used for taxing supplies of goods between countries within the EU means that the goods pass between countries free of tax and without physical border controls. This has given rise to significant opportunities for fraud, particularly what is known as MTIC (missing trader intra-Community) fraud or carousel fraud.   IAN ROXAN

variation of trusts   *see* **trusts**

vehicle tax   *see* **Environmental Taxes**

Venables, Jon   *see* **Thompson, Robert and Venables Jon**

vertical agreement   A vertical agreement is one between entities operating at different levels in relation to the production and distribution of goods and/or services. The form of vertical agreement most frequently falling to be reviewed under **competition law** is the distribution agreement between a manufacturer and retailer. Licensing agreements in respect of intellectual property are also viewed as being of a vertical nature. While such agreements are an essential part of the fabric of commerce they may have harmful effects where, for example, a retailer is limited by the manufacturer in the way in which they do business. The two areas that are of the greatest concern in the operation of competition law are territorial and pricing restraints imposed on retailers. In the leading case of *Consten and Grundig v Commission* (1966) the **European Court of Justice** held that such terms were capable of infringing Article 81(1) of the EC Treaty, and in so doing widened considerably the practical scope of competition law. Most terms that fall within vertical agreements, particularly those relating to the need to maintain the quality of the product, or those requiring the retailer to make fair efforts to promote the product, are unlikely to be caught by the operation of competition law. The principle remains however that setting minimum prices, and placing absolute territorial limits on where sales may be made, invites condemnation under both EC and UK competition law.
                                MARK FURSE

vertical equity in taxation   *see* **tax, ability to pay**

vexatious litigants   Vexatious litigants are those who repeatedly issue proceedings, or make repeated applications within proceedings, which are considered to be totally without merit. The Supreme Court Act 1981 gives the High Court the power to make an order (a 'Section 42 Order') preventing such litigants from instituting proceedings or making applications without the leave of the High Court. According to Her Majesty's Court Service, in 2007 there were 185 such orders in force, thirty-two of which had been made since 2002.

In addition to such orders, any judge can make a limited Civil Restraint Order, and certain judges can make Extended or General Civil Restraint Orders. Unlike a Section 42 Order, these orders are limited to a period not exceeding two years. These orders apply respectively to: the proceedings in which they are made; any matter relating to, or touching upon, the proceedings in which the order is made; or all claims and applications. All orders require the leave of a named judge for proceedings to be issued or applications to be made.

Moorhead and Sefton suggest that whilst vexatious or 'obsessive and difficult' litigants are relatively uncommon at first instance proceedings, they cause a disproportionate amount of disruption to the administration of justice. They also reported a tendency for such litigants to be fee exempt.
                    AVROM SHERR AND MARC MASON

R Moorhead and M Sefton, *Litigants in person: Unrepresented litigants in first instance proceedings. Department of Constitutional Affairs Research Series 2/05* (2005)

vicarious liability   In some circumstances a **person** may be liable for the wrongful acts of another. This form of liability is 'vicarious' and usually derives from the relationship between the person committing the act and the person upon whom vicarious liability is conferred. Typically, liability here is for civil wrongs; it is only in exceptional cases that vicarious—as opposed to personal—liability arises in relation to the commission of a crime.

Vicarious liability can encompass a range of relationships including the liability of partners for each other's acts and the liability of principals for the acts of their **agents**. However, in modern law, it is almost universally understood in terms of the liability of employers for the wrongful acts of their employees.

Thus, if an employee's carelessness results in injury to another, the injured party may have a legal claim, not only against the employee, but also against the employer—so long as certain conditions are met. These include (1) the employee must have committed legal wrong, in other words, a tort; (2) the employee must *be* an employee, that is, working under a **contract of employment** (in old legal parlance, a 'contract of service'); and (3) the tort/wrong must be committed in the 'course of employment'. The first condition is resolved by reference to **tort law** requirements; the second depends on contractual rules distinguishing a contract of employment (service) from a contract for services. Over the years this distinction has caused difficulties, particularly as, with changes in the nature and organization of work, the lines between employment and independent contractual status have blurred. The final requirement—that the tort be carried out in the course of employment—has also caused problems. Up to a point it is fairly straightforward: employers are not liable for what their employees do in their spare time. However, even within a work context, liability does not always arise. According to Salmond's formulation, liability was said to extend to the commission of wrongful acts authorized by the 'master' (read employer) or to authorized acts carried out in a 'wrongful and unauthorized mode'. For example, where a milkman, against his employer's orders, took a boy on his milk float to help him on his milk round, and the boy was injured by the milkman's negligence, the employer was held liable; the milkman had after all been doing his job, albeit in an unauthorized way (*Rose v Plenty* (1976)). By contrast, where a bus conductor attacked a passenger, the bus company was *not* held liable (*Keppel Bus Co Lt v Sa'ad bin Ahmad* (1974)). In these circumstances, the employee is said to be engaging in 'a frolic of his own'. Needless to say, the line between these two situations is far from easy to draw and the relevant case law is not really coherent. A lot depends on how one views the rationale for vicarious liability. Insofar as it is tied to risks created by the employer's business, one can understand a judicial approach seeking to limit liability to *anticipatable* risks. If, on the other hand, vicarious liability is understood as a distributive technique, a way of spreading loss sustained by one individual across an enterprise (through the employer's insurance), then wider liability makes more sense. This dilemma is illustrated in *Lister v Hesley Hall* (2002), a **House of Lords** decision about an employer's liability for sexual assaults on children carried out by the warden of a children's home. On the one hand, one could argue that such acts fall squarely within the category of 'frolics' for which employers should not be liable— this is hardly an 'unauthorized mode of doing an authorized act'. On the other hand, bearing in mind the employer's deeper pocket, the claimants' need, and the opportunity which employment created to commit the act, the imposition of liability on the employer here makes some sense. This was indeed the conclusion of the House of Lords who argued that liability should turn on showing a 'sufficiency of

connection' between the nature of the employment and the tort committed. This dilemma has been similarly faced in relation to employers' liability for acts of discrimination by employees. Here the **common law** approach to vicarious liability has been jettisoned in favour of a common sense literal approach to what constitutes the course of employment. Thus where employees subjected a fellow employee to racial abuse and assault, the employer was held liable (*Jones v Tower Boots* (1997)).

JOANNE CONAGHAN

See also: **abuse, liability for; civil liability, theories of**

victims   The second edition of *The Compact Oxford English Dictionary* offers a multiplex definition of *victim*:

'A **person** who is put to death or subjected to **torture** by another; one who suffers severely in body or property through cruel or oppressive treatment... One who is reduced or destined to suffer under some oppressive destructive agency . . . One who perishes or suffers in health, etc, from some enterprise or pursuit voluntarily undertaken.'

The word evidently has diffuse meaning. It tends to be used loosely and metaphorically to cover many circumstances, including ill health and accident, that are quite distinct from those of a person whose property or person has been subject to criminal attack. It refers to unpleasant conditions which few would willingly court; dwells on subjection, submissiveness, and passivity, states which are tainted by connotations of a devalued and degraded status; and makes no necessary connection with law, its range being clearly greater than that encompassed by the law alone. It is not remarkable that those who might call themselves victims have not always cared for such an apparently stigmatizing **identity**, preferring, in the case, say, of **women** who have been raped or subjected to **domestic violence**, to call themselves 'survivors' with its imagery of fortitude and resistance.

The law of England and Wales itself has had a long and ambivalent relation with the victims of criminal acts. People have not until very recently been addressed *as* victims in law or procedure. Neither are they recognized as parties. Mindful of the contested character of allegations in the **adversarial system**, judges and lawyers have been inclined to argue that they are no more than *alleged* victims until the conclusion of a trial, and by that time the title will not only have lost most of its practical effect but could also in principle have been denied in the some 97 per cent of cases where a suspected crime lacks any prospect of a **prosecution**. Victims of **violence** *have* been recognized as applicants for criminal injuries compensation; under the government's 'Victim's Charters' of 1990 and 1996, all victims are entitled to expect certain kinds of service from criminal justice agencies and from Victim Support, a **non-governmental organization**; and, at trial, they can appear as complainants and witnesses for the prosecution. However, they have only just been awarded formal rights, and those rights are modest and tangential. First there was section 2d of the Criminal Justice and Courts Service Act 2000, which laid down that the **probation** service must 'ensur[e] [the] offenders' awareness of the effects of crime on the victims of crime and the public'. In March 2001, there came into effect the European Framework Decision on the Standing of Victims in Criminal Procedure, binding on all Member States—including the UK—which talked about the rights of victims, but, at the urging of the governments of Britain and Ireland, waived any such formal rights in the procedure of **common law** countries. There is a statutory Code of Practice for Victims of Crime under the Domestic Violence, Crime and Victims Act 2004. Its wording is again tentative and oblique, echoing the two Victim's Charters which it replaces, and referring not to *rights* but to 'the precise standards of care and support that [victims] can expect to receive from criminal justice agencies'. Victims are not given a right to litigate themselves, being obliged to proceed through an **ombudsman**, and there are no penalties for non-compliance by agencies. But they *have* been formally recognized, after a fashion.

It is not difficult to account for such hesitancy and caution in the management of victims. Not only is *victim* a provisional status until there is an admission, **plea**, or finding at trial, but the word bears with it a taint of blame (consider, eg the 'just world' hypothesis which implies that bad things, like victimization, cannot and should not happen to good people, and that victims must in some fashion have deserved what befell them); contamination (the relatives of murdered people claim, for example, that they may be avoided because they are thought to bring bad luck); irrationality (the resistance to victims enjoying a fuller role in proceedings tends to underscore how their emotionality and impulsiveness are thought to undermine the calm and disinterested pursuit of **justice**); and vindictiveness (criminal injuries compensation was introduced into the UK in 1965 by liberal reformers anxious to buy off what were thought to be the vengeful victims of violence). Crimes tend disproportionately to be committed *within* social groups, and criminologists and practitioners in criminal justice argue that

there is a substantial overlap between victimized and offending populations. Crime, they say, may no longer be a confrontation between black and white, but of 'grey versus grey' (Antilla, (1964)). Victims are not then always attractive, innocent, deserving, or admirable people, falling as they do–in the words of David Downes—between the roles of pariah and saint, unless they conform to some of the features of what Nils Christie in 1986 called the 'ideal victim': those whose irreproachable blamelessness is apparent in their youthfulness or advanced age, and, perhaps, their **gender**.

Above all, there are powerful political and jurisprudential arguments which have kept the personal victim at a distance. Trials are conventionally presented as a contest between the state and the accused. The victim may be one whose possessions or body bear the marks of an offence, but crime is symbolically committed against the **community** metaphysically conceived; and the victim's somewhat paradoxical duty is to report and attest to how society has been hurt through his or her own suffering. Even in the heyday of private prosecutions, when the victim was responsible for bringing matters to trial, victims were regarded as venal and vengeful and crime itself was conceived to be an offence against something larger than, and independent of, the interests and person of an individual. That presumption has remained. The criminal law is not an instrument of what some lawyers take to be private vengeance, and the personal victim is held to have little formal part in it. Proposals floated in a consultation paper in late 2005 to introduce victims' advocates and victim impact statements in the courts of England and Wales (*Hearing the Relatives of Murder and Manslaughter Victims*, DCA, September 2005) met with the standard lawyerly riposte that, in the words of the director of the Legal Action Group in November 2005:

'The **criminal justice system** necessarily has the defendant rather than the victim, at the centre. The case is brought by the state on behalf of all society, not only the victims and their families… To give victims' families a direct voice in open court at the **sentencing** stage, presents a risk of exacerbating their stress while also posing problems of consistency and fairness for the defendant'

and, in the words of the Bar Council, 'The proposal that victims should have a say in decisions as to whether prosecutions are started, terminated, and what charges are brought is potentially inimical to justice'. That is a view often stated, and it has consistently stalled the more formal acknowledgement and representation of victims in criminal process.

PAUL ROCK

I Antilla, 'Victimology—A New Territory in Criminology' (1964) 5 *Scandinavian Studies in Criminology* 8

P Rock, *Constructing Victims' Rights* (Oxford: Clarendon Press, 2004)

See also: **criminal injuries compensation schemes**

victims' rights *see* **victims**

video evidence *see* **evidence, criminal**

Video Recordings Regulation *see* **Film and Video Recordings Regulation**

vigilantism Vigilantism derives from the Latin root *vigil*: a vigilante is one who watches or is observant. Vigilantism is more commonly used to refer to the rejection of state authority or competence for providing **security** by members of the public who coordinate to provide protection for themselves and others. It reflects a loss of faith in the protection offered by the **police** and so supplements this with organized self-help measures and local patrols. Vigilantism lies on a continuum with **community** or informal justice initiatives encouraged by the state. In Britain, when 'Guardian Angels' began patrolling the London Underground in the 1980s they received a cautious welcome. Similarly, government promotion of 'walking with a purpose' and Neighbourhood Watch Schemes in the 1990s were arguably an encouragement to quasi-vigilante activities. Yet it is difficult to prevent vigilantism declining into people taking the law into their own hands against particular groups or individuals on grounds of **race**, or social status. Other common targets are those suspected of crimes abhorred by the community in question, such as sexual offending, **child abuse**, or **terrorism**. Vigilantism may target suspect populations irrespective of the threat they actually pose. In its more extreme forms, vigilantism may result in intimidation, extortion, and **violence**. Lynching in the southern states of America; burning tyre or 'necklacing' in South Africa; punishment beatings in Northern Ireland; protection rackets and other activities of the Mafia in Italy, Russia, and America, and the Yakuza in Japan are all forms of vigilantism. LUCIA ZEDNER

L Johnston, 'What is Vigilantism?' (1996) 36/2 *British Journal of Criminology* 220–236

D Gambetta, *The Sicilian Mafia* (Cambridge, MA: Harvard University Press, 1993)

village greens The term 'village green' conjures up an image of Merrie England or the green at Auburn in Goldsmith's *The Deserted Village*. However, the reality is more prosaic. The term 'town or village green' is the term now used in statute. A combination of judicial decisions and Acts of Parliament have broadened its meaning. Inhabitants of a locality (or a neighbourhood within a locality) have the right to use the land for lawful games or recreation. This can be shown if there is a specific statute justifying that use; or if there is a customary right to use the land, or it is land on which the inhabitants have indulged in such sports or pastimes for not less than twenty years. Three **House of Lords** decisions have taken a broad view of what amounts to a town or village green, including, for example, 'an overgrown, rubble-strewn, semi-submerged area sandwiched between the canal and the railway', a car park, and a piece of land used for an annual Guy Fawkes bonfire. The Commons Act 2006 will make it easier for land to be registered as a village green or town green.

PETER CLARKE

violence To begin routinely, violence is a force capable of causing harm, injury, or death. But what is the relation between violence (force) and law? Violence (force) can be authorized by law, and performed in the name of the public. It can also, of course, be unleashed between individuals or groups in the form **of domestic violence**, various forms of assault, **homicide**, or **hate speech** ('horizontal violence'). Legal force—policing, imprisonment, the death penalty ('vertical violence')—is distinguished from horizontal violence through legal mediation or legal sanction. Violence in myriad forms can be sourced and legitimated by law, or it can be proscribed and become the object of law's violence. The latter also reflects Max Weber's definition of the state as the entity with a 'monopoly on the legitimate use of physical force'. Whether there can be a separation between law and violence, however, and the precise nature of this relation, are a more complicated and interesting matter. Legal scholar, Robert Cover, famously stated that: 'Legal interpretation takes place in a field of pain and death'. The statement asserts a relation between law's word (interpretation, judgment, decision) and violence. It also suggests a distinction between law and violence whereby violence takes place in some separate functional social context—such as in prisons, by warders, executioners, and so on. As Cover observes, 'Interpretations which occasion violence are distinct from the violent acts they occasion'. Suffice it to say that there is a relation between violence and law. But the separation of law and violence is less persuasive. So let's delve more deeply into this relation.

The relation between violence and law becomes more evident if we draw on the German term for 'violence', *Gewalt*. *Gewalt* signifies 'legitimate power, authority, public force'. The ambiguity that the term 'violence' invokes in German, can be amplified by exploring the relation between law and **justice**, and the centrality of violence to the legal enterprise of rendering justice, of doing justice, as well as to the very origin of law. How does law sustain the legitimacy of the violence it occasions? Jacques Derrida draws on Blaise Pascal to explain the significance of the links between violence (force), law, and justice. Law cannot be a mere calculation, Derrida tells us. Law lacks authority and legitimacy if the legal decision or order it proclaims is not just. Concretely, what is decreed in the general proclamation of the law must be made to apply, must be extended, to the singularity (uniqueness) of the predicament, culpability, or demand of the **person** who stands before the law. However, justice without some reference to legal authorization, to rule and **precedent,** or the customs that have gone before, is arbitrary. There is no law without justice—no justice without law; but the two cannot be without violence. Justice is superfluous if its decision or order is not enforced. And violence or force alone, without justice, is tyrannical. Violence (force) and justice are thus integral to law. The occasion of law's violence, as we have seen then, does not take place in some functionally differentiated 'other place', such as police custody, the prison, or the execution chamber. Enforceability, violence, is the currency of law's efficacy.

Violence also accompanies the foundation and preservation of law—what Walter Benjamin called 'law-making' and 'law-preserving violence': 'All violence as a means is either law-making or law-preserving. If it lays claim to neither of these predicates, it forfeits all validity'. The general strike or war are both examples of violence as a means of challenging, and if successful, supplanting the existing legal order. In both cases, a new order is the horizon of violence—thus the appellation 'law-making violence'. In the death penalty, and the **police**, Benjamin made the lasting observation that both law-making and law-preserving violence is present at once. What is 'rotten in law' is revealed in the death penalty: 'For if violence . . . is the origin of law, then it may be readily supposed that where the highest violence, that over life and death, occurs in the legal system, the origins of law jut manifestly and fearsomely into existence'. Such jutting violence is packed with significance. Although the 'highest violence' is ostensibly yet another sanction, law reaffirms itself by pointing to the origin where force asserted itself over the prior order with only the exigencies and demands

of the new order in mind. With war or **colonialism** in mind we could say that the origin of law demonstrates tremendous indifference to life—but with a new order as its end. The violence of the police, similarly, especially in the realm of what is deemed to be for 'security reasons', though no 'clear legal situation exists', will enable a discretionary violence that is at once law-making and law-preserving. The empirical ends of the particular legal system cease to be clear or determinative in the face of a threat to '**security**'.

The law, from contracts to **constitutions**, is intimately connected with violence; and the pretension of non-violence is just that. Benjamin offers two evocative examples which point to the centrality of violence to law. The first is the contract, which though originating in seemingly peaceful negotiations will ultimately see recourse to law's violence should either party break the agreement. The second is more powerful—parliamentarianism or the means of apparently non-violent agreement. The decay of parliamentarianism flows from forgetting the revolutionary violence that gave birth to it. **Parliaments**, representative institutions, are being replaced with pervasive regulation and inscrutable governance. But this only momentarily covers over the fate of all legal systems. They are preserved with violence and ultimately superseded in a violent eruption which has a new order as its end.   STEWART MOTHA

R Cover, 'Violence and the Word' (1986) 95 *Yale Law Journal* 1601
J Derrida, 'The Force of Law: The Mystical Foundations of Authority' in G Anidjar (ed), *Acts of Religion* (London: Routledge, 2002), 258–293

violence and crime   *see* **crime and violence**

visa   A 'visa' is a document issued at the discretion of a state, which authorizes a foreigner's entry into that state, stipulates the permitted duration and purpose of his or her stay, and prescribes any conditions attaching to that stay (such as the **right to work**). It is normally affixed to a person's **passport**, and may be issued for single or multiple entry. Possession of a valid visa is the basis by which a non-citizen's status is determined as lawful or unlawful. A person who does not possess a valid visa is liable to removal, and in some countries may be detained until removal is possible. Since visas are issued at the discretion of states, they remain liable to cancellation at any time, including after entry, subject to any constitutional or legislative substantive or procedural limitation on the power of cancellation.

A visa provides evidence of eligibility for entry, but is not itself a guarantee. The burden generally lies on the potential entrant to prove an entitlement to enter, and immigration officers may deny entry if they believe that the visa has been obtained fraudulently, that there has been a change of circumstances since the visa was issued (which has removed the basis of the holder's claim to admission), or that the holder will not comply with conditions attached to the visa (such as leaving the country at the end of the visa period, or refraining from working).

Visas are generally synonymous with 'entry permits', although traditionally the former were granted outside the destination country, while the latter were granted at the point of entry. This distinction is no longer strictly maintained in practice, and some visas can only be applied for once a person is within a particular country.

As a form of border control, visa regimes enable states to scrutinize foreigners seeking entry. Although the modern visa system did not begin until the early twentieth century, the British Aliens Act 1793 required foreigners to register on arrival in Britain, and obtain a locally-issued 'passport' bearing the name of the town or place to which he or she wished to go. Travel to other towns required a fresh 'passport' to be issued, and foreigners without this documentation were liable to imprisonment. Visas were first introduced as a requirement in the United States in 1924, and were described as evidencing the US's recognition of the validity of the bearer's passport (*Johanson v Phelps* (1926)), which itself constituted evidence of the issuing government's permission for the bearer to travel (*US v Rodriguez* (1960)).

Requirements as to *who* must possess a visa vary widely from country to country, and typically depend upon one's **nationality** (although Australia requires every non-citizen to hold a visa in order to lawfully enter the country, and anyone without one is liable to immigration detention). Some countries have reciprocal visa regimes in place; others refuse to issue visas to nationals of, or to those who have visited, certain countries (such as Israel). Some countries do not require certain foreign nationals to have a visa at all. Such 'visa waiver' schemes are usually determined on the basis of historical relationships between the countries, common membership of a regional organization (such as the European Union), or the statistical likelihood that those nationals will not overstay the period for which permission to enter has been granted. Some regions, like the European Union, operate a common visa regime for temporary entry, whereby a visa issued by one country within the region is recognized by others in that region

(see the **Schengen Agreement**). Diplomats are often exempted from visa requirements altogether, although this is more a convention of international comity than a rule of **international law**.

Visas may be issued for a variety of purposes, including transit, tourism, study, family reasons, employment, investment, medical treatment, and **refugee** protection. Failure to meet health and character criteria may be used to deny a person a visa, even if all other conditions are met.

Visa regimes have been criticized for failing to take account of the needs of **asylum** seekers. With the exception of the few states that choose to resettle refugees from abroad, asylum seekers are unable to secure protection visas outside countries in which they wish to obtain asylum. International refugee law prohibits states from penalizing refugees who enter without visas and from removing them to places where they risk persecution or other serious harm. However, since possession of a valid visa is increasingly a prerequisite for authorized departure on an aeroplane or ship (as carriers can be fined for transporting passengers who lack the necessary travel documentation), asylum seekers may be prevented from leaving their countries in the first place.

A few countries require their nationals to obtain an exit visa in order to leave their homeland. This is aimed at restricting access to countries with different political systems and ideologies, and has been acknowledged by the UN Human Rights Committee as a violation of the right to leave one's country.

JANE MCADAM

visitatorial jurisdiction   *see* **universities and higher education**

visual arts, law and   The law has always had a visual policy and understood the importance of the **governance** of images. For a large part of the Western tradition, **religion** and law have treated the visual arts and images more generally with caution if not hostility. The philosophical and religious traditions expressed a strong anxiety about the power of images. Plato excluded art and artists from the *Republic* and inaugurated the 'ancient quarrel' between art and philosophy. In his *Laws*, Plato stated that painters may represent men with contrasting characters and contradict themselves, but the legislator must not let his laws say two different things on the same subject. In the Judaeo-Christian tradition, the Second Commandment bans graven images and all likeness of things. Controversies about images permeate Western law. The iconoclastic wars in Byzantium and the Reformation reveal a deep-seated fear but also an ambiguity about the use of art. Modernity continues the quarrel. According to Kant's critical philosophy, three areas of inquiry and action, the cognitive, the practical, and the aesthetic are released in modernity to develop their own specific rationality, in separate institutions operated by distinct groups of experts. Modern law is born in this separation from aesthetic considerations.

After the Reformation and the fusion of secular and ecclesiastical jurisdictions iconophobic ideas became prominent in the **common law**. The image had come to be seen as too worldly, sensual, and potentially corrupt and was replaced by the word. In the same way that icons were excluded from churches, figures and imagery were banned from the law. The further linkage of imagistic language with rhetoric led to the subordination of rhetoric to logic and the elevation of logic to the proper method of law. The fear of images became the fear of plural interpretations, local and informal jurisdictions, different logics, and particular reasons. Art was assigned to imagination, creativity, and playfulness, law to control, discipline, and sobriety.

The law polices art and regulates images in a general and a specific sense. It treats works of art like any other object and artists like any other worker, imposing upon art and artists general restrictions and regulations. The law regulates the art market, the movement of artworks, the public funding of the arts and enforces contracts and agreements. More importantly, the law defines the boundaries of (good) art and regulates aesthetic considerations under the principles of freedom of speech and artistic expression and their limitations expressed in the laws of public order, **obscenity**, **copyright**, **blasphemy,** and **defamation**.

From the trial of Paolo Veronese by the Venetian inquisitors in 1573 for his liberal depiction of the *Last Supper*, to the 1878 **libel** case of *Whistler v Ruskin* about the artistic value of eight Whistler paintings, to the 1990 trial of seven Robert Mapplethorpe photographs for obscenity in Cincinatti and the trials over the Danish cartoons of the Prophet Muhammad in 2007, law has shown a constant interest in policing images in the name of decency, good taste, morals and, occasionally, political propriety. The boundaries of art have been defined pragmatically in the case law without too much concern about art's asserted ontological autonomy. As a result, art has habitually received less recognition than other values and its protection is based on general **freedom of expression** principles rather than on the specific contribution art makes to culture. Reputation and public morality have been valued over art in defamation.

In obscenity law, artworks are treated first as any obscene article and only if found obscene does the 'artistic merit' defence come into play. **Judges** often assert aesthetic neutrality, but the case law reveals that legal and aesthetic judgments are quite close in their effects despite their formal differences; legal reasoning easily cohabits with diverse (and often suspect) judicial tastes.

Law has often been asked to define what is (good) art. Were the Whistler *Nocturnes* art or a randomly flung pot of paint? Was Constantin Brancusi's *Bird in Space* the representation of a bird or too abstract for that and therefore not art? Was Jeff Koons' *String of Puppies* sculpture, a reproduction of a copyrighted kitsch postcard, or original art? In such cases, law's strategic intervention has been organized around the relationship between object, image, and text. The central question of aesthetic value and **representation** is intensely influenced here by the different legal considerations about originality and authorship as found, for example, in the law of **copyright**.

The law has not forgotten however the utility and effectiveness of carefully policed images. A language that carries the mainsprings of the social bond and transmits the commands of public order must both act on the emotions and persuade the intellect. Law's force has always relied on an economy of permitted and a criminology of dangerous images. Every major political change from Imperial Rome to Iraq was followed by the destruction or defilement of the emblems of the previous regime and the icons and statues of the defeated leaders. This historically changing combination of iconoclasm and iconophilia amounts to a complex and historically determined legal administration of aesthetics. The power of spiritual, edifying icons is celebrated and put into effect in every courtroom, in the wigs, the robes, and the other theatrical paraphernalia of legal performance and in the images of **justice** that adorn our public buildings. The law arranges, distributes, and polices its own image through icons of authority and **sovereignty**, tradition and fidelity, rationality and justice. The fear of idols is encountered in the renunciation of rhetoric, of obscene images and libellous words, non-representational and ugly forms, and in the claim that reason alone, without eloquence, passion, or ethics can deliver justice. If the relationship between words and image is political, the law has been called upon to arbitrate this ancient quarrel. COSTAS DOUZINAS

P Kearns, *The Legal Concept of Art* (Oxford: Hart, 1998)
C Douzinas and L Nead (eds), *Law and the Image: The Authority of Art and the Aesthetics of Law* (Chicago: Chicago University Press, 1999)

vocational legal education Legal education is traditionally divided into stages, each progressively preparing students for practice. A common pattern is an initial or academic stage, usually a law degree introducing legal doctrines and theory across a wide span of law. The 'vocational stage' follows, introducing more of the knowledge and skills required by practitioners. The requirements are similar, though not identical, throughout the British Isles. This entry sets out the current methods and structures of vocational legal education in England and Wales.

In England and Wales, the vocational stage begins with a year-long course, with content and delivery specified and monitored by the Law Society (for the solicitor's profession) or the Bar (for the barristers' profession). A period of supervised training in firms and chambers, working under the supervision of a qualified and approved practitioner, follows. Vocational legal education might also describe post-qualification education regimes, or Continuing Professional Development, undertaken by both branches.

Vocational legal education has deep historical roots. At the Bar, the ancient Inns of Court, to which all barristers must belong, a collegial-style legal education was offered until the fifteenth century, switching to apprenticeship after the Civil War. Formal training for the Bar began in 1852 when the four Inns standardized their training by creating the Council of Legal Education. Passing an examination for the Bar only became compulsory in 1872 and the process leading to it was haphazard. The Inns of Court School of Law ('ICSL') was created in 1925 and had a monopoly over the Bar's vocational course until 1996.

The Law Society instituted examinations in 1836 and used them to control access to the profession. The Solicitors' Act 1860 introduced a three-tier examination (with the preliminary examination including Latin) at the beginning, middle, and end of articles. The Law Society established the College of Law in 1961, having acquired the private law tutors Gibson and Weldon. The solicitors' vocational course, called the Law Society Finals, was offered by the College of Law at its branches and at nine other universities and polytechnics.

The vocational courses were frequently criticized both as crammers and a means of controlling the numbers entering the profession. The content was subject matter not necessarily required in degree courses, such as evidence and company law, although many students often studied these subjects.

In 1989 the Inns of Court School of Law launched a revised Bar Vocational Course ('BVC') to incorporate a new emphasis on skills and transactions. In 1993 the Law Society introduced the Legal Practice Course ('LPC'), replacing the Solicitors' Final Examination Course. The Law Society invited new providers to offer the course and approved additional providers. In 1993 the number of full-time places on the new course was 5,758, a slight increase on the number of places offered for the final year of the solicitors' final course. After 1993, sixteen institutions offered the LPC, a figure that grew to twenty-six in 2005–2006. There are currently nearly 9,000 LPC places. In 1996, the Bar also approved eight providers of the BVC, including the ICSL and the College of Law.

Both the LPC and BVC were built around content set by the professional bodies, reflecting the special emphasis of solicitors' or barristers' work respectively. This is currently civil and criminal litigation and evidence in the case of the BVC and business law and practice, **conveyancing,** and litigation in the case of the LPC. The most notable aspect of both new courses was an emphasis on the so-called DRAIN skills, the legal skills of drafting, research, advocacy, interviewing, and negotiation. Both course specifications require that these skills be assessed as part of the course. Providers of the LPC assess skills as competent or not competent, whereas the BVC required passing grades also to be classified as 'outstanding' or 'very competent' if appropriate. Some areas, such as professional ethics, are 'pervasive subjects' in the course, meaning that they are dealt with as they arise in other subjects.

The new vocational course regimes were extensively specified, even to the extent of library and staff resources, but providers were given considerable freedom in deciding how they would be delivered. There was an expectation that the generous staff–student ratios, typically set at 12.5:1, would be used to provide small-group work and intensive feedback on skills. Courses are subject to demanding regulatory regimes, including monitoring by panels of academics, practitioners, and administrators, who read materials, visit classes, and interview staff. Many providers charge relatively high fees (for the LPC, course fees for 2006–2007 range from £5,200 to over £9,000, and for the BVC from £7,430 to £11,185).

The final stage of education and training takes place under the guidance of a practitioner. Intending solicitors must enter a training contract with a firm approved by the Law Society for the purpose. Pupil barristers enter a pupillage contract under the guidance of an approved barrister. This was once the primary route to qualification and both branches of the legal profession retain a strong attachment to this form of training. In 1756, the Bar offered a two-year exemption from the qualification period for holders of university law degrees. The Law Society offered similar dispensation from its five-year articles of clerkship in 1821. Up until the 1960s, significant numbers of solicitors still qualified by the five-year route, but the popularity of the university route, and the recommendation of the Ormrod Report in 1971, caused it to be phased out in 1980. Increasing monitoring and reporting requirements on the firms of solicitors and chambers providing training are often blamed for shortages of training opportunities.

Each year, there are roughly 15,000 students eligible to enter the vocational stage, of which around 8,000 enrol on an LPC and 1,500 on a BVC. There are around 6,000 training contracts and 700 pupillages. The requirement that intending lawyers serve a period of training in the workplace, and the limited availability of such opportunities, particularly at the Bar, is seen as an artificial restriction. The distribution of opportunities to privileged applicants, by commercial chambers and large solicitors' firms, brought criticism and pressure on the profession. Other criticisms are that maintenance costs and high course fees are a disincentive to students from poorer backgrounds and that specialization in legal practice renders the generalist curriculum of the courses redundant. This has led to the creation of bespoke courses for the prospective trainees of the larger firms, a move criticized as privatization of what should be a public course and common platform for legal practice.

Between 2001 and 2006 the Law Society conducted an extensive review of the training framework for solicitors, including three consultations. The major proposal of the Training Framework Review was that the Law Society should specify only the outcomes of legal education and training, and not when or how it should be completed. Only a degree and a period of work-based learning would be required before qualification. Vocational courses would be retained, but students would no longer be required to meet the vocational outcomes by attendance. The proposals sparked considerable controversy and, although approved by the Law Society Council, it is unclear whether they will be implemented in full. The Bar reviewed its BVC, surveying pupils and newly qualified barristers as part of the process, and concluded with a consultation in 2006. While criticism of the BVC had been anticipated, both the course and much of the current content and specification received support, and significant changes are not anticipated.

A solicitor must complete the vocational course and traineeship before being admitted to the roll of solicitors and being allowed to use the title 'solicitor'

and to practice. A barrister is 'called to the Bar' having completed the BVC and undertaking twelve qualifying sessions. Formerly, these sessions were limited to eating dinners in the student's Inn. They now include lectures, advocacy training, moots, study weekends, and other events where students meet practising barristers and judges. On call to the Bar, a barrister is entitled to use the title 'barrister' but is not entitled to practice as such until completing pupillage. In January 2004 the Bar Council proposed to 'defer call' (ie withhold the title of barrister) until after pupillage is completed, but this proposal has yet to be implemented.

Continuing Professional Development ('CPD') requirements are applied by both barristers and solicitors to those wishing to practice. The standard requirement is that they undertake a set amount of approved educational activities annually, which are reported to the professional bodies. CPD is provided by a range of organizations and is often delivered by practitioners receiving CPD credit for this work. For example, in recent years, the Inns of Court have increased their role in post-qualification training. Barristers and judges, acting in a voluntary capacity, provide advocacy and other professional skills training.   ANDY BOON

Sir Alan Langlands, *Gateways to the Professions: A Consultation Paper* (Department for Education and Skills, January 2005)

A Boon, J Flood, and J Webb, 'Postmodern Professions?: The Fragmentation of Legal Education and the Legal Profession' (2005) 32 *Journal of Law and Society* 473

volenti non fit injuria *Volenti non fit injuria* is a complete defence to a tort. Often translated as 'voluntary assumption of **risk**', it is rarely used today because **damages** may instead be apportioned for **contributory negligence**. A court may find that the claimant voluntarily consented to conduct which would otherwise be a tort. A hospital patient will usually have given express consent to surgery and a boxer will usually be taken to have consented to being punched within the reasonable limits of the sport. Further, a claimant may have assumed the risk of a tort being committed. He must have had full knowledge of the nature and extent of the risk and must have voluntarily agreed, expressly or impliedly, to absolve the defendant from legal **responsibility** for the harm caused. A claimant who boards an aircraft operated by a pilot whom he knows is in a state of severe drunkenness is very likely to be *volens* (willing). For reasons of public policy, rescuers are unlikely to be *volens* as are employees claiming against their employers. Exceptionally, a participant in a crime may succeed in pleading *volenti non fit injuria* in a claim brought by a co-participant for injuries sustained during the perpetration of the crime. For torts under the Animals Act 1971, the defence of *volenti* is provided in section 5(2). *Volenti* is barred against passengers of motor vehicles on public roads by the Road Traffic Act 1988, section 149, and is generally unavailable for a breach of a statutory duty. Express agreements to assume a risk may be ineffective under the **Unfair Contract Terms** Act 1977 and the Unfair Terms in Consumer Contracts Regulations 1999. CAROL G S TAN

voluntary unemployment The 'work ethic' looms large in our society. The expectation is that, where one is capable of doing so, one should support oneself and one's family through work. Accordingly, social security benefits for the unemployed (whether **national insurance** or social assistance) have sought to keep out or penalize claimants whose conduct has brought about their unemployment or which conduces to its continuance. The rules punish voluntary unemployment. Part of the rationale lies in the insurance idea (you must not bring about the risk you are insured against), another part in a policy of promoting the work ethic and disciplining the 'work-shy'. The rules are the modern equivalent of the **Poor Law**'s requirement of giving up civil liberty and entering the workhouse to get poor relief and of its principle of 'less eligibility', designed to deter resort to the workhouse by making the conditions there much less attractive than ones which could be obtained by the lowest paid workers. The current benefit for the unemployed, jobseeker's allowance, reflects the idea in its very name; one is not simply unemployed (without work) one is actively trying to change that by taking positive steps to change one's unemployment into employment.

Two sets of rules relevant to jobseeker's allowance aim to deter voluntary unemployment. The first refer to what are called 'labour market' conditions. To get jobseeker's allowance for any week the applicant must throughout that week be available for a reasonable range of employment in a reasonably wide geographical area. Initially, one can confine one's availability to one's usual work and level of remuneration; but, after a few months, horizons will have to be broadened and expectations lowered. In addition, one must also take active steps to find the work for which one holds oneself out as available; one must actively seek work. Agreement with JobcentrePlus on the appropriate range of job search and the steps to take must be embodied in a Jobseeker's Agreement, the conclusion and signing of which is a precondition of getting benefit.

The second set of rules guarding against voluntary unemployment imposes sanctions in terms of non-payment of benefit for particular inappropriate behaviour or failure to follow a variety of instructions from Jobcentre staff. The period of sanction varies from a minimum of one week to a maximum of twenty-six weeks. In some cases the period is (within those limits) at the discretion of the decision-maker, in others it is fixed at two or four weeks. Sanctions will be imposed in respect of behaviour which has produced unemployment (losing one's job through misconduct or having voluntarily left it without just cause) or which conduces to its continuation (turning down a job offer without good cause, failing to attend for a job interview, attending for one but deliberately behaving in such a way that no employer would offer a job). A person cannot, however, be forced to strikebreak. To encourage attempting a new line of work, a person cannot be sanctioned for leaving a job within a statutory 'trial period'. DAVID BONNER

vulnerable suspects *see* **suspects**

vulnerable witnesses *see* **evidence, criminal**

W

wages and deductions Employers may make deductions from their workers' wages for a variety of reasons, ranging from **pension** contributions to penalties for disciplinary offences, such as lateness. Usually employers require contractual authority to make a deduction, but sometimes deductions are required by statute (such as employees' **income tax**). As in contracts generally, terms allowing money to be retained by (or payments made to) an employer in the event of specified misconduct must constitute a genuine attempt to pre-estimate the loss or damage that the employer may suffer in those circumstances rather than constituting an extravagant or unconscionable penalty. However this principle may not afford much protection to workers in a context where their resources are much less than those of their employer; also employers have the opportunity, which few workers have, to insure against loss or damage. In addition to deductions allowed expressly by the contract, employers may have implied authority to make deductions where a worker has breached the contract and the sum deducted or 'set off' represents the amount that the employer could claim in damages for that breach.

The dangers of abuse in this area were recognized by the legislature in the nineteenth century. The Truck Act 1896 sought to restrain the worst excesses by stipulating that fines or deductions for bad workmanship should be 'fair and reasonable' and proportionate to the loss caused to the employer. In 1986, these measures were repealed as inimical to freedom of contract and replaced by a statutory regime that seeks only to regulate the procedures to be followed by employers prior to making a deduction (or requiring a payment from a worker). In broad terms, it requires either that the employer has statutory or contractual authority (of which the worker must be notified) to make a deduction or that the worker has otherwise given written agreement to the deduction prior to the event or conduct which triggers it. Deductions for some purposes, such as recovering a previous overpayment of wages or because the worker has taken industrial action, are excluded altogether

from even these minimal requirements. Only in the case of retail workers are there any substantive constraints on deductions; in their case no more than 10 per cent of gross weekly earnings on a given pay day may be deducted for cash shortages and stock deficiencies, although if the worker leaves the job the full amount can be deducted on the final pay day.

A major difficulty with these provisions is that they do not require the employer to allow the worker a hearing before making a deduction, nor, indeed is there any requirement for the employer to demonstrate that the worker penalized was individually at fault if, for example, a till is short or stock is damaged. They therefore offer a crude disciplinary mechanism which circumvents the protections offered by **unfair dismissal** legislation. A worker may challenge the lawfulness of a deduction before an employment **tribunal**, which, if it upholds the claim, may order **restitution** of the sum in question.

GILLIAN MORRIS

Wales, law in A developing body of indigenous, lawyer-created Welsh law was in use in the Middle Ages, although Wales was not at that time a single, unified state. Although the earliest surviving manuscripts date from the thirteenth century, the laws are traditionally associated with the reign of Hywel Dda (Hywel 'The Good', died c.950) and take their common name ('Cyfraith Hywel') from him. The rich and varied manuscripts cluster around three textual traditions, the Cyfnerth, Blegywryd, and Iorwerth Redactions, and cover both procedure and substantive law, the latter notably balancing principles of compensation with ideas of punishment. The process of assimilation to English law began with a statute of 1284 (the Statute of Wales or Statute of Rhuddlan) which applied a modified version of English law to the areas of Wales associated with the insurrection of Llewelyn ap Gruffudd (from the suppression of which also derives the English 'Principality'), though the quasi-autonomous 'Marcher Lordships' and, to an extent, the Principality itself, continued to use their own customs.

Uniformity of law was achieved in 1536 when all 'sinister customs and usages of the Welsh' were abolished by statute, although a clause had originally promised an investigation into which native customs might continue. Ordinances under this Act initiated the establishment of a special superior tribunal, the Court of Great Sessions, which, confirmed by statute in 1543, exercised criminal, civil, and equitable jurisdiction in Wales (excluding Monmouthshire) until its controversial abolition in 1830. However the severance in 2007 of a traditional link with Chester in the designation of circuits means that Wales can now claim the status of a distinct administrative region of the court system. Another earlier specialist tribunal, The Council in the Principality and Marches of Wales, which can trace its origins to the reign of Edward IV, exercised a broad conciliar jurisdiction in the Principality and, until 1604, English border counties. It ceased to sit in the Civil War, but was revived at the Restoration only to be abolished in 1689 because of its association with prerogative rule. This association also led to the abolition in 1624 of an (unused) provision of the statute of 1543 which had allowed for legislation to be made for Wales without parliamentary approval. At the same time the 1543 Act ensured Welsh representation to the **Westminster Parliament**.

Thereafter law-making for the Principality had no special characteristics though it might have exclusive application, the Sunday Closing (Wales) Act 1881 being a significant symbolic measure in this respect. Wales has had a Secretary of State since 1964, following on from the office of Minister of Welsh Affairs from 1951. A scheme for devolution was contained in the Wales Act 1978 but was rejected in a referendum the following year. A narrow victory in a referendum in 1997 preceded the Government of Wales Act 1998, which created a new National Assembly for Wales with elected members. This Act conferred no primary legislative powers, but devolved certain areas of responsibility upon the new body. The Government of Wales Act 2006 gave the Assembly Government a defined status and paved the way for increased, though still not as yet autonomous, power in respect of legislation of the **Welsh Assembly**. This can now be created, as before, under specific Westminster statutes or (as an 'Assembly Measure', equivalent to statute) in relation to specified subject matter designated by an **Order in Council** mechanism within 'devolved fields'. A provision for legislating in such fields without the necessity of such Orders in Council is contained in the Act but requires approval by a referendum before it can be activated.

Welsh Assembly legislation is drafted bilingually, both languages having equal authority. This partially redresses an inequality in official recognition of the language ('a speech nothing like nor consonant to the natural mother tongue used within this Realm') which had appeared in the 1536 legislation, although the Welsh Courts Act of 1942 had allowed the language to be used in court where insistence on English would prejudice to a party or witness; and the Welsh Language Act 1967 had permitted the use of Welsh at the option of the party or witness within the Principality (though with a prior notice provision in higher courts). The Welsh Language Act 1993 confirms this right and provides for other public bodies to introduce schemes for bilingualism.

RICHARD IRELAND

TG Watkin, *The Legal History of Wales* (Cardiff: University of Wales Press, 2007)
Jenkins, *Hywel Dda: The Law* (Llandysul, 1986)

war and armed conflict The use of war as an instrument of national policy was prohibited by the General Treaty for the Renunciation of War 1928, to which many states then in existence were parties. A breach of this undertaking was the basis of some of the charges laid against a number of senior Nazi leaders charged before the International Military Tribunal at Nuremberg in 1945. Convictions of crimes against the peace followed. A similar process was undertaken by the International Military Tribunal for the Far East in Tokyo in relation to the foreign policy activities of the government of Japan.

The Charter of the **United Nations** (1945) avoids use of the term 'war' and prohibits the threat or use of force against the territorial integrity or political independence of any state. The UN Security Council was given the task of determining the existence of a threat to the peace, breach of the peace, or an act of aggression and of making recommendations or decisions to maintain or restore international peace and security. It can authorize the use of armed force (as in the Gulf War 1991) or, where appropriate, states can rely on the right of self-defence (Article 51 of the Charter) as in the Falklands/Malvinas conflict 1982.

Modern practice has seen the armed forces of states undertaking military action without a clear UN Security Council authorization to do so. The intervention in Kosovo in 1999 by the UK and other NATO states was based upon the perceived need to prevent 'an overwhelming humanitarian catastrophe' and did not follow from any authorization of the UN Security Council. The UK Government based its intervention in Iraq in 2003 on an interpretation of earlier UN Security Council resolutions relating to Iraq.

The practice of declaring war (and the use of the term 'belligerency') has now fallen into desuetude. Whatever the rights or wrongs of a use of armed force by one state against another, the laws of war (or **international humanitarian law**) will come into force as soon as an armed conflict between two or more states is taking place or where there is an occupation of territory. During the course of such a conflict enemy ships and aircraft can be seized as prize, subject to the jurisdiction of the prize court. The Hague Convention XII, 1907 attempted to provide an appeal court in prize cases, but it was never ratified.

During the course of the armed conflict civilians and wounded, sick, and shipwrecked members of the enemy armed forces must be rescued and given medical attention depending upon their needs. The dead must be buried, if possible according to the rites of the religion to which they belonged. In the course of conflict at sea hospital ships are protected vessels. Once merchant ships have been converted into hospital ships they are required to carry out this function for the duration of the armed conflict. A modern example of their use was during the Falklands/Malvinas conflict in 1982.

Members of the armed forces of a state engaged in the armed conflict are entitled to take part in the armed conflict as **combatants** and to be treated as prisoners of war if they are captured. States must release and repatriate them as soon as active hostilities have ceased. Modern practice has shown that in armed conflicts in which the UK has been involved prisoners of war have been held for relatively short periods or transferred to an ally.

It has become common for the greatest numbers of casualties during an international armed conflict to be among the civilian population. **International law** has attempted to provide protection to civilians during an occupation of territory and during attacks on military objectives in which civilians may be incidentally killed or injured, as so-called 'collateral damage'. The occupation of Iraq by the UK and the USA in 2003, and the aerial bombing of military objectives in Belgrade and Baghdad in recent years, illustrate how effective (or otherwise) this branch of international law is in protecting the civilian population from the effects of armed conflict.

Non-international armed conflicts occur more frequently than conflicts between or among states. It may, however, be unclear when criminal activity driven by a political goal has developed into an armed conflict. The UK took the view that it never did in Northern Ireland between 1969 and 1998. As long as the situation can be categorized as an 'armed conflict' (whether it is described as an insurgency or civil war or not) international law will apply. This law is much less detailed in this type of conflict, largely because states have recognized that their national law (particularly their criminal law) will apply to those who take up arms against the state. For this reason there is no concept of the prisoner of war. International law is concerned to ensure that those who do not take an active part in the hostilities are protected and that those who do and who are arrested are dealt with in accordance with internationally acceptable standards.

The outbreak of war can have a considerable effect on trans-national commercial activities. The Trading with the Enemy Act 1939 provides that it is an offence to trade with the enemy. An enemy is anyone who is resident in, or a person or company carrying on business in, enemy territory. The applicability of this legislation is, however, limited by the fact that that it only applies where there is a state of war in the UK. As shown above, this is an unlikely occurrence and the 1939 Act will not apply where the UK is involved in an international armed conflict 'not involving war in the technical sense'.

PETER ROWE

See also: **use of force; war crimes trials**

war crimes   War crimes are serious violations of **international humanitarian law** entailing individual criminal responsibility; ie serious violations of the customary or conventional laws governing the conduct of hostilities (*jus in bello*), which apply equally to all the parties to an armed conflict. War crimes presuppose the existence of armed conflict; but a crime committed during armed conflict is not necessarily a war crime. There must be a sufficient link between the crime and the conflict. Similarly, not every violation of international humanitarian law is a war crime. According to the **ICTY** Appeals Chamber, a 'serious' violation means the breach of a rule protecting important values with grave consequences for the victim. Article 8 of the Rome Statute of the **International Criminal Court** declares that 'war crimes' means grave breaches of the Geneva Conventions 1949 (eg wilfully killing protected persons) and other serious violations of the laws and customs applicable in international or non-international armed conflict (eg intentionally attacking civilians).

A distinction is sometimes drawn between war crimes established by treaty and those under **customary international law**, since a treaty binds only the states parties whereas customary international law generally binds all states. However, many 'treaty' war crimes codify customary international law. All war crimes have mental as well as physical elements. It must therefore be proved that the material element of the crime (*actus reus*) was committed with the necessary intent and knowledge (*mens rea*).

NICHOLAS GRIEF

war crimes trials   *see* **Barbie, Klaus; Demjanjuk, Ivan**

war crimes tribunals   The idea that morals, if not laws, control the waging of war dates back thousands of years. Following the Greek tradition, **Roman law** established prohibitions on the conduct of warfare; other important antecedents to modern war crimes tribunals include the trial and execution of Peter von Hagenbach in Austria in 1474 for atrocities committed during the siege of Breisach; and the promulgation of the 'Lieber Code,' a manual enumerating 'serious breaches of the law of war' that was distributed to the Union army during the American Civil War.

The Hague Conventions of 1899 and 1907 codified customary practice and established the general rules of conduct for belligerents in times of war. They remained silent, however, on the matter of punishments. In the century since the second Hague convention, jurists have experimented with four different forms of tribunals designed to try war criminals: *ad hoc* international courts, domestic national courts, hybrid tribunals, and a permanent **international criminal court**.

The first *ad hoc* international war crimes courts were established in the wake of World War II. Nuremberg's International Military Tribunal ('IMT') tried members of the Nazi leadership (1945–1946) and the International Military Tribunal for the Far East ('IMTFE') tried Japanese war criminals in Tokyo (1946–1948). Predating the IMTFE and conducted with greater competence, the IMT remains the more significant innovation in **international law**. As the first international war crimes trial in history, the IMT also marked the first time that waging a war of aggression and committing crimes against humanity had been formally recognized as incriminations in international law. Of equal significance, the IMT implemented a principle of individual **responsibility**, puncturing the immunity that had historically shielded state ministers.

As *ad hoc* courts, the IMT and the IMTFE disbanded with the end of their trials. The **United Nations**' Charter authorized the Security Council to create future international criminal tribunals exclusively on such an *ad hoc* basis. This power was not exercised until war in the Balkans, and genocide in Rwanda led to the establishment of the International Criminal Tribunal for the former Yugoslavia ('ICTY') in the Hague in 1993, and the International Criminal Tribunal Rwanda ('ICTR;') in Arusha, Tanzania in 1994. Although plagued by delays and cost overruns, the ICTY must be credited with establishing important precedents, such as holding that offences committed in 'internal armed conflicts' (as distinguished from international armed conflicts) can be considered war crimes in international law. The prosecution of Slobodan **Milosevic** also marked the first time that a former head of state had ever stood trial before an international court.

Domestic national courts have also served as war crimes tribunals. At the end of World War I, Germany was obliged to try soldiers accused of war crimes in the Leipzig Trials of 1921. The failure of these trials—most defendants were acquitted and those convicted received light penalties—remains emblematic of relying on domestic national courts to try domestic war criminals. As the trials of Adolf **Eichmann** in Jerusalem in 1961 and Klaus **Barbie** in Lyon in 1987 made clear, national courts perform better when asked to try non-nationals. More recently, the passage of statutes such as the UK's War Crimes Act of 1991 have established that war crimes can be tried under principles of universal jurisdiction. In such cases, a state may seek to prosecute conduct without regard to the nationality of the victim or perpetrator, or the place where the crime occurred. Domestic national courts in Sierra Leone, East Timor, and Cambodia have also worked with the UN to create hybrid tribunals capable of trying war criminals. These hybrid tribunals are designed to provide international expertise in helping underfunded or under-staffed domestic courts bring perpetrators to justice.

Finally, the creation of the **International Criminal Court** ('ICC'), a permanent institution with jurisdiction over war crimes, crimes against humanity, and genocide, may spell the end of the need for *ad hoc* tribunals such as the ICTY and the ICTR. The ICC is designed to function as a court of last resort, deferring to domestic national courts when such institutions are equipped and willing to try perpetrators of egregious international crimes. The ICC commenced operations on 1 July 2002 after the ratification of its enabling statute by the sixtieth state party. To date, over 100 states have ratified the statute; notably absent from this list are China, Russia, India, Pakistan, and the United States.

LAWRENCE DOUGLAS

GJ Bass, *Stay the Hand of Vengeance: The Politics of War Crimes Tribunals* (Princeton: Princeton University Press, 2000)

P Sands (ed), *From Nuremberg to the Hague: The Future of International Criminal Justice* (Cambridge: Cambridge University Press, 2003)

See also: **Nuremberg trials**

war pensions The term 'war pensions' can mislead. The main scheme applies where disablement or death is due to service of any kind as a member of the armed forces (not just during war or conflict) after 2 September 1939. Disablement **pensions** or gratuities, varying with the extent of disablement, are paid if any service factor was a cause of the disablement or aggravated an existing condition. Surviving spouses or civil partners receive pensions where death is due to or substantially hastened by service. Claimants must establish some connection between the disablement and the service; but very tenuous connections are sometimes accepted.

Legislation in 2004 and 2005 limited the existing scheme to the effects of service before 6 April 2005, while introducing a new, modernized, armed forces compensation scheme for the effects of post-April 2005 service. This gives fixed lump sums for specified categories of disablement, plus income payments to compensate for earnings loss at higher levels of disablement. A wider range of survivors can benefit on death. Proof of entitlement on the balance of probabilities is required. Claims must normally be made within five years of the event causing disablement. As there is no time limit for claiming under the old scheme, both will run in parallel for many years. Appeals from decisions of the Veterans Agency (an agency of the Ministry of Defence) lie to pensions appeal tribunals ('PATs'). PAT decisions after 5 April 2005 (except for assessments of disablement under the old scheme) can be appealed for error of law to the Social Security Commissioners.

JOHN MESHER

N Wikeley, *Wikeley, Ogus and Barendt's The Law of Social Security* (London: Butterworths Lexis Nexis, 5th edn, 2002), ch 21

warranties *see* **sale of goods; unfair contract terms**

Warren, Earl Earl Warren (9 March 1891–9 July 1974), Chief Justice, **United States Supreme Court**. An enormously popular Republican governor of California in the 1940s, Earl Warren ran for Vice-President in 1948. In 1952, Richard Nixon manoeuvered Warren into supporting Dwight Eisenhower's quest for the Republican nomination. In return, Eisenhower promised to nominate Warren to the first vacancy on the Supreme Court, which was created by Fred Vinson's death in 1953. Warren continued to resent Nixon's role: he announced his retirement in 1968, hoping in vain that Nixon would not have the chance to name his successor.

As governor a liberal Republican, Warren was a moderate liberal in his first years on the Court. Warren took his seat as the Court was considering ***Brown v Board of Education*** (1954), the school desegregation case. Firmly opposed to segregation, Warren cajoled some of his reluctant colleagues to join what became the Court's unanimous opinion. From 1962 to 1968, new members of the Court gave its liberals a firm majority, which aggressively promoted 1960s-style liberalism.

A former prosecutor, Warren was initially ambivalent about expanding the rights of criminal suspects, sympathizing with the problems **police** officers faced in enforcing the law. Influenced by his growing appreciation of the interaction between police procedures and **race** relations, Warren became a forceful advocate for enhanced protections for criminal suspects, believing that such protections would ultimately lead the police to become more professional. Warren was generally a strong supporter of **freedom of expression** rights, although, prudish in his personal views, he dissented from the Court's decisions restricting government's power to ban **obscenity**.

Warren, a genial chief justice, provided the social glue, though not the intellectual leadership, that created the Warren Court as the icon of 1960s judicial activism—a model for liberals and a foil for conservatives later in the century. MARK TUSHNET

See also: **segregation and desegregation**

waste A general definition of waste can be found in European and domestic **legislation** as being anything which 'the holder discards or intends or is required to discard' (Article 1(a) of the Waste Framework Directive). Beyond this basic definition, however, is the central issue of whether something has been 'discarded' and further detailed questions of classification connected to either the identity of the producer (eg household, commercial, or industrial waste) or the inherent properties of the waste itself (eg whether it is particularly hazardous) which are used in waste regulation systems to determine how waste is managed.

The question of whether something has been 'discarded' has come before the courts on many occasions. The underlying principle in these cases is that there is nothing inherent about the nature or characteristics of a substance or object which automatically makes it waste. The key issue is, therefore, the intention of the last holder of the material, substance, or object in question. This intention can only be determined by having regard to the factual circumstances of the material in question. In most situations the intention of the last holder is explicit. Thus if someone consigns waste for final disposal (eg by having it removed by a waste collection company), the subjective nature of 'discarding' is clear, notwithstanding the fact that the substance or object may be valuable to the person collecting it or to a third party. Alternatively, the holder of waste may be required to 'discard' an object because there is no further use for that object unless it is 'recovered' (ie treated or reprocessed in some way so that it can be used again).

In other circumstances, this intention to discard is not so easy to identify. In particular some waste treatment processes are the same as industrial processes (eg the recovery of energy from incineration and the use of raw material as a fuel). In such circumstances, the consignment of a material to such a process is not necessarily evidence of an intention to discard. In looking at these difficult cases, the courts have settled upon a flexible purposive interpretation and identified a range of factors to be taken into account. The most important of these is whether the purpose of waste legislation, ie to prevent the dangerous disposal of waste, would be undermined. Other relevant factors include whether the substance is a residue or product, whether there is a commercial price paid, and the likelihood of re-use without any further treatment.   STUART BELL

water law   Water has been a subject of legal regulation since early Mesopotamia, Egypt, and Rome. The Romans in particular developed intricate doctrines characterizing water in some situations as a *res communes* or natural good available in common to all, in other cases as an individual property right naturally attached to ownership of lands containing watercourses and ponds, or as additional incorporeal rights annexed to benefited land by agreement with neighbours or by long usage. There was little or no protection of access to water seeping through ground without forming a defined channel. The Romans distinguished navigation rights and rights to the sea from riparian or river rights, and they also developed a separate administrative and criminal law protecting orderly use of urban water supply carried in aqueducts. The elaborate Roman rules provided the basis not only of European codes but also of the English **common law**, which borrowed heavily and directly from Roman doctrine from the thirteenth to the nineteenth centuries.

Conflicts between riparian owners over in-stream access historically have provided the bulk of litigation over water rights. Conflict can arise from rival forms of consumption involving abstraction of the water from its course; or the water may be returned to the stream but in changed form, as where riparian owners use water for power or for industrial processes that alter the force of the stream or pollute its content. Litigation over water rights peaked in England and the north-eastern USA during the early industrial revolution up to around 1860, after which steam power began to lessen the demand for access to water streams. The common law courts adopted **Roman law** ideas to promote a reasonable use doctrine, allowing riparian owners a level of use of water that did not unreasonably cut into the like enjoyment of neighbours, and forbidding proprietary rights to persons who did not own riparian land. The law thus restrained commodification of natural water flows and prevented monopolistic rights emerging.

In the western USA a quite distinct doctrine of prior appropriation was developed, which had been adumbrated earlier by **Blackstone** and before him by Locke. The rationale for awarding exclusive rights to the first taker was that in drier areas both land and water use will best be promoted by giving the enterprising first possessor a right to own, and that a sharply defined property regime with little discretion would discourage litigation. Western states still employ prior appropriation doctrines, though the pure doctrine has been displaced in large part by statutory regulation.

It has been argued that the shifts and variations in riparian doctrine reflect the class interest of industrialists versus agrarians, or else the economic functions dictated by the local modes of production and consumption. It is at least as likely that an intellectual path dependence was at work, whereby doctrinal commitments derived from Roman law or eighteenth-century common law drove later legal mutations. Modern water law deals with a classically 'polycentric' set of issues that are increasingly resolved by statutory schemes of administration. Regulators most recently have used market trading of water entitlements to replace other legal and administrative methods of stinting access.

JOSHUA GETZLER

J Getzler, *A History of Water Rights at Common Law* (Oxford: Oxford University Press, 2004)

water quality standards   Water quality standards are set for Europe under a series of EEC directives concerning the Aquatic Environment, Groundwater, Surface Water Abstracted for Drinking Water, Freshwater Fisheries, Shellfish Waters, Bathing Waters and specific substances such as Waste Oils. These Directives will largely be replaced by a Framework Water Directive in either 2007 or 2013.

Part III of the Water Resources Act 1991 ('WRA') (control of **pollution** of water resources) applies to 'controlled waters', which are defined in section 104 of the WRA as relevant territorial waters, coastal waters, inland freshwaters, and ground waters. Under section 82, those waters are classified according to criteria established by Regulations. These Regulations implement the EC Directives, so that the Bathing Waters (Classification) Regulations 1991 sets a standard (BW1) for all bathing waters to which the Regulations apply. To meet the BW1 classification requirements, at least 95 per cent of the samples of waters taken and tested in accordance with the sampling regime under Schedule 2 to the Regulations must conform to the parametric values set out in Schedule 3. Schedule 3 requires, for example, that there must be fortnightly sampling for faecal coliforms and the parametric value assigned for the sample is 2,000 in 100ml.

The Secretary of State will issue a notice under section 83 of the WRA establishing water quality objectives by specifying applicable classifications under one of the classification regulations to the waters listed in the Schedule to the notice. Section 84 requires the Secretary of the State and the **Environment Agency** to use the powers they have been granted under Part III of the WRA in such a way that will, so far as practicable, ensure that the objectives specified in notices under section 83 are achieved at all times.

Drinking water standards are set under the EC 'Drinking Water' Directive 1998. In England and Wales this Directive is implemented by sections 67 to 86 of the Water Industry Act 1991 and the Water Supply (Water Quality) Regulations 2000 (England) and 2001 (Wales). These are concerned with public supplies of water. Private water supplies are regulated under the Private Water Supplies Regulations 1991. Water undertakers must supply 'wholesome' water to their customers and whether water supplies are 'wholesome' will be determined under regulation 4 of the 2000 or 2001 Regulations. Standards are enforced by the Drinking Water Inspectorate.

JOHN BATES

See also: **water law**

wealth tax A wealth tax charges a person by reference to that person's wealth at one particular time. The attraction of the tax is that it may be better than an income tax in determining a person's ability to pay. Such taxes are an accepted, if usually supplementary, feature of tax systems in other Organization for Economic Cooperation and Development ('OECD') countries, especially France and the Nordic countries. It was considered in the UK in the 1970s but, as Denis Healy, Chancellor of the Exchequer 1974–1979, wrote in his memoirs *The Time of My Life* (London: Michael Joseph, 1989, p 404), '[I]n five years I found it impossible to draft [a wealth tax] which would yield enough revenue to be worth the administrative cost and the political hassle'.

Policy decisions are needed on the questions (a) whether the tax should be single or multi rate; (b) whether it should be charged on individuals or on family units (however defined); (c) the point at which a person's wealth begins to attract liability (tax threshold); (d) whether the tax should be charged on assets outside the jurisdiction belonging to residents of the jurisdiction; (e) which assets should be included and which exempt—eg family home, rights to pensions, works of art, the family farm or business assets, not forgetting 'human capital'; and (f) whether the tax should be purely additional to the income tax charge or whether there should there be some offset (this naturally has an impact on rate structure). There are also traditional arguments for and against levying a tax which the taxpayer may only be able to pay by selling assets, as well as serious problems of valuation.

JOHN TILEY

CT Sandford, JRM Willis, and DJ Ironside, *An Annual Wealth Tax* (London: Heinemann for Institute for Fiscal Studies, 1975)

AR Prest, 'The Select Committee on a Wealth Tax' (1976) *British Tax Review* 7–15.

weapons, prohibited *see* **arms control**

weights and measures The interest of government in regulating weights and measures is largely concerned with maintaining confidence in markets, so that consumers are happy that they are getting what they pay for. Recognition of universal standards for measuring weight, length, and volume goes back to antiquity. In England the ambition to have common standards pre-dates the Norman invasion and is reflected in the Magna Carta (1215). A key element of standardization here is to end the usage of measures which are no longer regarded as appropriate. Thus the Weights and Measures Act 1824 had amongst its aims the elimination of alternative units of measurement in Scotland.

Similarly a key objective of the modern rules (found in the Weights and Measures Act 1985 and in the Weights and Packaged Goods Regulations 2006) is to fully replace the imperial measures of pounds and ounces, gallons and pints, miles and feet with the metric system which has gradually been introduced since the 1970s. The local authority officials charged with enforcing the rules face the difficulty that many smaller businesses and shoppers prefer to continue thinking in imperial quantities, and particularly for measures of weight, some market traders have resisted imperialization. Until 2009 the sale of loose food products is permitted simultaneously in imperial and metric, or solely in metric, but not solely in imperial. Between 2000 and 2002 a number of market traders were prosecuted for the offences relating to the failure to display prices using metric units for weights and the related offence concerning uses of scales which had only imperial measures. The 'metric martyrs' lost their claims that the legislation under which they were prosecuted was invalid, and whilst this *cause celebre* was sometimes characterized as resistance to the remote law-makers of Brussels, in fact it has been British government policy for more than thirty years to shift the basis for all weights and measures to the metric system. Cultural resistance to metrication in some contexts is sufficiently strong that old measures have been retained as a matter of legislative policy. The most notable example is the sale of beer and cider in pubs, which is still sold in pints.   COLIN SCOTT

welfare benefits for families The current system of welfare benefits for families has derived from the patriarchal vision of family set out by William Beveridge in his blueprint for the welfare state (*Social Insurance and Allied Services (The Beveridge Report)*, 1942). At this time, husbands were cast as the sole or primary breadwinners who were expected wherever possible to engage with the public world of work. The system introduced in 1946 was (unwisely) premised on **unemployment** being a short-term problem for a few families. Wives and children were dependants for whom husbands were obliged to provide. Wives therefore were not themselves expected to be gainfully employed, with their homemaking and childcaring activities confined to the private sphere of the home and to be rewarded not by the state but by their husbands. Thus, until 1980 when the 1979 European Equal Treatment Directive required a change in the law to avoid discrimination against women and with the exception of the Family Allowance (later **Child** Benefit, discussed below), only men were able to claim welfare benefits for the family as the designated 'head of household', it being assumed the money would be shared out by him to meet the household's needs.

Initially contributory benefits such as Unemployment Benefit paid on the basis of **national insurance** contributions included additional allowances for dependants, although during an era of high inflation it became necessary additionally to claim **means-tested benefits** such as Supplementary Benefit (which from 1966 represented the official poverty line) to meet the family's needs. Following radical New Right reforms in the 1980s signalling a retreat from the **welfare state**, contributory benefits became payable only for the contributor. Additional needs of other family members required a separate claim for supplementary benefit then renamed Income Support in 1986. Previously, families on supplementary benefit with no savings could apply for discretionary grants to meet 'exceptional needs' for themselves and their children which could not be met out of weekly benefit—examples are payment for a bed when a child grew out of a cot, payment for new school uniform or shoes, or for a much needed new cooker or fridge. However, this was replaced in 1986 **legislation** with a system of loans from the **Social Fund** which had to be repaid by weekly deductions from benefit over a fixed period of time. This aimed both to reduce the spiralling social security budget and to encourage thrift among the poor, but in an era of high unemployment throughout the 1980s and much of the 1990s, had the effect of greatly increasing child poverty. The Jobseekers Act 1995 replaced unemployment benefit and income support with respectively contribution-based and income-based Jobseekers Allowance which combine to provide the needs of the unemployed. This has left income support as a residual benefit for those who are not required to be actively seeking work, principally lone parents. The rising number of post-divorce and single lone parents has been seen as a burden on the welfare benefit system making lone parents a target of welfare reform.

From 2001, under New Labour's New Deal for Lone Parents, those whose youngest child reached school age, had to attend a work-focused meeting, as a condition of receiving income support and this was extended to all lone parents in 2004. Although at the current time lone parents are not obliged actively to look for work as a condition of receiving benefit until their youngest child is sixteen, it is proposed to make this a requirement when the youngest child is twelve.

This encouragement for parents to work is combined with the increased availability of in-work benefits now re-styled as **tax credits** for families. From the inception of the welfare state, it was accepted that working families with children needed extra financial help. This took the form initially of tax allowances paid directly to the married father plus Family Allowance. This was a universal non-means-tested benefit not linked to national insurance contributions paid (following a successful feminist lobby) directly to all mothers with children under sixteen. In 1977, it was renamed Child Benefit and initially a higher rate was payable to lone parents, although later withdrawn. At the same time Family Income Supplement (which became Family Credit) was a benefit introduced to ensure families in work were not worse off than those claiming benefits. Currently, low income families claim means-tested Working Tax Credit and Child Tax Credit, both paid directly into the pay packet, rather than claim a separate benefit, and may include an element for child-care.

ANNE BARLOW

See also: **welfare rights**

welfare principle   The welfare principle states that when a **court** decides any question about a child's upbringing or property, the child's welfare is the court's paramount concern. This is the guiding principle that the courts use to make decisions in **child** law and so of central importance to this area. The welfare principle was first introduced into the law in 1925, arguably originating as a means of avoiding giving mothers equal parental authority with fathers by subordinating both parents' interests to the interests of the child.

The welfare principle gives rise to several questions of interpretation. One is the meaning of 'paramount', which the **House of Lords** defined in 1970 as overriding: Lord MacDermott said in *J v C* (1970) that the child's welfare was the paramount consideration 'because it rules upon or determines the course to be followed'. In other words, when the welfare principle operates, the court will make whatever decision it regards as best for the child.

Another question is which decisions are covered by the welfare principle, given that a wide range of decisions may affect children's upbringing. The Court of Appeal gave the general answer to this in *Re Z* (1997) that a question of upbringing is determined when this is the central issue before the court. So for example, the welfare principle applies when a court is deciding which parent a child will live with after **divorce** but does not apply when a court is deciding whether to grant the divorce in the first place. Even when the child's upbringing is the central issue, there may be conditions that need to be met before the court considers the welfare principle; for example, a judge is not allowed to take a child into local authority care just because he or she views this as best for the child: the specific grounds for a care order have to be proved first.

Yet another issue of interpretation is how to identify the child whose welfare is paramount, given that court decisions about one child may have an impact on other children's welfare; for example, a decision that a brother should be allowed to visit his sister would be equally relevant to the brother's and sister's welfare. The House of Lords have decided that the answer depends on the wording of the legal provision under which the case is being considered. So for instance, if the brother applies for contact with his sister then he would be 'a **person**' applying for contact with 'a child', who would be his sister, and so his sister's welfare would determine the result. This makes the question of whose welfare is paramount depend on the vagaries of the procedure by which the case came to court, and sometimes on judicial fiat.

A big problem with the welfare principle is determining what is actually best for a child. In 1975, Mnookin famously argued that to make a rational decision, a judge would need considerable information, predictive ability, and some source for the values against which to measure the results, but that all three of these requirements presented difficulties. Expert witnesses such as court welfare officers or child psychiatrists often provide information and sometimes make predictions, and the judge is allowed to interview the child directly.

Decisions about children cannot be free of values. One source for these values is provided by section 1(3) of the Children Act 1989, which lays down a checklist of factors that a judge must in certain circumstances consider when deciding what is best for the child. These factors include the child's wishes and feelings and the likely effect on the child of any change of circumstances. Another source for these values is a variety of rules of thumb developed by courts in previous cases that give the judge guidelines about what is best for children; for example, the House of Lords confirmed in 2006 that it is generally best for a child to be brought up by his or her natural parent.

Some people have argued that these rules of thumb allow judges to consider other people's interests under the rubric of the welfare principle; for example, the principle that it is generally best for a child to be brought up by his or her natural parent could be viewed as giving covert protection to the natural parent's interests. Other people have argued that it would be better if these other interests were protected overtly because this would allow judges' reasons for their decisions to be more transparent.

On occasions, judges have overtly protected parents' interests in cases about children. A striking example is *Re E* (1997), in which the Court of Appeal decided that a condition that the child had to live at a particular address was an unwarranted imposition on the parent's right to choose where he or she would live within the United Kingdom. Judges have been encouraged to protect parents' rights by the **Human Rights Act 1998**, particularly under Article 8 of the European Convention on Human Rights, which provides that everyone has the right to respect for his or her **family life**.

Even so, judges have generally proclaimed that the Human Rights Act does not present any difficulty for the welfare principle. Some academics have agreed with this view, on the basis that children's interests are inextricably intertwined with their parents' interests, so that it is impossible to consider children's interests without protecting their parents' interests. However, other academics have worried that there is a conflict between the welfare principle, which demands that the child's interests should determine the result, and the Human Rights Act 1998, which requires a balancing of different interests.

Despite the Human Rights Act, the welfare principle continues to attract a wide consensus, perhaps because of its enormous symbolic appeal. When decisions are justified on the grounds that they are best for the child, this is a very powerful justification indeed.   HELEN REECE

H Reece, 'The Paramountcy Principle: Consensus or Construct?' (1996) 49 *Current Legal Problems* 267

J Eekelaar, 'Beyond the welfare principle' (2002) 14 *Child and Family Law Quarterly* 237

welfare rights   The welfare rights movement developed in both the US and the UK in the 1960s. The very notion of welfare rights is contentious amongst political and moral philosophers. Some argue that there is no parallel between the individual's right to private property, traditionally protected by **common law** rights and duties, and a person's interest in social welfare provided by the state. However, international conventions provide some support for the notion of welfare rights. For example, the **Universal Declaration of Human Rights** of 1948, as well as guaranteeing the classic individual civil and political rights, also refers to the right to security against risks over which one has no control such as unemployment, sickness and bereavement. The writings of TH Marshall have been particularly influential in this regard. Marshall argued that citizenship comprises a bundle of civil, political, and social rights, with social rights guaranteeing a

minimum level of income and security for all. Marshall envisaged a universal welfare scheme, based on the rights of citizenship, as an important means of promoting social integration. In the UK this led to welfare rights advocates, from the 1960s onwards, developing test case strategies to defend claimants' interests against discretionary decision-making, especially in the means-tested benefit schemes.

Similarly, the American scholar Charles Reich developed the concept of 'new property'. Reich's argument was that public sector largesse (such as welfare benefits and professional licences granted by the modern state) performed a function analogous to traditional property rights and so should be reconceptualized as 'new property' in order to protect individual autonomy. The notion of contributors having vested rights in social (or national) insurance programmes, earned by the payment of contributions, was relatively unproblematic, given the private law analogy with contract. Reich's innovation was to blur the distinction between insurance-based benefits and means-tested welfare benefits to extend the concept of rights to the latter type of programme, which had traditionally been seen as mere gratuities.

Reich's concept of a 'new property' soon had an impact on United States public law. For example, the **United States Supreme Court** in *Goldberg v Kelly* (1970) accepted that the receipt of welfare was not simply a privilege to be withdrawn at the will of the executive; instead a welfare claimant was entitled to a fair hearing before benefits could be terminated. However, the focus of Reich's analysis was primarily on procedural rather than substantive rights, reflecting the lawyer's traditional concerns with due process issues. In the UK in recent years the incorporation of the **European Convention on Human Rights** into domestic law through the Human Rights Act 1998 has given a new impetus to welfare rights arguments. Article 6 of the Convention, which guarantees of a fair trial in relation to civil rights and obligations, applies to most social security benefits, although the extent to which the Convention protects claimants against changes to substantive benefits rights is less clear.   NICK WIKELEY

CA Reich, 'The New Property' (1964) 73 *Yale Law Journal* 733

welfare state   The term 'welfare state' refers to the institutional framework under which the state assumes responsibility for the basic welfare of citizens and applies policies, operationalized via legislation, to that end. Social security, health, housing, and education are its main areas of provision. It is particularly associated with the meeting of basic needs;

and it thus operates as a redistributive mechanism for the inequalities that occur under a market economy. The UK's welfare state emerged in the first half of the twentieth century, notably as a result of the Liberal reforms on **pensions** and unemployment insurance prior to 1914 and Labour's post-Beveridge reforms. Beveridge had advanced the principle of welfare 'from cradle to grave' via universal social insurance, family allowances and a national health service (*Social Insurance and Allied Services*, Cmnd 217 (HMSO, 1942)).

There is an important dichotomy between 'institutional' and 'residualist' welfare states. Under the former, the state assumes a responsibility to ensure a reasonable standard of living for all and confers universal rights. The more conditional those rights and the weaker and less redistributive the framework of protection, the further from the institutional model is the welfare state. A 'residualist' welfare state steps in when other sources of welfare, including privately purchased provision, the family, and the voluntary sector, are inadequate. Thus it makes minimal or highly selective provision and places greater onus on the individual to make contingency arrangements, for example through insurance.

Another important typology is that identified by G Esping-Andersen (*Three Worlds of Welfare Capitalism* (Cambridge: Polity, 1990)). He sees welfare states as conservative, liberal, or social-democratic. The first broadly equates to the residualist model, but with specific support for traditional social structures such as the family. Liberal welfare states place an emphasis on **social insurance** and on welfare for all, but particularly the poorest, and thus on means-testing. Subject to its affordability, individuals can opt for private protection. The UK broadly fits into this model. Finally, the social-democratic welfare regime, associated with Scandinavian countries, is the most generous. It affords a degree of protection to the better off as well as the poorest, although maintains a strong emphasis on full employment.

When the UK and the US reduced state provision in the 1980s, in furtherance of economic neo-liberal policies, their welfare states became more residualist in character. Indeed, there was growing talk of a retreat from Beveridge in the UK, even of a 'crisis' in the welfare state. Since 1997, the Labour government has sought a 'Third Way', placing a greater onus on individual responsibility, more conditionality surrounding entitlement, and deeper private-sector involvement, with the state as 'manager'. The aim is to keep welfare spending within affordable limits and make citizens' rights and responsibilities more evenly balanced, while maintaining the basic functions of the welfare state. NEVILLE HARRIS

A Cochrane and J Clarke (eds), *Comparing Welfare States. Britain in International Context* (London: Sage, 2nd edn, 2001)

N Timmins, *The Five Giants. A Biography of the Welfare State* (London: Harper Collins, 2nd edn, 2001)

welfare-to-work The notion of 'welfare-to-work' reflects the basic idea that while the welfare state should provide security for those who are unable to support themselves or their family due to illness, disability, unemployment, or old age, it should also expect and encourage those who are capable of working to do so. Since 1911 social security law has incorporated this principle by, for example, providing that claimants classed as 'voluntarily' unemployed can be disqualified from benefit and denying entitlement to those who are not 'available for work'. Today, there is a policy assumption that many people not in employment could find work, particularly if they undergo training or receive work experience. Since the introduction of the jobseeker's allowance in 1996, participation in work-focused activities such as these is often required under the terms of a 'jobseeker's agreement' between the claimant and the state.

The Labour Government post-1997 has strongly promoted a policy of welfare-to-work. It identified as a fundamental problem within the social security system that 'people are trapped on benefit rather than being helped off' (*New Ambitions for Our Country: A New Contract for Welfare*, Cm 3805 (1998), 9). Work activation schemes such as the 'New Deal' programmes, targeted at different groups including young people, lone parents, and the disabled, have played an important part. So have regular agency reviews and interviews, designed, among other things, to ensure that a basic condition of 'actively seeking' employment is met. Welfare-to-work is also directed at incapacity benefit claimants, particularly through 'work-focused interviews'.

NEVILLE HARRIS

See also: **voluntary unemployment**

well-known trade marks Well-known **trade marks** enjoy a higher standard of legal protection due to the greater risk of unauthorized exploitation of their reputation. First, trade mark registries are obliged to refuse or cancel the later registration of a mark which constitutes a reproduction, imitation, or translation of a well-known mark, or which is likely to create confusion with an existing well-known mark, irrespective of whether or not the well-known mark is registered in the territory concerned or of whether or not the goods or services concerned are identical or similar.

Secondly, in cases of infringement of a well-known mark by use of an identical or deceptively similar mark, the claimant does not need to show likelihood of consumer confusion, irrespective of whether the goods or services are similar or dissimilar to those in respect of those for which the well-known mark is registered. The claimant need only show that the defendant has taken unfair advantage of or caused injury to the distinctive character or reputation of the well-known mark.

Finally, even if a well-known trade mark is unregistered in the United Kingdom, the owner may nonetheless obtain an injunction to prevent the unauthorized use of any mark that is identical or similar to the well-known mark and that is being used for identical or similar goods or services, provided the owner can show that the use in question is likely to cause confusion.

When determining whether or not a trade mark is well-known the court will take account of the knowledge of the mark in the relevant sector of the public, and the duration, extent, and geographical area of any use, promotion, or advertising of the mark.

GAIL EVANS

Welsh Assembly The National Assembly for Wales (to give it its formal name) is the devolved legislature for Wales, first established by the Government of Wales Act 1998. Its powers and functions were altered by the Government of Wales Act 2006, in particular by transferring its executive functions to a separate Welsh Assembly Government, and by extending its legislative powers.

Assembly members are elected from the UK parliamentary constituencies in Wales, with an additional twenty members elected from five Assembly electoral regions; at present the Assembly has sixty members.

Under the 2006 Act, the Assembly may enact, in English and Welsh, a new type of subordinate legislation ('Assembly Measures') for Wales on 'matters' specified by **Order in Council** relating to twenty 'fields' which encompass a wide range of state activity; the fields may be amended by Order. In the future, if supported by referendum held with the approval of both the UK Parliament and the Assembly, the Assembly would be empowered to enact primary legislation ('Acts' of the Assembly) in fields specified in Schedule 7 to the 2006 Act. However, an important limitation on the present and potential legislative competence of the Assembly is that it has no tax-raising powers. Public finance in Wales is by direct funding approved by the UK Parliament paid into a Welsh Consolidated Fund.

In addition to its legislative functions, the Assembly scrutinizes the policy and administration of the Welsh Assembly Government, and authorizes its expenditure and appropriation. The Assembly also nominates the First Minister of the Welsh Assembly Government.

T ST JOHN BATES

see also: **House of Commons; House of Lords; Northern Ireland Assembly; Scottish Parliament**

Westminster Parliament This is the legislative body for the whole of the **United Kingdom**, ie for England and, in respect of those powers which have not been devolved to the **Scottish Parliament**, the **Welsh Assembly** (but only delegated legislation), and the **Northern Ireland Assembly**, for the other components of the UK. It consists of two chambers, the elected **House of Commons** and the appointed **House of Lords**. The government is formed on the basis that it can command the confidence of the House of Commons. The **Prime Minister** is appointed by the sovereign under the **royal prerogative**, but this is regulated by constitutional convention so that she would appoint the leader of the largest party in the House of Commons. The parliament has a maximum duration of five years, although elections tend to be after four years when the Prime Minister advises the sovereign to dissolve the Parliament, thus triggering a general election. The House of Commons has 646 members ('MPs'), 529 from England, 59 from Scotland, 40 from Wales, and 18 from Northern Ireland. Each country has a boundary commission which reviews voting constituencies and has a duty to keep the constituencies of a similar size. The commissions make recommendations to redraw the boundaries so as to meet this and other criteria.

The members of the House of Lords are known as 'peers'. There are twenty-six 'Lords Spiritual', the most senior bishops in the Church of England. Since the House of Lords Act 1999 the Lords Temporal are people appointed to the chamber by being made a Life Peer. The 1999 Act was intended to remove from membership of the House all of the hereditary peers, but was amended to retain ninety-two hereditary peers. When the Constitutional Reform Act 2005 comes into full effect, the highest court will be the Supreme Court rather than (as formerly) the Appellate Committee of the House of Lords; and so future judges in this court will no longer be appointed to the House of Lords.

As the House of Commons is elected, and so accountable to the electors, it is more important than the House of Lords; and this is reflected in the fact that Prime Minister and the great majority of ministers will be MPs and that, in passing legislation, the

House of Lords may only delay the approval of a Bill, which can become an Act without the approval of the House of Lords if the provisions of the **Parliament Acts** 1911 and 1949 have been followed. If a Bill is a 'Money Bill' then it may not even be delayed by the House of Lords. Historically, gaining 'control of the purse' was an important factor in switching the balance of power from the sovereign to Parliament. As the government usually has a majority in the House of Commons, the importance of this control over the running of the country has diminished. Parliament now holds the government to account mainly through debate, the asking of questions and the scrutiny of legislation, policy, and administration by various committees, most of which reflect the composition of the House. They try to operate through consensus to maximize their effect but some issues result in division along party lines.

BRIAN THOMPSON

See also: **legislative and general committees; select committees**

Westminster system This phrase refers to a form of governmental structure developed in England, Westminster being the area of London where institutions of government were established after the Norman Conquest and the Palace of Westminster being the collection of buildings where the UK Parliament is housed. The Westminster system is alternatively referred to as 'parliamentary' or '**cabinet**' government, and may be contrasted with a 'presidential' system, of which the US provides the archetype. The key structural difference between Westminster and presidential systems is that in the former, but not the latter, members of the political (as opposed to the bureaucratic) element of the executive branch of government ('**ministers of state**') are appointed from amongst members of the legislature ('parliament'), predominantly elected members. A corollary is that ministers are 'responsible', both individually and collectively, to Parliament—hence the use of the term 'responsible government' to describe the Westminster system. In practical terms, it follows that in order to form and remain in government, an elected Member of Parliament (the **Prime Minister**) must be in a position to command a majority of votes in the Parliament or, in a bicameral legislature (with a lower and an upper house), in the lower house. According to the principle of collective **ministerial responsibility**, the members of a government stand or fall together. According to the principle of individual ministerial responsibility, ministers must account to Parliament for the way they perform their official functions and run their departments by

answering questions, providing information, remedying administrative failures and, in extreme cases of personal fault, resigning. PETER CANE

See also: **Westminster Parliament**

Westphalian system The Peace of Westphalia consists of the Treaties of Munster and Osnabrück signed in May and October 1648. These agreements ended a series of protracted wars in Europe (the 30 Years War and the 80 Years War). The conflicts in Europe preceding the Westphalian settlement were confused affairs, largely because the fault-lines were not at all clear. The impetus for war was partly religious: Protestant–Catholic rivalry in Europe had provoked innumerable, vicious wars in the period leading up to Westphalia. Cutting across these religious divisions, however, were classic inter-state wars such as that fought between the Hapsburgs and France in which Catholic France occasionally sided with Protestant interests. Finally, these wars were about the way in which political life in Europe should be organized. They represent, perhaps, the death-throes of a pan-European Holy Roman Empire struggling to preserve its prerogatives in the material and political realms in the face of the powerful sovereign states that were to dominate Europe thereafter.

For many international lawyers and political scientists, Westphalia has been viewed as a key transitional moment in which the sovereignty of states becomes the central normative idea anchoring the international (or, at least, European) system. Accordingly, the term 'Westphalia' characterizes an international legal order in which power is decentralized, authority is secularized, and empire is dissolved. States are the only sovereigns and they are sovereign in two senses; they can bar other forms of political authority or other states from exercising any control over their territories and, within these territories, they can pursue ideological and religious programmes of their own choice.

It is clear that the Westphalian political and legal order remains influential. The **United Nations** Charter, for example, contains provisions on the sovereign equality of states, on territorial integrity and political independence, and on the principles of self-determination and equal rights of states. Indeed, when officials or writers wish to refer to the current order they often describe it as 'Westphalian'.

British Prime Minster Tony Blair in a speech to his Sedgefield constituency in 2003 spoke of the need to replace the Westphalian order with a new international order based on global justice: 'So, for me, before September 11th, I was already reaching for a different philosophy in international relations from a traditional one that has held sway since the treaty of Westphalia in 1648'. What Blair meant was that the Westphalian assumptions about sovereignty had to be replaced by a commitment to **human rights** and peace that might involve dissolving sovereign rights when sovereigns, say, committed grave human rights abuses against their own people. But, for many thinkers, this is a post-Westphalian age in a more profound sense. Is it possible, they ask, to speak meaningfully about the territorial sovereignty of states in a period when the flow of capital and the movement of peoples have rendered such territory porous? Do sovereigns have the capacity to pursue independent political programmes in the face of highly intrusive mechanisms of oversight by international organizations or the dictates of the global financial markets?

Indeed, it may be that Europe again is the locus of a shift of a magnitude akin to that seen in 1648 as the **European Union**'s centralizing and supranational tendencies reverse the ascendance of sovereignty documented and constituted at Munster and Osnabrück.   GERRY SIMPSON

whistle-blowing   There is no universally accepted definition of whistle-blowing. Some define it narrowly as the reporting of illegal activities. Others prefer to take a more expansive view and would include a broad range of wrongdoing.

The Public Interest Disclosure Act 1998 only gives rights to workers. It sets out both the types of disclosure that can give rise to protection ('qualifying disclosures') and the circumstances in which such disclosures will be protected. A 'qualifying disclosure' is one which a worker *reasonably believes* tends to show: (i) a criminal offence; (ii) a failure to comply with any legal obligation; (iii) a **miscarriage of justice**; (iv) danger to the health and safety of any individual; (v) damage to the environment; (vi) the deliberate concealment of information tending to show any of the matters listed above. The matter disclosed may have occurred in the past, be currently occurring, or likely to occur.

Workers can be protected if they make qualifying disclosures in good faith to their employer or to another person responsible for the matter disclosed. Those in Government-appointed organizations can make a disclosure to a Minister. Additionally, workers can disclose to a person prescribed by the Secretary of State if they reasonably believe that the matter falls within that person's remit and that the information is substantially true.

External disclosures can be protected if workers: (i) act in good faith; (ii) reasonably believe that the information is substantially true; (iii) do not act for personal gain; (iv) have already disclosed substantially the same information to the employer or to a prescribed person (unless they reasonably believe that they would be subject to a detriment for doing so, or that the employer would conceal or destroy the evidence if alerted); (v) act reasonably. For these purposes regard shall be had in particular to: (a) the identity of the person to whom the disclosure is made; (b) the seriousness of the matter; (c) whether there is a continuing failure or one likely to recur; (d) whether the disclosure is made in breach of a duty of confidentiality owed by the employer to another person; (e) any action the employer (or prescribed person) has taken or might have been expected to take in relation to a previous disclosure; (f) whether the worker has complied with any procedure authorized by the employer for making a disclosure.

Finally, provision is made for disclosures about exceptionally serious wrongdoing. Again, in order to be protected: (i) workers must act in good faith; (ii) they must reasonably believe that the information is substantially true; (iii) they must not act for personal gain; (iv) the relevant failure must be of an exceptionally serious nature; and (v) in all the circumstances it must be reasonable to make the disclosure. Particular regard will be had here to the identity of the person to whom the disclosure is made.

Employment **tribunals** can provide **remedies** to workers who have been subjected to a detriment or been dismissed for making a protected disclosure.

                                              DAVID LEWIS

white-collar criminals   Who is a white-collar criminal? The answer is far from self-evident. One element is a vague type-of-activity category spanning, eg deception, illegal price-fixing, and—in some versions—health and safety violations that increase profits or reduce losses (although these latter have usually come to be defined as 'corporate crime'). A second element is a category of social status (eg including social security frauds by landlords but not by the poor), itself raising questions about the boundaries of white-collar status which has become far looser and more variegated in contemporary society than in the 1940s when the concept was first developed by Edwin Sutherland. The problem over who may be called a 'white-collar criminal' is compounded by international evidence-gathering difficulties and the use of discretion among **police** and non-police agencies to develop (or not develop) criminal-type investigations and to prosecute (or not) in the criminal courts; the more technically complex and morally ambiguous 'offences' may present problems securing a conviction, being therefore 'non-criminal' in practice. The rules of attribution of criminal liability to **companies** and to **directors** also affect the labelling process. In most countries, social security fraudsters are more likely than tax fraudsters to be prosecuted, but whereas Germany has special administrative courts for white-collar offences, Italy makes no distinction. The US has a relatively aggressive approach to the **prosecution** of fraudsters of all kinds, and some investigating magistrates in France, Italy, and Switzerland are active in prosecuting domestic and foreign elites; but the UK has a less activist attitude.

Criminal careers researchers lack interest in white-collar crimes as too ambiguous or ideological in denotation; and secondly, because studies generally start with juveniles and—although kids frequently lie and deceive—their early crimes seldom include fraud, still less corporate crimes. It is commonly asserted that people commit frauds and intellectual property ('IP') theft to get capital for drugs purchases, but one would have to query the pure economic rationality of offenders who chose to engage in high risk drugs trafficking when they could make huge sums of money from low risk fraud. Perhaps one difference between fraudsters and others is that the former see particular situations as enabling fraud and are able better to rationalize what they do as harmless or otherwise justifiable.

One systematic study conducted in the US by Weisburd, Waring, and Chayet (2001), showed that almost half of a broad range of federal fraud offenders convicted in the 1970s had been arrested previously for crimes other than fraud. The least diverse offenders were **securities** fraudsters. The average age of first **arrest** was thirty-five: higher for those less often arrested (who tended to be the more elite offenders, who are also better educated). Although it does not tell us what proportion of general criminal careers culminate in white-collar crime, fraud was the final event in the criminal history of half the data set. However, it is not clear whether offences (such as securities fraud or **antitrust**) committed over a lengthy period can, in any meaningful sense, be described as *one* offence, comparable to the more time-discrete offences such as thefts, robberies, and even violent crimes.

A study by KPMG (*Profile of a Fraudster* KPMG Holding, 2007) examined 360 'company fraud' cases which the forensic departments of KPMG in Europe, the Middle East, and Africa have investigated over recent years, whether or not prosecuted: the ability and willingness to hire KPMG means that frauds are more likely to be serious in impact and involve senior personnel, and that victims can afford to hire them. The patterns are similar right across geographical regions. The typical fraudster is aged between thirty-six and fifty-five and by the time the fraud begins, and he (85 per cent are male) has usually been employed by the company for six or more years. He typically works in the finance department and commits the fraud single-handed. In 86 per cent of cases he is at management level—and in two-thirds of cases he is a member of senior management. Over half commit twenty or more frauds, usually over some years. Indeed, whereas the media tend to focus on fraud/white-collar crimes by organized outsiders, surveys carried out by Ernst & Young, KPMG, and PriceWaterhouse Coopers suggest that the majority of big cases appear to be committed by insiders, sometimes colluding with outsiders. In sum, white-collar criminals are a heterogeneous group in terms of their backgrounds, their involvement with 'mainstream' offenders, their consciousness of transgressing social as well as legal norms, and the levels of social disapproval their offences elicit.

MICHAEL LEVI

D Weisburd, E Waring, and EF Chayet, *White-Collar Crime and Criminal Careers* (Cambridge: Cambridge University Press, 2001)

See also: **corporate criminal liability**

White Papers   White Papers are documents containing a public statement of government policy, presented to Parliament 'by command of Her Majesty', in practice by a Minister, on a subject considered to be of interest in the public domain, whose presentation is not required by statute, but where a published statement of policy is thought desirable.

The dissemination of information is essential to the effective working of Parliament and to public debate. Debate and the scrutiny of legislation in draft cannot take place without it. The right of Parliament to be informed is vital to the parliamentary process and from it flows that of asking questions of the government for the provision of information.

Historically, the term 'White Paper' referred to slimmer policy statements made by government, with white paper covers; while the expression 'Blue Books' covered bulkier government publications, bound in blue paper, which were often reports of Royal Commissions or important departmental committees.

The term 'Command Paper' refers to the procedure by which government papers are presented to Parliament by command of the Queen. They include statements of government policy, or proposals for legislation or administrative action; annual reports by government departments, exchange of notes and agreements with foreign governments and international organizations. Some major policy statements are presented annually, for example, the Defence White Papers, but others are made *ad hoc*, in answer to a specific need or in response to a public undertaking given in Parliament. Royal Commission reports and those of important departmental committees are also usually printed as Command Papers. Of recent years upward of 300 such papers have been presented annually.

Since 1833, each Command Paper has been given a serial number in a continuous sequence for ease of reference. In 1986 a new series with the abbreviation 'Cm' started (eg Cm 560). The great majority are printed but occasionally papers are presented, by command, without forming part of the printed numbered series. Some are presented to the House of Commons alone, for example the annual estimates, which are printed by order of the House.

Command Papers may be presented to Parliament on any date during the existence of a Parliament, though by practice this is not done on Saturdays, Sundays, and Bank Holidays. The presentation of a paper to Parliament is recorded in the Votes, Minutes, and Journals. Such papers are made available to Members and to the public, and parliamentary practice dictates that such information should not be released publicly before being made available to Parliament.

Green Papers are a comparatively recent development, used as an alternative to a White Papers when the government wishes to encourage public and parliamentary discussion of possible policy options, without commitment and before final decisions have been taken by the government and Parliament. They have been used to deal with a variety of public issues on which political opinion is divided. These have included, for example, central issues about the **European Union**, including entry into the European Monetary Union, and on a number of social issues.

MICHAEL WHEELER-BOOTH

Wilberforce, Richard Orme Lord Wilberforce (1907–2003) was educated at Winchester and New College, Oxford. He was called to the Middle Temple in 1932, appointed a Chancery judge in 1961 and, in 1964, was elevated to the **House of Lords**, where he remained until 1982. As an appellate judge, he stood for level-headedness, detachment, and the clear, common sense application of principle. Though he was essentially a cautious decision-maker, he was

not opposed to **common law** innovation. Among his memorable judgments are *DPP v Lynch* (1975), in which he argued that duress could amount to a defence in a charge of aiding and abetting murder; *McLoughlin v O'Brian* (1983), in which he ruled that someone not at the scene of an accident could nevertheless recover damages for 'nervous shock'; and *Bromley LBC v Greater London Council* (1983), in which it was held that the Greater London Council's 'cheap fares' scheme for London bus and tube transport breached its **fiduciary** duty to ratepayers. It is somewhat ironic, given Wilberforce's reputation for judicial restraint, that the 'two-stage test' for negligence which he expounded in *Anns v Merton* (1978) was eventually declared by the House of Lords to be an impermissible piece of judicial legislation. Although Wilberforce himself dealt firmly with lawmaking initiatives in the Court of Appeal, he often expressed his admiration for judicial innovators and was prepared to support their initiatives when those initiatives were taken up by Parliament. In retirement he lent his support to numerous legal and **human rights** reforms.   NEIL DUXBURY

See also: **assisting crime**

Wilde, Oscar That Oscar Wilde (1856–1900) is remembered as much for his public humiliation at the hands of the Victorian legal system as he is for his prodigious literary output is testimony both to the importance that law played in his life, and to the significance of his trials and conviction for twentieth-century campaigns to decriminalize homosexual activity between men.

Irish by birth and educated at Trinity College Dublin and Magdalen College Oxford, Wilde lived most of his life in London at a time when prostitution was characterized as the 'social evil', gonorrhoea and syphilis as 'social diseases', and sodomy the 'crime against nature' or the offence '*non nominandum inter christianos*'. The link between non-procreative sex, social disintegration, and moral abomination—especially where such sex took place between men—meant that Wilde felt compelled, like many others, to express his physical desires in secret with male prostitutes (Wilde called this 'feasting with panthers') while at the same maintaining the outward appearance of bourgeois heterosexual respectability through marriage and fatherhood. It was not, however, these dangerous liaisons which were the catalyst for Wilde's downfall but his love for Lord Alfred Douglas, the younger son of the Marquis of Queensberry. Incensed by the relationship, Queensberry accused Wilde, in writing, of 'posing as a somdomite' (sic) as a result of which Wilde felt obliged to instigate a prosecution for criminal **libel.**

Queensberry, whose defence was truth and justification, was acquitted and soon after, in the spring of 1895—the same time that Wilde's *Importance of Being Earnest*, a play about the perils of leading a double life was being staged—Wilde was charged with gross indecency under section 11 of the Criminal Law Amendment Act 1885. The first trial, in which Wilde's wit seduced the jury, was inconclusive; but at his second, the Crown appointed Sir Frank Lockwood, the **Solicitor-General**, as prosecuting counsel. His skill in getting Wilde to admit that his association with young men of a class entirely alien to his own was based on sexual attraction, rather than an innocent wish to be in the company of lively minds, as well as his right to give the closing speech (the only prosecutor entitled to do this) resulted in Wilde's conviction and sentencing to the maximum of two years imprisonment with hard labour.

Despite a petition to the **Home Secretary**, in which Wilde sought to explain his conduct in terms of the nascent medical model of homosexuality, Wilde served a full term—a period that provided inspiration for what many consider to be his finest non-dramatic work, *The Ballad of Reading Gaol*. In this, with a characteristic pun on his own name, he captured the tragic impact of the oppressive laws under which he had lived:

And the wild regrets, and the bloody sweats,
None knew so well as I:
For he who lives more lives than one
More deaths than one must die.

Oscar Wilde died in Paris in November 1900, aged forty-six, an exile and a bankrupt.

MATTHEW WEAIT

R Ellmann, *Oscar Wilde* (London: Hamish Hamilton, 1987)
M Foldy, *The Trials of Oscar Wilde: Deviance, Morality and Late-Victorian Society* (New Haven: Yale University Press, 1997)

Wilkes, John John Wilkes (1725–1797) was an MP who successfully fought for 'liberty' on three occasions. In 1763 the 23 April issue of his weekly political paper *The North Briton* was prosecuted for **libel** by the Grenville ministry. The constitutional significance of this event was that Wilkes was arrested under a general warrant, mocked by him as a 'ridiculous warrant against the whole English nation' because it named no suspects. There already existed doubts as to the legality of general warrants, long used by government against spies, libellers, and other unidentified persons. Wilkes now challenged this practice. On 6 December 1763, after Wilkes brought an action for **trespass**, Chief Justice Charles Pratt ruled in the Court of Common Pleas that general warrants could not be used as search warrants for unspecified buildings. The *St James's Chronicle* of 27 December celebrated this verdict. 'By this important decision every Englishman has the satisfaction of saying that "his home is his castle"'. This pronouncement was later complemented by judgments of Chief Justice Lord **Mansfield** in the Court of King's Bench on 18 June 1764 and 8 November 1765 that ended the use of general warrants for the arrest of persons.

Wilkes had long since fled to France, and during his self-imposed exile was expelled from Parliament and convicted of libel, being outlawed on his failure to return to Britain. He came back four years later to contest the general election of 1768, and won the seat of Middlesex. Although his outlawry was revoked on a technicality, he was sent to prison for two years for his libels, and remained there during the Middlesex elections controversy. On 3 February 1769 the Grafton ministry persuaded the **House of Commons** to expel him for various libels, new and old. After he was re-elected for Middlesex on 16 February the House of Commons next day declared him 'incapable' of election because he had been expelled. After a third by-election victory of Wilkes on 13 April the seat was awarded to his opponent. Wilkes returned to the Commons at the general election of 1774, and every session moved to rescind the resolution of 17 February 1769 until, after a change of ministry, his motion was carried on 3 May 1782, thereby establishing the right of parliamentary electors to choose any candidate not legally disqualified at the time of the poll, and ending the theoretical danger, often voiced in debate, that a ministry might purge the Commons of any MPs deemed undesirable.

The third victory for liberty also concerned Parliament, when in 1771 Wilkes established the right of the press to report debates. Hitherto reporting had been prevented by direct action against the printers of offending newspapers and magazines. Wilkes devised a scheme whereby printers were encouraged to take refuge in the City of London, where his partisans now held sway, and which claimed an exclusive right of arrest within its boundaries. City magistrates, including Wilkes, prevented the arrest of defiant printers, and the North ministry tacitly conceded defeat, although the formal ban on parliamentary reporting has never been rescinded. The freedom of the press to report Parliament was instrumental in ensuring the responsibility of MPs to their constituents.

PETER THOMAS

PDG Thomas, *John Wilkes: A Friend to Liberty* (Oxford: Clarendon Press, 1996)

Williams v Everett (1811)   Kelly, being indebted to several people, sent two bills of exchange to the defendants, his bankers, with instructions to apply the proceeds to several named creditors, including the claimant. Before the bills had been paid they were 'attached' in a lawsuit in the City of London courts by other creditors of Kelly, and the defendants refused to pay the claimant. The claimant brought an action for money had and received to his use. To short-circuit argument about whether the 'attachment' was legal, Lord Ellenborough, leading the Court of King's Bench, ruled that the money could not belong to the claimant—so as to make it money had and received to his use—unless there was 'privity', ie unless the defendants had undertaken *to the claimants* to pay; as the defendants had expressly refused to pay the claimants, the action would not lie.

The case was initially, probably correctly, received as being primarily a contribution to the then-very-tangled law of assignment of choses in action, but it gradually became a more general authority for various nineteenth-century 'privity of contract' dogmas. More recently it has been discussed as a **restitution** case.   MIKE MACNAIR

SJ Stoljar, *A History of Contract at Common Law* (Canberra: ANU Press, 1975), 140–143
LD Smith, 'Three-Party Restitution' (1991) 11 *Oxford Journal of Legal Studies* 481, 489–90

wills   *see* succession

winding up   Winding up or liquidation, as it is often known (the terms are commonly used interchangeably), is a process which involves a company's assets being collected and realized, with the resulting proceeds applied in discharging all debts and liabilities, and any balance which remains being distributed among the members according to their rights and interests, under the company's constitution, or otherwise dealt with as the constitution of the company directs. It is a process which prepares the company for its death, which is known as dissolution. Most often, winding up occurs where a company is not able to pay its debts, ie insolvent.

Winding up may be initiated by the decision of the shareholders of the company, who can vote for the company to enter that process. If the company is solvent this process will be known as 'members' voluntary winding up', but if the company is insolvent it is known as 'creditors' voluntary winding up'. If the members do not decide to wind up the company, a company can only be wound up by order of the court, a process known as compulsory winding up. The most common applicants for the winding up of companies by the **courts** are unsecured creditors who have not been paid what they are owed.

ANDREW KEAY

A Keay, *McPherson's Law of Company Liquidation* (London: Sweet & Maxwell, 2001)
IF Fletcher, *The Law of Insolvency* (London: Sweet & Maxwell, 3rd edn, 2001)

See also: **distribution of assets; insolvency, corporate; liquidator**

witchcraft trials, England   Although there were occasional trials for sorcery in the Middle Ages, England's witch-trials were mainly confined to the sixteenth and seventeenth centuries. A rise in accusations in the 1560s was a result of social conflict (caused by pressure of population upon resources), religious divisions and anxieties fomented by the Protestant Reformation and, most importantly, a burgeoning legal culture and the introduction of a law against witchcraft. The first statute (the Witchcraft Act) was passed in 1542, but repealed in 1547 and not replaced until 1563. Concerns about Catholic sorcery against Elizabeth I, and the demonological preoccupations of bishops exiled under Queen Mary, may well have spurred Parliament into action.

Poor survival of legal records makes it impossible to produce a comprehensive profile of prosecutions. There were around 1,000 trials, fewer than half of which resulted in execution. Between 80 and 90 per cent of defendants were women. Contrary to legend, the punishment was not burning, but hanging—as for all felonies. Indictments from the Home Circuit assizes show that although grand juries frequently approved cases at preliminary hearings, at trial only 22 per cent of arraigned witches were found guilty. Doubts about evidence, it seems, troubled petty jurors from the beginning.

There was little consensus about what witchcraft was, nor how best to prove it at law. Hundreds of cunning folk—wise men and women—were presented before the church courts, but here the offence was not diabolism but religious error, and punishments were mild. In the minds of the uneducated laity, however, a witch was not a faulty Protestant but a malevolent enemy who used demonic magic to commit anti-social crimes, or *maleficia*. Typically, this meant murder and inflicting illness (especially in infants), laming and killing livestock, and causing household enterprises, such as brewing and cheese-making, to fail. Many clergymen saw this response as an inability to accept God's providence; but the Witchcraft

Act provided an outlet for exactly the kind of grievance generated in communities nationwide.

In 1604 James I introduced a new statute, placing greater emphasis on the conjuration of evil spirits. By the time of the Lancashire trials in 1612, the Devil had started to play a more prominent role in accusations. The 1620s and 1630s marked a low point in witch-trials, reflecting Charles I's disdain for puritan obsessions with Satan. Popular desire, however, exploded in 1645–1647 when witch-finders Matthew Hopkins and John Stearne toured East Anglia, snaring some 300 suspects. Legal standards dipped and the evidence grew more outlandish—largely because of the unauthorized use of torture. Partly as a reaction, few trials ended in conviction after 1660, and the last execution occurred in the 1680s. A court found a witch guilty as late as 1712, but she was subsequently pardoned. The Witchcraft Act was repealed in 1736, and a statute proscribing the *pretence* to conjure evil spirits took its place. This Act was subsequently used against fortune-tellers and spiritualist mediums, most famously in the trial of Helen Duncan in 1944. In 1951 the Fraudulent Mediums Act replaced it.

MALCOLM GASKILL

J Sharpe, *Instruments of Darkness: Witchcraft in England, 1550–1750* (Philadelphia: University of Pennsylvania Press, 1996)

K Thomas, *Religion and the Decline of Magic: Studies in Popular Beliefs in Sixteenth and Seventeenth Century England* (London: Weidenfeld & Nicolson, 1971)

witchcraft trials, Scotland Often regarded as the 'continental' type, Scotland's witch-hunt actually mirrors England's in many respects. Certainly more people were tried. One study has uncovered almost 3,000 prosecutions, although archival gaps suggest that the true figure is higher. There were perhaps 1,000 executions—the earliest in 1542, the last in 1727—making Scotland the most prolific witch-hunting country in Europe, given that the population was under half-a-million. And yet few witches were officially tortured, 'sabbats' (festive meetings with Satan) were rarely heard of, and most crimes reported were acts of harm to person and property. Between two-thirds and three-quarters of witches were women, comparable to the English average.

Unlike the English legal system, the Scottish was largely based around Roman inquisitorial law. However, in practice, ordinary accusers reported suspects, who were then tried by juries—as was customary south of the border. The Presbyterian Church, or Kirk, dealt with complaints against all manner of magicians, healers, and witches, referring only the most serious cases to the civil courts. Mary,

Queen of Scots, introduced an Act against witchcraft in 1563, whereby anyone indulging in occult activities was liable to execution. And yet it seems that the courts were circumspect in their judgments. At the High Court of Justiciary in Edinburgh in the seventeenth century around half the accused were acquitted. The less fortunate were usually returned to their communities where they were strangled and burned at the stake.

How widespread accusations were before the Reformation, and in the Highlands even afterwards, the records do not allow us to say. Trials were mostly confined to the Lowlands and Borders, areas of intense religious and political conflict. But even here the distribution of trials was varied, both geographically and chronologically. There were several acute panics: 1590–1591, 1597–1598, 1628–1630, 1649 and 1659–1662. The first of these focused on witches said to have threatened King James, but at the heart of this episode—known as the North Berwick trials—simmered a political conspiracy involving the Earl of Bothwell. James took a personal interest in events and was inspired to write a treatise, *Daemonologie*, in 1597.

After 1600 accusations grew more demonic in character, as witchcraft came to be defined as the inversion of the Calvinist compact between Christ and people. This reached a climax during the civil wars. In 1649 Parliament and **Privy Council** issued numerous commissions of investigation, thereby asserting civil authority over the Kirk; excesses of unauthorized torture needed to be curbed in 1652. As ever, though, witch trials thrived on political instability, and in 1661–1662 there were 600 prosecutions, many orchestrated by 'witch-prickers'. Scepticism about the evidence for witchcraft, voiced by the **Lord Advocate** Sir George Mackenzie, helped to undermine the legal basis of trials in the later seventeenth century, even though accusations lingered well after 1700. The repeal of the Witchcraft Act in 1736 led to protests from the Kirk that Christianity was exposed to satanic attack. In remote regions witchbeliefs current in the sixteenth century survived into the twentieth century.

MALCOLM GASKILL

J Goodare (ed), *The Scottish Witch-Hunt in Context* (Manchester: Manchester University Press, 2002)

Christina Larner, *Enemies of God: the Witch-Hunt in Scotland* (London, 1981)

withholding and withdrawing life-prolonging treatment Medical progress means that life can now be sustained artificially, sometimes for many years. Inevitably this raises the question of whether steps must always be taken to prolong life for as long as possible, or whether there are circumstances in which it would be acceptable to withhold or withdraw treatment which is capable of prolonging the patient's life, such as mechanical ventilation or artificial nutrition and hydration ('ANH').

A competent adult patient has the right to refuse medical treatment, even if that refusal will lead to their death. This means that if a competent adult decides, for whatever reason, that they do not want life-prolonging treatment or they want it withdrawn, doctors *must* comply with their wishes, and to do otherwise would be to treat without consent, which would be unlawful.

In theory at least, a competent patient can also make a 'living will' or **advance directive**, refusing life-prolonging treatment in specified circumstances after they have lost the **capacity** to make this decision for themselves. Provided such an advance decision was made in writing, continues to be valid, and applies to the situation which has arisen, an advance refusal of life-prolonging treatment should have the same force as a contemporaneous one. In practice, however, there is often some uncertainty about whether the patient may have changed their mind since making the directive, rendering it invalid, or whether the advance refusal precisely covers the patient's circumstances. Where there is any doubt about an advance decision's validity or applicability, given that the consequences of following it will be the patient's death, it is probably unsurprising that doctors and the **courts** have been reluctant to treat it as binding.

Where the patient lacks capacity, and did not make a binding advance directive, the doctors and the courts will apply the best interests test when determining whether life-prolonging treatment should be withheld or withdrawn. Usually it is obvious that prolonging someone's life will be in her best interests, so it is only in cases where the patient's condition and prognosis is extremely grave that the withholding or withdrawal of life-prolonging treatment could plausibly be compatible with the best interests test.

Doctors proposing to withhold or withdraw life-prolonging treatment may apply to the court for a declaration as to whether such a course of action would be lawful. In these cases, the court is not *authorizing* the doctors to withhold or withdraw treatment, but is merely declaring that it would be lawful for them to do so, perhaps because life-prolonging treatment has become futile or too burdensome.

Of course, an obvious problem arises in cases where the decision is taken to withdraw treatment which is keeping the patient alive: namely, the doctors will *knowingly* be *doing something*, such as removing a gastrostomy tube, which will *cause* the patient's death. Might that not appear to satisfy both the *actus reus* (conduct which causes death), and the *mens rea* (intention to kill or to cause grievous bodily harm) of the crime of murder?

The courts' way around this conundrum has been to categorize the withdrawal of life-prolonging treatment as an *omission*, or a failure to act, rather than an *action*. The doctors who remove the tubes which connect the patient to treatment which is keeping them alive are said to be 'omitting to act' rather than acting. The act/omission distinction is very helpful for the law in this context, since otherwise it would be impossible to ever remove a patient from a ventilator without risking life imprisonment. It is, however, extremely controversial and was described by one of the Law Lords who decided the ground-breaking case of *Airedale NHS Trust v Bland* (1993) as 'intellectually and morally dubious'.

In the *Bland* case, the **House of Lords** were faced, for the first time, with the question of whether ANH could lawfully be withdrawn from a patient, Tony **Bland**, who was in a permanent vegetative state following injuries sustained at the Hillsborough stadium disaster in 1989. They unanimously decided that it could, because the treatment which was keeping Tony Bland alive had become 'futile'.

Some commentators have criticized the *Bland* judgment on the grounds that it necessarily involves the judgment that some lives are 'not worth living', and that this is incompatible with the principle of the **sanctity of human life**. Others have argued that it is illogical to allow doctors to effectively cause a patient's death by starvation and dehydration, and not to permit them to achieve the same outcome more quickly through administering a single lethal injection.

EMILY JACKSON

See also: **acts and omissions; best interests of patients; consent to treatment**

witnesses   *see* **evidence, criminal; evidence, civil**

WMDs   *see* **arms control**

Wolsey, Thomas (1471–1530)   Thomas Wolsey was appointed **Lord Chancellor** of England in December 1515 although he had no formal training in the **common law** or civil law. As Bishop, Archbishop (1514), and Cardinal (1515) at the same time he had authority over the **canon law**. The ambassadors reported his intentions to reform the laws and customs of the country and he is said to have interrupted the pleading of barristers on one occasion to complain of their want of knowledge and to have planned an institute to promote the study of law; but time and inertia were against him. He was active in the **Chancery Court** seeking to provide rapid and unbiased **justice** for all. He established the Court of Requests and other under-courts for poor suitors. He made more use of **Star Chamber** so that those responsible for administering justice in the provinces should not themselves be above the law, making examples of powerful aristocrats like the Earl of Northumberland. After his fall, his biographer, Cavendish, makes Wolsey say that a king 'ought to respect equity more than law for it is more honourable to do what is just than what is lawful'. As the equity courts could not enforce their judgments as the **common law courts** did, his reforms were only partially successful and although the Star Chamber supervised the common law courts he made no attempt to reform the King's Bench and Common Pleas. He did, however, attempt, largely unsuccessfully, to codify canon law. Contemporary writers like Polydore Vergil criticized his practices. Modern authors like John Guy see him as a plaintiff's judge; his biographer Peter Gwyn, as perhaps too lenient and flexible.   SYBIL M JACK

woman   The term 'woman' tends to be treated in law as a common sense biological concept and so is rarely legally defined. A woman, in law, is in essence characterized by the possession of female genitalia. And yet when used in a legal setting, the term 'woman' becomes a legal construct which means that it can vary from the biological definition. It is therefore possible, in theory, for a **person** to have a different legal sex for different legal purposes. The same individual could be a woman within one legal relationship (say a **pension** plan), a man in another (say an insurance contract). However, in the vast majority of cases, a person's legal sex is unproblematic and remains the same for their lifetime and within all their legal relations. A person's legal sex is registered at birth and the determination is made by a medical practitioner, rather than by a legal official.

Traditionally there have been serious legal disadvantages attached to being a woman which make it interesting to examine 'woman' as a distinct legal concept. Consistently, **judges** and law-makers have assumed that women are ill-suited for a wide variety of legal relations especially those associated with public life, and so have imposed on them certain incapacities. Law has therefore played a significant role in circumscribing the lives of women, particularly married women.

The most dramatic adverse consequence of **marriage** for women was a loss of independent legal existence. The **common law** principle of *couverture* entailed the legal fiction that the married man and woman were one. Marriage was therefore said to represent the 'civil death' of women. Famously, the eighteenth-century jurist, William **Blackstone**, declared (wrongly) that 'By marriage, the husband and wife are one person in law: that is the very being or legal existence of the woman is suspended during the marriage, or at least incorporated and consolidated into that of the husband' (*Commentaries on the Laws of England*).

In truth, married women remained legal persons for the purposes of much of the criminal law. For instance, they could still be charged with most criminal offences and fall victim to most of the crimes against the person. Married women, however, could not complain of **rape** by a husband because of the husband's immunity from **prosecution** for rape. This immunity persisted into the final decades of the twentieth century.

The largest practical effect of **couverture** for a married woman was to dispossess her of her property. Upon marriage, her husband acquired possession of her moveable goods and the right to manage her land and profit from it. This position was not reversed, in England, until the passage of the Married Women's Property Acts from 1870 to 1882.

From the late nineteenth century to the early twentieth century, women campaigned vigorously to be recognized as legal persons. They encountered strong and effective resistance. For example in 1869, a small group of women gained admission to Edinburgh University Medical School but were then denied the right to graduate (a denial judicially sanctioned). There followed a series of legal milestones at which women gained an increasing purchase on public life. Notoriously, England lagged behind the rest of the world in this process of reform. In 1861, South Australia granted restricted women's suffrage. In 1893, New Zealand became the first country to grant universal suffrage to women. Finland was the first European country to give women the vote in 1906. But it was not until 1928 that the United Kingdom granted women the right to vote on equal terms with men. And it was not until 1929 that the Judicial Committee of the English **Privy Council** finally concluded that the word 'persons' in statutory language (here it was the British North America Act) included women.

Women nevertheless remained effectively non-persons for many public purposes well into the twentieth century. The Royal Society remained closed to women until 1945. Cambridge University did not grant degrees to women until 1947.

The legal detriments imposed on women were based on a host of assumptions about their nature which went well beyond their basic biological reproductive functions to embrace their temperament, their **capacity** for independent rational thought, and their general suitability for public life. Rarely, if ever, were these assumptions verified in any manner, and time-honoured custom (women had always been regarded in this way) was invoked as supporting legal authority.

Such overt discrimination against women has now been, largely, formally eliminated by the removal of explicit legal incapacities and by the enactment of anti-discrimination **legislation**. A trend towards gender-neutrality in statutory language has strengthened this effort to make the sexes equal in law. The formal legal significance of being a woman has therefore contracted. Laws which specify the female (and male) sex are now expected to have a legitimate biological or related social reason. Typically, but not always, they refer to or relate to reproduction and sexual relations. Notably, the capacity to marry is still governed by biological sex and remains a legal relationship which is only permitted between the sexes.

According to modern feminists, however, the elimination of overt direct discrimination against women has not produced true legal equality. Most controversially, yet influentially, American legal theorist, Catharine MacKinnon, insists that the Anglo-American legal culture remains steeped in masculine values: that the very point of view adopted by law is male; that within law women remain subjugated and sexualized (especially by rape and **pornography** laws); and that law's person is still culturally and even physically a man. Other radical feminists have proposed that the division of persons in law into men and women either be abolished or be made a matter of personal choice. The legal distinction once drawn between women and persons means that this is technically possible. Because legal sex is a legal construction, it can be abolished or redefined by legal fiat.

A small body of jurisprudence on the legality of sex change, however, confirms a deep-seated legal commitment to the two-sex system and a profound reluctance to permit any departures from traditional biological definitions of women (and men) or to allow persons to choose or change their legal sex. England's Gender Recognition Act 2004 has gone some way to reversing this position.

NGAIRE NAFFINE

K O'Donovan, *Sexual Divisions in Law* (London: Weidenfeld & Nicolson, 1985)

C MacKinnon, *Feminism Unmodified* (Cambridge, MA: Harvard University Press, 1987)

women and crime Women commit only a modest proportion of officially recorded crime. This has been so for at least as long as such data has been collected and over many jurisdictions. While the female share of crime has risen in modern times, the increase has been slight. In 1984, in England and Wales, 16 per cent of known offenders were female; twenty years later, the proportion was 20 per cent. Similar figures are reported for the rest of the UK: women accounted for 14 per cent of those with a charge proved in Scotland in 2000 and for 12 per cent of all court **prosecutions** in Northern Ireland in 1999. Looking at the picture in more detail we find that women and girls contribute to almost all types of offences, including the most serious, such as **homicide**. However, they do so at lower levels, desist sooner, are less likely to be involved in organized and professional crime, and are mainly convicted of dishonesty offences. More than half of all women convicted or cautioned in England and Wales commit theft or fraud; 80 per cent of their criminal careers last less than one year (55 per cent for men).

Women are about 10 per cent of those found guilty of violent crimes, 2 per cent of those with convictions for sexual offences.

Younger women are more likely to become involved with the **criminal justice system**: 25 per cent of those referred to the Children's Reporter in Scotland on offence grounds in 2004–2005 were girls.

One increasingly used corrective to the known limitations of official statistics is crime surveys, both of **victims** and self-report studies, which are more relevant in measuring what is generally called 'the gender gap'. Such work is often focused on young people. Among recent findings are that half of young males and a third of young females reported taking an illegal drug, while 15 per cent of the former and 2 per cent of the latter acknowledged violent behaviour. One survey of schoolchildren aged ten to sixteen found little difference between the sexes; 55 per cent of boys and 49 per cent of girls admitted committing an offence in the previous year. An international study discovered two-thirds of boys but less than one-third of girls admitted violent behaviour.

Gender inequality before the law cannot explain these robust and persistent differences; very few sex-related provisions survive (eg the 1938 Infanticide Act—although there are hardly any **prosecutions** under this nowadays). For the most part, gender neutrality now applies as, for instance, in the Sexual

Offences Act 2003 where the old distinctions no longer apply: males as well as females can now be found guilty of soliciting for the purposes of prostitution.

Nevertheless, commentators have argued that the sexes are in practice treated differently in the criminal justice system. One view is that chivalry protects women from harsher penalties, another that once involved with the system, they experience more shame and stigma because they have transgressed as women and as offenders. Evidence supports both perspectives. Women are less likely to receive custodial sentences for some offences such as theft from a shop. Yet, their custody rate has increased much more sharply than that of men since the early 1990s. There was a much larger growth in the female **prison** population than the male from 1992 to 2004, up by 115 per cent as against 42 per cent. A series of reports have highlighted the plight of the small number of imprisoned women: their poor physical and mental health, histories of drug and alcohol abuse and **domestic violence**, and their own mainly non-violent offences. As such a small–5 per cent—proportion of inmates, they are shown to suffer more restrictions than men and to face penal regimes designed for men and only partially adapted to their needs.

FRANCES HEIDENSOHN

See also: **women as victims of crime**

women and gender in the legal profession Until the early 1980s when the first book on women lawyers appeared (Cynthia Fuchs Epstein's *Women in Law* (New York: Basic Books, 1981) about women practitioners in the US) women lawyers had been an ignored and neglected minority in all countries and jurisdictions. In the UK as anywhere else, the legal profession had been male dominated till late into the twentieth century. Professional rules which had been drafted in the course of the nineteenth century extended to men, as 'persons' referred to in Anglo-American legislation were men. Only at the beginning of the twentieth century it was decreed that women had to be considered as persons and could hold public office: in England by the Sex Disqualification (Removal) Act in 1919. Accordingly the first woman solicitors in the UK were admitted in 1920 in Scotland, in England and Wales in 1922. These early women lawyers were only tolerated and tended to practice in restricted areas which were considered suitable for women such as matrimonial and probate work.

During the first decades of the twentieth century the number of women lawyers rose slowly. Change occurred with the growing economic wealth of Western countries in the post-war period, which made it easier for women to get the chance of higher education. Modern methods of birth control helped women to plan their lives. In addition the growing rights-awareness associated with the civil rights movement attracted women to law. It also set the ground for the second women's movement in the 1970s. Equality and discrimination has become a leading subject of public discourse in recent decades, strongly promulgated by women lawyers. Today in almost all Western countries more women than men study law and they do at least as well as men in their examinations, ie they acquire the same 'academic capital'. However, legal education is still characterized by the traditional male culture, moulding the ideal lawyer by acculturation and assimilation.

In England and Wales the proportion of women in the number of new entrants to the profession of solicitor rose from 13 per cent in 1973 to more than 50 per cent in the 1990s. Meanwhile 43 per cent of qualified solicitors are women and 38 per cent in private practice. Figures for Scotland and Northern Ireland are comparable. Still considerably lower is the number of women barristers throughout the UK, not to speak of the number of female judges. The first woman judge was appointed in the 1960s to the County Court. They are still few. In 2007 only 10 per cent of High Court and Circuit Judges in England and Wales are women. The selection of judges from senior ranks and a non-transparent consultation process have worked against women and prevented a regular 'trickling up'.

In other formerly male domains, too, the number of women has risen in recent decades, but in none of them as dramatically as in law. This may be an indicator that law, as a subject closely related to the state power-structure and with good income possibilities, had formerly been particularly well-protected against female intrusion and competition.

In spite of the enormous rise in female participation in all key areas of law women have not altogether made their way. There is a gender-specific pay gap, the inequality beginning at the training stage and the gap widening with growing age. On entering the profession more men than women succeed in gaining the training place of their choice and subsequently their first job. Men enjoy greater network support, and are more readily granted respect and reputation in their professional work, which is rewarded as 'social capital'.

Women represent the law labour market's reserve army. They often work on insecure or temporary contracts, under less favourable working conditions, are often overqualified for the actual job they do, and are the first to be made redundant. In private practice they are more likely to work in the background, are less visible, and work more for individual than corporate clients. There are particular female-dominated segments in the legal services market, (horizontal segregation) such as family law and generalist fields characterized by little prestige and financial clout but greater emotional labour. Men are more likely to make it to partner status irrespective of any specific achievements such as experience, specialization, billable hours, and client structure (vertical segregation). Male bonding and images of a hegemonic masculinity characterized by assertiveness, objectivity, and efficiency, plus traditional breadwinner perceptions work for them. Women may feel rejected by traditional images of women, as found in barristers' chambers, or tangible male cultures.

Family responsibilities hinder women's careers in face of a profession which cherishes the philosophy and culture of total commitment and long hours. This leads to a particular female mobility— less upwards than sideways into other positions with working conditions more favourable to the combination of family and work, or downward and out (revolving-door effect). Or women forego a family. Many try to find their own niches outside the traditional professional order. In spite of all the difficulties, women lawyers enjoy high job satisfaction because of the importance of their work and a relatively high income compared to other women.

Discrimination may occur unwittingly or in the conviction that it can be rationally justified or attributed to individual failings rather than to gender-bias. But it is there. Equal opportunities and anti-discrimination programmes are more often of symbolic value than practical impact.

Although women lawyers perceive and describe differences between their own attitude to work and behaviour and that of their male colleagues, this does not basically affect the nature of their work. Women do not judge differently. However, they have changed the law by enforcing legislative measures which take into account modern notions of equality. Have they changed the profession? The former homogeneity of the legal profession has suffered serious erosion. There is a fracturing and a growing managerialism due to market forces associated with globalization. In the processes of post-modern change women lawyers are obviously just one factor; but they are a factor which influences and changes the appearance and image of the legal profession.

ULRIKE SCHULTZ

U Schultz and G Shaw, *Women in the World's Legal Professions* (Oxford: Hart, 2003)

See also: **judicial appointments**

women and legal education　*see* **gender issues in legal education**

women and property in developing countries

The subject of women and **property rights** in developing countries is often framed and defined in the negative, as deficient, lacking in protection, and consequently vulnerable. Whilst these are not experiences shared by all women in developing countries, they are pervasive and consistent to a majority of women who, due to their lower socio-economic status, ethnic background, and **race** are rendered even more vulnerable. This fact is attributed to a range of factors that place barriers to women seeking to control, administer, and own property. Cultural norms, marital property rights, tenure systems, and some women's lower socio-economic status have all had an adverse impact on women's property rights.

There are traditional norms, religious and cultural, that constitute barriers to women from accessing property rights. These norms also make it difficult for women to be allocated land on the same basis as men. Whilst there are variations to the manner in which land was historically held in a number of **communities,** the dominant narrative is that of land being held not on behalf of the individual but rather in the name of a clan, community, or family. These systems recognized a myriad of rights and interests in property without necessarily involving ownership of the land. However there have been and the still remain exclusions on the basis of **gender** that makes it difficult for property to be transferred to women through family networks, which incidentally is the most common form of passing property from one generation to the other in developing countries. The denial of women's rights to inheritance is the most pervasive form of this deprivation. In instances where the law protects women's rights to inheritance, there are still strong socio-cultural forces that do not recognize the newly acquired rights and proceed to dispossess the widow. This is also due to the fact that most of these laws aimed at altering social practices are not properly enforced. The existence of local norms that do not allow land to be allocated to women in their own names adds to constrain women's access to property rights.

Marital status is also used as a basis for precluding women from acquiring land. In instances where women are not married they may require another male member of the family to assist them in accessing or even purchasing land. There remain a number of countries that require women to be subject to the marital power of their husbands. In this instance, the law may require that property belonging to either spouse must be registered under the male partner's name regardless of when it was acquired and who acquired it. The existence of a combination of systems of law, mainly made up of religious laws, **customary laws**, and statutory laws that set up different proprietary consequences for each marital system creates a hierarchy of legal protections with the result that women who are married according to statutory law are often better protected than women who are not.

The introduction of laws and policies aimed at tenure reform has had the unintended consequence of changing the nature and form of property rights in a manner that heightens women's vulnerability. Tenure reform has sometimes taken the form of formalizing land rights by creating land registers and creating title deeds. Another variation in developing countries has been to change group or communal tenure into individual tenure. The new laws and policies have often failed to provide a model that is comparable to the one that existed before the reform process with the consequence that whatever undefined rights that women had under the informal systems are extinguished and inadvertently men's property rights are strengthened. Women's rights to property have also been undermined by the patriarchal assumption that the head of the household is the man. The consequence has been that when formal title is acquired, although granted to him to be held on behalf of the family, the law sets out different consequences by creating new rights that allow him ownership of the property.

Women's lower socio-economic status poses another barrier in that even when laws allow women to own and control property, women still lack the financial resources to purchase property. The growing trend of urbanization and women increasingly migrating to cities has given rise to the rapid growth of informal settlements and other forms of insecure tenure located in the periphery of the larger cities. This condition has given rise to the growth of systems that regulate property rights that run parallel to the legal system as access to judicial institutions remain constrained. The absence of laws and policies aimed at regulating the informal economy has made it possible for the legal vacuum to subsist.

A number of developing countries are currently involved in law reform processes that seek to change the prevailing inequities by providing for laws that enable women to acquire and own land regardless of their marital status. In countries where **equality** between men and women remains contested, there have been moves to change **constitutions** to provide a legal basis for equal treatment of men and women. There are other reform processes aimed at granting married women rights in the marital property by allowing for co-ownership of property. There are also attempts to scrap gender-discriminatory laws from the statute books and to stop the courts from applying traditional norms that do not protect women's rights to property. SIBONGILE NDASHE

women as victims of crime Politically and analytically, violent crime is the most interesting type of crime against **women**. The two most striking features of women's experience of violent crime are its location and the relationship of the victim to the offender. Women are most vulnerable to both sexual and non-sexual criminal **violence** in domestic settings and this is where they are most likely to suffer serious injury. Their assailant is likely to be someone they know, often a male sexual intimate. **Strangers** tend to account for a minority of **rapes** of women. This basic set of facts about women's criminal victimization has been confirmed by the British Crime Survey of private households which is regarded as the best measure of such crime in Britain. By contrast, the home is revealed to be the safest place for men. Although men, especially young men, are significantly more at **risk** of violent crime than women, their assailants are likely to be other young men (not women) and the violence is likely to occur outside the home.

The private location of the most serious crimes against women, crimes of violence, has made it less amenable to the interventions of criminal law and criminal justice and therefore less likely to enter the official statistics. By long tradition, criminal law and justice have been oriented towards anti-social acts which occur in public places and the home has been treated as a safe haven into which the state should intrude with the greatest reluctance. Liberal political philosophy has tended to support a fundamental right to **privacy** within the home. Patriarchal political and legal principles have further supported the right of men, treated as heads of families, to ensure order within the home and effectively govern its inhabitants. There remains a high level of state ambivalence about state intrusion into supposedly private family matters, and it is still the case that sexual crimes of violence committed by intimates in a domestic context are the hardest to prove.

Feminists have played a critical role in representing and asserting the interests of female victims of **domestic violence** and bringing the plight of such women to public attention. They have established women's refuges designed to provide **asylum** to women wishing to escape from violent men. They have established rape crisis centres to advise, support, and represent women complaining of sexual crimes. They have lobbied to change criminal law and practice in relation to rape and domestic violence, which are overlapping problems. They have also sought to extend the scope of behaviour covered by the criminal law and also to make the law more effective.

One particular concern of legal feminists (a concern shared by a number of criminal law theorists), has been the very low standard of male sexual conduct regarded as legally permissible. A mistaken and unreasonable belief by the accused that he had the victim's consent to sexual intercourse has constituted a full reply to a charge of rape. Legal feminists have met with some success in this area of law reform and there must now be reasonable grounds for such a belief.   NGAIRE NAFFINE

See also: **feminism and law reform**

women lawyers, distinguished Women were excluded from the legal profession in the UK until the passing of the Sex Disqualification (Removal) Act 1919. Several women have gone down in history for their unsuccessful petitions to the legal professional bodies prior to this date: among them, Bertha Cave, Christabel Pankhurst, and Gwyneth Bebb. Of these, only Bebb (who gave her name to the case, *Bebb v Law Society* (1914) holding that women were debarred from becoming lawyers because they always had been barred) eventually qualified and went into practice as a solicitor. Eliza Orme (1848–1937) was noteworthy for working all her life in legal practice despite being prevented from qualifying. The earliest woman law student in England, she set up her own **conveyancing** and **patent** agency where she and her female partner provided legal assistance to qualified male solicitors and barristers.

The first woman to qualify as a solicitor in England and Wales, in 1923, was Carrie Morrison (1888–1950), a lifelong advocate of legal independence for married women. The first woman to be called to the Bar was Ivy Williams (1877–1966). With the highest academic qualifications—she was the first woman to receive a non-honorary doctorate in law—she was called to the Bar in 1921 at the age of forty-three. She chose, however, not to enter legal practice, becoming the first woman legal academic. For twenty-five years she was the only woman tutor and lecturer in law at Oxford. The first woman to *practise* as a barrister was Helena Normanton (1882–1957). Admitted to Middle Temple 'within hours' of the passing of the Sex Disqualification (Removal) Act, she was called to the Bar in 1922, working up a busy practice— 'everything from **divorce** to murder'—and became

the first woman to prosecute in a murder trial. Later, as President of the Married Women's Association, Normanton fought for the right of married women to keep their maiden name for professional purposes (as she herself had done) and for divorce law reform. She wrote *Everyday Law for Women* (1932) to demystify law and empower women to take control of the legal aspects of their lives.

Normanton shared the honour of being the first woman appointed a King's Counsel (in 1949) with Rose Heilbron (1914–2004), a celebrated defence barrister in the 1950s and 1960s who in 1972 became the first woman judge to sit at the **Old Bailey**. Two years later she was appointed to the Family Division of the High Court and in 1975 chaired a committee on the reform of **rape** laws which recommended limitations on the cross-examination of women alleging rape.

Chrystal Macmillan (1872–1937), Scottish suffragette and pacifist, was called to the English Bar in 1924. In the inter-war period she was one of the most prominent spokeswomen for a range of feminist causes. Sybil Campbell (1889–1977), barrister, was appointed England's first woman stipendiary magistrate in 1945. Elsie Bowerman (1889–1973), Girton graduate, suffragette, and survivor of the Titanic disaster, was another early barrister who helped found the Women's Voluntary Service and headed the Status of Women section of the **United Nations** after the war. Eulalie Spicer (1906–1997) ran the Law Society's divorce services department set up during World War II to deal with the increase in **marriage** breakdown. In 1950, she took charge of the newly-created **Legal Aid** London division.

The first woman High Court judge was Elizabeth Lane (1905–1988), appointed in 1965 to the Probate, Divorce, and Admiralty division, having been the first woman County Court judge in 1962. Elizabeth Butler-Sloss (b.1933) was the first woman appointed to the Court of Appeal (in 1988). From a legal family, she chaired the Cleveland **child abuse** inquiry of 1987 and, in 1999, became the first woman President of the Family Division. A very different route to the judiciary was taken by Brenda Hale (b.1945), who spent twenty years as a law teacher (rising to Professor at the University of Manchester) before being appointed to the **Law Commission** in 1988, the first woman and youngest person to be so. Made a Queen's Counsel the following year, she became a judge in the Family Division in 1994; was promoted to the Court of Appeal in 1999; and in 2004 entered the House of the Lords as the first woman Lord of Appeal in Ordinary. A feminist and co-author of one of the first modern English books on women and law, she has already made a difference in several areas of law.

Helena Kennedy (b.1950) is one of the country's most distinguished barristers today. A Scot, she was called to the English Bar in 1972 and became a QC in 1991. In an influential book, *Eve Was Framed* (1993), she wrote about the male culture of the Bar and the sexism and racism she encountered as a student and practising lawyer, as well as the problems of women as litigants, defendants, and witnesses. Her practice has included a number of famous **miscarriage of justice** and criminal defence cases including those of battered wives who killed their husbands. A life peer since 1997, Kennedy is a powerful spokeswoman in debates on **justice** and **human rights** in the **House of Lords**.

Gareth Peirce (b.1940), solicitor, is another radical lawyer known for her miscarriage of justice and civil rights cases including the defence of terrorist suspects detained in **prison**. She led the successful Guildford Four appeal which became the subject of a Hollywood film, *In the Name of the Father*. Harriet Harman (b.1950) was the first woman—and first solicitor—to be appointed **Solicitor-General**; up to 2001 the post had always been occupied by male barristers. Finally, Patricia Scotland (b.1956) was born in Dominica into a large family that emigrated to England in 1958. A London graduate, she was called to the Bar in 1977, and in 1991, at the age of thirty-five, became the first black woman QC. Now a life peer, she has occupied a number of ministerial positions in the Labour government.

As late as 1970, only 3 per cent of practising solicitors and 0.5 per cent of practising barristers in England and Wales were women. Only in the closing years of the twentieth century did equal numbers of women begin to enter the legal professions although they continue to experience formidable barriers in progressing to higher levels. ROSEMARY AUCHMUTY

women's property rights before 1900 Women of all classes were less likely to own property than their male counterparts, on account of the practice of primogeniture in aristocratic families and, at the other end of the social spectrum, lower rates of remuneration for those in employment. Yet throughout all periods of history women did inherit and earn property in their own right: widows were often the major beneficiaries of their husband's wills, and daughters generally received a similar amount to sons (although they were more likely to receive their inheritance in the form of personal property than land). The right of single, widowed and, later, divorced women to deal with their property was not constrained by law.

Surveys of wills and probate accounts have shown that women were often nominated as executors and guardians as well as beneficiaries, and thus played an important role in owning and managing property.

It was **marriage**, rather than simply gender, that affected a woman's right to own and control property. The law took the view that the legal identity of a wife was merged with that of her husband during the marriage. As a consequence, control and ownership of the wife's property vested in the husband upon marriage. In practice, however, the apparent harshness of this rule was mitigated by a number of factors. First, the theory of marital unity was never fully reflected in the law, with different rules applying to different forms of property. An English husband became the absolute owner of his wife's personal property, with the exception of what was termed 'paraphernalia'—her clothes and jewellery—an exception that Trollope's Lizzie Eustace seeks to exploit in *The Eustace Diamonds*. By contrast, he was only a temporary guardian of any land that she owned: entitled to manage it, and to the income from it, but not permitted to sell it without her consent. Similar rules operated in Scotland: a husband became the absolute owner of his wife's moveable property—again, with an exception for paraphernalia—and acquired rights of control over other forms of property.

In turn, marriage imposed a number of obligations upon a husband and conferred certain rights upon wives. A husband acquired his wife's debts as well as her assets. He was required to maintain his wife, and she could pledge his credit in order to purchase necessaries. From one perspective this purchasing power was a necessary corollary to her management of the home and a means of ensuring the husband's comfort, but it also conferred upon wives considerable power as consumers. Upon his death she was entitled either to provision from his estate: either one-third of the land that her husband had owned—an entitlement termed dower in England and Wales and terce in Scotland—or such support as had been agreed.

Thirdly, wives were also daughters, and wealthy fathers were often concerned to ensure that their daughters' assets were protected from spendthrift sons-in-law. Such concerns resulted in the development of the 'separate use', whereby property could be transferred to trustees to be held for the benefit of the wife. To ensure that a wife would not be persuaded by her husband simply to transfer her separate property to him, the courts also developed the 'restraint on anticipation' to restrict what a wife could do with her property. Of course, while this ensured that wives would not be 'kicked or kissed' out of their separate property, it also limited their autonomy. Moreover, the practice of settling property for the separate use of a wife gave no protection to the vast majority of married women on whom no such settlements had been made.

It was not until the second half of the nineteenth century that there was any concerted attempt to reform the law. A campaign by a group of feminists in the 1850s revealed significant support for change; but the legislation passed by Parliament in 1857 dealt only with the position on separation or divorce, rather than with the property rights of married women in general. The publication of John Stuart Mill's *The Subjection of Women* in 1869 reinvigorated the debate, but the Married Women's Property Act 1870 was not the far-reaching measure that reformers were pressing for. It did, however, provide much-needed relief for poorer women, providing that a married woman's earnings, as well as certain investments and inheritances, would constitute her separate property. It was a further twelve years before the Married Women's Property Act of 1882 provided that any property owned by a wife before marriage or acquired thereafter would be her separate property. Contemporaneous reforms occurred in Scotland. As a result, married women were no longer deprived of their assets on account of their marital status, although they remained subject to the disadvantages faced by all women with regard to the acquisition of property.   REBECCA PROBERT

Woolmington v DPP   A decision of the House of Lords, *Woolmington v DPP* (1935) represents the first clear statement in English law that a person accused of a criminal offence is entitled to the protection of the presumption of innocence. It asserts very clearly that the burden of proof rests, as a matter of principle, with the prosecutor who brings the case to establish each element of that case to the satisfaction of the court. On a prosecution for **murder** of a man who had shot his wife, the trial judge told the jury that once the prosecutor had proved the fact of the killing, it was presumed to be murder unless the accused could establish otherwise. This was, at the time, an entirely standard direction. But the House held that it was wrong and contrary to the presumption of innocence.

There are several reasons why a criminal justice system should insist on the maintenance of the presumption. At a practical level, the decision-maker has a rule of thumb to follow in cases of doubt. If there is doubt, an acquittal is the appropriate outcome. There is also the consideration that the consequences

for the individual who is wrongly convicted are altogether more disastrous than is the wrongful acquittal of the guilty (undesirable though that might also be). When the criminal sanction is employed, the accused's liberty, dignity, and privacy are all jeopardized to a significant extent, and it is believed to be right that the state should be required to justify such intrusive invasions.

There are some well-established exceptions in which the defence does carry the burden, most notably in relation to the defence of insanity; and there are numerous situations where by statute Parliament has made it plain that it intends to depart from the basic principle, either expressly or by implication. Furthermore, the defence may be under an obligation to raise the issue in the first place (and may be required to adduce sufficient evidence to do that— the defendant is said to bear 'the evidential burden'). But subject to that, it follows from the presumption of innocence that the burden should rest ultimately with the prosecution, a principle described by Viscount Sankey in his speech (judgment) in the House of Lords as being 'one golden thread . . . always to be seen' in English criminal procedure.

The general principles are now reinforced by their articulation in Article 6 of the **European Convention on Human Rights** made part of English law through the **Human Rights Act 1998**, which enshrines the presumption as a fundamental **human right**. Although both the jurisprudence of the **European Court of Human Rights** and the English cases agree that Article 6 does not impose an absolute prohibition on the imposition of reverse onuses, there is considerable doubt about the circumstances in which this is permissible. The courts have taken the line that when Parliament has used language suggesting its intention to deviate from the standard, it will generally have imposed only an evidentiary burden.
                                          ATH SMITH

See also: **evidence, criminal**

work accidents   *see* **industrial injuries; prescribed diseases; tort system**

work permit   This is a phrase denoting legal authority to engage in employment. Although used most frequently in the context of immigrant workers seeking employment in a foreign country, in some jurisdictions work permits are a pre-condition for the employment of **children**, disabled people, or **minorities**. In the immigration context, work permits generally relate to **persons** granted temporary stay in a foreign country, either as business people, temporary workers, students, **working holiday** makers, persons granted temporary protection on humanitarian grounds, or other temporary migrants. However, the phrase can also apply to permanent **visa** classes granted on the basis of a migrant's skills and employability, as in the UK. The nature and function of work permits is as varied as the range of people to whom they apply. In many countries permits are granted by government to foreign workers with pre-existing offers to work. In other instances, the permits are part and parcel of a temporary migration visa. They may require the holder to work for a certain employer or in a certain industry; or they may restrict the number of hours of employment. Special conditions generally attach to work permits issued to working holiday makers (limiting both length of employment and employment with a single employer). Foreign students often face restrictions on hours worked: breach of the conditions can result in visa cancellation, detention, and expulsion from the country. Work permits can involve employer obligations determining wage levels and the terms and conditions of employment of a foreign worker.

MARY CROCK

See also: **migrant worker**

worker   *see* **contract of employment**

worker's compensation   Someone injured through work, or who has a work-related disease, can recover compensation from the employer at **common law** in the **tort system** if the employer's negligence caused the injury or disease or it was caused by the negligence of another employee in respect of whose negligence the employer is vicariously liable. The person injured can also recover compensation if the cause of the damage was a breach of statutory duty by the employer. Worker's compensation, in contrast, refers to statutory schemes under which an injured employee can make a 'no-fault' compensation claim (without proof of anyone's negligence) either against an employer or against the state.

Under the nineteenth-century Workmen's Compensation Acts, compensation from the employer was limited to half wages. The scheme, designed to be informal, proved very litigious. It was replaced in 1948 by the industrial injuries benefits scheme, part of the British **social security system**. Under it, state benefits are payable to an employee or office holder (eg policeman) (but not a self-employed person) who has suffered personal injury through accident arising out of and in the course of work. They are also payable in respect of a specified disease or injury linked to specific types of work (eg occupational deafness). Benefit is a weekly pension (the amount

varying according to the level of resulting disability), assessed by reference to the disparity between the claimant's condition and that of a person of the same age and sex whose condition is normal.

DAVID BONNER

N Wikeley, *Wikeley, Ogus and Barendt's Law of Social Security* (London: Butterworths, 5th edn, 2002), ch 20.
S Jones, 'Social Security and Industrial Injury' in N Harris (ed) *Social Security Law in Context* (Oxford: Oxford University Press, 2001), ch 15

working holiday   Working holiday maker ('WHM') schemes are like super-international exchange programmes for young people from selected countries. Agreements between the UK and **Commonwealth** countries allow young people aged between seventeen and thirty years (inclusively) who are either single or married to another WHM-eligible **person** to gain a two year **visa**. In the UK, visa holders cannot have dependent **children** aged five or over during their stay and must show that they have a healthy bank balance. Visa holders may work, but only in jobs that are incidental to their holiday in the UK and for no more than twelve months over the two years of their visa. In other Western countries, working holiday maker schemes operate on a reciprocal basis, although the length and terms of the schemes tend to be very similar to the UK scheme. In Australia, countries are chosen on the basis of statistical data kept on visa overstay and compliance rates (by country, age, and other criteria). In 2007, agreement was reached in Australia for visa programmes with the US and other non-traditional WHM countries, but with the further restriction that only tertiary-educated young people from participating countries would be eligible for the visas. The schemes are designed to add value to tourist programmes by fostering goodwill and building longer-term connections between the countries included in the scheme. Some young people convert to longer term work or study visas. Most make lifelong connections that bring both tangible and intangible benefits for the respective countries involved.   MARY CROCK

working time   *see* **hours of work**

working to rule   *see* **staff handbooks and works rules**

works councils   In broad terms, a works council is a body established within a **company**, or other place of work, to represent workers collectively in communications with management. The nature of works councils—the provision made for them in law, their constitution, roles, and functions—can vary between and within jurisdictions. Indeed, practice can vary from workplace to workplace in accordance with such variables as management and worker attitudes, the size and type of the workplace, and the wider political and economic climate. Nevertheless, it is possible to identify a number of features common to all works councils. First, works councils represent the employees of a particular workplace, not the employees within an industrial sector, or grade, or territorial area. Secondly, works councils represent all workers at a given workplace, regardless of **trade union** membership: a worker is represented by a works council simply by virtue of being employed at that workplace. Lastly, works councils represent workers collectively: they present the views of 'the workers' as one common voice.

In many European countries, comprehensive systems of works councils were introduced at the end of World War II through statute or collective agreement, to exist alongside centralized trade unions. No legal provision for works councils was ever made in the UK; however, bodies similar to works councils have existed in practice—at times, in large numbers. In 1992, a European Community Directive was passed to encourage the formation of works councils in large, trans-national companies (EC Directive 94/45).   RUTH DUKES

J Rogers and W Streeck, *Works Councils: Consultation, Representation, and Cooperation in Industrial Relations* (Chicago: University of Chicago Press, 1995)

See also: **collective bargaining**

World Bank   *see* **international monetary law**

world heritage sites   *see* **UNESCO World Heritage Centre**

World Intellectual Property Organization ('WIPO')   The World Intellectual Property Organization is a specialized agency within the **United Nations** system, with headquarters in Geneva, Switzerland. It was created in 1967 with the purpose of encouraging creative activity and promoting the protection of intellectual property throughout the world. Its roots go back to 1883, when the Paris Convention for the Protection of Industrial Property became the first international treaty enabling people from one country to obtain protection in other countries for their inventions, **trade marks,** and industrial **designs**. The Paris Convention entered into force in 1884 with the accession of fourteen member states, which set up an international administrative Bureau. In 1886, the **Berne Convention for the Protection of Literary and Artistic Works** was established to protect literary, musical, and artistic works. It too established an administrative Bureau. The two Bureaux joined in 1893 to form the Bureaux for the Protection of Intellectual Property ('BIRPI').

In 1970, BIRPI became WIPO following the entry into force of the Convention Establishing the World Intellectual Property Organization, and acquired a secretariat to serve the member states. In 1974, WIPO became a specialized agency of the United Nations system with a mandate to administer intellectual property matters recognized by member states of the UN. It moved in 1978 to the Headquarters building it now occupies in Geneva. Through 1996, WIPO expanded its role and further demonstrated the importance of intellectual property rights by entering into a Cooperation Agreement with the **World Trade Organization ('WTO')**.

Today WIPO is a dynamic entity with 184 member states, which administers twenty-four treaties and carries out a rich and varied programme of work. Its strategic goals are to promote an IP culture, to integrate IP into national development policies and programmes, to develop international IP laws and standards, to deliver quality services in global IP protection systems, and to increase the efficiency of WIPO's management and support processes. Unlike other branches of the United Nations, WIPO generates financial income independent of the contributions from member states. In 2006 over 90 per cent of its income of around 500m Swiss francs was expected to be generated from the collection of fees by the International Bureau under the intellectual property application and registration systems which it administers: the Patent Cooperation Treaty, the Madrid system for trade marks, and the Hague system for industrial designs.

Member states (as of 29 January 2006), serve as a public forum for IP discussion. Headquartered in Geneva, the Organization also operates Coordination Offices in Brussels, New York, Washington DC, Singapore, and Tokyo. As of 31 December 2006, the Organization employed 890 staff members. Much of WIPO's work is done through committees including the Standing Committee on **Patents**, the Standing Committee on **Copyright** and Related Rights, and the Advisory Committee on Enforcement. The Intergovernmental Committee on Access to Genetic Resources, **Traditional Knowledge**, and Folklore ensures that WIPO is actively engaged in policymaking in areas which have yet to be recognized by **international law** in establishment of new substantive intellectual property rights.

                    RUTH SOETENDORP

World Trade Organization The World Trade Organization ('WTO') is made up of both institutional elements and a set of nineteen major agreements that regulate trade between countries.

The general objective of the WTO is to promote free trade between states by seeking to minimize governmental barriers to trade. Examples of such barriers include taxation and customs duties beyond those allowed by the WTO Agreements; the discriminatory application of environmental standards in such a way as to affect trade; subsidies provided by a government to a domestic producer that may allow them to compete more successfully against foreign producers; and government measures that restrict or discriminate against foreign service providers (for example, banks, insurance companies, or telecommunication service providers) that wish to establish and operate business in a domestic market.

Beyond these examples the WTO Agreements seek to regulate and minimize trade barriers across the board by imposing obligations on WTO member states in a number of areas that include, for example, trade in goods (the 'General Agreement on Tariffs and Trade' or 'GATT'); trade in services (the 'General Agreement on Trade in Services' or 'GATS'); and Agreements on Agriculture, Textiles and Clothing, Technical Barriers to Trade (eg trade barriers that relate to product standards and labelling), Trade-Related Investment Measures, Dumping and Subsidies, and Sanitary and Phytosanitary Measures (trade barriers that relate to the health or life of humans, animals, or plants).

Two of the most common, and important, of the obligations imposed by these WTO Agreements on States are the Most Favoured Nation ('MFN') and National Treatment ('NT') obligations. The MFN obligation provides that if a WTO member state confers a trade advantage on one member state then it must afford the same (most favourable) standard of treatment to all other WTO member states. Consider, for example, if state X imposes a tariff rate of 15 per cent on imports of a specific type of marble from state Y, but later agrees to allow imports of the same type of marble from state Z into its country at a tariff rate of 10 per cent. The application of the MFN obligation in this case says that state X should only charge a tariff of 10 per cent on imports from state Y. The NT principle requires that the government of a WTO member state must not treat imports of goods, or foreign service-providers in its country, in a worse way than it treats domestically produced goods or domestic service-providers.

The MFN and NT obligations are in substance an application of the value of equality—that governments should ensure that like cases are treated equally. However, the WTO does not seek to ensure substantive equality in trade relations between states. The WTO is only concerned only with increasing the amount of global wealth generated through free trade by seeking to prevent trade barriers, and not to redistribute the resulting global wealth between different states. In part for this reason, the WTO has been the subject of severe criticism by some developing-country WTO members and non-governmental organizations; the WTO has also become the target of criticism by anti-globalization campaigners.

The institutional element of the WTO includes decision-making bodies constituted from the 151 WTO member states (eg the WTO Ministerial Conference, which heads the Organization and meets at least once every two years; and the WTO General Council, located in Geneva, which oversees the day-to-day operation and implementation of the WTO Agreements and decisions of the Ministerial Conference) and also notably the WTO Dispute Settlement System ('DISS') which is made up of first-order Panels that hear cases brought by Member States against each other and an Appellate Body that hears appeals against a Panel decision in a particular case.

The WTO DISS is one of the most efficient and effective mechanisms of inter-state dispute settlement that exists today. A reflection of this success has been its very frequent use by states to resolve successfully a large number of trade disputes. There have been over 365 cases brought by member states before WTO Panels since the WTO was established in 1994, and the Panels and Appellate Body have been used to resolve trade disputes between states in a large variety of areas that include, only by way of example, aircraft, automotive, cigarettes, computers, gambling and betting, genetically modified organisms ('GMOs'), hormones in beef, intellectual property rights, music, textiles, steel, and telecommunications equipment and services. Several of these cases have involved billions of dollars worth of trade.

DAN SAROOSHI

World Trade Organization Agreement on Trade Related Aspects of Intellectual Property Rights ('TRIPs') From the late 1970s there was a growing realization, particularly in the US, that the counterfeiting of trade-marked products was having a considerable adverse impact upon trade revenues. In 1979 the US and the European Community had reached agreement on a draft 'Agreement on Measures to Discourage the Importation of Counterfeit Goods'. This initiative was carried forward into the Ministerial meeting of 1982 for the preparations for the forthcoming **General Agreement on Tariffs and Trade ('GATT')** Round. In the face of a US suggestion that the Draft Code be adopted as part of the GATT, the developing countries led by Brazil and India argued that intellectual property issues were the exclusive territory of the **World Intellectual Property Organization ('WIPO')** and that, in any event, the GATT was concerned with trade in tangible goods and therefore, that the GATT had no jurisdiction over trade mark counterfeiting. The Resultant Ministerial Declaration requested the Director General of GATT to hold consultations with his counterpart at WIPO in order to clarify the appropriateness of joint action in relation to counterfeiting. Discussions within the GATT Council renewed the questioning of the relevance of intellectual property rights to the GATT and, additionally, raised the question of whether the allegations of the trade impacts of **trade mark** counterfeiting could be quantified. This challenge was taken up in the US, both through Congressional hearings and through studies conducted by trade associations submitting to those hearings.

Between 1982 and 1986 a Preparatory Committee of the GATT identified the issues which would be the concern of the forthcoming GATT Round. The US proposed that the Round consider all intellectual property rights, affirming that the GATT was the appropriate forum to seek the enforcement of intellectual property rights. Subsequent negotiations sought a compromise between opposing views on the jurisdiction of GATT in these matters, and produced a proposal which served as the basis for the Ministerial Declaration of 20 September 1986 which launched the Uruguay Round. This declaration referred to the 'need to promote effective and adequate protection of intellectual property rights' and 'elaborate as appropriate new rules and disciplines'.

A key factor in the ultimate success in securing the GATT TRIPs Agreement was the preparedness of the US to pursue its negotiating objectives through domestic trade legislation. Difficulties in the Uruguay Round over agriculture had resulted in the introduction in 1984 of an amendment to section 301 of the US Trade Act of 1974, which permitted the President to seek the elimination of 'unjustifiable or unreasonable' trade practices. The 1984 Trade and Tariff Act made intellectual property protection explicitly actionable under section 301. The Omnibus Trade and Competitiveness Act of 1988 introduced 'Special 301', which required an annual review by the US Trade Representative ('USTR') of the intellectual property practices of the country's trading partners. The USTR was required to identify 'priority foreign countries' which deny 'adequate and effective protection of intellectual property rights' or which 'deny fair and equitable market access' to US traders. The USTR is then obliged to place those countries on either a watch list or a priority watch list, with a view to a fast-track investigation, followed by trade retaliation in the form of increased duties or import restrictions.

A breakthrough in the deadlock over agriculture was achieved in the April 1989 meeting of the Trade Negotiations Committee, at which a Framework Agreement on the future direction of negotiations on intellectual property rights was settled. Further revisions were incorporated into a Draft Final Act which included a new TRIPs text. In the result the final draft of the TRIPs Agreement, which was adopted when the Uruguay Round was brought to a close at the Ministerial meeting at Marrakesh, 12–15 April 1994, was very close in form and content to this text.

The TRIPs Agreement came into effect on 1 January 1995. It contains general provisions and basic principles concerning intellectual property, as well as a catalogue of standards concerning the availability, scope, and use of intellectual property rights, which have to be adopted by Member countries. The principal provisions of the Paris and Berne Conventions are incorporated into the TRIPs Agreement, and the national treatment principle is re-affirmed as a basic tenet of intellectual property protection. The Agreement also contains the most-favoured-nation principle, which has not traditionally been provided for in the context of intellectual property rights on the multilateral level. This principle provides that any advantage, favour, privilege, or immunity granted by a Member to the nationals of any other country (whether a Member or not) shall be accorded immediately and unconditionally to the nationals of all other Members, with certain specified exemptions. Norms are laid down for national legislation on **copyright** and related rights, trade marks, geographical indications, industrial **designs**, **patents**, layout-designs (topographies) of integrated circuits, and undisclosed information.

A novel feature of the Agreement, compared with other international intellectual property conventions, is the requirement that specified enforcement procedures be available to permit effective action against any act of infringement of intellectual property rights covered by the Agreement, including expeditious civil remedies to prevent infringements and criminal remedies which constitute a deterrent to further infringements. The Agreement also provides for the border enforcement (customs enforcement) of intellectual property rights (see **border control of intellectual property**).

The negotiating parties appreciated that the exigencies of negotiation had produced a document which would require subsequent amendment and improvement, and that the speed of implementation would depend upon the level of economic development of a country. Thus, built in to the TRIPs Agreement itself was a reform agenda. Article 71 required the Council for TRIPs to review the implementation of the Agreement after the expiration of five years from its commencement and at two yearly intervals. Also influencing the reform agenda are the periodic meetings of trade ministers. The Doha Ministerial meeting, which was held in November 2001, instructed the Council for TRIPs, in pursuing its review programme 'to take fully into account the development dimension'. This was reiterated at the Hong Kong Ministerial in December 2005.

MICHAEL BLAKENEY

writs From the earliest periods for which we have written evidence, the writ was a principal means of communication between the **Crown** and individuals or groups who were a distance away. From the middle of the twelfth century it had a particular function as the mechanism by which **common law** litigation was initiated.

Original writs (by which litigation was commenced) were obtained from the Chancery. Writing in the first half of the thirteenth century, Bracton distinguished between writs of course, *brevia de cursu*, and magistral writs or writs of grace, *brevia magistralia*. The former were issued by Chancery clerks in more or less standard form, and were available as of right; the latter, by contrast, were issued by Chancery masters and had no set form, and they were available only as a matter of special grace. In practice, it was the writs of course which defined the remedies available at common law. Indeed, probably the commonest genre of English legal literature of the thirteenth and fourteenth centuries were Registers of Writs, collections of precedents of writs containing all of the standard forms together with variants upon them and sometimes a set of brief notes or commentaries; the canonical version of this was printed, reaching its final edition in 1687.

The system of writs defined the whole framework of common law learning until the eighteenth century, when English lawyers finally began to make explicit use of substantive legal categories (such as contract and tort) as their main method of organization. Nonetheless, the old system continues to exercise a considerable influence on legal thinking even

today. In formal terms, the writ as an originating mechanism was abolished in England in 1979.

DAVID IBBETSON

wrongful dismissal A 'wrongful dismissal' is a dismissal in breach of an employee's contract. It is critically important not to confuse wrongful dismissal, a **common law** wrong, with **unfair dismissal**, a statutory wrong. This is especially important because the demarcation between the two kinds of claim is a matter of some complexity and doubt.

Typically **contracts of employment** permit the employer (and employee) to terminate the contract by giving a certain period of notice. Even if this is not expressly agreed, the courts will often imply a 'notice term' of this kind. A typical wrongful dismissal therefore consists in an employer being dismissed either with no notice, or with less notice than the contract requires. Even where a termination of contract is wrongful for breaching another term of the contract, the **compensation** payable will often be limited by the presence of a notice term. This is because the law will calculate the loss for which the employee should be compensated according to what it would have cost the employer to take the easiest lawful route out of the contract.

Perhaps because these situations are so common, even very distinguished lawyers sometimes imply that the only way a dismissal can be wrongful (that is, in breach of contract) is if the employer breaks a notice term. But there are many ways an employer can breach a contract of employment when terminating it. For example, if a contractual disciplinary or performance management procedure is required before notice is given, failure to follow this will result in a dismissal being in breach of contract. Equally, an employment contract may specify the sorts of actions for which the employee is liable to be dismissed, so that dismissal for another reason would break the contract.

There is also an important category of wrongful dismissals called constructive dismissals in which the employer's breach will typically have nothing to do with a notice term. This covers situations in which the employer has broken the contract of employment in a way that is so fundamental that the law entitles the employee to treat it as immediately at an end. Note however that this is not the employee's only option. In fact, working out what an employee is best advised to do in these circumstances can be one of the most difficult aspects of modern employment law. Be that as it may, this category of dismissals demonstrates that a termination of employment can be wrongful in many more ways than because of a failure to give contractual notice.

Finally, it is important also to remember that not every summary dismissal is wrongful. In a mirror image of constructive dismissal, where an employee has committed a fundamental breach of contract, the employer has a common law right to treat the contract as terminated. Equally, the contract might spell out situations in which an employer is entitled to dismiss without notice. As for employees, however, it is worth exercising particular care before acting on either of these possibilities.

LIZZIE BARMES

See also: **discipline in the workplace; notice of termination of employment**

wrongful birth 'Wrongful birth' tort claims by parents must be distinguished from **'wrongful life'** cases where a **child** claims that s/he should never have been born. English law, like most **common law** jurisdictions, has rejected the concept of 'wrongful life' actions, as the **sanctity of human life** would be violated, and the values of non-existence and a disabled existence are impossible to compare (*McKay v Essex County Council* (1982)). A child can sue for **disabilities** resulting from negligent antenatal treatment of either parent (Congenital Disabilities (Civil Liability) Act 1976, section 1).

After initial conflation, 'wrongful birth' acquired a meaning distinct from 'wrongful conception' following a failed sterilization of either parent. In wrongful birth cases, the negligence is causally related not to the conception but to the birth, when the parents claim they would have terminated the pregnancy had they received competent medical services. The claimants may have wanted a child, but not with a disability sufficiently serious to justify termination under the Abortion Act 1967, section 1(1)(d), had the problem been detected through proper treatment of the expectant mother (eg diagnosis of rubella) or antenatal screening for foetal abnormality. A doctor may have failed to diagnose an undesired pregnancy in time for a lawful termination. More rarely, a failed termination procedure may result in a live birth.

The categories of recoverable **compensation** were developed in Scottish and English authorities about wrongful conception, notably *McFarlane v Tayside Health Authority* (2000); and *Rees v Darlington Memorial Hospital NHS Trust* (2003). The symbolic award of £15,000 for the tortious deprivation of parental **autonomy** in choosing not to conceive does not apply to wrongful birth cases; the same holds true for the mother's prenatal and postnatal expenses and loss of income and suffering associated with the pregnancy and birth, at least where she initially wished to have a child. More problematic are the parents' claims for raising the unwanted child. *McFarlane* characterized such expenses as pure economic loss (severed from the conception itself, as personal injury to the mother), and held that they are unrecoverable where a healthy child is born. *Rees* reached the same conclusion where the parent is disabled.

In *Parkinson v St James and Seacroft University Hospital NHS Trust* (2002) Hale LJ had distinguished *McFarlane* as being predicated upon a 'deemed equilibrium' between the benefits and burdens of healthy children, reasoning that this is disrupted by the additional expenses entailed by congenital disability and should be compensable. In *Rees,* the **House of Lords** rejected the 'deemed equilibrium' explanation of *McFarlane* but did not rule on *Parkinson*'s disability-related expenses exception. Thus, it has not been conclusively decided in English and Scottish law whether parents can recover the costs of caring for a disabled child in wrongful conception and, by analogy, wrongful birth cases. Where a termination due to foetal abnormality is unsuccessful, **damages** might be restricted to any additional injuries inflicted by the procedure, although had it been competently performed, the claimant would not have had this child and arguably the defendant should be liable for all of the disabilities (as with non-diagnosis of pregnancy (*Groom v Selby* (2001)). A wrongful birth case involving serious disability makes a more compelling appeal to distributive **justice** than a wrongful conception resulting in a healthy child.   LAURA HOYANO

L Hoyano, 'Misconceptions about Wrongful Conception' (2002) 65 *Modern Law Review* 883

JK Mason, 'Wrongful Pregnancy, Wrongful Birth and Wrongful Terminology' (2002) 6 *Edinburgh Law Review* 46

wrongful conception 'Wrongful conception' actions are one of a discrete species of lawsuit brought against medical professionals/health authorities following failures in the provision of family planning techniques (usually resulting in the birth of a **child**). Frequently brought under the tort of negligence, individuals claim that they would not have *conceived* the child, whether born healthy or disabled, but-for the negligence. Such claimants wished to avoid conception/**parenthood** entirely and accessed family planning methods such as vasectomy or sterilization. Such cases typically involve allegations of negligence in the performance of such procedures, or in the provision of advice (eg about the woman's or her partner's sterility).

Although the product of 'medical progress' and increased reproductive choice, these actions have proved particularly controversial in recent years in the UK (as elsewhere; see also the Australian case of *Cattanach v Melchior* (2003)). One question featuring prominently in cases involving 'healthy' children is whether the birth of a child can ever be viewed as compensable 'harm'. While English law appeared settled following *Emeh v Kensington, Chelsea and Westminster Area Health Authority* (1985), in permitting the recovery of **damages** for the pain and suffering and economic losses immediately associated with the physical events of pregnancy and childbirth ('mother's claim'), *and* for the child maintenance costs, this position changed after *McFarlane v Tayside Health Board* (2000). While not taking issue with the 'mother's claim', and also rejecting that a woman could be expected to mitigate her losses via **abortion** or **adoption** (*see Emeh*), in *McFarlane* the **House of Lords** unanimously determined that in cases of wrongfully conceived *healthy* children, the 'child maintenance' claim would be automatically non-actionable. Recognizing that on ordinary principles of **tort law** that the claim would otherwise succeed, their Lordships offered various policy/legal justifications for this departure, including the notion that a *healthy* child is to be regarded as a blessing, not a harm, as a matter of law.

Subsequent wrongful conception cases tested the reach of *McFarlane*, (eg *Greenfield v Irwin* (2001)). In *Parkinson v St James' and Seacroft University Hospital NHS Trust* (2002), the Court of Appeal awarded additional child maintenance damages relating to raising a 'seriously' *disabled* child (but not the ordinary costs which the Court considered that *McFarlane* excluded) born as a result of a failed sterilization. More surprisingly in light of *McFarlane*, in *Rees v Darlington Memorial Hospital NHS Trust* (2002), a Court of Appeal majority created a further exception by permitting recovery of additional damages by a disabled claimant who gave birth to a healthy child following a failed sterilization. This decision culminated in an appeal in *Rees v Darlington Memorial Hospital NHS Trust* (2003) in which the House of Lords was also invited (but refused) to depart from their decision in *McFarlane* under the *Practice Statement (Judicial Precedent)* (1966). Taking the opportunity to add depth to the policy reasoning in *McFarlane* (including concerns around awarding such damages against a cash-strapped NHS) by a 4:3 majority, the House overturned the Court of Appeal's decision, and substituted the additional maintenance award with a so-called 'conventional award' of £15,000. This award, said to acknowledge the denial of the parents' **autonomy** and lost opportunity to limit their family size, now applies to all wrongful conception cases involving healthy children.

Rees clarifies that irrespective of the health status of the parent, in the 'healthy' children cases, no child maintenance damages are available. Less certain is the position of wrongful conception cases involving *disabled* children (and **wrongful birth** cases). In *Rees*, their Lordships declined to rule on the question as to whether the 'conventional award' or additional damages would apply to the *Parkinson*-type case; therefore, until the matter is specifically visited by the House of Lords, *Parkinson* remains binding.

NICKY PRIAULX

N Priaulx, *The Harm Paradox: Tort Law and the Unwanted Child in an Era of Choice* (London: Routledge-Cavendish, 2007)

L Hoyano, 'Misconceptions about Wrongful Conception' (2002) 65 *Modern Law Review* 88

See also: **negligence in civil law; wrongful life**

wrongful life   Actions for 'wrongful life' are claims for **damages** by children born disabled who, but-for another's negligence, would not exist and endure the pain and suffering of their condition. An example is afforded by negligent failure to diagnose rubella in a woman who, if informed of the risk, would have lawfully terminated the pregnancy. Though recognized in a few North American States, Israel, and The Netherlands, such claims are not actionable under English **common law**, or in virtually all other jurisdictions. Criticized as logically incoherent and incompatible with legal doctrine, the 'wrongful life' action has also been deplored as inconsistent with the **sanctity of human life**, demeaning of the disabled, and a threat to familial relationships. Yet the emotive label, by appearing to impugn life itself, deflects attention from a defendant's culpable conduct.

The sanctity of life argument rests on the contestable assumption that life is invariably preferable to non-existence, which the law itself implicitly rejects, as when it permits withholding re-ventilation from severely afflicted infants. Moreover, the wrongful life action does not entail the termination of life. Nor does it demean the disabled if understood as a source of empowerment and dignity that provides corrective **justice** and sets medical standards. The alleged threat to familial relationships rests mainly on the spectre of negligence claims against mothers who had refused an **abortion**, a very unlikely prospect given the importance of their decision-making rights as to birth choices, and one which would not normally make sense financially.

The objections based on logic and legal doctrine seem more substantial. 'Normal' existence was never an alternative for wrongful life claimants, only non-existence. But does not the claim that one has 'suffered damage' logically entail one's prior existence? And if non-existence is the proposed comparator, how can a court calculate the damages which, in law, aim to restore claimants to their position prior to the negligent conduct? These objections, though weighty, are arguably surmountable if the starting point is the defendant's **responsibility** for the claimant's present suffering. It is then feasible to establish the basic elements of negligence—duty, breach, and damage. A putative duty of care is owed to the **foetus** by those responsible for **prenatal testing** and risk disclosure. Breach inheres in failure to take such care, and a right of action accrues for the **child** at birth. As for damages, a non-existent state entails no pain, suffering, or financial loss. In the exceptional context of 'wrongful life', the damages could appropriately seek to reflect any resultant medical and care costs plus pain and suffering, less any off-setting benefits of being alive.

The Congenital Disabilities (Civil Liability) Act 1976, although not designed to cover wrongful life claims, might possibly be so construed for negligence in embryo selection or in pre-conception genetic counselling. English law, like many legal systems, recognizes '**wrongful birth**' claims by parents for *their* emotional harm and financial loss when a child is born impaired due to negligence.

HARVEY TEFF

See also: **negligence in civil law; wrongful conception**

WTO   *see* **World Trade Organization**

Y

young offenders 'Young offenders' is the term commonly used in the UK to refer to children and young people above the age of criminal **responsibility** who have committed a criminal offence but who are below the age at which they will routinely be dealt with in adult **courts**. The age of criminal responsibility is currently set at ten for England, Wales, and Northern Ireland and, since 1998, there has been no presumption that children between ten and fourteen are *doli incapax* (incapable of being held criminally liable). Ten is one of the lowest ages in Europe although the **European Court of Human Rights**, in the case of *T v UK and V v UK* (2000) involving the boys convicted of murdering two-year-old James Bulger, held that this minimum age did not of itself breach Article 3. The minimum age for Scotland is eight (but see below) whilst the Republic of Ireland raised its minimum age from seven to twelve in 2006.

In all parts of the UK there are separate systems for dealing with children and young people who offend and in England, Wales, and Northern Ireland this is now called the Youth (formerly Juvenile) Justice System. Scotland has had a separate history in this respect since 1968. The importance of 'separateness' is clear in Article 40 of the UN **Convention on the Rights of the Child** ('UNCRC'): 'States Parties shall seek to promote the establishment of laws, procedures, authorities and institutions *specifically applicable* to children alleged as, accused of, or recognised as having infringed the penal law'. The UNCRC also enjoins diversion from judicial proceedings where possible. Separate systems and processes have been established in order to protect children from inappropriate adult systems but also to segregate children from adult offenders who might 'contaminate' them. However, ideas about what appropriate systems and procedures might look like have changed over time.

The Children Act 1908, which set up the first courts specifically for juveniles in the UK, was based on the view that young offenders are 'children in trouble' and, in line with this, the Children and Young Persons Act 1933 established the principle that still imposes a duty on 'every court' (including criminal courts) and, since 1985, the **Crown Prosecution Service** in England and Wales, to 'have regard to' the welfare of the child 'who is brought before it'. That principle also applies to Northern Ireland where it must be implemented 'with a view to furthering the child's personal, social and educational development'. Youth Offending Teams ('YOTs') are now listed in the Children Act 2004 as partners of Children's Services and the safeguarding duty in section 11 of that Act also applies to YOTs and the **police**: they must ensure functions are discharged 'having regard to the need to safeguard and promote the welfare of children'. When the child's **welfare principle** is perceived as the most important principle in practice the approach has been referred to as a 'welfare' model of youth justice, in contrast to the 'justice' model, when principles of due process take precedence. Arguably, developments in the last twenty years in all parts of the UK can be seen as a movement towards a justice model.

Today the Youth Justice System in England and Wales is overseen nationally by the Youth Justice Board ('YJB') whilst YOTs in each area provide staff and volunteers to run, for example, preventative schemes, provide 'appropriate adults' to accompany young offenders when questioned at the police station, do risk assessments, write pre-sentence reports, and supervise offenders on a variety of court orders. Most of the legal framework for this system was set up by the Crime and Disorder Act in 1998 after the Labour government came to power. Section 37(1) of that Act established the prevention of offending as the aim of the youth justice system in England and Wales and a similar aim is evident in the Justice (Northern Ireland) Act 2002: 'to protect the public by preventing offending by children' (sections 53(1) and (3)).

The White Paper, *No More Excuses—A New Approach to Tackling Youth Crime in England and Wales* (Home Office, 1997), by its very title indicated the more interventionist approach of the new Labour government to 'nip offending in the bud' and hold children and young people to account. *No More Excuses* also noted the government's intention to incorporate into the new processes the principles underlying **restorative justice**: restoration, reintegration, and responsibility. In particular it argued that 'reparation can be a valuable way of making young offenders face the consequences of their actions and see the harm they have caused'. The replacement of cautions by a more structured and statutorily-based system of reprimands and warnings in the Crime and Disorder Act 1998 was intended to achieve these aims. Administered by the police, the warning should if possible be done by means of a 'restorative conference' at which the **victim** is present. Further, the warning leads to referral to a youth offending team for a preventative programme. The new scheme means that normally young offenders have only two 'chances' before **prosecution** for a third offence.

The Youth Court has been the presumptive court for **minors** since 1991 when the non-criminal work of the old Juvenile Court was moved to a Family Proceedings Court. Since 2002, the most likely order for minors on their first appearance at the youth court has been the referral order This can last from three to twelve months and 'diverts' the young person from **punishment** to a Youth Offending Panel which has lay and YOT members. The young offender is expected to negotiate and agree with the Panel a contract of preventative activities to address his or her offending. Failure to agree or comply can mean a return to the youth court. If the contract is successfully 'signed off', the conviction is regarded as spent. In some respects there are similarities between this Panel and the Children's Hearings which have operated in Scotland since 1971 and which deal with referrals, via the Reporter, about children who might be in need of compulsory measures of supervision because of neglect and/or offending behaviour.

The Youth Court has a range of other orders at its disposal for offenders under the age of sixteen, including **fines**, reparation orders, supervision orders, and detention and training orders. For offenders aged sixteen to seventeen, there are also community **rehabilitation** and community punishment orders (involving supervision—with or without specified activities—and community work respectively). To discourage the use of custody by making community punishment more 'attractive' to youth courts, and, it is hoped, more effective at preventing re-offending, more intensive and controlling forms of supervision have been developed. In particular, the intensive supervision and surveillance programme ('ISSP') is aimed at fifteen to seventeen-year-old offenders and uses a combination of electronic and other forms of tracking, together with twenty-five hours of compulsory educational or other activity per week.

Despite a policy aim of reducing the use of custody for young offenders, provisions introduced since 1994 have given the courts more powers to impose custodial sentences. The detention and training order can currently be imposed on offenders aged twelve and above, subject to additional criteria for those under fifteen years of age. The length of the order has been increased to twenty-four months. Half of the time is spent in detention and the other half on supervision in the community. Except for younger offenders, the custodial period is normally spent in a **prison** service establishment. However, there are other provisions which allow longer sentences for serious offences and the equivalent of a life sentence for murder. The former sentence has been increasingly used: there was a tenfold increase in the period 1980–2000. The Criminal Justice Act 2003 also introduced new indeterminate sentences for offenders, adults, and minors, judged to be a risk to the public.

These trends have raised concerns in relation to both the welfare and the rights of young offenders and the UK has been subject to criticism for practices and conditions in the penal secure estate. Young prisoners are considerably more likely to have mental problems than their peers 'outside', and there has been a series of high profile **suicides**. Case law has recently established that the duties of the local authority in relation to the safeguarding of children do not end at the prison gates and procedures for implementing that duty are under review.

However, what is meant by 'youth justice' has also changed. The development and increased use of **anti-social behaviour orders**, parenting orders, and early intervention preventative schemes for those at risk of offending, together with parenting and acceptable behaviour contracts, have brought under the remit of the YJB children and young people who are not technically criminals, either because they are under ten years old or they have not committed an offence.

CHRISTINE PIPER

Yugoslav Tribunals   *see* **Milosevic, Slobodan**

Z

zero tolerance 'Zero tolerance' describes an intolerant attitude towards rule-breaking and a policy of strict enforcement against **transgression**. The idea is that maximal enforcement of minor infractions deters serious offending by 'nipping it in the bud'.

The term can be traced back to the US 'war on drugs', when, in 1988, Customs Commissioner, William Von Raab, described as 'zero tolerance' his policy of seizing vehicles, boats, or planes if a 'speck of any controlled substance' were found on board. In the UK, Edinburgh District Council Women's Committee in November 1992 used Zero Tolerance as a campaign slogan to highlight the unacceptability of male **violence** against women and children.

'Zero tolerance policing' is the best-known usage of the term. The New York 'miracle' in which **homicides** fell by two-thirds (from 2,245 to 767) between 1990 and 1997 was claimed by **police** officers to be achieved by aggressive enforcement of minor offences. The extent to which the crime drop can, in fact, be attributed to 'zero tolerance' is questionable, but the link has become firmly established in public consciousness. Critics contend that 'zero tolerance' is flawed in principle because it undermines the virtues of discretion and tolerance, and flawed in practice because it criminalizes minor wrongdoing and encourages overzealous policing.

Despite ambivalence, 'zero tolerance' is invoked as the solution to crime, failing schools, underperforming hospitals, late bill payment, and poor punctuation! This slippery phrase, born of authoritarian populism, is more a declaration of tough determination than a coherent approach to law enforcement.

BEN BOWLING

Sources of Illustrations

The images in the plate sections of this volume are reproduced by kind permission of the artist/photographer or copyright holder as follows:

Plates between pages 268 and 269:

JUSTICE

Goddess Ma'at, Late Dynastic Period, *c.* 600–400 BC, bronze, Egyptian, Late Period (715–332 BC), private collection. Photo © Heini Schneebeli/The Bridgeman Art Library.

Benin figures of justice, private collection, Vienna. Photo © Erich Lessing.

Hand of Justice, from the Treasure of St Denis (ivory and precious stones), French School, (10th century), Louvre, Paris, France. Photo © Peter Willi/The Bridgeman Art Library.

Justice (terracotta roundal), roundal from the Tomb of the Cardinal of Portugal, 1460s (glazed terracotta) by della Robbia, Luca (1400–82), San Miniato al Monte, Florence, Italy. Photo © The Bridgeman Art Library.

HUMAN RIGHTS

Declaration of the Rights of Man, the French Declaration of the Rights of Man and the Citizen, 1789 (coloured wood engraving), French School, (19th century), Musée de la Révolution Francaise, Vizille, France. Photo © The Bridgeman Art Library.

Universal Declaration of Human Rights, artwork by Octavio Roth. Photo © UN.

US Declaration of Independence, manuscript copy by Thomas Jefferson, Thomas Jefferson Papers, courtesy of the Massachussetts Historical Society.

THE LAW

Litigation cartoon, reproduced by permission of Wildy & Sons.

Clive Collins cartoon, *The Sun*, 21 November 1969. Courtesy of the British Cartoon Archive, University of Kent.

Peter Brookes cartoon, *The Times*, 16 July 1997. Courtesy of the British Cartoon Archive, University of Kent.

WOMEN AND THE LAW

Judge Thumb cartoon, *Rowlandson's Caricature Magazine*, Vol II, published by Thomas Tegg, *c.* 1782 (print), by Thomas Rowlandson (1756–1827), Guildhall Library, City of London. Photo © The Bridgeman Art Library.

Cat and Mouse Act poster, 1913, colour litho, English School, (20th century), private collection. Photo © The Bridgeman Art Library.

Indian suffragettes, Museum of London/Heritage Image Partnership.

WK Haseldon cartoon, *Daily Mirror*, 18 March 1920. Courtesy of the British Cartoon Archive, University of Kent.

LAWYERS (1)

Francis Bacon, by Paul van Somer (*c.* 1576–1621), from 'Gallery of Portraits', published in 1833, engraving, English School, (19th century), private collection. Photo © Ken Welsh/The Bridgeman Art Library.

Jeremy Bentham, Jeremy Bentham in an imaginary landscape, 1835, oil on paper, by George Frederick Watts (1817–1904), UCL Art Collections, University College London, UK. Photo © The Bridgeman Art Library.

Lord Denning, *Alfred Thomson ('Tom') Denning, Baron Denning* by Brian Organ. © National Portrait Gallery, London.

Friedrich August von Hayek, by Rodrigo Moynihan (1910–1990). © National Portrait Gallery, London.

LAWYERS (2)

Cicero bust 106–43 BC, marble, Roman, 1st century BC, Museo Capitolino, Rome, Italy. Photo © Giraudon/The Bridgeman Art Library.

Earl Warren, © MPI/Getty Images.

Oliver Wendell Holmes, engraving by American School, 20th century, private collection. Photo © Ken Welsh/The Bridgeman Art Library.

HLA Hart, photograph by Steve Pyke, reproduced courtesy of the photographer. Photograph held by the National Portrait Gallery, London.

LAWYERS (3)

Dame Brenda Hale, © Raveendran/AFP/Getty Images.

Dame Cornelia Sorabji, by Lafayette (Lafayette Ltd). © National Portrait Gallery, London.

Dame Rosalyn Higgins, photo by Max Koot, courtesy of the ICJ. All rights reserved.

Helena Normanton and Rose Heilbron, © The Women's Library/Mary Evans Picture Library.

LEADING CASES (1)

Carbolic Smoke Ball advertisment, reproduced with the permission of Carbolic Smoke Ball Co., Unusual Gifts for Lawyers, <http://www.carbolicsmokeball.com>.

Donoghue v Stevenson **bottle**, © CSBC Ltd, <http://www.carbolicsmokeball.com>.

M'Naghten's Case, © Mary Evans/ILN Pictures/Mary Evans Picture Library.

Plates between pages 524 and 525:

LEADING CASES (2)

De Keyser's Hotel, anon. engraving. Courtesy of the Guildhall Library, City of London Libraries.

Gaumont Picture Theatre, courtesy of Sandwell Community History and Archives Service.

Grand Junction Canal Company sign, photo by Stephen Dawson, courtesy of the photographer.

LAW COURTS (1)

Four Courts, Dublin, photo by Edwin Smith, courtesy of the RIBA Library Photographs Collection.

Supreme Court of India, by Simon Fieldhouse, courtesy of the artist.

US Supreme Court, © Paul Schutzer/Time Life Pictures/Getty Images.

Royal Courts of Justice, photo by Edwin Smith, courtesy of the RIBA Library Photographs Collection.

Fordwich Town Hall, © English Heritage, National Monuments Record/Heritage Image Partnership.

LAW COURTS (2)

International Court of Justice, PE Fotostudio, courtesy of the ICJ. All rights reserved.

European Court of Justice, courtesy of the Court of Justice of the European Union.

European Court of Human Rights, courtesy of the Council of Europe.

South African Constitutional Court, courtesy of the Constitutional Court of South Africa/David Krut Publishing.

COURTROOMS

The Old Bailey, George Cruickshank (1792–1878). Courtesy of the Guildhall Library Print Room, City of London Libraries.

Punjab court room, AFP Harcourt (1836–1910), from *Album of 409 Drawings Made In Delhi District, The Punjab, The Punjab States and on Board Ship 1861–1889*. Courtesy of the The British Library.

Hottentots trying a case, © Mary Evans Picture Library.

FAMOUS TRIALS (1)

Witchcraft trials, illustration from a collection of chapbooks on esoterica (woodcut), English School, private collection. Courtesy of the The Stapleton Collection/The Bridgeman Art Library.

The Trial of Warren Hastings, (1732–1818), Westminster Hall, 1788, watercolour on paper by James Nixon, (c. 1741–1812), private collection. Courtesy of The Bridgeman Art Library.

Titus Oates, from *Portraits, Memoirs, and Characters of Remarkable Persons, from the Reign of King Edward the Third, to the Revolution, etc*, London, 1813. Courtesy of The British Library.

Dr Hawley Crippen, Courtesy of Illustrated London News Ltd/Mary Evans/Mary Evans Picture Library.

FAMOUS TRIALS (2)

John Wilkes, (1727–97), 1763, etching by William Hogarth, (1697–1764), private collection. Photo © The Bridgeman Art Library.

Thomas Paine, (1737–1809), engraving, French School, (19th century), private collection. Photo © Ken Welsh/The Bridgeman Art Library.

Oscar Wilde, *The Illustrated Police Budget*, London, 1895. Courtesy of The British Library.

Edward Carson, by Alick P F Ritchie. Courtesy of The Print Collector/Hertage Image Partnership.

FAMOUS TRIALS (3)

Rosenbergs, © Keystone/Getty Images.

Lady Chatterley's Lover, © Keystone/Getty Images.

Oz trial, © Dennis Oulds/Central Press/Getty Images.

McLibel trial, © Madhuri Karia/Getty Images.

WAR CRIMES

Nuremberg Trials, © Hulton Archive/Getty Images.

Wandworth prison crowd, © Reg Speller/Fox Photos/Getty Images.

Adolf Eichmann, © Central Press/Getty Images.

Slobodan Milosevic, © Michel Porro/Getty Images.

Plates between pages 780 and 781:

MISCARRIAGES OF JUSTICE

Guildford Four, © John Stillwell/PA Archive/PA Photos.

Timothy Evans, © Keystone/Getty Image.

Stefan Kiszko, © Malcolm Croft/PA Archive/PA Photos.

Birmingham Six, © Sean Dempsey/PA Archive/PA Photos.

PROTEST

Tolpuddle Martyrs demonstration, Meeting of the Trade Unionists in Copenhagen Fields, 21 April 1834, engraving by W Summers, (fl.1833). Courtesy of Guildhall Library, City of London/The Bridgeman Art Library.

Match Girls' strike, © Hulton Archive/Getty Images.

Law Courts, © Brooke/Topical Press Agency/Getty Images.

Grunwick pickets, © Evening Standard/Getty Images.

PUBLIC ORDER

Tonypandy, © Hulton Archive/Getty Images.

Taff Merthyr Colliery, © Richards/Fox Photos/Getty Images.

Miners' strike, © George W Hales/Fox Photos/Getty Images.

Orgreave police, © Tom Stoddart/Getty Images.

EQUAL RIGHTS

MPs demonstration, © J Wilds/Keystone/Getty Images.

Public services equal pay demo, © Evening Standard/ Getty Images.

Bus conductors, © Homer Sykes/Getty Images.

Trico pickets, © Angela Deane-Drummond/Evening Standard/Getty Images.

CORPORATE RESPONSIBILITY

Thalidomide, © Leonard Mccombe/Time Life Pictures/ Getty Images.

Torrey Canyon, © Popperfoto/Getty Images.

Bhopal, © Sondeep/AP/PA Photos.

Paddington rail crash, © AFP/AFP/Getty Images.

COLONIALISM (1)

Punishment of a slave, A Letter, 1839, litho, private collection. Photo © Michael Graham-Stewart/The Bridgeman Art Library.

Slave traders, A group of Slaves being led to the West African Coast by Traders, from 'L'Afrique' by R Geoffroy, 1814, colour engraving, French School, (19th century). Courtesy of Bibliotheque de L'Arsenal, Paris, France/ Archives Charmet/The Bridgeman Art Library.

Children in the stocks, Courtesy of Heritage Image Partnership.

Eddie Mabo, 'The Age' courtesy of Jim McEwan/ Fairfaxphotos.

Les Gibbard cartoon, *The Guardian*, 30 July 1979, © Les Gibbard/British Cartoon Archive, University of Kent.

COLONIALISM (2)

British Empire map, image taken from *The Graphic*. Originally published/produced in London, 24 July 1886. Courtesy of The British Library.

The Huexotzinco Codex, Courtesy of Library of Congress Manuscript Division.

IMMIGRATION

Windrush, © Keystone/Getty Images.

Asian immigrants, © Evening Standard/Getty Images.

Registration queue, © William Vanderson/Fox Photos/ Getty Images.

Boat people, © John Minihan/Evening Standard/Getty Images.

Plates between pages 1036 and 1037:

RACE

David Low cartoon, *Evening Standard*, 7 September 1943. Courtesy of the British Cartoon Archive, University of Kent.

Children, © Carl Iwasaki/Time Life Pictures/Getty Images.

No coloured signs, © Terrence Spencer//Time Life Pictures/Getty Images.

I am a man, © Ernest C Withers, courtesy of Panopticon Gallery, Boston, MA.

NORTHERN IRELAND (1)

Anglo-Irish Treaty, © Topical Press Agency/Getty Images.

Bloody Sunday paratroopers, © Getty Images.

Bloody Sunday coffins, © M Stroud/Express/Getty Images.

NORTHERN IRELAND (2)

Bobby Sands protest, © Central Press/Getty Images.

Pub bombing, © Central Press/Getty Images.

Ian Paisley and Martin Guinness, © Paul Faith/AFP/ Getty Images.

Stormont, © Peter Muhl/AFP/Getty Images.

SOUTH AFRICA (1)

Sharpeville massacre, © Keystone/Getty Images.

Mandela outside court, © Jurgen Schadeberg/Getty Images.

Mandela's release, © Greg English/AP/PA Photos.

Leslie Illingworth cartoon, *Daily Mail*, 15 June 1964. Courtesy of the British Cartoon Archive, University of Kent.

SOUTH AFRICA (2)

Nelson Mandela, © Jurgen Schadeberg/Getty Images.

Truth and Reconciliation Commission, © Walter Dhladhla/AFP/Getty Images.

Albie Sachs, © Philip Littleton/AFP/Getty Images.

Yvonne Mokgoro, © Philip Littleton/AFP/Getty Images.

LIFE AND DEATH

Louise Brown, © Keystone/Getty Images.

Assisted suicide demonstration, © Karen Bleier/AFP/ Getty Images.

Abortion protest, © Cynthia Johnson/Time Life Pictures/Getty Images.

Diane Pretty, © Michael Crabtree/Getty Images.

FILMS

12 Angry Men, © AFP/AFP/Getty Images.

To Kill a Mockingbird, © Silver Screen Collection/Hulton Archive/Getty Images.

Inherit the Wind, © Hulton Archive/Getty Images.

Erin Brockovich, © Getty Images.

MISCELLANEOUS

Austin cartoon, David Austin, *The Guardian*, 15 July 1997. Courtesy of Janet Slee/British Cartoon Archive, University of Kent.

Joseph Lee cartoon, *The Evening News*, 21 August 1936. Courtesy of the British Cartoon Archive, University of Kent.

The New Compensation Act postcard, private collection, courtesy of Prof Wade Mansell.

Citizens' Advice Bureau, © Keystone/Getty Images.

Index of Names

(See also lists of contributors and cases)

Subject index

Public Order and Civil Liberties

Real and Personal Property